Text, Cases and Materials on Public Law and Human Rights

Text, Cases and Materials on Public Law and Human Rights

Third edition

Helen Fenwick and Gavin Phillipson

Routledge
Taylor & Francis Group

LONDON AND NEW YORK

Third edition published 2011 by Routledge
2 Park Square, Milton Park, Abingdon, Oxon, OX14 4RN
Simultaneously published in the USA and Canada
by Routledge
270 Madison Avenue, New York, NY 10016

Routledge is an imprint of the Taylor & Francis Group, an informa business

© 2011 Helen Fenwick and Gavin Phillipson

First two editions published by Cavendish Publishing Limited
First edition 1995
Second edition 2003

Typeset in Minion by
RefineCatch Limited, Bungay, Suffolk

Printed and bound in Great Britain by
MPG Books Group, UK

Parliamentary material is reproduced with the permission of the Controller of
HMSO on behalf of Parliament.

British Library Cataloguing in Publication Data
A catalogue record for this book is available from the British Library

Library of Congress Cataloging in Publication Data
Fenwick, Helen.
Text, cases, and materials on public law and human rights / Helen Fenwick and
Gavin Phillipson.—3rd ed.
p. cm.
1. Public law—Great Britain.   2. Civil rights—Great Britain.   I Phillipson,
Gavin.   II. Title.
KD3930.F46 2011
342.41—dc22

                                                                2010006936

ISBN10: 0-415-48431-6 (hbk)
ISBN13: 978-0-415-48431-2 (hbk)

ISBN10: 0-415-46214-2 (pbk)
ISBN13: 978-0-415-46214-3 (pbk)

To Paul and to Amelia

OUTLINE CONTENTS

DETAILED CONTENTS

PREFACE

The constitution of the United Kingdom is currently one of the most dynamic and controversial areas of law and practice to study and debate: the Blair government was elected on a manifesto promising the most radical and far-reaching package of constitutional reform in the 20th century, and, many would say, since the Great Reform Act of 1832. Thirteen years on, much of that programme has been implemented: devolution to Scotland, Wales, Northern Ireland and London; partial reform of the House of Lords; the introduction of the Freedom of Information Act 2000 and of the Human Rights Act 1998 (HRA), which incorporated the European Convention on Human Rights into domestic law, giving this country its first real Bill of Rights. The devolution process is still on-going: having been frozen for some time, the Northern Ireland settlement has been reanimated with the 2010 Agreement to restore the Assembly and put into effect the long-awaited passing of policing and justice powers to Stormont. The introduction of the Constitutional Reform Act, providing for changes in the office of Lord Chancellor and establishment of a new Supreme Court followed in 2005, and right at the end of the Labour reign in government from 1997–2010, the Constitutional Reform and Governance Act 2010 (discussed further below) was passed by Parliament. As this book went to press, the new Liberal-Conservative government announced the setting up of a Commission to review the possibility of introducing a Bill of Rights for Britain that would build on the rights contained in the European Convention on Human Rights and a referendum on the introduction of a more proportionate voting system for General Elections; other promised reforms include fixed term Parliaments, ending the right of the Prime Minister to call an election at the time of his or her choosing, an early Bill to establish a fully or elected House of Lords, and full implementation of the Wright reforms to strengthen the House of Commons, particularly its Select Committees; all these together give powerful proof that the process of radical constitutional reform is far from exhausted, although it is now taking a new turn, after the 2010 General Election. The new Government has also promised a Freedom (Great Repeal) Bill, which will repeal various liberty-invading measures and restore the right to peaceful protest that, the Government said, had been eroded by the Labour Government's range of public order and criminal justice measures (examined in chapters 19 and 20). This book aims to help the reader develop an informed critical insight into this reform programme through both a detailed consideration of the reforms themselves and an exploration of the historical roots and contemporary understandings of the constitutional arrangements in the UK.

It is widely recognised that any worthwhile study of this area of law requires perusal of a wide selection of materials lying beyond the law's domain; this is partly because large areas of the British constitution remain regulated, or at least strongly influenced, by conventions and shared understandings. Furthermore, this prevalence of non-legal rules in the constitution means that it is necessary to seek the views of those with first-hand knowledge or specialist expertise in the contentious areas: civil servants, MPs, government ministers, Ombudsmen, experts in public administration, as well as judges, barristers and academics. Thus the material in this book includes articles from journals on politics and administration as well as law, and extracts from reports of parliamentary committees and government papers as well as from the law reports.

The main aim of the book is to cover the areas that students taking the 'core' course in Public Law/ Constitutional and Administrative Law would normally encounter in their studies; however, it also contains material that would facilitate study or enquiry at other levels. In particular, its strong coverage of the Human Rights Act and that Act's impact on freedom of expression, police powers and public order law over the first ten years of its life make it useful reading for civil liberties courses, while it has sufficiently in-depth coverage of judicial review to make it a helpful supplementary text on administrative law courses. The depth of coverage of these areas is, we believe, unique in a book of this type.

Books of this type vary considerably in the amount of authorial input they contain. Some are literally just a collection of various materials, with virtually no commentary by the authors. Others contain almost equal amounts of authorial and source material. We have attempted to steer a middle course between these two extremes. In particular, the topics covered are presented in a structured way, with authorial introductions to the different sections, and a clear ordering of the different issues raised. Additionally, extensive commentary is provided, which not only explains basic issues where this is appropriate, but also provides additional insights and information, and in places takes a clear stance in an ongoing debate. Questions designed to provoke a critical and sceptical approach to the existing conventional and legal order are also included. To assist in encouraging such an approach, a variety of critical views are presented. Whilst the predominant ideological thrust of the authorial and source material is firmly within the tradition which Martin Loughlin has labelled 'liberal normativism', a conscious attempt has been made to give some space to the views of republican and functionalist critics of the more familiar liberal and conservative paradigms, especially in Part I.

This first part of the book explores basic concepts and principles of constitutionalism, using a strongly comparative approach, and examines how far the view that the UK is radically out of step with such principles requires modification in the light of the constitutional transformation outlined above. The peculiar prominence of constitutional conventions within the UK constitutional order is considered in Chapter 2. Chapter 3 considers the continuing evolution of the basic principles of the Rule of Law, now strongly influenced by the European Convention on Human Rights (ECHR). The ECHR has also had a considerable impact on the traditionally fuzzy separation of powers between executive and judiciary in the UK, culminating in the Constitutional Reform Act 2005. We now no longer have a powerful Cabinet Minister (the Lord Chancellor) sitting in our highest court (the House of Lords); our top judges (the Law Lords) no longer sit in the second chamber of Parliament; our senior judges are appointed by a body independent of the executive, instead of by one of the most senior members of it (the Lord Chancellor), and their institutional independence was thereby significantly enhanced. Chapter 3 includes full coverage of these highly significant developments, including the new Supreme Court, which opened its doors in October 2009 and the Judicial Appointments Commission, as well as the creation of the Ministry of Justice. Parliamentary sovereignty, including its historical and theoretical background, is examined in Chapter 4; challenges to traditional notions of sovereignty posed by the notion of common law fundamental rights as well as by the Human Rights Act are closely analysed. The House of Lord's decision in *A-G v Jackson* is also given detailed coverage, both for what it tells us about possible common limitations upon sovereignty and about the definition of an Act of Parliament. A separate chapter 5 is devoted to the impact of the European legal order on sovereignty, with particular prominence given to the analysis proffered by Laws LJ in *Thoburn v Sunderland City Council*. A new Chapter 6 introduces detailed analysis of the three devolution settlements, with discussion of the consequent evolution of the UK towards a form of quasi-federalism. The chapter considers the St Andrew's Agreement, the Northern Ireland Act 2009 and the 2010 Agreement to restore the Northern Ireland Assembly, the proposals for new primary legislative powers for the Welsh Assembly and the Calman proposals for devolution of more powers to Scotland.

The next chapter of the book traces the rapid growth in the power and influence of the institutions and law of the European Convention on Human Rights ECHR). Chapter 7 considers a number of the substantive rights and recent cases, such as *A v UK* (2009) on detention without trial and *Marper v UK* (2008) on DNA retention; it also examines the current method of challenging states' alleged violations of rights before the European Court of Human Rights. In this edition of the book we have omitted the chapter that provided a basic introduction to the institutions of the EU, the treaties and the notions of direct and indirect effect and the *Francovich* principle. This is partly for reasons of space but primarily because nearly all students taking Constitutional and Administrative Law courses will also be taking the core course in EU law, and it seemed to us increasingly futile to seek to cover in one chapter the subject matter of an entire, separate core course.

The third part of the book examines the changing role of Parliament, with a strong focus on the ongoing process of reform within both Houses. Chapter 8 on the House of Commons considers its overall role within the context of the party and electoral system. A number of rebellions in the Commons, including those over the Iraq war, tuition fees, and anti-terrorism powers are used to illustrate the paradox of the largely quiescent chamber that yet retains the potential to act as a powerful check, or even threat, to the government of the day. The first main section then considers its legislative role, and in particular, recent innovations in terms of pre-legislative scrutiny and the time-tabling of Bills. The second section examines the Commons' efforts to scrutinise the executive, with particular reference to the reforms of the Select Committees in 2002, and their growing importance within the Commons. This chapter includes full coverage of the Wright Committee reforms to the House of Commons, passed in 2010 in the wake of the MPs expenses scandal. The House of Lords is dealt with in Chapter 9; the peculiar value of its legislative work is illustrated in particular by detailed consideration of its role in amending Bills of constitutional significance. Around half of the chapter is devoted to consideration of reform of the Lords: analysis of issues arising from the proposals of Wakeham, the Public Administration Select Committee and the 2008 White Paper is placed firmly in a comparative context through extensive consideration of second chambers overseas. Particular emphasis is laid upon the arguments surrounding the composition of the House, the method of appointing any nominated members, and the powers of any new second chamber.

Chapter 10 deals with the issues raised by parliamentary privileges and standards, with particular reference to the important report of the Joint Committee on Parliamentary Privilege (1999) and the on-going input of the Committee on Standards in Public Life. In particular, this chapter offers full coverage of the reforms introduced in the wake of the MPs' expenses scandal by the Parliamentary Standards Act 2009, the Kelly Report 2009 and the Constitutional Reform and Governance Act 2010. The analysis of this episode is explored in the context of full discussion of the ever-contentious issue of standards in public life, and the ongoing evolution of standard-setting and enforcement mechanisms. The chapter also examines the parliamentary privilege of freedom of speech, including the recent controversy over the recent *Trafigura case.*

The fourth part of the book, concerning the Central Executive, Powers and Accountability, commences with Chapter 11 on prerogative powers, in which strong emphasis is placed on recent case law on judicial control of the prerogative, in particular *Bancoult* (2008) in the House of Lords; we also take a close look at the important reforms to the prerogative contained in the *Governance of Britain* package and 2010 Act. Chapter 12 examines first the system of Cabinet government and collective responsibility, looking in particular at innovations towards a stronger centre of government under the Blair and Brown Governments - the 'core executive' - together with the linked issue of the convention of collective responsibility. The 2010 reforms placing the civil service on a statutory basis are considered in detail. The second part of the chapter looks at the main mechanism for ensuring the accountability of central government: ministerial responsibility. A comprehensive analysis of the 'new' doctrine of ministerial responsibility is undertaken and the extent of the duty not to mislead Parliament is subjected to sustained analysis in the light in particular of the findings of the Scott Enquiry in 1996, the

Hutton and Butler inquires and the ongoing Chilcot inquiry on the run up to the war in Iraq and the use of intelligence on WMD.

Finally in this part, chapter 13 gives extensive consideration to access to government information. It begins by considering the changing and yet unchanged face of official secrecy in the UK and gives lengthy consideration to the House of Lords' decision in *Shayler*. The chapter moves on to examine the radical change brought about in access to official information by the introduction of the Freedom of Information Act 2000 (FoI Act), which came into force in 2005. The Act, which afforded UK citizens, for the first time, a right of access to information held by 'public authorities' is afforded extensive coverage, since it represents such an important change in the accountability of the state and public sector bodies. Key decisions under the Act, including over access to the details of MPs expenses, and the first two uses of the Ministerial veto in 2009, are given prominent coverage.

The fifth part of the book provides an introduction to key areas of administrative law. In Chapter 14, the procedural issues relating to judicial review are subjected to detailed analysis in the light of the introduction of CPR, Part 54, and the connection with the HRA test for amenability of public authorities to review. Chapter 15, which is very substantial, examines the grounds of judicial review. All the key principles are covered: particular emphasis is placed upon areas of current controversy and change, including review for error of fact after *E v Secretary of State for the Home Department* (2004), a thorough analysis of the common law duty to give reasons, the now established doctrine of substantive legitimate expectation as discussed and applied in *Abdi and Nadarajah* (2005), *Niazi* (2008) and, in the House of Lords, *BAPIO* (2008) and *Bancoult* (2008). Developments in the rule against bias driven by Article 6 ECHR are given close scrutiny: we examine in particular a series of House of Lords decision applying the test in *Porter v Magill* and *Locabail,* including *Al Hasan* (2005), *Lawal v Northern Spirit Ltd* (2003) and *R v Abdroikof (Nurlon)* (2007). A major section is devoted to the diversification of standards under the broad Irrationality head, including consideration of the House of Lords decision in *R (Ahmad) v Newham LBC* (2009) and there is discussion of the development of proportionality as a free-standing head of review (*R (on the application of Daly) v Secretary of State for the Home Department.* Chapter 16 examines the work and evaluates the effectiveness of the parliamentary and local Ombudsmen; discussion of progress on enacting the proposals for reform suggested in the Cabinet Office paper, *Review of the Public Sector Ombudsmen in England* (2000), is given particular prominence.

The last part of the book gives extensive consideration to the very significant changes in the protection of human rights that have come about since the second edition of this book was published. The Human Rights Act 1998 (HRA) came into force in 2000, so this part (chaps 17–20) evaluates judicial interpretations of its key provisions, and key aspects of the protection of civil liberties and human rights in Britain in the light of the impact of the HRA during the first decade of its life. Chapter 17 examines the Act itself in detail and goes on to give extensive consideration to a range of key decisions on it, including *R v A (No 2)* (2002), *Brown v Stott* (2001); *S and W (Children) (Care Orders)* (2002); *Ghaidan-Mendoza* (2004); *Belmarsh* (2004), *Huang* (2007); *YL* (2008); *Re P* (2009) and *Horncastle* (2010). As this book was in press, the new Conservative-Liberal coalition Government came to power in 2010, and announced the setting up of a Commission to examine the possibility of repeal of the Human Rights Act and its replacement by a new British Bill of Rights. This chapter contains evaluation of the HRA and coverage of the arguments surrounding the desirability or otherwise of a stronger Bill of Rights.

The further three chapters in this part cover, respectively, freedom of expression, freedom of protest and assembly, police powers in terms of crime control and counter-terrorism, and suspect's rights. The topics chosen within these areas and the emphasis placed on them highlight those issues which are of particular significance at the present time, including increases in police powers, erosion of safeguards for suspects, especially in the counter-terrorism field, and limitation of the freedom to protest. Prominent decisions in these fields, including *Pro-life Alliance v BBC* (2002), the public protest cases of

Laporte (2007); *Austin* (2009); *Animal Defenders* (2008) and *Gillan* (2006) are given extended coverage. The chapters consider in detail the extent to which the Convention rights protected under the HRA are being afforded real efficacy in the face of a range of rights-invading laws, including those recently created by the Terrorism Act 2000, as amended in 2006, the Police and Criminal Justice Act 2001, the Serious and Organised Crime Act 2005; the Prevention of Terrorism Act 2005. The extensive consideration of the state of freedom of expression and of protest in the UK, of police powers and suspects' rights, seeks to make the argument that from the beginning of the HRA era onwards the dangers of a decrease in state accountability and the creation of merely empty or tokenistic guarantees became apparent, partly due to the executive reaction to 9/11. The Labour governments, from 2001–2010 found that their own creation, the HRA, was hindering the use of a range of repressive laws, especially in the counter-terrorism field. The HRA as a result did not fully "bed" down.

We would like to thank our partners and family for their support and encouragement during the writing of this book. Langman Lloyd of Routledge Publishing has been invariably enthusiastic and helpful and shown great patience and flexibility during this third edition's long evolution. We would also like to thank all owners of copyright material who have given their permission to include such material in this book.

The law is stated as at 1 February 2010 but it has been possible to include some later material, including in particular provisions of the Constitutional Reform and Governance Act 2010.

TABLE OF CASES

TABLE OF STATUTES

D

TABLE OF STATUTORY INSTRUMENTS

TABLE OF EUROPEAN LEGISLATION

TABLE OF INTERNATIONAL LEGISLATION

ACKNOWLEDGEMENTS

Grateful acknowledgement is made to all the authors and publishers of copyright material which appears in this book, and in particular to the following for permission to reprint material from the sources indicated:

Cambridge University Press for extracts from *Cambridge Law Journal*, Adimbola A. Olowofoyeku, 'Bias and the Informed Observer: A Call for a Return to Gough' [2009] CLJ 68, ATH Smith, 'May Day, May Day: Policing Protest' [2008] CLJ 67.

Hart Publishing for extracts from Peter Leyland, *The Constitution of the United Kingdom: a Contextual Analysis* (2007).

Harvard University Press for extracts from John Rawls, *A Theory of Justice* (1972).

Lexis Nexis for extracts from *All England Reports*, *R v Devon County Council ex parte Baker; Durham County Council ex p Curtis* [1995] 1 All ER 73.

Oxford University Press for extracts from SE Finer, Vernon Bogdanor and Bernard Rudden, *Comparing Constitutions* (1995); Jeffrey Jowell, 'The Rule of Law today', in Jeffrey Jowell and Dawn Oliver (eds), *The Changing Constitution* (2000); Anthony King, *The British Constitution* (2007); Colin Munro, *Studies in Constitutional Law* (1999); Philip Norton, 'Parliament and policy in Britain: The House of Commons as a policy influence' in Philip Norton (ed) *Legislatures* (1990); Meg Russell, *Reforming the Lords: Lessons from Overseas* (2000); Colin Turpin, 'Ministerial responsibility', in Jeffrey Jowell and Dawn Oliver (eds), *The Changing Constitution* (1994); extracts from the *Oxford Journal of Legal Studies*, Eric Barendt, 'Is there a United Kingdom constitution?' (1997) OJLS 17 (1), R Stevens, 'A loss of innocence? Judicial independence and the separation of powers' (1999) OJLS 19; extracts from *Parliamentary Affairs*, Ann Abraham, 'The Ombudsman as part of the UK constitution: A contested role?' (2008) Parlt Aff 61(1), M Pythian, 'Hutton and Scott: A tale of two inquiries' (2005) Parlt Aff 58(1), FF Ridley, 'There is no British constitution: a dangerous case of the Emperor's clothes' (1988) Parlt Aff 41, Jennifer Smookler, 'Making a difference? The effectiveness of pre-legislative scrutiny' (2006) Parlt Aff 59(3).

Pearson Education for AW Bradley and KD Ewing, *Constitutional and Administrative Law* (2007).

Scottish Council for Law Reporting for extracts from *Whaley v Lord Watson* 2000 *SC* 340 and *Adams v Scottish Ministers* 2004 *SC* 665.

Sweet and Maxwell for extracts from Gabriele Ganz, *Understanding Public Law* (2001); extracts from *European Human Rights Reports*, *Handyside v United Kingdom* Series A No 24 (1976) 1 EHRR 737, *Hashman v Harrup v UK* (2000) 30 EHRR 241, *McGonnell v United Kingdom* (2000) 30 EHRR 289, *Sunday Times v United Kingdom* Series A, No 30 (1980) 2 EHRR 245, *SW & CW v UK* (1996) 21 EHRR 363 (1996), *The Observer and The Guardian v United Kingdom* (1991) 14 EHRR 153; extracts from *European Law Review*, A Arnull, 'From Opinion 2/94 to the future of Europe' (2002) EL Rev 27(1); extracts from *Law Quarterly Review*, TRS Allan, 'Parliamentary sovereignty: law, politics and revolution' (1997) LQR 113, Vernon Bogdanor, 'Our new constitution' (2004) LQR 242, Joseph Raz, 'The rule of law and its virtue' (1977) LQR 93, HWR Wade, 'Sovereignty—revolution or evolution?' (1996) LQR 112; extracts from *Public Law*, Eric Barendt, 'Separation of powers and constitutional government' [1995] PL 599, P Birkinshaw, '"I only ask for information"—the White Paper on Open Government' [1993] PL 557, 559, 560, DN Clarke and D Shell, 'Revision and amendment by the House of Lords: a case study' [1994] PL 409, 410–14, Lord Windelsham, 'The Constitutional Reform Act 2005: ministers, judges and constitutional change: Part 1' [2005] PL 806, R Williams, 'When is an error not an error? Reform of jurisdictional review of error of law and fact' [2007] PL 973; extracts from *Scots Law Times*, *Starrs and Chalmers v Procurator Fiscal, Linlithgow (Starrs v Ruxton)* 2000 SLT 42.

Taylor & Francis Group for extracts from Jeremy Waldron, *The Law* (1990).

John Wiley & Sons Ltd for extracts from *Legal Studies*, HM Fenwick and G Phillipson, 'Direct action, Convention values and the Human Rights Act' [2001] LS 21(4); extracts from *Modern Law Review*, John Griffith, 'The political constitution' (1979) 42 MLR 1; extracts from *The Political Quarterly*, Norman Bonney, 'Looming issues for Scotland and the union' (2008) *Political Quarterly* 79(4), Alan Doig and Mark Pythian, 'The national interest and the politics of threat exaggeration: the Blair government's case for war against Iraq' (2005) *Political Quarterly* 76(3), Editorial Commentary: 'The House of Lords (again)' (2009) *Political Quarterly* 80(1).

Every effort has been made to trace and contact copyright holders prior to publication. If notified, the publisher will undertake to rectify any errors or omissions at the earliest opportunity.

CHAPTER 1
CONSTITUTIONAL PRINCIPLES AND THE BRITISH CONSTITUTION

INTRODUCTION

In this chapter, the nature of constitutions in general is considered and the UK constitution is placed in this context. The impact of the Labour Government's extensive programmes of constitutional reform upon traditional ways of examining the UK's uncodified constitution will also be touched on. These reforms constitute by far the greatest change to the UK constitution in the 20th century. They are briefly described in the following extract from an article whose title is of clear significance.

V Bogdanor, 'Our new constitution' (2004) *Law Quarterly Review* 242 (extracts)

THE years since 1997 have seen an unprecedented and perhaps uncompleted series of constitutional reforms. They comprise:

1   The constitutional independence of the Bank of England from government in monetary policy.

2   Referendums, under the Referendums (Scotland and Wales) Act, 1997, providing for referendums on devolution to Scotland and Wales.

3   The Scotland Act, 1998, providing for a directly elected Scottish Parliament.

4   The Government of Wales Act, 1998, providing for a directly elected National Assembly in Wales.

5   The Northern Ireland Act, 1998, providing for a referendum on a partnership form of devolution to Northern Ireland.

6   The establishment, under the Northern Ireland Act, 1998, of a directly elected Assembly in Northern Ireland.[1]

7   A referendum, under the Greater London Authority (Referendum) Act, 1998, on a directly elected mayor and strategic authority for London.

8   The introduction of proportional representation for the elections to the devolved bodies in Scotland, Wales, Northern Ireland, and the London strategic authority.

9   The European Parliamentary Elections Act, 1999, providing for the introduction of proportional representation for elections to the European Parliament.

10   The requirement on local authorities, under the Local Government Act, 2000, to abandon the committee system and adopt a cabinet system, a city manager system or a directly elected mayor. A local authority which wished to choose the directly elected mayor option, however, would be required, first, to hold a referendum on this option. In addition, provision was made for 5% of registered electors to require a local authority to hold a referendum on a directly elected mayor—the first statutory provision for the use of the initiative in British politics.

11   The Human Rights Act, 1998, requiring public bodies to comply with the provisions of the European Convention on Human Rights, allowing judges to declare a statute

---

1   See also recently the Northern Ireland Act 2009—considered in Chapter 6. Note also the Justice and Security (Northern Ireland) Act 2007; Northern Ireland (St Andrew's Agreement) Act 2007.

incompatible with Convention rights and providing for Parliament to alter such legislation by means of delegated legislation.

12   The removal, under the House of Lords Act, 1999, of all but 92 of the hereditary peers from the House of Lords as the first phase of a wider reform of the Lords. At the time of writing, it is proposed to remove the remaining 92 hereditary peers.

13   The Freedom of Information Act, 2000.

14   The Political Parties, Elections and Referendums Act, 2000, requiring the registration of political parties, and control of political donations and national campaign expenditure, and providing for the establishment of an Electoral Commission to oversee elections and to advise on improvements in electoral procedure.

15   The abolition of the historic office of Lord Chancellor, the removal of the Law Lords from the House of Lords, and the establishment of a new Supreme Court [via the Constitutional Reform Act 2005].

Any one of these reforms would constitute, by itself a radical change. Taken together, they allow us to characterise the years since 1997 as a veritable era of constitutional reform. Indeed, the years since 1997 bear comparison with two previous periods of constitutional reform—the 1830s and the years immediately before the First World War. Each of those two periods, however, was dominated by a single major reform, the Great Reform Act of 1832 and the Parliament Act of 1911, statutorily restricting the powers of the House of Lords.

To the above list one may add, very recently, the Political Parties and Elections Act 2009[2] and, more significantly, the Parliamentary Standards Act 2009: in response to the MPs' expenses scandal[3] this statute broke new ground in terms of compromising the ancient principle of Parliamentary self-regulation—considered fully in Chapter 9.

Various aspects of the above package are considered in subsequent chapters of this book. The following five chapters concentrate on five key aspects of the British constitution: its unusually heavy reliance on constitutional conventions; the rule of law; the separation of powers; parliamentary sovereignty and devolution. To an extent, therefore, this first chapter serves to introduce themes examined in more detail in subsequent chapters.

FUNDAMENTAL IDEAS IN CONSTITUTIONAL THEORY

We might begin by asking what is the basic purpose of a constitution. One influential answer, at least in Western constitutional thought, has been that constitutions are necessary in order to control the power of the state; another strand in that train of thought emphasises the role constitutions play in ensuring that that power derives from a legitimate source. On the one hand, it tells us how power may be used; on the other, from where it should derive. To the first idea may be attributed the notions of the Rule of Law, and the separation of powers, whilst the second is clearly related to the notion of democratic

---

2   The Tribunals, Courts and Enforcement Act 2007 also introduced significant reform to the tribunals system.

3   See generally www.guardian.co.uk/politics/mps-expenses.

legitimacy. It is clear that there can be a tension between these two basic ideas. The following extract portrays that tension at work in history.

F Sejersted, 'Democracy and the Rule of Law: Some historical experiences of contradictions in the striving for good government', in J Elster and R Slagstad (eds), *Constitutionalism and Democracy* (1988), pp 131–33

The Rule of Law and democracy correspond to the two different concepts of liberty: the negative, which makes liberty dependent on the curbing of authority; and the positive, which makes it dependent on the exercising of authority. These two concepts of liberty are, according to Isaiah Berlin, 'two profoundly divergent and irreconcilable attitudes to the ends of life'. Each of them have, however, 'an equal right to be classed among the deepest interests of mankind' . . . Is there really such a contradiction between democracy and the Rule of Law?

Democracy and Rule of Law can be seen as two different means of overcoming the inherent contradiction between state and society. State-building is necessary to society, but also represents a threat. Rule of Law was meant to curb state authority, while democracy was meant to mobilise society in the exercising of state authority. This contradiction between state and society must have been strongly felt in the centuries following the Renaissance. There was a need for peace, order and public security, and it went along with a general distrust of human nature. Man was governed by passions and could not withstand the temptations of power. On the other hand there was a growing belief in the possibility of constructing a state where the power was bound and the passions were kept under control. This was the basis for all the intellectual energy which was put into the constitutionalist philosophy of that time. There were two main trends, the one recommending mixed government which opposed power with power, and the other recommending a Separation of Powers. The fundamental trait the two trends had in common was a purely negative approach to the exercise of power. This rather intense process of ideologisation seems to be important as a driving force behind the 'spontaneous outbreak of constitution-ma' in the late 18th and early 19th century in the American states and in Europe. This 'conservative element' is now commonly seen as an important element in the American Revolution. Although the European case is not so clear, it seems as if the general tendency in this time of revolutions was the same, namely to block power rather than to take power. Hannah Arendt has argued that the constitutions were not the result of revolutions. 'Their purpose was to stem the tide of revolution' (1963, p 143). It is certainly true that constitution-making could have this counter-revolutionary appearance. In the American Revolution it seems, however, to have been weak, and this is also the case in Norway. Constitution-making was not a reaction to a revolutionary situation; if anything, it was a revolution in itself, directed against the power of the king and furthered by the openness of the situation. The point is that constitution-making was directed against the power of the state, no matter who held power—a king or a democratically elected assembly.

Note

Constitutions, on the above account, are faced with a fairly Herculean role. To be able to function, they evidently need to be seen as both legitimate and authoritative. How can they lay claim to such attributes?

H Calvert, *British Constitutional Law* (1985), pp 4–5, 7, 8, 9, 14–15

So far as is known, the constitution of Al Capone's gang has never been published. Yet it undoubtedly had one. It probably contained little more than the basic rule or norm that 'what Big Al says, goes' and, in exercise of this 'authority', Big Al no doubt authorised lieutenants to issue instructions and to order that double-crossers be rubbed out. The appearances are that the Papa Doc regime in Haiti and Idi Amin's regime in Uganda functioned in much the same way.

They headed regimes which, for a while, and within the confines of the immediately pressing political environment, functioned effectively. Whether the Al Capone gang and the modern nation-state differ in other respects is something we must now consider.

It is tempting to seek to distinguish between 'proper' constitutions and other regimes of organisation. In much the same way that we all know an elephant when we see one without necessarily being able to proffer a very good definition of it, so also do we not all recognise a 'proper' state, 'properly' constituted when we see it? The Capone gang clearly fails; Papa Doc and Idi Amin were mere ephemeral aberrations. If there is such a distinction, however, wherein does it lie?

Suffice it to say for the present, that if the legality of the source of a constitution were the criterion of its validity, it would be a brave man who would assert that the UK has ever had a valid constitution. The modern constitution dates (with a few minor quibbles) from the revolution of 1688. Prior to that, the history of England at least is one of dubious claims to title to the Crown, conquests, schisms and broken treaties, all offering extremely unsure ground on which to base a legal title.

. . . So, legality of source will not serve to distinguish between 'proper' and 'improper' constitutions. Such a criterion condemns the constitutions of most of the world's oldest and most stable societies. What clearly is illustrated is that a regime illegal in its origins may nevertheless, in some mysterious way, come to generate its own legality. In international law, this event may be prompted by 'recognition' which, according to some schools of thought, confers legality whilst, according to others, merely declares a legality deriving otherwise. Within the 'state', and after a coup d'état purporting to establish a new constitution but without any initial basis in legality, the courts sometimes come to acknowledge the new 'validity' and consequent legality and offer a variety of reasons for so doing (see, e.g., *The State v Dosso* 1958 SC 533, re Pakistan). It will not do, however, to regard such decisions as constituting the legality of the new regime, as opposed merely to accepting it as a pre-existing fact. If we do so, we get into all sorts of logical difficulties— whence comes the authority of the court to constitute? Can it really be the case that a constitution firmly in place nevertheless remains invalid pending the caprice of an application to the courts? Perhaps the distinction is best sought elsewhere. If we are not to look to the pre-existing legal order for validity, perhaps we should look to another source. It is an established historical fact that the constitutions of many modern states were specifically adopted as constitutions intended and resolved to act as the foundation for the new order. There is a superabundance of such instances. Most of the old Commonwealth countries still have, as their constitutional cases, Acts of the old imperial Parliament— here legality and specific adoption meld. In the case of some newer Commonwealth countries, as in the case of the USA, a new constitution has been promulgated without regard for the pre-existing legal order but in title of some asserted natural right so to do. In some cases, such as that of the Republic of Ireland (formerly the Irish Free State) an old constitution has legitimately spawned a newer one. Even in the case of the UK, it may be possible to conjure such an instance out of the legislation of the revolutionary 'Parliament' of 1688–89 and the later Acts of Union with Scotland and Ireland.

In all cases of specific adoption, it is possible to point to a constitutional instrument of some sort. Whilst this is an extremely common phenomenon, however, it does not seem to be absolutely necessary. A few of the world's acknowledged states boast no such instrument yet it would be hard to deny any constitutional function for them. It is normal to rank the UK amongst them for, in truth, the legislation referred to above hardly amounts to a written constitution as the term is usually understood.

. . . Lawyers tend to yearn for legal criteria, and constitutional lawyers, or at least some of them, would like to be able to say when a constitution is 'in force'. This may be a practical problem where they have had to decide whether or not to regard a new regime as valid. The insuperable problem is, however, that there is no legal system to which one can refer for such questions. *Ex hypothesi*, the legality of a constitution cannot be found within itself. International law purports to offer criteria but they are inapt for the present purpose. Recognition, by which international law purports to confer or endorse constitutional validity, has frequently been withheld for long periods from 'states' undoubtedly functioning under constitutions of one sort or another. Constitutions are simply facts. As facts, we may well make all sorts of intelligent speculations about their origins, functions and prospects. A constitution may simply develop, or be imposed or adopted. It may regulate state activity in a variety of ways. It always stands to be overthrown; how likely this is depends upon how precariously it is in place. For one interested in studying the function of rules as regulating political behaviour within a state, the only relevant question is: 'Is a given constitution effective in this respect?' Effectiveness and stability are both greatly enhanced by acquiescence—the more the people (who are the potential rebels) are content with the existing regime, the more likely it is to remain in charge. To the extent that acquiescence is lacking, force is necessary. Recognition by other states may make economic and political life somewhat easier for the regime in question but will have only a marginal effect upon its stability. Little more can be said.

Note

On Calvert's account it appears that, in the last resort, constitutional legitimacy is parasitic upon efficacy and acquiescence. Is it therefore the case that, if the Capone gang had eventually become so powerful that it defeated the US Government and its agents and took effective control over the US, the rules governing the gang would (if Capone had so wished) have become its constitution? David Feldman suggests not:

> When St. Augustine asked, 'What are states without justice but robber-bands enlarged?' he was putting his finger on a key question for political theory. The difference between bands of robbers and states is that states are, or should be, organised through their constitutions in such a way as to limit the robber-band's capacity to use its powers in arbitrary, anti-social and unaccountable ways. In short, constitutions subject states to moral values and principles, thereby converting brute force into legitimate authority. They do this partly by adhering to traditional

modes of operation where those have acquired their own authority over time, and partly by explaining, interpreting, or changing those modes in the light of currently acceptable normative standards.[4]

DIFFERENT CONCEPTIONS OF 'CONSTITUTIONS'

Some of the complexity in discussing constitutions arises from the fact that the term is used in a number of different ways: Anthony King notes that the *Oxford English Dictionary* has a total of eight definitions.[5] He starts with the simplest and least contentious, whereby a 'constitution' refers to:

> The set of the most important rules and common understandings in any given country that regulate the relations among that country's governing institutions and also the relationship between [those] governing institutions and the people of that country.

As he notes, under this definition, all countries have constitutions, save for collapsed or 'failed states'.[6] Plainly also, under this definition, Britain has a constitution; moreover, it is 'wildly misleading', he argues, to say that it does not have a written constitution: 'What Britain lacks is not a written constitution but a *codified* Constitution, a Constitution with a capital "C", one that has been formally adopted.'[7]

King goes on to argue that the significance of the distinction between 'written' and 'unwritten' constitutions is generally exaggerated. He notes the 'hundreds of pages of constitutional legislation' existing in the UK and concludes that, 'To describe the UK Constitution, against that background, as unwritten, is simply bizarre'.[8]

A King, *The British Constitution* (2007), pp 6–9, 10–13

That said, much of Britain's constitution is, indeed, unwritten. The role of the prime minister is not provided for by statute, the cabinet is not mentioned anywhere in statute law, and a Civil Service Act regulating the relations between civil servants and their political masters has yet to be passed. Similarly, although the institutions and practices of local government are subject to innumerable statutes, no single statute defines the role of local government in Britain's overall constitutional structure. However, the fact that much of Britain's constitution is unwritten does not distinguish the UK from most other countries, including countries with codified, capital-C Constitutions. To take an obvious example, the US Constitution nowhere explicitly empowers US courts to strike down federal statutes and other acts of government on the grounds that they are unconstitutional (as distinct from merely illegal). Those who wrote the US Constitution did assume that the courts in the new

---

4   D Feldman, 'None, one or several? Perspectives on the UK's constitution(s)' [2005] 64(2) CLJ 329, 334–35.

5   *The British Constitution* (2007), p 11.

6   *Ibid*, p 3.

7   *Ibid*, p 5.

8   *Ibid*, p 6.

system would play such a role, but they felt no need, perhaps for that very reason, to draft a formal constitutional provision along those lines. They thought a 'common understanding' rather than a formal rule would suffice. And they were right. Led by Chief Justice John Marshall, the US Supreme Court in *Marbury* v. *Madison* in 1803 struck down a clause of the Judiciary Act 1789 on the grounds of its unconstitutionality. The court did not thereby amend the US Constitution, but it certainly amended the US small-c constitution (albeit along lines that had already been anticipated).

More generally, almost no country with a capital-C Constitution provides in its Constitution for one of the most significant features of any constitutional order: the country's electoral system. The US Constitution makes no provision for the simple-plurality, first-past-the-post electoral system even though that system is employed almost universally in America. The French Constitution is silent on what should be the nature of that country's electoral system, thus enabling French lawmakers to change the system frequently, sometimes at short intervals. Article 38 of the German Constitution states blandly that 'Details [of the electoral system] shall be regulated by a federal law'—and then stops. Yet clearly any democratic country's electoral system constitutes one of the most important rules regulating the relationship between that country's governing institutions and its citizens. The type of electoral system that a country has profoundly influences the structure of its party system, the perticular parties that people choose to vote for, the way in which shares of the people's vote are translated into parliamentary seats, the ways in which governments are formed and the ways in which, having been formed, they proceed to govern.

Not only do capital-C Constitutions quite commonly omit to cover matters of high constitutional importance: they quite commonly contain provisions relating to matters that are of no constitutional importance whatsoever. The aforementioned German Constitution solemnly declares that 'All German merchant vessels shall constitute a unitary merchant fleet.' Even better, the Austrian Constitution contains the following inconsequential provision, which might well have been drawn from an operetta libretto:

> The coat of arms of the Republic of Austria (the Federal coat of arms) consists of an unfettered single-headed, black, gilt-armed and red-tongued eagle on whose breast is imposed a red shield intersected by a silver crosspiece. On its head, the eagle bears a mural crown with three visible merlons. A sundered iron chain rings both talons. The right holds a golden sickle with inward turned blade, the left a golden hammer.

For its part, the Constitution of Iceland insists that 'the President of the Republic shall reside in or near Reykjavik' while the Constitution of Greece states that 'alteration of the contents or terms of a will, codicil or donations as to the provisions benefiting the State or a charitable cause is prohibited'. Capital-C Constitutions are not always the Solon-like documents they are sometimes made out to be.

None of this is to say that codified Constitutions do not matter. Of course they do—or may. The fact that the US Constitution provides that 'the President shall be Commander in Chief of the Army and Navy of the United States' gives the US president enormous power in times of international conflict, as the wars in Korea, Vietnam and Iraq amply demonstrated. It is merely to say that the observer needs to keep his or her eye on the Big Picture—a country's small-c constitution—and not be over-concerned with what happens to be written down and what happens not to be. In the specific case of Britain, although the country is far from acquiring a capital-C Constitution, more and more of its small-c constitution, as we shall see, has come to be written down in recent years.

II

It is worth exploring the implications of this distinction between constitutions and Constitutions a little further, if only in the interests of avoiding confusion.

Because the UK has no capital-C Constitution, it has no legal mechanism designed specifically for the purposes of bringing about changes in its constitution. All upper-case Constitutions contain provisions for their own amendment—usually provisions that call for quite complicated procedures outside the usual norm and requiring some kind of super-majority to be obtained—but a Constitution that does not exist cannot be amended in that sense. Indeed the British constitution is never 'amended'; it is only changed. It can be changed either as a result of changes in politicians' common understandings (often called 'conventions') or as a result of changes in ordinary statute law. In theory, the UK parliament could decide to distinguish between constitutional legislation and other kinds of legislation just as it now distinguishes between money bills and other kinds of bills. But it has never moved to make any such distinction, and, even if it did, the legislation embodying the distinction would itself be ordinary legislation and therefore subject to amendment and repeal. The result is that the British constitution is in many ways remarkably easy to change, and sometimes politicians and others do not even notice that constitutional change—as distinct from other kinds of change—is taking place. That which has not been specially flagged up may pass unnoticed; or, more precisely, its true significance may pass unnoticed.

III

Every country, apart possibly from failed states, has a constitution, but not every country enjoys what political theorists since at least the eighteenth century have called constitutional government. A constitution merely describes a state of affairs, which state of affairs may be good, bad or indifferent. Constitutional government denotes a type of political regime constructed in accordance with certain principles or ideals, which principles or ideals are judged to be good in themselves and against which a given constitutional regime's performance can be, and ought to be, judged.

The ideas of constitutional government and constitutionalism have formed a central part of Western political discourse throughout the modern era—the discourse of practising politicians as well as the discourse of political theorists. The politicians' and the theorists' concepts and language have not always been identical, but they have nevertheless had much the same ideas in mind. America's Founding Fathers set out in 1787 to ordain a constitutional form of government. Germany's founding fathers did the same in 1948 when they drafted the post-war German Constitution, that country's so-called Basic Law.

Constitutionalism as a normative political doctrine rests on three pillars. The first, the most explicitly normative, is that one of the principal purposes of any country's constitution should be to ensure that individuals and organizations are protected against arbitrary and intrusive action by the state. A properly written constitution should provide for the rule of law. It should make it impossible for a country's rulers to abuse their power—to act wilfully, corruptly and in their own interests rather than those of the nation as a whole. Ideally, it should also minimize the chances that incompetent individuals, if they come to power, will be able to inflict the consequences of their incompetence on their fellow citizens. A proper constitution is one that seeks to protect the freedom and autonomy of both individuals and organizations. The watchwords of a properly constituted state are—or should be—caution, moderation, restraint and a decent respect for individual citizens and for the citizenry as a whole.

Constitutionalism's second pillar is concerned specifically with the organization of the state. If the chances of the state's acting arbitrarily, incompetently or in violation of the rule of law are to be minimized, then there is everything to be said for creating a variety of separate state organs and for dispersing power and authority among them. To concentrate power is to increase the chances that it will be misused. The most efficacious means of preventing such misuse is to ensure that power is not concentrated. Hence constitutionalism's emphasis on 'checks and balances' and 'the separation of powers' (a phrase better rendered as 'separated institutions sharing powers'). The constitutionalist advocates the existence of a strong legislative assembly to act as a check on executive power and insists, in particular, on the independence of the judiciary from both the executive and the legislative branches of government. The constitutionalist may also press for the parcelling out of power, not only among the various organs of central government but away from central government to the periphery: to regional, state, provincial, and/or local governments. The constitution of practically every modern state embodies these tenets of constitutionalism—not least the independence of the judiciary—in one form or another.

The third pillar of constitutionalism concerns the relations between the state, however constituted, and the body of citizens. Obviously the rule of law is meant to act as the principal restraint on the state in its relations with citizens; in a constitutional state, the government is supposed to be bound by the law just like everybody else. But constitutionalism also recommends that there should be additional safeguards against the exercise of arbitrary and unwarranted state power. There is inevitably controversy about what the nature of those safeguards should be. There is controversy about whether the safeguards should rest on custom alone or should be enshrined in law. There is also controversy about whether the state should be confined within narrow bounds, as libertarians insist, or whether the state should be permitted a considerably wider remit, as socialists and social democrats insist. But at the beginning of the twenty-first century the prevailing view appears to be that there is no substitute in any properly constituted nation for a formally enacted bill of rights. Continuing debate centres, of course, on what precisely those rights should be.

It goes without saying that constitutional government and democracy are not the same thing—and, indeed, that the claims of constitutional government and those of democracy may conflict. What might be called radical or Jacobin democracy requires that the people should govern, full stop. If the rule of law is what the people want, fine. If not, not. If the separation of powers is what the people want, fine. If not, not. In fact, radical democracy points not towards a separation of powers but towards their concentration in the hands of the people or their appointed agents. Similarly, if the people want to entrench human rights in a formal bill of rights, fine. If not, not. And of course the people may change their minds, so that, if the people really are in charge, the very idea of entrenchment falls: under a radical form of democracy, the people, having introduced a bill of rights, are entitled to abolish that same bill at any time. In practice, of course, every liberal democracy has arrived at some sort of accommodation between the claims of democracy in its radical form and the claims of constitutional government. But the underlying tensions remain. They are perhaps most clearly exemplified in the United States, whose political arrangements embody both an extreme form of constitutionalism, manifested in its codified Constitution and the activities of the Supreme Court, and also, at the same time, a wide range of often extreme democratic claims, manifested in the use in many American states of referendums, popular initiatives and mechanisms for the recall of unpopular office-holders.

Notes

1. Thus the distinction between flexible and rigid constitutions is rather more important in practice than between unwritten and written. More useful ways of distinguishing between constitutions lie in the following: whether the executive and legislative sources of power in the country are separate (as in the USA) or fused; whether the constitution is flexible, that is, changeable like ordinary law, or inflexible, requiring special procedures; whether the state is unitary—controlled by one, sovereign legislature—or federal, in which there are separate spheres of power in the state, with the central government being unable to legislate in areas reserved to he regions. John F McEldowney, adopting Professor KC Wheare's classifications[9] (similar to those listed by Calvert), finds that 'it is at once apparent that the UK has a unitary, flexible constitution whose powers are fused'.[10]

2. King also very usefully distinguishes between the constitution simply as a description of how a country is organised—'what happens'—and the notion of *'constitutionalism'*—a set of propositions about how government *should* be limited, of the kind discussed by Sejersted above.

THE VARIETY OF CONSTITUTIONS

The *content* of constitutions, and their level of detail, tends to vary greatly as well. The following extract from a well-known work outlines the nature and content of three constitutions: those of the United States, France and the Federal Republic of Germany (FRG).[11]

SE Finer, V Bogdanor and B Rudden, *Comparing Constitutions* (1995), Chapter 2

Amendment

The provisions on the means by which a constitution may be amended are of both juridical and political importance, they are themselves an exercise of the constituent power in spelling out how its own creation may be changed; they divide the amending power among people, legislature, and executive, or between a federation and its components; and they may express basic values. The last are revealed in those features stated to be un-amendable: the republican form of government in France, and in Germany the basic human rights and the federal structure.

---

9   KC Wheare, *Modern Constitutions* (1966), pp 4–8.

10 John F McEldowney, *Public Law* (1994), p 4. We will consider in Chapter 6 whether the UK may now be described as having a 'quasi-federal' constitution, following the devolution settlements to Scotland, Wales and Northern Ireland.

11 As published, the book also includes analysis of the constitution of the Russian Federation; the authors have not included these parts.

In the USA, amendments require a special majority in Congress followed by ratification by three-quarters of the states. The last amendment dealt with members' salaries and was adopted in 1992; the 'equal rights amendment' has not yet succeeded. [The US Constitution has only been amended 6 times since 1945]. The French provisions give the President a certain leeway. The amendment bill must be passed by both Houses, but he or she may then either put it to the people or resubmit it to both Houses of Parliament convened together in one body (called Congress), in which case it requires three-fifths of the votes cast. . . .

. . .

By contrast to this process, and mindful of the Weimar provisions for referendum and initiative (which were alleged to have assisted the rise of Hitler), the German Constitution does not involve the people at all in the amendment procedure, but requires a special majority of each House.

. . .

General features

The American constitution is very brief. The founders' determination to limit government, both in range and procedure, explains the design of its first three articles, each devoted to a separate branch of federal power, and all interlocking with a system of checks and balances designed to ensure that neither legislature nor executive acquires undue might. . . . The brevity of the American text is largely offset by its age, by the accretions of customary procedures in the legislative and executive branches, and of course by the enormous achievements and awesome responsibility of the judicial branch of government. . . .

The. . .fundamental concerns of the Basic Law in the FRG [Federal Republic of Germany] are federalism and democracy, both victims of the unitary centralized state which Germany became after 1933. Consequently the text spells out and guarantees two main sets of rights: those of the Federation vis-à-vis the Länder and vice versa, and those of the people vis-à-vis the state. The essentials of both are, as it were, engraved for ever in provisions whose substance is immutable: according to art 9(3) (the 'perpetuity clause') the principles of art 1 (basic human rights) and art 20 (a democratic and social federal state) may not be amended. This is, at least in formal terms, quite different from the position elsewhere: in the UK a parliamentary majority (of votes cast) is sovereign; in the USA. . .no part of the constitution is declared to be unamendable (although there are procedural safeguards of varying strength); while in France only the republican form of government is immune from alteration (art 89, final paragraph).

USA

The American constitution created a federal Union. Secession was neither permitted nor forbidden, but South Carolina's attempt to leave triggered the Civil War of 1861–5. The Congress of the United States was given a list of matters on which it might legislate. The states were told that there were certain things they could not do. Everything else was, according to the Xth Amendment, 'reserved to the States respectively or to the people'. But Congress was given the important powers 'to regulate commerce with foreign nations and among the several states' and to make all laws 'necessary and proper' to carry out its tasks. In this way, the federal competence has grown enormously, although it is worth remembering that a constitutional amendment (the XVIth) was needed in order to permit a federal income tax. The Constitution is declared to be the supreme law of the land and so, in case of conflict, overrides any other federal or state provision. Nonetheless, it should be emphasized that, where the states have jurisdiction, this extends to all branches of government, legislative, executive, and judicial. One result of this is the fifty different versions of the basic areas of criminal and civil law (property, succession, contract, and the like).

Federal Republic of Germany

By contrast with the US text, the provisions dealing with the German federal structure are both lengthy and complex. The Länder have general legislative competence, but there is a list of exclusive federal powers, and a longer list of powers in art 74 which are described as 'concurrent' (a better rendering would be 'alternative'). . . . The provisions for the Land exercise of governmental powers and execution of federal laws (arts 30, 83) mean that—unlike the situation in the USA—there are few federal agencies, and no first or second-instance federal courts within the Länder. Although in theory the Länder have the general residual legislative power, federal law is supreme, and the erosion of local competence has provoked much discussion. . .

Governance

The 1789 French Declaration proclaimed that a society which lacked the separation of powers had no constitution at all. All the states dealt with in this book have, to a greater or lesser extent. . .In the United Kingdom, however, the principle refers mainly to the independence of the judiciary. Executive and legislative powers are at least as closely fused today as they were when Bagehot published *The English Constitution* in 1867.

Political parties find no formal mention in the US Constitution. Given the Nazi law of 1933 which permitted only one party in the Third Reich, it is not surprising that they are specifically mentioned in art 21 of the FRG Constitution (and can be ruled unconstitutional). They appear also in the French. . .texts. . . .

USA

The American Constitution devotes each of its first three articles to a separate branch of government. Legislative powers are vested in a bicameral Congress whose members are elected. The House of Representatives is composed of members apportioned among the states and elected for two years. Each state is represented by two senators, elected for a term of six years, and cannot be deprived of this right without its consent. The Lower House exemplifies the principle of the representation of individuals, the Upper House that of the representation of the geographical units comprising the Federation. The equality of representation in the Senate is, of course, out of all proportion to the size or population of the different states. . . . The Houses are equal in that both must concur to pass any law unlike, for instance, the position in Germany, France. . .and the UK where the Upper House may, in certain circumstances be overruled by the Lower.

The executive power is vested in a President, elected (in formal terms by an electoral college) for four years, who may not serve more than two terms. The Vice-President is elected in the same manner but separately. The American (and French. . .) President can be removed only by impeachment, a process in which the legislature becomes the court. The President selects his or her own cabinet, but presidential appointments require confirmation by the Senate. He or she may veto bills, but can be overruled by special majority of the legislature. Conversely, he or she has to persuade Congress to enact his or her own agenda into legislation.

In short, the main features of the presidential form of government as developed in the USA are the following. The President combines ceremonial status and political power. Legislature and executive are elected separately and for different terms, which means that the President may be of one political party and the majority of the legislature of another. The USA is well accustomed to this while, in the 1980s and 1990s, the French Constitution proved able to withstand the strain of cohabitation between a socialist President and a legislative majority of the right. The presidential system gives the chief executive length of tenure and wide control over subordinates. Furthermore, since the US executive is no part of Congress, there is little temptation for the latter to federalize the whole system and to overlook states' rights. The legislature cannot remove the President save by impeachment, in which the Lower House lays the charge and the Upper House tries the case.

Federal Republic of Germany

. . . Because of its federal structure, Germany has always had a bicameral system. The Bundestag, the Lower House, is elected by popular vote for a four-year term. In contrast to the provisions under both the Empire and Weimar, it can be dissolved only under the very exceptional circumstances of arts 63 and 68. The Upper House (Bundesrat) is selected by neither direct nor indirect elections. It is made up of sixty-eight members nominated by the sixteen Land governments, who are in effect delegates of the government rather than of the people or of the Land legislature. Unlike the US Senate, the number—and voting power—of the members (three, four, or five) depend on the population of the Land they represent. Legislation is by joint action of both Houses, although—as elsewhere—most bills are introduced by the government. The Bundesrat has an absolute veto in certain cases and can otherwise, in the last resort, merely suspend the passage of legislation. Bills duly passed go to the President for formal signature and counter-signature of the Chancellor. The office of President, allegedly abused by Hindenburg after 1930, is shorn of authority and preserved only as that of a largely ceremonial Head of State. The President is no longer directly elected by the people, but indirectly by a Federal Convention of members of the Federal and Land legislatures. He or she is not in charge of the armed forces, and has no emergency powers; appoints the federal judges and ministers, but does not select them and ratifies international Treaties, but usually only with the consent of the legislature. Like other Heads of State, the President's duties include the formal assent to federal statutes: but this is valid only on countersignature by the Chancellor. It is this latter office which carries the real power of Head of Government, and the Chancellor is—in legal terms— rather better protected than the British Prime Minister. The President must appoint to the office the person who obtains a majority of the votes of the members of the Bundestag. Only if no one has such a majority may the President choose whether to appoint the person with a majority of the votes cast or to dissolve the Bundestag. Once installed, the Chancellor nominates and demotes ministers (whose formal appointment and dismissal are for the President) and is well-protected against a 'no confidence' defeat in the legislature. It is not enough for the Bundestag to outvote him; a majority of the members must agree on the alternative Chancellor. Thus 'unnatural' combinations of left and right may defeat a Chancellor but they will not force a resignation as they could in the Weimar Republic. . . .

There is no unlimited power in the executive to dissolve the Bundestag and call an election. On the other hand, the Chancellor may use the 'no confidence' procedure in order to demonstrate ability to govern with authority. If his or her motion for a vote of confidence fails, the President may be asked to dissolve the Lower House; and the only way the Bundestag can stop this is by promptly electing another Chancellor by a majority of its members. This device was used by Willy Brandt after an unsuccessful attempt to oust him in 1972. He put a motion of confidence to the Bundestag, planning to lose it, asked the President to dissolve Parliament, and won the next election. . . .

France

The French system has features of both the presidential and the parliamentary models. . . . The President is far from being merely a titular Head of State. Since 1962 he or she is directly elected by the people, has arbitral powers under art 5, and emergency powers under art 16, and signs the regulations emanating from the executive's very extensive lawmaking powers (arts 37, 13). In association with the government he or she can present bills to the people to enact by referendum, thereby bypassing the parliament, and can dissolve the National Assembly and call new elections. By contrast, the legislature is trammelled. Its power to enact laws is laid down in terms not merely of form but of subject-matter, and (under art 41) the government may block any bill which does not fall within the areas listed in art 34. Much of its internal procedure is now defined in the constitution and this gives the Prime Minister and his or her Cabinet great procedural advantages over the Opposition.

. . .

The judicial branch

When it comes to the judiciary, separation of powers is taken quite seriously. . .In all the systems here dealt with, judges are independent and irremovable. . . .In the USA and UK it is not stated but is the case.

The only topic which merits brief discussion here is the relation between the constitution, the courts, and the legislature. For almost 200 years the USA has led the way in discussion and practice in this area. . .Art VI provides that the Constitution and federal laws made under it and treaties 'shall be the supreme law of the land' and shall bind state judges: thus the supremacy of federal over state law is clearly stated. But nothing expressly subordinates federal legislation to the federal constitution and art III on the judicial power does not in so many words confer jurisdiction to do this. Nonetheless the Supreme Court assumed such a jurisdiction and in 1803 held that 'an Act of the Legislature repugnant to the Constitution is void' (*Marbury v Madison*). As a result, any court of general jurisdiction seems to have power to declare any statute unconstitutional. . . .

The general continental European pattern is much more recent (dating from the 1920s) and tends to differ from the American model in a number of respects. First, the whole topic is expressly dealt with in the constitutional text. Second, the tribunal given a power of constitutional review is quite separate from the ordinary courts of general jurisdiction. Third, and a consequence of this, its jurisdiction is exclusive: other courts cannot decide issues of constitutionality but must, where such questions need to be settled to dispose of the case in hand, refer them to the Constitutional Court. Fourth, process may be instituted in a number of different ways: by ordinary courts in the manner just described; by ordinary citizens complaining that their individual constitutional rights are being infringed by some legislation; by certain high officials (President, Speaker etc.) seeking, in the absence of any particular dispute, to obtain a general and 'abstract' ruling on the constitutionality of a statute; and occasionally the constitutional tribunal is even given the power to review legislation on its own initiative. Finally, the Court's decision that a particular legislative provision is unconstitutional is itself given the force of law so as to bind all courts and officials. . .

The German Constitution sets up a Constitutional Court, the name emphasizing its main function. . . One most interesting function is that of ruling on the constitutionality of political parties (art 21(2)), though it can be seized only by legislature or government, and has in fact heard only two such cases: in 1952 the neo-Nazi Socialist Reich Party and in 1956 the Communist Party were held to be unconstitutional. It also handles disputes as to jurisdiction between Federal organs (art 93(1)(1) and between Federal and State organs (arts 93(1)(3), 84(4)). At the request of the government or one-third of the Bundestag members, it may rule on the compatibility of legislation with the constitution—and thus does so in the abstract, in the absence of any litigated case. During ordinary lawsuits, however, a German court which thinks that legislation might be unconstitutional, and needs to know in order to decide the dispute before it, must refer the question to the Constitutional Court (art 100). . . . A German court may also ask the Federal Constitutional Court whether a rule of international law directly creates rights for the litigants before it (arts 100(2), 25).

In all these types of proceeding, access to the German Constitutional Court is open only to governmental and parliamentary entities and the courts. But a 1969 amendment incorporated in the Constitution an avenue previously opened by statute (art 93.1(4a) and (4b)) whereby anyone who considers that his constitutional rights have been violated by the state may, after exhausting all other legal remedies, file a complaint directly with the Constitutional Court.

Just as the French institutional structure is unique, so is its forum for constitutional review. The body in question is, quite deliberately, not established as, or given the name of, a court: it is the Constitutional Council. Its members sit for only nine years, save for ex-Presidents who are ex officio members for life. Three of the appointed members are selected by the President of the Republic, and three each by the Speakers of each House. They are not necessarily trained lawyers, but tend to have held high ministerial or academic office.

This forum is an innovation of the Fifth Republic, and its primary functions may be summed up by saying that the Constitutional Council judges only the Parliament; and the Parliament is judged only by the Constitutional Council. . . .

The Constitution allows any bill—before promulgation—to be referred to the Council for an assessment of the bill's conformity with the Constitution (art 61 para. 2), and goes on to enact that a provision declared unconstitutional can be neither promulgated nor implemented. . . . The Constitutional Council has held a number of bills to be unconstitutional for contravention of human rights and has become, *de facto* if not *de jure*, a constitutional court.

However, the following points need to be stressed. First, statutes which have been promulgated are, as in the UK, entirely immune from constitutional challenge in any jurisdiction whatever. Second, and following from this, ordinary citizens and ordinary courts may not refer matters to the Council. That power is reserved to the President, the prime minister, the two Speakers, and (since a 1974 amendment) any sixty Deputies or Senators. But this last group is, of course, usually the Opposition which frequently refers Government bills in the hope that it will achieve by a lawsuit what it could not attain by a vote. . . .

Human rights
The first ten amendments to the US Constitution commit the Union to a respect for certain basic rights, and the XIVth Amendment subjects the states to the same discipline. The

rights in question are usually expressed by a negative: Congress shall make no law abridging the freedom of the press; the right to keep and bear arms shall not be infringed; the right to be secure shall not be violated; no person shall be deprived of life, liberty, or property without due process of law; no fact tried by a jury shall be otherwise re-examined than according to the rule of the common law.

The 1789 French Declaration, although somewhat more rhetorical, covers much the same ground and, as we have seen, operates via the 1958 preamble and the powers of the Constitutional Council to restrict the powers of the legislature. The Bill of Rights is deliberately placed at the very beginning of the German constitution (arts 1–19). The rights are acknowledged to be inviolable and inalienable, directly enforceable, and binding on legislature, executive, and judiciary. Furthermore the provisions which describe them are, as we have seen, entrenched against any amendment of their essentials. They are not all, however, expressed in absolute terms. On the contrary, the text seeks to balance the rights of any given individual against those of others, for instance to prevent their being used 'to offend against the constitutional order or against morality' (art 2(1)). But 'the essential content of a basic right may never be encroached upon' (art 19(2)). The society in which these rights are to be enjoyed is that of a representative democracy with separation of powers, described in art 20 as a democratic, social, and federal state in which all state authority emanates from the people, who exercise it by elections and voting and by specific legislative, executive, and judicial organs. Furthermore, the legislator is bound by the constitution, and the executive and judiciary by the law *stricto sensu*—and by justice.

. . . [The rights] are the standard commitments to freedom of personality, belief, expression, assembly, movement, occupation, and property, and the assertion of a right of privacy, of immunity from unauthorized search and seizure, and of a right to judicial protection against the state, the maxim that 'property imposes duties', the guarantee of trade union rights, the provision that the means of production may be nationalized, and the inclusion of the word 'social' in the constitutional description of the state. The Christian heritage ensured that the preamble mentions God, that freedom may not be used to offend against morality, and that the issue of private, including religious, education is fully covered.

. . . But the Bill of Rights is not, and is not intended to be, a set of merely procedural safeguards of the individual. The German constitution is imbued with a ranked set of values of which the most basic is the principle of human dignity, and comes equipped with a unique mechanism for its own and for their protection. Anyone who abuses his or her constitutional freedoms 'in order to combat the free democratic basic order shall forfeit these basic rights' (art 18), and 'all Germans have the right to resist anyone seeking to abolish the constitutional order' (art 20(4)).

Note

It will be noted that there is a great deal of variation in the above-described Constitutional orders. The supreme executive office of the President is, in France, far more powerful, vis-a-vis the legislature, than are the offices of President and Chancellor combined in Germany. The Constitutional Council in France has no counterpart in the other states described; the powers of the French President to legislate by putting measures direct to popular referendums would probably be seen as a usurpation of the legislature in the other countries. The UK is often criticised for its lax approach to the Separation of Powers doctrine (see Chapter 3), particularly in relation to the near fusion of the executive and legislative branches. However we can see already that there is much greater variation in the four states described concerning the relationship between the executive and legislative branches than in relation to the separation of powers as connoting the independence of the judiciary, which is much more strict and uniform.

THE EXISTENCE AND NATURE OF THE UK CONSTITUTION

The nature and content of the above constitutions give us a useful basis of comparison with the UK constitution. Given its uncodified nature, by necessity, constitutional rules and norms in the UK are drawn from a variety of domestic and international legal and non-legal sources; the following extract outlines the most important.

**P Leyland, *The Constitution of the United Kingdom:
A Contextual Analysis* (2007), pp 20–25**

STATUTE LAW

In the United Kingdom the basic principle of the constitution is the doctrine of parliamentary sovereignty. Since the Bill of Rights of 1689 the courts have recognised Acts of Parliament as the highest source of law. In one sense it might be true to say that all statutes passed by Parliament which have not been repealed are part of the constitution. This is because each one has been passed to set out or refine particular areas of law and there is a coincidence between ordinary law and the constitution. However, in practical terms, it is obvious that certain statutes are of special *constitutional* importance. The Petition of Right 1628 concerned the principle of no taxation without representation. The Bill of Rights 1689, although not a modern Bill of Rights, as discussed in chapter one secured a Protestant succession to the monarchy (a position that was confirmed by the Act of Settlement 1700). The Bill of Rights also formally confirmed that the seat of power had swung towards Parliament as part of a constitutional monarchy.

   The nature of constitutional statutes was considered in *Thoburn v Sunderland City Council* [[2003] 3WLR 247]. While Laws LJ did not set out any special test to determine the question of what would qualify, it was explained that constitutional statutes are pieces of legislation which condition the legal relationship between citizen and state in some general, overarching manner, or which enlarge or diminish the scope of what might be regarded as fundamental constitutional rights. A number of important constitutional statutes which will be the subject of discussion in later chapters were recognised by Laws LJ as falling into this category. The Acts of Union with Scotland in 1707 and with Ireland in 1800 dealt with arrangements for combining the English Parliament first with the Scottish Parliament and then the Irish Parliament. The Parliament Act 1911 set limits on the powers of the House of Lords in regard to legislation. The Representation of the People Act 1918 extended the vote to all men over 21 and women over 30, and the Representation of People Act 1969 reduced the voting age so that all adults over 18 could vote. The European Communities Act 1972 incorporated the Treaty of Rome and in so doing placed important limitations on the sovereignty of the Westminster Parliament. The Scotland Act 1998, the Government of Wales Act 1998, and the Northern Ireland Act 1998 set out the principles for devolution. The Human

Rights Act 1998 had the effect of incorporating the ECHR directly into English law and in so doing provides the United Kingdom with what is, in effect, a bill of rights.

THE COMMON LAW

In a system where judicial precedent applies, judicial decisions are binding and are used to develop the law on a case-by-case basis. The common law has always been an important source of the constitution. Certain aspects of private law, particularly concerning contract and tort, are comprised of rules originating from judicial decisions. There are particular landmark cases which have expanded the common law in a constitutional context. These decisions remain of constitutional significance. For example, the case of *Entick v Carrington* [(1765) 19 State Tr l029] concerned trespass and placed limits on powers of the Crown and Secretary of State to interfere with the person or property of the citizen without lawful authority. More recently, the UK Home Secretary was found to be in contempt of court for ignoring an order of the High Court in *M v Home Office* [[1994] 1 AC 377] (discussed in chapter three). However, it is important to note that decisions of the courts (including the House of Lords) may be amended and overridden by later statutes, eg the decision in *Burmah Oil v Lord Advocate* [[1965] AC 75] prompted the UK Parliament to pass the War Damage Act 1965, which had retrospective effect. The courts accept the validity of Acts of Parliament and thus validate the concept of parliamentary sovereignty. Although they do not directly challenge legislation, part of their role is to interpret statutes under established rules of statutory interpretation (see chapter seven).

EUROPEAN UNION LAW

The European Communities Act 1972, which came into force on 1 January 1973, made the law of the European Community (now the European Union (EU)) an important constitutional source. In *Van Gend en Loos* [Case 26/62 [1963] ECR 1 at 12] the European Court of Justice had explained the implications for member states of becoming a member:

The Community [now EU] constitutes a new legal order of international law for the benefit of which the States have limited their Sovereign rights . . . Independently of the legislation of member states, Community law therefore not only imposes obligations on individuals but is also intended to confer upon them rights which become part of their legal heritage.

Some categories of EU law have direct effect, which means that any rights or obligations enjoyed by or imposed on any individual under the Treaties can be enforced in the English courts. This body of law is confined to those areas covered by the Treaty of Rome 1957 and subsequent Treaties. Each Treaty (ie the Maastricht, Amsterdam, and Nice Treaties) has been incorporated into UK domestic law by statute. The law emanating from Europe which applies in the United Kingdom includes regulations, directives, and decisions. EU membership also means that rulings from the European Court of Justice can be binding on domestic courts within the United Kingdom. The importance of the EU was recognised by Lord Denning in *Bulmer v Bollinger* [[1974] 2 All ER 1226] when he famously described the Treaty of Rome as being 'like an incoming tide. It flows into the estuaries and up the rivers. It cannot be held back, Parliament has decreed that the Treaty is henceforth to be part of our law.' Where it applies, EU law operates as a higher order law and will have the effect of overriding domestic legal provisions.

EUROPEAN CONVENTION ON HUMAN RIGHTS

Since the Human Rights Act (HRA) 1998 came into force in October 2000 the ECHR is incorporated as part of UK law. The ECHR can be regarded as amounting to a constitutional charter of rights. As we shall see in later chapters, the ECHR is an international treaty setting out basic individual rights including: right to life; liberty and security; prohibition of torture and slavery; right to fair trial; no punishment without law; right to respect for privacy and family life; freedom of thought, conscience, and religion; freedom of expression; freedom of assembly and association; and prohibition of discrimination. All public bodies, including the courts, are legally required to act in a way which is compatible with the above rights, and a remedy may be sought if these citizen rights are breached.

LEGAL TREATISES

The lack of a codified constitution has meant that academic and legal treatises which describe and analyse the nature of the constitution as it has evolved assume special status. For example, there are classic works that may be cited with authority when seeking to establish how the constitution operates.

THE LAW AND CUSTOMS OF PARLIAMENT

The law and customs of Parliament refers to the resolutions of the two Houses of Parliament which establish parliamentary practice (standing orders of the House). This body of rules is of great political importance and it ranges from the regulation of debates to the functions of the leaders of the government and opposition. These rules can be changed by MPs and peers. For example, the recommendations of the Select Committee on Procedure (1978) were adopted following the 1979 general election resulting in the introduction of the House of Commons Departmental Select Committees to scrutinise the work of government departments. It is important to note that as parliamentary rules and procedures are established by standing orders, they fall outside the scope of both legislation and common law.

THE ROYAL PREROGATIVE

Many powers are exercised by ministers and officials under primary or secondary legislation, but the *royal prerogative* refers to those powers which have been left over from the period when the monarch was directly involved in the process of government These remaining powers, now mainly exercised by ministers, include: making treaties; declaring war; deploying the armed forces; regulating the civil service; and granting royal pardons. The prerogative powers continue to be important for the operation of government in these areas, and the prerogative powers have been recognised by judges in developing case-law. (The nature and extent of prerogative powers are discussed in more detail in chapter four.)

PART II: CONSTITUTIONAL CONVENTIONS

Conventions are a particularly important source of the UK constitution and they are also crucial to understanding how the constitution functions. [In the next chapter conventions will be discussed in more detail.] An observer of the UK constitution would build up a very incomplete account of its workings if attention was given only to legal rules, since conventions, in the words of one commentator, 'provide the flesh which clothes the dry bones of the law.' It is evident that: 'The legal structure of the constitution is everywhere penetrated, transformed and given efficacy by conventions.' Conventions are the source of the non-legal rules of the constitution. They may be characterised as being associated with laws but at the same time they are distinct from them. They lubricate the formal machinery of government and assist in making government work. In this sense they have an important *practical* dimension. It is very difficult to settle constitutional disputes without understanding them. Moreover, conventions allow what would otherwise be a rigid legal framework to be kept up to date with the changing needs of government because they are capable of evolving.

Aside from its diversity of sources, perhaps the most remarkable characteristic of the UK's constitution is its almost entirely flexible nature. This was noted by King above, and reflected in Jennings' vivid description of it as having 'not been made but. . .grown' and may be seen in the rather *ad hoc* mechanisms which the UK Government has for dealing with constitutional change, mechanisms that have received greater attention recently, due to the great outburst of reforming activity since 1997, described at the beginning of this chapter. When the Constitution Committee of the House of Lords wrote a report in 2001 on 'The Process of Constitutional Change',[12] it noted that there had been a major change to the way proposals for such change were handled within Government, and that the Lord Chancellor's Department (LCD) was the lead department, numerous responsibilities for constitutional change having been transferred to it from the Home Office. At the same time, the Constitutional Secretariat within the Cabinet Office was dismantled. The Committee comments:

> [The Secretariat had been] the unifying element at official level. . . set up immediately after the general election in 1997 to work alongside departments with lead responsibility for each element in the programme of constitutional reform. It had the task of servicing the collective decision-making necessary to deliver the Government's objectives and a co-ordinating role in bringing together interested departments and ensuring cohesion across the programme as a whole (para 8).

As the Committee went on to point out:

> the creation of the LCD as a Ministry of Justice and Constitutional Affairs was more by accident than design, resulting in a department that comes new to the culture of dealing with issues as 'constitutional' issues. . .
> 46 The evidence presented to us suggested that the transfer of responsibility for a number of constitutional issues to the LCD was the product of a desire to tidy up Government and to free the Home Office to concentrate on such issues as law and order and drug enforcement.. . .
> 48 Professor Hazell pointed out that the LCD's website has a promising button headed 'Constitutional Issues' but when you click on to it and go to the Constitutional Policy Division 'you find a wonderful ragbag of some of the functions that came over from the Home Office. . .I applaud the fact that the Lord Chancellor's Department has become in effect the Ministry of Justice and Constitutional Affairs. For the moment I lament that it has not yet fully recognised that or brought together constitutional affairs within the department in a much better integrated portfolio'.
> 49 This absence of expertise in dealing with constitutional issues as constitutional issues might not be so serious had the Constitution Secretariat of the Cabinet, which embodied such expertise, remained in existence. We are thus in a situation where there is no developed expertise to ensure co-ordination within the LCD and across Government.

---

12   The Constitution Committee, 'Changing the Constitution: The Process of Constitutional Change', HL 69 (2001–02).

Notes

1. The above description and analysis indicate clearly the casual and *ad hoc* nature of the UK's approach to its 'constitution'. In a delightfully revealing passage in the report, the Lord Chancellor said that: 'The Government...do not have a definition of the constitution and a pragmatic view is taken as to "whether any particular proposed measure should be regarded as constitutional"' [para 60].

2. Moreover, the pace of change to the institutional way in which Government handles constitutional reform has not slackened. As discussed in detail in Chapter 3, the 2003–05 constitutional changes culminating in the Constitutional Reform Act 2005 led at first to the creation of the Department of Constitutional Affairs—to which most of the business of the Lord Chancellor's department was transferred; however in May 2007 the DCA was itself discontinued and its business transferred to the Ministry of Justice (which also acquired certain responsibilities, including prisons, from the Home Office. The sequence may be delightfully illustrated by a little exercise in 'googling'. Enter a search for 'the Lord Chancellor's Department' and you are given a link to the DCA; that site announces in turn that its powers have been transferred to the Ministry of Justice (see further Chapter 12, pp 616–617).

3. There was an outburst of excited talk about radical constitutional reform in the wake of the MP's expenses scandal;[13] a good sample of the ideas being discussed may be found in the 'New Politics' section of the *Guardian* newspaper.[14] The episode strikingly epitomised the points made above about the *ad hoc* way in which constitutional change comes about in the UK: the proposals for constitutional reform floated after the scandal were raised primarily with the aim of repairing political damage and often appeared as short term tactics, rather than long term strategies for real change; moreover, it appears that certain specific proposals were introduced with the idea of 'wrong-footing' the opposition to gain political advantage rather than genuine constitutional improvement.[15] Moreover, while the Brown Government brought forward the rather grandly titled *Governance of Britain: Constitutional Renewal* Green[16] and White Papers,[17] later followed by a draft Bill, and, in 2009 a Bill that was enacted as the Consitutional Reform and Governance Act 2010, these changes do not amount to anything like a systematic constitutional renewal. Rather, the package amounts to a jumble of reforms, some of which are significant in principle (those in relation to the prerogative) but very cautious, some of which were minor (demonstrations near Parliament, flying the flag on public buildings) and some of which were dropped in the end (reform of the office of the Attorney General) and some that seemed unclear from the outset (proposals for a British Bill of Rights and Responsibilities). Those parts of the 2009 Bill that placed the Civil Service on a statutory footing are of real significance, and are considered in Chapter 12, pp 619–620). The particular provisions of this reform package are considered in the relevant chapters. But it is important to be clear at this point about their overall significance. As the House of Commons Public Administration Select Committee in 2008 noted:

---

13   Above, n 3. The episode and its aftermath in terms of reform of the regulatory mechanisms governing MPs' interests and expenses is considered in Chapter 10.

14   www.guardian.co.uk/commentisfree/series/politics-and-reform.

15   As will appear in subsequent chapters, there was much political jockeying for position both over ending the self-regulation of Parliament (Chapter 10) and Lords Reform (Chapter 9).

16   July 2007 Cm 7170.

17   March 2008 Cm 7343-I.

The proposals in the draft bill and white paper that we have examined would not, as the Prime Minister suggested last July, create 'a new British constitutional settlement that entrusts more power to Parliament and the British people'. They certainly do not involve the Prime Minister and Executive 'surrender[ing] or limit[ing] their powers' to any meaningful degree.[18]

4. Barendt discusses the indeterminate and—as some see it—unsatisfactory nature of the UK Constitution in the following essay, which is cast in the form of a review of Vernon Bogdanor's *Politics and the Constitution* (1996).

E Barendt, 'Is there a United Kingdom constitution?' (1997) 17(1) *Oxford Journal of Legal Studies* 137–46

. . . Bogdanor writes in his first essay, *The Political Constitution*, that the Constitution can be reduced to eight words: What the Queen in Parliament enacts is law. Leaving aside the consequences of accession to the European Community, there are no legal constraints on the legislative supremacy of Parliament. The legislature is controlled by the majority political party and every four or five years the electorate. (But provided the consent of the House of Lords is obtained, governments may lawfully postpone elections.) There are in short, as is well known, no legally enforceable guarantees against tyrannical government, or in other words we have what Lord Hailsham (when in opposition) termed an 'elective dictatorship'. There is a widespread, though not universal, view that this is profoundly unsatisfactory. . . .

Obviously there is a United Kingdom Constitution in some. . .senses. As Bogdanor, a political scientist, implies in his Introduction, there is clearly a constitution in the sense of a 'power map', outlining where power lies, explaining how it is exercised and so on. This is the constitution in the descriptive sense [i.e. by the simple definition noted by King above at p 7). There are also laws and decisions of a constitutional character, that is, rules which would form part of a codified constitution for the United Kingdom if it had one. To give just two straightforward examples, the common law concerning the existence and control of the Crown's prerogative powers, and the provisions in the Bill of Rights 1689 vindicating the (legislative) powers of Parliament, are clearly constitutional in substance. Moreover, these principles are normative. They limit the scope of the executive's power to legislate, as the House of Lords held recently in the *Fire Brigades Union* case, and have required the court to determine what counts as an Act of Parliament. So it will not do to say that the terms constitution and constitutional are only properly used in the United Kingdom in a descriptive sense. The complaint that there is no Constitution in the United Kingdom either means that only codified constitutions merit this description, or, more seriously, that in the absence of legally enforceable guarantees protecting the freedom of the citizen (and perhaps an effective separation of powers) it is improper to apply the term to our arrangements. The first charge can be dismissed relatively easily. . . .

Much more serious is the point that a constitutional text without legally enforceable guarantees of citizens' freedoms and a proper balance or separation of powers scarcely merits the description of a constitution. . .the rise of written constitutions in the nineteenth century occurred to meet the demand for limits on previously absolute government. The development was inspired by the principle of constitutionalism, a principle linked to, but

---

significantly different from, those of liberalism and democracy. Liberalism has clearly been concerned among other things with the province of law, but has little to say about the structure of government and the balance of powers. Democracy, with its emphasis on majority rule, is on one view fundamentally antithetical to the principal demand of constitutionalism, that the concentration of power in the hands of any institution of government is dangerous and that it should so far as practicable be dispersed. Indeed, the separation of powers in some form is arguably the essence of constitutionalism. However, there are plenty of countries which have constitutions but which do not observe the principles of constitutionalism. One-party States where opposition and the press are systematically repressed may still have a text described as 'the constitution'. Such States have what Giovanni Sartori has termed 'nominal' or 'facade' constitutions; the former are perhaps equivalent to Bogdanor's 'power maps', while the latter pretend to guarantee fundamental freedoms, but behind the facade it is a different story, as it was under the constitutions of the Soviet Union. Sartori argues persuasively that the terms 'constitution' and 'constitutional' should be limited to those arrangements which do observe the principles of constitutionalism: 'real'. . .constitutions. Otherwise we must conclude that a tyrannical government behaves constitutionally when it imprisons (or executes) the opposition, provided only it observes the legal forms.

. . . How should we characterize the UK Constitution? Is it to be viewed now as a 'facade', a curtain behind which some monstrous political melodrama is enacted? Vernon Bogdanor's essays fully chronicle the respects in which our arrangements fail to satisfy the principles of constitutionalism. Power is concentrated in the hands of the Prime Minister and Cabinet, almost always able through party discipline to secure the passage of its legislative programme. The present [Thatcher] Government has removed competing centres of power by abolishing the GLC and the metropolitan borough councils, and elsewhere has significantly cramped the freedom of local authorities. The financing and organization of the political parties, which in government exercise enormous power and influence, is almost entirely unregulated by law. In the final analysis the courts cannot protect fundamental rights when it is the clear intention of Parliament to remove them or to empower ministers to stop their exercise. . . . This looks like a 'facade' constitution. Moreover, its contours are uncertain, as is inevitable with uncodified and to some extent even unwritten arrangements. (Some (alleged) constitutional conventions are reduced to writing only in the texts of constitutional law books.)

Dicey would have disagreed with this assessment. Parliamentary supremacy would not in his view lead to authoritarian government because of the internal and external limits on its exercise, the existence of constitutional conventions, and the rule of law doctrine. Conventions ensure the responsibility of Ministers to Parliament, and through the House of Commons to the electorate, a role also discharged by the internal limit that legislation be politically acceptable (or at least not repugnant) to the majority of the public. The rule of law distinguishes proper legislation, Acts of Parliament, from executive decrees and from resolutions of one House. While the rule of law, for what it is worth, is guaranteed by the courts, Bogdanor is correct to point out that otherwise the values of constitutionalism are protected politically. The existence, scope, and application of conventions are determined by those bound by them, the politicians themselves. As Bogdanor puts it (at 26) '. . .the peculiarity of the British constitution is that it lacks an umpire. It is the players themselves, the government of the day, who interpret the way in which the rules are to be applied'. Indeed, the rules are made up as the game is played. Hence, Prime Ministers are free to determine when the principles of Cabinet collective responsibility apply, a freedom exploited by both Wilson and Callaghan to allow for dissent among members of their Governments over membership of the European Community. We can be quite sure that if a General Election produces a hung Parliament, politicians will debate in party political terms the appropriate conventions which 'regulate' the discretion of the Queen to choose her Prime Minister. [On this, see further Chapter 12, pp 604–608.

Notes

1. It should be noted that this piece has dated in some important respects, although its central thrust arguably remains still sound. Barendt noted that: 'The financing and organization of the political parties, which in government exercise enormous power and influence, is almost entirely unregulated by law.' Following the Political Parties, Elections and Referendums Act 2000, and Political Parties and Elections Act 2009, this is no longer the case. Chapter 2 notes the increasing recent tendency to codify constitutional conventions in codes of practice or resolutions of the Houses of Parliament, so that they are no longer simply made up by the players. The article was written before the Human Rights Act 1998: however, it remains the case under that instrument that, as Barendt pointed out: 'In the final analysis the courts cannot protect fundamental rights when it is the clear intention of Parliament to remove them or to empower ministers to stop their exercise. . .'. We shall return later in this chapter to the notion that in the UK, 'the values of constitutionalism are protected politically'.

2. It is, of course, the flexibility of the British constitution that is its most remarkable feature. Within the UK there is no written constitution which has a higher status than the rest of the law. The body of rules relating to the structure, functions and powers of the organs of state, their relationship to one another and to the private citizen, is derived from common law, statute and constitutional conventions. Therefore, the constitution does not impose express limits on what may be done by ordinary legislation in the way that many constitutions do. The legislative competence of the UK Parliament is formally unlimited (save to an extent that remains unclear by directly enforceable EU law (see Chapter 5)). The lack of any supreme constitutional law means that no Parliament may bind its successors or be bound by its predecessors and the courts cannot declare Acts of Parliament unconstitutional. Thus, every aspect of the constitution (with the possible exception of parliamentary sovereignty itself (see Chapter 4) is subject to change by ordinary Act of Parliament, a strong contrast to the constitutions of the USA, Germany and France, as we have seen. O Hood Phillips stresses that such flexibility cannot be directly attributable to the (largely) unwritten nature of the UK constitution, pointing out by way of example that 'the constitution of Singapore is written but entirely flexible'.[19] It should be noted, however, that the new legislatures set up in Scotland, Wales and Northern Ireland as part of the devolution settlement, bring to UK constitutional law the concept and practice of limited legislatures, since all are bound by EU law and the European Convention on Human Rights, as well as detailed rules governing their competency in terms of subject matter—and their legislation is subject to what is in effect constitutional review if it is thought that they may have acted outside their competence—see further Chapter 6.[20]

---

19 O Hood Phillips, *Constitutional and Administrative Law*, 7th edn (1987), p 7.

20 We are indebted to the anonymous reviewer for pointing out the significance of this point for the discussion here. S/he noted in particular ss 99 and 101 of the Government of Wales Act 2006 which permit the (Welsh) Counsel General, the (UK) Attorney General, or the Secretary of State for Wales to refer a proposed Assembly Measure to the Supreme Court to determine whether or not it is within the Assembly's legislative competence.

3. While this radical subjugation of all other aspects of the constitution, however fundamental, to parliamentary sovereignty leads Barendt to conclude only that the UK has an unsatisfactory constitution, some commentators go further.

FF Ridley, 'There is no British constitution: A dangerous case of the Emperor's clothes' (1988) 41 *Parliamentary Affairs* 340, 342, 359–60

Everywhere save Britain the constitution is defined as a special category of law. British usage dissolves the distinction between constitutional law and other laws because British courts recognise no such distinction. British political scientists, for their part, dissolve the distinction between law and other rules of behaviour because they are not much interested in law: for them, the constitution is practice. . .

Use of the word constitution as the manner in which a policy is organised, the main characteristic of its governmental system is undoubtedly the historic one. By the end of the 18th century, however, the word came to have another meaning. The American War of Independence and the French Revolution marked a turning point after which the new meaning became universal, Britain excepted. It applied to a special form of law embodied as a matter of convenience in a single document. As used elsewhere, it is now a term of law not politics. Constitutions therefore have certain essential characteristics, none of them found in Britain. Without these characteristics, it is impossible to distinguish a constitution from a description of the system of government in a way that is analytically precise. Without them, it is impossible to say that a country has a constitution in the current international sense of the word. More important, lest this be thought a linguistic quibble, without them a system of government lacks the legitimacy a constitution gives and a political system the protection it offers.

The characteristics of a constitution are as follows:

1 It establishes, or constitutes, the system of government. Thus it is prior to the system of government, not part of it, and its rules cannot be derived from that system.

2 It therefore involves an authority outside and above the order it establishes. This is the notion of the constituent power ('pouvoir constituant'—because we do not think along these lines, the English translation sounds strange). In democracies that power is attributed to the people, on whose ratification the legitimacy of a constitution depends and, with it, the legitimacy of the governmental system.

3 It is a form of law superior to other laws—because (i) it originates in an authority higher than the legislature which makes ordinary law and (ii) the authority of the legislature derives from it and is thus bound by it. The principle of hierarchy of law generally (but not always) leads to the possibility of judicial review of ordinary legislation.

4 It is entrenched—(i) because its purpose is generally to limit the powers of government, but also (ii) again because of its origins in a higher authority outside the system. It can thus only be changed by special procedures, generally (and certainly for major change) requiring reference back to the constituent power.

The term British constitution is near meaningless. . . It is impossible to isolate parts of the system of government to which the label constitutional may authoritatively be attached. There is no test to discriminate between constitutional and less than constitutional elements since labelling has no defined consequence, unlike countries where constitutions are a higher form of law. If used descriptively, as Wheare and others suggest, it is simply a fancy-dress way of saying the British system of government is at best redundant. More dangerous, those who talk of a British constitution may mislead themselves into thinking that there are parts of the system to which a special sanctity attaches. But in that normative sense the term is equally meaningless. When significant parts of the system are reformed, we have no test to tell us whether the outcome is an improper breach of the constitutional order, a proper amendment, or whether the reformed institutions were not part of the 'constitution' at all. I may be told that this is an academic quibble since our democratic politicians know what is of constitutional significance in our way of government, approach such matters differently from other reforms, and are politically if not legally constrained. That, however, is not the case. Our system of government is being changed, with increasing disregard for tradition, the only unwritten rules to which one might appeal as 'constitutional' principles.

There is cause for concern about the muddled way we think about the British 'constitution'; there is even greater cause for concern about the political consequences of its nature. It is sometimes said that our 'constitution' is now under stress as major changes occur far more rapidly than before in its written and unwritten parts. Is this due to changing ideas about how the British system of government should be organised, widely held, or is it simply that the Government of the day is using its power to change the system in the pursuit of its own political goals? Is the constitutional order evolving or is it under attack? We have moved from consensus to conflict in politics: have we moved in that direction, too, as regards our constitutional order, taking that to mean the broad principles underlying the way government is organised and power exercised? Many old principles no longer command universal agreement and there are well-supported demands for new principles. We have had debates on the entrenchment of rights; on federalism or regional devolution as against the unitary state; on the case for consensus rather than majority as a basis for government; on the relative weight of national versus local mandates and the independence of local government; on the duty of civil servants; on electoral reform with all its implications for the operation of government; on who should define the national interest; on open government and official secrecy; on complementing representative democracy by referenda and other forms of participation—and much else. Political disagreement and disagreement on the proper constitutional order are linked. An ideologically-committed Government, determined to implement its policies, will support different constitutional principles from those who want consensus policy-making; those concerned primarily with individual freedom and the rights of the public will support different principles from those who want strong government—and so on. Since opinion is now deeply divided on so many issues, one can probably no longer talk of the constitutional order as if it were a reflection of public opinion.

Notes

1. Two criticisms may be made of Ridley's analysis. First, due to its insistence that any constitution worth the name must be entrenched, it excludes constitutions, like those of Singapore, which are fully written (in a constitutional document) but entirely flexible. It may therefore be seen to distance academic analysis too far from political reality (though of course Ridley's whole thesis is that the word 'constitution', having been used politically, is in danger of becoming so vague a term as to be practically meaningless). Second, he arguably goes too far in alleging that there are no

parts of the British constitutional order to which any special sanctity attaches. It is surely not complacent to assert that if (say) a government procured the passing of an Act of Parliament which criminalised the publication of any matter critical of government, it would be universally, and with reason, regarded as having acted unconstitutionally. Similarly, it is clear that an Act of Parliament which plainly intruded into the legislative competence of the Scottish Parliament without the consent of that body would be unconstitutional in the conventional sense (see below). A more serious rupture in the conventional constitution—and serious political upheaval—would be caused were Westminster simply to abolish the Scottish Parliament, although such an Act would be valid as a matter of strict constitutional law (at least on the orthodox view). A more apt criticism of the present arrangements would be that the normative (conventional) aspects of the constitution would bite only in the most extreme (and therefore unlikely to materialise) cases. In more marginal instances, such as the response to curtailment of the right to silence in 1994),[21] or the enactment of the Prevention of Terrorism Act 2005, allowing for the imposition of draconian 'control orders' on terrorist suspects by the Home Secretary, albeit subject to judicial review,[22] the indeterminacy of the constitutional order prevents such a clear cut verdict.

2. We have just mentioned the Scottish Parliament—the product of course of the Labour Government's extensive programme of constitutional reform outlined at the beginning of this chapter. How far, if at all, has this radical set of changes changed Ridley's basic 'no constitution' thesis? The straightforward answer is that, from a narrow formal perspective it has made no difference at all. Neither of the two most dramatic changes—devolution, as represented for these purposes by the Scotland Act 1998 and the vesting in UK citizens of a set of basic civil rights enforceable in the national courts via the Human Rights Act 1998 (HRA)—create any 'higher' system of law. Both the Scotland Act and the HRA specifically affirm that they do not affect Parliament's continued ability to reverse the changes they make, either wholly or in part. Thus, the HRA makes no attempt to entrench itself, and further provides quite specifically that if the courts find a piece of legislation passed either before or after the HRA to be incompatible with one or more of the Convention rights, this will not affect the validity or continuing effect of that legislation (ss 3(2) and 4(6)). The White Paper on incorporation of the ECHR (Cm 3782) states clearly that the HRA is not intended to detract from the sovereignty of Parliament in any way. Similarly, the White Paper on Scottish devolution (Cm 3658) proclaims that 'The United Kingdom is and will remain sovereign in all matters', and this basic statement of principle is clearly enacted in the legislation. Section 28(7) of the Scotland Act states that the grant of legislative powers to the Scottish Parliament 'does not affect the power of the United Kingdom Parliament to make law for Scotland'. Westminster may, therefore, still legislate in the devolved areas and may also repeal or modify the Scotland Act itself by ordinary legislation. These two pieces of legislation introduce substantive, rights-based limitations on governmental power (the HRA) and devolution of that power to a specified region (the Scotland Act). These are matters which in most countries would be part of 'higher' constitutional law, subject to change only through extraordinary procedures themselves specified in the constitution. Instead, the opposite is provided for: following devolution and since the introduction of the HRA, Parliament is still, as a matter of law, able to invade basic rights or the legislative autonomy of Scotland as easily and readily as it may change the rate of income tax.

3. Thus, on one level, the 'no constitution' attack retains its basic force. But, on another level, its applicability to the UK has become more problematic. To take Scotland first, its Parliament and its government for most matters are now limited by what is in effect a codified constitution, made up

---

21 By virtue of ss 34–36 Criminal Justice and Public Order Act 1994. See Chapter 20, pp 1196–1199.

22 See Chapter 3, pp 97–99.

of the Scotland Act itself, the ECHR and EU law. This is because the Scotland Act provides that Acts of the Scottish Parliament or Executive which are outside the powers devolved to it by the Act or which infringe Convention rights or EU law will be *ultra vires* (s 29), and further that the courts have what can only be described as a power of constitutional review, being empowered to strike down legislation of the Scottish Parliament or actions of its Executive on those grounds. Of course, in the areas which are not devolved, the Scots continue to be governed by the unrestrained and unconstitutionalised Westminster government and Parliament. However, the day to day experience of the Scottish people is now to live under a government which, in most areas, is constrained by a written constitution, which will protect basic rights, specify the electoral system and set the basic shape of government. Those entrenched matters are above and beyond the reach of the Scottish government and Parliament (since neither may alter the Scotland Act itself).

4. In answer to this is may be said that, since the Westminster Parliament still has the legal right to legislate in the devolved areas against the will of the Scottish Parliament and even to abolish the devolved institutions entirely, the Scots still have no constitutionally limited government. This is true as a matter of strict law, but it is at this point that purely legal perspectives begin to give a misleading view of the constitution. For the fact is that these legal rights are, in reality, probably theoretical only. No one seriously expects either to be exercised: the system would be unworkable if Westminster interfered in the devolved matters in this way, while the outright abolition of devolution has become virtually a political impossibility, not least because the devolution proposals were strongly endorsed by the Scottish electorate in a referendum. The Conservative party, which bitterly opposed the Labour plans for devolution from the run up to the 1992 election onwards, some time ago bowed to reality and promised that it will not attempt to reverse devolution. Thus, the day to day experience of the Scottish people is now to live under a codified constitution for the first time.

5. Moreover, it is clear that the term 'unconstitutional' has started to have a very clear and definite meaning, certainly in relation to the Government of Scotland, but also in relation to Westminster. In relation to the former, it now means 'legislation or administrative decisions which violate the legal constraints on the government of Scotland'—there is no doubt as to that. Legislation on rights-related matters now falls to be discussed, and eventually adjudicated upon, in constitutional terms. As for Westminster, as devolution and the new Scottish Government have become firmly entrenched, a convention has become established to the effect that the Westminster Parliament will not legislate in the devolved areas without the consent of the Scottish Parliament, just as such a convention developed during the period of the Stormont Government of Northern Ireland between 1920 and 1972. As Bogdanor puts it, 'In practice. . .sovereignty is being transferred and Westminster will not be able to recover it, except under pathological circumstances.'[23] Indeed, in a Memorandum of Understanding drawn up between the UK Government and the devolved administrations, it is stated that 'the UK government will normally proceed in accordance with the convention that the UK Parliament would not normally legislate with regard to devolved matters except with the agreement of the devolved legislature', (the so-called Sewell Convention) implying that a convention to this effect was established with the setting up of the devolved legislatures.[24] So far, Westminster has not in fact legislated in the devolved areas without the consent of the Scottish Executive. Of course, legislation intruding into the areas of Scottish competency could not be legally condemned by the constitution, but the terminology of constitutionalism has entered into the competency of Westminster. Furthermore, this constitutional convention does not suffer

---

23 V. Bogdonor, 'Devolution—the Constitutional Aspects' in *Constitutional Reform in the UK* (1998), p 12.

24 See further on this, Chapter 2, pp 51–53.

from the indeterminacy of other more vague conventions, such as the principle of individual and collective responsibility of government to parliament, an indeterminacy that allows such principles to be manipulated by the government of the day and undercuts the confidence of any attempts to label a given act as clearly 'unconstitutional' (the problem discussed by McAuslan and McEl-downey, above). This is because the Scotland Act lays down in considerable detail the reserved powers of Westminster and thus the powers devolved. Devolution has thus become constitutional-ised: in a very concrete way as far as Scotland and its government are concerned; in a conventional but nevertheless real way for the Westminster Parliament.

6.   Much the same may be said of the HRA. We have noted that it is not in any formal way entrenched; nevertheless, for the first time, the rights of the UK citizenry have been authoritatively identified and stated to be fundamental. Executive actions are unlawful if they infringe such rights, unless primary legislation inescapably mandates or authorises the infringement (s 6). Case-law broadly confirms that this requires courts to assess for themselves whether Executive decisions have infringed Convention rights, affording a far higher level of protection for those rights than was available under judicial review, although there has been some vacillation about this point in some of the decided cases.[25] For the first time, statutory construction fully and unequivocally recognises the importance of basic rights—courts have to read both past and future legislation into conform-ity with the Convention rights if possible (s 3(1)). Cases such as *R v A (No 2)*[26] and *Ghaidan v Mendoza*[27] indicate the radical force of this provision, and how far it subordinates normal canons of statutory interpretation to the overriding imperative to uphold Convention rights if possible, though other cases, such as *Re W and B* indicate a less activist approach. Ministers now have to make a statement when introducing legislation into Parliament that it does not infringe Conven-tion rights, or that they believe it does, but they wish to proceed in any event (s 19). Statements of the latter kind would amount to a declaration that the UK intended quite deliberately to violate its Treaty obligations and breach international law; this requirement will inevitably act as a powerful deterrent against the introduction of such legislation. However, an instance of this has already arisen, albeit in relation to a relatively contentious issue of interpretation of Art 10: the UK refuses to accept the correctness of the Strasbourg court's finding that a complete ban on political advertis-ing in broadcasting is a violation of Art 10 and has maintained such a ban in the Communications Act 2003, making a negative (s 19) statement in relation to it when the Bill was introduced. Nevertheless, clear and serious legislative infringements of the Convention are still extremely unlikely, and inadvertent infringements will be avoided by the need to scrutinise the Bill prior to making the statement to Parliament mentioned above. Meanwhile, ambiguously worded legislation which may infringe rights can be dealt with via the interpretative obligation of the courts noted above. Together, and depending upon how rigorously the courts enforce the interpretative injunc-tion in s 3(1) of the HRA (as indicated above, the cases to date indicate that it is being taken very seriously, though the outcomes vary), this adds up to quite a strong guarantee that legislation will no longer, in practice, infringe basic rights. All this, however, can be removed, simply by repeal of the HRA. This is now official Conservative Policy, and given the trend of the opinion polls during 2008, currently looks likely. However, the Conservatives have promised instead a British Bill of Rights, which would also ensure that basic rights would remain to an extent constitutionalised. See further Chapter 17 on all the above.

7.   Thus, while no form of higher basic norms has, as a matter of law, been created, the effect of the

---

25   See, for example, I Leigh [2002] PL 265.

26   *R v A (Complainant's Sexual History) (No 2)* [2002] 1 AC 45, HL.

27   [2004] 3 WLR 113.

canvassed reforms may in practice be indistinguishable. The basic ability of Parliament to remove so called constitutional guarantees, perhaps only by express repeal, still remains, at least as a matter of strict law. However, Ridley's suggestion that the concept of 'constitutionalism' at the normative, conventional level cannot be deployed in the UK has lost much of its force, as certain notions of devolved power at least attain an authoritatively declared basis and become fenced round by strong inhibitory conventions. In that sense, these reforms inject a modest dose of normative constitutionalism into the UK Government and society while leaving us formally still in search of a capital 'C' constitution, in King's sense (above, at pp 7–9).

8. Munro's view is somewhat different; he does not accept that a constitution needs to be either codified or have a special higher order status to be worthy of the name.[28] To him, therefore, the question is not whether the constitutional reforms starting in 1997 represent a change in the basic classification of the UK constitution (they do not), but how they change its character. His conclusion is that the reforms 'are apt to require us to modify our view of the British constitution, which is less monolithic, less centralised and less political then before'. Instancing the growing influence and legal supremacy of European Community law, together with the HRA, devolution, the legal regulation of political parties[29] and the partial codification of the doctrine of ministerial responsibility which followed the Scott Enquiry (see Chapter 12), he goes on:

> In these various ways, the British constitution is becoming considerably more rule-based, rather less 'political' and rather more 'legal'. It will be interesting to see how much further these tendencies are taken, and whether there will be a reaction against them.[30]

9. Ridley's argument also rests upon the notion that fundamental attributes of the constitution could all be changed by ordinary Acts of Parliament, which is, after all, the orthodox view. However, this orthodoxy may not be quite as solidly based as when he wrote. First of all, it also arguably requires some revision in the light of the decision in *Factortame* in which the House of Lords held that a statute which contravened EC law should be disapplied (see further, Chapter 5). Moreover, recent articles indicate that members of the judiciary, including some very senior members, no longer accept this viewpoint. Lord Woolf has opined[31] that the courts would not apply an Act of Parliament which purported to remove the power of judicial review from the courts, on the basis that this would represent an intolerable attack upon the Rule of Law, on which the constitution is based. Similarly, Sir John Laws (now a judge in the Court of Appeal) has argued[32] that the constitution, not Parliament, is supreme, and that the 'higher order law' which the constitution represents would inhibit Parliament from successfully assailing fundamental human rights, democratic institutions and the Rule of Law. He acknowledges that 'constitutional theory has perhaps occupied too modest a place here in Britain', but urges that 'though our constitution is unwritten, it can and must be articulated'.[33] As we shall see, some recent encouragement for his view may be seen in certain,

---

28   C. Munro, *Studies in Constitutional Law*, 2nd edn (1999) pp 1–8.

29   Through the Registration of Political Parties Act 1998.

30   Munro, n 28 above, p 13.

31   See 'Droit public—English style' [1995] PL 57.

32   In 'Law and democracy' [1995] PL 72.

33   Extracts from both these articles appear in Chapter 4, pp 182–184. On the relevance of Britain's membership of the EU to this issue, see Chapter 5.

rather enigmatic dicta of their Lordships in the recent decision of *A-G v Jackson*.[34] The primary mover in the attempt to articulate liberal constitutional principles in the UK's constitution is TRS Allen. See, for example, his *Law, Liberty and Justice: the Legal Foundations of British Constitutionalism* (1993) and *Constitutional Justice: a Liberal Theory of the Rule of Law* (2001).[35]

10. Whilst the uncodified nature of the British constitution may not necessarily be related to the substantive deficiencies discussed above, this characteristic may be blamed for the *uncertainty* of many constitutional doctrines. Anthony King brings this out clearly.

A King, *The British Constitution* (2007), p 9

One consequence of the fact that Britain does not have a Constitution and that no distinction is made in British law between specifically constitutional matters and others is that the word 'unconstitutional' has no precise meaning in the UK, if indeed it has any meaning at all. A British government or a British minister may behave illegally; everyone knows what that means. But what would it mean to say that the government or an individual had behaved unconstitutionally? Certainly the word in this kind of context would have no generally understood meaning—it would probably amount to no more than a vague term of abuse—and in fact 'unconstitutional' and its cognates seldom feature in British political discourse. A rare instance occurred during the Westland affair in 1985–86 when the secretary of state for defence, Michael Heseltine, resigned from Margaret Thatcher's cabinet, protesting, among other things, that Thatcher as prime minister had violated the norms of constitutional government in refusing to allow the full cabinet to discuss properly the future of the Westland Helicopter Company. But, although everyone knew what Heseltine had in mind (Thatcher's whole style as prime minister), the specific charge that she had behaved unconstitutionally scarcely resonated among his fellow politicians and the media, and little more was heard of it. The simple truth was that the relevant constitutional norms, in so far as they existed, had not been spelt out anywhere and that, in any case, no authoritative tribunal existed to determine whether they had been violated. In the UK, as in other countries that lack capital-C Constitutions, the whole idea of constitutionality—and therefore of unconstitutionality—necessarily remains in limbo.

To put the same point another way, it is striking that in countries with capital-C Constitutions those Constitutions usually act as normative and legal standards. They constitute benchmarks against which the actions of governments and individuals can be tested. The Constitution in such countries can be 'violated' just as the ordinary law can be 'broken'. Constitutional courts usually exist in such countries precisely in order to determine whether in specific instances the country's Constitution has been violated. In the United States, the federal Supreme Court—in effect, America's constitutional court—is one of that country's pivotal political institutions. In the UK, by contrast, the constitution, not being a Constitution, is seldom understood as constituting any kind of normative or legal standard. The constitution in the UK is not in any sense a benchmark. It is simply, for better or worse, a state of affairs—'what happens'. Those who protest—as people occasionally do—that the British constitution has been violated are not saying anything precise. They are merely expressing disgruntlement with some new state of affairs.

---

34   *R (on the application of Jackson) v Attorney-General* [2005] UKHL 56; [2005] 3 WLR 733; [2006] 1 AC 262. See further Chapter 4 at pp 184–185.

35   For an extract from Allen, see pp 180–182. For critical commentary see I Harden [1996] PL 298; T Poole, 'Dogmatic Liberalism: TRS Allan and the Common Law Constitutionalism' (2002) 65 MLR 463 and, for a more general examination of the ideas in this school, 'Questioning Common Law Constitutionalism' [2005] 25(1) LS 142.

Note

McAuslan and McEldowney made a similar point back in 1985:[36]

> In considering the issue of legitimacy in relation to our constitutional arrangements and the exercise of governmental power, what has to be done is to examine a range of practices, decisions, actions (and non-practices, decisions and actions), statements and policies which between them can amount to a portrait of power, so that we can form a judgment or an assessment of that power set against the principles of limited government. . . It is not every failure to comply with law or every constitutional and non-constitutional short cut which adds up to an approach to powers which gives rise to questions of legitimacy. If that were so, there would scarcely be a Government in the last 100 years which could be regarded as legitimate, but it is those uses of power and law which seem to betray or which can only be reasonably explained by a contempt for or at least an impatience with the principles of limited government and a belief that the rightness of the policies to be executed excuse or justify the methods whereby they are executed. If, as we believe to be the case, powers are being so exercised, then the issue of constitutional legitimacy which arises is quite simply: what is the value or use of a constitution based on and designed to ensure the maintenance of a system of limited government if it can, quite lawfully and even constitutionally, be set on one side?

Notes

1. Contemporary examples of behaviour of uncertain constitutional legitimacy are not hard to find. To take just a few examples, the Conservative Party has been wont to refer to the entire Labour constitutional reform programme as amounting to 'vandalism' of the UK constitution. Persistent concerns focused on the Blair Government's centralisation of power within the Prime Minister's Office and the far greater use of unelected 'special advisers', who are specifically partisan, unlike the traditionally 'neutral' Civil Service.[37] There is a fear that the influence of 'special advisers' eclipses that of the Civil Service and even that of Ministers, while they themselves remain wholly unaccountable to Parliament.[38] Many saw it as 'unconstitutional' for the Prime Minister himself simply to decide and announce that Prime Ministers questions—a highly symbolic forum of constitutional accountability, perhaps the most famous in the UK constitution—would be changed from a twice to a once-weekly format, without even consulting Parliament, the other political parties or anyone else. The major reorganisation of central government, whereby 'Next Step' agencies, designed to operate at arm's-length from government, were set up without legislative discussion in Parliament to assume many of the tasks of government departments, with major implications for government accountability and responsibility, is another example (see further Chapter 12, pp 618–619 and 632–636).

---

36 'Legitimacy and the constitution: the dissonance between theory and practice', in P McAuslan and JF McEldowney (eds), *Law, Legitimacy and the Constitution* (1985), pp 12–15.

37 See the Report of the Public Administration Committee, *Special advisers: boon or bane*, HC 293 (2000–01).

38 Then Prime Minister Tony Blair Tony Blair reiterated his view on 16 July 2002 that they should not appear before Select Committees of Parliament in evidence to the Liaison Committee. For an example of a Select Committee complaint relating to the refusal of a high profile adviser—Lord Birt—to appear before it, see Chapter 8, pp 409–410.

2. What all these changes indicate is that, in the UK, the constitution, which in many other countries is policed by a constitutional court, or some other body independent of government, for example the French *Conseil D'Etat,* is in the UK an overtly *political* animal, as apt to be reformed to the convenience of government as social or economic policy. This theme, particularly in relation to the protection and enhancement of democracy, is developed in the final part of this chapter, by David Marquand.

THE POLITICS OF THE UK CONSTITUTION AND ITS REFORM

D Marquand, 'Democracy in Britain' (2000) 10(2) *Oxford International Review* 2–10 (extracts)

. . .

The old constitution—the constitution under which Amery and Crossman both grew up—is dissolving beneath our eyes. The only question is what will replace it. To that question the authors of the [Blair] revolution have no answer. On the contrary, they have reacted to the predictable consequences of their own achievement with a mixture of incredulity and indignation. Having created new opportunities for voices in Scotland, Wales, and London, they have expended large quantities of political capital on attempts to make sure that the voices merely echo the orthodoxies of the centre. Having abolished the voting rights of most hereditary peers in the name of democratic legitimacy, they have set their faces against an elected second Chamber that might possess sufficient legitimacy to challenge the executive-dominated House of Commons. Though this is not certain, they also appear to have contrived an overwhelmingly nominated House, scarcely more legitimate than the largely hereditary one it has replaced. Their proposals on freedom of information are a pale shadow of the commitments they made in opposition, while the proposed referendum on electoral reform has receded into a hazy, post-election distance.

The Democratisation of Britain

The most frequent explanation for this mixture of boldness and timidity is that Tony Blair is a control freak. That is psychobabble. He may well be a control freak. But I see no evidence that he is more freakish, or more anxious to exert control, than Gladstone, Salisbury, Lloyd George, Neville Chamberlain or Edward Heath, to mention only a few. Few people get to the top of the greasy pole of politics without a masterful ego and a strong appetite for power. The true origins of what I shall call the Blair paradox lie, I believe, in his inheritance, not in the accidents of personal psychology.

They lie, in the first place, in the long, convoluted and fiercely contested process through which Britain became a democracy in the first place. For the notion that this country is, in some sense, the cradle of democracy is a myth. Democracy came to Britain slowly, haltingly, and late. The best part of a century passed between the great Reform Act of 1832, which increased the size of the electorate from 4.5% to 7.0% of the adult population, and the arrival of manhood suffrage in 1918. Even then, women could not vote until they reached the age of 30. As late as 1945, my own parents had four votes between them—two as ordinary citizens and two as university graduates. The first general election in which every adult citizen had one vote, and no one had more than one, was that of 1950. In a different sphere, it was not until 1911 that the House of Lords lost its veto powers, and not until 1999 that most hereditary peers lost their seats within it.

. . . The history lived on in the mentalities of leaders and led. New groups were incorporated into the political nation; new men joined the political class. But the old, oligarchic order of the past changed the newcomers as much as they changed it.

. . . Of course, there were differences between left courtiers and their counterparts on the right. For the right, the British state—even in its new democratic incarnation—was clothed in a mystic patina of custom and memory, from which its authority ultimately derived. . .

. . . . . . By the same token, socialists and social democrats were as zealous in their commitment to the British tradition of autonomous executive power and to the doctrine of absolute parliamentary sovereignty that accompanied and sustained it as any Conservative. In effect, the left made a Faustian bargain with the old order: power within the existing system, in exchange for adherence to its norms.

. . . . . . The task, most social democrats believed, was to use the existing, now democratic constitution to change society from above. The young Aneurin Bevan saw Parliament as 'a sword, pointed at the heart of property power'. What mattered was to use the sword, not to waste time searching for a better one. . . . Most of the progressive left took it for granted that if the central executive were to complement political citizenship with social citizenship, to promote social justice, it would need all the autonomy it could lay its hands on. And so the court tradition reigned, throughout the inter-war years and well into the post-war period. . . .

. . .

Then came the Thatcher revolution—the second crucial element in Blair's inheritance. Mrs Thatcher was to the court tradition what Mr Toad was to motorcars. She drove it so hard that she smashed it up. Westminster absolutism and executive autonomy were essential to her whole project. Without the concentration of power that they made possible, her Governments could not have marginalised the trade unions, curbed the local authorities, privatised most of the nationalised industries or imposed market norms on the remaining public sector. But she and her colleagues ignored the intricacies of the apparatus they used with such enthusiasm. The autonomous executive that Amery extolled had been responsive, not pro-active; permissive, not coercive; discreet, not obtrusive. Concentrated power was always there in reserve, but with the unspoken proviso that it should be kept in reserve for as long as possible. In normal times its motto was 'live and let live'. With that motto and the delicate fabric of practices and understandings that embodied it the Thatcher Governments were soon at war: they had to be if they were to reconstruct a complex civil society, rich in intermediate institutions operating by non-market rules, in the stark image of an 'enterprise culture'. But they were using the forms of American democracy to snuff out its spirit.

They paid a heavy price. Their object was a liberal economy, centred on the rational, calculating, freely choosing consumer. But the constitution through which they tried to attain it derived its authority from un-chosen custom, beyond rational criticism. Thatcher herself saw no inconsistency in this. For her, free competition and traditional authority went together. She did not reckon with the social forces that she herself summoned up. Market forces were given freer reign; opportunities were widened; the already enfeebled old elites were further undermined; new men and the occasional new woman clawed their way to the top. But in the process, the mystique that had helped to legitimise the court tradition was stripped away. The hedonistic, tradition-scorning individualism that was fundamental to Thatcherite economics eroded the uncalculating respect for custom that was no less fundamental to its politics. The vulgar, vital, undeferential, bourgeois Britain that Thatcherite economics helped to bring into being became less and less willing to doff its cap to the monarchical state. By 1991 a Mori survey found that the proportion of those surveyed who thought the system 'needed a great deal of improvement' or could be improved 'quite a lot' had gone up to 63 per cent, while only 4 per cent thought it 'worked extremely well'. The core executive of ministers and officials at the heart of the state responded by becoming increasingly aggressive and determined to concentrate power in its own hands. For its pains, it became increasingly isolated from, and ever-more suspect to, the society for which it claimed to speak. The more vigorously the Thatcherites' capitalist renaissance roared ahead, the less legitimate became the institutions through which they had procured it.

The Blair Paradox

Against that background, the Blair paradox falls into place. New Labour inherited not so much a constitutional crisis as a constitutional vacuum. Confidence in the political system had plummeted. Accusations of 'sleaze' in high places were rife. In Scotland, the demand for home rule had become irresistible. Blair and his colleagues saw that if they were to fill the constitutional vacuum and stem the drain of legitimacy that had helped to undo their predecessors, they would have to reconstruct the political order on lines appropriate to a modern, post-imperial, late twentieth-century society. The trouble was that they had no coherent answer to the obvious consequential questions: What sort of modern society? What kind of reconstruction, informed by what vision of democracy? They sought diversity, openness, and the devolution of power. As Blair put it in a 1998 Fabian pamphlet,

> The demand for more democratic self-governance is fed by better educated citizens and the free-flow of information provided by new technology. . .We must meet this demand by devolving power. . .Devolution and local governance are not just important in themselves: open, vibrant, diverse democratic debate is a laboratory for ideas about how we should meet social needs.

That was the republican vision of Crossman and Tawney in a new guise. But Blair and his colleagues belonged to the Westminster village themselves. Its customs and assumptions were in their blood. If they were unwitting republicans they were also unwitting courtiers. They wished to reform the old order, but they also wished to renew the Faustian bargain that an earlier generation of social democrats had made with it. Like their political ancestors of seventy years before, they wanted to use the powers available to the autonomous executive of the court tradition to re-engineer society from the top—not, any longer, in the name of social ownership, or even social citizenship, but in the no less compelling names of equal opportunity and international competitiveness. Their critics on the left are apt to depict them as hopeless conservatives, seeking to fend off radical change. I don't believe that. I think they are torn between two kinds of radicalism, two visions of modernity and two conceptions of what democratic modernisation might mean—between modernisation as reinvented republicanism and modernisation as state-led adaptation to the pressures of the global market-place; between democracy as self-government and democracy as acquiescence.

That, roughly speaking, is where we are now. The strongest argument for any status quo—if it ain't broke, don't fix it—no longer applies. Manifestly, the old constitution is broke, partly by social change, partly by Thatcher, and partly by Blair. But, irrespective of party, Crossman's 'routine politicians' are still in thrall to it. So are the functionaries of Millbank and Smith Square and what is left of the mandarinate of Whitehall. As for ministers, they half-want to disperse power in the interests of modernisation from below, and half-want to concentrate it in the interests of modernisation from above. Plainly, this state of affairs cannot last. Further movement is inevitable. The only questions are: In which direction? And, under what banner?

. . . [One answer, Marquand suggests, lies in the republican tradition that has been confined to the sidelines of politics for so long. . .] The institutional implications of a republican alternative to populism are undeniably complex, but they are not in any way extraordinary. It would mean following through the logic of the constitutional changes that the Government has already made. There would have to be more spaces for voice; more diffusion of power and responsibility; more and stronger checks and balances to counter the inherent tendency of any central executive to limit voice and concentrate power. Thorny practical issues would have to be resolved. The primordial questions of nationhood and identity—fundamental to all modern states—would be on the table. The relationship between Scotland and Wales on the one hand, and England and the English regions on the other, would have to be settled. So would the relationship between all of these and a post-imperial Britain, inextricably involved in a proto-federal European Union. The democratic deficits in regional and local governance would have to be overcome. The octopoid 'quango state' whose growth has been one of the most remarkable features of the last thirty years would have to be democratised. The composition and powers of an elected second chamber would have to be determined. The form of a proportional electoral system would have to be determined. The form of a proportional electoral system would have to be decided. But none of these questions is unanswerable. Most of them are in the agenda already, though sometimes without acknowledgement, and equivalent questions have been posed and answered in most of the Member-States of the European Union. The really intractable problems lie elsewhere. A republican alternative would mean a change of mentality and assumption both among leaders and among led. The old Whig fetish of organic evolution would have to be jettisoned. The questions I listed a moment ago will in any case have to be answered sooner or later. But the piecemeal incrementalism of the Whig tradition is unlikely to produce consistent or coherent answers. A reinvented republicanism must be explicit, and the British (or perhaps I should say the English) have never been comfortable with constitutional explicitness.

Notes

1. Marquand usefully reminds us that issues of constitutionalism and democracy cannot be discussed as if hermetically sealed from quite another discipline—'politics'. However, this of course also means that specific theses, such as the first part of that set out above, risk becoming out of date as a result of political change. Consider Marquand's summary of the responses of the Blair government to its own radical programme in the first paragraph extracted above, concerning their reaction to devolution in Scotland, Wales and London and reform of the House of Lords. Some nine years after this article was written, much of this is already no longer the case. The Labour Government indeed made frantic and sustained efforts to ensure that the well known left-winger Ken Livingstone was blocked as standing from Labour's candidate for the London Mayor: Livingstone went on to run

and win as an independent in the first election in 2000, was subsequently brought back into the Labour fold and successfully ran again in the 2004 Mayoral election, this time as the Labour candidate but very much on this own terms. The same Government also sought to prevent the popular but 'maverick' MP Rhodri Morgan running as First Minister in the Welsh Assembly, instead forcing the loyalist Alun Michael on Wales; again, however, the attempt to control the leadership of a devolved body failed when the unpopular Michael was forced out by a vote of no confidence in the Assembly after less than a year.[39] Thus the attempts to 'control devolution' failed and the attempt has not been repeated—indeed Labour is now learning to live with the Scottish Nationalists—their arch enemies—being in power in Scotland, while it now shares power with the Liberal Democrats and Plaid Cymru in Wales. The Welsh Assembly quite quickly sought, and was given new powers, via the Government of Wales Act 2006.[40] Even while under Labour control, the Scottish and (to a lesser extent) Welsh assemblies quickly produced distinctive policies, breaking free of the shackles of Westminster Labour in crucial areas such as prescription charges, top up fees, free care for the elderly and school legal tables.[41] Meanwhile, the Government has recently come out in favour of a fully or substantially elected House of Lords, after repeated House of Commons votes made it clear that there was hardly any Commons support for a mainly appointed House.[42] It is true that the Government's original Freedom of Information Bill was very disappointing, but the measure enacted was much better than the Bill as a result of concessions granted in Parliament; in practice it has proved a far more effective mechanism for opening up government than many commentators predicted.[43] Meanwhile, of course, the Brown Government has proceeded to go further, in terms of enhancing parliamentary control over the prerogative.[44] As this book went to press, the Government was seeking legislation for a referendum on reform of the voting system for the Commons. In other words, constitutional change generates its own momentum: even when governments enact it half-heartedly, or with no clear narrative of where it wishes to go, other political actors will seize upon what has been granted and make it work more radically than government wanted; they will demand—and ultimately be granted—further reform.

2. As Munro observes, the UK constitution is becoming more 'legal' by which he means that questions which would hitherto have been decided by politicians on a purely discretionary basis have been placed in the hands of the courts. Thus, the above reforms represent a considerable transfer of power within the UK constitution—from the Westminster Parliament to the Scottish Parliament and Northern Ireland Assembly in the case of devolution, and from the executive to the courts in the case of the HRA.[45] If the argument made above (p 30) as to the operation of the HRA in practice is correct, there is also a *de facto* limitation of parliament's competency in the area of human rights. The transfer of what may be regarded as essentially 'political' questions—the proper scope of human rights and the point at which they should give way to societal interests—is deeply controversial, as the following extract from a well-known article by John Griffith indicates. The

---

39   Alun Michael assumed office on 12 May 1999; he lost the motion of confidence on 9 February 2000.

40   See Chapter 6, pp 284–288.

41   For the powers of these bodies, see Chapter 6.

42   See Chapter 9.

43   See Chapter 13.

44   See Chapter 11.

45   The courts also have an important role to play in determining the legislative competency of the devolved legislatures: see further, pp 246–255.

article was written partly in response to proposals for constitutional reform brought forward by Lords Hailsham and Scarman at the end of the 1970s, but its basic contentions are still of relevance today, both to the new constitutional settlement and to the ongoing debate as to whether the UK should adopt a codified and entrenched constitution or at least a Bill of Rights that, unlike the HRA, is protected from repeal in the ordinary way by Parliament.

J Griffith, 'The political constitution' (1979) 42 *Modern Law Review* 1 (extracts)

... As part of the recent movement to reintroduce natural law concepts into the theory and practice of politics, 'the law' has been raised from its proper and useful function as a means towards ends (about which it is possible to have differing opinions) to the level of a general concept. On this view, individual rules of law may be good or bad, but 'the law' is undeniably good and must be upheld or chaos will come again. There is more than a suspicion of sleight of hand here. For nobody, except committed anarchists, suggests that 'the law' should be dispensed with.

The ground is then shifted slightly and what becomes sacred and untouchable is something called the Rule of Law. The Rule of Law is an invaluable concept for those who wish not to change the present set up. A person may be said not to be in favour of the Rule of Law if he is critical of the Queen, the Commissioner of the Metropolitan Police, the Speaker of the House of Commons, or Lord Denning. Statutes may be contrary to the Rule of Law (like some, but not all, Indemnity Acts) but the common law, it seems, can never be. Objection to the rules of international law in their application to the UK is wholly excusable on proper occasions. Defiance of regulations and directives emanating from Brussels may often be accounted a positive virtue.

If the Rule of Law means that there should be proper and adequate machinery for dealing with criminal offences and for ensuring that public authorities do not exceed their legal powers, and for insisting that official penalties may not be inflicted save on those who have broken the law, then only an outlaw could dispute its desirability. But when it is extended to mean more than that, it is a fantasy invented by Liberals of the old school in the late 19th century and patented by the Tories to throw a protective sanctity around certain legal and political institutions and principles which they wish to preserve at any cost. ....

The proposals for a written constitution, for a Bill of Rights, for a House of Lords with greater powers to restrain governmental legislation, for regional assemblies, for a supreme court to monitor all these proposals, are attempts to write laws so as to prevent Her Majesty's Government from exercising powers which hitherto that Government has exercised.

The fundamental political objection is this: that law is not and cannot be a substitute for politics. This is a hard truth, perhaps an unpleasant truth. For centuries political philosophers have sought that society in which government is by laws and not by men. It is an unattainable ideal. Written constitutions do not achieve it. Nor do Bills of Rights or any other devices. They merely pass political decisions out of the hands of politicians and into the hands of judges or other persons. To require a supreme court to make certain kinds of political decisions does not make those decisions any less political.

I believe firmly that political decisions should be taken by politicians. In a society like ours this means by people who are removable. It is an obvious corollary of this that the responsibility and accountability of our rules should be real and not fictitious. And of course our existing institutions, especially the House of Commons, need strengthening. And we need to force Governments out of secrecy and into the open. So also the freedom of the Press should be enlarged by the amendment of laws which restrict discussion. Governments are too easily able to act in an authoritarian manner. But the remedies are political. It is not by attempting to restrict the legal powers of government that we shall defeat authoritarianism. It is by insisting on open government.

That is why these present proposals by Lord Hailsham, Lord Scarman and others are not only mistaken but positively dangerous. They seem to indicate a way by which potential tyranny can be defeated by the intervention of the law and the intervention of institutional devices. There is no such way. Only political control, politically exercised, can supply the remedy.

The philosophical objection to the new proposals stems from an unease about a formulation based exclusively on rights. I suspect I shall be misunderstood on this. So I had better begin by saying that my distrust of Governments and of the claims made by those in authority is as profound as any man's and more profound than most.

. . .I reject the notion that those who hold political power have any moral right or moral authority to do so, however they came to their positions. They are there and they have power. No more. [Next] following from what I have said, the power they exercise is not special. It is no different in kind from the power exercised by other groups in the community like the owners or controllers of large accumulations of capital or the leaders of large trade unions. [Finally], it is misleading to speak of certain rights of the individual as being funda-mental in character and inherent in the person of the whole individual. As an individual I make claims on the authorities who control the society in which I live. If I am strong enough—and I shall have to join with others to be so—my claim may be recognised within certain limits. It may even be given legal status. There is a continuous struggle between the rulers and the ruled about the size and shape of these claims and that is what is meant by Curran's statement, that the condition upon which God hath given liberty to man is eternal vigilance although, as you will have gathered, I am not persuaded that we have a divine donor in this respect.

. . .As an individual I may say that I have certain rights—the right to life being the most fundamental. But those who manage the society in which I live will reply: 'put up your claim and we will look at it; don't ring us, we'll ring you.'

In this political, social sense there are no over-riding human rights; no right to freedom, to trial before conviction, to representation before taxation; no right not to be tortured, not to be summarily executed. Instead there are political claims by individuals and by groups.

One danger of arguing from rights is that the real issues can be evaded. What are truly questions of politics and economics are presented as questions of law.

But paradoxically, arguments advanced avowedly for the protection of human rights are often concealed political propaganda. Those for a written constitution, a Bill of Rights, a supreme court and the rest are attempts to resolve political conflicts in our society in a particular way, to minimise change, to maintain (so far as possible) the existing distribution of political and economic power. . .

It seems to me that to call political claims 'inherent rights' is to mythologise and confuse the matter. The struggle is political throughout and moral only in the purely subjective sense that I may think I ought to be granted what I claim. Those in authority may think I ought not to be granted my claim. And there is no logic which says that their view is more based on their self-advancement (rather than, say, the public good) than mine is. . .

Similarly with lawmakers, like ministers and judges. They have regard to the political ends they serve. Party politicians being rather less homogeneous a group than judges are likely to make decisions more distinguishable than the decisions judges make. And the political ends which Ministers serve are not identical with those which judges serve. But it seems to me that to suggest ministers or judges are seeking abstractions like justice or the conscience of the community or whatever is 'nonsense on stilts'. They are political animals pursuing political ends which are far narrower, more limited and more short term, than those abstractions...

A further advantage in treating what others call rights as political claims is that their acceptance or rejection will be in the hands of politicians rather than judges, and the advantage of that is not that politicians are more likely to come up with the right answer but that, as I have said, they are so much more vulnerable than judges and can be dismissed or at least made to suffer in their reputation...

Question

When Griffith states that 'A person may be said to be not in favour of the Rule of Law if he is critical of the Queen, the Commissioner of the Metropolitan Police, the Speaker of the House of Commons or Lord Denning', is he criticising the substance of the doctrine or its misuse? If he is merely complaining that the doctrine is abused (like most theories), is he saying anything of interest?

Notes
1. Griffith's argument is that questions of rights are political and should be resolved by politicians, who are accountable. The problem with this approach appears to be this: rights are usually rights against government, for example, the right to freedom of information, giving the electorate access to information that may be embarrassing to the government, or the right to life or liberty of the person preventing the British government from e.g. using its armed forces to kill known members of the IRA in the absence of an immediate threat. Therefore, governments have a vested interest in eroding rights, in order to increase their freedom of action. If there are no legally entrenched rights, then the only sanction to prevent governments from eroding rights is the fear that this will result in political unpopularity. Unfortunately, at least in the UK, questions of rights are simply not major political issues. For example, the 1992 general election was fought almost entirely on social and economic issues,[46] in particular on taxation, the economy, education and health. The same can be said of the 1997, 2001 and 2005 elections. Indeed, certain issues, such as the rights of asylum seekers, appear to 'run' in the electoral struggle for mass public opinion primarily for the Right: political advantage appears to lie in being perceived as 'tough', that is, authoritarian and illiberal on such issues. Much the same may be said of measures to counter crime and, in particular, terrorism. The passage of the draconian Anti-Terrorism, Crime and Security Act 2001, which, along with a raft of other authoritarian measures, gave the Home Secretary the right to detain, without trial, those suspected of being international terrorists and posing a threat to the UK, caused no public outcry, even though it required the UK to derogate from (temporarily opt out of) the right to

46 For an analysis of the campaigning in that election, see D Kavanagh and B Jones, 'Voting behavior' in B Jones (ed), *Politics UK* (1994), pp 193 *et seq.*

liberty guaranteed by Article 5 of the European Convention on Human Rights. In this respect, it is worthy of note that the elected House of Commons did virtually nothing to ameliorate the most illiberal aspects of the Act. Such improvement as was achieved by Parliament was almost entirely the work of the unelected House of Lords.[47] It may be argued that the political accountability on rights issues which, in Griffith's scheme, both argues against 'legalising' rights and supposedly ensures their protection, simply does not exist in practice.[48] As Loveland has pithily put it, the difficulty with the 'political constitutionalism' school is that:

> This version of 'democracy' is evidently one which is either content to allow minority interests to be sacrificed to the wishes of Parliamentary majorities, or which assumes that our representative law-makers will always be blessed with a collective mindset which precludes the indulgence of such venal concerns.[49]

2. Griffith describes both judges and politicians as 'political animals, pursuing political ends'. Whatever the argument about the extent to which judges are affected by their personal political views (and Griffith's thesis, put forward elsewhere,[50] that the judges are strongly influenced by their ingrained conservatism, has been vigorously attacked),[51] Griffith surely fails to make a basic distinction: whilst judges purport to approach a politically contentious legal issue from a stand-point of neutrality, and must therefore at least *be seen* to be unbiased in their assessment, politicians make a profession out of constant, unremitting bias in favour of the policies of the party to which they owe their allegiance. In particular, judges are often required to enforce the provisions of laws which it is clear they do not themselves like; politicians will simply seek to change them.

3. A contemporary exponent of views in a similar tradition is Professor Tomkins. Tomkins begins his work by repudiating liberal-legalism—what may also be referred to as liberal constitutionalism—probably the dominant ideology that students will find in works on constitutional and administrative law. Tomkins contends that such theorists believe:

> (1) That law is both discrete from and superior to politics; (2) that the state can successfully be limited by law, although the law ought properly to allow for [public authorities] to enjoy a degree—albeit a controlled degree—of discretionary authority; (3) that the best way of controlling the state is through the judicial articulation and enforcement of broad principles of legality and (4) that the goal of this project is to safeguard a particular version of human rights.[52]

Tomkins rejects such a standpoint. This rejection is based partly on the reasons given by Griffiths above—that such a view seeks to make of law a substitute for what can only be done by politics. It is rejected also for the straightforward reason that Tomkins regards decision-making by judges as

---

47 On the contrast, see Chapter 9 at pp 451–454.

48 For an extended argument along these lines, see G Phillipson, 'Deference, Discretion and Democracy in the Human Rights Act Era' (2007) 60 *Current Legal Problems* 40–78.

49 I Loveland, 'Review of A. Tomkins', *Our Republican Constitution* (2006) 122 (Apr) LQR 340, 343.

50 *The Politics of the Judiciary,* 3rd edn (1985).

51 K Minogue, 'The Biases of the Bench', TLS, 6 January 1978, and S Lee, *Judging Judges* (1988).

52 A Tomkins, 'In Defence of the Political Constitution' (2002) 22(1) OJLS 157, 160.

inherently undemocratic—he therefore regards reforms like the Human Rights Act, which may be seen as transferring decision making in a large number of areas from politicians to lawyers, with hostility. But going beyond these practical matters, liberal-legalism is also rejected for more wide-wide ranging reasons. While liberal-legalists see the basic role of the constitution as being to place legal controls and limits on political decision making, particularly its impact on individual rights, Tomkins outlines a view of the constitution as resting primarily on political accountability.

A Tomkins, *Our Republican Constitution* (2005), pp 1–4

THE BRITISH CONSTITUTION is a remarkable creation. It is no exaggeration to say that there is nothing quite like it anywhere else in the world. Both in its famously 'unwritten' form and in aspects of its content it is extraordinary. At its core lies a simple—and beautiful—rule. It is a rule that has formed the foundation of the constitution since the seventeenth century. It is that the government of the day may continue in office for only as long as it continues to enjoy the majority support of the House of Commons. The moment such support is withdrawn is the very moment that the government is required to resign. By this one rule is democracy in Britain secured; by this one rule are 'we the British people' able, through our elected representatives in Parliament, to 'throw the scoundrels out'. The rule is known as the convention of ministerial responsibility or as the doctrine of responsible government. For now, the most important thing to note about the rule is that it stipulates that the government is constitutionally responsible *to Parliament*.

The extreme step of forcibly removing the government from office is not, of course, an everyday occurrence. This is not to say that it never happens. The Labour government led by prime minister James Callaghan fell in 1979 because it lost a vote of confidence in the House of Commons. Callaghan's successor as prime minister, Margaret Thatcher, reluctantly resigned from office eleven years later when it was explained to her by her Cabinet colleagues that they felt she had lost the support of the majority of backbench Conservative MPs. It is not only prime ministers who are responsible to Parliament: all government ministers are constitutionally responsible to Parliament.

Votes of no confidence and prime ministerial resignations are relatively rare but, in addition to providing the occasional drama of high political theatre, there is a second aspect to our rule. It is less spectacular, perhaps, but it is no less important The government is required to secure the support of a majority in Parliament not only when ministerial careers are on the line, but every single day. It is a routine obligation on the part of the government that it must ensure that its policies, decisions and actions enjoy parliamentary backing. Parliament is the institution through which the government must legislate; Parliament is the institution that controls the government's purse strings; and Parliament is the institution that will continuously inquire into the 'expenditure, administration and policy' of every government department. It follows that in order for it to realise its legislative ambitions, the government will have to persuade a majority in Parliament that its policies are the right ones; that in order for the government to enjoy financial freedom, it will have to persuade a majority in Parliament that its spending plans are the right ones; and that in order for government departments to achieve success they will have to ensure that their expenditure, administration and policy are sustainable.

The beauty of our rule lies in its recognition of what may be called the 'reality of government'. Government is not (or at least is not always) an especially attractive occupation: it can be cynical, even dirty. One way of expressing the 'reality of government' is to say that those in political office are liable to try to do whatever they can politically get away with. What is special about the British constitution is that it recognises this reality and acts on it. It does this by building it into the very heart of what the constitution tries to do. The purpose of all constitutions is to find ways of insisting that the government is held to account for its actions. What is unusual about the British constitution is the way it sets about accomplishing this task.

Most modern constitutions in the western world are not founded on an ideal of making government responsible to a political institution such as a Parliament. Most Western constitutions may *recognise* what I am calling the reality of government but they do not *act* on it in the way that the British constitution does. Rather than building constitutional structures of *political* accountability around this realisation, the bulk of Western constitutional practice has in modern times tended to focus instead on *legal* controls. Ideals of the 'rule of law' or of respect for 'fundamental' or 'human' rights form the backbone of today's constitutionalism in both continental Europe and North America. Ideals such as these are generally enforceable in courts of law rather than in political institutions such as Parliament. Accordingly it is to the judges, rather than to parliamentarians, that these constitutions look to provide the lead role in securing checks on government.

Instead of incorporating the fact that governments are liable to try whatever they think they can politically get away with into the fabric of constitutional accountability, such constitutions turn their backs on politics. It is as if they regard politics as part of the problem — as something that requires to be checked — rather than as part of the solution. What is beautiful about the British constitution is that it does not do this. It uses politics as the vehicle through which the purpose of the constitution (that is, to check the government) may be accomplished. This is beautiful for at least two reasons: first, because it is democratic; and secondly, because it can actually work. Politics really can stop governments from abusing their authority.

Turning instead to the courts to provide ways of holding the government to account endangers both democracy and effectiveness. No matter how democracy is defined, judges can never hope to match the democratic legitimacy of elected politicians. Whether you conceive of democracy in terms of the representativeness of the personnel or in terms of the openness and accessibility of the institution, Parliaments will always enjoy greater democratic legitimacy than courts. As for effectiveness, we shall come to examine this in more detail later, and when we do we shall see both how and why it is that courts — or at least British courts — are unable to secure the same results in terms of government accountability as Parliament can.

Before we come to consider this issue, it is important to add some further remarks on just how unusual the British prioritisation of political over judicial accountability is. It is easy to take one's routines for granted, but central constitutional traditions such as prime minister's question time are no mere habits. The weekly half-hour that the prime minister must endure at the despatch box in the House of Commons is one of the most important reminders of the constitution's core rule: that the prime minister and his government are accountable to Parliament and require its ongoing support if they are to continue in office. The prime minister may appear to be the most powerful politician in the country, but his power is not his to keep. He is but its temporary custodian. His power is held on trust. At election time it is the electorate itself that may, indirectly, remove it from him. But general elections normally occur only once every four or five years, and between elections it is Parliament, not the people themselves, to whom the prime minister must report if he is to be permitted to continue in office.

Traditions such as prime minister's question time and the doctrine of ministerial responsibility are so familiar to us in Britain and form such a central component of our political experience and expectations that we are in danger of assuming that they are shared everywhere. However, such an assumption would be sorely misplaced. There is simply no direct equivalent to the British system of political accountability in the United States, for example, in the traditions of many of our continental European neighbours or in the constitutional order of the European Union.

The US has in recent years suffered more than most from the absence of an effective mechanism of political accountability. Think, for example, of the protracted and hugely expensive procedures involved in the unsuccessful attempt to impeach President Clinton in the late 1990s. Bruce Ackerman, one of America's most astute constitutional commentators, has observed that:

> Bill Clinton would not have lasted a month as a prime minister in a parliamentary system. His backbenchers would have revolted, or his coalition partners would have ushered him out the door in a desperate effort to move into the next election with a new face at the head of the old government. In contrast, Americans had to waste a year on the politics of Clinton's personality. . . . [G]iven the American separation of powers, Bill Clinton's failings did not provide a constitutionally adequate basis for Congress to override the judgment rendered by the voters in 1996. But compared with the way a parliamentary system would have handled the affair, [the US Constitution] did a spectacularly bad job in dealing with this minor scandal.[B Ackerman, 'The New Separation of Powers' (2000) 113 *Harvard Law Review* 633, at 659.]

Under the terms of the US Constitution it is Congress, not a court of law, that is empowered to impeach the President. But short of this extreme step congressional powers to subject the executive branch to account are severely limited. Professor Ackerman's argument in the article just quoted from is that what he calls a 'constrained' form of parliamentarianism would make for a more suitable and more effective (as well as a more democratic) system of constitutional accountability than American presidentialism is capable of. We shall have cause to return to the United States at several points later in this book, but for now let us turn our attention briefly away from America and towards Europe.

It has been suggested that the English word 'accountability' does not even have an exact translation in some other European languages, such as French and German. But it is not just the word that is difficult to translate: British practices of political accountability have few parallels elsewhere in Europe. In France, for example, the current constitution (the Constitution of the Fifth Republic, dating from 1958) was expressly designed to limit the extent to which the National Assembly could subject the government to account. The Constitution provides that the prime minister is to be appointed by the President of the Republic, not by the National Assembly, [Constitution of 1958, Art 8] and stipulates that the government is accountable to the National Assembly only in strictly limited ways. Thus, while a government must resign if its general programme is defeated in a parliamentary vote, it is under no obligation to present such a programme to the National Assembly in the first place [*Ibid*, Art 49]. Further, the availability of censure motions is strictly curtailed, such that they may be passed only by an absolute majority of all members of the National Assembly.

British policy-makers and constitutional practitioners have been painfully slow to realise just how special our expectations of political accountability are.

Note

Commentators such as Tomkins evidently place a great deal of faith in the principle of the account-ability of government to Parliament. We examine the mechanics by which this takes place—parlia-mentary questions, select committees and so on, in Chapter 8; meanwhile in Chapter 12, we examine the principles that govern—or are meant to—this accountability—the notion of Ministerial Responsi-bility. It will be for those reading this work to compare and contrast these principles and mechanisms with those governing the legal accountability of government to the courts—in the chapters on the Human Rights Act, civil liberties, and judicial review—and decide what is the optimum balance of political and legal controls: all constitutional commentators agree that some mixture is needed, but disagree as to where the balance should lie.

POSTCRIPT

As noted above, the Brown Government's *Constitutional Renewal* package is flattered by its title (above, p 23). But on 2 February 2010, Gordon Brown, in a speech to the IPPR said the following:

> In the summer I announced that we would consult on the question of codifying our constitution as part of the consultation exercise on the British Bill of Rights and Responsibilities. There is, however, no consensus on what a codified constitution would be for, on what it would encompass and on what its status would be.
>
> But if we are to go ahead with a written constitution we clearly have to debate also what aspects of law and relationships between each part of the state and between the state and the citizen should be deemed 'constitutional'. I can therefore also announce today that a group will be set up to identify those principles and I hereby issue an invitation to all parties to be represented on this group. And if we are to decide to have a written constitution the time for its completion should be the 800th anniversary of the signing of the Magna Carta in Runneymede in 1215.
>
> The change of government in May 2010 leaves the above in doubt.

FURTHER READING

TRS Allan, *Law Liberty and Justice* (1995)

E Barendt, *An Introduction to Constitutional Law* (1998)

D Beetham, *The Legitimisation of Power* (1991)

R Bellamy, *Political Constitutionalism* (2007)

PP Craig, *Public Law and Democracy in the United Kingdom and United States of America* (1991)

CJ Friedrich, *Limited Government: A Comparison* (1991)

R Holme and M Elliot, *Time for a New Constitution* (1988)

IPPR, *A Written Constitution for the United Kingdom* (1991)

Sir WI Jennings, *The Law and the Constitution,* 5th edn (1959)

M Loughlin, *Public Law and Political Theory* (1992)

A Lyon, *Constitutional History of the United Kingdom* (2003)

G Marshall, *Constitutional Theory* (1981)

G Marshall and GC Moodie, *Some Problems of the Constitution* (1971)

P McAuslan and JF McEldowney (eds), *Law, Legitimacy and the Constitution* (1985) (essays)

R Slagstad, 'Liberal Constitutionalism and its Critics' (and other essays), in JK Wheare, *Modern Constitutions* (1966)

E Wicks, *The Evolution of a Constitution* (2006)

J Laws, 'Law and Democracy' [1995] PL 72

J Laws, 'The Constitution: Morals and Rights' [1996] PL 622

J Murkens, 'The Quest for Constitutionalism in UK Public Law Discourse' (2009) 29(3) OJLS 427

L Woolf-Phillips, 'A long look at the British Constitution' (1984) 37(4) *Parliamentary Affairs* 385

CHAPTER 2
THE NATURE AND ROLE
OF CONSTITUTIONAL
CONVENTIONS

INTRODUCTION

It is a characteristic of constitutions in general that they contain some areas which are governed by conventions, rather than by strict law. Constitutional Conventions may roughly be defined as non-legal, generally agreed rules about how government should be conducted and, in particular, governing the relations between different organs of government. Even where a country has a written constitution, conventions tend to evolve around the various rules. Since the UK has no comprehensive written constitution, it is particularly reliant on conventions, even to govern very important aspects of constitutional behaviour. The rule that the Queen will only exercise her very wide statutory and prerogative powers on and in accordance with the advice of Ministers is found in convention alone. It is generally known that, in a formal sense, the Queen appoints the Prime Minister. What is perhaps not generally appreciated is that when, for example, the Labour Party won the general election of 1997, that had no legal effect upon the Government. The UK did not have a Labour Government until Tony Blair was appointed Prime Minister by the Queen and asked to form a Government. Legally, the Queen can appoint whomsoever she chooses to be Prime Minister; it is only by convention that she must appoint as Prime Minister the person who is best able to command a majority in the House of Commons. The democratic basis of the UK's *government* (that is, the formation of its executive) therefore hangs upon convention, not law. The continuing placing of such heavy reliance on convention in a modern democracy purportedly governed by the Rule of Law is one of the more controversial features of the UK constitution. The historical explanation for why the UK constitution depends so heavily upon conventions is easy to find:

> Every constitution is likely to be based to some extent on convention as well as law. But conventions are likely to play a far larger and more prominent role in an uncodified constitution which is the product of a long period of evolution. There are likely to be fewer conventions in a country such as Israel, which, like Britain lacks a codified constitution, but is currently seeking to bring together its Basic Laws so as to enact one. For Israel did not begin as a state until 1948, and her history is not long enough for her to have acquired a substantial accretion of conventions. In the case of a country seeking to draw up a constitution *de novo* [from scratch] as, for example, with the German Basic Law in 1949, the problem of course does not exist.[1]

It should be noted that individual conventions will be examined in detail in subsequent chapters where relevant. Thus, important conventions concerning relations between the organs of government generally are considered in Chapter 3; those specifically governing the relations between the Lords and Commons will be examined in Chapter 9; and the key conventions of individual and collective ministerial responsibility are analysed in Chapter 12.

THE VARIETY OF CONVENTIONS

Conventions indeed rear their heads in a great many areas of the British constitution. A non-exhaustive list of the more important conventions would include the following:

---

1   V Bogdanor and S Vogenauer, 'Enacting a British Constitution: Some Problems' [2008] PL 38, 45.

- The Queen's powers under the Royal Prerogative relating to foreign affairs (e.g. the use of the armed forces) are to be exercised on the advice of Ministers (in reality, are exercised *by* Ministers);
- The Queen, when selecting a Prime Minister, must choose the party leader best able to command a working majority in the House of Commons (*or* the confidence of the Commons);
- The Queen's power to dissolve Parliament (resulting in a General Election) should be exercised on the advice of the Prime Minister (although there may be exceptions);
- The Queen's other prerogatives (other than her personal prerogatives) should be exercised on the advice of Ministers, or the relevant Minister, e.g. the Justice Secretary in effect exercises the prerogative of mercy;
- The Queen should give the Royal Assent (a necessary part of a valid Act of Parliament) to any Bill properly passed by Parliament;
- The Queen's power to appoint and dismiss Ministers is to be exercised on the advice of the Prime Minister (in effect, is exercised *by* the Prime Minister);
- A Government defeated on a motion of no confidence in the House of Commons must resign;
- Ministers are responsible and accountable to Parliament for the conduct, policy and administration of their departments; they must not knowingly mislead Parliament;
- Members of the Government must abide by collective responsibility; if they wish to publicly diverge from government policy they should resign (unless the PM licences such disagreement);
- Ministers should lay treaties before the House of Commons before they are ratified (the 'Ponsonby Rule');
- The House of Lords should not vote down at Second Reading, nor introduce wrecking amendments to government bills that implement a manifesto promise of the governing party (the 'Salisbury Convention');
- The UK Parliament will not normally legislate in the areas devolved to the relevant Scottish, Welsh, and Northern Ireland bodies without consent (the 'Sewell Convention');
- Parliament shall be summoned every year;
- Governments should not spend public money on government communications that have a party-political purpose;
- The advice of the law officers to the Government is confidential;
- Civil servants must be appointed and promoted strictly on merit and must remain impartial, serving each Government of the day;
- Government should seek the consent of Parliament before committing the armed forces to combat, save in urgent cases (this convention is of a doubtful status).

It should be noted that a number of the above are subject to exceptions and/or qualifications (some disputed), and even outright doubts as to their existence (e.g. the last stated, which is based upon the single precedent of the debate in the Commons in March 2003 before the Iraq war). Some of these issues are discussed further below. The list is not exhaustive: for example, there are a considerable number of important Conventions relating to the conduct of business in Parliament (e.g. in relation to the Speaker, and to the time given to government business). As Marshall notes:

> Amongst the conventions of the Constitution there are some whose formulation is reasonably precise and specific, and others whose formulation is in more general terms. An example of the first kind is the rule that the Queen must assent to Bills that have received the approval of both Houses. An example of the second kind is that the House of Lords should not obstruct the policy of an elected Government with a majority in the House of Commons. Many conventions fall into the second

category. This, perhaps, explains why so many questions of constitutional propriety remain unsettled. Might a British Government ever be dismissed by the Crown (comparably with what happened in Australia in 1975)? Is a Prime Minister entitled to dissolve Parliament and hold a general election whenever she wishes? Can a Government continue in office if its major legislation is defeated in the House of Commons? May a minister blame his civil servants if mistakes are made in the work of his department? The answers to all these questions are uncertain because, in each case, there is a general rule whose limits have not been fully explored; or possibly there may be two rules which are potentially in conflict.[2]

Notes

1. Examples of the uncertainty of many important conventions may be multiplied. To give just one example, Geoffrey Marshall and Graeme Moodie note[3] Ivor Jennings' suggestion that: '. . .in framing social legislation the appropriate department must consult the appropriate 'interest' and ask, 'what exactly is the rule?' Must every interest be consulted on every piece of social legislation? At what stage must they be consulted?' Even those Conventions which seem to the simplest and clearest may contain hidden ambiguities. For example, the notion that the Queen's Royal Assent to legislation must be granted to Bills passed by Parliament may not cover all circumstances: there is considerable disagreement as to whether, and if so, when, it might be proper for the Queen to refuse such assent. For discussion of this issue, covering also the similar position of Governors in Australian states, see Anne Twomey, 'The Refusal or Deferral of Royal Assent' [2006] PL 579.

2. As suggested above, great uncertainty also surrounds the conventional limits placed upon the extent to which it is constitutionally proper for the unelected House of Lords repeatedly to reject legislation, or particular provisions of legislation, approved by the Commons. There is one clear convention—the Salisbury Convention—to the effect that the Lords should neither reject nor radically amend legislation which puts into effect pledges made in the governing party's manifesto. But even this convention is now disputed by the Liberal Democrats[4] and others who contend that it ended with the removal of the bulk of the hereditary peers in 1999. Moreover, the conventional limitations on their powers in relation to non-manifesto legislation are far less clear. This matter is discussed in detail in Chapter 9, pp 442–445 in which the views of the Joint Committee on Conventions on the Lords-Commons Conventions[5] are considered; their findings are considered below under 'Codifying Conventions'.

3. An interesting and important question is whether conventions may be deliberately created: while seemingly not fitting well with the orthodox accounts of conventions considered below, in which there is heavy reliance on past practice, or 'precedents', the example of the so-called 'Sewel Convention' seems to indicate unequivocally that the answer is 'yes'. A new convention was deemed necessary upon the creation of the Scottish Parliament in 1998, exercising a wide range of legislative powers in Scotland. The legal doctrine of Parliamentary sovereignty—and the Scotland Act itself[6]—provide that the Westminster Parliament remains fully legally competent to legislate for Scotland, even in the areas devolved. However, if in practice, Westminster used this power against the wishes of the Scottish Parliament, then the intended result of devolution—governance of the devolved areas by the devolved institutions—would be frustrated. As a result, at the time that the

2   Geoffrey Marshall, *Constitutional Conventions* (1984), p 4.

3   *Some Problems of the Constitution*, 5th edn (1971), pp 31–32.

4   See, e.g. the speech of Lord Gresford, HL Debs, 23 May 2005, col 273 et seq.

5   2005–06, HL Paper 265-I/HC 1212-I.

6   Section 28(7).

Scotland Act was being considered by Parliament, the UK Government announced what became known as the 'Sewel Convention', now contained in the following document:

Memorandum of Understanding and Supplementary Agreements Between the United Kingdom Government Scottish Ministers, the Cabinet of the National Assembly for Wales and the Northern Ireland Executive Committee, Cm 5240 (2001) (extracts)

1 This Memorandum sets out the understanding of on the one hand, the United Kingdom Government, and on the other, Scottish Ministers, the Cabinet of the National Assembly for Wales and the Northern Ireland Executive Committee ('the devolved administrations') of the principles that will underlie relations between them. . .

2 This Memorandum is a statement of political intent, and should not be interpreted as a binding agreement. It does not create legal obligations between the parties. It is intended to be binding in honour only. . .

13 The United Kingdom Parliament retains authority to legislate on any issue, whether devolved or not. It is ultimately for Parliament to decide what use to make of that power. However, the UK Government will proceed in accordance with the convention that the UK Parliament would not normally legislate with regard to devolved matters except with the agreement of the devolved legislature. The devolved administrations will be responsible for seeking such agreement as may be required for this purpose on an approach from the UK Government.

14 The United Kingdom Parliament retains the absolute right to debate, enquire into or make representations about devolved matters. It is ultimately for Parliament to decide what use to make of that power, but the UK Government will encourage the UK Parliament to bear in mind the primary responsibility of devolved legislatures and administrations in these fields and to recognise that it is a consequence of Parliament's decision to devolve certain matters that Parliament itself will in future be more restricted in its field of operation.

Notes

1. Records kept by the Scottish Parliament show that the procedure by which the Westminster Parliament legislates on devolved areas, but with the consent of the Scottish Parliament—known as 'Sewel motions'—has been used regularly: so often indeed, that some commentators have referred to Westminster as 'Scotland's Other Parliament'.[7] Thirty-nine such motions were passed in the first session (1999–2003), thirty-eight in the second (2003–2007) and nine since 9 May 2007, in the third session. This heavy reliance on Westminster legislation even in the devolved areas has been queried by some in Scotland.[8] However, the point for present purposes is that the (new) convention has been adhered to without exception—Westminster has not legislated in the devolved areas without a consent motion. Evidently, therefore a convention *can* be deliberately created.[9]

---

7   'Scotland's other Parliament: Westminster Legislation about devolved Matters in Scotland since Devolution' [2002] PL 501.

8   E.g. N Burrows 'This is Scotland's Parliament; Let Scotland's Parliament Legislate' (2002) *Juridical Review* 213–36.

9   Though see the dissenting views of Munro, 'Thoughts on the Sewel Convention' 2003 SLT (News) 194 and Jaconelli, 'The Nature of Constitutional Convention' [1999] 19 LS 24, 39–40. Both argue that statements like Sewel only amount to something like statements of intent to create conventions—which can only actually come into being following a sustained period of obedience to the promised practice.

2. The Government recently proposed, as part of its Constitutional Renewal package[10] that 'the House of Commons should develop a convention', to be formalised by a Resolution of the House, to the effect that, save in cases of emergency, the consent of the Commons should be sought before committing the armed forces to conflict.[11] This issue is considered in detail in Chapter 11 on prerogative powers, at pp 565–571. For detailed and critical consideration of deliberate attempts to create Conventions, see A. McHarg, 'Reforming the United Kingdom Constitution: Law, Convention, Soft Law' (2008) 71(6) MLR 853.

ATTEMPTS TO DEFINE CONVENTIONS

Colin Munro has noted that Dicey's methodology in dealing with conventions was not 'to offer a definition'. Instead, 'Conventions were illustrated by examples, and negatively defined by the fact that they were not court-enforced'.[12] He considers the success of this method, and its critics, particularly Sir Ivor Jennings.

C Munro, *Studies in Constitutional Law*, 2nd edn (1999), pp 61–63, 65–66, 70–71

One technique employed by Jennings was to point to certain kinds of similarity or interaction between laws and conventions. Both sorts of rule rested upon general acquiescence, he suggested, and the major conventions were as firmly fixed and might be stated with almost as much accuracy as principles of common law [*The Law and the Constitution*, 5th edn, pp 72, 117]. The late Professor JOB Mitchell built up further arguments of this sort:

Conventions cannot be regarded as less important than rules of law. Often the legal rule is the less important. In relation to subject-matter the two types of rule overlap: in form they are often not clearly distinguishable. . .very many conventions are capable of being expressed with the precision of a Rule of Law, or of being incorporated into law. Precedent is as operative in the formation of convention as it is in that of law. It cannot be said that a Rule of Law is necessarily more certain than is a convention. It may therefore be asked whether it is right to distinguish law from convention [*Constitutional Law*, 2nd edn (1968), p 34]. . .

These statements appear to be of varying acceptability, but are apt to mislead. For example, there seems to be only a small number of conventions in this country whose existence and precise formulation are generally agreed, so that the statements about precision and certainty are very questionable. Sometimes there seems to be force in the assertion that the convention is more important than the law, but it is hard to see how their relative importance can be measured.

---

10 See *The Governance of Britain* 7170 (2007)—the Green Paper and Cm 7342-I (2008)—the White Paper.

11 Green Paper, at 18; White Paper, at 47–56.

12 *Studies in Constitutional Law* (1987), p 53.

Besides, the important point is that none of Mitchell's propositions, even if accurate, would entail the conclusion which he went on to derive from them, that any effort to distinguish laws and conventions is bound to fail. This is readily illustrated by applying some of the comparisons to other bodies of rules:

> Rules of morality cannot be regarded as less important than rules of law. . .in relation to subject-matter the two types of rules overlap. . .Very many religious edicts are capable of being expressed with the precision of a Rule of Law, or of being incorporated into law. Precedent is as operative in the formation of etiquette as it is in that of law. It cannot be said that a Rule of Law is necessarily more certain than is a rule of cricket.

These new statements are just as accurate as the others, to put it no higher. We cannot draw from them the conclusion that the laws are indistinguishable from rules of morality, religion, etiquette or cricket. In fact, the explanation of why conventions, and all these, reveal some similarities to laws is simple: they are all rules operating in society, and certain similarities, especially of form, are only to be expected.

A ginger ale, however, is not the same as a whisky, merely because each is amber in colour and liquid in form. The critical question is whether laws may be differentiated from conventions. Dicey, who was in no doubt that they might be, also suggested a means:

> The rules which make up constitutional law, as the term is used in England, include two sets of principles or maxims of a totally distinct character. The one set of rules are in the strictest sense 'laws', since they are rules which (whether written or unwritten, whether enacted by statute or derived from the mass of custom, tradition or judge-made maxims known as the common law) are enforced by the courts; these rules constitute 'constitutional law' in the proper sense of that term, and may for the sake of distinction be called collectively 'the law of the constitution'.
>
> The other set of rules consist of conventions, understandings, habits or practices which, though they may regulate the conduct of. . .officials, are not in reality laws at all since they are not enforced by the courts. This portion of constitutional law may, for the sake of distinction, be termed the 'conventions of the constitution', or constitutional morality [Dicey, p 23]. . .

Laws and enforcement

. . . What many have regarded as a more serious challenge to Dicey's test is posed by areas of law where the jurisdiction of the courts is apparently excluded, perhaps by an explicit provision that a duty may not be enforced in court proceedings or by the provision of an administrative channel as the exclusive remedy. Sometimes there are provisions of written constitutions in other countries which are expressed as non-justiciable, or are interpreted as such [for example, the Directive Principles of State Policy in the Constitution of India, which Article 37 declares not enforceable by any court]. Take the example that Jennings gives, a statutory duty upon local authorities to provide adequate sewers and disposal works, which was, under a statute, only remediable by means of complaint to the Minister of Housing and Local Government. When proceedings were brought in court, the House of Lords held that Parliament had deprived the courts of jurisdiction in that area, and that the complaint to the ministry was the sole means of redress (*Passmore v Oswaldwistle* UDC). The error that Jennings makes is in using the case as evidence that the law concerned was not court-enforced. The case is the best evidence possible that the law was court-enforced. Certainly a statutory duty was not judicially enforced, but that was precisely because the law said it should not be, and the courts obeyed the law and put it into effect. Other such examples may be explained in the same way. When provisions are unsusceptible to judicial enforcement, the correct analysis is either that no obligation is involved, as with some of the ideological pronouncements found in written constitutions, or is that an imperfect obligation has been created. None of this should surprise us. A legal system does not consist only of obligations for breach of which there is redress. . . These points are related to a larger contrast which may be drawn. Rules of law form parts of a system. Included in the system are rules about the rules: these are provisions about entry to, and exit from, the system, and procedures for the determination and application of the rules. We cannot conceive of a single legal rule, in isolation from a system. However, conventions do not form a system. There is no unifying feature which they possess, and no apparatus of secondary rules. They merely evolve in isolation from each other. Here, incidentally, lies the answer to Jennings's specious argument that laws and conventions are the same because both 'rest essentially upon general acquiescence' [*op cit*, p 117]. That is quite misleading. Conventions rest entirely on acquiescence, but individually. If a supposed convention is not accepted as binding by those to whom it would apply, then there could not be said to be a convention, and this is a test on which each must be separately assessed. Laws do not depend upon acquiescence. Individual laws may be unpopular or widely disobeyed, but it does not mean that they are not laws. No doubt the system as a whole must possess some measure of de facto effectiveness for us to recognise it as valid, although it might be stretching language to describe the citizens of any country occupied by enemy forces, or ruled by a brutal dictatorship as 'acquiescing' in the laws which govern them. In any event, is it obvious that the comparison is inapt.

Note

The distinction Munro draws as to the role which general acquiescence plays in relation to laws on the one hand and conventions on the other is a useful one. Jeremy Waldron has also considered this point, and draws a more general conclusion about the nature of conventions and the British constitution, after (in an earlier section of his essay) describing the appointment of Harold Macmillan's successor as Prime Minister.

J Waldron, *The Law* (1990), pp 62–67

It is important to say first that a convention is not just a regularity in political behaviour; it is not just a prediction of what reliably happens. Every year the Prime Minister moves to Chequers from Downing Street for Christmas. We can predict that she will do this, and we would be surprised if she didn't But surprise is all that would be occasioned by such an 'irregularity'. We wouldn't criticise the Prime Minister for not spending Christmas at Chequers. We don't see it as a principle or norm to judge her by. It is a regularity we have discerned in Prime Ministerial behaviour, not a standard Prime Ministers are supposed to live up to.

Now constitutional conventions are not like that They are normative. They are used for saying what ought to be done, and, as we saw, they are used as a basis for criticism if someone's behaviour does not live up to them. We use them to judge behaviour not merely to predict it.

But although they are norms, they would never be enforced by a court you could never get a judge to declare that a convention ought to be followed as a matter of law, and if someone decided to flout a convention the only remedy would be political not legal. (Either those in possession of political power— the people, the other office-holders, the military perhaps in the last resort—would put up with what had happened or they wouldn't. If they did, the convention would in effect have been changed. If they did not, there would be something akin to a revolution.) Most writers have said that since these are norms but not legal norms, the only conclusion possible is that they are moral norms—norms of political morality. AV Dicey, for example, wrote that conventions 'consisting (as they do) of customs, practices, maxims, or precepts which are not enforced or recognised by the courts, make up a body not of laws, but of constitutional or political ethics'. And Geoffrey Marshall says that they 'simply spell out the moral duties, rights, and powers of office-holders in relation to the machinery of government'.

But calling them 'moral' or 'ethical' doesn't really help. There are all sorts of different views about 'constitutional or political ethics' and about 'the moral duties, rights, and powers of office-holders'. Pacifists may think that MPs have a moral duty not to authorise expenditure on nuclear weapons. Radical democrats believe that no law should be passed without a referendum. Christian fundamentalists may believe that atheists should not be allowed to hold public office. All these are held by their proponents as moral norms, but I take it none of them would regard their principles as conventions of the constitution. Certainly, we think or we hope that there are moral justifications for the conventions we have. But there is no reason to be confident that they capture the best political morality. It is not their moral justification that makes them conventions of the British constitution. We have got to say something more specific.

Sir Kenneth Wheare once wrote that a convention is 'a rule of behaviour accepted as obligatory by those concerned in the working of the constitution'. That is an interesting definition because it suggests that, in the last resort these rules have no other basis than the fact that the people involved accept them as standards for their behaviour. They follow them in most cases; they feel guilt or compunction when they don't; they criticise deviations from them by others; and, what's more, everyone knows what is going on when these criticisms are made, for everyone has in mind roughly the same set of standards. They are not merely habits or regularities of behaviour; they enter into people's consciousness and become the subject-matter of reflection and of a sense of obligation. But they are not merely subjective views about morality either. They have a social reality, inasmuch as they capture a way in which people interact, a way in which people make demands on one another, and form attitudes and expectations about a common practice with standards that they are all living up to. They get mentioned in newspapers, in periodicals and in learned treaties. Politicians refer to them when they are evaluating one another's behaviour. They are social facts, not mere abstract principles, because they bind people together into a common form of life.

All this sounds very fragile compared with the robust reality of a statutory law or a written constitution. I have made it sound as though constitutional conventions are rules that pull themselves up by their own boot straps. They are rules because they are accepted as rules by those they bind, and if they weren't accepted by those they bind they wouldn't be rules at all. They have no other validity, no other force, than their common acceptance by the people they govern.

[Waldron then goes on to consider the jurisprudential aspect of this question, giving a brief outline of HLA Hart's theory that each system of law is based ultimately upon a supreme rule, which he terms 'The rule of recognition'.][13]

Rules of recognition

In Britain, the rule of recognition says (among other things) that a bill passed (in the appropriate way) by the two Houses of Parliament and assented to by the Queen has the force of law, and prevails over any earlier law or any other rule that conflicts with it. It tells us, in effect, to look at the institutional pedigree of a norm to see if it is a legal rule; look at its date, the process of its enactment and the formalities associated with it and that is all you need to know about its legal status. Other countries have more complicated rules of recognition; in the United States one has to look not only at how and when the Bill was passed (by both Houses of Congress, and with the President's assent or a fresh majority of two-thirds or more in each house of Congress) but also at its compatibility with the Bill of Rights embodied in the 1787 Constitution. And a full statement of the American rule of recognition would have to include the procedures for amending the constitution as well. Whatever the complexities, Hart's argument is that a legal system needs some such rule of recognition to identify what are to count at any time as its laws.

What gives the rule of recognition its legal force? What makes it the authoritative way of determining what the law is? The question does not really have an answer. It's a bit like asking what makes the US Constitution constitutional. The rule of recognition is just there. It is a social fact about the way people involved in the workings of our society—particularly lawyers, parliamentarians, judges, policemen, and so on—behave, and above all it's a fact about how they think they ought to behave. No doubt judges and so on have their reasons for thinking they should defer to the edicts of Parliament. Some of them may be democratic reasons; some of them may be reasons of tradition. But their practice of doing so—their practice of deferring to Parliament their practice of taking this as their standard—is not consecrated by any further authority. Their practice, their readiness to regard themselves as bound by this rule, is what makes our society a legal system; it's the fulcrum or the foundation of the rest. Without some social practice of this kind, there would be no legal system in Britain—that is, no shared sense among officials and people of which rules and commands they should expect to be upheld.

I brought up positivism and Hart's rule of recognition because I wanted to illustrate a general point about the foundations of political life. There is tradition, there is morality, there is affection, there is charisma, there is ideology, there is mystification, there are lies and—ultimately—there are bayonets and bullets. All of these are important in the analysis of politics, and all of them—including the last two (think of Northern Ireland)—have a part to play in explaining the stability of our political system. But there is also law and there is political order, regulating authority, succession, and the transfer and exercise of power. Law and political order matter an awful lot to us. But in the end they amount to an interlocking system of rules and practices that depend on nothing more concrete and nothing more secure than the readiness of those involved in political life to regulate and judge their own and others' behaviour by certain standards. Hart's theory of the rule of recognition implies

---

13   Hart's theory is set out in *The Concept of Law* (1961).

that something no more secure than this lies at the foundation of every legal system. What we have said about constitutional conventions indicates that they fall into this category as well. It is the fragile readiness of those involved in political life to order their conduct by certain implicit standards that forms the basis of whatever claim Britain has to be a constitutional regime.

What is different, then, about the British constitution is not that it rests in the last resort on a set of fragile understandings; that is true of every legal and constitutional system. Rather, the distinguishing fact about Britain is that so much of its constitutional law has that status. In other countries, there is a written charter whose authority rests implicitly on such a presupposition. Americans tacitly presuppose the authority of the delegates at the 1787 convention who began their document with 'We the People of the United States. . .' when they accept that document is binding. In Britain, however, the whole thing is a structure of tacit presuppositions from start to finish. There is no great charter whose authority is tacitly presupposed. There are just tacit presuppositions. That is the peculiar feature of our political life.

Notes

1. It should be noted that many jurists do not accept that the law can be identified solely by reference to its source, and that a legal system is thus based ultimately on a rule of recognition which identifies that source. The 'Natural Law' school argues that the ascertainment of whether a rule is a law is at bottom a moral exercise, whilst Ronald Dworkin has offered a 'third theory of law', in which interpretation and moral analysis play a key role in the identification of law, which, he argues, may exist before it is declared by any authoritative source.[14]

2. Crucial to the definition of conventions is the manner in which they are treated by the courts. Whilst at one time some commentators believed that 'the law courts can take no notice' of conventions at all, this notion has now been firmly scotched by the courts themselves. The Court of Appeal delivered an important judgment in a case arising out of the publication of the diaries of a former Cabinet Minister; the convention concerned was that of the collective responsibility of the Cabinet.

Attorney General v Jonathan Cape Ltd [1976] QB 752, 764, 770–71

Lord Widgery CJ: . . .It has always been assumed by lawyers and, I suspect, by politicians and the Civil Service, that Cabinet proceedings and Cabinet papers are secret, and cannot be publicly disclosed until they have passed into history. It is quite clear that no court will compel the production of Cabinet papers in the course of discovery in an action, and the Attorney General contends that not only will the court refuse to compel the production of such matters, but it will go further and positively forbid the disclosure of such papers and proceedings if publication will be contrary to the public interest.

The basis of this contention is the confidential character of these papers and proceedings, derived from the convention of joint Cabinet responsibility whereby any policy decision reached by the Cabinet has to be supported thereafter by all members of the Cabinet whether they approve of it or not, unless they feel compelled to resign. It is contended that Cabinet decisions and papers are confidential for a period to the extent at least that they must not be referred to outside the Cabinet in such a way as to disclose the

---

14   See *Taking Rights Seriously* (1977), Chapters 2–4, and for a more thorough exposition of R Dworkin's thesis, *Law's Empire* (1987).

attitude of individual ministers in the argument which preceded the decision. Thus, there may be no objection to a minister disclosing (or leaking, as it was called) the fact that a Cabinet meeting has taken place, or, indeed, the decision taken, so long as the individual views of ministers are not identified.

There is no doubt that Mr Crossman's manuscripts contain frequent references to individual opinions of Cabinet ministers, and this is not surprising because it was his avowed object to obtain a relaxation of the convention regarding memoirs of ex-ministers. . .There have, as far as I know, been no previous attempts in any court to define the extent to which Cabinet proceedings should be treated as secret or confidential, and it is not surprising that different views on this subject are contained in the evidence before me. . .

It is convenient next to deal with [the] submission. . .that the evidence does not prove the existence of a convention as to collective responsibility, or adequately define a sphere of secrecy. I find overwhelming evidence that the doctrine of joint responsibility is generally understood and practised and equally strong evidence that it is on occasion ignored. The general effect of the evidence is that the doctrine is an established feature of the English form of government, and it follows that some matters leading up to a Cabinet decision may be regarded as confidential. Furthermore, I am persuaded that the nature of the confidence is that spoken for by the Attorney General, namely, that since the confidence is imposed to enable the efficient conduct of the Queen's business, the confidence is owed to the Queen and cannot be released by the members of Cabinet themselves. I have been told that a resigning minister who wishes to make a personal statement in the House, and to disclose matters which are confidential under the doctrine, obtains the consent of the Queen for this purpose. Such consent is obtained through the Prime Minister.

The Cabinet is at the very centre of national affairs, and must be in possession at all times of information which is secret or confidential. Secrets relating to national security may require to be preserved indefinitely. Secrets relating to new taxation proposals may be of the highest importance until Budget day, but public knowledge thereafter. To leak a Cabinet decision a day or so before it is officially announced is an accepted exercise in public relations, but to identify the ministers who voted one way or another is objectionable because it undermines the doctrine of joint responsibility.

It is evident that there cannot be a single rule governing the publication of such a variety of matters. In these actions we are concerned with the publication of diaries at a time when 11 years have expired since the first recorded events. The Attorney General must show (a) that such publication would be a breach of confidence; (b) that the public interest requires that the publication be restrained; and (c) that there are no other facts of the public interest contradictory of and more compelling than that relied upon. Moreover, the court, when asked to restrain such a publication, must closely examine the extent to which relief is necessary to ensure that restrictions are not imposed beyond the strict requirement of public need.

Applying those principles to the present case, what do we find? In my judgment, the Attorney General has made out his claim that the expression of individual opinions by Cabinet ministers in the course of Cabinet discussion are matters of confidence, the publication of which can be restrained by the court when this is clearly necessary in the public interest.

The maintenance of the doctrine of joint responsibility within the Cabinet is in the public interest, and the application of that doctrine might be prejudiced by premature disclosure of the views of individual Ministers. . .

In the present case there is nothing in Mr Crossman's work to suggest that he did not support the doctrine of joint Cabinet responsibility. The question for the court is whether it is shown that publication now might damage the doctrine notwithstanding that much of the action is up to 10 years old and three general elections have been held meanwhile. So far as the Attorney General relies in his argument on the disclosure of individual ministerial opinions, he has not satisfied me that publication would in any way inhibit free and open discussion in Cabinet hereafter.

Notes

1. The Court of Appeal thus found that the convention in question *could* support an argument (based on breach of confidence) for legal restraint of publication, though, in the event, the action failed on the ground that, due to the lapse of time, the material had lost its confidential quality. The case is not the only example of conventions being taken into account by the courts. For example, in *Liversidge v Anderson* [1942] AC 206, HL and *Carltona Ltd v Commissioner of Works* [1943] 2 All ER 560 the courts supported the refusal to review the grounds on which executive discretionary powers had been exercised on the basis that a Minister is responsible to Parliament for the exercise of his power.

2. In considering the *Jonathan Cape* case, TRS Allan comments:

    . . . the recognition of convention by a court in the course of adjudication generally entails its acceptance as a rule which is legitimate. It is acknowledged as a rule of practice which is grounded in political principle. Curial 'recognition' implies judicial approval. In the result, the distinction between recognition and enforcement–that last refuge of orthodox theory–plainly dissolves. To recognise a convention is necessarily to endorse the principle which justifies it; and, in a context where legal doctrine is developed to reflect that principle, recognition means enforcement.[15]

    Jaconelli, however, flatly disagrees:

    [Allan's argument]. . .infer[s] too much from the occasional recognition, in cases such as this, of the existence of a constitutional convention. Allan's leap from recognition to enforcement, in particular, is totally unwarranted. Recall the typical example of a social rule: that men are to remove their hats in church. That standard of conduct may meet with widespread approval, including the approval of the judges. It does not follow that judges would be right to express their approval in the shape of inflicting a *legal* sanction on the occasional man who has refused to bare his head in church.[16]

3. In 1982, the Supreme Court of Canada had to consider a convention of the utmost importance, namely the understanding that the Senate and House of Commons of Canada would not seek to amend the constitution of Canada in such a way as to affect either the legislative role or the status of the provincial legislatures without first obtaining the consent of all Canada's provinces to such a change. The federal Government of Canada was seeking to make quite important changes to the federal system of Canada and had only obtained the assent of a small number of the provinces;

---

15   *Law, Liberty, and Justice: The Legal Foundations of British Constitutionalism* (1993), at 244.

16   J Jaconelli, 'Do Constitutional Conventions Bind?' [2005] 64(1) CLJ 149, 160–61.

a declaration was sought from the court to the effect that it would be unlawful for such changes to be made without seeking the consent of all the provinces. It was argued that the convention of obtaining such consent, which no one disputed, had 'crystallised' into a (constitutional) law. The court rejected this argument, finding that failure to obtain the necessary consents would not render any subsequent amendment unlawful. It was, however, prepared to say that 'the agreement of the Provinces of Canada, no views being expressed as to its quantification, is constitutionally required' and that acting without such consents 'would be unconstitutional in the conventional sense'. For an extract from the case see below at pp 64–65.

4. What therefore happened in this case was that a court made a non-binding finding as to what action a particular convention required, thereby giving it at least a degree of justiciability, and greatly increasing the likelihood that the conventional rule, once authoritatively declared, would be followed. Although the Canadian Government would, strictly speaking, have been free to ignore this judgment, it clearly did not wish to act in a way which the Supreme Court had described as 'unconstitutional' and therefore entered into negotiations with the provinces, eventually obtaining the consent of nine out of 10 of them to its plans. It may be noted that the Australian High Court has refused to make such declaratory judgments on the content of Conventions: *Judiciary and Navigation Acts* (1921) 29 CLR 257.

5. A more systematic attempt to define conventions has been attempted by Sir Ivor Jennings, as follows:

> We have to ask ourselves three questions. First, what are the precedents; secondly, did the actors in the precedents believe that they were bound by a rule; and thirdly, is there a reason for the rule? A single precedent with a good reason may be enough to establish the rule. A whole string of precedents without such a reason will be of no avail, unless it is perfectly certain that the persons concerned regarded them as bound by it.[17]

His analysis is considered by Marshall and Moodie below.

G Marshall and GC Moodie, *Some Problems of the Constitution*, 5th edn (1971), pp 28–33

Sir Ivor Jennings's account of conventions. . .is more convincing, but it is not entirely free from obscurity. . .For a convention to exist and operate the actors must obviously be aware of it and, in particular, of its obligatory character (even if in fact they conform to it for reasons other than self-conscious virtue). This awareness of obligation is a necessary characteristic of a convention, but it is a sure guide only if this obligation is felt very generally among those who work the constitution, i.e. among the authorities. Its absence may be conclusive, but not its presence. In and of itself it is not and cannot be a sufficient test: the actors may be divided in their opinions or they may be mistaken about their obligations. . .

4 Precedents
How then are reasons for conventional rules related to precedents? In the English legal system all cases decided in the highest courts of the judicial hierarchy are precedents, in the sense that these decisions are binding upon all other courts in all other similar cases.

---

17   *The Law and the Constitution*, 5th edn (1959) at p 136.

In this manner, judicial decisions, or precedents, may be said to establish rules of law. Where conventions are concerned, however, it seems that not even a series of similar precedent actions will always suffice to establish a conventional rule—if indeed it ever suffices. A distinction has therefore been drawn by Sir Ivor Jennings between precedents which do, and those which do not, establish a rule, i.e. between 'normative' and 'simple' precedents [Jennings, *Cabinet Government*, 2nd edn, p 7]. But in both legal and ordinary English we tend to use the word 'precedent' to refer to instances which, for some reason other than the fact of occurrence itself, are deemed to be relevant, desirable, or acceptable models for future action. Sir Ivor remarks at one point of the 'agreement to differ' amongst ministers in 1932: 'No harm was done by the precedent of 1932 provided that it is not regarded as a precedent' [*ibid*, 3rd edn, p 281]. A 'simple' precedent, in other words, could hardly be distinguished from no precedent at all. . .

The instance of 1924 is an instructive one. It is justifiable to query the opinion that King George V established a new rule (that the Prime Minister should always be a Member of the House of Commons) when he appointed Mr Baldwin instead of Lord Curzon. On the other hand, there now seems to exist a widespread view that a Prime Minister should not belong to a Chamber in which one party has little representation and in which few major debates or decisions occur. For some such reason, the King's action in 1924 may now be referred to as a precedent. But this reason would have existed whether or not there had existed a noble alternative to Mr Baldwin.

5 Obedience to conventions

Neither a general feeling of obligation among the authorities, nor precedents, therefore, suffice either to establish a rule or conclusively to demonstrate its existence and precise content.

The first part of the answer is contained in Jennings's suggestion that 'conventions are obeyed because of the political difficulties which follow if they are not' [*ibid*, p 129]. To complete the answer one must inquire what sort of political difficulties they are, for it is clear that political difficulties can arise from many actions which involve no breach of a convention. A Government runs into 'political difficulties' whenever it displeases some section of the community, whether it be by raising rents or refusing to issue a stamp commemorating the birth of Robert Burns, but it cannot seriously be claimed that either decision is in any sense 'unconstitutional'. Nevertheless it is by examining the effects of a breach of conventions that the reason for their existence is to be found. If a UK Government had, before 1931, legislated for a 'dominion', or had, since then, introduced legislation affecting the status of the Crown, without obtaining the consent of the countries concerned, it is likely that one or more members of the Commonwealth might have severed their connections with it; or, at least, that Commonwealth ties would have been imperilled. The serious breach in the conventions limiting the power of the House of Lords which occurred in 1909 resulted directly in the passing of the Parliament Act of 1911, just as Roosevelt's re-election for a third and fourth term led to the adoption of the 22nd Amendment to the American Constitution which makes a third term legally impermissible. . .These examples indicate that the conventions describe the way in which certain legal powers must be exercised if the powers are to be tolerated by those affected. The monarch's legal powers to rule, the House of Lords' legal powers to reject a bill passed by the Commons, the legal power of the UK Parliament to pass imperial legislation—all these powers are or were retained only for so long as they are exercised (or not exercised) in accordance with the conventions which have been established. Their potential abolition constitutes the 'political difficulties' which would probably follow upon a breach in the conventions of the constitution.

From this view of the nature of conventions it follows that a crucial question must always be whether or not a particular class of action is likely to destroy respect for the established distribution of authority.

Such an account of the relationship between law and convention bears a resemblance to that put forward by Dicey, but it differs therefrom in an important respect. According to Dicey, a breach in a convention involved the probability of a consequential breach of the law. But the truth is rather that a breach of a convention is likely to induce a change in the law or even in the whole constitutional structure. In this relationship, it may be suggested, is to be found the 'reason' for the conventions, stated in its most general form.

Notes

1. Joseph Jaconelli has recently re-considered Jennings' proposed tests.[18] He criticises the first requirement, that of precedent, noting that it may in practice amount to little more than 'a selective exercise in constitutional history'[19] and that it is not clear how 'history—in some cases. . .quite distant history [can] tell us what course of conduct *is required* of [the relevant person]'.[20] He also criticises Jennings for failing to provide any indication of what will count as a 'good' reason for a given alleged convention, when there may be strong reasons both for and against its continuance.[21]

2. A matter that is of obvious relevance to this debate is the reason(s) *why* conventions are obeyed by those who they purport to bind. This issue is considered by Marshall, below.

G Marshall, *Constitutional Conventions* (1984), pp 5–8

In the opening chapter of the Law of the Constitution Dicey, in discussing 'the rules that belong to the conventions of the Constitution', remarks that 'some of these maxims are never violated and are universally admitted to be inviolable. Others on the other hand have nothing but a slight amount of custom in their favour and are of disputable validity' [*Law of the Constitution*, 10th edn, p 26]. Confusingly, he goes on to explain this difference as one that rests upon the distinction between rules that bring their violators into conflict with the law of the land, and rules 'that may be violated without any other consequence than that of exposing the Minister or other person by whom they were broken to blame or unpopularity' [*ibid*]. This does not chime very easily with the thesis that the reason for obedience to all conventions is that breach of the conventions leads more or less directly to a breach of law. Dicey has often been criticised for holding this view, but it seems clear that he did not hold it in relation to all conventions. Indeed, it seems an explanation confined to a single contingency, namely the possibility that a Government might try to remain in office and raise taxes after losing the confidence of the House of Commons. But Dicey mentions a number of examples in which no illegal consequences would follow a breach of conventional principles. A Government that persuaded the House of Commons to suspend

---

18   J Jaconelli, 'The Nature of Constitutional Convention' (1999) 19 LS 24.

19   *Ibid*, p 28.

20   *Ibid*, p 29.

21   *Ibid*.

the Habeas Corpus Acts after one reading, or induced the House to alter the rules as to the number of times a Bill should be read would not, he said, come into conflict with the law of the land. Nor indeed would the House of Lords if it rejected a series of Bills passed by the Commons.

Some who have criticised Dicey's supposed explanation for obedience to conventions have suggested alternative reasons. Sir Ivor Jennings argued, for example, that conventions are obeyed 'because of the political difficulties which follow if they are not' [*The Law and the Constitution*, 5th edn, p 134]. Others have suggested that they are obeyed not because of the probability of a consequential breach of law, but because disregard of convention is likely to induce a change in the law or in the constitutional structure. But it could be objected that, in the case of many infringements of convention, legal or structural change would be an unlikely outcome. It may be more illuminating first to remember that widespread breach of political (as of linguistic) convention may itself sometimes lead to a change of convention, and secondly that conventions are not always obeyed. So, although we can sensibly ask what the uses or purposes of conventions are, it may be unnecessary to ask why they are obeyed when they are obeyed, since we pick out and identify as conventions precisely those rules that are generally obeyed and generally thought to be obligatory. Those who obey moral or other non-legal rules they believe to be obligatory, characteristically do it because of their belief that they are obligatory, or else from some motive of prudence or expected advantage. Those who disobey them do so because they do not regard them as obligatory, or wish to evade them, or wish to change them. In other words we do not need any special or characteristic explanation for obedience to the rules of governmental morality. Whatever we know about compliance with moral rules generally, will suffice.

Note

If the reason that conventions are obeyed is simply that they are thought obligatory by those affected by them, then it appears that the more important question is, what purposes do conventions serve? Whilst answers to this question have been touched on (Dicey—to avoid a breach of the law; Jennings—to avoid political difficulty), these are too general answers as they would also serve as plausible explanations for a great deal of human behaviour. Can more specific purposes for conventions be elucidated?

THE ROLE OF CONVENTIONS

The role of conventions was considered by the Supreme Court of Canada in the case mentioned below.

Reference re Amendment of the Constitution of Canada
(1982) 125 DLR (3d) 1 (extracts)

. . . The main purpose of constitutional conventions is to ensure that the legal framework of the constitution will be operated in accordance with the prevailing constitutional values or principles of the period. For example, the constitutional value which is the pivot of the conventions stated above and relating to responsible government is the democratic principle: the powers of the state must be exercised in accordance with the wishes of the electorate; and the constitutional value or principle which anchors the conventions regulating the relationship between the members of the Commonwealth is the independence of the former British colonies. . .

Perhaps the main reason why convention rules cannot be enforced by the courts is that they are generally in conflict with the legal rules which they postulate, and the courts are bound to enforce the legal rules. The conflict is not of a type which would entail the commission of any illegality. It results from the fact that legal rules create wide powers, discretions and rights which conventions prescribe should be exercised only in a certain limited manner, if at all.

[An] example will illustrate this point. As a matter of law, the Queen, or the Governor General or the Lieutenant Governor could refuse assent to every Bill passed by both Houses of Parliament or by a legislative assembly as the case may be. But by convention they cannot of their own motion refuse to assent to any such Bill on any ground, for instance, because they disapprove of the policy of the Bill. We have here a conflict between a legal rule which creates a complete discretion and a conventional rule which completely neutralises it. But conventions, like laws, are sometimes violated. And if this particular convention were violated and assent were improperly withheld, the courts would be bound to enforce the law, not the convention. They would refuse to recognise the validity of a vetoed bill. This is what happened in *Gallant v The King* (1949) 2 DLR 425. . .a case in keeping with the classic case of *Stockdale v Hansard* (1839) 9 Ad and El, 112 ER 1112, where the English Court of Queen's Bench held that only the Queen and both Houses of Parliament could make or unmake laws. The Lieutenant-Governor who had withheld assent in *Gallant* apparently did so towards the end of his term of office. Had it been otherwise, it is not inconceivable that his withholding of assent might have produced a political crisis leading to his removal from office, which shows that if the remedy for a breach of a convention does not lie with the courts, still the breach is not necessarily without a remedy. The remedy lies with some other institutions of Government; furthermore, it is not a formal remedy and it may be administered with less certainty or regularity than it would be by a court.

It should be borne in mind, however, that, while they are not laws, some conventions may be more important than some laws. Their importance depends on that of the value or principle which they are meant to safeguard. Also, they form an integral part of the constitution and of the constitutional system. . .

That is why it is perfectly appropriate to say that to violate a convention is to do something which is unconstitutional, although it entails no direct legal consequence. But the words 'constitutional' and 'unconstitutional' may also be used in a strict legal sense, for instance with respect to a statute which is found ultra vires or unconstitutional. The foregoing may perhaps be summarised in an equation: constitutional conventions plus constitutional law equal the total constitution of the country.

Questions

❶   Is it not rather a paradoxical state of affairs for any nation priding itself on upholding the Rule of Law that 'important parts of [its] constitution. . .more important than some laws' may be violated with 'no direct legal consequences'?

❷   The court found that the basic purpose of conventions is 'to ensure the legal framework of the Constitution in accordance with the prevailing constitutional values or principles of the period'. No doubt responsiveness to changing views as to what political morality demands is desirable. But take the case of a Minister whose department bungles the implementation of a new policy in such a way that there is room for doubt as to whether the policy or its implementation are at fault.[22] The Minister claims that the convention of ministerial responsibility has now developed in such a way that it only requires ministerial resignation if it is conclusively shown that policy, rather than its implementation, is to blame. Is it necessary that the person who would suffer through the imposition of a conventional rule upon them must be the person who also decides what that rule is?[23] Can flexibility be achieved without allowing people to be judges in their own cause in this way?

Notes

1. Marshall and Moodie note the prevalence of conventions in all constitutions and link this with what they see as their role.

   ... No general Rule of Law is self-applying, but must be applied according to the terms of additional rules. These additional rules may be concerned with the interpretation of the general rule, or with the exact circumstances in which it should apply, about either of which uncertainty may exist, and the greater the generality the greater will the uncertainty tend to be. Many constitutions include a large number of additional legal rules to clarify the meaning and application of their main provisions, but in a changing world it is rarely possible to eradicate or prevent all doubts on these points by enactment or even by adjudication. The result often is to leave significant degree of discretion to those exercising the rights or wielding the powers legally conferred, defined, or permitted. As Dicey pointed out, it is to regulate the use of such discretionary power that conventions develop [*op cit*, pp 426–29].

   The definition of 'conventions' may thus be amplified by saying that their purpose is to define the use of constitutional discretion. To put this in slightly different words, it may be said that conventions are non-legal rules regulating the way in which legal rules shall be applied.

2. In an illuminating article, Elliott offers a contemporary example of the effect of conventions upon the most important legal rule in the UK constitution: the sovereignty of Parliament. He argues that one effect of the Labour Government's radical programme of constitutional reform has been to widen the gap still further between the strict legal doctrine of parliamentary sovereignty, under which its powers are unlimited, and the political reality: it is, for example, inconceivable that Westminster would in reality simply abolish the Scottish Parliament (at least without the clear consent of the Scottish people). His suggestion is that constitutional conventions form a way of bridging the gap between legal theory and political reality, and may also come to have an influence on the *law* of the constitution as well.

---

22   The responsibility of the then Home Secretary Michael Howard for the problems in the Prison Service revealed by the Learmont Report in October 1995 is a case in point. See further Chapter 12, pp 638–642.

23   The views of the Prime Minister and other Ministers on the content of the convention will also obviously be important. However, since resignation (in the example given in the text) would amount to an admission of responsibility for the errors which have come to light, these other parties also have a clear vested outcome in the decision.

**M Elliott, 'Parliamentary sovereignty and new constitutional order:
legislative freedom, political reality and convention'
[2002] 22(3) *Legal Studies* 340 (extracts)**

As regional autonomy and human rights become increasingly embedded within the British constitutional order, so it is to be expected that conventions will emerge—indeed some have already begun to emerge [see below for discussion of the Sewel Convention] concerning the acceptable limitations of legislative action by the Westminster Parliament. In this way, convention comes to bridge the gap between a constitutional theory of unlimited legislative authority, and the reality of a political environment within which regional authority and fundamental rights are regarded as tracing the perimeter of acceptable legislative conduct.

The deployment of convention in this manner is already familiar. . .[Elliott cites those restraining the Monarch] and conventions already exist which regulate the exercise of legislative action. [Elliott cites the convention observed by the UK Parliament in not legislating in those areas devolved to Stormont during the period of devolution to Northern Ireland between 1920 and 1972.] Moreover, as. . .conventions. . .are inherently flexible, those conventions which emerge need not be static: as devolution becomes better established, conventions prohibiting unilateral legislation may well strengthen and may, in terms of the seriousness with which they are treated by the relevant political actors, harden. Similarly, different conventions may regulate the relationship between Westminster and each of the devolved institutions, reflecting the idea of the devolved institutions, reflecting the idea that the inappropriateness of unilateral interference in devolved matters is ultimately a function of the extent to which political autonomy has become an embedded feature of the region in question.

. . . Some writers view conventions in purely empirical terms. Hood Phillips, for instance, regards them as 'rules of political practice which are regarded as binding by those to whom they apply, but which are not laws' (*Constitutional and Administrative Law* (8th ed 2001) p 136). Others, however, recognise that conventions reflect both empirical and normative considerations—thus helping to explain why conventions are both descriptive of past practice and prescriptive of future conduct. These dual. . .aspects of convention find clear expression in the so-called Jennings Test, which requires not only that the practice is supported by precedent and that political actors feel bound to respect it, but also that there must be a reason for the practice. . .

In the present context, the 'practice' in question is legislative adherence to the principles of human rights and devolution: and it is submitted that there exists a compelling rationale for such adherence which (on Jennings' approach) supplies the 'reason' to support a convention, or which (applying Jaconelli's model) explains why pressure exists in favour of conforming to the practice. The position is self-evident in relation to human rights. The very classification of rights in such terms indicates their inherent worth and fundamental status: this, in turn, furnishes a strong normative reason for legislative adherence to such values, and also identifies the source of considerable pressure in favour of such practice. Similar conclusions may be drawn in relation to devolution. The normative value to be attached to regional autonomy is context-dependant, rather than (as in the case of human rights) inherent. However, in relation to those parts of the UK to which power has been devolved, the political context ascribes considerable weight to regional autonomy, as evidenced by the popular seal of support provided by the devolution referendums.[24] Consequently . . . self-determination [is] regarded as normatively valuable in Scotland, Wales and Northern Ireland, and this in turn supplies a strong reason for a mode of legislative behaviour, on the part of the UK Parliament, which respect the devolution settlement [and]. . .strong pressure [for such behaviour]. . .

Indeed it is said that that a convention has already emerged concerning the relationship between the UK and Scottish legislatures. In the House of Lords. . .Lord Sewel explained that:

> . . .we would expect a convention to be established that Westminster would not normally legislate with regard to devolved matters in Scotland without the consent of the Scottish Parliament. [HL Deb (5th series) col 791 (21 July 1998)].

This approach is acknowledged in the principal concordat—an informal, non-binding agreement—entered into following devolution. . .the Memorandum of Understanding [Cm 4444, 1999] [which repeats this undertaking].

. . . In this manner, constitutional convention serves to connect the disparate positions represented by the orthodoxy of unlimited legislative freedom and the political reality of a constitutional order within which the human rights and devolution schemes trace the perimeter of legislative action which is deemed to be constitutionally proper.

[Elliott then goes on to discuss the way in which the sharp distinction between convention and law is blurred when convention supplies a strong reason for the legal finding in a case.]

Prior to [conventional] rules is a foundation of constitutional principle which justifies and gives rise to them; as we saw earlier, this prescriptive aspect is reflected in Jennings' need for a reason for the rule, and also in Jaconelli's theory of conventions as social rules whose observance is directed by some underlying normative imperative.

If this richer conception of convention is adopted, then the justification for sharply distinguishing it from law, and for regarding it as wholly unenforceable judicially, is placed under a good deal of pressure. The law reports are replete with examples of constitutional principle shaping and determining the content of law. Thus the constitutional principle of access to justice requires strict interpretation of [clauses excluding judicial review; *Anisminic Ltd v Foreign Compensation Commission* [1969] 2 AC 147] and of statutory provisions which confer discretionary power [*ex parte Witham* [1998] QB 575]. . .[Elliott gives further examples]. These examples are given not as situations in which conventions have acquired legal recognition, but simply as instances of constitutional principle shaping the content of constitutional law.

[Thus] this approach. . .simply recognises that expression may be given to constitutional principles in different ways—by institutionalising them conventionally or legally—and that there need be no watertight dividing line between those two methodologies. As circumstances change—for instance as greater normative weight is ascribed to a given value—it may be appropriate and desirable to move from political enforcement of the value (by recognising it as giving rise to a convention) towards legal enforcement. This organic process, whereby the common law recognises and gives legal weight to values which are adjudged to be of sufficient normative importance, is well established; and it would be

---

24   The authors note here that the vote on Welsh devolution hardly provided a strong seal of popular support: see Chapter 6, pp 282–283.

illogical to exclude a given norm (which has hitherto been reflected by convention) from that process of the acquisition of legal weight simply because of a dogma that rigorously divorces convention and law.

Note

Jaconelli is critical of Elliott's argument:

> The idea that constitutional conventions could acquire the force of law through a process similar to prescription has, at present, no basis in legal authority. Elliott's thesis, nonetheless, appears to proceed by analogy with the recent history of judicial intervention in matters of the royal prerogative. From a situation where all prerogative powers were placed beyond judicial control the courts have moved to a position in which only those touching on matters of high policy will continue to be treated in this way. Those, by contrast, which involve matters of little political moment will now be subject to judicial review. By the same token, many constitutional conventions admittedly involve matters which would be regarded as not justiciable. The remainder, by implication, could in time become ripe for judicial enforcement.
>
> There are a considerable number of difficulties with this thesis. Why, for instance, should it hold only in regard to one particular category of constitutional conventions: namely, those limitative of the sovereignty of Parliament? If, to avoid such inconsistency, it were to apply to all constitutional conventions, it would raise the problem of identifying those conventions which are genuinely constitutional and those which are not. Clearly, the longer a convention has been followed, the less likely it is to be breached. It is difficult, moreover, to envisage a constitutional convention which would be apt for judicial enforcement—a matter on which Elliott does not offer any guidance. Therefore if the tests of length of observance and justiciability of subject-matter are to provide the twin criteria of enforcement, conceivably no situation would ever arise to test the validity of Elliott's hypothesis.[25]

SHOULD CONVENTIONS BE CODIFIED?

The uncertainty surrounding the content and even the existence of certain conventions has led a number of commentators to question whether conventions should now be set down in an authoritative text or even enshrined in law. It is supposed to be an advantage of conventions that they represent a means of bringing about developments in the constitution without the need for formal repeal or amendment of the law. The distinction between strict law and conventions grew up due to the need to effect a quiet erosion of the prerogative powers of the monarch. Such powers could by convention be vested in the Cabinet or Prime Minister, thereby avoiding the need for any formal statutory declaration that this had occurred. Conventions thus allow the constitution to evolve and keep up to date with changing circumstances. However, this very ease of change has for some time been generating unease amongst commentators. In this respect Johnson provides an important historical perspective. He notes

---

25 'Do Constitutional Conventions Bind?', n 18 above, at 162–163.

the strong influence of Dicey in this area, as in so many others—'it was he who gave such a large place to convention and attempted to explain how it operated as indispensable complement to constitutional law proper'—and then goes on:

N Johnson, *In Search of the Constitution* (1980), pp 32–34

But the crucial point is that the power of Victorian constitutional convention was incomparably greater than that of any contemporary convention of the same kind. In saying this I am to some extent doing no more than pointing out how much more seriously our forefathers were committed to the firm observance of a range of moral and political conventions far wider than would be conceivable today. In contrast it is a hallmark of our age that practically every aspect of social life is caught up in a process of change, is open to challenge and has lost the predictability which it once had. . .The large place [the Victorians gave] to convention was precisely the result of a belief that it was founded on habits and traditions expressive of the genius of the people which, like the rock of ages, would endure. . .

[But] in our present political life. . .there is no longer that degree of commitment to particular procedures, that respect of traditional values and habits, nor that breadth of agreement about how political authority should be exercised and for what purposes, which justify the belief that convention alone is a sheet-anchor on which we can rely for the protection of civil rights for the survival of a particular form of government. Flexible and adaptable the Constitution remains, but these are qualities that can be used for different purposes, and increasingly it becomes clear that they serve chiefly to justify the relentless extension of public power and the erosion of such notions as may survive of the limits within which it may properly be exercised. Thus what was a valuable element in the British constitutional tradition, a sign of political wisdom, has been perverted. . . Meanwhile, the virtues of trusting to convention are extolled as the vital principle of the Constitution by those whose chief interest it is to maintain just such a state of affairs.

. . . The chief effect of [the] famous flexibility [of the UK Constitution], of course, has been to spare us some of the conflict which might occur under a more formalized constitutional system when proposals for change are under debate, and thus to deprive us of the stimulus of having to argue seriously about the principles on which we claim to be acting. . .

Marshall and Moodie go on to consider the specific pros and cons of codifying conventions. The obvious pro, as they note, is greater certainty and clarity that would come from authoritative declaration of the content of a given convention. They continue.

G Marshall and GC Moodie, *Some Problems of the Constitution*, 5th edn (1971), pp 34–36

Let us try to draw up a 'balance sheet' of what it could and could not do.

1   Obedience to the rules would not become any more enforceable than it is now. There would undoubtedly be occasions when the mere clarification of a rule would ensure constitutional behaviour. The courts, moreover, can do much to secure observance of the law by such means as declarations and injunctions. But there are several limits

to the effectiveness of judicial, or even legislative, action in the face of determined opposition to the law by a Government or, for that matter, by any powerful social group. The sanctions behind constitutional law, as well as convention, are a compound of the desire to abide by the rules, to be 'constitutional', and of the political penalties of disobedience. Ultimately, revolution or civil war may be necessary to procure obedience, as has been amply demonstrated by the history of American legislation and adjudication upon the rights of Negro population in the south.

2   In the absence of a sufficient body of judicial decisions, even well-established legal principles may (at any given time) be of uncertain formulation and application; the principle of the sovereignty of Parliament itself is a case in point. However, in the event of an important dispute turning upon the interpretation of a legal rule, the machinery exists for an authoritative decision upon its meaning and precise application.

3   Legislation, as we have noted, would not prevent the growth of new conventions, about which uncertainty may exist.

4   It could not prevent dispute about what the rules ought to be. And it is important to realise that it is this type of dispute which underlies many arguments about (apparently) what the rules are. This was obviously the case, for example, in the argument about the royal power to 'veto' legislation which took place in 1913, or the Commons' debates about the extent of parliamentary privilege in 1958. It would be foolish to expect any-thing else, for convention may be described as the 'battleground' between conflicting political forces and constitutional beliefs in society. But this is true not only of disputes about conventional rules. It applies also to legal argument. To cite American experience again, it is evident that constitutional debates about racial segregation in education, or the powers of the federal government in the social and economic fields, have been more than mere scholarly disputations about the 'real' meaning of the 14th Amendment or the 'inter-state commerce clause', although this is the way in which they may be presented. Primarily, these debates have been attempts to persuade the Supreme Court Justices of what the documentary constitution ought to mean; and the standing of the court at any period will depend, in part, upon whether its interpretations conflict with the wishes and beliefs of the most powerful forces in society at the time. Conversely, it is at least arguable that the high standing of the British courts owes something to the fact that many of the most important constitutional rules are, at present, of a non-legal character. Another important factor is, of course, that the doctrine of parliamentary supremacy saves the British courts from having to give the last word on legal points. However, it is doubtful whether this would prevent the courts from a loss of prestige if they were constantly called upon to decide (even subject to parliamentary 'reversal') a whole series of constitutional controversies.

5   What has just been said suggests that the attempt to enact conventional rules might itself prove extremely difficult. It is likely that the fiercely disputed Parliament Act of 1911 rather than the Statute of Westminster would prove to be typical of the process. Even if agreement could be reached about what the rules are, it is hard to believe that no attempt would be made to formulate the rule with greater precision, in line with particular views as to what it should be. It can be argued, with come conviction, that this is in fact what happened with the Parliament Act and with the American 'third-term'

amendment. It is, moreover, most unlikely that in fact any attempt will be made to 'codify' the conventions until and unless their precise meaning has become a crucial factor in a constitutional crisis—in which case it might not be of very great significance whether the disputed rule was or was not a law, in that further legislation may anyway be needed to settle the dispute.

6   Enactment of the conventions may nevertheless be important, if once successfully achieved. Just as some course of action desired by a section of the community acquires a significant degree of legitimacy and authority simply by virtue of its acceptance as a convention, so a convention may acquire greater legitimacy and authority by its transformation into law. The exact significance of this 'evaluation' will probably vary with different rules.

Notes

1. It is important to note that in a typically British *ad hoc*, unsystematic way, a widespread codification of conventions regulating government behaviour is in fact occurring. An important example is *The Ministerial Code*, published by the Cabinet Office, which sets out in authoritative form a number of important constitutional principles relating to the conduct of Ministers, including crucially the convention of ministerial responsibility, as well as rules relating to ethical conduct in relation to gifts and hospitality. A resolution passed by both Houses of Parliament on the content of ministerial responsibility,[26] which the Code follows, reinforces its authority (for discussion, see Chapter 12, pp 628–629). Similarly, the *Rules Relating to the Conduct of MPs* sets out in detailed form the standards expected of MPs (considered in detail in Chapter 10), the *Civil Service Code* clarifies the duties of civil servants in relation to the provision of information to Parliament (Chapter 12, pp 662–663), and the Government's *Code of Practice on Access to Information*, previously gave the definitive account of what information Ministers could properly refuse to disclose to Parliament, replacing the previous position in which Ministers and their predecessors simply refused to answer questions on the basis of custom. (It has now been superseded by the Freedom of Information Act 2000, considered in Chapter 13). As Dawn Oliver commented in 1997:

> The upshot of [all] this. . .is that in the last two years or so the number of published codes regulating the conduct of Ministers, civil servants, and Members of Parliament has increased substantially and their importance to the discipline of constitutional law is growing, as the shortcomings of unarticulated understandings as mechanisms of control have come to be recognised.[27]

We noted above a further example—the proposed resolution of both Houses setting out a convention of consultation with Parliament before committing the UK's armed forces to battle (above, p 53).

2. One of the more cogent arguments *against* codification is the loss of prestige that the courts might face if forced to adjudicate on controversial issues of convention. However, this point obviously has far more force in relation to some conventions than others. Clearly, areas such as individual and collective ministerial responsibility should not be handed over to the courts for adjudication

---

26 HC Deb cols 1046–47 (19 March 1997); HL Deb cols 1055–62 (20 March 1997).

27 D Oliver, 'The Changing Constitution in the 1990s' [1997] NILQ 1.

(though there is no reason an independent committee, staffed, say, by judges, academics and MPs, should not be given the power to make nonbinding findings on whether a particular convention has or has not been breached). For one thing, collective, and on some occasions individeual responsibility, are generally in the interest of the Government and will therefore be enforced by it, within flexible limits. Additionally, individual ministerial responsibility is clearly at the heart of the notion of parliamentary accountability, and the stuff of everyday political conflict. As a result, a leading commentator has argued that, were the Convention of Ministerial Responsibility to be codified in a new UK Constitution, the courts would simply find the relevant provisions non-justiciable.[28] Other conventions, however, such as those relating to the powers of the monarch to refuse assent to legislation and to dissolve Parliament, or the obligation of a Government to resign upon being defeated in a general election, are in a different category. First, both because the situations would rarely arise at all, and because, if they did, the conventional rules would probably be followed, just as they are now, the fear that the courts would be 'constantly called upon to decide. . .constitutional controversies' is groundless. Second, these conventions are vital to democracy itself; as indicated above, it seems absurd to exclude constitutional fundamentals from the Rule of Law.

3. Codification would resolve the intolerable situation in which the very existence of some conventions has been in doubt. To give an historical example, in 1708 royal assent was withheld from a Bill of which the monarch in question, Queen Anne, disapproved, whereas in 1829 George IV gave consent to a Bill which he disliked. Sometime during those 100 years the convention in question must have come into being. However, it would be impossible to pinpoint the stage at which this occurred; if, during that time, the question had arisen as to whether withholding royal assent was unconstitutional, no answer would be available to the monarch in question; in effect it would not be available until after he or she had acted and even then might be challenged.

4. Some conventions, of course, benefit from their indeterminacy. The doctrine of collective Cabinet responsibility provides an example. Under the doctrine, Ministers are collectively responsible to Parliament for their actions in governing the country and therefore should be in accord on any major question. A Minister should resign if he or she is in disagreement with the policy of the Cabinet on any such question. Examples of such resignation include Sir Thomas Dugdale's in 1954 due to his disagreement with the Government as to the disposal of an area of land known as Crichel Down (this resignation is not always cited as an example of policy disagreement, but such appears to have been its basis), and Sir Anthony Eden's resignation in 1938 over Chamberlain's policy towards Mussolini. However, there appears to have been some blurring and weakening of the doctrine dating from the mid-1970s. In 1975 the Labour Cabinet was divided on the question of whether the UK should remain in the Common Market. It was agreed that, in the period before the referendum on the question, Cabinet Ministers should be able to express a view at variance with the official view of the Government that the UK should remain a member of the Common Market. Some weakening of the convention also appears from the Westland affair which, on the face of it, provides an example of its operation; when Michael Heseltine resigned from the Cabinet in 1986 due to his disagreement with government policy, he specifically stated that he did not do so as a result of his perception of an obligation arising from the convention. When John Major's administration was considering whether to allow a referendum on a single currency, the option of suspending collective Cabinet responsibility during the referendum campaign was canvassed as a legitimate possibility open to the Prime Minister, the 1975 suspension being cited as a precedent.

5. If the convention of collective responsibility were enshrined in a statute, departure from it as in 1975 might have been less readily undertaken, even if the provisions of the statute were made

---

28 Bogdanor and Vogenauer, n 1 above, at 50.

non-justiciable. In any event it would be difficult, and probably undesirable, to define the convention, as discretion in complying with it may be said to be endemic in it. Political inconvenience would clearly arise, and it might be argued that the democratic process would be endangered if Ministers could not at times express their views on exceptionally important issues with some freedom. Therefore, it may be argued that no advantage would be gained by enacting such a statute; such crystallisation of the convention would clearly reduce its value.

6. The only sensible conclusion seems to be that a selective approach towards further codification would be a prerequisite for reform. Some Conventions might be best left completely open and flexible. A few might be suitable for codification—even in the form of fairly loose statutory guidance: this might work well, for example, in relation to the current conventions surrounding the appointment of a Prime Minister: statutory guidance, directed to the Monarch, could at the very least state what matters should and should not be taken into account and might even specifically rule out specific choices of Prime Minister in particular situations. The question would then arise as to whether those provisions should be made justiciable or not. Other conventions still—perhaps the bulk—could certainly benefit from being authoritatively recognised and declared—but without being put into statutory form. Thus as two Australian academics have suggested, there could be a three-pronged approach to codification.

> Some conventions might appropriately be included in a written constitution, subject to enforcement in the courts; others might be included in the constitution as non-justiciable declarations of principle; others might be articulated outside the constitution by way of an informal agreement on the content of which is understood.[29]

7. Two examples of the latter process readily come to mind: the first is the Australian one, undertaken between 1976 and 1983 by a Constitutional Convention. The other, much more modest example is closer to home: the Joint Committee on Conventions recently made an attempt to declare the main conventions governing the use by the House of Lords of its powers over legislation. Both are considered further below.

8. In the following, Wood and Sampford describe the process undertaken in Australia by the (confusingly named) Australian Constitutional Convention—essentially a special cross-party forum.[30] It started with advice given by an academic, later judge, Professor Ryan. (UK readers should understand that the 'Governor-General' mentioned many times is the Queen's representative in Australia and exercises some of the powers that the Queen exercises in the UK).

D Wood and CG Sampford, 'Codification of constitutional conventions in Australia' [1987] *Public Law* 231 (extracts)

Ryan argued against incorporation because the necessary amendment would be difficult to pass. More fundamentally, he argued that incorporation would be undesirable if it made conventions legally enforceable, and unnecessary if it did not. Instead, Ryan argued for

---

29 'Identifying Conventions Associated with the Commonwealth Constitution', Australian Constitutional Convention, Standing Committee 'D', vol 2, 1982, p 1, cited in Heard, *Canadian Constitutional Conventions: The Marriage of Law and Politics* (1991), p 151.

30 Described by the authors as 'a forum of delegates from Commonwealth and State governments and oppositions which has met fairly regularly since 1973. . . founded to consider constitutional reform, and to try to build bipartisan support for amendments to the Constitution' (*ibid*, at p 231).

an authoritative statement of conventions without legal status, but with political and moral authority based solely on the 'reputations of those who drafted it' and 'its general acceptability. [The task was then given to a Standing Committee of the Convention, which requested opinions from 'distinguished academics and practitioners on what the Conventions were'.]

The politicians on the Standing Committee debated these in 1982, and provided some input to the content of the suggested conventions. The resulting views were drafted by academics into a set of 34 practices to be 'recognised and declared' as conventions of the Australian Constitution by a plenary session of the 1983 Constitutional Convention. The conventions dealt with the exercise of Australian constitutional powers by the Queen, the composition and operation of the Federal Executive Council, the power of the Queen to appoint the Governor-General, the power of the Governor-General to appoint and dismiss ministers, and his powers over, for instance, Parliament, legislation, and referenda. While the exercise was primarily one of recording conventions as they stood, it was freely admitted that some of the suggested practices were modifications of existing conventions where they were considered to be inadequate. . .

Most of the conventions were passed without a formal vote, which makes it difficult to gauge their exact degree of support. Where divisions were required conventions were passed by 48 to 39 and by 46 to 34, mainly on party lines. However, the most critical conventions, those concerning the Governor-General's powers over ministers and Parliament, proved to be unacceptable to many delegates. . .

These controversial conventions were returned to Standing Committee D, and other academics were called in to comment on them. The politicians discussed the issues and the academics drew up a revised list of 18 practices for the 1985 Convention. Given the shaky support that some conventions had received in 1983, more consideration was given to the appropriate criteria for recognition and declaration. The Standing Committee generally required clear supporting precedents and the likelihood of broad political agreement. Nonetheless, where general agreement was anticipated, some practices without clear precedent were recommended (although the committee were wise not to specify too precisely which conventions they considered new). Some of the most interesting innovations and/or new interpretations involved attempts to narrow the Governor-General's discretion and to shift responsibility under conventions from the Governor-General to the Prime Minister. Prime Ministers defeated in the House or at elections should advise the Governor-General, such advice to be published and almost always followed. Where the Prime Minister is defeated in the House and an alternative government possible, the Prime Minister should advise the commissioning of a new government rather than the calling of a new election. However, as agreement had been impossible on the Governor-General's powers, no conventions were produced in regard to them. When the Constitutional Convention met again, this failure was specifically noted in an amendment to the resolution adopting the conventions. It was hoped, however, that future Conventions would fill the gap by recognising further conventions. Regrettably, this hope is still to be fulfilled. . .

Perhaps the most striking and surprising feature of this attempt to codify constitutional conventions is its degree of success–it actually produced agreed texts for conventions.

Notes

1. The authors attribute this success largely to the involvement of academic experts, from whose non-partisan views the politicians found it difficult to dissent in the sense of putting forward an equally compelling alternative, and the pressure on the Standing Committee to agree proposals. It is interesting that it was impossible to reach consensus on some Conventions, with the vote splitting on party lines: given that the existence of conventions is meant to depend in part upon their being widely agreed, does this suggest that (a) there were in fact no Conventions in this area, merely competing arguments about what they should be, or (b) that there were Conventions albeit that some objected to them. Is the notion of a disputed Convention a contradiction in terms? A recent article on codifying the UK Constitution notes:

    > Tony Blair promised that there would be no change in the electoral system for House of Commons without a referendum; and in a recent research paper, the House of Commons Library claims that there is a 'constitutional convention that changes to the electoral system should be agreed as far as possible on an all-party basis'. It then goes on to declare in the next sentence, somewhat confusingly, that '[t]his convention is not universally observed'.[31]

2. Our other example of an attempt to clarify/codify a set of conventions is that of the attempt by a Joint Committee to reach authoritative agreement upon the Conventions governing the House of Lords. The substantive findings of the Committee are discussed in Chapter 9. Here it is its methodology and its views on what contribution 'codification' in different forms may make to the clarification and authority of Conventions that are of interest here.

Report of the Joint Committee on Conventions 2005–06, *HL Paper 265-I/HC 1212-I (extracts)*

253. 'Codification' may be taken in at least two senses: (i) the broad sense of an authoritative statement, and (ii) the narrow sense of reduction to a literal code or system. In the context of Parliament, an authoritative statement could take any of the following forms:

a)   a statement made anywhere, e.g. in a book
b)   some form of concordat or memorandum of understanding
c)   a statement made in Parliament, e.g. in Hansard or in evidence to a Committee
d)   a Committee report
e)   a report agreed to by one or both Houses of Parliament
f)   a resolution of one or both Houses of Parliament
g)   a literal Code, such as each House's Code of Conduct for Members
h)   a statement in the House of Lords' Companion to Standing Orders
i)   words in Erskine May
j)   a Standing Order
k)   an Act of Parliament

254. It might be felt that only the most formal of these—a Code, a Standing Order or an Act—would really constitute codification. But the Leader of the House of Commons

---

31   V Bogdanor and S Vogenauer, 'Enacting a British Constitution: Some Problems' [2008]PL 38, 43.

appeared to have a broader definition in mind when he noted, in the Commons debate on setting up this Committee, that '[t]he manner in which the conventions could be codified ranges from a codification in the body of the Committee's report, to a code that has been negotiated by both Houses and which we endorse in resolutions, through to its inclusion in Standing Orders or its enshrinement in law. That is a subsequent matter'. He later said that, in his opinion, 'it would be a grave error to put any description of the convention[s] into legislation'.

255. We are aware that our remit is to an extent self-fulfilling. The authoritative statements about conventions, by our witnesses and in this report, will be cited in future, even if the report leads to no further action. . .

263. The Clerk of the Parliaments distinguishes conventions from rules. Conventions evolve; rules are fixed. Rules require enforcement and sanctions; conventions have no sanctions. Conventions may evolve into fixed rules; those under consideration are 'too new to have become fixed'. If they were codified and fixed, they would cease to be conventions and become rules.

264. He gives examples of conventions described as such and set out in the Companion. One of them, the target rising time of 10pm, was substantially breached 53 times between its introduction in 2002 and the Whitsun recess 2006, showing that recording a convention in an agreed form may introduce clarity without ensuring observance.

265. The Clerk of the Parliaments draws attention to the question of who is bound by a convention and is in a position to deliver observance. For the Salisbury-Addison Convention, his answer is, the Leader of the Opposition. But for the reasonable time and delegated legislation conventions it is less clear, and in a self-regulating House any backbencher could provoke a breach.

266. If it were intended to embody a convention in a Standing Order or an Act, new clarity would be needed, e.g. in defining a manifesto Bill for the purposes of the Salisbury-Addison Convention. Formally defined powers might be used to the limit, rather than with restraint—though, as he pointed out, the Parliament Acts give the Lords a month to pass a Money Bill but they often do so within days. And legislation would raise the possibility of intervention by the courts, which would be undesirable and 'uncomfortable for both sides'.

267. In oral evidence, the Clerk of the Parliaments canvassed the more acceptable option of a unanimous report from this Committee endorsed by resolutions of both Houses. 'It does not mean to say that one cannot depart from the norm, but the clearer the norm is the more the House would have to justify, in the forum of public opinion, taking a different line'. Peer pressure would also operate. He denied that doing this would inhibit evolution.

268. The Clerk of the House of Commons, Sir Roger Sands, observed first that 'conventions must be understood in the context of the constitutional and political circumstances in which they have been forged . . . The "practicality" of codification . . . is not merely a matter of reviewing the technical options; it is a matter of considering whether the settled and predictable constitutional circumstances exist which would provide the necessary context for codification'.

269. He gave his own list of arguments against turning conventions into rules. This would involve difficulties of definition, and lead to loss of flexibility. It would imply a need for adjudication; for conventions governing relations between the Houses, this would have to be by either an extra parliamentary body or some kind of Conference of the two Houses. Paradoxically, codifying the conventions could lead to increased delay, while awaiting

adjudication. And if codification took the form of statute law, it would create a possibility of court intervention, which in his opinion could not be excluded, and which might be more likely with the creation of the new Supreme Court in 2009. Sir Roger agreed that this would be a 'substantial constitutional change'.

270. Commenting on the notion of embodying an agreed description of the conventions in resolutions, the Clerk of the House of Commons confirmed that this would be a weak form of codification. It would warrant entries in *Erskine May* and the *Companion*, 'but no more; and so the Speaker would find it very difficult to give rulings just on the basis of a codification in that form'. This is the process proposed by the Hunt report for codifying the Salisbury-Addison Convention, and the Hunt report envisaged eliminating 'any doubt or ambiguity as to their [the conventions'] application in all circumstances'. The Clerk of the House of Commons did not think that was 'a viable proposition'.

271. It was put to the Clerks that they might undertake the codification themselves. They agreed to do so if asked. But they could only produce a draft for the Houses' consideration; and in some areas, e.g. defining a manifesto commitment, they would be unable to help.

272. According to Lord Norton of Louth 'codifying conventions' is a contradiction in terms . . . If conventions are codified, they cease to be conventions'. This is because in his view codification by definition involves enforceability and a convention is by definition unenforceable. He admits however that one could adopt 'a soft definition of codification', i.e. 'simply listing what are agreed to be conventions'; but in his view this exercise would be 'nugatory'. He also admits that 'strong' codification, i.e. turning the conventions into enforceable rules, would be possible; but he argues against it. It would change the relationship between the Houses by taking from the Lords the leverage derived from reserve powers; it would require an enforcement mechanism; and in any case the present system works 'reasonably well'. Also it would reduce the capacity of the constitution to evolve in response to political reality.

274. . . Professor Bradley likewise sees two possible forms of codification: 'merely summarising past practice or an exercise in formulating rules for future conduct'. He argues against the rule-making approach. 'The British system is dynamic and flexible, rather than rigid'. Its lack of clarity may sometimes seem a nuisance, but it enables it to evolve as circumstances change. A convention may be the practical expression of a principle; in a certain situation it may be possible, even necessary, to appear to breach the convention while upholding the principle. The sovereignty of Parliament means that exceptions must be expected: 'a bill may raise a fundamental constitutional question such that it is not possible in advance to predict how the Lords should respond'. In the absence of rules, all this can 'come out in the political wash'.

275. Professor Bogdanor agrees with Professor Bradley in seeing the conventions as defined by, and changing in response to, the political situation, in which he includes public opinion. He agrees with Sir Roger Sands that now, 'when the constitution is in ferment', is a bad time to try to pin conventions down.

276. According to the Clerk of the Australian Senate, 'relations between the Houses in Canberra are governed entirely by the constitution and by standing orders. Various participants in the parliamentary processes have attempted at various times to invent conventions to suit their purposes, but no conventions have been established'. The Acting Clerk of the Australian House of Representatives provides an interesting illustration of the fact that a written constitution may still leave room for doubt and disagreement on important matters.

278. The Clerk of the Canadian Senate says, 'In many respects, the relations between the contemporary Senate and the House of Commons, as in the UK Parliament, have followed certain recognisable practices. These practices have never been codified and are not usually identified as conventions'.

Conclusions

279. In our view the word 'codification' is unhelpful, since to most people it implies rule-making, with definitions and enforcement mechanisms. Conventions, by their very nature, are unenforceable. In this sense, therefore, codifying conventions is a contradiction in terms. It would raise issues of definition, reduce flexibility, and inhibit the capacity to evolve. It might create a need for adjudication, and the presence of an adjudicator, whether the courts or some new body, is incompatible with parliamentary sovereignty. Even if an adjudicator could be found, the possibility of adjudication would introduce uncertainty and delay into the business of Parliament. In these ways, far from reducing the risk of conflict, codification might actually damage the relationship between the two Houses, making it more confrontational and less capable of moderation through the usual channels. This would benefit neither the Government nor Parliament.

280. However, we offer certain formulations for one or both Houses to adopt by resolution. In our view, both the debates on such resolutions, and the resolutions themselves, would improve the shared understanding which the Government seek.

281. We are unanimously agreed that all recommendations for the formulation or codification of conventions are subject to the current understanding that conventions as such are flexible and unenforceable, particularly in the self-regulating environment of the House of Lords. Nothing in these recommendations would alter the present right of the House of Lords, in exceptional circumstances, to vote against the Second Reading or passing of any Bill, or to vote down any Statutory Instrument where the parent Act so provides. The resolutions which we propose are couched in sufficiently general terms to make this self-evident. And a resolution can be amended or rescinded at any point, or even simply allowed to lapse. Therefore, while a resolution may improve clarity and increase shared understanding, it need not rule out exceptions or inhibit evolution.

Notes

1. In the result, the statements of Convention formulated by the committee were often in very broad terms. Nevertheless, the exercise was generally agreed to have been a helpful one—in some cases general agreement was found, while in others, the exercise sufficed to surface important areas of disagreement (e.g. about the Salisbury Convention).[32] The Committee's formulations were agreed by both Houses, as it had proposed.

2. Arguably, the numerous concerns expressed in the Committee's report about the dangers of 'codification' were greatly exaggerated: the primary purpose of the exercise is to achieve a greater level of clarity—the questions of sanctions for breach of conventions, or placing them on a legal basis are quite separate. Had the Committee and some of its witnesses paid greater attention to the three-fold classification suggested by the Australian academics cited above,[33] it might have been somewhat less anxious about the whole exercise.

3. On 2 February 2010, in a speech to the IPPR, Gordon Brown said the following:

---

32 See further, Chapter 9.

33 Above, text to note 29.

I can announce today that I have asked the Cabinet Secretary to lead work to consolidate the existing unwritten, piecemeal conventions that govern much of the way central government operates under our existing constitution into a single written document.

Whether this initative will bear any fruit post the 2010 Election remains to be seen.

FURTHER READING

A Heard, *Canadian Constitutional Conventions: The Marriage of Law and Politics* (1991)
I Jennings, *Cabinet Government,* 3rd edn (1959), esp. Chapter 1
N Johnston, *In Search of the Constitution* (1977), esp. Chapter 3
J Madison, *The Federalist Papers* (1987)
JDB Mitchell, *Constitutional Law,* 2nd edn (1968)
G Marshall, *Constitutional Conventions* (1984)

R Brazier, 'Government Formation from a Hung Parliament' [1986] PL 387
C Munro, 'Law and conventions distinguished' (1975) 91 LQR 218
CJG Sampford, '"Recognise and Declare": An Australian Experiment in Codifying Conventions' (1987) 7 OJLS 369
JG Wilson, 'American Constitutional Conventions: The Judicially Unenforceable Rules that Combine with Judicial Doctrine and Public Opinion to Regulate Political Behaviour' (1992) 40 *Buffalo Law Review* 645

CHAPTER 3
THE RULE OF LAW AND THE SEPARATION OF POWERS

INTRODUCTION—THE THEORETICAL BASIS OF THE RULE OF LAW[1]

The Rule of Law is a chameleon-like notion. Used by different people it may mean radically different things. As noted in Chapter 1 of this part, an influential commentator on the Left, John Griffith, objects to the notion being used to denote anything more substantive than a set of basic restraints on the powers of the state, particularly its ability to penalise it citizens.[2] Griffith complains that, contrary to his prescription, the doctrine is sometimes used in a much wider sense to create loyalty towards the status quo. Professor Joseph Raz notes that, in 1959, the International Congress of Jurists came up with a definition of the Rule of Law which effectively made it a shorthand for 'a complete social philosophy', prescribing a full panoply of civil, political, economic and social rights.[3]

However, both of these writers, and indeed the vast majority of commentators dealing with this subject, assume that the notion of the Rule of Law must mean at least that people should be ruled by rules (though even traditionalists have now disclaimed Albert Venn Dicey's notion that the granting of discretionary powers to the executive necessarily infringes the doctrine).[4] But is even this modest assumption justifiable? Frederick Schauer considers that the essence of a system run according to law is the notion that power must be *allocated* according to law. Whether that power must then be exercised according to a set of pre-ordained rules is another question.

F Schauer, *Playing by the Rules: A Philosophical Examination of Rule-Based Decision-Making in Law and in Life* (1991), pp 167–68, 10–11

. . .the relationship between rules and a 'legal system' is contingent, for decision according to rules is but one among several sorts of decision-making. As a result, although empowering rules create the institutions of dispute resolution and empower certain officials to resolve certain sorts of disputes, disputes could still be resolved largely without reference to mandatory rules imposing substantive constraint on the content of the decisions. Having been empowered to resolve a dispute, the adjudicator would be authorized. . .to come to a conclusion as open-endedly as appropriate in the circumstances.

. . . Consider child custody determinations, in which an open-ended 'best interests of the child' standard, rather than any more constraining set of rules, provides guidance for the decision-maker; the system of equity, no less part of the legal system for embodying flexibility and particularly as its method; the traditional sentencing process, in which the range of factors permissibly relevant to the decision is virtually unlimited; and the increasing use of substantially rule-free arbitration, mediation, and conciliation procedures as adjuncts to or substitutes for formal adjudication. These are but a few among many examples of forms of legal decision-making that, only with difficulty, can be characterised as rule-based. Consequently, I want to start with the assumption that rule-governed decision-making is a subset of legal decision-making rather than being congruent with it.

---

1   For the basic principles of the doctrine see, in this chapter, 'Principles deriving from the Rule of Law', below at p 85 *et seq*. This introduction considers the theoretical background to the doctrine.

2   See J Griffith, 'The Political Constitution' (1979) 42 MLR 15; quoted in Chapter 1, at p 39–41.

3   J Raz, 'The Rule of Law and its Virtue' (1977) 93 LQR 195; quoted below, pp 86–88.

4   See, for example, RFV Heuston, *Essays in Constitutional Law*, 2nd edn (1964), at 41–42; quoted below, at p 112.

Note

Schauer's distinction between power-allocating and power-exercising rules is useful in that it forces us to realise that a state—at least one like the UK with no fixed constitutional order—could dispense altogether with the idea of governing according to substantive rules without acting illegally. For example, Parliament could repeal the criminal law in its entirety and substitute for it an Act stating that certain government appointees were to have exclusive power to punish, as they thought fit, such acts as they thought ought to be punished within specified geographical areas allocated to them. Whilst such an Act would violate many of the fundamental doctrines of the Rule of Law as they are commonly understood to be—and be incompatible with various provisions of the European Convention on Human Rights (ECHR)[5]—such an Act would not be 'illegal', since Parliament would be exercising power allocated to it by law. (It is also worth noting that judicial review of decisions made under the Act would still be possible if, for example, an appointee purported to punish a citizen in respect of an act which was not committed in his or her allocated area.) Thus, Schauer's point both helps to clear up some confusion between illegal 'enactments' and ones which violate the principles of the Rule of Law, and also to make it clear that those principles are not the necessary attributes of any state established under law, but rather are contingent and therefore vulnerable to erosion.

THE BASIC IDEA OF THE RULE OF LAW: GOVERNMENT UNDER THE LAW OR 'LIMITED GOVERNMENT'

The basic notion that no one may exercise power unless that power has been granted to him or her by law can also be expressed in the notion of 'government under the law'. Jeremy Waldron explains why this notion has such significant connotations.

J Waldron, *The Law* (1990), pp 31–32

For many of us, the policeman on patrol is the most visible expression of the power of the British state. He represents an organisation that has the ability to overwhelm any of us with physical force if we resist its demands, and he can call on that force any time he wants...although the police in Britain are not armed as a matter of course except with truncheons, they do have access to firearms and, as events in Northern Ireland have shown, they can ask political leaders to deploy military force if that is necessary to resist some challenge to their authority. Their potential power, like that of any government official, is enormous, for in the last resort they can call upon all the organised force of the state. And the same is true of other officials as well—from taxation officials to social welfare clerks. They are all the agents of an immensely powerful organisation.

When you put it like that, it is hard to resist the image of one group of people—the

---

5   Notably the Art 6 guarantee of an 'independent and impartial tribunal' for the determination of criminal offences (see pp 137–140), and also the requirement that all legal restrictions upon Convention rights must be 'prescribed by law': see below, at p 118–120 the extracts from *Malone v UK* (1985) 7 EHRR 14 and *Hashman and Harrup v UK* (2000) 30 EHRR 241.

organised events of the state—wielding power over another, much larger group of people—the rest of us, relatively powerless in ourselves and abjectly vulnerable to their demands. Some are powerful, some are not. The state is the rule of one group of people by another. And that, of course, is an affront and an indignity to the people who are in the subordinate position, since it leaves us unfree and evidently unequal.

Ever since Aristotle, political philosophers have tried to mitigate or qualify that image. Politics, they have argued, need not be the arbitrary rule of man over man. Perhaps we can imagine a form of political life in which everyone is a subject and everyone is ruled, not by a person or by any particular group of people, but by a shared set of abstract rules. If I am subject to another person, then I am at the mercy of his whims and passions, his angers and prejudices. But if we are both subject to the law, then the personal factor is taken out of politics. By subjecting everyone to the law, we make ourselves, in a sense, equal again.

Notes

1. Waldron's conclusion, that the Rule of Law renders us 'in a sense equal again', refers to a notion of *formal* equality; it does not of course imply that the content of individual laws could not promote *substantive* inequality. As Jeffrey Jowell puts it, the concern of formal equality:

   is not with the content of the law but with its enforcement and application alone. As long as laws are applied equally, that is without irrational bias or distinction, then formal equality is complied with. Formal equality does not however prohibit unequal laws. It constrains, say, racially-biased enforcement of the law, but it does not inhibit racially discriminatory laws from being enacted [original emphasis].[6]

   However, it should be noted that the notion that the law, whatever its content, must apply equally to all, makes an important, albeit indirect contribution towards ensuring the fair *content* of laws. As Justice Jackson of the US Supreme Court pointed out in a seminal passage:

   there is no more effective practical guarantee against arbitrary and unreasonable government than to require that the principles of law which officials would impose upon a minority must be imposed generally. Conversely, nothing opens the door to arbitrary action so effectively as to allow those officials to pick and choose only a few to whom they will apply legislation and thus to escape the political retribution that might be visited upon them if larger numbers were affected. Courts can take no better measure to assure that laws will be just than to require that laws be equal in operation.[7]

   The recent decision in *Gillan v UK* (2010) (below, p 110) provides a clear example of this principle of the rule of law in operation.

---

6   J Jowell, 'The Rule of Law today', in J Jowell and D Oliver (eds), *The Changing Constitution*, 3rd edn (1994), p 76.

7   *Railway Express Agency Inc v New York* 336 US 106, 112–113 (1949), quoted by Lord Bingham, 'The Rule of Law' [2007] CLJ 67, at 74.

2. As well as promoting the notion of equality, the Rule of Law thus has perhaps a still more basic purpose: that of acting as a constraint on government power,[8] a power which, as Waldron remarks, 'has the ability to overwhelm any of us with physical force'.[9]

SPECIFIC PRINCIPLES DERIVING FROM THE RULE OF LAW

A basic principle: law applies to all

The notion that the executive is not above the law is related to the Diceyan notion that the Rule of Law includes the idea that there should be one law for all, governed and Government alike. Waldron discusses a practical application of this notion and the principles which may be derived from it, referring to the case of _Pedro v Diss_[10] in which Pedro was acquitted of assault after physically resisting an unlawful arrest made by Police Constable Diss.

J Waldron, *The Law* (1990), pp 37–38

[Constable] Diss grabs hold of Pedro, and Pedro punches him in the struggle to free himself. The magistrates say he is guilty of assault. On appeal, the High Court says (in effect): 'No. Unless the arrest is lawful, Pedro is entitled to defend himself against Martin Diss just as if he were any other citizen who tried to grab hold of him. Once they go beyond their specified powers, the police have no special privileges. The ordinary rules of self-defence apply. If it's wrong for me to attack Pedro, it's also wrong for Constable Diss to attack Pedro. The law is the same for everyone.' This requirement of universality—the idea of 'one law for all'—is a prominent feature of the normative ideal of the Rule of Law. But why is universality a good thing? Why is it desirable that there should be one law for everyone, irrespective of who they are, or their official status? One obvious application of universality is that we don't, on the whole, allow personalised laws; we don't have laws that make exceptions for particular people. In medieval England, there used to be things called 'Bills of Attainder', announcing that someone in particular (the Earl of Warwick, or the king's brother for example) was thereby banished from the realm and his estates confiscated. The idea of the Rule of Law is that the state should not use personalised mechanisms of that sort.

Moral philosophers link this requirement of universality with morality and with rationality. They say that if you make a moral judgment about someone or something, your judgment can't be based simply on that person or that incident in particular, or if it is, it's arbitrary. It

8   Two questions have been posed from the Left about this aspect of the doctrine. The first is whether the Rule of Law can actually achieve its aim of restraint. This question finds particularly strong expression within the 'Critical Legal Studies' school. See, e.g., Michael Tushnet, *Red, White and Blue: A Critical Analysis of Constitutional Law* (1988), pp 46–51. Some on the Left have also questioned whether it is *desirable* that government power should be constrained in this way. See Horowitz, 'The Rule of Law: An Unqualified Human Good?' (1977) 86 Yale LJ 591; EP Thompson, *Whigs and Hunters* (1975), p 266; discussed by Waldron below at 21–24.

9   J Waldron, *The Law* (1990), p 31.

10   [1981] 2 All ER 59, DC.

must be based on some feature of the person or action—something about what they did, something that might in principle be true of another person or another situation as well. In other words it must be based on something that can be expressed in a universal proposition. For example, if I want to say, 'It is all right for Diss to defend himself', I must say that because I think self defence is all right in general in that sort of case, not merely because I want to get at Pedro or say something special about Diss. So I must also be prepared to say that it would be all right for Pedro to defend himself in a similar circumstance. Unless I can point to some clearly relevant difference between the two cases, then I must accept that the same reasoning applies to both.

Another way of putting it is that universalisability expresses an important principle of justice: it means dealing even-handedly with people and treating like cases alike. If I am committed to treating like cases alike, then I ought to be able to state my principles in a universal form. If I cannot—that is, if I can't find a way to eliminate references to particular people from my legislation—that is probably a good indication that I am drawing arbitrary distinctions based on bias or self-interest or something of that sort.

Notes

1. There are numerous exceptions to the notion of one law applying equally to all. Members of Parliament enjoy complete civil and criminal immunity in respect of words spoken during 'proceedings in Parliament' by virtue of the Bill of Rights 1688,[11] while judges also enjoy various legal privileges. Diplomatic and consular immunities arise under the Diplomatic Privileges Act 1964 and the Consular Relations Act 1968, and these have been left undisturbed by the State Immunity Act 1978, s 16.

2. Waldron demonstrates how principles of justice (treating like cases alike) can be deduced from the simple notion of the law being addressed to, and applicable to, everybody. These ideas have found perhaps their most prominent proponents in the philosophical writings of Joseph Raz and John Rawls.

A cluster of formal principles

Raz is concerned to pare down the notion of the Rule of Law to what he sees as its logically necessary content (as we noted in the introduction to this chapter), whilst demonstrating that it yet prescribes a number of important principles about the application of coercive force within a legal system. Raz's exposition is followed by an extract from Rawl's *A Theory of Justice* (1972), in which he develops in detail the principles of justice that can be derived from the Rule of Law.

J Raz, 'The Rule of Law and its virtue' (1977) 93 *Law Quarterly Review* 195–98

FA Hayek has provided one of the clearest and most powerful formulations of the ideal of the Rule of Law: 'stripped of all technicalities this means that government in all its actions is bound by rules fixed and announced beforehand—rules which make it possible to foresee with fair certainty how the authority will use its coercive powers in given circumstances, and to plan one's individual affairs on the basis of this knowledge' [*The Road to Serfdom* (1944), p 54]. At the same time the way he draws certain conclusions from this ideal illustrates one

---

11 See Chapter 10.

of the two main fallacies in the contemporary treatment of the doctrine of the Rule of Law: the assumption of its overriding importance. My purpose is to analyse the ideal of the Rule of Law in the spirit of Hayek's quoted statement of it and to show why some of the conclusions which he drew from it cannot be thus supported. But first we must be put on our guard against the other common fallacy concerning the Rule of Law.

Not uncommonly when a political ideal captures the imagination of large numbers of people its name becomes a slogan used by supporters of ideals which bear little or no relation to the one it originally designated. . .In 1959 the International Congress of Jurists gave official blessing to a similar perversion of the doctrine of the Rule of Law:

> The function of the legislature in a free society under the Rule of Law is to create and maintain the conditions which will uphold the dignity of man as an individual. This dignity requires not only the recognition of his civil and political rights but also the establishment of the social, economic, educational and cultural conditions which are essential to the full development of his personality.

The report goes on to mention or refer to just about every political ideal which has found support in any part of the globe during the post-war years.

If the Rule of Law is the rule of the good law then to explain its nature is to propound a complete social philosophy. But if so, the term lacks any useful function. We have no need to be converted to the Rule of Law just in order to discover that to believe in it is to believe that good should triumph. The Rule of Law is a political ideal which a legal system may lack or may possess to a greater or lesser degree. That much is common ground. It is also to be insisted that the Rule of Law is just one of the virtues which a legal system may possess and by which it is to be judged. It is not to be confused with democracy, justice, equality (before the law or otherwise), human rights of any kind or respect for persons or for the dignity of man. A non-democratic legal system, based on the denial of human rights, on extensive poverty, on racial segregation, sexual inequalities and religious persecution may, in principle, conform to the requirements of the Rule of Law better than any of the legal systems of the more enlightened Western democracies. This does not mean that it will be better than those Western democracies. It will be an immeasurably worse legal system, but it will excel in one respect: in its conformity to the Rule of Law. . .

'The Rule of Law' means literally what it says: the rule of the law. Taken in its broadest sense this means that people should obey the law and be ruled by it. But in political and legal theory it has come to be read in a narrower sense, that the government shall be ruled by the law and subject to it. The ideal of the Rule of Law in this sense is often expressed by the phrase 'government by law and not by men'. . . . . . .Powerful people and people in government just like anybody else should obey the law. This is no doubt correct, and yet does it exhaust the meaning of the Rule of Law? There is more to the Rule of Law than the law and order interpretation allows. It means more even than law and order applied to the government. I shall proceed on the assumption that we are concerned with government in the legal sense and with the conception of the Rule of Law which applies to government and to law and is no mere application of the law and order conception.

The problem is that now we are back with our initial puzzle. If government is, by definition, government authorised by law, the Rule of Law seems to amount to an empty tautology, not a political ideal.

The solution to this riddle is in the difference between the professional and the lay sense of law. For the lawyer anything is the law if it meets the conditions of validity laid down in the system's rules of recognition or in other rules of the system [I am, here, following Hart, *The Concept of Law* (1961), pp 97–107]. This includes the constitution, parliamentary legislation, ministerial regulations, policeman's orders, the regulations of limited companies, conditions imposed in trading licences, etc. To the layman the law consists only of a sub-class of these. To him the law is essentially a set of open, general and relatively stable laws. Government by law and not by men is not a tautology if 'law' means general, open and relatively stable law. In fact the danger of this interpretation is that the Rule of Law might set too strict a requirement, one which no legal system can meet and which embodies very little virtue. It is humanly inconceivable that law can consist only of general rules and it is very undesirable that it should. Just as we need government both by laws and by men, so we need both general and particular laws to carry out the jobs for which we need the law.

The doctrine of the Rule of Law does not deny that every legal system should consist of both general, open and stable rules (the popular conception of law) and particular laws (legal orders), an essential tool in the hands of the executive and the judiciary alike. As we shall see, what the doctrine requires is the subjection of particular laws to general, open and stable ones. It is one of the important principles of the doctrine that the making of particular laws should be guided by open and relatively stable general rules.

This principle shows how the slogan of the Rule of Law and not of men can be read as a meaningful political ideal. The principle does not, however, exhaust the meaning of the Rule of Law and does not by itself illuminate the reasons for its alleged importance. Let us, therefore, return to the literal sense of the Rule of Law. It has two aspects: (I) that people should be ruled by the law and obey it; and (2) that the law should be such that people will be able to be guided by it. As was noted above, it is with the second aspect that we are concerned: the law must be capable of being obeyed. A person conforms with the law to the extent that he does not break the law. But he obeys the law only if part of his reason for conforming is his knowledge of the law. Therefore, if the law is to be obeyed it must be capable of guiding the behaviour of its subjects. It must be such that they can find out what it is and act on it.

This is the basic intuition from which the doctrine of the Rule of Law derives: the law must be capable of guiding the behaviour of its subjects. It is evident that this conception of the Rule of Law is a formal one. It says nothing about how the law is to be made: by tyrants, democratic majorities or any other way. It says nothing about fundamental rights, about equality or justice. It may even be thought that this version of the doctrine is formal to the extent that it is almost devoid of content. This is far from the truth. Most of the requirements which were associated with the Rule of Law before it came to signify all the virtues of the state can be derived from this one basic idea.

Notes

1. This chapter broadly follows Raz's assertion that '[the Rule of Law] is not to be confused with democracy, justice [or] human rights of any kind or respect for persons or for the dignity of man'; it therefore does not include consideration of substantive human rights sometimes associated with

the Rule of Law.[12] In a paper drafted for a committee of the House of Lords, Paul Craig summarises the argument (not his own) for this 'narrow conception' of the Rule of Law:

P Craig, *The Rule of Law,* Appendix 5, Sixth Report of the Select Committee on the Constitution, HL 115 (2006–07) (extracts)

We may all agree that laws should be just, that their content should be morally sound and that rights should be protected within society. The problem is that if the rule of law is taken to encompass the necessity for 'good laws' in this sense then the concept ceases to have an independent function. There is a wealth of literature devoted to the discussion of the meaning of a just society, the nature of the rights which should subsist therein, and the appropriate boundaries of governmental action. Political theory has tackled questions such as these from time immemorial. To bring these issues within the rubric of the rule of law would therefore rob this concept of an independent function. Laws would be condemned or upheld as being in conformity with, or contrary to, the rule of law when the condemnation or praise would simply be reflective of attachment to a particular conception of rights, democracy or the just society. The message is therefore that if you wish to argue about the justness of society do so by all means. If you wish to defend a particular type of individual right then present your argument. Draw upon the wealth of literature which addresses these matters directly. It is however on this view not necessary or desirable to cloak the conclusion in the mantle of the rule of law, since this will merely reflect the conclusion which has already been arrived at through reliance on a particular theory of rights or the just society.

2. Rawls in his famous work, *A Theory of Justice,* also sought to derive a set of basic principles deriving from the notion of law, which do not demand that *the content* of the law be good when judged by a particular philosophy.

J Rawls, *A Theory of Justice* (1972), pp 236–40

Let us begin with the precept that ought implies can. [Thus]. . .the actions which the rules of law require and forbid should be of a kind which men can reasonably be expected to do and to avoid. . .Laws and commands are accepted as laws and commands only if it is generally believed that they can be obeyed and executed. . .

The Rule of Law also implies the precept that similar cases be treated similarly. Men could not regulate actions by means of rules if this precept were not followed. . .The precept forces [judges] to justify the distinctions that they make between persons by reference to the relevant legal rules and principles. In any particular case, if the rules are at all complicated and call for interpretation, it may be easy to justify an arbitrary decision. But as the number of cases increases, plausible justifications for biased judgments become more difficult to construct. The requirement of consistency holds of course for the interpretation of all rules and for justifications at all levels. Eventually reasoned arguments

---

12 The distinction here is between what may be termed formal and substantive conceptions of the Rule of Law; on which see further Paul Craig, 'Formal and Substantive Conceptions of the Rule of Law: An Analytical Framework' [1997] PL 467. Lord Bingham has recently energetically dissented from the formal view: 'A state which savagely repressed or persecuted sections of its people could not in my view be regarded as observing the rule of law, even if the transport of the persecuted minority to the concentration camp or the compulsory exposure of female children on the mountainside were the subject of detailed laws duly enacted and scrupulously observed' (n 115 above, at 76).

for discriminatory judgments become harder to formulate and the attempt to do so less persuasive.

The precept that there is no offence without a law (*nulla crimien sine lege*), and the requirements it implies, also follow from the idea of a legal system. This precept demands that laws be known and expressly promulgated, that their meaning be clearly defined, that statutes be general both in statement and intent and not be used as a way of harming particular individuals who may be expressly named (Bills of Attainder), that at least the more severe offences be strictly construed, and that penal laws should not be retroactive to the disadvantage of those to whom they apply. These requirements are implicit in the notion of regulating behaviour by public rules. For if, say, statutes are not clear in what they enjoin and forbid, the citizen does not know how he is to behave. Moreover, while there may be occasional Bills of Attainder and retroactive enactments, these cannot be pervasive or characteristic features of the system, else it must have another purpose. A tyrant might change laws without notice, and punish (if that is the right word) his subjects accordingly, because he takes pleasure in seeing how long it takes them to figure out what the new rules are from observing the penalties he inflicts. But these rules would not be a legal system, since they would not serve to organise social behaviour by providing a basis for legitimate expectations.

Finally, there are those precepts defining the notion of natural justice. These are guidelines intended to preserve the integrity of the judicial process. If laws are directives addressed to rational persons for their guidance, courts must be concerned to apply and to enforce these rules in an appropriate way. A conscientious effort must be made to determine whether an infraction has taken place and to impose the correct penalty. Thus a legal system must make provisions for conducting orderly trials and hearings; it must contain rules of evidence that guarantee rational procedures of inquiry. While there are variations in these procedures, the Rule of Law requires some form of due process: that is, a process reasonably designed to ascertain the truth, in ways consistent with the other ends of the legal system, as to whether a violation has taken place and under what circumstances. For example, judges must be independent and impartial, and no man may judge his own case. Trials must be fair and open, but not prejudiced by public clamour. The precepts of natural justice are to insure that the legal order will be impartially and regularly maintained.

Now the connection of the Rule of Law with liberty is clear enough. . .The various liberties specify things that we may choose to do, if we wish, and in regard to which, when the nature of the liberty makes it appropriate, others have a duty not to interfere. But if the precept of no crime without a law is violated, say by statutes being vague and imprecise, what we are at liberty to do is likewise vague and imprecise. The boundaries of our liberty are uncertain. And to the extent that this is so, liberty is restricted by a reasonable fear of its exercise. The same sort of consequences follow if similar cases are not treated similarly, if the judicial process lacks its essential integrity, if the law does not recognise impossibility of performance as a defence, and so on. The principle of legality has a firm foundation, then, in the agreement of rational persons to establish for themselves the greatest equal liberty. To be confident in the possession and exercise of these freedoms, the citizens of a well-ordered society will normally want the Rule of Law maintained.

Notes

1. Perhaps the most important aspect of the Rule of Law, according to Rawls and Raz, is its freedom-promoting nature. In making known in advance and in a clear way what the restrictions on conduct are, the Rule of Law allows people to plan and thus control their own lives.

2. The principles which Rawls 'extracts' from the doctrine of the Rule of Law may be summed up as follows:

    - laws must not require the impossible;
    - like cases must be treated alike;
    - conduct can only be criminalised by law which is both reasonably ascertainable (and therefore non-retroactive) and of sufficient clarity;
    - cases must be tried fairly (therefore by an independent judiciary) and according to due process.

    To these principles, Raz[13] adds:

    - the procedure for the making of new laws should be governed by more general 'open stable and clear rules' [governing e.g. the procedures to be followed by Parliament to make statute law, the court hierarchy and rules of precedent governing the making of common law];
    - the courts must be readily accessible to all citizens;
    - the courts must have review power to ensure adherence by state authorites to the other principles.

3. When one compares the 'eight principles' of good law-making that Lon Fuller suggested,[14] there is a remarkable congruence. Fuller suggested that laws should be:

    1   general rules or norms, not aimed at particular persons (see Waldron's and Rawls' points above about the former use of Bills of Attainder);
    2   promulgated to the citizens through publication in some way;
    3   prospective, not retroactive;
    4   clear;
    5   not contradictory;
    6   not impossible to fulfil;
    7   stable;
    8   announced then followed—i.e. government action should be in accordance with the letter and spirit of the law.

    As to this last, the rule of law would plainly be futile if existing law did not in fact constrain and guide government action.

4. Lord Bingham has recently suggested that 'the core of the principle' is:

    > that all persons and authorities within the state, whether public or private, should be bound by and entitled to the benefit of laws publicly and prospectively promulgated and publicly administered in the courts.[15]

---

13 Raz, n 3 above, pp 199–201.
14 See *The Inner Morality of Law* (1964), esp. Chapter 2.

15 'The Rule of Law' [2007] CLJ 67, 69.

The remainder of this chapter will seek to ascertain how far these principles find legal expression in the UK.

THE RULE OF LAW IN THE BRITISH CONSTITUTION

The Constitutional Reform Act 2005 for the first time gave explicit statutory recognition to the rule of law as a constitutional principle. It provides, in section 1, that the Act does not adversely affect 'the existing constitutional principle of the rule of law'. Lord Chancellors also must take an oath, under s 17(1) of the Act, to respect the rule of law and defend the independence of the judiciary. However, as Lord Bingham pointed out in a recent important public lecture 'the Act does not define the existing constitutional principle of the rule of law', but merely refers to a pre-existing notion.[16] What shape does that notion appear to have in British legal discourse?

We assume from the outset that laws such as Bills of Attainder, described by Waldron above, are not passed in modern democracies such as the UK and that neither are laws passed that are impossible to obey; non self-contradiction within the law is also accepted as an obvious virtue. We concentrate on three particular principles: first, the requirement of legal justification for government action, particularly action that invades the rights or vital interest of citizens; second, the requirement that the law not be retrospective; third, the notion that law must be reasonably clear. As we shall see, this last requirement leads onto a well known controversy about the extent to which the granting of broad discretionary powers to Government infringes the rule of law.

The requirement of legal justification for government action

Historically, constitutional lawyers in this country have prided themselves on the UK's adherence to the Rule of Law, as upheld by the judges in a number of famous cases. One of these is *Entick v Carrington* (1765) 19 St Tr 1029, in which agents of the King, acting under a warrant issued by the Secretary of State, broke into the house of Entick, alleged to be the author of seditious writings, and removed certain of his papers. It was found that because the action was justified by no specific legal authority, it was a common trespass, for which the Secretary of State was liable in damages. Lord Camden CJ said:

> By the laws of England, every invasion of private property, be it ever so minute, is a trespass. No man can ever set his foot upon my ground without my licence, but he is liable to an action. . .If he admits the fact, he is bound to shew by way of justification, that some positive law has empowered or excused him.

If Government is under law, then since the courts are empowered to make the authoritative determination of what the law is, this must mean that the Government is in a sense under, and therefore obliged to obey orders of the courts, expressed in the form of injunctions. The normal sanction for failure to obey an order of the court is a finding of contempt of court. Perhaps surprisingly, the question whether Ministers of the Crown were obliged to obey court orders, and risked a finding of contempt if they did not, remained undecided in law until the following case in 1992.

---

16   *Ibid*, 67.

M v Home Office [1992] 2 WLR 73, 80, CA;
In Re M [1993] 3 WLR 433, 437–38 and 465–66, HL

In 1993, M, a citizen of Zaire, sought political asylum in the UK. His application was refused by the Home Office, and leave to apply for judicial review of the Home Office's decision was also refused. Just before his removal, a fresh application for judicial review, alleging new grounds, was made to Garland J in chambers; the judge indicated that he wished M's removal to be delayed pending consideration of the fresh application and understood counsel for the Home Office to have given an undertaking that this would be done. However, M's removal was not delayed, due to various mistakes and breakdowns in communication. Learning of this, Garland J then made an *ex parte* order requiring the Home Secretary to procure M's return to England. The Home Secretary, having taken legal advice, decided that the judge had no jurisdiction to make a mandatory interim injunction against him, as a minister of the Crown. Proceedings were then brought against the Home Secretary, alleging that he had been in contempt of court by virtue of his refusal to obey the *ex parte* order and the failure to comply with the terms of counsel's undertaking. The case was dismissed at first instance, and came to the Court of Appeal.

Lord Donaldson of Lymington MR: . . .this is a matter of high constitutional importance. Indeed I would say of the very highest. . .The system would be put under intolerable strain and would be likely to break down if a significant number of citizens treated the courts' orders as mere requests which could be complied with or ignored as they thought appropriate. I share [the] confidence [of Counsel for the Home Office] that, in the foreseeable future, governments and ministers will recognise their obligations to their opponents, to the courts and to justice. Where I have somewhat less confidence is in the suggestion that, were it ever otherwise, there would be a heavy political price to pay. There might well be, but I am not sure that there would be if, in particular circumstances, popular opinion was firmly on the side of the government and against the person who had obtained the order. Yet it is precisely in those circumstances that individual citizens should be able to look to the judiciary for protection under the law. I therefore do indeed think that it would be a black day for the Rule of Law and for the liberty of the subject if the first instance judge has correctly interpreted the law. I have reached the firm conclusion that he was mistaken. . .

The Court of Appeal found the Home Secretary personally to have been in contempt of court. He appealed to the House of Lords.

Lord Templeman: . . . My Lords, the argument that there is no power to enforce the law by injunction or contempt proceedings against a minister in his official capacity would, if upheld, establish the proposition that the executive obey the law as a matter of grace and not as a matter of necessity, a proposition which would reverse the result of the Civil War. For the reasons given by my noble and learned friend, Lord Woolf, and on principle, I am satisfied that injunctions and contempt proceedings may be brought against the minister in his official capacity and that in the present case the Home Office for which the Secretary of State was responsible was in contempt. I am also satisfied that Mr Baker was, throughout, acting in his official capacity on advice which he was entitled to accept and under a mistaken view as to the law. In these circumstances I do not consider that Mr Baker personally was guilty of contempt. I would therefore dismiss this appeal substituting the

Secretary of State for Home Affairs as being the person against whom the finding of contempt was made.

Lord Woolf: . . .The Court of Appeal were of the opinion that a finding of contempt could not be made against the Crown, a government department or a minister of the Crown in his official capacity. Although it is to be expected that it will be rare indeed that the circumstances will exist in which such a finding would be justified, I do not believe there is any impediment to a court making such a finding, when it is appropriate to do so, not against the Crown directly, but against a government department or a minister of the Crown in his official capacity.

Nolan LJ, at p 311, [in the Court of Appeal] considered that the fact that proceedings for contempt are 'essentially personal and punitive' meant that it was not open to a court, as a matter of law, to make a finding of contempt against the Home Office or the Home Secretary. While contempt proceedings usually have these characteristics and contempt proceedings against a government department or a minister in an official capacity would not be either personal or punitive (it would clearly not be appropriate to fine or sequest the assets of the Crown or a government department or an officer of the Crown acting in his official capacity), this does not mean that a finding of contempt against a government department or minister would be pointless. The very fact of making such a finding would vindicate the requirements of justice. In addition an order for costs could be made to underline the significance of a contempt. A purpose of the courts' powers to make findings of contempt is to ensure that the orders of the court are obeyed. . .

In cases not involving a government department or a minister the ability to punish for contempt may be necessary. However, as is reflected in the restrictions on execution against the Crown, the Crown's relationship with the courts does not depend on coercion and in the exceptional situation when a government department's conduct justifies this, a finding of contempt should suffice. In that exceptional situation, the ability of the court to make a finding of contempt is of great importance. It would demonstrate that a government department has interfered with the administration of justice. It will then be for Parliament to determine what should be the consequences of that finding.

. . .the object of the exercise is not so much to punish an individual as to vindicate the Rule of Law by a finding of contempt. This can be achieved equally by a declaratory finding of the court as to the contempt against the minister as representing the department.

Notes
1. It should be noted that counsel for the Home Secretary explicitly stated in argument that it was not part of his case to contend that the Crown was above the law, indeed, 'he accepted that the Crown has a duty to obey the law as declared by the courts'.
2. As TRS Allan notes,[17] the finding in this decision was of symbolic, rather than practical value, since '[t]he relationship between the courts and the Crown cannot . . .ultimately be a matter of coercion (as the current restrictions on execution against the Crown confirm)'. Nevertheless, its symbolic value should not be understated: to hold, as Simon Brown J did at first instance, that undertakings given by Crown officers were 'no more than unenforceable assurances', and that coercive orders were unavailable against them, would have driven a coach and horses through the notion of equality before the law.

---

17   [1994] 53 CLJ 1.

3. The notion, expressed in both the above cases, that exercises of governmental power, particularly those which impact upon the liberty of the citizen, must have a basis in law, has recently found a powerful reinforcement through the incorporation of the European Convention on Human Rights into UK law through the Human Rights Act 1998 (HRA). The Convention rights are now binding on all public authorities, including courts, which act unlawfully if they act incompatibly with them (s 6(1)). 'So far as is it is possible to do so, [all] legislation must be [construed compatibly] with the Convention rights' (s 3(1)), though if any primary legislation cannot be so construed, it remains valid and of full effect—the courts are given no strike-down power. Certain of the Convention rights permit interferences with them in limited circumstances: Art 2 (right to life); Art 5 (right to personal liberty); Art 8 (privacy); Art 9 (freedom of religion); Art 10 (freedom of expression); and Art 11 (freedom of assembly and association). In order for such interferences to be lawful under the Convention, the Government must first show that the interference was 'prescribed by' or 'in accordance with' the law, that is, that it had a basis in existing domestic law. In other words, an identifiable legal basis authorising the interference must be shown: mere executive discretion cannot suffice.

4. It was on this basis that the UK was held to be in violation of Art 8 of the European Convention in the case of *Malone v United Kingdom* (1985) 7 EHRR 14. Malone, an antiques dealer, was prosecuted for offences relating to dishonest handling of stolen goods. During the trial it emerged that the applicant's telephone had been tapped by the police acting on the authority of a warrant issued by the Home Secretary. Following his acquittal on the criminal charges, the applicant brought civil proceedings seeking to establish that the tapping of his telephone had been unlawful. He complained also of the practice of metering, whereby the Post Office would make available to the police the record of which numbers had been dialled by the suspect and the time and duration of each call. The extract below concerns only the latter complaint.

Malone v United Kingdom (1985) 7 *EHRR* 14 (extracts)

. . . .

62. Article 8 provides as follows:

1   Everyone has the right to respect for his private and family life, his home and his correspondence.

2   There shall be no interference by a public authority with the exercise of this right except such as is in accordance with the law. . .

B. Metering

[The Court first found that] release of [metering] information to the police without the consent of the subscriber also amounts, in the opinion of the Court, to an interference with a right guaranteed by Article 8. . .

   In England and Wales, although the police do not have any power, in the absence of a subpoena, to compel the production of records of metering, a practice exists whereby the Post Office do on occasions make and provide such records at the request of the police if the information is essential to police enquiries in relation to serious crime and cannot be obtained from other sources. . .

   Section 80 of the Post Office Act 1969 has never been applied so as to 'require' the Post Office, pursuant to a warrant of the Secretary of State, to make available to the police in connection with the investigation of crime information obtained from metering. On the other hand, no rule of domestic law makes it unlawful for the Post Office voluntarily to comply with a request from the police to make and supply records of metering. The practice described above, including the limitative conditions as to when the information may be provided, has been made public in answer to parliamentary questions.

However, on the evidence adduced before the Court, apart from the simple absence of prohibition, there would appear to be no legal rules concerning the scope and manner of exercise of the discretion enjoyed by the public authorities. Consequently, although lawful in terms of domestic law, the interference resulting from the existence of the practice in question was not 'in accordance with the law', within the meaning of Article 8(2).

. . . 89. There has accordingly been a breach of Article 8 in the applicant's case as regards [the]. . . release of records of metering to the police.

Notes
1. As a result of this decision, the UK had to pass the Interception of Communications Act 1985, which gave a statutory basis to the power to tap telephones. This has now been replaced by the Regulation of Investigatory Powers Act 2000.
2. It is ironic that in the unsuccessful *domestic* challenge to the legality of telephone tapping which preceded the challenge at Strasbourg, the judge dismissed Malone's case partly on the basis that, since in the UK everyone is free to do that which the law does not forbid, and there was no positive law forbidding telephone tapping, the Government was free to do it; in other words, a basic tenet of the Rule of Law was applied to *defeat* the claim. The judgment on this point missed the basic point that this freedom to do that which the law does not forbid should apply to *citizens,* who have a right to liberty, but not to *government,* which does not have such a general liberty of action, but only duties, a distinction eloquently brought out in the following case by Laws LJ (the facts are not material).

R v Somerset County Council ex parte Fewings and Others
[1995] 1 *WLR* 1037 (extracts)

. . . Public bodies and private persons are both subject to the Rule of Law; nothing could be more elementary. But the principles which govern their relationships with the law are wholly different For private persons, the rule is that you may do anything you choose which the law does not prohibit. It means that the freedoms of the private citizen are not conditional upon some distinct and affirmative justification for which he must burrow in the law books. Such a notion would be anathema to our English legal traditions. But for public bodies the rule is opposite, and so of another character altogether. It is that any action to be taken must be justified by positive law. A public body has no heritage of legal rights which it enjoys for its own sake; at every turn, all of its dealings constitute the fulfilment of duties which it owes to others; indeed, it exists for no other purpose. I would say that a public body enjoys no rights properly so called; it may in various contexts be entitled to insist that this or that procedure be followed, whether by a person affected by its decision or by a superior body having power over it; it may come to court as a judicial review applicant to complain of the decision of some other public authority; it may maintain a private law action to enforce a contract or otherwise protect its property. . .But in every such instance, and no doubt many others where a public body asserts claims or defences in court, it does so, if it acts in good faith, only to vindicate the better performance of the duties for whose fulfilment it exists. It is in this sense that it has no rights of its own, no axe to grind beyond its public responsibility: a responsibility which defines its purpose and justifies its existence. Under our law, this is true of every public body. The rule is necessary in order to protect the people from arbitrary interference by those set in power over them. . .

Notes

1. While the above would be broadly accepted as a basic principle governing the exercise of power by government, a qualification must be entered: as discussed in Chapter 11 on the prerogative, the very breadth and indeterminacy of some of the prerogatives, and in particular, the disquieting RAM doctrine,[18] would seem somewhat to undermine the clarity and certainty expressed by Laws J above. See further, pp 556–559.

2. At its narrowest, the above principle simply requires that governments, when acting, can point to specific legal authority to justify what they are doing. But it has also historically been associated with more resonant 'rule of law' principle prohibiting the executive from detaining or otherwise punishing those who have committed no crime, *even if* the detention is authorised by law (subject to various well-established exceptions, such as arrest on reasonable suspicion of having committed an offence and so on).[19] Executive internment has always been seen as anathema to the rule of law—as seen below, Dicey famously said:

> no man is punishable or can be lawfully made to suffer in body or goods except for a distinct breach of law established before the ordinary courts of the land.[20]

3. However, the perceived imperatives of fighting the terrorist threat have led the British Government to depart from this principle in relation to terrorist suspects. This is a major topic in civil liberties law and can only be briefly mentioned here. The point is to illustrate how quickly this supposedly fundamental principle may be departed from in the face of a new threat; of course internment had already been used against the IRA, but in Northern Ireland only. The problem arose originally because of the presence of foreign nationals in the UK whom the Government suspected of involvement in terrorism. It could not deport them because they would face torture at home[21]; conversely, the Government said, it could not put them on trial for terrorism offences, because this would mean revealing sensitive evidence in court that might put human sources of intelligence at risk, or reveal the capabilities of the intelligence services, thus enhancing the ability of terrorists to evade detection. Shortly after the 9/11 attacks in the USA, the Government decided to introduce a limited scheme of detention without charge for such foreign suspects, on the basis of the Home Secretary's reasonable suspicion of involvement with terrorism, subject to limited judicial review.[22] Since such detention would amount to a clear breach of Art 5 of the European Convention on Human Rights (the right to liberty of person),[23] the Government formally derogated from Art 5, on the basis that there was 'a state of emergency' in the UK, in order to allow them to detain these suspects without breaching the Convention.[24] However, the detention scheme was eventually found

---

18 The notion that the Crown (in effect, central government) has all the powers and freedom of action of natural or legal person.

19 Article 5 of the European Convention on Human Rights is the modern guarantee of this right to Liberty: see Chapter 7, pp 304–310.

20 AV Dicey, *An Introduction to the Study of the Constitution*, 10th edn (1959), p 18.

21 *Chahal v UK* (1996) 23 EHRR 413.

22 See Part IV, Anti-Terrorism Crime and Security Act 2001.

23 See Chapter 7, pp 304–310.

24 Article 15 allows for derogations from certain Convention rights where there is 'a state of emergency threatening the life of the nation', but only 'to the extent strictly required by the exigencies of the situation'.

to be unlawful in the seminal decision in *A v Secretary of State for the Home Department* (known as the *Belmarsh* case).[25] This decision, one of the most important made under the Human Rights Act, is discussed further in Chapter 17 (see pp 1001–1003 and 1010–1011). Here it may be noted that whilst there were more technical grounds for the decision,[26] their Lordships took the opportunity to express their strong disquiet at the very principle of executive of executive detention. For example, Lord Nicholls said:

> Indefinite imprisonment without charge or trial is anathema in any country which observes the rule of law. It deprives the detained person of the protection a criminal trial is intended to afford. Wholly exceptional circumstances must exist before this extreme step can be justified.[27]

Lord Hoffman went further in a passage that quickly became the most popularly quoted of the seminal *Belmarsh* judgment:

> The real threat to the life of the nation, in the sense of a people living in accordance with its traditional laws and political values, comes not from terrorism but from laws such as these. That is the true measure of what terrorism may achieve.

4. Following this decision, the detention regime was replaced by 'control orders' under the Prevention of Terrorism Act 2005; the Act's provisions dealt with the narrow basis of their Lordships' decision by applying to everyone suspected of involvement with terrorism activity, nationals and non-nationals alike. The Act gives the Secretary of State power to impose control orders on terrorist suspects, subject to judicial review, on the basis of 'reasonable suspicion' of 'involvement in terrorism-related activities'. The orders at first imposed were extremely invasive. A typical order involved:

> an 18 hour curfew, electronic tagging, a ban on use of the garden, requirements to report to a monitoring company twice a day, a ban on visitors and meetings with people other than those approved in advance by the Home Office, requirements to allow police to enter the house at any time and search and remove any item, and to allow the installation of monitoring equipment, prohibitions on phones, mobile phones and internet access, and restrictions on movement to within a defined area.[28]

However, in a series of cases, culminating in two House of Lords decisions, the courts have found both that the orders imposed have amounted to deprivation of liberty, contrary to Art 5 of the Convention[29] and that the procedures used, which usually involve secret evidence not disclosed to

---

25 [2005] 2 AC 68.

26 Essentially their Lordships found that since the scheme applied only to foreign nationals resident in the UK, but that the threat came substantially also from British nationals, the scheme was both disproportionate (because it was not an effective response to the threat) and discriminatory.

27 [2005] 2 AC 68, at [74], *per* Lord Nicholls.

28 12th Report, Joint Committee on Human Rights (2005–06), at [34].

29 From which the government had withdrawn the UK's derogation: see *Secretary of State for the Home Department v JJ and others* [2008] 1 AC 385.

the suspects or their lawyers, were fundamentally unfair, because they deprived suspects of the ability to challenge the core of the case against them.[30]

Law shall not be retrospective

In *Phillips v Eyre* (1870) LR 6 QB 1, 23, the strong presumption of the courts that Parliament does not intend to infringe the Rule of Law by penalising people retrospectively was made clear: 'the courts will not ascribe retrospective force to new laws affecting rights unless by express words or necessary implication it appears that such was the intention of the legislature.'

In the criminal sphere, the principle of non-retroactivity has been emphatically reaffirmed by the House of Lords. In *Waddington v Miah* [1974] 1 WLR 377, 378–80, their Lordships made it clear that they would be extremely loath to read any Act of Parliament as having retrospective criminal effect, Lord Reid saying, 'it is hardly credible that any government department would promote or that Parliament would pass retrospective criminal legislation'. This interpretative principle has now been bolstered, again by the Human Rights Act, in the field of criminal law.

Article 7 of the ECHR states:

1   No one shall be held guilty of any criminal offence on account of any act or omission which did not constitute a criminal offence under national or international law at the time when it was committed. Nor shall a heavier penalty be imposed than the one that was applicable at the time the criminal offence was committed.

2   This article shall not prejudice the trial and punishment of any person for any act or omission which, at the time when it was committed, was criminal according to the general principles of law recognised by civilised nations.

To many, the role of the judges in developing that part of the criminal law which is common law is open to question in the light of the requirements of certainty and non-retrospectivity made by the Rule of Law. This is because of the fundamental difference between a judgment by a court that has the effect of changing the law and an Act of Parliament that changes the law. Whereas changes made by legislation are virtually always framed so as to have only *prospective* effect, a court judgment may simultaneously change the law, and then apply that changed law to the person charged with the offence in question, who, axiomatically, carried out the act in question *before* the judgment was given.[31] Therefore, any change in the law made by that judgment is necessarily retrospective in effect. As ATH Smith has argued:

> being a common law system, [English criminal law] is in places highly uncertain, and. . .is therefore necessarily retrospective in character when the law is judicially developed. . .The enactment of a criminal code would provide a fixed and objective starting point for delineating the permissible restrictions on the right to personal freedom, even if it could not solve all the problems of certainty inherent in a government by laws and men.[32]

---

30   *Secretary of State for the Home Department v AF (No 3)* (2009) 3 WLR 74.

31   As ATH Smith argues: 'Comment; 1' [1985] PL 608.

32   *Ibid.*

The judges are of course well aware of this. Lord Bingham on this point said recently that the rule of law:

> preclude[s] excessive innovation and adventurism by the judges. It is one thing to alter the law's direction of travel by a few degrees, quite another to set it off in a different direction. The one is probably foreseeable and predictable, something a prudent person would allow for, the other not. . .Judicial activism, taken to extremes, can spell the death of the rule of law. . .These points apply with redoubled force in the criminal field. . .Judges may not develop the law to create new offences or widen existing offences so as to make punishable conduct of a type hitherto not subject to punishment.[33]

The case in which the issue of judicial change to the criminal law raised the greatest concern was the decision in *R v R*, in which the House of Lords effectively abolished the marital rape exemption—thus holding that husbands could thenceforth be guilty of raping their wives.

R v R [1991] 2 *WLR* 1065 (extracts)

The appellant was convicted of attempted rape; he was married to the victim, but she had left the matrimonial home two days earlier and left him a note saying she intended to petition for divorce. He forced his way into the house at which she was staying, assaulted her and attempted to rape her. He appealed against the decision on the basis that it was well established law that a man could not be guilty of raping his wife.

Lord Keith of Kinkel: Sir Matthew Hale, in his History of the Pleas of the Crown, (1736), wrote:

> But the husband cannot be guilty of a rape committed by himself upon his lawful wife, or by their mutual matrimonial consent and contract the wife hath given herself up in this kind [that is unto her husband] which she cannot retract.
>   [NB: 'given herself up in this kind' is an old-fashioned way of saying 'has agreed to have sexual intercourse upon demand']

> . . . In the first edition (1822) of *Archbold, Pleading and Evidence in Criminal Cases,* at p 259 it was stated, after a reference to Hale, 'A husband also cannot be guilty of a rape upon his wife'. For over 150 years after the publication of Hale's work there appears to have been no reported case in which judicial consideration was given to his proposition.
>   It may be taken that the proposition was generally regarded as an accurate statement of the common law of England. The common law is, however, capable of evolving in the light of changing social, economic and cultural developments. Hale's proposition reflected the state of affairs in these respects at the time it was enunciated. Since then the status of women, and particularly of married women, has changed out of all recognition in various ways which are very familiar and upon which it is unnecessary to go into detail. Apart from property matters and the availability of matrimonial remedies, one of the most important changes is that marriage is in modern times regarded as a partnership of equals, and no longer one in which the wife must be the subservient chattel of the husband. Hale's proposition involves that by marriage a wife gives her irrevocable consent to sexual intercourse with her husband under all circumstances and irrespective of the state of her health

---

33   See n 15 above, at 71.

or how she happens to be feeling at the time. In modern times any reasonable person must regard that conception as quite unacceptable.

In *S v HM Advocate* 1989 SLT 469, the High Court of Justiciary in Scotland recently considered the supposed marital exemption in rape in that country. . .[and] held that the exemption, if it had ever been part of the law of Scotland, was no longer so. . . The Lord Justice-General, Lord Emslie, who delivered the judgment of the court [said]:

> . . . A live system of law will always have regard to changing circumstances to test the justification for any exception to the application of a general rule. Nowadays it cannot seriously be maintained that by marriage a wife submits herself irrevocably to sexual intercourse in all circumstances. It cannot be affirmed nowadays, whatever the position may have been in earlier centuries, that it is an incident of modern marriage that a wife consents to intercourse in all circumstances, including sexual intercourse obtained only by force. There is no doubt that a wife does not consent to assault upon her person and there is no plausible justification for saying today that she nevertheless is to be taken to consent to intercourse by assault. . .The fiction of implied consent has no useful purpose to serve today in the law of rape in Scotland.

I consider the substance of that reasoning to be no less valid in England than in Scotland. On grounds of principle there is now no justification for the marital exemption in rape. It is now necessary to review how the matter stands in English case law. . .

In *R v Clarence*, 22 QBD 23 a husband who knew that he suffered from a venereal disease communicated it to his wife through sexual intercourse. He was convicted on charges of unlawfully inflicting grievous bodily harm contrary to section 20 of the Offences against the Person Act 1861 and of assault occasioning actual bodily harm contrary to section 47 of the same Act. The convictions were quashed by a court of 13 judges of Crown Cases Reserved, with four dissents. Consideration was given to Hale's proposition, and it appears to have been accepted as sound by a majority of the judges. However, Wills J said, at p 33, that he was not prepared to assent to the proposition that rape between married persons was impossible. Field J (in whose judgment Charles J concurred) said, at p 57, that he should hesitate before he adopted Hale's proposition, and that he thought there might be many cases in which a wife might lawfully refuse intercourse and in which, if the husband imposed it by violence, he might be held guilty of a crime.

[His Lordship then went on to consider subsequent cases which had whittled down the scope of the exemption; in *Rex v Clarke* [1949] 2 All ER 448 it was held that a husband could be guilty of rape 'in circumstances where justices had made an order providing that the wife should no longer be bound to cohabit with the husband'. In *R v Miller* [1954] 2 QB 282 'the husband was charged with rape of his wife after she had left him and filed a petition for divorce. He was also charged with assault upon her occasioning actual bodily harm'. It was found that he could not be charged with rape because 'the wife cannot refuse her consent', but that he could be charged with assault if he used 'force or violence in the exercise of that right' to intercourse with his wife; in *R v O'Brien (Edward)* [1974] 3 All ER 663, Park J held that a decree nisi effectively terminated a marriage and revoked the wife's implied consent to marital intercourse; the like finding was made by the Criminal Division of the Court of Appeal in *R v Steele* (1976) 65 Cr App R 22 as regards a situation where the spouses were living apart and the husband had given an undertaking to the court not to molest his wife. *R v Roberts* [1986] *Crim LR* 188 was similar (spouses had entered into a formal separation agreement)].

In *R v Sharples* [1990] *Crim LR* 198, however, it was ruled by judge Fawcus that a husband could not be convicted of rape upon his wife in circumstances where there was in force a family protection order in her favour and he had had sexual intercourse with her against her will. The order was. . .in the terms that 'the respondent shall not use or threaten to use violence against the person of the applicant'. . . .

There should be mentioned next a trio of cases which were concerned with the question whether acts done by a husband preliminary to sexual intercourse with an estranged wife against her will could properly be charged as indecent assaults. . .The effect of these decisions appears to be that in general acts which would ordinarily be indecent but which are preliminary to an act of normal sexual intercourse are deemed to be covered by the wife's implied consent to the latter, but that certain acts, such as fellatio, are not to be so deemed. Those cases illustrate the contortions to which judges have found it necessary to resort in face of the fiction of implied consent to sexual intercourse. In all of them lip service, at least, was paid to Hale's proposition. Since then there have been three further decisions by single judges.

[His Lordship considered them; in one, the judge followed the Scottish decision, holding that the marital exemption was no longer good law; his Lordship went on:]

A different view was taken in the other two cases, by reason principally of the terms in which rape is defined in section 1(1) of the Sexual Offences (Amendment) Act 1976, viz:

> For the purposes of section I of the Sexual Offences Act 1956 (which relates to rape) a man commits rape if—(a) he has *unlawful* sexual intercourse with a woman who at the time of the intercourse does not consent to it; and (b) at that time he knows that she does not consent to the intercourse or he is reckless as to whether she consents to it. . .[emphasis added]

In *R v J (Rape: Marital Exemption)* [1991] 1 All ER 759 a husband was charged with having raped his wife, from whom he was living apart at the time. Rougier J ruled that the charge was bad, holding that the effect of section 1(1)(a) of the Act of 1976 was that the marital exemption embodied in Hale's proposition was preserved, subject to those exceptions established by cases decided before the Act was passed. He took the view that the word 'unlawful' in the subsection meant 'illicit', i.e. outside marriage, that being the meaning which in *R v Chapman* [1959] 1 QB 100 it had been held to bear in section 19 of the Sexual Offences Act 1956.

Then in *R v S* (unreported), 15 January 1991, Swinton-Thomas J followed Rougier J in holding that section 1(1) of the Act of 1976 preserved the marital exemption subject to the established common law exceptions. Differing, however, from Rougier J, he took the view that it remained open to judges to define further exceptions. In the case before him the wife had obtained a family protection order in similar terms to that in *R v Sharples* [1990] *Crim LR* 198. Differing from Judge Fawcus in that case, Swinton-Thomas J held that the existence of the family protection order created an exception to the marital exemption.

The position then is that that part of Hale's proposition which asserts that a wife cannot retract the consent to sexual intercourse which she gives on marriage has been departed from in a series of decided cases. On grounds of principle there is no good reason why the whole proposition should not be held inapplicable in modern times. The only question is whether section 1(1) of the Act of 1976 presents an insuperable obstacle to that sensible course. The argument is that 'unlawful' in the subsection means outside the bond of marriage. That is not the most natural meaning of the word, which normally describes something which is contrary to some law or enactment or is done without lawful justification or excuse. Certainly in modern times sexual intercourse outside marriage would not ordinarily be described as unlawful. If the subsection proceeds on the basis that a woman on marriage gives a general consent to sexual intercourse, there can never be any question of intercourse with her by her husband being without her consent. There would thus be no point in enacting that only intercourse without consent outside marriage is to constitute rape.

. . . In my opinion there are no rational grounds for putting the suggested gloss on the word, and it should be treated as being mere surplusage in this enactment. . .

I am therefore of the opinion that section 1(1) of the Act of 1976 presents no obstacle to this House declaring that in modern times the supposed marital exemption in rape forms no part of the law of England. The Court of Appeal (Criminal Division) took a similar view. Towards the end of the judgment of that court Lord Lane CJ said, ante, p 611:

> The remaining and no less difficult question is whether, despite that view, this is an area where the court should step aside to leave the matter to the Parliamentary process. This is not the creation of a new offence, it is the removal of a common law fiction which has become anachronistic and offensive and we consider that it is our duty having reached that conclusion to act upon it.

I respectfully agree. My Lords, for these reasons I would dismiss this appeal.

Notes
1. It may be noted that their Lordships gave remarkably little consideration to the supposedly strong common law principle of non-retroactivity; the paragraph at the end of the judgment quoted from the Court of Appeal amounts to the only implied response to the charge of retrospective law-making.
2. The man convicted applied to the European Court of Human Rights on the grounds that at the time that he had forced intercourse with his wife this was not a criminal offence; that the Law Lords had only decided it was an offence after he committed the act, and that he therefore had been penalised for doing something which was not a crime when he did it. The principle of non-retroactivity, which is upheld by Art 7, ECHR, had therefore been violated. The judgment, which appears below, also concerned a man who had been convicted of raping his wife in relation to events which happened before the Court of Appeal judgment in *R v R*, but who was tried after it: the judge followed *R v R* and held that he could be convicted despite being married to the victim.

SW and CW v United Kingdom (1996) 21 *EHRR* 363 (extracts)

. . .

However clearly drafted a legal provision may be, in any system of law, including criminal law, there is an inevitable element of judicial interpretation. There will always be a need for elucidation of doubtful points and for adaptation to changing circumstances. Indeed, in the United Kingdom, as in the other Convention States, the progressive development of the criminal law through judicial law-making is a well entrenched and necessary part of legal tradition. Article 7 of the Convention cannot be read as outlawing the gradual clarification of the rules of criminal liability through judicial interpretation from case to case, provided that the resultant development is consistent with the essence of the offence and could reasonably be foreseen.

The applicant maintained that the general common law principle that a husband could not be found guilty of rape upon his wife, albeit subject to certain limitations, was still effective on 18 September 1990, when he committed the acts which gave rise to the rape charge. A succession of court decisions before and also after that date, for instance on 20 November 1990 in *R v J*, had affirmed the general principle of immunity. It was clearly beyond doubt that as at 18 September 1990 no change in the law had been effected, although one was being mooted.

. . .

Although the Court of Appeal and the House of Lords did not create a new offence or change the basic ingredients of the offence of rape, they were extending an existing offence to include conduct which until then was excluded by the common law. They could not be said to have adapted the law to a new kind of conduct but rather to a change of social attitudes. To extend the criminal law, solely on such a basis, to conduct which was previously lawful was precisely what Article 7 of the Convention was designed to prevent. Moreover, the applicant stressed, it was impossible to specify with precision when the change in question had occurred. In September 1990, change by judicial interpretation was not foreseen by the Law Commission, which considered that a parliamentary enactment would be necessary.

The Government and the [European Human Rights] Commission were of the view that by September 1990 there was significant doubt as to the validity of the alleged marital immunity for rape. This was an area where the law had been subject to progressive development and there were strong indications that still wider interpretation by the courts of the inroads on the immunity was probable. In particular, given the recognition of women's equality of status with men in marriage and outside it and of their autonomy over their own bodies, the adaptation of the ingredients of the offence of rape was reasonably foreseeable, with appropriate legal advice, to the applicant. He was not convicted of conduct which did not constitute a criminal offence at the time when it was committed.

The decisions of the Court of Appeal and then the House of Lords did no more than continue a perceptible line of case-law development dismantling the immunity of a husband from prosecution for rape upon his wife. . .There was no doubt under the law as it stood on 18 September 1990 that a husband who forcibly had sexual intercourse with his wife could, in various circumstances, be found guilty of rape. Moreover, there was an evident evolution, which was consistent with the very essence of the offence, of the criminal law through judicial interpretation towards treating such conduct generally as within the scope of the offence of rape. This evolution had reached a stage where judicial recognition of the absence of immunity had become a reasonably foreseeable development of the law (see paragraph 36 above).

The essentially debasing character of rape is so manifest that the result of the decisions of the Court of Appeal and the House of Lords—that the applicant could be convicted of attempted rape, irrespective of his relationship with the victim—cannot be said to be at variance with the object and purpose of Article 7 (Art 7) of the Convention, namely to ensure that no one should be subjected to arbitrary prosecution, conviction or punishment (see paragraph 34 above). What is more, the abandonment of the unacceptable idea of a husband being immune against prosecution for rape of his wife was in conformity not only with a civilised concept of marriage but also, and above all, with the fundamental objectives of the Convention, the very essence of which is respect for human dignity and human freedom. . .

47. In short, the Court, like the Government and the Commission, finds that the Crown

Court's decision that the applicant could not invoke immunity to escape conviction and sentence for rape upon his wife did not give rise to a violation of his rights under Article 7 para 1 of the Convention.

FOR THESE REASONS, THE COURT UNANIMOUSLY

Holds that there has been no violation of Article 7 para 1 (Art 7–1) of the Convention.

Notes

1. While it is impossible to feel any sympathy for the men involved in these cases, the decision of the court in this case arguably amounted to a dilution of the Art 7 guarantee. There was clearly a strongly arguable case that what had occurred did indeed amount to retroactive criminalisation. In its Working Paper 116, *Rape within Marriage*, 17 September 1990, the Law Commission had reviewed the state of the law in this area and concluded, at para 2.8:

   > It is generally accepted that, subject to exceptions (considered. . .below), a husband cannot be convicted of raping his wife. . .Indeed there seems to be no recorded prosecution before 1949 of a husband for raping his wife. . .

   The defendant was convicted in relation to events which happened in October 1989; if, almost a year *after* that date, the Law Commission, a body of distinguished experts, considered the marital exemption still to be good law, subject to some exceptions, it is hard to see how the defendant, even with advice, could have expected to foresee the change that was coming about.

2. A subsequent case, which in some ways raised the issues even more starkly than *R v R* itself, came several years later in *R v C* in 2004. In this case a man was convicted in 2002 of a number of serious violent and sexual offences, including having raped his then wife in 1970, in a particularly violent and degrading way. He appealed the conviction for the 1970 rape on the basis that:

   > it was not until the decision of the Court of Appeal in March 1991 in *R v R* [1992] 1 AC 599 that a man could be convicted of raping his wife during the subsistence of a marriage. Before then, in law a woman was deemed to have given irrevocable consent to sexual intercourse with her husband. This count, alleging rape, would not have been treated as an offence of rape at the time when it was committed, nor prosecuted. Therefore it was an abuse of process [to prosecute it now].[34]

   The man also claimed that his conviction violated Art 7(1) ECHR. His Counsel dealt with the seemingly contrary decision of the Strasbourg court in *SW v UK* (above) on the basis that:

   > the reasoning [in that decision] depended on the fact that by 1989 an individual husband who forced his wife to have sexual intercourse with him against her will would have been able to anticipate with 'reasonable certainty' that such actions would be regarded as criminal. That would not have been so in 1970, when this defendant raped his wife.[35]

   In response, the Court of Appeal re-surveyed the decisions relied on as showing acceptance of the marital rape exemption and went on to face squarely the issue of alleged retrospectivity:

---

34   *R v C* [2004] 1 WLR 1098, at [6].

35   *Ibid* at [8].

R v C [2004] 1 WLR 1098, 2013–15

The obstructed development of the common law, and the delayed identification of Hale's proposition as a fiction is readily understood. The issue was never taken to conclusion in a higher court. Faced with a count of rape by a husband on his wife, the court would be invited to quash the count, or to uphold a submission that there was no case for him to answer. If it did, or accepted the submission, the prosecution did not then enjoy any right of appeal. And even if a judge allowed the case to proceed to the jury, it still could not reach the Court of Appeal unless there was a conviction. So, by a series of decisions which did not require the principle to be addressed in this court, a number of exceptions were grafted onto the principle for which Hale provided the untested authority. [Those exceptions are surveyed above at pp 101–102].

. . .[Counsel for the Defendant] suggested that one way of testing the issue of foreseeability identified in the European Court of Human Rights' decision in *SW v United Kingdom* was to consider what his client would have been told if he had sought legal advice in about 1970. His solicitors would no doubt have warned him that it was morally wrong to force himself on his wife, and that he should not do so, but if they were to give him conscientious advice about the true state of the law, they would have to say that if he raped his wife he would not be committing a criminal offence. This represented the common understanding of the legal position.

We do not agree that this is anything like a complete statement of appropriate legal advice in 1970. The solicitor would have started by pointing out to his client that to rape his wife would be barbaric, and that he would not condone it. He would then have told his client that the courts had developed and could be expected to continue to develop exceptions to the supposed rule of irrevocable consent, and that if ever the issue were considered in this court, the supposed immunity of a husband from a successful prosecution for rape of his wife might be recognised for what it was, a legal fiction. He would in any event also have told his client that depending on the circumstances he might be convicted of indecent assault on his wife, punishable with imprisonment, and would be liable to be convicted of offences of violence ranging from common assault, by putting her in fear of violence, up to and including wounding or causing grievous bodily harm if he injured her in order to force her to have sexual intercourse. Any such offences, too, would be punishable by imprisonment. What is more, in 1970, the solicitor would have had to advise his client that persistent and unreasonable demands for sexual intercourse, if his wife was unwilling, and a single incident of rape, would have enabled her to found a petition for divorce on the grounds of cruelty, or depending on precisely when the incident occurred, his unreasonable behaviour. This conduct would also have entitled her either to a non-molestation order, or a non-cohabitation clause, depending on the jurisdiction in which she sought relief. The solicitor's advice would be that if he raped his wife after that, the supposed immunity would be gone, and he would then certainly be liable for the specific crime of rape. Before such an order, notwithstanding the repetition of Hale's principle in the authorities, he might be liable for rape, probably liable for indecent assault, and certainly liable for the appropriate offence of violence. On this view therefore he would have been told that he could not rape his wife with complete impunity. To the extent that the European Court of Human Rights in *SW v United Kingdom* proceeded on the basis that he could, its analysis was not fully informed.

[The Court went on to note the observations of the Strasbourg Court on the 'essentially debasing character of rape' (above at p 104) and continued]:

Accordingly, looking at article 7(1) and (2) together, and examining the entire purpose of the Convention, the wife was entitled to protection from inhuman or degrading treatment, and indeed from the 'destruction of any of the rights and freedoms protected by the Convention'. . .Article 7(2) provides ample justification for a husband's trial and punishment for the rape of his wife, according to the general principles recognised by civilised nations. Indeed, as it seems to us, it would be surprising to discover that the law in any civilised country protected a woman from rape, with the solitary and glaring exception of rape by the man who had promised to love and comfort her. . .

As a man may properly be convicted today of having raped his wife before the fiction of deemed consent was finally dissipated in March 1991, it cannot be said that a prosecution for rape [is] an abuse of process.

Notes

1. While the above decisions to some represented a judicial violation of the non-retroactivity principle, a far more straightforward—and less defensible—breach of that principle was seriously contemplated by the Blair administration in October 2001. In response to the terrorist attacks on America on 11 September, the Government announced that it would be bringing forward emergency antiterrorist legislation.[36] There had been a number of attacks carried out in the US and the UK using anthrax spores, which created widespread panic, and a number of hoaxers exploited this, giving false warnings to the police. It was initially announced that the Anti-Terrorism Bill would include a measure that would retrospectively increase the penalty for this kind of hoaxing from six months to seven years. Indeed, Ministers went as far as announcing that the increased penalty was in force, from 21 October 2001,[37] and that Parliament would 'later' pass legislation retrospectively making this change. This would clearly have amounted to an open and gross breach of Art 7 ECHR[38] and an unprecedented action as a matter of English law. Ministers, however, showed scant regard for the so called fundamental constitutional principles at stake. For example, Home Office Minister, Lord Rooker, reportedly said:

> Just because we are a tolerant liberal democracy does not mean we are going to have people wrecking that by using the very instruments that mean we are a tolerant and liberal democracy. We have not yet published the new legislation, but we have made it clear that we intend not to be . . .[hamstrung by]. . .human rights legislation which is clearly being abused—aided and abetted by the legal trade—by suspected terrorists.[39]

The same report described Oliver Letwin, shadow Home Secretary, as 'cautiously supportive'. When the Bill was published, the provision was not included; however, the reason given by Ministers was not that the Government had decided not, after all, to engage in such a blatant violation of its treaty obligations, but simply that the threat of the increased penalty had already had the effect of deterring would-be hoaxers, so that the Government considered the measure no longer necessary. Such a cavalier attitude, displayed by the very Government which introduced the Human Rights Act, indicates the remarkable lack of respect for the principles of constitutionalism

---

36   See HC Deb cols 924–39 (15 October 2001).

37   See 'Anthrax hoax law may breach human rights', *Daily Telegraph,* 22 October 2001.

38   See the view of the Joint Committee on Human Rights, *Second Report,* HL 37, HL 372 (2001–02), para 12.

39   See 'Anthrax hoax law may breach human rights', *Daily Telegraph,* 22 October 2001.

displayed by the British polity, in which the untrammelled ability of the Government of the day to respond to events in whatever way it sees fit appears to be the most valued attribute of the UK constitution.

2. The crisis in the banking system also produced a legislative proposal from the Government that amounted to a violation of the principle of non-retrospectivity, which this time was enacted in law. The case was a less grave one, because the matter concerned only civil liability, not criminal: clause 75 of the Banking Bill 2009 allowed the Treasury by order to disapply or modify the effect of a provision in an Act of Parliament, delegated legislation or rule of common law. It further provided that such orders 'may make provision which has retrospective effect in so far as the Treasury consider it necessary or desirable'. The Government justified this measure by reference to the extremely fast-moving nature of the crisis, and the need to take urgent action to safeguard the financial system, without having time to check whether there were any statutory impediments to the action taken (in other words, statutory bars to government action could be removed retrospectively). The Constitution Committee of the House of Lords[40] noted that, 'there is no absolute prohibition on retrospective legislation in British constitutional law or practice. There does, however, need to be a compelling reason in the public interest for a departure from the general principle that retrospective legislation is undesirable'; after a minor concession by the Government in response, it registered its concern[41] that 'desirability should not be a basis on which to allow ministers to change the law retrospectively' and that a precedent had been set that was 'not. . .acceptable'.

Laws must be sufficiently clear

The law must be accessible and so far as possible intelligible, clear and predictable.
(Lord Bingham)[42]

That laws must be sufficiently clear is an elementary characteristic that any good legal system should possess: laws that are not sufficiently clear cannot guide conduct. This is of particular importance in relation to criminal law. As noted above, doubts have been expressed in this regard on the basis that much criminal law is still derived from common law and is therefore 'in places, highly uncertain'.[43] Once again, in this area, the Rule of Law has been bolstered by the incorporation of the European Convention on Human Rights by the Human Rights Act 1998. As noted above, interference with Convention rights must be 'prescribed by law'. The European Court of Human Rights has found that such 'law' must have certain qualities, a matter which it addressed in a famous passage in *Sunday Times v United Kingdom* (1979) 2 EHRR 245, at [49]:

> . . .a norm cannot be regarded as a 'law' unless it is formulated with sufficient precision to enable the citizen to regulate his conduct; he must be able, if need be with appropriate advice, to foresee to a degree that is reasonable in all the circumstances, the consequences which a given action may entail. . .[However] those

---

40   'The Banking Bill 2009', Third Report of the Constitution Committee HL 19 (2008–09).

41   'The Banking Act 2009: Supplementary report on retrospective legislation' Eleventh Report of the Constitution Committee, HL 97 (2008–09).

42   See n 15 above, at 69.

43   ATH Smith, 'Comment; 1' [1985] PL 608.

consequences need not be attainable with absolute certainty, experience shows this to be unattainable. . .whilst certainty is highly desirable, it may bring in its train excessive rigidity and the law must be able to keep pace with changing circumstances. Accordingly many laws are inevitably couched in terms which, to a greater or lesser extent, are vague and whose interpretation and application are questions of practice.

Thus, the requirement that interferences be prescribed by law is not only a *formal* requirement, it says something about the qualities which that law must have.

One of the relatively rare cases in which an interference with a Convention right was found to be unlawful on this basis[44] was *Hashman and Harrup v UK* (2000) 30 EHRR 241. The application to the European Court of Human Rights was made by hunt saboteurs, complaining of a violation of their right to freedom of expression. They had blown a horn and engaged in 'halloo-ing' with the intention of disrupting a hunt. They succeeded in drawing some of the hounds away from the hunt, and one was killed when it ran across a road. Following a complaint to the local magistrates, they were bound over to keep the peace and be of good behaviour in the sum of £100 for 12 months under the Justices of the Peace Act 1361. The binding over was based on the finding that their behaviour had been *'contra bonos mores'* ('contrary to a good way of life'). The applicants' argument before the European Commission and then Court of Human Rights was that the convictions, which interfered with their right to freedom of expression under Article 10, could not be said to be prescribed by law, as the relevant domestic law was too vague and unclear to satisfy the requirement (in Article 10(2)) that any interference with the right under Article 10 must be 'prescribed by law'.

Hashman and Harrup v UK (2000) 30 *EHRR* 241, EctHR (extracts)

. . .13. Behaviour *contra bonos mores* has been described as 'conduct which has the property of being wrong rather than right in the judgment of the majority of contemporary fellow citizens' (per Lord Justice Glidewell in *Hughes v Holley* (1988) 86 Cr App R 130).
31. [The Court cited the principles laid down in the *Sunday Times* case, quoted above and went on:] The level of precision required of domestic legislation 'which cannot in any case provide for every eventuality' depends to a considerable degree on the content of the instrument in question, the field it is designed to cover and the number and status of those to whom it is addressed. . . .

The Court first recalls that in its *Steel* judgment, it noted that the expression 'to be of good behaviour' 'was particularly imprecise and offered little guidance to the person bound over as to the type of conduct which would amount to a breach of the order'. Those considerations apply equally in the present case, where the applicants were not charged with any criminal offence, and were found not to have breached the peace.

The Court next notes that conduct *contra bonos mores* is defined as behaviour which is 'wrong rather than right in the judgment of the majority of contemporary fellow citizens' (see paragraph 13 above). It cannot agree with the Government that this definition has the same objective element as conduct 'likely to cause annoyance', which was at issue in the case of *Chorherr* (1993) A 266-B. The Court considers that the question of whether conduct is 'likely to cause annoyance' is a question which goes to the very heart of the nature of the conduct proscribed: it is conduct whose likely consequence is the annoyance of others.

---

44 The complaint as to telephone tapping (as opposed to metering) in *Malone v UK* was also found to disclose a violation of Article 8 on this basis, since the applicable law, together with government statements explaining its practice in relation to telephone tapping, was found to be so vague and complex as not to fulfil the above requirements.

Similarly, the definition of breach of the peace given in the case of *Percy v Director of Public Prosecutions* (see paragraph 11 above) 'that it includes conduct the natural consequences of which would be to provoke others to violence' also describes behaviour by reference to its effects. Conduct which is 'wrong rather than right in the judgment of the majority of contemporary citizens', by contrast, is conduct which is not described at all, but merely expressed to be 'wrong' in the opinion of a majority of citizens.

Nor can the Court agree that the Government's other examples of behaviour which are defined by reference to the standards expected by the majority of contemporary opinion are similar to conduct *contra bonos mores* as in each case cited by the Government, the example given is but one element of a more comprehensive definition of the proscribed behaviour.

With specific reference to the facts of the present case, the Court does not accept that it must have been evident to the applicants what they were being ordered not to do for the period of their binding over. Whilst in the case of *Steel and Others* the applicants had been found to have breached the peace, and the Court found that it was apparent that the bind over related to similar behaviour, the present applicants did not breach the peace, and given the lack of precision referred to above, it cannot be said that what they were being bound over not to do must have been apparent to them.

The Court thus finds that the order by which the applicants were bound over to keep the peace and not to behave *contra bonos mores* did not comply with the requirement of Article 10(2) of the Convention that it be 'prescribed by law'. . . .

43. It follows that there has been a violation of Article 10 of the Convention.

Notes

1. It should be recalled that the requirement of the Convention that law must be sufficiently clear only applies to law which authorises interference with Convention rights.
2. As this book went to press, the European Court of Human Rights issued its judgment in the case of *Gillan v UK*, No 4158/05 (2010), which concerned a challenge to the law governing the use of stop and search under s 44 of the Terrorism Act 2000, which permits searches without reasonable suspicion of the individual concerned. The Court, considering a challenge under Art 8, the right to respect for private life, found that s 44 allowed for such arbitrary and unconstrained use of the power that the powers to search—and therefore to interfere with Art 8 rights—could not be considered to be 'prescribed by law'. As the Court observed, at para 85:

> there is a clear risk of arbitrariness in the grant of such a broad discretion to the police officer. . .the risks of the discriminatory use of the powers against [ethnic minorities] is a very real consideration.

See further Chapter 7, p 316 and Chapter 20, pp 1155–1156.

Dicey, the Rule of Law and discretionary powers

The most influential, though also one of the most controversial, expositions of the importance of the Rule of Law in the British constitutional scheme has been that put forward by Dicey. It is of interest today primarily as a starting point in a debate which has raged ever since over the compatibility of broad discretionary powers with the Rule of Law. This is also of course directly related to the preceding discussion on clarity in the law: the more narrow and precise rules are, the more clear and predictable they are in operation.

In Dicey's view the Rule of Law in the UK could be reduced to three propositions.

AV Dicey, *An Introduction to the Study of the Constitution*, 10th edn (1959), pp 188, 195, 202–03

We mean, in the first place, that no man is punishable or can be lawfully made to suffer in body or goods except for a distinct breach of law established before the ordinary courts of the land. In this sense the Rule of Law is contrasted with every system of government based on the exercise by persons in authority of wide, arbitrary or discretionary powers of constraint. . .It means. . .the absolute supremacy or predominance of regular law as opposed to the influence of arbitrary power, and excludes the existence of arbitrariness, of prerogative, or even of wide discretionary authority on the part of the government. . .a man may with us be punished for a breach of the law, but he can be punished for nothing else. [Second]. . . It means. . .equality of the law, or the equal subjection of all classes to the ordinary law of the land administered by the ordinary law courts; the 'Rule of Law' in this sense excludes the idea of any exemption of officials or others from the duty of obedience to the law which governs other citizens or from the jurisdiction of the ordinary tribunals. . .

[Third] from the general principles of the constitution (as for example the right to personal liberty, or the right of public meeting) are with us the result of judicial decisions determining the rights of private persons in particular cases brought before the courts; whereas under many foreign constitutions the security (such as it is) given to the rights of individuals results, or appears to result, from the general principles of the constitution.

Notes

1. In what follows, the discussion will focus on Dicey's first principle—the resistance to discretionary powers. His second, equality before the law, still, as Heuston points out, has some resonance in that 'the social or political or economic status of an individual is by itself no answer to legal proceedings, civil or criminal'[45] but has long been discredited, both as an accurate statement of the position in the UK, and insofar as it amounted to a critique of continental countries, such as France, where the *droit administratif* operated a separate form of justice for officials. As Jowell comments:

In 1928 William Robson wrote his celebrated book *Justice and Administrative Law,* in which he roundly criticised Dicey for his misinterpretation of both the English and French systems on that ground. He pointed out that there were in England 'colossal distinctions' [2nd edn (1947), p 343] between the rights and duties of private individuals and those of the administrative organs or government even in Dicey's time. Public authorities possessed special rights and special exemptions and immunities, to the extent that the citizen was deprived of a remedy against the State 'in many cases where he most requires it' [*ibid*, p 345]. Robson also convincingly showed how Dicey had misinterpreted French law, where the droit administratif was not intended to exempt public officials from the rigour of private

---

45   Heuston, n 4 above, p 44.

law, but to allow experts in public administration to work out the extent of official liability. Robson also noted the extent of Dicey's misrepresentation that disputes between officials and private individuals in Britain were dealt with by the ordinary courts. He pointed to the growth of special tribunals and inquiries that had grown up to decide these disputes outside the courts, and was in no doubt that a 'vast body of administrative law' existed in England [*ibid*].[46]

2. Dicey's third principle, that rights in the UK were the result of ordinary court decisions, is really an argument about the best way to protect civil liberties such as freedom of speech. Heuston notes that Dicey was above all a common law lawyer; he considered the specific guarantees of liberty offered by the common law to be of far more value than generally worded constitutions. However, the value which Dicey places upon common law rights over a Bill of Rights has been doubted, since the obvious correlation is that such rights are vulnerable to gradual erosion by statute. This position has been overtaken following enactment of the Human Rights Act, which for the first time gives UK citizens a general legislative statement of enforceable rights.

3. The applicability of the anti-discretionary element in Dicey's exposition of the Rule of Law to contemporary society is discussed further below, but a few comments are in order here. Heuston, a loyal supporter of Dicey, concedes that his view is no longer applicable in this respect, but attempts to place Dicey's opinion within its historical context:

> It must be recalled that Dicey's great work was written in the early 1880s, a period when the laissez faire state of the Victorians was only just beginning to give way to the welfare state of the modern world. Dicey. . .hardly foresaw the extent to which statutory powers of government would change the nature of English constitutional law. Today the fundamental problem is that of the control of discretionary powers, and it is indeed a serious criticism of Dicey's doctrine that he suggests that discretionary powers are in some way undesirable or unnecessary.[47]

4. As Heuston notes, Dicey's view was very much a product of its age. The 20th century attack on his model of the Rule of Law, which, in this respect at least, had received some support from Hayek[48] and Dickinson,[49] was two-fold. First of all, on the theoretical level, it was convincingly argued that it answered to an essentially conservative political viewpoint: Dicey's model, it was contended, was related to his ideal model of the state, as a minimalist facilitator of individual transactions and guarantor of individual rights. Dicey rightly foresaw that a Government which wished to devise and implement those major schemes of public provision for health, education and welfare to which he was opposed would require the granting to it of broad discretionary powers. His objection to the *type* of powers was therefore in reality rooted in his opposition to the *policies* which could be implemented through them. This argument thus reconstructed Dicey's account of the Rule of Law as rooted in a particular conception of government and pronounced that conception anachronistic and reactionary. As Murray Hunt has put it, 'the Rule of Law was nothing short of the encapsulation of his particular Whig conception of societal ordering, according to which the individual's

---

46   Jowell, 'The Rule of Law and its underlying values' in Jowell & Oliver (eds) *The Changing Constitution* (6th edn, 2007) at p 7.

47   Heuston, n 4 above, at 41–42.

48   See *The Road to Serfdom* (1944) and *The Constitution of Liberty* (1960).

49   See *Administrative Justice and the Supremacy of Law* (1927).

private rights, of property, personal liberty and freedom of discussion and association, ought to be sacrosanct from interference by the state'.[50]

5. The second part of the attack on this aspect of Dicey's argument was on the more practical level, by which the utility of Dicey's model as a prescription for modern government was subjected to a full-scale onslaught.[51] Discretionary powers, it was said, were a practical necessity if the government was to exercise wide-ranging interventionist powers for the public good. It would in many cases be wholly inappropriate and impracticable for officials attempting to implement complex schemes of social reform catering for the differing needs and circumstances of particular groups or individuals, sometimes on a local level and requiring local knowledge, to be fettered and encumbered by rigid rules of primary legislation. Such rules could only be changed with difficulty and delay, and could not be flexible enough to cater for local needs.[52] It was partly the perceived force of these arguments which paved the way for the proliferation of quasi- and non-legal rules which is such a distinctive feature of modern governance.[53]

Thus the central thrust of the argument against Dicey's view is that the immense complexity of the modern state, the desirability of decentralised decision-making, and the growth in sources of (corporate) economic power which can rival those of the state, all mean that a simplistic application of a rather rusty 19th century conception of the Rule of Law is both ineffective and inappropriate. Jowell considers both the continuing value of the doctrine and the aspects of it which warrant re-examination in contemporary society. His first point echoes that made by Schauer above—that there is often a choice to be made between the use of clear rules to constrain officials and the granting of broader discretion, to allow them the flexibility to come to the right, individualised decision in particular situations.

J Jowell, 'The Rule of Law today', in J Jowell and D Oliver (eds), The *Changing Constitution*, 4th edn (2000), pp 8–11

Certainty and the Rule of Law

An official possessed of discretion frequently has a choice about how it should be operated: whether to keep it open-textured, maintaining the option of a variety of responses to a given situation, or to confine it by a rule of standard—a process of legalisation. For example, officials administering welfare benefits could provide them on a case-by-case basis according to their conception of need, or they could announce precise levels of benefit for given situations. Similarly, laws against pollution could be enforced by a variable standard whereby the official must be satisfied that the polluter is achieving the 'best practicable means' of abatement. Alternatively, levels of pollution could be specified in advance, based on the colour of smoke emission, or the precise quantities of sulphur

---

50 'Constitutionalism and contractualisation', in M Taggart (ed), *The Province of Administrative Law* (1997), p 24. See further BJ Hibbits, 'The Politics of Principle: Albert Venn Dicey and the Rule of Law' (1994) 23 Anglo-Am LR 1.

51 KC Davis provides one of the most readable summaries of this attack, describing the Diceyan model as 'the extravagant version of the Rule of Law' (*Discretionary Justice* (1971), Chapter 1). Davis based his argument on both simple necessity and on the desirability of individualised justice, which often demands wide-ranging discretionary powers. He observes: 'The Franks Committee-Dickinson-Dicey-Hayek versions of the Rule of Law express an emotion, an aspiration, an ideal but none is based on a down to earth analysis of the practical problems with which modern governments are confronted.'

52 As Davis puts it, 'Discretion is indispensable for individualised justice, for creative justice, for new programs in which no one yet knows how to formulate rules, and for old programs in which some aspects cannot be reduced to rules. Eliminating discretionary power would paralyse governmental processes and would stifle individualised justice' (*ibid*, p 40). See further, R Unger, *Law in Modern Society* (1976).

53 For discussion, see I Harden and N Lewis, *The Noble Lie: The British Constitution and the Rule of Law* (1986), esp. pp 71–72.

dioxide. A policy of promoting safe driving could, similarly, be legalised by a rule specifying speeds of no more than 30mph on given streets.

Now for Dicey, and particularly for Hewart and Hayek, who mistrusted the grant of virtually any official discretion, the virtue of rule-bound conduct was principally that it allowed affected persons to know the rules before being subjected to them *ex post facto*. As a principle of justice, it was felt that no person should be condemned without a presumed knowledge of the rule alleged to have been breached. This assumes a penal law or criminal regulation of one form or another, and is understandable in that context where the lack of rules would involve risky guesses with serious consequences for non-compliance. It is fairer to a person prosecuted for a tax offence to have been made aware of the precise tax required than for the levels to be determined at the discretion of an official.

This argument, however, has a somewhat different compulsion when dealing not with penalties but with regulation involving the allocation of scarce resources. Should an applicant for a university place be entitled, out of fairness, to know the precise grades required for entrance? Should the applicant for welfare benefits be entitled to know the rules about allocations of winter coats? In cases such as these, the argument in favour of rules over discretion is an argument less from certainty than from accountability. This argument has two facets, the first being a concern to provide a published standard against which to measure the legality of official action and thus to allow individual redress against official action that does not accord with the rule or standard. Thus, an announced level of resources to qualify for welfare assistance ought to allow redress to a person who qualifies but is refused assistance. The second facet of accountability refers to the fact that the actual process of making rules and their publication generates public assessment of the fidelity of the rule to legislative purpose. Many statutes confer powers on officials to further the policy of the Act in accordance with wide discretion. The power may be to allocate council housing, or to provide for the needy, or to diminish unacceptable pollution of the air or water. The process of devising a points system for housing allocation, benefits for the needy, and acceptable emission levels of pollution thus forces the official into producing a formal operational definition of purpose. . .

The virtues of rules, as we have seen, include their qualities of legality, certainty, consistency, uniformity, congruence to purpose, and accountability loosely so called, all of which play an important part in the control of official discretion and may be seen as concrete manifestations of the Rule of Law. KC Davis, a leading American administrative lawyer, proposes in his book *Discretionary Justice* (1969) three main methods of controlling discretion. First is the 'confining' of discretion through rules akin to the legalisation we have just been discussing. He suggests that, wherever possible, discretion should be shaved down to the minimum compatible with the task to be performed. He proposes two other means of controlling discretion: its 'structuring' through open procedures, like the exacting federal rule-making procedures with which administrative agencies in the US must comply before issuing their regulations (Britain, incidentally, almost entirely lacks these procedures); and the 'checking' of discretion by means of a second look (not necessarily by the courts—internal administrative checks would suffice). . .

The limits of rules
Looking now a little closer at the arguments above about rules governing administrative action, we should consider whether. . .they. . .are after all wholly beneficial in the way that some constitutional theorists have assumed. Hayek gives an example:

it does not matter whether we all drive on the left or the right-hand side of the roads so long as we all do the same. The important thing is that the rule enables us to predict other people's behaviour correctly, and this requires that it should apply in all cases—even if in a particular instance we feel it to be unjust [*The Road to Serfdom* (1943), p 60].

We should start by challenging a central assumption of those in favour of rules, that their principal purpose is to constrain officials straining to escape from their legal shackles in order to indulge in discretion unconfined. Officials are well aware of the benefit of rules to their own efficiency. Rules announce or clarify official policies to affected parties, and thus facilitate obedience. They may also allow routine treatment of cases, thus increasing the speed of decision-making. A zoning system in planning, a list of features of 'sub-standard' housing, and a list of grades for university admission all allow decisions to be taken more quickly than a system that requires constant reappraisal of each case on its merits. Rules, therefore, reduce the anxiety and conserve the energy needed to reach decisions on a case-by-case basis. . .Despite the fact that rules may promote criticism, they also, in the short run at least, provide a shield behind which officials may hide, pleading consistent and uniform justice in response to criticism that the individual's case is unique.

So here we have the tension: the virtues of rules—their objective, even-handed features—are opposed to other administrative benefits, especially those of flexibility, individual treatment, and responsiveness. The virtue of rules to the administrator (routine treatment) may be a defect to the client with a special case (such as the brilliant applicant for a university place who failed to obtain the required grades because of a family upset or illness just before the examination). The administrator's shield may be seen as an unjustified protection from the client's sword. Officials themselves may consider that the job itself requires flexibility, or genuinely want to help a particular client, but feel unable to do so: hence the classic bureaucratic response, 'I'd like to help you—but there is this rule'.

Our administrative law itself recognises the limits of rule-governed conduct in terms of individual justice in its development of the principle against the 'fettering' of discretion. Where an official has wide discretion—for example, to provide grants to industry or to impose penalties upon overspending local authorities—a rule will often be introduced both to assist in the articulation of the standard and its even-handed application, and also to announce the standard to affected persons. The courts have not objected to the rule itself, but they have objected to its blanket application without giving a person with something new or special to say about his case the opportunity to put his argument to the decision-maker. The principle against the fettering of discretion acknowledges how rules can militate against good and fair public administration.

Notes

1. Lord Bingham has recently written:

    the essential truth of Dicey's insight stands. The broader and more loosely-textured a discretion is, whether conferred on an official or a judge, the greater the scope for subjectivity and hence for arbitrariness, which is the antithesis of the rule of law.

> This sub-rule requires that a discretion should ordinarily be narrowly defined and its exercise capable of reasoned justification.[54]

However, as Paul Craig has pointed out,[55] while certainty and clarity in the law are important virtues, they are not the only ones that a legal system must attain:

> It is also important to recognise. . . that the rule of law in the above sense [clear rules giving the minimum of discretion] is only one virtue of a legal system, and may have to be sacrificed to attain other desired ends. We may feel that the rule of law virtues of having clear, general laws should be sacrificed if the best or only way to achieve a desired goal is to have more discretionary, open-textured legal provisions. This may be so where it is not possible to lay down in advance in the enabling legislation clear rules in sufficient detail to cover all eventualities. Modifications to the rule of law in this manner are not somehow forbidden or proscribed. Given that it is only one virtue of a legal system it should not prevent the attainment of other virtues valued by that system.

2. The other principles of the Rule of Law mentioned above were that cases must be tried fairly (therefore by an independent judiciary) and according to due process. The issue of the independence of the judiciary is addressed in the second half of this chapter (p 141 *et seq*). The detail of the fair trial of cases obviously lies within the realm of criminal (and civil) procedure and therefore outside the scope of this work. Lord Bingham usefully summarises some 'core principles' in this area:

> that a matter should not be finally decided against any party until he has had an adequate opportunity to be heard; that a person potentially subject to any liability or penalty should be adequately informed of what is said against him; that the accuser should make adequate disclosure of material helpful to the other party or damaging to itself; that where the interests of a party cannot be adequately protected without the benefit of professional help which the party cannot afford, public assistance should so far as practicable be afforded; that a party accused should have an adequate opportunity to prepare his answer to what is said against him; and that the innocence of a defendant charged with criminal conduct should be presumed until guilt is proved.[56]

These general principles of fair procedures as expressed in administrative law are discussed below by Jowell. The notions put forward by Raz, that courts must be easily accessible and have review powers to ensure adherence by other public bodies to the principles of the Rule of Law, are clearly critical and are discussed elsewhere: for the availability of judicial review, and statutory attempts to exclude it, see Chapter 14.

3. For the principles governing the right of access to the courts, see the decision in *R v Lord Chancellor ex p Witham*,[57] an extract from which appears in Chapter 4, p 178. In brief, the case concerned a

---

54 See n 15 above, at 72.

55 See p 89 above.

56 See n 15 above, at 80–81.

57 [1998] QB 575.

challenge to changes to the rules governing court fees. The changes in the rules removed from litigants-in-person in receipt of income support their exemption from payment of such fees and the Lord Chancellor's power exceptionally to reduce or remit fees in cases of financial hardship. The applicant was an unemployed man in receipt of income support who wished to issue proceedings in person for defamation, for which legal aid was not available. Such proceedings have to be brought in the High Court and the fee would, under the new regime, be £500. He could not afford the fee and, by virtue of the changes to the rules, was no longer eligible for waiver. The basis of his argument was that the Lord Chancellor's actions had the effect of denying him access to the courts. His challenge succeeded. The judge remarked:

> . . .the right to a fair trial, which of necessity imports the right of access to the court, is as near to an absolute right as any which I can envisage. It seems to me, from all the authorities to which I have referred, that the common law has clearly given special weight to the citizen's right of access to the courts. It has been described as a constitutional right, though the cases do not explain what that means. In this whole argument, nothing to my mind has been shown to displace the proposition that the executive cannot in law abrogate the right of access to justice, unless it is specifically so permitted by Parliament; and this is the meaning of the constitutional right.

The Practical Implementation of the Rule of Law through Judicial Review

Chapters 14 and 15 of this book are devoted to the detailed rules and principles of judicial review. The following extract introduces the basic principles of judicial review and indicates how they may be seen as embodying some of the basic precepts of the rule of law discussed above. Jowell discusses, first of all, the way in which the requirement of fair procedure—a key aspect of the Rule of Law, going beyond the fairness of formal trials—is upheld, in terms very reminiscent of Rawls, and then goes on to consider the broader role of judicial review in policing adherence to requirements of legality and non-arbitrariness inherent in the Rule of Law.

**J Jowell, 'The Rule of Law today', in J Jowell and D Oliver (eds),
The Changing Constitution, 4th edn (2000), pp 13–19**

As we have seen, predetermined rules provide one way of controlling official discretion and achieving fairness for persons affected by public regulation. Procedural techniques provide another. I refer to these in connection with the notion contained in the Rule of Law that no person should be condemned unheard, a procedural protection also expressed in terms such as 'due process' or 'natural justice', the essence of which is the participation of affected persons in decisions affecting their rights or interests. This kind of 'structuring' or 'checking' of discretion attempts, like open rules, to promote fidelity to organisational purpose, both by permitting the persons affected to argue their case and, where a reasoned decision is required, giving, through the process of justification. . .The process itself does encourage 'purposive decisions'. . as justification must usually be made by reference to a general rule, standard, or principle. Overt reference to arbitrary or particularistic factors (such as the defendant's race or political views) will be difficult to sustain.

British public administration is deeply infused with the notion that adjudicative mechanisms of one form or another are necessary to provide procedural checks on discretion in order to comply with the Rule of Law. Some are provided through appeals—for example, in planning, from local to central government by means of written representations or a public inquiry. In other cases special tribunals exist to permit appeals from the decisions of a variety of officials upon issues as diverse as the registration of a new variety of rose to compensation for the acquisition of land. . . .

The practical application of the Rule of Law
. . . The day to day, practical implementation and enforcement of the Rule of Law is through the judicial review of the actions and decision of all officials performing public functions . . .There are three principal 'grounds' of judicial review: review for 'illegality', for 'procedural impropriety', and for 'irrationality' (or unreasonableness). The implementation of each of these grounds involves the courts in applying different aspects of the Rule of Law. Under the ground of illegality the courts act as guardian of Parliament's purpose, and may strike down official decisions which violate that purpose. Even when wide discretionary power is conferred upon an official, the courts are not willing to permit decisions which go outside its 'four corners'. Under the ground of procedural propriety the courts may, even where the statute is silent, supply the 'omission of the legislature' in order to insist that the decision-maker grant a fair hearing to the applicant before depriving him or her of a right, interest or legitimate expectation. The doctrine of legitimate expectation is itself rooted in the notion of legal certainty; the courts require a decision-maker at least to provide the affected person with a hearing before disappointing him of an expectation reasonably induced. At times the promised benefit itself may be required. In either case, certainty triumphs over administrative convenience.

It is perhaps more difficult to countenance the application of the Rule of Law in the third ground of judicial review, that of irrationality or unreasonableness, because it raises the question whether the principle governs the substance and not merely the procedure of official action.

To what extent does the Rule of Law touch on the substance, as well as the procedure, of official action. . .Laws in practice are not always enforced rigorously, but rather selectively, allowing for personal and other mitigating factors (as with the doctor speeding to the scene of an accident in the early hours of the morning). But suppose the police decide to charge only bearded male drivers with traffic offences and leave the clean-shaven and women drivers alone; or to charge only drivers of a particular race? Suppose an education authority chose to dismiss all teachers with red hair? Would these decisions infringe the Rule of Law on the ground of their substance? Courts in this country interfere with this kind of decision on the ground of its being an abuse of discretion, the term used being 'unreasonableness' in the sense set out in the celebrated *Wednesbury* case [*Associated Provincial Picture Houses v Wednesbury Corporation* [1948] 1 KB 223]. Is this judicial interference ultimately justified on the ground that the offending decision was a breach of substantive Rule of Law? If so justified, judges lay themselves open to accusations of improper interference with the substance of administration, about which they are reputed to know very little.

Those who deny that judges interfere with the substance of decisions contend that what the courts are doing when interfering with arbitrary, capricious, or oppressive decisions is ensuring that the official action is faithful to the law's purpose, thus achieving the containment of the administration in accordance with an implied legislative scheme. Even if a minister has power to act 'as he thinks fit', it is assumed that the statute conferring that power requires standards that are rationally related to purpose, and that the charging of only bearded drivers could not be related to the purpose of preventing unsafe driving. In practice, however, the legislation frequently has no clear 'purpose' itself, and to pretend otherwise is to adopt a fiction. Parliament often delegates enforcement to ministers, other authorities, or officials precisely in order to allow them to define and elaborate purpose. Implementation is often a process from the bottom up, rather than from the top down. When the Rule of Law allows judicial interference on grounds of 'unreasonableness', 'irrationality', or 'oppressiveness', it does become a substantive doctrine, one that is less easily accepted than the procedural, particularly in a society without a written constitution. Courts therefore tread warily on substantive Rule of Law and seek to exclude (or disguise) policy considerations from the decision. The 'unreasonableness' doctrine itself carefully avoids judicial second-guessing of the administration on the grounds of mere disagreement, and only permits interference if the official decision verges on the outlandish. . .

Notes

1. As discussed further in Chapters 15 and 17, nowadays, under both the developing common law of judicial review, and the HRA, the courts now extend their protection beyond acts without lawful authorisation, or undertaken without a fair procedure, or which are plainly irrational. The law now affords protection, through judicial review, for a set of substantive rights—personal liberty, freedom of speech, privacy, and the like (for the Convention articles, see Chapter 7). In this new guise, judicial review protects not just the Rule of Law (it will do so through the Convention requirement that interferences with Convention rights must be 'prescribed by law') but also a substantive set of civil and political rights.[58]

2. A recent, highly controversial case involving a Saudi arms deals, allegations of bribery and a surprising assertive High Court decision, well illustrates the interplay between judicial review and government policy, and starkly raised the issue of how far the courts are prepared to go in sensitive areas of government decision-making in order to protect the rule of law. The facts are stated below.

R (Corner House Research and another) v Director of the Serious Fraud Office [2008] *EWHC* 714, QB (extracts)

In 2004 the Director of the Serious Fraud Office, as authorised by section 1(3) of the Criminal Justice Act 1987, commenced an investigation into allegations of corruption against an United Kingdom company, [BAE Systems, the UK's largest arms company]. One aspect of the investigation concerned a valuable arms contract between the Government and. . .Saudi Arabia for which [BAE] was the main contractor. During the investigation the company represented to the Serious Fraud Office that disclosure of information required by a statutory notice served on it would adversely affect relations between the United Kingdom and Saudi Arabia and jeopardise the arms contract. Following communications and meetings, the Director took the view that he had a duty to investigate crime and that the investigation should continue, which it did. In the autumn of 2006 the Serious Fraud Office

---

intended to investigate bank accounts in Switzerland to ascertain whether payments had been made to an agent or public official of Saudi Arabia. That provoked an explicit threat by the Saudi authorities that if the investigation continued Saudi Arabia would withdraw from the existing bilateral counter-terrorism co-operation arrangements with the United Kingdom, withdraw co-operation from the United Kingdom in relation to its strategic objectives in the Middle East and end the negotiations then in train for the procurement of Typhoon aircraft. Following further discussion, the Director in December 2006 decided that the investigation should be discontinued. The claimants sought judicial review of his decision, contending that it had been unlawful for him to permit a threat to influence it.

[The investigation, then, was into allegations that the Saudi Government had been paid bribes by BAE Systems as part of a major arms deal; it was seemingly the threat of the revelation of such bribery that so exercised the Saudi Government. So concerned was that UK Government about the threatened Saudi response that the Prime Minister himself wrote to the Attorney General, warning of the dangers of continuing with the bribery investigation.

At first instance in the High Court the decision to discontinue the investigation was found to be unlawful. Most of the technical legal arguments in the case are outside the scope of this chapter; we consider here only the aspects of the courts' reasoning that were directly concerned with the rule of law. In this respect, the first two of the six grounds of challenge to the decision to cease the investigation are material and are as follows].

i) It was unlawful for the Director to accede to the threat made by [the Saudi government]; such conduct was contrary to the constitutional principle of the rule of law;

ii) the Director failed to take into account the threat posed to the UK's national security, the integrity of its system of criminal justice and the rule of law caused by surrender to the type of threats made in the instant case;[59]

Judgment of the Court

...The essential point, as we see it [is that] representatives of a foreign state had issued a specific threat as to the consequences which would flow from a refusal to halt the investigation. It is one thing to assess the risk of damage which might flow from continuing an investigation, quite another to submit to a threat designed to compel the investigator to call a halt. When the threat involves the criminal jurisdiction of this country, then the issue is no longer a matter only for Government, the courts are bound to consider what steps they must take to preserve the integrity of the criminal justice system.

The constitutional principle of the separation of powers requires the courts to resist encroachment on the territory for which they are responsible. In the instant application, the Government's response has failed to recognise that the threat uttered was not simply directed at this country's commercial, diplomatic and security interests; it was aimed at its legal system...That threat was made with the specific intention of interfering with the course of the investigation...

Had such a threat been made by one who was subject to the criminal law of this country, he would risk being charged with an attempt to pervert the course of justice. ...But whether or not a criminal offence might have been committed, the essential feature is that it was the administration of public justice which was traduced, it was the exercise of the Director's statutory powers which was halted.

---

59 [2008] EWHC 714, at [49].

60 Threats to the administration of public justice within the United Kingdom are the concern primarily of the courts, not the executive. It is the responsibility of the court to provide protection. . .

Mr Sales [Counsel for the Director of the SFO] argued that, in the context of the Director's decision, the rule of law requires no more than he should act in a manner consistent with the well-recognised standards which the courts impose by way of judicial review. The Director must exercise the powers conferred on him by the 1987 Act reasonably, in good faith, for the purposes for which they were conferred and without exceeding the limits of such powers . . .

63 At the heart of the obligations of the courts and of the judges lies the duty to protect the rule of law:—

> 'the rule of law enforced by the courts is the ultimate controlling factor on which our constitution is based' (per Lord Hope in R (Jackson) v Attorney-General [2006] 1 AC 262 paragraph 107). . .

65 The rule of law is nothing if it fails to constrain overweening power. The Honourable J.J Spigelman AC, Chief Justice of New South Wales has described judges and lawyers as 'boundary riders maintaining the integrity of the fences that divide legal constraint from the sphere of freedom of action. . .'

So too must the courts patrol the boundary between the territory which they safeguard and that for which the executive is responsible.

. . .We turn then to how the courts discharge that responsibility. The courts fulfil their primary obligation to protect the rule of law, by ensuring that a decision-maker on whom statutory powers are conferred, exercises those powers independently and without surrendering them to a third party. . . .

68 No revolutionary principle needs to be created. . .we can deploy well-settled principles of public law. In yielding to the threat, the Director ceased to exercise the power to make the independent judgment conferred on him by Parliament. There are many authorities which illustrate the proposition that by the surrender of independent judgment to a third party, a public body abdicates its responsibility. . .[the Court went on to cite a number of cases in which public authorities had been found to act unlawfully by surrendering to threats of disruption by pressure groups].

69 That line of well-established authority demonstrates how the courts protect the rule of law by ensuring the independence of the decision-maker, free from pressure and threat. . .

73 The Government's answer is that the courts are powerless to assist in resisting when the explicit threat has been made by a foreign state. Saudi Arabia is not under our control; accordingly the court must accept that there was nothing the Director could do, still less that the court can do now. Mr Sales said, as we have already recalled, that whilst it is a matter of regret, what happened was a part of life. The court cannot intervene but should leave the Government to judge the best course to adopt in response to the threat. . . .

77 Mr Sales' submission appears to us not to be one of principle but rather one of practicality: resistance is useless, the judgement of the Government is that the Saudi Arabian government will not listen and the authorities in the United Kingdom must surrender. That argument reveals the extent to which the Government has failed to appreciate the role of the courts in upholding and protecting the rule of law. . .

79 Surrender deprives the law of any power to resist for the future. . . .The context of the threat, in the present case, was the investigation of making bribes to foreign public officials, an offence introduced in 2001. If the Government is correct, there exists a powerful temptation for those who wish to halt an investigation to make sure that their threats are difficult to resist. Surrender merely encourages those with power, in a position of strategic and political importance, to repeat such threats, in the knowledge that the courts will not interfere with the decision of a prosecutor to surrender. After all, it was that appreciation which, no doubt, prompted the representatives of the Saudi Arabian government to deliver the threat. Had they known, or been told, that the threat was futile because any decision to cave in would be struck down by the courts, it might never have been uttered or it might have been withdraw.

. . .102 The Director failed to appreciate that protection of the rule of law demanded that he should not yield to the threat. Nor was adequate consideration given to the damage to national security and to the rule of law by submission to the threat. No-one took any steps to explain that the attempt to halt the investigation by making threats could not, by law, succeed. The Saudi threat would have been an exercise in futility, had anyone acknowledged that principle. We are driven to the conclusion that the Director's submission to the threat was unlawful.

Note

The Court accepted that there might be extreme situations, such as a threat to kill hostages, in which the justice system might have to be interfered with, e.g. by releasing prisoners, as demanded by the hostage-takers. But it found that such interference could only be justified where there was no alternative course open to the decision-maker (at [99]). This was not the case here, as it appeared that no attempt to consider other ways to deal with the Saudi threat other than discontinuing the investigation had been made.

The Government appealed this decision directly to the House of Lords and won.

R (Corner House Research and another) v Director of the Serious Fraud Office [2008] 3 *WLR* 568, HL (extracts)

Lord Bingham. . .My Lords. . .It is accepted that the decisions of the Director are not immune from review by the courts, but authority makes plain that only in highly exceptional cases will the court disturb the decisions of an independent prosecutor and investigator [his Lordship cited precedent and then went on to cite the Director's witness statement].

21. It was only following my first meeting with the ambassador on 30 November 2006 that I seriously began to entertain the thought that the national security public interest might be so compelling that I would have no real alternative. Ultimately, I was convinced by my discussions with the ambassador and the Prime Minister's minute that there was a very real likelihood of serious damage to UK national security.

It will be recalled that at the first meeting the ambassador had described the threats to national and international security as very grave indeed and had said that British lives on British streets were at risk. At the second meeting he had again said that lives would be at risk. At the third he had spoken of a real threat to British lives. The Assistant Director, in the light of those statements, envisaged that the withdrawal of co-operation might lead to 'another 7/7'. It is not suggested that the fears expressed by the ambassador and senior ministers were fanciful or ill-founded, or that the Director should have discounted them as being so. . .

[Lord Bingham went on to note that none of the authorities cited by the High Court were analogous on the facts and found that its formulation of a necessity test in para 99 (see above) was 'novel and unsupported by principle'. He went on]

The objection to the principle formulated by the Divisional Court is that it distracts attention from what, applying well-settled principles of public law, was the right question: whether, in deciding that the public interest in pursuing an important investigation into alleged bribery was outweighed by the public interest in protecting the lives of British citizens, the Director made a decision outside the lawful bounds of the discretion entrusted to him by Parliament.

[Lord Bingham then said that consideration *had* been given to other courses of action, such as dissuading the Saudis from going through with their threats, but that it was not in any event, the Director's job to consider other diplomatic courses of action, about which he had no expertise; he was entitled to rely on the advice given to him by the Prime Minister, the Ambassador, and the Attorney General. His Lordship concluded]:

The Director was confronted by an ugly and obviously unwelcome threat. He had to decide what, if anything, he should do. He did not surrender his discretionary power of decision to any third party. . .The issue in these proceedings is not whether his decision was right or wrong, nor whether the Divisional Court or the House agrees with it, but whether it was a decision which the Director was lawfully entitled to make. Such an approach involves no affront to the rule of law, to which the principles of judicial review give effect.

In the opinion of the House the Director's decision was one he was lawfully entitled to make. It may indeed be doubted whether a responsible decision-maker could, on the facts before the Director, have decided otherwise.

Baroness Hale . . .The great British public may still believe that it was the risk to British commercial interests which caused [the Director] to give way, but the evidence is quite clear that this was not so. He only gave way when he was convinced that the threat of withdrawal of Saudi security co-operation was real and that the consequences would be an equally real risk to 'British lives on British streets'. The only question is whether it was lawful for him to take this into account.

53 Put like that, it is difficult to reach any other conclusion than that it was indeed lawful for him to take this into account. But it is not quite as simple as that. It is common ground that it would not have been lawful for him to take account of threats of harm to himself, threats of the 'we know where you live' variety. That sort of threat would have been an irrelevant consideration. So what makes this sort of threat different? Why should the Director be obliged to ignore threats to his own personal safety (and presumably that of his family) but entitled to take into account threats to the safety of others? The answer must lie in a distinction between the personal and the public interest. The 'public interest' is often invoked but is not susceptible to precise definition. But it must mean something of importance to the public as a whole rather than just to a private individual. The withdrawal of Saudi security co-operation would indeed have consequences of importance for the public as a whole. I am more impressed by the real threat to 'British lives on British streets' than I am by unspecified references to national security or the national interest. 'National security' in the sense of a threat to the safety of the nation as a nation state was not in issue here. Public safety was.

55 I am therefore driven to the conclusion that he was entitled to take these things into account. I do not however accept that this was the only decision he could have made. He had to weigh the seriousness of the risk, in every sense, against the other public interest considerations. These include the importance of upholding the rule of law and the principle that no one, including powerful British companies who do business for powerful foreign countries, is above the law. It is perhaps worth remembering that it was BAE Systems, or people in BAE Systems, who were the target of the investigation and of any eventual prosecution and not anyone in Saudi Arabia. The Director carried on with the investigation despite their earnest attempts to dissuade him. He clearly had the countervailing factors very much in mind throughout, as did the Attorney General. A lesser person might have taken the easy way out and agreed with the Attorney General that it would be difficult on the evidence to prove every element of the offence. But he did not.

Notes

1. Two commentaries on these decisions take starkly opposing views. Hopkins and Yeginsu welcome the House of Lord's decision as upholding the legitimate discretion of the Director, given to him by Parliament; they support the Lords' rejection of the novel 'no alternative' standard applied by the High Court, about which they comment that, 'Given the breadth of discretion afforded to the Director by Parliament. . .[it] was a creative attempt to raise the bar for a lawful decision.'[60] A key difference between the High Court and House of Lords' decisions was that in the former, the rule of law was seen to act as an *independent* principle, requiring of the Director that he not surrender to the Saudi threats and break off the normal processes of legal investigation unless he had no alternative. In contrast, to the House of Lords, the rule of law is *encapsulated* in the grounds of judicial review—which, as Lord Bingham said, 'give effect' to the rule of law (para 41). Thus their Lordships' ruling 'declines to carve out a distinct legal category' occupied by rule of law concerns.[61] The authors conclude:

> The House of Lords' preference for conservatism over activism in this case has been lamented as 'downbeat'. . .Such gloom is misplaced. The abandonment of the investigation may be, as Baroness Hale observed, a distasteful outcome . . . As the House recognised, however, judicial review exists not to keep politics tasteful, but to keep executive discretion within the bounds set by Parliament. The *Corner House* judgment declares our current public law apparatus fit for this purpose. As such, the decision inspires rather than undermines confidence in our legal system. Admittedly, it highlights the limits of judicial review, and cases may yet arise which demand the rethinking of such limits. But this was not one of them. . .[62]

In contrast, Jeffrey Jowell is highly critical of the decision, noting that their Lordships paid little heed to the fact that the case involved two threats, not just one. While the first—the threat to public safety, was one properly for the Director to have broad discretion to consider:

> The second threat, however, [was] directed at a fundamental feature of the rule of law, namely that a person's criminal liability must depend on what he has done, and

---

60   R Hopkins and C Yeginsu, 'Storm in a Teacup: Domestic and International Conservatism from the Corner House Case' (2008) 13(4) JR 267, 269.

61   *Ibid*, p 270.

62   *Ibid*, p 272.

not his power or influence, here or abroad. Another element of the rule of law is that the process of investigation or prosecution should not be influenced by extraneous threats or inducements. Had the threats in this case been made by a British citizen, he would be liable at least to prosecution for perverting the course of justice. Baroness Hale's assertion (at para. 53) that a different approach may have been in order had the threats been made to the personal safety of the Director. . .rather than to the safety of the public seems, with respect, to be a distinction without any difference. Potential blackmailers will in future know to threaten the greatest ill for the greatest number.

   . . .The rule of law . . . is not absolute, but the courts should only countenance its limitation where strictly necessary for the preservation of some other important interest in a democratic society, of which public safety may be one. It is surprising that the House of Lords in *Corner House* positively encourages the view that the rule of law is on a par with any other 'relevant consideration' taken into account by the prosecutor. Lord Bingham has recently identified the various underlying elements of the rule of law, of which the core is that the law should be enforced; and enforced equally against all ('The Rule of Law' [2007] CLJ 67). . .And Lord Hoffmann has made the important point that government's duty to protect 'the life of the nation' requires regard not only to physical safety but also to our values of freedom and liberty (the *Belmarsh* decision).

2.   Jowell thus uses the arguments made by Lord Bingham in article already discussed against those made by his Lordship in his judgment in an actual case. It is noteworthy that in that article Lord Bingham stressed the importance of the statutory underpinning given to the rule of law in the Constitutional Reform Act (above, p 92):

> But the statutory affirmation of the rule of law as an existing constitutional principle. . .does have an important consequence: that the judges, in their role as journeymen judgment-makers, are not free to dismiss the rule of law as meaningless verbiage, the jurisprudential equivalent of motherhood and apple pie, even if they were inclined to do so.[63]

The question that irresistibly arises is: did the House of Lords' approach in the *Cornerhouse* case come close to treating the rule of law as mere verbiage?

3.   It must, however be recognised that the decision of the High Court was almost surprisingly idealistic and assertive for a British court. As we will see, the courts have traditionally been extremely loath to second guess the view of the executive on the requirements of national security. It is perhaps to be doubted whether the Saudis would have gone through with their threat, and whether the British Government even believed them or whether their real concern was the possibility of losing a highly lucrative arms deals and upsetting the Saudis generally. The idea that (a) the Saudis would definitely have broken off intelligence cooperation if the investigation was not stopped, (b) that this might well have led to an attack on Britain—'another 7/7'—being successful, when, with Saudi assistance, it would otherwise have been stopped, seems to be pure speculation. Nevertheless the possibility of British 'bodies on the street', however, remote, was enough. But in the end, from the point of view of the judiciary, the issue was this: remote the possibility may have been, but neither the Director nor the House of Lords was in a position to be able to assess the

---

63   Lord Bingham, 'The Rule of Law' [2007] CLJ 67, 69.

matter themselves: it was reasonable for the Director to rely on the advice he was given. In the end, as with so many other constitutional issues, the key issue is, not what the right answer is, but, who should properly decide the question.

4. Finally it should be noted that in certain instances, the Government has introduced legislation into Parliament seeking to place certain sensitive decisions beyond the reach of judicial review, through what are termed 'ouster clauses'. These are highly controversial since they amount, at their most extreme, to an attempt to put certain decisions above the law. An example is the Regulation of Investigatory Powers Act 2000. A special Tribunal is given exclusive jurisdiction to consider complaints relating to the Security Services, interception of communications and so on. Section 67(8) provides:

> Except to such extent as the Secretary of State may by order otherwise provide, determinations, awards, orders and other decisions of the Tribunal (including decisions as to whether they have jurisdiction) shall not be subject to appeal or be liable to be questioned in any court.

The courts' historical attitude has been to construe ouster clauses very strictly so that apparently attempts by Parliament to preclude judicial review do not have this effect. For example, the well known decision in *Anisminic Ltd v Foreign Compensation Commission* (1969) 2 All ER 147 concerned a statutory provision that gave jurisdiction to the Foreign Compensation Commission to determine compensation that should be paid to British nationals who had had property confiscated by foreign governments. An ouster clause stated: 'determinations by the Commissioners shall not be called into question in any court of law.' This sounded like an attempt to exclude judicial review, which does, after all, involve the 'questioning' of the decision of another body in a court of law. However, the courts found that the decision was only intended to limit appeals from decisions of the FCC made within its jurisdiction. But if it made an error of law in reaching its decision, that rendered its decision, not a 'determination' protected by review from the courts, but a mere 'nullity'. As Lord Reid said:

> I do not think that it is necessary or even reasonable to construe the word 'determination' as including everything which purports to be a determination but which is in fact no determination at all.

For further discussion of the courts' attitude towards ouster clauses and a recent governmental attempt to introduce an even more comprehensive ouster clause in relation to the Asylum and Immigration Tribunal,[64] see Chapter 14, pp 770–774.

The Rule of Law in the UK Constitution: conclusions

The above point about ouster clauses is really only a particular example of a more general point: that the rule of law is a broad principle of political morality, which Government and Parliament generally abide by and which the courts in particular seek to uphold. As the different approaches to it in the *Cornerhouse* case indicate, it may be seen as a background principle that simply forms the *rationale* for

---

64 In the Asylum and Immigration (Treatment of Claimants etc) Bill 2004.

general principles of statutory interpretation and the established grounds of judicial review (the House of Lords' view); at other times, judges portray see it as a free-standing constitutional principle that can be used to invalidate government action—the view of the High Court, and of Lord Bingham in his 2007 article quoted in a number of places in this chapter. But either way, like almost any other constitutional principle, it appears to be subject to parliamentary sovereignty. Parliament can pass legislation that expressly departs from general assumptions implicit in the rule of law—for example, by using ouster clauses to rule out legal challenges to certain types of executive decisions or passing legislation with retrospective effect. Courts are hostile to such departures from the rule of law, and will use their powers to interpret statutes and re-shape the common law to fight back against attempts by Parliament to remove the protection granted by the rule of law in specific areas. But as already noted in Chapter 1 and explored in more detail in Chapter 4, the essence of the doctrine of parliamentary sovereignty is that Parliament is supreme: if it expresses its meaning clearly enough in primary legislation, courts must bow to its will. So when talking about the courts' powers to enforce the rule of law against the other arms of government, one must always be careful to distinguish between instances in which a statute is being challenged and one where the challenge is to a lesser norm, such as bye-law or indeed an executive decision, as Paul Craig explains:

> The fact that a law is vague or unclear, and that it therefore provides little by way of real guidance for those affected by it, will not lead to a statute being invalidated in the UK. The courts may well interpret such a statute narrowly, in favour of the individual in such circumstances. They might also read it down pursuant to the Human Rights Act 1998, if the particular statute would otherwise infringe rights derived from the European Convention on Human Rights. . .
>
> The matter is different if the provision that fails to comply with the rule of law is something other than a statute. There is nothing to prevent the courts from invalidating other measures, whether they take the form of delegated legislation, individual ministerial decisions, acts of local authorities or decisions of agencies. If such a measure fails to comply with the requirements of the rule of law it is always possible for the courts to use one of the principles of judicial review to annul the measure. Thus if a minister purports to make a measure retrospective the courts will require express authorisation from the enabling statute, or something closely akin thereto, before they would be willing to accept that the minister's powers extended this far. Similarly, if the contested ministerial measure was very vague or unclear the courts would have a number of options at their disposal. They might decide that this was not consistent with the primary legislation; that it should be annulled under section 6 of the HRA; that the vagueness of the measure was indicative that the minister was acting for improper purposes; or that the challenged measure was an unreasonable exercise of the discretionary power vested in the minister.[65]

Some judges have recently started tentatively to suggest that, in sufficiently extreme situations, the traditional view that the rule of law is subject to parliamentary sovereignty may be reversed and that, as Lord Hope recently put it, 'the rule of law enforced by the courts is [now] the ultimate controlling factor on which our constitution is based'.[66] We will examine this issue in detail in Chapter 4, at pp 177–185.

---

65   Craig, p 89 above.

66   *R (Jackson) v Attorney-General* [2006] 1 AC 262 at [107].

THE SEPARATION OF POWERS

We are not prepared to accept that government can become, on the grounds of efficiency, or for any other reason, a single undifferentiated monolithic structure, nor can we assume that government can be allowed to become simply an accidental agglomeration of purely pragmatic relationships. . . .The diffusion of authority among different centres of decision-making is the antithesis of totalitarianism or absolutism . . . [67]

The accumulation of all powers, legislative, executive, and judiciary, in the same hands, whether of one, a few, or many, and whether hereditary, self-appointed, or elective, may be justly pronounced the very definition of tyranny. . .where the whole power of one department is exercised by the same hands which possess the whole power of another department, the fundamental principles of a free constitution are subverted.[68]

Reduced to its bare essentials, the doctrine of the separation of powers identifies three main organs of government—the legislature, the executive and the judiciary—and demands first that each should be separate and to an extent independent of each other, and second that each organ should be vested with only one main function of government. Thus, as Lord Templeman has put it, 'Parliament makes the law, the executive carry the law into effect and the judiciary enforce the law'.[69] It is immediately apparent that the doctrine is associated with that of the Rule of Law, which is strongly concerned with the manner in which the judiciary can keep the executive and (in the UK only to a very limited extent) the legislature within the bounds of its lawful authority. This issue has been explored above, while the practical means of enforcing such limitations—judicial review— is extensively discussed in Chapters 14 and 15. The other substantial concern of the doctrine is the relationship between the legislature and the executive, which is considered in detail in Parts III and IV. Therefore, what follows will confine itself to a discussion of the theoretical basis for the doctrine and its application in the UK. The latter part of the discussion will note the significant ways in which the growing influence of Article 6(1) of the ECHR has bolstered a vital aspect of both the separation of powers and the Rule of Law—the independence of the judiciary, and the functional separation between executive and judiciary. A brief comment will also be made on the overall impact of the HRA on the balance of powers between executive and judiciary.

The classic formulation of the doctrine is Montesquieu's:

When the legislative and executive powers are united in the same person, or in the same body of magistrates, there can be no liberty. . .Again, there is no liberty if the power of judging is not separated from the legislative and executive. If it were joined with the legislative, the life and liberty of the subject would be exposed to arbitrary control; for the judge would then be the legislator. If it were joined to the executive power, the judge might behave with violence and oppression. There would be an end to everything, if the same man, or the same body, whether of the nobles or of the people, were to exercise those three powers, that of enacting laws, that of executing public affairs, and that of trying crimes or individual causes. [Quoted in R Shackleton, 'Montesquieu, Bolingbroke and the separation of powers' (1949) 3 FS.]

---

67   MCJ Vile, *Constitutionalism and the Separation of Powers* (1967), pp 10 and 15.

68   James Madison, *The Federalist*, No XLVII.

69   *In Re M* [1993] 3 WLR 433.

Notes

1. As Colin Munro notes,[70] Montesquieu advocated that 'the three agencies of Government should perform their functions separately' but did not make it quite clear what form the separation should take, nor whether a 'complete separation of personnel' for the different agencies was required.

2. The classical or 'strict' version of the theory may be summarised as follows:

   (a)   The same people should not belong to more than one of the three main institutions of government; thus, for example, judges should not sit in Parliament.

   (b)   One organ of government should not control or interfere with the work of one of the other organs; thus ministers should not be able to interfere with the deciding of individual cases by judges.

   (c)   One organ of government should not be able to exercise the functions of another; thus judges should be only be able to interpret the law, not make new laws.

   As appears below, however, a modified version of the theory, known as the 'partial separation theory', has recently gained ground.

3. Apart from doubts as to the applicability of the doctrine to the British constitution (discussed below), considerable doubts have been expressed as to the value and coherence of the doctrine itself. These views are discussed and answered by Eric Barendt who first of all notes the criticisms of Sir Ivor Jennings, namely that 'there are no material differences between the three functions, so the separation principle fails to explain why certain functions should be given to one body rather than another'.[71] He also cites Marshall's arguments,[72] to similar effect, that, on the US version of the theory, judicial review of legislation is appropriate 'to check the legislative and executive branches, [which] would be an unwarrantable violation of . . . the pure theory' and concludes that the doctrine 'may be counted little more than a jumbled portmanteau of arguments for policies that should be supported or rejected on other grounds'.[73] In reply, Barendt first argues that Jennings exaggerated the difficulties of distinguishing genuinely different functions of government.[74] He then goes on to defend the doctrine on more fundamental grounds, and considers its wider significance.

E Barendt, 'Separation of powers and constitutional government' [1995] *Public Law* 599, 606–07

. . .the Separation of Powers is not in essence concerned with the allocation of functions as such. Its primary purpose. . .is the prevention of the arbitrary government, or tyranny, which may arise from the concentration of power. The allocation of functions between three, or perhaps more, branches of government is only a means to achieve that end. It does not matter, therefore, whether powers are always allocated precisely to the most appropriate institution—although an insensitive allocation would probably produce incompetent government. . .

---

70   C Munro, *Studies in Constitutional Law* (1987), p 191.

71   E Barendt, 'Separation of powers and constitutional government' [1995] PL 599, 603. Barendt here cites Jennings' *The Law and the Constitution*, 5th edn (1959), App I, pp 281–82 and 303.

72   *Ibid,* pp 603–04. Barendt refers to G Marshall's *Constitutional Theory* (1971), Chapter V.

73   Marshall, *ibid,* p 124; quoted in Barendt, *ibid,* at 604.

74   *Ibid,* 605–06.

This point is perhaps most clearly appreciated if we consider what has become one of the most complex areas for Separation of Powers analysis: the organisation, and control, of administrative authorities and agencies. These range from bodies which allocate social security and welfare benefits (such as public housing), to regulatory bodies, e.g. the Independent Television Commission and the Monopolies and Mergers Commission, and finally to supervisory or investigatory officers, such as the Comptroller and Auditor-General and the Parliamentary Commissioner for Administration (PCA). Now it can be asked whether these bodies perform legislative (or rule-making, to use the American term), administrative, or judicial functions. But these are impossible questions to answer. For, in truth many agencies perform at least two, and perhaps all three, functions. This is apparent in the US, where it is common for an independent regulatory agency to engage in rule-making, to formulate and apply policies, and to take individual decisions, often after a formal hearing. Perhaps in the UK the only authorities which consistently discharge all three functions are local authorities, which may make by-laws, formulate planning, highways and housing policies, and decide applications for planning permission which might be characterised as judicial, or at least quasi judicial, decisions. But certainly many agencies, including Government ministers, exercise a variety of functions, some of which can be characterised as executive and some as judicial.

Does this phenomenon mean that Separation of Powers analysis should be abandoned as hopeless? It would seem so, if the pure theory is adopted, with its rigid insistence that each function of government is discharged by a separate institution. But the answer may be quite different if we see the principle as essentially concerned with the avoidance of concentrations of power. For, then, questions may be asked about the relationship of the agency to the three traditional branches of government. Does Parliament or the Government have sole right to hire and fire members of the authority and its staff? Does the Government have exclusive power to issue directions or guidance to the agency? If the agency takes judicial or quasi-judicial decisions, how far is it subject to review by the ordinary courts? On this approach there would be a violation of the principle if the executive were entitled, without assent of the legislature, to give detailed directions to an agency, and appoint its members, when that agency takes decisions affecting individual rights and judicial review is (virtually) excluded. That would not be because an executive agency carried out judicial functions, but because it was so structured as to create or reinforce a concentration of power in the hands of the Government.

The partial separation theory

The argument in the previous section has shown that the Separation of Powers should not be explained in terms of a strict distribution of functions between the three branches of government, but in terms of a network of rules and principles which ensure that power is not concentrated in the hands of one branch. (In practice the danger now is that the executive has too much power, though it is worth remembering that at other times there was more anxiety about self-aggrandisement of the legislature.) That does not mean that the allocation of functions is wholly irrelevant. I will explain in the next section of this article how, in civil liberties cases, courts may properly insist that general rules be made by the legislature and that the executive does not act without legislative authorisation to deprive individuals of their rights. But the importance of a correct definition and allocation of functions should not be exaggerated. Madison for instance was not troubled by these questions, though nobody has argued so cogently for the Separation of Powers principle.

Outside the context of court rulings in civil liberties cases, the principle is most frequently applied in the architecture of the constitution itself. Powers are allocated to different institutions. The legislature is normally divided into two branches, a procedure recommended by Madison on the ground that otherwise it would be too powerful [Federalist Papers, No 51]. Each branch is empowered to check the others by exercising a partial agency or control over their acts [ibid, No 47]. That is why, for example, in the US constitution the Senate must give its advice and consent to the appointment of ministers, ambassadors and judges, and the President may veto Bills passed by the House of Representatives and the Senate, subject to an override by a two-thirds majority vote in each House. It is not very helpful to ask whether, in the former instance, the Senate is exercising an executive power and whether, in the latter, the President acts as a third branch of the legislature. What is important is that there is a system of checks and balances between institutions which otherwise might exercise excessive power. As Madison put it in Federalist Paper 51, the structure of government should be so arranged 'that its several constituent parts may, by their mutual relations, be the means of keeping each other in their proper places'.

Note

It was noted in Chapter 1 (pp 17–18) that the provisions in different constitutions dealing with relations between the executive and legislature show far more variation than those governing the independence of the judiciary. Indeed, the one part of the Separation of Powers doctrine that *does* command more or less universal acceptance is the independence of the judiciary—considered below. Two caveats should be noted however: first, this principle may be seen simply to flow from the notion of the rule of law, without the need to invoke 'the separation of powers'; second, there is quite wide variation in the ways that different constitutions seek to achieve judicial independence. For example, in the United States, the appointment of Supreme Court Judges is subject to the 'the advice and consent of the Senate'—in practice, openly partisan confirmation hearings, in which the appointment of particular judges becomes a party political struggle. This would be unthinkable in the UK, and indeed is seen as the very antithesis of preserving judicial independence. Other aspects of such independence, however, such as the necessity of security of tenure, are much more widely agreed. We explore these issues further below.

DOUBTS AS TO THE RELEVANCE OF THE SEPARATION OF POWERS DOCTRINE IN THE UK CONSTITUTION

C Munro, *Studies in Constitutional Law*, 2nd edn (1999), pp 302–04

Two initial observations may be made. The first is that the British constitution, with its long and largely unbroken history, is above all the product of experience and experiment. Its development has been characteristically pragmatic rather than principled, and so it is hardly likely absolutely to conform (or not to conform) to any ideal type. A second and related point is that the outlines of the modern British constitution had already been formed by the late 17th century. Therefore, even if earlier versions of the doctrine may not have been without some effect, Montesquieu's formulation of it in the mid-18th century could only have affected such developments as occurred after that date. . .

What about the 20th century constitution? Writers on the constitution seem to speak almost with one voice in denying that the Separation of Powers is a feature of the constitution. . .[75]

[Munro goes on to note, however, that the judiciary express a different view.]

. . .the House of Lords, in a case concerning an industrial dispute, felt it necessary to rebuke the Court of Appeal for having strayed beyond its proper constitutional function:

> At a time when more and more cases involve the application of legislation which gives effect to policies that are the subject of bitter public and parliamentary controversy, it cannot be too strongly emphasised that the British constitution, though largely underwritten, is firmly based on the Separation of Powers: Parliament makes the laws, the judiciary interpret them. [*Dupont Steels Ltd v Sirs* [1980] 1 All ER 529 at 541.]

Lord Scarman, in his speech in the same case, also remarked that 'the constitution's Separation of Powers, or more accurately functions, must be observed if judicial independence is not to be put at risk' [at 551]. In another case. . .Sir John Donaldson MR said:

> Although the UK has no written constitution, it is a constitutional convention of the highest importance that the legislature and the judicature are separate and independent of one another, subject to certain ultimate rights of Parliament over the judicature which are immaterial for present purposes. It therefore behoves the courts to be ever sensitive to the paramount need to refrain from trespassing on the province of Parliament.

Executive-Legislative relations: the doctrine denied?

Why, then, is there such a denial of the doctrine in the UK by academic commentators? It becomes apparent, when examining this issue, that the judiciary is concerned mainly with defining the correct relationship between itself and the legislative (and executive) arms, whilst academics speak of the broader picture, including the numerous glaring violations of the strict doctrine at least, which the UK constitution displays when the relationship between legislature and executive is considered. As Turpin and Tomkins point out, all mentions of the separation of powers doctrine in recent House of Lords judgments, regardless of the context, are related to one, narrow principle:

> All are concerned with demarcating *judicial* power (none is concerned, for example, with the relationship of legislative to executive power).[76]

---

75   Munro cites various commentators here, *Studies in Constitutional Law,* 2nd edn (1999), pp 304–05.

76   C Turpin and A Tomkins, *British Government and the Constitution,* 6th edn (2007), at 111. Here, the authors note an exception in *R v Secretary of State ex parte Fire Brigades Union* [1995] 2 AC 513. This decision is discussed in Chapter 11 on prerogative powers, pp 584–587.

Institutional overlap

One major problem in trying to apply any strict theory of the separation of powers arises when we come to the relationship between the Cabinet—the most important body in the executive—and the legislature, Parliament. First of all, there is a clear overlap of personnel: the Cabinet is made up almost entirely of Members of Parliament, the legislative body, though it should be noted that there is no legal requirement that government Ministers must also be MPs: Lord Carrington, Foreign Secretary in the early 80s, sat of course in the House of Lords, and a number of British Prime Ministers have not been MPs though there is now a clear convention to the effect that the Prime Minister should be a Member of Parliament. At the time of writing, many see the most powerful member of the Cabinet, after the Prime Minister, as being Peter Mandelson, a member of the House of Lords, and not an MP. Of course, the denial of the doctrine in this arrangement is not unique to the UK. It applies equally to all countries which have parliamentary governments, in which the government is drawn from the legislative body, as opposed to France and the US, where the President is elected entirely separately.

Moreover, the UK constitution does show some significant reflection of the doctrine in this area: civil servants, who make up the vast majority of the personnel of the executive, cannot stand as MPs under the House of Commons Disqualification Act 1975; under that Act, judges are also ineligible to stand as MPs, as are members of the armed forces and the police, the enforcement arms of the executive. Furthermore, the number of government Ministers eligible to sit in the House of Commons is limited by the Act to 95, limiting the overlap in numbers between Government and the Commons.

Functional overlap

So there is a substantial overlap of membership between the central executive and the legislature. More fatally for the strict doctrine, however, is the fact that, on the whole, one may describe central Government's relationship with Parliament not so much one of influence or even interference but of outright control. The extent to which central Government can determine the output of Parliament is explored in detail in Chapters 8 and 9. But one area must be briefly mentioned, where the concern is not of influence over Parliament by the Executive but of a near take-over by the latter of the former's function, through the means of delegated legislation.

Delegated legislation, often also known as secondary legislation, consists of rules made not *by* Parliament, but *under a power* in an Act of Parliament, which gives another body, normally a Minister, power to make rules in the area governed by the statute from which the rule-making power derives. Where the power is exercised by Ministers, the delegated legislation made is usually in the form of statutory instruments—governed by the Statutory Instruments Act 1946. As Turpin and Tomkins note:

> The reality is that the government, in drawing up a Bill for enactment by Parliament, decides how much detailed regulation of the subject matter to include in the Bill itself, and what powers to keep in its own hands for carrying out the purposes of the Bill.[77]

The Government cannot of course actually exercise the powers of Parliament: it cannot make primary legislation; only Parliament can do that. However, it can procure the passing of very widely drafted primary legislation, giving Ministers power to make regulations in a particular area. The regulations

---

77   Turpin and Tomkins, ibid at 445.

made by Ministers under such enabling legislation, known as delegated legislation, are an increasingly important source of laws. In fact, far more pages of delegated legislation are passed each year than primary legislation. The enactment of broad enabling powers by Parliament, which in effect give Ministers the power to legislate, may be seen as a significant erosion of parliamentary sovereignty and thus of the doctrine of the separation of powers. This issue is examined further in Chapter 8, but a few brief comments will be made here.

There are three restraints on this potential and partly realised power of Ministers to take legislative power for themselves.

- First of all, there is judicial control: the courts will review delegated legislation in order to ascertain whether it makes a proper use of the power given by the parent Act, for example by purporting to do things it was not authorised to do, or by serving a purpose which the courts find was not the purpose of the original Act.[78]
- Second, there is some parliamentary control over delegated legislation: the Statutory Instruments Act 1946 provides that such legislation must be laid before Parliament before coming into effect, though there is some doubt as to the legal effect of this requirement. The aim is clearly to allow Parliament to see whether the delegated legislation is making a reasonable use of the primary enabling legislation (see further Chapter 8, pp 380–384). However, the most common form of this procedure is the so-called 'negative resolution procedure': an order is laid before each House of Parliament and, unless either House votes to disapprove it, it automatically becomes law within a given period (e.g. 28 days). This method does not therefore *require* any actual debate or scrutiny of the measure—it merely provides for its possibility.
- Third, the power to grant Ministers effective legislative power is restrained by a generally observed *convention* that delegated legislation may not decide matters of important principle.

This principle is, however, threatened by the use of what are known as 'Henry VIII clauses', that is, provisions in an Act of Parliament which allow Ministers, by order, to revoke parts of primary legislation. An important recent example of such a clause appears in the Human Rights Act 1998. The HRA provides that all legislation, whenever acted, must be interpreted compatibly with Convention rights (s 3(1)); however, it provides that if it is not possible to do this, the higher courts may issue a formal declaration of incompatibility between the legislation itself and the Convention right (s 4). Such a declaration has no legal effect on the legislation, which remains valid and of full effect, but it does trigger a power under s 10 of the Act whereby a Minister may by order repeal the offending provision.

The Human Rights Act 1998 (extracts)

10(1)   This section applies if—

    (a)   a provision of legislation has been declared under section 4 to be incompatible with a Convention right. . .or

    (b)   it appears to a Minister of the Crown. . .that, having regard to a finding of the European Court of Human Rights. . .in proceedings against the United Kingdom, a provision of legislation is incompatible with an obligation of the United Kingdom arising from the Convention.

---

78   See, e.g. *Raymond v Honey* [1983] AC 1.

(2)   If a Minister of the Crown considers that there are compelling reasons for pro-
        ceeding under this section, he may by order make such amendments to the
        legislation as he considers necessary to remove the incompatibility.

. . .

Schedule 2 [which applies to s 10]
1.—(1) A remedial order may—

   (a)   contain such incidental, supplemental, consequential or transitional provision
         as the person making it considers appropriate;

   . . .

   (2) The power conferred by sub-paragraph (1)(a) includes—

   (a)   power to amend primary legislation (including primary legislation other than
         that which contains the incompatible provision);

   . . .

2.   No remedial order may be made unless—

   (a)   a draft of the order has been approved by a resolution of each House of
         Parliament made after the end of the period of 60 days beginning with the day
         on which the draft was laid; or
   (b)   it is declared in the order that it appears to the person making it that,
         because of the urgency of the matter, it is necessary to make the order without
         a draft being do approved.

[Urgent orders made without being approved in draft must be approved by a resolution of
both Houses within 120 days of being laid before Parliament or they will cease to have
effect (Sched 2, para 4(4)).]

Notes
1. This provision therefore allows Ministers to use delegated legislation to revoke provisions contained in primary legislation. The fact that the Government felt it was necessary to prevent the
   decision being made by the courts was explained by reference to the importance they attached to
   parliamentary sovereignty—they thought it undemocratic that the courts, rather than Parliament,
   should have the last word on such matters.[79] However, it was argued in Parliament that if this was
   genuinely the case, then it should actually be Parliament that takes the decision to change the
   legislation, not Ministers. The Government recognised the force of these arguments to some
   extent: it introduced an amendment to the effect that, as the Act now provides, the power only
   exists where there are 'compelling reasons' to act under s 10 and moreover orders made by
   Ministers under s 10 must (except in urgent cases) be positively approved by Parliament before
   coming into force and even in urgent cases, where they may come into force without so being
   approved, will lapse within 120 days if not approved. Thus, the paradoxical position is apparent
   that, even where the doctrine of the separation of powers is departed from, its influence cuts down
   the gravity of the departure.

---

79   See the White Paper which preceded the Human Rights Act, *Bringing Rights Home*, Cm 3782 (1997).

2. A similar pattern may be discerned in the most notorious recent attempt by the Executive to execute a power grab from Parliament, an episode that also reveals clearly the potential for parliamentary sovereignty simply to overwhelm other principles of the constitution. The Government introduced provisions in the unexcitingly titled Legislation and Regulatory Reform Bill 2006 that:

> Empower[ed] any Minister by order to make provision amending, repealing or replacing *any* legislation, primary or secondary, for *any* purpose, and to reform the common law to implement Law Commission recommendations. . .It [thus] [gave] Ministers a. . .general power to legislate.[80]

These provisions amounted to an open an attempt to transfer much of the legislative power of Parliament to the Executive:[81] indeed this 'astonishing proposal' became known as 'the abolition of Parliament Act'.[82] Although it passed the Commons up to the Committee stage largely unaltered, a string of negative Reports from various Parliamentary committees[83] and notice from the Chief Whip in the Lords that the Government faced defeat there on the Bill as currently drafted, forced the Government into a series of concessions. The enabling power was reduced to a power to make orders, including those repealing primary legislation, for the purpose of: '*removing or reducing any burden, or the overall burdens, resulting directly or indirectly for any person from any legislation*'. This was still an extremely broad delegated power, but it did at least row back from the wholesale transfer of legislative power to the executive represented by the original proposals.[84] The episode thus reveals the potential for the separation of powers to be *legally* undermined—but at the same time shows its potency as a *political* principle. This episode is considered further in Chapter 8.[85]

THE SEPARATION OF FUNCTIONS AS BETWEEN THE JUDICIARY, EXECUTIVE AND LEGISLATURE

Lord Styen, 'Democracy, the Rule of Law and the Role of the Judges' (2006) 3 *European Human Rights Law Review* 2006, 243, 247–48

It used to be said that the doctrine of separation of powers is a comparatively weak principle in the English constitution. As between the legislature and the executive that is still so. . .But the separation of powers as between the legislature and executive, on the one hand, and the judiciary, on the other hand, has been greatly strengthened. [In a decision of the Privy Council. . .Lord Bingham] observed:

---

80 House of Commons Regulatory Reform Committee (1ˢᵗ Special Report, 05–6)—emphasis added.

81 It was of course subject to some exceptions: rules made by Ministers under the provision would not have been able to make new criminal offences where the punishment exceeded 2 years; nor would they have been able to increase taxation.

82 See, e.g. David Howarth MP, 'Who Wants the Abolition of Parliament Bill?', *The Times*, 21 February 2006 www.timesonline.co.uk/tol/comment/columnists/guest_contributors/article733022.ece.

83 See Chapter 8, p 381.

84 For critical analysis of the final version of the clause see the Constitution Committee's Report: HL 194 (1005–06).

85 Another recent Henry VIII clause of note is that contained in the The Banking Act 2009 (above at 108).

> Whatever overlap there may be under constitutions on the Westminster model between the exercise of executive and legislative powers, the separation between the exercise of judicial powers on the one hand and legislative and executive powers on the other is total or effectively so. Such separation, based on the rule of law, was recently described . . . as 'a characteristic feature of democracies'.
>
> Under our constitution the separation of powers protecting judicial independence is now total and effectively so. This constitutional principle exists not to eliminate friction between the executive and judiciary. It exists for this reason only: to prevent the rise of arbitrary executive power. The importance of this exposition of this core principle in our constitution is enormous. The foundation of this development was broadly based: it was anchored on the rule of law.

The performance of judicial functions by the Executive

When we come to examine the functional separation between the judicial and executive roles, we can see a clear pattern of a strengthening separation in this regard, due primarily to the impact of the European Convention on Human Rights. An example of what Robert Stevens refers to as 'the casual British attitude to the separation of powers'[86] was the power of the Home Secretary to set the sentence to be served by juvenile killers.[87] Prior to October 1997, such offenders were detained for an indefinite period, wholly at the discretion of the Home Secretary. Under the Crime (Sentences) Act 1997, which came into force on 1 October, the Home Secretary set a 'tariff'—that part of a sentence designed to satisfy the demands of retribution and punishment—and upon its expiry, the prisoner became eligible for release by the Parole Board, and would be released unless it was thought that he or she still constituted a danger to society. In effect, therefore,[88] a sentencing function was being formed by a party politician and powerful member of the Cabinet. The obvious risks attendant upon such a state of affairs—the inability of the Home Secretary, as a politician seeking re-election, to put the impact on government popularity of media-driven populist sentiment out of his mind—were illustrated in *R v Secretary of State for the Home Department ex parte Venables and Thompson* [1998] AC 407. The Home Secretary, who had fixed a tariff of 15 years in relation to the child killers of Jamie Bulger (the trial judge had recommended eight years), was found to have acted unlawfully in taking into account a petition, organised by the *Sun* newspaper, which urged that the boys be detained for life. However, that decision left unchallenged the power of the Home Secretary to set the tariff in such cases, even though, as Lord Steyn remarked in the case: 'In fixing a tariff the Home Secretary is carrying out, contrary to the constitutional principle of the separation of powers between the executive and the judiciary, a classic judicial function.'

While a fresh decision on the tariff for this case was awaited from the Home Secretary, a more fundamental challenge—to his power to set such tariffs at all—was launched, this time before the European Court of Human Rights, in reliance upon Article 6(1) of the ECHR, which provides: 'In the determination of his civil rights and obligations or of any criminal charge against him, everyone is entitled to a fair and public hearing within a reasonable time by an independent and impartial tribunal established by law.'

---

86   Below, p 153.

87   This arose under s 53(1) of the Children and Young Persons Act 1933.

88   In setting the sentence, the Home Secretary has regard to the views of the trial judge and also consults with the Lord Chief Justice.

T v United Kingdom; V v United Kingdom (2000) 30 *EHRR* 121 (extracts)

The applicants alleged, *inter alia,* that the fact that their tariff had been set by the Home Secretary constituted a violation of Article 6, because he could not be considered an 'independent and impartial tribunal'. The Court first of all found, contrary to the submission of the government, that the fixing of the tariff period *did* engage Article 6 and then proceeded:

Both the applicant and the Commission were of the view that the tariff-fixing procedure had failed to comply with Article 6 § 1 in that the decision-maker was the Home Secretary rather than a court or tribunal independent of the executive. In addition the applicant pointed out that there had been no hearing and no opportunity for him to call psychiatric or other evidence, and that the Home Secretary retained a discretion to decide how much of the material before him he disclosed to the applicant.

The Government submitted that there were adequate safeguards to ensure that the procedure for the setting of the tariff was fair. Thus, the Secretary of State sought the views of the trial judge and the Lord Chief Justice, informed the applicant of the judges' views, and invited him to make representations as to the appropriate length of the tariff. The Secretary of State informed the applicant of the tariff fixed, and gave reasons in support of his decision. It was then open to the applicant to challenge the decision by way of judicial review.

The Court notes that Article 6 § 1 guarantees, *inter alia*, 'a fair. . .hearing. . .by an independent and impartial tribunal. . .'. 'Independent' in this context means independent of the parties to the case and also of the executive (see, amongst many other authorities, *Ringeisen v Austria* (1971) A13, p 39, § 95). The Home Secretary, who set the applicant's tariff, was clearly not independent of the executive, and it follows that there has been a violation of Article 6 § 1.

Notes
1. The result was that the function of setting tariffs for juveniles passed to the judiciary, in the person of the Lord Chief Justice.
2. This judgment clearly also cast into doubt the compatibility of Art 6(1) with the Home Secretary's continuing power to set the tariff for *adult* life prisoners. This was eventually challenged under the HRA in the following case.

R (on the application of Anderson) v Secretary of State for the Home Department [2002] 3 *WLR* 1800 (extracts)

In accordance with s 1(1) of the Murder (Abolition of Death Penalty) Act 1965, the trial judge imposed a mandatory sentence of life imprisonment. The trial judge and the Lord Chief Justice recommended a tariff of 15 years to be served by the appellant. Pursuant to his powers under s 29 of the Crime (Sentences) Act 1997, the Home Secretary rejected the judicial advice and fixed the tariff at 20 years. The appellant sought judicial review of the decision of the Home Secretary to increase the judicially recommended tariff and argued that the Home Secretary's role in fixing the tariff was incompatible with Article 6 of the ECHR. The Divisional Court dismissed the application and the Court of Appeal dismissed an appeal. The appellant appealed to the House of Lords.

Lord Bingham I return to the fixing of the convicted murderer's tariff term by the Home Secretary. . . The true nature of that procedure must be judged as one of substance, not of form or description. It is what happens in practice that matters. . . . What happens in practice is that, having taken advice from the trial judge, the Lord Chief Justice and departmental officials, the Home Secretary assesses the term of imprisonment which the convicted murderer should serve as punishment for his crime or crimes. That decision defines the period to be served before release on licence is considered. This is a classical sentencing function. It is what, in the case of other crimes, judges and magistrates do every day. . .

17. . . .in *Stafford v United Kingdom* (no. 46295/99) May 28, 2002, expressing its conclusions in paras 78–80 of the judgment [the European Court of Human Rights said]:

> . . . .
>
> the continuing role of the Secretary of State in fixing the tariff and in deciding on a prisoner's release following its expiry, has become increasingly difficult to reconcile with the notion of separation of powers between executive and judiciary, a notion which has assumed growing importance in the case-law of the Court. . .

20.   Mr Fitzgerald's argument for the appellant involved the following steps:

1   Under Art 6(1) of the Convention a criminal defendant has a right to a fair trial by an independent and impartial tribunal.

2   The imposition of sentence is part of the trial.

3   Therefore sentence should be imposed by an independent and impartial tribunal.

4   The fixing of the tariff of a convicted murderer is legally indistinguishable from the imposition of sentence.

5   Therefore the tariff should be fixed by an independent and impartial tribunal.

6   The Home Secretary is not an independent and impartial tribunal.

7   Therefore the Home Secretary should not fix the tariff of a convicted murderer.

I must review these steps in turn.

Step (1) is correct. The right to a fair trial by an independent and impartial tribunal is guaranteed by Art 6(1) of the Convention. . .and it is one of the most important rights to which domestic effect was given by the Human Rights Act 1998.

Step (2) is also correct. Strasbourg authority supporting the proposition is to be found in *Ringeisen v Austria* (No 1) (1971) 1 EHRR 455 [his Lordship cited other authority]. . .It makes good sense that the same procedural protections should apply to the imposition of sentence as to the determination of guilt.

Step (3) is a logical consequence of steps (1) and (2). But the point was clearly expressed by the Supreme Court of Ireland in *Deaton v Att-Gen and the Revenue Commissioners* [1963] IR 170 at 182–183:

> There is a clear distinction between the prescription of a fixed penalty and the selection of a penalty for a particular case. The prescription of a fixed penalty is the statement of a general rule, which is one of the characteristics of legislation; this is wholly different from the selection of a penalty to be imposed in a particular case. . .The Legislature does not prescribe the penalty to be imposed in an individual citizen's case; it states the general rule, and the application of that rule is for the Courts. . .the selection of punishment is an integral part of the administration of justice and, as such, cannot be committed to the hands of the Executive.

Examination of the facts has already led me to accept the correctness of step (4). . .The clearest authoritative statement of this proposition is in paragraph 79 of the European Court's judgment in Stafford, quoted in paragraph 17 above. . .It is clear beyond doubt that the fixing of a convicted murderer's tariff, whether it be for the remainder of his days or for a relatively short time only, involves an assessment of the quantum of punishment he should undergo.

If it be assumed that steps (1) to (4) are correct, step (5) necessarily follows from them.

The correctness of step (6) was accepted on behalf of the Home Secretary, and rightly so. The European Court has interpreted 'independent' in the context of Art 6(1) of the Convention to mean 'independent of the parties to the case and also of the executive': *V v United Kingdom* [above]. Far from being independent of the executive, the Home Secretary and his junior Ministers are important members of it. . . .Plainly, the Home Secretary is not independent of the executive and is not a tribunal.

Step (7) follows logically from the preceding steps and must be accepted. . . In *Benjamin and Wilson v United Kingdom* (Application No 28212/95) September 26, 2002) the European Court took a step further: it held that the Home Secretary's role in the release of two 'technical lifers' was objectionable because he was not independent of the executive and he could not save the day by showing that he always acted in accordance with the recommendation of the mental health review tribunal (para 36). The European Court observed (para 36):

> This is not a matter of form but impinges on the fundamental principle of separation of powers and detracts from a necessary guarantee against the possibility of abuse. . .The European Court was right to describe the complete functional separation of the judiciary from the executive as 'fundamental', since the rule of law depends on it.

28. Thus I accept each of Mr Fitzgerald's steps (1)–(7) save that, in the light of Benjamin and Wilson, it must now be held that the Home Secretary should play no part in fixing the tariff of a convicted murderer, even if he does no more than confirm what the judges have recommended. To that extent the appeal succeeds.

[The House then went on to find that because the Home Secretary's powers were contained in primary legislation, the only relief that could be granted was the issuing of a declaration of incompatibility under s 4, HRA].

Note

Following this decision, the statutory provision under which the Secretary of State had carried out his sentencing functions, s 29 of the Crime (Sentences) Act 1997, was repealed by the Criminal Justice Act 2003, which contained new provisions, giving the sentencing power to the judiciary. The above decisions thus resulted in the removal of the sentencing powers of the Home Secretary, and this particular functional overlap, strengthening the separation of powers.

JUDICIAL INDEPENDENCE AND THE *INSTITUTIONAL* OVERLAP   141

The performance of legislative functions by the judiciary?

The system of common law plainly allows the judges not only to decide individual cases, but to develop and change the law more generally, as seen above in the *R v R* (marital rape) case (pp 100–105). There are a few instances in which courts have been accused of going much further than 'development' by actually creating new laws: this would of course cause particularly acute concern were the new law to be a criminal offence. Such an instance was *Shaw v DPP*,[89] the accused had published a magazine containing the names and addresses of prostitutes and a description of their services. The House of Lords declared that the common law included a doctrine known as 'conspiracy to corrupt public morals', although no precedents were cited demonstrating that it had ever existed except as a variant of the power exercised by Star Chamber judges to punish offences against conventional morality. *Shaw* was later followed in *Knuller Ltd v DPP*.[90]

There is no doubt that the Human Rights Act has enhanced the judicial capacity for legal innovation (although it specifically provides that it does not create any new criminal offences). For example, s 3(1) of the Act provides that, '*so far as is possible to do so,* primary legislation and subordinate legislation must be read and given effect in a way which is compatible with the Convention rights.' This plainly provides a strong mandate for the courts to re-interpret legislation to achieve compatibility. This raises a concern around the separation of powers—the potential for the courts to exercise, in effect, a *legislative* function, by taking 'interpretation' so far that it changes legislation altogether: see further Chapter 4, pp 208–212 and Chapter 17, pp 957–970. The discussion in those chapters draw out the tension between the twin imperatives lying upon the judiciary to ensure Convention-compatible outcomes when deciding cases and to respect the separation of powers by not straying into the legislative realm. As discussed further in Chapter 17, the HRA ultimately retains parliamentary sovereignty and thus draws a limit to how far judicial creativity can go.[91]

JUDICIAL INDEPENDENCE AND THE *INSTITUTIONAL* OVERLAP BETWEEN THE JUDICIARY AND THE OTHER BRANCHES

The position of the Lord Chancellor[92]

The Traditional Roles and Office of Lord Chancellor

One of the most notorious features of the UK constitution has historically been the position of the Lord Chancellor. As Munro notes, he was referred to as 'a sort of dangerous one man band'.[93] This is because, up until very recently, the Lord Chancellor occupied important positions in all three of the main organs of government. He was entitled to, and did sit in the Judicial Committee of the House of

---

89   [1962] AC 220.

90   [1973] AC 435.

91   *Per* ss 3(2), 4 and 6(2).

92   See generally D Woodhouse, *The Office of Lord Chancellor* (2001).

93   Munro, n 75 at 328.

Lords, the highest court in the UK, thus holding high judicial office (although infrequently, only three times in 2002); he was an important Cabinet Minister and hence a key figure in the executive; and he was 'speaker' of the House of Lords, in which guise he performed an important and active legislative function. Moreover, the Lord Chancellor had the formal power to decide which judges heard which cases.[94] His position was, indeed, often seen as a living embodiment[95] of the denial of the doctrine of the separation of powers in the UK constitution.

It is nevertheless important to understand why the judges saw his position as an important guarantee of judicial independence. The classic defence of his position was given in 1943:

> The advantages which accrued to the Cabinet from the presence of a colleague who is not only of high judicial reputation but can represent to them the view of the judiciary; to the legislature from the presence in it of one who is both a Judge and a Minister; and to the judiciary from the fact that its President is in close touch with current political affairs, are enormous.[96]

As late as 1998, the then Lord Chief Justice, Lord Woolf said:

> As a member of the Cabinet he (the Lord Chancellor) can act as an advocate on behalf of the courts and the justice system. He can explain to his colleagues in the cabinet the proper significance of a decision which they regard as being distasteful in consequence of an application for judicial review. He can, as a member of the government, ensure that the courts are properly resourced. On the other hand, on behalf of the government, he can explain to the judiciary the realities of the political situation and the constraints on the resources which they must inevitably accept.
>
> As long as the Lord Chancellor is punctilious in keeping his separate roles distinct, the separation of powers is not undermined and the justice system benefits immeasurably. The justice system is better served by having the head of the judiciary at the centre of government than it would be by having its interests represented by a Minister of Justice who would lack these other roles.[97]

He was certainly a powerful figure. The last Lord Chancellor before reform, Derry Irvine:

> chaired a range of Cabinet committees and took an active role in Cabinet debates. He was responsible for the Queen's Speech, setting out the party policies, as well as being responsible for constitutional issues such as devolution, human rights and reform of the Lords. . . .It was said that he engineered a deal for a cadre of hereditary peers to remain in the Lords after reform.[98]

Similarly, his predecessor, Lord Mackay had seen himself as primarily an important member of the government, rather than a predominantly judicial figure. As Malleson puts it:

---

94   See further, JUSTICE, 'The judicial function of the House of Lords' (May 1999), at [33].

95   See, e.g. SA de Smith, 'The Separation of Powers in New Dress' (1966) 12 McGill LJ 491, 'Mention the theory of separation of powers to an English constitutional lawyer, and he will forthwith put on parade the Lord Chancellor [and] the Law Lords'.

96   Memorandum, LC02/3630, 31 January 1943.

97   H Woolf 'Judicial Review—The Tensions between the Executive and the Judiciary' (1998) 114 LQR 579.

98   Robert Stevens 'Reform in Haste and Repent at Leisure: Lolanthe, the Lord High Executioner and Brave New World' [2004] 24(1/2) LS 1, 21.

The combined effect of the Mackay and Irvine years, therefore, was that the ?
Lord Chancellor was transformed from that of senior judges exercising a su
executive function to that of Cabinet minister wearing an occasional judicia ...

However, as Malleson argues in the next extract, his position—together with the similarly overlapping role of the Law Lords, sitting in the House of Lords as both legislators and judges—was coming under increasing pressure in the last decade.

K Malleson, 'The Effect of the Constitutional Reform Act 2005 on the Relationship between the Judiciary, the Executive, and Parliament', Appendix 3, *Sixth Report of the Select Committee on the Constitution, HL 115 (2006–07) (extracts)*

The origins of the Constitutional Reform Act lie in the expanding role played by the higher courts in the UK over the last thirty years. The combined effect of the growth of judicial review, the development of the EU and, most recently, the Human Rights Act and devolution has been to give the courts a more central place in the British constitution. The senior judges are now required to police constitutional boundaries and determine sensitive human rights issues in a way which would have been unthinkable forty years ago. This new judicial role is still developing, but it is clear that the effect of this trend will be to reshape the relationship between the judiciary and the other branches of government. In the light of these changes, the main provisions of the Constitutional Reform Act—reforming the office of Lord Chancellor, establishing a new Supreme Court and restructuring the judicial appointments process—were designed to bring the institutional relationships between the judiciary and the other branches of government into line with the changing substantive role of the courts. In particular, the reforms were intended to secure the independence of the judiciary by 'redrawing the relationship between the judiciary and the other branches of government' and putting it on a 'modern footing'.

Although the timing of the introduction of the Constitutional Reform Bill in 2003 took many by surprise, its content did not. Concerns about the relationship between the judiciary and the other branches of government had been building up over a number of years. Where once there had been a general consensus that the Lord Chancellor's three roles as member of cabinet, head of the judiciary and speaker of the House of Lords enhanced the functioning of the political system and strengthened judicial independence, they increasingly came to be regarded as a potential source of abuse of executive power. In particular, the Lord Chancellor's responsibility for appointing the judges became a source of growing concern as the senior judges' role in scrutinising government decision-making increased. Likewise, the presence of the top appellate court in Parliament had once been widely regarded as an effective means of drawing on the legal expertise of the top judges during the law-making process so enhancing the quality of legislation. By the 1990s, however, many Law Lords themselves had come to regard the lack of separation between the two as problematic as the same senior judges who participated in passing the laws were increasingly asked to decide on the conformity of those acts with basic human rights.

By the late 1990s, far fewer voices were heard in support of the argument that these overlaps between the branches of government were a source of its stability. Increasingly,

---

99 K Malleson, 'Modernising the Constitution: Completing the Unfinished Business' [2002] LS 119, 126.

the interconnection was seen as endangering judicial independence, breaching basic constitutional principles and out of step with the rest of Europe. By the start of the second term of the Labour Government in 2001, the long debate about these issues had slowly generated broad support across the political spectrum for a 'clearer and deeper' separation of the functions and powers of the judiciary from the other branches of government. The decision to embark upon extensive institutional reform was therefore anticipated but [what was a] third surprising feature of the reforms is that they explicitly sought to promote constitutional principle above pragmatism. Whilst accepting that the previous arrangements had worked effectively, the changes were designed to restructure the relationship between the judiciary and the other branches of government so that it would conform more closely to the concept of the separation of powers. This elevation of principle above pragmatism is surprising given the traditional value ascribed to 'what works' in the British constitution.

Note

The final impetus for these changes seems to have come from a decision of the European Court of Human Rights. The rather unlikely facts of a case that was to result in a radical constitutional shake-up of the UK arose from a flower packing shed in Guernsey. Guernsey is one of the UK's dependent territories, but with a largely independent system of government. The decision was made under Art 6(1) of the European Convention on Human Rights (above, p 117).

McGonnell v United Kingdom (2000) 30 *EHRR* 289 (extracts)

McGonnell, a Guernsey flower grower, was refused planning consent to turn his flower-packing shed into a home. The refusal was based upon a development plan (DDP 6) passed by the Island's legislature (the States of Deliberation), which at that time was, as usual, presided over by the Bailiff of Guernsey. McGonnell's appeal against the refusal of planning consent was heard by the Royal Court, also presided over by the Bailiff.

The Bailiff is the senior judge of the Royal Court. . .In his judicial capacity, the Bailiff is the professional judge (with the lay Jurats) in the Royal Court, and is ex officio President of the Guernsey Court of Appeal. In his non-judicial capacity, the Bailiff is President of the States of Election, of the States of Deliberation, of four States Committees (the Appointments Board, the Emergency Council, the Legislation Committee and the Rules of Procedure Committee), and he plays a role in communications between the Island Authorities and the Government of the United Kingdom and the Privy Council. Where the Bailiff presides in his non-judicial capacity, he has a casting, but not an original, vote.

The applicant pointed to the non-judicial functions of the Bailiff, contending that they gave rise to such close connections between the Bailiff as a judicial officer and the legislative and executive functions of government that the Bailiff no longer had the independence and impartiality required by Article 6. As specific examples, the applicant pointed to three matters which were not referred to before the Commission. They are the facts that the Bailiff is invariably appointed from the office of the Attorney General, that he acts as Lieutenant Governor of the island when that office is vacant, and that the Bailiff who sat in the present case had also presided over the States of Deliberation when DDP 6, the very act which was at issue in the applicant's later case, was adopted.

The Government. . .underlined that when the Bailiff presides over the States of Deliberation or one of the four States Committees in which he is involved, his involvement is not that of an active member, but rather he is an independent umpire, who ensures that the proceedings run smoothly without taking part or expressing approval or disapproval of the matters under discussion.

7. The Court recalls that it [has previously] found. . .that in order to establish whether a tribunal can be considered as 'independent', regard must be had, inter alia, to the manner of appointment of its members and their term of office, the existence of guarantees against outside pressures and the question whether the body presents an appearance of independence. . .As to the question of 'impartiality', there are two aspects to this requirement. First, the tribunal must be subjectively free of personal prejudice or bias. Secondly, it must also be impartial from an objective viewpoint, that is, it must offer sufficient guarantees to exclude any legitimate doubt in this respect. . .The concepts of independence and objective impartiality are closely linked. . .

The Court can agree with the Government that neither Article 6 nor any other provision of the Convention requires States to comply with any theoretical constitutional concepts as such. The question is always whether, in a given case, the requirements of the Convention are met. The present case does not, therefore, require the application of any particular doctrine of constitutional law to the position in Guernsey: the Court is faced solely with questions of whether the Bailiff had the required 'appearance' of independence, or the required 'objective' impartiality.

In this connection, the Court notes that the Bailiff's functions are not limited to judicial matters, but that he is also actively involved in non-judicial functions on the island. The Court does not accept the Government's analysis that when the Bailiff acts in a non-judicial capacity he merely occupies positions rather than exercising functions: even a purely ceremonial constitutional role must be classified as a 'function'. The Court must determine whether the Bailiff's functions in his non-judicial capacity were, or were not, compatible with the requirements of Article 6 as to independence and impartiality.

The Court observes that the Bailiff in the present case had personal involvement with the planning matters at the heart of the applicant's case on two occasions. The first occasion was in 1990, when, as Deputy Bailiff, he presided over the States of Deliberation at the adoption of DDP 6. The second occasion was on 6 June 1995, when he presided over the Royal Court in the determination of the applicant's planning appeal. . .

. . .With particular respect to his presiding, as Deputy Bailiff, over the States of Deliberation in 1990, the Court considers that any direct involvement in the passage of legislation, or of executive rules, is likely to be sufficient to cast doubt on the judicial impartiality of a person subsequently called on to determine a dispute over whether reasons exist to permit a variation from the wording of the legislation or rules at issue. In the present case, in addition to the chairing role as such, the Deputy Bailiff could exercise a casting vote in the event of even voting. . .

The Court thus considers that the mere fact that the Deputy Bailiff presided over the States of Deliberation when DDP 6 was adopted in 1990 is capable of casting doubt on his impartiality when he subsequently determined, as the sole judge of the law in the case, the applicant's planning appeal. The applicant therefore had legitimate grounds for fearing that the Bailiff may have been influenced by his prior participation in the adoption of DDP 6. That doubt in itself, however slight its justification, is sufficient to vitiate the impartiality of the Royal Court, and it is therefore unnecessary for the Court to look into the other aspects of the complaint.

It follows that there has been a breach of Article 6 § 1.

Notes

1. Since the Lord Chancellor precisely acted as a judge in the House of Lords and presided over it in its legislative capacity, this judgment, if followed[100] by the UK courts, applying the Convention domestically,[101] would have prevented the Lord Chancellor from sitting as a judge on any case involving legislation passed or amended since the Labour Party came to power, or any legislation of the previous Government during the passage of which he played an active role as opposition spokesman. The earlier decision of *Procola v Italy*[102] had set out a much stricter approach to Art 6(1):

    > The mere fact that certain persons successively performed these two types of function [the pre-legislative review and hearing an appeal concerning the same legislative instrument] in respect of the same decisions is capable of casting doubt on the institution's structural impartiality.

2. The Lord Chancellor at the time, Lord Irvine, indicated that he did not intend to give up his role as a Law Lord as a result of the *McGonnell* judgment.[103] He indicated instead that he would not sit in any case concerning legislation he had been involved with, or in any case in which the Government's interests were concerned.[104] However, this was not enough to save him.

The Constitutional Reform Act 2005: reforming the office of Lord Chancellor

In 2003 the Government rather abruptly signalled a series of radical reforms in this area, including the abolition of the post of Lord Chancellor, whose role would pass to an ordinary Cabinet Minister. As the following extracts make clear, judges were angered and alarmed not only by the lack of consultation over these immensely important proposals, but also by the threatened loss of the post of Lord Chancellor, who was seen as a powerful guarantor for judicial independence and advocate for the judges at the heart of government.

Lord Hope, 'A phoenix from the ashes? Accommodating a new Supreme Court' (2005) 121(Apr) *Law Quarterly Review* 253 (extracts)

The press notice of June 12, 2003 gave few details. It was headed with the words 'Modernising Government'. We were told that there was to be a new Department of Constitutional Affairs, that the post of Lord Chancellor was to be abolished, that the first Secretary of State for Constitutional Affairs was to be Lord Falconer . . . and that a new Supreme Court was to be created to replace the existing system of Law Lords operating as a committee of the House of Lords. There was no suggestion that the Government were proposing that there should a period of consultation on any of these issues. The setting up of a new department

---

100   Courts are bound under the HRA to 'have regard' to judgments of the European Court and Commission but they are not instructed to follow them (s 2(1)).

101   As noted above, s 6(1) of the HRA states: 'it is unlawful for a public authority to act in a way which is incompatible with a Convention right'. Courts and tribunals are expressly included within the definition of 'public authority' (s 6(3)).

102   (1995) 22 EHRR 193 at [45].

103   'Irvine defends his dual role', *The Times*, 6 July 1999.

104   See further R Cornes, '*McGonnell v United Kingdom*, the Lord Chancellor and the Law Lords' [2000] PL 166.

might perhaps be said to have been a matter for the executive. But the abolition of the post of Lord Chancellor and the setting up of a new Supreme Court were not. They were fundamental constitutional changes, which would require discussion and legislation by Parliament. A period of consultation might have been advisable before the Government committed itself irrevocably to these proposals. But that was not to be.

Notes

1. As Lord Windelsham notes, 'a vehemently critical reaction to the government proposals was displayed by the Judges Council, representing 3,000 judges, as well as 28,000 magistrates'. He goes on:

> [Then Chief Justice] Woolf also was outspoken, although his language was more restrained. Asked if he had foreknowledge of the June announcement, he replied that he was given just a few minutes notice. He confirmed that Lord Bingham, the senior Law Lord had also not been consulted in advance. Woolf declared that he believed the abolition of the post of Lord Chancellor, without creating any new constitutional safeguards, posed the biggest threat to judicial independence for hundreds of years. The government's plans to retain policy over judicial appointments when setting up a judicial appointments commission was also inappropriate would amount to ministers having the power to pack the Bench with judges sympathetic to their policies. [105]
>
> [Calmer was] the 87-page considered response from the same Judges' Council to the government's Consultation Papers on judicial reform. It argued that as Head of the Judiciary, and a very senior member of the government, the Lord Chancellor had occupied a unique constitutional role binding together the three arms of the state: the legislature; the executive; and the judiciary. The government had decided to replace the Lord Chancellor with a Secretary of State whose role would be primarily political. He would no longer be constrained by judicial responsibilities and constitutional convention. The fact that the Lord Chancellor had presided over both the judiciary and the administration of the court system had enabled the development of constructive working relationships between the judiciary and the executive, without the necessity for a formal recognition of their different responsibilities. The abolition of the office created the need for a new constitutional settlement and for the respective roles of the executive and the judiciary to be set out in a legislative framework. Such an approach would protect the independence of the judiciary, maintain and promote the partnership that had been established, enhance the separation of powers, and increase transparency and public confidence. [106]

As Stevens puts it, the concern was simple:

> What if the Secretary of State for Constitutional Affairs, the substitute for the Lord Chancellor, were one day to be a layman? Many leading lawyers and judges are convinced the quality of MPs is on the decline. How could such a layman then protect the judiciary against the combined force of the other two branches of

---

105   Lord Windelsham, 'The Constitutional Reform Act 2005: Ministers, Judges and Constitutional Change: Part 1' [2005] PL 806, 815–16.

106   *Ibid* at 816.

government? . . .Who, in this new world, was going to protect the independence of the judiciary?" How could a layman appoint judges, even if recommended by an Appointments Commission?[107]

2. In response to such concerns, expressed not only by judges but the Conservative opposition, particularly in the House of Lords, the Government was forced to retreat from its original plan of abolishing the post of Lord Chancellor and reformulating his role into the post of Secretary of State for Constitutional Affairs. 'After intense debate, this was amended so that the title and the office of Lord Chancellor would remain, albeit in much reduced form',[108] so that the post's overlapping roles would be removed. First of all, the Lord Chancellor ceased to be speaker of the House of Lords, thus removing the legislative part of the post. It was agreed that it was for the House as a whole to elect a new Speaker, and this was duly done in July 2006 with the election of Baroness Hayman to the position. Second, his position as head of the judiciary passed to the most senior judge, the Lord Chief Justice, who became the head of the judiciary as President of the Courts of England and Wales. Finally, the responsibilities of the Lord Chancellor's department were transferred to the new Department of Constitutional Affairs. Not long after that, however, those responsibilities were in turn transferred to the new Ministry of Justice, with the addition of some functions that were transferred from the Home Office (see further below).

5. Anthony Bradley summarises the key changes brought about by the 2005 Act:

> The principal structural changes made by the CRA may be very briefly summarised. They have provided for greater formal separation between government and judiciary (and, as regards the new Supreme Court, between Parliament and judiciary) and for a new statutory interface in England and Wales between government, in the person of the Lord Chancellor, and the judiciary, represented by the Lord Chief Justice.
>
> (A) Contrary to the original intention of the Government, the Lord Chancellor remains in being, but he has lost his status as head of the judiciary in England and Wales and may not now sit as a judge. This greater separation between executive and judiciary made it essential for many functions of the Lord Chancellor to be re-assigned, some being transferred to the Lord Chief Justice, others being exercisable jointly by the Lord Chancellor and the Lord Chief Justice. The Lord Chancellor retains many important executive functions relating to the judiciary (including funding the system of justice, making judicial appointments in accordance with new statutory rules, and approving procedural rules for the courts). Many of these functions are ring-fenced, to ensure that they are not transferred to another Minister by the Prime Minister without further primary legislation. Under the CRA, the Lord Chancellor is not required to have had a legal career, nor to be a member of the House of Lords [he is merely required to be 'qualified by experience'—s 2 CRA].
>
> (B) The Lord Chief Justice is now President of the Courts and Head of the Judiciary of England and Wales. He is responsible:
>
> (i) for representing the views of the judiciary to Parliament, to the Lord Chancellor and to other Ministers;

---

107 Robert Stevens 'Reform in Haste and Repent at Leisure: Lolanthe, the Lord High Executioner and Brave New World' [2004] 24 (1/2) LS 1, 6.

108 K Malleson: Appendix 3 to the Report of the Select Committee on the Constitution (above, at 143).

(ii)   for maintaining appropriate arrangements for the welfare, training and guidance of the judiciary within resources made available by the Lord Chancellor; and

(ii)   for maintaining appropriate arrangements for the deployment of the judiciary and the allocation of work within courts.

These broad duties are accompanied by many specific responsibilities, some of which are exercisable jointly with the Lord Chancellor, or with the concurrence of the Lord Chancellor.

Alongside the statutory provisions has to be read a document known as the Concordat, entitled *Constitutional Reform: the Lord Chancellor's Judiciary-related Functions*, prepared in January 2004 while the Constitutional Reform Bill was before the House of Lords, at a time when the Government was proposing to abolish the office of Lord Chancellor and it was not known what the attitude of the judiciary would be to the proposals. The Concordat represented an agreement between the Lord Chancellor and the Lord Chief Justice (then Lord Woolf) regarding the future exercise of the Lord Chancellor's judiciary-related functions, and as such it facilitated the passage of the Constitutional Reform Bill through Parliament.[109]

6. Malleson explains why the agreement represented by the Concordat, which was then partly enacted by the 2005 Act, was necessary:

Before 2005, it was generally unnecessary to articulate whether the Lord Chancellor was acting in his judicial or executive capacity when carrying out a particular function. It was not clear whether, for example, decisions concerning the deployment of judges were a task which the Lord Chancellor performed as the head of the judiciary or a member of the executive. Under the terms of the Concordat it is now explicitly established that this role is for the Lord Chief Justice and therefore falls within the control of the judiciary. Perhaps the most interesting aspect of the Concordat was that it is not simply a carve up of power between the branches of government but is intended to create a form of partnership in which the two branches of government share in the decision-making affecting the governance of the judiciary and the running of the courts through the allocation of decision-making powers 'with appropriate constraints and mutual consultation'. Most decisions concerning the management of the courts and the judiciary are now formally ascribed to either the Lord Chief Justice or the Lord Chancellor, but in almost all cases there is a duty to consult with the other or obtain their agreement.[110]

Lord Windelsham notes that, following the agreement of the Concordat, Lord Woolf was prepared to announce that 'agreement had been reached with the government on the central issue of protecting judicial independence.'[111] The core of this agreement was the new statutory guarantee of judicial independence, which took the form of s 3 of the 2005 Act:

109   A Bradley, 'The New Constitutional Relationship between the Judiciary Government and Parliament'; and further paper: 'Changes in the Machinery of Government affecting the Department for Constitutional Affairs and the Home Office', Appendix 4 to the 6th Report of the Select Committee on the Constitution, HL 115 (2006–07).

110   Malleson, p 143 above.

111   Windelsham, n 105 above at 820. Lord Woolf made a statement to this effect in Parliament: HL Deb vol 658, col 1004, 8 March 2004.

The Constitutional Reform Act 2005 (extracts)

S 3 (1) The Lord Chancellor, other Ministers of the Crown and all with responsibility for matters relating to the judiciary or otherwise to the administration of justice must uphold the continued independence of the judiciary. . .

(4) The following particular duties are imposed for the purpose of upholding that independence.

(5) The Lord Chancellor and other Ministers of the Crown must not seek to influence particular judicial decisions through any special access to the judiciary.

(6) The Lord Chancellor must have regard to—

   (a) the need to defend that independence;
   (b) the need for the judiciary to have the support necessary to enable them to exercise their functions;
   (c) the need for the public interest in regard to matters relating to the judiciary or otherwise to the administration of justice to be properly represented in decisions affecting those matters.

(7) In this section "the judiciary" includes the judiciary of any of the following—

   (a) the Supreme Court;
   (b) any other court established under the law of any part of the United Kingdom;
   (c) any international court.

Notes

1. Hazell has a very clear view of the results of the above: 'The judges would not admit it, but they have emerged immensely stronger.'[112]

2. Despite this verdict, there remains concern that the Lord Chancellor, now also Secretary of State for justice, should be as effective an advocate for the judges as the previous historic office. The Constitution Committee of the House of Lords expressed concern at the failure of Lord Falconer to rebuke fellow Ministers for their criticisms of the sentence (unduly lenient in their view) given to a paedophile in a case that attracted particularly virulent media attacks on the judges.[113] The Committee commented:

   'The Lord Chancellor's duty, as the defender of judicial independence in the Cabinet, is both to ensure that ministers are aware of the need to avoid attacking individual judges and to reprimand them if they breach this principle.' The Lord Chief Justice has emphasised that this kind of intervention by the Lord Chancellor is 'a most valuable constitutional protection of judicial independence', because the only alternative would be for the Lord Chief Justice himself to intervene publicly, which would risk a high-profile dispute that would not be 'in the interests of the administration of justice.'

---

112 R Hazell, 'The Continuing Dynamism of Constitutional Reform' (2007) 60(1) *Parlt Aff* 3, 17.

113 E.g The *Daily Express* on 13 June 2003, described the judiciary as 'deluded, out-of-touch and frankly deranged' and 'combining arrogance with downright wickedness', suggesting that 'our legal system has not only lost touch with public opinion but with natural justice itself . . . [sentencing] now bears no relation at all to the seriousness of the crime.'

Noting the delay before Lord Falconer stepped in to defend the judges, the committee concluded that in this 'first big test of whether the new relationship between the Lord Chancellor and the judiciary was working properly. . .there was a systemic failure'.[114]

The Creation of the Ministry of Justice: renewed concerns about the independence of the judiciary

As noted above and in Chapter 1, the new Department for Constitutional Affairs was comparatively short-lived. The following critical paragraphs of the Constitution Committee's report chart the rapid take-over by the new Ministry of Justice.

Sixth Report of the House of Lords Constitution Committee, HL 151 (2006–07): 'Relations between the executive, the judiciary and Parliament' (extracts)

. . .20. A Home Office leak in *The Sunday Telegraph* on 21 January 2007 was the first public acknowledgement of the [new] plans. That article appeared to be the first that either the then Lord Chancellor or the Lord Chief Justice knew of the plans. The new MoJ has taken on all of the responsibilities of the Department for Constitutional Affairs (DCA) and the following responsibilities previously held by the Home Office:

- criminal law and sentencing;
- prisons;
- probation; and
- reducing re-offending.

Lord Falconer became the Secretary of State for Justice (the title of Secretary of State for Constitutional Affairs was abolished), a ministerial office he continued to combine with that of Lord Chancellor. These two posts were assumed by Jack Straw MP in the reshuffle after Gordon Brown became Prime Minister. . . .

59. So what constitutional impact might these reforms have? . . . They can be summarised as follows:

- Role of the Lord Chancellor: the impact of combining in one post the Lord Chancellor's responsibility to defend the independence of the judiciary and some of the Home Secretary's most controversial duties. The effect of having a Lord Chancellor in the House of Commons.
- Judicial Review: the impact of the Lord Chancellor being subject to a much greater number of judicial reviews upon his relationship with the Lord Chief Justice and the ongoing validity of the Concordat.
- Constitutional Affairs: the impact of constitutional affairs forming a much smaller part of the Lord Chancellor's department than previously.
- Funding of the Courts: the possibility of the courts budget being squeezed due to the demands of the resource-hungry prison system, and the impact of no longer having a judge on the board of the department.

---

114   Sixth Report, p 151, at [49].

67. We are disappointed that the Government seem to have learnt little or nothing from the debacle surrounding the constitutional reforms initiated in 2003. The creation of the Ministry of Justice clearly has important implications for the judiciary. The new dispensation created by the Constitutional Reform Act and the Concordat requires the Government to treat the judiciary as partners, not merely as subjects of change. . .

68. . . . . Clearly, if the roles of Lord Chancellor and Secretary of State for Justice continue to be combined, there is potential for conflict between the statutory duty to defend the independence of the judiciary and the temptation—to which home secretaries have regularly succumbed—to make intemperate remarks about judges and their judgments or sentencing decisions.

Notes

1. However, when the Committee reported again on this in October 2008, it was able to note with approval the fact that a satisfactory agreement between government and judiciary on the running of the courts system had been found.

> In January 2008, the Lord Chancellor and the then Lord Chief Justice reached agreement on a partnership model for the operation of Her Majesty's Court Service (HMCS), including the funding of the courts system. Subsequently, on 1 April, a formal Framework Document for HMCS was laid before Parliament. [Her Majesty's Courts Service Framework Document Cm. 7350.] Under the agreement, the Lord Chancellor and Lord Chief Justice would jointly agree the aims and objectives of HMCS and the priorities for, and division of, funding within HMCS. The Lord Chief Justice would also have the right to communicate to the Chancellor of the Exchequer the views of the judiciary on the provision and allocation of resources during Spending Review negotiations. HMCS staff would owe a joint duty to the Lord Chancellor and the Lord Chief Justice for the effective and efficient operation of the courts. Lord Phillips of Worth Matravers told us on 9 July 2008 that the agreement had resolved the tensions between the judiciary and ministers. He also stated that the HMCS budget would be subject to 'a kind of ring-fencing'.[115]

2. Bradley outlines the key features of the new agreement:

> In outline, the Lord Chancellor and the Lord Chief Justice will jointly agree the aims and objectives for the Courts Service, and the priorities for, and division of, funding within the Service. . ..
>
> A new Board of 11 members [including three judges] will give leadership and broad direction to the Courts Service, to be chaired by an independent non-executive chair (who is neither a judge nor a civil servant). . . The Framework Document describes the agreement reached over the financing and allocation of resources to the Courts Service, a matter of particular concern to the judges in the light of the creation of the Ministry of Justice; this includes scope for greater judicial engagement through the Courts Service Board in the resourcing of the courts. Moreover, the Lord Chief Justice will have a clear role in representing the views of the judiciary on provision and allocation of resources. . .The Lord Chief Justice will also be 'entitled to terminate the partnership if he concludes that it is no longer

---

115   House of Lords Constitution Committee, 'Relations between the executive, the judiciary and Parliament: Follow-up Report' HL 177 (2008–09) at [12].

compatible with his constitutional position or the independence of the judiciary' (at [15.6]. If for any reason the partnership is terminated:

> ' . . . [T]he governance of the [Courts Service] will revert to *a conventional agency model reporting directly to the Lord Chancellor,* unless and until a new model is agreed between the Lord Chancellor and Lord Chief Justice or a different legislative framework is put in place.' (at [15.7]) italics supplied).[116]

The Constitutional Reform Act 2005, the Law Lords and the Supreme Court

The Lord Chancellor is not the only senior judge whose position changed following *McGonnell* and under the resultant Constitutional Reform Act. The Law Lords, who made up both the Judicial Committee of the House of Lords and the Judicial Committee of the Privy Council, also, up until October 2009, sat in the House of Lords in its legislative capacity, and participated in its debates. On this basis, their adjudication in particular cases was also open to challenge under Article 6 of the ECHR, particularly if they had expressed a strong view in the Lords during the passage of legislation, the interpretation of which was at issue in the case now before them. In an attempt to minimise problems which could arise in this area, and also with an eye towards the preservation of the general reputation of the judiciary for political independence, the Law Lords, as recommended by the Wakeham Report,[117] made a statement of two principles to guide them in participating in the House of Lords' legislative and scrutinising activities.:

> first, the Lords of Appeal in Ordinary do not think it appropriate to engage in matters where there is a strong element of party political controversy; and secondly [they] bear in mind that they might render themselves ineligible to sit judicially if they were to express an opinion on a matter which might later be relevant to an appeal to the House.[118]

However, as Russell and Comes commented at the time, 'the only sure way of avoiding an Article 6(1) problem remains the removal of the Law Lords from the legislature'.[119]

Stevens considers that the advantages of barring the Law Lords from the legislative second chamber outweigh the disadvantages. He notes first of all the highly significant role that they have played, from time to time, in legislative matters:

R Stevens, 'A loss of innocence? Judicial independence and the separation of powers' (1999) 19 *Oxford Journal of Legal Studies* 366 (extracts)

Lord Goddard and his successor as Chief Justice, Lord Parker were strong advocates of hanging and flogging in the 40s and 50s. Lord Merriman and other divorce judges held up liberalisation in divorce law and procedure in the following decades. Perhaps the most

---

116   A Bradley, 'Relations between Executive, Judiciary and Parliament: An Evolving Saga?' [2008] PL 470, 485–6.

117   *A House for the future*, Cm 4534, Recommendation 59; available at www.official-documents.co.uk/ document/cm45/4534/4534.htm

118   HL Deb cols 419–20 (22 June 2000), Lord Bingham.

119   M Russell and R Comes, 'The Royal Commission on Reform of the House of Lords: A House for the Future?' (2001) 64 MLR 82.

dramatic political activities by the law lords, however, came in the late 80s as Lord Mackay introduced Green Papers designed to make the courts and the profession more efficient and responsive to the needs of the public, primarily by introducing market reforms. The retired law lords behaved in a remarkable manner during the legislative debates. No less than three—Lords Elwyn-Jones (a former Labour Lord Chancellor), Donaldson, and Lane (then retiring as Lord Chief Justice)—implied that the Conservative Lord Chancellor (Mackay) was guilty of Nazi tendencies—and of course violating the independence of the judiciary. . .Lord Hailsham, the then recently retired Conservative Lord Chancellor, expanded the notion of judicial independence far and wide. He regarded the Green Papers as 'an outrage' [*ibid*, at cols 1333–34].

[Stevens goes on to suggest that the arguments in favour of the Lords continuing to sit are outweighed by those to the contrary]:

The biggest disadvantage. . .is the appearance of judicial partiality—and confusion about the role of judges. When the *Fire Brigade* case [[1995] 2 AC 513] came before the Lords in 1995, a decision which eventually struck down Home Secretary Michael Howard's attempt to make cuts in the Criminal Injuries Compensation Scheme, it was difficult to find five law lords to sit judicially, since so many law lords had already spoken out, legislatively, against the Howard proposals. Rosenberg in *Trial of Strength* (1997) describes 27 January 1997 as the day when, in the morning, the law lords heard the judicial appeal about executive extension of the terms of imprisonment of children convicted of murder, and, in the afternoon, the same law lords were actively engaged in the legislative debates on the government's plan for mandatory and minimum sentences. As support for a totally or partially elected Second Chamber grows, the case for taking the law lords out of such a body becomes progressively stronger.

Notes

1.   While neither the Royal Commission on Lords Reform,[120] nor the Government's White Paper in response[121] called for removal of the Law Lords from the second chamber, this was the eventual path taken. Interestingly, the Law Lords themselves were divided on the proposals, with a majority opposing them. Lords Nicholls, Hoffmann, Hope, Hutton, Millet, and Rodger, said that 'on pragmatic grounds, the proposed change is unnecessary and harmful'. Lords Bingham, Steyn, Saville and Walker, saw the 'functional separation of the judiciary at all levels from the legislature and the executive as a cardinal feature of a modern, liberal, democratic state governed by the rule of law'.[122]

2.   Section 23(1) of the CRA provides for a Supreme Court of the United Kingdom to be established, to comprise 12 members (s 23(2)), each of whom will be called a 'Justice of the Supreme Court' (s 23(6)). The first members of the Supreme Court are those who at the commencement of the relevant part of the CRA 2005 are the Lords of Appeal in Ordinary (s 24(a)). A supplementary panel of judges will be available (s 39) comprising judges who are below the age of 75 (s 39(2)(c), and who previously, but do not now hold 'high judicial office' (s 39(2)(b)).

---

120   *A House for the Future*, Cm 4534.

121   *The House of Lords: Completing the Reform*, Cmd 529.

122   See House of Lords, *The Law Lords' response to the Government's consultation pages on Constitutional Reform: A Supreme Court for the United Kingdom* (2003).

3. Judicial Independence is preserved primarily through security of tenure. *Per* section 33: 'A judge of the Supreme Court holds that office during good behaviour, but may be removed from it on the address of both Houses of Parliament.' While serving as 'Justices of the Supreme Court', judges are precluded from being members of either House of Parliament (s 137). They are appointed by the procedure discussed below.

4. The jurisdiction of the Supreme Court will be largely the same as that of the Appellate Committee of the House of Lords (s 40) but with the addition of the 'devolution jurisdiction' of the Judicial Committee of the Privy Council (s 40(4)(b) and Schedule 9). Hazell, noting this, goes on to predict that the new Supreme Court will nevertheless come to differ importantly from the old House of Lords:

> The new court is likely over time to develop a significantly different mix of cases which it selects for hearing. Out will go the commercial and tax and private law cases, to leave room for cases of constitutional importance: human rights cases, cases about the right to die, privacy etc., our relationship with Europe, and devolution cases. That has been the experience of the Canadian Supreme Court over the last 25 years; our new Supreme Court will gradually follow suit and transform into more of a constitutional court.
>
> [Further], the court will have a much higher profile, when it starts to hear these more interesting cases. Once removed from the House of Lords, the court will come into its own. It will have its own website; it will need its own press officer to publicise and explain its decisions. Some of the judges might start to write their judgments in more user-friendly language. There will be more reporting of their decisions, and more discussion of the judges on the court, and their influence on the outcomes.[123]

Baroness Hale, the only female judge in the new court, asked whether it was not worth going further and re-thinking the role of the UK's highest court.

B Hale, 'A Supreme Court for the United Kingdom?' [2004] 24 (1/2) Legal Studies *36 (extracts)*

> If we are to have all the upheaval this will entail, is it not worth contemplating doing something a little more radical? President Barak, of the Supreme Court of Israel, says this of the role of a Supreme Court:
>
>> The primary concern of the supreme court in a democracy is not to correct individual mistakes in lower court judgments. That is the job of courts of appeal. The supreme court's concern is broader, system-wide corrective action. This corrective action should focus on two main issues: bridging the gap between law and society, and protecting democracy.
>
> By 'bridging the gap between law and society', he meant developing the law to meet the changing needs of society, in partnership with the legislature. By 'protecting democracy', he meant protecting not only formal democracy but substantive democracy in the shape of fundamental human rights, in particular to dignity and equality for all.

---

123   Hazell, n 112 above, at 17.

> What it could mean is taking away the ordinary criminal and civil cases, no matter how much money is involved, and leaving them to the domestic courts of each jurisdiction. Only cases of real constitutional importance would go to the Supreme Court. These would include the ground-breaking human rights cases, cases about our relationship with Europe or the rest of the world, including important cases interpreting international treaties or concepts such as sovereign immunity, and devolution cases. They might also include those public law cases which raised points of real significance even if the Human Rights Act 1998 was not invoked: the general approach to tax avoidance schemes or the amenability of Government ministers to sanctions for contempt of court might be examples. The Supreme Court might also take more ordinary cases, in both private and criminal law, but only on the basis that a serious inconsistency had arisen between two or more jurisdictions of the United Kingdom in the interpretation of United Kingdom legislation or the development of the common law on a subject where the law ought to be the same throughout the realm.

Note

The new Supreme Court assumed its jurisdiction on 1 October 2009. Its website may be found here: www.supremecourt.gov.uk/index.html and the new procedural rules governing its operation have been passed by Parliament as the Supreme Court Rules 2009.[124]

ENSURING JUDICIAL INDEPENDENCE FROM THE EXECUTIVE: THE APPOINTMENT AND DISMISSAL OF THE JUDGES

The position before the Constitutional Reform Act 2005

The previous section discussed the enhancing of the separation and independence of the judicial branch in terms of overlap of personnel—the Law Lords' dual role as legislators and judges. In this section we discuss the application of the principle that neither branch should control or improperly influence the work of the other in terms of the system for appointing and removing judges and ask: does the manner of their appointment and terms of their employment serve to guarantee their impartiality?

Previously, the most senior judiciary (the Law Lords, the Court of Appeal judges, President of the Family Division and Master of the Rolls) were appointed by the Queen on the advice of the Prime Minister. High Court, circuit and district judges were appointed by the Queen on the advice of the Lord Chancellor, as were recorders. In relation to the most senior positions (Law Lords and Court of Appeal judges), there was a system of 'secret soundings', whereby the Lord Chancellor would consult confidentially with existing judges at this level as to the merits of possible candidates for promotion.[125] This system had been subject to widespread criticism for its lack of transparency and for its tendency to limit membership of the senior judiciary to a small elite of senior barristers, overwhelmingly, white,

---

124   2009 No 1603 (L.17), available www.opsi.gov.uk/si/si2009/uksi_20091603_en_1

125   For a comprehensive account of the pre-reform system of appointments, see Sir Thomas Legg, 'Judges for the New Century' [2001] PL 62.

male and upper class.[126] Prior to the CRA, a limited, non-statutory reform was undertaken by way of the creation of a Commission for Judicial Appointments, which, despite its name, did not *make* appointments, but oversaw the process.

The UK's arrangements in relation to the appointment of certain low-level judges were recently found to fall foul of Article 6, ECHR. In this instance, the finding was made by the Scottish courts[127] applying s 57 of the Scotland Act 1998, which binds all members of the Scottish executive to act compatibly with the Convention rights.

Starrs and Chalmers v Procurator Fiscal, Linlithgow (Starrs v Ruxton)
2000 *SLT* 42 (extracts)

The complainers in this case were on trial for a criminal charge, heard by a temporary sheriff; the prosecution had been brought by a Procurator Fiscal. They raised the point that a trial before such a sheriff did not comply with Article 6, ECHR because the sheriff's manner of appointment meant that he could not be considered an 'independent and impartial tribunal'. When the point was dismissed, they appealed to the High Court.

Under the Sheriff Courts (Scotland) Act 1971, the Secretary of State was given very broad powers to appoint temporary sheriffs, which he used "to create a large pool of persons. . . available to supplement the permanent sheriffs as and when the need arises, to the extent of performing. . .25% of the total workload". Lord Reed noted the key provision in the statute.

Lord Reed: . . . Section 11(4) provides: 'The appointment of a temporary sheriff principal or of a temporary sheriff shall subsist until recalled by the Secretary of State.' The Solicitor General accepted that the effect of this provision is that a temporary sheriff holds office at pleasure. . .Section 11(4) can be contrasted with the provisions of section 12, which provide security of tenure to permanent sheriffs. Under section 12, a permanent sheriff can be removed from office only by an order which is subject to annulment in pursuance of a resolution of either House of Parliament. Such an order can only be made on a report by the Lord President and the Lord Justice Clerk to the effect that the sheriff is unfit for office by reason of inability, neglect of duty or misbehaviour. Such a report can only be made following an investigation by the Lord President and the Lord Justice Clerk. . . . Temporary sheriffs are expressly excluded from the scope of these provisions: section 12(7).

[Under] the current system of appointment of temporary sheriffs. . .membership of the pool of temporary sheriffs has increasingly come to be coveted as a step on the road towards a permanent appointment, and on the Lord Advocate's side it has equally come to be seen to some extent as, in effect, a probationary period during which potential candidates for a permanent appointment can be assessed.

In relation to section 11(4), the Solicitor General accepted that this impliedly conferred upon the Secretary of State a power to recall the appointment at will. . .It was common ground that section 11(4) in particular provided no security of tenure whatsoever for temporary sheriffs. The issue in dispute, so far as security of tenure was concerned, was whether the degree of protection which in practice existed, as a consequence of the involvement of the Lord Advocate and his independence from the political process, was sufficient to satisfy the requirements of Article 6 of the Convention.

---

126   See, for example, K Malleson [2004] PL 102.

127   The Appeal Court, the High Court of Justiciary.

[The consequence of the above arrangements is that] temporary sheriffs held office at pleasure, protected only by the integrity and good sense of the Lord Advocate.

I turn next to consider whether the temporary sheriff is an 'independent and impartial tribunal' within the meaning of Article 6 paragraph I of the Convention. . .

In order to establish whether a body can be considered to be 'independent', regard must be had, inter alia, to the manner of appointment of its members and their term of office, to the existence of guarantees against outside pressures and to the question whether the body presents an appearance of independence: see, inter alia, *Bryan* [(1995) A 335-A, para 37)]. . . .

Temporary appointments are. . .apt to create particular problems from the point of view of independence, particularly where the duration of the appointment is not fixed so as to expire upon the completion of a particular task or upon the cessation of a particular state of affairs (such as some emergency or exigency), but is a fixed period of time of relatively short duration. In particular, such a term of office is liable to compromise the judge's independence where the appointment can be renewed, as the European Court of Human Rights [has found]. As is stated in the European Charter on the statute for judges, adopted in Strasbourg in July 1998 under the auspices of the Council of Europe (DAJ/DOC (98) 23) (at para 3.3.):

> Clearly, the existence of probationary periods or renewal requirements presents difficulties if not dangers from the angle of the independence and impartiality of the judge in question, who is hoping to be established in post or to have his or her contract renewed.

Other international instruments demonstrate an equal awareness of these dangers. . . . [His Lordship cited similar provisions in the Universal Declaration on the Independence of Justice. . .]

It appears that in almost all the other systems surveyed the appointment of a temporary judge by the Executive for a period of one year, renewable at the discretion of the Executive, would be regarded as unconstitutional.

23. So far as temporary sheriffs are concerned. . .what to my mind is of critical importance, however, is that renewal is both possible and expected, but is at the discretion of the Executive. In effect, temporary sheriffs have their judicial careers broken up into segments of one year, so as to provide the Executive with the possibility of re-considering their appointment on an annual basis. This has obvious implications for security of tenure. . . . It also appears to me to be important that temporary sheriffs may well be potential candidates for a permanent appointment in the event of a vacancy occurring, as is recognised in the notes issued to candidates for appointment as temporary sheriffs. . . .

24. Given that temporary sheriffs are very often persons who are hoping for graduation to a permanent appointment, and at the least for the renewal of their temporary appointment, the system of short renewable appointments creates a situation in which the temporary sheriff is liable to have hopes and fears in respect of his treatment by the Executive when his appointment comes up for renewal: in short, a relationship of dependency. This is in my opinion a factor pointing strongly away from 'independence' within the meaning of Article 6. . .

26. The next matter to be considered is the existence of guarantees against outside pressures. In this regard, counsel for the appellants founded upon a number of factors. They submitted in the first place that the power to recall the appointment of a temporary

sheriff, or to decline to renew the appointment, is vested in the Scottish Executive, and in practice is exercised by the Lord Advocate. The temporary sheriff can even be deprived of his appointment in substance by being informally 'sidelined', without any formal recall or non-renewal, if he incurs the displeasure of officials. The consequence is to make the temporary sheriff entirely dependent upon the Scottish Executive, and in particular upon the Lord Advocate, for the continuation and renewal of his appointment. This, it was submitted, is particularly objectionable when the Scottish Executive, and in practice the Lord Advocate, is also responsible for making the permanent appointments which many temporary sheriffs are hoping to obtain. The objection becomes even more serious when it is appreciated that the Lord Advocate is also responsible for the criminal prosecutions which take place before temporary sheriffs. For the temporary sheriff to occupy a role subordinate to one of the parties to proceedings before him is, it was submitted, inconsistent with judicial independence. . .

It was common ground before us that, as a matter of law, a temporary sheriff can be removed from office at any time for any reason. It was also common ground that a temporary sheriff can be appointed on an annual basis and that his allocation to courts, and the renewal of his appointment, are thereafter within the unfettered discretion of the Executive. . .In these circumstances, I am prepared to proceed on the basis that a temporary sheriff does not, as a matter of law, enjoy anything which constitutes security of tenure in the normally accepted sense of that term.

. . .The Solicitor General emphasised that it is inconceivable that the Lord Advocate would interfere with the performance of judicial functions. I readily accept that; but that is not the point. Judicial independence can be threatened not only by interference by the Executive, but also by a judge's being influenced, consciously or unconsciously, by his hopes and fears as to his possible treatment by the Executive. It is for that reason that a judge must not be dependent on the Executive, however well the Executive may behave: 'independence' connotes the absence of dependence. It also has to be borne in mind that judicial independence exists to protect the integrity of the judiciary and confidence in the administration of justice, and thus society as a whole, in bad times as well as good. The adequacy of judicial independence cannot appropriately be tested on the assumption that the Executive will always behave with appropriate restraint: as the European Court of Human Rights has emphasised in its interpretation of Article 6, it is important that there be 'guarantees' against outside pressures. In short, for the judiciary to be dependent on the Executive flies in the face of the principle of the separation of powers which is central to the requirement of judicial independence in Article 6.

Notes

1. The result of the decision was that temporary sheriffs, who had been hearing about 25% of criminal cases in Scotland, could no longer do so. The Scottish Parliament passed an Act which placed the appointment of temporary sheriffs on a new basis, addressing the concerns as to security of tenure raised in the case.
2. The case raised questions for England and Wales as well. While there is no strict equivalent of the temporary sheriffs in England, the principle established in the case was felt to open the way to challenge the independence of a number of the part-time judiciary appointed by the Lord Chancellor, in particular assistant recorders and part-time judges in certain tribunals. New procedures were put in place in order to ensure that these appointments would have sufficient security of tenure in order to satisfy and be seen to satisfy the test of being 'independent and impartial' as required by Article 6. The essence of the new arrangements was a new five-year appointment, with

automatic renewal, subject only to narrow and specified grounds of misbehaviour, incapacity, redundancy and so on. Dismissal would similarly also be possible only on such grounds and a decision to dismiss or not to renew an appointment would be subject to the concurrence of the Lord Chief Justice and would be taken only following an investigation by a judge.

3. As Stevens notes, there is a general, and justified belief, that the judicial arm in the UK is independent of Government influence, but such independence is not as robustly protected as is commonly believed. His article must now be read as considering the historical position before the CRA 2005.

R Stevens, 'A loss of innocence? Judicial independence and the separation of powers' (1999) 19 *Oxford Journal of Legal Studies* 366 (extracts)

In England the concept of judicial independence, an integral part of the separation of powers, is an inchoate one. One might have thought that, since many of the early ideas about the separation of powers developed in England, the concept of judicial independence might be articulately analysed in the legal literature. Far from it. In modern Britain the concept of the separation of powers is cloudy and the notion of the independence of the judiciary remains primarily a term of constitutional rhetoric. Certainly its penumbra, and perhaps even its core, are vague. No general theory exists, although practically the English have developed surprisingly effective informal systems for the separation of powers; although it should never be forgotten that the system of responsible government is based on a co-mingling of the executive with the legislature. The political culture of the United Kingdom, however, provides protections for the independence of the judiciary, which are missing in the law.

It was these very issues—judicial independence, the significance of judicial views, the role of judges in cases with a significant political element—which were peaking in Britain as the country reached the millennium. . .For the previous 40 years, the courts had been directed or the judges had drifted back into those policy areas that they had largely left or been excluded from by the time of the First World War. In the 50s it was competition law, the 60s saw a formalized change to stare decisis, the 70s saw the renewed incursion into labour law, the renewal of judicial review of administrative decisions and the arrival of the EU. The 80s confirmed an increasingly creative approach to the common law while the early 90s provided a much wider approach to statutory interpretation. . .[In the late 1990s]. . .as The Economist warned, with the New Labour Government's constitutional changes, there would be 'a much wider array of cases' coming to the Lords:

> . . .many of these will be highly contentious, and will bring the law lords into conflict with politicians. . .like all senior judges, they are in effect appointed by the Lord Chancellor, who is the government's senior law officer and sits in the Cabinet, after secret consultations among judges and top lawyers. This is an untenable method of selection for judges who will be ruling on issues of great public and political interest. . . ['Judging the judges', *The Economist*, 23 January 1999].

The Independence of Individual Judges
It is acceptable, if not entirely accurate, to say that England has independence of the judiciary in the sense of independence of an individual judge. To take what are conventionally seen as the hallmarks of such independence—security of tenure, fiscal independence, impartiality and freedom from executive pressure—at the core, there is little doubt that

England qualifies under any reasonable standard of judicial independence with respect to individual judges.

Judicial Independence: The Judges as a Separate Branch of Government

. . . Another of the issues in judicial independence in England is that the judges are chosen, as they are in most other common law countries although normally with the assistance of a Judicial Appointments Commission, by a politician—basically the Lord Chancellor. While the English like to say that judicial appointments in their country are non-political, or even apolitical (and there are in fact no former MPs currently serving as judges), Europeans find it difficult to comprehend how a system which leaves the final say for choosing most judges with an active politician, the Lord Chancellor, with appointments to the House of Lords and Court of Appeal made by the Prime Minister, can be an apolitical system. Even the House of Commons Select Committee on Home Affairs has described the Prime Minister's involvement in senior judicial appointments as 'nothing short of naked political control' [Judicial Appointments Procedures, Vol 1, 5 June 1996, para 126].

. . . Yet in a sense the claims of the apolitical nature of the process are true. While the judiciary is chosen primarily from the English Bar, it is possible to argue that success and reputation at the Bar far outweigh other attributes. (Of course whether success as an advocate should be the primary criterion for judicial appointment is a different matter.) Once again political convention provides more support than legal rules might. With a relatively small and cohesive Bar, there is an argument that 'the judges select themselves'. . . It is also true that the days when politics played an important role in getting on the Bench have effectively gone. Lord Halsbury, at the turn of the century, was the last Lord Chancellor who blatantly appointed political supporters to the High Court Bench; and after the 1920s political service played little role in appointment to the House of Lords and Court of Appeal. Yet Mrs Thatcher rejected Lord Hailsham's report of the judges' preference and appointed Sir John Donaldson to be Master of the Rolls in the 1980s, and it was unlikely that she was unaware of Donaldson's work in the Tory cause in the Industrial Relations Court. Of course, what is political is always difficult to define. We should not forget that during the most radical government in Britain's history (the Attlee Government of 1945–51) Lord Chancellor Jowitt refused to appoint divorced persons to the Bench and, for a significant period, members of the Roman Catholic Church. While this latter was allegedly because they might have difficulty hearing divorce petitions on circuit, the real reason may well have been because he and the Home Secretary. . .were vigorously anti-Catholic. . .

There is an increasing consensus that allowing one politician in the Cabinet to choose judges is unacceptable. . .The problem remains, if the judges are not chosen by the Lord Chancellor, then by whom?

Note

The provisions in the Act of Settlement dealing with security of tenure were reproduced in the Senior Courts Act 1981, s 11(3). Senior judges (High Court judges and above) may only be dismissed by an address to the Crown passed by both Houses of Parliament. Section 33 of the Constitutional Reform Act extends this protection to the new Justices of the Supreme Court and to the senior judges in Northern Ireland (s 133). Judges below High Court level do not have this protection, but may be dismissed by the Lord Chancellor on the grounds of incapacity or misbehaviour, but following the Concordat, and the 2005 Act, only after the Lord Chancellor has consulted with the Lord Chief Justice, and in accordance with the procedures laid down by regulations made under the Constitutional

Reform Act, s 115. This duty to consult with the Lord Chief Justice was part of the agreement reached between Lord Woolf and the Lord Chancellor as a further guarantee of judicial independence following the reforms to the office of Lord Chancellor. Sections 108–121 also provide for the exercise of disciplinary powers by the Lord Chief Justice after investigation for misconduct, including a power to suspend judges from office.

The Judicial Appointments Commission

The New Appointments System

As we have seen above, the judiciary were gravely concerned at the thought that in future they would be appointed not by the quasi-judicial figure of the Lord Chancellor, but an ordinary party politician.[128] In response to such concerns, the Government introduced what to many was the long-overdue reform of setting up a proper Judicial Appointments Commission, which would take over from the Lord Chancellor the crucial role of *selecting* candidates; as seen below, the Lord Chancellor retains a very limited power of veto.

The CRA establishes a Judicial Appointments Commission of 15 members, a mixture of judges, lawyers and laypersons.[129] They are appointed by the Queen on the advice of the Lord Chancellor. Lord Mance, an existing Law Lord, has described its composition as 'more nuanced and subtle than any found in any other European jurisdiction'.[130] There are separate Commissions for appointments to Scotland and to Northern Ireland. For appointments within England and Wales, the procedure varies slightly as between appointments to the High Court and below, the Court of Appeal and the Supreme Court,[131] as does the composition of the selecting panel. Not all appointments are covered by the JAC: the Lord Chancellor still appoints some junior posts. For all other judicial appointments, the basic process is as described below.

Windelsham summarise the effect of the changes:

> Responsibility for making judicial appointments, a key function, [are] transferred from the Lord Chancellor to a new Commission, clearly independent of the government. This Commission [has] full responsibility for the process of advertising vacancies and evaluating candidates for judicial appointment. No candidate [will] be appointed to any judicial post for which the Commission [is] responsible unless recommended by the Commission. . . So as to ensure proper accountability to Parliament, the final decision on who to appoint or, more precisely, whose name to recommend to the Queen for appointment. . . remain[s] with the [Lord Chancellor]. Ministerial discretion [is] circumscribed, however, since only candidates who had been recommended by the Commission [can] be appointed, with no more than 'suitably restricted' powers for the minister to challenge any of its recommendations.[132]

---

128   See 146–151.

129   See Sched 12 of the Act for full details.

130   (2006) 25 CJQ 155.

131   The provisions for appointments to the Supreme Court are at ss 25–31; for appointments to the post of Lord Chief Justice and Heads of Divisions, at ss 67–75, for Court of Appeal judges (Lord Justices of Appeal) at ss 76–84 and others at ss 85–94.

132   Lord Windelsham, 'The Constitutional Reform Act 2005: Ministers, Judges and Constitutional Change: Part 1' [2005] PL 806, 820–821.

Thus the Commission does not actually appoint, but makes recommendations to the Lord Chancellor, who, in the case of the more senior appointments, then puts these to the Queen, or to the Prime Minister to put to the Queen (in the case of the Law Lords). Thus, formally speaking, senior politicians are still involved in the process; however, the Lord Chancellor's power to reject names put to him is highly restricted.

When an appointment is to be made, the Commission produces a Report, nominating one person. Turpin and Tomkins describe the somewhat elaborate provisions that detail what happens next:

> On receiving the Report (**stage 1**) the Lord Chancellor has three options: (a) to accept the selection; (b) to reject it; (c) to require the Commission to reconsider the selection. Following a *rejection* or *requirement to reconsider*, the Commission or panel must again make a selection. The Lord Chancellor has then (**stage 2**) the same three options: accept, reject or require reconsideration, but he may reject the selection only if it was made following a reconsideration at stage 1 and may require reconsideration of the selection only if it was made following a rejection at stage 1. Following a further selection after rejection or reconsideration at stage 2, the Lord Chancellor must, at **stage 3**, accept the selection.[133]

It should be noted that if the Lord Chancellor rejects a person at stages 1 or 2, the Commission, when making a further selection, may not re-select that person. However, where the Lord Chancellor has required reconsideration of a person, the Commission may decide to put that person forward again for the following stage.

The Lord Chancellor has, then, lost his power of *selection*; he has only a very limited power of rejection. The result of these rather complex procedures in fact is that he may only reject one candidate for any given post. We will briefly illustrate this. If the Lord Chancellor (LC) accepts at stage 1, then of course that candidate is selected. But what happens if the LC does reject one candidate? Let us consider the two possible scenarios: rejection at stage 1, or at stage 2.

- The Commission initially puts forward Erika at stage one. The LC rejects Erika, meaning that she cannot be put forward again. So the Commission then puts forward Clare at stage 2. Since the LC may only reject at stage 2 if he has not already rejected at stage 1, which he has, he cannot therefore reject Clare, but only require reconsideration. If the Commission, having reconsidered, decides to put forward Clare again, we are now at Stage 3, and the LC *must* now accept Clare.

The alternative scenario is as follows:

- The Commission initially puts forward Erika at stage one. The LC asks for reconsideration. The Commission, having reconsidered, puts forward Erika again, at stage 2. Since the LC may reject at stage 2 if he has asked for reconsideration at stage 1, which he did, he *can* reject Erika. But we are now at stage 3. Consequently, when the Commission now puts forward Clare at Stage 3, the LC *must* now accept Clare.

This of course assumes that the Commission is prepared to put forward names again following a request to reconsider. The point is to show the limits of the Lord Chancellor's power of rejection – only

---

133   Turpin and Tomkins, n 76 above, at 122–23.

one candidate per post. Given also that the LC may only reject on the narrow ground that 'in his opinion the person selected is not suitable for the office concerned',[134] and must give reasons for any rejection, it is not surprising that Lord Mance commented:

> The Lord Chancellor's powers to reject or require reconsideration [of names put to him] and his obligation to give reasons are restrictive to the point where it seems in practice to be almost inevitable that he will accept the Judicial Appointments Commission's recommendations.[135]

This appears to have been the case to date.

By virtue of ss 63 and 64, selection must be 'solely on merit', but the Commission may also 'have regard' to the need to encourage diversity. However, Jack Straw, the Secretary of State for Justice, was forced to admit in May 2008 that 'Expectations that the new system of appointing judges would lead to a more diverse judiciary have so far not been fulfilled.'[136] For reports on selection procedures adopted and on appointments to date see www.judicialappointments.gov.uk/.

The Constitutional Reform and Governance Bill 2009 contained provisions to make various changes to the above scheme. These would have removed magistrates from the remit of the JAC (this follows agreement on this between the Lord Chancellor, JAC, the Lord Chief Justice and the Magistrate's Association); moreover, the Prime Minister's (purely symbolic) role would have been removed from appointments made to the Supreme Court; however, earlier proposals to remove the Lord Chancellor's power to reject or require reconsideration of candidates nominated by the JAC were dropped by the Government. However, all these changes were dropped before the Bill became law in 2010.

Alternative Models for Judicial Appointments

As appears below, a number of lawyers, judges and commentators were critical both of the decision to give the Lord Chancellor such a restricted ability to reject JAC recommendations and to have a majority of judges on the JAC, considering that this carried the danger of the judges making conservative choices, thus tending to replicate the existing, narrow, make-up of the senior judiciary.

For example, Lord Lester, an eminent human rights QC and Liberal Democrat peer, commented in a Parliamentary debate on the new Supreme Court:

> The quality of independence is well provided by judges drawn from the independent Bar, for the Bar is a profession of self-governing and inner-directed individuals, trained to be robustly independent. But the Bar still lacks diversity and it has no monopoly for providing judges with such qualities. Judges and barristers need to recognise that experience of advocacy is not a necessary condition for a good judge. The qualities needed can be well provided on the basis of wider professional experience beyond the Bar, including solicitors, those who have chaired tribunals or who have been distinguished academics and civil servants.[137]

---

134   See, e.g. s 30(1).

135   Lord Mance, (2006) 25 CJQ 155.

136   See, e.g. 'Judicial diversity goes into reverse', *Guardian,* 19 May 2008.

137   652 HL Official Report (5th series) col 1 13, 8 September 2003.

Baroness Hale, currently the only female member of the Supreme Court, has similarly noted that:

> it is commonplace elsewhere in the world for members of the Supreme Court, whatever its constitutional role, to come from a much wider range of professional backgrounds and experience than our Law Lords do. They may come from the lower judiciary, but also from the Chief Prosecutor's or Attorney-General's Office, or other public service, or the universities, or private practice.[138]

Hazell[139] agrees that in this respect, 'the reforms took a wrong turning':

> The discretion previously enjoyed by the Lord Chancellor has been drastically restricted by the new arrangements for judicial appointments, so that in future he will be presented with a single name. Technically the Judicial Appointments Commission is an advisory commission, because the Lord Chancellor can reject the name and ask the commission to reconsider. In practice it will be an appointing commission, and it will be the judges appointing their own.
>
> Although there is a lay chair (Baroness Prashar) and lay membership of the Judicial Appointments Commission, it will be heavily influenced if not dominated by its judicial members. There is a risk of the commission playing safe, cloning the existing judiciary in terms of skills and experience, or worse still, operating Buggins' turn for the most senior appointments.

Thomas Legg, who worked for years as a civil servant in the Lord Chancellor's department on the appointment of judges, argues strongly that there needs to be greater democratic involvement in the appointment of senior judges as a matter of principle.

Sir Thomas Legg, 'Brave New World—The new Supreme Court and judicial appointments' [2004] 24 (1/2) *Legal Studies* 45, 46, 49, 52

I think there is now a strong case for requiring the candidate selected by the Prime Minister to be confirmed by a joint committee of both Houses of Parliament before his or her name is submitted to the Queen. This need not necessarily involve a public hearing, as happens in the Judiciary Committee of the United States Senate. The fact that MPs and peers are not competent to judge the professional qualities of the candidates is not relevant to this issue. The same will be true of the lay members of the Judicial Appointments Commission. . .Parliamentary confirmation will not bring the new Court into the political arena any more than it will be anyway, and may help to keep it out. The question is one of transparency and, above all, legitimacy—of which the new Supreme Court will need as much as it can get. It is not just fitting, but. . .necessary that both the other two branches of government, that is the legislature as well as the executive, should concur in the appointment of the nation's most senior judges. . .

With judges, we are not talking about ordinary jobs, but about state officials who are for good reasons virtually un-sackable, and who yet are armed with, and daily exercise,

---

138   B Hale, 'A Supreme Court for the United Kingdom?' [2003] LS 36, 43–44.

139   See n 112 above, at 18.

formidable powers over their fellow citizens. In appointing them, there is little room for experiment and none for political correctness for its own sake. . .

It is important to be clearer than the consultation paper is about the distinction between the independence of the judges and the independence of those who appoint them. Attempts to achieve absolute purity on the latter risk being self-defeating. Judicial independence rests on several pillars: law, convention, tradition, and the culture and spirit of the profession from which judges are drawn are more important than the location of the appointing authority. Certainly the appointers should be free of party political motives, as in fact they have been for many years. But the appointment of judges is properly a political act, in the broadest sense of the term, and I believe that it should be done by a political authority. Hence, my preference for a 'Recommending' Commission. Such a Commission should give the Secretary of State for Constitutional Affairs a **real** choice, for which he should take a **real** and accountable responsibility.

Notes

1. The argument for endowing the senior judges with greater legitimacy through the *symbolic* imprimatur of the legislature is understandable—although whether it would make any real difference to the perceived legitimacy of the top courts is open to question. But it is by no means clear what Legg means when he suggests that the Lord Chancellor should have a 'real choice' for which he would take 'a real and accountable responsibility'. First of all, given that the Lord Chancellor in future may not have any legal expertise, it is unclear on what basis the Lord Chancellor would choose *between* different candidates recommended as suitable by the JAC. This this could be done on the basis of seeking to increase judicial diversity, but as between, say, two white, male candidates (hardly an unusual scenario!) it is harder to imagine on what basis the selection would be made. Second, it is hard to envisage what form the proposed 'accountability' for the selection of senior judges would take: does Legg really envisage the Lord Chancellor appearing in front of a Select Committee and being required to explain why X was more suitable for promotion to the Supreme Court than Y? Or being summoned to defend his selection when an appointed judge makes a decision that displeases MPs or his colleagues? One wonders whether this supposed 'accountability' would be any more than a polite constitutional fiction, as it (sadly) often is.[140]

2. Kate Malleson highlights the division of opinion on these issues and the example of Canada's recent experiment.

It was in relation to these upper rank judicial appointments that opinion was most sharply divided over the new provisions. Many members of the judiciary argued that it was essential to remove all executive involvement in selecting the senior judiciary since it was at this level that the pressure to manipulate would be greatest. Others argued that it was precisely in relation to these appointments, where the judges were engaged in high-level decisions with policy-making implications, that there should be some real link to the democratic process and that the Lord Chancellor should be more than just a rubber stamp. Initially the Government supported the latter view in relation to the Supreme Court appointments and the Bill provided that the Supreme Court commission would nominate 2–5 names for the Lord Chancellor to choose from, so ensuring a degree of political input. In the end, however, the Bill

---

140   On Ministerial accountability, see Chapter 12.

was amended so that both the Supreme Court Commission and the Judicial Appointments Commission for England and Wales were given the ultimate decision-making power. . .The effect was to remove the danger of improper political interference from the system but it also removed the opportunity for democratic involvement in the selection of public decision-makers. . . .

[Malleson notes that the long-standing rejection of a role for Parliament in approving the appointment of judges stems sharply from hostility to US-style appointment-hearings and goes on]:

However, the decision of the Canadian Parliament to introduce nomination hearings for their Supreme Court judges in March 2006 as part of a reform designed to reduce party political influence, illustrates the growing awareness outside the UK of the need to explore new ways to enhance democratic accountability in the judicial appointments process whilst at the same time removing political patronage. The debate in Canada which took place before the hearings were introduced almost exactly mirrored that which took place at the time of the passage of the Constitutional Reform Act. The first Canadian parliamentary Supreme Court hearing was widely regarded to have been a success and future hearings will no doubt be watched with interest. It is possible therefore, that this is an option that may be revisited in the UK at some future date.[141]

THE SEPARATION OF POWERS AS A SYSTEM OF CHECKS AND BALANCES

It will be recalled that Barendt argued at the beginning of this part that the essence of the separation of powers doctrine is the avoidance of concentrations of power that threaten oppressive government. The key means by which the separation of powers doctrine is meant to achieve this is through the separation of functions and, to an extent, personnel, as between the three arms of government. But another important aspect of the doctrine is the notion that each branch of government has a legitimate role in checking the activities of the other. This is such an important theme within the notion of constitutional government that it will recur throughout this book—and indeed forms the background concern of whole chapters.

For example, the examination of Parliament's role will be very largely concerned with asking how far it is effective in acting as a check upon the executive by ensuring its political accountability, through conventions such as individual Ministerial responsibility (considered in Chapter 12) and through the practical means designed to ensure accountability: through Parliamentary Questions, debates, motions and Select Committees (considered in Chapter 8). Chapter 13, on freedom of information, considers how far the ordinary citizen can hold the Government to account through legal rights of access to information on the workings and activities of government. As discussed above (see pp 132–136), the other key function of Parliament, scrutinising and approving legislation put before it, is also examined through the lens of the separation of powers: in this case, the question asked (in Chapter 8 in relation to the Commons and Chapter 9 in relation to the Lords) is how far Parliament provides independent

---

141   Malleson, p 143 above.

assessment of the merits of proposed legislation, and therefore actually performs its putative role as a legislature, rather than simply passively approving measures put before it by the executive. Chapter 11 considers how far Parliament is able to hold Government to account for the exercise of its non-legislative powers—the royal prerogative. The system of Ombudsmen provides a means of a non-legal, non-Parliamentary remedy for poor government administration that causes injustice—a further, significant check upon executive power, which is examined in Chapter 16.

In the case of the courts, their 'checking' role has traditionally been seen as applying only to the executive through formal processes such as judicial review. Here, the key concern of the courts is to ensure that the executive does not exceed the bounds of its lawful authority, as discussed above. This crucial *legal* check upon executive action is considered in detail in Chapters 14 and 15. It is not entirely comprehensive, however: courts have traditionally held that there are certain areas of prerogative power whose exercise is not subject to judicial review. In the *GCHQ* case,[142] the following were said by Lord Roskill to be un-reviewable by the courts:

> The making of treaties, the disposal of the armed forces, the defence of the realm, the dissolution of Parliament. . .and the appointment of Ministers.

The width and significance of this area of non-reviewable executive power is considered in Chapter 11.

Meanwhile, throughout this book, but particularly in Chapter 17, the significance of the courts' still relatively new powers under the Human Rights Act is considered. Under s 6(1) of that Act: 'It is unlawful for a public authority to act in a way which is incompatible with one or more of the Convention rights.' Prior to the HRA, the judiciary acted as a significant, though strictly limited, check upon the executive, through the availability of judicial review. As discussed above, (see pp 117–119) under the traditional heads of judicial review, the judiciary ensures that Ministers and other public authorities do not act outside the powers lawfully given to them by Acts of Parliament, or by the accepted government prerogatives; that they do not misuse powers given for one purpose for another; that decisions are taken in a way which is procedurally fair (for example, through ensuring adequate consultation, giving both sides a chance to be heard and ensuring there is no bias in the decision-maker); and that their decisions are not grossly unreasonable.

The addition of a further head of review—to ensure that public authorities have not acted in violation of a Convention right, represents a significant strengthening and broadening of the court's powers vis-à-vis the executive: courts are now able to quash the decisions of public bodies not because they were outside their powers, or did not follow a fair procedure, but on the substantive basis that they violated human rights. The freedom of action of the executive—the area of discretion it enjoys—is, as a corollary, substantially curtailed. Prior to the HRA, the judges maintained that it was primarily for the executive to ensure that, in the exercise of their lawful discretion, they did not infringe upon basic rights, or did so no more than was strictly necessary. The judges would intervene only where, on a proper construction of legislation, there was no power to do what had been done,[143] or where no reasonable person could have considered that the rights violation entailed was justified by the aim pursued by the Minister—something that was very rarely shown.[144] Since 2000, primary responsibility for ensuring the protection of those basic rights enumerated in the ECHR has shifted to the judges.

---

142   *Council for Civil Service Unions v the Minister for the Civil Service* [1984] 3 All ER 935.

143   As, for example, in *ex parte Witham* [1998] QB 575.

144   See, e.g. the 'gays in the military case', *R v Ministry of Defence ex parte Smith* [1996] QB 517 for an instance in which a plainly discriminatory policy was found not to have violated the standard enumerated in the text.

Finally, Chapters 4 and 5 will consider how far there are any judicial checks upon Parliament. Traditionally, as readers will already have gathered, the view was taken that the courts' only role in relation to primary legislation was to apply it. However, as we will see in these chapters, and Chapter 17 on the HRA, courts now have an important role in scrutinising statutes for compatibility with the Convention rights; in the case of EU law, as we will see in Chapter 5, courts have decided that they have limited power to 'disapply' statutory provisions which contravene EU law.

As this brief survey shows, while the doctrine of separation of powers is only partly reflected in the UK's constitutional design, it is a strong influence, and one which provides the normative framework for much of any work on constitutional and administrative law. It will be returned to repeatedly throughout this book.

FURTHER READING

TRS Allan, *Constitutional Justice, A Liberal Theory of the Rule of Law* (2001)
KC Davis, *Discretionary Justice* (1971)
FA Hayek, *The Road to Serfdom* (1944)
M Loughlin, *Public Law and Political Theory* (1992)
A Tomkins, *Public Law* (2003), Chapter 2.
MJC Vile, *Constitutionalism and the Separation of Powers* (1967)

TRS Allan, 'The Rule of Law as the rule of reason: consent and constitutionalism' (1999) 115 LQR 221
N Barber, 'Prelude to the separation of powers' [2001] CLJ 59
E Barendt, 'Dicey and civil liberties' [1985] PL 596
P Craig, 'Dicey: unitary, self-correcting democracy and public law' (1990) 106 LQR 105
P Craig, 'Formal and substantive conceptions of the Rule of Law: an analytical framework' [1997] PL 467
P Craig, 'Competing Models of Judicial Review' [1999] PL 428
P Craig, 'Constitutional Analysis, Constitutional Principle and Judicial Review' [2001] PL 763
P Craig, 'Constitutional Foundations, the Rule of Law, and Supremacy' [2003] PL 92
P Craig, 'The Common Law, Shared Power and Judicial Review' (2004) 24 OJLS 237
C Munro, 'The Separation of Powers: Not such a Myth' [1981] PL 19
Report of the Committee on Ministers' Powers (Cmnd 4060)
SA de Smith, 'The separation of Powers in New Dress' (1966) 12 McGill LJ 491
A Tomkins, 'Of Constitutional Spectres' [1999] PL 325.

CHAPTER 4
PARLIAMENTARY
SOVEREIGNTY

INTRODUCTION

Parliamentary sovereignty has long been seen as the central feature of the UK constitution: simple, absolute and unalterable, even by Parliament itself; some have even argued that, as the fundamental norm at the basis of the UK legal system, a simple statement that 'what the Queen in Parliament enacts is law' amounted to our one-line constitution, with everything else being subject to change by Parliament itself and thus just current constitutional law, as opposed to the Constitution. However, as the essay on sovereignty in the latest edition of the influential collection, *The Changing Constitution* makes clear, in a number of very significant ways the principles of parliamentary sovereignty have changed markedly over the last 20 or so years; at the very least, they have remained the same only in a formal sense, which increasingly is out of step with reality.[1] This chapter therefore considers how far traditional understandings of sovereignty can and should remain applicable today. It does so in three main sections: the nature of parliamentary sovereignty; possible legal limitations on sovereignty; and the question of whether Parliament is able in any way to entrench legislation, so as to make it impossible or more difficult for subsequent Parliaments to repeal an Act they have passed. The next chapter will consider the impact of European Union law on the traditional doctrine of parliamentary sovereignty. The main concern will be the extent to which the legislative competence of Parliament has been restricted by the impact of EU law.

THE NATURE OF PARLIAMENTARY SOVEREIGNTY

The basic idea of sovereignty

The notion of 'parliamentary sovereignty' or the 'legislative supremacy of Parliament', as it is sometimes termed, can be seen to have both political and legal aspects. Given that the dominant body in Parliament, the Commons, is democratically elected, the notion can be seen as representing a description of the democratic basis for legislation in the UK. As used by constitutional lawyers, however, it means something much more specific: 'By the legislative supremacy of Parliament is meant that there are no *legal* limitations upon the legislative competence of Parliament.'[2]

As AW Bradley has summed up the doctrine:

> The sovereignty of Parliament describes in formal terms the relationship which exists between the legislature and the courts. As analysed by Dicey, the Queen in Parliament (the legislature) has 'the right to make or unmake any law whatever' and no person or body outside the legislature 'is recognised by the law of England as having a right to override or set aside the legislation of Parliament' [AV Dicey, *An Introduction to the Study of the Law of the Constitution*, 10th edn (1959), p 40]. In other words, there are no legal limits to the legislative authority of Parliament. When that authority is exercised in the form of an Act of Parliament, no court or other body

---

1   Hence the title of Professor AW Bradley's essay on sovereignty referred to: 'The Sovereignty of Parliament—Form or Substance?', in J Jowell and D Oliver (eds), *The Changing Constitution*, 6th edn (2007) (hereafter *Changing Constitution*, 6th edn).

2   AW Bradley and ECS Wade, *Constitutional and Administrative Law*, 11th edn (1993), p 69.

has power to hold such an Act to be void or invalid or in any respect lacking in legal effect.[3]

Notes

1. It will be seen that two distinct notions emerge from the above quotations. The first is the lack of legal, as opposed to conventional or moral, constraints on Parliament. Lord Reid has expressed this idea thus:

> It is often said that it would be unconstitutional for the UK Parliament to do certain things, meaning that the moral, political and other reasons against doing them are so strong that most people would regard it as highly improper if Parliament did these things. But that does not mean that it is beyond the power of Parliament to do such things. If Parliament chose to do any of them the courts would not hold the Act of Parliament invalid.[4]

The second is the fact that the doctrine, in its orthodox form,[5] apparently pays no heed to the make-up of Parliament, or its internal proceedings. Thus, for example, the doctrine is not concerned with whether the Commons is in fact representative of the electorate[6] or whether the balance of power between the Commons and the Lords is politically acceptable.

2. If it is accepted that there are conventional restraints upon Parliament's powers (the legal and political considerations referred to by Lord Reid) then does this mean that the concept of legislative supremacy is parasitic upon the more general distinction between law and convention already considered in Chapter 2?

Traditional doctrine scrutinised

Now that the basic parameters of the traditional doctrine have been indicated, the substantive content of the doctrine may be considered more closely. As Bradley indicated above, Dicey's conception of the doctrine has been easily the most influential and has to an extent marked out the parameters of the debate which has gone on ever since.

AV Dicey, *An Introduction to the Study of the Law of the Constitution*, 10th edn (1959), pp xxxiv–xxxv (introduction by ECS Wade)

The principle of parliamentary sovereignty was repeated by the author in each edition of this book up to 1914, when he emphasised that the truth of the doctrines had never been denied. They were:

1 Parliament has the right to make or unmake any law whatever [referred to as 'the positive aspect'].

---

3   AW Bradley, 'The sovereignty of Parliament: in perpetuity?', in J Jowell and D Oliver (eds), *The Changing Constitution*, 3rd edn (1994), p 81 (hereafter *Changing Constitution*, 3rd edn).

4   *Madzimbamuto v Lardner-Burke* [1969] 1 AC 645, 723.

5   But see the views of TRS Allen below, pp 180–181 and of P Craig, 'Public Law, Political Theory and Legal Theory' [2000] PL 211.

6   See Chapter 8, pp 349–355.

2   No person or body is recognised by the law of England as having a right to override or set aside the legislation of Parliament [referred to as 'the negative aspect'].

3   The right or power of Parliament extends to every part of the Queen's dominions.

Despite recent criticism, it is still true today as a proposition of the law of the UK to say that Parliament has the right to make or unmake any law whatever. Nor can any court within the UK set aside the provisions of an Act of Parliament. All that a court of law can do with such an Act is to apply it, ie to interpret the meaning of the enactment. This is enough to satisfy the lawyer, but it must be admitted that the conception is purely a legal one.

Notes

1. Whatever the controversies surrounding Dicey's views of sovereignty, one thing is certain: it is no longer true to say that '[No] court within the [UK] [can] set aside. . . an Act of Parliament'. This has in fact happened in relation to certain provisions of two statutes, the Merchant Shipping Act 1988 and the Employment Protection (Consolidation) Act 1978.[7] The impact of EC law on parliamentary sovereignty is discussed in the next chapter, but this important caveat to the traditional view must be borne in mind during this chapter.

2. Dicey's view is in fact not as monolithic as first appears. Munro 'unpacks' the various strands of the Diceyan conception of sovereignty after citing the classical formulation quoted above.

C Munro, *Studies in Constitutional Law*, 2nd edn (1999), pp 130–33

The negative aspect, more fully expounded, is that 'there is no person or body of persons who can, under the English constitution, make rules which override or derogate from an Act of Parliament, or which (to express the same thing in other words) will be enforced by the courts in contravention of an Act of Parliament' [Dicey, p 40]. We may notice that this is no more than a recognition that Acts of Parliament are supreme within the hierarchy of laws and a fortiori prevail over any principles or rules which are not laws. Dicey demonstrates the point by reference to the absence of any legislative power able to compete with Parliament [Dicey, pp 50–61]: the Crown's authority to legislate had, since the *Case of Proclamations* [(1611) 12 Co Rep 74] been restricted; judge-made law was recognisably subordinate to statute; one of the Houses of Parliament acting alone, even the House of Commons, could not make law, as *Stockdale v Hansard* [(1839) 9 Ad and El 1] showed; the electorate, which chose the members of the Commons, had no other role in the legislative process. All of these points were uncontroversial, for they were already well established.

The positive aspect of sovereignty, however, is made to carry much more weight. 'It means not only that Parliament may legislate upon any topic, but also that any parliamentary enactment must be obeyed by the courts' [Dicey, pp 87–91 and Chapter 2]. In a further reworking, sovereignty is said to involve first that there is no law which Parliament cannot change, so that even constitutional laws of great importance may be changed in the same manner as other laws; second, the absence of any legal distinction between

---

7   The cases were, respectively: *R v Secretary of State for Transport ex parte Factortame* [1990] 2 AC 85; *ex parte Factortame (No 2)* [1991] 1 AC 603; and *R v Secretary of State for Employment ex parte Equal Opportunities Commission* [1994] 2 WLR 409.

constitutional and other laws; and third, that there exists no person or body, executive, legislative or judicial, which can pronounce void any enactment of Parliament on the ground of its being opposed to the constitution or any other ground.

Dicey's treatment of all these points as attributes of a sovereign legislature, and his referring to the positive and negative 'sides' of sovereignty, imply that we have here a number of corollaries flowing from the same proposition. Such an inference, however, would be wrong. That statute law is superior to other forms of law in the hierarchy does not necessarily entail that Parliament may legislate upon any topic or repeal any law; for example, it would be possible to maintain (and some do) that some parts of the Acts of Union between England and Scotland are unalterable, without doubting that Acts of Parliament prevail over other kinds of law. Again, the absence of a judicial power to hold Acts of Parliament void does not of itself mean that the legislature is unlimited, for in some countries excess of legislative authority may be left as a matter between the legislature and the electors, or may be dealt with by a non-judicial process. Dicey did recognise this last point, but the general impression left by his account is that the different attributes he ascribes to Parliament are all of a piece. This is not so, and it is instructive to unpack Dicey's doctrine. When we do, we see that, while the 'negative side' of sovereignty was uncontroversial, the other propositions advanced by Dicey were more wide-reaching and not so obviously justified.

In purporting to show that Parliament's legislative authority was unlimited, Dicey offered evidence of a different sort [Dicey, pp 41–50, 61–80]. He cited the opinions of Coke, Blackstone and De Lolme. He exhibited historical instances of the width of Parliament's powers; it could alter the succession to the throne, as it did in the Act of Settlement; it could prolong its own life, as with the Septennial Act of 1715; it could make legal past illegalities by Acts of Indemnity. He argued that some supposed limitations on Parliament's capacity were not real—the existence of inalienable prerogative powers could no longer be maintained; that doctrines of morality or the rules of international law could prevail against Acts of Parliament found no support in case law. Finally, Dicey denied that earlier Acts had ever limited what a Parliament could do. The language of certain enactments, such as the Acts of Union, suggested an intention to restrict later Parliaments, but their subsequent history demonstrated the futility of the attempts. Therefore, Parliament's authority was not only unlimited, but illimitable, for attempts to bind succeeding Parliaments would be ineffective.

These matters, informative as they are, scarcely compel us to accept Dicey's case. . .Dicey does not really establish that Parliament is unlimited, still less that it is illimitable. But if his propositions are not verifiable, they are falsifiable by appropriate evidence. No evidence to that effect existed at Dicey's time. We may see whether it has been thrown up in the 100 years since.

Notes

1. The actual record of matters which have been affected by legislation is undoubtedly impressive:

> Parliament has in fact passed retroactive penal legislation, prolonged its own exist-ence, transformed itself into a new body by the Acts of Union with Scotland and Ireland, repealed and amended provisions of those Acts which were to have per-manent effect, altered the procedure for making laws (under the Parliament Acts)

and followed the new procedure, and changed the succession to the throne (by the Bill of Rights, the Act of Settlement 1700, and Declaration of Abdication Act 1936).[8]

However, as Professor Henry Calvert has pointed out: 'One no more demonstrates [that the powers of the UK Parliament are unlimited] by pointing to a wide range of legislative objects than one demonstrates the contrary by pointing to matters on which Parliament has not, in fact, ever legislated.'[9]

2. Clearly, a more systematic approach is required, in which all the main possible limitations on sovereignty are examined in turn. It is to this task that the rest of this chapter is devoted.

POSSIBLE LIMITATIONS ON SOVEREIGNTY

There are a number of ways in which, theoretically, Parliament's legislative omnipotence could be limited. These fall into three main categories: first, limitations based on the *substance* of the Act, for example, its conflict with other legal systems, or with fundamental constitutional principles; second, limitations as to the *form* of the measure passed by Parliament—such limitations would arise if the courts were empowered to make an authoritative determination as to what was to count as a valid Act of Parliament; third, limitations imposed on sovereignty by Parliament itself. These matters will be examined in turn.

Limitations based on substance

Possible limitations here could be based on two grounds: first, that the statute conflicted with laws derived from other legal systems; second, that it contravened fundamental liberties or other constitutional principles. It is important to note that such limitations could take the form of a refusal to apply the statute in question, the imposition of the requirement of express words on Parliament or the employment of a restrictive interpretation of the statute.

Conflict with other legal systems

If UK law conflicts with international law, or with a provision in a treaty to which the British Government is a signatory, the position seems clear. In the Scottish case of *Mortensen v Peters* (1906) 14 SLT 227, a direct conflict arose between domestic and international law. Mortensen, a Norwegian fisherman, was charged with illegal fishing in the Moray Firth, contrary to a bylaw passed under s 7 of the Herring Fishery (Scotland) Act 1889. The bylaw extended to the whole of the Moray Firth, even though much of the Firth comprised international waters. Mortensen had been fishing in international waters, but inside the banned area and was convicted under the bylaw. He appealed.

Mortensen v Peters (1906) 14 SLT 227 (extracts)

The Lord Justice General: In this court we have nothing to do with the question of whether the legislature has or has not done what foreign powers may consider a usurpation in a

---

8   SA de Smith, *Constitutional and Administrative Law*, 6th edn (1994), pp 77–78.

9   H Calvert, *Constitutional Law in Northern Ireland* (1968), p 14.

question with them. Neither are we a tribunal sitting to decide whether an act of the legis-lature is ultra vires as in contravention of generally acknowledged principles of international law. For us an Act of Parliament, duly passed by Lords and Commons and assented to by the King, is supreme, and we are bound to give effect to its terms. . .

It is said by the appellant. . .that international law has firmly fixed that a locus such as this is beyond the limits of territorial sovereignty; and that consequently it is not to be thought that in such a place the legislature could seek to affect any but the King's subjects.

It is a trite observation that there is no such thing as a standard of international law, extraneous to the domestic law of a kingdom, to which appeal may be made. International law, so far as this Court is concerned, is the body of doctrine regarding the international rights and duties of states which has been adopted and made part of the law of Scotland.

Notes

1. Lord Kyllachy in his judgment in the case noted that 'the language of the enactment. . .is fairly express. . .to the effect of making an unlimited and unqualified prohibition, applying to the whole area specified, and affecting everybody, whether British subjects or foreigners' *(ibid)*. It may be inferred that, if the words of the Act had been less unambiguous, the courts might have attempted an interpretation which either exempted foreign nationals or limited the ambit of the Act to territorial waters, or both. Indeed, it was confirmed in *Treacy v DPP* [1971] AC 537, 552 that: 'It is. . .a general rule of construction that, unless there is something which points to a contrary intention, a statute will be taken to apply only to the UK. . .clear and express terms [would be needed to go against this rule].'

2. The finding in *Mortensen* was confirmed by the Privy Council in *Croft v Dunphy PC* [1933] AC 156, in which it was said *(per* Lord MacMillan at p 164): 'Legislation of Parliament, even in contra-vention of generally acknowledged principles of international law, is binding upon, and must be enforced by, the courts of this country.' The point may be regarded as settled (the position is of course wholly different if the conflict is with European Union law—see Chapter 5).

3. The courts apply the same principle even if contravention of the international provision in question would result in the UK breaching its treaty obligations. In *Cheney v Conn* [1968] All ER 779, a taxpayer appealed against an assessment of income tax made under the Finance Act 1964 on the basis that part of the money would be used for the construction of nuclear weapons, contrary (so it was argued) to the Geneva Convention, to which the UK was a party. His appeal was dismissed and Ungoed-Thomas J said: 'What the statute itself enacts cannot be unlawful, because what the statute says and provides is itself the law, and the highest form of law that is known to this country.'

Question

Did this *dicta* go further than was necessary to decide the case?

Note

Numerous other decisions have confirmed that domestic law overrides conflicting treaty obligations; see, for example, *Re M and H (Minors)* [1988] 3 WLR 485, 498 and *R v Secretary of State for the Home Department ex parte Brind and Others* [1991] 1 AC 696. However, the latter case, amongst others, also confirmed that it is a general principle of statutory interpretation that the courts will strive to construe a statute in such a way as to be consistent with the UK's treaty obligations where possible.

Limitations based on protection of constitutional principles?

At first sight, the notion that the courts could refuse to apply a statute on the basis that it violated fundamental constitutional or moral principles seems both to fly in the face of theory, and to be flatly contradicted by authority. For example, the question of finding a statute to be invalid was rapidly dismissed in the following case:

R v Jordan [1967] *Crim LR* 483 (extracts)

The defendant was sentenced to 18 months' imprisonment for offences under the Race Relations Act 1965. He applied for legal aid to apply for a writ of *habeas corpus* on the ground that the Act was invalid as being a curtailment of free speech.

Held, dismissing the application, that Parliament was supreme and there was no power in the courts to question the validity of an Act of Parliament. The ground of the application was completely unarguable.

Notes

1. Such decisions highlight the apparently stark contrast between the UK and other jurisdictions where judicial review of legislation is a well accepted aspect of the constitution. For example, in the famous US case of *Marbury v Madison* (1803) 1 Cranch 137, 177, Chief Justice Marshall said:

   The constitution is either a superior paramount law, unchallengeable by ordinary means, or it is on a level with ordinary legislative acts, and, like other acts, is alterable when the legislature shall be pleased to alter it. If the former part of the alternative is true, then a legislative act contrary to the constitution is not law; if the latter part be true, then written constitutions are absurd attempts, on the part of the people, to limit a power in its own nature illimitable.

   As Bradley sums up the case: '[The finding was therefore that] it was for the court where necessary to hold that an Act of Congress was void should it conflict with the terms of the constitution.'[10] Bradley goes on to note that a similar approach is adopted in many other countries where there is a written constitution, including the Republic of Ireland, Canada, Australia and Germany.

2. However, the contrast may not be as stark as would first appear. Whilst there is no precedent for a refusal to apply a statute on such grounds, and many *dicta* against the notion, the courts are in certain cases prepared to impose on Parliament very strong presumptions that it cannot have intended to violate certain principles through the interpretation the courts give to statutes. This may lead them to require that Parliament must in some way make its meaning clear beyond doubt if it wishes to violate such principles.

3. Thus, in *Phillips v Eyre* (1870) LR 6 QB 1, 23 it was said: 'the courts will not ascribe retrospective force to new laws affecting rights unless by express words or necessary implication it appears that such was the intention of the legislature.' A similar rule relating to statutes intended to have extraterritorial effect has already been noted (above). Furthermore, in the administrative law field, the courts have shown themselves willing effectively to disregard an apparently clear statutory attempt to oust their power of supervisory review.[11]

---

10   Bradley, *Changing Constitution*, 3rd edn (1994), p 81.

11   *Anisminic Ltd v Foreign Compensation Commission* [1969] 2 All ER 147, see pp 702 and 710–11.

4. In a series of cases involving human rights, decided shortly before the Human Rights Act came into force, the courts began to develop what may be termed a jurisprudence of common law fundamental rights, independent of the European Convention on Human Rights and the Human Rights Act. The main areas in which this development has taken place are access to the courts and freedom of expression, as illustrated by the following two decisions. The first concerns a challenge to a provision of *delegated* legislation.

R v Lord Chancellor ex parte Witham [1998] QB 575 (extracts)

Laws LJ. . .

The common law does not generally speak in the language of constitutional rights, for the good reason that in the absence of any sovereign text, a written constitution which is logically and legally prior to the power of legislature, executive and judiciary alike, there is on the face of it no hierarchy of rights such that any one of them is more entrenched by the law than any other and if the concept of a constitutional right is to have any meaning, it must surely sound in the protection which the law affords to it. . .In the unwritten legal order of the British state, at a time when the common law continues to accord a legislative supremacy to Parliament, the notion of a constitutional right can in my judgment inhere only in this proposition, that the right in question cannot be abrogated by the state save by specific provision in an Act of Parliament, or by regulations whose vires in main legislation specifically confers the power to abrogate. General words will not suffice and any such rights will be creatures of the common law, since their existence would not be the consequence of the democratic political process but would be logically prior to it.

. . .the right to a fair trial, which of necessity imports the right of access to the court, is as near to an absolute right as any which I can envisage. . .It has been described as a constitutional right, though the cases do not explain what that means. In this whole argument, nothing to my mind has been shown to displace the proposition that the executive cannot in law abrogate the right of access to justice, unless it is specifically so permitted by Parliament; and this is the meaning of the constitutional right. But I must explain, as I have indicated I would, what in my view the law requires by such a permission. A statute may give the permission expressly; in that case it would provide in terms that in defined circumstances the citizen may not enter the court door. In *Ex parte Leech* [1994] QB 198 the Court of Appeal accepted, as in its view the ratio of their Lordships' decision in *Raymond v Honey* [1983] 1 AC 1 vouchsafed, that it could also be done by necessary implication. However for my part I find great difficulty in conceiving a form of words capable of making it plain beyond doubt to the statute's reader that the provision in question prevents him from going to court (for that is what would be required), save in a case where that is expressly stated. The class of cases where it could be done by necessary implication is, I venture to think, a class with no members. . .

R v Secretary of State for the Home Department ex parte Simms
[2000] 2 AC 115, 131–32

Lord Hoffman: Parliamentary sovereignty means that Parliament can, if it chooses, legislate contrary to fundamental principles of human rights. . .The constraints upon its exercise by Parliament are ultimately political, not legal. But the principle of legality means that Parliament must squarely confront what it is doing and accept the political cost.

Fundamental rights cannot be overridden by general or ambiguous words. This is because there is too great a risk that the full implications of their unqualified meaning may have passed unnoticed in the democratic process. In the absence of express language or necessary implication to the contrary, the courts therefore presume that even the most general words were intended to be subject to the basic rights of the individual. In this way the courts of the United Kingdom, though acknowledging the sovereignty of Parliament, apply principles of constitutionality little different from those which exist in countries where the power of the legislature is expressly limited by a constitutional document. . .

Note

This presumption was taken further in a series of *obiter* comments made by Laws LJ in a case which raised the issue of the impact of EC law on parliamentary sovereignty. That aspect of the decision is considered in the next chapter, but his Lordship also took the opportunity to make some more general remarks about the ability of the common law to impose certain restrictions upon Parliament.

Thoburn v Sunderland City Council [2002] 1 *CMLR* 50 (extracts)

In the present state of its maturity the common law has come to recognise that there exist rights which should properly be classified as constitutional or fundamental. [His Lordship cited authority, including *Simms, Pierson* [1998] AC 539 and *Witham* (above).] And from this a further insight follows. We should recognise a hierarchy of Acts of Parliament: as it were 'ordinary' statutes and 'constitutional' statutes. The two categories must be distinguished on a principled basis. In my opinion a constitutional statute is one which (a) conditions the legal relationship between citizen and State in some general, overarching manner, or (b) enlarges or diminishes the scope of what we would now regard as fundamental constitutional rights, (a) and (b) are of necessity closely related: it is difficult to think of an instance of (a) that is not also an instance of (b). The special status of constitutional statutes follows the special status of constitutional rights. Examples are the Magna Carta, the Bill of Rights 1689, the Act of Union, the Reform Acts which distributed and enlarged the franchise, the HRA, the Scotland Act 1998 and the Government of Wales Act 1998. Ordinary statutes may be impliedly repealed. Constitutional statutes may not. For the repeal of a constitutional Act or the abrogation of a fundamental right to be effected by statute, the court would apply this test: is it shown that the legislature's actual—not imputed, constructive or presumed—intention was to effect the repeal or abrogation? I think the test could only be met by express words in the later statute, or by words so specific that the inference of an actual determination to effect the result contended for was irresistible. The ordinary rule of implied repeal does not satisfy this test. Accordingly, it has no application to constitutional statutes.

This development of the common law regarding constitutional rights, and as I would say constitutional statutes, is highly beneficial. It gives us most of the benefits of a written constitution, in which fundamental rights are accorded special respect. But it preserves the sovereignty of the legislature and the flexibility of our uncodified constitution.

Notes

1. The propositions put forward in *Simms* find echoes in other cases concerning freedom of expression. In particular, in cases where journalistic material raises political issues, broadly

defined,[12] the courts have strongly emphasised the high status freedom of speech holds in the common law, as 'a constitutional right' or 'higher legal order foundation'.[13]

2. If the courts are thus, as Laws LJ asserts, prepared to impose requirements on the *form* in which Parliament expresses itself, in order to protect fundamental constitutional principles, might they be prepared to go further, *in extremis*? Bradley and Wade consider that:

> It is not possible, by legal logic alone to demonstrate the [the courts] have utterly lost the power to 'control' an Act of Parliament, or to show that a judge who is confronted with a statute fundamentally repugnant to moral principle (for example, a law condemning all of a certain race to be executed) must either apply the statute or resign his office.[14]

It is often not recognised that statements in cases such as *Simms* or others, to the effect that Parliament can enact any statute, however repugnant are, by their nature, strictly *obiter*.[15]

3. TRS Allan sees a direct link between the democratic foundation provided for the constitution by Parliament and the legal basis for the courts' obedience to statute; but he argues that the very nature of the link implies that that such obedience can never be absolute.

TRS Allan, 'The limits of parliamentary sovereignty' [1985] *Public Law* 614, 620–22, 623–24 and 627

The legal doctrine of legislative supremacy articulates the courts' commitment to the current British scheme of parliamentary democracy. It ensures the effective expression of the political will of the electorate through the medium of its parliamentary representatives. If some conception of the nature and dimensions of the relevant political Union provides the framework for the operation of the doctrine, equally some conception of democracy must provide its substantive political content. In other words, the courts' continuing adherence to the legal doctrine of sovereignty must entail commitment to some irreducible, minimum concept of the democratic principle. That political commitment will naturally demand respect for the legislative measures adopted by Parliament as the representative assembly, a respect for which the legal doctrine is in almost all likely circumstances a suitable expression. That respect cannot, however, be a limitless one. A parliamentary enactment whose effect would be the destruction of any recognisable form of democracy (for example, a measure purporting to deprive a substantial section of the population of the vote on the grounds of their hostility to Government policies) could not consistently be applied by the courts as law. Judicial obedience to the statute in such (extreme and unlikely) circumstances could not coherently be justified in terms of the doctrine of parliamentary sovereignty since the statute would plainly undermine the fundamental political principle which the doctrine serves to protect. The practice of judicial obedience to statute cannot itself be based on the authority of statute: it can only reflect a judicial choice based on an understanding of what (in contemporary conditions) political morality

---

12 *Reynolds v Times Newspapers* [1999] 4 All ER 60; *Derbyshire County Council v Times Newspapers* [1993] AC 534; *ex parte Simms* [2000] 2 AC 115.

13 *Reynolds, ibid,* at 628–29, *per* Lord Steyn; *Simms, ibid,* at 411, *per* Lord Steyn and 412, *per* Lord Hoffman.

14 Bradley and Wade, n 2 above, p 75.

15 See Goldsworthy, *The Sovereignty of Parliament: History and Philosophy* (1999) pp 239–240.

demands. The limits of that practice of obedience must therefore be constituted by the boundaries of that political morality. An enactment which threatened the essential elements of any plausible conception of democratic government would lie beyond those boundaries. It would forfeit, by the same token, any claim to be recognised as law.

Although, therefore, Dicey's sharp distinction between the application and interpretation of statute suffices for most practical purposes, it ultimately breaks down in the face of changing views of the contours of the political Union or of serious threats to the central tenets of liberal democracy. Presumptions of legislative intent, which draw their strength from judicial perceptions of widely held notions of justice and fairness, cannot in normal circumstances override the explicit terms of an Act of Parliament. This is because a commitment to representative government and loyalty to democratic institutions are themselves fundamental constituents of our collective political morality. Judicial notions of justice must generally give way to those expressed by Parliament where they are inconsistent. The legal authority of statute depends in the final analysis, however, on its compatibility with the central core of that shared political morality. If Parliament ceased to be a representative assembly, in any plausible sense of the idea, or if it proceeded to enact legislation undermining the democratic basis of our institutions, political morality might direct judicial resistance rather than obedience. Answers [to such questions] can only be supplied as a matter of political morality and in terms of the values which the judges accept as fundamental to our constitutional order. . .

A residual judicial commitment to preserving the essentials of democracy does not provide the only constraint on parliamentary supremacy. The political morality which underlies the legal order is not exhausted by our attachment to democratic government It consists also in attitudes about what justice and fairness require in the relations between government and governed, and some of these must be fundamental. If these attitudes authorise a restrictive approach to the interpretation of statutes which, more broadly construed, would threaten fundamental values, they might equally justify rejection of statutes whose infringement of such values was sufficiently grave. If an ambiguous penal provision should, as a matter of principle, be narrowly construed in the interests of liberty and fairness, a criminal statute which lacked all precision—authorising the punishment of whatever conduct officials deemed it expedient to punish—should, on the same principle, be denied any application at all. It would be sufficient for the court to deny its application to the particular circumstances of the case before it: there would in practice be no need to make a declaration of invalidity. The result, however, would be the same: the strength of the principle of interpretation, in effect denying the statute any application at all, would reflect the scale of the affront to the moral and political values we accept as fundamental.

Question

Allan states that: 'The practice of judicial obedience to statute cannot itself be based on the authority of statute: it can only reflect a judicial choice based on an understanding of what. . .political morality demands.' Might not such obedience be attributable rather to more mundane matters, such as historical fact, the weight of tradition and the inherent conservatism of the judiciary?[16]

---

16   For the best known analysis of alleged judicial Conservative bias, see JAG Griffith, *The Politics of the Judiciary,* 4th edn (1991).

Note

Allan's thesis could strike one as theoretically interesting, but unrealistic as a prediction of how the judiciary would react to abhorrent Acts of Parliament. But his view that sovereignty is itself subject to higher order considerations has recently received influential and important judicial support, albeit by judges speaking extra-judicially. Lord Woolf first of all considers how the courts would and should react if confronted with an Act of Parliament which purported to abolish the system of judicial review.

The Rt Hon Lord Woolf of Barnes, 'Droit public—English style' [1995] *Public Law* 57, 67, 68, 69

But what happens if a party with a large majority in Parliament uses that majority to abolish the courts' entire power of judicial review in express terms. . .? Do the courts then accept that the legislation means what it says? I am sure this is in practice unthinkable. It will never happen. But if it did, for reasons I will now summarise, my own personal view is that they do not. . .

Our parliamentary democracy is based on the Rule of Law. One of the twin principles upon which the Rule of Law depends is the supremacy of Parliament in its legislative capacity. The other principle is that the courts are the final arbiters as to the interpretation and application of the law. As both Parliament and the courts derive their authority from the Rule of Law so both are subject to it and cannot act in a manner which involves its repudiation. . .

There are, however, situations where already, in upholding the Rule of Law, the courts have had to take a stand. The example that springs to mind is the *Anisminic* case [1969] [2 AC 147]. In that case even the statement in an Act of Parliament that the Commission's decision 'shall not be called in question in any court of law' did not succeed in excluding the jurisdiction of the court. Since that case Parliament has not again mounted such a challenge to the reviewing power of the High Court. There has been, and I am confident there will continue to be, mutual respect for each other's roles.

However, if Parliament did the unthinkable, then I would say that the courts would also be required to act in a manner which would be without precedent. Some judges might chose to do so by saying that it was an unrebuttable presumption that Parliament could never intend such a result. I myself would consider there were advantages in making it clear that ultimately there are even limits on the supremacy of Parliament which it is the courts' inalienable responsibility to identify and uphold. They are limits of the most modest dimensions which I believe any democrat would accept. They are no more than are necessary to enable the Rule of Law to be preserved.

Notes

1. Lord Woolf thus issues quite a clear warning that Parliament, being itself bound by the Rule of Law, may not transgress its basic requirements. His warning that an attempt by Parliament to oust judicial review might be met with judicial disobedience to the relevant statute came close to being tested in the saga over the Asylum and Immigration Bill discussed in Chapter 3, p 126 and Chapter 14 at 770–774. In that constitutional confrontation, the Government blinked first.

2. Sir John Laws (now a Court of Appeal judge) has approached the same question of possible limitations on parliamentary sovereignty. He considers the issue from a rather broader perspective than Lord Woolf, examining the consequences following from the imperative of protecting

fundamental human rights and democracy itself, and the restraints placed upon Parliament by the fact that it is itself constituted by law.

Sir John Laws, 'Law and democracy'
[1995] *Public Law* 72, 84, 85–86, 87–88, 92

Now it is only by means of compulsory law that effective rights can be accorded, so that the medium of rights is not persuasion, but the power of rule; the very power which, if misused, could be deployed to subvert rights. We therefore arrive at this position: the constitution must guarantee by positive law such rights as that of freedom of expression, since otherwise its credentials as a medium of honest rule are fatally undermined. But this requires for its achievement what I may call a higher-order law: a law which cannot be abrogated as other laws can, by the passage of a statute promoted by a Government with the necessary majority in Parliament. Otherwise the right is not in the keeping of the con-stitution at all; it is not a guaranteed right; it exists, in point of law at least, only because the Government chooses to let it exist, whereas in truth no such choice should be open to any Government. . .

It is also a condition of democracy's preservation that the power of a democratically elected Government—or Parliament—be not absolute. The institution of free and regular elections, like fundamental individual rights, has to be vindicated by a higher-order law; very obviously, no Government can tamper with it, if it is to avoid the mantle of tyranny; no Government, therefore, must be allowed to do so.

But this is not merely a plea to the merits of the matter, which can hardly be regarded as contentious; the need for higher-order law is dictated by the logic of the very notion of government under law. If we leave on one side a form of society in which a single ruler rules only by the strength of his arm, and where the only law is the ruler's dictat, we can see that any Government holds office by virtue of a framework of rules. The application of the rules determines what person or party is entitled (or, under some imaginable systems, obliged) to become the Government. This is a necessary, not a contingent truth, since the institution of government is defined by the rules; were it otherwise, we are back to the case we have proposed to set aside. Richard Latham of All Souls said this over 40 years ago:

> When the purported sovereign is anyone but a single actual person, the designation of him must include the statement of rules for the ascertainment of his will, and these rules, since their observance is a condition of the validity of his legislation, are rules of law logically prior to him.

. . .The thrust of this reasoning is that the doctrine of Parliamentary sovereignty cannot be vouched by Parliamentary legislation; a higher-order law confers it, and must of necessity limit it. . .

Parliament. . .possesses what we may indeed call a political sovereignty. It is a sovereignty which cannot be objected to, save at the price of assaulting democracy itself. But it is not a constitutional sovereignty, it does not have the status of what earlier I called a sovereign text, of the kind found in states with written constitutions. Ultimate sovereignty rests, in every civilised constitution, not with those who wield governmental power, but in the conditions under which they are permitted to do so. The constitution, not the Parliament, is in this sense sovereign.

Note
Up until very recently, such judicial arguments were limited to academic utterances by the judges. However, in the recent decision of *Jackson* we see the UK's most senior judges for the first time questioning *in the course of a judgment* the traditional notion that Parliament's legislative powers may have general limitations going beyond those required by the ECA 1972. The facts and the main arguments in the case are set out below at 188–190; they are not necessary to explain the very general *dicta* that are quoted here.

Attorney-General v Jackson [2006] 1 AC 262 (extracts)

Lord Steyn: . . . We . . . have to come back to the point about the supremacy of Parliament. We do not have an uncontrolled constitution as the Attorney General implausibly asserts. In the European context the second *Factortame* decision made that clear. . .The settlement contained in the Scotland Act 1998 also points to a divided sovereignty. Moreover, the European Convention on Human Rights as incorporated into our law by the Human Rights Act 1998, created a new legal order . . . Instead it is a legal order in which the United Kingdom assumes obligations to protect fundamental rights, not in relation to other states, but towards all individuals within its jurisdiction. The classic account given by Dicey of the doctrine of the supremacy of Parliament, pure and absolute as it was, can now be seen to be out of place in the modern United Kingdom. Nevertheless, the supremacy of Parliament is still the general principle of our constitution. It is a construct of the common law. The judges created this principle. If that it so, it is not unthinkable that circumstances could arise where the courts may have to qualify a principle established on a different hypothesis of constitutionalism. In exceptional circumstances involving an attempt to abolish judicial review or the ordinary role of the courts, the Appellate Committee of the House of Lords or a new Supreme Court may have to consider whether this is a constitutional fundamental which even a sovereign Parliament acting at the behest of a complaisant House of Commons cannot abolish. It is not necessary to explore the ramifications of this question in this opinion. No such issues arise on the present appeal. [102]

Lord Hope of Craighead: 'Our constitution is dominated by the sovereignty of Parliament. But Parliamentary sovereignty is no longer, if it ever was, absolute. . . . It is no longer right to say that its freedom to legislate admits of no qualification whatever. Step by step, gradually but surely, the English principle of the absolute legislative sovereignty of Parliament which Dicey derived from Coke and Blackstone is being qualified [104].

Baroness Hale of Richmond: The concept of Parliamentary Sovereignty which has been fundamental to the constitution of England and Wales since the 17th Century . . . means that Parliament can do anything. The courts will, of course, decline to hold that Parliament has interfered with fundamental rights unless it makes its intentions crystal clear. The courts will treat with particular suspicion (and might even reject) any attempt to subvert the rule of law by removing governmental action affecting the rights of the individual from all judicial scrutiny. Parliament has also, for the time being at least, limited its own powers by the European Communities Act 1972 and, in a different way, by the Human Rights Act 1998. It is possible that other qualifications may emerge in due course. In general, however, the constraints upon what Parliament can do are political and diplomatic rather than legal. [159]

Note

It is important to recognise that it was wholly unnecessary for the Law Lords to include such general comments, given that they saw the point they had to decide as a fairly narrow one relating to the proper construction of the Parliament Acts (see below). Their comments of course are very general and one cannot deduce from them any clear and unequivocal view that the courts now regard Parliament as subject to judicially-determined limits stemming from the rule of law or fundamental rights. Perhaps Lord Steyn's assertion that the doctrine of sovereignty is 'a construct of the common law'—and thus changeable—is of greatest significance. By contrast, Lady Hale's comment (in parentheses!) that the courts 'might even reject' a statute purporting to abolish judicial review is almost teasingly elusive. It is possible that the Law Lords had in mind the Government's attempt a few years ago to persuade Parliament to pass legislation all but abolishing judicial review in asylum cases (see further Chapter 3)—an attempt that provoked a judicial and parliamentary outcry and on which the Government was eventually forced to retreat. Their Lordships' comments cannot be seen as announcing a clear departure from orthodoxy but rather as announcing its possibility (no longer 'unthinkable'): a warning shot across the bows of future Governments and the starting of a constitutional conversation about what further limits to parliamentary sovereignty should now be accepted, in the age of EU law, devolution and the Human Rights Act.

Limitations based on form: what is 'an Act of Parliament'?

An Act of Parliament is an expression of the sovereign will of Parliament. If, however, Parliament is not constituted as Parliament or does not function as Parliament within the meaning of the law, it would seem to follow that it cannot express its sovereign will in the form of an Act of Parliament. However, the courts have declined opportunities to declare an Act a nullity where it has been asserted that something which appears to be an Act of Parliament and which bears the customary words of enactment is not authentic, or is tainted by bad faith or fraud.

Nevertheless, the fact that any Act must bear the customary words of enactment is significant. The courts will not apply the doctrine of sovereignty to motions of the constituent bodies of Parliament that do not constitute actual enactments. Bradley and Wade note that:

> . . .the courts do not attribute legislative supremacy to. . . resolution[s] of the House of Commons[17]. . .[nor] instrument[s] of subordinate legislation which appear to be issued under the authority of an Act of Parliament,[18] even though approved by the resolution of each House of Parliament[19]. . .and will if necessary decide whether or not they have legal effect. Thus, for example: 'If it should appear that a measure has not been approved by one House, then (unless the Parliament Acts 1911–49 apply) the measure is not an Act.'[20]

---

17 *Stockdale v Hansard* (1839) 9 A & E 1; *Bowles v Bank of England* [1913] 1 Ch 57.

18 For example, *Chester v Bateson* [1920] 1 KB 829; [1920] Ch 27.

19 *Hoffman-La Roche v Secretary for Trade and Industry* [1975] AC 295.

20 Bradley and Wade, n 2 above, pp 70, 82.

Notes

1. Dicey considered that it was partly due to the fact that 'the commands of Parliament can be uttered only through the combined actions of its three constituent parts'[21] which made the doctrine of parliamentary sovereignty compatible with the Rule of Law. Parliament would not in practice wield arbitrary power because, as GW Keeton puts it, 'it was a combination of diverse elements, linked together by an intricate system of "checks and balances"'.[22] It should be noted that since Dicey wrote, this balance has been tipped markedly in favour of the Commons as a result of the Parliament Acts 1911–49 (see Chapter 9).

2. As already indicated, the courts combine this very limited but important role of distinguishing Acts of Parliament from other emanations of the legislature with a refusal to enquire into the manner and means by which an apparently authentic Act was passed by the constituent parts of Parliament (subject to consideration of the validity of the use of the Parliament Acts themselves—below). Thus courts will not entertain arguments that defects in internal legislative procedure invalidate what, on its face, is a valid Act of Parliament. The simple rule therefore appears to be that courts will not declare an Act a nullity if it bears the customary words of enactment:

   > BE IT ENACTED by the Queen's most Excellent Majesty, by and with the advice and consent of the Lords Spiritual and Temporal, and Commons, in this present Parliament assembled, and by the authority of the same, as follows:-

   The rationale for this refusal is partly the fear that such an enquiry, which could for example involve determining whether the House of Commons' own Standing Orders had been complied with, could bring the courts into conflict with Parliament, which would undoubtedly have made its own enquiry on the matter, the finding of which could differ from that made by the courts. The other reason is Article 9 of the Bill of Rights 1688, which provides that 'Freedom of speech and debates or proceedings in Parliament ought not to be impeached or questioned in any court or place out of Parliament', the most important effect of which is to confer complete civil and criminal immunity upon those speaking during proceedings in Parliament (for full discussion, see Chapter 10). However, Article 9 has also been construed so as to forbid any 'questioning' in the courts of the procedures used in Parliament to pass legislation: hence the refusal to consider finding an Act of Parliament to be invalid on the grounds of defective procedure, deception of the House, etc.

3. In *Edinburgh and Dalkeith Railway Co v Wauchope* (1842) 8 Cl and F 710, the court was asked to find that the legislation in question, a private Act, had been improperly passed in that Standing Orders of the House of Commons had not been complied with, and that the Act was therefore invalid. Lord Campbell said, *obiter,* that if according to the Parliament roll an Act has passed both Houses of Parliament and has received the royal assent, a court cannot enquire into the manner in which it was introduced into Parliament nor into what passed in Parliament during its progress through the various parliamentary stages.

4. This rule, now known as 'the enrolled Bill rule', was relied upon in *Pickin v British Railways Board* [1974] AC 765. Mr Pickin had sought to challenge a private Act of 1836 on the basis that Parliament had been misled by fraud. The House of Lords held that he was not entitled to examine proceedings in Parliament to show that the Act had been passed due to fraud. The action therefore failed.

---

21   AV Dicey, *An Introduction to the Study of the Law of the Constitution,* 10th edn (1959), p 402.

22   GW Keeton, *The Passing of Parliament* (1952), p 6.

Pickin v British Railways Board [1974] AC 765, 786–88

Lord Reid: . . . In my judgment the law is correctly stated by Lord Campbell in *Edinburgh and Dalkeith Railway Co v Wauchope* (1842) 8 Cl and F 710; 1 Bell 252. . .Mr Wauchope appears to have maintained in the Court of Session that the provisions of [the Act in question] should not be applied because it had been passed without his having had notice as required by Standing Orders. This contention was abandoned in this House. Lord Brougham and Lord Cottenham said that want of notice was no ground for holding that the Act did not apply. Lord Campbell based his opinion on more general grounds. He said, 1 Bell 252, 278–279:

> all that a court of justice can look to is the parliamentary roll; they see that an Act has passed both Houses of Parliament, and that it has received the Royal Assent, and no court of justice can inquire into the manner in which it was introduced into Parliament, what was done previously to its being introduced, or what passed in Parliament during the various stages of its progress through both Houses of Parliament I therefore trust that no such inquiry will hereafter be entered into in Scotland, and that due effect will be given to every Act of Parliament, both private as well as public, upon the just construction which appears to arise upon it.

No doubt this was obiter but, so far as I am aware, no one since 1842 has doubted that it is a correct statement of the constitutional position.

The function of the court is to construe and apply the enactments of Parliament. The court has no concern with the manner in which Parliament or its officers carrying out its Standing Orders perform these functions. Any attempt to prove that they were misled by fraud or otherwise would necessarily involve an inquiry into the manner in which they had performed their functions in dealing with the Bill which became the British Railways Act 1968.

In whatever form the respondent's case is pleaded he must prove not only that the appellants acted fraudulently but also that their fraud caused damage to him by causing the enactment of s 18. He could not prove that without an examination of the manner in which the officers of Parliament dealt with the matter. So the court would, or at least might, have to adjudicate upon that.

For a century or more both Parliament and the courts have been careful not to act so as to cause conflict between them. Any such investigations as the respondent seeks could easily lead to such a conflict, and I would only support it if compelled to do so by clear authority. But it appears to me that the whole trend of authority for over a century is clearly against permitting any such investigation.

Notes

1. Lord Reid might also have cited *Lee v Bude & Torrington Junction Railway Co* (1871) LR 6 CP 576, *per* Willes J in support of his finding: 'If an Act of Parliament has been obtained improperly, it is for legislature to correct it by repealing it; but so long as it exists in law, the courts are bound to obey it.'
2. Lord Reid appears to leave the possibility open that the courts might be prepared to question whether the purported statute before them was in fact an Act of Parliament, indeed this is arguably implicit in his reference to the fact that the courts will 'apply the *enactments* of Parliament'

(emphasis added). However, he also states that the courts will not enquire into 'the way in which' Parliament or its officers carry out its Standing Orders. The problem here is that it is the Standing Orders of the two Houses which go much of the way towards defining what 'enactments' of Parliament are. Lord Reid leaves it unclear whether the courts will enquire into whether Standing Orders had been complied with *at all*.

Questioning the validity of an Act of Parliament: Attorney-General v Jackson:[23] the formal issues

We saw above that in this decision, a number of their Lordships took the opportunity to cast doubt upon the notion that Parliament remains wholly unbound by any constitutional principles; below, we consider *dicta* in that case also casting doubt on the traditional view that no Parliament may bind its successor, even as to the form of future legislation on particular areas. In this section we consider the heart of the judgment: the challenge to the validity and nature of the Parliament Act procedure. It is necessary first of all briefly to explain the provisions of the Parliament Acts.

The Parliament Act 1911 removed the power of the House of Lords to veto primary legislation and replaced it with a power to delay legislation. The power of delay over Money Bills was set at one month, the power of delay over all other Public Bills was set at two years. Thus, if a bill was rejected on three separate occasions by the House of Lords over a period of two years, then that Bill would become 'an Act of Parliament'—note the terminology used—notwithstanding the fact that the House of Lords had refused its consent. Importantly, the power given to use the new procedure did *not* extend to a Bill to extend the life of a Parliament beyond five years. Section 2(1) of the 1911 Act reads:

> If any Public Bill (other than a Money Bill or a Bill containing any provision to extend the maximum duration of Parliament beyond five years) is passed by the House of Commons in three successive sessions (whether of the same Parliament or not), and, having been sent up to the House of Lords at least one month before the end of the session, is rejected by the House of Lords in each of those sessions, that Bill shall, on its rejection for the third time by the House of Lords, unless the House of Commons direct to the contrary, be presented to His Majesty and become an Act of Parliament on the Royal Assent being signified thereto, notwithstanding that the House of Lords have not consented to the Bill.

The Parliament Act 1949 then reduced the House of Lords power of delay over Public Bills to one year. The important point to note is that, whereas the 1911 Act was passed by the full Parliament, the Parliament Act 1949 was itself passed under the provisions made by the 1911 Parliament Act. Therefore, it had not gained the consent of the House of Lords. In other words, the special provision for making legislation while bypassing the Lords was itself used to reduce the power of the Lords further. It is this feature of the 1949 Act that was to give rise to the controversy in *Jackson*.

The 'new' Parliament Acts procedure, involving a delay of only one year, has been used to pass four Acts: the War Crimes Act 1991, European Parliamentary Elections Act 1999, Sexual Offences (Amendment) Act 2000 and the Hunting Act 2004. This last Act banned fox-hunting—specifically, the hunting of wild mammals with dogs. It had to be passed using the Parliament Act procedure because of its repeated rejection by the House of Lords. The Countryside Alliance, having fought the Hunting Act

---

23 [2005] 3 WLR 733; [2006] 1 AC 262.

all the way through Parliament, and in the court of public opinion, mounted one final challenge to it—this time in the courts. Their argument centered not around the substantive provisions of the Hunting Act, but the fact that it had been passed under the 1949 Act, which they contended was itself not a valid Act of Parliament. In doing so, they drew upon a considerable body of academic opinion, as Rodney Brazier describes.

Select Committee on the Constitution, 7th Report HL 141 (2005–06) Appendix One, by Rodney Brazier (extracts)

There is no doubt that the Parliament Act 1911 is a valid statute. It was passed by both Houses and received Royal Assent. But some constitutional lawyers have doubted the validity of the 1949 Act. . . The gist of the objection to the Act is as follows:

(i)   When enacting legislation under the 1911 Act the House of Commons and the Sovereign act as delegates of the Queen (or King) in Parliament—that is, as delegates of the Commons, Lords, and the Sovereign. Legislation passed under the 1911 Act is therefore delegated legislation;

(ii) There is a general legal principle that a delegate cannot enlarge his own power: that can only be done by the delegating authority itself;

(iii) But the Commons and the Crown, although only delegates, purported to enlarge their own authority in 1949. The Commons and the Crown sought to amend their constituent Act, the 1911 statute, by reducing the Lords' period of delay prescribed under that Act, and thereby increase their own. That is something which only the King in Parliament itself could have done;

(iv) Accordingly, the Parliament Act 1949 is not an Act of Parliament at all, and consequently measures passed under it are of doubtful validity.

35. By contrast, other constitutional lawyers, such as Professors S. A. de Smith and Rodney Brazier, and Anthony Bradley and Keith Ewing, believe that the 1949 Act is valid. The essence of their argument is as follows:

(a)   The Queen in Parliament has the power, recognised at common law, to enact primary legislation;

(b)   The Queen in Parliament can provide for alternative and simpler methods of enacting primary legislation for particular purposes. In doing so, the Queen in Parliament redefines itself for those specified purpose;

(c)   That has actually been done, by providing that a Regent can be substituted for an incapacitated Sovereign and can give Royal Assent (Regency Act 1937), and that the Commons and the Sovereign can enact primary legislation, in effect leaving out the House of Lords (Parliament Act 1911);

(d)   In such a redefinition, no question of delegation arises: rather, a redefined Parliament passes primary (and wholly valid) legislation under the specified, alternative procedure; and

(e)   In any case, where the 'delegation' argument has been raised in the context of colonial legislatures the courts have been reluctant to apply it to legislatures.

Notes

1. In essence, the applicant's arguments failed in the Divisional Court, which found the Parliament Act 1949 and therefore the Hunting Act passed under it valid. So did the Court of Appeal ([2005] QB 579), though it did so in a controversial judgment which placed significant restrictions upon future possible uses of the Parliament Act. Essentially, the Court of Appeal found that the Parliament Act procedure could not be used to make 'fundamental' constitutional changes (para 45), such as abolishing the House of Lords. The Court said that 'it does not necessarily follow that because there is compliance with the requirements in the 1911 Act, the result is a valid Act of Parliament'. However, it found no reason to hold that the 1949 Act had not been a valid use of the 1911 Act: reducing the delaying power from two years to one was a 'relatively modest and straight-forward amendment', not a fundamental constitutional change. Moreover, there had been general acceptance since the time the 1949 Act was passed that it, and legislation passed under it, was valid: this was now 'a political fact' (para 97).

2. The applicants appealed to the House of Lords. Recognising the significance of the decision, the case was heard by a special nine-member panel of Law Lords, instead of the usual five. Lord Bingham's speech recognised the novelty of a court entertaining a challenge to the validity of an Act of Parliament, given the clear authority of *Pickin*.

R (on the application of Jackson) v Attorney-General [2005] 3 WLR 733; [2006] 1 AC 262 (extracts)

Lord Bingham of Cornhill: Like the Court of Appeal . . . I feel some sense of strangeness at the exercise which the courts have (with the acquiescence of the Attorney General) have been invited to undertake in these proceedings. The authority of *Pickin*. . . is unquestioned, and it was there very clearly decided that 'the courts in this country have no power to declare enacted law to be invalid.'

[Lord Bingham went on to give two reasons for hearing the appeal.]

First, in Pickin, unlike the present case, it was sought to investigate the internal workings and procedures of Parliament to demonstrate that it had been misled and so had proceeded on a false basis. This was held to be illegitimate . . . Here the court looks to the parliamentary roll and see bills . . . which have not passed both Houses. . .

My second reason is more practical. The appellants have raised a question of law which cannot, as such, be resolved by Parliament. But it would not be satisfactory, or consistent with the Rule of Law, if it could not be resolved at all. So it seems to me necessary that the courts should resolve it, and that to do so involves no breach of constitutional propriety.

[In the following paragraphs, Lord Bingham decides the central point of the appeal]:

. . .Sections 1(1) and 2(1) of the 1911 Act provide that legislation made in accordance with those provisions respectively shall 'become an Act of Parliament on the Royal Assent being signified'. The meaning of the expression 'Act of Parliament' is not doubtful, ambiguous or obscure. It is as clear and well understood as any expression in the lexicon of the law. It is used, and used only, to denote primary legislation. If there were room for doubt, which to my mind there is not, it would be resolved by comparing the language of the second resolution, quoted in para 15, with the language of section 2(1) as enacted. The resolution provided that a measure meeting the specified conditions 'shall become Law without the consent of the House of Lords on the Royal Assent being declared'. Section 2(1), as just noted, provides that a measure shall become an Act of Parliament. The change can only have been made to preclude just such an argument as the appellants are advancing. The 1911 Act did, of course, effect an important constitutional change, but the change lay not in authorising a new form of sub-primary parliamentary legislation but in creating a new way of enacting primary legislation [para 24].

[As to the contention accepted by the Court of Appeal that there were implied limitations to the changes that could be introduced under the 1911 Act, Lord Bingham said]

Here, section 2(1) makes provision, subject to three exceptions, for any public Bill which satisfies the specified conditions to become an Act of Parliament without the consent of the Lords. The first exception relates to money Bills, which are the subject of section 1 and to which different conditions apply. The second relates to Bills containing any provision to extend the maximum duration of Parliament beyond five years. I consider this exception in detail below. The third relates to Bills for confirming a provisional order, which do not fall within the expression 'public Bill' by virtue of section 5. Subject to these exceptions, section 2(1) applies to 'any' public Bill. I cannot think of any broader expression the draftsman could have used. Nor can I see any reason to infer that 'any' is used in a sense other than its colloquial, and also its dictionary, sense of 'no matter which, or what' [para 29].

[His Lordship went on to cite historical evidence from Hansard in support of the conclusion that this in fact was what Parliament had intended and went on]

The known object of the Parliament Bill, strongly resisted by the Conservative party and the source of the bitterness and intransigence which characterised the struggle over the Bill, was to secure the grant of Home Rule to Ireland. This was, by any standards, a fundamental constitutional change. So was the disestablishment of the Anglican Church in Wales, also well known to be an objective of the Government. Attempts to ensure that the 1911 Act could not be used to achieve these objects were repeatedly made and repeatedly defeated (paras 15 and 20). Whatever its practical merits, the Court of Appeal solution finds no support in the language of the Act, in principle or in the historical record.

[On this point, a clear majority of their Lordships agreed with Lord Bingham. Lord Hope 'noted' the conclusion 'that there are no legal limits to what can be done under section 2(1)' of the Parliament Act 1911 [at 120]

Baroness Hale of Richmond: The Court of Appeal concluded that the 1911 Act procedure could not be used to effect fundamental constitutional change, but that the modifications to its procedure brought about by the 1949 Act were 'modest' rather than fundamental. On the contrary, it seems to me that the 1911 Act procedure can be used to effect any constitutional change, with the one exception stated. Section 2(1) of the 1911 Act applies to 'any Public Bill (other than a Money Bill or a Bill containing any provision to extend the maximum duration of Parliament beyond five years)'. There is no hint of any other exclusions.' [158].

'It is quite clear from the words used by Parliament in section 2 of the Parliament Act 1911 that it intended no limit on the Bills which might be passed under that procedure other than those expressly stated in that section.' [166].

Notes

1. It is important to note that Lord Rodger left this point open, while Lord Carswell found it a 'difficult' point, but said (at para 179):

   Despite the general lack of enthusiasm for the proposition espoused by the Court of Appeal, however, I incline very tentatively to the view that its instinct may be right, that there may be a limit somewhere to the powers contained in section 2(1) of the 1911 Act, though the boundaries appear extremely difficult to define.

2. It should be noted that the key reasons for the contrary view of the majority are not necessarily convincing: they rely upon a literal reading of s 2(1) of the Act—something that courts very readily depart from when key constitutional principles are at stake. They rely further upon the fact that it was plainly envisaged at the time that the 1911 Act was passed that it could and indeed would shortly be used for the purpose of bringing about undoubtedly fundamental constitutional change—namely Home Rule (that is, independence) for Ireland (then part of the UK in its entirety). But the views of parliamentarians at the early part of the 20th century should not necessarily be seen as binding on the courts at the beginning of the 21st: if the provision is interpreted by reference to constitutional principle, rather than original intention, the Court of Appeal's interpretation is readily supportable.

3. One reason for the Court of Appeal's view was its concern that if the 1911 Act really did give a power of legislation to the Commons and Monarch that was unconstrained save that it could not, acting without the Lords, extend the life of Parliament, including a power to amend the 1911 Act itself, then, as Anthony Bradley (above at p 189) comments, the door was in fact open for the extension of Parliament's life without the consent of the Lords:

> the 1911 Act could be used to extend the life of Parliament, contrary to the express language of the Act. All that would be required would be the enactment under the Parliament Acts of a bill to delete from the 1911 Act the express exclusion of bills seeking to extend the life of Parliament, after which the Commons and the Queen could pass a bill that would have this effect.

This argument, whereby the safeguard against extending the life of Parliament without the consent of the Lords could be easily bypassed, clearly troubled the House of Lords, so much so that a majority of their Lordships addressed it and, *obiter*, ruled out such a 'two-step' use of the Parliament Act procedure (Lord Nicholls, Lord Steyn, Lord Hope, Baroness Hale, Lord Carswell and Lord Brown, at paras 57–59, 79, 118, 164, 175, 194). As the headnote in the *Appeal Cases* Reports puts it:

> The 1911 Act in setting up the new procedure expressly excluded its use for legislation extending the duration of Parliament. That exclusion carried with it a like exclusion in respect of legislation aimed at achieving the same result by two steps rather than one.

Lord Nicholls put it thus (at paras 57–59):

> Section 7 of the 1911 Act substituted five years for seven years as the time fixed for the maximum duration of Parliament under the Septennial Act 1715. Section 2(1) of the 1911 Act makes clear beyond a peradventure that when enacting this statute Parliament intended the Commons should not be able, by use of the new section 2 procedure, unilaterally to extend the duration of Parliament beyond this newly-reduced limit of five years. The political party currently in control of the House of Commons, whichever it might be, could not use its majority in that House as the means whereby to postpone accountability to the electorate. The Government could not, of itself, prolong its period in office beyond a maximum of five years. Despite the 1911 Act, such an extension would still require the approval of the House of Lords.
>
> So much is apparent from the express language of the Act. But would it be open to the House of Commons to do indirectly by two stages what the House cannot do

directly in one stage? In other words, could the section 2 procedure be used to force through a Bill deleting from section 2 the words 'or a Bill containing any provision to extend the maximum duration of Parliament beyond five years'? If this were possible, the Commons could then use the section 2 procedure to pass a Bill extending the duration of Parliament.

In my view the answer to these questions is a firm 'no'. The Act setting up the new procedure expressly excludes its use for legislation extending the duration of Parliament. That express exclusion carries with it, by necessary implication, a like exclusion in respect of legislation aimed at achieving the same result by two steps rather than one. If this were not so the express legislative intention could readily be defeated.

Notes

1. The difficulty with this argument is that it tends to contradict the broader view of the majority that there are no limits other than those stated to what may be done using the Parliament Act procedure. First of all, one such implied limit has been introduced (albeit that its presence is deemed logically necessary from the terms of s 2(1) itself). But more importantly, the above view surely implies support for the notion that the Parliament Act procedure could not, after all, be used to abolish the House of Lords. For if that were done, then once the Lords was abolished, the life of Parliament could be extended without the consent of the Lords (since it would no longer exist). In this way, the Commons and Monarch would, by two steps, have achieved an extension of the life of Parliament without the consent of the Lords—precisely contrary to what Lord Nicholl's terms 'the express legislative intention' of the 1911 Act.

2. A more general point is raised by *Jackson*, as explained by Alison Young:

> It was unanimously held that the court had jurisdiction to ascertain whether the Hunting Act 2004 was an Act of Parliament. . .It might appear that this challenges Dicey's theory of continuing parliamentary legislative supremacy, which requires that 'no person or body is recognised by the law of England as having a right to override or set aside the legislation of Parliament'. Here, the House of Lords had jurisdiction to assess the validity of the Hunting Act 2004. The House of Lords could have determined that the Hunting Act 2004 was invalid; implying that the court could set aside legislation. However, this is not the case. The House of Lords had jurisdiction to determine whether the Hunting Act 2004 is an Act of Parliament. If the House of Lords were to have concluded that the Hunting Act 2004 was not an Act of Parliament, this would not amount to overriding or setting aside the legislation of Parliament. Rather, the courts would be concluding that a purported Act of Parliament was not an Act of Parliament.
>
> The jurisdiction of the court to determine whether a purported statute really is an Act of Parliament has been long-recognised by the common law. . .By determining whether a purported Act of Parliament has been validly enacted by the Queen in Parliament, the courts are reinforcing parliamentary legislative supremacy, ensuring that Parliament alone may enact statutes.[24]

For further reading on the *Jackson* decision, see the end of this chapter.

3. Some of their Lordships appeared to be of the view that the Parliament Act procedure amounted to an example of Parliament binding its successors, by stipulating the procedure to be used in passing

---

certain Bills—something that Parliament is generally deemed to lack the power to do (see, e.g. Lord Hope at para 113). Whether Parliament can indeed bind its successor, and thus limit its own powers is the complex question to which we now turn.

Can Parliament limit its own powers?

According to orthodox theory, Parliament cannot limit its own powers. Parliament can expressly repeal any Act which it has previously passed, and, by the doctrine of implied repeal, if there is any inconsistency between the provisions of two different statues, the later statute is deemed impliedly to repeal any inconsistent provisions of the earlier statute. No Parliament can protect its enactments from future express or implied repeal. As Munro explains:

> It is evident that, if every succeeding Parliament is to enjoy the same degree of legislative authority as its predecessors, then attempts to bind subsequent Parliaments do not succeed. Acts which purport to bind later Parliaments, assuming Dicey was correct in his view, are not invalid, but merely ineffective (like, in varying degrees many other provisions) and, like all other enactments, liable to repeal.[25]

Distinguishing form, manner and content-based restrictions

There is a clear distinction between three ways in which, theoretically, future Parliaments could be bound, in ascending order of restrictiveness. Let us imagine a fictitious statute setting up an English Parliament in 2020, which the 2020 Parliament wishes to protect against future repeal.

First, the 2020 statute could state that it could not be repealed save by legislation drafted in a particular *form* (for example, it could stipulate that it could only be repealed by express words, not through implied repeal).

Second, the 2020 Act could state that it could only be repealed by legislation passed using a special procedure—generally referred to as a requirement of *manner*—for example, by a two-thirds majority, or after the Bill had been approved in referendum.

Third, and most drastically, the 2020 Parliament could state simply that the English Parliament Act could not be repealed at all: this may be referred to as a restriction by reference to the *substance* or *content* of future enactments, since it defines the restriction not by the wording of any future statute (form) or the way in which it should be passed (manner) but by its content—does it seek to repeal the 2020 Act?

The above are not just abstract possibilities: they represent the three main ways in which codified Constitutions of other countries are protected from being changed by the legislature.

- *Form:* Section 33(1) of the Canadian Constitution protects the Charter of Rights within the Constitution (ss 2 and 7–15) by a requirement of form, as follows:

  > Parliament. . . .may expressly declare in an Act of Parliament. . .that the Act or a provision thereof shall operate notwithstanding a provision included in section 2 or section 7 to 15 of this Charter.

---

25   Munro (1987), p 173 above, pp 86–87.

In other words, the Canadian Parliament may change or repeal these constitutional rights, but only by an Act that expressly states that it has to have effect 'notwithstanding'—that is, in spite of—the rights declared in the Charter. This is a requirement of form because it requires such an Act to use a particular form of words.

- *Manner:* a large number of constitutions, including those of South Africa[26] and the United States, require special majorities for the passage of legislation to change all or part of the Constitution. Thus Art 5 of the US Constitution requires that constitutional amendments must be passed by a two-thirds vote in each House of Congress and also receive the consent of three-quarters of the states. These are practical examples of a restriction of *manner* upon legislative change; another common manner-based restriction is the requirement of a referendum to change the constitution, as in the Republic of Ireland.

- *Content-based restrictions:* For an example of an absolute restriction upon change—one based on content—we may look to the German Constitution. Art 79 deals with amendments to the Constitution (known as the Basic Law): it states that amendments to the federal and democratic nature of the constitution and 'the basic principles laid down in Arts 1 and 20 shall be inadmissible'. Article 1 gives the basic right to human dignity, while Art 20 declares Germany to be a 'democratic, social federal state' and states that 'all state authority shall emanate from the people' while state organs are subject to the rule of law and 'the constitutional order'.

The traditionally cited evidence that the UK Parliament may not bind its successors in any way

Of course, the position in the UK is different. Because there is no authoritative constitutional document that could protect certain aspects of the constitution from change by Parliament, any restrictions of this sort would have to come from Parliament itself. The difficulty is, however, that to allow Parliament to impose such restrictions upon its successors would impede or diminish its successor's sovereignty—and at the same time would involve Parliament changing the most fundamental rule of the constitution itself. Hence the traditional view that Parliament may not impose any such restrictions. But what is the evidence for this view?

The decisions usually cited for the proposition that Parliament cannot bind its successors in any of the above ways are *Vauxhall Estates v Liverpool Corporation* [1932] 1 KB 733 and *Ellen Street Estates v Minister of Health* [1934] 1 KB 590, CA, which, as Munro states:

> concerned a provision in the Acquisition of Land (Assessment of Compensation) Act 1919 which, in regulating the compensation to be paid when land was compulsorily acquired, said that if land was acquired under the terms of any other statute, then so far as inconsistent with this Act those provisions shall cease to have or shall nor have effect. These words could be read as an attempt to preclude repeal, and since the compensation allowed for under the later Housing Act 1925 was less generous, it was in the interests of the companies involved in the two cases to plead the invalidity of the 1925 Act on that ground.[27]

The argument was rejected by the courts. In *Vauxhall Estates* it was said (*per* Avory J):

> It must be admitted that such a suggestion as that is inconsistent with the principle of the constitution of this country. Speaking for myself, I should certainly hold, until

---

26   See s 74 of the Constitution of 1996.

27   *Ibid,* p 91.

the contrary were decided, that no Act of Parliament can effectively provide that no future Act shall interfere with its provisions.

In the *Ellen Street Estate* case, it was said (*per* Maugham LJ):

> The legislature cannot, according to our constitution, bind itself as to the form of subsequent legislation and it is impossible for Parliament to enact that in a subsequent statute dealing with the same subject-matter there can be no implied repeal. If in a subsequent Act Parliament chooses to make it plain that the earlier statute is being to some extent repealed, effect must be given to that intention just because it is the will of the legislature [(1934) 1 KB 590 at 597].

It should be noted that Avory J is hardly bullish about his view of sovereignty. He states only that he would hold it 'until the contrary were decided'.

Neither case of course dealt with an actual attempt by Parliament to impose the requirement that any future legislation on the same subject must bear a particular *form*, or indeed that it must be passed in a particular manner. If anything, the 1919 Act seemed to be seeking to entrench itself completely—by reference to its own content. Hence Bradley and Wade's comment that 'Maugham LJ went far beyond the actual situation' in stating that attempts to restrict future Parliaments, e.g. by reference to the wording that must be used to achieve repeal would fail. They also note that there were only 'very weak grounds for suggesting that in 1919 Parliament had been attempting to bind its successors'.[28] The decisions were hardly surprising therefore, in the circumstances. Munro agrees, remarking: 'It should, however, be said that the *dicta* in [these] cases hardly settle the question finally with regard to all possible circumstances. It is at best doubtful whether, in that instance, Parliament had intended to prevent repeal, and it was scarcely an issue which would tempt judges to break new ground.'[29] It seems therefore that the traditionally cited authority for the proposition that Parliament cannot bind itself as to either form or substance is not conclusive. The two possibilities will therefore now be considered in more detail.

Attempts to restrict Parliaments by reference to the *content* of protected legislation

The Acts of Union with Scotland (1707) and Ireland (1800) expressed certain aspects of the constitutions of the newly created states to be fixed, variously, 'for ever', for 'all time coming' or as 'established and ascertained for ever'.[30] The theory behind the argument that certain aspects of the Act of Union are not susceptible to repeal by the UK Parliament is simple. The Act was passed not by the UK Parliament but by the English and Scottish Parliaments.[31] By passing the Act, they abolished themselves and created a successor which was constituted from the start as limited by the provisions of the Act which created it. The problem with this theory is that, as Munro notes, the UK Parliament appears to have felt free to enact, and the courts appear to have felt themselves compelled to give effect to, legislation derogating from virtually all the fundamental principles of the Act of Union with Ireland and at least some of those contained in the Scottish Union Act.[32] However, it appears that the Scottish

---

28   Bradley and Wade, n 2 above, p 77.

29   Munro (1999), p 173 above, p 160.

30   For a general discussion of these Acts, see Munro (1999), ibid, pp 137–42.

31   Respectively, the Union with England Act 1707 and the Union with Scotland Act 1706.

32   Munro (1999), above, Chapter 4.

judiciary, at least, may regard certain aspects of the Act of Union with Scotland as immune from ordinary repeal.

MacCormick v Lord Advocate 1953 SC 396 (extracts)

The Lord President (Cooper): The principle of the unlimited sovereignty of Parliament is a distinctively English principle which has no counterpart in Scottish constitutional law. . . Considering that the Union legislation extinguished the Parliaments of Scotland and England and replaced them by a new Parliament, I have difficulty in seeing why it should have been supposed that the new Parliament of Great Britain must inherit all the peculiar characteristics of the English Parliament but none of the Scottish Parliament, as if all that happened in 1707 was that Scottish representatives were admitted to the Parliament of England. That is not what was done. Further, the Treaty and the associated legislation, by which the Parliament of Great Britain was brought into being as the successor of the separate Parliaments of Scotland and England, contain some clauses which expressly reserve to the Parliament of Great Britain powers of subsequent modification, and other clauses which either contain no such power or emphatically exclude subsequent alteration by declarations that the provision shall be fundamental and unalterable in all time coming, or declarations of a like effect I have never been able to understand how it is possible to reconcile with elementary canons of construction the adoption by the English constitutional theorists of the same attitude to these markedly different types of provisions.

The Lord Advocate conceded this point by admitting that the Parliament of Great Britain 'could not' repeal or alter such 'fundamental and essential' conditions. . .I have not found in the Union legislation any provision that the Parliament of Great Britain should be 'absolutely sovereign' in the sense that that Parliament should be free to alter the Treaty at will.

Notes

1. The Lord President went on to find the issue non-justiciable: 'The making of decisions upon what must essentially be a political matter is no part of the function of the court, and is highly undesirable that it should be.' For further debate on this, see Munro, *op cit*, Chapter 4 and I McLean and A McMillan, 'Professor Dicey's Contradictions' [2007] PL 435.
2. It is interesting to note that, in the devolution legislation granting differing measures of self-government to Scotland, Wales and Northern Ireland (considered in Chapter 6), Parliament chose to make a deliberate statement affirming its continuing sovereignty over the areas devolved to the subordinate legislatures created. Whether, despite such statements, Parliament has, as a matter of political reality, and perhaps as a matter of constitutional convention, ceded sovereignty at least over the areas devolved to the Scottish Parliament is considered in Chapters 1 and 6.
3. By contrast with the devolved areas, it is clear that when it came to granting independence to former colonies, Parliament clearly purported to divest itself of authority to legislate at all in respect of them. Section 2 of the Canada Act provides that, 'No Act of the Parliament of the UK passed after the Constitution Act 1982 (Canada) comes into force shall extend to Canada as part of its law'. No one doubts that the Canadian courts would ignore any legislation subsequently passed by the UK Parliament which purported to extend to Canada, but how would the British courts react? In *Manuel v Attorney-General* [1983] Ch 77, a case concerning the issue of whether the Canada Act had itself been properly passed, the following opinion was given (*per* Megarry VC).

Manuel v Attorney-General [1983] Ch 77, 87, 88

I do not think that, as a matter of law, it makes any difference if the Act in question purports to apply outside the UK. It matters not if a convention had grown up that the UK Parliament would not legislate for that colony without the consent of the colony. Such a convention would not limit the powers of Parliament, and if Parliament legislated in breach of the convention, 'the courts could not hold the Act of Parliament invalid': (*Madzimbamuto v Lardner-Burke* [1969] 1 AC 645, 723). Similarly if the other country is a foreign state which has never been British, I do not think that any English court would or could declare the Act ultra vires and void. No doubt the Act would normally be ignored by the foreign state and would not be enforced by it, but that would not invalidate the Act in this country. Those who infringed it could not claim that it was void if proceedings within the jurisdiction were taken against them. Legal validity is one thing, enforceability is another. . . Plainly, once statute has granted independence to a country, the repeal of the statute will not make the country dependent once more; what is done is done, and is not undone by revoking the authority to do it. Heligoland did not in 1953 again become British. But if Parliament then passes an Act applying to such a country, I cannot see why that Act should not be in the some position as an Act applying to what has always been a foreign country, namely, an Act which the English courts will recognise and apply but one which the other country will in all probability ignore.

Notes

1. Munro cites this *dicta* with approval, to support his view that if, using Sir Ivor Jennings' example, a law was passed in the UK Parliament making it an offence for Frenchmen to smoke in the streets of Paris, 'English courts, if a guilty Frenchman could be apprehended while visiting Folkestone, would enforce it'.[33] It should be noted however that Megarry VC's remarks were strictly *obiter* and that the Court of Appeal did not take the opportunity to endorse them.

2. Lord Denning, in *Blackburn v Attorney-General* [1971] 1 WLR 137, considers the case of the Acts 'which have granted independence to the dominions and territories overseas'. He asks: 'Can anyone imagine that Parliament could or would reverse those laws and take away their independence? Most clearly not. Freedom once given cannot be taken away. Legal theory must give way to practical politics [p 140].' Megarry VC in *Manuel,* however, opined that 'it is clear from the context that Lord Denning was using the word 'could' in the sense of 'could effectively'; I cannot read it as meaning 'could as a matter of abstract law'' (p 89). *Is* this clear?

3. The case of *Madzimbamuto v Lardner-Burke* [1969] 1 AC 526 concerned the attempt by Parliament to reassert its right to legislate for Southern Rhodesia, after that country, having 'in practice enjoyed self-government and legislative autonomy for many years'[34] unilaterally declared full independence. The Privy Council found that the UK Parliament was, as a matter of law, still competent to legislate for Rhodesia. It should be noted, however, that there had, in that case, been no formal renunciation by Parliament of legislative competence, along the lines of s 2 of the Canada Act. This case did not therefore really answer the question whether Parliament can deprive itself of legislative competence; it stated only that the unilateral act of a dependant territory could not do so, a scarcely surprising finding.

---

33   Munro (1999), p 173 above, p 153.

34   *Ibid,* p 151.

Attempts to bind as to the manner and/or form of future legislation

Evidence from decided cases

Section 1 of the Northern Ireland Act 1998[35] provides that Northern Ireland will not cease to be part of her Majesty's dominions without the consent of the majority of the people of Northern Ireland voting in a poll. How would the courts treat this provision? Some guidance may be gleaned from cases in which the Privy Council or courts in other common law jurisdictions have had to rule on the lawfulness of such provisions. One of the key cases is *Attorney-General for New South Wales v Trethowan* [1932] AC 526, PC, a decision of the Privy Council which concerned the New South Wales legislature. That legislature was subject to s 5 of the Colonial Laws Validity Act 1865, which provided:

> every representative legislature shall, in respect to the colony under its jurisdiction, have, and be deemed at all times to have had, full power to make laws respecting the constitution, power and procedure of such legislature; provided that such laws shall have been passed in such manner and form as may from time to time be required by any Act of Parliament, letters patent, order in council, or colonial law for the time being in force in the said colony.

The facts were as follows.

> In 1929 the Parliament of New South Wales passed an Act which provided that no Bill for abolishing the upper house of the legislature (the Legislative Council) should be presented for the royal assent unless it had been approved at a referendum by a majority of the electors. [It did this by amending the Constitution Act 1902, previously passed by that Parliament, adding a new s 7A.] It was further provided that this requirement of a referendum might not itself be repealed except by the same process. The aim of the right-wing Government which sponsored the legislation was to 'entrench' the position of the upper house, which the Labour Party had declared its intention to abolish. In 1930, however, a new Parliament was elected in which the Labour Party held the majority of seats in the lower house. Two Bills were passed through both Houses, the first purporting to repeal the referendum requirement, and the second purporting to abolish the Legislative Council. Neither Bill was submitted to the electors, and accordingly two members of the threatened Legislative Council sought an injunction to restrain the submission of these Bills for royal assent. The Supreme Court of New South Wales granted the injunction and the decision was appealed to the High Court of Australia, its highest court.[36]

Thus far then, it had been found that the New South Wales Parliament was bound by its previous Act requiring a referendum before the abolition of the Upper House. The High Court[37] made the same finding, dismissing the appeal. Dixon J stated clearly that he founded his judgment upon:

---

35   This is the Act which puts in place the legislative framework for the Good Friday Agreement (see further Chapter 1); the provision it contains was previously set out in s 1 of the Northern Ireland Constitution Act 1973.

36   Munro (1999), p 173 above, p 158.

37   *Attorney-General of New South Wales v Trethowan* (1931) 44 CLR 401.

> a consideration of the true meaning and effect of the written instruments from which the Parliament of New South Wales derives its legislative power. . . not. . .by the direct application of the doctrine of parliamentary sovereignty, which gives to the Imperial Parliament [the British Parliament] its supremacy over the law.

However, he went on to add that in his opinion, if an Act of the British Parliament had also laid down that a referendum must be held before it could be repealed, the courts 'would be bound to pronounce it unlawful' to allow a future Bill that repealed the Act without having held such a referendum to go to Royal Assent. In other words, the judge suggested that the UK Parliament could, after all, lay restrictions upon its future self.

The decision was then appealed to the UK Privy Council, then still Supreme Court for Australia on such matters. The Privy Council dismissed the appeal,[38] thus again upholding the right of the New South Wales Parliament to bind its successors. However, Viscount Sankey LC made it clear that 'The answer depends . . . entirely upon a consideration of the meaning and effect of s 5 of the [Colonial Laws Validity] Act of 1865'—the Act of the UK Parliament which gave legislative powers to the NSW Parliament. His Lordship said:

> Reading section [5] as a whole, it gives to the legislature of New South Wales certain powers, subject to this, that in respect of certain laws they can only become effectual provided they have been passed in such manner and form as may from time to time be required by any Act still on the statute book. Beyond that, the words 'manner and form' are amply wide enough to cover an enactment providing that a Bill is to be submitted to the electors and that unless and until a majority of the electors voting approve the Bill it shall not be presented to the Governor for His Majesty's assent.

In other words, the New South Wales Parliament was entitled, *because of s 5*, to prescribe that certain statutes could only be repealed using the procedure that those statutes laid down—in this case, a prior affirmative vote in a referendum. Further, if an attempt was made to repeal such a statute without following the procedure it had prescribed, the courts had the power to declare it unlawful.

Munro suggests that there are two possible views of this case:

> The first is that there is a general rule that legislation may be enacted only in such manner and form as is laid down by law, and that the UK Parliament is just as subject to that rule as was the New South Wales legislature. This view gains support from the dicta in the second paragraph of Dixon J's judgment in the High Court. However, the opposing view is that the decision has no relevance at all. The Privy Council said that the case depended 'entirely upon a consideration of the meaning and effect of s 5 of the Act of 1865' and it is hard to see how this can tell us anything about the UK Parliament, whose powers are not defined in or derived from any statute.[39]

It is hard not to agree with Munro.

---

38   [1932] AC 526, PC

39   (1999), p 173 above, p 158.

Questions

❶   In relation to the Northern Ireland Act 1998, how would the courts react if:

(a)   the UK Parliament passed an Act ceding Northern Ireland to the Republic of Ireland, and the Act did not recite that a majority of Northern Ireland citizens had approved the change in a poll?

(b)   the UK Parliament passed an Act repealing the s 1 guarantee without taking a poll?

❷   In relation to (b), would it make any difference if s 1 had stated that its own provisions could not be repealed without taking a poll?

Manner and form restrictions on sovereignty: the theory

A number of writers have taken the view that while Parliament may not bind itself in such a way as to prevent itself outright from changing the law in a given area (a content-based restriction), it may pass legislation (as did the New South Wales Parliament) which establishes that future legislation on a given area must conform to a 'manner and form' requirements laid down in the original statute. As Geoffrey Marshall puts it:

> Parliament. . .might conceivably bind the future or circumscribe the freedom of future legislators, not by laying down blanket prohibitions or attempting to enact a fundamental Bill of Rights, but by using their authority to provide different forms and procedures for legislation. A referendum or a joint sitting, for example, might be prescribed before certain things could be done. Or a two-thirds majority. Or a 75% or 80% majority. If it is also provided that any repeal of such provisions should not be by simple majority, the courts may be able to protect the arrangements laid down by declaring in suitable proceedings that any purported repeal by simple majority of a protected provision is ultra vires as being not, in the sense required by law, an 'Act of Parliament'. In this finding they would not be in any way derogating from parliamentary sovereignty but protecting Parliament's authority from usurpation by those not entitled for the purpose in hand to exercise it.[40]

This view, had, by the 1970s received support from a number of distinguished commentators.[41] RFV Heuston has produced a well known formulation of the theory.

RFV Heuston, *Essays in Constitutional Law*, 2nd edn (1964), pp 6–7

It is suggested that the new view can be summarised thus:

1   Sovereignty is a legal concept the rules which identify the sovereign and prescribe its composition and functions are logically prior to it.

---

40   *Constitutional Theory* (1971), p 42.

41   RFV Heuston, *Essays in Constitutional Law*, 1st edn (1961), 2nd edn (1964), Chapter 1; G Marshall, *Parliamentary Sovereignty and the Commonwealth* (1957); *ibid*, Chapter 3; JDB Mitchell, *Constitutional Law*, 2nd edn (1968), Chapter 4; and SA de Smith, *Constitutional and Administrative Law*, 2nd edn (1973), Chapter 4.

2 There is a distinction between rules which govern, on the one hand, (a) the com-position, and (b) the procedure, and, on the other hand, (c) the area of power, of a sovereign legislature.

3 The courts have jurisdiction to question the validity of an alleged Act of Parliament on grounds 2(a) and 2(b), but not on ground 2(c).

4 This jurisdiction is exercisable either before or after the Royal Assent has been signified—in the former case by way of injunction, in the latter by way of declaratory judgment.

Notes

1. The major difficulty with this view is that it does not provide an answer as to *what kinds* of laws Parliament should be able to protect in this manner. As we saw above, these kinds of restrictions are usually considered in relation to the protection of a Bill of Rights or other aspects of the constitutional order. The difficulty is that the assertion that Parliament can bind itself as to manner and form is not by its nature inherently limited in this way but is put *in general terms,* as if any law passed by Parliament could be thus protected. The problem with such a view, of course, is that to grant such a power to Parliament would amount to a direct and comprehensive threat to democracy. For if Parliament could, whenever it wished, provide that a given law could only be repealed by a two-thirds majority, then what would stop one Parliament, controlled, say, by a Conservative Government, from passing a Finance Act cutting income tax to 15% and including a provision that the Act could not be repealed or modified except by that majority? In such a case, a new Government, elected on a policy of increasing spending and raising tax, would find a statute increasing the level of income tax, but passed in the ordinary manner, declared *ultra vires* in the courts. Thus, the rule that Parliament cannot bind itself is not merely a technical matter of constitutional law: it protects the democratic rights of future majorities to reverse the decisions of previous ones. Any proponent of the 'manner and form' school must therefore incorporate within his or her argument some suggested definition as to the areas of law which Parliament should be able to protect and those which it must *not* be able to.

2. We have been discussing a possible 'rule' or 'law' that Parliament cannot bind itself. What is the source of this law? The answer, interestingly enough, is directly related to the question of whether Parliament can change or 'break' this law. As Bradley notes:

   In the absence of a written constitution for the UK, where is the source of the legal rule that there are no limits on the legislative capacity of Parliament and that the courts may not review the validity of legislation? For reasons of logic, we should not expect to find this rule created by an Act of Parliament. As was said by the jurist Salmond, 'No statute can confer this power upon Parliament, for this would be to assume and act on the very power to be conferred' [*Salmond on Jurisprudence* (PJ Fitzgerald (ed)), 12th edn (1966), p 111]. . .It is to the decisions of the courts that we must look to discover propositions about the legislative powers of Parliament.[42]

3. In his 2007 essay, Bradley goes on to note Dicey's formulation that the Queen in Parliament 'has *under the English constitution,* the right to make or unmake any law whatever'.[43] He points out that

---

42   Bradley, n 1 above, p 87.

43   Bradley, *Changing Constitution,* 6th edn (2004), p 30 (Bradley's emphasis).

in countries with a codified constitution, the power of the legislature to make law, and any limitations thereon, are laid down in that constitutional document. He goes on:

> By contrast, since the UK has no written constitution, for Dicey to refer to 'the constitution' as the source of Parliament's authority is but to create difficulty. What *is* the constitution in the absence of a written text? One political historian has written that constitution is a historical process, 'an integrated expression of historical experience, conferring a united meaning on political existence'. A senior Judge, Sir John Laws, has suggested that the absence of a written constitution 'means that the legal distribution of public power consists ultimately in a dynamic settlement, acceptable to the people, between the different arms of government'. Emphasis on a dynamic historical experience is important, since the 'constitution' of the UK is today experiencing a period of change. . .The substance of constitutional law reflects the evolutionary nature of the unwritten constitution. To quote Sir John Salmond. . .
>
>> The constitution as a matter of fact is logically prior to the constitution as a matter of law. In other words, constitutional practice is logically prior to constitutional law . . . Constitutional law follows hard upon the heels of constitutional fact.
>
> Just as the UK's constitutional law after 1945 came to reflect the end of Empire, so more recently it has adjusted to events that have taken the UK into the EU. Since 1998, the incorporation in national law or rights under the [ECHR] and the devolution of powers to Scotland and Wales are important political events to which the structure of constitutional law must also adjust.[44]

Notes

1. Bradley thus argues that in a state with an uncodified, flexible and evolving constitution, the powers that constitution affords to its legislature are necessarily subject to alteration as political and constitutional circumstances alter.
2. Sir Ivor Jennings has argued on this point as follows: the rules governing sovereignty are derived from the common law; Parliament can change the common law in any way; therefore Parliament can change the rules which relate to its own sovereignty.[45] Wade has replied to this argument as follows.

HWR Wade, 'The basis of legal sovereignty' *[1955] Cambridge Law Journal* 186–89

At the heart of the matter lies the question whether the rule of common law which says that the courts will enforce statutes can itself be altered by a statute. Adherents of the traditional theory, who hold that future Parliaments cannot be bound, are here compelled to answer 'no'. For if they answer 'yes', they must yield to Jennings' reasoning.

But to deny that Parliament can alter this particular Rule of Law is not so daring as it may seem at first sight; for the sacrosanctity of the rule is an inexorable corollary of Parliament's continuing sovereignty. If the one proposition is asserted, the other must be conceded. Nevertheless some further justification is called for, since there must be something peculiar about a rule of common law which can stand against a statute.

---

44   *Ibid* at 30–31, references omitted.

45   This formulation of Jennings' argument is given by Bradley and Wade, n 2 above, p 103.

The peculiarity lies in this, that the rule enjoining judicial obedience to statutes is one of the fundamental rules upon which the legal system depends. . .

Once this truth is grasped, the dilemma is solved. For if no statute can establish the rule that the courts obey Acts of Parliament, similarly no statute can alter or abolish that rule. The rule is above and beyond the reach of statute, as Salmond so well explains, because it is itself the source of the authority of statute. This puts it into a class by itself among rules of common law, and the apparent paradox that it is unalterable by Parliament turns out to be a truism. The rule of judicial obedience is in one sense a rule of common law, but in another sense — which applies to no other rule of common law — it is the ultimate political fact upon which the whole system of legislation hangs. Legislation owes its authority to the rule: the rule does not owe its authority to legislation. To say that Parliament can change the rule, merely because it can change any other rule, is to put the cart before the horse.

What Salmond calls the 'ultimate legal principle' is therefore a rule which is unique in being unchangeable by Parliament — it is changed by revolution, not by legislation; it lies in the keeping of the courts, and no Act of Parliament can take it from them. This is only another way of saying that it is always for the courts, in the last resort, to say what is a valid Act of Parliament; and that the decision of this question is not determined by any rule of law which can be laid down or altered by any authority outside the courts. It is simply a political fact. If this is accepted, there is a fallacy in Jennings' argument that the law requires the courts to obey any rule enacted by the legislature, including a law which alters this law itself. For this law itself is ultimate and unalterable by any legal authority.

Notes

1. Bradley notes the core of Wade's argument, 'If no statute can establish the rule that the courts obey Acts of Parliament, similarly no statute can alter or abolish that rule', and goes on: 'Wade's argument at this crucial point depends for its logical strength upon the word "similarly" (consider the argument "No person can bring his own life into being; similarly, no person can bring his own life to an end"), and it does not take adequate account of the fact that Parliament's legislative power includes power to make constitutional changes.'[46]

2. One key question then is how the rules of sovereignty may be altered. As seen above, Jennings argued that the rule that Parliament may not bind its successors is a common law rule that may be changed by Parliament, like any other rule. Others have suggested that as a common law rule, it may be changed by the courts,[47] while Wade, in the extract above, suggested that neither courts nor Parliament could change it, but only revolution. A more thorough examination of the argument that sovereignty is a common law doctrine and may therefore be changed by the judiciary or Parliament has been provided by Goldsworthy. His explanation depends upon an understanding of Hart's theory of a Rule of Recognition, advanced in his seminal work, *The Concept of Law* (1961).

---

46   Bradley, n 2 above, p 88.

47   E.g. the judgment of Sir John Laws in *Thoburn* (above, p 179).

JD Goldsworthy, *The Sovereignty of Parliament: History and Philosophy* (1999), pp 237–41, 243–46

Fundamental human laws can come into existence either by express agreement among the members of a Union, or at least the most powerful of them, as in the case of the adoption of a written constitution, or by the gradual development of customs, as in the case of rules of succession governing traditional monarchical systems. In both cases, the continued existence of such laws depends on their being accepted as binding, at least by people who are able to force others to comply with them. To accept that such a law is binding is to have what Hart called the 'internal point of view' towards the law: it is to believe that there are good reasons for insisting that it be obeyed, and for criticising those who fail to obey it.

Hart argued that for a legal system to exist, its most fundamental laws must be accepted as binding by its most senior officials, and the system as a whole must be generally obeyed, for whatever reason, by those subject to it. Indeed, the most fundamental laws of any legal system simply are whatever laws are accepted as binding, and routinely applied in administering the system, by its most senior officials. The most important of these laws is a 'rule of recognition', which specifies the criteria that determine what other laws should be recognised as members of the system or, in other words, as valid laws. While the existence, as valid laws, of all the other laws of the system depends on their satisfying those criteria, the existence of the rule of recognition itself depends on its being accepted as binding by the most senior officials of the system, and on their decisions being generally obeyed by everyone else. Those officials must adopt the internal point of view, but ordinary citizens need not.

According to Hart, the content of the rule of recognition, in any legal system, is entirely a matter of fact. It is whatever rule that system's most senior officials, including its judges, do in fact accept and apply in identifying valid laws of the system, irrespective of its merits from the perspective of political morality. That we might regard as morally repugnant the rule of recognition actually accepted and applied by the most senior officials of some legal system cannot alter the fact that it is a fundamental law of that system. If it confers sovereign law-making authority upon some person or institution, their unworthiness to exercise such authority cannot diminish the fact that they have it. Denying that fact would be as futile as denying that Hitler was Chancellor of Germany, because of the iniquity of his actions.

In Britain, the most senior legal officials, including judges, have for a very long time recognized as legally valid whatever statutes Parliament has enacted, and have often said that they are bound to do so. In applying Hart's theory to the British legal system, the ease for regarding the sovereignty of Parliament as a central component of its rule of recognition seems clear cut, as Hart himself apparently believed. Fear that Parliament might one day grossly abuse its authority might be a good reason to change the rule, but that is a different matter.

[Having set out this framework, Goldsworthy then goes on to consider what he regards as the fallacious argument that the rule of parliamentary sovereignty is judge-made law. While in doing so, he in part agrees with Wade in viewing the law of sovereignty as a unique kind of rule, he rejects Wade's view that it cannot be changed, save by revolution.]

Now it is true that Parliament did not, and could not, confer sovereign authority on itself by statute. But it is less often noted that for similar reasons the doctrine of parliamentary sovereignty cannot be a product of judicial law-making. The argument that it is judge-made consists of four steps: first, that there are only two kinds of law in Britain, statute law and common law: second, that the doctrine could not have been established by statute, because that would have been question-begging: third, that it must therefore be a matter of common law: and fourth, that the common law is judge-made law.

The argument fails because of the conjunction of the first and fourth steps. To say both that there are only two types of law in Britain, statute law and common law, and that the common law has been made by judges, is to say that all law in Britain has been deliberately made, either by Parliament, or by the judges. But if so, what could be the legal source of the judges' authority to make the common law? It could not be statute, because that would create a vicious circle (since the point of the argument is that Parliament's authority to enact statutes was conferred by the judges). The only alternative consistent with the argument is to think that the judges conferred authority on themselves. But that would be just as question-begging as the discredited idea that Parliament conferred authority on itself by statute.

The source of these logical difficulties is the Hobbesian assumption that every law, including those conferring authority on Parliament, and on the judges, must originally have been deliberately made by someone, and if it was not Parliament, then it must have been the judges. That assumption leads to the question-begging conclusion that either Parliament, or the judges, originally conferred legal authority on themselves. But the truth is that the judges are no more qualified than Parliament to be regarded as a Hobbesian sovereign, ultimately responsible for the creation of all law. The authority of either Parliament, or the judges, or both, must be based on laws that neither was solely responsible for creating. Those more fundamental laws are what Hart called the 'secondary rules' of the legal system, comprising rules of recognition, change, and adjudication. A necessary condition for the existence of such rules is a consensus among the most senior officials of the legal system, in all three branches of government, legislative, executive, and judicial. This avoids the question-begging that is implicit in any one branch of government purporting to confer law-making authority on itself. Parliament's sovereignty was not created by the judges alone, and its continued existence depends only partly, and not solely, on their willingness to accept it.

A common mistake in the interpretation of Hart's theory is to think that the rule of recognition is constituted by the practices and convictions of the judiciary alone. This is clearly not what Hart meant in the first edition of *The Concept of Law*. In describing the rule of recognition, he continually referred to its being constituted by the practices of legal officials in general: it 'rests simply on the fact that it is accepted and used as such a rule in the judicial and other official operations of a [legal] system whose rules are generally obeyed' [at p 117, emphasis added]. The reason why Hart insisted that no legal system can exist unless its officials adopt the internal point of view towards its most fundamental rules, and particularly its rule of recognition, is that 'the characteristic unity and continuity of a legal system' depends on the acceptance of 'common standards of legal validity' [at p 113].

He pointed out that if only some judges accepted the sovereignty of Parliament, and they made no criticisms of those who did not, ordinary citizens would sooner or later be faced with contradictory legal directives. The legal system would disintegrate into chaos. But this reasoning extends to all of the most senior officials of the system: the same disastrous consequences would flow from a rift between the judiciary as a whole, and the other branches of government.

... It follows that either the first or the fourth steps of the fallacious argument previously criticized must be rejected, either parliamentary sovereignty is a matter of neither statute law nor common law, or it is a common law doctrine that was not made by the judges. The second alternative is certainly arguable. The term 'common law' is now somewhat ambiguous. Until relatively recently, it meant customary law, which judges discovered and enunciated but did not make, whereas today, it usually means judge-made law. It is wrong to describe the doctrine of parliamentary sovereignty as a matter of common law in the modern sense of judge-made law. But it can be described as a matter of common law in the old sense of the term, meaning a custom that the courts have recognized, but did not create, and therefore cannot unilaterally change. It is indeed a creature of custom—or at least, of custom among senior legal officials—that gradually evolved from the sovereignty of the medieval King. Nevertheless, it might help prevent confusion if the doctrine were not described as one of common law, because its nature and status are so different from those of all other common law doctrines, as we understand them today.

... It does not follow that the doctrine of parliamentary sovereignty cannot be changed. There are many examples of fundamental legal rules changing as a result of official consensus changing. In the Australia Act 1986 (UK), the United Kingdom Parliament relinquished its authority to alter Australian law. If it attempted to resume that authority by repealing the Act, Australian courts would almost certainly refuse to accept the validity of the repeal, even if this meant repudiating the doctrine of parliamentary sovereignty that they themselves accepted many years ago. But this change in the allegiance of Australian courts is part of a change in the allegiance of all senior legal officials, and citizens in Australia, and would therefore be universally accepted there as legitimate. Indeed, a refusal by Australian courts to subscribe to that general change in allegiance would provoke political conflict between them and the other branches of government.

... Of course, a change in a fundamental legal rule has to start somewhere: someone has to initiate the requisite change in the official consensus that constitutes it. Parliament can do so, by enacting legislation such as the Australia Act, or the European Communities Act, provided that the courts are willing to accept the change. Alternatively, the courts can initiate change, provided that the other branches of government are willing to accept it. An example of this is the way in which the courts today are increasingly subjecting the exercise of royal prerogatives to judicial review. In past centuries, this would have been vehemently opposed by the executive branch of government, and blocked by legislation. The courts have been permitted to expand their authority to control the exercise of power by the executive government only because its attitudes, as well as their own, have changed.

It is sometimes suggested that any change in the fundamental rules of a legal system, brought about by a change in official consensus, must be described as 'extra-legal' or even 'revolutionary' [Wade, above]. This is debatable. There are important differences between abrupt changes to fundamental legal rules, imposed on many senior officials through their coercion or removal from office, and gradual changes resulting from a voluntary change of mind on their part in response to broader social developments. In the latter case, it may be appropriate to say that the rules have evolved legally. Be that as it may, there is nothing necessarily wrong with one group of officials attempting to initiate change in the fundamental rules of their legal system. But great caution is needed. If significant numbers of other officials are unlikely to agree with them, the result may be conflict endangering the stability of the system. . . A unilateral rejection by British courts of the doctrine of parliamentary sovereignty is unlikely to be meekly accepted by the other branches of government. Instead, they are likely to condemn it as an illegitimate attempt to alter the currently accepted balance of power, in favour of the courts. By unsettling what has for centuries been regarded as settled, the courts would risk conflict with the other branches of government that might dangerously destabilize the legal system.

Note

In summary, then, Goldsworthy's view is that alterations of the law of sovereignty lie beyond the unilateral action of either Parliament or the courts, since the law of sovereignty was produced by neither acting alone. However, Goldsworthy avoids Wade's implausible attitude that the law of parliamentary sovereignty is unalterable, save by revolution. Wade's view was placed in some difficulty by the decision in *Factortame,* which, as we have noted, amounted to a change to that law, whereas Goldsworthy is able to encompass it as an example of a change 'tacitly agreed' between Parliament and the courts.[48] The impact of that decision on traditional understandings of sovereignty is further explored below.

May Parliament now bind itself as to the *form* of future legislation? Recent evidence

As seen above, the literature in this area tends to discuss whether Parliament can bind itself as to 'manner and form', as if the two types of restrictions may readily be lumped together. In fact, they are very distinct, in two ways. First of all, there is now clear evidence that Parliament *can* bind itself, at least as to the *form* of future legislation; there is no such evidence in relation to restrictions as to *manner*. As we saw above, cases from the Commonwealth, such as *Attorney-General for New South Wales v Trethowan* [1932] AC 526, PC are inconclusive when applied to the UK Parliament. Second, it should be recognised that a restriction based merely on form—that is, a requirement that a future statute must use express words in order to undo a previous statute—amounts to no real restriction upon the freedom of action of a future Parliament. It is a moment's work for a draftsman to insert such words into a statute. As Goldsworthy puts it, 'a Parliament that can only effectively legislate if it uses a particular form of words, to ensure that its intentions are unmistakeable, is still free to legislate whenever it wishes to do so'.[49] By contrast, a requirement, say, that a two-thirds majority must be used to overturn a previous statute amounts to a very real fettering of future Parliaments, and thus a very real entrenchment of the provision in question, because such majorities, unlike the strokes of a draftsman's pen, are not at the disposal of a Government.

What then is the evidence that Parliament may now restrict itself as to the *form* of future legislation? The clearest example relates to the European Communities Act 1972 and its interpretation in the case of *R v Secretary of State for Transport ex parte Factortame (No 2)* [1992] 3 WLR 285. This issue is considered in detail in the next chapter.

The other area in which Parliament may have limited itself as to form is in the area of those rights guaranteed under the European Convention on Human Rights, now incorporated into UK law under the Human Rights Act 1998 (HRA) (see further Chapter 17). The Act does not make any formal attempt to entrench itself. Indeed it provides that if any statutes contain provisions found to be inconsistent with any of the Convention rights, such statutes will remain valid and of full effect (ss 3(2)(b) and 4(6)). Section 4 states:

---

48   See p 205 above, at p 244.

49   Ibid, at p 245.

(1) Subsection (2) applies in any proceedings in which a court determines whether a provision of primary legislation is compatible with a Convention right.

(2) If the court is satisfied that the provision is incompatible with a Convention right, it may make a declaration of that incompatibility.

. . .

(6) A declaration under this section ('a declaration of incompatibility')—

(a) does not affect the validity, continuing operation or enforcement of the provision in respect of which it is given. . .

In part, the Act in effect simply confirms the orthodox constitutional position, that later statutes override previous inconsistent ones. In this respect, the HRA is of the same status as any other Act of Parliament although it introduces the innovation of the formal judicial declaration of incompatibility under ss 4 and 10. Such a declaration can trigger the parliamentary 'fast track' procedure for amending the offending legislation by means of secondary legislation but this leaves Parliament entirely free as to whether to remedy the incompatibility which the courts have found to exist.

However, in relation to statutes passed *prior* to the HRA, the Act provides for a departure from orthodoxy. Under the doctrine of implied repeal, one would expect, where it was found that a provision in a statute *pre-dating* the HRA was incompatible with one or more of the Convention rights, that the provision would be impliedly repealed. However, ss 3(2)(b) and 4(6) do not take this route: by stating that the provisions of *any* statute found to be incompatible with Convention rights remain valid and in force, they have the effect that the doctrine of implied repeal will not apply to the HRA. In other words, where a provision of an *earlier* statute is found to be incompatible with a Convention right, it will nevertheless remain in force. In this respect, then, the HRA makes a quite clear alteration to the normal rules of parliamentary sovereignty. [50]

It may, however, make a further and more important alteration. Section 3(1) of the Act provides: 'So far as it is possible to do so, primary legislation and subordinate legislation must be read and given effect in a way which is compatible with the Convention rights.' The meaning and effect of this provision were considered by the House of Lords in *R v A (No 2)* [2001] 2 Cr App R 21, now the leading decision on s 3. The case concerned the interpretation to be given to s 41 of the Youth Justice and Criminal Evidence Act 1999 which prohibited the giving of evidence in a rape trial of the woman's sexual history, including any previous sexual history with the alleged rapist, except in very limited circumstances.[51] This was thought to raise an issue of compatibility with Art 6 of the European Convention on Human Rights (ECHR) which provides:

1. In the determination of his civil rights and obligations or of any criminal charge against him, everyone is entitled to a fair and public hearing within a reasonable time by an independent and impartial tribunal established by law. . .

3. Everyone charged with a criminal offence has the following, minimum rights:

. . .

(d) to examine or have examined witnesses against him and to obtain the attendance and examination of witnesses on his behalf under the same conditions as witnesses against him. . .

---

50   For discussion of the relevance of s 19 HRA to this issue, see Chapter 1 at 30.

51   These included instances where that history was said to be relevant to the defendant's *belief* in consent. The discussion in the text concerned the circumstances in which such evidence could be admitted as to whether the women *did in fact* consent.

The argument essentially was that to refuse to allow the defence to admit evidence of previous sexual relations between the alleged victim and the defendant would violate the defendant's right to a fair trial. The House of Lords found first of all, 'that on ordinary principles of construction, s 41 of the Youth Justice and Criminal Evidence Act 1999 was *prima facie* capable of preventing an accused person from putting forward evidence critical to his defence and, thus construed, was incompatible with Article 6 of the ECHR' (headnote). The key part of s 41 was s 41(3)(c) which permitted evidence of the women's previous sexual history with the defendant where:

> (c) it is an issue of consent and the sexual behaviour of the complainant to which the evidence or question relates is alleged to have been, in any respect, so similar. . .to any sexual behaviour of the complainant which. . .took place as part of the event which is the subject matter of the charge against the accused. . .that the similarity cannot reasonably be explained as a coincidence.

On its face, this allowed evidence to be given only in severely restricted circumstances. However, this was before the application of s 3(1) of the HRA.

R v A (No 2) [2001] 2 Cr App R 21 (extracts)

Lord Steyn: In my view ordinary methods of purposive construction of section 41(3)(c) cannot cure the problem of the excessive breadth of the section 41, read as a whole, so far as it relates to previous sexual experience between a complainant and the accused. . .

. . .The interpretative obligation under section 3 of the [HRA] is a strong one. It applies even if there is no ambiguity in the language in the sense of the language being capable of two different meanings. . . .In accordance with the will of Parliament as reflected in section 3 it will sometimes be necessary to adopt an interpretation which linguistically may appear strained. The techniques to be used will not only involve the reading down of express language in a statute but also the implication of provisions. A declaration of incompatibility is a measure of last resort. It must be avoided unless it is plainly impossible to do so. If a clear limitation on Convention rights is stated in terms, such an impossibility will arise. . .There is, however, no limitation of such a nature in the present case.

In my view section 3 requires the court to subordinate the niceties of the language of section 41(3)(c), and in particular the touchstone of coincidence, to broader considerations of relevance judged by logical and common sense criteria of time and circumstances. After all, it is realistic to proceed on the basis that the legislature would not, if alerted to the problem, have wished to deny the right to an accused to put forward a full and complete defence by advancing truly probative material. It is therefore possible under section 3 to read section 41, and in particular section 41(3)(c), as subject to the implied provision that evidence or questioning which is required to ensure a fair trial under Article 6 of the Convention should not be treated as inadmissible. The result of such a reading would be that sometimes logically relevant sexual experiences between a complainant and an accused may be admitted under section 41 (3)(c). On the other hand, there will be cases where previous sexual experience between a complainant and an accused will be irrelevant, e.g., an isolated episode distant in time and circumstances. Where the line is to be drawn must be left to the judgment of trial judges. On this basis a declaration of incompatibility can be avoided. If this approach is adopted, section 41 will have achieved a major part of its objective but its excessive reach will have been attenuated in accordance with the will of Parliament as reflected in section 3 of the 1998 Act. That is the approach which I would adopt.

[The House of Lords, by a majority, found that the HRA could be used to modify the meaning given to the 1999 Act, as Lord Styen had suggested].

[**Lord Hope,** dissenting took a different approach, considering that in this case s 41 (3)(c) did not in any event prevent the defendant from having a fair trial. But he went on]: I should like to add however that I would find it very difficult to accept that it was permissible under section 3 of the Human Rights Act 1998 to read into section 41(3)(c) a provision to the effect that evidence or questioning which was required to ensure a fair trial under Article 6 of the Convention should not be treated as inadmissible. The rule of construction which section 3 lays down is quite unlike any previous rule of statutory interpretation. There is no need to identify an ambiguity or absurdity. Compatibility with Convention rights is the sole guiding principle. That is the paramount object which the rule seeks to achieve. But the rule is only a rule of interpretation. It does not entitle the judges to act as legislators.. . .The compatibility is to be achieved only so far as this is possible. Plainly this will not be possible if the legislation contains provisions which expressly contradict the meaning which the enactment would have to be given to make it compatible. It seems to me that the same result must follow if they do so by necessary implication, as this too is a means of identifying the plain intention of Parliament: see Lord Hoffmann's observations in *R v Secretary of State for the Home Department, ex p Simms* [2000] 2 AC 115 at 131F–G.

In the present case it seems to me that the entire structure of section 41 contradicts the idea that it is possible to read into it a new provision which would entitle the court to give leave whenever it was of the opinion that this was required to ensure a fair trial. The whole point of the section, as was made clear during the debates in Parliament, was to address the mischief which was thought to have arisen due to the width of the discretion which had previously been given to the trial judge. A deliberate decision was taken not to follow the examples which were to be found elsewhere. . .of provisions which give an overriding discretion to the trial judge to allow the evidence or questioning where it would be contrary to the interests of justice to exclude it. Section 41(2) forbids the exercise of such a discretion unless the court is satisfied as to the matters which that subsection identifies. It seems to me that it would not be possible, without contradicting the plain intention of Parliament, to read in a provision which would enable the court to exercise a wider discretion than that permitted by section 41(2). I would not have the same difficulty with a solution which read down the provisions of subsections (3) or (5), as the case may be, in order to render them compatible with the Convention right. But if that were to be done it would be necessary to identify precisely (a) the words used by the legislature which would otherwise be incompatible with the Convention right and (b) how these words were to be construed, according to the rule which section 3 lays down, to make them compatible. That, it seems to me, is what the rule of construction requires.

Notes

1. Lords Steyn and Hutton were prepared to hold that the only way in which Parliament could legislate contrary to a Convention right would be by 'a clear limitation on Convention rights . . .stated in terms'. This approach lead them simply to read into s 41(3)(c) words which were not there, namely that evidence was to be admitted where that was necessary to achieve a fair trial. It may be noted that Lord Hope, in contrast, considered that this approach went too far, crossing the line from interpretation to legislating. He considered, in what is certainly the more usual understanding of the word 'interpretation', that the judge's task was limited to identifying specific words

which would otherwise lead to incompatibility and then re-interpreting those words, clearly not something which Lords Steyn and Hutton—and for that matter Lord Slynn—undertook.

2. Lord Hope's approach found more support in a more recent House of Lords' decision, *Re S and Re W (Care Orders)* [2002] 2 AC 291; [2002] 2 WLR 720 (also known as *Re S and W (Care Orders)*), endorsing a more restrained reading of s 3(1). Lord Nicholls observed that a reading of legislation under s 3(1) should not 'depart substantially from a fundamental feature of an Act of Parliament' (at para 40). To like effect are the *dicta* of Lord Woolf CJ in *Poplar Housing* [2002] QB 48, cited by Lord Hope in *R v A* (above) and of Lord Hope himself in *R v Lambert* [2002] AC 545; [2001] 3 WLR 206, 233–35. Similarly, whilst *Ghaidan Mendoza* [2004] 3 WLR 113 represents a bold use of s 3(1), again reading words in to a legislative provision, *Bellinger v Bellinger* [2003] 2 AC 467 shows that the Lords may refuse even a linguistically modest adjustment to the meaning of legislation if they consider that the change has far-reaching consequences that are better considered by Parliament. For further details on the HRA cases, see Chapter 17, pp 957–970.

3. The decision in *R v A* shows that where the judges chose to, they can use s 3(1) to require Parliament to use express words when it wishes to legislate incompatibly with the Convention rights.

4. All this could of course theoretically be removed simply by repeal of the HRA—something that is at present Conservative party policy. However, if the Conservatives do gain power at the next election, two fascinating questions will arise: first, what will they put in place of the HRA and what effect will that instrument have upon sovereignty; second, if the HRA is repealed and *not* replaced, will the courts develop the 'common law constitutional rights' jurisprudence noted above (pp 178–180) so that they are able, through the common law to afford as much protection to fundamental rights as they are now able to do under the Convention?

FURTHER READING

A Bradley, 'The Sovereignty of Parliament—Form or Substance?' in J Jowell and D Oliver, *The Changing Constitution*, 6th edn (2007)

R Cooke, 'A Constitutional Retreat' (2006) 122(Apr) LQR 224–31

R Ekins, 'Acts of Parliament and the Parliament Acts' (2007) 123(Jan) LQR 91–115

M Gordon, 'The Conceptual Foundations of Parliamentary Sovereignty: Reconsidering Jennings and Wade' [2009] PL 519.

J Jowell, 'Parliamentary Sovereignty under the new Constitutional Hypothesis' [2006] PL 562

KJ Keith , 'Sovereignty at the Beginning of the 21st Century: Fundamental or Outmoded?' [2004] 63(3) CLJ 581–604

CJS Knight, 'Bi-Polar Sovereignty Restated' [2009] 68(2) CLJ 361

S Lakin, 'Debunking the Idea of Parliamentary Sovereignty: The Controlling Factor of Legality in the British Constitution' (2008) 28(4) OJLS 709–34

G Marshall, 'Metric Measures and Martyrdom by Henry VIII Clause' (2002) 118(Oct) LQR 2002, 493–502.

A McHarg, 'What is Delegated Legislation?' [2006] PL 539

I McLean and A McMillan, 'Professor Dicey's Contradictions' [2007] PL 435

T Mullen, 'Reflections on *Jackson v Attorney General*: questioning sovereignty' (2007) 27(1) *Legal Studies* 1–25

M Plaxt, 'The Concept of Legislation: *Jackson v Her Majesty's Attorney General*' (2006) MLR 249

A Young, 'Hunting Sovereignty: *Jackson v. Her Majesty's Attorney-General* [2006] PL 187

CHAPTER 5
THE EUROPEAN UNION AND PARLIAMENTARY SOVEREIGNTY

INTRODUCTION

The previous chapter considered the doctrine of parliamentary sovereignty in general, and the possibility of restrictions deriving from within the UK constitutional order, in particular the possibility of those imposed by Parliament itself. The most important practical application of the debate as to whether the UK Parliament may limit its own powers or have legal limitations imposed upon it by external sources of legal authority arises from the UK's membership of the European Union. There has been no recent case-law on this matter, but the academic debate continues, although it is mainly focused at present on the implications of the *Jackson*[1] decision, discussed in the previous chapter, which shed little or no light on the European dimension.

The UK became a member of the European Community with effect from 1 January 1972 by virtue of the Treaty of Accession 1972. Treaties and Community law capable of having direct effect in the UK were given domestic legal effect by the European Communities Act 1972 (ECA) which, by s 2(1), incorporated all existing Community law into UK law.[2]

The problem posed by Britain's prospective membership of the Community was very obvious. The purposes of the Community meant that uniformity in the laws of the different Member States had to be guaranteed in those areas regulated by the Community. An Act of Parliament would obviously be required, providing that Community law was binding in Britain. That Act was the European Communities Act 1972. But, suppose that Parliament either deliberately, or inadvertently, later passed an Act that was inconsistent with Community law? The traditional doctrine of implied repeal states, as discussed above in Chapter 4, that if there is any inconsistency between the provisions of two different statutes, the later statute is deemed to repeal any provisions of the earlier statute that are inconsistent with it. Thus, no Parliament can protect its enactments from future express or implied repeal. So some device was needed in the European Communities Act to protect Community law from being gradually repealed in this way.

The device chosen was simple. No express declaration of the supremacy of Community law is included in the Act. The words intended to achieve this are contained in s 2(4), which reads as follows: 'any enactment passed *or to be passed*. . . shall be construed and have effect subject to the foregoing provisions of this section. . .' (emphasis added). 'The foregoing' are those provisions referred to in s 2(1) giving the force of law to 'the enforceable Community rights' there defined. Section 3(1) provides that questions as to the meaning or effect of Community law are to be determined 'in accordance with the principles laid down by any relevant decision of the European Court'.

Clearly, any Community law provision would prevail over UK legislation enacted before 1 January 1973. Authority for this can be found in rulings such as those in *Henn* [1981] 2 All ER 166 and *Goldstein* [1982] 1 WLR 804. This is uncontroversial and merely accords with the ordinary operation of the orthodox doctrine of parliamentary sovereignty. The problem arises in respect of statutes passed after 1 January 1972. By saying that any enactment 'to be passed', that is, any *future* enactment, must take effect 'subject to' the provisions of this Act, Parliament seemed to be suggesting that the courts must allow Community law to prevail over subsequent Acts of Parliament. This was evidently an attempt to suspend the normal doctrine of implied repeal—instead of any later statute which conflicted with EC law impliedly repealing it, such a later statute would have to be either 'construed', that is, interpreted so that it did not conflict with EC law, or if it could not be so interpreted, simply set aside ('have effect subject to'). In other words, Parliament was quite clearly seeking to bind its

---

1   *Jackson and others v Her Majesty's Attorney-General* [2005] UKHL 56; [2006] 1 AC 262; [2005] 3 WLR 733, HL.

2   The previous edition of this book contained in this chapter a brief discussion of the EU institutions and forms of EU law. Since such matters are covered extensively in a separate compulsory 'core' course in both LLB and GDL programmes, we have omitted this material in this edition for reasons of space.

successors. According to orthodox understandings of parliamentary sovereignty, as expressed in cases such as *Ellen Street Estates Ltd v Ministry of Housing* [1934] 1 KB 590 and *Vauxhall Estates v Liverpool Corporation Ltd* [1932] 1 KB 733, it had no legal power to do so (see pp 149–50, below).

THE POSITION OF THE EUROPEAN COURT OF JUSTICE

The European Court of Justice (ECJ) had early made clear its view that Community law should prevail over national law. Note that the following cases state the EU law position on the relationship between EU and domestic law; it does not necessarily follow that the ECJ's views on this matter have been fully accepted by the Member States.

Costa v ENEL (Case 6/64) [1964] ECR 585, 586, ECJ

By creating a Community of unlimited duration, having its own institutions, its own personality, its own legal capacity and capacity of representation on the international plane, and, more particularly, real powers stemming from a limitation of sovereignty or a transfer of powers from the states to the Community, the Member States have limited their sovereign rights and have thus created a body of law which binds both their nationals and themselves. The integration into the laws of each Member State of provisions which derive from the Community and, more generally the terms and the spirit of the Treaty, make it impossible for the states, as a corollary, to accord precedence to a unilateral and subsequent measure over a legal system accepted by them on a basis of reciprocity. Such a measure cannot therefore be inconsistent with that legal system. The law stemming from the Treaty, an independent source of law, could not because of its special and original nature, be overridden by domestic legal provisions, however framed, without being deprived of its character as Community law and without the legal basis of the Community itself being called into question.

The transfer by the states from their domestic legal system to the Community legal system of the rights and obligations arising under the Treaty carries with it a permanent limitation of their sovereign rights.

Amministrazione delle Finanze dello Stato v Simmenthal SpA (Case 106/77) [1978] ECR 629, 645–46, ECJ

[The Court ruled:] A national court which is called upon, within the limits of its jurisdiction, to apply provisions of Community law is under a duty to give full effect to those provisions, if necessary refusing of its own motion to apply any conflicting provision of national legislation, even if adopted subsequently, and it is not necessary for the court to request or await the prior setting aside of such provisions by legislative or other constitutional means.

Note
The far-reaching finding in this case was to the effect that conflict between provisions of national law and directly applicable Community law must be resolved by rendering the national law inapplicable, and that any national provision or practice withholding from a national court the jurisdiction to apply Community law even temporarily was incompatible with the requirements of Community law.

THE POSITION OF THE UK COURTS

The purposive approach

How have the UK courts approached this conflict? In *Felixstowe Dock and Railway Co v British Transport Docks Board* [1976] 2 CMLR 655, Lord Denning MR disposed of a challenge to UK law on the basis that 'once a Bill is passed by Parliament and becomes a statute, that will dispose of all discussion about the Treaty. These courts will have to abide by the statute without regard to the Treaty at all'. This was the traditional approach. However it then gave way to what has been termed a 'rule of construction' approach to s 2(4) ECA. In *Garland v British Rail Engineering* [1983] 2 AC 751, Lord Diplock suggested that, even where the words of the domestic law were on their face incompatible with the Community law in question, they should be construed so as to comply with it. He said that national courts must strive to make domestic law conform to Community law however 'wide a departure from the *prima facie* meaning may be needed to achieve consistency'. However, he added that they should do so only while it appeared that Parliament wished to comply with EC law.

This approach was applied in *Pickstone v Freemans* [1988] 3 WLR 265; [1988] 2 All ER 803[3] in the House of Lords, although not in the Court of Appeal. The Court of Appeal ruled that domestic legislation—the Equal Pay Amendment Regulations made under s 2(2) of the European Communities Act—was inconsistent with Art 119 of the EC Treaty. It then treated Art 119 as having more authority than the Amendment Regulations and made a ruling consistent with Art 119 (extracts from this case can be found in the next chapter). Thus, the House of Lords avoided the controversial approach of finding that EC law prevailed over national law but, by a less overtly contentious route, achieved the same result. It adopted a purposive interpretation of the domestic legislation which was not in conflict with Art 119. This was done on the basis that Parliament must have intended to fulfil its EC law obligations in passing the Amendment Regulations once it had been compelled to do so by the ECJ.

This decision provided authority for the proposition that plain words in a statute will be ignored if they involve departure from the provisions of European Community law, albeit under the guise of 'interpretation' rather than by a naked refusal to apply the words of an inconsistent UK statute. It might appear to follow that Parliament had succeeded in partially 'entrenching' s 2(1) of the European Communities Act, by means of s 2(4), by imposing a requirement of form (express words) on future legislation designed to override Community law. It should be noted that the House of Lords in *Pickstone* justified its disregard of statutory words by the finding that Parliament intended them to bear a meaning compatible with Community obligations.

The unequivocal primacy of Community law?

Lord Denning in *Macarthys v Smith* (Case 129/79) [1981] 1 All ER 111 suggested more clearly that partial 'entrenchment' of s 2(1) of the 1972 Act had occurred: 'we are entitled to look to the Treaty. . .not only as an aid but as an overriding force. If. . .our legislation. . .is inconsistent with Community law. . .then it is our bounden duty to give priority to Community law.' These *dicta* were to be tested in the decisive—and still leading—case on the issue, *R v Secretary of State for Transport ex parte Factortame (Nos 1–3)* (1989) and (1992). *Factortame* required the courts to go a significant step further than previous cases because the UK courts for the first time had to confront directly an

---

3   For comment see (1988) 51 MLR 221; [1988] PL 483.

irreconcilable conflict between EC law and domestic law. The UK statute, the Merchant Shipping Act 1988, was plainly incompatible with clear and fundamental principles of Community law and thus, since there was no question of 'interpreting' the two into compatibility, the courts were faced with a stark choice—either uphold the statute, thus plunging the UK into direct conflict with the Community authorities, or take the unprecedented step of simply refusing to follow provisions of primary legislation. The background to the case is described by Erika Szyszczak.

> Briefly, in order to prevent 'quota hopping', whereby the UK's fishing quotas were drained by ships registered in the UK but owned and operated by non-British companies, the UK introduced the Merchant Shipping Act 1988. This stipulated that, in order to register as British fishing vessels, ships had to be British owned and, in the case of ships owned by companies, 75% of shareholders had to be British citizens, resident and domiciled in the UK. As a result of this Act, 95 fishing vessels registered in the UK, but controlled by Spanish companies, were effectively banned from fishing in British waters. Facing economic ruin, the Spanish companies applied to the High Court for judicial review of the measures contained in the Merchant Shipping Act 1988 and for a declaration that the measures relating to nationality and residence requirements should not be applied since they contravened Community law.[4]

R v Secretary of State for Transport ex parte Factortame
[1990] 2 AC 85, HL (extracts)

The Community law rights in issue included the prohibition of discrimination on grounds of nationality, the prohibition of restrictions on exports between Member States, the provision for the free movement of workers and the requirement that nationals of Member States are to be treated equally with respect to participation in the capital of companies established in one of those states. A ruling on the substantive questions of Community law was requested from the European Court of Justice and pending that ruling, which could not be expected for another two years, the Divisional Court made an order by way of interim relief, setting aside the relevant part of the 1988 Regulations and allowing the applicants to continue to operate their vessels as if they were British registered.

This order was set aside by the Court of Appeal. Bingham LJ said, however, that where the law of the Community is clear 'whether as a result of a ruling given on an Article 177 [now 234] reference or as a result of previous jurisprudence or on a straightforward interpretation of Community instruments, the duty of the national court is to give effect to it in all circumstances. . .To that extent a UK statute is not as inviolable as it once was'. In the instant case it had not yet been established that the statute was inconsistent with Community law and in those circumstances it was held that the court had no power to declare a statute void.

The applicants appealed to the House of Lords which upheld the ruling of the Court of Appeal and referred to the European Court of Justice for a preliminary ruling the question whether Community law required a national court should grant the interim relief sought. Lord Bridge said that if it appeared after the European Court of Justice had ruled on the substantive issue that domestic law was incompatible with the Community provisions in question, Community law would prevail.

---

4   E Szyszczak, 'Sovereignty: Crisis, Compliance, Confusion, Complacency?' (1990) 15(6) EL Rev 480–81.

Lord Bridge: By virtue of s 2(4) of the Act of 1972, Part II of the Act of 1988 is to be construed and take effect subject to directly enforceable Community rights and those rights are, by s 2(1) of the Act of 1972, to be 'recognised and available in law, and . . . enforced, allowed and followed accordingly;'. . .This has precisely the same effect as if a section were incorporated in Part II of the Act of 1988 which in terms enacted that the provisions with respect to registration of British fishing vessels were to be without prejudice to the directly enforceable Community rights of nationals of any Member State of the EEC. Thus it is common ground that, in so far as the applicants succeed before the ECJ in obtaining a ruling in support of the Community rights which they claim, these rights will prevail over the restrictions imposed on registration of British fishing vessels by Part II of the Act 1988, and the Divisional Court will, in the final determination of the application for judicial review, be obliged to make appropriate declarations to give effect to these rights.

Note
The European Commission then successfully sought a ruling in the European Court of Justice that the nationality requirement of s 14 of the Merchant Shipping Act should be suspended (*Re Nationality of Fishermen: EC Commission v UK* (Case C248/89) [1989] 3 CMLR 601; [1991] 3 CMLR 706) pending the delivery of the judgment in the action for a declaration. This decision was given effect in the UK by means of the Merchant Shipping Act 1988 (Amendment) Order 1989. The European Court of Justice then ruled on the question of interim relief relying on *Amministrazione delle Finanze dello Stato v Simmenthal SpA* (Case 106/77) [1978] ECR 629. Predictably, it found that a national court must set aside national legislative provisions if that were necessary to give interim relief in a case concerning Community rights (*R v Secretary of State for Transport ex parte Factortame Ltd* (1989)).

As Szyszczak notes:

> Although invited to, the European Court did not issue any guidelines as to when interim relief should be available. Thus the circumstances and the form in which interim relief is granted are left to the discretion of the national courts, subject to the ruling in *Amministrazione delle Finanze dello Stato v SpA San Giorgio* [(Case 199/82) [1983] ECR 3595], that the conditions must not render the right to interim relief virtually impossible. It may be justifiable to subject the grant of interim relief against primary legislation to more stringent conditions than those applied to secondary legislation and administrative decisions. This may be a matter for the national court to assess alongside other issues such as whether damages may be an appropriate remedy.[5]

The House of Lords then considered the application for interim relief, in the light of the ruling of the ECJ. In an unprecedented move, their Lordships decided to grant the application, thus 'setting aside' the Merchant Shipping Act.

Factortame Ltd v Secretary of State (No 2) [1991] 1 AC 603 (extracts)

Lord Bridge of Harwich: My Lords, when this appeal first came before the House in 1989 (see *Factortame Ltd v Secretary of State for Transport* [1989] 2 All ER 692; [1990] 2 AC 85) your Lordships held that, as a matter of English law, the courts had no jurisdiction to grant

---

5   *Ibid*, p 482.

interim relief in terms which would involve either overturning an English statute in advance of any decision by the Court of Justice of the European Communities that the statute infringed Community law or granting an injunction against the Crown. It then became necessary to seek a preliminary ruling from the Court of Justice as to whether Community law itself invested us with such jurisdiction.

In June 1990 we received the judgment of the Court of Justice replying to the questions we had posed and affirming that we had jurisdiction, in the circumstances postulated, to grant interim relief for the protection of directly enforceable rights under Community law, and that no limitation on our jurisdiction imposed by any rule of national law could stand as the sole obstacle to preclude the grant of such relief. In the light of this judgment we were able to conclude the hearing of the appeal in July and unanimously decided that relief should be granted in terms of the orders which the House then made, indicating that we would give our reasons for the decision later.

Some public comments on the decision of the Court of Justice, affirming the jurisdiction of the courts of Member States to override national legislation, if necessary, to enable interim relief to be granted in protection of rights under Community law, have suggested that this was a novel and dangerous invasion by a Community institution of the sovereignty of the UK Parliament. But such comments are based on a misconception. If the supremacy within the European Community of Community law over the national law of Member States was not always inherent in the EEC Treaty it was certainly well established in the juris-prudence of the Court of justice long before the UK joined the Community. Thus, whatever limitation of its sovereignty Parliament accepted when it enacted the European Com-munities Act 1972 was entirely voluntary. Under the terms of the 1972 Act it has always been clear that it was the duty of a UK court, when delivering final judgment, to override any rule of national law found to be in conflict with any directly enforceable rule of Community law. Similarly, when decisions of the Court of Justice have exposed areas of UK statute law which failed to implement Council directives, Parliament has always loyally accepted the obligation to make appropriate and prompt amendments. Thus there is nothing in any way novel in according supremacy to rules of Community law in those areas to which they apply and to insist that, in the protection of rights under Community law, national courts must not be inhibited by rules of national law from granting interim relief in appropriate cases is no more than a logical recognition of that supremacy.

Notes

1. In *R v Secretary of State for Transport, ex parte Factortame Ltd (No 3)* [1992] QB 680, the ECJ had to consider the substantive issue in this case. It ruled that, while at present competence to determine the conditions governing the nationality of ships was vested in the Member States, such com-petence must be exercised consistently with Community law. It then determined that Part II of the Merchant Shipping Act 1988 was discriminatory on the grounds of nationality contrary to Art 52 and therefore did not so conform. Thus, the ECJ found that Art 52 had been breached due to the nationality and residence requirements laid down in the Act for registration of owners of fishing vessels. The ruling meant that Community law must be applied in preference to the Merchant Shipping Act 1988, which must be disapplied.

2. In relation to the grant of interim relief against a Minister of the Crown, Lord Bridge considered (i) that as a matter of domestic law injunctions could not be granted in judicial review proceedings against a Minister of the Crown, although he accepted (ii) (after the ruling of the ECJ on the matter) that there was an overriding principle of Community law requiring the grant of interim relief to a party whose claim to be entitled to directly effective rights under Community law was

seriously arguable. In the subsequent decision in *M v Home Office* [1994] 1 AC 377,[6] the Lords departed from this finding as regards point (i).

3. As Ian Loveland notes,[7] the *Factortame* decisions, radical though they were, left two practical issues open: first, could a statute be disapplied only after the ECJ on a reference had held that it was incompatible with EC law; second, was the novel power to 'disapply' statutes confined to the House of Lords, or could it be exercised by any court, however lowly? These questions were decisively answered, and the basic principle laid down in *Factortame* affirmed, in the House of Lords' decision in *R v Secretary of State for Employment ex parte EOC* [1995] 1 AC 377. Certain provisions of the Employment Protection (Consolidation) Act 1978 governed the right not to be unfairly dismissed, compensation for unfair dismissal and the right to statutory redundancy pay. These rights did not apply to workers who worked less than the specified number of hours a week. The Equal Opportunities Commission (EOC), considered that since the majority of those working for less than the specified number of hours were women, the provisions operated to the disadvantage of women, and were therefore discriminatory and in breach of EC law. The EOC accordingly wrote to the Secretary of State for Employment expressing this view. The Secretary of State replied by letter that the conditions excluding part-time workers from the rights in question were justifiable and therefore not indirectly discriminatory. The EOC applied for judicial review of the Secretary of State's refusal to accept that the UK was in breach of its obligations under EC law. The Secretary of State argued that no decision or justiciable issue susceptible of judicial review existed. However, the House of Lords found that, although the letter itself was not a decision, the provisions themselves could be challenged in judicial review proceedings. Judicial review was found to be available for the purpose of securing a declaration that certain UK primary legislation was incompatible with EC law, following *Factortame*. The requisite declarations were duly made.

4. After the *Factortame* litigation it may be said that the courts clearly have the power to refuse to obey an Act of Parliament if it conflicts with Community law, and Parliament is therefore effectively constrained in its freedom to legislate on any subject. If it wishes to avoid this restraint it will have to use express words demonstrating its intention to override any inconsistent EC law, though it is by no means clear that this would guarantee judicial obedience to such a statute. In contrast to *dicta* of Lord Denning in *Macarthys v Smith* [1979] 3 All ER 325 to the effect that a domestic court would give regard to express words in a statute requiring it to override Community law, Lord Bingham in *Factortame* did not enter a caveat that effect would have been given to express words used in the Merchant Shipping Act 1988 declaring that its provisions should prevail over those of Community law. He came close to suggesting that effect would not be given to such words in observing 'any rule of domestic law which prevented the court from giving effect to directly enforceable rights established in Community law would be bad'. In any event, since in practice it is highly improbable that such express words would be used, it appears to be impossible for Parliament to depart from the principle of the primacy of Community law unless it decides to withdraw from the Community.

Feldman believes that the answer is clear:

> Which view is correct? This question can be answered only if there is a means of authoritatively determining the outcome of the disagreement. In this case there is such a procedure. It is very likely that a court in the United Kingdom, faced with a

---

6   For the judgment see Chapter 3, pp 92–94.

7   I Loveland, *Constitutional Law, Administrative Law and Human Rights A Critical Introduction*, 5th edn (2009), p 411.

provision that is apparently inconsistent with directly effective Community law and expressed to be enforceable notwithstanding any such inconsistency, would quickly make a reference to the CJEC under Article 234 of the EU Treaty. There can be no doubt that the Court of Justice would say that Community law must be enforced notwithstanding the Act of Parliament, or that the court in the United Kingdom would accept that judgment as the final and authoritative word on the subject (unless and until the United Kingdom were to withdraw from the EU and repeal the European Communities Act 1972). Accepting that both Acts of Parliament and directly effective Community law are justiciable in courts in the United Kingdom entails accepting the need for some hierarchically superior judicial body to have the last word on such questions of law, and the combined effect of the European Communities Act 1972 and the EU Treaty is to makes it clear that the CJEC is that body.[8]

5. Loveland argues that insofar as *Factortame* introduced a hitherto unknown form of entrenchment into the UK Constitution:

> [it] is—it seems—of an extremely weak procedural kind. It does not take the form of requiring super-majorities within Parliament, not that there be resort to any extra-parliamentary device such as a referendum; it merely requires that a bare parliamentary majority expresses itself in unusually blunt language. A new Merchant Shipping Act which said in s 1 that it was intended to repudiate the UK's obligations under the Common Fisheries Policy would presumably have been applied by Lord Bridge and his colleagues. It is doubtful that it could have been disapplied through the judicial techniques ostensibly used in *Factortame No 2).*[9]

Loveland's point seems a good one: Lord Bridge's reasoning was based entirely on the notion of implied consent by Parliament to the duty of acting in conformity with EU law. But if Parliament legislated contrary to EU law, as in *Factortame,* the courts would assume that this was inadvertent, and that Parliament's overall intent was to remain in compliance. However, if the disputed statute stated on its face that it was *not* intended to be in compliance, this line of reasoning would not work. *Factortame* does not demonstrate clearly that such a statute would be applied by the courts: but fresh reasoning would be required if the courts were *not* minded to apply it.

6. Nevertheless, the change in attitude of the UK judiciary over the last 20 years is very notable. Like the judiciary in the other Member States, the UK judiciary has gradually come to a full realisation of the need to achieve a uniform application of Community law throughout the Member States. However, this has taken some time, as can be seen by comparing a case such as *HP Bulmer Ltd v J Bollinger SA* [1974] Ch 401 with *Factortame*. The *Bulmer* case is in this sense similar to a German case: *Internationale Handelsgesellschaft mbH* [1974] 2 CMLR 540.

7. What then is the final result of the *Factortame* and *EOC* cases? Do they amount to an unequivocal acceptance of the primacy of Community law by the British courts and the consequent fettering of the legislative competence of the UK Parliament? And on what basis did the House of Lords justify such an apparently radical departure from the orthodox, Diceyan understanding of sovereignty? These questions are considered in the following section.

---

8   D Feldman, 'None, one or several? Perspectives on the UK's constitution(s)' [2005] 64(2) CLJ 329, at 346.

9   Loveland, n 7 above, at 411–12.

Assessing *Factortame*; reconsidering sovereignty

The judicial reasoning and its critics

If Lord Bridge's explanation for what happened in the *Factortame* cases is examined, it is apparent that his reasoning represents a very typically British piece of judicial manoeuvring, allowing their Lordships to avoid facing up to the wider constitutional, even jurisprudential implications of the decision reached. It will be recalled that his Lordship justified what occurred on the basis that Parliament had accepted limitations on its sovereignty but that it had done so voluntarily. That explanation was clearly something of an exercise in pouring oil on politically troubled waters—as his comments made clear, there had been an angry response from the Euro-sceptic Right at the overriding of a UK statute by Community law and the loss of national sovereignty this indicated. In response, his Lordship was pointing out, if you like, that the UK may indeed have lost some of its sovereignty but that the loss had not been imposed from outside, but voluntarily accepted, since everyone had been fully aware of the consequences of joining the European Community before the UK made the decision to join in 1972. It does therefore answer one question: their Lordships indicated clearly that in their view the limitation placed upon parliamentary sovereignty came from *Parliament itself*, not from some outside body.

In other words, as far as the UK courts are concerned, the supremacy of EC law in the UK arises simply and solely from the provisions of a UK Act of Parliament, the European Communities Act 1972, not from the Treaties signed by the UK, nor from the judgments of the ECJ independently of the effect they are given in UK law via s 3(1) of the ECA. As Sir John Laws (now Laws LJ) put it, speaking extra-judicially, 'the law of Europe is not a higher-order law, because the limits which for the time being it sets to the power of Parliament are at the grace of Parliament itself'.[10] This therefore affirms one of the essential planks of the traditional view: Parliament's will cannot be overridden by any outside source of power. It should be noted that this is flatly contrary to the view of the ECJ in *Costa v ENEL* that the limitation of member states' sovereignty arises *not* from any particular statute they pass to incorporate EC law itself but from the unique nature and effect of EU law itself:

> The transfer by the states from their domestic legal system to the Community legal system of the rights and obligations arising under the Treaty *carries with it a permanent limitation of their sovereign rights.*[11]

The italicised words plainly imply that the UK would remain subordinate to EU law, regardless of the repeal or amendment of the European Communities Act 1972.

What the *Factortame* judgment completely fails to do, as Loveland points out,[12] is explain how it was that Parliament managed in 1972 to achieve this voluntary, partial surrender of its sovereignty. The orthodox view, or course, was that if Parliament tried to bind its successors by providing that later legislation would not override an earlier measure—as they did in s 2(4) of the ECA—the courts would simply not enforce it. So how was it that Parliament managed in 1972 to achieve the constitutionally impossible? Lord Bridge does not even attempt to answer this question. In fact he speaks as if the judgment represented nothing of any great significance, denying that it was in anyway 'novel'. His Lordship was also slightly disingenuous in asserting that it had always been absolutely obvious that

---

10   J Laws, 'Law and Democracy' [1985] PL 72, 89.

11   *Costa v ENEL* (Case 6/64) [1964] ECR 585, 586, above, p 221.

12   See n 7 above, p 411.

Parliament was accepting a limitation on its powers in 1972. In fact, in articles published shortly after the ECA was passed in 1972, Lord Diplock and Lord Denning both took the view that the rules of implied repeal would operate perfectly normally in relation to EC law.

It is also notable that their Lordships carefully placed all the responsibility for this change to the accepted constitutional order upon Parliament,[13] which, they implied, had freely chosen to limit its own sovereignty. The real issue, which their Lordships quite simply ducked, was that in the past Parliament had enacted provisions which appeared to have the aim of binding its successors—as perhaps in the *Ellen Street Estates* and *Vauxhall Estates* cases,[14] and in the Acts of Union with Scotland and Ireland[15]—but that, faced with later provisions that were incompatible with them, the courts had simply refused to uphold the purported binding force of the earlier statute and applied the later provisions in the normal manner. The courts in the *Factortame* case clearly decided to change *their* approach; but by pretending that they were simply and loyally enforcing the will of Parliament, they avoided having to explain what lay behind this change. As we will see below, Laws LJ, in a more recent decision, has provided an alternative, and much more explicit account of the effect of the ECA upon parliamentary sovereignty.

Two views as to the nature of the change to constitutional doctrine represented by *Factortame* are put forward below. In the first, Wade, who had earlier argued that sovereignty was the 'ultimate political fact' of the UK constitutional order, unchangeable by legal means, draws the conclusion logically required by such a stance: *Factortame* was a technical revolution. Since the change made could not take place legally, it was by definition an extra-legal shift in the constitutional order. TRS Allan offers an alternative view, arguing that *Factortame* rather represents an evolutionary adaptation of a legal principle, itself based on deeper political values, in legitimate response to changing political circumstances. Wade's argument is couched partly in response to the views of Sir John Laws, speaking extra-judicially. Laws has made it plain that, in his view, all that has occurred is a suspension of the doctrine of implied repeal in relation to directly effective EC law,[16] and, as he notes, the courts in other areas of law may require express words, for example, for a statute to have retrospective effect or impose a tax. The decision in *Factortame* is therefore, he suggests, 'hardly revolutionary'.

HWR Wade, 'Sovereignty—revolution or evolution?' (1996) 112 *Law Quarterly Review* 568 (extracts)

When in the second *Factortame* case the House of Lords granted an injunction to forbid a minister from obeying an Act of Parliament, and the novel term 'disapplied' had to be invented to describe the fate of the Act, it was natural to suppose that something drastic had happened to the traditional doctrine of Parliamentary sovereignty. . . The Parliament of 1972 had succeeded in binding the Parliament of 1988 and restricting its sovereignty, something that was supposed to be constitutionally impossible. . .

[Wade then cites a crucial part of Lord Bridge's speech in which he said that the effect of the 1972 Act was: 'as if a section were incorporated in Part II of the Act of 1988 which in terms enacted that the provisions with respect to registration of British fishing

---

13   As Craig points out: [1991] YBEL 221 at 252.

14   See Chapter 4, pp 195–196.

15   Ibid, pp 196–197.

16   Laws, n 10 above, at 89.

vessels were to be without prejudice to. . . directly enforceable Community rights' and comments:]

But this is much more that an exercise in construction. Lord Bridge's hypothetical section would take effect by authority of the Parliament of 1988, not the Parliament of 1972. To hold that its terms are putatively incorporated in the Act of 1988 is merely another way of saying that the Parliament of 1972 has imposed a restriction upon the Parliament of 1988. This is precisely what the classical doctrine of sovereignty will not permit. Sir John Laws [argues] that Parliament has only to provide expressly for the later Act to prevail over any conflicting Community law. But. . .if there had been any such provision in the Act of 1988 we can be sure that the [ECJ] would hold that it was contrary to Community law and that holding would be part of the Community law to which by the Act of 1972 the Act of 1988 is held to be subject. . . While Britain remains in the Community we are in a regime in which Parliament has bound its successors and which is nothing if not revolutionary.

[Wade goes on to note that Lord Bridge's speech in *Factortame (No 2)* (above) does not suggest a mere rule of construction but something much more radical.]

He takes it for granted that Parliament can 'accept' a limitation of its sovereignty which will be effective both for the present and for the future. It is a statement which could hardly be clearer: Parliament can bind its successors. If that is not revolutionary, constitutional lawyers are Dutchmen . . . Neither does Lord Bridge's theory fit well with any theory based upon statutory construction, such as the theory that every post-1972 statute is to be construed as impliedly subject to Community law, subject only to express provision to the contrary. Nothing of that kind is suggested by Lord Bridge's doctrine of 'voluntary acceptance' by Parliament of Community law as a 'limitation of its sovereignty'. The truth is, apparently, that so far from containing 'nothing in any way novel' the new doctrine makes sovereignty a freely adjustable commodity whenever Parliament chooses to accept some limitation. The effect may be similar to implying limitations into future statutes, as Lord Bridge himself explains. But 'voluntary acceptance' goes much deeper into the foundations of the constitution, suggesting by its very novelty that the courts are reformulating the fundamental rules about the effectiveness of Acts of Parliament. . .

But is 'revolutionary' the right word as a matter of law? Has the House of Lords adopted a new rule of recognition or ultimate legal principle as to the validity and effects of Acts of Parliament? As Craig puts it, 'The entry of the United Kingdom into the EEC might therefore be regarded as a catalyst for a partial change in the. . .ultimate legal principle, as it operates in the UK'. As previously supposed, the rule was that an Act of Parliament in proper form had absolutely overriding effect, except that it could not fetter the corresponding power of future Parliaments. It is a rule of unique character, since only the judges can change it It is for the judges, and not for Parliament, to say what is an effective Act of Parliament. If the judges recognise that there must be a change, as by allowing future Parliaments to be fettered, this is a technical revolution. This is what happens when the judges, faced with a novel situation, elect to depart from the familiar rules for the sake of political necessity. . .in *Factortame* the House of Lords elected to allow the Parliament of 1972 to fetter the Parliament of 1988 in order that Community law might be given the primacy which practical politics obviously required. This in no way implies that the judges. . .decided otherwise than for what appeared to be good legal reasons. The point is simply that the rule of recognition is itself a political fact which the judges themselves are able to change when they are confronted with a new situation which so demands.

Question

Does the *Factortame* case really establish, as Wade argues, that 'the new doctrine makes sovereignty a fully adjustable commodity whenever Parliament chooses to accept some limitation'?

TRS Allan, 'Parliamentary sovereignty: law, politics and revolution' (1997) 113 *Law Quarterly Review* 443 (extracts)

The difficulty with Professor Wade's thesis is immediately apparent from his reassurance that despite the change of fundamental rule [of parliamentary sovereignty] 'for reasons of political necessity'. . .we should not assume that in. . .*Factortame* the judges 'decided otherwise than for what appeared to them to be good legal reasons'. Now it is scarcely possible to argue both that changes in the rule of recognition are made or acknowledged for 'good legal reasons' and that such a rule constitutes only 'a political fact' subject to alteration for reasons of 'political necessity'. Legal reasons are usually understood to ground a legitimate judicial decision by invoking settled doctrine or principle: they serve to justify it by explaining the sense in which it was required by the standards of the existing legal order. A revolution occurs, or is cemented, only when a new source of authority is acknowledged, or fundamental rule adopted, which is not justified by the existing order, from which the courts have for whatever reason withdrawn their allegiance.

If legal reasons exist, drawn from accepted legal principles or constitutional doctrine, they can be inspected and weighed. If sufficiently strong they will justify a judicial decision: if not, the judges will either have erred in law or abandoned law for politics.

Which alternative does Professor Wade envisage as the appropriate explanation for *Factortame*? The preservation of a distinction between legal principle, on the one hand, and political expediency, on the other, is surely essential to any coherent understanding of the Rule of Law. Judges who make political decisions which violate accepted constitutional principles plainly act improperly: their conduct, when properly so described, should be condemned as illegitimate even if it is expedient or popular. . .

The existence of good legal reasons for the *Factortame* decisions shows that, far from any dramatic, let alone unauthorised, change in the 'rule of recognition', the House of Lords merely determined what the existing constitutional order required in novel circumstances. The view that the acknowledgments of exceptions or qualifications to the rule that courts should give unconditional obedience to statutes amounts to 'revolution' is simply dogmatic and ultimately incoherent. . .

However, it cannot really be supposed that the House of Lords was [as Wade argues] acknowledging an unrestricted freedom for Parliament to fetter the legislative authority of subsequent Parliaments. A Parliament which was strongly influenced by an authoritarian government might seek to entrench all kinds of provision whose vulnerability to repeal (by ordinary majority) it would be important for the courts to preserve on grounds of democratic principle. . .The principle of voluntary acceptance by Parliament of limits on sovereignty must clearly be confined to the present context. Whether any such voluntary acceptance of limits would be permitted in another context would depend on the circumstances: the reasons for and against such limits would have to be weighed. . .*Factortame* represents a rational attempt to explore the boundaries of legislative sovereignty within the contemporary constitution—even if each decision is presented in largely technical terms, with little serious attempt to articulate the constitutional considerations at stake.

Once we free ourselves of the idea that every qualification of the principle of judicial obedience to statutes constitutes a revolution inspired by political considerations which resist ordinary legal analysis, we can see that the reference to the 'rule of recognition' is really an excuse for shirking the explicit analysis of constitutional principle. The requirements of such a 'rule' are those which constitutional considerations dictate in the particular context under review. The absence of relevant discussion in the *Factortame* judgments can only be explained by the judge's understandable reluctance to risk political controversy, seeking to attribute all responsibility to Parliament, or else by the assumption that they were in some way bound by a 'rule of recognition' beyond the reach of rational, legal analysis. Neither explanation reflects much credit upon what is our highest, constitutional court. . .

. . . When constitutional debate is opened up to ordinary legal reasoning, based on fundamental principles, we shall discover that the notion of unlimited parliamentary sovereignty no longer makes any legal or constitutional sense. . .It is not so much, as [Craig] has suggested that the UK's entry into the EC might 'be regarded as a catalyst for a partial change in the. . .ultimate legal principle' [(1991) 11 YBEL 21 at 251] but rather that membership of the Community reveals the nature of the ultimate principle in all its existing complexity—integral to a larger, if mainly implicit, constitutional theory.

. . .

If therefore we are to treat the nature of parliamentary sovereignty as a matter for legitimate judicial exegesis, and not merely a matter of agreement between politicians, we cannot evade the task of developing a systematic theory of the constitution. Judicial decisions which settle doubts about the scope of parliamentary sovereignty must inevitably draw on such a theory, if they are rational and legitimate. . .Talk of revolution falsely implies that the courts' role is merely to accept, on grounds of expediency, whatever the politicians decide. The implications for the future of the legal order of insisting on the courts' inescapable constitutional role are surely profound. Wade's suggestion that 'the prudential course may be to follow the example of the House of Lords and turn a blind eye to constitutional theory altogether' must, then, be firmly rejected. Such a pusillanimous course would disarm us just when recourse to theory becomes more essential than even, when political change induces even orthodox lawyers to abandon the simple faith that parliamentary omnipotence can be the governing principle for a modern constitutional democracy.[17]

Question

Allen, then, suggests that the reasons which led the courts to decide *Factortame* as they did were 'legal' not 'political', but what, if any, criteria does he suggest to distinguish the two?

---

17   Allan's ideas are more fully developed in his book, *Law, Liberty and Justice* (1993).

Note

In the recent decision of *Thoburn v Sunderland City Council* [2002] 1 CMLR 50, Laws LJ put forward a quite different analysis of the position of the ECA. The facts are not particularly material: they concerned an alleged incompatibility between the Weights and Measures Act 1985 and the ECA 1972, which the judge found not to exist.[18] It should therefore be noted that his comments on whether a later incompatible act would nevertheless have prevailed are, strictly, *obiter*.

Thoburn v Sunderland City Council [2002] 1 CMLR 50 (extracts)

Parliament cannot bind its successors by stipulating against repeal, wholly or partly, of the ECA. It cannot stipulate as to the manner and form of any subsequent legislation. Thus there is nothing in the ECA which allows the Court of Justice, or any other institutions of the EU, to touch or qualify the conditions of Parliament's legislative supremacy in the United Kingdom. . .The British Parliament has not the authority to authorise any such thing. Being sovereign, it cannot abandon its sovereignty. . .

The present state of our domestic law is such that substantive Community rights prevail over the express terms of any domestic law, including primary legislation, made or passed after the coming into force of the ECA, even in the face of plain inconsistency between the two. This is the effect of *Factortame*. . .In *Factortame* Lord Bridge said this at 140:

> By virtue of section 2(4) of the Act of 1972 Part II of the [Merchant Shipping] Act of 1988 is to be construed and take effect subject to directly enforceable Community rights. . .This has precisely the same effect as if a section were incorporated in Part II of the Act of 1988 which in terms enacted that the provisions with respect to registration of British fishing vessels were to be without prejudice to the directly enforceable Community rights of nationals of any Member State of the EEC.

So there was no question of an implied pro tanto repeal of the ECA of 1972 by the later Act of 1988; on the contrary the Act of 1988 took effect subject to Community rights incorporated into our law by the ECA. In *Factortame* no argument was advanced by the Crown in their Lordships' House to suggest that such an implied repeal might have been effected. It is easy to see what the argument might have been: Parliament in 1972 could not bind Parliament in 1988, and section 2(4) was therefore ineffective to do so. It seems to me that there is no doubt but that in *Factortame* the House of Lords effectively accepted that section 2(4) could not be impliedly repealed, albeit the point was not argued.

[Laws LJ then went on to argue that the common law could denote certain statutes as 'constitutional' statutes, and thus not vulnerable to implied repeal (see the passage quoted in Chapter 4) and found]:

The ECA clearly belongs in this family. It incorporated the whole corpus of substantive Community rights and obligations, and gave overriding domestic effect to the judicial and administrative machinery of Community law. It may be there has never been a statute having such profound effects on so many dimensions of our daily lives. The ECA is, by force of the common law, a constitutional statute.

. . .

---

18   [2002] 1 CMLR 50, at para 50.

In my judgment (as will by now be clear) the correct analysis of that relationship involves and requires these following four propositions.

(1) All the specific rights and obligations which EU law creates are by the ECA incorporated into our domestic law and rank supreme: that is, anything in our substantive law inconsistent with any of these rights and obligations is abrogated or must be modified to avoid the inconsistency. This is true even where the inconsistent municipal provision is contained in primary legislation.

(2) The ECA is a constitutional statute: that is, it cannot be impliedly repealed.

(3) The truth of (2) is derived, not from EU law, but purely from the law of England: the common law recognises a category of constitutional statutes.

(4) The fundamental legal basis of the United Kingdoms relationship with the EU rests with the domestic, not the European, legal powers. In the event, which no doubt would never happen in the real world, that a European measure was seen to be repugnant to a fundamental or constitutional right guaranteed by the law of England, a question would arise whether the general words of the ECA were sufficient to incorporate the measure and give it overriding effect in domestic law. But that is very far from this case.

Notes

1. It is important to be clear about what Laws LJ means when he asserts that the specific rights and obligations created by EC law 'rank supreme'. It would seem that a UK statute which specifically stated that it was intended to override any such right or obligation would have that effect. But any other statute inconsistent with such rights or obligations would have no effect, even if passed *after* the ECA 1972.

2. Laws LJ argues that Parliament:

    > cannot stipulate as to the manner and form of any subsequent legislation. It cannot stipulate against implied repeal any more than it can stipulate against express repeal. . .The British Parliament has not the authority to authorise any such thing. Being sovereign, it cannot abandon its sovereignty [para 59].

    This, however, is not particularly persuasive. Laws LJ fails to draw the distinction between a mere restriction upon *form*, which, as argued in Chapter 4, leaves the legislature's freedom of action substantively unconstrained, and restrictions as to the *content* of acts or the manner of their passage. Moreover, if the UK Parliament is sovereign, he offers no justification as to why the courts, subordinate to Parliament precisely under that doctrine, may introduce a restriction upon form, while Parliament itself may not.

3. The novelty of Laws LJ's announcement of two classes of statutes is colourfully reflected in the reaction of two commentators who note that:

    > our feelings, on grasping the outlines of the constitutional architecture erected by Laws L.J., were of astonishment akin to that of Gulliver on first catching sight of Laputa, the 'island in the air'.[19]

---

19   J Young and D Campbell, 'The metric martyrs and the entrenchment jurisprudence of Lord Justice Laws' [2002] PL 399, 400. For criticism of the technical aspects of the judgment, see *ibid*.

4. It will be noted that Laws LJ's analysis is expressly opposed to that of the ECJ in *Costa v ENEL* and subsequent cases.[20] As Marshall puts it:

> In other words the ground for decision must be found not in the inherent supremacy of European law but in the provision made by Parliament in the European Communities Act 1972; in the recognition that that Act was to be treated as a constitutional statute; and in the acknowledgement that the traditional doctrine of sovereignty and implied repeal had been remoulded by the common law.[21]

5. Laws LJ's analysis of the position is considerably clearer than that in *Factortame*. In that decision, the House of Lords appeared to suggest that Parliament had somehow imposed a requirement of form upon future Parliaments, such that the ECA could not be impliedly repealed; however Laws LJ robustly rejects this suggestion. Instead, he suggests that the courts have the ability to designate certain statutes as 'constitutional', and thus immune from implied repeal. What he does not explain, however, is why it is any more acceptable for a sovereign body to have such a restriction imposed upon it from an outside body than it would be for it to be able to impose such a restriction upon itself. Only time will tell whether Laws LJ's analysis finds more favour.

Sovereignty after *Factortame*: How much has changed?

Some commentators take the view that, even where express words were used in a statute demonstrating Parliament's intention to legislate in conflict with EC law, a UK court might not give them effect. This suggests that if a UK statute is to override Community law, s 2(4) of the European Communities Act must first be repealed. The contrary view, that the doctrine of express repeal has been unaffected by the primacy of Community law, rests on the proposition that the judges, in disapplying statutory provisions, are simply carrying out Parliament's will as expressed in s 2(4) of the 1972 Act. This notion becomes harder to sustain in the face of provisions which appear to be intended to infringe Community law, such as the nationality requirements under the Merchant Shipping Act 1988. Nevertheless, in the face of such provisions, the judges appear to take the view that (i) Parliament in passing such provisions had in mind an interpretation of them which would render them compatible with Community law, and (ii) Parliament would not have wished the provisions to override Community law once the ECJ had ruled that they were incompatible.

If express words were used in a statute, such as 'these provisions are to take effect notwithstanding Art 52 of the Treaty', Parliament would appear to be expressing its intention that such provisions should be applied, regardless of a finding of the ECJ to the effect that they breach Art 52. In such an instance, as argued above,[22] judges would therefore be unable to hide behind the notion of fulfilling Parliament's will in disapplying the domestic provisions. If it is assumed that those provisions contained an implied term that the requirements they laid down were to be without prejudice to directly enforceable Community rights, such a term would directly contradict the express wording of the statute. Since a term may only be implied into a statute where there is room to do so under its express wording, it would seem that the judges would have to allow the express words to prevail and therefore the requirements in question would override Community law rights.

---

20   See above, p 215.

21   G Marshall, 'Metric Measures and Martyrdom by Henry VIII Clause' (2002) 118(Oct) LQR 493, 499.

22   See p 221.

Since Parliament retains the power to repeal the ECA expressly, it arguably still retains its ultimate sovereignty. It may be concluded that, where Community law conflicts with domestic law, the traditional doctrine of implied repeal will not be applied but, although the doctrine of parliamentary sovereignty has been greatly affected, it is arguable that it would revive in its original form if the UK withdrew from the EU.

It may be useful to conclude by examining how far the traditional Diceyan view of sovereignty can be said to have survived the ECA and its interpretation in *Factortame*. It will be recalled that under the traditional doctrine of the positive and negative aspects (see Chapter 4, pp 172–174) the following four propositions were advanced by Dicey:

(a) no person or body outside Parliament is recognised by the law as having a right to override or set aside any legislation of Parliament at all ('the negative aspect').

The positive aspect was said to entail three further propositions:

(b) there is no law which Parliament cannot change;
(c) there is therefore no distinction between constitutional and other laws;
(d) an enactment of Parliament cannot be pronounced void on the grounds that it conflicts with any principles of the constitution.

If these propositions are examined in turn, the results are instructive:

- **First** of all, then, is it still true to say that no person or body outside Parliament is recognised by the law as having a right to override or set aside any legislation of Parliament at all? **The answer is a clear no**. The courts have 'disapplied' an Act of Parliament, surely the equivalent of setting it aside.[23]
- **Second,** is it still the case that there is no law that Parliament cannot change? The answer is that we do not know for sure, but this is probably still the case, in the sense that Parliament can ultimately repeal the ECA and then proceed to legislate as it chooses, inconsistently with EC law.
- **Third**, it is now **no longer the case** that 'there is no distinction between constitutional and other laws.' Such a distinction now clearly exists: the law of the EC may be seen as 'constitutional' in character because, at the least, the doctrine of implied repeal does not apply. This is indeed expressly asserted by Laws LJ in *Thoburn*, as seen above. It may be that express repeal does not apply either—or rather that Parliament would have to repeal the ECA before the courts would allow EC law to be overridden by statute.
- **Fourth**—the proposition that an enactment of Parliament cannot be pronounced void on the grounds that it conflicts with any principles of the constitution—**remains technically correct.** In the *Factortame* and *EOC* cases, the courts 'disapplied' the offending legislation; they did not pronounce it void. It has been pointed out that the Merchant Shipping Act was not 'struck down' by the courts—indeed it remained of full effect in relation to all non-EC nationals.

---

23   The power of the Scottish Parliament to repeal legislation of the Westminster Parliament in the devolved areas is a further example of the erosion of this principle.

FURTHER READING

See p 212 above.

CHAPTER 6
DEVOLUTION[1]

---

1   This chapter is substantially researched and written by Alex Williams with contributions from Gavin Phillipson.

INTRODUCTION

This subject would comfortably occupy an entire book; indeed, whole works could be devoted to any one of the devolution schemes, in particular the Scottish settlement, which is the most radical in terms of the powers transferred from the UK Parliament at Westminster. In what follows, therefore, the discussion is confined to a broad outline of the schemes. The chapter's main focus is the scheme in Scotland. The Welsh Assembly's powers to enact primary legislation, granted by the Government of Wales Act 2006, are still awaiting a national referendum to trigger their entry into force. The Northern Ireland settlement is a very complex and distinctive one. Whilst the Northern Ireland Assembly has enjoyed uninterrupted operation since May 2007 following the St Andrews Agreement, the future of devolution in Northern Ireland, to a large extent, still hangs in the balance. In recent months the workings of the Assembly have been frustrated by bitter and protracted disagreements between the Democratic Unionist Party (DUP) and Sinn Fein over the timetabling for the transferral of policing and justice powers from Westminster. A deal has now been reached, but only after extensive talks between the Northern Ireland political parties and the British and Irish Governments. The Assembly still has a long way to go before it can function smoothly and independently. Although none of the devolution schemes are without their own constitutional significance, it is clear that the Scottish scheme is the most appropriate point of reference for present purposes because it enjoys the greatest overall combination of transferred power and political stability.

Before moving to consider the devolved schemes in greater detail, it is helpful to start with a basic idea of what devolution, as a concept, is. As Vernon Bogdanor explains:

> Devolution involves the transfer of powers from a superior to an inferior political authority. More precisely, devolution may be defined as consisting of three elements: the transfer to a subordinate elected body, on a geographical basis, of functions at present exercised by Ministers and Parliament. These functions may be either legislative, the power to make laws, or executive, the power to make secondary laws—statutory instruments, orders and the like—within a primary legal framework still determined at Westminster.[2]

Lord Bingham outlines the basic imperative, described below as the principle of subsidiarity, that drove the initiative in the UK:

Lord Bingham of Cornhill, 'The evolving constitution' [2002] I *European Human Rights Law Review* I (extracts)

> Decisions affecting the life and activities of the citizen should generally speaking be made at the lowest level of government consistent with economy, convenience and the rational conduct of public affairs. This is plainly akin to the European principle of sub-sidiarity. . .I shall call this 'the devolutionary principle'. . .
>
> While there is endless scope for argument about the application of this principle—what powers should be devolved and to what level?—I doubt if any rational person would challenge the principle as such. It would be obviously absurd if the central government were to concern itself with (for instance) local refuse collection, and equally absurd. . .if (say) foreign policy and defence were not conducted by the central government. So the

---

2   V Bogdanor, *Devolution in the United Kingdom* (1999), pp 2–3.

problem is where to draw the line, or lines. The devolutionary principle as I have expressed it is, I think, the ethical principle which underlies any federal or quasi-federal structure, and it recognises what I take to be a fact of political life: that the further removed from the citizen a government is, the more bureaucratic and out of touch with local problems the citizen tends to perceive it to be. The usual British perception of the not very swollen bureaucracy in Brussels illustrates the point.

It would seem clear that the devolutionary principle provides the rationale of the Government of Wales Act 1998, the Scotland Act 1998 [and] the Northern Ireland Act 1998.

Notes

1. Perhaps the most immediately striking feature of the schemes of devolution in the UK is their asymmetry, in that primary legislative power is devolved to Scotland and Northern Ireland whilst Wales must make do with secondary legislative powers unless and until a national referendum clearly indicates national dissatisfaction with that situation (below, pp 287–288). Alan Ward has criticised this aspect of devolution in the UK:

   > Indeed, one's overall impression of Labour's constitutional design is its incoherence. Some would see this as evidence of the genius of a flexible constitution, not a problem at all, but they are wrong. The constitutional innovation of recent years has produced a UK constitution that is so complex that it must be incomprehensible to most citizens, and constitutional incoherence surely contributes to the democratic deficit in the UK.[3]

   This is not to say, however, that the schemes lack anything in common. All of the devolved schemes create unicameral rather than bicameral bodies, which are elected by proportional representation, and all of the schemes are subordinate to the will of the Westminster Parliament.[4] The latter feature of the devolved schemes—the continuing sovereignty of the Westminster Parliament—is particularly interesting because it presents domestic judges with the difficult constitutional task of according sufficient recognition both to parliamentary sovereignty, on the one hand, and to the important democratic status of the newly-devolved bodies created by Westminster, on the other. Devolution, in all of its manifestations across the UK, is more than just a legal framework for the exercise of decentralised decision-making power. As Bogdanor remarks, the schemes generate 'a new locus of *political* power'.[5] The effect that this has had on the exercise by domestic courts of their powers to review the activities of the devolved bodies, which is illustrated by several challenges made in court to the validity of Acts of the Scottish Parliament, will be explored in the following section.

2. Bogdanor cautions against over-hasty assessments of the success or otherwise of devolution, remarking that:

   > New institutions and organisations take some years to settle down—a generation perhaps—and establish their distinctive patterns. Constitutional reforms take time to percolate and for their full effects to be understood.[6]

---

3   A Ward, 'Devolution: Labour's Strange Constitutional Design', in J Jowell and D Oliver, *The Changing Constitution*, 4th edn (2000), pp 134–35.

4   *Ibid*, pp 113–17.

5   V Bogdanor, *Devolution in the United Kingdom* (2001), p 288 (emphasis added).

6   V Bogdanor, *The New British Constitution* (2009), p 95.

This should not be taken to imply that the current system of national governance in the UK is somehow static in nature and immune from further refinement over the coming years. Indeed, another striking feature of the devolution schemes is their rapid speed of development. In particular, (as will be examined in detail below, pp 263–265) in the decade or so since the devolution schemes began to operate, there have already been serious calls by the nationalist Scottish Government to progress the Scottish scheme to full independence. Major reforms to the scheme for Wales (the Government of Wales Act 2006) were passed only eight years after the original statute (below, pp 287–288). Additionally, one plausible solution to the West Lothian question (the problem of MPs from devolved areas retaining full voting rights at Westminster) would involve further erosion of the union into a federal state comprised of national legislatures with their own fields of exclusive legislative competence (see below, pp 290–291). Curiously, what would make the idea of a federal UK all the more plausible is its broad similarity, in substance, to the current landscape of UK governance resulting from the devolution schemes. As Brazier remarks:

> [T]he old, centralized British state has passed away. . . It may be that a *de facto* federal constitution is [already] in place, if the United Kingdom Parliament and Government leave the devolved authorities in peace.[7]

An interesting point for readers to bear in mind when reading the following materials, therefore, is the huge evolutionary potential that the current schemes of devolution possess. It is impossible to rule out further enlargement of the devolved legislatures' powers or, more radically still, the break-away of one or more UK nations into independent states, over the next generation. We will be examining various key proposals for reform in greater detail below.

3. With these brief observations in mind, we can now turn to the overview and analysis of the various schemes.

SCOTTISH DEVOLUTION

Introduction[8]

Having been subject to partial rule from England, Scotland achieved complete independence from England by their victory in the battle of Bannockburn in 1314. Strife between the two nations continued, however, and was finally brought to an end at the beginning of the 18th century with the Treaty and Acts of Union 1707, which established full political and economic union. The treaty—which was enshrined in legislation passed by the English Parliament in 1706 and the Scottish Parliament the following year—made the two countries one, setting up a new parliament, the British Parliament, as the supreme legislative body of the new country. However, it was agreed at that time, and written into the treaties as unchangeable principles, that Scotland should retain its separate legal system, its separate established Church—the Presbyterian Church of Scotland—and its separate education system.[9] Once established, while the Westminster parliament legislated for Scotland,

---

7   R Brazier, *Constitutional Reform in the United Kingdom* (2008), p 121.

8   For a more detailed history, see C Munro, *Studies in Constitutional Law,* 2nd edn (2009), Chapter 2.

9   For analysis of the Treaties and Acts of Union in the context of parliamentary sovereignty, see Chapter 4, pp 196–197.

many Bills were 'Scottish' Bills, that is, concerned only with Scottish affairs, and there was a Scottish Office and Scottish Secretary of State. Before devolution, the Scottish Office, situated in Edinburgh, administered Scottish affairs. Scotland was allocated a block grant, which the Secretary of State was at liberty to allocate in accordance with what were thought to be local needs and priorities. Scotland thus had quite a high degree of executive devolution and preserved its separate legal system, church and education system.

The perceived problems with this state of affairs, however, were two-fold. First, as Mitchell observes, there was what could be termed a representational or legitimacy problem: the partially separate administration of Scotland could well be controlled by a political party that had been clearly rejected in the polls by the Scottish people. For example, throughout the 1980s and in the 1990s, up until the election of a Labour Government in 1997, Scotland was governed, like the rest of the UK, by a Conservative administration:

> While few would question the legality of Conservative rule, many questioned its justifiability... In February 1983, Gordon Brown, as vice-chairman of the Scottish Labour Party, questioned whether Conservative rule of Scotland would be legitimate if Labour won in Scotland again. The job of the Scottish Secretary should be made 'untenable', Brown argued... [This amounted to a] 'democratic deficit', and included the development of an understanding that devolution was required for legitimacy to be restored.[10]

As Mitchell observes, the first, 'democratic deficit' problem, was that Scotland had for many years consistently rejected the Conservative Party at the polls, preferring the Labour Party and, to a lesser extent, the Scottish Nationalist Party. For example, in 1987, the ruling Conservative Government won only 10 out of Scotland's 70 seats; in 1992, 12 seats. The system as it stood was seen as unrepresentative.

The second problem with Westminster rule of Scotland was that the Scottish Administration was neither sufficiently accountable nor *locally* accountable. While the Scottish Office was situated in Edinburgh, it was not accountable to any Scottish representative body, but solely to the Westminster Parliament, dominated by English MPs. It arguably received inadequate scrutiny there. As Colin Munro notes:

> The Scottish Office's appearance on the parliamentary question rota once every three weeks was hardly commensurate with the scale of their activities, and more generally it was obvious that the House of Commons had insufficient time for scrutiny of Scottish administration.[11]

Against the backdrop of these problems, a Constitutional Convention, comprised of representatives from the Labour Party, Liberal Democrats, trades union, churches and other small parties was established in the 1990s. The Convention proposed a Parliament for Scotland that would exercise substantial legislative powers. Its report, *Scotland's Parliament, Scotland's Right*, published in 1995, formed a blueprint for devolution which was reflected in many respects in the devolution scheme eventually devised by the Scotland Act 1998.

---

10   J Mitchell, 'Devolution's Unfinished Business' (2006) 77 *The Political Quarterly* 465.

11   Munro, n 8 above, at 39.

Scottish Devolution: basic principles

In July 1997, following the manifesto promise by the newly-elected Labour Government, the Scotland Office issued its White Paper, *Scotland's Parliament*, which set out the Government's key proposals for a Scottish Parliament and planned a referendum in Scotland on the issue the following autumn:

Scotland Office, Scotland's Parliament, Cm 3658 (1997) (extracts)

What the Scottish Parliament can do

The Scottish Parliament will have law-making powers over a wide range of matters which affect Scotland. There will be a Scottish Executive headed by a First Minister which will operate in a way similar to the UK Government and will be held to account by the Scottish Parliament. The Scottish Parliament and Executive will be responsible for [matters such as health; education and training; home affairs and the environment]. . .

Scotland in the United Kingdom

The legislation setting up the Scottish Parliament will specify those powers which are reserved to the UK Parliament. These matters include the **constitution** of the United Kingdom; **UK foreign policy** including relations with Europe; **UK defence** and **national security**; the stability of the UK's **fiscal, economic and monetary system**; **common markets** for UK goods and services; **employment legislation**; **social security**; and most aspects of **transport safety and regulation.**

The new constitutional arrangements

Scotland will remain an integral part of the United Kingdom, and The Queen will continue to be Head of State of the United Kingdom.

The UK Parliament is and will remain sovereign. Scotland's MPs will continue to play a full and constructive part at Westminster. The number of Scottish seats will be reviewed.

The Secretary of State for Scotland will work with the new Scottish Parliament and represent Scottish interests within the UK Government.

The Scottish Executive and the UK Government will work closely together at both Ministerial and official level.

There will be arrangements for resolving disagreements about whether legislation is within the powers of the Scottish Parliament. . .

Financial arrangements

The financial framework for the Scottish Parliament will be closely based on existing arrangements for financing The Scottish Office, and will allow the Scottish Parliament to approve spending decisions in accordance with Scottish needs and priorities.

The control of local authority expenditure, non-domestic rates and other local taxation will be devolved to the Scottish Parliament.

Subject to the outcome of the referendum, the Scottish Parliament will be given power to increase or decrease the basic rate of income tax set by the UK Parliament by up to 3p.

Notes

1. It should be stressed from the outset that the Government's plan was never to *cede* legislative authority to Scotland by making it independent. As the White Paper states, the Government's plan was for the Westminster Parliament to 'remain sovereign'. This is to be contrasted with the bolder recommendations of the Scottish Constitutional Convention, in *Scotland's Parliament, Scotland's*

Right: 'We, gathered as the Scottish Constitutional Convention, do hereby acknowledge the sovereign right of the Scottish people to determine the form of government suited to their needs'.

2. Following the White Paper, the proposal that there should be a Scottish Parliament was put to the Scottish people in the referendum of 11 September 1997. The proposal was approved by nearly 75% of those who took part, on a reasonable turnout of around 60%, and a second question—whether it should have limited tax-raising powers—was approved by a lower, but still convincing, majority of 63.5%.[12] Thus directly mandated by the people, the devolution scheme clearly acquired an important democratic legitimacy which has the effect of lending it a *de facto* entrenched status, a point returned to below.

3. The Scottish Parliament, which sits at Holyrood in Edinburgh, has at present 129 members (known as MSPs), though this number may fall as a result of boundary changes in future. Each elector has two votes. Seventy-three MSPs ('Constituency' MSPs) are elected in the same way as members of the Westminster Parliament; that is, each constituency elects the candidate who receives the most votes (the 'first past the post' system). The second vote, for a further 56 MSPs ('Regional List' MSPs), is cast for a party, rather than an individual candidate, under a proportional system known as the additional member system. The system is based around the current Euro-constituencies, which divide Scotland into 8 regions, each with 7 MSPs.[13] The Scottish Parliament is elected for fixed terms of four years. There is provision, however, for exceptional early dissolution if the Parliament resolves by a two-thirds majority that it should be dissolved, or if it is unable to agree upon a new First Minister within 28 days of the resignation or removal of the incumbent (see Scotland Act 1998, s 3(1)). It is thus clear, as Ward explains, that the devolved authorities lack:

> the kind of advantages possessed by the Prime Minister of the UK, who can dissolve, or threaten to dissolve, [the Westminster] Parliament at any time for partisan advantage or to bring party dissidents under control.[14]

There have so far been three general elections to the Scottish Parliament (1999, 2003 and 2007), the results of which were as follows:[15]

1999

Labour:	56	(of which 3 were Regional List MSPs)
SNP:	35	(of which 28 were Regional List MSPs)
Conservative:	18	(all of which were Regional List MSPs)
Liberal Democrats:	17	(of which 5 were Regional List MSPs)
Others:	3	(of which 2 were Regional List MSPs)

2003

Labour:	50	(of which 4 were Regional List MSPs)
SNP:	27	(of which 18 were Regional List MSPs)
Conservative:	18	(of which 15 were Regional List MSPs)
Liberal Democrats:	17	(of which 4 were Regional List MSPs)
Others:	17	(of which 15 were Regional List MSPs)

---

12   Source: www.scottish.parliament.uk/corporate/history/aDevolvedParliament/results.htm.

13   See further on electoral systems Chapter 8 at 349–354.

14   A Ward, 'Devolution: Labour's Strange Constitutional "Design"', in J Jowell and D Oliver (eds), *The Changing Constitution*, 4th edn (2000), p 124.

15   Source: www.scottish.parliament.uk/MSP/elections/2007/documents/Table1.pdf.

2007

SNP:	47	(of which 26 are Regional List MSPs)
Labour:	46	(of which 9 are Regional List MSPs)
Conservative:	17	(of which 13 are Regional List MSPs)
Liberal Democrats:	16	(of which 5 are Regional List MSPs)
Others:	3	(all of which are Regional List MSPs)

Notes

1. The Scottish Parliament's electoral system is inherently unlikely to produce overall majorities for a single party, as the figures show. In both the 1999 and 2003 elections, Labour was the largest single party, and formed a coalition with the Liberal Democrats, the third largest party. The SNP, which in 2007 became the largest single party (albeit only by a single seat), currently governs as a minority administration.

2. The 2007 electoral process, in which both local government and Scottish parliamentary elections were held on the same day, was widely reported to have been shambolic. Over 146,000 votes were rejected. The Electoral Commission undertook an independent investigation into the process, led by Canadian elections expert Ron Gould. His report[16] found that 'Almost without exception, the voter was treated as an afterthought by virtually all the other stakeholders.' A running theme throughout the Gould Report was the attribution of the electoral disorder to voter confusion, resulting in many inadvertently spoiled ballots, which was said in large part to be due to the combination of a new and unfamiliar design of ballot paper and the decision to hold both local government and Scottish parliamentary elections on the same day. Interestingly, and owing to the difference between 'reserved' and 'devolved' competences drawn by the Scotland Act (on this, see below, pp 241–242), the decisions to introduce the new ballot paper and to hold the local elections on the same day as the Scottish Parliamentary elections were made by authorities on different sides of the border. The Scotland Office had exercised its reserved powers in 2006 to determine the format of the ballot paper for the elections; the decision to combine the local with the general election polls, however, had been taken by the Scottish Executive in early 2007. The lack of co-ordination between Holyrood and Westminster when these decisions were made, Lardy explains, was a major cause of the ensuing voter confusion.

H Lardy, 'Explaining the failure of electoral democracy: devolution, election law design and the 2007 Scottish elections' [2008] *Public Law* 214 (extracts)

Although the Scotland Office chose to present this as a matter within the exclusive control of the devolved government, the law does not in fact grant final say on this to either institution. Rather it falls to the devolved institutions only by default. The current terms of the Scotland Act 1998 bind the UK government to four yearly terms for Scottish Parliament elections. The same Act devolves the administration of local elections to the Scottish government, but does not make any explicit reference to a power to combine the polls. That power arises from the incidental impact of the exercise of the devolved authority to set the cycle for local elections upon the reserved power regarding the Parliament's election timetable. The Scotland Act certainly does not forbid the Scottish government from taking steps which result in a combined poll. . .

---

16   Electoral Commission, Independent Review of the Local Government and Scottish Parliamentary Elections of 3rd May 2007 (2007).

> . . .What was lacking was a genuine dialogue in which both the reserved and devolved authorities tempered the exercise of their respective powers with reference to the likely consequences of the other's decision-making. The Scotland Office announced its intention to proceed with the new parliamentary ballot paper before the Scottish Executive had declared its intention to persist with a combined poll. The decision about the design of the ballot paper ought similarly to have been made in the context of the likely occurrence of a combined poll. As subsequent events demonstrated, the exercise of divided competence can pose a threat to the integrated functioning of the electoral process as a whole. . .
>
> It is to be hoped that the events of the 2007 elections, and the recommendations of the Gould report, will act as a prompt to full, regular and voluntary engagement in future.

Notes

1. Along these lines, the Gould Report recommended that 'assigning responsibility for both elections to one jurisdictional entity', and that the Scottish Government should be granted greater power to administer both elections (at p 111). Despite the then Secretary of State for Scotland, Des Browne MP, stating in his formal response to the Gould Report that a 'considered examination of the structures required for administering elections in Scotland is necessary',[17] it remains to be seen whether or not the Gould Report's recommendations will materialise into the transfer of greater authority to Holyrood to administer the Scottish Parliamentary elections.

2. As a practical solution to help avoid a repeat of the disorder in 2007, the Scottish Parliament has enacted the Scottish Local Government Elections Act 2009, which aims to decouple future Parliamentary and local government elections. The next local government elections will be held in 2012, the year after elections to the Scottish Parliament; they will then occur in 2017 and, thereafter, in four-year intervals at the mid-point of each Scottish Parliamentary term.

The competence of the Scottish Parliament

Devolved, Reserved and Excluded Matters

The operative provisions determining the legislative competence of the Scottish Parliament are ss 28–30 of the Scotland Act 1998 (SA 1998), which provide as follows:

28. Acts of the Scottish Parliament

1   Subject to section 29, the Parliament may make laws, to be known as Acts of the Scottish Parliament.

2   Proposed Acts of the Scottish Parliament shall be known as Bills; and a Bill shall become an Act of the Scottish Parliament when it has been passed by the Parliament and has received Royal Assent. . .

3   The validity of an Act of the Scottish Parliament is not affected by any invalidity in the proceedings of the Parliament leading to its enactment. . .

7   This section does not affect the power of the Parliament of the United Kingdom to make laws for Scotland.

---

17   Scotland Office, 'Written ministerial statement setting out formal response to the Gould report into the May 2007 Scottish Parliamentary elections' (24 June 2008).

29. Legislative competence

1   An Act of the Scottish Parliament is not law so far as any provision of the Act is outside the legislative competence of the Parliament.

2   A provision is outside that competence so far as any of the following paragraphs apply—

(a)   it would form part of the law of a country or territory other than Scotland, or confer or remove functions exercisable otherwise than in or as regards Scotland,

(b)   it relates to reserved matters [see below],

(c)   it is in breach of the restrictions in Schedule 4,

(d)   it is incompatible with any of the [ECHR] rights or with [European] Community law,

(e)   it would remove the Lord Advocate from his position as head of the systems of criminal prosecution and investigation of deaths in Scotland.

3   For the purposes of this section, the question whether a provision of an Act of the Scottish Parliament relates to a reserved matter is to be determined, subject to subsection (4), by reference to the purpose of the provision, having regard (among other things) to its effect in all the circumstances. . .

30. Legislative competence: supplementary

1   Schedule 5 (which defines reserved matters) shall have effect.

2   Her Majesty may by Order in Council make any modifications of Schedule 4 or 5 which She considers necessary or expedient.

3   Her Majesty may by Order in Council specify functions which are to be treated, for such purposes of this Act as may be specified, as being, or as not being, functions which are exercisable in or as regards Scotland. . .

Notes

1. The first and most important point to make about the Scottish Parliament is that it is, unequivocally, both a limited and subordinate legislature. Section 29(1) SA 1998, by providing that an Act of the Parliament 'is not law' so far as its provisions fall outside of the Parliament's legislative competence, gives judges a full strike-down power over legislation passed by it that is *ultra vires* (outside its powers).

2. Instead of setting out the specific powers to be passed to Scotland, the Act takes a different route: those powers not being transferred (known as 'reserved powers') are specified; anything not mentioned is deemed to be transferred. Competence is thus defined negatively: the Scottish Parliament may not legislate on 'reserved matters' (s 29(2)(b)), which remain within the exclusive competency of Westminster (this represents the reverse of the position adopted under the abortive Scotland Act 1978).

3. 'Reserved matters', as defined by Sched 5, include:

    •   constitutional issues, including the monarchy, the UK Parliament and the registration and funding of political parties and the Civil Service including the Scottish Civil Service;

- foreign and defence policy, including immigration and citizenship;
- the fiscal, economic and monetary system (that is, macro-economic issues, including interest rates and currency);
- common markets for UK goods and services;
- employment (including industrial relations) and social security;
- transport safety and regulation;
- energy, including the ownership and exploration of oil and gas;
- miscellaneous matters, including abortion, postal services, equal opportunities and broadcasting regulation.

4. The Scottish Parliament cannot legislate incompatibly with EU law or the European Convention on Human Rights (s 29(2)(d)), nor can it legislate extra-territorially (s 29(2)(a)) or remove the Lord Advocate (s 29(2)(e)). Matters in breach of the restrictions contained in Sched 4 will also be *ultra vires* (s 29(2)(c)). Schedule 4 sets out, *inter alia*, a detailed list of Westminster enactments specifically protected from amendment or repeal by the Scottish Parliament; these include the Human Rights Act 1998, core provisions of the European Communities Act 1972 and Scotland Act itself; and provisions relating to free trade under the Acts of Union.

5. Powers that are devolved to the Scottish Parliament therefore include:

- all areas of education;
- local government;
- land development and environmental regulation;
- many aspects of transport policy;
- the Scottish NHS;
- the legal system (civil and criminal law (save that the Scottish Parliament is bound by both EU law and the ECHR));
- agriculture and fisheries;
- sports, arts and culture.

6. The devolved areas may be altered by Order in Council (s 30(2) SA 1998), but the Order must be approved by both the Scottish and UK Parliaments. Devolved areas can also be changed by the Westminster Parliament by primary legislation, although that would require amendment of the Scotland Act itself. The budget that the Scottish Parliament and Scottish Executive dispose of is allocated as a block by the Westminster Parliament (ss 64–65). The Scottish Parliament may also vary income tax by 3p in the pound (s 73).

7. The Scottish Parliament is clearly a subordinate legislature in law. Not only is it created by Westminster statute, and thus (at least theoretically) subject to abolition, as the Greater London Council and metropolitan county councils were abolished in the 1980s, it is not even granted *exclusive* powers to legislate in the areas in which it is competent. Section 28(7) of the Scotland Act states that the grant of legislative powers to the Scottish Parliament 'does not affect the power of the UK Parliament to make law for Scotland', in line with the White Paper *Scotland's Parliament*, which proclaims that 'The United Kingdom is and will remain sovereign in all matters'. This, of course, would follow from the orthodox view of parliamentary sovereignty, under which Parliament cannot diminish its own powers. However, the fact that this was so baldly stated in the Scotland Act epitomises the way in which the devolution scheme, whilst on the one hand representing an important constitutional milestone of profound democratic significance, attempts to cleave resolutely, on the other hand, to an orthodox foundational UK constitutional principle. See further below at pp 246–254.

8. Significantly, it follows from the Scottish Parliament's general power to legislate in areas not reserved to Westminster that it has the power to amend or repeal Acts of the Westminster Parliament relating to devolved matters.[18] In effect, if the idea of the devolution settlement as a form of future governance for Scotland is not to be unduly frustrated, this means that all Acts of the Westminster Parliament applying to Scotland and relating to devolved matters, whether passed *or to be passed*, shall take effect in Scotland subject to the continuing will of the Scottish Parliament. The Scotland Act thus has interesting implications for the doctrine of parliamentary sovereignty and the courts' interpretation of future Westminster legislation. By conferring upon the Scottish Parliament a general power to amend or repeal Acts of the Westminster Parliament relating to devolved matters, Westminster is in substance imposing a restriction (known as restriction as to 'form': see Chapter 4, pp 194–195) on future Westminster Parliaments wishing to enact legislation relating to devolved matters—such legislation must state clearly on its face that it is intended to operate notwithstanding the powers of the Scottish Parliament to amend or repeal Westminster legislation; otherwise, an Act passed at Westminster on day one could simply be repealed by Scotland on day two. Assuming that such an attempt by Westminster to bind its successors would be valid according to contemporary perceptions of parliamentary sovereignty (such a restriction partially accords with the principle in *Thoburn v Sunderland City Council* [2002] 1 CMLR 1461 that constitutional statutes like the Scotland Act can only be expressly repealed),[19] these observations add force to Loveland's argument that the courts might require Westminster legislation purporting to legislate on devolved matters to state expressly that the Scotland Act shall be disregarded:

> A court which accepted the presumption that the Scotland Act was indeed intended to maximise the autonomy of the Scots electorate would not be sailing. . . into wholly uncharted constitutional waters if it held that s 28(7) [which preserves the ability of Westminster to legislate for Scotland] requires the courts to apply UK legislation affecting matters devolved to the Scots Parliament. . . only if the subsequent UK statute expressly states that the Scotland Act is being amended.[20]

9. It is important to remember, however, that such a conflict between the two Parliaments, where Westminster was intent to legislate for Scotland and Holyrood to repeal that legislation, would only arise in extreme circumstances in future, in which relations between the British and Scottish Governments had broken down. It appears that if such 'ping-pong' situations arose—whereby Parliament simply re-enacted the repealed legislation, the Scottish Parliament did likewise, and so on, it would have to be resolved politically, rather than legally.[21] As we will see in relation to the discussion of federalism and quasi-federalism (below, pp 256–258), Westminster has not so far legislated for Scotland without the Scottish Parliament's consent.

In relation to primary and secondary legislation passed by the Scottish Parliament, there will obviously be occasional borderline cases in which it is unclear whether that legislation is within the Parliament's competence as laid down by the Scotland Act. Section 101 provides as follows:

---

18   This was made clear by Lord Sewel during the passage of the Scotland Act: See HL Deb, col 789 (Lord Sewel) 21 July 1998. An amendment that would have prevented this was rejected. And see AW Bradley's 'The Sovereignty of Parliament—Form or Substance?', in J Jowell and D Oliver (eds), *The Changing Constitution*, 6th edn (2007) at p 51.

19   See Chapter 4, p 179. It only partially accords, because the *Thoburn* doctrine is that only the courts, not Parliament itself, can declare an Act 'constitutional' and so protected from implied repeal.

20   I Loveland, *Constitutional Law, Administrative Law and Human Rights: A Critical Introduction*, 5th edn (2009), p 441.

21   See HL Deb, *ibid.*

101. Interpretation of Acts of the Scottish Parliament etc.

1   This section applies to—

(a)   any provision of an Act of the Scottish Parliament, or of a Bill for such an Act, and

(b)   any provision of subordinate legislation made, confirmed or approved, or purporting to be made, confirmed or approved, by a member of the Scottish Executive, which could be read in such a way as to be outside competence.

2   Such a provision is to be read as narrowly as is required for it to be within competence, if such a reading is possible, and is to have effect accordingly. . .

In borderline cases, courts are therefore instructed by s 101(2) to go as far as possible, in terms of interpretation, to read down and give effect to legislation of the Scottish Parliament so as to ensure that the legislation remains within the Parliament's competence rather than being declared *ultra vires*. Section 101(2)'s aim is therefore to permit, rather than constrain, the Parliament's activities. This broadly reflects the purposive approach adopted by the Privy Council in *Edwards v Attorney-General for Canada* [1930] AC 124, PC to the interpretation of the British North America Act 1867, whose purpose was to create a union between Canada, New Brunswick and Nova Scotia. As Lord Sankey LC stated, at p 136:

The British North America Act planted in Canada a living tree capable of growth and expansion within its natural limits. Their Lordships do not consider it to be [their] duty . . . to cut down the provisions of the Act by a narrow and technical construction, but rather to give it a large and liberal interpretation so that [Canada] to a great extent may be mistress in her own house.

There is no provision in the Scotland Act relating to the interpretation of Westminster legislation that covers the devolved areas; however, as seen above, the courts may well take Westminster not to have intended to legislate in devolved areas unless that intention is made plain in the legislation in question.

10. Technically, the Scotland Act serves as a Constitution for Scotland in the orthodox sense (what Anthony King refers to as a 'capital C Constitution')[22] because it serves as a higher framework that cannot itself be repealed by the Scottish Parliament. The distinction between 'devolved' and 'reserved' matters is not without complication, however. Even if an Act of the Scottish Parliament can be interpreted (with or without the aid of the interpretative obligation under s 101(2)) as 'relating' to a devolved mater and therefore within the technical competence of the Parliament, what is the position if the legislation in question nevertheless *affects* reserved matters? Section 29(4) provides as follows:

(4)   A provision which—

(a)   would otherwise not relate to reserved matters, but

(b)   makes modifications of Scots private law, or Scots criminal law, as it applies to reserved matters,

---

22   See Chapter 1, pp 7–11.

is to be treated as relating to reserved matters unless the purpose of the provision is to make the law in question apply consistently to reserved matters and otherwise.

As Himsworth explains, s 29(4), along with Sched 4 to the Scotland Act, provide the answer to this question.

CMG Himsworth, 'Devolution and its Jurisdictional Asymmetries' (2007) 70 *Modern Law Review* 31 (extracts)

In the Scotland Act 1998, the need to accommodate the Scottish Parliament's responsibility for the specialities of Scots law has led to some of the Act's most sophisticated and complex provisions. The Act has to recognise two demands. One is the need for the Parliament to respect the reserved/devolved borderline the Act generally lays down. Secondly it has also to enable the Parliament to make general provision for the civil and criminal law of Scotland, the point being that such general provision may inevitably affect the law on both sides of the reserved/devolved divide. A 'legal system' competence [such as this], since it is based on quite different criteria from those which apportion competences on a functional basis, cuts across the initial divide in uncomfortable ways. The general rules of criminal law and criminal procedure affect the prosecution of offences related to both reserved and devolved subject matter. The general rules of contract and delict similarly cut across the subject divide and may, for instance, reach into the reserved areas of consumer protection or employment as well as the areas devolved to the Scottish Parliament. Judicial review procedures can plainly affect both devolved and reserved matters. The principal device for policing these cross-cutting competences is contained in section 29(4) of the Act which expressly permits the Parliament to modify Scots private law or Scots criminal law even where those modifications may relate to reserved matters, provided that 'the purpose of the provision is to make the law in question apply consistently to reserved matters and otherwise'. In other words, the legal system provisions have this necessary across-the-board characteristic. Additional, and more complex rules, are contained in Schedule 4 to the Act. These prevent the Parliament from modifying 'the law on reserved matters' but, in the case of a rule of Scots private or criminal law, only to the extent that the rule is 'special to a reserved matter' or relates to certain prescribed subject-matter. So far, these provisions appear to have operated in a trouble-free way. There has, at least, been no public challenge to a Bill or Act drafted in reliance upon them, although, as an aside, it should also be noted that there has been no challenge in the courts at all on the grounds that the Scottish Parliament has illicitly trespassed into the territory of reserved matters.

Note

The overall thrust of these provisions is to allow a certain amount of latitude to the Scottish Parliament, where Scots criminal and private law are concerned, to pass legislation on devolved matters which may nevertheless have a secondary impact on reserved matters. This is a sensible solution, given the historical independence of the Scots systems of criminal and private law.

Reviewing the *vires* of Acts of the Scottish Parliament: the case-law

Important constitutional questions arise when determining whether Acts of the Scottish Parliament have exceeded the Parliament's legislative competence. In particular, whilst the Scottish Parliament is a statutory body created by and subordinate to the Westminster Parliament in formal terms, does its status as a democratically elected legislature have any bearing on the jurisdiction of the domestic courts to scrutinise its behaviour according to ordinary principles of judicial review, such as improper purpose and irrationality? The issue has attracted much judicial comment, as the following cases demonstrate.

Whaley v Lord Watson 2000 SC 340 (extracts)

The case concerned the question whether the courts could review a decision by the Standards Committee of the Parliament as to whether Lord Watson, by introducing a Bill banning fox-hunting into the Scottish Parliament, had breached the Scotland Act 1998 (Transitional and Transitory Provisions) (Members' Interests) Order 1999, Art 6 of which forbade Members of the Parliament from carrying out Parliamentary activities in relation to affairs or interests in respect of which they had received remuneration from third parties. In a lower court, the Lord Ordinary refused to allow a legal challenge to the Committee's decision that Art 6 had not been breached.

The Lord President (Rodger)
These remarks of the Lord Ordinary contain some general observations about the relation-ship between the courts and the Scottish Parliament which had a bearing on his reasoning and which I am unable to endorse.

The Lord Ordinary gives insufficient weight to the fundamental character of the Parlia-ment as a body which—however important its role—has been created by statute and derives its powers from statute. As such, it is a body which, like any other statutory body, must work within the scope of those powers. If it does not do so, then in an appropriate case the court may be asked to intervene and will require to do so, in a manner permitted by the legislation. In principle, therefore, the Parliament like any other body set up by law is subject to the law and to the courts which exist to uphold that law. . .

Some of the arguments of counsel for the first respondent appeared to suggest that it was somehow inconsistent with the very idea of a parliament that it should be subject. . .to the law of the land and to the jurisdiction of the courts which uphold the law. I do not share that view. On the contrary, if anything, it is the Westminster Parliament which is unusual in being respected as sovereign by the courts. And, now, of course, certain inroads have been made into even that sovereignty by the European Communities Act 1972. By contrast, in many democracies throughout the Commonwealth, for example, even where the parlia-ments have been modelled in some respects on Westminster, they owe their existence and powers to statute and are in various ways subject to the law and to the courts which act to uphold the law. The Scottish Parliament has simply joined that wider family of parliaments. Indeed I find it almost paradoxical that counsel for a member of a body which exists to create laws and to impose them on others should contend that a legally enforceable framework is somehow less than appropriate for that body itself.

Lord Prosser: The contention that the court did not have jurisdiction to deal with the issues raised in this case was one I found hard to grasp. As I understood the submissions, the argument seemed to rest upon some broad view that since the Scottish Parliament was a parliament, rather than for example a local authority, the jurisdiction of the courts must be seen as excluded, as an unacceptable intrusion upon the legislative function which belonged to Parliament alone. A variant of this argument appeared to be that if the court's jurisdiction was not actually excluded as a matter of law, the court should nonetheless be slow or hesitant or reluctant or unwilling to use the jurisdiction which it had, in order to avoid an undesirable intrusion on Parliament's freedom in relation to legislation.

Both forms of argument appear to me to be entirely without foundation. If and in so far as a parliament may have powers which are not limited by any kind of legal definition, there is no doubt scope for concepts of 'sovereignty', with the courts unable to enforce boundaries which do not exist. But if and in so far as a parliament and its powers have been defined, and thus limited, by law, it is in my opinion self-evident that the courts have jurisdiction in relation to these legal definitions and limits, just as they would have for any other body created by law. If anything, the need for such a jurisdiction is in my opinion all the greater where a body has very wide powers, as the Scottish Parliament has: the greater the powers, the greater the need to ensure that they are not exceeded. But the jurisdiction of the courts and the legal definition of the body seem to me to be merely two sides of the same coin.

Faced with the suggestion that the courts might abstain from exercising a jurisdiction which they have, allowing the Parliament perhaps to exercise power beyond its legal limits, from a fear that enforcement of those limits might be seen as stopping Parliament from doing what it wanted to do, I am baffled: a defined parliament is there to do not whatever it wants, but only what the law has empowered it to do. In the odd, and perhaps unsatisfactory, context of 'sovereign' or undefined powers, the courts may be faced with problems; but these are very precisely problems of a kind which do not arise, and can afford no guidance, where the issue is one of law, and jurisdiction is its inevitable counterpart. The nature and functions of the Parliament, and of any particular provisions, will of course be matters which must be taken into account, whenever the courts in exercising their jurisdiction require to interpret or apply the provisions which the law has made in relation to the Parliament. But that is a quite different matter.

Notes

1. Although, as Lord Rodger observed, *Whaley* was significant because it was 'the first time that the court has had to consider the workings of the Scottish Parliament' (p 344), it is important not to lose sight of the context surrounding their Lordships' remarks. The Lord Ordinary's view that the domestic court somehow lacked the power under the Scotland Act to review the Standards Committee's decision would have effectively placed the activities of the Scottish Parliament, like the sovereign Westminster Parliament, beyond the reach of the courts. By drawing attention to the statutory *vires* placed around the Scottish Parliament by the Scotland Act 1998 and the concomitant role of the domestic courts to enforce that *vires* in accordance with Westminster's wishes, Lord Rodger and Lord Prosser evidently disagreed that the courts' powers of review were necessarily ousted in this way. Their remarks were directed towards correcting the Lord Ordinary's view that the Scottish Parliament's characteristics as a democratically elected legislature *necessarily* precluded review of its activities by domestic courts. Lord Rodger's view that the Parliament is a body 'like any other statutory body' does not, therefore, imply that its democratic characteristics have no bearing at all on how the courts exercise their powers of review. Indeed, as Lord Prosser observed, the courts would consider the 'nature and functions' of the Parliament when interpreting statutory provisions imposing constraints on its activities.

2. This important point is illustrated by the following case.

Adams v Scottish Ministers 2004 SC 665 (extracts)

According to ss 29(1) and 29(2)(d) of the Scotland Act 1998, an Act of the Scottish Parliament will be outwith the competence of the Scottish Parliament (and thus void) in so far as any of its provisions contravene the European Convention. The petitioners, all of whose livelihoods were dependent on the sport of foxhunting, alleged that the Protection of Wild Mammals (Scotland) Act 2002, which bans the hunting of foxes with dogs, was outwith the competence of the Scottish Parliament because it breached the Convention rights to respect for property (Art 1 of the First Protocol), respect for privacy and the right to a home life (Art 8), freedom of assembly (Art 11) and freedom from discrimination in the enjoyment of Convention rights (Art 14). The Lord Ordinary (Nimmo Smith) rejected the petition. The petitioners' reclaiming motion was dismissed.

The Lord Justice-Clerk (Gill) (giving the judgment of the court). . .
27 Although the concept of margin of appreciation does not apply in the domestic context, the supervisory role of the domestic court in its appraisal of legislation involves its conceding to the legislature a discretionary area of judgment. It will be easier for such an area of judgment to be recognised where, to a greater or lesser extent, the issues involve social or economic policy, much less so where the rights are of high constitutional importance or are of a kind where the courts are especially well placed to assess the need for protection. . .
46 If the Parliament was of the view that foxhunting was cruel, and was aware of the likely impacts of the legislation, the next question is whether the Parliament was entitled to make the judgment that foxhunting should be proscribed by law.
47 The starting point on this issue, in our opinion, is that the prevention of cruelty to animals has for over a century fallen within the constitutional responsibility of the legislature. The enactment of every statute on the subject has necessarily involved the making of a moral judgment. In our view, the 2002 Act should be seen as a further step in a long legislative sequence in which animal welfare has on numerous occasions been promoted by legislation related to contemporary needs and problems.
48 Looking at the Act in that context, we consider that it represents a considered decision by the Parliament on a long-standing and highly charged public controversy. In our view, any judgment on that controversy is pre-eminently one for MSPs. . . [who] are elected on their policies on matters such as this. Once elected, they have the means at hand to inform themselves on the factual and moral issues, and are open to representations from all interest groups. They are subject to the constraints of the legislative process, which requires, *inter alia*, that the principle of a Bill should be expressly considered and voted on before any question of the details of the proposal can arise. That consideration involves the formal reception of evidence and the analysis of the issues in the course of debates.
49 We consider that it was entirely within the discretion of the Parliament to make the judgment that the pursuit and killing of a fox by a mounted hunt and a pack of hounds for the purposes of recreation and sport and for the pleasure of both participants and spectators was ethically wrong; that the likely impacts of the legislation did not justify its continuing to be legal; that it was a fit and proper exercise of legislative power to proscribe such an activity; and that the criminal offences, and related sanctions, that the 2002 Act imposes were the appropriate means of doing so. Moreover, in deciding on the utility and appropriateness of the legislative response to the problem of animal cruelty, the Parliament was entitled to consider, *inter alia*, whether, apart from its sporting and recreational aspects, foxhunting was an efficient method of pest control.
50 The judgment of the Parliament in this case had the consequence that certain

individuals and groups would suffer economic loss without right to compensation. That was a material consideration, but not a decisive one. Most legislation that is enacted for some public benefit results in economic detriment to some persons or bodies. The lack of compensation is merely one of many material factors that go into the exercise by which the intended public benefit is balanced against adverse social, economic and other impacts and against private disadvantage. This is certainly not an area in which the courts have any special expertise. The considered judgment of the Parliament upon it lies squarely within the scope of that discretionary area into which, in our view, the court should not intrude.

51 For these reasons, we consider that the Lord Ordinary was right in his general approach to this matter. . . and in his conclusion that the prohibition of foxhunting was capable of being regarded as necessary in a democratic society for the protection of morals (Art 8(2)) and necessary in accordance with the general interest (Art 1, para 2 of the First Protocol).

52 That was pre-eminently a judgment for the legislature. In our opinion, there is no reason why we should conclude that the legislature exceeded or misapplied its discretionary area of judgment, still less substitute our own views on the matter.

Notes

1. For commentary on cases concerning the review of Acts of the Scottish Parliament up to and including *Adams*, see B Winetrobe, 'The Judge in the Scottish Parliament Chamber' [2005] PL 3. Whilst their Lordships ruled in *Whaley* that the nature of the Scottish Parliament as a democratic legislature would not of itself be enough to oust the courts' powers to review its activities, *Adams* indicates that the courts will nevertheless accord it significant weight when scrutinising the Parliament's behaviour, at least in the context of qualified Convention rights where courts are called upon to evaluate the balance that the Parliament has attempted to strike between the competing interests of different groups of individuals, or of the individual and (to use the term loosely in this context) the 'state'. This has the benefit of allowing the courts to retain their powers of review over the Parliament as a body created and constrained in its activities by a Westminster statute whilst at the same time recognising and giving effect to the Parliament's democratic mandate and expertise, on matters of sensitive social, economic or ethical policy, relative to the courts.

2. It is submitted that the courts should be wary of taking the principle of deference too far, however, particularly in the human rights context where the very purpose of the Convention is to guard against unjustified interference with fundamental rights by, *inter alia*, legislatures such as the Scottish Parliament. Baroness Hale made a similar point, again a reminder that the courts remain the ultimate judges of whether or not an Act of the Scottish Parliament has infringed the Convention, in *Whaley v Lord Advocate* [2007] UKHL 53 (which involved a further unsuccessful challenge on ECHR grounds to the competence of the Scottish Parliament to enact the Protection of Wild Mammals (Scotland) Act 2002)):

   [41] If we could confidently predict that the European Court of Human Rights would find that the hunting ban did engage these Convention rights and could not be justified, then in my view it would be our duty to say so. Even though it is the recently enacted Act of a democratic Parliament, we could not wash our hands of the matter.

The deferential approach by the courts to the legislature seen in *Adams* was appropriate in that case given the obvious, moral and ethical dimensions to the foxhunting issue and the related expertise possessed by the Parliament, but it remains to be seen how much weight judges reviewing the

Convention-compatibility of Acts of the Scottish Parliament relating to issues with which they are more familiar, such as procedure and evidence, will attribute to the Parliament's democratic character.

3. The recent first instance opinion in *Axa General Insurance Ltd v Lord Advocate* [2010] CSOH 2 broadly follows the *Adams* approach: whilst domestic courts retain their jurisdiction to review Acts of the Scottish Parliament on 'traditional' grounds of review such as irrationality, the democratic nature of the Scottish Parliament nevertheless has an important bearing on the *standard* of review. Readers may find it useful to refer to the explanation and discussion of the ground of review known as *Wednesbury* unreasonableness or 'irrationality' in Chapter 15, pp 870–883.

Axa General Insurance Ltd v Lord Advocate [2010] CSOH 2 (extracts)

In Scots law and the law of England and Wales, the question whether claimants developing 'pleural plaques' as a result of exposure to asbestos could show an actionable damage in tort had long been unclear. Whilst the development of pleural plaques is acknowledged medically as a consequence of exposure to asbestos, the condition of itself is not necessarily harmful. Dangerous and potentially fatal medical conditions can sometimes develop from pleural plaques, but it often takes decades for doctors to be able to tell whether or not this will happen to a given patient. Consequently, upon the diagnosis of pleural plaques, claimants wishing to sue tortfeasors in negligence for exposure to asbestos are usually only able to point to freestanding stress and anxiety resulting from their condition—and not personal injury as such—as their only 'damage'. Insurance companies in both jurisdictions, however, had usually conceded liability on this issue as a matter of course. The House of Lords recently decided *Rothwell v Chemical and Insulating Co Limited* [2008] 1 AC 281, which put it beyond doubt that the mere presence of pleural plaques, without more, would not constitute actionable damage in tort. Anticipating the possibility that domestic courts might apply *Rothwell* as persuasive in Scots law, the Scottish Parliament enacted the Damages (Asbestos-related Conditions) (Scotland) Act 2009 which, for the avoidance of doubt, designated pleural plaques (and similar conditions) conditions which *were* actionable for damages. The petitioners, all major insurance companies, sought judicial review of the Act on the grounds that it was irrational, and that it breached their Convention rights under Art 6 and Art 1 of the First Protocol. The Lord Ordinary dismissed the petition.

The Lord Ordinary (Emslie): [89] The question which arises for determination at this stage is whether the validity of the 2009 Act, as legislation emanating from the non-sovereign Scottish Parliament, is or is not susceptible to challenge on traditional common law grounds [i.e. illegality, irrationality and procedural impropriety]. . . [T]he question is: can the petitioners competently pursue an 'irrationality' challenge here? . . .

[His Lordship then examined domestic cases concerning the amenability of subordinate legislation to judicial review, and continued:]

[101] By 1998 it was clear from. . . [*R v Secretary of State for the Environment, ex parte Nottinghamshire County Council* [1986] AC 240 and *R v Secretary of State for the Environment, ex parte Hammersmith and Fulham London Borough Council* [1991] 1 AC 521] in particular that all subordinate legislation, whether formally approved by Parliament or not, was amenable to judicial review on traditional common law grounds including that of irrationality. . . *A fortiori* the traditional common law grounds of review extended to the acts and decisions of any public body created by Parliament and deriving its powers from statute. Only primary legislation enacted at Westminster could be thought to enjoy

complete immunity from the courts' supervisory jurisdiction at common law. All of these matters must have been known to Parliament at the time when SA 1998 was passed. . .

[Having discussed the Lord Ordinary's decision in *Adams v Scottish Ministers* 2003 SC 171, Lord Emslie continued:]

[125] With the utmost respect to the Lord Ordinary in *Adams*, I find myself unable to share his conclusion on competency in this case. To my mind the respondents' concession was well-founded, to the effect that SA 1998 [the Scotland Act] could not be regarded as embodying " . . . a comprehensive scheme . . . for the relationship between the courts and the Parliament", and so while section 29 of the Act plainly does not include irrationality among the specified limits on legislative competence I do not regard that as in any way fatal to the petitioners' position. The issue is surely not whether a duty on the Parliament or on Ministers to act rationally, or the availability of traditional common law grounds of review, is expressly spelled out. It would be unusual to find such provisions in any statute and, significantly, SA 1998 makes no such provision with respect to subordinate legislation where *ex concessu* both the duty and the remedy apply. In my judgment, the real question here is whether the Act contains anything sufficient, whether by clear words or necessary implication, to oust the fundamental supervisory jurisdiction of the courts at common law and thus—in the absence of any relevant procedural framework—make the Parliament the sole judge of the rationality of its own legislation. . .

[130] With such considerations in mind, it is appropriate to return to the traditional grounds on which the acts or omissions of any public authority created by statute may be subject to judicial review. These. . . embrace the three key categories of 'illegality', 'procedural impropriety' and 'irrationality'. Looking at the matter broadly, the concept of 'illegality' may appear to be the counterpart of the 'devolved' or 'legislative' competence for which express limits are set in SA 1998. Section 29 defines the scope of the Parliament's legislative powers, and there is no dispute here that an Act of the Scottish Parliament may be judicially reviewed on grounds of illegality, or excess of power, where the specified limits are exceeded. Similarly, 'procedural impropriety' may appear to match the 'procedural invalidity' which by section 28(5) is expressly excluded as a competent ground of review in that context. The question then arises as to whether, expressly or by necessary implication, SA 1998 excludes the possibility of judicial review under. . . [the] third head of 'irrationality'.

[131] As previously discussed, the statute was enacted against a background of (i) primary legislation of the sovereign Parliament of the United Kingdom at Westminster being altogether immune from review by the courts on any ground other than an alleged violation of European Community law or of Convention rights; (ii) subordinate legislation, whether approved by Parliament or not, being amenable to judicial review on *inter alia* all of the traditional common law grounds including irrationality; and (iii) every public body owing its existence and powers to statute being equally amenable to the common law supervisory jurisdiction of the courts. The new Scottish Parliament would be a non-sovereign public body owing its existence and powers to a statute liable to amendment or repeal. Its legislative competence extending to part of the United Kingdom would be subject to the continuing sovereignty of the Westminster Parliament. Even in a Scottish context, the legislative powers of the new parliament would be non-exclusive. Unlike the Westminster Parliament, the Scottish Parliament would be disabled from passing any enactment at variance with the European Convention on Human Rights. And in such circumstances there would inevitably be scope for debate on the true status of relevant legislation. If the Scottish Parliament was intended to be the first UK statutory body for two centuries or more to be

wholly immune from judicial review on traditional common law grounds, it would (assuming the competency of such a measure) have been easy for SA 1998 to spell that out in clear and unambiguous terms. Had the intention been for the new devolved legislature to enjoy all or even part of the immunity traditionally attaching to the sovereign Parliament at Westminster, this could equally have been made the subject of explicit provision. But that did not happen. SA 1998 contains no hint of an express provision bearing to exempt Acts of the new statutory Parliament from the possibility of judicial review on the ground of irrationality. . .

[132] As a matter of settled principle, fundamental rights of the subject (including appropriate recourse to the courts for review of parliamentary, executive or administrative acts or omissions) may not be overridden except by the express words of a statute or by necessary implication. . . Had Parliament intended to override that presumption here, and in so doing deny or even materially restrict fundamental common law rights of access to justice, it seems to me that SA 1998 would have had to spell that out in clear and unambiguous terms. . .

[136]. . . I consider that the disputed issue of competency in this case must. . . be resolved in the petitioners' favour. This conclusion seems to me to accord with principle and authority, with the legislative background to SA 1998, and with a fair and proper reading of the statute itself. Had the provisions of SA 1998 regarding primary legislation been framed along different lines, the respondents might have had a stronger argument at their disposal. It might not, in theory, have been inconceivable for the sovereign parliament at Westminster to intend the new devolved parliament in Edinburgh to enjoy the same level of immunity as it had itself always enjoyed, and some indication of that intention might have appeared in the Act. . .

[137] In my judgment, however. . . there is no reason to think that the Westminster Parliament intended to exclude the rule of law, the jurisdiction of the courts and the potential for review where no such exclusion had applied before. . .

Notes

1. Lord Emslie's opinion contains a commendably thorough analysis of both the scheme of the Scotland Act 1998 and the constitutional position, prior to its enactment, of the ordinary routes of judicial review open (or not) to applicants in respect of primary and secondary legislation in UK courts. Interestingly, his Lordship analyses the issue of the courts' powers to review Acts of the Scottish Parliament less in terms of the characteristics of the Parliament *itself* (i.e. as either an ordinary statutory body or, of greater constitutional significance, a democratic legislature), and more in terms of the right of the *petitioner* (applicant) in question to access to a court. Having taken this fundamental constitutional right of the applicant as his starting point, Lord Emslie then reasons that the Westminster Parliament would only have intended to abrogate it, by removing or reducing the powers of domestic courts to review Acts of the Scottish Parliament according to ordinary principles of judicial review, expressly or by necessary implication. Whilst the result of his Lordship's analysis—that domestic courts are able to review Acts of the Scottish Parliaments according to the same principles as for 'ordinary' statutory bodies—is substantially similar to that in *Whaley*, his Lordship's opinion in this case represents a stark reminder of the need, when analysing the legislative competences of the Scottish Parliament, to consider the relationship between Scottish Parliament and *the governed* as well as the relationship between the two Parliaments across the border. (See further on this issue K Armstrong, 'Contesting Government, producing Devolution: The Repeal of "Section 28" in Scotland' [2003] 23(2) LS 205).

2. Despite going to such lengths to explain that domestic courts *could* review Acts of the Scottish Parliament, Lord Emslie then went on to find that the institutional characteristics of the

Scottish Parliament nevertheless precluded any meaningful irrationality review of the Act under challenge.

Axa General Insurance Ltd v Lord Advocate [2010] CSOH 2 (extracts)

[142] Having reached the conclusion that the petitioners' common law challenge to the validity of the 2009 Act may competently be advanced, it now remains to consider the extent of review which may be thought appropriate in that context. While it is true that the Scottish Parliament is a non-sovereign public body owing its existence and powers to statute, it is nonetheless a democratically-elected parliament. The Acts which it passes are in the nature of primary legislation for Scotland, and except as provided in SA 1998 such Acts are not subject to supervision or control from Westminster. Their primary status is also confirmed by direct receipt of the Royal Assent. . . . On that basis, the scope for common law review of an Act of the Scottish Parliament can in my opinion be no wider, and may even be narrower, than the review permitted in respect of United Kingdom subordinate legislation carrying direct parliamentary approval. At best for the petitioners, therefore, and drawing strength from the guidance of the House of Lords in the *Nottinghamshire* and *Hammersmith* cases, I conclude that (in the words of Lord Bridge) the 2009 Act ' . . . is not open to challenge on the grounds of irrationality short of the extremes of bad faith, improper motive or manifest absurdity'.

[143] Like Lord Bridge in *Hammersmith*, I am persuaded of the constitutional propriety and good sense of the foregoing limitation, and would be concerned if any more liberal approach were to lead the courts into unwarranted scrutiny of the democratic legislative process. Demands for the recovery of parliamentary materials might prove difficult to control if the scope for 'irrationality' review were to be too loosely defined, and any departure from the clear line laid down by the House of Lords might risk leaving the courts with no workable stopping point short of the wide review appropriate to the acts and decisions of ministers, public bodies and administrative tribunals. To my mind such a result would be both undesirable and constitutionally inappropriate.

[144] Even if, in the particular circumstances of this case, I had been persuaded to take a contrary view in the respondents' favour, I would still not have been prepared to close the door on the possibility that, if extreme circumstances were ever to arise in the future, the courts would require to intervene in defence of the rule of law and the fundamental rights and liberties of the subject. In today's climate there is of course no reason to fear any such development, but if, hypothetically, a Scottish Parliament were ever to legislate in a manner which could be described as a flagrant and unconstitutional abuse of power, it is to my mind unthinkable that the courts should have no option but to hold themselves powerless to intervene. . .

Notes

1. In relying so heavily on the *Nottinghamshire* and *Hammersmith* cases, and in particular on the notion that the courts will only quash subordinate legislation approved by Parliament in extreme cases his Lordship did not advert to the decision of the Court of Appeal in *R (Asif Javed) v Secretary of State for the Home Department* [2001] 3 WLR 323. In that decision, the Court of Appeal held that the House of Lords in *Nottinghamshire* had *not* laid down any general rule that review of any order approved by Parliament by affirmative resolution would only be proper where there was bad faith or manifest absurdity; they had merely applied the test appropriate for the subject matter before them. See further Chapter 15, p 875.

2. His Lordship's conclusion therefore was that, as in *Adams*, whilst the democratic nature of the Scottish Parliament will not of itself oust the courts' powers of judicial review, it will nevertheless play a large part in setting the *standard* of review. However, as is a perennial problem given the blurred parameters of irrationality review and the common omission in legislation to indicate how competing incommensurable principles should be balanced against each other, it is far from clear why the individual's right of access to court should so readily be taken to yield to the need to give due respect to the Scottish Parliament's character as a democratically elected legislature. The high threshold of irrationality review set in cases like *Axa General Insurance* overwhelmingly favours the latter principle over the former without any indication by the Westminster Parliament that the balance between these two principles—both of which are said to be referable to its general intention when enacting legislation—should be resolved in this way.

3. Lord Emslie dismissed the petitioners' claims under Art 1 of the First Protocol and Art 6 ECHR on the basis that the provisions of the 2009 Act failed to engage either Convention right and, alternatively, that any interferences with those rights would be capable of justification in the public interest. In relation to Art 1 of the First Protocol, again couched in terms echoing the remarks of the Lord Justice-Clerk in *Adams*, Lord Emslie stated, at para 225:

> I am satisfied, not only that it was within the proper competence of the legislature to determine that the 2009 Act served a legitimate aim in the public interest, but also that in so doing the Parliament applied no inappropriate standards and came to a tenable view. Similarly, as regards proportionality and the duty to strike a fair balance between community interests and private rights, it seems to me not only that the Parliament was entitled to (and, on the evidence of the legislative papers, did) take the view that an appropriate balance had been struck, but also that there are no circumstances which would justify this court in reaching a different conclusion. Even if, as the petitioners contended, there had been no evidence of such issues being addressed, I would not have regarded that as a material cause for concern. On the authorities, what really matters is the objective nature and effect of legislation as enacted rather than any actual or imputed intent or belief. . . With that in mind I take the view, not only that [the] Act went no further than was necessary to fulfil the Parliament's legitimate aim in the public interest, but also that awards of damages against negligent employers, at appropriate levels and under settled rules, cannot be thought to constitute an unwarranted or disproportionate end result.

Challenging Acts of the Scottish Parliament—procedure

Since the Scotland Act gives the UK a new, limited legislature, in effect a constitutionalised, rather than an unconstrained legislature, it was clearly necessary to lay down a procedure for determining instances in which it is alleged that the Scottish Parliament has acted beyond its powers. Such procedures are common in other states, and generally take the form of allowing either pre-legislative challenge (as in France) or post-legislative challenge (as in the USA). The Scotland Act employs both techniques:

33.—Scrutiny of Bills by the Supreme Court

1   The Advocate General, the Lord Advocate or the Attorney General may refer the question of whether a Bill or any provision of a Bill would be within the legislative competence of the Parliament to the Supreme Court for decision. . .

35.—Power to intervene in certain cases

1   If a Bill contains provisions—

     (a)   which the Secretary of State has reasonable grounds to believe would be incompatible with any international obligations or the interests of defence or national security, or

     (b)   which make modifications of the law as it applies to reserved matters and which the Secretary of State has reasonable grounds to believe would have an adverse effect on the operation of the law as it applies to reserved matters,

     he may make an order prohibiting the Presiding Officer from submitting the Bill for Royal Assent.

2   The order must identify the Bill and the provisions in question and state the reasons for making the order. . .

Notes

1. In terms of *pre*-legislative challenge, if either a Scots or UK law officer raises an issue over whether a given Bill would be beyond the powers of the Parliament, it may, under s 33, be referred to the Supreme Court within 28 days for determination of its *vires* (originally, the final court was the Privy Council). If the Supreme Court determines that the Bill is outside the powers of the Scottish Parliament, it cannot be presented for Royal Assent un-amended. The UK Government, under s 35, can also block a legislative proposal if in its opinion it affects any reserved matter or would be incompatible with the UK's international obligations or defence or national security.

2. There is also a complex system for a Bill to be challenged once enacted, under the referral procedure in Sched 6 to the Scotland Act. If a devolution issue (i.e. an issue as to whether an Act of the Scottish Parliament is outside its powers and so void) arises in an ordinary case, a lower court has a discretion to refer the matter to a higher court for determination. Appeals from the higher courts lie to the Supreme Court, the rulings of which are made binding in all legal proceedings. Reed commented shortly after the scheme was set up that some within Scotland 'might regard it as ironical, to say the least, that the Scots having voted for self-government by a Scottish Parliament are now to be governed, in a sense, by judges'.[23] However, whilst this remains true in a theoretical sense, there have been no cases to date in which legislation of the Parliament has been annulled by the courts and, as appears above, the courts seem minded to adopt a deferential approach to review of its legislation.

DEVOLUTION, FEDERALISM AND 'QUASI-FEDERALISM'

Federalism is a complex concept and there is no universally agreed definition of it.[24] However, a rough definition might include three key elements: first, that there be *exclusive* areas of competence allocated to the federal and state/province legislatures; in those areas, only one body is competent to

---

23   Reed, 'Devolution and the Judiciary' in Cambridge Centre for Public Law, *Constitutional Reform in the United Kingdom: Practice and Principles* (1998), p 23.

24   See, for example, P King, *Federalism and Federation* (1982) and G Sawer, *Modern Federalism* (1976).

legislate and its legislation in that area cannot be overridden by the other body. Second, there is a written constitution, which defines and limits the jurisdiction of both legislatures, such that neither body can unilaterally abolish the other. Third, there is a court, or courts, with power to review the *vires* of the acts of *both* legislatures to ensure that they remain with their respective competencies. If this definition is applied to Scotland, it is immediately apparent that no federal system has been created. The Scottish Parliament has no *exclusive* areas of jurisdiction, since Westminster remains competent to legislate in all the devolved areas. While the Scotland Act could be seen as a written constitution that defines and limits the jurisdiction of the Scottish Parliament, there is no such instrument in relation to Westminster. Moreover, whilst the higher courts may review the *vires* of the Scottish Parliament, this is not possible in relation to the Westminster Parliament, at least under the orthodox interpretation of parliamentary sovereignty. Legally, therefore, the position is clear: the UK has not moved to a federal system. Bogdanor summarises the legal status of the devolution schemes:

> Devolution is to be distinguished from federalism, which would divide, not devolve, supreme power between Westminster and various regional or provincial parliaments. In a federal state, the authority of the central or federal government and the provincial governments is co-ordinate and shared, the respective scope of the federal and provincial governments being defined by an enacted constitution as, for example, in the United States or the Federal Republic of Germany. Devolution, by contrast, does not require the introduction of an enacted constitution.[25]

The political-conventional perspective presents a challenge to this position, however. We saw in Chapter 2 that the establishment of the devolution settlements prompted the 'creation' by Westminster of a constitutional convention known as the Sewel convention, according to which the UK Parliament will only legislate on the devolved areas with the consent of the devolved legislature.[26] This convention has been rigidly adhered to in practice: Westminster has not yet legislated on a devolved matter without a consent motion from the Scottish Parliament. Given the existence and strength of the Sewel convention, we might say, at the conventional level, that the first element of a federal system is present in the UK—the Scottish Parliament legislates for Scottish, devolved matters, the UK Parliament only for the reserved areas (or, with the permission of the Scottish Parliament, the devolved areas). As for the second element (the presence of a written constitution), the constitution for these purposes would be the Scotland Act. While it is clearly not 'higher law' in the sense that it remains subject to ordinary express repeal, if it becomes impossible to repeal or amend it as a matter of political reality without the consent of the Scottish Parliament then it becomes a form of *de facto* higher law. In this respect, the fact that the Parliament was established with the clear backing of the Scottish people as approved in a referendum is of great significance: it makes its abolition, or emasculation, without the consent of the Scottish people, virtually politically impossible. The power of democratic mandate is not to be underestimated, as Alan Ward emphasises:

> [T]he constitutional supremacy of the UK [Parliament] can be very hollow if a majority in a subordinate legislature backs a recalcitrant government which threatens to resign if it does not get its way. When faced with this challenge, the UK will have

---

25   V. Bogdanor, *Devolution in the United Kingdom* (1999), p 3.

26   See further, Chapter 2, pp 51–52.

only two, unpleasant, options: back down or abandon devolution and assume direct rule.[27]

The relative practical impotence of Westminster's powers to legislate for Scotland is evidenced by a further, historical, factor. As the Northern Ireland context (from 1922 onwards) demonstrates, Westminster has historically been extremely reluctant to exercise its powers over the Northern Ireland Assembly, only taking the reins following a breakdown in civil society. It is not clear whether anything less would prompt the suspension by Parliament of a functioning devolved legislature. With the foregoing in mind, it would not be unfair to say, then, that 'in constitutional theory alone. . . full power remains with Westminster.'[28] Parliament's political power to legislate for Scotland fails to match its technical supremacy as enshrined in the Scotland Act. As Tom Dalyell MP stated during the passage of the Scotland Bill through Parliament:

> [The statement made in s.28(7) that Westminster can legislate for Scotland] may conceivably be true in an arcane legal sense, but in the political reality of 1998 it is palpably misleading and about as true as it would be to say that the Queen can veto any legislation.[29]

Returning to the required elements of a federal system, and in particular the third element of a Supreme Court with powers of constitutional review, the new UK Supreme Court has full powers to review and indeed strike down Acts of the Scottish Parliament that exceed its *vires* (these powers were previously held by the Judicial Committee of the Privy Council). Although it has no power to do so in relation to Acts of the Westminster Parliament, it is nevertheless plausible to assume that courts will develop an interpretative presumption to the effect that the latter does not intend to legislate in the devolved areas without the consent of the Scottish Parliament (see above),[30] as the Sewel Convention states. While the formal *vires* of the UK Parliament would not be affected, this would amount to a strong *de facto* restriction upon its powers, as we have seen for example in relation to the ability of Parliament to enact effective ouster clauses.[31]

In conclusion, it is clear in law that the UK remains a unitary system: at the apex is 'a single agency or institutional complex, the [sovereign] Queen in Parliament, in a position of unimpeachable authority'.[32] The Westminster Parliament retains full legislative competence in relation to Scotland, so that no power, strictly speaking, has been 'transferred' to the Scottish Parliament; moreover the Scotland Act, whilst doubtless a 'constitutional statute',[33] undoubtedly remains subject at the very least to express repeal by Westminster. However, with the UK constitution, it is always necessary to view it from two perspectives—legal and political–conventional. In terms of the latter perspective, a marked change has occurred. The UK Parliament, as a matter of expressly declared, and so far faithfully followed, constitutional convention is now a limited Parliament—it will not legislate in the areas devolved to Scotland without the consent of the Scottish Parliament. Further the Scotland Act plainly has a special status as a matter of political fact—it will be impossible to repeal it or modify it in a way

27   A Ward, 'Devolution: Labour's Strange Constitutional "Design"', in J Jowell and D Oliver (eds), *The Changing Constitution*, 4th edn (2000), p 111, at p 132.

28   V Bogdanor, *Devolution in the United Kingdom* (1999), p 291.

29   HC Deb vol 305, col 366 (28 Jan 1998).

30   Above, pp 243–244.

31   See Chapter 14, pp 769–776.

32   N Walker, 'Beyond the Unitary Conception of the United Kingdom Constitution' [2000] PL 384, 387–88.

33   See Chapter 4, pp 179–180.

that reduces the scope of devolution without the consent of the Scottish Parliament. Moreover, the Scottish people are living, in relation to many areas of government, under what is in effect a codified constitution—the Scotland Act itself, which delimits the power of their legislature and Government and cannot be changed by them. Viewed through this second lens, devolution to Scotland has introduced what Bogdanor aptly refers to as 'quasi-federalism', i.e. a convention of federalism and a substantial degree of codification, to the UK constitution:

> [T]he relationship between Westminster and Edinburgh will be quasi-federal in normal times and unitary only in crisis times. For the formal assertion of parliamentary supremacy will become empty when it is no longer accompanied by a real political supremacy.[34]

This does not, of course, imply that the doctrine of parliamentary sovereignty is of no practical relevance at all in the devolution context. But as Bogdanor explains, it will:

> bear a highly attenuated meaning. It will probably mean no more than: (a) The more or less theoretical right to legislate on Scotland's domestic affairs against the wishes of the Scottish Parliament. . . and (b) The right to abolish the Scottish Parliament. It is, however. . . difficult to see this happening against the wishes of the Scottish Parliament and people. . .[35]

Notes

1. The relevance of the above for the traditional view of the UK constitution is discussed further in Chapter 1, pp 27–30.
2. As the foregoing indicates, there is a clear fracture in the devolution context between legal theory, according to which Parliament remains sovereign, and political reality, under which devolution to Scotland is virtually permanent. One author has argued that this may even come, in time, to undermine the legitimacy of the doctrine of parliamentary sovereignty itself as a key constitutional principle.

G Little, 'Scotland and Parliamentary Sovereignty'
[2004] *Legal Studies* 24(4) 540 (extracts)

The political reality of Scottish devolution has. . .presented powerful challenges to parliamentary sovereignty. Indeed, although it will take time for the full significance of this to become apparent, the political authority of parliamentary sovereignty is already limited in Scotland: while it remains possible that there could be a collapse of public confidence in the Scottish Parliament, and that support for direct rule from Westminster could regenerate, it is, in reality, very difficult to imagine Westminster abolishing the Scottish Parliament or legislating in devolved areas against its wishes. Secondly, for reasons which are expanded upon below, even if it is assumed that the relationship between Westminster and the Scottish Parliament will remain constructive, the political pressure on parliamentary sovereignty is likely to intensify as devolution evolves, rather than to decrease. Thirdly, in the event of future controversy over the issue of further constitutional reform for Scotland, this pressure could become acute, and may ultimately test the relationship between

---

34 V Bogdanor, *Devolution in the United Kingdom* (1999), p 291.

35 *Ibid*, p 292.

Westminster and the Scottish Parliament to breaking point. Fourthly, and more broadly, the political interaction between the Scottish Parliament and Westminster may be influenced by developments at European level which are inimical to traditional ideas of parliamentary sovereignty.

THE SCOTTISH EXECUTIVE

The Scotland Act creates and lays out detailed provisions for the formation of the Scottish Executive, which comprises the First Minister, Ministers appointed by the First Minister, and the Lord Advocate and Solicitor General for Scotland. The Scottish Executive is supported by the Scottish Administration, which is formally part of the UK Home Civil Service (s 51).

44.—The Scottish Executive

1   There shall be a Scottish Executive, whose members shall be—

(a)   the First Minister,
(b)   such Ministers as the First Minister may appoint under section 47, and
(c)   the Lord Advocate and the Solicitor General for Scotland.

2   The members of the Scottish Executive are referred to collectively as the Scottish Ministers.

3   A person who holds a Ministerial office may not be appointed a member of the Scottish Executive; and if a member of the Scottish Executive is appointed to a Ministerial office he shall cease to hold office as a member of the Scottish Executive.

4   In subsection (3), references to a member of the Scottish Executive include a junior Scottish Minister and 'Ministerial office' has the same meaning as in section 2 of the House of Commons Disqualification Act 1975.

The Scottish Parliament is required to nominate a First Minister within 28 days of an election or vacancy arising (s 46). The Presiding Officer recommends the Parliament's nominee to the Queen (s 46(4)), who formally appoints that person (s 45(1)) as First Minister. The First Minister then selects his or her Ministers from among the MSPs (s 47(1)) with the agreement of the Parliament (s 47(2)). These Minsters, like the First Minister, are formally appointed by the Queen and 'hold office at Her Majesty's pleasure' (s 47(3)(a)). The First Minister, with the Queen's approval, may also appoint junior Scottish Ministers to assist the Ministers in their tasks (s 49). Junior Scottish Ministers must also be MSPs and their recommendations to the Queen must be agreed by Parliament (ss 49(1) and 49(3)). The First Minister also recommends candidates for appointment to the positions of Lord Advocate and Solicitor General for Scotland (s 48(1)). Whilst these recommendations must be agreed by the Parliament, the Scottish Law Officers do not need to be MSPs.

As ss 43(3) and 43(4) make clear, nobody can become a member of the Scottish Executive or a junior Scottish Minister if they also hold 'Ministerial Office'. A person holds Ministerial Office, as defined by Sched 2 of the House of Commons Disqualification Act 1975, if they hold one or more of the designated positions of ministerial responsibility such as Prime Minister, Chancellor of the Exchequer,

Secretary of State, Minister of State, Attorney General, Solicitor General or Advocate General for Scotland.

Once appointed, Scottish Ministers and junior Scottish Ministers may be removed from office by the First Minister (ss 47(3)(b) and 49(3)(b)). The Scottish Law Officers, by contrast, are formally removed by the Queen upon recommendation by the First Minister (s 48(1)), but they are required to resign, along with the First Minister and any remaining members of the Executive, following a vote of no confidence in the Executive by the Parliament (ss 45(2), 47(3)(c), 48(2)). Junior Scottish Ministers, though they are not members of the Executive, must also resign in these circumstances (s 49(4)(c)). Hence, in law, the Scottish Executive is accountable to the Parliament. The Parliament can also require Ministers to appear before it or its committees to give evidence if summoned.

The Scottish Executive, like the Parliament, has all the powers and duties that formerly belonged to the Secretary of State for Scotland:

53.—General transfer of functions

1   The functions mentioned in subsection (2) shall, so far as they are exercisable within devolved competence, be exercisable by the Scottish Ministers instead of by a Minister of the Crown.

2   Those functions are—

(a)   those of Her Majesty's prerogative and other executive functions which are exercisable on behalf of Her Majesty by a Minister of the Crown,

(b)   other functions conferred on a Minister of the Crown by a prerogative instrument, and

(c)   functions conferred on a Minister of the Crown by any pre-commencement enactment. . .

Additional functions can be transferred by Orders in Council (s 63) and may, of course, be granted to the Executive under valid Acts of the Scottish Parliament. Section 56(1) expressly retains an assortment of functions to be exercised jointly by Ministers at Westminster. These include functions relating to road safety information and training, the funding of scientific research and the implementation of measures to give effect to UN Security Council decisions. Functions will also be retained for joint exercise by Ministers at Westminster if secondary legislation so provides (s 56(2)). Scottish Ministers must exercise any transferred functions 'within devolved competence', as s 53(1) states. The basic effect of this requirement, as indicated by s 54, is to prohibit the Scottish Ministers from doing anything which the Scottish Parliament would lack the competence to do through legislation:

54.—Devolved competence

1   References in this Act to the exercise of a function being within or outside devolved competence are to be read in accordance with this section.

2   It is outside devolved competence—

(a)   to make any provision by subordinate legislation which would be outside the legislative competence of the Parliament if it were included in an Act of the Scottish Parliament, or

(b)   to confirm or approve any subordinate legislation containing such provision.

3   In the case of any function other than a function of making, confirming or approving subordinate legislation, it is outside devolved competence to exercise the function (or exercise it in any way) so far as a provision of an Act of the Scottish Parliament conferring the function (or, as the case may be, conferring it so as to be exercisable in that way) would be outside the legislative competence of the Parliament.

The Scottish Ministers are also unable to act incompatibly with the European Convention rights or EU law (s 57(2)); an exception, provided for by s 57(3), is that the Lord Advocate, when prosecuting criminal offences or investigating deaths in Scotland, *can* act incompatibly with the Convention if he would be 'protected' from Convention challenge under s 6(2) of the Human Rights Act 1998 on the ground that his Convention-incompatible acts were compelled or authorised by primary legislation. A bare majority of the House of Lords ruled in *Somerville v Scottish Ministers* [2007] UKHL 44, [2007] 1 WLR 2734 that a victim bringing a damages claim against a member of the Scottish Executive for acting *ultra vires* by breaching the Convention *was not* required to respect the one year time limit for bringing claims against public authorities imposed by s 7(5) HRA. This was said to follow from s 100(3) SA 1998. By expressly providing that the Scotland Act 'does not enable a court or tribunal to award any damages. . . which it could not award if section 8(3) and (4) of the Human Rights Act 1998 applied', and by omitting to mention s 7(5) HRA, s 100(3) was taken to require compliance with ss 8(3) and 8(4) but *not* the time limit under s 7(5). The result, which would have left victims to take advantage of the potentially more generous time limits applied by the Scottish courts, has now been reversed by the Scottish Parliament through s 1 of the Convention Rights Proceedings (Amendment) (Scotland) Act 2009. The 2009 Act amends s 100(3) SA 1998 by inserting s 100(3B), which requires any proceedings to be brought by victims against Scottish Ministers for Convention breaches, as under the HRA, within one year of the date of the act complained of (or longer, if the court deems it equitable). This time limit does not apply to Convention challenges to the making of legislation by Scottish Ministers, but does apply to challenges by victims for *failure* by Ministers to make legislation: s 100(3D).

For obvious reasons it is expedient for the Secretary of State to be able to take pre-emptive action against breaches of European Convention or other international obligations by Scottish Ministers. Preserving the sanctity of the union between the UK's countries as a single state in international law, s 58 allows the Secretary of State to issue orders preventing or compelling action by the Scottish Ministers for the purpose of complying with the UK's international obligations:

58.—Power to prevent or require action

1   If the Secretary of State has reasonable grounds to believe that any action proposed to be taken by a member of the Scottish Executive would be incompatible with any international obligations, he may by order direct that the proposed action shall not be taken.

2   If the Secretary of State has reasonable grounds to believe that any action capable of being taken by a member of the Scottish Executive is required for the purpose of giving effect to any such obligations, he may by order direct that the action shall be taken. . .

Along these lines, international relations, including relations with the European Communities, are reserved matters under Sched 5. Nevertheless, Scottish Ministers are permitted by Sched 5 to assist Ministers of the Crown in the conduct of international affairs (Part I, para 7(2)(b)). This practically sensible provision allows Scottish Ministers their own input into these matters, to the extent that they relate to the devolved areas, in policy discussions at Westminster.

It should be stressed that the creation of the Scottish Executive has not rendered the role of Secretary of State for Scotland entirely redundant. There continues to be a Secretary of State for Scotland, who now takes primary responsibility for managing relations with the Scottish Executive. According to the Scotland Office's website, the role of the Secretary of State in the wake of the devolution settlement is now one of co-operation with, rather than control of, Scotland in its day-to-day affairs.[36]

Relations between the Scottish Executive and the UK Government are carried on under principles established in concordats signed between the two. This relatively novel framework for conducting inter-governmental relations is not without constitutional problems. In particular, concordats are statements of policy rather than legal agreements as such; indeed, as the *Memorandum of Understanding and Supplementary Agreements* between the UK Government and devolved administrations explicitly states, 'It is not intended that these agreements should be legally binding'.[37] As Rawlings argues, the decision by Governments to arrange their relations by concordats represents a 'deliberate constitutional choice' not to use more transparent and democratic methods such as primary and secondary legislation:[38]

> Co-operation and reciprocity may be all to the good in intergovernmental relations, but apple-pie sentiment should not be allowed to obscure the basic constitutional problems of transparency, diffusion of responsibility and political accountability that interlocking arrangements raise.[39]

Rawlings suggests that 'the rise of intergovernmental relations needs to be matched by a strong development of formal inter-parliamentary links' so as to increase the extent of Parliamentary supervision over inter-governmental affairs.[40]

DEVOLUTION IN SCOTLAND: PROPOSALS FOR REFORM

The Scottish Parliamentary elections of May 2007 opened up a new chapter in the history of the devolution scheme. For the first time since the enactment of the Scotland Act 1998, the Westminster and Holyrood Parliaments were governed by different parties. The Scottish National Party (SNP) won 47 seats in the Scottish Parliament and became the governing party, albeit a minority administration. This not only ended two terms of Labour-Liberal Democrat coalition, but it also had the real potential to upset the relatively amicable political relationship enjoyed between Westminster and Holyrood when Labour had been at the helm in both Parliaments.[41]

---

36 www.scotlandoffice.gov.uk.

37 Office of the Deputy Prime Minister, *Memorandum of Understanding and Supplementary Agreements Between the United Kingdom Government Scottish Ministers, the Cabinet of the National Assembly for Wales and the Northern Ireland Executive Committee*, Cm 5240 (2001), p 4.

38 R Rawlings, 'Concordats of the Constitution' (2000) 116 LQR 257, 279.

39 *Ibid*, p 285.

40 *Ibid*, pp 285–86.

41 See further N Bonney, 'The Settled Will of the Scottish People: What is Next for Scotland's Parliaments?' (2007) 78(2) *The Political Quarterly* 301, at 301.

J Bradbury and N McGarvey, 'Devolution: Problems, Politics and Prospects'
(2003) 56 *Parliamentary Affairs* 219 (extracts)

Similar priorities and a willingness to broach similar changes in delivery mechanisms meant that cross-border skirmishes between the Executive in Edinburgh and the UK government remained rare. When they had previously occurred, it was over issues not fundamental to the devolution settlement. Beyond the few headline differences (i.e. tuition fees, care for the elderly), critics suggested that the Executive had carried on the Scottish tradition of 'tartanising' Whitehall policy initiatives for Scottish consumption.

Following the election in 2007, the SNP wasted no time in forging towards its goal of Scottish independence. Shortly after assuming office, the Scottish Executive (restyled the 'Scottish Government' by the SNP) issued its consultation document entitled *Choosing Scotland's Future: A National Conversation*. The document reiterated the SNP's manifesto promise to the Scottish people to hold a referendum on Scottish independence before the end of the current Parliamentary term (2011), making the basic case for independence and advocating a 'national conversation' to allow for debate and consultation on the issue.

Scottish Executive, Choosing Scotland's Future (2007) (extracts)

The establishment of the Scottish Parliament under the Scotland Act 1998 gave the people of Scotland a direct democratic voice in decisions across a wide range of government activities already administered in Scotland. The devolution settlement explicitly recognised that the responsibilities given to the Scottish Parliament and Scottish Government in 1999 could be changed, and important mechanisms were included in the Act to allow for further devolution.

Significant powers are currently reserved to the United Kingdom Parliament and the United Kingdom Government. Further devolution in these important areas would allow the Scottish Parliament and Scottish Government to take their own decisions on these issues in the interests of Scotland and reflecting the views of the people of Scotland. In some areas, further devolution could also provide greater coherence in decision-making and democratic accountability for delivery of policy.

To go beyond enhanced devolution to independence would involve bringing to an end the United Kingdom Parliament's powers to legislate for Scotland, and the competence of United Kingdom Ministers to exercise executive powers in respect of Scotland. All of the remaining reservations in the Scotland Act would cease to have effect, and the Scottish Parliament and Scottish Government would acquire responsibility for all domestic and international policy, similar to that of independent states everywhere, subject to the provisions of the European Union Treaties and other inherited treaty obligations. . .

Enhanced devolution or independence would require legislation, probably at both Westminster and Holyrood. Substantially enhanced devolution would arguably, and independence would certainly, require the consent of the Scottish people through a referendum. Such a vote, while not constitutionally binding, has been accepted as the correct way of determining Scotland's constitutional future. There must, therefore, be due consideration of appropriate forms of legislation for such a vote, and of the question of how a referendum could be initiated by the Scottish Parliament.

In the Scottish Government's view there are three realistic choices. First, retention of the devolution scheme defined by the Scotland Act 1998, with the possibility of further evolution in powers, extending these individually as occasion arises. Second, redesigning devolution by adopting a specific range of extensions to the current powers of the Scottish Parliament and Scottish Government, possibly involving fiscal autonomy, but short of progress to full independence. Third, which the Scottish Government favours, extending the powers of the Scottish Parliament and Scottish Government to the point of independence. . .

This paper is the first step in a wide-ranging national conversation about the future of Scotland. This conversation will allow the people of Scotland to consider all the options for the future of the country and make informed decisions. This paper invites the people of Scotland to sign up for the national conversation and to suggest how the conversation should be designed to ensure the greatest possible participation.

Notes

1. Whilst the SNP's calls for independence, subsequently, have found favour with neither the Calman Commission nor the UK Government (see below), Bonney has gone further, even criticising the very idea that the Scottish Government is consulting on independence, arguing that such a matter, relating to the British Constitution, lays beyond the competence of the Executive as determined by the Scotland Act. This interesting observation serves as a further reminder that the Scottish Parliament and Executive, ultimately, remain bodies created and constrained in their activities by an Act of the Westminster Parliament.

N Bonney, 'Looming Issues for Scotland and the Union' (2008) *The Political Quarterly* 79(4) 560 (extracts)

Since the British Constitution is a reserved matter for the Westminster Parliament, which passed legislation following a referendum backing its principles, a strict interpretation of the 1998 Scotland Act might reasonably have ruled that consideration of such issues was beyond the competence of the Scottish Executive and Scottish Parliament. . . Nonetheless it is clear from the workings of the Scottish Parliament and the Scottish Executive that they are both at times willing to discuss, debate and expend public resources on issues that are not within their formal competence. Thus the Scottish Parliament has debated the Iraq War and the current First Minister has written to foreign governments about nuclear weapons policy.

Choosing Scotland's Future goes beyond the formal remit of the Scottish Executive by envisaging the Scottish Government, presumably itself, entering into negotiations about the terms, and procedures, for independence with the United Kingdom government following upon a Scottish referendum promoted by the Scottish or United Kingdom governments to approve such a step. Given the limited powers available to it, the Scottish Executive proposes to promote the course of independence by putting forward a referendum question in the form that 'the Scottish Government should negotiate a settlement with the Government of the United Kingdom so that Scotland can become an independent state'. It is stated that such a formulation is 'arguably' within the powers of the Scottish Parliament to approve—recognising that even this step may not be legitimate in the terms of the existing constitutional settlement enshrined in the Scotland Act 1988 [*sic*.]. It is even more strongly arguable that it may not be competent for the Civil Service and Scottish executive ministers to spend time developing and proposing this policy or for the Scottish Parliament to consider it when it is not a matter within their formal powers. . .

2. Bonney is also critical of the substance of the initial calls for independence made by the Scottish Government in *Choosing Scotland's Future*, referring to the document as a 'flimsy prospectus for independence that does not do justice to the seriousness of the issues with which it deals or with the manifold consequences that it might entail for the population of Scotland and the United Kingdom if it ever becomes the basis for serious political action and proposed constitutional change' (at p 564). In particular, Bonney regards demands by the Scottish Government for greater fiscal autonomy to lack foundation (at p 566):

> It has yet to be demonstrated that the Scottish Parliament and Executive have effectively managed the spending responsibilities they have before there should be consideration of additional taxation and spending powers. . . Until judgements are reached. . ., it is difficult to demonstrate that additional powers will result in improved outcomes for the Scottish population.

3. The Scottish Commission on Devolution was established in December 2007 by the Scottish Parliament and United Kingdom Government. Chaired by Professor Sir Kenneth Calman, the Calman Commission's task, as agreed by the Scottish Parliament, was 'To review the provisions of the Scotland Act 1998 in the light of experience and to recommend any changes to the present constitutional arrangements that would enable the Scottish Parliament to serve the people of Scotland better, improve the financial accountability of the Scottish Parliament, and continue to secure the position of Scotland within the United Kingdom.' The Commission issued its final report in June 2009.

Scottish Commission on Devolution, *Serving Scotland Better: Scotland and the United Kingdom in the 21st Century* (2009) (extracts)

There have always been some aspects of Scotland's national life which have been different from the rest of the UK. The distinctive Scottish legal system and the Scottish education system are good examples. In other respects, however, there is a continuity of approach between Scotland and the rest of the UK, for example in social security. The balance between these distinctive and shared elements, and how they have developed, has been determined by external circumstances, and by what Scottish people have aspired to. Empire, economic change, world wars, and social movements like the creation of the NHS have all played a part. For example, the growth of an integrated UK economy means the law affecting business and the taxation system is the same across the whole UK. On the other hand, many of the public services that have grown up over the 20th century have separate Scottish identities. . .

There have always been these two threads to Scotland's constitutional life. It has neither been absorbed into England, nor has it sought to cut itself off from the mainstream of British economic and social life. A Scottish Parliament in Edinburgh is the most recent step in the evolution of this relationship, and a very significant one. After 10 years of devolution we have been looking at how well it has worked, and how it should now change and develop further. . .

The first conclusion we have reached is that devolution has been a real success. The last 10 years have shown that not only is it possible to have a Scottish Parliament inside the UK, but that it works well in practice. Having a Scottish Parliament is in general popular with the people of Scotland, and they welcome the scope to have Scottish issues debated and decided in Scotland. The Scottish Parliament has embedded itself in both the constitution of the United Kingdom and the consciousness of Scottish people. It is here to stay. . .

In thinking about how devolution should develop further, we have looked very carefully at how it fits into the wider Union that is the United Kingdom. This is first of all a political Union, with a Parliament at Westminster where every part of the country is represented. Some things like defence and foreign relations can only be dealt with there if we are to have a Union at all. There should be no change in those. But we have considered what impact they have on matters that are now quite properly dealt with by the Scottish Parliament. For instance, working with the other members of the European Union critically affects agriculture and fisheries. This is an example of a recurring theme in our report—the different levels of government in the United Kingdom have to work more closely together. . .

The United Kingdom is an asymmetrical Union. Not only are the four nations very different in size, but devolution in Wales and Northern Ireland is different from devolution in Scotland, and there is no devolution for England. It is not our job to say whether this should change, or to make recommendations about how England is governed, but we cannot ignore the fact that the Parliament at Westminster is England's parliament as well as the Parliament for the whole of the UK. We can learn lessons from federal countries about how to help different levels of government to cooperate, but the tidy solutions that work where every part of a larger country can be governed in the same way cannot simply be applied here. . .

The UK is an economic Union with a very integrated economy, with goods and services traded within it all the time. We are absolutely clear that this economic Union is to Scotland's advantage and in considering how devolution should develop we have been very careful not to make recommendations that will undermine it. Many devolved powers are important for economic growth, and are most effectively run by the devolved bodies, but the Scottish Parliament and Government cannot run a separate macro-economic policy without threatening the benefits of this economic Union. This is also important for taxation, because the scope to have different rates of tax inside a single economy is limited. . .

Scotland also forms what we have called a social Union with the rest of the UK. This is not so obvious an idea as the economic Union, but it too has significant implications for how devolution should develop. There are many social ties that bind the UK together: family, professional and cultural. But there are also some common expectations about social welfare. Social security payments are available and are paid on the same basis to people across the country, according to their needs. This principle of fairness should not be undermined, though some benefits may have to be adjusted where they intersect with devolved policies like housing. . .

We think that there are certain social rights which should also be substantially the same, even when it is best that they are separately run in Scotland. The most important of these are that access to health care and education should be, as now, essentially free and provided at the point of need. And when taxes are shared across the UK they should take account of that need. Our first recommendation is therefore that the Scottish and UK Parliaments should confirm their common understanding of what those rights are, and the responsibilities that go with them. . .

This understanding of how devolution and the Union fit together is what guides our recommendations on improving the financial accountability of the Scottish Parliament, on what functions and responsibilities the Scottish Parliament and Ministers should have, and on how the different levels of government in the United Kingdom should work together. . .

Overall, however, we have been struck by how underdeveloped the inter-governmental and inter-parliamentary arrangements are. In other countries where there is more than one level of government these relationships tend to be better organised, and are seen as an important element of the constitution. . .

We therefore make a series of recommendations which are designed to emphasise the need for the two levels of government to work better together, in a transparent way, and to offer more opportunities for cooperation, which we think that the people of Scotland have a right to expect. The guiding principle is one of mutual respect, as each Parliament has its proper responsibilities, and each has its own democratic mandate. . .

The Scottish Parliament has very wide legislative powers. It can make law on anything that is not reserved to the UK Parliament. That enables it to deal with most domestic issues in Scotland—crime and justice, health, education, housing, transport and economic development, the environment, agriculture and fisheries and many other matters. Reserved issues include defence and foreign affairs, macro-economic management and social security. . .

The evidence we have had is that the division of responsibilities in the Scotland Act was well thought through and works well in practice. So we have not looked again at every element of these responsibilities, but instead at areas where there appear to be problems or pressures for change. These included: constitution and institutions; culture, charities, sport and gaming; employment and skills; energy; environment and planning; health and biosecurity; justice and home affairs; marine and fisheries; revenue and tax raising; science, research and higher education; social security; trade and commerce and others. . .

One important general theme in looking at these areas is that, although the split between devolved and reserved areas is well drawn at present, there will always be areas where the responsibilities of the different levels of government interact with one another. These are often the areas which are identified as areas for possible change. But it is clear that simply re-drawing the boundary will in many cases not solve the problem: there will always be interactions and overlaps wherever it is set. This emphasises that what is often needed is more effective arrangements for cooperation between the different levels of government.

Notes

1. The overall thrust of the Commission's recommendations, clearly, was to strengthen the relationship between the Scottish and Westminster Parliaments and facilitate the work of the Scottish Parliament within the current scheme of devolution.

2. To this end, the Calman Commission made a series of recommendations relating to various aspects of the work of the Parliament and Government. These included improving the Scottish Government's financial accountability (by e.g. tying Scotland's budget from the UK Exchequer more heavily to Scotland's own economic performance); strengthening the working relationship between the Holyrood and Westminster Governments (by e.g. emphasising 'mutual respect' between the two as a guiding principle in their relations and by encouraging deeper and broader programmes in UK Government departments to raise awareness and understanding of the devolution scheme); strengthening the devolution settlement (by e.g. devolving a number of further functions to Scotland such as the regulation of airguns and determination of the national speed limit) and strengthening the Scottish Parliament itself (in particular, by conducting a general

review of all provisions in the Scotland Act 'that constrain the Parliament in terms of its procedures or working arrangements to ensure they are proportionate, appropriate and effective').

3. One particular recommendation, to 'strengthen the Sewel Convention by entrenching it in the standing orders of each House [of Parliament at Westminster]', if carried through, would add credence to this chapter's arguments (above, pp 256–257) that the Sewel convention could lead, over time, to the crystallization of the Scotland Act 1998 into a *de facto* constitution binding on Westminster.

4. In November 2009, the Scottish Government published two documents. One was a direct response to the Calman Commission's final report; the other, entitled *Your Scotland, Your Voice: A National Conversation*, set out the results of the national conversation on independence proposed by the SNP in 2007.

Scottish Government, *The Scottish Government Response to the Recommendations of the Commission on Scottish Devolution* (2009) (extracts)

. . .

3   From the outset. . .it was clear that the Commission would not be able to consider the proposition that Scotland should be an independent country. Federalism was also outwith the Commission's remit.

4   Some commentators have noted that the Commission's Report is remarkable not so much for its recommendations as for its constitutional language, particularly in the early parts of the Report. The language of the Report normalises the language of distributed and popular sovereignty in the UK context for what is perhaps the first time in a UK wide document of this kind. The Report states that the UK has never been a unitary state and describes Parliamentary sovereignty as a 'convention'. The Commission Report points the way forward for effective extensions of Scottish sovereignty, but more in its framework and language than through its recommendations for actions, which are clearly the result of a compromise.

5   The report covers a lot of ground and is organised around a small number of themes:

•   Strengthening accountability in finance;
•   Strengthening co-operation (between Governments and Parliaments);
•   Strengthening the devolution settlement; and
•   Strengthening the Scottish Parliament.

Although the report is structured in accordance with these four themes it is difficult to see the Commission package as a coherent blueprint for the future.

6   Given the amount of ground it covers the Report touches on a range of issues. In that context there are certain recommendations which the Scottish Government supports and others—notably on taxation—which we believe would be damaging to Scotland and so strongly reject. There are still others which require further consideration by the Scottish Parliament, Scottish and UK Governments and the devolved administrations in Northern Ireland and Wales. . .

7   The Scottish Government made it clear shortly after publication in June that there were a number of recommendations in the Commission Report which had attracted widespread support and on which there ought to be immediate action:

'[The] Scottish Government believes their implementation would help to improve the government of Scotland and be in the interests of Scotland. Under the current constitutional arrangements it falls to the UK Government to initiate action on most of the recommendations concerned. The Scottish Government is ready to play its part in the spirit of mutual respect and co-operation advocated by the Commission and has made that clear to the UK Government.'

8   To date the Scottish Government has had no response from the UK Government to its request for co-operation other than a general statement that the Report is to be seen as a comprehensive package from which items cannot be 'cherry-picked'. As the recommendations do not represent a comprehensive or cohesive package in any real sense, the UK Government's insistence so far in treating it as such represents a missed opportunity.

Strengthening the devolution settlement

9   Six of the [Calman Commission's] recommendations relate to additions to the competence of the Scottish Parliament and the functions of Scottish Ministers and offer an extension of devolved responsibilities. To help take these recommendations forward Scottish Government officials prepared drafts of the orders necessary to transfer responsibility to the Scottish Parliament in the relevant areas. . .

12   Six other recommendations require new procedures and guidance within the UK Government and the Scottish Government has been pressing them to take the necessary action since the publication of the Commission Report. The changes would cover:

- Development of UK policy on the European Union. . .
- Scottish Ministers' engagement in EU business. . .
- Agreement to local variations on immigration policy. . .
- Consultation on welfare to work programmes. . .
- Appointments to the BBC Trust. . .
- Appointments to the Crown Estate. . .

13   These recommendations provide the opportunity to make real progress in areas of the Commission's Report on which there is broad consensus in Scotland. Action should be taken to implement those recommendations on which there is agreement rather than wait and risk losing momentum. . .

Strengthening accountability in finance

17   [The Report went on to strongly reject the Commission's proposals on increasing the financial accountability of the Scottish Government, alleging that] far from actually improving the financial framework for the Scottish Parliament, it is clear that moving in this direction would deliver less transparency, less accountability and would expose the Scottish Government budget to significant risks without adequate levers to offset these risks.

Notes

1. Whilst the Scottish Government was critical of the Calman Commission's recommendations on budgeting and taxation, which the Government claimed would decrease rather than increase

financial accountability, it was far more responsive, not surprisingly, to the Commission's recommendations that further competences should be devolved to the Parliament.

2. It is clear from the Government's response to the Calman report that the Government's preferred outcome for Scotland remains full independence. As its recent white paper reveals, the Scottish public will soon be able to have their say.

Scottish Government, *Your Scotland, Your Voice: A National Conversation* (2009) (extracts)

. . .Two things are clear. First, that there is a demand in Scotland to consider and debate our national future. Second, that the current arrangements do not meet the ambitions of our nation. Ten years on from devolution, almost all agree that it is time to expand the responsibilities of our Parliament. Ten years ago Donald Dewar [then First Minister for Scotland] said the Scottish Parliament was 'a new voice in the land, a voice to shape Scotland, a voice above all for the future'. He was right. But our Parliament is incomplete, unfinished. Its voice is muted or silent in many areas vital to our nation. . . Scotland cannot fully flourish until it takes responsibility for itself: for its economy, taxes, and spending; for its rich and its poor; for its natural resources and its waste; for its old and its young; for its roads and its seas; for its place in the world, for peace and war, for ties of friendship and common interest with the other nations of the earth. These are the matters with which normal, independent countries deal every day. They know the challenges and opportunities that come with that independence, as well as the responsibility. Scotland and its people are more than capable of doing so, too. We would benefit from the opportunities. . . [It] is time that Scotland reclaimed its place among the nations of Europe and the world. . .

Devolution was never intended as a fixed arrangement: it was and is a process which should respond to political, economic and social circumstances over time to ensure that Scotland is well-positioned to address the challenges it faces and take advantage of opportunities. Nor does devolution need to be Scotland's final constitutional destination. . .

The National Conversation has identified many areas for further devolution, as well as the arguments around independence. The National Conversation has illustrated that the constitutional debate raises issues across the whole range of government activity and Scottish life, from economic policy, taxation and benefits, foreign affairs and defence to human rights, broadcasting and responsibility for airguns and drink-drive limits. In these and many other areas, decisions for Scotland are not made by the Scottish Parliament and the Scottish Government, but by their United Kingdom counterparts. . .

The next step is to ensure that the whole of Scotland can give its view on the extension of the responsibilities of the Scottish Parliament. The Scottish Government proposes that a Referendum should be held in Scotland in 2010 to allow that view to be heard. . .

The Scottish Government believes that the future prosperity and development of Scotland is best served by becoming an independent country, a view shared in the Scottish Parliament by the Scottish Green Party. The Scottish Government favours a referendum which presents a clear choice between achieving that aspiration and the current devolution settlement. . .

Notes
1. At the time of writing, a date has not yet been set for the 2010 referendum on Scottish independence.

2. The Calman Commission's findings were also formally responded to in a White Paper published by the UK Government's Scotland Office, also in November 2009, entitled *Scotland's Future in the United Kingdom*. Whilst its purpose was to address the Commission's findings, the Scotland Office also took the opportunity to stress that Scottish independence does not currently feature in the UK Government's agenda:

> 2.2 The Government remains very firmly committed to Scotland's place in the United Kingdom. The Government believes that it brings benefits to all of the people of the UK. Together the nations in the United Kingdom are stronger. Working together, we are stronger internationally. Together we share resources and pool risks bringing benefits to all citizens, such as common standards of welfare. All the people of the UK benefit from this.

3. The Scotland Office welcomed and indicated that it would seek to facilitate the Calman Commission's recommendations:

> 6.1 The Government sees these [the Calman Commission's] plans as part of a coherent package for refreshing devolution in Scotland. Changes to the powers and financial accountability of the Scottish Parliament will require legislation. The Government envisages introducing legislation as soon as possible in the next Parliament. The legislation will require the consent of the Scottish Parliament under the Sewel Convention.
> 6.2 Discussions on improving intergovernmental cooperation have already begun in the Joint Ministerial Committee. The Government will wish to undertake detailed work with Scottish Ministers on the introduction of the new financial system and to discuss budgetary implications with them in due course.
> 6.3 The Government welcomes the commitment of the UK Parliament and the Scottish Parliament to take forward work on those of the Calman Commission's recommendations which are for them, and will continue to be involved in those discussions where they consider it helpful for us to do so.
> 6.4 We believe that these changes, once implemented, will provide a strong foundation for building on the Scottish Parliament's successful first ten years, to refresh devolution and reinvigorate Scotland's place at the heart of the United Kingdom.

4. It is pertinent to end our overview of the Scottish scheme with a reflection by Alan Trench on the current state of the reform proposals:

A Trench, 'The Calman Commission and Scotland's disjointed constitutional debates' [2009] *Public Law* 686 (extracts)

Two big constitutional issues loom following publication of the Calman report. First, will it be delivered . . . [?] While much can be done by secondary legislation, a number of key issues would appear to need primary legislation. As well as legislative time to be found at Westminster, there is the question of ensuring political support as well. With a UK general election due by June 2010, time is tight.

Secondly, how does the report relate to a possible referendum on Scottish independence? The SNP Government remains committed to a referendum in 2010, and to publishing a White Paper with a referendum Bill on St Andrew's Day (November 30) 2009. The issue will therefore be a running theme in Scottish politics for the rest of 2009 and throughout 2010. . . For his part, [First Minister] Alex Salmond repeated immediately after publication of the report that a referendum could include the Calman recommendations as an option. This raises the prospect of a 'preferential referendum', in which three (or more) options would be presented, either as different responses to a single question or as separate, sequential questions. The Scottish Government is keen to keep the pressure up; 10 days after publication of the Calman report, the Scottish Government lodged in the Parliament illustrative draft orders to transfer to the Parliament and Scottish Government the extra powers recommended in the report (though not to transfer to London the powers recommended to be 'un-devolved').

The constitutional conservatism of the Calman report narrows the political options—the choice will clearly be between an updated version of the status quo, and whatever 'independence' actually means. A more radical version of devolution is only on the cards as a longer-term option if Calman is implemented, and pressure for further change is sustained. However, it is the prospect of a referendum (and the accompanying debates at Holyrood about holding one) that offers the best hope of joining up what has so far been a disjointed constitutional debate. That will, at last, force the proponents of the various options to engage with each other, and to take the debate to the wider public. That can only be for the good. The fact that the people will shortly have their say—if not by way of a referendum, then at the 2010 UK and 2011 Scottish general elections—should focus minds on making the various cases as strongly as possible.

5. At the time of print, the new Conservative–Liberal Democrat Government intends to implement the Calman recommendations.

THE SCHEME IN NORTHERN IRELAND

Historical background and the peace process

It is impossible to understand the scheme of devolution to Northern Ireland without some awareness of its troubled history. The following is a very brief account.[42] Ireland was conquered by England and ruled by it, as a colony, from the 12th century. From the 15th century the Irish Parliament accepted laws passed by the English Parliament as law there; any Bills passed by it had to be submitted to the King of England and his Council for approval. Once England became Protestant under Henry VIII a vigorous attempt was made to suppress the Catholic religion in Ireland, involving, amongst other things, Protestant settlers from England and Scotland being handed estates in Northern Ireland during the 17th century.[43] Ireland's Parliament, as well as remaining subordinated to the British Parliament, still excluded Catholic members. In 1800, the country was united with Britain, the Irish Parliament being induced to accept the union by heavy bribery and the promise of Catholic emancipation as a *quid pro quo*. One hundred Irish members sat in the UK Parliament. A growing Irish Nationalist

---

42 See, for further accounts, M Mulholland, *Northern Ireland: A Very Short Introduction* (2002) and C Turpin and A Tomkins, *British Government and the Constitution*, 6th edn (2007), pp 228–34; Munro, n 8 above.

43 BBC History, 'The Road to Northern Ireland 1167–1921' (accessible at www.bbc.co.uk).

movement gradually increased its representation to a majority of Irish members in Westminster. Attempts to give Home Rule to Ireland were defeated by strikes and threatened insurrection by Protestants in the north of Ireland, who did not want to be governed by a Catholic country. Following the brutal suppression of the Easter Rising, in 1918 Sinn Fein won all but four of the now 128 seats outside the northern counties but, refusing to sit at Westminster, instead set up the Irish Dail. The attempted repression of this attempt at self-government led to a two-year war with the IRA. An eventual compromise was negotiated whereby Ireland would be partitioned. This prevented all-out civil war but at the cost of the Catholic minority in the six Northern counties being subject to continuing, unwanted government by the UK.

In 1920, partition took place: the South obtained (effective) independence and became the Irish Free State (later the Irish Republic); the six Northern Counties, dominated by Protestants, exercised their option to remain part of the UK as Northern Ireland.[44] The Government of Ireland Act established a devolved system of government for Northern Ireland, giving it its own Parliament (known as Stormont) and Executive, though subject to the supremacy of the Westminster Parliament. Stormont had the power to make laws 'for the peace, order and good government of Northern Ireland'; certain subjects, including defence, foreign policy and so on, were reserved to the UK Parliament. A convention was soon established, and followed, that Westminster would not interfere in the matters devolved to Stormont, which allowed it a substantial degree of autonomy.

The essential problem during the devolved period, which lasted from 1921 to 1972, was that the Unionists held a permanent majority in the Parliament and therefore always formed the Government. They also controlled local government. The result was serious discrimination against Catholics in various areas, including housing, education and policing policy, the police service (the RUC) being dominated by Protestants.[45] Eventually, increasing civil disorder forced the UK Government to re-impose direct rule, including the despatch of British troops, and the introduction of internment. The powers of Stormont were vested in the Secretary of State for Northern Ireland; legislation for Northern Ireland was introduced by him in the form of Orders in Council under the Northern Ireland (Temporary Provisions) Act 1972. However, direct rule did not bring an end to sectarian violence between armed Catholic and Protestant groups; the IRA attacked both British troops in Northern Ireland and targets in England, and killings by the British Army, including most notoriously the Bloody Sunday episode, kept nationalist feelings high. Various attempts up until the mid-1980s to restore devolved government and bring the conflict to an end all failed.

The lead-up to the Good Friday Agreement in 1998, which eventually achieved a ceasefire and restored devolved governance (albeit temporarily), started with the Anglo-Irish Agreement, negotiated between the UK and Irish Governments. It stated that there would be no constitutional change to the position of Northern Ireland without the consent of a majority of the Northern Irish population (something enshrined in UK law but long rejected in principle by the Irish Government) and it established closer cooperation between the two Governments. In a Joint Declaration (1993), the UK Government declared it had 'no selfish, strategic or economic interest' in Northern Ireland remaining part of the UK, moving to a position of neutrality on the province's constitutional position. It looked forward to all-party talks provided that those taking part were committed to peaceful means. Following this, the IRA commenced a ceasefire from 1994. This was broken in 1996 with the Canary Wharf bombing, but resumed in 1997 with the election of a Labour Government. The Blair administration reversed the previous policy of refusing to hold substantive talks until the IRA had disarmed, and persuaded the Unionists to engage in talks. Although boycotted by the hard-line Democratic Unionist

---

44 Turpin and Tomkins, n 42 above, p 229.

45 *Ibid*, p 231.

Party (DUP), these eventually culminated in the Good Friday Agreement (Cm 3833/1998), which was implemented in the UK by means of the Northern Ireland Act 1998 (NIA).[46]

THE GOOD FRIDAY AGREEMENT AND THE NIA 1998

Agreement between the Government of the United Kingdom and the Government of Ireland (1998) (extracts)

1   The participants endorse the commitment made by the British and Irish Governments that, in a new British-Irish Agreement replacing the Anglo-Irish Agreement, they will:

(i)   recognise the legitimacy of whatever choice is freely exercised by a majority of the people of Northern Ireland with regard to its status, whether they prefer to continue to support the Union with Great Britain or a sovereign united Ireland;

(ii)   recognise that it is for the people of the island of Ireland alone, by agreement between the two parts respectively and without external impediment, to exercise their right of self-determination on the basis of consent, freely and concurrently given, North and South, to bring about a united Ireland, if that is their wish, accepting that this right must be achieved and exercised with and subject to the agreement and consent of a majority of the people of Northern Ireland;

(iii)   acknowledge that while a substantial section of the people in Northern Ireland share the legitimate wish of a majority of the people of the island of Ireland for a united Ireland, the present wish of a majority of the people of Northern Ireland, freely exercised and legitimate, is to maintain the Union and, accordingly, that Northern Ireland's status as part of the United Kingdom reflects and relies upon that wish; and that it would be wrong to make any change in the status of Northern Ireland save with the consent of a majority of its people;

(iv)   affirm that if, in the future, the people of the island of Ireland exercise their right of self-determination on the basis set out in sections (i) and (ii) above to bring about a united Ireland, it will be a binding obligation on both Governments to introduce and support in their respective Parliaments legislation to give effect to that wish;

(v)   affirm that whatever choice is freely exercised by a majority of the people of Northern Ireland, the power of the sovereign government with jurisdiction there shall be exercised with rigorous impartiality on behalf of all the people in the diversity of their identities and traditions and shall be founded on the principles of full respect for, and equality of, civil, political, social and cultural rights, of freedom from discrimination for all citizens, and of parity of esteem

---

46   For detailed analysis of the political climate in the run-up to the Good Friday Agreement and a comprehensive overview of the Agreement's principal aims, see C McCrudden, 'Northern Ireland and the British Constitution since the Belfast Agreement', in J Jowell and D Oliver (eds), *The Changing Constitution*, 6th edn (2007), pp 227–70.

and of just and equal treatment for the identity, ethos, and aspirations of both communities;

(vi) recognise the birthright of all the people of Northern Ireland to identify themselves and be accepted as Irish or British, or both, as they may so choose, and accordingly confirm that their right to hold both British and Irish citizenship is accepted by both Governments and would not be affected by any future change in the status of Northern Ireland.

2   The participants also note that the two Governments have accordingly under-taken in the context of this comprehensive political agreement, to propose and support changes in, respectively, the Constitution of Ireland and in British legislation relating to the constitutional status of Northern Ireland.

Note

The fundamental principles of the Good Friday Agreement were as follows:

- Northern Ireland was to remain part of the UK unless and until a majority of its citizens by referendum decided otherwise.
- The Republic of Ireland agreed to amend its Constitution to abandon its territorial claim to Northern Ireland.
- A power-sharing Assembly and Executive were established: unlike in a normal democracy where one party, provided it received a sufficient share of the votes, could govern on its own, the agreement was structured in such a way that all the main parties would be guaranteed a share in government, in an attempt to avoid the problems arising under the previous Unionist-dominated Stormont Government.
- A North-South Ministerial Council was established to coordinate relations between the Republic and Ulster. This was regarded as highly controversial by the Unionists as it involved giving the Republic a greater say in Northern Irish affairs, something Unionists have always bitterly resisted. However, the NIA provided that all agreements reached by the Council must be approved by the Assembly.
- A Council of the Isles was established to consider matters of mutual interest to Wales, Scotland, Northern Ireland, England and the Channel Islands.
- All parties were to use their best endeavours to secure decommissioning of para-military weapons; a deadline of May 2001 was set for total disarmament of all paramilitary organisations (this deadline was not met).

The Good Friday Agreement was endorsed by referenda in both Northern Ireland and the Republic: in the North by 71.1% on an 81.1% turnout; in the South, by 94.4% on a 56% turnout.[47]

Under the NIA, the Assembly has 108 members elected by a proportional voting system—the single transferable vote—using multi-member constituencies. Like the Scottish Parliament, it is elected for a four-year term. It can be prematurely dissolved, however, by an Assembly vote with a two-thirds majority (s 32(1) and (2)), and must be dissolved if the offices of First or Deputy First Minister or the Northern Ireland Ministerial offices are left unfilled more than seven days from the first meeting of the Assembly following a general election, or if a vacancy for the posts of First and/or Deputy First Minister arises and the post is not filled within seven days (s 32(3)). The most recent (2007) Assembly elections yielded the following results on a 62.3% turnout:[48]

---

47   Source: Northern Ireland Office (www.nio.gov.uk).

48   Source: Northern Ireland Assembly (www.niassembly.gov.uk).

Democratic Unionist Party (DUP):   36
Sinn Fein: 28
Ulster Unionist Party: 18
Social Democratic and Labour Party (SDLP):   16
Alliance Party of Northern Ireland: 7
Others: 3

The current First and deputy First Ministers are Peter Robinson (DUP) and Martin McGuinness (Sinn Fein) respectively.

The competencies of the Assembly and the Executive

Turning in greater detail to the framework of the Act, the NIA begins by making the constitutional position of Northern Ireland and the right of the people to self-determination clear.[49]

1.— Status of Northern Ireland.

1   It is hereby declared that Northern Ireland in its entirety remains part of the United Kingdom and shall not cease to be so without the consent of a majority of the people of Northern Ireland voting in a poll held for the purposes of this section in accordance with Schedule 1.

2   But if the wish expressed by a majority in such a poll is that Northern Ireland should cease to be part of the United Kingdom and form part of a united Ireland, the Secretary of State shall lay before Parliament such proposals to give effect to that wish as may be agreed between Her Majesty's Government in the United Kingdom and the Government of Ireland.

Section 5(1) permits the Assembly to pass primary legislation known, like that of the Westminster and Scottish Parliaments, as Acts (the Assembly can also pass secondary legislation). In similar fashion to the Scotland Act 1998, the NIA expressly reserves to Westminster the power to legislate for Northern Ireland notwithstanding the Assembly's ordinary power to amend or repeal Acts of the Westminster Parliament falling within the Assembly's legislative competence:

5.—Acts of the Northern Ireland Assembly.

. . .

6   This section does not affect the power of the Parliament of the United Kingdom to make laws for Northern Ireland, but an Act of the Assembly may modify any provision made by or under an Act of Parliament in so far as it is part of the law of Northern Ireland.

The Assembly's legislative competence is determined by ss 6–8 NIA.

---

49   As Brazier observes, s 1 is an interesting provision because it expressly recognises the possibility of future break-up of the union: R Brazier, *Constitutional Reform in the United Kingdom* (2008), p 116.

6.—Legislative competence.

1   A provision of an Act is not law if it is outside the legislative competence of the Assembly.

2   A provision is outside that competence if any of the following paragraphs apply—

(a)   it would form part of the law of a country or territory other than Northern Ireland, or confer or remove functions exercisable otherwise than in or as regards Northern Ireland;

(b)   it deals with an excepted matter and is not ancillary to other provisions (whether in the Act or previously enacted) dealing with reserved or transferred matters;

(c)   it is incompatible with any of the Convention rights;

(d)   it is incompatible with Community law;

(e)   it discriminates against any person or class of person on the ground of religious belief or political opinion;

(f)   it modifies an enactment in breach of section 7 . . .

Unlike the Scotland Act, which only distinguishes two categories of matter ('reserved' and 'devolved') when determining legislative competence, the NIA establishes three: *transferred matters* are those upon which the Assembly is competent to legislate. These include agriculture and rural development, education, environment, health, social services, culture, training and employment. *Excepted matters* (listed in Sched 2) are those that *cannot* be transferred to the Assembly without an amendment of the NIA by Westminster. These are similar to the reserved matters under the Scotland Act and include the main provisions of the NIA itself. The *reserved matters* (in Sched 3) are those that are not within the competence of the NIA but *may* be transferred to it by Order in Council approved by both Houses of Parliament, following a request by the Assembly for such a transfer by a resolution passed with cross-community support (see below). They include financial services and markets, firearms and explosives and broadcasting.

The NIA must obtain the consent of the Secretary of State to pass legislation containing either a provision dealing with an excepted matter that is ancillary to other provisions dealing with reserved or transferred matters (s 8(1)(a)), or a provision dealing with a reserved matter (s 8(1)(b)). As under the Scotland Act, Assembly legislation breaching the ECHR or EU law will be *ultra vires* (ss 6(2)(c) and (d)), as will legislation purporting to modify any Westminster legislation listed in s 7; this list includes the Human Rights Act 1998 and core provisions of the European Communities Act 1972. An additional restriction upon the NIA, reflecting Northern Ireland's sectarian history, is that it may not enact legislation discriminating against any person on the grounds of religious or political belief (s 6(2)(e)). In a further bid to safeguard fundamental rights and values such as equality and freedom from discrimination, s 68 of the NIA also created the Northern Ireland Human Rights Commission, a body corporate whose purposes include 'keep[ing] under review the adequacy and effectiveness in Northern Ireland of law and practice relating to the protection of human rights' (s 69(1)), advising the Secretary of State, Assembly and Executive of legislative measures appropriate for safeguarding human rights, and advising the Assembly on the compatibility of Assembly Bills with human rights.

As Turpin and Tomkins note:

The Commission was also given the task of advising the Secretary of State on the scope for defining a Bill of Rights for Northern Ireland, supplementing the

'Convention Rights' included in the Human Rights Act 1998 and reflecting, as provided in the Belfast Agreement, 'the particular circumstances of Northern Ireland' and 'principles of mutual respect for the identity and ethos of both communities and parity of esteem'. It has published draft proposals for consultation and has engaged in discussions with political parties, human rights lawyers and other representatives of civil society on the terms of a Bill of Rights. These have proved contentious, but the Commission is continuing its efforts [in its own words] 'to build political consensus around a strong and inclusive Bill of Rights.[50]

The Commission's Bill of Rights project in Northern Ireland is ongoing. Its formal advice to the Secretary of State for Northern Ireland was presented in December 2008.[51] As well as reiterating the importance and application of certain rights already granted by the European Convention and the Human Rights Act 1998, the Commission also recommended supplementing those rights with others such equality of opportunity in public service and a general right to freedom from violence and harassment extending, in particular, to freedom from domestic and sexual violence. These recommendations could serve as a useful starting point for building on the basic Bill of Rights proposals previously advanced by the Conservative and Labour parties at Westminster.[52]

Section 11 establishes a similar process as the Scotland Act for referring Bills to the Supreme Court (formerly the Judicial Committee of the Privy Council) in order to assess their potential validity as Acts of the Assembly. All Bills must be presented by the Secretary of State to the Queen for Royal Assent. The Secretary of State can refuse to present for Royal Assent, and can therefore block the enactment of, any Bill which he considers would breach the UK's international obligations (s 14(5)(a), or be incompatible with the interests of, e.g. defence or national security (s 14(5)(b)) or harm the single market of goods and services within the UK (s 14(5)(b)).

The procedures that the Assembly must follow in terms of the passage of legislation and the construction of its executive are designed to prevent one-party domination. Thus, the passage of the annual budget requires cross-community support (s 63); but any 30 members can demand that any vote be made subject to the same requirement (s 42(1)). 'Cross-community support' means either a majority of both Unionists and Nationalists ('parallel consent') or the support of 60% of all members including at least 40% from each side ('weighted majority') (s 4(5)).

There are complex rules governing the formation of the Executive, again designed to ensure power-sharing.[53] After a general election, the largest political party of the largest political designation (i.e. 'unionist', 'nationalist' or 'other') nominates a First Minister and the largest party of the second largest designation a deputy First Minister (ss 16A(3)–(4)). Nominees must decide whether or not to take up their positions within periods specified by Standing Orders but there is an absolute deadline of seven days from the first meeting of the Assembly for the positions to be filled (s 16A(3) and 16A(8)). Within this seven-day deadline, the Northern Ireland Ministerial offices must also be filled in accordance with the procedure laid down in s 18 (s 16A(3)(b)). Should nominees to the posts of First or deputy First Minister decline, the nomination process continues in the same fashion until the positions are filled (ss 16A(6)–(7)). Should the positions of First or deputy First Minister or the

---

50   *British Government and the Constitution*, 6th edn (2007) at 241.

51   Northern Ireland Human Rights Commission, *A Bill of Rights for Northern Ireland* (2008).

52   For analysis of the current Bill of Rights debate, see Chapter 17, pp 944–949 and 1012–1015.

53   For critical analysis of the procedure for forming the Executive, see J McGarry and B O'Leary, 'Stabilising Northern Ireland's Agreement' (2004) *The Political Quarterly* 213.

ministerial offices be left unfilled seven days after the first meeting of the Assembly, the Secretary of State must propose a further general election (s 32(3)). A similar procedure applies if a vacancy for the position of First or deputy First Minister arises (it should be noted that if one resigns, the other ceases to hold office: s 16B(2)). For the sake of the Assembly, therefore, clear pressure exists upon unwilling nominees to decline their nominations as quickly as possible so that further nominations can be made before the deadline passes.

Section 16A NIA, which was inserted by the Northern Ireland (St Andrews Agreement) Act 2006 in place of the (original) s 16, puts it beyond doubt that 'no person may take up office as First Minister, deputy First Minister or Northern Ireland Minister by virtue of this section after the end of the period mentioned in subsection (3)' (s 16A(8)). This is an evident attempt by Parliament to clarify the procedure surrounding the (repealed) s 16, which omitted to explain what would happen if the specified time period (then six weeks) elapsed without ministerial appointments being made. This issue was the subject of an appeal to the House of Lords in the following case:

Robinson v Secretary of State for Northern Ireland
[2002] UKHL 32 (extracts)

In 2001, David Trimble and Mark Durkhan were elected as First and deputy First Minister respectively. Following an initial failure to gain the required level of cross-community support within the Assembly for their nominations, they were eventually elected two days after the expiry of the statutory time period. Peter Robinson, Member of the Assembly and leader of the DUP, sought to challenge the appointments on the basis that the Northern Ireland Assembly lacked the power to make them out of time. The House of Lords ruled by a bare majority (Lords Hutton and Hobhouse dissenting) that the appointments were lawfully made.

Lord Bingham:
'10. The 1998 Act, as already noted, was passed to implement the Belfast Agreement, which was itself reached, after much travail, in an attempt to end decades of bloodshed and centuries of antagonism. The solution was seen to lie in participation by the unionist and nationalist communities in shared political institutions, without precluding (see section 1 of the Act) a popular decision at some time in the future on the ultimate political status of Northern Ireland. If these shared institutions were to deliver the benefits which their pro-genitors intended, they had to have time to operate and take root.
(1) The 1998 Act does not set out all the constitutional provisions applicable to Northern Ireland, but it is in effect a constitution. So to categorise the Act is not to relieve the courts of their duty to interpret the constitutional provisions in issue. But the provisions should, consistently with the language used, be interpreted generously and purposively, bearing in mind the values which the constitutional provisions are intended to embody. Mr Larkin [QC, for Peter Robinson] submitted that the resolution of political problems by resort to the vote of the people in a free election lies at the heart of any democracy and that this democratic principle is one embodied in this constitution. He is of course correct. Sections 32(1) and (3) expressly contemplate such elections as a means of resolving political impasses. But elections held with undue frequency are not necessarily productive. While elections may produce solutions they can also deepen divisions. Nor is the democratic ideal the only constitutional ideal which this constitution should be understood to embody. It is in general desirable that the government should be carried on, that there be no governmental vacuum. . .'

Notes

1. Whilst the result itself in *Robinson* has been reversed by s 16A, the reasoning in the judgments is nevertheless instructive; interestingly, it reveals how the political background to the NIA may affect the courts' interpretation of its provisions. Lord Bingham was clearly concerned that declaring the appointments void on the basis that they were made out of time could frustrate the purpose of the Northern Ireland Act to facilitate democracy and political harmony after 'decades of bloodshed and centuries of antagonism'. By contrast, Lord Hutton, dissenting, adopted a more legalistic approach that focused to a greater extent on the technical status of the Assembly as a body created by statute and strictly bound to act within the *vires* set by Westminster:

    > '54. My Lords, despite the attractiveness of the respondents' argument based on the purpose of the Belfast Agreement, I have come to the conclusion that the appeal should succeed. The Northern Ireland Assembly is a body created by a Westminster statute and it has no powers other than those given to it by statute. Section 16(1) and section 16(8) expressly require that the election of the First Minister and deputy First Minster shall take place within a period of six weeks beginning either with the first meeting of the Assembly or, if the offices become vacant at any time, within a period of six weeks beginning with the time of the vacancy. Therefore once the period of six weeks has expired the Assembly has no express power under the Act to elect the First Minister and deputy First Minister. Does the Assembly then have an implied power to elect a First Minister and deputy First Minister outside the six weeks' period? Where a statute gives power to a statutory body to perform a certain act within a specified period the normal rule is that the body has no power to perform that act outside the period, and I see nothing in the provisions of the Act pointing to a different conclusion.'

2. How *do* courts accord sufficient recognition both to the legal truth that the Assembly is a body created and constrained in its activities by Westminster statute, on the one hand, and to the political truth that the Assembly is an elected legislature with a profoundly democratic mandate to its activities, on the other? As we saw above (pp 246–254), this thorny issue has arisen before in relation to challenges brought in domestic courts to the validity of Acts of the Scottish Parliament. Although the democratic status of the Assembly will be an important factor for courts to consider when scrutinising its activities (see, in particular, the recent *Axa General* case above, pp 250–254, in relation to Scotland), it should not be taken too far; Parliament was well aware of the political climate in Northern Ireland and Parliament's intention, as expressed through its language, ought to be the courts' chief concern. With respect, the minority approach of Lord Hutton in *Robinson* is preferable to that of Lord Bingham. Just as the duty upon the Assembly under s 16 to select *a* First Minister and *a* deputy First Minister could not sensibly have been construed as allowing the Assembly to elect more than one of each, it represented a similarly strained construction of the language of s 16, which required those elections to be made *within six weeks*, to read it as permitting the Assembly to make them out of time.

    Once validly elected to office, a Minister may, by Assembly resolution, be temporarily excluded from office on the basis, *inter alia*, that that person or their party is no longer committed to exclusively democratic and peaceful means (s 30); such a resolution needs cross community support. All Ministers must take the pledge set out in Schedule 4, which affirms their 'commitment to non-violence and exclusively peaceful means. . .to serve all the people of Northern Ireland equally, and. . .to promote equality and prevent discrimination'.

The Secretary of State for Northern Ireland can also suspend the Assembly and Executive. This has happened four times since the NIA came into force: in February 2000, August 2001, September 2001 and, most recently, October 2002. Here, the Assembly was suspended by John Reid, then Secretary of State for Northern Ireland, after both Unionist Parties stated that they would withdraw from the power-sharing Executive unless Sinn Fein was excluded from it, something unacceptable to the British Government and to the nationalist SDLP. Rather than allowing the collapse of the Executive, the British Government decided to suspend it and the Assembly. The Unionist ultimatum came after police found evidence that the IRA was operating a spy ring within Sinn Fein at Stormont.[54]

The St Andrews Agreement and the Restoration of the Assembly

Following suspension of the Assembly and the imposition of direct rule from Westminster in 2002, the British and Irish Governments renewed their efforts to restore the Assembly to operation and fresh talks with the Northern Ireland political parties resumed from 2003–2004. In 2005, the independent De Chastelain Commission verified the IRA's claims to have decommissioned its arms; this represented official confirmation that the IRA's campaign of violence had ended and paved the way for fresh progress in Northern Ireland to be made. In further preparation for the restoration of the Assembly, Parliament enacted the Northern Ireland Act 2006, s 1 of which conferred upon the Secretary of State the broad power to refer to the suspended Assembly any matter as he thought fit in order to prepare for its restoration. The Act's purpose was to bring Assembly Members together for talks which, it was hoped, would result in the nomination of an Executive comprised of a new First Minister, deputy First Minister and Northern Ireland Ministers. The deadline set by the Act for nominating an Executive was 24 November 2006. The immediate talks broke down after Ian Paisley (DUP) refused the proposal by Sinn Fein for him to be appointed First Minister alongside Martin McGuinness (Sinn Fein) as Deputy First Minister.

The St Andrews agreement was reached on 13 October 2006 following talks between the British and Irish Governments and Northern Ireland political parties. The Agreement provided, most importantly, for commitment between the parties to the restoration of the Assembly and, in particular, commitment by the DUP to power-sharing within the Executive and acceptance by Sinn Fein of the Police Service of Northern Ireland:

> 13. It is clear to us that all the parties wish to see devolution restored. It is also clear to us that all parties wish to support policing and the rule of law. We hope they will seize this opportunity for bringing the political process in Northern Ireland to completion and establishing power-sharing government for the benefit of the whole community.[55]

The St Andrews Agreement was given legislative effect by Parliament via the Northern Ireland (St Andrews Agreement) Act 2006. The Act created a 'Transitional Assembly' to sit from 24 November

---

54   For a detailed account of the climate leading up to the suspension in 2002, see J Bradbury and N McGarvey, 'Devolution: Problems, Politics and Prospects' (2003) 56 Parlt Aff 219, 227–30.

55   British and Irish Governments, *Agreement at St Andrews* (2006) (available on www.nio.gov.uk).

2006 to 26 March 2007 (the latter being the revised deadline for restoration) and specified various other measures to facilitate restoration by Westminster. The Act required the Secretary of State to dissolve the Assembly if the restoration deadline elapsed with no Executive appointed. The Transitional Assembly was dissolved on 30 January 2007 and the election campaign began for the current Assembly. The election was held on 7 March 2007. The two largest parties were the DUP (with 35 seats) and Sinn Fein (28). The deadline for appointing the Executive was looming, however, and it soon became apparent after the election that the deadline would be missed. Following legislative extension of the deadline to the 8 May so as to postpone the mandatory dissolution of the Assembly by the Secretary of State,[56] the Assembly was restored by Westminster and remains in operation.

The initial progress made by the St Andrews Agreement was dealt an almost fatal blow from late 2009 to early 2010, however, when bitter disagreements between the DUP and Sinn Fein over the timetable for the transfer of policing and justice powers from Westminster reached their climax. After extensive talks between the parties and the British and Irish Governments in early 2010, a deal was eventually reached on 5 February whereby policing and justice powers would be transferred to Stormont in April 2010. Almost certainly, this deal has saved the Assembly from what could have been further suspension by Westminster. As Gerry Adams (Sinn Fein) wrote in *The Guardian* the following day:

> It was another 'Good Friday' in the peace process yesterday. Hillsborough Castle was the setting for the final piece of the jigsaw of devolution which saw agreement between Sinn Féin and the Democratic Unionist party on the transfer of policing and justice powers and other outstanding matters arising from the Good Friday and St Andrews agreements.
>
> Many had thought it wouldn't, couldn't happen. That our respective positions were too far apart. But it did, and it was achieved primarily as a result of very intense discussions between Sinn Féin and the DUP. This is a hugely important, as well as symbolic moment. This is the political parties in the north of Ireland demonstrating our ability to negotiate a successful agreement together. It marks a new phase in the process. . .[57]

Note

The powers were transferred on 12th April 2010. Whilst it remains to be seen how effectively they can be exercised in practice, the political breakthrough made by the deal, as Adams writes, is of itself a source of much optimism.

DEVOLUTION TO WALES

England and Wales became a single state-like entity in the 13th century via the Statute of Wales Act 1284 and Wales has been ruled from England ever since, through the office of what became, in 1964, the Secretary of State for Wales. Historically, demand for devolution and independence has been much lower in Wales than in Scotland. The vote in support of Welsh devolution in 1997 was much lower than in Scotland, at a mere 50.3%. The margin of support was thus only 0.3%. Moreover

---

56 The deadline was revised by the Northern Ireland (St Andrews Agreement) Act 2007, which amended the 2006 St Andrews Agreement Act.

57 G Adams, 'Another Good Friday', *The Guardian*, 6 February 2010.

the turnout was low, at 51%. Thus barely a quarter of the Welsh people expressed a positive preference for devolution.[58]

The Welsh Assembly has 60 members, elected, like those of the Scottish Parliament, under a system of mixed proportional representation and first past the post. The Assembly is currently governed by a coalition between the Welsh Labour and Plaid Cymru parties, which is led by First Minister Carwyn Jones AM (Labour). The most recent (2007) general election results were as follows:[59]

Labour:	26	(of which 2 are Regional List AMs)
Plaid Cymru:	15	(of which 8 are Regional List AMs)
Conservative:	12	(of which 7 are Regional List AMs)
Liberal Democrats:	6	(of which 3 are Regional List AMs)
Other:	1	(this is a Constituency AM)

The Assembly, as it now stands, owes its existence to two main pieces of legislation: the Government of Wales Act 1998 and the Government of Wales Act 2006. Each Act represents a distinct stage in the Assembly's development.

In contrast to the Scotland Act 1998, which created a devolved legislature capable of enacting legislation on any matters not reserved to the UK Parliament at Westminster, the Government of Wales Act 1998 created an 'Assembly' with relatively limited powers. The Assembly, unlike the Scottish Parliament, was only permitted by the Act to operate in the areas specifically transferred to it by the Secretary of State for Wales. More importantly, the Assembly was unable to pass primary legislation. Again in contrast to the Scottish Parliament, the Assembly had no separately identifiable 'executive' and 'legislative' organs. The scheme devised by the 1998 Act came widely to be known as one of 'executive' rather than 'legislative' devolution. In essence, the Assembly merely took over the role of Secretary of State for Wales in passing delegated legislation ('Assembly Measures') to flesh out policies the broad frameworks of which were devised by Acts of Parliament passed at Westminster. Areas of competence devolved to the Assembly included education and training; local government; the environment; regulation; many aspects of transport policy; housing; the health service, agriculture and fisheries; social services; and sports, arts and culture.

Why were the powers granted to the Welsh Assembly less extensive than those granted to the Scottish Parliament and Northern Ireland Assembly? The answer, as Turpin and Tomkins explain, lies in the less objectively compelling need for devolution to Wales in the first place:

> From the beginning there was a marked contrast in the success of devolution in Scotland compared with Wales. Unlike in Scotland, it was never clear that the Government of Wales Act 1998 solved the problem it was designed to address. Perhaps this was because (again, unlike Scotland) it was not clear what the problem was in the first place. It was as if Wales was being dragged along in Scotland's wake, offered something of devolution but never as much as was offered to (or demanded by) the Scots. This was nothing new: as Sir David Williams put it ('Devolution: the Welsh Perspective', in A. Tomkins (ed), *Devolution and the British Constitution* (1998), pp 21–2), 'In the 1970s the dominance of Scotland in the devolution debates largely obscured the Welsh dimension, and the process has been repeated in the later 1990s.' Further, he continues, 'there is little or no constitutional framework or context in which the proposals for executive devolution can

58   Source: wwww.electoralgeography.com.

59   Source: www.ukpolitical.info.

properly be assessed.' What led Welsh devolution in the later 1990s, it seems, was not an echo of the consistent and coherent demand for home rule that had been heard so resoundingly in Scotland, but an inchoate and far from unanimous sense within the Labour party that, in the light of developments in Scotland, *something* ought also to be offered to Wales. Exactly what that something should amount to, it seems, was determined as much by reference to internal squabbles within the Labour Party as to any constitutional road map.[60]

Notes

1. The authors' emphasis on the differing constitutional strengths of the calls for devolution in Scotland and Wales is also relevant to our analysis of the conferral of primary law-making powers upon the Assembly by the Government of Wales Act 2006 (see below, pp 287–288).

2. In July 2002, Rhodri Morgan AM, then First Minister for Wales, appointed a Commission led by Lord Richard of Ammenford QC to report on the powers and electoral arrangements of the Assembly. The Richard Commission issued its report in March 2004, concluding that there was scope for various aspects of improvement to the current devolution scheme.

Commission on the Powers and Electoral Arrangements of the National Assembly for Wales (2004) (extracts)

The Government of Wales Act 1998 established the National Assembly for Wales and enabled the transfer of devolved powers and responsibilities from the Secretary of State for Wales to the Assembly on 1 July 1999 . . . These powers, which include powers to make secondary (or delegated) legislation, allow the Assembly to make rules and regulations, set standards and issue guidance in areas such as health, education and the environment, within the basic framework of primary legislation that is made by the UK Parliament. . .

Real-life problems rarely fit into the definitions of the Assembly's devolved powers and, as a result, the Assembly Government has been pushing against the limits of the powers in a number of areas. The complexity of the devolved powers—knowing what the Assembly Government can and can't do—is becoming less of a problem for those close to government, but this remains a central issue for accountability to the people of Wales. . .

The Assembly Government benefits from close engagement with Whitehall departments in developing policy and legislation affecting Wales, and goodwill and co-operation are important in making the relationship work. However, the Assembly Government is the junior partner in the relationship and making different arrangements for Wales is a complication for hard-pressed central departments—which can cause delay even when there is no objection to giving the Assembly Government what it wants. . .

Notes

1. The Commission went on to make a series of recommendations in each of the fields ('powers' and 'electoral' arrangements) of investigation. Most significantly, the Commission recommended reconstituting the Assembly as a separate legislature and executive and, in preparation for an eventual shift towards full legislative competence, recommended progressive widening of the Assembly's fields of competence by the Secretary of State for Wales at Westminster. Noting the constitutional significance of gaining powers to pass primary as opposed to merely secondary

---

legislation, the Commission noted the possible need for a Welsh referendum on the issue but left that question, ultimately, for the UK Government and Westminster Parliament to decide. In order to cope with the heightened workload which the Commission envisaged its recommendations would generate, the Commission called for an increase in the number of Assembly Members from 60 to 80 and recommended reforming the Assembly's electoral system to a single transferrable vote (STV) system to prevent the potential windfalls to larger political parties that the recommended increase in Assembly Members risked bringing. (The STV system is designed to encourage greater competition within constituencies by allowing parties to field more than one candidate in a given constituency and voters to rank candidates in order of preference.)

2. For commentary on the various recommendations made by the Richard Commission, see T Jones and J Williams, 'The Legislative Future of Wales' (2005) 68(4) MLR 642. In particular, the authors welcome the Commission's recommendation to reconstitute the Welsh Assembly into separate legislature end executive:

T Jones and J Williams, 'The Legislative Future of Wales' (2005) 68(4) *Modern Law Review* 642 (extracts)

The Richard Commission was clear that the structure of the National Assembly should be changed from a single corporate body to a separate legislature and executive. This is presented as an 'implication' of the conferring of primary legislative powers on the Assembly, but the Commission does acknowledge that there is a strong case for changing the Assembly's legal structure in any event, that is, with the powers it currently has. The Commission found that the concept of a single unitary body was no longer sustainable and had contributed to the public's confusion about responsibility for decisions. In practice, using powers in the Government of Wales Act 1998, the Assembly delegates the exercise of almost all its functions to the First Minister, who in turn delegates the majority of them to other Assembly Ministers in the Cabinet. . .

It would be difficult to find anyone who would dissent from the Commission's recommendation that there should be a Welsh (Assembly) Government, responsible for executive acts and decisions, separate from the National Assembly, but directly answerable and accountable to it. The Assembly's corporate structure is the result of a political compromise that involved a serious blurring of constitutional principle. The Richard Commission referred to the 'tension between the original design of an executive body subordinate to the UK Parliament at Westminster, and the aspirations of a body with its own democratic mandate'. The nomenclature 'executive devolution' may have satisfied those who needed to minimise the changes that were being elected for Wales, especially in comparison with Scotland, but in so doing it disguised the actual and potential legislative functions of the Assembly *within the existing settlement*. . . [This has] been resolved as best may be within the corporate structure, to the credit of the officials and Assembly Members who have worked out the *de facto* separation of. . . the parliamentary and governmental functions within the Assembly. It can hardly be satisfactory, however, for this 'divorce within a marriage' to be forced to subsist, whether or not the Assembly is granted primary legislative powers. . .

The Government of Wales Act 2006

The Richard Commission's recommendations did not go unnoticed at Westminster. The Government White Paper entitled *Better Governance for Wales* (2005) (Cm 6582), issued by the Secretary of State for Wales, formed the blueprint for the Government of Wales Act 2006 that followed.[61] Under the 2006 Act, in accordance with the Richard Commission's recommendations, Parliament duly re-established the Assembly with a separate legislature and Government (the 'Welsh Assembly Government').

45. Welsh Assembly Government

1   There is to be a Welsh Assembly Government, or Llywodraeth Cynulliad Cymru, whose members are–

(a)   the First Minister or Prif Weinidog (see sections 46 and 47),

(b)   the Welsh Ministers, or Gweinidogion Cymru, appointed under section 48,

(c)   the Counsel General to the Welsh Assembly Government or Cwnsler Cyffredinol i Lywodraeth Cynulliad Cymru (see section 49) (referred to in this Act as "the Counsel General"), and

(d)   the Deputy Welsh Ministers or Dirprwy Weinidogion Cymru (see section 50).

2   In this Act and in any other enactment or instrument the First Minister and the Welsh Ministers appointed under section 48 are referred to collectively as the Welsh Ministers.

This creation of the Assembly Government was accompanied by changes to the procedure for selection by the Assembly of its executive officers. Under the 1998 Act (s 53), the leader of the Assembly (the Assembly First Secretary) was *elected* by the Assembly and then went on to *appoint* the remaining members of the Executive Committee. Under the 2006 Act however, the Assembly *nominates* a leader (now 'First Minister') to the Queen. The First Minister 'holds office at Her Majesty's pleasure' and may appoint Welsh Ministers and Deputy Ministers *with the monarch's permission* (ss 46–48). These arrangements, which now more closely resemble the procedure for forming a Government under the Scottish scheme,[62] have the technically retrogressive effect of placing ultimate control over the appointment of the leader into the hands of the monarch rather than the Assembly. Whilst the practical chances of the Queen refusing to endorse the appointment of a Welsh First Minister might be considered minimal, Ward observes that it may nevertheless amount to a trump card to be played by Westminster:

> [E]very opening for the Royal Prerogative of the kind we see in the Scotland Act [and now the Government of Wales Act 2006] represents a reserve power for the UK government through its advice to the sovereign. . . [She will], no doubt, regard the Prime Minister as her primary adviser if the two executives disagree on an important issue.[63]

---

61   For brief commentary on some key aspects of the White Paper's proposals, see R Whitaker, 'Ascendant Assemblies in Britain? Rebellions, Reforms and Inter-Cameral Conflict' (2006) 59(1) Parlt Aff 173, at 177–78.

62   The arrangements still differ, however, in that nominations to the Scottish Executive must be approved by the Parliament: Scotland Act, s 47(2). See further, on government formation, Chapter 12, pp 603–608.

63   See n 3 above, p 121.

Aside from implementing the Richard Commission's recommendation of a separated executive and legislature, the 2006 Act also provided—again following the Commission's recommendation—for the progressive expansion of the Assembly's competences in relation to designated matters within various fields such as agriculture and fisheries, culture and economic development (see Schedule 5). Like the Scottish Parliament, the Welsh Assembly is (and remains) unable to pass Assembly Measures incompatible with the European Convention or Community law (s 94(6)).

Perhaps the most significant change made by the 2006 Act was to invest the Assembly with the power to enact primary legislation (see ss 103–116). As stipulated by ss 103 and 104 however, these provisions will only come into force once a Welsh referendum, proposed by not less than two thirds of Assembly Members, indicates that the public wish them to. The latter requirement, as Rawlings describes, represents one of various 'locks on the door' to primary law-making powers for the Assembly.

R Rawlings, 'Hastening Slowly: the next phase of Welsh Devolution' [2005] *Public Law* 824 (extracts)

. . .The most striking feature of the. . . [process of granting primary law-making powers] is the array of locks on the door to full legislative powers for Wales. To this effect, the commitment to hold a referendum has been developed into an elongated legal and administrative scheme in the name of establishing 'consensus'. . .

At the heart of this will be the peculiar requirement in British constitutional practice of a two-thirds majority in the Assembly in favour of a referendum. There is no point here being in political denial: given the local electoral mathematics this represents the Welsh Labour Party veto, a device for ensuring a broad spread of backing inside the dominant political interest. . .

The requirement, however, does have broader appeal, especially given what has been called the 'quasi-autochthonous' quality of the Welsh constitutional enterprise; more prosaically, the need to convince the power-brokers in London to cede full-blown legislative devolution. A loud and clear voice for Wales, grounded in the fact of an established institutional consensus for 'changing the current settlement', clearly would be useful. . .

In this regard, the second main lock, a free-standing gatekeeper role for the Secretary of State, is the more objectionable. If it be the settled will of the democratically elected representatives in the National Assembly to consult the people in a referendum, why should the principle of automaticity not apply, so ensuring that this most high constitutional question for Wales is put to Parliament? A proposed duty on the minister, if minded to table the order, 'to undertake such consultation as he considers appropriate' [see s 103(6) of the 2006 Act], only serves to compound matters. . .

Note

Whilst the second 'lock on the door' does seem rather unnecessary given the democratic force that must necessarily underlie the Assembly's request for a referendum, the first lock, as Rawlings observes, may be seen as an appropriate procedural hurdle to granting primary law-making power to the Assembly given the constitutional significance of doing so. This interesting point illustrates the differing context surrounding devolution in Wales compared to Scotland (and also to Northern Ireland), a theme which was noted briefly (above, pp 282–283) in relation to the original devolution scheme under the 1998 Act. In Wales, the need for a scheme of devolution was less objectively compelling because the country has for centuries shared its legal and judicial system with England. As Rawlings pertinently observes (at pp 826–27):

> [The White Paper] supplied a clear constitutional vision, more especially in terms of legal and political accountability, where in their different ways both the corporate body concept and the extravagant disaggregation of the law-making function were rightly seen to offend, and also of coherence and intelligibility, as viewed against the backdrop of the patchwork of functions. Again, neatly illustrating the peculiarities of the Welsh condition, Richard's chief proposal of full legislative powers on the basis of a devolved parliamentary system could be seen, at one and the same, as a radical recipe in light of the territorial history (of close integration with England), and in comparative terms as a modest package, one designed to bring Wales into the constitutional mainstream.

Although the 2006 Act broadly endorsed the Richard Commission's recommendations, it did not give effect to all of them. In particular, Parliament ignored the Commission's calls for an increase in the number of Assembly Members. Alan Trench has argued that the 2006 Act 'is unlikely to be the end of the story'; there is some way to go, it would seem, before the Welsh Assembly becomes a fully-fledged legislature like its counterparts in Scotland and Northern Ireland.

A Trench, 'The Government of Wales Act 2006: the next steps on devolution for Wales' [2006] *Public Law* 687 (extracts)

Although the Act has been presented as an attempt to settle Wales's constitutional position for the long term, it leaves significant business unfinished. The Assembly still has only 60 members, not the 80 recommended by the Richard Commission and considered by many as necessary to scrutinise legislation properly. (With 16 members on the payroll vote as ministers or deputy ministers, there are only 44 available for committee and backbench duties—and that includes leaders and business managers for the opposition parties.) The UK government strenuously resisted calls for the Bill to provide for 80 members, or at least to create a mechanism to increase the size of the Assembly in due course. If the Assembly becomes at all active as a legislature, it is hard to see how the issue of its size can be avoided, and so fresh Westminster legislation will be needed.

THE WEST LOTHIAN QUESTION AND REGIONAL DEVOLUTION

The schemes of devolution to Scotland, Wales and Northern Ireland, as Brigid Hadfield observes, generate the result that 'England is the only UK nation all of whose laws are made and all of whose polices are formulated by a UK body and never by a solely English-elected body.'[64] This has potentially problematic consequences, collectively termed the 'West Lothian' or 'English question.' In what

---

64   B Hadfield, 'Devolution, Westminster and the English Question' [2005] PL 286, 291.

follows, the different aspects of this issue will be systematically presented and analysed; possible solutions will then be explored.

The English question arises not only because of the presence of representative institutions in the other nations of the UK, and the absence of an English equivalent, but because of the fact that the UK Parliament, as a result, has to serve as the Parliament for England, but with the problematic feature of containing a significant proportion of MPs from the non-English nations. Out of a total of 650 MPs, 117 represent non-English constituents: Scotland has 59 (a number recently reduced from 72 in partial recognition of the English question), Wales has 40 and Northern Ireland 18. There are two distinct consequences that follow from this: first, what might be termed the government-formation issue; second, the legislation-legitimacy issue. As to the first, the problem is simply that it is possible that in future, there will be a UK Government that only holds power due to the presence in Westminster, as part of the governing party's majority, of Scottish and Welsh MPs (hereafter the 'Celtic MPs'). (The issue does not arise with Northern Irish MPs, since they belong to separate parties.) There would be nothing wrong with such a situation save for the fact that the UK Government also has to act as the English Government (since there is no other). Thus the English face the possible future of being governed by an administration which is a minority one in terms of seats: in blunt terms, by a Labour Government when they voted Conservative.

An initial point sometimes made is that this is not significant because it was precisely the fate of Scotland and Wales during the 1980s: both consistently rejected the Conservatives in the polls (over-whelmingly so towards the end of the 80s and during the 90s before 1997) and yet were still governed by them. The English, it might be said, are simply grumbling about something that has already happened for long periods of time to their brethren in the Celtic nations. But this would be a poor rejoinder. The position just described was widely recognised as unjust, and it was partly in order to remedy it that Scottish and Welsh devolution was introduced. Two wrongs do not make a right.[65]

It should be noted that the situation just described has not in fact happened since devolution was introduced, the current Labour administration having had, since 1997, a majority of the English MPs, as well as an overall majority (although their majority amongst English MPs is only around 30 at present). Under a Conservative Government, the problem could not practically arise, because the Conservatives tend to do much better in England than Scotland and Wales. It would only be likely to occur if a Labour Government was formed, with a majority so small that it was numerically less than the number of Celtic MPs it had. This being the case, this part of the English question is strictly a potential, rather than an actual problem.

In contrast, the second part of the West Lothian question *has* already materialised. This more well-known aspect points out that, as a result of legislative devolution in Scotland, Scottish MPs at Westminster can and do vote on legislation passed at Westminster that only applies to England (hereafter 'English laws' or 'English Bills'), while English MPs cannot vote on equivalent laws applying to Scotland, because such laws are now passed by the Scottish Parliament. (As the Welsh Assembly does not yet enjoy the power to pass primary legislation, the issue is less acute in relation to Welsh constituency MPs.) This, it is suggested, is a conspicuous constitutional unfairness in principle. The problem is at its most acute where legislation which could not command a majority amongst English MPs is yet passed because of the votes of Scottish MPs; in such a situation it may be said that legislation has been imposed upon England that its representatives, as a whole, did not vote for. Instead, Scottish MPs, who are, as Hadfield puts it, 'Unelected by [English voters] and unaccountable to [them]'[66] determine the policies that will apply to those voters. Notoriously, this is precisely what happened

65   See also J Mitchell, 'Devolution's Unfinished Business' (2006) 77(4) *The Political Quarterly* 465, 471–72.

66   Hadfield, n 64 above, 286.

in relation to two highly controversial Government bills: those introducing foundation hospitals and student tuition (or 'top-up') fees in England. In the foundation hospitals vote in November 2003, the Labour Government achieved a narrow win of 302 to 285 votes, relying on the support of 43 Scottish Labour MPs to do so.[67] The Bill only applied to England and Wales because health is a matter devolved to the Scottish Parliament. In the top-up fees vote of January 2004, the Labour Government relied on 46 Scottish MPs in order to win by a majority of only five votes.[68] In both votes, not only were Scottish MPs voting on issues related only to England and Wales, but they were also voting in support of policies that Holyrood, exercising its devolved powers over health and education, had already considered and rejected as unsuitable for Scotland! As Hadfield observes:

> In such a situation, education law and policy for Scotland is decided by the Scottish Parliament without any input from elected representatives from England. Conversely, if all MPs at Westminster contribute to the debate and vote on English education law and policy, then Scottish MPs are exercising vis-à-vis English law a role not given to English elected representatives vis-à-vis Scots law.[69]

What then are the possible solutions and how satisfactory would they be? In short order, they may be summarised as: first, reduction of the representation at Westminster of the Scottish (and possibly Welsh) MPs; second, an English Parliament; third, the policy popularly known as 'English votes for English laws'; fourth, English regional devolution. The first option may readily be dismissed. Scottish representation has recently already been reduced so that it fairly represents its population. The Westminster Parliament still decides many crucial issues relevant to the UK as a whole, including macro-economic policy, virtually all taxation issues, immigration and citizenship and energy policy; moreover, of course, it forms the UK Government and holds the UK Government to account on issues such as the conduct of foreign policy and the deployment of UK forces abroad. This being the case, it would seem unfair for Scotland to be under-represented in a legislative body—in danger of becoming what Hadfield has termed a '*de facto* English legislature'[70]—that decides these crucial issues affecting Scottish as much as English voters. Furthermore, it would not solve the fundamental problem, since Scottish MPs (albeit fewer of them) would still vote on Bills affecting only England.

The second solution would be an English Parliament, which might, though it would not need to, lead to a federal UK.[71] It was briefly put forward by former Conservative leader William Hague. It is the most comprehensive solution, in the sense that, if the powers of the English Parliament more or less mirrored those of the Scottish Parliament, and assuming that the Westminster Parliament no longer passed legislation in the English devolved areas, Scottish MPs would no longer vote on English laws; moreover the UK Parliament and Government, formed by Celtic MPs would only deal with UK-wide matters. Practically speaking, the main drawback with this solution is simply that there seems to be little public support for it. Even nationalists such as the SNP might oppose these plans on the basis that they would be more likely to result, in Brazier's words, in the 'freezing of Scotland (or Wales) within a

---

67   BBC News, 'Anger over hospitals reform vote' (20 November 2003).

68   BBC News, 'Scots MPs attacked over fees vote' (27 January 2004).

69   See n 64 above, 288.

70   *Ibid*, p 296.

71   This, in turn, 'could well add to pressures for break-up of the UK': N Bonney, 'The Settled Will of the Scottish People: What is Next for Scotland's Parliaments?' (2007) 78(2) *The Political Quarterly* 301, at 306.

permanent federation' rather than the nationalists' goal of formal independence.[72] The other objection to it is that the federation created by an English Parliament—whether a quasi-federation or a legal federation (which would require the UK Parliament to surrender its sovereignty)—would be unbalanced and dominated by England. The Report of the Royal Commission on the Constitution in 1973 (Cmnd 5460), said of this possibility:

> [531] A federation consisting of four units—England, Scotland, Wales and Northern Ireland—would be so unbalanced as to be unworkable. It would be dominated by the overwhelming political importance and wealth of England. The English Parliament would rival the UK Federal Parliament; and in the Federal Parliament itself, the representation of England could hardly be scaled down in such a way as to enable it to be out-voted by Scotland, Wales and Northern Ireland, together representing less than one-fifth of the [UK] population.

These objections, however, are not wholly persuasive. The Westminster Parliament, which in some senses currently acts as a federal Parliament for the UK in the sense that it decides policies normally decided by the federal legislature, is *already* dominated by English MPs and thus English voters. Thus if this is a problem in this respect, it already exists, and the introduction of an English Parliament would make no difference to it. As for the contention that the English Parliament would 'rival' the Westminster Parliament, why this would matter? The English Parliament would undoubtedly be a major institution, and would have to be given a huge budget to dispense. But why this would be problematic is not clear. It is possible, perhaps, that the English Parliament would draw away the political talent, in terms of personnel from Westminster; however, despite its importance in terms of determining English policies on things like health, education and criminal justice—the bread and butter of politics—the UK Parliament and Government would remain just that: the institutions determining not just UK foreign policy and the use of the armed forces but nearly all taxation issues and macro-economic policy. The US Federal Government, and Congress and Senate are extremely important and prestigious institutions and would remain so, even if there were a very large State representing most of the population, provided that that State's governing institutions did not wield the same powers. This solution then, seems less problematic than generally assumed.

The third and most likely solution, which would require far less constitutional upheaval and expense than the second, would be some variant of the Conservative party policy of 'English votes for English laws': all Bills introduced into Westminster would need to be somehow designated as either 'UK' in nature (e.g. if it implemented a treaty) or as affecting only Wales, or only Scotland or only England.[73] In the latter case, Scottish and Welsh MPs would be barred from voting on it. If this new system were enshrined in law, issues around court-enforceability would arise, since the doctrine of parliamentary privilege is generally thought to preclude the courts from challenging the validity of an Act of Parliament on the basis of the procedure by which it is enacted.[74] However, it could, at least as a first step, be

---

72   R Brazier, *Constitutional Reform in the United Kingdom* (2008), p 122.

73   Hadfield, *op cit*, 299.

74   The decision in *Jackson v Attorney-General* [2005] UKHL 56; [2006] 1 AC 262 has made a limited exception to this principle: judicial review of statute is permitted on the limited basis required to ascertain whether laws passed under the Parliament Act procedure have followed the relevant legislation—the Parliament Acts 1911–1949. Legislation that those statutes state cannot be passed under the procedure, including a Bill to extend the life of Parliament, can be challenged in the courts. However, this is a simple case of examining the Parliamentary roll, to see whether the House of Lords has or has not assented to the legislation (see detailed discussion in Chapter 4, pp 188–194). An Act that allowed the courts to examine which MPs had voted on legislation and to declare the Act null and void if, e.g. Scottish MPs had voted on an 'English' bill would be much more controversial, as would permitting challenge to the parliamentary determination (e.g. by the Speaker) that a given Bill was, or was not, an 'English' Bill.

adopted merely by resolution of the House of Commons, as a constitutional convention to be followed by all MPs. The solution seems elegant because of its economy and simplicity: effectively a new, but intermittently existing, English Parliament would be created within the Westminster Parliament: the latter would morph into the former whenever an English Bill was being considered. It would not of course deal with the issue of Government formation, but that problem is likely to arise extremely rarely; indeed, under this solution, a Government with an overall majority, but no majority amongst English MPs, would be unlikely to survive to trouble constitutional observers with its lack of legitimacy vis-à-vis the English electorate.

Like the other solutions, 'English votes for English laws' is not without potential problems. It is objected first, that it would introduce an invidious division between MPs and violate the principle that all MPs are equal at Westminster.[75] As against this however, it might be said that the principle would not be 'violated' as such, but simply replaced with another one: that to avoid unfairness to English voters, a limited exception would be introduced to the principle that MPs are equal at Westminster. Second, and more (though not wholly) plausibly, it is said that defining an 'English Bill' would be practically impossible. Whether this were done by the Speaker, as the House of Commons Procedure Committee has proposed, or by another committee of Parliament, legislation considered by Westminster often involves Scotland, Wales and England and might be thought difficult to disentangle it into its constituent parts. Against this however, Hadfield observes that in the Planning and Compulsory Purchase Bill, all but three clauses applied to England and Wales, three applied to Scotland and three to the UK as a whole.[76] On its face, the simple solution here would be to divide this Bill into three, each containing the relevant clauses: a three clause UK Planning Bill—on which all MPs would vote, a longer Planning (England and Wales) Bill on which English and Welsh MPs would vote, and a three clause Planning (Scotland) Bill on which only Scottish MPs would vote (assuming that the Bill lay outside the competence of the Scottish Parliament—if not, that body should deal with it). Hadfield has pointed out that the greater use of framework Bills for Wales, whereby only the bare bones of principle are set out, and the Welsh Assembly then passes detailed delegated legislation to flesh out the policies, would also force the use of separate Bills for Wales, thus going a long way towards obviating the problem whilst only enhancing the powers of the Welsh Assembly. Overall, to conclude, the definitional problem is far from insuperable.

The final, and most important objection to 'English votes for English laws', is known as the 'in-out' Government scenario.[77] In brief, were Scottish MPs to be prevented from voting on 'English laws', the possible scenario could arise of a Government that was dependent upon Scottish MPs for its majority losing that majority when Parliament was dealing with an English-only Bill. Since much of the important work of Westminster consists of dealing with Bills mainly or exclusively affecting England, this, it might be thought, would fatally undermine that Government. Once again however, this objection is more apparent than real. First, the scenario would arise in only one limited circumstance: the election of a Labour Government with a very small majority. But more importantly, this argument could be dismissed as simply spurious: a Government one of whose main concerns is the formation of English policy *ought* to be fatally undermined if it has no majority amongst English MPs. Moreover, as Hadfield observes, if such a Government cannot pass legislation concerning England that does not command a majority amongst English MPs, this is not a problem, but a desirable outcome. 'Why should [such legislation] become law?'[78] In reality, all this objection amounts to is the observation that

---

75   Hadfield, n 64 above, 302.

76   *Ibid*, p 300.

77   *Ibid*, p 301.

78   *Ibid*.

a Labour Government with no majority amongst English MPs (which has very rarely happened, historically) would no longer be able to impose legislation upon England without the support of a majority of English MPs. Thus put, the 'problem' sounds rather a desirable state of affairs. Such a Government would simply have to work with other parties to get its English legislation through (as the minority SNP Government is currently doing rather successfully in Scotland) and, at a later point, go to the country and seek to gain this time a majority amongst English MPs. If it could not, 'so be it'.[79]

The Greater London Authority Act 1999 established the Greater London Authority, a city-wide governing body for the boroughs of London comprising the elected office of the Mayor of London and the elected 25-member London Assembly to scrutinise the Mayor's actions. The GLA is responsible for areas such as transport, development and policing. A fourth (compromise) solution to the West Lothian question involves granting the English regions greater autonomy and direct representation, in a similar fashion to London, through the creation of Regional Assemblies extending across the country. In 2002, the Labour Government announced such a scheme with referenda to be held concerning the establishment of such assemblies in the North East, North West and Yorkshire, the areas most enthusiastic for some form of devolved governance.[80] Eventually only a single referendum was held, in the North East in 2004, where the proposal was rejected by 78% of voters on a 47.8% turnout.[81] Whilst the House of Commons Justice Committee recently countenanced in its Fifth Report that support for regional assemblies could increase in future,[82] it is clear that the idea has been sidelined by the Government for the foreseeable future. HM Treasury published its *Review of sub-national economic development and regeneration* in July 2007, which proposed to make existing bodies such as local authorities and regional development agencies responsible for devising and implementing regional economic, environmental and social strategy.[83]

> 6.100 The Government will therefore bring forward proposals to give the Regional Development Agencies the executive responsibility for developing the integrated regional strategy, working closely with local authorities and other partners. Regional Assemblies in their current form and function will not continue. Instead, local authorities in the regions will be responsible for agreeing the regional strategy with the RDAs. . .

The scheme proposed by the Government for developing regional strategy is broadly enshrined in the Local Democracy, Economic Development and Construction Act 2009, much of which is awaiting entry into force at the time of writing. It should be stressed that regional assemblies, even had the plans for them been carried through by the Government, would merely have eased the West Lothian problem rather than solved the puzzle as such; above all, regional assemblies would still have lacked the extensive powers enjoyed by the Scottish Parliament.

In conclusion, therefore, *none* of the solutions suggested above, on their own, are perfectly capable of satisfactorily solving the West Lothian question. A viable overall solution, as Hadfield argues, might be to combine the 'English votes for English laws' idea with a further, procedural, modification to the legislative process at Westminster modelled on the Parliament Acts:

---

79   *Ibid.*

80   See Office of the Deputy Prime Minister, *Your Region, Your Choice: Revitalising the English Regions* (2002) (Cm5511).

81   BBC News, 'North East votes 'no' to assembly' (5 November 2004).

82   House of Commons Justice Committee, Fifth Report of Session 2008–2009, *Devolution: A Decade On* (HC 529–I) [209].

83   For criticism of previous local democracy reform initiatives, see N Bonney, 'Local Democracy Renewed?' (2004) *The Political Quarterly* 43.

B Hadfield, 'Devolution, Westminster and the English question' [2005] *Public Law* 286 (extracts)

[In terms of implementing the 'English votes for English laws' idea, it might be possible to]. . . draw on the provisions of the Parliament Acts 1911–49 concerning the delaying powers of the House of Lords. This would mean that if a Speaker-certified English Bill were passed on Third Reading *in the Commons* against the wishes of a majority of English M.P.s, the Bill would be delayed for, say, six months. On its reintroduction, however, no such vote could prevent it from proceeding and the House of Lords would not be able to use its present delaying powers under the Parliament Acts. All M.P.s would, if called, be able to *speak* on the debates on the floor of the House on such Bills and under this recommendation could vote on all occasions. This would thus preserve a 'union-element' in the proceedings whilst giving greater recognition to an English dimension. . .

Note

The Conservative Party's Democracy Task Force, chaired by Kenneth Clarke MP, issued its short report entitled *Answering the Question: Devolution, the West Lothian Question and the Future of the Union* in July 2008. The report recommended adopting the 'English votes for English laws' idea, but applying the principle only to the Committee and Report stages of a Bill's passage through Parliament; *all* MPs would continue to vote at Second and Third Reading. This, it was argued, would aim to strike a balance between solving the West Lothian question and avoiding the political instability of the 'in-out' arrangement that could result from a purely English procedure. According to the Conservative Party's website, the Party policy in relation to the West Lothian question is to 'give English MPs a decisive say on laws that affect only England'.[84] It remains to be seen whether this will involve the Task Force's recommendation. The Conservative–Liberal Democrat coalition agreement states that a commission will be established 'to consider' the question.

FURTHER READING

R Brazier, *Constitutional Reform: Reshaping the British Political System* (2008).

V Bogdanor, *The New British Constitution* (2009), esp. Chapter 4

B Hadfield, 'Devolution and the Changing Constitution: Evolution in Wales and the Unanswered English Question', in J Jowell and D Oliver (eds), *The Changing Constitution*, 6th edn (2007)

A Tomkins (ed), *Devolution and the British Constitution* (1998)

R Brazier, 'The Scottish Government' [1998] PL 212

R Brazier, The Constitution of the UK' [1999] CLJ 98

A Brown, 'Designing the Scottish Parliament' (2000) 53 Parlt Aff 542

N Burrows, 'Unfinished Business: The Scotland Act 1998' (1999) 62(2) MLR 241

P Craig and M Walters, 'The Courts, Devolution and Judicial Review' [1999] PL 274

M Laffin, and A Thomas, 'Designing the National Assembly for Wales' (2000) 53 Parlt Aff 557

J Mitchell, 'New Parliament, New Politics in Scotland' (2000) 53 Parlt Aff 605

M O'Neill, 'Great Britain: From Dicey to Devolution' (2000) 53 Parlt Aff 70

A Ward, 'Devolution: Labour's Strange Constitutional Design', in J Jowell and D Oliver (eds), *The Changing Constitution*, 4th edn (2000)

R Wilford, 'Designing the Northern Ireland Assembly' (2000) 53 Parlt Aff 577

84 www.conservatives.com/Policy/Where_we_stand/Democracy.aspx.

CHAPTER 7
THE EUROPEAN CONVENTION ON HUMAN RIGHTS

INTRODUCTION

The European Convention on Human Rights was originally conceived after the Second World War as a means of preventing the kind of extreme violation of human rights seen in Germany during and before the war. It came into force in 1953.[1] Drafted in 1949, it was based on the United Nations Declaration of Human Rights,[2] and partly for that reason, and partly because it was only intended to provide basic protection for human rights, it appears today as quite a cautious document, less far-reaching than the 1966 International Covenant on Civil and Political Rights. However, the idea that the way a state treated its own nationals was a matter of international concern was revolutionary at the time of the European Convention's conception. The rights listed in the Convention and the means of protecting them reflected the human rights concerns of the allied powers in the post-war years. The rights were intended as a safeguard against the type of atrocities perpetrated by Nazi Germany and as a protection against the spread of communism. The Convention system includes the right of individual petition— the right of individuals to bring petitions to the Commission on Human Rights alleging violations of a Convention right by their own state. This was highly significant since normally only sovereign states have standing in international law. Its machinery for enforcement includes a Court with the power to deliver a ruling adverse to the Government of a Member State.

The role of the European Convention on Human Rights has changed dramatically since 1953.[3] Its impact has grown immeasurably in a range of ways. Far more states are now members; a huge rise in the number of states who became parties to the Convention occurred after the fall of communism and the dissolution of the Soviet Union when Eastern block states, such as Poland, the Czech Republic, Hungary began to join. Therefore the Convention's influence now extends across Eastern Europe. The Council of Europe now has almost 50 members[4] and the total population affected by the Convention now runs into hundreds of millions. Its influence has increased due to the impact of Protocol 11 (discussed below) which came into force in 1998, making it impossible for States to exclude the right of individual petition. But prior to 1998 there had been a huge jump in the number of states accepting the right of individual petition—only three had done in 1950. The Convention itself has grown by way of additional Protocols, as discussed below.

In the first twenty years of its existence the system received relatively little attention and the Court decided very few cases. When individual petition was first adopted in 1959 (the UK did not accept it until 1966) the Court received only a handful of cases. By 1964 it had decided only two cases and by 1974, seventeen. Only 3% of cases were found admissible between 1955 and 1982, making it clear how extremely difficult it was to satisfy the admissibility criteria. In that period 1955–1982—27 years— there were in total 22,158 applications, or an average of 791 a year. A staggering increase in the Court's workload since then is apparent: applications rose to around 3,000 a year by the mid-eighties; by 1982 the figure was nearly 6,000, but by 1998 it had risen to over 16,000. Once into the 2000s the increase became even more dramatic—the 1998 figure had doubled to over 31,000 by 2001—only three years

---

1   On the history of the Convention, see Lord Lester, 'European Human Rights and the British Constitution', in J Jowell and D Oliver *The Changing Constitution*, 4th edn (2000).

2   The Declaration was adopted on 10 December 1948 by the General Assembly of the United Nations.

3   See further on the history of the Convention, C Ovey and R White, *Jacobs and White European Convention on Human Rights*, 4th edn (2006), Chapter 1.

4   Currently, the Western European members include: Albania, Andorra, Austria, Belgium, Cyprus, Denmark, Finland, France, Germany, Greece, Iceland, Ireland, Italy, Liechtenstein, Luxembourg, Malta, The Netherlands, Norway, Portugal, San Marino, Spain, Sweden, Switzerland, Turkey, UK. Eastern European members include: Bulgaria, Croatia, the Czech Republic, Estonia, Georgia, Hungary, Latvia, Lithuania, Macedonia, Moldova, Poland, Romania, Russia, Slovakia and Slovenia and Ukraine. The numbers increased owing to the disintegration of the Soviet Union and Yugoslavia.

later. By 2004 it was 44,000. That is, in a single year in 2004, the court received twice as many applications as it had received in the first 27 years of its existence. Currently, 4% of applications that go forward to the admissibility stage are deemed admissible. The court is giving 733 judgments a year, compared to two in the first five years. There is a backlog of 80,000 cases, meaning that the Court must take a tactical approach to managing its caseload. In 2010 that load is around 250,000 cases.[5] The Protocol 14 reforms, discussed below, may alleviate the problem somewhat, but it is fair to say that the success of the Convention system is currently placing it in jeopardy.

The Court insists upon the dynamic nature of the Convention and adopts a teleological or purpose-based approach to interpretation, which has allowed the substantive rights to develop until they can cover situations unthought of in 1949. There is general agreement that its jurisprudence has had an enormous impact, not only through the outcome of specific cases, but in a general symbolic, educative and preventative sense. At the same time, the Court is greatly influenced by general practice in the Member States as a body and will interpret the Convention to reflect such practice, so that a state which is clearly out of conformity with the others may expect an adverse ruling. Where practice is still in the process of changing, and may be said to be at an inchoate stage as far as the Member States generally are concerned, it may not be prepared to place itself at the forefront of such changes. The Court views the primary responsibility for the protection of human rights as lying with the member state. On certain sensitive matters the Court affords the state a degree of discretion (a 'margin of appreciation')— see pp 316 and 336, below.

The Convention has had far more effect on UK law than any other human rights treaty. The machinery for the enforcement of the Convention is impressive compared to that used in respect of other human rights treaties, particularly the 1966 International Covenant on Civil and Political Rights which, as far as the UK is concerned, has been enforceable only through a system of assessment of national reports. Its function in raising awareness of human rights was of particular significance in the UK since, until the enactment of the Human Rights Act 1998, no equivalent domestic instrument had such a role. Since the Human Rights Act has afforded the Convention further effect in UK law, its interpretation, the values it encapsulates and the development of the control machinery have become of even greater significance. An understanding of the workings of the Convention is crucial due to its influence on the development of human rights in the UK and because the jurisprudence is now being very frequently relied on in the domestic courts.[6] Despite the inception of the Human Rights Act (HRA), cases are still being referred to Strasbourg. When the Conservative Party came to power in 2010, it appeared that plans to repeal the HRA, as it had pledged to do, had been de-prioritised, due to the agreement with the Liberal-Democrats. If repeal eventually does occur, it would be expected that there would be an increase in cases coming from the UK; the back-log of cases discussed provides another argument for retaining the HRA. The Strasbourg jurisprudence relating to a number of the Convention guarantees is considered further, in relation to domestic law, in Part VI.

THE CONVENTION AND ITS PROTOCOLS[7]

Article 1 of the Convention provides that 'The High Contracting Parties shall secure to everyone within their jurisdiction the rights and freedoms defined in s 1 of this Convention.' This is the general

---

5   See further S Greer, *The European Convention on Human Rights: Achievements, Problems and Prospects* (2006).

6   See Chaps 17–20, and in particular, Chap 17, p 972.

7   Note that we do not comment in the text on two Articles: Art 4 prohibits slavery and forced labour, subject to very narrow exceptions in relation to forced labour. It is rarely claimed. Art 12 has also been of little significance. It provides that 'Men and women of marriageable age have the right to marry and to found a family, according to the national laws governing the exercise of this right.'

duty to ensure to all citizens the substantive rights. The substantive rights may be said to fall into two groups: Arts 2–7, covering the most fundamental human rights and containing no express exceptions, or narrow express exceptions; and Arts 8–12, which may be said to cover a more sophisticated or developed conception of human rights and which are subject to a broad range of express exceptions. Thus, under Arts 2–7, argument will tend to concentrate on the question of whether a particular situation falls within the compass of the right in question, whereas under Arts 8–11 it will largely concentrate on determining whether the interference with the guarantee can be justified (Art 12 only contains one exception, but of a very broad nature). There is an enormous amount of overlap between the Articles and it may be found that weaknesses or gaps in one can be remedied by another, although the Convention will be interpreted as a harmonious whole.[8] It will also be found that invocation of a substantive right in order to attack a decision in the national courts on its merits may sometimes fail, but that a challenge to the *procedure* may succeed under one of the Articles explicitly concerned with fairness in the adjudicative process—Arts 5, 6 and 7.[9] The rights and freedoms are largely concerned with civil and political rather than social and economic matters; the latter are governed by the 1961 European Social Charter and the 1966 International Covenant on Economic, Social and Cultural Rights.

The Convention has grown by way of additional protocols so that it now creates a more advanced human rights regime based on Arts 2–14 with the First Protocol[10] in conjunction with the Fourth,[11] Sixth[12] and Seventh[13] Protocols. The very significant Protocol 12,[14] creating a free-standing right to freedom from discrimination, was opened for ratification in November 2000. The UK has not yet ratified the rights contained in the Fourth and Seventh Protocols, and at present does not intend to ratify the Twelfth Protocol, indicating that although there is a measure of harmony between the basic Convention regime and the UK legal system, that is not the case as far as aspects of the more advanced regime is concerned. The Joint Committee on Human Rights in 2005 recommended that the Government should ratify the fourth and twelfth Protocols.[15] The UK has ratified Protocol 13 which abolishes the death penalty in all circumstances. The other Protocols are concerned with the procedural machinery of the Convention, including Protocol 14, which the UK has ratified; it provides for a number of changes to the structure and procedures of the ECtHR, intended to deal with its growing caseload and to enable it to process cases more efficiently.[16]

---

8   P Van Dijk and GJH Van Hoof, *Theory and Practice of the European Convention on Human Rights* (1998), Chapter II.

9   See C Gearty, 'The European Court of Human Rights and the Protection of Civil Liberties: An Overview' [1993] CLJ 89.

10 Cmnd 9221. All the parties to the Convention, except Switzerland, are parties to this Protocol, which came into force in 1954. See p 341, below.

11 Cmnd 2309. It came into force in 1968; the UK is not yet a party. It covers freedom of movement.

12 (1983) 5 EHRR 167. It came into force in 1985. The UK is now a party to it and it is included in the Human Rights Act, Sched 1. See below, Chapter 17, p 957. It covers removal of the death penalty.

13 (1984) 7 EHRR 1. It came into force in 1988. The UK is not a party but in 1997 proposed to ratify it imminently: see the White Paper, *Rights Brought Home: the Human Rights Bill*, Cm 3782, 1997, paras 4.14–4.15, and the Home Office Review of Human Rights Instruments (amended) 26 August 1999. However, 13 years later it has not yet done so.

14 See below, p 335.

15 Seventeenth Report of Session 2004–5 HL Paper 99, HC 264, paras 34 and 37.

16 Protocol 14 was agreed by the Council of Europe Member States on 13 May 2004, and signed by the UK two months later. It was laid before Parliament on 15 November 2004. For discussion of Protocol 14 see Xavier-Baptiste Ruedin (2008) EHRLR 81.

ARTICLES 2–6

Article 2 Right to life

1   Everyone's right to life shall be protected by law. No one shall be deprived of his life intentionally save in the execution of a sentence of a court following his conviction of a crime for which this penalty is provided by law.

2   Deprivation of life shall not be regarded as inflicted in contravention of this Article when it results from the use of force which is no more than absolutely necessary:

    (a)   in defence of any person from unlawful violence;

    (b)   in order to effect a lawful arrest or to prevent the escape of a person lawfully detained;

    (c)   in action lawfully taken for the purpose of quelling a riot or insurrection.

Notes

1.   The right to life under Art 2 can be viewed as the most fundamental of all human rights. Its significance receives recognition under all human rights' instruments and its vital importance is recognised under UK common law.[17] Article 2 provides non-derogable protection of the right to life.[18] The Court has said: 'The first sentence of Article 2 enjoins the State not only to refrain from the intentional and unlawful taking of life, but also to take appropriate steps to safeguard the lives of those within its jurisdiction.'[19] Thus, while the State must not order or empower its agents to kill its subjects, except within the specified exceptions, it also has further responsibilities under Art 2 to protect the right to life by law.

2.   The European Court of Human Rights has so far avoided the question whether the foetus is protected by Art 2—in other words, whether it would come within the term 'everyone'. In *Open Door Counselling v Ireland*, the Court deliberately left open the possibility that Art 2 might place some restrictions on abortion.[20] If it was to find that the foetus is protected, the result, in terms of changes to almost all the State parties' laws on abortion, would be far-reaching, since only abortion falling within the exceptions to Art 2 would be permitted. There would be an immense increase in dangerous illegal abortions and women would travel outside the Member States for abortions, leading to an increase in later terminations. It has been found in the context of national legislation on abortion that the woman seeking abortion can rely on Arts 2 and 8, since her life and physical and mental health are in question.[21]

The Commission has, however, committed itself to the view that the foetus is not protected under Art 2. In *H v Norway*,[22] the Commission found that the lawful abortion of a 14-week foetus on social grounds did not breach Art 2. It took this stance partly on the basis that otherwise, a

---

17   It is recognised in the crimes of murder, manslaughter and infanticide. The deliberate killing of another human being is viewed as requiring to be marked out from other crimes by means of the mandatory life sentence penalty. For a full discussion, see Clayton and Tomlinson, 'further reading', p 347 below, Chapter 7.

18   See Art 15(2). Derogation is not allowed in times of emergency or war; derogation is only possible in respect of death resulting from acts of war themselves.

19   *LCB v UK* (1998) 27 EHRR 212, para 36.

20   ECtHR, Judgment of 29 October 1992; (1992) 15 EHRR 244. For comment, see (1992) 142 NLJ 1696. See also *Vo v France* (2005) 40 EHRR 12.

21   *X v UK*, Appl No 8416/78; 19 D & R 244 (1980).

22   Appl No 17004/90 (1992) 73 DR 155.

conflict with the mother's Art 8 rights might arise, and partly because, since the State Parties' laws on abortion differ considerably from each other, a wide margin of discretion should be allowed.

3. Decisions under Art 2 indicate that two, usually distinct, duties are placed on the national authorities, although their scope is unclear. First, as indicated, Art 2 places the public authorities under a duty not to take life except in certain specified circumstances. This duty covers intentional, officially sanctioned killings (executions, deliberate killing to save life) and unintentional killings (where the risk of killing is taken by using lethal force in a riot situation). Where State agents do take life, the obligation to protect the right to life by law requires that 'there should be some form of effective official investigation'.[23] This requirement was found to be breached in *Jordan, Kelly, Arthurs, Donelly and Others v UK*[24] in respect of the killing of eight IRA members by the SAS in 1987.

4. Second, Art 2 places a positive obligation on the State authorities to protect the right to life by law. This positive obligation may take a number of forms. It requires that reasonable steps be taken in order to enforce the law in order to protect citizens (*X v UK and Ireland*).[25] It was held in *W v UK*[26] that these measures will not be scrutinised in detail. Clearly, the State may not be able to prevent every attack on an individual without an enormous expenditure of resources.[27] Therefore the Convention will leave a wide margin of discretion to the national authorities in this regard, although the State will be under some duty to maintain reasonable public security.[28]

   Where State agents' actions are very closely linked to the preservation of a known individual's life as, for example, the actions of police officers are during a hostage situation, the State will be under a positive obligation not only to seek to preserve life, but also to act reasonably in so doing. The need to preserve life in the immediate situation would appear to override the general duty to maintain State security and prevent crime. These notions seem to underlie the findings of the Commission in *Andronicou and Constantinou v Cyprus*.[29] Article 2 was found to have been violated by Cypriot police when, in attempting to deal with a siege situation in which a hostage had been taken, they fired a number of times at the hostage taker, killing the hostage. The number of bullets fired reflected, it was found, a response which lacked caution.

5. Generally, the para 2 exceptions are reasonably straightforward and are aimed mainly at unintentional deprivation of life. This was explained in *Stewart v UK*,[30] which concerned the use of plastic bullets in a riot. It was found that para 2 is concerned with situations where the use of violence is allowed as necessary force and may, as an unintended consequence, result in loss of life. On this basis, the use of plastic bullets was found to fall within its terms. However, paras 2(a), (b) and (c) also cover instances where the force used was bound to endanger life and was intended to do so, but was necessary in the circumstances. Thus, national laws recognising the right to use

---

23 *McCann v UK* (1995) 21 EHRR 97, para 161.

24 (2001) *The Times*, 18 May.

25 Appl 9829/82 (not published).

26 Appl 9348/81, 32 D & R (1983), p 190.

27 It was accepted in *Osman v UK* (1998) 29 EHRR 245 that the obligation to protect the right to life had to be interpreted 'in a way that does not impose an impossible or disproportionate burden on the authorities' (para 116). In that instance, the police had failed to take measures to prevent a murder taking place despite very strong indications that the victim was in imminent danger. See further below, on the Art 6 issue in the case, n 72 p 311.

28 Appl 7145/75, *Association X v UK* (1978) Appl 7154/75; 14 DR 31.

29 (1996) 22 EHRR CD 18.

30 Appl 10044/82; D & R 39 (1985); (1985) 7 EHRR 453; see also *Kelly v UK* (1993) 16 EHRR 20, in which the European Commission found that the use of force to prevent future terrorist acts was allowable. For criticism of the decision in *Kelly*, see (1994) 144 NLJ 354.

self-defence are, in principle, in harmony with para 2(a). Clearly, the State can use lethal force where absolutely necessary in order to quell a riot. But, the necessity will be carefully scrutinised: State agents must act with caution in resorting to lethal force.[31]

6. The Court addressed the question of the strictness of the 'absolutely necessary' test in *McCann, Farrell and Savage v UK*,[32] the first judgment of the Court to find a breach of Art 2. The case concerned the shooting by SAS soldiers of three IRA members on the street in Gibraltar. The main question for the Court was the extent to which the State's response to the perceived threat posed by the IRA members was proportionate to that threat. The Court found that the use of force could be justified where 'it is based on an honest belief which is perceived for good reason to be valid at the time but which subsequently turns out to be mistaken. To hold otherwise would be to impose an unrealistic burden on the State and its law enforcement personnel'. Following this finding, the Court found that the actions of the soldiers who carried out the shooting did not amount to a violation of Art 2.

However, the organisation and planning of the whole operation had to be considered in order to discover whether the requirements of Art 2 had been respected. The Court focused on the decision not to arrest the suspects when they entered Gibraltar. This decision was taken because it was thought that there might have been insufficient evidence against them to warrant their charge and trial. However, this decision subjected the population of Gibraltar to possible danger. The Court considered that taking this factor into account and bearing in mind that they had been shadowed by the SAS soldiers for some time, the suspects could have been arrested at that point. Further, there was quite a high probability that the suspects were on a reconnaissance mission at the time of the shootings and not a bombing mission. This possibility, the possibility that there was no car bomb or that the suspects had no detonator, was not conveyed to the soldiers and since they were trained to shoot to kill, the killings were rendered almost inevitable. All these factors were taken into account in finding that the killing of the three constituted a use of force which was more than absolutely necessary in defence of persons from unlawful violence within the meaning of para 2(a) of Art 2. The State had sanctioned killing by State agents in circumstances which gave rise to a breach of Art 2.

Article 3 Prohibition of torture

No one shall be subjected to torture or to inhuman or degrading treatment or punishment.

Notes

1. The right to freedom from torture or inhuman or degrading treatment or punishment under Art 3 is recognised in international human rights Treaties[33] and in many, although not all, domestic human rights instruments.[34] The right is also protected by specific Conventions, the United Nations Convention Against Torture and Other Cruel, Inhuman or Degrading Treatment or Punishment 1984[35] and the European Convention for the Prevention of Torture and Inhuman and

---

31   A breach of Art 2 was found in *Gulec v Turkey* (1999) 28 EHRR 121: gendarmes had fired into a crowd to disperse it; less forceful means could have been used.

32   (1995) 21 EHRR 97, A 324, Council of Europe Report.

33   Article 5 of the Universal Declaration and Art 7 of the ICCPR.

34   For discussion of this right as recognised in other jurisdictions, see Clayton and Tomlinson, 'further reading' p 347 below, Chapter 8, esp pp 412–29.

35   Cmnd 9593, 1985; it came into force in 1987 and it was ratified by the UK in December 1988.

Degrading Treatment or Punishment 1987.[36] Torture is a crime under international law.[37] Thus, there is strong international recognition of the fundamental values enshrined in this right.

2. Article 3 contains no exceptions and it is also non-derogable. Thus, on the face of it, once a State has been found to have fallen within its terms, no justification is possible.[38] The Court has made it clear that the use of forms of Art 3 treatment in order to extract information, even in order to combat terrorism, is unjustifiable.[39]

3. The responsibility of the State extends beyond prohibiting the use of Art 3 treatment by State agents. It includes a duty to ensure that individuals within their jurisdiction are not subjected to Art 3 treatment by other individuals.[40] It also includes an obligation not to deport a person who needs medical treatment to a country where he will not receive it.[41] The State also has a positive obligation to carry out an effective investigation into allegations of breaches of Art 3.[42]

4. In determining the standard of treatment applicable below which a State will be in breach of Art 3, a common European standard is applied, but also all the factors in the situation are taken into account.[43] The Court has found that such factors include: 'the nature and context of the treatment, its duration, its mental and physical effects and, in some instances, the sex, age and state of health of the victim.'[44] It is clear that, in order to determine this issue, present views must be considered rather than the views at the time when the Convention was drawn up. The three forms of treatment mentioned represent three different levels of seriousness. Thus, torture, unlike degrading treatment, has been quite narrowly defined to include 'deliberate inhuman treatment causing very serious and cruel suffering'.[45] Clearly, treatment which could not come within the restricted definition of torture could still fall within one of the other two heads, especially the broad head—'degrading treatment'. In order to characterise treatment as inhuman, it must reach a minimum level of severity.[46] Physical assault,[47] the immediate threat of torture,[48] and interrogation techniques causing psychological disorientation,[49] have all been found to amount to inhuman treatment.

---

36 Cm 1634, 1991; it was ratified by the UK in June 1988. For discussion, see Evans and Morgan, *Preventing Torture: A Study of the European Convention for the Prevention of Torture* (1998).

37 See *R v Bow Street Stipendiary Magistrate ex parte Pinochet Ugarte (No 3)* [1999] 2 WLR 827.

38 *Ireland v UK* (1978) 2 EHRR 25.

39 *Tomasi v France* (1992) 15 EHRR 1.

40 In *A v UK* (1999) 27 EHRR 611, a violation of Art 3 was found since the law had failed to protect a child from excessive chastisement by his stepfather.

41 In *D v UK* (1998) 24 EHRR 423, a violation of Art 3 was found since the UK proposed sending D back to the West Indies after he had contracted AIDS, where he would not receive appropriate treatment for his condition.

42 *Aksoy v Turkey* (1996) 23 EHRR 533; *Selmouni v France* (2000) 29 EHRR 403.

43 The *Greek* case (1969), Yearbook XII 186–510.

44 *A v UK* (1998) 27 EHRR 611, para 20.

45 *Ireland v UK* (1978) 2 EHRR 25.

46 *A v UK* (1998) 27 EHRR 611, para 20.

47 *Ireland v UK* (1978) 2 EHRR 25.

48 *Campbell and Cosans v UK* (1982) 4 EHRR 293.

49 *Ireland v UK* (1978) 2 EHRR 25.

5. *Chahal v UK* laid down a very significant principle which extended the reach of Art 3.[50] Originally an illegal immigrant, Mr Chahal obtained leave to remain in Britain indefinitely in 1974. In 1984, he visited the Punjab for a family wedding and met the chief advocate of creating an independent Sikh State. Later, he was arrested by Indian police and allegedly tortured. He escaped from India and became the founder of the International Sikh Youth Federation in the UK. In 1990, he was arrested after a meeting at a Southall temple. The Home Office accused him of involvement in Sikh terrorism and decided to deport him on national security grounds. He sought asylum on the ground that he would be tortured if sent back to India and applied to the European Commission, alleging *inter alia* a breach of Art 3. The Court found that since there were strong grounds for believing that Mr Chahal would indeed have been tortured had he been returned to India, a breach of Art 3 had occurred.[51] This principle was reaffirmed in *Saadi v Italy*, below, which concerned the question whether deportation of an applicant who arguably posed a threat to national security to a country where he alleged that he faced the risk of Art 3 treatment would breach Art 3. He was sentenced to imprisonment for crimes and the order of deportation was to be carried out once he had served his sentence.

Saadi v Italy (2008) No 37201/06

3. The applicant alleged that enforcement of a decision to deport him to Tunisia would expose him to the risk of being subjected to treatment contrary to Article 3 of the Convention. . .

35. . . . the Minister of the Interior ordered him to be deported to Tunisia. . . observing that 'it was apparent from the documents in the file' that the applicant had played an 'active role' in an organisation responsible for providing logistical and financial support to persons belonging to fundamentalist Islamist cells in Italy and abroad. Consequently, his conduct was disturbing public order and threatening national security.

35. the applicant requested political asylum. He alleged that he had been sentenced in his absence in Tunisia for political reasons and that he feared he would be subjected to torture

122. the United Kingdom [intervening in the case] argued that, in cases concerning the threat created by international terrorism, the approach followed by the Court in the *Chahal* case (which did not reflect a universally recognised moral imperative and was in contradiction with the intentions of the original signatories of the Convention) had to be altered and clarified. In the first place, the threat presented by the person to be deported must be a factor to be assessed in relation to the possibility and the nature of the potential ill-treatment. That would make it possible to take into consideration all the particular circumstances of each case and weigh the rights secured to the applicant by Article 3 of the Convention against those secured to all other members of the community by Article 2. Secondly, national-security considerations must influence the standard of proof required from the applicant. In other words, if the respondent State adduced evidence that there was a threat to national security, stronger evidence had to be adduced to prove that the applicant would be at risk of ill-treatment in the receiving country. In particular, the individual concerned must prove that it was 'more likely than not' that he would be subjected to treatment prohibited by Article 3.

---

50 (1997) 23 EHRR 413.

51 The Art 5 issue is considered below, p 307.

134. According to the Court's settled case-law, ill-treatment must attain a minimum level of severity if it is to fall within the scope of Article 3. The assessment of this minimum level of severity is relative; it depends on all the circumstances of the case, such as the duration of the treatment, its physical and mental effects and, in some cases, the sex, age and state of health of the victim. . .[52]

138. Accordingly, the Court cannot accept the argument of the United Kingdom Government, supported by the respondent Government, that a distinction must be drawn under Article 3 between treatment inflicted directly by a signatory State and treatment that might be inflicted by the authorities of another State, and that protection against this latter form of ill-treatment should be weighed against the interests of the community as a whole. Since protection against the treatment prohibited by Article 3 is absolute, that provision imposes an obligation not to extradite or expel any person who, in the receiving country, would run the real risk of being subjected to such treatment. . . . It must therefore reaffirm the principle stated in the *Chahal* judgment that it is not possible to weigh the risk of ill-treatment against the reasons put forward for the expulsion in order to determine whether the responsibility of a State is engaged under Article 3, even where such treatment is inflicted by another State. In that connection, the conduct of the person concerned, however undesirable or dangerous, cannot be taken into account, with the consequence that the protection afforded by Article 3 is broader than that provided for in Articles 32 and 33 of the 1951 United Nations Convention relating to the Status of Refugees. . . .

139. The Court considers that the argument based on the balancing of the risk of harm if the person is sent back against the dangerousness he or she represents to the community if not sent back is misconceived. The concepts of 'risk' and 'dangerousness' in this context do not lend themselves to a balancing test because they are notions that can only be assessed independently of each other. Either the evidence adduced before the Court reveals that there is a substantial risk if the person is sent back or it does not. The prospect that he may pose a serious threat to the community if not returned does not reduce in any way the degree of risk of ill treatment that the person may be subject to on return. For that reason it would be incorrect to require a higher standard of proof, as submitted by the intervener, where the person is considered to represent a serious danger to the community, since assessment of the level of risk is independent of such a test.

140. With regard to the second branch of the United Kingdom Government's arguments, to the effect that where an applicant presents a threat to national security, stronger evidence must be adduced to prove that there is a risk of ill-treatment (see paragraph 122 above), the Court observes that such an approach is not compatible with the absolute nature of the protection afforded by Article 3 either. It amounts to asserting that, in the absence of evidence meeting a higher standard, protection of national security justifies accepting more readily a risk of ill-treatment for the individual.

149. . . . the decision to deport the applicant to Tunisia would breach Article 3 of the Convention if it were enforced.

Article 5 Right to liberty and security

1   Everyone has the right to liberty and security of person. No one shall be deprived of his liberty save in the following cases and in accordance with a procedure prescribed by law:

---

52   The Court referred to *Price v the United Kingdom*, No 33394/96, § 24, ECHR 2001-VII; *Mouisel v France*, No 67263/01, § 37, ECHR 2002-IX; and *Jalloh v Germany* [GC], No 54810/00, § 67, 11 July 2006.

(a) the lawful detention of a person after conviction by a competent court;

(b) the lawful arrest or detention of a person for non-compliance with the lawful order of a court or in order to secure the fulfilment of any obligation prescribed by law;

(c) the lawful arrest or detention of a person effected for the purpose of bringing him before the competent legal authority on reasonable suspicion of having committed an offence or when it is reasonably considered necessary to prevent his committing an offence or fleeing after having done so;

(d) the detention of a minor by lawful order for the purpose of educational supervision or his lawful detention for the purpose of bringing him before the competent legal authority;

(e) the lawful detention of persons for the prevention of the spreading of infectious diseases, of persons of unsound mind, alcoholics or drug addicts or vagrants;

(f) the lawful arrest or detention of a person to prevent his effecting an unauthorised entry into this country or of a person against whom action is being taken with a view to deportation or extradition.

2   Everyone who is arrested shall be informed promptly, in a language which he understands, of the reasons for his arrest and of any charge against him.

3   Everyone arrested or detained in accordance with the provisions of paragraph 1(c) of this Article shall be brought promptly before a judge or other officer authorised by law to exercise judicial power and shall be entitled to trial within a reasonable time or to release pending trial. Release may be conditioned by guarantees to appear for trial.

4   Everyone who is deprived of his liberty by arrest or detention shall be entitled to take proceedings by which the lawfulness of his detention shall be decided speedily by a court and his release ordered if the detention is not lawful.

5   Everyone who has been the victim of arrest or detention in contravention of the provisions of this Article shall have an enforceable right to compensation.

Notes

1. The guarantee under Art 5 refers to protection from deprivation of physical liberty, not to protection for physical safety.[53] The presumption embodied in the Article is that liberty and security must be maintained. However, it then sets out the two tests which must be satisfied if it is to be removed. First, exceptions are set out where liberty can be taken away; second, under paras 2–4, the procedure is set out which must be followed when a person is deprived of liberty. Thus, if the correct procedure is followed, but an exception does not apply, Art 5 will be breached, as, conversely, it will if an individual falls within an exception but, in detaining him or her, the correct procedure is not followed. It will be found that a number of successful applications have been brought under Art 5 with the result that the position of detainees in Europe has undergone improvement. It should be noted that Art 5 is concerned with total deprivation of liberty, not restriction of movement, which is covered by Art 2 of Protocol 4 (at the time of writing, the UK is not yet a party to Protocol 4).

---

53   *X v Ireland* (1973) 16 YB 388.

2. In general, the case law of the Court discussed below suggests that the circumstances in which liberty can be taken away under para 5(1)(a)–(f) will be restrictively interpreted, although the instances included are potentially wide. Article 5(1) not only provides that deprivation of liberty is only permitted within these exceptions, it also requires that it should be 'in accordance with a procedure prescribed by law'. In *Winterwerp v Netherlands*,[54] the Court found that this meant that the procedure in question must be in accordance with national and Convention law, taking into account the general principles on which the Convention is based, and it must not be arbitrary.

3. *Art 5(1)(b): Detention to fulfil an obligation.* This exception refers to deprivation of liberty in order to 'secure fulfilment of an obligation prescribed by law'. This phrase raises difficulties of interpretation and is clearly not so straightforward as the first form of such deprivation permitted under para 5(1)(a). It is very wide and appears to allow deprivation of liberty in many instances without intervention by a court. It might even allow preventive action before violation of a legal obligation. However, it has been narrowed down; in *Lawless*,[55] it was found that a specific and concrete obligation must be identified. Once it has been identified, detention can in principle be used to secure its fulfilment. A requirement to submit to an examination on entering the UK has been found to be specific enough.[56]

4. *Art 5(1)(c): Detention after arrest but before conviction.* This provision refers to persons held on remand or detained after arrest. Article 5(3) requires that in such an instance, a person should be brought 'promptly' to trial; in other words, the trial should occur in reasonable time. A level of suspicion below 'reasonable suspicion' will not be sufficient; in *Fox, Campbell and Hartley*,[57] the Court found that Art 5(1)(c) had been violated on the basis that no reasonable suspicion of committing an offence had arisen, only an honest belief (which was all that was needed under s 11 of the Northern Ireland (Emergency Provisions) Act 1978). The only evidence put forward by the Government for the presence of reasonable suspicion was that the applicants had convictions for terrorist offences and that when arrested, they were asked about particular terrorist acts. The Government said that further evidence could not be disclosed for fear of endangering life. The Court said that reasonable suspicion arises from 'facts or information which would satisfy an objective observer that the person concerned may have committed the offence'. It went on to find that the Government had not established that reasonable suspicion was present in justifying the arrests in question. The Court took into account the exigencies of the situation and the need to prevent terrorism; however, it found that the State Party in question must be able to provide some information which an objective observer would consider justified the arrest. It was found that the information provided was insufficient and therefore a breach of Art 5 had occurred. This ruling suggests that in terrorist cases, a low level of reasonable suspicion is required and this test was applied in *Murray v UK*.[58] The Court found that no breach of Art 5(1)(c) had occurred, even though the relevant legislation (s 14 of the Northern Ireland (Emergency Provisions) Act 1987) required only suspicion, not reasonable suspicion, since there was some evidence which provided a basis for the suspicion in question.

---

54   Judgment of 24 October 1979, A 33; (1979) 2 EHRR 387.

55   Report of 19 December 1959, B 1 (1960–61) p 64; Judgment of 1 July 1961, A 3 (1960–61); (1961) 1 EHRR 15.

56   *McVeigh, O'Neill and Evans v UK* (1981) Report of 18 March 1981, D & R 25; (1981) 5 EHRR 71.

57   Judgment of 30 August 1990, A 178; (1990) 13 EHRR 157.

58   (1994) 19 EHRR 193.

5. *Promptly informing of the reason for arrest.* Paragraph 5(2) provides that a detainee or arrestee must be informed promptly of the reason for arrest. This information is needed so that it is possible to judge from the moment of its inception whether the arrest is in accordance with the law so that the detainee could theoretically take action straight away to be released. All the necessary information—the factual and legal grounds for the arrest—need not be given at the point of arrest; it can be conveyed over a period of time, depending on the circumstances. A period of two days between the arrest and the conveying of the information has been found not to breach Art 5(2).[59] The Commission's view is that this information need not be as detailed and specific as that guaranteed by para 6(3) in connection with the right to a fair trial.[60]

6. *Promptness of judicial hearing.* Article 5(3) confers a right to be brought promptly before the judicial authorities; in other words, not to be held in detention for long periods without an independent hearing. It refers to persons detained in accordance with Art 5(1)(c) and therefore covers both arrest and detention, and detainees held on remand. The significance of Art 5(3) rests on its strong link to the purpose of Art 5 itself.[61] There will be some allowable delay in both situations; the question is, therefore, what is meant by 'promptly'. Its meaning was considered in *Brogan v UK*[62] in relation to an arrest and detention arising by virtue of the special powers under s 12 of the Prevention of Terrorism (Temporary Provisions) Act 1989. The UK had entered a derogation under Art 15 against the applicability of Art 5 to Northern Ireland, but withdrew that derogation in August 1984. Two months later, the *Brogan* case was filed. The applicants complained, *inter alia*, of the length of time they were held in detention without coming before a judge, on the basis that it could not be termed prompt. The Court took into account the need for special measures to combat terrorism; such measures had to be balanced against individual rights. However, it found that detention for four days and six hours was too long. The Court did not specify how long was acceptable; previously, the Commission had seen four days (in ordinary criminal cases) as the limit.[63] Following this decision, the UK Government ultimately chose to derogate from Art 5 and this decision was eventually found to be lawful by the European Court of Human Rights.[64]

7. *Review of detention.* Article 5(4) provides a right to review of detention, whatever the basis of the detention. The detainee must be able to take court proceedings in order to determine whether a detention is unlawful. This is an independent provision: even if it is determined in a particular case by the Commission that the detention was lawful, there could still be a breach of Art 5(4) if no possibility of review of the lawfulness of the detention by the domestic courts arose. The review must be by a court and it must be adequate to test the lawfulness of the detention. This requirement was found not to have been satisfied by judicial review proceedings or by habeas corpus in *Chahal v UK*:[65] neither procedure provided a sufficient basis for challenging a deportation decision.

---

59 *Skoogstrom v Sweden* (1981) 1 Dig Supp para 5.2.2.1.

60 It was determined in Appl 8828/79, *X v Denmark* D & R 30 (1983), p 93 that para 5(2) does not include a right to contact a lawyer.

61 See *Bozano v France* (1986) 9 EHRR 297; *Assenov v Belgium* (1999) 28 EHRR 652; *T v Malta* (1999) 29 EHRR 185.

62 Judgment of 29 November 1988; (1989) 11 EHRR 117; A 145.

63 *X v Netherlands* (1966) 9 YB 564.

64 *Brannigan and McBride v UK* (1993) 17 EHRR 594.

65 (1997) 23 EHRR 413.

The most significant recent decision on this point—set out below—was made by the Grand Chamber of the Court in 2009 in a case brought against the UK by some of those foreign nationals detained without charge on suspicion of being involved in international terrorism under Part IV of the Anti-Terrorism, Crime and Security Act 2001. The facts appear below and see also Chapter 17, p 975. In the part of the judgment that follows, the Court was concerned with the fairness of the procedure by which the applicants were able to challenge the decisions by the Secretary of State to detain them before SIAC—the Special Immigration Appeals Commission. Sensitive intelligence evidence against the suspects was treated as 'closed material'.

A v United Kingdom (2009) 3455/05
Judgment of the Grand Chamber

214. The applicants' second ground of complaint under Article 5 § 4 concerns the fairness of the procedure before SIAC under section 25 of the 2001 Act to determine whether the Secretary of State was reasonable in believing each applicant's presence in the United Kingdom to be a risk to national security and in suspecting him of being a terrorist. This is a separate and distinct question, which cannot be said to be absorbed in the finding of a violation of Article 5 § 1, and which the Court must therefore examine.

215. The Court recalls that although the judges sitting as SIAC were able to consider both the 'open' and 'closed' material, neither the applicants nor their legal advisers could see the closed material. Instead, the closed material was disclosed to one or more special advocates, appointed by the Solicitor General to act on behalf of each applicant. During the closed sessions before SIAC, the special advocate could make submissions on behalf of the applicant, both as regards procedural matters, such as the need for further disclosure, and as to the substance of the case. However, from the point at which the special advocate first had sight of the closed material, he was not permitted to have any further contact with the applicant and his representatives, save with the permission of SIAC. In respect of each appeal against certification, SIAC issued both an open and a closed judgment.

216. The Court takes as its starting point that, as the national courts found and it has accepted, during the period of the applicants' detention the activities and aims of the al'Qaeda network had given rise to a 'public emergency threatening the life of the nation'. It must therefore be borne in mind that at the relevant time there was considered to be an urgent need to protect the population of the United Kingdom from terrorist attack and, although the United Kingdom did not derogate from Article 5 § 4, a strong public interest in obtaining information about al'Qaeda and its associates and in maintaining the secrecy of the sources of such information. . .

217. Balanced against these important public interests, however, was the applicants' right under Article 5 § 4 to procedural fairness. . . .In the circumstances of the present case, and in view of the dramatic impact of the lengthy—and what appeared at that time to be indefinite—deprivation of liberty on the applicants' fundamental rights, Article 5 § must import substantially the same fair trial guarantees as Article 6 § 1 in its criminal aspect. . .

218. Against this background, it was essential that as much information about the allegations and evidence against each applicant was disclosed as was possible without compromising national security or the safety of others. Where full disclosure was not possible, Article 5 § 4 required that the difficulties this caused were counterbalanced in

such a way that each applicant still had the possibility effectively to challenge the allegations against him.

219. The Court considers that SIAC, which was a fully independent court. . .and which could examine all the relevant evidence, both closed and open, was best placed to ensure that no material was unnecessarily withheld from the detainee. In this connection, the special advocate could provide an important, additional safeguard through questioning the State's witnesses on the need for secrecy and through making submissions to the judge regarding the case for additional disclosure. On the material before it, the Court has no basis to find that excessive and unjustified secrecy was employed in respect of any of the applicants' appeals or that there were not compelling reasons for the lack of disclosure in each case.

220. The Court further considers that the special advocate could perform an important role in counterbalancing the lack of full disclosure and the lack of a full, open, adversarial hearing by testing the evidence and putting arguments on behalf of the detainee during the closed hearings. However, the special advocate could not perform this function in any useful way unless the detainee was provided with sufficient information about the allegations against him to enable him to give effective instructions to the special advocate. While this question must be decided on a case-by-case basis, the Court observes generally that, where the evidence was to a large extent disclosed and the open material played the predominant role in the determination, it could not be said that the applicant was denied an opportunity effectively to challenge the reasonableness of the Secretary of State's belief and suspicions about him. In other cases, even where all or most of the underlying evidence remained undisclosed, if the allegations contained in the open material were sufficiently specific, it should have been possible for the applicant to provide his representatives and the special advocate with information with which to refute them, if such information existed, without his having to know the detail or sources of the evidence which formed the basis of the allegations. An example would be the allegation made against several of the applicants that they had attended a terrorist training camp at a stated location between stated dates; given the precise nature of the allegation, it would have been possible for the applicant to provide the special advocate with exonerating evidence, for example of an alibi or of an alternative explanation for his presence there, sufficient to permit the advocate effectively to challenge the allegation. Where, however, the open material consisted purely of general assertions and SIAC's decision to uphold the certification and maintain the detention was based solely or to a decisive degree on closed material, the procedural requirements of Article 5 §4 would not be satisfied.

221. The Court must, therefore, assess the certification proceedings in respect of each of the detained applicants in the light of these criteria.

[The Court then noted that the allegations against some of the applicants made in the open material were sufficiently specific as to allow them to be challenged. But it found to the contrary in relation to certain other applicants including, the third and fifth.]

224. The open allegations in respect of [these] . . . applicants were of a general nature, principally that they were members of named extremist Islamist groups linked to al'Qaeda. SIAC observed in its judgments dismissing each of these applicants' appeals that the open evidence was insubstantial and that the evidence on which it relied against them was largely to be found in the closed material. . . The Court does not consider that these applicants were in a position effectively to challenge the allegations

against them. There has therefore been a violation of Article 5 §4 in respect of the third and fifth applicants.

The challenge on this point could also of course have been brought under the fair trial guarantee, Art 6(1) (below). The court however found that it was not necessary additionally to consider the Art 6(1) claim as in this instance it raised no separate issues. This decision was of great importance: it not only dealt with the past actions of the UK Government but led directly to a House of Lords judgment that found incompatible the use of the same procedure under the Prevention of Terrorism Act 2005 for challenging the imposition of control orders on terrorist suspects: see Chapter 17, p 975. It also laid down general guidance on when the use of secret evidence and special advocates to challenge it can be considered still to amount to a fair procedure: the Court found clearly that such procedures cannot be fair when the decisive evidence is contained in closed material that the suspect himself has no chance to challenge.

8. *Compensation.* Paragraph 5(5) provides for compensation if the arrest or detention contravenes the other provisions of Art 5.[66] This provision differs from the general right to compensation under Art 50[67] because it exists as an independent right: if a person is found to have been unlawfully arrested under domestic law in the domestic court, but no compensation is available, he or she can apply to the European Court of Human Rights on the basis of the lack of compensation. As far as other Convention rights are concerned, if a violation of a right occurs which is found unlawful by the national courts, but no compensation is granted, the applicant cannot allege breach of the right.

Article 6 Right to a fair trial

1   In the determination of his civil rights and obligations or of any criminal charge against him, everyone is entitled to a fair and public hearing within a reasonable time by an independent and impartial tribunal established by law. Judgment shall be pronounced publicly but the press and public may be excluded from all or part of the trial in the interests of morals, public order or national security in a democratic society, where the interests of juveniles or the protection of the private life of the parties so require, or to the extent strictly necessary in the opinion of the court in special circumstances where publicity would prejudice the interests of justice.

2   Everyone charged with a criminal offence shall be presumed innocent until proved guilty according to law.

3   Everyone charged with a criminal offence has the following minimum rights:

(a)   to be informed promptly, in a language which he understands and in detail, of the nature and cause of the accusation against him;

(b)   to have adequate time and facilities for the preparation of his defence;

(c)   to defend himself in person or through legal assistance of his own choosing or, if he has not sufficient means to pay for legal assistance, to be given it free when the interests of justice so require;

---

66   See the reference to Art 5(5) in the HRA, s 9(3).

67   Appl No 6821/74, *Huber v Austria* 6 D & R 65 (1977), p 65.

(d) to examine or have examined witnesses against him and to obtain the attend-
    ance and examination of witnesses on his behalf under the same conditions as
    witnesses against him;

(e) to have the free assistance of an interpreter if he cannot understand or speak
    the language used in court.

Notes

1. Article 6 is one of the most significant Convention Articles and the one which is most frequently
   found to have been violated. Paragraph 1 imports a general requirement of a fair hearing, applying
   to criminal and civil hearings which covers all aspects of a fair hearing. Paragraph 3 lists minimum
   guarantees of a fair hearing in the criminal context only. Since para 3 contains minimum guarantees, the para 1 protection of a fair hearing goes beyond para 3. In investigating a fair hearing, the
   Strasbourg Court is not confined to the para 3 guarantees; it can consider further requirements of
   fairness. Thus, if para 1 is not violated, it will be superfluous to consider para 3 and if one of the
   para 3 guarantees is violated, there will be no need to look at para 1. However, if para 3 is not
   violated, it will still be worth considering para 1. It follows that although civil hearings are expressly
   affected only by para 1, the minimum guarantees may also apply to such hearings too.

2. *Article 6(1): Fair hearing.* The term 'criminal charge' has an autonomous Convention meaning.
   The question of what is meant by 'a criminal charge' has generated quite a lot of case law.
   'Charge' has been described as 'the official notification given to an individual by the competent
   authority of an allegation that he has committed a criminal offence'.[68] The proceedings in question must be determinative of the charge. Therefore, proceedings ancillary to the determination
   of the charge do not fall within Art 6.[69] The term 'civil rights and obligations' also has an
   autonomous Convention meaning and therefore cannot merely be assigned the meaning of 'private' as understood in UK administrative law. Thus, the meaning of 'civil rights and obligations'
   does not depend upon the legal classification afforded the right or obligation in question by the
   national legislator; the question is whether the content and effect of the right or obligation
   (taking into account the legal systems of all the contracting States) allows the meaning 'civil right'
   or 'civil obligation' to be assigned to it.[70] This wide provision allows challenge to decisions taken
   in the absence of legal procedures in a disparate range of circumstances.[71] The civil right must
   have some legal basis as established in the State in question, but assuming that there is such a
   basis, Art 6 may apply to immunities or procedural constraints preventing the bringing of claims
   to court.[72]

3. *An independent and impartial tribunal established by law.* All courts and tribunals falling within Art
   6 must meet this requirement. The tribunal must be established by law[73] and be independent of the
   executive.[74] Factors to be taken into account will include the appointment of its members, their

---

68 Judgment of 15 July 1982, *Eckle* A 51; (1982) 5 EHRR 1, p 33.

69 See, e.g. *X v UK* (1982) 5 EHRR 273 (appointment of a legal aid lawyer was found to fall outside Art 6).

70 Judgment of 16 July 1971, *Ringeisen v Austria*, A 13, p 39; (1971) 1 EHRR 455.

71 E.g. *O v UK* (1987) 10 EHRR 82 concerned a decision to terminate access to a child in care although no legal procedure was in place allowing
    consideration of its merits.

72 See *Osman v UK* (1998) 5 BHRC 293; *Fayed v UK* (1994) 18 EHRR 393.

73 *Zand v Austria* (1978) 15 DR 70 (this means law emanating from Parliament, although aspects of the judicial organisation may be delegated to
    the executive).

74 *Benthem v Netherlands* (1985) 8 EHRR 1.

terms of office, and guarantees against outside influence.[75] Impartiality is judged both subjectively and objectively.[76] In other words, actual bias must be shown, but also the existence of guarantees against bias.[77] The decision in *McGonnell v UK*[78] left open the question whether a judge having both legislative and executive functions could be viewed as independent and impartial. In a number of cases against the UK, military discipline as exercised by way of court martial has not been found to satisfy the requirement of impartiality.[79]

4. *Hearing within a reasonable time.* The hearing must take place within a reasonable time. These are the same words as are used in Art 5(3), but here, the point is to put an end to the insecurity of the applicant who is uncertain of the outcome of the civil action or charge against him or her rather than with the deprivation of liberty.[80] Thus, the ending point comes when the uncertainty is resolved either at the court of highest instance or by expiry of the time limit for appeal. In determining what is meant by 'reasonable', fairly wide time limits have been applied so that in some circumstances, as much as seven or eight[81] years may be reasonable. The Court has approved a period of nearly five years[82] and the Commission a period of seven-and-a-half.[83]

5. *Other aspects of fairness.* Apart from access to legal advice and the other minimal guarantees of Art 6(3), what other rights are implied by the term a 'fair hearing'? It has been found to connote equality between the parties,[84] and in principle, entails the right of the parties to be present in person,[85] although criminal trial *in absentia* does not automatically violate Art 6: the right can be waived[86] and does not normally extend to appeals.[87] The hearing should be adversarial[88] in the sense that both parties are given an opportunity to comment on all the evidence that is adduced.[89] A refusal to summon a witness may constitute unfairness,[90] as may a failure to disclose

---

75   *Bryan v UK* (1995) 21 EHRR 342.

76   *Fey v Austria* (1993) 16 EHRR 387; *Pullar v UK* (1996) 22 EHRR 391.

77   *Remli v France* (1996) 22 EHRR 253.

78   (2000) 8 BHRC 56.

79   See *Findlay v UK* (1997) 24 EHRR 221; *Hood v UK* (2000) 29 EHRR 365, Judgment of 25.2.97; see also *Coyne v UK*, Judgment of 24.10.97, RJD 1997-V 1842; *Cable and Others v UK*, App No 24436/94 (1999) *The Times*, 11 March.

80   See, generally, Van Dijk and Van Hoof, 'further reading' p 347 below, pp 446–47.

81   In *Vernillo v France* 12 HRLJ 199, seven-and-a-half years in respect of civil proceedings was not found too long owing to the special responsibilities of the parties.

82   *Buchholz*, Judgment of 6 May 1981, A 42.

83   Report, 12 July 1977, in *Haase* D & R 11 (1978), p 78.

84   *Neumeister*, Judgment of 27 June 1968; (1979–80) 1 EHRR 91; *De Haes and Gijsels v Belgium* (1997) 25 EHRR 1.

85   *Colloza v Italy*, Judgment of 12 February 1985, A 89 (1985); *Zana v Turkey* (1998) 4 BHRC 242.

86   *Colloza v Italy*, Judgment of 12 February 1985, A 89 (1985).

87   *Ekbatani v Sweden* (1988) 13 EHRR 504, cf *Monnell and Morris v UK* (1987) 10 EHRR 205.

88   *Ruiz-Mateos v Spain* (1993) 16 EHRR 505.

89   *Mantovanelli v France* (1997) 24 EHRR 370.

90   *X v Austria* Appl No 5362/72, Coll 42 (1973), p 145.

evidence.[91] The court must give a reasoned judgment.[92] These and further significant aspects of fairness are discussed further in Chapter 20.[93]

6. *Article 6(2): The presumption of innocence in criminal cases.* Paragraph 2 'requires inter alia that when carrying out their duties, members of a court should not start with the preconceived idea that the accused has committed the offence charged; the burden of proof is on the prosecution and any doubt should benefit the accused. It also follows that it is for the prosecution to inform the accused of the case that will be made against him so that he may prepare and present his defence accordingly and to adduce evidence sufficient to convict him'.[94] It follows from the presumption of innocence that the court must base its conviction exclusively on evidence put forward at trial.[95] Thus, a conviction based on written statements which were inadmissible breached para 6(2).[96] This provision is very closely related to the impartiality provision of para 6(1). The expectation that the State bears the burden of establishing guilt requires that the accused should not be expected to provide involuntary assistance by way of a confession. Thus, the presumption of innocence under para 6(2) is closely linked to the right to freedom from self-incrimination which the Court has found to be covered by the right to a fair hearing under para 6(1) (*Funke v France*).[97]

In *Murray (John) v UK*,[98] on the other hand, the Commission did not find that para 6(1) had been breached where inferences had been drawn at trial from the applicant's refusal to give evidence. The Court in *Murray* also found no breach of Art 6 due to such drawing of inferences in the particular circumstances of the case, taking into account the fact that 'the right to silence' could not be treated as absolute, the degree of compulsion exerted on the applicant and the weight of the evidence against him.[99] However, the Court did find that Art 6(1) had been breached by the denial of access to a lawyer since such access was essential where there was a likelihood that adverse inferences would be drawn from silence. In *Saunders v UK*,[100] the Commission found that the applicant's right to freedom from self-incrimination had been infringed in that he had been forced to answer questions put to him by inspectors investigating a company takeover or risk the imposition of a criminal sanction. The ruling of the Court was to the same effect, taking into account the special compulsive regime in question for Department of Trade and Industry inspections.[101]

---

91   *Edwards v UK* (1992) 15 EHRR 417 (it was found that the hearing in the Court of Appeal remedied this failure). In *Rowe and Davis v UK* (2000) 30 EHRR 1, the failure of the prosecution to make an application to the trial judge to withhold material caused a breach of Art 6. Review of the material later by the Court of Appeal could not remedy the breach.

92   *Hadjianastassiou v Greece* (1992) 16 EHRR 219, para 33.

93   See pp 1204–1209, 1217, 1222, 1226, 1229. Also, for further discussion, see Ashworth, A, 'Article 6 and the fairness of trials' [1999] Crim LR 261; *Harris, O'Boyle and Warbrick* (2009), p 347 below, Chapter 6.

94   Judgment of 6 December 1988, *Barbéra, Messegué and Jabardo*, A 14 6(2) (1989) p 33. See also *Salabiaku v France* (1988) 13 EHRR 379.

95   *X v Federal Republic of Germany* D & R 17 (1980), p 231.

96   *Barbéra* [1987] 3 All ER 411.

97   (1993) 16 EHRR 297.

98   (1996) 22 EHRR 29. For comment, see Munday [1996] Crim LR 370.

99   *Murray (John) v UK* (1996) 22 EHRR 29. See also *Averill v UK* (2001) 31 EHRR 36.

100   No 19187/91 Com Rep paras 69–75.

101   *Saunders v UK* (1997) 23 EHRR 313. See further Chapter 20, p 1205–6.

Article 7 No punishment without law

1   No one shall be held guilty of any criminal offence on account of any act or omission which did not constitute a criminal offence under national or international law at the time when it was committed. Nor shall a heavier penalty be imposed than the one that was applicable at the time the criminal offence was committed.

2   This Article shall not prejudice the trial and punishment of any person for any act or omission which, at the time when it was committed, was criminal according to the general principles of law recognised by civilised nations.

Note
This article, and one of the leading cases on it, is discussed in Chapter 3, pp 99–103.

ARTICLES 8–12

Article 8 Right to respect for family and private life

1   Everyone has the right to respect for his private and family life, his home and his correspondence.

2   There shall be no interference by a public authority with the exercise of this right except such as is in accordance with the law and is necessary in a democratic society in the interests of national security, public safety or the economic well-being of the country, for the prevention of disorder or crime for the protection of health or morals, or for the protection of the rights and freedoms of others.

Article 9 Freedom of thought, conscience and religion

1   Everyone has the right to freedom of thought, conscience and religion; this right includes freedom to change his religion or belief and freedom, either alone or in community with others and in public or private, to manifest his religion or belief, in worship, teaching, practice and observance.

2   Freedom to manifest one's religion or beliefs shall be subject only to such limitations as are prescribed by law and are necessary in a democratic society in the interests of public safety, for the protection of public order, health or morals, or for the protection of the rights and freedoms of others.

Article 10 Freedom of expression

1   Everyone has the right to freedom of expression. This right shall include freedom to hold opinions and to receive and impart information and ideas without interference by public authority and regardless of frontiers. This Article shall not prevent States from requiring the licensing of broadcasting, television or cinema enterprises.

2   The exercise of these freedoms, since it carries with it duties and responsibilities, may be subject to such formalities, conditions, restrictions or penalties as are prescribed by law and are necessary in a democratic society, in the interests of national security territorial integrity or public safety, for the prevention of disorder or crime, for the protection of health or morals, for the protection of the reputation or rights of others, for preventing the disclosure of information received in confidence, or for maintaining the authority and impartiality of the judiciary.

Article 11 Freedom of assembly and association

1   Everyone has the right to freedom of peaceful assembly and to freedom of association with others, including the right to form and to join trade unions for the protection of his interests.

2   No restrictions shall be placed on the exercise of these rights other than such as are prescribed by law and are necessary in a democratic society in the interests of national security or public safety, for the prevention of disorder or crime, for the protection of health or morals or for the protection of the rights and freedoms of others. This Article shall not prevent the imposition of lawful restrictions on the exercise of these rights by members of the armed forces, of the police or of the administration of the State.

General restrictions on the rights and freedoms contained in Arts 8–11

Notes

1. These Articles have a second paragraph enumerating certain restrictions on the primary right. The interests covered by the restrictions are largely the same: national security, prevention of disorder or crime, protection of morals, the rights of others, public safety. As indicated above, the State is allowed a 'margin of appreciation'—a degree of discretion—as to the measures needed to protect the particular interest.[102]

2. To be justified, State interference with Arts 8–11 guarantees must be prescribed by law, have a legitimate aim, be necessary in a democratic society and be applied in a non-discriminatory fashion. In most cases under these Articles, Strasbourg's main concern has been with the 'necessary in a democratic society' requirement; the notion of 'prescribed by law' has been focused upon to some extent, but almost always with the result that it has been found to be satisfied. The 'legitimate aim' requirement will normally be readily satisfied; as Harris, O'Boyle and Warbrick point out, the grounds for interference are so wide that 'the State can usually make a plausible case that it did have a good reason for interfering with the right'.[103] The provision against non-discrimination arises under Art 14; it has proved to be very significant.[104]

3. The 'prescribed by law' requirement means that the restriction must be in accordance with a rule of national law which satisfies the Convention meaning of 'law'. Also, the law on which the restriction is based is aimed at protecting one of the interests listed in para 2; in other words, the restriction falls within one of the exceptions. Interpreting 'prescribed by law' in *Sunday Times v UK*,[105] the European Court of Human Rights found that 'the law must be adequately accessible' and 'a norm cannot be regarded as a "law" unless it is formulated with sufficient precision to enable the citizen to regulate his conduct'. This finding has been flexibly applied; for example, in *Rai, Allmond and 'Negotiate Now' v UK*,[106] the Commission had to consider the ban on public demonstrations or

---

102   See above, p 297. See also p 336, below.

103   *Law of the European Convention on Human Rights* (1995), p 290.

104   See below, pp 334–5.

105   A 30, para 49 (1979).

106   81-A D & R 46 (1995).

meetings concerning Northern Ireland in Trafalgar Square. The ban was the subject of a statement in the House of Commons and many refusals of demonstrations had been made subsequent to it. The Commission found that the ban was sufficiently prescribed by law: 'It is compatible with the requirements of foreseeability that terms which are on their face general and unlimited are explained by executive or administrative statements, since it is the provision of sufficiently precise guidance to individuals . . . rather than the source of that guidance which is of relevance.'[107] In *Steel and Others v UK*[108] the Commission introduced a very significant qualification: 'The level of precision required depends to a considerable degree on the content of the instrument, the field it is designed to cover, and the number and status of those to whom it is addressed'.[109] Although the term 'margin of appreciation' was not used, this finding appears to allow the Member State a certain leeway in relation to the 'prescribed by law' requirement.

4. As this book went to press, the European Court of Human Rights issued its judgment in the case of *Gillan v UK*, No 4158/05 (2010), which concerned a challenge to the law governing the use of stop and search under s 44 of the Terrorism Act 2000, which permits searches without reasonable suspicion of the individual concerned (see Chapter 20, pp 1153–1155). The Court, considering a challenge under Art 8, the right to respect for private life, found that s 44 allowed for such arbitrary and unconstrained use of the power that the powers to search—and therefore to interfere with Art 8 rights—could not be considered to be 'prescribed by law'. As the Court observed, at para 85:

> there is a clear risk of arbitrariness in the grant of such a broad discretion to the police officer. . .the risks of the discriminatory use of the powers against [ethnic minorities] is a very real consideration.

5. The Court has interpreted 'necessary in a democratic society' as meaning that: 'an interference corresponds to a pressing social need and, in particular, that it is proportionate to the legitimate aim pursued'.[110] Thus, in the particular instance, it can be said that the interference is necessary in the sense that it is concerned with a particular restriction such as the protection of morals, and in the particular case, there is a real need to protect morals—a pressing social need—as opposed to an unclear or weak danger to morals. Further, the interference must be in proportion to the aim pursued; in other words, it does not go further than is needed, bearing in mind the objective in question.

   But the doctrine of proportionality is strongly linked to the principle of the margin of appreciation: the Court has stated that the role of the Convention in protecting human rights is subsidiary to the role of the national legal system[111] and that since the State is better placed than the international judge to balance individual rights against general societal interests, Strasbourg will operate a restrained review of the balance struck. The notion of a margin of appreciation conceded to States permeates the Art 8(2), 9(2), 10(2) and 11(2) jurisprudence, although it has not strongly influenced the interpretation of the substantive rights.

---

107 *Ibid*, p 152.

108 (1998) 28 EHRR 603.

109 Paragraph 145. The Commission based these findings on the judgments of the Court in *Chorherr v Austria* Series A 266-B, para 23 (1993) and in *Cantoni v France*, para 35 (1996) 96 ECHR 52.

110 *Olsson v Sweden*, A 130, para 67 (1988).

111 *Handyside v UK*, A 24, para 48 (1976).

Article 8

Notes

1. Article 8 seems to cover four different areas, suggesting that, for example, private life can be distinguished from family life. However, the case law suggests that these rights usually need not be clearly distinguished from each other.[112] There will tend to be a clear overlap between them; for example, it is often unnecessary to define 'family', because the factual situation might so obviously fall within the term 'private'. The inclusion of the wide (and undefined) term 'private' means that rights other than those arising from the home, family life and correspondence may fall within Art 8(1). It should be noted that Art 8 only provides a right to *respect* for private life, etc. Thus, the extent of the respect required can vary to an extent in view of the various practices in the different States. In contrast to Art 10, finding that a claim is covered by para 1 is not a simple matter: attention cannot merely focus on the exceptions.

2. The negative obligation—to refrain from interference—is central,[113] but a number of requirements to take positive action have been accommodated within Art 8. Where a positive obligation is claimed, Strasbourg has traditionally afforded a wide margin of appreciation. The margin can widen or narrow depending on the circumstances of the case, resulting in a variation of the intensity of the Court's review of the States' actions. Two further factors may also be present in this context and may influence Strasbourg in conceding a particularly wide margin of appreciation where a complainant seeks to lay a positive obligation on the State. First, this is the case where the harm complained of flows from the action of a private party, rather than the State itself, so that the so-called 'horizontal effect' of the Convention is in issue and, second, where there is a potential conflict with another Convention right.

3. *Exceptions and justification under Art 8(2).* There must be an interference by the public authorities. But, as the discussion above indicates, this can include the failure to carry out a positive obligation. In the absence of a positive obligation, however, a failure to act would not constitute an interference.[114] Where an interference occurs, proper safeguards must be in place to protect individuals from arbitrary interfere; there must be a legal framework which satisfies the 'in accordance with the law' test and strict limits must be placed on the power conferred.[115] If the exception in respect of national security is invoked, the State may find that is relatively easy to justify the interference.[116] But where interferences, such as searches or surveillance, occur in respect of criminal activity, a higher standard will be required. Thus, judicial authorisation of searches or surveillance may be required.[117] Where a grave invasion of privacy has occurred, judicial authorisation and a warrant may not be enough.[118]

4. *The concept of respect for private life—privacy of personal information.* Respect for the privacy of personal information clearly falls within the notion of private life; initially, the Court approached this aspect cautiously, tending to be satisfied if a procedure was in place allowing the interest in

---

112   In *Mialhe v France* (1993) 16 EHRR 332 it was made clear that the four aspects of private life tend to constitute overlapping concepts.

113   See, e.g. *Gul v Switzerland* (1996) 22 EHRR 93, para 38.

114   *Airey v Ireland* (1979) 2 EHRR 305.

115   *Camenzind v Switzerland*, RJD 1997-III 2880.

116   See *Leander v Sweden* (1987) 9 EHRR 433.

117   *Funke v France* (1993) 16 EHRR 297.

118   *Niemietz v Germany* (1992) 16 EHRR 97.

such control to be weighed up against a competing interest. Thus, in *Gaskin v UK*,[119] the interest of the applicant in obtaining access to the files relating to his childhood in care had to be weighed up against the interest of the contributors to it in maintaining confidentiality, because this interference with privacy had a legitimate aim under the 'rights of others' exception. It was held that the responsible authority did not have a procedure available for weighing the two. Consequently, the procedure automatically preferred the contributors and that was disproportionate to the aim of protecting confidentiality, and therefore could not be 'necessary in a democratic society'.

5. The opposite result was reached, but by a similar route, in *Klass v FRG*,[120] brought in respect of telephone tapping. It was found that although telephone tapping constituted an interference with a person's private life, it could be justified as being in the interests of national security and there were sufficient controls in place (permission had to be given by a Minister applying certain criteria including that of 'reasonable suspicion') to ensure that the power was not abused. In the similar *Malone* case,[121] however, there were no such controls in place and a breach of Art 8 was therefore found, which led to the introduction of the Interception of Communications Act 1985.

6. As is well known, recently the Court has broadened the protection for personal information by recognizing a positive obligation on the state to provide a remedy for misuse of personal information by the media. In the following, landmark case, the court found, unanimously, that the failure of the German courts to provide Princess Caroline with a remedy in relation to pictures published without her consent of her engaged in everyday activities amounted to a breach of Art 8.[122]

Von Hannover v Germany (2005) 40 EHRR 1

[53] In the present case, there is no doubt that the publication by various German magazines of photos of the applicant in her daily life either on her own or with other people falls within the scope of her private life. . .

[57] The Court reiterates that although the object of Article 8 is essentially that of protecting the individual against arbitrary interference by the public authorities, it does not merely compel the State to abstain from such interference: in addition to this primarily negative undertaking, there may be positive obligations inherent in an effective respect for private or family life. These obligations may involve the adoption of measures designed to secure respect for private life even in the sphere of the relations of individuals between themselves. . . The boundary between the State's positive and negative obligations under this provision does not lend itself to precise definition. The applicable principles are, nonetheless, similar. In both contexts regard must be had to the fair balance that has to be struck between the competing interests of the individual and of the community as a whole; and in both contexts the State enjoys a certain margin of appreciation.

[as to the balance to be struck between Arts 8 and 10, the Court said:]

[43] The Court considers that a fundamental distinction needs to be made between reporting facts—even controversial ones—capable of contributing to a debate in a democratic society, relating to politicians in the exercise of their functions, for example,

119 (1990) 12 EHRR 36.

120 (1978) 2 EHRR 214; see also *Ludi v Switzerland* (1993) 15 EHRR 173.

121 Report of 17 December 1982, A 82; (1984) 7 EHRR 14. See above, Chapter 3, pp 95–96.

122 For extended analysis of this decision, see Fenwick and Phillipson, *Media Freedom under the Human Rights Act* (2006), Chapter 13.

and reporting details of the private life of an individual who, moreover, as in this case, does not exercise official functions. While in the former case the press exercises its vital role of 'watchdog' in a democracy by contributing to 'impart[ing] information and ideas on matters of public interest. . .it *does not do so* in the latter case. . .

[46] The situation here does not come within the sphere of any political or public debate because the published photos and accompanying commentaries relate exclusively to details of the applicant's private life . . .

[65]. . . the publication of the photos and articles in question, of which the sole purpose was to satisfy the curiosity of a particular readership regarding the details of the applicant's private life, cannot be deemed to contribute to any debate of general interest to society despite the applicant being known to the public

Bodily integrity

Notes

1. Under Art 8, physical intrusions on the bodily integrity of individuals by State agents may be justified if the requirements of Art 8(2) are satisfied. Equally, UK law also recognises a need to create a balance between the interest of the State in allowing physical interference with individuals for various purposes, including the prevention of crime and the interest of the individual in preserving his or her bodily integrity. UK law determines that in certain circumstances, bodily integrity may give way to other interests—see Chapter 20. Articles 3 and 8 together provide substantive guarantees against certain types of custodial ill treatment. But, clearly, Art 3 will cover only the grossest instances of ill treatment. It is notable that the Convention contains no provision equivalent to that under Art 10 of the International Covenant on Civil and Political Rights which provides 'persons deprived of their liberty shall be treated with humanity and with respect for the inherent dignity of the human person'.

2. In the *Greek* case,[123] the conditions of detention were found to amount to inhuman treatment due to overcrowding, inadequate food, sleeping arrangements, heating, toilets and provision for external contacts. Failure to obtain medical treatment after a forcible arrest was found to infringe Art 3 in *Hurtado v Switzerland*.[124] Conduct which grossly humiliates is degrading treatment contrary to Art 3.[125] Art 8 may be viewed as overlapping, to an extent, with Art 3, but it also covers some matters which would not be serious enough to amount to Art 3 treatment.[126] In order to bring Art 8 into play, it must be found that its protection extends to the matter in question—in the context of detention, including police detention, it would probably be that 'private or family life' is affected. Certain conditions or incidents of detention may fall outside Art 8, such as a failure to provide an interpreter. But a failure to allow a juvenile or a mentally disturbed person to consult privately with a member of his or her family, acting as an appropriate adult, might be viewed as an interference with either private or family life.

3. The most significant recent case on Art 8 follows. It concerns both control over personal information and bodily integrity.

---

123   12 YB 1 (1969) Com Rep.

124   A 280-A (1994) Com Rep.

125   The *Greek* case, 12 YB 1 (1969) Com Rep.

126   See the findings in the corporal punishment case of *Costello-Roberts v UK* (1993) 19 EHRR 112. The Court found that the treatment was not severe enough to fall within Art 3; in the particular circumstances it did not fall within Art 8, but the Court considered that there might be circumstances in which Art 8 could be viewed as affording a wider protection to physical integrity than that which is afforded by Art 3.

S v United Kingdom (2009) 48 EHRR 50 (extracts)

The first applicant, a British national, had been arrested in January 2001 at the age of 11 and charged with attempted robbery. His fingerprints and DNA samples were taken. He was acquitted in June 2001. The second applicant, also a British national, was arrested in March 2001 and charged with harassment of his partner. His fingerprints and DNA samples were taken. The case against him was formally discontinued in June 2001. Both applicants asked for their fingerprints and DNA samples to be destroyed. The police authorities refused. Under domestic law the police authorities were entitled to retain indefinitely the fingerprints and DNA samples of those suspected but later not convicted of a criminal offence.

The applicants sought to challenge the refusal through the domestic courts. However, their application was rejected in turn by the Administrative Court, the Court of Appeal and the House of Lords. The House of Lords held that the mere retention of fingerprints and DNA samples did not constitute an interference with the applicants' right under art. 8 to respect for private life. Neither, it held, did it amount to a breach of art. 14 in that the difference of treatment between the applicants and the general body of persons who had not had their fingerprints and DNA samples taken and retained by the police was not a difference based on a relevant 'status'.

The applicants complained, relying on art. 8, that the retention of their fingerprints, cellular samples and DNA profiles amounted to a violation of their right to respect for private life.

68 The Court notes at the outset that all three categories of the personal information retained by the authorities in the present cases, namely fingerprints, DNA profiles and cellular samples, constitute personal data within the meaning of the Data Protection Convention as they relate to identified or identifiable individuals. The Government accepted that all three categories are ' personal data' within the meaning of the Data Protection Act 1998 in the hands of those who are able to identify the individual . . .

Cellular samples and DNA profiles

70 In *Van der Velden* (App. No. 29514/05, 7.12.06), the Court considered that, given the use to which cellular material in particular could conceivably be put in the future, the systematic retention of that material was sufficiently intrusive to disclose interference with the right to respect for private life. . .

71 The Court maintains its view that an individual's concern about the possible future use of private information retained by the authorities is legitimate and relevant to a determination of the issue of whether there has been an interference. Indeed, bearing in mind the rapid pace of developments in the field of genetics and information technology, the Court cannot discount the possibility that in the future the private-life interests bound up with genetic information may be adversely affected in novel ways or in a manner which cannot be anticipated with precision today. Accordingly, the Court does not find any sufficient reason to depart from its finding in the *Van der Velden* case.

72 Legitimate concerns about the conceivable use of cellular material in the future are not, however, the only element to be taken into account in the determination of the present issue. In addition to the highly personal nature of cellular samples, the Court notes that they contain much sensitive information about an individual, including information about his or her health. Moreover, samples contain a unique genetic code of great relevance to both the individual and his relatives.

73 Given the nature and the amount of personal information contained in cellular

samples, their retention per se must be regarded as interfering with the right to respect for the private lives of the individuals concerned. That only a limited part of this information is actually extracted or used by the authorities through DNA profiling and that no immediate detriment is caused in a particular case does not change this conclusion.

74 As regards DNA profiles themselves, the Court notes that they contain a more limited amount of personal information extracted from cellular samples in a coded form. The Government submitted that a DNA profile is nothing more than a sequence of numbers or a bar-code containing information of a purely objective and irrefutable character and that the identification of a subject only occurs in case of a match with another profile in the database. It also submitted that, being in coded form, computer technology is required to render the information intelligible and that only a limited number of persons would be able to interpret the data in question.

75 The Court observes, nonetheless, that the profiles contain substantial amounts of unique personal data. While the information contained in the profiles may be considered objective and irrefutable in the sense submitted by the Government, their processing through automated means allows the authorities to go well beyond neutral identification. The Court notes in this regard that the Government accepted that DNA profiles could be, and indeed had in some cases been, used for familial searching with a view to identifying a possible genetic relationship between individuals. It also accepted the highly sensitive nature of such searching and the need for very strict controls in this respect. In the Court's view, the DNA profiles' capacity to provide a means of identifying genetic relationships between individuals is in itself sufficient to conclude that their retention interferes with the right to the private life of the individuals concerned. The frequency of familial searches, the safeguards attached thereto and the likelihood of detriment in a particular case are immaterial in this respect. This conclusion is similarly not affected by the fact that, since the information is in coded form, it is intelligible only with the use of computer technology and capable of being interpreted only by a limited number of persons.

76 The Court further notes that it is not disputed by the Government that the processing of DNA profiles allows the authorities to assess the likely ethnic origin of the donor and that such techniques are in fact used in police investigations. The possibility the DNA profiles create for inferences to be drawn as to ethnic origin makes their retention all the more sensitive and susceptible of affecting the right to private life.

77 In view of the foregoing, the Court concludes that the retention of both cellular samples and DNA profiles discloses an interference with the applicants' right to respect for their private lives, within the meaning of art. 8(1) of the Convention.

[The Court then went on to consider whether the interference was justified, finding that the interference was both prescribed by law and served legitimate aim.]

105 The Court finds it to be beyond dispute that the fight against crime, and in particular against organised crime and terrorism, which is one of the challenges faced by today's European societies, depends to a great extent on the use of modern scientific techniques of investigation and identification. . .

106 However, while it recognises the importance of such information in the detection of crime, the Court must delimit the scope of its examination. . .

107 The Court will consider this issue with due regard to the relevant instruments of the Council of Europe and the law and practice of the other contracting states. The core principles of data protection require the retention of data to be proportionate in relation to the purpose of collection and insist on limited periods of storage. These principles appear to have been consistently applied by the contracting states in the police sector in

accordance with the Data Protection Convention and subsequent Recommendations of the Committee of Ministers.

108 As regards, more particularly, cellular samples, most of the contracting states allow these materials to be taken in criminal proceedings only from individuals suspected of having committed offences of a certain minimum gravity. In the great majority of the contracting states with functioning DNA databases, samples and DNA profiles derived from those samples are required to be removed or destroyed either immediately or within a certain limited time after acquittal or discharge. A restricted number of exceptions to this principle are allowed by some contracting states.

109 The current position of Scotland, as a part of the United Kingdom itself, is of particular significance in this regard. . . .the Scottish Parliament voted to allow retention of the DNA of unconvicted persons only in the case of adults charged with violent or sexual offences and even then, for three years only, with the possibility of an extension to keep the DNA sample and data for a further two years with the consent of a sheriff.

110 This position is notably consistent with Committee of Ministers' Recommendation R(92)1, which stresses the need for an approach which discriminates between different kinds of cases and for the application of strictly defined storage periods for data, even in more serious cases. Against this background, England, Wales and Northern Ireland appear to be the only jurisdictions within the Council of Europe to allow the indefinite retention of fingerprint and DNA material of any person of any age suspected of any recordable offence.

112 . . .The Court observes that the protection afforded by art. 8 of the Convention would be unacceptably weakened if the use of modern scientific techniques in the criminal-justice system were allowed at any cost and without carefully balancing the potential benefits of the extensive use of such techniques against important private-life interests. In the Court's view, the strong consensus existing among the contracting states in this respect is of considerable importance and narrows the margin of appreciation left to the respondent State in the assessment of the permissible limits of the interference with private life in this sphere. . .

113 In the present case, the applicants' fingerprints and cellular samples were taken and DNA profiles obtained in the context of criminal proceedings brought on suspicion of attempted robbery in the case of the first applicant and harassment of his partner in the case of the second applicant. The data were retained on the basis of legislation allowing for their indefinite retention, despite the acquittal of the former and the discontinuance of the criminal proceedings against the latter.

114 The Court must consider whether the permanent retention of fingerprint and DNA data of all suspected but un-convicted people is based on relevant and sufficient reasons. . . .

119 In this respect, the Court is struck by the blanket and indiscriminate nature of the power of retention in England and Wales. The material may be retained irrespective of the nature or gravity of the offence with which the individual was originally suspected or of the age of the suspected offender; fingerprints and samples may be taken—and retained—from a person of any age, arrested in connection with a recordable offence, which includes minor or non-imprisonable offences. The retention is not time limited; the material is retained indefinitely whatever the nature or seriousness of the offence of which the person was suspected. Moreover, there exist only limited possibilities for an acquitted individual to have the data removed from the nationwide database or the materials destroyed; in particular, there is no provision for independent review of the justification for the retention according to defined criteria, including such factors as the seriousness of the

offence, previous arrests, the strength of the suspicion against the person and any other special circumstances. . .

122 Of particular concern in the present context is the risk of stigmatisation, stemming from the fact that persons in the position of the applicants, who have not been convicted of any offence and are entitled to the presumption of innocence, are treated in the same way as convicted persons. In this respect, the Court must bear in mind that the right of every person under the Convention to be presumed innocent includes the general rule that no suspicion regarding an accused's innocence may be voiced after his acquittal. It is true that the retention of the applicants' private data cannot be equated with the voicing of suspicions. Nonetheless, their perception that they are not being treated as innocent is heightened by the fact that their data are retained indefinitely in the same way as the data of convicted persons, while the data of those who have never been suspected of an offence are required to be destroyed. . . .

124 The Court further considers that the retention of the unconvicted persons' data may be especially harmful in the case of minors such as the first applicant, given their special situation and the importance of their development and integration in society. . .

125 In conclusion, the Court finds that the blanket and indiscriminate nature of the powers of retention of the fingerprints, cellular samples and DNA profiles of persons suspected but not convicted of offences, as applied in the case of the present applicants, fails to strike a fair balance between the competing public and private interests and that the respondent State has overstepped any acceptable margin of appreciation in this regard. Accordingly, the retention at issue constitutes a disproportionate interference with the applicants' right to respect for private life and cannot be regarded as necessary in a democratic society. This conclusion obviates the need for the Court to consider the applicants' criticism regarding the adequacy of certain particular safeguards, such as too broad an access to the personal data concerned and insufficient protection against the misuse or abuse of such data.

126 Accordingly, there has been a violation of art. 8 of the Convention in the present case.

Note

This ruling caused considerable dismay to the UK Government, and it appears determined that its compliance will be the most minimal possible. At the time of writing, it appears that the Government will seek to legislate so as to allow it to keep the DNA profiles of innocent people (those arrested but never convicted) for only six years, instead of indefinitely.[127]

Autonomy

Notes

1. Personal autonomy has been recognised for some time in the USA as strongly linked to the concept of privacy. In *Doe v Bolton*,[128] Douglas J said that 'the right to privacy means freedom of choice in the basic decisions of one's life respecting marriage, divorce, procreation, contraception, education and upbringing of children'. At Strasbourg, the value of personal autonomy has also received quite clear recognition.[129] Personal autonomy connotes an interest not only in preventing physical intru-

---

127   www.guardian.co.uk/politics/2009/nov/11/police-dna-profiles-bill.

128   (1973) 410 US 179; (1973) 35 L E 2d 201.

129   *Dudgeon v UK* (1982) 4 EHRR 149; *Lustig-Prean v UK* (1999) 7 BHRC 65.

sion by others, but also with the extent to which the law allows an individual a degree of control over his or her own body.

2. The choice of adults as to the disposal of their own bodies in the member states tends to be highly circumscribed. In the Member States, although in general suicide is no longer a crime, in the vast majority of them aiding and abetting suicide has not been de-criminalised. Thus, for example, a relative of a person who is unable to commit suicide because she is incapacitated through illness cannot help her to die in order to avoid severe pain and suffering without risking prosecution for murder or manslaughter. Euthanasia is legal in Holland and in Belgium. It is not recognised in UK law[130] except in the very narrow sense that allowing a patient in a persistent vegetative state to die will be acceptable if it can be said, objectively speaking, to be in his or her best interests because no improvement can be expected.[131] Also, under the so called 'double effect' doctrine, a doctor will not be guilty of murder if she administers a very high level of a pain-killing drug which she knows is likely to cause death, so long as the primary intention is to relieve pain.[132] A conflict with Art 2 might arise[133] if euthanasia was allowed in other situations; it has merely been found at Strasbourg that passively allowing a person to die need not attract criminal liability in order to satisfy Art 2.[134] The consent of the victim would be irrelevant; euthanasia is not covered by any of the Art 2 exceptions.

3. In 2001, an action was brought in the UK under the Human Rights Act against the Director of Public Prosecutions in relation to his decision that a husband who wishes to help his wife to die once her terminal Motor Neurone Disease reaches a certain stage would be liable to the risk of prosecution.[135] The woman wanted a declaration that her husband would not be prosecuted and argued that the State has a responsibility to make such a declaration since otherwise, Arts 3 and 8 would be breached. The claim was backed by the UK group *Liberty*. The claim was rejected by the House of Lords, and Diane Pretty took the case to Strasbourg.[136] She complained under a number of Articles, including Art 8.

Pretty v United Kingdom (2002) No 2346/02

3. The applicant, who is paralysed and suffering from a degenerative and incurable illness, alleged that the refusal of the Director of Public Prosecutions to grant an immunity from prosecution to her husband if he assisted her in committing suicide and the prohibition in domestic law on assisting suicide infringed her rights under Articles 2, 3, 8, 9 and 14 of the Convention. . . .

58. The applicant argued that, while the right to self-determination ran like a thread through the Convention as a whole, it was Article 8 in which that right was most explicitly recognised and guaranteed. It was clear that the right to self-determination encompassed the right to make decisions about one's body and what happened to it. She submitted that this included the right to choose when and how to die and that nothing could be more

---

130   For discussion, see S Orst 'Conceptions of the Euthanasia Phenomenon' [2000] JCIVLIB 155.

131   *Airedale NHS Trust v Bland* [1993] AC 789, HL.

132   *Cox* [1992] BMLR 38.

133   See pp 299–300.

134   *Widmer v Switzerland*, No 20527/92 (1993), unreported. See also p 299.

135   The claim was rejected on appeal to the HL: *R (On the Application of Diane Pretty) v DPP and Secretary of State for the Home Dept* [2001] UKHL 61.

136   *Pretty v UK* (2002) 35 EHRR 1; 23 HRLJ (2002), 194

intimately connected to the manner in which a person conducted her life than the manner and timing of her death. It followed that the DPP's refusal to give an undertaking and the State's blanket ban on assisted suicide interfered with her rights under Article 8(1). . . .

61. As the Court has had previous occasion to remark, the concept of 'private life' is a broad term not susceptible to exhaustive definition. It covers the physical and psychological integrity of a person. . . . the Court considers that the notion of personal autonomy is an important principle underlying the interpretation of its guarantees.

62. . . . The Court would observe that the ability to conduct one's life in a manner of one's own choosing may also include the opportunity to pursue activities perceived to be of a physically or morally harmful or dangerous nature for the individual concerned. The extent to which a State can use compulsory powers or the criminal law to protect people from the consequences of their chosen lifestyle has long been a topic of moral and jurisprudential discussion, the fact that the interference is often viewed as trespassing on the private and personal sphere adding to the vigour of the debate. However, even where the conduct poses a danger to health or, arguably, where it is of a life-threatening nature, the case-law of the Convention institutions has regarded the State's imposition of compulsory or criminal measures as impinging on the private life of the applicant within the meaning of Article 8 § 1 and requiring justification in terms of the second paragraph. . . .

65. The very essence of the Convention is respect for human dignity and human freedom. Without in any way negating the principle of sanctity of life protected under the Convention, the Court considers that it is under Article 8 that notions of the quality of life take on significance. In an era of growing medical sophistication combined with longer life expectancies, many people are concerned that they should not be forced to linger on in old age or in states of advanced physical or mental decrepitude which conflict with strongly held ideas of self and personal identity. . . .

67. The applicant in this case is prevented by law from exercising her choice to avoid what she considers will be an undignified and distressing end to her life. The Court is not prepared to exclude that this constitutes an interference with her right to respect for private life as guaranteed under Article 8(1) of the Convention. It considers below whether this interference conforms with the requirements of the second paragraph of Article 8.

68. An interference with the exercise of an Article 8 right will not be compatible with Article 8 § 2 unless it is 'in accordance with the law', has an aim or aims that is or are legitimate under that paragraph and is 'necessary in a democratic society' for the aforesaid aim or aims. . . .

69. The only issue arising from the arguments of the parties is the necessity of any interference, it being common ground that the restriction on assisted suicide in this case was imposed by law and in pursuit of the legitimate aim of safeguarding life and thereby protecting the rights of others.

70. According to the Court's established case-law, the notion of necessity implies that the interference corresponds to a pressing social need and, in particular, that it is proportionate to the legitimate aim pursued; in determining whether an interference is 'necessary in a democratic society', the Court will take into account that a margin of appreciation is left to the national authorities, whose decision remains subject to review by the Court for conformity with the requirements of the Convention. The margin of appreciation to be accorded to the competent national authorities will vary in accordance with the nature of the issues and the importance of the interests at stake.

71. The Court recalls that the margin of appreciation has been found to be narrow as regards interferences in the intimate area of an individual's sexual life (see *Dudgeon* (1982)

4 EHRR 149, p. 21, §52, and *A.D.T. v. the United Kingdom*, no. 35765/97, §37, ECHR 2000-IX). Although the applicant has argued that there must therefore be particularly compelling reasons for the interference in her case, the Court does not find that the matter under consideration in this case can be regarded as of the same nature, or as attracting the same reasoning.

72. The parties' arguments have focused on the proportionality of the interference as disclosed in the applicant's case. The applicant attacked in particular the blanket nature of the ban on assisted suicide as failing to take into account her situation as a mentally competent adult who knows her own mind, who is free from pressure and who has made a fully informed and voluntary decision, and therefore cannot be regarded as vulnerable and requiring protection. This inflexibility means, in her submission, that she will be compelled to endure the consequences of her incurable and distressing illness, at a very high personal cost.

74. . . . the Court finds, in agreement with the House of Lords. . . that States are entitled to regulate through the operation of the general criminal law activities which are detrimental to the life and safety of other individuals. . . . The more serious the harm involved the more heavily will weigh in the balance considerations of public health and safety against the countervailing principle of personal autonomy. The law in issue in this case, section 2 of the 1961 Act, was designed to safeguard life by protecting the weak and vulnerable and especially those who are not in a condition to take informed decisions against acts intended to end life or to assist in ending life. Doubtless the condition of terminally ill individuals will vary. But many will be vulnerable and it is the vulnerability of the class which provides the rationale for the law in question. It is primarily for States to assess the risk and the likely incidence of abuse if the general prohibition on assisted suicides were relaxed or if exceptions were to be created. Clear risks of abuse do exist, notwithstanding arguments as to the possibility of safeguards and protective procedures.

76. The Court does not consider therefore that the blanket nature of the ban on assisted suicide is disproportionate. The Government have stated that flexibility is provided for in individual cases by the fact that consent is needed from the DPP to bring a prosecution and by the fact that a maximum sentence is provided, allowing lesser penalties to be imposed as appropriate. The Select Committee report indicated that between 1981 and 1992 in twenty-two cases in which 'mercy killing' was an issue, there was only one conviction for murder, with a sentence of life imprisonment, while lesser offences were substituted in the others and most resulted in probation or suspended sentences. . . . It does not appear to be arbitrary to the Court for the law to reflect the importance of the right to life, by prohibiting assisted suicide while providing for a system of enforcement and adjudication which allows due regard to be given in each particular case to the public interest in bringing a prosecution, as well as to the fair and proper requirements of retribution and deterrence.

77. Nor in the circumstances is there anything disproportionate in the refusal of the DPP to give an advance undertaking that no prosecution would be brought against the applicant's husband. Strong arguments based on the rule of law could be raised against any claim by the executive to exempt individuals or classes of individuals from the operation of the law. In any event, the seriousness of the act for which immunity was claimed was such that the decision of the DPP to refuse the undertaking sought in the present case cannot be said to be arbitrary or unreasonable.

78. The Court concludes that the interference in this case may be justified as 'necessary in a democratic society' for the protection of the rights of others and, accordingly, that there has been no violation of Article 8 of the Convention.

Notes (continued)

4. The Courts' arguments under Art 8(1) in *Pretty* would also appear to be applicable to a woman's claim of a right to an abortion,[137] although so far no such right has been clearly established under Art 8(1). In *Tysiac v Poland*[138] the Court found an infringement of Art 8 when a restrictive consent procedure prevented a woman having an abortion, where pregnancy was likely to—and did— result in the serious deterioration of the woman's health. Tysiac had argued that her rights had been 'violated substantively, by failing to provide her with a legal abortion, and . . . [procedurally,] . . . by the absence of a comprehensive legal framework to guarantee her rights by appropriate procedural means' (para 61). The Court found 'that it has not been demonstrated that Polish law as applied to the applicant's case contained any effective mechanisms capable of determining whether the conditions for obtaining a lawful abortion had been met in her case. It created for the applicant a situation of prolonged uncertainty. As a result, the applicant suffered severe distress and anguish when contemplating the possible negative consequences of her pregnancy and upcoming delivery for her health'.[139] Thus the Court avoided addressing Tysiac's argument on the substantive right issue. But it is apparent that the Court is prepared to find that an abortion that is potentially legal should be in practice possible.

5. On a question concerning an irreconcilable conflict of moral views there are grounds for conceding a margin of appreciation to the national legislatures, but it cannot be unlimited and a state which is out of line with the rest, most obviously Ireland, may fall outside that margin,[140] especially where it also appears to be in breach of international agreements such as The Convention on the Elimination of All Forms of Discrimination against women 1979. The stance taken in a number of other jurisdictions suggests that where this human rights issue comes before the highest national courts, the woman's right to security of the person and to freedom of choice is viewed as paramount[141] and it has been found that the right to life does not extend to the foetus.[142]

6. *Sexual autonomy.* The Court has made it clear that the choice to have sexual relations with others falls within Art 8. In this sphere, it is suggested that the Court has gradually abandoned its initially cautious approach. In *Dudgeon*,[143] the Northern Ireland prohibition of homosexual intercourse was found to breach Art 8. However, this case concerned a gross interference with privacy since it allowed the applicant no means at all of expressing his sexual preference without committing a criminal offence. In 1984,[144] the Commission declared inadmissible an application challenging s 66 of the Army Act 1955, which governs conviction for homosexual practices in the armed forces, on the basis that it could be justified under the prevention of disorder or protection of morals clauses.[145]

---

137   See JM Gher and C Zampas, 'Abortion as a Human Right' (2008) HRLR 249.

138   (2007) 45 EHRR 42.

139   At para 126.

140   See p 297. For discussion, see R Dworkin, *Life's Dominion* (1993).

141   See the decision of the Canadian Supreme Court in *Morgentaler v R* [1988] 1 SCR 60; the decision of the US Supreme Court in *Planned Parenthood of Southeastern Pennsylvania v Casey* (1992) 505 US 833.

142   *Christian Lawyers Assoc of South Africa v The Minister of Health* 1998 (11) BCLR 1434; *Borowski v AG of Canada* (1987) 39 DLR (4th) 731.

143   Judgment of 22 October 1981, A 45; (1982) 4 EHRR 149.

144   *B v UK* 34 D & R 68 (1983); (1983) 6 EHRR 354; A 9237/81.

145   The charges had involved a soldier under 21. See, now, *Smith and Grady v UK* (2000) 29 EHRR 493 in which it was found that the ban breached Art 8. The ban is no longer being applied.

This stance has now been abandoned, and the Court has taken a much more interventionist stance in relation to the sexual autonomy of homosexuals.[146]

7. The 'Bolton Seven' case brought against the UK led to significant changes in the law.[147] The applicants were prosecuted in 1998 on the basis of a video which showed them engaging in consensual group sex. They were convicted of gross indecency. One of the men, Williams, and another, Connell, admitted to having had sex with one of the other five who was, at the time, six months under the then age of consent, 18. Williams was convicted of buggery, although his suspended sentence was later revoked by the Court of Appeal. At the time of the convictions, the court was warned that the prosecutions breached Art 8. Five of the men applied to the European Court of Human Rights and, in July 2001, in order to avoid defeat in the Court, the Government offered each of them compensation in an out of court settlement. The Sexual Offence Act 2003 brought about equalization of the position. By these incremental steps, legal acceptance of the sexual autonomy of homosexuals was brought about, in the sense of achieving equality with heterosexuals.

Sexual identity

Article 8 recognises the fundamental interest of individuals in determining their own identity in terms of gender. This significant aspect of private life arose in a number of cases brought under the European Convention on Human Rights against the UK by transsexuals. In *Rees v UK*[148] the applicant, who was born a woman but had had a gender re-assignment operation, complained that he could not have his birth certificate altered to record his new sex, thereby causing him difficulty in applying for employment. However, the court refused to find a breach of Art 8, because it was reluctant to accept the claim that the UK was under a positive obligation to change its procedures in order to recognise the applicant's identity for social purposes. It followed a similar route in *Cossey v UK*,[149] although it did consider whether it should depart from its judgment in *Rees* in order to ensure that the Convention could reflect societal changes. However, it decided not to do so because developments in this area in the Member States were not consistent and still reflected a diversity of practices. In *B v France*[150] it was found that although there had been development in the area, no broad consensus among Member States had emerged. Nevertheless, the civil position of the applicant in terms of her sexual identity was worse than that of transsexuals in the UK and on that basis, a breach of Art 8 could be found. In *Goodwin v UK*[151] the Court finally took the step of affording full recognition to the status of transsexuals under Art 8.

Article 10

Notes

1. Article 10 obviously overlaps with Art 9's protection for freedom of thought, but it is broader, since it protects the means of ensuring freedom of expression. There is also an obvious overlap

---

146 In *Lustig-Prean* v UK (1999) 29 EHRR 548 it was found that the army ban breached Art 8; see also *Sutherland v UK*, App No 25186/94 (1997) EHRLR 117, in which an application regarding the age of consent for homosexual relations (8 September 1999) was postponed since the Government assured the Commission that the Sexual Offences (Amendment) Bill would proceed equalising the age of consent (see, now, the Sexual Offences (Amendment) Act 2000 s 1).

147 *ADT v UK* (2000) 2 FLR 697; see *The Guardian*, 27 July 2001.

148 (1986) 9 EHRR 56.

149 A 184; (1990) 13 EHRR 622. A similar application also failed in *Sheffield and Horsham v UK* (1999) 27 EHRR 163.

150 (1992) 13 HRLJ 358; for comment see [1992] PL 559.

151 [2002] ECHR 583.

with Art 11 which protects freedom of association and assembly. The stance taken under Art 10 is that while almost all forms of expression will fall within the primary right, all expression is not equally valuable—there is a clear hierarchy of expression. It was found in *X and Church of Scientology v Sweden*[152] that commercial speech is protected by Art 10, but that the level of protection should be less than that accorded to the expression of political ideas, thereby indicating that political speech should receive special protection. As Harris, O'Boyle and Warbrick put it in *Law of the European Convention on Human Rights*:[153] 'The privileged position of political speech derives from the Court's conception of it as a central feature of a democratic society'. Thus the 'political' speech cases of *Sunday Times v UK*,[154] *Jersild v Denmark*,[155] *Lingens v Austria*,[156] *Thorgeirson v Iceland*,[157] all resulted in findings that Art 10 had been violated and all were marked by an intensive review of the restriction in question in which the margin of appreciation was narrowed almost to vanishing point.

2. The Court has stressed that Art 10 applies not only to speech which is favourably received, but also to speech which shocks and offends. In *Jersild v Denmark*,[158] the Commission accepted that this may include aiding in the dissemination of racist ideas. In that instance, the applicant had not himself expressed such views; his conviction had arisen due to his responsibility as a television interviewer for their dissemination. This factor was also taken into account by the Court in finding that the conviction constituted an interference with freedom of expression in breach of Art 10.[159] The television programme in question had included an interview with an extreme racist group, the Greenjackets; such interviews were found to constitute an important means whereby 'the press is able to play its vital role as public watchdog' and therefore strong reasons would have to be adduced for punishing a journalist who had assisted in the dissemination of racist statements by conducting the interview, bearing in mind that the feature taken as a whole was not found by the Court to have as its object the propagation of racist views. The Court pointed out that the racist remarks which led to the convictions of members of the Greenjackets did not have the protection of Art 10.

3. Article 10 includes an additional guarantee of the freedom to receive and impart information. However, it was thought until recently that the seeking of information did not appear to connote an obligation on the part of the Government to make information available; the words 'without restriction by public authority' do not imply a positive obligation on the part of the authority to ensure that information can be received. So the right appeared to be restricted in situations where there was no willing speaker. Article 10 was not, therefore, viewed as a full freedom of information measure.[160] In fact, the freedom to seek information was deliberately omitted from Art 10—

---

152 Appl No 7805/77 (1979); YB XXII.

153 (1995), p 397.

154 (1979) 2 EHRR 245.

155 (1994) 19 EHRR 1.

156 (1986) 8 EHRR 103. *Lingens* concerned the defamation of a political figure. See further, *Lombardo v Malta* (2009) 48 EHRR 23 which concerned a comment by a newspaper on the lack of public consultation by Figura Local Council.

157 (1992) 14 EHRR 843. *Thorgeirson* concerned newspaper articles reporting allegations of brutality against the Reykjavik police. See further *Selisto v Finland* [2005] EMLR 8, which concerned a newspaper article reporting allegations of professional misconduct by a member of the medical profession.

158 (1992) 14 HRLJ 74; see also *Open Door Counselling and Dublin Well Woman Centre Ltd* (1992) 15 EHRR 244 (below, p 331).

159 (1994) 19 EHRR 1.

160 This was supported in the *Gaskin* case (1990) 12 EHRR 36: the Art 10 claim failed on this basis.

although it appears in the Universal Declaration of Human Rights—in order to avoid placing a clear positive obligation on the Member States to communicate information. However, in a recent decision on an application's admissibility, the European Court of Human Rights for the first time, applied Art 10 of the Convention in a case where a request for access to administrative documents was refused by the authorities.[161] Thus, the Court recognised for the first time that Art 10 provides a right to receive information from an unwilling Government—in other words, a freedom of information right. Obviously the right is subject to the para 2 exceptions, but this departure is obviously quite significant since it recognises that access to information, even from an unwilling speaker, is an important aspect of free expression.

4. Mediums other than written publications can be subjected to a licensing system under Art 10(1) and because this restriction is mentioned in para 1, it appears that a licensing system can be imposed on grounds other than those outlined in para 2, thereby broadening the possible exceptions. However, this provision has been restrictively interpreted.[162] Any such exceptions must, of course, be considered in conjunction with the safeguard against discrimination under Art 14: for example, if the State has a monopoly on a medium, it must not discriminate in granting air time to different groups.

5. The restrictions of Art 10(2) are wide and two, 'maintaining the authority of the judiciary' and 'preventing the disclosure of information received in confidence', are not mentioned in Art 10's companion Articles, Arts 8, 9 and 11. The first of these exceptions was included bearing in mind the contempt law of the UK, but it was made clear, in the well known *Sunday Times* case,[163] that in relation to such law, the margin of appreciation should be narrow due to its 'objective' nature. In other words, what was needed to maintain the authority of the judiciary could be more readily evaluated by an objective observer than could measures needed to protect morals.

A very different approach was taken in the *Handyside* case[164] arising from a conviction under the Obscene Publications Act 1959 and concerning the more subjective nature of the 'protection of morals' exception. The applicant put forward certain special circumstances—that the prohibited material in question was circulating in most other countries and so suppression could not be very evidently necessary in a democratic society—but such circumstances were barely discussed. A wide margin of appreciation was left to the national authorities as to what was 'necessary'. One possible reason for this was that the authority of the judiciary is a more objective notion than the protection of morals and this may have led to a variation of the necessity test. A similar approach was taken in *Müller v Switzerland*,[165] the Court stating: 'it is not possible to find in the legal and social orders of the Contracting States a uniform European conception of morals. By reason of their direct and continuous contact with the vital forces of their countries State authorities are in a better position than the international judge to give an opinion on the exact content of these requirements.'

However, *Vereinigung Bildender Kunstler v. Austria* (2007), No 68354/01 indicates that the Court may be prepared to take a stricter stance towards explicit expression. The case concerned extremely explicit paintings, satirizing various public figures, using blown up newspaper pictures of their faces. One of those thus depicted brought proceedings in copyright and obtained an injunction

---

161   *Matky v Czech Republic* 5th section 19101/03 (Unreported, 10 July 2006); see also the decision of the Human Rights Committee in *Gauthier v Canada* Communication no 633/195, UN doc CCPR/C/65/D/633/1995 (1999) .

162   It means merely that states may impose a licensing system outside the para 2 exceptions (see *Groppera Radio AG v Switzerland* (1990) 12 EHRR 321).

163   Judgment of 26 April 1979, A 30; (1979) 2 EHRR 245 (discussed in full in Chapter 18, pp 1049–1051).

164   Judgment of 7 December 1976, A 24; (1976) 1 EHRR 737. See further Chapter 18, pp 1077–1078.

165   (1991) 13 EHRR 212.

restraining the showing of the painting. On the application to Strasbourg, relying on Art 10, the Court was prepared to rely only on the 'rights of others' (a form of copyright claim) exception and not on the aim, the 'protection of morals'. This was interesting as the Government tried to rely on 'protection of morals' and the Court would not allow it to do so; this indicates some narrowing of the notion of 'protection of morals'. The case is also of interest since the applicant won—so to an extent it reverses the trend on artistic but explicit speech cases. At least it indicates that the Court may be prepared to narrow the margin of appreciation conceded in this context and so indicates a change in trend. However, its significance may be limited in that the Court took the view that the protection of morals was not involved, since domestic legal proceedings had been concerned solely with the copyright claim.

6. The Court has also considered the question of restricting expression where it offends against religious sensibilities. This was a key factor in the ruling in *Otto-Preminger Institut v Austria*.[166] The decision concerned the showing of a satirical film depicting God as a senile old man and Jesus as a mental defective erotically attracted to the Virgin Mary. Criminal proceedings for the offence of disparaging religious doctrines were brought against the manager of the Institute which had scheduled the showings of the film. The film was seized by the Austrian authorities while criminal proceedings were pending. The European Court of Human Rights found that the seizure of the film could be seen as furthering the aims of Art 9 of the Convention and therefore it fell within the 'rights of others' exception. In considering whether the seizure and forfeiture of the film was 'necessary in a democratic society' in order to protect the rights of others to respect for their religious views, the Court took into account the lack of a discernible common conception within the Member States of the significance of religion, and therefore considered that the national authorities should have a wide margin of appreciation in assessing what was necessary to protect religious feeling. In ordering the seizure of the film, the Austrian authorities had taken its artistic value into account, but had not found that it outweighed its offensive features. The Court found that the national authorities had not overstepped their margin of appreciation and therefore decided that no breach of Art 10 had occurred. This decision left a very wide discretion to the Member State, a discretion which the dissenting judges considered to be too wide.[167]

7. The stance taken in *Otto-Preminger* and in *Müller* echoes the view expressed in *Cossey v UK*[168] that where a clear European view does emerge, the Court may well be influenced by it, but it also suggests a particularly strong reluctance to intervene in this very contentious area. The margin of appreciation in respect of the protection of morals will not be unlimited, however, even in the absence of a broad consensus. The Court so held in *Open Door Counselling and Dublin Well Woman v Ireland*,[169] ruling that an injunction which prevented the dissemination of any informa-tion at all about abortion amounted to a breach of Art 10. This accords with the view expressed in *B v France*[170] that what can be termed the common standards principle is only one factor to be taken into account and must be weighed against the severity of the infringement of rights in question.

8. Actions in respect of both prior and subsequent restraints on freedom of expression may be brought under Art 10, but pre-publication sanctions will be regarded as more pernicious and thus

---

166   (1994) 19 EHRR 34.

167   See also *Wingrove v UK* (1997) 24 EHRR 1.

168   (1990) 13 EHRR 622.

169   (1992) 15 EHRR 244.

170   (1992) 13 HRLJ 358.

harder to justify as necessary (*Observer and Guardian v UK*).[171] In relation to post-publication sanctions, criminal actions will be regarded as having a grave impact on freedom of expression, but civil actions which have severe consequences for the individual may also be hard to justify. In *Tolstoy Miloslavsky v UK*,[172] the European Court of Human Rights considered the level of libel damages which can be awarded in UK courts. Libel damages of £1.5 m had been awarded against Count Tolstoy Miloslavsky in the UK in respect of a pamphlet he had written which alleged that Lord Aldington, a high ranking British army officer, had been responsible for handing over 70,000 people to the Soviet authorities without authorisation, knowing that they would meet a cruel fate. The Count argued that this very large award constituted a breach of Art 10. Was the award necessary in a democratic society as required by Art 10? The Court found that it was not, having regard to the fact that the scope of judicial control at the trial could not offer an adequate safeguard against a disproportionately large award. Thus, a violation of the applicant's rights under Art 10 was found.

The Strasbourg approach to Art 10 is discussed further in Chapter 18.

Article 11

Notes

1. Article 11 protects freedom of association and of assembly. The addition of the word 'peaceful' has restricted the scope of para 1: there will be no need to invoke the para 2 exceptions if the authorities concerned could reasonably believe that a planned assembly would not be peaceful. Thus, assemblies can be subject to permits so long as the permits relate to the peacefulness of the assembly and not to the right of assembly itself. However, a restriction of a very wide character relating to peacefulness might affect the right to assemble itself and might therefore constitute a violation of Art 11 if it did not fall within one of the exceptions.

2. It should be noted that freedom of assembly may not merely be secured by a lack of interference by the public authorities; they may have positive obligations to intervene in order to prevent an interference with freedom of assembly by private individuals, although they will have a very wide margin of appreciation in this regard.[173] It has been held in respect of the guarantees of other Articles that States must secure to individuals the rights and freedoms of the Convention by preventing or remedying any breach thereof. If no duty was placed on the authorities to provide such protection, then some assemblies could not take place.

   It will be argued in Chapter 19 that the freedom of assembly jurisprudence under Art 11 is cautious. In finding that applications are manifestly ill-founded, the Commission has been readily satisfied that decisions of the national authorities to adopt quite far reaching measures, including complete bans, in order to prevent disorder, are within their margin of appreciation.[174] The Court has also found 'the margin of appreciation extends in particular to the choice of the reasonable and appropriate means to be used by the authority to ensure that lawful manifestations can take place peacefully'.[175]

---

171   (1991) 14 EHRR 153.

172   (1995) 20 EHRR 422.

173   Appl 1012/82, *Plattform 'Ärzte für das Leben' v Austria* D & R 44 (1985); (1988) 13 EHRR 204 (it was not arguable that Austria had failed in its obligation to prevent counter-demonstrators interfering with an anti-abortion demonstration).

174   See *Christians against Racism and Fascism v UK* No 8440/78, 21 DR 138; *Friedl v Austria* No 15225/89 (1995) 21 EHRR 83.

175   *Chorherr v Austria* Series A 266-B, para 31 (1993).

3. The term 'association' need not be assigned its national meaning. Even if a group such as a trade union is not an 'association' according to the definition of national law, it may fall within Art 11. The term connotes a voluntary association, not a professional organisation established by the Government. It should be noted that it is only with respect to trade unions that the right to form an association is expressly mentioned, albeit non-exhaustively. Such a right in respect of other types of association is clearly implicit—a necessary part of freedom of association. The key rights protected by Art 11 include the basic right to form associations[176] and the right to autonomy of an association.[177] An association itself can exercise Convention rights, including freedom of expression (*Socialist Party and Others v Turkey*).[178]

4. The earlier Strasbourg jurisprudence tended to be protective of State interests,[179] but the more recent 'association' jurisprudence of the Court is more interventionist. In *Socialist Party and Others v Turkey*,[180] the Court allowed only a very narrow margin of appreciation in finding that the dissolution of the Socialist Party of Turkey had breached Art 11. The Court linked the three freedoms of expression, association and assembly together in finding that democracy demands that diverse political programmes should be debated, 'even those that call into question the way a State is currently organised'. The Court did not accept that the message of the group that a federal system should be put in place which would ensure that Kurds would be put on an equal footing with Turkish citizens generally, amounted to incitement to violence. The dissolution of the party was thus disproportionate to the aim in view—the preservation of national security. This stance is in accordance with the Convention jurisprudence, which has quite consistently recognised the need to protect the interests of minority and excluded groups.[181]

Similar findings were made in *Sidiropoulos v Greece*[182] in respect of an association formed to promote the interests of the Macedonian minority in Greece. The Court said that one of the most important aspects of freedom of association was that citizens should be able to form a legal group with the aim of acting collectively in their mutual interest. In *Vogt v Germany*[183] the Court held that a woman who was dismissed from her teaching post because of her membership of an extreme left wing group had suffered a violation of both Arts 10 and 11. These decisions suggest that where political associations are in question, the Court will take a strict stance, in accordance with its stance on political expression.[184] But these decisions may be contrasted with that in *Ahmed v UK*.[185] The applicants were local government officers who were active in local politics. Regulations were introduced with a view to ensuring local government impartiality; they restricted the political activities of certain categories of local government officers; thereupon the applicants had to resign

---

176   *X v Belgium* (1961) 4 YB 324.

177   *Cheall v UK* (1985) 8 EHRR 74.

178   Judgment of 25 May 1998, Appl No 20/1997/804/1007; (1999) 27 EHRR 51, paras 41, 47, 50.

179   See *Glasenapp v FRG* A 104 (1986); *Kosiek v FRG* A 105 (1986); *CCSU v UK* (1988) 10 EHRR 269.

180   Judgment of 25 May 1998 (App No 20/1997/804/1007); (1999) 27 EHRR 51, paras 41, 47, 50.

181   Such groups have included criminals: *Soering v UK* A 161 (1989); prisoners: *Ireland v UK* A 25 (1978), *Golder v UK* A 18 (1975); racial minorities: *East African Asians cases* (1973) 3 EHRR 76, *Hilton v UK* Appl No 5613/72, 4 DR 177 (1976) (no breach found on facts); sexual minorities: *Dudgeon v UK* A 45 (1982), *B v France* A 232-C (1992); political minorities: *Arrowsmith v UK* Appl No 7050/75, 19 DR 5 (1978); religious minorities: *Kokkinakis v Greece* A 260-A (1993).

182   No 57/1997/841/1047; 10 July 1998.

183   (1995) 21 EHRR 205.

184   See p 329, above.

185   (1998) 5 BHRC 111; [1999] IRLR 188.

from their political parties and cease canvassing for elections. The Court found that the interference with their Art 10 and 11 rights was proportionate to the aims in view since it was intended to ensure that the traditional political neutrality of council officers was maintained. Thus, unless a countervailing Convention value is also in issue, it may be assumed that political associations will receive particular protection.

ARTICLES 13–17, FIRST PROTOCOL; MARGIN OF APPRECIATION DOCTRINE

Article 14

Prohibition of discrimination

The enjoyment of the rights and freedoms set forth in this Convention shall be secured without discrimination on any ground such as sex, race, colour, language, religion, political or other opinion, national or social origin, association with a national minority, property, birth or other status.

Notes
1. Article 14 does not provide a general right to freedom from discrimination, only that the rights and freedoms of the Convention must be secured without discrimination. Thus, if discrimination occurs in an area which is *not* covered by the Convention, such as most contractual aspects of employment, Art 14 will be irrelevant. Thus, Art 14 remains of limited value since it is not free standing and does not cover social and economic matters lying outside the protected rights.
2. An applicant may allege violation of a substantive right taken alone and also that he or she has been discriminated against in respect of that right. However, even if no violation of the substantive right taken alone is found, and even if that claim is manifestly ill-founded, there could still be a violation of that Article and Art 14 taken together, so long as the matter at issue is covered by the other Article. This was found in *X v Federal Republic of Germany*:[186] 'Article 14 of the Convention has no independent existence; nevertheless, a measure which in itself is in conformity with the requirement of the Article enshrining the right or freedom in question, may however infringe this Article when read in conjunction with Article 14 for the reason that it is of a discriminatory nature.' In this sense, the Court has granted more autonomy to Art 14 than appeared to be intended originally.[187]

   This ruling allowed more claims to be considered than the 'arguability' principle applying under Art 13. For example, in *Abdulaziz, Cabales and Balkandali*,[188] the female claimants wanted their non-national spouses to enter the UK and alleged a breach of Art 8, which protects family life. That claim was rejected. But a violation of Art 14 was found because the way the rule was applied made it easier for men to bring in their spouses. It was held that: 'Although the application of Art 14 does not necessarily presuppose a breach [of the substantive provisions of the Convention and the Protocols]—and to this extent it is autonomous—there can be no room for its application unless the facts at issue fall within the ambit of one or more of the rights and freedoms.' In

---

186 Appl 4045/69 (1970) Yearbook XIII.

187 For comment on the increasing autonomy of Art 14, see S Livingstone, 'Article 14 and the Prevention of Discrimination in the ECHR' (1997) 1 EHRR 25.

188 A 94; (1985) 7 EHRR 471.

response to this ruling, the UK Government 'equalised down', placing men and women in an equally disadvantageous position as regards their non-national spouses.

3. Under Art 14, discrimination connotes differential treatment which is unjustifiable. The differential treatment may be unjustifiable, either in the sense that it relates to no objective and reasonable aim, or in the sense that there is no reasonable proportionality between the means employed and the aim sought to be realised.[189] In *Abdulaziz*, the aim was to protect the domestic labour market. It was held that this was not enough to justify the differential treatment because the difference in treatment was out of proportion to that aim. The outcome in this case illustrated the limitations of Art 14 which it shares with all anti-discrimination measures: it is concerned only with procedural fairness and can only ensure equal treatment which may be unjustifiable. Unjustifiable equal treatment is, however, unlikely to occur when the group in question is comparing itself with the dominant group since the dominant group will ensure, through the democratic process, that it does not experience a lower standard of treatment. However, where, as in *Abdulaziz*, the differentiation is occurring within a non-dominant group, the way is opened for equally poor treatment. This can be averted only by comparing the group as a whole with the dominant group. However, this argument was rejected by the European Court of Human Rights, which found that the treatment was not racially discriminatory.

4. Protocol 12 will eventually address the weaknesses of Art 14 since it provides a free-standing right to freedom from discrimination in relation to rights protected by law.[190] Thus it is not necessary to argue that another *Convention* right is engaged. The protection from discrimination under the Twelfth Protocol will eventually render Art 14 redundant. However, at present, the UK Government has not ratified it and it does not currently intend to do so on the basis that the Protocol contains unacceptable uncertainties. In particular, the Government views the potential application of the Protocol as too wide, since it covers any difference in treatment and applies to all 'rights set forth by law' in both statute and common law. The Labour Government considered that it could therefore lead to an 'explosion of litigation'. On its face this was a surprising position for a Labour Government apparently committed to anti-discrimination policies to take. It remains to be seen whether the Con-Lib government takes a different position.

Article 13

Right to an effective remedy

Everyone whose rights and freedoms as set forth in this Convention are violated shall have an effective remedy before a national authority notwithstanding that the violation has been committed by persons acting in an official capacity.

Note
Article 13 provides a right to an effective remedy for breach of another Convention right before a national authority. Even if no violation of the other Article is eventually found, it can still be argued that the national courts should have provided an effective means of considering the possible violation. In *Leander v Sweden* it was found that 'the requirements of Art 13 will be satisfied if there exists domestic machinery whereby, subject to the inherent limitations of the context, the individual can secure compliance with the relevant laws'.[191] This machinery may include a number of possible

---

189   *Geïllustreerde Pers NV v Netherlands* D & R 8 (1977).

190   For further discussion of Protocol 12, see G Moon (2000) 1 EHRLR 49.

191   (1987) 9 EHRR 433. Note that if such machinery exists, but is of doubtful efficacy, a challenge under Art 6(1) may be most likely to succeed (*de Geouffre de la Pradelle v France* (1993) HRLJ 276).

remedies. It has been held that judicial review proceedings will not be sufficient. In *Smith and Grady v UK*, the Court said of the concept of *Wednesbury* unreasonableness:

> . . .the threshold at which the. . . Court of Appeal could find the Ministry of Defence policy irrational was placed so high that it effectively excluded any consideration by the domestic courts of the question whether the interference with the applicants' rights answered a pressing social need or was proportionate to the national security and public order aims pursued, principles which lie at the heart of the Court's analysis of complaints under Art 8 of the Convention.'[192]

The margin of appreciation doctrine

Notes

1. As the discussion so far has mentioned, the state is allowed a 'margin of appreciation'—a degree of discretion—as to the measures needed to protect an interest which falls within one of the exception clauses. The doctrine of the margin of appreciation has a particular application with respect to para 2 of Arts 8–11, but it can affect all the guarantees. In different cases, a wider or narrower margin of appreciation has been allowed. A narrow margin may be allowed, in which case a very full and detailed review of the interference with the guarantee in question will be conducted. This occurred in *Sunday Times v UK*.[193] It was held that Strasbourg review was not limited to asking whether the state had exercised its discretion reasonably, carefully and in good faith; its conduct must also be examined in Strasbourg to see whether it was compatible with the Convention. If a broader margin is allowed, Strasbourg review will be highly circumscribed. For example, the minority in the *Sunday Times* case (nine judges) wanted to confine the role of Strasbourg to asking only whether the discretion in question was exercised in good faith and carefully, and whether the measure was reasonable in the circumstances.

2. It is quite hard to predict when each approach will be taken to the margin of appreciation doctrine, but it seems to depend on a number of factors. Some restrictions are seen as more subjective than others, such as the protection of morals. It is therefore thought more difficult to lay down a common European standard, and the Court and Commission have, in such instances, shown a certain willingness to allow the exceptions a wide scope in curtailing the primary rights. Some restrictions, particularly national security, fall more within the state's domain than others, and therefore the Strasbourg authorities may think that the state authorities are best placed to evaluate the situation and determine what is needed. In *Civil Service Unions v UK*,[194] the European Commission of Human Rights, in declaring the unions' application inadmissible, found that national security interests should prevail over freedom of association, even though the national security interest was weak, while the infringement of the primary right was very clear; an absolute ban on joining a trade union had been imposed. The margin of appreciation doctrine clearly has the power to undermine the Convention, and therefore its growth has been criticised.[195]

---

192 (2000) 29 EHRR 493 para 138.

193 (1979) 2 EHRR 245 (see further Chapter 18, pp 1049–51).

194 (1987) 10 EHRR 269.

195 See T Jones, 'The Devaluation of Human Rights under the European Convention' [1995] PL 430; P Mahoney, 'Marvellous Richness or Invidious Cultural Relativism?' (1998) 19 HRLJ 1. See also *Harris, O'Boyle and Warbrick* (2009), p 347 below, at 11–14.

Articles 15 and 17

Article 15 Derogation in time of emergency

1. In time of war or other public emergency threatening the life of the nation any High Contracting Party may take measures derogating from its obligations under this Convention to the extent strictly required by the exigencies of the situation, provided that such measures are not inconsistent with its other obligations under international law.
2. No derogation from Article 2, except in respect of deaths resulting from lawful acts of war, or from Articles 3, 4 (paragraph 1) and 7 shall be made under this provision.
3. Any High Contracting Party availing itself of this right of derogation shall keep the Secretary-General of the Council of Europe fully informed of the measures which it has taken and the reasons therefor. It shall also inform the Secretary-General of the Council of Europe when such measures have ceased to operate and the provisions of the Convention are again being fully executed.

Article 17 Prohibition of abuse of rights

Nothing in this Convention may be interpreted as implying for any State, group or person any right to engage in any activity or perform any act aimed at the destruction of any of the rights and freedoms set forth herein or at their limitation to a greater extent than is provided for in the Convention.

Notes

1. Further general restrictions on Convention rights are allowed under Arts 17, 15 and 64. Under Art 15(2), derogation is allowed in respect of most, but not all, of the rights. In order to derogate, the state in question must show that there is a state of war or public emergency, and in order to determine the validity of this claim two questions should be asked. First, is there an actual or imminent exceptional crisis threatening the organised life of the state? Second, is it really necessary to adopt measures requiring derogation from the Articles in question and do the measures go no further than the situation demands? A margin of discretion is allowed in answering these questions because it is thought that the state in question is best placed to determine the facts, but it is not unlimited; Strasbourg will review it if the State has acted unreasonably.
2. The UK entered a derogation in the case of *Brogan*[196] after the European Court of Human Rights had found that a violation of Art 5, which protects liberty, had occurred. At the time of the violation there was no derogation in force in respect of Art 5 because the UK had withdrawn its derogation. However, after the decision in the European Court, the UK entered the derogation, stating that there was an emergency at the time. This was challenged as an invalid derogation but the claim failed on the basis that the exigencies of the situation did amount to a public emergency,[197] and the derogation could not be called into question merely because the Government had decided to keep open the possibility of finding a means in the future of ensuring greater conformity with Convention obligations. The fact that the emergency measures had been in place since 1974 did not mean that the emergency was not still in being. That derogation formed part of the Human Rights Act 1998 (Sched 3, Part I), but the Act was amended once the derogation was withdrawn.
3. The Anti-Terrorism, Crime and Security Act 2001, introduced as a response to the 11 September

---

196   (1989) 11 EHRR 117.

197   *Brannigan and McBride v UK* (1994) 17 EHRR 539.

attacks in New York, contained provisions in Part 4 allowing for the indefinite detention without trial of non-British citizens subject to immigration controls suspected of international terrorism, with an initial appeal to the Special Immigration Appeals Tribunal (SIAC) set up under the Special Immigration Appeals Commission Act 1997. The Government considered that the new provisions would be incompatible with Art 5(1) of the Convention, which protects the right to liberty and security of the person, afforded further effect in domestic law under the Human Rights Act, and therefore entered a derogation to Art 5(1), under s 14 of the Human Rights Act[198] within the terms of Art 15 of the Convention. The Government made an Order under s 14, the Human Rights Act (Designated Derogation) Order 2001.[199] The Schedule to the Order stated that there was a domestic public emergency, which was especially present on the basis of the presence of foreign nationals in the UK who threatened its national security. On this basis, therefore, the Labour Government argued, the measures in Part 4 were clearly and strictly required by the very grave nature of the situation. The derogation was however found to be invalid by the House of Lords in *A and Others v Secretary of State for the Home Dept*[200] on the basis that the measure taken—indefinite detention without trial—was not necessary and proportionate, as Art 15 requires. See further on the House of Lord's decision, Chapter 3, pp 97–98, Chapter 17, p 970. As noted above, in February 2009, the European Court handed down a decision on this matter, dealing with a number of complaints of breaches of Articles of the Convention. Its finding in relation to the derogation itself was as follows. It is quoted at some length, as it sets out clearly the Court's general approach in this area.

A v United Kingdom (2009) 3455/05
Judgment of the Grand Chamber

173. The Court recalls that it falls to each Contracting State, with its responsibility for 'the life of [its] nation', to determine whether that life is threatened by a 'public emergency' and, if so, how far it is necessary to go in attempting to overcome the emergency. By reason of their direct and continuous contact with the pressing needs of the moment, the national authorities are in principle better placed than the international judge to decide both on the presence of such an emergency and on the nature and scope of the derogations necessary to avert it. Accordingly, in this matter a wide margin of appreciation should be left to the national authorities.

Nonetheless, Contracting Parties do not enjoy an unlimited discretion. It is for the Court to rule whether, *inter alia*, the States have gone beyond the 'extent strictly required by the exigencies' of the crisis. The domestic margin of appreciation is thus accompanied by a European supervision. In exercising this supervision, the Court must give appropriate weight to such relevant factors as the nature of the rights affected by the derogation and the circumstances leading to, and the duration of, the emergency situation. . .

174. . . .In the unusual circumstances of the present case, where the highest domestic court has examined the issues relating to the State's derogation and concluded that there was a public emergency threatening the life of the nation but that the measures taken in response were not strictly required by the exigencies of the situation, the Court considers that it would be justified in reaching a contrary conclusion only if satisfied that the national

---

198   Section 14(1)(b), (4) and (6) provide power for the Secretary of State to make a 'designation order', designating any derogation from an Article or Protocol to the Convention; it can be made in anticipation of the making of the proposed derogation.

199   SI 2001/3644. It was laid before Parliament on 12 November 2001, coming into effect on the following day. It designated the proposed derogation as one that was to have immediate effect.

200   [2005] 2 AC 68; [2005] 2 WLR 87; [2005] 3 All ER 169.

court had misinterpreted or misapplied Article 15 or the Court's jurisprudence under that Article or reached a conclusion which was manifestly unreasonable. . .

ii. Whether there was a 'public emergency threatening the life of the nation'

177. Before the domestic courts, the Secretary of State adduced evidence to show the existence of a threat of serious terrorist attacks planned against the United Kingdom. Additional closed evidence was adduced before SIAC. All the national judges accepted that the danger was credible (with the exception of Lord Hoffmann, who did not consider that it was of a nature to constitute 'a threat to the life of the nation'). Although when the derogation was made no al'Qaeda attack had taken place within the territory of the United Kingdom, the Court does not consider that the national authorities can be criticised, in the light of the evidence available to them at the time, for fearing that such an attack was 'imminent', in that an atrocity might be committed without warning at any time. The requirement of imminence cannot be interpreted so narrowly as to require a State to wait for disaster to strike before taking measures to deal with it. Moreover, the danger of a terrorist attack was, tragically, shown by the bombings and attempted bombings in London in July 2005 to have been very real. Since the purpose of Article 15 is to permit States to take derogating measures to protect their populations from future risks, the existence of the threat to the life of the nation must be assessed primarily with reference to those facts which were known at the time of the derogation. The Court is not precluded, however, from having regard to information which comes to light subsequently. . . .

178. While the United Nations Human Rights Committee has observed that measures derogating from the provisions of the ICCPR must be of 'an exceptional and temporary nature', the Court's case-law has never, to date, explicitly incorporated the requirement that the emergency be temporary, although the question of the proportionality of the response may be linked to the duration of the emergency. Indeed, the cases cited above, relating to the security situation in Northern Ireland, demonstrate that it is possible for a 'public emergency' within the meaning of Article 15 to continue for many years. The Court does not consider that derogating measures put in place in the immediate aftermath of the al'Qaeda attacks in the United States of America, and reviewed on an annual basis by Parliament, can be said to be invalid on the ground that they were not 'temporary'. . . .

180. As previously stated, the national authorities enjoy a wide margin of appreciation under Article 15 in assessing whether the life of their nation is threatened by a public emergency. While it is striking that the United Kingdom was the only Convention State to have lodged a derogation in response to the danger from al'Qaeda, although other States were also the subject of threats, the Court accepts that it was for each Government, as the guardian of their own people's safety, to make their own assessment on the basis of the facts known to them. Weight must, therefore, attach to the judgment of the United Kingdom's executive and Parliament on this question. In addition, significant weight must be accorded to the views of the national courts, who were better placed to assess the evidence relating to the existence of an emergency.

181. On this first question, the Court accordingly shares the view of the majority of the House of Lords that there was a public emergency threatening the life of the nation.

iii Whether the measures were strictly required by the exigencies of the situation
. . .

183. The Government contended, first, that the majority of the House of Lords should have afforded a much wider margin of appreciation to the executive and Parliament to

decide whether the applicants' detention was necessary. A similar argument was advanced before the House of Lords, where the Attorney General submitted that the assessment of what was needed to protect the public was a matter of political rather than judicial judgment.

184. When the Court comes to consider a derogation under Article 15, it allows the national authorities a wide margin of appreciation to decide on the nature and scope of the derogating measures necessary to avert the emergency. Nonetheless, it is ultimately for the Court to rule whether the measures were 'strictly required'. In particular, where a derogating measure encroaches upon a fundamental Convention right, such as the right to liberty, the Court must be satisfied that it was a genuine response to the emergency situation, that it was fully justified by the special circumstances of the emergency and that adequate safeguards were provided against abuse. . .The doctrine of the margin of appreciation has always been meant as a tool to define relations between the domestic authorities and the Court. It cannot have the same application to the relations between the organs of State at the domestic level. As the House of Lords held, the question of proportionality is ultimately a judicial decision, particularly in a case such as the present where the applicants were deprived of their fundamental right to liberty over a long period of time. In any event, having regard to the careful way in which the House of Lords approached the issues, it cannot be said that inadequate weight was given to the views of the executive or of Parliament.

185. The Government also submitted that the House of Lords erred in examining the legislation in the abstract rather than considering the applicants' concrete cases. However, in the Court's view, the approach under Article 15 is necessarily focussed on the general situation pertaining in the country concerned, in the sense that the court—whether national or international—is required to examine the measures that have been adopted in derogation of the Convention rights in question and to weigh them against the nature of the threat to the nation posed by the emergency. Where, as here, the measures are found to be disproportionate to that threat and to be discriminatory in their effect, there is no need to go further and examine their application in the concrete case of each applicant.

186. The Government's third ground of challenge to the House of Lords' decision was directed principally at the approach taken towards the comparison between non-national and national suspected terrorists. The Court, however, considers that the House of Lords was correct in holding that the impugned powers were not to be seen as immigration measures, where a distinction between nationals and non-nationals would be legitimate, but instead as concerned with national security. Part 4 of the 2001 Act was designed to avert a real and imminent threat of terrorist attack which, on the evidence, was posed by both nationals and non-nationals. The choice by the Government and Parliament of an immigration measure to address what was essentially a security issue had the result of failing adequately to address the problem, while imposing a disproportionate and discriminatory burden of indefinite detention on one group of suspected terrorists. As the House of Lords found, there was no significant difference in the potential adverse impact of detention without charge on a national or on a non-national who in practice could not leave the country because of fear of torture abroad. . . .

190. In conclusion, therefore, the Court, like the House of Lords, and contrary to the Government's contention, finds that the derogating measures were disproportionate in that they discriminated unjustifiably between nationals and non-nationals. It follows there has been a violation of Article 5 § 1 in respect of the first, third, fifth, sixth, seventh, eighth, ninth, tenth and eleventh applicants.

Notes (continued)

4. This is a highly significant decision by the Court. It indicates in particular that, where a national court finds against its Government on a Convention issue, the court will only make a contrary finding if convinced that the national court had misinterpreted the Convention or reached a conclusion that was 'manifestly unreasonable.' The practical significance of the judgment lay partly in the Art 6 implications it had for the control order scheme under the 2005 Prevention of Terrorism Act (above, pp 308–310) and partly in the award of damages it was able to make in favour of those detained under the now discredited 2001 provisions.

First Protocol

(1952) Cmnd 9221

Article 1 Protection of property

Every natural or legal person is entitled to the peaceful enjoyment of his possessions. No one shall be deprived of his possessions except in the public interest and subject to the conditions provided for by law and by the general principles of international law.

The preceding provisions shall not, however, in any way impair the right of a State to enforce such laws as it deems necessary to control the use of property in accordance with the general interest or to secure the payment of taxes or other contributions or penalties.

Article 2 Right to education

No person shall be denied the right to education. In the exercise of any functions which it assumes in relation to education and to teaching, the State shall respect the right of parents to ensure such education and teaching in conformity with their own religious and philosophical convictions.

Article 3 Right to free elections

The High Contracting Parties undertake to hold free elections at reasonable intervals by secret ballot, under conditions which will ensure the free expression of the opinion of the people in the choice of the legislature.

THE INSTITUTIONS FOR THE SUPERVISION OF THE CONVENTION AND THE RIGHT OF COMPLAINT

The European Commission of Human Rights and the European Court of Human Rights

Under Art 19 the Convention set up the European Commission of Human Rights and the European Court of Human Rights. This machinery for the enforcement of the Convention was impressive compared to that used in respect of other human rights treaties, particularly the 1966 International Covenant on Civil and Political Rights, which, as far as the UK is concerned, has been enforceable only through a system of assessment of national reports.[201]

---

201   The Optional Protocol to the Covenant governs the right of individual petition; but it has not been ratified by the UK. For comment on the general efficacy of the reporting system, see (1980) HRLJ 136–70.

The main role of the Commission, which has now been abolished, was to filter out applications as inadmissible, thereby reducing the workload of the Court. However, it also had another role; it tried to reach a friendly settlement between the parties and could give its opinion on the merits of the case if it was not intended that a final judgment should be given. It also referred the case to the Court or (occasionally) the Committee of Ministers for the final judgment. Creation of the Commission represented a compromise: when the Convention was drafted in 1949 it was thought too controversial merely to allow citizens to take their Governments before the Court. There was a feeling that a political body composed of government representatives might be more sympathetic to states' cases; the state might feel less on trial than in the Court. Therefore, the Commission was created as an administrative barrier between the individual and the Court and has been used as a means of filtering out a very high proportion of cases, thus considering far more cases than the Court.

The role of the Commission came under review for a number of reasons. It was barely able to deal with the number of applications it received, and as states which used to be part of the Soviet Union became signatories to the Convention, this problem was exacerbated. Moreover, although the notion of involvement of an administrative body in dealing with cases may have been acceptable in 1950, it arguably detracted from the authority of the Convention. The Parliamentary Assembly of the Council of Europe therefore recommended that the Commission should be abolished. The arrangements governing the control mechanism are contained in the Eleventh Protocol,[202] which has had a radical effect on the Convention procedure. Its most significant reform was to set up the single Court of Human Rights[203] which now sits full time in place of the Court and Commission (under Art 19); thus, the functions of the two were merged. Once the Court and Commission merged, it is arguable that the authority of the Convention increased because its jurisprudence was no longer be influenced by the decisions of an administrative body; the control system has become, in this respect, more akin to that of a domestic legal system. But although the Commission has been abolished, it has had a considerable influence on the Strasbourg jurisprudence.

In general, the European Court of Human Rights has increased enormously in standing and efficacy over the last 30 years, partly due to its activism and creativity in interpreting the Convention[204] and its willingness to find that Member States have violated the rights of individuals. It has already brought about a number of important reforms in human rights matters in the UK.[205]

The right of complaint: individual applications

Article 34, widely viewed as the most important Article in the Convention since it governs the right of individual complaint, enables citizens of Member States to seek a remedy for a breach of Convention rights by petitioning the European Court. The right of complaint was not intended to mimic the working of a domestic legal system. The Court hears very few cases in comparison with the number of applications made.[206] The route to Strasbourg is lengthy and discourages applicants from using it. It is still a slow and cumbersome route owing to the number of applications, despite improvements in the

---

202   For comment, see A Mowbray [1993] PL 419.

203   See 'Reform of the control systems' (1993) 15 EHRR 321.

204   For discussion of the role of the Court in interpreting the Convention, see *Harris, O'Boyle and Warbrick* (2009), p 347 below, at chap 1.4.

205   See DJ Harris, M O'Boyle and C Warbrick, *Law of the European Convention on Human Rights* (1995), p 648.

206   In 1991, the Commission registered 1,648 applications; it referred 93 cases to the Court, which gave judgment in 72: European Court of Human Rights, Survey of Activities 1959–91. Currently, around 4% of cases are found admissible; see p 297, above.

mechanisms for considering them.[207] The fact that an application may take, at present, five years or more to be heard is perhaps one of the main deficiencies of the Convention enforcement machinery.[208]

Section II of the Convention

European Court of Human Rights
Article 27
Committees, Chambers and Grand Chamber

1   To consider cases brought before it, the Court shall sit in committees of three judges, in Chambers of seven judges and in a Grand Chamber of 17 judges. The Court's Chambers shall set up committees for a fixed period of time.

. . .

Article 28
Declarations of inadmissibility by committees

A committee may, by a unanimous vote, declare inadmissible or strike out of its list of cases an individual application submitted under Article 34 where such a decision can be taken without further examination. The decision shall be final.

Article 29
Decisions by Chambers on admissibility and merits

1   If no decision is taken under Article 28, a Chamber shall decide on the admissibility and merits of individual applications submitted under Article 34.

. . .

Article 30
Relinquishment of jurisdiction to the Grand Chamber

Where a case pending before a Chamber raises a serious question affecting the interpretation of the Convention or the protocols thereto or where the resolution of a question before it might have a result inconsistent with a judgment previously delivered by the Court, the Chamber may, at any time before it has rendered its judgment, relinquish jurisdiction in favour of the Grand Chamber, unless one of the parties to the case objects.

Article 31
Powers of the Grand Chamber

The Grand Chamber shall

(a) determine applications submitted either under Article 33 or Article 34 when a Chamber has relinquished jurisdiction under Article 30 or when the case has been referred to it under Article 43; and

(b) consider requests for advisory opinions submitted under Article 47.

---

207   Apart from the Prot. 11 reforms, new procedures were introduced under the Eighth Protocol, including a summary procedure for rejecting straightforward cases.

208   The average time was a little over four years in the early 1990s: see 'Reform of the control systems', n 203 above, at 360, para 7. See further above, as to the current position, regarding the case-load, p 297.

Article 32
Jurisdiction of the Court

1   The jurisdiction of the Court shall extend to all matters concerning the interpret-
         ation and application of the Convention and the protocols thereto which are referred
         to it as provided in Articles 33, 34 and 47.

2   In the event of dispute as to whether the Court has jurisdiction, the Court shall
         decide. . . .

Article 34
Individual applications

The Court may receive applications from any person, non-governmental organisation
or group of individuals claiming to be the victim of a violation by one of the High Contracting Parties of the rights set forth in the Convention or the protocols thereto. The
High Contracting Parties undertake not to hinder in any way the effective exercise of this
right.

Article 35
Admissibility criteria

1   The Court may only deal with the matter after all domestic remedies have been
         exhausted, according to the generally recognised rules of international law, and
         within a period of six months from the date on which the final decision was taken.

2   The Court shall not deal with any individual application submitted under Article 34
         that

         (a)   is anonymous; or
         (b)   is substantially the same as a matter that has already been examined by the
                Court or has already been submitted to another procedure of international
                investigation or settlement and contains no relevant new information.

3   The Court shall declare inadmissible any individual application submitted under
         Article 34 which it considers incompatible with the provisions of the Convention or
         the protocols thereto, manifestly ill-founded, or an abuse of the right of application.

4   The Court shall reject any application which it considers inadmissible under this
         Article. It may do so at any stage of the proceedings.

Article 36
Third party intervention

1   In all cases before a Chamber or the Grand Chamber, a High Contracting Party
         one of whose nationals is an applicant shall have the right to submit written
         comments and to take part in hearings.

. . .

Article 38 [which replaced Article 28]
Examination of the case and friendly settlement proceedings

1   If the Court declares the application admissible, it shall

(a)   pursue the examination of the case, together with the representatives of the parties, and if need be, undertake an investigation, for the effective conduct of which the States concerned shall furnish all necessary facilities;

(b)   place itself at the disposal of the parties concerned with a view to securing a friendly settlement of the matter on the basis of respect for human rights as defined in the Convention and the protocols thereto.

2   Proceedings conducted under paragraph 1.b shall be confidential.

Article 40
Public hearings

. . . Hearings shall be public unless the Court in exceptional circumstances decides otherwise.

Article 41
Just satisfaction

If the Court finds that there has been a violation of the Convention or the protocols thereto, and if the internal law of the High Contracting Party concerned allows only partial reparation to be made, the Court shall, if necessary, afford just satisfaction to the injured party.

. . .

Article 43
Referral to the Grand Chamber

1   Within a period of three months from the date of the judgment of the Chamber, any party to the case may, in exceptional cases, request that the case be referred to the Grand Chamber.

2   A panel of five judges of the Grand Chamber shall accept the request if the case raises a serious question affecting the interpretation or application of the Convention or the protocols thereto, or a serious issue of general importance.

3   If the panel accepts the request, the Grand Chamber shall decide the case by means of a judgment.

Article 46
Binding force and execution of judgments

1   The High Contracting Parties undertake to abide by the final judgment of the Court in any case to which they are parties.

2   The final judgment of the Court shall be transmitted to the Committee of Ministers, which shall supervise its execution.

Notes

1. The requirement that domestic remedies must have been exhausted refers to the 'legal remedies available under the local law which are in principle capable of providing an effective and sufficient means of redressing the wrongs for which [the respondent state is said to be responsible]'.[209] If there is a doubt as to whether a remedy is available, Art 35 (previously Art 26) will not be satisfied unless the applicant has taken proceedings in which that doubt can be resolved.[210] This generally

---

209   *Nielsen v Denmark* Application No 343/57, (1958–59) 2 YB 412.

210   *De Vargattirgah v France* Application No 9559/81.

means that judicial procedures must be instituted up to the highest court which can affect the decision but also, if applicable, appeal must be made to administrative bodies.

2. An application is found to be manifestly ill-founded if the facts obviously fail to disclose a violation. In the past, when the Commission decided on this matter, the ill-founded character of the application was not always as manifest as this would imply. Under the current arrangements, it is necessary to have unanimity if a committee declares the application inadmissible (r 53(3) of the Rules of the Court), but a majority if a Chamber of the Court does so. Although it is more satisfactory that the decision is being taken judicially, it is arguable that it should have been necessary to have unanimity or a two-thirds majority as to a finding of manifest ill-foundedness by a Chamber, even though a bare majority suffices in respect of the other conditions.

3. The proceedings before the Chamber of seven judges consist of a written stage, followed by a hearing.[211] Chambers designate Judge Rapporteurs to examine applications. The arrangements are characterised by their flexibility: within the Rules, the Court is free to decide on a procedure which can be tailored to the nature of a particular application (see r 42(2)) and this may include visiting a particular place, such as a prison. An on-the-spot inquiry can be conducted by a delegate of the Court. The Court can also order a report from an expert on any matter. After this initial stage, the Chamber will normally conduct an oral hearing if there has been no oral admissibility hearing.

4. The Court is not bound by its own judgments (r 51, para 1). Nevertheless, it usually follows and applies its own precedents unless departure from them is indicated in order to ensure that interpretation of the Convention reflects social change. Under Art 46, the judgment of the Court is binding on the State Party involved. The Court is not ultimately a coercive body and relies for acceptance of its judgments on the willingness of states to abide by the Convention. The Court can award compensation under Art 41. The purpose of the reparation is to place the applicant in the position he or she would have been in had the violation not taken place. It will include costs unless the applicant has received legal aid. It can also include loss of earnings, travel costs, fines and costs unjustly awarded against the applicant. It can also include intangible or non-pecuniary losses which may be awarded due to unjust imprisonment or stress.[212] There is, in effect, a right of appeal in exceptional cases to the Grand Chamber, under Art 43.

5. *Protocol 14 reforms.* Protocol 14 follows on from Protocol 11 in introducing changes designed to improve the efficiency of operation of the Court. The volume of cases remains a huge problem and the Courts' case load is unacceptably high, resulting in long back-logs and the possibility of the whole system collapsing under sheer weight of numbers (above, pp 296–297).

Now that Protocol 14 is in force (it came into force in 2009 once it was ratified by Russia) it changes para 3 of Art 35 so that it reads:

> The Court shall declare inadmissible any individual application submitted under Article 34 if it considers that:
>
> a. the application is incompatible with the provisions of the Convention or the Protocols thereto, manifestly ill-founded, or an abuse of the right of individual application; *or*
> b. the applicant has not suffered a significant disadvantage, unless respect for human rights as defined in the Convention and the Protocols thereto requires an

---

211 Under Art 55, the Court shall draw up its own rules and determine its own procedure.

212 E.g. in *Young, James and Webster v United Kingdom* (1981) 4 EHRR 38, pecuniary and non-pecuniary costs were awarded: the Court ordered £65,000 to be paid. See further Part VI Chapter 17, pp 992–4.

examination of the application on the merits and provided that no case may be rejected on this ground which has not been duly considered by a domestic tribunal.

Under Protocol 14, cases will be 'filtered' out that have less chance of succeeding as will those that are broadly similar to cases brought previously against the same Member State. Moreover, a case will not be considered admissible where an applicant has not suffered a 'significant disadvantage'. The UK Joint Committee on Human Rights broadly welcomed the contents of Protocol 14, since it considered that it included many positive aspects which should improve the functioning of the control system of the Convention. But it found that the introduction of a new requirement that an applicant to the European Court of Human Rights must have suffered a 'significant disadvantage', was 'very controversial' because it restricts the right of individual petition.[213]

Significantly, a new mechanism is introduced with Protocol 14 to assist enforcement of judgments by the Committee of Ministers. Under it, the Committee can ask the Court for an interpretation of a judgment and can even bring a Member State before the Court for non-compliance of a previous judgment against that state. Thus adverse judgments against Member States will have a higher chance of being implemented. Protocol 14 also amends Art 59 of the Convention, allowing for the European Union to accede to it.

6. The Committee of Ministers consists of one representative from the Government of each Member State of the Council of Europe, usually the Minister for Foreign Affairs. Under Art 46, the Committee is charged with supervising the execution of the Court's judgment. If the state fails to execute the judgment, the Committee decides what measures to take: it can bring political pressure to bear, including suspension or even, as a final sanction, expulsion from the Council of Europe. However, doubts have been raised over the fitness of the Committee to oversee one of the key stages in the whole Convention process, namely the implementation of national law to bring it into line with the findings of the Court.

FURTHER READING

D Harris, M O'Boyle and C Warbrick, *Law of the European Convention on Human Rights* (1995); 2nd edn (2009) D Harris, M O'Boyle, E Bates, C Buckley

M Janis, R Kay and A Bradley, *European Human Rights Law, Texts and Materials,* 3rd edn (2008)

C Ovey and R White, *Jacobs and White European Convention on Human Rights,* 4th edn (2006)

AR Mowbray, *Cases and Materials on the European Convention on Human Rights* 2nd edn (2007)

R Clayton and H Tomlinson, *The Law of Human Rights,* 2nd edn (2006); 3rd edn (2009)

H Fenwick, *Civil Liberties and Human Rights,* 4th edn (2007), Chapter 2

S Greer, *The European Convention on Human Rights: Achievements, Problems and Prospects* (2006)

E Bates, *The Evolution of the European Convention on Human Rights from its Inception to the Creation of a Permanent Court of Human Rights* (2009)

D Feldman, *Civil Liberties and Human Rights,* 2nd edn (2002), Chapter 2

P Van Dijk and F Van Hoof, *Theory and Practice of the European Convention on Human Rights,* 3rd edn (1998)

M O'Boyle 'On reforming the operation of the European Court of Human Rights' (2008) EHRLR 1

O De Shutter *International Human Rights Law* (2010)

Reports of cases are available from the Court's website, www.dhcour.coe.fr.

---

213   1st Report Session, 2004–5.

CHAPTER 8
THE COMMONS: ELECTIONS, PARTIES, LEGISLATION AND SCRUTINY[1]

---

1   General reading for this part may be found at the end of this chapter.

INTRODUCTION

This chapter considers the role of the House of Commons in the UK constitution in relation to the legislative process and, importantly, scrutiny of the executive. Its emphasis will be on the constitutional relationship between the Commons and Government, on the functions Parliament can realistically be attempted to perform, the extent of its domination by government and an evaluation of its work. Recent reforms and proposals for further reform will also be considered, particularly those made in the aftermath of the 2009 MPs expenses scandal. Since the Commons is also the principal democratic forum of the UK, from which governments are formed, and which ultimately holds the key to their continued existence, this chapter also considers the effect of the electoral system which plays such an important part in determining the make-up and behaviour of both Commons and government and the vital role of political parties, not least in subverting the traditional, constitutional relationship between MPs and Government. Because of the vast range and scale of changes elsewhere in the UK constitution which this book must cover, and the fact that there is currently little realistic prospect of reform to the UK Parliament's electoral system, this chapter does not consider alternatives to the 'first past the post' electoral system used in the UK for elections to the Westminster Parliament in detail.

THE ELECTORAL SYSTEM[2]

What then is that system, how does it work in practice, and what are some of the alternatives to it?

**G Ganz, *Understanding Public Law*, 3rd edn (2001),
pp 4–8 (updated by the authors)**

Historically the electoral system is based on the representation of communities. This is still reflected in the qualification for voting and the method of voting. Everyone who is 18, a Commonwealth citizen (who is legally in the UK) or a citizen of [Ireland], not a peer who is entitled to sit in the House of Lords and not serving a sentence of imprisonment or held in a mental institution as a consequence of criminal activity is entitled to be placed on the electoral register in a constituency where he is resident. Residence does not now involve a qualifying period or residence on a particular date (formerly October 10). . .

Those who cannot satisfy the residence qualification may be entitled to be registered in a constituency where they were resident, e.g. if they are absent because they are members of the armed forces or British citizens living abroad who have been registered there within the preceding 20 years (Representation of the People Act 1989). In such cases entitlement to vote is based on citizenship rather than residence to which lip-service is paid through registration in the constituency where the citizen was previously resident. Such a notional residence is essential as all voters must be on an electoral roll in a constituency.

The constituency is the linchpin of our electoral system. Its origin lies in the representation of communities which is still an important part of an MP's work. There is, however, a constant tension between this concept of representation and the modern party system which affects so many facets of our representative democracy. It manifests itself at the

---

2   For a recent, detailed study, see B Watt, *UK Election Law: A Critical Examination* (2006). See also D Butler, 'Electoral Reform' (2004) 57(4) Parlt Aff 734.

outset when the constituency boundaries are drawn. These [have been] reviewed every eight to twelve years by four politically impartial Boundary Commissions, one for each part of the United Kingdom [but, from 2006, their functions in this respect were] taken over. . .by the Electoral Commission set up under the Political Parties, Elections and Referendums Act 2000. [The four impartial Boundary Committees established by the Electoral Commission must exercise their powers so as to] create constituencies as near as possible to the electoral quota which is obtained by dividing the electorate of that part of the United Kingdom by the number of constituencies in it without crossing county or London borough boundaries (unless there are exceptional circumstances) and taking into account local ties. The number of seats has increased with each review [until recently] and is now [650], but the changes in population are not evenly spread throughout the country. This has profound implications for the political parties but political considerations cannot be taken into account by the Commissions and, therefore, political arguments are put to them cloaked in arguments about local ties (Home Affairs Committee Report, HC 97 (1986–87), p 80). Not surprisingly nearly every review since 1945 has given rise to political controversy. In 1969 the Labour government refused to implement the Boundary Commissions' recommendations and in 1983 unsuccessfully challenged them in Court (*R v Boundary Commission for England ex parte Foot,* 1983).

The crucial importance of constituency boundaries to the outcome of elections is the result of our electoral system, called first past the post, under which an MP is elected for a constituency if he receives one vote more than his nearest rival however small his percentage of the total vote. This not only enables MPs to be elected on a minority vote (312 MPs in 1997) but on two occasions since the war (1951 and February 1974) the party gaining most seats polled fewer votes than the main opposition party. Most disadvantaged by our electoral system are the Liberal Democrats, whose support is fairly evenly spread throughout the country and who come second in a large number of seats but only win a handful of seats where their support is concentrated. In 1997 they gained 46 seats for 17 per cent of the vote, whilst Labour gained 418 seats for 43 per cent and the Conservatives 165 seats with 31 per cent of the vote. It is this glaring discrepancy between seats and votes since the revival of the Liberal party in 1974 which has fuelled the pressure for electoral reform. The result of the 2001 election has left this situation virtually unchanged. [For detailed figures see below.]

As these figures illustrate, the system can also be unfair to the major parties. Labour obtained over 60 per cent of the seats with 43 per cent of the vote whilst the Conservatives gained 25 per cent of the seats with 31 per cent of the vote. Even more startling is that Labour polled fewer votes in 1997 (13.5 million) than the Conservatives in 1992 (14 million) and achieved an overall majority of 179 seats, whereas the Conservatives only managed a majority of 21 in 1992. There were several reasons for this. The turnout of voters was much lower in 1997 (only 71.5 per cent against 77.7 per cent in 1992) and some of the lowest polls were in Labour seats. Liberal Democrat voters switched to Labour in greater numbers than to Conservatives. Most importantly the election was won in approximately 100 seats where the lowest swing of votes was needed to win the seat. By targeting these seats Labour achieved better than average results where they counted most. Election campaigns have, therefore, become highly professional operations focused on a narrow band of voters, who are canvassed and cajoled, often at the expense of the party's traditional supporters. The 2001 election with a record low turnout of 59 per cent confirmed these trends.

The concentration on these marginal seats highlights the importance of constituency boundaries and their review by the Boundary [Committees]. These reviews have to reflect the movement of population from the North to the South and out of the cities to the rural hinterland. . .

In fulfilment of a pre-election agreement with the Liberal Democrats, which was embodied in its manifesto, Labour set up a Commission under the chairmanship of Lord Jenkins, a leading Liberal Democrat peer and former Labour Minister, to recommend the best alternative system to the existing system of voting. They thus became the first government elected triumphantly under the present system to set in train the process of reform. Whether the choice between the existing system and an alternative system is put to the electorate in a referendum after the 2001 election remains to be seen.

The fairness of an electoral system must be judged not only by the proportionality of votes to seats but by the proportionality of power. If seats had been allocated in proportion to votes in Britain, the third party (now the Liberal Democrats) would have held the balance of power since 1974, as its counterpart did in Germany for 30 years. This gives disproportionate power to a minority party. The Jenkins Commission was asked to take into account both proportionality of votes and stable government (which is not the hall-mark of coalitions) as well as the link between an MP and a geographical constituency.

The Commission in its report (Cm 4090, 1998) rejected the Alternative Vote which retains single member constituencies but where voters list candidates in order of preference and which ensures that an MP is elected by more than 50 per cent of the votes including second-preference votes. One of its main reasons was that it would have disadvantaged the Conservatives in 1997 disproportionately because of the strength of the anti-Conservative vote. It also rejected the Single Transferable Vote, where votes are cast for candidates in order of preference in multi-member constituencies and seats are allocated according to a complicated formula, partly because of its complexity. It came down in favour of a version of the Additional Member System used in Germany, where a proportion of MPs are elected in single member constituencies and these are then topped-up by MPs elected from a party list so as to achieve proportionality—each voter having two votes, one for a constituency MP and one for the party. The constituency MP would be elected by the Alternative Vote system. For the top-up MPs Britain would be divided into 80 areas returning one or two MPs so as to provide between 15 per cent and 20 per cent of MPs. The Commission calculated that this degree of proportionality would have produced single party majority governments in three out of the last four elections and a hung Parliament, where no party has a majority only in 1992. The Liberal Democrat party would be the main beneficiary of the change by receiving a more proportional share of seats. The boundary changes necessitated by these recommendations made it impossible for it to come into effect at the next election regardless of when the referendum was held.

Notes

1. For further detail on the law and practice of boundary changes, see C Turpin and A Tomkins, *British Government and the Constitution*, 6th edn (2007) at 497–506. The points made above as to the dramatic lack of correspondence between percentage of votes won and percentage of Commons seats won under the first past the post system may be illustrated by looking at the results from the three general elections of 1997, 2001 and 2005.

1997 General Election (71.5% turnout).

Party	% of total votes	Seats won	% of total seats (659)
Conservative	30.7	165	25.03%
Labour	43.2	418	63.43%
Liberal Democrats	16.8	46	6.98%
Nationalists	2.5	10	1.52%
Others	6.8	20	3.03%

2001 General Election (59.4% turnout).

Party	% of total votes	Seats won	% of total seats (659)
Conservative	31.7	166	25.18%
Labour	40.7	412	62.51%
Liberal Democrats	18.3	52	7.89%
Nationalists	2.5	9	1.36%
Others	6.8	20	3.03%

2005 General Election (61.3% turnout).

Party	% of total votes	Seats won	% of total seats (659)
Conservative	32.3	197	30.5%
Labour	35.2	356	55.10%
Liberal Democrats	22.1	62	9.04%
Nationalists	2.2	9	1.39%
Others	8.2	22	3.41%

[Figures adapted from Turpin and Tomkins, *British Government and the Constitution*, 6th edn (2007) at 516–17.]

2. It is particularly striking that, in the 2005 General Election, Labour achieved only 2.9% more of the popular vote than the Conservatives—35.2% compared to 32.3% —but obtained a whopping 25% more of the seats. Given the turnout of 61.3%, this meant that only around one fifth of the population actually voted for the party that then governed them for five years. This was indeed the lowest share of the popular vote ever obtained by a government. Meanwhile, the gross unfairness of the system to the third party, the Liberal Democrats, discussed above, is immediately apparent: on each occasion the party's percentage of seats was less than half its percentage of the vote. In 1992, it was even worse, as the party obtained nearly 18% of the total vote but only 3% of the seats (20). At the level of individual MPs, many are also unrepresentative of their constituents: most MPs are elected on considerably less than 50% of the popular vote—they simply have more than any other one candidate.

3. Moreover, as the following table shows,[3] the distribution of seats currently strongly favours the Labour party, making it difficult for the Conservatives to gain an overall majority:

2. Outcomes at the next election

Con (%)	Lab (%)	Con MP's	Lab MP's	Other MP's	Majority
35	35	234	330	86	Lab +4
36	34	252	305	93	Lab −21
37	33	269	292	89	Lab −34
38	32	287	274	87	Con −39
39	31	302	261	87	Con −24
40	30	319	245	86	Con −7
41	29	336	231	83	Con +10

Kalitowki comments:

> While the electoral system currently favours Labour, boundary changes in 2007 have reduced its majority by around a half, giving the party only between 30 and 40 seats more than the other parties rather than the 64 seats they enjoy at the moment. Thus, even a small swing against the incumbent party to the opposition would see Labour's overall majority disappear. Yet, while it may be relatively easy for the Conservatives to deprive Labour of their majority, it will be more difficult for them to secure an overall majority, as they would need to win over 42 per cent of the popular vote. This is no easy feat, considering that Labour clearly won the last election with only 35.3% of the vote.[4]

4. Below, Bogdanor considers the variety of electoral systems now used in the UK following devolution (see further, Chapter 7) and the pressure this creates for reform of the electoral system used for Westminster.

V Bogdanor, 'Our New Constitution' (2004) Law Quarterly Review 242 (extracts)

[As a result of the various devolution settlements] It has now come to be accepted that elections to any body other than the House of Commons or a local authority should be by proportional representation.

This is a quite unexpected development. Until the 1970s, it was generally assumed that the plurality or 'first past the post' electoral system was the natural one for Britain to use. Opposition to it was confined almost wholly to the Liberal Party and the arguments of Liberals were generally dismissed as special pleading. . . .By the end of the century, however, there were no less than four electoral systems in operation in Britain in addition to the first past the post system. They were:

---

3   Taken from S Kalitowski, 'Hung-up over Nothing? The Impact of a Hung Parliament on British Politics' (2008) 61(2) Parlt Aff 396, 398.

4   *Ibid.*

1   The single transferable vote method of proportional representation used in all elec-
    tions in Northern Ireland, except elections to the House of Commons. This is also the
    electoral system used in all elections in the Irish Republic.

2   A system of proportional representation based on the German method, used for
    elections to the Scottish Parliament, the National Assembly of Wales and the London
    strategic authority.

3   The regional list method of proportional representation used for elections to the
    European Parliament.

4   The supplementary vote used in elections for the mayor of London.

At the beginning of the 20th century, Britain enjoyed a uniform electoral system, the
plurality or the first past the post system, but a diversified franchise, there being no less
than seven different ways in which a man could qualify for the vote. By the end of the 20th
century, in contrast, the qualification for the franchise was uniform, but there were a wide
variety of electoral systems. Indeed, an elector in London could use four different electoral
systems. In voting for a Member of Parliament, he or she would use first past the post;
in voting for a Mayor of London, he or she would use the supplementary vote; in voting
for the London strategic authority, he or she would use a variant of the German system
of proportional representation; and in voting for Europe, he or she would use regional list
proportional representation.

Notes

1. 'Hung Parliaments', in which no one party has an overall majority, requiring either a minority
    Government or a coalition, by necessity produce a different kind of politics, in which a greater
    degree of accommodation between the political parties is often required. For analysis see S Kali-
    towski, 'Hung-up over Nothing? The Impact of a Hung Parliament on British Politics' (2008)
    61(2) *Parliamentary Affairs* 396.

2. At the time of writing, reform to the electoral system of Westminster seems to be unlikely, with
    the probable winners of the next election, the Conservative Party, remaining opposed. Labour has
    now promised a referendum on introducing the Alternative Vote system, which is not, strictly, a
    form of PR,[5] if re-elected, while the Liberal Democrats remain firmly in favour of radical reform.
    Thus reform would be most likely if the Labour Party loses its overall majority and needs to form
    a coalition with the Liberal Democrats, or possibly if it is returned with a very small majority,
    such that it needs Liberal Democrat support in order to secure the passage of at least some of its
    legislation.

3. The workings and effect of the electoral system, as described above, are crucial to the work of the
    Commons: the basic fact of the Commons is that the government will normally have a majority of
    its own party in the House; hence the struggle of Parliament against the executive tends to play very
    much second fiddle to the struggle between the parties.

4. The role of the Opposition receives some recognition in the constitution. The Leader of Her
    Majesty's Opposition (invariably the Leader of either the Conservative or Labour Parties) is paid a

---

5   Clauses to guarantee this were included in the Constitutional Reform and Governance Bill 2009 but dropped in the 'wash up' before the Bill
    became the 2010 Act.

salary and public funding, known as 'Short money', assists the Opposition in its task.[6] As Ganz notes,[7] in debate, the Speaker must call for contributions alternately from the Opposition parties and the Government, while the membership of parliamentary committees is proportionate to party strengths. It remains rare for Independents to be elected to the House, although there have been four since 1997, when Martin Bell, an 'anti-sleaze' candidate, beat Neil Hamilton in a previously rock-solid Conservative seat.[8] For a historical overview of the importance of political parties within the UK Constitution, see V Bogdanor, 'The Constitution and the Party System in the Twentieth Century' (2004) 57(4) *Parliamentary Affairs* 717. For the detailed rules that govern the conduct of political parties, including election spending, party political broadcasts and the financing and registration of parties, including rules laid down by the Political Parties, Elections and Referendums Act 2000, see Turpin and Tomkins (above at 351) at 507–14, and 539–46. Changes to the rules governing donations to parties and expenditure on campaigning by parliamentary candidates have also been made by the Political Parties and Elections Act 2009.

5. Philip Norton has summarised the four main changes to Parliament generally since the early 1970s as: increased independence (of backbench MPs); greater professionalism (that is, more MPs are now career politicians); increased specialisation (the introduction of permanent Select Committees has given MPs the opportunity to build up expertise in particular areas); and greater accessibility (both greater visibility, through broadcasting of the Commons' proceedings, and a more active relationship between MPs and the public and pressure groups).[9]

6. One recent change to the Commons worthy of note is the setting up of Westminster Hall, which functions as a parallel but subordinate chamber to the Commons. The report below recommending its establishment also notes some of the pressures and problems the current Commons labours under. The establishment of Westminster Hall was recommended in the *Second Report of the Select Committee on Modernisation of the House of Commons*, HC 194 (1998–99) and was approved by the House on 24 May 1999. Sittings in Westminster Hall began on Tuesday 30 November 1999. After the experiment had been running for some time, the Committee found that 'Westminster Hall has provided valuable additional opportunities for both private Members and select committees. . .[and that] the business taken in Westminster Hall has been additional business which would otherwise not have taken place at all.'[10] The Committee also made a number of recommendations including increasing the proportion of time available for debate of Select Committee reports, seen as one of the most important and well-attended types of debate carried out by Westminster Hall. The issue of debating Select Committee reports is returned to below. The Westminster Hall experiment is now firmly established.

---

6   See HC Deb col 1869 (20 March 1975), and col 427 (26 May 1999).

7   G Ganz, *Understanding Public Law,* 3rd edn (2001), at p 30.

8   For discussion of the role and work of independent MPs in the Commons, see P Cowley and M Stuart, ' There was a Doctor, a Journalist and Two Welshmen: the Voting Behaviour of Independent MPs in the United Kingdom House of Commons, 1997–2007' (2009) 62(1) Parlt Aff 19–31.

9   P Norton, 'Parliament's changing role', in Pyper and Robins, *Governing the UK in the 1990s* (1995) above, esp. at 85–95.

10   Fourth Report, HC 906 (1999–2000) paras 24 and 25.

THE COMMONS: APPROVAL OF LEGISLATION

The role of the Commons in relation to executive policy

The doctrine of the separation of powers, which demanded that a body separate from the executive be vested with legislative power, has been extremely influential in general terms but seldom has a constitution been fashioned which accords with its precepts (for discussion, see Chapter 3). At least in theory, Parliament is pre-eminently a legislative body, and as the dominant partner in Britain's tri-partite legislature,[11] the contribution of the Commons should be of great importance. It is, however, elementary that a Government with an overall majority will be able to ensure that the vast majority of its Bills will reach the statute books, often with little modification. For example, up until 2003, there had been five full sessions of Parliament since the Labour Government came to power in 1997; during that time there were 1,640 Divisions in the House of Commons,[12] without a single defeat on a whipped vote, let alone defeats on the Second Reading of a Bill (that is, wholesale rejection of the entire Bill). As we shall see, from 2005 on, the Government with its reduced majority suffered defeats on a few clauses, and came close to defeat on numerous other occasions, but the overall pattern remains the same. If Parliament is not then in fact a separate legislature, what is its proper role? In order to be able to analyse properly the functions that the Commons performs in relation to legislation, it is necessary to place it into a comparative perspective, by examining how legislatures can be classified.

P Norton, 'Parliament and policy in Britain: the House of Commons as a policy influencer', in P Norton (ed), *Legislatures* (1990) (extracts)

. . . I would distinguish between legislatures which have a capacity, occasionally or regularly exercised, for policy-making, for policy-influencing, and for having little or no policy impact.

1 Policy-making legislatures are those which can not only modify or reject Government measures but can themselves formulate and substitute a policy for that proposed by Government.

2 Policy-influencing legislatures can modify or reject measures put forward by Government but cannot substitute a policy of their own.

3 Legislatures with little or no policy impact can neither modify or reject measures, nor generate and substitute policies of their own.

'Policy' has been subject to different definitions. I would define it as a related set of proposals which compromise a recognisable whole, based ideally but not necessarily (in practice probably rarely) on conscious and tested assumptions as to costs, needs, end products and implications. 'Policy-making' is the generation of that recognisable whole. Once 'made', policy can then be presented for discussion, modification, acceptance or

---

11 Commons, Lords, Monarch.

12 See the speech of Lord Phillips, HL Deb col 627 (21 January 2003).

rejection, application and evaluation. 'Policy influence' can be exerted at these later stages. It may take the form of formal modification or even rejection. It may work through a process of anticipated reaction: that is, the policy-makers may be influenced by expectations of whether or not a particular policy will gain approval. In such instances, the 'making' of policy is influenced by, but is not in the hands of, the legislature. In cases of little or no policy impact, a legislature has no appreciable influence upon policy-making nor upon the later stages of the policy cycle.

If we liken policy to a small (or not so small) jigsaw the picture becomes clearer. Policy-makers put the jigsaw together. They may do so in a clumsy and haphazard manner. They may produce a well-structured piece. Whichever, the responsibility for putting it together is theirs. A policy-making legislature can modify or reject that jigsaw, substituting one it has compiled itself. A policy-influencing legislature can reject the jigsaw or, more likely, reject or move about some of the pieces, but has not the capacity to reconstruct it or create a new jigsaw. A legislature with little or no policy impact looks upon and approves the jigsaw, with or without comment.

This classification of legislatures has two advantages. Firstly, it provides a useful frame-work for distinguishing between the US and UK legislatures. Congress is a policy-making legislature. That is, not only can it amend or reject executive policy, it can—and occasion-ally does—substitute a policy of its own. It has the leadership capable of formulating a policy as a substitute to that of the executive. In the House of Commons, the equivalent leadership is the executive. Though it has the capacity, recently exercised, to modify and even reject executive proposals, the House does not have the capacity to generate alterna-tive policies. It is a policy influencer, not a policy-maker.

Question

Elsewhere, Norton notes that his second category—policy-influencing legislatures—is 'the most crowded of the three'; into it fall 'most legislatures of Western Europe. . .of the Commonwealth [and] of the new legislatures of east and central Europe' whilst the first category—policy-making legislatures—'is almost empty', its only members being the US Congress and the US state legislatures.[13] Why has Montesqueiu's model been so overwhelmingly rejected?

Notes

1. Norton states that the House of Commons does not have a leadership 'capable of formulating a policy as a substitute to that of the executive', but on one level this is inaccurate. The Opposition can and does formulate alternative policies. What it does not have is the administrative back-up (civil servants, parliamentary draftsmen) to allow it to produce a large volume of alternative legislation, though it could presumably produce some. The essential difference is that the Opposition will only rarely have a majority in the Commons whereas the US Congress is quite often controlled by a party which does not also make up the executive. MPs of course can and do introduce what are called 'Private Member's Bills'. Time is set aside for these in Standing Order 14

---

13   P Norton, *Does Parliament Matter?* (1993), pp 50–51.

(generally, on Fridays) but usually Bills can only become law if they have support from the government, which can ensure that the Bill has adequate time to pass all its stages. Notable reforms have been achieved through private member's bills, historically in areas that are morally contentious and seen, to an extent as 'matters of conscience': examples are the de-criminalisation of homosexuality, the liberalisation of abortion and the ending of capital punishment. As Turpin and Tomkins point out, more recent examples include the Public Interest Disclosure Act 1998 (giving limited protection to 'whistleblowers'), the Female Genital Mutilation Act 2003, and the Gangmaster's (Licensing) Act 2004. They go on to note that even where such a Bill fails, if it attracts strong support within and outside Parliament, this may result in the Government bringing forward its own legislation on the subject—they instance the Disability Discrimination Act 1995.[14] See further on private member's Bills, Brazier, 'Enhancing the Backbench MP's Role as a Legislator: The Case for Urgent Reform of Private Members Bills' (2010) 63(1) *Parliamentary Affairs* 201–11.

2. Even if it is accepted that the legislative role of the Commons lies in *responding* to government measures, if it is thought that this role demands that the House provide independent assessment of the merit of government Bills and make numerous amendments to them, then clearly it is not fulfilling this role. As Henry Calvert puts it, 'the substantial task of legislating will have been largely discharged before the Bill is read in the House', or again, 'Before the formally dramatic part of the legislative process even begins almost all the terms of almost all [government] Bills are settled'.[15] However, on one view, the argument which states that the Commons is redundant because it is largely powerless to amend or reverse the Government's programme is wrongheaded; it is contended that the Commons would be undermining democratic accountability if it substantially changed Government Bills, since the legislative programme of the party which attracted the greatest proportion of votes should be enacted, in accordance with the electorate's presumed wishes. This argument was undoubtedly what Professor Bernard Crick had in mind when he wrote, 'the phrase "parliamentary control" should not mislead anyone into asking for a situation in which Governments can have their legislation changed or defeated'.[16]

3. Crick's point of view is clearly open to a number of objections: it can be plausibly argued that many people vote, not after a careful assessment of which legislative programme they would like to see enacted, but on the basis of traditional loyalty, misinformation, misunderstanding or their reaction to politicians' perceived personalities. Further, it is undoubtedly true that people may vote for a party even though they may object to some of its specific legislative proposals.[17] Finally, Crick's argument applies in its purest form only to manifesto Government Bills; as Michael Zander notes (below), these in fact form only a small percentage of enacted legislation; the argument is certainly wholly inapplicable to legislation which actually appears to reverse the policies which the electorate thought the party introducing it stood for: an example can be seen in the increases in taxation introduced by the Major administration subsequent to the 1992 General Election in which a key Conservative campaigning theme was its opposition to the higher taxes it alleged Labour would introduce.

4. During the last years of the Major Government (ending in 1997), when its overall majority dwindled in the end to only one, the force of Crick's argument was perhaps more apparent than usual. As a Government's majority decreases, it must perforce have more regard to the views of its backbenchers. However, when a majority reaches a low enough level, small groups of dissident MPs

---

14   Turpin and Tomkins, *British Government and the Constitution*, 6th edn (2007) at 600.

15   *British Constitutional Law* (1985), p 84.

16   *The Reform of Parliament* (1964), p 80.

17   For general discussion of voting patterns, see D Kavanagh and B Jones, 'Voting behaviour', in B Jones (ed), *Politics UK* (1994).

become able to force the Government to depart from its pre-planned policy which was the platform on which it was elected. Of course, most of its legislative policies are not directly mandated (see below) but, to take the example of the Major Government's policy on the European Union, the Government stood on a platform of a general attitude towards Europe which could perhaps be described as cautious engagement. This was the publicly declared, official policy of the Conservative Party. If a number of anti-EU MPs are able to force the Government into a far more thorough-going scepticism, this could be viewed as a welcome example of greater parliamentary control over the executive. But it may also be seen, in Crick's terms, as an undermining of the democratic mandate.

The Commons and Party Loyalty

In another sense, it is of course wholly unrealistic to expect the House of Commons to subject Government Bills to independent scrutiny. The Government is the Government precisely because it is the party with an overall majority in the Commons. Therefore, by definition, the majority of MPs in the House will be pre-disposed to support legislation introduced by the Government, so that it is built into the nature of the Commons that most of its members will precisely *not* be impartially minded. The House can be seen to be poised between two possible roles, fulfilling neither of them. Because, formally, the Commons is the law-making body, it must be composed of democratically elected members, that is, those tied to political parties, thus ensuring that in practice the Cabinet legislates. But again, because MPs are tied to political parties, they are unable to carry out properly the actual task of the House, scrutiny of legislation, in a fair-minded and impartial manner. Moreover, as explored further below, Standing Orders give Government strong control over Parliament in practice. Both these points are well brought out in the following commentary.

Hansard Society Commission on Parliamentary Scrutiny, *The Challenge for Parliament: Making Government Accountable (2001), Chapter 2 (extracts)*

2.7 . . .At Westminster the two most important factors which determine activity are the dominance of the governing party over the activity of the Commons, and the influence of the parties over their MPs.

2.8 Westminster is characterised by the dominance of the executive. Although this is common in many democracies, especially where the executive is drawn from the legisla-ture. . .the extent of executive dominance at Westminster is far greater than for many other parliaments. The extent of this control is conveyed in Standing Order 14 of the House of Commons which states that 'save as provided in this order, government business shall have precedence at every sitting'.

2.9 The organisation of business in the chamber of the Commons is determined by the governing party. It allocates the timing for all debates and legislation, and although in practice this relies on negotiation with the Opposition parties through the 'usual channels', the Government will time debates to its own advantage. The notion that the Government shall get its business dominates procedures in the chamber and standing committees. This has a number of implications for Parliament as an institution. It means that Parliament is informed of its business by a Cabinet minister, the Leader of the House, on a weekly basis who announces the content for each day the following week and provisional business for the week after. Although the Labour Government has introduced reforms which seek to bring a greater predictability to parliamentary business, the current system means that it is impossible for MPs to plan their work too far ahead.

2.10 The effect on the ethos of the Commons is to emphasise the distinction between executive and legislature. MPs conceive their role according to their position, and the position of their party, in relation to the Government. There is little sense that Parliament owns its business or determines its own workload, nor much sense of Parliament acting collectively as an institution. In some respects this atomises and individualises the work of MPs, with each MP acting as 'his own public relations officer'. Although Parliament has certain collective functions, its ability to deliver them is limited by the fact that it has no collective ethos, 'The idea of 'Parliament' as a political force, or as a whole, is simply a myth. Parliament in this sense simply does not exist.'

2.11 The only collective activity inside the Commons is orchestrated by the political parties and the only realistic career path for the ambitious MP is through the structures of the political party. The vast majority of activity in the Commons chamber is organised along party lines and the whips on both sides play a significant role in marshalling the contributions of their MPs. The knowledge that whips and party leaders will determine their political career has a significant bearing on MPs' behaviour, and it is those traits which emphasise the party political divide that are most likely to get a backbencher noticed. Promotion is more likely to be the result of partisan activity—toeing the party line, asking the right questions, scoring points off the Opposition—than pursuing the accountability functions of Parliament.

Notes

1. It should be borne in mind that the Commons still provides a constitutional safeguard, albeit one of mainly theoretical importance, in that governments could presumably not rely on it to pass legislation which removed the basic liberties of the citizen. However, confidence in this safeguard was for many people gravely weakened when, in November 2001, the Commons passed the Government's Anti-Terrorism, Crime and Security Bill 2001, which, *inter alia*, allowed for the detention without trial for an indefinite period of suspected international terrorists.[18] The Bill was purportedly an emergency measure, introduced into Parliament in response to the perceived greater threat from international terrorism following the attacks on America on 11 September 2001. However, a very large number of its provisions did not in fact deal with specifically anti-terrorism measures. It included a new offence of incitement to religious hatred, which, in itself would clearly provide no assistance in the fight against terrorism, new powers of the police compulsorily to photograph criminal suspects—not just suspected terrorists (Part 10), a new procedure whereby Third Pillar EU criminal measures would become part of UK law via secondary legislation (Part 13) and measures to put in place a new Code of Practice on retention of communications data—websites visited, mobile phone calls made and so on (Part 11).[19] The Bill was a very lengthy one—126 clauses and eight lengthy schedules—and indeed took the Government two months to prepare. Nevertheless, it was rushed through the Commons with almost indecent haste: MPs first of all accepted a timetable of only 16 hours in which to scrutinise a Bill of 124 pages and then imposed not a single defeat on the Government, though the Government did accept amendments

---

18   Very broadly defined, using the definition in the Terrorism Act 2000, for which see H Fenwick, *Civil Rights, New Labour and the Human Rights Act* (2000), Chapter 3.

19   For analysis of the Act's provisions, see A Tomkins, 'Legislating against Terror: the Anti-Terrorism, Crime and Security Act 2001' [2002] PL 205 and H Fenwick, 'The Anti-Terrorism, Crime and Security Act 2001: A Proportionate Response to 11 September?' (2002) 65(5) MLR 724.

tabled by chairs of Select Committees which had scrutinised the Bill in draft. The Common's spineless performance in relation to this Bill caused one respected commentator to remark: 'In a long record of shaming fealty to whips, never have so many MPs showed such utter negligence towards so impressive a list of fundamental principles.'[20] Its performance in relation to the 2005 Anti-Terrorism Act was little better: all the improvements to the initially highly draconian scheme were made in the Lords. However, as noted below, it was in relation to further terrorism legislation in 2006 that the Government finally tasted defeat (see p 365 below).

2. There are in fact many precedents for draconian and illiberal legislation being passed by the Commons in such indecent haste. The most dramatic example was the Official Secrets Act 1911, which made it a criminal offence to reveal virtually any official government information without proper authorisation. Its passage is described by the Minister responsible for piloting it through the Commons.

EB Seely, *Adventure* (1930), p 145[21]

I got up and proposed that the bill be read a second time, explaining, in two sentences only, that it was considered desirable in the public interest that the measure should be passed. Hardly a word was said and the bill was read a second time; the Speaker left the Chair. I then moved the bill in committee. This was the first critical moment; two men got up to speak, but both were forcibly pulled down by their neighbours after they had uttered a few sentences, and the committee stage was passed. The Speaker walked back to his chair and said: 'The question is, that I report this bill without amendment to the House.' Again two or three people stood up; again they were pulled down by their neighbours, and the report stage was through. The Speaker turned to me and said: 'The third reading, what day?' 'Now, sir,' I replied. My heart beat fast as the Speaker said: 'The question is that this bill be read a third time.' It was open to anyone of all the members in the House of Commons to get up and say that no bill had ever yet passed through all its stages in one day without a word of explanation from the minister in charge. . . . But to the eternal honour of those members, to whom I now offer, on behalf of that and all succeeding Governments, my most grateful thanks, not one man seriously opposed, and in a little more time than it has taken to write these words that formidable piece of legislation was passed.

Notes

1. It is fair to say that whilst the above passage indicates the dramatic extent to which scrutiny in the Commons may be curtailed to vanishing point, it is inconceivable that a Bill could be passed in this way today. John F McEldowney suggests that the main role of the Commons is to legitimise legislation (echoing Norton's view that most legislatures exist not to make laws but to assent to them) and also to provide the 'life blood of party politics' through its 'debates, votes and censure[s]'.[22] This latter suggestion may be seen as a variant on the publicising role of Parliament suggested by some commentators (see below).

2. If it is accepted that due to its make-up and the party system, the Commons cannot be expected either to take on the role of policy-maker or provide genuinely independent assessment of

---

20   Hugo Young, 'Once Lost, These Freedoms will be Impossible to Restore', *The Guardian,* 11 December 2001.

21   This passage was cited in M Zander, *The Law-Making Process* (1994).

22   *Public Law* (1994), p 45.

Government Bills, by what criteria may it be assessed? Putting it another way, what can we reasonably expect it to do? It is suggested that four main functions may be identified. The first is the education of both the Government and electorate through the publicising effects of debate in Parliament: the electorate will become aware of the issues surrounding a particular policy, whilst the reaction of newspapers, commentators and the public to debates on the proposed legislation will help keep the Government informed of the drift of public opinion. The second is the influence on the pre-legislative process which both backbenchers and Opposition MPs may have. The third is the limited amount of improvement and amendment which, despite the partisan nature of the Commons, still does take place. The fourth is the clarification as to the meaning and operation of a given piece of legislation which may take place during debate. This may, since *Pepper v Hart* [1993] 1 All ER 42, go to the interpretation a Bill receives in the courts; it may also provide ammunition for future political attack if things do not go as planned. It is clear that in relation to the first, third and fourth of these functions, the amount of time and resources which Members have available to them to devote to scrutiny of legislation will be crucial; the importance of the second and third will be closely tied to the size of the Government's majority.

3. The ability of backbench MPs to influence government policy is obviously dependent upon the degree to which (within the context of the basic loyalty which the party system demands) they are prepared to view their own party's policy with a critical eye, and vote against legislation it has brought forward. Philip Norton notes an interesting trend here.

Philip Norton, *Does Parliament Matter?* (1993), p 21

The behaviour of MPs has changed in recent decades. Most significantly of all. . .has been the change in behaviour in the division (voting) lobbies. Members have proved relatively more independent in their voting behaviour. As we have seen, cohesion was a marked feature of parliamentary life by the turn of the century. That cohesion has been maintained throughout the 20th century, reaching its peak in the 1950s. In the 1960s, one distinguished American commentator was able to declare that cohesion had increased so much 'until in recent decades it was so close to 100% that there was no longer any point in measuring it' (Beer, 1969:350–51). Shortly afterwards, it did become relevant to measure it.

The early years of the 1970s saw a significant increase in cross-voting by Conservative MPs. They voted against their own leaders more often than before, in greater numbers and with more effect. On six occasions, cross-voting resulted in the Government being defeated. Cross-voting also became a feature of Labour MPs after the party was returned to office in 1974, contributing to most of the 42 defeats suffered by the Government in the 1974–79 Parliament. The number of defeats on the floor of the House, combined with defeats in standing committee, ran into three figures. Some degree of independent voting has been maintained in succeeding Parliaments. In 1986, the Government lost the second reading of the Shops Bill, the first time in the 20th century a Government with a clear overall majority had lost a second reading vote.

Notes

1. There was a widespread perception, at least during the Parliament of 1997–2001, that Labour backbenchers were amongst the most party-minded in recent history, a perception challenged below by Philip Cowley. As he notes, Labour MPs were criticised as '"Daleks", "clones" and "spineless". . .for leaking [critical] Select Committee reports [to assist the Government in rebutting

them and]. . .asking patsy questions for Ministers.'[23] He notes that, in some ways, the accusation may be seen to be true, but it leaves out of account the effect which the damaging lack of cohesion had on a Labour Party out of power for 18 years on attitudes of MPs and also the huge size of Mr Blair's majority (179) which tended to mask the quite large rebellions that did in fact occur: a third of Labour MPs in fact voted against the Government at some point.

2. The backbenchers of the post-election 2001 Parliament proved somewhat more assertive than even their colleagues of 1997. As Philip Cowley and Mark Stuart noted:

> . . .the Government faces a potentially tougher ride from its backbenchers this Parliament. . .The first 44 votes saw 10 backbench Labour rebellions against the whips; the comparable figure for the last Parliament was zero.[24]

Such predictions of greater backbench independent-mindedness were spectacularly borne out by the parliamentary reaction to the Blair Government's policy on military action against Iraq in early 2003. The UN Security Council on 25 November 2002 passed resolution 1441, which found Iraq to be in material breach of its disarmament obligations under numerous previous resolutions and threatened 'serious consequences' if Iraq failed fully to co-operate with UN Inspectors seeking to investigate whether Iraq had, as it claimed, fully dismantled its prohibited nuclear, chemical and biological weapons programmes. Blair's policy, in the light of less than full cooperation from the Iraqi Government was to seek to obtain a further Security Council resolution, expressly endorsing military action against Iraq to disarm it of such weapons. However, he also repeatedly refused to rule out taking such action, in partnership with the US, even if there was no such further resolution because, for example, of what he termed an 'unreasonable veto' by one of the five permanent members of the Security Council. In a debate held shortly before conflict began, but by which time it was looking as if Blair might fail to secure a second UN resolution, a rival motion was put forward by Chris Smith, a former Labour Cabinet Minister, stating that the case for military action was 'as yet unproven'.

3. In the event, the rebellion of Labour MPs came to 122, apparently the largest single rebellion against a Government since the modern party system was put in place. There was a further debate on 18 March 2003[25] on the eve of military action; by this time, the attempt to obtain a Security Council resolution explicitly authorising the use of force had been abandoned in the face of implacable opposition from France, Germany and Russia and lack of support from other members of the Security Council, representing a major failure of Anglo-American diplomacy and a serious reverse for the Government. It was now faced with its worst case scenario—taking the country to war with no explicit UN backing, without even a majority of the UN Security Council in favour, and with massive protests sweeping the country and the rest of Europe. An anti-war march in March 2003 attracted over a million protestors, making it the largest ever demonstration in Britain; the polls showed a majority of the public against war in the absence of explicit UN authorisation. Robin Cook, former Foreign Secretary, and now Leader of the House of Commons—a Cabinet post—resigned, and made a powerful speech attacking government policy on war with Iraq.[26]

---

23   P Cowley, 'The Commons: Mr Blair's Lapdog?' (2001) 54 Parlt Aff 815, at 818–19.

24   P Cowley and M Stuart, 'Parliament: Mostly Continuity, but More Change than You'd Think' (2002) 55 Parlt Aff 271, at 284.

25   HC Deb cols 760 et seq (18 March 2003).

26   For Robin Cook's resignation statement, see Chapter 12 at 624–625.

4. It was in these circumstances that the Government asked Parliament to back it in going to war against Iraq. The Prime Minister opened the debate with an impassioned plea for support, having intimated that he would resign should the party fail to back him. One of the principal Government defences of its actions in taking action without explicit UN backing was that the French President, by expressly stating that his Government would veto *any* resolution authorising force, whatever the circumstances, had made it effectively impossible for the Security Council to enforce the 'final' demand to the Iraqi regime to disarm contained in resolution 1441, since there was now no credible threat of UN-mandated force to back it up. Thus, it could be argued that the French Government had stymied the UN process, rendering it pointless to pursue it further, given the plausible assumption that it was only the threat of such force which had forced Saddam Hussein to allow the UN inspectors back into Iraq (they had left in 1998 in the face of the regime's persistent failure to cooperate with them). In the event, the rebellion—those voting for a backbench amendment opposing war—was even larger than last time (139 Labour MPs voted for the anti-war amendment), but not as bad as had been feared, given the fact that a number of Labour MPs who voted with the Government in the previous debate did so because at that point it was hoped that the Government would still obtain explicit Security Council authorisation for the use of force. On the separate vote on the substantive government motion, the Government won by 412 votes to 149, a majority of 263. This outcome meant that Blair could lead the country into war with the legitimacy of a clear parliamentary mandate for military action.

5. The episode, to many commentators, represented a major reassertion of parliamentary power against the executive: whilst in theory it would have been possible for the Government to take the country to war without parliamentary approval, given that the power to do so resides in the Royal Prerogative (see further Chapter 10), given the enormity of the issues at stake, and the huge unease in the Labour Party and the country at large, such an action would have been politically unthinkable. To many, the fact that the Blair Government had refused to give Parliament a chance to vote on a substantive motion[27] on the military action in Kosovo in 1999[28] was evidence of the administration's contempt for Parliament, and the weakness of Labour MPs in allowing Parliament thus to be sidelined. In retrospect, however, it is perhaps apparent that the Government only felt able to take such action in the knowledge that its policy on Kosovo had broad support in the Parliamentary Labour Party and, indeed, across the parties. Where such support was lacking, the Government was forced to bow to Parliament's will, in giving MPs the chance to vote against war *before* military action was taken: in fact, by so doing, Blair's premiership was actually placed at risk and he was faced with the prospect of resigning should his policy have been opposed by a majority of the Parliamentary Labour Party.[29] The episode thus reveals the simple truth that, as Adam Tomkin has argued,[30] there *is* in fact no *government* majority in Parliament at any time. The 'government vote' in Parliament in fact consists only of the payroll of government *Ministers,* who are bound by the convention of collective responsibility to vote for government policy or resign. Backbench MPs do not, strictly, form part of this majority: whilst they are arguably under an obligation to vote for measures contained in the Government's manifesto, they are free to use their judgement on other matters, although, of course, the normal expectation will be that they will vote

---

27 That is a motion explicitly approving government policy, as opposed to a motion simply to adjourn the House, which allows dissent to be expressed, but not a chance to vote directly against the government.

28 Debates were held after the conflict began, on 24 March and 19 April, 1999.

29 Mr Blair had drawn up contingency plans for his resignation and the withdrawal of British forces from the Gulf, should the vote in the Parliamentary Labour Party have gone against him.

30 A Tomkin, 'Conclusion', in *Government Unwrapped: The Constitution after Scott* (1998).

with their party. But the episode illustrates that all that is needed for Parliament to re-assert its will over the executive is for MPs to have the necessary resolve to do so, a resolve that can be generated where, as in this case, Members feel sufficiently strongly about the issue in question and there is widespread and deeply-felt public opposition to government policy. The episode presented the relationship between Parliament and the executive in a markedly different light from that normally seen: rather than Parliament as the obedient lapdog of the Government, the public saw the Prime Minister forced to seek Parliament's assent, having to persuade by force of argument, not just by invoking party loyalty, and with a credible threat to his premiership should he lose that argument. As Mr Blair put it:

> At the outset, I say that it is right that the House debate this issue and pass judgement. That is the democracy that is our right, but that others struggle for in vain. . . .[31]

6. In the same year as the Iraq vote, the Government also found itself in trouble in relation to its controversial policy of introducing Foundation Hospitals, designed to free hospitals from governmental control. As the Health and Social Care (Community Health and Standards) Bill was passing through Parliament in 2003, there were repeated, serious rebellions at all stages of the Bill's progress, so that, 'In order to stave off possible defeats, the Government was repeatedly forced to make concessions to its backbench critics'.[32]

7. Cowley and Stuart conclude, looking back on the huge rebellions over the Iraq war, Foundation Hospitals, and the Criminal Justice Bill in that year:

> The idea, fashionable just a year ago, that the Government Whips face an acquiescent parliamentary party. . .is now just laughable. By the end of the second session, the 2001 Parliament had witnessed more backbench rebellions by government MPs than at the comparable point of any postwar Parliament. In just over two years, it had seen almost two-thirds of its backbenchers vote against it.[33]

8. The Blair Government did not lose any Bills in the House of Commons; however, towards the end of its life, it was defeated on a handful of votes on particular clauses in committee. It lost in its attempt to have overturned certain Lords amendments to the Racial and Religious Hatred Bill 2005, designed to restrict the ambit of the new offence of incitement to religious hatred, and protect free speech; it was also defeated in the Commons on its proposal to extend the time for which terrorism suspects can be held without charge for questioning. In November 2005, the Government's proposed 90-day time limit was defeated and a compromise, of an extension to only 28 days, was passed instead. Nevertheless, these were the only legislative defeats inflicted on the Blair Government in its 10 years in power, and this in the context of a Government that passed thousands of pages of legislation a year (3,500 in 2004 alone) and created over 3,000 new criminal offences since 1997. Moreover, in June 2008 Gordon Brown managed partially to reverse the defeat on extending the period of pre-charge detention for terrorism suspects. Brown managed to persuade MPs to vote for an increase to 42 days, albeit only after extensive pressure was applied by the Whips and he suffered a major back-bench rebellion; the measure was rejected in the Lords.

---

31   HC Deb col 761 (18 March 2003).

32   P Cowley and M Stuart, 'Parliament in 2003: More Bleak House than Great Expectations' (2004) 57(2) Parlt Aff 301 at 309.

33   *Ibid*, p 312.

The legislative process in the Commons

The following table shows the volume and increase in the number of pages of legislation enacted each year between 1992 and 2004:

Table 1: Volume of primary legislation, 1992–2004

Year	No of Acts	No. of pages of law
1992 (election year)	55	1,288
1993	65	2,041
1994	42	2,005
1995	48	2,290
1996	57	2,248
1997 (election year)	62	1,534
1998	47	2,357
1999	35	2,063
2000	45	3,610
2001 (election year)	25	1,232
2002	43	2,848
2003	44	3,435
2004	38	3,470

Source: Ev 77 and Acts & Statutory Instruments: Volume of UK legislation 1950 to 2005. House of Commons

The pre-legislative stage

As Zander points out:

> The belief that most bills derive from a Government's manifesto commitments is mistaken. It has been estimated that only 8% of the Conservative Government's bills in the period from 1970 to 1974 came from election commitments and that in the 1974–79 Labour Government the proportion was only a little higher at 13% (Richard Rose, *Do Parties Make a Difference?*, 2nd edn (1984), pp 72–73). The great majority of bills originated within Government departments, with the remainder being mainly responses to particular and unexpected events such as [terrorism legislation].[34]

In terms of parliamentary influence, Governments must take account of the likely response of its own backbenchers to legislation, as ascertained by the Whips, at the pre-legislative stage. If backbenchers are aware of widespread public discontent at proposed legislation, this will be relayed to the Government

---

34   Zander, n 49 below, at 2.

which will wish to avoid the embarrassment of hearing its own supporters expressing public dissent—dissent which, as Norton remarks, 'provides good copy for the press'.[35] The effect of this anticipated response may be to force the Government into modifying its proposals, the most dramatic example being the Labour Government's abandonment of its proposed industrial relations legislation in 1969 when it became clear to it that its own MPs did not support the measure. Similarly, in October 1992, John Major's administration was forced to abandon its plans for immediate closure of 31 coal pits in order to avoid near certain defeat by Conservative backbenchers, whilst Michael Heseltine's plans to sell off the Post Office suffered a similar fate in 1994. A more recent example relates to legislation on asylum proposed by the Blair Government in 1999.[36] While the Blair Government, cushioned by a succession of large majorities, generally felt strong enough to disregard such threatened rebellions; indeed, it did so shortly after taking power when it forced through a cut in single parent benefit despite a threatened back bench revolt which, when it duly appeared, generated considerable adverse publicity for the Government and the measure in question. On other occasions, however, the threat of rebellion did force concessions from Government. Following the 2005 election, in which the Government's majority was cut to around 60, it had to engage far more in such pre-legislative negotiation with potential rebels. Gordon Brown's unpopularity forced him into a still more emollient approach. The most striking example occurred in 2008 when widespread opposition both in the media and amongst back-benchers forced Chancellor Darling to bring forward a mini-budget, to compensate those rendered worse off by the abolition of the 10p tax band.

The Modernisation Committee noted in 1997 that very few Bills were published in draft form for scrutiny before being formally introduced to the House. It noted that, partly as a result, consultations between government and those outside Parliament with a legitimate concern in the legislation has been criticised as patchy and spasmodic.[37] One aspect of the Labour Government's modernisation reform programme for the House of Commons has been a very significant increase in the number of Bills published in draft for pre-legislative scrutiny by committees of the House. The opportunities of both back benchers and the Opposition to exert pre-legislative influence on Bills are markedly increased when the Government publishes Bills in draft, to allow more detailed comment on them from Select Committees and other interested bodies. This tendency was welcomed by the Modernisation Committee, which commented that such practice provides 'a real chance for the House to exercise its powers of pre-legislative scrutiny in an effective way'.[38] Important examples have included Bills on the Food Standards Agency, Freedom of Information, Tobacco Advertising, Financial Services and Anti-Terrorism; in a number of cases, amendments proposed by Select Committees were accepted by the Government. It has been commented that this process is 'far less partisan and far more open to analysis and debate, and, as a consequence, makes, where it is possible, for far better law'.[39] The Joint Committee on Human Rights now plays a particularly significant role in advising the Government and parliament as to whether proposed Bills are compatible with the European Convention on Human Rights: on occasions, its reports have resulted in pre-legislative concessions from the Government.[40]

---

35   *The Commons in Perspective* (1981) p 119.

36   On which, see Cowley, n 23 above.

37   Modernisation Committee, HC 190 (1997–98), paras 5 and 6.

38   HC 382, 2000–01, para 19.

39   HC Deb, 26 June 2006, col 43.

40   For comparative discussion of the role and work of the Committee, see C Evans and S Evan, 'Legislative Scrutiny Committees and Parliamentary Conceptions of Human Rights' [2006] PL 785.

The practice of publishing Bills in draft is being used more frequently: 18 were treated this way in the five years between 1992 and 1997; 39 between 2000 and 2005.

In its Annual Report for 2002,[41] the Liaison Committee noted that: 'there are already encouraging signs that one of the preconditions for pre-legislative scrutiny—a steady flow of draft Bills—is beginning to be met (para 30).' It picked out in particular the pre-legislative scrutiny of the important, and controversial, Communications Bill 2002:

> By common consent, this was a highly successful exercise, at least defined in terms of the thoroughness and openness of the process and the extent to which the Committee was able to secure the Government's agreement to significant and wide-ranging changes in the draft bill [para 31].

In 2006, the Modernisation Committee found:

> There is little doubt that pre-legislative scrutiny produces better laws. As the Law Society told us, 'it would probably be difficult to prove scientifically that more prelegislative scrutiny has improved legislation, but it would seem unarguable in practice that it has . . . Effective consultation procedures and processes such as publication and consideration of Bills in draft would appear to have greatly improved the text which is presented to Parliament or to have identified drawbacks in the draft text which require its rethinking'. This view was echoed by the Hansard Society, the Members of Parliament who gave evidence to us, and by academic witnesses. Witnesses from the CBI, the TUC and the Law Society all suggested that pre-legislative scrutiny could play a significant part in improving the quality of bills.[42]

A 2006 study of the impact of pre-legislative scrutiny focused on two important statutes that were subject to such scrutiny—the Civil Contingencies Act 2004 and the Disability Discrimination Act 2005 and the extent to which they were improved by it. We include extracts below in relation to the former.

J Smookler, 'Making a Difference? The Effectiveness of Pre-Legislative Scrutiny' (2006) 59(3) *Parliamentary Affairs* 522, 523–26 (extracts)

The Civil Contingencies Bill became an Act of Parliament on 18 November 2004 and has major implications for the Government's response to serious emergencies such as a terrorist attack or an environmental disaster. It is divided into two sections: Part 1 makes provision for civil contingencies in the UK including contingency planning at local and regional level; Part 2 provides for the drafting and use of emergency powers by Government Ministers. It was published by the Cabinet Office as a draft Bill in June 2003 and underwent pre-legislative scrutiny by a Joint Committee of 22 Members. The Committee reported to the Government in November 2003, making 50 recommendations for changes to the draft Bill, based on over 350 written consultation responses and evidence from 30 oral witnesses. At the publication of their report, the Joint Committee expressed serious concerns about the content of the draft Civil Contingencies Bill, noting that: 'in the wrong hands, [the Bill] could be used to undermine or even remove legislation underpinning the

---

41   HC 558 (2002–03).

42   First Report (2005–06) HC 1097 at [20].

British Constitution and infringe human rights. Our democracy and civil liberties could be in danger if the Government does not take account of our recommended improvements'. The revised Civil Contingencies Bill was [then] introduced into the House of Commons in January 2004 . . .

[The author notes that the Government claimed to have accepted 75% of the Joint Committee's recommendations and goes on]: Upon more detailed examination, the Government actually accepted only 13 recommendations in full (24%), partially accepted or deferred 19, disagreed with 16, failed to address one and one was no longer relevant in the light of other changes.

The 13 recommendations accepted in full by the Government at a pre-legislative stage included some key concessions and some significant changes in policy. They agreed, for instance, to remove a clause that would prevent emergency regulations from being subject to judicial Review [including review under the Human Rights Act]. . . The Government also accepted, in full or in part, 12 of the Committee's 14 recommendations curtailing the draft Bill's definition of an emergency. The Committee had criticised the definition as 'unduly broad', containing 'ambiguous terminology and unclear thresholds and triggers' and raising 'concerns about the Bill's potential for misuse'. One such recommendation was instrumental in leading the Government to reassess a policy intention and considerably narrow the powers they had initially considered necessary. . .Crucially, in order to make emergency regulations, a situation would first have to be considered a threat to 'human welfare' under the revised definition of emergency. This was a marked change of emphasis in line with the Committee's recommendation. . . .

Although a greater number of the Joint Committee's recommendations were rejected by the Government at a pre-legislative stage, they included fewer of significance. . . . In some cases, a recommendation was agreed to in theory, but implemented differently from how the Committee had envisaged. It recommended, for instance, that the conditions that must be met before a state of emergency could be declared—known as the 'triple lock'—should be explicitly stated in a single or adjoining clauses on the face of the Bill, rather than mentioned in discrete sections. The triple lock included seriousness, necessity and geographical proportionality, and was reflected in four separate clauses in the draft Bill. The Committee's primary concern was a practical one: 'Given the confused and hurried circumstances in which an emergency is likely to be declared, when the only guidance to the Government of the day may be the legislation itself, it is vital that safeguards against misuse are made as clear on the face of the Bill as possible'. The Government agreed with [this principle of transparency], but their subsequent amendments to the Bill resulted in the 'triple-lock' still being scattered across three separate clauses. Although the Government voiced their agreement, their changes did not reflect the spirit of the Committee's recommendation.

The revised Bill was introduced in the House of Commons during January 2004. There was mixed opinion about whether pre-legislative scrutiny had significantly influenced the new version of the Bill. The Government considered that 'taken together, the public consultation and the pre-legislative scrutiny have made a real difference to the Bill . . . '. Lord Condon, a former member of the pre-legislative committee, also considered the process to have been a useful one: 'I was very impressed with the thoroughness of the process . . . [and] pleased that the Government responded so positively to so many of the 50 recommendations made by the Committee. The Bill before your Lordships' House is now in much better shape than the original'. The human rights organisation Liberty responded to the changes with a very guarded welcome: 'The government has taken a step in the right direction. Their initial proposals were quite terrifying. But these present proposals remain worrisome.'

Notes

1. The author goes on to point out that while further, unimplemented proposals of the Committee were picked up during the Parliamentary process, only two further such proposals found their way into the Bill: the main impact was during the pre-legislative stage. However, she notes that 'This was virtually reversed in the case of the Disability Discrimination Bill, where the more significant concessions were acceded to only as a result of pressure during the legislative stages.'[43] But either way, the process had proved valuable.

2. As part of the modest package of measures announced in the *Constitutional Renewal* papers, the Government in 2007 published not just individual Bills in draft but 'a Draft Legislative Programme, providing a summary of its legislative intentions for the next Parliamentary session in advance of the Queen's Speech.' See the following reports of the Modernisation Committee: First Report (2007–08), HC 81; First Special Report (2007–08) HC 497; see also the comments in The Liaison Committee's review of the 2007–08 year, which worked earlier publication of the programme, to give more time for the Government to take account of the Committees' comments.[44]

3. In terms of scrutiny of individual draft Bills, however, the Liaison Committee found that 06–07 had been a historically low year for the number of Bills published in draft. The Hansard Society recently noted that:

   of the 23 bills announced in the first ever draft programme in July 2007 only one bill was then subsequently published in draft (the draft Constitutional Renewal Bill) and referred for full pre-legislative scrutiny to a parliamentary committee.[45]

   This indicates the infuriatingly patchy nature of the process still and, of course, the fact that the decision whether to subject a Bill to such scrutiny remains entirely for the government.

4. The Liaison Committee was also critical of the fact that often pre-legislative scrutiny had been allocated by the Government to specially appointed Joint Committees of both Houses, rather than Select Committees, thus wasting the latter's expertise, and causing considerable delays while the Joint Committees were appointed.[46] We note in chapter 11 that the findings of the Joint Committee on the draft Constitutional Renewal Bill seemed bland and uncritical compared to those made by Lords and Commons' Select Committees, which provided far more penetrating analysis.[47]

5. Recently the Hansard Society concluded that:

   [Ministers] do not tend to regard the need to make changes to a *draft* bill as a political defeat. Less political capital is expended at the draft end of the law making process. Indeed, it can often be politically advantageous to accept amendments at this stage as the bill may then secure a smoother and more expeditious passage

---

43   Smookler, at 532.

44   First Report (2007–08),HC 291 at [39].

45   Hansard Society, *Representative Democracy: Briefing Paper 1: House of Commons Reform* (2009), para 1.2.

46   *Ibid* at [23]–[32].

47   See pp 570–571 and 572–574.

later on. In contrast, once a bill enters the formal legislative process ministers 'tend to adopt a proprietary attitude towards them' . . .

We believe that pre-legislative scrutiny by parliamentary committee should be the norm for most bills. Where possible, MPs who take part in pre-legislative scrutiny should also subsequently become members of the public bill committee thereby ensuring that specialist knowledge of the legislation at draft stage is carried over into formal consideration of the final bill.[48]

Legislation: the formal process in the House of Commons

Legislation must go through several stages to pass the Commons. The first reading is formal only. The second reading is the main debate on the overall policy of a Bill and its key principles. If defeated at that point (which is extremely rare), that is the end of the Bill. After the Second Reading comes the Committee stage, in which the Bill goes to what used to be called Standing Committees (see below); these are in fact appointed specially for that Bill, in proportion to party strengths. At this stage, the Bill is considered clause by clause and amendments are moved to it (usually by Opposition MPs, nearly always unsuccessfully), though back-benchers from the governing party may rebel, and Government itself may put forward amendments to its Bill at this point. If it emerges wholly unamended it goes straight to Third Reading—a debate on the whole Bill on the floor of the House. But any amendments must be considered at Report Stage, during which further amendments may be moved; there may be attempts to restore clauses removed in Committee or indeed remove clauses added there. Governments often use this stage to introduce amendments intended to answer concerns raised at Committee stage, or elsewhere, e.g. by Select Committees. Once it passes the Commons it goes to the Lords:

> After a Commons bill has been through the Lords, it is returned with the Lords amendments to it, which then must be considered in the House. On any bill, the two Houses must finally reach agreement on the amendments made by each other if the bill is not to fall during that session. Under the Parliament Acts 1911 and 1949, disagreement between the two Houses can delay a bill only for a year if the Commons persist with it; and in the case of a money bill, a bill passed by the Commons can go for Royal Assent after only one month's delay. Where one House cannot agree to the other's amendments, it sends a message to that effect giving reasons. A bill can go back and forth several times but it is only rarely that a bill has had to be reintroduced in a second session in order to become law, because of the failure of the two Houses to agree. . . The final stage in the enacting process is Royal Assent. [49]

The whole process can take anything from a few days (in urgent cases) to six months.

Notes

1. Clarification as to the meaning and implementation of a Bill was put forward at the beginning of this chapter as a useful product of parliamentary debate; the passage of the Prevention of Terrorism (Additional Powers) Act 1996 is instructive in this respect. Despite the fact that the Bill was guillotined (see below), a few important points emerged from the Home Secretary's speeches

---

48   Hansard Society, n 45 above.

49   M Zander, *The Law-Making Process* (1994), pp 63–64.

during the debate. The most controversial provision in the Bill allowed for the police to stop and search persons for items related to terrorist offences without any reasonable suspicion. In response to numerous questions during the debate about the safeguards balancing the new power, two key points were made: first, guidance as to the operation of the powers would be issued by the Home Secretary to the police;[50] second, and more specifically, the Home Secretary would instruct the police to apply the PACE Code for stop and search to all searches under the new power.[51] The second point is particularly important, and given the silence of the new Act itself as to the applicability of the Code, may enable the courts to decide, through perusal of *Hansard*,[52] that Parliament's intention was that the Code should be applied. Thus, significant legal consequences could flow from this assurance.

2. The committee stage is often perceived as a time in which party loyalties are less strong and more constructive debate may take place. However, as appears from Zander's account, MPs lack the resources that would give them the expertise required to challenge increasingly complex government legislation from a position of sufficient knowledge. As Griffith and Ryle comment, 'the Opposition has no back up comparable to that of the minister's departmental staff'.[53] Norton, whilst noting that MPs' resources have increased dramatically since 1960, remarks that: 'By international standards [their] office, secretarial and research facilities remain poor.'[54]

3. Adversarial debate may be used in committee as on the floor of the House and the style is particularly unsuited to examining the factual and technical background to the Bill. Vernon Bogdanor has described Standing Committees as 'mere ad *hoc* debating committees within which second reading speeches are repeated at tedious length interspersed with the reading of well-rehearsed briefs helpfully supplied by interested organisations'.[55] In general therefore, the committee stage results in the acceptance of Government amendments only because, as Griffith's examination of Standing Committees found, 'party discipline is largely maintained'.[56] One recent study noted that: 'at. . .Committee stage (and indeed at subsequent stages) it is extremely rare—in the case where the Government has a majority—for any amendment, other than one moved by the minister, to be accepted.'[57] Further, many Opposition amendments are designed not to increase the effectiveness of the Bill but to embarrass the Government; the political role of Opposition MPs can prevent them undertaking *constructive* criticism. The Standing Committee stage for the poll tax legislation—a hugely controversial change to local government finance, which eventually had to be scrapped, at a total cost of £1.5 billion, and which was so unpopular that it lead to rioting in London and contributed heavily to the downfall of Margaret Thatcher—has been described as 'a futile marathon. . .mostly a matter of posturing. . .scrutiny by slogan and sound bite'.[58] However,

---

50 HC Deb col 265 (2 April 1996).

51 *Ibid.*

52 *Pepper v Hart* [1993] 1 All ER 42 provides that the court may look to *Hansard* to assist it in construing ambiguous statutes.

53 See n 59 below, at 16.

54 P Norton, *Does Parliament Matter?* (1993), p 20.

55 'The Westminster malaise', *The Independent,* 15 May 1996.

56 'Standing Committees in the House of Commons, in Walkland and Ryle, *The Commons Today* (1985), at 130.

57 P Davis, 'The Significance of Parliamentary Procedures in Control of the Executive: A Case Study: The Passage of Part 1 of the Legislative and Regulatory Reform Act 2006' [2007] PL 677, 685.

58 Butler, *Failure in British Government,* quoted in HC Deb col 1098 (13 November 1997).

where Opposition MPs are able to offer constructive criticism, it may have an indirect effect; whilst nearly all Opposition amendments are rejected, 'Ministers in committee do agree to reconsider proposals from the Opposition (often in order to make progress), and this sometimes results in government amendment at a late stage which more or less accept the Opposition's argument'.[59] The Hansard Society has commented that standing committees 'fail to deliver genuine and analytical scrutiny of [bills], their political functions are neutered, dominated almost exclusively by government . . . , they fail to engage with the public and the media (in contrast to select committees) and they do not adequately utilise the evidence of experts or interested parties'.[60]

4. Nevertheless, where Government majorities are smaller, the Opposition is united, and there is considerable public opposition to a Bill, back-bench opposition may have greater effect. A recent commentary noted the effect of opposition during the passage of the ID cards Bill in the House of Commons in terms of the concessions granted by then Home Secretary Charles Clark.[61] Meanwhile, as noted above, the Government was defeated outright on the attempt to increase pre-charge detention from 14 to 90 days, while the controversial new offence of 'glorifying terrorism' was also 'watered down' in the face of strong Commons opposition.[62]

5. Suggestions have recently been made for improving the way in which the Commons handles Bills of constitutional significance. Traditionally, Bills classed as of 'first class constitutional importance' use a Committee of the Whole House (CWH) during the Committee stage. Hazel has argued that this procedure does not make for improved scrutiny,[63] in particular because the pressure on time on the floor of the House results in a much shorter Committee stage, with only on average a fifth of the number of amendments being considered, compared to when the normal Committee procedure.[64] He suggests a number of ways of improving the scrutiny of such Bills, including publication in draft, scrutiny at Committee stage by a Committee empowered to take evidence and the use of checklists, as advocated by Dawn Oliver[65] as in Australia and New Zealand 'to ensure observance of legal and constitutional principles'[66]

6. It should be noted that The Study of Parliament Group had previously recognised the problems with Standing Committees, particularly MPs' lack of expertise, and, on a very few occasions, the Standing Committees have been allowed to follow the recommendations of the group and call expert witnesses, Ministers and records before going on to the usual clause-by-clause examination of the Bill and amendments. This procedure was followed during the passing of the Criminal Attempts Act 1981, and substantial changes were made during the committee stage. Such Committees are known as 'Special Standing Committees' (SO 91). In 2007, the Modernisation Committee made a series of suggestions designed to enhance the scrutiny at Committee stage: essentially they advocated adopting this special procedure for all Standing Committees, which they said should be renamed 'Public Bill Committees'.

---

59   JAG Griffith and M Ryle, *Parliament: Functions, Practice and Procedures* (1989), p 317.

60   Quoted in the Select Committee on Modernisation of the House of Commons, First Report, 1995–06, HC 1097 para 50.

61   See R Whitaker, 'Backbench Influence on Government Legislation? A Flexing of Parliamentary Muscles at Westminster' (2006) 59(2) Parlt Aff 35, 352–53.

62   *Ibid*, p 353–55.

63   R Hazel, 'Time for a New Convention: Parliamentary Scrutiny of Constitutional Bills 1997–2005' [2006] PL 247.

64   *Ibid*, 276–77.

65   D Oliver. 'Improving the Scrutiny of Bills: The Case for Standards and Checklists' [2006] PL 219.

66   Hazel, 'Time for a New Convention', at 297.

Modernisation Committee The Legislative Process, *First Report*, 2005–06, HC 1007

53. Most of our witnesses favoured those committee arrangements which provided for an evidence-taking, as well as a deliberative stage. There are several benefits that an evidence-taking stage could provide. It is first and foremost a mechanism for ensuring that Members are informed about the subject of the bill and that there is some evidential basis for the debate on the bill. Evidence-gathering is also, by its nature, a more consensual and collective activity than debate, and there is evidence that those outside Parliament have a more positive view of select committee proceedings than of debate. So there is a reputational benefit to Parliament in being seen to engage in a more open, questioning and consensual style of law-making, before moving on to the necessary partisan debate.

54. An evidence-taking stage is also an effective way of engaging the wider public directly in the legislative process [as well as interest groups]. . .

56. All these benefits, of course, are there to be had at the pre-legislative stage and pre-legislative committees usually (though not always) allow a rather longer inquiry than is possible once a bill has begun its passage through the House. But, as we have already noted, there is often a disjunction between the pre-legislative stage and the legislative stage, with few Members of pre-legislative committees finding their way onto the standing committee considering the bill. Furthermore, the bill which is presented is might differ significantly from the original draft, so that parts of it will not have been subject to the pre-legislative stage. Unlike the other stages of a bill, pre-legislative scrutiny is in the gift of the Government. . .

58. We recommend that special standing committees should, with some important modifications to the current Standing Order which we set out below, be the norm for Government bills which originate in the Commons [and be renamed 'Public Bill Committees. [The Committee suggested certain exceptions, including urgent or very short Bills. . .]

69. It is. . .likely that providing for evidence sessions on the bill will reduce the time needed and taken for debate on the bill. For example, many of the 'probing' amendments tabled in standing committee for the purpose of testing a particular piece of wording, most of which are in any event withdrawn, could be dispensed with if Members had an opportunity at the outset to question the Minister and officials on the bill. Direct questioning is perhaps a more efficient means for Members to examine the bill than the use of probing amendments, which often require officials to guess what the amendment might be getting at when preparing the Minister's brief, and then lead to debate on the technical merits of the proposed amendment rather than on the merits of the bill. . . .

71. The simple purpose of [previous, set time restrictions on the evidence gathering phrase]—to stop [it] from becoming unduly drawn-out and unnecessarily delaying the passage of the bill can now adequately be met by a sensible programme order. We recommend that public bill committees should hold at least one evidence session, with the Minister and officials, in all cases. Beyond that, the general restrictions on the number, duration and timing of oral evidence sessions held by public bill committees should be lifted. Appropriate out-dates should be applied instead on a case-by-case basis in the programme order.

Note

The Committee also suggested that the Public Bill Committees (PBCs) should start with any pre-legislative report produced by a previous committee, rather than re-examining witnesses on matters already considered; it also recommended changes to the papers used by a Committee to make the whole process more transparent and easy to follow by those outside Parliament. The Committee's recommendations, including necessary changes to standing orders, were accepted. In its review of 2007–08, the Liaison Committee commented very favourably on the new system, finding that 'In the 2007–08 session, twelve PBCs held a total of 35 oral evidence sessions and received 164 pieces of written evidence.' Moreover, the PBC procedure had not limited the opportunities for pre-legislative scrutiny of draft Bills nor of examination of Bills before Parliament by Select Committees.[67] In 2009, the Hansard Society suggested further minor reforms to the system.[68] Hazell, who believes that 'The inadequate scrutiny of legislation is the greatest single scandal in the House of Common', comments that the advent of PBCs is 'certainly an improvement' on the old Standing Committees but adds:

> it must be asked if legislative scrutiny will ever really improve until Select Committees are also involved in the process. That is what happens in Scotland, where the task of scrutinising bills goes to the unified subject committees. They struggle because of the increase in their workload, but it does mean that the bill is scrutinised by members with some interest and feel for the policy background.[69]

Government control over the parliamentary timetable

The key aspect of Government dominance over Parliament, other than its majority, and the greatest threat to the ability of the Commons properly to scrutinise Government Bills, comes from the devices available to the Government to reduce the time available for debate. The use of the 'closure' allows debate to be simply cut off at the instance of Government Whips (if supported on a vote which must be passed with at least 100 members in favour), while the 'guillotine' allows the Government to allocate a set amount of time for each stage of debate. Nowadays, most Government Bills are timetabled in advance.

As Ganz comments, the use of the guillotine or timetabling of Bills goes to the heart of our democratic process, i.e. the relationship between Government and Parliament.[70] It is by no means unknown for the guillotine to be used in relation to legislation with serious implications for civil liberties. In 1996 the Commons passed in a single day the Prevention of Terrorism (Additional Powers) Bill, introduced in the wake of the IRA's bomb attack on Canary Wharf, and allowing for stop and search without reasonable suspicion for terrorist offences.[71] The episode vividly illustrates that if both main parties are behind a populist measure, scrutiny can be reduced to negligible proportions, leaving individual backbenchers largely impotent. Since, in fact, measures which are seen as 'tough' on crime or terrorism often have all party support, given their populist appeal, it can be seen how the party system not only facilitates executive dominance of the Commons at the expense of the Opposition, but perhaps as importantly can result in the almost total withdrawal of sustained backbench scrutiny if such an action is perceived to be politically advantageous by the Opposition leadership. Similarly rushed Bills were passed in the wake of the Omagh bombing in 1998[72] and the 11 September attacks

---

67   Liaison Committee, First Special Report (2007–08) HC 291 at [40].

68   Hansard Society, *Representative Democracy: Briefing Paper 1: House of Commons Reform* (2009), para 2.2

69   Hazel, 'The Continuing Dynamism of Constitutional Reform' (2007) 60(1) Parlt Aff 3, at 12.

70   p 349 above, at 32–33.

71   See HC Deb cols 159–66, 181 (2 April 1996).

72   See C Walker, 'The Bombs in Omagh and their Aftermath: The Criminal Justice (Terrorism and Conspiracy) Act 1998' (1999) 62(6) MLR 879.

on America in 2001, in spite of the fact that, only a year before, the UK Parliament had passed the Terrorism Act 2000 which had placed on a permanent basis, and massively extended the scope of, the UK's previous 'temporary, emergency' antiterrorism legislation. See further on the passage of this legislation, Chapter 9 at 451–454).

An alternative to the imposition of the guillotine or closure are 'programming' Bills, whereby a timetable for the Bill's passage is agreed between the party Whips. This technique is discussed in a series of reports from the Modernisation Select Committee.

Second Report of the Modernisation Committee: *Programming of Legislation and Timing of Votes*, HC 589 (1999–2000)

5   . . . The basic requirements of a reformed system as identified in our First Report were:

- The Government of the day must be assured of getting its legislation through in reasonable time (provided that it obtains the approval of the House).
- The Opposition in particular and Members in general must have a full opportunity to discuss and seek to change provisions to which they attach importance.
- All parts of a bill must be properly considered.

12   Our own analysis confirms that even with programme motions the third of our aims—scrutiny of all parts of a bill—is hardest to deliver. Although it is clear that programmed bills have been rather more comprehensively discussed than have old-style guillotined bills, there remain some gaps and omissions.

The case for agreed programming

13   While we acknowledge that there remain deficiencies in the agreed programming procedures used since 1997, it remains our firm judgment that, whilst voluntary informal agreements will continue to have a role to play, agreed programming of legislation can have a role to play in ensuring a more effective and efficient use of parliamentary time and improvement in the scrutiny of legislation. Its benefits extend across the range of interests in Parliament and beyond:

- It allows the Government to know when it can obtain approval of each piece of its programme.
- It offers the Opposition the opportunity to determine the structure and focus of the debate.
- Backbenchers from all parties may be given more certainty of voting times.
- In the longer term legislation will be better drafted because of the pressure on the Government to reduce the number of amendments which are tabled at the last minute.

Notes

1. The Committee's recommendation in this Report that programming be used for all Bills was only made at the cost of splitting the Committee. The non-Labour minority on the Committee issued a scathing minority Report. Nevertheless, the use of programming as an experiment for

one session was approved by the House on 7 November 2000.[73] The Committee was later forced to report, however,[74] that the attempt to find overall support for programming had failed:

> Despite all party agreement on the value of programming early in the Parliament and strong attempts to reach agreement in preparing our Second Report of last Session, it was not possible to reach agreement across the House or with all backbenchers on the current Sessional Orders. In practice, every programme motion in this Session has faced opposition, irrespective of content.

2. In fact, considerable hostility had been raised towards programming, which was widely perceived across the parties as amounting in practice to merely another means whereby Government limited and controlled opposition in Parliament. A particularly notorious incident occurred in relation to the Criminal Justice and Police Bill in 2001, described here by two Conservative members of the Modernisation Committee:

Appendix to a Report of the Modernisation Committee on Programming of Legislation, HC 382 (2000–01): Memorandum submitted by Mrs Angela Browning MP and Mr Richard Shepherd MP

. . .Every bill this session has been guillotined. Few enquiries if any are made of the Official Opposition or opposition parties as to what time may be necessary to properly discharge the duty of scrutiny. This may perhaps best be illustrated by reference to the Criminal Justice and Police Bill. The out time from Standing Committee, which had been set immediately after Second Reading and without any reference to the weight of issues raised at Second Reading, simply proved inadequate. When the guillotine fell at 7 pm in standing Committee, the Committee had only reached Clause 90 out of 132. There were amendments yet to be considered, including Government amendments. . . .The whole of Part III, from Clause 49 to Clause 69, had also not been considered. The Guillotine arrangements for Report Stage were also so tight that clauses and amendments which had not been considered in Standing Committee were not considered at Report.

. . .As the House knows, the Government tabled a Motion stating that:

> . . .the Bill shall be deemed to have been reported to the House, as amended by the Committee and as if those Clauses and Schedules the consideration of which has not been completed by the Committee has been ordered to stand part of the Bill with the outstanding Amendments which stood on the Order Paper in the name of Mr Charles Clarke.

The Speaker advised the House that there is no precedent for such a Motion (Hansard, col 728) . . .

We do not believe that it is in the interest of the House and of its standing among those whom we are elected by to pass a motion that is an untruth. Nor is it proper to consign to the Lords an unconsidered bill.

---

73   HC Deb cols 209 *et seq.*

74   HC 382 (2000–01), para 3.

The Select Committee in writing its Report would permit no analysis of what has actually happened to consideration of bills under the Sessional Order of 7 November 2000. We believe this would have been a helpful exercise to the Select Committee and the House in assessing whether the Sessional Order has achieved the aim of properly scrutinising bills.

Of the 'beliefs' expressed in the Select Committee Majority Report, in paragraph 7: *We believe that if these procedural approaches are supported by all we will have improved the legislative 'terms of trade' to the benefit of everyone.*

We reject the view that it improves the 'terms of trade' for everyone. It is clearly to the disadvantage of the Official Opposition, to the expressed disadvantage of back-benchers and minorities and to the balance between the majority and the minority within the House. It has strengthened the Government's control over procedures with no discernible concession to the Opposition. It is true that the Government will get greater certainty for this legislative timetable. The proposition that Opposition parties and backbenchers will get greater opportunities to debate and vote on the issues of most concern to them simply has not been borne out by experience in this Session of the experiment of systematic guillotining of all bills. Similarly the evidence of this Session is that the House has not scrutinised legislation better and we would refer back to the Government Motion of 12 March, to which we have previously made reference, as indicative of this failure.

Notes

1. One reform which has helped relieve a little pressure on parliamentary time is the introduction of carry-over, whereby instead of Bills automatically falling if they have not completed all their stages by the end of the Session, they may be carried over to complete their passage in the next session.[75] For further discussion of the mechanics and implications of carry-over, see the Third Report of the Modernisation Committee: HC 543 (1997–98). Carry-over of Bills, subject to certain safeguards, was agreed by the Commons in 2002.

2. Despite Opposition dissatisfaction, programming has remained. As Hazel notes: 'since 2001, programme motions have become normal for all government Bills'.[76]

   The Hansard Society commented in 2009 that 'Programming motions are regarded as one of the most fundamental reforms undertaken in the House of Commons in the last decade'[77] and was highly critical of the way they had been used in a partisan way by Government to limit scrutiny.

3. The MPs Expenses Scandal, considered fully in Chapter 10, led to sustained calls in the media and from within Parliament and the Opposition Parties for the renewal of Parliament. One concrete result was the setting up of a Committee on Reform of the House.[78] One of its key suggestions is greater independence for Select Committees (below). The other is, broadly, to give the Commons greater control over its own timetable and business. These ideas for reform are considered at the end of this chapter, but here we note the Committee's eloquent explanation of the extent and nature of Governmental control over Parliament.

---

75   *Modernisation of the House of Commons: A Reform Programme for Consultation,* HC 440 (2001–02).

76   Hazel, n 63 above, at 275.

77   Hansard Society, *Representative Democracy: Briefing Paper 1: House of Commons Reform* (2009), para 1.3.

78   See House of Commons Reform Committee, *Rebuilding the House*

House of Commons Reform Committee, *Rebuilding the House,*
***First Report* (2008–09) (extracts)**

109. The single greatest cause of dissatisfaction which we have detected with current scheduling of legislative business in the House arises from the handling of the report stage of government bills—technically the "consideration" stage when a Bill has been reported back to the House from a public bill committee. In the majority of cases, the programme motion decided without debate immediately after Second Reading allows for a single day for report and Third Reading. It also usually specifies that the report stage will end one hour before the moment of interruption, leaving at most one hour for Third Reading. Even where no other business is taken first, such as a Ministerial Statement, that leaves around five hours for a report stage.

110. The report stage is a highly valued opportunity for scrutiny of legislation for a number of reasons.

- It offers all Members of the House at least a theoretical opportunity to propose amendments to a Bill or speak to them.
- It provides the one opportunity for the House as a whole to vote on a major specific provision of a Bill or a closely connected issue, including issues of public concern which might have been dealt with in a Bill but are not. Because it is on the floor of the House, debates on report stage represent the only opportunity for detailed participation in scrutiny of the Bill for senior backbenchers such as select committee chairmen who have not served on the public bill committee, for dissenting backbenchers who have not been chosen to serve on it and those members who for other reasons have been unable to serve on it.
- It represents what in many cases will be the only opportunity for Members from the smaller parties to participate in legislative scrutiny.

The report stage is the only opportunity for the House as a whole to engage with proposed legislation and debate and decide its principal provisions in any detail.

111. Practice and procedure on report have a significant effect on outcome. New Clauses moved by Ministers are taken first. They may well be grouped for discussion with related new Clauses and amendments moved by the Opposition or other parties or individual Members. Ministers—and only Ministers—may move a motion to take new Clauses and amendments in a different order so as to prioritise one "topic" over another. Ministers—and only Ministers—may move a motion to provide for end-times—'knives'—for particular groups of amendments so as to give time to others further down the list.

112. In practice, as a result of the programme motion proposed by Ministers and approved with little or no debate, the situation is that on many report stages several groups of amendments from Opposition parties or backbencher amendments selected by the Chair and grouped for a joint debate are not even reached for debate, let alone a decision. The practice of the Chair is only to allow a vote on a non-Ministerial amendment or new Clause if it has been part of a group which has at least had some debate. At the end of the time allowed for report, there is a ritual whereby Government amendments within the last group to be debated, and those relating to later unreached and undebated parts of a Bill are put without any explanation and routinely agreed to, while other amendments are simply lost.

113. This is an issue which causes great dissatisfaction in the Opposition parties and on the backbenches...

Note

We turn to the Committee's proposals for reform at the end of this chapter. It is worth noting that, despite the critical content of much of the discussion above, the clear direction of travel in recent times has been positive as Hazel notes:

> The legislative process has undergone steady improvement in recent years, with more to come. . . More Bills are published in draft, there is a growing array of specialist parliamentary committees to scrutinise them, and growing recognition that most serious scrutiny takes place in committee, and not on the floor of the House.[79]

Proposals for more radical reform are considered at the end of this chapter.

Delegated legislation

The Modernisation Committee has noted:

> In terms of volume alone, the majority of legislation is made not by acts of Parliament (primary legislation) but by secondary or delegated legislation, also known as statutory instruments (SIs). In 2003, for example, there was a total of 8,942 pages of SIs, compared to 3,435 pages of non-consolidation acts. Typically, delegated legislation is made by the Government using powers granted by an Act of Parliament. It can take a variety of forms, including Orders in Council, Rules, Regulations and Codes of Practice. . .
>
> 10. Secondary legislation has the same force in law as primary legislation, except that a court may consider whether the Government was properly exercising the powers conferred on it by Parliament in making the legislation, whereas it cannot look at the processes leading up to the passage of an Act of Parliament.[80]

Notes

1. There is a broader issue of constitutional principle at stake in the increasing use of Acts that lay down merely a skeletal framework for legislation whereby extremely important matters are decided by secondary legislation (the most important contemporary example is undoubtedly the Legislative and Regulatory Reform Act 2006—below).[81] The enactment of broad enabling powers by Parliament which give Ministers *de facto* powers to legislate may also be seen as a significant erosion of parliamentary sovereignty. So called 'Henry VIII' clauses, in giving Ministers the power to amend primary legislation by regulations which may never be seen or debated by Parliament,[82] offend against one of the fundamental principles of parliamentary sovereignty, that 'no person or body is recognised by the law of England as having a right to override or set aside the legislation of Parliament'.[83]

---

79   Hazel, 'Time for a new Convention' at 296.

80   Modernisation Committee, *The Legislative Process,* First Report (2005–06) HC 1097 at [9].

81   On previous similar legislation, see D Miers, 'The Deregulation Procedure: An Expanding Role' [1999] PL 477.

82   On the power to make such Orders contained in s 10 of the Human Rights Act 1998, in order to repeal or amend legislative provisions found to be incompatible with the European Convention on Human Rights, see Chapter 3, at 134–135.

83   AV Dicey, *An Introduction to the Study of the Law of the Constitution,* 10th edn (1959), pp xxxiv.

2. The 2006 Act was discussed in Chapter 3 in terms of the Separation of Powers, but it is important to consider it here also, in order to assess the response of the Commons to it.[84] In the words of the Regulatory Reform Committee, the original Bill:

> Empower[ed] any Minister by order to make provision amending, repealing or replacing *any* legislation, primary or secondary, for *any* purpose, and to reform the common law to implement Law Commission recommendations. . . It [thus] [gave] Ministers a. . .general power to legislate.[85]

As the House of Lord's Constitution Committee commented on the original Bill:

> the breadth of Ministers' powers to change the statute book was astonishingly wide. [Cl 1 of the Bill] established no effective legal boundaries to the scope of the power. Had this provision become law, it would have eroded the principal difference between an order made by a Minister under delegated powers and an Act of Parliament, namely that a Minister's powers, unlike Parliament's, are limited.[86]

3. The Regulatory Reform Committee suggested introducing additional safeguards into the Bill, including a Parliamentary veto on use of the procedure, restrictions on the scope of the power that the Bill gave to Ministers to legislate by SI and the beefing up of the procedures under which the House would consider Orders made under the Act. However, the Bill went through the Committee stage virtually unscathed.[87] At that point, though, other Committees weighed in with significant criticisms of the Bill, and suggested both hugely scaling up parliamentary checks under the suggested new procedure, and excluding certain statutes from the Act's scope (so that e.g. the Human Rights Act could not be abolished or modified using the procedure).[88] Faced with growing adverse media coverage and a warning from the chief Whip in the Lords that the Government faced defeat there on the Bill as currently drafted, the Government made a series of concessions, including, crucially, reducing the power under the Bill to one to make orders, including those repealing primary legislation, for the purpose of: *'removing or reducing any burden, or the overall burdens, resulting directly or indirectly for any person from any legislation.'* This was still an extremely broad delegated power, but it did at least row back from the wholesale transfer of legislative power to the executive represented by the original proposals. Moreover, various safeguards suggested by the Committees were included, and further were added during the passage in the Lords, including the use of the 'super-affirmative' method of approving instruments made under the Act, described below.

---

84   For a full account, see P Davis, 'The Significance of Parliamentary Procedures in Control of the Executive: A Case Study: The Passage of Part 1 of the Legislative and Regulatory Reform Act 2006' [2007] PL 677, to whom we are indebted for the brief account that follows here.

85   House of Commons Regulatory Reform Committee (1st Special Report, 05–6)—emphasis added.

86   11th Report (2005–06) HL 194, at [8].

87   Davis, n 84 above, at 686.

88   See Reports of the House of Commons Procedure Committee (First Report, (2005–2006) HC 894); the Joint Committee on Human Rights (Seventeenth Report, (2005–2006) HL 164, HC 1062); Public Administration Select Committee (Third Report, (200–2006) HC 1033).

Scrutiny of delegated legislation: efficacy

The following report from the Procedure Committee outlines the standard methods of scrutiny for delegated legislation, and the special methods used for the scrutiny of European Union legislation (all of which is delegated legislation under the European Communities Act 1972) and for Orders made under the Deregulation and Contracting Out Act 1994 (and now also the Regulatory Reform Act 2006) which are of special significance because they amend primary legislation.

**First Report of the Procedure Committee, Delegated Legislation,
HC 48 (1999–2000) (extracts)**

5 . . . The present system, which has grown up over many years, is founded on the distinction between two categories of statutory instrument: 'affirmative instruments', which require a positive Resolution of each House to come into effect, and 'negative instruments', which can be annulled by a Resolution of either House if passed within 40 days of their laying.

6 An affirmative instrument stands automatically referred for debate in a Standing Committee on Delegated Legislation ('DL Committee') unless the Government agrees that it be debated on the Floor of the House. Debate in Committee arises on a formal and unamendable motion, 'That the Committee has considered the draft XYZ Order 2000', and after a maximum of one and a half hour's debate, the Chairman reports the instrument to the House irrespective of whether or not the motion has been agreed to. A motion to approve the instrument is then put to the House, without further debate. Instruments taken on the Floor are debated for up to an hour and a half, also on an un-amendable motion.

7 Negative instruments are not debated unless a motion is tabled seeking ('praying') that the instrument be annulled, and the Government agrees either that the instrument be debated in a DL Committee or, much more rarely, on the Floor of the House. For many years the Government has accepted no obligation so to agree. Proceedings in committee are the same as for an affirmative instrument; however, in the case of negatives referred to committee there are no subsequent proceedings on the Floor (a point of some significance given that negatives can only effectively be annulled by a vote on the Floor).

8 All statutory instruments laid before Parliament are scrutinised by the Joint Committee on Statutory Instruments (JCSI). The committee's task is to consider technical but important issues such as whether the instrument is made within the powers conferred by the parent legislation, and whether its drafting is defective. The committee is precluded from considering the actual merits of instruments or the policy underlying them. It has the assistance of Speaker's Counsel and regularly reports to both Houses.

9 In the last complete Session, 1998–99, 178 affirmative instruments were laid before the House, of which 150 were considered in committee, 21 were considered on the Floor, and seven were withdrawn. In the same Session, 1,266 negative instruments were laid before the House, of which 28 were considered in committee and one on the Floor.

48 **The European Scrutiny Committee** (until 1998 the European Legislation Committee) is charged with the task of considering a range of EU documents, as defined in Standing Order No 143. These include EU Regulations, Directives, Decisions of the Council, budgetary documents, Commission proposals, reports and recommendations, documents submitted to the European Central Bank, various inter-governmental proposals, and reports of the Court of Auditors. About 1,000 EU documents a year are deposited in Parliament for scrutiny. The Committee's functions are to assess the political and/or legal importance of these documents and decide which merit further scrutiny, either

in European Standing Committee or on the Floor; to report in detail on each document the Committee considers important (some 475 a year), taking written and oral evidence if necessary; to monitor business in the Council of Ministers and the negotiating position of UK Ministers; to review EU legal, procedural and institutional developments which may have implications for the UK and the House; and to police the scrutiny system.

49 When a document is referred by the Committee to one of the three European Standing Committees, that committee will meet to hear a Government Minister make a statement and answer questions put by Members for up to 1 hour (extendable by a further 30 minutes at the Chairman's discretion); this is followed by a debate on an amendable motion for up to a further 1 hour 30 minutes. The Chairman reports to the House any resolution to which the committee has come, or that it has come to no resolution. A Government motion couched in similar terms is usually moved in the House a few days later; the Question on this is put forthwith.

Notes

1. There has been a long history of parliamentary committees complaining that the system for parliamentary scrutiny and control of delegated legislation is grossly inadequate. In 1978, the Select Committee on Procedure 1977–78 warned, 'the system provides only vestigial control of statutory instruments and is in need of complete reform'. The fundamental problem identified with the system was that instruments subject to negative affirmation were increasingly becoming law without ever having been debated by the Commons. Since that Report, this phenomenon increased sharply: in 1978–79, 71.7% of prayers for annulment were debated; in the 1985–86 Session, this percentage had dropped to 30.6%.

2. As mentioned above, an important mechanism for the scrutiny of delegated legislation is the Joint Committee on Statutory Instruments, whose remit is to draw the attention of Parliament to any statutory instrument (other than those made under the HRA or the Legislative and Regulatory Reform Act 2007) (below) on a number of narrow grounds, including retrospective effect, delay, attempted ouster of judicial review, imposing charges on public funds or where it appears to be *ultra vires.*[89]

3. JD Hayhurst and P Wallington argue that the use of delegated legislation has changed significantly, especially in the previous decade or so. 'It is no longer the technical implementation of detail in a legislative mosaic, although undoubtedly the majority of statutory instruments are in this category. More of the policy of a legislative proposal is likely to be delegated, the legislation being enabling not just at a specific but at the broadest level.'[90] For a sustained analysis of the inadequacies of the current system, and proposals for reform, see the First Report of the Procedure Committee, *Delegated Legislation,* HC 48 (1999–2000).[91]

4. In 2001 the Commons established a Regulatory Reform Committee, whose remit is to examine and report on all draft legislative reform orders proposed by the Government under the Regulatory Reform Act 2001—now the Legislative and Regulatory Reform Act 2006 (above). As noted by the Modernisation Committee, the 2006 now provides for a special procedure for scrutinising instruments made under it, also used for instruments made under the 'fast track' procedure laid down in the Human Rights Act for amending legislation found by the courts to be incompatible with Convention rights.

---

89   Standing Order 151.

90   'The Parliamentary Scrutiny of Delegated Legislation' [1988] PL 547–76, at p 573.

91   For further comments on this issue and suggestions for reform, see P Tudor (clerk to the House of Lords Delegated Powers and Deregulation Committee), 'Secondary Legislation: Second Class or Crucial?' (2000) 21(3) SLR 149.

Under the 'super-affirmative' procedure, used for Regulatory Reform Orders (RROs) and Remedial Orders made under the Human Rights Act, a proposal for a draft Order is laid before Parliament and examined by the relevant select committee (Regulatory Reform or Human Rights); a draft Order is then laid and proceeded with in a similar way to an affirmative SI, depended, in the case of an RRO, on how the Committee voted on it.[92]

THE COMMONS AS SCRUTINEER OF THE EXECUTIVE

It is an axiom of any theory of responsible government that thorough scrutiny of the executive arm of the state is vital to a democratic system; an important part of this scrutiny is undertaken by Parliament, to which, at least theoretically, all Ministers are responsible.[93] As Norton has pointed out, in the House of Commons, 'Unlike [in] many legislatures, the Government of the day is obliged to explain its actions continually and open itself to constant criticism. The US President does not face a critical Congress and can even hide away from the press if he so chooses. The British Prime Minister, however, has to face the Leader of the Opposition twice a week over the despatch box.'[94] Chapter 12 considers the normative content of the doctrine of Ministerial responsibility and its underpinnings in the Ministerial Code. However, as Tomkins points out:

> It would be all very having rules and conventions of ministerial responsibility, but without adequate parliamentary means to apply those rules in practice, the doctrines would be useless.[95]

It is the adequacy and effectiveness of those means that are explored in this chapter. However, there is a central problem for the Commons in an acting as a scrutiniser of the executive: that MPs from the governing party—nearly always that majority in the House—tend to place their loyalty to their political party above their rather abstract duty, as members of the legislature, to hold the executive to account. In addition, the dual imperative driving opposition members—to exact such accountability, but also to score as many political points as they can—tends to make the Government overly defensive in relation to the Commons. It can also have the effect of causing MPs from the governing party to 'rally round' the Government in its defence, thus siding with the very body they are supposed to be scrutinising and holding to account. Tomkins refers to party loyalty as 'the fault line that has the potential to run deepest through the system of political accountability'.[96] As we will see below, it is when backbench MPs can develop a sense of collective identity independent of party, and some real expertise in particular fields, that scrutiny is likely to be most effective.

---

92   First Report, (2005–06) HC 1097, at [9].

93   It should be noted that changes in the organisation of the Civil Service, the 'Next Steps' initiative, and the rise in the number of government services carried out by semi-autonomous agencies, has raised serious questions as to the extent to which Ministers in charge of the relevant departments can still be held accountable to Parliament. This issue is discussed in the chapter on the executive (Chapter 11).

94   Norton, 'Parliament I: the House of Commons', in Jones, n 17 above, at 319. Prime Minister's Questions now only takes place once a week, but for the same total time period.

95   A Tomkins, *Public Law* (2003) 160.

96   *Ibid*, at 164.

Scrutiny on the floor of the Commons

Opportunities for scrutiny on the floor of the House include 20 Opposition Days, the debate on the Queen's Speech, motions of censure, emergency debates (rarely granted), Adjournment Motions, Prime Minister Questions, and Departmental Questions. As Michael Ryle points out, the opportunities for scrutiny in the Commons have increased markedly over the last 50 years.[97] He instances the right to table Early Day Motions: 'little used until the mid-1960s, today up to 2,000 such motions are tabled each session.'

As noted above, Standing Order 14(1) provides that '*Save as provided in this order, government business shall have precedence at every sitting*'. The Commons Reform Committee noted[98] that the exceptions provided for in SO 14 include:

- Opposition days each session, allotted on days determined by the Government: and ;
- oral questions for an hour on Mondays to Thursdays and Urgent Questions [SO No 21];
- motions for leave to bring in Bills under the 'ten-minute rule', on Tuesdays and Wednesdays [SO No 23];
- emergency debates [SO No 24];
- end of day 30 minute adjournment backbench debates every sitting day [SO No 9];
- three Estimates days each year, for debates under the auspices of the Liaison Committee [SO No 54];
- [Westminster Hall] is used on Tuesdays and Wednesdays for five separate 30 or 90 minute backbench debates selected by ballot and on Thursdays for debates on either select committee reports or other matters chosen by the Government. The same Standing Order provides for the Speaker to appoint six days in Westminster Hall for debates on select committee reports chosen by the Liaison Committee.

Whilst the floor of the House now has increased potential as a forum for scrutiny of the executive, it is here that scrutiny can still sometimes be at its most ineffective. Adjournment debates provide opportunities for backbenchers to make extended criticisms of government policy. Unfortunately, the House tends to be almost empty at this time, and very little publicity is afforded to these debates, which consequently lose much of their sting. Emergency debates allow a further opportunity to raise urgent issues on the floor of the House, but requests for such debates are rarely granted. Similarly, Early Day Motions allow for cross-party expressions of concern or criticism of government policy; opportunities for debate of these Motions have markedly increased with the advent of Westminster Hall as an alternative forum for debate, but the situation is still far from satisfactory.

Far more publicity is given to the questioning of Ministers on the floor of the House; 1 hour a day is set aside every day, except Friday, for oral answers to be given to Members' questions. A recent report by the Procedure Committee revealed the enormous growth in the use of questions for both oral and written answers[99] from just 3,525 in 1946–47 to 28,739 in 1999–2000. The latest report[100] found that, by March 2009, the average daily number of questions tabled was 515, more than double the number tabled in any session of the 1997–2001 Parliament; it recommended that Members be reminded not to

---

97 Michael Ryle, 'The Changing Commons' (1994) Parlt Aff 647, pp 658–59.

98 *Rebuilding the House* at [121]–[123].

99 Annex C to the Third Report of the Procedure Committee, Parliamentary Questions, HC 622 (2001–02).

100   First Special Report Written Parliamentary Questions: Government Response to the Committee's Third Report of Session 2008–09 HC 129.

table questions, the answers to which are obtainable elsewhere. The Government remarked that it was inevitable, with over 500 questions a day, that answers may not always be up to the standards MPs want nor answered within the normal time limit.

Limitations on the obligation to reply to parliamentary questions

The basic principles governing ministerial replies to any form of questioning in Parliament are set out in the Ministerial Code (Cabinet Office, 2007) which replicates the wording of a resolution passed by Parliament in 1997:[101]

(b) Ministers have a duty to Parliament to account and be held to account, for the policies, decisions and actions of their Departments and Agencies.

(c) It is of paramount importance that Ministers give accurate and truthful information to Parliament, correcting any inadvertent error at the earliest opportunity. Ministers who knowingly mislead Parliament will be expected to offer their resignation to the Prime Minister.

(d) Ministers must be as open as possible with Parliament and the public, refusing to provide information only when disclosure would not be in the public interest, which should be decided in accordance with the relevant statutes, and the Freedom of Information Act 2000.

(e) Ministers should similarly require civil servants who give evidence before Parliamentary Committees on their behalf and under their direction to be as helpful as possible in providing accurate, truthful and full information in accordance with the duties and responsibilities of civil servants as set out in the Civil Service Code.

These excluded areas have been cut down a little—Ministers may no longer withhold information on the basis of 'established parliamentary convention', but instead only 'when disclosure would not be in the public interest and relevant statutes. Previously, the matter had to be decided in accordance with the Government's Code of Practice on Access to Government Information, which was non-statutory and legally unenforceable. The content of the duty of ministerial responsibility and accountability are explored in Chapter 12, pp 627–663, while the Freedom of Information Act itself is covered in Chapter 13 and readers are referred to those chapters at this point. However, a few brief comments will be made here.

The Freedom of Information Act 2000 for the first time introduced a general right of access to government information, policed by an independent Information Commissioner and which is ultimately enforceable through the contempt jurisdiction of the High Court (s 52). MPs of course are able to make as much use of the Act as anyone. The Act therefore dealt with the basic previous problem that Ministers could not ultimately be compelled to release information. However, the Act is riddled with extremely wide ranging exemptions—broader even than those in the Code, in the view of some commentators. In particular, there is a class exemption in s 35 in relation to all information relating to 'the formulation or development of government policy'. The only limitation to this astonishingly broad exemption—which is not subject to any burden on Ministers to prove that any harm would be caused by releasing the information in question—is that statistical information relating to a decision is no longer exempted once the decision is made. But, for example, evidence of other policy options considered, and the reasons for rejecting them, would be covered by the exemption. The Information Commissioner can order release of the information concerned if satisfied that the public interest

---

101   HC Deb cols 1046–47 (19 March 1997).

in withholding information does not outweigh the interest in its reception (s 2); however, because the information relates to a central government department, its release can ultimately be vetoed by a Cabinet Minister (s 53). In practice, the Commissioner has been much more bullish and FOI-oriented in interpreting and enforcing the Act than many had predicted; however, the Ministerial veto has also been used—twice in about five years; see further, Chapter 13 at 725–730.

Parliamentary questions will also of course be refused if they do not relate to a matter within the Minister's area of responsibility. Thus questions on areas of competency devolved to the Scottish, Wales and Northern Ireland assemblies will be ruled out of order, as will matters falling within the purview of local authorities, the Greater London Assembly, or other bodies, such as Chief Constables of Police, or privatised industries.

In relation specifically to parliamentary questions, in addition to the specific grounds for refusing questions set out in the Act, there is also the ground of excessive cost: successive Governments have refused to answer questions deemed disproportionately expensive to research. The figure above which a question will be deemed too expensive to answer is currently £600.[102] There are also more general limitations on the use of questioning, explained by the Public Administration Committee, which also goes on to note problems with the use of these restrictions by Ministers as well as complaints as to the promptness and quality of answers.[103]

Public Administration Committee, *Ministerial Accountability and Parliamentary Questions*, HC 61 (2000–01)

4 The House's principal rules on what may be asked in a written Parliamentary Question are derived from decisions by successive Speakers on individual Questions, endorsed from time to time by Select Committees on Procedure. They can be crystallised in three essential points:

- Questions should seek information or press for action, i.e. they should not become a form of debate, giving Members the opportunity to make statements, or political points, directly;
- Questions should be on matters for which the Government has responsibility, and should be directed to the Minister within the Government who is responsible; and
- Questions should not repeat recently answered Questions.

The last of these points is one of the reasons for the operation of the system of what has been generally known as 'blocking'. A Question may not be asked if that same Question has already been asked and answered in the current Session (unless there is a reason to believe that the situation has changed). If a Minister declines to provide information in answer to a Parliamentary Question (or refuses to take a particular action, if that is what has been asked), the same Question cannot be asked again for the next three months (again, unless there is reason to believe that circumstances have changed). . .

[The evidence before the Committee showed that departments blocked between 0.37 and 2.52% of questions asked]

. . . 11 We have said in our two latest reports that in many cases, when a Department withholds information in response to a question on the grounds that the information is confidential, it fails to mention the relevant exemption of the Code of Practice on Access to

---

102   Third Report of the Procedure Committee, HC 622 (2001–02), para 20.

103   HC 61 (2000–01), para 4.

Government Information. This happens despite the fact that the Government accepted a recommendation of the Public Service Committee in July 1996 that the relevant exemption should be specified when departments gave such answers.

12 We. . .recommend again that the Government ensure that where Departments withhold information under an exemption in the Code of Practice (or later under the Freedom of Information Act 2000) they invariably cite the relevant exemption. . .

17 Only a small proportion of questions in reality elicit 'disproportionate cost' answers. When they are given they undoubtedly cause disproportionate annoyance. In 1997–1998, out of 51,982 written questions, 1,441 received such answers; in 1998–1999 it was 732 out of 32,286 and in 1999–2000, 871 of 36,850.

18 Perhaps inevitably, Members and others suggested to us that 'disproportionate cost' is sometimes used as an excuse for not answering. . .

19 We recommend that when Departments are considering refusing to answer a question on the grounds of 'disproportionate cost', there should be a presumption that any of the requested information which is readily available should be given.

Notes

1. The Government's response to this report[104] accepted the recommendations it made. However, subsequent reports found that some departments were *still* failing to cite the relevant Code exemption when refusing answers.[105] In response,[106] the Government pledged again to tackle this problem. However, in its Report in 2005, the Committee again had to take the Government to task:

   > More than 98% of the Questions in the last two sessions received an answer (although these include holding replies and questions not answered for reasons of disproportionate cost). However, of those where an answer has been refused between sessions 2000–01 and session 2003–04, just over half (52.5%) of the responses have cited the Code exemption. The Home Office. . .has only managed an average of 13%, reaching a low of 9% in the last Session. Overall this has been a poor performance by Whitehall, not least since departments have invariably proved quite capable of coming up with the relevant exemption when we asked them do so subsequently.[107]

2. Oral questioning of Ministers is now often afforded live television coverage, and Prime Minister's questions are always covered on terrestrial television stations. Oral questions and their supplementaries tend to be used as an opportunity to probe Ministers' grasp of their portfolios or to attack government policy. They thus have some effect in ensuring that Ministers are kept up to the mark; they provide an opportunity for weak elements in government policy to be publicly exposed, and are one of the few times in which ordinary backbenchers can raise matters directly with Cabinet Ministers.

3. The ability of members to put down really probing questions is reduced by the lack of information and support staff available to backbenchers. Ministers, by contrast, have the aid of a skilled team of civil servants who provide them with answers to the tabled questions and undertake research into

---

104 HC 464 (2001–02).

105 Public Administration Committee, Ninth Report of the Committee for 2001–02 HC 1086.

106 First Report, *Ministerial Accountability and Parliamentary Questions: The Government Response to the Committee's Ninth Report of Session 2001–02*, HC 136 (2002–03).

107 Public Administration Select Committee, Fifth Report (2004–05) HC 449-I at [4].

the questioner's known interests and concerns in an attempt to anticipate and prepare the Minister for possible supplementaries. This inequality has led some observers to call for the establishment of a Department of the Opposition to improve the efficiency of Opposition MPs by giving them a staff of civil servants which would go some way to redressing the imbalance between Ministers and MPs. Needless to say, no such department has yet been created.[108]

4. This is perhaps one area in which television coverage has, whilst being helpful in terms of publicity, perhaps given a misleading impression. The kind of 'Commons clash' at Prime Minister's Question Time (PMQT) between the Leader of the Opposition and the Prime Minister which routinely gains television coverage may give the impression that ritual baiting, party point scoring and, above all, a complete lack of information transmission are the outstanding characteristics of PMQT. What needs to be borne in mind is that PMQT is by far the most politicised of all oral questioning of Ministers. A more comprehensive examination of parliamentary questions generally reveals that, whilst oral questions are often put and dealt with on a purely party political basis, they can yield useful results in terms of scrutiny as well. Information can be gained; useful concessions or statements of intent to which the Government can later be held are extracted; inadequacies in government thinking is exposed.

5. The Hansard Society Commission's 2001 report[109] was highly critical of Question Time, particularly Prime Minister's Questions:

> [Question Time] is dominated by point scoring and the vast majority of questions on both sides of the House are planted by the whips. The high level of political management of questions is illustrated by the fact that in the first 21 PMQs in 1997 the Prime Minister's 'standard reply to [planted questions]—'My honourable friend is absolutely right'—was used 35 times' [S Weir and D Beetham, *Political Power and Democratic Control in Britain: The Democratic Audit of the United Kingdom* (1999), p 432].

6. A fairly typical example of a recent exchange between then Prime Minister Gordon Brown and the leader of the Liberal Democrats follows:

HC Deb 20 Jan 2010, col 297

> **Mr Clegg**: I should like to return to the issue of Cadbury's. Last month, Lord Mandelson declared that the Government would mount a huge opposition to the Kraft takeover of Cadbury's, so why does the Royal Bank of Scotland, which is owned by this Government, now want to lend vast amounts of our money to Kraft to fund that takeover?
>
> **The Prime Minister:** If the right hon. Gentleman is really suggesting that the Government can step in and avoid any takeover that is taking place in this country overnight, and then tell a bank that it has got to deprive a particular company of money by Government dictate, his liberal principles seem to have gone to the wall.
>
> **Mr. Clegg**: I thank the Prime Minister for the little economics lecture, but there is a simple principle at stake. Tens of thousands of British companies are crying out for that money to protect jobs, and instead RBS wants to lend it to a multinational with a record of cutting jobs. When British taxpayers bailed out the banks, they would never have

---

108   But see Turpin, *British Government and the Constitution,* 3rd edn (1993), p 451 for possible disadvantages.

109   See p 359 above, at paras 4.19–4.23.

believed that their money would be used to put British people out of work. Is that not just plain wrong?

The Prime Minister: Putting the words 'liberal' and 'principle' together seems very difficult now—[Interruption.] I have to tell the right hon. Gentleman that no Government are doing more to try to protect and increase jobs than this country's. Unemployment is falling today as a result of the actions we have taken. If we had taken the advice of the Liberal party, unemployment would be a great deal higher than it is now. He has nothing to offer the debate on the economy at all—[Interruption.]

Mr. Speaker: Order. The House really must calm down. . .

Note

As a way of simply obtaining information, questions for written answers are generally to be much more effective.

HC Written Answers to Questions, Wednesday, 3 July 2002

Mr Beard: To ask the Secretary of State for Defence what the latest estimate is of the cost of the Trident Acquisition Programme; and if he will make a statement. [67206]

Mr Hoon: The current estimate of the total acquisition cost of the Trident programme, with payments already made expressed at the prices and exchange rates actually incurred and future spend at the current financial year rate (the hybrid) estimate, is now £9,800 million. Since the 2001 estimate and leaving aside the effects of price inflation and exchange rate variation (+£11 million), there has been a real cost increase of £25 million. This increase derives principally from additional costs associated with dockyard projects and with missiles and related equipment, offset by a reduced acquisition cost for the four submarines. Expenditure on the Trident acquisition programme to 30 September 2001 represented over 98 per cent of the total estimate. If all expenditure, past and projected, is brought up to this current year's economic conditions (the non-hybrid estimate) the estimate is £14,376 million.

The programme continues to show an overall reduction in real terms on its original 1982 estimate. This reduction, including the savings resulting from the decision to process missiles at the United States facility at Kings Bay, Georgia, now stands at over £3.7 billion at current prices.

The proportion of the estimate for work undertaken in the United Kingdom continues to be around 70 per cent Three in-service Vanguard class submarines are successfully maintained continuous at-sea deterrence, with the fourth, HMS Vanguard, now undergoing planned major overhaul. . .

Dr Tonge: To ask the Secretary of State for Defence what new agreements have been reached regarding the Ballistic Missile Early Warning Station at RAF Fylingdales following the end of the 1972 ABM Treaty. [66684]

Mr Ingram: None.

Notes

1. It may be seen from the above that the style of answering written questions is far more straight-forward and factual, and a great deal of information of use both in informing debate about public policy in particular areas and in assisting backbenchers and the Opposition in pressing for action from Government, as well as exposing flaws in government policy, may be obtained. Tomkins

comments that, in contrast to the drama of oral questions, which are often simply a party-political joust, 'written questions. . .are a vital ingredient of contemporary parliamentary practice and contribute a great deal to the system of parliamentary accountability.'[110]

2. Whilst, in general, questions of Ministers, speeches and debates on policy may have little impact, they may on occasions be decisive. The careers of Ministers, even Prime Ministers, can be severely damaged or destroyed during such occasions, whilst the reputation of an administration as a whole may be dented. One example is the famous speech of Norman Lament, made after his forced resignation, in which he described the Major administration as giving the impression of being 'in office, but not in power'; a similarly wounding attack was made by Sir Geoffrey Howe on Mrs Thatcher in his unexpectedly ferocious resignation speech in November 1990. Conversely, if a Minister manages to acquit him or herself with aplomb during a testing debate, his or her stature may be increased.

3. The Modernization Committee recently made a series of suggestions for enhancing the role of the back-bench MP in *Revitalizing the chamber: the role of the Back-Bench MP*.[111]These relatively modest proposals included: allocating part of most question times to topical questions; extra debates on topical matters on a weekly basis; a weekly half-hour slot for debating Select Committee Reports in Westminster Hall; and shorter speeches, including from front benchers. They were not all accepted and have to an extent been superseded by the far more radical proposals from the Commons Reform Committee—see below at 419–424.

THE SELECT COMMITTEES

Introduction

It was precisely to give backbenchers more in-depth knowledge of government departments that 14 Select Committees were set up in 1979, covering between them each of the major government departments with the exception of the Law Officers' Department and the Lord Chancellor's Department which were brought within the system later.

The current list of Select Committees is as follows:

Departmental Committees: Business; Innovation and Skills; Children; Schools and Families Committee; Communities and Local Government Committee; Culture; Media and Sport; Defence; Energy and Climate Change ; Environment, Food and Rural Affairs; Foreign Affairs; Health; Home Affairs; International Development; Justice (covering the successor department to the old Lord Chancellor's Department, which briefly became the Department for Constitutional Affairs); Northern Ireland Affairs; Scottish Affairs; Transport; Treasury; Welsh Affairs; Work and Pensions.

The following committees cut across departments: Deregulation; Environmental Audit; European Scrutiny; Public Accounts; Public Administration (which is also the committee for the Parliamentary Ombudsman); Regulatory Reform; Science and Technology; Statutory Instruments; Joint Committee on Human Rights.

Eight Regional Committees, one for each of England's administrative regions apart from London

---

110   Tomkins, *Public Law* at 161.

111   HC 337 (2005–06).

were established by Order of the House on 1 Jan 2009: East Midlands, East of England; North East; North West; South East; South West; West Midlands; Yorkshire and The Humber. There was a pre-existing Committee for London.

The Liaison Committee exists to oversee and coordinate the work of the other Select Committees. The Modernisation Committee's remit is to consider improvements to House of Commons' working practices, something also covered by the Procedure Committee. The remit of the Standards and Privileges Committee is matters of privilege and member's conduct and financial interests.

The Committees were set up due to widespread dissatisfaction with procedures on the floor of the House of Commons as a means of scrutinising the workings of Government and a consequent perception that the balance of power between the executive and Parliament was not being maintained under the then current arrangements, as Ryle explains below.

Memorandum by Mr Michael Ryle (SC 35)

At the heart of the functions of the House of Commons today lies the task of scrutinising the policies and acts of the Government. Ministers must explain and defend—or be prepared to explain and defend—everything they do or propose to do. Their principal critics, the Opposition parties, must equally explain and defend their alternative policies. Parliament is essentially a critical forum through which the powers of Government are exercised and in which they are publicly examined. The influence of Parliament depends on the extent to which its critical process both reflects and conditions public opinion. To be effective the House of Commons must both listen to and speak to the people it represents. This public criticism, to be effective, requires the use of procedures which enable ministers, civil servants and others to be examined in detail on their responsibilities and, above all, which provide access to the information necessary to assets their conduct. The great growth in this century in the range, volume and complexity of modern government has meant that this criticism in depth can no longer be achieved by the simple process of debate followed by vote, and that there is not enough time for the actions of ministers to be fully considered on the floor of the House. Hence the development of a range of committee systems.

Note

The new Committees were better equipped and organised than their predecessors, set up in the 1966–70 Parliament. Their function was expressed to be 'to examine the expenditure, administration and policy of the principal government departments'. The Committees allow officials and Ministers to be questioned in a systematic and searching manner, which is not always possible on the floor of the House of Commons. Furthermore, the members of the Committees are comparatively well informed and can call on the assistance of expert advisors. The published reports of Committees constitute a significant and valuable source of information about the workings of Government. The Committees show an impartiality remarkable in the contentious atmosphere of the Commons; they 'seek to proceed by a more non-partisan approach',[112] conducting their business in an inquisitorial as opposed to adversarial manner on party lines. As the Hansard Society Commission found:

> The strength of the select committees is that they are largely free from the interfer-
> ence of the political parties. . .once they are established, the committees tend to

---

112   P Craig, *Administrative Law*, 2nd edn (1989), p 69.

derive their influence from effective cross-party collaboration. As a result, the committees provide a forum which allows MPs from all parties to reconcile their conflicting roles in the pursuit of the public interest.[113]

Determining membership of the Select Committees: their independence

This relative lack of partisanship, widely seen as one of the most valuable aspects of the Select Committees, can be partly explained by the fact that the Committees' members are chosen from the backbenches: by Convention, no front bench spokespersons are appointed to them, although former Ministers may be. However, members of the Committee of Selection, which nominates the MPs to the Committees, are themselves chosen by the whips, so that the Government can still exercise partial control in an attempt to keep known outspoken and independently minded MPs off the Committees. Turpin and Tomkins assert that 'government and Opposition Whips [have] exercised a covert and decisive influence' on selection.[114] The role of the Committee of Selection in seeking to manipulate the membership of Select Committees to the (perceived) advantage of governments has come under sustained scrutiny over the last few years, particularly from the Liaison Committee, made up of the chairs of each departmental Select Committee to oversee and evaluate their work and remit. The following report, which received much publicity and support for its proposals outside Parliament,[115] analyses the problem and proposes a solution.

First Report of the Liaison Committee, *Shifting the Balance: Select Committees and the Executive*, HC 300 (1999–2000)

10 When the 1979 system was introduced, the Committee of Selection was given the responsibility of picking Members to serve on the departmental select committees. If the committees were to be independent monitors of Government, the argument ran, then their membership should not be in the hands of government or party organisation— in practice the Whips. They should be selected to do a job on behalf of the House as a whole. . .

11 In practice, however, the Committee of Selection—itself heavily influenced by the Whips—has nominated Members to serve on select committees in the same way as Members to serve on standing committees or private bill committees—primarily on the basis of lists supplied by the Whips.

12 This has had three unwelcome results:

- on some occasions there have been long delays—whatever their cause—in setting up select committees at the beginning of a Parliament, at the very time when committees need to put in maximum effort to establish their approach, plan their programme and begin work. These delays are of course convenient for the government of the day.

---

113   See p 359 above, at para 2.25.

114   Turpin and Tomkins, n 14 above, at 614.

115   See, e.g. M Brown, 'Withdraw the whip and give backbenchers power', *The Independent*, 6 March 2000.

when a Member decides to leave a committee there have been long delays—for no good reason—in making the change of membership. Some committees have been as many as three Members short for a matter of months, when there has been no shortage of volunteers.

Members have undoubtedly been kept off committees, or removed from them, on account of their views. Oppositions as well as governments have been guilty of this, but of course if committees are to be effective scrutineers of government it is the influence of the governing party that causes us the greater concern.

13 It is wrong in principle that party managers should exercise effective control of select committee membership.

Notes

1. The Committee went on to suggest acting as a committee of selection for members of Select Committee, to remove the power of the Whips. This report was debated in the House on 9 November 2000 and again on 12 February 2001. In the latter debate, the House endorsed the Government's view that 'concentrating patronage in the hands of three senior Members of the House' would not 'increase the transparency or effectiveness of the Committee system'.

2. However, further impetus for change to the present system was given by events in July 2001, following the June 2001 General Election. The Government sought to remove two chairs of Select Committees whom it saw as being particularly critical of government policy: Gwyneth Dunwoody, previously chair of the Transport Committee; and Donald Anderson, former chair of the Foreign Affairs Committee: see HC Deb cols 50 (16 July 2001). The Government was defeated on the motions relating to the composition of the Foreign Affairs Committee (that is, on the chairmanship of Anderson) by 301 votes to 232 and the Transport Committee (chairmanship of Dunwoody) by 308 to 221. Well over 100 Labour MPs rebelled. While this was widely seen in the media as evidence of a new vigour and independent spirit amongst the previously 'robotic' Parliamentary Labour Party, it should be noted that the vote was a free one, and not on a matter of policy.[116]

3. Whatever the wider significance of this rebellion, it helped keep the issue of selection of Select Committee members firmly on the parliamentary agenda. The matter was returned to by the Liaison Committee in 2002,[117] considering a report by the Modernisation Committee on the matter. It suggested an alternative, a Committee of Nomination, made up of senior backbench MPs, with no whips. The proposal to change to the new system was debated by the House on 14 May 2002[118] but was narrowly defeated, by 209 votes to 195. As an example of attempts by the Government to control and limit the independence of Select Committees (ironically enough, since that was the very mischief which the change was designed to limit) it should be noted that, although the proposal was brought forward by Robin Cook, a member of the Government, not one Cabinet Minister voted in favour of the change and, as one Member pointed out after the vote, although it was a free vote, members of the whips office were present, directing members of the Labour Party to vote against this proposal (see Mr Prentice's point of order at col 720).

4. The Committee set up to consider reforms to the House's procedures, in the wake of the MPs expenses scandal (see above at 378) returned to this matter in November 2009.

---

116 See further, Cowley and Stuart, n 24 above, at 282–84.

117 Second Report of the Liaison Committee, *Select Committees: Modernisation Proposals*, HC 692 (2001–02).

118 HC Deb cols 666 *et seq.*

House of Commons Reform Committee, Rebuilding the House,
***First Report* (2008–09) (extracts)**

56 . . .We consider that under any system the principal select committees should be nominated within no more than six weeks of the Queen's Speech and that this should be laid down in Standing Orders and capable of being enforced by the Speaker. . . .

72. It should be for the House and not for the Executive to choose which of its Members should scrutinise the Executive: the House should also have a strong if not decisive influence on the identity of the Chair. It is unacceptable that the power of the whips has on some occasions in the past been used to keep off select committees those members of their own party who are seen as unsound or too critical. . .It is also unacceptable that the Whips can in effect offer chairs as a reward or "consolation prize" to former Ministers, and that favoured candidates are parachuted into committees when a vacancy occurs. . .

73. The system by which parties select names to put forward to the Committee of Selection, and by which the whips divide up chairs between the parties, is very far from transparent. While on occasions the internal selection procedures of the parliamentary parties have been discussed or revealed, they remain a mystery to many within Westminster as well as to those outside. The criteria for selection are unknown. . .

74. The credibility of select committees could be enhanced by a greater and more visible element of democracy in the election of members and Chairs. Cross-party working is the basis of the success of select committees. That has been achieved under the current system of appointment. But the sense that a committee membership place is merely a form of party patronage—albeit formally endorsed by the House—may adversely affect Members' sense of duty to attend meetings. There is a danger that appointment to a salaried select committee chair if it remains largely controlled and influenced by the whips might on occasion be less and "alternative career path" and more of an extension of the massive patronage that already exists through the appointment of ministers. . .

80. We recommend an initial system of election by the whole House of Chairs of departmental and similar select committees, and thereafter the election by secret ballot of members of those committees by each political party, according to their level of representation in the House, and using transparent and democratic means. . .We have concluded that of the four options we considered this is the system most likely to demonstrate the determination of the House more effectively to hold the executive to account, to give more authority to the scrutiny function of Parliament and at the same time to preserve the effective functioning of select committees. We also believe that it is likely to command widespread support in the House as a major step forward, but short of more radical proposals. It should give a major boost to these select committees, help establish the position of their Chairs, and increase the standing of their elected members.

Election within party groups
87. We propose that in the new Parliament members of departmental and similar select committees should be elected by secret ballot within party groups, by trans-parent and democratic processes, with the outcome reported to and endorsed by the House. . .The method chosen should be one approved by the Speaker, following independent advice, as transparent and democratic: "kite-marked" as legitimate in effect. Officers nominated by the Speaker would be obliged to assure themselves that

the processes followed by each party, as notified by its Leader, were indeed in accordance with these norms. And each party would be obliged to publish the method it had adopted.

Note

As noted above, this is the latest in a series of attempts to wrest control over membership of the Committees from the Whips. If implemented, it would be important, both symbolically and practically. See further below at 419–424 for the report of this Committee and the prospects for implementation.

The remit and work of the Select Committees

Jurisdiction of the Committees

Second Report from the Select Committee on Procedure, HC 19–11 (1989–90), para 5

The general terms of reference of these committees are as set out in Standing Order No 130. . . .The committees are responsible for the interpretation of their own terms of reference. The committees are entitled to examine the expenditure, administration and policy of the principal Government departments, and also of their 'associated public bodies'. The terms of the standing orders do not define 'associated public bodies', but the then Chancellor of the Duchy of Lancaster said in his speech on 25 June 1979 that 'The Government also accept the Procedure Committee's view that the committees must be able to look at the activities of some public bodies that exercise authority of their own and over which ministers do not have the same direct authority as they have over their own departments. The test in every case will be whether there is a significant degree of ministerial responsibility for the body concerned.'

Associated public bodies therefore include all nationalised industries, fringe bodies and other Governmental organisations within the responsibilities of the department or departments concerned for which ministers are ultimately answerable. They do not, however, include bodies for which ministers are not answerable to Parliament, even though these bodies may be in receipt of Government funds. There will no doubt be borderline cases, but in general the existing principles of parliamentary accountability can be applied.

Notes

1. As the Liaison Committee noted:[119]

> All committees examine the work of non-departmental public bodies within their remit. For some, such as the Culture, Media and Sport Committee, this is a considerable task: the Department of Culture, Media and Sport is a small department but sponsors more such bodies than any other; and 95% of its programme expenditure is spent by quangos. The Agriculture Committee and the Defence Committee have begun rolling programmes to examine the agencies for which they are responsible, and other committees are following a similar pattern.

---

119   First Report of the Liaison Committee, *Shifting the Balance: Unfinished Business* HC 321–11 (2000–01), para 79.

2. Parliament agreed on 14 May 2002 upon a set of 'core tasks' for Select Committees, following suggestions of the Liaison[120] and Modernisation[121] Committees. This was also something strongly recommended by the Hansard Society Commission,[122] which argued that this would make 'scrutiny more systematic'. The following extract sets out those tasks, together with guidance on them from the Liaison Committee.

**Departmental Select Committee Objectives and Tasks: An Illustrative Template,
Appendix 3 to the First Report of the Liaison Committee for 2002–03,
Annual Report, HC 558 (2002–03)**

OBJECTIVE A: TO EXAMINE AND COMMENT ON THE POLICY OF THE DEPARTMENT

Task 1: To examine policy proposals from the UK Government and the European Commission in Green Papers, White Papers, draft Guidance etc, and to inquire further where the Committee considers it appropriate

This calls for more systematic scrutiny of proposals made. It is not intended to involve formal written or oral evidence as a matter of course, but to ensure that a Committee is at least apprised of proposals and has the opportunity to consider whether detailed scrutiny of them should form part of their programme of work. . .

Task 2: To identify and examine areas of emerging policy, or where existing policy is deficient, and make proposals. . .

Task 3: To conduct scrutiny of any published draft bill within the Committee's responsibilities

This calls for Committees to commit time for necessary oral evidence and reporting, subject to its timetable for other inquiries. . .

Task 4: To examine specific output from the department expressed in documents or other decisions

This calls for a formal framework for being informed of secondary legislation, circulars and guidance, treaties and previously identified casework decisions, so that they can if needed be drawn to a Committee's attention.

OBJECTIVE B: TO EXAMINE THE EXPENDITURE OF THE DEPARTMENT

Task 5: To examine the expenditure plans and out-turn of the department, its agencies and principal NDPBs

This calls for a systematic framework for committee scrutiny of the Department's Main and Supplementary Estimates: its expenditure plans; and its annual accounts. . .

OBJECTIVE C: TO EXAMINE THE ADMINISTRATION OF THE DEPARTMENT

Task 6: To examine the department's Public Service Agreements, the associated targets and the statistical measurements employed, and report if appropriate.

Task 7: To monitor the work of the department's Executive Agencies, NDPBs, regulators and other associated public bodies.

---

120   HC 692 (2001–02), para 16.

121   HC 224 (2001–02), para 34.

122   See p 359 above, at paras 3.23–3.46.

Task 8: To scrutinise major appointments made by the department.

Task 9: To examine the implementation of legislation and major policy initiatives
This would call for a framework of detailed annual progress reports from departments on Acts and major policy initiatives so that committees could decide whether to undertake inquiry. . .

OBJECTIVE D: TO ASSIST THE HOUSE IN DEBATE AND DECISION

Task 10: To produce Reports which are suitable for debate in the House, including Westminster Hall, or debating committees. This could call for committees to come to an explicit view when deciding on an inquiry as to whether a debate was in due course envisaged.

Notes
1. One area of Select Committee work that has been of increasing importance over the last few years has been the examination of treaties which the Government proposes to enter into. This area was reformed under the Constitutional Reform and Governance Act 2010 – see Chapter 11 for details.
2. A new role for Select Committees has been found in holding confirmation hearings for key public appointments made by Government, though the Committees have no veto over the decision.[123] As seen above, this is now one of the core tasks of Select Committees. The Liaison Committee in 2003 noted by way of example that 'The Treasury Committee has already established an effective role by scrutinising each appointment made by the Chancellor to the Bank of England's Monetary Policy Committee. During 2002 there were three such appointments'.[124]
3. In 2007, the Government suggested extending this role as part of Gordon Brown's package of constitutional reforms to encompass *pre-appointment* hearings.

The Governance of Britain, Cm 7170 (2007)

72. Public bodies at arm's-length from Ministers play an important role in public life across a range of areas ranging from the regulation of key utilities to health service bodies and from the boards of museums and galleries to those who can investigate complaints about the way key public services are provided. All in all there are some 21,000 such appointments and ultimately they are the responsibility of Ministers, who are accountable to Parliament for these appointments. . . .

74 . . .The Government believes the time is now right to go further and seek to involve Parliament in the appointment of key public officials. The role of Parliament, and specifically the issue of Committee hearings with those nominated for office, has been the subject of considerable debate over the past decade . . .

75 . . . .There are a number of positions in which Parliament has a particularly strong interest because the officeholder exercises statutory or other powers in relation to protecting the public's rights and interests. Some of these appointments are not subject to oversight by the Commissioner for Public Appointments or other form of independent scrutiny.

76. The Government therefore believes that Parliament, through its select committees, should play this role. It therefore proposes that the Government nominee for key positions such as those listed below should be subject to a pre-appointment hearing with the

---

123   See the First Report of the Liaison Committee, *Shifting the Balance: Unfinished Business*, HC 321–11 (2000–01), paras 90–93.

124   HC 558 (2002–03), para 20.

relevant select committee. The hearing would be non-binding, but in the light of the report from the committee, Ministers would decide whether to proceed. The hearings would cover issues such as the candidate's suitability for the role, his or her key priorities, and the process used in selection.

77. The Government, in consultation with the Liaison Committee, will prepare a list of such appointments for which these hearings will apply. Where responsibility is devolved, it will be for the respective administration to consider the appointment. . . .

78. This list will be kept under review and discussed with the Liaison Committee, and, where appropriate, the Commissioner for Public Appointments.

79. For market-sensitive and certain other appointments, including the Governor and the two Deputy Governors of the Bank of England, the Chairman of the Financial Services Authority, and some utility regulators, there is a particular set of issues around confirmation hearings. But the Government does believe that it is important to ensure greater account-ability than currently exists. So, for these positions, once the appointment has been approved, the relevant select committee will be invited to convene a hearing with the nominee before he or she takes up post. The relevant department will consult with the select committee as to what such hearings might usefully cover.

Notes

1. This is an important step forward in expanding the role of the Select Committees, though it should be noted that the hearings are advisory only those held for Judges in the US Senate for example. In the 2008 White Paper (CM 7342-I), the Government decided to proceed with this experiment on a pilot basis and noted that its approach:

    > has been supported by the Public Administration Select Committee, which has recommended that pre-appointment hearings should apply to 'major auditors, ombudsmen and other complaint investigators, regulators and inspectors, as well as to those responsible for the appointments system itself'.[125] The Liaison Commit-tee published their views on the Government's initial list on 5 March 2008 (Session 2007–08 HC 384).The Government will continue to work with the Liaison Commit-tee to agree a final list of suitable posts.

2. The new system has not been without its controversy, as one might expect. In 2009, the Children, Schools and Family Committee recommended against the appointment of the Secretary of State's proposed candidate for Children's Commissioner, Maggie Atkinson, but the appointment went ahead.[126] The Committee also complained that no appointment hearing had been held for the appointment of the head of Ofqual, the body that oversees the testing regime in schools.[127] Behind this, however, lay a partial victory for the Committee, which had succeeded in its aim that four key players in this area *not* included in the Government's original list of posts subject to pre-appointment hearings *should* be so subject: they were the head of Ofqual, HM Chief Inspector of Education, Children's Services and Skills (Ofsted), the Chair of the Qualifications and Curriculum Agency and the Children's Commissioner.[128]

---

125   Third Report of Session 2007–08, HC 152.

126   See the Eight Report of the Committee (2008–09) HC 998.

127   Uncorrected transcript of Oral Evidence given by Ed Balls MP and David Bell (2009–10) HC 277-i.

128   See *ibid.*

Scrutiny of departmental expenditure

Clearly, scrutiny over the national finances is a vital link in the chain of Commons' control of the executive; it is, however, patchy.[129] Turpin commented in 1990 that government borrowing 'largely escapes scrutiny' while detailed parliamentary examination of departmental supply expenditure 'was abandoned long ago'.[130] However, in the area of verifying the authorisation of expenditure and ascertaining that value for money has been obtained, the Public Accounts Committee has been notably effective. It is, as Stanley de Smith notes, 'scrupulously non-partisan',[131] while the value of its investigations is greatly enhanced by the fact that the Comptroller and Auditor-General, an officer of the House and therefore independent from the Government and assisted by a staff of several hundreds, sits with it. One of its most influential recent reports, which received a great deal of attention, was concerned with the controversial issue of the effectiveness of the Private Finance Initiative (PFI).[132]

There have been a number of moves recently for departmental Select Committees to make greater efforts in terms of financial scrutiny. Reporting in 2001–02, the Liaison Committee found that the situation remained unsatisfactory, with only 'some limited examination of expenditure plans. . .undertaken by most departmental select committees'.[133] Additional specialist support staff to assist committees should be appointed from the Scrutiny Unit,[134] it found. Reporting in 2009 on the previous parliamentary year, the Liaison Committee saw some improvements, with room for much more.

Liaison Committee, *First Report* (2008–09)
***The Work of Committees in 2007–08*, HC 291**

43. Departmental Annual Reports (DARs) remain the lynchpin of committees' scrutiny of expenditure. Standard operating procedure is for committees to receive an analysis of their department's DAR from the Committee Office Scrutiny Unit, the substance of which is followed up through written questions, which in turn form the basis of a subsequent oral evidence session with Ministers and senior officials. The lines between expenditure, policy and administration are not always clear, and quite often an oral evidence session on an Annual Report will touch upon questions of policy or administration which have financial consequences. Select committees continue to demonstrate the useful impact that effective scrutiny of expenditure can have on their wider work programmes, and that 'expenditure, policy and administration' need not fall into discrete silos.

44. In our last report, we encouraged all departmental select committees to hold evidence sessions on their target department's DAR. We welcome the fact that in the 2007–08 session, for the first time all the departmental select committees took oral evidence on their departments' Departmental Annual Reports. . .

46. Estimates are the vehicle by which departments request 'supply' to fund their spending programmes. As with APRs, most committees conduct scrutiny of Estimates by way of correspondence. A notable exception is the Defence Committee, which informs

---

129   See further J McEldowney, 'The control of public expenditure', in J Jowell and D Oliver, *The Changing Constitution,* 6th edn (2007).

130   *British Government and the Constitution* (1990), p 482.

131   SA de Smith, *Constitutional and Administrative Law,* 6th edn (1994), p 287.

132   Forty-Second Report of the Public Accounts Committee, *Managing the Relationship to Secure a Successful Partnership in PFI Projects,* HC 460 (2001–02).

133   Second Report of the Liaison Committee, Select Committees: Modernisation Proposals HC 692 (2001–02) at [10]–[14].

134   This is a central resource for all Committees.

the House by reporting on all of the Ministry of Defence's Main and Supplementary Estimates before the House is asked to agree them. The reason for the Defence Committee's detailed scrutiny of Estimates lie in the titles of their reports: *Costs of operations in Iraq and Afghanistan: Winter Supplementary Estimate 2007–08* and *Operational costs in Afghanistan and Iraq: Spring Supplementary Estimate 2007–08*. Historically, figures for costs of specific operations have not featured in the Main Estimates. This is something to which the Committee took exception, and it has succeeded in securing an assurance from the MoD that in future, operational costs will be included in some detail in the Main Estimates.

47. Estimates Memoranda, prepared by departments for select committees, were introduced in 2004 to explain the changes in figures from the previous Estimate and how they related to spending limits and departmental targets. We produced a report in 2006 which sought to ensure that Departments made them more consistently helpful, and in October 2007 the Treasury issued new guidance on Estimates Memoranda, with advice from the Scrutiny Unit. Select committees continue to use the services of the Scrutiny Unit in understanding and interpreting Estimates and Estimates Memoranda.

48. ...The Scrutiny Unit considers that in general the quality of the memoranda has improved as a result of the evolving guidance and committees' influence on departments. **We welcome the general improvement in the quality of the explanatory memoranda about Estimates provided by Government departments to departmental select committees...**

50. Financial scrutiny is an increasingly important issue for the Liaison Committee itself. In our last report we noted that a group of our members was working on ways in which the financial information provided by Government could be improved, and how committees might use that information. In April 2008 we published a report based on the work of the group, *Parliament and Government Finance: Recreating Financial Scrutiny.* Its key recommendations included:

- simplification of the Government's over-complex financial system, to the benefit of Government as much as Parliament;
- improving the quality of the financial information provided to Parliament, including providing more information to select committees about PFI contracts; and
- creating more opportunities for Members to challenge the Government on financial matters and hold it to account.

Our report also took account of the Government's 'Alignment' Project, which is intended to bring the Estimates, departmental budgets and Resource Accounts framework closer together, and to recast all the financial reporting documents currently presented to the House, with a view to providing greater consistency between different financial reporting documents and therefore greater simplicity and transparency for users, including Parliament. We noted that this was 'potentially a historic development' in parliamentary scrutiny of government finances.

51. In its reply, the Government agreed that the financial system and associated documentation should provide Parliament with the detailed information it needs, and that the overall shape of the Government's finances and changes in it should be presented comprehensibly. But it rejected changing PFI contracts to increase the ability to pass information to committees; providing more time to debate the Comprehensive Spending Review; letting the House debate and vote on individual government programmes or items

of expenditure; and allowing motions which propose increased expenditure or transfers between budgets.

Notes

The Liaison Committee returned to this topic in a Report published in 2009. Only a summary can be given here:

Liaison Committee, Financial Scrutiny: *Parliamentary Control over Government Budgets, Second Report* (2008–09), HC 804

The Treasury has now, in a White Paper published in March (the Alignment Project), published plans to improve the quality and clarity of the financial information. The objective is to bring consistency to what is included in the budgets which the Government sets individual departments, the Estimates which are put to Parliament to approve government spending, and the accounts of departmental spending audited by the National Audit Office. At present, these differ considerably—for example there is £129bn of spending for 2008–09 currently included in departmental budgets but not in the Estimates presented to Parliament.

Alignment will require significant adjustments—most prominently the ending by the House of legal (but not practical) control over the income which departments generate themselves and then use directly in support of their spending (as opposed to income from general taxation). Gains will include the inclusion of capital controls within the sums voted by Parliament.

Overall, we support the package of detailed proposals by the Treasury to achieve alignment. A system will be needed to ensure these benefits are not lost through any future changes to the budgeting process.

We welcome the principle of alignment because it will:

- allow the controls exercised by Parliament to reflect those exercised within Government, and
- enable the House to track spending plans clearly as they are translated from plans for future years into precise figures requiring legislative authority for each year, and into actual spending recorded in the accounts.

This change would be a significant contribution to remedying one of the major gaps identified by this and other committees, that of the House's inability to examine effectively the spending plans of the future years of each Government Spending Review. Existing procedures are closely geared towards examination by the House of the current year's spending plans. Given that this is usually after the year has started, it is generally too late to have any effect. Better aligned and clearer figures will enable the various select committees of the House to examine the budget figures provided for years to come on the basis that they are 'draft Estimates' for those future years.

But this in itself is not enough. The opportunities for committees and the House to debate and influence these figures need to be developed further. We propose that:

- the Procedure Committee should examine how Estimates could be better examined in committee (perhaps using a procedure akin to that for European legislation, allowing all Members to participate in scrutinising and debating a department's Estimate);

- the motions which can be debated on the days set aside in the House for consideration of Estimates be broadened to include substantive motions expressing the House's opinion on future spending plans.

We also recommend that, to reflect the additional kinds of business which can be debated, the number of Estimates Days should be increased to 5 (from 3). In addition, as has been recommended before, we consider that it should be standard practice for there to be debates both on Spending Reviews and on the annual Pre-Budget Report. We also believe strongly that the Main Estimates ought to be published as closely as possible to the beginning of the financial year to which they relate.

Note
The Hansard Society recently made further proposals for reform in this area.

Hansard Society, *Representative Democracy: Briefing Paper 1: House of Commons Reform* (2009)

Financial scrutiny generally needs to be given a much higher priority by parliamentary committees. Because the Treasury Committee is currently overburdened, we recommend the establishment of a separate HM Revenue and Customs Committee in the House of Commons, building on the Treasury Committee's HMRC sub-committee. Consideration should also be given to the creation of a separate Tax Administration or Taxation Committee or a Joint Committee on Tax Administration involving MPs and peers.

Designated departmental sub-committees should carry out a clearer set of functions in relation to following up National Audit Office and Public Account Committee recommendations as well as scrutinising spending plans, and a Finance and Audit Sub-Committee should be piloted in a number of committees. Additionally, we recommend that Parliament should increase its impact on the Budget process by enabling select committees in the period between the pre-budget report and the main Budget, to take expert and public evidence on the Government's plans, make a case for the priorities it wishes government to consider, and ensure the government provides full information and explanations for its proposals. The entire Finance Bill should also be subject to pre-legislative scrutiny by parliamentary committee and the interim Comprehensive Spending Review report should be made available at a time in the parliamentary calendar that allows for consideration by parliamentary committee.[135]

Powers of the Select Committees

The Procedure Committee sets out the basic position:[136]

7 Select Committees (and their sub-committees) normally have the power to 'send for persons, papers and records'. This power is understood as a power to 'order' the attendance of persons and the submission of papers. . .

---

135   See further, A Brazier and V Ram, *The Fiscal Maze. Parliament, Government and Public Money* (2006).

136   HC 19–11 (1989–90).

8 Any official who appears before a Select Committee or who submits papers to it does so on behalf of his ministers. As the Procedure Committee emphasised in its report:

> The over-riding principle concerning access to Government information should be that the House has power to enforce the responsibility of ministers for the provision of information or the refusal of information. It would not, however, be appropriate for the House to seek directly or through its committees to enforce its rights to secure information from the executive at a level below that of the ministerial head of the department concerned (normally a Cabinet minister), since such a practice would tend to undermine rather than strengthen the accountability of ministers to the House.

In practice, committees normally proceed on the basis of 'requests' for departmental witnesses and evidence rather than through the exercise of formal powers. . .

. . .with the exception of the Committee on Standards and Privileges with regard to Members of the Commons, a committee cannot order the attendance of Members of either House of Parliament; but Members may attend voluntarily. While a committee cannot, therefore, insist on Ministers attending one of its hearings, Ministers will normally accept an invitation to give evidence. Similarly the committees can only request that government departments send papers and records. The Government has frequently reaffirmed that ministers and civil servants will attend committees when requested and provide committees with the information necessary to their inquiries . . .

The ability to obtain Government documents

The record of the Committees in obtaining the Government records they require gives rise to most concern: in the words of the 1997 Liaison Committee Report, 'It is in [this area] that most difficulties have arisen'.[137] Select Committees have the formal power to send for papers; however, Parliament can compel the production of documents from a department headed by a Secretary of State (that is, most departments) only through an address to the Crown.[138] Furthermore, as Tomkin notes,[139] the current draft of the Cabinet Office memorandum *Departmental Evidence and Response to Select Committees* states (at para 50):

> The Government's commitment to provide as much information as possible to Select Committees is met largely through the provision of memoranda, written replies to Committees' questions and oral evidence from Ministers and officials. It does not amount to a commitment to provide access to internal files, private correspondence, including advice given on a confidential basis or working papers.

The Liaison Committee found in 1997 that governmental promises to make time for a Commons debate on a refusal to provide requested documentation have not been honoured: 'There have been a significant number of cases where committees have been refused specific documents but the

---

137   See n 140 below, at para 14.

138   Erskine May, *Treatise on the Law, Privileges, Proceedings and Usage of Parliament*, 21st edn (1989), p 630.

139   See n 95 above, at 79–80.

Government has not provided time for the subject to be debated.' The reference to a debate is to the House's formal power to make a finding that a refusal to supply requested documents—or indeed a refusal to attend a Committee at all—represented a contempt of Parliament. Such a finding could only be made after a debate and the Committee recommended that 'The onus should be shifted onto the government to defend in the House its refusal to disclose information to a select committee' and that the power of the Privileges Committee 'to require that specific documents or records in the possession of a Member relating to its inquiries be laid before the Committee' be extended to all Committees.[140]

As explored further below, significant problems again became apparent during the investigations by the Foreign Affairs Committee into the extremely sensitive issue of the decision to go to war in Iraq in 2003. The Committee complained of inadequate cooperation by Government in supplying it with witnesses and intelligence material (below at 406).

There is a Committee devoted to examining the work of the Security and Intelligence Agencies, although special rules govern its appointment and its work. Its members are appointed by the Prime Minister, it meets within the Cabinet Office and deliberates in secret, although its reports, once redacted of sensitive material, are published. It has enjoyed 'unprecedented access to the intelligence and security agencies,'[141] in terms of both personnel and documentation; as a result its members have acquired considerable expertise in an area traditionally fenced in with great secrecy by Government; however, a recent analysis concludes that 'it is less clear whether it has served to educate parliament more broadly about intelligence'.[142] The author notes that while 'in its report on intelligence on Iraqi WMD, the ISC was critical of the Government's presentation of the intelligence in the dossiers':

> what is striking about the ISC's examination of the Government's publication of intelligence material is the lack of any suggestions regarding how intelligence material might be placed in the public domain. . . .Moreover. . .ISC offered no comment on the manner in which intelligence material was presented to, and assessed by, Members of Parliament, to whom the dossiers were in the first instance presented, and who were asked to vote on military action on the basis of the information in them. The failure of the ISC to provide a deeper understanding of the nature of intelligence was thrown into sharp relief by the publication of the report of the Butler Inquiry into intelligence on Iraqi WMD [which] quite deliberately set out to address the lack of understanding of intelligence beyond Whitehall by providing a layman's guide to the nature, uses and limitations of intelligence. . . In terms of educating parliamentarians about intelligence, the impact of the Butler report may well prove to be far greater than over ten years of reports from the ISC.[143]

Notes
1. The Governance of Britain package initiated certain limited reforms of this Committee, intended to make it slightly more independent of Government.[144]
2. The Butler report is considered further in Chapter 12 in the context of the obligation not to mislead Parliament; it may be noted here however, that it provides another example, like the Scott Inquiry before it, and the Chilcott Inquiry, which is ongoing at the time of writing, of the

---

140   First Report (2006–07) HC 323-I.

141   A Defty, 'Educating Parliamentarians about Intelligence: The Role of the British Intelligence and Security Committee' (2008) 61(4) Parlt Aff 621, 628.

142   *Ibid*, p 631.

143   *Ibid*, p 636–37.

144   Discussed by the House of Commons Reform Committee: First Report at [58].

significantly superior ability of outside Inquiries to obtain information and documentation from the Executive as compared to the select committees. The Foreign Affairs Committee noted that:

> The following papers, requested by this Committee and refused by the Government, were provided to Lord Hutton's Inquiry:
>
> - drafts of the September 2002 dossier;
> - the JIC assessments which were used in compiling the dossier;
> - other records relevant to the dossier and to Iraqi WMD assessments, such as e-mails, notes of meetings and internal memoranda.
>
> All these papers have been published, some with deletions.[145]

3. This was despite the fact that the Hutton Inquiry had no legal powers to compel production of these documents. A note by the Clerks of the House for the Liaison Committee brings out the point further:

Scrutiny of Government: Select Committees after Hutton
Note by the Clerks (2004)

14. The Hutton Inquiry had access to a wide range of written material submitted by government departments and agencies, other organisations and individuals. The evidence was voluntarily submitted, in response to a general request for all relevant material, equivalent to the discovery of papers in a civil court. It includes a mass of e-mails between officials, drafts of official papers, confidential correspondence, minutes of private meetings and personnel records. The evidence is listed on the Inquiry website, with reference numbers: it can be viewed in the original form, having been scanned in. There are some words or passages blacked out.

15. This presents a striking contrast to the regime for select committees:

- a select committee would not be given the *form* of documentary evidence supplied to Hutton: most strikingly perhaps the correspondence or loose minutes between senior officials and the mass of emails, which constitute the richest source for an audit trail
- a select committee would not be given the *nature* of documentary evidence supplied to Hutton, much of which would fall into the categories of advice to Ministers or paper whose release would adversely affect the candour of internal discussion, where release would be blocked under the terms of the 1997 Code of Practice [and now under the FOI Act]
- above all a select committee would not be given (and might not ask for) *documentary evidence* as opposed to information [due to the Osmotherly rules].

16. Committees have to live within the framework of the existing rules. There are therefore not many cases of Committees requesting specific documents and encountering a straight refusal. In its post-Scott July 1996 Report the Public Service Committee noted several such instances, including the refusal of reports, commissioned by departments from outsiders. Recent experience has thrown up some further examples:

---

145   First Special Report, HC 440 (2003–04) at [10].

- The Defence Committee asked for copies of 'Lessons learnt' reports from Commanding Operations in Operation Telic which were prepared as part of MoD's overall assessment of the operation. This was refused. The Chairman expressed his displeasure at the refusal in the course of an evidence session in September 2003. The MoD has subsequently reiterated its refusal.
- The Environmental Audit Committee has complained of the refusal of departments to publish their sustainable development reports. The Treasury claimed that these were an internal part of the spending review process.
- The FAC had difficulty in procuring actual FCO telegrams (i.e. official correspondence) in its Sierra Leone inquiry and more recently was refused access to official papers relating to the Bali bombing, on the grounds that these were being supplied to the Intelligence and Security Committee.
- The International Development Committee eventually resorted to an appeal to the Ombudsman under the Code of Practice to seek copies of ministerial correspondence between FCO and DTI/ECGD on the Ilisu Dam.

The Quadripartite [4 Select Committees acting together] has encountered a refusal to provide—even in confidence—an analysis of the costs and benefits to Tanzania of acquiring a military air traffic control system, with the FCO claiming that to do so would risk either breaching commercial confidences or harming the frankness and candour of internal discussion.

Note

At present, there seems little likelihood of any major shift in the preparedness of Government to make actual documents, as opposed to information, available to Committees. The experience of the Foreign Affairs committee on the Iraq issue is returned to below, in relation to the issues of witnesses.

The ability to call witnesses

The power to question members of the executive is clearly crucial to the efficacy of the Committees and, not surprisingly, has caused controversy. As Tomkin notes,[146] whilst MPs and Ministers can be required to attend by committees if an initial request is refused, and, in the last resort, ordered to attend by the House, no MP has been ordered to attend 'this century' and no Minister has ever been ordered to attend. In 1979, the Leader of the House pledged that '. . .every minister. . .will do all in his or her power to co-operate with the new system of committees'. Despite this promise, the Committees have sometimes found themselves frustrated when investigating areas of acute sensitivity by the refusal of certain key witnesses to attend. For example, in 1984, the Government would not allow the Director of Government Communications Headquarters (GCHQ) to give evidence to the Select Committee on Employment which was enquiring into the trade union ban at GCHQ. Similarly, in 1986, the Defence Committee, in the course of its enquiry into the Westland affair, wished to interview certain officials; again the Minister in question would not allow them to attend.

Up until 2002 , a convention prevented the Select Committees from questioning the most important member of the executive—the Prime Minister. However, the PM now faces a twice yearly Q&A session with the Liaison Committee.[147] They were generally seen as providing for far more revealing, probing

---

146   See n 95 above, at 75.

147   This was proposed in First Report of the Liaison Committee, Shifting the Balance: Unfinished Business, HC 321– 11 (2000–01), paras 143–45.

questioning of the Prime Minister than that allowed for by parliamentary questions. The Liaison Committee itself has commented[148] that the sessions 'met our aim of achieving a 'more productive and informative' event than is possible under the current operation of Prime Minister's Questions in the Chamber'.[149] However, save for this innovation, the Commons has not adequately adapted its methods and structures of scrutiny to cater for the growth in the structures and power of the centre of Government, sometimes referred to as the 'core executive' (see Chapter 12, pp 611–616). In particular, Special Advisers play an enhanced role within Government (though perhaps less so under Gordon Brown then Tony Blair but, as seen below, the Commons has encountered particular difficulty when seeking to scrutinise their activities and influence.

Successive administrations have set out their views on the attendance of civil servants before Select Committees in the following document, first issued by the Cabinet Office in 1994 and subsequently updated a number of times. It is traditionally know as 'the Osmotherly rules'.

Cabinet Office, *Departmental Evidence and Response to Select Committees* (2005) (extracts)[150]

2 In providing guidance, the memorandum attempts to summarise a number of long-standing conventions that have developed in the relationship between Parliament, in the form of its Select Committees, and successive Governments. As a matter of practice, Parliament has generally recognised these conventions. It is important to note, however, that this memorandum is a Government document. Although Select Committees will be familiar with its contents, it has no formal Parliamentary standing or approval, nor does it claim to have. . .

40 Civil servants who give evidence to Select Committees do so on behalf of their Ministers and under their directions.

41 This is in accordance with the principle that it is Ministers who are accountable to Parliament for the policies and actions of their Departments. Civil servants are accountable to Ministers and are subject to their instruction; but they are not directly accountable to Parliament in the same way. It is for this reason that when civil servants appear before Select Committees they do so, on behalf of their Ministers and under their directions because it is the Minister, not the civil servant, who is accountable to Parliament for the evidence given to the Committee. This does not mean, of course, that officials may not be called upon to give a full account of Government policies, or indeed of their own actions or recollections of particular events, but their purpose in doing so is to contribute to the central process of Ministerial accountability, not to offer personal views or judgements on matters of political controversy or to become involved in what would amount to disciplinary investigations which are for Departments to undertake. . .

Summoning of Named Officials

43 The line of ministerial accountability means that it is for Ministers to decide which official or officials should represent them.

---

148 In its Annual Report for 2002, HC 558 (2002–03) at para 9.

149 See generally on Prime Ministerial accountability to Parliament, P Riddell, 'Prime Ministers and Parliament' (2004) 57(4) Parlt Aff 814–29.

150 The full text of the Code is available from the Cabinet Office website: www.cabinetoffice.gov.uk/propriety_and_ethics/civil_service/select_committees.aspx.

44 Where a Select Committee indicates that it wishes to take evidence from a particular named official, including special advisers, the presumption should be that Ministers will agree to meet such a request. However, the final decision on who is best able to represent the Minister rests with the Minister concerned and it remains the right of a Minister to suggest an alternative civil servant to that named by the Committee if he or she feels that the former is better placed to represent them. In the unlikely event of there being no agreement about which official should most appropriately give evidence, it is open to the Minister to offer to appear personally before the Committee. . . .

46 It has also been agreed that it is not the role of Select Committees to act as disciplinary tribunals. . . A Minister will therefore wish to consider carefully a Committee's request to take evidence from a named official where this is likely to expose the individual concerned to questioning about their personal responsibility or the allocation of blame as between them and others. This will be particularly so where the official concerned has been subject to, or may be subject to, an internal departmental inquiry or disciplinary proceedings. Ministers may, in such circumstances, wish to suggest either that he or she give evidence personally to the Committee or that a designated senior official do so on their behalf.

Notes

1. This ability of Ministers to control which of their officials appear before Select Committees is justified in terms of ministerial responsibility; since Ministers, not civil servants, are responsible to Parliament and civil servants give advice only on behalf of Ministers, it is for Ministers to choose which civil servants they think are appropriate to 'represent' them. The guidance adds that retired officials should not normally be asked to give evidence. During the Scott Inquiry, two retired officials in the Ministry of Defence (MoD), Mr Primrose and Mr Harding, had important first-hand information about aspects of the Supergun affair, and the Trade and Industry Select Committee (TISC), which was investigating the affair, wished to interview them. The MoD refused to allow them to attend.[151] Sir Richard Scott has commented that in his view 'ministerial accountability does require Ministers to facilitate Select Committees obtaining first-hand evidence from those with first-hand knowledge of the matter in question'.[152]

2. More recent examples of refusals by Ministers and others to appear before Committees are not hard to find. In a Special Report of the Transport, Local Government and the Regions Committee, *The Attendance of a Minister from HM Treasury before the Committee*,[153] the Committee was enquiring into London Underground and was informed that the decision to adopt a public private partnership (PPP) method of financing it had been entirely driven by the Treasury, against virtually unanimous outside advice. Its subsequent request for a Treasury Minister to appear before it was refused. The Committee concluded that, as a result, 'Treasury Ministers have treated this Committee with disdain'.

3. A further important example of refusal to appear before a Committee, in this case in relation to one of the Prime Minister's more controversial former 'special advisers', Lord Birt was documented critically by the Transport, Local Government and the Regions Committee.[154] It concluded:

---

151   See *Inquiry into Exports of Defence Equipment and Dual-Use Goods to Iraq and Related Prosecutions*, HC 115 I (1995–96), paras F4 61–F4 66.

152   Minutes of evidence taken before the Public Services Committee on 8 May 1996, HC 313 (1995–96), QQ 394–97.

153   HC 771 (2001–02).

154   Fourth Report, *The Attendance of Lord Birt at The Committee*, HC 655 (2001–02).

17 One of the most surprising aspects of this episode is that the Prime Minister and his Department should take it upon themselves to decide who should give oral evidence to Select Committees. . . .We consider that No 10 Downing Street's refusal to allow Lord Birt to attend this Committee to discuss the future of transport amounts to a deliberate attempt to undermine the Departmental Select Committee system. . .

19 There are a growing number of units and staff attached to No 10 Downing Street. In effect a Prime Minister's Department has been created. It, and the advisers within it, like Lord Birt, are increasingly influential. . .

21 The Prime Minister's advisers should be accountable to departmental Select Committees . . .

22 Unfortunately, this is not possible because Lord Birt, like so many of the Prime Minister's advisers, is a Member of the Other House. He is therefore able to take advantage of the ancient convention, established in quite different circumstances, that he will not be summoned to appear before a Commons' Committee. **We recommend that this convention be modified to ensure that the Prime Minister's or other Minister's advisers do not abuse it to evade scrutiny.** We endorse the recommendation of the Modernisation Committee that the Procedure Committees of both Houses examine this matter.

Note

The Foreign Affairs Committee, when investigating the decision to take part in the invasion of Iraq in March 2003, wrote a specific report about the refusal of the Government to cooperate with it in terms of the attendance of key witnesses.

First Special Report, *Implications for the Work of the House and its Committees of the Government's Lack of Co-operation with the Foreign Affairs Committee's Inquiry into The Decision to go to War in Iraq*, HC 440 (2003–04)

2   When we began our Inquiry in June 2003, we were hopeful that we would receive full co-operation from the Government. As we set out below, this was not forthcoming.

3   We commented in paragraph 6 of our Report on *The Decision to go to War in Iraq,* as follows:

> We are strongly of the view that we were entitled to a greater degree of co-operation from the Government on access to witnesses and to intelligence material. Our Chairman wrote to the Prime Minister (requesting his attendance and that of Alastair Campbell); the Cabinet Office Intelligence Co-ordinator; the Chairman of the Joint Intelligence Committee; the Chief of Defence Intelligence; the Head of the Secret Intelligence Service; and the Director of GCHQ. None of them replied. It was the Foreign Secretary who informed us that they would not appear. The Chairman wrote a further letter to Alastair Campbell and after an initial refusal he agreed to appear. We asked for direct access to Joint Intelligence Committee (JIC) assessments and to relevant FCO papers. That was refused, although some extracts were read to us in private session. We are confident that our inquiry would have been enhanced if our requests had been met.

4   The only way in which the Committee could have sought to insist on the attendance of official witnesses or the production of official papers would have been to make a Special Report to the House, or to table an appropriate Motion. Either course of action would have required the Government's agreement for a debate to be held in government time.

The Government's evidence to the Intelligence and Security Committee

5   The following witnesses, requested by this Committee and refused by the Government, gave evidence to the Intelligence and Security Committee's inquiry into Iraqi Weapons of Mass Destruction—Intelligence and Assessments:

- the Prime Minister;
- the Cabinet Office Security and Intelligence Co-ordinator;
- the Chairman of the Joint Intelligence Committee;
- the Chief of Defence Intelligence;
- the Head of the Secret Intelligence Service ('C');
- the Director of GCHQ.

The evidence of all these was given in private but some of that given by the Cabinet Office Security and Intelligence Co-ordinator has since been published by Lord Hutton.

6   The following papers, requested by this Committee and refused by the Government, were provided to the Intelligence and Security Committee:

- drafts of the September 2002 dossier;
- the JIC assessments which were used in compiling the dossier;
- other records relevant to the dossier and to Iraqi WMD assessments.

Many of these papers have been published by Lord Hutton, some with deletions.

7   We note that the Intelligence and Security Committee has no powers to compel the attendance of witnesses or to require the production of papers and records.

8   The Government chose to co-operate with the inquiry carried out by the Intelligence and Security Committee in ways in which it did not co-operate with a select committee of the House.

9   The following witnesses, requested by this Committee and refused by the Government, gave evidence to Lord Hutton's Inquiry into the Circumstances Surrounding the Death of Dr David Kelly CMG:

- the Prime Minister;
- the Cabinet Office Security and Intelligence Co-ordinator;
- the Chairman of the Joint Intelligence Committee;
- the Head of the Secret Intelligence Service.

The evidence of all these was given in public and has been published.

. . .

11   We note that Lord Hutton's Inquiry was not established by Parliament under the

Tribunals and Inquiries Act. It was established administratively, by the Prime Minister. The Inquiry therefore had no powers to compel the attendance of witnesses or to require the production of papers and records. All those who co-operated with Lord Hutton's Inquiry—including this Committee—did so willingly and no formal sanction could have been applied against any person who refused to co-operate.

12   The Government chose to co-operate with Lord Hutton's Inquiry in ways in which it did not co-operate with a select committee of the House.

Power to send for persons, papers and records

13   The House has given this Committee, in common with other Committees, power under its Standing Orders to send for persons, papers and records. **The experience of the Foreign Affairs Committee in the course of its Inquiry into The Decision to go to War in Iraq suggests that these powers are, in practice, unenforceable in relation to the Executive.** (emphasis added).

Notes

The Committee concluded in its substantive report that Ministers did not mislead Parliament in relation to the intelligence or otherwise in relation to the decision to go to war.[155] However, its conclusions were weakened by its inability to obtain access to crucial witnesses and documents. See further on whether Parliament was misled, Chapter 12 at 651–662.

It is noteworthy that the Standards and Privileges Committee has recently been given power to order the attendance of any Member. The Liaison Committee recommended in its 1997 Report that this power should be given to the departmental Select Committees[156] but this recommendation has not to date been implemented, despite being echoed by other committees many times since.

Pressure from select committees, amongst others, led to the revision of the 'Osmotherly rules' in 2005 to provide for the attendance of special advisors, and assurances were given to the Liaison Committee in 2004 that Special Advisors would now be allowed to give such evidence.[157] However, the Public Administration Select Committee found in late 2005 that there was still marked resistance from the then Prime Minister on this matter, concluding:

> It is clear that there is strong resistance to the appearance of Special Advisers from No. 10 Downing Street. We are disappointed that the Prime Minister appears to feel that there is no presumption that his own key Advisers will appear before select committees when they are requested to do so, notwithstanding the general under-takings that have recently been given to select committees on this matter.[158]

The questioning of witnesses present before the Committee

The main restrictions upon what witnesses will disclose are those set out in the Freedom of Information Act (above). Additional restrictions, purportedly designed to protect civil service neutrality and the principles of ministerial responsibility, apply to civil servants, as explained below.

---

155   Foreign Affairs Committee, *The Decision to go to War in Iraq,*HC 813-I (2002–03) esp. at [183]–[186].

156   HC 323–1 (1996–97), para 12.

157   Minutes of Evidence, HC 1180–i, Q 26.

158   1st Special Report, HC 690 (2005–06) at [15].

Cabinet Office, *Departmental Evidence and Response to Select Committees* (2005) (extracts)

9. Select Committees have a crucial role in ensuring the full and proper accountability of the Executive to Parliament. Ministers have emphasised that, when officials represent them before Select Committees, they should be as forthcoming and helpful as they can in providing information relevant to Committee inquiries. In giving evidence to Select Committees, officials should take care to ensure that no information is withheld which would not be exempted if a parallel request were made under the Freedom of Information Act.

. . .

55. Officials should as far as possible confine their evidence to questions of fact and explanation relating to government policies and actions. They should be ready to explain what those policies are; the justification and objectives of those policies as the Government sees them; the extent to which those objectives have been met; and also to explain how administrative factors may have affected both the choice of policy measures and the manner of their implementation. Any comment by officials on government policies and actions should always be consistent with the principle of civil service political impartiality. Officials should as far as possible avoid being drawn into discussion of the merits of alternative policies where this is politically contentious. If official witnesses are pressed by the Committee to go beyond these limits, they should suggest that the questioning should be referred to Ministers.

. . .

79. There are well established conventions which govern the withholding of policy papers of a previous Administration from an Administration of a different political complexion. These were set out in a Parliamentary answer from the Prime Minister on 24 January 1980 (Official Report, Columns 305–307). Since officials appear before Select Committees as representatives of their Ministers, and since Select Committees are themselves composed on a bipartisan basis, it follows that officials should not provide a Committee with evidence from papers of a previous Administration which they are not in a position to show to their present Ministers.

Notes

1. The guidance goes on to stress that questioning by Committees must not be permitted to turn effectively into disciplinary hearings of individuals; such hearings are carried on only in Departments and are confidential.
2. Failure to attend has generally been less of a problem than failure to answer questions properly. As Norton puts it, 'Whilst the committees normally get the witnesses they want, they do not always get the answers they want. . .'.[159] As the above extract made clear, the areas on which officials will refuse to answer questions are wide, and constitute a severe restriction on freedom of information.[160] How far they are justified by the doctrines of civil service neutrality and ministerial responsibility to Parliament is a question considered elsewhere in this book (see Chapter 12, at pp 628–637). Nevertheless, the overall verdict of the Liaison Committee in 2003 was that, 'Overall the relationships between committees and departments are reported as good, with a high level of cooperation and openness'.[161] This positive verdict was repeated in the Liaison Committee's review of the Committees in 2007–08.

---

159   P Norton, *Does Parliament Matter?* (1993), p 108.

160   R Brazier, *Constitutional Practice* (1994), p 227.

161   HC 558 (2002–03), para 42.

3.   Where the Committees seek to question individuals about suspected serious wrongdoing, a conflict may arise between the public interest in seeking the information in question, and the individual privilege against self-incrimination. This problem arose out of the investigation by the Social Security Select Committee of the Maxwell pension fund. When the Committee called Kevin and Ian Maxwell, both refused to answer certain key questions: see First Special Report from the Social Security Committee, HC 353 (1991–92). However, this has not proved to be a general problem with the Select Committees. [162]

Evaluation of the Select Committees and Reform

Commenting on the work of the Committees during the 80s and 90s, Giddings thought that while of some value, it 'has been unsystematic and its coverage of the work of Government patchy, not to say idiosyncratic' and that the Committees had not really changed the basic nature of the Commons—primarily adversarial and party-based, and Executive dominated. He recommended involvement of the Committees in the legislative process, while recognising that of course this would carry the risk of their becoming more adversarial.[163]

Professor Peter Hennessy has argued[164] that, leaving aside formal changes to their powers and jurisdiction, the Select Committees could still achieve far more simply by being more bold in their aspirations: 'I have always thought that, in the end, if Select Committees really pushed this, perhaps having to go to votes in the House or orders from the floor and so on for people to attend, the whole climate would change.'[165] Griffith and Ryle's blunt conclusion is that 'Select Committees have not made a general impact on Government policies'.[166] As Norton notes, they are essentially 'advisory bodies' only[167] and, as Gavin Drewry comments, 'in the business of scrutiny and exposure, not government'.[168] Where their activities do impact on policy, this is more likely to happen in relatively 'non political' areas. To expect Select Committees to be able to change contentious party-driven policies is clearly unrealistic.

It can be difficult to assess the impact of the Committees on departmental policy making because Committee reports may merely contribute to debate which is already taking place, but it is clear that, particularly where reports are unanimous, as is generally the case, they may have some impact on the policy debate. One of the few examples of a Select Committee report apparently resulting in a clear change in government policy can be seen in the decision to repeal the 'sus' law by means of the Criminal Attempts Act 1981 after a critical report from the Home Affairs Select Committee. In more recent times, the Labour Government responded very positively to the

---

162   Any punishment imposed by the House for contempt, in refusing to answer questions which the witness believed would incriminate him or her, would be likely to infringe Art 6 of the European Convention on Human Rights, which guarantees the presumption of innocence. However, However, an action could not be brought directly against Parliament under the Human Rights Act 1998, since Parliament is expressly included from the definition of 'public authorities' which are bound by the Convention rights: See s 6(1) and (3).

163   P Giddings, 'Select Committees and Parliamentary Scrutiny: Plus Ça Change?' (1994) 47(4) Parlt Aff 668, 682.

164   See the minutes of evidence taken before the Public Services Committee on 20 March 1996, HC 313 (1995–96).

165   *Ibid*, Q 90.

166   See n 59 above, at, 430.

167   *Does Parliament Matter?* (1993), p 108.

168   *The New Select Committees* (1989).

report of the Home Affairs Select Committee on police complaints and the disciplinary procedure for officers guilty of misconduct (HC 258–1 (1997–98)); the Government's response appears as HC 683. The Government accepted a large number of the Committee's findings and recommendations, including the broad thrust of the Committee's report that the present procedures of the Police Complaints Authority were inadequate and that significant reform was required to strengthen the complaints system.

Further examples of Select Committee influence are provided below.

Liaison Committee, *The work of committees in 2007–08, First Report* (2008–09), HC 291

Table 4: Examples of the impact of select committee scrutiny

Committee	Policy area	Committee approach	Impact
Business and Enterprise	Energy prices and fuel poverty	Inquiry and Report [1]	Ofgem probe into energy markets; implementation of Committee's recommendations
Environment, Food and Rural Affairs	Veterinary Surgeons Act 1966	Inquiry and Report [2]	Stimulated vigorous debate within the veterinary profession
Home	Domestic Violence	Inquiry and Report [3]	Government accepted recommendations on identifying cases of forced marriage abroad and in the United Kingdom, and on the effectiveness of schemes to ensure the safety of victims in their homes
Treasury	Abolition of 10 pence tax rate	Inquiry and Report [4]	Influenced Government decision to reduce the impact of the change on low-income households

[1] Business and Enterprise Committee, Eleventh Report of Session 2007–08, *Energy prices, fuel poverty and Ofgem, HC 293-I*. [2] Environment, Food and Rural Affairs Committee, Sixth Report of Session 2007–08, *The Veterinary Surgeons Act 1966, HC 348*. [3] Home Affairs Committee, Sixth Report of Session 2007–08, *Domestic Violence, Forced Marriage and "Honour"-Based Violence, HC 263-I*. [4] Treasury Committee, Thirteenth Report of Session 2007–08, *Budget Measures and Low-income households*, HC 326, and Third Report of Session 2007–08, *Work of the Committee, 2007–08*, HC 173

Table 5: Committee impact on emerging or deficient policy

Committee	Inquiry report	Impact
Communities and Local Government	Existing housing and climate change [1]	Government acepted amendment to the Climate Change Bill enabling the introduction of financial inicentives for microgeneration
Environment Audit	Biofuels [2]	Government announced a consultation on the reduction of biofuel targets
Foreign Affairs	Overseas Territories [3]	Following a Committee recommendation, commission of inquiry on Turks and Caicos Islands appointed
Health	Dental Services [4]	Revealed that the Department's original goal that patient access to dental services would improve from April 2006 had not been realised
IUSS	Biosecurity [5]	Government accepted two recommendations: that at inter-agency body with the role of improving strategic planning and co-ordination of high containment laboratories be created, and that a Ministerial group should meet to discuss biosecurity

[1] Communities and Local Government Committee, Seventh Report of Session 2007–08, *Existing Housing and Climate Change*, HC 432–1, [2] Environmental Audit Committee, First Report of Session 2007–08, *Are Biofuels Sustainable?*, HC 76–1 and Environmental Audit Committee, Fourth Report of Session 2007–08, *Are Biofuels Sustainable? The Government Response*, HC 528. [3] Foreign Affairs Committee, Seventh Report of Session 2007–08, *Overseas Territories*, HC 147-I. [4] Health Committee, Fifth Report of Session 2007–08, *Dental Services*, HC 289-I. [5] Innovation, Universities, Science and Skills Committee, Sixth Report of Session 2007–08, *Biosecurity in UK Research Laboratories*, HC 360-I.

Notes

1. There is no doubt that a number of recent Select Committee reports that were critical of government policy have had a very marked impact, receiving extensive publicity in the media, always forcing the Government further to explain and defend its policies from the criticisms made and, on occasion, causing it to reconsider its policies. Particularly influential were a number of trenchant reports by the Transport Committee. Its most important[169] was a forensic dissection of the Government's 10 Year Transport Plan—its master-plan for tackling the hugely difficult issue of reducing car usage and improving public transport as an alternative. The Report[170] was widely viewed in the media as sounding the death knell for the plan as originally conceived by John Prescott, while some viewed it as partly responsible for the resignation, in June 2002, of the then Transport Secretary, Stephen Byers.[171]

---

169   Another hard-hitting report concerned the adoption of a Public Private Partnership for the London Underground: HC 680 (2001–02).

170   Eighth Report of the Select Committee on Transport, Local Government and the Regions, *Ten Year Plan for Transport*, HC 558–1 (2001–02).

171   See further Chapter 12 at p 644.

2. More recently, the Liaison Committee, in its Annual Report for 2004, noted that: 'The Culture, Media and Sport Committee's inquiry into the Government's plans for reform of the national lottery concluded that multiple licences were a recipe for disaster and identified a number of other ways for encouraging effective competition for a single operating licence.' As a result, 'The Government reconsidered its policy and subsequently published the National Lottery Bill, which provided for a "clear and firm presumption" for a single licence, awarded by competition'. The Secretary of State subsequently wrote to the Committee stating that, 'The work the Government undertook . . . was hugely influenced by the work of the Committee.'

3. A notable victory was scored recently by the Health Committee in relation to the smoking ban introduced by the Health Act 2006. The Bill as originally published allowed for smoking to continue in private members' clubs and, much more controversially, in pubs that did not serve food. The Health Committee came out strongly for a total ban in public places, and the Committee's Chair then 'led a group of MPs preparing an amendment to the legislation along these lines'.[172] This was of course the eventual result when the legislation was finalised, with the Government forced to concede a free vote in Parliament in order to avoid a possible defeat on a whipped vote. Of course the Committee was by no means the sole reason why this result was achieved (some members of the Cabinet, including the then Health Secretary apparently favoured this result) but it plainly had important influence. Similarly, as noted above, Select Committees played a significant role in raising strong concerns about the Legislative and Regulatory Reform Bill 2006;[173] as Kalitowski notes: 'the work of several select committees examining the Bill proved to be of particular value and largely made up for the absence of formal pre-legislative scrutiny.'[174]

4. The Hansard Society Commission was strongly of the view that, in order to enhance their impact, the Committees should pursue recommendations made in their reports with much greater perseverance:

> The impact of committee reports will be determined by the assiduity with which their recommendations are monitored and followed up. Committees should publish a periodic review (two to three years after the original report) assessing how far their recommendations have been implemented.[175]

5. Ganz argues that whilst Select Committee reports can be influential, especially when unanimous, the key problem is that 'they exist as an oasis in an adversarial system'. This gives rise to 'the most fundamental weakness. . .the difficulty in transferring the consensus of the committee to the House itself'. Thus, when Select Committee reports on proposed legislation are cited on the floor of the House, and an acute conflict arises between loyalty to the Committee on the one hand and to the party on the other, the party almost invariably[176] triumphs. Ganz instances the 'open disagreement' between members of the Trade and Industry Committee on the interpretation of their unanimous report on proposed pit closures and the ease with which the Government was able to buy off the rebels with the minimum of concessions,[177] a pattern repeated when a hostile report by

---

172 Whitaker, above n 61 at 357.

173 See above at 381.

174 S Kalitowski, 'Rubber Stamp or Cockpit? The Impact of Parliament on Government Legislation' (2008) 61(4) Parlt Aff 694, 701.

175 See p 359 above, at para 3.40.

176 A notable exception, as Ganz points out (p 349 above, at 32) was during the debate on the 'sus' report (HC Deb col 1763 (5 June 1980)).
177 HC Deb col 25 (29 March 1993).

the same Committee[178] over rail privatisation was considered during the report stage of the legislation.[179]

6. In 2002, a package of proposals to strengthen Select Committees was agreed[180] between the Liaison and Modernisation Committees.[181] This included: greater support for Committees through the Scrutiny Unit; greater involvement in pre-legislative scrutiny; greater support for the Chairs of Committees; the establishment of core tasks for Committees (above at 397–398); considering giving all Committees the powers possessed by the Committee on Standards and Privileges to require the attendance of witnesses; the clarification of the rules governing the attendance of Ministerial special advisors as witnesses when summoned by Committees, and the creation of an 'alternative career structure' for the Chairs of Committees by paying a salary to them.

7. Then Leader of the House Robin Cook described the above proposals as: 'The most comprehensive package to strengthen the Select Committee system in the 20 years since it was set up.'[182] They were debated by the House of Commons on 14 July 2002. The House rejected the proposal that minority parties (the SNP, Plaid Cymru) and the Northern Ireland parties should be guaranteed some places on Select Committees (col 712). However, it then accepted the main proposal regarding core tasks for Select Committees, greater resources and more specialist support staff (cols 715–16) and was also in favour of payment for Chairs of Select Committees in an attempt to encourage members to see this as an alternative career path, something also strongly recommended by the Hansard Commission.[183] The proposals should represent a significant enhancement of the effectiveness of Select Committees, although the extra salary voted for Chairs (£12,500) though welcome, is perhaps unlikely to lure many away from their ambitions for Ministerial office. The most recent report from the Liaison Committee[184] stated: 'Much of our earlier agenda for improvement has been accepted. Our main focus is no longer campaigning on the principles, but monitoring progress in their implementation.'

8. It may be noted that, with the recent innovations to Select Committees both already agreed and implemented by the Commons in May 2002, many suggestions made previously by commentators such as Giddings for improving the system have been met: there is an attempt at greater co-ordination of the Committee's activities; a much greater involvement in pre-legislative scrutiny and an extension of resources and availability of the services of the National Audit Office to the Committees. The Liaison Committee found that the new Scrutiny Unit, as proposed above:

> has already established itself as a useful source of support to select committees in their pre-legislative and financial scrutiny roles. It comprises ten staff at present and will expand during 2003 to the 18 approved by the House of Commons Commission. The current staff include one Estimates specialist, two auditors, a statistician, a lawyer and a social policy expert.[185]

---

178   HC 375 and 245 (1992–93).

179   HC Deb cols 758 *et seq* (25 May 1993).

180   There were some areas of disagreement, notably over a recommendation to increase the size of Select Committees and to rename them 'Scrutiny Committees'.

181   See Second Report of the Liaison Committee, Select Committees: Modernisation Proposals, HC 692 (2002).

182   HC Deb col 655 (14 July 2002).

183   See p 359 above, at paras 2.34–2.36.

184   First Report, *Annual Report for 2002*, HC 558 (2002–03), para 2.

185   HC 558 (2002–03).

THE MP's EXPENSES SCANDAL AND FURTHER IMPETUS FOR PARLIAMENTARY REFORM

This matter was mentioned above. The Report from the Reform Committee, set up in the wake of the MPs expenses scandal largely speaks for itself.

House of Commons Reform Committee, *Rebuilding the House, First Report* (2008–09) (extracts)

1. We have been set up at a time when the House of Commons is going through a crisis of confidence not experienced in our lifetimes. This is largely, but not exclusively, because of the revelations about Members' expenses, bringing with it a storm of public disapproval and contempt. Public confidence in the House and in Members as a whole has been low for some time, but not as low as now. It is not too much to say that the institution is in crisis. . .

4. Without the shock of recent events, it is unlikely that this Committee would have been established. Yet the case for an inquiry such as ours was already strong, and becoming ever stronger. Since 1997 the Modernisation Committee has presided over a number of reforms, some of which—such as sittings in Westminster Hall and oral questions without notice to Ministers—have proved successful. However, a number of the proposals from that Committee, and the Procedure Committee and others, have been shelved, sidelined or simply disregarded, often without being put to the House, which is dispiriting for reform and reformers. A steady stream of reports from outside bodies have made the case for significant parliamentary reform. . .

19. It became clear in June that the House was dependent on the Government to provide time for debate on the motion of no confidence in the former Speaker, something which was quintessentially a House matter. This incident crystallised concerns expressed for some time about Members' inability to control the business in their own House. . .

23. The most important common theme is the House's lack of control over its own business. There is a well-established concern (dating back many decades) that Government in general is too dominant over parliamentary proceedings. The House is notionally in charge but, partly because of difficulties of collective decision-making, partly due to imbalance of resources, and partly as a result of its own Standing Orders, the coordination of decisions often rests with the executive. There is a feeling that the House of Commons, as a representative and democratic institution, needs to wrest control back over its own decisions rather than delegating so much (as it does now) to Ministers and frontbenchers. Where the House does retain at least notional control, such as the approval by the Chamber as a whole of select (but not public bill) committee membership, that must not be compromised.

[The Committee notes widespread dissatisfaction with Government timetabling of Bills, particularly the Report stage discussed above (at 379).] It then noted the time set aside for questions, adjournment debates, Opposition Days etc (noted above at 385) and continued]

126. The default position is therefore that time "belongs" to the Government, subject to a number of exceptions and practices which allow others to influence and even determine the agenda. Put crudely, and subject to maintaining a majority, the Government enjoys not merely precedence but exclusive domination of much of the House's agenda, and can stop others seeking similar control. . .

161. The system fails in several ways to match the basic principles set out at the beginning of this Report. We set out below five ways in which it fails to meet these tests.

PARLIAMENTARY CONTROL OF BUSINESS

(ix) It is wrong in principle that, in addition to controlling its own legislative timetable, the Government rather than the House decides what is discussed, when, and for how long.

162. It is entirely right that a democratically elected Government should have a priority right to put its legislative and other propositions before the House at a time of its own choosing, and to be able to plan for the conclusion of that business. But it should be for the House as a whole to determine how much time to devote to such debate and scrutiny. It is also right in a democratic Chamber that the Government is free to deploy its majority to pass its business. But the procedures and practices which have grown up over the past two centuries have delegated to Government too much power to fix the agenda, and to take too many decisions without reference to its notional majority in the Chamber. We consider it for example unacceptable that Ministers can determine the scheduling of Opposition Days without reference to others; that they have an untrammelled power to decide the topics for general and topical debates; that they can determine which issues in major bills are debated on the floor of the House and by corollary which issues are not; that they can determine the fate of backbench legislation by procedural means rather than by decision of the House; and that they determine which pieces of secondary legislation are or are not debated in the Chamber. It is not easy for Members to bring on a debate—as opposed to a 30 minute exchange between a Member and a Minister—on a topic which Ministers do not want to have debated, irrespective of the strength of feeling across the House: let alone a debate on a substantive motion. Nor does the House have a mechanism to establish its own inquiry, beyond existing select committees, when the Government is unwilling to do so.

CROSS-PARTY WORKING

(x) The current framework provides protected time in the Chamber for the Government, Opposition and individual Members, but scarcely recognises the cross-party work of select committees, let alone other groups of Members.

. . .

TRANSPARENCY

> (xi) The system for scheduling business is not transparent to many inside the House, let alone those outside.

164. Even the term "the usual channels" has a distinct air of mystery which demonstrates the difficulty of establishing who has made or can make a particular decision. There is no consultation with minority parties or backbenchers. Most decisions are taken in private, do not have to be justified in public and can sometimes only be gleaned after the event. Naturally much of the detailed planning and negotiation needs to be conducted in private, but the process itself needs to be clear in order to be legitimate.

TOPICALITY

(xii) The House is not systematically using its time to debate those matters of current concern which the nation expects its elected Chamber to be debating, nor is it responding flexibly to a swiftly moving political agenda, nor setting a long term policy agenda.

165. . . .As a result controversial select committee reports are often not debated promptly; and other controversial issues are avoided.

USE OF TIME

(xiii) Time in the House is frequently described as a scarce commodity; but it is often wasted on business stretched out artificially to a pre-determined voting time or on arid debate on subjects on which backbenchers on neither side much wish to speak.

F Five elements of a reformed system

. . .

I. . . THE HOUSE SHOULD DETERMINE ITS OWN AGENDA AND SITTING PATTERN

168. Time in the House belongs to the House. At present the House has no mechanism for determining its own business and therefore takes no responsibility for it and for the difficult choices which have to be made. It is then all too easy to blame the Government for not providing time for debate: the Business Statement is followed by a raft of suggestions for additional debates but no proposal as to where the time is to come from. The current system infantilises Members and demonises Government: ending it would be to the advantage of both Ministers and Parliament.

169. The agenda should therefore fall to be decided by the House, if need be by a majority. The straightforward way of doing that is by putting a motion to the House on a set day and time each week. That is standard practice in many parliaments around the world and has operated in the Scottish Parliament without problems for the last decade. No extra time would be required as it would take the place of the Business Statement and subsequent questions. This Motion would:

- set out the basic details of the agenda in the House for the week ahead;
- be open to amendment, subject to the Chair's powers of selection;
- be put formally to the vote after the elapse of a period set in Standing Orders, such as 45 minutes.

. . .

174. A votable motion on the agenda provides a traditional accountability mechanism for such decisions, and ultimately a sanction were the wishes of a majority of the House to be misjudged or ignored. Any programme which requires the positive approval of the House will necessarily be drawn up—and we deal below with how and by whom it is to be drawn up—with the intention of satisfying a clear majority of members and delivering to the Government sufficient time to get the business it initiates through the House.

. . .

II. BACKBENCH BUSINESS SHOULD BE SCHEDULED BY BACKBENCHERS AND THE HOUSE

176. Backbenchers should schedule backbench business. Ministers should give up their role in the scheduling of any business except that which is exclusively Ministerial business, comprising Ministerial-sponsored legislation and associated motions, substantive non-legislative motions required in support of their policies and Ministerial statements The rest of the business currently scheduled by Ministers—such as House domestic business, select committee reports and general and topical debates—is for backbenchers to propose and the House to decide. . . .

180. We therefore recommend that a Backbench Business Committee be created. It

should be comprised of between seven and nine members elected by secret ballot of the House as a whole, with safeguards to ensure a due reflection of party proportionality in the House as a whole. The Chair would also be elected by ballot of the whole House. Front-bench members of all parties and PPSs would be ineligible for membership of the commit-tee. . .The committee would meet weekly to consider the competing claims for time made by select committees and backbenchers in groups or as individuals for the protected days and/or time-slots [see below] available in the two weeks ahead, and then to come to a firm view on the backbench business in the week immediately ahead.

181. . . .[This] will be a major step forward. . .It will create new opportunities for all Members, giving them a greater sense of ownership and responsibility for what goes on in their own House. It will make debates more responsive to public concerns, as fed in to Members by their constituents. It will strengthen the position of the widely-respected select committees. We feel that this is an essential reform which will have many benefits for Members, for Parliament as a whole, and for the esteem in which it is held.

III THE GOVERNMENT SHOULD RETAIN THE INITIATIVE ON SCHEDULING MINISTERIAL BUSINESS

Ministerial business

182. Ministers should continue to have the first call on House time for Ministerial business, meaning Ministerial-sponsored primary and secondary legislation and associated motions, substantive non-legislative motions required in support of their policies and Ministerial statements on major policy changes. Ministers would for example retain the right to determine the date of second reading of a Government Bill, and the day by which the Bill was to conclude its passage through the House.

Ministerial control of timing

183. Ministers should also continue to be entitled to put to the House for its assent the order in which items of Ministerial business are scheduled and the day on which they are to be taken.

184. The Government's right to have the opportunity to put its legislative and other propositions to the House, at a day of its choosing, should not however extend to deciding without any reference to the House for how long these are to be debated by the House. Scheduling must allow for Ministers to have a proper opportunity to present their case; for Opposition parties to present theirs; and for backbenchers to speak. But it cannot be right that Ministers effectively decide with little or no consultation the length of a Second Reading debate or the report stage of a Bill or the time to be devoted to Lords amendments. There needs to be some means of consultation with Members speaking for the House and not just front-benchers.

185. Under programming of most Government Bills, the time allowed for the report stage is put to the House in the programme motion moved immediately after Second Reading. These motions are effectively unamendable and are not open to separate debate. It is unnecessary for the House to be asked to agree so peremptorily *before* a Committee stage how long the report stage should last.

IV THE OPPOSITION ARE ENTITLED TO MORE SAY IN WHEN OPPOSITION DAYS ARE SCHEDULED AND HOW THEY ARE USED

. . .

V SELECT COMMITTEES AND INDIVIDUAL MEMBERS SHOULD BE GIVEN ENHANCED OPPORTUNITIES, WHILE RETAINING THEIR EXISTING RIGHTS OF INITIATIVE

Select committee debates

191. [Noting the opportunities for debating Select Committee reports at present, the Committee continues] But. . .it is hard for select committees to get the attention of the House itself. Debates are not held until a Government Reply is received, which can take two months to compile, and sometimes more. And where there are debates there is no opportunity for a committee to test its conclusions in a vote of substance, based on a draft resolution it can put forward, itself then subject to amendment. . .These are the sort of opportunities which should be possible under a reformed system.

Individual Member initiatives

192. Individual backbenchers must continue to be able to raise subjects as adjournment debates in the Chamber and in Westminster Hall, and to press legislation through Private Members' Bills, as well as participating in debate and questioning. In addition, any revised system must respond to the widespread sense that the right should be restored to Members to get a substantive motion put to the House and decided. We propose below the introduction of a regular slot for debate on a heavily signed motion from the back-benches, separate from the EDM system. That would offer a return to backbenchers of the right to move a motion in the House which was lost in 1994. We also propose some other new forms of business which might be introduced, to be scheduled within backbench time.

. . .

Private Members Bills

194. One essential test of the House's control of its own business is whether the handful of legislative propositions tabled by those backbenchers fortunate enough to win one of the top 7 places in the sessional ballot should be able to see their bills progress in the House unless and until defeated by a majority. The House should be responsible for ensuring that merely procedural devices cannot obstruct Private Members' Bills, and that they are brought to a decision. This could among other things mean scheduling Private Members' Bills at some other time in the week than Fridays, such as Wednesday evenings. As a corollary to this, the Government and other parties should be free to whip against those Bills it opposes; but the outcome should be clearly dependent on a decision of the House one way or another.

Notes

1. The Committee also sought ways of achieving greater public access to and involvement in Parliament and in contributing to and indeed initiating law-making and reform through petitions and the like:

> The Committee calls for the primary focus of the House's overall agenda for engagement with the public to be shifted towards actively assisting a greater degree of public participation.
>
> It calls for urgent discussions on the currently stalled process of introducing an e-petitions system, and for the Procedure Committee to become for a trial period a Procedure and Petitions Committee, dealing with petitions submitted under existing rules. It recommends a number of changes designed to give presentation of petitions greater significance in the House's proceedings, including the

possibility of a debate. The Committee also calls for the working up of a scheme for identifying a monthly backbench Motion suitable for debate, alongside the existing Early Day Motions.

The report looks at the prospects for some form of "agenda initiative" which might enable the public to ensure that a given issue is debated in the House. It calls for the House to commission an investigation of the practicalities of such a procedure at national level, drawing on local and international experience, and concludes that the opportunities should be seized for nourishing representative democracy by the exploration of other democratic possibilities.[186]

2. This report seeks to do something quite fundamental—give the Commons back a substantial degree of control over its own business. However, as Hazel makes clear, a precedent for such reforms exists in other UK legislatures:

> [In Scotland and Wales the business [of the devolved assemblies] is planned by a committee, chaired by the Presiding Officer, on which all the parties are represented. It is more inclusive, more transparent, and less dominated by the government. It is the business committee which allocates bills to committees and decides on the timetable, and it is the business committee which decides on the membership of committees and their chairs: unlike the Commons, where again these matters are controlled by the party whips.[187]

3. Votes were taken in the Commons on the Wright proposals on 4th March 2010 and they were accepted, including the proposals on selection of Select Committees members. However, the standing order changes needed were lost in the 'wash up' before the May 2010 election. The new Conservative–Liberal Government has however pomised to implement the changes in full.

FURTHER READING

P Bennet and S Pullinger, *Making the Commons Work* (1991)

R Blackburn and A Kennon, *Griffith & Ryle on Parliament: Functions, Practice and Procedures*, 2nd edn (2002)

M Franklin and P Norton, *Parliamentary Questions* (1993)

Hansard Commission, *The Challenge for Parliament: Making Government Accountable* (2001)

J McEldowney, 'The control of public expenditure', in J Jowell and D Oliver, *The Changing Constitution*, 6th edn (2007)

P Norton, *Legislatures* (1990)

Norton Commission, *Strengthening Parliament* (2000)

R Pyper and L Robins (eds), *Governing the UK in the 1990s* (1995), Part II

M Ryle and P Richards (eds), *The Commons under Scrutiny* (1988)

A Tomkin, 'Conclusion', in *Government Unwrapped: The Constitution after Scott* (1998)

S Kalitowski, 'Rubber Stamp or Cockpit? The Impact of Parliament on Government Legislation' (2008) 61(4) Parlt Aff 694

---

186   *Ibid*, Summary.

187   Hazel, 'Continuing Dynamism', at 12.

CHAPTER 9
THE HOUSE OF LORDS
AND REFORM

INTRODUCTION

Reform of the House of Lords, at the time of writing, remains firmly on the political agenda. Labour's first term of office saw it achieve an historic Labour Party goal with the passage of the House of Lords Act 1999, which removed all but 92 of the hereditary peers, who, for centuries, had comprised the large majority of the membership of the Lords. The process of reform, following reports from the Royal Commission on Reform of the House of Lords, under the chairmanship of Lord Wakeham[1] (hereafter 'Wakeham') the Government's White Paper in response,[2] an influential report from the Public Administration Select Committee,[3] two from the new Joint Committee on Lords Reform[4] and three White Papers since then, culminating in the latest in 2008[5] is still seemingly ongoing, although the Conservatives, likely to win the 2010 Election, seem unlikely to move swiftly to engage in radical reform. This chapter will consider the constitutional role of the House of Lords. It will examine its membership, the pattern and extent of party control over it, its effectiveness in scrutinising legislation and policy, and the constraints, both legal and conventional, which restrict its powers. In the context of that inquiry it will then consider the various proposals for reform discussed above and lessons from overseas that may help resolve the debate as to the best way forward for this still unfinished part of Labour's constitutional reform programme.

COMPOSITION OF THE HOUSE OF LORDS AND PARTY BALANCE

The composition of the House before 1999

As indicated above, the make-up of the Lords has recently undergone a significant change; this extends both to its membership and to the method of appointing independent ('cross-bench') peers. To most commentators in this area, the outstanding feature of the unreformed House of Lords was its wholly undemocratic character and particularly the presence of some 750 hereditary peers. As Shell remarks, 'That most of those entitled to sit, to speak, and to vote in the second chamber do so simply because they inherited this right seems extraordinary.'[6] As to the remainder:

> every single one of them has become a member of the second chamber because the Prime Minister of the day had decided to recommend them for a peerage-
> . . .[while] whatever the complexion of the government of the day, the Conservative

---

1   Wakeham Report, *A House for the Future,* Cm 4534 (2000), available at www.officialdocuments.co.uk/ document/cm45/4534/4534.htm.

2   This appeared in the White Paper, *The House of Lords: Completing the Reform,* Cmd 5291 (2001) available at www.lcd.gov.uk/constitution/hol-ref/holreform.htm and in a further document published by the Lord Chancellor's Department, *House of Lords Reform: Supporting Documents* (6 December 2001), available at www.lcd.gov.uk/whatsnfr.htm.

3   Fifth Report, HC 494–i (2001–02), esp. at paras 6 and 36 (hereafter PAC).

4   For the resolutions appointing it see: HC Deb cols 338–80 (19 June 2002); HL Deb cols 354–62 (4 July 2002). Its terms of reference may be found at: www.parliament.uk/ parliamentary_committees/joint_committee_on_house_of_lords_reform.cfm. Its reports are discussed below.

5   *An Elected Second Chamber,* Cm 7438 (2008).

6   Donald Shell, 'The House of Lords: Time for a Change?' (1994) 47(4) Parlt Aff 721, 721.

> Party always enjoys control in the House of Lords. . . To say that such a House is
> deeply offensive to democratic values is. . .a truism.[7]

The membership of the House of Lords was thus drawn from a number of sources: the hereditary peers, 26 Bishops of the Church of England (other Christian denominations and non-Christian faiths are not represented); the Law Lords, and the life peers. On the creation of life peerages in 1958, Griffith and Ryle comment:

> Life peers have transformed the House. Instead of a House consisting predomin-
> antly of landowners and retired politicians (with a sprinkling of lawyers and bishops)
> the range of occupations and interests has been vastly increased.[8]

2. The following description was given by a peer during a recent debate on reform of the Lords:

> You form a unique pool of expertise and experience. Casual research reveals that
> 20 per cent of you came from the [Commons], including two former Prime Ministers,
> five former Chancellors of the Exchequer and more than 60 other former Ministers;
> another 20 per cent come from business, international commerce and financial
> services; and some 14 per cent are lawyers and judges. Other well represented
> sectors are local government, the Civil and Foreign Services, trades unions,
> teachers, professors, doctors, nurses, the voluntary services, the armed forces and
> police, agriculture, the religious faiths and the media.[9]

3. The political make-up of the House of Lords prior to the removal of the hereditary peers was set out in the following White Paper, which preceded the House of Lords Act 1999.

Modernising Parliament — Reforming the House of Lords, Cm 4183 (1999), Chapter 3 (extracts)

Political parties operate within the overall structure of the House of Lords. But unlike the House of Commons, there is a significant independent element — the cross-bench peers. At 4 January 1999, the political make-up of the House. . .was:

Party	Life Peers	Hereditary Peers of first creation	by succession	Bishops	Total
Conservative	172	4	300		476
Labour	157	1	17		175
Liberal	45	0	24		69
Democrat					

---

7   *Ibid*, 722.

8   JAG Griffith and M Ryle, *Parliament: Functions, Practice and Procedures* (1989), p 462.

9   HL Deb col 651 (9 January 2002).

Party	Life Peers	Hereditary Peers of first creation	Hereditary Peers by succession	Bishops	Total
Cross-bench	119[1]	0	198		317
Other[2]	10	4	88	26	128
TOTAL	503	9	627	26	1,165

1 Includes 28 Law Lords
2 Peers who have not taken a party whip

As can be seen, the Conservatives have a clear majority over the other parties overall, and an overwhelming majority among the hereditary peers. They constitute nearly 50 per cent of the total of hereditary peers, including the politically non-affiliated. They also form the largest single party among the life peers. The Conservatives' share of the House of Lords far exceeds the Party's vote in recent general elections (which was 34% in 1997 and 44.5% in 1992).

Notes
As the above analysis highlights, when one looks instead of total membership, at those who attended more than 50% of the sessions, a slightly different picture emerges. First, only about a third of peers attended 50% or more—the figures were 399 for 1996–97. Second, the peers were distributed as follows: Conservatives have 195, or 49%; Independents (cross-benchers) 21%; Labour 83 or 21%; Liberal Democrats 37 or 9%. So to defeat the Conservatives, nearly all the Independents had to vote with Labour and the Liberal Democrats—given that these three put together only have a bare 51% of the votes. So unless the Independents voted overwhelmingly with the non-Conservative parties (which they very seldom did—see below), the Conservatives always had a majority.

The composition of the Lords after the removal of the hereditary peers

The first part of the reform of the House of Lords came with the removal of most hereditary peers from the House of Lords. This was achieved through the short House of Lords Act 1999, which provided, in s 1, that 'No-one shall be a member of the House of Lords by virtue of a hereditary peerage'.

As Stephen Tierney notes:

> Labour's attempt to remove the right of hereditary peers to sit and vote in the House of Lords was only a partial success. . .the Act, which in the end preserved the right of ninety-two hereditary peers to remain in the House of Lords, emerged as the result of an agreement between the Government and Lord Cranborne, leader of the Conservative Party in the Lords. . .The Government was prepared to reach a settlement with the dominant Conservative Party in the Lords in order to avoid disruption not only to this proposal but to other important elements of the Government's legislative programme.[10]

The deal over how many hereditaries to retain was apparently the subject of some remarkable haggling between Irvine and Cranborne and indicates the utter *'ad hocery'* that constitutional reform in the

10   S Tierney, 'The Labour Government and Reform of the House of Lords' (2000) 6(4) EPL 506, at 508–09.

UK can descend into. The latter could threaten 'the complete buggerisation of your legislative programme'[11] if Labour didn't come to a compromise; the former, the dismissal of the entire grouping of hereditaries if the price for buying Conservative cooperation in their demise became too high. Irvine's initial offer was for 10 hereditaries to be retained; Cranborne demanded 150. After conferring, negotiations resumed.

A Rawnsley, *Servants of the People: The Inside Story of New Labour* (revised edn, 2001), p 202

Irvine was sanctioned to up his offer to the survival of 75 of the hereditary peers pending the second stage of Lords' reform. 'We really do want a deal.' Cranborne had come down to 100. To bridge the gap between them, the Viscount wondered if the government would throw in the 15 hereditaries who held offices. 'I'll talk to young Blair,' replied Irvine. The next day, Cranborne heard from Irvine: 'Done.' Cranborne asked: 'Will you give me the Earl Marshall and the Lord Great Chamberlain?' Irvine: 'Done.' The Viscount and the Cardinal, these peers of the realm, bargained about the future composition of one half of parliament with the sophistication of a couple of used-car dealers. Thus was British constitutional history made.

To seal the bargain, on Thursday 26 November, Cranborne was smuggled into Downing Street and up to the Prime Minister's flat. . .Blair frowned at him: 'But will Hague [then Conservative Leader] back this?' Cranborne was operating behind enemy lines: . . .Hague and his fellow Tories in the Shadow Cabinet had told him they didn't want a deal with the government. Cranborne. . . expressed himself relaxed. He. . .expected Hague to come round. . .

When the deal was announced, Hague renounced it and sacked Cranborne. Then, confronted with a rebellion by Conservative peers, Hague was abjectly forced to swallow the fix done with the government. . .A year later, 650 of the hereditaries were gone from the Lords. . .

Notes

1. As Tierney notes, '[This] was widely perceived as a tactical deal compromising the principle of no hereditary representation which Labour had categorically and repeatedly asserted in the manifesto, the Queen's Speech and the White Paper'.[12]

2. One of the few plausible arguments made for the retention of the hereditary peers was that the work of some talented and distinguished peers (such as the Russell family) would be lost to the nation as a result of the reform. The retention of the 92, assuming that peers voted for those with a proven record as able and committed scrutinisers, answered this concern, as well as easing the passage of the Bill through the Lords.

3. The reform made a striking difference. As Bogdanor puts it:

   At the beginning of the twentieth century, the Lords was primarily a hereditary and aristocratic institution, but by the end of the century it had become a predominately nominated body, comprising both party politicians and also experts. The name of the chamber was the same, but its role and function had become quite different.[13]

---

11   A Rawnsley, *Servants of the People: The Inside Story of New Labour* (2000), p 202.

12   Tierney, n 10 above.

13   V Bogdanor, *The New British Constitution* (2009) at 157.

4. A second point is also of importance. Given that all life peers are appointed by the Prime Minister of the day, this reform actually *increased* executive influence over Parliament. However, an examination of the party balance immediately after the 1999 Act revealed that fears that removal of the hereditary peers would lead to the House overnight becoming packed with 'Tony's cronies', thus becoming 'the Government's poodle', were proved to be largely groundless. Immediately after the departure of the hereditaries, the party balance was as follows: Conservatives 35%, Labour 27.5%, cross-benchers 24.5%, Liberal Democrats, 8%, Bishops and others, 5%. The Conservatives thus remained the biggest group by a comfortable margin; Labour were only slightly ahead of the cross-benchers—indeed the independent members outnumbered Labour if the Bishops were counted in. Thus, in theory, in order to move its legislation through the House, the Government still needed to persuade no less than 151 non-Labour peers to support it. The figures also reveal that the strong cross-bench element in the Lords, far from being reduced, was strengthened, in terms of proportion of membership. Around 14% of the total eligible membership of the unreformed Lords were cross-benchers (1998 figures); as a result of the House of Lords Act, that figure rose to 24.5%, or virtually a quarter of the total.

5. Clearly, however, the use of prime ministerial patronage, in relation to the transitional House was, and continues to be crucial. It would have been quite possible for this power, unrestrained save by some rather vague conventions relating to the appointment of peers from other parties, to have been used over time to pack the Lords with Labour placemen, giving Labour an eventual overall majority. To counter this fear, the Government set out a series of principles in the White Paper to govern Mr Blair's appointments to the transitional House.[14]

> In our manifesto we said:
> *'Our objective will be to ensure that over time party appointees as life peers more accurately reflect the proportion of votes cast at the previous general election. We are committed to maintaining an independent cross-bench presence of life peers. No one political party should seek a majority in the House of Lords.'*
> Our present intention is to move towards broad parity between Labour and the Conservatives. The principle of broad parity and proportionate creations from the Liberal Democrat and other parties would be maintained throughout the transitional period.

6. In pursuit of this goal of broad parity with the Conservatives the Government appointed a much higher number of life peers per year than under previous governments. As Tierney notes: 'By June 2000 [Blair] had appointed 214 peers compared to a total of 203 appointed by Margaret Thatcher in her eleven years in office.'[15] By November 2001, this had risen to 248 peers, meaning, as *The Times* commented, that 'In a House. . .containing just over 700 peers, more than a third owe their places in Parliament to one Prime Minister'.[16] However, fewer than half of these peers, 113, are Labour peers. Bogdanor notes that:

> It seems rapidly to have become an accepted convention that in future no single party should ever again enjoy an overall majority in the House of Lords. The government of the day therefore, whether Labour or Conservative, will have to persuade the House by argument; it will not be able, like Conservative governments in

---

14 *Modernising Parliament: Reforming the House of Lords,* Cm 4183 (1999), Chapter 6.

15 Tierney, n 10 above, at 509.

16 *The Times,* 8 November 2001.

the past, to take the assent of the Lords for granted. In practice, it is the cross-benchers and the Liberal Democrats who often find themselves in a pivotal position. . .The House of Lords is therefore, permanently hung.[17]

7.   The more important concern with the present House is that it is, and always has been, objectionable on constitutional grounds that the Prime Minister, the effective head of the executive, should appoint members of one chamber of the legislature, and this objection gains far more force now that the large majority of that chamber—rather than as, previously, a minority—are appointed. In response to this concern, the Government proposed a new, non-statutory, independent appointments commission, which would appoint the cross-bench peers.

Modernising Parliament—Reforming the House of Lords, Cm 4183 (1999), Chapter 6 (extracts)

The Commission will be an advisory non-departmental public body. It will consist of representatives of the three main political parties, and independent figures who will comprise a majority, one of whom will become the Chairman. It will operate an open and transparent nominations system for cross-bench peers, both actively inviting public nominations and encouraging suitable bodies to make nominations. The general qualities being sought and the type of information required to support a nomination will be made public. It will seek to cast its net wider than the present system to achieve successful nominations. . . .

The Appointments Commission will also take on and reinforce the present function of the Political Honours Scrutiny Committee in vetting the suitability of all nominations to life peerages. It will continue to include scrutiny on the grounds of propriety in relation to political donations, as endorsed by Lord Neill in his report on the funding of official parties. . .The Prime Minister will have no right to refuse a nomination the Commission had passed.

The Appointments Commission itself will be appointed in accordance with the rules of the Commissioner for Public Appointments. It will also seek his advice about best practice in the area of attracting and assessing potential nominees.

Awards of peerages will continue to be made by The Queen. In accordance with the normal conventions for the exercise of the prerogative, the names of those recommended will have to be submitted by the Prime Minister. The Prime Minister will decide the overall number of nominations to be made to The Queen and the Commission will be asked to forward to the Prime Minister the same number of recommendations. The Prime Minister will pass these on to Her Majesty in the same way as he will pass on the recommendations of other party leaders to fill the vacancies on their benches. Therefore, except in the most exceptional of circumstances, such as those endangering the security of the realm, the only nominations which the Prime Minister will be able to influence are those from his own party. . .

Notes

1.   Thus, the current position is that the Prime Minister still appoints all those peers who take a party whip (the large majority) while the non-statutory Appointments Commission appoints the others; this nevertheless represents an appreciable diminution of the PM's power of patronage and also a form of guarantee that the cross-benchers appointed genuinely will be independent of party.

---

17   Bogdanor, n 13 above at 157–58.

2.   The political composition of the House of Lords at 1 Feb 2010 was as follows:

By Party Strength

Party	Life Peers	Elected by Party	Hereditary Elected Office Holders	*Royal Office Holder	Bishops	Total
Conservative	141	39	9	0	0	189
Labour	207	2	2	0	0	211
Liberal Democrat	67	3	2	0	0	72
Crossbench	149	29	2	2	0	182
Bishops	0	0	0	0	26	26
Other**	23	2	0	0	0	25
TOTAL	587	75	15	2	26	705

NB Excludes 12 Members who are on leave of absence, 16 disqualified, a senior members of the judiciary and 1 disqualified as an MEP

3.   It may be seen that Labour is now the largest party, though only by around 20 seats out of 705, having 211 seats, to the Conservatives' 189 seats. No one party is anywhere near a majority, Labour having a little under 30% of the total seats, with the Conservatives having a fraction under 28%. The independent element, at 182 members, is only slightly smaller than the Conservative contingent, indeed it is larger, if the 26 Bishops are counted in. It is hard not to conclude that in removing (most of) those with no claim at all to be there, the hereditary peers, reducing the permanent dominance of the Conservative party, whilst denying dominance to any other party, and retaining a strong independent element, the new House is a significant improvement over the old. The hereditary peers were the most objectionable feature of the Lords since they had nothing at all to recommend them as a class, though of course individual hereditary peers might happen to be useful members of the House. The transitional House is not more democratic, but it is more meritocratic. This theme will be returned to at the end of this chapter.

4.   The actual appointments made by the new Appointments Commission were subject to some criticism for elitism,[18] one Labour MP describing the appointments as 'a complete farce'[19]—though mainly, it seems, because the phrase 'people's peers', apparently used by one Labour spin doctor to describe the expected creations of the Commission, had created expectations that ordinary people, including working class people with no particular achievements, would be appointed. In fact, the Commission appointees represented, roughly speaking, 'the great and the good' who might have been expected to have been rewarded peerages anyway.[20] It is suggested, however, that the criticism of the Commission's choices is misplaced: the work of the Lords is often technical and requires expertise; no one questions the calibre of those appointed, nor their ability to make useful

---

18   See, e.g. 'No Joe Soaps among the people's peers', *The Telegraph,* 27 April 2001; 'Lords: business as usual', *The Guardian,* 27 April 2001.

19   Gordon Prentice, on BBC R4 'The World at One', quoted in *The Telegraph,* 27 April 2001.

20   The 15 appointed included seven knights and three professors.

contributions to the work of the Lords. The Chairman of the Commission said that 'the process unearthed a wider variety of candidates than the old system'.[21] However, the Commission has not made many appointments. As the Joint Committee on Lords Reform recently remarked, 'There is, therefore, a growing need to top up the stock of expertise and of younger members'.[22]

The following extract provides a contemporary look at the appointees of the Commission.

M Russell and M Sciara, 'Independent parliamentarians en masse: The changing nature and role of the "crossbenchers" in the House of Lords' (2009) 62(1) *Parliamentary Affairs* 32, 36, 37

In practice, the prime minister has continued to appoint the most senior office holders, leaving the Commission to take over appointing other leading figures. The Commission was established in 2000, under the chairmanship of Lord Stevenson of Coddenham, a Crossbench peer. It created an open system of appointment, inviting self-nominations, with candidates assessed by application form and interview. The Commission's creation was much publicised (not least by Alastair Campbell's promise of 'people's peers'), and it received over 3,000 applications in its first year. By November 2007, the Commission had made five rounds of nominations, totalling 42 individuals (one since deceased), and its recommendations are automatically accepted. These 'Stevenson peers' have a broadly similar profile to those appointed under the old system, including many high achievers from the public and voluntary sectors, in particular. But it is clear under the new system that appointment is principally a job rather than an honour, and these independents are expected to play some active role in the work of the House. Following severe press criticism of the first round of appointees for low attendance, members are questioned about the commitment that they can make to parliamentary work, and are conscious of the danger of public censure.

The levels of professional expertise for which the Lords is known are at their most concentrated on the Crossbenches. Many on the party benches have achieved high political office, and others have been high achievers in their professions. However, the great majority of Crossbenchers have earned a place in the House without any connection to party, and have had to prove their qualifications in other fields.

Note

While the removal of most of the hereditary peers and the setting up of the Appointments Commission clearly represented an improvement on the unreformed House, it is worth noting the enormous problems, in terms of legitimacy, that still dog the Lords. It remains entirely unelected, dominated by the legally unrestrained patronage of the Prime Minister, and not very representative of the votes cast at the last general elections. It is also male-dominated (though this has improved somewhat recently to nearly 20% female representation),[23] very under-representative of ethnic minorities, of the working class, of most of the regions of England and, with a membership whose average age is 68, of the young and indeed the middle-aged.

---

21   *The Telegraph,* 27 April 2001.

22   HL 97, HC 668 (2002–03), para 30.

23   C Eason, 'Women Peers and Political Appointment: Has the House of Lords Been Feminised Since 1999?' (2009) 62(3) Parlt Aff 399.

LIMITATIONS ON THE POWERS OF THE HOUSE OF LORDS

Legal limitations

The *legal* constraints on the power of the Lords arise under the Parliament Act 1911, as amended by the Parliament Act 1949. As AW Bradley and ECS Wade note, the Act of 1911 was brought in after the 'rather uncertain convention' that the Lords should give way to the Commons when the people's will was behind that body broke down when the Lords rejected Lloyd George's budget in 1909.[24]

Directly in response to that rejection, section 1 provided that if a Bill is a money Bill as defined in s 1(2) of the Parliament Act 1911,[25] and is passed by the Commons but is not passed by the Lords without amendment within one month after their receiving it, it shall be presented to the Queen for the Royal Assent and become an Act of Parliament. This provision was adopted with a view to stopping the Lords blocking the passing of essential financial legislation in future. Section 2 of the Act deals with other Bills.

Parliament Act 1911 (as amended by the Parliament Act 1949)[26]

2.(1) If any Public Bill (other than a Money Bill or a Bill containing any provision to extend the maximum duration of Parliament beyond five years) is passed by the House of Commons [in two successive sessions] (whether of the same Parliament or not), and having been sent up to the House of Lords at least one month before the end of the session, is rejected by the House of Lords in each of those sessions, that Bill shall, on its rejection [for the second time] by the House of Lords, unless the House of Commons direct to the contrary, be presented to His Majesty and become an Act of Parliament on the Royal Assent being signified thereto, notwithstanding that the House of Lords have not con-sented to the Bill: Provided that this provision shall not take effect unless [one year has elapsed] between the date of the second reading in the first of those sessions of the Bill in the House of Commons and the date on which it passes the House of Commons [in the second of those sessions].

(2) When a Bill is presented to His Majesty for assent in pursuance of the provisions of this section, there shall be endorsed on the Bill the certificate of the Speaker of the House of Commons signed by him that the provisions of this section have been duly complied with.

3. Any certificate of the Speaker of the House of Commons given under this Act shall be conclusive for all purposes, and shall not be questioned in any court of law.

Notes

1. Thus the Parliament Act allows the House of Commons to assert political supremacy over the Lords. For non-money Bills, when a Bill has been passed by the Commons in two successive

---

24 See AW Bradley and ECS Wade, *Constitutional and Administrative Law*, 11th edn (1993), p 204.

25 'A Money Bill means a Public Bill which in the opinion of the Speaker of the House of Commons contains only provisions dealing with all or any of the following subjects, namely, the imposition, repeal, remission, alteration, or regulation of taxation; the imposition for the payment of debt or other financial purposes of charges on the Consolidated Fund, or on money provided by Parliament, or the variation or repeal of any such charges; supply; the appropriation, receipt, custody, issue or audit of accounts of public money; the raising or guarantee of any loan or the repayment thereof; or subordinate matters incidental to those subjects or any of them'.

26 Amendments made by the 1949 Act appear in square brackets.

sessions and it is rejected for a second time by the Lords it can be presented on its second rejection for the Royal Assent. One year must elapse between the second reading of the Bill in the Commons at the first session and its passing in the Commons in the second. Note that a Bill is deemed rejected by the Lords if it is either not passed un-amended by it, or only with such amendments as are agreed to by both Houses (s 2(3)).

2.   However, the limits on the Lords' power under the Parliament Acts are not as significant as may at first appear. First, not all Bills are subject to the Parliament Acts. Exemption extends to private Bills, Statutory Instruments, Bills prolonging the life of Parliament beyond five years and Bills originating in the House of Lords (around a third of Government Bills). Second, in practice, the Government will not want to wait for over a year before securing the passage of its legislation and so will normally be prepared to accept compromise amendments. The fact that the Parliament Act procedure has been used only 7 times since 1911 is decisive evidence of this.

3.   As previously mentioned, the Lords are generally circumspect in the use of their formal powers. They will, however, on occasion use their powers of suspension fully as in relation to the Trade Union and Labour Relations (Amendment) Bill 1974–75. In the debate in the Lords in relation to their amendments to this Bill, Lord Carrington said:

> In our system we have hitherto taken the view that the will of the elected house must in the end prevail, but that there should be a second House which has the opportunity. . .to enforce a delay in which there can be reassessment by Government. . .If we now decide to use that very limited power we are not thwarting the will of the people for, in so far as it is represented by the House of Commons, it will and must prevail in a comparatively short time. [HL Deb vol 365 col 1742 (11 November 1975).]

The Lords eventually allowed the Bill to go for Royal Assent only because the Government threatened to pass it under the Parliament Acts procedure. By delaying the Bill the Lords had ensured that it would receive greater scrutiny. The suspensory powers were again used to the full in relation to the War Crimes Bill 1991, which had to be passed under the Parliament Acts procedure, as did the European Elections Act 1999, the Sexual Offences (Amendment) Act 2000 and of course the Hunting Act 2004 (see further below).[27]

5.   As Meg Russell points out, while it is commonly thought that the Parliament Acts allow the Lords to impose a delay of one year to a Bill, in practice, the period of delay may be much shorter:

> . . .the European Parliamentary Elections Bill. . .was only the second bill since 1949 to be forced through the house under the Parliament Act procedures. However, objections in the House of Lords, which repeatedly tried to amend the bill to provide for 'open' rather than 'closed' lists of candidates delayed the bill by only about a month. Although the bill was introduced in the House of Commons in October 1997, it did not pass to the Lords until the spring of 1998. Its third reading in the house was then not until October that year. This is when the disagreement between the chambers became clear. During the months of October and November 1998 the bill was repeatedly amended in the Lords, and shuttled back and forth to the House of Commons, where the amendments were rejected each time. The Houses failed to agree by the end of the parliamentary session in November. However the bill was

---

27   This gave rise to the litigation in the *Jackson* case on the legality of the Parliment Act procedure, discussed in Chapter 4 at 188–194.

able to be reintroduced only eight days later, at the start of the new session. The inconvenience caused to government by this episode in the end was relatively minor, and the elections held in June 1999 used the 'closed' list system.[28]

6. Examination of the powers of the House of Lords should be put in comparative context. The following table indicates the powers of second chambers overseas over ordinary legislation. It should be noted that virtually all second chambers overseas have additional powers over legislation altering the constitution, a matter discussed further below.

M Russell and R Cornes, 'The Royal Commission on Reform of the House of Lords: a House for the future?' (2001) 64 *Modern Law Review* 82, 84

Table 1: Power of the upper house over ordinary and financial Bills in 10 democracies

Country	Power over ordinary Bills	Power over financial Bills
Australia	Total veto	As for ordinary Bills
Canada	Total veto	As for ordinary Bills
France	6–12 months' delay	As little as 1–5 days' delay
Germany	Total veto over Bills affecting states, delay over others	As for ordinary Bills
Ireland	Three months' delay	Three weeks' delay
Italy	Total veto	As for ordinary Bills
Japan	Two months' delay	One month's delay
Spain	Two months' delay	As for ordinary Bills
Switzerland	Total veto	As for ordinary Bills
UK	Approximately one year's delay	One month's delay
USA	Total veto	As for ordinary Bills

The Bryce Commission. . .wisely stated that one of the four main functions of an upper house was 'The interposition of so much delay (and no more) in the passing of a Bill into law as may be needed to enable the opinion of the nation to be adequately expressed upon it.' The chamber's current powers could be said to meet this requirement.

Conventional restraints upon the Lords

The conventions and their observation

The Lords accept a number of self-imposed informal constraints that have developed into conventions designed to avoid accusations that they are thwarting the will of the people. One of the most important conventions has been termed 'the doctrine of the mandate', know known as the 'Salisbury' or 'Government Bill convention.' This doctrine was explained by Lord Salisbury in 1964: 'as a guiding

---

28   M Russell, *Reforming the House of Lords: Lessons from Overseas* (2000), p 266.

principle, where legislation had been promised in the party manifesto, the Lords would not block it on the ground that it should be regarded as having been approved by the British people.'[29] This doctrine was developed during the post-war Labour administration but now normally applies to 'mandated' Bills of either party. However, this doctrine has not always meant that the Lords will refrain from insisting on an amendment to a Bill even though the effect will almost certainly be to kill it. This occurred in relation to the House of Commons (Redistribution of Seats) Bill in 1968–69.

When the Lords oppose a Bill sent up by the Commons they nearly always propose amendments at the committee stage rather than vote against the second reading, but there is a (weak) convention that amendments at the committee stage should not re-open matters of principle already accepted by the Commons. The Lords will rarely insist on their amendments to a Government Bill if a compromise can be reached, although of course they may do so when the Government lacks an effective majority to ensure their rejection in the Commons. O Hood Phillips has also argued[30] that there is almost a convention that the Lords will not return a Government Bill to the Commons for reconsideration more than once, though the behaviour of the Lords in relation to legislation sponsored by the Labour administration since 1997 (below) casts this assertion into doubt. Writing in the mid-90s, Donald Shell considered that the combined effect of these legal and conventional restraints on the Lords meant that it was unable to provide an appreciable check on the Government-dominated Commons. The experience of the Thatcher Government was again used as an example:

> To the Thatcher Governments of the 1980s the House was frequently an irritant but never a serious obstacle. In particular, legislation relating to local government and its various responsibilities, notably education and housing, was frequently amended against the will of the government. Ministers regularly gave ground to the Lords, with the House even being described as the real opposition during the 1983 Parliament when the Labour opposition in the Commons was at its lowest ebb. But in the late 1980s there appeared to a hardening of ministerial attitudes to the Lords, with the Government endeavouring wherever possible to overturn any defeat it suffered there. This culminated in the used of the Parliament Act procedures to pass the War Crimes Act of 1991, a Bill which the Government chose to persist with notwithstanding strong opposition in the Lords. . .[31]

Notes

1. Shell has elsewhere expressed the view that by 1985 the Thatcher Government was experiencing 'real difficulties' with the Lords.[32] The inference is presumably that the 'more determined and self-confident mood amongst peers' in 1983 which he noted in his earlier article was a product of the peers' knowledge that the Commons opposition was at that time relatively ineffectual, given the huge Conservative majority after the 1983 General Election; and further that as the Conservatives' majority was progressively reduced in subsequent elections, the peers retreated towards a more facilitative and anodyne approach. If this explanation is correct, it may be concluded that the Lords are capable of taking a flexible approach towards their self-imposed restraints, adopting a more bullish approach when the political situation seems to demand it. This is one argument in favour of leaving such restraints on a self-imposed basis only.

---

29   HL Deb vol 261 col 66 (4 November 1964).

30   *Constitutional and Administrative Law,* 7th edn (1987), p 148.

31   D Shell, 'The House of Lords: Time for a Change?' (1994) Parlt Aff 721, 733.

32   D Shell, 'The House of Lords and the Thatcher Government' (1985) Parlt Aff 16, 28.

2. However, any notion that as a government's majority decreases[33] the House of Lords is content to leave real opposition to government proposals to the Commons seems hard to square with the important series of defeats inflicted by the Lords on the Major Government's legislation—defeats on matters of controversial policy relating to television rights to sport (described as 'the biggest Government upset in the Lords since 1988'),[34] pensions and rights of asylum seekers. While it is tempting to try to formulate general rules about the behaviour of the Lords which relate it to the situation in the Commons, it is quite possible that, the Salisbury Convention excepted,[35] the most important factor in determining the assertiveness of the Lords is simply the nature of the legislation put before them.

3. The House of Lords has shown a fair degree of assertion in relation to the Labour Government of 1997–2010, even before the removal of the hereditary peers. One peer recently compared the performance of the Lords with the Commons since 1997.

HL Deb cols 627–628 (21 January 2003)

Lord Phillips of Sudbury: What is the best demonstration of effective holding to account of a Government? Most people would say that it is the ability of the Opposition in the House of Commons to vote down measures by the Government which they think are bad or misconceived. . . In the five Sessions of Parliament since the present Government came to power in 1997, there have been 1,640 Divisions in the House of Commons. On how many occasions were the Government defeated in a whipped vote? The answer is not one.

In the same period, in this place, we had 639 whipped votes. The Government won 475; they were defeated in 164 Divisions. Therefore, in one in four Divisions throughout the five-year period, the Government in this place have been defeated, whereas in another place, on not one single occasion have they been defeated in a whipped Division. In the past year, the number of defeats has risen from one in four to one in three.

Notes

1. A striking example of the Lords' assertiveness was the European Elections Bill 1998 discussed by Russell above. Defending themselves against the charge that their insistence on the amendment to introduce 'open' rather than 'closed lists' for the elections breached the Convention, Lord Mackay cited the relevant pledge in Labour's 1997 manifesto: 'We have long supported a proportional voting system for election to the European Parliament.' He commented: 'There is no mention of the system to be used. There is no mention of a closed list [or of]. . .an open list. Therefore this Bill, if we amend it with the open list, honours in every possible way the commitment given by the Labour Party in its manifesto. . .your Lordships are not breaching [the Salisbury] Convention.'[36] Eventually, the Bill was passed using the Parliament Acts procedure.

2. The Lords took a similarly assertive stance over the Teaching and Higher Education Bill 1998; widespread opposition in the Lords to a provision in the Bill which waived the payment of fees for the fourth year of a degree taken at a Scottish university for Scottish students, but not those from the rest of the UK, led the Lords to restore on three occasions an amendment rejected by the

---

33   John Major's administration was reduced to a majority of just one in 1996.

34   'Peers inflict huge defeat on TV sport', *The Independent*, 7 February 1996. The defeat in 1988 referred to was the 133 vote defeat over the 'poll tax' in May of that year.

35   See pp 436–437, above.

36   HL Deb cols 1343–34 (18 November 1998).

Commons which equalised the position for students from all parts of the UK. The Government was eventually forced to promise an independent review of the system within six months of its establishment, an important concession.

3. Much more controversially, the House of Lords in 1998 and again in 2000 decisively rejected the Commons' attempt to legalise the age of consent between homosexuals and heterosexuals.[37] Their Lordships were warned in clear terms by both Lord Lester and Lord Williams for the Government that a failure to equalise the age of consent would almost certainly result in the UK being found in breach of the ECHR, but undeterred, the House voted by 290 to 122 against the clause to equalise. When the Government again brought the change in under the Sexual Offences Amendment Bill 2000, the Lords again voted it down.[38] Eventually the Government used the Parliament Acts procedure to make the reform without the Lords' consent, only the fifth time that the procedure had been used at that time.

The effect of removal of the hereditary peers

What was unknown at the time that the House of Lords Act 1999 was passed was whether the reformed House would react to its small increase in legitimacy by becoming more assertive in its relations with the Commons. As seen above, it is the *conventional* restraints on the exercise of its own powers that, in practice, keep it firmly subordinate to the Commons, and thus the Government. One aspect of this restraint, which figures as at the least an entrenched *custom*, if not exactly a constitutional *convention*, was the notion that the Lords would not use their powers—left untouched by the Parliament Acts—to vote down subordinate legislation. It appears that the Lords had only in fact rejected secondary legislation once in the 20th century,[39] in 1968 in relation to a sanctions order against Rhodesia. That in fact was an order requiring positive approval from the Lords: Erskine May reveals that they have *never* voted down orders requiring only the negative approval procedure. Up until recently, the Lords had not voted on any item of subordinate legislation submitted to them for consideration. However, when this was pointed out to them and it was suggested that a convention had come into being that the Lords would not vote down items of subordinate legislation, their Lordships response was bullish: a motion by Lord Simon of Glaisdale to the effect that the House had unfettered freedom to vote on any subordinate legislation before them was overwhelmingly approved.[40]

Nevertheless, the Lords still held back from exercising this freedom until after the partial reform of their House. The dispute which eventually caused them to exercise it related to the refusal of the Government, in its legislation governing the London Mayor and Assembly, to give candidates a free 'mail shot' to the electorate. The Lords chose to express their discontent on the matter in a novel way: they voted upon a piece of delegated legislation (the Greater London authority (Election Expenses) Order 2000), which dealt with the nuts and bolts of the London mayoral and assembly elections, in particular the amount of electoral expenditure which candidates would be allowed to incur; the Order required only negative approval, that is, it would go through automatically unless voted against. To the consternation of the Government, the Lords threw the Order out and in doing so quite clearly relied upon their newly reformed status. During the debate, there was some disagreement about whether the practice of the Lords not to reject secondary legislation had achieved the status of a constitutional

---

37   For the 1998 debate, see HL Deb vol 592 cols 936 *et seq* (22 July 1998).

38   HL Deb vol 619 cols 19 *et seq* (13 November 2000).

39   See R Brazier, *Constitutional Practice*, 2nd edn (1994), p 254, n 119.

40   HL Deb vol 559 col 356 (20 October 1994).

convention. Some peers certainly took this view. Lord Hughes, for example, said: 'in relation to orders [it was my understanding] that secondary legislation may be challenged only on the grounds that it is not in accord with primary legislation.'[41] Others firmly rejected such a notion, pointing to the House's resolution of October 1994 cited above. Others still, such as Lord Cranbourne, for the Conservatives,[42] appeared to believe that while there may have been convention that the House would not reject such legislation, it would not apply now, the House being a reformed chamber which was not necessarily bound by the conventions of the unreformed House.

In general, there was strong support for a more assertive attitude on the part of the new House. Lord Mackay noted that a Government spokesperson (the Lord Privy Seal) had stated in the *House Magazine* on 27 September 1999 that the 'new' House of Lords 'will be more legitimate, because its members have earned their places, and therefore more effective'.[43]

Such attitudes could also be seen in the response of the Lords to a controversial piece of *primary* legislation, which would have restricted the right of a defendant to choose trial by jury. The heart of the Government's Criminal Justice (Mode of Trial) Bill was clause 1, which removed the right of defendants to choose jury trial in 'either way' offences, such as theft and burglary. The crucial part of the debate took part in Committee stage in January 2000[44] and only got as far as clause 1. The very first amendment put down restored the right of the defendant to be tried by a jury in such cases at his election, and thus ripped the heart out of the Bill. It was therefore what is commonly referred to as a 'wrecking amendment' since it altered the fundamental principle of the legislation. This amendment was carried by the Lords by a large majority: 222 votes to 126. The Government spokesperson, Baroness Jay, immediately announced that since the Bill 'no longer represented Government policy' it would be withdrawn.[45] It is important to note that the Bill started life in the Lords, not the Commons. Therefore, by effectively throwing out the Bill, the Lords had prevented the Commons being able even to see it. A report in *The Times* remarked that this was the 'first time in memory' that 'a mainstream Bill' had been 'killed...before it had reached the elected House'. As Lord Windlesham put it: 'This [was] a significant moment in the short life of the reformed House.'[46]

A further example of assertiveness by the Lords, which provoked rather less enthusiasm by many constitutional observers, was its rejection of the notorious 'section 28' of the Local Government Act. This provision is actually contained in s 2A of the LGA 1986 and it prohibits local authorities from 'promoting homosexuality' generally and in particular from 'promoting the teaching in any maintained school of the acceptability of homosexuality as a pretended family relationship' (sub-s (2)). This provision had long been controversial, with many seeing it as enshrining discrimination against, or at least official disapproval for homosexuality in the law. Labour sought to remove this through a clause in what became the Local Government Act 2000. This was opposed by many—particularly Conservative—peers in the Lords. Baroness Young, proposing an amendment to keep clause 2A, said: 'Lady Jay [of the Government]...has said on more than one occasion that the new House is more legitimate. We are perfectly entitled to take a view on this matter.'[47]

---

41   HL Deb col 164 (22 February 2000).

42   *Ibid*, cols 151–52.

43   *Ibid*, col 143.

44   HL Deb col 1246 *et seq* (20 January 2000).

45   *Ibid*, col 1297.

46   *Ibid*, col 1273.

47   HL Deb vol 616 col 103 (24 July 2000).

The attempt to abolish the clause was defeated by 270 to 228 votes in a debate that illustrated that whilst the Lords can act as a bulwark against the erosion of civil liberties they also have a tendency to be much more conservative—even reactionary—in matters of morality, perhaps not surprisingly, given that the average age of those who sit in the Lords is 68. For the full debate see HL Debs vol 616 cols 97–130 (24 July 2000). Since then, the Lords have continued their assertive behaviour, concentrating mainly on matters affecting civil liberties. The 2008 White Paper gives some more recent figures:

> In the 1997–98, 1998–99 and 1999–2000 sessions, the Government suffered 39, 31 and 36 defeats in the House of Lords respectively. (The 2000–2001 session was very short and has therefore been omitted.) From the 2001–02 to the 2006–07 session inclusive, the average number of such defeats in each session was almost 60. The House of Lords very rarely rejects a statutory instrument and it has done so on only three previous occasions. The last occasion was on 28 March 2007 and concerned the Gambling (Geographical Distribution of Casino Premises Licenses) Order 2007 [affirmative instrument]. [48]

R Whitaker, 'Ping-pong and policy influence: Relations between the Lords and Commons, 2005–06' (2006) 59(3) *Parliamentary Affairs* 536

> Since the 2005 general election, the Lords have inflicted 32 defeats on the Government, many of which concern anti-terrorism and related policies. These losses represent a continuation of the Lords' behaviour in the six parliamentary sessions from 1999–2000 to 2004–05, which saw an increase in government defeats as a proportion of government-whipped votes. In the current parliamentary session, the upper and lower houses managed a comparatively long rally in their game of ping-pong on the Identity Cards Bill during February and March 2006. Objections from Conservative and Liberal Democrat peers clearly forced the government to make compromises. The Terrorism Bill similarly had a rough ride through the Lords and was then passed back and forth between the two houses of parliament. There were also problems for the government's Racial and Religious Hatred proposals when defeats inflicted by the Lords were confirmed by MPs. All of these cases have demonstrated the Lords' willingness to defeat the government and, to varying degrees, their ability to influence the content of legislation.

Notes

1. The Lords indeed did valuable work in relation to the Prevention of Terrorism Bill 2005 and its introduction of 'control orders', voting for amendments to beef up significantly judicial oversight of the scheme and the safeguards within it. In relation to the Racial and Religious Hatred Bill 2006 referred to, the Lords succeeded in imposing important liberalising amendments to the proposed new offence of incitement to religious hatred which, in a rare rebellion, were accepted by the House of Commons against the will of the Government; a similar amendment was inserted into the new offence of incitement to hatred on grounds of sexual orientation in May 2008. Hazell comments:

> In the Lords, the government is defeated in 35 per cent of all divisions. In the 2004–05 session, more than half of the divisions resulted in a government defeat. Although Labour is now the largest party in the Lords, no single party commands an

---

48   See n 5 above, at p 12.

overall majority, and to win votes in the Lords the government must generally rely on the support of the Liberal Democrats. The Liberal Democrats and the cross benchers between them hold the balance of power, but the Liberal Democrats are a more cohesive group who attend and vote more often, so that they generally have the swing votes. [49]

One of the most significant recent defeats imposed upon the Government was the extension of the new offence of corporate manslaughter in the Manslaughter and Corporate Homicide Bill to include prison and police officers—a course of action rejected by the Commons and Government four times but finally forced upon them by the Lords in July 2007. Finally, of course, the Lords threw out the Government's renewed attempt in the Terrorism Bill 2008 to extend the period of pre-charge detention for terrorism suspects. Brown managed to persuade MPs to vote for an increase to 42 days; the measure was rejected in the Lords, and the Government abandoned that part of the Bill.

2. Given the large number of Government defeats that happen in the Lords compared to the very small number of uses of the Parliament Acts (7 since 1911) it is plain that the most important factor determining how much the Lords opposes government bills is the conventions generally held to govern its behaviour. This matter was recently explored in a joint committee of both houses.

Joint Committee on Conventions, *Conventions of the UK Parliament*, 2005–06 HL Paper 265-I/HC 1212-I (extracts)

Salisbury Convention

91. Lord Wallace of Saltaire, the Deputy Leader of the Liberal Democrats in the House of Lords, emphasised that, in the Liberal Democrats' view, "the Salisbury-Addison Convention was a historical negotiation between the Labour Party in the Commons and the Conservative Party in the Lords" and therefore not relevant to current circumstances.

92. Donald Shell, Senior Lecturer in Politics, Bristol University, regards the definition of the Salisbury-Addison Convention as accurate and adequate but would not describe it as a true convention of the constitution. "It was an understanding between party leaders in the House of Lords formulated to meet a particular situation, and an understanding which has endured so long as those circumstances have prevailed."

93. Professor Rodney Brazier, Professor of Constitutional Law, University of Manchester, refers to a "well-known view that the Salisbury-Addison convention ceased to exist when most of the hereditary peers were excluded from membership of the House of Lords in 1999. This view is accepted in Conservative, Liberal Democrat, and other circles, although I understand that it is not the view of the Government." He too was persuaded that the Salisbury-Addison Convention ended impliedly in 1999.

[The Committee's conclusions were as follows]:

98. The Convention now differs from the original Salisbury-Addison Convention in two important respects. It applies to a manifesto Bill introduced in the House of Lords as well as one introduced in the House of Commons. It is now recognised by the whole House, unlike the original Salisbury-Addison Convention which existed only between two parties.

99. The Convention which has evolved is that:

---

49   R Hazell, 'The Continuing Dynamism of Constitutional Reform' (2007) 60(1) Parlt Aff 3.

In the House of Lords:
A manifesto Bill is accorded a Second Reading;
A manifesto Bill is not subject to 'wrecking amendments' which change the Government's manifesto intention as proposed in the Bill; and
A manifesto Bill is passed and sent (or returned) to the House of Commons, so that they have the opportunity, in reasonable time, to consider the Bill or any amendments the Lords may wish to propose.

100. In addition the evidence points to the emergence in recent years of a practice that the House of Lords will usually give a Second Reading to any Government Bill, whether based on the manifesto or not. We offer no definition of situations in which an attempt to reject a Bill at Second Reading might be appropriate, save that they would include free votes. But to reject Bills at Second Reading on a regular basis would be inconsistent with the Lords' role as the revising chamber. In practice the Lords have the means to express their views on the principles of a Bill without rejecting it at Second Reading, by tabling a non-fatal motion or amendment at Second Reading.

[The Committee concluded that no further codification than the above, e.g. by seeking to define a 'manifesto bill' was desirable or practicable. For its views on the general issue of codifying conventions, see Chapter 2 at 76–79.]

120. The convention 'that Government business in the Lords should be considered in reasonable time' is set out in the Wakeham report, in the context of the Parliament Acts and linked with discussion of the Salisbury-Addison convention. ' . . . [T]he reformed second chamber should maintain the House of Lords convention that all Government business is considered within a reasonable time. Traditionally, the convention applies to all business, but it is particularly important that there should be no question of Government business being deliberately overlooked.'

Reasonable time
The Committee noted the view of the Hunt Report on this:

> A reasonable time limit for the Lords to scrutinise a bill would not in any way under-mine the principle of the Parliament Acts. A time limit would impose a discipline on all sides of the House, including the Government, to deal with legislation in an efficient manner. Large bills or bills to which the Government proposed to add a considerable number of amendments would trigger a longer period for consideration in the Lords. Further detailed work will be required on the actual time limit, though the 60 parliamentary days limit which received considerable support in 1968 would be a good starting point for discussion. The aim would be to set a reasonable time limit which reflects current experience with bills in the Lords. In the light of our later recommendations on changing the legislative procedure, some of the current intervals between different stages should be revisited to allow more flexibility.

133. The Opposition acknowledge the reasonable time convention, and consider that it is fully observed. In their view, when Bills run slow, it is normally to suit the Government. A guillotine would obstruct the Lords' work as a revising chamber, and would leave parts of Bills unscrutinised in either House. If it were subject to negotiated exceptions, it would replicate the present system; if exceptions were up to the Government, it would be 'a massive increase in executive power'. If the limit were statutory, it would breach the

convention that neither House interferes in the other's internal workings. They oppose any codification in this area, and would vote against any Bill.

[Similarly the Liberal Democrats and Cross Benchers opposed such a limit].

148. Our. . . academic witnesses came out unanimously against transforming the reasonable time convention into a 60-day rule. The convention is observed as it stands. How long is reasonable varies, depending on the context, e.g. whether the Bill had pre-legislative scrutiny, whether it was fully scrutinised in the Commons, and the Government's own priorities. Flexibility is helpful. . .

The Committee concluded:

153. Everyone agrees that the Lords should consider Government business in reasonable time, and **in our view there is indeed such a convention**. And no-one except the Government sees a problem in this area. . .

154. **There is no conventional definition of 'reasonable', and we do not recommend that one be invented.** The Government wants to define 'reasonable' or set a time limit; but in our view there is no problem which would be solved by doing so.

Secondary legislation

227. On the basis of the evidence, we conclude **that the House of Lords should not regularly reject Statutory Instruments, but that in exceptional circumstances it may be appropriate for it to do so**. . .

229. For the Lords to defeat SIs frequently would be a breach of convention, and would create a serious problem. But this is not just a matter of frequency. **There are situations in which it is consistent both with the Lords' role in Parliament as a revising chamber, and with Parliament's role in relation to delegated legislation, for the Lords to threaten to defeat an SI. For example:**

(a) where special attention is drawn to the instrument by the Joint Committee on Statutory Instruments or the Lords Select Committee on the Merits of SIs

(b) when the parent Act was a 'skeleton Bill', and the provisions of the SI are of the sort more normally found in primary legislation

(c) orders made under the Regulatory Reform Act 2001, remedial orders made under the Human Rights Act 1998, and any other orders which are explicitly of the nature of primary legislation, and are subject to special 'super-affirmative' procedures for that reason

(d) the special case of Northern Ireland Orders in Council which are of the nature of primary legislation, made by the Secretary of State in the absence of a functioning Assembly

(e) orders to devolve primary legislative competence, such as those to be made under section 95 of the Government of Wales Act 2006 and

(f) where Parliament was only persuaded to delegate the power in the first place on the express basis that SIs made under it could be rejected.

230. This list is not prescriptive. But if none of the above, nor any other special circumstance, applies, then opposition parties should not use their numbers in the House of Lords to defeat an SI simply because they disagree with it. This would be contrary to the fundamental conventions which govern the relationship between the Houses, [in terms of] the primacy of the Commons.

Note

The above findings of the Committee were approved in resolutions of both Houses: HL Deb 16 January 2007, col 638; HC 17 January 2007, col 887. In its 2008 White Paper, the Government:

> agreed with the Joint Committee's views that legislation, or any other form of codification that would turn conventions into rules, was not the way forward. Codification would remove flexibility, exclude exceptions and inhibit evolution in response to political circumstances.

THE WORK OF THE HOUSE OF LORDS

The work of the House and its effectiveness will be examined in this section. Broadly, the House has two roles, undertaking detailed scrutiny of both legislation and government policy and administration. These roles include the House's important functions of initiating legislation and scrutinising and reporting on the policy and legislative output of the institutions of the European Union. As Brigid Hadfield notes:

> The White Paper of 1968 on reform of the Lords listed the following main functions:
>
> (a) the provision of a forum for full and free debate on matters of public interest;
> (b) the revision of public bills brought from the House of Commons;
> (c) the initiation of public legislation, including in particular those Government bills which are less controversial in party political terms, and private members' bills;
> (d) the consideration of subordinate legislation;
> (e) the scrutiny of the activities of the executive; and
> (f) the scrutiny of private legislation.
>
> To this must now be added—most importantly—the scrutiny of (proposed) legislation emanating from the European Economic Community...which last function takes place mainly in Committee and sub-committee rather than on the floor of the House.[50]

It is important to note that while the Lord Chancellor was previously the Speaker of the House of Lords, this role was removed from him in 2006 (see p 148 above). The Speaker of the House 'has no effective and controlling powers, and the standing orders of the House deny him power to maintain order. His role is "ornamental and symbolic";[51] the responsibility for maintaining order rests with the House as a whole.'[52]

Scrutiny of legislation

The work of the House in considering public Bills constitutes its single most time-consuming task, reflecting the fact that such scrutiny is generally regarded as the Lords' most important role. Philip Norton has suggested three main features of the House of Lords which render it 'particularly suitable' for the task of detailed consideration of legislation.

---

50   B Hadfield, 'Whither or Whether the House of Lords' (1994) 35(4) NILQ 320.

51   HL 9 (1987–88), para 13.

52   Griffith and Ryle, n 8 above, p 464.

P Norton, 'Parliament II: the House of Lords', in B Jones (ed),
***Politics UK* (1994), p 354**

First, as an unelected House, it cannot claim the legitimacy to reject the principle of measures agreed by the elected House. Thus, basically by default, it focuses on the detail rather
than the principle. Secondly, its membership includes people who have distinguished
themselves in particular fields—such as the sciences, the law, education, industry industrial
relations—who can look at relevant legislation from the perspective of practitioners in the
field rather than from the perspective of party politicians. And, third, the House has the time
to debate non-money bills in more details than is usually possible in the Commons—unlike
in the Commons there is no provision for a guillotine and all amendments are discussed.
The House thus serves as an important revising chamber, trying to ensure that a bill is well
drafted and internally coherent. In order to improve the bill, it will suggest amendments,
most of which will be accepted by the Commons. In terms of legislative scrutiny, the House
has thus developed a role which is viewed as complementary to, rather than one competing
with (or identical to) that of the Commons.

Notes

1. Two of the positive attributes which Norton identifies arise from the fact that the House is not
   elected; the first directly, the second from the fact that it cannot consider money Bills, which is a
   reflection of its lower, because undemocratic, status. (Such a wide disability does not apply,
   for example, to the elected US Senate.) The paradoxical notion that much of the value which
   commentators perceive in the Lords is attributable to the one characteristic which most lays it open
   to attack—its unelected status—is a recurring theme in the literature on the subject.

2. To the above positive attributes can be added the following: the greater age of members in the
   Lords, which arguably gives them a more mature and experienced outlook; their long terms of
   office, which mean they can take a more independent line, not being subject to re-selection; their
   comparative lack of political ambition, flowing from the fact that most peers are at the end of their
   political careers.[53] This point in particular is emphasised by a recent commentator:

   Life peers are free to make relatively independent judgements about government
   proposals and actions because they are appointed for life. Even if they are nominated to the Lords by a party and take that party's whip, their life appointment means
   that they are not thereafter dependent on the party for patronage, unlike MPs. In the
   case of the Crossbenchers, they are not dependent at all on parties, and thus can
   exercise a judgement that is even free of the bonds of identity and loyalty.[54]

3. What is the *nature* of the legislative work of the Lords?:

   The legislative work of the Lords relates mainly to public Bills, on the consideration
   of which it expends half its time. The formal delaying power of the House is probably less important in real terms than the fact that its presence means a prolongation of the parliamentary consideration of Bills, providing opportunity for more

---

53   See, e.g. Russell, n 28 above, p 248–49.

54   J Parkinson, 'The House of Lords: A Deliberative Democratic Defence' (2007) *Political Quarterly* 78(3) 374.

detailed scrutiny and for second thoughts on the part of the Government, in the light of comments made both inside and outside Parliament. Also, its existence enables Bills to be initiated elsewhere than in the Commons, which tends to suffer from a glut of Bills at the beginning of a session (especially after a general election) and from the Finance Bill in the second part of a session.

. . .it would seem from a consideration of the 12 parliamentary sessions since 1972 that the Lords do have a valuable revising role, albeit a more limited role than is usually appreciated.

It should be noted, first, that many of the Commons' Bills go through the Lords 'on the nod'. This is probably best explained by the subject-matter of those Bills, although a partial explanation may be found in the fact that these Bills arrive in the Lords later rather than earlier in the parliamentary session. The conclusion is, however, that the Lords concentrate their revising efforts on only a limited number of Commons' Bills. Secondly, the majority of amendments proposed and accepted are of the technical or drafting kind; these cause no difficulties to any Government of any complexion and this is the main explanation for their high level of acceptability to the Commons. Some amendments are, however, of substantive importance.[55]

4.   The picture that emerges from examining the Lords' legislative work is one of a House that is concerned not so much with the broad policy behind Bills, but rather with ensuring that measures will be workable in practice. In this sense, the Lords may be seen as complementary to the House of Commons, which is regarded as unsuitable for the detailed scrutiny of legislation, due to its combative style of debate, and the fact that the opposition will oppose much government legislation as a matter of course.[56] However, such a division of labour by the two Houses arguably leaves a lacuna in the scrutiny provided by Parliament as a whole: if the Commons opposition attacks policy wholesale, whilst the Lords largely ignore it, measured and discriminating criticisms of policy may never receive consideration.

5.   Clarke and Shell compare the ability of the House of Lords to revise and amend legislation with that of the Commons.

DN Clarke and D Shell, 'Revision and amendment by the House of Lords: a case study' [1994] *Public Law* 409, 410–14

The House of Lords and government legislation
Increasingly in recent years attention has focused on the role of the House in making a seemingly ever growing number of amendments to an ever expanding quantity of legislation. In the early 1950s the number of pages of primary legislation enacted each year rose to around 1,000; by the 1970s it had reached almost 2,000, and in the 1980s up to 1987 the average was over 2,500, after which the page size for legislation altered, though it would seem volume continued to increase. Far from reducing the quantity of legislation, and improving its quality, as the Conservatives in opposition in the 1970s had argued was necessary, the Conservatives in office since 1979 steadily increased the quantity. Nor would many accept that there had been any improvement in quality in the sense of clarity

---

55   Hadfield, 'Whither or Whether the House of Lords' (1994) 35(4) NILQ 320, p 325, 326.

56   See Chapter 8.

and precision and the avoidance of unnecessary complexity and obscurity. It has been widely argued that this has been the main reason underlying the vast growth in the number of amendments made to Bills in the revising chamber. [In the three sessions 1970–73 the House of Lords made (on average) some 950 amendments per session to government Bills; by 1979–82 the average had risen to almost 1,300 per session, but by 1987–90 it had gone up to an average of over 2,600.] Overwhelmingly these were amendments introduced by ministers themselves, though many were of course responses to representations made to Government by the many interests typically affected by legislation, such representations being made both within and outside of parliament. Twenty years ago a major study of parliamentary scrutiny of legislation concluded that many Bills emerge from the House of Commons 'in a state unfit to be let loose on the public' [JAG Griffith, Parliamentary Scrutiny of Government Bills (1974), p 231]. Since then the situation has deteriorated considerably. As a result the House of Lords sits longer hours and spends an increasing proportion of its time tidying up legislation brought to it from the Commons in a highly unsatisfactory form. In the 1992–93 session the House of Lords spent almost half its sitting time dealing with Government legislation, and made 2,056 amendments to Government Bills, of which only 18 were subsequently rejected by the Commons.

The ability to revise and amend
. . .it is the way the legislative procedure operates in the Upper House which facilitates the submission and consideration of amendments. The student of Parliament is taught at an early stage that a Bill goes through the same stages in each House; a second reading to debate the principles of the Bill, a committee stage to consider the detail, a report stage to report on and consider final amendments before the third reading completes the process. The keen student may even take note that the Lords always sits as a committee of the whole House, the Commons rarely so. The reality is that the procedure is similar only in form. In the case of the passage of the [Leasehold Reform, Housing and Urban Development Act 1993] through the Commons, for example, only 32 MPs were assigned to the Standing Committee. Though the report stage occupied about 10 hours, the third reading debate, following on immediately [the usual practice], lasted barely 40 minutes. Some of the themes and concerns that were to surface in the Upper House had an earlier rehearsal in the Commons—but by no means all. Amendments to the Bill in the Commons were few; at the committee stage, some threats were headed off by promises to reconsider and then by making no change at the report stage. Where divisions were called at report the House divided largely on party lines. This procedure is, in reality, highly ritualised. The Government has its majority, even in committee; the divisions called by the Opposition at report stage on the 1993 Act were set pieces on a few issues of principle. Where amendments were put down by Conservative back-bench opponents at the report stage, the arguments were largely markers for later debate in the Lords.

It is the different way the same format of committee stage, report, and third reading is used that permits the Lords to make the best use of the time to consider amendments. Since the committee stage involves the whole House and amendments are also allowed at the third reading stage in the Lords [four and a half hours on the 1993 Act], any peer who has a concern can put down an amendment at the committee stage knowing that there are two further occasions to return to the issue. Indeed, many such amendments are acknowledged to be 'probing'; seeking to elucidate the meaning of a particular section; or to judge the Government's attitude to some change; or, by listening to other contributions to the debate, to gauge the degree of support from elsewhere in the House. Many amendments are withdrawn, with consent, without a vote thus enabling private discussions, redrafting and resubmission at report or third reading. These three genuine opportunities permit a process which allows proposals to be aired, reconsidered and reformulated in a way that is not possible in the Commons.

Notes

1. The House of Lords recently agreed an important package of proposals designed to render its scrutiny more effective.[57] As well as changes to the timing of sittings and the parliamentary year, the changes include:

> scrutinising virtually all major government Bills in draft; carry-over of Bills that have received pre-legislative scrutiny (so that they do not fall automatically at the end of a parliamentary session if not passed), subject to certain safeguards; scrutiny of the Finance Bill (the Bill implementing the Budget) by a sub-committee of the Economic Affairs Committee; creation of a new Select Committee to scrutinise the merits of all statutory instruments subject to parliamentary scrutiny, the latter proposal being designed to ensure that statutory instruments of political importance were properly considered by [the] House.[58]

2. The Lords are often seen as having a particularly important role to play in the protection of civil liberties, an issue to which the Commons may often show little sensitivity when both main parties feel obliged to show their 'toughness' on law and order issues. The Lords inserted an important amendment to the Police and Criminal Evidence Bill 1984 allowing evidence unfairly obtained to be excluded; this eventually prompted the Government to put forward its own amendment which became s 78 of the Act. The War Crimes Bill 1990 was rejected outright by the Lords, on the grounds that the convictions of former Nazi war criminals, which it aimed to facilitate, would be inherently unsafe. The Government was forced to use the Parliament Act procedure to enable the Bill to become law. Similarly, in January 1997, the Lords defeated the Government to procure an important amendment of principle to the Police Act 1997. As originally conceived, the Bill gave police officers power to enter premises to plant listening devices to assist in the detection of crime. Authorisation was to be given by the Chief Constable; by contrast when the police want to tap phones they must obtain a warrant from the Home Secretary. There was also no exception in relation to bugging premises where conversations involving legal professional privilege might take place—listening devices could therefore have been planted at lawyer's offices. The Lords inserted amendments to force the police to seek prior *judicial* approval before installing listening devices, forcing the Government to bring forward its own, similar proposals. More recent examples have already been noted above (at 440–442).

3. One of the most important recent parliamentary innovations in relation to the protection of civil liberties and human rights is the Joint Committee on Human Rights, whose basic remit is to scrutinise Bills for compatibility with the ECHR, and report on changes that may be needed to achieve some compatibility. The Committee was particularly influential in relation to the Anti-Terrorism Bill 2001 and detailed examples of its work on that Bill are discussed below. For further detail of the Committee's work, see D Feldman, 'Parliamentary scrutiny of legislation and human

---

57 First proposed by a Leader's Group to consider the working practices of the House; its report was considered by the House on 21 May 2002: HL Deb cols 641 *et seq*. Their recommendations were remitted to the Procedure Committee, which arrived at detailed proposals to put them into practice in their Fifth Report: HL 148 (2001–02). They were approved by the House on 24 July 2002: HL Deb cols 373 *et seq*.

58 HL Deb col 656 (21 May 2002), Lord Roper.

rights' [2002] PL 323 and Lord Lester, 'Parliamentary scrutiny of legislation under the Human Rights Act 1998' (2002) 4 EHRLR 432.

4. The legislative role of the House of Lords is not confined to scrutiny of measures originating in the Commons. Bills which are not seen as contentious in party political terms are regularly introduced into the Lords, thus relieving pressure on the Commons. This work is by no means small in scale: Griffith and Ryle have compiled figures showing that in 1978, 58 Public General Acts were introduced in the Lords, 60 in 1979, 67 in 1980 and 57 in 1982.[59] From consideration of Acts from some sessions between 1978 and 1982, Hadfield has identified four (not exclusive) broad categories into which Public Bills introduced in the Lords can be placed:

   (a) law reform measures, including consolidating Acts and Acts dealing with the administration of justice;
   (b) international Acts, including the implementation of treaties;
   (c) Acts relating solely to Northern Ireland or Scotland; and
   (d) matters of non-controversial substance (in the party-political sense).[60]

5. Members of the Lords, unlike members of the Commons, are free to introduce Private Members' Bills into the House and there is usually enough time for them to be debated fully, although of course if they are passed this does not ensure that time will be found for them in the Commons. As the Lords have no constituents to whom they are accountable they may feel free to bring forward Private Members' Bills on emotive and contentious subjects such as homosexuality and abortion. The initiative for relaxing the law relating to homosexual conduct, which eventually resulted in the passing of the Sexual Offences Act 1967, came from the Lords, not the Commons. Similarly, the Anti-Discrimination (No 2) Bill 1972–73 raised interest when being discussed by the Lords' Select Committee. This led to espousal of the Bill first by backbenchers and then by the Government. The eventual result was the Sex Discrimination Act 1975.

6. In 1992, the House of Lords created for itself an important new scrutinising mechanism for overseeing the use of delegated legislation, the scrutiny of which, as noted above, is generally thought to be inadequate in the Commons.[61] This is a new Select Committee on the Scrutiny of Delegated Powers (DPSC), since renamed the Delegated Powers and Regulatory Reform Committee. The remit of the Committee is 'to report whether the provisions of any Bill inappropriately delegate legislative powers; or whether they subject the exercise of legislative power to an inappropriate degree of parliamentary scrutiny';[62] the Committee itself has indicated that it will pay particular attention to Bills containing 'Henry VIII' clauses (giving ministers powers to repeal or amend primary legislation through order) and skeleton legislation which in effect gives ministers power to 'legislate' their own chosen policy through secondary legislation. The Committee has expressed satisfaction with its own work; Government has co-operated with it by producing a memorandum for most pieces of delegated legislation, which explains the purpose of a given provision and why delegated legislation has been used for it. The Committee has a particularly significant role examining orders made under the Henry VIII clause in the Regulatory

---

59 Griffith and Ryle, n 8 above, p 353.

60 Hadfield, n 55 above, p 325.

61 We give here only a very brief summary of the Committee's work, drawing on C Himsworth's interesting analysis, 'The Delegated Powers Scrutiny Committee' [1995] PL 34. All quotes in the text are from this article, unless otherwise indicated.

62 First Report of the Select Committee on the Procedure of the House, HL Deb col 11 (1992–93) quoted *ibid*, p 36.

Reform Act 2001 and now under the Legislation and Regulatory Reform Bill 2006 Act (see Chapter 3 at 136 and Chapter 8, p 381). As a briefing note on the Committee explains:

> regulatory reform orders may be made by any minister to amend or repeal any enactment of primary legislation with a view to removing or reducing any administrative or bureaucratic burden. Both Houses of Parliament must be satisfied that the technical requirements of the 2001 Act have been met. The 2001 Act provides for a two-stage process of parliamentary scrutiny:
> 1. The proposal, together with explanatory material is laid before Parliament in the form of a draft order. The Committee and its Commons equivalent have 60 days in which to report.
> 2. The government lays a draft order before Parliament, either in its original form or amended to take account of the two Committees' views, for approval by resolution of each House. This can only be done in the Lords after the Committee has made a second report on it.[63]

The Committee may be regarded as having made an important contribution to the scrutiny provided by the Lords, and to have provided a welcome focusing of attention on the increasing use of delegated legislation for matters of principle and substance.

The work of the House of Lords in practice: a case study

The response of the House of Lords to the Anti-Terrorism, Crime and Security Bill 2001, introduced into Parliament in response to the perceived greater threat from international terrorism following the attacks on the United States on 11 September 2001, illustrate the work of the second chamber in scrutinising and revising Government legislation. The Bill was a long one: 126 clauses and eight lengthy Schedules. Much of it did not in fact deal with specifically anti-terrorism measures. It included a new offence of incitement to religious hatred which, in itself, would clearly provide no assistance in the fight against terrorism, new powers of the police compulsorily to photograph criminal suspects—not just suspected terrorists (Part 10), a new procedure whereby Third Pillar EU criminal measures would become part of UK law via secondary legislation (Part 13) and measures to put in place a new Code of Practice on retention of communications data—websites visited, mobile phone calls made and so on (Part 11). Its most controversial part, which was aimed at terrorism, was Part 2. This gave power to the Home Secretary to detain non-British nationals suspected of involvement with international terrorism, who, it is thought, could not be convicted of any offence, but who also could not be deported to their country of origin because there were grounds to think that they would there be subject to torture or inhuman and degrading treatment, because to do so would violate Article 3 of the European Convention on Human Rights (ECHR), which is not derogable. In order to allow for such detention, the Government decided to derogate from Art 5 ECHR which provides for the right to personal liberty. The Bill provided that the Home Secretary's determinations that a person was involved with international terrorism and his decisions to detain them could not be questioned in any court, but only in the Special Immigration Appeals Commission (SIAC), which is, however, a fully-fledged judicial tribunal.[64]

---

63   Available at www.parliament.the-stationery-office.co.uk/pa/ldl99798/ldbrief/lddeleg.pdf.

64   Joint Committee on Human Rights, Second Report, HL 37, HC 372 (2001–02), para 46.

The approach of the Lords may be contrasted with the Commons, which first of all accepted a timetable of only 16 hours in which to scrutinise a Bill 124 pages long and containing an important derogation from the UK's international obligations under the ECHR, and then imposed not a single amendment on the Government. One peer himself remarked upon the far heavier burden the Lords had taken up in scrutinising the legislation:[65]

> What concerns me most is that, had this House not had the time and the ability to scrutinise it, the legislation would have gone through. It is a matter of concern that a Bill containing 126 clauses should be sent to this House without most of them having been properly considered. It is no good the Home Secretary or any other Cabinet Minister complaining about this House, when it has done its job—a job which should have been done by the House of Commons in the first place, it having been elected to do so. It is entirely reprehensible that an elected House of Commons should have less concern than this House for the freedoms and the rights of the people of this country. . .unless the House of Commons does its job, this House has to spend a great deal more time on the Bill—more than three times as much—and has to do the job for it.

In contrast, their Lordships imposed a series of major defeats on the Government; these included: restricting the scope of information sharing by government agencies to that relevant to possible terrorist offences; rejecting the proposed offence of incitement to religious hatred; insisting on shorter 'sunset clauses' for controversial parts of the Bill (provisions whereby they automatically lapsed after a space of time); rejecting the proposed exclusion of judicial review; on transposing EU criminal legislation into domestic law via secondary legislation; on retention of communications data. As is apparent from any reading of the debates, this was done in no narrow partisan spirit—imposing defeats on a governing party just because they are the other side—but out of genuine concern for basic liberties. For example, the defeat on information sharing related to clause 17 of the Bill, which applied to some 66 existing statutes which allowed disclosure of information by one public authority to another (clause 19 gave similar powers to Customs and Excise). It amounted to an enormous broadening of that power, allowing any public authority to require from another information for an extraordinarily broad range of grounds connected with criminal investigations, not limited to possible terrorism offences.

On some points, the Government was in the end forced to accept complete defeat: the proposed creation of an offence of incitement to religious hatred was repeatedly rejected by the Lords[66] and eventually dropped from the Bill altogether. The Lords also procured the insertion of 'sunset' clauses against Government resistance, whereby the more draconian aspects of the legislation would automatically lapse after a specified period,[67] as well as statutory provision for a review of the detention powers specifically by a person appointed by the Home Secretary[68] and a full review of the operation of the whole legislation by Privy Counsellors.[69] On retention of communications data, the Lords scored

---

65   HL Deb col 1155 (10 December 2001), Lord Stoddart.

66   See, e.g. HL Deb vol 629 cols 1163–95 (10 December 2001) and HL Deb vol 629 cols 1449 *et seq* (13 December 2001).

67   Sections 21–23, giving the power of detention without trial, therefore required extension 15 months after the date on which the Act was passed.

68   Section 28.

69   Their report may specify particular provisions which will then lapse within six months, unless the report is debated in each House within that period: s 122.

a significant victory by insisting on their amendment[70] that the Code of Practice which the Secretary of State would draw up could only contain provisions necessary 'for the purposes of prevention or detection of crime or the prosecution of offenders *which may relate directly or indirectly to national security*',[71] not any criminal offences as the Government had wanted.

The Lords eventually accepted compromises from the Government on other issues. On provisions to allow EU criminal legislation to become law in the UK without primary legislation, the Government dropped its original proposal whereby the provisions would cover all such legislation, accepting instead that they would cover only a limited and specified set of measures agreed by EU leaders[72] and would lapse in July 2002.[73] The Lords also eventually accepted the exclusion of judicial review of SIAC decisions in return for a Government concession—to make the SIAC a superior court of full record[74]— which essentially gives it the same powers as the High Court, as well as placing its reasons on the public record.[75] On s 17—the extraordinarily broad powers given to public authorities to share information (above)—a weak compromise was reached which was designed to ensure that large amounts of information could not be gathered purely on the basis of a fishing expedition by police or other prosecuting authorities: the Bill as amended by the Lords provides that public authorities may not disclose information unless satisfied 'that the making of the disclosure is proportionate to what is sought to be achieved by it'.[76] This in particular represented a major climbdown by the Lords. The crucial point on which they had repeatedly insisted was that the clause as drafted did not restrict the scope of the information-sharing provision to terrorist-related offences;[77] this amendment left that problem substantially untouched. The requirement on the public authority to consider proportionality adds nothing as a matter of law—Lord Lester described it as 'window dressing'[78] because s 6(1) HRA[79] would impose the same obligation via Article 8 ECHR.[80] The amendment thus 'merely restate[d] the existing duty under the Human Rights Act'[81] so that on the major issue—the breadth of the power— the Lords essentially collapsed.[82]

Nevertheless, the contrast between the approach of the elected—and thoroughly whipped—Commons and the unelected, and relatively independent-minded Lords was marked. As one respected commentator remarked: 'In a long record of shaming fealty to whips, never have so many MPs showed

---

70   See HL Deb vol 629 cols 1474 *et seq* (13 December 2001).

71   Section 102(3)(b).

72   Listed in s 111(2).

73   Section 111(1).

74   Section 35(1).

75   See HL Deb vol 629 cols 1435 *et seq* (13 December 2001).

76   This is now sub-s (5) of s 17; an identical provision was also included as sub-s (3) of s 19, which deals with disclosure of information held by revenue departments.

77   The Lords inserted an amendment at report stage as follows: 'Information may only be disclosed. . .if the public authority concerned believes or suspects that the disclosure may be of information which directly or indirectly relates to a risk to national security or to a terrorist.' See HL Deb vol 629 cols 949–75 (6 December 2001). For the debate in which the Lords accepted instead the government amendment, see HL Deb vol 629 cols 1142 *et seq* (13 December 2001).

78   *Ibid*, col 1425.

79   Section 6(1) states: 'It is unlawful for a public authority to act in a way that is incompatible with a Convention right.'

80   That is, assuming that the disclosure in question related to private life and so engaged Art 8. If it did so, under para 2 of that Article, the disclosure could only lawfully be made if it pursued a legitimate aim and was 'necessary in a democratic society, i.e. proportionate to the pressing social need that the legislation sought to address.

81   HL Deb vol 629 col 1423 (13 December 2001), Lord Thomas of Gresford.

82   As one peer remarked: 'It is rather sad that we. . .have been seen to cave in to what I would describe as waffle.' *Ibid*, col 1424, the Earl of Onslow.

such utter negligence towards so impressive a list of fundamental principles.' In contrast, as he noted, the Lords engaged in a thorough and painstaking examination of the Bill: 'Their debate is serious, their resilience formidable and their morality alive. They don't oppose the anti-terrorism campaign, but they want to keep it within sane limits. They scrutinise, question and amend.'[83] This contrast between the approach of the two Houses must be borne in mind when considering the debate as to the democratic element within any reformed second chamber (below).

Scrutiny of EU policy and legislation

Given the ever-growing impact of EU legislation, this task is clearly of great importance, particularly as it has been suggested that the British MEPs in the European Parliament are not particularly effective in this role.[84] The main responsibility for this area of the Lords' work lies with the House of Lords Select Committee on the European Communities. Vernon Bogdanor has commented that:

> There is widespread agreement that the scrutiny procedures adopted by the Lords are amongst the most effective in the Community. In 1977, a Committee established by the Hansard Society for Parliamentary Government was 'struck by the relevance and businesslike nature of the results of the Lords' work in this field, and think it significant that the Commons, who are meant to represent the people of this country, have taken in contrast to the Lords, a largely inward-looking and conservative attitude where the opposite was required.' And in 1982 a Report of the Study Group of the Commonwealth Parliamentary Association on 'The Role of Second Chambers' concluded that the Lords offered 'the only really deep analysis of the issues that is available to the parliamentary representatives of the [then] ten countries in the Community. . .The Lords' reports are far more informative and comprehensive than those produced by the Commons committee on European legislation.' The Study Group attributed this to the greater specialist knowledge of peers and comparative absence of partisanship.
>
> [The Committee] has the advantage, because of the system of nominating to life peerages men and women of eminence, of containing experts in almost every field covered by Community activity. Whether the subject-matter be agriculture, law, or economics, some of the leading authorities in the country will be found in the Lords; and since much Community legislation is technical, this means that the Lords is peculiarly suited to considering it. Thus the scrutiny procedures of the House of Lords owe their effectiveness to factors which it would be difficult to replicate in any legislature dominated primarily by party politicians.[85]

Dawn Oliver agrees, noting that 'the reports [of the Committee] are widely regarded in Europe as being of extremely high quality and are capable of having a significant influence on European policy development'.[86]

Once again the conclusion is reached that the Lords' effectiveness in this area is strongly linked to its undemocratic nature. It is *not* of course dependent on the particular method for selecting life peers,

---

83   H Young, 'Once lost, these freedoms will be impossible to restore', *The Guardian*, 11 December 2001.

84   See V Bogdanor, 'Britain and the European Community', in J Jowell and D Oliver (eds), *The Changing Constitution*, 3rd edn (1994), p 18–19.

85   *Ibid* at 12–13.

86   D Oliver, 'The 'modernization' of the United Kingdom Parliament', in J Jowell and D Oliver (eds), *The Changing Constitution*, 6th edn (2007) at 178.

that is, prime ministerial patronage. Philip Norton broadly concurs with Bogdanor's favourable assessment of the work of the Lords in this area:

> The EC Committee has built up an impressive reputation as a thorough and informed body, issuing reports which are more objective and extensive than its counterpart in the Commons, and which are considered authoritative both within Whitehall and the institutions of the EC. The House, like the chambers of other national legislatures, has no formal role in the EC legislative process, and so has no power, other than that of persuasion, to affect outcomes. The significance of the reports, therefore, has tended to lie in informing debate rather than in changing particular decisions.[87]

Similarly, the Hansard Society Commission has praised the scrutiny of EU issues by the above Committees as 'an example of very highly effective scrutiny work undertaken by the Lords'.[88]

Scrutiny of domestic administration and policy

The House also scrutinises government policy. Peers can debate policy in a less partisan atmosphere than the Commons and are not subject to the constituency and party influences that dominate in the elected House. They are therefore in a position to debate issues of public policy that may not be at the heart of the partisan battles and which, consequently, receive little attention in the Commons. Given their backgrounds, peers are also often—though not always— able to debate public policy from the perspective of those engaged in the subject.

> The House, for example, is able to debate science policy with an authority denied the lower House—it contains several distinguished scientists. When discussing education, the House will normally hear from peers who are professors, university chancellors, vice-chancellors, and former Secretaries of State for Education.'[89]

The Lords have other methods by which they scrutinise policy: questions of Ministers and the Select Committees. These are intended to complement, not duplicate the work of the Commons Select Committees and so are not departmental, but rather cross-cutting in their remit. Of these, as Rodney Brazier observes, those on the European Union, considered above, and on Science and Technology 'are generally acknowledged to be outstanding successes'.[90] Recent additions to the Lords committees include the Constitution Committee, whose remit, as well as reporting on the process of ongoing constitutional reform, requires them to report on Bills that raise an important question of principle about a principal part of the constitution, and the Economic Affairs Committee. However, since the methods of scrutiny used are broadly similar to those in the House of Commons, considered in detail in Chapter 8, no further material is offered here, due to constraints of space. Methods of making Lords scrutiny more effective are considered under reform proposals, below.

87   Philip Norton, 'Parliament II: the House of Lords', in B Jones (ed), *Politics UK* (1994), p 359.

88   *The Challenge for Parliament: Making Government Accountable* (2001), para 6.21. Though note a more sceptical note was struck by a member of the EU Committee in a recent debate, noting that many of the Committee's excellent reports get little attention in the media and thus achieve little input into public debate: HL Deb cols 576–77, Lord Harrison.

89   Norton, n 87 above, p 354.

90   R Brazier, *Constitutional Reform*, 2nd edn (1998), p 90.

FURTHER REFORM OF THE HOUSE OF LORDS

Labour's programme of reform for the Lords was never meant to finish with removal of the hereditary peers. Certainly, a considerable amount of Government attention has been paid to the issue of further reform since the House of Lords Act 1999. The Royal Commission on Reform of the House of Lords, under the chairmanship of Lord Wakeham produced a comprehensive, if unpopular blueprint for reform;[91] there have been four White Papers since then, moving from one that broadly accepted Wakeham's proposals but weakened them[92] to the latest in 2008, which supports a fully or mainly accepted House. A powerfully argued Public Administration Select Committee[93] (PAC) report criticised the White Paper strongly and called for a majority elected House instead. A Joint Committee of both Houses,[94] set up to find a way forward for reform, produced a report giving various options on composition of a reformed second chamber at the end of December 2002.[95] Free votes in both Houses on these options were held in January 2003[96] and again in 2007.[97]

This section will consider the possibilities for further reform of the House of Lords. It will first set out a series of general principles to guide reform that may be gleaned from second chambers overseas; it will then consider the proposals set out in the Wakeham report. Criticism of Wakeham and the counter-proposals set out in the Fifth Report of the PAC and in particular the 2008 White Paper will also be considered. The final main section will explore particular aspects of the reform proposals now on the table.

Reform: general principles and lessons from overseas

The following extract from Russell's authoritative study of overseas second chambers is illuminating both in pointing out how some of the valuable features which one might assume were unique to the Lords are in fact shared by other second chambers, and in helping to pin-point factors common to such second chambers which make them distinctive and valuable.

M Russell, *Reforming the Lords: Lessons from Overseas* (2000) (extracts, references omitted)

Many. . .factors mean that, despite the diverse nature of these chambers [those in France, Canada, Australia, Spain, Italy, Ireland and Germany] in measurable terms, there is a certain atmosphere that tends to be common to them all. This is critical to their work and the impact that they have.

---

91   Wakeham Report, n 1 above.

92   Cmd 5291 (2001); see sources at n 2.

93   Fifth Report, HC 494–1 (2001–02), esp. at paras 6 and 36.

94   For the resolutions appointing it see the references given in n 4.

95   First Report, HL 17, HC 171 (2002–03).

96   For the debate in the Lords see HL Deb vol 643 cols 575–688 (21 January 2003) and 721–838 (22 January 2003). For debate in the Commons see HC Deb vol 398 cols 187–274 (21 January 2003) and for the debates and votes on composition specifically, HC Deb vol 399 cols 152–243 and HL Deb vol 644 cols 115–40.

97   See below, at 472–73.

First, they are all smaller than their respective first chambers, some considerably so. This results in a more intimate atmosphere, in the chamber itself and in both party groups and committees. Coupled with longer parliamentary terms, which apply in Canada, France and Australia, this means that the members of the chamber are likely to know each other better than the members of the lower house. Once the higher average age of Senators is taken into account a picture already begins to emerge of more mature and deliberative parliamentary chambers with a less adversarial atmosphere. [Moreover]. . .in several cases the power of the upper house over legislation, and particularly over making and breaking governments, tends to be less than that of the first chamber . . .This means that the outcome of votes in the second chamber may be less critical, and that political leaders will tend to be concentrated in the first chamber. Even in Italy and Australia, where the power of the chambers over legislation is more or less equal, party leaders and senior cabinet members will tend to be drawn more from the lower house. These factors tend to add to a calmer, less adversarial chamber, which is not under such intense media scrutiny as the lower house. This could certainly be said to apply to all the chambers considered here.

Party discipline in upper chambers may also be less strict. This particularly applies where the upper house can be overridden by the lower chamber, as has been demonstrated on occasion by the British House of Lords. But this can also be a result of the stature of upper house members. The House of Lords is an example of a chamber where members are less bound by the party whip because they are at the end of their political careers, are not subject to re-selection, and have confidence in their own mature judgment. A similar situation applies, for example, in the French Senat, where members are mature and well-established political figures. The slower, more stately, pace of the Senat is also influenced by the nine-year terms served by its members. . .

In Canada a similar situation applies. Here, as in Britain, France, Germany, and Australia (other than in exceptional circumstances) the chamber cannot be dissolved. This helps to give it an independent authority. The long-serving members of the Canadian Senate are socialised over time into a less partisan culture. There is thus a higher incidence of 'cross voting' in the Senate, as compared to the lower house where party discipline is extraordinarily strict. This is one factor which makes Canadians a little more tolerant of their otherwise unpopular, unelected Senate.

The Irish Seanad, which generally has a weak position within the parliamentary system, also exhibits similar traits. The lack of pressure and adversarialism in the Seanad, its very small size and its independent members, all help provide 'a less hurried forum for discussion of the issues facing Irish society and the implications of legislative proposals.' The Seanad, which is less subject to media attention, is often used to debate new and controversial issues on which the parties do not have established positions. The university Senators regularly play a leading role in such debates.

The Australian Senate offers a counter-example on party discipline, given that the outcome of votes in the upper house is crucial to the success of the government's legislation. The political numbers in the Senate generally mean that its members must attend every vote and stick rigidly to the party line—something which need not apply in the lower house. However, the fact that political negotiations must take place in the Senate, whilst the lower house is strictly adversarial, means that relations between its members are none the less better. The rowdy debates and question periods in the House of Representatives lead Senators to dub it 'the monkey house', whilst its members refer to the Senate as 'the mortuary'. The following quote further emphasises the distinct personality of the Australian Senate, and could refer to any one of these seven second chambers:

> Candidates with Prime Ministerial aspirations, with talent for scoring points from the opposing party and divining the moods of the electorate, will recognise the House of Representatives as the place where they can shine. Candidates whose aspirations lie in the direction of independent thought and research, who really want to come to grips with the issues confronting the nation, and to do something about them will see the Senate as the place where they can be most effective (Lucy, *The Australian Form of Government* (1993), p 195).

. . . In all seven parliaments, even where the upper house has less time available for legislative consideration than the lower house, it generally has a reputation for more detailed scrutiny. This is a product both of the chamber's composition and its powers. The concentration of party leaders and ministers in the lower house, and consequently the focus of media attention on that chamber, means that lower houses tend to focus on big political issues, and high-profile point-scoring and debate. Thus although most bills may start their legislative passage in the lower house, many details often remain ill-considered when they reach the upper house. Meanwhile, by the time the bill arrives, groups both inside and outside of parliament will have had time to consider its detail and bring forward proposed amendments. These will often be debated in the less frenetic atmosphere of the upper house.

The fact that the upper house has lesser powers than the lower house also places it, at times, in a stronger position to negotiate legislative changes. Whilst members of the lower house must toe the party line, and government defeats may be seen as a confidence issue, the same pressure does not apply in the upper house. Thus even members of the government side in the second chamber may be more prone to question the content of bills, and threaten to vote against the government. In upper houses where government does not have a majority, the threat of defeat is very real. Although the chamber may have only a limited delaying power, the inconvenience and embarrassment which is caused by government defeats may result in compromise. Governments will, in any case, often make concessions more easily in the upper house than they can in the lower house, where every amendment may be viewed by the media as a defeat or a U-turn. For all of these reasons the upper house is often the site of genuine negotiation between the parties, and a higher degree of consensus than is generally found in the lower house. . .

[Russell later summarises the effectiveness of the lower chambers in dealing with legislative detail as being dependent on four key factors: longer terms of office and rolling membership; non-renewable terms of office; no ministers (or less important) ministers in the chamber; more mature members. She then goes on to consider public perceptions of her seven chambers.]

The most embattled of the chambers is probably the Senate of Canada. Although it is responsible for much detailed legislative and investigative work, the 'accepted image of the Senate [is] as a dusty, obscure Arcadia filled with aged and retired political war horses. . .whose main concern, apart from enjoying a good, comfortable, life, is to preserve private wealth and the interests of big business.' This is an image that is perpetuated by the media, who periodically question the working hours and lifestyles of Senators. The upper house is also widely criticised by the provinces, which have no involvement in choosing its members, despite its formal role as the territorial house. These criticisms are damaging to the Senate, whose views are less likely to be listened to as a result. The results of many Senate committee investigations, for example, have been left to gather dust. As Franks has observed, 'it is clear that appointment by the Prime Minister from among party supporters has by now reduced the legitimacy of the Senate to the point where it harms not only the Senate but also parliament as a whole and even the government'.

In Ireland 'mainstream opinion is tolerant of the Seanad rather than supportive of it.' . . .However, there are times when the media focuses on the Seanad, and helps to generate negative feelings towards it. For example during the 1997 election campaign the Irish Times ran a piece entitled 'There is no point in the Seanad' and opening 'Hundreds of candidates are engaged in another frenetic election campaign, this time for a redundant institution.' It remarked that 'if there is to be no fundamental change in the Seanad's role and composition there is no reason to retain it' (*Irish Times*, 2 July 1997).

Viewed as equally pointless is the powerful Italian Senate. Generally controlled by the same political parties as the lower house, and carrying out identical functions, the upper house is seen to add little to the system apart from delay. In a system where parliament is generally considered inefficient and problematic, 'the sternest criticisms of bicameralism have stemmed from its having come to be identified as one of the major causes of the malfunctioning of the whole institutional system'. Although this may not be entirely justified, 'for the most part—and here there is substantial agreement—it is the structure of a perfectly equal bicameralism that is held responsible for the crisis of representation—in Italian polities'.

Of the seven chambers, the German Bundesrat is the only one that receives general public support. Germany appears to be almost unique in having no campaign that seeks to reform the upper house. In fact there are even moves to extend the structure of the Bundesrat to create second chambers in the states, attended by representatives of local government. This is because the Bundesrat is acknowledged as a genuine forum where state and federal interests are represented, and agreements are reached. Although disputes between the chambers can be fuelled by party politics, this is not seen as an overriding concern.

This is in stark contrast to the situation in Spain, where 'the Senate, initially intended as a chamber for territorial representation in central government, is widely seen as a useless body'. Even senior officials of the upper house are prepared to admit that 'practically since the moment the constitution was approved, there has been talk of a less-than-ideal Senate, proposing the need for its reform, because it is felt that the chamber does not meet the requirements of full territoriality'. It had been hoped that the addition of autonomous community Senators, as devolution progressed, would strengthen the territorial basis of the house. However, these Senators make up only one in five of the total, and after almost 20 years there is a lively debate in Spain on upper house reform.

In some countries the view of the upper house is more equivocal. France is an example. Despite some attempts by the Senat authorities to modernise its image, most commentators recognise that the upper house is essentially a conservative institution. For example, on the day after the Senat blocked the Parite legislation to give women equal rights to elected office the leader column of Le Monde was headed 'A Senat from another age'. The piece said that:

. . .the Senat boasts that it is a temple of 'wisdom' against the extremes of the [lower house] and the swings of universal suffrage. Carefully protecting a mode of scrutiny from another age, the Senators themselves are not unhappy to present themselves as the guardians of a sepia, rural, unchanging France. . .at the [Senat], 'wisdom' becomes conservatism.' [*Le Monde*, 27 January 1999.]

These sentiments echoed the earlier comments of Lionel Jospin, who has described the Senat as 'an anomaly amongst modern democracies'. [*Le Monde*, 21 April 1998.]

However, the French public seem less convinced about the need to reform the upper house. The only two constitutional referendums that have ever been rejected by the French people—in 1946 and 1969— included weakening or removal of the Senat. The second of these resulted in the fall of President de Gaulle. Opinion polls demonstrate that the Senat is relatively popular. In 1990, 46 per cent of voters believed the upper house performed its role well, compared to 38 per cent who believed the same about the lower house. This may, however, simply indicate a lack of understanding of the work of the Senat—because of its claimed role in protecting liberties it may be confused by some people with the Constitutional Council.

Opinions over the Australian Senate are equally split Governments never welcome the powerful interventions of the elected Senate, which they do not politically control. However, oppositions always embrace the opportunity to use the Senate—in partnership with minor parties—to modify government proposals. Thus the major parties tend to have a schizophrenic attitude to the upper house—in government they resent its interference, but in opposition they appreciate its benefits. Prime Minister Paul Keating famously referred to members of the Senate as 'unrepresentative swill' and to the house itself as a 'spoiling chamber'. Nevertheless his party, upon entering opposition in 1996, began to use exactly the same tactics as the previous opposition in the Senate to rein back government. This fluctuating attitude to the upper house is shared by the press, which at times lambasts and at other times celebrates its role. Much of the debate in Australia centres around the concept of mandate with the government claiming that its majority in the lower house gives it a mandate to govern, and the opposition and minor parties claiming that their combined forces in the proportionally elected Senate have a mandate to question and modify government proposals. The press keenly joins in the debate, with headlines such as 'Will of the people: yes, but which people?' and 'End the mandate muddle' [*The Sunday Telegraph*, 4 October 1998].

All the evidence suggests that voters in Australia are fairly happy with the way things are. Votes for small parties are always higher for the Senate than for the lower house, and analysis of voting patterns shows that some Australians operate 'split ticket' voting— supporting one party in the lower house elections and another in the Senate. It has been suggested that voters do this in order to ensure that, even if their own party is elected, the Senate operates as a brake on government.

When polled, 45 per cent of voters say they believe it is better when government does not control both houses of parliament, compared to 41 per cent who would prefer government to do so.

[Russell later summarises what her research has indicated are the key factors in ensuring a successful upper house.]

That the upper house should represent the territorial nature of the state.
Probably the most striking aspect of reform debates overseas is the extent to which there is a movement towards 'territorial' upper houses. In these systems the second chamber represents the provinces, regions, or states in the national parliament. The proposal to move towards a more territorial model has emerged in reform debates in

both federal and unitary states. This remains an aspiration in Italy, for example, where the original intention that the Senate should be a house of the regions has never been realised. Even in countries where the upper house is nominally territorial—such as Canada and Spain—there is strong pressure for reform to create a more genuine connection to sub-national institutions.

The two chambers should have distinct functions.
It is relatively common in parliaments overseas—as at Westminster—for the lower chamber to focus on the broad direction of policy, while the upper house takes more responsibility for detailed legislative scrutiny. However, where the upper house is territorial this offers an added opportunity for specialisation, which helps make it distinctive from the lower house. Proposals in Italy and Spain, for example, would give the upper house particular responsibility for territorial matters. This builds on the German model. In Ireland it has been proposed that the upper chamber specialises by concentrating on European and delegated legislation, and detailed inquiries, whilst government ministers are restricted to membership of the lower house.

No powers to remove government from office.
   A specialisation that receives universal support is the system whereby government must retain the confidence of the lower house only. Like the UK, most countries follow this model. The exception is Italy, where the upper house can vote government out of office. However, reform proposals include the removal of this power from the Senate.

Lesser powers over financial legislation, more over constitutional change.
   As in Britain, most parliaments give reduced powers to the upper house over financial legislation. Australia is an exception, but since a constitutional crisis was caused by the Senate in 1975 it has been proposed that its powers be reduced in this area. On the other hand, it is common for the upper house to have powers to block constitutional change. These powers have only been weakened (for example in Canada) where other constitutional safeguards apply.

Government should not control the chamber.
   An important way in which the two chambers may be distinct in composition is through their political balance. Government generally has a majority in the lower house, but this need not apply in the upper house. In countries where government does have a majority in the upper house—notably Ireland and Spain—the limited impact of the chamber is criticised. In contrast, the distinct political complexion of the Australian upper house adds to its impact. In Australia government is frustrated by its lack of control over the Senate, but the Australian people seem largely to support the existing party balance, which results in legislative negotiation and compromise. Polls in other countries suggest that this is a common public response.
   Direct election is supported, although indirect election may provide better territorial links.
   In countries where the upper chamber is directly elected, this feature generally has public support. For example, the reform debate in Italy emphasises the importance of a distinct upper house, but few would suggest that the Senate cease to be directly elected. Neither have any serious reform proposals of this type been made in Australia. Meanwhile most recent proposals in Canada have focused on the need for an elected chamber, and directly elected Senators were also included in the recent proposals in Ireland. However, in Spain, where the majority of upper house members are directly elected, it is proposed by some

that territorial links would be strengthened through an expansion in the number of indirectly elected members in the chamber.

The second chamber should be smaller than the first.
In all countries except the UK, the second chamber of parliament is smaller than the first. This is a completely non-controversial feature, and is generally cited as one of the upper house's assets. A smaller chamber is generally more manageable and efficient, more friendly and courteous, and has smaller and more effective committees.

Long parliamentary terms, and a chamber renewed in parts.
Many second chambers have a membership which is renewed in parts—for example the French Senat, where one-third of members are elected every three years, and the Australian Senate, where half are elected every three years. This means that the chamber has a rolling membership, and cannot be dissolved by government. Where this system applies it appears to be supported, and in some countries where it does not apply there are suggestions that it be introduced.

Note
Many of the specific points made by Russell above are returned to below. With the broad outline of what she sees as the generally agreed features of an effective second chamber in mind, we may turn to consideration of the Royal Commission's proposed outline of a new second chamber.

The Wakeham Report—basic recommendations[98]

A House for the Future, Cm 4534 (2000) (extracts)

Roles
12. The new second chamber should have four main roles:

- It should bring a range of different perspectives to bear on the development of public policy.
- It should be broadly representative of British society. People should be able to feel that there is a voice in Parliament for the different aspects of their personalities, whether regional, vocational, ethnic, professional, cultural or religious, expressed by a person or persons with whom they can identify.
- It should play a vital role as one of the main 'checks and balances' within the unwritten British constitution. Its role should be complementary to that of the House of Commons in identifying points of concern and requiring the Government to reconsider or justify its policy intentions. If necessary, it should cause the House of Commons to think again. . .
- It should provide a voice for the nations and regions of the United Kingdom at the centre of public affairs.

---

98   The Commission's terms of references were: '*Having regard to the need to maintain the position of the House of Commons as the pre-eminent chamber of Parliament* and taking particular account of the present nature of the constitutional settlement, including the newly devolved institutions, the impact of the Human Rights Act 1998 and developing relations with the European Union: To consider and make recommendations on the role and functions of the second chamber; To make recommendations on the method or combination of methods of composition required to constitute a second chamber fit for that role and those functions [emphasis added].'

Powers

13. No radical change is needed in the balance of power between the two Houses of Parliament. . .[see further on powers, below at 489–494].

Making law

16. There should be no significant changes in the second chamber's law-making functions. Parliament should continue to derive the benefits of being bicameral, with a second chamber capable of bringing a distinctive range of perspectives to bear. There should be more pre-legislative scrutiny of draft Bills. . .

Protecting the constitution

The second chamber's role in protecting the constitution should be maintained and enhanced. It should no longer be possible to amend the Parliament Acts using Parliament Act procedures, as was done in 1949. Such a change would maintain the current balance of power between the two Houses of Parliament and reinforce the second chamber's power of veto over any Bill to extend the life of a Parliament.

There should be no extension of the second chamber's formal powers in respect of any other matter, whether 'constitutional' or concerning human rights. But an authoritative Constitutional Committee should be set up by the second chamber to scrutinise the constitutional implications of all legislation and to keep the operation of the constitution under review.

A Human Rights Committee should be set up by the second chamber to scrutinize all Bills and Statutory Instruments for human rights implications. . .

Giving a voice to the nations and regions

20. The new second chamber should be able to play a valuable role in giving a voice to the nations and regions, whatever pattern of devolution and decentralisation may emerge in future. The chamber must serve the interests of the whole of the United Kingdom and contain people from all over the United Kingdom. It should contain a proportion of 'regional members' to provide a direct voice for the nations and regions of the United Kingdom at the centre of national affairs. These 'regional members' should not be drawn from the devolved administrations, or from the Scottish Parliament and the other devolved Assemblies, but should be able to speak for each national or regional unit of the United Kingdom. Because the 'regional members' would share a regional perspective with MEPs, members of the devolved institutions, the English Regional Chambers and the existing local government groupings, they could encourage and facilitate greater contact across different levels of Government and a stronger 'regional' voice, in Europe as well as at Westminster.

[Wakeham recommended that the Lord's existing important and important work on secondary legislation, EU business and scrutiny of government policy and administration should continue and be improved.]

Characteristics

28. Taking account of the roles and functions we think the new second chamber should perform, we believe it should, above all, be:

- authoritative;
- confident; and
- broadly representative of the whole of British society.

It should also contain members with:

- a breadth of experience outside the world of politics and a broad range of expertise;
- particular skills and knowledge relevant to the careful assessment of constitutional matters and human rights;
- the ability to bring a philosophical, moral or spiritual perspective to bear;
- personal distinction;
- freedom from party domination. A significant proportion of the members should belong to no political party and sit on the Cross-Benches, so that no one party is able to dominate the second chamber;
- a non-polemical and courteous style; and
- the ability to take a long-term view.

29. A new second chamber with these characteristics should remedy the deficiencies of the old House of Lords, which lacked the political legitimacy and confidence to do its job properly, while preserving some of its best features.

Composition
30. . . .we do not recommend:

- a wholly or largely directly elected second chamber;
- indirect election from the devolved institutions (or local government electoral colleges) or from among United Kingdom MEPs;
- random selection; or
- co-option.

While the principle of vocational or interest group representation is attractive, the objective would be more effectively achieved through an independent appointments system. On the other hand, total reliance on an independent appointments system to nominate members of the new second chamber would leave no voice for the electorate in its composition. It would be unsatisfactory as a basis for identifying people to provide a voice for the nations and regions of the United Kingdom.

We also believe the proposed arrangements for making appointments to the interim House of Lords through the mechanism of an independent Appointments Commission would not be satisfactory as a long-term solution. They leave too much power in the hands of the Prime Minister of the day and they confine the role of the Appointments Commission to the nomination of Cross-Benchers.

33. We therefore recommend that a new second chamber of around 550 members should be made up as follows:

- A significant minority of the members of the new second chamber should be 'regional members' chosen on a basis which reflects the balance of political opinion within each of the nations and regions of the United Kingdom. The regional electorates should have a voice in the selection of members of the new second chamber. Those members in turn will provide a voice for the nations and regions.
- Other members should be appointed on the nomination of a genuinely independent Appointments Commission with a remit to create a second chamber which was broadly representative of British society and possessed all the other characteristics mentioned above.

- The Appointments Commission should be responsible for maintaining the proportion of independents ('Cross-Benchers') in the new second chamber at around 20 per cent of the total membership.
- Among the politically-affiliated members, the Appointments Commission would be required to secure an overall political balance matching the political opinion of the country as a whole, as expressed in votes cast at the most recent general election.

35. Untrammelled party patronage and Prime Ministerial control of the size and balance of the second chamber should cease. The Appointments Commission should ensure that the new second chamber is broadly representative of British society. It should make early progress towards achieving gender balance and proportionate representation for members of minority ethnic groups. In order to identify appropriate candidates for the second chamber it should maintain contacts with vocational, professional, cultural, sporting and other bodies. It should publish criteria for appointment to the chamber and invite nominations from the widest possible range of sources.

We present three possible models for the selection of the regional members. Each model has the support of different members of the Commission. Model B has the support of a substantial majority of the Commission.

- Model A—a total of 65 regional members, chosen at the time of each general election by a system of 'complementary' election.
- Model B—a total of 87 regional members, elected at the time of each European Parliament election. One-third of the regions would choose their regional members at each election.
- Model C—a total of 195 regional members elected by thirds, using a 'partially open' list system of PR, at the time of each European Parliament election.

37. To promote continuity and a longer-term perspective, all members (under all three models) should serve for three electoral cycles or 15-year terms, with the possibility of being reappointed for a further period of up to 15 years at the discretion of the Appointments Commission.

Notes
1. Specific aspects of the Wakeham proposals will be examined in more detail below. We do not consider the government's White Paper in response to Wakeham because it was quickly discredited and abandoned.[99]
2. Wakeham's proposals on the role of a reformed chamber now command widespread acceptance. The Government's 2008 White Paper said simply:

   In its three main functions of scrutinising legislation, conducting investigations and holding Government to account, the second chamber should complement the work of the Commons. Irrespective of its membership, this should continue to be the case in a reformed second chamber.[100]

---

99 Members of the Wakeham Commission, including Lord Hurd, Lord Wakeham, Baroness Dean and Gerald Kaufman MP all said they could not support the White Paper as it stood.

100 *An Elected Second Chamber*, Cm 7438 (2008), Executive Summary.

3. The proposals of the PAC in 2002,[101] which appeared to represent the views of most MPs, were also for a mixed House, made up of elected and appointed members, independents and party political members. It backed Wakeham over the remit of the independent Appointments Commission, the 20% independent element, who should be picked for their expertise and authority in their fields, especially human rights and constitutional matters, and the targets for making the House more representative in terms of gender, race etc, aiming by these methods to preserve the House's current qualities of relative independence from party and expertise in a variety of fields. It sided with Wakeham against the government in recommending two parliament terms for all classes of members to bolster their independence, and on barring second terms. Where the PAC's report made a major departure from Wakeham was in its suggestion that 60% of its membership should be elected, a figure which the Committee thought represented the 'centre of gravity' amongst the views of MPs.[102] These members would be elected using an open list PR system based on the European constituencies. The existing life peers would be compulsorily retired to make room for the new elected members, while, in line with the recommendation of both Wakeham and the government, the rump of the hereditary peers would be removed from the House. A further 20% of the House would be nominated party-political members, appointed by the Appointments Commission in proportion to the parties' share of the vote at the most recent second chamber election, in order to allow for the inclusion in the House of former senior Ministers and backbenchers and of distinguished experts who also take a party whip.[103]

    The Reports of the Joint Committee may also be mentioned, although they were short on specific recommendations. Clear recommendations included the following: that no one party should dominate the House;[104] that a strong independent element should be retained in any new House;[105] that there should be no greater control by the parties over peers taking a whip than at present, if possible;[106] that the remaining hereditary peers should be removed as part of a further reform package; that the Committee was 'not attracted to' compulsory retirement for existing life peers (para 55), so that the House would number around 600 (para 46); and that there should be a statutory Appointments Commission, as recommended by the Royal Commission (para 52). Thereafter:

> All three main parties included pledges in their 2005 manifestos in favour of further reform of the Lords. A cross-party group (with representatives of Crossbenchers and the Bishops) was established in June 2006, and met regularly over the following eight months. In February 2007 the Government published its White Paper *The House of Lords: Reform* [(2007, Cm 7027)] which took full account of the discussions in the cross-party group, which informed the two-day debate which took place in the Commons and the Lords in March 2007.[107]

---

101   HC 494–1 (2001–02).

102   *Ibid,* paras 96 and 97.

103   The PAC instanced Lord Winston, Professor of Gynaecology (Labour), Lord Wallace, Professor of International Relations (Liberal Democrat), and Lord Norton, Professor of Government (Conservative).

104   First Report, HL 17, HC 171 (2002–03), para 34.

105   *Ibid,* para 40.

106   *Ibid* and para 35.

107   Forewood, *An Elected Second Chamber,* Cm 7438 (2008).

5. In terms of moving towards a more general, preliminary evaluation of the Wakeham proposals, it is worth recalling Russell's analysis above as to the crucial factors which make for an effective second chamber. As summarised by the PAC,[108] the reformed Lords should have:

> **Distinct composition:** There are various ways in which the membership of the new upper house can be made distinct from that of the House of Commons. The method of composition may be different, but the party balance in the chamber will also be particularly important.
>
> **Adequate powers:** If the new upper house is to be able to make an impact, and have bargaining power with the government and the lower house, it will need to have moderate to strong powers.
>
> **Perceived legitimacy:** In order to use its powers the new chamber—unlike the existing House of Lords—will need to be seen to have legitimacy, and be able to carry public support.[109]

The Joint Committee arrived at five key qualities that a reformed House should have: legitimacy; representativeness; no domination by one party, independence and expertise.[110] In substance, it is suggested, these coincide with the first two of Russell's criteria: representativeness goes to legitimacy, while independence, freedom from party domination and expertise are qualities that render the Lords distinct from the Commons.

A consensus emerges from all the major reports so far on these key points:

- No major changes in the powers of the new chamber are needed.
- The reformed chamber should be subordinate to Commons.
- No one party should have a majority.
- A strong independent element should be retained.
- A significant elected element should be present.

6. The Government's 2008 White Paper suggested four key principles to guide composition of the second chamber:

An Elected Second Chamber, Cm 7438 (2008) (extracts)

3.3 The representative basis for elected members of the reformed second chamber should be different from that for members of the House of Commons. This is not necessarily to say that the voting system would be different but that the arrangements for elections taken as a whole, including the size of constituencies and the frequency and timing of elections, should not duplicate those for the House of Commons. Different voting arrangements should encourage diversity in the membership of the two chambers.

Members of the reformed second chamber should be able to bring independence of judgement to their work. Members who are elected will, for the most part, achieve membership on the basis that they represent a particular political party, although there will be scope for independent candidates. While most of the elected members will have party affiliations, the intention is that they should exercise their independent judgement in the

---

108 Fifth Report, HC 494 (2001–02), para 8.

109 *Ibid*.

110 See n 104 above, para 30.

second chamber. Some of this will be a matter for the parties, but Chapter 4 of this White Paper considers how electoral systems could help achieve this, including by providing that members of the reformed second chamber should serve a single term of around 12–15 years. If there is to be an appointed element in the reformed second chamber, appointments should be made on an independent basis, reflecting the merits of the particular individual. No party appointments are envisaged. (3.4)

3.5 Long tenure. The work of any legislature is challenging. If all the members of the second chamber at a particular point in time were newly appointed or elected, it would take some time for them, individually and collectively, to understand their new roles and maximise their effectiveness in carrying them out. Significant continuity in the membership of the House of Commons is maintained by virtue of the fact that, even when there is a change of Government, many of those elected will have been Members of Parliament previously. There is a need to ensure similar continuity in the second chamber.

3.6 The reformed second chamber should take account of the prevailing political view amongst the electorate, but also provide opportunities for independent and minority views to be represented. The Government wants the reformed second chamber to complement the House of Commons. The composition of the Commons will reflect the prevailing political view of the country and if the second chamber is to have increased legitimacy, it should do so too. However, it should also reflect a diversity of views. Chapter 6 of this White Paper considers further how this might be achieved through voting systems for the second chamber. Chapter 6 considers how any appointed element could be used to ensure that the reformed second chamber reflects a wide range of views.

Notes

1. The Wakeham proposals clearly fulfilled the criterion of *distinct composition*: the proposed membership would be markedly different from that of the Commons in a number of ways. First, the 20% independent members would provide a bedrock of expertise, experience and alternative perspectives from those held by professional politicians. Second, the exclusive jurisdiction of the Appointments Commission over the party political appointments should also have the effect of providing at least some party members of a different character from those found in the Commons: strong party loyalty would not be a key criterion for the Appointments Commission, as it is for the political parties themselves, so that those it selected might well tend to be those more experienced and independently-minded party members who might not recommend themselves to the parties but who yet could make a valuable contribution to the work of the second chamber. Long, non-renewable terms would further bolster their independence from party. Third, and just as significantly, party balance in the Lords would, under the Wakeham proposals, form a strong contrast to the position in the Commons, since neither the government, nor any other party in the Lords would have an overall majority, the position which, as discussed below, research suggests is the best option.[111] The Wakeham proposals thus also fulfil each of the three 'distinctiveness' criteria of the Joint Committee—no domination by one party, independence and expertise.

2. It is Russell's third factor and the Joint Committee's first—legitimacy—that is problematic in relation to the Wakeham proposals. Certainly the general response to Wakeham and *a fortiori* the White Paper in the press and elsewhere suggests that a House with only a small elected element would simply not be seen as sufficiently legitimate; however, the current political climate suggests that if the elected element were increased to half, this would probably suffice. But any reformed

---

111   See below, pp 469–470.

House that had some elected element and a significant element appointed by an independent body would have overwhelmingly greater legitimacy than the unreformed, or even the current, House.

3. In the next section, specific issues that would need to be resolved in any reform programme are examined in the light of academic and parliamentary viewpoints.

Party balance

M Russell, *Reforming the Lords: Lessons from Overseas* (2000) (extracts)

In modern systems the most important difference between the chambers is liable to be in terms of political balance. This will have a critical impact on the relationship between the two chambers, and the relationship between the upper house and government. We have seen that there are three patterns of party balance demonstrated by the seven chambers surveyed. The first is for government to control the upper house, as well as the lower house—this is generally the case in Ireland, Italy, and Spain. This holds the danger that the upper house will simply act as a 'rubber stamp' for government decisions. In France and Canada, as in the UK, the upper house is sometimes dominated by the governing party and at other times by the opposition. This leads to the prospect of periods of great tension, interspersed with periods where the upper house does not play a particularly effective scrutiny role. The most interesting pattern is that in Australia and Germany, where neither government nor opposition generally win control of the upper house. This provides an opportunity for genuine bargaining between the upper house and the government. . .

Critically, political balance has at least as great an effect on an upper house's impact as [its formal powers and legitimacy]. Upper chambers which are controlled by government will tend to be of limited impact, whilst those which are sometimes controlled by the opposition win occasional bloody victories. But an upper house will tend to be at its most genuinely influential when controlled by neither government nor opposition. When the balance of power is held by other forces, government will be more inclined, and more able, to negotiate in order to secure its bills. This is seen in particular in the Australian and German upper houses. Whilst governments may find this process frustrating, a powerful upper house which is controlled by forces independent of government can help create a form of consensus politics which results in better political outcomes in the longer term.

Notes

1. There are, then, three logical alternatives for party balance in a parliamentary chamber:

    Government control: Spain, Italy and Ireland are examples, and as Russell notes above, are some of the most widely derided chambers with the lowest levels of public confidence and satisfaction in them. 'It is difficult for a chamber with a permanent government majority to play an effective review role.'[112]

    Opposition control: as Russell notes, 'while providing a strong check upon government, this amounts to a potentially unstable situation as an opposition-controlled chamber may seek to disrupt all government legislation. The unreformed Lords, which often faced Labour governments with a House effectively under the control of the Conservative Opposition, has not on the

---

112   Russell, at p 298.

whole sought to do this, because of the conventions noted above, which proceed partly from a widely shared recognition of its own lack of legitimacy. The Canadian Senate is similar'.

Neither opposition nor government controlled. According to Russell, this 'appears to be the most effective option according to overseas experience'. It is frustrating to governments, as in Australia, but popular with the public and approved by commentators. 'Even in Ireland, where the upper house has weak powers, the chamber worked effectively during one isolated period when independent members had control'.[113] It is, of course, the position in the current House of Lords, which may go some way to explaining why it is a relatively effective body, even though lacking democratic legitimacy.

2. The Wakeham report essentially agreed with this view, arguing that while:

> 'it would be unrealistic to think that the second chamber could somehow be insulated from party politics. . . It is nevertheless crucial that no one political party should be able to dominate the second chamber.' Moreover, a strong independent element such as that represented in the present House of Lords by the Cross-Benchers—members who are not affiliated to any political party [should be retained.]. [This would help secure] a second chamber which was more broadly representative of British society [and help ensure that governments would need] to win any arguments on their merits rather than by appealing to party loyalty or partisan interests.[114]

3. Wakeham also noted that papers commissioned from the Public Policy Group at the London School of Economics:

> They used general and European election data going back to 1974 to model the outcomes that might be expected from the use of different electoral systems to select members of the second chamber. One of the points to emerge most clearly was that if the overall political balance of the second chamber had been determined by reference to the parties' shares of the vote at national or regional level in any general or European election since the mid-1970s, it would always have produced a chamber in which every party had a proportional share of the seats, the Government party was normally the largest but no single party ever had a majority. This observation holds true for every general election since 1901, except for the two in the 1930s in which governing coalitions won more than 50 per cent of the popular vote.[115]

4. While neither the government nor Wakeham received much praise or even positive recognition for this aspect of their plans for reform of the Lords, their proposal that that the government of the day would never control the Lords, so that the balance of power will lie either with independents, or with smaller parties, deserves to be welcomed by those wishing to see an effective and assertive second chamber. This recommendation has been approved by both the PAC in its Fifth Report,[116] which, in arguing for a 20% appointed independent element, and a proportional electoral system, wished to minimise the possibility of one party gaining overall control of the chamber. Under this

---

113   *Ibid,* p 299.

114   Wakeham, at [10.24] and [10.26].

115   *Ibid* at [11.14].

116   HC 494 (2001–02), para 80.

system, the largest party, with a typical 43% or 44% of the national vote, would have around a third of the seats in the second chamber, compared to a possible very large majority in the first, as at present. The Joint Committee recommended that: 'any arrangements for the reformed House must take account of the importance of maintaining the principle that no one political party should be able to be dominant in it,'[117] and this principle now seems to command universal acceptance.[118]

An elected, appointed or a mixed House?

Ultimately, it has been in failing to decide this crucial question in votes held in 2003 and 2007 that the two Houses of Parliament have so far stymied the current drive towards comprehensive reform of the Lords. The options on which they voted were as follows: *Option 1*—fully appointed; *Option 2*—fully elected; *Option 3*—80% appointed, 20% elected (the Wakeham option); *Option 4*—80% elected, 20% appointed; *Option 5*—60% appointed, 40% elected; *Option 6*—60% elected, 40% appointed (the PAC option); *Option 7*—50% appointed, 50% elected. An amendment in the Commons called for the Lords to be abolished.

Votes were held on the seven options for reform in the Commons and Lords in February 2003 as follows:

	Abolition	100% appt'd	100% elected	80% appt'd	80% elected	60% appt'd	60% elected	50/50
Lords								
For		335	106	39	93	60	91	84
Against		110	329	375	338	358	317	322
Commons								
For	172	245	272		281		253	
Against	390	323	289	[no vote]	284	[no vote]	316	[no vote]

Essentially, then, the Lords backed a wholly appointed House, while the Commons rejected that option, but also failed to agree upon either a wholly elected House, or any of the 'hybrid' options. In this section, the arguments on this essential matter of composition, which were essentially echoed in the debates in both Houses, are examined.

Following these votes, in September 2003, the Government produced a consultation paper, *Next Steps for the House of Lords*,[119] proposing interim reforms including the removal of the remaining hereditary peers from the Lords. The original aim of making the House of Lords 'more democratic and representative' was replaced by the goal of making the Lords 'more legitimate and more representative.' Thus the proposals would have kept the Lords fully appointed, but removed some powers of the PM over the party balance of the Lords. 'However, this was derided by reformers as a backward step that

---

117   First Report, HL 17, HC 171 (2002–03), para 36.

118   See, e.g. the Joint Committee Report HL 97, HC 668 (2002–03), para 24.

119   CP 14/03, http://www.dca.gov.uk/consult/holref/index.htm

sought to cement the all-appointed house that the Commons had rejected'[120] and in March 2004, the Government announced that it would not at that time proceed with legislation to enact the proposals. An attempt at cross party agreement was made by in *Reforming The House of Lords: Breaking the Deadlock* in February 2005, proposing a 70/30 elected appointed House, with all appointed Peers to be nominated by a statutory appointments commission, and all other members elected by the Single Transferable Vote system for 12 year terms. A Bill giving effect to these proposals was abandoned after first reading in the Lords.

In May 2005 Labour won its third General Election. The Queen's speech contains continued commitment to introduce legislation to reform the House of Lords. In July 2006, the then Leader of the House of Commons indicated a willingness to seek consensus around a proposed 50% elected, 50% appointed Upper House.

> I will be working with colleagues on all sides of both Houses over the coming months as part of an intensive effort to reach consensus on how a future Upper Chamber may look. I think a consensus is achievable and I believe this: if we do not seize the opportunity before us now, I fear that reform will be placed on the back-burner for decades to come. My sense is that we should be able to build consensus around the idea of a House which is split 50% elected and 50% appointed, phased in over a long period, perhaps as long as 12 or 15 years. Crucially the shift must be one which leads to a House which does not threaten the primacy of the Commons, but which is more representative of the society we live in today.[121]

In February 2007, the Government published a White Paper: *The House of Lords: Reform*[122] suggesting a 50/50 elected/appointed House as a model around which consensus might be achieved. It argued that key principles for reform included: the primacy of the House of Commons; that the House of Lords should play a complementary role; but be more legitimate; that there should be no overall majority for any party, but a significant non party-political element.

However, in March 2007, votes were held in both Houses on these proposals, but giving the same options as in 2003. Both Houses overwhelmingly rejected the proposed 50/50 split but reached radically opposing conclusions.

	100% appt'd	80% appt'd	60% appt'd	50/50	60% elected	80% elected	Fully elected
Lords							
For	361			46	45	114	122
Against	121	Defeated*	Defeated*	409	392	336	326
Commons							
For	196			155	178	305	337
Against	375	Defeated*	Defeated*	418	392	267	224

* Defeated without vote

---

120   M Russell, 'House of Lords reform: Are we nearly there yet?' (2009) 80(1) *Political Quarterly* 119.

121   Jack Straw, *The Future for Parliament*, Speech at the Hansard Society AGM, 11 July 2006, www.hansardsociety.org.uk/assets/Hansard_society_speech.pdf

122   Cm 7027.

On this occasion, therefore the House of Commons at least expressed a clear preference, but it was directly opposed to that of the Lords. As noted above, the Government's 2008 proposals reflected the view of the Commons, in putting forward a wholly or mainly elected House.[123] However, Meg Russell sees cause for optimism in that at least the three main parties have now converged:

> Until now the most obvious obstacle to Lords reform has been the failure to agree if election or appointment is the most appropriate form of composition. This was what sank the Royal Commission's report, and the government's second, third and fourth White Papers. It was the sole focus of both rounds of parliamentary votes. Finally this issue appears to be resolved. The Liberal Democrats have long been committed to election, and the Conservatives first officially embraced a largely elected house several years ago. The government's change in position on this issue thus seems to be the last bit of the puzzle.[124]

However, she concludes that there still several new obstacles to be overcome as soon as this initial one is out of the way.

An objection to any mixed House?

Since the two solutions of an entirely appointed or entirely elected House both seem to have obvious drawbacks one might expect that the obvious solution would have been some form of mixed House. The Royal Commission, three White Papers and the PAC all recommended such a proposal; one might therefore expect that such an option would be seen as commending a clear consensus. Unfortunately, in the authors' view, this is not the case. Phillipson explains and refutes one of the objections to mixed chambers:

> The first main argument is the so-called 'Strathclyde paradox':[125] 'If election is so good, why should the public not elect *all* our political Members? If it is bad, why elect any at all?'[126] This piece of school-boy logic has, mystifyingly, gained con- siderable support in the Lords.[127] It is flawed because it rests upon the false premise that electing members is straightforwardly either good or bad. In fact, if the three criteria for an effective second chamber are borne in mind, it becomes apparent that election has some advantages and some drawbacks. Election *is* 'good' in terms of legitimacy: if there were to be *no* elected members, this would prevent the House from having sufficient democratic legitimacy to assert itself effectively against the Executive-dominated Commons. This would particularly be the case were the House to be deliberately reformed on a non-democratic basis.[128] However, the issue of the composition of the Lords does not rest solely upon legitimacy. As canvassed above, in addition to being legitimate, it should also be distinct from the

---

123   The above is only a brief summary; for a comprehensive history, see P Dorey, 'Stumbling through "stage two"': New Labour and House of Lords reform' (2008) 3 *British Politics* 22–44.

124   Russell, n 120 above at 120.

125   After Lord Strathclyde, the Conservative Leader in the Lords.

126   HL Deb col 830 (22 Jan 2003).

127   See 'Irvine gloom on Lords reform', *Guardian*, 8 January 2003.

128   See below, at 480–83.

Commons, more independent from party control and to have the expertise to aid it in its sometimes highly technical work. Once these factors are considered, we can see why we might not want *all* the chambers members to be elected, desirable though this would be in terms of legitimacy: such a course of action would preclude the appointment of members who would add expertise, independence and thus distinctive value to the House. Having different classes of members—in other words a hybrid House—ensures that these different requirements are *all* met. The so-called Strathclyde paradox only has any force if it is assumed that reform of the Lords is to be judged by one criterion alone.[129]

The other key argument is that a hybrid House would be unworkable in practice. This view was first expressed by Bogdanor.

V Bogdanor, 'Reform of the House of Lords: a sceptical view' (1999) 70(4) *Political Quarterly* 375 (extracts)

There are especial difficulties, it may be suggested, in a mixed second chamber, combining directly or indirectly elected members with a nominated element. For a mixed chamber would, by definition, contain members enjoying different degrees of democratic legitimacy. The danger then is that any vote carried by a group with a lesser degree of democratic legitimacy will be seen as less valid than a vote carried by a group with greater democratic legitimacy. In the past, the Labour party has regarded votes carried by the hereditary peers as having less weight than votes carried by the life peers, since it regards the former as less legitimate than the latter. In a new second chamber composed of an elected element and a nominated element, votes carried by the latter would be regarded as carrying less weight than those carried by the former. Who elected you? would be the cry directed at the hapless nominated members whenever they carried a vote against their elected colleagues.

Note

1. Russell cautiously agrees that this could be a problem:

    The greatest potential difficulty in a new upper house that combines elected and appointed members is that it could become controversial whenever the appointed members decide the outcome of a vote. . .A similar situation applied towards the end of the life of the previous House of Lords, when commentators were quick to point out the occasions that the hereditary members were in this decisive position. Hereditary members were seen as less legitimate than life members, and it is possible that appointed members would bear the same stigma in a new chamber where most members had been elected.[130]

She points out that the only parallel here would be the Italian Senate, which has a small number of *ex officio* appointed members; because their numbers are small, their votes are rarely determinate. However, 'On the one recent occasion when this happened, in 1994, it caused considerable controversy'. Phillipson sets out the counter-arguments:

---

129   G Phillipson, '"The Greatest Quango of them All", "A Rival Chamber" or "A Hybrid Nonsense"? Solving the Second Chamber Paradox' [2004] PL 352, at 359–60.

130   Russell, 'Second Chambers Overseas' (1999) 70 *Pol. Quart* 411, 417.

G Phillipson, '"The greatest quango of them all", a "rival Chamber" or "a hybrid nonsense"? Solving the Second Chamber Paradox' [2004] *Public Law 352*, at 360–2

This point was echoed in Parliament by some of the more thoughtful objectors to a mixed House in the parliamentary debates on the Joint Committee report in January 2003 and indeed seemed to be used as the chief argument against having a mixed House. 'The compromises of part-election are the worst option, with the invidious outcome of two classes of members—elected and appointed'.[131] 'A partly elected second Chamber would. . .create two classes of Member. We can imagine the cries of 'Foul!' when elected Members are outvoted by unelected Members'.[132] 'It will be the nominated upper Members of Parliament who will be responsible for stopping the popular will of the elected Members of the House of Lords.[133]

However, the extent to which this would be a problem for a hybrid House has been too readily assumed. First of all, the reaction of the elected members to such an eventuality is a matter of speculation. As Russell has pointed out, only two chambers out of 58 bi-cameral legislatures world-wide have a substantial amount of appointed members in the second chamber, so there is little evidence from which to predict with any confidence the dynamics of such chambers.[134] If a mixed House had been approved by both Houses of Parliament on a free vote, and so had received all-party endorsement, it would be difficult for elected members to carp at the presence and influence of the non-elected members which Parliament itself had agreed should be there. Second, there are ways of minimising the problem. Both the Royal Commission and the PAC[135] recommended that in a mixed House everything should be done to ensure that all members enjoy parity of esteem, whether elected or appointed. Thus as the Royal Commission put it:

> Once members have arrived in the chamber, by whatever route, they should so far as possible serve the same terms, benefit from the same allowances and facilities and be treated in all respects identically.[136]

This very clear recommendation was completely ignored by many of the opponents of mixed House in parliament.[137]

Finally, the proponents of this view miss a simple, but crucially important point: if the elected members constituted a *majority* of the House, as the PAC suggested should be the case, and as this article will argue, then the elected would rarely or never be defeated

---

131   HC Deb col 204 (21 January 2003).

132   *Ibid*, col 250, Mr Clelland.

133   HL Deb col 631 (21 January 2003), Lord Hughes.

134   'Second Chambers Overseas' (1999) 70(4) *Political Quarterly* 411, 417.

135   See n 93 above, paras 98–99.

136   See n 74 Wakeham, para 12.5.

137   See, e.g. HL Deb col 648 (21 January 2003), Lord Sheldon: elected members 'will still claim a greater legitimacy with secretaries, research assistants and offices.' 'Imagine the ill-feeling if you have a hybrid House and elected Members get salaries and appointed Members do not.' (*Ibid*, col 649 (Lady Saltoun). See also the similar fears of Baroness Seccombe, *ibid*, col 653 and of Lord Gilbert, *ibid*, col 818 (22 January 2003).

by the un-elected; thus the danger Bogdanor foresees would simply never materialise. This relatively obvious point seemed, however, to escape the notice of many Peers. As one said,

> The crucial point about a hybrid system is that, *whatever* the percentage—20/80, 60/40, 50/50—it would not be stable. The first time the unelected Members defeated the elected Members there would be increasing pressure to have more elected Members (emphasis added).[138]

How his Lordship envisaged, say, a 20% un-elected contingent defeating an 80% elected one is not clear. Moreover, it is unlikely that any given issue would split the two groups of members squarely down the middle as Bogdanor suggests. In nearly all cases, there would be bound to be some elected members (particularly perhaps Liberal Democrat and non-partisan party members generally) siding with their independent colleagues. This would preclude the isolation and exposure of the un-elected members. However, a modified version of this objection, that could still apply where the elected members were in a majority, was advanced by Lord Butler, former Cabinet secretary, in debate:

> Let us envisage that on a controversial issue the government of the day and the opposition parties are in conflict, but one side has a small majority which is over-turned by the votes of the minority of appointed Members. If we have accepted election as a necessary condition for legitimacy, where is legitimacy then?[139]

It is clear that in such a case, there would be no straightforward clash between the elected and the un-elected, as Bogdanor envisages. But the only response to Butler's question, 'where would legitimacy be then?' is that legitimacy should be seen as a condition for the House as a whole: if it has a majority of elected members, it is the House in which the democratic will can always prevail and thus a legitimate institution. While, if the situation Butler envisages were to materialise, it could cause awkward questions to be asked, it is ironic that this objection is nearly always made by those who favour a wholly appointed House. Such a House, when it disagrees with the Commons, precisely pits the appointed, as a body, against the elected Commons, and therefore raises in a far more stark and extreme way the problem at issue.

It is possible therefore that a mixed House *could* raise some legitimacy issues in this way, but this does *not* provide, as Bogdanor and others suggest, a conclusive argument against such a chamber. Rather it may represent the only real drawback in what is otherwise the best solution to a notoriously difficult problem; a drawback to be balanced against the numerous advantages to be discussed below.

What proportion (if any) of the new House should be elected?

In this section we consider the arguments advanced for and against the four main options of a fully elected, fully appointed, mainly elected and mainly appointed House. We start with Wakeham, which advocated a mainly appointed House.

---

138   *Ibid*, col 726, Lord Higgins.

139   *Ibid*, col 770.

A House for the Future, Cm 4534 (2000) (extracts)

11.5 A second chamber which was wholly or largely directly elected would certainly be authoritative and confident, but the source of its authority could bring it into direct conflict with the House of Commons. There would be a risk that the second chamber would have a different political complexion from the House of Commons. Such a divergence would, whatever the formal distinctions between the chambers in terms of their powers and pre-eminence, be bound to give rise to constitutional conflicts. A different risk would arise if the second chamber had the same political complexion as the House of Commons because that could cause it to act as a compliant rubber stamp for whatever any future Government might want to do.

11.6 ... There would, in particular, be no justification for a continuation of the Salisbury Convention (see Chapter 4). If a directly elected second chamber were to be opposed to a Bill, it would not be easy to argue that it should, save in exceptional circumstances, defer to the views of the other directly elected chamber.

...

11.8 A wholly directly elected second chamber could not be broadly representative of the complex strands of British society. The fact is that elections can only be fought effectively by organised political parties which can attract large blocks of voters and who have the resources to organise television broadcasts, publicity, canvassing, public meetings and the like... Successful candidates for any direct elections to the second chamber would almost certainly come from a narrow class of people who are politically aware and highly partisan and who have to a very considerable degree already committed their lives to political activity. Putting it bluntly but accurately, a wholly elected second chamber would in practice mean that British public life was dominated even more than it is already by professional politicians.

11.9 By the same token, total reliance on direct election would in practice be incompatible with securing membership for people with relevant experience of and expertise in other walks of life. Such people would generally be reluctant to commit themselves to a party platform or engage in electioneering and would therefore be unlikely to put themselves forward as candidates for election. They would also be unlikely to be successful if they did so. While they might be well known in their field, such people rarely achieve widespread popular recognition or support. They lack the skills necessary to fight an electoral battle. Direct election would therefore be unlikely to produce members with the ability to speak directly for the voluntary sector, the professions, cultural and sporting interests and a whole range of other important aspects of British society.

11.10 In addition, most systems of direct election deliver results which may be geographically representative but which are seldom gender-balanced or provide appropriate representation for ethnic, religious or other minorities.

11.11 Direct elections are also not well suited to securing membership of the second chamber for those with specific expertise and authority in constitutional matters and the protection of human rights.

11.12 Another fundamental criticism of any proposal that the membership should be wholly or largely elected is that it would significantly reduce the prospects for securing a second chamber which was relatively independent of the influence of political parties. Very few independents, if any, would secure election, even using a highly proportional system such as Single Transferable Vote (STV). Successful candidates for election would nearly all be closely associated with political parties and essentially dependent on those parties.

Notes

1. A critical weakness in the arguments expressed above are that they are often expressed as being arguments directed against 'a wholly or mainly' elected body, as if the same considerations apply to each, while in other instances it is not made clear which scenario is being envisaged; however the two clearly have profoundly different implications. Exactly the same, possibly deliberate confusion can be seen in a recent comment of the Lord Chancellor:

> . . .a wholly or substantially elected House. . .would be a House of equal legitimacy to the House of Commons, since it would be elected. The rationale for the conventions by which this House came to accept that it is subordinate to the House of Commons, as the sole elected Chamber, would be gone for ever.[140]

The points made in paras 11.5 and 11.6—the challenge to the pre-eminence to the Commons—in reality applies only to a wholly elected second chamber or one in which all but a very small minority were elected. If, for example, 60% of the second chamber were elected, the House of Commons, as wholly elected body, could still claim a significantly stronger democratic mandate for its decisions. The arguments in paras 11.8 and 11.9 about representativeness and expertise are only expressed to apply to a *wholly* elected chamber, and this is clearly the case. The same is true of para 11.11, since a minority of appointed members could provide the necessary constitutional expertise; they could also supply the independent members whose admitted desirability is canvassed in para 11.12. The concern as to gender and ethnic representation (para 11.10) could be answered by having a substantial minority of appointed members, where a duty lay upon the appointing body to secure such equality of representation (as Wakeham in fact proposes). The 'voter fatigue' concern, aired in para 11.13, since it goes to the process of having to engage in a further round of electioneering and voting, rather than the proportion of elected to non-elected members in the chamber for which the elections were held, would presumably apply to *any* elections for a second chamber, regardless of that proportion. Ironically, voter apathy would probably in fact be most marked if the elected element of the second chamber was so small as to give rise to a perception that the elected element was tokenistic and the elected members impotent, because constantly out-voted by appointees, a point made recently by the Joint Committee: 'We cannot see an election for a small proportion of the new House raising any enthusiasm or contributing to a sense of the importance of the reformed House in the eyes of the electorate'.[141] This point, rather ironically in view of Wakeham's actual proposals, therefore argues for at the least a substantially elected element.

2. In the result, Wakeham's arguments against an elected House do not appear to apply with any force against a chamber composed of the 60% elected element that the PAC recommended.

3. The PAC report was representative of the Commons' attitudes in its robust dismissal of such fears:

> The Government, and some members of the Lords, have laid particular stress on the threat which would allegedly be posed to the pre-eminence of the Commons by a more legitimate reformed second chamber. We are satisfied that the Parliament Acts provide sufficient safeguards against that. [Moreover] Governments are formed, tested and held to account in the Commons. They have to retain the

140 *Ibid*, col 832 (22 January 2003) (emphasis added).

141 First Report, HL 17, HC 171 (2002–03), para 70.

confidence of the Commons if they are to retain office. Only the Commons can make or break governments. We therefore do not believe that a reformed, more representative second chamber will pose a threat to that status.[142]

Seemingly the Labour Government was finally convinced by these arguments. One of the most important passages in the 2008 White Paper says:

> The Government welcomes a confident and assertive second chamber. It sees this as further enhancing our democracy and something that is entirely consistent with the primacy of the House of Commons. That primacy rests in the fact that the Government of the day is formed from the party or parties that can command a majority in the House of Commons. It also rests in the Parliament Acts and in the financial privilege of the House of Commons. The Prime Minister and most senior ministers are also drawn from the House of Commons. A more assertive second chamber, operating within its current powers, would not threaten primacy.[143]

4. A more sophisticated argument against an elected House is put forward by Dawn Oliver, one of the members of the Royal Commission. Oliver notes the arguments put forward by Wakeham against a fully or largely elected House and goes on.

> The reformed second chamber will be a hybrid body in many respects: in protecting the constitution and human rights it will be performing functions that non-political, non-elected, unaccountable bodies such as constitutional courts or councils perform elsewhere: it is accepted that such bodies should not be democratically accountable. In much of what it does it will be performing a technical scrutiny function and holding government to account, activities that are also performed by other non-elected bodies such as the press and pressure groups, advisory committees, and the like, and in which political affiliation or accountability is not essential. And its powers are limited—in primary legislation to a one-year suspensory veto. This is quite different from the position in the Commons, whose consent is always required for legislation. The true legislator in the system, or at least the body which has the last word on legislation, is— and under the proposals will remain—the House of Commons. This is the body that needs to be accountable to the electorate. In other words, the arguments surrounding the reform of the House of Lords also raise issues about what makes an institution a 'legislative chamber' and when the notion of 'legislative chamber' ends and runs into that of council of state, constitutional court or constitutional council.[144]

Notes
1. The weakness in the Commission's argument on this point, more articulately put forward here by Oliver than in the report itself, is clear. As Russell and Comes put it: 'Whilst there are arguments for the inclusion of both groups within the House, the Commission does little to justify the *dominance* of the chamber by appointed members, the majority of whom would continue to take a party whip.'[145]

---

142   See n 116 above, para 51.

143   See n 100 above, at 4–5.

144   D Oliver, 'The reform of the UK Parliament', in J Jowell and D Oliver (eds), *The Changing Constitution,* 4th edn (2000), p 288–89.

145   M Russell and R Cornes, 'The Royal Commission on Reform of the House of Lords: A House for the Future?' (2001) 64 MLR 82, at 86.

2. Oliver's argument above justifies the predominance of non-elected members on the basis that they will primarily be undertaking a technical, scrutinising function, which does not require an impeccable democratic mandate. A similar point was made by Robin Cook, for the government:

> The limited functions of a second Chamber do not require it to mirror the democratic mandate of the House of Commons. On the contrary, the second Chamber will be better able to fulfil its role of deliberation and a more valuable forum in which difficult issues can be discussed openly if its debates are informed by the expertise and authority of people with a lifetime of distinction.[146]

However, if this is the justification for a mainly non-elected House, with the implication that the skills required are those of expertise and objectivity, rather than those of the politician, then it would surely point to the non-elected element being made up of independent rather than party political members, whereas Wakeham suggests a mainly appointed House but with only a 20% independent element: in other words one would have party members deciding constitutional and human rights issues—but without the legitimacy given by election. This seems a crucial weakness in the Wakeham proposals.

It is in relation to the third criterion—*perceived legitimacy*—that the Royal Commission model and, *a fortiori*, proposals for a fully appointed Chamber fall down. The view of the PAC was that the general response to Wakeham and the White Paper in the press and Parliament proved that a House with only a small elected element would simply not be seen as sufficiently legitimate. As one MP put it:

> Why should a small group choose the representatives of 60 million people? We have. . .got rid of Old Sarum, where seven people elected two MPs, and Dunwich under the sea, where 14 did. . . do they really want to go back not just centuries but to a different millennium?[147]

Or as Lord Goodhart put it, an all appointed House would mean: 'one House of Parliament being elected by an electorate of eight, nine or 10 people. . .a totally incredible idea.'[148] The strongly expressed conviction of the PAC was that a reformed House needs not a small, but a majority elected element, in order to give it the legitimacy it needs to make full and proper use of its existing powers to amend and delay legislation where it considers that the Government needs to think again.[149] The PAC argued that, 'second chamber reform is. . .about strengthening Parliament as a whole in relation to an executive that is uniquely powerful in the British system.'[150] As Lord Goodhart put it:

> What is the greatest problem of the British constitution today and what has been the greatest problem for many years past. . .? When the Government have a large

---

146   HC Deb (10 March 2002).

147   HC Deb col 239 (21 January 2003), Malcom Savidge.

148   HL Deb col 825 (22 January 2003).

149   See n 116 above, Part One and paras 81–98.

150   *Ibid*, para 6.

majority in the House of Commons, as it has for 19 of the last 24 years, there are no effective checks on the abuse of executive powers.[151]

In opposition to such views, the Royal Commission and many in the Lords argued that, given the role of an expert and revising chamber which the Royal Commission envisaged for the reformed Lords, there were other routes to legitimacy other than election. As Viscount Tenby put it: 'there are other legitimacies: the legitimacy of expertise, of experience and. . .even the legitimacy of age. All these are not only useful in an amending and examining Chamber, but essential if the role assigned to it is to be discharged effectively.'[152] Lord Winston made a similar point:

> A huge number of British institutions, by their very nature, do a fine service in supporting this country, but they are essentially not democratic. The Law Lords are not democratic. The universities are not democratic. The monarchy is not democratic. The regulatory bodies, such as the Human Fertilisation and Embryology Authority and the Human Genetics Commission, are not democratically elected. The research councils are not democratic, but they need to be transparent in their working. Most important in terms of government, the Civil Service is not democratic either.[153]

This kind of argument, especially the comparision with the judiciary, is frequently made, the notion being that judges are not elected and yet derive legitimacy for the considerable power they exercise through other means: independence, integrity, expertise in the law. As Lord Forsyth said: 'No one argues that our judges need to be elected to have legitimacy and to command respect.'[154] The Lord Chancellor echoed this comparision: 'We do not, in this country, maintain that the only legitimate route to public office is election. We do not, for example, elect our judges.'[155]

The objection to this argument, however, is clear: it pays no regard to the quite different roles of the judges and that of the second chamber of Parliament. In comparison to the legally unlimited power wielded by Parliament,[156] the judicial branch exercises only a relatively narrow band of power, which is ultimately either given to it by parliament (in the case of statutory interpretation) or confined to issues that Parliament has acquisced in leaving in judicial hands (the common law). Even in relation to their powers under the Human Rights Act, which Gearty argues transferred 'a huge and open-ended portion of [parliament's] legislative function to the judiciary',[157] the courts remain bound by unambigous incompatible primary legislation[158] and cannot, through purported interpretation, 'legislate' to cover gaps in the law that arguably give inadequate protection for Convention rights.[159] Moreover, in exercising their powers under the HRA, the judiciary are

---

151   HL Deb col 823 (22 January 2003).

152   *Ibid*, col 781; see the like view of Baroness Carnegy, *ibid*, col 659 (21 January 2003).

153   *Ibid*, col 661 (21 Januay 2003), Lord Winston.

154   *Ibid*, col 674.

155   See n 151 above, col 834 (22 January 2003).

156   Subject perhaps to the supremacy of EU law: however it is probably the case that the UK courts would follow an Act of Parliament expressly derogating from EU law or withdrawing from the Union (see Chapter 5).

157   C Gearty, 'What are Judges are For?', Inaugural Lecture, Kings College London, 11 December 2000.

158   Section 3(2) HRA.

159   *Re S and Re W* [2002] 2 All ER 192, HL.

exercising powers explicitly given to them by Parliament and capable of revocation through repeal of the Act. Thus in making their decisions, judges are not called upon to exercise their own unconfined judgement, still less their party political views. They are not asked to decide, *de novo*, what they think desirable for society. The House of Lords as a legislative body is, precisely, asked to do this: to bring Peers' individual political views to bear upon issues such as foundation hopitals, equalisation of the age of consent for homosexuals, cross-media ownership and so on.

Of the unreformed House, Donald Shell wrote in 1994 that its lack of legitimacy meant that: 'It would now be foolish to rely on the House to provide satisfactory protection for the fundamentals of the constitution.' This view was arguably borne out by the response of the Lords in April 1996 to the Prevention of Terrorism (Additional Powers) Act, passed in the wake of the IRA's bomb attack on Canary Wharf, breaking its ceasefire; *inter alia*, the Act gives the police new powers to stop and search pedestrians for terrorist-related items without having to have reasonable suspicion (s 1). The fundamental principle at stake (it has of course been violated before) was that measures threatening the liberty of the subject should be given a decent period for scrutiny and that debate should not be subject to severe time constraints. The Act passed all its stages in the Commons in a single day and the Lords were requested by the government to follow suit. As the debate made clear, many peers expressed considerable disquiet at what they were being asked to do, but ultimately appeared to think it their duty to acquiesce.[160] Thus the House felt itself unable either to reject the Bill or to extend time for consideration, although peers clearly expressed a sense of constitutional impropriety in the way in which the matter had been handled.

5. However, as suggested above, the response of the Lords to the 2001 AntiTerrorism Bill was much more bullish; the greater preparedness to resist the government on crucial issues probably flowed from the Lords' own perception of their greater legitimacy, following the removal of the hereditary peers. Ministers were no longer able to lambast the House simply as an anachronistic impediment to the democratic process, dominated by Conservative hereditary peers; as commentators pointed out, the government was now dealing with an institution which it had reformed, albeit limitedly, precisely to make it more legitimate and representative.[161] Nevertheless, as seen above, the Lords did give way on a number of crucial issues; doubtless this was, at least in part, due to the Lords' own perception of their lack of legitimacy. A fully-reformed Lords, with a substantially elected element, would no doubt have felt far more able to stick to its guns. The clear lesson to be learned is that the crucial factor in the readiness of the Lords to provide a substantial check upon the government is not so much its formal powers—which are, in any event, likely to remain substantially unchanged in any process of further reform—but its own perception of its legitimacy. Increasing its legitimacy will markedly increase its impact as a constitutional check in practice even without any formal increase in its powers.

6. *Perceived* legitimacy is therefore crucial. The Royal Commission, as seen above, recognised this. However, in the view certainly of the PAC, the Commission simply misjudged the public mood in considering that a mainly appointed House with a small elected element would garner to itself sufficient apparent legitimacy to be truly effective. While their arguments as to other means of obtaining legitimacy and authority (expertise, representativeness, personal distinction, independent-mindedness and so on)[162] are not without some merit, they arguably fail to recognise that the direct political power that the House of Lords exercises requires it to have a direct electoral mandate from the people, as the press and parliamentary reaction to Wakeham and the White

---

160   See HL Deb vol 571 no 73 cols 298, 301–04, 337–38 (3 April 1996).

161   See 'Blunkett "bully on terror bill"', *The Guardian*, 10 December 2001.

162   See Wakeham Report, para 10.6.

Paper indicated. As the PAC put it, in proposing a predominately appointed chamber, Wakeham and the government 'are bravely swimming against the tide of political and public opinion'. In the following extract, the PAC explains this point and puts forward an alternative suggestion.

Select Committee on Public Administration, *Fifth Report*, HC 494 (2001–02) (extracts)

85. The debate in the House of Commons on 9 January, the support for the Early Day Motion, our own survey of MPs, and public opinion surveys show that having a minority elected element is no longer a credible option. . .there has been a revulsion against party patronage. The main criticism of the White Paper voiced again and again in the parliamentary debates and in the media was that it is no longer acceptable for most of the second chamber to be party placemen, who owe their place to their party leader. Even if these appointments were not made directly by party leaders but mediated by the Appointments Commission, a largely appointed second chamber would still be 'the biggest quango in the land'. The public is no longer willing to accept patronage on that scale.[163]

Without sufficient legitimacy, the second chamber will not be as effective as it needs to be. This consideration has also led us to conclude that the superficially attractive option of parity between election and appointment, reflecting the merits and purposes of each, is not sufficient to guarantee legitimacy and effectiveness.

That is why we have concluded that the new second chamber must be predominantly elected. But we also believe that there should still be a significant appointed element. The cross-benchers will only get there by appointment. Scientists, industrialists, public servants, academics and other experts who would not normally stand for election will only get there by that means. We are proposing the continuation of an appointed element not simply to accommodate those opposed to election, but because there are those who genuinely believe that the appointed members add value through their distinct expertise and experience from outside politics, which should not be lost. . .

Note

1. The elected element in the new chamber was designed partly to ensure proper regional representation, one of the classical functions of a second chamber (see Russell, above, at p 460). Some chambers in federal systems use a system of indirect election to achieve this, whereby regional assemblies elect members to serve in the second chamber: such members thus act at least partly as representatives of their region, rather than their party only. The problem with seeking to implement such a proposal in the UK at present, as all the reports considered above recognised, was that in the absence of English regional assemblies, there would be no bodies that could elect members to represent the regions of England. There would be little point in having members nominated by the Scottish Parliament if there were no equivalents from Northumberland or Yorkshire

Practical issues: the electoral system, terms of office, timings of elections

There remains considerable argument as to the mechanics of elections to the second chamber, whatever the proportion of the elected element, which cannot be addressed in detail here. The key one is probably is the electoral system to be used. As one MP remarked:

---

163   Wakeham Report, paras 85 and 86.

> If the. . .elected element is elected using the closed-list system that operates for the European Parliament, the power of patronage would apply not just to the political appointments but to the elected element as well. The party bosses would determine who was top of the list. The second Chamber would be almost entirely created by patronage and appointment.[164]

The PAC also came out strongly against the use of a closed list system, which they described as 'not acceptable and a turn-off for voters'.[165] They added a number of useful principles which should guide the selection of an electoral system. It should, they said:

- be complementary to the voting system for the House of Commons;
- minimise the risk of one party gaining an overall majority;
- maximise voter choice, by enabling voters to vote for individual candidates, within and across parties;
- encourage a more diverse chamber; and
- encourage the election of independent-minded people.

They concluded that:

> These principles will best be realised by using multi-member constituencies, and a proportional voting system. This could be either STV [single transferable vote] or regional lists, so long as the lists are fully open lists, which maximise voter choice. We would not support limited open lists, which present an appearance of choice for the voter, but almost never affect the outcome.[166]

These recommendations were taken up by the Joint Committee, which recommended that any elections should use open regional list or STV, *not* first past the post.[167] As Russell recently noted:

> Most proposals to date, including the Royal Commission's report, the earlier White Papers, a report from the Commons Public Administration Committee, and various others from outside bodies, have proposed that elections be based on a proportional representation system. This makes sense as it ensures that the second chamber is distinct from the House of Commons and has its own different logic of composition. It also has the benefit of ensuring that no party would have a majority in the chamber (so that neither government nor the main opposition would be in control), and of bringing a degree of proportionality to Westminster which many have long sought. The current chamber, which resulted from the hereditary peers' removal in 1999, is far more proportional than its predecessor, and now more or less reflects the balance of votes cast at recent general elections (with the complicating factor of a large number of independent Crossbenchers). In the past all three parties have expressed a desire that this kind of 'no overall control' situation in the chamber

---

164   HC Deb col 770 (10 March 2002), Norman Lamb.

165   HC 494 (2001–02), para 110.

166   *Ibid*, paras 111–12.

167   See n 141 above, para 53.

should be retained. Yet just as a new consensus becomes visible on method of composition, this more established consensus seems to be breaking down.[168]

Meg Russell goes on to provide a clear explanation of the problems with the Conservative proposal:

> Many campaigners outside parliament would be completely opposed to reform based on a non-proportional system. If the purpose of the second chamber is to act as a modifying influence on executive power in the Commons, rather than to be the creature of either the government or the main opposition (threatening, in turn, to create either a rubber stamp or gridlock), PR is essential. This means tacit support for government decisions is needed from those outside the governing party. Faced with a choice between a reformed chamber elected by first past the post, or the appointed but proportional chamber we have currently got, the status quo far better provides for the kind of consensual decision making desirable to counterbalance exaggerated government majorities.[169]

Another important issue is the length of the terms of office that members should serve. Wakeham proposed 15 years for both elected and appointed members, with no right of re-election for the elected members. The aim was clearly to bolster members' independence. The PAC favoured Wakeham, though it suggested a compromise:

> 121. We believe that a renewable term as short as five years would both seriously jeopardise the independence of second chamber members and increase the risk of conflict with the members of the Commons. There would be greater likelihood of claims that the second chamber members were as legitimate as the MPs. Such a move would be a fundamental departure from the Royal Commission recommendations. . .
>
> 126. We recommend that elected second chamber members should serve a single term extending to two Parliaments. No member of the second chamber should be permitted to stand for election to the Commons for ten years after leaving the second chamber. These restrictions would apply from the next general election. Political parties should not be allowed to nominate for appointment anyone who has served as an elected member of the second chamber.[170]

7. Its suggested compromise of two parliamentary terms would mean an average term of eight years, while the Joint Committee recommended in its First Report a term of 12 years with members then being banned from standing for the Commons for three years.[171]

8. By 2008, the Government felt able to say:

> A key recommendation of Lord Wakeham's Royal Commission, which has since enjoyed widespread consensus, is that elected members of the second chamber

---

168   Russell, n 120 above, at 120.

169   *Ibid*, at 121.

170   See n 116 above.

171   First Report, HL 17, HC 171 (2002–03), para 48.

should normally serve a single, non-renewable term of 12–15 years. They should be elected in thirds, with each member serving three electoral cycles.[172]

9.   There is also doubt as to the timing of elections, with both main parties currently proposing that it should take place on the same day as the general election, bearing in mind of course that since the elections would be staggered, each such election would only return a third of the members of the House.[173] Thus, as the 2008 White Paper put it:

> Staggered elections would . . .reduce the scope for the membership of the second chamber to 'mirror' that of the House of Commons. In particular, they would damp the effect of substantial swings between the support for the main political parties and hence reduce the scope for one particular party to gain an overall majority in the second chamber. A party is likely to have to win the majority of seats at a succession of elections to be guaranteed a majority in the chamber overall under all four voting systems modelled, particularly under a list or STV system.[174]

10.   Russell comments:

> On this point there have been various proposals over the years, ranging from a minimum of five-year terms in the 2001 White Paper, to the fifteen-year terms proposed by the Royal Commission. Here there was general agreement by those at the cross-party talks that elected members (and appointed members, if included) should serve relatively long terms of twelve–fifteen years, and that these should be non-renewable. This is a sensible proposal, ensuring that members are relatively free of pressure both from their party leaderships and from constituents. It would therefore help to preserve another of the best elements of the present culture in the House of Lords and. . .distinct from the. . .Commons.[175]

The appointment of members

The Appointments Commission

A House for the Future, Cm 4534 (2000) (extracts)

Number of Appointments Commissioners
13.14 The interim Appointments Commission will include representatives of the three main political parties and a number of independents. The latter will form a majority among the Commissioners and will provide the chairman, implying a total of at least seven Commissioners. Experience from other public bodies working in politically controversial areas, such as the Committee on Standards in Public Life, suggests that there would be significant merit in including nominees from each of the main political parties. While they would be expected not to behave in a partisan manner, their understanding of how

---

172   See n 100 above, at 4.1.

173   See further *ibid* at [4.2]–[4.4].

174   *Ibid* at [4.14].

175   Russell, n 120 above at 122.

Parliament and the political parties work and think would be of considerable benefit to the Appointments Commission. We therefore recommend that three of the Appointments Commissioners should be nominees from the main political parties. A Commissioner nominated by the convenor of the Cross-Benchers would be a logical corollary. These four members should be balanced by four independent members, of whom one should be the chairman. The resulting total of eight should allow scope for representation from Scotland, Wales or Northern Ireland, thereby ensuring that the Appointments Commission was not a solely English body.

Selection of Appointments Commissioners

13.15 Since the first report of the Nolan Committee in 1995, both Conservative and Labour Governments have committed themselves to filling the majority of public appointments according to what have become known as the 'Nolan principles', notably that appoint-ments should be made strictly on merit and should be free of the taint of favouritism or bias. . .

Appointment of Commissioners

13.18 . . . Since the Appointments Commission will operate in respect of the second chamber, it would be most appropriate for it to be that chamber whose approval is required, on a motion moved by the Leader of the House, following the normal consultation with the leaders of the other party groupings and the Convenor of the Cross-Benchers.

Length and Security of Tenure

13.19 All Appointments Commissioners, including party nominees, should have a long period in office with security of tenure in order to protect them against undue influence and encourage them to bring a long-term perspective to bear on their work.

Notes

1. The PAC commented:

    . . . For the new second chamber to be credible and have authority, its appointed members must be independent minded people, not just perceived as the recipients of party patronage. They must bring expertise from the professions, science, the arts and other walks of life which are under-represented in politics. And they must help to redress the imbalances amongst the elected members and to promote diversity.[176]

2. However, the Committee's view that there should also be party affiliated nominated members seems now to have fallen out of favour.

An Elected Second Chamber, Cm 7438 (2008) (extracts)

6.1. The Government considers that the key argument for any appointments in the second chamber is that they would preserve a significant independent element. Given this, the Government proposes that there should be no party political appointments to a reformed second chamber. However, there should not be a bar on those who have or who have had party-political affiliations or connections being considered.

---

176   See n 116 above at [128].

6.4 The Government proposes that if there is an appointed element in a reformed second chamber, there should continue to be an Appointments Commission, which would seek applications and nominations, against published criteria. Appointments would be made on merit, with the key focus being an individual's ability, willingness and commitment to take part in the full work of the second chamber. The Government also proposes that any appointed members of a reformed second chamber should take part fully in its work, in general terms devoting the same amount of time to that work as elected members.

6.5 The Government proposes that, as for elected members, appointed members of a reformed second chamber should serve for three electoral cycles without the possibility of reappointment. One-third of appointed members would be replaced at each set of elections to the second chamber.

. . .

6.8 The Government proposes that there should be no reserved seats for Church of England Bishops in a wholly elected second chamber. It also proposes that if there is an appointed element in a reformed second chamber, there should be a proportionate number of seats reserved for Church of England Bishops.

6.9 After careful consideration, the Government proposes to endorse the recommendations of the Wakeham Commission that providing reserved places for other churches and faith communities other than the Church of England in a reformed second chamber would be problematic. Any appointments to represent other churches and faith groups should be made through the Appointments Commission in the usual way

6.15 The Government considers that any appointed element in a reformed second chamber would be an effective way of securing the continuation of a number of independent members. The presence of a significant minority of independent members would both distinguish the second chamber clearly from the House of Commons and complement the work of the Commons by providing non-partisan viewpoints in the legislative revision process. The size of any appointed element should be at the level of the 20% voted for by the House of Commons in March 2007.

6.18 Given the Government's view that the primary purpose of any appointed element in a reformed second chamber should be to secure the continuation of a number of independent members, it believes that, subject to paragraph 6.23, there should be no party-political appointments to that chamber. The existence of a substantial number of elected members in a reformed second chamber will ensure proper representation for political parties, which are the cornerstone of democracy in this country.

Principles for appointment

6.25 The criteria used currently by the House of Lords Appointments Commission for non-party political appointments are attached at Annex 6. They include that applicants and nominees should:

- have a record of significance that demonstrates a range of experience, skills and competencies;
- be able to make an effective and significant contribution to the work of the House across a wide range of issues;
- have some understanding of the constitutional framework and the skills and qualities needed to be an effective member of the House;
- have the time available to make an effective contribution within the procedures of working practices of the House; and

- be able to demonstrate outstanding personal qualities, in particular integrity and independence.

6.26 If there is to be an appointed element in a reformed second chamber, the Government proposes that the key focus in assessing potential appointees should be their ability, willingness and commitment to take part in the full range of the work of the chamber. Both elected and any appointed members will bring these qualities. While account should be taken of achievement or expertise, those appointed to a reformed second chamber should hold their membership because they are the best people for the job and will make an effective contribution to the work of the chamber, rather than because they are the most successful in their chosen field. . . .

6.32 In 2006–07, the House of Commons Public Administration Select Committee considered the possible future status, role and operation of the House of Lords Appointments Commission, in the context of considering the policy and regulatory issues arising from matters investigated by the police in response to allegations concerning the possible offer of peerages in exchange for financial assistance to political parties. The Committee reported in December 2007. It recommended, in advance of the introduction of any elected element, that the current Appointments Commission should be put onto a statutory footing, to clarify its remit and remove the Prime Minister from decisions on the size and composition of the House of Lords.

6.33 In its February 2007 White Paper The House of Lords: Reform, the Government set out its view that: 'Whilst it would be acceptable for the Appointments Commission to remain on a non-statutory basis if its current role were to continue, it would not be appropriate if its role were to increase significantly.' It remains the Government's view that if there is to be an appointed element in a reformed second chamber, with an appointments commission as a permanent part of the arrangements, that commission should be on a statutory basis. However, any legislation providing for an appointments commission should contain only broad parameters in relation to its role and operation, to give the Commission flexibility to respond effectively to changing needs and circumstances.

Note
Meg Russell comments:

> most previous reports from government and elsewhere have suggested inclusion of a 20 per cent independent appointed element. This would ensure that the Crossbenchers were retained. . . The presence of independent members is one of the things the public appreciates about the House of Lords. This factor was considered important to Lords legitimacy by 83 per cent of respondents in a recent survey commissioned by the Constitution Unit. [177]

Changing the *powers* of the Lords?

The current *powers* of the Lords are recognisably in the moderate end of the international spectrum (above at 436). As Hadfield[178] has pointed out, the powers of a second chamber cannot be

---

177   Russell, n 120 above at 121.

178   See n 50 above, p 349.

considered in isolation from its composition and legitimacy. Broadly speaking, the more legitimate a second chamber is, the greater its powers may permissibly be. Now since, the aim of any reform to the Lords, in particular the introduction of some elected element, would be greatly to increase its legitimacy, one might have expected that increases in the powers of the Lords would be on the agenda. But in this area, as in others, Wakeham was cautious. The report said:

> The second chamber's role in protecting the constitution should be maintained and enhanced. It should no longer be possible to amend the Parliament Acts using Parliament Act procedures, as was done in 1949. Such a change would maintain the current balance of power between the two Houses of Parliament and reinforce the second chamber's power of veto over any Bill to extend the life of a Parliament.
>
> There should be no extension of the second chamber's formal powers in respect of any other matter, whether 'constitutional' or concerning human rights (from the Executive Summary)

There now seems little prospect of any substantial change to the powers of the Lords, in particular giving it special powers over legislation that alters the constitution or abrogates fundamental rights, as is the norm in other Western democracies. Indeed, the PAC stated in their report that one of the areas of consensus was that 'there should be no major change in the powers of either House'.[179] The Joint Committee, having considered the possibility of giving the reformed House special powers over 'constitutional legislation' simply recommended that 'no new powers [be] given to the House of Lords at this stage'.[180]

The Government similarly seems to consider the current powers of the Lords about right:

> The reformed second chamber should be confident in challenging both the executive and the House of Commons. The second chamber should be able to make the government pause and reconsider. Ultimately, however, the government should be able to get its business through the legislature, through effective resolution of disagreements between the two Houses and, if necessary in the most exceptional cases, by using the Parliament Acts. This ensures the primacy of the House of Commons and means that, ultimately, any gridlock between the two Houses can be resolved.[181]

What seems to be going unrecognised in Parliament is that such a no-change policy, even if reform in other areas occurs, would leave the Lords in a glaringly anomalous position compared to nearly all second chambers overseas. As Russell remarks:

> The most basic constitutional role which a new upper house could play would be to exert a greater power over bills to amend the constitution than over ordinary bills. This is standard practice overseas. . .[Out of] 20 Western democracies. . .aside from the UK, the only countries where the upper house does not have special powers over constitutional amendments are those where other safeguards—such as automatic referendums on constitutional change—are built into the system.

---

179   *Ibid.*

180   HL 17, HC 171 (2002–03), para. 29. The Committee left open the possibility of returning to the Royal Commission's proposal to amend the Parliament Acts to prevent their change without the Lords' approval: *ibid,* note 36.

181   (2008) at [3.1].

The following table indicates the position overseas; comment on this matter by the author follows.

M Russell and R Cornes, *'The Royal Commission on reform of the House of Lords: A house for the future?'* (2001) 64 MLR 82, p 86

Table 2: Procedures for constitutional change in 10 democracies

Australia	Must be passed by referendum.
Canada	Must be passed by provincial assemblies.
France	Must pass both chambers, then either joint sitting by 3/5 majority, or a referendum.
Germany	Must pass both chambers by 2/3 majority.
Ireland	Must be passed by referendum.
Italy	Must pass both chambers by absolute majority, and if not by 2/3 majority referendum may be called by 1/5 of members of either house, 500,000 electors or five regional assemblies.
Japan	Must pass both chambers by 2/3 majority.
Spain	Must pass both chambers by 3/5 majority, or lower house by 2/3 majority and upper house by absolute majority. Referendum may be requested by 1/10 of members of either house.
Switzerland	Must pass both chambers, else referendum.
UK	Treated as ordinary legislation.
USA	Must pass both chambers by 2/3 majority, plus States' approval by referendum.

**G Phillipson, *'The powers of a reformed second chamber'*
[2003] PL 32 (extracts)**

The Royal Commission's sole ground of principle for rejecting any proposal to bring the Lords into line with this almost unanimous Western consensus is as follows:

> Our fundamental concern about any such proposal is that it would alter the current balance of power between the two chambers and could be exploited to bring the two chambers into conflict. It would be inconsistent with the requirement in our terms of reference 'to maintain the position of the House of Commons as the pre-eminent chamber of Parliament' and with our view of the overall role that the second chamber should play. [para 5.7]

The Commission put forward this remarkable position even though they clearly recognised the risk of the Parliament Acts being used to push through ill-considered constitutional change. The weaknesses of this argument are, it is suggested, three-fold. First, giving the

House extra powers over constitutional legislation would not as the Commission asserts (without argument) be 'inconsistent' with maintaining the Commons as the 'pre-eminent' House. In the vast majority of legislative instances—all those unconnected with significant constitutional or human rights matters—the Commons would remain the superior House, able to bypass Lords opposition after the delay of only a year, or, in the case of money bills, a month only. This would clearly maintain its pre-eminence, whatever the position was in relation to 'constitutional' legislation.

Second, the Lords already have special powers under the Parliament Acts in relation to one type of constitutional legislation—a Bill to extend the life of a Parliament—and the Royal Commission supported retention of this power and indeed, strengthening it, so that the Parliament Acts themselves could not be amended to remove or weaken this safeguard using the procedure they themselves provide for bypassing the Lords [paras 5.13–5.16]. The Royal Commission supported the retention of this power, presumably because it represents an important democratic safeguard. But once it is accepted that the Lords should have special powers to safeguard democracy in this basic manner, then logic suggests extending the scope of such powers to cover other matters equally important to the maintenance of a liberal democracy, such as rights to freedom of expression and assembly, habeas corpus, the franchise and the like. The Royal Commission proposals would leave the Lords with an absolute veto over a proposal, say, to extend a Parliament by a year during wartime, but with nothing but their normal delaying power over a peacetime Bill abolishing habeas corpus or criminalizing all public protest. Such a position is hard to defend on principled grounds.

Third, and perhaps most importantly, the Royal Commission fails to situate its reasoning on this matter within the wider constitutional context that the UK, unusually amongst Western democracies, has no provision for primary legislation that abrogates fundamental human rights to be annulled on such grounds in the courts or even to be subject to pre-legislative audit in some form of Constitutional Council, as in France. There are numerous recent examples of Parliament being asked to rush through legislation threatening civil liberties in hasty response to short term crises, legislation which, once on the statute book, cannot be challenged in the courts. [The author cites the Prevention of Terrorism (Additional Powers) Bill 1996, Criminal Justice (Terrorism and Conspiracy) Bill 1998, and the 2001 Anti-Terrorism, Crime and Security Bill—all discussed above at p 365–72—and goes on]:

Such casual attitudes towards internationally recognised human rights norms arguably spring from the historic absence of a codified constitution and a Bill of Rights. The UK's entrustment of the protection of such rights to the unfettered discretion of a governing party representing the majority of the day—or rather, typically around 43–45% of it—has traditionally meant that there has been no set of clearly constitutionalised standards around which the different political parties and political commentators can unite. Neither the ECHR nor the Human Rights Act yet represents such a unifying point: the Conservatives and much of the right-wing press remain sceptical about the HRA, and it and the Convention is often presented in the tabloid newspapers as a 'foreign', European imposition, frequently confused with the EU and thus a target for the Euro-scepticism of much of the popular press. Even the Labour Government that introduced the HRA appears profoundly ambivalent about the limitations on governmental power that it seeks to impose. Commentators on other state-power legislation introduced by this Government, including the Terrorism Act 2000 and the Regulation of Investigatory Powers Act 2000, have concluded that the Government has, at best, a highly qualified attitude of respect for fundamental human rights, especially where they clash with crime control values [see, eg, H Fenwick, Civil Rights: New Labour and the Human Rights Act (2000)].

In short, within the context of a political order that both culturally and constitutionally represents the principle of unbridled majoritarianism, it is of particular importance that the second chamber should be able to enforce at the least a thoughtful and considered decision in relation to the abridgement of basic human rights and the necessity of garnering a broad consensus that such action is truly necessary. [The PAC was open to this proposal: *op cit*, paras 74 and 75.]

The practical problem that the Royal Commission highlighted—the lack of a mechanism for identifying the provisions that should trigger the Lords' special powers in a country without a codified constitution— does not seem an insuperable problem. Perhaps the best practical solution would be to give the power to certify a Bill as 'constitutional' to the Constitution Committee of the second chamber. . .There would be numerous instances in which the classification of the Bill would be obvious, for example, changes to any of the devolution Acts, the franchise, the Freedom of Information Act, the European Communities Act 1972, the Human Rights Act, any legislation introduced with a negative statement under section 19 HRA [meaning that the Government thinks some of its provisions may be incompatible with the ECHR], any further derogation Orders in relation to the ECHR, and the legislation establishing the new second chamber itself. In order to avoid the special powers being triggered where no real issue was at stake, legislation could state that the changes made to such legislation or generally to the constitution must be 'significant' or 'of principle' to activate those powers, so that they would not be brought into play by, say, minor consequential amendments to the devolution legislation, or Bills which raised only doubtful claims of incompatibility with the ECHR. The power triggered by a positive finding of the Constitution Committee could be any one of the following: an extended power of delay—say two years; the removal of the application of the Parliament Acts (ie, an absolute veto); the need for special majorities in both Houses; or for a referendum.

Notes

1. The author also argued against the only substantive proposal made by Wakeham on powers: to reduce the Lords' powers of delegated legislation. This proposal now seems to have fallen out of favour and so is not further considered here.

2. In relation to the highly important conventional restraints upon the Lords, discussed above,[182] both the government and Wakeham suggested that the Salisbury Convention should continue to be observed: this is arguably a sensible compromise between the need for an effective check upon government and the necessity for a government of the day to be able to implement, at least in substance, the main points of its manifesto programme, thus ensuring that the basic link between elections and subsequent policy changes remains in place, provided it did not apply to 'constitutional' legislation, as discussed above. But there are some strong objections to the convention.

> [It] grants, in my view, undue weight to the idea of the mandate, something that is both conceptually shaky and inherently majoritarian. The Salisbury doctrine has no place in a democracy that works along more deliberative than majoritarian lines,

---

182   See pp 436–445.

and the upper house should be able to scrutinise vigorously the government's programme in whatever shape it comes.[183]

Anthony King has also recently argued strongly against the Salisbury doctrine.[184]

4. It seems inevitable that if the House of Lords is radically reformed the question of these conventions will be re-opened. The Joint Committee said:

> If the Lords acquired an electoral mandate, then in our view their role as the revising chamber, and their relationship with the Commons, would inevitably be called into question, codified or not. Given the weight of evidence on this point, should any firm proposals come forward to change the composition of the House of Lords, the conventions between the Houses would have to be examined again.[185]

5. The Lords do not often have a key role in relation to manifesto commitments, which at least have been thought through to some extent and formulated after consultation within the party concerned and sometimes more widely, rather their checking function is at its most valuable when government, reacting to political pressures, seek to rush through Parliament ill-considered and short-termist legislation. The Anti-Terrorism Act 2001 is a prime example. Wakeham said:

> it should continue to consider all Government business within a reasonable time. . .and be cautious about challenging the clearly expressed views of the House of Commons on major issues of public policy.[186]

The Joint Committee's view on this was that:

> The continuing operation of the existing conventions in any new constitutional arrangement will be vital in avoiding deadlock between the Houses—which could all too easily become an obstacle to continuing good governance. **We therefore strongly support the continuation of the existing conventions.**[187]

6. In terms of new mechanisms for scrutiny, here again, save for some modest proposals for extensions of the House's Committee system to include new Committees on constitutional matters,[188] devolution, human rights[189] and the scrutiny of treaties, Wakeham had nothing very new to suggest. Its most interesting idea was that 'a mechanism should be developed which would require Commons Ministers to make statements to, and deal with, questions from members of the second chamber',[190] although cautiously again the Commission proposed that this would have to meet off the floor of the House, in order to respect the long-standing convention that members of one

---

183   J Parkinson, 'The House of Lords: A Deliberative Democratic Defence' (2007) *Political Quarterly* 78(3) 374, 381.

184   See *The British Constitution* (2008) at 299–300.

185   HL 265-I; HL 1212-II above, at [61].

186   Wakeham, at [14].

187   First Report, HL 17, HC 171 (2002–03), para 12.

188   See Wakeham Report, Chapter 5.

189   Wakeham suggested that the devolution and human rights committees could be sub-committees of an overarching Constitutional Committee.

190   Wakeham Report, Recommendation 45 (para 8.7).

House do not speak in another.[191] This would significantly enhance ministerial accountability: at present, because of the convention that Cabinet Ministers[192] must be drawn from the Commons, the House of Lords is often able to scrutinise only relatively junior Ministers, who have to answer questions on a very wide area, due to the relatively small number of Ministers who are members of the Lords. As Russell notes, 'the convention barring House of Commons ministers from the House of Lords is highly unusual. In most countries ministers may speak in either chamber, irrespective of whether they are a member of that chamber'.[193] The Hansard Society Commission approved this proposal, remarking that it would allow much greater use to be made of the Lords' expertise, enhancing parliamentary scrutiny of the executive overall.[194]

Prospects for reform[195]

Bogdanor, writing in 2009, surveys the key difficulties in finding an alternative representative basis for the Lords: territory is the obvious one, but very hard to apply in the UK where the English regions have little identity; however, non-democratic reforms of the Lords will not be supported by MPs. There is also the key problem that a more democratic second chamber would undoubtedly be more assertive, making governments reluctant to accept this without limits on its powers. He concludes that democratic reform may be as far away as ever.[196] Other commentators, recognising these difficulties, urge some modest but important reforms as an interim measure:

Editorial Commentary, 'The House of Lords (again)'
(2009) 80(1) *Political Quarterly* 165, 166

The 1999 reform which removed most hereditary peers does look, in retrospect, to be much more important than most people realised at the time. It has created a chamber that is relatively proportional, with no single party in control, and is more confident to challenge the government on controversial policies. It has had many victories, on issues such as detention of terrorist suspects and limitations on trial by jury. In future it would challenge a conservative government just as it challenges Labour. The other problem created by the endless disagreements about ambitious, large-scale reform is that small-scale reforms which could be implemented quickly, and further enhance the present house, tend to be overlooked. For example, the House of Commons Public Administration Committee suggested in 2007 (after the 'cash for honours' controversy) that more extensive powers should be given to the House of Lords Appointments Commission, at least until further reform is reached. In this way we could end the increasingly anomalous practice whereby the prime minister decides how many peers are created and when, and how these are balanced between the parties (a situation that, at least in theory, would allow a prime minister to do away with proportionality and 'pack' the Lords with party supporters). The Commission

---

191   *Ibid*, paras 8.7–8.8.

192   Save for the Lord Chancellor.

193   Russell, n 28 above, p 274.

194   *The Challenge for Parliament: Making Government Accountable* (2001), para 6.15.

195   A number of other issues are raised by the debate over Lords reform, including religious representation and the resources and payment to be devoted to members of the Lords. On grounds of space, these have not been discussed here.

196   Bogdanor, n 13 above, at 160–64.

could also be given a greater role in choosing between nominees put forward by the parties, for example, to ensure gender and ethnic balance. A bigger (but still small) step would be to move from life appointments to a fixed term of office for second chamber members, which would halt the currently spiralling size of the chamber.

Yet another, long overdue, would be to break the link between the peerage and membership of the upper house—making clear that membership is now a job, no longer just an honour.

The time has finally come to remove the hereditaries, a relic of the previous half-reform. But the issue of patronage needs to be tackled too. This means that the Lords Appointment Commission, which should now be put on a statutory basis, should extend its proprietary role in relation to party nominations so that it selects from the names submitted on the basis of clear criteria. This will curb patronage, improve the quality of those sent to the Lords by the parties, and deal with the kind of problems revealed by the recent allegations of peerages being traded for donations and loans.

Goes on that also need to reduce the size of the Lords by introducing retirement and fixed terms of office. And also break the link between the award of a peerage as an honour and being appointed to the second chamber as a Parliamentarian. 'There are many members of the House of Lords who wanted the title but did not want the legislative service; and there are some who claim to want the legislative service, but not the title. The whole issue of party dominations has been contaminated by this confusion.'

Notes
1. The Constitutional Reform and Governance Bill 2009 included clauses that: put an end to the mini-elections for hereditary peers, held when one of their number dies (thus if passed, hereditary peers who die would not be replaced, and they would eventually therefore die out from the House); provided for the House to have powers to expel peers who bring the House into disrepute; provided that Peers who commit certain serious criminal offences or become bankrupt may no longer sit in the House; gave Peers the right to resign from the House. However, these parts of the Bill were lost in the 'wash-up' before the May 2010 Election.
2. In February 2010, the Government promised finally to publish a Bill in draft to put the House of Lords on a substantially elected basis.[197] This did not happen before the 2010 Election. The new Conservative–Liberal Coalition Government promises a wholly or mainly elected House.

FURTHER READING

R Blackburn and A Kennon, *Griffith & Ryle on Parliament: Functions, Practice and Procedures,* 2nd edn (2002)
B Dickson and P Carmichael (eds), *The House of Lords: Its Parliamentary and Judicial Roles* (1999)
D Oliver, *Constitutional Reform in the UK* (2003)
I Richards and D Welfare, *Unfinished Business: Reforming the House of Lords* (1999)

A Kelso, 'Reforming the House of Lords: Navigating Representation, Democracy and Legitimacy at Westminster' (2009) 59(4) Parlt Aff 563

197   Gordon Brown, Speech to the IPPR, 2 February 2010.

CHAPTER 10
PARLIAMENTARY PRIVILEGE

INTRODUCTION

This chapter will consider the privileges of Parliament. The examples used will mainly relate to the House of Commons, but the privileges of the two Houses are generally substantially identical[1]— differences will be pointed out in appropriate places. It will touch on all the main privileges, concentrating on freedom of speech as by far the most important and contentious privilege claimed. Conflict between Parliament and the courts will also be discussed and criticisms of the current state of affairs in this field will be considered. The effect of the 2009 expenses scandal, the Parliamentary Standards Act 2010 and the Kelly Report[2] will be considered in full.

'The sole justification for the present privileges of the House of Commons is that they are essential for the conduct of its business and maintenance of its authority', according to one clerk of the House of Commons. If the constant general purpose has been the maintenance of Parliament's independence, the threats to that independence have come from various quarters: at times from the ordinary courts seeking to enforce the general law of the land, at times from the Crown, at times from other persons or bodies, including the mass media. Sometimes the enemy is within, and then privilege enables the House to deal with members who abuse their office or seek to obstruct its business.[3]

The Joint Committee on Parliamentary Privilege summarised parliamentary privilege thus:

> Parliamentary privilege consists of the rights and immunities which the two Houses of Parliament and their members and officers possess to enable them to carry out their parliamentary functions effectively. Without this protection members would be handicapped in performing their parliamentary duties, and the authority of Parliament itself in confronting the executive and as a forum for expressing the anxieties of citizens would be correspondingly diminished.

As Colin Munro emphasises, parliamentary privilege has a unique status in law; while some parts of it may be found in statute,[4] and some in common law,[5] others are part of the law of Parliament itself:

> Its origin is customary; it is recognised as having the status of law; but it will be found, for the most part, not in statutes or cases, but in parliamentary proceedings. . .Since it is enforced primarily by the Houses themselves, it is defined principally in resolutions of the Houses and rulings by the Speakers. Of course, like any other part of the law, parliamentary privilege is subject to the supremacy of Acts of Parliament. Acts have curtailed the scope of privilege [and]. . .may regulate the exercise of privilege. . .But it is also possible for statute to maintain or extend the scope of privileges. The privileges of freedom of speech and exclusive cognisance of internal proceedings were given a statutory foundation when included as Article 9 of the Bill of Rights: 'That the freedom of speech, and debates or proceedings in

---

1   E May, *Treatise on the Law, Privileges, Proceedings and Usage of Parliament*, 1st edn (1844), p 44, referring to W Hakewill, *Modus Tenendi Parliamentum*, All the privileges which do belong to those of the Commons House of Parliament *a fortiori* do appertain to all the Lords of the Upper House.'

2   *Twelth Report from the Kelly Committee on Standards in Public Life*, Cm 7724 (2009).

3   C Munro, *Studies in Constitutional Law*, 2nd edn (1999), p 216.

4   E.g. the Defamation Act 1996, s 13; Art 9 Bill of Rights 1689, Parliamentary Papers Act 1844.

5   Cases such as *Bradlaugh v Gossett* (1884) 12 QBD 271, as well as numerous cases on the interpretation of Article 9, Bill of Rights.

Parliament, ought not to be impeached or questioned in any court or place out of Parliament.'[6]

Notes

The justification for privilege offered by the clerk of the Commons cited by Munro offers a stringent test: only those matters which are 'essential' for the proper conduct of the business of the House should be claimed as privileges. The Committee on Standards and Privileges has given its own view of the *raison d'être* of parliamentary privileges (in its report on the 'cash for questions affair'). It regards their purpose as 'not to protect individual Members of Parliament but to provide the necessary framework in which the House in its corporate capacity and its Members as individuals can fulfil their responsibilities to the citizens they represent',[7] a definition which also stresses that 'privileges' are not in fact to do with the personal aggrandisement of MPs but simply necessary adjuncts to their role as public servants. Given that one of the fundamental principles of the British Constitution is supposed to be equality before the law, it seems right that those who argue in favour of placing some in a uniquely privileged position should have to adduce compelling evidence that such protection is indeed necessary. It is worth bearing these tests in mind when examining the arguments put forward in cases in which the proper scope of privilege has been contested.

THE 'INTERNAL' PRIVILEGES OF PARLIAMENT

The privileges in general

Many questions of privilege have been relatively un-contentious; those which affect only members of Parliament in their capacity as MPs have been agreed by Parliament and the courts to be under the sole jurisdiction of Parliament. As Coleridge J said in *Stockdale v Hansard* (1839) 9 Ad & El 233:

> . . .that the House should have exclusive jurisdiction to regulate the course of its own proceedings and animadvert upon any conduct there in violation of its rules or derogation from its dignity, stands upon the clearest ground of necessity.

The case of *Bradlaugh v Gossett* (1884) 12 QBD 271 is also instructive; it was summarised in *Rost v Edwards* [1990] 2 WLR 1280.

Rost v Edwards [1990] 2 WLR 1280, 1287

In *Bradlaugh v Gossett* (1884) 12 QBD 271 the Parliamentary Oaths Act of 1866 required Charles Bradlaugh, who had been elected to Northampton as a Member of the House of Commons, to take the oath. The question had arisen whether Mr Bradlaugh was qualified himself to sit by making an affirmation instead of taking the oath. Subsequently, following re-election, he was prevented from taking the oath by order of the House. The sergeant was ordered to exclude him from the House until he undertook not to disturb the proceedings further. Mr Bradlaugh sought a declaration from the courts that the order of the House was ultra vires and also an injunction restraining the Sergeant at Arms from preventing him from entering the House and taking his oath. The court decided against Mr Bradlaugh, taking the

---

6   Munro, n 3 above, at 217.

7   Quoted in D Oliver, 'The Committee on Standards in Public Life: Regulating the Conduct of Members of Parliament' (1995) PA 590, 596.

view that what was in issue was the internal management of the House procedure and therefore the court had no jurisdiction. Lord Coleridge CJ said at p 275:

> What is said or done within the walls of Parliament cannot be inquired into in a court of law. On this point all the judges in the two great cases which exhaust the learning on the subject—*Burdett v Abbott* (1811) 14 East 1, 148 and *Stockdale v Hansard*, 9 Ad & El 1—are agreed, and are emphatic. The jurisdiction of the Houses over their own members, their right to impose discipline within their walls, is absolute and exclusive. To use the words of Lord Ellenborough, 'They would sink into utter contempt and inefficiency without it'.

> The House of Commons is not subject to the control of. . .[the] courts in its administration of that part of the statute law which has relation to its own internal proceedings. . .Even if that interpretation should be erroneous, [the] court has no power to interfere with it, directly or indirectly (at 278, 286).

Note
As Munro notes, whilst disputed elections (an area previously falling within the House's right to regulate its own proceedings) are now determined by High Court judges, the 'form' of privilege is preserved, as their findings are merely certified to the Speaker for him to act as he thinks fit; in fact the findings of the court are invariably complied with.[8] Despite this erosion of privilege in the area of elections, the question of whether a candidate may take his seat having been clearly elected still falls to be determined solely by the House,[9] as recent examples make clear.

C Munro, *Studies in Constitutional Law*, 2nd edn (1999), pp 227 et seq

The House of Commons may also expel a member for grounds other than disqualification, if it considers him unfit to continue in that capacity. A sufficient cause would be conviction of a criminal offence involving turpitude. . .In 1947 when Garry Allighan was expelled, it was his gross contempt of the House which caused it. He had made unsubstantiated allegations that details of confidential party meetings, held within the precincts of Parliament, were being revealed by members to journalists for money or while under the influence of drink. He was himself receiving payments for doing just that, and had lied to the Committee of Privileges.

It is interesting to consider that, if the Government were to use its majority in the House to vote to expel all members who opposed it, no objection could be heard by the courts in this country. It is usually said in response to this that there is nothing to prevent expelled members, if not disqualified from standing, from being re-elected, as John Wilkes was by the electors of Middlesex in the eighteenth century. That is true, but the real protection against abuse lies in conventional self-restraint. The calling of an election is itself at the wish of a Commons majority, for another aspect of privilege is the House's right to determine when casual vacancies will be filled. When a vacancy arises through a member's death, expulsion or disqualification, it is for the House to resolve that a writ be issued for the holding of a by-election.

---

8   Munro, n 3 above, at 227.

9   *Ibid.*

Exclusive cognisance of internal affairs
Each House collectively claims the right to control its own proceedings and to regulate its internal affairs and whatever takes place within its walls. The claim was partly protected by the provision in the Bill of Rights to the effect that 'the freedom of speech and debates or proceedings in Parliament ought not to be impeached or questioned in any court or place out of Parliament', and so this aspect of privilege is linked to the freedom of speech. It is also linked to the privilege concerning composition, for the Houses regard their membership as their own affair.

The claim has been accepted by the courts, at least provided they can agree that 'internal concerns' are involved. 'Whatever is done within the walls of either assembly must pass without question in any other place', said Lord Denman in *Stockdale v Hansard* [at 114]. In *Bradlaugh v Gossett*, Stephen J observed that 'the House of Commons is not a court of justice, but the effect of its privilege to regulate its own internal concerns practically invests it with a judicial character', and held that 'we must presume that it discharges this function properly and with due regard to the laws, in the making of which it has so great a share' [at 285]. Indeed, the doctrines upon which claims to privilege are based, and upon which the jurisdiction of courts is denied or restricted have much in common with those which are expressed as the sovereignty of Parliament. When, for example, the validity of an Act of Parliament is challenged on the ground of alleged defects of parliamentary procedure, and the courts refuse to investigate, their refusal might be justified on grounds of sovereignty or privilege. In *British Railways Board v Pickin* [1974] 1 All ER 609. . .the sovereignty aspect was emphasised, but privilege was also adduced as a justification in the speeches of Lord Simon of Glaisdale and Lord Morris of Borth-y-Gest. . .

However, if matters happen 'within the walls', but are unconnected with the business of Parliament, the ordinary courts may be entitled to assume jurisdiction without being in breach of privilege, or at least are allowed to. 'I know of no authority for the proposition that an ordinary crime committed in the House of Commons would be withdrawn from the ordinary course of criminal justice', said Stephen J in *Bradlaugh v Gossett* [at 283]. In practice it has been left to the ordinary authorities and courts to deal with incidents such as the killing of the Prime Minister by a madman in the lobby of the House of Commons (in 1812) and the projection of CS gas into the chamber by a protester in the public gallery (in 1970).

Sometimes there would be concurrent jurisdiction, as where one member assaults another in the course of proceedings. . .

Notes
1. It is hard to see why the House requires its ability to allow or disallow Members at its pleasure. Apart from the hypothetical (but still disturbing) possibility that the House *could* resolve, quite legally, to expel all Opposition MPs, a more realistic concern relates to its power to determine when vacancies (caused by death or bankruptcy) should be filled. Complaints have been directed at government dilatoriness in moving writs for by-elections at which they expect to be defeated, and it is not fanciful to suggest that a Government with a majority of only one could procure a delay in a by-election which could wipe out its majority so that the election only took place after a crucial Commons vote which was expected to be very close. There seems to be no reason why the law should not provide that all by-elections must take place within a fixed time of a seat becoming vacant.

2. A case which, as Munro puts it,[10] took a 'generous' view of the scope of the House's internal affairs was *R v Graham-Campbell ex parte Herbert* [1935] 1 KB 594, in which the High Court considered whether a magistrate had been right in finding that he lacked the jurisdiction to prosecute Members for selling alcohol without a licence in the Members' Bar.

R v Graham-Campbell ex parte Herbert [1935] 1 KB 594, 602

Lord Hewart CJ: Here, as it seems to me, the magistrate was entitled to say, on the materials before him, that in the matters complained of the House of Commons was acting collectively in a matter which fell within the area of the internal affairs of the House, and, that being so, any tribunal might well feel, on the authorities, an invincible reluctance to interfere. To take the opposite course might conceivably be, in proceedings of a somewhat different character from these, after the various stages of those proceedings had been passed, to make the House of Lords the arbiter of the privileges of the House of Commons.

Notes
1. This decision cannot be justified by arguing that the privilege found here to exist, of flouting the licensing laws,[11] was necessary to allow the House to carry on its business properly. (Such a notion could, for example, justifiably be used to protect Members from criminal liability incurred by speeches or questions in the House.) Even if some notion of protecting the dignity of Parliament is invoked, it is hard to see how that is protected by shielding Members from the ordinary criminal law in a matter as unrelated to their constitutional activities as illegal drinking.
2. It seems almost certain that if more serious offences were committed, the House would hand over the matter to the courts, for as Stanley de Smith comments, its penal powers 'are inadequate to deal with ordinary crime';[12] in any event Parliament would be anxious to avoid the unfavourable publicity that would undoubtedly ensue from an attempt to protect such an offender through an assertion of immunity by virtue of privilege. In the unlikely event of such an assertion being made by the Commons, the outcome must be in doubt.
3. The Joint Committee on Parliamentary Privilege has made a series of recommendations on the possible immunity of Members from the ordinary criminal law. It recommended that MPs should be included within the scope of future legislation on bribery[13] a proposal energetically backed by the Wicks Report,[14] supported by the Government,[15] and enacted in the Bribery Act 2010.[16] The Joint Committee also made more general recommendations:

> Each House of Parliament should continue to exercise control over its own affairs. Statute should provide that the privilege of each House to manage its internal affairs within its precincts applies only to activities directly and closely relating to proceedings in Parliament.

10 See n 3 above, p 230.

11 Note that Avory J also found that the Licensing Acts were not intended to apply to Parliament.

12 SA de Smith, *Constitutional and Administrative Law,* 6th edn (1994), p 325.

13 For the Government's proposals, see Cm 4759 (2000).

14 Wicks Committee, Sixth Report, Cm 4557–1 (2000), paras 3.8–3.11.

15 In evidence to the Wicks Committee, see *ibid,* para 3.10.

16 See further below at 529.

It should also be made clear in statute that every law applies to Parliament unless Parliament has been expressly excluded. The precincts of Parliament should not be a statute-free zone.[17]

Notes

1. The reasoning and recommendations of the Joint Committee show a clear attempt to pare away from the ambit of privilege those areas of parliamentary activity which do not require protection. It should be remembered that a basic principle of the Diceyan version of the Rule of Law is equality before the law; as the Joint Committee notes, exempting law-makers from the laws they make which bind others appears a particularly unfortunate derogation from this principle and not one which can be justified by arguments as to the sovereignty and efficacy of the legislature.

2. The relationship between parliamentary privilege and police powers was raised by the dramatic events surrounding Damian Green in November 2008, discussed here by Bradley and Ewing:

Mr Green, the Opposition front bench spokesman on Home Office affairs, was the subject of action taken after the Cabinet Office had asked the Metropolitan Police to investigate the repeated leaking of secret Home Office papers to the press. The request was said to be based on security implications, and the police were wrongly told that the leaks had already caused substantial injury to national security. Following the arrest of Christopher Galley, a civil servant in the Home Office, Mr Green was arrested by a police team that included anti-terrorist officers; his home and constituency office were searched and papers removed under a search warrant; and he was charged with the little-known offence at common law of conspiracy to commit misconduct in public office and with aiding and abetting such misconduct. His office at Westminster was searched by the police, acting without a warrant, and all his parliamentary papers were removed.

This sensational seizure was possible because the police chose to act on the basis of a purported consent that was given by an official of the House of Commons, the Serjeant at Arms. . . Neither the Speaker of the House (Michael Martin MP) nor the Clerk of the House of Commons was informed or asked to consent, and it is doubtful whether any consent given could have extended to search and removal of the MP's files. The Speaker promptly told the House that a warrant would in future always be required and that the Speaker must be notified before it was executed. The sequence of events meant that the issue of whether, given the historic privileges of Parliament, a warrant for search and seizure of Mr Green's papers would have been lawful did not come before a court. There followed a period of deadlock. The police attempted to proceed with the investigation, despite the privilege difficulties, and the government successfully prevented the Standards and Privileges Committee of the Commons from considering the affair.

Some months later, the situation eased when the Crown Prosecution Service decided that neither the civil servant nor Mr Green would be subject to criminal proceedings. By then, the Home Affairs Committee of the Commons had taken evidence relating to the police conduct, and found that the Cabinet Office's request to the police had exaggerated the security implications. Another Commons committee concluded that to invoke the

---

17   HLP 43–41 (1998–99), paras 19 and 20.

offence of misconduct in public office for leaking official secrets would in general, and apart from any financial corruption, be contrary to the intention of Parliament when the Official Secrets Act 1989 removed the protection of the criminal law from many categories of official papers (10th Report of the House of Commons Public Administration Committee, Leaks and Whistleblowing in Whitehall (HC 83, 2008–09) After the forced retirement of Speaker Martin over the affair of MPs' expenses (see below), the House appointed an ad hoc select committee to examine these events from the viewpoint of parliamentary privilege.[18]

Note

That committee is the Committee on Issue of Privilege (Police Searches on Parliamentary Estate) www.parliament.uk/parliamentary_committees/policesearches.cfm. At the time of writing, the Committee has published details of evidence it has taken, but not yet its report.

Members' financial interests

The problem of Members' outside interests

One further, important aspect of the Commons' internal regulatory rules lies in the regulations governing Members' financial interests. As Alan Doig notes, this issue has implications which go well beyond mere internal self-regulation.

> It is generally accepted, and certainly among MPs, that MPs may have other occupations and sources of income in addition to their parliamentary salary. It is also not in dispute that in representing interests and opinions, MPs can help bridge the gap between government and organisations affected by its activities. Government policy-making and decision-taking need a continuing bilateral relationship of information, cooperation and mutual understanding. . . . Such organisations, ranging from multinationals like ICI or British Airways to representative organisations like the National Farmers' Union or the Royal College of Nursing will have offices and staff to monitor, liaise with and report back on the decision-making processes of Whitehall and Westminster. Those without a permanent governmental relations office can hire professional lobbyists. Whatever the means, however, the purpose is to get that interest's message to the policymakers and the legislators.
>
> Concern about the activities of interests and of professional lobbyists and the involvement of MPs with those activities has been growing. . .in representing the views of interests, what [MPs] say and do may be felt to be compromised because they are being paid to sell the interest's views to colleagues, ministers and civil servants, whether or not they themselves are convinced of the intrinsic value of that interest's case.[19]

---

18   Bradley and Ewing, *Constitutional and Administrative Law,* 14th edn (2007), 'Update'—August 2009. For further details see HC Debs, col. 2, 3 December 2008 and col 255, 8 December 2008.

19   A Doig, 'Full circle or dead end? What next for the Select Committee on Members' Interests?' (1994) 47(3) Parlt Aff 355, 356.

N Allen, 'Voices from the shop floor: MPs and the domestic effects of ethics reforms' (2009) 62(1) *Parliamentary Affairs* 88, 89

Writing in the early 1990s, one commentator concluded that: 'The House of Commons is fast becoming a market-place with the politician as the commodity. Instead of representing the public and their constituents, MPs are increasingly hiring themselves out to the business world' [M. Hollingsworth, *MPs for Hire: The Secret World of Political Lobbying*, (1991), p. 1]. Some behaviour was especially egregious. In July 1994, the Sunday Times revealed that two Conservative MPs, Graham Riddick and David Tredinnick, had been prepared to accept money for tabling parliamentary questions in a 'cash for questions' sting. Three months later, the Guardian alleged that the lobbyist Ian Greer had paid thousands of pounds to two Conservative MPs, Tim Smith and Neil Hamilton, for tabling parliamentary questions on behalf of Mohamed Al Fayed, the owner of Harrods. The allegations related to a period in the 1980s when Smith and Hamilton had been backbench MPs, but both men were now junior ministers. Smith resigned immediately. Hamilton denied he had done anything wrong but was sacked.

More significantly, this second 'cash for questions' scandal prompted the then prime minister John Major to appoint a Committee on Standards in Public Life (the Nolan Committee) to examine the arrangements for maintaining standards of conduct among all holders of public office, including MPs. In turn, the Committee's First Report, published in May 1995 [Cm 2850 (1995)] prompted the House of Commons to examine its arrangements for regulating MPs' conduct. In response, the House instituted a Code of Conduct, new rules relating to MPs' outside interests and two new in-house bodies to police the rules, a Parliamentary Commissioner for Standards and a Select Committee on Standards and Privileges. Rules were better defined, enforcement was strengthened and a new, more pro-active regulatory regime was established.

Note

The Code of Conduct recommended by Nolan was drafted by the new Committee on Standards and Privileges, which reported in July 1996.[20] Its proposed draft of the Code was accepted by the House after a short debate without a division.[21] The Code itself, in line with Nolan's recommendation that it amount to a statement of broad principle accompanied by detailed guidance, is relatively brief —and accompanied by a much more lengthy *Guide to the Rules relating to the Conduct of Members*, which also includes the text of all relevant House resolutions. It has been amended on a number of occasions following a series of reports both by the Committee on Standards in Public Life[22] and the Committee on Standards and Privileges. It has been amended since then, in 2002 and most recently in February 2009, in response to a report from the Standards and Privileges Committee,[23] which was partly concerned with ending the dual reporting that had been necessary since the Political Parties, Elections and Referendums Act 2000 (PPERA) had required reporting of certain MPs' interests to the Electoral

---

20   Third Report, HC 604 (1995–96).

21   HC Deb cols 392–407 (24 July 1996).

22   In two main reports, the first known as the Neill Report after its then Chair: Sixth Report, Vol 1, Cm 4557–1 (2000); the second known as the Wicks Report under Lord Wicks: Eighth Report, Cm 5663 (2002).

23   *Dual Reporting and Revised Guide to the Rules* 4th Report (2008–09), HC 208 at [4].

Commission.[24] As a result, it introduced a new category of interests—loans that had previously been registerable under PPERA—and amended the requirements under some of the other categories of registerable interests, as well as adding a new category 12 of interests, namely employment of family members. Specific sections of the Guide that deal with the advocacy rule, the Register of Members' interests and the procedure to be used for investigating alleged infringements of the Rules are quoted below in the relevant sections of this chapter. The Code itself is as follows:

The Code of Conduct for Members of Parliament prepared pursuant to the Resolution of the House of 19 July 1995

I. Purpose of the Code

The purpose of the Code of Conduct is to assist Members in the discharge of their obligations to the House, their constituents and the public at large by:

(a) Providing guidance on the standards of conduct expected of Members in discharging their parliamentary and public duties, and in so doing

(b) Providing the openness and accountability necessary to reinforce public confidence in the way in which Members perform those duties.

II. Scope of the Code

2. The Code applies to Members in all aspects of their public life. It does not seek to regulate what Members do in their purely private and personal lives.

. . .

III. Public duty

4. By virtue of the oath, or affirmation, of allegiance taken by all Members when they are elected to the House, Members have a duty to be faithful and bear true allegiance to Her Majesty the Queen, her heirs and successors, according to law.

5. Members have a duty to uphold the law, including the general law against discrimination, and to act on all occasions in accordance with the public trust placed in them.

6. Members have a general duty to act in the interests of the nation as a whole; and a special duty to their constituents.

IV. Personal conduct

7. In carrying out their parliamentary and public duties, Members will be expected to observe the following general principles of conduct identified by the Committee on Standards in Public Life in its First Report as applying to holders of public office. These principles will be taken into consideration when any complaint is received of breaches of the provisions in other sections of the Code.

'Selflessness

Holders of public office should take decisions solely in terms of the public interest. They should not do so in order to gain financial or other material benefits for themselves, their family, or their friends.

---

24 As the Committee explained: An unintended consequence of the PERPA was to require Members to register certain interests both with the Registrar of Members' Interests and with the newly formed Electoral Commission. This led to confusion and duplication, with Members facing criticism or sanctions for registering an interest with one body but not with the other. This is turn created pressure to streamline procedures, cutting out the duplication without prejudicing transparency. In response to that pressure, provision was included in section 59 of the Electoral Administration Act 2006 for donations to be reported to the Registrar of Members' Interests only. This provision could commence only once the Electoral Commission had signalled that it was satisfied that the House's arrangements would provide it with the information it required. A corresponding provision to align reporting requirements for loans is to be found at para 16 of Sched 7A of PPERA, which was inserted by the Electoral Administration Act.

Integrity
Holders of public office should not place themselves under any financial or other obligation to outside individuals or organisations that might influence them in the performance of their official duties.

Objectivity
In carrying out public business, including making public appointments, awarding contracts, or recommending individuals for rewards and benefits, holders of public office should make choices on merit.

Accountability
Holders of public office are accountable for their decisions and actions to the public and must submit themselves to whatever scrutiny is appropriate to their office.

Openness
Holders of public office should be as open as possible about all the decisions and actions that they take. They should give reasons for their decisions and restrict information only when the wider public interest clearly demands.

Honesty
Holders of public office have a duty to declare any private interests relating to their public duties and to take steps to resolve any conflicts arising in a way that protects the public interest.

Leadership
Holders of public office should promote and support these principles by leadership and example.'

V. Rules of Conduct

8. Members are expected in particular to observe the following rules and associated Resolutions of the House.

9. Members shall base their conduct on a consideration of the public interest, avoid conflict between personal interest and the public interest and resolve any conflict between the two, at once, and in favour of the public interest.

10. No Member shall act as a paid advocate in any proceeding of the House.

11. The acceptance by a Member of a bribe to influence his or her conduct as a Member, including any fee, compensation or reward in connection with the promotion of, or opposition to, any Bill, Motion, or other matter submitted, or intended to be submitted to the House, or to any Committee of the House, is contrary to the law of Parliament.

12. In any activities with, or on behalf of, an organisation with which a Member has a financial relationship, including activities which may not be a matter of public record such as informal meetings and functions, he or she must always bear in mind the need to be open and frank with Ministers, Members and officials.

13. Members must bear in mind that information which they receive in confidence in the course of their parliamentary duties should be used only in connection with those duties, and that such information must never be used for the purpose of financial gain.

14. Members shall at all times ensure that their use of expenses, allowances, facilities and services provided from the public purse is strictly in accordance with the rules laid down on these matters, and that they observe any limits placed by the House on the use of such expenses, allowances, facilities and services.

15. Members shall at all times conduct themselves in a manner which will tend to maintain and strengthen the public's trust and confidence in the integrity of Parliament and never undertake any action which would bring the House of Commons, or its Members generally, into disrepute.

VI. Registration and Declaration of Interests

16. Members shall fulfil conscientiously the requirements of the House in respect of the registration of interests in the Register of Members' Interests and shall always draw attention to any relevant interest in any proceeding of the House or its Committees, or in any communications with Ministers, Government Departments or Executive Agencies.

VII. Duties in respect of the Parliamentary Commissioner for Standards and the Committee on Standards and Privileges

17. The application of this Code shall be a matter for the House of Commons, and for the Committee on Standards and Privileges and the Parliamentary Commissioner for Standards acting in accordance with Standing Orders Nos 149 and 150 respectively.

18. Members shall cooperate, at all stages, with any investigation into their conduct by or under the authority of the House.

19. No Member shall lobby a member of the Committee on Standards and Privileges in a manner calculated or intended to influence their consideration of a complaint of a breach of this Code.

We now turn to the two main areas of controversy: first, employment of Members by outside bodies and its influence on their conduct; second, the issue of disclosure of outside interests. These issues will be dealt with in turn.

Parliamentary consultancies: permissibility, payment for advocacy

Nolan first of all recommended that 'Members should remain free to have paid employment unrelated to their role as MPs'[25]—a freedom which remains today —and then went on to consider the thorny issue of Members entering into agreements with and receiving payment not from ordinary employment, such as law or journalism, but as part of consultancy agreements made with lobbying firms (what Nolan referred to as 'multi-client consultancies') and campaigning groups, which were clearly related to their activities in Parliament.

First Report of the Committee on Standards in Public Life, Cm 2850 (1995)

We would consider it thoroughly unsatisfactory, possibly to the extent of being a contempt of Parliament, if a Member of Parliament, even if not strictly bound by an agreement with a client to pursue a particular interest in Parliament, was to pursue that interest solely or principally because payment, in cash or kind, was being made. A Member who believes in a cause should be prepared to promote it without payment; equally a Member ought not to pursue a cause more forcefully than might otherwise have been the case as a result of a financial interest. We believe that such action would breach the spirit if not the letter of the 1947 resolution, and we cannot be confident that all Members are as scrupulous in this respect as some have claimed to be.[26]

---

25   See Cm 2850 (1995) hereafter 'Nolan Report', para 21.

26   In the event, Nolan recommended against a general advocacy ban (paras 51–55) but only on multi-client consultancies.

Second Report from the Select Committee on Standards in Public Life, HC 816 (1994–95) (extracts)

11. The main source of public anxiety, as identified by Nolan, is the notion that influence, whether real or imagined, can be bought and sold through Members. This suggests that any remedial action, rather than seeking to draw a line of legitimacy between different types of outside body with which Members should or should not be allowed to have paid relationships, ought to concentrate on defining as closely as possible those actions by Members which, because they give rise to suspicions about the exercise—or attempted exercise—of improper influence, need to be prohibited. . .

12. We propose that the rules of the House should now distinguish between paid advocacy in Parliament (unacceptable for the reasons outlined above) and paid advice (acceptable provided it is properly registered and declared).

Note

The recommendations of the Committee in this area, specifically the addendum to the 1947 Resolution, were accepted by the House on 6 November 1995,[27] amended on 14 May 2002 and now appear in the Rules of the House. The Guide to the Rules deals with these matters as follows.

Guide to the Rules Relating to the Conduct of Members (2009)

3. Lobbying for reward or consideration

53. On 6th November 1995 the House agreed to the following Resolution relating to paid advocacy.

It is inconsistent with the dignity of the House, with the duty of a Member to his constituents, and with the maintenance of the privilege of freedom of speech, for any Member of this House to enter into any contractual agreement with an outside body, controlling or limiting the Member's complete independence and freedom of action in Parliament or stipulating that he shall act in any way as the representative of such outside body in regard to any matters to be transacted in Parliament; the duty of a Member being to his constituents and to the country as a whole, rather than to any particular section thereof: and that in particular no Members of the House shall, in consideration of any remuneration, fee, payment, or reward or benefit in kind, direct or indirect, which the Member or any member of his or her family has received is receiving or expects to receive—

(i) advocate or initiate any cause or matter on behalf of any outside body or individual, or
(ii) urge any other Member of either House of Parliament, including Ministers, to do so,

by means of any speech, Question, Motion, introduction of a Bill or Amendment to a Motion or a Bill or any approach, whether oral or in writing, to Ministers or servants of the Crown.

(Resolution of the House of 15th July 1947, amended on 6th November 1995 and on 14th May 2002)

27   HC Deb cols 659–61.

90. This Resolution prohibits paid advocacy. It is wholly incompatible with the advocacy rule that any Member should take payment for speaking in the House. Nor may a Member, for payment, vote, ask a Parliamentary Question, table a Motion, introduce a Bill or table or move an Amendment to a Motion or Bill or urge colleagues or Ministers to do so.

91. The Resolution does not prevent a Member from holding a remunerated outside interest as a director, consultant, or adviser, or in any other capacity, whether or not such interests are related to membership of the House. Nor does it prevent a Member from being sponsored by a trade union or any other organisation, or holding any other registerable interest, or from receiving hospitality in the course of his or her parliamentary duties whether in the United Kingdom or abroad. However, if a financial interest is required to be registered in the Register of Members' Financial Interests, or declared in debate, it falls within the scope of the ban on lobbying for reward or consideration.

92. The Resolution in its current form extends and reinforces an earlier Resolution of the House in 1947 that a Member may not enter into any contractual arrangement which fetters the Member's complete independence in Parliament by any undertaking to press some particular point of view on behalf of an outside interest. Nor, by virtue of the same Resolution, may an outside body (or person) use any contractual arrangement with a Member of Parliament as an instrument by which it controls, or seeks to control, his or her conduct in Parliament, or to punish that Member for any parliamentary action.

93. The rule regarding lobbying for reward or consideration applies equally in the case of benefits received by family members by blood or by marriage or a relationship equivalent to marriage.

94. In addition to the requirements of the ban on lobbying for reward or consideration, Members should also bear in mind the long established convention that interests which are wholly personal and particular to the Member, and which may arise from a profession or occupation outside the House, ought not to be pursued by the Member in proceedings in Parliament.

Guidelines on the application of the ban on lobbying for reward or consideration
. . .
96. The Committee on Standards and Privileges has provided the following *Guidelines to assist Members in applying the rule:*

- **Parliamentary proceedings**: When a Member is taking part in any parliamentary proceeding or making any approach to a Minister or servant of the Crown, advocacy is prohibited which seeks to confer benefit exclusively upon a body (or individual) outside Parliament, from which the Member has received, is receiving, or expects to receive a financial benefit, or upon any registrable client of such a body (or individual). Otherwise a Member may speak freely on matters which relate to the affairs and interests of a body (or individual) from which he or she receives a financial benefit, provided the benefit is properly registered and declared.
- **Constituency interests**: Irrespective of any relevant interest which the Member is required to register or declare, he or she may pursue any constituency interest in any proceeding of the House or any approach to a Minister or servant of the Crown, except that:
  - where the Member has a financial relationship with a company in the Member's constituency the guidelines above relating to parliamentary proceedings shall apply;

— where the Member is an adviser to a trade association, or to a professional (or other representative) body, the Member should avoid using a constituency interest as the means by which to raise any matter which the Member would otherwise be unable to pursue.

97. The Committee on Standards and Privileges has made it clear that it would regard it as a very serious breach of the rules if a Member failed to register or declare an interest which was relevant to a proceeding he or she had initiated. Similar considerations would apply in the case of approaches to Ministers and others.

[Note: 'Initiating a parliamentary proceeding' includes: presenting a Bill; presenting a Petition; tabling and asking a Parliamentary Question; asking a supplementary question to one's own Question; initiating, or seeking to initiate an adjournment (or other) debate; tabling or moving any Motion (e.g. an 'Early Day Motion', a Motion for leave to introduce a Bill under the 'Ten Minutes Rule' or a Motion 'blocking' a Private Bill; tabling or moving an Amendment to a Bill; proposing a draft Report, or moving an Amendment to a draft Report, in a Select Committee; giving any written notice, or adding a name to such notice, or making an application for and introducing a daily adjournment debate, or an emergency debate. A similar consideration applies in the case of approaches to ministers or civil servants.]

100. **The financial interests of Members are extremely varied, as the Register demonstrates. Each Member will need to apply the rule and the Guidelines to his or her particular circumstances. When in doubt, Members will be able to seek the advice of the Registrar, the Commissioner, or the Committee on Standards and Privileges.**

However, some illustrative examples of the application of the Guidelines may be of value —

(a) A Member who is director of a company may not seek particular preference for that company (e.g. tax relief, subsidies, restriction of competition) in any proceeding of the House or any approach to Ministers or officials.

(b) In the case of trade associations, staff associations, professional bodies, charities (or any similar representative organisation):

(ii) Membership alone of any representative organisation does not entail any restrictions under the rule.

(iii) A Member who is, for example, a remunerated adviser:

— may not advocate measures for the exclusive benefit of that organisation; nor speak or act in support of a campaign exclusively for the benefit of the representative organisation or its membership (e.g. a campaign for special tax relief, or for enhanced pay and numbers);

— may speak or act in support of a campaign which is of particular interest to the representative organisation (e.g. in the case of an animal welfare organisation, a campaign to prohibit the importation of animal fur, or prohibit blood sports; in the case of a charity for cancer research, a campaign for the prohibition of smoking).

Note

This reform was probably the most important change to the rules of the House resulting from the Nolan Report. As noted above, it was changed in May 2002[28] by a resolution of the House approving the Ninth Report of the Committee on Standards and Privileges, which included a draft new Code of Conduct and Guide.[29] Instead of drawing a distinction between *initiating* a parliamentary proceeding and simply *participating* in a debate started by others, the rule for taking part in any proceedings in the House or approach to a Minister or civil servant, as seen above, is that:

> advocacy is prohibited which seeks to confer benefit exclusively upon a body (or individual) outside Parliament, from which the Member has received, is receiving, or expects to receive a pecuniary benefit, or upon any registrable client of such a body (or individual). Otherwise a Member may speak freely on matters which relate to the affairs and interests of a body (or individual) from which he or she receives a pecuniary benefit, provided the benefit is properly registered and declared (Guide to the Rules, above).

Disclosure of interests

The detail of the requirements on MPs to disclose interests is laid down in the Code of Conduct together with the Guide to the Rules Relating to the Conduct of Members. This covers the types of interests that must be registered; the means by which disclosure must be made in the Register; the obligation to disclose interests orally and by notice during parliamentary proceedings; the special rules relating to parliamentary consultancy agreements; guidance on all the above.

Guide to the Rules Relating to the Conduct of Members, as approved by Parliament on 14 May 2002 [30]

. . .

6. The House has two distinct but overlapping and interdependent mechanisms for the disclosure of the personal financial interests of its Members: registration of interests in a Register which is open for public inspection; and declaration of interest in the course of debate in the House and in other contexts.

7. The main purpose of the Register is to give public notification on a continuous basis of those financial interests held by Members which might be thought to influence their parliamentary conduct or actions.

8. The main purpose of declaration of interest is to ensure that Members of the House and the public are made aware, at the appropriate time when a Member is making a speech in the House or in Committee or participating in any other proceedings of the House, of any past, present or expected future financial interest, direct or indirect, which might reasonably be thought by others to be relevant to those proceedings.

---

28 See: Committee on Standards in Public Life, Sixth Report, Vol 1, Cm 4557-I (2000), summarised in A Doig, 'Sleaze: Picking up the Threads or 'Back to Basics' Scandals?' (2001) 54 Parlt Aff 360, 370; Committee on Standards and Privileges, Fifth Report, HC 267 (2000–01). For the debate approving the motion see HC Deb cols 730 *et seq* (14 May 2002).

29 HC 763 (2001–02).

30 For commentary on the interpretation of the latest changes to the rules see: Committee on Standards and Privileges, *Dual Reporting and Revised Guide to the Rules* 4th Report (2008–09), HC 208.

1. Registration of Members' Financial Interests

Rules of the House

> 'Every Member of the House of Commons shall furnish to a Registrar of Members' Financial Interests such particulars of his registrable interests as shall be required, and shall notify to the Registrar any alterations which may occur therein, and the Registrar shall cause these particulars to be entered in a Register of Members' Interests which shall be available for inspection by the public.'
> *(Resolution of the House of 22 May 1974, amended on 9 February 2009)*
>
> 'For the purposes of the Resolution of the House of 22 May 1974 in relation of disclosure of interests in any proceeding of the House or its Committees, any interest declared in a copy of the Register of Members' Financial Interests shall be regarded as sufficient disclosure for the purpose of taking part in any division of the House or in any of its Committees.'
> *(Part of the Resolution of the House of 12 June 1975, amended on 9 February 2009)*

Duties of Members in respect of registration

14. Any Member who has a registrable interest which has not at the time been registered, shall not undertake any action, speech or proceeding of the House (except voting) to which the registration would be relevant until he or she has notified the Commissioner of that interest.

15. Members are responsible for making a full disclosure of their interests, and if they have relevant interests which do not fall clearly into one or other of the specified categories, they are nonetheless expected to register them, normally under Category 11.

16. [This para sets out varying minimum thresholds below which interests are not registrable except in Categories 1, 2 and 3.]

The Categories of Registrable Interest
[The Code then sets out 12 categories of interests:]

1   renumerated directorships;

2   remunerated employment;

3   consultancies providing service as an MP;

4   sponsorships or any other form of financial or material support including from trade unions and trade associations;

5   gifts, benefits and hospitality;

6   overseas visits related to MP's status;

7   overseas benefits and gifts;

8   land/property other than a home;

9   shareholdings greater than a specified value (over 15% of the issued share capital of the company or greater in value than the current MPs salary);

10 loans and credit arrangements that fall within Schedule 7 of the Political Parties, Elections and Referendums Act 2000 (PPERA) as amended by the Electoral Administration Act 2006 [loans over £1,500 must be entered]. In relation to all loans

of over £1,500, members must check that they come from a 'permissible source'— essentially from a UK-based individual, company or organisation;

11   other interests not falling within one of the other categories, but which fall within the main purpose of register namely 'financial interests or other material benefits. . . which might reasonably be thought by others to influence his or her actions, speeches, or votes in Parliament, or actions taken in his or her capacity as a Member of Parliament,' (see above); this will generally mean that non-remunerative interests do not have to be registered unless 'a Member considers that an unremunerated interest which the Member holds might be thought by others to influence his or her actions in a similar manner to a remunerated interest'.

12   Family members employed and remunerated through parliamentary allowances.

[All the above categories are subject to detailed rules and exceptions.]

2. Declaration of Members' Interests
RULES OF THE HOUSE

> 'In any debate or proceeding of the House or its Committees or transactions or communications which a Member may have with other Members or with Ministers or servants of the Crown, he shall disclose any relevant pecuniary interest or benefit of whatever nature, whether direct or indirect, that he may have had, may have or may be expecting to have.'
> (*Resolution of the House of 22 May 1974*)
>
> 'For the purposes of the Resolution of the House of 22 May 1974 in relation to disclosure of interests in any proceeding of the House or its Committees,
>
> (i) Any interest declared in a copy of the Register of Members' Financial Interests shall be regarded as sufficient disclosure for the purpose of taking part in any division of the House or in any of its Committees.
> (ii) The term "proceeding" shall be deemed not to include the asking of a supplementary question.'
> . . .

37. In 1974 the House replaced a long standing convention with a rule that any relevant pecuniary interest or benefit of whatever nature, whether direct or indirect, should be declared in debate, or other proceeding. The same rule places a duty on Members to disclose to Ministers, or servants of the Crown, all relevant interests. The term 'servants of the Crown' should be interpreted as applying to the staff of executive agencies as well as to all staff employed in government departments.

Note

Two new categories of interest have been added since 2002, namely, loans of over £1,500 and details of the employment of family members to work on parliamentary business, reflecting increasing public concern over these areas.[31]

---

31   As for example in relation to the employment by the former leader of the Conservative Party, Iain Duncan Smith of his wife as his diary secretary, which was investigated in 2003. See Standards and Privileges Committee, *Employment of Family Members through the Staffing Allowance*, 7th Report (2008–09) HC 436.

Agreements for the provision of services

Such agreements, whereby Members enter into a contract to provide parliamentary assistance to a particular firm were seen as requiring particular transparency, since it is such agreements that are thought to be most likely to influence Members in their actions as MPs. Again, the new rules approved by the resolution of 14 May 2002 had the effect of relaxing the old rules significantly so that agreements do not need to be registered if the remuneration gained from them is seen as *de minimis*—specifically, no more than 1 per cent of the current parliamentary salary.

Guide to the Rules Relating to the Conduct of Members

Agreements for the provision of services

> 'Any Member proposing to enter into an agreement which involves the provision of services in his capacity as a Member of Parliament shall conclude such an agreement only if it conforms to the Resolution of the House of 6th November 1995 relating to Conduct of Members; and a full copy of any such agreement including the fees or benefits payable in bands of: up to £5,000, £5,001–£10,000, and thereafter in bands of £5,000, shall be deposited with the Parliamentary Commissioner for Standards at the same time as it is registered in the Register of Members' Financial Interests and made available for inspection and reproduction by the public.
> [Existing agreements also to be placed in such form by 31 March 1996.]
>   Provided that the requirement to deposit a copy of an agreement with the Commissioner shall not apply—
>
> (a) if the fees or benefits payable do not exceed one per cent of the current parliamentary salary [currently around £600]; nor
> (b) in the case of media work (but in that case the Member shall deposit a statement of the fees or benefits payable in the bands specified above).'
> (*Part of a Resolution of the House of 6 November 1995, amended on 14 May 2002 and on 9 February 2009*)

. . .

67. 'Services in the capacity of a Member of Parliament' is usually taken to mean advice on any parliamentary matter or services connected with any parliamentary proceeding or otherwise related to the House. Essentially, when Members are considering whether an agreement is necessary they should ask themselves 'Would I be doing this job in this way if I were not a Member of Parliament', and seek an agreement if the answer is 'No'.

Notes
1. The House of Commons accepted in the debate of 6 July 1995 'the extension of the requirement for. . .relevant interests to be declared by means of symbols on the Order Paper, previously applied only to the proposers of Early Day Motions, to all written parliamentary Proceedings except Division lists', also recommended by Nolan.[32] In political terms, this was seen as uncontroversial, as merely extending the range of a given type of disclosure to encompass other activities. In fact, this was quite an important change, allowing possible motivations behind the initiation of written parliamentary proceedings to be immediately ascertained.

---

32   As summarised in the Second Report from the Committee on Standards in Public Life, HC 816 (1994–95), para 3.

2. When the Committee on Standards in Public Life, now chaired by Sir Christopher Kelly, produced its most recent report (hereafter 'the Kelly Report'), it re-considered the issue of member's outside interests. Aside from its recommendation to reverse the changes made by the Parliamentary Standards Act 2009 (see below), its recommendations on the substantive issue were brief and as follows:

Recommendation 34
MPs should remain free to undertake some paid activity outside the House of Commons, provided it is kept within reasonable limits and there is transparency about the nature of the activity and the amount of time spent on it.

Recommendation 37
All candidates at parliamentary elections should publish, at nomination, a register of interests including the existence of other paid jobs and whether they intend to continue to hold them, if elected. The Ministry of Justice should issue guidance on this in time for the next general election. Following the election, consideration should be given as to whether the process should become a statutory part of the nominations process.[33]

Enforcement of the rules—the mechanisms and compliance by MPs

The enforcement procedures

It is important to appreciate that the ability of the House to enforce the standards rules is merely part of both Houses' general jurisdiction to punish both Members and non-Members for breaches of privilege—contempts of Parliament. As Munro puts it:

The Houses are able to deal with offenders and enforce their privileges because they are the High Court of Parliament, and so have an inherent jurisdiction. . .[34]

The mechanisms to police adherence to the rules are a Committee on Standards and Privileges (hereinafter 'the Committee') and a Parliamentary Commissioner for Standards ('the Commissioner'). The Committee also has the general role of investigating contempts of the House not related to breaches of the Code of Conduct. Complaints alleging a breach of the Code entail an initial investigation by the Commissioner, whose report then forms the basis of the Committee's own investigation.

Guide to Rules relating to the Conduct of Members (extracts)

4. Procedure for Complaints
103. The Parliamentary Commissioner for Standards will consider complaints whether from Members or from members of the public, alleging that a Member has breached the Code of Conduct and associated rules. . . .

---

33 *Twelfth Report from the Kelly Committee on Standards in Public Life*, Cm 7724 (2009), pp 87–90.

34 Munro, n 3 above, p 216.

108. If the Commissioner is satisfied that sufficient evidence has been tendered in support of the complaint to justify his taking the matter further, he will ask the Member to respond to the complaint. If he decides, having received the Member's response and on the basis of any further enquiries he may decide are necessary, that the complaint of a breach of the rules of the House has not been substantiated, he will dismiss the complaint and report that conclusion briefly to the Committee on Standards and Privileges. If after enquiry he finds that there has been a breach of the rules of the House or that the complaint raises issues of wider importance, he will normally report the facts and his conclusions to the Committee. Under Standing Order No. 150, however, he may decide that the matter can be resolved through the rectification procedure. If so, he will determine the complaint on that basis and report the fact briefly to the Committee. In the case of non-registration, rectification requires a belated entry in the current Register, with an appropriate explanatory note; in the case of non-declaration, it requires an apology to the House by means of a point of order. In cases involving parliamentary facilities or allowances the rectification procedure normally requires the Member to make appropriate repayment. . .

109. The Committee on Standards and Privileges will consider any matter relating to the conduct of Members, including specific complaints in relation to alleged breaches of the Code of Conduct or Guide to which the House has agreed and which have been drawn to the Committee's attention by the Commissioner.

110. It is a requirement of the Code of Conduct that Members cooperate at all stages with any inquiry by the Committee on Standards and Privileges or the Commissioner into their conduct. It is also a requirement that Members do not lobby members of the Committee on Standards and Privileges or the Commissioner in a manner calculated to influence their consideration of complaints.

111. The Committee has power under its Standing Order to send for persons, papers and records; to order the attendance of any Member before it; and to require that specific documents in the possession of a Member relating to its inquiries or to the inquiries of the Commissioner be laid before it . . .

113. On specific complaints for which the Commissioner has concluded that there has been a breach of the rules, and the Committee agrees in whole or in part, the Committee may make recommendations to the House on whether further action is required. It may also report to the House on other complaints if it thinks fit.

114. If the Commissioner concludes that a complaint is frivolous or vexatious, or that an inquiry would be disproportionate given the nature and seriousness of the allegation made, he may decide not to inquire into it. In such cases he would report the circumstances briefly to the Committee.

Note

It is important to note the unique powers enjoyed by the Committee, those over and above those enjoyed by Parliament's other Select Committees. The Committee may order the attendance of Members and require papers to be laid before it. In contrast, other Select Committees may force the attendance of a Member before it only though obtaining a Resolution of the House as a whole. The Committee has a wide remit: it may consider any matter relating to the conduct of Members.

The efficacy of the procedures[35]

It was presumed when the new procedures were set up that the Committee would be reluctant to overturn findings made by the Commissioner, particularly where doing so would lay it open to charges of party political bias. While the Committee does not often overturn such findings, it has done so in a number of cases[36] and in some cases, where the Commissioner reported that she had been unable to obtain satisfactory co-operation from the Member in question, has reacted simply by admonishing the Member, but dropping the complaint. An example occurred when, after the 1997 election, the Labour-dominated Committee was investigating complaints against Labour Members, including Labour Ministers in some cases.[37] One of the most important cases was the report on Dr John Reid, a senior Labour Minister, and Mr John Maxton.[38] The limited powers of the Commissioner—unable to send for persons or papers, and with no power to compel Members to answer questions—raised the question as to whether the Commissioner has sufficient powers to investigate cases involving recalcitrant 'suspects' satisfactorily. The most notorious case in which this issue was raised was the investigation into a total of 18 complaints against Keith Vaz, then Minister for Europe in the Labour Government. See Third Report HC 314–I (2000–01) and Fifth Report, HC 605–1 (2001–02). There have been a number of cases in which adverse findings by the Commissioner have not been upheld by the Committee. Oliver noted, that in the May 1995 debate on Nolan, 'some hostility [was shown by Members] directed mainly to concern that the House's 'sovereignty' might be undermined if independent outsiders were involved in policing conduct';[39] which suggested that at least some Members may be minded to view the work and findings of the Commissioner with a sceptical eye. Hostility amongst many members to one of the more energetic Commissioners, Elizabeth Filkin, led to her being in effect eased out of her office in 2001 after serving only one term. [40]

Moreover, there is evidence to suggest that many MPs have little awareness of the content of the Code. Research carried out in 2008 including the finding:

> MPs are fully aware of the Code's existence, but judging by the responses of those interviewed, most MPs rarely consult it. A senior select committee chairman noted that the Code was something of a fixture: 'Once you've seen it there's no need to return to it'. Some MPs never consult the Code. A former member of the Standards and Privileges Committee declared: 'I've no idea what the Code says, I'm entirely indifferent. I've never read it; it's balls and bullshit. Ninety-five per cent of MPs haven't read it'. It is, of course, virtually impossible to verify his estimate, but the fact that eight other MPs—nine in total—admitted to never having read it suggests there may be some truth in it.[41]

Of course, those MPs who have no outside interests have no need to be aware of the code, and the same research indicated that this was the approach of some. However, the procedures have certainly not been

---

35 For a recent survey of the Commissioner's work, see Doig, n 28 above, at 360–75.

36 Some recent examples were the rejection by the Committee of the Commissioner's findings on Roy Beggs (Third Report, HC 320 (2000–01)) and on John Maxton (Second Report, HC 319 (2000–01)). A more recent investigation concerned John Prescott, a Cabinet Minister: Standards and Privileges Committee, Thirteenth Report: Conduct of Mr John Prescott, HC 1553, 2006.

37 See, e.g. the report of the Committee on Keith Vaz, Third Report HC 314–I (2000–01).

38 Second Report, HC 89 (2000–01).

39 Oliver, [1995] PL 497, 499.

40 See H Young, 'A brilliant public servant is being hounded from office', The Guardian, 3 July 2001.

41 Allen, p 505 above, at 91.

little used. The same research found that 'Between April 2002 and March 2003, some 43 Members were the subject of a specific complaint (Table 1). Over the next five years, the comparable figures were 79, 93, 79, 116 and 137'.[42] Unfortunately, there is some evidence that the ethics rules have been used for partisan ends, both by the media and by individual MPs.[43] The new paragraphs 108 and 112 above of the guidance is intended to allow for early informal rejection of a complaint that is not considered well-founded.

Some concerns have also been raised as to the compliance of the Committee with basic standards of procedural fairness, although the decision in *Demicoli v Malta* (1992) 14 EHRR 47 seems to suggest that 'types of breach of privilege proceedings, which may be said to be disciplinary in nature in that they relate to the internal regulation and orderly functioning of the House', would not fall within Article 6 of the Convention. Furthermore, even if it could be argued that the Committee's activities were *prima facie* covered by Art 6, it appears that no action could be brought under the HRA, quite apart from the fact that one would expect a court to be minded to refuse jurisdiction in a matter affecting Parliament's regulation of its own affairs. This is because while the Act makes it 'unlawful for a *public authority* to act in a way which is incompatible with a Convention right' (s 6(1)) and s 6(3) specifically states that neither House of Parliament nor 'a person exercising functions in connection with proceedings in Parliament' count as 'public authorities' for the purposes of the Act. No action could therefore be brought against either the Committee or the House itself by an aggrieved Member.

Various recommendations for improving the fairness of proceedings of investigations by the Privileges Committee have been made by the Joint Committee on Parliamentary Privilege, HLP 43–41 (1998–99), the Wicks Report, Cm 5663 (2002) at 6.25–6.28 and the Eighth Report of the Committee on Standards and Privileges, HC 403 (2002–03). However, even were the procedures made fairer, with a greater independent element, the problem remains that the Commons does not always follow the Committee's recommendations, nor is it bound by its previous decisions, drawbacks illustrated by the case of *GR Strauss*,[44] considered below at p 539. Whilst the Commons as a whole is not ideally suited to make the final decisions on matters of privilege, the Committee itself has been subject to criticisms as a forum for trying issues which, at least theoretically, could result in the imprisonment of those it finds to have been in breach of privilege or to have committed contempts. First, it is nominated in proportion to party strengths. It is, as de Smith notes,[45] unusual for it to divide along party lines, but it did so in the *WJ Brown* case,[46] in delivering a verdict which favoured the government MP concerned, and more recently split dramatically over the Nolan Report. One could envisage such considerations intruding in the case of, for example, a senior government figure sued for libel; in determining whether the minister's publishing of the libel was covered by privilege, government MPs might well be more concerned with possible embarrassment to the Government than with following expert recommendation. A similar issue could arise where the Committee determined a complaint of a breach of the rules governing Members' interests by a government minister: the complaint would be determined by a Committee with a majority (in some cases a large majority) of MPs of the same party as the Minister. As noted above, this happened in relation to the cases against Keith Vaz, Dr John Reid, and

---

42   *Ibid* at 94.

43   *Ibid* at 97–98.

44   See Report of the Committee of Privileges, HC 308 (1956–57).

45   See n 12 above, p 320.

46   HC 188 (1946–47).

also Geoffrey Robinson, the former Paymaster General.[47] If the Committee reports are unanimous, this may be sufficient to rebut the suspicion of bias in observers' minds—though this may not satisfy the requirements of Art 6 of the ECHR. This problem—inherent in the system of self-regulation—would only be solved if the contempt jurisdiction were transferred altogether to another body, perhaps the ordinary courts, or the Judicial Committee of the Privy Council. However, as the attitude of the Joint Committee on Parliamentary Privilege towards giving the Privy Council any role in hearing appeals from decisions of the Commons on privilege indicates, this is an unlikely course of action.

THE EXPENSES SCANDAL, THE PARLIAMENTARY STANDARDS ACT 2009 AND THE KELLY REPORT

At first sight, one might conclude that the expenses scandal that burst upon Parliament in 2009, whilst politically dramatic, had little effect upon Parliamentary privilege. It has long been accepted that the assessment of and payment to MPs of expenses incurred in doing their duties as MPs is not an aspect of 'proceedings in Parliament' under Art 9 of the Bill of Rights (see below at 536). Hence the partial removal of this aspect of regulation of MPs from the House of Commons to an outside body, the Independent Parliamentary Standards Authority ('IPSA'—see below) did not formally intrude into Parliamentary privilege. However, the episode is of significance for this area this for two reasons: first, the 2009 Act also had the effect of endowing IPSA, an outside standards body, with the power to draw up a new code relating to member's interests, registration and disclosure. The Bill as originally introduced also gave IPSA powers to enforce the registration and disclosure rules and created new criminal offences of failing to abide by these rules. These offences were withdrawn from the Bill during its passage in Parliament. Moreover, by virtue of clauses hurriedly included in the Constitutional Reform and Governance Act 2010, IPSA's jurisdiction over members' outside *interests*, as opposed to their expenses, was abolished only a few months after the Act was passed.[48] Paradoxically, therefore, the episode has reaffirmed the principle of self-regulation in this area: it was briefly waived aside in the face of the panic induced by the scandal, but quickly reasserted itself. Second, while the claiming and payment of MPs' salaries and expenses do not amount to a 'proceeding in Parliament', the 2009 Act and the establishment of IPSA are further aspects of the move from full self-regulation of MPs conduct to the imposition of externally-generated standards and oversight. Moreover, the Kelly Report has suggested changes to the operation of the Commons' privilege Committee and the new Speaker's Committee, which represent a departure in a limited sense from full self-regulation, since non-MPs will now sit on these bodies.

The background: the expenses scandal[49]

Peter Leyland explains the factual background to the scandal:

> Against a background of the steady introduction of private sector disciplines throughout the public sector, with the incentivisation of pay at executive level now

---

47   See First Report of the Committee, HC 297 (2001–02).

48   See below, at 529–531.

49   For a more detailed overview of the crisis and the expenses system, see A Kelso, 'Parliament on its Knees: MP's Expenses and the Crisis of Transparency at Westminster' (2009) 80(3) *Political Quarterly* 329.

widely taken for granted, Westminster MPs are paid a relatively modest annual salary of £65,000. On top of this, however, they are allowed to claim for office expenses, which include the payment of secretarial staff of up to £100,000. Also, MPs with constituencies outside London are entitled to certain expenses related to a secondary home. The House of Commons publishes a Green Book with a preface from the Speaker which is intended to provide detailed guidelines about the rules concerning the financial allowances available to MPs. The Department of Resources, formerly the Fees Office, is responsible for administering the rules and ensuring compliance. The principles set out in this Green Book leave little doubt that elected politicians are expected to set an example of probity and honesty. Claims should be above reproach and reflect actual usage and therefore they should be based on proper records. They must be expenses necessary for members to incur to ensure that they could properly perform their parliamentary duties.[50]

Notes

1. As Bradley and Ewing explain, from 1971:

> MPs from constituencies outside London became able to claim an additional costs allowance (ACA) to compensate them for 'expenses wholly, exclusively and necessarily incurred when staying overnight away from their main UK residence . . . for the purposes of performing Parliamentary duties'. In the years after 1971, the scope of this self-regulatory scheme widened until in effect the ACA came to be seen by most MPs as part of their salary. By 2007–08, a maximum tax-free payment per year of £23,083 could be charged to such items as a second mortgage, rent, furnishings, home maintenance and a food allowance of £400 per month.[51]

The following extract from an article investigating the views of MPs to the standards and rules governing them reveals the attitude of MPs to their expenses before the scandal broke:

> Interestingly, the most vocal complaints against regulation were in the area of parliamentary allowances and expenses. . .Several of those interviewed expressed their dislike at the scrutiny of their expense claims and an apparent decline in the deference shown to them by House of Commons staff. 'In the good old days', explained one long-serving Conservative, 'they [the Fees Office, which is responsible for processing expenses claims] were there for you. Now the relationship's almost been reversed'. Or, as a senior official put it, staff are now more willing to say 'no' to MPs. To be fair, the long-serving Conservative felt that the new relationship was 'for the good'. Others did not share this view. A Labour MP insisted: 'we're in the situation where officials are telling us what we can and cannot do'. She described the Fees Office as 'trying to police the system when they should be administering it'. She added, scornfully, how 'the Fees Office is now run by a former tax inspector'. Such comments just go to show how sensitive many MPs are when it comes to scrutiny of their work and finances.[52]

---

50   P Leyland, 'Freedom of Information and the 2009 Parliamentary Expenses Scandal' [2009] PL 675.

51   Bradley and Ewing, *Constitutional and Administrative Law,* 14th edn (2007), 'Update'—August 2009.

52   N Allen, 'Voices from the Shop Floor' (2008) 61(1) Parlt Aff 88, 99.

It should be noted that under the old system, even if the Fees Office refused a claim, the member could appeal to the Committee on Member's Allowances and thence to the Member's Estimate Committee (SO 152D). So MPs had the final word on their own expenses.

2. Leyland notes the role of freedom of information in forcing the scandal into the open.

> Three journalists. . .requested further information on MPs' expenses, including the disclosure of claim forms and supporting documents. [It was refused by the Commons but] the Information Commissioner upheld their claim, as did the Tribunal and the High Court, which confirmed the Tribunal decision [*Corporate Officer of the House of Commons v Information Commissioner* [2009] 3 All ER 403] at [34]:
>
> > once it emerged, as the Tribunal has found, that the operation of the ACA [additional costs allowance] system was deeply flawed, public scrutiny of the details of individual claims [was] inevitable.
>
> This FOI ruling can be regarded as the prelude to an extraordinary catalogue of revelations concerning MPs' expenses which have shaken the foundations of the entire political establishment.[53]

The ruling is extracted in Chapter 13 at 715–718.

3. 'Weaknesses with the system' started to emerge in 2008, with the suspension from the House of Derek Conway MP for misusing his allowances to pay members of his family. This 'fuelled wider concerns that MPs were using their allowances and expenses to bolster their salaries'.[54] In response, the House brought forward some recommendations to reform the system. As Kelly explains:

> 1.14 A first set of changes was agreed in July 2008 following an internal review conducted by the House of Commons Members Estimate Committee (MEC). The proposals put forward by that Committee were at that stage relatively limited in scope. Even so, 7 of the 18 recommendations were rejected by the House of Commons. The rejected recommendations included the proposals that receipts should be required for all claims, that claims for furnishings and capital improvements should no longer be allowed and that for the first time expenditure should be subject to annual full scope audit by the National Audit Office (NAO). The existing external audit was very limited, not seeking to investigate beyond the Member's confirmation that expenses had been properly claimed. It is clear that at that stage many MPs had failed to understand the urgent need for reform.

4. However, such defiance was not to last much longer. Leyland continues the story:

> The first tremor occurred in February 2009 with accusations that Jacqui Smith MP, the then Home Secretary, had allegedly claimed £116,000 in second home expenses for her constituency house. This matter was duly referred to the Parliamentary Commissioner for Standards to see if there had been any serious wrongdoing. From May 8, 2009 the Daily Telegraph newspaper followed this up with an unprecedented flood of individual allegations directed at MPs from all political parties: 88 Labour MPs, 71 Conservative MPs, 10 Liberal Democrat MPs and 4 MPs

---

53   Leyland, n 50 above, at 677.

54   N Allen, 'Voices from the Shop Floor' at 105.

from other parties, out of a total of 645 MPs, had been named by the middle of June. It was apparent that this extremely detailed information had been deliberately leaked by an individual working within Parliament. The itemised breakdown in some cases unearthed allegations of serious dishonesty. For example, claims for interest payments on mortgages that had already been paid off or for mortgage interest payments where the property had been purchased outright and there was no mortgage to pay back. It became apparent from these disclosures that many MPs whose constituencies are outside London have maximised financial gain by regularly changing the designation of their second home, a practice referred to as 'flipping'. They were able to sell off the original property at a profit while claiming back the full cost of renovation. Some MPs, including one Cabinet minister, sold these secondary properties at a profit after having received repayments and mortgage relief, but avoided payment of capital gains tax on the sale. The payment of family members as staff is another practice which has been called into question. The publication of details has also revealed what might be termed 'creative abuse of the rules' with inappropriate claims, some of which appear almost comical in the light of the principles set out in the Green Book for Members referred to above. These included: clearing the moat around a country mansion, maintaining a duck island, and fitting mock Tudor beams.

The abuse of at least the spirit if not the letter of these rules by dozens of MPs from all parties has prompted an unprecedented wave of public anger and hostility against the political class.[55]

Notes

1. A number of Ministers and shadow Ministers were directly or indirectly forced out of power as a result of the scandal.[56] 'The Speaker himself, Michael Martin MP, was forced to retire when it appeared that he had lost the confidence of the House and of the public generally, largely because of a failure to give leadership in the complex wrangling over the publication of MPs' expenses.'[57] In fact, Martin had led attempts to exempt Parliament from the FOI Act on this matter,[58] and generally appeared wholly out of touch, and unable to deal with, the degree of public anger on the issue. A large number of MPs made clear that they would stand down at the next general election as a result of the scandal.

2. The Kelly Report found that:

> There has been a profound crisis of public confidence in the integrity of MPs brought about by successive revelations about the nature of their self-determined and self-policed expenses scheme and the way they have used it. The public are understandably angry about a major systemic failure in an area where they are justified in expecting the highest standards. MPs have been able to misuse for personal gain an expenses regime which was intended simply to reimburse them for the additional costs necessarily incurred in performing their jobs. Anger has been fuelled further by a perception that ordinary citizens are subject to restrictions in their own working lives which were not being applied in the same way to MPs,

---

55   Leyland, n 50 above, at 677–78.

56   For details, see Kelso, n 49 above. See Chapter 13 at 715–718.

57   Bradley and Ewing, 'Update' n 51 above.

58   See Kelso, n 49 above, at 332–34.

and by the reluctance of the House of Commons to recognise the need for reform until forced to do so.[59]

3. Some interim measures, designed to stop the worst of the abuses, were agreed by the party leaders in April and May 2009, including proper 'full scope' external audit beginning with spending in 2009–10, and the curbing of certain ACA claims. As a further interim measure, Sir Thomas Legg, a retired civil servant, was appointed to review expense claims going back to 2004, and require repayments where he found claims to have been excessive. He did this in some instances by applying retrospective rules as to the amount that could be claimed under certain categories. This caused great discontent amongst MPs and large numbers appealed against the initial findings.[60] Legg has no means of enforcing his findings other than via pressure from media and public opinion—they will go to the Member's Estimate Committee.[61] A more permanent solution was sought in a major investigation carried out by the Committee on Standards in Public Life. However, such was the panic induced by the relentlessly hostile media criticism and the seemingly catastrophic loss of public confidence in Parliament that the Government decided to legislate before Kelly reported. [Note, the provisions below do not take account of changes made by the Constitutional Reform and Governance Act 2010.]

The Parliamentary Standards Act 2009

1 Bill of Rights
Nothing in this Act shall be construed by any court in the United Kingdom as affecting Article IX of the Bill of Rights 1689.

2 House of Lords
(1) Nothing in this Act shall affect the House of Lords.

    . . .

3 Independent Parliamentary Standards Authority etc
(1) There is to be a body corporate known as the Independent Parliamentary Standards Authority ('IPSA').
(2) Schedule 1 (which makes provision about the IPSA). . .has effect.
(3) There is to be an officer known as the Commissioner for Parliamentary Investigations ('the Commissioner').
(4) Schedule 2 (which makes provision about the Commissioner) has effect.

4 MPs' salaries
(1) The IPSA is to pay the salaries of members of the House of Commons in accordance with the relevant resolutions of the House.
(2) That is subject to anything done in exercise of the disciplinary powers of the House.

5 MPs' allowances scheme
(1) The IPSA is to pay allowances to members of the House of Commons in accordance with the MPs' allowances scheme.
(2) In this Act 'the MPs' allowances scheme' means the scheme prepared under this section as it is in effect for the time being.

---

59   Kelly Report, Executive Summary, at [4].

60   See 'At least 70 MPs challenge expenses payback rulings from Commons auditor', *The Guardian,* 17 December 2009. The appeals went to a retired judge.

61   See http://news.bbc.co.uk/1/hi/8301884.stm.

(3) The IPSA must—

    (a) prepare the scheme;
    (b) review the scheme regularly and revise it as appropriate.

(4) In preparing or revising the scheme, the IPSA must consult [various bodies including the Speaker and the Committee on Standards in Public Life, hereafter 'Standards Committee'].
(5) The Speaker must lay the scheme (or revision) before the House of Commons.
(6) The scheme (or revision) comes into effect on the date specified in the scheme (or revision).

6 Dealing with claims under the scheme

(1) No allowance is to be paid to a member of the House of Commons under the MPs' allowances scheme unless a claim for the allowance has been made to the IPSA.
(2) The claim must be made by the member (except where the scheme provides otherwise).

(3) On receipt of a claim, the IPSA must—

    (a) determine whether to allow or refuse the claim, and
    (b) if it is allowed, determine how much of the amount claimed is to be allowed and pay it accordingly.

[(4) and (5) provide that IPSA must review a refusal upon request.]
[Section 7 provides that IPSA must provide advice about relevant taxation matters to MPs.]

8 MPs' code of conduct relating to financial interests

(1) The IPSA must prepare a code to be observed by members of the House of Commons, the content of which is provision made by virtue of subsections (7) and (8).
(2) In this Act 'the MPs' code of conduct relating to financial interests' means the code prepared under this section as it is in effect for the time being.
(3) The IPSA must review the code regularly and revise it as appropriate.
(4) In preparing or revising the code, the IPSA must consult [similar bodies to those above].
(5) The Speaker must lay the code (or revision) before the House of Commons.
(6) The code (or revision) does not come into effect until it is approved by a resolution of the House of Commons.
(7) The code must require members to register specified information about specified financial interests in a register maintained by the IPSA.
(8) The code must prohibit a member from—

    (a) by any specified means, advocating or initiating any cause or matter on behalf of any person in consideration of any specified payment or specified benefit in kind, or
    (b) in consideration of any specified payment or specified benefit in kind, urging any other member to advocate or initiate, by any specified means, any cause or matter on behalf of any person.

9 Investigations

(1) The Commissioner may conduct an investigation if the Commissioner has reason to believe that a member of the House of Commons—

(a) may have been paid an amount under the MPs' allowances scheme that should not have been allowed, or

(b) may have failed to comply with a requirement included by virtue of section 8(7) (registration of interests) in the MPs' code of conduct relating to financial interests.

(2) An investigation may be conducted—

(a) on the Commissioner's own initiative,

(b) at the request of the member, or

(c) in response to a complaint by an individual.

. . .

(4) If, after conducting an investigation, the Commissioner finds that the member was paid an amount under the scheme that should not have been allowed, the Commissioner must refer the Commissioner's findings to the [Standards Committee].

(5) But the Commissioner need not refer the findings if—

(a) the member accepts the findings,

(b) such other conditions as may be specified by the IPSA are, in the Commissioner's view, met in relation to the case, and

(c) the member repays to the IPSA, in such manner and within such period as the Commissioner considers reasonable, such amount as the Commissioner considers reasonable.

[(6) and provides for reference to the Standards Committee of a finding of breach of code governing Member's interests.]

(7) But the Commissioner need not refer the findings if—

(a) the member accepts the findings,

(b) the Commissioner considers that the financial interest concerned was minor or that the failure was inadvertent,

(c) such other conditions as may be specified by the IPSA are, in the Commissioner's view, met in relation to the case, and

(c) the member takes any steps required by the Commissioner to correct the register.

(8) If the Commissioner finds that a member who is the subject of an investigation has not provided the Commissioner with information the Commissioner reasonably requires for the purposes of the investigation, the Commissioner may refer the finding to the [Standards Committee].

(9) The IPSA must determine—

(a) procedures in relation to investigations under subsection (1),

(b) procedures in relation to complaints under subsection (2)(c),

(c) procedures in relation to the circumstances in which the Commissioner's findings are to be published.

(10) [IPSA must consult as above in relation to these.]

(11) The procedures must be fair and, in particular, provide a member who is the subject of an investigation or complaint with an opportunity—

(a) to make representations to the Commissioner about the investigation or complaint,
(b) to make representations to the Commissioner, before the Commissioner's findings are referred to the [Standards Committee].

(12) Procedures by virtue of subsection (11)(a) must include—

(a) an opportunity to be heard in person,
(b) an opportunity, where the Commissioner considers it appropriate, to call and examine witnesses.

10 Offence of providing false or misleading information for allowances claims
(1) A member of the House of Commons commits an offence if the member—

(a) makes a claim under the MPs' allowances scheme, and
(b) provides information for the purposes of the claim that the member knows to be false or misleading in a material respect.

[the penalty is a year's imprisonment or a fine].
[Schedule 1 deals with IPSA. The members of IPSA are appointed by the Queen on an address from the Commons; one must have held high judicial office and another must be a former member of the House. No current members may sit on it. Members have security of tenure. Under Schedule 2, The Commissioner also has security of tenure and is appointed by the Queen following nomination with the Speaker, consulting the new Speaker's Committee—8 MPs chaired by the Speaker.]

Notes
1. Bradley and Ewing comment:

> This Act is of great constitutional significance, but it was enacted by an accelerated procedure that made it impossible for all the implications of the proposals to be fully considered . . . Strong criticism of aspects of the bill, both in the Commons and the Lords, caused several clauses to be withdrawn by the government [and the addition of section 1].[62]

2. The Act as passed in 2009 is indeed nothing like as strong as was intended when the Bill was introduced into Parliament. In some important respects, self-regulation has been preserved: notably, the Commissioner has no powers of enforcement. He may only refer findings of a breach of the rules to the Standards Committee to deal with. Thus MPs will still ultimately police themselves. Moreover, as the Explanatory Notes to the Act make clear, the Commissioner has no role in relation to policing either the advocacy rule or disclosure requirements (since these were dropped from the Bill). Section 9(1) provides for investigations by the Commissioner only in relation to breaches of the rules governing allowances, and breaches of the requirements to *register* financial interests (s 9(1)(b)). (The registration jurisdiction was itself subsequently abolished—see below.) Again, in the original legislation, the Commissioner was entitled to investigate any breach of the rules governing financial interests; these were the registration requirements, the ban on paid advocacy and the disclosure requirements: as originally introduced the rules had to 'require a member who

---

62 'Update', n 57 above.

has a specified financial interest in any matter to declare specified information about that interest before taking part in any specified proceedings relating to that matter;[63] echoing the disclosure requirements of the House of Commons Code. These were withdrawn from the Bill, after protests about infringements of parliamentary privilege.

3. In terms of *rule-making* as opposed to enforcement, the Act draws a distinction between rules regarding expenses and those regarding member's interests. Only in relation to the rules governing expenses does IPSA have the final word: it produces a code and lays it before the Commons, but the House has no power to reject it (s 5(5) and (6)). Conversely, in relation to the new Code on members' interests, while IPSA draws up the code, it 'does not come into effect until it is approved by a resolution of the House of Commons' (s 8(6)). Thus in relation to expenses, the House has surrendered rule-making and investigation but not enforcement to an outside body.

4. In relation to member's interests, the following is the case: (a) the Act provides that the rules are to be drawn up by IPSA but that the House retains a veto; (b) investigations relate only to registration of interests, not disclosure or the ban on paid advocacy; (c) all enforcement remains with the Commons. Thus the Prime Minister's statement on 10 June 2009 that the Bill would mean the movement 'from the old system of self-regulation to independent, statutory regulation' has turned out to be only half-true. The Act is hardly a revolutionary change, although it does represent a modest departure from the ancient rule of the House's exclusive cognisance of its own affairs. As the Justice Committee remarked: 'the creation of a body to administer allowances and pay need not affect privilege because these matters are not proceedings in Parliament'.[64]

5. The Bill as originally introduced gave powers to the Commissioner to require MPs to repay expenses wrongly paid and to correct entries on the register of member's interests. However these were withdrawn after protests that, since such findings would have to be subject to judicial review or appeal, this would inevitably involve courts investigating and passing judgement on proceedings in Parliament. This would have represented an incursion into Article 9 and so was rejected.

6. The original Bill also would have introduced offences of (1) failing, without reasonable excuse, to comply with the rules on registration and (2) breaching the rules that prohibit paid advocacy. The former could perhaps have been retained, since the register of member's interest can be considered not to be part of proceedings in parliament (see *Rost v Edwards*, below at 540–541). Therefore, offences relating to the register can be prosecuted without bringing into question proceedings in Parliament. However, as we have seen, doubt has been cast on this finding in *Rost*. A criminal offence of breaching the rules prohibiting paid advocacy, on the other hand, would plainly base liability squarely on words spoken in Parliament and would certainly therefore have violated Art 9. The offence was withdrawn after protests on this point from the House of Lords Constitutional Committee.[65]

7. Finally, the original Bill contained the following controversial clause:

10 Proceedings in Parliament

No enactment or rule of law which prevents proceedings in Parliament being impeached or questioned in any court or place out of Parliament is to prevent—

---

63 Clause 5(8).

64 *Constitutional Reform and Renewal: Parliamentary Standards Bill* 7th Report (2008–09), HC 791, at [5]. See also the remark of then Standards Commissioner Sir Philip Mawer, in the *Trend* case: 'The decision whether . . . any Member who may be shown to have wrongfully claimed parliamentary allowances should face a criminal prosecution is one for the police and the prosecuting authorities, not for me. . . . Claiming an allowance is not a proceeding in Parliament and the provisions of parliamentary privileges do not apply.' (HC 435 (2002–03) Appendix, para 46).

65 See paras 40 and 41.

(a) the IPSA from carrying out any of its functions;
(b) the Commissioner from carrying out any of the Commissioner's functions;
(c) any evidence from being admissible in proceedings against a member of the House of Commons for an offence under section 9.

This made it clear that the original Bill would have constituted a significant erosion of parliamentary privilege; however, once the clauses that would have interfered with privilege were dropped, this clause became redundant, and was also withdrawn.

8. As the Constitution Committee pointed out,[66] findings by the IPSA, e.g. refusing an allowance may be subject to judicial review. However, we would suggest that its procedures may not now be subject to Art 6 because it can make no binding findings other than on allowances: all it can do is refer cases to the Standards Committee. It should also be noted that the draft Bribery Bill published in March 2009 provided in clause 15 that the words or conduct of an MP or peer will be admissible in a prosecution for bribery notwithstanding Art 9. However, this provision was not included in the Bill enacted by Parliament as the Bribery Act 2010. Moreover, as this book went to press, the DPP announced that charges would be brought against three MPs and one Peer for the offence of false accounting in relation to their expenses claims.[67] The MPs have raised the issue of parliamentary privilege; it will be determined in court, but appears baseless, given the views expressed above that the claiming and payment of expenses are not 'proceedings in Parliament'.

Changes to the new governance system recommended by the Kelly Report

Leyland's view is that 'the original Bill was emasculated in the face of criticism in both Houses during its parliamentary stages'.[68] However, as it turned out, having only been in existence a few months, the new legislation was amended by Parliament in 2010. Essentially, Kelly proposed four key changes to the legislation:

(a) the removal of jurisdiction over members' outside interests from IPSA;
(b) the consequent abolition of the Commissioner for Parliamentary Investigations;
(c) the restoration of the enforcement powers of IPSA in relation to expenses originally included in the Bill but removed during its passage through Parliament;
(d) the adding of independent members to the Speaker's Committee and (not a matter addressed in the Act) to the Committee on Standards and Privileges.

These points are addressed in turn. The Government made these changes through amendments to the Constitutional Reform and Governance Bill 2009 which was enacted in 2010.

Removal of jurisdiction over MPs' interests

There was widespread criticism of the inclusion of the provisions about Member's outside interests in the Parliamentary Standards Act, since it was not these, but the expenses system that had been

---

66   18th Report (2008–09) HL 134 at [18].

67   See *The Guardian*, 5 February 2009: www.guardian.co.uk/politics/2010/feb/05/mps-expenses-charges.

68   Leyland at 680.

discredited by the scandal. Picking up on this argument, when the Kelly Committee on Standards in Public Life reported, it found against the transfer of the power to draw up rules governing these outside interests from the Commons Standards and Privileges Committee to IPSA. Kelly found that giving IPSA the dual function of regulating both expenses and outside interests would make it a hybrid body, and that this would be 'unsatisfactory' in a number of respects, as follows:

Twelfth Report from the Committee on Standards in Public Life, Cm 7724 (2009) (the Kelly Report) (extracts)

- The additional responsibility for financial interests risks distracting the new body from its core function of operating the new expenses scheme.
- MPs would be required to abide by two separate codes of conduct, one statutory and the other non-statutory.
- The creation of a new Commissioner for Parliamentary Investigations, separate from the existing Parliamentary Commissioner for Standards, risks a blurring of their respective responsibilities and difficulty in maintaining demarcation lines. . .

13.19 Moreover, there are two more fundamental reasons for rethinking the remit of the independent body. The first is that the issue of parliamentary privilege could still arise if responsibility for financial interests, a standards issue, is taken from the House and vested in an outside body. The code of conduct on financial interests relates to how MPs behave as Members of the House, including whether they have financial or other interests which might affect their judgments or conduct as legislators or in holding the Executive to account. This is potentially a privilege issue.

13.20 The determination and payment of expenses, on the other hand, are in a different category. They do not bear on how individual Members operate in the House in their role as MPs. They are common to all Members and do not have any direct influence on their judgments or behaviour as legislators or in holding the Executive to account. They are practical matters best determined and operated by an independent body which is demonstrably not self-serving.

13.22 The second fundamental reason for limiting the independent body's remit here is that it is vital that the House buys into the standards of conduct and behaviour it considers acceptable in relation to financial and other standards issues. Such behaviour is a key part of the culture of the House, and cannot effectively just be imposed from outside.

13.23 To be robust and effective, standards and values have to be developed from within. What is now required is leadership from the top, reinforcing for MPs an ethos of public service and a culture of personal responsibility for their own behaviour. At this juncture, the House needs to regain not only public credibility but its own self-respect. Taking responsibility for its own code of conduct on financial interests, and enforcing it robustly, would be an important step in that direction.

13.24 Returning responsibility for the register and code of conduct on financial interests to the House of Commons may seem counter-intuitive in view of the failure, under self-regulation, of the House to police the expenses scheme properly. But since the power of sanction in relation to matters related to the code of conduct on financial interests remains largely in the hands of the House of Commons, the form of external regulation proposed in the Act is a chimera and offers a misleading sense of reassurance.

13.25 For all these reasons, the Committee believes that responsibility for the register of financial interests and the code of conduct should be returned to the House of Commons.
13.26 The Committee recognises that if that is to happen the independence and effectiveness of the House's internal regulatory arrangements need to be strengthened. We make a number of suggestions about that later in this chapter.

Notes
1. Some of the arguments above (those in paras 13.22 and 13.23) seem manifestly unpersuasive. The Report baldly urges that the House will not buy into rules and values concerning 'financial issues' if they are externally imposed. This in itself is highly questionable: isn't precisely the underlying problem that the expenses scandal revealed that MPs are obsessed with the idea that, unlike everyone else, they must be regulated by no-one but their sweet selves? But in any event the Report makes no argument in this respect for distinguishing between rules concerning expenses and those concerning outside interests—both concern rules about financial issues after all. It also notes rightly that the House needs to regain its self-respect and then makes the strange assertion that 'taking responsibility for its own code of conduct on financial interests. . .would be an important step in that direction', as if this would be a new thing for the House to do. It's not clear how simply *retaining* the old position of being responsible for outside interests will help *restore* lost self-respect. Kelly is on stronger ground when making the arguments about hybridity, about duplication, and the fact that without external enforcement, the drawing up of a code on MPs' interests by IPSA would indeed be 'a chimera'.
2. In response to the above, the Government, in a written statement by Harriet Harman said: 'The Government propose to repeal section 8 of the 2009 Act and the consequential references to it.'[69] Since this was achieved in the 2010 Act, the consequence is that, aside from the minor recommendations of Kelly regarding publication, at election time, of a register of each MPs outside interests, this aspect of parliamentary privilege has emerged unscathed from the expenses scandal.

Abolition of the Commissioner for Parliamentary Investigations

Since the outside bodies were therefore to lose their role in relation to privileged matters, the Committee also found that it was unnecessary to have a separate Commissioner for Parliamentary Investigations appointed by the House, 'with all the resulting potential for confusion and duplication of roles with the Parliamentary Commissioner for Standards' (at 13.38). Kelly recommended instead that IPSA should appoint a 'a compliance officer tasked with policing the expenses system, advising MPs on claims and promoting best practice.' Furthermore, 'Since the compliance officer. . .needs to be demonstrably independent of the House of Commons, it would be appropriate if he/she were appointed by the independent regulator, rather than through the Speaker's Committee, as laid down in the Act' (at 13.39). The officer 'should be able to conduct an investigation on his or her own initiative, at the request of the independent regulator, or in response to a complaint from a member of the public or an MP' (Recommendation 44). The Government agreed to this proposal also and provisions to this effect were enacted in the 2010 Act, which replaced the Commissioner with a Compliance Officer—see ss 26, 33, 34 and Schedule 4. Decisions of the Officer were made subject to appeal to a Tribunal—see s 31(5).

---

69   HC Deb 10 Dec 2009 : Column 35WS.

New enforcement powers for IPSA

Twelfth Report from the Committee on Standards in Public Life, Cm 7724 (2009)

13.41 If it is to carry out its functions effectively, it is essential that the independent regulator is given sufficient powers. It needs to be able to respond flexibly and robustly to a range of situations of differing degrees of seriousness including, a lack of cooperation from MPs, ensuring that wrongly claimed amounts are repaid, dealing with breaches of the expenses regime where repayment alone is not sufficient but where evidence of a criminal offence is not strong enough for a prosecution, and taking appropriate action in those cases where criminality is suspected.

13.42 In the Committee's view the Parliamentary Standards Act falls short of this requirement in a number of ways.

13.43 Under the Act, the new body has no power to require an MP either to repay an overpaid or wrongly claimed sum or to provide it with relevant information it has reasonably requested—though it does have the power to insist that claims are supported by docu-mentary evidence. Powers to this effect were included in the original Bill, but they were later removed in response to concerns about possible infringements of parliamentary privilege. Instead, the independent regulator must make a report of its findings in cases of non-cooperation to the House's Standards and Privileges Committee. This places it in the highly invidious position of relying for its ability to exercise its basic administrative functions on the very institution from which it is meant to be independent. It also puts the independent regulator at odds with other organisations charged with paying out (or taking in) public money, such as the DWP [Department of Work and Pensions] and HMRC [Revenue and Customs]. Both have powers without recourse to any other body to demand information and require repayment, backed by a range of statutory sanctions. The Committee's under-standing is that, in principle, these powers apply to MPs in their capacity as taxpayers or benefit claimants in the same way as to anyone else. There is no obvious reason why MPs should be in any different position when they claim expenses.

13.45 ...Any failure on the part of an MP, without reasonable excuse, to comply with those duties to cooperate should, consistent with the procedural safeguards laid out in the Act, be subject to an appropriate range of sanctions to be imposed by the independent regulator, along the lines of those available to HMRC and DWP. We are satisfied that no issue of privilege arises here as claiming expenses is not a proceeding of Parliament. In deciding whether or not sanctions were justified in a particular expenses-related case the independent regulator would not have to rely on evidence of what an MP had said or done in the House or any of its committees.

13.46 If the independent regulator believes that a case in which it has imposed a sanction on an MP also raises parliamentary standards issues, it should make a public report to that effect. It would then be up to the Commissioner for Standards to investigate the case and, if applicable, it would be up to the Standards and Privileges Committee to decide whether a parliamentary sanction (e.g. suspension from the House) was appropriate.

Recommendation 45
The independent regulator's enforcement regime should be strengthened by giving it the power to:

- **Compel MPs to cooperate with the new body, including through the provision of relevant information.**

- **Require the repayment of wrongly paid or misclaimed sums, with associated costs if appropriate.**
- **Impose, subject to the procedural safeguards laid out in the Act, its own non-parliamentary sanctions for breaches of the expenses regime (including where necessary of a financial nature). . .without the need to report to the Commissioner for Parliamentary Standards.**

Note

The Government accepted this recommendation, which was essentially aimed at restoring the enforcement powers that had been included in the original Bill but removed under protest:

> As it now appears that allowing sanctions to be imposed directly by the regulator is acceptable, the Government will introduce amendments to the 2009 Act to give the compliance officer the power to impose sanctions, namely a civil penalty, as well as requiring restitution of wrongly paid allowances. Repayments, monetary penalties and costs will also be made recoverable as a civil debt. In addition, the Government will provide a route of appeal from the decisions of the compliance officer to the first-tier tribunal. Since allowances claims are not covered by privilege, there should not be any difficulty in this regard.
>
> Cases could still be referred to the Committee on Standards and Privileges if it is felt that parliamentary sanctions are also needed or to the prosecuting authorities if the offence of making false declarations may have been committed.[70]

These provisions were passed and became ss 26, 33, 34 and Schedule 4 of the 2010 Act.

Introducing an independent element into the relevant Commons' committees

Twelfth Report from the Committee on Standards in Public Life, Cm 7724 (2009)

Recommendation 48

The Speaker's Committee on the independent regulator should include three lay members drawn from outside Parliament who have not previously been MPs or peers. They should be chosen through the official public appointments process and formally approved by the House.

Recommendation 51

There should be at least two lay members who have never been Parliamentarians on the Standards and Privileges Committee. Their appointment should be made in the same way as that of the lay members of the Speaker's Committee of the independent regulator.

Recommendation 52

The external members of both the Standards and Privileges Committee and the Speaker's Committee of the independent regulator should have full voting rights. If the House authorities are of the opinion that clarifying the question of parliamentary privilege in that regard requires an amendment to the Parliamentary Standards Act, the Government should facilitate this.

---

70   HC Deb 10 Dec 2009: Column 35WS.

Note

For the response of the Committee on Standards and Privileges to these recommendations, see its 2nd Report of 2009–10, *Implementing the Twelfth Report from the Committee on Standards in Public Life* HC 67. These proposals were given effect through Section 27 of the 2010 Act.

Changes to the substantive rules governing entitlement to claim expenses

Kelly also made a number of recommendations in relation to the actual rules governing expenses. These are far less constitutionally significant, but the proposed new rules include the following:

> MPs would be banned from claiming towards the cost of their mortgages and employing relatives at public expense. Sir Christopher says mortgage claims should be stopped after an "appropriate transitional" period and employing relatives should be phased out within five years. MPs would be allowed to claim for rent instead of mortgage payments. The practice of "flipping" which of their properties an MP calls their second home would be banned. Any MP making a capital gain over the next five years on the sale of a subsidised home will have to give it up. Generous resettlement grants for MPs who stand down would also be axed under the proposals. In future, MPs would get eight weeks' pay instead— under the current system some long-serving MPs can get up to £64,000.[71]

For a summary of these, see the Executive Summary, paras 16–26, and, for the detail of the proposals, the body of the report itself. Kelly also set out a set of principles in Chapter 3 of the Report to govern the expenses system in future:

- Members of Parliament should always behave with probity and integrity when making claims on public resources. MPs should be held, and regard themselves, as personally responsible and accountable for expenses incurred, and claims made, and for adherence to these principles as well as to the rules.
- Members of Parliament have the right to be reimbursed for unavoidable costs where they are incurred wholly, exclusively, and necessarily in the performance of their parliamentary duties, but not otherwise.
- Members of Parliament should not exploit the system for personal financial advantage, nor to confer an undue advantage on a political organisation.
- The system should be open and transparent, and should be subject to independent audit and assurance.
- The details of the expenses scheme for Members of Parliament should be determined independently of Parliament.
- There should be clear, effective and proportionate sanctions for breaches of the rules, robustly enforced.
- The presumption should be that, in matters relating to expenses, MPs should be treated in the same manner as other citizens. If the arrangements depart from those which would normally be expected elsewhere, those departures need to be explicitly justified.

---

71   http://news.bbc.co.uk/1/hi/uk_politics/8301443.stm

- The scheme should provide value for the taxpayer. Value for money should not necessarily be judged by reference to financial costs alone.
- Arrangements should be flexible enough to take account of the diverse working patterns and demands placed upon individual MPs, and should not unduly deter representation from all sections of society.
- The system should be clear and understandable. If it is difficult to explain an element of the system in terms which the general public will regard as reasonable, that is a powerful argument against it.

The scandal and the House of Lords

As seen above, the new Act does not apply to the House of Lords, which was largely untouched by the expenses scandal. However, as Bradley and Ewing note:

> In 2009 the House through its Committee for Privileges had to deal with allegations that certain peers had told journalists that parliamentary services could be provided to commercial interests in return for payment. An investigation into the conduct of four members of the House established that two peers had breached the House's code of conduct. The question then arose as to what sanction the House could impose on the two peers. The House accepted the view of the Committee for Privileges that the House has always since before 1705 had the power to discipline its members; although the House may not exclude a member entirely (as the House of Commons may do), the House has an inherent power to suspend a member from the House for a period not exceeding the life of the current Parliament. This was considered an appropriate sanction to be exercised today, unlike the power of the House to detain or to fine someone who had breached the privileges of the House. The two peers were suspended for the remainder of the current session.[72]

Notes

1. As a result of the discovery the Lords had no power to expel Members, provision to allow for the automatic exclusion of Peers who had committed serious offences or their expulsion by resolution of the House were tabled by the Government as amendments to add to the Constitutional Reform and Governance Bill 2009. However, as noted in Chapter 9, at 496, these provisions were *not* passed.
2. In relation to expenses in the Lords, Kelly said:

> 3.5 The arrangements for providing financial support to members of the House of Lords is currently being considered by the [Senior Salary's Review Board]. There are a number of important differences between the House of Commons and House of Lords. Peers, for example, do not currently receive a salary. But on matters relating to expenses there ought to be a consistent approach between the two chambers. The principles we have set out in this chapter should also, mutatis mutandis, in our view apply to the expenses system for members of the House of Lords.

---

72   Bradley and Ewing, 'Update' above.

Conclusions on the expenses episode

Kelso comments:

> For much of its history, Parliament functioned on the basis that it presided over a deferential and ill-informed electorate, and that the secretive and elitist way in which it conducted its affairs was justified because MPs were honourable individuals who knew best about how to fulfil their jobs and run the House. . . . Any remnants of that sentiment have now been entirely blown away.[73]

The expenses scandal undoubtedly shook public confidence in Parliament to the core, and appeared utterly to discredit the long cherished notion of self-regulation in the eyes of the media and the public. This may prove to have longer term repercussions. Yet, as we have seen, attempts to use the episode to make further inroads on self-regulation, in terms of outside rule making and enforcement of the rules regarding member's interests were first emasculated during the passage of the Bill, while the weak changes that were left in have been reversed, returning the issue of member's outside interests to full self-regulation once again. Article 9 of the Bill of the Rights continues to be upheld as a kind of constitutional super-norm, which may not be called into question. It remains to be seen how much longer this can carry on being the case.

FREEDOM OF SPEECH

The general parameters of the privilege

In terms of creating conflict outside Parliament it is, not surprisingly, those privileges that, in their exercise, can affect the legal *rights* of those outside Parliament which have caused difficulties. Principal amongst these is freedom of speech, as Munro explains.

C Munro, *Studies in Constitutional Law,* 2nd edn (1999)

The privilege. . .was effectively secured at the Revolution. Its inclusion in the Bill of Rights gave it a statutory foundation. Article 9 of the Bill of Rights proclaimed: That the freedom of speech, and debates or proceedings in Parliament ought not to be impeached or questioned in any court or place out of Parliament'. . . .

Article 9 applies equally to both Houses, and its effect is that no action or prosecution can be brought against a Member for anything said or done in the course of proceedings in Parliament The most important application of this is that it invests members with an immunity from the law of defamation, when they are speaking in Parliament and on some other occasions. So, when an action for defamation was brought against a Member of the Commons for words spoken in the House, the court recognised that it had no jurisdiction in the matter, and ordered that the writ should be removed from the records [*Dillon v Balfour* (1887) 20 LR Ir 600]. In the same way, the courts would be unable to entertain prosecutions or actions of other kinds. In 1938, when Mr Duncan Sandys raised a matter of national

---

security in a parliamentary question, and refused to reveal the sources of his information, a prosecution on an Official Secrets charge was threatened. The House asserted its privilege in order to avert the threat [HC 146 (1937–38), HC 173 (1937–38)]. In 1977, at a trial on Official Secrets Act charges, a judge had allowed a witness, an officer in the Security Services, to be identified only as 'Colonel B'. When some organs of the press referred to the officer by his real name, in disregard of the judge's wishes, proceedings for contempt of court were brought against them. However, four Members of the Commons, who named the officer during questions in the House, were, under the shelter of privilege, immune from such proceedings themselves. Article 9 also means that matters arising in the course of parliamentary proceedings cannot be relied on for the purpose of supporting an action or prosecution based on events occurring elsewhere. For example, the Church of Scientology, bringing a libel suit against an MP for remarks made in a television interview, was unable to refer to his speeches in the House of Commons in seeking to prove his malice [*Church of Scientology of California v Johnson-Smith* [1972] 1 QB 522; [1972] 1 All ER 378.]

Parliament's official reports and papers enjoy a corresponding privilege. Following *Stockdale v Hansard* [(1839) 9 Ad & El 1], the Parliamentary Papers Act 1840 was passed, which bars proceedings, criminal or civil, against persons for the publication of papers or reports printed by order of either House of Parliament, or copies of them. . .

Notes

1. Extracts from *Hansard* are thus covered by absolute privilege under s 3 of the Parliamentary Papers Act 1840; however, protection does not extend to headlines under which the extract appears (*Mangena v Lloyd* (1908) 99 LT 824).

2. Section 15 and Sched 1 of the Defamation Act 1996 provide that fair and accurate *reporting* of proceedings in Parliament—in fact of any proceedings of any legislature in the world—are covered by qualified privileges. The interpretation of this privilege was recently considered in *Curistan v Times Newspapers Ltd* [2008] EMLR 17 by the Court of Appeal. It was held that:

   H11 One of the requirements of a fair and accurate report was that the quality of fairness should not be lost by intermingling extraneous material with the material for which the privilege was claimed. A report could be selective and concentrate on one aspect, as long as it reported fairly and accurately the impression that the reporter would have received as a reasonable spectator in the proceedings. A report did not cease to be fair and accurate because it contained slight inaccuracies, but if there was a substantial or material misstatement of fact prejudicial to the claimant's reputation then the report would not be privileged.

A parliamentary sketch will also be covered by qualified privilege if it is fair and accurate and published without malice (*Cook v Alexander* [1974] 1 QB 279).

The inter-relationship between injunctions, parliamentary privilege and the above qualified privilege to report proceedings in Parliament was recently raised by the quickly notorious *Trafigura* case in October 2009. The lawyers Carter-Ruck served the *Guardian* newspaper with an injunction preventing it from publishing an allegedly confidential document that related to ongoing libel litigation concerning claims that the company Trafigura had dumped toxic waste in the Cote d'Ivoire in Africa, causing thousands to become ill. (Trafigura later agreed to pay £30 million in compensation to the victims.) Carter-Ruck obtained and served on the *Guardian* a so-called 'Super Injunction' that forbade not only mention of the report, but also of the fact that an injunction had been obtained or on whose behalf. A question was subsequently asked in Parliament about it. It appears clear that such an injunction could not stop an MP, under cover of Parliamentary privilege, from asking a question in Parliament: this would be protected under Art 9. A memorandum prepared by Carter-Ruck and submitted to the Committee on Culture Media and Sport, states:

> There is and never has been any suggestion on the part of my firm, nor, I am sure, have the *Guardian*'s lawyers ever been under the misapprehension, that the interim Orders made in the Trafigura case could or would have the effect of restraining debate within Parliament itself. Under Article 9 Bill of Rights 1688 no court order could have such an effect.[74]

However, in such cases, the Speaker could choose not to allow the question, on the basis of the House's *sub judice* rule, which provides that 'matters awaiting adjudication in a court of law should not be brought forward in motions, debates, questions or supplementary questions'.[75]

The real issue at stake in this case was whether the *Guardian* could be prevented by the injunction from reporting a question asked in the House by an MP about the injunction. Such reporting is covered neither by Art 9 itself, nor by the Parliamentary Papers Act; as the Joint Committee on Privileges confirmed 'in the case of court injunctions restraining publicity, these bind the media but not either House'.[76] In this case, Carter-Ruck agreed to the *Guardian*'s request and obtained from the court a variation of the injunction, in order to allow for reporting of the question in Parliament.

Areas of uncertainty and controversy

Wason v Walter (1868) QB 73 confirmed that Art 9 of the Bill of Rights provides complete civil and criminal immunity for Members in respect of words spoken by them during proceedings in Parliament.[77] Members are free, for example, to reveal information in Parliament in breach of the Official Secrets Act.[78] Members have deliberately sometimes revealed information in Parliament protected by court injunction in order to protest against the fact that the media are being prevented from reporting it, as recently in the *Trafigura* case, and in relation to the naming of 'child Z', contrary to an injunction restraining revelation of the child's name in an Early Day Motion in the 1995–96 session.[79] This is thus a remarkably wide privilege, considering the numerous constraints on freedom of expression of the rest of the population (see Chapter 18). Regrettably, however, as was evident from the above, the scope of the privilege is by no means clear. This is partly due to the fact that, as Munro noted, the phrase

---

74   Select Committee on Culture Media and Sport, Memoranda PS 143 (2009–10).

75   For discussion of the *sub judice* rule see First Report of the Joint Committee on Parliamentary Privilege, HC 43-I (1998–99) www.publications.parliament.uk/pa/jt199899/jtselect/jtpriv/43/4308.htm esp. at paras 203–11.

76   See the Joint Committee report, *ibid* at 204.

77   Note, however, the interesting comment of Laws J on Art 9 (speaking extra-judicially): 'I am not myself convinced that if [an MP] were motivated by reasons of actual personal malice to use his position to defame, in the course of debate, an individual outside Parliament, he should not as a result be subject to the ordinary laws of defamation, and Article 9 could readily be construed comfortably with such a state of affairs' (J Laws, 'Law and democracy' [1995] PL 72, 76, n 14).

78   See the Joint Committee (1999), at [212]–[216].

79   That case led the then Procedure Committee to state that: If there were strong evidence to suggest that breaches of court orders as a result of proceedings of the House represented a serious challenge to the due process of law, we would not hesitate to recommend a further limitation on the rights of free speech enjoyed by members. . .We urge members to exercise the greatest care in avoiding breaches of court orders (Second Report, HC (1995–96), at [16]).

'proceedings in Parliament' is of uncertain meaning. It is fairly clear, as the Joint Committee on Parliamentary Privilege remarked, that it covers:

> . . . Debates (expressly mentioned in Article 9), motions, proceedings on bills, votes, parliamentary questions, proceedings within committees formally appointed by either House, proceedings within sub-committees of such committees, and public petitions, once presented, statements made and documents produced in the course of these proceedings, and notices of these proceedings. . . internal House or committee papers of an official nature directly related to the proceedings, and communications arising directly out of such proceedings, as where a member seeks further information in the course of proceedings and another member agrees to provide it [as well as]. . . the steps taken in carrying out an order of either House.[80]

The difficulty really arises over what may be counted as 'proceedings in Parliament'. Something is not a 'proceeding in Parliament' merely because it happens there. A defendant's defamatory statements about his former wife, put in letters to MPs, were not protected by reason of having been posted within the Palace of Westminster (*Rivlin v Bilankin* [1953] 1 All ER 534). Even a conversation between Members, if on private affairs, would probably not be privileged (HC 101 (1938–39)). Rather the phrase seems intended to cover what is the business of Parliament or its Members. The matter has been considered by the Commons, but decisions by the House on matters of privilege set no binding precedent. The London Electricity Board case in 1958 is one well-known example:

> Mr George Strauss MP, in a letter written to a minister, described the Board's practices in selling scrap metal as 'a scandal which should be instantly rectified'. The letter was passed on to the Board, which threatened to sue Mr Strauss for libel. The House determined that the letter was not a 'proceeding in Parliament', although the Committee of Privileges had taken the opposite view [HC 305 (1956–57), HC 227 (1957–58), 591, HC Official Report (5th series), col 208]. However, it is difficult to infer much from this, for the vote was narrow and the decision is not binding on the House. It may too have been significant that the subject of the letter (being a matter of day-to-day administration of a nationalised industry) was not within ministerial answerability, and therefore could not have formed the basis of a parliamentary question. The Speaker ruled that if a Member tabled a question, and a minister invited him to discuss it with him, the correspondence or discussions were covered by privilege [591 HC Official Report (5th series), col 808].[81]

Subsequent events have suggested that the matter would now be differently decided. In 1967 the Select Committee on Parliamentary Privilege strongly recommended that legislation be enacted to reverse the Commons decision in *Strauss* (1970); the Joint Committee on Publication of Proceedings in Parliament proposed a definition of 'proceedings in Parliament', which *included* letters sent between MPs for the purpose of allowing them to carry out their duties. Their proposed definition was subsequently approved by the Faulks Committee on Defamation 1975, and the Committee of Privileges 1976–77. Further, in the *Strauss* case, the vote on whether the Electricity Board had committed a breach of privilege, which went against Strauss, an Opposition MP, divided substantially along party lines. This

---

80   See n 75 above, para 102.

81   Munro, n 3 above, p 222

phenomenon was seen even more clearly in the Report of the Committee of Privileges on implementation of the Nolan Committee's recommendations: both the Committee and the House as a whole split on clearly defined party lines.[82] If the Commons is going to be influenced by party political principles when making such determinations, this will clearly hinder any attempt to deduce a set of consistent principles from its decisions.

The problem of whether a particular speech or letter is covered by absolute privilege assumes a more pressing aspect when a litigant sues in defamation in respect of words which Parliament has deemed to be absolutely privileged, that is, immune from civil or criminal proceedings. When this happens, Parliament can regard the action as a contempt and attempt to prevent the litigant from exercising his legal right to sue and enforce the judgment of the court. As Munro points out:

> In the London Electricity Board case, it was taken for granted in parliamentary discussion that the commencement of proceedings in a court in respect of a 'proceeding in Parliament' was in itself a breach of privilege. That assumption may be criticised, and the assumption that a mere threat to institute proceedings amounts to a breach of privilege is even more doubtful. It may be noted too that the Select Committee on Parliamentary Privilege recommended in 1967 that, save in exceptional circumstances, such matters should be left to the ordinary processes of the courts [HC 34 (1967–68)]. But it is by no means certain that the House might not take a similar view again.[83]

Notes

1. The difficulty was illustrated in 1839 in the case of *Stockdale v Hansard* (1839) 9 Ad & El 1. Stockdale brought an action in respect of allegedly defamatory words in a report of prison inspectors published by Hansard, by order of the Commons. When the action was tried, the court decided that Hansard's reports were *not* covered by absolute privilege, so that Stockdale could proceed. Parliament, however, refused to accept this judgment and so an impasse developed (see below), which was finally resolved only when the Parliamentary Papers Act 1884 was passed. Alternatively, as in the *Church of Scientology* case mentioned above, the issue can arise where a defendant to a libel action wishes to defend the proceedings brought against him by referring to matters which have taken place in Parliament: in such a case it will be necessary to ascertain what amounts to 'proceedings in Parliament'. This issue arose in *Rost v Edwards* [1990] 2 WLR 1280, in which Popplewell J had 'no hesitation' in saying *(obiter)* that correspondence between Members was covered, but cited no authority, and indeed no argument of principle to support his view.

2. The Joint Committee on Parliamentary Privilege, HLP 43–41 (1998–99) saw insufficient justification for extending Art 9 to cover MPs' correspondence.

3. A part of the judgment in *Rost* which was later to become controversial was Popplewell J's finding that the Register of Members' Interests was *not* part of 'proceedings in Parliament' for the purposes of Art 9. This issue arose again in *Hamilton v Al Fayed* [1999] 1 WLR 1569; [1999] 3 All ER 317, CA; [2001] 1 AC 395. Neil Hamilton made a number of parliamentary interventions, including questions in the defendant Al Fayed's interests, and on October 20, 1994 the *Guardian* published a front page story which alleged that Al Fayed had paid tens of thousands of pounds to the plaintiff through the agency of Ian Greer Associates (IGA), in return for asking questions in

---

82 As noted above, the issue which split the parties was the proposed disclosure of the *amount* of outside earnings. All of the Conservative Members on the Committee voted against the proposal, whilst all Opposition Members voted in favour. For the debate, see HC Deb cols 608–82 (6 November 1995); for the crucial divisions showing how the Committee and the House voted, see the Second Report from the Select Committee on Standards in Public Life, HC 816 (1994–95), pp xx–xxi and HC Deb cols 661–62.

83 C Munro, *Studies in Constitutional Law* (1987), p 140.

Parliament on his behalf. The article also alleged that the plaintiff and his wife had enjoyed a week's stay at the Ritz Hotel in Paris free of charge, and had had free shopping trips to Harrods at the defendant's invitation. The plaintiff issued proceedings for libel against the *Guardian,* as did IGA and Mr Ian Greer, on the same day as the publication, October 20, 1994. The *Guardian* pleaded justification, alleging *inter alia* that over the two-year period 1987 to 1989 the plaintiff sought and received from the defendant in the form of either cash or Harrods gift vouchers a total of £28,000, for the most part in cash, and that such sums represented payments by the defendant for the plaintiff's services in tabling parliamentary questions and motions and other parliamentary services. In his reply the plaintiff asserted that he had never received any payment in cash or kind for any action taken by him in support of the defendant's cause.

On July 21, 1995 May J (as he then was) stayed both the plaintiff's and Greer-IGA's actions, holding that 'the claims and defences raised issues whose investigation would infringe parliamentary privilege to such an extent that they could not fairly be tried'. A significant part of his ratio was that The Guardian would be inhibited in presenting its plea of justification since it would be precluded on grounds of parliamentary privilege from linking the alleged payments made to the plaintiff with the admitted tabling of the parliamentary questions. That seemed to be the end of the matter. But on July 4, 1996 the Defamation Act 1996 received Royal Assent. Section 13 [of the Act] was prompted by the stay of Mr Hamilton's action in the preceding July. It allows Members to waive privilege so as to allow them to take proceedings which would otherwise be stayed as contrary to Article 9. On July 31, 1996 May J lifted the stay imposed by him on July 21, 1995. Section 13 of the Defamation Act 1996 provides as follows:

Defamation Act 1996, s 13

1 Where the conduct of a person in or in relation to proceedings in Parliament is in issue in defamation proceedings, he may waive for the purposes of those proceedings, so far as concerns him, the protection of any enactment or rule of law which prevents proceedings in Parliament being impeached or questioned in any court or place out of Parliament.

2 Where a person waives that protection:

(a) any such enactment or rule of law shall not apply to prevent evidence being given, questions being asked or statements, submissions, comments or findings being made about his conduct; and

(b) none of those things shall be regarded as infringing the privilege of either House of Parliament.

3 The waiver by one person of that protection does not affect its operation in relation to another person who has not waived it. . .

4 Nothing in this section affects any enactment or rule of law so far as it protects a person (including a person who has waived the protection referred to above) from legal liability for words spoken or things done in the course of, or for the purposes of or incidental to, any proceedings in Parliament.

5 Without prejudice to the generality of subsection (4), that subsection applies to:

(a) the giving of evidence before either House or a committee;

(b) the presentation or submission of a document to either House or a committee;

(c)   the preparation of a document for the purposes of or incidental to the trans-
acting of any such business;

(d)   the formulation, making or publication of a document, including a report, by or
pursuant to an order of either House or a committee; and

(e)   any communication with the Parliamentary Commissioner for Standards or any
person having functions in connection with the registration of members'
interests.

In this subsection 'a committee' means a committee of either House or a joint committee of
both Houses of Parliament.

Notes

1. After the end of the *Guardian* case, the Standards Commissioner investigated the allegations
concerning Hamilton and in his report of July 1997, concluded that Hamilton had indeed received
cash payments from the defendant and hospitality at the Ritz as a reward for lobbying. In its report
of November 1997 the Standards Committee held that Hamilton's conduct had fallen seriously and
persistently below the standards which the House was entitled to expect, and this finding was
approved by the House. Meanwhile in January 1997 Channel 4 broadcast a programme in its
Dispatches strand which contained an interview with the defendant in which he repeated his
allegations concerning the cash payments, the holiday in the Ritz and the shopping trips to Harrods. In January 1988 the plaintiff commenced fresh proceedings for libel against the defendant.
The defendant applied to strike out the action on the grounds that (1) to allow the action to
proceed would necessarily involve questioning proceedings in Parliament in contravention of Art 9
of the Bill of Rights 1689 or a wider rule of which Art 9 was merely one manifestation and/or (2)
the action constituted a collateral attack upon Parliament's decision upon allegations of misconduct against the plaintiff in resolving to adopt the Standards Committee's report.

2. One point that the litigation raised was whether the investigation and report of the Commissioner
and Committee which had both made findings against Hamilton in the 'cash for questions affair'
were 'proceedings in Parliament' and so protected under Art 9 from being 'impeached or questioned' in court. Some doubt was cast on the contention that they were such 'proceedings' by the
findings of Popplewell J at first instance. Indeed his conclusion was that the findings (or as he saw
it, non-findings) of the Committee on the key issue and the investigation of the Commissioner
were not 'proceedings in Parliament' such as to oust the jurisdiction of the court to consider them
critically. These matters were then considered in the Court of Appeal (*Hamilton v Al Fayed* [1999]
1 WLR 1569, CA, which found that: 'The [Commissioner's] inquiry and report, the hearings before
the CSP [the Committee] and its report, as well as the resolution of the House, amounted individually and collectively to 'proceedings in Parliament' whether for the purposes of Article 9 of the
Bill of Rights or of any wider rule which enjoins the protection of such proceedings.' This part of
the Court of Appeal judgment was explicitly endorsed by the House of Lords [2001] 1 AC 395. In
R (On the application of Mohammed Al Fayed) v Parliamentary Commissioner for Standards,[84] the
Court of Appeal had to consider whether a report made by Commissioner to the House of
Commons Standards and Privileges Committee was amenable to judicial review. The Court had no
hesitation in finding that it was.

3. The Joint Committee on Parliamentary Privilege made a number of recommendations on what
should amount to 'proceedings in Parliament' for the purposes of Art 9 and recommended that
the term should be defined in statute. The Joint Committee recommends the enactment of a
definition on the following lines:

---

84   [1998] 1 WLR 669.

(1)   For the purposes of Article 9 of the Bill of Rights 1689 'proceedings in Parlia-
         ment' means all words spoken and acts done in the course of, or for the
         purposes of, or necessarily incidental to, transacting the business of either
         House of Parliament or of a committee.

(2)   Without limiting (1), this includes:

         (a)   the giving of evidence before a House or a committee or an officer
               appointed by a House to receive such evidence;
         (b)   the presentation or submission of a document to a House or a com-
               mittee or an officer appointed by a House to receive it, once the document
               is accepted;
         (c)   the preparation of a document for the purposes of transacting the busi-
               ness of a House or a committee, provided any drafts, notes, advice or the
               like are not circulated more widely than is reasonable for the purposes of
               preparation;
         (d)   the formulation, making or publication of a document by a House or a
               committee;
         (e)   the maintenance of any register of the interests of the members of a House
               and any other register of interests prescribed by resolution of a House.[85]

Three points in particular may be noted about this definition: first, it explicitly *includes* the Register of
Members' Interests in what would be a direct statutory reversal of the decision in *Rost* on the point;
second, it is intended, as noted above, to *exclude* letters sent by MPs whether to constituents or
Ministers; third, it *excludes* the matter of MPs' expenses. It has not been enacted.

'Impeached or questioned'

It is not merely the phrase 'proceedings in Parliament' which has caused disagreement. Article 9 of the
Bill of Rights states that freedom of speech, debates and proceedings in Parliament ought not to be
'impeached or questioned in any court or place outside Parliament'. It is accepted that this means that
no legal liability may arise in respect of words spoken in Parliament, but what further meanings do
the words have? Do they mean that words spoken, or matters taking place in Parliament cannot even
be adduced in evidence in legal proceedings? Or that they may be so adduced, but cannot be
subject to *critical* scrutiny? While *Rost v Edwards* [1990] 2 WLR 1280, 1289–90 suggested the former
interpretation, it now appears tolerably well settled that the second is correct. The Privy Council in
Prebble v Television New Zealand Ltd [1994] 3 All ER 407 said that '[i]t is questionable whether *Rost*
was rightly decided' and confirmed that:

> parties to litigation, by whomsoever commenced, cannot bring into question any-
> thing said or done in the House by suggesting (whether by direct evidence, cross-
> examination, inference or submission) that the actions or words were inspired by
> improper motives or were untrue or misleading. Such matters lie entirely within the
> jurisdiction of the House. . .
>
> However, their Lordships wish to make it clear that. . .there could be no objection
> to the use of Hansard to prove what was done and said in Parliament as a matter of
> history. . .

---

85   HLP 43–1 (1998–99), para 129.

The House noted also that:

> there may be cases in which the exclusion of material on the grounds of parliamentary privilege makes it quite impossible fairly to determine the issue between the parties. In such a case the interests of justice may demand a stay of proceedings. But such a stay should only be granted in the most extreme circumstances. . .

Notes

1. Thus the Privy Council said that where it was impossible to determine the matter at issue between the parties, a stay might be ordered so that Parliament could determine whether it wished to waive privilege in the interests of justice. Libel actions in which most of the matters of justification were covered by privilege might fall within that special rule. However, in the instant present case, in which the defendant would still be able to put forward most of the matters relied on in justification, that exceptional procedure should not be followed.

2. The *Prebble* view was questioned by the Court of Appeal in *Hamilton v Al Fayed* [1999] 1 WLR 1569, which proposed a narrower scope for Art 9 in this respect. However, the House of Lords emphatically re-affirmed the *Prebble* view in the same case:

Hamilton v Al Fayed [2001] 1 AC 395 (extracts)

Lord Browne-Wilkinson: . . . The normal impact of parliamentary privilege is to prevent the court from entertaining any evidence, cross-examination or submissions which challenge the veracity or propriety of anything done in the course of parliamentary proceedings. Thus, it is not permissible to challenge by cross-examination in a later action the veracity of evidence given to a parliamentary committee. If that approach had been adopted in the present case, there can be no doubt that, apart from section 13, the trial of the action would from the outset have proved completely impossible. All evidence by Mr Hamilton that he had not received money for questions would have conflicted directly with the evidence of Mr Al Fayed which was accepted by the parliamentary committees. Any attempt to cross-examine Mr Al Fayed to the effect that he was lying to the parliamentary committees when he said that he had paid money for questions would have been stopped forthwith as an infringement of parliamentary privilege.

Notes

1. Thus, the decision was that the courts were unable to hear any evidence or permit any cross-examination which implied any criticism of MPs *or others giving evidence to Parliament* about what had gone on in Parliament, without Parliament's permission, unless the MP concerned decided to waive privilege under the Defamation Act 1996, s 13. Whether the evidence should be admitted would therefore be decided by a resolution of the House of Commons, which could be subject to party political considerations. It seems far from satisfactory that matters of admissibility of evidence should be decided by such a partisan body.

2. For a similar case in which the defendant newspaper wished to rely upon pleading impropriety connected with the handling of certain Early Day Motions in Parliament in defending an action brought by an MP, see *Allison v Haines, The Times,* 25 July 1995. The defence was found to be contrary to Article 9, but it was held that since the defence pleaded was the only one available to the defendant, it would be manifestly unfair to allow the action to proceed; it was therefore struck out.

3. Recently in *Toussaint v Attorrney General of St Vincent* [2007] 1 WLR 2825, the Privy Council confirmed that a statement in Parliament could be relied upon simply as a record of what was said

by the Prime Minister explaining why a particular decision had been made, provided that the statement itself was not impugned.

The case of *R (Asif Javed) v Secretary of State for the Home Department* [2002] QB 129, is discussed in Chapter 15 at 875. The Court of Appeal of England and Wales found that Art 9 did not prevent the courts from annulling subordinate legislation that had been tabled and approved by Parliament, even though the result appeared discordant with statements approving the legislation made in parliamentary debate. In *Bradley* [2007] EWHC 242 (Admin), a case concerning a challenge to the findings of the Parliamentary Commissioner for Administration, the court found that the litigant could not rely on oral evidence given by the PCA to a parliamentary committee, but that it could cite from the report produced by that Committee (see paras 25–35). A similar finding was made in *Office of Government Commerce v Information Commissioner* [2008] EWHC 774 in the context of a finding by the Information Tribunal (which hears appeals on freedom of information requests) that had in effect found a Ministerial reply to a parliamentary question to have been inadequate and relied on findings by a Select Committee to support its findings in favour of disclosure.

4. The Joint Committee on Parliamentary Privilege took a firmly conservative view on this point: they recommended a statutory definition of the meaning of 'impeached or questioned' based on s 16 of the Parliamentary Privileges Act 1987 (Commonwealth legislation), namely:

> a statutory enactment to the effect that no court or tribunal may receive evidence, or permit questions to be asked or submissions made, concerning proceedings in Parliament by way of, or for the purpose of, questioning or relying on the truth, motive, intention or good faith of anything forming part of proceedings in Parliament or drawing any inference from anything forming part of those proceedings.

5. It is evident from *Prebble* and *Fayed* taken together that the Privy Council and the House of Lords (Lord Browne-Wilkinson delivered the relevant speeches in both cases) saw two reasons as to why critical scrutiny of proceedings in Parliament cannot take place. One was that, if the courts found that the Member had lied to the House (a contempt of Parliament) but Parliament found he or she had not, there would be a conflict between Parliament and the courts. But all the serious conflicts which have arisen between the courts and Parliament (see below) have arisen because the courts have tried to attach *legal liability* to things done or said in Parliament and Parliament has sought to protect its Members from such liability. No such liability was in question in this case. The second reason given was that, if Members anticipated that their statements made in the House would later be subject to 'challenge' or questioning, they would not have the confidence to speak out freely. Two things may be said about this. First, it seems, with respect, simply incorrect. If a Member is telling the truth, or giving his honest opinion, why should the realisation that his statements may later be scrutinised inhibit him from speaking? Maybe such a realisation would inhibit him from telling lies, but is this a bad thing? Presumably, no one wishes to encourage members to be dishonest. But second, what members say in the House is *already the subject of critical and probing scrutiny,* as carried on by journalists and political commentators. What possible justification is there for saying that a member who may be savaged in the press for misleading the House—as William Waldegrave was repeatedly[86] in respect of misleading answers given by him to the House in relation to government policy on arms sales to Iraq—must be exempt from such criticism if it would be voiced by a barrister in a courtroom? In neither case is he or she in danger of incurring legal liability for what he or she says.

---

86   See, e.g. 'Five steps to save us from the contempt of our rulers', *The Independent,* 16 February 1995.

6. The arguments of the Joint Committee on this point seem manifestly unpersuasive: reacting to a proposal by Dr Marshall that statute should make clear that Art 9 only had the effect of forbidding the imposition of actual legal liability in respect of words spoken in Parliament, it said:

> [Such] a provision. . .would mean that members, although not facing legal liability, could find themselves called to account in court for what they said in Parliament and why they said it. We believe that, in general, this would not be desirable. Legal immunity may be the principal function of Article 9 today, but it is not the only purpose. Although the phrase 'impeached or questioned' perhaps supports the view that the Article 9 prohibition is co-terminous with legal liability, a wider principle is involved here, namely, that members ought not to be called to account in court for their participation in parliamentary proceedings. This is, and should remain, the general rule.[87]

It may be noted that no argument is given for allowing MPs to be fully exposed to the vitriolic and often inaccurate or politically biased criticism of MPs' conduct which may appear in the press, but prohibiting the far more measured and scrupulous criticism which might take place in court.

7. Thus, it is suggested that the arguments for maintaining such a draconian bar on, for example, any suggestion being made in court that a parliamentary committee may have received untruthful or inaccurate evidence from a person who may not even be an MP come nowhere near supporting it.

8. The injustice which appears to arise from privilege, where the person claiming privilege is the one who has made the defamatory statements concerned, was adverted to in *Wright and Advertiser Newspapers Ltd v Lewis* (1990) 53 SASR 416, 421–22; it was pointed out that if a Member of Parliament 'sued for defamation in respect of criticisms of his statements or conduct in the Parliament. The defendant would be precluded however from alleging and proving that what was said by way of criticism was true. This would amount to a gross distortion of the law of defamation'.

9. Section 13 of the Defamation Act 1996, which in essence allows an MP to waive privilege in relation to defamation proceedings, was designed to remedy the apparent injustice which occurs when MPs are forced out of office as a result of allegations relating to their parliamentary conduct, but have no way of clearing their name through defamation proceedings (any action would be struck out as contrary to Art 9). It was confirmed in *Hamilton v Al Fayed* [2001] 1 AC 395, HL that s 13 allowed Hamilton to waive privilege in this case.

10. Whilst many MPs and peers welcomed the advent of s 13, two clear objections to it are apparent. The first is the apparent unfairness of the new position: if an MP is defamed about his parliamentary activities, he or she can lift the cloak of privilege to sue. By contrast, a newspaper or journalist defending an action brought by an MP, who needs to adduce evidence as to proceedings in Parliament as part of his defence (as in *Prebble*) will find that privilege will prevent him from doing so. In addition, of course, citizens defamed by MPs will continue to be unable to clear their names as only MPs will be able to waive privilege.

11. The second main objection to the change was argued by Lords Lester and Richards in the debate on s 13; as the former put it, '[t]he immunities written into Article 9 were not included simply for the personal. . .benefit of Members. . .but to protect the integrity of the legislative process by ensuring the independence of individual legislators'.[88] Since the rationale for privilege is supposed to be its necessity to each House as a whole, it follows that waiver of its protection should be a

---

87   See n 85 above, para 77.

88   Quoted *ibid*.

matter for the House only, not a power in the hands of individual Members to be used for their personal benefit.

12. The Joint Committee found this criticism of s 13 persuasive and recommended:

> Section 13 should be replaced by a short statutory provision empowering each House to waive Art 9 for the purpose of any court proceedings, whether relating to defamation or to any other matter, where the words spoken or the acts done in proceedings in Parliament would not expose the speaker of the words or the doer of the acts to any legal liability.[89]

13. A final problem with the embargo on any form of questioning of proceedings in parliament is that it may represent a violation of Art 6 of the ECHR. Article 6(1) states: 'In the determination of his civil rights and obligations. . .everyone is entitled to a fair and public hearing within a reasonable time by an independent and impartial tribunal established by law.' As we have seen above, it is possible that the judicial interpretation of Art 9 of the Bill of Rights (as precluding any evidence to be given, or cross-examination engaged in which expressly or impliedly constitutes any kind of criticism of anyone engaged in parliamentary proceedings) may effectively prevent a litigant from being able to have his or her cause of action determined. The action may be struck out, *not* on the basis that the litigant has no cause of action, but that the hearing of it would involve an infringement of parliamentary privilege. Since the litigant would be wholly denied judicial determination of his or her rights, there would seem to be an argument that this would violate Art 6 of the ECHR (on which see Chapter 7, at 310–313).

14. The Court of Appeal in *Fayed v Hamilton* did not need to consider the point, since it allowed the action to proceed, but it did at least mention the issue, unlike the House of Lords. They said simply, 'had we been of the view that this libel action ought to be stayed as an assault on the privileges of Parliament, we do not believe that the Strasbourg jurisprudence would have required the court to disapply a rule or principle of such general constitutional importance'. This judgment now seems to have been vindicated by the decision in *A v United Kingdom* (2003), No 35373/97, in which the European Court of Human Rights heard a complaint from a woman who claimed to have been defamed during proceedings in the UK Parliament, which had been reported in the press. She argued that her inability to bring proceedings in court violated both her right to privacy under Art 8 and her right to a fair trial under Art 6 and to a remedy under Art 13. The Court found no violation: the privilege which blocked her action was necessary to protect free speech in Parliament and was narrower in scope than the comparable rules existing in other European countries.[90]

15. The *Trafigura* affair (above at 537) raises a further question: would the *Guardian* have been protected by Art 9 from an action in contempt of court had it published details of the question in Parliament about the injunction? On its face, as suggested above, the answer is no: Art 9 protects not *reporting of* Parliament, but only *proceedings in* Parliament. But in such a case, the newspaper would be being punished for reporting such proceedings. Thus, at least indirectly, its liability would arise on the basis of words spoken in Parliament, which it had merely reported. It seems at least arguable that this could amount to a breach of Art 9.

16. In conclusion, it is suggested that Art 9 of the Bill of Rights, as currently interpreted, is both riddled with anomalies in its interpretation and, more importantly, contains a serious and arguably

---

89   Joint Committee on Parliamentary Privilege, HLP 43–41 (1998–99), at [89].

90   For criticism, see A Barber (2003) 119 LQ 557–60.

unjustifiable restriction on access to justice. In what appears to be an obsessive quest to prevent courts from having to entertain any criticism of any actor in parliamentary proceedings, the courts have contrived to undermine one of the basic tenets of the rule of law: the right of a citizen to have his or her rights determined in an ordinary court, or as Art 6 of the ECHR puts it, to have his or her civil rights 'determined by an independent and impartial tribunal'.

Competing jurisdictions over the scope of privilege: Parliament versus the courts

One peculiar characteristic of parliamentary privilege is the fact that both the courts and Parliament have at times claimed the right to determine what is the law in this area. As Leopold puts it, in the context of the scope of the privilege of free speech, 'the problem is that [a ruling on the matter] could be made by both Parliament and the courts with not necessarily the same result'.[91] Should conflict flow from such a different result, the outcome remains uncertain, as illustrated by a case already mentioned, *Stockdale v Hansard* (1834) 9 Ad & El 1.[92] Stockdale brought an action in respect of allegedly defamatory words in a report of prison inspectors published by Hansard, by order of the Commons. When the action was tried, the court decided that Hansard's reports were not covered by absolute privilege, so that Stockdale could proceed. The court further adjudged that the House did not 'have the power to declare what its privileges are', while the House passed a resolution affirming that it was the sole judge of its own privileges. The House showed its readiness to back up its resolution with force by imprisoning the Sheriff of Middlesex for contempt when he attempted to enforce the court's judgment in favour of Stockdale by levying execution upon Hansard's property; the courts backed away from confrontation by refusing to grant the Sheriff a writ of habeas corpus. The court stated that it refused the writ because the Speaker's warrant did not state the facts which allegedly constituted the contempt, and it would not be seemly for them to enquire further since, as De Smith puts it, although 'the House of Commons was not a superior court . . . it was entitled to as much respect as if it were'. It is not certain that the matter could again be resolved as it was in Stockdale. Calvert considers it uncertain 'that a court of law would meekly accept a general return to a writ' in similar circumstances'.[93] Keir and Lawson, in contrast, take the view that the courts 'yielded the key to the fortress' by refusing to question the legality of imprisonment for contempt where no reason is given, implying that a precedent has been set (*Cases in Constitutional Law*, 6th edn, 1979, p 225). Further, if the Lords was asked to grant a writ of *habeas corpus*, it could not avoid questioning the Commons' actions on the grounds that the Commons was a superior court. An appeal was in fact made to the Lords in *Paty's case* (1704), but the counsel preparing it was promptly imprisoned by the Commons. However, as noted above, in *Prebble* and *Al Fayed*, the House of Lords appeared to accept that parliamentary privileges could not be questioned in court except in exceptional circumstances. The whole area may therefore still be said to be encased in a web of ambiguity; conflicts could arise in the future because two different bodies may claim competing jurisdictions over the ambit of privilege. No precedent has been set as to how to resolve these conflicts other than the frustrating by Parliament of the powers of the courts by imprisoning its officers, which in fact is not a resolution but merely a stalemate; further, it is not even certain whether such an outcome would be repeated if the issue arose again.

---

91   [1990] PL 30.

92   For a full analysis, see E May, *Treatise on the Law, Privileges, Proceedings and Usage of Parliament*, 20th edn (1983), pp 151–54.

93   *Introduction to British Constitutional Law* (1985), p 115.

How should this conflict be resolved? De Smith has suggested that jurisdiction over breaches of privilege and contempts should be handed over to the courts.[94] It seems clear that the present state of affairs is unsatisfactory, as discussed above. It has been noted that the present competition for jurisdiction makes for uncertainty in this area, whilst the view that the party political nature of the Commons renders it unsuitable for deciding what are in effect legal issues has also been touched on. But, as discussed above, there are also serious grounds for dissatisfaction with the Commons as a decision-making body itself; its procedures not only fall foul elementary principles of natural justice; they may also constitute a breach of Art 6 ECHR.

FURTHER READING

C Boulton (ed), *Erskine May's Treatise on the Law, Privileges, Proceedings and Usage of Parliament*, 23rd edn (2004)

A Doig, 'Cash for Questions: Parliament's Response to the Offence that Dare Not Speak its Name' (1998) 51(1) Parlt Aff 36

A Doig, 'Sleaze: Picking up the Threads or 'Back to Basics' Scandals?' (2001) 54 Parlt Aff 360

A Doig, 'Sleaze Fatigue in 'The House of Ill-repute'' (2002) Parlt Aff 389

A Doig, 'Sleaze, Ethics and Codes: The Politics of Trust' (2004) 57(2) Parlt Aff 435.

O Gay, 'The Development of Standards Machinery in the Commons' in O Gay and P Leopold (eds), *Conduct Unbecoming: The Regulation of Parliamentary Standards* (2004).

D Oliver, 'The Committee on Standards in Public Life: Regulating the Conduct of Members of Parliament' (1995) Parlt Aff 591

D Oliver, 'Standards of Conduct in Public Life—What Standards?' [1995] PL 497

A Sharland and I Loveland, 'The Defamation Act 1996 and Political Libels' [1997] PL 113

D Woodhouse, 'The Parliamentary Commissioner for Standards: Lessons from the Cash for Questions Inquiry' (1998) 51(1) Parlt Aff 51–61.

---

94 *Constitutional and Administrative Law*, 6th edn (1994), p 332.

CHAPTER 11
PREROGATIVE POWERS

INTRODUCTION

In his *Commentaries on the Laws of England*, Blackstone wrote that the prerogative is 'that special pre-eminence which the King has, over and above all other persons, and out of the ordinary course of the common law, in right of his royal dignity'. The term 'prerogative', then, refers to powers that are unique to the sovereign and which were not granted by statute; as we will see, they are recognised, rather than granted by the common law. Prerogative powers are sometimes referred to as the 'royal prerogative'; this is technically correct, as in law these powers belong to the monarch. However, by convention, they are in practice exercised by the Prime Minister; in some cases by the Cabinet. However, certain prerogatives remain which are generally exercised by the monarch personally. These are sometimes known as the 'personal prerogatives' and will be examined below.

It should be stressed at the outset that it is one of the unique and disturbing features of the UK constitution that, by means of this historical relic, it allows powers of such great breadth, magnitude and importance to be wielded by the executive alone: as a Labour Party paper of 1993 commented:

> It is where power is exercised by government under the cover of royal prerogative that our concerns are greatest. . . Massive power is exercised by executive degree without accountability to Parliament.[1]

Ironically enough, this area, which most concerned Labour in 1993, remained untouched by the great wave of constitutional reform enacted by the Blair administration from 1997 on, save for the impact of the Human Rights Act 1998 on judicial control of the prerogative. However, as this chapter discusses, the Brown Government brought forward proposals, as part of its *Constitutional Renewal*[2] package for reform in three areas: to give Parliament a statutory role in approving treaties; to establish a convention that armed forces will only be committed to battle after a vote in Parliament; to place the civil service on a statutory basis. The first two of these is considered below; the changes relating to the civil service are considered in the next chapter, at 619–621.

This chapter first considers the nature of prerogative powers, and then goes on to examine the more important prerogatives: the power to dissolve Parliament, to assent to Bills, to declare war, to dismiss and appoint Ministers; personal prerogatives of the monarch; and various immunities such as the Queen's personal immunity from suit or prosecution, and property rights.[3] Second, it considers the extent to which the prerogative, traditionally largely unchecked by Parliament, may be subjected to greater political control, as a result of the *Constitutional Renewal* changes. Third, it examines the extent to which *legal* control of the prerogative through judicial review continues to develop.

---

1   Labour Party, *A New Agenda for Democracy* (1993), p 33.

2   See the White Paper *The Governance of Britain: Constitutional Renewal,* Cm 7341-I and the Constitutional Reform and Governance Bill introduced before Parliament in 2009, and passed (in part) in 2010.

3   This chapter does not consider the arcane and rarely invoked prerogative power known as 'act of state', defined by O Hood Phillips as 'an act done by the Crown as a matter of policy in relation to another state, or in relation to an individual who is not within the allegiance to the Crown' (O Hood Phillips and P Jackson, *Constitutional and Administrative Law,* P Jackson and P Leopold (eds), 8th edn (2001), p 321. For discussion, see *ibid*, pp 320–26.

THE NATURE AND EXTENT OF THE PREROGATIVE

Prerogative acts and prerogative legislation

The exercise of prerogative powers generally consists simply in taking action—e.g. using armed force against another country, or signing a treaty. These are readily identifiable as executive acts. However, the prerogative also includes a power to legislate, through what are known as Orders in Council. 'Council' here refers to the Privy Council, formerly an important institution, nowadays a largely ceremonial body made up of senior politicians,[4] which in effect allows Ministers to enact non-parliamentary legislation that nominally emanates from the Crown. Orders in Council are signed by the Queen. As Moules explains:

> English law recognises two types of Order in Council: first, Orders in Council made under statutory powers (such as those made pursuant to s. 2(2) of the European Communities Act 1972 in order to implement Community obligations) and secondly, Orders in Council made under the royal prerogative. The former count as delegated legislation. The latter are technically primary legislation, but are not subject to parliamentary consent or scrutiny. Instead, they are approved by the sovereign at a meeting of the Privy Council attended normally only by four members.[5]

Because Orders in Council are in some respects a form of primary legislation, there has been a long-standing view that they are not subject to judicial review. This question has now been resolved by the decision in *Bancoult*,[6] considered below.

The nature of the prerogative generally

C Munro, *Studies in Constitutional Law*, 2nd edn (1999), pp 256–59 (extracts)

The royal prerogative may be defined as comprising those attributes peculiar to the Crown which are derived from common law, not statute, and which still survive.

Some of these points need to be amplified, so that we may see what sort of creature we are dealing with. First, notice that the prerogative consists of legal attributes, not matters merely of convention or practice. The courts will recognise, in appropriate cases, that these attributes exist, and, when necessary, enforce them. So, when a university archaeological team excavated a treasure hoard from St Ninian's Isle in the Shetlands, an action was brought to establish that the treasure belonged to the Crown [*Lord Advocate v University of Aberdeen* 1963 SC 533]. The courts will rule, in other cases, that a prerogative which has been claimed does not exist or that Government action falls outside the scope of the prerogative. . .

---

4   Not to be confused with the Judicial Committee of the Privy Council, in effect a supreme court for former colonies that still use it as their highest court.

5   R Moules, 'Judicial Review of Prerogative Orders in Council: Recognising the Constitutional Reality of Executive Legislation' [2008] 67(1) CLJ 12.

6   *R (On The Application of Bancoult) v Secretary of State For Foreign and Commonwealth Affairs* [2008] UKHL 61; [2009] 1 AC 453

Strictly speaking, the prerogatives are recognised, rather than created, by the common law, for their source is in custom. By origin, royal prerogatives were attributes which of necessity inhered in kings as the governors of the realm. It is natural to think of the prerogative as composed of powers, for it is in the exercise of the Crown's discretionary powers, and the control of that exercise, that our chief interest lies. But rules affected the Crown in a variety of ways. Some gave rights to the Crown, such as the right to treasure trove. Some gave immunities, such as the Crown's immunity from being sued. Some even imposed duties, such as the Crown's duty to protect subjects within the realm.

Strictly speaking, it may be maintained that the term 'prerogative' should be reserved for rules peculiar to the Crown, as Blackstone expounded:

> It signifies. . .something that is required or demanded before, or in preference to, all others. And hence it follows, that it must be in its nature singular and eccentrical; that it can only be applied to those rights and capacities which the king enjoys alone, in contradistinction to others, and not to those which he enjoys in common with any of his subjects; for if once any one prerogative of the Crown could be held in common with the subject, it would cease to be prerogative any longer [Commentaries, 1, p 239].

On this view, the prerogative properly describes matters, such as the power to declare war or the granting of royal assent to Bills, which are peculiar to the Crown. . . These special legal attributes are a residue, a remnant of what was possessed by medieval kings and queens. What remains is left to the executive by the grace of Parliament, for Parliament can abrogate or diminish the prerogative, like any other part of the common law. The prerogatives that remain are relics. But they are not unimportant relics.

Notes

1. Munro admits that there is more than one view on the scope of the prerogative but arguably understates the definitional vacuum surrounding the term. Moreover, it is not as if there has not been more than adequate time for clarification. As John F McEldowney and Patrick McAuslan put it:

> Notwithstanding that the royal prerogative as a source of power of the government antedates Acts of Parliament, has been at the root of a civil war and a revolution in England and has been litigated about on countless major occasions in respect of its use both at home and overseas, its scope is still unsure.[7]

Rather extraordinarily, as an important report by the Public Administration Select Committee, *Taming the Prerogative,* pointed out:

> . . .in an era of increasing freedom of information, Parliament does not even have the right to know what these powers are. Ministers have repeatedly answered parliamentary questions about Ministers' prerogative powers by saying that records are not kept of the individual occasions on which those powers are used, and that it

---

7   'Legitimacy and the constitution: the dissonance between theory and practice', in P McAuslan and JF McEldowney, *Law, Legitimacy and the Constitution* (1985), p 12.

would not be practicable to do so. Ministers have also said that it would be impossible to produce a precise list of these powers. . .[8]

As one of their witnesses commented, 'this last statement is incredible. It means that at the heart of British Government there is a kind of constitutional black hole'.[9]

2. Professor HWR Wade believes that this lack of clarity (for which he partly blames Dicey—see below) has resulted in many exercises of power being wrongly labelled as examples of the prerogative. He notes a number of examples of government actions that have been mis-described by the courts as acts of 'prerogative' power.

HWR Wade, *Constitutional Fundamentals* (1989), pp 58–66

But what does 'prerogative' mean? I have felt disposed to criticise the use of this term in some recent judgments and other contexts where, as it seemed to me, no genuine prerogative power was in question at all. If prerogative power is to be brought under judicial control, and if ministers are to be condemned for abusing it unlawfully, it is worth finding out what it really is. In the first place, the prerogative consists of legal power—that is to say, the ability to alter people's rights, duties or status under the laws of this country which the courts of this country enforce. Thus when Parliament is dissolved under the prerogative it can no longer validly do business. When a man is made a peer, he may no longer lawfully vote in a parliamentary election. When a university is incorporated by royal charter, a new legal person enters the world. All these legal transformations are effected in terms of rights, duties, disabilities, etc, which the courts will acknowledge and enforce. The power to bring them about is vested in the Crown by the common law, so it clearly falls within the definition of the royal prerogative as 'the common law powers of the Crown'.

[Wade then goes on to consider actions mis-described as being taken under the prerogative]: Another example shows another species of inaccuracy. The Criminal Injuries Compensation Board is an instance of the practice, dear to the administrative heart, of doing things informally and extra-legally if means can be devised. This Board pays out several million pounds of public money annually to the victims of violent crime. But until recently it had no statutory authority. [The Board was made statutory by the Criminal Justice Act 1988.] Parliament simply voted the money each year, and the Board dispensed it under the rules of the scheme, which were laid before Parliament by the Home Secretary but had no statutory force. Nevertheless, by a feat no less imaginative than in the Laker Airways case, the courts assumed jurisdiction to quash decisions of the Board which did not accord with the rules of the scheme. In doing so, they described the Board as 'set up under the prerogative' [*R v Criminal Injuries Compensation Board ex p Lain* [1967] 2 QB 864, at 881, 883]. But one essential of 'prerogative', if I may be forgiven for saying so, is that it should be prerogative. Its etymology means that it should be some special power possessed by the Crown over and above the powers of an ordinary person, and by virtue of the Crown's special constitutional position.

. . . Now if we apply this test to the constitution of the Criminal Injuries Compensation Board, it is surely plain that the Government, in establishing it, was merely doing

---

8 Public Administration Select Committee, 'Taming the Prerogative: Strengthening Ministerial Accountability to Parliament', 4th Report (2003–04), HC 422, at [12].

9 *Ibid*, Ev 7 (Peter Browning).

what. . .any of us could do if we had the money ready to hand. We could set up a board, or a committee, or trustees with authority to make grants according to whatever rules we might please to lay down. Thousands of foundations or trusts have been set up in the exercise of exactly the same liberty that the Government exercised in the case of the criminal injuries scheme. So far as the Crown came into the picture at all, it was exercising its ordinary powers as a natural person, which of course include power to transfer property, make contracts and so on. [In *R v Panel on Take-overs and Mergers ex p Datafin plc* [1987] QB 815, at 848, Lloyd LJ expressed his agreement with this argument.] Blackstone was quite right, in my opinion, in saying that such powers are not prerogative at all.

Much the same might be said of other powers of the Crown which writers on constitutional law are fond of cataloguing as prerogative, without regard to Blackstone's doctrine. The power to appoint and dismiss ministers, for instance, appears to me to be nothing else than the power which all legal persons have at common law to employ servants or agents, so that it lacks any 'singular and eccentrical' element. Ministers as such have no inherent powers at common law and must therefore be counted as ordinary servants. It is otherwise with judges, who have very great legal powers, and their appointment and dismissal were undoubtedly within the true prerogative before Parliament gave them a statutory basis. I will not go through the whole catalogue of the powers commonly classed as prerogative in textbooks and elsewhere, though I suspect that a number of them would not pass the Blackstone test. A collector's piece comes from a hopeless case of 1971. Mr Clive Jenkins, the trade union leader, sued the Attorney General in an attempt to stop the Government from distributing a free pamphlet on the Common Market at a cost to the taxpayer of £20,000. The judge is reported to have held that the issue of free information is 'a prerogative power of the Crown' which the court cannot question [*Jenkins v Attorney General* (1970) 115 SJ 674]. Since all the Crown's subjects are at liberty to issue as much free information as they like (and many of them issue much too much of it), I offer you this as a choice example of a non-prerogative.

The truth seems to be that judges have fallen into the habit of describing as 'prerogative' any and every sort of Government action which is not statutory. It may be, also, that the responsibility for this solecism can be loaded onto that popular scapegoat, Dicey. For his well known definition of prerogative is 'the residue of discretionary power left at any moment in the hands of the Crown'. He makes no distinction between the Crown's natural and regal capacities, indeed at one point he says [*The Law of the Constitution*, 10th edn, p 425]:

> 'Every act which the executive Government can lawfully do without the authority of an Act of Parliament is done in virtue of this prerogative.'
> So the judges and authors whose wide statements I have ventured to criticise could quote Dicey against me. But if we match Dicey against Blackstone, I think that Blackstone wins. Nor do I think that the criticism is mere pedantry. The true limits of the prerogatives of the Crown are important both in constitutional and in administrative law. This is all the more so now that the courts are showing signs, as in the Laker Airways case, of bringing the exercise of the prerogative under judicial control. It may well be easier to extend control to the few genuine prerogative powers which may possibly admit it, for example an improper use of nolle prosequi, if the court is not by the same token committed to extend it to all sorts of pretended prerogatives, such as the control of the civil service and the making of contracts or treaties.

Note

Wade's contention that 'Ministers as such have no inherent powers at common law' is perhaps open to question. Whilst theoretically all prerogative powers are vested in the sovereign, the courts recognise clearly enough that the powers are in fact exercised by Ministers: in *R v Secretary of State for the Home Department ex parte Northumbria Police Authority*[10] (discussed below), the court referred to 'the prerogative powers available to the Secretary of State [for the Home Department] to do all that is reasonably necessary to preserve the peace of the nation'. Nor is this a case where the courts were mistakenly labelling 'prerogative' a power in fact belonging to any ordinary citizen.

Prerogative and 'third source' powers

The most important point Wade makes is that a number of actions that Ministers take on behalf of the Government, such as entering into contracts, are not done under the prerogative, but are simply examples of the power to do anything that a legal or natural person can do. Under Wade's view, the setting up of the non-statutory criminal injury compensation scheme was an example of such an action. As Cohn points out:

> A series of studies have. . .pointed at the parallel existence of other non-statutory, non-prerogative powers. The titles given to these powers differ; whether 'new prerogatives', 'common law' , 'de facto', 'residual' or 'third source' powers, all refer to powers that do not enjoy the status of prerogative but are similarly exercised by governments in the absence of an empowering statute. . . .Indeed, in a series of British and Commonwealth studies, commentators have reminded their readers (governments required no reminder) that governments often operate outside of statute, and that not all such powers could (nor, indeed, should) be awarded the title ' prerogative.' In Harris's words, these powers emanate from 'a third source'—neither statute, neither prerogative—and are found, inter alia, in 'thousands of government actions', including governance through contract, the instatement of subsidy programmes and other types of policy decisions [BV Harris, 'The "Third Source" Revisited' (2007) 123 LQR 225, 226–27].[11]

The basic proposition, that the Crown has all the powers of a natural or legal person is sometimes called 'the Ram doctrine',[12] although it goes much further than the proposition by a civil servant after which it was named.[13] This 'third source' of powers, non-prerogative, but non-statutory, was recently considered by the courts in two cases, the second of which, *ex p C*, is considered by the first, which follows. The facts are not strongly material, and concerned the power of the Secretary of State to undertake preparatory actions for a proposed merger of two different layers of local government. The legal basis of the power to do this was challenged. The Court of Appeal starts by considering the decision of the lower court.

---

10   [1988] 2 WLR 590, at 609.

11   M Cohn, 'Judicial Review of Non-statutory Executive Powers after *Bancoult*: A Unified, Anxious Model' [2009] PL 260, at 260.

12   See further, A Lester and M Weait 'The Use of Ministerial Powers without Parliamentary Authority: The Ram Doctrine' [2003] PL 415.

13   It is named after a memo written in 1945 by Sir Granville Ram, then First Parliamentary Counsel. As Lester and Weait (*ibid* at n 2 comment): 'The existence of the Ram doctrine was revealed in para 3.46 of a Report on Privacy and Data Sharing, issued by the Performance and Innovation Unit of the Cabinet Office.'

Shrewsbury & Atcham Borough Council, Congleton Borough Council v The Secretary of State for Communities and Local Government [2008] EWCA Civ 148 (extracts)

Carnwath LJ. . .

21 On [the issue of *vires*] [Underhill J at first instance] held, that, apart from any express or implied statutory restriction, there was no relevant limit on the powers of the Secretary of State to do what she had done. This conclusion followed the decision of this court in *R v Secretary of State for Health ex p. C* [2000] 1 FLR 627, concerning the legality of a non-statutory list of sexual offenders maintained by the Secretary of State for Health. The court held that the Secretary of State, as representative of the Crown, enjoyed non-statutory powers analogous to those of a natural person, not confined to those conferred by statute, or to her traditional prerogative powers. Hale LJ, with the agreement of the other members of the Court of Appeal (Lord Woolf MR, and Lord Mustill), said:

> The Crown is not a creature of statute and in one respect at least is clearly different from a local authority. The Crown has prerogative powers. But what does this mean? Professor Sir William Wade, in Wade and Forsyth, *Administrative Law* (Clarendon Press, 7th edn, 1994), at pp 248–249, draws a clear distinction between prerogative and other powers:
>
> > 'Prerogative' power is, properly speaking, legal power which appertains to the Crown but not to its subjects. . . .Although the courts may use the term 'prerogative' in this sense, they have fallen into the habit of describing as 'prerogative' every power of the Crown which is not statutory, without distinguishing between powers which are unique to the Crown, such as the power of pardon, from powers which the Crown shares equally with its subjects because of its legal personality, such as the power to make contracts, employ servants and convey land.
>
> There is no suggestion of a specific prerogative power in this case but *Halsbury's* Laws of England, vol. 8 (2), at note 6 to para 101, confirms that 'At common law the Crown, as a corporation possessing legal personality, has the capacities of a natural person and thus the same liberties as the individual'. It was on this ground that Richards J [at first instance in *Re C*] declined to hold that the [Sex Offenders Register] was unlawful.

22 The judge regarded himself as bound by this reasoning. As 'the most workmanlike description' of this third category of powers, he adopted the term 'common law powers' (in line with some of the speeches in *R. (Hooper) v. Secretary of State for Work and Pensions* [2005] 1 WLR 1681). He rejected Mr Arden's argument that the reasoning in *C* did not extend to acts of 'a governmental character' , as inconsistent with the facts of *C* itself:

> The maintaining of the Index . . . was not, as the Court of Appeal will certainly have appreciated, an act like renting office accommodation or buying paper-clips. It cannot realistically be regarded as anything other than . . . a governmental act, and one whose exercise would . . . have a profound adverse impact on the persons included in the list (para 16).

He summarised the position in the light of that judgment:

> . . . the fact that the Crown enjoys legal personality means that it is *prima facie* entitled — so far as *vires* in the strict sense are concerned — to do any lawful act,

even if the act in question is plainly governmental. I say '*prima facie*' because such power is limited in a number of important ways. In particular:

- It does not. . .extend to any act involving interference with the rights and liberties of the subject.
- Its exercise is reviewable on ordinary public law grounds.
- It does not operate in any ' field' in which Parliament has chosen to legislate: . . . (para 17).

. . .

45. . .Hale LJ found support for a more general 'common law' power (or ' third source' power, as Professor Harris describes it) in a passage in Wade and Forsyth. However, the examples given in that extract ('the power to make contracts, employ servants and convey land') do seem to me, with respect, of limited assistance. They are in the nature of ancillary powers, necessary for the carrying out of any substantive governmental (or indeed non-governmental) function, whether statutory, corporate or common law. Similarly, the passage cited from Halsbury's Laws refers to an earlier passage. . .dealing with the ' general legal capacity' of the Crown as a 'corporation sole or aggregate', which also gives as examples the power to enter contracts or own property. The obvious need for such powers to my mind throws no light on what, if any, non-statutory substantive functions the Crown retains beyond the scope of the 'prerogative', as traditionally understood. . .

47. . .*Northumbria Police Authority* ([1989] QB 26) seems to support a narrower approach. The issue was whether the Secretary of State could maintain a central store of police riot equipment for the use of Chief Constables, even without the approval of their local police authorities. It was held that the Secretary of State had the necessary powers both under the Police Act 1964 and under the Crown's traditional prerogative of keeping the peace. It is notable that there was no suggestion that the Secretary of State could rely on some 'third source' power. That omission can be readily understood in the context of the authorities mentioned in the judgments. It is sufficient to cite two examples:

(1)   Lord Parmoor, *A-G v De Keyser's Hotel* [1920] AC 508, 568: 'The growth of constitutional liberties has largely consisted in the reduction of the discretionary power of the executive, and in the extension of Parliamentary protection in favour of the subject, under a series of statutory enactments. The result is that, whereas at one time the Royal prerogative gave legal sanction to a large majority of the executive functions of the Government, it is now restricted within comparatively narrow limits. The Royal prerogative has of necessity been gradually curtailed, as a settled rule of law has taken the place of an uncertain and arbitrary administrative discretion.'

(2)   Lord Denning MR, *Laker Airways Ltd v Department of Trade* [1977] QB 643, 705: 'The prerogative is a discretionary power exercisable by the executive government for the public good, in certain spheres of governmental activity for which the law has made no provision, such as the war prerogative (of requisitioning property for the defence of the realm), or the treaty prerogative (of making treaties with foreign powers). The law does not interfere with the proper exercise of the discretion by the executive in those situations: but it can set limits by defining the bounds of the activity: and it can intervene if the discretion is exercised improperly or mistakenly. This is a fundamental principle of our constitution . . .'

Lord Denning referred to Blackstone's definition of the prerogative (following Locke) as—
'the discretionary power of acting for the public good, where the positive laws are silent . . .'
(*Commentaries* Vol I p 252).

It is not easy to reconcile such statements of high authority with the existence of a residual category of substantive 'third source' powers, apart from the prerogative. At the very least, they suggest that any such category is exceptional, and should be strictly confined.

48 Reference to the status of a Minister as 'corporation sole', or to analogies with the powers of natural persons, seem to me unhelpful. In the case of an artificial person, it may be important to distinguish between the power to act, as a matter of corporate capacity, and the legal constraints limiting the exercise of the power.

Unlike a local authority, the Crown is not a creature of statute. As a matter of capacity, no doubt, it has power to do whatever a private person can do. But as an organ of government, it can only exercise those powers for the public benefit, and for identifiably 'governmental' purposes within limits set by the law. Apart from authority [i.e. the decision of the Court of Appeal in *ex parte C,* above], I would be inclined respectfully to share the view of the editors of De Smith *De Smith's Judicial Review* (6th ed) para 5–025) that: 'The extension of the Ram doctrine beyond its modest initial purpose of achieving incidental powers should be resisted in the interest of the rule of law'.

49 Following [*ex parte C*], this is not a debate which can be continued usefully at this level. . .

Note

In other words, Carnwarth LJ clearly disagreed with the approach of the Court of Appeal in *ex parte C,* but since the Court of Appeal is bound by its previous judgments, was not able to disagree with it. The matter can only be resolved by the House of Lords. Readers may at this point wish to cross refer to the Rule of Law chapter at 96–97 and the well known quote by Laws LJ in *ex parte Fewings*[14] to the effect that for public authorities, the position is that they must justify their actions by positive law, *unlike the position of ordinary citizens,* for whom the rule is that they may do anything that the law does not forbid. The converse notion, of treating the Government as being able to do anything that law did not forbid, was the doctrine that the Government relied on in the *Malone* case,[15] to argue successfully that they could tap telephones because there was no law to prohibit it. (It will be recalled that the case was subsequently lost at Strasbourg).[16] The dicta of Laws LJ in *Fewings* was generally regarded as a decisive and welcome disposal of the mistaken approach in *Malone.* But the approach of the Court of Appeal in *ex parte C*—going to something as serious as the establishment of the Sex Offenders Register—seems to take us back towards the widely criticised approach in *Malone.*

The range of prerogative powers

The prerogative covers a quite startlingly wide range of areas. No definitive list exists, but the Public Administration Select Committee attempted one in the following report and included in its evidence a rather more comprehensive list supplied by government lawyers.

---

14   *R v Somerset County Council ex parte Fewings and Others* [1995] 1 All ER 513, 523.

15   *Malone v Commissioner for the Metropolitan Police (No 2)* [1979] 2 All ER 620.

16   *Malone v United Kingdom* (1985) 7 EHRR 14.

Public Administration Select Committee, *Taming the Prerogative:*
Strengthening Ministerial Accountability to Parliament,
4th Report (2003–04), HC 422 (extracts)

9. The principal royal prerogative, or Ministerial executive, powers exercised by Ministers include the following:

(a) The making and ratification of treaties.

(b) The conduct of diplomacy, including the recognition of states, the relations (if any) between the United Kingdom and particular Governments, and the appointment of ambassadors and High Commissioners.

(c) The governance of British overseas territories.

(d) The deployment and use of the armed forces overseas, including involvement in armed conflict, or the declaration of war. (The Royal Navy is still maintained by virtue of the prerogative; the Army and the RAF are maintained under statute.)

(e) The use of the armed forces within the United Kingdom to maintain the peace in support of the police.

(f) The Prime Minister's ability to appoint and remove Ministers, recommend dissolutions, peerages, and honours (save for the four Orders within The Queen's own gift), patronage appointments (e.g. in the Church of England), and the appointment of senior judges.

(g) Recommendations for honours by the Foreign and Commonwealth Secretary and the Defence Secretary.

(h) The organisation of the civil service.

(i) The grant and revocation of passports.

(j) The grant of pardons (subject to recommendations by the Criminal Cases Review Commission) and the Attorney-General's power to stop prosecutions.

Memorandum by Treasury Solicitor's Department

Domestic Affairs

4. Although this is the area in which legislation has increasingly been introduced thereby limiting the extent of the prerogative, some significant aspects of the prerogative survive in the area of domestic affairs. These include:

— the appointment and dismissal of Ministers;
— the summoning, prorogation and dissolution of Parliament;
— royal assent to Bills;
— the appointment and regulation of the civil service;
— the commissioning of officers in the armed forces;
— directing the disposition of the armed forces in the UK;
— the appointment of Queen's Counsel;
— the prerogative of mercy. . .
— the issue and withdrawal of UK passports;
— the granting of honours;
— the creation of corporations by Charter;
— the King (and Queen) can do no wrong (for example the Queen cannot be prosecuted in her own courts)

Foreign affairs

5. The conduct of foreign affairs remains very reliant on the exercise of prerogative powers. Parliament and the courts have perhaps tended to accept that this is an area where the Crown needs flexibility in order to act effectively and handle novel situations.

6. The main prerogative powers in this area include:

— the making of treaties;
— the declaration of war;
— the deployment of the armed forces on operations overseas;
— the recognition of foreign states;
— the accreditation and reception of diplomats.

Note

1. Both lists omit, (as Alder points out) the prerogative to govern overseas territories, and the second omits the Attorney General's power to terminate particular legal proceedings by entering a plea of *nolle prosequi*. The White Paper promised the removal of this power,[17] but it did not appear in the Constitutional Reform and Governance Bill 2009. The power to issue passports is still, anomalously, governed by the royal prerogative. The Government has promised to bring forward legislation to place this power on a statutory basis, but has not yet done so.[18]

2. Calvert's concentration on the treaty-making aspect of the prerogative's ambit in foreign affairs deflects attention from the rather more drastic actions which may be taken in under it. Heuston quotes Walter Bagehot on the subject:

> I said in this book it would very much surprise people if they were really told how many things the Queen could do without consulting Parliament. Not to mention other things, she could. . . .dismiss all the sailors [and] sell off all our ships of war and all our navy stores; she could make a peace by the sacrifice of Cornwall and begin a war for the conquest of Brittany. . . She could make every parish in the United Kingdom a university. . . In a word, the Queen could by prerogative upset all the action of civil government.[19]

Of course, these powers are, by convention, exercised on the advice of Ministers, but since conventions are not enforced by the courts, it is still correct to say that the Queen *could*, as a matter of strict legal theory, do all the above.

PERSONAL PREROGATIVES

There are however some prerogatives that the Monarch exercises personally; these relate to her powers over Parliament, the appointment of a Prime Minister, and the award of certain honours. Sir Ivor Jennings notes:

---

17   *Governance of Britain* at [90]–[95].

18   *Constitutional Renewal* White Paper: 'the Government will remove the prerogative in relation to granting passports and place the power on a statutory basis in other legislation'. See paras 20–24 of Rodney Brazier's paper in Appendix 1 of *Taming the Prerogative*.

19   W Bagehot, *The English Constitution*, pp 282–84, quoted *ibid*, p 72.

There are, however, certain prerogative powers which the Queen exercises on her own responsibility, and which may fitly be called 'the personal prerogatives'. Exactly what they are is by no means clear; for there are differences of opinion in respect of several of them. There is no controversy that she need not accept advice as to the appointment of a Prime Minister or as to the creation of peers so as to override the opposition of the House of Lords. There is controversy as to whether she can dismiss a Government or dissolve Parliament without advice, or whether she can refuse to dissolve Parliament when advised to do so.[20]

In the following report, the PAC sought a systematic classification.

Public Administration Select Committee, *Taming the Prerogative: Strengthening Ministerial Accountability to Parliament*, 4th Report (2003–04), HC 422 (extracts)

4. In preparing for our inquiry we identified three main groups of prerogative powers. . . [which] are described in the following paragraphs.

5. **The Queen's constitutional prerogatives** are the personal discretionary powers which remain in the Sovereign's hands. They include the rights to advise, encourage and warn Ministers in private; to appoint the Prime Minister and other Ministers; to assent to legislation; to prorogue or to dissolve Parliament; and (in grave constitutional crisis) to act contrary to or without Ministerial advice. In ordinary circumstances The Queen, as a constitutional monarch, accepts Ministerial advice about the use of these powers if it is available, whether she personally agrees with that advice or not. That constitutional position ensures that Ministers take responsibility for the use of the powers. . . .

7. **The legal prerogatives of the Crown**, which The Queen possesses as the embodiment of the Crown. There are many such prerogatives which are legal (rather than constitutional) in character. Several are historical remnants, such as the Crown's rights to sturgeon, certain swans, and whales, and the right to impress men into the Royal Navy. But two legal prerogatives have more modern legal significance, namely, the principle that the Crown (or the state) can do no wrong, and that the Crown is not bound by statute save by express words or necessary implication. Many of these legal prerogatives have been amended by parliamentary legislation; others are in need of reform; some others may be obsolete. It has been suggested that the Law Commission should review this group of prerogatives.

8. **Prerogative executive powers**. . .Historically, the Sovereign by constitutional convention came to act on Ministerial advice, so that prerogative powers came to be used by Ministers on the Sovereign's behalf. As Ministers took responsibility for actions done in the name of the Crown, so these prerogative powers were, in effect, delegated to responsible Ministers. But Parliament was not directly involved in that transfer of power. This constitutional position means that these prerogative powers are, in effect though not in strict law, in the hands of Ministers. Without these ancient powers Governments would have to take equivalent authority through primary legislation. As with the legal prerogatives just outlined, the connection between these powers and the Crown, or The Queen, is now tenuous and technical, and the label 'royal prerogative' is apt to mislead. Indeed, Members have been prevented from raising certain matters in the House (such as honours) on the ground that these matters involve a royal connection, even though it may be merely formal.

---

20   *Cabinet Government*, 3rd edn (1959), p 394, quoted in R Brazier, *Constitutional Texts* (1990), p 437.

It makes more sense to refer to these powers not as 'royal prerogative' but as 'Ministerial executive powers'.

Note

The power to dissolve Parliament, independently of a request to do so by the Prime Minister, is by no means obsolete. As Brazier points out:

> In the wholly unlikely events of a Government losing a vote of confidence in the House of Commons but refusing either to recommend a dissolution or to resign, or of a Government which tried improperly to extend the life of Parliament beyond the statutory maximum of five years, the Queen would be justified in insisting on an immediate dissolution. There has been royal insistence on a dissolution twice this century in the context of the Prime Minister's request to create peers so as to coerce the House of Lords: in both cases the Prime Minister unreservedly acquiesced.[21]

The conventions governing the relationship between the monarch, Parliament and the Prime Minister are further discussed in Chapter 12 at 603–608.

PARLIAMENTARY CONTROL OVER THE PREROGATIVE AND REFORM

One of the most remarkable features of the prerogative, to foreign observers, must be the way in which it allows:

> almost the whole terrain of foreign policy in the UK [to be] carried on by the government. . .[without] the need to secure any formal [parliamentary] approval to its diplomatic agreements and executive decisions.[22]

Perhaps the most striking aspect of this situation is the complete absence of any formal parliamentary control over two of the most important types of decision which Government may make: the signing of treaties, and the deployment of the armed forces abroad. As to the former, Blackburn notes:

> The UK now has the only Parliament in the European Union that lacks any formal mechanism for securing scrutiny and approval to treaties. The 1924 Ponsonby 'Rule'—now a Foreign Office circular—is clearly inadequate as a basis for effective scrutiny. It involves the voluntary practice of governments laying treaties signed by the UK before Parliament as Command Papers after their entry into force, and in the case of treaties requiring legal ratification a copy being placed on the Table of the house 21 days beforehand.[23]

---

21 *Constitutional Texts* (1990), pp 438–39. These instances concerned requests made by Asquith to Edward VII and George V.

22 R Blackburn, 'The House of Lords', in R Blackburn and R Plant (eds), *Constitutional Reform: The Labour Government's Constitutional Reform Agenda* (1999), p 33.

23 *Ibid.*

He notes the complaint of the Labour Party, when in opposition:

> Treaty after treaty is concluded without the formal consent of Parliament. Indeed foreign policy as a whole is an area virtually free from democratic control and accountability.[24]

There has now been limited reform in the area of treaties: see below at 571–574.

The lack of any necessity to seek approval from, or even consult with Parliament before committing the country's armed forces to battle abroad, whether in a formal state of war or not, is perhaps the other most remarkable feature of the use of the prerogative, as Brazier notes.

R Brazier, *Constitutional Reform*, 2nd edn (1999), p 123

On three occasions since 1945 the Cabinet has committed large military forces to actual or possible armed conflict, although not, in legal parlance, to war. In none of these cases was Parliament formally consulted before the decision to send forces was made. Suez, the Falklands, and the Gulf all received British armed forces on ministerial direction under the royal prerogative power to dispose those forces as the Crown thinks fit. How odd—perhaps bizarre—it is that the approval of both Houses of Parliament is required for pieces of technical, and often trivial, subordinate legislation, whereas it is not needed at all before men and women can be committed to the possibility of disfigurement or death! Speed of military response may, of course, be vital. . . To insist on prior approval of all military deployments would be absurd, especially when Parliament is in recess, as it was at start of the Gulf emergency. But the commitment of military forces is an act which may have such terrible consequences that the approval of Parliament ought to be required within a specified period. Even under the present arrangements, no British government is going to take the country to the brink of, or to actual, fighting unless it is reasonably confident that it can carry Parliament with it. . . The UK needs a War Powers Act, under which Parliament would have to be informed and its consent obtained with in a specified number of days in order that the armed services could be deployed lawfully overseas. . .

Notes

1. To Brazier's examples could be added the deployment and use of the RAF in Bosnia in the 1990s by the Major Government, and the prolonged campaign of air-strikes against the targets in Kuwait and Serbia authorised by the Blair Government, neither of which were the subject of formal parliamentary approval. It was in fact not until the Iraq war in 2003 (below) that the Government decided that a formal vote should be held in Parliament before committing troops to battle.

2. To make matters worse, in the absence of legal requirements to obtain parliamentary approval of actions taken under the prerogative, there are not even any clear *conventions* on the matter. As Munro notes: 'John Major, as Prime Minister, was merely stating how things were when he replied to a question by saying that "it is for individual Ministers to decide on a particular occasion whether and how to report to Parliament on the exercise of prerogative powers".'[25]

3. The most recent example, at the time of writing, relates to commencement of the war in Iraq in Spring 2003. The Prime Minister, Tony Blair, found himself in the position of having a foreign

---

24   Labour Party, *A New Agenda for Democracy* (1993), p 33.

25   C Munro, *Studies in Constitutional Law*, 2nd edn (1999), p 276.

policy—favouring military action against Iraq, even in the absence of specific Security Council authorisation—that was sharply opposed to the views of many within the parliamentary Labour Party. He was questioned on the issue of whether Parliament would be given a chance to debate and vote on military action before any was taken, and the wider issue of whether the historical power to use the royal prerogative to commit the country to war without Parliament's approval now required reform.[26] While acknowledging that 'I cannot think of a set of circumstances in which a Government can go to war without the support of Parliament', he refused to give an undertaking that he would consult Parliament *before* undertaking military action against Iraq. Of course, in the event, several debates took place, the most important being on 26 February 2003, when there was a full scale vote on a substantive motion, in which no less than 122 Labour MPs rebelled against a three-line whip by voting for an anti-war amendment to the government motion (see further, Chapter 8, at 363–365). It seems to have been generally accepted within the Government that Blair would have resigned had he lost the vote.

4. As Munro notes, there are a number of prerogatives upon which it is not even possible to raise a question in Parliament:

> When Members have tried to ascertain. . .what advice the Prime Minister has given to the Queen as to the dissolution of Parliament, the question is ruled out on the ground that the Prime Minister is not responsible to Parliament for that advice. . . Questions cannot be asked which bring the name of the Sovereign or the influence of the Crown before Parliament. The advice given to the Sovereign about some wider matters has similarly been ruled out of bounds: not only the dissolution of Parliament, but also the grant of honours, the ecclesiastical patronage of the Crown, and the appointment and dismissal of Privy Councillors.[27]

Reform: enhancing accountability to Parliament for using armed forces

As was pointed out to the Constitution Committee, since the end of the Second World War 'Britain has been involved in more military operations than any other country, including the United States. . . [including] more than sixty deployments since 1990.'[28] Virtually all of these operations were undertaken without obtaining prior parliamentary approval. While the decision to hold a full debate and vote on the Iraq are in 2003 *may* have set a precedent, it was done more as a matter of political necessity than out of a sense of constitutional obligation. As the Attorney General commented at the time:

> The decision to use military force is, and remains, a decision within the Royal Prerogative and as such does not, as a matter of law or constitutionality, require the prior approval of Parliament.[29]

---

26 Oral Evidence Given by the Prime Minister to the Liaison Committee, 21 January 2003; available www.publications.parliament.uk/pa/cm200203/cmselect/cmliaisn/334-i/3012102.htm.

27 See n 25 above, at p 277.

28 The Constitution Committee: *Waging War: Parliament's Role and Responsibility* 5th Report (2005–06) HL 236-I at [26] (hereafter *Waging War*).

29 Answer to a Parliamentary question 19 February 2003. Cited in Ev 4 to Public Administration Select Committee, 'Taming the Prerogative: Strengthening Ministerial Accountability to Parliament', 4th Report (2003–04), HC 422 at [57] (David Gladstone)—hereafter this report is referred to as *Taming the Prerogative*.

As the Constitution Committee commented:

> In summary, the deployment power's status as a prerogative power means that there are few restrictions to its use, other than those that have arisen from precedent or convention. Parliament has no formal role in approving deployments, although governments have usually kept Parliament informed about the decision to use force and the progress of military campaigns. The decision to invade Iraq in 2003 was the first time Parliament had voted on a substantive motion to deploy forces into conflict before fighting had begun since the Korean War in 1950. . . . Generally speaking. . .the deployment power is one to which no statutory or legal standards can be applied. . .[30]

A legal requirement for Parliamentary assent?

There are two basic options for reform. First, at least some of the prerogatives could be replaced by legislation, such as a War Powers Act, setting out the lawful powers of the Government to use armed force, and the procedures to be followed. These could include a requirement that a vote be held in Parliament to be held prior to the commencement of hostilities, unless necessity precluded it, in which case, such a vote would have to be held within a fixed period, say fourteen days. There have been a number of attempts to achieve such reform by Private Members Bill, most recently in one put forward by Lord Lester. The Public Administration Select Committee recently stated that:

> any decision to engage in armed conflict should be approved by Parliament, if not before military action then as soon as possible afterwards. A mere convention is not enough when lives are at stake.[31]

It recommended a public consultation exercise on legislation to give effect to this proposal. However, the Select Committee on the Constitution recently took a different stance, arguing that the fear of exposing members of the armed forces to prosecution for taking part in what could be found an illegal war and the possibility of judicial review, once the power to use force was placed on a statutory footing, both pointed strongly away from a statutory solution.

The Constitution Committee: *Waging War: Parliament's Role and Responsibility* 5th Report (2005–06) HL 236-I (extracts)

81. In summary, the key benefits of legislation to provide the right of prior parliamentary authorisation have been argued to be:

- democratic legitimacy; democratic accountability; and confirmation of widespread political backing, leading to greater confidence on the part of the Chiefs of Staff in the legitimacy of the deployment and higher morale of the Armed Forces;
- the creation of 'safer' arrangements for decision-making and facilitation of a more cohesive Government strategy on military action;
- following an international trend towards increasing standards of democratic governance and bring the United Kingdom into line with other countries' arrangements.

---

30   *Waging War,* at [16].

31   *Taming the Prerogative,* at [57].

82. By contrast, the main disadvantages have been argued to be:

- the decision to authorise deployments would be dictated by the immediate views and reactions of public opinion, while they should be taken by the executive;
- a curtailment of the necessary flexibility of action in order to defend national security; procedures leading to delayed decision making would allow more media influence and intervention; and there could be possible confusion about authorisation if events changed quickly on the ground;
- a lack of clarity in identifying those deployments to which legislation would apply; the legislation could open the door to judicial review, appeal and challenge in a way that might have adverse operational consequences;
- the outcome of a parliamentary vote might lead to damaging levels of uncertainty as to the legality of the actions of the armed forces and might weaken the resolve of the Government; this would be particularly acute if the two Houses failed to agree;
- formal requirements for prior approval have often been circumvented elsewhere.

. . .

84. While we were taking evidence, there was a notable contrast between the announcement of the decision to deploy British troops to Afghanistan by a ministerial statement on 26 January 2006 and the prolonged process of achieving parliamentary support in the Netherlands in order to allow the participation of Dutch troops in the same operations, which was only completed in February 2006 after 6 months of negotiation. . .

104. . . .We have not been persuaded that the difficulties of putting the deployment power on a statutory basis could easily be overcome, and consider that the problems of the uncertainty generated outweigh any constitutional merits. In our view, the possibility— however remote—of, for example, subjecting forces of the Crown to criminal prosecution for actions taken in good faith in protecting the national interest is unacceptable. We also see no merit in legislative architecture which creates the possibility of judicial review of Government decisions over matters of democratic executive responsibility. In addition, the need to provide for 'emergency' exceptions would create loopholes that could be readily exploited by a future administration with ambitions less benign than those to which we are accustomed. . .

Notes

1. The concerns of the Constitution Committee are, it is suggested, overstated. First of all, there is already the possibility of legal consequences for waging unlawful war under the jurisdiction of the International Criminal Court. The Bill could in any event simply rule out criminal liability for the armed forces when acting under orders from the Government. Second, if in future the UK Government were only to use armed force when it was certain that it could justify such action as lawful, many would see this, following the Iraq war, as a positive rather than a negative result. Finally, the argument that any legislation would leave loopholes that could be exploited is a perverse one indeed: at present the entire position consists of one giant loophole, placing no constraints upon governments at all. Any control would surely be an improvement. It is suggested therefore that an overwhelming case can be made for legislative reform in this area.

2. Numerous Bills have been put forward to achieve a legal requirement for Parliamentary assent. Professor Brazier's, prepared for the *Taming the Prerogative* report, was one of the simplest:

5 *Armed conflict*

. . . .

(2)   Her Majesty's armed forces shall take part in armed conflict only if participation in it is approved by resolution of each House of Parliament.

(3)   But section 5(2) shall not apply in case of action taken by those armed forces in their immediate and personal self-defence.

(4)   Resolutions under this section must be obtained—

(a)   before those armed forces participate in armed conflict, or
(b)   if Her Majesty's Government is of the opinion that such participation is necessary as a matter of urgency before resolutions could be obtained, within seven days of the beginning of that participation.

(5)   If Parliament is prorogued or is dissolved when such resolutions are needed then resolutions under this section must be obtained as soon as practicable.

6 Declaration of war

No declaration of war shall be made on behalf of the United Kingdom unless that declaration has been approved by resolution of each House of Parliament.

The way forward—a Convention

Not surprisingly, in view of the concerns of the military and the views of the Constitution Committee (above), it is only a convention that the Brown Government proposed, to be concretised by way of a parliamentary resolution. This is in itself disappointing, but the suggested way forward also appears to be designed to allow for maximum governmental control over the process. The proposal is for the approval of the House of Commons to be sought by way of debate and vote before committing the armed forces to conflict, but with important caveats, as appears below.

The Constitution Committee argued for a parliamentary convention, whereby Governments would be required to seek parliamentary approval before committing forces to actual or potential armed conflict as follows:

(1)   Government should seek Parliamentary approval (for example, in the House of Commons, by the laying of a resolution) if it is proposing the deployment of British forces outside the United Kingdom into actual or potential armed conflict;

(2)   In seeking approval, the Government should indicate the deployment's objectives, its legal basis, likely duration and, in general terms, an estimate of its size;

(3)   If, for reasons of emergency and security, such prior application is impossible, the Government should provide retrospective information within 7 days of its commencement or as soon as it is feasible, at which point the process in (1) should be followed;

(4)   The Government, as a matter of course, should keep Parliament informed of the progress of such deployments and, if their nature or objectives alter significantly should seek a renewal of the approval.[32]

---

32   *Waging War*, at [110].

The Government proposals (below) were considerably more cautious.

The Governance of Britain: Constitutional Renewal, Cm 7341-I (extracts)

216 ... The Government believes it essential that any new mechanism contains exceptions to the requirement for parliamentary approval that will allow the Government to respond swiftly in an emergency or carry out an operation in secrecy if necessary. This is vital to ensure that our national security, our ability to conduct effective operations and the safety of the UK Forces are not compromised by the implementation of the new mechanism. . .

218 The Government also proposes that there should not be a requirement to obtain retrospective approval for a conflict where prior approval had not been sought because of the secret or urgent nature of the deployment. . . .It believes that there could be some very serious and undesirable consequences of a failure to gain parliamentary approval for an operation which was underway. A requirement to seek retrospective approval for operations which are underway has the potential to call into question the credibility of the UK's use of force, our international relations and crucially, the safety and morale of the UK Forces, were a retrospective approval denied. It would, however, be the intention of the Government always to seek the prior approval of the Commons.

221 Given the well recognised imperative of the safety and effectiveness of our Armed Forces, and the many and various circumstances which could lead to the consideration of entering into armed conflict, the Government believes that the Prime Minister is the most appropriate authority to decide what information should be supplied to Parliament in the approval process.

222 . . .In common with standard practice the Government does not propose that the actual advice of the Attorney General should be made available to Parliament, although Parliament would be informed about the legal basis of the proposed conflict. . .

223 For similar reasons the Government proposes that it is for the Prime Minister to determine the most appropriate timing for seeking parliamentary approval in relation to the build up and deployment of forces or the progress of international negotiations [bearing in mind]. . .the need not to compromise safety of troops stationed abroad or continuing diplomatic efforts by too early a declaration that the Government intend to initiate armed conflict. . .

Note

All agree that it is necessary to allow the government to waive the requirement in cases of urgency or where surprise is required. However, under the above proposals, there is no requirement for retrospective approval of a decision to use armed force in such cases: the government would simply inform the House without, seemingly, permitting either debate or vote. Second, it is entirely for the Prime Minister to decide (a) *when* in the process of the build up to conflict to seek approval from Parliament and (b) what information to give Parliament on the background to the situation and the government's reasons for wishing to use armed force. In relation to the former, it is of course far harder politically for Parliament to vote against the use of armed force, when troops have already been deployed in a neighbouring country and war is imminent, as in the case of Iraq in 2003. In such circumstances, a negative vote would be likely to force the Prime Minister to resign, as Tony Blair was prepared to do had he lost the vote on the Iraq war; this is something which is obviously likely to deter many MPs from the governing party from voting against the use of force. Third, in particular, the Attorney General's advice on the legality of the proposed use of force will *not* be revealed—despite the huge controversy over this point in relation to the Iraq war and calls for such advice to be revealed in full on future occasions. In short, the Prime Minister, in deciding how to present the case for war to Parliament, is left entirely judge in his own case, as the Report below notes.

Public Administration Select Committee: *Constitutional Renewal: Draft Bill and White Paper*, 10th Report of the 2007–8 Session, HC 499 (extracts)

In effect, the Prime Minister is made the 'guarantor of the probity' of this part of the constitution. Peter Hennessy suggested to us that 'in the City that would be called "insider trading"':

> [Prime Ministers]. . .are the last people in the world who are going to be in a fit state of mind to judge, I think, what is proper for Parliament to have and what not; it is asking too much for a human being who is in a state of hyper anxiety to do that, and I think that is the single greatest weakness in what the Government has brought forward.

. . .

74. We are concerned that the terms of the resolution as drafted leave too much discretion in the hands of the Prime Minister. We would be more reassured if there were independent endorsement of information provided by the Prime Minister on a conflict, and of any decision that a conflict was too urgent or too secret to allow a prior debate and vote in the Commons. One option might be for this endorsement to come from the cross-party Intelligence and Security Committee. This Committee already has access to information, 'disclosure of which', as the Government admits, 'would be gravely damaging to the national interest and could put individuals at risk'.

75. We also are not convinced by the Government's arguments against the House holding a debate and vote on an urgent conflict once it was already under way. It is notable that all but one of the respondents to the Government's own consultation 'thought that the Government should seek retrospective approval from Parliament if it had deployed troops for reasons of urgency or secrecy'. The Government is concerned that [this could]. . . call into question the credibility of the UK's use of force, our international relations and crucially, the safety and morale of the UK Forces'. This is the price of democracy, and is a risk that Prime Ministers should have to weigh up before taking the extraordinary step of entering into a conflict without a prior mandate from the House of Commons. . . .

77. Peter Hennessy made [a] further forceful point in his evidence to us:

> the full legal advice of the Attorney General on conflict decisions should be made available to Parliament—'make sure that, unless there is very good reason not to, the full opinion on the legality of the war is given you, not some shrivelled inadequate summary'.

78. Michael Wills put the Government's counter-argument:

> I think it is clear that any lawyer, the Attorney General or whoever, knowing that their full legal opinion following the logic of their argument all the way through, is going to be put in full in the public domain, not necessarily as we all know happens treated objectively and faithfully in the public domain, could well end up being inhibited. It could have what we call a chilling effect on the advice.

What is clear, and what all parties seem to agree, is that there must be a 'full, frank statement of the legal basis' for military action. The contradiction we see is in how a statement can be full and frank, but yet less full and frank than the Attorney's verbatim legal advice (else why not publish it?). One person's 'full and frank' may be another person's 'shrivelled inadequate summary'. . . . The publication of the advice could well be the most straight-forward solution.

Note

However, the Joint Committee on the Draft Bill essentially backed the Government's inadequate proposals.[33] In doing so, they ignored the findings of the Constitution Committee, which had echoed the objections of the PAC to giving Governments this degree of control over the whole process:

> 42. . .Some witnesses questioned the effectiveness of these accountability meas-ures in practice. The Rt Hon Kenneth Clarke MP considered that parliamentary discussion preceding both the Falklands and Kosovo engagements curtailed real accountability:
>
> > . . .The whole thing was used more as a process of explanation and persuasion than it was of giving Parliament a real way to challenge the decision and to be accountable fully, which I think means throw-ing down before Parliament the opportunity to reject this policy if it wants to before any military action takes place.
>
> . . .
>
> 43. This view was echoed in other evidence. Professor John McEldowney. . . thought the lessons of the Iraq war were that the Government could set the agenda, identify the issues and provide its own publicity on the need for military action and its subsequent outcome, leaving Parliament relatively weakened. Accountability was also described as problematic because, in line with all prerogative power, it is 'dependent on the goodwill of the executive or the existence of a convention that Parliament should be informed'. Dr Ziegler told us that parliaments could be marginalised by lack of information (at any rate in time to influence their decisions) or by being confronted by *faits accomplis*: 'this is known as the de-parliamentarisation of decision-making'.[34]

No resolution was passed before the May 2010 General Election.

The Parliamentary scrutiny of treaties: the Constitutional Reform and Governance Act 2010

Here, the Brown Government put forward legislation, the Constitutional Reform and Governance Bill 2009. As the White Paper that accompanied it made clear, the proposal was for a statutory requirement to follow the Ponsonby requirements, with the stipulation that Treaties would not be deemed ratified until this has been done. All well and good. However, numerous aspects of the scheme dilute this prima facie requirement considerably as appears below.

---

33   Joint Committee, 'Draft Constitutional Renewal Bill' (2007–08) HL 166-I; HC 551-I at [332].

34   The Constitution Committee: *Waging War*, at [43].

The Governance of Britain: Constitutional Renewal, Cm 7341-I (extracts)

158 . . .In the event of a vote by the House of Commons against ratification of a treaty, the Government could not proceed to ratify it. If the Government later wished to re-present the same treaty to Parliament for ratification, it would have to lay an explanatory statement before both Houses and re-start the 21 sitting-day laying period from the beginning, in which a further debate and vote could be triggered. Another negative vote would again block ratification. In other words, the House of Commons would have the last word. In the event of a vote by the House of Lords against ratification of a treaty, the Government could not proceed to ratify it, unless it first laid an explanatory statement before both Houses explaining why the treaty should be ratified notwithstanding the views of the Lords. The Government believes that this approach would respect the primacy of the House of Commons, while recognising the importance of the role of the Lords in treaty scrutiny.

159 The legislation should make provision for alternative procedures for consulting and informing Parliament so as to provide flexibility when needed in exceptional circumstances. [There are]. . .examples where the Government has informed and consulted Parliament on a treaty using various alternative procedures, in circumstances where it was not possible to publish and lay the treaty for 21 sitting days prior to ratification. These examples show that such cases are very rare, but that they still can and do occur; for example, a treaty may need to be ratified during a Parliamentary recess, in circumstances where delay would be detrimental to the national interest. Other cases of urgency may occur, very rarely, when Parliament is sitting. In such cases, the Government would inform and consult Parliament by the most expeditious and practical means available (see paragraphs 148–155 of the consultation document for examples of such alternative procedures which have been used in the past. These examples include making an oral announcement to Parliament, laying a written statement, and consulting Opposition leaders during a recess).

160 In such exceptional cases, the Government proposes that the legislation would require it to lay a statement before Parliament at the earliest opportunity to explain why the treaty requires ratification without completing the normal period of Parliamentary scrutiny, and the steps taken or to be taken to consult Parliament by an alternative more rapid means. This would ensure that Parliament is able to call Government to account for any treaty where it has invoked this alternative procedure. This requirement to lay a written statement would not preclude Government from informing and consulting Parliament by any additional procedural means practically available.

Public Administration Select Committee, Constitutional Renewal: Draft Bill and White Paper, 10th Report of the 2007–8 Session, HC 499 (extracts)

81. . . .Essentially, the Government proposes to formalise the 'Ponsonby Rule', under which treaties are normally laid before Parliament for 21 sitting days before ratification. There is also provision in the draft bill, however, for ratification of a treaty to be delayed if the House of Commons resolves that it should not be ratified.

82. The Government does not propose that there should be a debate and vote on every treaty, or indeed on any treaty. It would be for Members to demand a vote, and for the Government, if willing, to find the opportunity for this vote to take place.

83. Once again, there are exceptions to the standard procedure:

- Certain classes of treaty would not be covered by the procedure, either because the Orders in Council which implement them are already subject to a vote (e.g. double taxation agreements) or because an Act of Parliament already provides that they may not be ratified without a further Act of Parliament (e.g. treaties to increase the powers of the European Parliament). These exemptions give us no cause for concern. However, two other kinds of exemption deserve closer consideration.
- Under clause 22 of the draft bill, 'if the Secretary of State is of the opinion that, exceptionally, the treaty should be ratified without the conditions . . . having been met', the treaty could be ratified without being laid before Parliament, or before 21 sitting days had elapsed.
- If the House of Commons were to vote that a treaty should not be ratified, the Secretary of State could lay a statement indicating that he 'is of the opinion that the treaty should nevertheless be ratified and explaining why', following which the House would have a further 21 sitting days in which to vote once again if it wished to insist that the treaty should not be ratified. The Secretary of State could then lay a further statement, and the procedure would be repeated once again, or many more times, until either the House or the Secretary of State gave way.

84. The Government's commitment to transferring power from the Executive to Parliament in this area has apparently waned since July 2007, when the Prime Minister spoke of 'put[ting] on to a statutory footing Parliament's right to ratify new international treaties'. As we have shown, the draft bill would instead give Parliament a right to object to the ratification of treaties, but only if the Government decides to provide the opportunity for Parliament to object; and would then allow the Government to overrule any objection Parliament might make. This part of the draft bill thus establishes a very weak form of parliamentary safeguard, which, if it proves uncomfortable, the Government can short-circuit anyway.

85. In most other countries, Parliaments hold considerable powers over the making of treaties. For example:

- In the United States, the President may only make a treaty with the concurrence of the Senate by a two-thirds majority.
- In France, an Act of Parliament is required before the President may approve or ratify peace treaties, commercial treaties, treaties or agreements relating to international organisations, those that commit the finances of the State, those that modify provisions which are matters for statute, those relating to the status of persons, and those that involve the cession, exchange or addition of territory.

86. There are no exceptions to these provisions in these countries. Parliamentary approval must always be gained before a treaty can be ratified. This leads us to question the value of clause 22 of the draft bill, and the Government's suggestions that there may be rare cases in which delaying the ratification of a treaty could be detrimental to the national interest. Why should it be open to the Secretary of State to ratify a treaty without meeting a very slight obligation to Parliament, when this option is not available to his international counterparts, where the parliamentary requirements to be met are much stronger? . . .

88. The procedure proposed following a vote against ratification of a treaty is also suspect. The proposal seems to be that a Secretary of State could repeatedly ask the House of Commons to revisit its decision. This is constitutionally dangerous territory. If

there is a debate and vote on a treaty, we assume that the Minister will have made his best arguments for the treaty in the course of that debate. He should not be allowed to second-guess the Chamber. If the House of Commons rejects a bill, the Minister cannot come back with the same bill a few days later, saying 'here is why I think this should become law despite you'.

The House also has a long-standing rule that the same question should not be put to it twice in the same parliamentary session. We see no reason why that rule should be cast aside in this case.

Notes

1. The Joint Committee on the draft Bill[35] was again much more cautious. It expressed broad support for the Government's proposals. On the issue of the Government being able to re-present a Treaty repeatedly, it simply recited that some witnesses were in favour, some against, and then, with no reasoning, sided with the Government. On the ability to side-step the laying requirements altogether the Committee agreed that the Government might reasonably need to do this and asked only that the Government should provide detailed information. The Committee noted Democratic Audit's comment:

> the Ponsonby Rule does not in practice lead to debates, let alone votes, being held on treaties. Indeed, it pointed out that the Government had admitted as much in its consultation paper. Therefore the proposals 'would have no practical impact, since . . . the opportunity to reject a treaty that the government proposal seems to provide would not arise. Parliament will have to change its organisation and procedures if it is to turn this latent power into a reality' (*ibid* at 233).

The Committee noted various suggestions for improving this—a new 'sifting committee' specific-ally to consider treaties, a means of scrutinising treaties prior to signature and, perhaps most importantly, a mechanism whereby Parliament could trigger a debate and vote, rather than simply relying on requests through the usual channels. It suggested (at para 238) that a new Joint Committee on Treaties be established.

2. The Government's proposals were given effect through ss 20–25 of the 2010 Act, in substantially the form discussed above. The provisions, while a small advance on the previous position, represent a very weak reform, shot through with exceptions. It is noteworthy that Professor Brazier, in his report for *Taming the Prerogative,* considered this issue and produced proposals for a Bill that would have given Parliament a far more muscular role. First of all, it did not allow for the Secretary of State simply to re-present a treaty that Parliament had rejected. Second, it only allowed the Government to dispense with Parliamentary consent where ratification was 'urgently needed'. And perhaps most importantly it divided treaties into two groups, and for the more significant, provided that they would not become law without a positive vote in their favour in the House of Commons.[36]

3. The Constitutional Renewal and Governance Bill contains provisions placing parts of the prerogative relating to the Civil Service on a statutory basis. These are considered in the following chapter at 619–620.

---

35   Joint Committee, 'Draft Constitutional Renewal Bill' (2007–08) HL 166-I; HC 551-I.

36   *'Taming the Prerogative,* Appendix 1.

CONTROL OF THE PREROGATIVE BY THE COURTS

Two basic questions arise here. First, will the courts be prepared to make a finding as to whether the prerogative claimed actually exists in law; second, will they be prepared to adjudge whether an admittedly existent power was properly exercised?

Determining the *existence* of a prerogative power

The courts have clearly answered the first question in the affirmative. As far back as the early 17th century, in the famous *Case of Proclamations*,[37] it was said that: '. . .the King hath no prerogative, but that which the law of the land allows him'. Furthermore, the courts will not allow new prerogatives to be created by executive fiat, although they may allow a recognised prerogative to broaden in adapting itself to new situations. In *BBC v Johns*,[38] the BBC claimed that a new prerogative had come into existence; in response Diplock LJ said, 'It is 350 years and a civil war too late for the Queen's courts to broaden the prerogative. The limits within which the executive government may impose obligations or restraints on the citizens of the United Kingdom without any statutory authority are now well settled and incapable of extension'. However, Lord Diplock's statement must be treated with some caution: in *Malone v Metropolitan Police Commissioner*,[39] the assertion that a prerogative power existed to authorise telephone tapping was based on the argument that no new power was being created although an old one was being extended to a new situation. It could be argued that the boundary between creating a new power and adapting an old one is not always clear, and that *Malone's* case is an example of an instance in which it is arguable that a new power was being claimed since it was very doubtful whether a prerogative power to intercept communications between citizens had ever existed.

How do the courts decide whether a claimed prerogative power exists?

It appears that in some instances the courts may approach the question of whether a prerogative to do a certain act exists not by considering whether it is authorised by some clearly defined and specific aspect of the prerogative but rather by first accepting the presence of a rather expansive and broadly defined general prerogative power and then finding that the specific act in question falls within that broad power. In the following case,[40] one issue which arose was whether there was, as the Home Secretary claimed, a general prerogative to do all that is reasonably necessary to keep the Queen's peace:

R v Secretary of State for the Home Department ex parte Northumbria Police Authority [1988] 2 WLR 590, 609–10

Purchas LJ: Mr Keene referred us to Chitty's *Prerogatives of the Crown* (1820) for the purposes of demonstrating that there was then no recognisable 'prerogative to provide or equip a police force'. With respect to Mr Keene, in my judgment this argument begs the

---

37 (1611) 12 Co Rep 74.

38 [1964] 1 All ER 923, at 941.

39 [1979] Ch 344.

40 The facts appear below, at p 583.

question. One is not seeking a prerogative right to do this. The prerogative power is to do all that is reasonably necessary to keep the Queen's peace. This involves the commissioning of justices of the peace, constables and the like. The author clearly identifies the prerogative powers inherent in the Crown in relation to the duty placed on the Sovereign to protect his dominions and subjects. . .

After considering the principle and transcendent prerogatives with respect to foreign states and affairs, as supreme head of the church as the fountain of justice the author turns to the question of the protection of the realm in these terms, at p 71:

> The duties arising from the relation of sovereign and subject are reciprocal. Protection, that is, the security and governance of his dominions according to law, is the duty of the sovereign; and allegiance and subjection, with reference to the same criterion, the constitution and laws of the country, form, in return, the duty of the governed, as will be more fully noticed hereafter. We have already partially mentioned this duty of the sovereign, and have observed that the prerogatives are vested in him for the benefit of his subjects, and that His Majesty is under, and not above, the laws.

The up-to-date position is summarised in Halsbury's *Laws of England* (4th edn, 1981), vol 36, p 200, para 320:

> General functions of constables. The primary function of the constable remains, as in the 17th century, the preservation of the Queen's peace. . .

. . . In my judgment, the prerogative powers to take all reasonable steps to preserve the Queen's peace. . .include the supply of equipment to police forces which is reasonably required for the more efficient discharge of their duties.

Nourse LJ. . . References in reported cases and authoritative texts to a prerogative of keeping the peace within the realm are admittedly scarce. The police authority relied especially on Chitty's silence as to that matter in his *Prerogatives of the Crown* (1820). I do not think that the scarcity is of any real significance. It has not at any stage in our history been practicable to identify all the prerogative powers of the Crown. It is only by a process of piecemeal decision over a period of centuries that particular powers are seen to exist or not to exist, as the case may be. . . The scarcity of references in the books to the prerogative of keeping the peace within the realm does not disprove that it exists. Rather it may point to an unspoken assumption that it does.

Notes

1. This case reveals the weakness of the UK Constitution in enforcing a very basic aspect of the rule of law in relation to the prerogative. Because it is accepted that prerogative powers are residual—that is, recognised rather than created by the common law —it can therefore be plausibly argued by the Crown that the absence of prior positive recognition by the courts of a particular prerogative is not necessarily fatal to a claim that it exists, as the above case, and the next one, *Bancoult*, demonstrates. Moreover, if the Crown is doubtful about finding evidence of a specific power, then instead it can be argued that it is merely an aspect of a very general prerogative. Thus in the above case, the power to supply equipment to police forces was argued to be but a particular aspect of a broad, undefined power to keep the peace. In the case below, this type of reasoning—subsuming the power to do a specific act within a very general power—is also followed.

2. The *Bancoult* litigation, to which we now turn, resulted in a whole series of cases, culminating in an important House of Lords' decision. As a major decision in this area, it covers a number of aspects of law, not all of which are relevant to this chapter.[41] But two broad issues arising from the case *are* considered in this chapter. The first was the controversy as to the claimed existence of the power in question—to deny the right of abode to the inhabitants of an overseas territory, considered here. The second was the correct approach of the courts to reviewing the *exercise* of that power, considered below (at 593–598). The facts are unfortunately somewhat complex. Cohn explains the background:

> The *Bancoult* decisions were part of the struggle of the. . .Chagossians, some of them British citizens. . .who had been former inhabitants of the Chagos Archipelago in the Indian Ocean [known as] the British Indian Ocean Territory (BIOT). . .Under a British-American accord signed in the 1960s, Britain permitted the United States to establish defence facilities on the largest island, Diego Garcia, and undertook to evacuate the population of any island on which the United States wished to provide military facilities. All local inhabitants of the archipelago were removed by 1973. By the time of the hearings in the High Court, more than 30 years after the evacuation, the facilities established on Diego Garcia had become a major American strategic asset. . .Originally, the eviction was effected by a [1971] Ordinance made under the 1965 BIOT Constitution Order in Council, which authorised legislation in the territory for its 'peace, order and good government'.[42]

In 2000, the 1971 Ordinance was quashed by the Divisional Court on the ground that the exclusion of an entire population from its homeland lay outside the purposes of the 1965 Order under which the Ordinance had been made (*Bancoult No 1*).[43] At the time, the Foreign Office, in a written statement, said that it accepted the court's ruling and that a new Immigration Ordinance would be put in place that would allow the islanders to return to the islands other than Diego Garcia (it being impossible, because of treaty agreements with the US, to restore them to Diego Garcia). It said further that it would continue to explore the practical feasibility of restoring the Chagossians to these islands. It was not possible in practice for such return to happen without substantial economic support from the UK Government. Thus the quashing of the 1971 Ordinance made no immediate difference in that no Chagossians, as a result, attempted to re-settle the islands.

A feasibility study then concluded that it would be very difficult to restore the islanders, especially given the looming threat of rising sea levels, due to global warming. As to providing further assistance to this end, the Government noted that in 1982 it had reached a final settlement with the islanders on financial compensation for their removal; the courts held in 2002 that the Chagossians had no enforceable right to further compensation to enable them to fund re-settlement.[44] There were also concerns about the effect of re-settlement of the other islands on the security of US bases on Diego Garcia.

Therefore, in 2004, without further consulting the islanders, or Parliament, the Government made two Orders in Council which had the effect of removing the legal rights of the Chagossians to return to any of the islands. As Cohn explains, 'the British Government opted to bypass the judicial ruling

---

41   The doctrine of substantive legitimate expectations is considered in Chapter 15 at 850–870.

42   Cohn, 'Unified Anxious' at 267–68.

43   *R (Bancoult) v Secretary of State for Foreign and Commonwealth Affairs* [2001] QB 1067.

44   Judgment of Ouseley J in *Chagos Islanders v Attorney General* [2003] EWHC 2222, QB.

[in 2000] by elevating the legal status of the provision that denied the right of abode'. Instead of relying on an ordinance made *under* a general Order in Council giving the right to make laws 'for the peace, order and good government of the Territory', the Government made new Orders in Council—in effect making a new constitution for the territory. Section 9 of the British Indian Ocean Territory (Constitution) Order 2004 ('the Constitution Order') indeed provided:

(1) Whereas the territory was constituted and is set aside to be available for the defence purposes of the Government of the United Kingdom and the Government of the United States of America, no person has the right of abode in the territory.

(2) Accordingly, no person is entitled to enter or be present in the territory except as authorised by or under this Order or any other law for the time being in force in the territory.

As Cohn puts it, 'Evacuation was now formally authorised, and return effectively forbidden, by a direct edict of the Crown, a measure designed to protect the Government from further judicial meddling'.[45]

When these Orders in Council were themselves challenged by the islanders, the Government's first line of defence was to argue that the Orders were immune from judicial scrutiny, having been made by the Queen exercising her sovereign powers in respect of the governance of a colony.[46] In other words, this was a legislative, not an executive act: the Orders in Council should be treated as primary legislation, and therefore immune from review (see above at 552).

The Divisional Court however quashed the orders in Council and this was upheld by the Court of Appeal,[47] mainly on the grounds that the Government had not had sufficient regard to the legitimate expectations of the islanders, created by the Government statement in 2000, that they would be allowed to return: the decision to deny this right was therefore an abuse of power. The Court also held that 'exiling an entire population while citing "the peace, order and good government" of the very same population as a basis for the evacuation was "repugnant" and therefore irrational'. In so doing, as Cohn notes, 'judicial review was applied to an Order in Council—a formal expression of the prerogative that had never before been subject to such treatment'.[48]

This was a radical decision, given that it concerned a sensitive area of foreign policy, and relations with the UK's most important ally, the United States. Not surprisingly, the Government appealed this defeat to the House of Lords. The judgment is a long and technical one: at this point we consider only the challenge to the very existence of a power to legislate by Order in Council to deny the right of abode to a whole people.

R (On The Application of Bancoult) v Secretary of State For Foreign and Commonwealth Affairs [2008] UKHL 61; [2009] 1 AC 453 (extracts)

Lord Hoffman. . .
42 Sir Sydney's [Counsel for the Chagossians] proposition that the Crown does not have power to remove an islander's right of abode in the territory is in my opinion also too extreme. He advanced two reasons. The first was that a right of abode was a fundamental

---

45 Cohn, at 268–69.

46 There was a further argument that the Orders in Council were barred from review save on very limited grounds by the Colonial Laws Validity Act—but this was found not to apply by the majority: see e.g. [2009] 1 AC 453 at [36]–[41], *per* Lord Hoffman; Lord Rogers and Lord Carswell dissented on this point.

47 [2007] EWCA Civ 498; [2008] QB 365.

48 Cohn, at 269.

constitutional right. He cited the 29th chapter of Magna Carta: 'No freeman shall be taken, or imprisoned . . . or exiled, or any otherwise destroyed . . . but by the lawful judgment of his peers, or by the law of the land.'

43 'But. . .by the law of the land' are in this context the significant words. Likewise Blackstone (*Commentaries on the Laws of England*, 15th ed (1809), vol 1, p 137): 'But no power on earth, except the authority of Parliament, can send any subject of England *out of* the land against his will; no, not even a criminal.'

44 That remains the law of England today. The Crown has no authority to transport anyone beyond the seas except by statutory authority. At common law, any subject of the Crown has the right to enter and remain in the United Kingdom whenever and for as long as he pleases: see *R v Bhagwan* [1972] AC 60. The Crown cannot remove this right by an exercise of the prerogative. That is because since the 17th century the prerogative has not empowered the Crown to change English common or statute law. In a ceded colony,[49] however, the Crown has plenary legislative authority. It can make or unmake the law of the land.

45 What these citations show is that the right of abode is a creature of the law. The law gives it and the law may take it away. In this context I do not think that it assists the argument to call it a constitutional right. The constitution of BIOT denies the existence of such a right. I quite accept that the right of abode, the right not to be expelled from one's country or even one's home, is an important right. General or ambiguous words in legislation will not readily be construed as intended to remove such a right: see *R v Secretary of State for the Home Department, Ex p Simms* [2000] 2 AC 115, 131–132. But no such question arises in this case. The language of section 9 of the Constitution Order [above at 578] could hardly be clearer. . .There seems to me no basis for saying that the right of abode is in its nature so fundamental that the legislative powers of the Crown simply cannot touch it.

46 Next, Sir Sydney submitted that the powers of the Crown were limited to legislation for the 'peace, order and good government' of the territory. Applying the reasoning of the Divisional Court in *Bancoult (No 1)*, he said that meant that the law had to be for the benefit of the inhabitants, which could not possibly be said of a law which excluded them from the territory.

47 There are two answers to this submission. The first is [that] the prerogative power of the Crown to legislate for a ceded colony has never been limited by the requirement that the legislation should be for the peace, order and good government or otherwise for the benefit of the inhabitants of that colony. That is the traditional formula by which legislative powers are conferred upon the legislature of a colony or a former colony upon the attainment of independence. But Her Majesty exercises her powers of prerogative legislation for a non-self-governing colony on the advice of her ministers in the United Kingdom and will act in the interests of her undivided realm, including both the United Kingdom and the colony: see *Halsbury's Laws of England*, 4th ed reissue, vol 6, para 716. . .

. . .

49 Her Majesty in Council is therefore entitled to legislate for a colony in the interests of the United Kingdom. No doubt she is also required to take into account the interests of the colony. . .but there seems to me no doubt that in the event of a conflict of interest, she is entitled, on the advice of Her United Kingdom ministers, to prefer the interests of the United Kingdom. I would therefore entirely reject the reasoning of the Divisional Court which held the Constitution Order invalid because it was not in the interests of the Chagossians.

---

49   That is one that has been gained not by conquest, but by being handed over by another colonial power.

50 My second reason for rejecting Sir Sydney's argument is that the words 'peace, order and good government' have never been construed as words limiting the power of a legislature. . .They have always been treated as apt to confer plenary law-making authority. For this proposition there is ample authority in the Privy Council: [his Lordship cited authority]. . .the courts will not inquire into whether legislation within the territorial scope of the power was in fact for the 'peace, order and good government' or otherwise for the benefit of the inhabitants of the territory. So far as *Bancoult (No 1)* departs from this principle, I think that it was wrongly decided.

[Lord Rodgers and Lord Carswell agreed with Lord Hoffman.]

Lord Bingham (dissenting). . .

69 It is for the courts to inquire into whether a particular prerogative power exists or not, and, if it does exist, into its extent: *Council of Civil Service Unions v Minister for the Civil Service* [1985] AC 374, 398e. Over the centuries the scope of the royal prerogative has been steadily eroded, and it cannot today be enlarged: *British Broadcasting Corpn v Johns* [1965] Ch 32, 79e. As an exercise of legislative power by the executive without the authority of Parliament, the royal prerogative to legislate by Order in Council is indeed an anachronistic survival. When the existence or effect of the royal prerogative is in question the courts must conduct an historical inquiry to ascertain whether there is any precedent for the exercise of the power in the given circumstances. 'If it is law, it will be found in our books. If it is not to be found there, it is not law': *Entick v Carrington*. . .In *Burmah Oil Co Ltd v Lord Advocate* [1965] AC 75 , 101, Lord Reid said:

> The prerogative is really a relic of a past age, not lost by disuse, but only available for a case not covered by statute. So I would think the proper approach is a historical one: how was it used in former times and how has it been used in modern times?

70 The House was referred to no instance in which the royal prerogative had been exercised to exile an indigenous population from its homeland. Authority negates the existence of such a power. Sir William Holdsworth, *A History of English Law*, (1938), vol X, p 393, states: 'The Crown has never had a prerogative power to prevent its subjects from entering the kingdom, or to expel them from it.' Laws LJ, in para 39 of his *Bancoult (No 1)* judgment. . .cited further authority:

> for my part I would certainly accept that a British subject enjoys a constitutional right to reside in or return to that part of the Queen's dominions of which he is a citizen. [Laws LJ cites the Blackstone quote above at 579). . . *Plender, International Migration Law*, 2nd ed (1988), ch 4, p 133 states: 'The principle that every state must admit its own nationals to its territory is accepted so widely that its existence as a rule of law is virtually beyond dispute . . .' and cites authority of the European Court of Justice in *Van Duyn v Home Office* (Case 41/74) [1975] Ch 358 , 378–379 in which the court held that 'it is a principle of international law . . . that a state is precluded from refusing its own nationals the right of entry or residence'. Dr Plender further observes, *International Migration Law*, p 135: 'A significant number of modern national constitutions characterise the right to enter one's own country as a fundamental or human right' , and a long list is given. . .

It is not, I think, suggested that those whose homes are in former colonial territories may be treated in a way which would not be permissible in the case of citizens in this country.

Hence the disingenuous pretence, in the 1960s–1970s, that there was no population which belonged to the outer islands of the Chagos Archipelago, to which alone this dispute relates. It is unnecessary to consider whether some power such as that claimed might be exercisable in the event of natural catastrophe or acute military emergency, since none such existed. Nor is it to the point that the Queen in Parliament could have legislated to the effect of section 9: it could, but not without public debate in Parliament and democratic decision. 71 I accordingly conclude that there was no royal prerogative power to make an Order in Council containing section 9, and it is accordingly void.

Lord Mance (dissenting) . . .

156 Mr Crow's further and principal submission that any common law right of abode in BIOT that Chagossians may have had could always be and was overridden and removed by Her Majesty in Council. This, Mr Crow submits, is what section 9 of the [2004 Constitution Order] on any view achieves. Within the United Kingdom, such a result could only be achieved by Parliament, whereas in territories such as BIOT it is submitted that the royal prerogative reigns unlimited in scope, subject only (Mr Crow's contrary submission being already rejected) to judicial review.

157 This submission treats BIOT and the prerogative power to make constitutional or other laws relating to BIOT as if they related to nothing more than the bare land, and as if the people inhabiting BIOT were an insignificant inconvenience (a phrase which reflects the flavour of some of the Government's internal memoranda in the 1960s), liable to be dispossessed at will for any reason that might seem good to the executive in the interests of the United Kingdom. . .But enacting a constitution for a conquered or ceded colony which has the aim of depopulating the whole of a habitable territory in the interests of the United Kingdom or its allies is another matter. A colony, whether conquered, ceded or settled, consists, first and foremost, of people living in a territory, with links to a parent state. The Crown's 'constituent' power to introduce a constitution for a ceded territory is a power intended to enable the proper governance of the territory, at least among other things for the benefit of the people inhabiting it. A constitution which exiles a territory's inhabitants is a contradiction in terms. The absence of any precedent for the exercise of the royal prerogative to exclude the inhabitants of a colony from the colony is significant, although to my mind entirely unsurprising. Until the present case, no-one can have conceived of its exercise for such a purpose. Territories, such as Gibraltar or Malta, have been conquered or ceded with military purposes in mind, but never, so far as appears, has there been either an original purpose or a subsequent attempt compulsorily to exclude their natural inhabitants. It may not have been necessary in the present case to use force to empty BIOT, but the logic of the Government's position is that this too would have been permissible. . .

159. . . . No doubt it is true, and I accept, that Parliament could by statute achieve the result at which the BIOT Order 2004 aimed. But that is not, as Mr Crow urged in his written case and oral submissions, a reason for holding that the Queen in Council can or must 'logically' be able to do the same. On the contrary, as Waller LJ rightly observed in the Court of Appeal (para 106), there are fundamental differences between legislation enacted by the executive through Her Majesty in Council and legislation subject to democratic debate in Parliament. . .

160 In my opinion, the royal prerogative to legislate in relation to BIOT did not extend to enacting legislation aimed at depriving BIOT of its inhabitants' right to enter and be present there. . .

Note

As discussed above, the answer to the question of whether a claimed prerogative power actually exists depends upon how narrowly or broadly it is framed. In this case, Lords Bingham and Mance ask, 'is there a prerogative power to exclude an entire people from their homeland?' and answer no—there being indeed no reference to such a power 'in the law books'. Lord Hoffman asks instead, 'is there a prerogative power to legislate generally for overseas territories' and finds that there is—finding also no reason to limit that power. In other words, Lord Hoffman, despite finding Orders in Council open to judicial review, essentially sees no limits to what they can do—finding them in that sense, to be the same as Acts of Parliament. As Lord Rodgers says: 'Assuming, then, that Her Majesty's constituent power can properly be described as a power to make "laws for the peace, order and good government of the territory", such a power is equal in scope to the legislative power of Parliament.'[50] Lord Bingham, rather more consistently, does *not* assume that Orders in Council for overseas territories can do anything— rather there needs to be past evidence for the exercise of specific powers. In this case, he finds none— 'The House was referred to no instance in which the royal prerogative had been exercised to exile an indigenous population from its homeland.' (*ibid* at [70]). It will be seen therefore that the apparently simple exercise of 'looking in the law books' to see whether a claimed prerogative power exists, in fact depends on at least two important assumptions: first, whether there is a fundamental difference between the power to legislate for overseas territories by means of orders in council and Parliament's unlimited power to legislate; second, whether the power to legislation by orders in council should be taken to be limited by fundamental principles of international human rights law. The majority answered 'no' to both questions, and the Government therefore won its appeal.

The effect of statute upon a claimed prerogative power

At times, the question of whether a claimed prerogative power is recognised by the law will be complicated by the enactment of a statute covering the same area. What happens when an area formerly regulated by the prerogative becomes covered by a statute?

Attorney-General v De Keyser's Royal Hotel Ltd [1920] AC 508, 526, 539, 575

Lord Dunedin: Inasmuch as the Crown is a party to every Act of Parliament, it is logical enough to consider that when the Act deals with something which before the Act could be effected by the prerogative, and specially empowers the Crown to do the same thing, but subject to conditions, the Crown assents to that, and by that Act, to the prerogative being curtailed.

. . .

Lord Atkinson: It is quite obvious that it would be useless and meaningless for the Legislature to impose restrictions and limitations upon, and to attach conditions to, the exercise by the Crown of the powers conferred by a statute, if the Crown were free at its pleasure to disregard these provisions, and by virtue of its prerogative do the very thing the statutes empowered it to do. One cannot in the construction of a statute attribute to the Legislature (in the absence of compelling words) an intention so absurd. It was suggested that when a statute is passed empowering the Crown to do a certain thing which it might theretofore have done by virtue of its prerogative, the prerogative is merged in the statute. I confess I do not think the word 'merged' is happily chosen. I should prefer to say that when such a statute; expressing the will and intention of the King and of the three estates of the realm, is

---

50   *Ibid* at [109].

passed, it abridges the Royal Prerogative while it is in force to this extent: that the Crown can only do the particular thing under and in accordance with the statutory provisions . . .and subject to all the limitations, restrictions and conditions by [them] imposed.

. . .

Lord Parmoor: The constitutional principle is that when the power of the executive to interfere with the property or liberty of subjects has been placed under Parliamentary control, and directly regulated by statute, the executive no longer derives its authority from the Royal Prerogative of the Crown but from Parliament, and that in exercising such authority the executive is bound to observe the restrictions which Parliament has imposed in favour of the subject.

Notes

1. In the *Northumbria Police Authority* case (above), the court had to consider whether s 4 of the Police Act 1964, which authorised Police Authorities to maintain vehicles, apparatus and equipment required for police purposes, effectively granted them a monopoly of this power, so that the Home Secretary had had his pre-existing prerogative power to keep the peace (which included the power to maintain and supply equipment to the police) abridged by the statute. Section 4(4) of the Police Act 1964 provided that the police authority for a police area 'may. . .provide and maintain such vehicles, apparatus, clothing and other equipment as may be required for police purposes of the area'. It was argued that since the Home Secretary had an undoubted power under the statute to supply equipment, subject to certain requirements, he could not claim a parallel prerogative power to supply such equipment without any safeguards. The court rejected this argument on the basis that the statute did not expressly state that equipment was not to be supplied under any other power. Purchas LJ held:

   > Where [an exercise of the prerogative is directed towards the benefit or protection of the individual. . .express and unequivocal terms must be found in the statute which deprives the individual from receiving the benefit or protection intended by the exercise of prerogative power. . .

   This appears to come close to stating that statute will only oust the prerogative if it uses express words in doing so; this would make it actually harder to abolish parts of the prerogative than to repeal previous Acts of Parliament, since previous Acts can be impliedly repealed, and thus seem to elevate the status of the prerogative over Acts of Parliament in direct opposition to the basic principle that statute is the highest form of law known in this country.

2. Croom-Johnson LJ's judgment was less controversial. He thought that s 4 'does not expressly grant a monopoly' and that in the circumstances 'there [was] every reason not to imply' such a monopoly, which does at least appear to admit of the possibility that the monopoly necessary to oust the prerogative could have been impliedly granted. Clarity appears to be lacking in this case, but the impression gained is that the courts were reluctant to allow erosion of the prerogative in the absence of a clear intent (express *or* implied?) to do so. In other words, any ambiguity—and there clearly was ambiguity in this case—seems to be resolved in favour of preservation of the prerogative. As Cohn comments (at 272):

   > Even detailed statutes need not be considered as precluding non-statutory powers. Courts can identify such statutes as non-inclusive arrangements beset by lacunae, and rule that a non-statutory action pertaining to a field covered by statute can still emerge unscathed [citing the *Northumbria* decisions].

3. Will the disabling of the prerogative by statute still take effect even where the statute in question only gives 'enabling' powers, allowing a scheme under the statutory provisions to be set up in the future? If it does not, could the Government set up an alternative scheme, inconsistent with the statutory one, acting under the prerogative? These were the issues which the House of Lords had to consider in *R v Secretary of State for the Home Department ex parte Fire Brigades Union and others* [1995] 2 WLR 464. The Criminal Justice Act 1988, ss 108–17 and Scheds 6 and 7 provided for a statutory scheme to replace the old non-statutory scheme for compensating victims of violent crime. The statutory scheme would have compensated victims under the tort measure of damages. Section 171 of the Act permitted the Secretary of State for the Home Department to choose when the scheme was to come into force. He decided not to bring it in and instead set up a tariff system (acting under the prerogative) which was radically different from the scheme envisaged by the Act.

4. Ian Leigh describes the background to the case:[51]

> The applicants in the Fire Brigades Union case argued that introduction of a new non-statutory scheme was unlawful in the sense either that the minister was in breach of the provisions for the introduction of the 1988 scheme, or that the existence of the unimplemented, but unrepealed, statutory scheme prevented the introduction of a wholly different scheme. . . . Either the case could be understood as an attack on the (non)use of the Home Secretary's power to make a commencement order under the Criminal Justice Act 1988, s 171. Or it could be understood as being concerned with limiting the prerogative power to introduce a new scheme, because of the existence of unimplemented amending legislation. Broadly, the second was the view taken by the majority in the Court of Appeal ([1995] 1 All ER 888), while the majority in the House of Lords preferred the first approach. A majority of the Court of Appeal held that the commencement section created no enforceable duty in the Home Secretary to bring the legislation into force at any particular time. However, a different majority held (Hobhouse LJ dissenting) that the Home Secretary had acted unlawfully in using the prerogative to introduce the new scheme since the 1988 Act suspended the prerogative in this area. Both points were cross-appealed to the House of Lords.

R v Secretary of State for the Departments ex parte Fire Brigades Union [1995] 2 WLR 464 (extracts)

[Lord Browne-Wilkinson found that the Home Secretary did not have an absolute duty to bring the scheme in, but continued as follows]:

Lord Browne-Wilkinson: It does not follow that, because the Secretary of State is not under any duty to bring the section into effect, he has an absolute and unfettered discretion whether or not to do so. So to hold would lead to the conclusion that both Houses of Parliament had passed the Bill through all its stages and the Act received the royal assent merely to confer an enabling power on the executive to decide at will whether or not to make the parliamentary provisions a part of the law. Such a conclusion, drawn from a section to which the sidenote is 'Commencement', is not only constitutionally dangerous but flies in the face of common sense. The provisions for bringing sections into force under s 171(1) apply not only to the statutory scheme but to many other provisions. For example, the provisions of Pts I, II and III relating to extradition, documentary evidence in criminal proceedings and other evidence in criminal proceedings are made subject to the same provisions. Surely, it cannot have been the intention of Parliament to leave it in the entire discretion of the Secretary of State whether or not to effect such important changes to the criminal law. In the absence of express provisions to the contrary in the Act, the plain intention of Parliament in conferring on the Secretary of State the power to bring certain sections into force is that such power is to be exercised so as to bring those sections into force when it is appropriate and unless there is a subsequent change of circumstances which would render it inappropriate to do so.

If, as I think, that is the clear purpose for which the power in s 171(1) was conferred on the Secretary of State, two things follow. First, the Secretary of State comes under a clear duty to keep under consideration from time to time the question whether or not to bring the section (and therefore the statutory scheme) into force. In my judgment he cannot lawfully surrender or release the power contained in s 171(1) so as to purport to exclude its future exercise either by himself or by his successors. In the course of argument, the Lord Advocate accepted that this was the correct view of the legal position. It follows that the decision of the Secretary of State to give effect to the statement in para 38 of the 1993 White Paper (Cm 2434) that 'the provisions in the 1988 Act will not now be implemented' was unlawful. The Lord Advocate contended, correctly, that the attempt by the Secretary of State to abandon or release the power conferred on him by s 171(1), being unlawful, did not bind either the present Secretary of State or any successor in that office. It was a nullity. But, in my judgment, that does not alter the fact that the Secretary of State made the attempt to bind himself not to exercise the power conferred by s 171(1) and such attempt was an unlawful act.

There is a second consequence of the power in s 171(1) being conferred for the purpose of bringing the sections into force. As I have said, in my view, the Secretary of State is entitled to decide not to bring the sections into force if events subsequently occur which render it undesirable to do so. But if the power is conferred on the Secretary of State with a view to bringing the sections into force, in my judgment, the Secretary of State cannot himself procure events to take place and rely on the occurrence of those events as the ground for not bringing the statutory scheme into force. In claiming that the introduction of the new tariff scheme renders it undesirable now to bring the statutory scheme into force, the Secretary of State is, in effect, claiming that the purpose of the statutory power has been frustrated by his own act in choosing to introduce a scheme inconsistent with the statutory scheme approved by Parliament.

THE LAWFULNESS OF THE DECISION TO INTRODUCE THE TARIFF SCHEME
The tariff scheme, if validly introduced under the Royal Prerogative, is both inconsistent with the statutory scheme contained in ss 108 to 117 of the 1988 Act and intended to be permanent. In practice, the tariff scheme renders it now either impossible or at least more expensive to reintroduce the old scheme or the statutory enactment of it contained in the 1988 Act. The tariff scheme involves the winding up of the old Criminal Injuries Compensation Board together with its team of those skilled in assessing compensation on the common law basis and the creation of a new body, the Criminal Injuries Compensation Authority, set up to assess compensation on the tariff basis at figures which, in some cases, will be very substantially less than under the old scheme. All this at a time when Parliament has expressed its will that there should be a scheme based on the tortious measure of damages, such will being expressed in a statute which Parliament has neither repealed nor (for reasons which have not been disclosed) been invited to repeal.

My Lords, it would be most surprising if, at the present day, prerogative powers could be validly exercised by the executive so as to frustrate the will of Parliament expressed in a statute and, to an extent, to pre-empt the decision of Parliament whether or not to continue with the statutory scheme even though the old scheme has been abandoned. It is not for the executive, as the Lord Advocate accepted, to state as it did in the White Paper (para 38) that the provisions in the 1988 Act 'will accordingly be repealed when a suitable legislative opportunity occurs'. It is for Parliament, not the executive, to repeal legislation. The constitutional history of this country is the history of the prerogative powers of the Crown being made subject to the overriding powers of the democratically elected legislature as the sovereign body. The prerogative powers of the Crown remain in existence to the extent that Parliament has not expressly or by implication extinguished them. But under the principle in *A-G v De Keyser's Royal Hotel Ltd* if Parliament has conferred on the executive statutory powers to do a particular act, that act can only thereafter be done under the statutory powers so conferred: any pre-existing prerogative power to do the same act is pro tanto excluded. . .

In his powerful dissenting judgment in the Court of Appeal, Hobhouse LJ decided that, since the statutory provisions had not been brought into force, they had no legal significance of any kind. He held, in my judgment correctly, that the *De Keyser* principle did not apply to the present case: since the statutory provisions were not in force they could not have excluded the pre-existing prerogative powers. Therefore the prerogative powers remained. He then turned to consider whether it could be said that the Secretary of State had abused those prerogative powers and again approached the matter on the basis that since the sections were not in force they had no significance in deciding whether or not the Secretary of State had acted lawfully. I cannot agree with this last step. In public law the fact that a scheme approved by Parliament was on the statute book and would come into force as law if and when the Secretary of State so determined is in my judgment directly relevant to the question whether the Secretary of State could in the lawful exercise of prerogative powers both decide to bring in the tariff scheme and refuse properly to exercise his discretion under s 171(1) to bring the statutory provisions into force.

I turn then to consider whether the Secretary of State's decisions were unlawful as being an abuse of power. In this case there are two powers under consideration: first, the statutory power conferred by s 171(1); second, the prerogative power. In order first to test the validity of the exercise of the prerogative power, I will assume that the 1988 Act, instead of conferring a discretion on the Secretary of State to bring the statutory scheme into effect, had specified that it was to come into force one year after the date of the royal assent. As Hobhouse LJ held, during that year the *De Keyser* principle would not apply and the prerogative powers would remain exercisable. But in my judgment it would plainly have been an improper use of the prerogative powers if, during that year, the Secretary of State had discontinued the old scheme and introduced the tariff scheme. It would have been improper because in exercising the prerogative power the Secretary of State would have had to have regard to the fact that the statutory scheme was about to come into force: to dismantle the machinery of the old scheme in the meantime would have given rise to further disruption and expense when, on the first anniversary, the statutory scheme had to be put into operation. This hypothetical case shows that, although during the suspension of the coming into force of the statutory provisions the old prerogative powers continue to exist, the existence of such legislation basically affects the mode in which such prerogative powers can be lawfully exercised.

Does it make any difference that the statutory provisions are to come into effect, not automatically at the end of the year as in the hypothetical case I have put, but on such day as the Secretary of State specifies under a power conferred on him by Parliament for the purpose of bringing the statutory provisions into force? In my judgment it does not. The Secretary of State could only validly exercise the prerogative power to abandon the old scheme and introduce the tariff scheme if, at the same time, he could validly resolve never to bring the statutory provisions and the inconsistent statutory scheme into effect. For the reasons I have already given, he could not validly so resolve to give up his statutory duty to consider from time to time whether to bring the statutory scheme into force. His attempt to do so, being a necessary part of the composite decision which he took, was itself unlawful. By introducing the tariff scheme he debars himself from exercising the statutory power for the purposes and on the basis which Parliament intended. For these reasons, in my judgment the decision to introduce the tariff scheme at a time when the statutory provisions and his power under s 171(1) were on the statute book was unlawful and an abuse of the prerogative power.

Notes

1. The House of Lords held by a majority of three to two (Lord Keith and Lord Mustill dissenting) that it was an abuse of power for the Home Secretary to purport to use the prerogative to set up a scheme inconsistent with the statutory one. The decision to do so was therefore unlawful.

2. As Leigh notes:

   The Lords' decision in effect treats the prerogative as a source of law equivalent to legislation: it can only be repealed by later legislation which is itself in force. This is appealing on grounds of symmetry and logic, but can be criticised as an overly mechanical approach, which attributes more clarity and certainty to prerogative power than is justified. Although it may be too late to create new prerogatives, the exact scope of many prerogative powers remains wholly unclear until litigated. In effect, therefore, as a source of law, the prerogative is given a latent potential which greatly exceeds that of unimplemented (but precise and detailed) statutory provisions.[52]

3. It will be noted that notwithstanding the view of Professor Wade (above) that the whole Criminal Injuries Compensation Scheme had nothing to do with the prerogative, it was common ground that the prerogative was in fact being used.

4. One important argument of the dissenting minority was that, since any scheme the Minister put in place could be changed (albeit with difficulty) by Parliament in the future, the Minister could not be said to be frustrating Parliament's intent as he had not put an end to the statutory scheme, something only Parliament itself could do.[53] With respect, this view seems to be clearly mistaken. By bringing in a scheme which differed radically from that envisaged by Parliament, the Minister was clearly contravening their will: the fact that such contravention could later be reversed is beside the point. Lord Mustill seems to think that Parliament's will is not frustrated as long as it is not permanently frustrated.[54]

---

52   I Leigh, 'The Prerogative, Legislative Power, and the Democratic Deficit: The *Fire Brigades Union* case' [1995] 3 Web JCLI.

53   *Per* Lord Mustill at p 267

54   For further comment on the decision, see *TRS Allan* [1995] CLJ 491.

Reviewing the *exercise* of prerogative powers

Our second question was how far the courts would be prepared to question the *exercise* of prerogative powers as opposed to their legal existence. The traditional view was, as Munro puts it, 'that courts lacked jurisdiction to review the manner of exercise of prerogative powers, or the adequacy of the grounds upon which they had been exercised'.[55] In relation to prerogative powers which are not classifiable as 'acts of state', before the decision in the *GCHQ* case (*CCSU v Minister for Civil Service*[56] below), the most important revision of the non-reviewability principle was made by Lord Denning in the following case.

Laker Airways Ltd v Department of Trade [1977] QB 643, 705

Lord Denning: . . .The prerogative is a discretionary power exercisable by the executive Government for the public good, in certain spheres of governmental activity for which the law has made no provision, such as the war prerogative (of requisitioning property for the defence of the realm), or the treaty prerogative (of making treaties with foreign powers). The law does not interfere with the proper exercise of the discretion by the executive in those situations: but it can set limits by defining the bounds of the activity: and it can intervene if the discretion is exercised improperly or mistakenly. That is a fundamental principle of our constitution. It derives from two of the most respected of our authorities. In 1611 when the King, as the executive Government, sought to govern by making proclamations, Sir Edward Coke declared that: 'the King hath no prerogative, but that which the law of the land allows him': see the *Proclamations Case* (1611) 12 Co Rep 74, 76. In 1765 Sir William Blackstone added his authority, *Commentaries*, vol 1, p 252: 'For prerogative consisting (as Mr Locke has well defined it) in the discretionary power of acting for the public good, where the positive laws are silent, if that discretionary power be abused to the public detriment, such prerogative is exerted in an unconstitutional manner.'

Note
In *GCHQ*, the House of Lords had to consider a challenge to an Order in Council made by the Prime Minister which prevented staff at GCHQ belonging to national trade unions. Six members of staff and the union involved applied for judicial review of the Prime Minister's instruction on the ground that she had been under a duty to act fairly by consulting those concerned before issuing it. It had first to be determined whether the decision was open to judicial review. In general, a person affected by a decision concerning public law matters made under statutory powers may challenge it by way of judicial review.

CCSU v Minister for Civil Service [1985] AC 374, 417–18, HL

Lord Roskill: . . . If the executive in pursuance of the statutory power does an act affecting the rights of the citizen, it is beyond question that in principle the manner of the exercise of that power may today be challenged on one or more of the three grounds [of judicial review]. If the executive instead of acting under a statutory power acts under a prerogative power and in particular a prerogative power delegated to the respondent under Article 4 of the Order in Council of 1982, so as to affect the rights of the citizen, I am unable to see,

---

55 *Studies in Constitutional Law,* at 279.

56 [1985] AC 374.

subject to what I shall say later, that there is any logical reason why the fact that the source of the power is the prerogative and not statute should today deprive the citizen of that right of challenge to the manner of its exercise which he would possess were the source of the power statutory.

In either case the act in question is the act of the executive. To talk of that act as the act of the sovereign savours of the archaism of past centuries.

But I do not think that that right of challenge can be unqualified. It must, I think, depend upon the subject matter of the prerogative power which is exercised. Many examples were given during the argument of prerogative powers which as at present advised I do not think could properly be made the subject of judicial review. Prerogative powers such as those relating to the making of treaties, the defence of the realm, the prerogative of mercy, the grant of honours, the dissolution of Parliament and the appointment of ministers as well as others are not, I think, susceptible to judicial review because their nature and subject matter are such as not to be amenable to the judicial process. The courts are not the place wherein to determine whether a treaty should be concluded or the armed forces disposed in a particular manner or Parliament dissolved on one date rather than another.

In my view the exercise of the prerogative which enabled the oral instructions of 22 December 1983 to be given does not by reason of its subject matter fall within what for want of a better phrase I would call the 'excluded categories' some of which I have just mentioned. It follows that in principle I can see no reason why those instructions should not be the subject of judicial review.

Notes

1. The House of Lords went on to find that the applicants had had a legitimate expectation that they would be consulted, and that the Prime Minister had, *prima facie*, 'acted unfairly'[57] in failing so to consult, but that reasons of national security justified the failure. Diplock LJ, in a well known *dicta*, remarked:

   National security is the responsibility of the executive government; what action is needed to protect its interest is. . .a matter on which those on whom the responsibility rests, and not the courts of justice must have the last word. It is par excellence a non-justiciable process. The judicial process is totally inept to deal with the sort of problems which it involves.

2. *GCHQ* then set out an *(obiter)* list of prerogatives which were to remain not subject to review. These included 'the making of treaties, the defence of the realm, the prerogative of mercy, the grant of honours, the dissolution of Parliament and the appointment of ministers as well as others. . .'. *R v Secretary of State for the Foreign Office ex parte Rees Mogg* [1994] QB 552 confirmed that the courts would not entertain challenges to the prerogative power to conclude treaties (in this case the Treaty of Maastricht). However, in other cases, the courts have begun to whittle away at that list.

3. *R v Secretary of State for Foreign and Commonwealth Affairs ex parte Everett* [1989] 2 QB 540 concerned a challenge to the refusal to issue a passport. Passports are issued by the Passport Office (now a government agency, then a government department) under the royal prerogative. The Government can therefore exercise a discretion to withhold a passport where a person wishes to travel abroad to engage in activities which are politically deplored, although legal. Because these powers arise under the royal prerogative, it was thought that they would not be open to review until

the ruling noted above in the *GCHQ* case. The applicant, who was living in Spain, applied for a new passport when his old one expired. The Secretary of State refused to grant him one, on the basis that there was an outstanding warrant for his arrest in the UK and it was government policy not to give passports to such people. The applicant applied for judicial review on the basis that no details of the warrant had been given to him. It was held that the Secretary of State was obliged to provide the applicant with details of the warrant and that if there were exceptional reasons why the normal policy should not be applied, they would be taken into account. The Government had argued that the grant of a passport came under the umbrella of foreign policy and so was in the area of 'high policy' in which courts could not interfere. Taylor J said that he agreed that matters of high policy would not now be reviewable. But, he argued, the grant of passport was an administrative decision, affecting the rights of individuals and their freedom of travel.

4. A further incursion into previously excluded territory occurred in *R v Secretary of State for the Home Department ex parte Bentley* [1994] QB 349, which concerned the prerogative of mercy, one of the prerogatives on Lord Roskill's list. The issue was whether the Home Secretary's refusal to recommend a posthumous pardon for Derek Bentley, executed in 1953 for the murder of a policeman, was subject to judicial review. The Home Secretary had said that his personal view was that Bentley should not have been hanged, but that he could not exercise the prerogative of mercy since he had not been given any evidence indicating that Bentley was innocent. The court found, plainly against Lord Roskill's *dicta* in *GCHQ*, that the prerogative of mercy *was* reviewable, though on rather limited grounds. While they said it would be difficult or impossible to assess the complex balancing act of political, moral and legal motives which the Home Secretary might engage in, in deciding whether to grant a pardon, in this case the issue was narrower and more technical, thus more suited to judicial oversight: that is, had the Home Secretary misdirected himself in failing to consider all the different types of action he could take under the prerogative. The court found that he had wrongly considered that the only option open to him was a full pardon; instead he should have considered whether some lesser action—a formal, public declaration that an injustice had been done to Bentley—could properly be carried out. It was thus held that the decision was at least partially open to review; the court dealt with Roskill's suggestion in *GCHQ* by simply dismissing it as *obiter*. However, the court was cautious when it came to remedies: instead of making any order, it simply issued a formal 'invitation' to the Home Secretary to reconsider his decision, an invitation which the Home Secretary did not decline.

5. A much more assertive approach was taken very recently in *R (On the Application of Page) v Secretary of State for Justice*,[58] in which a prisoner sought judicial review of a decision of the Secretary of State not to exercise the prerogative of mercy to allow his release at the correct date. There is detailed, written guidance on what is termed 'special remission': the ability of the Minister to cancel part of a sentence via the exercise of the prerogative. This had not been properly taken into account and Collins J found that it was a 'rare case' in which the decision had been therefore unlawful and could be quashed.

6. *R v Ministry of Defence ex parte Smith*[59] is a well known decision concerning a challenge to the then ban on homosexuals serving in the armed forces, a policy which it was found was maintained by the prerogative. The policy was dropped by the Government after eventually losing an application to Strasbourg[60] and the approach of the court to the substantive issue would now be different since such challenges would be brought under the Human Rights Act (below). The point of interest here

58 [2007] EWHC 2026 (Admin).

59 [1995] 4 All ER 427.

60 *Smith and Grady v UK* (2000) EHRR 493.

is that it was argued for the Ministry of Defence that *(inter alia)* the case was 'concerned with the exercise of a prerogative power in an area—the defence of the realm— recognised by the courts to be unsuitable for judicial review' This contention was directly addressed by the court of first instance, and Simon Brown LJ said (at 446):

> To my mind only the rarest cases will today be ruled strictly beyond the court's purview—only cases involving national security properly so-called and where in addition the courts really do lack the expertise or material to form a judgment on the point at issue. This case does not fall into that category. True, it touches on the defence of the realm but it does not involve determining 'whether. . .the armed forces [should be] disposed of in a particular manner' (which Lord Roskill in CCSU thought plainly unreviewable—as indeed had been held in *China Navigation Co Ltd v A-G* [1932] 2 KB 197, [1932] All ER Rep 626). No operational considerations are involved in this policy. Now, indeed, that the 'security implications' have disappeared, there appears little about it which the courts are not perfectly well qualified to judge for themselves.

7. Having found the issue justiciable, the court went on to find that the policy of excluding homosexuals could not be held to be *Wednesbury* unreasonable. Clearly, the last part of the judge's remarks were *obiter;* when the Court of Appeal heard the appeal of the servicemen and women it made no such general remarks about the availability of review against the prerogative, but nor did it disapprove of Simon Brown LJ's comments, and indeed it appeared to take it for granted that the issue was justiciable. Clearly, therefore, *ex parte Smith* indicates that the unreviewable areas of the prerogative were perhaps smaller than had been previously thought, whilst Simon Brown LJ's *dicta* that only 'the rarest cases' will be non-justiciable is an emphatic statement of judicial intention to enforce the fundamentals of the Rule of Law through the courts save in those cases where it would be clearly inappropriate.

8. Support for this view can be found in *R on the Application of Abbasi and another v Secretary of State for Foreign and Commonwealth Affairs and Secretary of State for the Home Department,*[61] an important recent decision of the Court of Appeal. The case arose from the detention by the US military authorities of a British national, Abbasi, whom they suspected of being a member of Al Qa'eda, in Guantanamo Bay. The US Government's position was that those being held were 'unlawful combatants' and so could be held by the US throughout the duration of the 'war on terrorism', which in practice could well mean indefinite detention. Detainees at that point had no access to a court to challenge their detention, US courts having refused jurisdiction up until that time, and nor had their status been determined by a competent tribunal, as the Geneva Convention arguably requires. Abbasi argued that, since he was being subject, in effect, to arbitrary detention, in violation of habeas corpus, the Foreign Office had a duty either to make representations on his behalf to the US Government or, at the least, to explain why they had in fact taken no action in relation to his case. The court first of all found that it was obliged to approach the application for judicial review on the basis that: 'in apparent contravention of fundamental principles recognised by both jurisdictions and by international law, Mr Abbasi is at present arbitrarily detained in a 'legal black-hole' (at para 64). However, one of the apparent stumbling blocks in the way of the applicant was the Government's argument that the exercise of prerogative powers in the field of foreign affairs was non-justiciable (in reliance on the *dicta* from *GCHQ,* considered above). The Court's finding was that the mere fact that the prerogative power in relation to foreign affairs was

---

61   [2002] EWCA Civ 1598; [2003] UKHRR 76.

in issue was not enough to oust the jurisdiction of the court—it was the particular subject matter that was determinative. Moreover, in an extreme case where the Foreign Office appeared to be refusing even to consider making representations to the US Government about someone in the position of the applicant, judicial review would lie; however, such consideration had been given in this case, and there was no question of the court ordering the Government to make representations.

9. This judgment is evidently a mixture of boldness and caution: the court accepted that there were still 'forbidden areas' of prerogative immune from review; but it was bold in carving out an exception to an area traditionally thought forbidden in this case, and left open the possibility that it might be possible to require 'more than that the Foreign Secretary give due consideration to a request for assistance': a radical proposition, given that this could potentially amount to a direct intervention by the courts in the conduct of foreign affairs.

10. *R (Al Rawi) v Foreign Secretary*[62] took a similar approach in relation to a non-British national detained at Guantanamo, who had been granted permanent leave to remain, save that in this case, the Secretary of State was entitled to refuse to make representations, since the applicants were not British nationals. The court stressed that in such cases, it was for the Secretary of State to determine what considerations were relevant in making his decision, effectively, part-insulating such decisions from challenge, and added that he should be granted an especially broad margin of discretion.

11. In a third recent decision, *CND v The Prime Minister of the United Kingdom and others*,[63] CND requested the court to determine the correct legal interpretation of UNSC Resolution 1441, which gave Iraq a final chance to comply with previous resolutions as to disarmament and threatened serious consequences if it did not. It was of course not in dispute that the court did not have the lawful power to prevent the UK Government from commencing hostilities against Iraq by way of injunction or a quashing order: the question was whether the court could declare whether the Resolution did, or did not give the UK Government lawful grounds, as a matter of international law, to take such action, in the event of non-compliance by the Iraqi Government. The court in this case firmly disclaimed the invitation to enter upon any such determination on a number of grounds. In terms of the issues discussed here, the key reason was that any declaration by the court would be damaging to the UK's national interest in terms of international relations and defence, since it could embarrass or tie the hands of the UK Government. It was therefore non-justiciable. This finding was unsurprising, since it would have involved the court entering directly into a highly sensitive issue of international relations.[64]

12. The *Abbasi* decision is perhaps the most interesting of these: it exemplifies the contemporary approach of the courts that it is not the broad area under consideration that determines justiciability, but rather whether the particular issues raised by the challenge involve questions unsuited to judicial determination. To that extent, the relatively crude 'list' approach of Lord Roskill in *GCHQ* has been quite substantially modified. It certainly seems that the position has moved on markedly since 1987, when Munro suggested that 'the propriety of *most* exercises of prerogative power will still continue to be unsusceptible to challenge in the courts'.[65]

13. The most important recent decision on review of prerogative powers is *Bancoult,* the facts of which have already been given. We considered above the House of Lord's approach to determining

---

62 [2007] 2 WLR 1219.

63 [2002] EWHC 2759, QB.

64 On the court's attitude towards ruling on the legality of the state's use of force in international relations (in the context of an attempt to use as a defence to charges of criminal damage and aggravated trespass at military bases) see also *R v Jones* [2007] 1 AC 136, which confirms a conservative approach.

65 *Studies in Constitutional Law* (1987), p 182, emphasis added.

the existence of the claimed power. Here we focus on two further issues. First, is an Order in Council subject to judicial review at all, or is it in effect primary legislation, as the Government argued? Second, how assertive should the courts be in reviewing it? As to the first, the High Court had acknowledged that historically '[a]n Order in Council made by the Queen for a ceded colony, now an overseas territory . . . attracted at least the same sovereign immunity as that of Parliament, provided that it is not repugnant to an Act of Parliament or delegated legislation'.[66]

R (On The Application of Bancoult) v Secretary of State For Foreign and Commonwealth Affairs [2008] UKHL 61; [2009] 1 AC 453 (extracts)

Lord Hoffman. . . It is true that a prerogative Order in Council is primary legislation in the sense that the legislative power of the Crown is original and not subordinate. It is classified as primary legislation for the purposes of the Human Rights Act 1998 . . . But the fact that such Orders in Council in certain important respects resemble Acts of Parliament does not mean that they share all their characteristics. The principle of the sovereignty of Parliament, as it has been developed by the courts over the past 350 years, is founded upon the unique authority Parliament derives from its representative character. An exercise of the prerogative lacks this quality; although it may be legislative in character, it is still an exercise of power by the executive alone. Until the decision of this House in *Council of Civil Service Unions v Minister for the Civil Service* [1985] AC 374, it may have been assumed that the exercise of prerogative powers was, as such, immune from judicial review. That objection being removed, I see no reason why prerogative legislation should not be subject to review on ordinary principles of legality, rationality and procedural impropriety in the same way as any other executive action. Mr Crow rightly pointed out that the Council of Civil Service Unions case was not concerned with the validity of a prerogative order but with an executive decision made pursuant to powers conferred by such an order. That is a ground upon which, if your Lordships were inclined to distinguish the case, it would be open to you to do so. But I see no reason for making such a distinction. I see no reason why prerogative legislation should not be subject to review on ordinary principles of legality, rationality and procedural impropriety in the same way as any other executive action.

[None of their Lordships saw Orders in Council as being *per se* unreviewable. Cohn comments that 'this part of the decision spells an important development in constitutional review of prerogative, reflecting the victory of a modern, functional attitude towards administrative powers. It has also weakened the distinction between prerogative and other non-statutory powers: both are now equally amenable to regular review.'[67] The next major issue is the standard of review of the Orders in Council and the substantive grounds of challenge.]

Lord Hoffman: On this question there was a radical difference in the approaches advocated by the parties. Mr Crow said that because the Crown was acting in the interests of the defence of the realm, diplomatic relations with the United States and the use of public funds in supporting any settlement on the islands, the courts should be very reluctant to interfere. Judicial review should be undertaken with a light touch and the Order set aside only if it appeared to be wholly irrational. Sir Sydney, on the other hand, said that because the Order deprived the Chagossians

---

66   [2006] EWHC 1038; [2006] ACD 81 at [143] (Hooper LJ).

67   Cohn, at 270.

of the important human right to return to their homeland, the Order should be subjected to. . .an 'anxious' degree of scrutiny in requiring the public body in question to demonstrate that the most compelling of justifications existed for such measures.'

I would not disagree with this proposition, which is supported by a quotation from. *Ex p Smith*. . .However, I think it is very important that in deciding whether a measure affects fundamental rights or has 'profoundly intrusive effects', one should consider what those rights and effects actually are. If we were in 1968 and concerned with a proposal to remove the Chagossians from their islands with little or no provision for their future, that would indeed be a profoundly intrusive measure affecting their fundamental rights. But that was many years ago, the deed has been done, the wrong confessed, compensation agreed and paid. The way of life the Chagossians led has been irreparably destroyed. The practicalities of today are that they would be unable to exercise any right to live in the outer islands without financial support which the British Government is unwilling to provide and which does not appear to be forthcoming from any other source. During the four years that the Immigration Ordinance 2000 was in force, nothing happened. No one went to live on the islands. Thus their right of abode is, as I said earlier, purely symbolic. If it is exercised by setting up some camp on the islands, that will be a symbol, a gesture, aimed at putting pressure on the Government . . . When one considers the rights in issue in this case, which have to be weighed in the balance against the defence and diplomatic interests of the state, it should be seen for what it is, as a right to protest in a particular way and not as a right to the security of one's home or to live in one's homeland. It is of course true that a person does not lose a right because it becomes difficult to exercise or because he will gain no real advantage by doing so. But when a legislative body is considering a change in the law which will deprive him of that right, it cannot be irrational or unfair to consider the practical consequences of doing so. Indeed, it would be irrational not to.

My Lords, I think that if one keeps firmly in mind the practical effect of section 9 of the Constitution Order, the issues in this appeal fall into place. The Government does not consider that it is in the public interest that an unauthorised settlement on the islands should be used as a means of exerting pressure to compel it to fund a resettlement which it has decided would be uneconomic. That is a view it is entitled to take. . .

In addition. . .the Government had to give due weight to security interests. The United States had expressed concern that any settlement on the outer islands would compromise the security of its base on Diego Garcia. A representative of the State Department wrote a letter for use in these proceedings, giving details of the ways in which it was feared that the islands might be useful to terrorists. Some of these scenarios might be regarded as fanciful speculations but, in the current state of uncertainty, the Government is entitled to take the concerns of its ally into account.

58 Policy as to the expenditure of public resources and the security and diplomatic interests of the Crown are peculiarly within the competence of the executive and it seems to me quite impossible to say, taking fully into account the practical interests of the Chagossians, that the decision to impose immigration control on the islands was unreasonable or an abuse of power.

Lord Rodgers: It is not open to the courts to hold that legislation enacted under a power described in those terms does not, in fact, conduce to the peace, order and good government of the territory. Equally, it cannot be open to the courts to substitute their judgment for that of the Secretary of State advising Her Majesty as to what can properly be said to conduce to the peace, order and good government of BIOT. This is simply because such questions are not justiciable. The law cannot resolve them: they are for the determination of the responsible ministers rather than judges. In this respect, the legislation made for the colonies is in the same position as legislation made by Parliament for this country, as the High Court of Australia pointed out. In both cases, the sanction for inappropriate use of the legislative power is political, not judicial. The difference— and it is, of course, very important— is that Orders in Council are made without the concurrence of Parliament or of any other representative legislature and so the political control is less direct. That lack of direct political control over them may well be considered undesirable in today's world. If so, the appropriate remedy is for Parliament, not the courts, to get involved in scrutinising the substance of such Orders in Council.

Lord Carswell. . .I accordingly agree with Lord Rodger in holding that it is not for the courts to substitute their judgment for that of the Secretary of State advising Her Majesty as to what can properly be said to conduce to the peace, order and good government of BIOT. A court might understandably be strongly attracted to the view that a law which removes the Chagossians from their homeland cannot be said to be for the peace, order and good government of the colony. But it is not for the courts to declare the law invalid on that ground. Once they enter upon such territory they could very easily get into the area of challenging what is essentially a political judgment, which is not for the courts of law. However distasteful they may consider a provision such as those under consideration in the present case, I think that the rule of abstinence should remain unqualified and the courts should not pronounce on the validity of such a provision on the ground that it is not for the peace, order and good government of the colony in question.

[In other words, both Lord Rodgers and Lord Carswell thought that the courts could not 'look behind' the power to issue the order. The only question that could be asked was, 'can it be said that no reasonable Secretary of State could have decided to have s 9 enacted?' Given the difficulties of re-settling the islanders, and the concerns of the Americans he had no difficulty in answering this question in the negative. **Lord Carswell** said]:

The feasibility reports make it abundantly plain that resettlement in the Chagos Islands, even with substantial financial support, would have been impracticable. The whole substructure of their economy had disappeared and could not be recreated. The practicability of starting replacement occupations was extremely doubtful. The wisdom of settling in the atolls, given the ecological factors now pertaining, was questionable. Looming over all considerations were the twin issues of prohibitive cost and the United Kingdom's interests in co-operation with an important ally in maintaining a secure defence installation. The Secretary of State was quite justified in taking all these factors into account. Criticisms have been advanced of the validity of the reasons advanced on behalf of the United States for wanting to keep the whole of the territory free from settlement, but even if it might be said that the concerns expressed appear exaggerated, the fact remains that the US clearly desired to keep a large clear area around the base. Decisions about how far to accommodate such concerns and wishes are very much a matter for ministers, who have access to a range of information not available to the courts and are accountable to Parliament for their actions.

[Lords Bingham and Mance dissented strongly. Both had found that there was simply no prerogative power to deny the right of abode to an entire population. **Lord Bingham** went on to find that, if there was such a power, its exercise, which all agreed was open to judicial review, could be successfully challenged under normal grounds]:

First, section 9 was irrational in the sense that there was, quite simply, no good reason for making it. (1) It is clear that in November 2000 the re-settlement of the outer islands (let alone sporadic visits by Mr Bancoult and other Chagossians) was not perceived to threaten the security of the base on Diego Garcia or national security more generally. Had it been, time and money would not have been devoted to exploring the feasibility of resettlement. (2) The United States Government had not exercised its treaty right to extend its base to the outer islands. (3) Despite highly imaginative letters written by American officials to strengthen the Secretary of State's hand in this litigation, there was no credible reason to apprehend that the security situation had changed. It was not said that the criminal conspiracy headed by Osama bin Laden was, or was planning to be, active in the middle of the Indian Ocean. In 1968 and 1969 American officials had expressly said that they had no objection to occupation of the outer islands for the time being. (4) Little mention was made in the courts below of the rumoured protest landings by LALIT [a group of Chagossian protestors]. Even now it is not said that the threatened landings motivated the introduction of section 9, only that they prompted it. Had the British authorities been seriously concerned about the intentions of Mr Bancoult and his fellow Chagossians they could have asked him what they were. (5) Remarkably, in drafting the 2004 Constitution Order, little (if any) consideration appears to have been given to the interests of the Chagossians whose constitution it was to be. (6) Section 9 cannot be justified on the basis that it deprived Mr Bancoult and his fellows of a right of little practical value. It cannot be doubted that the right was of intangible value, and the smaller its practical value the less reason to take it away.

Lord Mance. . . Arguments that any right of abode is symbolic, since it would be impracticable to exercise without expensive government support to which it is accepted that there is no right and which would not be forthcoming, in my view miss the point. If anything, they indicate that the right claimed could be recognised without this being likely to have any practical effect on the present state of the Chagos Islands [or] the operations of the United States base at Diego Garcia many miles away. . .

The letters [from US officials] appear all to have been addressed to the possibility of permanent and extensive re-settlement of the outer islands, an unlikely future event in June 2000 or 2004 or 2006. In any event, it is clear that the United Kingdom Government in 2000 either did not share the United States' assessment or did not consider that it bore on or precluded the grant to the Chagossians of a right to enter and be present in the outer islands. This is clear from the terms of Mr Robin Cook's press statement and the BIOT Ordinance issued on 3 November 2000 after the decision in *Bancoult (No 1)*. The United States authorities themselves also appear to have recognised a reality in somewhat different terms to that indicated in their letter of 21 June 2000, in view of the affirmative answer given. . .by Mr John Battle, Minister of State, Foreign and Commonwealth Office, on 9 January 2001 to the Parliamentary question: 'has the United States agreed that the islanders may return to any of the outlying islands? The letter of 21 June stated that that could imperil the base's status. Has that now changed?' (Hansard (HC Debates), col 193WH).

[As to the feasibility of re-settlement, his Lordship noted that by 2004, separate legal proceedings had determined that the Government had no obligation to fund the substantial costs of re-settlement.[68] He went on]:

In the absence of any legal obligation to fund resettlement, the prospective cost of doing so appears to me (as it did to Sedley LJ in the Court of Appeal: para 71) an unconvincing reason for withdrawing any right of abode and any right to enter or be present in BIOT. . .

In the light of what I have already said any order removing the Chagossians' right of abode in the Chagos Islands was abrogating what Sedley LJ. . .described, in my opinion appropriately, as 'one of the most fundamental liberties known to human beings, the freedom to return to one's homeland, however poor and barren the conditions of life'. I do not think that one needs to go as far back in history as Sedley LJ did (para 58) to recognise how enduring and strongly held a human instinct this is. Assuming that such a right can be removed by the Crown in Council, none the less it is one the removal of which calls for both careful consideration and good reason. The situation is one where an anxious or heightened review is called for. . .It is mistaken, and in my opinion conflates quite separate considerations, to dismiss from consideration the legal freedom to return and all that it represents for the human spirit on the basis that return is impractical or uneconomic; or that the existence of legal freedom to return might be used as a moral pressure point on the United Kingdom to provide funds which it would be uneconomic to provide and which the Government has established in court that it has no duty to provide; or that the right may in practice remain symbolic. Symbols can themselves be important, more so in some cultures than others. Recognition of a wrong can be as valuable as, sometimes valued more than, concrete compensation. The denial of a legal right to return, however remote the prospects of its exercise in practice, may add insult to injury. In any event, if the right is likely to remain symbolic, most of the reasons advanced for removing it lose force.

Notes

1. Cohn comments that 'In this. . .decision, the House of Lords has finally dealt a fatal blow to government reliance on the royal insignia as an impermeable shield against review.'[69] However, she also notes the very cautious nature of the approach of the majority:

The decision seems to have been coloured by one central consideration: the sensitivity of the issue involved. All majority judges emphasised, in different degrees of force, the importance of judicial restraint in contexts pertaining to national security, foreign affairs, and the expenditure of public resources. For Lord Hoffmann, these

68   See p 578 above.

69   Cohn at 261.

fields were 'peculiarly within the competence of the executive'; Lord Rodger squarely identified the questions as 'not justiciable' and Lord Carswell referred to judicial 'abstinence' as a guiding principle (at [58] (Lord Hoffmann); [109] (Lord Rodger); [130] (Lord Carswell).[70]

2. What appears quite extraordinary is the treatment by the majority of the fact that, because of the prior destruction of their way of life by the British Government, the islanders were now most unlikely to return. One might have thought that this fact would function solely as a means of rendering irrelevant the US security fears, and the concerns of the UK Government that it did not want to fund such large scale re-settlement. Instead, it was used by the majority as a reason for saying (in effect) that since the Islanders couldn't exercise their right to return it was of little or no importance. For detailed, critical comment on this decision, and proposals for how the courts should properly approach review of the exercise of such powers, particularly where they impact on rights, see Cohn (above) and M Elliott and A Perreau-Saussine, 'Pyrrhic public law: Bancoult and the sources, status and content of common law limitations on prerogative power' [2009] PL 697.

Impact of the Human Rights Act 1998

The Human Rights Act 1998 (HRA) is considered fully in Chapter 17, but it would be wrong to leave any discussion of judicial control of the prerogative without at least a reference to the changes the Act has brought about. The relevant provision is s 6(1), which simply provides: 'It is unlawful for a public authority to act in a way which is incompatible with a Convention right' (that is, a right contained in the European Convention on Human Rights, as defined in the HRA itself). The partial definition of 'public authority' includes courts (s 6(3)) and will clearly also include the Crown exercising the prerogative. What effect has this had? The most important and basic effect has been to put an end to the notion of there being areas of prerogative powers that are non-justiciable *per se*. The HRA states that it is unlawful for public authorities to contravene Convention rights and gives a right to bring proceedings for such a breach (s 7) and to seek remedies (s 8). An exercise of the prerogative which breaches a Convention right is now therefore as justiciable as any other executive action, simply because there has been no attempt to exclude the prerogative from the general duty under s 6(1): such an attempt would plainly have been incompatible with the Convention itself.

On the face of it, this sounds like a radical change, and it is, in principle. However, a number of factors reduce the impact of the HRA. The most stark and obvious of these is the fact that the HRA specifically protects acts of the prerogative from being annulled by the courts where they are expressed as Orders in Council. This is because such Orders are included within the definition of 'primary legislation' (s 21(1)) which, by virtue of ss 3(2)(b) and 4(6), may not be struck down by the courts if found to be incompatible with Convention rights. *Bancoult* has now established that Orders in Council made under the prerogative may be struck down by the courts on non-HRA grounds; what is clear is that the HRA will allow acts of prerogative power made in this way to be insulated from successful assault on Convention grounds. While the courts may make a purely declaratory finding that the Order in question is in breach of the Convention, the sections cited provide that such a declaration will not affect the Order's continuing effect and validity.[71]

---

70   *Ibid* at 270.

71   For criticism of this provision see P Billings and B Pontin [2001] PL 21.

The second factor is a simple one: the exercise of many, perhaps most, of the areas of the prerogative currently regarded as non-justiciable will not engage the Convention at all. It is hard to see, for example, how the powers to conclude treaties, appoint Ministers, grant honours, and for that matter, dissolve Parliament could raise serious Convention points.

The third factor is a little more complex. While the HRA will require the courts to decide whether ministerial action breached a Convention right, *as a matter of law,* it is already clear that in certain areas they will take a deferential approach to this assessment, particularly in relation to Arts 8–11 of the ECHR which set out broad exceptions allowing lawful interference with the primary rights granted, provided that the interference is prescribed by law, in pursuit of an aim specified in the Article in question and is 'necessary in a democratic society', by which it is meant that there was a 'pressing social need' to take the complained of action and the interference was proportionate to the legitimate aim pursued.[72] In determining whether a given interference *was* 'necessary', it is apparent that courts may consider themselves bound to recognise and respect an 'area of discretionary judgment'[73] when reviewing the decisions of Ministers in some areas. A deferential approach may be taken to their decisions, either on democratic grounds, or on the well-established and familiar basis that the courts do not have the ability to assess the complex policy considerations in play (see further Chapter 17, pp 999–1012). It may be noted that in the pre-HRA era, while the areas excluded from review were shrinking, the approach of the courts in a number of the key cases above was very cautious. This trend has largely continued.

RADICAL REFORM OF THE PREROGATIVE

Is the existence of the prerogative itself satisfactory? Rodney Brazier is in no doubt that it is not:

> [T]he state of executive powers is unsatisfactory. Ministers rely daily on those powers to do what would otherwise lack legal foundation, in circumstances which are very agreeable for ministers. For in relying on the prerogative as authority, ministers, obviously, are not limited by the terms of any Act of Parliament . . . Ministers do not have to consult, or even to inform, Parliament when they have it in mind to do things by virtue of the prerogative. They do not have to worry in every case whether the courts might review the manner in which they use those powers . . . [T]he royal prerogative is an elastic concept, the apparent limits of which may be stretched by ministers; and in doing so they are safe in the knowledge that anyone aggrieved will have to mount a challenge, after the event, through judicial means—if such means are open, and if the citizen has the inclination and perseverance to do so. Once again, an old constitutional notion has proved itself to be exceptionally helpful to governments. If ministerial responsibility to Parliament amounted to a real

---

72 *Olsson v Sweden* (1988) 11 EHRR 259.

73 In *R v DPP ex parte Kebilene* [1999] 3 WLR 972, Lord Hope rejected any domestic application of the margin of appreciation doctrine but went on: 'In some circumstances it will be appropriate for the courts to recognise that there is an area of judgment within which the judiciary will defer, on democratic grounds, to the considered opinion of [the democratic body or person] whose act or decision is said to be incompatible with the Convention.' This approach has now been confirmed in a number of cases decided after the HRA came into force: see, e.g. *R (On the application of Alconbury Developments Ltd) v Secretary of State of the Environment, Transport and the Regions and Other Cases* [2001] 2 WLR 1389, HL; *Brown v Stott* [2001] 2 WLR 817, PC, at 835.

check on executive power then this would matter less. But on the whole it does not amount to very much.[74]

Cohn emphatically agrees:

> The choice of a non-statutory path enables government to act freely, without passing the cumbersome legislative process; to design and apply rules without necessarily publishing them, thereby evading subjection to accountability mechanisms; and to reshape these rules as it finds proper.[75]

We have already seen above that the much vaunted reforms contained in the Constitutional Reform and Governance Act 2010 have produced only a marginal increase in Parliamentary control and accountability in this area.

What then, is to be done? A number of commentators have suggested that the answer lies in simply abolishing certain prerogatives, and the codification of others in statute. The Labour Party in 1993 committed itself to:

> . . .[ensuring] that all actions of government are subject to political and parliamentary control, including those actions now governed by the arbitrary use of the Royal Prerogative to legitimize actions which would otherwise be contrary to law. [The party reaffirms its] intention to review the Royal Prerogative and to identify particular areas of government activity which should be regulated by statute or excluded from its protection.[76]

Munro gives the example of the power to dissolve Parliament:

> The prerogative, nominally exercised by the Crown, is in reality exercised on the Prime Minister's advice, at least in the ordinary course of events. This effectively enables the Prime Minister to choose the date of the next general election, and it is notorious that the choice is influenced not by considerations of the public interest but by calculations of party advantage. That is surely an abuse of power, but it is a power the exercise of which seems to be impossible to challenge, whether in Parliament or in the courts.[77]

In this respect, it may be noted that the Government, in legislating for a Scottish Parliament, did not give the Queen (and thereby the Scottish First Minister), the power to dissolve it. Instead, the Parliament may be dissolved only upon its own vote, and then requires a two-thirds majority, or if the First Minister dies or resigns and no replacement can be found within 28 days (s 3 of the Scotland Act 1998). The deliberate choice not to replicate the unfettered power of the UK Prime Minister in designing the new institutions surely reflects an implicit acceptance that the UK position cannot be defended in terms of principle. The new Coalition Government in 2010 announced the introduction of

---

74 R Brazier, 'Constitutional Reform and the Crown', in M Sunkin and S Payne (eds), *The Nature of the Crown: A Legal and Political Analysis* (1999), p 356.

75 Cohn, at 265.

76 *A New Agenda for Democracy* (1993)

77 Munro, n 25 above, pp 290–91.

fixed term, five year Parliaments, with a power of the Commons to dissolve Parliament on a 55% vote. At the time of writing it remains to be seen whether this will be successfully implemented.

FURTHER READING

R Brazier, *Ministers of the Crown* (1997)

T Daintith and A Page, *The Executive in the Constitution: Structure, Autonomy, and Internal Control* (1999)

T Daintith, 'The Executive Power Today: Bargaining and Economic Control', in J Jowell and D Oliver (eds), *The Changing Constitution* (1985)

C Harlow (ed), *Public Law and Politics* (1984)

IPPR, *The Constitution of the United Kingdom* (1991)

I Jennings, *The Law and the Constitution*, 5th edn (1959) and *Cabinet Government* (1959)

JF McEldowney and P McAuslan, *Law, Legitimacy and the Constitution* (1985)

G Marshall and GC Moodie, *Some Problems of the Constitution* (1971)

R Pyper and L Robins (eds), *Governing the UK in the 1990s* (1995), Part I

S Sunkin and S Payne, *The Nature of the Crown* (1999)

R Blackburn, 'The Prerogative Power of Dissolution of Parliament: Law, Practice, and Reform' [2009] PL 766

M Cohn, 'Medieval Chains, Invisible Inks: On Non-Statutory Powers of the Executive' (2005) 97 OJLS 118

T Daintith, 'Regulation by Contract' (1979) 32 CLP 41.

BV Harris, 'The "Third Source" of Authority for Government Action Revisited' (2007) 123 LQR 225, 248

BS Markesinis, 'The Royal Prerogative Revisited' [1973] 32 CLJ 287

G Winterton, 'The Prerogative in Novel Situations' (1983) 99 LQR 407

G Zellick, 'Government beyond Law' [1985] PL 283

CHAPTER 12
THE CENTRAL EXECUTIVE: STRUCTURES AND ACCOUNTABILITY

INTRODUCTION

This chapter does not attempt a description of the everyday workings of the institutions that make up the central executive, for that would amount to a description of a system of government, rather than an analysis of the constitution. Insofar as a distinction can be maintained,[1] a work on the constitution should be looking for a normative framework within which government is supposed to be carried on; simply describing the practice of government *per se* is not therefore the aim. What we are looking for, then, are informing and pervasive ideas and conventions which purport to regulate government activity according to an idea of constitutionalism.[2] Since the core of the notion of constitutionalism are the ideas of limited government, checks on government power, and the accountability of government, these themes determine the topics considered here. Attention will focus therefore on two main themes: first, the increased concentration of power into a few hands within government and, second, a cluster of concepts about responsibility and accountability—the responsibility of ministers for their departments, their responsibility to be open with Parliament and not to mislead it and the responsibilities of civil servants to ministers and possibly to Parliament. The impact on traditional notions of accountability of the 'Next Steps' reforms will be considered also. The whole topic of accountability will be informed by the evidence thrown up by the Scott Inquiry and its conclusions and by developments in ministerial responsibility under the Blair Government, particularly in relation to ministerial resignations and the information given to Parliament in relation to intelligence on Iraq's WMD programme before the war in 2003.

THE PRIME MINISTER, CABINET AND THE CIVIL SERVICE

Five main issues will be discussed here. First, the process and rules governing the appointment of a Prime Minister and formation of a Government; second, the debate as to where the actual centre of power lies within the UK Executive; third, and clearly connected to the second matter, the ways in which the Prime Minister can (a) control and manipulate, and (b) effectively bypass Cabinet; fourth, the governance of the civil service and its independence including the historic step of placing the service on a statutory basis; fifth, the relevance of collective responsibility to the second and third issues.

The appointment of a Prime Minister and Government formation

Harry Calvert, *An Introduction to British Constitutional Law* (1986), pp 150–51, 155

Legally, the position is simple. The monarch may, if he wishes, appoint any number of persons he likes to be 'Minister of the Crown' and may, if he wishes, appoint one of them to

---

1   There is some debate as to what matters properly belong in a work on constitutional law. For a critical analysis of recent trends in this respect, see FF Ridley, 'There is No British Constitution: A Dangerous Case of the Emperor's Clothes' (1988) 41 Parlt Aff 40, esp. pp 342 *et seq.*

2   See Chapter 1.

be his 'Prime' Minister. Acts of Parliament assume, but do not require that there will be a 'Prime Minister'.

The efficient functioning of the constitution, however, does require that there should be a Prime Minister and, since any Government is heavily dependent upon Parliament, and particularly the House of Commons, especially for the authority to raise taxes, it follows that if a Prime Minister is to do the job properly, he must be a person who enjoys the confidence or support of a stable majority of the House of Commons. Under the modern party system, a party leader is that party's candidate for the office of Prime Minister and when, in a general election, the electorate returns to the House of Commons a majority of members of a particular party it in substance elects a Prime Minister. The words 'in substance' have been used because formally the choice remains that of the monarch but the constitutional role of the monarch in this regard is now accepted as being nothing more than formally appointing the person who commands a majority in the House of Commons, and in the usual situation above envisaged there will be no room for doubt on the matter. The electorate will have made it abundantly clear who should be appointed.

In exceptional situations, however, it may be less clear. Suppose:

. . .a Prime Minister resigns or dies in office and the majority party is divided as to who his successor shall be; or although a particular party secures a majority in a general election, its leader is defeated. Who is to be appointed?

For the monarch, the basic criterion remains the same. He must seek to ensure that he appoints a person who will enjoy the confidence of a majority of Members of the House of Commons. Usually, the monarch will be spared a controversial decision. All major political parties now have procedures for electing a leader and would, if circumstances compelled it, find ways of removing an old one and appointing a new. Once the leaders of the various factions are identified, then either one commands a majority, in which case, the problem disappears; or, if there is no majority, a wise monarch will await reliable information as to what has emerged as a result of the horse-trading and dealing which would inevitably attend the business of trying to form a coalition or, at least, a minority Government with the tacit support of a majority.

There is no 'proper' course for a monarch in such unusual circumstances, there is merely a prudent course. If the monarch made the 'wrong' choice, i.e. appointed a person who, in the event, could not command the support of a majority in the House of Commons, that appointment would nevertheless remain valid although effective government would be impossible and crisis would result. The monarch would then have to consider a dissolution if advised or, if not, consider whether to dismiss the Prime Minister wrongly chosen and appoint another in his place, or to muddle on. Controversy would attend any chosen course of action and the stature of the monarch would be demeaned. In an extreme case, the existence of the monarchy itself would be threatened. These considerations effectively mean that in exceptional cases, the monarch's role might well go beyond simply doing what he is told. There can be room for substantial individual judgment by a monarch and if caution does not attend its exercise, crisis with unpredictable consequences may result.

Notes

1. As noted in Chapter 2, on Conventions:

It is generally known that, in a formal sense, the Queen appoints the Prime Minister. What is perhaps not generally appreciated is that when, for example, the Labour

Party won the general election of 1997, that had no legal effect upon the Government. The UK did not have a Labour government until Tony Blair was appointed Prime Minister by the Queen and asked to form a government. Legally, the Queen can appoint whomsoever she chooses to be Prime Minister; it is only by convention that she must appoint as Prime Minister the person who is best able to command a majority in the House of Commons. The democratic basis of the UK's *government* (that is, the formation of its executive) therefore hangs upon convention. . .

And, one might add, the exercise of the Monarch's judgement. This is supposed to be constrained or at least guided by precedents, but as Brazier points out, after surveying them: they are few, since the UK Election system normally gives majority governments, and 'unhelpful'.[3] For discussion of the role of precedents in evidencing constitutional conventions, see Chapter 2, pp 61–62.

2. The only post-war precedent, in fact is 1974, described here by Tomkins:

> Before the election, the Conservatives had been in office, with Edward Heath as Prime Minister. But the largest party in the Commons was Labour, led by Harold Wilson. [The Liberals, led by Thorpe 'had the balance of power'.] In the event the politicians played their roles in such a way as to prevent the Queen from having to make a choice. Heath initially refused to resign as Prime Minister, instead going into coalition negotiations with Thorpe. Only when those broke down, two or three days after the election, did Heath resign. At that point the Queen had no alternative but to call for Wilson, which she did. He formed a minority administration, which survived until autumn at which point a second election was called, in October, which Labour won with a small overall majority. . .
>
> In the days immediately following the February 1974 election, before Heath resigned, Wilson kept quiet, biding his time. He could have jumped up and down, demanding to be called to the Palace [to be asked to form a government] and making life difficult for Heath and for the Queen. Equally, Health could have resisted resignation for longer, despite the collapse of his coalition negotiations, in the vain hope that Parliament might support him. But again, he did not. Both played their hands like statesmen, rather than careerist party hacks, deliberately keeping the monarchy away from having to intervene.[4]

Tomkins goes on to point out that even if Heath had not resigned, the Queen could have been kept out of controversy by the simple means of Parliament passing a motion of no confidence in Heath's Government at which point, by convention, he would have had to resign. Wilson could then have been appointed as PM.

3. Brazier, a leading commentator in this area, emphatically advocates the desirability of such situations being resolved by the politicians, allowing the Monarch to stand clear of politically contentious situations:

> . . . the guiding light ought to be that the political crisis should if possible be resolved by politicians—in a phrase, that there should be political decisions, politically arrived at. . . .[This] would help to refute any allegation that a non-elected head of state had imposed a particular solution on the elected House, instead of

---

3   R Brazier, 'The Constitution in the New Politics' [1978] PL 117, 118.

4   Tomkins, *Public Law* (2003) at 66–67.

allowing that House, through the party leaders, to arrive at a conclusion. It would also enhance the Queen's impartiality as between the political parties and between individuals, which would be crucially important if a political compromise were to prove impossible, when only the Queen could end the political crisis.[5]

4. Turpin and Tomkins[6] posit a situation in which the following is the result after a Labour Prime Minister calls an election.

Conservative	260
Labour	240
Liberal Democrats	120
Others	26

They posit further that the Labour PM resigns, after telling the Queen that the Liberal Democrats are willing to join Labour in a coalition Government, led by the deputy leader of the Labour party, who is to be confirmed as the new party leader. Meanwhile 'the Conservative Leader. . .declares that he is prepared to form a minority government'. Whom should the Queen invite to form a Government? The authors note that:

> the precedents, (especially those of [government formation in hung Parliaments] in 1923, 1929 and February 1974), suggest that the Sovereign should send for the Conservative leader, as leader of the largest party in the House of Commons, to form a minority government.

They cite in support of this Bogdanor's reading of the precedents—that 'the sovereign [does] not require a government in a hung parliament to command majority support'.[7] However, they also note Brazier's objection that the precedents represent nothing other than 'political accommodations arrived at as the result both of the political realities of the day and of the personal relationships between the party Leaders'[8] and make the point that a Lib-Lab coalition would be far more stable than a minority Conservative Government, which would have no majority to defeat a motion of no confidence, which could be called at any time. They comment:

> The view seems to be gaining ground that, in the event of a hung Parliament, the leader of the largest single party should have no overriding claim to be appointed as Prime Minister if it were clearly demonstrated to the Sovereign that a 'copper bottomed coalition agreement' had been reached between other parties and that their chosen leader was assured of majority support.

5. Brazier, who supports this view, is indeed emphatic that the so-called precedents 'should certainly not be taken as rule-constitutive precedents'.[9] His view is that the Queen should make clear in advance that she would only appoint the leader of a coalition as Prime Minister if satisfied of its

---

5   *Constitutional Practice*, 3rd edn (1999) at 33.

6   *British Government and the Constitution*, 6th edn (2007) at 359.

7   V Bogdanor, *The Monarchy and the Constitution* (1997), p 153.

8   R Brazier, *Constitutional Practice*, 3rd edn (1999), p 31.

9   *Constitutional Reform*, 3rd edn (2008) at 99.

stability, to be ascertained by requiring a list of proposed appointments to the Cabinet, 'an agreed Queen's speech, and a guarantee that the coalition would not seek a dissolution [of Parliament] within a stated time'.[10]

6. Our comment is a simpler one: that the UK Constitution deals with this extraordinarily important issue—who should be appointed Prime Minister—extremely poorly. First of all, it falls to be decided by a hereditary Monarch, who is supposed, these days, to be merely a dignified figurehead; second, it is underpinned by no *law* linking the decision to the result of the general election, meaning that the democratic basis of the UK executive is not guaranteed by the law; third, in the event of a hung parliament, the rules are extremely ambiguous. If the UK were ever to move to a system of proportional representation for General Elections—which would be likely to lead to far more hung Parliaments—it seems plain that the imperative would grow to remove this decision from the hands of a hereditary Monarch, guided only by such scanty, contested and inconclusive precedents. Either the Monarch would have to be replaced with an elected Head of State[11] or at the least, some statutory, or Conventional guidelines would surely have to be laid down to govern the matter.[12]

7. Brazier notes the difficulty of formulating any conventional rules in this area: the leaders of the Conservative and Labour parties generally refuse to discuss the issue, 'but when cornered. . .have insisted that [in such a case] the leader of the largest single party would be entitled to form a minority Government'—a position that plainly favours their parties. He notes that in contrast, the Liberal Democrats favour government by a coalition—the position normally taken by third party leaders.[13] The present situation is plainly one of the least satisfactory aspects of the UK's uncodified constitution,[14] and this may well become painfully apparent, next time the UK's Parliament is 'hung'.[15]

8. As another commentator notes, there are plenty of options for reform:

> The Fabian Society's Commission on the Future of the Monarchy called for dissolution of Parliament to be strictly regulated by statute and for the appointment of the prime minister to be a matter for Parliament [*The Future of the Monarchy*, Fabian Society, 2003]. It has been suggested elsewhere that the Speaker of the House could appoint the prime minister [T. Hames and M. Leonard, *Modernising the Monarchy*, Demos, 1998]. The Institute for Public Policy Research made a similar recommendation in its 1991 report, [*The Constitution of the United Kingdom*].
> (S. Kalitowski. 'Hung-up over Nothing? THe Impact of a Hung Parliament on British Politics' (2008) 61(2) *Parlt. Aff* 396, 399).

9. It is illuminating to contrast the position in relation to the appointment of the Prime Minister, the leader of the UK Government, governed as it is entirely by convention, with the statutory provisions of the Scotland Act, which govern the choice of the First Minister of the Scottish

---

10   *Ibid*, p 101.

11   On the possibilities for replacing the Queen as Head of State, see Chapter 7 of Brazier's *Constitutional Reform*, 3rd edn (2008), esp. at 93–97.

12   For discussion of the issues surrounding the codification of constitutional conventions, see Chapter 2, pp 67–79.

13   *Constitutional Reform*, at 99–100.

14   For a more positive view of the position, see R Blackburn, 'Monarchy and the Personal Prerogatives' [2004] PL 546.

15   Some similar issues are raised by the lack of clear rules for dealing with the instance in which a Prime Minister dies or becomes incapacitated by illness during his Premiership: for critical discussion and suggestions for reform see A Vannard, 'Prime Ministerial Succession' [2008] PL 302.

Executive, in some sense Scotland's Prime Minister. In the UK, as we have seen, the position in law is very simple: the Prime Minister is simply the Queen's chief minister. He becomes Prime Minister not by virtue of the results of general elections, which simply determine the make up of the House of Commons, but solely and simply by being chosen by the Queen. It is only through the conventions discussed above that the Queen's unfettered legal powers are exercised so as to match up the appointment of the Prime Minister with the democratic will of the people. Under the Scotland Act, in contrast, the First Minister is nominated by the Scottish Parliament within 28 days of an election or vacancy and appointed by the Queen (s 46). While the Queen is not legally *obliged* to appoint the nomination of the Parliament, there is at least a clear legal role for the Parliament to play in nominating the First Minister and the Queen may in law appoint only a member of the Scottish Parliament as First Minister (s 45(1)), something that is only a matter of convention in relation to the House of Commons and the Prime Minister. It is perhaps rather incongruous that, in shaping a Parliament for the 21st century, the Queen was still given the legal power to appoint. By contrast, the Welsh and Northern Ireland assemblies *elect* rather than nominate ministers— there is no role for the Queen to play at all. The experience of devolution in Wales and Scotland (the Northern Ireland settlement *requires* coalition and so is a special case)[16] shows that the political parties have been able to adapt both to governing in coalition and minority governments: for example, the Scottish Executive was for the first eight years formed by a Labour-Liberal pact, but since May 2007, has been run by a stable minority SNP administration. Such experience may prove valuable when the next UK Parliament is 'hung.' See further on the Scottish and Welsh executives, Chapter 6.

The changing role of the Cabinet

> . . .the Cabinet, as an institution, does not rest on parliamentary authority but rather on practice developed over the centuries. . . . Important consequences attend the fact that the composition, powers and procedures of the Cabinet are not fixed by law. . . . It may meet more or less regularly; it may discharge business in plenary session or sit in committees. We are told that decisions are usually arrived at by consensus, but there is nothing to stop a vote being taken, or simply for the Prime Minister to divine the 'sense of the meeting' and proceed accordingly. . . .[17]

Notes

1. Walter Bagehot, writing in 1867, called the Cabinet 'the most powerful body in the nation'[18] and considered that collective responsibility meant that every member of the Cabinet had the right to take part in Cabinet discussion but was bound by the decision eventually reached. In contrast, John Mackintosh in *The British Cabinet* (1977) wrote: 'the principal policies of a government may not be and often are not originated in Cabinet.'

2. A number of writers, including Richard Crossman, have considered that Cabinet government has shown signs of developing into Prime Ministerial government and that therefore collective decision making has suffered (see, for example, his *Diaries of a Cabinet Minister* (1975)). Crossman argued that the power of the Prime Minister to sack ministers, to determine the Cabinet agenda and the existence and membership of Cabinet committees meant that his or her control over the

---

16   See further Chapter 16, pp 272–281.

17   Harry Calvert, *An Introduction to British Constitutional Law* (1986), p 146.

18   *The English Constitution* (1963 edn).

Cabinet was the most important force within it. Mrs Thatcher, Prime Minister between 1979 and 1990, is generally considered to have (at least temporarily) increased the power of the Prime Minister by using the available power to the full. The Blair premiership is also generally seen to be marked by the sidelining of Cabinet. While it may tentatively be suggested that Gordon Brown's administration saw a return to a more collegiate style of decision making, this may have been simply a symptom of Brown's relative political weakness, rather than a principled change in direction.

3. However, other commentators point out that in diluting and fragmenting the power of the Cabinet in this fashion it might be argued that Thatcher and Blair were merely taking further a process which had already begun. The use of gatherings other than Cabinet to make decisions—inner Cabinets, Cabinet committees, ministerial meetings—had been growing for the last 30 years and had arguably undermined the Cabinet as a decision-making body, though many considered this inevitable.

4. As Rodney Brazier notes, 'Meeting only once a week for a couple of hours. . .and being composed entirely of Ministers with heavy departmental responsibilities, the Cabinet could not possibly now be the forum either for the close control of activities of Government or for the co-ordination of the departments of state'.[19] Neither, clearly does it have time either to formulate, approve or even discuss much policy. 'Since the Second World War all but a tiny proportion of decisions have been taken by individual ministers, by correspondence and by committees.'[20] These last have assumed an increasingly important role: much of the major policy-making work of Government which requires either the co-operation of more than one department or is so important that it requires wider discussion has long been carried out through the Cabinet committee system which in its formal guise 'has been in existence since the First World War, [comprising] some 30 to 40 standing committees. . .and well over 100 *ad hoc* committees' which both settle points of detail and isolate fundamental questions for decision by Cabinet.[21]

5. The Ministerial Code, the official statement of rules and principles governing ministerial conduct, issued by the Cabinet Office, and redrafted by the Prime Minister of the day,[22] has this to say about the role of the Cabinet:

> 2.3 The business of the Cabinet and Ministerial Committees consists in the main of:
>
> a. questions which significantly engage the collective responsibility of the Government because they raise major issues of policy or because they are of critical importance to the public;
> b. questions on which there is an unresolved argument between Departments.
>
> 2.4 Matters wholly within the responsibility of a single Minister and which do not significantly engage collective responsibility as defined above need not be brought to the Cabinet or to a Ministerial Committee unless the Minister wishes to inform his colleagues or to have their advice. No definitive criteria can be given for issues which engage collective responsibility.

---

19   R Brazier, *Constitutional Practice,* 2nd edn (1994), p 104.

20   S James, 'The Cabinet system since 1948: Fragmentation and Integration' (1994) 47(4) Parlt Aff 613, 619.

21   R Brazier, 'Reducing the Power of the Prime Minister' (1991) 44(4) Parlt Aff 453, 456.

22   For comment on the status of the Code, see below at 628.

6. However, the Code does later give some fairly clear guidance on when Cabinet consultation is required:

> 2.6 Before publishing a policy statement (white paper) or a consultation paper (green paper), departments should consider whether it raises issues which require full collective ministerial consideration through the appropriate Cabinet Committee. The expectation is that most such papers will need collective agreement prior to publication. Any Command Paper containing a major statement of Government policy should be circulated to the Cabinet before publication. This rule applies to Papers containing major statements even when no issue requiring collective consideration is required.

For now it is sufficient to note the Cabinet's relative lack of importance, except perhaps *in extremis*. What are the consequences of this for the exercise of power within Government?

Prime Ministerial control over Cabinet and Government

Two main issues are in play here: first, the Prime Minister's power of patronage; and second, his or her control over the agenda and meeting of Cabinet and its committees—crudely speaking, over who discusses what and when.

Prime ministerial patronage

Whilst the Queen formally appoints all ministers of the Crown, this power is of course exercised in practice by the Prime Minister who has the absolute power of appointment and dismissal of ministers. The Prime Minister's freedom to choose who he or she wants will be limited by the need to maintain some sort of balance in the Cabinet between different wings of the parties and to appease powerful personalities within it, but still the Prime Minister, and the Prime Minister alone, makes these decisions. Similarly, the Prime Minister may—subject to political constraints—get rid of any ministers he or she does not want at any time in response to major mistakes made by that minister or simply because he or she finds their views uncongenial. This is of course normally achieved through 'reshuffling' rather than outright dismissal, which is comparatively rare. The skill and judgment—and ruthlessness—of a Prime Minister in exercising this power is of key importance: Clement Atlee famously observed that a vital characteristic of any Prime Minister was the ability to be a good butcher.

The political constraints on this power are most marked in one area. As James remarks:

> This discretion [to dismiss or reshuffle] may be less when dealing with the most senior two or three members of the Cabinet who can more or less insist on one of the top jobs. For something like two-thirds of the post-war era, the Exchequer and the Foreign Officer have been held by party magnates who were effectively irremovable. Once someone has reached that level in the Cabinet, there are few other places to which they can be transferred.[23]

---

23   James, n 20 above, at 625.

Such would certainly appear to have been the case in relation to the Chancellor under Tony Blair's administration, Gordon Brown. So important was Brown to the Government that it seemed impossible to move him against his will from the Treasury, and indeed, Blair never did so, despite periods of intense conflict between the two and the urging of Blair's advisors.

Nevertheless, in spite of this exception, the Prime Minister, if determined enough, can make quite extensive use of this power in order to achieve a Cabinet which reflects the Prime Minister's particular political outlook. Mrs Thatcher, as is well known, made particular use of this power, having come to power in 1979 with a Cabinet initially balanced between moderates and Thatcherites. However, by 1981 Mrs Thatcher had shuffled five of the seven moderates out of her Cabinet, leaving her with a Cabinet that reflected her own political convictions pretty closely.[24] But this cannot be put down merely to the excesses of an extreme ideology. As Brazier notes,[25] there were clear precedents for this type of behaviour. When Neville Chamberlain came to power in 1937, he ruthlessly excluded from his Cabinet anyone who was opposed to his policy of appeasing the European dictators. This power that the Prime Minister has over the careers of ministers obviously gives him or her enormous influence over ministers, aware as they are that their continuing in office is, broadly speaking, dependent upon their retaining the Prime Minister's favour. Blair did not perhaps use his powers of appointment and dismissal as ruthlessly as Thatcher, partly because he always felt the need not to alienate his exceptionally powerful Chancellor by openly removing ministers loyal to the Chancellor from key positions.

Prime Ministerial control over government business and 'the core executive'

The Prime Minister can determine what the Cabinet does and does not discuss, both specifically, in that its written agenda for its weekly meetings is set by him or her, and more generally, through the manipulation of Cabinet committees. As well as using the official Cabinet committees, which have formal procedures and are serviced by the Civil Service in respect of minutes, agendas etc, the Prime Minister can make use of *ad hoc* informal groups of ministers, convened to discuss a particular issue. Meetings of these groups will not be attended by civil servants and they will often not have formal agendas or minutes. The use of the formal committees is, as noted above, well established, and, given that it allows proper discussion of the issue by a fair number of ministers, is generally seen as a necessary and reasonable way of doing business. However, the particularly heavy use made by Mrs Thatcher of *ad hoc* groups of ministers to discuss key issues raised more concern.[26] But the use of such informal groups was not an innovation of Thatcher, as James notes:[27]

> In the 1960s and 70s. . . [Prime Ministers] managed [issues] by secret committees. Barbara Castle's diaries recorded that for years Wilson prevented his Cabinet from discussing Rhodesia and devaluation; similarly, the head of Callaghan's policy unit recalls his Prime Minister running economic policy through a secret committee called 'the seminar'.

Mrs Thatcher appears to have taken this technique further, by making much greater use of such groups as a deliberate means of disabling the views of those opposed to her policies. Because Prime

---

24   See Brazier (1994), n 19 above, at 79.

25   *Ibid*, pp 72–73.

26   M Doherty, 'Prime Ministerial Power and Ministerial Responsibility' (1988) 41(1) Parlt Aff 49, 54

27   See n 20 above, at 621.

Ministers can hand-pick these groups, they can (within limits) ensure that a given sensitive issue is discussed only by those ministers with whom they wish to discuss it. Thus, for example, in the early 1980s Michael Heseltine put forward proposals for a radical programme of investment in the inner cities, to tackle the poverty, unemployment and crime which was causing serious social unrest. Mrs Thatcher, who was opposed to the plan, convened a special group of ministers to discuss it, selecting ministers she knew would be hostile to Heseltine's proposals. The group duly came up with recommendations that involved nothing like the investment Heseltine had proposed.[28]

The point is that Mrs Thatcher's way of doing business starkly illustrated the enormous powers which the flexible nature of the Cabinet and committee system gives to *any* Prime Minister. As Brazier notes, the power to decide 'whether to set up a committee and when to dissolve it...its terms of reference...members and chairman [and to] lay down rules which restrict appeal to the full Cabinet' means that 'Significant parts of the British machinery of Government are...within the personal control of the Prime Minister'.[29] Cabinet Committees may exist but not meet; or they may meet only to rubber-stamp decisions already made by a small group. The treatment of the budget provides a vivid illustration of this point:

> ...the Chancellor's budget proposals are of major economic and political impor-tance, but they are arrived at in great secrecy in the Treasury, in consultation with the Prime Minister. Individual ministers can and do make representations to the Chancellor...which may or may not be heeded. But the first which the Cabinet hears of the detail of the budget are on the morning... the Chancellor presents it to the House [by which time] it is obviously too late...for ministers to be able to insist on more than minor changes. This astonishing procedure is justified by the need for secrecy [to prevent] damaging leaks.[30]

As noted above, the general view is that the Blair premiership was even more presidential than Thatcher's, that the Cabinet was marginalised as never before and that the Prime Minister sought and gained control over the rest of Government to a greater extent than any previous premier. For example, the crucial decision in May 1997 to give the Bank of England independence and the power to set interest rates—one of the most important decisions in economic policy for decades—was apparently taken by the Prime Minister and the Chancellor of the Exchequer alone, in consultation with their special advisers. Other members of the Cabinet were not even consulted. Foster, in a major article, notes that under Blair, at least up to 2003, 'There were to be no Cabinet decisions',[31] and Clare Short, formerly International Development Secretary, does not recall any being made up to 2003, when she resigned. Cabinet meetings were short and had no formal papers. Indeed:

> 'Consulting cabinet', as frequently reported in the media, became a euphemism, put out by the press office, for Blair consulting those he chose to consult. In 2000 he was to be openly dismissive of cabinet government, recalling the 1970s 'the old days of Labour governments where meetings occasionally went on for two days and you had a show of hands at the end'.[32]

---

28   See P Hennessy, *Cabinet* (1986), p 102.

29   Brazier (1991), n 21 above, at 456–57.

30   *Ibid*, p 456.

31   C Foster, 'Cabinet Government in the Twentieth Century' (2004) 67(5) MLR 753, 764.

32   *Ibid*, p 766

It was Clare Short who made the most bitter attack upon Blair's style of governing, upon her resignation from the Cabinet. Her resignation concerned the UN resolution to reconstruct Iraq (see below), but she also took the opportunity to attack the Government's general style:

> The problem is the centralisation of power into the hands of the Prime Minister and an increasingly small number of advisers who make decisions in private without proper discussion. It is increasingly clear, I am afraid, that the Cabinet has become, in Bagehot's phrase, a dignified part of the constitution—joining the Privy Council. There is no real collective responsibility because there is no collective; just diktats in favour of increasingly badly thought through policy initiatives that come from on high.
>
> The consequences of that are serious. Expertise in our system lies in Departments. Those who dictate from the centre do not have full access to that expertise and do not consult. That leads to bad policy. In addition, under our constitutional arrangements, legal, political and financial responsibility flows through Secretaries of State to Parliament. Increasingly, those who are wielding power are not accountable and not scrutinised. Thus we have the powers of a presidential-type system with the automatic majority of a parliamentary system. My conclusion is that those arrangements are leading to increasingly poor policy initiatives being rammed through Parliament, which is straining and abusing party loyalty and undermining the people's respect for our political system.[33]

Notes

1. It should be noted that Blair was careful to gain the full formal backing of the Cabinet for the highly controversial policy of taking military action against Iraq in Spring 2003 (on which see further below). Moreover, in May/June 2003, Blair and Brown were careful to consult fully with Cabinet ministers before formally announcing the Government's decision not to join the euro at this stage, a decision which was formally endorsed by the full Cabinet, as was the decision to bid for the 2012 Olympics; in the later years of the Blair Government, there were also 'heated discussions' over the controversial policies of student 'top up fees' and foundation hospitals. [34]

2. Some further correctives to the picture of prime ministerial power being painted should also be noted: first of all, the power of Prime Ministers depends greatly on (a) the size of their majority in Parliament, and (b) their perceived popularity and the popularity of their policies. This is vividly illustrated by the eventual fate of Margaret Thatcher: having been one of the most dominant premiers the UK has known, she was eventually brought down by her Ministers, once they became convinced that was doing serious damage to the Government's popularity and chances of winning the next General Election.[35] Second, the powers outlined above do not mean that the Prime Minister has the capacity to control the detailed policy-making and day-to-day administration of all government departments. Simple lack of knowledge and insufficient time preclude this—although the increasing grip of the centre of Government over the work of departments is noted below. Finally, and specifically in relation to Blair's administration, Hennessey noted that:

---

33   HC Deb col 38 (12 May 2003).

34   Foster, n 31 above, at 767.

35   See further, Alderman and Carter, 'A Very British Coup: The Ousting of Mrs Thatcher' (1991) 41 Parlt Aff 125; Brazier, 'The Downfall of Margaret Thatcher' (1991) 54 MLR 471.

> Second. . .the Prime Minister's. . .neighbour, Gordon Brown, is a contender for the title of most commanding Chancellor of the Exchequer since 1945. . .To a remarkable degree, Blair's is a twin-stellar government. The Chancellor's constellation revolves around the comprehensive spending reviews and their detailed public service agreements which give the Treasury a degree of control over departmental policy outcomes of a kind previous Chancellors could only dream of. [36]

It was of course sustained pressure from Gordon Brown and his supporters in the Cabinet that eventually led Tony Blair to resign and hand over the Premiership to him in June 2007.[37]

3. The ability of the Prime Minister, or of a small group of Ministers, to bypass Cabinet is of significance: it may reduce internal consultation and scrutiny: if an issue is discussed in a small, informal and carefully selected group, the number of people—and particularly un-persuaded, possibly sceptical people—to whom proposed government policy has to be explained is decreased, as is the variety of critical perspectives which have the chance of influencing that policy. This might be seen as a negative effect in constitutional terms since the effect is that power is concentrated in fewer hands and policy (arguably) becomes less honed and tested.

4. The most controversial decision made by the Blair Government was of course its decision to participate in the US-led invasion of Iraq in 2003. The Butler Inquiry into the (faulty) intelligence used as the basis for the invasion raised clear concerns about the effect of Blair's informal style of government on the way the decision to go war was made.

Review of Intelligence on Weapons of Mass Destruction HC 898 (2003–04) (extracts)

606. We received evidence from two former Cabinet members, one of the present and one of a previous administration, who expressed their concern about the informal nature of much of the Government's decision-making process, and the relative lack of use of established Cabinet Committee machinery.

[Butler then noted that although Cabinet discussed Iraq numerous times in the run up to the decision to go to war, these were often simply oral briefings by the PM or Foreign Secretary.]

By contrast, over the period from April 2002 to the start of military action, [there were] some 25 meetings attended by the small number of key Ministers, officials and military officers most closely involved provided the framework of discussion and decision-making within Government.

610. One inescapable consequence of this was to limit wider collective discussion and consideration by the Cabinet to the frequent but unscripted occasions when the Prime Minister, Foreign Secretary and Defence Secretary briefed the Cabinet orally. Excellent quality papers were written by officials, but these were not discussed in Cabinet or in Cabinet Committee. Without papers circulated in advance, it remains possible but is obviously much more difficult for members of the Cabinet outside the small circle directly involved to bring their political judgement and experience to bear on the major decisions for which the Cabinet as a whole must carry responsibility. The absence of papers on the Cabinet agenda so that Ministers could obtain briefings in advance from the Cabinet Office, their own departments or from the intelligence agencies plainly reduced their ability to

---

36   Hennessy, n 40 below, at 389.

37   See further on Blair's premiership, P Hennessy, 'Rulers and Servants of the State: the Blair Style of Government 1997–2004' (2005) Parlt Aff 58(1) 6–16.

prepare properly for such discussions, while the changes to key posts at the head of the Cabinet Secretariat lessened the support of the machinery of government for the collective responsibility of the Cabinet in the vital matter of war and peace.

611. We do not suggest that there is or should be an ideal or unchangeable system of collective Government, still less that procedures are in aggregate any less effective now than in earlier times. However, we are concerned that the informality and circumscribed character of the Government's procedures which we saw in the context of policy-making towards Iraq risks reducing the scope for informed collective political judgement. Such risks are particularly significant in a field like the subject of our Review, where hard facts are inherently difficult to come by and the quality of judgement is accordingly all the more important.

Notes

1. Gordon Brown gave indications when he became Prime Minister in 2007 that he wanted to have a more collegiate, formal method of Government, with less influence from unelected Special Advisors. To this end, instead of the Prime Minister's office being run by a political special advisor acting as Chief of Staff as under Blair (Jonathan Powell), Brown appointed Jeremy Howard, a civil servant, to be permanent secretary,[38] and a senior official in Cabinet Office to oversee collective government, used career civil servants, rather than the more political special advisers, as his top advisers on Europe and foreign affairs, and revoked the 1997 Order in Council that had allowed special advisors executive powers to give orders to civil servants.[39]

2. Hennessey has noted:

   A shrewd and careful inside observer spoke privately about this in early 1999:

   > Do we need a Prime Minister's Department? It's largely an academic debate now because we already have one. It's a properly functioning department with a departmental head [Mr Blair's chief of staff, Jonathan Powell; a political appointee, not a career civil servant], with a sense of being the central machinery of government. We do now, in effect, have a PMD, but (and it's a crucial 'but') it is not formalised. This is an advantage because it makes it extremely flexible.

   Not only does the Prime Minister agree an annual work programme with each of his Cabinet ministers. . .he has instituted an equivalent system for the permanent secretaries at the head of the more important departments [to ensure that they] have personal objectives, on which their performance will be assessed, for taking forward the government's modernisation agenda and ensuring delivery of the government's key targets.[40]

3. This structural strengthening of the centre may also be seen in the creation of the Prime Minister's Delivery Unit in 2001, 'with a remit to strengthen the Government's ability to deliver the Prime

---

38   See The Constitution Committee, *The Cabinet Office and the Centre of Government,* Fourth Report (2009–10) HL 30, Chapter 2.

39   See *The Governance of Britain* (2008) Cm 7342-I, at [193]. For commentary on the role of Special Advisors, particularly under the Blair Government, see the Public Administration Committee, *Special Advisers: Boon or Bane?* (2000–01), HC 293.

40   P Hennessy, 'The Blair Style and the Requirements of Twenty-first Century Premiership' (2000) PQ 386, 388–89.

Minister's key public service priorities' in four key areas—education, health, crime and transport [and the establishment of] The Strategy Unit. . .in 2002 to improve the Government's capacity to address long term and/or cross-cutting strategic issues.[41]

4. Turpin and Tomkins note that political scientists have recently suggested shifting the focus of debate from bemoaning the 'decline' or 'decay' of Cabinet Government—as if such a thing 'is always and necessarily to be lamented and even, in some sense, improper or unconstitutional,'[42] and instead focusing attention on the strengthening power of the centre—the 'core executive thesis'.[43] Given the complexities and time pressure of modern government, more decision making is naturally taking place within a strengthened centre of government, comprising the 'Prime Minister's office, the Treasury, the Cabinet Office, the Foreign Office, the Law Officers and offices managing the governing party's parliamentary and mass support bases'.[44] These central bodies are also better coordinated, and exercise much stronger control over policy formation in the Departments, partly through the new Delivery and Strategy Units. Burch and Holliday comment that 'the British core is increasingly coordinated and coherent, and increasingly proactive and performance-driven'.[45] For a major recent report on this issue, see The Constitution Committee, *The Cabinet Office and the Centre of Government*, Fourth Report (2009–10) HL 30: the report concluded that the strengthening of the centre was both necessary and desirable, although it raised issues about how the activities of the centre of government could be held to account—something explored further below.

Prime Ministerial power to re-organise Government

A further aspect of Prime Ministerial power is the ability to reorganise government departments themselves, without reference to Parliament—since the power to do so derives from the prerogative.[46] This is emphasised by the Ministerial Code, which states that 'The Prime Minister is responsible for the overall organisation of the executive and the allocation of functions between Ministers in charge of departments' (4.1) and requires the PM's permission for changes to this allocation.

The Labour Government from 1997 has engaged in such reorganisations very frequently; the most recent example is the creation of the Department of Justice in May 2007 to replace the short lived Department of Constitutional Affairs (which itself replaced the Lord Chancellor's Department in 2003), and the hiving off to the new Ministry of Justice many of the functions of the Home Office, including the prison service and probation.[47] It is now generally acknowledged that the abolition of the Lord Chancellor's Department, and the attempted abolition of the post itself, was a shambles, embarked upon hastily, without proper consultation and advice and with a glaring lack of understanding of the profound constitutional and legal implications (see further on this Chapter 3, pp 146–153).

---

41   Constitution Committee, HL 30, at [44]. See further on the Prime Minister's office, M Burch and I Holliday, 'The Prime Minister's and Cabinet Offices: An Executive Office in all but Name' (1999) 52 Parlt Aff 32.

42   Turpin and Tomkins at 398.

43   They cite P Dunleavy and R Rhodes, 'Core Executive Studies in Britain' (1990) 68 *Pub Admin* 3 and *Prime Minister, Cabinet and Core Executive* (1995); M Smith, *The Core Executive in Britain* (1999).

44   Turpin and Tomkins, at 398.

45   M Burch and Holliday, 'The Blair Government and the Core Executive' (2004) 39 *Government and Opposition* 1, at 20.

46   See generally, the PAC, Seventh Report (2006–07), HC 672.

47   See further Chapter 1, pp 21–22. For further examples of such departmental re-organisations, see Turpin and Tomkins at 406.

Having examined the course of events and taken evidence from the key players, the Constitution Committee concluded:

> 214. In the case of the proposal to abolish the Office of Lord Chancellor in June 2003, the Cabinet Office was unable to ensure compliance with proper constitutional norms in the adoption of a change of such constitutional significance. It is particularly disturbing that these failures occurred without there being any external crisis which might explain, far less justify, such failures. . .
>
> 215. Whilst we accept the general proposition that the ability to undertake machinery of government changes should remain as a prerogative power of the Prime Minister on behalf of the Crown, this should be subject to a number of provisos. In the case of the proposal to abolish the Office of Lord Chancellor, the fact that it marked a constitutional change of great significance, with implications for both Parliament and the judiciary and that the post could only be removed by statute, meant that it required totally different handling.
>
> 216. We recommend that the Cabinet Office should play a formal role in investigating the likely consequences of any machinery of government changes, particularly those with constitutional implications.
>
> 217. We further recommend that parliamentary scrutiny of machinery of government changes should be enhanced, and that, as a minimum requirement, the Government, advised by the Cabinet Office, should be required to set before Parliament a written analysis of the relevant issues and consequences relating to a proposed machinery of government change with constitutional implications, and that an oral ministerial statement be made in Parliament. We affirm the value of the scrutiny work of parliamentary committees in this context, and recommend that relevant committees of both Houses be given the opportunity to scrutinise proposed changes, both before and after they take place.[48]

Note

It remains to be seen whether the new Government will accept these proposals.

Ministers, Civil Servants and Government Agencies

Introduction

The Civil Service is around half a million strong, permanent and therefore politically neutral—serving the policies of the Government of the day, and responsible to Ministers, not to Parliament (see further below, pp 662–663). Historically it has been governed by the prerogative under a long-standing Order in Council. A more detailed Civil Service Management Code, last updated in January 2009,[49] is made under the authority of the Order itself. Hence up until 2010, the rules governing the civil service could be altered without reference to Parliament, as happened when Tony Blair amended the Order in Council to give Special Advisers the executive powers later revoked by Gordon Brown (above, p 615). Other rules and principles governing the civil service, including the core values of integrity, honesty,

---

48 *The Cabinet Office and the Centre of Government* (above).

49 For the latest version, see www.civilservice.gov.uk/about/resources/csmc/CSMC-Intro.aspx

objectivity and impartiality, were set out only in non-legal documents, including in particular the Civil Service Code, the so-called Armstrong Memorandum and the Ministerial Code. The Ministerial Code states, at para 1.2j:

> *Ministers must uphold the political impartiality of the Civil Service and must not ask any civil servant to act in a way which would conflict with the Civil Service Code.*

More specifically, the Code provides that:

> 3.1 Ministers have a duty to ensure that influence over Civil Service and public appointments is not abused for partisan purposes. Civil service appointments must be made in accordance with the requirements of the Civil Service Order in Council and the *Civil Service Commissioners' Recruitment Code*. Public appointments should be made in accordance with the requirements of the law and, where appropriate, the Code of Practice issued by the Commissioner for Public Appointments.

As Tomkins comments, 'What is noteworthy about this complex net of codes and Memorandum. . .is that both Parliament and the courts are effectively excluded from the whole process.'[50] One commentator giving evidence given to the Public Administration Committee (PAC) said:

> . . .British civil servants—unlike their counterparts in France and Germany in particular—are not independent. The Civil Service is regulated by Orders-in-Council issued by a Minister under delegated prerogative powers. Its members consequently enjoy no statutory rights (or indeed existence), owe no allegiance to the public and answer solely to the government of the day.[51]

At present, a non-statutory but independent Civil Service Commission regulates the appointment of civil servants, deals with disciplinary matters, and hears complaints brought by civil servants under the Civil Service Code. The Constitutional Reform and Governance Act 2010 (below) places the Commission on a statutory basis (section 2).

An important change to the organisation of the civil service came in the 1980s when the Thatcher Government introduced what came to be known as 'Next Step Agencies'. The thinking behind their creation was expressed at the time as follows:

> The aim should be to establish a quite different way of conducting the business of government. The central civil service should consist of a relatively small core engaged in the function of servicing ministers and managing departments, who will be the 'sponsors' of particular government policies and services. Responding to these departments will be a range of agencies employing their own staff, who

---

50 Tomkins, *Public Law* at 77. The courts are excluded because in law Ministers, not civil servants, are responsible for the actions of government: while everyone knows perfectly well that many decisions entrusted by statute to 'the Secretary of State' are in fact taken by civil servants, for the purposes of legal challenges, the decisions of civil servants are attributed to Ministers, by the so-called *Carltona* doctrine. There is a Civil Service (Management Functions) Act 1992, however this very short statute merely 'provides authorisation for delegation by ministers of powers in relation to the management of the civil service to particular departments or agencies' (P Jackson and P Leopold, O. Hood Phillips and Jackson, Constitutional and Administrative Law, 8th edn (2001) at 378); in practice, this means that the power to appoint and dismiss civil servants is delegated by Ministers to the Head of the Civil Service and the permanent Heads of Department (Explanatory Notes to the Constitutional Reform and Governance Bill (20 July 2009), at [3].

51 Paper submitted by Mr David Gladstone (Ev 3).

may or may not have the status of Crown servants, and concentrating on the delivery of their particular service, with clearly defined responsibilities between the Secretary of State and the Permanent Secretary on the one hand and the Chairmen or Chief Executives of the agencies on the other. Both departments and their agencies should have a more open and simplified structure.[52]

Tomkins notes that by the time the Conservatives left office in 1997, about 135 Agencies had been created, employing around 75% of all civil servants.[53] The important issues around securing parliamentary accountability for the Agencies are explored below.

Placing Civil Service governance on a statutory basis: The Constitutional Reform and Governance Act 2010

The *Governance of Britain* reforms proposed placing key aspects of Civil Service management, including the service's 'role, management and values' and the existing Civil Service Commission on a statutory basis[54] and enshrining in law 'the historic principle of appointment on merit on the basis of fair and open competition' (except for Special Advisers). Clauses to this effect made up Part 1 of the Constitutional Reform and Governance Bill, which was originally introduced into the Commons in the 2008–09 session, carried over, and re-presented to Parliament on 19 November 2009. This part of the Bill was passed into law by Parliament just before the 2010 General Election. The legislation also enshrined the Commission's power to hear complaints from Civil Servants and gave the Minister for the Civil Service (the PM) the ability to manage it (s 3); it also lays down rules about the permissible numbers and the role and powers of Special Advisers, who give political advice to Ministers.[55] This statutory statement of the power of the Minister to manage the service is not apparently intended to give Ministers a general power to appoint and dismiss civil servants, except for their Special Advisers—this power will continue to be delegated to Permanent Secretaries and the Head of the Civil Service.[56] The Act provides that the Prime Minister must publish and lay before Parliament the Civil Service Code, which will form part of the terms and conditions of service of any civil servant (s 5). Separate Codes must be published to deal with the Diplomatic Service and Special Advisers (ss 6 and 8).

The establishment of a statutory footing for the Civil Service represents a reform long advocated by a number of commentators including the PAC[57] and the Committee on Standards in Public Life,[58] and is to be welcomed as an extension of the rule of law and a diminution of the almost untrammelled executive power represented by regulation of the service under the prerogative by Order in Council[59] and non-statutory codes, guidance and memoranda. The PAC said:

---

52   Prime Minister's Efficiency Unit, *Improving Management in Government: The Next Steps* (1988), at [44].

53   For a look back at the original rationale for the reforms, and an assessment of them, see K Jenkins, 'Politicians and Civil Servants: Unfinished Business—The Next Steps Report, Fulton and the Future' (2008) 79(3) *Political Quarterly* 418.

54   *The Governance of Britain*, Cm 7342-I (2008), at [168]

55   *Ibid* at [188]–[193].

56   *Ibid.*

57   See, e.g. its response to the Government's previous draft Civil Service Bill: Third Report, HC 336 (2004–05).

58   See its Ninth Report, *Defining the Boundaries within the Executive: Ministers, special advisors, and the permanent civil service* (2003).

59   On Orders in Council, see generally Chapter 11.

There is much to welcome in the Government's proposals for the civil service. The First Civil Service Commissioner told us that she welcomed the publication of the Bill and 'agree[d] with the broad thrust of the provisions'. In Peter Hennessy's view, 'the current Prime Minister deserves an enormous amount of credit for bringing this forward'; while Robert Blackburn wanted 'to congratulate the Government on actually grasping this nettle and bringing forward constitutional reform in this area'.[60]

It should be noted however, that the legislation is only a skeleton, containing broad principles. All the detailed rules will continue to be laid down in the Civil Service Management Code. Moreover, even though the Civil Service Code must be laid before Parliament, no procedure attaches to this—in other words, Parliament is given no power in the Act to approve or negative the Code, still less to amend it (see ss 6 and 8). The PAC was concerned also that the Bill did not set out clearly all the key values of the civil service that should appear in the Code. The Committee noted that the Government's previous draft Civil Service Bill in 2004 stated that the Code must include the requirements that civil servants should carry out their duties: a) efficiently; b) with integrity and honesty; c) with objectivity and impartiality; d) reasonably; e) without maladministration; f) according to law. Only b) and c) appear in the Act (as s 7(4)). The Committee was also concerned that the provisions concerning Special Advisors left too much to be determined by the Code to be drawn up by Ministers and urged:

> It needs to be absolutely clear in primary legislation that no special advisers should be able to authorise expenditure, or to exercise either management functions or statutory powers.[61]

This now appears as section 8(5) of the 2010 Act. The Committee was also concerned that the Bill gave Ministers a general power to manage the Civil Service, explicitly including powers of appointment, discipline and dismissal. It noted that the Government had changed its position 'dramatically' on this and concluded that 'giving Ministers the general power to appoint and dismiss civil servants does not seem in keeping with the Government's commitment to a civil service recruited on merit and able to serve administrations of different political persuasions'.[62]

The Joint Committee on the draft Bill agreed, saying:

> while Ministers can legitimately be consulted about particular moves within the civil service, Ministers should not be involved in appointment or dismissal of individual civil servants without the express approval of the Prime Minister. We invite the Lord Chancellor to follow up on his offer to look again at the drafting of [the relevant clause] to reflect this.

The Act as passed omits the reference to dismissal or disciplining of civil servants as being within the management power of the Prime Minister: see section 3(3):

The PAC also recommended provisions to strengthen the independence of the Civil Service Commissioners, both in terms of appointment and operations,[63] a point on which they were strongly supported by the Joint Committee that examined the Bill in draft.

---

60   Tenth Report (2007–08) HC 499, at [8].

61   *Ibid*, p [44].

62   *Ibid*, p [22].

63   *Ibid*, p [46]–[64].

Prime Minister, Cabinet and collective responsibility

Collective responsibility as an aspect of government accountability will be considered briefly below. Here, its significance in relation to the issues discussed above is considered. According to Brazier:

> The doctrine of collective ministerial responsibility requires that all ministers, and usually parliamentary private secretaries, must accept Cabinet decisions, or dissent from them privately while remaining loyal to them publicly, or dissent publicly and resign, unless collective responsibility is waived by the Cabinet on any given occasion. If a minister does not resign over an issue of policy or procedure he will be collectively responsible for it, in the sense that he will have to support it publicly through his votes in Parliament and through his speeches.[64]

As the Ministerial Code puts it:

> 2.1 Collective responsibility requires that Ministers should be able to express their views frankly in the expectation that they can argue freely in private while maintaining a united front when decisions have been reached. This in turn requires that the privacy of opinions expressed in Cabinet and Ministerial Committees, including in correspondence, should be maintained. . . .
> 2.3 The internal process through which a decision has been made, or the level of Committee by which it was taken, should not be disclosed. Decisions reached by the Cabinet or Ministerial Committees are binding on all members of the Government. . . .

Some version of collective responsibility is clearly a prerequisite for any kind of recognisable government. Any collection of individual people is inevitably going to disagree over at least some important issues, and if all those disagreements were on public show, if ministers could constantly disclaim responsibility for decisions they did not like, then we would hardly have recognisable 'government' policy at all—only different policies, held by different individuals. Nor would Parliament be able to hold Ministers to account for their polices, if one Minister was simply able to blame another for a policy that he or she disapproved of, or was proving unpopular. But it is important nevertheless to recognise clearly all the implications and which consequences of the convention, necessary as it may be to an extent.

C Turpin, 'Ministerial responsibility', in J Jowell and D Oliver (eds),
The Changing Constitution, 3rd edn (1994), pp 147–50

The rigour of collective responsibility is, as is well known, mitigated by the practice of 'unattributable leaking' by ministers to the press, in this way rallying support outside for their position in arguments within Government, or letting it be known that they have opposed a decision unwelcome to sections of their party or to interest groups. Gordon Walker defended this practice as necessary to the preservation of collective responsibility

---

64   Brazier (1994), n 19 above, at 129–30.

[*The Cabinet* (1972), p 32]. It has not diminished in frequency since his time and must be counted an established, if not entirely 'correct', feature of the constitutional system. Prime Ministers try to curb the practice, but have been known to resort to it themselves.

A more radical remedy for the strains which may be caused in party and government by the demands of collective solidarity is the suspension of the obligation, so as to allow open dissent, within specified limits, on a strongly contested question. The 1932 'agreement to differ' was seen as something unique until collective responsibility was again suspended in 1975 for the referendum campaign on membership of the European Communities, and in 1977 for the second reading of the European Assembly Elections Bill. There are those who deprecate this sort of expedient as undermining the basis of parliamentary government, but it is questionable whether the public interest is always well served by the concealment of differences on policy within government. In particular, when the Opposition leadership is in agreement with the official Government view on an important issue facing the country, public debate is devalued if the dissenting opinions of senior politicians on both sides are stifled by insistence on collective responsibility.

In any event it may be impossible to maintain a public show of ministerial solidarity when there are sharp ideological differences, or an especially keen contest on some particular question of policy, between Cabinet ministers. This became evident in the periods of Labour government in the 1960s and 1970s. In the earlier years of Mrs Thatcher's premiership there were ministers who openly expressed their disagreement with Government policies and who were not, with one or two exceptions, visited with immediate loss of office as a result Leading dissentients were, however, progressively removed in Cabinet reshuffles and dissension became less persistent—but when it occurred, was more portentous. . . When Mr Nigel Lawson resigned as Chancellor of the Exchequer in 1989, he did so on the ground that the exchange-rate policy he was seeking to further was not being supported by the Prime Minister, who was instead giving rein to the contrary opinions of her personal economic adviser, Sir Alan Walters. Mr Lawson too, in his resignation speech, insisted on the need for the collective resolution of policy differences in government. Disagreement between ministers on policy towards the European Community precipitated the resignation in 1990 of Sir Geoffrey Howe, Leader of the House of Commons and Deputy Prime Minister, who protested in his letter of resignation that 'Cabinet government is all about trying to persuade one another from within' [*The Times*, 2 November 1990].

. . .Although, as we have seen, the responsibility of ministers does not depend on their having taken part in the making of the decision or policy in question, the convention of collective solidarity finds its most secure anchorage, and its most convincing justification, in executive arrangements which allow for full discussion and the representation of contrary viewpoints. A style of administration—like that of Mrs Thatcher's premiership—which is not favourable to collective decision-making may be seen as undermining the basis of the convention.

Notes

1. A recent example of the flexibility of the doctrine of collective responsibility lay in the attitude of Clare Short, Secretary of State for International Development, to government policy on the use of force against Iraq,[65] specifically the Government's eventual, and hugely controversial, decision to

---

65   See Chapter 8 for more on Parliament and the Iraq conflict, at pp 363–365.

take military action against Iraq in March 2003 without an explicit mandate from the UN Security Council.[66] The Security Council on 25 November 2002 had passed resolution 1441, which found Iraq to be in material breach of its disarmament obligations under numerous previous resolutions and threatened 'serious consequences' if Iraq failed fully to cooperate with UN inspectors seeking to investigate whether Iraq had, as it claimed, fully dismantled its prohibited nuclear, chemical and biological weapons programmes. Government policy, in the light of less than full cooperation from the Iraqi Government, was to seek to obtain a further Security Council resolution, expressly endorsing military action against Iraq to disarm it of such weapons. However, by mid-March, the attempt to obtain a Security Council resolution explicitly authorising the use of force had been all but abandoned in the face of implacable opposition from France, Germany and Russia and lack of support from other members of the Security Council, representing a major failure of Anglo-American diplomacy and a serious reverse for the Government. The Government was now faced with the prospect of taking the country to war with no explicit UN backing, without even a majority of the UN Security Council in favour, and with massive protests sweeping the country and the rest of Europe. At this point, Clare Short launched an extraordinary public attack on the Government's policy—a policy for which she had collective responsibility—warning that she would resign from the Government if no such resolution was secured. In a radio interview she said:

> The whole atmosphere of the current situation is deeply reckless; reckless for the world, reckless for the undermining of the UN in this disorderly world, which is wider than Iraq, reckless with our government, reckless with his own future, position and place in history. It's extraordinarily reckless. I'm very surprised by it.[67]

2. However, once the Government finally decided that it would take military action even without such a UN resolution, Short did *not* resign, losing a great deal of political credibility thereby, but then resigning over a related issue only a few months later (see below). The episode demonstrates, it is suggested, that there is no *automatic* sanction of enforced resignation, or dismissal, for breaches of collective responsibility: all will depend upon the Prime Minister's calculation of the best course of action for the Government (and/or his or her own position) at the time. Blair obviously took the view that it would be better to keep Short in the Cabinet, at least for the present, despite her extraordinary attack upon government policy.

3. As Turpin notes, collective responsibility implies not only a duty of public acquiescence to official government policy but, as a corollary to this, a reasonable chance for government ministers to at least discuss key policies which the convention will demand they later defend. As the Ministerial Code now puts it, 'Collective responsibility requires that Ministers should be able to express their views frankly in the expectation that they can argue freely in private while maintaining a united front when decisions have been reached' (above). As James notes, the lesson of the Heseltine affair is that 'the enforcement against ministers of the rule of collective responsibility implies an obligation on the Prime Minister. . .to ensure that colleagues are consulted, at least on major issues'.[68] Brady comments that Thatcher did not recognise these two aspects of the convention, rather regarding 'collective responsibility as something owed to a Prime Minster and not

---

66   Clare Short and Robin Cook were the two Cabinet ministers to resign; there were a number of lower level resignations also over the issue.

67   See 'Short spearheads rebellion with threat to quit over war', *The Guardian,* 10 March 2003.

68   James, n 20 above, at 627.

something which had to be earned and nurtured'.[69] The problem is that these two basic aspects of the convention (the duty to present a united front and the duty on the PM to consult) derive unequal levels of support from the political imperatives of government. Whilst, with exceptions, the basic survival of Government depends upon the first aspect, giving maximum incentive for its enforcement by the Prime Minister, by contrast, as discussed above, the Prime Minister may often have strong reasons *not* to allow fulfilment of the second, since denial of full ministerial participation in policy formation will clearly assist a Prime Minister bent on forcing through controversial policies. Further, the first part of the convention arguably provides a disincentive for honouring the second: the Prime Minister's motivation for allowing full participation is hardly increased by his knowledge that (provided things are not pushed too far) ministers will have to support a given policy regardless of whether they supported, opposed or even discussed it. Once again, in an important aspect of British governmental practice, politics may be seen to trump constitutionalism.

4. Tony Blair's Government was unusual in seeing two high profile resignations—by Robin Cook and (eventually) Clare Short—made on a point of principle: a policy of the Government which members of the Cabinet felt that they could not support. When the Government finally decided to support US military action against Iraq without a second UN resolution, Robin Cook, Leader of the House of Commons, resigned. His statement follows:

Personal Statement of Robin Cook, HC Deb cols 736 et seq (17 March 2003)

This is the first time for 20 years that I have addressed the House from the Back Benches . . .I have chosen to address the House first on why I cannot support a war without international agreement or domestic support.

I applaud the heroic efforts that the Prime Minister has made in trying to secure a second resolution. I do not think that anybody could have done better than the Foreign Secretary in working to get support for a second resolution within the Security Council. But the very intensity of those attempts underlines how important it was to succeed. Now that those attempts have failed, we cannot pretend that getting a second resolution was of no importance.

. . . It is not France alone that wants more time for inspections. Germany wants more time for inspections; Russia wants more time for inspections; indeed, at no time have we signed up even the minimum necessary to carry a second resolution. We delude ourselves if we think that the degree of international hostility is all the result of President Chirac. The reality is that Britain is being asked to embark on a war without agreement in any of the international bodies of which we are a leading partner—not NATO, not the European Union and, now, not the Security Council.

To end up in such diplomatic weakness is a serious reverse. Only a year ago, we and the United States were part of a coalition against terrorism that was wider and more diverse than I would ever have imagined possible. History will be astonished at the diplomatic miscalculations that led so quickly to the disintegration of that powerful coalition. The US can afford to go it alone, but Britain is not a superpower. Our interests are best protected not by unilateral action but by multilateral agreement and a world order governed by rules. Yet tonight the international partnerships most important to us are weakened: the European Union is divided; the Security Council is in stalemate. Those are heavy casualties of a war in which a shot has yet to be fired.

---

69   C. Brady, 'Collection Responsibility of the Cabinet' (1999) 52(2) Parlt. Aff 214, 221.

. . . [It is unfair] to accuse those of us who want longer for inspections of not having an alternative strategy. For four years as Foreign Secretary I was partly responsible for the western strategy of containment. Over the past decade that strategy destroyed more weapons than in the Gulf war, dismantled Iraq's nuclear weapons programme and halted Saddam's medium and long-range missiles programmes. Iraq's military strength is now less than half its size than at the time of the last Gulf war.

Iraq probably has no weapons of mass destruction in the commonly understood sense of the term—namely a credible device capable of being delivered against a strategic city target. It probably still has biological toxins and battlefield chemical munitions, but it has had them since the 1980s when US companies sold Saddam anthrax agents and the then British Government approved chemical and munitions factories. Why is it now so urgent that we should take military action to disarm a military capacity that has been there for 20 years, and which we helped to create? Why is it necessary to resort to war this week, while Saddam's ambition to complete his weapons programme is blocked by the presence of UN inspectors?

Only a couple of weeks ago, Hans Blix told the Security Council that the key remaining disarmament tasks could be completed within months. I have heard it said that Iraq has had not months but 12 years in which to complete disarmament, and that our patience is exhausted. Yet it is more than 30 years since resolution 242 called on Israel to withdraw from the occupied territories. We do not express the same impatience with the persistent refusal of Israel to comply. I welcome the strong personal commitment that the Prime Minister has given to Middle East peace, but Britain's positive role in the Middle East does not redress the strong sense of injustice throughout the Muslim world at what it sees as one rule for the allies of the US and another rule for the rest.

. . . From the start of the present crisis, I have insisted, as Leader of the House, on the right of this place to vote on whether Britain should go to war. It has been a favourite theme of commentators that this House no longer occupies a central role in British politics. Nothing could better demonstrate that they are wrong than for this House to stop the commitment of troops in a war that has neither international agreement nor domestic support. I intend to join those tomorrow night who will vote against military action now. It is for that reason, and for that reason alone, and with a heavy heart, that I resign from the Government [Applause.]

Note

Clare Short, having failed to resign over the failure to secure UN backing for the conflict, resigned only a few months later over the terms of a proposed UN resolution on the reconstruction and interim Government of Iraq, after Saddam Hussein's Government had been overthrown in the conflict. Her resignation statement made plain her reasons for so doing.

Personal Statement of Clare Short, HC Deb cols 736 et seq (12 May 2003)

. . . I believe that it is the duty of all responsible political leaders right across the world—whatever view they took on the launch of the war—to focus on reuniting the international community in order to support the people of Iraq in rebuilding their country, to re-establish the authority of the UN and to heal the bitter divisions that preceded the war. I am sorry to say that the UK Government are not doing this. They are supporting the US in trying to bully the Security Council into a resolution that gives the coalition the power to establish an Iraqi Government and control the use of oil for reconstruction, with only a minor role for the UN. . .

I am ashamed that the UK Government have agreed the resolution that has been tabled in New York and shocked by the secrecy and lack of consultation with Departments with direct responsibility for the issues referred to in the resolution. I am afraid that this resolution undermines all the commitments I have made in the House and elsewhere about how the reconstruction of Iraq will be organised. Clearly this makes my position impossible and I have no alternative [other] than to resign from the Government.

Note

The Brown Government lost a number of Ministers who felt that they could no longer support the Government; however it appears that these Ministers did not in general resign because of their disagreement over a particular area of government policy. Rather, they appeared to have been motivated at least partly by the desire to force the resignation of the Prime Minister, Gordon Brown, who rapidly came to be regarded as an electoral liability for the Labour party. The clearest example of this is the resignation of James Purnell as Work and Pensions Secretary in June 2009;[70] Purnell left the Cabinet and called on Brown to step aside in the interests of the Government and the Labour party. But if there was a concerted 'plot', it was botched[71] and Brown managed to survive the departure of five cabinet ministers in a week. Hazel Blears resigned as Communities Secretary shortly before Purnell, in a move that seemed clearly designed to destabilise the Government; however, she was by then deeply unpopular as a result of her part in the MPs expenses scandal (she had avoided paying capital gains tax on a home paid for by the second homes' allowance and been forced to repay thousands of pounds); moreover, it seemed that she may merely have resigned to avoid the humiliation of being sacked or demoted: Gordon Brown had described her conduct in relation to her expenses as 'completely unacceptable'.[72] In the same week, John Hutton resigned as Defence Secretary, but claimed it was for family reasons, lessening the impact of his departure,[73] while Geoff Hoon resigned as Transport Secretary, again, seemingly due to criticisms of his expenses claims.[74] Jacqui Smith's resignation of the post of Home Secretary was seemingly also due to the expenses scandal.[75] Caroline Flint also resigned as Europe Minister, attacking Brown's Government style,[76] but was reported to be furious because she had not been given a Cabinet post in a reshuffle. It was claimed in the media that the resignations had weakened the Prime Minister so much that he could not carry out the re-shuffle he wanted, in particular forcing him to leave Alastair Darling as Chancellor, when Brown allegedly wanted to replace him with his close ally Ed Balls. The episode underlined that ultimately senior Ministers can bring down the Prime Minister, but that to do so, they must act in a coordinated way; high profile resignations for personal reasons, or because of personal scandals foster a sense of crisis round the Government, but do not directly threaten the Prime Minister.

70   www.guardian.co.uk/politics/2009/jun/04/james-purnell-resigns-gordon-brown-cabinet.

71   www.guardian.co.uk/politics/2009/jun/10/plot-to-oust-gordon-brown-failed.

72   www.guardian.co.uk/politics/2009/jun/03/hazel-blears-resignation.

73   www.telegraph.co.uk/news/newstopics/politics/gordon-brown/5451115/John-Hutton-resigns-piling-pressure-on-Gordon-Brown.html.

74   www.telegraph.co.uk/news/newstopics/mps-expenses/5454920/Geoff-Hoon-resigns-amid-expenses-controversy.html.

75   See p 645 below.

76   For her resignation letter, see www.guardian.co.uk/politics/2009/jun/05/caroline-flint-resignation-letter.

GOVERNMENT ACCOUNTABILITY AND RESPONSIBILITY

What then are the conventions and practices by which the exercise of the vast powers of central government may be scrutinised by, and made accountable to Parliament? First of all, it should be noted that government as a whole is responsible to, and holds office at the pleasure of, the House of Commons and, by convention, must resign if defeated on a motion of no confidence. However, only two Governments, both in a minority in the Commons, have lost the confidence of the House since 1924. In 1924, Ramsay MacDonald's first Labour Government was deserted by its Liberal allies, while in 1976, the Labour Government lost its small majority, partly through by-election defeats, and was defeated on a Conservative vote of no confidence in 1979. Apart from these examples, governments that lose in the House on particular issues have managed to muster their majorities and procure a reversal of the vote. For example, in July 1992, the Major Government suffered a defeat due to a back-bench rebellion in a vote relating to the Maastricht Treaty. However, the Prime Minister put down a motion of confidence the following day, and secured a majority.

The collective responsibility of Government for its decisions and policies may be undermined where a particular minister is held individually responsible in order to divert the adverse consequences arising from a strict application of collective responsibility. The resignation of the Secretary for Trade and Industry, Mr Brittan, in 1986 during the Westland affair could be characterised as such an instance; his acceptance of responsibility deflected demands for the resignation of the Prime Minister herself. It was arguable that a similar thing happened over the resignation of Peter Mandelson in January 2001 in relation to the Hinduja passports affair. While the decision to grant the Hinduja brothers passports in an expedited manner was almost certainly not a decision made by the Cabinet, there was a strong sense amongst commentators that Mandelson's resignation was forced in order to keep the affair from damaging the Prime Minister himself.[77] In other words, individual responsibility may at times act as a proxy for collective responsibility.

Conversely, the convention of collective responsibility can prevent individual Ministers from having to take responsibility: no-one was forced to resign either over the misleading information given to Parliament on Iraq's alleged WMD, or over the disastrous aftermath of the Iraq war, partly because, as Robin Butler's inquiry into the intelligence and presentational failings found,[78] the errors made were collective ones. In this instance, collective responsibility has in effect shielded Mr Blair from taking individual responsibility for the decision to go to war which, it now appears fairly clear, was to a large extent driven by him personally (see further below, pp 651–663).

Aside from the 'nuclear option' of bringing down a Government—extremely unlikely in the case of a Government with a working majority in the Commons—the traditional doctrine for ensuring the accountability of the Executive is the convention of individual Ministerial responsibility, which in practice means the accountability of ministers to Parliament. The detailed *mechanisms* by which the actions of ministers and their departments are scrutinised (Parliamentary Questions, Select Committees, etc) were examined and evaluated in Chapter 8. The normative content of the convention itself, the means by which it treats the different positions of Minister and Civil Servants and sanctions for its breach are examined here.

The contemporary concept of ministerial responsibility is complex. Essentially it involves two concepts: first, the duty of ministers to give an account and explanation of their actions and of the decisions taken by their department to Parliament; second, the obligation to accept responsibility for

---

77   See, for example, A Rawnsley, *Servants of the People: The Inside Story of New Labour,* 2nd edn (2001), Chapter 22.

78   *Review of Intelligence on Weapons of Mass Destruction,* HC 898 (2003–04).

mistakes made personally by them or by their department. A corollary to both these aspects of the doctrine is the duty of ministers not to mislead Parliament. The above summary indicates the order in which the various elements of this topic will be considered.

The duty of accountability

We start then with the duty to give an account. The traditional doctrine will be considered first, possible modification of it in the light of the increasing complexity of government business and the 'Next Steps' reforms will then be noted and, finally, areas of uncertainty and difference of opinion relating to the 'new' position will be considered. In this section, therefore, we are considering what the duty of accountability means, by contrasting it with the notion of personal responsibility for policy or other failings and the implications of that distinction for the accountability split between ministers and officials. In the last major section of this chapter, the *content* of the duty to give an account is explored, by which is meant an examination of *what* ministers must tell Parliament and their duty not to mislead it.

The accountability/responsibility distinction

What exactly, then, is a minister *accountable* for? Theoretically, the answer is everything that goes on in his or her department. That this obligation is indeed formally present can be seen in the official government definition of ministerial responsibility, which we will return to again later in this chapter. That definition, appearing in the Ministerial Code, a Cabinet Office document containing guidance for Ministers, formerly known as Questions of Procedure for Ministers (QPM) is as follows:

> 1.2b. Ministers have a duty to Parliament to account for, and be held to account, for the policies, decisions and actions of their departments and agencies.

It should be noted that, whilst as the Nolan report remarked, 'QPM has no particular constitutional status',[79] Professor Hennessy, giving evidence to the Public Service Committee in April 1996[80] described QPM as the 'strand of DNA which determines the proper conduct of central government. . .as both the Nolan and Scott Inquiries discovered as they went along'. Moreover, the above paragraph (together with others relating to the extent of the duty to account to Parliament considered below) was approved by a resolution of both Houses in 1997,[81] giving it far greater significance than mere guidance from the executive to its own. Tomkins comments:

> No longer is ministerial responsibility merely an unwritten constitutional Convention. . . It is now a clear parliamentary rule, set down in resolutions by both Houses of Parliament. . . The government acting on its own cannot now change the terms on ministers' responsibility to Parliament in the way that the Conservative government did throughout its period in office.[82]

---

79   First Report of the Committee on Standards in Public Life, Cm 2850–1 (1995), Chapter 3, p 92.

80   HC 313–1 (1995–96), Minutes of Evidence, 20 March 1996, Q 66.

81   HC Deb vol 292 cols 1046–47 (19 March 1997); HL Deb vol 579 col 1055 (20 March 1997).

82   A Tomkin, *The Constitution after Scott: Government Unwrapped* (1998), p 62.

It is noteworthy that the latest edition of the Code explicitly accepts this, saying (para 1.6):

> Ministers must also comply at all times with the requirements that Parliament itself has laid down in relation to the accountability and responsibilities of Ministers [referring to the resolution of the Commons on 19 March 1997].

This change was introduced in 2005 and re-affirmed in the 2007 version. The wording of the relevant parts of the Code mirror those of the parliamentary resolutions, but it is important for it to be affirmed that the obligations are imposed by Parliament *independently* of the Executive.

The PAC recently described the Code as 'an integral part of the new constitutional architecture' and called for 'it to be recognised as such'.[83] The Ministerial Code, as it now is, is also a useful starting point, partly because it gives the governmental view of its own responsibility and partly because it is interesting to note what it leaves unsaid. As a matter of fact and common sense, clearly a minister will not be able to give an account of everything going on within a large and complex government department in which hundreds of decisions may be taken every day by civil servants, often at quite a low level. But the Code does not say how this affects the minister's accountability. Presumably, a minister is accountable for the actions of civil servants in that he or she can be required to investigate a matter and report to the House on it, but can there be a parallel accountability of the civil servants themselves? In the chapter on the House of Commons (Chapter 8, pp 408–409 and 413–414), the restrictions on what kinds of questions civil servants would respond to when being questioned by Select Committees—restrictions which suggested that they did not need to account for their own personal decisions—were noted and will not be rehearsed here. As the Government sees the position from the point of view of the convention of ministerial responsibility, the civil servant is accountable not to Parliament but to the minister. Meanwhile, the Minister is not 'responsible' for the actions of civil service, though he or she is accountable for them. This view is summed up—and critiqued—in the following important Select Committee report which starts by considering the basic problem that it is unrealistic to expect ministers to take responsibility for every action taken in their departments.

Second Report from the Public Service Committee, HC 313 (1995–96) (extracts)

16. The most recent, and most elaborate, interpretation of the doctrine [of Ministerial responsibility]. . .has come in the Government's reply to the Treasury and Civil Service Committee's 1994 Report on the Role of the Civil Service. The Government says that:

> In the Government's view, a Minister is 'accountable' to Parliament for everything which goes on within his department, in the sense that Parliament can call the Minister to account for it. The Minister is responsible for the policies of the department, for the framework through which those policies are delivered, for the resources allocated, for such implementation decisions as the Framework Document may require to be referred or agreed with him, and for his response to major failures or expressions of Parliamentary or public concern. But a Minister cannot sensibly be held responsible for everything which goes on in his department in the sense of having personal knowledge and control of every action taken and being personally blameworthy when delegated tasks are carried out incompetently, or when mistakes or errors of judgement are made at operational level. It is not possible for Ministers to

---

83   Third Report, HC 235 (2000–01), at [15].

handle everything personally, and if Ministers were to be held personally responsible for every action of the department, delegation and efficiency would be much inhibited. It was for this reason that evidence suggested the use of the word 'accountable' for the first of these two meanings of the word responsible, to distinguish it from the second.

. . . The Government's distinction now receives some support. Professor Rodney Brazier has recommended its acceptance:

> . . . The principle that a Minister is responsible to Parliament and public, and that he or she should bear personal blame for acts and omissions (and in appropriate cases resign), should be narrowed down to cases in which the Minister has some personal responsibility for, or some personal involvement in, a blameworthy act or omission. It is absurd nowadays to try to continue the fiction that a Minister is personally responsible, and should bear personal obloquy, for every occurrence in the department, even if he was unaware of it and had no reason to be aware of it.

. . .We are less certain that the distinction between 'accountability' and responsibility' is always a useful one. For the substance of it is a distinction between those matters on which Ministers have merely to provide an explanation to the House, and those matters on which failures may be regarded as their own fault and which may justifiably lead to the Minister's resignation. In many, probably most, cases that distinction is easily made. A Minister is obviously responsible for deciding on what policy to follow, or the resources allocated to particular budgets, for example. But in other cases, the distinction is hard to draw. The most difficult area is the one with which Maxwell-Fyfe grappled: to what extent can Ministers be said to be responsible (in the sense that it may be regarded proper that they lose their job if something goes wrong) for essentially administrative failures within a department?

. . .Ministers must accept in some degree that they are personally responsible for the overall way in which their Department is administered. They cannot, indeed, be blamed for individual failures at operational level; but they might be blamed for a broader pattern of incompetence [and the] organisation and resource framework of a Department. Ministers cannot be blamed for each failure connected with the work of the department; but if such a failure were great enough, many may feel it proper that the Minister resign.

What Ministers must never do is to put the blame onto civil servants for the effects of unworkable policies and their setting of unrealistic targets. If, when things go wrong, it is held that Ministers are not to blame because they did not (knowingly) mislead Parliament, and civil servants are not to blame because they acted as servants of Ministers, then the unsatisfactory outcome is that nobody is to blame. There is clearly something unsatisfactory about a doctrine of Ministerial Responsibility that can issue in such a conclusion.

. . .**It is not possible absolutely to distinguish an area in which a Minister is personally responsible, and liable to take blame, from one in which he is constitutionally accountable. Ministerial responsibility is not composed of two elements with a clear break between the two. Ministers have an obligation to Parliament which consists in ensuring that government explains its actions. Ministers also have an obligation to respond to criticism made in Parliament in a way that seems likely to satisfy it—which may include, if necessary, resignation.**

... We believe that the following represents a working definition of 'Ministerial responsibility'. Ministers owe a fundamental duty to account to Parliament. This has, essentially, two meanings. First, that the executive is obliged to give an account—to provide full information about and explain its actions in Parliament so that they are subject to proper democratic scrutiny. This obligation is central to the proper functioning of Parliament, and therefore any Minister who has been found to have knowingly misled Parliament should resign. While it is through Ministers that the Government is properly accountable to Parliament, the obligation to provide full information and to explain the actions of government to Parliament means that Ministers should allow civil servants to give an account to Parliament through Select Committees when appropriate—particularly where Ministers have formally delegated functions to them, for example in the case of Chief Executives of Executive Agencies. Second, a Minister's duty to account to Parliament means that the executive is liable to be held to account: it must respond to concerns and criticism raised in Parliament about its actions because Members of Parliament are democratically-elected representatives of the people. A Minister's effective performance of his functions depends on his having the confidence of the House of Commons (or the House of Lords, for those Ministers who sit in the upper House). A Minister has to conduct himself, and direct the work of his department in a manner likely to ensure that he retains the confidence both of his own party and of the House. It is for the Prime Minister to decide whom he chooses as Ministers; but the Prime Minister is unlikely to keep in office a Minister who does not retain the confidence of his Parliamentary colleagues.

Notes

1. In its response to this report,[84] the Government rejected the suggestion in the final sentence of the first paragraph of this definition of ministerial responsibility, saying that it was not prepared to breach:

> the longstanding basic principle that civil servants, including the Chief Executives of Next Step Agencies [see below] give an account to Parliament on behalf of the Ministers whom they serve. Were civil servants to go beyond this, they would inevitably be drawn into matters on which, as the Committee itself acknowledges (para 114) they must refer Select Committees to the Minister.

2. Lord Justice Scott indicated in his report (below) that he accepted the 'new' doctrine, saying he found it 'difficult to disagree' with Sir Robin Butler's view that:

> the conduct of government has become so complex and the need for ministerial delegation of responsibilities to and reliance on the advice of officials has become so inevitable as to render unreal the attaching of blame to a minister simply because something has gone wrong in the department of which he is in charge.[85]

3. It is important to be clear that the duty on *ministers* to explain extends to answering criticisms, to defending the record of the department in question, even to promising investigation and remedial

---

84 First Special Report, HC 67 (1996–97).

85 *Inquiry into Exports of Defence Equipment and Dual-Use Goods to Iraq and Related Prosecutions,* HC 115–I (1995–96), at K8.15.

action if necessary. The duty to explain therefore goes beyond the mere neutral transmission of information: 'accountability' means not only 'giving an account' but also 'being held to account' with the proviso that this kind of being held to account does not include the acceptance of personal fault by the minister. (Acceptance of such fault means acceptance of 'responsibility' and resignation may then become an issue—a matter we will examine below.) Lord Armstrong explained it thus to the Public Service Committee. 'In cases in which the minister cannot fairly be held to be personally responsible. . .the responsibility of the minister is to take the action which is required to ensure that it does not happen again.'[86]

4. Woodhouse, writing in 2002, sees recognition by Robin Cook (in relation to the Sandline affair in 1998) and Straw (in relation to the passports crisis of 1999) of this principle of what she calls 'explanatory and amendatory responsibility', in that both ministers provided a full account of what had gone wrong (though Cook is criticised for some initial obstruction of the investigation by the Foreign Affairs Select Committee) and put in place remedial action which, in turn, they invited Parliament to scrutinise, thus 'completing the accountability cycle'.[87]

5. Woodhouse also insists that, for accountability to be satisfactory, Ministers must accept what she terms 'role responsibility', which means the duty effectively to supervise the overall performance of their departments, something that 'requires ministers to be aware of what is going on in their departments, ignorance being no excuse, and proactive in preventing errors and in taking appropriate action to correct mistakes'.[88] This echoes the view of the Public Service Committee (above) that Ministers must have responsibility for the overall performance of their departments and accept culpability when that performance is seriously sub-standard.

6. An area of particular contemporary concern is the patchy extent of parliamentary accountability of ministerial special advisers. The parliamentary view of the fact that ministers have often refused to allow special advisers to appear for questioning before Select Committees, despite their undoubted great influence on policy formation, was given in Chapter 8, at pp 407–412. A further point to note is that, while the strengthening of the centre of government referred to above is probably inevitable and not necessarily improper or undesirable, ministerial accountability to Parliament is structured on the basis of scrutiny of *departments* and the Ministers overseeing them. Aside from the relatively new appearances of the Prime Minister before the Liaison Committee, there are no real mechanisms to scrutinise the activities of the 'core executive'. Parliament may thus need to re-orient its scrutinising mechanisms to account for the reality of where power and policy making lies in government.

The impact of the Next Steps Agencies

The nature of the reforms that created the so-called 'Next Steps Agencies' was briefly explored above. The key question surrounding the introduction of the reforms from the constitutional point of view was what effect they would have on the traditional accountability of ministers to Parliament for the work of their departments. If ministers were no longer running the departments, who would answer to Parliament for their work? The original Next Steps report recognised that the issue was of concern.

---

86   Minutes of Evidence, HC 313 (1995–96), 3 April 1996, Q 115. Lord Armstrong is a former Secretary to the Cabinet, and Head of the Home Civil Service. He held these positions during the launch of the 'Next Steps' initiative.

87   'The Reconstruction of Constitutional Accountability' [2002] PL 73, 83–85.

88   A Woodhouse, 'UK Ministerial Responsibility in 2002: The Tale of Two Resignations' (2004) 82(1) Pub Admin 1, 9.

Prime Minister's Efficiency Unit, Improving Management in Government: The Next Steps (1988), Annex A: Accountability to Ministers and Parliament on Operational Matters

The precise form of accountability for each agency would need to be established as part of drawing up the framework for agencies. Any change from present practice in accountability would, of course, have to be acceptable to ministers and to Parliament. It is axiomatic that ministers should remain fully and clearly accountable for policy. For agencies which are Government departments or parts of departments ultimately accountability for operations must also rest with ministers. What is needed is the establishment of a convention that heads of executive agencies would have delegated authority from their ministers for operations of the agencies within the framework of policy directives and resource allocations prescribed by ministers. Heads of agencies would be accountable to ministers for the operations of their agencies, but could be called—as indeed they can now—to give evidence to Select Committees as to the manner in which their delegated authority had been used and their functions discharged within that authority. In the case of agencies established outside departments, appropriate forms of accountability to ministers and to Parliament would need to be established according to the particular circumstances.

Notes

1. How have these suggested new arrangements for scrutiny of the agencies been realised in practice and what impact have these changes had? A parliamentary question which is perceived as raising matters within the remit of the Chief Executive of an agency will be answered by the Executive (subject to an exception, below), and his or her answers have (from October 1992) been published in *Hansard*. Chief Executives give evidence to the Public Accounts Committee in relation to their Agency's accounting policies. But what exactly *is* the allocation of responsibility between minister and Chief Executive, and does the fact that the Chief Executive has taken on greater levels of responsibility than civil servants were ever admitted to have relieve the minister of accountability for those areas? The Government position is reiterated in the 1995 Next Steps Review:[89]

   > The introduction of Next Steps agencies has not changed the normal framework of ministerial accountability to Parliament. Ministers account to Parliament. The Next Steps programme has, however, built on the conventional relationships between ministers and those carrying out the executive functions of Government. The aim is that operational responsibilities should be clearly delegated, with the Chief Executive being personally responsible to the minister for the management and performance of the agency. The form and extent of this delegation is determined case by case in published framework documents. However, for ministers to provide an adequate account to Parliament and others, they need to keep in touch and do, of course, retain the right to look into, question and even intervene in the operations of an agency if public or Parliamentary concerns require it.

2. The Government considers that the reforms have 'emphasised delegation and clarity of responsibility' and thus 'strengthened accountability'.[90] The Treasury and Civil Service Select Committee disagrees.

---

89   Cm 3164, p iv.

90   Memorandum submitted by the Office of Public Science and Service, at [12].

Treasury and Civil Service Select Committee Fifth Report
(1993–94) HC 27 (extracts)

171. We do not believe that ministerial power to intervene in the actions and decisions of agencies justifies the retention of ministerial accountability for the actions and decisions of agencies for which Chief Executives are responsible. The theoretical separation of accountability and responsibility is nowhere more untenable than in the operation of agencies; continued adherence to the theory behind such a separation might jeopardise the durability of the delegation at the heart of Next Steps. The delegation of responsibility should be accompanied by a commensurate delegation of accountability. **We recommend that agency Chief Executives should be directly and personally accountable to select committees in relation to their annual performance agreements. Ministers should remain accountable for the framework documents and for their part in negotiating the annual performance agreement, as well as for all instructions given to agency Chief Executives by them subsequent to the annual performance agreement. To this end, we recommend that all such instructions should be published in agency annual reports, subject only to a requirement to preserve the personal confidentiality or anonymity of individual clients.**

Notes
1. It will be seen that the Select Committee made quite a radical proposal—to end the ministerial obligation to answer for all operational matters within Agencies. This would be replaced by a corresponding obligation upon Chief Executive, which would be enforced by Select Committees, in effect ending the 'parallel' system of accountability which currently exists.[91] The Public Service Committee agreed.[92] However, the proposal was rejected by the Government—on the grounds that it would undermine ministerial accountability.
2. The situation as it relates to accountability therefore seems to be this: Chief Executives answer parliamentary questions on operational matters and give evidence to Select Committees, but the minister can be asked all the same questions as the Chief Executive if Parliament is dissatisfied with the latter's replies. Also, the minister can intervene in any aspect of the running of agencies, though the expectation is that he or she will not do so and as we shall see, when errors and blunders in operational matters come to light, ministers will often distance themselves from mistakes which they claim are due to mistakes in running the agencies, not in the original policies themselves. Only the minister can be asked about matters of high policy. Although the Chief Executive gives an account to Parliament about operational matters, any disciplinary action against the Chief Executive is a matter for the minister only, not Parliament.
3. Is this a logically satisfactory position? Arguably not. The whole point of these agencies is that they are supposed to operate with a large degree of independence from ministers; thus, they can determine their own spending priorities, and negotiate pay levels with the civil servants they employ. This is supposed to lead to greater efficiency and better delivery of public services, since the agencies should be run on much more business-like lines and be free from constant political interference by ministers. As Lord Armstrong said in evidence before a Select Committee:

> It seemed to me absolutely clear at [the time the first agencies were set up] that. . . Chief Executives were going to be given responsibility for day to day

---

91 See p 629 above, 20 March 1996, Q 92.

92 *Ibid,* Report.

management. . . and they would be left to get on with it and the letters of complaints and that kind of thing would be dealt with by the Chief Executive and the minister would not expect to be involved.[93]

Given that this is the whole point of the changes, it seems futile and illogical still to maintain that the minister should be accountable for everything going on in the agencies. Nevertheless, the present Government, reformist in other areas of the constitution, has firmly maintained the traditional view on this matter, 'refusing to accept arguments that Chief Executives should be personally and directly accountable to Parliament for the matters assigned to them'.[94]

4. Oliver has gone further and alleges that there are reasons of principle, as well as internal consistency, for discarding, or at least radically revising, the doctrine of ministerial accountability.

D Oliver, 'Parliament, ministers and the law' (1994) 47(4) *Parliamentary Affairs* 630, 644–45

. . . There are civilised countries in the world. . .which manage, indeed are relatively effectively governed, without our level of reliance on this convention, our rejection of legal regulation in central government. . . and our tendency to reject fully-fledged or full-blooded alternatives.

In New Zealand for example—the closest relative of the United Kingdom system—much of the public sector has been corporatised in state owned enterprises independent of ministers, thus breaking the unity of the Crown. Almost the whole of the remaining civil service is organised into executive agencies and ministers are responsible for formulating the policy within which these operate. Ministers, not Chief Executives, are responsible to Parliament. Appointments of Chief Executives and staff are on the recommendation of the State Services Commission, which is independent of the Government department, by the Governor General in Council—effectively the Cabinet; the Chief Executive is the employer of agency staff. In Sweden executive agencies are independent of Government, they have representative boards, they report directly to Parliament and they are subject to audit by a range of independent auditing agencies. Ministers are not responsible to Parliament for them, although Sweden has a parliamentary executive.

Note

In its latest parliamentary report on the issue, the PAC returned to the idea of enhancing civil service accountability to Parliament.

Public Administration Committee, Ministers and Civil Servants, Third Report (2006–07), HC 122 (extracts)

The doctrine of ministerial accountability means that when civil servants appear before Parliament it is as ministers' proxies. They get neither credit nor blame. By contrast, in both Finland and Sweden, civil servants operate under legal frameworks which give them a considerable degree of autonomy and accountability. . . .Political and constitutional

---

93 *Ibid*, Minutes of Evidence, 3 April 1996, Q 109. Lord Armstrong was Cabinet Secretary and Head of the Home Civil Service during the launch of the Next Steps initiative.

94 See C Turpin, *British Government and the Constitution*, 5th edn (2002), p 466.

systems are complex, and must be considered in their entirety. In the United Kingdom, the legal assumption is that civil servants act on ministers' behalf, and exercise ministers' powers. In contrast, in Sweden and Finland civil servants are legally accountable themselves for the decisions they take, and will personally be held to account for those decisions. We have argued against the feasibility or desirability of a formal separation of accountability of this kind. Nonetheless, we believe that civil servants could be considerably more open with Parliament without threatening the doctrine of ministerial responsibility.

57. [Although] times are changing. . .the formal position [on Ministerial responsibility] has not altered since the 1997 Resolution on ministerial responsibility. We consider it is time for it to do so. **We consider that increasing the expectation that civil servants will account honestly to Parliament does not undermine the principle of ministerial responsibility, but strengthens accountability as a whole.**

Note

The Committee went on to propose a new public service bargain, something the Government rejected, maintaining that the existing Civil Service and Ministerial Codes were sufficient. There is little really new in the above report, and the Government's response to it was not favourable to the idea of enhanced accountability of civil servants to Parliament.[95] There has thus been no real development in this field for some years, save for the agreement by the Government that Special Advisors should attend and give evidence to Select Committees, which, as Chapter 8 demonstrates, has been far from consistently honoured.[96]

The obligation to accept responsibility for errors and failures

The constitutional position

Here, we examine how developments in the duty to explain have affected responsibility for error and consider whether, as many commentators argue, a contraction of responsibility has occurred. As seen above, governments have at certain times argued that ministers should not have to accept personal blame—and therefore possibly resign—unless matters of policy (sometimes 'high policy') are involved. Certainly, resignations in the absence of such fault have always been few and far between.

The resignation of Sir Thomas Dugdale in respect of the Crichel Down Affair in 1954 is usually cited as an example of a resignation due to responsibility accepted by the minister for departmental errors. Land in Devon was acquired by compulsory purchase in 1938 for use as a bombing range. It was then transferred to the Ministry of Agriculture and by it to the Commissioners for Crown Lands who let it to a tenant of their choice. The former owner of the land was denied the right to buy it back and neighbouring landowners who had been led to believe that they would be able to bid for it were denied the opportunity to do so. When these events led to an enquiry it was concluded that civil servants in the Department of Agriculture had acted in a deceitful and high-handed manner. The Minister for Agriculture then resigned and said in the House: 'I as Minister must accept full responsibility to Parliament for any mistakes or inefficiency of officials in my Department.' In fact, this example of the

---

95   See Tenth Special Report, HC 1057 (2007–08).

96   See Chapter 8, at 407–412.

operation of the doctrine may not be as clear cut as this example suggests: it became apparent that the minister had played a personal part in the decisions made.

One rare example of a ministerial resignation in the absence of personal fault was Lord Carrington's, in the aftermath of the Argentinian invasion of the Falkland Islands in 1982, though it was apparent that Carrington's decision was taken at least partly for political reasons—to assist the Government in the difficult times ahead. In any event, if there ever was a time when ministers accepted that they should resign to atone for mistakes which were not their own, that time has certainly passed. The previous Conservative Government's position has been summarised thus:[97]

> The Government contended that 'It has never been the case that ministers were required or expected to resign in respect of any and every mistake made by their departments, though they are clearly responsible to Parliament for ensuring that action is taken to put matters right and prevent a recurrence'. . .The Government's position was broadly consistent with that outlined by Sir David Maxwell-Fyfe in the Crichel Down debate in July 1954. He listed categories of actions or events for which, in the view of the Government, it would and would not be appropriate to hold a minister responsible. He contended that 'a minister is not bound to defend action of which he did not know, or of which he disapproves', but he concluded that a minister 'remains constitutionally responsible to Parliament for the fact that something has gone wrong, and he alone can tell Parliament what has occurred and render an account of his stewardship'. Lord Jenkins and Lord Callaghan endorsed the Government's view that ministers should not be expected to resign for administrative failures in which they are not directly involved, the latter remarking that 'if we were to apply Thomas Dugdale's approach today we would not have the same Cabinet for three weeks running'.

Notes

1. The 'new' doctrine of responsibility for policy only appears to have gained ground: not only have the last Conservative and Labour Governments both asserted it, but Parliament seems at times to have at least partially accepted it. As Woodhouse notes,[98] when the 'new' doctrine was put forward by the then Home Secretary, James Prior, in 1983, after a break-out from the Maze Prison by IRA prisoners, in response to calls for his resignations, many MPs were not impressed. For example, Enoch Powell protested that the minister could not say to the House and to the public that the policy was excellent and was his, but that the execution was disastrous or defective and had nothing to do with him. However, when Kenneth Baker put forward the same argument in a similar situation in 1984, 'the House seemed to accept his division between policy and administration and the corresponding limitation of his responsibility'.[99]

2. The following questions are raised by the 'new' position on responsibility: (a) is the operational/policy division sustainable, an issue considered above; (b) is it liable to be abused by ministers anxious to avoid responsibility; and (c) how should persons other than ministers be held responsible? Points (b) and (c) are considered in turn.

---

97   Fifth Report from the Treasury and Civil Service Select Committee, HC 27 (1993–94), at [121.

98   D Woodhouse, 'When do Ministers Resign?' (1993) 46(3) *Parliamentary Affairs* 277, 286–87.

99   *Ibid*, p 287.

Ministerial abuse of the operational/policy divide?

It is clear that there is room for doubt in trying to locate the operational/policy divide. Without being unduly cynical, it might be suggested that ministers are happy to leave the matter vague, in order to give themselves maximum scope for argument when faced with criticisms about failures in their department. The advantages of this confusion to beleaguered ministers anxious to stay in government seems to be two-fold. First, it will very often be arguable as to whether failures in a given area are due to policy or its implementation. As Professor Hennessy had recently pointed out. 'There is not actually a proper division between [the two]... These are seamless garments. If operationally you hit real trouble, it is usually because the policy is flawed.'[100] Woodhouse agrees:

> The distinction between policy and operations is thus flawed because of the difficulty, in many cases, in making a clear split between the two and the assumption that ministers are necessarily removed from operational matters. The result is that blame may be wrongly located. There may also be an accountability gap in cases of recurring operational errors or poor performance which have arisen from the failure of ministers adequately to supervise their departments.[101]

In other words, the day to day problems which occur in a department may in actuality be attributable to overall—but hidden—policy problems, such as insufficient funding. So, policy mistakes may be *inferred* from widespread operational difficulties. Government has, however, tended to take the opposite line, relying on a 'bright line' distinction between the two, which serves in practice to exonerate ministers from blame after departmental failings have come to light. In particular, commentators saw a tendency during the last Conservative administration to narrow down the areas of 'policy' for which ministers conceded they were personally responsible to 'high government policy and overall political strategy'.[102] The suspicion that the area of departmental activity for which ministers will accept responsibility is an ever-shrinking one is, to an extent, borne out by events during the 18 years of the previous Conservative administration. Although there were a number of major failings in government policy, including the arms to Iraq affair, the BSE crisis, the poll tax and the Pergau Dam affair, only one minister, Lord Carrington, actually accepted responsibility for error in his department (the Foreign Office) and resigned; this took place in the wholly exceptional circumstance of the actual loss of British territory—the Falkland Islands—by an armed invasion. Other than this, the only examples of the areas for which ministers will take responsibility are negative ones, where the particular problems that had occurred in the department were found by the minister *not* to be ones which would engage his or her responsibility.

The reaction of ministers to the appalling performance in its first year of the Child Support Agency is also instructive, as Woodhouse points out.[103] Ministers refused to take any blame for the Agency's failure to meet its performance targets and its already long record of maladministration, despite the fact that, as Woodhouse argues, 'the ministers' failure to ensure that the Agency was properly established, staffed and resourced directly affected the ability of the Agency to operate effectively'. Similarly, Cook, in relation to the Sandline affair in 1998 and Straw, in relation to the passports crisis of 1999, both stated that essentially operational decisions were to blame for the problems that

---

100   HC 27 (1993–94).

101   Woodhouse, 'A Tale of Two Resignations', n 88 above, at 8.

102   D Woodhouse, 'Ministerial Responsibility: Something Old, Something New' [1997] PL 262, 268.

103   *Ibid*, at 269–270.

arose in their departments, assertions which to be fair to them were largely accepted by independent commentators.[104] Cook did recognise systemic and cultural problems with the Foreign Office but, given that he had been Foreign Secretary for less than a year, could not reasonably be expected to take personal responsibility for these. Woodhouse, writing in 2002, observed that 'in the second half of the 20th century, only the resignations of Dugdale (1954), Carrington (1982) and Brittan (1986) can, with any degree of certainty, be attributed to departmental fault'.[105] A 2007 study by academics at the LSE found no clear instances of resignations from the Blair Government on issues of departmental policy, although 14 calls for such resignation were made.[106]

Estelle Morris's resignation as Education Secretary in October 2002 appeared to come about partly as a result of major administrative problems over the marking of A and A/S levels and the vetting of new teachers and at first sight might therefore appear to be a rare instance of a Minister taking responsibility for problems within her department or Agency. Moreover, one of her stated reasons for resigning was the failure of the Government to reach its targets for literacy and numeracy in 11 year olds. The previous Secretary of State, David Blunkett had said he would resign if these were not met. However, it is not a clear-cut instance, because Morris did not acknowledge that the above grounds *impelled* her resignation; rather—and very unusually—her stated grounds for quitting her post were that she thought she did not have the political and strategic skills to do it as well as she would like. Tomkins however regards her resignation as driven by 'the high media profile given to a series of failings and difficulties in her departments'; seen in this sense, her resignation comes close to the classic model of taking responsibility for the overall performance of her department.

Woodhouse sees in Morris's resignation, and in Byers', an acceptance of what she terms 'role responsibility'—discussed above.[107] Another possible instance is Charles Clarke. He did not resign in 2006, but lost his job in a re-shuffle and declined to take any of the lesser posts offered to him. However, his exit from Government seems to have been due to his admission of serious difficulties at the Home Office, not least over its failure to deport about 1,000 foreign criminals upon their release from prison—he had offered to resign a few weeks earlier and said in a statement to the Commons that he accepted responsibility for this systemic failure at the Home Office.[108]

A further problem with the operational/policy split is that in the common case in which both policy and its application are at fault, ministers, because they control the flow of information to Parliament, can often ensure that only evidence of *administrative* failings reach Parliament. Civil servants may know first hand that policy was to blame as well, but will be unable to bring this to Parliament's attention against the wishes of their minister. As the FDA has pointed out:

> Operational failures. . .could all be laid at the door of Government agencies failing to deliver Government policies. . . At the same time, policy failures and the reasons for them, for example lack of resources, remaining impenetrable because of the confidentiality which binds a civil servant to ensure that any difference in the advice which she or he gives the Minster and the Government's ultimate decision is never revealed.[109]

---

104   See, e.g. Woodhouse, above n 87 at 84–86.

105   *Ibid*, p 74.

106   www.lse.ac.uk/collections/pressAndInformationOffice/newsAndEvents/archives/2007/MinisterialResignations.htm.

107   At p 632.

108   HC Deb, col 573 (26 April 2006).

109   See n 86 above, (Memorandum), 20 March 1996, at [24].

Dawn Oliver agreed,[110] while Derek Lewis, in a memorandum submitted to the Public Services Committee in 1996,[111] voiced similar concerns. Derek Lewis was formerly Chief Executive of the Prisons Service and was sacked by the then Home Secretary, Michael Howard, over what Howard said were operational failures. Noting that, at present, 'in speaking publicly about agencies, Chief Executives are either required to avoid comment on. . .policy or to expound the policy of the Government of the day', he goes on to argue that the Chief Executive should be permitted to comment publicly and to Parliament on policy:

> If this is not permitted, the principle of ministerial responsibility is seriously distorted. Ministers would be free to impose half-baked impractical policies or to set wholly unrealistic performance targets, and then simply load the blame onto those running the agency for any failure to implement or achieve as a mere operational matter.

He notes by way of example that both chief constables of police and the Chair of the Bank of England are able, within limits, to express their views on government policies which they are actively involved in implementing, and expresses the view that, far from merely provoking 'destructive and intolerable conflict' between Chief Executives and ministers, allowing such 'reasoned public debate' would improve the quality of our democracy.[112]

Lord Justice Scott made an important point which addressed precisely this concern. Noting Sir Robin Butler's distinction between 'accountability' and 'responsibility', he argues that it has:

> . . .an important bearing on the obligation of ministers to provide information to Parliament If ministers are to be excused blame and personal criticism on the basis of the absence of personal knowledge or involvement, the corollary ought to be an acceptance of the obligation to be forthcoming with information about the incident in question. Otherwise Parliament (and the public) will not be in a position to judge whether the absence of personal knowledge and involvement is fairly claimed or to judge on whom responsibility for what has occurred ought to be placed. Any re-examination of the practices and conventions relied on by Government in declining to answer, or to answer fully, certain Parliamentary Questions should, in my opinion, take account of the implications of the distinction drawn by Sir Robin between ministerial 'accountability' and ministerial 'responsibility' and of the consequent enhancement of the need for ministers to provide, or to co-operate in the provision of, full and accurate information to Parliament.[113]

While the Freedom of Information Act 2000 in theory gives both MPs and the public a means of ascertaining the facts about such matters, there is a class exemption in s 35 in relation to all information relating to 'the formulation or development of government policy'. The only limitation to this astonishingly broad exemption—which is not subject to a burden on ministers to prove that harm would be caused by releasing the information in question—is that statistical information relating to a

---

110   D Oliver, 'Parliament, Ministers and the Law' (1994) 47(4) Parlt Aff 630 at 643.

111   See n 86 at [132] above.

112   *Ibid,* [10]–[12].

113   *Inquiry into Exports of Defence Equipment and Dual-Use Goods to Iraq and Related Prosecutions,* HC 115–I (1995–96), at K8.16.

decision may be released once the decision is made. But, for example, evidence of other policy options considered and the reasons for rejecting them may not be. While the Information Commissioner can order release of the information concerned if satisfied (*per* s 2) that the public interest in withholding information does not outweigh the interest in its reception because the information relates to a central government department, its release can ultimately be vetoed by a Cabinet minister (s 53). See further on the Freedom of Information Act, Chapter 13.

The other main advantage to ministers of the ambiguity surrounding the operational policy divide is this: because ministers have repeatedly asserted (particularly in relation to the Next Steps agencies) that operational matters are not their primary responsibility, it appears that they can have the best of both worlds. They can interfere with the day-to-day running of the agency in order to satisfy short-term political imperatives, but then if things go wrong step back and rely on the principle that policy only is their concern to deflect criticism on to the Chief Executive concerned. To many, this is what the Derek Lewis saga illustrates. When the highly critical Learmont Report on the state of Britain's prisons came out in October 1995, Michael Howard, the Home Secretary, found that all the problems identified therein were due not to his policies but to the way they had been put into practice by the head of the Prison Service, Derek Lewis, whom he promptly sacked. Lewis complained in vain that in fact much of his day-to-day work had been directed and controlled by Michael Howard and launched an action for wrongful dismissal against the Home Office which it eventually settled, paying the claimed damages in full.

There was evidence that Howard had in fact intervened in matters of day-today running. The Learmont Report contained a section devoted to the difficulties encountered by the Prison Service because of the political demands made on Lewis. The report found that 'ways and means must be found to overcome the problem' and that a new relationship was needed to 'give the Prison Service the greater operational independence that agency status was meant to confer'.[114] A newspaper reported a prison governor as saying, 'The idea that Howard has not been meddling is just nonsense. . . . We all know he's been messing everywhere'.[115] In an interview,[116] Lewis claimed that documents which he would demand from the Home Office to support his action would prove extensive ministerial interference: 'Lewis is calling for minutes of meetings which he says will show how he was summoned virtually every day to the Home Office by one minister or another, interfering in operational matters.' Examples he gave include the personal intervention of Mr Howard to try to procure the movement of Private Lee Clegg (the soldier convicted of murder following a shooting at a security checkpoint in Northern Ireland) to an open prison after a campaign on his behalf by the right-wing press. Further allegations were that 'ministers challenged the punishments meted out to particular prisoners—a matter that is the sole legal prerogative of prison governors' and also decisions on home leave for prisoners and the disciplining of staff.[117] When the Learmont Report came out, and the Opposition called for Mr Howard's head, Howard was protected politically by the support of his party and the Prime Minster, whilst constitutionally he was assisted in making his claim that the mistakes did not concern him by the presumption that operational matters were always the sole concern of Chief Executives. The problem is that the type of interference described above will often be covert: Parliament will not usually have access to the evidence which would reveal it.

---

114   Quoted in 'Bitter revenge of the uncivil servant', *Sunday Times,* 22 October 1995.

115   *Ibid.*

116   'My life with Michael Howard', *Independent,* 3 June 1996.

117   *Ibid.*

Most interestingly, Lord Armstrong, giving his views on these matters before the Public Service Committee[118] in April 1996 said:

> I think that if you had asked me that day before I retired whether I thought the Prison Service should be made into an agency, I would have doubted it, because I should have felt that not only the objectives and the budget are matters of great political moment but there are many aspects of day to day management which inevitably become politically controversial. . .

He contrasts the Prison Service with the Driver and Vehicle Licence Centre (DVLC) which was ideal because its work was only 'management activity'. The highly political nature of all aspects of penal policy and practice make it inevitable that ministers will be unable to resist the pressure to intervene in day-to-day management decisions, thus both undermining the basis of the Next Steps principle and creating confusion about responsibility and accountability. Interestingly, when the present Labour Government came to power in 1997, Jack Straw announced that the Home Secretary and other Home Office ministers would take back responsibility for answering parliamentary questions on the Prison Service, perhaps in recognition of the particular problems thrown up by prisons policy.[119] (The Prison Service is now run, along with probation, by the National Offender Management Service (NOMS).)

A recent episode concerning the Scottish Qualifications Agency, in which tens of thousands of examination marks for Scottish Highers were found to be suspect, shows that the issue of the extent of ministerial responsibility for 'arm's-length' agencies is not going away. The head of the agency, Ron Tuck, accepted responsibility and resigned; ministers denied responsibility.

E Clarence, *'Ministerial responsibility and the Scottish Qualifications Agency'* (2002) 80(4) Public Administration 91 (extracts)

The SQA incident clearly illustrates that the responsibility and accountability structures between ministers and NDPBs [Non-Departmental Public Bodies] as they currently exist are unsatisfactory. There is an inherent tension between the use of agencies, NDPBs and [Individual Ministerial Responsibility]. Davis and Willman have argued, convincingly, that the agency model cannot function 'within the present system of public accountability through Ministers'. . . . As Wilding makes clear, the accountability of fringe bodies is ultimately a dilemma: increased accountability will involve increased ministerial activity, as ministers will seek to ensure that they are satisfactorily discharging their responsibilities. . . . This runs counter to the purpose of NDPBs and agencies. . . . 'You can have public accountability or you can have independence; you can usually achieve. . .a balance of the two; but you cannot push one beyond a certain point without sacrificing the other. . . .'

Note

The above leads directly to the issue of how officials and staff at departments, agencies and NDPBs can be held responsible.

This penchant of ministers to attribute failure not to their policy but to operational matters, and thus to officials, raises a question as to whether Parliament should have any part to play in protecting

---

118   See n 86 above [132], QQ 109–11, 116–20.

119   HC Deb col 397 (19 May 1997).

officials in danger of being scapegoated by ministers or even in disciplining them itself. Civil servants are employed under the royal prerogative which, as the FDA (First Division Association, representing Senior Civil Servants) recently noted,[120] 'legally. . .gives the right to dismiss a civil servant at will and without compensation. . . The Government in practice exercises [that] right'. The FDA went on to voice its concern over the manner in which Derek Lewis was dismissed:

> The Home Secretary dismissed Mr Lewis summarily, for no stated disciplinary reasons and outside the terms of the Civil Service Management Code and departmental procedures. Mr Lewis was given no notice of his dismissal [*ibid*].

That problems continue is evident in the report of the Select Committee on Environmental, Food and Rural Affairs[121] into the serious problems encountered at the Rural Payments Agency. The Committee noted that while the Chief Executive of the agency had been dismissed, another official who shared responsibility for the governance of the agency had not been, while the Permanent Secretary remained in post. The Government in response[122] regretted the naming of civil servants in the Committee's report, reiterating the view that Select Committees have no role to play in disciplining civil servants, and denying the need to reformulate the guidance on these matters in the Ministerial Code.

Ministerial resignation in practice

It is important to note that it would be naive to talk of the above factors as if they were determinative of a minister's decision whether or not to resign. Whether or not a resignation actually occurs will of course depend upon a wide variety of other factors, and the actual record of resignations will not be seen to marry well with any constitutional theory that supposedly dictates when resignation should occur. One well known empirical study of resignations was Finer's:[123]

> SE Finer's classic analysis on this subject shows that three variables have to come into alignment: the minister must be compliant, the Prime Minister firm, and the party clamorous. Finer suggests that this conjunction is rare—and is quite fortuitous. Furthermore, from a normative (or constitutionalist) viewpoint, it is also indiscriminate in the sense that which ministers escape and which are caught has very little to do with the gravity of the offence.[124]

Notes
1. A more recent study,[125] citing a number of cases (Edwina Currie, David Mellor, Cecil Parkinson) in which the Prime Minister of the day tried unsuccessfully to hang on to the minister in question suggests that Finer's second requirement is not always necessary.[126]

---

120   *Ibid,* p [10]. For the prerogative generally, see Chapter 11.

121   HC 107 (2006–07).

122   HC 056 (2006–07).

123   SE Finer, 'The Individual Responsibility of Ministers' (1956) 34 *Public Administration* 377.

124   M Loughlin, *Public Law and Political Theory* (1992), pp 52–53.

125   Woodhouse (1993), n 98 above, at 277. See also her 'A Tale of Two Resignations' at 12–17.

126   See further K Dowding and W-T Kang, 'Ministerial resignations 1945–97' (1998) 76(3) *Public Administration* 411.

2. As is well known, there were no resignations over the Scott Report, despite the findings that Sir Nicholas Lyell was 'personally at fault' and William Waldegrave had signed a string of untrue letters and deliberately chosen not to inform Parliament of the change in policy on arms-related exports to Iraq (see below). However, even though there were no resignations, the point about the constitutional factors discussed above is that the Government still has to justify a refusal to accept responsibility to the public and to Parliament in normative, constitutional terms. It must put a case forward as to *why* the minister does not need to resign: there was no intention to mislead Parliament; the Attorney General's advice on PIIs is a matter of legal opinion and so on. The constitutional convention thus sets the parameters for the debate. Further, whilst a minister may cling on to power, if the Government is seen to have a weak case in constitutional terms this will be apparent to the public, which will draw conclusions accordingly.[127]

3. A difficult case to classify, perhaps, is the resignation in May 2002 of the Secretary of State for Trade and Industry, Stephen Byers. Byers was forced out after months of hostile press coverage, particularly surrounding the circumstances of the dismissal of Byers' former press officer, Martin Sixsmith, and his refusal to sack another press adviser, Jo Moore, over her notorious 'good day to bury bad news' memo of 11 September 2001. It is not clear that serious problems in his department's *policy* can be laid at his door, though there was extreme discontent in various quarters over his decision to place Railtrack in administration and his plans for its replacement, as well as the state of the railways generally. Moreover he had, through inept presentation (in particular, by apparently misleading Parliament and the public over exactly when Sixsmith had been dismissed), lost the trust of the general public— principally by relentless media attacks upon him—and so had become a liability to the Government. In that sense, Byers' resignation may be seen to reflect the 'realist' interpretation of ministerial 'responsibility': that ministers will be forced to resign only when, on a hard-headed political calculation, their staying on will cause more damage to the governing party than their resignation.[128] As seen above, the exit of Charles Clarke from the Government in 2006 appears also to reflect a mixture of realist and constitutional considerations.

4. Aside from resignation out of responsibility for errors and failures of policy, or for misleading Parliament, ministers may also be forced to resign because of personal errors of judgment, if sufficiently serious or, indeed, simply for personal reasons.[129] A recent example was the resignation of Ron Davies in October 1998, after an indiscretion of some sort took place on Clapham Common. However, the minister might of course be reinstated when it was thought that his misconduct had expiated itself. The prime example is the reinstatement of Peter Mandelson to the Cabinet less than two years after he had resigned in December 1998 following the revelation that he had been lent a very large sum of money from a fellow Government minister, Geoffrey Robinson, and concealed the loan from the Prime Minister.

5. Breach of the Ministerial Code or misuse of public office to do a personal favour may also force a resignation—as in the two resignations of David Blunkett. His first resignation from the Government, in December 2004, appears to have been over a mixture of embarrassment to the Government over his personal life, and alleged misuse of his office to fast-track a visa application for his ex-lover's nanny. His position had also been weakened after he published a book which

---

127   Opinion polls taken shortly after the Scott Report showed that majorities of over 60% thought Waldegrave and Lyell should resign.

128   But *cf* the view of Woodhouse, at p 639 above.

129   Alan Milburn, the Health Secretary, resigned in June 2003 simply because he found that the job allowed him hardly any time with his family.

contained numerous attacks upon fellow Ministers. His second resignation, from the post of Work and Pensions Secretary, in November 2005, came after he was accused of breaking the Ministerial Code by taking paid work while he was out of the Cabinet, without seeking advice from the relevant watchdog. More recently, Peter Hain was forced out of the Cabinet in 2008 after the Electoral Commission referred to the police allegations that he had broken the law governing declaration of donations to his Deputy Leadership campaign—a more clear-cut case since alleged criminality, rather than mere breach of the Ministerial code, was in issue. A number of Ministers were also caught up in the MPs expenses scandal and either resigned or were sacked. The most high profile of these was Jacqui Smith, who stepped down from the post of Home Secretary shortly before a reshuffle, following a series of humiliating revelations about her husband's claim for pay-as-you-view adult films, and her decision to claim her family home as a second home while lodging with her sister in London; there had also been a series of difficulties at the Home Office, which had weakened her position.[130] Other Ministerial victims of the expenses scandal were Hazel Blears (see p 626 above); Tony McNulty resigned during a Cabinet reshuffle in June 2009 after he was accused of abusing the second homes' allowance,[131] while Kitty Ussher was sacked from her position as a junior Treasury Minister in the same month, after being accused of 'flipping' her second designated home, in order to maximise her claims.

Enforcing ministerial responsibility: a new mechanism?

Under the current position, save for the highly unusual and uncertain sanction of enforced resignation, discussed above, the only person who can enforce the constitutional duties of ministers is the Prime Minister. The Ministerial Code stresses this, stating that ministers can only remain in office 'for as long as they retain the Prime Minister's confidence'. In response to a recommendation from the Neil Committee on Standards in Public Life,[132] the 2001 version of the Ministerial Code and subsequent versions made it clear that the ultimate responsibility for judging compliance with the Code lies with the Prime Minister: 'He is the ultimate judge of the standards of behaviour expected of a Minister and the appropriate consequences of a breach of those standards' (para 1.5).

However, commentators have argued for some time that leaving assessment of compliance purely to the Prime Minister is no longer a satisfactory state of affairs. When ministers are accused of some form of impropriety, particularly where it is impropriety committed by a number of ministers, such as misleading Parliament on a number of occasions, the Prime Minister as leader of the Government has an enormous vested interest in refuting the accusation. Moreover, using the Cabinet Secretary to investigate highly sensitive, political matters can also be unsatisfactory, as seen in the case of Peter Mandelson and the Hinduja brothers' passport applications. This episode, discussed briefly above, led to Mandelson's enforced second resignation over the issue of whether he had misled the public and the Prime Minister by denying having used his ministerial position to intervene with the Home Office in order to expedite the granting of passports to the Hinduja brothers as an informal quid pro quo for their large donation to the Millennium Dome. The Cabinet Secretary was asked to investigate, at great

---

130 See www.guardian.co.uk/politics/2009/jun/02/darling-hoon-expenses-reshuffle.

131 He was later ordered to re-pay over £13,000 in misclaimed expenses and apologise to the House by the Standards and Privileges Committee.

132 Sixth Report of the Committee on Standards in Public Life, *Reinforcing Standards*, Cm 4557–1 (2000), at [4.72]–[4.78], and Recommendation 13.

speed, what was an extremely politically sensitive matter,[133] but Mandelson's resignation was forced on him primarily on the basis of a political judgment by Blair that it was necessary as a way of killing the story, which was obsessing the media at the time. An independent investigator would take some of the immediate political heat out of such situations by announcing what would quite evidently be an impartial investigation, and newspapers would find it much harder to attack its actual findings because, unlike the Prime Minister, the investigator would evidently have no vested interest in either the departure or survival of the minister concerned. This might also reduce the power of the media to force out Ministers by repeated negative coverage, as in the cases of Mandelson, and arguably, Byers (above).

When the PAC investigated this issue it recommended that the Parliamentary Commissioner for Standards be given the role of investigating alleged breaches of the Ministerial Code and reporting to the PM and the House.[134] This was rejected at the time, but the Committee on Standards in Public Life then changed its mind on its earlier stance, and in its 2003 Report 'advocated independent mechanisms to investigate alleged misconduct by Ministers'[135] in order to avoid civil servants being drawn into such controversial territory. The PAC returned to the issue in 2006 Report[136] and the Government gave way later that year. First Blair appointed an (unused) adviser, then Gordon Brown decided to appoint the then Parliamentary Commissioner for Standards, Sir Philip Mawer, as his Independent Adviser, with the duty to investigate allegations of breaches of the Code at the instigation of the Prime Minister, starting in January 2008, after he had ceased to be the Parliamentary Commissioner. The role is limited to investigating and advising *the Prime Minister* on alleged breaches of the Ministerial Code[137]—there is no reporting role to Parliament as some have advocated and no power to investigate independently. For the latest reports by the PAC, with suggestions for ways of strengthening the position of the Adviser, and the Government's response, see Seventh Report, *Investigating the Conduct of Ministers* HC 381 (2007–08) and Ninth Special Report, *Government Response* HC 1056 (2007–08).

The content of the duty to give an account and not mislead Parliament

Until November 1995—and therefore during the time in which the events which gave rise to the Scott inquiry took place—the Ministerial Code, then known as Questions of Procedure for Ministers (QPM) had this to say about the duty not to mislead Parliament:

> [Ministers' responsibility for their department] includes the duty to give Parliament. . .and the public as full information as possible about the policies, decisions and actions of the Government, and not to deceive or mislead Parliament and the public [para 27].

The importance of the obligation to give full and truthful information to Parliament is clear, as noted in the Scott Report:[138]

---

133   For an excellent account, see A Rawnsley, *Servants of the People: The Inside Story of New Labour* (2001), Chapter 22.

134   PAC, Third Report, *The Ministerial Code: Improving the Rule Book*, HC 235 (2000–01).

135   O Grey, 'Briefing on the Ministerial Code' SN/PC/03750 (2007), Parliament and Constitution Centre, p 6.

136   *The Ministerial Code: the case for independent investigation* (2005–06) HC 1457.

137   *Ibid*, p 1.

138   See n 113 above.

D4.58 . . .Without the provision of full information it is not possible for Parliament, or for that matter the public, to hold the executive fully to account. It follows, in my opinion, that the withholding of information by an accountable minister should never be based on reasons of convenience or for avoidance of political embarrassment and should always require special and strong justification.

The findings of the Scott Report

By far the most comprehensive and authoritative inquiry into the compliance by government with its duty to give an account in the context of a controversial defence exports policy, an enquiry which had unique access to highly confidential government papers and to government officials, was that undertaken by Lord Justice Scott into the export of defence-related equipment to Iraq. The report's[139] conclusion was that:

> Government statements made in 1989 and 1990 about policy on defence exports to Iraq consistently failed. . .to discharge the obligations imposed by the constitutional principle of ministerial accountability.[140]

The affair resolved around Government guidelines governing the granting of export licences for sale of defence-related equipment to both Iran and Iraq. Essentially, previous guidelines, which prevented the supply of both 'lethal equipment' and (Guideline (iii)) equipment that 'would significantly enhance the capability of either side to prolong or exacerbate the conflict' were secretly changed following the ending of the Iran–Iraq are in 1988. First Guideline (iii) above was liberalised so that it now only prohibited the export of equipment that *'would be of direct and significant assistance to either country in the conduct of offensive operations in breach of the ceasefire'*. Then, following the Iranian *fatwa* (sentence of death) against Salman Rushdie in 1989, the policy was secretly tilted in favour of Iraq by applying the new, more liberal guideline to sales to Iraq but reverting to the previous, stricter guidelines in relation to Iran.[141]

This new policy was agreed upon by ministers. However, as Scott found, 'A conscious decision was taken by the junior ministers that there should be no public announcement [of the new policy]'. He goes on to find that:

> . . . The answers to PQs [Parliamentary Questions]. . .failed to inform Parliament of the current state of government policy on non-lethal arms sales to Iraq. This failure was deliberate. . .[142]

The Scott Report then went on to consider the defence of the Ministers who stood accused of misleading Parliament, in particular William Waldegrave, that there had in fact been no new policy adopted, but just a flexible (re)interpretation of the old one.

---

139   *Ibid.* For articles generally on the Scott Report, see the Autumn 1996 edition of *Public Law,* and I Leigh and L Lustgarten, 'Five Volumes in Search of Accountability: The Scott Report' (1996) 59(5) MLR 695.

140   *Ibid,* D4.63.

141   *Ibid,* D3.65–D3.90.

142   *Ibid,* D4.42.

Inquiry into Exports of Defence Related Equipment and Dual-Use Goods to Iraq and Related Prosecutions, HC 115–I (1995–96) (extracts)

To describe this revised formulation as no more than an interpretation of the old, is, in my opinion, notwithstanding the many advocates who espoused the thesis, so plainly inapposite as to be incapable of being sustained by serious argument. In my opinion, the [new policy] was, on any ordinary use of language, an agreement to adopt a new and more liberal policy towards sales of non-lethal defence equipment than had been in place during the conflict and to do so by applying a revised formulation of guideline (iii) in place of the original. The intended effect of applying the revised guideline was to release a certain class of non-lethal defence equipment from the Guidelines.

D3.124 I accept that Mr Waldegrave and the other adherents of the 'interpretation' thesis did not, in putting forward the thesis, have any duplicitous intention and, at the time, regarded the relaxed interpretation, or implementation, of guideline (iii) as being a justifiable use of the flexibility believed to be inherent in the Guidelines.

D4.42 . . . Having heard various explanations as to why it was necessary or desirable to withhold knowledge from Parliament and the public of the true nature of the Government's approach to the licensing of non-lethal defence sales to Iran and Iraq respectively, I have come to the conclusion that the overriding and determinative reason was a fear of strong public opposition to the loosening of the restrictions on the supply of defence equipment to Iraq and a consequential fear that the pressure of the opposition might be detrimental to British trading interests.

Note

Scott thus found that Ministers had misled Parliament, by adopting a new policy, and then concealing it, but that, because they had honestly believed the 'interpretation' thesis, they had not 'knowingly' misled Parliament—because they did not, as he puts it above, 'have any duplicitous intention'; this was a finding that many believed to have been generous, not to say naïve.

After the Scott Report the duty not to mislead Parliament

The findings of Scott take us to four key questions at the heart of the current debate over the duty not to mislead Parliament. The first is the question whether, and if so when, the giving of incomplete information is to be regarded as misleading; the second is when, if ever, it may be justifiable to lie to Parliament; the third is the significance of the minister's own belief as to whether he or she is saying something misleading; and the fourth is the constitutional position of civil servants who are asked to co-operate with the misleading of Parliament or become aware that it is occurring.

Since the time of the Scott Report, the obligation as set out in QPM, now the Ministerial Code, has changed quite significantly. The accountability obligation now reads as follows:

> 1.2 c. It is of paramount importance that Ministers give accurate and truthful information to Parliament, correcting any inadvertent error at the earliest opportunity. Ministers who knowingly mislead Parliament will be expected to offer their resignation to the Prime Minister;
> d. Ministers should be as open as possible with Parliament and the public, refusing to provide information only when disclosure would not be in the public interest, which should be decided in accordance with the relevant statutes and the Freedom of Information Act 2009;

e. Ministers should similarly require civil servants who give evidence before Parliamentary Committees on their behalf and under their direction to be as helpful as possible in providing accurate, truthful and full information in accordance with the duties and responsibilities of civil servants as set out in the Civil Service Code.

'Ministers must not knowingly mislead Parliament'

Fifth Report from the Treasury and Civil Service Select Committee, HC 27 (1993–94), paras 124–26

. . .There has been considerable concern recently about the adequacy of, and adherence to [the guidance in Questions of Procedure for Ministers regarding openness with Parliament].

Sir Robin Butler informed the Scott Inquiry that there was a category of Parliamentary answers 'where it is necessary to give an incomplete answer, but one should, in these circumstances, seek not to mislead'. Mr Waldegrave, in evidence to the sub-committee, vividly asserted the need, in certain circumstances, not to disclose all relevant information:

> 'There are plenty of cases over the years, with both Governments, where the minister. . .will not mislead the House and will take care not to mislead the House, but may not display everything he knows about that subject. . . Much of Government activity is much more like negotiation, much more like playing poker than it is like playing chess. You do not put all the cards up all the time in the interests of the country.'

. . .Both Mr Waldegrave and Sir Robin Butler gave examples of answers which they held to be incomplete but not misleading. In such cases there was a general duty 'to make clear that you have information which you cannot disclose', although there were circumstances when even this would not be appropriate. Even in the latter circumstances, ministers and civil servants had to 'frame their answer in a way which avoids misleading, if they possibly can'.

126. Sir Robin stressed that it was wrong for a minister or a civil servant to lie, to mislead intentionally or to give an answer which was known to be false. The Prime Minister has made it clear in a letter to the Chairman of the Sub-Committee that, in such circumstances, a minister would usually be expected to relinquish his office. However, Sir Robin Butler and Mr Waldegrave also contended that there were 'very rare occasions' when the wrong of lying to the House would be outweighed by the greater wrong consequent upon not lying. Three instances were adduced in support of this contention. First, Sir Stafford Cripps did not mislead Parliament over devaluation but said after the devaluation in 1949 that, if he had been asked just before devaluation whether he was going to devalue he would have told a lie to Parliament. Second, Mr Peter Thomas gave an untrue answer about whether Mr Greville Wynne, who had just been arrested by Soviet authorities, was working for British Intelligence; this was untrue but was considered necessary to save Mr Wynne's life. [The Committee noted that it was also argued that Lord Callaghan had lied to, or at least misled the House, about an impending devaluation in 1967].

134. . . .The knowledge that ministers and civil servants may evade questions and put the best gloss on the facts but will not lie or knowingly mislead the House of Commons is one of the most powerful tools Members of Parliament have in holding the executive to

account. Not only is the requirement laid down clearly in Government guidance to ministers, it is a requirement which the House of Commons itself expects from all its Members, departure from which standard can be treated as a contempt. We accept that the line between non-disclosure and a misleading answer is often a fine one, not least because the avoidance of misleading answers requires not only strict accuracy but also an awareness of the interpretations which could reasonably be placed upon an answer by others, but ministers should be strengthened in their determination to remain the right side of that line by certainty about the consequences of a failure to do so. **Any minister who has been found to have knowingly misled Parliament should resign.**

Notes

1. A senior member of the FDA in evidence to the Public Service Committee commented that: 'there is a commonly accepted culture that the function of [an answer to a PQ] is to give no more information than the minister thinks will be helpful to him or her, the minister, in the process of political debate in the House.'[143]

2. The giving of selective information is thus routine. During the Scott Inquiry, Sir Gore-Booth [a very senior civil servant] opined, in a similar manner to Sir Robin Butler and William Waldegrave, that giving such incomplete information was not necessarily misleading—'half a picture can be true'. Scott's comment on this view is as follows:

   > D4.55 The problem with the 'half a picture' approach is that those to whom the incomplete statement is addressed do not know, unless it is apparent from the terms of the statement itself, that an undisclosed half is being withheld from them. They are almost bound, therefore, to be misled by the statement, notwithstanding that the 'half a picture' may, so far as it goes, be accurate.[144]

3. However, Scott was unworried about the reformulation of QPM noted above:

   > K8.5 The qualification of 'mislead' by the addition of the adverb 'knowingly' does not, to my mind, make any material difference to the substance of the obligation resting on ministers not to mislead Parliament or the public. It must, I believe, always have been the case that misleading statements made in ignorance of the true facts were not regarded as a breach of a minister's obligation to be honest with Parliament and the public. Questions might, of course, arise as to why the minister was ignorant of the true facts and thus unable to have rendered to Parliament an accurate account of his stewardship.

4. While a genuinely inadvertent mistake of fact should not be viewed as serious misconduct (though as Scott notes, it may raise issues of competence) it is worth remembering the case of Waldegrave himself: Scott found that he persisted in his view that the Guidelines had not changed 'in the face of overwhelming evidence to the contrary'. The position potentially is, therefore, that a minister who holds an honest but manifestly unreasonable—even bizarre—view that government policy has not changed is entitled simply to tell Parliament that there has been no change. Clearly the risk is that a

---

143   See n 86 above, 20 March 1996, Q 21.

144   Scott Report, at D4.55.

minister will be able to refute charges of knowingly misleading the House as long as he or she is able to make up some argument, however flimsy, that he or she did not *realise* that that was what he or she was doing. The duty ought surely to be based on the requirement for a more objective assessment by the minister. To take the example of the change in the export guidelines: if the minister realised or ought to have realised that, despite his or her honest belief that government policy had not changed, others might well take a different view, and the information which gives rise to the possible inference that there has been a change ought to be disclosed to Parliament. Parliament can then make its own judgment on the matter. In short, ministers' duty should be neither to knowingly *or recklessly* mislead Parliament. As Leigh and Lustgarten put it, the real issue is whether 'a minister, who, though not intending to deceive, has failed in his duty to inform Parliament for reasons that are found to be indefensible and illogical should remain in post?'[145] Tomkin agrees:

> . . .should William Waldegrave have been allowed to have continued in office simply because he wrongly failed to realise that his answers and letters were misleading?. . .What happened to the days when ministers were constitutionally responsible to Parliament for their incompetence as well as for their dishonesty? . . . Limiting ministers' culpability to situations where they have knowingly and deliberately lied to Parliament is confining their responsibilities too narrowly and the Scott report erred in not saying so. . . If ministers are only constitutionally responsible when they know that Parliament is being misled, who is constitutionally responsible when ministers do not know?[146]

Note

More recently, Stephen Byers sought to rely on the defence that he had not 'knowingly' misled Parliament after he had wrongly announced in February 2002 that his former press officer, Martin Sixsmith, had agreed terms for his resignation, when in fact this had not been agreed. Byers' story, seemingly accepted by Labour colleagues during a Commons debate in May 2002, was that this had been his genuine, though mistaken, understanding at the time from discussions with his permanent secretary. Byers refused to resign, or even apologise, stating that at all times he had acted in good faith, representing to Parliament—and to the public—the position as he believed it to be. He escaped censure by Parliament, but was forced to resign later in the month. As discussed above (p 644), the causes of his resignation were complex but, in part, came from a widespread perception that he had in fact been duplicitous. The lesson drawn by commentators was, however, that it was the press and not Parliament that had forced the resignation, by making Byers a liability for the Government through constant, negative reportage which served to prevent transport policy from being anything other than a 'bad news' story whilst he was in charge of it.[147]

The Iraq War, Hutton, Butler and Chilcott

No findings of equivalent authority to those of the Scott Report have yet been made in relation to what has undoubtedly been the most controversial foreign policy decision in decades—the invasion of Iraq. Evidence to the Foreign Affairs Committee noted the background facts:

---

145 See n 139 above, at 706.

146 Tomkin, n 4 above, at 43–44. See also the Public Service Committee HC 313 (1995–96), 20 March 1996; FDA memorandum, at [38]–[41].

147 See, e.g. 'Pressure that proved too much for the rubber man', *The Guardian,* 29 May 2002.

A central element of the justification offered by the British and US Governments for military action against Iraq was the need to disarm the Saddam Hussein regime of its proscribed weapons of mass destruction (WMD).

On 24 September 2002 the British Government published a dossier containing its assessment of Iraq's programmes to develop WMD (the 'September Dossier'). The dossier drew on existing publicly available information, such as UN reports and testimony from Iraqi defectors, and on analysis of secret intelligence sources. The executive summary declared that the judgements made in the report "reflect[ed] the views of the Joint Intelligence Committee (JIC). The Prime Minister declared in the foreword that: 'I and other Ministers have been briefed in detail on the intelligence and are satisfied as to its authority'.

A further dossier released by the Prime Minister's Office on 3 February 2003 provided information on the infrastructure put in place by the Iraqi regime to conceal its WMD programmes (the 'February Dossier') The introduction stated that the document drew on a number of sources, 'including intelligence material'. Some media commentators have labelled it the 'dodgy dossier' due to its apparent reliance on, and rewording of, academic articles and the reported absence of ministerial consultation prior to publication.[148]

Note
The February dossier was indeed rapidly found to have consisted partly of plagiarised material from an academic article available on the internet. The verdict of the Foreign Affairs Committee, published before it became clear that in fact there were no WMD in Iraq, was critical in some respects but ultimately benign:

Foreign Affairs Committee, The Decision to go to War in Iraq, HC 813-I (2002–03) (extracts)

183. This inquiry into the information which the Government presented to Parliament in the period leading up to war in Iraq has focused on the two dossiers which were published in September 2002 and in February 2003. . .It was these documents, and particularly the first, which were seen as forming the basis of the Government's case against the regime of Saddam Hussein.

184. On the evidence before us, we reject the serious allegations which have been made that the September dossier was the object of political interference. We conclude that the September dossier was probably as complete and accurate as the Joint Intelligence Committee (JIC) could make it, consistent with protecting sources, but that it contained undue emphases for a document of its kind. We further conclude that the jury is still out on the accuracy of the September dossier until substantial evidence of Iraq's weapons of mass destruction, or of their destruction, is found.

185. On the second dossier, there can be no dispute that, whatever the accuracy of the information it contains, it was a disaster. We conclude that the February dossier was badly handled and was misrepresented as to its provenance and was thus counter-productive. The furore over the process by which the document was assembled and

148   Foreign Affairs Committee, *The Decision to go to War in Iraq*, HC 813-I (2002–03), Appendix 1 (extracts).

published diverted attention from its substance. This was deeply unfortunate, because the information it contained was important.

186. The central charge has been that Ministers misled Parliament. We have not been permitted to question the Prime Minister, although our Chairman and his colleagues on the Liaison Committee will have such an opportunity the day after we publish this Report. We have based our conclusions on the totality of the oral and written evidence available to us, alongside our own judgment as Members of Parliament who read or heard almost every word of the Government's case in the period leading up to the war. **Consistent with the conclusions reached elsewhere in this Report, we conclude that Ministers did not mislead Parliament.**

Note

Many now disagree with this conclusion, although it is arguable whether Parliament was 'knowingly' misled, since Blair certainly convinced himself about the evidence of Iraq's WMD programme. Perhaps the most important lesson to be learned from this report is that the Committee was obliged to form a judgment without being able to interview key witnesses or read key documents—which were later disclosed to some or all of the Hutton, Butler and Chilcott Inquiries (see further Chapter 8, pp 404–412). It demonstrates therefore that, as long as the Executive controls the circumstances under which it is held to account, really penetrative parliamentary scrutiny may be evaded. Below, two commentaries analyse the manner in which the Government's presentation of the evidence about Iraq exaggerated the threat, the second in particular focusing on political influence over the dossier produced for public consumption by the JIC.

A Doig and M Pythian, 'The national interest and the politics of threat exaggeration: the Blair Government's case for war against Iraq' (2005) *Political Quarterly* 368 (extracts)

The background: cause and camouflage

The 2004 Butler Report was the fourth inquiry to consider aspects of the war against Iraq, including the role of intelligence. The first of the inquiries, by the Foreign Affairs Committee, had been critical yet limited by the nature of the evidence available to it. However, one unforeseen outcome of its hearings was the series of events that culminated in the suicide of MoD biological weapons expert Dr David Kelly. He had given an off-the-record interview to Andrew Gilligan, a BBC journalist, about the government's September 2002 dossier on the threat posed by Iraqi weapons of mass destruction (WMD) which was used to suggest, in an interview broadcast by the BBC, that the threat had been exaggerated, or 'sexed up', during the dossier's production. Gilligan had already been quizzed about his source before the Committee. Both he and Kelly, who had been identified in the media through a bizarre naming process approved by Downing Street, appeared before further hearings of the Foreign Affairs Committee. Kelly also appeared before the second inquiry—that held by the Intelligence and Security Committee; within two days of this last public appearance he had committed suicide. By the time the Intelligence and Security Committee report (which was critical of the government's use of the dossier in devaluing the work of the intelligence agencies) was published in September 2003, Blair had been obliged to set up a third inquiry into the circumstances of Kelly's death under a former Lord Chief Justice of Northern Ireland, Brian Hutton. The public hearings conducted by the Hutton Inquiry and evidence available to it (notably internal Downing Street email traffic concerning the production of the dossier) suggested a critical outcome. However, when the report finally appeared in

January 2004, it exonerated the government of any bad faith in relation to the creation of the dossier and focused its criticisms on the collective failures of BBC management that had allowed the allegations to be broadcast and then defended them in the face of attacks from Downing Street spokesmen.

However, on the same day that the Hutton report was published, in Washington DC arms expert David Kay, charged with leading the postwar hunt for Iraq's WMD, was admitting to the Senate Armed Services Committee that 'we were all wrong' and that Saddam had destroyed such weapons, possibly even as early as 1991. The intelligence that Blair had consistently cited as indicating the urgency of the task ahead was thus called into question. Pressure quickly built in the USA for an inquiry into prewar intelligence on Iraq, and having failed to dissuade the United States from holding its own inquiry, Blair felt obliged to follow suit and announce the fourth and final inquiry, chaired by former Cabinet Secretary Sir Robin Butler.

The Butler Report derived much of its impact from direct access to the relevant intelligence reports, clearly demonstrating that the summaries provided by the Prime Minister in the lead-up to war went beyond the level of threat indicated in intelligence reports (themselves questionable in terms of provenance and evaluation) in both description and tone. The report suggested that Downing Street officials, aware of the Prime Minister's commitment to the United States to participate in the invasion and an approaching deadline, sought intelligence and an approach to its presentation that would convey their account of why the UK *should* press for an invasion in appropriately stark terms, but without revealing any prior agreement to such an invasion. In other words, intelligence was being sought to support political judgements already arrived at.

The Report does gently suggest the possibility that one failure in the lead-up to war was that the 'ultimate users of intelligence' — by virtue of his *modus operandi* essentially the Prime Minister and a small group of Downing Street advisers — did not fully understand some of the limitations inherent in intelligence. This may not be a far-fetched idea in relation to a Prime Minister who had not previously held an office where he would come into contact with it and was said to be somewhat in thrall to the world of espionage and intelligence. On the other hand, the need for an informed customer for intelligence would be of less importance if intelligence was not driving policy but seized upon to provide a publicly defensible *raison d'être* at a point in time to provide both cause — and camouflage — to justify siding with the USA over a decision to invade but without revealing earlier commitments to President Bush to do so.

The Butler Report provides evidence to suggest that a war to remove Saddam was decided on for reasons not associated with UK-gathered intelligence material, and that from April 2002 until the eve of war the Prime Minister pursued a policy of threat exaggeration in a bid to persuade the British public and members of the UN Security Council of the necessity and urgency of war. . .

In his parliamentary response to the Butler Report, Blair was equally at pains to point out his judgement over the 'real' choices that had to be made:

> there was no conspiracy. There was no impropriety. The essential judgment and truth, as usual, does not lie in extremes. We all of us acknowledge that Saddam was evil and his regime depraved. Whether or not actual stockpiles of weapons are found, there was not and is not any doubt that Saddam used weapons of mass

destruction and retained every strategic intent to carry on developing them. The judgment is this: would it have been better or more practical to have contained him through continuing sanctions and weapons inspections, or was this inevitably going to be, at some point, a policy that failed; and was removing Saddam a diversion from pursuing the global terrorist threat or part of it?

Why now? Deadline politics

The Butler Report was, however, clear that, whatever the reason, it was not as a result of the intelligence of a worsening WMD picture in Iraq. As the Report stated:

> When the government concluded that action going beyond the previous policy of containment needed to be taken, there were many grounds for concern arising from Iraq's past record and behaviour. There was a clear view that, to be successful, any new action to enforce Iraqi compliance with its disarmament obligations would need to be backed with the credible threat of force. But there was no recent intelligence that would itself have given rise to a conclusion that Iraq was of more immediate concern than the activities of some other countries.

The invasion would appear to be a long-developing strategy whose time had come but which required evidence of break-point circumstances to justify the specific need to act in early 2003, and the genesis for the decision to join in the US action is now becoming clearer. In April 2002, the Prime Minister travelled to meet the US President on his ranch in Crawford, Texas. It is at this meeting that a number of commentators and observers locate a commitment to participate in enforced regime change in Iraq, despite the advice and intelligence picture presented prior to departure for the United States. This is a view supported by the content of memos dating from this period and leaked to the *Daily Telegraph* in September 2004. In one of these, Blair's foreign policy adviser, David Manning, reports back on a meeting with Bush National Security Advisor Condoleezza Rice: 'I said that you would not budge in your support for regime change but you had to manage a press, a Parliament and a public opinion that was very different from anything in the States. And you would not budge on your insistence that, if we pursued regime change, it must be very carefully done and produce the right result. Failure was not an option.'

A further leaked memo, published by the *Sunday Times* in May 2005, fills in another piece of this chronology. A record of a meeting held in Downing Street in July 2002 and attended by senior military and intelligence figures as well as the Foreign Secretary, Defence Secretary and Attorney General, it reveals the head of MI6 reporting back on a visit to Washington where 'military action was now seen as inevitable'. Nevertheless, Foreign Secretary Jack Straw conceded that, 'the case was thin. Saddam was not threatening his neighbours, and his WMD capability was less than that of Libya, North Korea or Iran'. While the Attorney General warned that regime change was not a legal basis for military action, the memo shows both Prime Minister and Foreign Secretary suggesting that weapons inspectors could be used to help generate a legal justification.

The reality of this planning was kept from the wider Cabinet and public. Clare Short's diary entry of 9 September 2002 records Blair assuring her that no final decisions had been taken and so there was no need to discuss Iraq in Cabinet—only for Short to find out from Gordon Brown later that day that Blair had asked for 20,000 British troops to be made available for the Gulf. As the date for the invasion came closer, so the frequency of Blair's references to the threat posed by Iraq increased and the language used became more emphatic, while at the same time he continued to insist in public that no decisions had been taken on Iraq.

. . .

Prior to the publication of the Butler report, with the intelligence assessments still secret, Blair's public justification for the invasion, both before and after it took place, lay in the apparently compelling nature of intelligence on the threat posed by Saddam's WMD, implying an immediacy that necessitated undertaking military action without delay. As he told the Hutton Inquiry in August 2003, his justification for the production of the September 2002 dossier and, by implication, for going to war with Iraq, was rooted in concerns arising from intelligence:

> What changed was really two things which came together. First of all, there was a tremendous amount of information and evidence coming across my desk as to the weapons of mass destruction and the programmes associated with it that Saddam had . . . There was also a renewed sense of urgency, again, in the way that this was being publicly debated . . . Why did we say it was a big problem? Because of the intelligence. And the people were naturally saying: produce that intelligence then.
>
> And again, later: 'So, in a sense, the 24 September dossier was an unusual—the whole business was unusual, but it was in response to an unusual set of circum-stances. We were saying this issue had to be returned to by the international com-munity and dealt with. Why were we saying this? Because of the intelligence.'

The Butler Report is rightly scathing about the whole dossier concept: 'in translating material from JIC assessments into the dossier, warnings were lost about the limited intelligence base on which some aspects of these assessments were being made'. This cannot have been accidental—the dossier had to succeed in evoking a sense of threat to garner public support for enforced regime change where scepticism was widespread, and also to present a case sufficiently robust to prevent the government being knocked off course from going into a war it was already committed to. Hence, neither can it have been accidental that, as Butler concluded, 'the language in the dossier may have left readers with the impression that there was fuller and firmer intelligence behind the judgements than was the case'. Or, as he put it subsequently in the House of Lords, the dossier 'did not make clear that the intelligence underlying those conclusions was very thin, even though the JIC assessments had been quite clear about that'. The dossier, Butler concluded, went to 'the outer limits of the intelligence available'.

In a sense, it had to. Blair's interest in other possible justifications for invading Iraq such as human rights or the promotion of democracy, either when in opposition or as Prime Minister, was underwhelming. On the other hand, there can be little doubt that Blair himself believed that prohibited weapons existed and would be found at some point after the war, otherwise his strategy of threat exaggeration makes no sense—postwar searches would simply have exposed his prewar position and himself to subsequent political risk. On that basis it is arguable that he, and certainly those around him on his behalf, allowed the issue of WMD, and the intelligence that underpinned it as a threat, to become the defining catalyst that would underwrite the public decision of the government to call for an invasion it already knew was to take place.

On the other hand, a distinction needs to be made between what the Prime Minister believed in September 2002 and what he believed on the eve of war. Butler, in presenting his report, admitted to being 'surprised' that UK intelligence on the Iraqi threat was not reassessed in the wake of Hans Blix's failure to find any WMD. It is notable that in his eve of war parliamentary speech, Blair chose not to repeat any of the more alarmist assertions contained in the September dossier. Yet he remained unwilling to allow weapons inspectors any more time. Perhaps, as Robin Cook suggested, 'the real reason why invasion was urgent was the growing realisation that Hans Blix was about to remove [the] principal pretext for war'. In this context, and facing a sceptical domestic audience, he exploited whatever information he had in order to maintain his commitment to the US administration. But for a series of uncontrollable events, of which the suicide of Dr David Kelly was key, few if any of the changes in justifications, and their exaggeration, that characterised his case for war would have become the subject of inquiry, analysis and criticism. . .

Buoyed to the point of arrogance by his self-view of his ability to lead from the front and define political issues, Blair seems to have taken on the mantle of the national interest and fast became embroiled in a series of events and timetable he could not control, and over which he exercised less influence than he thought he might. To give himself a current and overwhelming reason to support invasion, he knowingly exaggerated existing intelligence. From this, controversy has arisen over whether or not he may have misled Parliament and the public and, in so doing, undermined those domestic democratic principles and processes he claimed he wanted for Iraq. It may be argued that it is a controversy of his own making and one for which he will have to accept the consequences. In this, he may share the decision to go to war with the Saddam Hussein regime, and to exaggerate the threat the regime posed to do so, with his US counterpart, but both must also address the consequences not only for Iraq but also for their two countries in whose interest they professed to act. As James Pfiffner says of Bush, Blair's colleague-in-arms:

> the issue here is not whether the war with Iraq was wise; whether it was a wise war will become clear only with the passage of years. At issue here is a matter of democratic leadership. Citizens must trust the president because they do not have all of the information that he has. If the president misrepresents the nature of crucial information, he undermines the democratic bonds between citizens and president upon which this polity is based. Insofar as President Bush misled the Congress and the citizenry, either from deliberate misstatements or through creating an atmosphere in which he was not well informed by his advisors, he undermined the crucial trust upon which the nation depends.

M Pythian, 'Hutton and Scott: a tale of two inquiries' (2005) 58(1) *Parliamentary Affairs* 124, at 130–31 and 132

Many of the subsequent difficulties with regard to [the September dossiers] are rooted in the question of ownership, compounded by the lack of distance between unelected officials in Downing Street and the man charged with taking responsibility for the intelligence content of the dossier, the Chairman of the Joint Intelligence Committee, John Scarlett. Whose dossier was it? Downing Street's or, via the Joint Intelligence Committee, the intelligence community's? Awkwardly for the government, the Hutton inquiry unearthed a minute of a meeting attended by both Downing Street and intelligence officials towards the end of the drafting process stating that 'ownership lay with No.10'. The Treasury Solicitor's office wrote to the inquiry to seek clarification, to be reassured that it had 'spoken to John Scarlett about the reference to ownership of the Dossier. He has confirmed that he had ownership until the approved text was handed to No.10 on 20 September'. Given the proximity between Downing Street and John Scarlett during the drafting stage, the confusion is understandable. That the intelligence services owned the text was of course crucial to the government's defence of the dossier. Yet a trail of emails and memos to and from Downing Street staffers show that well before this date they were unhappy with what they called the 'Scarlett version' of the dossier, and were discussing amendments that would heighten the sense of threat beyond a level supported by the original intelligence.

In a 10 September email from Daniel Pruce [No 10 Press Officer] to Mark Matthews [Foreign Office Press Officer], he advises: 'We make a number of statements about Saddam's intentions/attitudes. Can we insert a few quotes from speeches he has made which, even if they are not specific, demonstrate that he is a bad man with a general hostility towards his neighbours and the West? Much of the evidence we have is largely circumstantial so we need to convey to our readers that the cumulation of these facts demonstrates an intent on Saddam's part—the more they can be led to this conclusion themselves rather than have to accept judgements from us, the better.' The common thread running through these exchanges is the need to demonstrate Saddam's malign intent, ideally towards the UK. Hence, on 11 September Daniel Pruce emailed Alastair Campbell [the Government's Director of Communications]: 'I think we need to personalise the dossier onto Saddam as much as possible—e.g. by replacing references to Iraq with references to Saddam. In a similar vein I think we need a device to convey that he is a bad and unstable man. A few quotes from Saddam to demonstrate his aggressive intent and hatred of his neighbours and the West would help too.' The same day Tom Kelly [No 10 Spokesperson] emailed Alastair Campbell, commenting on the current draft and again emphasising the importance of demonstrating intent: 'This does have some new elements to play with, but there is one central weakness—we do not differentiate enough between capacity and intent. We know that he is a bad man and has done bad things in the past. We know he is trying to get WMD—and this shows those attempts are intensifying. But can we show why we think he intends to use them aggressively, rather than in self-defence. We need that to counter the argument that Saddam is bad, but not mad . . . The key must be to show that Saddam has the capacity, and is intent on using it in ways that threaten world stability, and that our ability to stop him is increasingly threatened.'

In a subsequent email from Jonathan Powell [Chief of Staff] to John Scarlett, copied to Campbell, Powell made the point that in launching the document 'we do not claim that we have evidence' that Saddam 'is an imminent threat'. However, this is precisely the case that the revisions to the text were effectively seeking to make. The bid to show 'intent', and hence imply imminence, involved moving beyond a position supported by the available intelligence—spinning it up. The cumulative impact of heightening the sense of threat through the use of more emotive language and other devices was to suggest a sense of imminence that simply did not exist. In the dossier's Foreword, issued in Tony Blair's name, the language was of a 'current and serious threat to the UK national interest' and a threat that was 'serious and current'. The key paragraph explaining just why the threat extended to the UK made its link by a general reference to 'today's inter-dependent world' where 'a major regional conflict does not stay confined to the region in question'. Hence, unless the UK faced up to the threat, 'in the longer term, we place at risk the lives and prosperity of our own people'. As John Morrison, a former deputy chief of defence intelligence, put it: 'In moving from what the dossier said Saddam had, which was a capability possibly, to asserting that Iraq presented a threat, then the Prime Minister was going way beyond anything any professional analyst would have agreed.' In Hans Blix's characterisation, exclamation marks were inserted where there should have been question marks.

. . .

In making the unscripted live broadcast, Gilligan (see p 653 above) had to fill broadcast space that required him to go beyond or expand on this cue, and it was here that the claim that the document was 'sexed up' was made. Moreover, later in the broadcast Gilligan said he had been told that the government knew that the infamous 45-minute claim 'was questionable'. When Lord Hutton came to assess whether it was indeed the case that the dossier had been 'sexed up' he offered himself the choice of deciding whether 'sexing up' referred to the possibility implied by Gilligan's unscripted assertion that the government included claims that it knew or suspected to be questionable; or whether it referred to the process of redrafting so as to heighten the sense of threat and imminence of threat posed by Saddam, as illustrated above. Hutton concluded: 'If the term is used in this latter sense, then because of the drafting suggestions made by 10 Downing Street for the purpose of making a strong case against Saddam Hussein, it could be said that the government "sexed-up" the dossier. However, in the context of the broadcasts in which the "sexing-up" allegation was reported, and having regard to the other allegations reported in those broadcasts, I consider that the allegation was unfounded as it would have been understood by those who heard the broadcasts to mean that the dossier had been embellished with intelligence known or believed to be false or unreliable, which was not the case.'

Note

It will be seen immediately that the above commentaries are far more critical than was the Foreign Affairs Committee: indeed they convict Blair and his inner ring both of exaggerating the evidence for war and, more seriously, of pursuing a policy that was concealed not only from Parliament, but from most of the Cabinet also and at variance with the British Government's declared policy. The Butler Inquiry followed Hutton, which, as noted above, had a narrow focus on the events surrounding the death of David Kelly. Its remit was to examine specifically the intelligence that had underpinned the public case for war, and the way that intelligence was used by the Government. Brief extracts follow.

Review of Intelligence on Weapons of Mass Destruction, HC 898 (2003–04) (extracts)

5.5 The Government's dossier of September 2002.

310. It is. . .fair to say at the outset that the dossier attracted more attention after the war than it had done before it. When first published, it was regarded as cautious, and even dull. Some of the attention that it eventually received was the product of controversy over the Government's further dossier of February 2003 [the 'dodgy dossier, which Butler does not comment on]. Some of it arose over subsequent allegations that the intelligence in the September dossier had knowingly been embellished, and hence over the good faith of the Government. Lord Hutton dismissed those allegations. We should record that we, too, have seen no evidence that would support any such allegations.

311. The September dossier also subsequently attracted attention because of the fact that, contrary to the expectation reflected in it, military forces entering Iraq did not find significant stocks of chemical or biological weapons or evidence of recent production of such weapons . . .

315. We have considered carefully whether the dossier was explicitly intended to make a case for war. We have seen no evidence that this was the Government's purpose. The dossier was a broadly-based document which could support a range of policy options. . .

327. The Government wanted a document on which it could draw in its *advocacy* of its policy. The JIC sought to offer a dispassionate *assessment* of intelligence and other material on Iraqi nuclear, biological, chemical and ballistic missile programmes. The JIC, with commendable motives, took responsibility for the dossier in order that its content should properly reflect the judgements of the intelligence community. They did their utmost to ensure that this standard was met. But this will have put strain on them in seeking to maintain their normal standards of neutral and objective assessment. . .

[Butler then noted that each JIC assessment contained warnings about the limitations of the intelligence, highlighting in particular a statement by the JIC in March 2002 that *'Intelligence on Iraq's weapons of mass destruction (WMD) and ballistic missile programmes is sporadic and patchy'* and goes on]

331 . . .But the public, through reading the dossier, would not have known of [such warnings]. The dossier did include a first chapter on the role of intelligence, as an introduction for the lay reader. But, rather than illuminating the limitations of intelligence. . .the language in that Chapter may have had the opposite effect on readers. Readers may, for example, have read language in the dossier about the impossibility for security reasons of putting all the detail of the intelligence into the public domain as implying that there was fuller and firmer intelligence behind the judgements than was the case: our view, having reviewed all of the material, is that judgements in the dossier went to (although not beyond) the outer limits of the intelligence available. The Prime Minister's description, in his statement to the House of Commons on the day of publication of the dossier, of the picture painted by the intelligence services in the dossier as 'extensive, detailed and authoritative' may have reinforced this impression.

332. We believe that it was a serious weakness that the JIC's warnings on the limitations of the intelligence underlying some of its judgements were not made sufficiently clear in the dossier.

. . .

397. [The Committee then found that prior to the war Iraq 'had the strategic intention of resuming the pursuit of prohibited weapons programmes, including if possible its nuclear weapons programme' when possible in future and was carrying out 'illicit research and development, and procurement, activities' but had no stocks of WMDs.]

Conclusion on Iraq

427. The developing policy context of the previous four years, and especially the impact of the events of 11 September 2001, formed the backdrop for changes in policy towards Iraq in early 2002. The Government's conclusion in the spring of 2002 that stronger action (although not necessarily military action) needed to be taken to enforce Iraqi disarmament was not based on any new development in the current intelligence picture on Iraq. In his evidence to us, the Prime Minister endorsed the view expressed at the time that what had changed was not the pace of Iraq's prohibited weapons programmes, which had not been dramatically stepped up, but tolerance of them following the attacks of 11 September 2001. **When the Government concluded that action going beyond the previous policy of containment needed to be taken, there were many grounds for concern arising from Iraq's past record and behaviour. There was a clear view that, to be successful, any new action to enforce Iraqi compliance**

with its disarmament obligations would need to be backed with the credible threat of force. But there was no recent intelligence that would itself have given rise to a conclusion that Iraq was of more immediate concern than the activities of some other countries.

The treatment of intelligence material

449. **In general, we found that the original intelligence material was correctly reported in JIC assessments. A [rare] exception was the '45 minute' report....We should record in particular that we have found no evidence of deliberate distortion or of culpable negligence.**

The effect of departmental policy agendas

450. We examined JIC assessments to see whether there was evidence that the judgements inside them were systematically distorted by non-intelligence factors, in particular the influence of the policy positions of departments. **We found no evidence of JIC assessments and the judgements inside them being pulled in any particular direction to meet the policy concerns of senior officials on the JIC.**

Notes

1. Despite the widespread popular perception that the Government, in particular Mr Blair, simply lied about the issue, it appears that the more accurate view is that the intelligence evidence was over-presented and that some of the fault lay with the Joint Intelligence Committee in allowing significant reservations in its earlier reports to be omitted from the dossier. It may be seen that the Report did not focus much on presentation of the intelligence to Parliament but, found that at times caveats and doubts over specific claims were not passed on. Thus, as seen above, the report concludes that the impression was given that the intelligence supporting the claims about Iraq's WMD threat was 'firmer and fuller' than it actually was. But Butler—to widespread scepticism— found that there had been 'no deliberate distortion' of the available information.[149] This allowed Blair and his Government largely to escape Parliamentary censure for misleading it, although there is overwhelming evidence that the public has rejected Butler's findings and believes that Blair was disingenuous.[150]

2. It is noteworthy that it was the same Sir Robin Butler who argued previously that giving only 'half a picture' to Parliament can be both necessary and not misleading who in this inquiry found no evidence that Ministers had misled Parliament. However, it is evident from reading the full report that Butler was only tangentially concerned with the presentation of the dossier to Parliament. For example, there is virtually no commentary on the Prime Minister's Foreword to the dossier (in Annex B it is put alongside the dossier itself and the previous JIC reports, in a long table putting extracts from the 3 documents side by in a presentation that is well worth reading). In particular, the Foreword stated:

---

149 For comment, see S Case and C Haddon, 'Something Old, Something New: An Historical Perspective on the Butler Review' (2004) *Political Quarterly* 417.

150 A further issue raised by the Iraq affair related to the position of the Attorney General, whose eventual advice that the war was lawful was crucial in allowing the participation of British forces. *The Governance of Britain,* Cm 7170 (July 2007) had raised expectation of real changes to his role, to strengthen his independence from government; one proposal made by a Parliamentary Committee was to split the role in two, so that the person giving supposedly 'independent' advice on matters of acute political controversy was not also a 'political' government Minister (see the report of the Constitutional Affairs (now Justice) Committee, *The Constitutional Role of the Attorney General* Fifth Report, HC 307 (2006–07); another issue was whether his advice should be made public, given its enormous public importance, rather than the fiction being maintained that his position was analogous to a lawyer giving confidential advice to a private client (see also the Report of the Constitution Committee on the issue (Seventh Report, HL 93 (2007–08). The Government first decided against radical change—the draft *Constitutional Reform and Governance Bill* 'ma[de] no substantial change to the current situation' (Justice Committee, Fourth Report, HC 698 (2007–08) and then decided to scrap any legislative change entirely: see Cm 7689 (July 2009)). The Bill put before Parliament contained no provisions on the matter.

> What I believe the assessed intelligence has established *beyond doubt* is that Saddam has continued to produce chemical and biological weapons, that he continues in his efforts to develop nuclear weapons, and that he has been able to extend the range of his ballistic missile programme (emphasis added).

3. Butler makes no comment on this at all, although it was a point of central importance and it is very hard to maintain that it does not amount to a misleading gloss on the contents of the dossier itself and the previous JIC reports. It can of course be taken simply as a statement of belief: had the first three words 'What I believe' been omitted, it would have been more obviously misleading. Possibly, the wording was deliberate in this respect.

4. The Chilcott Inquiry,[151] which was launched on 30 July 2009, and is holding highly publicised hearings as this book goes to press, has a much wider remit. Its terms of reference are to:

> consider the period from the summer of 2001 to the end of July 2009, embracing the run-up to the conflict in Iraq, the military action and its aftermath. . . considering the UK's involvement in Iraq, including the way decisions were made and actions taken, to establish, as accurately as possible, what happened and to identify the lessons that can be learned.

The impression so far is that this much wider remit has allowed the Inquiry to focus, as its predecessors could not, on the issues of most concern: whether Blair mislead the country on the threat from Iraq, in part by 'sexing up' the first dossier; whether he did indeed make a secret agreement with the US to go to war (as alleged above); whether the war was unlawful, as many contend, and whether the Attorney General had been subject to pressure resulting in his changing his mind in favour of the legality case; how far the Cabinet was involved in making the decision to go to war; why the post-war planning for reconstruction and governance went so badly wrong. Readers will be able to form their own view when Chilcott reports on how far it has succeeded in answering these questions to the public's satisfaction. But the simple and important point remains: parliamentary accountability failed to get answers to these questions, which is partly why Chilcott (and Butler) was needed.

Misleading Parliament: the position of civil servants

Two questions arise here. First, what does a civil servant do if he or she is asked to draft answers to Parliamentary Questions which he or she considers misleading, or is instructed to withhold certain information from Select Committees? Second, if civil servants willingly collude with ministers to mislead Parliament, can they be brought to account? One of the extremely rare cases in which a civil servant actually went public with allegations of ministerial deception of Parliament was the celebrated case of Clive Ponting, considered briefly in Chapter 13. Ponting revealed to an MP his view that Parliament had been misled by Ministers in relation to information given to Parliament concerning the sinking by a British submarine of the Argentinian naval ship *The General Belgrano* with considerable loss of life in May 1982, during the Falklands Conflict. Ponting had been asked to draft a reply to a parliamentary question that he considered to be misleading. He was prosecuted under the Official Secrets Act in respect of the leak.[152]

---

151   For full details, including transcripts of oral evidence given by Blair and others, see www.iraqinquiry.org.uk.

152   See G Marshall, 'Ministers, civil servants, and open government', in C Harlow (ed), *Public Law and Politics* (1986), pp 86–89.

Until recently, civil servants owed no general duty not to mislead Parliament or the public. However, since 1996, when a new Civil Service Code was published, this is no longer the case. The Code states (para 8) that civil servants 'must not knowingly mislead. . .Parliament or others'.[153] Moreover, as noted above, the new formulation of the Ministerial Code instructs Ministers that they should:

> similarly require civil servants who give evidence before Parliamentary Committees on their behalf and under their direction to be as helpful as possible in providing accurate, truthful and full information in accordance with the duties and responsibilities of civil servants as set out in the Civil Service Code.

Nevertheless, it is clear that if civil servants are asked to collude in deceiving Parliament, or become aware of such deception by ministers, they are in 'no circumstances' to go public with this information: 'the civil servant should not leak information to the British public'. Instead, civil servants have the right under the Code to appeal ultimately to the Civil Service Commissioners but only after departmental procedures have failed to resolve the issue (the Code, paras 15–18). As one witness to a Parliamentary committee explained,[154] civil servants do see this as a 'very substantial benefit. . .because one cannot suppose that the. . . Commissioners will turn down such an appeal simply because they think that the information which is not being released is embarrassing to ministers and their party policy. . . [but only] if they [thought]. . .it was not in the public interest, properly so defined for that information to be released'.

Of course, if civil servants do not complain, this may not always be for fear of the consequences to them. They may simply not be concerned about whether Parliament is being misled or not, as long as they are carrying out instructions. Civil servants interviewed by Scott were quite blunt about where their loyalties lay. Mark Higson, for example, said, 'It was simply a matter of us not telling the truth, of knowingly not telling the truth to the public and Parliament. The policy was bent and we concealed that policy'. In such cases, civil servants' lack of accountability to Parliament means that they can effectively escape being brought to account in any way for colluding with ministers to deceive. Under the present constitutional understanding, only ministers, not Parliament, can 'punish' civil servants. But whilst ministers may be prepared to discipline civil servants for errors of administration, they are hardly likely to punish civil servants for carrying out their instructions to draft incomplete or misleading answers to questions. Another lacuna in Parliamentary accountability is thus apparent.

FURTHER READING

R Brazier, *Ministers of the Crown* (1997)

R Brazier, *Constitutional Practice*, 3rd edn (1999)

P Craig and A Tomkins (eds), *The Executive and Public Law: Power and Accountability in Comparative Perspective* (2006)

T Daintith and A Page, *The Executive in the Constitution: Structure, Autonomy, and Internal Control* (1999)

G Drewery, 'The Executive: Towards Accountable Government and Effective Governance?', in J Jowell and D Oliver, *The Changing Constitution*, 6th edn (2007)

---

153   This came into force on 1 January 1996 for the latest version, see n 48 above.

154   See evidence given before the Public Service Committee, HC 313 (1995–96), 20 March 1996, QQ 33–35.

C Foster, *British Government in Crisis* (2005).

JP Mackintosh, *The British Cabinet* (1977)

M Sunkin and S Payne, *The Nature of the Crown* (1999)

C Foster, 'Cabinet Government in the Twentieth Century' (2004) 67(5) MLR 753

P Hennessy, 'Rulers and Servants of the State: The Blair Style of Government 1997–2004' (2005) 58(1) Parlt Aff 6–16

K Jenkins, 'Politicians and Civil Servants: Unfinished Business—The Next Steps Report, Fulton and the Future' (2008) 79(3) *Political Quarterly* 418

C Polidano, 'The Bureaucrats Who Almost Fell under a Bus: A Reassertion of Ministerial Responsibility?' (2000) *Political Quarterly* 177

CHAPTER 13
OFFICIAL SECRECY
AND FREEDOM OF
INFORMATION

INTRODUCTION

It has often been said that the UK is more obsessed with keeping government information secret than any other Western democracy.[1] It is clearly advantageous for the party in power to be able to control the flow of information in order to prevent public scrutiny of certain official decisions and in order to be able to release information selectively at convenient moments.

The British Government has available a number of methods of keeping official information secret, including the deterrent effect of criminal sanctions under the Official Secrets Act 1989, use of the doctrine of Public Interest Immunity (PII), the Civil Service Conduct Code,[2] around 80 statutory provisions engendering secrecy in various areas, and the civil action for breach of confidence. (The use of the doctrine of confidence in this context is discussed in Chapter 18.) The situation of the civil servant in the UK who believes that disclosure as to a certain state of affairs is necessary in order to serve the public interest may therefore be contrasted with the situation of his or her counterpart in the US, where he or she would receive protection from detrimental action flowing from whistle-blowing[3] under the Civil Service Reform Act 1978. A weak form of a public interest defence might have been adopted under proposals in the Government White Paper on freedom of information, published in July 1993.[4] It was proposed that the disclosure of information would not be penalised if the information was not 'genuinely confidential'. But when the Labour Government introduced the Public Interest Disclosure Act 1998, crown servants involved in security and intelligence activities, or those whose 'whistle-blowing' breaches the 1989 Act, were expressly excluded from its ambit, leaving them unprotected from employment detriment.

The justification traditionally put forward for maintaining a climate of secrecy, which goes beyond protecting specific public interests such as national security, is that freedom of information would adversely affect 'ministerial accountability'. In other words, Ministers are responsible for the actions of civil servants in their departments and therefore must be able to control the flow of information emanating from the department in question. However, it is usually seen as essential to democracy that government should allow a reasonably free flow of information so that citizens can be informed as to the government process and can therefore assess government decisions in the light of all the available facts, thereby participating fully in the workings of the democracy. A number of groups, including the Campaign for Freedom of Information, have therefore advocated freedom of information and more 'open' government in Britain, as in most other democracies. They accept that certain categories of information should be exempt from disclosure, but argue that those categories should be as restricted as possible compatible with the needs of the interest protected, and that the categorisation of any particular piece of information should be open to challenge.

The citizen's 'right to know' is recognised in most democracies, including the US, Canada, Australia, New Zealand, Denmark, Sweden, Holland, Norway, Greece and France. In such countries, the general principle of freedom of information is subject to exceptions where information falls into specific categories. Perhaps responding to the general acceptance of freedom of information, there was a shift in the attitude of the Conservative Government of 1992–97 to freedom of information in the UK: that

---

1   See, e.g. G Robertson, *Freedom, the Individual and the Law* (1989), pp 129–31.

2   See G Drewry and T Butcher, *The Civil Service Today* (1991). It should be pointed out that the Civil Service Code, which came into force on 1 January 1996, contains a partial 'whistle-blowing' provision in paras 11–12. See below, p 685.

3   For discussion of the situation of UK and US civil servants and developments in the area, see Y Cripps, 'Disclosure in the Public Interest: The Predicament of the Public Sector Employee' [1983] PL 600; G Zellick, 'Whistle-blowing in US law' [1987] PL 311–13; JG Starke (1989) 63 ALJ 592–94.

4   *Open Government* (1993). See below, p 689.

is, the principle was accepted, but the traditional stance as to the role of the law hardly changed. The UK has traditionally resisted freedom of information legislation and, until 1989, criminalised the unauthorised disclosure of any official information at all, however trivial, under s 2 of the Official Secrets Act 1911, thereby creating a climate of secrecy in the Civil Service which greatly hampered the efforts of those who wished to obtain and publish information about the workings of Government.

The 1989 Official Secrets Act decriminalised the disclosure of a range of government information, but did *not* provide rights of access to that information. Such rights were finally provided under the Freedom of Information Act 2000 (FoI Act), introduced in the early years of the Blair Labour Government, which therefore created a dramatic break with the traditional culture of secrecy: 'the principle that communication was the privilege of the State rather than of the citizen was at last. . . reversed.'[5] The Act operates only within the categories of information unaffected by the Official Secrets Act, and does *not* simply allow access to information uncovered by that Act. Much information uncovered by the 1989 Act can and does fall within the extensive exemptions of the FoI. At the same time it extends well beyond government departments. It came fully into force in 2005, so it is still in the early years of its operation. The part it is playing in introducing a climate of openness in the Civil Service, and in public authorities more generally, is one of the central concerns of this chapter.

OFFICIAL SECRECY

Introduction

During the 19th century, as government departments grew larger and handled more official information, the problem of confidentiality grew more acute. Internal circulars, such as the Treasury minute entitled 'The premature disclosure of official information' 1873, urged secrecy on all members of government departments. The perceived need to enforce secrecy led to the passing of the Official Secrets Act 1889 which made it an offence for a person wrongfully to communicate information obtained owing to his employment as a civil servant. However, the Government of the time grew dissatisfied with this measure; under its terms the state had the burden of proving both *mens rea* and that the disclosure was not in the interests of the state. It was thought that a stronger measure was needed and eventually the Government passed the Official Secrets Act 1911, s 2(1) of which provided:

> . . . If any person having in his possession or control [any information. . .] which has been entrusted in confidence to him by any person holding office under His Majesty or which he has obtained [or to which he has had access] owing to his position as a person who is or has held of office under His Majesty, or as a person who holds or has held a contract made on behalf of His Majesty, or as a person who is or has been employed under a person who holds or has held such an office or contract. . . (a) communicates the [code word, pass word,] sketch, plan, model, article, note, document, or information to any person, other than a person to whom he is authorised to communicate it, or a person to whom it is in the interest of the state his duty to communicate it, . . .that person shall be guilty of a misdemeanour.

---

5   D Vincent, *The Culture of Secrecy, Britain 1832–1998* (1998), p 321.

The criticism frequently levelled at s 2 was that it lacked any provision regarding the *substance* of the information disclosed, so that technically it criminalised, for example, disclosure of the colour of the carpet in a Minister's office. There were surprisingly few prosecutions under s 2; it seems likely that it created an acceptance of secrecy in the Civil Service which tended to preclude disclosure. In one of the few cases which did come to court, *R v Fell*,[6] the Court of Appeal confirmed that liability was not dependent on the contents of the document in question or on whether the disclosure would have an effect prejudicial to the interests of the state.

The decision in *R v Ponting*[7] is usually credited with finally bringing about the demise of s 2.[8] Clive Ponting, a senior civil servant in the Ministry of Defence, was responsible for policy on the operational activities of the Royal Navy at a time when Opposition MPs, particularly Tam Dalyell, were pressing the Government for information relating to the sinking of the *General Belgrano* in the Falklands conflict. Michael Heseltine, then Secretary of State for Defence, decided to withhold such information from Parliament and therefore did not use a reply to Parliamentary Questions drafted by Ponting. He used instead a much briefer version of it and circulated a confidential minute indicating that answers on the rules of engagement in the Falklands conflict should not be given to questions put by the Parliamentary Select Committee on Foreign Affairs. Feeling that Opposition MPs were being prevented from doing their job of scrutinising the workings of Government, Ponting sent the unused reply and the minute anonymously to the Labour MP, Tam Dalyell, who disclosed the documents to the press.

Ponting was charged with the offence of communicating information under s 2. His defence rested on the provision in s 2(1)(a) of the 1911 Act that the information had been communicated 'to a person to whom it is in the interests of the state his duty to communicate it, or to a person to whom it is in the interests of the state his duty to communicate it'. The judge directed the jury that 'duty' meant official duty, meaning the duty imposed upon Mr Ponting by his position. In relation to the words, 'in the interests of the state', the judge said:

> I direct you that these words mean the policies of the state as they were in July 1984. . . and not the policies of the state as Mr Ponting, Mr Dalyell, you or I might think they ought to have been. . . The policies of the state mean the policies laid down by those recognised organs of Government and authority. . . While it has [the support of a majority in the House of Commons], the Government and its policies are for the time being the policies of the state.

Thus, the judge in *Ponting* effectively directed the jury to convict. Despite this direction they acquitted, presumably feeling that Ponting should have a defence if he was acting in the public interest in trying to prevent Government suppression of matters of public interest. The prosecution and its outcome provoked a large amount of adverse publicity, the public perceiving it as an attempt at a cover-up which had failed, not because the judge showed integrity but because the jury did.[9]

---

6   [1963] Crim LR 207. See D Hooper, *Official Secrets* (1987) for the history of the use of s 2.

7   [1985] Crim LR 318. See also [1985] PL 203, at 212 and [1986] Crim LR 491.

8   It may be noted that, although a conviction was obtained in *R v Tisdall*, *The Times*, 26 March 1984, the decision created some adverse publicity for the Government due to what was perceived as a draconian use of s 2. Sarah Tisdall worked in the Foreign Secretary's private office and in the course of her duties came across documents relating to the delivery of cruise missiles to the RAF base at Greenham Common. She discovered proposals to delay the announcement of their delivery until after it had occurred and to make the announcement in Parliament at the end of Question Time in order to avoid answering questions. Considering that this political subterfuge was morally wrong, she leaked the documents to *The Guardian* but they were eventually traced back to her. She pleaded guilty to an offence under s 2 and received a prison sentence of six months—an outcome which was generally seen as harsh: see Cripps, n 3 above.

9   For comment on the case, see C Ponting, *The Right to Know* (1985); G Drewry, 'The Ponting case' [1985] PL 203.

The outcome of the *Ponting* case may have influenced the decision not to prosecute Cathy Massiter, a former officer in the security service, in respect of her claims in a Channel 4 programme screened in March 1985 *(MI5's Official Secrets)* that MI5 had tapped the telephones of trade union members and placed leading CND members under surveillance.[10] Section 2's perceived lack of credibility may also have been a factor in the decision to bring civil as opposed to criminal proceedings against *The Guardian* and *The Observer* in respect of their disclosure of Peter Wright's allegations in *Spycatcher*: civil proceedings for breach of confidence were in many ways more convenient and less risky than a s 2 prosecution (see Chapter 18, pp 1023–1031).

There is a long history of proposals for the reform of s 2. The Franks Committee, which was set up in response to Caulfield J's comments in *R v Aitken* (1971), recommended that s 2 should be replaced by narrower provisions which took into account the nature of the information disclosed.[11] The Franks proposals formed the basis of the Government's White Paper on which the Official Secrets Act 1989 was based.

The Official Secrets Act 1989[12]

Once the decision to reform the area of official secrecy had been taken, an opportunity was created for radical change which could have included freedom of information legislation along the lines of the instruments in America and Canada. However, it was made clear from the outset that the legislation was unconcerned with freedom of information.[13] It de-criminalises disclosure of some official information, although an official who makes such disclosure may of course face an action for breach of confidence as well as disciplinary proceedings, but it does not in itself make any provision for affording access to official information. Thus, claims made, for example, by Douglas Hurd (the then Home Secretary) that it is 'a great liberalising measure' clearly rest on other aspects of the Act. Aspects which are usually viewed as liberalising features include the categorisation of information covered, the introduction of tests for harm, the *mens rea* requirement of ss 5 and 6, the defences available, and decriminalisation of the receiver of information. In all these respects the Act differs from its predecessor, but it is arguable that the changes have not brought about any real liberalisation. Other features of the Act have also attracted criticism: the categories of information covered are very wide and do not admit of challenge to the categorisation; the Act contains no defences of public interest or of prior disclosure, and no general requirement to prove *mens rea*.

The Official Secrets Act 1989

Security and intelligence
1.–(1) A person who is or has been—

    (a)   a member of the security and intelligence services; or
    (b)   a person notified that he is subject to the provisions of this subsection,

---

10   The IBA banned the programme pending the decision as to whether Massiter and the producers would be prosecuted. The decision not to prosecute was announced by Sir Michael Havers on 5 March 1985.

11   Report of the Committee on s 2 of the Official Secrets Act 1911, Cmnd 5104; see W Birtles, 'Big Brother Knows Best: The Franks Report on s 2 of the Official Secrets Act' [1973] PL 100.

12   For comment on the 1989 Act see: S Palmer, 'Tightening secrecy law' [1990] PL 243; J Griffith, 'The Official Secrets Act 1989' (1989) 16 JLS 273; D Feldman, *Civil Liberties and Human Rights,* 2nd edn (2002), Chapter 15.3; *Bailey, Harris and Jones* (2009), Chapter 12.2 (for full reference, see p 347).

13   See White Paper on s 2, Cmnd 7285; Green Paper on Freedom of Information, Cmnd 7520; White Paper, Reform of the Official Secrets Act 1911, Cmnd 408.

is guilty of an offence if without lawful authority he discloses any information, document or other article relating to security or intelligence which is or has been in his possession by virtue of his position as a member of any of those services or in the course of his work while the notification is or was in force.

...

(3) A person who is or has been a Crown servant or government contractor is guilty of an offence if without lawful authority he makes a damaging disclosure of any information, document or other article relating to security or intelligence which is or has been in his possession by virtue of his position as such but otherwise than as mentioned in subsection (1) above.

(4) For the purposes of subsection (3) above a disclosure is damaging if—

(a) it causes damage to the work of, or of any part of, the security and intelligence services; or

(b) it is of information or a document or other article which is such that its un-authorised disclosure would be likely to cause such damage or which falls within a class or description of information, documents or articles the unauthorised disclosure of which would be likely to have that effect.

(5) It is a defence for a person charged with an offence under this section to prove that at the time of the alleged offence he did not know, and had no reasonable cause to believe, that the information, document or article in question related to security or intelligence or, in the case of an offence under subsection (3), that the disclosure would be damaging within the meaning of that subsection.

...

Defence

2.–(1) A person who is or has been a Crown servant or government contractor is guilty of an offence if without lawful authority he makes a damaging disclosure of any information, document or other article relating to defence which is or has been in his possession by virtue of his position as such.

(2) For the purposes of subsection (1) above a disclosure is damaging if—

(a) it damages the capability of, or of any part of, the armed forces of the Crown to carry out their tasks or leads to loss of life or injury to members of those forces or serious damage to the equipment or installations of those forces; or

(b) otherwise than as mentioned in paragraph (a) above, it endangers the interests of the United Kingdom abroad, seriously obstructs the promotion or protection by the United Kingdom of those interests or endangers the safety of British citizens abroad; or

(c) it is of information or of a document or article which is such that its unauthorised disclosure would be likely to have any of those effects.

(3) It is a defence for a person charged with an offence under this section to prove that at the time of the alleged offence he did not know and had no reasonable cause to believe, that the information, document or article in question related to defence or that its disclosure would be damaging within the meaning of subsection (1) above.

...

International relations

3.–(1)   A person who is or has been a Crown servant or government contractor is guilty of an offence if without lawful authority he makes a damaging disclosure of—

(a)   any information, document or other article relating to international relations; or

(b)   any confidential information, document or other article which was obtained from a state other than the United Kingdom or an international organisation, being information or a document or article which is or has been in his possession by virtue of his position as a Crown servant or government contractor.

(2)   For the purposes of subsection (1) above a disclosure is damaging if—

(a)   it endangers the interests of the United Kingdom abroad, seriously obstructs the promotion or protection by the United Kingdom of those interests or endangers the safety of British citizens abroad; or

(b)   it is of information or of a document or article which is such that its unauthorised disclosure would be likely to have any of those effects.

(3)   In the case of information or a document or article within subsection (1)(b) above—

(a)   the fact that it is confidential; or

(b)   its nature or contents, may be sufficient to establish for the purposes of subsection (2)(b) above that the information, document or article is such that its unauthorised disclosure would be likely to have any of the effects there mentioned.

(4)   It is a defence for a person charged with an offence under this section to prove that at the time of the alleged offence he did not know, and had no reasonable cause to believe, that the information, document or article in question was such as is mentioned in subsection (1) above or that its disclosure would be damaging within the meaning of that subsection.

(5)   In this section 'international relations' means the relations between states, between international organisations or between one or more states and one or more such organisations and includes any matter relating to a state other than the United Kingdom or to an international organisation which is capable of affecting the relations of the United Kingdom with mother state or with an international organisation.

Crime and special investigation powers

4.–(1)   A person who is or has been a Crown servant or government contractor is guilty of an offence if without lawful authority he discloses any information, document or other article to which this section applies and which is or has been in his possession by virtue of his position as such.

(2)   This section applies to any information, document or other article—

(a)   the disclosure of which—

(i)   results in the commission of an offence; or

(ii)   facilitates an escape from legal custody or the doing of any other act prejudicial to the safekeeping of persons in legal custody; or

(iii)   impedes the prevention or detection of offences or the apprehension or prosecution of suspected offenders; or

(b)   which is such that its unauthorised disclosure would be likely to have any of those effects.

(3)   This section also applies to—

(a)   any information obtained by reason of the interception of any communication in obedience to a warrant issued under section 2 of the Interception of Communications Act 1985 [or under the authority of an interception warrant under section 5 of the Regulation of Investigatory Powers Act 2000],[14] any information relating to the obtaining of information by reason of any such interception and any document or other article which is or has been used or held for use in, or has been obtained by reason of, any such interception; and

(b)   any information obtained by reason of action authorised by a warrant issued under section 3 of the Security Service Act 1989 [or under section 5 of the Intelligence Services Act 1994 or by an authorization under section 7 of that Act],[15] any information relating to the obtaining of information by reason of any such action and any document or other article which is or has been used or held for use in, or has been obtained by reason of, any such action.

(4)   It is a defence for a person charged with an offence under this section in respect of a disclosure falling within subsection (2)(a) above to prove that at the time of the alleged offence he did not know, and had no reasonable cause to believe, that the disclosure would have any of the effects there mentioned.

(5)   It is a defence for a person charged with an offence under this section in respect of any other disclosure to prove that at the time of the alleged offence he did not know, and had no reasonable cause to believe, that the information, document or article in question was information or a document or article to which this section applies.

Information resulting from unauthorised disclosures or entrusted in confidence

5.–(1)   Subsection (2) below applies where—

(a)   any information, document or other article protected against disclosure by the foregoing provisions of this Act has come into a person's possession as a result of having been—

(i)   disclosed (whether to him or another) by a Crown servant or government contractor without lawful authority; or

---

14   Inserted by Sched 4, para 5 to the 2000 Act.

15   Inserted by Sched 4, para 4 to the 1994 Act.

      (ii)   entrusted to him by a Crown servant or government contractor on terms requiring it to be held in confidence or in circumstances in which the Crown servant or government contractor could reasonably expect that it would be so held;

      (iii)   disclosed (whether to him or another) without lawful authority by a person to whom it was entrusted as mentioned in sub-paragraph (ii) above; and

  (b)   the disclosure without lawful authority of the information, document or article by the person into whose possession it has come is not an offence under any of those provisions.

(2)   Subject to subsections (3) and (4) below, the person into whose possession the information, document or article has come is guilty of an offence if he discloses it without lawful authority knowing, or having reasonable cause to believe, that it is protected against disclosure by the foregoing provisions of this Act and that it has come into his possession as mentioned in subsection (1) above.

(3)   In the case of information or a document or article protected against disclosure by sections 1 to 3 above, a person does not commit an offence under subsection (2) above unless—

  (a)   the disclosure by him is damaging; and

  (b)   he makes it knowing, or having reasonable cause to believe, that it would be damaging; and the question whether a disclosure is damaging shall be determined for the purposes of this subsection as it would be in relation to a disclosure of that information, document or article by a Crown servant in contravention of sections 1(3), 2(1) or 3(1) above.

. . .

(5)   For the purposes of this section information or a document or article is protected against disclosure by the foregoing provisions of this Act—

  (a)   it relates to security or intelligence, defence or international relations within the meaning of section 1, 2 or 3 above or is such as is mentioned in section 3(1)(b) above; or

  (b)   it is information or a document or article to which section 4 above applies and information or a document or article is protected against disclosure by sections 1 to 3 above if it falls within paragraph (a) above.

(6)   A person is guilty of an offence if without lawful authority he discloses any information, document or other article which he knows, or has reasonable cause to believe, to have come into his possession as a result of a contravention of section 1 of the Official Secrets Act 1911.

Information entrusted in confidence to other states or international organisations
6.–(1) This section applies where—

  (a)   any information, document or other article which—

(i) relates to security or intelligence, defence or international relations; and

(ii) has been communicated in confidence by or on behalf of the United Kingdom to another state or to an international organisation, has come into a person's possession as a result of having been disclosed (whether to him or another) without the authority of that state or organisation or, in the case of an organisation, of a member of it; and

(b) the disclosure without lawful authority of the information, document or article by the person into whose possession it has come is not an offence under any of the foregoing provisions of this Act.

(2) Subject to subsection (3) below, the person into whose possession the information, document or article has come is guilty of an offence if he makes a damaging disclosure of it knowing, or having reasonable cause to believe, that it is such as is mentioned in subsection (1) above, that it has come into his possession as there mentioned and that its disclosure would be damaging.

(3) A person does not commit an offence under subsection (2) above if the information, document or article is disclosed by him with lawful authority or has previously been made available to the public with the authority of the state or organisation concerned or, in the case of an organisation, of a member of it. . . .

(5) For the purposes of this section information or a document or article is communicated in confidence if it is communicated on terms requiring it to be held in confidence or in circumstances in which the person communicating it could reasonably expect that it would be so held.

Authorised disclosures

7.–(1) For the purposes of this Act a disclosure by—

(a) a Crown servant; or

(b) a person, not being a Crown servant or government contractor in whose case a notification for the purposes of section 1(1) above is in force, is made with lawful authority if, and only if, it is made in accordance with his official duty.

(2) For the purposes of this Act a disclosure by a government contractor is made with lawful authority if, and only if, it is made—

(a) in accordance with an official authorisation; or

(b) for the purposes of the functions by virtue of which he is a government contractor and without contravening an official restriction.

(3) For the purposes of this Act a disclosure made by any other person is made with lawful authority if, and only if, it is made—

(a) to a Crown servant for the purposes of his functions as such; or

(b) in accordance with an official authorisation.

(4) It is a defence for a person charged with an offence under any of the foregoing provisions of this Act to prove that at the time of the alleged offence he believed that

he had lawful authority to make the disclosure in question and had no reasonable cause to believe otherwise.

(5) In this section 'official authorisation' and 'official restriction' mean, subject to subsection (6) below, an authorisation or restriction duly given or imposed by a Crown servant or government contractor or by or on behalf of a prescribed body or a body of a prescribed class.

(6) In relation to section 6 above 'official authorisation' includes an authorisation duly given by or on behalf of the state or organisation concerned or, in the case of an organisation, a member of it.

. . .

Notes

1. *Section 1(1): Information relating to the security services disclosed by members or former members.* Section 1(1) is intended to prevent members or former members of the security services (and any person notified that he or she is subject to the provisions of the subsection) disclosing anything at all relating or appearing to relate to the operation of those services.[16] It is a wide category and is not confined only to work done by members of the security and intelligence services. All persons covered thus come under a lifelong duty to keep silent even though their information might reveal a serious abuse of power by the security services or some operational weakness. There is no need to show that any harm will or may flow from the disclosure, and so all information, however trivial, is covered. In *R v Shayler*, below, it was argued that since s 1(1) and s 4(1) are of an absolute nature, they are incompatible with Article 10 of the Convention, under the Human Rights Act 1998 (HRA), owing to the requirement that interference with expression should be proportionate to the legitimate aim pursued. In other words, it was argued that using s 3 of the HRA in a creative fashion to seek to resolve the incompatibility would be unfruitful, since compatibility could not be achieved. This argument was rejected by the House of Lords (below).

2. *Section 1(3): Information relating to the security services disclosed by Crown servants.* In contrast to s 1(1), s 1(3) is only satisfied if harm results from the disclosure, but taken at its lowest level under s 1(4)(b) it is clear that this test may be very readily satisfied: it is not necessary to show that disclosure of the *actual* document in question would be likely to cause harm, merely that it belongs to a class of documents disclosure of which would be likely to have that effect. Disclosure of a document containing insignificant information and incapable itself of causing the harm described under s 1(4)(a) can therefore be criminalised, suggesting that the importation of a harm test for Crown servants as opposed to members of the security services may not in practice create a very significant distinction between them. However, harm must be likely to flow from disclosure of a specific document where, due to its unique nature, it cannot be said to be one of a class of documents. The fact that there is a test for harm at all under s 1(3), however weak, affirms a distinction of perhaps symbolic importance between two groups of Crown servants because the first step in determining whether a disclosure may be criminalised is taken by reference to the *status* of the person making the disclosure rather than by the nature of the information, suggesting that s 1(1) is aimed at underpinning a culture of secrecy in the security services rather than at ensuring that no damaging disclosure is likely to be made.

3. *Information relating to defence.* The harm test under s 2 is also potentially extremely wide due to its open-textured wording. The first part of this test under s 2(2)(a), which is fairly specific and deals with quite serious harm, may be contrasted with that under (b), which is much wider. Bearing

---

16 Under s 1(2), misinformation falls within the information covered by s 1(1) as it includes 'making any statement which purports to be a disclosure of such information or which is intended to be taken as being such a disclosure'.

s 2(2)(c) in mind, the test, at its lowest level, would be satisfied by showing that a disclosure of information in the category would be likely to endanger the interests of Britain abroad or seriously obstruct them. Again, in many cases it would be difficult for a Crown servant to determine beforehand whether or not a particular disclosure would be criminal.

4. *Section 3(1)(b): Information obtained from a foreign state or international organisation.* The harm test relating to information falling within s 3(1)(b), contained in s 3(3), is somewhat curious; once the information is identified as falling within this category, a fiction is created that harm *may* automatically flow from its disclosure. This implies that there are circumstances in which the only ingredient which the prosecution *must* prove is that the information falls within the category. Given that s 3(3) uses the word 'may', thereby introducing uncertainty into the section, there is greater leeway for imposing a Convention-friendly interpretation on it under s 3 of the HRA. If the word 'may' is interpreted strictly, the circumstances in which it would be unnecessary to show harm would be greatly curtailed. It could then be argued that since harm or its likelihood must be shown, the harm test itself must be interpreted compatibly with Article 10. It would have to be shown that the interference in question answered to a pressing social need (*Sunday Times v UK*).[17] Depending on the circumstances, it could be argued that if, ultimately, the 'interests of the UK abroad' would be benefited by the disclosure, or on balance little affected, no pressing social need to interfere with the expression in question could be shown.

5. *Information obtained by use of intercept and security service warrants.* Section 4(3) covers information obtained by the use of intercept and security service warrants. There is no harm test under this category. It therefore creates a wide exception to the general need to show harm under s 1(3) when a Crown servant who is not a member of the security services makes a disclosure about the work of those services. But although s 4(1) appears to impose an absolute ban on disclosures falling within s 4(3), it is not incompatible with Art 10 under the HRA, according to the House of Lords in *Shayler*, since, as noted above, there are avenues which can be used to allow for disclosures of information falling within the category, in the public interest. This point is pursued below.[18]

6. *Section 5: Information resulting from unauthorised disclosures.* Section 5 does not refer to a new category of information. The section is primarily aimed at journalists who receive information leaked to them by Crown servants, although it could of course cover anybody in that position. Since s 5 is aimed at journalists and potentially represents an interference with their role of informing the public, it requires a very strict interpretation under s 3 of the HRA, in accordance with Art 10, bearing in mind the emphasis placed by Strasbourg on the importance of that role.[19] In contrast to disclosure of information by a Crown servant under one of the six categories, s 5 imports a requirement of *mens rea* under s 5(2). This provision affords some recognition to media freedom; nevertheless the burden of proof on the prosecution would be very easy to discharge if the information fell within ss 1(3), 3(1)(b) or 4(3) due to the nature of the tests for damage included in those sections; it would only be necessary to show that the journalist knew that the information fell within the category in question. Another apparent improvement in terms of media freedom is the decriminalisation of the receiver of information. However, this improvement might be said to be more theoretical than real in that it was perhaps unlikely that the mere receiver would be prosecuted under the 1911 Act, even though that possibility did exist. The fact that journalists were included at all in the net of criminal liability under s 5 has been criticised on the basis that some recognition should be given to the important role of the press in informing the public about

---

17   (1979) 2 EHRR 245.

18   See pp 684–685.

19   See, e.g. *Goodwin v UK* (1996) 22 EHRR 123.

government actions.[20] In arguing for a restrictive interpretation of s 5 under s 3 of the HRA, a comparison could be drawn with the constitutional role of the press recognised in America by the *Pentagon Papers* case:[21] the Supreme Court determined that no restraining order on the press could be made so that the press would remain free to censure the Government. A court could afford recognition to the significance of the journalistic role, as required by Article 10, by placing a strong emphasis on the *mens rea* requirement. Where a journalist appeared to be acting in the public interest in making the disclosure, it would be possible for a court to interpret the *mens rea* requirement as disproved on the basis that it would be impossible to show that the defendant knew or should have known that the disclosure was damaging to the interest in question if on one view (even if mistaken) it could be seen as beneficial to it, and that was the view that the journalist took.

7. *Unauthorised publication abroad of information.* Section 6 covers the unauthorised publication abroad of information which falls into one of the other substantive categories apart from crime and special investigation powers. It covers the disclosure to a UK citizen of information which has been received in confidence from the UK by another state or international organisation. Typically, the section might cover a leak of such information to a foreign journalist who then passed it on to a UK journalist. However, liability will not be incurred if the state or organisation (or a member of the organisation) authorises the disclosure of the information to the public (s 6(3)). Again, since this section is aimed at journalists, a requirement of *mens rea* is imported: it must be shown under s 6(2) that the defendant made 'a damaging disclosure of [the information] knowing or having reasonable cause to believe that it is such as is mentioned in subsection (1) above and that its disclosure would be damaging'. However, it is important to note that under s 6(4), the test for harm under this section is to be determined 'as it would be in relation to a disclosure of the information, document or article in question by a Crown servant in contravention of s 1(3), 2(1) and 3(1) above'. Thus, although it appears that two tests must be satisfied in order to fulfil the *mens rea* requirement, the tests may in fact be conflated as far as s 3(1)(b) is concerned because proof that the defendant knew that the information fell within the relevant category may satisfy the requirement that he or she knew that the disclosure would be damaging. The requirement that *mens rea* be established is not, therefore, as favourable to the defendant as it appears to be because— as noted in respect of s 5—it may be satisfied even where the defendant believes that no damage will result. Once again, aside from this particular instance, this applies in all the categories due to the objective element in the *mens rea* arising from the words 'reasonable cause to believe'.

8. The following decision is not on the 1989 Act but concerns the civil action for breach of confidence. However, it indicates the approach that can be taken under s 5 of the 1989 Act.

Lord Advocate v Scotsman Publications Ltd [1989] 2 All ER 852, at 859, 860, 861

Lord Templeman: My Lords, in this appeal the Lord Advocate, acting on behalf of the Crown, claims to restrain the respondent newspapers and television companies from disclosing certain information contained in a book written by one Cavendish, that information having been obtained by him in the course of his employment with the British security and intelligence services.

Any such restraint is an interference with the right of expression safeguarded by the Convention for the Protection of Human Rights and Fundamental Freedoms, Article 10. . .

---

20   See, e.g. KD Ewing and CA Gearty, *Freedom Under Thatcher* (1990), pp 196–201.

21   *New York Times Co v US* (1971) 403 US 713.

The question. . .is whether the restraint sought to be imposed on the respondents is 'necessary in a democratic society in the interests of national security' [para 2 of Article 10]. Similar questions were considered in *A-G v Guardian Newspapers Ltd (No 2)* [1988] 3 All ER 345, [1988] 3 WLR 776 (the *Spycatcher* case) but at that time Parliament had not provided any answer to the questions posed by the conflict between the freedom of expression and the requirement of national security.

In my opinion it is for Parliament to determine the restraints on freedom of expression which are necessary in a democratic society. The courts of this country should follow any guidance contained in a statute. If that guidance is inconsistent with the requirements of the convention then that will be a matter for the convention authorities and for the UK Government. It will not be a matter for the courts.

The guidance of Parliament has now been provided in the Official Secrets Act 1989. In my opinion the civil jurisdiction of the courts of this country to grant an injunction restraining a breach of confidence at the suit of the Crown should not, in principle, be exercised in a manner different from or more severe than any appropriate restriction which Parliament has imposed in the 1989 Act. . .

In my opinion the respondents fall into the category described by s 5.

The information derived from Cavendish which the respondents may wish to publish and disclose is information embedded in a book of memoirs by Cavendish. Part of that book relates to the period between 1948 and 1953 when Cavendish was a security employee and is protected against disclosure by s 1 of the 1989 Act. The Crown concedes, however, that publication of that information by the respondents will not cause or be likely to cause damage to the work of the security or intelligence services, presumably because the information is inaccurate or unenlightening or insignificant. . . . Nevertheless, the Crown contends that it is entitled to restrain the respondents from publishing this harmless information because the information is contained in the memoirs of a security employee. It is said that the publication of harmless information derived from a former security employee and protected by s 1 against disclosure by him, though not damaging in itself, would cause harm by encouraging other security employees to make disclosures in breach of s 1 of the 1989 Act and by raising doubts as to the reliability of the security service.

. . . If the 1989 Act had been in force when Cavendish circulated his book to a chosen band of readers, he would have committed an offence under s 1 of the Act notwithstanding that the information disclosed in his book is harmless. But it does not follow that third parties commit an offence if they disclose harmless information. Were it otherwise, the distinction between an offence by a security employee and an offence by a third party which appears from the 1989 Act would be eradicated. A security employee can commit an offence if he discloses any information. A third party is only guilty of an offence if the information is damaging in the sense defined by the Act. I would affirm the decision of the Court of Session and dismiss the appeal of the Crown.

Note

The leading decision on the 1989 Act follows. It is a very significant decision since it indicates that ss 1(1) and 4(1) of the 1989 Act are not incompatible with Article 10 scheduled in the Human Rights Act 1998.[22] It is the only decision of the House of Lords on the 1989 Act. The facts and legal background appear in the speech of Lord Bingham.

---

22   For full discussion of the Human Rights Act 1998, see Chapter 17.

R v Shayler [2003] 1 AC 247 (extracts)

Lord Bingham My Lords,

1. Mr David Shayler, the appellant, is a former member of the Security Service. He has been indicted on three counts charging him with unlawful disclosure of documents and information contrary to sections 1 and 4 of the Official Secrets Act 1989. Moses J, exercising a power conferred by section 29(1) of the Criminal Procedure and Investigations Act 1996, ordered that a preparatory hearing be held before him. At that hearing the judge ruled under section 31(3)(b) of that Act that no public interest defence was open to the appellant under those sections, which he held to be compatible with article 10 of the European Convention for the Protection of Human Rights and Fundamental Freedoms. The appellant appealed to the Court of Appeal (Criminal Division) which upheld those rulings. The appellant now challenges these rulings of the judge and the Court of Appeal before the House.

. . .

The facts

5. On 24 August 1997, The Mail on Sunday published an article written by the appellant himself (according to the by-line) and a number of other articles by journalists purporting to be based on information disclosed by the appellant. The prosecution allege that the appellant was paid a substantial sum of money by the newspaper for these activities. The prosecution also allege that the information contained in and referred to in the articles relates to matters of security and intelligence to which the appellant could only have had access by reason of his employment with the service.

In reply to the charge he said: 'I have been living in Paris for three years and I have decided voluntarily to return to Britain to face charges under the Official Secrets Act. . . . Any disclosures made by me were in the public and national interests. In my defence I will rely on my right of freedom of expression as guaranteed by the common law, the Human Rights Act and Article 10 of the European Convention on Human Rights.'

. . .

8. At the preparatory hearing before the judge the first issue was whether, in law, the appellant would be entitled to be acquitted of the charges against him if (as he asserted on his arrest) his disclosures had (or, one should add, might have) been made in the public and national interest.

. . .

20. It is in my opinion plain, giving sections 1(1)(a) and 4(1) and (3)(a) their natural and ordinary meaning and reading them in the context of the OSA 1989 as a whole, that a defendant prosecuted under these sections is not entitled to be acquitted if he shows that it was or that he believed that it was in the public or national interest to make the disclosure in question or if the jury conclude that it may have been or that the defendant may have believed it to be in the public or national interest to make the disclosure in question. The sections impose no obligation on the prosecution to prove that the disclosure was not in the public interest and give the defendant no opportunity to show that the disclosure was in the public interest or that he thought it was. The sections leave no room for doubt and if they did the 1988 white paper quoted above, which is a legitimate aid to construction, makes the intention of Parliament clear beyond argument.

The right to free expression

21. The fundamental right of free expression has been recognised at common law for very many years. . .Modern democratic government means government of the people by the people for the people. But there can be no government by the people if they are ignorant of the issues to be resolved, the arguments for and against different solutions and the facts underlying those arguments. The business of government is not an activity about which only those professionally engaged are entitled to receive information and express opinions. It is, or should be, a participatory process. But there can be no assurance that government is carried out for the people unless the facts are made known, the issues publicly ventilated. Sometimes, inevitably, those involved in the conduct of government, as in any other walk of life, are guilty of error, incompetence, misbehaviour, dereliction of duty, even dishonesty and malpractice. Those concerned may very strongly wish that the facts relating to such matters are not made public. Publicity may reflect discredit on them or their predecessors. It may embarrass the authorities. It may impede the process of administration. Experience however shows, in this country and elsewhere, that publicity is a powerful disinfectant. Where abuses are exposed, they can be remedied. The role of the press in exposing abuses and miscarriages of justice has been a potent and honourable one. But the press cannot expose that of which it is denied knowledge.

22. Despite the high value placed by the common law on freedom of expression, it was not until incorporation of the European Convention into our domestic law by the Human Rights Act 1998 that this fundamental right was underpinned by statute. Section 12 of the 1998 Act reflects the central importance which attaches to the right to freedom of expression. The European Court of Human Rights for its part has not wavered in asserting the fundamental nature of this right. [His Lordship quoted from *Vogt v Germany* (1995) 21 EHRR 205] and went on. . .

23. Despite the high importance attached to it, the right to free expression was never regarded in domestic law as absolute. The European Convention similarly recognises that the right is not absolute: article 10(2) qualifies the broad language of article 10(1) by providing, so far as relevant to this case:

> The exercise of these freedoms, since it carries with it duties and responsibilities, may be subject to such formalities, conditions, restrictions or penalties as are pre-scribed by law and are necessary in a democratic society, in the interests of national security, territorial integrity or public safety, for the prevention of disorder or crime, . . .,for the protection of the. . .rights of others, for preventing the disclosure of infor-mation received in confidence. . .

[His Lordship explained the basic approach to interpreting para 2 (for general discussion of Act 10(2) see Chapter 7, at pp 315–316, 330–332.

24 . . .It was common ground below, in my view, rightly, that the relevant restriction was prescribed by law. It is on the question of necessity, pressing social need and pro-portionality that the real issue between the parties arises.

25. There is much domestic authority pointing to the need for a security or intelligence service to be secure. . .members of the service will feel unable to rely on each other; those upon whom the service relies as sources of information will feel unable to rely on their identity remaining secret; and foreign countries will decline to entrust their own secrets to an insecure recipient see, for example, *Attorney General v Guardian Newspapers Ltd (No 2)* [1990] 1 AC 109, 118C, 213H–214B, 259A, 265F; *Attorney General v Blake* [2001] 1 AC 268, 287D–F. In the *Guardian Newspapers Ltd (No 2)* case, at p 269E–G, Lord Griffiths expressed the accepted rule very pithily:

The Security and Intelligence Services are necessary for our national security. They are, and must remain, secret services if they are to operate efficiently. The only practical way to achieve this objective is a brightline rule that forbids any member or ex-member of the service to publish any material relating to his service experience unless he has had the material cleared by his employers. . . .What may appear to the writer to be trivial may in fact be the one missing piece in the jigsaw sought by some hostile intelligence agency.

The need to preserve the secrecy of information relating to intelligence and military operations in order to counter terrorism, criminal activity, hostile activity and subversion has been recognised by the European Commission and the Court in relation to complaints made under article 10 and other articles under the convention: [his Lordship cited authority]. . .

26. The thrust of these decisions and judgments has not been to discount or disparage the need for strict and enforceable rules but to insist on adequate safeguards to ensure that the restriction does not exceed what is necessary to achieve the end in question. The acid test is whether, in all the circumstances, the interference with the individual's convention right prescribed by national law is greater than is required to meet the legitimate object which the state seeks to achieve. The OSA 1989, as it applies to the appellant, must be considered in that context.

27. The OSA 1989 imposes a ban on disclosure of information or documents relating to security or intelligence by a former member of the service. But it is not an absolute ban. It is a ban on disclosure without lawful authority. It is in effect a ban subject to two conditions. First of all, the former member may, under section 7(3)(a), make disclosure to a Crown servant for the purposes of his functions as such. . . .

(1.) The former member may make disclosure to the staff counsellor, whose appointment was announced in the House of Commons in November 1987 . . .

(2.) If the former member has concerns about the lawfulness of what the service has done or is doing, he may disclose his concerns to (among others) the Attorney General, the Director of Public Prosecutions or the Commissioner of Metropolitan Police.

(3.) If a former member has concerns about misbehaviour, irregularity, maladministration, waste of resources or incompetence in the service he may disclose these to the Home Secretary, the Foreign Secretary, the Secretary of State for Northern Ireland or Scotland, the Prime Minister, the Secretary to the Cabinet or the Joint Intelligence Committee. He may also make disclosure to the secretariat, provided (as the House was told) by the Home Office, of the parliamentary Intelligence and Security Committee. He may further make disclosure, by virtue of article 3 of and Schedule 2 to the Official Secrets Act 1989 (Prescription) Order 1990 (SI 200/1990) to the staff of the Controller and Auditor General, the National Audit Office and the Parliamentary Commissioner for Administration.

28. Since one count of the indictment against the appellant is laid under section 4(1) and (3) of the OSA 1989, considerable attention was directed by the judge and the Court of Appeal to the role of the commissioners appointed under section 8(1) of the Interception of Communications Act 1985, section 4(1) of the Security Service Act 1989 and section 8(1) of the Intelligence Services Act 1994. The appellant submits, correctly, that none of these commissioners is a minister or a civil servant, that their functions defined by the three statutes do not include general oversight of the three security services, and that the secretariat serving the commissioners is, or was, of modest size. But under each of the three Acts, the commissioner was given power to require documents and information to be supplied to him by any crown servant or member of the relevant services for the purposes of his functions (section 8(3) of the 1985 Act, section 4(4) of the 1989 Act, section

8(4) of the 1994 Act), and if it were intimated to the commissioner, in terms so general as to involve no disclosure, that serious abuse of the power to intercept communications or enter premises to obtain information was taking or had taken place, it seems unlikely that the commissioner would not exercise his power to obtain information or at least refer the warning to the Home Secretary or (as the case might be) the Foreign Secretary.

29. One would hope that, if disclosure were made to one or other of the persons listed above, effective action would be taken to ensure that abuses were remedied and offenders punished. But the possibility must exist that such action would not be taken when it should be taken or that, despite the taking of effective action to remedy past abuses and punish past delinquencies, there would remain facts which should in the public interest be revealed to a wider audience. This is where, under the OSA 1989 the second condition comes into play: the former member may seek official authorisation to make disclosure to a wider audience.

30. As already indicated, it is open to a former member of the service to seek authorisation from his former superior or the head of the service, who may no doubt seek authority from the secretary to the cabinet or a minister. . . . If the document or information revealed matters which, however, scandalous or embarrassing, would not damage any security or intelligence interest or impede the effective discharge by the service of its very important public functions, [authorisation] might be appropriate. Consideration of a request for authorisation should never be a routine or mechanical process: it should be undertaken bearing in mind the importance attached to the right of free expression and the need for any restriction to be necessary, responsive to a pressing social need and proportionate.

31. One would, again, hope that requests for authorisation to disclose would be granted where no adequate justification existed for denying it and that authorisation would be refused only where such justification existed. But the possibility would of course exist that authority might be refused where no adequate justification existed for refusal, or at any rate where the former member firmly believed that no adequate justification existed. In this situation the former member is entitled to seek judicial review of the decision to refuse, a course which the OSA 1989 does not seek to inhibit. In considering an application for judicial review of a decision to refuse authorisation to disclose, the court must apply the same tests as are described in the last paragraph. It also will bear in mind the importance attached to the convention right of free expression. It also will bear in mind the need for any restriction to be necessary to achieve one or more of the ends specified in article 10(2), to be responsive to a pressing social need and to be no more restrictive than is necessary to achieve that end.

32. For the appellant it was argued that judicial review offered a person in his position no effective protection, since courts were reluctant to intervene in matters concerning national security and the threshold of showing a decision to be irrational was so high as to give the applicant little chance of crossing it. Reliance was placed on the cases of *Chahal v United Kingdom* (1996) 23 EHRR 413 and *Tinnelly & Sons Ltd v United Kingdom* (1998) 27 EHRR 249, in each of which the European Court was critical of he effectiveness of the judicial review carried out.

33. There are in my opinion two answers to this submission. First the court's willingness to intervene will very much depend on the nature of the material which it is sought to disclose. If the issue concerns the disclosure of documents bearing a high security classification and there is apparently credible unchallenged evidence that disclosure is liable to lead to the identification of agents or the compromise of informers, the court may very well be unwilling to intervene. If, at the other end of the spectrum, it appears that while

disclosure of the material may cause embarrassment or arouse criticism, it will not damage any security or intelligence interest, the court's reaction is likely to be very different. Usually, a proposed disclosure will fall between these two extremes and the court must exercise its judgment, informed by article 10 considerations. The second answer is that in any application for judicial review alleging an alleged violation of a convention right the court will now conduct a much more rigorous and intrusive review than was once thought to be permissible. . . [His Lordship quoted from *Daly* to illustrate this (see Chapter 17 at 000–00) and went on]

This approach contrasts sharply with that adopted in the authorities on which the appellant based his submission. In *Chahal*, on applications for both habeas corpus and judicial review, there was no effective judicial enquiry into the legality of the applicant's detention, and this was of even greater importance where the applicant faced the risk of torture or inhuman or degrading treatment: (1996) 23 EHRR 413, paras 132, 150–151. In *Tinnelly* the issue of conclusive certificates had effectively prevented any judicial determination of the merits of the applicants' complaints: (1998) 27 EHRR 249, para 77.

34. The appellant contended that even if, theoretically, judicial review offered a means of challenging an allegedly wrongful refusal of authorisation to disclose, it was in practice an unavailable means since private lawyers were not among those to whom disclosure could lawfully be made under section 7(3)(a), and a former member of the service could not be expected to initiate proceedings for judicial review without the benefit of legal advice and assistance. I would for my part accept that the fair hearing guaranteed by article 6(1) of the convention to everyone in the determination of their civil rights and obligations must ordinarily carry with it the right to seek legal advice and assistance from a lawyer outside the government service. But this is a matter to be resolved by seeking official authorisation under section 7(3)(b). The service would at that stage, depending on the nature of the material sought to be disclosed, be fully entitled to limit its authorisation to material in a redacted or anonymised or schematic form, to be specified by the service; but I cannot envisage circumstances in which it would be proper for the service to refuse its authorisation for any disclosure at all to a qualified lawyer from whom the former member wished to seek advice. If, at the hearing of an application for judicial review, it were necessary for the court to examine material said to be too sensitive to be disclosed to the former member's legal advisers, special arrangements could be made for the appointment of counsel to represent the applicant's interests as envisaged by the Court of Appeal in *Secretary of State for the Home Department v Rehman* [2000] 3 WLR 1240, 1250–1251, paras 31–32.

. . .

36. The special position of those employed in the security and intelligence services, and the special nature of the work they carry out, impose duties and responsibilities on them within the meaning of article 10(2): *Engel v The Netherlands (No 1)* (1976) 1 EHRR 647, para 100; *Hadjianastassiou v Greece* (1992) 16 EHRR 219, para 46. These justify what Lord Griffiths called a bright line rule against disclosure of information of documents relating to security or intelligence obtained in the course of their duties by members or former members of those services. (While Lord Griffiths was willing to accept the theoretical possibility of a public interest defence, he made no allowance for judicial review: *Attorney General v Guardian Newspapers Ltd (No 2)* [1990] 1 AC 109, 269G.) If, within this limited category of case, a defendant is prosecuted for making an unauthorised disclosure it is necessary to relieve the prosecutor of the need to prove damage (beyond the damage inherent in disclosure by a former member of these services) and to deny the defendant a

defence based on the public interest; otherwise the detailed facts concerning the disclosure and the arguments for and against making it would be canvassed before the court and the cure would be even worse than the disease. But it is plain that a sweeping, blanket ban, permitting of no exceptions, would be inconsistent with the general right guaranteed by article 10(1) and would not survive the rigorous and particular scrutiny required to give effect to article 10(2). The crux of this case is whether the safeguards built into the OSA 1989 are sufficient to ensure that unlawfulness and irregularity can be reported to those with the power and duty to take effective action, that the power to withhold authorisation to publish is not abused and that proper disclosures are not stifled. In my opinion the procedures discussed above, properly applied, provide sufficient and effective safeguards. It is, however, necessary that a member or former member of a relevant service should avail himself of the procedures available to him under the Act. A former member of a relevant service, prosecuted for making an unauthorised disclosure, cannot defend himself by contending that if he had made disclosure under section 7(3)(a) no notice or action would have been taken or that if he had sought authorisation under section 7(3)(b) it would have been refused. If a person who has given a binding undertaking of confidentiality seeks to be relieved, even in part, from that undertaking he must seek authorisation and, if so advised, challenge any refusal of authorisation. If that refusal is upheld by the courts, it must, however reluctantly, be accepted. I am satisfied that sections 1(1) and 4(1) and (3) of the OSA 1989 are compatible with article 10 of the convention; no question of reading those sections conformably with the convention or making a declaration of incompatibility therefore arises. On these crucial issues I am in agreement with both the judge and the Court of Appeal. They are issues on which the House can form its own opinion. But they are also issues on which Parliament has expressed a clear democratic judgment.

. . .

38. I would dismiss the appeal.

Lord Hope, Lord Hutton, Lord Hobhouse of Wood-Borough and Lord Scott of Foscote agreed that the appeal should be dismissed.

Notes

1. The 1989 Act contains no explicit public interest defence and it follows from the nature of the harm tests that one cannot be implied into it; on the face of it, any good flowing from disclosure of the information in question cannot be considered, merely any harm that might be caused. The information may concern corruption at such a high level that internal methods of addressing the problem would be ineffective. However, s 3 of the HRA could be used creatively to seek to introduce such a defence—in effect— through the back door, by relying on Art 10. Whether or not this is possible in respect of categories of information covered by a harm test, it appears that it is not possible in respect of s 1(1) and s 4(1) following the decision in *Shaylor* (above).

2. The Lord's decision in *Shaylor* means that s 3 HRA need not be used in relation to s 1(1) and s 4(1). It is probable that the same arguments would apply if, in respect of disclosure of information falling within other categories, the defence sought to introduce a public interest defence, relying on Article 10. It can be concluded therefore that there is now very little prospect of relying on s 3 of the HRA to imply some form of public interest test into the Act.

3. The problem with the House of Lords' analysis in *Shaylor* is that the avenues available to members or former members of the security services to make disclosures are unlikely to be used. It seems, to say the least, highly improbable that such a member would risk the employment detriment that might be likely to arise, especially if he or she then proceeded to seek judicial review of the decision.

One of the most important principles recognised at Strasbourg is that rights must be real, not tokenistic or illusory. It is argued that the right to freedom of expression—one of the central rights of the Convention—is rendered illusory by ss 1(1) and 4(1) of the 1989 Act in relation to allegedly unlawful activities of the security services—a matter of great significance in a democracy.

4. *Whistle-blowing.* As mentioned above, a civil servant in the UK who believes that disclosure as to a certain state of affairs is necessary in order to serve the public interest does not have the protection available to his or her counterpart in the US where he or she is protected from detrimental action flowing from whistleblowing[23] under the Civil Service Reform Act 1978. However, the Civil Service Code, which came into force on 1 January 1996 and was revised in 1999, contains a partial 'whistle-blowing' provision in paras 11 and 12 (see Hansard, HL Deb (9 January 1996)). The duty of civil servants remains not to disclose any information to which they have acquired access as civil servants, without authorisation (para 10 of the Code). However, paras 11 and 12 provide that if a civil servant believes that he or she is being asked to act in a way which *inter alia* is improper, unethical or which raises fundamental issues of conscience, he or she should report the matter in accordance with departmental guidance (para 11). If the matter has been reported in this manner and the civil servant does not believe that a response is a reasonable response, he or she should report the matter to the Civil Service Commissioners (para 12). Where the matter cannot be resolved by resort to these procedures the civil servant should either resign or carry out his or her instructions (para 13 of the Code).[24] This is therefore a very limited provision since it only allows ultimate disclosure of information to the Civil Service Commissioners. No protection is offered in the Code if the disclosure is to an Opposition MP, as in *Ponting*.

5. *A defence of prior publication?* No express defence of prior publication is provided by the 1989 Act; the only means of putting forward such a defence would arise in one of the categories in which it was necessary to prove the likelihood that harm would flow from the disclosure; the prosecution might find it hard to establish such a likelihood where there had been a great deal of prior publication because no further harm could be caused. Prior publication would be irrelevant under s 1(1). Thus, where a member of the security services disclosed information falling within s 1 which had been published all over the world and in the UK, a conviction could still be obtained. If such publication had occurred but the information fell within s 1(3), the test for harm might be satisfied on the basis that, although no further harm could be caused by disclosure of the *particular document,* it nevertheless belonged to a class of documents disclosure of which was likely to cause harm. Where harm flowing from publication of a specific document is relied on, *Lord Advocate v Scotsman Publications Ltd* (above) suggests that a degree of prior publication may tend to defeat the argument that further publication can still cause harm. However, this suggestion must be treated with care as the ruling was not given under the 1989 Act and the link between the Act and the civil law of confidence may not form part of its ratio.[25]

6. *Circumventing the Act?* In 2008 the Conservative MP Damian Green was arrested on suspicion of conspiracy to commit misconduct in public office, under an obscure and little-used provision, after the leaking to him by a civil servant of information that was embarrassing to the Government, but which did not fall within any of the categories covered by the 1989 Act.[26] The police questioned him on the basis that he had not merely received 'leaked' information but had 'groomed' a civil

---

23   For discussion of the situation of UK and US civil servants and developments in the area, see Cripps, n 3 above; Zellick, n 3 above.

24   See further *Hansard,* HL Deb (29 November 1995).

25   Only Lord Templeman clearly adverted to such a link.

26   See *The Times,* 28 November 2008; the *Guardian,* 28 November 2008.

servant to pass it to him. This incident raised the possibility that the benefits of criminalising only the leaking or receipt of information within those categories might be undermined; a return to the catch-all coverage of the old s2 appeared to be possible if punishment was available in respect of receipt of leaked information merely embarrassing to the Government. In the event the Crown Prosecution Service (CPS) decided that Damian Green would not face charges relating to the information leaks from the Home Office.[27] There is no precedent for the arrest of an MP and a search of his office by police in relation to a leak inquiry. The incident raised concerns that the police were being used to silence critics of the Government and to prevent disclosure of material embarrassing to the Government, but not harmful to the public interest as reflected in the categories under the 1989 Act.

Questions

❶   How far, if at all, has the 1989 Act afforded any recognition to the important constitutional role of the journalist?

❷   As things stand, a journalist who repeated allegations made by a member of the security services as to corruption or treachery in MI5 could be convicted if it could be shown, first, that he or she knew that the information related to the security services and, second, that disclosure of that type of information would be likely to cause damage to the work of the security services, regardless of whether the particular allegations would cause such damage. What would be the position under the Act, taking into account the impact of the HRA, of a journalist who repeated allegations made by a future Cathy Massiter after they had been published in other countries?

FREEDOM OF INFORMATION[28]

Almost all democracies have introduced freedom of information legislation[29] within the last 30–45 years. For example, Canada introduced its Access to Information Act in 1982 while America has had such legislation since 1967. The UK now has the Freedom of Information Act 2000 (FoI Act) which came into force in 2005. Certain developments suggest that even prior to the introduction of the FoI Act 2000 a gradual movement towards more open Government was taking place in the UK. The Data Protection Act 1984, followed by the 1998 Act, allowed access to personal information held on computerised files. The Campaign for Freedom of Information had, from 1985 onwards, brought about acceptance of the principle of access rights in some areas including local government. Disclosure of a range of information was, as discussed above, decriminalised under the Official Secrets Act 1989.

---

27   See, e.g. the *Guardian*, 16 April 2009.

28   See generally: H Fenwick, *Civil Liberties and Human Rights*, 4th edn (2007), Chapter 7; SH Bailey, N Taylor, *Bailey, Harris and Jones: Civil Liberties: Cases and Materials*, 6th edn (2009), Chapter 12; D Feldman, *Civil Liberties and Human Rights in England and Wales*, 2nd edn (2002), Chapter 15; P Birkinshaw, *Freedom of Information: The Law, the Practice and the Ideal*, 3rd edn (2001); J Beatson, and Y Cripps, *Freedom of Expression and Freedom of Information* (2000).

29   See LJ Curtis, 'Freedom of Information in Australia' (1983) 14 Fed LR 5; HN Janisch, 'The Canadian Access to Information Act' [1982] PL 534. For the US, see M Supperstone, *Brownlie's Law of Public Order and National Security* (1982), pp 270–87; P Birkinshaw, *Freedom of Information: The Law, the Practice and the Ideal*, 2nd edn (1996), Chapter 2.

A White Paper on Open Government (Cm 2290) was published in July 1993. In this section we will look briefly at the US freedom of information legislation and will go on to consider the current arrangements for affording access to information held by public authorities, including government departments, in the UK. Prior to the coming into force of the FoI Act in 2005, such access largely depended on a Code of Practice, the Code of Practice on Access to Government Information, which was policed by the Ombudsman (the Parliamentary Commissioner for Administration—PCA).[30] The Code provisions will be considered briefly in order to provide a context for the consideration of the arrangements in place under the Freedom of Information Act 2000, which will follow. Finally the section will consider examples of the operation of the FoI Act in practice over the last five years.

Freedom of information in the US

Freedom of Information Act 1967 (US)

5 US Code §552

§ 552.(a) Each agency shall make available to the public information as follows:

(1) Each agency shall separately state and currently publish in the Federal Register for the guidance of the public—

   (A) descriptions of its central and field organisation and the established places at which, the employees (and in the case of a uniformed service, the members) from whom, and the methods whereby, the public may obtain information, make submittals or requests, or obtain decisions;
   (B) statements of the general course and method by which its functions are chan-nelled and determined, including the nature and requirements of all formal and informal procedures available;
   (C) rules of procedure, descriptions of forms available or the places at which forms may be obtained, and instructions as to the scope and contents of all papers, reports, or examinations;
   (D) substantive rules of general applicability adopted as authorised by law, and statements of general policy or interpretations of general applicability formu-lated and adopted by the agency; and
   (E) each amendment, revision, or repeal of the foregoing.

(3) Except with respect to the records made available under paragraphs (1) and (2) of this subsection, each agency, on request for identifiable records made in accord-ance with published rules stating the time, place, fees to the extent authorised by statute, and procedure to be followed, shall make the records promptly available to any person. On complaint, the district court of the United States in the district in which the complainant resides, or has his principal place of business, or in which the agency records are situated, has jurisdiction to enjoin the agency from withholding agency records and to order the production of any agency records improperly with-held from the complainant. In such a case the court shall determine the matter de

---

novo and the burden is on the agency to sustain its action. In the event of non-compliance with the order of the court, the district court may punish for contempt the responsible employee, and in the case of a uniformed service, the responsible member.

(4)(b) This section does not apply to matters that are—

(1) specifically required by executive order to be kept secret in the interest of the national defence or foreign policy;

(2) related solely to the internal personnel rules and practices of an agency;

(3) specifically exempted from disclosure by statute;

(4) trade secrets and commercial or financial information obtained from a person and privileged or confidential;

(5) inter-agency or intra-agency memorandums or letters which would not be available by law to a party other than an agency in litigation with the agency;

(6) personnel and medical files and similar files the disclosure of which would constitute a clearly unwarranted invasion of personal privacy;

(7) investigatory files compiled for law enforcement purposes except to the extent available by law to a party other than an agency.

**P Birkinshaw, *Freedom of Information:
The Law, the Practice and the Ideal,* 1st edn (1988), pp 36–8**

Freedom of information—overseas experience
The USA has possessed a Freedom of Information Act (FOIA) since 1966. All agencies in the executive branch of the federal government, including administrative regulatory agencies, are subject to FOIA. Excluded from the operation of the Act are the judicial and legislative branches of government. State government and local and city government are not included in this legislation. The aim of the Act, as amended in 1974, is to provide public access to an agency's records if it is covered by the Act. An applicant does not have to demonstrate a specific interest in a matter to view relevant documents—an idle curiosity suffices. Although the basic thrust of the Act is positive and supportive of openness, there are nine exemptions from the FOIA. Mandatory secrecy requirements rather than permissive ones have become more common, the 'balancing test' requiring the weighing of public access against the government need for secrecy has been eliminated, and systematic declassification has been cancelled. The order allows for its own mandatory 'review requests' of classified information as an alternative to FOIA actions. Internal rules and practices of an agency will be exempt but not the manuals and instructions on the interpretation of regulations. Other important exemptions include: trade secrets; commercial and financial information obtained by the Government that is privileged or confidential; inter- or intra-agency memoranda or letters which are not available by law, information protected by other statutes; personnel or medical files disclosure of which would constitute an invasion of privacy; and investigatory records compiled for law enforcement purposes if disclosure would result in certain types of harm.

Freedom of information in the UK prior to the Freedom of Information Act

Public Records Act 1958, as amended by the Public Records Act 1967

5.—(1) Public records in the Public Record Office, other than those to which members of the public had access before their transfer to the Public Record Office, shall not be available for public inspection until they have been in existence for 30 years . . . or such other period, either longer or shorter, as the Lord Chancellor may, with the approval, or at the request, of the Minister or other person, if any, who appears to him to be primarily concerned, for the time being prescribe as respects any particular class of public records.

Geoffrey Robertson has suggested that information is withheld under the 1958 Act to prevent embarrassment to bodies such as the police or civil servants rather than to descendants of persons mentioned in it; and in support of this he cites examples such as police reports on NCCL (1935–41), flogging of vagrants (1919), decisions against prosecuting James Joyce's *Ulysses* (1924) as instances of material which in January 1989 was listed as closed for a century.[31]

In 1992–93, a review was conducted of methods of ensuring further openness in government and its results were published in a White Paper on Open Government (Cm 2290). The White Paper stated that a Code of Practice on Access to Information would be adopted (the Code is compared below to the FoI Act) and there would be a reduction in the number of public records withheld from release beyond 30 years. A review group established by Lord Mackay in 1992 suggested that records should only be closed for more than 30 years where their disclosure would: cause harm to defence; national security, international relations and economic interests of the UK; information supplied in confidence; personal information which would cause substantial distress if disclosed. Under s 3(4) of the 1958 Act records may still be retained within departments for 'administrative' reasons or for any other special reason.[32]

The Freedom of Information Act (FoI Act) 2000 (see below), Part VI and Sched 8 amended the 1958 Act. Part VI amends the exemptions of Part II of the 1958 Act in respect of historical records, with a view to enhancing the ease of access to them. The Constitutional Reform and Governance Act 2010 Sched 7 amended s 62 FoI Act so that a record becomes a 'historical record' 20 years after its creation, not 30. Section 63(1) of the FoI Act reduces the number of exemptions that apply to such records. This is done in three tranches. First, exemptions are removed after 30 years in respect of a number of categories of information, including information prejudicial to the economic interests of the UK, information obtained with a view to prosecution, court records, information prejudicial to public affairs and commercial interests. Second, one exemption is removed after 60 years—in respect of information concerning the conferring of honours. Third, a large number of exemptions under s 31 relating to various investigations and the maintenance of law and order are removed after 100 years. These modest provisions are to be welcomed, as easing the task of historians, but their limited nature should be questioned; it must be asked why any absolute exemptions, in particular those relating to intelligence information, remain.[33]

---

31   See *Media Law* (1990), p 338.

32   The White Paper proposals in relation to public records are considered by Birkinshaw, "I only ask for information'—the White Paper on Open Government' [1993] PL 557.

33   *Cf* the provision in respect of intelligence information held in the Public Record Office of Northern Ireland, which is no longer be subject to an absolute exemption, under the FoI Act, s 64(2).

A Code of Practice on Access to Government Information was introduced from April 1994 as promised in the White Paper on Open Government. It was revised in 1997 but has now been superseded by the 2000 Act.

THE FREEDOM OF INFORMATION ACT 2000

Introduction

The criminalisation of the disclosure of official information under the Official Secrets Acts discussed above may be contrasted with the position in other democracies which have introduced freedom of information legislation within the last 45 years. Canada introduced its Access to Information Act in 1982, while, as indicated above, the US has had such legislation since 1967.

With the example set by other democracies in mind, commentators argued for a number of years that the voluntary Code should be replaced by a broad statutory right of access to information, enforceable by another independent body or through the courts.[34] In particular, many commentators considered that one of the messages of the Scott report, published in February 1996, was that the UK needed an FoI Act, although it is impossible to know whether freedom of information could have prevented the Matrix Churchill affair which concerned a secret change of policy in relation to selling arms to Iraq.[35] The report tellingly revealed the lack of 'openness' in government: the system appeared to accept unquestioningly the need to tell Parliament and the public as little as possible about subjects which were seen as politically sensitive. It was apparent that the voluntary Code could not provide a sufficient response to the concerns which the report aroused. The Matrix Churchill affair, which led to the Scott Inquiry, would not, it seems, have come to the attention of the public but for the refusal of the judge in the *Matrix Churchill* trial to accept that the information covered by the Public interest immunity (PII) certificates,[36] relating to the change in the policy of selling arms to Iraq, could not be revealed. As the Select Committee on the PCA pointed out in its second report, an FoI Act would tend to change the culture of secrecy in government departments.

For the reasons given above, the general consensus was that merely placing the Code on a statutory basis was not a satisfactory course of action. The Conservative Governments of 1979–97 had no plans to enact freedom of information legislation. The Select Committee on the PCA recommended the introduction of an FoI Act (para 126), but this proposal was rejected by the then Conservative Government.[37] The Labour Government which came into office in 1997 had made a manifesto commitment to introduce an FoI Act. The White Paper, *Your Right to Know* (Cm 3818) was published on 11 December 1997. The White Paper stated: 'Unnecessary secrecy in government leads to arrogance in governance and defective decision-making. . .the climate of public opinion has changed: people expect much greater openness and accountability from government than they used to.' The FoI Act 2000, which received royal assent on 30 November 2000 and came into force in 2005, is one of the Labour Government's major measures of constitutional reform.[38] As will be indicated below, the White Paper

---

34 See Birkinshaw (2001), n 28 above; A Tomkins, *The Constitution Unwrapped: Government after Scott* (1998), Chapter 3, pp 124–26.

35 See P Birkinshaw, 'Freedom of Information' (1997) 50 Parlt Aff 166; Tomkins, *ibid,* Chapter 3, pp 123–26.

36 Certificates imposing a ban on revealing information in a trial.

37 HC 75, HC 67 (1996–97).

38 The best source of detailed critical analysis of the Bill may be found on the website of the Campaign for Freedom of Information (www.cfoi.org.uk), which contains numerous briefing notes and press releases. Those prepared for the House of Lords' Committee, Report and Third Reading stages are extremely useful, provided they are read alongside the Act itself. The following analysis has relied partly on those notes.

proposed a freedom of information regime that would have had a radical impact.[39] Had it been implemented, not only would it have brought the UK into line with other democracies as regards its freedom of information provision, but also in a number of respects the legislation would have been more bold and radical than that in place in other countries. When the Bill appeared, it was viewed as a grave disappointment,[40] but a number of improvements were made to it during the parliamentary process. The Act that has emerged cannot be termed radical, but it shows an adherence to the principle of openness which was absent in the Bill. The FoI Act 2000 gives citizens, for the first time, a statutory right to official information, which extends to all such information except that which the Act defines as exempt. The Act does not extend to Scotland, with the exception of a few cross-border bodies. The Scottish Parliament passed its own freedom of information legislation in 2002 which was viewed as more liberal than the FoI Act.

In interpreting the FoI Act, s 3 of the Human Rights Act has a role. As mentioned in Chapter 7, Art 10 includes an additional guarantee of the freedom to receive and impart information. However the right appeared to be restricted in situations where there was no willing speaker. Article 10 was not, therefore, viewed as a full freedom of information measure.[41] However, in a recent decision[42] the European Court of Human Rights recognised for the first time that Art 10 does provide a right to receive information from an unwilling Government in certain circumstances; the right is not of course absolute since it is subject to the para 2 exceptions. Thus, s 3 of the HRA and Art 10 could be relied upon to seek to persuade a court that the exceptions under the FoI Act should receive a narrow interpretation. Further, all the public authorities recognised by s 6 of the HRA (which would normally also be public authorities for FoI purposes) are bound by Art 10, which, taking account of this new departure of the Strasbourg Court, is now a significant factor.

Basic rights under the Act and its scope

Freedom of Information Act 2000

PART I

ACCESS TO INFORMATION HELD BY PUBLIC AUTHORITIES

General right of access to information held by public authorities.
1.–(1) Any person making a request for information to a public authority is entitled—

    (a) to be informed in writing by the public authority whether it holds information of the description specified in the request, and

    (b) if that is the case, to have that information communicated to him.

  (2) Subsection (1) has effect subject to the following provisions of this section and to the provisions of sections 2, 9, 12 and 14.

  . . .

  (6) In this Act, the duty of a public authority to comply with subsection (1)(a) is referred to as 'the duty to confirm or deny'.

---

39   See P Birkinshaw, 'An "All Singin' and All Dancin' Affair": New Labour's Proposals for Freedom of Information' [1998] PL 176.

40   See P Birkinshaw and N Parry, 'Every Trick in the Book: The Freedom of Information Bill 1999' (1999) 4 EHRLR 373.

41   This was supported in the *Gaskin* case (1990) 12 EHRR 36. See Chapter 7, p 329.

42   *Matky v Czech Republic* 5th section 19101/03 (Unreported, 10 July 2006); see also the decision of the Human Rights Committee in *Gauthier v Canada* Communication no 633/195, UN doc CCPR/C/65/D/633/1995 (1999) .

Effect of the exemptions in Part II.

2.–(1) Where any provision of Part II states that the duty to confirm or deny does not arise in relation to any information, the effect of the provision is that where either—

    (a)   the provision confers absolute exemption, or

    (b)   in all the circumstances of the case, the public interest in maintaining the exclusion of the duty to confirm or deny outweighs the public interest in disclosing whether the public authority holds the information, section 1(1)(a) does not apply.

  (2)   In respect of any information which is exempt information by virtue of any provision of Part II, section 1(1)(b) does not apply if or to the extent that—

    (a)   the information is exempt information by virtue of a provision conferring absolute exemption, or

    (b)   in all the circumstances of the case, the public interest in maintaining the exemption outweighs the public interest in disclosing the information.

  (3)   For the purposes of this section, the following provisions of Part II (and no others) are to be regarded as conferring absolute exemption—

    (a)   section 21,

    (b)   section 23,

    (c)   section 32,

    (d)   section 34,

    (e)   section 36 so far as relating to information held by the House of Commons or the House of Lords,

    (f)   in section 40—

        (i)   subsection (1), and

        (ii)   subsection (2) so far as relating to cases where the first condition referred to in that subsection is satisfied by virtue of subsection (3)(a)(i) or (b) of that section,

    (g)   section 41, and

    (h)   section 44.

Public authorities.

3.–(1) In this Act 'public authority' means—

    (a)   subject to section 4(4), any body which, any other person who, or the holder of any office which—

        (i)   is listed in Schedule 1, or

        (ii)   is designated by order under section 5, or

    (b)   a publicly-owned company as defined by section 6. . . .

Fees.

9.–(1) A public authority to whom a request for information is made may, within the period for complying with section 1(1), give the applicant a notice in writing (in this Act referred to as a 'fees notice') stating that a fee of an amount specified in the notice is to be charged by the authority for complying with section 1(1).

. . .

(3) Subject to subsection (5), any fee under this section must be determined by the public authority in accordance with regulations made by the Secretary of State.

Time for compliance with request.

10.–(1) . . .a public authority must comply with s 1(1) . . .not later than the 20th working day following the date of receipt . . .

Exemption where cost of compliance exceeds appropriate limit.

12.–(1) Section 1(1) does not oblige a public authority to comply with a request for information if the authority estimates that the cost of complying with the request would exceed the appropriate limit.

(2) Subsection (1) does not exempt the public authority from its obligation to comply with paragraph (a) of section 1(1) unless the estimated cost of complying with that paragraph alone would exceed the appropriate limit.

. . .

Vexatious or repeated requests.

14.–(1) Section 1(1) does not oblige a public authority to comply with a request for information if the request is vexatious.

(2) Where a public authority has previously complied with a request for information which was made by any person, it is not obliged to comply with a subsequent identical or substantially similar request from that person unless a reasonable interval has elapsed between compliance with the previous request and the making of the current request. . . .

The Information Commissioner and the Information Tribunal.

18.–(1) The Data Protection Commissioner shall be known instead as the Information Commissioner.

(2) The Data Protection Tribunal shall be known instead as the Information Tribunal.

Publication schemes.

19.–(1) It shall be the duty of every public authority—

(a)   to adopt and maintain a scheme which relates to the publication of information by the authority and is approved by the Commissioner. . .

Notes

1. *The scope of the Act.* The Act covers 'public authorities'. Section 3 sets out the various ways in which a body can be a public authority. Instead of using the method adopted in the HRA, which, similarly, covers only 'public authorities' and which defines them by means of a very broad and general, non-exhaustive definition,[43] the FoI Act takes the different route of listing a number of public authorities in Sched 1. The list is divided into two halves. First, Parts I–V list those bodies that are

---

43   See Chap 17, pp 976–989.

clearly public authorities; under s 6 of the HRA they would be standard public authorities. Second, Parts VI–VII list those bodies that are only public authorities so long as they continue to meet the conditions set out in s 4(2) and (3)—that they have been set up by Government and their members appointed by central government. Such bodies would probably also be viewed as standard public authorities under the HRA. But the list is not exhaustive, since s 4(1) gives the Secretary of State the power to add bodies to the list in Parts VI–VII if they meet the conditions set out in s 4(2) and (3), by Order. Under s 3(1)(b), a publicly owned company as defined in s 6 is automatically a public body; no formal designation is needed. Section 6 defines such bodies as those wholly owned by the Crown or any public authority listed in Sched 1, other than government departments. Some public authorities are covered only in respect of certain information they hold, in which case the Act only applies to that class of information (s 7(1)). Rather disturbingly, under s 7(3), the Secretary of State can amend Sched 1 so that a particular public authority becomes one which is subject only to such limited coverage by the Act—in effect potentially drastically limiting the range of information which can be sought from that authority.

2. *Public authorities covered.* The Act covers, in Sched 1, all government departments, the House of Commons, the House of Lords, quangos, the NHS, administrative functions of courts and tribunals, police authorities and chief officers of police, the armed forces, local authorities, local public bodies, schools and other public educational institutions, public service broadcasters. Under s 5, private organisations may be designated as public authorities in so far as they carry out statutory functions, as may the privatised utilities and private bodies working on contracted-out functions. The coverage of the Act is therefore far greater than that under the previous Code, and it is notable that some private sector bodies are covered, although it should be noted that the Government made it clear in debate on the Bill that the distinction between private and public bodies in terms of their obligations under the FoI Act should be strictly maintained and that s 5 should be used only to designate bodies discharging public functions.[44] The FoI Act is clearly *not* to be extended into the realm of business. The Act has been praised for the very wide range of bodies which it covers; in comparison with freedom of information regimes abroad, the coverage is very generous. But it should be noted that, in fact, its coverage of private bodies discharging public functions is subject to the exercise of a discretion by the Secretary of State.

The following decision mainly concerned the question of 'hybrid authorities' under the Act.

Sugar v British Broadcasting Corporation and another [2009] UKHL 9, on appeal from [2008] EWCA Civ 191 (extracts)

Lord Phillips of Worth Matravers
1 The Freedom of Information Act 2000 ('the Act') provides for a general right of access to information held by public authorities . . . Schedule 1 to the Act lists the public authorities to which the Act applies. A small number of these are listed in respect only of certain specified information. One of these is the first respondent ('the BBC'), which is listed as 'The British Broadcasting Corporation in respect of information held for purposes other than those of journalism, art or literature'.
2 The BBC holds a report that it commissioned in respect of its coverage of the Middle East ('the Balen Report'). The appellant, Mr Sugar asked the BBC to provide him with a copy of this report. He contended that the report was held by the BBC for purposes other than journalism, art or literature and that, in consequence, the BBC held it as a

public authority and was bound by the Act to communicate its contents to him. The BBC disagreed. It contended that it held the report for the purposes of journalism and not as a public authority and that, in consequence, the Act had no application. I shall call the issue of whether or not the BBC held the report for journalistic purposes 'the journalism issue'. Mr Sugar challenged the BBC's response before the Commissioner. The Commissioner upheld the BBC's contention. Mr Sugar appealed to the Tribunal. The BBC and the Commissioner argued that the Tribunal had no jurisdiction. The Tribunal held that it had jurisdiction and purported to exercise this by reversing the Commissioner's decision on the journalism issue. The BBC then brought, simultaneously, an appeal under the provisions of the Act and a claim for judicial review. The claim succeeded [2007] EWHC 905 (Admin); [2007] 1 WLR 2583 . . . The Tribunal had acted without jurisdiction and its decision could not stand. I shall describe the issue of whether the Tribunal had jurisdiction as 'the jurisdiction issue'.

3 Mr Sugar had anticipated the possibility of this result by making a cross-application for judicial review, challenging the Commissioner's decision on the journalism issue. This challenge failed. Davis J upheld the Commissioner's finding that, for the purposes of Mr Sugar's application to it, the BCC was not a public authority. He held that the Commissioner had rightly held that he had no jurisdiction. He added that he would not have granted relief in any event, for further material events had occurred since the date of the Commissioner's decision.

4 Mr Sugar appealed to the Court of Appeal on the jurisdiction issue alone. His appeal failed. In the leading judgment Buxton LJ upheld Davis J's decision that neither the Commissioner nor the Tribunal had had any jurisdiction to entertain Mr Sugar's challenges— [2008] EWCA Civ 191; [2008] 1 WLR 2289.

. . . The broad issue is whether the Commissioner was correct, on his view of the merits of the journalism issue, to conclude that he had no jurisdiction under the Act. That is an issue of general importance. . . .

25 The seminal question is whether Mr Sugar made a request for information to a public authority under section 1 of the Act.

26 When a request for information is specifically made under the Act to a hybrid authority it is axiomatic that the maker of the request is making it to the hybrid authority in its capacity as a public authority. That is because the obligations under the Act only apply to public authorities. So far as Mr Sugar was concerned, the terms of his letter of request made it quite clear that he was asserting that the BBC owed him a duty to provide the Balen Report in its capacity as a holder of public documents. He was well aware that the BBC would be under no duty to provide him with the information if it did not hold it as a public document and thus in its capacity as a public authority.

27 It follows that, on the facts of this case, it was quite wrong to treat Mr Sugar as having made a request to the BBC other than in its capacity as a public authority simply because of the nature of the information that he was requesting. More generally, it would be quite impractical to adopt such an approach to a request for information made to a hybrid authority. What if the request was in generic terms and the authority purported to hold some information covered by the request for journalistic purposes and other such information as public information?

28 I now adopt the alternative approach to the construction of 'public authority' as used in the Act, namely that it embraces hybrid authorities for all purposes. On that approach it is clear that Mr Sugar's request for information was made to a public authority within the terms of section 1.

31 . . . the request for information made by Mr Sugar to the BBC was made to a public authority and section 1 of the Act applied to it. What was the BBC's obligation on receipt of the request? That depends upon the answer to the journalism issue. If Mr Sugar is correct on this issue, the BBC was under an obligation under section 1(1)(b) to communicate the Balen Report to him. What if the BBC is correct, and the Balen Report was excluded information?

32 The duty of a public authority under section 1(1) is to inform the inquirer in writing whether or not it holds 'information of the description specified in the request'. That is 'the duty to confirm or deny' — see section 1(6) . How does this apply in the case of the hybrid authority which holds the information as excluded information. If the BBC's approach to the construction of 'public authority' is adopted, the answer is easy. The application is made to the hybrid authority in its capacity as a holder of public information. Its reply is that, in that capacity, it does not hold the information.

33 What if one adopts the alternative approach to the construction of public authority? My initial reaction was that the appropriate response will be to say that it holds the information but does not have to communicate it because it is not information to which its obligations under the Act apply. This is not, however, a satisfactory solution. In the present case the BBC was well aware that it held the information requested. But a hybrid authority will not always know whether it holds information of the description requested. Considerable time, trouble and expense may be involved in ascertaining whether it does. The hybrid authority may have a separate system for filing public information and excluded information. A request under section 1(1) cannot require the hybrid authority to search through its excluded information, simply in order to be in a position to tell the inquirer that it holds the information but has no obligation to disclose it. Nor does it. Section 7 confines the hybrid authority's obligations to public information. Thus, its obligation under section 1 is to ascertain whether or not it holds information of the description requested as part of its public information, as specified in Schedule 1. If it does not, it is entitled to answer the inquirer 'information of the description that you have requested does not form part of the information that I hold in respect of. . .' followed by the description of public information specified in Schedule 1.

34 This response to an inquiry differs significantly from that required where a public authority is asked for information that it holds that is exempt information. This perhaps answers the question why the draftsman of the Act did not adopt the same approach to excluded information that he adopted to exempt information.

35 The response given by the BBC in this case was more detailed than necessary if, as it claimed, the Balen Report was excluded information. On that premise, the response more than satisfied the BBC's obligation under section 1 to 'confirm or deny'. The issue raised by Mr Sugar was, however, whether that premise was correct. That was an issue that he was entitled to raise by his complaint to the Commissioner under section 50 and the Commissioner had jurisdiction to entertain that complaint.

36 By way of summary I shall set out the three short paragraphs of the Tribunal's decision on jurisdiction that encapsulate lucidly, succinctly and correctly the conclusions that I have reached at rather greater length:

'22. In our view Mr Sugar made an information request to the BBC, which is a public authority within the meaning of FOIA. There was nothing in the formulation of the request to take it outside the ambit of FOIA. It was a request for information that was properly made under s.1 of FOIA.

23. The basis for the BBC's rejection of his request was that, upon careful examination of the factual circumstances, the report which he asked for was (in the BBC's
view) held for the purposes of journalism. If the BBC was right in taking this view, that
did not mean that Mr Sugar had not made an information request to the BBC as a
public authority. In our judgment when, following the rejection, Mr Sugar applied to
the IC, his application was made under s.50(1).
24. We consider that the IC's duty under s.50(1) to consider whether a request
has been dealt with in accordance with the requirements of Part I can include, in
appropriate cases, consideration of whether Part I lays down any requirements
for the particular information in question. The Commissioner was entitled to decide
that failure to produce the report was not a contravention of the requirements of Part
I. In the present case he effectively so decided. That was in substance a decision
under s.50.'

38 For these reasons I am satisfied that the Tribunal had jurisdiction to make the decision
that it did. I would allow this appeal. If the appeal is allowed it will follow that the governing
decision on the journalism issue is that of the Tribunal, and that the only possible appeal
from that decision lies to the High Court on a point of law. The BBC's outstanding appeal
should therefore be remitted to the Administrative Court for determination. Davis J has, of
course, already ruled on the journalism issue, but he approached that issue as one raised in
a judicial review challenge by Mr Sugar of the Commissioner's decision on the point. He
applied the *Wednesbury* test, asking himself whether the decision of the Commissioner
was 'a lawful and rational one, properly open to him on the material before him', para 59.
That is not the test that he should have applied had he concluded, as he should have
done, that the Tribunal's decision was made with jurisdiction and that BBC's only right to
challenge it was on the ground that it was wrong in law. It follows that the result of allowing
this appeal will be to restore the Tribunal's decision.

Notes (cont.)
3. The House of Lords thus rejected the claim that on the basis of the nature of the information
    sought the BBC could not be viewed as a public authority for the purposes of the Freedom of
    Information Act 2000. Therefore a *request* for information held by the BBC was not *excluded* from
    the requirements of disclosure, and was subject to the jurisdiction of the Information Commis-
    sioner and, on appeal, the Information Tribunal. This is significant since certain public authorities
    in Schedule 1 of the FoI Act were qualified by reference to the class of information held, of which
    one was the BBC. Those were referred to as 'hybrid authorities'. The information held by them in
    their capacity as public authorities could be described as 'public information'. The other informa-
    tion held by them would be described as 'excluded information'. Section 1 of Part I of the Act
    applied, the Lords found, whenever a request for information was made to a public authority,
    whatever the nature of the information sought, whether the public authority held the information
    or not and, in the case of a hybrid authority, whether the information was public or excluded
    information. When a request for information was specifically made under the Act to a hybrid
    authority, it was found to be axiomatic that the maker of the request was making it to the hybrid
    authority in its capacity as a public authority. The BBC was to be treated as a public authority for
    the purposes of the request and so the Commissioner, and Tribunal had jurisdiction to consider the
    complaint of the requester.
    Clearly, if the decision had gone the other way, it would never have been possible to scrutinise
    the BBC (or another hybrid authority's) claim that *at the stage of making the request* it was not a

public authority. If that had been found to be the case, if part of the information requested was not in fact held for the purposes of journalism etc, the requester would have had no means of discovering that that was the case. It was important to afford the Commissioner and Tribunal jurisdiction to consider the claim, by designating the BBC as a public authority at the stage of making the request, whether or not it later turned out that the information was held for the purposes of journalism, meaning that the BBC did not hold it as a public authority and so was not subject to FoI in relation to that information. The next question to be decided – as indicated above—will be whether the information *was* held for the purposes of journalism; if so it will be excluded from the duty of disclosure under the Act.

4. *The rights granted by the Act.* The Act grants two basic rights under s 1(1): the right of the citizen to be informed in writing by the public authority whether it holds information of the description specified in the request and, if that is the case, to have that information communicated to him or her. It may be noted that the right conferred under s 1(1)(b) can cover original documents as well as 'information',[45] and in this respect the Act is clearly an improvement on the previous Code, which only covered 'information'. Both these fundamental rights are subject to the numerous exemptions the Act contains. Thus, where an authority is exempt from providing information under the Act, it is also entitled to refuse even to state whether it holds the information or not, although in some cases, it may only do this where stating whether it holds the information would have the effect of causing the prejudice that the exemption in question is designed to prevent. Such cases will be indicated below.

Exemptions under the Act

Seven specified interests were indicated in the White Paper, which took the place of the exemptions under the Code. The test for disclosure was based on an assessment of the harm that disclosure might cause and the need to safeguard the public interest. The test was: will this disclosure cause substantial harm to one of these interests? The first of these interests covered national security, defence and international relations. Obviously, this interest covered a very wide range of information. A further five interests were: law enforcement, personal privacy, commercial confidentiality, the safety of the individual, the public and the environment, and information supplied in confidence. Finally, there was an interest termed 'the integrity of decision-making and policy advice processes in government'. In this category, a different test was used: it was not necessary to show that disclosure of the information would cause substantial harm; a test of simple harm only was used.

The exemptions proposed under the White Paper were relatively narrow and were subject to quite a strict harm test. They may be sharply contrasted with those that emerged under the Act which include a number of 'class'-based exemptions. The exemptions under the Act rely on the key distinction between 'class' and 'harm-based' exemptions mentioned above. The harm-based exemptions under the Act are similar to those indicated in the White Paper: they require the public authority in question to show that the release of the information requested would, or would be likely to, cause prejudice to the interest specified in the exemption. But a number are class-based, meaning that in order to refuse the request, the authority only has to show that the information falls into the class of information covered by the exemption, not that its release would cause or be likely to cause harm or prejudice. It may be noted that the class exemptions can be further divided into two groups: those that are content-based, in the sense that no access to the information under the FoI Act or any other

---

45   Section 84 defines information broadly to cover information 'recorded in any form', and in relation to matters covered by s 51(8) this includes unrecorded information.

instrument is available; and others, which relate not to the content of the information, but to the process of acquiring it. These distinctions are made clear below, in the first group of exemptions considered.

The Act complicates matters further by providing that, in relation to some, but not all, of the class exemptions, and almost all the 'harm exemptions', the authority, having decided that the information is *prima facie* exempt (either because the information falls into the requisite class exemption, or because the relevant harm test is satisfied, as the case may be), must still then go on to consider whether it should be released under the public interest test set out in s 2. This requires the authority to release the information unless 'in all the circumstances of the case, the public interest in maintaining the exemption outweighs the public interest in disclosing the information'. It should be noted that this provision was amended in the Lords so as to require release unless the interest in maintaining secrecy *'outweighs'* the interest in disclosure. This was thought to provide greater protection for freedom of information, since it must be demonstrated that the need for secrecy is the more compelling interest in the particular case. The Campaign for Freedom of Information (CFoI) noted that where information falls into a class exemption, and an authority objects to disclosure even under the public interest test, it is able not only to argue that the specific disclosure would have harmful effects, *but also that the public interest would be harmed by any disclosure from within the relevant class of documents, regardless of the consequences of releasing the actual information in question.*[46] By contrast, under a prejudice test, the authority must be able first to identify the harm that would be caused by releasing the *specific information* requested, and then go on to show that that specific harm outweighs the public interest in disclosure. For consideration of the public interest test see the 2007 decision of the Tribunal against the BBC, and the 2009 decision relating to publication of Cabinet minutes concerning the Iraq war, both extracted below.

In the result, the exemptions under the Act can actually be broken down into four different categories, starting with the most absolute exemptions and moving to the least. It is helpful to consider them in the order suggested by this categorization, because the Act does not set out the exemptions in any systematic way, but rather randomly, so that class exemptions are mixed in with 'harm-based' exemptions, and 'absolute exemptions' with both. It should be noted that the following categorisation relates to categories of exemptions not necessarily to categories of information, although the two may be synonymous. The four suggested categories are as follows, and are described in order of their illiberality.

(a)   'Total' exemptions: that is, class exemptions to which the public interest test in s 2 *does not apply*. Thus, the public authority concerned only has to show that information sought falls into the exempt class, not that its disclosure would cause any harm or prejudice; and, there is no duty to consider whether the public interest in maintaining the exemption outweighs the public interest in disclosing the information.

(b)   Class exemptions to which the s 2 public interest test does apply. This is self-explanatory.

(c)   Harm-based exemptions to which the s 2 public interest test does not apply. In these exemptions, the authority has to show that the release of the particular information concerned would cause or be likely to cause the relevant prejudice, but then need not go on to consider whether this prejudice outweighs the public interest in disclosure: once prejudice is established, that is the end of the matter.

---

46   Freedom of Information Bill, House of Lords, Third Reading, 21 November 2000, briefing notes, p 10.

(d)   Harm-based exemptions to which the s 2 public interest test *does* apply. These are the exemptions under which it is hardest for the public authority concerned to resist the release of information. To do so, it must first demonstrate prejudice or likely prejudice from the release of the particular information request and then, even if prejudice is shown, go on to consider whether the public interest in forestalling that prejudice outweighs the public interest in disclosing the information under s 2.

These categories are important, not only in terms of the substantive legal tests which must be satisfied before information may be withheld: they also have crucial practical consequences in terms of time limits and enforcement. As explained below, the 20 day deadline for releasing information does not apply to information released only on public interest grounds. More importantly, the Commissioner's decision to order release on such grounds can, in relation to information held by certain governmental bodies, be vetoed by Ministers (a matter discussed further below). Extracts from the statute containing the exemptions follow.

Freedom of Information Act 2000 (extracts)

PART II
EXEMPT INFORMATION

Information accessible to applicant by other means.
21.–(1) Information which is reasonably accessible to the applicant otherwise than under section 1 is exempt information.
   (2)   For the purposes of subsection (1)—

         (a)   information may be reasonably accessible to the applicant even though it is accessible only on payment. . . .

Information intended for future publication.
[This exemption covers information intended for future publication where it is reasonable that information should be withheld until that future date is exempt and the duty to confirm or deny does not apply to the extent that complying with it would itself entail disclosing such information.]

Information supplied by, or relating to, bodies dealing with security matters.
23.–(1) Information held by a public authority is exempt information if it was directly or indirectly supplied to the public authority by, or relates to, any of the bodies specified in subsection (3).
   (2)   A certificate signed by a Minister of the Crown certifying that the information to which it applies was directly or indirectly supplied by, or relates to, any of the bodies specified in subsection (3) shall, subject to section 60, be conclusive evidence of that fact.
   (3)   The bodies referred to in subsections (1) and (2) are [the intelligence and security services, GCHQ, the special forces and the various tribunals to which complaints may be made about their activities and about phone tapping.]
   . . .
   (5)   The duty to confirm or deny does not arise if, or to the extent that, compliance with section 1(1)(a) would involve the disclosure of any information (whether or not

already recorded) which was directly or indirectly supplied to the public authority by, or relates to, any of the bodies specified in subsection (3).

National security.

24.–(1) Information which does not fall within section 23(1) is exempt information if exemption from section 1(1)(b) is required for the purpose of safeguarding national security.

(2)   The duty to confirm or deny does not arise if, or to the extent that, exemption from section 1(1)(a) is required for the purpose of safeguarding national security.

(3)   A certificate signed by a Minister of the Crown certifying that exemption from section 1(1)(b), or from section 1(1)(a) and (b), is, or at any time was, required for the purpose of safeguarding national security shall, subject to section 60, be conclusive evidence of that fact.

. . .

26. [this exemption covers information the disclosure of which would prejudice or would be likely to prejudice **defence and the armed forces**]

27 [This is a like exemption in relation to **international relations**]

28. [This is a like exemption concerning relations between administrations in the UK (for example, between the government and the Scottish Executive]

29. [This is a like exemption covering information the disclosure of which would prejudice or would be likely to prejudice **the economy**]

33. . . .[This exemption covers cover information the disclosure of which would prejudice or would be likely to prejudice **auditing functions** of any public authorities]

Investigations and proceedings conducted by public authorities.

30.–(1) Information held by a public authority is exempt information if it has at any time been held by the authority for the purposes of—

(a)   any investigation which the public authority has a duty to conduct with a view to it being ascertained—

(i)   whether a person should be charged with an offence, or
(ii)   whether a person charged with an offence is guilty of it,

(b)   any investigation which is conducted by the authority and in the circumstances may lead to a decision by the authority to institute criminal proceedings which the authority has power to conduct, or

(c)   any criminal proceedings which the authority has power to conduct.

(3)   The duty to confirm or deny does not arise in relation to information which is (or if it were held by the public authority would be) exempt information by virtue of subsection (1) or (2).

31.–(1) Information which is not exempt information by virtue of section 30 is exempt information if its disclosure under this Act would, or would be likely to, prejudice—

(a)   the prevention or detection of crime,
(b)   the apprehension or prosecution of offenders,
(c)   the administration of justice,
(d)   the assessment or collection of any tax or duty or of any imposition of a similar nature,

    (e)   the operation of the immigration controls,

    (f)   the maintenance of security and good order in prisons or in other institutions where persons are lawfully detained,

    (g)   the exercise by any public authority of its functions for any of the purposes specified in subsection (2),

    (h)   any civil proceedings which are brought by or on behalf of a public authority and arise out of an investigation conducted, for any of the purposes specified in subsection (2), by or on behalf of the authority by virtue of Her Majesty's prerogative or by virtue of powers conferred by or under an enactment. . . .

(2)   The purposes referred to in subsection (1)(g) to (i) are—

    (a)   the purpose of ascertaining whether any person has failed to comply with the law,

    (b)   the purpose of ascertaining whether any person is responsible for any conduct which is improper,

    (c)   the purpose of ascertaining whether circumstances which would justify regulatory action in pursuance of any enactment exist or may arise,

    (d)   the purpose of ascertaining a person's fitness or competence in relation to the management of bodies corporate or in relation to any profession or other activity which he is, or seeks to become, authorised to carry on,

    (e)   the purpose of ascertaining the cause of an accident. . .

(3)   The duty to confirm or deny does not arise if, or to the extent that, compliance with section 1(1)(a) would, or would be likely to, prejudice any of the matters mentioned in subsection (1).

Court records, etc.

32.–(1) Information held by a public authority is exempt information if it is held only by virtue of being contained in—

    (a)   any document filed with, or otherwise placed in the custody of, a court for the purposes of proceedings in a particular cause or matter,

    (b)   any document served upon, or by, a public authority for the purposes of proceedings in a particular cause or matter, or

    (c)   any document created by—

        (i)   a court, or

        (ii)   a member of the administrative staff of a court, for the purposes of proceedings in a particular cause or matter.

(2)   Information held by a public authority is exempt information if it is held only by virtue of being contained in—

    (a)   any document placed in the custody of a person conducting an inquiry or arbitration, for the purposes of the inquiry or arbitration, or

    (b)   any document created by a person conducting an inquiry or arbitration, for the purposes of the inquiry or arbitration.

(3) The duty to confirm or deny does not arise in relation to information which is (or if it were held by the public authority would be) exempt information by virtue of this section.

Parliamentary privilege.
34.–(1) Information is exempt information if exemption from section 1(1)(b) is required for the purpose of avoiding an infringement of the privileges of either House of Parliament. . . .

Formulation of government policy, etc.
35.–(1) Information held by a government department or by the National Assembly for Wales is exempt information if it relates to—

    (a)   the formulation or development of government policy,
    (b)   Ministerial communications,
    (c)   the provision of advice by any of the Law Officers or any request for the provision of such advice, or
    (d)   the operation of any Ministerial private office.

  (2)   Once a decision as to government policy has been taken, any statistical information used to provide an informed background to the taking of the decision is not to be regarded—

    (a)   for the purposes of subsection (1)(a), as relating to the formulation or development of government policy, or
    (b)   for the purposes of subsection (1)(b), as relating to Ministerial communications.

  (3)   The duty to confirm or deny does not arise in relation to information which is (or if it were held by the public authority would be) exempt information by virtue of subsection (1).
  (4)   In making any determination required by section 2(1)(b) or (2)(b) in relation to information which is exempt information by virtue of subsection (1)(a), regard shall be had to the particular public interest in the disclosure of factual information which has been used, or is intended to be used, to provide an informed background to decision-taking.

Prejudice to effective conduct of public affairs.
36.–(1) This section applies to—

    (a)   information which is held by a government department or by the National Assembly for Wales and is not exempt information by virtue of section 35, and
    (b)   information which is held by any other public authority.

  (2)   Information to which this section applies is exempt information if, in the reasonable opinion of a qualified person, disclosure of the information under this Act—

    (a)   would, or would be likely to, prejudice—

        (i)   the maintenance of the convention of the collective responsibility of Ministers of the Crown, or

(ii) the work of the Executive Committee of the Northern Ireland Assembly, or

(iii) the work of the executive committee of the National Assembly for Wales,

(b) would, or would be likely to, inhibit—

(i) the free and frank provision of advice, or

(ii) the free and frank exchange of views for the purposes of deliberation, or

(c) would otherwise prejudice, or would be likely otherwise to prejudice, the effective conduct of public affairs.

(3) The duty to confirm or deny does not arise in relation to information to which this section applies (or would apply if held by the public authority) if, or to the extent that, in the reasonable opinion of a qualified person, compliance with section 1(1)(a) would, or would be likely to, have any of the effects mentioned in subsection (2).

(4) In relation to statistical information, subsections (2) and (3) shall have effect with the omission of the words 'in the reasonable opinion of a qualified person'.

(5) In subsections (2) and (3) 'qualified person' [means Ministers, the Speaker of the House re the Commons or the Clerk of Parliament re the Lords].

Personal information.
40.–(1) Any information to which a request for information relates is exempt information if it constitutes personal data of which the applicant is the data subject.

Information provided in confidence.
41.–(1) Information is exempt information if—

(a) it was obtained by the public authority from any other person (including another public authority), and

(b) the disclosure of the information to the public (otherwise than under this Act) by the public authority holding it would constitute a breach of confidence actionable by that or any other person.

(2) The duty to confirm or deny does not arise if, or to the extent that, the confirmation or denial that would have to be given to comply with section 1(1)(a) would (apart from this Act) constitute an actionable breach of confidence.

Notes
As noted above, the exemptions can be broken down into four categories. We take them in order.

1 Class exemptions not subject to the public interest test

These exemptions can be referred to as 'total' or absolute exemptions: that is, class exemptions to which the public interest test in s 2 *does not* apply. The public authority concerned only has to show that information sought falls into the exempt class, not that its disclosure would cause any harm or prejudice, and there is no duty to consider whether the public interest in maintaining the exemption outweighs the public interest in disclosing the information. Most of these exemptions, such as those under ss 12, 14, 32, 34, 40 and 41 are self-explanatory. Section 21 covers information that is reasonably accessible to the applicant from other sources. Section 23(1) covers information supplied by or which relates to the intelligence and security services, GCHQ, the special forces and the various tribunals to which complaints may be made about their activities and about phone tapping. It should be noted that, as indicated above, the bodies mentioned in this exemption are not themselves covered by the Act at all. This exemption therefore applies to information which is held by *another public authority,* but which has been supplied by one of these bodies. Because it is a class exemption, it could apply to information which had no conceivable security implications, such as evidence of a massive overspend on MI5 or MI6's headquarters. The duty to confirm or deny does not apply to information in this category where complying with it would itself involve disclosure of information covered by this exemption. Bearing in mind the complete exclusion of the security and intelligence services from the Act, the use of this exemption unaccompanied by a harm test and not subject to the public interest test is likely to mean that sensitive matters of great political significance remain undisclosed, even if their disclosure would ultimately benefit those services or national security.

Information the disclosure of which would contravene any other Act of Parliament (for example, the Official Secrets Act 1989), or would be incompatible with any EU obligation, or constitute a contempt of court (s 44) is exempt, and the duty to confirm or deny does not apply to the extent that compliance with it would amount to a contravention, as described above. This exemption ensures that the FoI Act cannot be seen impliedly to repeal the numerous provisions that criminalise the release of information, but rather preserves them all.

2 Class exemptions subject to the public interest test

This second category covers class exemptions subject to the public interest test. In relation to these exemptions, in practice, while the Commissioner always has the last word on whether the information falls into the class in question, he/she will not always be able to enforce a finding that it should nevertheless be released on public interest grounds if the information is held by certain governmental bodies, since the ministerial veto may be used.

The Commissioner has given guidance as to what 'the public interest' in the Act means (in Guidance Note 3):

> It is important to bear in mind that the competing interests to be considered are the public interest favouring disclosure against the public (rather than private) interest favouring the withholding of information. There will often be a **private** interest in withholding information which would reveal incompetence on the part of or corruption within the public authority or which would simply cause embarrassment to the authority. However, the public interest will favour accountability and good administration and it is this interest that must be weighed against the public interest in not disclosing the information.

Information relating to investigations that may lead to criminal proceedings. This class exemption subject to the public interest test arises under s 30(1); it is a sweeping exemption, covering all information, whenever obtained, which relates to investigations that may lead to criminal proceedings. It represents a specific rejection of the recommendation of the MacPherson Report[47] that there should be no class exemption for information relating to police investigations. It overlaps with the law enforcement exemption of s 31, which does include a harm test. The exclusion of police operational matters and

---

47   The MacPherson Report on the Stephen Lawrence Inquiry, Cm 4262 (1999), proposed that all such matters should be covered by the FoI Act, subject only to a 'substantial' harm test.

decisions echoes the approach under s 4 of the Official Secrets Act, but unlike s 4, no harm test is included. There are certain aspects of information relating to investigations which would appear to require disclosure in order to be in accord with the principle of openness enshrined in the Act. For example, a citizen might suspect that his or her telephone had been tapped without authorisation or that he or she had been unlawfully placed under surveillance by other means. Under the Act, no satisfactory method of discovering information relating to such a possibility exists. It is therefore unfortunate that telephone tapping and electronic surveillance were not subjected to a substantial harm, or even a simple harm, test.

This exemption extends beyond protecting the police and the CPS and covers all information obtained by safety agencies investigating accidents. Thus, it covers bodies such as the Health and Safety Executive, the Railway Inspectorate, the Nuclear Installations Inspectorate, the Civil Aviation Authority, the Marine and Coastguard Agency, environmental health officers, trading standards officers and the Drinking Water Inspectorate. It covers routine inspections as well as specific investigations, since both can lead to criminal prosecution. Thus, anything from an inspection of a section of railway track by the Railway Inspectorate to a check upon hygiene in a restaurant by the Health and Safety Executive can be covered. The duty to confirm or deny does not apply (s 30(3)). As the CFoI commented:

> Reports into accidents involving dangerous cars, train crashes, unsafe domestic appliances, air disasters, chemical fires or nuclear incidents will go into a permanently secret filing cabinet. The same goes for reports into risks faced by workers or the public from industrial hazards. The results of safety inspections of the railways, nuclear plants and dangerous factories would be permanently exempt. This is the information that most people assume FoI legislation exists to provide.[48]

The need for such a sweeping class exemption is hard to justify since s 31 specifically exempts information which could prejudice the prevention or detection of crime, or legal proceedings brought by a public authority arising from various forms of investigation. That exemption ensures that no information is released which could damage law enforcement and crime detection and it has been noted above that information which could amount to a contempt of court is also exempted. The CFoI noted that the recently retired Director General of the Health and Safety Executive has said publicly that the work of the HSE does not require such sweeping protection.[49] It should be noted that, where it has been decided that the information falls into the protected class, the authority must then go on to consider whether it should be released under the public interest test. Since most of the information above will not be held by a government department (see below), the Commissioner will be able to order disclosure if she thinks the information should be released under this provision, with no possibility of a ministerial veto.

The other major class exemption in this category, under s 35, has been just as criticised. Section 35 amounts to a sweeping exemption for virtually all information relating to the formation of government policy. The duty to confirm or deny does not apply. This exemption was presumably intended to prevent government from having to decide policy in a goldfish bowl— to protect the freeness and frankness of Civil Service advice and of internal debate within government—but, once again, it appears to go far beyond what would sensibly be required to achieve this aim. As appears above, section

---

48   Freedom of Information Bill, House of Lords, Committee Stage, 19 October 2000, briefing notes.

49   *Ibid.*

36 contains a harm-based exemption which covers almost exactly the same ground. Since this covers all information whose release might cause damage to the working of government—and is framed in very broad terms—it appears to be unnecessary to have a sweeping class exemption covering the same ground. Moreover, this exemption is not restricted to Civil Service advice; it covers also the background information used in preparing policy, including the underlying facts and their analysis. As the CFoI commented:

> There would be no right to know about purely descriptive reports of existing practice, research reports, evidence on health hazards, assumptions about wage or inflation levels used in calculating costs, studies of overseas practice, consultants' findings or supporting data showing whether official assertions are realistic or not.[50]

The sole exception to this exemption appears in s 35(2); it applies only 'once a decision as to government policy has been taken' and covers 'any statistical information used to provide an informed background to the taking of the decision'. This was a concession made by the Government fairly late in the Bill's passage through Parliament and is very limited. First, unlike most other freedom of information regimes, by excluding only statistical information from the exemption, s 35(2) allows the *analysis* of facts to be withheld. Second, it only applies once a decision has been taken. Thus, where the Government gives consideration to introducing a new policy but then shelves the matter without a decision, statistics used during the consideration process remain exempt. The White Paper preceding the Bill proposed that there should be no class exemption for material in this area, but rather that, as under the previous Code, a harm test would have had to be satisfied to prevent disclosure. While information in this category is subject to a public interest test, it is important to note that, because, by definition it will generally be information held by a government department, if the Commissioner orders disclosure on public interest grounds, the ministerial veto will be available to override her.

The exemption under s 35(1) is much more restrictive than the equivalent exemption under the previous, voluntary Code of Practice on Access to Government Information. The latter required in para 2 that both facts and the analysis of facts underlying policy decisions, including scientific analysis and expert appraisal, be made available once decisions are announced. Material relating to policy formation could only be withheld under a harm test if disclosure would 'harm the frankness and candour of internal discussion'. However, as appears below, the interpretation by the Commissioner has been robust in allowing the public interest to prevail over this, and other class exemptions. In addition, the Commissioner has issued a Guidance Note (no 24) dealing specifically with this exemption, and evidently intended to narrow its scope. The Information Commissioner's view is that there must be some clear, specific and credible evidence that the formulation or development of policy would be materially altered for the worse by the threat of disclosure under the Act. The Note adds specific factors to be taken into account in deciding whether the exemption is made out:

- In this particular case, would release of this information make civil servants less likely to provide full and frank advice or opinions on policy proposals?
- Would it, for example, prejudice working relationships by exposing dissenting views?
- Would the prospect of future release inhibit the debate and exploration of the full range of policy options that ought to be considered, even if on reflection some of them are seen as extreme?

---

50   *Ibid*, p 1.

- Would the prospect of release place civil servants in the position of having to defend everything that has been raised (and possibly later discounted) during deliberation?
- On the other hand, would the possibility of future release act as a deterrent against advice which is ill-considered, vague, poorly prepared or written in unnecessarily brusque or defamatory language? Would the prospect of release in fact enhance the quality of future advice?
- Is the main reason for exempting the information to spare a civil servant or a minister embarrassment? If so, then it is not appropriate to use this exemption.

The guidance states—on the exception to the exemption relating to statistics:

> Statistical information incorporates analyses, projections and meta-data, as well as the statistics themselves; numerical data which may take the form of a table or graph or simply be a sum total. Statistics must be derived from a recorded or repeatable methodology, and commentary on this is also statistical information.

Further class exemptions. Information subject to legal privilege (s 42) is exempt. The duty to confirm or deny does not apply if compliance with it would itself breach legal privilege. Trade secrets (s 43(1)) are exempt, but the duty does apply. 'Communications with Her Majesty, with other members of the Royal Family or with the Royal Household', or information relating to 'the conferring by the Crown of any honour or dignity' (s 37) are exempt and the duty to confirm or deny does not apply. It is unclear why it was necessary to bestow a class exemption relating to the royal household and honours and dignities, although this follows the previous Code of Practice. A separate class exemption covers information obtained for the purposes of conducting criminal proceedings and a very wide variety of investigations (specified in s 31(2)) carried out under statute or the prerogative, and which relate to the obtaining of information from confidential sources.

3 Harm-based exemptions not subject to the public interest test

This third category of exemptions has only one member. There is a general, harm-based exemption under s 36 for information the disclosure of which would be likely to prejudice the effective conduct of public affairs or inhibit free and frank discussion and advice. This exemption is subject to the general public interest test with one exception: for a reason that is not readily apparent, where the information in question is held by the Commons or Lords, the public interest test cannot be considered. In order to invoke this exemption, the authority has to show that the release of the particular information concerned would cause or be likely to cause the relevant prejudice, but then need not go on to consider whether this prejudice outweighs the public interest in disclosure: once prejudice is established, that is the end of the matter.

4 Harm-based exemptions which are subject to the public interest test

This category covers a vast range of exemptions. These are the exemptions under which it is hardest for the public authority concerned to resist the release of information. To do so, it must first demonstrate prejudice or likely prejudice from the release of the particular information requested and then, if prejudice is shown, go on to consider whether the public interest in forestalling that prejudice outweighs the public interest in disclosing the information under s 2. As harm-based exemptions, these are in one respect the least controversial aspect of the Act. But it is extremely important to note that the Act departed from one of the most liberal and widely praised aspects of the White Paper, namely, the requirement that in order to make out such exemptions, the authority concerned would have to demonstrate 'substantial' harm. This was changed to a test of simple prejudice, although government spokespersons have attempted to deny that the change makes any difference in practice. In each case, the duty to confirm or deny does not apply if, or to the extent that, compliance with it in itself causes the prejudice which the exemption seeks to prevent.

The Law Commissioner has a guidance note (note 20) the 'prejudice' test, indicating how the term should be interpreted, in general terms:

> In legal terminology, prejudice is commonly understood to mean harm and the Information Commissioner regards them as being equivalent. So, when considering how disclosure of information would prejudice the subject of the exemption being claimed, the public authority may find it more helpful to consider issues of harm or damage. Although prejudice need not be substantial, the Commissioner expects that it be more than trivial. Strictly, the degree of prejudice is not specified, so any level of prejudice might be argued. However, public authorities should bear in mind that the less significant the prejudice is shown to be, the higher the chance of the public interest falling in favour of disclosure.

As appears above, these exemptions cover information the disclosure of which would prejudice or would be likely to prejudice: defence and the armed forces (s 26); international relations (s 27); the economy (s 29); the mental or physical health or safety of any individual (s 38); auditing functions of other public authorities (s 33); the prevention, detection of crime, legal proceedings brought by a public authority arising from an investigation conducted for any of the purposes specified in s 31(2) (above) and carried out under statute or prerogative; the collection of tax, immigration controls, good order in prisons; the exercise by any public authority of its functions for any of the purposes specified in s 31(2) (above), and relations between administrations in the UK (for example, between the Government and the Scottish Executive) (s 28). These exemptions are relatively straightforward, although they go beyond the information covered by the Official Secrets Act 1989.

National security. The use of the national security exemption, albeit accompanied by the harm test, may mean that sensitive matters of great political significance remain undisclosed. In particular, the breadth and uncertainty of the term 'national security' may be allowing matters which fall only doubtfully within it to remain secret. Had the Act been in place at the time of the change in policy regarding arms sales to Iraq, the subject of the Scott report, it is likely that information relating to it would not have been disclosed since it could have fallen within the exception clauses. The whole subject of arms sales appears to fall within the national security exception and possibly within other exceptions as well.[51]

Commercial interests under s 43. The CFoI commented that under this exemption, the prejudice referred to could be caused by consumers refusing to buy a dangerous product. Thus, they noted, that the fact that a company had sold dangerous products, or behaved in some other disreputable manner, could be suppressed if disclosure would lead customers to buy alternative products or shareholders to sell their shares.[52] This is clearly correct; however, in the case of unsafe products, the public interest test surely requires disclosure.

Effective conduct of public affairs—s 36 (above). Two main criticisms of this exemption can be made. First, the test is not a wholly objective one, but is dependent upon 'the reasonable opinion of a qualified person'. The intention behind this provision is apparently to allow a person representing the department or body in question to make the primary determination of prejudice, with the

---

51   See further the Minutes of Evidence before the Public Service Committee, HC 313–1 (1995–96), 13 66 *et seq.*

52   Freedom of Information Bill, House of Lords, Committee Stage, 19 October 2000, briefing notes, p 1.

Commissioner being able to take issue with such a finding only if it is irrational in the *Wednesbury* sense. The second main objection to this section is the 'catch-all' provision covering information the release of which could 'prejudice the effective conduct of public affairs', a phrase which is so vague and broad that it could mean almost anything. For consideration of the term 'prejudice the effective conduct of public affairs' under s36, see the 2007 decision of the Tribunal against the BBC, extracted below.

5 Expiry of certain exemptions.

As indicated above, the Act, through amendments to the Public Records Act 1958, provides that some of that Act's exemptions will cease to apply after a certain number of years,[53] although these limitations are hardly generous. The following exemptions cease to apply at all after 30 years (s 63(1)): s 28 (inter-UK relations), s 30(1) (information obtained during an investigation), s 32 (documents generated in litigation), s 33 (audit functions), s 35 (information relating to internal government discussion and advice), s 36 (information which could prejudice effective conduct of public affairs), s 37(1)(a) (communications with royal household), s 42 (legal professional privilege) and s 43 (trade secrets and information which could damage commercial interests). The exemptions under s 21 (information accessible by other means) and s 22 (information intended for future publication) cease to apply after 30 years where the relevant document is held in a public record office (s 64(1)). Still less generously, information relating to the bestowing of honours and dignities (s 37(1)(b)) only ceases to be exempt after 60 years, while we will have to wait 100 years before the expiry of the exemption for information falling within s 31, that is, information which might prejudice law enforcement, the administration of justice, etc. Additionally, one of the absolute exemptions— information provided by the security, intelligence, etc services (s 23(1))—will cease to be absolute after 30 years, that is, the public interest in disclosure must be considered once 30 years has expired. The Constitutional Reform and Governance Act 2010, Sched 7 made some minor changes to certain of these provisions, in particular that information covered by s 37(1)(a) would no longer be exempt after 20 years.

Applying for information—time limits

Information requested must generally be supplied within 20 days of the request (s 10(1)). However, there is an important exception to this: where an authority finds that information is *prima facie* exempt, either because it falls within a class exemption, or the requisite prejudice is thought to be present, but then goes on to consider whether the information should nevertheless be released under the public interest test, it does not have to make a decision within the normal 20-day deadline. Instead, it must release the information only within an unspecified 'reasonable period'.

In a press release in 2005, the Campaign for Freedom of Information (hereafter usually referred to as CFoI) said 'the Government's figures showed that a "disturbing" level of requests were not being dealt with within the Act's time limits'.[54] Overall, more than a third (36%) of Government departments failed to meet the deadline of 20 working days (25% failed even to tell the applicant that they needed extra time, as required by the Act). The Home Office had by far the worst record amongst government departments. In 60% of all requests it failed either to respond to the request within 20 days, or even to inform the applicant that it needed more time within that period. The Campaign said this represented 'routine disregard for the Act's requirements'.[55]

---

53   See p 689.

54   Press Release, dated 23 June 2005, available on the Campaign's website: www.cfoi.org.uk.

55   *Ibid.*

Other important Ministries did much better. The Department for Transport and the Department for Constitutional Affairs both answered 83% of their requests within the basic 20 working day period. The Department for Work and Pensions met this time limit in 81% of cases, and the Ministry of Defence, which received far more requests than any other department, met the 20 day limit for 71% of its requests.[56]

Applying for information—practical problems

There are a number of practical problems in using the Act. Requests for information must be in writing (s 8) and, under s 9, a fee may be charged. The citizen can have difficulty in obtaining the document he or she requires. He or she may not be able to frame the request for information specifically enough in order to obtain the particular documents needed. The request may be met with the response that 3,000 documents are available touching on the matter in question; the citizen may lack the expert knowledge needed to identify the particular document required. If so, under s 1(3), the authority need not comply with the request and can continue to postpone its compliance until and if the requester succeeds in formulating the request more specifically. Section 1(3) does not allow the authority to postpone the request until it has had a chance to obtain further information, enabling it to deal with the request.

The authority may not provide full information in response to the request. CFoI found a disturbing variation in the extent to which the department concerned answered the requests put to it in full.[57] The Department of Transport provided full answers in 76% of cases, followed by the MOD, which managed 67%. However, 'at the other end of the scale the Department of Trade and Industry provided full answers in only 21% of cases, the Home Office in 28% and the Cabinet Office in 29% of cases'. The Campaign said 'it's. . .clear that some parts of Whitehall are more committed to freedom of information than others'.

In 2006 the Department for Constitutional Affairs ordered an independent review of the economic cost of the Act.[58] Implementation of FoI is estimated to cost roughly £35m a year. Under the current financial regime, public bodies do not make a charge for considering requests if the work involved does not exceed £600 of a civil servant's time. The independent report looking at the economic impact of the legislation, found that journalists make up 10 per cent of the volume of central government requests and 21% of the cost.

The relevant existing Regulations are the Freedom of Information and Data Protection (Appropriate Limit and Fees) Regulations 2004, which came into force in January 2005. Their key provisions are: the 'appropriate limit', above which public authorities may decline to comply with a request for information, is set at £600 for central Government and Parliament, and £450 for the wider public sector; when estimating whether the costs of complying with a request for information would exceed the appropriate limit, public authorities may only include the costs of determining whether the information is held, and then locating, retrieving and extracting it; where those costs relate to the time spent by officials or other people carrying out the relevant activities on behalf of the authority, they must be calculated at a standard rate of £25 per hour; and when estimating whether the costs of complying with a request for information would exceed the appropriate limit, public authorities may aggregate the costs of two or more requests received from the same person, or persons who appear to be acting in concert or in pursuance of a campaign, provided the requests relate to the same or similar information and are received within a period of 60 working days.

---

56   *Ibid.*

57   See CFoI's press release, n 34 above.

58   *An independent review of the impact of FoI*, A Report for the Dept of Constitutional Affairs, October 2006.

In response to the Review mentioned above, the Government took the view that implementing the Act had become too expensive and in December 2006 the Department for Constitutional Affairs published draft Regulations intended to restrict use of the Act.[59] The draft Regulations would have allowed restrictions to be placed on the type of information requested based on cost. Restrictions could also have been placed on the frequency of requests from any one individual or body (the aggregation proposal). Under that proposal any one organisation would have been limited in the number of requests that could be made when the aggregated costs of dealing with requests from that organisation exceeded the cost limits. Thus, if a very large media organisation, such as the BBC, had made a request, that would have meant that further requests from a member of that organisation, even working in a completely separate sector of the organisation and pursuing a very different story, could have been refused once the cost limit had been reached. The restrictions also would have created leeway for delay and for the creation of bureaucratic obstacles to obtaining access to the information while, for example, costs of obtaining it were worked out. The proposed restrictions indicated that the Government, in the very early life of the Act, was already becoming concerned about its use. The Act appeared to be being used more successfully than the Government had predicted that it would be. However, the proposals were dropped in October 2007 after many representations had been made against them.

Enforcing the rights under the Act

The enforcement mechanisms

The enforcement review mechanism under the Act is far stronger than the mechanism established under the previous Code. The internal review of a decision to withhold information, established under the Code, was formalised under the Act and the role of the Ombudsman in policing the Code was, under the Act, replaced by that of the Information Commissioner (formerly the Data Protection Commissioner). The Commissioner's powers are also much more extensive than those of the Ombudsman. As indicated below, she has the power to order disclosure of the information and can report a failure to disclose information to the courts who can treat it in the same way as a contempt of court. Under the White Paper, it was to be a criminal offence to destroy, alter or withhold records relevant to an investigation of the Information Commissioner. It was also to become a criminal offence to shred documents requested by outsiders, including the media and the public. However, the two offences are omitted from the Act. No civil liability is incurred if a public authority does not comply with any duty imposed by the Act (s 56).

The rights granted under the Act are enforceable by the Information Commissioner. Importantly, the Commissioner has security of tenure, being dismissable only by the Crown following an address by both Houses of Parliament. An appeal lies from decisions of the Commissioner to the Information Tribunal which is made up of experienced lawyers and 'persons to represent the interests' of those seeking information and of public authorities (Sched 2, Part II). (See further below on the work of the Commissioner in relation to decided cases.)

Under s 50, 'Any person (in this section referred to as 'the complainant') may apply to the Commissioner for a decision whether, in any specified respect, a request for information made by the complainant to a public authority has been dealt with in accordance with [the Act]'. The Commissioner must then make a decision unless the application has been made with 'undue delay', is frivolous or vexatious, or the complainant has not exhausted any complaints procedure provided by the public authority (s 50(1)). If the Commissioner decides that the authority concerned has failed to

---

59 Draft FoI and Data Protection (Appropriate Limit and Fees) Regulations 2007, Consultation Paper 28/06, 14 December 2006.

communicate information or confirm or deny its existence when required to do so by the Act, she must serve a 'decision notice' on the authority stating what it must do to satisfy the Act. She may also serve 'Information Notices' upon authorities, requiring the authority concerned to provide her with information about a particular application or its compliance with the Act generally. The Commissioner may ultimately force a recalcitrant authority to act by serving upon it an enforcement notice, which, *per* s 52(1), 'requir[es] the authority to take, within such time as may be specified in the notice, such steps as may be so specified for complying with those requirements'. If a public authority fails to comply with a Decision, Enforcement or Information Notice, the Commissioner can certify the failure in writing to the High Court, which, the Act provides (s 52(2)), 'may inquire into the matter and, after hearing any witness who may be produced against or on behalf of the public authority, and after hearing any statement that may be offered in defence, deal with the authority as if it had committed a contempt of court'. In other words, the Commissioner's decisions can, in the final analysis, be enforced just as can orders of the court. These powers are buttressed by powers of entry, search and seizure to gain evidence of a failure by the authority to carry out its obligations under the Act or comply with a Notice issued by the Commissioner (detailed in Sched 3).

The Commissioner's decisions are themselves subject to appeal to the Tribunal and this power of appeal is exercisable upon the broadest possible grounds. The Act provides that either party may appeal to the Tribunal (s 60) against a decision notice and a public authority against an enforcement or information notice (s 57(2) and (3)), either on the basis that the notice is 'not in accordance with the law', or 'to the extent that the notice involved an exercise of discretion by the Commissioner, that he ought to have exercised his discretion differently' (s 58(1)). The Tribunal is also empowered to review 'any finding of fact on which the notice in question was based' and, as well as being empowered to quash decisions of the Commissioner, may 'substitute such other notice as could have been served by the Commissioner'. The nature of the Tribunal's appeal jurisdiction is indicated below in the 2007 decision against the BBC, requiring release of the minutes of the BBC Governors' meeting regarding the Director-General.

There is a further appeal from the Tribunal to the High Court, but on a 'point of law' only (s 59). In practice, this will probably be interpreted so as to allow review of the Tribunal's decisions, not just for error of law, but also on the other accepted heads of judicial review.

The ministerial veto of the Commissioner's decisions

The ministerial veto is viewed as a highly controversial aspect of the Act. The White Paper made no provision for such a power of veto, on the basis that to do so would undermine confidence in the regime. Such a veto clearly dilutes the basic freedom of information principle that a body independent from Government should enforce the rights to information and since, in cases where the release of information could embarrass Ministers, it constitutes them judge in their own cause, it is objectionable in principle. For the veto to be exercisable, two conditions must be satisfied under s 53(1): first, the Notice which the veto will operate to quash must have been served on a government department, the Welsh Assembly or 'any public authority designated for the purposes of this section by an order made by the Secretary of State'; second, the Notice must order the release of information which is *prima facie* exempt but which the Commissioner has decided should nevertheless be released under the public interest test in s 2. (By *prima facie* exempt, it will be recalled, is meant information that either falls into a class exemption or, where prejudice is required to render it exempt, the Commissioner has adjudged the prejudice to be present.) The veto is exercised by means of a certificate signed by the Minister concerned stating that he or she has 'on reasonable grounds formed the opinion that, in respect of the request or requests concerned, there was no failure' to comply with the Act. The decision must be made at a relatively senior level. If the information is sought from a department of the

Northern Irish Executive or any Northern Ireland public authority, it must be exercised by the First and Deputy Minister acting together; if a Welsh department or any Welsh public authority, the Assembly First Secretary; if from a government department or any other public authority, a Cabinet Minister. The reasons for the veto must be given to the complainant (s 56), unless doing so would reveal exempt information (s 57) and the certificate must be laid before Parliament or the Welsh/Northern Ireland Assembly as applicable. As noted below, the veto had been used twice by the end of 2009.

Publication schemes

Under ss 19 and 20, public authorities have to adopt 'publication schemes' relating to the publication of information by that authority. This is a significant aspect of the Act since more citizens can thereby gain access to a wider range of information. The difficulty and expense of making a request can thereby be avoided. The scheme can be devised by the authority or, under s 20, a model scheme devised by the Information Commissioner can be used. If a tailor-made scheme is used, it must be approved by the Commissioner (s 19(1)(a)). Use of the model scheme is probably desirable as promoting consistency between authorities and thereby enhancing access to information. Further information on the implementation of these schemes is provided below, in the Lord Chancellor's report.

Preliminary assessment

Rodney Austin described the draft Bill as 'a denial of democracy'.[60] It is suggested that the improvements made to the Bill during its passage through Parliament, while still leaving it a far weaker and more illiberal measure than proposed by the widely praised White Paper which preceded it, render this view inapplicable to the Act itself. In particular, the public interest test has been strengthened, and applies to most of the exemptions in the Act, including, crucially, the key class exemptions relating to investigations and to the formation of government policy. However, as the CFoI points out, it is misleading to view this as converting class exemptions into 'harm-based' ones, since the very existence of a class exemption is based upon a presumption, built into the Act, that such information is, *as a class*, of a type which generally should not be released. Despite its weaknesses, this is a constitutional development whose significance can hardly be overstated. The FoI Act, enforceable by the Information Commissioner, is a clear improvement on the Code introduced by the Major Government since it introduces a statutory right to information, its coverage is far wider and the enforcement mechanism is stronger. Ultimately, the right is enforceable if necessary through the courts.

The Act represents a turning point in British democracy since, for the first time in its history, the decision to release many classes of information has been removed from government departments and public authorities and placed in the hands of an independent agency, the Information Commissioner. However, as seen, the Act fences round the statutory 'right' to information with so many restrictions that, depending upon its interpretation, much information of any conceivable interest can still be withheld. How far this is turning out to be the case in practice depends primarily upon the robustness of the stance taken by the Commissioner, particularly in applying the public interest test to the class exemptions under the Act, where it provides the only means of obtaining disclosure. As the decisions below indicate, the Commissioner has taken a very robust line in this respect, forcing two exercises of the Ministerial veto. We contend that the decisions below render Austin's view now wholly untenable. Examples of FoI claims are given below.

---

60   R Austin, 'Freedom of Information: A Sheep in Wolf's Clothing?', in J Jowell and D Oliver (eds), *The Changing Constitution*, 5th edn (2004), p 237.

Decided cases under the FOI Act

The decision below, made by the Commissioner under the Act was made under s 31, not s 30, but, since the two categories cover such similar ground, it is a useful indicator in relation to both.

An individual requested from Bridgend County Borough Council 'A copy of the last hygiene inspection report of the Heronston Hotel'; the Council refused the request,[61] arguing that to reveal it would prejudice the exercise of its function of 'ascertaining whether circumstances which would justify regulatory action in pursuance of any enactment exist or may arise'.[62] The enactment in question was the Food Safety Act 1990. The Council's argument was that:

Decision Notice dated 9 December 2005; ref: FS50073296

. . .the release of inspection reports would undermine the way it carries out food hygiene inspections. It promotes an informal approach to the inspection of premises, where advice and practical assistance is given to businesses. . . .If information was publicly available, businesses would no longer be willing to have open discussions with inspectors. The Council would then be forced to adopt a formal inspection regime without the ability to protect the public by what it believes to be more effective means. This, it argues, would be prejudicial to the purpose at section 31(2)(c) of the Act.

The Commissioner rejected the Council's view. It is important that she did so without having to rely on the public interest test: she decided that the exemption itself was not fulfilled. This was because she took the view that 'that the release of this information would bring greater clarity to, and reinforce public confidence in, the inspection system'.[63] She also found that whilst release of the information might, as the Council argued, prejudice its informal inspections system, it would not affect the specific duties the Council had under the Food Safety Act, because it would still be obliged to carry out inspections and, if necessary, 'pursue formal regulatory action'.

Note
The following, highly significant decision arose out of the MPs expenses scandal, which is discussed in Chapter 10. The background was that three journalists requested further information on MPs' expenses, including the disclosure of claim forms and supporting documents. It was refused by the Commons but the Information Commissioner upheld their claim, as did the Tribunal. The Commons then appealed the decision to the High Court.

Corporate Officer of the House of Commons v The Information Commissioner, and others [2008] EWHC 1084 (Admin) (extracts)

This is the judgment of the Court
1 This appeal is concerned with the right of access under the Freedom of Information Act 2000 (FOIA) to information relating to the Additional Costs Allowance (ACA), an allowance payable to Members of Parliament (MPs) who represent constituencies outside London or outer London constituencies who are eligible to receive ACA rather than the London supplement payable to MPs representing inner London constituencies.

---

61   Citing s 31(1)(g).

62   A function listed in s 31(2)(c).

63   The Statement of Reasons.

Parliamentary Privilege

2 [The Court noted that 'specific provision is made for information held by the House to be exempted from the provisions of the Act if any of its privileges may be infringed' under s34(1) but that 'None has been signed.']

Narrative of the present proceedings

3 The ACA was introduced in 1971. It is one of several allowances available to MPs and reimburses them 'for expenses wholly, exclusively and necessarily incurred when staying overnight away from their main UK residence . . . for the purposes of performing Parliamentary duties. This excludes expenses that have been incurred for purely personal or political purposes'.

4 The House of Commons published information about the total sums paid annually in respect of this allowance to each of the fourteen MPs expressly identified in these proceedings. However further details including the claim forms and supporting documents were then requested.

[The Court listed the detailed information sought, which related to claims made by particular MPs, including those by Tony Blair and a number of Cabinet Ministers, as well as David Cameron.] The particular applications were:

5 The applications were refused. Complaint was made under section 50 of FOIA to the Information Commissioner (the Commissioner). After a fairly protracted process he decided that the applicants should be provided with a breakdown of the total annual amounts claimed by each MP for accommodation allowances in the specified years. The breakdown was to be given by reference to twelve categories of expense set out in the 'Green Book', a House of Commons publication giving details, among other information, about allowances and pensions. Acting through the Corporate Officer of the House of Commons, the House appealed to the Information Tribunal (the Tribunal) under s 57 of FOIA, suggesting that the order for disclosure should not have been made, or alternatively, that the categories of the breakdown of the total annual amounts should be varied. The applicants resisted this appeal and cross-appealed on the basis that the relevant information in respect of each of the four applications should be disclosed in full in accordance with the original or, in the case of Ms Brooke, the amended request.

6 The Tribunal disagreed with the Commissioner. The appeal by the House of Commons was dismissed and the cross appeals were effectively allowed by decision dated 26th February 2008. The Corporate Officer appeals against the Tribunal's decision under section 59 of FOIA . This provides for an appeal from the decision of the Tribunal 'on a point of law'. Unlike an appeal from the decision of the Commissioner to the Tribunal, this appeal is not a re-hearing nor what is sometimes described as an appeal on the merits. This court has no jurisdiction to interfere with the decision of this specialist Tribunal unless it is *legally* flawed.

. . .

The decision of the Information Tribunal

14 The carefully structured decision of the Tribunal covers 28 pages of closely reasoned judgment. . . . it led to the conclusion which is now criticised by the Corporate Officer that the rules of the House for addressing accommodation allowances during the relevant periods were 'redolent of a culture very different from that which exists in the commercial sphere or in most other public sector organisations today'. No less important, the Tribunal found that 'coupled with the very limited nature of the checks' the system as operated constituted a recipe for confusion, inconsistency and the risk of misuse. Seen in relation to

the public interest that public money should be, and be seen to be properly spent, the Tribunal found that the ACA system was deeply unsatisfactory, and its shortcomings both in terms of transparency and accountability were acute. These findings are not open to challenge in this appeal.

15 We have no doubt that the public interest is at stake. We are not here dealing with idle gossip, or public curiosity about what in truth are trivialities. The expenditure of public money through the payment of MPs' salaries and allowances is a matter of direct and reasonable interest to taxpayers.

16 The Tribunal examined the effect of the provision for exemption in the context of 'personal data' within the DPA. Even if the disclosure was amply justified in the public interest, the question arose whether it was unwarranted in the context of possible prejudice to the rights or legitimate interests of any individual MPs . . . the Tribunal concluded that, notwithstanding the entitlement of MPs to their privacy, the disclosure was not unwarranted, and should therefore be given.

17 In reaching its conclusion on these issues the Tribunal reflected on the very large number of considerations advanced on behalf of the Corporate Officer. These included the existence of a scheme for publication of the system for payment of ACA expenses and the annual audit which meant that the need for public scrutiny was sufficiently fulfilled. It was suggested that it would be unfair for MPs to be exposed to criticism for claims properly made within the rules as they existed at the time. Disclosure would lead to further questioning of MPs by the media and if disclosed the figures would be liable to be misunderstood and false comparisons might be drawn. This would distract from more important parliamentary business. Many of the issues arising from the disclosure went more to the principles governing the payment of ACA, rather than the details of the expenditure themselves. These needed no further disclosure as there was ample informa-tion available to the public. It was further suggested that wider disclosure would be liable to discourage the most able citizens from seeking election to the House. It was pointed out that MPs themselves were not public authorities subject to FOIA. Moreover there would be a perverse risk that those MPs who provided most supporting information for their claims to allowances would be those most greatly exposed to public scrutiny. We have noted this wide ranging series of suggestions, relied on by the Corporate Officer and rejected by the Tribunal as sufficient to outweigh the public interest in disclosure, before recording, in the language of the decision, that it was 'suggested that further disclosure would be unfair, having regard to the history of MPs, expectations'.

Reasonable expectations

18 The principal ground of appeal asserts that the Tribunal misdirected itself by failing to recognise the existence of and therefore give appropriate weight to the reasonable expect-ations of MPs about precisely how information about the ACA claims would be made available to the public . . . this constituted an error of law which infected the entire decision, and although the Tribunal purported to conduct the necessary balancing exercise, this highly relevant consideration was not addressed or was inadequately addressed.

[The Court went on to note the Tribunal's findings that MPs could not reasonably claim to have been unaware of what the requirements of the Act would mean for them in terms of disclosure of details of their expenses claims.]

31 In view of our narrative of the critical facts it is impossible for us to conclude that the Tribunal simply ignored the issue of MPs' reasonable expectations. This conclusion is reinforced by the careful listing of the argument as the second of a total of ten

considerations advanced on behalf of the House in support of the contention that disclosure would be inappropriate. Each was addressed in turn by the Tribunal, and albeit briefly, a clear readily understood reason given for its conclusion.

32 In our judgment the submission that the Tribunal failed to address the arguments advanced to it in the context of the reasonable expectation of MPs is unrealistic. The judgment speaks for itself. The Tribunal expressly recorded the argument, and expressly rejected it. It did so by reference to the facts, including the publication scheme itself and the relevant letters. We can find no misdirection or other error of law which would justify interfering with the decision of the Tribunal.

33 In the light of the importance of the point we add our own conclusions. Despite Mr Giffin's endeavours, we were unable to ascertain which representations made to MPs would have enabled them reasonably to expect that the detailed information ordered to be disclosed by the Tribunal would not enter the public arena. To the extent that it may have been suggested that information beyond the publication scheme would *never* be disclosed, such a representation would conflict with the fundamental purpose of section 1(1) of FOIA which was a distinct obligation to the publication scheme obligations imposed under section 19. That indeed was conceded before the Tribunal. . . . Once legislation which applies to Parliament has been enacted, MPs cannot and could not reasonably expect to contract out of compliance with it, or exempt themselves, or be exempted from its ambit. Such actions would themselves contravene the Bill of Rights, and it is inconceivable that MPs could expect to conduct their affairs on the basis that recently enacted legislation did not apply to them, or that the House, for its own purposes, was permitted to suspend or dispense with such legislation without expressly amending or repealing it. Any such expectation would be wholly unreasonable.

34 . . . Even if (which we do not accept) MPs were justified in anticipating that the details of their claims for ACA would not normally be disclosed, once it emerged, as the Tribunal has found, that the operation of the ACA system was deeply flawed, public scrutiny of the details of individual claims were inevitable. In such circumstances it would have been unreasonable for MPs to expect anything else.

[The Court then noted a particular argument based on privacy and data protection, that details should not be released that revealed MPs addresses.]

39 Having closely examined the privacy issue, not only as it related to the MPs claiming ACA, but also to anyone living with them, the Tribunal concluded that 'the ACA system is so deeply flawed, the shortfall in accountability is so substantial, and the necessity of full disclosure so convincingly established, that only the most pressing privacy needs should in our view be permitted to prevail'. It may be that the system will be revised, and subject to much more robust checking to ensure, for example, that the addresses to which ACA relates do in fact exist, and that the claims for them are within the scheme and not excessive. If so, the case for specific disclosure of such addresses may be rather less powerful. As it seems to us, all the necessary elements to the decision making process were properly recognised and carefully balanced by the Tribunal. No basis has been shown to justify interference.

45 The appeals by the Corporate Officer of the House of Commons are dismissed.

Note
For discussion of this decision and its aftermath, see P Leyland, 'Freedom of Information and the 2009 Parliamentary Expenses Scandal' [2009] *Public Law* 675. The episode is discussed in Chapter 10, pp 520–536.

Guardian Newspapers Ltd and Heather Brooke v Information Commissioner and BBC EA/2006/0011 and EA/2006/0013

Introduction

1. A Government dossier was published in September 2002 entitled IRAQ'S WEAPONS OF MASS DESTRUCTION. In March 2003 the United Kingdom went to war against Iraq. In May 2003 Mr Andrew Gilligan during a BBC broadcast made criticisms of the accuracy and truthfulness of the dossier which in some respects went beyond what his source, Dr David Kelly, had told him. In July 2003 Dr Kelly took his own life. Lord Hutton's 'Report of the Inquiry into the Circumstances Surrounding the Death of Dr David Kelly CMG', published on 28 January 2004, made certain criticisms of the BBC in relation to the report by Andrew Gilligan.

2. Later the same day the Governors of the BBC met to consider the Hutton Report. The Chairman and the Director General of the BBC resigned.

3. This appeal is concerned with whether the BBC must release the minutes of the Governors' meeting pursuant to the Freedom of Information Act 2000 ('FOIA' or 'the Act').

4. We are not directly concerned with the September dossier, the Iraq war, Mr Gilligan's remarks, the conduct of the BBC, or Lord Hutton's report: for our purposes those matters are general background to the appeal and we express no view on them. Nor are we concerned with whether the resignations were an appropriate or inappropriate response to the Hutton report. The only matter for our decision is the withholding or release of the Governors' minutes. . . .

6. In February 2005 Heather Brooke, who is a campaigner for open government and a freelance writer, requested of the BBC *'all minutes from meetings held by the BBC's Board of Governors during the time period January 16–31, 2004'*. In March 2005 Matt Wells of The Guardian requested *'complete copies of the agenda and minutes of the special board of governors meeting of 28 January, 2004'*.

7. The BBC declined the requests, contending that disclosure would inhibit the free and frank exchange of views for the purposes of deliberation, and citing FOIA s 36(2)(b)(ii). The BBC's reasoning was set out in two letters of 17 March 2005 and a further letter of 20 May 2005.

The complaints to the Information Commissioner

8. Ms Brooke and The Guardian complained to the Information Commissioner. He issued a Decision Notice in both cases on 15 February 2006. He agreed with the BBC that the s 36 exemption applied, and decided *'the public interest in maintaining this exemption currently overrides the public interest in disclosing the requested information'*.

. . . .

53. The exemption requires a degree of likelihood that the free and frank exchange of views for the purposes of deliberation will be inhibited by such disclosure. We interpret the phrase *'would or would be likely to'* in the same sense as in *Hogan v Information Commissioner* EA/2005/0026 and 0030 at paragraphs 34–35, derived from *R (On the application of Lord) v Secretary of State for the Home Office* [2003] EWHC 2073 (Admin) per Munby J at paragraphs 99–100. It means that inhibition would probably occur (i.e., on the balance of probabilities, the chance being greater than 50%) or that there would be a 'very significant and weighty chance' that it would occur. A 'real risk' is not enough; the degree of risk must be such that there 'may very well be' such inhibition, even if the risk falls short of being more probable than not.

54. The first condition for the application of the exemption is not the Commissioner's or the Tribunal's opinion on the likelihood of inhibition, but the qualified person's *reasonable opinion*'. If the opinion is reasonable, the Commissioner should not under s 36 substitute his own view for that of the qualified person. Nor should the Tribunal.

. . .

64. On this point we consider that the Commissioner is right, and that in order to satisfy the sub-section the opinion must be both reasonable in substance and reasonably arrived at. We derive this conclusion from the scheme of the Act and the tenor of s 36, which is that the general right of access to information granted by s 1 of the Act is only excluded in defined circumstances and on substantial grounds. The provision that the exemption is only engaged where a qualified person is of the reasonable opinion required by s 36 is a protection which relies on the good faith and proper exercise of judgment of that person. That protection would be reduced if the qualified person were not required by law to give proper rational consideration to the formation of the opinion, taking into account only relevant matters and ignoring irrelevant matters. In consideration of the special status which the Act affords to the opinion of qualified persons, they should be expected at least to direct their minds appropriately to the right matters and disregard irrelevant matters. Moreover, precisely because the opinion is essentially a judgment call on what might happen in the future, on which people may disagree, if the process were not taken into account, in many cases the reasonableness of the opinion would be effectively unchallengeable; we cannot think that that was the Parliamentary intention.

. . .

67. It should be noted that the BBC's view was not merely that there was a very significant and weighty chance that the free and frank exchange of views would be inhibited, but that it would indeed be inhibited.

. . .

78. Mr Tomlinson further submitted that the BBC's opinion was mere assertion, not based on evidence as to the effect on the free and frank exchange of views. We consider there is considerable force in this criticism. The material before us did not show that any Governor actually said that disclosure of the minutes of 28 January 2004 would, or would be likely to, inhibit the free and frank exchange of views in future deliberations. Nevertheless, the Governors did give consideration to the exemption at their meeting in February 2005, and we are unable to regard the absence of specific evidence as necessarily invalidating the judgment that was made, which related to the future and was therefore necessarily hypothetical.

. . .

101. In considering where the public interest lies, we give weight to the BBC's opinion that disclosure of the information would inhibit the free and frank exchange of views for the purposes of deliberation.

102. However, in order to weigh the balance of public interest, we have to form a view on the severity, extent and frequency with which such inhibition would or might occur, and in our view the evidence from the BBC on that aspect was unimpressive.

. . .

113. It does not seem to us that the likelihood of inhibition of future discussions, resulting from disclosure of the minutes of 28 January 2004, would be particularly high, or that any such inhibition would be particularly severe or frequent. The more sensitive the future material at the time of an information request, the greater the prospect that the public interest represented by the exemption will be held to outweigh the public interest in dis-

closure of that particular material. Future cases arising under s 36 can be considered on their own merits, in light of their own particular circumstances.

Between Cabinet Office and Information Commissioner
EA/2008/0024 and EA/2008/0029
Tribunal decision 27 Jan 2009

Decision

The Tribunal upholds the decision notice dated 19 February 2008 and dismisses the appeal by the Cabinet Office against the Information Commissioner's direction to disclose (subject to the redactions specified) the Minutes for the Cabinet Meetings that took place on 13th and 17th March 2003.

The Tribunal dismisses the appeal by Dr Lamb seeking disclosure of the other records of the Cabinet Meetings that took place on 13th and 17th March 2003, as identified in its preliminary decision dated 11 August 2008.

Reasons for Decision

Introduction

We have decided that the public interest in maintaining the confidentiality of the formal minutes of two Cabinet meetings at which Ministers decided to commit forces to military action in Iraq did not, at the time when the Cabinet Office refused a request for disclosure in April 2007, outweigh the public interest in disclosure. We have reached that decision by a majority and not without difficulty. We concluded that there was a strong public interest in maintaining the confidentiality of information relating to the formulation of government policy or Ministerial communications, (including in particular the maintenance of the long standing convention of cabinet collective responsibility). However, this is an exceptional case, the circumstances of which brought together a combination of factors that were so important that, in combination, they created very powerful public interest reasons why disclosure was in the public interest. It was this that led the majority of the panel to conclude that they were at least equal to those in favour of maintaining the exemption and that, subject to certain redactions designed to avoid unnecessary risk to the UK's international relations, the minutes should be disclosed.

We have decided, unanimously, that the public interest in maintaining the confidentiality of certain informal notes taken during the same Cabinet Meetings did outweigh the public interest in their disclosure. They are therefore not to be disclosed at all and, of course, no question of redaction therefore arises in respect of that information. . . .

34. As the quotation from section 2(2)(b) in paragraph 6 above makes clear disclosure of information covered by a qualified exemption must be ordered unless the public interest factors in favour of confidentiality outweigh the public interest in disclosure. Those arguing for disclosure therefore have a slight advantage in that they do not have to show that the factors in favour of disclosure exceed those in favour of maintaining the exemption. They only have to show that they are equal. . .

37. The general factors were said to arise in this way. The Cabinet Office relied on both sub-sections (1)(a) and (1)(b) of section 35, but it concentrated on the fact that all the disputed information fell squarely within subsection (1)(b), because it concerned policy discussions between ministers in Cabinet. This brought into consideration the long established constitutional convention of collective responsibility. As this lies at the heart of the Appeal we set out in the following paragraphs our understanding of what the convention involves and the manner it which it has developed over the years. . . .

50. The Cabinet Office relied in particular on the importance of maintaining the convention of Cabinet collective responsibility and confidence, as described above, and stressed its importance to the effective functioning of a central element of the nation's system of government. The evidence of Sir Gus O'Donnell stressed that the danger to the convention lay, in particular, in the risk that if Ministers anticipated that Cabinet Minutes would be prematurely disclosed they would disrupt genuine debate by speaking for the official record and/or ensure that sensitive issues were addressed in small group discussions outside the Cabinet. However, the Cabinet Office did accept that the section 35 exemption was qualified, not absolute. It acknowledged that there might therefore be occasions when the public interest in disclosing particular information was at least equal to the public interest in maintaining confidentiality. But it argued that cogent reasons must nevertheless be given to establish that, in a given case, the public interest lay in favour of disclosure.

51. For his part the Information Commissioner accepted, in both his Decision Notice and in the submissions made to us by his counsel, Mr Pitt-Payne, that the maintenance of Cabinet confidentiality was a strong factor favouring the maintenance of the exemption. He acknowledged, too, that disclosure shortly after any meeting as a matter of routine would damage policy making and collective Cabinet responsibility and that it was relevant to take into account the possible indirect consequences of particular information being disclosed. That is to say that the potential consequences for future decision-making processes lay at the heart of the public interest test (*Export Credits Guarantee Department v Friends of the Earth* [2008] EWHC 638 (Admin) at paragraph 38). The Information Commissioner qualified his concession by adding that in his view the question must always be to what extent will disclosure of the particular information in dispute have the relevant indirect adverse consequences. He encouraged us to focus on the damage to Cabinet collective responsibility that might be caused by the disclosure of these particular minutes in the particular circumstances of this case (including the passage of time between the events in question and the date when Dr Lamb's request was refused). The Information Commissioner's own Decision Notice had stressed that he considered that the circumstances were exceptional and that the disclosure of the two specific and unusual sets of Cabinet minutes would not have the detrimental effects that the Cabinet Office feared. . .

56. The Information Commissioner also argued that Cabinet collective responsibility would actually be enhanced by the disclosure of material showing how the Cabinet operated. We note the point but do not place any great weight on it.

57. Finally, we should mention the specific reasons for maintaining the exemption. These were that British military forces were still active within Iraq and that the content of the disputed information may impact present and future decisions relating to the disposition of those forces. We can say that, having read the Minutes (and again without disclosing their detailed content), we do not believe that their publication would cause any particular harm in either of those two respects.

Factors in favour of disclosure

58. In his Decision Notice the Information Commissioner stated that the public interest factors in favour of disclosure were:

(a) The gravity and controversial nature of the subject matter;
(b) Accountability for government decisions;
(c) Transparency of decision making; and
(d) Public participation in government decisions.

He accepted that there was a degree of overlap between those factors and it may be said that the desirability of establishing factors (b) to (d), inclusive, stems from the importance of factor (a). Or, put another way, that the public interest is in knowing, not only whether the UK had been right to go to war, but also how that decision had been reached.

59. The Information Commissioner laid stress on the fact that the decision to go to war was controversial at the time, and remains so, because it was not one that was based on self defence or a united international response to aggression. It had caused the resignation from the Government of one senior Minister, two other more junior members of the Government and one Civil Servant as well as public dissent by another Cabinet Minister. It had been opposed by a mass public demonstration. It had been based on a decision to remove or destroy weapons of mass destruction, a strategy that was not supported by many other nations and is now perceived as having been based on incorrect intelligence. It had also been based on legal advice which has been challenged by a number of knowledgeable commentators. The Cabinet Office accepted the importance of the decision that had been made but sought to persuade us that it was not so exceptional as to justify the convention of Cabinet collective responsibility being put at risk. . . .

62. There may be cases in the future where the particular circumstances do require a consideration of the public interest in support of disclosure of legal advice given during the course of military conflict. But it is not an issue in this case. All we are required to do is to give appropriate weight to, among other factors, the public interest in disclosure at the relevant time of certain specific information about the Cabinet's consideration of the particular legal advice involved in this case. That advice dealt with the initial commitment of forces. The weight we apply to that factor does not imply any judgment as to the weight that might be applied in any future case where the relevant advice relates, not to the initial decision to commit forces to action, but to the detailed conduct of the resulting military action thereafter. Even more clearly, our decision does not contribute anything to the consideration of any other factors that may be required to be applied, on one side of the scale or the other, in any such future case.

63. There was also said to remain a concern that the stated reasons for taking the decision were not genuine, that UK policy was being dominated by the strategy adopted by the USA and that the style of government adopted by the Prime Minister at the time had the effect of emasculating Cabinet as the central forum for decision making on major issues. As we have already noted the last of these points has been supported by statements made by Clare Short, one of the members of the Cabinet at the time and, more significantly, by the conclusions of the Butler Report.

Notes

1. In the hotel food inspection decision above the points made by the Commissioner indicate a robust upholding of transparency as a good in itself and a sceptical attitude to the arguments of public authorities against it. More strikingly still, whilst the Commissioner did not formally have to consider the argument based on the public interest, since she did not find the exemption to apply at all, she did 'note that there is an overwhelming public interest in the disclosure of this category of information'. This is a significant statement, and indicates that robust policing by the Commissioner, who will not in this area be subject to the Ministerial veto, may lay to rest some of the fears generated by s 30, as to the transmission of information to the public about issues affecting health and safety.

2. The phrase 'likely to prejudice' used in certain FoI exemptions (above)[64] has been considered by the courts in the case of *R (On the application of Alan Lord) and The Secretary of State for the Home*

Department. Although this case concerns the Data Protection Act, the Commissioner regards this interpretation as persuasive. The judgment reads:

> 'Likely' connotes a degree of probability where there is a very significant and weighty chance of prejudice to the identified public interests. The degree of risk must be such that there 'may very well' be prejudice to those interests, even if the risk falls short of being more probable than not.

In other words, the probability of prejudice occurring need not be 'more likely than not', but there should certainly be substantially more than a remote possibility. Once again, this approach will help to rule out flimsy or implausible claims of prejudice.

3. The case of *Corporate Officer of the House of Commons v The Information Commissioner* (above) concerned requests under the FoI Act by journalists Ben Leapman and Jon Ungoed-Thomas and freedom of information campaigner Heather Brooke. All three asked for details of the expenses claimed by certain MPs to be released. The requests were refused by the Commons and referred to the Information Commissioner, who joined the three journalists' cases together and ordered the release of some information on 15 June 2007. MPs had, in May 2007, voted in favour of the Freedom of Information (Amendment) Bill which sought to exempt MPs from the 2000 FoI Act. The House of Commons voted 96 to 25 in favour of the Exemption of the House of Commons amendment. The Bill was then withdrawn prior to second reading in the House of Lords since it appeared that the Bill would be defeated in the Lords. In February 2008, after referral to the Information Tribunal, it was held that Commons authorities would release information on 14 MPs. This decision was appealed, meaning that the release of the information was delayed. The appeal was heard at the High Court, which ruled on 16 May 2008 in favour of releasing the information on the basis that the Tribunal's decision was not flawed in law as had been argued. As regards the FoI claim, the argument that the Tribunal's decision gave insufficient weight to the reasonable expectations of MPs was rejected on the basis that the evidence did not support that claim. Disclosure of the information in question in the media had by this time made the appeal academic. However, it remains an important precedent as to the relevant exemption under the FoI Act. The separate privacy claim under the DPA was also found to fail on the basis that the Tribunal had been right to conclude that the public interest in knowing of the MPs' addresses outweighed their private interests (interpreted in accordance with the principles under Art 8 ECHR) in keeping the addresses private.

4. In January 2009, Harriet Harman, then Leader of the House of Commons, tabled a motion which would exempt MPs' expenses from being disclosed under a Freedom of Information request, in order to prevent any further disclosure of information. Labour MPs were placed under a three line whip in order to force the motion through the Commons. However, opposition parties stated that they would vote against the proposals. Strong public and media opposition was also evident. The proposals were then dropped on 21 January 2009. The Commons authorities announced that full disclosure of all MPs' expenses would be published on 1 July 2009, which occurred, causing great controversy when the details became known. The incident is illustrative of the significance of FoI; it demonstrates that various aspects of public life remained unscrutinised until its advent.

5. *Use of the exemption under s 36(2)(b)(ii).* This exemption applies to information to where 'in the reasonable opinion of a qualified person, disclosure "(a) would, or would be likely to, prejudice . . . ." the free and frank exchange of views for the purposes of deliberation'. The 2007 decision of the Tribunal (above) that the BBC should disclose the minutes of the Governors' meeting represented a highly significant interpretation of the public interest test. The BBC had argued that minutes of all governors' meetings should remain secret as the governors would be hesitant to

express their real opinions if they knew that these accounts would be published. It was found that the exemption applied, but that in balancing the competing values at stake under the public interest test the tribunal agreed with the *Guardian*'s argument that the governors' meeting after the Hutton report was a 'unique and highly unusual' event in the BBC's history. Therefore it found that the public interest in disclosure outweighed the argument in favour of maintaining confidentiality.

6.   The findings of the Tribunal in January 2009, extracted above, regarding the disclosure of the Cabinet minutes relating to the decision to engage in military action in Iraq, is obviously of great significance due to the importance of the decision. The Tribunal determination also clearly has important implications for the use of FoI in relation to Cabinet decisions in future. Since information of this nature is covered by an exemption under s 35 which is subject to a public interest test, the Tribunal had to engage in a careful balancing exercise, weighing up the public interest in disclosure against the interest in maintaining confidentiality. That balancing exercise came down against disclosure of the informal notes of the meeting. As regards the minutes, a number of the factors weighing on each side are set out in the extracts above. Under the FoI Act, the Government does not generally have to release information relating to the formulation of policy due to the s 35 exemption—if challenged as to the use of the exemption, it is normally able to argue that the public interest in confidentiality prevails. But the tribunal found that this was an exceptional case due to the strong public interest in knowing what was said as Ministers discussed the decision to approve the invasion.

7.   *First uses of the Ministerial veto.* Once the Tribunal had decided in the 2009 Iraq war Cabinet minutes decision in favour of disclosure, however, the Ministerial veto was used by Jack Straw, the Justice Secretary, to override the decision—the first time the veto has been used. His statement, made to the House of Commons on Tuesday 24 February 2009 was as follows:

> Following the Information Tribunal's decision upholding the Information Commissioner's decision that a redacted version of the Cabinet minutes of 13 and 17 March 2003 should be disclosed, and having taken the view of Cabinet, I have today given a certificate under section 53 of the Freedom of Information Act 2000 to the Information Commissioner. The effect of my certificate is that the disputed information—these Cabinet Minutes relating to Iraq—will not be disclosed.
>
> The conclusion I have reached has rested on the assessment of the public interest in disclosure and in non-disclosure of these Cabinet minutes. I have placed a copy of that certificate, and a detailed statement of the reasons for my decision in the Libraries of both Houses. I have also published today the criteria against which I decided to exercise the veto in this case.
>
> To permit the Tribunal's view of the public interest to prevail would risk serious damage to Cabinet government; an essential principle of British Parliamentary democracy. That eventuality is not in the public interest.

8.   The above is a summary, published by the Ministry of Justice. The full statement is available on Hansard.[65] This was obviously the type of situation the veto was designed for. Thus the strong public interest grounds identified by the Tribunal for disclosure were obviously afforded no weight—in effect—by the Government in deciding to use the veto. This use of the veto graphically illustrates the extent to which its existence is opposed to the values underlying FoI since persons who have an interest in preventing disclosure have the last word on release of the information, not

---

the Independent Commissioner or Tribunal. In the House of Commons, Jack Straw said that he had not taken the decision 'lightly'. He went to add that the public interest in disclosure of the minutes could not 'supplant the public interest in maintaining the integrity of our system of government . . . it is a necessary decision to protect the public interest in effective cabinet government'. His decision was supported by the Conservatives.[66] Thus, it may be assumed that FoI requests for disclosure of Cabinet minutes in future are very unlikely ever to be successful.

9.   The second use of the veto to date occurred in December 2009 and related to minutes of a Cabinet Committee on Devolution. The original decision of the Commissioner was as follows:

Freedom of Information Act 2000 Decision Notice Date 23 June 2009, Public Authority: Cabinet Office

The complainant made his request to the Cabinet Office on 3 October 2005 for the following request information:

> I would like to make a request under Freedom of Information to see all the minutes of the Cabinet Sub-Committee on Devolution Scotland, Wales and the Regions (DSWR).

[The complainant subsequently refined his request to]:

> the briefing papers and supporting documentation prepared by civil servants and ministerial advisers for the first meeting of the Cabinet Sub-Committee (DSWR). My understanding is that the Committee met for the first time in early May 1997.

6. On 4 November 2005 the Cabinet Office issued a refusal notice in respect of the refined request of 6 October 2005. The Cabinet Office confirmed it holds relevant information but found that the papers directly concerned the work of the Cabinet Committee and, like some of the information identified in the first part of the complainant's request, found this information to be exempt by virtue of section 35(1)(a) and (b). In applying the public interest test the Cabinet Office found the public interest in maintaining the exemption outweighed the public interest in disclosure of the information.

Findings of fact

12. The withheld information is the minutes of the Cabinet Committee on Devolution, Scotland, Wales and the Regions from 1997. This Committee was chaired by Lord Irvine of Lairg and was charged to give collective consideration to the details of the devolution proposals which had been outlined in broad terms in the Labour Party's manifesto for the 1997 election. The committee was also to consider the promotion of legislation to effect the devolution proposals and how such legislation could be implemented. [The Commissioner went on to find that the minutes were covered by the class exemptions in section 35(1)(a) and (b) but then went on to consider whether nevertheless the public interest in disclosure overrode those exemptions.]

The Cabinet Office acknowledge that there is a public interest in disclosing information which would enable: greater transparency in how government operates; the public

---

66   See House of Commons debates, 23 February 2009.

to assess the quality of debate between ministers and the quality of decision making; improved capability for the public to contribute knowledgeably to debate and also a strong public interest in ensuring that decision making is based upon full consideration of all the possible options.

21. However, the Cabinet Office argued that the requirements of openness must be balanced against the proper and effective functioning of government. They state that:

> the very existence of the exemption at section 35(1) (b) is designed to protect the way in which government Ministers communicate with each other and conduct the business of government through the Cabinet and Cabinet Committee system. At the very heart of this system is the constitutional convention of collective responsibility (the convention). The maintenance of this convention is fundamental to the continued effectiveness of cabinet government, and its continued existence if there-fore manifestly in the public interest. To release details of discussions between ministers in Cabinet committees would undermine this. Ministers should be able to discuss freely and frankly in private in the expectation that when decisions have been reached, they will present a united front. In order to safeguard the convention it must be applied consistently and therefore if it were only information that revealed dis-agreement between ministers that was withheld then it would soon become apparent that where information is withheld there must have been disagreement. The principle of collective responsibility would then have been breached.

. . .

23. The Cabinet Office argue that the harm caused by disclosure of Cabinet and Cabinet Committee minutes will in most cases by twofold: the specific relating to the subject under discussion; and the general, relating to damage to the doctrine of collective responsibility through the impact on future behaviour. If Ministers cannot be confident that their discussions will be protected they may be inhibited in their deliberations. They may seek to have key discussions outside of the confines of meetings, or encourage minimal recording of discussions. This would be contrary to good government; which requires Ministers and their officials to engage in full, frank and uninhibited consideration of policy options.

24. The Cabinet Office state that there is a place for public participation in the policy making process and for public debate of policy options, however it is not in the best interest of policy formulation that every stage of the policy making process and every aspect of ministerial discussion should be exposed to public scrutiny.

25. The Commissioner recognises that the Cabinet Office's main argument for main-taining the exemption is that disclosure could undermine the convention of collective Cabinet responsibility.

26. In reaching a decision as to where the balance of the public interest lies the Commissioner has considered the findings of the Information Tribunal in *Scotland Office vs. Information Commissioner EA/2007/0070* in which the Tribunal stated:

> To the extent that the Appellant is suggesting that because of the impor-tance of the convention, there is some form of presumption against dis-closure of such information implicit in that exemption, or that the public

interest in maintaining the exemption under section 35(1) (b) is inherently weighty, we must disagree. . . . Furthermore not all information coming within the scope of section 35(1) (b) will bring the convention of collective Cabinet responsibility into play. Some communication may be completely anodyne or may deal with processes rather than policy issues. Communications may also be purely for information purposes, such as when reports are circulated. The very fact that certain information constitutes Ministerial communications, does not, therefore, mean that there is a public interest in non disclosure. Even where Ministerial communications engage the collective responsibility of ministers (where, for example, it reveals actual deliberations and exchanges of views), that in itself does not mean that the public interest against disclosure will inevitably be weighty. The maintenance of the convention of collective responsibility is a public interest like any other.

27. The Tribunal went onto explain that:

Where Ministerial communication does engage the convention of collective responsibility, it is necessary in particular, to assess whether and to what extent the collective responsibility of Ministers would be undermined by disclosure. Factors such as the content of the information, whether it deals with issues that are still 'live', the extent of the public interest and debate in those issues, the specific view of different Ministers it reveals, the extent to which Ministers are identified, whether those Ministers are still in office or in politics as well as the wider political context, are all matters that are likely to have a bearing on the assessment of the public interest balance.

28. In this case the Committee minutes do not deal with 'live' policy issues as devolution as proposed in the Labour Party 1997 manifesto has been realised. Specifically the remit of the Committee was:

To consider policy and other issues arising from the Government's policies for devolution to Scotland and Wales and the regions of England and to promote and oversee progress of the relevant legislation through Parliament and its subject implementation.

The relevant legislation was enacted and devolution in Scotland and Wales has long since been implemented.

29. The Commissioner has also considered the members of the Committee and notes that of those only one remains active in the government. Some have passed away and only a handful remain in any way involved in politics. In any event, the Commissioner also does not consider that the minutes attribute any specific opinions to any individual Minister.

30. The Commissioner also considered the findings of the Tribunal in relation to the notion of collective responsibility in *FoE vs Information Commissioner and The Export Credit Guarantee Department EA/2006/0073.* In considering the public interest the Tribunal found that:

There is not and can be no immutable rule in terms of reliance upon the collective ministerial responsibility and/or the individual accountability of ministers to Parliament. The Tribunal refutes any suggestion that those notions, either singly or together represent some form of trump card in favour of maintaining the particular exemption.

Whilst the Tribunal decision in this case related to regulation 12(4)(e) under the Environmental Information Regulations to all intents and purposes the consideration of the public interest in that case were equally applicable to section 35(1)(b).

31. Having viewed the withheld information the Commissioner does not consider that disclosure of the minutes in this case would undermine the convention of collective responsibility. The minutes themselves do not offer much insight into the nature of the debate or the contributions of individual ministers which would, as suggested by the Cabinet Office, undermine the convention.

32. The Commissioner notes that there are competing arguments as to whether the specific policy issue under discussion at the Committee is still 'live'. The Commissioner accepts that political debate may continue on the nature of devolution in general. In that respect there is a strong public interest in disclosure to inform current or future debate. However, the topics specifically under discussion in 1997 were no longer live at the time of the request as the resultant decisions in relation to the withheld information had been taken and implemented. The Commissioner considers that the policies discussed and the discussions themselves relate to historic decisions and that the current political climate differs significantly to the one in which the Committee operated. The devolved administrations have been in place since 1999 and the different options discussed within the sub-committee meetings were either rejected or implemented at the time.

33. The Commissioner's approach in this case in consistent with that advocated in the majority Tribunal decision in the *Iraq Cabinet minutes case* (EA/2008/0024 & 0029). The focus of the decision must turn on the facts of the each case and in particular the subject-matter of the issues under consideration. The Commissioner has weighed the competing public interest factors in this case. In line with the Tribunal decisions referred to above, he rejects the blanket approach taken by the Cabinet Office which is that disclosure of the minutes, regardless of content is not in the public interest as it would undermine the convention of collective responsibility. Whilst the convention and it maintenance is one of the public interest factors to be considered, and it is a factor that the Commissioner places much weight upon, it is only one element of the public interest test.

34. In this case, the issues discussed and recorded in the minutes continue to be of significant public interest, but the sensitivity of the specific content has reduced with the passage of time. The Commissioner finds that, on balance, the public interest in maintaining the exemption does not outweigh the public interest in disclosure of the information.

The Decision

35. The Commissioner's decision is that the public authority did not deal with the request for information in accordance with the Act.

(i) The Cabinet Office incorrectly applied section 35(1) (a) and (b) to the withheld information, namely the minutes of the meetings held in 1997 of the Cabinet Committee on Devolution, Scotland, Wales and the Regions.

(ii) The Cabinet Office breached the requirements of section 1(1)(b) by failing to disclose the requested information to the complainant.

Steps required

36. The Commissioner requires the public authority to take the following steps to ensure compliance with the Act: Disclose the information withheld under sections 35(1) (a) and (b) as described in paragraph 35 (i) above.

37. The public authority must take the steps required by this notice within 35 calendar days of the date of this notice.

Notes (cont.)

10. As with the order for the production of the Cabinet Minutes relating to the Iraq War, the Labour Government decided not to comply, and instead use the Ministerial veto. In a statement in the House of Commons, on Thursday 10 December 2009, The Right Honourable Jack Straw MP, Lord Chancellor and Secretary of State for Justice said:

> I have today given the Information Commissioner a certificate under section 53 of the Freedom of Information Act 2000 ('the Act'). The certificate relates to case FS50100665 from 23 June 2009 in which, in my opinion, the Information Commissioner wrongly found that the Cabinet Office had failed to comply with section 1(1)(b) of the Act by withholding copies of the minutes of the Cabinet Ministerial Committee on Devolution to Scotland and Wales and the English Regions (DSWR) of 1997. The consequence of my giving the Information Commissioner a certificate is that the Commissioner's decision notice ceases to have effect.
>
> This is only the second time this power (the 'veto') has been exercised since the Act came into force in 2005 and over that period of time central government has received approximately 160,000 non-routine requests for information. The decision to exercise the veto in this case was not taken lightly but in accordance with the Statement of Government Policy on the use of the executive override as it relates to information falling within the scope of section 35(1) of the Act.
>
> In accordance with the policy, my conclusion rests on an assessment of the public interest in disclosure and non-disclosure of these Cabinet minutes, and of the exceptional nature of the case. Whilst the convention of collective Cabinet responsibility is only one part of the public interest test, in my view disclosure of the information in this case would put the convention at serious risk of harm. As an integral part of our system of government the maintenance of the convention is strongly in the public interest and must be given appropriate weight when deciding where the balance of the public interest lies.
>
> Having done that, and having taken into account all of the circumstances of this case, I have concluded that the public interest falls in favour of non-disclosure and that this is an exceptional case where release would be damaging to the convention of collective responsibility and detrimental to the effective operation of Cabinet government. Consequently, this case warrants the exercise of the veto.[67]

---

67   Ministry of Justice 10 December 2009. Available www.justice.gov.uk/news/announcement101209a.htm.

FURTHER READING

R Austin, 'The Freedom of Information Act 2000: A Sheep in Wolf's Clothing?', in J Jowell and D Oliver, *The Changing Constitution*, 6th edn (2007)

SH Bailey, N Taylor, *Bailey, Harris and Jones: Civil Liberties: Cases and Materials*, 6th edn (2009), Chapter 12

J Beatson and Y Cripps, *Freedom of Expression and Freedom of Information* (2000)

P Birkinshaw, *Government and Information* (1990)

P Birkinshaw, *Freedom of Information: The Law, the Practice and the Ideal*, 3rd edn (2001)

KD Ewing and CA Gearty, *Freedom under Thatcher* (1990), Chapter 6

D Feldman, *Civil Liberties and Human Rights in England and Wales*, 2nd edn (2002)

H Fenwick, *Civil Liberties and Human Rights*, 4th edn (2007), Chapter 7

P Gill, *Policing Politics: Security, Intelligence and the Liberal Democratic State* (1994)

T Hartley and J Griffiths, *Government and Law* (1981), Chapter 13

D Leigh, *The Frontiers of Secrecy—Closed Government in Britain* (1980)

L Lustgarten and I Leigh, *In From the Cold: National Security and Parliamentary Democracy* (1994)

J Michael, *The Politics of Secrecy* (1982)

G Robertson, *Public Secrets* (1982)

S Shetreet (ed), *Free Speech and National Security* (1991)

N Whitty, T Murphy and S Livingstone, *Civil Liberties Law* (2001), Chapter 7

CHAPTER 14
JUDICIAL REVIEW:
AVAILABILITY, APPLICABILITY,
PROCEDURAL EXCLUSIVITY

INTRODUCTION

Judicial review is the procedure whereby the High Court is able to review the legality of decisions made by a wide variety of bodies which affect the public, ranging from Government Ministers exercising prerogative[1] or statutory powers, to the actions of certain powerful self-regulatory bodies. In the following chapter, the principles which the courts apply in making this assessment are considered. This chapter is concerned with the principles which determine whether review will be available or whether the complainant must rely on private law remedies; it examines the important procedural implications for the complainant which result from this public/private divide. The reforms to judicial review procedure represented by the Civil Procedure Rules (CPR), Part 54 are explored. These rules came into force on 2 October 2000, the same day as the Human Rights Act 1998 (HRA). It should be noted that cases concerning applications made before this date will be governed by Order 53 of the Rules of the Supreme Court, and so will often refer to 'Ord 53'. Much of the case law decided under Ord 53 remains a reliable guide to how things will be conducted under the new CPR. As Fordham comments: 'Part 54 [CPR] is not identical to RSC Order 53 but its practical effect on key points remains the same.'[2] The issue of who may apply for review is also given thorough discussion, with particular reference to the position of campaigning groups, which are increasingly turning to legal methods as a way of attacking decisions to which they are opposed. Related matters, such as the circumstances in which review may be excluded, are also explored.

What limitations, then, are there on the availability of judicial review? Five main factors are used to decide whether aggrieved persons can challenge decisions. First, is the body which had made the decision one which it is appropriate to subject to review? Second, even if the body is in general terms subject to review, is the particular decision complained of reviewable? Third, does the person who seeks to challenge the decision have standing *(locus standi)* to do so? Fourth, what is the procedural relevance for the applicant of answers to the above questions? Does he or she have to proceed in a particular way depending on whether review is available? What will be the consequences for the applicant's case if he or she uses a procedure deemed inappropriate by the court for challenging the decision in question? Finally, we will briefly consider some instances in which Parliament has tried to exclude or limit the right to judicial review, and the courts' response to these attempts. These issues are examined below.

WHAT KINDS OF BODY ARE SUSCEPTIBLE TO REVIEW?

It is important to understand first of all that judicial review involves the imposition of a set of standards for lawful decision making upon public bodies. Hence the court, before reviewing a body, must ascertain whether it is truly 'public' in nature. But why does the law impose such requirements on governmental bodies? Peter Cane explains:

> First, because the institutions of governance have the job of running the country they must have some functions, powers, and duties which private citizens do not

---

1 For discussion specifically of the courts' ability to review the exercise of the prerogative, see Chapter 11 at 575–599.

2 M Fordham, 'Judicial Review: The New Rules' [2001] PL 4.

have; obvious examples are the waging of war and issuing of passports. Secondly, because of the very great power government institutions can wield over its citizens (most particularly because government enjoys a monopoly of legitimate force) we may want to impose on them special duties of procedural fairness that do not normally apply to private citizens and special rules about what organs of governance may do and decide. Thirdly, because certain institutions of governance have a monopoly over certain activities and the provision of certain goods and service, it might be thought that the exercise of such powers ought to be subject to forms of 'public accountability' to which the activities of private individuals are usually not subject.[3]

Access to judicial review is now governed by the Civil Procedure Rules, Part 54, along with s 31 of the Supreme Court Act 1981 (quoted below, pp 746–749). CPR 54.1 provides:

> (2) In this Part—
>   (a) a 'claim for judicial review' means a claim to review the lawfulness of
>   (i) an enactment; or
>   (ii) a decision, action or failure to act in relation to the *exercise of a public function* [emphasis added].

Not all decision-making bodies will be subject to review. There are clear examples of those which are. Many applications for judicial review are concerned with bodies such as local authorities carrying out statutory duties, which are quite clearly subject to public law remedies. The fact that a body derives its authority from statute will generally be conclusive—though not always: see the *Lloyds* case below. So statutory regulatory bodies, such as Ofcom, will generally be subject to judicial review, unless there is some particular reason why not (for example that judicial review has been excluded or restricted by statute).[4] Thus recently in *R (On the application of Siborurema) v Office of the Independent Adjudicator for Higher Education*,[5] the Adjudicator, who now deals with certain complaints by staff and students from universities (in this case a decision by a university to require a student to withdraw) was found to be subject to review.

Difficulties arise in the case of bodies that are created in some other way, such as self-regulatory bodies set up by persons with a common interest, or where a public authority contracts out its services. As David Pannick[6] notes:

> That public law does not regulate the decisions of bodies with which the applicant has voluntarily entered into a consensual relationship is well established. As Lord Parker CJ explained in 1967, 'private or domestic tribunals have always been outside the scope of certiorari since their authority is derived solely from contract, that is, from the agreement of the parties concerned' [*ex parte Lain* [1967] 2 QB 86 at 882B-C].

---

3   P Cane, *An Introduction to Administrative Law* (2004), pp 13–14.

4   See e.g. below at 764–774.

5   [2007] EWCA Civ 1365; [2008] ELR 209.

6   D Pannick, 'Who is Subject to Judicial Review and in Respect of What?' [1992] PL 1.

This might appear to rule out self-regulatory bodies, since they technically depend upon voluntary submission to their findings. However, at least in some decisions, the courts have taken a more realistic view of the situation.

In the leading case in this area, the Court of Appeal had to consider whether the Panel on Takeovers and Mergers, a self-regulating body without statutory, prerogative or common law powers, was subject to the supervisory jurisdiction of the High Court as performing a public function. The Panel operated a Code regulating takeovers and mergers in the City.

R v City Panel on Takeovers and Mergers ex parte Datafin plc
[1987] 2 WLR 699, 702–05, 712–15

Sir John Donaldson MR [quoting from the Introduction to the Code]:

> The code has not, and does not seek to have, the force of law, but those who wish to take advantage of the facilities of the securities markets in the United Kingdom should conduct themselves in matters relating to take-overs according to the code. Those who do not so conduct themselves cannot expect to enjoy those facilities and may find that they are withheld. . .

The provisions of the code fall into two categories. On the one hand, the code enunciates general principles of conduct to be observed in take-over transactions: these general principles are a codification of good standards of commercial behaviour and should have an obvious and universal application. On the other hand, the code lays down a series of rules; some of which are no more than examples of the application of the general principles whilst others are rules of procedure designed to govern specific forms of take-over. Some of the general principles, based as they are upon a concept of equity between one shareholder and another, while readily understandable in the City and by those concerned with the securities markets generally, would not easily lend themselves to legislation. The code is therefore framed in non-technical language and is, primarily as a measure of self-discipline, administered and enforced by the panel, a body representative of those using the securities markets and concerned with the observance of good business standards, rather than the enforcement of the law. . .

'Self-regulation' . . .can connote a system whereby a group of people, acting in concert, use their collective power to force themselves and others to comply with a code of conduct of their own devising. . .

The panel is a self-regulating body in [this] sense. Lacking any authority de jure, it exercises immense power de facto by devising, promulgating, amending and interpreting the City Code on Take-overs and Mergers, by waiving or modifying the application of the code in particular circumstances, by investigating and reporting upon alleged breaches of the code and by the application or threat of sanctions. These sanctions are no less effective because they are applied indirectly and lack a legally enforceable base. Thus, to quote again from the introduction to the code:

> . . . If the panel finds that there has been a breach, it may have recourse to private reprimand or public censure or, in a more flagrant case, to further action designed to deprive the offender temporarily or permanently of his ability to enjoy the facilities of the securities markets. The panel may refer certain aspects of a case to the Department of Trade and Industry, the Stock Exchange or other appropriate body.

No reprimand, censure or further action will take place without the person concerned having the opportunity to appeal to the appeal committee of the panel.

The unspoken assumption, which I do not doubt is a reality, is that the Department of Trade and Industry or, as the case may be, the Stock Exchange or other appropriate body would in fact exercise statutory or contractual powers to penalise the transgressors. Thus, for example, rules 22 to 24 of the Rules of the Stock Exchange (1984) provide for the severest penalties, up to and including expulsion, for acts of misconduct and by rule 23.1 [these include actions found by the Panel to breach the Code].

The principal issue in this appeal, and only issue which may matter in the longer term, is whether this remarkable body is above the law. Its respectability is beyond question [and]. . . I am content to assume for the purposes of this appeal that self-regulation is preferable in the public interest. But that said, what is to happen if the panel goes off the rails? Suppose, perish the thought, that it were to use its powers in a way which was manifestly unfair. What then? Mr Alexander submits that the panel would lose the support of public opinion in the financial markets and would be unable to continue to operate. Further or alternatively, Parliament could and would intervene. Maybe, but how long would that take and who in the meantime could or would come to the assistance of those who were being oppressed by such conduct?

. . .In *Criminal Injuries Compensation Board ex p Lain* [1967] 2 QB 864. . .Diplock LJ [had to consider] the Board [which], in the form which it then took, was an administrative novelty. Accordingly it would have been impossible to find a precedent for the exercise of the supervisory jurisdiction of the court which fitted the facts. Nevertheless the court not only asserted its jurisdiction, but further asserted that it was a jurisdiction which was adaptable thereafter. This process has since been taken further. . .[his Lordship considered subsequent cases]. In all the reports it is possible to find enumerations of factors giving rise to the jurisdiction, but it is a fatal error to regard the presence of all those factors as essential or as being exclusive of other factors. Possibly the only essential elements are what can be described as a public element, which can take many different forms, and the exclusion from the jurisdiction of bodies whose sole source of power is a consensual submission to its jurisdiction.

. . . The panel. . .is without doubt performing a public duty and an important one. This is clear from the expressed willingness of the Secretary of State for Trade and Industry to limit legislation in the field of take-overs and mergers and to use the panel as the centrepiece of his regulation of that market. The rights of citizens are indirectly affected by its decisions, some, but by no means all of whom, may in a technical sense be said to have assented to this situation, e.g., the members of the Stock Exchange. At least in its determination of whether there has been a breach of the code, it has a duty to act judicially and it asserts that its raison d'être is to do equity between one shareholder and another. Its source of power is only partly based upon moral persuasion and the assent of institutions and their members, the bottom line being the statutory powers exercised by the Department of Trade and Industry and the Bank of England. In this context, I should be very disappointed if the courts could not recognise the realities of executive power and allow their vision to be clouded by the subtlety and sometimes complexity of the way in which it can be exerted. . .

Notes

1. Sir John Donaldson also considered whether the Panel could be controlled by the use of private law remedies. Since it was clear that it could not be, he and the other members of the Court of Appeal took the view that the Panel was subject to judicial review for the reasons given.
2. It appears clear, at any rate, that the fact that the source of a body's power is non-statutory should not be decisive (a finding confirmed by *R v Royal Life Saving Society ex parte Howe etc*).[7] Indeed in a decision that the judges expressly contrasted with *Datafin*, a statutory body, Lloyds of London, was found to be *not* subject to review.

R (on the application of West) v Lloyds of London [2004] EWCA (Civ) 506 (extracts)

Lloyds is incorporated by a private Act of Parliament and its powers are set out in various Acts. This is because of its enormous importance within the insurance market. A challenge by way of judicial review was made to a decision of the Business Committee of Lloyds, alleging that it had approved buy outs of the applicant's shares at an under-value.

Brooke LJ

29 It was an important, but not an essential, part of [Counsel's] submissions that Lloyd's derived its powers from an Act of Parliament. . .and that] while the FSA [Financial Services Authority]; now possessed extensive reserve powers, Lloyd's was itself exercising regulatory powers for the protection of its members qua consumers of financial services which government would be exercising itself if Lloyd's fell short in the way it exercised its powers.
30 I cannot accept these submissions. The fact that Lloyd's corporate arrangements are underpinned by a private Act of Parliament and not by the Companies Acts makes it in no way unique and is certainly not dispositive of the matter. Mr Walker Q.C., who appeared for Lloyd's, told us that a number of insurance companies were incorporated by private Act of Parliament, and he showed us one such example. I am entirely satisfied that the line of cases at Divisional Court level which related to the private law status of Lloyd's in relation to functions such as are in issue in this case were correctly decided.
31 The decisions under challenge were concerned solely with the commercial relationship between Dr West and the relevant managing agents, and this was governed by the contracts into which he had chosen to enter. Those decisions were of a private, not a public, nature. They have consequences for Dr West in private, not public, law.
32 . . .It seems to me that the functions of Lloyd's which are under review in this case are totally different from the functions of the Takeover Panel that were under consideration in *Ex p. Datafin*. The Panel exercised regulatory control in a public sphere where governmental regulatory control was absent. This case is concerned with the working out of private contractual arrangements at Lloyd's which is itself subject to external governmental regulation.

Notes

1. As Pannick comments:

> Since *Datafin* the issue for public lawyers is not whether one can identify a private law agreement in order to exclude judicial review, but whether the respondent body (as the Divisional Court acknowledged was the case in relation to the Jockey Club)

---

7   [1990] COD 497.

has such a de facto monopoly over an important area of public life that an individual has no effective choice but to comply with their rules, regulations and decisions in order to operate in that area.[8]

2. However, as will become apparent, this principle has not been applied consistently. While Campbell[9] argues that the control of monopoly power should be the key principle underpinning the control of public power by judicial review, he acknowledges that there are cases that do not conform to this principle—which he therefore finds to be 'wrongly decided'; these concern religious or sporting bodies, as we will see below (at 741–743). Campbell argues for the monopoly principle by starting with the premise that judicial review is intended to ensure fair and rational decision-making that upholds the rule of law[10] (referred to in the quote as treating others 'morally'); from this, he continues:

> An individual who is subjected to an exercise of power that is not monopolistic, and who is of the view that he is not being treated morally in the relevant sense, can, *if* he is concerned so to be treated, choose to deal with another decision-making body. . . *if* people wish to be treated in accordance with the principles of good administration by an alternate decision-making body that operates in a market, and that market is in any way competitive, there is at least some prospect that they will be so treated, and the more competitive the market is, and the greater the number of people who wish to be so treated, the greater that prospect will be. . .
>
>   By contrast, if a decision-making body that exercises monopoly power does not act [in accordance with good administration]. . .and there are no alternate decision-making bodies, then, absent judicial review, there is no possibility of those who wish to be treated in accordance with the principles of good administration being so treated. That. . .provides a rational basis for the subjection to judicial review of power that is monopolistic in the sense understood here.[11]

3. Besides using the notion of monopoly power, another criterion used by the courts is to ask whether, if the body in question did not exist, some state body would be required to regulate the area of activity in question (sometimes referred to as the 'but for' or 'governmental' test). As Rose J remarked in *R v Football Association Ltd ex parte Football League Ltd*,[12] when considering an application to review the FA:

> Despite its virtually monopolistic powers and the importance of its decisions to many members of the public who are not contractually bound to it, it is, in my judgment, a domestic body whose powers arise from and duties exist in private law only. I find no sign of underpinning directly or indirectly by any organ or agency of the state or any potential government interest, as Simon Brown J put it in [*ex parte*

---

8   Pannick, n 6 above.

9   C Campbell, 'Monopoly Power as Public Power for the Purposes of Judicial Review' (2009) 125(Jul) LQR 491, n 60 and p 503.

10   For the connection between judicial review and the rule of law, see Chapter 15, pp 777–778 and Chapter 3, pp 117–126.

11   Campbell, at 510–11.

12   [1993] 2 All ER 833.

> *Wachmann* [1992] 1 WLR 1306], nor is there any evidence to suggest that if the FA did not exist the state would intervene to create a public body to perform its functions.

Conversely, in *R v Advertising Standards Authority ex parte Insurance Services*,[13] the ASA, a self-regulatory body which deals with complaints in relation to advertising, and has no coercive powers at all, was found to be amenable to review, on the basis that it was the practice of the Director of Fair Trading to intervene on a complaint about misleading advertising only if the ASA had not dealt satisfactorily with the complaint. This provided the 'governmental underpinning' sufficient to demonstrate a 'public element' to the ASA's functions.[14] The notion that a body has been 'woven into the fabric' of government, or 'enmeshed' with goverment in this way—which also plainly applied in the *Datafin* case—has also been identified as a key principle used by the courts in determining whether a body should be subject to review.[15]

4. Considering the finding in the *Datafin* decision, that to be reviewable a body needs to have 'a public element' or be under some 'public duty', Fredman and Morris comment, 'even a cursory look at this formulation demonstrates that the dividing line between public and private remains elusive'.[16] What, after all is a 'public element' or 'public duty?' They go on to note that the test developed in later cases (and deployed by Rose J above) that the body 'should be governmental in nature so that if it did not exist the Government would be likely to step in and create a replacement' (the 'but for' test) is 'singularly difficult to apply with any degree of certainty' because of the lack of consensus as to the proper functions of government'.[17] Fredman and Morris are arguably under-stating the matter here: there is not so much a 'lack of consensus' as to the proper functions of government as a heated political debate. Indeed, the scope and proper role of government could be said to be one of *the* defining controversies between Left and Right. As Lord Woolf has noted (commenting extra-judicially): 'Increasingly services which, at one time, were regarded as an essential part of Government are being performed by private bodies.' This growth in the 'contracted-out state' has caused intense controversy and great legal difficulty.[18] Lord Woolf there-fore disapproves the governmental test.[19] It has been noted that:

> political parties disagree. . .about the proper role of the State, particularly in the context of privatisation, and political theorists hav[e] widely divergent views about the distinction between that which is public and that which is private and the role of the State.[20]

---

13   (1990) 2 Admin LR 77.

14   It has also been held that the Press Complaints Commission, a similar body, whose function is self-explanatory is probably amenable to review: *R v Press Complaints Commission ex parte Stewart-Brady* (1997) 9 Admin LR 274.

15   C Campbell, 'The Nature of Power as Public in English Judicial Review' [2009] 68(1) CLJ 90, at 96–99 and 108–109 respectively; he is critical of the test, which he finds leads to inconsistent results. It was used in the context of s 6 HRA in the *Poplar Housing* case (below at 744).

16   S Fredman and GS Morris, 'The Costs of Exclusivity: Public and Private Re-examined' [1994] PL 69.

17   *Ibid*, p 72.

18   For a trenchant analysis, see Craig (2002) 118 LQR 564–67.

19   Lord Woolf, '*Droit Public*—English Style' [1995] PL 57, 63 and 64.

20   Campbell, n 15 above, at 92–93.

It has been argued that English courts are particularly ill-placed to apply the governmental test, since English law lacks any 'prevailing and well-developed theory of the state'.[21] As a result:

> . . .In purporting to apply the but-for test, judges will, to a very large extent, be required to rely on their own conceptions of the appropriate role of the government. Because judges are not political scientists, these conceptions, where they exist at all, will be largely intuitive and unexamined. Accordingly, the judges' conclusions as to whether the government would undertake a particular function will tend to be ad hoc and unprincipled.[22]

5. On the other hand, Pannick[23] notes that the 'governmental' test is closely analogous with the test adopted by the European Court of Justice for deciding whether a respondent is a 'state body' with the result that directives may be directly invoked against it. The Community law principle applies to:

> . . .a body, whatever its legal form, which has been made responsible, pursuant to a measure adopted by the state, for providing a public service under the control of the state and has for that purpose special powers beyond those which result from the normal rules applicable in relations between individuals. . .[24]

6. The trend has generally been to hold that private bodies performing contracted-out services on behalf of public bodies are *not* subject to judicial review, although the matter is to an extent a case-sensitive one. In *R v Servite Houses and Wandsworth LBC ex parte Goldsmith and Chatting*,[25] residents of a care home sought to challenge a decision to close it, in breach of promises made to them and therefore arguably, of their legitimate expectations.[26] The care home was run by a private company, under contract with a local authority under the National Assistance Act 1948, s 26. The local authority funded the patients and was able to discharge its statutory duty to arrange for the provision of care accommodation by means of the contract with the private provider. Nevertheless, the court found that the provider was *not* exercising a public function for the purposes of judicial review. Moses J found that judicial review would only be available if there was 'sufficient statutory penetration which goes beyond the statutory regulation in the manner in which the service is provided'. This was not the case here because the nature of the contracting out regime meant that 'not only is the relationship between Servite and [the Council] governed solely by the terms of the contract between them, but the relationship between Servite and the [claimants] is solely a matter of private law'. Since the residents had no contractual remedy, this left them powerless to challenge the decision.[27] The decision was thus based at least partly on the fact that the the body in question was not sufficiently 'enmeshed' into government.

---

21 Campbell, *ibid*, at 92, quoting JWF Allison, *A Continental Distinction in the Common Law*, revised edn (2000) at 37.

22 Campbell, *ibid* at 93.

23 See n 6 above.

24 *Foster v British Gas plc* [1991] 1 QB 405 at 427G-H (ECJ). For recent comment on this case-law, see Campbell, n 15 above, at 113–115.

25 (2001) 33 HLR 35.

26 For the doctrine of substantive legitimate expectations, see Chapter 15, at 850–870.

27 The same scenario was considered under the 'public authority' provisions of the HRA by the House of Lords in *YL v Birmingham City Council* [2007] UKHL 27, with the same result (discussed in Chapter 17 at 983–984 and 986–987). This led Parliament to provide explicitly that private providers in this situation *were* performing a public function for the purposes of the HRA in the Health and Social Care Act 2008, s 145.

7. However, very recently in *R (On the Application of Weaver) v London & Quadrant Housing Trust*[28] the Court of Appeal confirmed that a publicly funded housing trust *was* performing a public function for the purposes of judicial review when evicting a tenant. The case is mainly concerned with the proper interpretation of s 6 HRA, but at first instance, the factors treated as relevant were that the trust was publicly funded, subject to intense government regulation, had to carry out government policy and cooperate with the local authority, and that it in effect stood in the place of the local authority.[29] Both the 'but for' and the 'enmeshment with government tests' were thus satisfied.[30]

8. A further recent case concerns a council transferring a function to a private company. In *Regina (Beer (Trading as Hammer Trout Farm)) v Hampshire Farmer's Markets Ltd*[31] the Court of Appeal heard an appeal against the finding that a private company, Hampshire Farmer's Markets Ltd, to whom the local council had transferred the function of running farmers markets, *was* subject to judicial review. The claimant had applied for a licence to run a stall in the 2002 programme (as he had in previous years) but was refused; he successfully sought judicial review to quash the decision. On appeal, the Court of Appeal found that the crucial factors were, first, that Council would itself have been subject to review if still running the market; second that the markets took place on public land to which the public had access, third, that the company was set up by the Council with the specific aim of running the market, and thus 'stepped into the Council's shoes' (it used the same criteria for determining applications as the Council had); and fourth, that the Council substantially assisted the company in carrying out its activities (including providing premises, finance and the use of staff). These were sufficient to render running the markets a public function, despite the fact that in doing so the company was not carrying out any statutory function for the Council. Whether it is possible to defend the distinction between this case and *Servite* homes (above) or (under the HRA) *YL v Birmingham* (below at 744), both of which also concerned private bodies exercising hitherto public functions, may however be doubted. The fact that company in the Farmer's Market case was *created* by the council was certainly one relevant difference;[32] the company could thus be seen as 'woven into the fabric' of government.[33] The close involvement of the local authority in its running also meant that it satisfied the 'enmeshment' criteria.[34]

9. One body which has generated a great deal of litigation on this issue is the Jockey Club, which regulates horse-racing in the UK. A number of inconsistent first instance decisions on the matter[35] led to an appeal (on the third decision) to the Court of Appeal, which was thus given the opportunity to sort out the 'confusion' left by those decisions.

---

28 [2009] EWCA Civ 587.

29 The decision was appealed to the Supreme Court, but leave was refused.

30 The 'enmeshment' phrase is noted by Campbell, n 15 above at 108. A similar decision is *R (On the Application of A v Partnerships in Care Ltd*, in which a private psychiatric hospital was held to be exercising 'functions of a public nature' for the purposes of judicial review [2002] 1 WLR 2610.

31 [2004] 1 WLR 233. The authority of its findings in general terms may be vitiated by the fact that appeal proceeded on the basis that the test for amenability under judicial review and the 'public authority' definition in the Human Rights Act were the same—a finding that has since been disapproved by the House of Lords (see below at 744).

32 For the situation in which the Council itself is carrying out the function of running a market and was also found to be subject to review, see *R (Agnello and others v Hounslow London Borough Council* [2003] EWHC 3112.

33 See Campbell, n 15 above, at 96

34 *Ibid* at 108–09.

35 *Jockey Club ex parte Massingberd-Mundy* (1990) 2 Admin LR 609; *Jockey Club ex parte RAM Racecourses Ltd* (1990) 3 Admin LR 265 and *Jockey Club ex parte the Aga Khan* [1993] 2 All ER 853.

R v Jockey Club ex parte Aga Khan [1993] 2 All ER 853, 866–87

Lord Justice Bingham MR: . . .I have little hesitation in accepting the applicant's contention that the Jockey Club effectively regulates a significant national activity, exercising powers which affect the public and are exercised in the interest of the public. I am willing to accept that if the Jockey Club did not regulate this activity the Government would probably be driven to create a public body to do so.

But the Jockey Club is not in its origin, its history, its constitution or (least of all) its membership a public body. While the grant of a royal charter was no doubt a mark of official approval, this did not in any way alter its essential nature, functions or standing. Statute provides for its representation on the Horseracing Betting Levy Board, no doubt as a body with an obvious interest in racing, but it has otherwise escaped mention in the statute book. It has not been woven into any system of governmental control of horse racing, perhaps because it has itself controlled horse racing so successfully that there has been no need for any such governmental system and such does not therefore exist This has the result that while the Jockey Club's powers may be described as, in many ways, public they are in no sense governmental I would accept that those who agree to be bound by the Rules of Racing have no effective alternative to doing so if they want to take part in racing in this country. It also seems likely to me that if, instead of Rules of Racing administered by the Jockey Club, there were a statutory code administered by a public body, the rights and obligations conferred and imposed by the code would probably approximate to those conferred and imposed by the Rules of Racing. But this does not, as it seems to me, alter the fact, however anomalous it may be, that the powers which the Jockey Club exercises over those who (like the applicant) agree to be bound by the Rules of Racing derive from the agreement of the parties and give rise to private rights on which effective action for a declaration, an injunction and damages can be based without resort to judicial review. It would in my opinion be contrary to sound and long-standing principle to extend the remedy of judicial review to such a case.

Question

Lord Justice Bingham finds (a) that the Jockey Club exercises powers 'which affect the public and are exercised in the interests of the public'; (b) that it is in practice impossible to take part in racing in Britain unless one accepts the jurisdiction of the club; (c) that the government would have to do the job the Club does now if the Club did not; but that (d) whilst the Club's powers are 'public' they are not 'governmental'. He therefore concludes that it is not subject to public law. Can any coherent set of factors to determine the private/public issue be derived from these findings?

Notes

1. It may well be the case that the above decision is attributable simply to the fact that 'English courts have generally declined to regard activities of the bodies controlling sport as coming within public law.'[36]

---

36   C Munro, 'Sport in the Courts' [2005] PL 681. Munro explores the somewhat different approach taken under Scots Law.

2. One clear point that appears to emerge from the *Jockey Club* decision is Bingham LJ's finding that access to private rights will preclude the availability of public law remedies. A second crucial factor is whether persons aggrieved by the decisions of the body in question would have some other, private law remedy, for example in contract. Thus, in *R v Code of Practice etc ex parte Professional Counselling Aids*,[37] the fact that the Code of Practice Committee played a part in a system that operated in the public interest rendered it subject to review, while in *R v Football Association of Wales ex parte Flint Town United Football Club*,[38] the existence of a contractual relationship between the Club and the Association was decisive in the court's decision that judicial review would be inappropriate. This point has not met with universal acclaim:

> The reliance on contract as the key to the availability or lack of availability of the Order 53 procedure in relation to regulatory bodies has some serious drawbacks. First, it distinguishes somewhat arbitrarily between those non-statutory bodies whose source of power is derived from contract and those whose power is not so derived. However, it is difficult to see why such bodies should be public while others with regulatory functions of similar significance should be private. Secondly, and more importantly, the equation of contract with private law is based upon the misguided belief in the voluntary, consensual nature of contract, obscuring the reality of underlying power relations. . .
>
> The second context in which contract has been deployed in order to prevent the use of the Order 53 procedure relates to bodies who, despite having an avowedly public character, have exercised their powers through the medium of contract. [This] equation of contract with private law reveals a further problem; it implies that even avowedly public bodies have 'private lives' which are beyond the scrutiny of the courts in their public-law jurisdiction.[39]

3. Lord Woolf has suggested that the existence of a private law remedy should not by itself exclude judicial review; rather the test should be whether the issue in respect of which review is sought is '*satisfactorily protected* by private law' (emphasis added).[40] This seems a more sensible test as it would take into account the cases in which a contract may be theoretically present but in which it would be either impractical or ineffective to sue on it.

Influence of the Human Rights Act

As noted above, the CPR introduced a new test for amenability of 'public function'. Section 6(1) of the HRA states that it is 'unlawful for a public authority' to act in a way which is incompatible with a Convention right';[41] 'public authority' is not defined in the Act, but s 6(3)(b) provides that it includes any person certain of whose functions are functions of a public nature. This test appeared to introduce

---

37   *The Times*, 7 November 1990.

38   [1991] COD 44.

39   Fredman and Morris, n 19 above, at 74, 76.

40   See n 22 above, at 64.

41   That is, a right under the European Convention on Human Rights, as defined by s 1 HRA 1998.

a more inclusive definition of public bodies ('public authorities') for the purposes of cases brought under the HRA than was being applied by the courts under judicial review prior to the advent of the CPR in 2000. Indeed, Ministers in Parliament accepted that a wide variety of non-statutory bodies would be public authorities for the purposes of the HRA, including the Jockey Club itself,[42] the water companies,[43] the Royal National Lifeboat Institution[44] and the British Board of Film Classification.[45] At one point it appeared that the seemingly more generous test in the HRA might have the effect of broadening the interpretation of public body in judicial review. In *Poplar Housing and Regeneration Community Association Ltd and Secretary of State for the Environment v Donoghue*,[46] however, the court found that:

> While HRA section 6 requires a generous interpretation of who is a public authority, it is clearly inspired by the approach developed by the courts in identifying the bodies and activities subject to judicial review. The emphasis on public functions reflects the approach adopted in judicial review by the courts and text books since the decision of the Court of Appeal. . .in . . . *ex parte Datafin*.

Subsequent case-law has decisively rejected the notion that the two tests should be harmonised. In *YL v Birmingham City Council*,[47] Lord Bingham observed that:

> Section 6(3)(b) [HRA] extends the definition of public authority to cover bodies which are not public authorities but certain of whose functions are of a public nature, and it is therefore likely to include bodies which are not amenable to judicial review.

This in fact confirmed earlier House of Lords authority in *R (SB) v Governors of Denbigh High School*[48] and *Aston Cantlow and others v Wallbank*;[49] in the latter, Lord Hope observed (at para 52) that, although the domestic case law on judicial review might be helpful, it could not be determinative of what is a core or hybrid public authority, a question that 'must be examined in the light of the jurisprudence of the Strasbourg Court as to those bodies which engage the responsibility of the state for the purposes of the Convention'. Lord Mance observed in *YL* that while some authorities (including *Poplar Housing*) had 'assimilated' the two tests:

> . . .it is clear from the House's decision in *Wallbank*. . .and *Denbigh High School*- . . .that, while authorities on judicial review can be helpful, section 6 has a different rationale, linked to the scope of state responsibility in Strasbourg.

The interpretation given to s 6 HRA is explored in Chapter 17 at 976–989.

---

42   HC Deb col 1020 (20 May 1998).

43   *Ibid*, col 409.

44   HC Deb col 407 (7 June 1998).

45   HC Deb col 413 (17 June 1998).

46   [2002] QB 48.

47   [2007] UKHL 27 at [12].

48   [2007] 1 AC 100.

49   [2004] 1 AC 546.

It is important to note that **not all decisions of public bodies are open to review.** Even where it is clear that the decision-making body may be described as a public body, particular decisions made by it may not be susceptible to judicial review if they are not seen to have a clear 'public' element. So for example, employees of public bodies will generally be required to resolve employment disputes such as dismissal by ordinary civil actions, in the same way as employees of private bodies, although this may not apply if the person in question is an office holder rather than an employee (see *McClaren v Home Office*)[50] and depending on whether he is seeking to enforce contractual rights or not.[51] For a recent case dealing with such a matter see *R (Tucker) v Director General of the National Crime Squad,*[52] in which the Court of Appeal found that the decision by the deputy director of the Senior Crime Squad to summarily terminate a detective inspector's secondment to the squad was not susceptible to judicial review. To have been so, the Court found that:

> . . .Three things had to be identified, namely, whether the defendant was a public body exercising statutory powers, whether the function being performed in the exercise of those powers was a public or a private one and whether the defendant was performing a public duty owed to the claimant in the particular circumstances under consideration; that, applying those criteria, it was clear that the third criterion was not met, since the deputy director general had not been performing a public duty owed to the applicant when he sent him back to his home force because the decision taken in relation to the applicant was specific to him; that there was a clear line between disciplinary issues where an officer had the right to public law safeguards such as fairness, and operational or management decisions where the police were entitled to run their own affairs without the intervention of the courts.[53]

PROCEDURAL IMPLICATIONS OF THE PUBLIC/PRIVATE DIVIDE

Applications for judicial review follow a procedure which differs in many important respects from the ordinary civil procedure. In order to understand it, it is necessary briefly to consider the remedies available upon judicial review proceedings. If it is found, upon review, that an authority has acted unlawfully, there are a number of remedies that can be granted. Detailed discussion of these remedies lies outside the scope of this book;[54] a very brief summary only will be given. The following are known as the prerogative remedies. They were renamed, as part of the Woolf reforms to judicial review. The old names, which will be found in decisions pre-dating the reforms, are given in brackets:

---

50   [1990] ICR 824

51   See below re the decision on this point in *Roy* at 753–757. *Cf* the position of 'core' or 'standard' public authorities under s 6(1) HRA, which appear to be bound by the Convention rights in respect of *all* of their activities: see Chapter 17, pp 977–979.

52   [2003] EWCA Civ 57; [2003] ICR 599.

53   [2003] ICR 599, headnote.

54   Readers are referred to P Craig, *Administrative Law,* 6th edn (2008), Chapters 24–27; Wade and C Forsyth, *Administrative Law,* 8th edn (2000), Chapters 16–22 for a full exposition.

(a) *quashing order (certiorari):* quashes an unlawful decision;
(b) *prohibitory order (prohibition):* prohibits an authority from performing a proposed unlawful act;
(c) *mandatory order (mandamus):* compels an authority to perform a particular act.

Prerogative remedies may not be granted against the Crown, though they can be granted against individual Government Ministers; additionally, they have not been used in relation to delegated legislation found to be unlawful.

In addition, the following remedies, which are non-prerogative (and thus not unique to judicial review) may be sought:

(a) *injunction:* restrains an unlawful action, and may be interim or final; for their use against the Crown and against Government Ministers, see *Re M* [1993] 3 WLR 433, HL (Chapter 3, pp 93–94) and *R v Secretary of State of Transport ex parte Factortame (No 2)* [1990] 1 AC 604 (Chapter 5, pp 218–219);
(b) *declaration:* an authoritative statement by the court, for example, that a given act is unlawful; often used in relation to the Crown, or delegated legislation;
(c) *damages* are *not* available per se on judicial review. They may be awarded only if the applicant has claimed one of the above remedies *and* if he or she can show that the authority has committed a breach of contract, a tort or a breach of s 6(1) of the Human Rights Act 1998 (see Chapter 17, pp 991–996). The Law Commission has recently recommended that courts should be able to award damages in judicial review cases in limited circumstances.[55]

Supreme Court Act 1981, s 31

Application for judicial review

31.–(1) An application to the High Court for one or more of the following forms of relief, namely—

(a) an order of mandamus, prohibition or certiorari;
(b) a declaration or injunction under subsection (2); or
(c) an injunction under section 30 restraining a person not entitled to do so from acting in an office to which that section applies,

shall be made in accordance with rules of court by a procedure to be known as an application for judicial review.

(2) A declaration may be made or an injunction granted under this subsection in any case where an application for judicial review, seeking that relief, has been made and the High Court considers that, having regard to—

(a) the nature of the matters in respect of which relief may be granted by orders of mandamus, prohibition or certiorari;
(b) the nature of the persons and bodies against whom relief may be granted by such orders; and
(c) all the circumstances of the case,

---

55 See The Law Commission, *Administrative Redress: Public Bodies and the Citizen* (2008), Paper No 187, available at www.lawcom.gov.uk/remedies.htm. For comment, see T Cornford, 'Administrative Redress: The Law Commission's Consultation Paper' [2009] PL 70; M Fordham, 'Monetary Awards in Judicial Review' [2009] PL 1.

it would be just and convenient for the declaration to be made or the injunction to be granted, as the case may be.

(3)   No application for judicial review shall be made unless the leave of the High Court has been obtained in accordance with rules of court; and the court shall not grant leave to make such an application unless it considers that the applicant has sufficient interest in the matter to which the application relates.

(4)   On an application for judicial review the High Court may award damages to the applicant if—

(a)   he has joined with his application a claim for damages arising from any matter to which the application relates; and

(b)   the court is satisfied that, if the claim had been made in an action begun by the applicant at the time of making his application, he would have been awarded damages.

(5)   If, on an application for judicial review seeking an order of certiorari, the High Court quashes the decision to which the application relates, the High Court may remit the matter to the court, tribunal or authority concerned, with a direction to reconsider it and reach a decision in accordance with the findings of the High Court.

(6)   Where the High Court considers that there has been undue delay in making an application for judicial review, the court may refuse to grant—

(a)   leave for the making of the application; or

(b)   any relief sought on the application

if it considers that the granting of the relief sought would be likely to cause substantial hardship to, or substantially prejudice the rights of, any person or would be detrimental to good administration.

(7)   Subsection (6) is without prejudice to any enactment or rule of court which has the effect of limiting the time within which an application for judicial review may be made.

Note

Judicial review has now been brought within the CPR; the detailed rules which apply to judicial review proceedings are set out below. For the sake of clarity the following should be noted: the Act above uses old terminology. Under the CPR, (b) an order of mandamus is now known as a 'mandatory order', 'prohibition' is now called a 'prohibiting order' and 'certiorari' is now known as a 'quashing order'.

Civil Procedure Rules, Part 54

PART 54 JUDICIAL REVIEW

54.1 Scope and interpretation

(1)   This Part contains rules about judicial review.

(2)   In this Part—

(a)   a 'claim for judicial review' means a claim to review the lawfulness of—

    (i)   an enactment; or

    (ii)   a decision, action or failure to act in relation to the exercise of a public function.

. . .

(e)   'the judicial review procedure' means the Part 8 procedure as modified by this Part;

(f)   'interested party' means any person (other than the claimant and defendant) who is directly affected by the claim; and

(g)   'court' means the High Court, unless otherwise stated. . . .

54.2 When this Part must be used

The judicial review procedure must be used in a claim for judicial review where the claimant is seeking—

(a)   a mandatory order.

(b)   a prohibiting order.

(c)   a quashing order; or

(d)   an injunction under section 30 of the Supreme Court Act 1981 (restraining a person from acting in any office in which he is not entitled to act).

54.3 When this Part may be used

(1)   The judicial review procedure may be used in a claim for judicial review where the claimant is seeking—

    (a)   a declaration; or

    (b)   an injunction. . . .

    (Where the claimant is seeking a declaration or injunction in addition to one of the remedies listed in rule 54.2, the judicial review procedure must be used.)

(2)   A claim for judicial review may include a claim for damages restitution or the recovery of a sum due but may not seek such a remedy alone.

54.4 Permission required

The court's permission to proceed is required in a claim for judicial review whether started under this Part or transferred to the Administrative Court.

54.5 Time limit for filing claim form

(1)   The claim form must be filed—

    (a)   promptly; and

    (b)   in any event not later than 3 months after the grounds to make the claim first arose.

(2)   The time limit in this rule may not be extended by agreement between the parties.

(3)   This rule does not apply when any other enactment specifies a shorter time limit for making the claim for judicial review.

. . .

54.16 Evidence

(1)   Rule 8.6 does not apply.

(2)   No written evidence may be relied on unless—

    (a)   it has been served in accordance with any—

        (i)   rule under this Part; or
        (ii)   direction of the court; or

    (b)   the court gives permission.

54.17 Court's powers to hear any person

(1)   Any person may apply for permission—

    (a)   to file evidence; or
    (b)   make representations at the hearing of the judicial review.

(2)   An application under paragraph (1) should be made promptly.

54.18 Judicial review may be decided without a hearing

The court may decide the claim for judicial review without a hearing where all the parties agree.

54.19 Court's powers in respect of quashing orders

(1)   This rule applies where the court makes a quashing order in respect of the decision to which the claim relates.

(2)   The court may—

    (a)   remit the matter to the decision-maker; and
    (b)   direct it to reconsider the matter and reach a decision in accordance with the judgment of the court.

(3)   in so far as any enactment permits, substitute its own decision for the decision to which the claim relates.

    (Section 31 of the Supreme Court Act 1981 enables the High Court, subject to certain conditions, to substitute its own decision for the decision in question.)

54.20 Transfer

The court may—

    (a) order a claim to continue as if it had not been started under this Part; and

    (b) where it does so, give directions about the future management of the claim.

(Part 30 (transfer) applies to transfers to and from the Administrative Court.)

Note

For a discussion of CPR 54, see T Cornford, 'The New Rules of Procedure for Judicial Review' (2000) 5 Web JCLI.

Procedural exclusivity

The most important implication of the public/private divide is the principle now known as 'procedural exclusivity': this principle governs the situation if a person brings an ordinary action when he or she should have used judicial review. CPR, R54.20 (above) and 30.5 give the courts broad powers to transfer cases to and from the Administrative Court, but the problem is that judicial review has an exceptionally tight time limit (three months) compared to ordinary actions in contract or tort (six years). The person mistakenly thinking that he or she can sue in tort or contract when judicial review was required is unlikely to take action within three months and is thus liable to find him- or herself out of time for a judicial review action.

The basic rule: O'Reilly v Mackman and after

The leading authority in the field is the House of Lords' decision in the following case, in which prisoners at Hull Prison, alleging that decisions made by the prison's Board of Visitors were bad for want of natural justice, attempted to proceed by way of writ or originating summons, rather than under RSC, Ord 53 (the previous rules governing applications for judicial review). Their proceedings were struck out and they appealed to the House of Lords.

O'Reilly v Mackman [1983] 2 AC 237, 283–85

Lord Diplock: . . .Order 53 since 1977 has provided a procedure by which every type of remedy for infringement of the rights of individuals that are entitled to protection in public law can be obtained in one and the same proceeding by way of an application for judicial review, and whichever remedy is found to be the most appropriate in the light of what has emerged upon the hearing of the application, can be granted to him. If what should emerge is that his complaint is not of an infringement of any of his rights that are entitled to protection in public law, but may be an infringement of his rights in private law and thus not a proper subject for judicial review, the court has power under r 9(5), instead of refusing the application, to order the proceedings to continue as if they had begun by writ [see now CPR, r 54.2(a)—above]. There is no such converse power under the RSC to permit an action begun by writ to continue as if it were an application for judicial review. . .

My Lords, at the outset of this speech, I drew attention to the fact that the remedy by way of declaration of nullity of the decisions of the Board was discretionary—as are all the remedies available upon judicial review. Counsel for the plaintiffs accordingly conceded that the fact that by adopting the procedure of an action begun by writ or by originating summons instead of an application for judicial review under Ord 53 (from which there have now been removed all those disadvantages to applicants that had previously led the courts to countenance actions for declarations and injunctions as an alternative procedure for obtaining a remedy for infringement of the rights of the individual that are entitled to protection in public law only) the plaintiffs had thereby been able to evade those protections against groundless, unmeritorious or tardy harassment that were afforded to statutory tribunals or decision-making public authorities by Ord 53, and which might have resulted in the summary, and would in any event have resulted in the speedy disposition of the application, is among the matters fit to be taken into consideration by the judge in deciding whether to exercise his discretion by refusing to grant a declaration; but, it was contended, this he may only do at the conclusion of the trial.

[But] to delay the judge's decision as to how to exercise his discretion would defeat the public policy that underlies the grant of those protections: viz the need, in the interests of good administration and of third parties who may be indirectly affected by the decision, for speedy certainty as to whether it has the effect of a decision that is valid in public law. An action for a declaration or injunction need not be commenced until the very end of the limitation period; if begun by writ, discovery and interlocutory proceedings may be prolonged and the plaintiffs are not required to support their allegations by evidence on oath until the actual trial. The period of uncertainty as to the validity of a decision that has been challenged upon allegations that may eventually turn out to be baseless and unsupported by evidence on oath, may thus be strung out for a very lengthy period, as the actions of the first three appellants in the instant appeals show. Unless such an action can be struck out summarily at the outset as an abuse of the process of the court the whole purpose of the public policy to which the change in Ord 53 was directed would be defeated. . .

Now that. . . all remedies for infringements of rights protected by public law can be obtained upon an application for judicial review, as can also remedies for infringements of rights under private law if such infringements should also be involved, it would in my view as a general rule be contrary to public policy, and as such an abuse of the process of the court, to permit a person seeking to establish that a decision of a public authority infringed rights to which he was entitled to protection under public law to proceed by way of an ordinary action and by this means to evade the provisions of Ord 53 for the protection of such authorities.

My Lords, I have described this as a general rule; for though it may normally be appropriate to apply it by the summary process of striking out the action, there may be exceptions, particularly where the invalidity of the decision arises as a collateral issue in a claim for infringement of a right of the plaintiff arising under private law, or where none of the parties objects to the adoption of the procedure by writ or originating summons. Whether there should be other exceptions should, in my view, at this stage in the development of procedural public law, be left to be decided on a case to case basis. . .

In the instant cases where the only relief sought is a declaration of nullity of the decisions of a statutory tribunal, the Board of Visitors of Hull Prison, as in any other case in which a similar declaration of nullity in public law is the only relief claimed, I have no hesitation, in agreement with the Court of Appeal, in holding that to allow the actions to proceed would be an abuse of the process of the court. They are blatant attempts to avoid the protections for the defendants for which Ord 53 provides. I would dismiss these appeals.

Notes
1. On the same day, judgment was given in *Cocks v Thanet District Council*.[56] The plaintiff had applied to the Council, which was also the local housing authority, for permanent accommodation, but was supplied only with temporary accommodation. He sued in the county court for a declaration that the Council owed him a duty to house him permanently under the Housing (Homeless Persons) Act 1977, and was in breach of that duty. The issue that eventually reached the House of Lords was whether the plaintiff was entitled to proceed in the county court or should proceed by judicial review. The judge at first instance in the High Court—to which the case was removed—had held that the plaintiff could proceed in the county court. The finding of the House of Lords on appeal

was that where a person has a possible statutory right to a benefit (for example, housing), if he or she is found to satisfy the relevant criteria, he or she will have a *private* right to the benefit. However, a decision that the criteria are *not* satisfied is a matter of public law only and may be challenged only by the judicial review procedure. As Fredman and Morris put it, 'the. . .decision as to whether an applicant was homeless was a public discretion, but once the discretion had been exercised in the applicant's favour it became a private right'.[57] In Lord Bridge's words:

> Once a decision has been reached by the housing authority which gives rise to the. . .housing duty, rights and obligations are immediately created in the field of private law. [This] duty. . .once established, is capable of being enforced by injunction and the breach of it will give rise to a liability in damages. But it is inherent in the scheme of the Act that an appropriate public law decision of the housing authority is a condition precedent to the establishment of the private law duty.[58]

2. Fredman and Morris go on to note that in *Ali v Tower Hamlets*,[59] a 'third dimension was added': the applicant had a private law right to accommodation but, if he wished to challenge the *type* of accommodation offered, his remedy lay only in public law.
3. The doctrine of 'procedural exclusivity' established in these cases has been widely criticised, first for flawed reasoning, second for its tendency to lead to meritorious cases being struck out simply because the wrong procedure has been used. Fredman and Morris consider that 'the public/ private barrier articulated in *O'Reilly* cannot be defended' and has produced 'deleterious consequences'. Their critique of the decision follows.

S Fredman and GS Morris, *'The costs of exclusivity: public and private re-examined'* [1994] PL 69, 70–71, 80–81

Recent cases demonstrate yet more strongly that the doctrine of procedural exclusivity makes it likely that meritorious claims will fail for no reason other than the wrong choice of procedure [Note that there is no provision for changing from the writ procedure to Ord 53]. One way in which this is manifested is in the fact that litigants are tempted to use the confusion for tactical advantage. The public employment cases again are a good example. The Crown has been a prime mover in this regard. In a series of cases begun by civil servants by an application for judicial review, the Crown argued that leave should not be granted on the grounds that civil servants had contracts of employment and therefore the issue was private [*R v Civil Service Appeal Board ex parte Bruce* [1988] 3 All ER 686]. At the same time, the Crown has applied to strike out cases begun by civil servants under the writ procedure on the grounds that these employees did not have contracts and therefore the issue was one of public law [*McClaren v Home Office* [1990] ICR 824]. A similar point can be made in respect of the voluntary regulation cases. Thus in *Law,* the applicant was content with the writ procedure, but the Greyhound Racing Club asserted the public nature of its

---

57 See n 16 above, at 80.

58 [1983] 2 AC 286.

59 [1992] 3 All ER 512.

function in order to block the claim at the threshold. In *ex p Aga Khan*, the converse was the case: the Jockey Club asserted the private nature of its functions in order to block the Aga Khan's attempt to use public law. This phenomenon is not always deliberate: the luckless applicant in *Ali* could be forgiven for assuming that his remedy lay in private law. Yet his of all cases appears on the face of it meritorious: how could it not be unreasonable to allocate a sixth-floor flat to a disabled person?

Possibly more problematic still is the recognition in recent cases of the possibility of pursuing substantially the same argument but in a different forum. Thus, as noted above, the Court of Appeal which refused to consider the Aga Khan's claims of breach of natural justice in public law was willing to concede that the same claim could have been entertained as a private-law claim of breach of an implied term in the contract. The only difference it seems, lies in the nature of the remedies. The result is inordinate cost and expense, with case after case being struck out or refused leave for no reason other than that the incorrect procedure had been chosen. . .

Notes

1. By contrast, Lord Woolf comments that he 'would be loath to see the effect of [*O'Reilly v Mackman*] undermined,'[60] contending:

    . . . It did, and still does, seem to me to be illogical to have a procedure which is designed to protect the public from unnecessary interference with administrative action, and then allow the protection which is provided to be by-passed. However, it is quite wrong to assume that the necessary price of that decision is drawn-out litigation over issues as to whether a particular action has been commenced in the wrong court. . .

2. The most important decision in this area since *O'Reilly* was the following, in which the House of Lords appeared to show some concern to restrict the *O'Reilly* principle.

    Dr Roy was a general practitioner providing general medical services within the NHS. The Committee, acting under statutory powers, withheld a proportion of his basic practice allowance on the ground that he had not been devoting a substantial amount of his time to his practice. Under the relevant statutory rules, the full rate of the allowance was payable only if in the opinion of the Committee he was so devoting a substantial amount of his time. Dr Roy issued a writ claiming, *inter alia,* payment of the withheld sum, contending that he *had* devoted himself to his practice as required by the regulations. The Committee applied to have the action struck out as an abuse of the process of the court on the ground that Dr Roy should have proceeded by way of an application for judicial review under RSC, Ord 53.[61]

---

60   'Judicial Review: A Possible Programme for Reform' [1992] PL 221, 231.

61   P Cane, 'Private Rights and Public Procedure' [1992] PL 193.

Roy v Kensington and Chelsea and Westminster Family Practitioner Committee [1992] 1 AC 624 (extracts)

Lord Lowry: . . .I have already referred to the judgment of the Court of Appeal [in this case] [1990] 1 Med LR 328, which concluded that there was a contract for services between Dr Roy and the committee and that it was therefore in order for Dr Roy to sue the committee for a declaration of his rights and an order for payment. I cannot altogether accept the reasoning which led the members of the Court of Appeal to conclude that there was a contract. . . At the same time, I would be foolish to disregard the fact that all the members of a distinguished Court of Appeal held that a contract for services existed between Dr Roy and the committee. It shows, to say the least, that there are 'contractual echoes in the relationship,' as Judge White [1989] 1 Med LR 10, 12, put it and makes it almost inevitable that the relationship. . .gave rise to 'rights and obligations' and that Dr Roy's rights were private law rights. . .arising from the statute and regulations and including the very important private law right to be paid for the work that he has done. . .

The judge, however, held that, even if the doctor's rights to full payments under the scheme were contractually based, the committee's duty was a public law duty and could be challenged only on judicial review. Mr Collins admitted that, if the doctor had a contractual right, he could. . .vindicate it by action. But, my Lords, I go further: if Dr Roy has any kind of private law right, even though not contractual, he can sue for its alleged breach.

. . .Even if one accepts the full rigour of *O'Reilly v Mackman*, there is ample room to hold that this case comes within the exceptions allowed for by Lord Diplock. It is concerned with a private law right, it involves a question which could in some circumstances give rise to a dispute of fact and one object of the plaintiff is to obtain an order for the payment (not by way of damages) of an ascertained or ascertainable sum of money. If it is wrong to allow such a claim to be litigated by action, what is to be said of other disputed claims for remuneration? I think it is right to consider the whole spectrum of claims which a doctor might make against the committee. The existence of any dispute as to entitlement means that he will be alleging a breach of his private law rights through a failure by the committee to perform their public duty. If the committee's argument prevails, the doctor must in all these cases go by judicial review, even when the facts are not clear. I scarcely think that this can be the right answer.

My Lords, whether Dr Roy's rights were contractual or statutory, the observations made by the Court of Appeal concerning their enforcement are important. Balcombe LJ said [1990] 1 Med LR 328, 331:

> Since Dr Roy's rights against the committee sound in contract, on the face of it there would appear to be no reason why he should not sue on the contract by ordinary action. Of course, as Mr Briggs accepts, the court will not substitute its opinion for that of the committee in deciding whether Dr Roy did devote a substantial amount of time to general practice. What the court can do is to decide whether the committee, in forming its opinion, did so on an incorrect view of the law and, if so, remit the question to the committee for reconsideration.

Nourse LJ said, at p 332:

> . . . In order that there may be no doubt about the matter, I will add that if a practitioner wishes to question an initial decision by the committee not to accept his application to be included on their list of doctors, he must in that case take pro-ceedings for judicial review. At that stage no contract has come into existence and

the practitioner's only right is a public law right to have his application properly considered. . .

In the present case, the public law decision of the FPC to include Dr Roy's name on the medical list brought into existence private law rights and duties. These duties included a duty imposed on the FPC to consider fairly any issues which might arise for determining whether Dr Roy was eligible for the full rate of basic practice allowance. In the present case, the matter on which the FPC had to form an opinion was whether Dr Roy was devoting a substantial amount of time to general practice under the National Health Service.

The judgments to which I have referred effectively dispose of an argument pressed by the committee that Dr Roy had no right to be paid a basic practice allowance until the committee had carried out their public duty of forming an opinion under paragraph 12.1(b), with the supposed consequence that, until that had happened, the doctor had no private law right which he could enforce. The answer is that Dr Roy had a right to a fair and legally correct consideration of his claim. Failing that, his private law right has been infringed and he can sue the committee.

. . . With regard to *O'Reilly v Mackman* [Mr Lightman, for Roy] argued in the alternative. The 'broad approach' was that the rule in *O'Reilly v Mackman* did not apply generally against bringing actions to vindicate private rights in all circumstances in which those actions involved a challenge to a public law act or decision, but that it merely required the aggrieved person to proceed by judicial review only when private law rights were not at stake. The 'narrow approach' assumed that the rule applied generally to all proceedings in which public law acts or decisions were challenged, subject to some exceptions when private law rights were involved. There was no need in *O'Reilly v Mackman* to choose between these approaches, but it seems clear that Lord Diplock considered himself to be stating a general rule with exceptions. For my part, I much prefer the broad approach. . . which would also, if adopted, have the practical merit of getting rid of a procedural minefield. I shall, however, be content for the purpose of this appeal to adopt the narrow approach, which avoids the need to discuss the proper scope of the rule. . .

Whichever approach one adopts, the arguments for excluding the present case from the ambit of the rule or, in the alternative, making an exception of it are similar and to my mind convincing.

1   Dr Roy has either a contractual or a statutory private law right to his remuneration in accordance with his statutory terms of service.

2   Although he seeks to enforce performance of a public law duty under paragraph 12.1, his private law rights dominate the proceedings.

3   The type of claim and other claims for remuneration (although not this particular claim) may involve disputed issues of fact.

4   The order sought (for the payment of money due) could not be granted on judicial review.

5   The claim is joined with another claim which is fit to be brought in an action (and has already been successfully prosecuted).

6   When individual rights are claimed, there should not be a need for leave or a special time limit, nor should the relief be discretionary.

7   The action should be allowed to proceed unless it is plainly an abuse of process.

8   The cases I have cited show that the rule in *O'Reilly v Mackman* [1983] 2 AC 237, assuming it to be a rule of general application, is subject to many exceptions based on the nature of the claim and on the undesirability of erecting procedural barriers.

. . . In conclusion, my Lords, it seems to me that, unless the procedure adopted by the moving party is ill suited to dispose of the question at issue, there is much to be said in favour of the proposition that a court having jurisdiction ought to let a case be heard rather than entertain a debate concerning the form of the proceedings.
For the reasons already given I would dismiss this appeal.

Notes
1. Peter Cane summarises Lord Lowry's reasons why 'it was right to allow Dr Roy to bring his claim by writ rather than by application for judicial review':

> The most important of these reasons were that: (1) Dr Roy was seeking to protect private law rights (this was also the basis of Lord Bridge's speech in Dr Roy's favour); (2) those private law rights 'dominate[d] the proceedings'; (3) the remedy sought by Dr Roy, namely an order for the payment of money due, could not be granted under Ord 53; and (4) if Dr Roy's complaint against the Committee succeeded, he would be entitled to the payment of the money withheld, and a person should not be required to use Ord 53 to claim a non-discretionary remedy.[62]

2. Cane goes on to ask whether *Roy* helps to clarify the definition of 'private law rights', so relied on in *Roy*.

> Contractual and property rights are obviously private law rights, as are rights to obtain monetary awards for private law wrongs or to obtain restitution on some other basis than wrongful conduct (such as mistake of fact). The really difficult cases are those in which the right in question arises out of a statutory provision. Dr Roy's right was such: the Court of Appeal held that there was a contract between Dr Roy and the Committee [(1990) 1 Med LR 328] but the House of Lords declined to decide this issue and instead treated Dr Roy's right as a private law statutory one. Are all statutory 'rights' private law rights? Surely not! It is quite clear that not all statutory duties are actionable in private law. We know from *Cocks v Thanet DC* [[1983] 2 AC 286] that the statutory right of certain homeless persons to be housed by a local authority is a private law right; and we know from Roy that the statutory right of a registered GP, under certain circumstances, to receive a full basic practice allowance is a private law right. But just as the courts have found it impossible to provide much guidance in general terms on the question of which statutory duties are actionable in the tort of breach of statutory duty, so it seems unlikely that much general guidance will ever be available on the question of which rights are private law rights for present purposes.[63]

---

62 *Ibid.*

63 *Ibid.*

3. Fredman and Morris see four main advantages to the approach of the House of Lords in *Roy*:[64] first, the explicit recognition of the fact that a single claim could (as in *Roy* itself) contain a mixture of public and private law elements; second, the 'move away from procedural rigidity' represented by the Lords' preparedness to allow a writ action in a case concerning some public law elements, provided the private elements dominated; third, the recognition that the choice of procedure should be at least partly dictated by whether it would be suitable for the type of claim in question; fourth, the move away from contract as a key factor for locating the public/private divide. They consider the first point to be the most important in that it recognises and allows for the complexity of a mixed case to be accommodated within a single action: 'having begun his action by writ, Dr Roy's case may then depend upon invoking public law principles in order to establish his private rights and obtain a private law remedy' (p 82).

4. The third point they mention appears to have received some recognition in the House of Lords' decision in *Mercury Communications v Director General of Telecommunications*.[65] In refusing to strike out Mercury's application challenging decisions of the Director General relating to its operational agreement with BT brought by originating summons on the grounds that Mercury should have proceeded by way of an application for judicial review, the House of Lords stated, *inter alia*, that: (a) a crucial question was whether the proceedings constituted an abuse of the procedures of the court; and (b) that in determining (a) it should be borne in mind that the procedure selected by Mercury was at least as well suited and possibly better suited for determining the issues raised than an application for judicial review. This seems to represent a move towards a pragmatic view of procedure, based on efficacy and convenience rather than some elusive public/private divide.

5. In *Steed v Secretary of State for the Home Department*,[66] Steed made an application to the Secretary of State for compensation under the Firearms (Amendment) Act 1997 on 29 July 1997 after handing in to the authorities various firearms. On 27 October he issued a county court summons for the sum allegedly due, claiming that there had been excessive delay in paying him the compensation due. The claims submitted under options A and B of the scheme were paid on 26 November 1997 and the Secretary of State then sought to strike out the summons as disclosing no reasonable cause of action. The application was dismissed, as were two subsequent appeals. The Secretary of State appealed to the House of Lords, contending, *inter alia*, that a challenge other than by judicial review was an abuse of process at any time prior to final determination of the individual claim. It was held, dismissing the appeal, that once all conditions of the scheme had been satisfied an applicant was clearly entitled to payment under the terms of the scheme; and that since the proceedings had not sought to challenge the lawfulness of the scheme itself nor sought to take the place of a discretionary decision specifically reserved to the administration, they could not be said to constitute an abuse of process.[67]

6. A decision taken after CPR 54 came into force follows. It concerned a student 'who had been denied the possibility of obtaining a degree of higher than third class in breach, she alleged, of university regulations. She sued on the contract between herself and the university but her claim was struck out as non-justiciable. At her appeal to the Court of Appeal, the university argued that

---

64 See n 16 above, at 82–83.

65 [1995] 1 All ER 575.

66 [2000] 1 WLR 1169.

67 On abuse of process see further *Carter Commercial Developments v Bedford Borough Council* [2001] EWHC Admin 669 in which the bringing of an ordinary action to determine a public law issue was found to be an abuse of process: the claimant, it was found, had deliberately sought to avoid the time limits contained in CPR 54 and *Phonographic Performance Ltd v Dept of Trade and Industry* [2004] EWHC 1795 at [36].

she ought to have proceeded by way of judicial review.'[68] It is important to note that, as a 'new' university, the University of Hull and Lincolnshire (ULH) was not established by royal charter, and so such disputes did not, as they would with an 'old' university, fall within the jurisdiction of the University Visitor.[69] As Sedley LJ explained: 'ULH is simply a statutory corporation with the ordinary attributes of legal personality and a capacity to enter into contracts within its powers. The arrangement between a fee-paying student and ULH is such a contract.'

Clark v University of Lincolnshire and Humberside [2000] 1 WLR 1988 (extracts)

Woolf MR: . . .A university is a public body. This is not in issue on this appeal. Court proceedings would, therefore, normally be expected to be commenced under Order 53. . .The courts today will be flexible in their approach. . . When considering whether proceedings can continue the nature of the claim can be relevant. If the court is required to perform a reviewing role or what is being claimed is a discretionary remedy, whether it be a prerogative remedy or an injunction or a declaration the position is different from when the claim is for damages or a sum of money for breach of contract or a tort irrespective of the procedure adopted. . . .

Similarly if what is being claimed could affect the public generally the approach of the court will be stricter than if the proceedings only affect the immediate parties. It must not be forgotten that a court can extend time to bring proceedings under Order 53. The intention of the CPR is to harmonise procedures as far as possible and to avoid barren procedural disputes which generate satellite litigation.

Where a student has, as here, a claim in contract, the court will not strike out a claim which could more appropriately be made under Order 53 solely because of the procedure which has been adopted. It may however do so, if it comes to the conclusion that in all the circumstances, including the delay in initiating the proceedings, there has been an abuse of the process of the court under the CPR. . .

The emphasis can therefore be said to have changed since *O'Reilly v Mackman*. What is likely to be important when proceedings are not brought by a student against a new university under Order 53, will not be whether the right procedure has been adopted but whether the protection provided by Order 53 has been flouted in circumstances which are inconsistent with the proceedings being able to be conducted justly in accordance with the general principles contained in Part I. . .

Notes
Cornford notes:

> It was clearly Lord Woolf's purpose to emphasise the court's flexibility and minimise the importance of the choice between procedures. It is unlikely, however, that the judgment will much reduce the importance of the exclusivity principle. If the scope of the judgment is confined to litigants who have contractual rights then it breaks no new ground. As mentioned above, it is well established that holders of private rights are entitled to use private law procedure. As Sedley LJ pointed out in his judgment in *Clark* (at p 757d), the claimant's position was stronger than that of the plaintiff in the Roy case. At the same time, if the scope of the judgment is confined in this way,

---

68   Cornford, n 70 below.

69   Though note that the Higher Education Act 2004, s 20, has excluded from the Visitorial jurisdiction complaints by former students.

there will remain a large class of claimants who do not possess a private right or anything like it and who will continue to be obliged to use judicial review.

If, on the other hand, the judgment is applied beyond the contractual context, it gives very uncertain guidance.[70]

Collateral challenge

One exception to the general rule that public law issues should be raised only in judicial review proceedings mentioned by Lord Diplock in *O'Reilly* was collateral challenge. It was established in *Wandsworth London Borough Council v Winder*[71] that a tenant who was being sued in ordinary civil proceedings for arrears in rent by his local authority was entitled to use in his defence the public law plea that the increase was *ultra vires* and therefore void. In the following case, the issue arose in the criminal context: the defendant was convicted of an offence under a bylaw prohibiting smoking on trains and wished to be able to challenge the validity of the bylaw as a collateral challenge to the charges against him.

Boddington v British Transport Police [1999] 2 AC 143 (extracts)

Lord Irvine: . . .In every case it will be necessary to examine the particular statutory context to determine whether a court hearing a criminal or civil case has jurisdiction to rule on a defence based upon arguments of invalidity of subordinate legislation or an administrative act under it. There are situations in which Parliament may legislate to preclude such challenges being made, in the interest, for example, of promoting certainty about the legitimacy of administrative acts on which the public may have to rely.

The recent decision of this House in *R v Wicks* [1998] AC 92 is an example of a particular context in which an administrative act triggering consequences for the purposes of the criminal law was held not to be capable of challenge in criminal proceedings, but only by other proceedings. The case concerned an enforcement notice issued by a local planning authority and served on the defendant under the then current version of section 87 of the Town and Country Planning Act 1971. The notice alleged a breach of planning control by the erection of a building and required its removal above a certain height. One month was allowed for compliance. The appellant appealed against the notice to the Secretary of State, under section 174 of the Town and Country Planning Act 1990, but the appeal was dismissed. The appellant still failed to comply with the notice and the local authority issued a summons alleging a breach of section 179(1) of the Act of 1990. In the criminal proceedings which ensued, the appellant sought to defend himself on the ground that the enforcement notice had been issued ultra vires, maintaining that the local planning authority had acted in bad faith and had been motivated by irrelevant considerations. The judge ruled that these contentions should have been made in proceedings for judicial review and that they could not be gone into in the criminal proceedings. The appellant then pleaded guilty and was convicted. This House upheld his conviction. Lord Hoffmann, in the leading speech, emphasised that the ability of a defendant to criminal proceedings to challenge the validity of an act done under statutory authority depended on the construction of the statute in question. This House held that the Town and Country Planning Act 1990 contained an elaborate code including provision for appeals against notices, and that on the proper

---

70   T Cornford, 'The New Rules of Procedure for Judicial Review' (2000) 5 Web JCLI.

71   [1985] AC 461.

construction of section 179(1) of the Act all that was required to be proved in the criminal proceedings was that the notice issued by the local planning authority was formally valid.

. . . However, in approaching the issue of statutory construction the courts proceed from a strong appreciation that ours is a country subject to the rule of law. This means that it is well recognised to be important for the maintenance of the rule of law and the preservation of liberty that individuals affected by legal measures promulgated by executive public bodies should have a fair opportunity to challenge these measures and to vindicate their rights in court proceedings. There is a strong presumption that Parliament will not legislate to prevent individuals from doing so

The particular statutory scheme in question in *Wicks* . . .did justify a construction which limited the rights of the defendant to call the legality of an administrative act into question. But in my judgment it was an important feature of [the case] that [it was] concerned with [an] administrative act specifically directed at the defendants, where there had been clear and ample opportunity provided by the scheme of the relevant legislation for those defendants to challenge the legality of those acts, before being charged with an offence.

By contrast, where subordinate legislation (eg, statutory instruments or byelaws) is promulgated which is of a general character in the sense that it is directed to the world at large, the first time an individual may be affected by that legislation is when he is charged with an offence under it: so also where a general provision is brought into effect by an administrative act, as in this case. A smoker might have made his first journey on the line on the same train as Mr Boddington; have found that there was no carriage free of no smoking signs and have chosen to exercise what he believed to be his right to smoke on the train. Such an individual would have had no sensible opportunity to challenge the validity of the posting of the no smoking signs throughout the train until he was charged, as Mr Boddington was, under byelaw 20. In my judgment in such a case the strong presumption must be that Parliament did not intend to deprive the smoker of an opportunity to defend himself in the criminal proceedings by asserting the alleged unlawfulness of the decision to post no smoking notices throughout the train. I can see nothing in [the relevant legislation,] section 67 of the Transport Act 1962 or the byelaws which could displace that presumption. . . .

Accordingly, I consider that the Divisional Court was wrong in the present case in ruling that Mr Boddington was not entitled to raise the legality of the decision to post no smoking notices throughout the train, as a possible defence to the charge against him.

. . . In my judgment only the clear language of a statute could take away the right of a defendant in criminal proceedings to challenge the lawfulness of a byelaw or administrative decision where his prosecution is premised on its validity.

Notes

1. The procedure for judicial review, as well as the draconian three-month time limit, differs in two important respects from an ordinary civil action. Instead of discovery of documents and cross-examination of witnesses being the norm, they will be ordered only in strictly limited, exceptional circumstances, though here, too, the new CPR may have some influence. As to cross-examination, Lord Diplock said in *O'Reilly v Mackman* that 'it will only be upon rare occasions that the interests of justice will require that leave be given for cross-examination of deponents on their affidavits in applications for judicial review,' because, as he said, disputes of fact are likely to be rare. He added however, that 'it should be allowed whenever the justice of the particular case so requires'.

2. As to discovery, the importance for the applicant of being able to obtain sight of certain documents was emphasised by Lord Diplock in the same case. Referring to *Anisminic Ltd v Foreign*

Compensation Commission (below) he noted that it was only through discovery that 'the minute of the Commission's decision which showed that they had asked themselves the wrong question was obtained'. It was the fact that the Commission had asked itself the wrong question which established that it had erred in law and thus exceeded its jurisdiction.[72] Discovery therefore played a vital role in that case.

3. Nevertheless, as Cornford notes:

> It soon became clear however that discovery would be ordered in only very limited circumstances . . . The applicant would bring his challenge and the respondent authority would be entitled to defend and explain its actions by means of affidavits. The court would then only accede to any application for discovery by the applicant if he could already point to evidence in his possession which cast doubt on the veracity of the affidavit. The applicant was thus in a Catch-22 situation. He could only obtain evidence to disprove the authority's version of events if he already possessed it.[73]

4. *R v Secretary of State for Foreign Affairs ex parte the World Development Movement*[74] provided a good example of the courts' restrictive approach. The applicant was seeking discovery of the minutes of certain meetings: summaries of those minutes had been set out in affidavits filed on behalf of the respondent. The applicant argued that only disclosure of the minutes themselves would reveal fully the grounds on which the decision being challenged (to grant aid to fund the Malaysian Pergau Dam project) had been made and suggested that 'that the affidavit summaries [were] at best incomplete, and at worst misleading.' However, the judge found insufficient reason to believe that the affidavits were misleading and refused discovery.

5. Michael Fordham sees the position on oral evidence and cross-examination as being even more restrictive under the CPR:

> The problem is this. Part 54 adopts and modifies Part 8. The rules regarding oral evidence and cross-examination of a witness are contained in CPR, r 8.6(2) and (3). But far from incorporating or referring to these, CPR, 54.16(1) provides that 'Rule 8.6 does not apply'. This is most unfortunate.[75]

WHO MAY APPLY FOR JUDICIAL REVIEW?

Persons seeking leave—'permission' as it is now called—to apply for judicial review will only be granted it if, per s 31 of the Supreme Court Act 1981, they can show that they have 'sufficient interest in the matter to which the application relates' (above, p 747). This requirement has not been altered by CPR, Part 54 which, as Cornford notes, 'say nothing about standing at all'.[76] Thus, the pre-CPR case-law continues to govern this area.

---

72 For the decision itself, see below, pp 769–770 and Chapter 15, pp 826–828.

73 See n 70 above.

74 [1995] 1 All ER 615, see esp. 620–22.

75 M Fordham, 'Judicial Review: The New Rules' [2001] PL 4, 5.

76 Cornford, n 70 above.

A person who is individually and directly concerned with the decision he or she disputes, for example, if it relates to his or her employment (as in *Roy*) or application for housing (as in *Ali v Tower Hamlets*) will always be found to have 'sufficient interest'. The controversial issue in this area is whether groups or individuals with no personal concern in the decision in question (for example, pressure groups, local associations, etc) have standing to question it.[77]

It was found in *R v Secretary of State for the Environment ex parte Rose Theatre Trust Co*[78] that pressure groups whose only interest in a decision is concern about the issues involved will not in general have *locus standi* to challenge the decision. The law has moved on considerably from that position, partly as a result of an approach derived from *R v IRC ex parte National Federation of Self Employed* [1982] AC 617. In that case, their Lordships were unanimous in stressing that the question of standing is inextricably linked with the substantive merits of the application.

The appellants were a body of taxpayers who wished to challenge arrangements made by the Inland Revenue for the taxation of casual employees of certain Fleet Street newspapers, which, *inter alia*, involved a partial amnesty on previous tax evasion. The appellants argued that the arrangements treated the employees in question in an overly generous manner, and that they had never been given such concessions. The issue for the House of Lords was whether the appellants had standing to challenge the IRC's decision and seek an order for *mandamus* compelling the Inland Revenue to collect taxes in the usual way.

R v IRC ex parte National Federation of Self Employed [1982] AC 617, 649–50, 653–55

Lord Scarman: . . .I pass now to the. . .nature of the interest which the applicant has to show. . .The sufficiency of the interest is, as I understand all your Lordships agree, a mixed question of law and fact. The legal element in the mixture is less than the matters of fact and degree: but it is important as setting the limits within which, and the principles by which, the discretion is to be exercised.

My Lords, I will not weary the House with citation of many authorities. Suffice it to refer to. . .words of Lord Wilberforce in *Gouriet v Union of Post Office Workers* [1978] AC 435, 482, where he stated the modern position in relation to prerogative orders: 'These are often applied for by individuals and the courts have allowed them liberal access under a generous conception of locus standi.' The one legal principle, which is implicit in the case law and accurately reflected in the rule of court, is that in determining the sufficiency of an applicant's interest it is necessary to consider the matter to which the application relates. It is wrong in law, as I understand the cases, for the court to attempt an assessment of the sufficiency of an applicant's interest without regard to the matter of his complaint. If he fails to show, when he applies for leave, a prima facie case, or reasonable grounds for believing that there has been a failure of public duty, the court would be in error if it granted leave. The curb represented by the need for an applicant to show, when he seeks leave to apply, that he has such a case is an essential protection against abuse of legal process. It enables the court to prevent abuse by busybodies, cranks, and other mischief-makers. I do not see any further purpose served by the requirement for leave.

But, that being said, the discretion belongs to the court: and, as my noble and learned friend, Lord Diplock, has already made clear, it is the function of the judges to determine the way in which it is to be exercised.

---

77   For an interesting and in-depth analysis of this issue, see C Hilson and I Cram, 'Judicial Review and Environmental Law—Is There a Coherent View of Standing?' (1996) 16(1) LS 3. See also J Alder, *Constitutional and Administrative Law*, 7th edn (2009) at 358–59; Craig, n 54 above, Chapter 24.

78   [1990] 1 All ER 754.

[Lord Scarman then went on to find that, in fact, the appellant had failed to make out a *prima facie* case that the IRC had acted unfairly. He also noted that the Court of Appeal had been 'misled' into treating *locus standi* as an issue separate from the merits]:

The federation, having failed to show any grounds for believing that the revenue has failed to do its statutory duty, have not, in my view, shown an interest sufficient in law to justify any further proceedings by the court on its application. Had they shown reasonable grounds for believing that the failure to collect tax from the Fleet Street casuals was an abuse of the revenue's managerial discretion or that there was a case to that effect which merited investigation and examination by the court, I would have agreed with the Court of Appeal that they had shown a sufficient interest for the grant of leave to proceed further with their application. I would, therefore, allow the appeal.

Notes

1. On the question of the standing of individual tax-payers to challenge decisions of the Inland Revenue, see further *R v HM Treasury ex parte Smedley*.[79]

2. In *R (Bulger) v Home Secretary*,[80] relatives of a murdered child were found not to have standing to challenge the sentence given to him, largely on public policy grounds. This was partly because the impact on the family had already been taken into account at the original sentencing stage, and partly because the family were not a party to the original case, and it would be contrary to the public interest to allow sentencing decisions to be challenged by way of judicial review by victims' and defendants' families.

3. The courts appeared to move beyond the position taken in *Rose Theatre* in *R v Her Majesty's Inspectorate of Pollution ex parte Greenpeace Ltd (No 2)*,[81] discussed here by Ivan Hare. Greenpeace was seeking review of the decision of Her Majesty's Inspectorate of Pollution (HMIP) to allow testing at the THORP nuclear reprocessing plant without further consultation.

... Greenpeace sought to impugn the substantive decision to vary [British Nuclear Fuel Limited's] authorisation on the ground that an entirely new authorisation was required before testing at THORP could lawfully commence. This application was also dismissed but of general importance was the rejection of BNFL's claim that Greenpeace lacked sufficient standing to initiate the proceedings. In accepting that Greenpeace had *locus standi,* Otton J was influenced by a number of factors including the international reputation of the group and its significant local membership in the affected area. He also stressed that Greenpeace represented the best, and possibly the only, means by which the issues raised by the application could be addressed by a court. Two further points require some comment. First, Otton J took account of the fact that Greenpeace was seeking an order of certiorari and held that 'if mandamus were sought that would be a reason to decline jurisdiction'. In other words, the test of standing will vary according to the remedy sought by the applicant. This statement was purportedly based on the decision of the House of Lords in IRC *ex p National Federation of Self-Employed and Small Businesses Ltd* [above]. In fact, Lord Wilberforce was the only member of the House to adopt a clear position in favour of this view with Lord Diplock equally clearly opposed to it

79   [1985] 1 All ER 589 at 594, 595; [1985] QB 657, 670, 667 *per* Slade LJ and Lord Donaldson MR.

80   [2001] EWHC 119 (Admin).

81   [1994] 4 All ER 329.

and the other Lords appearing to express somewhat equivocal support for Lord Diplock's position. There is a very strong argument that the purpose of the introduction of the unified Ord 53 procedure was to remove exactly this sort of distinction between the different forms of relief. Any return to the adjectival complexity of the prerogative orders is to be regretted.

Secondly, the court expressly declined to follow *ex p Rose Theatre Trust Co*, a case which many feared marked a rejection of the prevailing liberal attitude to locus standi. . ..Otton J emphasised that Greenpeace, 'with its particular experience in environmental matters, its access to experts in the relevant realms of science and technology (not to mention the law), is able to mount a carefully selected, focused, relevant and well-argued challenge'.[82]

4. Another issue of importance in the case was the fact that the interest Greenpeace had in the matter went clearly beyond the merely ideological. Otton J stressed the local health interest of the 2,500 supporters in the Cumbria region, whose health might be effected by emissions from the nuclear plant.[83] Thus, members of the group had a personal interest in a matter of substantial general concern—public health. Thus, although the court expressly declined to follow *Rose Theatre*, the decision was clearly distinguishable anyway: in the earlier case the group seeking to challenge the decision not to list the theatre site was only interested in the case because of its general concern about the preservation of this country's historical heritage. As Hilson and Cram remark, 'Had a substantial number of the individuals in the [Rose Theatre pressure group] lived locally, the position might well have been different'.[84]

5. A similar approach was adopted in *R v Secretary of State for the Environment ex parte Friends of the Earth*[85] where the group and its director were granted leave to challenge a decision related to the quality of drinking water in certain specified areas. The fact that the director lived in one of those areas— London—gave him a personal local interest in the matter.

6. However, in other cases involving decisions of *national* importance, the courts have been prepared to move beyond this stance and allow challenges by persons whose only concern with the decision is intellectual or ideological. The rationale appears to be that, in these cases, there is no one who will be personally affected and who could therefore claim a greater interest in the matter than the applicant. The result would therefore be that if the applicant were denied leave, no one else would be able to come forward to challenge the decision so that the courts would have no opportunity to test the legality of an important decision, a position that the courts seem increasingly minded to avoid. Thus, for example, in *R v Secretary of State for Foreign and Commonwealth Affairs ex parte Rees-Mogg*,[86] it was found that the applicant had standing 'because of his sincere concern for constitutional issues'.

7. *R v Secretary of State for Employment ex parte EOC*[87] concerned in part the standing of the Equal Opportunities Commission (EOC), a quango with the remit of curbing discrimination, to

---

82 I Hare [1995] 54(1) CLJ 1, 2–3.

83 Hilson and Cram, n 77 above, at 18.

84 *Ibid*, p 19.

85 [1994] CMLR 760.

86 [1994] 1 All ER 457 (*cf* the remarks of Lord Donaldson MR in *ex parte Argyll Group plc* [1986] 2 All ER 257, 265–66).

87 [1994] 2 WLR 409.

challenge statutory provisions. Certain provisions of the Employment Protection (Consolidation) Act 1978 governed the right not to be unfairly dismissed, compensation for unfair dismissal and the right to statutory redundancy pay. These rights did not apply to workers who worked less than a specified number of hours a week. The EOC considered that since the majority of those working for less than the specified number of hours were women, the provisions operated to the disadvantage or women and were therefore discriminatory. It was held, *inter alia,* that the EOC was entitled to bring judicial review proceedings in order to secure a declaration that UK law was incompatible with EC law. Declarations were made that the conditions set out in the provisions in question were indeed incompatible with EC law. The case also illustrates the point that where both an individual *and* a group have an interest in a given decision, the courts may favour the group.[88]

8. In the following case, the question was whether the pressure group concerned had standing to challenge an allegedly unlawful grant of foreign aid.

R v Secretary of State for Foreign Affairs ex parte the World Development Movement [1995] 1 WLR 386 (extracts)

Rose LJ: Internationally, [the World Development Movement] has official consultative status with UNESCO and has promoted international conferences. It has brought together development groups within the OECD. It tends to attract citizens of the United Kingdom concerned about the role of the United Kingdom Government in relation to the development of countries abroad and the relief of poverty abroad.

Its supporters have a direct interest in ensuring that funds furnished by the United Kingdom are used for genuine purposes, and it seeks to ensure that disbursement of aid budgets is made where that aid is most needed. It seeks, by this application, to represent the interests of people in developing countries who might benefit from funds which otherwise might go elsewhere.

If the applicants have no standing, it is said that no person or body would ensure that powers under the 1980 Act are exercised lawfully. For the applicants, Mr Pleming QC submitted that the Foreign Secretary himself, in a written statement of 2 March 1994, has expressly accepted that the matter is '. . .clearly of public and Parliamentary interest'. It cannot be said that the applicants are 'busybodies', 'cranks' or 'mischief makers'. They are a non-partisan pressure group concerned with the misuse of aid money. If there is a public law error, it is difficult to see how else it could be challenged and corrected except by such an applicant. He referred the court to a number of authorities: *National Federation of Self-Employed and Small Businesses Ltd*, in particular the speech of. . . Lord Diplock, where there appears this passage:

It would, in my view, be a grave lacuna in our system of public law if a pressure group, like the federation, or even a single public spirited taxpayer, were prevented by outdated technical rules of *locus standi* from bringing the matter to the attention of the court to vindicate the Rule of Law and get the unlawful conduct stopped. The Attorney General, although he occasionally applies for prerogative orders against public authorities that do not form part of central Government, in practice never does so against Government departments. It is not, in my view, a sufficient answer to say that judicial review of the actions of officers or departments of central Government is

---

88 See further on this issue, Hilson and Cram, n 77 above at 21–25.

unnecessary because they are accountable to Parliament for the way in which they carry out their functions. They are accountable to Parliament for what they do so far as regards efficiency and policy, and of that Parliament is the only judge; they are responsible to a court of justice for the lawfulness of what they do, and of that the court is the only judge ([1982] AC 617 at 644).

. . . The question of lawfulness being for the court, Mr Pleming submitted that the court in its discretion should accept the standing of the applicants. If they cannot seek relief, he said, who can? Neither a Government nor citizen of a foreign country denied aid is, in practical terms, likely to be able to bring such a challenge. . .

. . .I find nothing in *IRC v National Federation of Self-Employed and Small Businesses Ltd* to deny standing to these applicants. The authorities referred to seem to me to indicate an increasingly liberal approach to standing on the part of the courts during the last 12 years. It is also clear from [that decision] that standing should not be treated as a preliminary issue, but must be taken in the legal and factual context of the whole case (see [1982] AC 617 at 630, 649. . .).

Furthermore, the merits of the challenge are an important, if not dominant, factor when considering standing. In Professor Sir William Wade's words in *Administrative Law* (7th edn, 1994), p 712: '. . .the real question is whether the applicant can show some substantial default or abuse, and not whether his personal rights or interests are involved.'.

Leaving merits aside for a moment, there seem to me to be a number of factors of significance in the present case: the importance of vindicating the Rule of Law, as Lord Diplock emphasised in *IRC*. . .; the importance of the issue raised, as in *ex p Child Poverty Action Group;* the likely absence of any other responsible challenger, as in *ex p Child Poverty Action Group* and *ex p Greenpeace Ltd;* the nature of the breach of duty against which relief is sought (see *IRC* [1982] AC 617 at 630); and the prominent role of these applicants in giving advice, guidance and assistance with regard to aid (see *ex p Child Poverty Action Group*. . . All, in my judgment, point, in the present case, to the conclusion that the applicants here do have a sufficient interest in the matter to which the application relates within s 31 (3) of the 1981 Act and Ord 53, r 3(7).

Notes

1. The case is clearly not a charter for the tiresomely officious: the applicants were a body whose work was of international repute and whose concern for the issue in hand was genuine.[89] Further, the fact that there was no one more closely affected by the decision in question who could have brought the case was clearly instrumental in the court's finding. The requirement that no such person or persons be available to mount a challenge will often operate to protect what Hilson and Cram term 'local autonomy';[90] the idea is that if a particular community or individual is content to acquiesce in a decision, it would show disrespect for their autonomy if other bodies, not affected by the decision, were to be allowed to challenge it. Thus, it is argued that in the case of decisions which are *only* of local significance, the courts are right to insist as they do that any challenger must have a local interest.[91] By contrast, in cases in which decisions have particular local interest but are also of

---

89   See also the finding that Rees-Mogg's concern for constitutional issues was 'sincere' and that Greenpeace was genuinely exercised about testing at THORP.

90   n 77 above, at 10–12 and 15–21.

91   *Ibid* at 17.

national significance (for example, the *Rose Theatre* case itself), it is argued that 'the autonomy of those personally affected or locally connected ought to be overridden and standing granted to those with [only] a general interest'.[92] This does not, however, represent the current legal position.[93]

2. In *Broadmoor Special Hospital Authority v Robinson*,[94] Lord Woolf MR said:

> 'Sufficient interest', has been approached by the courts in a generous manner so that almost invariably if an applicant can establish a case which deserves to succeed, standing will not constitute a bar to the grant of a remedy.

3. It is important to note that the *motive* of the applicant in bringing a case is still treated as a potentially relevant factor by the court: an illegitimate motive, such as ill-will, may lead to standing being refused, even where the court has accepted that the case raises a matter of significant public concern. Thus in *R (Feakins) v Secretary of State for the Environment, Food and Rural Affairs*[95] Dyson LJ said:

> In my judgment, if a claimant has no sufficient private interest to support a claim to standing, then he should not be accorded standing *merely* because he raises an issue in which there is, objectively speaking, a public interest. As Sedley J said in *R v Somerset County Council, Ex p Dixon* [1997] JPL 1030, when considering the issue of standing, the court had to ensure that the claimant was not prompted by an ill motive, and was not a mere busybody or a trouble-maker. Thus, if a claimant seeks to challenge a decision in which he has no private law interest, it is difficult to conceive of circumstances in which the court will accord him standing, even where there is a public interest in testing the lawfulness of the decision, *if* the claimant is acting out of ill-will or for some other improper purpose. It is an abuse of process to permit a claimant to bring a claim in such circumstances. If the real reason why a claimant wishes to challenge a decision in which, objectively, there is a public interest is not that he has a genuine concern about the decision, but some other reason, then that is material to the question whether he should be accorded standing.

The court however noted the caution expressed by Auld LJ in the Court of Appeal in *R (Mount Cook Land Ltd) v Westminster City Council*[96] in relation to treating motive as important in this context, in particular where he said:

> I do not say that considerations of a claimant's motive in claiming judicial review could never be relevant to a court's decision whether to refuse relief in its discretion, for example, where the pursuance of the motive in question goes so far beyond the advancement of a collateral purpose as to amount to an abuse of process. The

---

92 *Ibid*, at 15–16 and see pp 19–20.

93 *Rose Theatre; R v Pools Borough Council ex parte Beebee* [1991] JPL 643.

94 [2000] QB 775, 787.

95 [2004] 1 WLR 1761, CA at [23].

96 [2003] EWCA Civ 1346 at [45] and [46].

court should, at the very least, be slow to have recourse to that species of conduct as a basis for discretionary refusal of relief.

Standing was not in fact denied in the *Feakins* case, despite the court remaining unsure about the claimant's motive. It is submitted that, given the difficulty of establishing a subjective state of mind, motive should only very exceptionally (if at all) be treated as relevant: if an application raises an arguable point of unlawful conduct by a public body on a matter of public importance, it is hard to see why the applicant's state of mind should lead to the court refusing to hear the case.

4. Recent decisions indicate that the liberal approach to standing continues. The *Corner House* case was considered in the chapter on the rule of law,[97] but the standing point was that it allowed two charities, Corner House Research and the Campaign against Arms Trade, to challenge a decision by the Serious Fraud Office to stop an investigation into alleged serious bribery by BAE systems of Saudi government officials: *R (Corner House Research and another) v Director of the Serious Fraud Office*.[98] Similarly, in *Regina (Refugee Legal Centre) v Secretary of State for the Home Department*,[99] the Refugee Legal Centre (RLC), an independent not-for-profit organisation concerned with the provision of legal services to asylum seekers, was found to have standing to challenge, on behalf of asylum seekers, the decision of the Home Secretary to introduce a fast-track pilot scheme for the adjudication of asylum applications made by single male applicants arriving in the United Kingdom from countries where the Secretary of State believed there to be no serious risk of persecution. The scheme was alleged to be unfair, because it severely compressed the decision-making process into only three days. Although the point was not contested, Sedley LJ said that the Home Office had been right not to challenge the RLC's standing, pointing out that, precisely because of the exceptionally tight time-scale imposed on asylum seekers, it was much better placed than any such individual to bring a challenge to the system itself. [100]

5. To bring a claim under the HRA, applicants must show that they are 'a victim' of the action, or proposed action of the public authority (s 7(1)), clearly a more restrictive test than that considered above. The test is discussed further in Chapter 17, pp 991–992.

6. While, as noted at the beginning of this section, the CPR do not purport to alter the law of standing, the changes they make to the obtaining of permission to bring a challenge are quite significant, in a way which may influence the courts' jurisprudence in this area. Previously, as Lord Diplock said in *ex parte National Federation of Self Employed* at 644A:

> If, on a quick perusal of the material then available, the court thinks that it discloses what might on further consideration turn out to be an arguable case in favour of granting to the applicant the relief claimed, it ought, in the exercise of judicial discretion, to give him leave to apply for that relief.

As Tom Cornford and Maurice Sunkin comment:

> The single most important aspect of these reforms is the way the permission stage has been re-crafted from an essentially summary ex parte filter of arguability to a

---

97 See Chapter 3, pp 119–126.

98 [2008] EWHC 714 (QB).

99 [2005] 1 WLR 2219.

100 *Ibid* at [4] and [5]. For another generous case, this time involving an individual, see *R (Edwards) v Environment Agency* [2004] 3 All ER 21.

procedure which is both a filter of access and an inter partes procedure of the sort familiar in ordinary civil litigation.[101]

This has seemingly encouraged the courts to scrutinise the issue of standing much more rigorously at the permission stage, rather than leaving main consideration of it to the full hearing, as previously. Indeed, a later study highlights the fact that there has been a sharp decline in the proportion of applications for judicial review that are given leave to proceed, from 71% in 1981 to only 22% in 2006,[102] and expresses concern at the inconsistencies that arise in granting or refusing permission.

CAN JUDICIAL REVIEW BE EXCLUDED?

The basic position

It is a fundamental principle of English law that the courts always have a duty to ensure that a body exercising power does so within the parameters set for it in the provisions (often primary legislation) which established it or gave it power in the area under consideration. In *Anisminic* (below), it was held that this power of the court to keep the deciding body within the remit defined in the Act which gave it its powers could not be excluded, despite apparently clear words in a statute to the contrary. To allow the court's supervisory jurisdiction to be ousted would be to accede to the proposition that the body in question had arbitrary powers, and the court was not prepared to believe that such powers are ever granted, since the granting of them would undermine the basic principle of the Rule of Law.

Anisminic Ltd v Foreign Compensation Commission [1969] 2 AC 147, 170

Lord Reid: . . .Let me illustrate the matter by supposing a simple case. A statute provides that a certain order may be made by a person who holds a specified qualification or appointment, and it contains a provision. . .that such an order made by such a person shall not be called in question in any court of law. A person aggrieved by an order alleges that it is a forgery or that the person who made the order did not hold that qualification or appointment. Does such a provision require the court to treat that order as a valid order? It is a well established principle that a provision ousting the ordinary jurisdiction of the court must be construed strictly—meaning, I think, that, if such a provision is reasonably capable of having two meanings, that meaning shall be taken which preserves the ordinary jurisdiction of the court.

Statutory provisions which seek to limit the ordinary jurisdiction of the court have a long history. No case has been cited in which any other form of words limiting the jurisdiction of the court has been held to protect a nullity. If the draftsman or Parliament had intended to introduce a new kind of ouster clause so as to prevent any inquiry even as to whether the document relied on was a forgery, I would have expected to find something much more specific than the bald statement that a determination shall not be called in question in any court of law. Undoubtedly such a provision protects every determination which is not a nullity. But I do not think that it is necessary or even reasonable to construe the word

---

101   T Cornford and M Sunkin, 'The Bowman Report, Access and the Recent Reforms of the Judicial Review Procedure' [2001] PL 11, 15.

102   V Bondy and M Sunkin 'Accessing Judicial Review' [2008] PL 647, 648.

'determination' as including everything which purports to be a determination but which is in fact no determination at all. And there are no degrees of nullity. There are a number of reasons why the law will hold a purported decision to be a nullity. I do not see how it could be said that such a provision protects some kinds of nullity but not others: if that were intended it would be easy to say so.

Notes

1. The basic idea behind the *Anisminic* decision is that by making an error in law, the body asked itself the wrong question, determined a point it was not authorised to decide and thus exceeded its *vires*. Its decision was therefore *ultra vires* and a nullity. The idea of a body being empowered to err in law within certain limits was rejected.

2. Section 12(1) of the Tribunals Act 1992 now provides that the supervisory functions of the superior courts will not be excluded by Acts passed prior to 1 August 1958. This or course implies that effect may be given to ouster clauses in later statutes.

Tribunals and Enquiries Act 1992

12.–(1) As respects England and Wales—

   (a)   any provision in an Act passed before 1st August 1958 that any order or determination shall not be called into question in any court, or

   (b)   any provision in such an Act which by similar words excludes any of the powers of the High Court,

shall not have effect so as to prevent the removal of the proceedings into the High Court by order of certiorari or to prejudice the powers of the High Court to make orders of mandamus. Supervisory functions of superior courts not excluded by Acts passed before 1 August 1958.

Note

1. However, where a different means for resolving disputes has been provided by Parliament, the starting point of the courts is that applicants should use it. In *R (Cowl v Plymouth City Council (Practice Note)*, Lord Woolf said:

   The court should not permit, except for good reason, proceedings for judicial review to proceed if a significant part of the issues between the parties could be resolved outside the litigation process. . .Today, sufficient should be known about alternative dispute resolution to make the failure to adopt it, in particular when public money is involved, indefensible.[103]

Attempts to restrict/exclude judicial review of asylum decisions: the 'super ouster'

By the early years of the 21st century, successive Governments had for some time been expressing acute frustration with the effect of judicial review upon the asylum system. Desperate to gain credibility for

---

103   [2002] 1 WLR 803, CA. There is, for example a statutory procedure for challenging Compulsory Purchase Orders under the Acquisition of Land Act 1981, which courts have found should be followed instead of judicial review.

being 'tough' on an issue on which they were subject to relentless media and opposition attacks, the Blair Government engaged in a series of attempts to 'streamline' the whole system of legal challenges to decisions to refuse asylum, with the aim of speeding up the deportation of unsuccessful asylum claimants, and reducing the number of challenges.[104] Prior to the reforms considered below, a person contesting a decision by a Home Office official denying them entry to the UK could appeal at first instance to an Adjudicator. There was then an appeal with leave on point of law to the Immigration Appellate Authority ('IAT'). But 'the vast majority' of applications for leave to appeal were refused.[105] Many people were therefore seeking judicial review at this point—of the decision to refuse leave to appeal. Since the Government could not deport anyone who had given notice that they were intending to make a judicial review application,[106] this alone was causing significant delays to the process of deporting such people. The Government therefore brought forward what became section 101 of the Nationality, Immigration and Asylum Act 2002, which removed judicial review of IAT decisions to refuse leave to appeal, replacing them with a statutory right of appeal on the basis of written sub-missions only, under very strict time limits and with no further right to appeal to the Court of Appeal.[107] This reform was challenged in the following case by asylum seekers whose applications for asylum had been rejected by the Adjudicator, and their applications for leave to appeal to the IAT refused. They sought to bring judicial review of the decision of the IAT to refuse leave; their application was unsuccessful at first instance, so they appealed.

R (on the application of G) v Immigration Appeals Tribunal
[2005] 1 WLR 1445 (extracts)

12 The common law power of the judges to review the legality of administrative action is a cornerstone of the rule of law in this country and one that the judges guard jealously. If Parliament attempts by legislation to remove that power, the rule of law is threatened. The courts will not readily accept that legislation achieves that end: see *Anisminic* . . .

The complaint that is made of statutory review on this appeal is, essentially, that it does not offer procedural advantages that attend judicial review, namely a right to an oral hearing and a right, with permission, to appeal to the Court of Appeal.

15 . . .Collins J [at first instance] considered that the right to seek statutory review by a High Court judge was a remedy that catered adequately for the possibility that the IAT might err in law in refusing permission to appeal against an immigration decision. . .

20 [The court must] consider whether an alternative remedy is proportionate when deciding whether to exercise its power of judicial review. The consideration of proportional-ity involves more than comparing the remedy with what is at stake in the litigation. Where Parliament enacts a remedy with the clear intention that this should be pursued in place of judicial review, it is appropriate to have regard to the considerations giving rise to that intention. The satisfactory operation of the separation of powers requires that Parliament should leave the judges free to perform their role of maintaining the rule of law but also that, in performing that role, the judges should, so far as consistent with the rule of law, have regard to legislative policy.

---

104   For a comprehensive account of the whole issue see R Rawlings, 'Review, Revenge and Retreat' (2005) 68(3) MLR 378.

105   A Le Suer, 'Three Strikes and its Out? The UK Government's Strategy to Oust Judicial Review from Immigration and Asylum Decision Making' [2004] PL 225, 228.

106   See *M v Home Office* [1993] 3 WLR 433, discussed Chapter 3, pp 93–94.

107   The application must be made within 14 days, instead of the normal three month period for judicial review.

21 . . .In the present case it is the clear intention of Parliament. . .that statutory review under section 101 of the Act should be used in place of judicial review. The reason for that intention is the wish to process asylum applications with expedition. That is a legitimate objective and. . .it is right to have regard to [it], but this cannot justify refraining from the use of judicial review if the alternative of statutory review will not provide a satisfactory safeguard for those who are, or may be, entitled to asylum.

26 . . .We have concluded, in agreement with Collins J, that the statutory regime, including statutory review of a refusal of permission to appeal, provides adequate and proportionate protection of the asylum seeker's rights. It is accordingly a proper exercise of the court's discretion to decline to entertain an application for judicial review.

Notes

1. This decision is an excellent example of the care with which a court will evaluate the satisfactoriness of any remedy that has been provided in statute in place of judicial review.
2. However, what happened next was altogether more stark and dramatic. While the above new provision dealt with a large number of previous judicial review claims, this still did not satisfy the Government. After only a very brief consultation period, the Home Office proposed a much more radical reform:

> It. . .proposed to replace the existing two-tier tribunal appeal structure (adjudicators plus the IAT) with a new, single-tier tribunal to be called the Asylum and Immigration Tribunal (AIT), with most cases being heard by a single judge.[108]

It also sought to all but remove judicial review of decisions of the new AIT, leaving only a reference procedure by which the president of the AIT, but not the parties, could seek guidance on questions of law from the Court of Appeal.[109] It also appeared to immunise from judicial review related enforcement measures taken by the Home Office[110] and removed HRA challenges as well.[111] The clause designed to achieve all this read:

Asylum and Immigration (Treatment of Claimants, etc) Act Bill 2003

108A Exclusivity and finality of Tribunal's jurisdiction

(1)   No court shall have any supervisory or other jurisdiction (whether statutory or inherent) in relation to the Tribunal.

(2)   No court may entertain proceedings for questioning (whether by way of appeal or otherwise)—

(a)   any determination, decision or other action of the Tribunal (including a decision about jurisdiction and a decision under section 105A [that is the Tribunal's review of its own decisions).

---

108   Le Suer, n 105 above at 231.

109   *Ibid.*

110   R Rawlings, 'Review, Revenge and Retreat' (2005) 68(3) MLR 378, 382.

111   By providing that s 7(1) HRA—which gives a cause of action against public authorities for breach of Convention rights (see Chapter 17, pp 990–992) was to have effect 'subject to' the new statutory provisions.

(b) any action of the President or a Deputy President of the Tribunal that relates to one or more specified cases. . .

(e) a decision to remove a person from the United Kingdom, a decision to deport a person or any action in connection with a decision to remove a person from the United Kingdom or to deport a person, if the removal or deportation is in consequence of an immigration decision.

As Rawlings comments:

> The clause was then judge-proofed by the not so subtle device of lifting the words of Lord Reid's famous speech in *Anisminic* [above at 769]. . .Effectively driven by the realisation that anything less would be vulnerable to such manoeuvrings by the senior judiciary, the clause was thus designed to knock out legal principles grounding and maintaining court supervision one by one.[112]

Thus the clause continued:

> (3) Subsections (1) and (2)—
>
> (a) prevent a court, in particular, from entertaining proceedings to determine whether a purported determination, decision or action of the Tribunal was a nullity by reason of—
>
> (i) lack of jurisdiction,
> (ii) irregularity,
> (iii) error of law,
> (iv) breach of natural justice, or
> (v) any other matter [though not where it was alleged that a decision had been made in bad faith].

This unprecedented attempt to shield from review even blatant errors of law and procedure resulted in a torrent of criticism from Parliament[113] and from the legal establishment, including previous Lord Chancellors and senior judges; critics even threatened the 'nuclear option' that the courts would ultimately declare the clause unconstitutional if enacted, as a fundamental breach of the rule of law.[114] Le Suer notes the response of the Bar Council:

> The intended effect of that clause is to 'oust' the jurisdiction of the High Court to review the new Tribunal's decisions, even where the Tribunal has got the law wrong or acted in breach of natural justice. This is a startling proposition. It would be startling if done in a dictatorship. It is incredible that it is proposed in the United Kingdom—the so-called mother of the Common Law.[115]

---

112   Rawlings n 110 above at 383.

113   See, e.g. the Commons Constitutional Affairs Select Committee, HC 211 (2003–04) at [70].

114   The case was set out in full by Fordham, now published as 'Common Law Illegality of Ousting Judicial Review' [2004] JR 86.

115   Le Suer, n 105 above at 233.

The eventual outcome was a government retreat:

> In the event, having struggled through the Commons, ministers abandoned the ouster on reaching the House of Lords, where the list of speakers lined up to do battle reads like a 'who's who' of the legal establishment, headed by two former Lords Chancellor (Mackay and Irvine) and Lord Woolf. ... [The Government] announced that it would 'bring forward amendments to replace the judicial review ouster with a new system allowing oversight by the administrative court'.[116]

The eventual result was a streamlined system of statutory review of decisions of the AIT,[117] similar to that achieved by the earlier statute in relation to review of decisions to refuse to leave to appeal to the old IAT. Rawlings describes it as a 'complicated set of routings, reeking of high-level political and legal compromise,'[118] including three routes of review to the Court of Appeal.[119]

It may be pointed out that in cases involving national security the courts have historically tended to find either that review is not available or that it is very marginal. However, since the HRA this tendency has been partially reversed, particularly in the famous *Belmarsh* decision.[120] The notion of deference in the context of national security is considered in Chapter 15, pp 831–832, in relation to the prerogative in Chapter 11, pp 589–599 and in the context of the HRA, pp 999–1012.

A number of statutes governing national security concerns contain exclusion clauses, which direct complaints to specialised tribunals, often with far less satisfactory due process guarantees than the ordinary courts, and exclude the courts from reviewing the decisions of such tribunals. The Security Services Act 1989 contains such a clause in s 5(4). If a member of the public has a grievance concerning the operation of the 1989 Act, complaint to a court is not possible; under s 5 it can only be made to a tribunal and under s 5(4) the decisions of the tribunal are not questionable in any court of law. Similarly, Section 65(2) of the Regulation of Investigatory Powers Act 2000 excludes the ordinary courts from hearing HRA actions in relation to, *inter alia*, proceedings against the intelligence services, vesting jurisdiction instead in the Investigatory Powers Tribunal (IPT). While at first instance recently this was found not to exclude judicial review on HRA grounds,[121] this was very recently overturned by the Court of Appeal.[122] The Court of Appeal's decision was affirmed one of the first judgments of the new Supreme Court.[123]

---

116   Rawlings n 110 above at 406.

117   Asylum and Immigration (Treatment of Claimants, etc) Act 2004, s 26; Asylum and Immigration Tribunal (Procedure) Rules 2005, SI No 230.

118   Rawlings at 407.

119   For full details of the new system, see R Thomas, 'After the Ouster: Judicial Review and Reconsideration in a Single Tier Tribunal' [2006] PL 674. For parliamentary commentary see the Joint Committee on Human Rights, HL 102, HC 240 (2003–04).

120   *A v Secretary of State for the Home Department* [2004] UKHL 56.

121   *A v B (Investigatory Powers Tribunal: Jurisdiction* [2008] 3 All ER 511.

122   [2009] EWCA Civ 24; [2009] 3 All ER 416.

123   [2009] UKSC 12.

FURTHER READING

JWF Allison, *A Continental Distinction in the Common Law* (2000)

P Craig, *Administrative Law,* 6th edn (2008), Chapters 24–27

M Elliott, *Beatson, Matthews and Elliott's Administrative Law: Text and Materials,* 3rd edn (2005), Chapters 5, 14 and 15

S Halliday, *Judicial Review and Compliance with Administrative Law* (2003)

P Leyland and G Anthony, *Textbook on Administrative Law,* 6th edn (2009)

M Taggart (ed), *The Province of Administrative Law* (1997)

M Arshi and C O'Cinneide, 'Third Party Intervention: the Public Interest Re-affirmed' [2004] PL 69

C Campbell, 'Monopoly Power as Public Power for the Purposes of Judicial Review' (2009) 125(Jul) LQR 491

C Campbell, 'The Nature of Power as Public in English Judicial Review' [2009] 68(1) CLJ 90

R Rawlings, 'Review, Revenge and Retreat' (2005) 68(3) MLR 378

R Thomas, 'After the Ouster: Judicial Review and Reconsideration in a Single Tier Tribunal' [2006] PL 674

CHAPTER 15
GROUNDS OF JUDICIAL REVIEW

INTRODUCTION

The system of judicial review allows the judges to interfere in the decisions made by central and local government and a vast range of other public bodies. Using this self-made weapon, judges have struck down numerous important decisions, from the policy of the Greater London Council to reduce public transport fares in the capital by 25%,[1] to the decision of the Home Secretary to introduce a new criminal injuries compensation scheme.[2] What is the justification for this interference?

One of the traditional answers to this question is the doctrine of *ultra vires:* the judges in striking down decisions on judicial review are merely upholding the will of Parliament; either in an obvious and clear way, as when they hold that a public authority's action was not permitted by the statute under which it has purported to act, or impliedly. In the latter type of case, the notion is that when the courts 'supply the omission of the legislature' and imply rules of procedural fairness into a statutory scheme that contains no such provision expressly, they are also carrying out the implicit will of Parliament, since Parliament must be taken to be aware of the developed principles of natural justice applied by the courts, and by not excluding them, has impliedly stamped them with its approval. This school of thought is referred to, broadly as the *'ultra vires'* school. An alternative justification for judicial review has been put forward by a number of scholars including Sir John Laws, as he then was.

Sir John Laws, 'Law and democracy' [1995] Public Law 72, 78

Lord Diplock's judicial review criterion of illegality is plain enough: no subordinate body may exceed the express bounds of its statutory power: that is, the power which on its proper construction the Act confers. But what of the other heads of review, *Wednesbury* unreasonableness and procedural unfairness? They are now as elementary as illegality. In the elaboration of these principles the courts have imposed and enforced judicially created standards of public behaviour. But the civilised imperative of their existence cannot be derived from the simple requirement that public bodies must be kept to the limits of their authority given by Parliament. Neither deductive logic nor the canons of ordinary language, which are the basic tools of statutory construction, can attribute them to that ideal, since although their application may be qualified by the words of any particular statute, in principle their roots have grown from another seed altogether. In some formulations, it is true, they have purportedly been justified by the attribution of an intention to the legislature that statutory decision-makers should act reasonably and fairly; but this is largely fictitious. In recent times, before *Ridge v Baldwin* it was not generally thought (to put it crudely) that administrative, non-judicial, bodies owed such duties as to hear the other side. Before *Padfield* it was not generally thought that it was an enforceable function of every statute conferring public power that it only justified action to promote the distinct purposes of the Act, even though the Act did not state them. Before the concept of legitimate expectation assumed the status of a substantive legal principle (whose precise date may be nicely debated), it was not generally thought that decision-makers should be prevented from departing from previous assurances as to their actions without giving those affected an opportunity to make representations. Wednesbury itself reaches back to older law; but its fruition and its maturity came 20 years and more after it was decided. It cannot be

---

1   *Bromley LBC v GLC* [1983] AC 768.

2   *R v Secretary of State for the Home Dept ex parte Fire Brigades Union and others* [1995] 2 All ER 244, HL.

suggested that all these principles, which represent much of the bedrock of modern administrative law, were suddenly interwoven into the legislature's intentions in the 1960s and 70s and onwards, in which period they have been articulated and enforced by the courts. They are, categorically, judicial creations. They owe neither their existence nor their acceptance to the will of the legislature. They have nothing to do with the intention of Parliament, save as a fig-leaf to cover their true origins. We do not need the fig-leaf any more.

Notes

1. For criticism of Laws' view and a defence of *ultra vires* as the fundamental basis of judicial review, see C Forsyth, 'Of fig-eaves and Fairy Tales: The *Ultra Vires* Doctrine, The Sovereignty of Parliament and Judicial Review' [1996] CLJ 122, esp. 127–40; for further discussion of these issues see J Jowell, 'The rule of law today', in J Jowell and D Oliver (eds), *The Changing Constitution*, 6th edn (2007), pp 17–22; P Craig, *Administrative Law*, 6th edn (2008), Chapter 1 and 'Competing Models of Judicial Review' [1999] PL 428–47; HWR Wade, *Administrative Law*, 8th edn (2000), Chapters 1 and 2. A modified version of the *ultra vires* doctrine has recently been put forward by Mark Elliott, *The Constitutional Foundations of Judicial Review* (2001). For extended discussion and criticism, see P Craig and N Bamforth, 'Constitutional Analysis, Constitutional Principle and Judicial Review' [2001] PL 763; for a recent rejoinder by C Forsyth and M Elliott, see 'The Legitimacy of Judicial Review' [2003] PL 286–307. For a critical overview of the debate, see TRS Allan, 'The Constitutional Foundations of Judicial Review: Constitutional Conundrum or Interpretative Inquiry' [2002] CLJ 87. For a sustained critique of the rights-based justification for judicial review put forward by Laws LJ, Jowell and Oliver, Allan and Craig, see T Poole, 'Questioning Common Law Constitutionalism' (200) 25 LS 142 and 'Legitimacy, Rights and Judicial Review' (2005) 25 OJLS 697.

2. Judicial review is to be distinguished from review of the merits of the decision itself. It is concerned only with the legality of the decision, which will itself depend on whether it falls within any of the three main heads of review discussed below. Sir John Laws[3] gives a clear explanation as to why constitutional principle makes the simultaneous demand that judges ensure decisions are made legally but do not assess their merits:

> [This demand] arises as a matter of definition from the very nature of the public power respectively lying in the hands of the courts and those whom they review. The paradigm of a public body subject to the public law jurisdiction is one whose power is conferred by statute. The statute is logically prior to it; and by the constitution it is for the courts to police the statute. But they do not act under the statute. They are altogether outside it. Their power is not derived from it, nor ultimately from any Act of Parliament. This state of affairs has two consequences. First, the judges have to see that the power given by the statute is not transgressed by its donee; secondly, they have no business themselves to exercise the powers conferred by it, precisely because they are not the donee. Hence the essence of the judicial review jurisdiction. It vindicates the Rule of Law not only by confining statutory power within the four corners of the Act, but also ensuring that the statute is not usurped by anyone—including the courts themselves.[4]

---

3   J Laws, 'Law and Democracy' [1995] PL 72.

4   *Ibid,* pp 77–78. Laws' analysis is not applicable in terms to cases in which the body which the court is reviewing does not receive its powers from statute, but it can apply by analogy; whichever source of power gave the jurisdiction to the decision-making body, it did not give a simultaneous jurisdiction to the courts.

3. In the seminal *GCHQ* case, Lord Diplock summed up the grounds for judicial review in the following statement:

CCSU v Minister for Civil Service (the GCHQ case) [1985] AC 374, 410

Lord Diplock: Judicial review has I think developed to a stage today when without reiterating any analysis of the steps by which the development has come about, one can conveniently classify under three heads the grounds upon which administrative action is subject to control by judicial review. The first ground I would call 'illegality,' the second 'irrationality' and the third 'procedural impropriety. 'That is not to say that further development on a case by case basis may not in course of time add further grounds. I have in mind particularly the possible adoption in the future of the principle of 'proportionality' which is recognised in the administrative law of several of our fellow members of the European Economic Community.

Note

To these grounds should now be added breach of rights under the European Convention on Human Rights, as defined by s 1 of the Human Rights Act 1998 (HRA). The HRA is dealt with in Chapter 17 but s 6(1) of the Act makes it 'unlawful for a public authority to act in a way which is incompatible with a Convention right'.

THE RULE AGAINST BIAS

One of the two key principles of procedural impropriety, or rules of natural justice, *nemo judex in causa sua,* is commonly expressed to forbid bias on the part of the decision-maker. The central principle is the famous dicta of Chief Justice Lord Hewart that justice should not only be done but be seen to be done" (*R v Sussex Justices* [1924] 1 KB 256, 259). It is now clear that there are two basic classes of bias: direct and indirect interests on the part of the decision-maker in the case in question, though the dividing line between the two will not always be clear. In the former type of case, once it is shown that the direct interest was present, the judge is automatically disqualified from hearing the case; in the second kind of case, it is not enough to show that the interest was there. It must be shown that the presence of the interest was such as to cause a fair-minded observer to conclude that there was a real danger that the decision-maker was biased.

Direct interest—the automatic disqualification rule

A financial interest

The simplest cases are those in which the decision-maker has some financial interest in the outcome. If the decision-maker has such an interest—that is, he stands to profit if the case is decided one way but not another—there is no need for the challenger to show that there was any actual risk of the financial interest influencing the outcome of the decision; he or she simply has to show that the decision-maker has a financial interest in the outcome of the decision. If he or she can show this, this will automatically invalidate the decision. In the leading case, *Dimes v Grand Junction Canal Co Proprietors* [1852] 3 HLC 759, a decision of the Lord Chancellor was set aside because he owned shares in one of the parties. The House of Lords made a point of stressing that they did not believe that the Lord Chancellor had in fact been influenced by his ownership of shares, but that this was not the point. As Lord Goff commented in *R v Gough* [1993] AC 646:

> In such a case therefore, not only is it irrelevant that there was in fact no bias on the part of the tribunal, but there is no question of investigating, from an objective point of view, whether there was any real likelihood of bias, or any reasonable suspicion of bias, on the facts of the particular case. The nature of the interest is such that public confidence in the administrating of justice requires that the decision should not stand.

This principle still remains and the same applied if it is a close relative of the decision-maker who has the interest. However, as the Court of Appeal stressed in the recent case of *Locabail (UK) Ltd v Bayfield Properties Ltd* [2000] QB 451, 'the link had to be so close and direct as to render the interest of that other person for all practical purposes indistinguishable from an interest of the judge'. The Court noted that the rule is also subject to a *de minimis* exception: if the financial interest is so small or slight that it could not reasonably be thought to have any chance of affecting the judge's mind, it will be ignored (at 473).[5]

Another class of direct interests?

Until recently, it was considered that it was only financial interests that gave rise to automatic disqualification. However, the *Pinochet* case, below, added another category. The background to the case was the arrest in the UK of Senator Pinochet, after Spain had requested that he be extradited to Spain to face charges of torture, extra-judicial killings, kidnapping and 'disappearances'. The House of Lords heard an appeal from a challenge by Pinochet against his continuing detention. Pinochet argued that, as a former head of state, he was immune from prosecution and extradition. During the hearing of this case, Amnesty International was given leave to intervene and argued that no immunity should be granted to Pinochet. The House of Lords decided 3:2 that he was not immune, meaning that the extradition process could proceed. One of the judges who voted against immunity was Lord Hoffman. It then transpired that Lord Hoffman was a Director and Chairperson of Amnesty International Charity Limited (AICL), a registered charity incorporated to undertake those aspects of the work of Amnesty International Limited (AI) which are charitable under UK law. In other words, he was a director of an organisation which was, as Lord Browne-Wilkinson found in *Pinochet,* 'a constituent part' of Amnesty International, one of the actual parties to the appeal. Pinochet then petitioned the House of Lords to set aside its own earlier judgment on the grounds of an appearance of bias on the part of Lord Hoffman.

R v Bow Street Metropolitan Stipendiary Magistrate and Others ex parte Pinochet Ugarte (No 2) [2000] 1 AC 1 19 (extracts)

Lord Browne-Wilkinson: . . . In my judgment, this case falls within the first category of case, viz where the judge is disqualified because he is a judge in his own cause. In such a case, once it is shown that the judge is himself a party to the cause, or has a relevant interest in its subject matter, he is disqualified without any investigation into whether there was a likelihood or suspicion of bias. The mere fact of his interest is sufficient to disqualify him unless he has made sufficient disclosure . . .I will call this 'automatic disqualification.'

---

5   The cases cited in support of this are *BTR Industries South Africa (Pty) Ltd v Metal and Allied Workers' Union* 3 SA 673, 694 (1992); *R v Inner West London Coroner ex p Dallaglio* [1994] 4 All ER 139, 162; *Auckland Casino Ltd v Casino Control Authority* [1995] 1 NZLR 142, 148.

. . . By seeking to intervene in this appeal and being allowed so to intervene, in practice AI became a party to the appeal. Therefore if, in the circumstances, it is right to treat Lord Hoffmann as being the alter ego of AI and therefore a judge in his own cause, then he must have been automatically disqualified on the grounds that he was a party to the appeal. Alternatively, even if it be not right to say that Lord Hoffmann was a party to the appeal as such, the question then arises whether, in non-financial litigation, anything other than a financial or proprietary interest in the outcome is sufficient automatically to disqualify a man from sitting as judge in the cause.

Are the facts such as to require Lord Hoffmann to be treated as being himself a party to this appeal?

[His Lordship found that Lord Hoffman himself could not be treated as personally being a party to the appeal and went on:]

Then is this a case in which it can be said that Lord Hoffmann had an 'interest' which must lead to his automatic disqualification? Hitherto only pecuniary and proprietary interests have led to automatic disqualification. But, as I have indicated, this litigation is most unusual. It is not civil litigation but criminal litigation. Most unusually, by allowing AI to intervene, there is a party to a criminal cause or matter who is neither prosecutor nor accused. That party, AI, shares with the government of Spain and the CPS, not a financial interest but an interest to establish that there is no immunity for ex-heads of state in relation to crimes against humanity. The interest of these parties is to procure Senator Pinochet's extradition and trial, a non-pecuniary interest So far as AICL is concerned, clause 3(c) of its memorandum provides that one of its objects is 'to procure the abolition of torture, extra-judicial execution and disappearance'. AI has, amongst other objects, the same objects. Although AICL, as a charity, cannot campaign to change the law, it is concerned by other means to procure the abolition of these crimes against humanity. In my opinion, therefore, AICL plainly had a non-pecuniary interest, to establish that Senator Pinochet was not immune.

That being the case, the question is whether in the very unusual circumstances of this case a non-pecuniary interest to achieve a particular result is sufficient to give rise to automatic disqualification and, if so, whether the fact that AICL had such an interest necessarily leads to the conclusion that Lord Hoffmann, as a director of AICL, was automatically disqualified from sitting on the appeal? My Lords, in my judgment, although the cases have all dealt with automatic disqualification on the grounds of pecuniary interest, there is no good reason in principle for so limiting automatic disqualification. The rationale of the whole rule is that a man cannot be a judge in his own cause. In civil litigation the matters in issue will normally have an economic impact; therefore a judge is automatically disqualified if he stands to make a financial gain as a consequence of his own decision of the case. But if, as in the present case, the matter at issue does not relate to money or economic advantage but is concerned with the promotion of the cause, the rationale disqualifying a judge applies just as much if the judge's decision will lead to the promotion of a cause in which the judge is involved together with one of the parties. Thus in my opinion if Lord Hoffmann had been a member of AI he would have been automatically disqualified because of his non-pecuniary interest in establishing that Senator Pinochet was not entitled to immunity. . .

Can it make any difference that, instead of being a direct member of AI, Lord Hoffmann is a director of AICL, that is of a company which is wholly controlled by AI and is carrying on much of its work? Surely not. The substance of the matter is that AI, AIL and AICL are all various parts of an entity or movement working in different fields towards the same goals. If the absolute impartiality of the judiciary is to be maintained, there must be a rule which automatically disqualifies a judge who is involved, whether personally or as a director of a company, in promoting the same causes in the same organisation as is a party to the suit. There is no room for fine distinctions if Lord Hewart CJ's famous dictum is to be observed: it is 'of fundamental importance that justice should not only be done, but should manifestly and undoubtedly be seen to be done:' see *R v Sussex Justices, Ex parte McCarthy* [1924] 1 KB 256, 259.

. . . It is important not to overstate what is being decided. It was suggested in argument that a decision setting aside the order of 25 November 1998 would lead to a position where judges would be unable to sit on cases involving charities in whose work they are involved. It is suggested that, because of such involvement, a judge would be disqualified. That is not correct. The facts of this present case are exceptional. The critical elements are (1) that AI was a party to the appeal; (2) that AI was joined in order to argue for a particular result; (3) the judge was a director of a charity closely allied to AI and sharing, in this respect, AI's objects. Only in cases where a judge is taking an active role as trustee or director of a charity which is closely allied to and acting with a party to the litigation should a judge normally be concerned either to recuse himself or disclose the position to the parties. However, there may well be other exceptional cases in which the judge would be well advised to disclose a possible interest.

Lord Goff of Chieveley: . . .The effect. . .for present purposes is that Lord Hoffmann, as chairperson of one member of that organisation, AICL, is so closely associated with another member of that organisation, AI, that he can properly be said to have an interest in the outcome of proceedings to which AI has become party. . . It follows that Lord Hoffmann had an interest in the outcome of the present proceedings and so was disqualified from sitting as a judge in those proceedings.

Lord Hope: . . .I think that the connections which existed between Lord Hoffmann and Amnesty International were of such a character, in view of their duration and proximity, as to disqualify him on this ground. In view of his links with Amnesty International as the chairman and a director of Amnesty International Charity Ltd. he could not be seen to be impartial. There has been no suggestion that he was actually biased. He had no financial or pecuniary interest in the outcome. But his relationship with Amnesty International was such that he was, in effect, acting as a judge in his own cause. I consider that his failure to disclose these connections leads inevitably to the conclusion that the decision to which he was a party must be set aside.

Notes

1. The principle laid down in this case is not as clear as it could be, partly because four different speeches were given. However, it appears that there is a clear narrow *ratio* from the case. The narrow rule established is that:

> If the absolute impartiality of the judiciary is to be maintained, there must be a rule which automatically disqualifies a judge who is involved, whether personally or as a Director of a company, in promoting the same causes in the same organisation as is a party to the suit (*ibid* at 135, *per* Lord Browne-Wilkinson).

In other words, Lord Hoffman was a director of an organisation that was a constituent part of one of the parties to the appeal. That party to the appeal clearly had an interest in the outcome, that is, it wanted it to be established that Pinochet was not immune from prosecution. Since Lord

Hoffman was the director of an organisation which in effect was a party to the appeal and had an interest in a particular outcome, he must be automatically disqualified. So the narrow, clear rule is confined to cases where a judge belongs to and has the same interest as an organisation *which is a party to the hearing*. That is clear.

2. At one point it seemed possible that the decision might be taken as standing for a wider principle: that a judge who had an interest in the outcome of a hearing because he belonged to an organisation which campaigned on the matter would also be treated as automatically disqualified. However, it does not now seem that the *Pinochet* principle will be extended any further than the narrow ruling. Indeed the case could today have been decided quite comfortably under the *Porter v Magill* test (below), without casting any aspersions on Lord Hoffman's actual impartiality. For comment and criticism of the *Pinochet* decision, see K Malleson, 'Judicial Bias and Disqualification after *Pinochet (No 2)*' (2000) 63 MLR 119 and A Olowofoyeku, 'The *Nemo Judex* Rule: The Case Against Automatic Disqualification' [2000] PL 456.

The Rule against bias: indirect interests

The basic test to be applied

In contrast to the position with 'direct interests' where the automatic disqualification rule applies, where the interest is 'indirect', it had always been the position that it must be shown that there was, objectively, some risk, or danger of bias, or that there could be a reasonable apprehension of such a danger. The test for bias has changed quite recently under the influence of Art 6 ECHR. Previously the leading case on this was *R v Gough* [1993] AC 646, which set out the following test:

> the court should ask itself whether. . .there was a real danger of bias on the part of the relevant member of the tribunal in question, in the sense that he might unfairly regard (or have unfairly regarded) with favour, or disfavour, the case of a party to the issue under consideration by him.

However, this test fell to be reassessed in the light of the coming into force of the Human Rights Act 1998, which makes Art 6 of the ECHR binding upon all UK public authorities who are determining a person's 'civil rights and obligations'. Article 6 provides: 'In the determination of his civil rights and obligations, or of any criminal charge against him, everyone is entitled to a fair and public hearing within a reasonable time by an independent and impartial tribunal established by law.' See Chapter 7 at 310–313.

The Court of Appeal decision in *Medicaments and Related Classes of Goods (No 2)* [2001] 1 WLR 700, contains an exhaustive analysis of Strasbourg case law on bias, under Art 6(1).

> . . .83 We would summarise the principles to be derived from the [Strasbourg] line of cases as follows:
>
> (1) If a judge is shown to have been influenced by actual bias, his decision must be set aside.
> (2) Where actual bias has not been established the personal impartiality of the judge is to be presumed.
> (3) The court then has to decide whether, on an objective appraisal, the material facts give rise to a legitimate fear that the judge might not have been impartial. If they do the decision of the judge must be set aside.

(4) The material facts are not limited to those which were apparent to the applicant. They are those which are ascertained upon investigation by the court.

(5) An important consideration in making an objective appraisal of the facts is the desirability that the public should remain confident in the administration of justice.

84 This approach comes close to that in *Gough*. The difference is that when the Strasbourg court considers whether the material circumstances give rise to a reasonable apprehension of bias, it makes it plain that it is applying an objective test to the circumstances, not passing judgment on the likelihood that the particular tribunal under review was in fact biased.

Note

The leading case on this issue is now the House of Lords' decision in *Porter v Magill* [2002] 2 AC 357. The background facts appear below, p 840. The issue of bias arose because of the role of the district auditor, Magill, in investigating the 'home for votes' scandal in Westminster City Council, and in particular the statutory liability for wilful misconduct of Porter and others personally to make good the losses sustained by the Council as a result of the unlawful sale of Council houses, a liability of several million pounds. In particular, the auditor was said, in effect, to combine the roles of investigator, prosecutor and judge. Moreover, in the press conference in which he announced his preliminary findings, he was said to have effectively prejudged the issue and made it clear that, although he had not yet reached a final conclusion, his mind was effectively made up. This was argued to raise issues both under the common law of bias and to preclude the auditor from being an independent and impartial tribunal under Art 6(1) of the ECHR (above). It was found that the issue under Art 6(1) was satisfactorily answered by there being a full statutory right of appeal against the district auditor's findings to the High Court, which clearly did satisfy the requirements of Art 6(1). Lord Hope then dealt with the issue of common law bias, taking the opportunity to lay down a general modification of the *Gough* test, starting with a quotation from the *Re Medicaments* decision set out above:

Porter v Magill [2002] 2 AC 357, 493–95

Lord Hope:

85. When the Strasbourg jurisprudence is taken into account, we believe that a modest adjustment of the test in Gough is called for, which makes it plain that it is, in effect, no different from the test applied in most of the Commonwealth and in Scotland. The court must first ascertain all the circumstances which have a bearing on the suggestion that the judge was biased. It must then ask whether those circumstances would lead a fair-minded and informed observer to conclude that there was a real possibility, or a real danger, the two being the same, that the tribunal was biased.

I respectfully suggest that your Lordships should now approve the modest adjustment of the test in *R v Gough* set out in that paragraph. . . . I would however delete from it the reference to 'a real danger'. Those words no longer serve a useful purpose here, and they are not used in the jurisprudence of the Strasbourg court. The question is whether the fair-minded and informed observer, having considered the facts, would conclude that there was a real possibility that the tribunal was biased.

Turning to the facts. . . I think that it is plain. . .that the auditor made an error of judgment when he decided to make his statement in public at a press conference. The main impression which this would have conveyed to the fair-minded observer was that the purpose of this exercise was to attract publicity to himself, and perhaps also to his firm. It was an exercise in self-promotion in which he should not have indulged. But it is quite another matter to conclude from this that there was a real possibility that he was biased. Schiemann LJ said, at p 1457d–e, that there was room for a casual observer to form the view after the press conference that the auditor might be biased. Nevertheless he concluded, at p 1457h, having examined the facts more closely, that there was no real danger that this was so. I would take the same view. The question is what the fair-minded and informed observer would have thought, and whether his conclusion would have been that there was real possibility of bias. The auditor's conduct must be seen in the context of the investigation which he was carrying out, which had generated a great deal of public interest. A statement as to his progress would not have been inappropriate. His error was to make it at a press conference. This created the risk of unfair reporting, but there was nothing in the words he used to indicate that there was a real possibility that he was biased. He was at pains to point out to the press that his findings were provisional. There is no reason to doubt his word on this point, as his subsequent conduct demonstrates. I would hold, looking at the matter objectively, that a real possibility that he was biased has not been demonstrated.

Notes

1. Olowofoyeku comments:

    > The principle of apparent bias is common in the Anglo-American legal traditions . . .
    > For example, in parts of the Commonwealth, the principle of apparent bias refers to
    > a 'reasonable apprehension' or 'reasonable suspicion' of bias, while it refers in US
    > Federal law to cases in which a judge's impartiality might reasonably be questioned
    > [28 U.S.C.§455(a).]. The aim in all cases is to ensure that justice is 'seen' to be done.
    > This principle, 'of fundamental importance', is widespread, enshrined in the juris-
    > prudence of the European Court of Human Rights, and is all about appearances.[6]

2. In principle, the above test applies to all decisions subject to judicial review, whether taken by an administrative body, such as a local authority or by a judicial or quasi-judicial one: *R v Secretary of State for the Environment ex parte Kirkstall Valley Campaigning* [1996] 3 All ER 304. However, as we shall see below, where the decision is taken by a political body, such as a local authority or Government Minister, its application is rather more flexible, to cater for the fact that such bodies are inevitably entitled to prefer their own political polices.

3. Although the following case has been superseded by *Porter v Magill* as a definitive statement of the law, it contains very useful general guidance on the circumstances in which the courts are likely to find a reasonable apprehension of bias.

Locabail (UK) Ltd v Bayfield Properties Ltd [2000] 2 WLR 870, CA (extracts)

Lord Woolf MR and Sir Richard Scott V-C [giving the judgment of the court:] . . . It would be dangerous and futile to attempt to define or list the factors which may or may not give rise to a real danger of bias. Everything will depend on the facts, which may include the nature of the issue to be decided. We cannot, however, conceive of circumstances in which an objection could be soundly based on the religion, ethnic or national origin, gender, age, class, means or sexual orientation of the judge. Nor, at any rate ordinarily, could an

---

6   A. Olowofoyeku, 'Bias and the Informed Observer: A Call for a Return to Gough' [2009] 68(2) CLJ 388, 391.

objection be soundly based on the judge's social or educational or service or employment background or history, nor that of any member of the judge's family; or previous political associations; or membership of social or sporting or charitable bodies; or Masonic associations; or previous judicial decisions; or extra-curricular utterances (whether in textbooks, lectures, speeches, articles, interviews, reports or responses to consultation papers); or previous receipt of instructions to act for or against any party, solicitor or advocate engaged in a case before him; or membership of the same Inn, circuit, local Law Society or chambers. . . By contrast, a real danger of bias might well be thought to arise if there were personal friendship or animosity between the judge and any member of the public involved in the case; or if the judge were closely acquainted with any member of the public involved in the case, particularly if the credibility of that individual could be significant in the decision of the case; or if, in a case where the credibility of any individual were an issue to be decided by the judge, he had in a previous case rejected the evidence of that person in such outspoken terms as to throw doubt on his ability to approach such person's evidence with an open mind on any later occasion; or if on any question at issue in the proceedings before him the judge had expressed views, particularly in the course of the hearing, in such extreme and unbalanced terms as to throw doubt on his ability to try the issue with an objective judicial mind (see *Vakauta v Kelly* (1989) 167 CLR 568); or if, for any other reason, there were real ground for doubting the ability of the judge to ignore extraneous considerations, prejudices and predilections and bring an objective judgment to bear on the issues before him. The mere fact that a judge, earlier in the same case or in a previous case, had commented adversely on a party or witness, or found the evidence of a party or witness to be unreliable, would not without more found a sustainable objection. In most cases, we think, the answer, one way or the other, will be obvious. But if in any case there is real ground for doubt, that doubt should be resolved in favour of recusal. We repeat: every application must be decided on the facts and circumstances of the individual case. The greater the passage of time between the event relied on as showing a danger of bias and the case in which the objection is raised, the weaker (other things being equal) the objection will be.

We do not consider that waiver, in this context, raises special problems. . . If, appropriate disclosure having been made by the judge, a party raises no objection to the judge hearing or continuing to hear a case, that party cannot thereafter complain of the matter disclosed as giving rise to a real danger of bias. It would be unjust to the other party and undermine both the reality and the appearance of justice to allow him to do so.

Note

Obvious examples of bias may arise from family relationships. In *Metropolitan Properties v Lannon* [1969] 1 QB 577, the issue was whether Mr Lannon could sit as a member of a rent assessment committee, determining the fairness of a rent set by a Landlord, when his father was in dispute with the same landlord. It was held that he could not. This was extended to friendship in *AWG Group Ltd and another v Morrison and another* [2006] 1 WLR. 1163. A judge informed the parties that a witness at imminent civil trial was a long standing family acquaintance. He refused the subsequent application by the other side to recuse himself. On appeal it was found that he should have done, as his relationship with the witness was enough to give rise to a reasonable apprehension of bias in the fair minded observer. In what follows, we consider some other, more problematic categories of indirect bias.

Judge has previously expressed strong views

Locabail (UK) Ltd v Bayfield Properties Ltd [2000] 2 WLR 870, CA (extracts)

This concerned the hearing of a number of cases. In the third case [*Timmins v Gormley*] the defendant admitted liability for personal injuries sustained by the claimant but disputed the quantum of damage. Trial of that issue was heard by a member of the Bar, sitting as a recorder, who was a specialist practitioner in personal injury cases and had, by regular contributions to specialist literature, shown consistent support for claimants in obtaining damages from defendants and their insurers. . . Following judgment in the claimant's favour the defendant learnt of an article written by the recorder and published shortly after trial in which he had expressed views in trenchant terms in favour of claimants and critical of defendants and their insurers.

Lord Woolf MR and Sir Richard Scott V-C [giving the judgment of the court:]
. . .It is not inappropriate for a judge to write in publications of the class to which the recorder contributed. The publications are of value to the profession and for a lawyer of the recorder's experience to contribute to those publications can further rather than hinder the administration of justice. There is a long established tradition that the writing of books and articles or the editing of legal textbooks is not incompatible with holding judicial office and the discharge of judicial functions. There is nothing improper in the recorder being engaged in his writing activities. It is the tone of the recorder's opinions and the trenchancy with which they were expressed which is challenged here. Anyone writing in an area in which he sits judicially has to exercise considerable care not to express himself in terms which indicate that he has preconceived views which are so firmly held that it may not be possible for him to try a case with an open mind. . . .The specialist judge must therefore be circumspect in the language he uses and the tone in which he expresses himself. It is always inappropriate for a judge to use intemperate language about subjects on which he has adjudicated or will have to adjudicate.
. . .We have. . .to ask, taking a broad common sense approach, whether a person holding the pronounced pro-claimant anti-insurer views expressed by the recorder in the articles might not *unconsciously* have leaned in favour of the claimant and against the defendant in resolving the factual issues between them. Not without misgiving, we conclude that there was on the facts here a real danger of such a result. We do not think a lay observer with knowledge of the facts could have excluded that possibility, and nor can we. We accordingly grant permission to appeal on this ground, allow the defendant's appeal and order a retrial (emphasis added).

Notes

1. Recently, in *Helow v Advocate General for Scotland* 2008 SLT 967, an asylum seeker of Palestinian origin, who averred that her family had been involved in massacres in the Lebanon and that she had been involved in the preparation of a lawsuit in Belgium alleging the personal responsibility of the Israeli Prime Minister, sought asylum in the United Kingdom. Lady Cosgrove dismissed her petition for review of the refusal of leave to appeal by the Immigration Appeal Tribunal against the rejection of her claim to asylum. Cosgrove was a member of the International Association of Jewish Lawyers and Jurists; she received its journal, which took a strongly pro-Israeli line in some articles. It was held that, although a judge who had expressed or supported the views expressed in such articles would not be eligible to hear and determine H's claim, the fair-minded and informed observer would not impute the published views of *others* to Cosgrove and according would not perceive a real possibility of bias.

2. An easier case, in which the apprehension of bias in the judge came from remarks made directly in the proceedings was *El-Farargy v El-Farargy* [2007] EWCA Civ 1149, which concerned Justice Singer's role in divorce proceedings involving a Saudi Sheik. It was found that comments he had made before he came to make his final judgment indicating that he had already formed a view about the case were permissible and did not cross the line, since judges were entitled to express preliminary views and it should be realised that they could change their minds as a hearing progressed. However, a number of remarks he had made about the Sheik, to his departing 'on his flying carpet', to 'every grain of sand [being] sifted', to the case being 'a bit gelatinous . . . like Turkish Delight', and to a 'relatively fast-free time of the year' were disparaging and mocking on both religious and racial grounds and would rise to reasonable apprehension of bias in a fair-minded observer. It was found that Justice Singer's refusal to recuse himself had been wrong and his decision was quashed.

Institutional bias caused by overlap of roles

Into this category fall those instances in which there is nothing about the decision-maker personally that is objected to. Rather the objection in these cases is that the decision-maker has carried out another role in relation to the decision she is now sitting on that might reasonably be thought to cast doubt on her impartiality. This has been found to arise, for example, where a panel hearing an appeal or review includes the person who made the original decision against which the appeal is being made. So in *Hannam v Bradford Corporation* [1970] 1 WLR 937, a decision to recommend that a school teacher be sacked was made by a School's Governing Body. That recommendation had to be confirmed by a Council Committee. Three of the members of the committee had sat on the body which made the original recommendation. The Committee's decision was quashed for bias.

A similar, much more recent case was *R (Al-Hasan) v Secretary of State for the Home Department* [2005] 1 WLR 688, HL. The appellants were prisoners who had refused to squat following a general order for a squat search of prisoners (i.e. an intimate search). In subsequent disciplinary proceedings, the deputy governor of the prison (D) ruled that in both cases the order to squat was lawful and he accordingly found each of the appellants guilty of an offence against discipline. D had been present when the general order for a squat search had been approved by the prison's governor. The applicants argued that this meant that he could not bring the necessary degree of independence and impartiality to the task of deciding whether the order had been lawful. It was held that by the very fact of his presence when the search order was confirmed, D had given it his tacit assent and endorsement. When thereafter, the order was disobeyed and D had to rule upon its lawfulness, a fair minded observer could reasonably suspect that he was predisposed to find it lawful, since for him to have decided otherwise would have amounted to a contention on his part that the governor ought not to have confirmed the order and that he himself had been wrong to acquiesce in it.

A similar institutional problem arose in the following decision of the House of Lords.

Lawal v Northern Spirit Ltd (2003) UKHL 35

The claimant had appealed to the Employment Appeal Tribunal (EAT). The other side was represented by QC, who was also a part time judge who had who had previously sat with one of the lay members of the EAT panel before whom the appeal was being heard. On a subsequent judicial review, alleging an appearance of bias for this reason, the Court of Appeal rejected the application, describing it as based on:

> merely a speculative and remote possibility based on an unfounded and, some might think, condescending assumption that a lay member sitting with another judge

on the hearing of an appeal cannot tell the difference between the impartial decision-making role played by a tribunal panel of a judge and two lay members and the adversarial role of the partisan advocates appearing for the parties.

Pill LJ dissented. He explained, at para 39 that:

The fair-minded and informed lay observer will readily perceive. . . the degree of trust which lay members repose in the presiding judge. It is in my judgment likely to diminish public confidence in the administration of justice if a judge who enjoys that relationship with lay members, with the degree of reliance placed on his view of the law, subsequently appears before them as an advocate. The fair-minded observer might well reasonably perceive that the litigant opposed by an advocate who is a member of the Tribunal and has sat with its lay members is at a disadvantage as a result of that association . . .

Opinion of the Committee of the House

21 The principle to be applied is that stated in *Porter v Magill*, namely whether a fair minded and informed observer, having considered the given facts, would conclude that there was a real possibility that the tribunal was biased. Concretely, would such an observer consider that it was reasonably possible that the wing member may be subconsciously biased? The observer is likely to approach the matter on the basis that the lay members look to the judge for guidance on the law, and can be expected to develop a fairly close relationship of trust and confidence with the judge. The observer may also be credited with knowledge that a Recorder, who in a criminal case has sat with jurors, may not subsequently appear as counsel in a case in which one or more of those jurors serve. Despite the differences between the two cases, the observer is likely to attach some relevance to the analogy because in both cases the judge gives guidance on the law to laymen. But the observer is likely to regard the practice forbidding part-time judges in the Employment Tribunal from appearing as counsel before an Employment Tribunal which includes lay members with whom they had previously sat as very much in point.

22 . . .What the public was content to accept many years ago is not necessarily acceptable in the world of today. The indispensable requirement of public confidence in the administration of justice requires higher standards today than was the case even a decade or two ago. . .

23 . . .Like Pill L.J. in the Court of Appeal we consider that the present practice in the EAT tends to undermine public confidence in the system. It should be discontinued. . .

Appeal allowed

Notes

1. For two further cases on intermingling of functions, see *R (Bennion) v Chief Constable of Merseyside Police* [2002] ICR 136, CA and *R (McNally) v Secretary of State for Education and Metropolitan Borough of Bury* [2001] ELR 773.

2. In 2003, following a review by Lord Justice Auld, the Criminal Justice Act removed the previous exemption from jury service from various classes of lawyers and police. All citizens are now eligible to serve save those of unsound mind. The reforms have, however rapidly given rise to a number of challenges from defendants convicted who discovered that their juries contained such persons. The following leading case also seems to indicate that the *Porter v Magill* test does not give rise to a satisfactory level of legal certainty in practice.

R v Abdroikof (Nurlon) [2007] 1 WLR 2679, HL (extracts)

These appeals, involving three different claimants, concerned challenges to police officers and a Crown Prosecution Service (CPS) solicitor serving on juries. Abdroikov had been convicted by a jury whose foreman was a serving police officer—a fact unknown to the court until the jury had retired to consider its verdict. Green had been convicted by a jury that included a police officer serving in the same borough as the police officer who had conducted a stop and search on Green, and who had been a prosecution witness at Green's trial. The two officers had also once served in the same police station at the same time, although they did not know each other. Williamson had been convicted by a jury whose foreman was a solicitor working for the CPS. The trial judge had overruled the objections of defence counsel to the presence of this solicitor on the jury. The Court of Appeal dismissed Abdroikov's, Green's and Williamson's appeals against their convictions based on apparent bias and they appealed to the House of Lords.

Lord Bingham. . .
24 . . .It is not a criticism of the police service, but a tribute to its greatest strength, that officers belong to a disciplined force, bound to each other by strong bonds of loyalty, mutual support, shared danger and responsibility, culture and tradition. The Morris Committee [on Juries, 1965] thought it self-evident that officers could not be, or be seen to be, impartial participants in the prosecution process, a disqualification which in the judgment of ACPO [the Association of Chief Police Officers]. . .extended to civilian employees of the police. Serving police officers remain ineligible for jury service in Scotland, Northern Ireland, Australia, New Zealand, Canada, Hong Kong, Gibraltar and a number of states in the United States, the remainder of the states providing a procedure to question jurors on their occupations and allegiances. But Parliament has declared that in England and Wales police officers are eligible to sit, perhaps envisaging that their identity would be known and any objection would be the subject of judicial decision.
25 In the case of the first appellant. . .had the matter been ventilated at the outset of the trial, it is difficult to see what argument defence counsel could have urged other than the general undesirability of police officers serving on juries, a difficult argument to advance in face of the parliamentary enactment. It was not a case which turned on a contest between the evidence of the police and that of the appellant, and it would have been hard to suggest that the case was one in which unconscious prejudice, even if present, would have been likely to operate to the disadvantage of the appellant, and it makes no difference that the officer was the foreman of the jury. In the event, confronted with this question at very short notice, defence counsel raised no objection. I conclude, not without unease, that having regard to the parliamentary enactment the Court of Appeal reached the right conclusion in this case, and I would dismiss the appeal.
26 The second appellant's case is different. Here, there was a crucial dispute on the evidence between the appellant and the police sergeant, and the sergeant and the [police] juror, although not personally known to each other, shared the same local service background. In this context the instinct (however unconscious) of a police officer on the jury to prefer the evidence of a brother officer to that of a drug-addicted defendant would be judged by the fair minded and informed observer to be a real and possible source of unfairness, beyond the reach of standard judicial warnings and directions. The second appellant was not tried by a tribunal which was and appeared to be impartial. It cannot be supposed that Parliament intended to infringe the rule in the *Sussex Justices* case, still

less to do so without express language. I would allow this appeal, and quash the second appellant's conviction.

27 In the case of the third appellant, no possible criticism is to be made of [the juror in question], who acted in strict compliance with the guidance given to him and left the matter to the judge. But the judge gave no serious consideration to the objection of defence counsel, who himself had little opportunity to review the law on this subject. It must, perhaps, be doubted whether Auld LJ or Parliament contemplated that employed Crown prosecutors would sit as jurors in prosecutions brought by their own authority. It is in my opinion clear that justice is not seen to be done if one discharging the very important neutral role of juror is a full-time, salaried, long-serving employee of the prosecutor. . . . The third appellant was entitled to be tried by a tribunal that was and appeared to be impartial, and in my opinion he was not. The consequence is that his convictions must be quashed. This is a most unfortunate outcome, since the third appellant was accused of very grave crimes, of which he may have been guilty. But even a guilty defendant is entitled to be tried by an impartial tribunal and the consequence is inescapable. I would allow the appeal and remit the case to the Court of Appeal with an invitation to quash the convictions and rule on any application which may be made for a retrial.

   Baroness Hale agreed with the approach and conclusions of Lord Bingham]

Lord Roger (dissenting).

[His Lordship found first that the fictional fair minded observer might well be surprised to learn that serving police officers and CPS lawyers can sit on juries. He went on]:

32 But then, being fair minded and informed, the observer will think a little more about the matter. He will reflect that, up and down the land, day in day out, we take risks when we hand the critical decisions on guilt or innocence to juries. We take the risk that, consciously or subconsciously, men on juries may be unduly sympathetic to a man charged with rape who claims that he and the woman just got carried away by their physical urges; [or that]. . .a juror who has herself been the victim of sexual abuse may tend to side with the woman who claims that she was sexually assaulted by the defendant; [or that] a gay juror may tend to believe the gay man who says that he was assaulted by the defendant in a homophobic attack [or]. . .a homophobic juror may just reject the gay man's evidence. We take the risk that, consciously or subconsciously, a black juror may tend to believe the evidence of a black witness as opposed to the account given by an Asian defendant. . . [and that]. . .a juror who was convicted of drug dealing and was sentenced to four years in prison in the early 1990s may sympathise with a defendant accused of supplying drugs. Having reflected on these and similar situations, the observer will realise that, in effect, Parliament has now added two to the long list of situations where there is indeed a risk, where it is indeed possible, that, consciously or subconsciously, a juror may be partial. But he will also realise that Parliament must have considered that in these two situations, like so many others, the risk is manageable within the system of jury trial as we know it.

33 . . .The law is not naïve: it stipulates that there should be 12 men and women on a jury. The assumption is that, among them, the 12 will be able to neutralise any bias on the part of one or more members and so reach an impartial verdict—by a majority, if necessary. If any of the jurors consider that the jury will be unable to do so, then they must tell the judge, who can then deal with the matter—by discharging the jury, if necessary. So the mere fact that there is a real possibility that a juror may be biased does not mean that there is a real possibility that the jury will be incapable of returning an impartial verdict.

34 The reality therefore is that the jury system operates, not because those who serve are free from prejudice, but despite the fact that many of them will harbour prejudices of various kinds when they enter the jury box

Lord Mance

80 . . .the fair minded and informed observer—a reasonable member of the public—is neither unduly compliant or naive nor unduly cynical or suspicious. . .But the fair minded and informed observer is him or herself in large measure the construct of the court. Individual members of the public, all of whom might claim this description, have widely differing characteristics, experience, attitudes and beliefs which could shape their answers on issues such as those before the court, without their being easily cast as unreasonable. The differences of view in the present case illustrate the difficulties of attributing to the fair minded and informed observer the appropriate balance between on the one hand complacency and naivety and on the other cynicism and suspicion.

Note

Olowofoyeku comments:

> The facts of the three appeals in *Abdroikov* were straightforward, and the applicable legal principles were supposedly clear. The judges did not disagree as to the facts, and they did not disagree as to the law. Yet, in applying accepted facts to accepted principles of apparent bias, the outcome was an almost even split (3/5 overall) between senior judges (Court of Appeal and House of Lords). The arguments supporting these different decisions are all reasonable, and, sometimes, compelling, as one would expect of the rationalisations of senior judges. Such splits would be understandable, and, indeed, almost inevitable, if the issue were novel, the facts disputed, or the law unclear. But this was not the case here.[7]

He points out that:

> In *R v Bakish Alla Khan* [2008] EWCA Crim 531, Lord Phillips. . .admitted that the Court had "not found it easy to deduce on the part of the majority of the [Lords in *Abdroikov*] clear principles that apply where a juror is a police officer". . .This is a poor reflection on the state of the law. . .

Notes

1. The problems have continued. In *R v Pintori* [2007] EWCA Crim 1700, the Court of Appeal quashed a conviction where a juror had worked alongside three police officers who gave evidence and knew them reasonably well. The court considered that in these circumstances there was a real possibility that the jury's verdict had been affected by bias.

2. *Gillies v Secretary of State for Work and Pensions* [2006] 1 WLR 781 similarly had to go all the way to the House of Lords to settle whether the fair-minded observer would perceive a real possibility of bias arising from the fact that the medical member of a disability appeal tribunal deciding whether the applicant could receive disability benefits was a doctor employed by the Benefits Agency. This meant that she was paid to produce reports for the Agency: the suspicion was therefore that she might be inclined to side with the Agency against claimants. The House of Lords

---

7   Olowofoyeku, *ibid* at 397.

agreed with the lower Scottish court that there was *no* reasonable apprehension of bias in this case. The doctor's relationship with the Benefits Agency was that of an independent expert adviser and so there could be no reasonable fear that the doctor had a predisposition to favour the Benefits Agency. A fair minded and informed observer would have appreciated that professional detachment and an ability to exercise her own judgment on medical issues were at the centre of the doctor's relationship with the Agency, and that she was just as capable of exercising those qualities when sitting as the medical member of a disability appeal tribunal.

Decisions taken by non-judicial bodies—the place of policy

This problem arises from the fact that many decisions subsequently challenged on judicial review are taken by politicians—local or central—who are of course in office to carry out the policies of their political party. How then can such decisions be subject to challenge for bias without imposing a false impartiality on those elected to be partial? An early example was provided by *Franklin v Minster of Town and Country Planning* [1948] AC 87. A Government Minister had to decide whether to build a new town, Stevenage after hearing evidence and a report from a public enquiry. Before the enquiry had reported to him he made it clear that it was Government policy for the town to be built. It was found that, while the Minister had to give genuine consideration to the report of the enquiry, he clearly could not be expected to be impartial in a judge-like way. The general solution to this problem has been to hold that such political decision makers are entitled to be predisposed in favour of their own policies, but that they must not close the minds to contrary arguments or evidence, as this would amount to something equivalent to fettering their discretion:[8] see for example *R v Secretary of State for the Environment ex p Kirkstall Valley Campaign Ltd* [1996] 3 All ER 304. A recent example arose in *R (On the application of Lewis) v Redcar and Cleveland Borough Council* [2009] 1 WLR 83, which concerned a challenge to the planning committee of a local authority. It was alleged that the Labour members of the committee had their minds made up in advance on the application. It was found that, when taking such decisions, the members of the committee had to have regard to material considerations, but they were not required to cast aside their views on planning policy that they would have formed when seeking election. What was objectionable was predetermination. A decision maker in the planning context was not acting in a judicial or quasi-judicial role but in a situation of democratic accountability. He had to address the planning issues before him fairly and on their merits, even though he might approach them with a predisposition in favour of one side of the argument. Jackson J said:

> In the context of decisions reached by a council committee, the notional observer is a person cognisant of the practicalities of local government. He does not take it amiss that councillors have previously expressed views on matters which arise for decision. In the ordinary run of events, he trusts councillors, whatever their pre-existing views, to approach decision making with an open mind. If, however, there are additional and unusual circumstances which suggest that councillors may have closed their minds before embarking upon a decision, then he will conclude that there is a real possibility of bias or predetermination.

For a similar decision see *Condron v National Assembly for Wales* [2006] EWCA Civ 1573.

Recent academic commentary has been highly critical of the law in this area. Atrill[9] argues that in practice the 'fair-minded observer' test only works by imputing far too much specialist knowledge on

---

8   See below, pp 848–850.

9   S Atrill, 'Who is the "Fair-minded and Informed Observer"? Bias after Magill' (2003) 62(2) CL 279.

the part of the informed observer and fails to take account of a wider bundle of policy interests by allowing for more balancing to take place between perceived bias and other important interests. Blom-Cooper,[10] commenting on *Davidson v Scottish Ministers* [2004] UKHL 34, argues that the test can be far too sensitive—allowing litigants to trawl through cases they have lost to find any possible objection to the decision maker. *Davidson* concerned a decision by the Court of Session, finding that coercive orders could not be made against the Scottish Executive. It was set aside on the grounds that one of the judges in the panel, Lord Hardie had previously, as Lord Advocate, advised the House of Lords during the passage of the Scotland Act, on this very point of law and indeed moved an amendment, intended to ensure that such orders could not be made—an opinion contrary to the one urged upon the court by the applicant. The decision was taken under Article 6, on the same grounds as that applied in *McGonnell v United Kingdom* (2000) 30 EHRR 289, namely that 'a risk of apparent bias is liable to arise where a judge is called upon to rule judicially on the effect of legislation which he or she has drafted or promoted during the parliamentary process'[11] (see Chapter 3, pp 144–146). Blom-Cooper concludes:

> The current law in the United Kingdom is wildly unhelpful and irrational. It should be reappraised and given a rational basis. The alleged apparent bias in the *Davidson* case points up the lengths to which disgruntled litigants will go to anticipate or, on appeal, undermine a thoroughly correct decision of the court by unearthing previously undiscovered material suggestive of partiality.[12]

The author of the following article is highly critical of the *Porter v Magill* test, contending that 'It is not right' for court decisions on bias 'to be predicated, not on some point of principle (which can be unpacked), but entirely on whatever judges may imagine that some fictional characters would think'.[13] His critique of the recent case law follows.

A Olowofoyeku, *'Bias and the Informed Observer: a call for a return to Gough'* [2009] 68(2) Cambridge Law Journal 388 (extracts)

This outcome of apparently sidelining reasonable, impartial, reviewing judges in favour of reasonable, impartial, ordinary lay members of the public would be fine enough if the legal construct developed to support it were realistic. However, the combined wisdom of global common law jurisprudence on the 'informed observer' produces an extraordinary and wholly unrealistic creature—howbeit, one that may be deemed a logical necessity in this context, given that this invisible lay member of the reviewing panel has an absolute veto (in that his or her judgement in the matter is taken to be determinative.

[The author gives numerous examples from the case-law of what the courts have found it necessary to deem the fair-minded observer to know. These include: the structure of police disciplinary panels and the Chief Constables' statutory duties in [*Re Purcell* [2008] NICA 11], that judges do sit on matters which they have dealt with on previous occasions, that deference must be given to the will of Parliament, and the practical realities of decision

---

10   [2005] PL 225.

11   *Davidson* at [17], *per* Lord Bingham.

12   Blom Cooper at 225.

13   Olowofoyeku, at 389.

making in the local housing authority's department (all said in *Feld v. London Borough of Barnet* [2004] EWCA Civ 1307). He goes on]:

In *Re Bothwell's application (No 2)* [2007] NIQB 25 at [19] Weatherup J. felt that the informed observer would note 'the specialist nature' of the Tuberculosis and Brucellosis Valuation Appeals Panel and the appointment of a specialist from the Department of Agriculture and Regional Development (DARD) 'to reflect the need for such expertise to contribute to decision making, the separation of powers within the Department so that the DARD member is appointed from a different stream to those engaged in processing claims and the non involvement of the DARD member with any aspect of the matters giving rise to the claim, which matters would of themselves not indicate any real possibility of bias or legitimate doubt.' In *Bolkiah & Ors v. The State of Brunei Darussalam & Anor (Brunei Darussalam)* [2007] UKPC 62 at [21], Lord Bingham attributed the following knowledge to the informed observer:

> [The observer must] be taken to understand that the Chief Justice [of Brunei] was a judge of unblemished reputation, nearing the end of a long and distinguished judicial career in more than one jurisdiction, sworn to do right to all manner of people without fear or favour, affection or ill-will and already enjoying what he described as 'reasonably adequate' pension provision. Such an observer would dismiss as fanciful the notion that such a judge would break his judicial oath and jeopardise his reputation in order to curry favour with the Sultan and secure a relatively brief extension of his contract, or to avoid a reduction of his salary which has never (so far as the Board is aware) been made in the case of any Brunei judge at any time. The Chief Justice must be seen as a man for whom all ambition was spent, save that of retiring with the highest judicial reputation.

. . .Finally, in. . .*Redcar and Cleveland Borough Council* [above, p 793], Jackson J. said:

> In the context of decisions reached by a council committee, the notional observer is a person cognisant of the practicalities of local government. He does not take it amiss that councillors have previously expressed views on matters which arise for decision.

The clear trend in the cases has been that, as the complexities of the factual situations or the 'grey areas' increase, the informed observer is imbued with increased knowledge and understanding in order for the courts to be able to arrive at the right outcome. This is inconsistent with the rationales for interposing a lay person, for, in the end, the courts will attribute to the informed observer all the knowledge which they consider necessary in order for them to reach the right decision. In fact, if one were to attempt to articulate the knowledge and experience of judges, one could do no better than what we have just seen being attributed to the impartial observer. As such, this impartial observer might as well be a judge.

The reasons for wanting to replace the evaluations of judges with the perspective of an ordinary lay member of the public are laudable. However, the task assigned to the observer, when all its parameters are fully engaged, is beyond the ken of an ordinary lay member of the public. The task was expressed succinctly by Kerr LCJ in *Re Purcell's* application:

> The concept of apparent bias does not rest on impression based on an incomplete picture but on a fair and reasoned judgment formed as a result of composed and considered appraisal of the relevant facts.
>
> This is a straightforward description of what judges do on a day-to-day basis. The task is, in essence, a normal judicial function. This is the reason why the courts have been at pains (incrementally) to attach increasingly unrealistic and unachievable attributes to the unfortunate lay person to whom they have endeavoured, for all the noblest reasons, to hive off the task. The difficulties experienced by the courts in constructing the informed lay observer require that this construct either be thought through in order to provide a realistic basis for decision-making on the issue of apparent bias, or be killed off and buried.
>
> As Mummery LJ rightly said in *AWG Group Ltd v. Morrison* [above, p 786], 'an appellate court is well able to assume the vantage point of a fair-minded and informed observer with knowledge of the relevant circumstances.' He then went on to say that the appellate court 'must itself make an assessment of all the relevant circumstances and then decide whether there is a real possibility of bias'. The next logical step is what he did not say—that the appellate court, consisting of fair-minded and informed observers with knowledge of the relevant circumstances, must draw its conclusions, not by reference to what another fictitious fair-minded and informed observer with knowledge of the relevant circumstances would conclude, but by reference to what itself as an embodiment of fair-mindedness and relevant knowledge had concluded.

Note

The sheer number of decisions that have had to be made by the Court of Appeal or House of Lords[14] noted above appear to indicate that the law in this area is in a state of crisis.

THE DUTY TO ACT FAIRLY

Procedural impropriety is one of the three main grounds of review identified by Lord Diplock in *Council of Civil Service Unions v Minister for the Civil Service* [1985] AC 374; [1984] 3 All ER 935; other than the rule against bias, it can denote both a failure to observe express procedural requirements (most commonly consultation) and a breach of the common law rules of natural justice, also known as the 'duty to act fairly'. In this area also, Art 6 has had influence, as appears below.

Statutory consultation

When dealing with the effects of failure to undertake statutory consultation, the courts have tended to classify such requirements as either mandatory or directory. Breach of a mandatory requirement will render the decision or act in question invalid, in contrast to breach of a directory requirement which will not.[15] The terminology was recast in *Wang v Commissioner of Inland Revenue* [1994] 1 WLR 1286, in which the court said that it was preferable to approach the issue by enquiring as to the legislative

---

14   See also *Panday v Virgil (Senior Superintendent of Police)* [2008] 1 AC 1386 by the Privy Council.

15   For a recent application of this approach, see *R v Sekhon* [2003] 1 Cr App R 34.

intent behind laying down procedural requirements. The problem here is that the statute generally gives little guidance as to whether a given requirement should be complied with and absolutely none as to the consequences if it is not. So finding Parliament's intention becomes, in reality, a question of the courts asking whether it is fair or desirable in all the circumstances to quash the decision.

A more helpful approach entails examination of the *impact* of the alleged procedural breach on the person who should have been consulted and on the public at large. Courts following this approach will first ask what was the *purpose* of the consultation requirement in question? Having established this, they will then go on to consider whether the failure to take the step in question substantially detracted from the expressed purpose. In *R v Lambeth London Borough Council ex parte Sharp* (1986) 55 P & CR 232, a Council was obliged by statute to give people living in its area the opportunity to comment on plans for a new development. The notice it put up in purported compliance with this obligation was defective as first, it did not say the time period during which representations had to be received to be considered, and second, it did not state that representations, to be considered, had to be in writing. The court found that the purpose of the provision was to enable local people to have a say in the question of planning permission; the deficiencies in the notice made it likely that this purpose would be hindered. It therefore quashed the eventual decision to grant planning permission.[16] Recently, in *R (C (A Minor)) v Secretary of State for Justice* [2009] 2 WLR 1039, the importance of the disregarded duties to consult were also considered. The Secretary of State brought in new rules governing the treatment of trainees at secure training centres, providing that a trainee could be physically restrained for the purpose of ensuring good order and discipline. Under the negative resolution procedure, the new rules were debated in the House of Lords, which did not resolve to annul them, so that they took effect. Judicial review was sought on the basis that the new rules were *ultra vires* because the Secretary of State had unreasonably failed to consult with the Children's Commissioner for England and failed to carry out a race equality impact assessment, as required by statute, before laying them before Parliament. The Court of Appeal found that the rules were unlawful and should be quashed. Particular emphasis was laid on the importance of carrying out a race equality impact analysis. The fact that Parliament had approved the rules despite the failures of the Secretary of State was found to be irrelevant—it was the courts' constitutional duty to police adherence to these rules, not Parliament's. Importantly, it was observed that as a general rule, once delegated legislation had been found to be unlawful it should normally be quashed.

What, however, will be the position if there are no statutory requirements about consultation or other types of procedures or if there are provisions but these do not state what kinds of procedures are required? In other words, when must a person affected by a decision be consulted about it (and allowed to make representations, in whatever form) and what kind of consultation, consideration or hearing must take place? These questions will be addressed in turn.

When is a duty to act fairly required by the common law?

The courts have to decide this question in two kinds of cases: first, where there is no statute governing the area (for example, where dealing with a non-statutory body) or second where there *is* a relevant statute but it makes no provision for procedural fairness. For much of the first half of this century, the courts drew a distinction between administrative decisions and 'judicial' type decisions, allowing the right to a hearing, or consultation, only in the latter type of case. This distinction led to many cases

---

16   For a similar approach, see *R v Immigration Appeal Tribunal ex parte Jeyeanthan* [1999] 3 All ER 231.

being decided on this rather unhelpful and artificial distinction. It was artificial because, with the complexities of modern government and the way it makes decisions, it was often exceedingly difficult to classify a particular decision confidently as one or the other. It was unhelpful as a tool for deciding when fair procedures should be followed because it appeared to ignore what was surely the key point, namely the importance of the decision concerned for the individual affected by it. As one judge has remarked, it is not much comfort for someone who attends a court case on a parking offence where, because the proceedings were judicial, a rigidly fair and careful procedure was followed, to come home and find a letter from the Council to say that his house is going to be demolished because of a planning decision and be told by this lawyer that he has no right to be consulted on this because it is an administrative decision. This distinction was largely swept away by the decision in *Ridge v Baldwin* [1964] AC 40, described by Wade as 'the turning point of judicial policy'.[17] *Ridge* made it clear that it was not so much the type of decision being made, or the status of the person making it, that was important, so much as whether fairness demanded consultation. In determining this issue, the primary matter to look at is the *impact* of the decision on the person affected and, in particular, what rights or interests of the person are affected by the decision.

If the decision affects a person's legal rights, then the decision-maker will generally be required to follow a high standard of fairness—as in civil or criminal trials.[18] More difficult are those cases where the decision will affect an interest, for example, a person's business, but will not infringe his or her rights. A classic example would be a case where the decision in question was to revoke a licence allowing a person to run their business. In general, the individual interest will have to be balanced against the cost and inconvenience to the decision-maker of holding hearings and following lengthy procedures. But sometimes in cases of this sort, a person affected by a decision may also be able to claim a right to a hearing or consultation simply by virtue of the importance of the decision for his or her livelihood, reputation or some other vital interest. The following well known case illustrates the principle well. A market trader, Harry Hook, was banned for life following an incident in which he had urinated in the street and been abusive to a security guard who had remonstrated with him. A key question was whether the hearings concerning his case had to be run in accordance with principles of procedural fairness.

R v Barnsley Metropolitan Borough Council ex parte Hook
[1976] 1 WLR 1052, 1055–57

Lord Denning MR: . . . .

I do not think that the right of a stallholder arises merely under a contact or licence determinable at will. It is a right conferred on him by the common law under which, so long as he pays the stallage, he is entitled to have his stall there; and that right cannot be determined without just cause. I agree that he has to have the permission of the market-holder to start with. But once he has it and has set up his stall there, then so long as he pays the stallage, he has a right to keep it there. It is not to be taken away except for just cause and then only in accordance with the provisions of natural justice. I do not mind whether the market-holder is exercising a judicial or an administrative function. A stall-holder counts on this right in order to enable him to earn his living.

---

17   See *Constitutional Fundamentals*, p 79.

18   Though note that this is not invariable. In cases of urgency, for example, arrest, the courts have not found that the police have any duty to allow the person concerned to make any statement in their defence.

Notes

1. Thus a crucial aspect of the decision was the simple fact that it deprived Mr Hook of his livelihood. Where someone complains of a decision not to give them a licence in the first place, he or she is far less likely to be able to attack the procedure surrounding such a decision successfully. This is because he or she is seen not as having been deprived of any benefit he or she previously had, but merely as not having had a benefit granted to him or her. Furthermore, as compared with cases where people have been deprived of a pre-existing benefit as a result of wrong-doing of some sort, there generally is no question of a 'case against them' which it appears fair to allow them to reply. In many cases, it will simply be the case that there were more deserving applicants for the benefit.

2. In *McInnes v Onslow Fane* [1974] 1 WLR 1520, Megarry VC said that in mere application cases the standard was far lower than in revocation cases. In his view, in application cases, all that the applicant could reasonably demand was that the decision-maker should reach an 'honest conclusion without bias and not in pursuance of any capricious policy', that is any wrongful or fanciful policy. But he or she could demand nothing in the way of any particular procedure. However, it is not now a matter of clear law that in so-called application cases there can never be some duty to follow a fair procedure. Where an application being made results in evidence being put in by third parties against the application, or, particularly the applicant, the courts have found that fairness requires that the applicant be given the substance of the objections and a chance to reply to them: *R v Huntingdon District Council ex parte Cowan* [1984] 1 WLR 501. Thus, if a body charged with deciding upon an application receives submissions from one side, it may have to disclose them to the other, in accordance with the classic principle, *audi alteram partem.*[19] *R v Secretary of State for the Home Department ex parte Al Fayed* [1997] 1 All ER 228, discussed below, illustrates the same principle.

3. In cases involving interests rather than rights, an important concept often used to determine whether a hearing is required is the concept of legitimate expectation. This is especially helpful where the case does not involve a clear right. These decisions tend to lie somewhere between simply being refused a benefit at one extreme and having one's rights infringed on the other.[20] This notion was first formulated by Lord Denning MR in *Schmidt v Home Secretary* [1969] 2 Ch 149 and its principles clarified in the *GCHQ* case, in which the Civil Service unions sought review of the decision, made by the Prime Minister to ban trade unions at GCHQ. One argument was that the trade unions had a legitimate expectation of being consulted before such an important change to their terms of service were made.

Council of Civil Service Unions v Minister for the Civil Service (the GCHQ case) [1985] AC 374, 400–01, 412–13

Lord Fraser: . . .Even where a person claiming some benefit of privilege has no legal right to it, as a matter of private law, he may have a legitimate expectation of receiving the benefit or privilege, and, if so, the courts will protect his expectation by judicial review as a matter of public law.

[Such] expectation may arise either from an express promise given on behalf of a public authority or from the existence of a regular practice which the claimant can reasonably expect to continue . . .The submission on behalf of the appellants is that the present case is of the latter type. The test of that is whether the practice of prior consultation of the staff on

---

19 Literally, 'hear the other side'.

20 See generally on legitimate expectation, the very useful analysis by P Craig (1992) 108 LQR 79.

significant changes in their conditions of service was so well established by 1983 that it would be unfair or inconsistent with good administration for the Government to depart from the practice in this case. Legitimate expectations such as are now under consideration will always relate to a benefit or privilege to which the claimant has no right in private law, and it may even be to one which conflicts with his private law rights. In the present case the evidence shows that, ever since GCHQ began in 1947, prior consultation has been the invariable rule when conditions of service were to be significantly altered. Accordingly in my opinion if there had been no question of national security involved, the appellants would have had a legitimate expectation that the minister would consult them before issuing the instruction of 22 December 1983. . .

Lord Diplock: . . .Prima facie. . .civil servants employed at GCHQ who were members of national trade unions had, at best in December 1983, a legitimate expectation that they would continue to enjoy the benefits of such membership and of representation by those trade unions in any consultations and negotiations with representatives of the management of that Government department as to changes in any term of their employment. So, but again prima facie only, they were entitled, as a matter of public law under the head of 'procedural propriety', before administrative action was taken on a decision to withdraw that benefit, to have communicated to the national trade unions by which they had therefore been represented the reason for such withdrawal, and for such unions to be given an opportunity to comment on it.

Notes
1. Their Lordships went on to find that, though the failure to consult had been unfair, the decision was justified on national security grounds.
2. The requirement that if a practice is to give rise to legitimate expectation, the fact that it must be regular was stressed in the case. As Baldwin and Horne note: 'It is to be anticipated, therefore, that where a body is engaged in irregular, non-recurring forms of decision-making it will be deemed less likely to create expectations than where it deals with a series of similar decisions.'[21]
3. In the *GCHQ* case, the legitimate expectation arose from a regular practice but it was acknowledged of course that an express undertaking could also give rise to the expectation. One such case, described by Baldwin and Home[22] is *R v Liverpool Corporation ex parte Liverpool Taxi Fleet Operator's Association* [1972] 2 WLR 1262: The corporation had limited the number of taxi-cab licences in Liverpool to 300 and had assured the owners that they would not change the policy without hearing representations. When the corporation resolved to increase the number, the Court of Appeal said that this could not be done without hearing the owners. The basis of the decision was fairness rather than either estoppel or a general duty to consult when rule-making. An expectation (and, it seems, one that had been relied upon) could not be dashed with impunity, especially one accompanied by an undertaking to pursue a particular course of action or procedure. In a more recent decision, *R (On the application of Greenpeace Ltd) v Secretary of State for Trade and Industry* [2007] EWHC 311, a Government White Paper on the future of nuclear energy had promised 'the fullest public consultation'. In the event, the consultation process was seriously flawed and did not provide for respondents to comment on the main matters of substance. The court quashed the Government's subsequent decision to build new nuclear power stations, Sullivan J remarking (at para 48):

---

21 'Expectations in a Joyless Landscape' (1986) 49 MLR 685, 700.

22 *Ibid*, at 699.

the promise. . .was given at the highest level: in a Government White Paper. It would be curious, to say the least, if the law was not able to require the Government to honour such a promise, absent any good reason to resile from it.

4. A useful attempt at setting out the law in this area in a systematic way can be found in the following case, concerning a decision by Durham council to shut down certain residential homes for the elderly. The council had only specifically made the residents aware of the plan five days before the final decision was made to go ahead with it. Residents from both homes claimed that they had had a legitimate expectation of proper consultation, which had been frustrated by the Councils' actions. Simon Browne LJ found that cases of legitimate expectation could be broken down into four different categories. The first was expectation of continuing to receive a substantive benefit as opposed to a procedural one (known as substantive legitimate expectations and dealt with below). His Lordship went on to consider the others.

R v Devon County Council ex parte Baker; Durham County Council ex parte Curtis [1995] 1 All ER 73, 88–91

[Category 2] The concept of legitimate expectation is used to refer to the claimant's interest in some ultimate benefit which he hopes to retain (or, some would argue, attain). Here, therefore, it is the interest itself rather than the benefit that is the substance of the expect-ation. In other words the expectation arises not because the claimant asserts any specific right to a benefit but rather because his interest in it is one that the law holds protected by the requirements of procedural fairness; the law recognises that the interest cannot properly be withdrawn (or denied) without the claimant being given an opportunity to comment and without the authority communicating rational grounds for any adverse decision. . .

[His Lordship dismissed Category 3—the third notion of simply expecting fairness in procedure,]

[Category 4]: The final category of legitimate expectation encompasses those cases in which it is held that a particular procedure, not otherwise required by law in the protection of an interest, must be followed consequent upon some specific promise or practice. Fair-ness requires that the public authority be held to it. The authority is bound by its assurance, whether expressly given by way of a promise or implied by way of established practice. [The judge cited the *Liverpool Taxi Owners*, *GCHQ* and *A-G of Hong Kong v Ng Yuen Shiu* [1983] 2 AC 629 case as illustrative of this line of authority.]

. . The legitimate expectation argument in the Durham case is advanced in these terms:

The County Council's decision deprived the appellants of a benefit or advantage which they had hitherto been permitted by the County Council to enjoy and which they could legitimately expect either to continue indefinitely, or at least to continue unless and until the County Council communicated to them some rational ground for withdrawing the benefit on which they were given an opportunity to comment.

This, of course, is asserting a legitimate expectation in category 2. . .[which] comprises those interests which the law recognises are of a character which require the protection of procedural fairness. What then is the touchstone by which such interests can be identified?

Thus the only touchstone of a category 2 interest emerging from Lord Diplock's speech in GCHQ] is that the claimant has in the past been permitted to enjoy some benefit or advantage. Whether or not he can then legitimately expect procedural fairness, and if so to what extent, will depend upon the court's view of what fairness demands in all the circumstances of the case. That, frankly, is as much help as one can get from the authorities. In short, the concept of legitimate expectation when used, as in the Durham case, in the category 2 sense seems to me no more than a recognition and embodiment of the unsurprising principle that the demands of fairness are likely to be somewhat higher when an authority contemplates depriving someone of an existing benefit or advantage than when the claimant is a bare applicant for a future benefit. . .

With these thoughts in mind I return to the Durham case. That the appellants have hitherto been enjoying some benefit or advantage of which the county council now proposes to deprive them cannot be doubted. On the authorities they accordingly get to first base in terms of asserting a legitimate expectation of some procedural fairness in the decision-making process. But it is no good pretending that the authorities carry them or the courts a single step further than that. The fact is that it still remains for the court to say, unassisted by authority save only in so far as there may exist other cases analogous on their facts, whether that legitimate expectation ought to be recognised and, if so, precisely what are the demands of fairness in the way of an opportunity to comment and so forth.

As stated, I share Dillon LJ's view on the facts of this case that five days' notice of the proposed closure of Ridgeway House gave the residents wholly insufficient opportunity to make such representations as they would have wished to make in favour of their home being kept open in preference to others.

Note
It is interesting to note Simon Browne LJ's frankness as to the limited amount of precise guidance which can be gained from the authorities. His judgment amounts to an assertion that the courts can merely apply common sense and reasonableness, unencumbered—and unassisted—by any more detailed guidance.

What is required for a fair hearing?

The issue here then is the manner in which a person affected by a decision must be permitted to make his case; to put it another way, what, in different circumstances will be the *content* of the duty to act fairly. Jowell considers the kinds of factors that may weigh with the court in determining what level of procedural protection should be afforded in a particular case:

> . . . As with rules, adjudication is not appropriate in all situations. Where speed and administrative despatch are required, it may be excluded: could one really allow a pavement hearing before a police officer is able to tow away an illegally parked car? In some situations it is felt that an authoritative judgment without the opportunity of challenge is required (the marking of examination scripts may serve as an example here, or admission to a university). Sometimes parties who have to live with each other after the dispute prefer techniques of mediation or conciliation to negotiate an acceptable solution. These forms of resolving disputes differ from adjudication where the final decision is taken by the independent 'judge' and is imposed rather than agreed, a feature not acceptable in all situations and which also partially explains the move to negotiated solutions noted above. Finally, it should be borne

in mind that the opportunity for a hearing may not easily be taken: hearings take time, may need expertise, and are often costly (legal aid is generally not provided to parties before administrative tribunals or inquiries).[23]

Note

In ascending order of seriousness, the different procedural safeguards which the courts may find required are as follows: notice of the charge or case against a person; the right to a hearing; the right to call witnesses and cross-examine the other party's witnesses; the right to legal representation.

Notice of the case against

The first of these safeguards then is notice of the case against a person, or of the decision that a person may wish to object to. This is the lowest level of procedural protection; if a person has no notice of the case against him/her, then clearly he or she cannot make any effective representations on his or her own behalf. In *R v Governing Body of Dunraven School and Another ex parte B (by his Mother and Next Friend), The Times*, 3 February 2000, a 15-year-old boy was excluded from his school. He applied for judicial review on the basis that he had not been informed of the main evidence against him (provided by another boy). His parents had a right to make representations about the decision. It was held that the duty to act fairly required him to have been informed of the allegations against him, since otherwise it would be impossible for his parents to argue effectively against the decision to exclude. Because this right is so basic, it is only likely to be denied either for very pressing reasons of public policy (for example, national security) or where the applicant is a mere applicant for a benefit, for example, the applicants in *McInnes* (above). This is for two reasons. First, in these cases, no wrong-doing has usually been alleged against the applicant. The case is therefore radically different from one in which someone is facing a sanction of some sort—disciplinary proceedings for example, or expulsion from a school—and needs notice of the case against him or her in order to be able to defend him or herself. Second, if the applicant is asking why his or her application has been turned down, in the hope of being able to persuade the decision-maker to change his or her mind, the courts may treat his or her request as one for reasons for a final decision—and as noted below, there is no general duty to give reasons for decisions. As Craig notes, in these kinds of cases, 'there has been a tension between two principles operating within this area, the right to notice, and the absence of any general duty to give reasons'.[24]

However, in cases where it becomes evident that the reason a benefit is being withheld is because of allegations or evidence given by a third party, then this brings the case into the position where there is a 'case against' someone. In such cases, there may be a duty to disclose at least the substance of the allegations or case against that person, or his or her application, as in *R v Huntingon District Council ex parte Cowan*, discussed above.

The only other circumstance in which the right to notice may be excluded is if the court takes the view that even if notice been given, it would have been pointless as nothing the applicant could have said in response would have made a difference. *R v Chief Constable of North Wales Police ex parte Thorpe* [1998] 3 WLR 57, CA is an example. The applicants were paedophiles, recently released from prison after serving long sentences for sexual offences against children and were having difficulties finding somewhere to live. They eventually hired a caravan on a site in North Wales. Unfortunately, there were numerous children in the caravan park from time to time. The police therefore asked them to move; when they refused, the police showed the site owner press cuttings revealing the applicants' past; the owner then made them leave the site. In the Court of Appeal, the applicants argued that they

---

23   J Jowell, 'The Rule of Law today', in J Jowell and D Oliver (eds), *The Changing Constitution*, 4th edn (2000), pp 14–15.

24   Craig (2008), p 396.

had been treated unfairly as they had not been shown the police information and given opportunity to comment. It was held that while the gist of the police case should have been disclosed, nothing the applicants could have said would have made any difference to the police decision: therefore there had been no substantial injustice.

The right to make representations: written or oral proceedings?

The next question which arises is whether a person must be allowed to make representations in response to the case against him or her, and if so whether he or she must be allowed to do so at an oral hearing or whether it will be sufficient to allow a person to make his or her representations in writing only. Plainly, an oral hearing is a much more burdensome procedure, and in many cases, unlikely to be necessary. Conversely, as with the right to notice, the situations in which a person is likely not to be granted a right to make written representations is in the bare application cases; this follows logically from the refusal to grant him or her notice of the case against him or her. However, again, if the refusal of a benefit amounts to an implied slur on his or her character, it may be held that representations should have been allowed. A good example is *R v Secretary of State for the Home Department ex parte Al Fayed* [1997] 1 All ER 228. The Fayed brothers applied to the Home Secretary to be naturalised (awarded British citizenship). They clearly satisfied all the conditions laid down under the relevant statute except for one which was nebulous: the requirement that they be of good character. The Home Secretary refused citizenship and gave no reasons. Section 44(2) of the British Nationality Act stated that the Home Secretary 'shall not be required to assign any reason' for such a decision. It was held that the Home Secretary ought to have identified to the Al Fayeds the areas which were causing him difficulty in granting nationality and given them a chance to respond, since the decision clearly amounted to an implied slur upon their good name. The decision was clearly based on the principle that reputation is something the applicant has already and if the net result of his or her application is to lower that reputation then he or she is in danger of being *deprived* of something; therefore, the standards of fairness ought to be higher.

Clearly, as with other areas of procedural fairness, such as reasons, if vital rights or interests are at stake, the right to make representations will generally be upheld. So in *R v Secretary of State for the Home Dept ex parte Harry* [1998] 1 WLR 1737, the applicant was a mental patient detained under conditions of security which would mean minimal liberty. Following a review of his case, the Home Secretary was advised by an advisory board that a recommendation by a mental health review tribunal that he be transferred to a lower security hospital, with considerably more freedom, be refused, with the result that Harry would stay at a maximum security classification. The Home Secretary did not disclose the advice to the detainee, or allow him to make representations. It was found that he should have done both in the circumstances. A similar decision is *R (Hirst) v Secretary of State for the Home Department.*[25]

In other cases, where the nature of the interest of the applicant would not be enough by itself to give him or her a right to be heard, the concept of legitimate expectation may require this, as in *GCHQ* (above).

Alder points out that particular issues can arise where a decision maker relies on an expert assessor:

> . . .where the judge disagrees with an assessor on an important matter, he should give the parties a chance to comment: *Ahmed v Governing Body of Oxford University* (2003). If any inquiry is held, the decision-maker cannot subsequently take

new evidence or advice received from an outside source into account without giving
the parties an opportunity to comment: see *Elmbridge BC v Secretary of State for
the Environment, Transport and the Regions* [2002] Envir LR 1; *AMEC Ltd v White-
friars City Estates* [2005] 1 All ER 723.[26]

In terms of deciding whether an oral hearing should have been permitted, one strand of thinking the
courts have employed is to look to the *purpose* any such hearing would have served. In some cases, this
brings the courts perilously close to admitting into consideration the argument that giving a hearing
would have made no difference. In such cases (*Thorpe*, above, is an example) the courts do not seem to
have fully worked out whether they are concerned with upholding substantive fairness (that is, a fair
outcome) or procedural fairness (that is, a fair procedure, regardless of the likely outcome of the case).
Thus, they sometimes seem to use the test of 'fairness' to mean, was the result 'fair'? The reasoning will
be that if the court thinks that in fact allowing the applicants to make representations, or call witnesses,
as the case may be, could have made no difference to the applicant, then he or she has suffered no real
unfairness. Such tendencies can be seen in the following, leading case.

Lloyd and Others v McMahon [1987] 1 AC 625 (extracts)

Liverpool City Council had been late in setting a rate and, as a result, the Council had
lost income—the rates it would have collected had the rate been set at the proper time.
The district auditor (DA) wrote to the councillors warning them that due to their wilful
misconduct they were in danger of being held personally liable—surcharged—to make up
this loss. The individual councillors were informed that they could make written representations to the DA before he reached his decision. They did so. He then found them jointly
and severally liable for the sum lost, namely £106,103. The case was an appeal against
the DA's decision under the Local Government Act 1982, s 20. The main issue was whether
the DA's decision should be struck down because he had not allowed the councillors to
make representations in their defence at an oral hearing.

Lord Keith of Kinkel: . . .My Lords, if the district auditor had reached a decision adverse to
the appellants without giving them any opportunity at all of making representations to him,
there can be no doubt that his procedure would have been contrary to the rules of natural
justice and that . . .the decision would fall to be quashed. In the event, written representations alone were asked for. These were duly furnished, in very considerable detail, and an
oral hearing was not requested, though that could very easily have been done, and there is
no reason to suppose that the request would not have been granted. . . The true question is
whether the district auditor acted fairly in all the circumstances. It is easy to envisage cases
where an oral hearing would clearly be essential in the interests of fairness, for example
where an objector states that he has personal knowledge of some facts indicative of wilful
misconduct on the part of a councillor. In that situation justice would demand that the
councillor be given an opportunity to depone to his own version of the facts. [Lord Keith
found that all relevant documents and evidence, including the appellants' evidence had
been considered by the district auditor.]
      . . .If the appellants had attended an oral hearing they would no doubt have reiterated the
sincerity of their motives from the point of view of advancing the interests of the inhabitants
of Liverpool. [But] . . .the sincerity of the appellants' motives is not something capable of

---

26 J Alder, *Constitutional and Administrative Law,* 7th edn (2009) at 342.

justifying or excusing failure to carry out a statutory duty, or of making reasonable what is otherwise an unreasonable delay in carrying out such a duty. In all the circumstances I am of opinion that the district auditor did not act unfairly, and that the procedure which he followed did not involve any prejudice to the appellants

Lord Browne-Wilkinson: . . .My Lords the so-called rules of natural justice are not engraved on tablets of stone. To use the phrase which better expresses the underlying concept, what the requirements of fairness demand when any body, domestic, administrative or judicial, has to make a decision which will affect the rights of individuals depends on the character of the decision-making body, the kind of decision it has to make and the statutory or other framework in which it operates. In particular, it is well-established that when a statute has conferred on any body the power to make decisions affecting individuals, the courts will not only require the procedure prescribed by the statute to be followed, but will readily imply so much and no more to be introduced by way of additional procedural safeguards as will ensure the attainment of fairness. . .

Notes
1. The decision at first sight seems open to criticism: the councillors' reputations were at stake and they were also in danger of suffering the equivalent of a criminal sanction—a fine, indeed a heavy one. These factors would generally point to a high level of procedural fairness. The real basis of the decision seemed to have been that, first, the councillors had not requested an oral hearing at the time, which cast some doubt on their subsequent contention that it was essential for a fair decision to be made. Second, as seen above, the House of Lords found that the applicants had lost nothing by not having an oral hearing; they had been given a full opportunity to make written representations with full knowledge of the case against them, and an oral hearing would have added nothing of relevance.
2. *McMahon* may be contrasted with the recent House of Lords decision in *R (On the application of Smith) v Parole Board* [2005] 1 WLR 350. The appellants (S and W), had both been released on licence from prison, meaning that if they breached the terms of their licence, they could be recalled to prison. Both were recalled for breach, and the Parole Board revoked their licences. They brought judicial review proceedings, arguing that the refusal of the Parole Board to hold oral hearings before deciding to revoke their licences was a breach of the duty to act fairly. In one case, the licence was revoked because the man, convicted of rape, had been found to be using crack cocaine after his release; in the other, because he had missed an appointment with his probation officer, and was accused of having been involved in an incident of damage to property and assault while drunk, something he denied. The effect of the recalls was that both had to serve substantial further periods of imprisonment. The relevant statutory rules permitted but did not require oral hearings in these circumstances. Both men sought judicial review of the decision to revoke their licences without granting them an oral hearing and the decision went all the way to the Lords.

R (West) v Parole Board; R (Smith) v Parole Board [2005] 1 WLR 350, HL (extracts)

Lord Bingham
1 My Lords, these appeals concern the procedure to be followed by the Parole Board when a determinate sentence prisoner, released on licence, seeks to resist subsequent revocation of his licence. The appellant claimants contend that such a prisoner should be offered an oral hearing at which the prisoner can appear and, either on his own behalf or through a legal representative, present his case, unless the prisoner chooses to forgo such a hearing.

The respondent Parole Board accepts that in resolving challenges to revocation of their licences by determinate sentence prisoners it is under a public law duty to act in a procedurally fair manner. It accepts that in some cases, as where there is a disputed issue of fact material to the outcome, procedural fairness may require it to hold an oral hearing at which the issue may be contested. It accepts, through leading counsel, that it may in the past have been too slow to grant oral hearings. But it strongly resists the submission that there should be any rule or presumption in favour of an oral hearing in such cases. . .

30 In considering what procedural fairness in the present context requires, account must first be taken of the interests at stake. On one side is the safety of the public, with which the Parole Board cannot gamble. . .On the other is the prisoner's freedom. This is a conditional, and to that extent precarious, freedom. . . It is noteworthy that a short-term prisoner who has served half his sentence and a long-term prisoner who has reached his non-parole date have a statutory right to be free: a conditional right, but none the less a right, breach of which gives an enforceable right to redress: see *R v Governor of Brockhill Prison, Ex p Evans (No 2)* [2001] 2 AC 19.

31 While an oral hearing is most obviously necessary to achieve a just decision in a case where facts are in issue which may affect the outcome, there are other cases in which an oral hearing may well contribute to achieving a just decision. The possibility of a detainee being heard either in person or, where necessary, through some form of representation has been recognised by the European court as, in some instances, a fundamental procedural guarantee in matters of deprivation of liberty: [his Lordship cited Strasbourg case-law]. . . .

32 In Canada. . .and New Zealand. . .statutory provision is made for oral revocation hearings. In the United States, most states had already made such provision when the Supreme Court held such hearings to be necessary. . .In Australia, courts have repeatedly held that there must be an oral hearing. . .In this country, as already noted, revocation hearings are routinely held in the cases of life sentence prisoners and Her Majesty's pleasure detainees.

. . .In the 19-month period from 1 April 2003 to 31 October 2004, the House was informed, the [Parole] board considered representations against the recall of determinate sentence prisoners in 1,945 cases but held oral hearings in only four.

. . .35 The common law duty of procedural fairness does not, in my opinion, require the board to hold an oral hearing in every case where a determinate sentence prisoner resists recall. . .But. . .even if important facts are not in dispute, they may be open to explanation or mitigation, or may lose some of their significance in the light of other new facts. While the board's task certainly is to assess risk, it may well be greatly assisted in discharging it (one way or the other) by exposure to the prisoner or the questioning of those who have dealt with him. It may often be very difficult to address effective representations without knowing the points which are troubling the decision-maker. The prisoner should have the benefit of a procedure which fairly reflects, on the facts of his particular case, the importance of what is at stake for him, as for society. . . .

45 In his representations against revocation the appellant West offered the board explanations, which he said he could substantiate, of his failure to keep an appointment with his probation officer and of the incident at his ex-partner's hostel. The board could not properly reject these explanations on the materials before it without hearing him. . .His challenge could not be fairly resolved without an oral hearing and he was not treated with that degree of fairness which his challenge required.

46 The resort to class A drugs by the appellant Smith clearly raised serious questions, and it may well be that his challenge would have been rejected whatever procedure had

been followed. But it may also be that the hostels in which he was required to live were a very bad environment for a man seeking to avoid addiction. It may be that the board would have been assisted by evidence from his psychiatrist. The board might have concluded that the community would be better protected by encouraging his self-motivated endeavours to conquer addiction, if satisfied these were genuine, than by returning him to prison for two years with the prospect that, at the end of that time, he would be released without the benefit of any supervision. Whatever the outcome, he was in my opinion entitled to put these points at an oral hearing. Procedural fairness called for more than consideration of his representations, on paper, as one of some 24 such applications routinely considered by a panel at a morning session.

47 I would allow both appeals. I would in each case make a declaration that the Parole Board breached its duty of procedural fairness owed to the appellant by failing to offer him an oral hearing of his representations against revocation of his licence.

Lord Slynn. . .

50 There is no absolute rule that there must be an oral hearing automatically in every case. Where, however, there are issues of fact, or where explanations are put forward to justify actions said to be a breach of licence conditions, or where the officer's assessment needs further probing, fairness may well require that there should be an oral hearing. If there is doubt as to whether the matter can fairly be dealt with on paper then in my view the board should be predisposed in favour of an oral hearing.

[The appeal was allowed in favour of the applicants.]

Notes

1. This decision gives some useful guidance. In particular, given that the right to liberty of a person recalled back to prison for breach of their licence is clearly engaged, *but* the House of Lords made clear that not all decisions finding such a breach require a hearing, it is plain that on their own the importance of the rights of the claimant alone may not require an oral hearing: it will generally be necessary to show how the matter cannot be fairly determined without a hearing, although this is not confined solely to resolving disputed matters of fact.

2. In the above case, Lord Bingham appeared to take the view that Art 6 and the common law duty of fairness would probably lead to the same requirements. However, other recent cases concerning fair procedure have been decided entirely under Art 6. A recent example in the House of Lords concerned the question whether care workers had a right to a hearing before being placed by the Home Secretary on a list indicating that they may pose a risk to vulnerable adults, even though the statute (the Care Standards Act 2000) did not provide for a hearing. The House of Lords found that the Art 6 guarantee of a fair hearing was engaged—often a tricky and technical question—and had been breached and made a declaration of incompatibility under the HRA:[27] *R (Wright) v Health Secretary.*[28]

3. In a further recent decision of the House of Lords concerning a challenge to the absence of an oral hearing, Art 6 was the primary issue, but some of the strands of reasoning would be applicable to the common law duty to act fairly. *R (Dudson) v Secretary of State for the Home Department* [2006] 1 AC 245 concerned the redetermination by the Lord Chief Justice of the sentence to be served by a juvenile murderer, D, following the finding by the European Court of Human Rights that it was

---

27 See Chapter 17, pp 960–961.

28 [2009] 2 WLR 267; for comment see R Moules [2009] CLJ 251.

unlawful for the Home Secretary, who had previously set the sentence, to do so.[29] No hearing was held, the Lord Chief Justice deciding the matter on the papers and in fact recommending a reduction of two years, which was accepted. D contended that there should have been an oral hearing under Article 6. It was found that all relevant matters, including the representations of the offender, had been fully considered. The LCJ was not deciding fresh matters of fact, which had been decided at the original trial, but rather deciding where to place D on the sentencing scale. Consequently an oral hearing would not have added anything and D did not contend that he had lost the opportunity to dispute matters of fact by not having one. Nor had his lawyers raised the absence of an oral hearing in their written representations made in response to the LCJ's decision. As Lord Hope put it:

> it was not suggested by the appellant's solicitors that an oral hearing was required so that the appellant could appear in person before the Lord Chief Justice and give evidence. The request for an oral hearing was made solely on the ground that this procedure was a normal part of the sentencing exercise.[30]

His Lordship found no violation of Art 6; moreover, although the common law issues were not directly addressed, it may be assumed that their Lordships also considered there to have been no violation of the common law duty to act fairly. The decision thus re-illustrates the key point that to successfully argue for an oral hearing, the applicant must show that one was necessary for the fair disposal of his case.

The right to call witnesses and to cross-examine opposing witnesses

The first issue—witnesses— is the simplest and most important. The whole *point* of an oral hearing, as opposed to one conducted on paper, is to resolve disputed issues of fact (including intention and motive); to allow for the credibility of witnesses to be examined, for each side to convince the 'judge' of their good faith, conviction and sincerity; to allow for inconsistencies or omissions in one side's account to be probed through questioning by the other side, or their lawyer—known as cross-examining. Therefore in most instances it would make little point to conduct an oral hearing but refuse to allow for the presence of witnesses or their cross-examination. So the essential test here is generally the same as that for an oral hearing: is the calling of witnesses, and allowing their cross-examination by the applicant, necessary to ensure a fair hearing of the applicant's case? Generally, therefore, an oral hearing should provide for the calling of witnesses and cross-examination, if this is necessary for the fair disposal of the hearing. But in a case which involves merely the interpretation of rules, or the law, or an examination of one person's isolated conduct, a public authority will not generally be required to permit their use. If it is thought the request is in bad faith it may also be declined. Both points are illustrated by *R v Board of Visitors of Hull Prison ex parte St (No 2)* [1979] 3 All ER 545. It was held that a Board of Visitors must be able to exercise a discretion to refuse a prisoner's request for witnesses if it is felt that he or she is purposely trying to obstruct or subvert the proceedings by calling large numbers of witnesses or if, where the request is made in good faith, it is felt that the calling of large numbers of witnesses is unnecessary. However, mere administrative inconvenience would not support a decision to refuse such a request and so, if the only reason for the refusal was, for example, the inconvenience involved in recalling the witnesses from other prisons, that would be insufficient. The principles

---

29   See Chapter 3, pp 137–138.

30   [2009] 2 WLR 267, at [37].

established in the above case were confirmed in *R v Board of Visitors for Nottingham Prison ex parte Moseley, The Times,* 23 January 1981; it was held that if it were established that a prisoner had asked for and been refused permission to call witnesses that would, *prima facie,* be unfair.

In many instances it would seem essential that a prisoner should be able to call witnesses in order to challenge the evidence against him or her. Moreover, it may be unlikely that a case will often be so straightforward as to require only one witness for the defence. Therefore, if a prisoner can demonstrate that calling more than one witness was necessary due to the nature of his or her defence, it would follow that he or she should have been allowed to call them. In *St Germain (No 2),* Lane LJ also considered whether the prisoners must be allowed to cross-examine those who had given evidence against them, or whether such evidence could be given by way of written statements only.

R v Board of Visitors of Hull Prison ex parte St Germain (No 2)
[1979] 3 All ER 545, 552–53

. . . It is clear that the entitlement of the board to admit hearsay evidence is subject to the overriding obligation to provide the accused with a fair hearing. Depending upon the facts of the particular case and the nature of the hearsay evidence provided to the board, the obligation to give the accused a fair chance to exculpate himself, or a fair opportunity to controvert the charge. . . or a. . full opportunity of presenting his case. . .may oblige the board not only to inform the accused of the hearsay evidence but also to give the accused a sufficient opportunity to deal with that evidence. Again, depending upon the nature of that evidence and the particular circumstances of the case, a sufficient opportunity to deal with the hearsay evidence may well involve the cross-examination of the witness whose evidence is initially before the board in the form of hearsay.

We again take by way of example the case in which the defence is an alibi. The prisoner contends that he was not the man identified on the roof [and breaking prison rules]. . .In short the prisoner has been mistakenly identified. . .The prisoner may well wish to elicit by way of question all manner of detail, e.g. the poorness of the light, the state of the confusion, the brevity of the observation, the absence of any contemporaneous record, etc, all designed to show the unreliability of the witness. To deprive him of the opportunity of cross-examination would be tantamount to depriving him of a fair hearing.

We appreciate that there may well be occasions when the burden of calling the witness whose hearsay evidence is readily available may impose a near impossible burden upon the board. However, it has not been suggested that hearsay evidence should be resorted to in the total absence of any first-hand evidence and this is the usual practice. Accordingly where a prisoner desires to dispute the hearsay evidence and for this purpose to question the witness, and where there are insuperable or very grave difficulties in arranging for his attendance the board should refuse to admit that evidence, or, if it has already come to their notice, should expressly dismiss if from their consideration. . . .

Notes
1. The refusal of witnesses and of cross-examination led to the quashing of six findings of guilt by way of *certiorari.* See also *R v Deputy Governor of Long Lartin Prison ex parte Prevot* [1988] 1 All ER 485, HL. It should be noted that disciplinary hearings in prisons are basically adversarial procedures where the purpose of the procedures in question is the determination of a person's guilt or innocence. In this respect, they are very similar to court proceedings and so one would expect that the ability to call and examine witnesses would be the norm. But hearings may take place in very different circumstances, such as planning enquiries; these are not adversarial proceedings, but

polycentric disputes, where an adjudicator is attempting to reach a conclusion on an administrative matter, after hearing evidence from numerous sources, and weighing up the conflicting priorities bearing upon his decision. In such circumstances, the courts are much more reluctant to impose formal, judicial style practices, such as cross-examination.[31]

2.   The leading case here is *Bushell v Secretary of State for the Environment* [1981] AC 75. The procedure in question was a public enquiry, the purpose of which was to allow an inspector holding the enquiry to hear local objections to the plan to build a new motorway which he would then take account of in advising the Minister whether the scheme should go ahead. One of the key factors in the decision by the Department of Environment (DoE) whether to build new motorways, and if so where, was their projections of what the increase in traffic on existing roads would be over the next 15 years. The method of making these projections, which was highly complicated, was set out in a publication called the Red Book. Some of those who were objecting to the plan to build the motorway believed that the method set out in the Red Book of predicting increases in traffic flow was flawed and overestimated the probable growth. At the enquiry, they were allowed by the inspector holding it to call witnesses who attacked the methodology set out in the Red Book. These criticisms were set out by the inspector in his eventual report to the Minister. However, the inspector did not allow the objectors to cross-examine representatives from the DoE on the Red Book methodology. Some of the objectors, including those whose property values would be affected by the motorway, applied for an order quashing the road-building schemes on the ground that they had been wrongfully deprived of the opportunity to cross-examine the experts. The judgment contains valuable comment on the issue of procedural fairness generally.

Bushell and Another v Secretary of State for the Environment [1981] AC 75 (extracts)

Lord Diplock: . . .Proceedings at a local inquiry at which many parties wish to make representations without incurring the expense of legal representation and cannot attend the inquiry throughout its length ought to be as informal as is consistent with achieving those objectives. To 'over-judicialise' the inquiry by insisting on observance of the procedures of a court of justice which professional lawyers alone are competent to operate effectively in the interests of their clients would not be fair. It would, in my view, be quite fallacious to suppose that at an inquiry of this kind the only fair way of ascertaining matters of fact and expert opinion is by the oral testimony of witnesses who are subjected to cross-examination on behalf of parties who disagree with what they have said. Such procedure is peculiar to litigation conducted in courts that follow the common law system of procedure, it plays no part in the procedure of courts of justice under legal systems based upon the civil law, including the majority of our fellow member states of the European Community. . . So refusal by an inspector to allow a party to cross-examine orally at a local inquiry a person who has made statements of facts or has expressed expert opinions is not unfair per se.

Whether fairness requires an inspector to permit a person who has made statements on matters of fact or opinion, whether expert or otherwise, to be cross-examined by a party to the inquiry who wishes to dispute a particular statement must depend on all the circumstances. In the instant case, the question arises in connection with expert opinion upon a technical matter. Here the relevant circumstances in considering whether fairness requires that cross-examination should be allowed include the nature of the topic upon which the opinion is expressed, the qualifications of the maker of the statement to deal with that topic,

---

31   See, e.g. *R v City Panel on Mergers and Takeovers ex parte Guinness plc* [1990] 1 QB 46.

the forensic competence of the proposed cross-examiner, and, most important, the inspector's own views as to whether the likelihood that cross-examination will enable him to make a report which will be more useful to the minister in reaching his decision than it otherwise would be is sufficient to justify any expense and inconvenience to other parties to the inquiry which would be caused by any resulting prolongation of it.

The circumstances in which the question of cross-examination arose in the instant case were the following. Before the inquiry opened each objector had received a document containing a statement of the minister's reasons for proposing the draft scheme. . . The second paragraph of the minister's statement of reasons said: 'The government's policy to build these new motorways [sc for which the two schemes provided] will not be open to debate at the forthcoming inquiries [sic]: the Secretary of State is answerable to Parliament for this policy.'

Because of the time that must elapse between the preparation of any scheme and the completion of the stretch of motorway that it authorises, the department, in deciding in what order new stretches of the national network ought to be constructed, has adopted a uniform practice throughout the country of making a major factor in its decision the likelihood that there will be a traffic need for that particular stretch of motorway in 15 years from the date when the scheme was prepared. . . The propriety of adopting it is clearly a matter fit to be debated in a wider forum [than a local inquiry] and with the assistance of a wider range of relevant material than any investigation at an individual local inquiry is likely to provide; and in that sense at least, which is the relevant sense for present purposes, its adoption forms part of government policy. . .

But whether the uniform adoption of particular methods of assessment is described as policy or methodology, the merits of the methods adopted are, in my view, clearly not appropriate for investigation at individual local inquiries by an inspector whose consideration of the matter is necessarily limited by the material which happens to be presented to him at the particular inquiry which he is holding. It would be a rash inspector who based on that kind of material a positive recommendation to the minister that the method of predicting traffic needs throughout the country should be changed and it would be an unwise minister who acted in reliance on it.

At the local inquiry into the M42 Bromsgrove and the M40 Warwick. . .the objectors were allowed to voice their criticisms of the methods used to predict traffic needs for the purposes of the two schemes and to call such expert evidence as they wanted to in support of their criticisms. What they were not allowed to do was to cross-examine the department's representatives upon the reliability and statistical validity of the methods of traffic prediction described in the Red Book and applied by the department for the purpose of calculating and comparing traffic needs in all localities throughout the country. This is the only matter in relation to the conduct of the inquiry by the inspector of which complaint is made.

Was this unfair to the objectors? For the reasons I have already given. . . I do not think it was. I think that the inspector was right in saying that the use of the concept of traffic needs in the design year assessed by a particular method as the yardstick by which to determine the order in which particular stretches of the national network of motorways should be constructed was government policy in the relevant sense of being a topic unsuitable for investigation by individual inspectors upon whatever material happens to be presented to them at local inquiries held throughout the country. . .

Lord Edmund-Davies (dissenting): . . .The general law may, I think, be summarised in this way: (a) In holding an administrative inquiry (such as that presently being considered), the inspector was performing quasi-judicial duties, (b) He must therefore discharge them in accordance with the rules of natural justice, (c) Natural justice requires that objectors (no less than departmental representatives) be allowed to cross-examine witnesses called for the other side on all relevant matters, be they matters of fact or matters of expert opinion, (d) In the exercise of jurisdiction outside the field of criminal law, the only restrictions on cross-examination are those general and well-defined exclusionary rules which govern the admissibility of relevant evidence; beyond those restrictions there is no discretion on the civil side to exclude cross-examination on relevant matters. . . .

Then is there any reason why those general rules should have been departed from in the present case? We have already seen that the parameters of the inquiry, as agreed to by the department representatives, embraced need as a topic relevant to be canvassed and reported upon. We have already considered the unacceptable submission that the Red Book was 'government policy.' And, while I am alive to the inconvenience of different inspectors arriving at different conclusions regarding different sections of a proposed trunk road, the risk of that happening cannot in my judgment, have any bearing upon the question whether justice was done at this particular inquiry, which I have already explained was, in an important respect, unique of its kind.

There remains to be considered the wholly novel suggestion, which has found favour with your Lordships, that there is a 'grey area'—existing, as I understand, somewhere between government policy (which admittedly may not be subjected to cross-examination) and the exact 'line' of a section of a motorway (which may be)—and that in relation to topics falling within the 'grey area' cross-examination is a matter of discretion. I find that suggestion to be too nebulous to be grasped. Furthermore, why such an area should exist has not been demonstrated—certainly not to my satisfaction—nor have its boundaries been defined, unlike those existing restrictions on cross-examination to which I have already referred and I confess to abhorrence of the notion that any such area exists. For the present case demonstrates that its adoption is capable of resulting in an individual citizen denied justice nevertheless finding himself with no remedy to right the wrong done to him.

My Lords, it is for the foregoing reasons that I find myself driven to the conclusion that the refusal in the instant case to permit cross-examination on what, by common agreement, was evidence of cardinal importance was indefensible and unfair and, as such, a denial of natural justice. But, even so, can it be said that no prejudice to the respondents resulted? [His Lordship found that there was a 'very real possibility that cross-examination of the department witnesses on the lines projected might have created serious doubts in his mind regarding their traffic forecasts and therefore as to whether need for the motorways had been established and those doubts. . .could well have led him to different conclusions and findings.] That the objectors were in truth prejudiced is, in my judgment, clear. Professor Wade has warned (*Administrative Law*, 4th edn, p 454): '. . .in principle it is vital that the procedure and the merits should be kept strictly apart, since otherwise the merits may be prejudged unfairly' and Lord Wright said in *General Medical Council v Spackman* [1943] AC 627, 644–645:

If the principles of natural justice are violated in respect of any decision, it is, indeed, immaterial whether the same decision would have been arrived at in the absence of the departure from the essential principles of justice. The decision must be declared to be no decision.

[His Lordship in dissent found that the decision should have been quashed.]

Notes

1. The reasoning of the majority is clearly open to criticism. First, no reason was given as to why it was thought that informality of procedure, which it is plausible to suppose, encourages people to participate would be undermined by allowing representatives from the DoE to be questioned. Second, the reasoning is arguably contradictory: if the use of the Red Book with its assumptions was not a subject on which criticism should be allowed at all because it was government policy, then on what basis did the inspector allow witnesses to be called to attack that policy, but not allow cross-examination of witnesses defending it? No basis is given for the drawing of such a distinction.

2. This decision, then, seems to leave law in a fairly confused state as it applies to enquiries, rather than adversarial proceedings. Do those arguing that they should have been permitted cross-examination have to prove that they would have derived positive advantage from it? Will a plea of 'policy' always defeat a claim for cross-examination? Do applicants have to prove it was likely that the decision in question would have been different had cross-examination been permitted? For critical discussion of the state of the law, see A Samuels, 'A Right to an Oral Hearing in Quasi-judicial Proceedings?' [2005] 64(3) CLJ 523.

Legal representation

The approach here has been very much to deny any clear right to legal representation except in courts and in certain tribunals (in statutory tribunals, the position is that legal representation should normally be permitted, in the absence of statutory provision to the contrary). This has been so even in cases where the nature of the proceedings in question is virtually identical, for example, the trying of prisoners for disciplinary offences by Boards of Visitors. In *R v Board of Visitors of HM Prison, the Maze ex parte Hone* [1988] 1 AC 379, the applicant had been convicted of assaulting prisoner officers at a hearing in which he had had no legal representation. He appealed to the House of Lords on the question whether legal representation should be available as of right due to the requirements of natural justice. The House of Lords found that in some cases legal representation ought to be allowed but that there was no general right to it. The House of Lords took into account the delay and cost of obtaining legal advice which the House thought would be prejudicial to the administration of discipline in the prison, and also that, once granted, it would be difficult to deny the right in governors' hearings. If legal advice were imported into governors' hearings it was thought that difficulties would arise as such hearings would not be sufficiently expeditious.

In another prisoners' rights case, *R v Secretary of State for the Home Dept ex parte Tarrant* [1984] 2 WLR 613; [1985] QB 251, the court put forward a number of factors which it said the Board of Visitors ought to consider in deciding in its discretion whether to grant permission for legal advice. These were (a) the seriousness of the charge and of the penalty, (b) the likelihood that points of law might be likely to arise, (c) the ability of the prisoner to conduct his own case, and (d) the need for speed in making the adjudication. In less serious cases, clearly it will be very difficult to claim a right to legal advice. Thus, for example, in *Pett v Greyhound Racing Association Ltd (No 2)* [1970] 1 QB 46, a greyhound owner was facing a serious disciplinary charge after traces of drugs had been found in his dog's urine. It was found that he had not been entitled to legal representation despite the clear threat to his livelihood and reputation.

Failure to give reasons for the final decision

It is important to distinguish this head of review from the allegation that the applicant was not given notice of the case against him or her, dealt with above. In the latter head, the applicant is arguing that there was a stage in the decision-making process in which he or she should have been given the opportunity to hear the case against him or her, so that he or she could make representations against it, prior to any final decision being made. In the former, with which we are concerned here, the applicant is arguing that the *final decision eventually made* should be quashed, regardless of the fairness of the procedure leading up to its being made, simply because he or she was not given any reasons for it. The leading case follows.

R v Secretary of State for the Home Department ex parte Doody and Others [1994] 1 AC 531, 560–65 (extracts)

The four applicants had each received mandatory life sentences for murder. The Home Secretary, after consulting with the Lord Chief Justice and the trial judge (referred to in the judgment as 'the judges'), had set the 'penal element'[32] in the sentence, which reflected the demands of retribution and deterrence. Once the penal part of the sentence had been served, the case would then go to the Parole Board which could then recommend whether it was safe to release the prisoner on licence or whether further imprisonment was needed to protect the public from the prisoner (referred to as 'the risk element'). In this case, the Home Secretary determined the penal period without consulting the prisoners; he then informed them of his decision, but did not give them any reason for it, or tell them whether he had fixed a period which differed from that recommended by the judges. The applicants sought, *inter alia,* declarations that (a) they were entitled to make representations to the Home Secretary on the matter; (b) the Home Secretary was required to inform them what period had been recommended by the judges and their reasons; (3) he was also required to inform them, if he had differed from the judges, of his reasons for so doing. On appeal, the first two declarations were granted by the Court of Appeal. The Home Secretary appealed to the House of Lords and the applicants cross-appealed. The extract below is concerned only with issue (c)—reasons.

Lord Mustill: . . .I begin by inquiring what requirements of fairness, germane to the present appeal, attach to the Home Secretary's fixing of the penal element. As general background to this task, I find in the more recent cases on judicial review a perceptible trend towards an insistence on greater openness, or if one prefers the contemporary jargon 'transparency', in the making of administrative decisions. This tendency has been accompanied by an increasing recognition. . .that a convicted offender should be aware what the court has in mind for his disposal. Whilst the current law and practice concerning discretionary life sentences conform entirely with this trend the regime for mandatory life prisoners conspicuously does not. Should this distinction be maintained in its entirety?

. . .I accept without hesitation, and mention it only to avoid misunderstanding, that the law does not at present recognise a general duty to give reasons for an administrative decision. Nevertheless, it is equally beyond question that such a duty may in appropriate circumstances be implied, and I agree with the analyses by the Court of Appeal in *Civil Service Appeal Board, ex p Cunningham* [1991] 4 All ER 310 of the factors which will often be material to such an implication.

Turning to the present dispute. . . I prefer simply to assert that within the inevitable constraints imposed by the statutory framework, the general shape of the administrative regime which ministers have lawfully built around it, and the imperatives of the public

---

32   Also referred to as the 'tariff sentence'.

interest, the Secretary of State ought to implement the scheme as fairly as he can. The giving of reasons may be inconvenient, but I can see no ground at all why it should be against the public interest: indeed, rather the reverse. This being so, I would ask simply: Is refusal to give reasons fair? I would answer without hesitation that it is not. As soon as the jury returns its verdict the offender knows that he will be locked up for a very long time. For just how long immediately becomes the most important thing in the prisoner's life. . . Where a defendant is convicted of, say, several armed robberies he knows that he faces a stiff sentence: he can be advised by reference to a public tariff of the range of sentences he must expect; he hears counsel address the judge on the relationship between his offences and the tariff; he will often hear the judge give an indication during exchanges with counsel of how his mind is working; and when sentence is pronounced he will always be told the reasons for it. So also when a discretionary life sentence is imposed. . . Contrast this with the position of the prisoner sentenced for murder. He never sees the Home Secretary; he has no dialogue with him: he cannot fathom how his mind is working. There is no true tariff, or at least no tariff exposed to public view which might give the prisoner an idea of what to expect. The announcement of his first review date arrives out of thin air, wholly without explanation. The distant oracle has spoken, and that is that.

My Lords, I am not aware that there still exists anywhere else in the penal system a procedure remotely resembling this. I. . .simply ask, is it fair that the mandatory life prisoner should be wholly deprived of the information which all other prisoners receive as a matter of course. I am clearly of the opinion that it is not. . .

. . .My Lords, I can moreover arrive at the same conclusion by a different and more familiar route, of which ex p Cunningham provides a recent example. It is not, as I understand it, questioned that the decision of the Home Secretary on the penal element is susceptible to judicial review. To mount an effective attack on the decision, given no more material than the facts of the offence and the length of the penal element, the prisoner has virtually no means of ascertaining whether this is an instance where the decision-making process has gone astray. I think it important that there should be an effective means of detecting the kind of error which would entitle the court to intervene, and in practice I regard it as necessary for this purpose that the reasoning of the Home Secretary should be disclosed. If there is any difference between the penal element recommended by the judges and actually imposed by the Home Secretary, this reasoning is bound to include, either explicitly or implicitly, a reason why the Home Secretary has taken a different view.

Notes

1. As NR Campbell observes,[33] with Craig,[34] this last 'justification [for requiring reasons] could apply to all administrative decisions potentially susceptible to. . . judicial review'. Campbell continues:

   It must be compared with the House of Lords' previous view on this issue, expressed by Lord Keith in *Lonrho plc v Secretary of State for Trade and Industry* [[1989] 2 All ER 609 at 620]:

   The only significance of the absence of reasons is that if all other known facts and circumstances appear to point overwhelmingly in

---

33   NR Campbell, 'The Duty to Give Reasons in Administrative Law' [1994] PL 184.

34   (1994) 110 LQR 12.

favour of a different decision, the decision-maker, who has given no
reasons cannot complain if the court draws the inference that he had
no rational reason for his decision.

On this previous view, the absence of reasons was irrelevant
unless the decision was prima facie unreasonable.[35]

2. Campbell goes on to propose tentatively that *Doody* may now be taken to require reasons to
be given in all cases by the authorities when making decisions which directly affect the liberty
of the applicant, instancing *R v Secretary of State for the Home Department ex parte Duggan*
[1993] 3 All ER 277 in which it was held that a category A prisoner was entitled to be given reasons
for the decision that he should remain in this category and therefore remain very unlikely
to be released on licence. A recent similar decision is *R (On the application of Wooder) v Feggetter*
[2003] QB 219, concerning a patient detained under the Mental Health Act, who sought
judicial review of the decision to treat him with drugs without his consent. It was held that that
where a decision to administer medical treatment sanctioned the violation of the autonomy
of a competent, non consenting adult patient, the common law implied a duty to give reasons as of
right.
3. In decisions lacking such implications for personal liberty 'it is suggested that the duty to provide
reasons may arise only where, because of the circumstance of the decision [it] is in particular need
of explanation'.[36] Campbell gives three such exceptional instances:[37]

First, a decision is in particular need of explanation where, by itself, it is prima facie
unreasonable. This may arise because all the known facts point to a decision different from that reached by the decision-maker [as] in *Sinclair* [*The Times*, 5 February
1992].

Prima facie unreasonableness may also arise where a decision is substantially
different from that which the applicant reasonably or legitimately expected [as in]
Cunningham. Secondly, a decision may be in particular need of explanation where,
by itself, it is prima facie unlawful [as in] *R v Northavon District Council, ex p Smith*
[[1993] 3 WLR 776, CA].

Thirdly, a decision may be in particular need of explanation where there is
some conflict of evidence, and it is unclear what view of the evidence the decision-
maker has taken in reaching its conclusion. Without knowledge of those factual
conclusions a person adversely affected by the decision may be unable to determine whether the decision-maker has acted lawfully or reasonably, and thus
whether there are grounds for review. So much seems implicit in *R v Criminal
Injuries Compensation Board, ex p Cummins* [*The Times*, 21 January 1992].

4. *Doody* certainly moved English law a little closer to imposing a general duty to give reasons for
administrative decisions. However, the following case, in which the duty was found not to be
present, demonstrates that much will depend on the particular circumstances of the case.

---

35 Campbell, n 33 above, 186.

36 *Ibid*, 188.

37 Only the skeleton of Campbell's argument is given here; n 33 above, at 188–89.

R v Higher Education Funding Councill ex parte Institute of Dental Surgery [1994] 1 WLR 651

The applicant institution wished to challenge the decision of the HEFC to award it a lower-than-hoped-for rating for its research, likely to result in a £270,000 cut in its funding.

Sedley J: . . .In the present state of the law there are two classes of case now emerging: those cases, such as Doody's case, where the nature of the process itself calls in fairness for reasons to be given; and those, such as Cunningham's case, where (in the majority view) it is something peculiar to the decision which in fairness calls for reasons to be given.

. . .We unhesitatingly reject Mr Beloff's submission that the judicial character of the Civil Service Appeal Board and the quasi-judicial function of the Home Secretary in relation to life sentence prisoners distinguish the cases requiring reasons from cases of purely administrative decisions such as the present one. In the modem state the decisions of administrative bodies can have a more immediate and profound impact on people's lives than the decisions of courts, and public law has since *Ridge v Baldwin* been alive to that fact. While the judicial character of a function may elevate the practical requirements of fairness above what they would otherwise be, for example by requiring contentious evidence to be given and tested orally, what makes it 'judicial' in this sense is principally the nature of the issue it has to determine, not the formal status of the deciding body.

The first limb of [counsel for the applicant's] submission is accordingly that the decision of the respondent was of a kind for which fairness requires that reasons be given. His written contention is that this will be the case—

> when the relevant decision has important consequences for the individual or body concerned, especially if the absence of reasons makes it very difficult for the applicant and the court to know whether the respondent has acted by reference to irrelevant factors, and especially if there is no justification for withholding reasons.

In our view this formula will not do. The absence of reasons *always* makes it difficult to know whether there has been an error of approach. The question of justification for withholding reasons logically comes after the establishment of a prima facie duty to give them. Neither can therefore add to the principal ground advanced, which is of such width that it would make a duty to give reasons a universal rule to which the only exception would be cases of no importance to anybody. There are certainly good arguments of public law and of public administration in favour of such a rule, but it is axiomatically not, or not yet, part of our law.

. . . .We must therefore look also at the other indicia: the openness of the procedure, widely canvassed in advance and published in circular form, the voluntary submission of self-selected examples of work; the judgment of academic peers. These, it seems to us, shift the process substantially away from the pole represented by *Doody*'s case, not on mere grounds of dissimilarity (there will be many dissimilar cases in which reasons are nevertheless now required) but because the nature of the exercise was that it was open in all but its critical phase, and its critical phase was one in which, as Professor Davies deposes, 'the grade awarded to a particular institution was not determined by a score against specific features' . . .In the result, the combination of openness in the run-up with the proscriptively oracular character of the critical decision makes the respondent's allocation of grades inapt, in our judgment, for the giving of reasons, notwithstanding the undoubted importance of the outcome to the institutions concerned.

... Purely academic judgments, in our view, will as a rule not be in the class of case, exemplified (though by no means exhausted) by Doody's case, where the nature and impact of the decision itself call for reasons as a routine aspect of procedural fairness. They will be in the *Cunningham* case class, where some trigger factor is required to show that, in the circumstances of the particular decision, fairness calls for reasons to be given.

Is there then such a trigger factor here? The second limb of Mr Pannick's submission is that the applicant institute has been confronted with a decision which, on the evidence, is inexplicable: the institute's excellence is widely acknowledged and attested. We lack precisely the expertise which would permit us to judge whether it is extraordinary or not. It may be a misfortune for the applicant that the court, which in Cunningham's case could readily evaluate the contrast between what the board awarded and what an industrial tribunal would have awarded, cannot begin to evaluate the comparative worth of research in clinical dentistry; but it is a fact of life. The applicant's previous grading, the volume and frequency of citation of its research and the high level of peer-reviewed outside funding which it has attracted, to all of which Mr Pannick points, may well demonstrate that the applicant has been unfortunate in the grading it has received, but such a misfortune can well occur within the four corners of a lawfully conducted evaluation.

Notes

1. TRS Allan has criticised this decision; he notes that 'the court rejected the council's stated objections to giving reasons'—that it would undermine the assessment exercise—as 'casuistic and disingenuous'.[38] The judge could not see why distinguished academics were unable to give reasons for their individual and collective judgments. The judge also found the procedure for assessment to be somewhat defective. Noting this, and the fact that 'the importance of the rating to the Institute's standing and morale could scarcely be exaggerated', Allan concludes that 'the court's refusal to require the council to explain its decision seems hard to justify'.[39]

2. Article 6 has started to have some impact on this area of judicial review also, as the following two cases reveal. Both concern appeals from the General Medical Council to the Privy Council on the grounds of failure to give reason for decisions in the circumstances of the particular case. There was no provision in the governing rules for reason-giving. In the first, a doctor had her registration to practice suspended indefinitely on grounds of ill-health, but 'No reason was given to support the conclusion that there was still a serious impairment of fitness due to the appellant's medical condition nor why an indefinite suspension was appropriate.'

Stefan v General Medical Council [1999] 1 WLR 1293, PC

...Their Lordships adopt the observation of Lord Donaldson in *ex p Cunningham* ... that:

> I do not accept that, just because Parliament has ruled that some tribunals should be required to give reasons for their decisions, it follows that the common law is unable to impose a similar requirement upon other tribunals, if justice so requires.

The trend of the law has been towards an increased recognition of the duty upon decision-makers of many kinds to give reasons. This trend is consistent with current developments

38   [1994] 52(2) CLJ 207, 209.

39   *Ibid.*

towards an increased openness in matters of government and administration. But the trend is proceeding on a case by case basis. . . and has not lost sight of the established position of the common law that there is no general duty, universally imposed on all decision-makers. But it is well established that there are exceptions where the giving of reasons will be required as a matter of fairness and openness. These may occur through the particular circumstances of a particular case. Or, as was recognised in *ex. p. Institute of Dental Surgery*. . .there may be classes of cases where the duty to give reasons may exist in all cases of that class. . . There is certainly a strong argument for the view that what were once seen as exceptions to a rule may now be becoming examples of the norm, and the cases where reasons are not required may be taking on the appearance of exceptions. But the general rule has not been departed from and their Lordships do not consider that the present case provides an appropriate opportunity to explore the possibility of such a departure. . . .

Turning to the particular circumstances of the present case their Lordships are per-suaded that there was a duty at common law upon the Committee in the present case to state the reasons for their decision. In the first place there is the consideration that the decision was one which was open to appeal under the statute. The appeal was only on a ground of law but, as has already been mentioned, the existence of such a provision points to the view that as matter of fairness in deciding whether there are grounds for appeal, and as matter of assistance in the presentation and determination of any appeal, the reasons for the decision should be given. Secondly, a consideration of the whole procedure and function of the Committee prompts the conclusion that the procedures which it follows and the function which it performs are akin to those of a court where the giving of reasons would be expected. . . .But the carrying out of a judicial function remains, as was recognised [in] . . . *ex p Cunningham*. . .[and] *ex p Murray* [1998] COD 134 at 136, 'a consideration in favour of a requirement to give reasons'.

Thirdly, the issue was one of considerable importance for the practitioner. . .the sus-pension causes Dr Stefan considerable hardship, not only in financial terms through her inability to work as a registered practitioner, but also in respect of her own natural desire to spend the remaining years of her professional career in some fulfilling and satisfying capacity in the medical service. The importance of the issue may not closely equate with the importance of personal liberty, but the matter is of very real significance in her own eyes and deserves to be respected. In *R v City of London Corporation, ex p Matson* (1995) 94 LGR 443 at 457 the effect on the reputation of the complainer of a rejection from office without the disclosure of reasons was one factor in requiring an explanation to be given. It is not obvious why it was considered that Dr Stefan's fitness for the work which she sought to do was not only impaired but seriously impaired.

Fourthly, Dr Stefan has repeatedly asked for an explanation of the Committee's view and for the diagnosis which they have reached of her condition. . . .The Committee stated that they were deeply concerned about her mental condition, but they do not explain precisely what the nature of that concern was, nor how it impaired her fitness to practise.

Fifthly, the only expert witness who had examined Dr Stefan and appeared to give evidence before the Committee, Dr Adams, stated in his written report that she was now well able to control the expression of her attitudes to race and gender, which had been matter of earlier concern, and that the passage of time had reduced the intensity of her distress and anger. He stated that her 'paranoid ideas have less emotional drive behind them and are less expressed' and that she 'is at present fit to practice on a limited basis as a Clinical Assistant in Ophthalmology or in the pharmaceutical industry'. In cross-examination and in response to questions from members of the Committee he modified his view, but still appeared to be saying that she was fit to practise albeit under stringent conditions of supervision. The risk appeared to be one of paranoid behaviour under stress. But it is not evident that he was retracting his view that her condition had improved and it is not clear why in the light of his evidence the Committee reached the decision which they did.

Sixthly, this was the first time that an indefinite suspension was decided upon. The departure from the periodic suspensions which had been imposed before was certainly a legitimate course under the amended legislation but, particularly in light of an apparently less serious condition, the selection of it called for an explanation. . .

In addition, however, to that narrow approach their Lordships are also persuaded that in all cases heard by the Health Committee there will be a common law obligation to give at least some brief statement of the reasons which form the basis for the decision. Plainly the Health Committee are bound to carry out their functions with due regard to fairness. The first two of the grounds already mentioned will apply to any case coming before the Committee: the provision of a right of appeal and the judicial character of the body point to an obligation to give reasons. Furthermore in every case the subject matter will be the future right of the doctor to work as a registered practitioner, and while there may be differences between individual cases as to the significance of that from the point of view of the particular practitioner, the general consideration will remain that the Committee are adjudicating upon the right of a person to work as a registered practitioner.

Notes

1. Clearly, the most significant passage in this judgment for general purposes is as follows:

   There is certainly a strong argument for the view that what were once seen as exceptions to a rule may now be becoming examples of the norm, and the cases where reasons are not required may be taking on the appearance of exceptions [at 1301].

2. For the interrelationship of Art 6 ECHR and the common law duty to give reasons, see further the Privy Council decision in *Gupta v GMC* [2002] 1 WLR 1691, which concerned a decision by the Professional Conduct Committee that the doctor had been guilty of serious professional misconduct. The Privy Council first found that Art 6 of the ECHR now required that 'either the Committee itself had to be an independent and impartial tribunal or, if not, that its processes had to be subject to control by an appellate body with full jurisdiction to reverse its decision' (at para 8). That appellate body was the Privy Council. The argument essentially was that any body which, like the GMC, determined a person's 'civil rights and obligations', if it could not itself satisfy the requirement of being 'an independent and impartial tribunal established by law' it had to be subject to review by a body which did, and was of full jurisdiction, that is, able to overturn the decisions of the subordinate body on questions of fact as well as law. To be able to exercise this function, the Privy Council needed to know the reasons for the Committee's decision and therefore it should be required to give them. This argument, as one of general principle, was not rejected; rather it was found that in the particular circumstances of the case, the manner in which the Committee made its findings sufficiently revealed its reasons for them for the Privy Council to carry out its review function, particularly bearing in mind the deference that it would inevitably extend to the findings of the Committee on the facts, the credibility of witnesses, etc.

3. What is important about the decision, then, is the seeming acceptance of the basic argument, outlined above. The appellant lost, simply because it was found that, on the facts, she knew enough of the reasons for the Committee's decision to be able to mount an effective challenge to it. But in cases where this was not so, the argument from Art 6 of the ECHR now amounts to a powerful one in the applicant's favour, but only of course where the applicant's 'civil rights and obligations' are engaged.

4. In the following case, the court provided a useful summary as to the principles governing the giving of reasons (these exclude the Art 6 argument).

R v Ministry of Defence ex parte Murray **[1998] COD 134 (extract)**

(a) The law does not at present recognise a general duty to give reasons (*Doody* at 564E).

(b) When a statute has conferred on any body the power to make decisions affecting individuals, the court will not only require the procedure prescribed by statute to be followed, but will readily imply so much and no more to be introduced by way of additional procedural standards as will ensure the attainment of fairness (*Cunningham*, *per* Donaldson LJ at 318, quoting *Lloyd v McMahon* [1987] 1 AC 625 at 702–703 and *Doody* at 564F).

(c) In the absence of a requirement to give reasons, the person seeking to argue that reasons should have been given must show that the procedure adopted of not giving reasons is unfair (*Doody* at 561 A).

(d) There is a perceptible trend towards an insistence on greater openness. . . or transparency in the making of administrative decisions (*Doody* at 561E).

(e) In deciding whether fairness requires a tribunal to give reasons regard will be had not only to the first instance hearing but also to the availability and the nature of any appellate remedy or remedy by way of judicial review:

  (i)   the absence of any right of appeal may be a factor in deciding that reasons should be given (*Cunningham* at 322j); and

  (ii) if it is important that there should be an effective means of detecting the kind of error [by way of judicial review] which would entitle the court to intervene, then the reasoning may have to be disclosed (*Doody* at 565H and also *Cunningham* at 323a).

(f) The fact that a tribunal is carrying out a judicial function is a consideration in favour of a requirement to give reasons (*Cunningham* at 323a) and particularly where personal liberty is concerned (*Institute of Dental Surgery* at 263A).

(g) If the giving of a decision without reasons is insufficient to achieve justice then reasons should be required (*Cunningham* at 323a) as also where the decision appears aberrant (*Institute of Dental Surgery* at 263a, cited with approval in *ex p Matson* (1996) 8 Admin LR 49 at 62).

(h) In favour of giving reasons are the following factors: the giving of reasons may among other things concentrate the decision-maker's mind on the right questions; demonstrate to the recipient that this is so; show the issues have been conscientiously addressed and how the result has been reached; or alternatively alert the recipient to a justiciable flaw in the process (*Institute of Dental Surgery* at 256H, cited with approval in *ex p Matson* at 71).

(i) In favour of not requiring reasons are the following factors: it may place an undue burden on decision-makers; demand an appearance of unanimity where there is diversity; call for articulation of sometimes inexpressible value judgments; and offer an invitation to the captious to comb the reasons for previously unsuspected grounds of challenge (*Institute of Dental Surgery* at 257A).

(j) Although fairness may favour a requirement for reasons, there may be considerations of public interest which would outweigh the advantages of requiring reasons (*Cunningham* at 323b).

(k) The giving of reasons will not be required if the procedures of the particular decision-maker would be frustrated by a requirement to give reasons, even short reasons (*Cunningham* at 323b).

Note

For further comments see A Le Sueur, 'Legal Duties to give Reasons' (1999) 52 CLP 150 and PP Craig, 'The Common Law, Reasons and Administrative Justice' [1994] 53 CLJ 282.

ILLEGALITY

As Lord Diplock explained it in the *GCHQ* case, 'By "illegality" as a ground for judicial review I mean that the decision-maker must understand correctly the law that regulates his decision-making power and must give effect to it' (at 410). The head of 'illegality' is perhaps the broadest head of judicial review; it may be summarised as including the following four types of illegality:

(a) Doing an act with no legal authority—what may be known as 'simple illegality'.

(b) *Misinterpreting* the law governing the decision.

(c) Failure to *retain* a discretion by: (i) improper delegation; or (ii) fettering of discretion through adoption of rigid policy.

(d) *Abuse* of discretion: (a) using a power for an improper purpose; (b) taking into account irrelevant considerations or failing to take account of relevant ones.

To these well established heads may now be added the violation of substantive legitimate expectations, dealt with below. Each of the above heads are now examined in turn.

'Simple' illegality

The first head, then, is doing an act for which the public body concerned has no legal authority. An old and clear case is *Attorney General v Fulham Corporation* [1921] Ch 440. In this case Fulham was empowered to provide facilities for local poor people to wash their own clothes. They set up a commercial washing service, whereby people could bring in their clothes and the Council would wash them for them. The Council said this would 'relieve Housewives to a great extent of this most laborious work'. The Attorney General brought an action against Fulham, and it was found that it had no power to set up commercial laundries. The following decision is another example.

Laker Airways v Dept of Trade [1977] QB 643, 704, CA

Laker Airways had been granted a licence by the Civil Aviation Authority (CAA) under statutory authority. The Secretary of State had power to issue guidance to the CAA as to its duties. As a result of a change in Government, and consequent change in policy, the Secretary of State issued 'guidance' to the CAA as he was entitled to; the guidance, how-ever, instructed the CAA to revoke Laker's licence. The result would have been to give the then state-owned British Airways a monopoly, in line with government policy. Laker sought judicial review of the decision.

Lord Denning MR: The first [question] is whether the Secretary of State was acting beyond his lawful powers when he gave the new policy guidance to the Civil Aviation Authority.

In determining this point, I have found much help from the well reasoned decisions of the Civil Aviation Authority, not only in 1972, when they granted the licence to Laker Airways, but also in 1975 when they refused to revoke it. It is plain that they applied most conscientiously and sensibly the four general objectives set out in s 3(1)(a), (b), (c) and (d) of the statute, as amplified and supplemented by the 1972 policy guidance. The new policy guidance of 1976 cuts right across those statutory objectives. It lays down a new policy altogether. Whereas the statutory objectives made it clear that the British Airways Board was not to have a monopoly, but that at least one other British airline should have an opportunity to participate, the new policy guidance says that the British Airways Board is to have a monopoly. No competition is to be allowed. And no other British airline is to be licensed unless British Airways had given its consent. This guidance was not a mere temporary measure. It was to last for a considerable period of years.

Those provisions disclose so complete a reversal of policy that to my mind the White Paper cannot be regarded as giving 'guidance' at all. In marching terms it does not say 'right incline' or 'left incline'. It says 'right about turn'. That is not guidance, but the reverse of it.

There is no doubt that the Secretary of State acted with the best of motives in formulating this new policy—and it may well have been the right policy—but I am afraid that he went about it in the wrong way. Seeing that the old policy had been laid down in an Act of Parliament, then, in order to reverse it, he should have introduced an amending Bill and got Parliament to sanction it. He was advised, apparently, that it was not necessary, and that it could be done by 'guidance'. That, I think, was a mistake. And Laker Airways are entitled to complain of it, at any rate in its impact on them. It was in this respect ultra vires and the judge was right so to declare.

Notes

1. In *R v Manchester City Council ex parte Stennett*, [2002] 4 All ER 124, the House of Lords found that a policy of charging those who needed after-care after discharge from mental hospitals was unlawful: s 117 of the Mental Health Act, which placed a duty upon local authorities to provide such care, did not give authority to charge for it.[40]

2. *R (On the application of S) v Secretary of State for the Home Department*[41] was a complex case

---

40   See A Scully [2003] 62(1) CLJ 1–3 for comment.

41   [2006] EWCA Civ 1157. The full case title follows the form above—*R (On the application of X) v Secretary of State for the Home Department* but also including M, A, K, D and is also known in the same form but using J, H and N.

concerning Afghan hijackers, which led to widespread media and political condemnation.[42] However, the actual basis for the decision was not generally understood by those commenting on it. The applicants had originally hijacked a plane and flown it to Britain where they had claimed asylum. This was unsuccessful, but it was found that they could not be returned to Afghanistan because of the risk of torture contrary to Art 3 ECHR. Under the Government's then current policy they were entitled to remain for an initial six month period. The Secretary of State then however changed his own policy so that he could instead give them a grant of only temporary admission, as allowed for under Sched 2, para 16 of the Immigration Act 1971 for those who might be required to submit to further examination. It was held that his decision was *ultra vires*, since it was not in fact contemplated that any such further examination would take place. The Court of Appeal found that someone who successfully maintained that their removal would constitute a violation of their Convention rights should be entitled to leave to remain for however limited a period. That status could not be taken away from them by the Secretary of State conferring on them a new status that was not contemplated by the statutory scheme he relied on. In other words, the case was one of fairly simple illegality: because public opinion found it distasteful that hijackers could get leave to remain because of the fear of torture if they were returned, the Secretary of State had sought to find a way to deny them this by changing his own policy in a way that was not compatible with the statute. The decision could also be seen in terms of violation of substantive legitimate expectations—see below, p 850–870.

In a number of cases prior to the Human Rights Act 1998, the courts, in an attempt to provide protection for certain basic rights, including access to a court, and freedom of expression, were prepared to strike down delegated legislation that interfered with such rights on this basis of simple illegality. The argument used was that abrogation of such rights required specific authorisation in the enabling legislation, and that, absent such authorisation, the delegated legislation, in interfering with basic rights, was *ultra vires*. In other words, where basic rights were at stake, the legal authorisation required for acts that interfered with them had to be precise and specific. As Lord Hoffman put it in *ex parte Simms* [2000] 2 AC 115, 131, 'fundamental rights cannot be overridden by general or ambiguous words'. See, for example, *R v Lord Chancellor ex parte Witham* [1997] 2 All ER 799, an extract from which appears in Chapter 4, at 178.

3. *In ex parte Pierson* [1998] AC 539, 575, Lord Browne-Wilkinson summarised the principle thus:

> A power conferred by Parliament in general terms is not to be taken to authorise the doing of acts by the donee of the power which adversely affect the legal rights of the citizen or the basic principles on which the law of the United Kingdom is based unless the statute conferring the power makes it clear that such was the intention of Parliament.

4. Many such cases would now be decided under the HRA. But in *Daly*,[43] Lord Cooke remarked:

> . . .while this case has arisen in a jurisdiction where the European Convention for the Protection of Human Rights and Fundamental Freedoms applies, and while the case is one in which the Convention and the common law produce the same result,

---

42 See 'Judges overrule Reid in Afghan hijack case', *Guardian*, 4 August 2006; www.guardian.co.uk/uk/2006/aug/04/immigration.immigrationpolicy. The Shadow Home Secretary, David Davis, called the decision 'crazy', while a spokesman for the previous Home Secretary David Blunkett had called a previous decision in the saga 'mind-boggling' and the Prime Minister himself dubbed it 'an abuse of common sense'.

43 *R v Secretary of State for the Home Department ex parte Daly* [2001] 2 AC 532, at para 30.

it is of great importance, in my opinion, that the common law by itself is being recognised as a sufficient source of the fundamental right to confidential communication with a legal adviser for the purpose of obtaining legal advice. Thus the decision may prove to be in point in common law jurisdictions not affected by the Convention. Rights similar to those in the Convention are of course to be found in constitutional documents and other formal affirmations of rights elsewhere. The truth is, I think, that some rights are inherent and fundamental to democratic civilised society. Conventions, constitutions, bills of rights and the like respond by recognising rather than creating them.

See further Chapter 17, pp 1003–1012.

Error of law: are *all* errors of law reviewable?

This principle is elementary: a public authority must correctly construe the legal authority under which it acts. However, an important preliminary question that has arisen is whether *any* error of law made by the decision maker will result in it being held to have exceeded its jurisdiction and thus to have acted unlawfully. The issue is that there may be mistakes that a body is entitled to make in coming to a decision—mistakes which do not render its decision unlawful. As we shall see, if the decision-making body—a tribunal—makes a 'mistake' in the sense that it gives more weight to a particular consideration than the court would have, or if it makes a mistake as to whether a fact is proven or not, the courts will view such mistakes as being within the tribunal's jurisdiction. But are mistakes as to the law which governs a tribunal ever of this type? Or do all errors of law made by a tribunal mean that it has exceeded its rightful jurisdiction? The leading case in this area follows.

Anisminic Ltd v Foreign Compensation Commissioners **[1969] AC 147, 171–75**

Anisminic Ltd had had certain of its property sequestered by the Egyptian Government, and had later sold it to TEDO, an Egyptian organisation, for considerably less than its actual value. Anisminic applied for compensation to the Foreign Compensation Commission, which had the duty, under Art 4 of the Foreign Compensation etc Order 1962, of distributing compensation to businesses such as Anisminic which had suffered loss by virtue of the confiscation of their property. Article 4 stated that the Commission was to treat a claim as good if they were satisfied of the following:

(a) the applicant was the person referred to in the relevant part of Annex E of the Order as 'the owner of the property or the successor in title of such a person'; and
(b) the person referred to in that part of Annex E 'and any person who became successor in title of such person. . .were British Nationals'.

The Commission's initial finding was that Anisminic Ltd was not entitled to compensation because TEDO (its successor in title) was not a British national.

Lord Reid: It has sometimes been said that it is only where a tribunal acts without jurisdiction that its decision is a nullity. But in such cases the word 'jurisdiction' has been used in a very wide sense, and I have come to the conclusion that it is better not to use the term except in the narrow and original sense of the tribunal being entitled to enter on the inquiry in question. But there are many cases where, although the tribunal had jurisdiction to enter on the inquiry, it has done or failed to do something in the course of the inquiry which is of such a nature that its decision is a nullity. It may have given its decision in bad faith. It may have made a decision which it had no power to make. It may have failed in the course of the inquiry to comply with the requirements of natural justice. It may in perfect good faith have misconstrued the provisions giving it power to act so that it failed to deal with the question remitted to it and decided some question which was not remitted to it. It may have refused to take into account something which it was required to take into account. Or it may have based its decision on some matter which, under the provisions setting it up, it had no right to take into account. I do not intend this list to be exhaustive. But if it decides a question remitted to it for decision without committing any of these errors it is as much entitled to decide that question wrongly as it is to decide it rightly.

I can now turn to the provisions of the Order under which the commission acted, and to the way in which the commission reached their decision. The effect of the Order was to confer legal rights on persons who might previously have hoped or expected that in allocating any sums available discretion would be exercised in their favour.

The main difficulty in this case springs from the fact that the draftsman did not state separately what conditions have to be satisfied (1) where the applicant is the original owner and (2) where the applicant claims as the successor in title of the original owner. It is clear that where the applicant is the original owner he must prove that he was a British national on the dates stated. And it is equally clear that where the applicant claims as being the original owner's successor in title he must prove that both he and the original owner were British nationals on those dates, subject to later provisions in the article about persons who had died or had been born within the relevant period. What is left in obscurity is whether the provisions with regard to successors in title have any application at all in cases where the applicant is himself the original owner. If this provision had been split up as it should have been, and the conditions to be satisfied where the original owner is the applicant had been set out, there could have been no such obscurity.

This is the crucial question in this case. It appears from the commission's reasons that they construed this provision as requiring them to inquire, when the applicant is himself the original owner, whether he had a successor in title. So they made that inquiry in this case and held that TEDO was the applicant's successor in title. As TEDO was not a British national they rejected the appellants' claim. But if, on a true construction of the Order, a claimant who is an original owner does not have to prove anything about successors in title, then the commission made an inquiry which the Order did not empower them to make, and they based their decision on a matter which they had no right to take into account. If one uses the word 'jurisdiction' in its wider sense, they went beyond their jurisdiction in considering this matter. It was argued that the whole matter of construing the Order was something remitted to the commission for their decision. I cannot accept that argument. I find nothing in the Order to support it. The Order requires the commission to consider whether they are satisfied with regard to the prescribed matters. That is all they have to do. It cannot be for the commission to determine the limits of its powers. Of course if one party submits to a tribunal that its powers are wider than in fact they are, then the tribunal must deal with that submission. But if they reach a wrong conclusion as to the width of their powers, the court must be able to correct that—not because the tribunal has made an error of law, but because as a result of making an error of law they have dealt with and based their decision on a matter with which, on a true construction of their powers, they had no right to deal. If they base their decision on some matter which is not prescribed for their adjudication, they are doing something which they have no right to do and, if the view which I expressed earlier is right, their decision is a nullity. So the question is whether on a true construction of the Order the applicants did or did not have to prove anything with regard to successors in title. If the commission were entitled to enter on the inquiry whether the applicants had a successor in title, then their decision as to whether TEDO was their successor in title would I think be unassailable whether it was right or wrong: it would be a decision on a matter remitted to them for their decision. The question I have to consider is not whether they made a wrong decision but whether they inquired into and decided a matter which they had no right to consider.

[His Lordship then went on to consider whether the FCC had in fact misconstrued the Order. He found that it had, by inquiring whether TEDO was a British-owned company, something which had no relevance in this case. He concluded:] I would therefore hold that the words 'and any person who became successor in title to such person' in art 4(1)(b)(ii) have no application to a case where the applicant is the original owner. It follows that the commission rejected the appellants' claim on a ground which they had no right to take into account and that their decision was a nullity. I would allow this appeal.

Notes

1. While a number of cases subsequent to *Anisminic* appeared to cast doubt on the notion that every error of law takes a body outside its jurisdiction, two decisions of the House of Lords, *R v Lord President of the Privy Council ex parte Page* [1993] 1 All ER 97, and *Boddington v British Transport Police* [1999] 2 AC 143 confirmed that all errors of law will be *prima facie* reviewable. As Lord Browne-Wilkinson said, in *Page,* it was to be assumed that 'Parliament had only conferred the decision-making power on the basis that it was to be exercised on the correct legal basis: a misdirection in law in making the decision therefore rendered the decision *ultra vires*' (at 108).

2. The case also set out a number of exceptions to this general rule. These are, first, where the error of law is not relevant to the decision challenged; second, where the decision was made by an inferior court. Here, it was said that if there is legislation providing that the decision of such a court is final, then it will be allowed to err within its jurisdiction[44] though it is unclear whether this distinction survives and what the justification would be—why differentiate courts and tribunals? The third exception is specialised areas, where jurisdiction has been handed to another body, such as ecclesiastical courts, or University Visitors, as in *Page* itself.[45]

3. A further question arises: can the body under review come to a different decision on what the law requires from what the court would have thought without having been found to have 'erred' and so to have acted unlawfully? In many cases, the answer to what the law requires will be one on which reasonable people could disagree. Will the court invariably substitute its opinion of what the law is or what it demands for the opinion of the tribunal? The answer is that the courts appear to draw a distinction between two things: (a) what is the correct interpretation of the law and (b) what is the 'right answer' when applying that legal test to the facts of the situation? It appears that courts will invariably regard a failure to reach what they regard as the correct conclusion in relation to (a) as tainting a decision with illegality. However, in relation to (b), where the legal test to be applied is inherently somewhat open-ended, the courts may not always quash the body's decision if they would have reached a different conclusion. Instead, it may find that as long as the conclusion

---

44   *Re Racal Communications Ltd* [1981] AC 374.

45   But see now statutory reform in this area—Chapter 14, p 758, note 69.

reached is one that is within the range of conclusions open to a reasonable decision maker apply-ing the law in question, it can stand: *Edwards v Bairstow* [1956] AC 14.

4. A classic example is *R v Monopolies and Mergers Commission ex parte South Yorkshire Transport Ltd* [1993] 1 All ER 289. Here, the Home Secretary could refer a proposed merger to the Commission if the merger would mean that the supply of over 25 per cent of the service in question 'in a substantial part of the United Kingdom' would be in the hands of only one person. The question at issue was whether the test of 'substantial part of the UK' was satisfied. The House of Lords said that it was the court's role to decide what 'substantial' meant in the context of that statute. But then having defined it, if the meaning was so imprecise that different decision-makers, applying it to the facts in front of them, might reasonably come to different conclusions, only if the conclusion reached was not within that range of reasonable responses would the court intervene. On the facts, the Home Secretary had not come to a conclusion that was aberrant. The correctness of this approach was recently reaffirmed by the House of Lords in *R v Ministry of Defence ex parte Walker* [2000] 1WLR 806.

Can decisions be reviewed for errors of fact?

The *South Yorkshire Transport* case nicely illustrates the difficulty of deciding what amounts to a question of fact, as opposed to law. Clearly, certain questions, such as whether a contract exists, will require consideration of legal questions. However, it is often unclear where, for example, a word such as 'dwelling house' or 'substantial proportion' appears in a statute, whether it should be interpreted as a question of law or fact. One approach is to ask whether the word in the statute in question was intended to be used in its ordinary, English sense or whether it is to be understood in some technical, artificial sense. Which category it falls into is a question of law for the courts. If it is held to be the former, then it is a question of fact. An example was the word 'offensive' in public order legislation.[46] Up until recently, as Jones noted, 'there [were] very few English cases where mistake of fact has been accepted as a ground for judicial review, and an even smaller number which appear to have been decided on this ground alone'.[47] Traditionally, the limited instances in which mistake of fact could give rise to unlawfulness were as follows:

- *Jurisdictional fact.* A fact will be considered jurisdictional if the decision maker is only entitled to enter upon his enquiry if the particular fact exists. In such a case, the court must itself decide whether the fact existed.[48] Wade gives the example of a tribunal having power to reduce the rent of 'a dwelling house'. If it mistakenly finds a property to be a dwelling house when in fact it is business property, it will have acted *ultra vires*, because the objective conditions that are required to be satisfied before it can enter in upon its enquiry—the property being a dwelling house—are not present.[49]
- *No evidence justifying a decision.* Where a decision rests upon a factual basis, it may be seen as an error of law, if there is no evidence for the facts found by the decision maker.[50] In *Coleen*

---

46 See *Brutus v Cozens* [1973] AC 854.

47 T Jones, 'Mistake of Fact in Administration' [1990] PL 507.

48 *White and* Coffins *v Minister of Health* [1939] 2 KB 838.

49 HWR Wade and C Forsyth, *Administrative Law* (1994), p 286.

50 See, e.g. *R v Secretary of State for Education ex parte Tameside* [1977] AC 1014, though there has been some doubt as to the justiciability of the point.

Properties v Minister of Housing and Local Government [1971] 1 WLR 433, a Minister had disagreed with an inspector's recommendation that it was not reasonably necessary to purchase a given property in order to redevelop an area but without citing any evidence to justify his disagreement with him. Thus, making a decision with no, or insufficient, evidence may be an error of law.

- *Mistake of fact equating to an irrelevant consideration.* As Jones notes,[51] 'a mistake of fact by an administrative decision-maker [may] fall to be regarded as the taking into account of an irrelevant consideration', as in *Simplex GE (Holdings) Ltd v Secretary of State for the Environment and the City of St Albans District Council* [1988] COD 160, a planning case in which a Minister mistakenly thought that a study by a planning inspector had been taken into account by a Council whose decision he had heard an appeal against. 'The Court of Appeal [found] that the mistake had been a significant factor in the minister's decision. It was sufficient for the appellant to show, as had been done in this case, that the decision might have been different had the irrelevant consideration not been taken into account.'

Aside from these areas, the traditional rule has been that assessment of matters of fact is not for the court to second-guess. As Lord Brightman remarked in *Puhlhofer v Hillingdon LBO* [1986] AC 484:

> Parliament intended the Local Authority to be the judge of fact. . . Where the existence or non-existence of fact is left to the judgement and discretion of a public body and that fact involves a broad spectrum ranging from the obvious to the debatable to the just conceivable, it is the duty of the court to leave the decision of that fact to the [Local Authority] save where it is obvious that the public body, consciously or unconsciously, is acting perversely.

In the recent decision of *R v Criminal Injuries Compensation Board ex parte A* [1999] 2 AC 330, 344–45, four members of the House of Lords were prepared to agree with Lord Slynn's *obiter* finding that there could be review of the Board's decision on a matter of fact, namely inaccurate evidence given to it by a policewoman about the findings of a medical examination aimed at ascertaining whether A had in fact suffered the injuries (rape and buggery) that she claimed. The policewoman's testimony was to the effect that the examination suggested that A's claims were probably false, whereas the report of that examination—not seen by the Board—was in fact consistent with the injuries A claimed to have suffered. This evidence was obviously of critical importance to A's claim and the Board had clearly proceeded on the basis of a mistake as to an established fact (the actual findings of the medical examination). The House of Lords in fact decided the case on the alternative basis of a breach of the rules of natural justice, so the comments made were *obiter* only. However, they are readily explicable: this was not a case where forming a view as to the 'facts' is in reality an exercise in expert, or political opinion, as, say in *Rehman* (below), with which the court would, rightly be reluctant to interfere. There was no doubt but that the evidence given to the Board was inaccurate. As such, finding an error of law on the basis of this mistake of fact could readily be analysed under traditional grounds of judicial review, as either having regard to an irrelevant matter—the inaccurate evidence given to the Board— or as failing to have regard to a relevant matter—the actual findings of the medical evidence not considered by the Board.

In cases that concern a grave threat to the applicant's liberty, courts have traditionally looked much more closely to see whether the decision-maker could have reasonably decided as he or she did on the

---

51   T Jones, 'Mistake of Fact in Administration' [1990] PL 507, 512

evidence before him. In *R v Secretary of State for the Home Department ex parte Khawaja* [1984] AC 74, immigration authorities had power to arrest and detain as a preliminary step to deporting a person thought to be an illegal immigrant. A preliminary question raised was whether the term 'illegal immigrant' could cover a person who had obtained leave to enter by deception or fraud. It was held that it could. The next question was what standard of proof the immigration officer needed to satisfy. The Home Department contended it was enough that there were some grounds on which he could reasonably have made the decision. The court found, however, that this was inadequate in the circumstances: the immigration officer's belief had to be supported by evidence which established the matter to a high probability. The court would determine whether that standard was met. In *R v Home Secretary ex parte Budgaycay* [1986] AC 484, one of the issues was whether a person deported would be in danger of life or limb; the court found that it would decide for itself whether certain factual evidence that the applicant would be in such danger had been given sufficient weight by the Home Secretary. A recent instance of this approach is provided by the Court of Appeal decision in *Besnik Gashi* [1999] INLR 276.

The *Rehman* decision by the House of Lords seemed to row back on this approach somewhat, by emphasising that findings of fact often involve an exercise of judgment, and that the courts should be slow to interfere with such judgments made by the original decision maker. The House of Lords was considering an appeal from the Special Immigration Appeals Tribunal (SIAC) which had found, *inter alia*, that the Home Secretary had not satisfied it, to 'to a high civil balance of probabilities', that the deportation of the applicant was justified on public good grounds because he had engaged in conduct that endangered the national security of the UK and, unless deported, was likely to continue to do so. SIAC, under the Special Immigration Appeals Commission Act 1997, was given power to review the findings of the Secretary of State on points of law, on matters of fact and where it considered that his discretion should have been exercised differently (see s 4 of the 1997 Act).

R v Secretary of State for the Home Department ex parte Rehman
[2001] 3 WLR 877 (extracts)

Lord Hoffman. . .

48. [The Court of Appeal found that] it was wrong to treat the Home Secretary's reasons as counts in an indictment and to ask whether each had been established to an appropriate standard of proof. The question was not simply what the appellant had done but whether the Home Secretary was entitled to consider, on the basis of the case against him as a whole, that his presence in the United Kingdom was a danger to national security. When one is concerned simply with a fact-finding exercise concerning past conduct such as might be undertaken by a jury, the notion of a standard of proof is appropriate. But the Home Secretary and the Commission do not only have to form a view about what the appellant has been doing. The final decision is evaluative, looking at the evidence as a whole, and predictive, looking to future danger. As Lord Woolf MR said, at p 1254, para 44:

> [T]he cumulative effect may establish that the individual is to be treated as a danger, although it cannot be proved to a high degree of probability that he has performed any individual act which would justify this conclusion.

My Lords, I will say at once that I think that on each of these points the Court of Appeal were right. In my opinion the fundamental flaw in the reasoning of the Commission was that although they correctly said that section 4(1) gave them full jurisdiction to decide questions of fact and law, they did not make sufficient allowance for certain inherent limitations-. . .,first. . . . however broad the jurisdiction of a court or tribunal, whether at first instance or on appeal, it is exercising a judicial function and the exercise of that function must recognise the constitutional boundaries between judicial, executive and legislative power. Secondly, the[re are] limitations on the appellate process [which].arise from the need, in matters of judgment and evaluation of evidence, to show proper deference to the primary decision-maker.

[Lord Hoffman then asked what the proper role of SIAC was, and in relation to matters of fact, said:]

> . . . the factual basis for the executive's opinion that deportation would be in the interests of national security must be established by evidence. It is therefore open to SIAC to say that there was no factual basis for the Home Secretary's opinion that Mr Rehman was actively supporting terrorism in Kashmir.

Notes

1. This decision nicely illustrates how even a statutory scheme, which very clearly gives a judicial body—SIAC—the power to review findings of fact made by the executive, can be read down so as to limit and curtail that power to one of merely establishing an evidentiary basis for the Secretary of State's finding of fact. In like manner, the House of Lords also read down SIAC's power in the statute to strike down the Secretary of State's finding on the basis that it would have exercised the discretion differently into an ability only to 'reject the Home Secretary's opinion on the ground that it was one which no reasonable minister advising the Crown could in the circumstances reasonably have held' (*per* Lord Hoffman, para 52).

2. Since then, however, the courts have progressed the notion of review for error of fact substantially. In *E v Secretary of State for the Home Department* [2004] QB 1044, the Court of Appeal established that it was no longer necessary to characterise the relevant error as a failure to have regard to relevant considerations. Rather, review for error of fact was now a separate ground for review based on unfairness; Carnwath LJ held that to succeed on this ground, a claimant must show:

    (i)   a mistake as to a existing fact (including a mistake as the availability of evidence);
    (ii) the fact or evidence must be uncontentious and objectively verifiable;
    (iii) the claimant/the claimant's lawyers must not have been responsible for the mistake; and
    (iv) the mistake must have played a material part in the tribunal's reasoning.[52]

3. It should be noted further that where statute gives an advisory, fact-finding body, such as an Ombudsman a clear investigative role, the scope for a Minister to reject the factual findings of such a body may be quite limited—see below, p 879.

4. The following commentary explains the crucial differences between different kinds of factual errors that a decision-maker may make and the consequences for the appropriate level of review of those errors by a court.

---

52   Nathalie Lieven QC, 'Judicial Review: Trends and Forecasts' [2009] JR 9. He notes that the *E* decision was further considered by the Court of Appeal in *Kaydanyuk v Secretary of State for the Home Department* [2006] EWCA Civ 368 and *Shaheen v Secretary of State for the Home Department* [2005] EWCA Civ 1294; [2006] Imm AR 57.

R Williams, *'When is an error not an error? Reform of jurisdictional review of error of law and fact'* [2007] Public Law 973, 978–99, 804–08

The key point about all such cases is that once it is accepted that there is an objectively right answer to such a question. . .concerns. . .about the court substituting its judgment for that of the decision-maker [vanish], because the correctness of the answer is independent of the entity pointing it out. If a decision-maker wrongly assesses an individual's age and fails to make a grant, it does not much matter who points that mistake out to it; the mistake is undeniable and must be corrected. . .

However, where there is no objectively right answer the court must accept that it is not detecting errors at all, rather it is reviewing the exercise of the initial decision-maker's discretion. This process will indeed require the court to use rationality review, just as it does when it is reviewing the substantive result produced by the decision-maker through the exercise of its discretion. Unlike the 'right answers' category, where the answer itself justifies the intervention, review of discretionary judgment requires the court to justify its control and to establish the precise level of that intervention in the usual way. At this stage various factors can be taken into account. Obviously, for example, if Parliament has clearly located the power to define a statutory term with one body rather than another, that will be the most important consideration, but even where this has not been done explicitly the courts should consider and articulate openly their own institutional competence relative to that of the original decision-maker.

For example, if. . .it is thought particularly important to have a consistent and thus centrally-determined definition of a particular statutory term, this will indicate that responsibility for defining that term should lie with the courts, rather than with several different original decision-makers. In other cases, the greater scientific, economic or other expertise of the original decision-maker will be such that the courts are relatively less well placed to define the statutory term. Thus in some cases the decision-maker's assessment of what is required to satisfy a jurisdictional condition will be allowed to stand unless that assessment is wholly irrational, while in other cases the court might intervene even in the absence of such outright irrationality. The point is that in each case the reviewing court accepts that it is engaging in rationality review and thus that it must openly consider and articulate these kinds of concerns, rather than hiding them behind an ex post facto label. Once a court has established in a particular case that it is entitled to intervene it will not, strictly speaking, be doing so on the basis that the original decision-maker was wrong, or in error, nor on the basis that the court's definition is objectively correct in the sense of being scientifically measurable, even though the court may well be tempted to frame its judgment in these terms. Rather the court will have intervened because, as between the competing definitions offered by the initial decision-maker and the court there are more factors (such as consistency, expertise etc.) in favour of the court's definition. Conversely when it decides not to intervene, this does not render the original decision inherently 'right' in an objectively or scientifically verifiable way, it is simply that the court feels less well placed to offer a definition than was the original decision-maker. . . .

[Williams goes to suggest a blueprint for how errors of law and fact should be dealt with in future. She suggests first getting rid of the difficult term 'jurisdictional'; instead '*all* errors would be prima facie reviewable' and goes on]:

2. Second, we should also dispense with the distinction between issues of fact and issues of law, i.e. between the meaning of a term in the abstract and its application or not to

a particular set of facts. Any such distinction is impossible to draw in practice. . . and arguably all such issues are in any case reviewable since *E*.

3. Thus instead of using the earlier, problematic terminology we should distinguish between three categories of case:

3. (a) Where the definition of a statutory term has one correct meaning or application in fact and the decision-maker fails to reach that meaning or application, the court can intervene automatically and substitute its judgment for that of the decision-maker (for example where a statute refers to engines with a particular capacity). . .we may prefer to call this category something like 'review of objectively verifiable errors in the assessment of jurisdiction'.

3. (b) Where the definition or application of a statutory term contains an element of discretion, either in the present (such as 'illegal entrant' in *Khawaja*), or because it requires a prediction of future events (as in *E* itself), the court should interfere with the original decision only where the decision-maker's conclusion on that meaning or application was f)irrational or aberrant. . .

3. (c) The third category of cases are those in which the focus is not on the definition of a jurisdictional condition at all, but rather on the decision-maker's treatment of the evidence. The point to note about this category is that it need not relate solely to jurisdictional matters (i.e. to the definition or application of terms such as 'illegal immigrant' or 'engine capacity'). It is equally possible for decision-makers to deal incorrectly with evidence in relation to other matters, such as the relevant considerations to be taken into account at the substantive stage of their decision. This suggests that it may well be desirable to separate such evidential matters from those concerning jurisdictional issues per se. Within this third category three further subdivisions can then be made.

3. (c) (i) The first concerns cases such as *Ex p. A* [above] in which the Board simply failed to consider a piece of evidence. Conversely, the decision-maker may have considered a piece of evidence from the wrong case. [She instances *R (on the application of Haile) v Immigration Appeal Tribunal* [2001] EWCA Civ 663 and *R (on the application of Ahmed (Naeem)) v Secretary of State for the Home Department* [2004] EWCA Civ 552].

3. (c) (ii) The second concerns cases in which there seems to be no evidence at all to support the decision-maker's conclusion on a particular issue [She instances *Reid v Secretary of State for Scotland* [1999] 2 AC 512.]

3. (c) (iii) Cases in which there is evidence to support one conclusion, but the decision-maker has reached the opposite conclusion. . .[In this category] the standard of review seems fairly weak; the courts must only see whether the evidence 'tends' to show what the decision-maker thinks it does. The evidence need not be *consistent* with the decision reached, it apparently needs only to avoid being 'self-contradictory'. [This is because] if the complaint is that this evidence was not sufficient, or indeed that the reviewing court would have come to a different conclusion on the basis of it, then we have re-entered the sphere of review of discretion.

Notes

1. The above commentary usefully brings out the central point that mistakes of fact by a decision maker may amount to very different kinds of error, requiring different standards of review by a court. The two crucial distinctions are: first whether the error is objectively manifest (thinking an

asylum seeker is from one country when in fact she is from another), or whether it is in reality an alleged error of judgment (considering a person to be a risk to national security when someone else might well draw a different conclusion). The second is whether the error goes to a jurisdictional matter or is simply one relating to a number of facts that must be considered.[53]

2. The influence of Art 6 ECHR has been noted in a number of places in this chapter. It has directly affected the standard of review applied in indirect bias cases (above). However, it may start to have a more general impact upon the intensity of judicial review generally. Many decisions made by local authorities, Ministers or other non-judicial bodies may affect a person's 'civil rights and obligations' and so require a 'fair hearing by an independent and impartial tribunal' under Art 6(1). This does not mean that all such decisions must be taken by courts or tribunals instead (plainly an impossible requirement) but rather, as the House of Lords has found (following Strasbourg) that Art 6 is satisfied even where the original decision-maker is not an independent and impartial tribunal provided that the decision maker is subject to review by a court, which was of 'full jurisdiction', that is, 'full jurisdiction to deal with the case *as the nature of the decision requires*'.[54] As the courts are starting to realise, this may require a greater willingness to correct errors of fact as well as law than is usual in judicial review. Further discussion of what judicial review requires to comply with Art 6 is beyond the scope of this work, but for full consideration see *Begum (ibid) R (Alconbury Developments Ltd) v Secretary of State for the Environment, Transport and the Regions* [2001] 2 WLR 1389 and *R (Hammond) v Home Secretary* [2005] 3 WLR 1229 esp. at [27], *per* Lord Hoffman. Most recently *Tsfayo v United Kingdom* (No. 60860/00) 14 November 2006 appears to have re-opened this issue, suggesting again the English judicial review may not provide adequate protection for Art 6. For full analysis see J Howell QC, 'Alconbury Crumbles' [2007] JR 9.

Abuse of discretion: improper purposes

In this area, as in that of irrelevant considerations, the tests applied by the courts place under scrutiny the reasoning process used by the public body under challenge. What then is the rationale for holding that the taking into account of irrelevant considerations, or acting for a purpose not authorised by the governing statute, renders a decision unlawful? The case of *R v Somerset County Council ex parte Fewings* [1995] 1 All ER 513, QB; [1995] 3 All ER 20, CA is particularly instructive. It concerned the decision of Somerset County Council to ban stag hunting on its land and the challenge thereto. The Councillors, in making their decision, appeared to have been motivated primarily by the view that stag hunting was morally repellent; in acting for such a reason, they seemed to have assumed that they could simply act on their moral principles as if they were private citizens. The courts reminded them that as public bodies they were required to justify their acts by reference to some positive law which gave them power to do what they did. That power, the judge pointed out, would have been granted for some purpose. Parliament does not simply hand out powers which allow authorities to act because they feel like it or to serve whatever private purposes they happen to have in mind. It is a fundamental axiom of public law that power is always granted for a purpose; this is because power is granted to

---

53   Recently in *R (On the application of Lim) v Secretary of State for the Home Department* [2007] EWCA Civ 773, a Malaysian national was to be removed from the UK on the ground of breach of his conditions of his residence. Whether he had indeed breached those conditions was found to be a question of precedent fact; however it was found that judicial review was not the appropriate means of challenging it, since the statutory mechanisms for challenging such decisions set out in s 82 of the Nationality, Immigration and Asylum Act 2002 were specifically designed to deal with such appeals. See further on review of fact: *IBA Health Ltd v Office of Fair Trading* [2004] 4 All ER 1103; *R (MH) v Bedfordshire County Council* [2007] EWHC 2435 (Admin), [2008] ELR 191 and *R (Ali) v Secretary of State for the Home Department* [2007] EWHC 1983 (Admin).

54   *Per* Lord Bingham in *Runa Begum v Tower Hamlets London Borough Council* [2003] 2 WLR 388, at [5].

public authorities to serve the public interest, not to please themselves with. That basic point—the duty to serve the public interest—will rule out the use of powers for certain purposes which do not serve the particular public interests that the power in question was granted to serve. One of the basic challenges to a discretionary decision therefore is that the power was used for the wrong purpose.

To ascertain whether a public body has acted for an improper purpose, there generally must be some way of establishing authoritatively what would have been a proper purpose, though this may not always be necessary in cases of blatant misuses of power: the courts may be able to say, in effect, whatever the purpose of the statute may have been, it cannot have been to allow you to do what you did. However, in most cases, the courts need to ascertain the purpose of the statute which gave the power, if only in a broad way. These can be divided into cases where the statute states the purpose of the power granted and those where it does not. The former cases are fairly straightforward: thus, for example, in *Sydney Municipal Council v Campbell* [1925] AC 338 a statute allowed the Council to purchase land for the specific purposes of 'carrying out improvements in or remodelling any protection of the city'. It was clear that the Council had purchased the particular piece of land in question not for these purposes but simply in order to make money by benefiting from an increase in land values.

However, in most cases, there will be no clear statement of statutory purpose; but the principle that where an authority is endowed with power for one purpose, it must not use it for another applies even where the statute sets out no apparent purpose. In such cases it will be for the courts to construe such a purpose from considering the statute as a whole. They may, since *Pepper v Hart* [1993] AC 593, have regard, in certain circumstances, to what was said by the sponsor of the Bill (usually the Government Minister responsible) in debate in Parliament. However, *R v Secretary of State for the Environment, Transport and the Regions ex parte Spath Holme Limited* [2001] 2 AC 349 subsequently emphasised that resort to *Hansard* must be strictly justified by reference to the criteria laid down in that decision. It is clear, following that decision, that resort to *Hansard* by the courts will be relatively rare, and, as their Lordships stressed, only for the purpose of construing ambiguous provisions, *not* for determining the overall policy behind such provisions. However, even without such assistance, as the following case illustrates, the courts are prepared to infer a purpose from the general scheme of the legislation and then hold a decision *ultra vires* for failing to conform with that purpose.

Padfield v Minister of Agriculture, Fisheries and Food [1968] AC 977, 1029–32, 1034

Section 19 of the Agricultural Marketing Act 1958 provided that if persons complained to the Secretary of State about relevant matters, he could refer the complaints to a Committee of Investigation. The plaintiffs, whose complaint had not been so referred, sought judicial review of the decision not to refer their complaint.

Lord Reid: The question at issue in this appeal is the nature and extent of the minister's duty under s 19(3)(b) of the Act of 1958 in deciding whether to refer to the committee of investigation a complaint as to the operation of any scheme made by persons adversely affected by the scheme. The respondent contends that his only duty is to consider a complaint fairly and that he is given an unfettered discretion with regard to every complaint either to refer it or not to refer it to the committee as he may think fit. The appellants contend that it is his duty to refer every genuine and substantial complaint, or alternatively that his discretion is not unfettered and that in this case he failed to exercise his discretion according to law because his refusal was caused or influenced by his having misdirected himself in law or by his having taken into account extraneous or irrelevant considerations.

In my view, the appellants' first contention goes too far. There are a number of reasons which would justify the minister in refusing to refer a complaint. For example, he might consider it more suitable for arbitration, or he might consider that in an earlier case the committee of investigation had already rejected a substantially similar complaint, or he might think the complaint to be frivolous or vexatious. So he must have at least some measure of discretion. But is it unfettered?

It is implicit in the argument for the minister that there are only two possible interpretations of this provision—either he must refer every complaint or he has an unfettered discretion to refuse to refer in any case. I do not think that is right. Parliament must have conferred the discretion with the intention that it should be used to promote the policy and objects of the Act; the policy and objects of the Act must be determined by construing the Act as a whole and construction is always a matter of law for the court. In a matter of this kind it is not possible to draw a hard and fast line, but if the minister, by reason of his having misconstrued the Act or for any other reason, so uses his discretion as to thwart or run counter to the policy and objects of the Act, then our law would be very defective if persons aggrieved were not entitled to the protection of the court.

Notes

1. It was found that the Minister had acted unlawfully, because his actions pursued a purpose not authorised by the statute. Wade notes that in this case the House of Lords emphasised 'in broad terms that unfettered discretion is something which the law does not admit. If it were otherwise, everyone would be helpless in the face of the unqualified powers which Ministers find it so easy to obtain from Parliament'.[55]

2. Despite such approving views, the courts have been accused of using their practice of inferring a purpose as a means whereby to interfere with policy. Often the purpose inferred is uncontroversial or the courts only go so far as stating, in effect, that whatever the purpose of the body's power may be, it is not to enable it to do the act complained of (as in the well known case of *R v Barnsley MBC ex parte Hook* [1976] 1 WLR 1052 (discussed below). In other cases, however, the judiciary has been accused of inferring an unwarrantably narrow purpose from an Act which appears to grant broad discretion, and then holding a decision unlawful because it is not in conformity with this purpose. Arguably, this technique was adopted by the House of Lords in *Bromley London Borough Council v Greater London Council* [1983] 1 AC 768, discussed by Jeremy Waldron below.

J Waldron, *The Law* (1990), pp 117–19

'Within six months of winning the election, Labour will cut fares on London Transport buses and tubes by an average of 25%.' The Labour Party made that commitment in its manifesto for the 1981 elections to the Greater London Council (GLC). It won the election and within six months bus and tube fares were reduced as promised. The move necessitated an increase in the rates (i.e. property taxes) levied on the London boroughs. Bromley (a Conservative-controlled council), brought an action in the High Court to challenge the decision. The GLC did not take the challenge very seriously, and were not surprised when the High Court judge rejected the Bromley application.

---

55   HWR Wade, *Constitutional Fundamentals* (1989), pp 53–54.

A few weeks later, the Bromley council appealed, and three judges sitting in the Court of Appeal reversed the original decision and upheld the Bromley challenge. The judges condemned the fare reduction as 'a crude abuse of the poor' and they quashed the supplementary rate that the GLC had levied on the London boroughs to pay for it. The GLC appealed to the House of Lords, the highest court in the land, but to no avail.

The Law Lords held unanimously that the GLC was bound by a statute requiring it to 'promote the provision on integrated, efficient and economic transport facilities and services in Greater London', and they interpreted this to mean that the bus and tube system must be run according to 'ordinary business principles' of cost effectiveness. The Labour council, they said, was not entitled to lower the fares and increase the deficit of London Transport in order to promote their general social policy, and they were certainly not entitled simply to shift a large percentage of the cost of travel in London from commuters to ratepayers.

The fact that the policy had been announced in advance and had secured majority support, carried little weight with the courts. According to the Law Lords and the judges in the Court of Appeal, members of the GLC should not have treated themselves as 'irrevocably bound to carry out pre-announced policies contained in election manifestos', particularly when it became apparent that central Government would penalise the move to bodies like the GLC. So, though the voters had supported in their thousands, the fare reduction was reversed, the supplementary rate quashed, and the policy frustrated, by the order of five judges.

It is fair to say the GLC and their lawyers were taken aback by the Court of Appeal and House of Lords decisions, 'shell-shocked' was the term one lawyer used. More than anything else, the Labour councillors were flabbergasted by the Law Lords' intrusion into a decision so clearly legitimated by electoral democracy. . .As they saw it, the electorate had been given a choice: to subsidise London Transport in the interest of social and environmental policy or to persist with the existing fare structure. The electorate had made their choice, and councillors couldn't understand why the judges—who knew almost nothing about the detailed policy issues involved—would want to overturn their decision. Council solicitors were at a loss to explain the vehement unanimity of the Lords' decision: 'There is always room for argument where there is discretionary power.' The only thing they could see was that the courts were indulging in a gut-level reaction to Labour policy, to the beginning of some apprehended revolutionary socialist challenge.

Note

Ambiguity as to whether a decision is tainted with illegality through the influence of 'improper purposes' can arise in the case of decisions made for a plurality of purposes—some proper, some improper—as in the following case.

R v Inner London Education Authority ex parte Westminster Council
[1986] 1 All WLR 28

The Inner London Education Authority (ILEA) was opposed to government policy on rate-capping which it believed would adversely affect education provision in London. It was empowered by statute (s 142(2) of the Local Government Act 1972) to incur expenditure in the course of publicising matters within its area of information on matters relating to local government. The case arose from the decision of ILEA to retain an advertising agency in order to mount a campaign to generate 'awareness of the authority's views of the needs of the education service and to alter the basis of public debate about the effect of. . . government actions'. ILEA admitted that the campaign had the dual purpose of educating the public and persuading them to share ILEA's opposition to rate-capping.

Glidewell J: If a local authority resolves to expend its ratepayers' money in order to achieve two purposes, one of which it is authorised to achieve by statute but for the other of which it has no authority, is that decision invalid? I was referred to the following authorities: (i) *Westminster Corporation v London and North Western Railway Co* [1905] AC 426. [Glidewell J considered the decision and concluded:] This suggests that a test for answering the question is, if the authorised purpose is the primary purpose, the resolution is within the power . . . (ii) More recently in *Hanks v Minister of Housing and Local Government* [1963] 1 QB 999, Megaw J . . . quoted part of the dissenting judgment of Denning LJ in *Earl Fitzwilliam's Wentworth Estates Co Ltd v Minister of Town and Country Planning* [1951] 2 KB 284, 307:

> If Parliament grants a power to a government department to be used for an authorised purpose, then the power is only validly exercised when it is used by the department genuinely for that purpose as its dominant purpose. If that purpose is not the main purpose, but is subordinated to some other purpose which is not authorised by law, then the department exceeds its powers and the action is invalid.

It had been submitted to Megaw J that, although Denning LJ had dissented from the decision of the majority, this passage in his judgment did not differ from the view of the majority. Megaw J went on [[1963] QB 999, 1020]:

> . . . In the end, it seems to me, the simplest and clearest way to state the matter is by reference to 'considerations'. A 'consideration', I apprehend, is something which one takes into account as a factor in arriving at a decision. I am prepared to assume, for the purposes of this case, that, if it be shown that an authority exercising a power has taken into account as a relevant factor something which it could not properly take into account in deciding whether or not to exercise the power, then the exercise of the power, normally at least, is bad. . . I say 'normally' because I can conceive that there may be cases where the factor wrongly taken into account, or omitted, is insignificant, or where the wrong taking into account, or omission, actually operated in favour of the person who later claims to be aggrieved by the decision.

Professor Evans, in de Smith's *Judicial Review of Administrative Action*, 4th edn (1980), p 329. . .distils from the decisions of the courts five different tests upon which reliance has been placed at one time or another, including, at pp 330–2:

(1)   What was the true purpose for which the power was exercised? If the actor has in truth used his power for the purpose for which it was conferred, it is immaterial that he was thus enabled to achieve a subsidiary object. . .

(5)   Was any of the purposes pursued an unauthorised purpose? If so, and if the unauthorised purpose has materially influenced the actor's conduct, the power has been invalidly exercised because irrelevant considerations have been taken into account.

. . . I gratefully adopt the guidance of Megaw J, and the two tests I have referred to from de Smith's *Judicial Review of Administrative Action*.

It thus becomes a question of fact for me to decide, upon the material before me, whether in reaching its decision of 23 July 1984, the staff and general sub-committee of ILEA was pursuing an unauthorised purpose, namely, that of persuasion, which has materially influenced the making of its decision. I have already said that I find that one of the sub-committee's purposes was the giving of information. But I also find that it had the purpose of seeking to persuade members of the public to a view identical with that of the authority itself, and indeed I believe that this was a, if not the, major purpose of the decision. In reaching this decision of fact, I have taken into account in particular the material to which I have referred above in AMV's 'presentation' of 18 July 1984, the passages I have quoted from the report of the Education Officer to the sub-committee, particularly the reference to 'changing the basis of public debate', and the various documents which have been published by AMV since 23 July with the approval of ILEA. I accept that some of these documents do inform, but in my view some of them contain little or no information and are designed only to persuade. This is true in particular, in my view, of the poster slogan 'Education Cuts Never Heal' (skilful though I think it is) and it is also true of the advertisement 'What do you get if you subtract £75 million from London's education budget?'

Adopting the test referred to above, I thus hold that ILEA's subcommittee did, when making its decision of 23 July 1984, take into account an irrelevant consideration, and thus that decision was not validly reached.

Notes

1. Glidewell J thus found that a decision would be unlawful if 'materially influenced' by an unauthorised purpose. Purchas LJ put forward an arguably less strict test in *Simplex GE (Holdings) Ltd v Secretary of State for the Environment* [1988] COD 160[56] where he held that, on the issue of whether an unauthorised purpose had influenced a decision, the applicant did not need to show that the decision-maker 'would or even probably would have come to a different conclusion [if he had not been influenced by the improper purpose]. He has only to exclude the. . . contention. . . that the [decision-maker] necessarily would still have made the same decision'. This test implies that once an unauthorised consideration can be shown to have been present, the onus of proof shifts to the decision-maker to show that he or she would clearly have made the same decision without taking account of that consideration. Glidewell J's test seemed to envisage that it was for the applicant to show 'material influence' by the consideration.

2. Recently, in *Porter v Magill* [2002] AC 357, the House of Lords had to consider a complex case on improper purposes arising from the Shirley Porter affair. It appeared that Porter, the Conservative leader of Westminster Council at the relevant time, had formulated a policy of designating certain blocks of Council houses to be sold to approved applicants, rather than being re-let, with the aim of increasing the number of likely Conservative voters in key marginal wards; the aim, in short, being electoral advantage. Capital grants of £15,000 were made available to tenants to encourage them to move. It was argued that this was an improper purpose for the Council to follow, thus rendering its actions unlawful. Porter argued that the realities of party politics were that party considerations were bound to intrude upon decisions made by elected councillors, and that provided they also had a proper purpose for any decisions they made, this in itself did not render the decision unlawful. This argument was rejected by the House of Lords.

---

56   The facts of the case appear above at 830..

Porter v Magill [2002] 2 AC 357, 466–67

Lord Bingham: Elected politicians of course wish to act in a manner which will commend them and their party (when, as is now usual, they belong to one) to the electorate. Such an ambition is the life-blood of democracy and a potent spur to responsible decision-taking and administration. Councillors do not act improperly or unlawfully if, exercising public powers for a public purpose for which such powers were conferred, they hope that such exercise will earn the gratitude and support of the electorate and thus strengthen their electoral position. The law would indeed part company with the realities of party politics if it were to hold otherwise. But a public power is not exercised lawfully if it is exercised not for a public purpose for which the power was conferred but in order to promote the electoral advantage of a political party. The power at issue in the present case is section 32 of the Housing Act 1985, which conferred power on local authorities to dispose of land held by them subject to conditions specified in the Act. Thus a local authority could dispose of its property, subject to the provisions of the Act, to promote any public purpose for which such power was conferred, but could not lawfully do so for the purpose of promoting the electoral advantage of any party represented on the council.

The House was referred to a number of cases in which the part which political allegiance may properly play in local government has been explored. . . . These cases show that while councillors may lawfully support a policy adopted by their party they must not abdicate their responsibility and duty of exercising personal judgment. There is nothing in these cases to suggest that a councillor may support a policy not for valid local government reasons but with the object of obtaining an electoral advantage.

Abuse of discretion: relevant and irrelevant considerations

This ground is very similar to that of improper purpose, but it focuses upon examining the matters taken into account by an authority in coming to its decisions (which may or may not be the same enquiry as asking what its purposes were). In *R v Somerset County Council ex parte Fewings* [1995] 3 All ER 20, CA,[57] the local authority banned stag-hunting on an area of its land, which, under s 10(2)(b) of the Local Government Act 1972, they were to manage 'for the benefit of their area'. On appeal to the Court of Appeal, the decision was found to be unlawful on the grounds that, *inter alia:*

(a)   the councillors, in making their decision, at no point had their attention drawn to the governing statutory provision; and

(b)   that they had made their decision largely on the basis that they considered stag-hunting cruel and morally repulsive, a consideration which, though relevant, was not the only factor they should have considered under the test.

In the same case Simon Browne LJ in the Court of Appeal discussed the three kinds of considerations which logically may present themselves to a decision maker exercising a discretion. These are: (a) factors which a decision maker *must* take into account ('mandatory factors'); (b) factors which he or she must *not* take into account ('prohibited factors'); (c) factors which the decision maker *may* at

---

57   For comment, see G Nardell [1995] PL 27.

his or her discretion take into account. Thus, decisions which fail to take into account factors in the first category, or take into account those in the second category, will clearly be unlawful. However, the third category is there to allow for the exercise of discretion by the decision maker: there are some factors that it is permissible, but not necessary, to have regard to, though it should be noted that courts do not always recognise this intermediate category.

The leading decision in this area follows: it concerns the setting by the Home Secretary of the 'tariff' part of the sentence to be served by the notorious teenage killers of a six-year-old child, James Bulger. As explained in the judgment of Lord Browne-Wilkinson:

> . . .In essence, the tariff approach is this. The life sentence is broken down into component parts, viz, retribution, deterrence and protection of the public. The trial judge and the Lord Chief Justice advise the Secretary of State as to the sentence which would be appropriate for the crime having regard to the elements of retribution and deterrence. In the light of that advice (and not being in any way bound by it) the Secretary of State makes his own decision as to the minimum period which the prisoner will have to serve in order to satisfy the requirements of retribution and deterrence. This is the tariff period.

The challenge to the Home Secretary's decision was made on a large number of grounds; the grounds considered here were that he took into account an irrelevant consideration—public opinion—and, through his adoption of a 'tariff' policy for child offenders, ruled out consideration of relevant factors.

R v Secretary of State for the Home Department ex parte Venables and others [1998] AC 407 (extracts)

Lord Goff: . . .Having received this advice from the trial judge and the Lord Chief Justice, the Home Secretary. . .proceeded to consider the question of the penal element in the sentence for the two boys, and decided that it should be increased to 15 years. . . . In his Decision Letters, dated 22 July 1994, it was stated that the Home Secretary had regard (inter alia) to:

> the public concern about this case, which was evidenced by the petitions and other correspondence the substance of which were disclosed to your solicitors by our letter of 16 June 1994, and to the need to maintain confidence in the system of criminal justice.

The letter dated 16 June 1994 referred in particular to a petition, signed by some 278,300 members of the public (with some 4,400 letters in support) urging that the two boys should remain in detention for life; a petition, signed by nearly 6,000 members of the public, asking for a minimum period of detention of 25 years; and over 20,000 coupons, cut out of a popular newspaper, together with over 1,000 letters, demanding a life tariff. There were only 33 letters agreeing with the judiciary, or asking for a lower tariff.

. . . That there was public concern about this terrible case, there can be no doubt. But events such as this tend to provoke a desire for revenge, and calls for the infliction of the severest punishment upon the perpetrators of the crime. This elemental feeling is perhaps natural, though in today's society there is a tendency for it to be whipped up and exploited by the media. When this happens, it can degenerate into something less acceptable. Little credit can be given to favourable responses to a campaign that the two respondents should 'rot in jail' for the rest of their lives, especially when it is borne in mind that those who responded may well have been unaware that, even after the penal element in their sentences had been served, their release would not be automatic but would be the subject of very careful consideration by the responsible authorities. It was the submission of Mr Fitzgerald for Venables that material such as that which the Secretary of State had regard to in the present case was no more than public clamour, and as such worthless. It should therefore have been disregarded by the Secretary of State. In the Court of Appeal this submission was accepted by Lord Woolf MR and Hobhouse LJ, but rejected by Morritt LJ.

... when it comes to fixing the penal element. . .the Secretary of State. . .is deciding what in future will be the period of time which a prisoner must serve, compassionate considerations apart, before he may be released, if it is then thought fit. It is scarcely surprising that, in *Ex parte Doody*, at p 557, Lord Mustill said of this exercise that:

> Even if the Home Secretary still retains his controlling discretion as regards the assessment of culpability the fixing of the penal element begins to look much more like an orthodox sentencing exercise, and less like a general power exercised completely at large.

Furthermore this approach derives strong support from the statutory context in which the discretion is now to be found. For in the same Part [II] of the same statute, the fixing of the penal element for discretionary life prisoners is, by section 34 of the Act of 1991, performed by the judges. They will undoubtedly act in a judicial manner when doing so; and indeed that they should do so must have been the intention of Parliament when entrusting this function to them. In so doing, they will disregard any evidence of the kind now under consideration as irrelevant and prejudicial. It follows that, if the Secretary of State was right to have regard to it, there will exist an extraordinary and anomalous conflict between neighbouring sections, sections 34 and 35, in the same statute.

... the only way in which the conflict can be resolved is by recognising that, if the Secretary of State implements a policy of fixing a penal element of the sentence of a mandatory life prisoner pursuant to his discretionary power under section 35, he is to this extent exercising a function which is closely analogous to a sentencing function with the effect that, when so doing, he is under a duty to act within the same constraints as a judge will act when exercising the same function. In particular, should he take into account public clamour directed towards the decision in the particular case which he has under consideration, he will be having regard to an irrelevant consideration which will render the exercise of his discretion unlawful.

Lord Browne-Wilkinson: [considered the Home Secretary to have acted unlawfully in excluding from consideration the welfare of the child offenders]. . . I would add a word on the issue whether it was procedurally improper for the Secretary of State to take into account the petitions and other material sent to him. The Court of Appeal and, I understand, the majority of your Lordships take the view that this was improper. I find it unnecessary to express any final view but I would sound a word of caution. Parliament has entrusted decisions relating to the future of these applicants to the executive, not to the judiciary. Whilst it is right for the courts to ensure that in making his decision the Secretary of State acts in accordance with natural justice, in my view the court should be careful not to impose judicial procedures and attitudes on what Parliament has decided should be an executive function. I understand it to be common ground that the Secretary of State, in setting the tariff, is entitled to have regard to 'broader considerations of a public character' including public respect for the administration of justice and public attitudes to criminal sentencing. How is the Secretary of State to discover what those attitudes are except from the media and from petitions? To seek to differentiate between the Secretary of State discovering public feeling generally (which is proper) and taking into account distasteful public reactions in a particular case (which is said to be unlawful) seems to me too narrow a distinction to be workable in practice. Public attitudes are ill-defined and are usually only expressed in relation to particular cases. . .

Lord Steyn: . . . may the Home Secretary take into account public clamour about the tariff to be fixed in a particular case?

. . . For my part the matter can be decided on a twofold basis. First, the material in fact taken into account by the Home Secretary was worthless and incapable of informing him in a meaningful way of the true state of informed public opinion in respect of the tariff to be set in the cases of Venables and Thompson. . . It was therefore irrelevant. But the Home Secretary was influenced by it. He gave weight to it. On this ground his decision is unlawful. But the objection to the course adopted by the Home Secretary is more fundamental. . .

In fixing a tariff the Home Secretary is carrying out, contrary to the constitutional principle of separation of powers, a classic judicial function. . . Parliament entrusted the underlying statutory power, which entailed a discretion to adopt a policy of fixing a tariff, to the Home Secretary. But the power to fix a tariff is nevertheless equivalent to a judge's sentencing power. Parliament must be assumed to have acted, have entrusted the power to the Home Secretary on the supposition that, like a sentencing judge, the Home Secretary would not act contrary to fundamental principles governing the administrator of justice. Plainly a sentencing judge must ignore a newspaper campaign designed to encourage him to increase a particular sentence. It would be an abdication of the rule of law for a judge to take into account such matters. The same reasoning must apply to the Home Secretary when he is exercising a sentencing function. . . I would therefore hold that public protests about the level of a tariff to be fixed in a particular case are legally irrelevant and may not be taken into account by the Home Secretary in fixing the tariff. I conclude that the Home Secretary misdirected himself in giving weight to irrelevant considerations. . .

Notes

1. Lord Lloyd broadly agreed with Lord Browne-Wilkinson that the petitions were not irrelevant matters for the Home Secretary; Lord Hope agreed with Lord Woolf that setting a mandatory sentence for a child precluded the Home Secretary from taking account of relevant matters, namely 'the child's development and progress while in custody'. He also agreed with Lord Goff that 'the public clamour' was an irrelevant matter.

2. The different grounds of decision by their Lordships reveal how far judicial opinion may differ upon what are relevant and irrelevant considerations in a particular case. Three of their Lordships considered the public clamour irrelevant; Lord Browne-Wilkinson expressed doubts as to this conclusion; while Lord Lloyd disagreed with it. Lord Browne-Wilkinson and Lord Hope thought that the fixing of a tariff period for a child, in the same way that a tariff period would be fixed for an adult murderer, was itself unlawful since it precluded the Home Secretary from taking into account, during the tariff period, relevant considerations—namely the welfare and development of the child offenders. But this was not the basis of the decision of the remainder of their Lordships.

3. In the recent House of Lords decision in *R (On the application of Mehanne) v City of Westminster Housing Benefit Review Board* [2001] 2 All ER 690, the Board was required by statute not to grant

the full amount of housing benefit claimed if it considered the rent unreasonably high. The statute said that the Board should have regard 'in particular to the cost of suitable accommodation elsewhere'. It was held that the Board should have (as it had not) had regard to the particular circumstances of the applicant, including the pregnancy of his wife and his reduced level of benefits as an asylum seeker. Lord Bingham gave some general guidance on when a matter should be viewed as a relevant one under statute, saying, that absent 'very clear [statutory] language, I would be very reluctant to conclude that the. . .board were precluded from considering matters which could affect the mind of a reasonable and fair minded person'. It was also found that such an interpretation served the underlying policy objective of the legislation, namely to ensure that the housing needs of society's most disadvantaged sector were met.

4. A recurring question over the last few years has been whether local authorities in making various decisions which involve resources, for example, provision for old people and for children with special educational needs, may take into account their own limited financial resources, and if so, at what stage of the decision-making process. Local authorities have found resources increasingly tight and have often explained that in making decisions to limit or restrict services, they have been influenced by their need to preserve scarce resources. This has led to a number of challenges from those adversely affected on the grounds that the resources available were, in the context of the particular decision, not a matter to which the authority should have had regard.

5. The courts' response to such arguments has varied. In *R v Gloucester County Council ex p Barry* [1997] 2 WLR 459, the Council, if it considered a disabled person had certain 'needs', was under a statutory duty to make arrangements to cater for him or her. B had been previously assessed as having certain needs, which were fully catered for in 1992 and 1993. In 1994, the Council told him that, due to central Government cuts in their funding, it was no longer able to provide for his full needs. The House of Lords held, by a 3:2 majority, that in assessing 'need', the Council had to consider what was an acceptable standard of living. In assessing that, the Authority could have regard to its own resources, and so had not acted unlawfully.

6. In *R v Sefton Metropolitan Borough Council ex parte Help the Aged* [1997] 4 All ER 532, the court drew a distinction between (a) assessing a person's needs, and (b) deciding what to provide in order to meet those needs. In determining the first question, the court said that an authority could, following *Barry,* take into account resources, but once it had decided that a particular person was in need, it came under a binding duty to provide for those needs and lack of resources was not relevant. *Barry* was distinguished again in *R v East Sussex County Council ex parte Tandy* [1998] 2 All ER 769, HL. Here, a local authority had a duty to provide 'suitable education' for the children in its area. T had been unable to attend school and had received tuition of five hours a week, funded by the Council. In 1996, the authority reduced this to three hours because of financial constraints. On its face, the situation seemed very similar to *Barry*—an initial provision being reduced to save money. However, the House of Lords found that the concept of 'suitable education', unlike a person's 'needs' (as in *Barry*), was objective, and did not vary according to resources. In taking account of its own resources in deciding what was 'suitable', the authority had had regard to an irrelevant consideration. Alder comments: 'In [cases other than *Barry*] the courts have interpreted the governing legislation as imposing an absolute duty, with *Barry* being confined to its statutory context.'[58]

7. It should be noted that the general attitude of the courts is that, where resources are found to be a relevant matter, it is not for the courts to substitute their judgment for that of the public authority

---

58 J Alder, 'Incommensurable Values and Judicial Review: The Case of Local Government' [2001] PL 717, 731. See also *R v Manchester City Council ex parte Stennett* [2002] UKHL 34; [2002] 4 All ER 124; noted A Scully [2003] 62(1) CLJ 1.

in question as to the most efficient or desirable distribution of resources: that is a matter of policy and discretion.[59]

8. What does 'taking into account' a consideration mean? Does the authority have to satisfy the court that it has given a consideration found to be relevant at least a threshold, minimum weight.[60] In *Tesco Stores Limited v Secretary of State for the Environment* [1995] 1 WLR 759, Lord Hoffman gave a firm 'no' to this question: Provided that the. . .authority has regard to all material considerations, it is at liberty (provided that it does not lapse into *Wednesbury* irrationality) to give them whatever weight the. . .authority thinks, or indeed no weight at all. The fact that the law regards something as a material consideration therefore involves no view at all about the part, if any, which it should play in the decision-making process.[61]

9. Abuse of discretion, as well as including improper purposes and irrelevant considerations, also includes the notion of acting arbitrarily. It is difficult to pin down what is meant by this and it may be that such decisions should be categorised as a species of *Wednesbury* unreasonableness, but the following example may be illuminating. In *R (On the application of S) v Secretary of State for the Home Department* [2007] EWCA Civ 546, R had applied for asylum in 1999. His application was never dealt with and in January 2001, a policy decision was made to defer consideration of older asylum applications in order to meet performance targets. There was then a policy change regarding applicants from Afghanistan following the removal of the Taliban regime. He was eventually interviewed in March 2004 and his claim for asylum rejected; discretionary leave to remain was also refused. He had now been in the UK for over seven years and had proved himself a model citizen. It was found that in the exceptional circumstances of the case it would be an abuse of power to remove him and the court so held. His application had been severely prejudiced by the political decision to delay considering old cases on grounds that had nothing to do with their merits and was therefore arbitrary. The court stressed that this was an exceptional decision: an arbitrary decision that would have had an extremely harsh effect upon the applicant had been made.

Failure to *retain* discretion

Improper delegation

The basic principle here is that if one body is given a power to make decisions in an area, it may not delegate that power to another body. Thus, a board given power to dismiss workers at a port may not give that power to dismiss the port manager. Nor indeed may it lawfully ratify his or her decisions. The most it can do is to take *recommendations* from the manager and then decide *itself* whether to follow them.[62] The major exception to this provision is that Ministers may delegate decisions to civil servants or other Government officials, as decided by the following case.[63]

---

59   See generally on this: J King, 'The Justiciability of Resource Allocation' (2007) 70 MLR 197; K Syrett, 'Of Resources, Rationality and Rights: Emerging Trends in the Judicial Review of Allocative decisions' [2001] Web JCLI.

60   As Laws J suggested in *ex parte Fewings* [1995] 1 All ER 513.

61   *Ibid*, p 780.

62   *Barnard v National Dock Labour Board* [1953] 2 QB 18.

63   See generally D Lanham, 'Delegation and the Alter Ego Principle' (1984) 100 LQR 587.

Carltona Ltd v Works Commissioners [1943] 2 All ER 560, 563

The Commissioners of Works had power under wartime regulations to requisition property, and Carltona's factory was requisitioned. A requisition notice in respect of Carltona's factory was made by a civil servant, of the rank of assistant secretary, for and on behalf of the Commissioners of Works (at the head of which was a Minister).

Lord Greene MR: In the administration of Government in this county the functions which are given to ministers (and constitutionally properly given to ministers because they are constitutionally responsible) are functions so multifarious that no minister could ever personally attend to them. . . It cannot be supposed that [the regulation in question] meant that, in each case, the minister in person should direct his mind to the matter. The duties imposed upon ministers and the powers given to ministers are normally exercised under the authority of the ministers by responsible officials of the department. Public business could not be carried on if that were not the case. Constitutionally, the decision of such an official is of course the decision of the minister, the minister is responsible. It is he who must answer before Parliament for anything his officials have done under his authority and if for an important matter he selected an official of such junior standing that he could not be expected competently to perform the work, the minister would have to answer for that in Parliament.

Notes

1. In some cases, the courts have indicated a readiness to scrutinise the *Carltona* principle more carefully. *R v Secretary of State for the Home Department ex parte Oladehinde* [1991] 1 AC 254 concerned a challenge to the legality of the practice of the Home Secretary to delegate to immigration inspectors (officials of some seniority and considerable experience) the decision to serve notices of intention to deport. Following such a notice, deportees had a highly restricted right of appeal; the final deportation order was made by the Secretary of State. In the Court of Appeal, it was said, *per* Woolf LJ, that the *Carltona* principle was to be 'regarded as an implication which is read into a statute in the absence of [contrary] legislative intent'. Here, however, Woolf LJ noted that the whole scheme of legislation was to divide responsibilities and to assign some specific responsibilities to the Secretary of State and some to particular categories of officials. In these circumstances, it was not appropriate to allow the Secretary of State to delegate to officials powers which had in fact been conferred on him. The House of Lords agreed that the *Carltona* principle could be 'negatived or confined by clearly necessary implication' in a statute (at 278). But this, the Lords held, could only be done on *Wednesbury* grounds. In other words, the court would find the *Carltona* principle to be displaced only if the scheme of delegation was one which no reasonable Minister would have put in place. The House of Lords said that the court should be slow to find further *implied* restrictions on the right to delegate where the governing statute had certain *express* prohibitions on delegation. Delegation would be appropriate provided that the decisions delegated 'were suitable to [the] grading and experience' of the official concerned and did not lead to a conflict of interest for the officials (at 303). So, for the House of Lords, the principle in favour of *Carltona* was difficult to displace. Thus, the mere fact that certain divisions of responsibilities are expressly laid down in a statute does not prevent further delegation from Ministers to civil servants, though it might be thought that this made the efforts of the draftsman in setting out an explicit division of responsibilities in the statute somewhat futile. The Lords did emphasise, however, that the courts would be prepared to find that a particular scheme of delegation was unlawful, on the facts, though it was unclear whether it would have to be *Wednesbury* unreasonable or not.

2. It should be noted that local authorities, under s 101 of the Local Government Act 1972 may, subject to express provision in that, or any other Act, delegate functions to (a) a committee, sub-committee or officer of the authority, or (b) any other authority.

Over-rigid application of a predetermined policy — 'fettering'

It is commonplace for public authorities to react to the granting of a broad discretion given to them by statute by adopting a fairly detailed policy, partly in order to ensure that individual decisions represent a predetermined policy which reflects that authority's priorities and partly to speed up decision making; without such policies, each decision would have to be made on an individual, discretionary basis, and inconsistencies would be bound to arise. It is important to note that, under the principles of judicial review, there is nothing objectionable about the adoption of a policy *per se*; a problem arises only if the authority applies a given policy so rigidly that it refuses to consider whether exceptions to it should be made in atypical individual cases. The classic decision here is *British Oxygen Co Ltd v Minister of Technology* [1971] AC 610. The ministry had a discretion to make grants to those buying new plant; however, it had formed a policy of not awarding any grants in respect of items which cost less than £25 each. British Oxygen had bought a large number of cylinders over three years, at a cost of £4 million; however, the price of one individual cylinder was £20. British Oxygen did not therefore qualify for a grant and challenged the policy. Lord Reid said that, in such cases, the authority 'will almost certainly have evolved a policy so precise that it could well be called a rule. There can be no objection to that, provided the authority is always willing to listen to anyone with something new to say'. Because the Ministry had considered British Oxygen's application carefully, it had not therefore acted unlawfully.

A recent application of the doctrine by the Court of Appeal may be found in the following case, in which it was found that a health authority's policy of refusing to fund gender reassignment surgery for transsexuals was flawed. Although it acknowledged transsexualism as an illness, it failed to deal with it as such and thus operated what amounted to a blanket ban on the treatment.

R v North West Lancashire Health Authority ex parte A and others
[2000] 1 WLR 977, CA

Auld LJ: . . .A, D and G suffer from an illness called 'gender identity dysphoria', commonly known as transsexualism. Each was born with male physical characteristics, but psychologically has a female sexual identity. Each has been living as a woman for some years. At the material time A and G had each been diagnosed by a specialist consultant to have a clinical need for surgery substituting female for male characteristics, a procedure known as 'gender re-assignment surgery'. D was awaiting assessment of suitability for such surgery. They all challenge the Authority's refusal to fund their treatment, including surgery, under the National Health Service because of its policy not to do so in the absence of 'overriding clinical need' or other exceptional circumstances. They maintain that they are ill and that the Authority's policy, and refusals pursuant to it, to fund treatment for them are irrational. The Authority justifies its policy and refusals on the ground that it has a statutory obligation to care for all within its area and limited financial resources with which to do so, requiring it to give a lower priority to some medical conditions than to others and that transsexualism rightly has a low priority. [The policy had an exception for overriding clinical need, as Auld LJ pointed out.]

. . . the only material illustration in the Policy of the degree of overriding clinical need that might justify an exception is serious mental illness which the treatment could be expected substantially to improve.

. . . It is proper for an Authority to adopt a general policy for the exercise of such an administrative discretion, to allow for exceptions from it in 'exceptional circumstances' and to leave those circumstances undefined; see *In re Findlay* [1985] 1 AC 318, HL, per Lord Scarman at 335H–336F. In my view, a policy to place transsexualism low in an order of priorities of illnesses for treatment and to deny it treatment save in exceptional circumstances such as overriding clinical need is not in principle irrational, provided that the policy genuinely recognises the possibility of there being an overriding clinical need and requires each request for treatment to be considered on its individual merits.

However, in establishing priorities—comparing the respective needs of patients suffering from different illnesses and determining the respective strengths of their claims to treatment—it is vital for an Authority: 1) accurately to assess the nature and seriousness of each type of illness; 2) to determine the effectiveness of various forms of treatment for it; and 3) to give proper effect to that assessment and that determination in the formulation and individual application of its policy.

Conclusions

[The] basic error, one of failure properly to evaluate such a condition as an illness suitable and appropriate for treatment, is not mitigated by the allowance in both Policies for the possibility of an exception in the case of overriding clinical need or other exceptional circumstances. [The Policies] gave no indication of what might amount to an overriding clinical need or other exceptional circumstances. . .[save for emphasising]. . .the likely rarity and unpredictability of such circumstances, and instanced as a possibility when 'the problem'. . .was the cause of serious mental illness. [Hence] Given the Authority's reluctance to accept gender reassignment as an effective treatment for transsexualism— and it would follow logically any condition caused by it—the provision for an exception in a case of 'overriding clinical need' was in practice meaningless, as Mr Blake observed. It was as objectionable as a policy which effectively excluded the exercise by the Authority of a medical judgment in the individual circumstances of each case. . .

In my view, the stance of the Authority, coupled with the near uniformity of its reasons for rejecting each of the respondents' requests for funding was not a genuine application of a policy subject to individually determined exceptions of the sort considered acceptable by Lord Scarman in Findlay. . .The ostensible provision that it makes for exceptions in individual cases and its manner of considering them amount effectively to the operation of a 'blanket policy' against funding treatment for the condition because it does not believe in such treatment.

Notes

1. This decision indicates that it is not enough for a public authority, in settling upon a policy, simply to *assert* that it is prepared to consider departing from it in exceptional cases: it must be able to show that such preparedness is real, not a legal fiction, designed merely to safeguard it from legal challenge. For a similar decision, see *Rogers* [2006] EWCA Civ 392; [2006] 1 WLR 2649, noted below, pp 876).

2. In *R (On the application of Ealing LBC) v Audit Commission* [2005] EWCA Civ 556, a local authority challenged the decision of the Audit Commission to rate their overall performance as 'poor', because they had been given a zero rating from the Commission for Social Care (CSC) Inspection in respect of its social services performance. Ealing contended that the Audit Commission had thereby used a rigid rule and had also in effect subordinated its decision to that of the CSC; either way it had failed to retain and exercise the discretion given to it. The Court of Appeal agreed with

the lower court that the challenge failed: the Audit Commission had decided to use the score given by the CSC in a particular way that did not amount to a failure to exercise its own discretion and had been entitled to do so.

3. In contrast, a rule in the Prison Rules that babies born to mothers in prison could only stay with them until they were 18 months was found to be unlawful when applied rigidly. The court found that whilst the provision was sensible and lawful as a general rule, it must be applied flexibly and with provision for exceptional cases. In the case of Q, a mother who had given birth in prison, she was on a short sentence and there was no suitable placement available for her child: it was unlawful to have made no exception in her case: *R(Q) v Secretary of State for the Home Department* [2001] 1 WLR 2002.

4. Making rules to govern cases will not be unlawful if Parliament has expressly provided for the body to make rules; in such a case the only question will be whether the rules are *intra vires* the statutory power, rational and proportionate: *R (On the application of Nicholds) v Security Industry Authority* [2007] 1 WLR 2067.

5. For critical analysis of the 'no-fetter' principle, see C Hilson, 'Judicial Review, Policies, and the Fettering of Discretion' [2002] PL 111.

Substantive legitimate expectations: the principle of legal certainty[64]

The concept of a legitimate or justified expectation has been used by the courts as a way of imposing on decision-makers duties to follow fair procedures, as noted above at 799–802. In this section, however, we are concerned with a person who is claiming that he or she had been lead to believe that if he or she did *x*, he or she would receive a particular benefit, *y*, or continue to receive it, that they did not get *y*, or *y* was withdrawn from them, and should not have been. The doctrine is usually traced to the decision in *R v Secretary of State for the Home Department ex parte Khan* [1984] 1 WLR 1334, in which its own published criteria for adoption from abroad were not followed by the Home Office. The court found that the Home Office could not change the criteria without doing two things, one procedural and one substantive. The first was to give the applicant an opportunity to argue that the old criteria should apply to him—in effect a right to consultation on the change, which is uncontroversial. But the second and more significant finding the court made was that:

> the Secretary of State. . .should not in my view be allowed to resile from [the published criteria] without affording interested persons a hearing, *and then only if the overriding public interest demands it* [at 1337, emphasis added].

This represented the beginning of a slow and hesitant development of this new head of review. It was immediately apparent that it was controversial because, at its strictest, it appears to prevent authorities from changing their policies unless the courts think the overriding public interest demands it. This is a form of fettering of discretion, which, as just noted above, the courts normally consider to be a form of unlawfulness. In *R v Secretary of State for Transport ex parte Richmond upon Thames London Borough Council* [1994] 1 All ER 577, 596 Laws J said that:

---

64   On this issue generally, see P Craig [1996] 55 CLJ 289; see also his *Administrative Law* 6th edn (2008), Chapter 20.

> . . .such a doctrine would impose an obvious and unacceptable fetter upon the power (and duty) of a responsible public authority to change its policy when it considered that that was required in fulfilment of its public responsibilities.

Law J said that to hold that a change in policy contrary to assurances that it would not be changed must be justified by reference to 'the overriding public interest'

> would imply that the court is to be the judge of the public interest in such cases, and thus the judge of the merits of the proposed policy change. [This]. . .must be rejected. The court is not the judge of the merits of the decision-maker's policy.

The views of Laws J were, however, challenged by Sedley J in *R v Ministry of Agriculture Fisheries and Food ex parte Hamble Fisheries* [1995] 2 All ER 714, 723–24. It is strongly arguable that Laws J overstates the extent of the restriction that the recognition of a doctrine of substantive legitimate expectations would place upon public authorities. Such a doctrine would not, in effect, say that once a policy—such as the circumstances in which children will be allowed into the UK for adoption—has been formulated and announced, it cannot be changed unless the court considers it in the public interest. It is only saying that *in relation to those people to whom it has been announced and who have relied upon it*, a departure from it may have to be justified. That will be a limited group of people. So all that protection for legitimate expectation would mean would be that where an authority wanted to change its policy, it still could, but it might have to make special transitional arrangements for particular people who had relied upon the old policy.

Steele, noting this controversial element, sets out the ways in which in principle the courts could limit the application of the substantive expectations head so as to avoid wrongly interfering with the discretion of decision-makers:

> [The courts'] slow acceptance of the beguilingly simple principle that what is promised must sometimes be delivered stems from reluctance to dictate to decision-makers how they should allocate limited resources. Judges feel far more comfortable telling public bodies what procedures they should follow rather than what outcomes they should procure. However, there are various ways in which the concept of substantive legitimate expectations can be kept within acceptable bounds. First, we could make the basic definitions do the work, narrowly construing the terms 'legitimate' and 'expectation.' Secondly, even if we employed a fairly wide definition of 'legitimate expectation', we could put the emphasis on the standard of review, ensuring that decisions to frustrate legitimate expectations are reviewed on rationality or fairness grounds only to the appropriate intensity. Thirdly, even if we employed a fairly intensive form of review, leading to many instances in which we would say that a body abused its power by frustrating a legitimate expectation, we could decide not to grant full substantive protection—giving the applicant what he was promised—in every case.[65]

The above limiting factors will be considered in detail in what follows. It is important to note that in many cases the applicant is not seeking to claim anything based on a change in general policy at all. Craig divides the cases into four categories:

---

65   I Steele, 'Substantive Legitimate Expectations: Striking the Right Balance?' (2005) 121(Apr) LQR 300.

  (i) A general norm or policy choice which an individual has relied on has been replaced by a different policy choice;
 (ii) A general norm or policy choice [upon which an applicant has relied], is departed from in the circumstances of a particular case;
(iii) There has been an individual representation relied on by a person which the administration seeks to resile from in the light of a shift in general policy;
(iv) There has been an individual representation which has been relied upon. The administration then changes its mind and makes an individualised decision which is inconsistent with the original representation [the original representation may have been that certain criteria will be used to make a decision or simply that a particular benefit will be granted or will not be withdrawn].[66]

It is clear that it is only cases in categories (i) and (iii), in particular the former, that would impose a real restriction upon public bodies; and in fact, as appears below, restrictions based on substantive expectations are far less likely to be imposed in such cases. Conversely, it is clear that the individual will have the strongest claim in category (iv) cases. Appreciating the critical importance between these very different categories is probably the only way of making sense of a body of case law that often does not itself keep them distinct.

It has recently been emphasised by the House of Lords that the person seeking to rely upon an expectation that a given policy would not be changed must have been personally aware of the terms of that policy; without that, no expectation that it will not change can arise. In *R v Ministry of Defence ex parte Walker* [2000] 1 WLR 806, a case concerning a change in criteria for the payment of compensation to members of the armed forces injured whilst on service, Lord Slynn observed:

> It is, however, common ground that the Ministry [of Defence] made no express representation to Sgt Walker that he would be paid compensation under the initial criteria, or at all. Although Sgt Walker said that he believed that he would be compensated, it is not established that he knew the terms of the original criteria, or what he believed to be the circumstances in which he would be compensated, or that he relied on any representation as to compensation in going to Bosnia. Accordingly, it does not seem to me that he can say that any legitimate expectation was frustrated.

Knowledge of a policy is one thing, reliance upon it to one's detriment is another. *R v Secretary of State for Education and Employment ex parte Begbie* [2000] 1 WLR 1115 esp at 1124 confirmed that it is not necessary for a person to have changed his position as a result of a representation in order for an obligation to fulfil a legitimate expectation to come into play. This was said to be because the principle of good administration *prima facie* requires adherence by public authorities to their promises. However, it was added that 'it would be wrong to understate the significance of reliance in this area of the law. It is very much the exception, rather than the rule, that detrimental reliance will not be present when the court finds unfairness in the defeating of a legitimate expectation'. It was subsequently confirmed in *R (Bibi) v Newham LBC* [2002] 1 WLR 203 that detrimental reliance is not always necessary.

Moreover, we can now say, as a result of two recent Court of Appeal decisions, that even the requirement of *knowledge* by the claimant is not insisted upon when the complaint is not that one policy has been changed to another, but simply that the current official policy was erroneously not applied to the claimant's case, to his or her disadvantage. This emerged in two cases in which asylum

---

66   Craig (2008), n 64 above, 649–50.

seekers, as a result of major administrative errors, were simply not assessed at all under the relevant policy. In *R (Rashid) v Secretary of State for the Home Department* [2005] EWCA Civ 744, the Home Office had failed to apply the relevant policy to an Iraqi Kurdish asylum seeker, with the result that his application had been refused. Once the mistake was discovered, the Home Office sought to justify the original decision on the basis (a) that the facts on the ground had changed since then (because the Saddam Hussein regime had been overthrown) and (b) that the applicant had not been aware of the original policy. It was accepted that he would have been granted asylum had the correct policy been applied. The Court of Appeal accepted that the correct test was whether there had been 'such conspicuous unfairness by the Secretary of State as to amount to an abuse of power' and found it satisfied in this case. [67]

The two key points that have caused difficulty are as follows: first, in what circumstances will a person have a *legitimate* expectation as opposed to an expectation *simpliciter*? Second, if there is a legitimate expectation that a given benefit will be applied, what is to be the test to decide when the decision-maker may depart from it? In *Kahn*, above, it was suggested that the test should be that an expectation found to be legitimate may only be frustrated if there was 'an overriding public interest', the judge of which was to be the court. However, later cases doubted this, reverting to a *Wednesbury* test; it appears that we have now moved back closer to something like the *Khan* approach, although the matter is not clearly settled.

When does a *legitimate* expectation arise?

In *R v Devon County Council ex parte Baker* and *ex parte Curtis* [1995] 1 All ER 73, 88 Simon Browne LJ said,

> The ... authorities show that the claimant's right will only be found established when there is a *clear and unambiguous representation upon which it was reasonable for him to rely* (emphasis added).

An expectation can, however, also be based upon a regular practice. In *R v Inland Revenue Commissioners ex parte Unilever plc* [1996] STC 681, the IRC had for over 20 years allowed Unilever to claim relief for trading loss even though the relief was not properly sought, being out of time. Without warning, the IRC then revoked this practice, at a cost to Unilever running into millions of pounds. It was held that Unilever was entitled to rely upon the well-established practice of the Revenue and it was unlawful, as an abuse of power, to withdraw the policy without notice. Note, however, that this was a category (iv) case—of an individual promise (in effect) being altered to a new individualised decision—something that probably explains the applicant's success.

However, in other cases, particularly those falling in categories (i) and (iii), it may not be reasonable for a person to expect that a given policy will not be changed. In such cases, the courts may use the fact that the expectation has to be *legitimate*— that is justified in their eyes—to deny it almost any content at all. As Sedley J said in *R v Ministry of Agriculture, Fisheries and Foods ex parte Hamble Fisheries* [1995] 2 All ER 714, 731, legitimacy is 'not an absolute. It is a function of expectations induced by Government and of policy considerations which militate against their fulfilment'. Therefore, if the applicant is demanding that the old policy be applied to them, his or her expectation that policy will remain the same must be balanced both against the general desirability of allowing policy to be freely changed and also any particular factors in favour of change which apply in the particular case.

---

67 See also *R (S) v Secretary of State for the Home Department* [2007] EWCA Civ 54; [2007] Imm AR 781.

In *R v Department for Education and Employment ex parte Begbie* [2001] 1 WLR 1115 it was held that promises made by prominent members of the Labour Party, both while in Opposition and in power, that children already benefiting from the assisted places scheme[68] would continue to receive this until they finished their schooling, could not then be imposed upon the (Labour) Secretary of State, as this would fetter his discretion under the relevant statute.[69] In particular, it was said that it was clear that a party in opposition would not know all the facts and ramifications of a promise until it achieved office and to hold that a pre-election promise bound a new Government could be inimical to good government. In other words, once again, the applicants failed at the first stage: they could not show that their expectation was *legitimate*. This was not surprising, given that this case fell into category (iii): the applicants were seeking to object to a shift in general policy, albeit one contrary to a representation made to them.

Thus, if there are powerful public interests at stake—as there often will be where a general change in policy has been made—it may be very difficult for the applicant to convince the court that he or she had any *legitimate* expectation that the policy in question would remain unchanged. In other words, an expectation will not be regarded as legitimate if the applicant could have foreseen that the policy or promise was likely to change. An important example is *Findlay v Secretary of State for the Home Department* [1985] AC 318, HL, in which the Minister announced changes to parole policy, motivated by public concern about prisoners obtaining parole seemingly too soon into their sentences and also about prisoners committing offences while on parole. The changes meant that, amongst other things, life prisoners would have to serve much longer sentences than they had been lead to believe under the old policy. They claimed a legitimate expectation that the old policy would be applied to them. The House of Lords rejected their claim and Lord Scarman said:

> . . . but what was [the prisoners'] *legitimate* expectation? Given the substance and purpose of the legislative provisions governing parole, the most that a convicted prisoner can legitimately expect is that this case will be examined individually in the light of whatever policy the Secretary of State sees fit to adopt [provided the new policy] is a lawful exercise of. . . discretion. . . Bearing in mind the complexity of the issues which the [Minister has to consider and the importance of the public interest in the administration of parole I cannot think that Parliament intended the discretion to be restricted in this way [at 388].]

The reasoning was presumably that because public safety was in issue, the public interest must be overriding. Note that in this case, therefore, the concept of public interest in unfettered discretion was deployed not to overcome the expectation and allow change but to deny that any 'legitimate', that is, reasonable, expectation that no change would be made arose in the first place.

Change of policies and transitional provisions

We have noted above that, using Craig's classification, it is hardest to maintain that any legitimate expectation has been frustrated where one general policy is changed for another. As Steele puts it:

> where the administration puts in place a new overall policy after an individual has anticipated the previous policy applying to himself. . .the administration must be free to change from one *intra vires* policy to another. It would therefore appear to

---

68   Whereby members of poor families are given subsidised places at private schools.

69   Education (Schools) Act 1997, s 2(2)(b).

be extremely difficult for an applicant to establish a legitimate expectation in this type of case.[70]

The following case addresses precisely this scenario. *R (Bhatt Murphy (a Firm) and others) v Independent Assessor; R (Niazi) v Secretary of State for the Home Department* [2008] EWCA Civ 755 concerned disappointed applicants to a Government scheme for compensating victims of miscarriages of justice. The scheme was abolished; the claimants had suffered such miscarriages and instructed lawyers to make a claim, but had not put in their applications by the time the scheme was wound up. The applicants sought judicial review on the basis that they had a legitimate expectation of having their claims considered under the scheme and, in the alternative, to have been consulted before it was brought to an end. The court stated that the mere existence of a Government scheme was not by itself sufficient to create a legitimate expectation that the scheme would be continued. There was also no right to notice or consultation. This was a category 1 case: a general policy was replaced by another. There had been no individualised representations, assurances, or decisions. In this sense it is not surprising that the challenge failed.

What is interesting about the case is not therefore the outcome but the remarks of Laws LJ and Sedley LJ in their judgments. Laws LJ noted that:

> Authority shows that where a substantive legitimate expectation is to run, the promise or practice which is its genesis is not merely a reflection of the ordinary fact. . .that a policy with no terminal date or terminating event will continue in effect until rational grounds for its cessation arise. Rather it must constitute a specific undertaking, directed at a particular individual or group, by which the relevant policy's continuance is assured (para 46).

He added that, to give rise to substantive and enforceable expectations, such undertakings or assurances must be of 'a pressing and focused nature' and summarised:

> The power of public authorities to change policy is constrained by the legal duty to be fair. . .A change of policy which would otherwise be legally unexceptionable may be held unfair be reason of prior action, or inaction, by the authority. If it has distinctly promised to preserve existing policy for a specific person or group who would be substantially affected by the change, then ordinarily it must be kept to its promise (substantive expectation). If, without any promise, it has established a promise distinctly and substantially affected a specific person or group who in the circumstances was in reason entitled to rely on its continuance and did so, then ordinarily it must consult before effecting any change (the secondary case of procedural expectation). To do otherwise, in any of these instances, would be to act so unfairly as to perpetuate an abuse of power (para 46).

Knight notes that Laws LJ said that, 'it is difficult to imagine a case in which government will be held legally bound by a representation or undertaking made generally or to a diverse class' (para 46). He goes on:

> Laws L.J. suggested that the wider the class of person affected the greater possibility of there being a countervailing public interest. This is probably the most

---

> accurate summary of the position taken by the courts, but it is interesting to note the gloss of Sedley L.J. in *Bhatt* stressing [at para 69] that it is now entirely orthodox for a legitimate expectation to be founded upon a policy.[71]

Sedley LJ also pointed out, however, that where it is a change from one policy that has been relied upon to another, the expectation may well be limited to the way in which the alternation between the two policies is handled. He noted that:

> government has for many years routinely made transitional provisions to cushion those who would otherwise be unfairly affected by a change of policy. Such provision may take the simple form of giving prior warning that the change is coming. Where that is not possible, it commonly takes the form of transitional provisions for the temporary continuation of certain of the benefits of the policy (para 70).[72]

In this case, Sedley LJ found that the transitional measures taken were adequate although they 'must seem parsimonious and largely arbitrary to the firms affected, and few would dispute that the government could have acted more handsomely'.

Knight agrees that it now seems apparent from both *Bhatt* and *BAPIO* (below), first that transitional measures should be used in such circumstances, and second that 'the courts will not examine the details of those provisions, with suggestions that perfection is not required so long as manifest unfairness is avoided'.[73] It should of course be noted that where the only 'transitional arrangement required' is notification of the change in policy, that this amounts only to a procedural, not a substantive requirement. [74]

Lieven, however, is uncertain whether, in the case of transitional arrangements from one policy change to another, the doctrine of legitimate expectations should be used at all.

> The content of the substantive legitimate expectation which Sedley LJ held arose from policy was that 'if the policy is altered to his disadvantage, the alteration must not be effected so as to unfairly frustrate any reliance that he has legitimately placed on it' (*Bhatt* at [68]). Such a generalised 'expectation' of fair treatment consequent upon a policy change unnecessarily extends the doctrine of legitimate expectations beyond its core concern with promises and representations. The same result could readily be achieved by saying that the court will review policy changes on a *Wednesbury* basis and that it would hold the manner in which a policy has been changed to have been unreasonable if it did not adequately protect the interests of those who had relied on the policy prior to the change.[75]

The authors are inclined to agree: it is important not to confuse the notion that citizens have a legitimate expectation that public bodies will act fairly towards them—which is saying nothing more

---

71   Knight n 73 below, at 20–21.

72   This approach is in line with that previously suggested by Steele: n 65 above, at 308.

73   CJS Knight, 'Expectations in Transition: Recent Developments in Legitimate Expectations' [2009] PL 15, 24.

74   For an instance in which it was held only that the Secretary of State was obliged to give notice of a proposed departure from policy, and hear representations on the matter, see *R (Mullen) v Secretary of State for the Home Department* [2005] 1 AC 1.

75   Lieven, n 52 above, at 19.

than that such bodies have a general duty to do so—and instances in which a specific representation or conduct by a body generates a specific legitimate expectation by an individual or group. [76]

What is the standard of review when a decision-maker overrides an admittedly legitimate expectation?

The second issue, logically, after deciding whether a legitimate expectation exists, is the circumstances in which a decision-maker is allowed to frustrate the expectation by departing from the policy, and in particular who is to be the judge of that question. Since it is a legally recognised interest, there must be some public interest justification for overriding it. Without such a justification, therefore, the authority will be held to have acted unlawfully. [77] But suppose it claims that there *was* such a justification? Steele sets out the basic choices:

> Once the applicant has established that he held a legitimate expectation which has been frustrated, the respondent body will usually attempt to justify its decision to frustrate the expectation by invoking a countervailing public interest. Here the court is faced with a 'standard of review' question—how intensively should it review the balance struck by the primary decision-maker between the two conflicting values, the private interest of the applicant in the expectation being upheld and the (alleged) public interest in the expectation being frustrated? Should the court accept the view taken by the decision-maker as to which interest must take priority or should it impose its own view? The former position would make it impossible for an applicant to succeed in establishing an abuse of power in any case where the body could point to a countervailing public interest, while the latter position would cross the sacrosanct line between review and appeal. English law therefore takes a position somewhere on the spectrum between these extremes. Precisely where on the spectrum it falls has been a matter of some controversy. [78]

As noted above, in *Khan,* the court thought that the standard was that departure was only allowed where the 'overriding public interest' demanded it and that the court was to be the judge of whether that overriding interest was present. This view was also supported by Sedley LJ in *ex parte Ha*mble. There he said that the matter of when a decision maker could override a legitimate expectation was a matter for the court. However, this approach was then expressly condemned by the Court of Appeal in *R v Secretary of State for the Home Department ex parte Hargreaves* [1997] 1 WLR 906[79] as 'heresy', the court asserting that in substantive cases, the test should always be *Wednesbury*. If adopting this approach, courts would only intervene if it thinks that no reasonable decision maker would have decided to frustrate the expectation in question, an approach which leaves the doctrine of

---

76 Other unsuccessful cases include: *R (Bloggs 61) v Secretary of State for the Home Department* [2003] EWCA Civ 686; [2003] 1 WLR 2724 (no legitimate expectation created by a promise made by the police to the effect that a prisoner would, following his co-operation as a police informer, serve his sentence in a protected witness unit run by the Prison Service); *R (Association of British Civilian Internees: Far East Region) v Secretary of State for Defence* [2003] EWCA Civ 473; [2003] QB 1397 (see Chapter 16 at 900–901); *Rowland v Environment Agency* [2003] EWCA Civ 1885; [2005] Ch 1 (invalidity of a proposed course of action negates the possibility of an individual claiming that his expectation of that course of action being pursued should be protected by the court); *R (On the application of Wheeler) v Office of the Prime Minister* [2008] EWHC 1409 (no legitimate expectation of a referendum on the Lisbon Treaty generated by prior Ministerial promises of a referendum on the European Constitution). See also *Henry Boot Homes Ltd v Bassetlaw District Council* [2002] EWCA Civ 983.

77 As, e.g. in *R v IRC ex parte Unilever plc* [1996] STC 681; *R v Inland Revenue Commissioners ex parte MFK* [1990] 1 WLR 1545, 1577.

78 Steele, n 65 above, at 314.

79 For comment, see C Forsyth, '*Wednesbury* Protection of Substantive Legitimate Expectations' [1997] PL 375.

substantive legitimate expectations as merely one means of falling foul of the *Wednesbury* test and thus robs it of any independent bite.[80] This, however, was a case involving a generalised change of policy (category (i)) and so the decision was not surprising. The above *dicta*, however, sought to exclude any protection, save *Wednesbury* unreasonableness, in *all* cases of substantive expectations. However, such a blanket exclusion of proper protection for such expectations was rejected in the subsequent, leading case.

R v North and East Devon Health Authority ex parte Coughlan
[2000] 2 WLR 622 (extracts)

The applicant, who was severely disabled was moved with seven other patients, from Newcourt Hospital, which it was desired to close, to a purpose-built facility, Mardon House, on the clear understanding that Mardon House would be their home for life. Individual flatlets were specifically tailored to their needs and the General Manager of the Health Authority assured them: 'the Health Authority has made it clear to the Community Trust that it expects the Trust to continue to provide good quality care for you at Mardon House for as long as you choose to live there.' The case concerned a challenge to the subsequent decision of the Health Authority to close Mardon House, one argument was that the closure represented a violation of *Coughlan*'s (substantive) legitimate expectation that it would be a home for life and that the Health Authority had advanced no overriding public interest to justify such a violation. The Court found that the Health Authority had taken into account—and given weight to—its own previous promise to the applicant and others in now deciding whether to close Mardon House.

Lord Woolf MR, Mummery and Sedley LJJ:
. . .There are at least three possible outcomes (a) The court may decide that the public authority is only required to bear in mind its previous policy or other representation, giving it the weight it thinks right, but no more, before deciding whether to change course. Here the court is confined to reviewing the decision on *Wednesbury* grounds [as in *Re Findlay* and *ex parte Hargreaves*. (b) [The court then noted that in other instances 'the court may decide that the promise or practice induces a legitimate expectation of, for example, being consulted before a particular decision is taken'.] (c) Where the court considers that a lawful promise or practice has induced a legitimate expectation of a benefit which is substantive, not simply procedural, authority now establishes that here too the court will in a proper case decide whether to frustrate the expectation is so unfair that to take a new and different course will amount to an abuse of power. Here, once the legitimacy of the expectation is established, the court will have the task of weighing the requirements of fairness against any overriding interest relied upon for the change of policy.

In many cases the difficult task will be to decide into which category the decision should be allotted. In what is still a developing field of law, attention will have to be given to what it is in the first category of case which limits the applicant's legitimate expectation (in Lord Scarman's words in *Re Findlay*) to an expectation that whatever policy is in force at the time will be applied to him. . .most cases of an enforceable expectation of a substantive benefit (the third category) are likely in the nature of things to be cases where the expectation is

---

80   For critical comment on this case see P Craig, 'Substantive legitimate expectations and the principles of judicial review', in M Andenas, *English Public Law and the Common Law of Europe* (1998); TRS Allan, 'Procedure and Substance in Judicial Review' [1997] CLJ 246; S Foster, 'Legitimate Expectations and Prisoners' rights' (1997) 60 MLR 727.

confined to one person or a few people, giving the promise or representation the character of a contract. . . .

We consider that [both Counsel] are correct, as was the judge, in regarding the facts of this case as coming into the third category. . . Our reasons are as follows. First, the importance of what was promised to Miss Coughlan, (as we will explain later, this is a matter underlined by the Human Rights Act 1998); second, the fact that promise was limited to a few individuals, and the fact that the consequences to the Health Authority of requiring it to honour its promise are likely to be financial only.

The court's task in all these cases is not to impede executive activity but to reconcile its continuing need to initiate or respond to change with the legitimate interests or expectations of citizens or strangers who have relied, and have been justified in relying, on a current policy or an extant promise. The critical question is by what standard the court is to resolve such conflicts. . . The present decision may well pass a rationality test; the Health Authority knew of the promise and its seriousness; it was aware of its new policies and the reasons for them; it knew that one had to yield, and it made a choice which, whatever else can be said of it, may not easily be challenged as irrational.

In the ordinary case there is no space for intervention on grounds of abuse of power once a rational decision directed to a proper purpose has been reached by lawful process. The present class of case is visibly different. It involves not one but two lawful exercises of power (the promise and the policy change) by the same public authority, with consequences for individuals trapped between the two. . .In such a situation a bare rationality test would constitute the public authority judge in its own cause, for a decision to prioritise a policy change over legitimate expectations will almost always be rational from where the authority stands, even if objectively it is arbitrary or unfair. . . . One approach is to ask not whether the decision is ultra vires in the restricted Wednesbury sense but whether, for example through unfairness or arbitrariness, it amounts to an abuse of power.

[The court went on to found that the attempt in *Hargreaves* to confine review of frustration of substantive expectations to a weak *Wednesbury* standard was *obiter* and went on]. . .*Hargreaves* can. . .be distinguished from the present case. . . In this case it is contended that fairness in the statutory context required more of the decision maker than in *Hargreaves* where the sole legitimate expectation possessed by the prisoners had been met. It required the Health Authority, as a matter of fairness, not to resile from their promise unless there was an overriding justification for doing so. Another way of expressing the same thing is to talk of the unwarranted frustration of a legitimate expectation and thus an abuse of power or a failure of substantive fairness. Again the labels are not important except that they all distinguish the issue here from that in *Hargreaves*. They identify a different task for the court from that where what is in issue is a conventional application of policy or exercise of discretion. Here the decision can only be justified if there is an overriding public interest. Whether there is an overriding public interest is a question for the court [citing further authority in support, including *ex parte Khan* and dicta of Lord Diplock in *GCHQ* at 408, referring to 'benefits or advantages which the applicant can legitimately expect to be permitted to continue to enjoy'.]

The fact that the court will only give effect to a legitimate expectation within the statutory context in which it has arisen should avoid jeopardising the important principle that the executive's policy-making powers should not be trammelled by the courts. . . . Policy being (within the law) for the public authority alone, both it and the reasons for adopting or changing it will be accepted by the courts as part of the factual data—in other words, as not ordinarily open to judicial review. The court's task—and this is not always understood— is then limited to asking whether the application of the policy to an individual who has been led to expect something different is a just exercise of power. In many cases the authority will already have considered this and made appropriate exceptions (as was envisaged in *British Oxygen*. . .and as had happened in *Hamble Fisheries*), or resolved to pay compensation where money alone will suffice. But where no such accommodation is made, it is for the court to say whether the consequent frustration of the individual's expectation is so unfair as to be a misuse of the authority's power.

Fairness and the Decision to Close

[The] promise that Mardon House would be [Coughlan's] home for life. . .was an express promise or representation made on a number of occasions in precise terms. It was made to a small group of severely disabled individuals who had been housed and cared for over a substantial period in the Health Authority's predecessor's premises at Newcourt. It specifically related to identified premises which it was represented would be their home for as long as they chose. It was in unqualified terms. It was repeated and confirmed to reassure the residents. It was made by the Health Authority's predecessor for its own purposes, namely to encourage Miss Coughlan and her fellow residents to move out of Newcourt and into Mardon House, a specially built substitute home in which they would continue to receive nursing care. The promise was relied on by Miss Coughlan. Strong reasons are required to justify resiling from a promise given in those circumstances. This is not a case where the Health Authority would, in keeping the promise, be acting inconsistently with its statutory or other public law duties. A decision not to honour it would be equivalent to a breach of contract in private law.

The Health Authority treated the promise as the 'starting point' from which the consultation process and the deliberations proceeded. It was a factor which should be given 'considerable weight', but it could be outweighed by 'compelling reasons which indicated overwhelmingly that closure was the reasonable and the right course to take'. The Health Authority, though 'mindful of the history behind the residents' move to Mardon House and their understandable expectation that it would be their permanent home', formed the view that there were 'overriding reasons' why closure should nonetheless proceed. The Health Authority wanted to improve the provision of reablement services and considered that the mix of a long stay residential service and a reablement service at Mardon House was inappropriate and detrimental to the interests of both users of the service. The acute reablement service could not be supported there without an uneconomic investment which would have produced a second class reablement service. It is, however, clear from the Health Authority's evidence and submissions that it did not consider that it had a legal responsibility or commitment to provide a home, as distinct from care or funding of care, for the Applicant and her fellow residents. It considered that. . .the provision of care services to the current residents had become 'excessively expensive', having regard to the needs of the majority of disabled people in the Authority's area and the 'insuperable problems' involved in the mix of long term residential care and reablement services at Mardon House. . .

. . . But the cheaper option favoured by the Health Authority misses the. . .fact that [it] has not offered to the Applicant an equivalent facility to replace what was promised to her. The Health Authority's undertaking to fund her care for the remainder of her life is substantially different in nature and effect from the earlier promise that care for her would be provided at Mardon House. That place would be her home for as long as she chose to live there. We have no hesitation in concluding that the decision to move Miss Coughlan against her will and in breach of the Health Authority's own promise was in the circumstances unfair. It was unfair because it frustrated her legitimate expectation of having a home for life in Mardon House. There was no overriding public interest which justified it.

Notes

1. It should be noted that this decision only comes into play if it has already been determined that there is a *legitimate* expectation (that is, the applicant has satisfied the criteria of the representation being clear and unequivocal, that is was reasonable for him or her to rely upon it, etc). This is likely to happen only in cases falling within category (iv), and (a weaker claim) category (ii). But if the legitimacy of that expectation can be established, and a public authority asserts that an overriding public interest justifies frustrating it, the decision lays down a radically different test from *Hargreave*. *Coughlan* found that the *Hargreave* approach should be applied only in some cases. In others, the court should decide itself whether the public interest should have properly overridden the legitimate expectation.

2. The court said that in order to decide which approach to take, courts should use the following criteria:

    (a) whether 'the expectation is confined to one person or a few people, giving the promise or representation the character of a contract' (that is, category (iv) cases);
    (b) the importance of the promise to the individual;
    (c) the level of detriment to the public authority of being forced to honour promise.[81]

    This detriment will clearly be greater if the authority is seeking to resile from the promise because of a generalised change in policy (category (iii) cases).

3. Laws LJ in *ex parte Begbie* [2001] 1 WLR 1115[82] took the opportunity to make some cautionary remarks about the application of the principles enunciated in *Coughlan*. As Elliott puts it,[83] he argued that 'substantive review operates on a sliding scale' between the deferential *Wednesbury* approach on the one hand and high intensity proportionality review on the other and that this scale:

    embraces many different levels of judicial intervention with the standard of review being determined by the specific features of the case. Thus, if the matter in question lies in the 'macro-political' field, raises 'wide-ranging issues of general policy' or is likely to have 'multi-layered effects' which substantially reduce the government's freedom to formulate policy, a less intrusive form of review is called for.[84]

4. In *R (Abdi and Nadarajah)* v *Home Secretary* (2005) EWCA Civ 1363 a claim of substantive expectations failed on the facts but Laws LJ took the opportunity to confirm the *Coughlan* approach (at para 68):

---

81   For general comment, see P Craig and S Schonberg. 'Substantive legitimate expectations after *Coughlan*' [2000] PL 684.

82   See M Elliott, 'The Human Rights Act 1998 and the Standard of Substantive Review' [2001] CLJ 301, 315–22.

83   M Elliott, 'Legitimate Expectation: The Substantive Dimension' [2000] CLJ 421, at 424.

84   *Ibid.*

Where a public authority has issued a promise or adopted a practice which represents how it proposes to act in a given area, the law will require the promise or practice to be honoured unless there is good reason not to do so. [This] is said to be grounded in fairness, and no doubt in general terms that is so. I would prefer to express it rather more broadly as a requirement of good administration, by which public bodies ought to deal straightforwardly and consistently with the public. In my judgment this is a legal standard which, although not found in terms in the European Convention on Human Rights , takes its place alongside such rights as fair trial, and no punishment without law. That being so there is every reason to articulate the limits of this requirement — to describe what may count as good reason to depart from it — as we have come to articulate the limits of other constitutional principles overtly found in the European Convention. Accordingly a public body's promise or practice as to future conduct may only be denied. . .in circumstances where to do so is the public body's legal duty, or is otherwise, to use a now familiar vocabulary, a proportionate response (of which the court is the judge, or the last judge) having regard to a legitimate aim pursued by the public body in the public interest. The principle that good administration requires public authorities to be held to their promises would be undermined if the law did not insist that any failure or refusal to comply is objectively justified as a proportionate measure in the circumstances.

Steele notes that 'we have moved from the rather crude *Coughlan* dichotomy, which would admit of only two different types of review, to a sliding scale of review. This is a logical step since. . . proportionality is itself a flexible standard of review.' What is important is that *Hargreaves*' attempt to emasculate the doctrine of substantive expectations has now been clearly rejected. It has now been accepted that it is for judges, albeit in a limited category of case, to make the primary judgment as to whether a legitimate expectation was outweighed by the public interest, precisely the approach that had been described not just as mistaken but as 'heresy' in *Hargreaves*. Shortly after it was decided, *Coughlan* was cited in a couple of House of Lords decisions[85] with no hint of disapproval, indeed with apparent endorsement and in *R (Reprotech (Pebsham) Ltd) v East Sussex County Council* [2003] 1 WLR 348, 358, Lord Hoffmann accepted *Coughlan* as correct. The two latest House of Lords decisions follow; it will be apparent that it does not decisively resolve some of the above questions.

R (BAPIO Action Ltd) v Secretary of State for the Home Department
[2008] 1 AC 1003 (extracts)

The House of Lords had to consider the lawfulness of new guidance issued in 2006 by the Department of Health that effectively barred doctors who had qualified in another country, but who were present legally in the UK under the Immigration Rules, from getting work in an English hospital. Before this, Governments had actively encouraged overseas doctors to come to the UK because they were highly skilled migrant workers under the Immigration Rules and thus allowed to work in the UK without the need to apply for a work permit. The Department of Health had not altered the Immigration Rules, which would have required

---

85   See *R v MOD ex parte Walker* [2000] 1 WLR 806, *per* Lord Hoffmann: 'This is not a case like *R v North and East Devon Health Authority ex p Coughlan* [1999] Lloyd's Rep (Medical) 306, in which a public authority made a specific promise and then withdrew it.' *Dicta* in *R v Secretary of State for the Home Department ex parte Hindley* [2001] 1 AC 410 left the status of *Coughlan* carefully open, while not explicitly endorsing it (*ibid*, at 419, *per* Lord Steyn and at 421, *per* Lord Hobhouse).

parliamentary approval, but had altered their impact by the guidance issued. The applicants claimed that their legitimate expectation of being able to work as doctors in the UK had been frustrated by the change in policy by the Department of Health. Lords Bingham and Carswell ruled in favour of the applicants on grounds other than legitimate expectations.

Lord Scott. . .

26 The 'legitimate expectations', on which the respondents rely, can reasonably be described, in my opinion, as an expectation that the employment policy of the Department of Health, so far as junior doctors from outside the UK and EEA and post-graduate training positions at NHS hospitals are concerned, would remain unaltered. I am not clear, however, on what basis this expectation, whether or not described as 'legitimate', should be treated as fettering the ability of the Secretary of State for Health to adjust departmental policy so as to afford priority in offers of post-graduate training positions first to suitable UK and EEA [European Economic Area] junior doctors if in her judgment the discharge of her statutory duties under the 1977 Act, now the 2006 Act, required that adjustment. The reasons. . .for the adjustment in policy that the guidance represents seem to me very powerful [and have]. . .not been challenged.

30 . . .It is not, in my opinion, open to the Department of Health to fetter its ability to adjust its policy from time to time so as to continue to discharge its statutory duty to ensure the proper functioning of NHS hospitals. [The claimant's expectations] do not justify elevating those expectations to the point at which they can succeed in challenging the sensible and, to my mind, well justified [new] guidance. . .to NHS employers.

Lord Rodgers. . .

35. . . .In my view, [the change] was unfair to the IMGs with HSMP status in this country because the Government thereby dashed the legitimate expectations which it had fostered and on which they had acted. The advice was accordingly unlawful.

Lord Mance. . .

59. But the grant of HSMP [Highly Skilled Migrant Programme] status to IMGs [International Medical Graduates] within category (i) [already practising in the UK] undoubtedly gave them a legitimate expectation that they would be able to seek and obtain employment in the fields of their skill; and that may in public law itself preclude the Crown from acting inconsistently with the expectation so created.

60 For IMGs already in the United Kingdom with HSMP status (category (i)), the guidance would. . .have undermined their legitimate expectations in a very fundamental way. They would have come here intending to make the United Kingdom their main home. Their decision to come would necessarily have taken account of the prospect of employment in the NHS. Prior to the guidance, the normal practice was for leave to stay with HSMP status to be renewed without difficulty, provided the requirements for renewal were met. IMGs with that status would have expected to be able if they wished to stay here and be employed in the NHS until the time came when their leave could be made indefinite. The introduction of a resident labour market test for those whose limited leave expired before the end of the post on offer would radically undermine this expectation. That could have been done by amending the immigration scheme, which would at least have involved a measure of parliamentary scrutiny. But, by issuing the guidance, the Secretary of State for Health as one emanation of the Crown was exercising her prerogative to give informal guidance inconsistently with the legitimate expectations generated by the

Immigration Rules and practice adopted by another emanation of the Crown, the Home Secretary. In my opinion, the inconsistency and its effects were so profound as to render such guidance invalid.

Notes

1. Elliott notes:

> Lord Scott thought that the claimants' case fell at the first hurdle: although IMGs reasonably expected to be allowed to remain and work in the UK, those expectations were not legitimate because so characterising them would have had the effect of 'elevating' them so as to render unlawful the Health Secretary's 'sensible and . . . well-justified guidance'. Lord Scott was right to recognise that the enforcement of expectations as to the conferral or continued enjoyment of substantive benefits has important implications for the width of ministerial discretion, and that courts should be wary of eviscerating such discretion by enforcing substantive expectations too readily. However, his analysis blurs the distinction recognised by lower courts between considerations of legitimacy and protection—a distinction which allows for greater analytical clarity by enabling courts to acknowledge openly that even though a claimant is entitled to expect a given outcome, countervailing public interests may exert a stronger pull. This is precisely the sort of structured, transparent analysis which English administrative law—wedded for so long to the opaque concept of *Wednesbury* unreasonableness—is now striving to embrace, and it is regrettable that Lord Scott's analysis signally fails to contribute to that enterprise.[86]

2. As to Lord Mance, Elliott comments that his reasoning that the expectation of IMGs already in the UK under the HSM Programme, should be protected because of 'profound' effects which IMGs would otherwise suffer:

> appears to come dangerously close to impugning a ministerial decision because it is judicially regarded as wrong on the merits. Lord Mance failed to explain *why* the Health Secretary's policy was insufficiently important to justify overriding certain individuals' interests; the fact that Lord Scott, as noted above, reached the opposite conclusion makes this omission all the more striking. Existing case law rightly indicates that whether substantive expectations should be protected turns on the balance of fairness as between the expectation-holder and the wider public, requiring the court to identify and ascribe weight to those competing interests and to determine by reference to an articulated standard whether the decision-maker has struck an acceptable balance between them. This approach, under the rubric of proportionality, is now commonplace where other highly-regarded interests such as human rights are at stake, and it is disappointing that their Lordships missed this opportunity to anchor the doctrine of legitimate expectation within English law's increasingly sophisticated mainstream jurisprudence concerning substantive review.[87]

86 M Elliott [2008] 67(3) CLJ 453, 454.

87 *Ibid*, p 455.

3. The other dispute between their Lordships was whether the Health Secretary's guidance could be impugned on the basis of expectations generated by another Ministers' policy—the *Home Secretary's* HSMP. Lord Scott thought that it could not 'because, as existing case law establishes, an undertaking by one entity cannot bind another'. Lord Mance and Rodgers however took the more traditional view that as Lord Rodgers put it, at para 34:

> it would be wrong, not only as a matter of constitutional theory, but as a matter of substance, to put the powers, duties and responsibilities of the Secretary of State for the Home Department into a separate box from those of the Secretary of State for Health. Both are formulating and implementing the policies of a single entity, Her Majesty's Government.

Elliott comments that:

> holding that one central government department can never be subject to legitimate expectations arising from the statements or policies of another is incompatible with a system of public law which effectively holds the executive to account.[88]

The most recent decision of the House of Lords in this area follows.

R (On The Application of Bancoult) v Secretary of State For Foreign and Commonwealth Affairs [2008] UKHL 61; [2009] 1 AC 453

The facts of this case appear in Chapter 11, pp 577–578. It will be recalled that one argument put forward by the Chagossian/Illios Islanders was that they had a substantive legitimate expectation that their legal right to return to the Islands would be honoured by the Government, based on a statement made by the Foreign Secretary in November 2000; this expectation was, they argued, then wrongfully frustrated in 2004 when, without further consulting the islanders, or Parliament, the Government made two Orders in Council which had the effect of removing the legal rights of the Chagossians to return to any of the islands. The Secretary of State's 2000 statement had been as follows:

> I have decided to accept the court's ruling and the Government will not be appealing. The work we are doing on the feasibility of resettling the Ilois now takes on a new importance. We started the feasibility work a year ago and are now well underway with phase two of the study. Furthermore, we will put in place a new Immigration Ordinance which will allow the Ilois to return to the outer islands while observing our Treaty obligations. . .

The statement was followed by a new Immigration Ordinance that granted the right to the islanders to return to the islands other than Diego Garcia.

Lord Hoffman
60 . . .It is clear that in a case such as the present, a claim to a legitimate expectation can be based only upon a promise which is 'clear, unambiguous and devoid of relevant qualification'. . . It is not essential that the applicant should have relied upon the promise to

---

his detriment, although this is a relevant consideration in deciding whether the adoption of a policy in conflict with the promise would be an abuse of power and such a change of policy may be justified in the public interest, particularly in the area of what Laws LJ called 'the macro-political field': *Ex p Begbie* [2000] 1 WLR 1115 , 1131.

61 In my opinion this claim falls at the first hurdle, that is, the requirement of a clear and unambiguous promise. The Foreign Secretary said that the Crown accepted the decision in *Bancoult (No 1)* that the 1971 Immigration Ordinance was outwith the powers of the BIOT Order and that a new Ordinance would be made which would allow 'the Ilois to return to the outer islands'. This was done. Nothing was said about how long that would continue. But the background to the statement was the ongoing study 'on the feasibility of resettling the Ilois'. If that resulted in a decision to resettle, then one would expect the right of abode of the Chagossians on the outer islands to continue. On the other hand, if it did not, the whole situation might need to be reconsidered. It was obvious that no one contemplated the resettlement of the Chagossians unless the Government, taking into account the findings of the feasibility study, decided to support it. If they did not, a new situation would arise. The Government might decide that little harm would be done by leaving the Chagossians with a theoretical right to return to the islands and for two years after the feasibility report, that seems to have been the view that was taken. But the Foreign Secretary's press statement contained no promises about what, in such a case, would happen in the long term.

62 No doubt the Chagossians saw things differently. As we have seen, they tried to persuade the Government that the press statement amounted to the adoption of a policy of resettlement. They realised that what mattered was whether the Government was willing to fund resettlement. Otherwise they had secured an empty victory. But the question is what the statement unambiguously promised and in my opinion it comes nowhere near a promise that, even if there could be no resettlement, immigration control would not be reimposed.

63 Even if it could be so construed, I consider that there was a sufficient public interest justification for the adoption of a new policy in 2004. For this purpose it is relevant that no one acted to their detriment on the strength of the statement, that the rights withdrawn were not of practical value to the Chagossians and that the decision was very much concerned with the 'macro-political field'.

Lord Bingham. . .

73 [The new policy] contradicted a clear representation made by the then Secretary of State in his press release of 3 November 2000. There was no representation that the outer islands would be resettled irrespective of the findings of the feasibility study, or that Her Majesty's Government would finance resettlement, and it was implicitly acknowledged that observance of its Treaty obligations might in future oblige the Government to close the outer islands. But there was in my opinion a clear and unambiguous representation, devoid of relevant qualification, that (1) the Government would not be challenging the Divisional Court's decision that Mr Bancoult and his fellow Chagossians had been unlawfully excluded from the outer islands for nearly 30 years, (2) the Government would introduce a new Immigration Ordinance which would allow the Chagossians to return to the outer islands unless or until the United Kingdom's treaty obligations might at some later date forbid it, and (3) the Government would not persist in treating the Chagossians as it had reprehensibly done since 1971. This representation was clearly addressed to Mr Bancoult and those associated with him in the litigation. It was fortified by the making, on the same

day, of the Immigration Ordinance 2000 which made special provision for persons (like Mr Bancoult and the Chagossians) who were British Dependent Territories citizens under the British Nationality Act 1981 by virtue of their connection with the British Indian Ocean Territory, together with their spouses and dependent children. Mr Bancoult and his fellows were clearly intended to think, and did, that for the foreseeable future their right to return was assured. The Government could not lawfully resile from its representation without compelling reason, which was not shown. It is not in such circumstances necessary for the representee to show that he has relied on or suffered detriment in reliance on the representation. In any event, by analogy with the law of estoppel, it is enough if the representee would suffer detriment if the representor were to resile from his representation (*Grundt v Great Boulder Pty Gold Mines Ltd* (1937) 59 CLR 641).

[Lord Rodgers made the same finding as Lord Hoffman, that the representation was not sufficiently clear and unambiguous.]

Lord Carswell. . .

The principles governing what is now known as substantive legitimate expectation were outlined by the Court of Appeal in *Ex p Coughlan* in a judgment which has now become very familiar. . .I would. . .prefer not to express a concluded opinion on the limits of the concept. I am content, however, for present purposes to accept that breach of such an expectation can give rise to an actionable claim and to consider the issue on that basis.

124 . . . For the reasons given by Lord Hoffmann and Lord Rodger, I also consider that the Government did not give the Chagossians a clear and unambiguous promise that they would be allowed to return and resettle permanently on the outer islands. I might add two other points. The press statement was not an assurance directed towards one individual or a small number of people, whereas in *Coughlan*, para 60, the Court of Appeal regarded such a limitation as a significant feature in favour of the applicant's claim. Secondly, if the Government were obliged to resettle the Chagossians, the consequences could be more than financial, as it could give rise to friction with the United States: see *Coughlan*, para 60.

135 The basis of the jurisdiction is abuse of power and unfairness to the citizen on the part of a public authority. . .On this basis it has been held that two factors, both present in the case before the House, tend to show that there has not been an abuse of power. The first is when the authority changes its policy on sufficient public grounds. If there is an overriding public interest behind its change of policy, it will not be an abuse of power. . . The second factor is whether the claimant has relied on the promise or representation, in particular whether he has thereby suffered any detriment. [His Lordship cited *Begbie* and *Bibi* as showing that this is generally required and went on]: If it could be said, contrary to my opinion, that the press statement of 3 November 2000 did contain a sufficiently clear and unambiguous promise or representation, these factors would militate against affording a remedy to the Chagossians.

Lord Mance

174 [Noted the key parts of the press release and that it was "issued by the Foreign Secretary on behalf of the United Kingdom Government."] All these statements are only consistent with a clear policy decision taken by the United Kingdom to recognise and give legal effect to a right to return on the part of the Chagossians, while continuing the feasibility study which had already been started, in order to assess the feasibility of any resettlement programme which the Government might or might not in due course support.

176 Mr Crow [for the Government]'s main submission was, however, that the press statement was subject to the outcome of the ongoing feasibility study. Again, I do not

consider that this corresponds in any way with its natural meaning. The statement amounted to an unconditional recognition, coupled with an assurance that this would be given effect, of a legal right to enter and to be present, whether on a temporary or long-term basis. So too, the subsequent Parliamentary statement by Mr Battle as well as other later statements, as for example that of Baroness Amos in a letter to Mr Bancoult's solicitors dated 28 April 2003. None of these statements was made conditional on or subject to the feasibility study. The feasibility study went to a different question, whether resettlement would be economically feasible, so that the Government as a matter of broader policy or outsiders might be encouraged and prepared to fund it. Accordingly, withdrawal in June 2004 of any right of abode and any right to enter and be present in [the islands] has to be seen against a background in which the Government in November 2000 assured Chagossians that they would have such a right, without undertaking any commitment to fund it.

178 . . . In *Ex p Begbie* Laws LJ. . .underlined the importance that may attach to whether the decisions in question affect only a few individuals or involve wide-ranging questions of general policy, moving into the 'macro-political' field, where judges may well be in no position to adjudicate save at most on a bare *Wednesbury* basis: pp 1130a–1131d.

179 [His Lordship noted that in *Ex p Begbie* it was found that detrimental reliance on a representation 'was not a pre-condition' but that it would 'normally be required' and that Sedley LJ, in the same case had]

> no difficulty with the proposition that in cases where the Government has made known how it intends to exercise powers which affect the public at large it may be held to its word irrespective of whether the applicant had been relying specifically upon it. . .

181 In *Nadarajah*, Laws LJ giving the only full judgment identified six factors. . .as relevant to the existence or otherwise of any substantive legitimate expectation: (1) a promise specifically communicated to an individual or group, which is then ignored, as in *Coughlan*, (2) the clarity of the representation, (3) the singling out of an individual who is then treated less favourably than others also affected by the representation, (4) detrimental reliance, (5) whether the original promise was the result of an honest mistake, which is being corrected and (6) maladministration. But Laws LJ also sought to carry the law's development and the search for principle beyond terms such as abuse of power or even fairness and beyond a list of a range of factors 'which might make the difference': paras 67–68. He identified the underlying principle as a requirement of good administration, by which public bodies ought to deal straightforwardly and consistently with the public, and the litmus test for departures from a previously announced promise or practice as being whether the depart-ure represented 'a proportionate response (of which the court is the judge, or the last judge) having regard to a legitimate aim pursued by the public body in the public interest': para 68. He added that this approach made no distinction between procedural and substantive expectations, but noted that proportionality itself involved an assessment of factors such as those included in Mr Underwood's list: para 69.

182 For my part, I have no difficulty in accepting as the underlying principle a require-ment of good administration, by which public bodies ought to deal straightforwardly and consistently with the public. I prefer to reserve for another case my opinion as to whether it is helpful or appropriate to rationalise the situations in which a departure from a prior decision is justified in terms of proportionality, with its overtones of another area of public

law. It is on any view necessary to make an assessment of the relevant factors on each side. . .The nature and clarity of the promise or practice and of the legitimate expectation which it engenders combine with the circumstances and reasons giving rise to the proposed change of practice as factors which have to be weighed together in order to consider whether and how far justice requires that the public authority should be held to a position consistent with the promise or practice.

183 On the facts of the present case, I have come to the conclusion that the courts below reached the right result. First, there is no indication that the Government gave any real weight to the common law right of abode which the Chagossians, Mr Bancoult in particular, in my view still enjoyed in 2004 by virtue of their birth and connections with BIOT. Second, there is no indication that the Government gave any real weight to the legitimate expectation generated by its words and conduct in 2000. This is a particularly powerful consideration on the facts of this case, where such words and conduct would have been seen as righting a historic wrong and resolving the Chagossians' legal entitlement. Third, there was no consultation with the Chagossians or anyone before the [2004 Order] was issued. Fourth, the factors relied upon as justifying [the Order] (defence and the outcome of the feasibility study) are factors directed on their face to a remote and unlikely risk of large scale resettlement of the outer Chagos Islands. Both appear now to be related by the Secretary of State to some extent to a risk, not substantiated in legal or, to any realistic extent, practical terms in either 2004 or now, that the United Kingdom Government would have positively to fund and arrange such resettlement, or that a right of resettlement could cause friction with the United States of America. The defence considerations (some hard to follow in themselves, though that is not critical to the view I have formed) were not regarded as any bar to the recognition of a legal right to enter and be present in the outer islands in 2000 or after the events of 11 September 2001, and nothing has been shown to suggest any significant change in such considerations since then. The outcome of the feasibility study was known from June 2002 without any steps being felt necessary for two years. Its bearing is not on the legal right of abode, entry or presence, but on the feasibility of the United Kingdom or others deciding to support a positive programme of resettlement. That, for reasons I have given, is not what is in issue in these proceedings. The practical likelihood of any large-scale resettlement serves also to counter any argument (based on Coughlan, para 60) that the Chagossians number considerably more that a 'few' individuals— a most unattractive argument anyway against the background of the determined pretences lying at the origins of this matter 40 years ago that there were no Chagossians at all. . .

185 [Finally]. . .the present case concerns an unequivocal assurance and conduct, on a matter on which it is not suggested that there can have been any mistake. The assurance was directed at Chagossians as defined by the Ordinance of 3 November 2000. It was intended to right an historic grievance, and was understood and no doubt relied upon (in the sense that it was given credence) accordingly. The sense of grievance likely to arise from its revocation without the most careful consideration and strong reason is obvious. The Secretary of State's argument that no-one acted upon his statement and Ordinance to his or her detriment between 3 November 2000 and 10 June 2004 is in my view answered by the considerations that specific detriment is not an absolute pre-condition and that in the context of a general public statement proof of individual reliance may not be expected (see per Sedley LJ in *Ex p Begbie* quoted in para 179 above). . . But the dominant consideration in my opinion is that the Government's statement and conduct were intended and understood to resolve the long-standing controversy regarding the Chagossians' right to

enter and be present in the outer Chagos Islands, and that it would be and in the circumstances was maladministration to go back on that resolution without any consultation and
without strong cause, which has not been shown.

Notes

1. The following points are apparent from the above decision: (i) the House of Lords plainly accepted
    substantive expectations as a valid ground of review; (ii) it was agreed that detrimental reliance on
    the representation was not always required, but that the absence of such reliance weakened a
    claimant's case; (iii) where a representation was not made to a small group, the case for reliance on
    it was weaker; (iv) the decision does not settle the issue of the correct standard of review when a
    public body resiles from a legitimate expectation; (v) in practice, the method used seems to have
    been a rough balancing act, rather than mere *Wednesbury*; (vi) Lord Mance expressed some doubt
    about using proportionality for such purposes, while Lord Bingham posited that the test should be
    whether there were 'compelling reasons' for frustrating a legitimate expectation. Once again there-
    fore the House of Lords, whilst affirming this head of review, failed to take the opportunity to
    define firmly and clearly its contours.

2. Steele suggests:

    > In light of the realisation in *Begbie* that substantive review is best conceived of as a
    > sliding scale of intensity rather than a choice between two alternative intensities,
    > and the possibility that that sliding scale will soon be explained entirely using the
    > language of proportionality. . .the legitimacy of the expectation is simply a factor
    > which pushes the case towards a higher-intensity application of the proportionality
    > test. . .Deciding whether an expectation was 'legitimate' mainly entails assessing
    > the conduct of the parties in the events which culminated in the promise, whereas
    > setting the standard of review requires a broader examination of the administrative
    > context in which the promise is located. The former inquiry focuses on the situation
    > when the expectation arose, while the latter is concerned with the situation when
    > the body seeks to frustrate the expectation.[89]

3. For a comprehensive assessment of this area of law, though written before some of the most recent
    cases considered above, see P Craig, *Administrative Law*, 6th edn (2008), Chapter 20.

IRRATIONALITY

The conceptual basis of the doctrine

It must be stated at the outset that some confusion exists as to whether this is a kind of mixed-bag
category, which encompasses a number of diverse matters such as improper considerations, basing a
decision on no evidence, etc or properly speaking refers only to 'pure unreasonableness'. Indeed, this
may be because, in fact, unreasonableness or irrationality as a wholly separate head arguably has no
independent conceptual life, and, unless made more substantive in its scope, may as well be subsumed
into 'illegality', a point returned to below. Lord Diplock's formulation of this head in the *GCHQ* case
[1985] AC 374, 410 (in which he referred to it as 'irrationality') was as follows:

---

89   Steel, n 65 above, at 318.

> By 'irrationality' I mean what can by now be succinctly referred to as 'Wednesbury unreasonableness. . .' It applies to a decision which is so outrageous in its defiance of logic or of accepted moral standards that no sensible person who had applied his mind to the question to be decided could have arrived at it.

The notion of unreasonableness, as indicated, found its genesis in the following decision.

Associated Provincial Picture Houses v Wednesbury Corporation
[1948] 1 KB 223, 228–29, 231, CA

The Wednesbury Corporation had power to grant licences for the opening of cinemas on Sundays 'subject to such conditions as the authority think fit to impose'. The Corporation imposed a condition in a Sunday licence that no children under 15 should be admitted to the cinema.

Lord Greene MR: When discretion of this kind is granted, the law recognises certain principles upon which that discretion must be exercised, but within the four corners of those principles the discretion, in my opinion, is an absolute one and cannot be questioned in any court of law.

It is true the discretion must be exercised reasonably. Now what does that mean? Lawyers familiar with the phraseology commonly used in relation to exercise of statutory discretions often use the word 'unreasonable' in a rather comprehensive sense. It has frequently been used and is frequently used as a general description of the things that must not be done. For instance, a person entrusted with a discretion must, so to speak, direct himself properly in law. He must call his own attention to the matters which he is bound to consider. He must exclude from his consideration matters which are irrelevant to what he has to consider. If he does not obey those rules, he may truly be said, and often is said, to be acting 'unreasonably'. Similarly, there may be something so absurd that no sensible person could ever dream that it lay within the powers of the authority.

It appears to me quite clear that the matter dealt with by this condition was a matter which a reasonable authority would be justified in considering when they were making up their mind what condition should be attached to the grant of this licence. Nobody, at this time of day, could say that the well-being and the physical and moral health of children is not a matter which a local authority, in exercising theirs powers, can properly have in mind when those questions are germane to what they have to consider. Here Mr Gallop [for the plaintiff] did not, I think, suggest that the council were directing their mind to a purely extraneous and irrelevant matter, but he based his argument on the word 'unreasonable', which he treated as an independent ground for attacking the decision of the authority; but once it is conceded, as it must be conceded in this case, that the particular subject-matter dealt with by this condition was one which it was competent for the authority to consider, there, in my opinion, is an end of the case.

Once that is granted, Mr Gallop is bound to say that the decision of the authority is wrong because it is unreasonable, and in saying that he is really saying that the ultimate arbiter of what is and is not reasonable is the court and not the local authority. It is just there, it seems to me, that the argument breaks down. It is clear that the local authority are entrusted by Parliament with the decision on a matter which the knowledge and experience of that authority can best be trusted to deal with. The subject-matter with which the condition deals is one relevant for its consideration. They have considered it and come to a decision upon it. It is true to say that, if a decision on a competent matter is so unreasonable that no reasonable authority could ever have come to it, then the courts can interfere. That, I think, is quite right; but to prove a case of that kind would require something overwhelming, and in this case, the facts do not come anywhere near anything of that kind. I think Mr Gallop in the end agreed that his proposition that the decision of the local authority can be upset if it is proved to be unreasonable, really meant that it must be proved to be unreasonable in the sense that the court considers it to be a decision that no reasonable body could have come to. It is not what the court considers unreasonable, a different thing altogether.

Notes

1. *Wednesbury* is sometimes seen as implying a test of bare rationality. However, it clearly has a substantive dimension, at least in Diplock's reformulation in *GCHQ* (above). As Jowell and Lester point out:

    > Lord Diplock's third ground of review, 'irrationality', identifies a way in which the substance of official decisions may be challenged by the courts. By separating irrationality from illegality, he made the point that even though a decision may be legal (in the sense of being within the scope of the legislative scheme), it may nevertheless be substantively unlawful. In other words, he recognised that the courts may strike down a decision because it offends substantive principles, independent of those provided for by the statute in question.[90]

2. Clayton points out:

    > it is now apparent that a decision may be irrational on two different bases:
    >
    > - either that the conclusion reached by the public body is unsustainable as one which no decision maker could reasonably take; or
    > - because the reasoning process itself was logically flawed.[91]

    He cites Lord Woolf in *ex parte Coughlan* [2001] QB 213 at [65]:

    > Rationality, as it has developed in modern public law, has two faces: one is the barely known decision which simply defies comprehension; the other is a decision which can be seen to have proceeded by flawed logic (though this can often be equally well allocated to the intrusion of an irrelevant factor).

3. An important case concerned the decision of Leicester City Council to withdraw certain facilities from Leicester City Football Club on the ground that it had failed to condemn the 1984 Rugby Tour of South Africa or to discourage its members from playing. The Council had asked the club four questions: does the club support the Government's opposition to the tour; does the Club agree that the tour is an insult to a large proportion of the Leicester population; will the Club press the RFU to call off the tour; will the Club press the players to pull out of the tour? The Council made it clear that only an affirmative answer to all four questions would be acceptable. The stance of the club was that it was a matter of opinion whether a sporting boycott assisted in breaking down apartheid, and that it was a matter of individual conscience for its members whether they took part in the tour.

---

90   J Jowell and A Lester, 'Beyond *Wednesbury*: Substantive Principles of Administrative Law' [1987] PL 368, 369–70.

91   R Clayton and K Ghaly, 'Shifting Standards of Review' [2007] JR 210, 211.

Wheeler v Leicester City Council [1985] AC 1054, 1077–79, HL

Lord Roskill: The council's main defence rested on s 71 of the Race Relations Act 1976. That section appears as the first section in Part X of the Act under the cross-heading 'Supplemental'. For ease of reference I will set out the section in full:

Without prejudice to their obligation to comply with any other provision of this Act, it shall be the duty of every local authority to make appropriate arrangements with a view to securing that their various functions are carried out with due regard to the need—

(a) to eliminate unlawful racial discrimination; and
(b) to promote equality of opportunity, and good relations, between persons of different racial groups.

[His Lordship considered argument on the construction of the statute and concluded:]

I do not doubt that the council were fully entitled in exercising their statutory discretion under, for example, the Open Spaces Act 1906 and the various Public Health Acts, which are all referred to in the judgments below, to pay regard to what they thought was in the best interests of race relations.

The only question is, therefore, whether the action of the council of which the club complains is susceptible of attack by way of judicial review. It was forcibly argued by Mr Sullivan QC for the council, that once it was accepted, as I do accept, that s 71 bears the construction for which the council contended, the matter became one of political judgment only, and that by interfering the courts would be trespassing across that line which divides a proper exercise of a statutory discretion based on a political judgment, in relation to which the courts must not and will not interfere, from an improper exercise of such a discretion in relation to which the courts will interfere.

To my mind the crucial question is whether the conduct of the council in trying by their four questions, whether taken individually or collectively, to force acceptance by the club of their own policy (however proper that policy may be) on their own terms, as for example, by forcing them to lend their considerable prestige to a public condemnation of the tour, can be said either to be so 'unreasonable' as to give rise to 'Wednesbury unreasonableness' or to be so fundamental a breach of the duty to act fairly which rests upon every local authority in matters of this kind and thus justify interference by the courts.

I do not for one moment doubt the great importance which the council attach to the presence in their midst of a 25% population of persons who are either Asian or of Afro-Caribbean origin. Nor do I doubt for one moment the sincerity of the view expressed in Mr Soulsby's affidavit regarding the need for the council to distance itself from bodies who hold important positions and who do not actively discourage sporting contacts with South Africa. Persuasion, even powerful persuasion, is always a permissible way of seeking to obtain an objective. But in a field where other views can equally legitimately be held, persuasion, however powerful, must not be allowed to cross that line where it moves into the field of illegitimate pressure coupled with the threat of sanctions. The four questions, coupled with the insistence that only affirmative answers to all four would be acceptable, are suggestive of more than powerful persuasion. The second question is to my mind open to particular criticism. What, in the context, is meant by 'the club?' The committee? 90 playing members? 4,300 non-playing members? It by no means follows that the committee would all have agreed on an affirmative answer to the question and still less that a majority of their members, playing or non-playing, would have done so. Nor would any of these groups of members necessarily have known whether 'the large proportion', whatever that phrase may mean in the context, of the Leicester population would have regarded the tour as 'an insult' to them.

I greatly hesitate to differ from four learned judges on the Wednesbury issue but for myself I would have been disposed respectfully to do this and say that the actions of the club were unreasonable in the Wednesbury sense.

Note

The following case concerned a challenge by Nottinghamshire County Council to a decision of the Secretary of State for the Environment relating to the rate support grant for the authority, which had been laid before, and approved by Parliament. One ground of challenge was that the decision was unreasonable because it was disproportionately disadvantageous to a small group of authorities.

Nottinghamshire County Council v Secretary of State for the Environment
[1986] 2 AC 240, 246–50

Lord Scarman: The submission raises an important question as to the limits of judicial review. We are in the field of public financial administration and we are being asked to review the exercise by the Secretary of State of an administrative discretion which inevitably requires a political judgment on his part and which cannot lead to action by him against a local authority unless that action is first approved by the House of Commons.

. . .My Lords, I think that the courts below were absolutely right to decline the invitation to intervene . . .I cannot accept that it is constitutionally appropriate, save in very exceptional circumstances, for the courts to intervene on the ground of 'unreasonableness' to quash guidance framed by the Secretary of State and by necessary implication approved by the House of Commons, the guidance being concerned with the limits of public expenditure by local authorities and the incidence of the tax burden as between taxpayers and ratepayers. Unless and until a statute provides otherwise, or it is established that the Secretary of State has abused his power, these are matters of political judgment for him and for the House of Commons. They are not for the judges or your Lordships' House in its judicial capacity.

For myself, I refuse in this case to examine the detail of the guidance or its con-sequences. My reasons are these. Such an examination by a court would be justified only if a prima facie case were to be shown for holding that the Secretary of State had acted in bad faith, or for an improper motive, or that the consequences of his guidance were so absurd that he must have taken leave of his senses. The evidence comes nowhere near establish-ing any of these propositions. . . .[The] guidance. . . complied with the terms of the statute [which]. . .has inevitably a significant bearing upon the conclusion of 'unreasonableness' in the Wednesbury sense. If, as your Lordships are holding, the guidance was based on principles applicable to all authorities, the principles would have to be either a pattern of perversity or an absurdity of such proportions that the guidance could not have been framed by a bona fide exercise of political judgment on the part of the Secretary of State. And it would be necessary to find as a fact that the House of Commons had been misled: for their approval was necessary and was obtained to the action that he proposed to take to implement the guidance.

In my judgment, therefore, the courts below acted with constitutional propriety in reject-ing the so-called 'Wednesbury unreasonableness' argument in this case.

Notes

1. In *R (Asif Javed) v Secretary of State for the Home Department* [2001] 3 WLR 323, CA the Court of Appeal held that the House of Lords in *Nottinghamshire* had not laid down any general rule that review of any order approved by Parliament by affirmative resolution would only be proper where there was bad faith or manifest absurdity; they had merely applied the test appropriate for the subject matter before them. In that case the challenge was to delegated legislation designating Pakistan, for the purposes of returning asylum seekers, as a country in which there was 'in general no serious risk of persecution'. The court quashed the legislation on ordinary *Wednesbury* grounds. It appears that in that case the Secretary of State's determination of fact in making the finding about the lack of risk of persecution in Pakistan for woman was so unsupportable as to be perverse. See Chapter 6, pp 250–253, for the approach recently taken to an attempted irrationality challenge to an Act of the Scottish Parliament.

2. In *R v Secretary of State for the Environment ex parte Hammersmith LBC* [1991] 1 AC 521, another case on economic policy, Lord Bridge held that the decision 'was not open to challenge on grounds of irrationality short of the extremes of bad faith, improper motive or manifest absurdity'. Have these cases laid down that in certain areas of decision making—for example, matters of economic policy which had been approved by Parliament—a 'super *Wednesbury*' test should be applied? In *R v Ministry of Defence ex parte Smith and others* [1995] 4 All ER 427, HL; [1996] 1 All ER 257, CA,[92] which concerned a challenge by homosexual servicemen and women to the ban on homosexuals serving in the armed forces, Simon Browne LJ, without commenting on whether 'super *Wednesbury*' was a legitimate development, considered that it would not in any event apply in a case where like the instant, human rights were at stake; he appeared to believe that national economic policy issues could raise the reasonableness threshold but that the mere fact that the policy in question had been debated by Parliament would not. When the case came to the Court of Appeal, Sir Thomas Bingham MR took a clear stance on the matter.

R v Ministry of Defence ex parte Smith and others [1996] 1 All ER 257, 264, CA

Sir Thomas Bingham MR: . . .It was argued for the ministry, in reliance on [the Nottinghamshire and Hammersmith] decisions, above, that a test more exacting than Wednesbury was appropriate in this case. The Divisional Court rejected this argument and so do I. The greater the policy content of a decision, and the more remote the subject matter of a decision from ordinary judicial experience, the more hesitant the court must necessarily be in holding a decision to be irrational. That is good law and, like most good law, common sense. Where decisions of a policy-laden, esoteric or security-based nature are in issue, even greater caution than normal must be shown in applying the test, but the test itself is sufficiently flexible to cover all situations.

Notes

1. Clayton and Ghaly note, at p 210, that *Wednesbury*, although always hard to prove, has become more flexible:

> The full rigour of the *Wednesbury* test (sometimes known as the test of 'perversity') has however been softened recently, [citing Lord Cooke in *R v Chief Constable of Sussex ex parte ITF* [1999] 2 AC 418 at 482] and reformulated into a test which asks whether the decision is 'within the range of reasonable responses' under

---

92   The phrase 'super-*Wednesbury*' originated in this case.

the relevant power. In some cases under this head the question is asked whether the decision-maker struck a 'fair' or 'proportionate' balance between competing considerations, or between means and ends. This kind of common law 'proportionality' is, however, different from the 'structured proportionality' [used for EC law or HRA challenges].

2. Recent examples of successful challenges[93] include courts holding that there has been: an unreasonable refusal of interim housing (*Paul-Coker* [2006] EWHC 497 (Admin); [2006] HLR 32); an unreasonable decision against a residential care assessment (*LH* [2006] EWHC 1190); an unreasonable removal of an asylum seeker (*Ahmadzai* [2006] EWHC 318 (Admin)); and an unreasonable refusal of a cancer drug (*Rogers* [2006] 1 WLR 2649). It should be noted, however that the *Ahmadzai* decision was reversed by the Court of Appeal: [2006] EWCA Civ 1550.

3. Of these, the *Rogers* case is worth noting briefly: it is unusual for courts to find that policies by health authorities as to the use of particular drug treatments are irrational, because they normally turn on decisions about the best allocation of available resources,[94] a matter on which courts are rightly reluctant to second-guess primary decision makers. However, in this instance, a challenge by a woman with breast cancer to a decision by the health authority not to supply her with Herceptin, cost was not an issue. The court found that the claimant fell within the group who were eligible to be given treatment with the drug but that the health authority had a policy of withholding assistance save in unstated exceptional circumstances. It found that such a policy would be rational in the legal sense, provided that it was possible to envisage, and the decision maker did envisage, what the exceptional circumstances might be. But if it was not possible to envisage any such circumstances, the policy would be in practice a complete refusal to fund the drug treatment, and as such would be irrational, in the sense of being illogical, or not rationally justified. This was first of all because the reasoning given by the authority was incomplete, in that it relied on the notion of exceptional circumstances but was unable to give an indication of what these might be and how they would justify refusing the drug to one patient and granting it to another; and second because it purported to be a policy of allowing treatment in exceptional circumstances but in practice was a policy of always refusing treatment.

4. However, another recent Court of Appeal decision emphasises the difficulty of mounting a *Wednesbury* challenge when there are no such obvious flaws in reasoning: *Secretary of State for the Home Department v BUAV* [2008] EWCA Civ 417. An anti-vivisection organisation had sought to challenge a Government Inspector's report on apparent severe regulatory failings in relation to the care of monkeys in medical experiments at Cambridge University that caused them severe pain, distress and in some cases death. The inspector broadly gave the regulatory regime and procedures at Cambridge a clean bill of health. The High Court found that the Inspector had reached perverse conclusions. On appeal, the Court of Appeal stressed the dangers of the court seeking to substitute its inexpert view for those of the Government Inspector and an expert witness at trial and allowed the Secretary of State's appeal. For strong criticism of this decision, see D Thomas, 'How Irrational Does Irrational Have To Be?: *Wednesbury* in Public Interest, Non-Human Rights Cases' [2008] JR 258.

5. The following very recent decision of the House of Lords illustrates well the reluctance of courts to substitute their views on the reasonableness of a particular policy adopted for those of the body responsible for dealing with the area in question. A challenge reached the house by an applicant

---

93   One could also add *R (Javed) v Secretary of State for the Home Department* [2001] EWCA Civ 789; [2002] QB 129.

94   See, e.g. *R v Cambridge Health Authority ex parte B* [1995] 1 WLR 898; *R v North West Lancashire Health Authority ex parte A, D and G* [2000] 1 WLR 977.

who had not been allocated social housing by his local authority, although he was in considerable need. As Lord Neuberger noted (para 57 of the judgment below):

> courts have held on a number of occasions that authorities were acting irrationally by having schemes which did not effectively prioritise different degrees of need between applicants who satisfied [the statutory criteria]: *R v Islington LBC Ex p Reilly and Mannix* (1999) 31 HLR 651 and *R v Westminster City Council Ex p Al-Khorsan* [2001] 33 HLR 6 (both of which were approved by the *Court of Appeal in R (on the application of A) v Lambeth LBC; R (on the application of Lindsay) v Lambeth LBC* [2002] HLR 57.

The House of Lords took the occasion to remind courts of the restraints that the *Wednesbury* doctrine deliberately lays upon them.

R (On the Application of Ahmad) v Newham LBC [2009] UKHL 14; [2009] HLR 31

Under the Housing Act 1996, as amended, an authority must have a scheme for determining priorities and procedures in the allocation of it social housing and must not allocate housing except in accordance with that scheme. The Act provides for priority to be given to various classes of vulnerable or particularly needy persons, such as the homeless, and those who need to move on medical or disability grounds.

Lord Neuberger. . .

35 There were two reasons why the courts below considered that the Scheme was unlawful. The first, and principal, reason was well summarised in the Court of Appeal by Richards L.J. (who gave the only reasoned judgment), at [2008] EWCA Civ 140 at [69]. He said that the [housing allocation scheme] 'places all those who qualify for reasonable preference under s.167(2) in a single group, that of Priority Homeseeker, and . . . their relative priority in bidding for available accommodation is determined not by relative need, but by the length of time they have been registered on the housing list'. In agreement with the deputy judge, he said that this was 'plainly an insufficient mechanism for identifying those in greatest need and giving them priority'. At [para 70]. . .he rejected the argument that the existence of [other priority groupings] 'ma[d]e good the deficiency of the [CBL]', because of the 'highly restrictive' criteria which have to be satisfied in order to qualify for those groups.

46 . . . as a general proposition, it is undesirable for the courts to get involved in questions of how priorities are accorded in housing allocation policies. Of course, there will be cases where the court has a duty to interfere, for instance if a policy does not comply with statutory requirements, or if it is plainly irrational. However, it seems unlikely that the legislature can have intended that judges should embark on the exercise of telling authorities how to decide on priorities as between applicants in need of rehousing, save in relatively rare and extreme circumstances. Housing allocation policy is a difficult exercise which requires not only social and political sensitivity and judgement, but also local expertise and knowledge. . .

Baroness Hale. . .

15 . . .The earlier decisions in the High Court and Court of Appeal [above]. . . concluded that a policy was irrational if it did not contain 'a mechanism for identifying those with the greatest need and ensuring that so far as possible and subject to reasonable countervailing

factors (for example, past failure to pay rent etc) they are given priority'. There are numerous problems with that approach. The Act only requires a 'reasonable preference' to be given to particular groups of people. It cannot be said that a scheme for identifying which individual households are in greatest need *at any particular time* is the only way in which a reasonable council might decide to give reasonable preference to those groups [emphasis added]. It is the groups rather than the individual households within them which have to be given reasonable preference. Identifying the individual households in greatest need could only be done through some sort of points based system and experience has shown that these too may be open to attack, either on the ground that they are too rigid and therefore unduly fetter the council's discretion or on the ground that the particular distribution of points is for some reason irrational. . . The trouble is that any judicial decision, based as it is bound to be on the facts of the particular case, that greater weight should be given to one factor, or to a particular accumulation of factors, means that lesser weight will have to be given to other factors. The court is in no position to rewrite the whole policy and to weigh the claims of the multitude who are not before the court against the claims of the few who are. Furthermore, relative needs may change over time, so that if the council were really to be assessing the relative needs of individual households, it would have to hold regular reviews of every household on the waiting list in order to identify those in greatest need as vacancies arose. No-one is suggesting that this sort of refinement is required. It would be different, of course, if the most deserving households had a right to be housed, but that is not the law.

16 . . .One can, of course, imagine policies that would be irrational. It is dangerous to give examples which have not been tested by argument. But one possibility might be a policy which ensured that small families had priority over large ones, or that people coming from outside the borough had priority over those living within it, or that people who had been waiting the shortest time had preference over those waiting the longest. But it is not irrational to have a policy which gives priority to some tightly defined groups in really urgent need and ranks the rest of the 'reasonable preference' groups by how long they have been waiting. These definitions are of course open to criticism, and no doubt when the council come to rewrite their policy they will give careful thought to the points which have been made in these proceedings, but it is not for the courts to pick detailed holes in the definitions which the council have chosen. [The statutory provisions] make it clear that, subject to the express provisions, it is for the council to decide on what principles the scheme is to be framed.

22 It is fitting to conclude by endorsing these words of the deputy judge ([49] of his judgment):

> . . .Judges must be particularly slow in entering the politically sensitive area of alloca-
> tions policy by over-broad use of the doctrine of irrationality. A particular scheme
> cannot be castigated as irrational simply because it is not a familiar one to the court
> or is not considered to be the perfect solution to a difficult, if not impossible, ques-
> tion to resolve.

Castigating a scheme as irrational is of little help to anyone unless a rational alternative can be suggested. Sometimes it may be possible to do this. But where the question is one of overall policy, as opposed to individual entitlement, it is very unlikely that judges will have the tools available to make the choices which Parliament has required a housing authority to make.

Notes

1. The other side of *ex parte Smith* is Lord Bingham's explanation that the more substantial the interference with human rights, the more the court will require by way of justification before it is satisfied that the decision is reasonable. Lord Woolf MR explained the reasoning process to be used more fully in *R v Lord Saville ex parte A* [2002] 1 WLR 1855 at [37]:

> What is important to note is that when a fundamental right such as the right to life is engaged, the options available to the reasonable decision-maker are curtailed. They are curtailed because it is unreasonable to reach a decision which contravenes or could contravene human rights unless there are sufficiently significant countervailing considerations. In other words it is not open to the decision-maker to risk interfering with fundamental rights in the absence of compelling justification. Even the broadest discretion is constrained by the need for there to be countervailing circumstances justifying interference with human rights. The courts will anxiously scrutinise the strength of the countervailing circumstances and the degree of the interference with the human right involved and then apply the test accepted by Sir Thomas Bingham MR in *ex p Smith*.

2. The statutory context may affect the standard of *Wednesbury* to be applied. In considering findings by the Parliamentary Commissioner for Administration (PO), it might be assumed a Minister is entitled to reject them outright simply on the basis of preferring his or her own view, provided that such a rejection is not *Wednesbury* unreasonable in the orthodox sense. There is certainly nothing in the statute that lays any duty on Ministers to accept PO findings, or enumerating any criteria that should be applied by the Minister in deciding whether to accept or reject PO findings. However, in the recent decision of *Bradley*,[95] the Court of Appeal found that a Minister may only reject the findings of the PO for 'cogent reasons'—a significantly higher standard than *Wednesbury*. This finding, which has been objected to by one commentator,[96] plainly indicates the inherent capacity of this head to impose higher standards on a decision-maker where the courts consider that the overall legal and constitutional context justify this. For a similar decision, limiting the ability of the Mayor of London to reject an Inspector's findings, see *The Mayor of London v Enfield LBC* [2008] EWCA Civ 202; [2008] Env LR 33.

3. Clayton and Ghaly sum up (at p 210):

> In English public law there are now **four** tests the court may apply when undertaking the substantive review of primary decisions:
>
> (a) Reasonableness review. [i.e. standard *Wednesbury*]. . .
> (b) Anxious scrutiny reasonableness review. Where 'domestic' human rights are in issue (i.e. rights implied outside of Convention rights), the courts have applied stricter or more 'anxious' scrutiny of the primary decision than that applied under the pure Wednesbury formula [see *ex p. Smith*]
> (c) Constitutional rights review. Where implied 'constitutional rights' are engaged (based, e.g. on the rule of law *ex p. Pierson* [1998] AC 539 or free

---

95   *R (Bradley) v Secretary of State for Work and Pensions* [2008] EWCA Civ 36; [2008] 3 WLR 1059.

96   See Chapter 16, at 916..

expression *ex p. Simms* [2000] 2 AC 115, the 'principle of legality' is applied. Under this principle the courts make the presumption that the rights will apply unless revoked by Parliament expressly or by necessary implication.

(d) Structured justification proportionality review. Here the courts apply a structured set of questions relating to the balance, necessity and suitability of the public authority's decision.

Notes

1. This last ground of review only appears to apply when the courts are within the scope of application of EU law, or when applying the law of the European Convention on Human Rights[97] under the Human Rights Act.[98] The authors reject however, any notion that *Wednesbury* has become assimilated into proportionality, castigating *R (Suleiman) v Secretary of State for the Home Department* [2006] EWHC 2431 (Admin) as wrong in suggesting otherwise. Ultimately, however as Steele comments, the experience of dealing with proportionality in HRA and EU cases may well be decisive:

> The realisation in rights cases that the proportionality test can be applied with varying degrees of intensity is at last assuaging fears that adopting the test in non-rights cases will lead to excessively close scrutiny of decisions by the courts. It therefore seems likely that the House of Lords will in the future extend the more structured form of inquiry which that test provides to non-rights cases.[99]

2. The issue therefore is whether proportionality may come to 'spill over' into judicial review in cases not involving either the HRA or EU law: may it come to function as a free standing general head of English judicial review? This is a large topic, considered only briefly here.[100]

Proportionality—the future?

In the *GCHQ* case [1985] AC 374, Lord Diplock, after his seminal summary of the current heads of judicial review as illegality, procedural impropriety and irrationality, added, in a well-known passage (at 410):

> That is not to say that further development on a case by case bias may not in course of time add further grounds. I have in mind particularly the possible adoption of future of the principle of proportionality, which is recognised in the administrative law of several of our fellow members of the [EEC].

However, in *Brind and another v Secretary of State for the Home Department* [1991] 1 All ER 720, HL, this possibility appeared to recede. Lord Bridge and Lord Roskill were prepared to leave the possibility

---

97   See further Chapter 7, pp 315–316.

98   See further Chapter 17, pp 1003–1111.

99   Steel, n 65 above, at 318.

100   For further guidance, see J Jowell, 'Beyond the Rule of Law: towards constitutional judicial review' [2000] PL 671; D Feldman, 'Proportionality and the Human Rights Act 1998', in *The Principle of Proportionality in the Laws of Europe* (1999), pp 117, 127 *et seq*; G Wong, 'Towards the Nutcracker Principle: Reconsidering the Objections to Proportionality' [2000] PL 92.

open for the future (at 724 and 725), but Lord Ackner thought it should be ruled out, in the absence of its introduction in legislation by Parliament (at 735) and it was also disapproved by Lord Lowry, who observed:

> . . .there can be very little room for judges to operate an independent judicial review proportionality doctrine in the space which is left between the conventional judicial review doctrine and the admittedly forbidden appellate approach [i.e. review on the merits].

These *dicta* appeared to misunderstand the principled basis for the proportionality doctrine, which is *not* the equivalent of 'merits' review. Paul Craig provides a very clear explanation:

P Craig, *Administrative Law*, 6th edn (2008), pp 627–28

It is important at the outset to ascertain the place of proportionality within the general scheme of review, and its relationship with other existing methods of control. It is clear, as a matter of principle, that to talk of proportionality at all assumes that the public body was entitled to pursue its desired objective. The presumption is, therefore, that the general objective was a legitimate one, and that the public body was not seeking to achieve an improper purpose. If the purpose was improper then the exercise of discretion should be struck down upon this ground, without any investigation as to whether it was disproportionate. Proportionality should then only be considered once the controls [represented by the existing heads of 'Illegality' review]. . .have been satisfied.

Let us turn now to the meaning of the concept itself. It is obvious that at a general level proportionality involves some idea of balance between competing interests or objectives, and that it embodies some sense of an appropriate relationship between means and ends. We must therefore identify the relevant interests and ascribe some weight to them. A decision must then be made as to whether the public body's decision was indeed proportionate or not, in the light of the preceding considerations. The most common formulation is a three part analysis. The court considers:

(i)   Whether the measure was suitable to achieve the desired objective.
(ii) Whether the measure was necessary for achieving the desired objective.
(iii) Whether it none the less imposed excessive burdens on the individual. The last part of this inquiry is often termed proportionality *stricto sensu* [in a strict sense].

It will be apparent from the subsequent analysis that the court will have to decide how *intensively* to apply these criteria. It should also be recognised that the criteria may require the court to consider *alternative strategies* for attaining the desired end. This follows from the fact that the court will, in fundamental rights cases, consider whether there was a less restrictive measure for attaining the desired objective. . .

Note

Recent judicial observations on this matter appear in the following case. Lord Steyn's comments are mainly directed towards the approach required under the Human Rights Act 1998, but are of wider interest; Lord Cooke's plainly are of general application.

R v Secretary of State for the Home Department ex parte Daly
[2001] 2 AC 532, 547, 549

Lord Steyn: . . .The contours of the principle of proportionality are familiar. In *de Freitas v Permanent Secretary of Ministry of Agriculture, Fisheries, Lands and Housing* [1999] 1 AC 69 the Privy Council adopted a three stage test. Lord Clyde observed, at p 80, that in determining whether a limitation (by an act, rule or decision) is arbitrary or excessive the court should ask itself: whether: (i) the legislative objective is sufficiently important to justify limiting a fundamental right; (ii) the measures designed to meet the legislative objective are rationally connected to it; and (iii) the means used to impair the right or freedom are no more than is necessary to accomplish the objective.

Clearly, these criteria are more precise and more sophisticated than the traditional grounds of review. What is the difference for the disposal of concrete cases? The starting point is that there is an overlap between the traditional grounds of review and the approach of proportionality. Most cases would be decided in the same way whichever approach is adopted. But the intensity of review is somewhat greater under the proportionality approach. Making due allowance for important structural differences between various convention rights, which I do not propose to discuss, a few generalisations are perhaps permissible. I would mention three concrete differences without suggesting that my statement is exhaustive. First, the doctrine of proportionality may require the reviewing court to assess the balance which the decision maker has struck, not merely whether it is within the range of rational or reasonable decisions. Secondly, the proportionality test may go further than the traditional grounds of review inasmuch as it may require attention to be directed to the relative weight accorded to interests and considerations. Thirdly, even the heightened scrutiny test developed in *R v Ministry of Defence, Ex p Smith* [1996] QB 517, 554 is not necessarily appropriate to the protection of human rights. It will be recalled that in Smith the Court of Appeal reluctantly felt compelled to reject a limitation on homosexuals in the army. The challenge based on article 8 of the Convention for the Protection of Human Rights and Fundamental Freedoms (the right to respect for private and family life) foundered on the threshold required even by the anxious scrutiny test. The European Court of Human Rights came to the opposite conclusion: *Smith and Grady v United Kingdom* (1999) 29 EHRR 493. The court concluded, at p 543, para 138:

> the threshold at which the High Court and the Court of Appeal could find the Ministry of Defence policy irrational was placed so high that it effectively excluded any consideration by the domestic courts of the question of whether the interference with the applicants' rights answered a pressing social need or was proportionate to the national security and public order aims pursued, principles which lie at the heart of the court's analysis of complaints under article 8 of the Convention.

In other words, the intensity of the review, in similar cases, is guaranteed by the twin requirements that the limitation of the right was necessary in a democratic society, in the sense of meeting a pressing social need, and the question whether the interference was really proportionate to the legitimate aim being pursued.

The differences in approach between the traditional grounds of review and the proportionality approach may therefore sometimes yield different results. It is therefore important that cases involving convention rights must be analysed in the correct way. This does not mean that there has been a shift to merits review. On the contrary, as Professor

Jowell [2000] PL 671, 681 has pointed out the respective roles of judges and administrators are fundamentally distinct and will remain so. To this extent the general tenor of the observations in *Mahmood* [2001] 1 WLR 840 are correct. And Laws LJ rightly emphasised in Mahmood, at p 847, para 18, 'that the intensity of review in a public law case will depend on the subject matter in hand'. That is so even in cases involving Convention rights. In law context is everything.

Lord Cooke: . . .I think that the day will come when it will be more widely recognised that [the *Wednesbury* decision] was an unfortunately retrogressive decision in English administrative law, insofar as it suggested that there are degrees of unreasonableness and that only a very extreme degree can bring an administrative decision within the legitimate scope of judicial invalidation. The depth of judicial review and the deference due to administrative discretion vary with the subject matter. It may well be, however, that the law can never be satisfied in any administrative field merely by a finding that the decision under review is not capricious or absurd.

Notes

1. In *R (On the application of Alconbury Developments) v Secretary of State for the Environment* [2001] 2 WLR 1389; [2001] 2 All ER 929, Lord Slynn observed that 'even without reference to the [HRA] the time has come to recognise that [proportionality] is part of English Administrative law, not only when judges are dealing with [EU law] but also when they are dealing with acts subject to domestic law' (at 976). If *Wednesbury's* days are numbered, as Lord Cooke suggests (it should be noted that his remarks were not endorsed by any of the other Law Lords deciding the case), then the obvious replacement would be some form of proportionality. In *R v Secretary of State for the Home Department ex parte Hindley* [2001] 1 AC 410, one of the arguments advanced by the applicant was that the imposition upon her by the Secretary of State of a 'whole life tariff', that is, a sentence that she spend the rest of her natural life in custody was unlawful because it was disproportionate. It is worthy of note that the response of their Lordships to this argument was not simply to observe that proportionality is not a recognised head of review in English law, outside the context of EU and ECHR law; rather it was found merely that, on the facts, the sentence could not be considered disproportionate.[101] Similarly, in *R v Secretary of State for the Environment, Transport and the Regions ex parte Spath Holme Limited* [2001] 2 AC 349, one of the arguments advanced was that Ministers had acted 'unreasonably, unfairly and disproportionately'; again the argument was not rejected on grounds of principle by their Lordships but simply dealt with on the facts of the case (see at 396, *per* Lord Bingham). While clearly not a positive endorsement of the use of proportionality as a free-standing ground of review, these decisions appear to indicate a much greater readiness to countenance it than was apparent 10 years ago in *Brind* [1991] 1 All ER 720, HL.

2. However, *Assn. of British Civilian Internees Far Eastern Region v SS for Defence* [2003] 3 WLR 80 has confirmed that, outside cases concerning the HRA or EU law, *Wednesbury* remains the appropriate standard. The Court of Appeal indicated its dissatisfaction with the *Wednesbury* test and its view that it should be replaced with a proportionality test but said that only the House of Lords could perform the 'burial rites' of *Wednesbury*. As Fordham notes: 'The Law Lords, failing to take the hint, refused permission to appeal, and put the development of the common law back a decade.'[102]

---

101   See the speech of Lord Steyn, at 412, and of Lord Hobhouse, at 421: 'I agree with your Lordships that this aspect of the appellant's case fails on the facts.'

102   M Fordham, 'Wednesbury' [2007] JR 266, 267.

FURTHER READING

R Clayton, 'Principles of Judicial Deference' [2006] JR 109

R Clayton, 'Shifting Standards of Review' [2007] JR 210

P Craig, 'Judicial Review, Appeal and Factual Error' [2004] PL 788

M Elliott, 'Legitimate Expectations and Unlawful Representations' [2004] CLJ 261

M Fordham, 'Wednesbury' [2007] JR 266

S Hannett and L Busch 'Ultra vires representations and illegitimate expectations' [2005] PL 729

T Hickman, 'The Reasonableness Principle: Reassessing its Place in the Public Sphere' [2004] CLJ 166

C Hilson, 'Policies, the Non-Fetter Principle and the Principle of Substantive Legitimate Expectations: Between a Rock and a Hard Place' [2006] JR 28

C Knight 'The Test that Dare Not Speak its Name: Proportionality Comes Out of the Closet?' [2007] JR 117

C Knight, 'Proportionality, the Decision-Maker and the House of Lords' [2007] JR 221

A Le Sueur, 'The Rise and Ruin of Unreasonableness' [2005] JR 32

T Poole, 'The Reformation of English Administrative Law' [2009] 68(1) CLJ 142

R Williams, 'When is an Error not an Error? Reform of Jurisdictional Review of Error of Law and fact' [2007] PL 973

CHAPTER 16
OMBUDSMEN

INTRODUCTION

The following description of the concept of ombudsmen is taken from a leading international reference work on the subject:

> The ombudsman is an independent and non-partisan officer. . .often provided for in the Constitution, who supervises the administration. He deals with specific complaints from the public against administrative injustice and maladministration. He has the power to investigate, report upon, and make recommendations about individual cases and administrative procedures. He is not a judge or tribunal, and he has no power to make orders or to reverse administrative action. He seeks solutions to problems by a process of investigation and conciliation. His authority and influence derive from the fact that he is appointed by and reports to one of the principal organs of state, usually either the parliament or the chief executive.[1]

The Ombudsman concept has proved hugely popular, and there are now Ombudsmen in more than 90 countries round the world. The following extract from an article written by the current UK Parliamentary Ombudsman, shows both the unifying features they all share and some quite important variations—that may be borne in mind when considering arguments as to the particular scheme of the UK Ombudsmen and possible reforms. In it, Abraham refers to work by Professor Kucsko-Stadlmayer.

A Abraham, 'The future in international perspective: the ombudsman as agent of rights, justice and democracy' (2008) 61(4) *Parliamentary Affairs* 681 (extracts)

What [Professor Kucsko-Stadlmayer] refers to as 'the basic model' is to be found in countries such as Norway, the Netherlands, Cyprus and Israel, and replicated in the institution of the European Union's own 'European Ombudsman'. The basic model comprises coverage of the entire administrative system, supervision against standards of 'good administration', together with powers of investigation, inspection, recommendation and public report, but in the absence of binding findings. In other words, the basic model covers the classical Ombudsman activity of detecting maladministration and using powers of exhortation and moral authority to produce individual remedy and future systemic change.

The basic model is, however, subject to variation in a number of ways. First, coverage is in some cases extended to supervision of private sector entities close to the State (e.g. in Austria, Albania and France) or to the justice system (e.g. in Sweden, Finland and Poland). Secondly, the supervisory criteria can be focused, for example, to include the explicit protection of human rights (e.g. in Spain and Slovenia) or the explicit promotion of human rights in other ways (e.g. in Finland, Hungary, Romania, Denmark and several of the former Soviet states). Thirdly, the powers available to the Ombudsman can be extended to include the ability to bring challenges before the constitutional court (e.g. in Austria, Poland, Portugal, Hungary), the ability to refer or even institute criminal prosecution against civil servants (e.g. in Greece, Finland, Bosnia, Poland), to introduce proposals for legislation (e.g. in France, Greece and Portugal) or to exercise a wide range of 'amicus curiae' [friend

---

1   GE Caiden (ed), *International Handbook of the Ombudsman* (1983), p 13.

of the court] powers of intervention in court cases (e.g. in Poland, Finland, Croatia and Romania).

Notes

1. The first UK ombudsman was the Parliamentary Commissioner for Administration—now known simply as the Parliamentary Ombudsman (PO); that office was set up under the Parliamentary Commissioner Act 1967. Since then the system has been extended to other areas (see below), suggesting that it has shown itself to be of value. It is important to bear in mind the role the PO was set up to fulfil. Pre-existing judicial and parliamentary remedies did not, it appeared, provide adequate redress for members of the public who had suffered as a result of maladministration in central government. Defective administrative action was going un-remedied either because it fell outside the jurisdiction of the courts or because MPs did not have sufficient powers to investigate it satisfactorily.

2. There will be some overlap between the range of administrative actions the ombudsman can consider and those which can be considered where there is a statutory right of appeal or in judicial review proceedings (see below). However, in a number of respects the ombudsman system may be more effective as a means of providing redress for the citizen mistreated by government authorities than judicial and Parliamentary remedies, principally, perhaps, because use of the PO is free to the complainant. However, it should be borne in mind that the ombudsman system was not set up as a *replacement* for other remedies, but in order to fill gaps they created.

3. A note on abbreviations and terminology: this chapter, as well as referring to the Parliamentary Ombudsman ('PO') will also mention the Commissioner for Local Administration—the ombudsman who oversees local government, known either as the CLA or, as in this chapter, the Local Government Ombudsman (LGO). The Health Service Commissioner's office has now been merged with that of the PO, and both will be referred to by that abbreviation. Where 'the Ombudsman' is mentioned, the reference is to the PO unless the context indicates otherwise. Note that all PO reports are available online at www.ombudsman.org.uk/improving_services/index.html

4. A wide-ranging and radical review of the work of the PO and other public sector ombudsmen was carried out by the Cabinet Office in 2000,[2] sometimes referred to as the Calcutt Report, after the name of its Chair. The principal recommendations for reform of this important report are considered in the final section of this chapter. However, where earlier sections deal with issues on which the report made a recommendation (for example, on access to the PO), that recommendation is considered at that point.

THE POSITION, ROLE AND WORK OF THE PO

The position and role of the PO

Parliamentary Commissioner Act 1967, as amended

Appointment and tenure of office

1.–(1) For the purpose of conducting investigations in accordance with the following provisions of this Act there shall be appointed a Commissioner, to be known as the Parliamentary Commissioner for Administration.

---

2 *Review of the Public Sector Ombudsmen in England,* Cabinet Office, April 2000.

(2)   Her Majesty may by Letters Patent from time to time appoint a person to be the Commissioner, and any person so appointed shall (subject to subsections (3) and (3A) of this section) hold office during good behaviour.

(3)   A person appointed to be the Commissioner may be relieved of office by Her Majesty at his own requestor may be removed from office by Her Majesty in consequence of Addresses from both Houses of Parliament, and shall in any case vacate office on completing the year of service in which he attains the age of sixty-five years.

(3A) [provision for removal for ill-health] . . .

Matters subject to investigation
5.–(1) Subject to the provisions of this section, the commissioner may investigate any action taken by or on behalf of a Government department or other authority to which this Act applies, being action taken in the exercise of administrative functions of that department or authority, in any case where—

(a)   a written complaint is duly made to a member of the House of Commons by a member of the public who claims to have sustained injustice in consequence of maladministration in connection with the action so taken; and

(b)   the complaint is referred to the commissioner, with the consent of the person who made it, by a member of that House with a request to conduct an investigation thereon.

[For s 5(2)–(3), see below, p 895.]

(5)   In determining whether to initiate, continue or discontinue an investigation under this Act, the commissioner shall, subject to the foregoing provisions of this section, act in accordance with his own discretion; and any question whether a complaint is duly made under this Act shall be determined by the commissioner.

Provisions relating to complaints
6.–(1) A complaint under this Act may be made by any individual, or by any body of persons whether incorporated or not, not being—

(a)   a local authority or other authority or body constituted for purposes of the public service or of local government or for the purposes of carrying on under national ownership any industry or undertaking or part of an industry or undertaking;

(b)   any other authority or body whose members are appointed by Her Majesty or any minister of the Crown or Government department, or whose revenues consist wholly or mainly of moneys provided by Parliament.

(3)   A complaint shall not be entertained under this Act unless it is made to a member of the House of Commons not later than 12 months from the day on which the person aggrieved first had notice of the matters alleged in the complaint; but the commissioner may conduct an investigation pursuant to a complaint not made within that period if he considers that there are special circumstances which make it proper to do so.

. . .

Obstruction and contempt

9.–(1) If any person without lawful excuse obstructs the commissioner or any officer of the commissioner in the performance of his functions under this Act, or is guilty of any act or omission in relation to an investigation under this Act which, if that investigation were a proceeding in the Court, would constitute contempt of court, the commissioner may certify the offence to the Court. . . .

Interpretation

12. . . . (3) It is hereby declared that nothing in this Act authorises or requires the Commissioner to question the merits of a decision taken without maladministration by a government department or other authority in the exercise of a discretion vested in that department or authority.

Notes

1. As provided in s 1, the PO has security of tenure. She is appointed by the Government, but, by convention, only following consultation with the chair of the Select Committee on the PO (now the Public Administration Select Committee, hereafter PAC) and the Leader of the Opposition. She appoints her own staff, around 100 in number.[3] Court decisions challenging the PO for refusing to investigate have confirmed that the PO has complete discretion in this matter and cannot be compelled to investigate.[4]

2. There are clear advantages for the aggrieved citizen in using the ombudsman rather than relying on an MP to resolve the problem. Although MPs are of course able to hear a wide range of complaints, their powers of investigation are limited. The PO, in contrast, has broad powers of investigation. Under s 7 of the Act, she may examine all documents relevant to the investigation, and the duty to assist her overrides the duty to maintain secrecy under the Official Secrets Act 1989. The PO does not, however, have access to Cabinet papers.

3. Parliamentary procedures such as Questions and Select Committees operate within the doctrine of ministerial responsibility; in other words the expectation is that the Minister in question will remedy matters. As Harlow points out, and Chapter 12 discusses, the doctrine may actually shelter more administrative blunders than it exposes.[5] The PO can be more effective in practice as she on the other hand looks behind that expectation and considers the workings of the administrative body itself.

4. The PO was given the ability to investigate a wider range of complaints than could be investigated in a court and given greater investigative powers than those available to MPs. In some instances of maladministration there may be a statutory right of appeal to a tribunal. Where a court or tribunal could consider such defective administration, the PO will not investigate the matter unless it would be unreasonable to expect the complainant to seek redress in litigation.

5. The PO is empowered to consider maladministration under s 10(3) of the Act as opposed to illegality. Maladministration has been described by Richard Crossman in the debate on the Parliamentary Commissioner Bill 1967 as including 'bias, neglect, inattention, delay, incompetence, ineptitude, perversity, turpitude, arbitrariness'.[6] It must not be forgotten that once

---

3   See G Drewry, 'The ombudsman: parochial stopgap or global panacea?', in P Leyland and T Woods (eds), *Administrative Law: Facing the Future* (1997), p 98.

4   *Re Fletcher's Application* [1970] 2 All ER 527.

5   'Ombudsmen in Search of a Role' (1978) 41 MLR 452.

6   HC Deb vol 754 col 51 (1966).

maladministration is found, it must be shown that it caused 'injustice'. It was recently clarified in the case of *ex p Balchin (No 2)*,[7] that 'injustice' is specifically *not* limited to identifiable loss or damage, but includes 'a sense of outrage caused by unfair or incompetent administration'. See further below, pp 922–925.

6. The third report from the Select Committee on the PO for the Session 1993–94 noted that the PCA has produced an expanded list of forms of maladministration.

Third Report from the Select Committee on the Parliamentary Commissioner for Administration, HC 345 (1993–94)

Maladministration

10 ... The commissioner has always made clear his preference for the term mal-administration, included in the statute without definition, in that it gives him considerable freedom and flexibility in interpretation. ...At paragraph 7 of his annual report Mr Reid produced an expanded list in the language of the 1990s [PO Annual Report for 1993, para 7]:

- rudeness (though that is a matter of degree);
- unwillingness to treat the complainant as a person with rights;
- refusal to answer reasonable questions;
- neglecting to inform a complainant on request of his or her rights or entitlement;
- knowingly giving advice which is misleading or inadequate;
- ignoring valid advice or overruling considerations which would produce an uncomfort-able result for the overruler;
- offering no redress or manifestly disproportionate redress;
- showing bias whether because of colour, sex, or any other grounds;
- omission to notify those who thereby lose a right of appeal;
- refusal to inform adequately of the right of appeal;
- faulty procedures;
- failure by management to monitor compliance with adequate procedures;
- cavalier disregard of guidance which is intended to be followed in the interest of equitable treatment of those who use a service;
- partiality;
- failure to mitigate the effects of rigid adherence to the letter of the law where that produces manifestly inequitable treatment.

Note

In investigating maladministration, the ombudsman system may have some advantages over a court hearing. Its informality in investigation may be more effective at times in discovering the truth than the adversarial system in the courts. Moreover, in court, the Crown may plead public interest immunity to avoid disclosing documents, whereas the PO can look at all departmental files. Such flexibility is also reflected in the fact that the ombudsman procedure is not circumscribed by rules as regards time limits and therefore may provide a remedy in instances which cannot be considered by a court. The current PO draws out these points:

---

7   (2000) LGLR 87.

A Abraham, 'The Ombudsman as part of the UK Constitution: a contested role?' (2008) 61(1) *Parliamentary Affairs* 206, 207

...The performance of [the PO's] quasi-judicial functions is marked by characteristics that put clear blue water between the Ombudsman approach and that of the courts and tribunals, especially those of a common law jurisdiction like that of England and Wales. First, my investigative process is inquisitorial, not adversarial; it is normally conducted in correspondence and by face to face or telephone interviews, rather than in the combative environment of a courtroom. Secondly, my findings are not confined by strict judicial precedent; instead I reach conclusions that are just and reasonable in the particular circumstances of the case, informed by principle no doubt, but far less overtly legalistic than the judgment of a court or tribunal. Thirdly, the remedy imposed will not be enforceable against the respondent by the complaint, but will instead derive its authority from its cogency and moral force; on the other hand, the remedy will very frequently extend beyond the sort of financial redress that is the staple fare of the courts and tribunals, effecting instead a degree of future prevention as well as retrospective cure.

This amounts to a process that has all the hallmarks of a developed system of justice but one that is different from the...system in operation in the civil courts of England and Wales. The formality, legalism and inflexibility that characterise the legal process are absent from the Ombudsman system, being replaced instead by relative informality, equitable principle and flexibility, all in the cause of producing a process of dispute resolution that is responsive to the needs of citizens, fair to both parties and effective in delivering appropriate remedies.

Notes

1. Although maladministration is a wide concept, it does mean that the PO is generally concerned with administrative defects rather than with the merits of a government decision or are of policy. This distinction is contained in s 12(3) of the Act which provides that the PO may not investigate the merits of a decision taken without maladministration. This raises the important distinction between policy (which Ombudsmen may not question) and administration is generally maintainable; however, it has on occasion caused disagreement. Because parts of the statutory scheme are virtually identical in wording, cases on the LGO can provide useful guidance as to how the powers and duties of the PO should be interpreted.[8] The policy/administration distinction is clearly of the greatest importance in terms of defining the proper ambit of both the PO and the LGO's investigations; it arose for consideration in *R v Local Commissioner ex parte Eastleigh Borough Council*.[9] Michael Jones comments:[10]

   > *Eastleigh*'s first importance, perhaps, is that it helps to clarify the impact which s 34(3) of the 1974 Act has upon the scope of the commissioner's jurisdiction [s 34(3) is in the same terms as s 12(3) PCA 1967, above p 889]... In *Eastleigh*, the court's interpretation of s 34(3) affirms the orthodox view, and the legislature's

---

8   In *R (On the application of Bradley) v Secretary of State for Work and Pensions* [2008] EWCA Civ 36; [2009] QB 114 (considered below), a case concerning the PO, it was found (at para 43) that consideration of 'relevant provisions of the Local Government Act 1974...form[ed] an important part of [the claimant's] argument'.

9   [1988] 3 WLR 116.

10   M Jones, 'The Local Ombudsmen and Judicial Review' [1988] PL 608.

intent, that the commissioners ought not to usurp the policy-making discretions of democratically elected authorities. . . .

But how far does the prohibition in s 34(3) extend? Parker LJ. . .recognised that the immunity conferred by s 34(3) is not absolute: the terms of s 34(3) do not preclude the ombudsman from questioning the merits of all discretionary policy decisions, but only those taken without maladministration [ibid, at 123]. In other words, the local ombudsmen (and their parliamentary colleague) may continue to find maladministration in the processes by which discretionary decisions are made upon grounds which closely resemble the *Wednesbury* principles of review employed by the courts: relevancy, proper purposes and so on. And there may still be room for a finding of maladministration where a commissioner considers that the terms of an authority's policy transcend the bounds of reasonableness, and step into perversity, capriciousness, or what the courts now term irrationality. After all, the Parliamentary Commissioner, prompted by his Select Committee, has developed the analogous concept of the bad rule.

2. As the above makes clear, whilst the jurisdiction of the PO is, strictly speaking, limited to investigating specific cases of maladministration, she can and does make general findings and recommendations to improve the administration of a given department. The most recent PO to hold the post, Ms Ann Abrahams, has made it clear that she is firmly of the view that her remit does *not* include making recommendations on specific policy issues not arising from complaints made to her.[11] Plainly, however, she *does* see a role for the PO in using investigations and reports on complaints to improve administration and the application of particular policies.

A Abraham, 'The Ombudsman as part of the UK Constitution: A contested role?' (2008) 61(1) Parliamentary Affairs 206, 210–12

The grievances that citizens bring to my Office put me on notice of where things are going wrong and of where improvement is most needed; they make it possible for me to prescribe values and behaviours that will reduce the likelihood of repetition; and they also enable me to tackle future breaches. In this way a virtuous circle is established, the ultimate objective being not so much the retrospective eradication of maladministration but the prospective promotion of good administration, prevention rather than cure.

This codifying function, albeit derived from and closely implicated with my core complaint-investigating function, marks out a very distinctive role that sets me apart from either the courts and tribunals or other forms of [Alternative Dispute Resolution]. It is a function that is also complementary to my ability to issue 'special reports', concerned not so much with individual grievances but rather with the underlying and systemic defects that have given rise to an entire cluster of complaints. It is the sort of function to which the common law mentality with its inherent individualism is a stranger, constrained from looking beyond the facts of the particular case, compelled invariably to resort to a simplistic 'rotten apple' theory of organisational malfunction instead of a more realistic analysis that makes room for systemic and institutional failure.

Secondly, there is my wider-reaching ability to influence and contribute to the improvement, not just of administration and complaint handling, but of public service delivery itself.

---

11   Oral Evidence before PAC, 11 March 2003, HC 506–1.

In part, this ability is the natural concomitant of improving internal administration: there is a necessary link between good administration and the improvement of service delivery. Yet beyond that, there is also scope to extract the lessons yielded by a comprehensive 'database' of complaints in such a way that I can present a compelling narrative of ineffective service delivery and so bring about Insight, a shift in awareness and, if necessary, a change of 'culture' within the public sector. This 'influencing' work is no doubt more remote from the resolution of individual complaints than a more conventional 'system of justice' role might entail, but it is nevertheless part and parcel of the remedial action available to me and ultimately rooted in the core activity of complaint handling. Thirdly, and most ambitiously, there is the prospect of drawing upon the experience of complaint handling not just to improve administration and change culture, but to inform policy debate on aspects of public service delivery.

A recent example suggests how this cumulative remedial action can work in practice to the public benefit. In June 2005, I completed a special report into the UK Government's then new system for operating tax credits. That report focused in particular on the social group intended to benefit from the reform: low-income families with children, and low-income earners. Drawing directly on the experience of the individual complaints referred to me, I identified an underlying pattern of dissatisfaction that stemmed to a large extent from the Government having adopted a 'one size fits all' system, a system designed to require minimum human intervention and relying instead on IT. In short, I found that this 'blanket' approach took no account of the very different circumstances and needs within the target group. The result was that the new system often had harsh and unintended consequences for the most vulnerable users of the system, frequently leading to debt recovery action by the Government to retrieve overpayments caused by the malfunctioning of its own reforms and, irony of ironies, casting into debt those most in need of financial support and intended to benefit from the reform in the first place . . .The picture that emerges is one of a tax credits system that, even when working as intended, in some respects runs counter to the key policy objectives of helping tackle child poverty and of encouraging more people to work by 'making work pay'.

Question

Do not these findings by the PO as to the overall effectiveness of the tax credits scheme amount to questioning the merits of government policy?

THE JURISDICTION OF THE PO: EXCLUDED AREAS

Although the jurisdiction of the PO has recently been extended to cover a much wider range of governmental bodies (below), much of the ongoing debate continues to concern the areas of governmental activity that are excluded from her remit. Schedules 2 and 3 to the Act, as amended, list, respectively, the bodies generally subject to her jurisdiction and the areas of work within those bodies that are specifically excluded.

Parliamentary Commissioner Act 1967, ss 4, 5 and Scheds 2 and 3

Departments etc subject to investigation

4.–(1) Subject to the provisions of this section and to the notes contained in Schedule 2 to this Act, this Act applies to the government departments, corporations and unincorporated bodies listed in that Schedule; and references in this Act to an authority to which this Act applies are references to any such corporation or body.

(2) Her Majesty may by Order in Council amend Schedule 2 to this Act by the alteration of any entry or note, the removal of any entry or note or the insertion of any additional entry or note.

(3) An Order in Council may only insert an entry if—

    (a) it relates—

        (i) to a government department; or

        (ii) to a corporation or body whose functions are exercised on behalf of the Crown; or

    (b) it relates to a corporation or body—

        (i) which is established by virtue of Her Majesty's prerogative or by an Act of Parliament or an Order in Council or order made under an Act of Parliament or which is established in any other way by a Minister of the Crown in his capacity as a Minister or by a government department;

        (ii) at least half of whose revenues derive directly from money provided by Parliament, a levy authorised by an enactment, a fee or charge of any other description so authorised or more than one of those sources; and

        (iii) which is wholly or partly constituted by appointment made by Her Majesty or a Minister of the Crown or government department.

[Section 4(3A) and (3B) preclude bodies being investigated that are covered by the Welsh Administration Ombudsman and the Scottish Administration and 'any Scottish public authority with mixed functions or no reserved functions within the meaning of the Scotland Act 1998'.]

(4) No entry shall be made in respect of a corporation or body whose sole activity is, or whose main activities are, included among the activities specified in subsection (5) below.

(5) The activities mentioned in subsection (4) above are—

    (a) the provision of education, or the provision of training otherwise than under the Industrial Training Act 1982;

    (b) the development of curricula, the conduct of examinations or the validation of educational courses;

    (c) the control of entry to any profession or the regulation of the conduct of members of any profession;

(d)   the investigation of complaints by members of the public regarding the actions of any person or body, or the supervision or review of such investigations or of steps taken following them.

(6)   No entry shall be made in respect of a corporation or body operating in an exclusively or predominantly commercial manner or a corporation carrying on under national ownership an industry or undertaking or part of an industry or undertaking.

(7)   Any statutory instrument made by virtue of this section shall be subject to annulment in pursuance of a resolution of either House of Parliament. . . .

5.–(2) Except as hereinafter provided, the commissioner shall not conduct an investigation under this Act in respect of any of the following matters, that is to say:

(a)   any action in respect of which the person aggrieved has or had a right of appeal, reference or review to or before a tribunal constituted by or under any enactment or by virtue of Her Majesty's prerogative;

(b)   any action in respect of which the person aggrieved has or had a remedy by way of proceedings in any court of law;

provided that the commissioner may conduct an investigation notwithstanding that the person aggrieved has or had such a right or remedy if satisfied that in the particular circumstances it is not reasonable to expect him to resort or have resorted to it.

(3)   Without prejudice to subsection (2) of this section, the commissioner shall not conduct an investigation under this Act in respect of any such action or matter as is described in Schedule 3 to this Act.

. . .

Schedule 3
Matters not subject to investigation:

- Action taken in matters certified by a Secretary of State or other Minister of the Crown to affect relations or dealings between the Government of the United Kingdom and any other Government or any international organisation of States or Governments.
- Action taken, in any country or territory outside the United Kingdom, by or on behalf of any officer representing or acting under the authority of Her Majesty in respect of the United Kingdom, or any other officer of the Government of the United Kingdom other than action which is taken by an officer (not being an honorary consular officer) in the exercise of a consular function on behalf of the government of the United Kingdom.
- Action taken in connection with the administration of the Government of any country or territory outside the United Kingdom which forms part of Her Majesty's dominions or in which Her Majesty has jurisdiction.
- Action taken by the Secretary of State under the Extradition Act 1870, the Fugitive Offenders Act 1881 or the Extradition Act 1989.

- Action taken by or with the authority of the Secretary of State for the purposes of investigating crime or of protecting the security of the state, including action so taken with respect to passports.
- The commencement or conduct of civil or criminal proceedings before any court of law in the United Kingdom, of proceedings at any place under the Naval Discipline Act 1957, the Army Act 1955 or the Air Force Act 1955, or of proceedings before any international court or tribunal.

6A. Action taken by any person appointed by the Lord Chancellor as a member of the administrative staff of any court or tribunal, so far as that action is taken at the direction, or on the authority (whether express or implied), of any person acting in a judicial capacity or in his capacity as a member of the tribunal.

6B.(1) Action taken by any member of the administrative staff of a relevant tribunal, so far as that action is taken at the direction, or on the authority (whether express or implied), of any person acting in his capacity as a member of the tribunal.

6C. Action taken by any person appointed under section 5(3)(c) of the Criminal Injuries Compensation Act 1995, so far as that action is taken at the direction, or on the authority (whether express or implied), of any person acting in his capacity as an adjudicator appointed under section 5 of that Act to determine appeals.

7. Any exercise of the prerogative of mercy or of the power of a Secretary of State to make a reference in respect of any person to. . .the High Court of Justiciary or the Courts-Martial Appeal Court

8. (1) Action taken on behalf of the Minister of Health or the Secretary of State by [various health bodies].

9. Action taken in matters relating to contractual or other commercial transactions, whether within the United Kingdom or elsewhere, being transactions of a government department or authority to which this Act applies or of any such authority or body as is mentioned in paragraph (a) or (b) of subsection (1) of section 6 of this Act and not being transactions for or relating to—

   (a) the acquisition of land compulsorily or in circumstances in which it could be acquired compulsorily;
   (b) the disposal as surplus of land acquired compulsorily or in such circumstances as aforesaid.

10. (1) Action taken in respect of appointments or removals, pay, discipline, super-annuation or other personnel matters, in relation to—

   (a) service in any of the armed forces of the Crown, including reserve and auxiliary and cadet forces;
   (b) service in any office or employment under the Crown or under any authority to which this Act applies; or
   (c) service in any office or employment, or under any contract for services, in respect of which power to take action, or to determine or approve the action to be

taken, in such matters is vested in Her Majesty, any Minister of the Crown or any such authority as aforesaid.

. . .

11. The grant of honours, awards or privileges within the gift of the Crown, including the grant of Royal Charters.

Notes
1. Some of the departments listed in Sched 2 contract out certain of their functions to private companies and these are covered by the PO.[12] Prior to 1987, the PO's jurisdiction was limited to central government departments and agencies, but the Parliamentary and Health Service Commissioners Act 1987 amended the 1967 Act in order to add about 50 non-departmental public bodies such as the Arts Council and the Equal Opportunities Commission to its remit. Subsequent Statutory Instruments have added or removed governmental bodies from the list, as the machinery of government changes and currently over 300 bodies are covered. In 2006 the PO acquired a new area of work, in hearing complaints from victims of crime in relation to the criminal justice system under the new Victims Code (2006).
2. Below, a Select Committee gives the reasons for various exclusions.

Evidence Taken Before the Select Committee on the PO, HC 64 (1993–94), Vol II, Annexes A and B

PO: subject areas outside jurisdiction
Means of referring a complaint (s 5(1))
Implications of s 5(1) are that it excludes from jurisdiction (a) bodies which are distinct entities from those in Schedule 2 and which are exercising functions of their own, and (b) legislative, judicial and quasi-judicial functions.

Right of appeal to tribunal (s 5(2)(a))
Any action in which a right of appeal to a tribunal exists is excluded. A tribunal is not defined in the Act. They were considered outside the scope of PO at the outset, because (a) their functions are quasi-judicial, not administrative, and (b) they are distinct from departments listed in Schedule 2 and exercise functions of their own. This was seen to conform with the underlying policy of the Act, that PO was not to replace existing institutions or safeguards, but to supplement them by providing protection for the citizen in his/her dealings with the executive where otherwise they do not exist.

Legal remedy (s 5(2)(b))
Actions where a legal remedy exists are excluded, again reflecting the principle that PO should not usurp the functions of existing institutions which provide protection for the citizen. (The proviso to the clause recognised the fact that there are few situations where there is ground for complaint of maladministration and where legal proceedings in some form or another cannot be instituted.)

Contractual or commercial transactions (Schedule 3, para 9)
The original reason for this exclusion was that PO was intended to operate in the field of relationships between the Government and the governed. Commercial judgments are by

---

12   Deregulation and Contracting Out Act 1994, s 72.

nature discriminatory, so the justification ran, and so allowing the commercial judgments of departments to be open to examination by private interests while leaving those interests themselves free from investigation would amount to putting departments, and with them the taxpayer, at a disadvantage.

In its response to the fourth report of the select committee 1979–80, the Government repeated this argument in rejecting the Committee's conclusion that the continued exclusion of these matters would not be justified, and stated more generally that only these activities unique to Government should be subject to PO. (The committee felt that all Government activities should be examinable unless there was a compelling argument otherwise.). . .

Exercise of extradition orders (Schedule 3, para 4)
In the exercise of extradition orders, the Secretary of State is acting in a quasi-judicial capacity as a final appellate authority. Adding, in effect, a further appeal an investigation by PO would, the argument ran, be inappropriate and inconsistent with the Government's responsibility for compliance with international obligations.

Power of Secretary of State to intercept communications and withhold or withdraw passports when investigating crime (Schedule 3, para 5)
The exclusion of complaints relating to the above was justified because (a) the use of the power ought to be kept secret, and (b) its use must form part of criminal investigations which are not, in other respects, a matter for central government and thus outside the PO's scope.

Note
Most controversial has been the exclusion from the PO's remit of contractual and commercial matters although, despite this criticism, the same matters have been excluded in the Scottish Public Services Ombudsman Act 2002 (see Sched 4, para 7). Drewry comments that, 'Looking at other ombudsman systems, such exclusions are rare—and the Northern Ireland PO (whose office is modelled closely on that of the mainland PO) does exercise jurisdiction in this area, without this causing any apparent difficulties'.[13] The Government's justification for the exclusion, as appears above, is based both on a theoretical contention that such matters are not in themselves governing activities, but only incidental to them, and also on the more practical ground that such scrutiny would place government departments at a commercial disadvantage, compared to the private interests which would not be open to scrutiny in the same way. The exemption clearly excludes a potentially wide range of decisions from the ambit of the PO, though as Mary Seneviratne notes, 'it has in practice. . . accounted for few rejections, perhaps because its scope has been limited by successive POs, who have decided that a service does not become commercial [merely] because a charge is made for it'.[14] In the following report the committee considered that the exclusion of commercial matters was unjustified.

Fourth Report from the Select Committee on the PO, HC 593 (1979–80)

4 In his evidence the [PO] placed much emphasis on a point made by the Select Committee in 1978, namely that s 5 of the Parliamentary Commissioner Act provided that the commissioner would not take up a case where a legal remedy was available, save in exceptional circumstances, and so if [the commercial exclusion were abolished] there

---

13   Above, n 3, at 99.

14   M Seneviratne, *Ombudsman in the Public Sector* (1994), p 23.

would still be no danger of the commissioner being involved in disputes about the performance of contracts. He believed, as his predecessors had, that paragraph 9 was unnecessary and undesirable in addition to s 5, and by its sweeping scope has had the effect of excluding many complaints which may have been found on investigation to be entirely justifiable. What he was concerned about was the way in which a department conducted the administrative side of Government buying and selling, where there was considerable scope for maladministration that could not be brought before the courts. He cited the case of a small office cleaning company, which had as the mainstay of its business a contract with a Government department; when the contract came up for renewal the company was not invited to tender, and on making enquiries it was told that another Government department had communicated confidential information of a damaging nature about the company to the department with which it had held the contract. The commissioner told us that he could investigate a complaint about the communication of confidential information because that was an administrative matter, but he would not be able to look into whether the information was used to remove the company from the list of tenderers for the contract because that was a commercial matter excluded by paragraph 9 of the Schedule.

. . . 8 We do not accept the Government's contention that only those activities, which are unique to the function of government, should be subject to review by the Parliamentary Commissioner; rather we believe that in principle all areas of government administration should be investigable by him unless in particular cases a compelling argument can be made out for their exclusion. Accordingly the claim that the Government's commercial activities should be exempt from examination because private contractors are exempt is in our view beside the point. The Government has a duty to administer its purchasing policies fairly and equitably, and if those policies are the subject of complaint then the complaints should be investigated; this is particularly important if any future Government were again to use the award of contracts as a political weapon. Section 12(3) of the Act would prevent the commissioner from questioning a bona fide commercial decision to purchase goods or services from one firm rather than another, or the legitimate exercise of a department's discretion to give selective assistance to one firm or one industry rather than another, but if decisions of this kind are taken with maladministration then it is right that they should be reviewed. . . We are satisfied that ss 5 and 12(3) of the Parliamentary Commissioner Act are sufficient on their own and that the further exemption from investigation conferred by paragraph 9 of Schedule 3 is not justified.

Notes

1. It is apparent that one of the main fears of the Committee in relation to the commercial exclusion was that the Government's immense public purchasing power could be used as a political weapon; for example, it could reward businesses which were pursuing policies in line with government recommendations (for example, on wage levels) with lucrative contracts.

2. Witnesses giving evidence to PAC in 2000 took a strong view on removal of the contractual exemption:

> [This is] a real problem because in this country public contracts are not subjected to any legal scrutiny through the courts, as there was hardly any litigation until very recent years. . . . Public money should be followed wherever it is spent and however it is spent and through whatever form it is spent. The problem with a contractual exemption is, if you say that a contractor is performing with maladministration then

you can go for that and criticise it. If the contractor turns around and says, 'This relates to the terms of our contract and this is a contractual dispute that I have with the public authority contractor', then it may well be able to get itself out of the framework.

The reason why the contract exemption was put there in the first place was for the Ministry of Defence, as I understand it, who are very sensitive about defence procurement. [But the exemption]. . .covers a whole range of public expenditure of money and the delivery of public services and public goods. . . I would prefer to have [the exemption] out altogether and to leave something along the lines, 'If there is a legal remedy then you pursue that. [But] the Ombudsman might be asked by third parties to investigate matters where there is no contractual nexus, so there is no legal remedy'.[15]

3. The point being made here is that while an actual contractor with the Government, who had a complaint about the Government's performance of that contract, should be required to pursue any complaint through the courts, where it had the prospect of a remedy, such an option would not be available to a third party, complaining about abuse of the Government's contractual power, since the third party would have no contract upon which to sue.

4. The exclusion in relation to actions in respect of which the claimant may have had a legal remedy in s 5(2) of the Act (above at 895) recently came under scrutiny as a result of the *Debt of Honour* case,[16] concerning the refusal by the MoD to pay *ex gratia* compensation to former British internees. As Kirkham points out, it could have been argued (and the MoD implied) that the PO should not have investigated those parts of the case in respect of which legal action could or had been brought (it had failed in *Association of British Civilian Internees: Far East Region v Secretary for Defence*).[17] Kirkham goes on:[18]

> However, there are good reasons why section 5(2)(b) cannot mean that the PO is prevented from investigating a complaint simply because the complainant has the option of bringing a case by way of judicial review. As one former ombudsman has been quoted as saying, there is 'an argument that nearly all actions which could amount to maladministration . . . could also be the subject of an application for leave to move for judicial review'. This is because the relatively liberal interpretation that the Administrative Court applies to the rules on standing and the broad range of administrative law grounds available, means that most complaints to the ombudsmen could be expressed in terms that are amenable to judicial review. Taken to its logical conclusion, therefore, a strict interpretation of section 5(2)(b)would deprive the PO of most of her elective purpose. Fortunately, such an absurd result is prevented by a line at the end of section 5(2) that allows the PO some flexibility. Thus the PO can investigate a complaint where a legal remedy is also available to a claimant, if she is 'satisfied that in the particular circumstances it is not reasonable to expect him to have resorted to it'. It is on the basis of these

---

15   PAC, 3rd Report, HC 612 (1999–2000), Evidence, 28 June 2000, 16 56–59 (Professor Patrick Birkinshaw).

16   Fourth Report of the Parliamentary Commissioner for Administration HC 324 (2004–05).

17   [2003] QB 1397.

18   R Kirkham, 'Challenging the Authority of the Ombudsman: The Parliamentary Ombudsman's Special Report on Wartime Detainees' (2006) 69(5) MLR 792, 798.

rather vague and unsatisfactory words that the PO conducts many of her investigations.

Kirkham goes on to offer an extensive analysis of when the existence of JR or other legal remedies means that it is improper, or possibly unlawful for the PO (or LGO) to investigate;[19] he also illustrates how the PO may effectively impose higher standards of good administration than do the courts on judicial review. It may be noted that the Law Commission in its paper on *Administrative Redress*[20] proposed the removal of the s 5(2) bar and its replacement with a provision whereby ombudsman would be able to 'conduct an investigation, notwithstanding that the person aggrieved has or had a legal remedy, if in all the circumstances it is in the interests of justice to investigate'.[21]

ACCESS TO THE PO: THE 'MP FILTER'[22]

Complaints cannot be made directly to the PO by a Member of Parliament. Under s 5(1) of the PO 1967 the PO may investigate a written complaint made by a member of the public to a Member of Parliament if the complaint is referred by the MP and both he and the complainant agree to investigation by the PO. Some amelioration of this system of making complaints occurred: since 1978, when the PO receives a complaint directly from a member of the public, the complainant's MP will be contacted and, if he or she is in agreement, the PO will investigate. This system does not, however, encourage citizens to complain directly to the PO and, due to his low profile, many will in any event be unaware that complaint is possible. This filter role played by MPs has been the subject of much controversy. It was intended initially as a experimental measure, to be reviewed after five years, but it is still in place at the time of writing. The filter system is virtually unique amongst the other countries in the world which have created ombudsmen; only the French ombudsman is subject to a similar filter. A summary of the problems with the present system appears below.

First Report from the Select Committee on the PO, HC 33 II (1993–94)

65 Objections to the MP filter can be summarised as follows:

(1) The public should have direct access to the commissioner as a matter of right.

(2) The filter is an anomaly, almost unknown in other ombudsman systems. No such requirement exists, for instance, in the case of the Health Service Commissioner.

(3) Individuals with complaints may be unwilling to approach an MP, while desiring the ombudsman's assistance.

(4) The filter means that the likelihood of individuals cases being referred to the commissioner will largely depend on the views and practice of the particular constituency MP. Some look with more favour on the Office of the commissioner than others.

---

19 See *ibid*, esp. at 799 *et seq.*

20 (2008) Paper No 187, available at www.lawcom.gov.uk/remedies.htm.

21 *Ibid* at [5.71].

22 For general discussion of the relationship between the PO and MPs, see G Drewry and C Harlow, 'A Cutting Edge? The Parliamentary Commissioner and MPs' (1990) 53 MLR 745.

(5)   The filter acts as an obstacle to the commissioner effectively promoting his services.

(6)   The filter creates an unnecessary bureaucratic barrier between the complainant and the commissioner involving considerable paperwork for MPs and their offices.

Notes

1. Evidence that the MP filter may reduce the number of complaints received by the PO came in a paper submitted to the above Select Committee:

    The number of complaints received by the Parliamentary Ombudsman is far lower than envisaged when the Parliamentary Ombudsman was introduced. The level is still more surprising when compared with the number of complaints received by ombudsmen in other countries. For example:

    Figures for 1991 show:
Danish ombudsman	5 million population:	2,000 complaints
Swedish ombudsman	8 million population:	4,000 complaints
British ombudsman	55 million population:	766 complaints

    The jurisdiction and constitutional position of the Scandinavian ombudsmen is very different from the Parliamentary Ombudsman. Even so, the number of complaints received by the ombudsmen in this country still appears low.[23]

2. The following extract indicates the chief objections MPs have to the removal of the MP filter.

    The work of the Parliamentary Ombudsman, acting at the behest of MPs and reporting to them the details of his investigations, has a vital role in equipping the Member for the tasks of Parliament. The knowledge of the details of and problems in administration has an important part in any effective scrutiny of the executive. The publication of anonymised reports can never be a genuine substitute for direct involvement in the case which the Member has referred. Direct access will result in the denial to Members of expertise in the problems facing their constituents as they come into contact with the executive. This is to impoverish parliamentary, and thus political, life.[24]

3. A number of points may be made in response to this. First of all, the argument, even if sound, seems rather self-serving. One may fairly predict that most constituents would consider that gaining a more efficient system for remedying their grievances easily outweighed this rather speculative harm. Second, the argument seems flawed in its own terms: it fails to recognise that direct access by the public to the PO need not necessarily cause any decrease at all in either the involvement of MPs in the matters raised or in the flow of information to them, the second of which is certainly vital to their role as scrutinisers of the executive. The Committee says that the publication of anonymised reports can never be a genuine substitute for direct involvement in the case which the Member has referred. But this is not the only alternative to the present system. If direct access were introduced, the continued involvement and knowledgability of MPs could be ensured very simply; the PO would simply copy the appropriate MP into any complaint received, and with news of the investigation of the complaint (if he or she decided to take it up) as it

---

23   Appendix to the Minutes of Evidence Taken before the Select Committee on the PO, HC 64 (1993–94), vol II, at [3.7].

24   First Report from the Select Committee on the PO, HC 33 11 (1993–94) at [75] and [76].

proceeded.[25] It does not seem clear that MPs' constitutional role necessarily demands that they should have to make the *decision* as to whether a complaint should be investigated, particularly as it may reasonably be feared that their political allegiance could distort their judgment in sensitive cases. Third, MPs would, of course, continue to receive numerous complaints on a variety of matters, many of which would be outside the PO's jurisdiction. Finally as a former PO, put it, Parliament would retain its expertise derived from the PO because the PO would 'draw to the attention of Parliament what we find in terms of general problems or general features of public administrations'.[26]

4. The Cabinet Office Review went on to note that one of the main problems with the MP filter system is simple ignorance amongst MPs of the jurisdiction of the PO:

> In 1998/99 nearly half the cases put to the PO by Members of Parliament were outside jurisdiction, or were not about administrative actions or were cases in which the PO thought it reasonable that the complainant go to a court or tribunal. . . In these cases particularly, the time wasted by the complainant, the MP and the PO is considerable and, for the complainant, the experience must often have been frustrating or distressing.

5. This relative ignorance by MPs of the Ombudsman and the possibility that some are reluctant to refer complaints to the PO was the subject of scathing criticism in evidence submitted to the Select Committee on the PO, which concluded that:

> . . .The existing system puts the interest of MPs above the interests of individual consumers with a grievance. If the MP filter does serve the interests of MPs, it does so at the expense of individual consumers and citizens for whom it constitutes a barrier to accessing a very important system of redress.[27]

6. As the Cabinet Office Review pointed out, the problem here is the unaccountable and unreviewable[28] discretion of MPs as to whether to refer a complaint to the PO:

> 3.46. . .how MPs use the PO is up to them—they can bar all access, refer complaints mechanically or operate strictly as a filter. They can filter out the frivolous but they do not have to. They can take an active interest in the investigation and any report, or simply act as a post box for the complainant. What happens depends on the MP—each sets his or her own policy for the gatekeeper role.

In the Australian state of New South Wales, in which complaints to the Ombudsman can come directly from the public or from MPs, the vast majority of complaints come directly from the public. The British system, as JUSTICE pointed out in 1979,[29] weakens the PO because she is unable

---

25   The Cabinet Office Review, see below, made a similar recommendation: see para 3.51. This might require permission from the complainant, in order to comply with the Data Protection Act 1998, but presumably this would not be problematic.

26   PAC, 3rd Report, HC 612 (1999–2000), Evidence, 21 June 2000, Q 7.

27   Appendix to the Minutes of Evidence Taken before the Select Committee on the PO, HC 64 (1993–94), Vol II, para 3.7.

28   The decision of an MP as to whether or not to refer a case to the PO would be regarded as non-justiciable and so not amenable to judicial review.

29   JUSTICE report, HC 593 (1979–80).

to publicise herself as available directly to receive complaints when she is not so available. It may be noted that the authors of a comparative study of ombudsmen consider that 'direct access. . .is an essential requirement of the office'.[30]

7. It appears that the above arguments have eventually won the day and that the days of the MP filter are probably numbered. The Cabinet Office Review, the PO herself and the PAC agreed that it had outlived its usefulness and should be removed. It is particularly significant that the PAC, whose predecessor Committees, as seen above, had consistently argued for the retention of the filter, has now changed its view, and expressed it in such firm terms:

> We believe that the idea of an MP filter, which was inserted at the genesis of the ombudsman scheme to assuage the sensibilities of MPs about a new form of redress, is now inconsistent with the world of public service charters and ought to be replaced by direct public access to the public sector ombudsmen.[31]

The Law Commission has also recently supported this reform.[32]

8. Before and after the expected removal of the filter, it is evident that increasing knowledge by both MPs and consumers of the existence and worth of the PO is the key to increasing his practical accessibility to the public. While the PO and government departments covered by her work are making much greater efforts in this respect, relatively low public awareness of the PO has remained a problem. As the Cabinet Office Review noted:

> A survey by MORI for the Citizen's Charter Unit in 1997 showed that less than half the population were aware of the PO or the CLA. A similar figure was found by MORI in a survey for the CLA in 1995. In 1996 a survey by the Consumers' Association found that 41% of all respondents in a sample of 1000 adults had no awareness of the PO, HSC or CLA. The figure rose to 51% in social group C2DE [para 3.6].

THE WORK OF THE PO: PROCESS, REMEDIES AND EXAMPLES

Number of cases investigated

In 2008–09, 16,137 enquiries were received by the office of the PO. However, a relatively small proportion of these were actually investigated. First of all, 2,830 were found to be out of the PO's remit and complainants were referred elsewhere. Thousands more were referred back to the complained-of body, on the grounds that the internal complaints procedures had not been exhausted. As the 2008–09 Annual Report noted: 'this year we closed some 9,583 cases which were either not properly made or otherwise premature, including referring many back to the relevant bodies. Overall, in 2008–09 some 79 per cent of the enquiries we closed did not satisfy these basic checks'. Overall the PO 'closed 15,639

30 See Drewry, n 3 above, at 96.

31 Third Report, n 26 above, at [12].

32 See above, n 20.

enquiries, of which 108 were resolved through intervention short of an investigation' (47 in 2007–08). There are now fewer concluded statutory investigations because other—often simpler and faster—means of resolving complaints short of concluding a statutory investigation are increasingly being used. In a growing number of cases this enables the Ombudsman to achieve the same outcome for a complainant more quickly and cheaply than using the statutory process.[33]

Investigations: process and procedure

Parliamentary Commissioner Act 1967, as amended

Procedure in respect of investigations
7.–(1) Where the commissioner proposes to conduct an investigation pursuant to a complaint under this Act, he shall afford to the principal officer of the department or authority concerned, and to any other person who is alleged in the complaint to have taken or authorised the action complained of, an opportunity to comment on any allegations contained in the complaint.

    (2)   Every such investigation shall be conducted in private, but except as aforesaid the procedure for conducting an investigation shall be such as the commissioner considers appropriate in the circumstances of the case; and without prejudice to the generality of the foregoing provision the commissioner may obtain information from such persons and in such manner, and make such inquiries, as he thinks fit, and may determine whether any person may be represented, by counsel or solicitor or otherwise, in the investigation.

. . .

Evidence
8.–(1) For the purposes of an investigation under this Act the commissioner may require any minister, officer or member of the department or authority concerned or any other person who in his opinion is able to furnish information or produce documents relevant to the investigation to furnish any such information or produce any such document.

    (2)   For the purposes of any such investigation the commissioner shall have the same powers as the Court in respect of the attendance and examination of witnesses (including the administration of oaths or affirmations and the examination of witnesses abroad) and in respect of the production of documents.

    (3)   No obligation to maintain secrecy or other restriction upon the disclosure of information obtained by or furnished to persons in Her Majesty's service, whether imposed by any enactment or by any rule of law, shall apply to the disclosure of information for the purposes of an investigation under this Act; and the Crown shall not be entitled in relation to any such investigation to any such privilege in respect of the production of documents or the giving of evidence as is allowed by law in legal proceedings.

---

33 HC 897 (2001–02).

(4) No person shall be required or authorised by virtue of this Act to furnish any information or answer any question relating to proceedings of the Cabinet or of any committee of the Cabinet or to produce so much of any document as relates to such proceedings; and for the purposes of this subsection a certificate issued by the Secretary of the Cabinet with the approval of the Prime Minister and certifying that any information, question, document or part of a document so relates shall be conclusive.

(5) Subject to subsection (3) of this section, no person shall be compelled for the purposes of an investigation under this Act to give any evidence or produce any document which he could not be compelled to give or produce in proceedings before the Court.

10.–(1) In any case where the commissioner conducts an investigation under this Act or decides not to conduct such an investigation, he shall send to the member of the House of Commons by whom the request for investigation was made (or if he is no longer a member of that House, to such member of that House as the commissioner thinks appropriate) a report of the results of the investigation or, as the case may be, a statement of his reasons for not conducting an investigation.

(2) In any case where the commissioner conducts an investigation under this Act, he shall also send a report of the results of the investigation to the principal officer of the department or authority concerned and to any other person who is alleged in the relevant complaint to have taken or authorised the action complained of.

Notes

1. It is important to appreciate that, for the complainant, the PO is not the beginning of his or her complaint process but probably the end. Some government departments have set up arrangements for independent review—these might be independent review panels as is the case with the Benefits Agency or independent complaints examiners such as the Adjudicator for the Inland Revenue, Customs and Excise and Contributions Agency and the Independent Complaints Examiner for the Child Support Agency. Generally, complainants must exhaust an internal complaints system before being referred to its independent review tier.

2. The first stage of the PO's work is deciding whether or not to investigate a complaint referred to her and if a positive decision is taken, what kind of investigation to adopt. In a Memorandum sent by the PO to PAC in 2008, she described the new working process:[34]

> The year 2006–07 saw us developing a new strategic approach to complaint handling which differentiates much more clearly between: (i) complaints which are either inappropriate for my Office to take on or can be dealt with in a different way other than by an investigation; and (ii) those cases which are sufficiently serious or complex to justify the full attention and force of an Ombudsman's investigation. A consequence of this is that while we continue to assess substantial volumes of complaints, we will now conduct a much smaller number of investigations than in the past, but ones which on average are likely to take longer and have a greater

---

34 www.publications.parliament.uk/pa/cm200708/cmselect/cmpubadm/1144/1144we03.htm.

impact. This new way of working, together with looking in a much more focused way at alternative opportunities for resolving complaints, has inevitably had an impact on the time taken to complete our casework. However, I am clear that this will ultimately provide a much better service and individual benefit for our customers, and help us to better achieve the wider public benefit set out in our objectives.

Our new processes involve a new concept of assessment panels — where enquiries to the Office are considered by me or senior members of my staff to consider whether full investigation is appropriate, or whether there are better routes to achieving positive outcomes. The way we do this is to consider whether in each case there is:

- prima facie evidence of administrative fault or service failure;
- injustice or hardship as a consequence of that fault; and
- a reasonable prospect of delivering what the complainant is seeking by making their complaint, or some other overriding issue why I should investigate.

3. As the above reveals, the PO has continuously developed new working methods, including in particular informal attempts to dispose of cases quickly:

Thanks to the willing cooperation of departments and agencies in dealing with, in some cases, numerous informal enquiries, often by telephone, those informal methods have proved their worth. Such work can be time-consuming for the department or agency concerned; but it is worthwhile if it achieves a satisfactory resolution to the complaint without a costly full investigation.[35]

4. In his Annual Report for 2000, the PO noted that:

In an increasing proportion of cases it is possible to resolve complaints without completing a statutory report; in those cases, the investigator sends to the referring Member and the body complained against a brief account setting out the main points agreed (2000–01).[36]

Elliott notes that, 'in 2003–04, only 4.5 per cent of the 1,877 concluded cases resulted in a statutory report; almost half were concluded simply by making inquiries of the department concerned.'[37] The system for handling NHS complaints has recently been simplified, moving from a 3-tier system, to a 2-tier one.[38]

5. Overall, the PO found in favour of 62% of complaints in 06–07, 55% in 07–08 and 52% in 08–09. This leads onto the important issue of remedies and the non-enforceability of the PO's recommendations.

---

35   Annual Report for 1997–98, at [2.8].

36   Annual Report for 2000–01, HC 5 (2001–2002), at [2.10].

37   M Elliott, 'Asymmetric Devolution and Ombudsman Reform in England' [2006] PL 84 at 87.

38   See www.ombudsman.org.uk/news/hot_topics/changes_nhs_complaints_system.html

Remedies[39]

The General Position

Findings and recommendations made by the PO are not enforceable in law. The PO can neither order compensation nor apply to a court to enforce her findings (though see below on judicial review); compliance is therefore voluntary. Thus the adverse publicity generated by a refusal to comply with a recommendation is the only sanction for non-compliance. However, it appears that the influence of the PO is far greater in practice than her formal powers. Government in practice generally accepts that the PO's findings should be complied with as the following Treasury Guidance indicates:

> The PO's recommendations on remedies are not legally binding on departments and could be rejected. However, the Financial Secretary to the Treasury in giving evidence to the Select Committee on the PO on 18 December 1991 said, 'I am not aware of any circumstances in which the (the PO's) recommendations have been ignored. This is the basis on which the Government has tended to work—and has, as far as I am aware always worked—in that we do accept and implement the recommendations that are made'.[40]

The PO's main weapon in the face of intransigence from Government is to lay a ' special report' under section 10(3) of the Act:

> If, after conducting an investigation under this Act, it appears to the commissioner that injustice has been caused to the person aggrieved in consequence of maladministration and that the injustice has not been, or will not be, remedied, he may, if he thinks fit, lay before each House of Parliament a special report upon the case.

Although the PO's lack of formal powers might appear to weaken the institution, it has been argued that the need for such a limitation is inherent in the role, as suggested in the definition above in the introduction to this chapter. If the PO could award compulsory remedies, it would be necessary to give the department complained about a full and formal opportunity to answer the allegations made. Probably some of the procedures would have to be conducted in public. The fact that the PO operates informally and privately has been thought to enhance her powers of persuasion. Where a particular complaint seems to be merely symptomatic of a deep-seated problem in a department, the PO can sometimes persuade it to change its general procedure. This occurred in the *Ostler* case: the Department of the Environment was persuaded to introduce new procedures in order to prevent a repetition of the situation that led to Ostler's complaint. Similarly, in her report for 2006, the PO noted that the Department of Health intended to integrate the handling of health and social care complaints, something which was recommended in the PO's 2005 report on the NHS complaints system. Thus, this apparent weakness in the PO's powers may underlie one of his main strengths. As the authors of a recent commentary put it:

> The suggestion is. . .that Ombudsmen working in constructive partnerships with public bodies are in a stronger position to secure workable solutions than if the

---

39   For a recent survey of the PO's success in securing *ex gratia* payments for complainants, see M. Amos, 'Devolution and the applicability of statutes to the Crown in the inter-governmental context' [2000] PL 7, 21–30.

40   Official Guidance to Departments and Agencies concerning *ex gratia* financial compensation, DAO (GEN) 15/92, para 8.

Ombudsmen were seen as a hostile force imposing solutions. Moreover, any short-term gains in securing redress would have to be offset against the long-term costs involved in discouraging public bodies from being amenable partners in the process of resolution and in working towards future improvements in the quality and fairness of administration.[41]

On the other hand, the lack of a power to award a remedy may in some situations appear to amount to a weakness in the PO system. In *Congreve v Home Office*,[42] the applicant succeeded in showing that the Home Office had acted unlawfully as regards television licence fees and a refund was awarded. The situation had already been investigated by the PO which had found inefficiency on the part of the Home Office but had not recommended a remedy for licence holders.

However, as the Cabinet Office Review noted at para 6.76:

Resolution in favour of the complainant will almost always involve some form of redress. This might be an action following intervention to solve a problem (for example, providing the service which has not been delivered or the benefit which has been delayed) or retrospective redress such as an explanation, apology or compensation. Sometimes both may be involved — both restoration of benefit including arrears and perhaps interest and consolatory payments.

Ex gratia payments to individuals adversely affected by maladministration appear to be made in roughly half of the cases in which the PO makes a finding of maladministration (in 92 out of 177 cases in 1992 and in 108 out of 236 cases in 1995). Apologies, reconsideration of an individual case and/or changes to administrative rules and procedures may also result. Remedies may also be offered to other members of the public known to have been affected by a problem similar to that of the complainant.

As Austin has noted, compliance with the PO's recommendations usually involves the payment of *ex gratia* compensation, an apology or the reconsideration of a prior decision by the correct process. Rarely does it involve reversal on merits of an important policy decision.[43] Indeed, in certain cases the Government will explicitly state that it does not accept the PO's finding of maladministration but is prepared to offer payment or an apology as a gesture of goodwill or out of respect for the PO. This occurred in relation to the notorious Barlow Clowes affair: the PO found five areas of serious maladministration by the Department of Trade and Industry in relation to the affair, in which many investors lost their life savings when Barlow Clowes—a brokerage business—collapsed. The Government rejected the findings, but nevertheless, 'out of respect for the office of Parliamentary Commissioner'[44] offered very considerable *ex gratia* payments to the victims totalling £150 million, an outcome which Wade and Forsyth describe as 'his most spectacular single achievement thus far'.[45] (There was a similar outcome in the Channel Tunnel rail link case (below, p 919–920).)

---

41   Kirkham *et al* (2008) at 522.

42   [1976] 2 QB 629.

43   'Freedom of information: the constitutional impact', in J Jowell and D Oliver (eds), *The Changing Constitution*, 3rd edn (1994), p 443.

44   HC Deb 164 cols 201–11 (19 December 1989).

45   HWR Wade and C Forsyth, *Administrative Law*, 8th edn (2000), p 100.

A further problem with the remedial system operated by the PO is that of delay: whilst departments nearly always accept the PO's recommendations in the end, considerable time may be spent in haggling over the compensation suggested. PAC's report on the PO's Annual Report for 1998–99 commented:

> We are particularly concerned that the delays mentioned above can still be attributed in part to 'prolonged delays before departments accepted our recommendations for redress in cases in which we had found complaints of mal-administration to be justified'.[46]

Later commentary of the Committee suggested that this situation had, if anything, got worse: when he published his annual report last year, [the PO] said 'We have noticed a tendency for departments to take a harder line and be less co-operative' adding that investigations into mismanagement by departments were 'uphill work'.[47] Certainly, delay in responding to PO recommendations has been a major feature of the three big reports in recent times, *A Debt of Honour, Trusting in the Pensions Promise* and *Equitable Life*, considered further below.

The PO will often enter into extended consultation with a department over the compensation it proposes to offer, especially in complex cases, such as that concerning the disastrous advice and mismanagement by a previous Government over the State Earnings Repayment Scheme, is an example. In the Annual Report for 2000–01,[48] the PO noted that following a critical report, the Department concerned consulted with him on their proposals for redress and 'as a result of those discussions. . . substantially revised their original plan' to make it more generous. Following the PO's approval of the new plan in a report (HC 271) the proposals were formally introduced by regulation.

Government resistance in particular instances

While there is a general pattern that PO recommendations are nearly always implemented in the end by Government, there are a few high profile instances of rejections by the Government of PO findings. Two occurred in only 12 months recently and a third remains unresolved at the time of completing this chapter.[49] The first related to a report entitled *A Debt of Honour*,[50] dealing with *ex-gratia* payments to former British civilian internees in the Far East. However, while initially rejecting the PO's findings, the Government eventually relented, and by the time the PO produced her annual report for 2006, she was able to report that the MOD had agreed to expand the eligibility criteria for compensation, as recommended.

The second recent instance related to more widespread problem. In *Trusting in the Pensions Promise*, 125,000 people lost significant parts of defined benefit occupational pensions when such schemes wound up between April 1997 and March 2004 without sufficient funds to pay the benefits promised', due, the PO found, to Government maladministration.[51] Information provided by the Government

---

46   HC 106, para 9.

47   PAC, Third Report, *Ombudsman Issues*, HC 448 (26 February 2003) at [32]002E.

48   HC 5 (2001–02), at [12].

49   The Equitable Life investigations. See pp 911 and 916–917.

50   Fourth Report (2005–06) HC 234.

51   PAC Sixth Report (2005–06).

had been, she said, 'incomplete, unclear and inconsistent'.[52] She recommended that the Government consider restoring benefits to those affected, a recommendation brusquely rejected by the Government. As the PO describes it:

> I recommended that the Government consider doing the decent thing by itself paying, or at least arranging for the payment of, meaningful compensation, not just for the financial losses suffered by individuals but for their sense of outrage, their distress, anxiety and uncertainty. The Government in no uncertain terms made it clear that it would not do so. What it seemed to be saying was that the Ombudsman was an optional source of advice whose findings could be weighed up on a 'take it or leave it' basis. The Secretary of State's view of maladministration was, in other words, to have equal weight to that of the Ombudsman, leaving the executive in effect as judge in its own cause.[53]

However, in the end, though only after two adverse court decisions on the Government's rejection of the PO's report,[54] the Government relented. On 17 December 2007, the Secretary of State announced that a review would enable the terms of the Government's Financial Assistance scheme to be extended.[55] The PO said that this amounted to 'full compliance with [her] key recommendation and . . . also remedie[d] the deficiencies in the Financial Assistance Scheme identified in [her] report'.[56]

The final recent instance, the *Equitable Life* report, is discussed below, but to date, the Government has not complied with the PO recommendations. Given that the entire system depends upon the Government of the day accepting an obligation to implement PO recommendations, and that this sense of obligation rests partly upon the practice of successive Governments to do so, such instances might be seen as threatening gradually to undermine the whole basis of the PO system. However it is clear that such instances are extremely rare. In her 2007 Annual Report, the PO was able to report that 'in every one of the cases reported on in 2006/07, the parties complied with the Ombudsman's recommendations'. Overall, the current PO sees a pattern of only 'occasional conflict [with the Government] when the going gets tough'.[57] In the 08–09 Annual Report the PO noted:

> Despite the high profile government rejection of [PO]'s recommendations on Equitable Life, over 99 per cent of the recommendations PO made during the year have been accepted or are currently being considered by the body or practitioner complained about (99 per cent in 2007–08).

It may be noted that within the UK, other Ombudsmen have been given greater powers by legislation. When the Commissioner for Complaints in Northern Ireland finds that an individual has sustained injustice as a result of maladministration, the individual concerned can apply to the county court under s 7(2) of the Commissioner for Complaints Act (Northern Ireland) 1969, which may award damages at its discretion. The new Welsh Ombudsman (above) may, if s/he is satisfied that a public

---

52   Annual Report, 2006 HC 1363.

53   A Abraham, 'The Ombudsman and the Executive: The Road to Accountability' (2008) 61(3) Parlt Aff 535, 536–37.

54   See below, pp 912–916.

55   HC Debs vol 469, col 100WS (17 December 2007).

56   Press release 07/07, 17 December 2007.

57   Abraham, 'Contested Role' at 213.

authority has disregarded a report served on it without lawful excuse, issue a certificate to that effect to the High Court (s 20).

Indirect enforcement of PO findings via the courts?

As just noted, the Government only agreed to implement the PO's report, *Trusting in the Pensions Promise*, after litigation. As Kirkham *et al* note:

> To be vindicated through a process of dispute resolution and then to find that the public body complained against has dismissed the outcome of that process. . . increases the possibility of redress being pursued in the courts, an option which was explored in a novel form in the *Occupational Pensions* affair. It has long been recognised that ombudsman reports can be subject to judicial review by either the complainant or the public body involved [see below, pp 922–925], but before *Bradley* no one had ever sought judicial review of a public body's decision to reject an ombudsman report. Following the Department of Work and Pensions' continued refusal to accept the full implications of the PO's report, four people affected by the winding-up of their occupational pension schemes did just this.[58]

This then was the first time that a decision by a Minister to reject findings by the PO had been challenged in the courts. The core of the challenge was that the Government had acted unlawfully in rejecting the findings of the PO. As appears below, at first instance this challenge was successful.[59] The court also held that the findings of the PO as to maladministration were binding on the government department concerned unless they could be shown to be flawed or irrational. The Government appealed both findings, to the Court of Appeal.

R (On the application of Bradley) v Secretary of State for Work and Pensions [2008] EWCA Civ 36; [2009] QB 114 (extracts)

Sir John Chadwick. . .

44 It is, I think, impossible to contend that there is anything in the 1967 Act which, in terms, requires the body whose conduct is the subject of an investigation under section 5(1) to accept the [PO]'s findings of maladministration. Parliament could have enacted such a provision; but it did not. Had that been its intention, it might have been expected to say so. . .

51 I would conclude that. . .the Secretary of State, acting rationally, is entitled to reject a finding of maladministration and prefer his own view. . .

72 [His Lordship cited this paragraph in the skeleton argument of the claimants]:

> For the avoidance of doubt, the relevant test is not whether a reasonable Secretary of State could *himself conclude that failure to disclose risks in official leaflets was [not] maladministrative.* Such a test would fail to take into account the fact that Parliament has conferred on the ombudsman the function of making findings of maladministration and that the decision under review is a decision to reject that

---

58 R Kirkham, B Thompson, T Buck, 'When Putting Things Right goes Wrong: Enforcing the Recommendations of the Ombudsman' [2008] PL 510, 517.

59 [2007] EWHC 242 (Admin); [2007] Pens LR 87 (QBD (Admin))

conclusion. The question is not whether the defendant himself considers that there was maladministration, **but whether in the circumstances his rejection of the ombudsman's finding to this effect is based on cogent reasons.**

. . .I would agree with that statement of the test by which the court should determine whether the Secretary of State's rejection of the ombudsman's first finding of maladministration should be quashed.

91 [Thus]. . .it is not enough that the Secretary of State has reached his own view on rational grounds: it is necessary that his decision to reject the ombudsman's findings in favour of his own view is, itself, not irrational having regard to the legislative intention which underlies the 1967 Act: he must have a reason (other than simply a preference for his own view) for rejecting a finding which the ombudsman has made after an investigation under the powers conferred by the Act. . .

95 . . .The judge observed. . .that no reasonable Secretary of State could rationally disagree with the ombudsman's view that the information [in Government leaflets] was incomplete and potentially misleading. I am satisfied that the judge was correct in that observation; but, for my part, I prefer to say that, in the circumstances of this case, it was irrational for the Secretary of State to reject the ombudsman's finding to that effect. For that reason I would hold that the judge was correct to conclude that the Secretary of State's decision to reject the first finding of maladministration should be quashed. It follows that I would dismiss the Secretary of State's appeal.

Wall LJ

135 By far the most important [point here], in my judgment, is Sir John Chadwick's rejection of the proposition that the decision of this court in *Eastleigh* is authority for the proposition that the Secretary of State is bound by the parliamentary ombudsman's findings of maladministration and must treat them as correct unless and until they are quashed in judicial review proceedings. This is, in my judgment, a fundamental point, and in para 5 of her written reply (undated, but received by the court on 14 August 2007, after the conclusion of the argument) the ombudsman stated:

> . . .The ombudsman submits that in considering the report and what action to take in respect of it, the Secretary of State must proceed on the basis that the ombudsman's findings of injustice caused by maladministration are correct unless they are quashed in judicial review proceedings. If this is accepted then that is the end of the matter as no application for judicial review has been made seeking to quash the report. . . .

136 For the reasons which Sir John Chadwick sets out in paras 37–71 of his judgment, and with great respect to the ombudsman, I am unable to agree with [this].

137 . . .under the 1967 Act, a minister who rejects the Ombudsman's findings of maladministration will have to defend him or herself in Parliament, and will be subject to parliamentary control. The ultimate remedy for aggrieved citizens such as the complainants in the instant case, whose complaints to their Members of Parliament have led to the ombudsman's report, will-ultimately-be through political action rather than judicial intervention.

138 In making these observations, I have not lost sight of the fact that the decision of the minister/Secretary of State to reject the parliamentary ombudsman's findings of maladministration is itself, capable of being judicially reviewed on conventional public law

grounds. However, in this context, the remedy—if the application for judicial review is successful— is procedural rather than substantive. The decision is quashed as unlawful, and the minister must think again. The limitations on judicial review as a remedy do not need to be spelled out.

141 ...It is clear to me that this case comes as close as it is possible to come to the clear line which divides the areas in which political and judicial decisions hold sway. Nobody reading the papers in this case could have anything but the utmost sympathy for the plight of the complainants, all of whom, it seemed to me, were decent, hardworking people who, through no fault of their own, had been—or were at serious risk of being—deprived of that for which they had worked throughout their lives, namely a modestly comfortable retirement. But in my judgment, judicial review principles apart, their remedy is political, not juridical...

142 In my judgment, the role of the ombudsman under the 1967 Act is not only to report to Parliament, but, where appropriate, vigorously to alert Parliament to an injustice which has occurred through maladministration. It is, therefore, for Parliament to provide the remedy, subject only to the role of the courts in ensuring that the acts of the ombudsman herself and the role of the relevant departments in responding to her reports are themselves lawful.

Notes

1. On the challenge raised in the particular case, the Court of Appeal therefore found that the Government did not have rational grounds for rejecting the PO's first finding of maladministration (that government leaflets on the pension schemes had been misleading) while finding that the Government was entitled to reject other findings made by the PO (though the court was careful to say that in so finding they were casting no doubt on the PO's findings in this regard). It was just before the Department's appeal to the Court of Appeal that it agreed to implement the PO's findings, indicating that the legal proceedings acted as an effective means of indirect enforcement.

2. On the wider issue, Kirkham *et al* sum up the judgment as providing the 'minimum requirement, therefore, is that if the Government wishes to reject an ombudsman's finding, it is required to provide rationally defensible reasons that directly address the PO's report'[60]—what Sir John Chadwick referred to as 'cogent reasons'. They support this finding on the basis that:

> ... Significant moral and financial energy has been invested in establishing ombudsman schemes. They have become a vital part of the administrative justice system serving the dual function of upholding the rights of citizens in their dealings with the public sector, while encouraging the promotion of good administration. Both of these roles map on to wider constitutional agendas. The government has made much in recent years of its move towards establishing a system of more proportionate redress, and a regular refrain of constitutional lawyers is the need to put in place stronger accountability mechanisms. In its contribution towards these tasks the Ombudsmen have been granted extensive powers of investigation. Given all of this it would be strange were the reports of Ombudsmen to be granted only advisory legal status, so that it is at the whim of public bodies whether or not to accept them. In *Bradley*, the Court of Appeal provided legal support for these arguments, and in so doing confirmed that the role of the public body is to respect the statutory status of the ombudsman, to focus on the outcome of an ombudsman

60 Kirkham *et al*, at 528.

report and accept the spirit within which this dispute resolution mechanism was established.[61]

3. The PO has commented:

> My own view is that the Court of Appeal's decision establishes a viable framework for the future relationship between the Ombudsman, Parliament and the Executive, and that it does so in a way that properly observes the constitutional role of the Ombudsman in holding the executive to account.
>
> I say that because at the core of the judgment was what I take to be a deep respect not just for the plight of the aggrieved individuals involved, but for the institution of Parliamentary democracy itself.
>
> By taking the course that approximates to requiring the executive to have 'due regard' to the Ombudsman's findings, I suggest that the Court of Appeal in effect reaffirmed the Ombudsman's privileged role, exercised on behalf of Parliament itself and therefore indirectly on behalf of citizens at large, in the process of deliberation about the polycentric issue of resource allocation that lies at the heart of so much of our political discourse. In the end, it is not, of course, for the Ombudsman in any way to usurp the proper place of the executive in determining and delivering public policy. It is, though, very much the Ombudsman's job to play a distinctive part within the constitutional framework as an assistant to Parliament in its task of holding the executive to account and in facilitating the deliberative exercise that underpins our democratic practice.[62]

4. Kirkham *et al* argue that compliance with Ombudsmen recommendations cannot be taken for granted, noting that 'there have. . .been many LGO cases in the past where local authorities have been forthright in their criticism of ombudsman reports and refused to implement the report's recommendations as a result'.[63] They conclude that there is a strong argument for going further than the Court of Appeal did and finding the PO findings to be binding in law:

> The central justifying argument behind granting some form of legal authority to the findings of an ombudsman is relatively simple. While there are several roles that an ombudsman can perform, all the Ombudsmen in the United Kingdom were introduced to act as a form of dispute resolution mechanism and were thus established to investigate and report upon complaints. According to standard liberal conceptions of justice, in order to maintain the fairness and legitimacy of this process, a minimum requirement is that the final proclamation as to the validity of the complaint is given by an independent body or person. To maximise the effect of the ombudsman scheme, therefore, this is the role that should be the sole prerogative of the ombudsman. By contrast, were the body complained against to have the final say on the findings of an ombudsman report then this would devalue the process; objectivity would not be secured and public confidence in the strength of the ombudsman system would be much reduced. In the words of the former Select

---

61   *Ibid* at 527.

62   Abraham, 'Road to Accountability' at 540.

63   Kirkham *et al* at 519.

Committee on the Parliamentary Commissioner for Administration: 'There would be no point in having an Ombudsman if the Government were to show disregard for his Office, his standing as an impartial referee, and for the thoroughness of his investigation.'[64]

5. Conversely, another commentator considers that the Court of Appeal actually went too far in *Bradley*, arguing that:

> If the courts were to engage in searching scrutiny of the government's response this could displace Parliament as the central institution for ensuring accountability, and would run against the grain of the system of political accountability created by the Act. An over-active role for the courts could also lead to the legalisation and thus impoverishment of the political discourse the PO's reports are intended to spark. It would be an unwelcome development if a court's account of the rationality of a Minister's decision were to become the dominant or determinative one, so that if the court declared the Minister's decision rational then the Minister could use that as a defence to parliamentary accountability, while in the case of a finding of irrationality the Minister would be forced to accept findings which he bona fide disagrees with. In the end this could cast the courts as the primary forum for deliberating the rightness or wrongness of the Minister's decision, thereby completely undermining the political nature of the Ombudsman process.[65]

6. Kirkham *et al* disagree and consider that it remains the case that when the Government digs its heels in, ultimately the resolution remains firmly a political matter.

> . . .Disputes occur when an ombudsman report is initially resisted on various grounds by the government. In response, the PO is able to increase the pressure on the government by submitting a formal report to Parliament and making her findings publicly available. Parliament can then provide its opinion on the affair. If at this stage it becomes clear that there is little political support for its position, the government ordinarily finds some way to change its position and comply with at least the key features of the PO's report. Thus the effectiveness of the ombudsman scheme is maintained, albeit on occasion a significant period of time elapses before a solution is arrived at and sometimes the government continues to dispute certain aspects of the original ombudsman report.[66]

7. However, instances in which the Government of the day continues to reject or resist PO findings raise in stark form the relationship not only between the PO and the Executive, but the wider constitutional question concerning Parliament-Executive relationships. This issue was recently discussed by the PO during questioning by the PAC in the context of the ongoing refusal by the Government to implement PO recommendations in the Equitable Life case. This case concerned substantial losses sustained by hundreds of thousands of policy holders, following the effective

---

64   *Ibid* at 523.

65   J Varuhas, 'Governmental Rejections of Ombudsman Findings: What Role for the Courts?' (2009) 72(1) MLR 91, 110–111.

66   Kirkham *et al*, at 513.

collapse of the company in 2000. After an initial investigation by Lord Penrose in 2004, which found maladministration and delays in remedying them described *at that point* as 'iniquitous and unfair',[67] the matter was reported to the PO. After an exhaustive investigation, the PO reported in July 2008[68] and found 10 counts of maladministration and that in six of them, individuals had suffered injustice. These essentially related to the failings of the Department of Trade and Industry, the FSA and the Government Actuary's Department to oversee the company properly:

> The 'central story' of the Ombudsman's investigation is the failure of regulators to exercise their powers to ensure that a company with a sound reputation was in fact observing minimum standards.[69]

The PO's findings were accepted by PAC, which backed the PO in a series of reports,[70] in particular her recommendation for the creation of a compensation scheme to pay for the loss that has been suffered by Equitable Life's members as a result of maladministration and the administering of this system by a body independent from government, 'a compensation scheme that is independent, transparent and simple, administered by a tribunal'. However, the Labour Government was still declining to comply with many of the PO's important recommendations, although a court case forced it to widen its proposed compensation scheme to include further classes of persons affected by the effective collapse of the company.[71] During the last debate on this matter,[72] many Labour MPs voted on party lines, supporting the Government against the PO, causing some concern as to the ability of Parliament to enforce findings of the PO, discussed here by the PO and members of PAC.

Public Administration Select Committee, Transcript of Oral Evidence HC 1079-I (5 November 2009)

. . .On two major recent occasions people have come to you, you have dealt with their cases and then, because of the nature of the Government's response, they have felt obliged to go to the courts. You expressed grave concern about this as a trend and as a development, and you say, 'Unless a parliamentary solution is found to cope with situations, however rare they might be, and one of my reports is contested by the Government, resort to litigation by complainants looks likely to be repeated in the future'. You go on to say, 'This has the potential to undermine faith in the parliamentary process and the ombudsman system for the resolution of grievances which Parliament has created on its behalf.' You obviously feel that this is an extremely serious development. . .

Ms Abraham: Indeed. . .this promotion and safeguarding of the constitutional position of

---

67   HC Deb, 21 Oct 2009, col 922.

68   'Equitable Life: A Decade of Regulatory Failure' 4th Report (2007–08) 815.

69   PAC, 'Justice Delayed: The Ombudsman's Report on Equitable Life', 2nd Report (2008–09) HC 14-I (summary).

70   See *ibid* and 'Justice Denied? The Government's Response to the Ombudsman's Report on Equitable Life' 6th Report (2008–09) HC 219. The Committee published further reports commenting on the Government's resistance to the PO's findings: 3rd Special Report (2008–09) HC 569 and 4th Special Report (2008–09) HC 953.

71   *R (On the application of Equitable Members Action Group) v HM Treasury Divisional Court* [2009] EWHC 2495, Admin.

72   HC Deb, 21 Oct 2009, cols 918–975.

Parliament's Ombudsmen has given me huge pause for thought in recent times and very particularly, I think, in relation to recent events with Equitable Life, but not exclusively. . . . If I could perhaps take some words from a complainant who wrote to us, who says, 'What happens now? The Ombudsman upheld our complaint after a long but thorough investigation. A parliamentary committee has reinforced that, but the Government, the guilty party, has rejected this independent assessment. We know that Parliament's role is to scrutinise the Government, but nobody can tell us what happens next. We feel like we are left in limbo and we wonder whether it was worth it.' I think my question to Parliament is: what am I supposed say to the complainant who says, 'What happens next?' What we have seen happen does not seem to me to answer the question in the way that is likely to leave our complainant feeling rather less bewildered.

Q22 Chairman: What about an answer which says that Parliament in 1967 expressly said that it did not want the Parliamentary Ombudsman's recommendations to be binding? Is that not the answer?
Ms Abraham: . . .[But] I cannot imagine that Parliament intended that government should be allowed to be judging its own cause . . . . . .I think what the court. . .in *Equitable Life* recently [said] is say that. . .on questions of remedy, the Government is entitled to have a different view here but that is a matter for Parliament. . .[So] what happens in a situation where the Government decides that a different remedy is appropriate and explains its reasons for taking that view? What I heard one member say is, 'Surely this is the kind of instance in which the Government should be introducing the debate, presenting it to the House and allowing the House the final word. Is that a forlorn hope?'
Mr Walker: Yes. . . .

Q25 Paul Flynn: . . .Your decision . . . on Equitable Life was one taken on the merits of the case but you are free of any obligation to consider the financial consequences, which might involve. . .a figure of four billion pounds, and the Government, whatever colour, is going to have to take a decision in a matter of months' time whether it is reasonable for them to pay the compensation, entirely justified as it may be, while they are actually cutting in essential areas. Is it not right that the supreme judgment has to be made by the Government of the day?
Ms Abraham: I thought the supreme judgment had to be made by Parliament, but maybe I need to go back and re-read my constitution.

Q26 Paul Flynn: That is a very quaint old-fashioned view.
Ms Abraham: But I like to hang on to it.

Note
The eventual outcome remains to be seen, but the huge financial implications of compensating former members of Equitable Life, estimated as amounting to up to £4 billion will obviously be a major consideration for the current and future Governments in devising a compensation scheme, especially given the current highly adverse state of the public finances.

Further Examples of the PO's work

The following extracts from PO Annual Reports give a flavour of the kinds of cases investigated by the PO, and the outcomes his office can procure.

[C.373/00]
Benefits Agency

Mr W complained that the Benefits Agency had refused to pay him invalid care allowance backdated to May 1995 when his wife had claimed disability living allowance. After our informal enquiry, the Agency said that they recognised that the claim pack for invalid care allowance in circulation between April 1991 and April 1995 had misdirected customers by telling them not to make a claim until the person they looked after had been awarded disability living allowance at the middle or highest rate. On this basis the Agency made on ex gratia payment to Mr W of £6,496.20 for the period May 1995 to September 1998 to compensate him for the invalid care allowance he should have received.

[C.551/99]
Child Support Agency: loss of entitlement to child support maintenance

The Ombudsman upheld Mrs X's complaint that she had no enforceable right to child support maintenance for a period of more than a year because an interim maintenance assessment which CSA had imposed was defective. Subsequently the non-resident parent had told CSA that he had become employed and had provided the details of his employer; but CSA had taken no action to make a full maintenance assessment or to obtain payment from him during the period of 13 months while he was employed. Following a report on the case by the Independent Case Examiner, CSA agreed to make Mrs X a payment of £160 for the trouble she had been caused and for her out-of-pocket expenses, but they refused to compensate her for loss of entitlement to child support maintenance on the grounds that the non-resident parent had not established a regular pattern of payments. Following the Ombudsman's intervention, CSA accepted that a regular payment pattern would have been established but for their maladministration. CSA agreed to make Mrs X an advance payment of £9,447.91 in respect of arrears owed by the non-resident parent, and compensatory payments totalling £3,745.41 for her lost entitlement to child support maintenance and interest.

HM Revenue & Customs

Ms A complained on behalf of her partner, Mr F, who has mental health problems, about overpayments amounting to £2,445.24 on his tax credit awards for 2005–06 and 2006–07. Because of Mr F's mental health problems he had sought help from Jobcentre Plus staff when he made his initial claim for tax credits, and they had completed the form for him.

When HM Revenue & Customs (HMRC) reconsidered the circumstances of the overpayment at our request, they concluded that staff at Jobcentre Plus had filled in Mr F's claim form incorrectly by not indicating that he had a partner, and that they had not questioned Mr F appropriately when he had told them he was sharing a house with someone. They also said that Mr F had made it clear at the time that he had been unable to fill in the forms himself or to understand the award notices that he had received. HMRC accordingly agreed to remit the full overpayment of £2,445.24. They also paid Mr F £50 compensation in recognition of delays during the complaints process.[73]

Notes

1. An important recent investigation by the PO concerned a number of complaints by those whose property has been affected by the Channel Tunnel rail link. The investigation was notable in being

---

the largest undertaken to that date by the PO;[74] it also involved the PO in the unusual step of examining the Transport Department's handling of the project as a whole, albeit in the context of five individual complaints. The problems generated concerned peoples' homes, the value of which had been blighted by the prospect that the rail link would run past or near them. The PO's report[75] found that there had been maladministration, causing widespread blight for which the Government had not, in line with existing policy, made any provision; however, it also found that there were a number of cases of exceptional hardship, in respect of which it recommended that compensation should be offered. The Select Committee on the PO backed the PO's findings and recommendations.[76] The department denied that there had been any maladministration, and, unusually, refused to implement the PO's recommendations. Neither the PO nor the Select Committee were impressed by the department's arguments; in particular, both denied strongly that in asking the department to look again at exceptional cases, they were criticising the general government policy of not offering compensation for generalised blight. On this point, the Select Committee said:

> At the heart of this debate is a definition of maladministration found in the [PO's 1993 Annual Report] failure to mitigate the effects of rigid adherence to the letter of the law where that produces manifestly inequitable treatment. . . The definition, which we fully support, implies an expectation that, when an individual citizen is faced with extraordinary hardship as a result of strict application of law or policy, the executive must be prepared to look again and consider whether help can be given.[77]

2. The department, faced with the embarrassing prospect of a debate in the Commons on the matter, in which it would have been opposed by a unanimous, cross-party Select Committee, eventually agreed to look again at the possibility of a compensation scheme for those affected to an exceptional or extreme degree by the generalised blight. However, the Government made it clear that it agreed to this only out of respect for the PO Select Committee and the office of PO and without admission of fault of liability, a concession described by Diane Longley and Rhoda James as grudging.[78] Nevertheless, in terms of winning compensation, the PO had prevailed again.

ACCOUNTABILITY OF THE PO

Parliamentary accountability

Parliamentary Commissioner Act, 1967 section 10

. . .

---

74 Annual Report of the PO for 1995, Cm 296, p 3, para 7.

75 Fifth Report of the PO, HC 193 (1994–95).

76 Sixth Report of the Select Committee on the PO, HC 270 (1994–95).

77 *Ibid*, para 20; quoted in D Longley and R James, *Administrative Justice: Central Issues in UK and European Administrative Law* (1999), p 42.

78 *Ibid*, p 44.

(4)   The commissioner shall annually lay before each House of Parliament a general report on the performance of his functions under this Act and may from time to time lay before each House of Parliament such other reports with respect to those actions as he thinks fit.

(5)   For the purposes of the law of defamation, [such reports and related parliamentary reports] shall be absolutely privileged. . . .

Notes

1. The current PO, Ann Abraham notes:

> With Parliament the relationship is robust. The founding legislation placed the Ombudsman fairly and squarely in the Parliamentary context, with the Ombudsman having Officer of the House status, being subject to the MP filter, and having the chance to make report directly to Parliament in case of an injustice caused by maladministration not being remedied. The existence of a Select Committee with responsibility for examining the work of the Ombudsman has reinforced the interdependence of Ombudsman and Parliament, even though since 1997 the Public Administration Select Committee has had the task of combining scrutiny of the Ombudsman with its myriad other duties.[79]

2. The most recent examples show PAC engaging in vigorous, strongly critical scrutiny of Ann Abraham re the disappointing performance of the PO in the last year, demanding explanations and improvement.[80]

3. The PO's Annual Reports and reports on special and on selected cases are laid before Parliament and provide a means of explaining the PO's role and work. As part of the Cabinet Office Review, MPs were asked how often they read these reports: 12% of those replying to the survey never read them, 35% hardly ever, 47% occasionally, and only 5% frequently read the reports.[81]

4. Perhaps justifiably therefore, the current PO, Ann Abraham, perceives an under-valuing of her role by MPs—even lingering feelings of usurpatation of MPs role that were expressed when the office was introduced, of which the most extreme manifestation occurred when 'Quentin Hogg, the future Lord Hailsham, put the Opposition view that the Ombudsman marked in effect the end of parliamentary democracy'. She continues:

> What all this suggests is an urgent need to re-engage the interest of MPs in the work of the Ombudsman and to reignite the feeling that the Ombudsman makes available to MPs an important resource at a time when discussion about the accountability of the executive has become especially acute.[82]

Abraham argues in particular that their needs to be greater 'buy-in' by MPs to the PO's role and work:

---

79   'Contested Role' (2008) 61(1) Parlt Aff 206, at 213.

80   See Oral Evidence, October 2008 www.publications.parliament.uk/pa/cm200708/cmselect/cmpubadm/c1143-i/c114301.htm and November 2009 www.publications.parliament.uk/pa/cm200809/cmselect/cmpubadm/uc1079-i/uc107901.htm.

81   Cabinet Office Review, para 3.24.

82   'Road to Accountability', at 541.

The true sign of its achievement is likely to be MPs' increased awareness of, and engagement with, the reports of the Ombudsman that are laid before Parliament for their consideration. It is only occasionally that such reports lead to debate on the floor of the House. . . . If the Ombudsman is, on behalf of MPs and their constituents, to play a significant part in the democratic process by contributing to debate and deliberation, it is through her individual, special and annual reports that such a contribution is most likely to be made. That contribution can only come to life if MPs themselves ensure that the Ombudsman's findings are regularly reflected in the general mix of debate on the issues of the day.[83]

Judicial control

The decision in *R v Parliamentary Commissioner for Administration ex parte Dyer*[84] had indicated that, in principle, the decisions of the PO were subject to judicial review, though Simon Brown LJ 'emphasised that the court was not readily to be persuaded to interfere with the exercise of the Commissioner's discretion. Indeed he went so far as to wonder whether in reality the end result is much different from that arrived at by Lord Bridge of Harwich in *ex parte Hammersmith and Fulham'*,[85] in other words that review would lie only to correct the extremes of bad faith, improper motive or manifest absurdity (see Chapter 15, pp 874–875). Subsequent case law has indicated a somewhat less deferential approach to review of the PO. The two *ex parte Balchin* decisions have pushed forward the extent and depth of judicial scrutiny of decisions of the PO.

R v Parliamentary Commissioner for Administration ex parte Balchin (No 2)[86]

A proposed new bypass, approved by the Department of Transport (DOT), caused serious blight to the Balchins' £400,000 home, rendering it worthless, and thus causing the Balchins to become bankrupt when banks called in the loans secured on the house and Mr Balchin's business failed as a consequence. Norfolk local authority did not compulsorily purchase the property, deciding instead to follow a scheme whereby compensation would be paid to the Balchins only once the road was completed. In fact, the road scheme was abandoned.

The Balchins complained to the PO on the basis that the minister responsible had been guilty of maladministration in approving the scheme without seeking assurances from the local authority that it would compensate the Balchins. The PO's finding was that the DOT had not been guilty of maladministration because the minister was under no obligation to seek such assurances, and even though his officials could have pointed out to the Council its statutory discretionary power to purchase the property under s 246(2A) of the Highways Act, it was evident that the Council would not have acted under it (it had rejected an invitation from the Balchins' bank to exercise its powers under this provision). The Balchins sought judicial review of the PO's decision, arguing, *inter alia,* that he had

---

83   *Ibid* at 543

84   [1994] 1 WLR 621.

85   [1994] 1 WLR 621, 626. N Marsh, 'The Extent and Depth of Judicial Review of the Decisions of the Parliamentary Commissioner for Administration' [1994] PL 347.

86   Reported at (2000) LGLR 87.

misdirected himself in relation to the DOT's failure to point out to the Council its powers under s 246(2A).

In the first decision[87] Sedley J found that the PO had:

> been led by a scrupulous regard for his jurisdictional remit, excluding as it does local government, into a failure to consider the relevant fact of Norfolk's attitude. . .in order to decide, as his own findings made it necessary for him to do, whether the Department of Transport ought in response to have drawn the council's attention to its new power to acquire blighted property [s 246(2A)] and perhaps also to its obligation to consider exercising it. . .Once Norfolk's apparent disregard of its obligations was established by him, the [PO] could not properly avoid the question whether correct advice with the imprimatur of central government might have made a difference.

The ruling was thus that the PO should reconsider the Balchins' complaint, taking into account this time the failure of the DOT to draw the attention of the Council to their power under s 246(2A). It was careful not to give any indication as to whether, had the PO taken this into account, he would be bound to have made a finding of maladministration, as that would have been to invade the PO's discretionary area of judgment. Nevertheless, as Giddings points out, 'This ruling was the first time a finding by the Parliamentary Ombudsman had been overturned in the courts.'[88]

In the light of this decision, the case was then reconsidered by the new PO; his fresh report indicated that he had explicitly considered whether the Secretary of State had been at fault in not specifically drawing the Council's attention to the new power, and whether it would have made any difference if he had.

The PO concluded that the minister had not acted maladministratively, principally because the Council had been informed of the new power by a standard government circular, and the minister was entitled to assume that the Council were therefore aware of their new powers. This decision was once again challenged by way of judicial review. One of the arguments relied upon was that the PO had given no reason for finding, as he had, that the DOT had in fact borne in mind the s 246(2A) power in relation to the Balchins' home.

Dyson J: . . .It would appear that the PO did not explore with the Permanent Secretary [of the DOT] the state of knowledge of those in the DOT who were actually dealing with the Balchins' case. But, in my view, if he had thought about the picture that was disclosed by the contemporaneous documents that were before him, he would surely have pressed the Permanent Secretary on this point. This is because the documents pointed very strongly to the conclusion that those involved with the case had indeed overlooked the existence of the power.

. . . As we have seen, the first PO did raise with the DOT the question of why section 246(2A) was not mentioned in these documents, and was given the explanation of 'over-stepping the mark', which he found 'unconvincing'. The second PO did not raise this question. But it was a critical question, since the answer to it would cast shafts of light on

---

87   [1998] PLR 1

88   P Giddings [2000] PL 201.

the issue of whether those in the Department who were handling the Balchins' case were aware of section 246(2A).

In the result, the PO made no finding as to whether any, and if so which, of the officials in the Department who were handling the Balchins' case were aware of section 246(2A). In my judgment, this is a crucial omission. It was immaterial that there were some officials within the Department who were aware of the section at the material time. What mattered, for the purpose of an inquiry into whether there had been maladministration in failing to seek to persuade the Council to exercise its power under section 246(2A), was whether those who were dealing with this case were aware of it. The reason why this omission is so important is that the documents make it overwhelmingly likely that all of those persons overlooked the existence of the power at the material time.

In short, the finding that the DOT did not overlook section 246(2A) was at the heart of the PO's conclusion that there was no maladministration. It was this finding that enabled him to conclude that the decision reached by the DOT was 'within the reasonable range of responses open to them given their knowledge' and 'one they were entitled to take' (paragraph 29). It is not possible to say what conclusion he would have reached on the issue of maladministration if he had found that those handling the Balchins' case had overlooked section 246(2A). I think that the PO was unwittingly led into error by the rather unspecific evidence of the Permanent Secretary. It is possible that, as Mr Elvin suggests, there were persons in the DOT handling the Balchins' case who had not overlooked section 246(2A). But if that is so, there is no trace of them in any of the material that has been placed before me. Moreover, given the close interest shown by the Minister, and the terms in which his various letters were expressed, the hypothesis suggested by Mr Elvin is inherently unlikely. This emphasises the shortcomings in the reasoning of the PO's decision.

In reaching the conclusion that the decision on maladministration is flawed, I am very conscious of what Sedley J referred to as 'the very wide areas of judgment and discretion given to the PO by the Act' (page 929). . . .

Mr Elvin. . .submits that the court should be particularly reluctant to interfere with decisions of the PO, since they are 'policy laden'. I would not quarrel with this as a general rule. But where the court finds that there is a real shortcoming in the reasoning of the PO, it seems to me that it is not passing judgment on the substance of a policy decision. It is criticising the reasoning on grounds which do not depend in any way on the policy element of the decision.

[Dyson J went on to consider a further ground of challenge, based on the argument that the PO had impliedly concluded that no injustice, within the meaning of the 1967 Act had been caused to the Balchins because, even had the DOT specifically drawn the attention of the Council to the s 246(2A) power, the Council would not have exercised it.]

At page 926 of his judgment, Sedley J said this of injustice:

> Less judicial attention had been devoted so far to the meaning of injustice' in the legislation, but de Smith, Woolf and Jowell, *Judicial Review of Administrative Action* (5th ed) write at paragraph 1–102: 'Injustice' has been widely interpreted so as to cover not merely injury redressible in a court of law, but also 'the sense of outrage aroused by unfair or incompetent administration, even where the complainant has suffered no actual loss' (citing Mr RHS Crossman, speaking as Leader of the House of Commons). It follows that the defence familiar in legal proceedings, that because the outcome would have been the same in any event there has been no redressible wrong, does not run in an investigation by the PO. . .

. . .the Balchins had a very strong case on outrage. They had been financially ruined by the proposed scheme, and the Minister had made it clear to his officials that he wanted to ensure that the Council helped them. And yet, ex hypothesi, in its dealings with the Council over the Balchins' case, the DOT overlooked the existence of the only power which, if invoked, could have helped them. It is not possible to know what view the PO had as to how bad a case of maladministration this would have been, and how intense a sense of outrage it would have aroused, on the assumption (contrary to his findings) that the DOT did overlook the power and was guilty of maladministration.

This leads me straight to the question of the adequacy of the PO's reasons. He could have simply refused to deal with the issue of injustice on the grounds that his findings of maladministration were sufficient to dispose of the matter. But I have rejected Mr Elvin's argument that this is what he did. . . It is clear that the issue of injustice was one of the principal controversial issues, and the PO was required to give reasons in relation to it, which were sufficient to enable the parties to know what he decided, and why. In my judgment, since the case on outrage was so strong, the PO should have made it clear that he had considered it, and why he had decided that it did not involve injustice in this case. The failure to mention it leads to the reasonable suspicion that he failed to have regard to it at all, or that, if he did, his reasons for concluding that there was no injustice would not bear scrutiny. In my view, this reasons challenge is justified. I would rest this part of my decision on the simple fact that the PO should have dealt expressly with the outrage point.

Notes

1. Giddings concludes that the case:

    clarifies in two important respects the reach of judicial review of the [PO]. . .and those two aspects lie at the heart of the Ombudsman's statutory remit: to determine whether the complainant has suffered injustice in consequence of maladministration. First, the Ombudsman's process for finding maladministration has been held to be amenable to judicial review—and in this case was found wanting by the court in two respects: investigative failure and shortcomings in subsequent reasoning. Secondly, the meaning of injustice has been clarified to include not only loss but also a sense of outrage and indignation.[89]

2. The extent of the amenability of decision making by the PO to judicial review is now such that in the 2000 Cabinet Office Review,[90] the authors said simply: 'The Ombudsman's entire process is subject to judicial review.' However, there is no evidence that such cases are more than occasional: the PO noted in her last Annual Report that: 'During 2008–09, seven judicial reviews were issued against PHSO; six were refused permission to proceed and one was still awaiting a decision at the year end.'[91] Moreover, as Kirkham *et al* conclude: 'the case law on the Ombudsmen is generally very respectful of their discretionary authority'.[92]

---

89 [2000] PL 201 at 204.

90 *Review of the Public Sector Ombudsmen in England,* April 2000, para 1.24.

91 Annual Review 2008–09.

92 Kirkham *et al* (2008) at 523.

OTHER OMBUDSMEN

Evidence submitted to the Select Committee on the PO[93] demonstrates the growth of the ombudsman system. In the public sector, the PO has been joined by the following: the Health Service Commissioner for England, Scotland, Wales; the Commission for Local Administration in England; the Commission for Local Administration in Wales; the Commissioner for Local Administration in Scotland; the Northern Ireland Parliamentary Commissioner for Administration and Commissioner for Complaints; the Prisons Ombudsman for England and Wales (from end of 1993). In the private sector, ombudsmen include the following: the Banking Ombudsman; the Building Societies Ombudsman; the Ombudsman for Corporate Estate Agents; the Insurance Ombudsman; the Investment Ombudsman; the Legal Services Ombudsman; the Legal Services Ombudsman for Scotland; the Pensions Ombudsman.

The Scotland Act 1998 requires the Scottish Parliament to legislate for the creation of an Ombudsman to investigate actions of the Scottish Executive (s 91), and the Scottish Public Services Ombudsman Act 2002 created an Ombudsman with a much broader remit than the PO, encompassing the devolved institutions, local government and the Scottish NHS. In relation to Northern Ireland, an Assembly Ombudsman was established under the Northern Ireland Act 1998.[94] The Public Services Ombudsman for Wales, introduced by the Public Services Ombudsman (Wales) Act 2005 is able to investigate matters relating to local government, social housing, health, the Welsh Assembly, certain Welsh public authorities and (so far as their conduct impacts upon Wales) certain other public authorities.

Consideration of these ombudsmen is outside the remit of this book, but a few brief remarks may be made about the LGO.[95] The LGO scheme broadly resembles that of the PO; there is no equivalent of the MP filter, but the attention of the body complained of must have been brought to the complaint before the LGO will investigate. Again, there are certain exclusions from the LGO's remit, and the LGO cannot compel compliance with its reports, although decisions such as *Eastleigh* and *Bradley* (above) have come close to making LGO findings enforceable via judicial review. Its remit was formally expanded in 2007 so that it 'can now investigate failures in service and failures to provide a service, in addition to the existing powers to investigate maladministration'.[96] It may also 'investigate matters which come to [its] attention during an investigation, where it appears that someone, other than the original complainant, may have suffered injustice'.[97]

Seneviratne notes that the following bodies are subject to investigation by the Local Government Ombudsmen (LGO): district, borough, city, or county councils (not town or parish councils); the Commission for New Towns or new town development corporations (housing matters only); housing action trusts; police authorities; fire authorities; any joint board of local authorities, including the National Park Boards; the National Rivers Authority (flood defence and land drainage matters only); and the Broads Authority. In practice, the vast majority of investigations involve local councils.[98] The changes made in 2007 add non-statutory bodies providing contracted out services on behalf of Local

---

93 HC 42 (1993–94), Vol II.

94 See SI 1996/1298 (NI 8).

95 See further DCM Yardley, 'Local Ombudsmen in England: Recent Trends and Developments' [1983] PL 522.

96 M Seneviratne, 'Updating the Local Government Ombudsman' [2008] PL 627 at 627.

97 *Ibid* at 632.

98 Seneviratne, n 14 above, at 85.

Authorities to the jurisdiction of the LGO and allowed for more flexible and informal methods of investigating and resolving complaints. The Cabinet Office Review drew favourable conclusions as to the work of the LGO. Stage II of the Financial Management and Policy Review of the CLA in 1996, which drew on polls by MORI in 1995, concluded that the work of the LGO was generally well respected by complainants, their advisers and local authorities; although there was widespread concern about delays.

REFORM OF THE PUBLIC SECTOR OMBUDSMEN: THE CABINET OFFICE REVIEW 2000

The problems of the present system

In its overall review of the ombudsmen, which examined the PO, the LGO and the Health Service Commissioner, the Cabinet Office found as follows:

Review of the Public Sector Ombudsmen in England, April 2000 [from appendix A— paper submitted by Ombudsmen]

11. The present arrangements are unhelpful to complainants. Complaints do not necessarily relate only to the actions of a body within one ombudsman's jurisdiction. For example:

   a. an elderly or mentally ill person may have a complaint about the way a hospital and a social services authority dealt with his or her discharge from hospital; or
   b. parents may be aggrieved by the delay in issuing a Statement of their child's Special Educational Needs partly because of tardiness by the education authority and partly because of dilatoriness by the health authority in providing reports for the child's assessment or may be aggrieved by the subsequent failure of both types of authority to secure the provision of the speech therapy specified in the Statement;
   c. a claimant of Housing Benefit may have been caused injustice because of faults not only by the council but also by the DSS or the Rent Officer Service.

Increasingly, partnerships are being forged between, for example, NHS bodies and local authorities so as to achieve better assessment of the client's needs and the delivery of services to meet them. . . . This is welcome but the present jurisdictions of the English Ombudsmen do not sit easily with this trend.

   Complainants find it difficult to know to which Ombudsman to complain and rarely complain to more than one at the same time even though they would have good grounds to do so. . .

   At present, far from having only 'one door' to knock on, the complainant (often vulnerable, inarticulate and poor) is faced with at least three. . . Information and publicity about getting redress is fragmented because the PO, HSC and LGOs produce separate brochures, complaint forms and press notices. It seems likely, therefore, that awareness and understanding about what the English Ombudsmen can do is impaired. . .

[extract from the Review]

2.29 The effect of this complex environment can be to lead to a sense of confusion. The public on the whole do not understand how it all fits together. If they have a problem, it is often not clear where to go and frequently only part of their problem can be dealt with by any single body. A complaint which crosses boundaries between agencies (for example, a discharge from a hospital to local authority social services which goes wrong) may need to be pursued through two or more complaints processes, eventually to two or more ombudsmen. Complainants in these circumstances are often vulnerable and may have disadvantages such as language or literacy difficulties which make it difficult to pursue their complaints to a satisfactory conclusion.

All of the public sector ombudsmen and perhaps the Independent Housing Ombudsman might find themselves involved in such a complaint, dealing with them as four separate complaints each of which might have been pursued through separate internal complaints processes before arriving on each ombudsman's desk. . .

2.31 . . .In one group of 6 cases, 3 involved multiple agencies and the words 'being pushed from pillar to post' were used frequently. Because each agency feels itself responsible for its own transactions, but not for an entire activity, slip-ups occur and arrangements for resolving the problems are lacking. If a complaint does reach an ombudsman he or she can deal only with the element involving bodies within jurisdiction. When the problem giving rise to the complaint has arisen because of the boundary (for example, a communication failure) it may be difficult to resolve the matter satisfactorily and obtain redress—particularly if the major fault lies with the body out of jurisdiction on the other side of the boundary.

Note

In order to combat these problems, the Review recommended a radical solution— the restructuring of the PO, LCA and HSC into one, collegiate structure of public sector ombudsmen, able to take complaints about any matter within jurisdiction regardless of whether it concerned a local authority, the NHS or a government department.

Restructuring the Ombudsmen: a single new Commission for the public sector

Review of the Public Sector Ombudsmen in England, April 2000

At present, the ombudsmen are defined by function—central government, health service and local government—and each is confined in his or her jurisdiction to that particular function. This will be too rigid in future. All ombudsmen should be able to cover the complete jurisdiction, any functional divides being purely an administrative arrangement in the same way as areas of the country are at present with the CLA. Structural arrangements within the new organization will need to allow for new partnerships cutting across functions but we envisage that a functional focus will predominate. This would provide advantages by maintaining expertise and engagement with the various areas of government. We see advantages in retaining specific Local Government and Health Service Ombudsman roles to underpin this focus but neither they nor their colleagues should be confined by law to particular areas of the jurisdiction. By building in this flexibility from the start we believe that the new Commission could be easily reshaped to accommodate changing government structures and it would allow other functional allocations to be made (e.g. an Education Ombudsman) if appropriate. We recommend that a collegiate structure (the new Commission) is put in place. . .

As long as the external requirements of accountability, service to the public, value for money and transparency are met we recommend that the ombudsmen should be able to manage the internal arrangements of the new Commission, including the location of offices, to adapt it to the changing external environment over time. . . .We recommend that the following framework is adopted in planning the legislation for, and organisation of, the new Commission:

- The organisation must be resilient in its ability to respond to developments in the delivery of public services by central and local government. If it is 'government shaped' it may be too inflexible when the shape of government changes.
- The internal organisation must operate as a single entity for the management of work and generally for accountability, policy-making, funding and resource management.
- The individual ombudsmen must be appointed as office-holders with a personal jurisdiction across the entire work of the new Commission. They should not be appointed to have particular functional or geographical responsibilities. However by agreement within the new Commission they would each be identified with a particular group of the bodies under jurisdiction. Thus, for example, local authorities will know which member of the new Commission will deal with them individually or corporately on questions of policy and practice.
- The staff of the new Commission should specialise in aspects of the functions of bodies under jurisdiction and as necessary form teams to deal with partnership working by those bodies. Such partnerships may involve bodies not under jurisdiction, or under the jurisdiction of another complaints investigation scheme, and innovative collaborative arrangements will be needed.
- The new Commission must work closely with central and local government authorities and the National Health Service, as appropriate through the central unit (which we recommend later in this chapter) to address the jurisdictional issues raised by partnerships, franchises, contracted out services or other developing mechanisms for the delivery of public services.
- The responsibilities of the ombudsmen for bodies under jurisdiction or for the geographical division of work should be agreed within the new Commission. . .

5.4 In suggesting a new Commission we are proposing two major changes: a new Act to replace three separate pieces of legislation, and a new organisation formed from three separate though related organisations. This will be a substantial task though made easier by commonality between the different legislation and existing close working relationships between the three ombudsmen.

The jurisdiction and powers of the new Commission will in the first instance be derived from those of the existing ombudsmen.

Notes

1. What was being aimed at is indicated by the comments of witnesses to the Select Committee:

   > Presumably in the public sector you could just invite complainants, 'If you have a complaint against virtually any public body, just write to the Ombudsman, London.' Maybe you would not even need the 'London'.
   >
   > When we went to Sweden we went into the public end of the Ombudsman's office and there was a desk with somebody at the back of it taking complaints off the street and he was there for all the Ombudsmen, local government, this one and the other. . .that would be the ideal situation, taking the MPs away from it, taking the councillors away from it and letting members of the public come into a National Ombudsman's shop to make their complaint there and then.[99]

2. As to jurisdiction, the Review was relatively cautious, merely recommending that there should be no overall reduction in the jurisdiction of the new Commission and that any changes to jurisdiction should not be made in piecemeal way, but as part of a higher level review of the overall role and powers of the public sector ombudsmen (para 5.9).

3. By contrast PAC, in its report on the Review, took a more radical line: in answering the question, '*Should the legislation specify the bo*dies which a*re not within the ombudsmen's jurisdiction, rather than those which are*', it answered, firmly, 'This change has been consistently recommended by our predecessor committees[100] and it should be seen as a basic principle of any new system'.[101] One of their witnesses put it thus: 'The onus of jurisdiction needs to be shifted in favour of the complainant. All state agencies and their activities should be in jurisdiction unless otherwise specifically excluded. That is the complainant's citizen-friendly way of addressing the question.'[102]

4. Another important issue for the Review was whether the new Commission should, unlike the present ombudsmen, be allowed to conduct investigations off her own bat, so called 'own initiative investigations'. On this, the Review was again conservative, observing, 'An ombudsman's function must remain grounded in addressing injustice caused to an individual and own-initiative investigation appears inconsistent with impartiality' (para 6.15); it may be noted that two witnesses giving evidence to PAC took a different line. Professor Birkinshaw observed that 'The great majority of ombudsmen in other countries do have this power [and] I have never heard it said that this has undermined the sense of confidence in them as being independent.'[103] Professor Seneviratne agreed: 'I think that is essential if an Ombudsman is going to have an over-arching searching out of systemic problems.'[104]

5. The Review also considered the relationship of the new Commission, which would have jurisdiction only in England, with the ombudsmen for Scotland and Wales. It noted that 'cases sometimes cross borders (for example, a complaint by a person living in Wales using medical services in England or concerning a child moving countries involving two sets of social services)' and concluded that '"associate" arrangements for public sector ombudsmen in the other three countries

---

99 Third Report of the Select Committee on Public Administration, HC 612 (1999–2000), Evidence, 21 June 1999, Q 10 (Mr Campbell).

100 That is, previous Select Committees on the PO.

101 Third Report, n 99 above, para 15.

102 *Ibid,* Evidence, 28 June 2000, Q 48 (Prof Giddings).

103 *Ibid,* Q 77.

104 *Ibid,* Evidence, 9 November 1999, 16 26–27.

[should be] put in place' (para 7.11) to allow one body to investigate, by agreement with the other, such cross-border cases. It further pointed out that, 'There may. . . occasionally, be instances of serious maladministration, which apply beyond England and where the new Commission may wish to address the matter on a United Kingdom basis, perhaps making a special report to Parliament. We recommend that the new Commission remains able to report to Parliament on a United Kingdom basis.' (para 7.12).

Access to the new Commission and working methods

As discussed above, the Review was clear that the MP filter was an outdated, obstructive anomaly that should be removed, a view now backed by PAC (see above, pp 901–904). The public should have direct access to the new Commission, whatever the subject matter of their complaint, via a single entry point, to be known as **'the gateway'**:

> All complaints whether about central or local government, health services, other public bodies within jurisdiction or partnerships will be submitted through the gateway. The gateway will also provide information and advice to enquirers, taking over the current ombudsmen's advice line functions. . .[and also deal with premature complaints].
> 6.50 The gateway will belong to the new Commission as a whole and will act in an informal manner, with customer service principles at the heart of its operation. The aim will be to route a complaint to the right place as quickly as possible.

How far the new Commission should be permitted, even encouraged to move away from the relatively formal, thorough, but time-consuming method of the PO is a question intimately related to a broader question—its overall role. A tension lies at the heart of the PO between two competing conceptions of her role: on the one hand, the imperative to provide a rapid, cheap and satisfactory remedy *to the particular complainant.* This aspect of her role is often served best by informality, by flexibility in dealing with complaints and a non-confrontational approach to the respondent of the complaint. On the other hand, the PO can carry out major investigations into serious policy failures, acting as a tool of parliamentary accountability, and as primarily an *investigative* and *critical* agency, rather than a remedy providing one. As the Review noted, such a role requires fidelity to the formal, thorough—but time-consuming procedure—laid down in the PO1967 itself:

> Investigations are the 'big-stick' which keeps Parliament engaged and ultimately underpins the ombudsman's ability to ensure redress for complainants. MPs and organisations like Citizens Advice Bureaux can assist complainants with interventions and settlements but the ombudsman has unique powers to investigate complaints.
> 6.10 Formal investigations are likely to be required in three circumstances: where the investigation is the resolution (this is particularly likely with health cases), where a respondent body has not co-operated in trying to achieve resolution and where the wider public interest means that full details of what happened need to be exposed.

Professor Giddings, in evidence to PAC expressed the view that the Ombudsman could be seen to have as many as four different roles:

> Is the Ombudsman primarily a complaint handling facility, a way of enabling individuals who have a problem to get that problem resolved, or is the Ombudsman there not to do that, as you have other complaint handling mechanisms internally, but as a way of using complaints to identify and remedy systemic faults in an organisation that is being made accountable? Is the Ombudsman there to in a sense stand aside, monitor and review other complaint handling procedures? For example, to use a generic term, the adjudicators are dealing with the mass business of all the complaints which have not been successfully resolved by the internal mechanisms and then the Ombudsman would be seen as monitoring the adjudicators, ensuring that they are acting effectively or, fourthly, is the Ombudsman there as a sort of super advocate for the individual citizen, in international terms, the citizen's protector concept? Those four roles are not mutually exclusive but they do have different implications for the way you organise and deliver the service.[105]

Interestingly, the National Association of Citizens Advice Bureaux, when giving evidence to PAC, was very clear that it was the audit, rather than the individual complaint resolution aspect of the PO's work, that to them was the most important—'seeking out systemic problems and dealing with systemic problems'.[106]

The Review was concerned that the working methods of the new body should be suitably flexible to allow all these aspects of the ombudsmen's roles to be continued (see paras 6.16 and 6.71).

It was not proposed that the new Commissioner should have the power to award compulsory remedies. Aside from the other issues, canvassed above, it was feared that, if the Commissioner had such a power, it could become subject to Art 6 of the European Convention on Human Rights, thus imposing a more formal, court-like procedure.[107]

In essence, then, the proposals recognise the value of the new, informal approach taken by the PO in some cases to complaints resolution, but advocate a revised statutory framework which would give explicit recognition and sanction to such an approach, whilst preserving the legal ability of the PO to insist upon the formal, heavyweight, investigative process where that seemed appropriate to the complaint or to the problems it *prima facie* revealed.

Considerable concern has been expressed both by PAC and the PO at the failure of Government to introduce concrete legislative proposals to give effect to the reforms recommended by the Cabinet Office Review.[108]

In 2005, a further report, *Cabinet Office, Reform of the Public Sector Ombudsmen in England* (2005) advocated making certain changes to streamline the English Ombudsmen system by way of regulatory reform through secondary legislation.[109] This has now been done, via the Regulatory Reform Order of 2007, which allows for joint working between various public sector Ombudsmen, As Elliott explains it, the Order:

> [allows] ombudsmen to share information, undertake joint investigations and issue joint reports. . .[something] be facilitated, in part, by permitting ombudsmen to

---

105   *Ibid*, Q 2.

106   *Ibid*, Evidence, 28 June 2000, Q 79 (Mrs Edwards).

107   *Ibid* (answer to consultation Q 11).

108   See the *Annual Review* HC 5 (2001–02), paras 6 and 7 and PAC Report, HC 897 (2001–02), para 11.

109   See M Elliot, 'Asymmetric devolution and ombudsmen reform in England' [2006] PL 84, for comment and criticism.

delegate their functions to each other's staff, enabling 'a single officer to interview witnesses, research files on behalf of two or more of the Ombudsmen, call for documentary evidence, obtain specialist professional advice, and produce a final report'.[110]

However, the reforms are relatively modest compared to the 2000 proposals for two main reasons: first, the MP filter remains; second, the reforms as Elliot points out, 'leave intact the three separate public sector ombudsmen's jurisdictions, albeit that they will be able to co-operate to a greater extent than at present'.[111]

FURTHER READING

M Seneviratne, *Ombudsmen: Public Services and Administrative Justice* (2002)

A Abraham, 'The Ombudsman and "Paths to Justice": A Just Alternative or Just an Alternative?' [2008] PL 1–10.

T Cornford, 'Administrative Redress: The Law Commission's Consultation Paper' [2009] PL 70

M Elliott, 'Asymmetric Devolution and Ombudsman Reform in England' [2006] PL 84

The Kirkham Report: *Withstanding The Test of Time* HC 421 (2006–07)

N O'Brien, 'Ombudsmen and Social Rights Adjudication' [2009] PL 466

The Law Commission, *Administrative Redress: Public Bodies and the Citizen* (2008), Paper No 187, available at www.lawcom.gov.uk/remedies.htm.

M Seneviratne, '"Joining Up" The Ombudsmen—The Review of the Public Sector Ombudsmen in England' [2000] PL 582

---

110 *Ibid* at 88.

111 *Ibid* at 89.

CHAPTER 17
THE TRADITIONAL PROTECTION OF CIVIL LIBERTIES IN BRITAIN AND THE IMPACT OF THE HUMAN RIGHTS ACT 1998

INTRODUCTION

In many Western democracies, the rights of citizens are enshrined in a constitutional document sometimes known as a Bill or Charter of Rights. Until the inception of the Human Rights Act 1998 (HRA), the UK had no similar charter of rights since the ancient Bill of Rights 1688 does not contain a list of rights comparable to those of modern Bills of Rights. In 2000, when it came fully into force, the HRA afforded further effect to the European Convention on Human Rights (see Chapter 7) in domestic law. Thus, UK citizens could rely for the first time on an instrument resembling a Bill of Rights. This chapter will contrast the current methods of protecting human rights and freedoms under the HRA with the methods used pre-HRA. It will try to show that although the HRA has brought about significant changes, it can be viewed as forming part of a process as opposed to creating abrupt and radical change in that protection. Further, its inception was not intended to entail fundamental constitutional change.

Traditionally, pre-HRA, in order to discover which freedoms were protected and the extent of that protection, it was necessary to examine the common law, statutes and the influence of treaties to which the UK is a party, especially the European Convention on Human Rights. Certain characteristics of the UK constitution determined the means of protecting fundamental freedoms in the UK. The doctrine of the supremacy of Parliament meant that constitutional law could be changed in the ordinary way—by Act of Parliament. As every student of constitutional law knows, Parliament has the power to abridge freedoms that in other countries are seen as fundamental rights. It follows from this that all parts of the law are equal—there is no hierarchy of laws and therefore constitutional law cannot constrain other laws. This fundamental characteristic of the UK constitution has been preserved in the HRA in ss 3(2) and 6(2), as explained below.

Further, judges could not strike down provisions in Acts of Parliament, and that position is maintained under the HRA. So if, for example, a statute was passed containing a provision that in some way limited freedom of speech, a judge merely had to apply it, whereas in a country with an 'entrenched' Bill of Rights (one given special constitutional protection—a protection greater than that afforded to 'ordinary' law), the statutory provision might be struck down as unconstitutional—as in the US. However, there was, prior to the inception of the HRA, a possible constraint on this process. If the judge considered that the provision in question was at all ambiguous, he or she could interpret it in such a way that freedom of speech was maintained, by relying on Article 10 of the Convention. An exception to the lack of a strike-down power was created by EU law. If the domestic provision came into conflict with an EU provision protecting human rights, e.g. in the sphere of equality law, the judge could decide to 'disapply' it, unless the conflict could be resolved. Thus, parliamentary sovereignty had suffered some limitation in the pre-HRA era. Where the EU had (and has) an impact on human rights, it could provide a protection which could broadly be said to have removed certain fundamental freedoms, or aspects of them, from the reach of Parliament.[1]

Civil liberties thus were traditionally defined as residual, not entrenched, as in other countries: they were seen as the residue of freedom left behind after the legal restrictions had been defined. Thus, it was often said that civil liberties in the UK were in a more precarious position than they were in other democracies, although this did not necessarily mean that they were inevitably less well protected: some Bills of Rights offered only a theoretical protection to freedoms which was not reflected in practice. These constitutional arrangements have not been fundamentally changed under the HRA; a judge is not able to declare a statutory provision invalid because it conflicts with a Convention right protected by the Act. It might appear then that the HRA has not affected the traditional methods of protecting

---

1   See Chapter 5, in particular pp 217–223.

liberties. However, as will become apparent below, that is not the case: under s 3 of the HRA, judges have a much greater obligation than they had previously to seek to ensure that statutory provisions are consistent with the Convention rights.

That is the constitutional background to the HRA. That background is still of great significance since it was crucial in the development of civil liberties in this country and because the HRA has been greatly influenced by the domestic constitutional traditions: its main provisions represent a compromise between maintaining those traditions and giving greater protection to human rights. This chapter begins by considering the nature and adequacy of the traditional domestic arrangements which protected fundamental freedoms only as liberties and will go on to consider the extent to which the Convention influenced the domestic protection of civil liberties in the pre-HRA era. It will then examine the instrument that has afforded the Convention further effect in domestic law—the HRA.

At the present time the Liberal-Conservative government has declared its intention, after the 2010 general election, to consider repeal of the HRA and the introduction of a 'Bill of Rights' for Britain.[2] Clearly, it is quite possible that if repeal of the HRA occurred, in around 2012–14, there might be a reluctance to follow it by the introduction of a Bill of Rights. The possibility of repeal of the HRA and introduction of a Bill of Rights affords the following discussion a particular pertinence at the present time. If the HRA was repealed, the methods of protecting human rights in the UK would—at least for a time—reflect the pre-HRA arrangements discussed below, although the judiciary might also be likely to develop common law doctrines that afforded the ECHR rights greater protection than was available in the pre-HRA era. The impact of a Bill of Rights, if one was eventually introduced, would depend, obviously, on the mechanism used for protecting the rights listed in it and on the choice of rights. But if *less* protection for human rights was provided than is available under the ECHR, the UK would probably find itself faced with an increase in applications to Strasbourg, meaning that UK citizens would be more likely than under the HRA to suffer rights-violations.

The HRA was introduced under the Labour Government in 1998 on the basis that rights were, finally, to be 'brought home'.[3] There were expectations at that time that the HRA would revive the civil liberties tradition—there was a sense of a break with the erosions of liberty associated with the Conservative Governments of 1979–97.[4] But the post-HRA period is also the post 9/11 period. Legislation passed after the HRA, which is considered in this Part, including the Terrorism Acts 2000 and 2006, the Anti-Terrorism Crime and Security Act 2001, the Prevention of Terrorism Act 2005, the amendments to the Police and Criminal Evidence Act 1984,[5] is in a number of respects more authoritarian and less human rights-regarding than much of the legislation passed in the pre-HRA years. Thus, the fact that the UK now has a document that looks something like a Bill of Rights, in the tradition of other democracies, should not obscure the tendency of the executive to sacrifice human rights at a time viewed as a time of crisis due to terrorist activity.

---

2   Prior to the election the Conservatives had decided to repeal the HRA. David Cameron in a speech to the Centre for Policy Studies, London 26 June 2006 *Balancing freedom and security—A modern British Bill of Rights* stated that the HRA should be repealed. . . 'The Human Rights Act has a damaging impact on our ability to protect our society against terrorism. . . . I am today committing my Party to work towards the production of a Modern Bill of Rights'. He also stated that the new Bill of Rights should be entrenched. He accepted that the UK would remain bound by the decision in *Chahal v UK* (the decision preventing deportation of terrorist suspects if they would be at risk of Art 3 treatment in the receiving country—see Chapter 7, p 303) but considered that repeal of the HRA would curb delays and cost in the criminal justice system. He did not explain what would occur if a person sought to rely on their Convention rights under the new Bill of Rights' fair trial Article, or what would occur if there was a successful application to Strasbourg under Art 6 which would also have succeeded domestically under the HRA but which failed under the new Bill of Rights due to the modifications to the fair trial right that Cameron presumably had in mind in speaking of the hindrance created by the HRA in terms of using criminal justice measures.

3   See *Bringing Rights Home: Labour's plans to incorporate the ECHR into UK Law: A Consultation Paper,* December 1996 (1997) and the White Paper, *Rights Brought Home,* Cm 3782, October 1997; see also J Straw and P Boateng (1997) 1 EHRR 71.

4   See Lord Cooke, 'The British Embracement of Human Rights' (1999) EHRLR 243; D Feldman, 'The Human Rights Act and Constitutional Principles' (1999) 19(2) LS 165.

5   See Chapter 20, esp p 1146 *et seq,* 1169 *et seq,* 1181 *et seq.*

THE TRADITIONAL PROTECTION OF CIVIL LIBERTIES UNDER THE BRITISH CONSTITUTION

The Diceyan tradition

AV Dicey, *The Law of the Constitution* (1959), pp 197–98

In Belgium, which may be taken as a type of countries possessing a constitution formed by a deliberate act of legislation, you may say with truth that the rights of individuals to personal liberty flow from or are secured by the constitution. In England the right to individual liberty is part of the constitution, because it is secured by the decisions of the courts, extended or confirmed as they are by the Habeas Corpus Acts. If it be allowable to apply the formulas of logic to questions of law, the difference in this matter between the constitution of Belgium and the English constitution may be described by the statement that in Belgium individual rights are deductions drawn from the principles of the constitution, whilst in England the so called principles of the constitution are inductions or generalisations based upon particular decisions pronounced by the courts as to the rights of given individuals.

This is of course a merely formal difference. Liberty is as well secured in Belgium as in England, and as long as this is so it matters nothing whether we say that individuals are free from all risk of arbitrary arrest, because liberty of person is guaranteed by the constitution, or that the right to personal freedom, or in other words to protection from arbitrary arrest, forms part of the constitution because it is secured by the ordinary law of the land. But though this merely formal distinction is in itself of no moment, provided always that the rights of individuals are really secure, the question whether the right to personal freedom or the right to freedom of worship is likely to be secure does depend a good deal upon the answer to the inquiry whether the persons who consciously or unconsciously build up the constitution of their country begin with definitions or declarations of rights, or with the contrivance of remedies by which rights may be enforced or secured. Now, most foreign constitution-makers have begun with declarations of rights. For this they have often been in no wise to blame. Their course of action has more often than not been forced upon them by the stress of circumstances, and by the consideration that to lay down general principles of law is the proper and natural function of legislators. But any knowledge of history suffices to show that foreign constitutionalists have, while occupied in defining rights, given insufficient attention to the absolute necessity for the provision of adequate remedies by which the rights they proclaimed might be enforced.

TRS Allan, 'Constitutional rights and common law'
(1991) 2 *Oxford Journal of Legal Studies* 453, pp 456–60

Contemporary reluctance to view the common law as a source of constitutional rights may be partly the consequence of defective legal analysis. At the root of common misunderstanding lies a confusion about the residual nature of liberty.

If common law liberty is merely residual, it is argued, it may be eaten away by ever-encroaching restrictions and restraints until deprived of all substance. The argument benefits here from the failure to distinguish between liberty and liberties.

It is important to make the distinction between liberty and liberties in understanding the common law. The common law does, of course, recognise a general right to liberty—in the sense that every encroachment by the state (or by another) on one's freedom must be justified. There need not be special moral justification of the kind which permits restriction of a basic liberty, such as freedom of speech. But there must be lawful authority for coercive action, and legislative restrictions on individual freedom must be duly enacted in the appropriate constitutional manner. If, then, liberty is residual, in the sense that everything which is not expressly forbidden the individual is permitted, the foundation of constitutional rights is laid. The burden is on the government or public authority to justify coercion. This is the aspect of the Rule of Law illuminated by *Entick v Carrington* [(1765) 19 St Tr 1029]: every coercive act of government which is not shown to be authorised is automatically illegal.

Notes

1. The Diceyan tradition holds that the absence of a written constitution in Britain is not a weakness but a source of strength. This is because the protection of the citizen's liberties is not dependent on vaguely worded constitutional documents but, rather, flows from specific judicial decisions which give the citizen specific remedies for infringement of his or her liberties.[6] Dicey regarded one of the great strengths of the British constitution as lying in the lack of broad discretionary powers vested in the executive. Citizens could only be criminalised for clear breaches of clearly established laws. Where there was no relevant law, they could know with absolute confidence that they could exercise their liberty as they pleased without fear of incurring any sanction. The Diceyan thesis finds support in the seminal decision of *Derbyshire County Council v Times Newspapers.*[7] The House of Lords found, without referring to Article 10 of the European Convention, that the importance the common law attached to free speech was such that defamation could not be available as an action to local (or central) government.

2. The traditional reluctance of judges to intervene in the politically important areas of state governance, such as national security or deportation was evidenced by the decisions in *Council of Civil Service Unions v Minister for the Civil Service*[8] and *R v Secretary of State for the Home Department ex parte Hosenball.*[9]

3. Contrary to the Diceyan view, it may be found that where an attempt has been made in a statute (perhaps due to decisions of the European Court of Human Rights or the European Court of Justice) to give the law some coherence with a view to ensuring that a particular freedom is protected, as is the case with freedom of speech in the Contempt of Court Act 1981, the common law may begin to take on a role which in some respects undermines the statutory provisions.[10] Or the common law provisions may in some respects curtail liberty more than the statutory ones; this may be said in

---

6   See p 937 above, ibid, at p 190.

7   [1993] AC 534.

8   [1985] AC 374.

9   [1977] 1 WLR 766.

10   See Chapter 18, pp 1062–1069.

particular of the common law doctrine of breach of the peace.[11] Keith Ewing and Conor Gearty have argued that for this reason a Bill of Rights may be undesirable as the people need Parliament to protect them from the judges, not merely the judges to protect them from Parliament.[12]

Judicial review and civil liberties

In one area—judicial review—the judges have shown a general determination to develop the common law with the basic aim of preventing the exercise of arbitrary power. Traditionally, in the pre-HRA era, the doctrine was fundamentally limited in that as long as a Minister appeared to have followed a correct and fair procedure, to have acted within his or her powers and to have made a decision which was not clearly unreasonable, the decision had to stand regardless of its potentially harmful impact on civil liberties. Thus, the fact that basic liberties were curtailed in the *GCHQ*[13] and *Brind*[14] cases did not in itself provide a ground for review. In other words, the courts were confined to looking back at the method of arriving at the decision rather than forward to its likely effects. In cases which touched particularly directly on national security, so sensitive were the judges to the executives' duty to uphold the safety of the realm, that they might define their powers even to look back on the decision as almost non-existent (see *R v Secretary of State for Home Department ex parte Stitt*).[15] Pre-HRA Sir John Laws considered, however, that judicial review might develop in such a way that it would provide greater protection for civil liberties.[16] If the HRA is repealed, continuance of the operation of the doctrine of proportionality in relation to matters covered by the ECHR would depend on judicial acceptance of this argument. The judges might be prepared to find, by analogy with the decision in *Anisminic*,[17] that even clear words in a statute purporting to oust application of the doctrine could be disapplied.

Sir John Laws, 'Is the High Court the guardian of fundamental constitutional rights?' [1993] *Public Law* 59, 71–75

Now there has been much reference in the recent public law learning to [the concept of proportionality], but the courts have in fact only flirted with it. The first stage is to see why it has not taken root so far. What has happened is that the courts have only recognised proportionality as a facet or species of *Wednesbury* (eg *R v Secretary of State for Health ex parte United States Tobacco* [1992] 1 QB 353 at 366G). The difficulty is that if proportionality is merely a facet of irrationality, it adds nothing to *Wednesbury*. . . if it is to take its place as a distinct concept, then there must be cases where it may succeed as a ground of substantive challenge, where *Wednesbury* would not; and this means that the court must be willing to strike down a decision on substantive and not merely procedural grounds

---

11 See Chapter 19, pp 1120–1135.

12 KD Ewing and CA Gearty, *Freedom under Thatcher: Civil Liberties in Modern Britain* (1989), pp 270–271.

13 *Council of Civil Service Unions v Minister for Civil Service* [1984] 3 All ER 935 (the Prime Minister's decision struck directly at freedom of association).

14 [1991] 1 All ER 720, HL (political speech was directly curtailed).

15 *The Times*, 3 February 1987.

16 See also Chapter 15, pp 875–883 in relation to developments in judicial review.

17 See Chapter 14, pp 769–774.

where ex hypothesi the decision is not an irrational one. The reason why so far the courts have been unwilling to take this step is surely the received wisdom that to do so would be to turn the public law court into a court of merits, and so to usurp the primary function of the decision-maker under review.

The truth is that the most interesting, and important, types of challenge to discretionary decisions—certainly those involving fundamental rights—are not usually about simple irrationality, or a failure to call attention to relevant matters. They are much more likely to be concerned with the way in which the decision-maker has ordered his priorities; the very essence of discretionary decision-making consists, surely, in the attribution of relative importance to the factors in the case. And here is my point: this is precisely what pro-portionality is about. . . .if we are to entertain a form of review in which fundamental rights are to enjoy the court's distinct protection, the very exercise consists in an insistence that the decision-maker is not free to order his priorities as he chooses. . .an insistence that he accord the first priority to the right in question unless he can show a substantial, objective, public justification for overriding it. Proportionality is surely the means of doing this. It is a ready-made tool in our hands.

It will be said that this approach falls foul of one of the received nostrums in our public law, . . .the rule that the relative weight to be accorded to the factors in play is always and only for the decision-maker to decide. . . . But if the issue is freedom of speech, or person, or the like, the application of this principle would mean that the decision-maker is at liberty to accord a high or low importance to the right in question, as he chooses. This cannot be right. What is therefore needed is a preparedness to hold that a decision which over-rides a fundamental right without sufficient objective justification will, as a matter of law, necessarily be disproportionate to the aim in view.

Notes

1. In the years immediately preceding the inception of the HRA, the judiciary showed a determin-ation to use judicial review to protect fundamental rights in a large number of instances. In *R v Secretary of State for the Home Department and Another ex parte Norney and Others*[18] the Secretary of State had made a determination that he would not refer the cases of the applicants, IRA life sentence prisoners, to the parole board until after the expiry of the tariff period of the sentences. Given the timetable of the parole board, this meant that in effect every tariff period was increased by 23 weeks. The applicants sought judicial review of the decision of the Secretary of State. It was found that the practice flouted common law principle and Art 5(4) ECHR. A declar-ation was therefore granted that the Home Secretary should have referred the applicants' cases to the parole board at such a time as would have ensured as far as possible that they would be heard immediately after expiry of the tariff period.

2. In *R v Ministry of Defence ex parte Smith and Others*,[19] the argument used by the Master of the Rolls in reaching the decision has some apparent affinity with that advanced by Sir John Laws above. The applicants had sought judicial review of the policy of the Ministry of Defence in maintaining a ban on homosexuals in the armed forces. The applicants had been dismissed due to the existence of the ban. In conducting such review the court applied the usual *Wednesbury* principles of reasonable-ness. This meant that the court could not interfere with the exercise of an administrative discretion

---

18   (1995) 7 Admin LR 861.

19   [1996] 1 All ER 257. See also *R v Cambridge Health Authority ex parte B* [1995] TLR 159, CA; [1995] 1 WLR 898.

on substantive grounds save where it was satisfied that the decision was unreasonable in the sense that it was beyond the range of responses open to a reasonable decision-maker; but it was found that in judging whether the decision-maker had exceeded that margin, the human rights context was important; the more substantial the interference with human rights, the more the court would require by way of justification before it was satisfied that the decision was reasonable. Applying such principles and taking into account the support of the policy in both Houses of Parliament, it was not found that the policy crossed the threshold of irrationality. Thus, the appeal was dismissed.

3. In the immediate pre-HRA era, a number of decisions recognised certain common law rights which, it was found, could not be abrogated except by express words or necessary implication—where there is only one way of reading the legislation in question. These cases are considered above (p 941) and included the rights of access to the courts,[20] to free speech,[21] and to basic subsistence.[22] The rule of construction in these instances was described in one of the most significant of these decisions, *R v Secretary of State for the Home Department ex parte Simms*,[23] by Lord Hoffman, as follows, at 412:

> Parliamentary sovereignty means that Parliament can if it chooses legislate contrary to fundamental principles of human rights. . . But the principle of legality means that Parliament must squarely confront what it is doing and count the political cost. Fundamental rights cannot be overridden by general or ambiguous words. . . because there is too great a risk that the full implications of their unqualified meaning may have passed unnoticed in the democratic process. . . In this way the courts of the UK, though acknowledging the sovereignty of Parliament, apply principles of constitutionality little different from those which exist in countries where the power of the legislature is expressly limited by a constitutional document.

In *R v Lord Chancellor ex parte Witham*,[24] Laws J found that the power of the Lord Chancellor to prescribe court fees was not based on sufficiently precise words to allow him to deny the right of access to a court by preventing an applicant on income support from issuing proceedings for defamation.

The influence of the European Convention on Human Rights pre-HRA

The influence of the European Convention on Human Rights increasingly provided further protection for civil liberties, domestically, even *prior* to the inception of the HRA.[25] The rulings of the European Court of Human Rights had led to better protection of human rights in such areas as prisoners'

---

20   *R v Lord Chancellor ex parte Witham* [1998] QB 575. But *cf R v Lord Chancellor ex parte Lightfoot* [2000] 2 WLR 318. For comment on the first instance decision [1998] 4 All ER 764, see M Elliott, '*Lightfoot*: Tracing the Perimeter of Constitutional Rights' [1998] JR 217.

21   *R v Secretary of State for the Home Dept ex parte Simms* [1999] 3 All ER 400, CA; [1999] 3 WLR 328, HL.

22   *R v Secretary of State for Social Security ex parte Joint Council of Welfare of Immigrants* [1996] 4 All ER 835; Lord Saville in *Criminal Injuries Compensation Board ex parte A* [1999] 2 AC 300; [1999] 4 All ER 860.

23   [1999] 3 All ER 400.

24   [1998] QB 575.

25   The Treaty on European Union, Art 6 provides that the EU will respect fundamental rights as recognised by the Convention.

rights,[26] freedom of expression[27] and privacy.[28] Each state decides on the status the Convention enjoys in national law; there is no obligation under Art 1 ECHR to allow individuals to rely on it in *national* courts. In some states it has the status of constitutional law;[29] in others of ordinary law.[30] In Britain, until the inception of the HRA, it had no binding domestic force. Successive UK Governments considered that it was not necessary for the Convention to be part of British law; they maintained that the UK's unwritten constitution was in conformity with it. Thus, until the HRA came into force in 2000, a UK citizen could not go before a UK court and simply argue that a Convention right had been violated. But in the ten years prior to the inception of the HRA the ECHR was increasingly having a significant influence within domestic law since the judges were increasingly prepared to take it into account in reaching a decision.

Brind v Secretary of State for the Home Department
[1991] 1 All ER 720, 722–23, 733–35

Lord Bridge of Harwich: It is accepted, of course, by the applicants that, like any other treaty obligations which have not been embodied in the law by statute, the Convention is not part of the domestic law, that the courts accordingly have no power to enforce Convention rights directly and that, if domestic legislation conflicts with the Convention, the courts must nevertheless enforce it. But it is already well settled that, in construing any provision in domestic legislation which is ambiguous in the sense that it is capable of a meaning which either conforms to or conflicts with the Convention, the courts will presume that Parliament intended to legislate in conformity with the Convention, not in conflict with it. Hence, it is submitted, when a statute confers upon an administrative authority a discretion capable of being exercised in a way which infringes any basic human right protected by the Convention, it may similarly be presumed that the legislative intention was that the discretion should be exercised within the limitations which the Convention imposes. I confess that I found considerable persuasive force in this submission. But in the end I have been convinced that the logic of it is flawed.

But I do not accept that this conclusion means that the courts are powerless to prevent the exercise by the executive of administrative discretions, even when conferred, as in the instant case, in terms which are on their face unlimited, in a way which infringes fundamental human rights. Thus, Article 10(2) of the Convention spells out and categorises the competing public interests by reference to which the right to freedom of expression may have to be curtailed. In exercising the power of judicial review we have neither the advantages nor the disadvantages of any comparable code to which we may refer or by which we are bound. But again, this surely does not mean that in deciding whether the Secretary of State, in the exercise of his discretion, could reasonably impose the restriction he has imposed on the broadcasting organisations, we are not perfectly entitled to start from the premise that any restriction of the right to freedom of expression requires to be justified and that nothing less than an important competing public interest will be sufficient to justify it.

---

26 *Golder v United Kingdom*, Series A No 18, (1975) 1 EHRR 524.

27 *Sunday Times v United Kingdom* (1979) 2 EHRR 245.

28 *Gaskin v United Kingdom* (1989) 12 EHRR 36.

29 E.g. Austria.

30 This includes Belgium, France, Italy, Luxembourg and Germany.

Derbyshire County Council v Times Newspapers Ltd [1992] 3 WLR 28, 60–61, CA

Butler-Sloss LJ: In *Attorney-General v Guardian Newspapers Ltd (No 2)* [1990] 1 AC 109, Lord Goff of Chieveley said (in relation to breach of confidential information), at p 283:

> . . . I wish to observe that I can see no inconsistency between English law on this subject and Article 10 of the European Convention on Human Rights. This is scarcely surprising, since we may pride ourselves on the fact that freedom of speech has existed in this country perhaps as long as, if not longer than, it has existed in any other country in the world. The only difference is that, whereas Article 10 of the Convention, in accordance with its avowed purpose, proceeds to state a funda-mental right and then to qualify it, we in this country (where everybody is free to do anything, subject only to the provisions of the law) proceed rather upon an assump-tion of freedom of speech, and turn to our law to discover the established exceptions to it. In any event I conceive it to be my duty, when I am free to do so, to interpret the law in accordance with the obligations of the Crown under this treaty.
>
> Adopting, as I respectfully do, that approach to the Convention, the principles governing the duty of the English court to take account of Article 10 appear to be as follows: where the law is clear and unambiguous, either stated as the common law or enacted by Parliament, recourse to Article 10 is unnecessary and inappropriate. . . . But where there is an ambiguity, or the law is otherwise unclear or so far undeclared by an appellate court, the English court is not only entitled but, in my judgment, obliged to consider the implications of Article 10. . .

Notes

1. The decision in *Brind* reaffirmed the accepted principle in the pre-HRA era that the Convention should be taken into account where domestic legislation is ambiguous. It also determined that state officials are *not* bound by the Convention in exercising discretionary power. The ruling in *Brind* relied on the general principle of construction that statutes will be interpreted if possible so as to conform with international treaties to which Britain is a party on the basis that the Government is aware of its international obligations and would not intend to legislate contrary to them. The position as regards the Convention was reiterated in *Re M and H (Minors)*[31] by Lord Brandon of Oakbrook: 'while English courts may strive where they can to interpret statutes as conforming with the obligations of Britain under the Convention, they are nevertheless bound to give effect to statutes which are free from ambiguity. . . even if those statutes may be in conflict with the Convention.' Thus, if a statute unambiguously violated fundamental rights the courts merely had to apply it in the pre-HRA era.

2. Applying Art 10, the Court of Appeal found in the *Derbyshire* case that a local authority cannot sue for libel. However, the House of Lords considered that in the particular instance, the common law could determine the issues in favour of freedom of speech.[32]

3. Lord Scarman in *Attorney-General v BBC*[33] considered the influence of the Convention on the common law. He said that where there was some leeway to do so, a court which must adjudicate on the relative weight to be given to different public interests under the common law should try to

---

31 [1988] 3 WLR 485.

32 [1993] AC 534, esp. at 551.

33 [1981] AC 303, 354.

strike a balance in a manner consistent with the treaty obligations accepted by the Government. 'If the issue should ultimately be. . .a question of legal policy, we must have regard to the country's international obligation to observe the Convention as interpreted by the Court of Human Rights.'[34]

4. Should a Conservative Government repeal the HRA, the above cases might once again become influential in legitimising continued judicial reference to the EHCR. The principles of 'common law constitutionalism', considered above at 937–941, would also once again become of great relevance.

Questions

❶   How far does Laws' thesis, above, fit with the decision in *Brind v Secretary of State for the Home Department?*

❷   Simon Lee in *Judging Judges* (1989), p 160 stated, 'We already have a Bill of Rights in the European Convention', as part of an argument that the whole Bill of Rights debate was misguided. Do you agree that this was the case pre-HRA?

❸   Is the decision in the *Smith* case, above, as regards the relevance of the Convention to the exercise of administrative discretion, distinguishable from Lord Bridge's findings on this point in *Brind?*

THE BILL OF RIGHTS QUESTION

In the latter half of the 20th century, support grew for the notion that there was a need for some constitutional change to safeguard civil liberties and that that change should take the form of a Bill of Rights. This issue is discussed by Dworkin and Waldron below, from entirely opposed perspectives.

R Dworkin, A Bill of Rights for Britain (1990), pp 32–38

The argument for parliamentary supremacy is often thought to rest on a more important and fundamental argument, however, according to which Britain should not have subscribed to the European Convention in the first place. This is the argument: that it is undemocratic for appointed judges rather than an elected Parliament to have the last word about what the law is. People who take that view will resist incorporation, because incorporation enlarges the practical consequences of what they regard as the mistake of accepting the Convention. They will certainly resist the idea that domestic judges should have the power to read the Convention more liberally and so provide more protection than Strasbourg requires.

Their argument misunderstands what democracy is, however. In the first place, it confuses democracy with the power of elected officials. There is no genuine democracy, even though officials have been elected in otherwise fair elections, unless voters have had access to the information they need so that their votes can be knowledgeable choices

---

rather than only manipulated responses to advertising campaigns. Citizens of a democracy must be able to participate in government not just spasmodically, in elections from time to time, but constantly through informed and free debate about their Government's performance between elections. Those evident requirements suggest what other nations have long ago realised: that Parliament must be constrained in certain ways in order that democracy be genuine rather than sham. The argument that a Bill of Rights would be undemocratic is therefore not just wrong but the opposite of the truth.

The depressing story of the Thatcher Government's concentrated assault on free speech is more than enough to prove that point. In the *Harman, Ponting* and *Spycatcher* cases, in denying a public interest exception in the new Official Secrets Act, in the broadcasting bans, in the Death on the Rock matter, government tried to censor information of the type citizens need in order to vote intelligently or criticise officials effectively. . . true democracy is not just statistical democracy, in which anything a majority or plurality wants is legitimate for that reason, but communal democracy, in which majority decision is legitimate only if it is a majority within a community of equals. That means not only that everyone must be allowed to participate in politics as an equal, through the vote and through freedom of speech and protest, but that political decisions must treat everyone with equal concern and respect, that each individual person must be guaranteed fundamental civil and political rights no combination of other citizens can take away, no matter how numerous they are or how much they despise his or her race or morals or way of life.

That view of what democracy means is at the heart of all the charters of human rights, including the European Convention. It is now the settled concept of democracy in Europe, the mature, principled concept that has now triumphed throughout Western Europe as well as in North America. It dominates the powerful movement towards democracy in Eastern Europe and Russia, and it was suppressed only with the most horrible tyranny in China. The rival, pure statistical concept of democracy, according to which democracy is consistent with oppressing minorities, was the concept proclaimed as justification by the Communist tyrannies after the Second World War: they said democracy meant government in the interests of the masses. The civilised world has recoiled from the totalitarian view, and it would be an appalling irony if Britain now embraced it as a reason for denying minorities constitutional rights.

This seems to me a decisive answer to the argument that incorporation would be undemocratic. . . Even people who do not think of themselves as belonging to any minority have good reasons for insisting that a majority's power to rule should be limited. Something crucially important to them—their religious freedom or professional independence or liberty of conscience, for example—might one day prove inconvenient to the Government of the day. Even people who cannot imagine being isolated in that way might prefer to live in a genuine political community, in which everyone's dignity as an equal is protected, rather than just in a state they control. . .

J Waldron, 'A right-based critique of constitutional rights'
(1993) 13 *Oxford Journal of Legal Studies* 18, 46–47, 50–51

. . .the fact that there is popular support, even overwhelming popular support, for an alteration in constitutional procedures does not show that such alteration therefore makes things more democratic. Certainly, my arguments entail that if the people want a regime of

CHAPTER 17 TRADITIONAL PROTECTION OF CIVIL LIBERTIES IN BRITAIN AND THE HRA 1998   946

constitutional rights, then that is what they should have: democracy requires that. But we must not confuse the reason for carrying out a proposal with the character of the proposal itself. If the people wanted to experiment with dictatorship, principles of democracy might give us a reason to allow them to do so. But it would not follow that dictatorship is democratic. Everyone agrees that it is possible for a democracy to vote itself out of existence; that, for the proponents of constitutional reform, is one of their great fears. My worry is that popular support for the constitutional reforms envisaged by Dworkin and other members of Charter 88 amounts to exactly that voting democracy out of existence, at least so far as a wide range of issues of political principle is concerned.

Dworkin also suggests that the democratic argument against a Bill of Rights is self-defeating in a British context, 'because a majority of British people themselves rejects the crude statistical view of democracy on which the argument is based'. But although democracy connotes the idea of popular voting, it is not part of the concept of democracy that its own content be fixed by popular voting. If a majority of the British people thought a military dictatorship was democratic (because more in tune with the 'true spirit of the people' or whatever), that would not show that it was, nor would it provide grounds for saying that democratic arguments against the dictatorship were 'selfdefeating'. If Dworkin wants to make a case against 'the crude statistical view' as a conception of democracy, he must argue for it . . .In the end, I think, the matter comes down to this. If a process is democratic and comes up with the correct result, it does no injustice to anyone. But if the process is non-democratic, it inherently and necessarily does an injustice, in its operation, to the participatory aspirations of the ordinary citizen. And it does this injustice, tyrannises in this way, whether it comes up with the correct result or not.

If we are going to defend the idea of an entrenched Bill of Rights put effectively beyond revision by anyone other than the judges, we should try and think what we might say to some public-spirited citizen who wishes to launch a campaign or lobby her MP on some issue of rights about which she feels strongly and on which she has done her best to arrive at a considered and impartial view. She is not asking to be a dictator; she perfectly accepts that her voice should have no more power than that of anyone else who is prepared to participate in politics. But—like her suffragette forebears—she wants a vote; she wants her voice and her activity to count on matters of high political importance.

In defending a Bill of Rights, we have to imagine ourselves saying to her: 'You may write to the newspaper and get up a petition and organise a pressure group to lobby Parliament. But even if you succeed, beyond your wildest dreams, and orchestrate the support of a large number of like-minded men and women, and manage to prevail in the legislature, your measure may be challenged and struck down because your view of what rights we have does not accord with the judges' view. When their votes differ from yours, theirs are the votes that will prevail.' It is my submission that saying this does not comport with the respect and honour normally accorded to ordinary men and women in the context of a theory of rights.

Notes

1. Dworkin argues that the implications of Waldron's thesis are themselves contrary to true democracy. Further, the refusal to disable the majority by entrenchment of rights includes a refusal to entrench democracy itself. This refusal in effect means that Waldron will not deny the right of the majority of the day to destroy democracy by disenfranchising a group such as all non-whites, or even by voting itself out of existence, thereby denying democracy to future generations.

2. A further paradox in Waldron's argument, the existence of which he concedes (at p 46), is that if the majority vote in a referendum for an entrenched Bill of Rights they must, on his argument, be allowed to have one. Clearly, the only way to prevent the majority from entrenching a Bill of Rights would be to have an entrenched law forbidding the entrenchment of laws. This would obviously be impossible on its own terms.

3. Dworkin's main argument is that a Bill of Rights is ultimately concerned with *preserving* a worth-while democracy for the future, and therefore that entrenched basic rights show *more* respect for democratic principles than do the advocates of retaining the untrammelled power of the majority of the day.[35]

Possible methods of protecting rights under a Bill of Rights

In the pre-HRA era, it was generally accepted that if a 'Bill of Rights' were introduced, it would afford domestic protection to the guarantees of the European Convention on Human Rights. A number of commentators considered possible methods of protecting the rights—a debate which will re-arise if the current Conservative-Liberal Government persuades Parliament to repeal the HRA with a view to introducing a Bill of Rights. The extent to which democracy might seem to be infringed if unelected judges had to apply the Bill of Rights was clearly partly dependent on its authority and on the availability of review of legislation. The most contentious possibility was the adoption of the American model. It would have meant that judges would be empowered to strike down prior and subsequent legislation in conflict with the Bill of Rights. It would also have meant giving the Bill of Rights higher authority than other Acts of Parliament by entrenching it, so that no possibility of correction of judicial decisions by subsequent legislation arose, except in so far as provided for by the method of entrenchment.

A much less contentious possibility, in democratic terms, which was considered, was that of allowing the rights listed in a Bill of Rights to prevail only over prior inconsistent legislation. A 'middle way', which was also the most likely possibility, would have been to protect the Convention rights only by a so-called 'notwithstanding clause' on the Canadian model—on that model subsequent legislation would only have been able to override the rights if the intention of doing so was clearly stated in the legislation; that is, a statutory provision would be included in such legislation stating, for example, 'the provisions of s 6 are to take effect notwithstanding the requirements of Article 6 of Schedule 1 to the Bill of Rights'. This 'middle way' undermines the argument against a Bill of Rights as undemocratic since under it the legislative body, at least in theory, remains free to pass legislation that is contrary to one of the rights; since the Bill of Rights is not entrenched, it also retains the power to amend or repeal part or all of it.

R Dworkin, *A Bill of Rights for Britain* (1990), pp 28–30

> Several influential supporters of a Bill of Rights (including Lord Scarman, a former member of the House of Lords, who has been a pioneer in the argument for incorporation) have proposed that in the first instance incorporation should take what is technically a weaker form: the incorporating statute should provide that an inconsistent statute is null and void

---

35   See further R Dworkin, 'Liberalism', in *A Matter of Principle* (1985). See also HLA Hart, *Law Liberty and Morality* (1963), and Lord Lester, *Democracy and Individual Rights* (1968).

unless Parliament has expressly stated that it intends the statute to override the Convention. In practice this technically weaker version of incorporation would probably provide almost as much protection as the stronger one. If a Government conceded that its statute violated the Convention, it would have no defence before the Commission or Court in Strasbourg. In any case, quite apart from that practical point, no respectable Government would wish to announce that it did not care whether its legislation or decisions violated the country's domestic promises and international obligations. If a Government felt itself able to make such an announcement, except in the most extraordinary circumstances, the spirit of liberty would be dead anyway, beyond the power of any constitution to revive.

Should Parliament be Supreme?
The politicians say that the very idea of a Bill of Rights restricting the power of Parliament is hostile to the British tradition that Parliament and Parliament alone should be sovereign. That supposed tradition seems less appealing now, when a very powerful executive and well-disciplined political parties mean less effective power for back-bench MPs than it did before these developments. The tradition has already been compromised in recent decades, moreover. It was altered by the European Communities Act, for example, under which judges have the power to override parliamentary decisions in order to enforce directly effective Community rules.

In any case, quite apart from these considerations, incorporating the European Convention would not diminish Parliament's present power in any way that could reasonably be thought objectionable. Parliament is already bound by international law to observe the terms of that Convention. . . It is hard to argue that this further limitation would be wrong in principle, however. Britain agreed when it accepted the European Convention and the jurisdiction of the European Court of Human Rights, that it would be bound by the principles laid down in the Convention as these principles were interpreted not by Parliament but by a group of judges. If that limitation on the power of Parliament is acceptable, how can it be unacceptable that the principles be interpreted not by mainly foreign judges but by British judges trained in the common law and in the legal and political traditions of their own country?

The argument for parliamentary supremacy would be irrelevant, moreover, if the Convention were incorporated in the weaker form I suggested should be the initial goal. For then Parliament could override the Convention by mere majority vote, provided it was willing expressly to concede its indifference about doing so. No doubt that condition would, in practice, prevent a Government from introducing legislation it might otherwise enact. That is the point of incorporation, even in the weak form. But forcing Parliament to make the choice between obeying its international obligations and admitting that it is violating them does not limit Parliament's supremacy, but only its capacity for duplicity. Candour is hardly inconsistent with sovereignty.

Note
The possibility of this form of weak entrenchment, by reference only to the form of wording required to allow Parliament to depart from a Convention right (or from a House of Lords' interpretation of such a right), is considered further in Chapter 4, pp 208–212.

THE HUMAN RIGHTS ACT 1998: INTRODUCTION[36]

After the 1997 General Election, the Labour Government committed itself in the Queen's Speech to introducing a Bill incorporating the 'main provisions' of the European Convention on Human Rights into UK law. The Human Rights Bill, receiving the 'main provisions' of the Convention into domestic law, was introduced into Parliament in October 1997. The HRA had to find a place within a strongly established, if unwritten, constitution. The following section considers and analyses the HRA and certain very significant decisions on the effect of its key provisions. It is intended to provide a framework for the discussion of the impact of the Act, which pervades Part VI. The discussion seeks to show that the HRA represents a compromise between parliamentary supremacy and protection for human rights, but that difficulties in the creation of that compromise are apparent.[37] The discussion below should be read in conjunction with the discussion of the European Convention on Human Rights in Chapter 7 since the HRA does not set out a new list of rights; it merely lists the main Convention rights in Sched 1 and is intended to give domestic effect to them. Thus, the rights themselves and the Strasbourg jurisprudence interpreting them, much of which pre-dated the inception of the HRA, are obviously of crucial significance.

The Green Paper, *Bringing Rights Home*,[38] concluded: 'We aim to change the relationship between the State and the citizen, and to redress the dilution of individual rights by an over-centralising government that has taken place over the past two decades.' This aim was to be achieved by means of the European Convention on Human Rights as afforded further effect in domestic law under the HRA. The Act came fully into force on 2 October 2000. The Convention thus received into domestic law creates a transformation in constitutional terms in the sense that it provides positive rights in place of negative liberties. Since, traditionally, the constitution recognised only negative liberties as opposed to positive rights, the judicial focus of concern always tended to be on the content and nature of the restrictions in question rather than on the value and extent of the right. This was a bold, imaginative constitutional change. However, such boldness had limits, which are reflected in the HRA. A seminal constitutional decision involving a choice between judicial and parliamentary checks on executive power and therefore as to the allocation of power, had to be taken regarding the choice of model for the enforcement of the Convention. The choice made was, as indicated below, to leave parliamentary power formally unchecked: judicial rulings remain (at least theoretically) subject to primary legislation (see further, Chapter 4, pp 210–211). The HRA therefore seeks to reconcile a transfer of power to the judiciary with parliamentary supremacy. It is readily apparent, then, that there is a contradiction between the liberal aim of affording the Convention rights efficacy in domestic law in order to aid in reversing the effects of the over-centralisation of power, and the aim of preserving the key feature of the constitution which gave rein to that power—parliamentary supremacy.[39]

Although the European Convention on Human Rights contains a list of rights that are very similar to those contained in a number of Bills or Charters of Rights, the HRA does not create a Bill or Charter of Rights in the way that, for example, the US Amendments to the Constitution can be said to constitute a Bill of Rights, since those rights have a higher status than 'ordinary law' and other laws conflicting with the rights can be struck down as unconstitutional. Further, unlike the German Basic Law or the US Amendments, the HRA can simply be repealed or amended like any ordinary statute

---

36   See texts referred to under 'Further Reading' p 1017, below for general reading and background.

37   See Chapter 4, pp 210–212.

38   J Straw and P Boateng, *Bringing Rights Home: Labour's Plans to Incorporate the ECHR into UK Law: A Consultation Paper*, December 1996 (1997).

39   See further, Chapter 4.

and it is, therefore, in a far more precarious position. The HRA is modelled on the New Zealand Bill of Rights which uses a rule of construction under s 6 to the effect that a court is obliged, wherever an enactment can be given a meaning that is consistent with the rights and freedoms contained in the Bill of Rights, to prefer that meaning to any other meaning.[40] In so far as a Bill of Rights might be expected to demonstrate a strong commitment to human rights, demanding, if necessary, constitutional changes to provide such protection, the HRA, like the New Zealand Bill of Rights, does not have the characteristics of a Bill of Rights. The HRA does *not* 'incorporate' the Convention rights into substantive domestic law, since it does not provide that they are to have the 'force of law', the usual form of words used when international treaties are incorporated into domestic law.[41] Instead, under s 1(2) of the HRA, certain of the rights discussed in Chapter 7 are to 'have effect for the purposes of this Act'. On the other hand, the reaction of both judiciary and executive to the HRA has meant that in some respects it *can* be viewed as having the status of a Bill of Rights, as discussed below.

One relevant question is whether the HRA was merely intended to give domestic effect to the Convention rights, as interpreted at Strasbourg, or whether the courts were free to create a domestic human rights jurisprudence, providing a more generous interpretation of the rights—if free to do so within the HRA constraints discussed below—than had yet been accepted at Strasbourg. The House of Lords in the case of *Re P*[42] in the context of subordinate legislation arguably incompatible with Art 14 read with Art 8, decided that the UK courts could take their own view of the content of the rights. Baroness Hale said on this:

> How should the courts of this country respond where a provision in subordinate legislation is said to be incompatible with the Convention rights, but the European Court of Human Rights in Strasbourg might well regard the matter as within the margin of appreciation allowed to member states? Should the courts form their own view of the content of the Convention rights or should they leave it to the legislators? Are the 'Convention rights' for the purpose of section 1(1) of the 1998 Act, the rights as defined by Strasbourg but given effect in UK law, or are they the rights defined by United Kingdom law within the parameters defined by Strasbourg?'[43] In response to her question she said: ' . . . if there is a clear and consistent line of Strasbourg jurisprudence, our courts will follow it. But if the matter is within the margin of appreciation which Strasbourg would allow to us, then we have to form our own judgment'.[44]

This was a highly significant decision since it is likely to give encouragement to further developments within a domestic human rights jurisprudence that may reach further than Strasbourg has yet done. As Herring finds on the decision: 'the Human Rights Act does not *just* give citizens rights that are established in the ECHR by the ECtHR. It also enables the English courts to generate rights found to exist in the ECHR, that would not be found by the ECtHR'.[45]

---

40 For discussion as to the use of this model, see M Taggart, 'Tugging on Superman's Cape: Lessons from the Experience with the New Zealand Bill of Rights' [1998] PL 266; A Butler, 'Why the New Zealand Bill of Rights is a Bad Model for Britain' (1997) OJLS 332; H Schwartz, 'The Short and Happy Life and Tragic Death of the New Zealand Bill of Rights' [1998] NZLR 259.

41 See, e.g. the Carriage of Goods by Sea Act 1971, s 1(2).

42 [2008] UKHL 38; [2008] 3 WLR 76.

43 At [84].

44 At [120].

45 Jonathan Herring 'Who Decides on Human Rights?'(2009) LQR 125(Jan), 1–6.

Below, certain extracts from the text of the HRA are set out; this is followed by headings dealing with the most significant sections—ss 2, 3, 4, 6; each section is followed by notes on those provisions. After the notes, extracts from a number of the most significant cases on those key HRA provisions are provided. These cases are grouped under the particular headings, but they should also be read as indicating in a more general way the approaches that the courts have taken to the HRA over the first 10 years of its existence.

Human Rights Act 1998 (extracts)

Chapter 42
Introduction
1. The Convention Rights
(1) In this Act 'the Convention rights' means the rights and fundamental freedoms set out in—

(a) Articles 2 to 12 and 14 of the Convention;
(b) Articles 1 to 3 of the First Protocol; and
(c) Articles 1 and 2 of the Sixth Protocol,

as read with Articles 16 to 18 of the Convention.

(2) Those Articles are to have effect for the purposes of this Act subject to any designated derogation or reservation (as to which see sections 14 and 15).

. . .

(4) The Secretary of State may by order make such amendments to this Act as he considers appropriate to reflect the effect, in relation to the United Kingdom, of a protocol.

. . .

Remedial action
10. Power to take remedial action
(1) This section applies if— remedial action.

(a) a provision of legislation has been declared under section 4 to be incompatible with a Convention right and, if an appeal lies—

(i) all persons who may appeal have stated in writing that they do not intend to do so;
(ii) the time for bringing an appeal has expired and no appeal has been brought within that time; or
(iii) an appeal brought within that time has been determined or abandoned; or

(b) it appears to a Minister of the Crown or Her Majesty in Council that, having regard to a finding of the European Court of Human Rights made after the coming into force of this section in proceedings against the United Kingdom, a provision of legislation is incompatible with an obligation of the United Kingdom arising from the Convention.

(2)   If a Minister of the Crown considers that there are compelling reasons for proceeding under this section, he may by order make such amendments to the legislation as he considers necessary to remove the incompatibility.

(3)   If, in the case of subordinate legislation, a Minister of the Crown considers—

(a)   that it is necessary to amend the primary legislation under which the subordinate legislation in question was made, in order to enable the incompatibility to be removed; and

(b)   that there are compelling reasons for proceeding under this section, he may by order make such amendments to the primary legislation as he considers necessary.

(4)   This section also applies where the provision in question is in subordinate legislation and has been quashed, or declared invalid, by reason of incompatibility with a Convention right and the Minister proposes to proceed under paragraph 2(b) of Schedule 2.

(5)   If the legislation is an Order in Council, the power conferred by subsection (2) or (3) is exercisable by Her Majesty in Council.

(6)   In this section 'legislation' does not include a Measure of the Church Assembly or of the General Synod of the Church of England.

(7)   Schedule 2 makes further provision about remedial orders.

Other rights and proceedings
11. Safeguard for existing human rights
A person's reliance on a Convention right does not restrict—

(a)   any other right or freedom conferred on him by or under any law having effect in any part of the United Kingdom; or

(b)   his right to make any claim or bring any proceedings which he could make or bring apart from sections 7 to 9.

12. Freedom of expression
(1)   This section applies if a court is considering whether to grant any relief which, if granted, might affect the exercise of the Convention right to freedom of expression.

(2)   If the person against whom the application for relief is made ('the respondent') is neither present nor represented, no such relief is to be granted unless the court is satisfied—

(a)   that the applicant has taken all practicable steps to notify the respondent; or
(b)   that there are compelling reasons why the respondent should not be notified.

(3)   No such relief is to be granted so as to restrain publication before trial unless the court is satisfied that the applicant is likely to establish that publication should not be allowed.

(4)   The court must have particular regard to the importance of the Convention right to freedom of expression and, where the proceedings relate to material which the

respondent claims, or which appears to the court, to be journalistic, literary or artistic material (or to conduct connected with such material), to—

(a)   the extent to which—

(i)   the material has, or is about to, become available to the public; or
(ii)   it is, or would be, in the public interest for the material to be published;

(b)   any relevant privacy code.

(5)   In this section— 'court' includes a tribunal; and 'relief' includes any remedy or order (other than in criminal proceedings).

13. Freedom of thought, conscience and religion

(1)   If a court's determination of any question arising under this Act might thought, affect the exercise by a religious organisation (itself or its members collectively) conscience of the Convention right to freedom of thought, conscience and religion, it must have particular regard to the importance of that right.

Derogations and reservations

14. Derogations

(1)   In this Act 'designated derogation' means—

(1)   In this Act 'designated derogation' means any derogation by the United Kingdom from an Article of the Convention, or of any protocol to the Convention, which is designated for the purposes of this Act in an order made by the [Secretary of State].

(3)   If a designated derogation is amended or replaced it ceases to be a designated derogation.

(4)   But subsection (3) does not prevent the Secretary of State from exercising his power under subsection (1)(b) to make a fresh designation order in respect of the Article concerned.

(5)   The Secretary of State must by order make such amendments to Schedule 3 as he considers appropriate to reflect—

(a)   any designation order; or
(b)   the effect of subsection (3).

(6)   A designation order may be made in anticipation of the making by the United Kingdom of a proposed derogation.[46]

15. Reservations

(1)   In this Act 'designated reservation' means—

---

46   Sections 14 and 16 and Sched 3, Part I were amended by the Human Rights Act (Amendment) Order (No 1), SI 2001/1216. The amendment reflected the withdrawal of the derogation to Art 5(3) which had been necessary as a result of the decision of the European Court of Human Rights in *Brogan v UK* (1988) 11 EHRR 117. Changes effected under the Terrorism Act 2000 allowed for the withdrawal of the derogation; see Chapter 20, pp 1189–1190.

(a)   the United Kingdom's reservation to Article 2 of the First Protocol to the Convention; and

(b)   any other reservation by the United Kingdom to an Article of the Convention, or of any protocol to the Convention, which is designated for the purposes of this Act in an order made by the Secretary of State.

(2)   The text of the reservation referred to in subsection (1)(a) is set out in Part II of Schedule 3.

(3)   If a designated reservation is withdrawn wholly or in part it ceases to be a designated reservation.

(4)   But subsection (3) does not prevent the Secretary of State from exercising his power under subsection (1)(b) to make a fresh designation order in respect of the Article concerned.

(5)   The Secretary of State must by order make such amendments to this Act as he considers appropriate to reflect—

(a)   any designation order; or
(b)   the effect of subsection (3).

16. Period for which designated derogations have effect

(1)   If it has not already been withdrawn by the United Kingdom, a designated derogation ceases to have effect for the purposes of this Act. . . at the end of the period of five years. . . beginning with the date on which the order designating it was made.

(2)   At any time before the period—

(a)   fixed by subsection (1). . .; or
(b)   extended by an order under this subsection, comes to an end, the Secretary of State may by order extend it by a further period of five years.

(3)   An order under section 14(1) . . .ceases to have effect at the end of the period for consideration, unless a resolution has been passed by each House approving the order.

(4)   Subsection (3) does not affect—

(a)   anything done in reliance on the order; or
(b)   the power to make a fresh order under section 14(1).

(5)   In subsection (3) 'period for consideration' means the period of 40 days beginning with the day on which the order was made.

(6)   In calculating the period for consideration, no account is to be taken of any time during which—

(a)   Parliament is dissolved or prorogued; or
(b)   both Houses are adjourned for more than four days.

(7)   If a designated derogation is withdrawn by the United Kingdom, the Secretary of State must by order make such amendments to this Act as he considers are required to reflect that withdrawal.

17. Periodic review of designated reservations

(1)   The appropriate Minister must review the designated reservation referred to in section 15(1)(a)—

. . .

(3)   The Minister conducting a review under this section must prepare a report on the result of the review and lay a copy of it before each House of Parliament.

. . .

Parliamentary procedure

19. Statements of compatibility

(1)   A Minister of the Crown in charge of a Bill in either House of Parliament must, before Second Reading of the Bill—

(a)   make a statement to the effect that in his view the provisions of the Bill are compatible with the Convention rights ('a statement of compatibility'); or

(b)   make a statement to the effect that although he is unable to make a statement of compatibility the government nevertheless wishes the House to proceed with the Bill.

(2)   The statement must be in writing and be published in such manner as the Minister making it considers appropriate.

. . .

21. Interpretation, etc.

(1)   In this Act—

        . . .

        'primary legislation' means any—

        (a)   public general Act;
        (b)   local and personal Act;
        (c)   private Act;
        (d)   Measure of the Church Assembly;
        (e)   Measure of the General Synod of the Church of England;
        (f)   Order in Council—

                (i)   made in exercise of Her Majesty's Royal Prerogative;
                (ii)   made under section 38(1)(a) of the Northern Ireland Constitution Act 1973 or the corresponding provision of the Northern Ireland Act 1998; or
                (iii)   amending an Act of a kind mentioned in paragraph (a), (b) or (c); and includes an order or other instrument made under primary legislation (otherwise than by the National Assembly for Wales, a member of the Scottish Executive, a Northern Ireland Minister or a Northern Ireland department) to the extent to which it operates to bring one or more provisions of that legislation into force or amends any primary legislation;

. . .

'subordinate legislation' means any—

(a)   Order in Council other than one—

    (i)   made in exercise of Her Majesty's Royal Prerogative;

    (ii)   made under section 38(1)(a) of the Northern Ireland Constitution Act 1973 or the corresponding provision of the Northern Ireland Act 1998; or

    (iii)   amending an Act of a kind mentioned in the definition of primary legislation;

(b)   Act of the Scottish Parliament;

(c)   Act of the Parliament of Northern Ireland;

(d)   Measure of the Assembly established under section I of the Northern Ireland Assembly Act 1973;

(e)   Act of the Northern Ireland Assembly;

(f)   order, rules, regulations, scheme, warrant, byelaw or other instrument made under primary legislation (except to the extent to which it operates to bring one or more provisions of that legislation into force or amends any primary legislation);

(g)   order, rules, regulations, scheme, warrant, byelaw or other instrument made under legislation mentioned in paragraphs (b), (c), (d) or (e) or made under an Order in Council applying only to Northern Ireland;

(h)   order, rules, regulations, scheme, warrant, byelaw or other instrument made by a member of the Scottish Executive, a Northern Ireland Minister or a Northern Ireland department in exercise of prerogative or other executive functions of Her Majesty which are exercisable by such a person on behalf of Her Majesty;

'transferred matters' has the same meaning as in the Northern Ireland Act 1998; and 'tribunal' means any tribunal in which legal proceedings may be brought.

22. Short title, commencement, application and extent

(1)   This Act may be cited as the Human Rights Act 1998.

. . .

(4)   Paragraph (b) of subsection (1) of section 7 applies to proceedings brought by or at the instigation of a public authority whenever the act in question took place; but otherwise that subsection does not apply to an act taking place before the coming into force of that section.

(5)   This Act binds the Crown.

(6)   This Act extends to Northern Ireland.

(7)   Section 21(5), so far as it relates to any provision contained in the Army Act 1955, the Air Force Act 1955 or the Naval Discipline Act 1957, extends to any place to which that provision extends.

SCHEDULES

Schedule 1
[Schedule 1 includes Arts 2–12 and 14–18 of the Convention and the Sixth Protocol, covering removal of the death penalty (the Articles are set out in Chapter 7).[47]]
Schedule 2 REMEDIAL ORDERS—see discussion in Chapter 3, pp 134–135.

THE INTERPRETATIVE OBLIGATION UNDER SECTION 3; THE REMEDIAL PROCESS UNDER SECTIONS 4 AND 10; PRE-LEGISLATIVE SCRUTINY UNDER SECTION 19

Under the Human Rights Act 1998, the Convention[48] receives a subtly crafted but robust form of constitutional protection. The key provision in creating this form of protection for the Convention under the Human Rights Act is s 3(1). It is clear from s 3 that the Convention rights have, in one sense, a lower status than ordinary statutory provisions have in that they cannot *automatically* override pre-existing law. But, more significantly, s 3 places an obligation on the judges to ensure that all statutory provisions should be rendered, if possible, compatible with the Convention rights. If they cannot be, the provisions will remain valid (s 3(2)(b). Significantly, s 3(2)(a) makes it clear that the obligation imposed by s 3 arises in relation to both previous and subsequent enactments. The requirement to construe legislation 'so far as it is possible to do so' consistently with the Convention rights makes it clear that a very determined stance under s 3 best reflects the intention of Parliament, although it may also be pointed out that since Parliament has enacted s 4, it clearly contemplated some limits on what could be achieved by means of s 3. Therefore, by imposing this interpretative obligation on the courts, the rights become capable of affecting subsequent legislation in a way that is not normally possible.[49] If legislation cannot be rendered compatible with the rights, a declaration of the incompatibility can be made under s 4.[50] Remedial legislation can then be introduced into Parliament to modify or repeal the offending provisions, under s 10.[51]

This subtle form of protection avoids full incorporation of the Convention and therefore appears to create an acceptable compromise between the protection of rights and preservation of the democratic process via the doctrine at Parliamentary sovereignty. Sections 3 and 4 on their face appear to leave the ultimate decisions as to rights-protection to Parliament. However, the use of ss 3 and 4 *in practice* has, it is argued, led to quite a clear transfer of power to the judiciary. This point is explored below, but it led one commentator to conclude in 2007 that the HRA is a 'wolf masquerading as a sheep'.[52]

---

47   See pp 299–315.

48   The term 'the Convention' will be used to refer to the Convention rights currently included in Sched 1 to the HRA 1998.

49   For extensive consideration of this point, see Clayton and Tomlinson, 'further reading' below, p 1017, Chapter 4.

50   See below, p 970 *et seq.*

51   See below, p 971.

52   See Leigh and Masterman, 'further reading' below, p 1017.

Legislation

3. Interpretation of legislation

(1)   So far as it is possible to do so, primary legislation and subordinate legislation must be read and given effect in a way which is compatible with the Convention rights.

(2)   This section—

(a)   applies to primary legislation and subordinate legislation whenever enacted;

(b)   does not affect the validity, continuing operation or enforcement of any incompatible primary legislation; and

(c)   does not affect the validity, continuing operation or enforcement of any incompatible subordinate legislation if (disregarding any possibility of revocation) primary legislation prevents removal of the incompatibility.

4. Declaration of incompatibility

(1)   Subsection (2) applies in any proceedings in which a court determines whether a provision of primary legislation is compatible with a Convention right.

(2)   If the court is satisfied that the provision is incompatible with a Convention right, it may make a declaration of that incompatibility.

(3)   Subsection (4) applies in any proceedings in which a court determines whether a provision of subordinate legislation, made in the exercise of a power conferred by primary legislation, is compatible with a Convention right.

(4)   If the court is satisfied—

(a)   that the provision is incompatible with a Convention right; and

(b)   that (disregarding any possibility of revocation) the primary legislation concerned prevents removal of the incompatibility, it may make a declaration of that incompatibility.

(5)   In this section 'court' means—

(a)   the House of Lords;

(b)   the Judicial Committee of the Privy Council;

(c)   the Courts-Martial Appeal Court;

(d)   in Scotland, the High Court of Justiciary sitting otherwise than as a trial court or the Court of Session;

(e)   in England and Wales or Northern Ireland, the High Court or the Court of Appeal.

(6)   A declaration under this section ('a declaration of incompatibility')—

(a)   does not affect the validity, continuing operation or enforcement of the provision in respect of which it is given; and

(b)   is not binding on the parties to the proceedings in which it is made.

5. Right of Crown to intervene

(1)   Where a court is considering whether to make a declaration of incompatibility, the Crown is entitled to notice in accordance with rules of court.

(2)   In any case to which subsection (1) applies—

    (a)   a Minister of the Crown (or a person nominated by him);
    (b)   a member of the Scottish Executive;
    (c)   a Northern Ireland Minister;
    (d)   a Northern Ireland department,

is entitled, on giving notice in accordance with rules of court, to be joined as a party to the proceedings.

(3)   Notice under subsection (2) may be given at any time during the proceedings.

(4)   A person who has been made a party to criminal proceedings (other than in Scotland) as the result of a notice under subsection (2) may, with leave, appeal to the House of Lords against any declaration of incompatibility made in the proceedings. . . .

Notes

1. Section 3(1) HRA can be used to reinterpret primary legislation to render it compatible with the ECHR rights 'if at all possible'. If it is not possible the legislation remains valid and must be enforced; a declaration of the incompatibility (DOI) can be made if in a court able to make DOIs (s 4). Section 21(1) defines 'primary legislation' to include Orders in Council made under the royal prerogative. Thus, executive power as well as parliamentary sovereignty is preserved under the HRA.[53] This is clearly an anomalous provision, since it renders individual rights subordinate to powers which may be used to infringe them and which cannot claim legitimacy derived from the democratic process.

2. Subordinate legislation covers Orders in Council not made under the royal prerogative, and orders, rules, regulations, bylaws or other instruments made under primary legislation unless the rule etc 'operates to bring one or more provisions of that legislation into force or amends any primary legislation'. The last provision is significant, since it means that where provision is made under primary legislation for amendment by executive order, subject to the negative, or even the affirmative resolution procedure, the amendment, which will almost certainly have received virtually no parliamentary attention, will still be able to override Convention provisions.

3. If legislation cannot be rendered compatible with the rights by use of s 3(1)HRA, its validity is unaffected (s 3(2)(b) and (c)), but a declaration of the incompatibility can be made by a higher court under s 4. Parliament may then modify the offending provisions under s 10. The incompatible legislation must continue to be enforced. The declaration of incompatibility also does not affect the validity of the legislation. This subtle form of protection avoids formal entrenchment and therefore creates a compromise between leaving the protection of rights to the democratic process and entrusting them fully to the judiciary.[54]

4. *The position of the Scottish Parliament, the Northern Ireland Assembly and the Welsh Assembly.* The devolution legislation places the Scottish Parliament, the Northern Ireland Assembly and the Welsh Assembly in a different position from that of the Westminster Parliament as regards the legal status

---

53   For discussion of the effect of treating this exercise of prerogative powers as primary legislation, see N Squires, 'Judicial Review of the Prerogative after the HRA' (2000) 116 LQR 572–75.

54   It is argued in Chapter 1, p 30 that the HRA may be *de facto* entrenched as a result of the interrelationship between ss 3 and 19.

of the Convention rights. The Welsh Assembly is not able to pass primary legislation and it is bound by the Convention under s 107(1) of the Government of Wales Act 1998. The Scottish Parliament cannot act incompatibly with the Convention under s 29(2)(d) of the Scotland Act 1998. The Executive and law officers in Scotland are also bound.[55] Under s 21 of the HRA, legislation passed by the Scottish Parliament and by the Northern Ireland Assembly is regarded as secondary legislation. Under s 3 of the HRA, any primary legislation[56] passed by the Westminster Parliament and applicable to Scotland, Northern Ireland and Wales will be binding, even if it is not compatible with the Convention. These arrangements mean that Scotland has, in effect, a Bill of Rights in the traditional sense since the Scottish Parliament is bound by the Convention and therefore cannot pass primary legislation which conflicts with it.[57] The references to 'legislation' in this chapter, so far and below, are to legislation emanating from the Westminster Parliament.

5. *The 'declaration of incompatibility' and the remedial process.*[58] Section 4(2) applies under s 4(1) when a court is determining in any proceedings whether a provision of primary legislation is incompatible with a Convention right. If a court is satisfied that the provision is incompatible with the right, 'it may make a declaration of that incompatibility'—a declaration that it is not possible to construe the legislation in question to harmonise with the Convention. Section 4(4) applies to incompatible secondary legislation where incompatible primary legislation prevents the removal of the incompatibility. Again, the incompatibility can be declared.

6. There are certain limitations on the use of s 4. First, only certain higher courts can make the declaration (s 4(5)). Second, such courts have a *discretion* to make a declaration of incompatibility. Section 4(2) clearly leaves open the possibility that such a court, having found an incompatibility, can nevertheless decide *not* to make a declaration of it. In *Wilson v First County Trust Ltd,*[59] the Court of Appeal found that s 127(3) of the Consumer Credit Act 1974 was incompatible with Art 6 and Art 1 of the First Protocol to the Convention. The Court considered that, having found an incompatibility, it *should* make a declaration of it for three reasons (at para 47). First, the question of the incompatibility had been fully argued at a hearing appointed for that purpose. Second, the order required by s 127(3) could not lawfully be made on the appeal unless the court was satisfied that the section could not be read in such a way as to give effect to the Convention rights, and that fact should be formally recorded by a declaration that 'gives legitimacy to that order'. Third, a declaration provides a basis for a Minister to consider whether the section should be amended under s 10(1) (see below). The Court duly went on to make the declaration. The declaration can be overturned on appeal to a higher court, as occurred in *R (On the application of Alconbury Developments) v Secretary of State for the Environment and Other Cases.*[60] The Divisional Court made a declaration of incompatibility which was overturned on appeal to the House of Lords. Once a declaration of incompatibility has been made, the legislative provision in question remains valid (s 4(6)). The Convention guarantee in question will in effect be disapplied by the court in relation to that incompatible provision.

---

55 See the Scotland Act, s 57. Thus, in Scotland and Wales, the Convention became binding from 1 July 1999, when the devolution legislation came into force, over a year before the HRA came fully into force.

56 The Scotland Act 1988, s 29(2)(b) and Sched 5, and the Government of Wales Act 1998, Sched 2. See further, Chapter 6.

57 See further S Tierney, 'Devolution Issues and s 2(1) of the HRA' (2000) 4 EHRLR 380–92.

58 For further discussion of the significance of the ministerial power to make remedial orders, see Chapter 3, pp 134–135.

59 [2001] 3 All ER 229.

60 [2001] 2 WLR 1389.

7. If a declaration of incompatibility is made, s 10 will apply which *allows* a Minister to make amendments to the offending legislation by means of the 'fast track' procedure. Section 10 may also be used where a decision of the European Court of Human Rights suggests that a provision of legislation is incompatible with the Convention. However, as indicated above, the Minister is under no obligation to make the amendment(s), either after any such decision or after a declaration of incompatibility under s 4, and may only do so if he or she considers that there are 'compelling reasons for proceeding under this section'. In other words, the fact that a declaration of incompatibility has been made will not necessarily in itself provide a compelling reason, although the circumstances in which it is made may do so. Schedule 2, set out above, provides two procedures for making a 'remedial order' which must, under s 20, be in the form of a statutory instrument. In *R (On the Application of H) v London North and East Mental Health Review Tribunal*,[61] a declaration of incompatibility was made between s 73 of the Mental Health Act 1983 and Art 5. Once the declaration had been made, the Secretary of State for Health, acting under s 10 of the HRA, made a remedial order amending s 73 in order to achieve compatibility.

8. *Declarations as to the compatibility of new Bills with the Convention rights.* Under s 19(1)(a) of the HRA, a Minister must state that any future Bill is compatible with the Convention or that while unable to make such a declaration, the Government nevertheless wishes to proceed with the Bill. When the relevant Minister has made a declaration of compatibility under s 19(1)(a), its effects may be viewed as additional to the duty the courts are already under, arising from s 3(1), to ensure that the legislation is rendered compatible with the guarantees if at all possible. The Lord Chancellor has said: 'Ministerial statements of compatibility will inevitably be a strong spur to the courts to find the means of construing statutes compatibly with the Convention.'[62] All legislation passed since the obligation to make a statement regarding compatibility came into force[63] has been accompanied by a declaration of its compatibility with the Convention rights, under s 19, except the Communications Act 2003. But this need not mean that all such legislation is in fact compatible: the mere fact that a declaration is made does not mean that it can be assumed that compatibility was in fact achieved.

Decisions on ss 3 and 4 of the HRA

The following case is one of the leading decisions on the meaning of s 3 of the HRA.

R v A (Complainant's Sexual History) [2002] 1 AC 45, HL (extracts)

R v A concerned interpretation of s 41 Youth Justice and Criminal Evidence Act 1999 which forbade any evidence to be given in a rape trial of the woman's sexual history, including any previous sexual history with the alleged rapist except in very limited circumstances. The issue concerned compatibility with Article 6 ECHR, which provides: '(1) everyone is entitled to a fair and public hearing' and '6 in part(3) (d) to examine, or have examined witnesses against him.' Section 41(3)(c) permitted evidence of the women's previous sexual history

---

61   [2001] QB 1.

62   Lord Irvine [1998] PL 221.

63   The obligation to make a statement of compatibility came into force on 24 November 1998, under the Human Rights Act 1998 (Commencement) Order 1998, SI 1998/2882.

where: '(c) it is an issue of consent [i.e. the question for determination is, did the woman actually consent to sexual intercourse] and the sexual behaviour of the complainant to which the evidence or question relates is alleged to have been, in any respect, so similar. . .to any sexual behaviour of the complainant which. . .took place as part of the event which is the subject matter of the charge against the accused . . . that the similarity cannot reasonably be explained as a coincidence.'

Lord Steyn: . . .the interpretative obligation under section 3 of the 1998 Act is a strong one. It applies even if there is no ambiguity in the language in the sense of the language being capable of two different meanings . . . The White Paper made clear that the obligation goes far beyond the rule which enabled the courts to take the Convention into account in resolving any ambiguity in a legislative provision: see Rights Brought Home: The Human Rights Bill (1997) (Cm 3782), para 2.7. The draftsman of the Act had before him the slightly weaker model in section 6 of the New Zealand Bill of Rights Act 1990 but preferred stronger language. Parliament specifically rejected the legislative model of requiring a reasonable interpretation. Section 3 places a duty on the court to strive to find a possible interpretation compatible with Convention rights. Under ordinary methods of interpretation a court may depart from the language of the statute to avoid absurd consequences: section 3 goes much further. Undoubtedly, a court must always look for a contextual and purposive interpretation: section 3 is more radical in its effect. . . . In the progress of the Bill through Parliament the Lord Chancellor observed that 'in 99% of the cases that will arise, there will be no need for judicial declarations of incompatibility' (HL Deb, 5th Feb, 1998, col. 840) . . . It will sometimes be necessary to adopt an interpretation which linguistically may appear strained. The techniques to be used will not only involve the reading down of express language in a statute but also the implication of provisions. A declaration of incompatibility is a measure of last resort. It must be avoided unless it is plainly impossible to do so. If a clear limitation on Convention rights is stated in terms, such an impossibility will arise . . . There is, however, no limitation of such a nature in the present case. In my view section 3 requires the court to subordinate the niceties of the language of section 41(3)(c), and in particular the touchstone of coincidence, to broader considerations of relevance judged by logical and common sense criteria of time and circumstances . . .

[Section 41(3)(c) was interpreted as follows]:

> It is therefore possible under section 3 to read section 41, and in particular section 41(3)(c), as *subject to the implied provision that evidence or questioning which is required to ensure a fair trial under article 6 of the Convention should not be treated as inadmissible* [emphasis added]. The result of such a reading would be that sometimes logically relevant sexual experiences between a complainant and an accused may be admitted under section 41(3)(c). On the other hand, there will be cases where previous sexual experience between a complainant and an accused will be irrelevant, e.g. an isolated episode distant in time and circumstances. Where the line is to be drawn must be left to the judgment of trial judges. On this basis a declaration of incompatibility can be avoided . . . (at pp 369–70).

Lord Hope (dissenting): A fair balance must be struck 'between the demands of the general interest of the community and the requirements of the protection of the individual's fundamental rights': *Sporrong and Lönnroth v Sweden* (1982) 5 EHRR 35, 52, para 69. . . . The question whether a legitimate aim is being pursued enables account to be taken of the public interest in the rule of law. The principle of proportionality directs attention to the question whether a fair balance has been struck between the general interest of the community and the protection of the individual.

. . . It is plain that the question is in the end one of balance. Has the balance between the protection of the complainant and the accused's right to a fair trial been struck in the right place? . . . The area is one where Parliament was better equipped than the judges are to decide where the balance lay. . . . But two important factors seem to me to indicate that prima facie the solution that was chosen was a proportionate one. The first is the need to restore and maintain public confidence in the system for the protection of vulnerable witnesses. Systems which relied on the exercise of a discretion by the trial judge have been called into question. . . . The second is to be found in a detailed reading of the section as a whole. As I have tried to show in my analysis of the various subsections, it contains important provisions which preserve the defendant's right to ask questions about and adduce evidence of other sexual behaviour by the complainant where this is clearly relevant. . . . I emphasise the words 'every case', because I believe that it would only be if there was a material risk of incompatibility with the Article 6 right in all such cases that it would be appropriate to lay down a rule of general application as to how, applying section 3 of the Human Rights Act 1998, section 41 (3) ought to be read in a way that is compatible with the Convention right or, if that were not possible, to make a declaration of general incompatibility. I do not accept that there is such a risk. This is because I do not regard the mere fact that the complainant had consensual sexual intercourse with the accused on previous occasions as relevant to the issue whether she consented to intercourse on the occasion of the alleged rape.

For these reasons I consider that it has not been shown that, if the ordinary principles of statutory construction are applied to them, the provisions of section 41 which are relevant to the respondent's case are incompatible with his Convention right to a fair trial.

Re S and Re W (Care Orders) [2002] 2 AC 291 (extracts)

It was argued that once children who had been taken into care were placed under a care plan by the local authority under the Children Act 1989, the inability of the courts to intervene to protect children, if they thought the care plan had been breached and the child's welfare thus threatened, amounted to a breach of the child's (and possibly the parent's) rights under Art 8 (right to respect for private and family life) and Art 6 (right to have civil rights and obligations determined by an independent and impartial tribunal established by law). The CA, using s 3(1) HRA, read into the Children Act an ability for the courts to supervise the care plan and allow interventions by guardians if the care plan was being breached.

Lord Nicholls: [Section 3(1) HRA] is a powerful tool whose use is obligatory. It is not an optional canon of construction. Nor is its use dependent on the existence of ambiguity. Further, the section applies retrospectively. So far as it is possible to do so, primary legislation 'must be read and given effect' to in a way which is compatible with Convention rights. This is forthright, uncompromising language. . .

But the reach of this tool is not unlimited. Section 3 is concerned with interpretation. This is apparent from the opening words of section 3(1): 'so far as it is possible to do so'. The side heading of the section is 'Interpretation of legislation'. Section 4 (power to make a declaration of incompatibility) and, indeed, section 3(2)(b) presuppose that not all provisions in primary legislation can be rendered Convention compliant by the application of section 3(1). The existence of this limit on the scope of section 3(1) has already been the subject of judicial confirmation, more than once: see, for instance, Lord Woolf CJ in *Poplar Housing*. . .and Lord Hope of Craighead in *R v Lambert* [2001] 3 WLR 206, 233–235, paras 79–81. . . .

In applying section 3 courts must be ever mindful of this outer limit. The Human Rights Act reserves the amendment of primary legislation to Parliament. By this means the Act seeks to preserve parliamentary sovereignty. The Act maintains the constitutional boundary. Interpretation of statutes is a matter for the courts; the enactment of statutes, and the amendment of statutes, are matters for Parliament . . .

The boundary line [between the two] may be crossed even though a limitation on Convention rights is not stated in express terms. Lord Steyn's observations in *R v A* [above] are not to be read as meaning that a clear limitation on Convention rights in terms is the only circumstance in which an interpretation incompatible with Convention rights may arise.

Note

In *Bellinger v Bellinger* [2003] 2 AC 467, HL W, a post-operative transsexual, appealed against a decision under the Matrimonial Causes Act 1973 that she was not lawfully married to her husband, H, because she, W, was in fact a man. Section 11 of the Act states: '11(c): A marriage . . . shall be void on the following grounds only, that is to say . . . that the parties are not respectively male and female . . .'. W argued that the word 'female' should be interpreted as including her and other post-op transsexuals, relying on her right to private and family life under Article 8 ECHR. It was held that it was not possible to interpret the word 'female' in the Act as referring to a transsexual:

> Such a fundamental change in the law, which would interfere with the traditional concept of marriage and give rise to complex and sensitive issues, should be made only by Parliament after careful deliberation and not by judicial intervention (*ibid* at 467).

This can be compared with the findings in the leading decision:

Ghaidan v Mendoza [2004] 3 WLR 113 (extracts)

On the death of a protected tenant of a dwelling-house his or her surviving spouse, if then living in the house, becomes a statutory tenant by succession. But a person who was living with the original tenant 'as his or her wife or husband' is treated as the spouse of the original tenant as so also succeeds to the tenancy: Rent Act 1977, Schedule 1, para 2(2). Mendoza had lived with his gay partner for 18 years in a stable and monogamous relationship in the relevant property. Following his partner's death in 2001, the landlord, Ghaidan, sought to evict Mendoza on the basis that he was not entitled to succeed to the tenancy, since he had not been living with his partner 'as his or her wife or husband'. Mendoza argued that to treat him differently from a heterosexual partner of a deceased tenant would violate his rights under Art 8 ECHR read with Art 14 (the right to non-discrimination in the exercise of Convention rights). He invoked s 3(1) HRA. The House of Lords held by 4:1 that that the words living with the tenant 'as his or her wife or husband' could be interpreted as meaning: 'living with the tenant, as *if they were* his or her wife or husband'.

Lord Nicholls. . . the mere fact the language under consideration is inconsistent with a Convention-compliant meaning does not of itself make a Convention-compliant interpretation under section 3 impossible. Section 3 enables language to be interpreted restrictively or expansively. But section 3 goes further than this. It is also apt to require a court to read in words which change the meaning of the enacted legislation, so as to make it Convention-compliant. In other words, the intention of Parliament in enacting s 3 was that, to an extent bounded only by what is 'possible', a court can modify the meaning, and hence the effect, of primary and secondary legislation.'

'Parliament, however, cannot have intended that in the discharge of this extended interpretative function the courts should adopt a meaning inconsistent with a fundamental feature of legislation. That would be to cross the constitutional boundary s 3 seeks to demarcate and preserve. Parliament has retained the right to enact legislation in terms which are not Convention-compliant. The meaning imported by application of s 3 must be compatible with the underlying thrust of the legislation being construed. Words implied must, in the phrase of my noble and learned friend Lord Rodger of Earlsferry, "go with the grain of the legislation". Nor can Parliament have intended that s 3 should require courts to make decisions for which they are not equipped. There may be several ways of making a provision Convention-compliant, and the choice may involve issues calling for legislative deliberation. Both these features were present in *Re S and Re W* . . .'

R (On the Application of Hammond) (FC) v Secretary of State for the Home Department [2006] 1 AC 603, HL (extracts)

[The relevant provision] should be read subject to an implied condition that the High Court judge has the discretion to order an oral hearing, where such hearing is required to comply with a prisoner's rights under article 6(1) of the Convention. Thus the discretion may be exercised when, and only when, an oral hearing is necessary to meet the requirement of fairness. . . no argument was addressed to the scope of the interpretative duty imposed by section 3 of the 1998 Act, and it is unnecessary to form an opinion whether the Divisional Court's interpolation, if challenged, would be sustainable.

Notes

1. It was always clear that the courts should not imply the word 'reasonably' into s 3.[64] They are expected to find a *possible*, not a reasonable, interpretation, according to its wording. An opposition amendment which would have imported the word 'reasonably' into the section was opposed by the Government.[65] The selected key decisions above on the use of s 3(1) indicate the approaches that the courts are taking to this strong interpretative obligation.

2. *Re S and Re W* does not have the same authority as *R v A, Ghaidan* or *Hammond* in stating the current position regarding the use of s 3. Lord Nicholls found that there was in any event no incompatibility between Arts 6 and 8 and the relevant provisions of the Children Act, necessitating a re-interpretation of those provisions. His remarks are therefore strictly speaking *obiter* since reliance on s 3, demanding consideration of its effects, was not determinative of the outcome in that instance. In contrast, in *R v A* and in *Ghaidan* the findings on s 3 must be viewed as part of the *ratio* of the case since they led to a change to the statutory provision in question. In *R v A*, Lord Clyde, Lord Slynn and Lord Hutton concurred with Lord Steyn in considering that s 41 of the Youth Justice and Criminal Evidence Act could be rendered compatible with Art 6 by reading s 41(3) as 'subject to the implied provision that evidence or questioning which is required to ensure a fair trial under Article 6 of the Convention should not be treated as inadmissible'.

---

64   This was confirmed by the House of Lords in *R v A* [2001] 2 WLR 1546 by Lord Steyn, para 44.

65   Vol 313, HC Deb Col 421, 3 June 1998.

3. In *R v A* the Law Lords, especially Lord Steyn, used an extremely bold interpretative technique. In so doing, they in fact went beyond using interpretative techniques and—in effect—rewrote the legislation. The stance of the Lords—apart from Lord Hope—in that instance, and the stance taken in *Ghaidan* and *Hammond* suggests that the judiciary are prepared to take an extremely vigorous stance when interpreting existing law in the light of Convention provisions: they are prepared to ensure that the outcome which allows the Convention to prevail is achieved even if that involves a significant disregard for statutory language. In *R v A*, the House of Lords very clearly accepted that a declaration of incompatibility was a last resort and that s 3 could be used in an extremely creative fashion in order to avoid having to make one. It is suggested that this approach tends to marginalise the democratic process: if s 3 is used, even if it emasculates a legislative provision, as in *R v A*, Parliament has not been asked—under the s 4 procedure—to amend the provision. The whole process remains in the hands of the judiciary. Moreover, in *R v A* it is arguable that the Convention itself did not demand the change to the statute which Lord Steyn imposed upon it since no case at Strasbourg had indicated that such a 'rape-shield' law was incompatible with Article 6. In this sense, *R v A* has, it is contended, placed the whole carefully crafted scheme of the HRA in jeopardy. The tensions inherent in the scheme were explored and heightened, since s 3 can be used to outflank ss 4 and 10, where incompatibility appears to arise. The idea, which seemed to be inherent in s 4, that the making of declarations of incompatibility even in criminal cases might be preferred to the use of s 3(1) seems to have been shown to be misconceived.

4. In response to *R v A*, it would have seemed on the face of it possible for Parliament merely to reinstate the offending provision, using words that left no leeway at all for the bold 'interpretation' placed upon s 41(3)(c) of the Youth Justice and Criminal Evidence Act 1999. It should be noted that the House of Lords considered that the provision had provided a 'gateway' for the very creative interpretation adopted.[66] However, so doing might have invited a declaration of incompatibility; if no amendment had been forthcoming under s 10 of the HRA, a defendant affected by the legislation would have been likely to apply to Strasbourg. If at some point the European Court of Human Rights in response found a breach of Art 6 (which is in fact arguably unlikely since a wide margin of appreciation is accorded to the state in respect of admission of evidence), the Government would probably have viewed itself as obliged to amend the legislation. Thus, the application of s 3 of the HRA, combined with the UK's international obligations, has made an inroad into the principle of parliamentary supremacy.

5. A more cautionary note was sounded regarding the application of s 3 in *Poplar Housing and Regeneration Community Association Ltd and Secretary of State for the Environment v Donoghue*.[67] Lord Woolf said that s 3 'does not entitle the court to legislate; its task is still one of interpretation but interpretation in accordance with the direction contained in s 3' (paras 75 and 76). He went on to say that the most difficult task facing the courts is that of distinguishing between interpretation and legislation. This approach was confirmed by Lord Nicholls in *Re S and Re W (Care Orders)*, above. Clearly, 'the precise limits of the s 3 rule of construction remain controversial'.[68] But those limits are now beginning to become apparent. Deference will be shown to Parliament except in areas that the judges regard as peculiarly their own domain, such as admission of evidence. The question of deference is addressed in a number of cases, below.

---

66 *R v A (No 2)* [2002] 1 AC 45, *per* Lord Steyn, para 42.

67 [2001] 3 WLR 183.

68 Clayton and Tomlinson, 'further reading', below, p 1017, 1st edn, p 169.

6. In *Anderson*[69] the incompatibility lay in the involvement of the Secretary of State in sentencing adult life prisoners. The Secretary of State's role in the legislation was a pervasive feature of it. The Secretary of State's role in sentencing was found to be incompatible with Art 6 since he could not be viewed as the equivalent of an 'independent and impartial tribunal'. A declaration of incompatibility was made rather than seeking to use s 3(1) since the Secretary of State's role was such a fundamental feature of the statute as a whole—any other approach would have been against the grain of the statute. Since the use of s 3 was therefore rejected, the House of Lords instead issued a declaration of incompatibility on the ground that a power conferred on the Home Secretary by s 29 of the Crime (Sentencing) Act 1997 to control the release of mandatory life sentence prisoners was inconsistent with the right to have a sentence imposed by 'an independent and impartial tribunal', under Art 6 ECHR.

Secretary of State for the Home Department (Respondent) v MB (FC) (Appellant) [2007] UKHL 46; [2007] 3 WLR 681 (extracts)

Lord Bingham. . . . 44. Since a majority of my noble and learned friends are of my opinion on the principles relevant to this issue, it is necessary to consider the question of remedy. In receiving and acting on closed material not disclosed to MB and AF, the courts below acted in strict accordance with the Act and the Rules. It was suggested in argument that the relevant provisions should be read down under section 3 of the Human Rights Act 1998, so that they would take effect only when it was consistent with fairness for them to do so. This would be a possible course, and it is plain that the provisions do not operate unfairly in all cases, as where the open material is sufficient to support the making of an order. But I question whether section 3 should be relied on in these cases, first, because any weakening of the mandatory language used by Parliament would very clearly fly in the face of Parliament's intention, and, secondly, because it might be thought preferable to derogate from article 6, if judged permissible to do so (on which I express no opinion whatever), than to accept any modification of the terms of the Act and the Rules. I therefore see force in the argument that a declaration of incompatibility should be made and the orders quashed. Having, however, read the opinions of my noble and learned friends Baroness Hale of Richmond, Lord Carswell and Lord Brown of Eaton-under-Heywood, I see great force in the contrary argument, and would not wish to press my opinion to the point of dissent. I therefore agree that section 3 should be applied, and the cases referred back, as they propose, for consideration in each case by the judge in the light of the committee's conclusions.

Lady Hale:[70] On the face of it, therefore, the judge is precluded from ordering disclosure even where he considers that this is essential in order to give the controlled person a fair hearing . . . In my view, therefore [the relevant parts of the Act and Rules] should be read and given effect 'except where to do so would be incompatible with the right of the controlled person to a fair trial'.

---

69   *R (On the application of Anderson) v Secretary of State for the Home Department* [2003] 1 AC 837.

70   At [69–76].

Notes

1. Following the lead of the House of Lords in the key decisions mentioned, in particular *R v A*, *Donoghue, Alconbury*,[71] *Bellinger, Ghaidan*, it is apparent that a number of steps are being taken when the argument is put that a legislative provision is incompatible with a Convention right. Section 3 may be used in a very bold fashion, as indicated by Lord Steyn in the majority in *R v A*, and by Lord Nicholls in *Ghaidan*, in order to avoid a finding of incompatibility unless, according to *Donoghue*, so doing would mean crossing the boundary between interpreting and legislating. *Bellinger* and *Ghaidan* indicate that the word 'possible' in s 3(1) impliedly relates to matters ranging well beyond linguistic possibility. Clearly, they appear to view it as denoting something that is possible linguistically but that may be undesirable, for a range of reasons. So when will the courts be prepared to read words into a statute, or to reinterpret an existing word, in order to avoid incompatibility? In other words, which factors will persuade them to the more radical approach adopted in *R v A* and in *Ghaidan*? Their approach appears to be that they will adopt that more radical approach where it appears to them to be proper and desirable to do so. Kavanagh points out that the courts will take a more radical approach to compatibility under s 3, not where it is 'possible' to do so, but where they think it is *appropriate*, taking various matters into account, to do so.[72]

2. The following discussion is partly based on Dr Kavanagh's analysis of the s 3(1) cases.[73] Kavanagh argues that the decision in *Re S and Re W*[74] shows that, while the courts are prepared to read words into statutes, as in *R v A*, or *Ghaidan*, they will not do so, 'as a way of radically reforming a whole statute or writing a quasi-legislative code granting new powers and setting out new procedures to replace that statute'.[75] As discussed, the Court of Appeal had written a number of provisions into the statute in *Re S* under s 3—an approach that was rejected by the House of Lords. Another aspect of this stance is to find that the change proposed, to ensure compatibility, will probably be rejected where it would run counter to a pervasive feature of the statute—where the objectionable provisions permeate the statute. This factor was decisive in *Anderson*.[76] Lord Hope took a similar stance in *R v Lambert*.[77] He said as to section 3 that, 'Resort to it will not be possible if the legislation contains provisions, either in the words or phrases which are under scrutiny or elsewhere, which expressly contradict the meaning which the enactment would have to be given to make it compatible. The same consequence will follow if legislation contains provisions which have this effect by necessary implication. . . .It does not give power to the judges to overrule decisions which the language of the statute shows have been taken on the very point at issue by the legislator'.[78] In *R v A, Lambert* or *Ghaidan* the objected-to provision was *not* viewed as fundamental

---

71 *R (On the application of Alconbury Ltd) v Secretary of State for the Environment, Transport and the Regions and other cases* [2001] 2 All ER 929; (2001) NLJ 135.

72 'Statutory Interpretation and Human Rights after Anderson: A More Contextual Approach' [2004] PL 537 at 544–45.

73 See A Kavanagh, 'Unlocking the Human Rights Act: The 'Radical Approach' to Section 3(1) Revisited' (2005) 3 EHRLR 259; see in particular 'The Elusive Divide between Interpretation and Legislation under the HRA' (2004) 24(2) OJLS 259; and 'Statutory Interpretation and Human Rights after Anderson: A More Contextual Approach' [2004] PL 537, which is a response, in part, to D Nicol, 'Statutory Interpretation and Human Rights after Anderson' [2004] PL 273. See also Alec Samuels 'The Human Rights Act 1998 Section 3: A New Dimension to Statutory Interpretation?' (2008) Stat LR 130; I Leigh and R Masterman *Making Rights Real: The Human Rights Act in its First Decade* (2008), Chapters 4 and 5.

74 [2002] 2 AC 291. This decision was reversed unanimously by the House of Lords.

75 'Statutory Interpretation and Human Rights after Anderson: A More Contextual Approach' [2004] PL 537 at 540.

76 *R (On the application of Anderson) v Secretary of State for the Home Department* [2003] 1 AC 837.

77 *R v Lambert* [2001] 3 All ER 577.

78 At [79].

to the statute as a whole or a substantial part of it. Where the change *is* viewed as fundamental it would require extensive change to achieve compatibility. Clearly, different views could be taken as to the fundamental nature or otherwise of a provision.

3. The subject matter of the provision at issue is relevant to the use made of s 3. If the area in question is one that is clearly within the judicial domain in terms of constitutional competence and role the judges are also more inclined to boldness.[79] Matters peculiarly within the judicial domain include the ordering of the criminal or civil justice system, matters of sentencing, or admissibility of evidence. In that context, the judges are more likely to be prepared to take a radical approach, as they did in *R v A*, in *R v Offen* and in *Hammond*.[80] In taking such a stance in that context they tend not to view themselves as stepping outside their own area of constitutional responsibility. The argument will be aided if Parliament is not otherwise addressing this issue—there are no plans to reform the objected-to provision, and no issues of resource allocation arise. In such circumstances there will be positive reasons for activism and none for deference.

4. If a case involves issues of social policy or resource allocation, the courts are much less likely to be bold. This factor was of relevance in *Re S:* the proposed 'interpretation' of the statute that had been accepted in the Court of Appeal would also have had 'far-reaching practical ramifications for local authorities and their care of children, including the authority's allocation of scarce financial and other resources'.[81] Those policy and resource factors were also of relevance, as indicated above, in *Bellinger v Bellinger* and persuaded the court to take a cautious approach to s 3.[82] The change brought about in *Ghaidan v Godin-Mendoza*[83] was not viewed as engaging significant counter-vailing policy or resource-based factors. In *Ghaidan* Lord Nicholls said that Parliament could not have intended that under s 3 judges should make decisions for which they are not equipped.[84] As Leigh and Masterman point out, this indicates that the courts are required to make an assessment as to whether Parliament is 'better placed than the judges to remedy the incompatibility claimed'.[85] In the cases of *Lambert* and *Sheldrake*[86] the judges were arguably pulled in opposing directions; in confronting reverse onus clauses aimed at combating organised crime or terrorism, both decisions concerned matters that could be viewed as within the judicial area of particular competence, but they also related to resource allocation in terms of the costs and difficulties of combating organised crime and bringing those allegedly involved to trial, as the culmination of a resource-intensive process.

5. Kavanagh further argues, referring to Lord Steyn's judgment in *Ghaidan*, that the key to understanding the trend in the use of s 3 is to see it as a remedial provision.[87] In other words, where the use of s 3 rather than s 4 is the *only* means of providing a remedy in the particular situation, the judges will tend to employ s 3. As she notes, in *Bellinger*, a remedy was about to be provided for the applicant by planned legislation, whereas in *Ghaidan* Mr Mendoza would have had no means of succeeding to a statutory tenancy had s 3 not been employed as it was. It now appears that the

---

79 The context is relevant in terms of both expertise and constitutional role: *R v A* [2002] 1 AC 45; *R v Offen* [2001] 1 WLR 253.

80 [2001] 1 WLR 253. The case concerned the 'reading down' of provisions governing mandatory sentences for repeat offenders.

81 A Kavanagh, 'Statutory Interpretation and Human Rights after Anderson: A More Contextual Approach' [2004] PL 537 at 540.

82 [2003] 2 AC 467, HL.

83 [2004] 2 AC 557, HL.

84 *Ibid* at para 33.

85 See Leigh and Masterman (2008), n 73 above, p 104.

86 *Sheldrake v DPP* [2004] UKHL 43; [2005] 1 AC 264; [2005] 1 All ER 237.

87 See Fenwick, Phillipson and Masterman (eds), *Judicial Reasoning under the HRA* (2007), Kavanagh, Chapter 5.

courts tend to view s 3, not s 4, as the main remedial mechanism of the HRA, only turning to s 4 exceptionally as a last resort, so normally this fourth step will not be needed.[88] If no remedy is available or in prospect, *except* by way of s 3, it appears that the courts may be strongly inclined towards the more radical use of s 3. This tendency to use s 3 rather than s 4 marginalises the idea of setting up a dialogue between courts and Parliament that arguably underlies s 4, and leads to a transfer of power to the judiciary, and away from the legislature.

Declarations of incompatibility under s4 HRA

Notes

1. This is an innovative provision. 'For the first time Parliament has invited the judges to tell it that it has acted wrongly by legislating incompatibly with a Convention right'.[89] Nevertheless, the House of Lords has made it clear, in *R v A*, as indicated above, that it views the making of a declaration as a last resort to be avoided if at all possible, and this was reaffirmed in *Ghaidan*.[90] An early declaration of incompatibility was made by the Divisional Court in respect of four planning cases: *R (On the application of Alconbury Developments) v Secretary of State for the Environment and Other Cases,*[91] but the declaration was then reversed by the House of Lords,[92] on the basis that a close reading of the Convention jurisprudence revealed that no incompatibility arose. A further early declaration was made by the Court of Appeal in relation to the system of appeals for prisoners detained on mental health grounds in *R(H) v London North and East Region Mental Health Review Tribunal.*[93] The Court found that s 73 of the Mental Health Act was incompatible with Art 5 since it in effect reversed the burden of proof against the detained person. The declaration was surprising in the sense that s 3 could have been used more strenuously to find that the system of appeals in such mental health cases could be viewed as compliant with the Convention.

2. The most well known and far-reaching declaration was made by the House of Lords in *A v Secretary of State for the Home Department;*[94] it is discussed below.[95] The declaration was accepted by the Government, and the offending provisions in the Anti-Terrorism, Crime and Security Act 2001 were repealed. A significant declaration was made by the Court of Appeal in *Westminster City Council v Morris.*[96] The Court of Appeal held that the Housing Act 1996, s 185(4) was incompatible with Art 14. Section 185(4) permitted a difference in treatment based on national origin or on a combination of nationality, immigration control, settled residence and social welfare which, the Court found, could not be justified.

3. A declaration is clearly an empty remedy as far as the majority of litigants is concerned, even though it does eventually bring about a change in the law. Clearly, it cannot be viewed as an

---

88   See Lord Steyn's remarks on this point in *Ghaidan* [2004] 2 AC 557, HL at [50].

89   D Feldman, 'The Human Rights Act 1998 and Constitutional Principles' (1999) 19(2) LS 165, 187.

90   See *Ghaidan* [2004] 2 AC 557, HL at [50].

91   [2001] HRLR 2.

92   [2001] 2 WLR 1389.

93   [2002] QB 1.

94   [2004] QB 335.

95   See p 1001 *et seq.*

96   [2006] 1 WLR 505.

effective remedy in Convention terms and this was affirmed in the Chamber judgment in *Burden v United Kingdom*.[97] It was found that the applicants had not needed to exhaust that remedy. The Court stated that it did not consider that the applicants could have been expected to have brought a claim for a declaration of incompatibility under s 4 of the 1998 Human Rights Act before bringing their application to the European Court of Human Rights, since it was a remedy that was dependent on the discretion of the executive and so ineffective on that ground. The Court expressed the view, however, that it was possible that at some future date, evidence of a long-standing and established practice of Ministers giving effect to the courts' declarations of incompatibility might be sufficient to persuade it of the effectiveness of the procedure. Since the Government has so far accepted that declarations should be responded to and has not resisted a declaration, it appears quite possible that the Court may find eventually that a declaration amounts to an effective remedy. But it is impossible not to conclude that this aspect of the system of remedial action is inadequate to the task of providing a domestic remedy for violation of Convention rights.[98] If, at the least, legislation is not forthcoming within the next few years to amend s 4 of the HRA with a view to allowing certain lower courts to make declarations, the pressure on the judiciary to find compatibility, already very high, will become increasingly severe.

4.   The most important point to note about s 4 declarations is that they are not binding—the Government is not legally bound to respond (s 10 HRA). In this sense they provide a weaker means of judicial intervention[99] than s 3 since s 3 places remedial action in the judges' own hands. Nevertheless, s 4 is having a significant impact in ensuring compatibility between statutory provisions and Convention rights. The Government's stance appears to be that it will seek to bring forward amending legislation once a declaration has been made; it has not sought to argue that a declaration should be ignored. Since October 2000 there have been 24 declarations of incompatibility, 15 of which have not been reversed on appeal. All the declarations so far made under the HRA have either been remedied or are currently under consideration with a view to being remedied.[100]

The remedial process under s 10

This is discussed in Chapter 3, pp 134–135. The response of the Labour Governments to the declarations of incompatibility made so far indicates that they accepted this argument. The government has moved to address all of them and in no instance has it stated that it merely intends to maintain the incompatibility[101]—although the HRA clearly allows it to do so. So although the HRA theoretically leaves the last word to Parliament in terms of creating compatibility, thereby preserving Parliamentary sovereignty, in practice the executive appears to accept the ECHR constraints, rather than the broader HRA ones. The ECHR *itself* allows for no exception in order to recognise Parliamentary sovereignty. It is unlikely that this stance will change under the current Lib-Con government.

---

97   Appl 13378/05; (2008) 47 EHRR 38.

98   See I Leigh and L Lustgarten, 'Making Rights Real: The Courts, Remedies and the Human Rights Act' [1999] 58(3) CLJ 509, 543.

99   See A Young on this point and on s 4 generally: 'A Peculiarly British Protection of Human Rights' (2005) 68 MLR 858, at 862.

100   See for examples of declarations, n 101 below.

101   E.g. in *R (H) v London North and East Region Mental Health Review Tribunal (Secretary of State for Health intervening)* [2002] QB 1 the Mental Health Act 1983 s. 73 was found to be incompatible with Arts 5(1) and 5(4); the Mental Health Act 1983 (Remedial Order) 2001 was introduced to address the incompatibility by way of the fast track procedure. In *A and Others* [2004] QB 335 the House of Lords declared Part 4 ACTSA 2001 incompatible with Arts 5 and 14 ECHR; Part 4 was repealed by the Prevention of Terrorism Act 2005. In *Smith v Scott* (2007) CSIH 9 the Representation of the People Act 1938, s 3(1) was declared incompatible with Art 3 First Protocol; the Labour Government stated that the appropriate remedial action was being considered.

TAKING ACCOUNT OF THE STRASBOURG JURISPRUDENCE UNDER SECTION 2

2. Interpretation of Convention

(1)   A court or tribunal determining a question which has arisen in connection with a Convention right must take into account any rights—

    (a)   judgment, decision, declaration or advisory opinion of the European Court of Human Rights;

    (b)   opinion of the Commission given in a report adopted under Article 31 of the Convention;

    (c)   decision of the Commission in connection with Article 26 or 27(2) of the Convention; or

    (d)   decision of the Committee of Ministers taken under Article 46 of the Convention, whenever made or given, so far as, in the opinion of the court or tribunal, it is relevant to the proceedings in which that question has arisen.

Notes

1. In seeking to interpret statutory provisions compatibly with the Convention rights under the Human Rights Act, the domestic judiciary 'must take into account' any relevant Strasbourg jurisprudence,[102] under s 2. Thus, they are not bound by it. In *R (On the application of Ullah) v Special Adjudicator,*[103] in the context of s 2, Lord Bingham said: 'In determining the present question, the House is required by section 2(1) of the Human Rights Act 1998 to take into account any relevant Strasbourg case law. While such case law is not strictly binding, it has been held that courts should, in the absence of some special circumstances, follow any clear and constant jurisprudence of the Strasbourg court[104] . . .it follows that a national court subject to a duty such as that imposed by section 2 should not without strong reason dilute or weaken the effect of the Strasbourg case law. The duty of domestic courts is to keep pace with the Strasbourg jurisprudence as it evolves over time: no more but certainly no less'.[105] Masterman finds: 'the potential for UK *courts* to engage in a meaningful dialogue on the scope of the Convention rights has been restricted by the general tendency to 'take their lead from Strasbourg'.[106]

2. Similar findings were made in a decision on the retention of fingerprints and samples under the Police and Criminal Evidence Act 1984 by the House of Lords in *Marper.*[107] Lord Steyn followed *Ullah* in rejecting the idea, which had been put forward by Lord Woolf in the Court of Appeal, that domestic cultural traditions should determine the ambit of the Convention rights.[108] However, he

---

102   See the definition in s 2 above.

103   [2004] UKHL 26; [2004] 2 AC 323; [2004] 3 WLR 23; [2004] 3 All ER 785.

104   He relied on *R (Alconbury Developments Ltd) v Secretary of State for the Environment, Transport and the Regions* [2001] UKHL 23; [2003] 2 AC 295, at para 26.

105   At [20].

106   See R Masterman, 'Interpretations, Declarations and Dialogue: Rights Protection under the Human Rights Act and Victorian Charter of Human Rights and Responsibilities' [2009] PL 112.

107   *R (On the application of Marper) v Chief Constable of South Yorkshire* [2004] 1 WLR 2196, e.g. at [78], *per* Baroness Hale.

108   At para 27. Lord Woolf CJ in the Court of Appeal had expressed this view at [2002] 1 WLR 3223, para 34.

considered that such traditions would be relevant in determining whether the *infringement* of the right was justified: 'I do accept that when one moves on to consider the question of objective justification under article 8(2) the cultural traditions in the United Kingdom are material. With great respect to Lord Woolf CJ the same is not true under article 8(1). . .' Similarly, in *N v Secretary of State for the Home Department*,[109] which concerned the deportation of an AIDS sufferer to a country that would not have the medical facilities of the UK, the House of Lords, having criticized the reasoning of the Strasbourg court,[110] accepted that the case law 'had to be applied'.

3. The view that the purpose of the HRA is not to enlarge the rights or remedies offered at Strasbourg, but only to ensure that those rights and remedies can be enforced by the domestic courts, also finds a basis in *Aston Cantlow v Wallbank*;[111] *R (Greenfield) v Secretary of State for the Home Department*;[112] and *R (Quark Fishing Ltd) v Secretary of State for Foreign and Commonwealth Affairs*.[113] That view was also reiterated and afforded further explanation in *R(SB) v Denbigh High School*.[114] In *Kay v Lambeth London Borough Council; Leeds City Council v Price*,[115] discussed below, Lord Bingham, with whom the other Law Lords agreed on this issue, said that domestic courts are not strictly required to follow rulings of the Strasbourg court, but that they must give practical recognition to the principles it expounds.

    As Masterman argues, the minimalist approach taken in *Ullah* towards the jurisprudence, which does not allow domestic courts to expand the ambit of a Convention right where clear and constant Strasbourg jurisprudence stands in the way, creates a tension with the status of the HRA as a constitutional instrument.[116] Clayton similarly finds that there is a tension between 'established perceptions of the judicial role' and the constitutional status of the HRA.[117] The over-generous and over-expansive approach of Lord Steyn to Art 6 in *R v A* was criticised above, but that was on the basis that there were strong countervailing Convention-based and constitutional objections to the course taken on the particular facts at issue. That approach, absent those objections, is in keeping with the redefined role of the judges now mapped out for them under the HRA, but it is clearly in tension with the approach in *Ullah* since it did much more than *keep pace* with the Strasbourg jurisprudence.

4. If the jurisprudence in question is *not* clear and constant it can be disregarded. Also it can be disregarded where a domestic precedent stands in the way. This was made clear by the House of Lords in *Kay & Anor v London Borough of Lambeth & Ors; Leeds City Council v Price*.[118] The case concerned rights to possession of property in domestic law which appeared to violate Art 8. The

---

109   [2005] 2 WLR 1124.

110   Lord Steyn at [11–13]: 'the Strasbourg jurisprudence, it has to be said, is not in an altogether satisfactory state'.

111   [2004] 1 AC 546, paras 6–7, 44.

112   [2005] 1 WLR 673, paras 18–19.

113   [2005] 3 WLR 837, paras 25, 33, 34, 88 and 92.

114   [2006] 2 WLR 719, para 29.

115   [2006] UKHL 10; [2006] 2 AC 465; [2006] 2 WLR 570; [2006] 4 All ER 128.

116   See further R Masterman, 'Aspiration or Foundation? The Status of the Strasbourg Jurisprudence and the Convention Rights in Domestic Law' in H Fenwick, R Masterman and G Phillipson (eds), *Judicial Reasoning under the UK Human Rights Act* (2007).

117   See R Clayton 'Judicial Deference and Democratic Dialogue': The Legitimacy of Judicial Intervention under the HRA' [2004] PL 33, 34.

118   [2006] UKHL 10; [2006] 2 AC 465; [2006] 2 WLR 570; [2006] 4 All ER 128.

Court of Appeal in the *Leeds* case had concluded that the decision in *Connors v United Kingdom*,[119] which was relied upon by the applicants in resisting possession proceedings, was inconsistent with the earlier House of Lords decision in *Harrow London Borough Council v Qazi*[120] and that they were bound to apply the House of Lords decision.[121] Lord Hope agreed on the precedent issue. He found that *Connors* was not incompatible with *Qazi*, but that *Qazi* should not in any event be departed from.

5. It is interesting to compare the restrained stance taken in *Ullah*, as discussed, with the more expansive findings as to the Strasbourg jurisprudence in a very different context in the 2008 adoption case in the House of Lords of *Re P*,[122] which was mentioned above and is extracted below. Lord Bingham said in *Ullah* that 'a national court subject to a duty such as that imposed by s 2 should not without strong reason dilute or weaken the effect of the Strasbourg case law'. Lord Hope said in *Re P* on those words in *Ullah*—'[Lord Bingham] said that the duty of the national courts is to keep pace with the Strasbourg jurisprudence as it evolves over time: "no more, but certainly no less." Not, it should be noted, "certainly no more". The Strasbourg jurisprudence is not to be treated as a straightjacket from which there is no escape'. *Re P* forms part of the domestic Human Rights Act jurisprudence that has given a lead to Strasbourg, that has treated the Strasbourg jurisprudence as a floor, not a ceiling.

6. In certain circumstances the House of Lords may not follow the Strasbourg case law even where it is clear and (arguably) constant. In the *Animal Defenders* case[123] the House of Lords put forward certain somewhat unconvincing reasons for refusing to follow Strasbourg. In *R v Horncastle*[124] the Supreme Court went further, finding:

> 108 In these circumstances . . . it would not be right for this court to hold that the sole or decisive test [from the Strasbourg decision] should have been applied rather than the provisions of the 2003 Act, interpreted in accordance with their natural meaning. I believe that those provisions strike the right balance between the imperative that a trial must be fair and the interests of victims in particular and society in general that a criminal should not be immune from conviction where a witness, who has given critical evidence in a statement that can be shown to be reliable, dies or cannot be called to give evidence for some other reason. In so concluding I have taken careful account of the Strasbourg jurisprudence. I hope that in due course the Strasbourg court may also take account of the reasons that have led me not to apply the sole or decisive test in this case.

The UK was appealing the decision in question (*Al-Khawaja*)[125] to the Grand Chamber. The Supreme Court decided that the European Court's decision insufficiently appreciated or accommodated particular aspects of the domestic process, and determined that in those rare circumstances it could decline to follow the decision, as it did.

---

119   (2004) 40 EHRR 189.

120   [2004] 1 AC 983.

121   See *Price v Leeds CC* [2005] 1 WLR 1825.

122   [2008] UKHL 38; [2008] 3 WLR 76; [2009] 1 AC 173 Lord Hoffmann, Lord Hope of Craighead, Lord Walker of Gestingthorpe, Baroness Hale of Richmond, Lord Mance, 23, 24 April 2008; 18 June, para 50.

123   See Chapter 18, pp 1038–1042.

124   [2010] 2 WLR 47.

125   (2009) 49 EHRR 1.

In re P and others (AP) (Appellants) (Northern Ireland) [2009] 1 AC 173 (extracts)

Lord Hoffmann

33. As this House affirmed in *In re McKerr* [2004] UKHL 12; [2004] 1 WLR 807, 'Convention rights' within the meaning of the 1998 Act are domestic and not international rights. They are applicable in the domestic law of the United Kingdom and it is the duty of the courts to interpret them like any other statute. When section 6(1) says that it is unlawful for a public authority to act incompatibly with Convention rights, that means the domestic rights set out in the Schedule to the Act and reproducing the language of the international Convention.

34. In the interpretation of these domestic rights, the courts must 'take into account' the decisions of the Strasbourg court. This language makes it clear that the United Kingdom courts are not bound by such decisions; their first duty is to give effect to the domestic statute according to what they consider to be its proper meaning, even if its provisions are in the same language as the international instrument which is interpreted in Strasbourg.

Notes (continued)

7. Where the jurisprudence is clear *and* is of particular authority it may be treated as—in effect—binding. In the counter-terrorism case of *Secretary of State for the Home Department v AF and others*[126] the stance taken by Lord Carswell, and accepted by the majority, was to the effect that the principle espoused by the Grand Chamber's judgment differed from that adopted by the majority in the previous House of Lords' decision in *Secretary of State for the Home Department v MB*,[127] which might be viewed as 'preferable', but that 'whatever 'latitude' might be permitted to the courts by the duty to take Strasbourg judgments into account under s 2(1) HRA, *'the authority of a considered statement of the Grand Chamber is such that our courts have no option but to accept and apply it'*.[128] The decision being applied was the very significant judgment of the Strasbourg Court in *A v United Kingdom*[129]—the case brought against the UK by the Belmarsh detainees detained without trial under Part 4 ACTSA, claiming compensation for their detention.[130]

8. *MB* was a case in which the House of Lords had to consider the imposition of a control order on a person suspected of terrorism-related activity—an order obtained outside the criminal justice system imposing obligations on the controlee including house detention for a period every day and other surveillance measures, such as tagging. The House of Lords decided—although the findings were somewhat equivocal and ambiguous—that in the proceedings imposing the control order there was no irreducible minimum disclosure of the case against him that had to occur so long as the proceedings in general could be viewed as fair. The Strasbourg Court in *A and others v UK* decided on that issue in relation to Art 5(4), that given the 'dramatic impact of the lengthy, and at the time, apparently indefinite, deprivation of liberty' on the fundamental rights of the applicants, Art 5(4) must import substantially the same fair trial guarantees as Art 6(1) in its criminal aspect

---

126   [2009] UKHL 28; [2009] 3 WLR 74.

127   [2008] AC 440.

128   'Views may differ as to which approach is preferable, and not all may be persuaded that the Grand Chamber's ruling is the preferable approach. But I am in agreement with your Lordships that we are obliged to accept and apply the Grand Chamber's principles in preference to those espoused by the majority in *MB*' (emphasis added). At para 108.

129   *A v United Kingdom* (3455/05) (2009) 49 EHRR, 29 ECHR (Grand Chamber)

130   In all, 11 applications were referred to the Grand Chamber; the applicants had been detained pursuant to the provisions of the ATCSA. They complained of violation of a number of their Convention rights, including their right to liberty under Art 5(1), relying upon the findings in their favour by the House of Lords in the *A* case in 2004. The United Kingdom was permitted by the Court to challenge those findings, but did so without success.

(*Garcia Alva v Germany*,[131] and see also *Chahal*).[132] In the crucial paragraph (220) of the judgment the Court found: '*where, however, the open material consisted purely of general assertions and SIAC's decision to uphold the certification and maintain the detention was based solely or to a decisive degree on closed material, the procedural requirements of Article 5(4) would not be satisfied*'[133] (emphasis added). Thus the Court found that although a balance could be struck, the national security interest could not demand that *no* disclosure of the basis for suspicion need occur.

9. Thus the Strasbourg Court in *A v UK* upheld a higher standard of fair trial rights than the House of Lords had upheld in *MB*, meaning that despite the HRA, and the reliance on the Strasbourg jurisprudence demanded by s 2, the Lords had failed to interpret the Strasbourg jurisprudence in a way with which Strasbourg would have concurred. It is fair to say that the relevant Strasbourg jurisprudence pre-*A v UK* did not give an entirely clear answer to the question before the Lords as to the minimum disclosure required, but there were a number of indications within it that fair trial values as understood at Strasbourg would not be satisfied if no disclosure at all occurred.[134] So it was an instance in which the Lords should have sought to take a more activist stance under s 2 HRA, applying such jurisprudence at Strasbourg as was available in order to answer the question posed to them in a way that would tend to uphold fair trial values, recognised under Arts 6 and 5(4), rather than in a way that afforded them a very limited recognition.

THE POSITION OF PUBLIC AUTHORITIES UNDER THE HRA; REMEDIES; HORIZONTAL EFFECT

'Public authorities' and 'public functions'

Section 6 HRA provides:

6.–(1) It is unlawful for a public authority to act in a way which is incompatible with a Convention right.

(2) Subsection (1) does not apply to an act if—

(a) as the result of one or more provisions of primary legislation, the authority could not have acted differently; or

(b) in the case of one or more provisions of, or made under, primary legislation which cannot be read or given effect in a way which is compatible with the Convention rights, the authority was acting so as to give effect to or enforce those provisions.

(3) In this section 'public authority' includes—

---

131   (2001) 37 EHRR 335, para 39.

132   (1996) 23 EHRR 413, paras 130–31.

133   Para 220, *GC* judgment.

134   See Chapter 7, pp 307–310, 312–313.

    (a)   a court or tribunal; and

    (b)   any person certain of whose functions are functions of a public nature, but does not include either House of Parliament or a person exercising functions in connection with proceedings in Parliament.

(4)   In subsection (3) 'Parliament' does not include the House of Lords in its judicial capacity.

(5)   In relation to a particular act, a person is not a public authority by virtue only of subsection (3)(b) if the nature of the act is private.

(6)   'An act' includes a failure to act but does not include a failure to—

    (a)   introduce in, or lay before, Parliament a proposal for legislation; or

    (b)   make any primary legislation or remedial order.

Notes

1. Section 6 is the central provision of the HRA. It is the main provision giving effect to the Convention rights: rather than incorporation of the Convention, it is made binding against public authorities. Under s 6(6), 'an act' includes an omission, but does not include a failure to introduce in or lay before Parliament a proposal for legislation or a failure to make any primary legislation or remedial order. Section 6(6) was included in order to preserve parliamentary sovereignty and prerogative power: in this case, the power of the executive to introduce legislation. Thus, apart from its impact on legislation, the HRA also creates obligations under s 6 which bear upon 'public authorities'. Such obligations have a number of implications. Independently of litigation, public authorities must put procedures in place in order to ensure that they do not breach their duty under s 6.

2. An exception had to be made under s 6 in order to bring it into harmony with s 3 and to realise the objective of preserving parliamentary sovereignty. This is accomplished in s 6(2)(a) and (b). Thus, s 6(2)(a) creates a strong obligation requiring public authorities to do their utmost to act compatibly. It may be noted that s 6(2)(a) applies to primary legislation only, whereas s 6(2)(b) applies also to subordinate legislation made under incompatible primary legislation. This is implicit in the use of the words 'or made under' used in the latter sub-section, but not the former. The exception under s 6 applies to legislation only (which, as indicated above, includes Orders in Council made under the royal prerogative, under s 21(1)). If a common law provision conflicts with the duty of a public body under s 6, the duty will prevail. Therefore, certain common law reforms under s 6 may occur more readily than statutory reform; as indicated above, no provision has been included in the Act allowing the common law to override the Convention or creating restrictions as to those courts which can find incompatibility between the two.

3. *'Standard' and 'functional' public authorities; purely private bodies.* Under s 6, Convention guarantees are binding only against 'public authorities'. Under s 6(3)(a), the term 'public authority' includes a court or, under s 6(3)(b), a tribunal, and under s 6(3)(c), 'any person certain of whose functions are functions of a public nature'. Parliament 'or a person exercising functions in connection with proceedings in Parliament' is expressly excluded from the definition. This refers to the Westminster Parliament; the Scottish Parliament, the Northern Ireland Assembly and the Welsh Assembly will be public authorities. Not only is the definition under s 6(3) non-exhaustive, it also leaves open room for much debate on the meaning of 'functions of a public nature'.[135] The terms

---

135   For discussion as to the way that this test interacts with the existing test for amenability to judicial review, see Chapter 14, pp 741, 743–744.

'public authority' and 'public function' were left deliberately undefined in the HRA. The interaction between the terms 'public authorities' and 'public functions' was explained in the Notes on
Clauses accompanying the Bill as indicating that where a body is clearly recognisable as a public
authority, there is no need to look at the detailed provisions of s 6(3)(a)–(c). Thus, the term 'public
authority' includes bodies which are self-evidently of a public nature, such as the police, government departments, the Probation Service, local authorities, the security and intelligence services.
They are referred to as 'standard or "core" public bodies'. Below, key decisions on the terms 'public
authority' and 'public function' indicate the approach that the courts are taking to these terms.

4. Under s 6(5), 'in relation to a particular act, a person is not a public authority by virtue only of
   s 6(3)(c) if the nature of the act is private'. Since, in relation to standard public authorities, there is
   no need to consider s 6(3)(c), this provision refers to functional public authorities and has the
   effect of excluding the private acts of functional public authorities from the scope of the HRA (but
   see the discussion of 'indirect horizontal effect', below). This is a very significant matter, since the
   private acts of standard public authorities are *not* excluded. Therefore, for example, assuming that
   acts relating to employment are private acts, an employee of a standard public authority could use
   the HRA directly against the authority, as explained below, while the employee of a functional
   public authority could not.

5. Thus, under the generally accepted view of s 6(3) and (5), the provisions create three categories of
   body in relation to the Convention rights. First, there are standard ('pure') public authorities which
   can *never* act privately, even in respect of matters governed by private law, such as employment
   relations. Such bodies are obliged under s 6 to act in accordance with Convention rights in relation
   to all of their activities, whether they can be accounted public or private functions. Second, there
   are functional (quasi-public) authorities which have a dual function and which can act privately;
   these are bodies having several functions, some public and some private; they are caught by the
   Convention in respect of the former functions but not the latter. In other words, they are not
   bound by the Act to adhere to the Convention rights when engaged in *private* acts. It is possible, it
   is suggested, that they could operate privately in respect of *aspects* of carrying out their public
   functions, while they would always act privately respect of their private functions. Classic functional bodies include privatised fuel or water companies and other contracted-out services. Third,
   there are purely private bodies which have no public function at all. It was accepted in Parliament
   in debate on the Human Rights Bill that this was the correct reading of s 6.[136]

6. An example of a body in the second category arose in respect of Railtrack (now abolished and re-
   nationalised), which had a public function in respect of rail safety *(see Cameron v Network Rail)*,[137]
   but might also have dealt with ancillary matters linked to safety, including employment, which
   could have been viewed as private. The other, private, function of such bodies (British Telecom and
   British Gas may provide examples) would relate, *inter alia*, to their dealings with shareholders and
   property development and in respect of those functions it is probable that such bodies could never
   act publicly.[138] A further example was given by the Lord Chancellor; he stated in debate on the
   Human Rights Bill that 'doctors in general practice would be [functional] public authorities in
   relation to their National Health Service functions, but not in relation to their private patients'.[139]
   Similarly, a private security company that has a contract with the Government to transport

---

136   See Straw, HC Official Report Cols 409–10 (1998).

137   [2006] EWHC 1133, QB.

138   See HL Deb Col 811, 24 November 1997.

139   *Hansard*, HL Deb, Vol. 583; col. 811 (24 November 2001). See further Clayton and Tomlinson, *The Law of Human Rights*, 1st edn (2000), para
      5–03.

prisoners to and from court and especially if it has a statutory duties in so doing, is probably a functional public authority for the purposes of the HRA when it is transporting prisoners, but not when it is guarding private property under a contract with a private organisation, since that is a private function. Therefore, when performing that latter function, it is not under a direct duty to respect Convention rights.

Key decisions on s 6 of the Human Rights Act

The term under s 6(3)(b) 'functions of a public nature' has—unsurprisingly—created difficulties of interpretation. Not only is the definition under s 6(3) non-exhaustive, it also left open room for much debate on the meaning of this phrase.

Poplar Housing and Regeneration Community Association Ltd and Secretary of State for the Environment v Donoghue [2001] 3 WLR 183[140] (extracts)

The defendant's property was transferred to the claimant housing association from the local authority which had been created by the local authority in order to transfer to it a substantial proportion of the authority's housing stock. The housing association then notified her that possession of the property was required and, subsequently, it issued a summons for possession under s 21(4) of the Housing Act 1988, as amended by s 98 of the 1996 Act. The defendant applied for an adjournment to enable her to place before the court evidence that the housing association was a public authority, or performing a public function, for the purposes of s 6 of the HRA and that, therefore, it was unlawful for it to act in a way which was incompatible with the European Convention on Human Rights, as scheduled to the HRA, and that in seeking an order for possession under s 21(4) of the 1988 Act, it was contravening her right to respect for her private and family life and her home under Article 8(1) of the Convention. The application for an adjournment was refused. The defendant appealed.

Lord Woolf CJ:
Public bodies and public functions
The importance of whether Poplar was at the material times a public body or performing public functions is this: the Human Rights Act 1998 will only apply to Poplar if it is deemed to be a public body or performing public functions. Section 6(3) HRA means that hybrid bodies, which have functions of a public and private nature, are public authorities, but not in relation to acts which are of a private nature. The renting out of accommodation can certainly be of a private nature. The fact that through the act of renting by a private body a public authority may be fulfilling its public duty, does not automatically change into a public act what would otherwise be a private act. The purpose of section 6(3)(b) is to deal with hybrid bodies which have both public and private functions. It is not to make a body, which does not have responsibilities to the public, a public body merely because it performs acts on behalf of a public body which would constitute public functions were such acts to be performed by the public body itself. An act can remain of a private nature even though it is performed because another body is under a public duty to ensure that that act is performed.

In coming to our conclusion as to whether Poplar is a public authority within the Human Rights Act 1998 meaning of that term, we regard it of particular importance in this case that:

(i) While section 6 of the Human Rights Act 1998 requires a generous interpretation of who is a public authority, it is clearly inspired by the approach developed by the courts in identifying the bodies and activities subject to judicial review. The emphasis on public functions reflects the approach adopted in judicial review by the courts and textbooks since the decision of the Court of Appeal (the judgment of Lloyd LJ) in *R v Panel on Take-overs and Mergers ex p Datafin plc* [1987] QB 815.

(ii) Tower Hamlets, in transferring its housing stock to Poplar, does not transfer its primary public duties to Poplar. Poplar is no more than the means by which it seeks to perform those duties.

(iii) The act of providing accommodation to rent is not, without more, a public function for the purposes of section 6 of the Human Rights Act 1998. Furthermore, that is true irrespective of the section of society for whom the accommodation is provided.

(iv) The fact that a body is a charity or is conducted not for profit means that it is likely to be motivated in performing its activities by what it perceives to be the public interest. However, this does not point to the body being a public authority. In addition, even if such a body performs functions, that would be considered to be of a public nature if performed by a public body, nevertheless such acts may remain of a private nature for the purpose of sections 6(3)(b) and 6(5).

(v) What can make an act, which would otherwise be private, public is a feature or a combination of features which impose a public character or stamp on the act. Statutory authority for what is done can at least help to mark the act as being public; so can the extent of control over the function exercised by another body which is a public authority. The more closely the acts that could be of a private nature are enmeshed in the activities of a public body, the more likely they are to be public. However, the fact that the acts are supervised by a public regulatory body does not necessarily indicate that they are of a public nature. This is analogous to the position in judicial review, where a regulatory body may be deemed public but the activities of the body, which is regulated, may be categorised private.

(vi) The closeness of the relationship which exists between Tower Hamlets and Poplar. Poplar was created by Tower Hamlets to take a transfer of local authority housing stock; five of its board members are also members of Tower Hamlets; Poplar is subject to the guidance of Tower Hamlets as to the manner in which it acts towards the defendant.

(vii) The defendant, at the time of transfer, was a sitting tenant of Poplar and it was intended that she would be treated no better and no worse than if she remained a tenant of Tower Hamlets. While she remained a tenant, Poplar therefore stood in relation to her in very much the position previously occupied by Tower Hamlets.

While these are the most important factors in coming to our conclusion, it is desirable to step back and look at the situation as a whole. As is the position on applications for judicial review, there is no clear demarcation line which can be drawn between public and private bodies and functions. In a borderline case, such as this, the decision is very much one of fact and degree. Taking into account all the circumstances, we have come to the conclusion that while activities of housing associations need not involve the performance of public functions, in this case, in providing accommodation for the defendant and then seeking possession, the role of Poplar is so closely assimilated to that of Tower Hamlets that it was performing public and not private functions.

[Poplar was found to be a functional public authority.]

R (On the Application of Heather) v Leonard Cheshire Foundation; R (On the Application of Ward) v Leonard Cheshire Foundation [2002] 2 All ER 936, CA (extracts)

H and W, residents of a home for the disabled, owned and run by Leonard Cheshire Foundation (LCF), a charity, appealed against the dismissal of their application for judicial review of L's decision to redevelop the home. As a consequence of the redevelopment, H would no longer be accommodated at the home.

LCF is the United Kingdom's leading voluntary sector provider of care and support services for the disabled.

'. . . 6 In the proceedings for judicial review the claimants contended that in making these decisions LCF was exercising functions of a public nature within the meaning of s 6(3)(b) of the HRA and so, as a public authority, was required not to act in a way which was incompatible with Article 8 of the European Convention on Human Rights. It was argued that instead the trustees had contravened Article 8 by not respecting the claimants' right to a home and failing to take into account, inter alia, promises made to them that Le Court would be their "home for life". In our judgment the role that LCF was performing manifestly did not involve the performance of public functions. The fact that LCF is a large and flourishing organisation does not change the nature of its activities from private to public. . .

There is no other evidence of there being a public flavour to the functions of LCF or LCF itself. LCF is not standing in the shoes of the local authorities. Section 26 of the NAA provides statutory authority for the actions of the local authorities, but it provides LCF with no powers. LCF is not exercising statutory powers in performing functions for the appellants.

LCF is clearly not performing any public function.

. . .We dismiss this appeal.'

Parochial Church Council of the Parish of Aston Cantlow and Wilmcote v Wallbank [2004] 1 AC 546 (extracts)

Was the action of a parochial church council seeking to enforce liability to repair a church the action of a public authority? Lord Nicholls first considered whether the PCC should be viewed as a core public authority, finding that there no single test was available to determine whether a public body carried out a public function.

Lord Nicholls

6. The expression 'public authority' is not defined in the Act, nor is it a recognised term of art in English law, that is, an expression with a specific recognised meaning. The word 'public' is a term of uncertain import, used with many different shades of meaning: public policy, public rights of way, public property, public authority (in the Public Authorities

Protection Act 1893), public nuisance, public house, public school, public company. So in the present case the statutory context is all important. As to that, the broad purpose sought to be achieved by section 6(1) is not in doubt. The purpose is that those bodies for whose acts the state is answerable before the European Court of Human Rights shall in future be subject to a domestic law obligation not to act incompatibly with Convention rights. If they act in breach of this legal obligation victims may henceforth obtain redress from the courts of this country. In future victims should not need to travel to Strasbourg.

7. Conformably with this purpose, the phrase 'a public authority' in section 6(1) is essentially a reference to a body whose nature is governmental in a broad sense of that expression. . . . under the Human Rights Act a body of this nature is required to act compatibly with Convention rights in everything it does. The most obvious examples are government departments, local authorities, the police and the armed forces. Behind the instinctive classification of these organisations as bodies whose nature is governmental lie factors such as the possession of special powers, democratic accountability, public funding in whole or in part, an obligation to act only in the public interest, and a statutory constitution. . . . One consequence of being a 'core' public authority, namely, an authority falling within section 6 without reference to section 6(3), is that the body in question does not itself enjoy Convention rights. . . . A core public authority seems inherently incapable of satisfying the Convention description of a victim: 'any person, *non-governmental organisation* or group of individuals' (article 34, with emphasis added). Only victims of an unlawful act may bring proceedings under section 7 of the Human Rights Act, and the Convention description of a victim has been incorporated into the Act, by section 7(7). . . . It must always be relevant to consider whether Parliament can have been intended that the body in question should have no Convention rights.

8. What, then, is the touchstone to be used in deciding whether a function is public for [the purpose of s 6(3)?] Clearly there is no single test of universal application. There cannot be, given the diverse nature of governmental functions and the variety of means by which these functions are discharged today. Factors to be taken into account include the extent to which in carrying out the relevant function the body is publicly funded, or is exercising statutory powers, or is taking the place of central government or local authorities, or is providing a public service (para 12).

The essential characteristic of a [core] public authority is that it carries out a function of government which would engage the responsibility of the United Kingdom before the Strasbourg organs (para 160).

Note

Applying these tests, the House of Lords found in *Wallbank* that parochial church councils (PCCs) are not 'core' public authorities. Lord Nicholls noted that as the established church, the Church of England has special links with central government, but he considered that it remains essentially a religious organisation. He found that the constitution and functions of PCCs do not support the view that they should be characterised as core public authorities. Lord Nicholls said that the essential role of a PCC is to provide a formal means, prescribed by the Church of England, whereby *ex officio* and elected members of the local church promote the mission of the Church and discharge financial responsibilities in respect of their own parish church; he viewed these as acts of self-governance and PCCs as far removed from the type of body whose acts engage the responsibility of the state under the European Convention. As indicated, he further noted that if PCCs could be characterised as core public authorities that would mean that they would not be capable of being victims within the meaning of the Human Rights Act and, *inter alia*, would not be able take advantage of s 13, which gives express mention to the exercise by religious organisations of the Art 9 right of freedom of thought, conscience and religion.[141] Lord Hope noted that the Strasbourg jurisprudence supports this approach.[142] He also considered that the case law on judicial review might not provide much assistance as to functions of a public nature because the cases were not decided for the purposes of identifying the liability of the state in international law.[143]

YL v Birmingham City Council [2008] 1 AC 95 (extracts)

Lord Mance: [under the ECHR jurisprudence] the State may in some circumstances remain responsible for the manner of performance of essentially state or governmental functions or powers which it has chosen to delegate to a private law institution. Examples are provided by *Wós v Poland* (Application No 22860/02) (unreported) 1 March 2005 and *Sychev v Ukraine* (Application No 4773/02) (unreported) 11 October 2005. . . . [this] principle recognises that there may be certain essentially state or governmental functions, particularly involving the exercise of duties or powers, for the manner of exercise of which the State will remain liable, notwithstanding that it has delegated them to a private law body. It is necessary to consider whether the provision of care and accommodation in a private care home under an arrangement made with a local authority falls within this principle. The above analysis confirms that Strasbourg case law contains no case directly in point. In contrast with *Sychev*, a private care home does not acquire or exercise any obvious State power or duty. In contrast with both *Wós* and *Sychev*, it is not established and capitalised by the State for state purposes. The ambit and significance of the reasoning in *Costello-Roberts* is less clear, but the case concerns the very different field of education, where the court may, on one view, have considered that any activity bearing centrally on the provision of education was a non-delegable State function, whether it is provided by a state or under private contractual arrangements in a private school. The case does not indicate that the same can or should be said of the provision of care and accommodation.

Lord Bingham (dissenting): An argument heavily relied on in support of the appeal has been a comparison of the management by a local authority care home with the management of a privately owned care home. There is no relevant difference, it is pointed out, between the activities of a local authority in managing its own care homes and those of the managers of privately owned care homes. The function of the local authority is unquestionably a function of a public nature, so how, at least in relation to residents the charges for whom are being paid by the local authority, can the nature of the function of the managers of a privately owned care home be held to be different? So the argument goes. There are, in my opinion, very clear and fundamental differences. The local authority's activities are carried out pursuant to statutory duties and responsibilities imposed by public law. The costs of doing so are met by public funds, subject to the possibility of a means tested recovery from the resident. In the case of a privately owned care home the manager's duties to its residents are, whether contractual or tortious, duties governed by private law. In relation to those residents who are publicly funded, the local and health authorities become liable to pay charges agreed under private law contracts and for the recovery of which the care home has private law remedies. The recovery by the local

---

141   See [13]–[15].

142   At [62]. *Holy Monasteries v Greece* (1995) 20 EHRR 1 and *Hautanemi v Sweden* (1996) 22 EHRR CD 156.

143   *Ibid*, para 52.

authority of a means tested contribution from the resident is a matter of public law but is no concern of the care home (para 29).

Notes

1. The House of Lords held by a 3–2 majority in *YL* that private care homes are not discharging a public function for HRA purposes, and so are not bound by the European Convention on Human Rights, even when they are looking after clients on behalf of a local authority. That was the view of Lords Scott, Mance and Neuberger. Lord Bingham and Baroness Hale dissented. This decision has now been over-turned legislatively, as discussed below, but that does not aid in determining the meaning of 'public function' in general since only care homes are affected.

2. In *Poplar* the finding of a public function in the particular case was not based on whether the function should be viewed as inherently 'public' in nature—using the wording of the statutory test. Instead, the Court of Appeal stressed a number of factors other than that of taking over the role of a public authority providing a public service, the provision of accommodation, although that factor was obviously of great significance. It stressed that the definition of what is a public authority should be given a generous interpretation, but the approach, it said, 'is clearly inspired by the approach developed by the courts in identifying the bodies and activities subject to judicial review.

3. In *Poplar* the Court identified a number of factors which would suggest that a function was public. If the function was carried out under statutory authority and there was control over the function by another body which was a public authority that would be of significance. If there were acts which could be of a private nature—providing accommodation for rent—which were enmeshed in the activities of a public body that would also aid in finding that the function was public, as would the closeness of the relationship with the public body, and that a transfer of responsibilities between the public and private sectors had occurred. The problem with this decision is that it demanded that a number of criteria should be satisfied other than the inherently 'public' nature of the role in question. The provision of social housing is a public service that serves the public interest since it addresses the problem of homelessness. On the face of it the function appears to be 'public'. The demand that other criteria should be satisfied obviously limits the potential generosity of the statutory term which, it is argued, invites, and was intended to invite, an expansive interpretation. The Government's intervention in *R (On the application of Johnson) v Havering London Borough Council/YL v Birmingham City Council and Others*,[144] discussed below, confirms that this was the intention.

    A recent decision giving a more expansive interpretation to the notion of 'public function' is *R (On the Application of Weaver) v London & Quadrant Housing Trust*.[145] The Court of Appeal confirmed that a publicly funded housing trust was performing a public function for the purposes of judicial review and the HRA. Moreover, the act of terminating a tenancy was not a 'private act' within the meaning of s 5(6); the factors relied on in making these findings were, broadly, those enumerated in *Poplar*, *YL* and *Aston-Cantlow*, including in particular the fact that the trust was publicly funded, subject to intense government regulation, had to carry out government policy and cooperate with the local authority, and that it in effect stood in the place of the local authority.[146]

---

144   [2007] All ER 271.

145   [2009] EWCA Civ 587.

146   But note that at the time of writing, it is believed that the decision is being appealed to the Supreme Court.

4. The purpose behind ss 6–9 HRA was stressed by Lord Hope in *Aston-Cantlow*:[147]

> 'There is one vital step that is missing from the Court of Appeal's analysis. It is not mentioned expressly in the Human Rights Act 1998, but it is crucial to a proper understanding of the balance which ss 6 to 9 of the Act seek to strike between the position of public authorities on the one hand and private persons on the other. The purpose of these sections is to provide a remedial structure in domestic law for the rights guaranteed by the Convention. It is the obligation of states which have ratified the Convention to secure to everyone within their jurisdiction the rights and freedoms which it protects. . . .The source of this obligation is article 13. It was omitted from the articles mentioned in section 1(1) which defines the meaning of the expression "the Convention rights", as the purpose of sections 6 to 9 was to fulfil the obligation which it sets out. But it provides the background against which one must examine the scheme which these sections provide.'

5. Section 6 was obviously intended to impose Convention obligations on those carrying out public functions and to disallow the avoidance of those obligations simply because functions had been transferred from the public to the private sector. But in making 'public function' the central criterion under the HRA, the intention was to single out only those functions that should be accounted public—and which therefore should be discharged in a Convention-compliant fashion. So the function in question, *not* the nature of institution discharging it, should be the crucial factor.

    Dawn Oliver argues: 'The problem here is that not all of the considerations and criteria identified by Lord Woolf relate to the nature of the functions or acts in question, which is what s 6 is about, but are institutional (the institutional arrangements of the housing association) and relational (the relationship of the local authority with the housing association and the prior relationship between the local authority and the tenant).'[148]

6. In *R (On the application of Heather and others) v Leonard Cheshire Foundation and Another*[149] in which it was found that the body in question was not carrying out a public function, the Court identified three decisive factors which led it to the conclusion that LCF's functions were not public. The home was publicly funded, but there was no other evidence of a 'public flavour' to the activities of LCF. It was not, it was found, standing in the shoes of the local authority. It was noted that the nature of the service provided by LCF did not differ between those residents of the Home who were publicly funded and those who were privately funded. The fact that the claimants would lose the protection of Art 8 against LCF if it was not viewed as performing a public function was viewed as a circular argument. It was observed that the need to secure the protection of Art 8 could not in itself change the classification of a function.

7. Public interest factors were found to be relevant in the decision of the House of Lords in *Parochial Church Council of the Parish of Aston Cantlow and Wilmcote v Wallbank* (extracted above).[150] *Core* public authorities, it was pointed out, had 'governmental' functions, such as 'democratic accountability, public funding, an obligation to act only in the public interest, a statutory

---

147   At [44].

148   'Functions of a Public Nature under the Human Rights Act' [2004] PL 329–51.

149   [2002] 2 All ER 936; [2002] EWCA Civ 366. For discussion see V Sachdeva [2002] JR Law 249. See for the first instance decision: [2001] EWHC Admin 429; [2001] ACD 75. For discussion see Johnston [2001] JR 250. See also Monica Carss-Frisk QC, 'Public Authorities: The Developing Definition' (2002) EHRLR 319.

150   [2004] 1 AC 546; [2003] WLR 283.

constitution'.[151] The majority of the House of Lords found that the parochial church council (PCC) was not a governmental body but was a functional authority; but went on to decide that the PCC was not carrying out a public function in this particular instance. Lord Hope found that 'The nature of the act is to be found in the nature of the obligation which the PCC is seeking to enforce. . .[namely] a civil debt. The function it is performing has nothing to do with the responsibilities which are owed to the public by the state.'[152] The Court of Appeal had seen the liability as a tax and therefore as pertaining to a public function because it was enforced on people who were not necessarily church-members and, using circular reasoning, because it was imposed by a public authority. The House of Lords saw it as a civil liability that arose from occupation of a particular type of land. It was stressed in particular that the liability was taken on with notice—and therefore voluntarily—when purchasing the land. This, it was found, distinguished it from a tax,[153] which would apply generally. The Lords, as the passages quoted above indicate, found that a PCC could be a functional, but not a 'core' public authority since if it had been viewed as a governmental organisation—as the Court of Appeal found—it could not have fallen within the meaning of Art 34 ECHR and so could not have been a 'victim' at Strasbourg. The PCC had some governmental functions but that did not make it a core public authority in general. The essential factor in determining 'core' public authority status appeared to be whether the body was 'governmental', such that the UK would be responsible for its actions under Art 34 of the Convention.[154]

8. The Lords in *Wallbank* appeared to focus more on a functional approach than the Court of Appeal had been doing. But in *R v Hampshire Farmers Market ex parte Beer*,[155] the Court of Appeal returned to its largely institutional approach. It noted that neither *Poplar* nor *Leonard Cheshire* had been overruled or expressly disapproved by the House of Lords.[156] Having done so, it went on to apply an approach in which institutional factors played an important part. It held that the question under the HRA would remain the same as that under judicial review unless the Strasbourg case law required otherwise. The Court of Appeal concluded that the farmers' market was a public authority. This was first because the power of access to a public market had a public element or flavour.[157] Second it was because the market owed its existence to the local authority and had stepped into its shoes, in the sense that it performed functions which had previously been performed by the local authority.[158] Further, the company exercised public functions so as to be amenable to judicial review, and therefore it was also a public authority under the HRA.

9. In the case of *YL v Birmingham City Council and Others* (extracted above),[159] the House of Lords took the *Wallbank* approach. The key point of the appellants' complaint was that as a result of the transfer they would lose a remedy that they would have been able to deploy to assert Art 8 protection against the local authority directly. The council, it was argued, would be removing or diminishing the human rights that they formerly guaranteed to the claimants. Therefore in

---

151   Para 7.

152   *Ibid* at [64].

153   *Ibid* at [66], *per* Lord Hobhouse.

154   See the test for 'victims' under s 7 HRA, discussed below.

155   [2004] 1 WLR 233; [2003] EWCA Civ 1056.

156   *Hampshire*, n 155 above, at [15].

157   At paragraph 30.

158   At paragraphs 35–36.

159   [2007] UKHL 27, CA; [2007] EWCA Civ 26. For analysis of the decision and its wider implications for the courts' approach to 'contracting out' and the HRA, see A Williams, '*YL v Birmingham City Council*: Contracting Out and Functions of a Public Nature' (2008) EHRLR 524.

discharging its statutory obligations to the claimants under ss 21 and 26, the council would be failing to ensure real and effective protection of their rights and so it would be acting incompatibly with the Convention and unlawfully under s 6 HRA. The Lords took a functional approach and found that the function in question should not be viewed as public, largely on the basis that the function was one governed by private, not public, law. Lord Mance found that the Convention jurisprudence on the delegation of state powers to private bodies, meaning that the state would retain responsibility for the discharge of the powers, did not determine the issue. The possibility therefore that the state might have responsibility (outside the field of positive obligations) for a private body's actions at Strasbourg but that that body might avoid liability under the HRA, was continued. It is pointed out, however, that the purpose of ss 6–9 HRA was to provide for the delivery of effective remedies in the domestic courts. If the term 'public function' is defined too narrowly, that creates a situation where claimants could obtain a remedy at Strasbourg, by claiming against the state, but could not obtain it directly, under the HRA. It is suggested that the Lords did not take that factor fully into account.

10. The Lords in *YL* concluded that the private care home in accommodating the appellants was not performing the functions of a public authority under s 6(3)(b) of the 1998 Act. In so finding it reaffirmed its own previous approach to the public function issue, despite the attempt by the Secretary of State of Constitutional Affairs, intervening in the case, to persuade it that its approach was out of kilter with that of the Lords in *Aston-Cantlow*. It had been hoped in the *Johnson* case, given the intervention of several key parties, including the Secretary of State of Constitutional Affairs, that the confusion surrounding the 'public function' test might be resolved and a clear test might emerge. The case however failed to produce such a test.[160] Subsequently, legislation, the Health and Social Care Act 2008, s145, was brought forward to reverse the decision in *YL*. Private and voluntary sector organisations providing residential care services under contract to local authorities are now designated 'public authorities' for s 6 HRA purposes.[161] But that does not lay down a test applicable in other contexts. The change is of interest, however, since it provides in effect a new provision to be read alongside the HRA s 6, and also indicates to the courts Parliament's intention that s 6(3)(b) should not be afforded an overly restrictive interpretation.

11. It is clear that the House of Lords' approach to the public function test in s 6(3)(b) focuses more upon whether the *function* in question should be seen as public, and less upon the institutional factors relied upon in the Court of Appeal, most notably by Lord Woolf in *Poplar* and in *Leonard Cheshire*. The Joint Committee on Human Rights noted in its Fourth Report[162] that Lord Nicholls said that the definition of 'public function' in the HRA should be given a 'generously wide' interpretation,[163] while Lord Hope found that: 'It is the function that the person is performing that is determinative of the question whether it is, for the purposes of the case, a "hybrid" public authority.'[164]

---

160   See further H Quane, 'The Strasbourg Jurisprudence and the Meaning of 'Public Authority' under the HRA' [2006] PL 106; D Oliver, 'The Frontiers of the State: Public Authorities and Public Functions under the HRA' [2000] Autumn PL 476, 477; J Landau 'Functional public authorities after *YL* [2007] PL 630.

161   The Health and Social Care Act 2008, s 145. The Health and Social Care Act 2008 (Commencement No 4) Order 2008, SI 2008/2994 brought s 145 of the Health and Social Care Act 2008 into force. Section 145(1) provides: 'A person ('P') who provides accommodation, together with nursing or personal care, in a care home for an individual under arrangements made with P under the relevant statutory provisions is to be taken for the purposes of subsection (3)(b) of section 6 of the Human Rights Act 1998 (c. 42) (acts of public authorities) to be exercising a function of a public nature in doing so.'
       (2) The 'relevant statutory provisions' are—
           (a) in relation to England and Wales, sections 21(1)(a) and 26 of the National Assistance Act 1948 (c. 29). . .'.

162   'The Meaning of Public Authority under the Human Rights Act' HC 382, HL 39 (2003–04) 12.

163   *Wallbank*, at [11]. See M Sunkin 'Pushing Forward the Frontiers of Human Rights Protection: The Meaning of Public Authority under the HRA' [2004] PL 643.

164   *Ibid* at [41].

12. From the case law discussed it is apparent that a variety of factors are currently being taken into account in order to determine whether a body has a public function, but the most significant one is, in the Court of Appeal decisions, consideration of the principles deriving from judicial review case law on the question whether the decision-maker is a public body.[165] Commentators agree that this is the case[166] and it was contemplated that it would be from the debates on the Human Rights Bill.[167] Most commentators considered at the inception of the HRA that this would be the primary, or at least a very significant method, of answering the question[168] whether a body was discharging a public function. However, the House of Lords indicated in *Aston-Cantlow* that the judicial review cases should not be definitive, partly because the Strasbourg jurisprudence takes an autonomous approach to the nature of public bodies that differs from the judicial review approach. This was also pointed out by a number of commentators pre-HRA.[169] The starting point used in judicial review cases is the finding that the body is statutory or is acting under prerogative powers. But the source of a body's power is now viewed as far less significant than the public element in its functions.[170] However, in the cases considered so far the question whether there is statutory authority for or underpinning the function in question has been viewed as near-decisive or as significant (*Poplar, Aston-Cantlow*). Clearly, the *Aston-Cantlow* approach, in which amenability to review is taken into account but is not conclusive, is the more authoritative and also the more appropriate one.

13. Where a body is non-statutory, a further determining factor in terms of amenability to judicial review concerns the question whether there is evidence of government support or control for the body,[171] while a relevant, although not a conclusive factor, is whether it has monopoly power.[172] A further factor concerns the question whether, had the body not existed, the Government would have set up an equivalent body.[173] Similarly, the cases considered on s 6 HRA have taken account of whether the body is publicly funded and whether it is controlled by a public authority (*Aston-Cantlow, Poplar*). The strength of the link between the two bodies is relevant; in *Poplar* it was relevant that board members were also members of the public authority. It can also be asked whether the function is being exercised over public land and whether there is a difference between the way a service is provided when it is publicly funded and when it is privately funded, as in *YL*. The Joint Committee has concluded that, absent a situation in which the body in question is exercising coercive powers or powers of a public nature directly assigned to it by statute, its

---

165   See generally on this point D Oliver, 'The Frontiers of the State: Public Authorities and Public Functions under the HRA' [2000] PL 476.

166   See M McDermont, 'The Elusive Nature of the 'Public Function': *Poplar Housing and Regeneration Community Association Ltd v Donoghue*' (2003) 66(1) MLR 113; J Morgan 'The Alchemist's Search for the Philosopher's Stone: The Status of Registered Social Landlords under the Human Rights Act' (2003) 66(5) MLR 700; P Cane 'Church, State and Human Rights: Are Parish Councils Public Authorities?' (2004) 120(Jan) LQR 41–48.

167   See Straw, HC Deb Cols 408, 409, 17 June 1998.

168   See Clayton and Tomlinson, p 1017, below, 1st edn, p 194; Lester and Pannick, p 1017, below, 1st edn, para 2.6.3.

169   See Grosz, Beatson and Duffy, *Human Rights – the 1998 Act and the ECHR* (2000), para 4–04; see further N Bamforth, 'The Application of the HRA to Public Authorities and Private Bodies' [1999] 58 CLJ 159.

170   This can now be said due to the influence of the finding to this effect in *R v Panel of Take-Overs and Mergers ex parte Datafin* [1987] QB 815, 838. See further N Bamforth, 'The Scope of Judicial Review: Still Uncertain' [1993] PL 239.

171   *R v Disciplinary Committee of the Jockey Club ex parte Aga Khan* [1993] 1 WLR 909. See pp 742–743, above.

172   *R v Football Assoc ex parte Football League* [1993] 2 All ER 833.

173   *R v Disciplinary Committee of the Jockey Club ex parte Aga Khan* [1993] 1 WLR 909. Even if that is case, if the source of the body's power is contractual, that will be a strong indication that it is a private body: *Aga Khan, ibid*.

institutional connection with Government is likely to remain a significant factor in determining whether any of its functions are public.[174]

14. A number of arguments can be put forward to the effect that the courts should be prepared to take a generous stance towards the public function test in order to avoid excluding bodies from the direct scope of the HRA. So doing seems to reflect the intention underlying the Act[175] and would be consonant with the general approach taken to human rights instruments. It would also mean that the contracting out of public services to the private sector would not result in a failure of that sector to observe Convention standards in respect of such services. This is a very significant matter due to the diminution of the public sector that has occurred over the last 25 years and is still occurring.

15. Many commentators have criticized the failure of the Courts in the cases extracted above to take the more generous approach to the interpretation of 'public function'.[176] The Joint Committee on Human Rights concluded in 2003 that: 'A serious gap has opened in the protection which the Human Rights Act was intended to offer, and a more vigorous approach to re-establishing the proper ambit of the Act needs to be pursued.'[177] The group *Liberty* argued in 2006: 'gaps in human rights protection have arisen because some courts have sought to identify Functional Public Authorities by looking at the character of the institutional arrangements of the body, i.e. the extent to which the body is controlled or funded by a core public body, rather than the character of the function that it is performing. . . . The appropriate question for the courts to ask is, however, whether the function in question is one for which the state has taken responsibility in the public interest. . . . the best response to ill-informed and misleading claims that the HRA is no more than a charter for terrorists and criminals. . . . [is that] the Act [while offering traditional protection in those contexts against state abuse of power] must be shown also to provide visible and accessible protection for children, disabled people and older people at the most vulnerable times in their lives'.[178] The *YL* case, which was expected to provide a more workable test and to accept the more generous approach of the House of Lords in *Aston Cantlow*, failed, as discussed above, to do so. This matter remains problematic and may demand further legislative intervention.

16. In 2007 the Joint Committee on Human Rights published its Ninth Report of Session 2006–07 on *The Meaning of Public Authority under the Human Rights Act*.[179] The Committee recommended that urgent consideration should be given to the amendment of existing statutes to ensure that the sectors most seriously affected by the narrow interpretation of 'public authority' were made subject to the HRA.[180] As an alternative, the Committee proposed that Bills providing for the contracting-out or delegation of public functions to private bodies should provide that the body performing the functions will be a public authority for the purposes of the HRA.[181]

---

174 Seventh Report 2003–4, at [16].

175 The Lord Chancellor said at Second Reading of the Bill in the House of Lords: 'We . . . decided that we should apply the Bill to a wide rather than a narrow range of public authorities so as to provide as much protection as possible for those who claim that their rights have been infringed'. HL Official Report Cols 1231–32, 3 November 1997.

176 See the Seventh Report of the Joint Committee on Human Rights, 2003–4, HL Paper 39/HC 382, in particular at paras 41–44 and paras 45–74; JCHR, Thirty-Second Report, *The Human Rights Act: the DCA and Home Office Reviews*, especially para 92. See also Kate Markus, in 'What is Public Power: the Courts' Approach to the Public Authority definition under the Human Rights Act', in *Delivering Rights*, Jowell and Cooper (eds) (2003), at pp 106–114. See also A Williams (2008) n 159, above.

177 Seventh Report of JCHR for 2003–4 at [43].

178 Evidence from Liberty to the JCHR, December 2006.

179 HL Paper 77, HC 410. Published on 28 March 2007.

180 Para 142.

181 Para 143.

Proceedings and remedies

7.–(1) A person who claims that a public authority has acted (or proposes to act) in a way which is made unlawful by section 6(1) may—

   (a)   bring proceedings against the authority under this Act in the appropriate court or tribunal; or

   (b)   rely on the Convention right or rights concerned in any legal proceedings, but only if he is (or would be) a victim of the unlawful act.

  (2)   In subsection (1)(a) 'appropriate court or tribunal' means such court or tribunal as may be determined in accordance with rules; and proceedings against an authority include a counterclaim or similar proceeding.

  (3)   If the proceedings are brought on an application for judicial review, the applicant is to be taken to have a sufficient interest in relation to the unlawful act only if he is, or would be, a victim of that act.

  (4)   If the proceedings are made by way of a petition for judicial review in Scotland, the applicant shall be taken to have title and interest to sue in relation to the unlawful act only if he is, or would be, a victim of that act.

  (5)   Proceedings under subsection (1)(a) must be brought before the end of—

   (a)   the period of one year beginning with the date on which the act complained of took place; or

   (b)   such longer period as the court or tribunal considers equitable having regard to all the circumstances, but that is subject to any rule imposing a stricter time limit in relation to the procedure in question.

  (6)   In subsection (1)(b) 'legal proceedings' includes—

   (a)   proceedings brought by or at the instigation of a public authority; and

   (b)   an appeal against the decision of a court or tribunal.

  (7)   For the purposes of this section, a person is a victim of an unlawful act only if he would be a victim for the purposes of Article 34 of the Convention if proceedings were brought in the European Court of Human Rights in respect of that act.

  (8)   Nothing in this Act creates a criminal offence.

8. Judicial remedies

  (1)   In relation to any act (or proposed act) of a public authority which the court finds is (or would be) unlawful, it may grant such relief or remedy, or make such order, within its powers as it considers just and appropriate.

  (2)   But damages may be awarded only by a court which has power to award damages, or to order the payment of compensation, in civil proceedings.

  (3)   No award of damages is to be made unless, taking account of all the circumstances of the case, including—

    (a)   any other relief or remedy granted, or order made, in relation to the act in question (by that or any other court); and

    (b)   the consequences of any decision (of that or any other court) in respect of that act, the court is satisfied that the award is necessary to afford just satisfaction to the person in whose favour it is made.

(4)   In determining—

    (a)   whether to award damages; or

    (b)   the amount of an award, the court must take into account the principles applied by the European Court of Human Rights in relation to the award of compensation under Article 41 of the Convention.

9. Judicial acts

(1)   Proceedings under section 7(1)(a) in respect of a judicial act may be brought only—

    (a)   by exercising a right of appeal;

    (b)   on an application (in Scotland a petition) for judicial review; or

    (c)   in such other forum as may be prescribed by rules.

(2)   That does not affect any rule of law which prevents a court from being the subject of judicial review.

(3)   In proceedings under this Act in respect of a judicial act done in good faith, damages may not be awarded otherwise than to compensate a person to the extent required by Article 5(5) of the Convention.

(4)   An award of damages permitted by subsection (3) is to be made against the Crown; but no award may be made unless the appropriate person, if not a party to the proceedings, is joined.

Notes

1. *Use of ss 7 and 8 of the HRA.* Sections 7 and 8 HRA allow for proceedings to be brought by a person who is or would be a victim, against a public authority which has acted or is proposing to act unlawfully by breaching the Convention rights, and provide a remedy if the proceedings are successful in the sense of finding such a breach. In *Re S and Re W (Care Orders)*,[182] Lord Nicholl had to consider whether ss 7 and 8 of the HRA provide a statutory basis for demanding that the authority should put in place procedures designed to avoid a breach of the rights where no such finding has been made. He said 'sections 7 and 8 [cannot] be pressed as far as would be necessary if they were to bring the introduction of the starring system within their embrace'. He found that the question whether the authority has acted unlawfully, or was proposing to do so, is a matter to be decided in the proceedings under s 7. 'Relief can be given against the authority only in respect of an act, or a proposed act, of the authority which the court finds is or would be unlawful. For this purpose, an act includes a failure to act. But the starring system would impose obligations on local authorities in circumstances when there has been no such finding.' He considered that the non-fulfilment of a 'starred event' could not necessarily be equated with a breach or threatened breach of a Convention right. Assuming that the failure to introduce a system such as the starring system would constitute

---

a breach of Art 8 (Lord Nicholl did not consider that this was the case), then the authority in question would be failing in its duty under s 6 of the HRA if it did not introduce such a system, unless it was unable to do so due to the operation of primary legislation (s 6(2)).

2. *Victims.* Section 7(1)(a) of the Act allows a person who claims that a public authority has acted or proposes to act in breach of a Convention right to bring proceedings against the public authority. Section 7(1)(b) allows a person to rely on the Convention in any legal proceedings. But in either case, the person must be (or would be) a 'victim' of the unlawful act. Section 7(7) provides: '. . .a person is a victim of an unlawful act only if he would be a victim for the purposes of Article 34 of the Convention if proceedings were brought in the European Court of Human Rights in respect of that act.' It was accepted in Parliament that the Strasbourg interpretation of 'victim' would be used, rather than the wider test for standing under the UK judicial review doctrine which allows pressure groups to bring actions so long as they satisfy the 'sufficient interest' test.[183] The Strasbourg test was considered in Chapter 7.[184] As Joanna Miles points out, it cannot be said that the concept of 'victim' has been interpreted consistently at Strasbourg, although it is clear that those indirectly affected may be covered.[185]

3. *Actions under s 7(1)(a).* Section 7(1)(a) allows a victim of a breach or threatened breach of a Convention right to bring an action against a standard public authority or a functional body acting in its public capacity[186] on that basis. The action must be brought in 'the appropriate court or tribunal' which will be determined 'by rules' (s 7(2)). Under s 7(9), the term 'rules' means: '. . .in relation to proceedings in a court or tribunal outside Scotland rules made by the Lord Chancellor or the Secretary of State for the purpose of this section or rules of court. . .'. Thus, the HRA creates a new form of action based on a liability of public authorities to provide a remedy for breaching the Convention rights—a new public law wrong. The claim may take the *form* of a complaint such as to a specialised tribunal. The use of the ECHR under the HRA in judicial review proceedings is covered in Chapter 15, pp 879–883.

4. *Invoking the Convention under s 7(1)(b).* Unlike s 7(1)(a), which provides for a new cause of action against public authorities, s 7(1)(b) allows for Convention points to be raised once an action has begun under an existing cause of action, where the other party is a public authority. Therefore, s 7(1)(b) is invoked far more frequently. Under s 7(1)(b), there are a number of possible instances in which a victim can raise Convention arguments in proceedings in which a public authority is involved. In the contexts covered by this book, the Convention is frequently invoked in criminal proceedings.

5. *Remedies.* Assuming that a breach of the Convention is found, all the familiar remedies, including damages, certiorari (now a quashing order), a declaration or mandamus (a mandatory order), a prohibiting order (now a prohibition) are available so long as they are within the jurisdiction of the relevant court or tribunal. Traditionally, the courts have been reluctant to award damages in public law cases and s 8(3) of the HRA encourages the continuance of this tradition in requiring consideration to be given first to any 'other relief or remedy granted or order made', the consequences of the court's decisions, and the necessity of making the award. If damages are awarded it is on the basis of 'just satisfaction' (s 8(3)). A line of authorities seeks to emphasise that a declaration of a breach of human rights should be considered 'just satisfaction' and no more

---

183   See Chapter 14, pp 763–768.

184   For extensive discussion, see Clayton and Tomlinson, n 168 above, pp 1484–1498.

185   J Miles, 'Standing under the Human Rights Act: Theories of Rights Enforcement and the Nature of Public Law Adjudication' [2000] 59(1) CLJ 133–67, 137.

186   The term 'public authority' will be used to encompass both types of body for the purposes of the rest of the discussion.

should be required by way of redress. In *Anufrijeva and Another v Southwark London Borough Council; R (Mambakasa) v Secretary of State for the Home Office; R(N) v Secretary of State for the Home Office*[187] it was held that: 'Where an infringement of an individual's human rights has occurred, the concern will usually be to bring the infringement to an end and any question of compensation will be of secondary, if any, importance.' The Court of Appeal found that there was a wide discretion as to whether damages should be awarded, and that an award should be made only when it was 'necessary' (s 8(3) HRA) so to do in order to afford just satisfaction. The finding of a violation would often itself be just satisfaction, it found, and damages were to be viewed as a 'remedy of last resort'.[188] The Court further found that the exercise of the discretion as to damages should include consideration of the balance between the interests of the victim and of the public as a whole.[189]

6. It was reaffirmed in *R (Greenfield) v Home Office*[190] that damages need not be awarded. A prisoner who failed a mandatory drugs test was charged and convicted under the Prison Rules 1999 and ordered to serve an additional 21 days' imprisonment. The prisoner alleged that in being denied legal representation at the hearing before the deputy controller of the prison his right to a fair trial had been infringed. The Divisional Court and Court of Appeal dismissed the prisoner's appeal on the grounds that the offence was a prison disciplinary offence and not a criminal offence for the purposes of Art 6. In the Lords, following a decision of the Strasbourg Court, it was conceded that the proceedings did involve a criminal charge; the deputy controller was not an independent tribunal and the prisoner was wrongly denied legal representation. On the prisoner's claim for damages, the Lords held that the approach at Strasbourg that a finding that Art 6 had been violated was, in itself, just satisfaction, and should be followed; so there should be no award of damages to the prisoner.

7. A somewhat similar approach was taken in *Re P.*[191] The Court of Appeal considered whether the judge at first instance had been correct in considering that a declaration of a breach of Art 8 amounted to 'just satisfaction' where a breach of Art 8 had been found on the basis that a mother had been insufficiently involved in the decision by the local authority to abandon a care plan for her rehabilitation with her child. The mother had appealed on the basis of a number of Strasbourg authorities which she claimed entitled her to damages in addition to the declaration. The appeal was ultimately unsuccessful, but their Lordships did indicate that such loss of opportunity cases could attract a damages award.

8. Under s 8(4), the court in deciding to award damages must take into account the principles applied by the European Court of Human Rights. The Strasbourg Court can award compensation under what is now Art 41.[192] The purpose of the reparation is to place the applicant in the position he would have been in had the violation not taken place. Compensation will include costs unless the applicant has received legal aid, although where only part of a claim is upheld, the costs may be diminished accordingly.[193] It can also include loss of earnings, travel costs, fines and costs unjustly

---

187   [2004] QB 1124; [2004] 2 WLR 603.

188   At para 56.

189   *Ibid.*

190   [2005] 2 WLR 240.

191   *C (A Child), Re* [2007] EWCA Civ 2; [2007] 1 FLR 1957.

192   Previously Art 50 under the old numbering of the Articles.

193   *Steel v UK* (App no 24838/94) (1999) 28 EHRR 603, para 125.

awarded against the applicant.[194] Compensation is also available for intangible or non-pecuniary losses such as loss of future earnings[195] or opportunities,[196] unjust imprisonment,[197] stress or loss of personal integrity.[198]

9. There are difficulties in following the principles of the European Court of Human Rights. One is, as Mowbray has pointed out, that the method of determining the award in any particular judgment is frequently unclear.[199] Also, the Court, prior to the changes introduced under Protocol 11, had no independent fact finding role[200] and therefore, where it was unclear that the breach had occasioned the effect in question, it had at times refused to award compensation. The October 2000 Law Commission report 'Damages Under The Human Rights Act 1998'[201] noted that the Strasbourg Court normally applied a strict causation test which barred the majority of claims for pecuniary loss; it argued that the tort measure should be employed under the HRA. Awards at Strasbourg have tended to be modest and its practice is not to award exemplary damages.[202] This is a clear instance in which domestic courts can create higher standards than those maintained at Strasbourg, both in terms of dealing with this issue of causality and in creating a clearer rationale for awards, although they are able to derive guidance from post-1998 Strasbourg decisions taken under the Protocol 11 reforms.

10. In *R (Greenfield) v Home Office*,[203] the House of Lords held that at least in cases involving a breach of Art 6, damages should not be assessed on the same basis as in tort cases. There was no need, it was found, to go beyond the level of damages that would be awarded at Strasbourg. Lord Bingham said:[204]

> The routine treatment of a finding of violation as, in itself, just satisfaction for the violation found reflects the point already made that the focus of the Convention is on the protection of human rights and not the award of compensation.[205]

---

194 See as to heads of loss Burns, N (2001) NLJ 164.

195 E.g. in *Young, James and Webster v UK*, Judgment of 13 August 1981, A 44 (1981), pecuniary and non-pecuniary costs, taking such loss into account, were awarded: the Court ordered £65,000 to be paid.

196 *Weeks v UK* (App no 9787/82) (1987) 10 *EHRR* 293.

197 In *Steel v UK*, at para 122, the three successful applicants were each imprisoned for seven hours. The Court, without giving reasons, awarded them £500 each in compensation for non-pecuniary damage.

198 See further A Mowbray 'The European Court of Human Rights' Approach to Just Satisfaction' [1997] PL 647; Feldman, 'Remedies for Violation of Convention Rights under the HRA' (1998) EHRLR 691; M Amos, 'Damages for Breach of the Human Rights Act' (1999) EHRLR 178; D Fairgrieve, 'The Human Rights Act 1998, Damages and Tort Law' [2001] PL 695–716; Sir Robert Carnwath, 'ECHR Remedies from a Common Law Perspective' (2000) 49 ICLQ 517.

199 Mowbray, *ibid*, p 650.

200 As Leigh and Lustgarten point out in 'Making Rights Real: The Courts, Remedies and the Human Rights Act' [1999] 58(3) CLJ 509, 529.

201 Report No 266, 2000.

202 *BB v United Kingdom* (2004) 39 EHRR 635, para 36.

203 [2005] 1 WLR 673.

204 At [9]–[12].

205 He further said: 'Thus the Court of Appeal (Lord Woolf CJ, Lord Phillips of Worth Matravers MR and Auld LJ) were in my opinion right to say in *Anufrijeva v Southwark London Borough Council* [2003] EWCA Civ 1406; [2004] QB 1124, paras 52–53: 'The remedy of damages generally plays a less prominent role in actions based on breaches of the articles of the Convention, than in actions based on breaches of private law obligations where, more often than not, the only remedy claimed is damages. 53. Where an infringement of an individual's human rights has occurred, the concern will usually be to bring the infringement to an end and any question of compensation will be of secondary, if any, importance.'

He noted that where Art 6 is found to have been breached, the outcome will often be that a decision is quashed and a retrial ordered, which will vindicate the victim's Convention right. He noted that the Court has 'acknowledged the principle of *restitutio in integrum*'.[206] As he found, the Court has

> ordinarily been willing to depart from its practice of finding a violation of Art 6 to be, in itself, just satisfaction under Art 41 only where the Court finds a causal connection between the violation found and the loss for which an applicant claims to be compensated. Such claim may be for specific heads of loss, such as loss of earnings or profits, said to be attributable to the violation. The Court has described this as pecuniary loss, which appears to represent what English lawyers call special damage. This head does not call for consideration here. It is enough to say that the Court has looked for a causal connection, and has on the whole been slow to award such compensation.

He considered the question of general damages, that the Strasbourg Court tends to call non-pecuniary damage. He found that,

> A claim under this head may be put on the straightforward basis that but for the Convention violation found the outcome of the proceedings would probably have been different and more favourable to the applicant, or on the more problematical basis that the violation deprived the applicant of an opportunity to achieve a different result which was not in all the circumstances of the case a valueless opportunity. While in the ordinary way the Court has not been easily persuaded on this last basis, it has in some cases accepted it.[207]

In other words, it has made an award if it considers that the applicant had been deprived of a real chance of a better outcome. He further found[208] that where,

> having found a violation of article 6, the Court has made an award of monetary compensation under Art 41, under either of the heads of general damages considered in this opinion, whether for loss of procedural opportunity or anxiety and frustration, the sums awarded have been noteworthy for their modesty.[209]

On the question whether reliance should be placed on the tort measure of damages or the Strasbourg standard, he said:

---

206 He referred to numerous Strasbourg authorities including a statement of particular authority given by a Grand Chamber on a reference specifically directed to the issue of just satisfaction under Art 41: *Kingsley v United Kingdom* (2002) 35 EHRR 177, para 40: 'The Court recalls that it is well established that the principle underlying the provision of just satisfaction for a breach of Article 6 is that the applicant should as far as possible be put in the position he would have enjoyed had the proceedings complied with the Convention's requirements. The Court will award monetary compensation under Article 41 only where it is satisfied that the loss or damage complained of was actually caused by the violation it has found, since the State cannot be required to pay damages in respect of losses for which it is not responsible.'

207 He referred to numerous cases using the phrase 'a loss of real opportunities' including most recently *Delta v France* (1990) 16 EHRR 574, para 43.

208 At [17].

209 He relied on numerous Strasbourg authorities including in particular *Curley v United Kingdom* (2000) 31 EHRR 401, in which it was said, at para 46: 'It does not, however, consider that the domestic scales of compensation applicable to unlawful detention apply in the present case where there has been no equivalent finding of unlawfulness.'

First, the 1998 Act is not a tort statute. Damages need not ordinarily be awarded to encourage high standards of compliance by member states, since they are already bound in international law to perform their duties under the Convention in good faith. . . Secondly, the purpose of incorporating the Convention in domestic law through the 1998 Act was not to give victims better remedies at home than they could recover in Strasbourg but to give them the same remedies without the delay and expense of resort to Strasbourg. Thirdly, section 8(4) requires a domestic court to take into account the principles applied by the European Court under article 41 not only in determining whether to award damages but also in determining the amount of an award. There could be no clearer indication that courts in this country should look to Strasbourg and not to domestic precedents. . . . . [domestic judges] should not aim to be significantly more or less generous than the Court might be expected to be, in a case where it was willing to make an award at all.[210]

Notes (continued)

11. The Department of Constitutional Affairs 2006 *Review of the Implementation of the Human Rights Act*[211] considered the tiny handful of reported cases where HRA damages have been awarded: *R(Bernard) v Enfield LBC*[212] where £10,000 was awarded to two claimants to reflect the impact of the profoundly disabled wife living in unsuitable accommodation; *R(KB) v Mental Health Review Tribunal*[213] where damages of £750 to £4,000 were awarded for delays in tribunal hearings.

12. In *Van Colle v Chief Constable of Hertfordshire*[214] substantial HRA damages were awarded for breaches of Articles 2 and 8. The award was to parents of a witness murdered due to inadequate police protection and despite pleas to the police for greater protection. In assessing HRA damages Cox J took account of the character and conduct of the parties and the extent and seriousness of the breach; this included: the failure of the police to appreciate the escalating pattern of intimidation or to consider the need to protect the witness; the failure to implement the witness protection protocol. Also relevant was the minor disciplinary sanction imposed on the police officer concerned (a fine of 5 days' pay), the enormous distress and grief of the parents, and the failure of the police to make a suitable apology. Cox J therefore awarded HRA damages of £15,000 for the son's distress in the weeks leading up to his death and £35,000 for the claimants' own grief and suffering.

Private bodies and indirect horizontal effect

What is the position if a private body or person wishes to sue another private body relying on a Convention right? This issue has arisen in the context of Art 8; citizens have sought to obtain remedies against the press for publication without consent of private information. If the citizen could take the newspaper to court relying directly on Art 8, the HRA would create direct 'horizontal' effect. But s 6 appears to prevent the creation of full direct 'horizontal' effect since it only binds public authorities to

---

210   At [19].

211   At 17.

212   (2003) HRLR 111.

213   [2004] QB 836.

214   [2006] EWHC 360 QB.

abide by the ECHR rights. It has been established in a series of cases, extracted below, that legal effects between private parties (for example, citizens, newspapers) are limited to the creation of indirect horizontal effect, that is, the use of the Convention in relation to an *existing* cause of action.

Statutes which affect the legal relations between private parties are affected by s 3 of the HRA and therefore, in this sense, the Act clearly creates indirect horizontal effects.[215] The position was less clear in relation to the common law. As regards the effect of s 6 HRA, this was the area of greatest uncertainty under the Act and it has therefore proved to be a focus for academic debate.[216] Initially the academic debate became polarised, Professor Wade perceiving no distinction between the obligations of private and public bodies[217] and Buxton LJ taking the stance that no horizontal effects are created.[218] In the decisions below, the doctrine of indirect horizontal effect was established, but so far only in the context of Art 8. It became clear that the Court's own duty as a public authority under s 6(1) HRA to act compatibly with Convention rights did not lead to the creation of a free-standing cause of action relying on the Convention rights (as claimed by Wade)—where there was no existing cause of action: there would be no unlawful act by the newspaper entitling the court to grant a remedy. The majority of commentators considered pre-HRA, and in the early post-HRA years, that the inclusion of courts as public authorities under s 6 would at the least heighten the impact of the Convention on the common law,[219] but the nature of that impact remained uncertain for some time.

Venables and Thompson [2001] Fam 430 (extracts)

Butler-Sloss LJ: in my view, the claimants in private law proceedings cannot rely upon a free-standing application under the Convention.

A v B plc [2003] QB 195 (extracts)

Lord Woolf: Under section 6 of the [HRA], the court, as a public authority, is required not to act 'in a way which is incompatible with a Convention right'. The court is able to achieve this by absorbing the rights which articles 8 and 10 protect into the long-established action for breach of confidence.

---

215 It could have been argued that as private individuals do not have Convention rights against each other, there is no need to construe the statute in question compatibly with the rights under s 3. The courts have not taken this stance: *Wilson v the First County Trust Ltd* [2001] 3 All ER 229 is authority for the proposition that where a statute is being interpreted and applied in a dispute between two private parties, the obligation in s 3(1) applies as it would if one of them was a public authority. On this point see N Bamforth, 'The True "Horizontal Effect" of the HRA' (2001) 117 LQR 34.

216 See, e.g. M Hunt, 'The "Horizontal" Effect of the Human Rights Act' [1998] PL 423; I Leigh, 'Horizontal Rights, the Human Rights Act and Privacy: Lessons from the Commonwealth' (1999) 48 ICLQ 57; W Wade, 'The United Kingdom's Bill of Rights', 1998, pp 62–64, and on the Convention generally: A Clapham, *Human Rights in the Private Sphere* (1993); A Clapham, 'The Privatisation of Human Rights' (1995) EHRLR 20; G Phillipson, 'The Human Rights Act, Horizontal Effect' and the Common Law: A Bang or a Whimper' (1999) 62 MLR 824; Buxton LJ, 'The Human Rights Act and Private Law' (2000) 116 LQR 48. Clayton and Tomlinson, n 168 above, provide a very full discussion of the various aspects of 'horizontal effect' that also considers the position in a variety of jurisdictions (pp 204–238).

217 *The United Kingdom's Bill of Rights* (1998), pp 62–63.

218 'The Human Rights Act and Private Law' (2000) 116 LQR 48. Wade, having set out his position in favour of full direct horizontal effect returned to the attack, replying to Buxton LJ in 'Horizons of Horizontality' (2000) 116 LQR 217.

219 See Hunt 'The "Horizontal" Effect of the Human Rights Act' [1998] PL 423; G Phillipson, 'The Human Rights Act, "Horizontal Effect" and the Common Law: A Bang or a Whimper' (1999) 62 MLR 824; Lord Lester and Pannick, n 168 above, p 32 and by Clayton and Tomlinson, n 168 above, pp 236–238. This was precisely the basis of the findings in the early post-HRA decision in *Thompson and Venables v Associated Newspapers and Others* [2001] 1 All ER 908.

Campbell v MGN [2004] 2 AC 457 (extracts)

Lord Hoffman: Even now that the equivalent of article 8 has been enacted as part of English law, it is not directly concerned with the protection of privacy against private persons or corporations. It is, by virtue of section 6 of the 1998 Act, a guarantee of privacy only against public authorities (at [49]).

[Lady Hale approved the above dicta from *A v B* and said]:

> The 1998 Act does not create any new cause of action between private persons. Neither party to this appeal has challenged the basic principles which have emerged from the Court of Appeal in the wake of the Human Rights Act 1998. The 1998 Act does not create any new cause of action between private persons. But if there is a relevant cause of action applicable, the court as a public authority must act compatibly with both parties' Convention rights (at [132]).

[Lord Hope said]:

> In the present case it is convenient to begin by looking at the matter from the standpoint of the respondents' assertion of the article 10 right and the court's duty as a public authority under section 6(1) of the Human Rights Act 1998, which section 12(4) reinforces, not to act in a way which is incompatible with that Convention right.[220]

[Lord Nicholl however said only that]:

> The *values embodied in* articles 8 and 10 are as much applicable in disputes between individuals or between an individual and a non-governmental body such as a newspaper as they are in disputes between individuals and a public authority (at [17], emphasis added).

In the following case, Buxton LJ appeared to accept something akin to an absolute duty under s 6 HRA to develop the common law consistently with the Convention rights, at least in the context of Arts 8 and 10:

McKennitt v Ash [2007] 3 WLR 194 (extracts)

. . . . difficulty has been experienced in explaining how that state obligation is articulated and enforced in actions between private individuals. However, judges of the highest authority have concluded that that follows from section 6(1) and (3) of the Human Rights Act, placing on the courts the obligations appropriate to a public authority. . .

The effect of this guidance is, therefore, that in order to find the rules of the English law of breach of confidence we now have to look in the jurisprudence of articles 8 and 10. Those articles are now not merely of persuasive or parallel effect but, as Lord Woolf says [in *A v B* (*above*)], are the very content of the domestic tort that the English court has to enforce. Accordingly, in a case such as the present, where the complaint is of the wrongful publication of private information, the court has to decide two things. First, is the information private in the sense that it is in principle protected by article 8? If no, that is the end of the case. If yes, the second question arises: in all the circumstances, must the interest of

---

220   *Ibid* at [114].

the owner of the private information yield to the right of freedom of expression conferred on the publisher by article 10? The latter enquiry is commonly referred to as the balancing exercise, and I will use that convenient expression.

Notes

1. The courts have been reluctant to take an explicit position on this matter, but it is implicit in *Campbell* that a form of indirect horizontal effect has been accepted, which appears from *McKennitt* to impose something close to an absolute duty of the courts as public authorities under s 6 HRA to develop the common law compatibly with the rights, rather than a requirement merely to have regard to them.[221] The result has been the dramatic transformation of the pre-existing domestic doctrine of confidence into a remedy for misuse of private information (a 'privacy' remedy). The demands that the duty imposes appear to be determined by the scope of the Convention rights, at least in the context of Arts 8 and 10, following *McKennitt*.

2. The decisions discussed clearly do not mean that *direct* horizontal effect is created—that citizens can simply take another private person or body to court in reliance solely on a claim of breach of a Convention right. Under the HRA litigants can rely on an obligation of the court to develop the common law compatibly with the ECHR rights under s 6 HRA. There is still not a complete consensus on this matter, either among academics[222] or the judiciary. But this appears to be the stance that the courts are taking as the HRA beds in.

3. At present reliance must be placed on an existing cause of action in order to be able to invoke the court's s 6 duty in private common law adjudication. Although it would seem hard for a court to resist the argument that indirect horizontal effect cannot be confined to the context of privacy, the question of the courts' duty in relation to the other Convention rights has not yet been settled.

PROPORTIONALITY, DEFERENCE AND THE 'DISCRETIONARY AREA OF JUDGMENT'[223]

Since the decision of the House of Lords in *Rehman v Secretary of State for the Home Dept*[224] the Home Secretary has been accorded a broad latitude in determining when a risk to national security arises. A broad view was taken by the House of Lords in *Rehman* of the meaning of a threat to national security; it was found that such a threat should be broadly defined to include the possibility of future threats, including those to the UK's allies. However, the degree of deference to the executive shown in *Rehman* has not been as apparent in contexts outside that of national security in decisions taken under the HRA and even within that context less deference has been shown since s 6 HRA and the ECHR jurisprudence have been employed to give the courts a stronger role in curbing executive excess.

---

221   See further. *Murray v Big Pictures Ltd* [2008] EWCA Civ 446.

222   J Beatson and S Grosz: 'Horizontality: A Footnote' (2000) 116 LQR 385; N Bamforth, 'The True "Horizontal Effect" of the Human Rights Act 1998' (2001) 117 LQR 34; D Beyleveld and S Pattinson, 'Horizontal Applicability and Horizontal Effect' (2002) 118 LQR 623; J Morgan 'Questioning the True Effect of the Human Rights Act' [2002] LS 259, and his 'Privacy, Confidence and Horizontal Effect: "Hello" Trouble' [2003] CLJ 443. See Fenwick and Phillipson, *Media Freedom under the HRA* (2006), Chapter 14 which broadly takes the stance that indirect horizontal effect is being created.

223   For the notion of respect for a 'discretionary area of judgment' see D Pannick, 'Principles of Interpretation of Convention rights under the Human Rights Act and the Discretionary Area of Judgement' [1998] PL 545. See further also: P Craig, 'The Courts, the Human Rights Act and Judicial Review' (2001) 117 LQR 589; R Edwards, 'Judicial Review under the Human Rights Act' [2002] 65 CLJ. See further R Edwards, 'Judicial Deference under the Human Rights Act' (2002) 65(6) MLR 859; F Klug, 'Judicial Deference under the Human Rights Act' (2003) 2 EHRLR 125; T Hickman, 'Constitutional Dialogue, Constitutional Theories and the Human Rights Act 1998' [2005] PL 306; C O'Cinneide, 'Democracy and Rights: New Directions in the Human Rights Era' (2004) 57 CLP 175.

224   [1999] INLR 517 (SIAC); [2000] 3 All ER 778, CA; [2001] 3 WLR 877, HL.

As discussed in Chapter 7, decisions at Strasbourg in certain sensitive areas of morality, social policy or relating to national security tend to be influenced by the margin of appreciation doctrine, meaning that Strasbourg is reluctant to interfere with the decision of the Member State.[225] A central issue under the HRA concerns the part to be played, domestically, by the margin of appreciation doctrine. Since it has probably been the key dilutant of Convention standards, as Chapter 7 indicated,[226] it has been essential that UK judges and other public authorities should reject it as a relevant factor in their own decision-making under the Convention, although there are some instances, as indicated below, when it is seen as appropriate to recognise a 'discretionary area of judgment'. As indicated in Chapter 7, the margin of appreciation doctrine is a distinctively international law doctrine, based on the need to respect the decision making of nation states within defined limits. Therefore, it has no application in national law.

When the UK judges apply decisions influenced by the doctrine under the HRA s 2, they can consider whether it is possible and desirable to avoid applying the margin of appreciation aspects of the jurisprudence.[227] While it was clear at the time of the inception of the HRA that the doctrine itself had no application in national law,[228] the obligation to disapply it can be viewed as going much further than merely refusing to import it into domestic decision making. The judiciary have accepted that they should not import the doctrine wholesale into domestic law, but they have shown that they are prepared to rely on decisions at Strasbourg which have been influenced by it. To an extent, this was the approach adopted in the leading pre-HRA case of *R v DPP ex parte Kebilene*:[229] although the doctrine itself was rejected, the outcomes of applications at Strasbourg were taken into account without adverting to the influence the doctrine had had on them.[230]

Thus, the judges have shown at times some unawareness as to the hidden effects of the doctrine. Where they are inclined to show deference, application of Strasbourg decisions influenced by the doctrine, may aid them in doing so. However, where there is a gap in the Strasbourg jurisprudence and it is likely that the ECHR claim at issue might be found to fall within the margin of appreciation accorded to the Member State, the House of Lords has determined, in the recent case of *Re P*[231] (below), that it should itself decide on the claim, even if that means going further in developing the rights than Strasbourg has done or would do.

Ex parte Kebilene [2000] AC 326 (extracts)

Lord Hope: This technique [the margin of appreciation] is not available to the national courts when they are considering Convention issues arising within their own countries [but] ... In some circumstances it will be appropriate for the courts to recognise that there is an area of judgment within which the judiciary will defer, on democratic grounds, to the considered opinion of [the democratic body or person] whose act or decision is said to be incompatible with the Convention.

---

225   See p 336.

226   See p 333, n 2.

227   See M Hunt, R Singh and M Demetriou, 'Is There a Role for the Margin of Appreciation in National Law after the Human Rights Act?' (1999) EHRLR 15.

228   In *R v Stratford JJ ex parte Imbert, The Times*, 21 February 1999, Buxton LJ confirmed *obiter* that the doctrine had no such application. This was also the advice given by the Judicial Studies Board.

229   [1999] 3 WLR 372.

230   Such applications included *H v UK*, App No 15023/89 and *Bates v UK*, Appl No 26280/95.

231   [2008] UKHL 38; [2009] 1 AC 173; [2008] 3 WLR 76.

Brown v Stott [2001] 2 All ER 97, PC (extracts)
(This case is also discussed in Chapter 20, p 126.)

The case arose from a charge of drink-driving. It concerned the compatibility of a statutory provision with a Convention right—Article 6. Under the Scotland Act 1998, acts of members of the Scottish Executive on devolution issues are invalid if they are incompatible with Convention rights (s 57(2)). No declaration of incompatibility is available. A vehicle belonging to Miss Brown was parked in a car park. In reliance on s 172(2) of the Road Traffic Act 1988, a police officer asked Miss Brown who had been the driver of her vehicle when it entered the car park. She answered: 'It was me.' The issue arose whether the procurator fiscal could lead evidence of the admission which Miss Brown had been compelled by law to make under s 172(2).

Lord Steyn: Under the Convention system the primary duty is placed on domestic courts to secure and protect Convention rights. The function of the ECHR is essential but supervisory. In that capacity it accords to domestic courts a margin of appreciation, which recognises that national institutions are in principle better placed than an international court to evaluate local needs and conditions. That principle is logically not applicable to domestic courts. On the other hand, national courts may accord to the decisions of national legislatures some deference where the context justifies it: see *R v DPP ex parte Kebilene*, per Lord Hope of Craighead at pp 993–94 . . .

  This point is well explained in Lester and Pannick (*Human Rights Law and Practice*, 1999, p 74): 'Just as there are circumstances in which an international court will recognise that national institutions are better placed to assess the needs of society, and to make difficult choices between competing considerations, so national courts will accept that there are some circumstances in which the legislature and the executive are better placed to perform those functions.' . . .

  'In my view this factor is of some relevance in the present case. Here s 172(2) addresses a pressing social problem, namely the difficulty of law enforcement in the face of statistics revealing a high accident rate resulting in death and serious injuries. The legislature was entitled to regard the figures of serious accidents as unacceptably high. It really then boils down to the question whether in adopting the procedure enshrined in s 172(2), rather than a reverse burden technique, it took more drastic action than was justified. While this is ultimately a question for the court, it is not unreasonable to regard both techniques as permissible in the field of the driving of vehicles. After all, the subject invites special regulation; objectively the interference is narrowly circumscribed; and it is qualitatively not very different from requiring, for example, a breath specimen from a driver. Moreover, it is less invasive than an essential modern tool of crime detection such as the taking of samples from a suspect for DNA profiling.'

A and others v Secretary of State for the Home Department
[2004] UKHL 56; [2005] 2 AC 68 (extracts)

The case concerned indefinite detention of non-nationals without trial under ss 21 and 23 of Part 4, Anti-Terrorism, Crime and Security Act 2001, a measure adopted to avert the threat of terrorism, taking account of the fact that the suspects could not be deported due to the risk of Art 3 treatment in the receiving country. Section 14 HRA preserves the possibility of escaping from the effects of the Convention rights, within limits. The government considered that the new provisions would be incompatible with Art 5(1) of the Convention, which protects the right to liberty and security of the person, and therefore entered a derogation to Art 5(1), under s 14[232] within the terms of Art 15 of the Convention.[233] Although there is an exception under Art 5(1)(f) allowing for detention of 'a person against whom action is being taken with a view to deportation or extradition', it would not cover the lengthy detentions envisaged during which deportation proceedings would not be in being and attempts to find a safe third country had manifestly failed.[234] This case concerned the challenge of the detainees to their detention. In this instance, in the very sensitive context of national security—one in certain respects more within the area of competence of the executive rather than that of the judiciary—Lord Bingham in the majority gave indications as to the circumstances in which a degree of deference would be appropriate. Rather than accept that deference should be paid to the legislature or executive in a general sense, he considered that different institutional competences might make *degrees* of deference appropriate. He considered that the Home Secretary was entitled to take the view that an emergency situation was in being, on the basis that a degree of deference should be paid on the grounds of 'institutional competence,' in the sense that the Home Secretary had to make an essentially political judgment.

Lord Bingham: . . .I would accept that great weight should be given to the judgment of the Home Secretary, his colleagues and Parliament on this question, because they were called on to exercise a pre-eminently political judgment. It involved making a factual prediction of what various people around the world might or might not do. . . It would have been irresponsible not to err, if at all, on the side of safety (at 29).

[Nevertheless, he went on to find that the measures taken to meet it were disproportionate to the aims pursued.]

32. The evidence before SIAC was that the Home Secretary considered 'that the serious threats to the nation emanated predominantly (albeit not exclusively) and more immediately from the category of foreign nationals'. In para 95 of its judgment SIAC held: 'But the evidence before us demonstrates beyond argument that the threat is not so confined [i.e. is not confined to the alien section of the population]. There are many British nationals already identified—mostly in detention abroad—who fall within the definition of "suspected international terrorists," and it was clear from the submissions made to us that in the opinion of the [Home Secretary] there are others at liberty in the United Kingdom who could be similarly defined.'

This finding has not been challenged, and since SIAC is the responsible fact-finding tribunal it is unnecessary to examine the basis of it. There was however evidence before SIAC that 'upwards of a thousand individuals from the UK are estimated on the basis of intelligence to have attended training camps in Afghanistan in the last five years,' that some British citizens are said to have planned to return from Afghanistan to the United Kingdom and that 'The backgrounds of those detained show the high level of involvement of British citizens and those otherwise connected with the United Kingdom in the terrorist networks.' It seems plain that the threat to the United Kingdom did not derive solely from foreign nationals or from foreign nationals whom it was unlawful to deport. Later evidence, not

---

232   The Human Rights Act (Designated Derogation) Order 2001, SI 2001/3644.

233   See Chapter 7, pp 336–341.

234   See *Chahal v UK* (1996) 23 EHRR 413, para 113. Deportation proceedings should be in being and it should be clear that they are being prosecuted with due diligence.

before SIAC or the Court of Appeal, supports that conclusion. The Newton Committee recorded the Home Office argument that the threat from Al-Qaeda terrorism was predominantly from foreigners but drew attention (para 193) to 'accumulating evidence that this is not now the case. The British suicide bombers who attacked Tel Aviv in May 2003, Richard Reid ("the Shoe Bomber"), and recent arrests suggest that the threat from UK citizens is real. Almost 30% of Terrorism Act 2000 suspects in the past year have been British. We have been told that, of the people of interest to the authorities because of their suspected involvement in international terrorism, nearly half are British nationals.'

33. It is plain that sections 21 and 23 of the 2001 Act do not address the threat presented by UK nationals since they do not provide for the certification and detention of UK nationals.

[Lord Bingham refused to accept the *full* claim made for deference by the executive]:

37 . . . the Attorney General . . . directed the weight of his submission to challenging the standard of judicial review for which the appellants contended. . . . He submitted that as it was for Parliament and the executive to assess the threat facing the nation, so it was for those bodies and not the courts to judge the response necessary to protect the security of the public. These were matters of a political character calling for an exercise of political and not judicial judgment. . . . .

As will become apparent, I do not accept the full breadth of the Attorney General's argument on what is generally called the deference owed by the courts to the political authorities. It is perhaps preferable to approach this question as one of demarcation of functions or what Liberty in its written case called 'relative institutional competence'. The more purely political (in a broad or narrow sense) a question is, the more appropriate it will be for political resolution and the less likely it is to be an appropriate matter for judicial decision. The smaller, therefore, will be the potential role of the court. . . The present question seems to me to be very much at the political end of the spectrum: . . . the appellants have shown no ground strong enough to warrant displacing the Secretary of State's decision on this important threshold question . . . Even in a terrorist situation the Convention organs have not been willing to relax their residual supervisory role . . . [in *Korematsu v United States]*: '. . . in times of distress the shield of military necessity and national security must not be used to protect governmental actions from close scrutiny and accountability.'

It follows from this analysis that the appellants are in my opinion entitled to invite the courts to review, on proportionality grounds, the Derogation Order and the compatibility with the Convention of section 23 and the courts are not effectively precluded by any doctrine of deference from scrutinising the issues raised. . .

But the function of independent judges charged to interpret and apply the law is universally recognised as a cardinal feature of the modern democratic state, a cornerstone of the rule of law itself. The Attorney General is fully entitled to insist on the proper limits of judicial authority, but he is wrong to stigmatise judicial decision making as in some way undemocratic. It is particularly inappropriate in a case such as the present in which Parliament has expressly legislated in section 6 of the 1998 Act to render unlawful any act of a public authority, including a court, incompatible with a Convention right, has required courts (in section 2) to take account of relevant Strasbourg jurisprudence, has (in section 3) required courts, so far as possible, to give effect to Convention rights and has conferred a right of appeal on derogation issues. The effect is not, of course, to override the sovereign legislative authority of the Queen in Parliament, since if primary legislation is declared to be incompatible the validity of the legislation is unaffected (section 4(6)) and the remedy lies with the appropriate minister (section 10), who is answerable to Parliament. The 1998 Act gives the courts a very specific, wholly democratic, mandate. As Professor Jowell has put it, 'The courts are charged by Parliament with delineating the boundaries of a rights-based democracy'.

Huang v Secretary of State for the Home Dept [2007] 2 AC 167, HL (extracts)

19. In *de Freitas v Permanent Secretary of Ministry of Agriculture, Fisheries, Lands and Housing* [1999] 1 AC 69, 80, the Privy Council, drawing on South African, Canadian and Zimbabwean authority, defined the questions generally to be asked in deciding whether a measure is proportionate: 'whether: (i) the legislative objective is sufficiently important to justify limiting a fundamental right; (ii) the measures designed to meet the legislative objective are rationally connected to it; and (iii) the means used to impair the right or freedom are no more than is necessary to accomplish the objective.'

   This formulation has been widely cited and applied. But counsel for the applicants (with the support of Liberty, in a valuable written intervention) suggested that the formulation was deficient in omitting reference to an overriding requirement which featured in the judgment of Dickson CJ in *R v Oakes* [1986] 1 SCR 103, from which this approach to proportionality derives. This feature is (p 139) the need to balance the interests of society with those of individuals and groups. This is indeed an aspect which should never be overlooked or discounted. The House recognised as much in *R (Razgar) v Secretary of State for the Home Department* [2004] UKHL 27; [2004] 2 AC 368, paras 17–20, 26, 27, 60, 77, when, having suggested a series of questions which an adjudicator would have to ask and answer in deciding a Convention question, it said that the judgment on proportionality 'must always involve the striking of a fair balance between the rights of the individual and the interests of the community which is inherent in the whole of the Convention. The severity and consequences of the interference will call for careful assessment at this stage' (see para 20). If, as counsel suggest, insufficient attention has been paid to this requirement, the failure should be made good.

20. In an article 8 case where this question is reached, the ultimate question for the appellate immigration authority is whether the refusal of leave to enter or remain, in circumstances where the life of the family cannot reasonably be expected to be enjoyed elsewhere, taking full account of all considerations weighing in favour of the refusal, prejudices the family life of the applicant in a manner sufficiently serious to amount to a breach of the fundamental right protected by article 8. If the answer to this question is affirmative, the refusal is unlawful and the authority must so decide. . . .

21. Mrs Huang was successful in her appeal to an adjudicator, but that decision was reversed on the Secretary of State's appeal to the Immigration Appeal Tribunal. Mr Kashmiri was unsuccessful before both the adjudicator and the Immigration Appeal Tribunal. The Court of Appeal ([2006] QB 1, para 63) found the decisions of the Tribunal in each case to be legally defective, since both, following the approach laid down in *M (Croatia) v Secretary of State for the Home Department* [2004] INLR 327, adopted a review approach incorrectly based on deference to the Secretary of State's view of proportionality.

In re P and others (AP) (Appellants) (Northern Ireland) [2009] 1 AC 173 (extracts)

One of the key issues that arose in this case concerned the employment of the Human Rights Act in this instance in which the Strasbourg—if it had heard the claim—might well have found that the claim lay within a state's margin of appreciation. The Lords could have found that if the claim would probably not succeed before the Strasbourg Court (although that was not certain) then the English courts should also find that it would fail before the domestic courts under the Human Rights Act on the basis that the domestic courts under the HRA need do no more than Strasbourg would have done. Lord Hoffmann did *not* take this stance: 'In such a case, it for the court in the United Kingdom to interpret articles 8 and 14 and to apply the division between the decision-making powers of courts and Parliament in the way which appears appropriate for the United Kingdom. The margin of appreciation is there for division between the three branches of government according to our principles of the separation of powers. There is no principle by which it is automatically appropriated by the legislative branch.'[235]

[Lord Hope of Craigenhead considered the question of deference to the legislature in relation to the claim that unmarried couples should be allowed to adopt even though an Order of the Northern Ireland Assembly did not allow them to. He did *not* consider that deference should be shown to the legislature on the issue]:

In the light of this background it is clear that the choices that would have to be made, if a measure about eligibility for adoption were to be put before the Assembly, would be choices on an aspect of social policy. I think that it is clear too that these are choices about which opinions may reasonably differ in a modern democratic society. The choice is a particularly sensitive one because it is plain that it would not be possible, compatibly with articles 8 and 14 of the Convention, for the Assembly to extend eligibility to unmarried couples of the opposite sex without extending it to same sex unmarried couples also: see *EB v France*, application no 43546/02, 22 January 2008. In that case the Strasbourg court said that where a State had gone beyond its obligations under article 8 in creating a right to adopt it could not, in the application of that right, take discriminatory measures within the meaning of article 14: para 49. My first instinct therefore was to regard the issue of principle as one that ought to be taken by the legislature and not by the courts, for the reasons that I gave in *R v Director of Public Prosecutions, ex p Kebilene* [2000] 2 AC 326, 381.

The Court of Appeal adopted the approach which I suggested in *Kebilene*. But I have come to the view that it is not determinative in this case. It is, of course, now well settled that the best guide as to whether the courts should deal with the issue is whether it lies within the field of social or economic policy on the one hand or of the constitutional responsibility which resides especially with them on the other: see, for example, *R (Pro Life Alliance) v British Broadcasting Corporation* [2003] UKHL 23; [2004] 1 AC 185, para 136, per Lord Walker of Gestingthorpe. The fact that the issue is a political issue too adds weight to the argument that, because it lies in the area of social policy, it is best left to the judgment of the legislature. But the reason why I differ from the Court of Appeal's approach is that it lies in the latter area as well. Cases about discrimination in an area of social policy, which is what this case is, will always be appropriate for judicial scrutiny. The constitutional responsibility in this area of our law resides with the courts. The more contentious the issue is, the greater the risk is that some people will be discriminated against in ways that engage their Convention rights. It is for the courts to see that this does not happen. It is with them that the ultimate safeguard against discrimination rests.

I am not persuaded that extending eligibility to the appellants would give rise to practical difficulties of a kind that would make intervention by the courts inappropriate. All we would be saying is that they were to be treated, for the purposes of eligibility for adoption, as if

---

235   At [37].

they were married to each other. The assessment of their suitability as a couple is an entirely different matter. The facts must be examined as they are. Regard must be had to all the circumstances in deciding on any course of action, as article 9 of the 1987 Order makes clear. A major revision of the law of adoption, such as that which has taken place in Great Britain, would no doubt require much additional work to be done by way of subordinate legislation and departmental guidance. But I do not see this as being made necessary by the decision about eligibility which we are being asked to make in this case. In *Bellinger v Bellinger (Lord Chancellor intervening)* [2003] 2 AC 467 the House declined to recognise the acquired gender of a transsexual person for the purposes of the right to marry. But this would have represented a major change in the law with far-reaching ramifications, not the least of which was where the line was to be drawn to mark the transition from one sex to another, as Lord Nicholls of Birkenhead pointed out in paras 37–41. In my opinion the problems that would have followed from it were of a wholly different order from those which would follow from a decision that the appellants are eligible to be considered as the child's adoptive parents although they are unmarried.

Baroness Hale . . . So what did Parliament mean when it required the courts to act compatibly with the Convention rights? Did it mean us only to go as far as Strasbourg would go? Or did it mean us, in at least some cases, to be able to go further? It seems clear that Parliament recognised the problem and intended the latter. . .

Lord Mance. . . In the case of subordinate legislation like the Adoption (Northern Ireland) Order 1987, the application of s 6(1) is not constrained by s 6(2) of the 1998 Act (and no question therefore arises of making a declaration of incompatibility under s 4). In performing their duties under ss. 3 and 6, courts must of course give appropriate weight to considerations of relative institutional competence, that is 'to the decisions of a representative legislature and a democratic government within the discretionary area of judgment accorded to those bodies': see *Brown v. Stott* [2003] 1 AC 681, 703, though the precise weight will depend on inter alia the nature of the right and whether it falls within an area in which the legislature, executive or judiciary can claim particular expertise: see *R v. DPP, ex p. Kebilene* [2000] 2 AC 326, 381 per Lord Hope of Craighead.

The House's attention was drawn in argument to the review of the Northern Irish legislative position regarding adoption, which has been under way for a considerable period and to which my noble and learned friend Lord Walker refers at paragraphs 72 to 78. The House was asked to allow this process to proceed, and the desirability of such an issue being resolved by the legislature was a significant factor in the judgments of both Gillen J at first instance in April 2006 and the Court of Appeal in June 2007. But it was not suggested that, if the House formed the view that the regime governing adoption in force in Northern Ireland under the Adoption (Northern Ireland) Order 1987 was objectively unjustified, it could on the facts of this case be an answer to the complaint of discrimination that national authorities had required time to adapt their laws to meet changing patterns of behaviour or attitudes (cf *M v. Secretary of State for Work and Pensions* [2006] UKHL 11; [2006] 2 AC 91). The absolute exclusion from eligibility for adoption of unmarried opposite sex couples in all circumstances in Northern Ireland represents discrimination which has been identified as unjustified for a long period.

Note

For detailed analysis of this decision, see A Kavanagh, 'Strasbourg, the House of Lords or Elected Politicians: Who decides about Rights after *Re P*?' (2009) 72(5) MLR 828.

Lord Steyn, 'Deference: a tangled story' (2005) *Public Law* 346

Acting within its jurisdiction, a court may in certain circumstances consider it right to defer to the views of the other branches of government. That itself is, of course, a judicial decision. While in the British constitution the disentangling of the legislature and the executive is not always easy, it may be right to say that the courts will more readily defer to Parliament than to the executive. But the decision to defer is by law a matter entrusted to the discretion of the courts.

The principle underlying cases where the court decides to refrain from arriving at its own view on the merits of an issue is usually discussed under the general rubric of deference. It refers to the idea of a court, exceptionally, out of respect for other branches of government and in recognition of their democratic decision-making role, declining to make its own independent judgment on a particular issue. . . . .

Lester and Pannick state, in the framework of the ECHR, what the underlying principle is. They say:

> This doctrine concerns not the legal limits to jurisdiction but the wise exercise of judicial discretion having regard to the limits of the courts' institutional capacity and the constitutional principle of separation of powers. It is essential that the courts do not abdicate their responsibilities by developing self-denying limits on their powers.

This observation encapsulates much of what deference is about.

First, separation of powers requires judges to concentrate on disputes which properly come before them and to avoid straying into legislative and executive business. Secondly, the court must sometimes consider in the context of the particular case before it, where an issue of deference arguably arises, whether the context and circumstances of the case require the court to defer on a specific issue to the view of the legislature or the executive. It is not a matter of law: it is a matter of discretion to be exercised in the objective circumstances of the particular case. Thirdly, what courts may not do is to abdicate any part of their jurisdiction. That is so under the 1998 Act where Parliament itself has entrusted a constitutional role to the court. The same is true outside the scope of the 1998 Act.

Parliament itself laid upon our courts the duty to decide whether Convention rights have been breached. In Roth Simon Brown L.J. (now Lord Brown of Eaton-under-Heywood) said: 'The court's role under the Human Rights Act is as the guardian of human rights. It cannot abdicate this responsibility.' In point of principle there cannot be any no-go areas under the ECHR and for the rule of law. On the other hand, the courts may recognise that in a particular case and in respect of a particular dispute, Parliament or the executive may be better placed to decide certain questions. The courts ought not to take such decisions on a priori grounds without scrutiny of the challenged decision since nobody can know in advance whether it has been infected by manifest illegality. This is a balanced approach well suited to the needs of our mature democracy.

There are powerful policy reasons why courts should never abdicate their democratic and constitutional responsibilities. The truth is that even democratic governments sometimes flagrantly abuse their powers and need to face open and effective justice. . . .

At the risk of over-simplification I would summarise the position as follows. The rule of law requires that courts do not surrender their responsibilities. So far as the courts desist from making decisions in a particular case it should not be on grounds of separation of powers, or other constitutional principle. Deference may lead courts not to make their own judgments on an issue. The degree of deference which the courts should show will, of course, depend on and vary with the context. The true justification for a court exceptionally declining to decide an issue, which is within its jurisdiction, is the relative institutional competence or capacity of the branches of government.

Lord Hoffmann observed:

Under the constitution of the United Kingdom and most other countries, decisions as to whether something is or is not in the interests of national security are not a matter for judicial decision. They are entrusted to the executive.

Lord Hoffmann explained this approach as follows:

It is not only that the executive has access to special information and expertise in these matters. It is also that such decisions, with serious potential results for the community, require a legitimacy which can be conferred only by entrusting them to persons responsible to the community through the democratic process.

. . . The structure of the ECHR makes clear that an interference with the relevant Convention right is only justifiable if it is in accordance with the law and necessary in a democratic society, criteria upon which the view of the executive cannot possibly be conclusive. Indeed it is the very ethos of the ECHR that the courts will be the arbiters of these criteria. In one sense all these concepts involve matters of policy under Lord Hoffmann's formulation in ProLife Alliance. But it cannot be right to say that these are issues which constitutional principle withdraws from decision by the courts.

Numerous other decisions of the European Court show that issues of national security do not fall beyond the competence of national courts. But, self evidently, national courts must give substantial weight to the views of the executive on matters of national security. So far I have examined the reasoning of Lord Hoffmann mainly in the context of national security, public safety and related concepts. I have done so first because the occasion for deference will perhaps most frequently and credibly arise in this area. But Lord Hoffmann's reasoning strikes wider. He states that 'the principle that majority approval is necessary for a proper decision on policy or allocation of resources is also a legal principle'. On this reasoning such decisions are beyond the competence of the courts.

. . . there cannot be a legal principle requiring the court to desist from making a judgment on the issues in such cases [on policy or resource allocation]. In interpreting legislation the courts must simply, with the aid of all relevant internal and external sources, try to find the contextual meaning of a given text. There is in my view no justification for a court to adopt an a priori view in favour of economic conservatism.

In common law adjudication it is an everyday occurrence for courts to consider, together with principled arguments, the balance sheet of policy advantages and disadvantages. It would be a matter of public disquiet if the courts did not do so. Of course, in striking the balance the courts may arrive at a result unacceptable to Parliament. In such cases Parliament can act with great speed to reverse the effect of a decision. It has done so in the past. That is in the spirit of our constitution, and is wholly in accord with the democratic ideal. But there is no need to create a legal principle requiring the courts to abstain from ruling on policy matters or allocation of resource issues. On the other hand, the objective circumstances will dictate whether there is a need for deference to the view of other branches of government on the particular issue. It is obvious that the courts may only develop the law in the spaces left by Parliament. What does this mean? The context is all important. The only possible generalisation is this: when Parliament has spoken on the matter, there is no scope for judicial innovation. On the other hand, when Parliament has not spoken, the position is different. Parliamentary inaction is usually explicable on many different grounds. It is generally not a sure foundation for courts to refuse to decide cases in accordance with their constitutional duties.

There is a valuable body of academic literature on this subject. A recent analysis by Professor Jeffrey Jowell Q.C. is particularly persuasive. After setting out Lord Hoffmann's views in some detail he summarised his conclusion as follows:

> In so far as the courts . . . concede competence to another branch of government, it seems to me that such a concession is not a matter of law, nor based upon any legal principle as Lord Hoffmann contends. Lord Hoffmann is right that it is for the courts to decide the scope of rights, but there is no magic legal or other formula to identify the 'discretionary area of judgment' available to the reviewed body. In deciding whether matters such as national security, or public interest, or morals should be permitted to prevail over a right, the courts must consider not only the rational exercise of discretion by the reviewed body but also the imperatives of a rights-based democracy. In the course of some of the steps in the process of this assessment the courts may properly acknowledge their own institutional limitations. In doing so, however, they should guard against a presumption that matters of public interest are outside their competence and be ever aware that they are now the ultimate arbiters (although not ultimate guarantors) of the necessary qualities of a democracy in which the popular will is no longer always expected to prevail.

This passage encapsulates a balanced approach. I would respectfully commend it.

Notes

1. *The discretionary area of judgment.* In *R v DPP ex parte Kebilene*[236] (above) Lord Hope said that the margin of appreciation doctrine is not available to the national courts when considering Convention issues. Nevertheless, he considered that there would be circumstances which would make it appropriate for the courts to show deference. He considered that there could be an area of judgement within which the judiciary would defer 'to the considered opinion of [the democratic body or person] whose act or decision is said to be incompatible with the Convention'. In the context of the case, which concerned the compatibility of primary terrorist legislation with the Convention, these findings were used to justify a deferential approach. The approach was one which sought to introduce qualifications into a guarantee which on its face was unqualified. The term used by Lord Hope to describe the area in which choices between individual rights and societal interests might arise was 'the discretionary area of judgment'; he found that it would be easier for such an area of judgment to be recognised 'where the Convention itself requires a balance to be struck, much less so where the right [as in Article 6(2)] is stated in terms which are unqualified. . . But even where the right is stated in [such] terms. . .the courts will need to bear in

---

mind the jurisprudence of the European Court which recognises that due account should be taken of the special nature of terrorist crime and the threat which it poses to a democratic society'.[237]

2. In support of his balancing approach, Lord Hope referred to Lord Woolf's findings in *Attorney-General of Hong Kong v Lee Kwong-kut*.[238] Lord Woolf considered the Canadian approach when applying the Canadian Charter of Rights and Freedoms, Article 1 of which states that the rights and freedoms which it guarantees are: '. . .subject only to such reasonable limits prescribed by law as can be demonstrably justified in a free and democratic society.' He said: 'In a case where there is real difficulty, where the case is close to the borderline, regard can be had to the approach now developed by the Canadian courts in respect of section 1 of their Charter.'

    The approach of Lord Hope in *ex parte Kebilene* towards the development of a broad domestic doctrine of deference was based on a watering down of the Convention rights since a provision equivalent to Art 1 of the Charter was omitted from the basic Convention rights under Arts 2–7. Thus, a minimalist approach to the rights, aided by interpretations of the European Court or Commission of Human Rights influenced by the margin of appreciation doctrine, allows the courts, in certain circumstances, to adopt a deferential stance accorded to the democratically elected legislature. But Lord Hope's doctrine of deference depends on the area of policy under consideration. In *Re P* (extracted above and see also below) Lord Hope considered that in the area in question—discrimination in relation to a social policy—deference was not required.

3. In *Brown v Stott,* as seen above, the Lords adopted an approach of according an area of discretion to the legislature in coming to its decision. Bearing that doctrine in mind, it was argued that Art 6 itself does not expressly require that coerced statements should be excluded from evidence and that although a right to freedom from self-incrimination could be implied into it, the right had not been treated at Strasbourg as an absolute right. The Lords relied on decisions to that effect at Strasbourg that had been influenced by the margin of appreciation doctrine. Lord Bingham found: 'Limited qualification of [Art 6] rights is acceptable if reasonably directed by national authorities towards a clear and proper public objective and if representing no greater qualification than the situation calls for.' The objective in question was the laudable one of curbing traffic accidents. On that basis, by importing a form of balancing test into Art 6, it was found that answers given under s 172 could be adduced in evidence at trial. The decision, it is suggested, exemplified a minimalist approach in the sense that it required a 'reading down' of the Convention right in question. The combination of the uses of the doctrine of deference to the legislature, combined with the use of Strasbourg decisions affected by the margin of appreciation doctrine, led, it is argued, to a decision that afforded the right a lesser significance than Strasbourg has accorded it.

    If the intention had been to balance the rights in Art 6 against a range of societal interests, a paragraph could have been included, as in Arts 8–11, setting out the exceptions and the tests to be applied in using them. Alternatively, a general exception could have been included, as in Art 1 of the Canadian Charter. The decision not to adopt either of these courses implies that there is little or no room for the use of implied exceptions. In so far as Strasbourg has suggested that the Art 6 rights are qualified, the Lords should have considered whether adoption of that stance was due to the use of the doctrine of the margin of appreciation.

4. *Proportionality*. In *A and others*—probably the most significant decision under the HRA—the appellants founded on the proportionality principles discussed in Chapter 15, adopted by the Privy Council in *de Freitas v Permanent Secretary of Ministry of Agriculture, Fisheries, Lands and*

---

237   He gave the example of the ruling of the Court in *Murray v UK* (App no 14310/88) (1994) 19 EHRR 193, p 222, para 47.

238   [1993] AC 951, at 966.

239   [1999] 1 AC 69, 80.

Housing.[239] As to the second test from *de Freitas*, the appellants argued that ss 21 and 23 of Part 4, Anti-Terrorism, Crime and Security Act 2001 did not rationally address the threat to the security of the United Kingdom presented by Al-Qaeda terrorists and their supporters because (a) it did not address the threat presented by UK nationals, (b) it permitted foreign nationals suspected of being Al-Qaeda terrorists or their supporters to pursue their activities abroad if there was any country to which they were able to go, and (c) the sections permitted the certification and detention of persons who were not suspected of presenting any threat to the security of the United Kingdom as Al-Qaeda terrorists or supporters.

As to the third test from *de Freitas*—the 'less intrusive means' proportionality test—the appellants argued that if the threat presented to the security of the United Kingdom by UK nationals suspected of being Al-Qaeda terrorists or their supporters could be addressed *without* infringing their right to personal liberty, it had not been shown why similar measures could not adequately address the threat presented by foreign nationals.[240] In other words, less intrusive means were available, and were being used, which could therefore also have been used against foreign nationals suspected of terrorist activity. Lord Bingham viewed these arguments as to the disproportionality of the Part 4 scheme with the aims pursued as sound. Lord Bingham was not prepared to accept that the grave intrusion into liberty represented by indefinite detention could be justified by the harm sought to be averted—the terrorist threat.[241]

5. An activist approach recognises the existence of a discretionary area of judgment, but does so on carefully scrutinised grounds, as Lord Steyn indicates above (Deference: A tangled story). In *A and others*—the *Belmarsh* case—Lord Bingham's findings indicate that where deference is demanded due to the very political nature of a security-based decision, that does not mean that deference should be extended equally to all aspects of that decision. He therefore created differentiation in terms of the deference to be accorded to the threshold decision as to the existence of an emergency and to the decision as to the measures required to be adopted to meet it. *A and others* indicates that the discretionary area of judgment accorded to the executive or legislature is narrowing considerably, in some contexts almost to vanishing point, which is in accordance with s 6 HRA.[242] Clearly, if a court accepts that a decision-maker is acting within a discretionary area of judgment, and then proceeds as a result to choose a weak proportionality test, then it is deliberately disabling itself from being able to discover whether the rights-infringing decision was genuinely necessary. Since the Convention itself allows for exceptions to the rights, the building in of further deference is unnecessary, except where there are compelling reasons to do so, such as that, in the national security context, the decision-maker is in possession of sensitive information not available to the judiciary.

6. In *Re P* the Lords took a similarly activist stance, finding not only that domestic courts could take a more expansive stance to the scope of ECHR rights than would be likely to be taken at Strasbourg, but also that in so doing deference need not be accorded to the Northern Ireland Assembly. Lord Hope (see above) stated that the Lords did not need to take a deferential stance because the matter—discrimination—was one that fell peculiarly within the sphere of judicial responsibility: 'Cases about discrimination in an area of social policy, which is what this case is, will always be appropriate for judicial scrutiny. The *constitutional responsibility in this area of our law resides with the courts*' (emphasis added). Thus, in a strikingly bold move, the Lords decided to quash a legislative order for Northern Ireland.

---

240 At [31].

241 At [36].

242 See further Clayton, 'Judicial Deference and 'Democratic Dialogue': The Legitimacy of Judicial Intervention under the Human Rights Act 1998' [2004] PL 33.

7. *Huang* (above) confirms that the proportionality analysis under the HRA should be fully conducted and that any doctrine of deference cannot stand in the way of carrying out that analysis. Thus, even where the relevant legislation appears to have taken account of factors that allow an interference with Art 8 (or one of the other materially qualified rights—Arts 9, 10, 11) to be justified under Art 8(2), on the basis that the measure is viewed as necessary in a democratic society, which includes the need to show that the measure is proportionate to the aims pursued,[243] that does not absolve the court from carrying out the exercise afresh itself.

Conclusions on the HRA

F Klug, 'A bill of rights: do we need one or do we already have one?' (2007) *Public Law* 701

Surveying the literature on bills of rights across the globe, Alston. . . points to three common characteristics:

- they provide protection for those human rights which are considered, at a given moment in history, to be of particular importance;
- they are binding upon governments and can only overridden with significant difficulty (Alston avoids the phrase 'judicial entrenchment' and does not exclude the possibility that they *can* be overridden);
- they provide some form of redress in the event that violations occur.

All these characteristics, I would maintain, co-exist to some degree in the HRA. As with most post-war bills of rights, the HRA draws its inspiration and principles from the 1948 Universal Declaration of Human Rights and the broad, ethical values it proclaims, aimed at establishing fair and tolerant societies. This is explicit in the preamble to the ECHR, most of whose rights are incorporated in the HRA. As such, the HRA does indeed uphold a swathe of the fundamental rights considered to be important—the first of Alston's defining characteristics—although, admittedly, the ECHR lags behind some of the more recent human rights instruments; for example, in its characterisation of equality and in its neglect of children's rights. . .

Crucially, however, British courts can develop their *own* interpretation of the broad values in the HRA, provided this does not *'weaken'* the protection afforded by the ECHR. This capacity is an essential hallmark that distinguishes the HRA from an incorporated treaty typical of monist systems, of which there are many in Europe, where ratification of a treaty *automatically* binds the national authorities, including the courts, to comply with its provisions. Contrary to recent, *misleading* statements by the Leader of the Conservative Party that the HRA 'obliged British courts to base their judgements on the ECHR and [its] case law . . . giving them no scope to develop their own principles', judges are required under HRA s 2 to 'take account of' the European Court case-law, but are not *bound* by it. . . .

Recently, however, the courts have started to row back on Parliament's intention to allow them to develop their own jurisprudence under the HRA. [Klug considers cases such as

---

Ullah and goes on]. . . As. . .Masterman, has pointed out, the Convention *itself* 'assumes that the domestic courts will *also* take a progressive approach' to rights and should be 'free to develop an enhanced protection within their national legal system'. This argument is given force by the 'margin of appreciation' doctrine which means there are many issues on which there is no persuasive Strasbourg authority at all. Sir Andrew Morritt V.C. got to the heart of the matter when he said in *Aston Cantlow* that the judges' task 'is not to cast around in the European Human Rights Reports like black letter lawyers seeking clues. In the light of s.2(1) of the HRA, it is to draw out the broad principles which animate the Convention.' This approach is what distinguishes the HRA from an incorporated treaty. It is what places it in the realm of a bill of rights that takes its source from a regional human rights treaty but is interpreted by domestic judges, who also draw from the human rights jurisprudence of *other* jurisdictions where appropriate. As. . .Wintemute has commented, 'if a country voluntarily incorporates the exact wording of the Convention into its national law, the Convention ceases to be a European text and becomes a *national* text, to which national courts are free to give a more generous interpretation'.

Alston's second indicator—that bills of rights should be binding on the executive—is another defining principle of the HRA. Governments, like the courts and all public authorities, are explicitly prohibited from acting incompatibly with the rights it upholds. The HRA is the only domestic statute (excluding the European Communities Act) that is determinative of *future* legislation, as well as past, and it is governments, of course, that are the prime initiator of laws. There is, as is well established, a significant caveat to this requirement under the Act. Whilst exhibiting many features of a 'higher law' to which all other laws and policies must conform where '*possible*', the HRA prohibits courts from striking down Acts of Parliament. . . .Lord Hope, in *Shayler,* correctly stated that where legislation cannot be interpreted to remove an incompatibility under HRA s.3, 'the position whether it should be amended so as to remove the incompatibility must be left to Parliament' and the only option left to the courts is to issue a DOI. In reality, however, the government has never ignored such declarations. Of the 16 DOIs issued by the higher courts and still standing (out of 22 made altogether) the government has responded either by amending, or committing to amend, the legislation or policy at issue, or changing the offending practice. They might refuse to do so in the future, but this is likely to be far from usual.

And whilst it is quite true that Parliament can still theoretically pass any domestic legislation it wishes (exempting EU-driven law and subject to the censure of the ECtHR), breaches of fundamental rights have become far more *transparent,* as we are seeing with the current tussles over control orders. Ministers are now statutorily bound to declare whether Bills they introduce respect fundamental rights and the courts are constitutionally empowered to review Acts of Parliament for the *first time in British history.*

With the establishment of the increasingly authoritative parliamentary Joint Committee on Human Rights, whose self-defined remit now includes evaluating government responses to DOIs, the executive, legislature and judiciary each have a role in rights compliance. They are effectively engaged in a dialogue about the nature of human rights and how they should be applied, as Jack Straw predicted they would be when piloting the Human Rights Bill through Parliament nearly 10 years ago.

It is wrong to assume, as some constitutional lawyers do, that this approach to rights compliance, sometimes referred to as the 'dialogue model', was introduced *solely* to protect the *'doctrine of parliamentary sovereignty '* and hence retain the ultimate authority of government. It was adopted partly for this reason but also to address the perceived 'democratic deficit' characteristic of bills of rights with judicial strike down powers, notably in the United States, South Africa and Germany. In these jurisdictions the power to determine the meaning of broad values such as liberty or privacy—and to rewrite or repeal laws which do not conform to that meaning—are handed from elected politicians to unaccountable judges who effectively become *legislators* in the process.

The 'dialogue model' was a response to this stumbling block to support for bills of rights within the Labour Party, which, as we saw, was largely sceptical about handing judges the power to strike down legislation and so hamper the policies of a future Labour government. The model reflected a considered view, given clear expression by Geoffrey Palmer, the former New Zealand Minister of Justice, in the White Paper that heralded the 1990 New Zealand Bill of Rights, that 'in a great many cases where controversial issues arise . . . there is no 'right' [human rights] answer'. Many of us who were involved in the campaign for a bill of rights in the early 1990s, including myself, held the view that the interpretation of broad values inherent in all bills of rights—such as the right to life or the legitimate limits of free speech—often involves philosophical or quasi-political judgments that are better determined by elected representatives, with the courts acting as a *check on the executive,* rather than as a primary decision-taker or law-maker.

Jack Straw emphasised from the outset that higher courts 'could make a Declaration [of Incompatibility] that, subsequently, Ministers propose and Parliament accepts, should *not* be accepted'. The example he gave was abortion law, but he might have added advertising restrictions, gun controls and election expenditure limits, all issues that courts with strike down powers in other jurisdictions have determined breach their bills of rights. As . . . Gearty has put it 'the genius of the HRA' model invites 'the political back in to control the legal at just the moment when the supremacy of the legal discourse seems assured'. The fact that Parliament (or more accurately, the government acting through Parliament) still has 'the final say' under the HRA should not be confused with 'business as usual'. The HRA clearly *refines*—though does not *overturn*—the doctrine of 'parliamentary sovereignty', as successive Home Secretaries have volubly complained. Governments and parliaments are now accountable for their actions to a set of internationally recognised human rights values enshrined in the HRA, which they can no longer ignore with impunity, using the will of the electorate as 'cover'. Alston's qualification, that it should only be possible to override a bill of rights *'with difficulty'*, applies to the HRA.

Alston's third defining feature—redress for rights violations—is also present in the HRA. . . .there is now a growing list of people who have benefited, when prior to the HRA they would have had no remedy at all—from the Belmarsh detainees who were subject to indefinite detention without trial to disabled people subject to undignified treatment in their own home. . . .

[But] Bills of rights are not just legal and constitutional documents. They have a symbolic role in highlighting the fundamental values that signify what a country stands for. They are intended to act as a baseline of common principles in a diverse society.

Assessed against these criteria, the HRA has clearly failed to past muster. Support for introducing a bill of rights, at nearly 80 per cent, has remained fairly consistent over the last 15 years, according to the ICM 'State of the Nation' polls; the inference being that the HRA is generally *not* considered *to be one*. The reality is that the Act has never been sufficiently 'owned' by British people as '*their* bill of rights'. Three main factors account for this, in my view.

First, the HRA appeared like a bolt out of the blue to most people. Whereas years of local and national public consultation preceded bills of rights in Canada, New Zealand and South Africa in the 1980s and 1990s (and, more recently, in the Australian Capital Territories and the state of Victoria) there was no prior consultation in the United Kingdom. Very little groundwork was done to prepare for the introduction of the HRA beyond the publication of *Bringing Rights Home,* the discussion document Labour issued before it came to power and a large-scale training programme for the judiciary prior to the Act coming into force.

This has been compounded, *until recently,* by an absence of consistent political leadership and no statutory Human Rights Commission to explain the role and purpose of the HRA. Whilst the Act was always promoted as a means of 'bringing rights home', early references to it as a major constitutional innovation, acting as Britain's bill of rights, were soon buried. The more the HRA revealed its potency, the more the government seemed intent on playing down its significance, in the hopes it might wither away. In 1998 Jack Straw described the HRA as 'one of the most important pieces of constitutional legislation the UK has seen'. Lord Irvine suggested it 'occupies a central position in our integrated programme of constitutional change'. But by 2002 ministers were insisting that 'the Act is primarily about access to justice in our own courts'. The accompanying narrative suggested this was no more than a 'tidying up' measure to complete the process that had begun in the 1950s with the ratification of the ECHR. For anyone who didn't much like anything with the title European in it, this was hardly a convincing selling point!

Secondly, the lack of a strong narrative about the HRA left the field wide open for the furtive imagination of the tabloids, in search of easy copy, to exploit with fervour. Once the inevitable reality dawned that the HRA, as a 'higher law', was far more potent than the 'bringing rights home' narrative suggested, the tabloid press had a field day, inventing stories based on cases that never happened or had little to do with the Act itself, with no government rebuttal unit, until recently, to counter these urban myths. The tabloids have effectively created a subtitle to the Act in the public's mind which reads: human rights for FTPs: foreigners, terrorists, and paedophiles—law abiding citizens need not apply. Much of this is reminiscent of the media frenzy that accompanied the introduction of race and sex discrimination legislation in the 1970s. Time will tell whether the Lord Chancellor's recently launched campaign—*Human Rights are Common Sense*—and the new Commission for Equality and Human Rights (CEHR), the first British statutory body charged with promoting the values in the HRA, will succeed in rehabilitating it.

The third, and possibly most important reason why the HRA has failed to bed down smoothly, is that it has been rather *too* successful at challenging the executive for the government's comfort. In an inverse imitation of Frankenstein's monster, the Act's own creator has increasingly turned against it.

CONCLUSIONS

Traditionally, it is expected in the UK that the courts and Parliament will control badly thought-out repressive laws introduced in the face of a crisis. The current crisis caused by terrorist activity in the post-9/11 years is viewed by the Government as of particular magnitude. But the UK judiciary has controlled the executive to quite a surprising extent; indeed, they have responded to draconian legislation introduced in this crisis *more* robustly than in relation to previous ones, as a comparison between *Rehman* and the Belmarsh case of *A and others* reveals. The reason for the difference lies in the inception of the Human Rights Act which has encouraged the judges to take a more active role as the protectors of human rights. Nevertheless, it could be said at the same time that the Human Rights Act has been shown to have failed since in two instances, in the counter-terrorism context, the House of Lords under the HRA has not upheld standards as high as those upheld at Strasbourg and has had to be 'corrected' by Strasbourg.[244]

But although that is the case, it would be premature to conclude that the HRA has failed in that it did not fully bring rights home. It has had a general ameliorating effect on counter-terrorist legislation; had it not been in place *greater* deference would have been likely to be accorded to the executive. In contexts *outside* the counter-terrorism one, it has often had a significant impact in upholding human rights, as Klug argues above, and as is apparent, to an extent, from the discussions in the succeeding chapters.[245] Now that a Liberal-Conservative Government is in power it is possible that it will eventually repeal the HRA, since that was Conservative policy prior to the 2010 General Election. If so, human rights will be safeguarded by the methods discussed at the beginning of this chapter (unless a new British Bill of Rights is introduced instead of the HRA). But that would tend to mean that in some instances lower standards of human rights would be maintained and that the UK would be more likely to be found to have violated the European Convention on Human Rights at Strasbourg. Thus, while the HRA has not fully brought rights home as it was intended by the Labour Government in 2000 to do, the humiliation in human rights terms that may await the UK if the HRA is repealed would be likely to be greater than it has been in the last ten years—from 2000–2010.

Questions

1   Assume that the Government wishes to reinstate the 'rape shield' provisions affected by the ruling of the Lords in *R v A;* it intends to introduce legislation in Parliament with this object in mind. What, if anything, could be done to safeguard such legislation from further judicial intervention based on s 3 HRA?

2   A statute is passed in 2011 which contains the following provision: 'Section 3 of the Human Rights Act is hereby repealed.' How might the courts react to the provision when deciding cases raising Convention points and how might they react to subsequent legislation which appeared to be inconsistent with one or more of the Convention rights?

3   Indications have emerged as to those bodies which are bound by the Convention rights since they have public functions within the meaning of s 6 HRA, and as to those bodies which have no such functions and so are not bound by the rights. Do you find the bases for distinguishing between these bodies convincing and coherent? Is there a convincing rationale underlying this distinction between private and public bodies?

---

244 In *Gillan and Quinton v UK* (App no 4158/05), judgment of 12 January 2010—see pp 1155–1156—which in effect corrected the Lords in *R (On the application of Gillan) v Commissioner of Police for the Metropolis* [2006] UKHL 12; [1964] 2 WLR 689—see pp 1151–1152—and in *A and others v UK* (above pp 308–310) which in effect corrected the Lords in *MB* (see p 967 above).

245 See in particular pp 1125–1128 and p 1191 for examples of this tendency.

❹ How much force, if any, is there in Waldron's argument (above) in relation to the protection for the Convention rights under the Human Rights Act, as opposed to making provision for their formal entrenchment?

❺ Consider the following position: after election of a Conservative Government the UK adopts a new domestic Bill of Rights 2013, stating (in s 1) that all future enactments of Parliament will take effect subject to its terms unless they expressly state that they are to have effect notwithstanding its provisions. Subsequently, statute A is enacted, s 9 of which provides that it is to take effect notwithstanding the provisions of Art 10 of the UK Bill of Rights, which protects a right to respect for private life. In the following year, statute B, s 3 of which makes further provision in the same area as s 9, is enacted, but without a notwithstanding clause. Statute A has impliedly repealed part of Art 10.

Assuming that s 3 of statute B is incompatible with the impliedly repealed area of Art 10, would the courts give effect to s 3? Would the answer to this question differ if statute A was later repealed? Would it matter whether statute A was impliedly or expressly repealed?

FURTHER READING

S Bailey and N Taylor, *Bailey, Harris and Jones: Civil Liberties: Cases and Materials*, 6th edn (2009), Chapter 1

R Clayton and H Tomlinson (eds), *The Law of Human Rights* 2nd edn (2008), esp. Chapters 3, 4, 5

C Donnelly (2007) *Delegation of Governmental Power to Private Parties*

D Feldman, *Civil Liberties and Human Rights*, 2nd edn (2002), Chapter 2

H Fenwick, *Civil Liberties and Human Rights*, 4th edn (2007), Chapters 3 and 4

H Fenwick, G Phillipson and R Masterson, *Judicial Reasoning under the UK Human Rights Act* (2007)

J Jowell and J Cooper (eds), *How the Human Rights Act is Working and for Whom* (2003)

A Kavanagh, *Constitutional Review under the Human Rights Act* (2009)

I Leigh and R Masterman, *Making Rights Real—The Human Rights Act in its First Decade* (2008)

A Lester, D Pannick and J Herberg: *Human Rights Law and Practice* 3rd edn (2009)

R Stone, *Textbook on Civil Liberties and Human Rights*, 7th edn (2008)

AL Young, *Parliamentary Sovereignty and the Human Rights Act* (2008)

M Arden, 'Human Rights in the Age of Terrorism' (2005) 121 LQR 604

Colin D Campbell, 'The Nature of Power as Public in English Judicial Review' [2009] CLJ 90

R Clayton, 'Judicial Deference and "Democratic Dialogue"' [2004] PL 33

R Clayton, 'The Human Rights Act Six Years On: Where are we Now?' (2007) EHRLR 11

R Edwards, 'Judicial Deference under the Human Rights Act' (2002) 65 MLR 859

K Ewing, 'The Futility of the Human Rights Act' [2004] PL 829

K Ewing, 'The Human Rights Act and Parliamentary Democracy' (1999) 62 MLR 79

S Fredman, 'From Deference to Democracy' [2006] LQR 53

A Kavanagh, 'The Elusive Divide between Interpretation and Legislation under the Human Rights Act 1998' (2004) OJLS 259

A Kavanagh, 'Unlocking the Human Rights Act: "The Radical" Approach to Section 3(1)' (2005) EHRLR 260

A Kavanagh, 'The Role of Parliamentary Intention in Adjudication under the HRA 1998' (2006) OJLS 153

R Kay, 'The ECHR and the Control of Private Law' (2005) EHRLR 466

F Klug, 'Judicial Deference under the Human Rights Act 1998' (2003) EHRLR 125

F Klug and K Starmer, 'Standing Back From the Human Rights Act: How Effective is it 5 Years On?' [2005] PL 716

F Klug, 'The Long Road to Human Rights Compliance' [2006] NILQ 186

F Klug, 'A Bill of Rights: Do We Need One or Do We Already Have One?' [2007] PL 701

J Landau, 'Functional Public Authorities after *YL*' [2007] 630

T Lewis, 'The European Ceiling on Human Rights' [2007] PL 720

M McDermott, 'The Elusive Nature of the Public Function' (2003) 66 MLR 113

D Nicol, 'Statutory Interpretation and Human Rights after *Anderson*' [2004] PL 274

C O'Brien, 'Judicial Review under the Human Rights Act: Legislative or Applied Review?' (2007) EHRLR 550

T Poole, 'Legitimacy, Rights and Judicial Review' (2005) OJLS 697

J Steyn, 'Dynamic Interpretation amidst an Orgy of Statutes' (2004) EHRLR 245

J Steyn, '2000–2005: Laying the Foundations of Human Rights Law in the United Kingdom' (2005) 4 EHRLR 349

A Williams 'A Fresh Perspective on Hybrid Public Authorities under the Human Rights Act: Private Contractors, Rights-Stripping and "Chameleonic" Horizontal Effect' [2010] PL, forthcoming

CHAPTER 18
FREEDOM OF EXPRESSION

INTRODUCTION

Freedom of expression is widely regarded as one of the most significant human rights. For example, in the US the first amendment to the constitution provides: 'Congress shall make no law. . .abridging the freedom of speech or of the press.' The justifications for according this particular freedom such significance have been much debated. One of the most significant is that citizens cannot participate fully in a democracy unless they have a reasonable understanding of political issues; therefore, open debate on such matters is essential. In *Derbyshire County Council v Times Newspapers*,[1] Lord Keith, in holding that neither local nor central government could sustain an action in defamation, said: 'It is of the highest importance that a democratically elected governmental body. . .should be open to uninhibited public criticism.' Barendt considers that this theory is 'probably the most attractive. . .of the free speech theories in modern Western democracies', and concludes that 'it has been the most influential theory in the development of 20th century free speech law'.[2] Barendt also accepts the validity of the thesis that freedom of speech is necessary to enable individual self-fulfilment.[3] It is argued that individuals will not be able to develop morally and intellectually unless they are free to air views and ideas in debate with each other.

These justifications have received recognition within the Strasbourg and UK expression of jurisprudence. The European Court of Human Rights has repeatedly asserted that freedom of expression 'constitutes one of the essential foundations of a democratic society',[4] and that it is applicable not only to 'information' or 'ideas' that are favourably received or regarded as inoffensive or as a matter of indifference, but also to those that 'offend, shock or disturb'.[5] Particular stress has been laid upon the pre-eminent role of the press in a state governed by the Rule of Law which, in 'its vital role of public watchdog' has a duty 'to impart information and ideas on matters of public interest' which the public 'has a right to receive'.[6] It is a marked feature of the Strasbourg jurisprudence that clearly political speech receives a much more robust degree of protection than other types of expression. Thus the 'political' speech cases of *Sunday Times v UK*,[7] *Jersild v Denmark*,[8] *Lingens v Austria*,[9] *Thorgeirson v Iceland*,[10] all resulted in findings that Art 10 had been violated and all were marked by an intensive review of the restriction in question in which the margin of appreciation was narrowed almost to vanishing point.[11]

---

1 [1993] AC 534.

2 E Barendt, *Freedom of Speech* (1987), pp 20 and 23 respectively.

3 *Ibid*, p 15.

4 *Observer and Guardian v UK*, Series A No 216; (1991) 14 EHRR 153, para 59.

5 See, e.g. *Thorgeirson v Iceland* (1992) 14 EHRR 843, para 63.

6 *Castells v Spain*, Series A No 236, (1992) 14 EHRR 445, para 43.

7 (1979) 2 EHRR 245.

8 (1994) 19 EHRR 1. *Jersild v Denmark* concerned an application by a Danish journalist who had been convicted of an offence of racially offensive behaviour after preparing and broadcasting a programme about racism which included overtly racist speech by the subjects of the documentary.

9 (1986) 8 EHRR 103. *Lingens* concerned the defamation of a political figure. See further, *Lombardo v Malta* (2009) 48 EHRR 23 which concerned a comment by a newspaper on the lack of public consultation by Figura Local Council.

10 (1992) 14 EHRR 843. *Thorgeirson* concerned newspaper articles reporting allegations of brutality against the Reykjavik police. See further *Selisto v Finland* [2005] EMLR 8, which concerned a newspaper article reporting allegations of professional misconduct by a member of the medical profession.

11 See the discussion of the doctrine in Chapter 7, p 336.

A similar pattern may be found in the domestic free speech jurisprudence. Earlier pronouncements to the effect that 'The media. . .are an essential foundation of any democracy'[12] were emphatically reinforced by pronouncements in the House of Lords' decision in *Reynolds v Times Newspapers*,[13] which afforded an explicit recognition to their duty to inform the people on matters of legitimate public interest. Media freedom in relation to political expression has clearly been recognised as having a particularly high value in UK law and Convention jurisprudence. The argument from self-development—that the freedom to engage in the free expression and reception of ideas and opinions in various media is essential to human development—has received some recognition at Strasbourg[14] and in the House of Lords.[15]

However, freedom of expression is not absolute in any jurisdiction; other interests can overcome it, including the interests in protecting morals, the reputation of others, national security, fair trials and public order. In fact, freedom of expression comes into conflict with a greater variety of interests than any other liberty and is therefore in more danger of being curtailed. Most Bills of Rights list these interests as exceptions to the primary right of freedom of expression, as does the European Convention on Human Rights (ECHR), Art 10. This obviously does not mean that the mere invocation of the other interest will lead to displacement of freedom of expression; there must be strong reasons for allowing the other interest to prevail. Under Article 10 of the Convention it is necessary to show that there is a pressing social need to allow the other interest to prevail.[16]

Prior to the inception of the Human Rights Act 1998 (HRA), Art 10 of the ECHR was taken into account by the courts in construing ambiguous legislation on the basis, as Chapter 17 indicated, that as Parliament must have intended to comply with its treaty obligations, an interpretation should be adopted which would allow it to do so.[17] Article 10 was also, pre-HRA, taken into account where there was ambiguity in the common law.[18] Combined with the effects of certain very significant decisions finding against the UK at Strasbourg,[19] Art 10 had a greater impact on UK law than its fellow article, Art 11, even pre-HRA. However, its impact has been variable. It has not had as much impact as might perhaps have been expected as far as the laws of obscenity and decency are concerned. As Chapter 19 explains, it has also had little effect on expression in the form of public protest. As Chapter 13 indicates, access to information was not found to be covered by Art 10 until recently, although such access is viewed as associated with expression.

Under s 3 HRA, the obligation to interpret legislation compatibly with Art 10, and the related Arts 9 and 11 (see Chapter 7), is much stronger than it was in the pre-HRA era, while the courts and other public authorities, including the police, are bound by the Convention under s 6 to uphold freedom of expression. Section 12 HRA has an impact when a court is considering granting a remedy in civil proceedings which affects freedom of expression.[20] Article 10 provides a strong safeguard for freedom

---

12   *Francome v MGN* [1984] 2 All ER 408, 898, *per* Sir John Donaldson.

13   [1999] 3 WLR 1010.

14   The European Court of Human Rights has frequently asserted that freedom of expression is one of the essential foundations for the 'development of everyone' (in, e.g. *Otto-Preminger v Austria* (1994) 19 EHRR 34, para 49).

15   *Per* Lord Steyn in *Secretary of State for the Home Department ex parte Simms* [2000] AC 115; [1999] 3 WLR 328, at 498.

16   See Chapter 7, pp 330–332 and below, pp 1050–1051.

17   See pp 939–944.

18   See p 943.

19   See below pp 1050–1051 and Chapter 7 pp 331–332.

20   See Chapter 17 p 952, and below, p 1024.

of expression in relation to competing interests, since it takes the primary right as its starting point. The content of speech will rarely exclude it from the protection of Art 10, although not all speech is included.[21] Article 10(2) demands that interferences with the primary right should be both necessary and proportionate to the legitimate aim pursued. But interferences with expression have not all been subject to the same intensity of scrutiny at Strasbourg due to the hierarchy of expression recognised under Art 10, political expression being viewed as of the highest value.

This chapter will indicate that there are two methods of protecting those interests which compete with freedom of expression: prior and subsequent restraints. Prior restraints, including censorship, are generally seen as more pernicious. Subsequent restraints operate after publication of the article in question: the persons responsible may face civil or criminal liability. The trial may then generate publicity and the defendants may have an opportunity of demonstrating why the publication was in the public interest. However, the distinction between the two kinds of restraint may not be as stark as this implies. Subsequent restraints may have a chilling effect on publications; editors and others may well not wish to risk the possibility of incurring liability.

A judicial willingness to respect the values of freedom of expression became apparent in the 1990s.[22] This chapter considers the judges' concern, in the context of both prior and subsequent restraints, to strike a balance between free expression and a variety of other interests in the pre-HRA era, and then goes on to indicate the impact that Art 10, as given further effect under the HRA, has been having in this area over the last ten years since 2000. The main concern of this chapter and the next one (which concerns free expression in the context of public protest) is to evaluate the changes in this 'balance' which are occurring under the HRA. Obviously, in a book of this nature, it is not possible to address such a vast topic comprehensively. In particular, for reasons of space, we have not been able to deal with 'hate speech' offences.[23] It should however be noted that the ancient common law offence of blasphemy, very rarely prosecuted, was finally abolished in 2008.[24]

RESTRAINING FREEDOM OF EXPRESSION TO PROTECT THE STATE OR GOVERNMENT

Introduction

Broadly speaking, speech criticising or attacking the Government or purporting to reveal state abuse of power will not attract criminal or civil liability.[25] However, there are a number of qualifications to this general rule. Journalists revealing material covered by the Official Secrets Act 1989 risk prosecution. Information on which such criticism or attacks might be based may not be available either because, as

---

21 In *Jersild v Denmark* (1994) 19 EHRR 1 it was assumed that the actual racist utterances of racists in a broadcast were not protected.

22 See the House of Lords' decision in the *Derbyshire* case [1993] AC 534 and *ex parte Simms* [1999] QB 349.

23 Recently extended to cover inciting hatred on grounds of religious belief (Racial and Religious Hatred Act 2006) and sexual orientation (Criminal Justice and Immigration Act 2008, s 74 and Sched 17).

24 By s 79 Criminal Justice and Immigration Act 2008; for commentary on blasphemy, see Fenwick and Phillipson, *Media Freedom under the Human Rights Act* (2006), Chapter 15.

25 See Lord Keith's comments in the *Derbyshire* case [1993] AC 534.

discussed in Chapter 13, it is covered by the Official Secrets Act 1989 or because, although the Act does not apply, it is unavailable under the Freedom of Information Act 2000.[26]

However, apart from the methods of controlling the release of state information discussed in Chapter 13, there are certain other disparate means available to the Government in order to suppress or constrain speech which may be viewed as undermining the state, emanations of the state or Government. Two such means are discussed in this section, and the regulation of political broadcasting is also considered.

Breach of confidence

Introduction[27]

Breach of confidence is a civil remedy affording protection against the disclosure or use of information which is not generally known, and which has been entrusted in circumstances imposing an obligation not to disclose it without authorisation from the person who originally imparted it. This area of law developed as a means of protecting secret information belonging to individuals and organisations. However, it can also be used by the Government to prevent disclosure of sensitive information and is in that sense a substitute for or complementary to the other measures available, including the Official Secrets Act 1989.[28] It is clear that governments are prepared to use actions for breach of confidence against civil servants and others in instances falling outside the categories of information covered by that Act—or within them. In some respects, breach of confidence actions may be more valuable than the criminal sanctions provided by the 1989 Act. Their use may attract less publicity than a criminal trial, no jury will be involved and they offer the possibility of quickly obtaining an interim injunction.

However, where the Government, as opposed to a private individual, is concerned, the courts have not been prepared to accept readily that it is in the public interest that the information should be kept confidential. It has to be shown that the public interest in keeping the information confidential due to the harm its disclosure would cause is not outweighed by the public interest in disclosure. This issue was considered in *Attorney-General v Jonathan Cape*,[29] below. The nature of the public interest defence—the interest in disclosure—was clarified in *Lion Laboratories v Evans and Express Newspapers*.[30] The Court of Appeal held that the defence extended beyond situations in which there had been serious wrongdoing by the plaintiff. Even where the plaintiff was blameless, publication would be excusable where it was possible to show a serious and legitimate interest in the revelation.

Under the HRA, since use of this doctrine in this context may create a direct interference with political speech, Art 10 demands that its use should be subject to careful scrutiny, and the public interest question tended to become, post-HRA, a matter to be looked at within Art 10 parameters. Since this is a common law doctrine, s 3 HRA does not apply. But the courts have a duty under s 6 HRA to develop the doctrine compatibly with Art 10. In cases concerning state information this is of less significance than in cases concerning the private information of individuals since the state body in

---

26   Seditious libel is still theoretically an offence but there are no recent cases. See *Burns* (1886) 16 Cox 355; *Aldred* (1909) 22 Cox CC 1; *cf Caunt* (1947) unreported, but see (1948) 64 LQR 203; for comment see Barendt, n 2 above, pp 152–60.An attempt to extend it to cover attacks on Islam failed in *R v Chief Metropolitan Magistrate ex parte Choudhury* [1991] 1 QB 429 (see M Tregilgas-Davey (1991) 54 MLR 294–99).

27   General reading: SJ Bailey, N Taylor *Bailey, Harris and Jones: Civil Liberties: Cases and Materials*, 6th edn (2009), pp 803–22; D Feldman, *Civil Liberties and Human Rights*, 2nd edn (2002), pp 872–89.

28   See Chapter 13, p 669 *et seq.*

29   [1976] QB 752.

30   [1985] QB 526.

question will also be a public authority and so *itself* bound by s 6 to abide by the ECHR rights. Thus the court can be viewed as adjudicating on the state's claim to prevent disclosure of the information in the context of the state body's own duty to comply with the demands of Art 10.

Section 12 HRA is also applicable where interference with the right to freedom of expression is in issue as it inevitably will be in this context (see Chapter 17, pp 952–953). Section 12(4) requires the court to have particular regard to the right to freedom of expression under Art 10. Thus, s 12(4) provides added weight to the argument that in the instance in which the state seeks to suppress the expression of an individual using this doctrine, the court must carefully consider the pressing social need to do so and the requirements of proportionality under Art 10(2), interpreting those require-ments strictly. In considering Art 10 the court should, under s 12(4)(a), take into account the extent to which the material is or is about to become available to the public, and the public interest in publica-tion. These two matters are now central in breach of confidence actions. As *Attorney-General v Times Newspapers*[31] (below) demonstrates, s 12(4) has made it more difficult for the state to obtain an injunction where a small amount of prior publication has taken place.

Interim injunctions

In breach of confidence actions the Attorney-General, as indicated below, typically seeks an interim injunction and then, if it is obtained, the case may proceed to the trial of the permanent injunction. This possibility was very valuable to the Government because, in many instances, the other party (usually a newspaper) did not pursue the case to a trial of the permanent injunction since the secret was often no longer newsworthy by that time. However, s 12(3) of the HRA provides that no relief which, if granted, might affect the exercise of the Convention right to freedom of expression is to be granted so as to restrain publication before trial, unless the court is satisfied that the applicant is likely to establish that publication should not be allowed. The leading case on the interpretation of s 12(3) is now *Cream Holdings Limited and others v Banerjee and others*.[32] The House of Lords had to consider the proper test to be applied in deciding whether to grant an injunction against publication of confidential information, taking account of the terms of s 12(3) HRA. The old test was that, as a threshold test, the applicant had to show that he or she had a 'real prospect of success' at final trial. If so, the court would consider where the 'balance of convenience' lay[33] between the case for granting an injunction and that of leaving the applicant to his or her remedy in damages. So in *Banerjee* the Lords had to consider the modification of that test under the HRA. Lord Nicholls noted that press concerns under the old 'balance of convenience' test lay behind the enactment of s 12(3). The leading speech was delivered by Lord Nicholls, with whom all their Lordships agreed. His Lordship said:

> 'Likely' in section 12(3) cannot have been intended to mean 'more likely than not' in all situations [emphasis added]. . . the general approach should be that courts will be exceedingly slow to make interim restraint orders where the applicant has not satisfied the court he will probably ('more likely than not') succeed at the trial. In general, that should be the threshold an applicant must cross before the court embarks on exercising its discretion, duly taking into account the relevant juris-prudence on article 10 and any countervailing Convention rights. But there will be cases where it is necessary for a court to depart from this general approach and a

---

31 [2001] 1 WLR 885.

32 [2004] 3 WLR 918. For comment see ATH Smith 'Freedom of the Press and Prior Restraint' [2005] 64(1) CLJ 4.

33 *American Cyanamid Co v Ethicon Ltd* [1975] AC 396.

> lesser degree of likelihood will suffice . . .[34] cases may arise where the adverse consequences of disclosure of information would be extremely serious, such as a grave risk of personal injury to a particular person. Threats may have been made against a person accused or convicted of a crime or a person who gave evidence at a trial. . .Despite the potential seriousness of the adverse consequences of disclosure, the applicant's claim to confidentiality may be weak.[35]

Lord Nicholls further had in mind the less contentious instance in which an injunction of short duration (days or hours) is required in order to give a judge time to consider the case properly:

> an application [may be] made to the court for an interlocutory injunction to restrain publication of allegedly confidential or private information until trial. The judge needs an opportunity to read and consider the evidence and submissions of both parties. Until then the judge will often not be in a position to decide whether on balance of probability the applicant will succeed in obtaining a permanent injunction at the trial. In the nature of things this will take time, however speedily the proceedings are arranged and conducted. . . . Confidentiality, once breached, is lost for ever.[36]

Moreover, *ex parte* injunctions cannot be granted under s 12(2) unless there are compelling reasons why the respondent should not be notified or the applicant has taken all reasonable steps to notify the respondent.

Changes in the doctrine

All these requirements under the HRA must now be taken into account in adjudicating on Government claims that information should not be disclosed under the doctrine of confidence. The result is that the doctrine appears post-HRA to be undergoing quite a significant change from the interpretation afforded to it in the *Spycatcher* litigation (below). The series of cases set out below begins with the decision in *Jonathan Cape* in which the ingredients of the breach of confidence action in this context are reiterated, and an indication is given as to the approach taken by the courts pre-HRA to the balance to be struck between the public interest in maintaining confidence and the interest in disclosure. It moves on to the changes evident in the post-HRA cases.

Attorney-General v Jonathan Cape [1975] 3 WLR 606[37] (extracts)

The Attorney-General invoked the law of confidence to try to stop publication of Richard Crossman's memoirs on the ground that they concerned Cabinet discussions. The diaries of Mr Crossman, a Cabinet Minister in the Wilson Government, included detailed accounts of Cabinet and Cabinet Committee meetings, including the attribution to members of views which they expressed there. The Lord Chief Justice accepted that such public secrets could be restrained, but only on the basis that the balance of the public interest came down

---

34   See n 32 above at [22].

35   *Ibid*, at [19].

36   *Ibid* at [17]–[18].

37   [1976] QB 752; [1975] 3 All ER 484.

in favour of suppression. As the discussions had taken place 10 years previously it was not possible to show that harm would flow from their disclosure; the public interest in publication therefore prevailed.

Lord Widgery CJ: The Attorney-General contends that all cabinet papers and discussions are prima facie confidential, and that the court should restrain any disclosure thereof if the public interest in concealment outweighs the public interest in a right to free publication.

. . .in *Coco v AN Clarke Ltd* [1969] RPC 41 at 47 Megarry J, reviewing the authorities, set out the requirements necessary for an action based on breach of confidence to succeed:

> In my judgment three elements are normally required if, apart from contract, a case of breach of confidence is to succeed. First, the information itself. . .must 'have the necessary quality of confidence about it'. Secondly, that information must have been imparted in circumstances importing an obligation of confidence. Thirdly, there must be an unauthorised use of that information to the detriment of the party communicating it. . . .

In my judgment, the Attorney General has made out his claim that the expression of individual opinions by Cabinet ministers in the course of Cabinet discussion are matters of confidence, the publication of which can be restrained by the court when this is clearly necessary in the public interest. . . .

[However The court should intervene only in the clearest of cases where the continuing confidentiality of the material can be demonstrated. In less clear cases—and this, in my view, is certainly one—reliance must be placed on the good sense and good taste of the Minister or ex-Minister concerned.

For these reasons I do not think that the court should interfere with the publication of volume 1 of the diaries and I propose, therefore, to refuse the injunctions sought. . .

Attorney-General v Guardian Newspapers Ltd [1987] 1 WLR 1248 (extracts)

In 1985 the Attorney-General commenced proceedings in New South Wales[38] in an attempt (which was ultimately unsuccessful)[39] to restrain publication of *Spycatcher* by Peter Wright. The book included allegations of illegal activity engaged in by MI5 and alleged that some MI5 officers had conspired to destabilise the Labour Government under Harold Wilson. In the UK on 22 and 23 June 1986, *The Guardian* and *The Observer* published reports of the forthcoming hearing which included some *Spycatcher* material, and on 27 June the Attorney-General obtained temporary *ex parte* injunctions preventing them from further disclosure of such material. *Inter partes* injunctions were granted against the newspapers on 11 July 1986 by Millet J. On 12 July 1987, the *Sunday Times* began publishing extracts from *Spycatcher* and the Attorney-General obtained an injunction restraining publication on 16 July. On 14 July 1987 the book was published in the United States and many copies were brought into the UK. *The Guardian* and *The Observer* applied to the Vice-Chancellor for discharge of the injunctions.

Sir Nicolas Browne-Wilkinson VC: There are three applications. The first two are made by *The Guardian* and *The Observer* newspapers to discharge interlocutory junctions made

---

38 (1987) 8 NSWLR 341.

39 High Court of Australia (1988) 165 CLR 30; for comment, see M Turnbull (1989) 105 LQR 382.

against them in two orders made by Millett J on 11 July 1986 and confirmed (subject to minor modifications) by the Court of Appeal on 25 July 1986. . . .

In my judgment, there has been a most substantial change in circumstances. In 1986, as I have said, the publication in *The Guardian* and *The Observer* was, so far as that court was aware and so far as I am aware, the only breach in the security walls. Otherwise the matter had not hit the press in any way, save that the action was pending in Australia. Of the allegations made by Mr Wright in the book there had been no other indication.

[Due to the change in circumstances, the Vice-Chancellor discharged the Millet injunctions, but they were restored by the Court of Appeal ([1987] 3 All ER 316) in modified form. The newspapers appealed to the House of Lords ([1987] 3 All ER 316, 346–47).]

Lord Brandon of Oakbrook: I was a party to the majority decision of this House given on 30 July 1987 that the injunctions in issue should not be discharged but should be continued until trial. My reasons for being a party to that decision can be summarised in nine propositions as follows.

1 The action brought by the Attorney General against *The Guardian* and *The Observer* has as its object the protection of an important public interest, namely the maintenance so far as possible of the secrecy of the British security service.

2 The injunctions in issue are interlocutory, that is to say temporary injunctions, having effect until the trial of the action only.

3 Before the publication of *Spycatcher* in America the Attorney General had a strong arguable case for obtaining at trial final injunctions in terms similar to those of the temporary injunctions.

4 While the publication of *Spycatcher* in America has much weakened that case, it remains an arguable one.

5 The only way in which it can justly be decided whether the Attorney General's case, being still arguable, should succeed or fail is by having the action tried.

6 On the hypothesis that the Attorney General's claim, if tried, will succeed, the effect of discharging the temporary injunctions now will be to deprive him, summarily and without a trial, of all opportunity of achieving that success.

7 On the alternative hypothesis that the Attorney General's claim, if tried, will fail, the effect of continuing the temporary injunctions until trial will be only to postpone, not to prevent, the exercise by *The Guardian* and *The Observer* of the rights to publish which it will in that event have been established that they have.

8 Having regard to (6) and (7) above, the discharge of the temporary injunctions now is capable of causing much greater injustice to the Attorney General than the continuation of them until trial is capable of causing to *The Guardian* and *The Observer*.

9 Continuation of the injunctions until trial is therefore preferable to their discharge.

Lord Bridge (in the minority): Having no written constitution, we have no equivalent in our law to the First Amendment to the constitution of the United States of America. Some think that puts freedom of speech on too lofty a pedestal. Perhaps they are right—we have not adopted as part of our law the European Convention on Human Rights. . .to which this country is a signatory. Many think that we should. I have hitherto not been of that persuasion, in large part because I have had confidence in the capacity of the common law to safeguard the fundamental freedoms essential to a free society including the right to freedom of speech which is specifically safeguarded by Article 10 of the Convention. My confidence is seriously undermined by your Lordships' decision . . . Freedom of speech is always the first casualty under a totalitarian regime. Such a regime cannot afford to allow the free circulation of information and ideas among its citizens. Censorship is the indispensable tool to regulate what the public may and what they may not know. The present attempt to insulate the public in this country from information which is freely available elsewhere is a significant step down that very dangerous road. The maintenance of the ban, as more and more copies of the book *Spycatcher* enter this country and circulate here, will seem more and more ridiculous. If the Government are determined to fight to maintain the ban to the end, they will face inevitable condemnation and humiliation by the European Court of Human Rights in Strasbourg. Long before that they will have been condemned at the bar of public opinion in the free world.

Note
By a 3:2 majority the House of Lords upheld the interim injunctions.

Attorney-General v Guardian (No 2) [1990] 1 AC 109 (extracts)

On 21 December 1987 in the trial of the permanent injunctions, Scott J discharged the interlocutory injunctions. The Court of Appeal upheld this decision. The Attorney-General appealed to the House of Lords.

Lord Keith of Kinkel: In so far as the Crown acts to prevent [disclosure of confidential information] or to seek redress for it on confidentiality grounds, it must necessarily, in my opinion, be in a position to show that the disclosure is likely to damage or has damaged the public interest. How far the Crown has to go in order to show this must depend on the circumstances of each case. In a question with a Crown servant himself, or others acting as his agents, the general public interest in the preservation of confidentiality, and in encouraging other Crown servants to preserve it, may suffice. But where the publication is proposed to be made by third parties unconnected with the particular confidant, the position may be different. The Crown's argument in the present case would go the length that, in all circumstances where the original disclosure has been made by a Crown servant in breach of his obligation of confidence, any person to whose knowledge the information comes and who is aware of the breach comes under an equitable duty binding his conscience not to communicate the information to anyone else irrespective of the circumstances under which he acquired the knowledge. In my opinion that general proposition is untenable and impracticable, in addition to being unsupported by any authority. . .it can scarcely be a relevant detriment to the Government that publication of material concerning its actions will merely expose it to public discussion and criticism. It is unacceptable in our democratic society that there should be a restraint on the publication of information relating to Government when the only vice of that information is that it enables the public to discuss, review and criticise Government action.

Accordingly, the court will determine the Government's claim to confidentiality by reference to the public interest. Unless disclosure is likely to injure the public interest, it will not be protected. . . .

I am of the opinion that the reports and comments proposed by *The Guardian* and *The Observer* would not be harmful to the public interest, nor would the continued serialisation by *The Sunday Times*. I would therefore refuse an injunction against any of the newspapers. I would stress that I do not base this upon any balancing of public interest nor upon any considerations of freedom of the press, nor upon any possible defences of prior publication or just cause or excuse, but simply upon the view that all possible damage to the interest of the Crown has already been done by the publication of *Spycatcher* abroad and the ready availability of copies in this country.

The majority in the House of Lords concurred in dismissing the appeal of the Attorney-General.

The Observer and The Guardian v United Kingdom (1991) 14 EHRR 153, 190–95

The Guardian and *The Observer* applied to the European Commission on Human Rights alleging, *inter alia,* a breach of Art 10 in respect of the temporary injunctions. The Commission referred the case to the Court, having given its unanimous opinion that the injunctions constituted a breach of Art 10.

56 The Court is satisfied that the injunctions had the direct or primary aim of 'maintaining' the authority of the judiciary, which phrase includes the protection of the rights of litigants [see *Sunday Times v United Kingdom* (1980) 2 EHRR at para 56].

It is also incontrovertible that a further purpose of the restrictions complained of was the protection of national security.

57 The interference complained of thus had aims that were legitimate under paragraph (2) of Article 10.

. . .

Was the interference 'necessary in a democratic society?

59 The Court's judgments relating to Article 10, starting with *Handyside v United Kingdom* (1976) 1 EHRR 737, concluding most recently, with *Oberschlick v Austria*, Series A No 204. . .announce the following major principles.

(a) Freedom of expression constitutes one of the essential foundations of a democratic society.

(b) These principles are of particular importance as far as the press is concerned. Whilst it must not overstep the bounds set, inter alia, in the 'interests of national security' or for 'maintaining the authority of the judiciary', it is nevertheless incumbent on it to impart information and ideas on matters of public interest. Not only does the press have the task of imparting such information and ideas: the public also has a right to receive them. . . .

60 . . .the court would only add to the foregoing that Article 10 of the Convention does not in terms prohibit the imposition of prior restraints on publication, as such. This is evidenced. . .by the *Sunday Times* judgment of 26 April 1979 and its *Markt Intern Verlag GmbH and Klaus Beerman* judgment of 20 November 1988 [(1990) 12 EHRR 161]. On the other hand, the dangers inherent in prior restraints are such that they call for the most careful scrutiny on the part of the court. This is especially so as far as the press is concerned, for news is a perishable commodity and to delay its publication, even for a short period, may well deprive it of all its value and interest.

2 The period from 11 July 1986 to 30 July 1987

In forming its own opinion, the Court has borne in mind its observations concerning the nature and contents of *Spycatcher* and the interests of national security involved; it has also had regard to the potential prejudice to the Attorney General's breach of confidence actions, this being a point that has to be seen in the context of the central position occupied by Article 6 of the Convention and its guarantee of the right to a fair trial [see *Sunday Times v United Kingdom*, para 55]. Particularly in the light of these factors, the court takes the view that, having regard to their margin of appreciation, the English courts were entitled to consider the grant of injunctive relief to be necessary and that their reasons for so concluding were 'sufficient' for the purposes of paragraph (2) of Article 10. [The Court also found the injunctions proportionate.]

3 The period from 30 July to 13 October 1988

66 On 14 July 1987 *Spycatcher* was published in the USA. This changed the situation that had obtained since 11 July 1986. In the first place, the contents of the book ceased to be a matter of speculation and their confidentiality was destroyed. Furthermore, Mr Wright's memoirs were obtainable from abroad by residents of the UK. . . .

68 The fact that the further publication of *Spycatcher* material could have been prejudicial to the trial of the Attorney General's claims for permanent injunctions was certainly in terms of the aim of maintaining the authority of the judiciary, a 'relevant' reason for continuing the restraints in question. The court finds, however, that in the circumstances it does not constitute a 'sufficient' reason for the purposes of Article 10.

It is true that the House of Lords had regard to the requirements of the Convention even though it is not incorporated into domestic law. It is also true that there is some difference between the casual importation of copies of *Spycatcher* into the UK and mass publication of its contents in the press. On the other hand, even if the Attorney General had succeeded in obtaining permanent injunctions at the substantive trial, they would have borne on material the confidentiality of which had been destroyed in any event—and irrespective of whether any further disclosures were made by *The Observer* and *The Guardian*—as a result of the publication in the US. Seen in terms of the protection of the Attorney General's rights as a litigant, the interest in maintaining the confidentiality of that material had, for the purposes of the Convention, ceased to exist by 30 July 1987 [see, *mutatis mutandis*, *Weber v Switzerland* (1990) 12 EHRR 508, at para 51].

69 As regards the interests of national security relied on, the Court observes that, in this respect, the Attorney General's case underwent, to adopt the words of Scott J, 'a curious metamorphosis' [*Attorney-General v Guardian Newspapers (No 2)* [1990] AC 109]. As emerges from Sir Robert Armstrong's evidence. . .injunctions were sought at the outset, inter alia, to preserve the secret character of information that ought to be kept secret. By 30 July 1987, however, the information had lost that character and, as was observed by Lord Brandon of Oakbrook. . .the major part of the potential damage adverted to by Sir Robert Armstrong had already been done. By then, the purpose of the injunctions had thus become confined to the promotion of the efficiency and reputation of the security service, notably by: preserving confidence in that service on the part of third parties; making it clear that the unauthorised publication of memoirs by its former members would not be countenanced; and deterring others who might be tempted to follow in Mr Wright's footsteps.

Notes

1. The Court of Human Rights in *The Observer and The Guardian* concluded unanimously that the objectives considered were insufficient to justify continuing the restriction after July 1987 since it prevented newspapers exercising their right to purvey information which was already available on a matter of legitimate public interest. Thus, a breach of Art 10 was found in respect of the maintenance of the injunctions after, but not before, 30 July 1987.

2. The European Court concluded that once publication of *Spycatcher* had occurred in the US the objectives considered were insufficient to justify continuing the restriction since it prevented the newspapers exercising their right to purvey information which was already available on a matter of legitimate public interest. The test put forward by the House of Lords at the interlocutory stage thus breached Art 10: it allowed an injunction to be granted, even where disclosure would not cause clear damage to the public interest, on the basis that confidentiality had to be preserved until the case could be fully looked into. This test left open the possibility that the other party would not pursue the case to the permanent stage and therefore that freedom of speech could be suppressed on grounds which were not well founded.

3. In *Attorney-General v Blake (Jonathan Cape Ltd, Third Party)*,[40] Blake a former member of the SIS who became a double agent working for the Soviet Union published a book about his experiences. Although the Attorney-General's claim of breach of confidence was rejected, because the information was no longer confidential, the House of Lords found that Blake's actions were in breach of contract and that, in the exceptional circumstances, the Attorney-General was entitled to restitutionary damages for the breach—essentially, an account of profits from the book. This was a significant judgment since it found what appeared to be a novel basis for the decision. It creates a deterrent discouraging members of the intelligence and security services from making disclosures, even in instances in which the disclosure of confidential information is not in question.

4. The so-called 'DA' Notice Committee was set up with the object of letting the press know which information could be printed and at what point. Press representatives sit on the Committee as well as civil servants and officers of the armed forces. The existence of the 'DA' notice system[41] may tend to deter or dissuade the press and others from the publication of confidential or sensitive Government information.[42] In the Third Report from the Defence Committee in 1979,[43] the system, then known as the 'D' notice system, was examined and it was concluded that it was failing to fulfil its role. It was found that major newspapers did not consult their 'D' notices to see what was covered by them and that the wording of 'D' notices was so wide as to render them meaningless. The system conveyed an appearance of censorship which had provoked strong criticism. The review which followed this report reduced the number of notices and confined them to specific areas. The system was reviewed again in 1992 (*The Defence Advisory Notices: A Review of the D Notice System*, MOD Open Government Document No 93/06), leading to a reduction in the number of notices to six. P Sadler conducted a survey in 2007 which found that the system had not changed significantly since the changes prompted by the 1992 review.[44]

5. In *A-G v Times Newspapers*, Tomlinson, a former M16 officer, wrote a book, *The Big Breach*, about his experiences in M16,[45] which the *Sunday Times* intended to serialise. There had been a small amount of publication of the material in Russia. The Attorney-General sought an injunction to restrain publication. The key issue concerned the duty of a newspaper to demonstrate that a degree of prior publication had occurred whereby it could be said that the material had lost its quality of confidentiality. The A-G's case was that the newspaper had to get clearance from the A-G or the

---

40   [2001] 1 AC 268.

41   On the system generally, see J Jaconelli, 'The "D" Notice System' [1982] PL 39.

42   See P Sadler, *National Security and the D-Notice System* (Ashgate, 2001); for recent comment see S Bailey, N Taylor, *Bailey, Harris and Jones: Civil Liberties Cases, Materials, and Commentary*, 6th edn (2009), pp 798–803.

43   HC 773 (1979–80), para 640 i–v, *The 'D' Notice System*.

44   'Still keeping secrets? The DA Notice system post 9/11', Comms L 205.

45   [2001] 1 WLR 885, CA. Tomlinson was charged with an offence under s 1 of the Official Secrets Act 1989, pleaded guilty and was imprisoned for six months.

court that anything they wished to publish was indeed in the public domain before they would be entitled to publish it. The Court noted the jurisprudence of the Strasbourg court on the particular importance of protecting speech dealing with matters of public interest and quoted with approval Eady J's view at first instance that:

> It is in practical terms for the Attorney General to demonstrate. . .that any restriction on freedom of expression sought to be imposed, or continued, can itself be justified by some countervailing and substantial public interest. In the light of what is today going to be readily available in the public domain in Russia, the United States and elsewhere in the world, I am afraid I am not persuaded that the public interest requires the *Sunday Times* to be restricted, for reasons based on a duty of confidence, to any greater extent than any other organ of the media. . . .

The Court of Appeal concluded that the newspaper was not required to obtain the A-G's permission before publication.

The findings in this decision suggested that Art 10 is having a somewhat greater impact in breach of confidence actions than it had at Strasbourg in relation to the *Spycatcher* material. The case did not, however, decide the question of granting an injunction restraining publication where *no* prior publication has taken place, but the material is of public interest (which could clearly have been said of the Wright material). Following *Bladet-Tromso v Norway*,[46] it is suggested that an injunction should not be granted where such material is likely, imminently, to come into the public domain, a position consistent with the demands of s 12(4) of the HRA which refers to such a likelihood. Even where this cannot be said to be the case, it would be consonant with the requirements of Art 10 and s 12 to refuse to grant an interim injunction on the basis of the duty of newspapers to report on such material. The burden would be placed on the state to seek to establish that a countervailing pressing social need was present and that the injunction did not go further than necessary in order to serve the end in view.

Controls over political broadcasting

Government influence over broadcasting is of enormous significance due to the importance of broadcasting as the main means of informing the public as to matters of public interest. The openly partisan nature of the popular press means that broadcasting (including the web-sites of broadcasters) provides the main impartial source of information for most people. The press provides highly opinionated news coverage—the opinions of journalists and editors strongly affect commentaries, and also 'spin' is often placed on news stories.

Ofcom, the current broadcast regulator, was set up under powers provided for in the Office of Communications Act 2002 and with the powers and duties designated under the Communications Act 2003.[47] They include the licensing[48] and regulation of broadcasting. Ofcom also affects public sector broadcasting.[49] The current statutory regime represents a compromise between BBC editorial freedom

---

46   RJD 1999–III.

47   s 2 (1), (2), 2003 Act.

48   Television Licensable Content Services and the licensing regime which applies to them are described in ss 232–240 of the Communications Act 2003.

49   See further H Fenwick *Civil Liberties and Human Rights* (2007) Chapter 6, pp 520–22.

and greater regulation by a Government regulator[50] since the regime for the BBC has to operate within the parameters of its Charter and Agreement. Previously, the Broadcasting Standards Commission (BSC) regulated all the broadcast media, while the Independent Television Commission (ITC) regulated the non-BBC channels. The BBC Trust has replaced the Board of Governors of the BBC as the body responsible for maintaining standards of taste and decency in BBC programmes. The recently revised Charter and Agreement of the BBC (2007) sets out in more detail the obligations of the BBC as a public broadcaster, in particular its obligation to maintain independence. The BBC and Ofcom now share responsibility for regulating the BBC in terms of the content of programmes.

Communications Act 2003 s 198 (1)

It shall be a function of OFCOM , to the extent that provision for them to do so is contained in—

    (a) the BBC Charter and Agreement, and
    (b) the provisions of this Act and of Part 5 of the 1996 Act,

to regulate the provision of the BBC's services and the carrying on by the BBC of other activities for purposes connected with the provision of those services.

The BBC Agreement states (inter alia):

The BBC must observe Relevant Programme Code Standards in the provision of the UK Public Broadcasting Services [and] 'Relevant Programme Code Standards' means those standards for the time being set under section 319 of the Communications Act 2003 [see below] (s 46).

Communications Act 2003 s 198(2):

For the purposes of the carrying out of that function OFCOM:

    (a) are to have such powers and duties as may be conferred on them by or under the BBC Charter and Agreement; and
    (b) are entitled, to the extent that they are authorised to do so by the Secretary of State or under the terms of that Charter and Agreement, to act on his behalf in relation to that Charter and Agreement.

S319 (1): It shall be the duty of OFCOM to set, and from time to time to review and revise, such standards for the content of programmes to be included in television and radio services as appear to them best calculated to secure the standards objectives. s 319(2) The standards objectives include:

    (a) that persons under the age of eighteen are protected;
    (f) that generally accepted standards are applied to the contents of television and radio services so as to provide adequate protection for members of the public from the inclusion in such services of offensive and harmful material.

S320 (1) The requirements of this section are—(a) the exclusion, in the case of television and radio services (other than a restricted service within the meaning of section 245), from

---

50   See further First Report of Select Committee on Culture, Media and Sport (2004) *A Public BBC* HC 82-I.

programmes included in any of those services of all expressions of the views or opinions of the person providing the service on any of the matters mentioned in subsection (2); (3) Subsection (1)(a) does not require—(a) the exclusion from television programmes of views or opinions relating to the provision of programme services; or (b) the exclusion from radio programmes of views or opinions relating to the provision of programme services.

S320 Special impartiality requirements

(1)   The requirements of this section are. . . . .

(b)   the preservation, in the case of every television programme service, teletext service, national radio service and national digital sound programme service, of due impartiality, on the part of the person providing the service, as respects all of those matters;

(c)   the prevention, in the case of every local radio service, local digital sound programme service or radio licensable content service, of the giving of undue prominence in the programmes included in the service to the views and opinions of particular persons or bodies on any of those matters.

(2)   Those matters are—

(a)   matters of political or industrial controversy; and
(b)   matters relating to current public policy.

S321(2) [provides that for the purposes of section 319(2)(g) an advertisement will contravene the prohibition on political advertising if it is]—

(a)   an advertisement which is inserted by or on behalf of a body whose objects are wholly or mainly of a political nature; (b) an advertisement which is directed towards a political end; or (c) an advertisement which has a connection with an industrial dispute.

S321(3) [provides a non-exhaustive definition of 'objects wholly or mainly of a political nature'], which covers: influencing the outcome of elections, bringing about changes in the law, influencing political policy and influencing persons with public functions, including functions conferred via international agreements.

S336(5): The Secretary of State may, at any time, by notice require OFCOM to direct the holders of the Broadcasting Act licences specified in the notice to refrain from including in their licensed services any matter, or description of matter, specified in the notice.

Notes

1. The BBC Agreement now allows Ofcom to impose penalties, including financial ones, on the BBC or require it to carry a correction or statement of findings if it contravenes a 'relevant enforceable requirement'.[51] A 'relevant enforceable requirement' includes the Broadcasting Code policed by Ofcom. The maximum penalty that can be imposed is £250,000 (s 198(5) of the 2003 Act). Section 325 Communications Act 2003 covers observance of the Code in licensed TV services. Under s 325

---

51   Cl 93 and 94.

the conditions included in Broadcasting Act licences ensure that the s 319 standards for offence avoidance (see below) are observed in the service provision and that procedures for handling and resolving complaints regarding adherence to the standards are established. Section 237 allows for the imposition of penalties, including financial penalties, for the contravention of licence conditions or of directions given by Ofcom (not exceeding £250,000). If a complaint is made regarding a licensed TV service, it must be considered by Ofcom; if it is made in relation to the BBC, it will be considered by both the BBC and Ofcom.

2. Broadcasting must observe due impartiality requirements which are now contained in the Communications Act 2003, ss 319(c) and 320; they are reflected in s 5 of Ofcom's Broadcasting Code which came into force in 2005. There are three key statutory requirements. First, under s 319(2)(c) news included in television and radio services must be presented with due impartiality. Second, under s 320(1)(a) the opinions of persons providing a programme service on matters of industrial or political controversy or current public policy must be excluded, and third, under s 320(1)(b), all programming should preserve due impartiality on those matters, although this last requirement can be satisfied in relation to 'a series of programmes taken as a whole'.[52] Under the 2003 Act the BBC is drawn further into the external regulatory scheme *except* on the question of impartiality.[53] The due impartiality provision in s 5 of Ofcom's Code does *not* apply to the BBC, and so it remains unenforceable as far as the BBC is concerned. Thus a complaint regarding due impartiality can be made only to the BBC, not to Ofcom; in this respect due impartiality stands in contrast to the other matters of content regulation in which responsibility is shared. Leaving the BBC outside the regulatory scheme under the 2003 reforms in relation to the due impartiality provisions of Ofcom's Code provides a significant means of maintaining the BBC's dwindling independence. The key difference, then, between independent television and the BBC is that the BBC Trust has the responsibility of ensuring due impartiality and accuracy. The BBC Trust was created when the BBC's Charter was renewed at the end of 2006;[54] it took on the oversight role previously discharged by the Governors.[55]

3. The Government had a direct power of censorship in relation to independent television under s 10(3) of the Broadcasting Act 1990.[56] Section 10(3) was repealed by the Communications Act 2003, but a very similar provision was included in the 2003 Act in s 336(5)—above. This power places the Government at one remove from the broadcasting organisations since it operates through Ofcom. The power under s 10(3) of the 1990 Act was of the widest possible nature since it allowed a ban on broadcasting 'any matter' or class of matter. Section 336(5) is equally wide; it uses the term 'description' rather than 'class' of matter, but this does not appear to be a significant difference—the term 'description' is possibly wider than the term 'class'. Under s 336(7) Ofcom must comply with a direction issued under s 336(5). The Government also possesses such a power in relation to the BBC via the BBC's Licence Agreement, as amended.[57] These powers are not

52 Section 320(4)(a).

53 The BBC Agreement, as amended, allows Ofcom to impose penalties, including financial ones, on the BBC if it contravenes a 'relevant enforceable requirement'.

54 The Green Paper that reviewed the BBC's Royal Charter stated that the government intended to create a new body called the BBC Trust (Review of BBC's Royal Charter *A strong BBC, independent of government*, published May 2005). The White Paper was published in 2006, and the Charter came into force in January 2007. It may be noted that parts of the Green Paper are to be treated as 'White', including the part on governance and accountability. See HL Paper 50-I, 15 March 2005 at [47].

55 *Ibid* at p 10, para 3.1.

56 Previously the power arose under the Broadcasting Act 1981, s 29(3).

57 Under s 8.2 'The Secretary of State may from time to time by notice in writing require the Corporation to refrain at any specified time or at all times from broadcasting or transmitting any matter or matter of any class specified in such notice; and the Secretary of State may at any time or times vary or revoke any such notice'.

expressed as emergency powers, but so far they have only been used to impose a ban in relation to national security (see *Brind,* below). The Home Secretary also retains a further emergency power under s 133 of the 2003 Act of ordering that a particular licensed service should cease or restrict its broadcasting.[58] Emergency powers to take control over BBC broadcasting are contained in the BBC's Agreement.

4. Political advertising, sometimes referred to as 'advocacy advertising', refers to an advertising genre distinct from that covering the promotion of specific consumer products—consumer advertising—although the two verge into each other at the margins. Advocacy advertising covers a wide spectrum of forms of publicity, overlapping with consumer advertising at the one end and party political advertising at the other. It includes so-called 'cause-related' marketing—the promotion of a product by associating it with a particular social or political cause.[59] It covers at its heart issue-based advertising—the advertising of single issue interest groups seeking to sway public opinion towards a particular point of view, but it also covers the advertising of formal political parties and groupings.[60] Parliament has made it clear in successive Acts of Parliament concerning broadcast regulation that political advertising should not be permitted on television or radio. This has been the case ever since commercial broadcasting began in the UK in the 1950s. Thus commercial advertising is permitted,[61] but advertising on behalf of pressure groups such as Amnesty continues to be forbidden. Under the statutory scheme governed by the Broadcasting Act 1990 the broadcasting of political advertising by a licensed service was prohibited.[62] The term 'political advertising' covered advertising by a body whose 'objects were wholly or mainly of a political nature'. The Independent Television Commission (ITC) and Radio Authority (RA) were under duties as regulatory bodies to ensure that this rule was complied with. In practice this ban meant that advertising from bodies of a political nature was automatically refused by the licensed services.

5. The ban was continued with some modification under the Communications Act 2003. The use of the broadcast media for paid political advertising is now prohibited by ss 319 and 321 of the Communications Act 2003. Section 319(2)(g) imposes a duty on Ofcom to ensure that political advertising is not included in television or radio services. Section 321(2) provides that the ban applies to advertisements of a political body or that is directed towards a political end. The ban appears to be even wider than these rules would warrant.

6. Ofcom has the duty of ensuring that the ban is observed.[63] Section 319(1) of the 2003 Act requires Ofcom to set standards to ensure that the 'standards objectives' are met and those objectives

---

58 Section 132 (1): If the Secretary of State has reasonable grounds for believing that it is necessary to do so—

(a) to protect the public from any threat to public safety or public health, or (b) in the interests of national security, he may, by a direction to OFCOM, require them to give a direction under sub-section (3) to a person ('the relevant provider') who provides an electronic communications network or electronic communications service or who makes associated facilities available.

59 See S Adkins, *Cause-related Marketing* (2000). This form of advertising is especially associated with the companies Benetton and Monsanto.

60 See for further discussion of the forms of advertising covered, A Scott '"A Monstrous and Unjustifiable Infringement?" Political Expression and the Broadcasting Ban on Advocacy Advertising' (2003) 66(2) MLR 224–44 at 225–6.

61 It might be banned if it had mixed commercial and political objects. Scott (*ibid,* at 226) notes that when Monsanto launched an advertising campaign associating its products with a particular political message, it chose not to seek to place the advertisements with the broadcast media, placing them in the press instead.

62 Broadcasting Act 1990, ss 8(1)(a) and 92.

63 Rule 4 of the TV advertising Standards Code and section 2, Rule 15 of the BCAP Radio Advertising Standards Code reflect the ban. The Broadcast Advertising Clearance Centre ('BACC') and Ofcom are both bound to ensure that Rule 4 is observed. The TV and Radio Codes are administered by the Advertising Standards Authority (ASA) and BCAP. Ofcom, however, remains responsible under the terms of a Memorandum of Understanding, between Ofcom and the ASA, for enforcing s 4 of the TV Code and s 2, Rule 15 of the Radio Code.

include preventing the broadcasting of advertising that infringes the prohibition on political advertising in s 321(2).

7. Ofcom also has duties relating to offence avoidance in broadcasting and the protection of children under s 319. The BBC has produced a code of Editorial Guidelines, s 8 of which deals with issues of taste and decency and imposes standards similar to those imposed on independent broadcasting. Ofcom's broadcasting Code reflects those standards objectives in clauses 1 and 2. These 'offence avoidance' provisions do not normally relate to political broadcasting, but they may do, where the broadcasting makes its political point due to the use of explicit images.

The pre-2003 Communications Act direct government power of censorship

Brind and Others v Secretary of State for the Home Department
[1991] 1 AC 696 (extracts)

The current power of the Secretary of State to control broadcasting under s 336(5) of the 2003 Act previously arose under s 29(3) of the Broadcasting Act 1981. This power was invoked by the Secretary of State in 1988 in order to issue directives requiring the Independent Broadcasting Authority (IBA) to refrain from broadcasting words spoken by persons representing certain extremist groups or words spoken supporting or inviting support for those groups. The very similar power under clause 13(4) of the 1981 licence and agreement between the Home Secretary and the BBC was invoked in order to apply the same ban to the BBC. The ban covered organisations proscribed under the Northern Ireland (Emergency Provisions) legislation as well as Sinn Fein, Republican Sinn Fein and the Ulster Defence Association. The ban was challenged by the National Union of Journalists and others, but not by the broadcasting organisations themselves.

Lord Bridge of Harwich: I find it impossible to say that the Secretary of State exceeded the limits of his discretion. In any civilised and law-abiding society the defeat of the terrorist is a public interest of the first importance. That some restriction on the freedom of the terrorist and his supporters to propagate his cause may well be justified in support of that public interest is a proposition which I apprehend the appellants hardly dispute. The Secretary of State, for the reasons he made so clear in Parliament, decided that it was necessary to deny to the terrorist and his supporters the opportunity to speak directly to the public through the most influential of all the media of communication and that this justified some interference with editorial freedom. I do not see how this judgment can be categorised as unreasonable. What is perhaps surprising is that the restriction imposed is of such limited scope. . . The viewer may see the terrorist's face and hear his words provided only that they are not spoken in his own voice. . . . [the complaints of the journalists] fall very far short of demonstrating that a reasonable Secretary of State could not reasonably conclude that the restriction was justified by the important public interest of combating terrorism.
The House of Lords unanimously dismissed the appeal.

Note
As Chapter 17 explained, the inception of the HRA had the effect of reversing the decision in *Brind* in relation to the domestic effect of the ECHR. If the power of censorship is invoked again, it will have to be used within Convention limits. This would not necessarily mean that such a ban would breach Art 10: it may be noted that the challenge to the ban failed at Strasbourg: *Brind and McLaughlin*

v UK.[64] The ban remained in place until September 1994 when it was lifted after the IRA declared the cessation of violence. When the ceasefire broke down in 1996, the ban was not re-imposed.

The current ban on political advertising

R (On The Application of Animal Defenders International) v Secretary of State For Culture, Media and Sport [2008] UKHL 15 (extracts)

Lord Bingham of Cornhill: 1. In these proceedings the appellant, Animal Defenders International, seeks a declaration under section 4 of the Human Rights Act 1998 that section 321(2) of the Communications Act 2003 is incompatible with article 10 of the European Convention on Human Rights as given effect in this country by the 1998 Act. The section is said to be incompatible as imposing an unjustified restraint on the right to freedom of political expression.

2. The appellant is a non-profit company whose aims include the suppression, by lawful means, of all forms of cruelty to animals, the alleviation of suffering and the conservation and protection of animals and their environment. It campaigns against the use of animals in commerce, science and leisure, seeking to achieve changes in law and public policy and to influence public and parliamentary opinion towards that end. Because of its campaigning objectives it is not eligible for registration as a charity.

3. In 2005 the appellant launched a campaign entitled 'My Mate's a Primate' with the object of directing public attention towards the use of primates by humans and the threat presented by such use to the survival of primates. The campaign was to include newspaper advertising, direct mailshots, and also an advertisement on television.

7. In enacting the 2003 Act, Parliament paid close attention to the important decision of the European Court of Human Rights in *VgT Verein gegen Tierfabriken v Switzerland* (2001) 34 EHRR 159. . .

9. The facts in *VgT* were very similar to those in the present case. The applicant was an association dedicated to the protection of animals. . .In reaction to television commercials broadcast by the meat industry it prepared a TV advertisement contrasting the behaviour of pigs in their natural environment with their treatment in the course of industrial production. The theme of the advert was 'eat less meat, for the sake of your health, the animals, and the environment'. . . The Commercial Television Company, responsible for handling commercial advertising on behalf of the Swiss Radio and Television Company, declined to broadcast the advert because of its clear political character. . .

12. . . .In *Vgt* the margin of appreciation was reduced: what was at stake was not an individual's purely commercial interest but his participation in a debate affecting the general interest. In considering proportionality, (para 72) the court had to balance the applicant's freedom of expression on the one hand with the reasons adduced by the Swiss authorities on the other, 'namely to protect public opinion from the pressures of powerful financial groups and from undue commercial influence; to provide for a certain equality of opportunity between the different forces of society; to ensure the independence of the broadcasters in editorial matters from powerful sponsors; and to support the press'. The court acknowledged (para 73) that powerful financial groups could obtain competitive advantages in the areas of commercial advertising and noted the Federal Court's view

---

(para 74) that television had a stronger effect on the public on account of its dissemination and immediacy, but was of opinion (*ibid*) that while the domestic authorities might have had valid reasons for this differential treatment, a prohibition of political advertising applicable only to certain media and not to others did not appear to be of a particularly pressing nature. The court summarised its thinking in para 75 of its judgment:

> Moreover, it has not been argued that the applicant association itself constituted a powerful financial group which, with its proposed commercial, aimed at endangering the independence of the broadcaster; at unduly influencing public opinion; or at endangering the equality of opportunity between the different forces of society. Indeed, rather than abusing a competitive advantage, all the applicant association intended to do with its commercial was to participate in an ongoing general debate on animal protection and the rearing of animals. The Court cannot exclude that a prohibition of 'political advertising' may be compatible with the requirements of Article 10 of the Convention in certain situations. Nevertheless, the reasons must be 'relevant' and 'sufficient' in respect of the particular interference with the rights under Article 10. . .In the Court's opinion, however, the domestic authorities have not demonstrated in a 'relevant and sufficient' manner why the grounds generally advanced in support of the prohibition of political advertising also served to justify the interference in the particular circumstances of the applicant association's case.

The court pointed out (para 77) that the applicant had no means other than through the Swiss Radio and Television Company of reaching the entire Swiss public and was not concerned (para 78) with the mechanics of programming. It concluded (para 79) that the ban was not necessary in a democratic society and so violated article 10. . . .

13. On the introduction of the Bill which became the 2003 Act, the Secretary of State felt unable to make a statement pursuant to section 19(1)(a) of the Human Rights Act 1998 that in her view the provisions of the Bill were compatible with the Convention rights scheduled to the 1998 Act . . .The government's position was that it believed and had been advised that the ban on political advertising in what became sections 319 and 321 was compatible with article 10, but because of the European Court's decision in *VgT* [below] it could not be sure. . .

27. Freedom of thought and expression is an essential condition of an intellectually healthy society. The free communication of information, opinions and argument about the laws which a state should enact and the policies its government at all levels should pursue is an essential condition of truly democratic government. These are the values which article 10 exists to protect, and their importance gives it a central role in the Convention regime, protecting free speech in general and free political speech in particular.

28. The fundamental rationale of the democratic process is that if competing views, opinions and policies are publicly debated and exposed to public scrutiny the good will over time drive out the bad and the true prevail over the false. It must be assumed that, given time, the public will make a sound choice when, in the course of the democratic process, it has the right to choose. But it is highly desirable that the playing field of debate should be so far as practicable level.

Hypothetical examples spring readily to mind: adverts by well-endowed multi-national companies seeking to thwart or delay action on climate change; adverts by wealthy groups seeking to ban abortion; or, if not among member states of the Council of Europe, adverts by so-called patriotic groups supporting the right of the citizen to bear arms. Parliament was entitled to regard the risk of such adverts as a real danger, none the less so because legislation has up to now prevented its occurrence.

30. The question necessarily arises why there is a pressing social need for a blanket prohibition of political advertising on television and radio when no such prohibition applies to the press, the cinema and all other media of communication. The answer is found in the greater immediacy and impact of television and radio advertising. This was recognised by the European Court in *Jersild v Denmark* (1994) 19 EHRR 1, para 31, and again in *Murphy v Ireland* [No 44179/98 (2003)] in the passages referred to in para 24 above, although the court appeared to discount the point somewhat in para 74 of its judgment in *VgT*.

31. Since, in principle, no restriction may be wider than is necessary to promote the legitimate object which it exists to serve, it is necessary to ask whether any restriction on political advertising less absolute than that laid down in sections 319 and 321 would suffice to meet the mischief in question. The possibility suggests itself of regulating political advertising by time or frequency or expenditure or by the nature and quality of the adverts in question. It is, I think, unnecessary to explore this possibility in detail, for four main reasons. First, Mr Fordham for the appellant has not, clearly advisedly, advanced such an argument although, as I understand, he did so below. Secondly, it is difficult to see how any system of rationing or capping could be devised which could not be circumvented, as, for instance, by the formation of small and apparently independent groups pursuing very similar political objects. In its judgment in *Murphy*, para 77, the European Court recognised the difficulty of invigilating religious adverts fairly, objectively and coherently on a case by case basis and exactly the same difficulty would arise here, perhaps even more embarrassingly. It is hard to think that any such system would not accord excessive discretion to officials, and give rise to many legal challenges. Thirdly, the important duty of broadcasters to present a fair, balanced and reasonably comprehensive cross-section of public opinion on the issues of the day across the range of their programmes, hard as it is to discharge in any event, would be rendered even harder to discharge if account had to be taken of what might well be a considerable volume of political advertising. Fourthly, despite an express request by the Joint Human Rights Committee to consider compromise solutions, the government judged that no fair and workable compromise solution could be found which would address the problem, a judgment which Parliament accepted. I see no reason to challenge that judgment.

34. If, as in *VgT*, a body with aims similar to those of the applicant in that case or the appellant in this had grounds for wishing to counter the effect of commercial advertising bearing on an issue of public controversy, it would have strong grounds for seeking an opportunity to put its case in the ordinary course of broadcast programmes. The broadcaster, discharging its duty of impartiality, could not ignore such a request. But that is not this case. A question of compatibility might arise if a body whose objects were wholly or mainly of a political nature sought to broadcast an advertisement unrelated to its objects, or if an advertisement were rejected as of a political nature or directed towards political ends when it did not fall within section 321(3)(a), (b), (c), (d), (e) or (g) but only within section 321(3)(f). But the present is not such a case. The appellant's proposed advertisement was, as one would expect, consistent with its objects and, as the appellant's chief executive makes plain in her evidence, its object is to persuade Parliament to legislate. If such a limited challenge were to arise, there might well be scope for resort to section 3 of the 1998 Act, agreed to be inappropriate in the present case.

35. In *Murphy*, para 81, the European Court observed that there appeared to be no clear consensus between member states as to the manner in which to legislate for the

broadcasting of religious advertisements and that there appeared to be no uniform conception of the requirements of the protection of the rights of others in the context of the
legislative regulation of the broadcasting of religious advertising. The same may be said
of political advertising. While the laws of some states, notably the Scandinavian states
and Ireland, appear to resemble those of the UK, those of some other states do not. The
European Court has regarded such a lack of consensus as tending to widen the margin of
appreciation enjoyed by member states: *Petrovic v Austria* (1998) 33 EHRR 307, para 38;
Stambuk v Germany (2002) 37 EHRR 845, para 40. There is here no settled practice among
European states, and it may be that each state is best fitted to judge the checks and
balances necessary to safeguard, consistently with article 10, the integrity of its own
democracy.

36. For these reasons, reflecting those of Ouseley J and, in the main, those of Auld LJ,
I conclude that the ban on political advertising in sections 319 and 321 is necessary in a
democratic society and so compatible with the Convention. I would accordingly dismiss
this appeal.

The appeal was dismissed.

Notes

1. For further discussion of the *Animal Defenders* decision, see T Lewis and P Cumper, 'Balancing
   Freedom of Political Expression Against Equality of Political Opportunity: The Courts and the
   UK's Broadcasting Ban on Political Advertising' [2009] PL 89. The House of Lord's decision has
   been placed in renewed doubt by the recent *TV Vest v Norway*[65] decision at Strasbourg which
   affirmed the stance taken in *VGT* to the effect that total bans on political advertising contravene Art
   10. The Court found that such bans are disproportionate to the aim sought to be achieved—to
   prevent undue interference in the democratic process by powerful interest groups paying for
   broadcast adverts—since other, less intrusive, methods of achieving that aim are available. As far as
   the UK courts are concerned the decision in *TV Vest* does not affect the domestic position under
   the Human Rights Act, even assuming that a domestic court would accept that *Animal Defenders*
   and *TV Vest* are incompatible with each other. The House of Lords in *Kay & Anor v London
   Borough of Lambeth & Ors; Leeds City Council v Price*[66] noted that *Connors v United Kingdom*[67] was
   arguably inconsistent with the earlier House of Lords decision in *Harrow London Borough Council v
   Qazi*.[68] The Court of Appeal had found that it was bound to apply the House of Lords decision.[69]
   Lord Bingham, with whom the other Law Lords agreed on this issue, said that under s 2 HRA
   domestic courts must give effect to principles expounded by the Strasbourg court. However, adherence to precedent, he said, is a cornerstone of the domestic legal system whereby some degree of
   certainty in legal matters is most effectively achieved. He found that therefore where judges consider that a binding domestic precedent is inconsistent with a Strasbourg decision, they should
   follow the ordinary rules of precedent, except in an extreme case where the pre-HRA decision of a
   superior court could not survive the introduction of the HRA. Lord Hope agreed on the precedent

---

65   *TV Vest AS & Rogaland Pesnjonistparti v Norway* (ECHR) (App No 21132/05); (2009) 48 EHRR 51. The UK intervened as a third party in the
     case to present the argument for the ban and referred to the *Animal Defenders* case (at paras 54–7) but this argument was not successful.

66   [2006] UKHL 10.

67   (2004) 40 EHRR 189.

68   [2004] 1 AC 983.

69   See *Price v Leeds CC* [2005] 1 WLR 1825.

issue. He found that *Connors* was not incompatible with *Qazi,* but that *Qazi* should not in any event be departed from.

2. However, the decision in *TV Vest* puts greater pressure on the Government to reconsider the broadcasting ban in the 2003 Act. The ban on political advertising clearly hits most hard at pressure groups and minority parties expressing non-mainstream views—it has a far greater adverse effect on them than it has on the main political parties. Excluded from the airwaves and often (for different reasons) from the press, they have traditionally been able to seek expression for their message by means—such as direct action—which tend to alienate them further from the majority and re-emphasise their marginal status. The internet is changing this position, but the broadcast ban on political advertising still has great significance given the continuing and powerful influence of broadcasting. On the other hand, the possibility that powerful interest groups could unduly influence the democratic process, possibly drowning out the voices of less well-funded groups, remains significant. The Government is now under pressure to consider the possibility of introducing a more limited ban based, for example, on placing limits on the amount single interest groups could spend on advertising to promote a particular cause.

Application of 'taste and decency' requirement to Party Political Broadcasts

As indicated, political advertising is banned in broadcasting (ss 319, 321 Communications Act 2003) and prohibited in the BBC also. There is an exception for Party Political Broadcasts (PPBs)— allowed at election times for parties which have fielded a certain number of candidates. But the general 'taste and decency' (now arising with some modification under the 2003 Act) provisions applied to them, pre-2003 Act, imposed under s 6(1) Broadcasting Act 1990, under the ITC Code and under the Broadcasting Standards Commission Code. Similarly, the BBC *Producers' Guidelines* 'Impartiality and Accuracy',[70] state: 'The content of party political broadcasts, party election broadcasts, and ministerial broadcasts (together with Opposition replies) is primarily a matter for the originating party or the Government and therefore it is not required to achieve impartiality. The BBC remains responsible for the broadcasts as publisher, however, and requires the parties to observe proper standards of legality, taste and decency.' Paragraph 4.2 of the ITC *Programme Code* was to similar effect.

R (On the application of ProLife Alliance) v BBC [2003] 2 WLR 1403 (extracts)

Facts

The ProLife Alliance is a registered political party which opposes abortion. At the 2001 General Election the ProLife Alliance—the applicant—put up enough parliamentary candidates to qualify for a party election broadcast ('PEB') in Wales.[71] The applicant submitted a modified form of the video which it had submitted in 1997, which had been edited to remove the most distressing graphic images of abortions but still showed aborted late-stage foetuses in a mutilated state. The broadcasters refused to broadcast the video (as they had in 1997) on the ground that it offended against good taste and decency and would cause widespread offence. Representatives of the broadcasters refused to screen the images as part of the proposed broadcast but did not raise any objection, however,

---

70 www.bbc.co.uk/guidelines/editorialguidelines/edguide/impariality.

71 The six Alliance candidates in Wales received a total of 1,609 votes, or 0.117% of the total votes cast.

to the soundtrack proposed. Therefore the ProLife Alliance was able to make various anti-abortion points verbally. Eventually a version of the video was submitted by the Alliance and unanimously approved by the broadcasters. It replaced the offending images with a blank screen on which the word 'censored' appeared, and which was accompanied by a sound track describing the images shown in the banned pictures. This version was then broadcast in Wales before the General Election.[72] The pre-Ofcom taste and decency provisions of the BSC Standards Code, the ITC Code and the BBC Agreement applied to all forms of broadcasting expression, including political expression. Therefore PPBs and PEBs were covered (and are still covered under the current regime, above).

The ProLife Alliance then applied for permission to seek judicial review of the broadcasters' refusal to broadcast the original version of the video, showing the offending images. The challenge was not to s 6(1)(a) of the Broadcasting Act 1990, imposing the requirement to adhere to the taste and decency standards, itself, or the equivalent standards of the BBC's Licensing Agreement, as inconsistent with Art 10 under the HRA; so a declaration of the incompatibility of s 6(1)(a) with Art 10 was not sought under s 4HRA. (Given that the case was brought against the BBC which was not subject to s 6(1)(a) it is hard to see that a declaration could have been made, in any event. This point was avoided by the judges in the proceedings.) The applicant argued rather that the broadcasters had not properly *applied* those standards, on the basis that they had failed to attach sufficient significance to the electoral context—a context in which freedom of expression was especially crucial.

Lord Nicholls of Birkenhead: 1. Television broadcasters must ensure, so far as they can, that their programmes contain nothing likely to be offensive to public feeling. This 'offensive material restriction', as it may be called, is a statutory obligation placed on the independent broadcasters by section 6(1)(a) of the Broadcasting Act 1990. The BBC is subject to a comparable, non-statutory obligation under paragraph 5.1(d) of its agreement with the Secretary of State for National Heritage. This appeal concerns the operation of the offensive material restriction in the context of a party election broadcast. It is common ground that nothing in the present case turns on the fact that the obligation on independent television companies is statutory in form, whereas the obligation on the BBC is contained in an agreement. . .
3. Early in May 2001 ProLife Alliance submitted a tape of its proposed broadcast to BBC, ITV, Channel 4 and Channel 5. The major part of the proposed programme was devoted to explaining the processes involved in different forms of abortion, with prolonged and graphic images of the product of suction abortion: aborted foetuses in a mangled and mutilated state, tiny limbs, a separated head, and the like. Unquestionably the pictures are deeply disturbing. Unquestionably many people would find them distressing, even harrowing. Representatives of each broadcaster refused to screen these pictures as part of the proposed broadcast. The broadcasters did not then, or at any stage, raise any objection regarding the proposed soundtrack. ProLife Alliance was not prevented from saying whatever it wished about abortion. The objection related solely to still and moving pictures of aborted foetuses.
4. On 22 May 2001 ProLife Alliance commenced judicial review proceedings against the

---

72 It may be noted that had the Alliance succeeded in the application discussed below, and put the offending version of the same video forward for broadcasting in the 2005 election campaign, the broadcasters would have had to broadcast it if the Alliance had put up enough candidates to qualify for a PEB.

BBC. At an expedited hearing, on 24 May Scott Baker J refused permission to proceed with the challenge. ProLife Alliance then submitted further versions of the proposed broadcast to BBC, ITV and S4C. . . On 2 June a fourth version was submitted and unanimously approved. This version replaced the offending pictures with a blank screen bearing the word 'censored'. The blank screen was accompanied by a sound track describing the images shown on the banned pictures. This version was broadcast in Wales on the evening of the same day. Five days later, on 7 June, the general election took place.

5. In January 2002 an appeal by ProLife Alliance was heard by the Court of Appeal . . . [2002] 3 WLR 1080. The court made a declaration that the BBC's refusal to broadcast ProLife Alliance's party election broadcast was unlawful.

6. Freedom of political speech is a freedom of the very highest importance in any country which lays claim to being a democracy. Restrictions on this freedom need to be examined rigorously by all concerned, not least the courts. The courts, as independent and impartial bodies, are charged with a vital supervisory role. Under the Human Rights Act 1998 they must decide whether legislation, and the conduct of public authorities, are compatible with Convention rights and fundamental freedoms. Where there is incompatibility the courts must grant appropriate remedial relief.

7. In this country access to television by political parties remains very limited. Independent broadcasters are subject to a statutory prohibition against screening advertisements inserted by bodies whose objects are of a political nature. The BBC is prohibited from accepting payment in return for broadcasting. Party political broadcasts and party election broadcasts, transmitted free, are an exception. These 'party broadcasts' are the only occasions when political parties have access to television for programmes they themselves produce. In today's conditions, therefore, when television is such a powerful and intrusive medium of communication, party broadcasts are of considerable importance to political parties and to the democratic process.

8. The foundation of ProLife Alliance's case is article 10 of the European Convention on Human Rights. . . . On its face prior restraint is seriously inimical to freedom of political communication.

9. That is the starting point in this case. In proceeding from there it is important to distinguish between two different questions. Once this distinction is kept in mind the outcome of this case is straightforward. The first question is whether the content of party broadcasts should be subject to the same restriction on offensive material as other programmes. The second question is whether, assuming they should, the broadcasters applied the right standard in the present case.

10. It is only the second of these two questions which is in issue before your Lordships. I express no view on whether, in the context of a party broadcast, a challenge to the lawfulness of the statutory offensive material restriction would succeed. For present purposes what matters is that before your Lordships' House ProLife Alliance accepted, no doubt for good reasons, that the offensive material restriction is not in itself an infringement of ProLife Alliance's convention right under article 10. The appeal proceeded on this footing. The only issue before the House is the second, narrower question. The question is this: should the court, in the exercise of its supervisory role, interfere with the broadcasters' decisions that the offensive material restriction precluded them from transmitting the programme proposed by ProLife Alliance?

11. On this ProLife Alliance's claim can be summarised as follows. A central part of its campaign is that if people only knew what abortion actually involves, and could see the reality for themselves, they would think again about the desirability of abortion. The

disturbing nature of the pictures of mangled foetuses is a fundamental part of ProLife Alliance's message. Conveying the message without the visual images significantly diminishes the impact of the message. . . .

12. In my view, even on the basis of the most searching scrutiny, ProLife Alliance has not made out a case for interfering with the broadcasters' decisions. Clearly the context in which material is transmitted can play a major part in deciding whether transmission will breach the offensive material restriction. . . . the broadcasters remain subject to their existing obligation not to transmit offensive material. Parliament has imposed this restriction on broadcasters and has chosen to apply this restriction as much to party broadcasts as to other programmes. The broadcasters' duty is to do their best to comply with this restriction, loose and imprecise though it may be and involving though it does a significantly subjective element of assessment.

13. The present case concerns a broadcast on behalf of a party opposed to abortion. Such a programme can be expected to be illustrated, to a strictly limited extent, by disturbing pictures of an abortion. But the ProLife Alliance tapes went much further. In its decision letter dated 17 May 2001 the BBC noted that some images of aborted foetuses could be acceptable depending on the context: 'what is unacceptable is the cumulative effect of several minutes primarily devoted to such images'. None of the broadcasters regarded the case as at the margin. Each regarded this as a 'clear case in which it would plainly be a breach of our obligations to transmit this broadcast.' In reaching their decisions the broadcasters stated they had 'taken into account the importance of the images to the political campaign of the ProLife Alliance'. In my view the broadcasters' application of the statutory criteria cannot be faulted. There is nothing, either in their reasoning or in their overall decisions, to suggest they applied an inappropriate standard when assessing whether transmission of the pictures in question would be likely to be offensive to public feeling.

14. I respectfully consider that in reaching the contrary conclusion the Court of Appeal fell into error in not observing the distinction between the two questions mentioned above, one of which was before the court and the other of which was not. Laws LJ said the 'real issue' the court had to decide was 'whether those considerations of taste and offensiveness, which moved the broadcasters, constituted a legal justification for the act of censorship involved in banning the claimant's proposed PEB'. The court's constitutional duty, he said, amounted to a duty 'to decide for itself whether this censorship was justified'. . . .

15. The flaw in this broad approach is that it amounts to re-writing, in the context of party broadcasts, the content of the offensive material restriction imposed by Parliament on broadcasters. It means that an avowed challenge to the broadcasters' decisions became a challenge to the appropriateness of imposing the offensive material restriction on party broadcasts. As already stated, this was not an issue in these proceedings. Had it been, and had a declaration of incompatibility been sought, the appropriate government minister would need to have been given notice and, no doubt, joined as a party to the proceedings. Then the wide-ranging review of the authorities undertaken by the Court of Appeal would have been called for.

16. As it was, the Court of Appeal in effect carried out its own balancing exercise between the requirements of freedom of political speech and the protection of the public from being unduly distressed in their own homes. That was not a legitimate exercise for the courts in this case. Parliament has decided where the balance shall be held. The latter interest prevails over the former to the extent that the offensive material ban applies without distinction to all television programmes, including party broadcasts. In the absence of a successful claim that the offensive material restriction is not compatible with the

Convention rights of ProLife Alliance, it is not for the courts to find that broadcasters acted unlawfully when they did no more than give effect to the statutory and other obligations binding on them. Even in such a case the effect of section 6(2) of the Human Rights Act 1998 would have to be considered. I would allow this appeal. The broadcasters' decisions to refuse to transmit the original version, and the first and second revised versions, of Prolife Alliance's proposed broadcasts were lawful.

Lord Hoffman

52. The Alliance has never argued that section 6(1)(a) of the 1990 Act, in its application to PEBs, is inconsistent with its rights under article 10 of the Convention. But this is lip-service, because the thrust of its submissions, which found favour in the Court of Appeal, is that the statute should be disregarded or not taken seriously.

56. In the present case, that primary right [under Art 10] was not engaged.

57. There is no human right to use a television channel. Parliament has required the broadcasters to allow political parties to broadcast but has done so subject to conditions, both as to qualification for a PEB and as to its contents.

61. The emphasis, therefore, is on the right not to be denied access on discriminatory grounds . . .

64. That was the question in the recent controversial ECHR case of *VgT Verein Gegen Tierfabriken v Switzerland* (2002) 34 EHRR 159, which concerned the prohibition of political advertising by section 18(5) of the Swiss Federal Radio and Television Act.

   (c) Are conditions as to taste and decency discriminatory?

65. A condition concerning standards of taste and decency is neutral in the sense that applies across the board to all political parties wishing to broadcast PPBs.

71. Is there anything in European law which suggests that a taste and decency require-ment would be regarded as unreasonable or discriminatory? In the *VgT* case the court made it clear that it was not considering a case in which the objection to an advertisement was that its content was offensive . . . And at this point it is also relevant to consider the response of the ECHR to the complaint of the Alliance about the rejection of its PEB in the 1997 election. On 26 June 2000 the Registrar of the ECHR wrote to the Alliance saying that 'in accordance with the general instructions received from the Court' he drew their atten-tion to 'certain shortcomings' in the application. The indication given by the Registrar was that the court might consider that the taste and decency requirements were not an 'arbi-trary or unreasonable' interference with their access to television. Subsequently the court, after noting that the Alliance had been informed of 'possible obstacles' to the admissibility of the application, rejected it as not disclosing 'any appearance of a violation of the rights and freedoms set out in the Convention . . .'

72. The Court of Appeal treated this decision as an aberration . . . [but] it is more in accordance with the jurisprudence of the ECHR and a proper analysis of the nature of the right in question than the fundamentalist approach of the Court of Appeal.

73. In my opinion therefore, there is no public interest in exempting PEBs from the taste and decency requirements on the ground that their message requires them to broadcast offensive material.

78. If, as I think, Parliament was entitled to impose standards of taste and decency which were meant to be taken seriously, the next question is whether the broadcasters acted lawfully in deciding that the Alliance PEB did not comply.

79. Once one accepts that the broadcasters were entitled to apply generally accepted standards, I do not see how it is possible for a court to say that they were wrong.

Notes

1. It is argued that the majority judges in the House of Lords in *ProLife* failed to apply Art 10 correctly since the effect of s 3(1) HRA was misunderstood. The striking thing about their ruling was the extraordinarily contorted reasoning; the Lords assumed that Pro-life was challenging the statute itself—seeking to set it aside. Section 3(1)'s very function is to create compatibility with the Convention rights and as discussed this would not have involved damaging the statute, let alone setting it aside.

2. The failure to deal with the impact of the margin of appreciation doctrine in *ProLife* was significant. The stance of the UK judiciary in relation to the implications of the effects of this doctrine arguably amounts to one of their most significant failures in confronting the application of the HRA. The line of cases on explicit expression at Strasbourg stemming from *Handyside*[73] is deeply affected by this doctrine, which is not applicable at the national level. Therefore the admissibility decision against ProLife, part of that line, relied upon by Lord Hoffman, should have been applied—as far as that is possible—after stripping away the effects of the doctrine upon it. Since it was a decision upon admissibility alone, the decision would have been rendered almost an empty one once that process had been undertaken. It may be noted that the Court of Appeal accepted—correctly—that this admissibility decision was non-determinative of the issue before it. Had the Lords taken that stance that would have left the judges with little guidance as to the Strasbourg stance on the matter, except from the *Handyside* line of authority and from general Strasbourg free speech principles.

3. Lord Hoffman found that *VGT Verein gegen Tierfabriken v Switzerland*,[74] (above) in which a breach of Art 10 was found in relation to discrimination in allocation of broadcast time, did not deal with an instance in which the objection to an advertisement was that its content was offensive. However, that left the point at issue open. Therefore the general principle from *Handyside* should have been applied, bearing in mind that *Handyside* was itself to an extent in point in relation to the instant case. It dealt with speech that could be termed political, if that term is broadly interpreted, including information about abortion, taking impliedly a pro-abortion stance. The book in question in *Handyside* informed children and teenagers about matters related to sexuality, and its implicit message could be viewed as a liberal one. The Court took a strong stance in favour of offensive speech under Art 10(1) but then applied the tests of necessity and proportionality under Art 10(2) in a manner that was heavily influenced by the margin of appreciation doctrine. If the influence of that doctrine on the decision was to be disapplied at the domestic level, the decision could be taken to endorse a very restrictive role for rules aimed at avoidance of offence in relation to semi-political speech. *A fortiori* the decision would endorse such a role in relation to political speech of *higher* value—as in the *ProLife Alliance* case.

    Therefore, if the effects on the findings of the margin of appreciation doctrine could have been disapplied, *Handyside* would arguably favour a stance closer to that of the Court of Appeal than that of the House of Lords, although whether, bearing in mind the view taken by the BBC of the gravity of the offence that would be caused by the video, it could have supported the findings of the Court of Appeal as to the *outcome*, is debatable. It is concluded that the treatment of the Strasbourg jurisprudence in both the House of Lords and Court of Appeal was flawed: Lord Hoffman did not take account of the effects of the margin of appreciation doctrine and severely under-stated the value placed by Strasbourg on speech in general and political speech in particular, while the Court of Appeal failed to analyse the implications of the jurisprudence relating to such speech, choosing instead to rely on more familiar common law principles.

---

73   Eur Ct HR, A 24; (1976) 1 EHRR 737.

74   34 EHRR 159, at para 76, p 177.

5. Journalists, film-makers and groups such as Amnesty, can challenge Ofcom directly, by invoking s 7(1)(a) of the HRA,[75] since Ofcom is a public authority under s 6 HRA. Decisions as to licensing, political advertising, and adjudications regarding impartiality may be subjected thereby to scrutiny based on the ECHR standards. Since the independent television companies are not public authorities, they can also bring such proceedings, as 'victims' under the HRA. Proceedings under s 7(1)(a) cannot be brought *against* the independent companies, but decisions of the public service broadcasters—the BBC and possibly Channel 4[76]—as to programming policy etc can be challenged directly by invoking s 7(1)(a) of the HRA, so long as the person bringing the action satisfies the victim requirement under s 7(3) of the HRA. The use of s 7(1)(a) could in theory mean that such decisions are tested more directly against Convention standards than they have been in the past by means of judicial review. Section 12 of the HRA is applicable. The application of the Ofcom Code (2005) can also be challenged in such proceedings. Provisions of such Codes can be struck down by the courts unless primary legislation prevents the removal of the incompatibility. Given that the detailed provisions are commonly contained in the Codes, this is a significant possibility.

6. The principle of non-interference with political expression, except in exceptional circumstances, is well established under the Convention. The Strasbourg standard as regards political expression is very strict, as the Introduction to this chapter indicated. Nevertheless, reliance on Art 10 in these instances is unlikely to prove fruitful due to the deference the courts pay to the expert regulator—Ofcom or the BBC (when acting as a regulator). *R (On the application of ProLife Alliance)* indicated the stance of the courts as regards deference and set the standard of deference to be adopted post-HRA. The House of Lords found that the court should not substitute its decision for that of the broadcaster, and the broadcaster had decided that the broadcast offended against the regulations on taste and decency. The application of such regulations was not found in itself to breach Art 10. The findings of the House of Lords in *Animal Defenders* also indicated that there is a judicial unwillingness to interfere with the decisions of Parliament in this context, despite the value Strasbourg places on political expression, which was reaffirmed in the *VgT* case, at Strasbourg. It may be said that after the *Animal Defenders* and *ProLife* decisions it seems unlikely that the ECHR via the HRA will have a significant impact in the context of broadcast regulation.

RESTRAINING FREEDOM OF EXPRESSION TO PROTECT THE ADMINISTRATION OF JUSTICE

Introduction[77]

This section considers two interests which are frequently perceived as being in conflict: the interest in protecting the administration of justice and the interest in media freedom. Domestically, the interest in the administration of justice has been protected by the law of contempt. A number of aspects of

---

75   See Chapter 17, pp 990–992.

76   The BBC is clearly a functional public authority, while Channel 4 probably is: both bodies have a public function in respect of their public service remit which is especially significant in the case of the BBC. Channel 4's role is governed by statute—s 25 of the 1990 Act. See above, Chapter 17, pp 977–989, on the meaning of 'public function' in s 6(3)(b) HRA.

77   General reading: H Fenwick and G Phillipson, *Media Freedom under the Human Rights Act* (2006), Chapters 6, 7; H Fenwick, *Civil Liberties and Human Rights*, 4th edn (2007), Chapter 5, esp. pp 319–82; E Barendt, *Freedom of Speech*, 1st edn (1987), 2nd edn (2007), Chapter 8; B Sufrin and N Lowe, *The Law of Contempt* (1996) (new edition 2010); G Robertson and A Nichol, *Media Law* (1999), Chapter 6; *Arlidge, Eady and Smith on Contempt*, 2nd edn (1999).

contempt law are discussed below, including its use in curbing discussions and publicity in the media which might influence those involved in forthcoming proceedings, specific reporting restrictions, and requirements to disclose journalistic sources.

It should be pointed out that within UK law the protection of the administration of justice is viewed as a general societal concern rather than as a means of protecting an individual's right to a fair trial, although it may have that effect. Nevertheless, the fact that many aspects of the law of contempt can be seen as having as their *ultimate* rationale the protection of the right to fair trial leads to the conclusion that in so far as this other individual right is clearly at stake, free speech may be compromised to a certain extent. Such a conclusion would be in accord with the European Convention on Human Rights (ECHR), which guarantees both the right to free speech (Art 10) and the right to a fair trial (Art 6). Interferences with the guarantee of free speech under Art 10, as afforded further effect in domestic law under the HRA, may be justified where they have the legitimate aim of 'maintaining the authority and impartiality of the judiciary' under para 2. This phrase may be taken to cover the preservation of the integrity of the administration of justice, including the rights of litigants. Since contempt law has a role to play in preventing prejudice to proceedings or deterring the media from causing such prejudice, it may be viewed as a means of protecting Art 6 rights (see Chapter 7, pp 310–313), although the main responsibility for providing such protection falls on the trial judge.[78] Viewed as exceptions to Art 10, such rights fall within the rubric 'the rights of others' in para 2, as well as that of 'maintaining the authority of the judiciary'. Contempt law therefore comes into conflict with free expression, either on the basis of protecting general societal interests and/or other individual rights.

Publications prejudicing particular criminal or civil proceedings

Contempt of court at common law prior to the inception of the Contempt of Court 1981 curtailed the freedom of the media to discuss and report on issues arising from criminal or civil proceedings on the basis that those proceedings might suffer prejudice. The elements of common law contempt consisted of the creation of a real risk of prejudice (the *actus reus*) and an intention to publish. The period during which the risk in question might arise was known as the *sub judice* period. In *R v Savundranayagan and Walker*,[79] it was found that the starting point of this period occurred when the proceedings were 'imminent'. *Attorney-General v Times Newspapers Ltd*,[80] however, moved the balance towards the protection of the administration of justice and away from protection for free expression. The case concerned litigation arising out of the thalidomide tragedy. The parents of the children affected by thalidomide (which caused severe deformities to the developing foetus) wished to sue Distillers, the company that had manufactured the drug, because they believed that it was responsible for the terrible damage done to their unborn children. Distillers resisted the claims and entered into negotiation with the parents' solicitors. Thus, the litigation was dormant while the negotiations were taking place.

Meanwhile, the Sunday Times wished to publish an article accusing Distillers of acting ungenerously towards the thalidomide children. The article came close to alleging that Distillers had been negligent, although it was balanced in that it did consider both sides. The Attorney-General obtained an injunction in the Divisional Court preventing publication of the article on the ground that it amounted to a

---

78 See the comments of Simon Brown LJ regarding the differing roles of the judge in contempt proceedings and at trial: *Attorney-General v Birmingham Post and Mail Ltd* [1998] 4 All ER 49. But *cf* the findings in *Attorney-General v Guardian Newspapers* [1999] EMLR 904.

79 [1968] 1 WLR 1761.

80 [1974] AC 273.

contempt of court. The Court of Appeal then discharged the injunction but it was restored on appeal by the House of Lords on the ground that the article dealt with the question of negligence and therefore prejudged the case pending before the court. It held that such prejudgment was particularly objectionable as coming close to 'trial by media' and thereby leading to an undermining of the administration of justice; a person might be adjudged negligent by parts of the media with none of the safeguards available in court. This ruling created the 'prejudgment' test, which seemed to be wider than the test of real risk of prejudice, in that little risk to proceedings might be shown, but it might still be possible to assert that they had been prejudged. This test had a potentially grave effect on freedom of speech because it was very difficult to draw the line between legitimate discussion in the media of issues of possible relevance in civil or criminal actions and prejudgment.

After the decision of the House of Lords was found to breach Art 10 of the ECHR in the following decision of the Strasbourg Court, reform of this area of contempt law was undertaken.

Sunday Times v United Kingdom (1980) 2 EHRR 245, 275–81

The European Court of Human Rights found that the injunction clearly infringed freedom of speech under Article 10(1); the question was whether one of the exceptions within Article 10(2) could be invoked. [The Court considered the reasoning of the House of Lords courts and the submissions of the UK Government justifying the injunction and said]:

The Court regards all these various reasons as falling within the aim of maintaining the 'authority . . .of the judiciary' as interpreted by the court in the second paragraph of Article 10. Accordingly, the interference with the applicants' freedom of expression had an aim that is legitimate under Article 10(2).

Was the interference 'necessary in a democratic society' for maintaining the authority of the judiciary? [The court cited *Handyside* as authority that 'necessary' in this context referred to pressing social need, and for the margin of appreciation doctrine and went on]

Again, the scope of the domestic power of appreciation is not identical as regards each of the aims listed in Article 10(2). The *Handyside* case concerned the 'protection of morals'. The view taken by the contracting states of the 'requirements of morals', observed the Court, 'varies from time to time and from place to place, especially in our era', and 'state authorities are in principle in a better position than the international judge to give an opinion on the exact content of these requirements' [*ibid*, para 48]. Precisely the same cannot be said of the far more objective notion of the 'authority' of the judiciary. The domestic law and practice of the contracting states reveal a fairly substantial measure of common ground in this area. This is reflected in a number of provisions of the Convention, including Article 6, which have no equivalent as far as 'morals' are concerned. Accordingly, here a more extensive European supervision corresponds to a less discretionary power of appreciation.

The draft article was nonetheless the principal subject-matter of the injunction. It must therefore be ascertained in the first place whether the domestic courts' views as to the article's potential effects were relevant in terms of the maintenance of the 'authority of the judiciary'.

One of the reasons relied on was the pressure which the article would have brought to bear on Distillers to settle the actions out of court on better terms. However, even in 1972, publication of the article would probably not have added much to the pressure already on Distillers. . . .The speeches in the House of Lords emphasised above all the concern that the processes of the law may be brought into disrespect and the functions of the courts usurped either if the public is led to form an opinion on the subject-matter of litigation before adjudication by the courts or if the parties to litigation have to undergo 'trial by newspaper'. Such concern is in itself 'relevant' to the maintenance of the 'authority of the judiciary'. . .

Nevertheless, the proposed Sunday Times article was couched in moderate terms and did not present just one side of the evidence or claim that there was only one possible result at which a court could arrive. . . Accordingly, even to the extent that the article might have led some readers to form an opinion on the negligence issue, this would not have had adverse consequences for the 'authority of the judiciary', especially since, as noted above, there had been a nationwide campaign in the meantime.

At the time when the injunction was originally granted and at the time of its restoration, the Thalidomide case was at the stage of settlement negotiations. The applicants concur with the Court of Appeal's view that the case was 'dormant' and the majority of the Commission considers it unlikely that there would have been a trial of the issue of negligence.

As the Court remarked in its *Handyside* judgment, freedom of expression constitutes one of the essential foundations of a democratic society; subject to paragraph 2 of Article 10, it is applicable not only to information or ideas that are favourably received or regarded as inoffensive or as a matter of indifference, but also to those that offend, shock or disturb the state or any sector of the population [*ibid*, para 49]. As the Court has already observed, Article 10 guarantees not only the freedom of the press to inform the public but also the right of the public to be properly informed. In the present case, the families of numerous victims of the tragedy, who were unaware of the legal difficulties involved, had a vital interest in knowing all the underlying facts and the various possible solutions. They could be deprived of this information, which was crucially important for them, only if it appeared absolutely certain that its diffusion would have presented a threat to the 'authority of the judiciary'.

Notes

1. In the light of these findings, the court ruled that the injunction was not 'necessary in a democratic society'. Thus, the exception under Art 10(2) could not apply: Art 10 had been breached.
2. The UK Government responded to this decision in the enactment of the Contempt of Court Act 1981, which was intended to take account of the ruling of the European Court of Human Rights and was also influenced to an extent by the proposals of the Phillimore Committee on reform of contempt law.[81]

Contempt of Court Act 1981

1. In this Act 'the strict liability rule' means the rule of law whereby conduct may be treated as a contempt of court as tending to interfere with the course of justice in particular legal proceedings regardless of intent to do so.

2.–(1) The strict liability rule applies only in relation to publications. . .

(2) The strict liability rule applies only to a publication which creates a substantial risk that the course of justice in the proceedings in question will be seriously impeded or prejudiced.

(3) The strict liability rule applies to a publication only if the proceedings in question are active within the meaning of this section at the time of the publication.

---

81 See Report of the Committee on Contempt of Court, Cmnd 5794 (1974).

(4)   Schedule 1 applies for determining the times at which proceedings are to be treated as active within the meaning of this section.

3.–(1)   A person is not guilty of contempt of court under the strict liability rule as the publisher of any matter to which that rule applies if at the time of publication (having taken all reasonable care) he does not know and has to reason to suspect that relevant proceedings are active.

(2)   A person is not guilty of contempt of court under the strict liability rule as the distributor of a publication containing any such matter if at the time of distribution (having taken all reasonable care) he does not know that it contains such matter and has no reason to suspect that it is likely to do so.

(3)   The burden of proof of any fact tending to establish a defence afforded by this section to any person lies upon that person. . .

4.–(1)   Subject to this section a person is not guilty of contempt of court under the strict liability rule in respect of a fair and accurate report of legal proceedings held in public, published contemporaneously and in good faith.

(2)   In any such proceedings the court may, where it appears to be necessary for avoiding a substantial risk of prejudice to the administration of justice in those proceedings, or in any other proceedings pending or imminent, order that the publication of any report of the proceedings, or any part of the proceedings, be postponed for such period as the court thinks necessary for that purpose. . . .

5. A publication made as or as part of a discussion in good faith of public affairs or other matters of general public interest is not to be treated as a contempt of court under the strict liability rule if the risk of impediment or prejudice to particular legal proceedings is merely incidental to the discussion.

6. Nothing in the foregoing provisions of this Act—

. . .(c)   restricts liability for contempt of court in respect of conduct intended to impede or prejudice the administration of justice.

Schedule 1
Times when proceedings are active for purposes of section 2
Criminal proceedings
Subject to the following provisions of this Schedule, criminal proceedings are active from the relevant initial step specified in paragraph 4 until concluded as described in paragraph 5.
    The initial steps of criminal proceedings are—

(a)   arrest without warrant;
(b)   the issue, or in Scotland the grant, of a warrant for arrest;
(c)   the issue of a summons to appear, or in Scotland the grant of a warrant to cite;
(d)   the service of an indictment or other document specifying the charge. . .

5. Criminal proceedings are concluded—
(a)   by acquittal or, as the case may be, by sentence;
(b)   by any other verdict, finding, order or decision which puts an end to the proceedings;
(c)   by discontinuance or by operation of law.

12. Proceedings other than criminal proceedings and appellate proceedings are active from the time when arrangements for the hearing are made or, if no such arrangements are previously made, from the time the bearing begins, until the proceedings are disposed of or discontinued or withdrawn. . . .

Appellate proceedings

15. Appellate proceedings are active from the time when they are commenced

    (a) by application for leave to appeal or apply for review, or by notice of such an application;

    (b) by notice of appeal or of application for review;

    (c) by other originating process, until disposed of or abandoned, discontinued or withdrawn.

Note

The 1981 Act modified the common law without bringing about radical change. It introduced various liberalising elements but it was intended, as a number of commentators observed, to maintain the stance of the ultimate supremacy of the administration of justice over freedom of speech, while moving the balance further towards freedom of speech.[82] In particular, it introduced stricter time limits, a more precise test for the *actus reus*, as proposed by the Phillimore Committee, and under s 5 allowed some publications dealing with matters of public interest to escape liability, even though a risk of prejudice to proceedings had been created.

Attorney-General v English [1983] 1 AC 116 (extracts)

This judgment is the leading case on a number of aspects of the use of the 1981 Act.

Lord Diplock: My Lords, this is an appeal brought by the editor and publishers of the Daily Mail . . . holding them to be guilty of contempt of court by publishing an article entitled 'The vision of life that wins my vote' on 15 October 1980, which was published the morning of the third day of the trial in the Crown Court at Leicester of a well-known paediatrician, Dr Arthur, on a charge of murdering a three-day-old mongoloid baby boy.

    . . . Next for consideration is the concatenation in the subsection [s 2(2)] of the adjective 'substantial' and the adverb 'seriously', the former to describe the degree of risk, the latter to describe the degree of impediment or prejudice to the course of justice. . . . In combination I take the two words to be intended to exclude a risk that is only remote.

    My Lords, that Mr Malcolm Muggeridge's article was capable of prejudicing the jury against Dr Arthur at the early stage of his trial when it was published seems to me to be clear. It suggested that it was a common practice among paediatricians to do that which Dr Arthur was charged with having done, because they thought that it was justifiable in the interests of humanity even though it was against the law. . . . The judge thought at that stage of the trial that the risk was substantial, not remote. So, too, looking at the matter in retrospect, did the Divisional Court despite the fact that the risk had not turned into an actuality since Dr Arthur had by then been acquitted. For my part I am not prepared to dissent from this evaluation. I consider that the publication of the article on the third day of what was to prove a lengthy trial satisfied the criterion for which s 2(2) of the 1981 Act provides.

    [Having found that s 2(2) was satisfied Lord Diplock went on to consider s 5.]

---

82   For comment on the 1981 Act at the time when it was passed, see CJ Miller [1982] Crim LR 71; JC Smith [1982] Crim LR 744.

The article, however, fell also within the category dealt with in s 5. It was made, in undisputed good faith, as a discussion in itself of public affairs, viz Mrs Carr's candidature as an independent 'pro-life' candidate in the North West Croydon by-election. . . It was also part of a wider discussion on a matter of general public interest that had been proceeding intermittently over the last three months, on the moral justification of mercy killing and in particular of allowing newly born hopelessly handicapped babies to die. So it was for the Attorney General to show that the risk of prejudice to the fair trial of Dr Arthur, which I agree was created by the publication of the article at the stage the trial had reached when it was published, was not 'merely incidental' to the discussion of the matter with which the article dealt.

My lords, the article that is the subject of the instant case appears to me to be in nearly all respects the antithesis of the article which this House (pace a majority of the judges of the European Court of Human Rights) held to be a contempt of court in *A-G v Times Newspapers Ltd* [1974] AC 273. There the whole subject of the article was the pending civil actions against the Distillers Co arising out of their having placed on the market the new drug Thalidomide, and the whole purpose of it was to put pressure on that company in the lawful conduct of their defence in those actions. In the instant case, in contrast, there is in the article no mention at all of Dr Arthur's trial. It may well be that many readers of the Daily Mail who saw the article and had read also the previous day's report of Dr Arthur's trial, and certainly if they were members of the jury at that trial, would think 'That is the sort of thing that Dr Arthur is being tried for; it appears to be something that quite a lot of doctors do'. But the risk of their thinking that and allowing it to prejudice their minds in favour of finding him guilty on evidence that did not justify such a finding seems to me to be properly described in ordinary English language as 'merely incidental' to any meaningful discussion of Mrs Carr's election policy as a pro-life candidate in the by-election due to be held before Dr Arthur's trial was likely to be concluded, or to any meaningful discussion of the wider matters of general public interest involved in the current controversy as to the justification of mercy killing. To hold otherwise would have prevented Mrs Carr from putting forward and obtaining publicity for what was a main plank in her election programme and would have stifled all discussion in the press on the wider controversy about mercy killing from the time that Dr Arthur was charged in the magistrates' court in February 1981 until the date of his acquittal at the beginning of November of that year; for those are the dates between which under s 2(3) and Schedule I, the legal proceedings against Dr Arthur would be 'active' and so attract the strict liability rule.

Such gagging of bona fide public discussion in the press of controversial matters of general public interest, merely because there are in existence contemporaneous legal proceedings in which some particular instance of those controversial matters may be in issue, is what s 5 of the Contempt of Court Act 1981 was in my view intended to prevent. I would allow this appeal.

The other four Law Lords agreed.

Note
The following judgments give helpful guidance as to the meaning of s 2(2) of the 1981 Act.

Attorney-General v News Group Newspapers [1986] 3 WLR 365, 375, CA

Sir John Donaldson MR: . . .[T]here has to be some risk that the proceedings in question will be affected at all. Second, there has to be a prospect that, if affected, the effect will be serious. The two limbs of the test can overlap, but they can be quite separate. I accept Mr Laws' submission that 'substantial' as a qualification of 'risk' does not have the meaning of 'weighty,' but rather means 'not insubstantial' or 'not minimal.' The 'risk' part of the test will usually be of importance in the context of the width of the publication. To declare in a speech at a public meeting in Cornwall that a man about to be tried in Durham is guilty of the offence charged and has many previous convictions for the same offence may well carry no substantial risk of affecting his trial, but, if it occurred, the prejudice would be most serious. By contrast, a nationwide television broadcast at peak viewing time of some far more innocuous statement would certainly involve a substantial risk of having some effect on a trial anywhere in the country and the sole effective question would arise under the 'seriousness' limb of the test. Proximity in time between the publication and the proceedings would probably have a greater bearing on the risk limb than on the seriousness limb, but could go to both.

A-G v Guardian Newspapers (1999) EMLR 904 (extracts)

The case concerned the trial of one Kelly for stealing body parts, apparently for artistic purposes; during the trial *The Observer* published an article suggesting in strong terms that Kelly had had no artistic purpose in stealing the parts, but was motivated merely by a morbid fascination with dead people. The writer linked Kelly's fascination to that experienced by a number of named serial killers. Since Kelly's honesty was a key issue in the trial, the article was very damaging to his case since in the jury's eyes it could have undermined his credibility. Both Collins LJ and Sedley LJ concluded that the article therefore created a risk of serious prejudice. The Court of Appeal considered that it was placing a strong reliance on the Article 10(2) tests as interpreted in *Worm v Austria*[83] in finding that although a risk of serious prejudice arose, it was not certain that it could be viewed as a substantial one. Sedley LJ wrestled with the question whether the risk should be described as substantial:

> in the end, and not without anxiety, I have concluded that it is simply not possible to be sure that the risk created by the publication was a substantial risk that a jury, properly directed to disregard its own sentiments and any media comment, would nevertheless have its own thoughts or value judgments reinforced by the article to a point where they influenced the verdict. As a first cross-check, I doubt whether an appeal would have been allowed had the jury which convicted Mr Kelly read the article. As a second cross-check, it seems to me that the threat from this article, published when it was, to the course of justice in Mr Kelly's trial was not sufficient to make either prior restraint or subsequent punishment a proportionate response in a society which, as a democracy, values and protects the freedom of the press.

Notes

1. Collins LJ in *Guardian* felt that the issue was so finely balanced that he would not dissent from Sedley LJ's conclusion on this point. It was therefore found that the test of 'serious prejudice,' but not that of 'substantial risk,' in s 2(2) was satisfied. The test under s 2(2) has also been considered in quite a large number of cases, mainly in the 1980s and 1990s. The ruling in *Attorney-General v News Group Newspapers*[84] made it clear that the proximity of the article to the trial will be relevant

---

83   (1998) 25 EHRR 454.

84   [1987] 1 QB 1.

to the question of risk. The Court of Appeal held that a gap of 10 months between the two could not create the substantial risk in question because the jury would be likely to have forgotten the article by the time the trial came on. Even if the article were faintly recollected at the time of the trial it might be likely to have little impact. In *Attorney-General v Independent TV News and Others*,[85] TV news and certain newspapers published the fact that a defendant in a forthcoming murder trial was a convicted IRA terrorist who had escaped from jail where he was serving a life sentence for murder. It was found that s 2(2) was not satisfied since the trial was not expected to take place for nine months, there had only been one offending news item and there had been limited circulation of only one edition of the offending newspaper items. The risk of prejudice was found to be too small to be termed substantial. A publication during the trial is clearly most likely to create a risk. If the case will be very much in the public eye due to the persons or issues involved (as was the case in respect of the article in *Hislop and Pressdram*[86] concerning Sonia Sutcliffe, wife of the Yorkshire Ripper) the article is more likely to make an impact, although the mere fact that the issue attracts a great deal of media coverage will not mean that jurors will be viewed as unable to put it from their minds.

2. Serious prejudice can arise in various ways. In *Attorney-General v Morgan*,[87] an article in *The News of the World* referred to the criminal record of one of the defendants and to the criminal background of both defendants. These references were given great prominence and were repeated throughout the article. Despite the lapse of time before the trial—eight months—a substantial risk of serious prejudice was found to have been created. However, in *Attorney-General v Guardian Newspapers*,[88] the publication of the fact that one unidentified defendant out of six in a Manchester trial was also awaiting trial elsewhere was not found to satisfy s 2(2) since it was thought that it would not cause a juror of ordinary good sense to be biased against the defendant.

3. There have been few post-HRA cases on s 2 of the 1981 Act, and Art 10 has had little impact on the application of the 1981 Act. This may partly be because the failure of the prosecution in *A-G v Guardian* (above) has led to a perception that the s 2(2) bar is so high that it can only be reached in clear-cut cases. An example of a post-HRA decision arose in *A-G v MGN*.[89] In that instance liability was not disputed and the articles in question were apparently published in error. The articles, in the *Sunday Mirror*, concerned the trial of certain Premiership footballers for affray and causing grievous bodily harm with intent. The article revived allegations that the attack was racially motivated. The article was published at the time when the jury was considering its verdicts and, as the publishers recognised, its thrust was at variance with the evidence as presented in the criminal trial. The publishers recognised that the judge had given a clear direction that there was no evidence of a racial motive. The second article concerned a co-accused, Duberry. He had been acquitted, but his credibility and his evidence were still relevant in relation to the guilt or innocence of the four remaining defendants, in respect of whom verdicts had not been returned. Liability was not disputed, but the court gave some consideration to the s 2(2) tests, finding that they were satisfied due to the timing of the article and the probability that the jurors might have been influenced for or against the four defendants. The trial had been abandoned as a result of the article and a re-trial ordered. It was found that: '"substantial" in that context connotes a risk which is more than remote and not merely minimal . . . and it has to be accepted that within the range of

---

85   [1995] 2 All ER 370.

86   [1991] 1 QB 514.

87   [1998] EMLR 294.

88   [1992] 3 All ER 38.

89   [2002] EWHC 907.

strict liability contempts, this case is towards the top end.' This indicates that a test akin to that of Lord Diplock in *A-G v English* is still influencing judges, particularly at first instance. The HRA was not mentioned and the fine imposed was high but not excessive.

4. Recently, in *Attorney-General v Random House Group Ltd*,[90] s 2(2) was found to be satisfied, s 5 found not to apply, and an injunction was granted (unusually) to restrain publication of the book in question until after the trial had finished. The case concerned the retrial of those suspected of carrying out the so-called airline plot, to blow up planes using explosives concealed in soft drinks bottles. A book was written by a very senior police officer about the investigation of terrorist plots, including 7/7 and the airline plot, which was covered in five pages in the book. It was published days before the trial of the suspects was concluding, an injunction was swiftly sought and gained and it was withdrawn from sale. Parts had been serialised in *The Times*, but no extracts of the crucial five pages had been published. It was not thought that the book had come to the attention of any of the jurors as things stood. However, the question was—were the injunction to be lifted, and the book to go back on sale, was there a substantial risk that jurors might encounter it and be seriously prejudiced by it?

Attorney-General v Random House Group Ltd [2009] EWHC 1727, QB (extracts)

Tugenhadt J. . .

27. The Act does not in terms provide for injunctions. While it is common ground that an injunction may be granted to restrain what would be a contempt of court under s 2 of the Act, there is an issue as to the conditions which the Attorney-General must satisfy if such an injunction is to be granted. There is no authority governing the standard of proof that is to be met by the Attorney-General, and certainly none since the coming into force of The Human Rights Act 1998 ('HRA').

[The Judge then considered and rejected the *American* Cyanamid approach (above at n 33), noted the provisions of s 12(3) HRA and the speech of Lord Nicholls in *Cream Holdings* (above at pp 1024–1025) and went on]:

41. The editors of *Arlidge Eady & Smith* [*On Contempt of Court* (3rd edn 2005) conclude their consideration of this subject at para 6–18 by stating that the test in *ex p HTV Cymru (Wales) Ltd* [2002] EMLR 11 applies. Ms Evans adopts this, and I accept her submission.

42. In that case Aikens J. . .said this at paras 24 and 25:

'24. What standard of proof has to be satisfied by the applicant before it can obtain an injunction?

25. . .the applicant must demonstrate:

(1) that the court is sure that the alleged acts are going to be carried out, if not restrained;

(2) that the court is sure that if the alleged acts are carried out, then they would amount to a contempt of court. For the present case the test must be that the acts would create a substantial risk that the course of justice in this trial will be seriously impeded or prejudiced.'

43. In the present case there is no dispute, and I am sure, that further sales of the Book will be made if not restrained. So the question for me to decide is whether I am sure that that would create a substantial risk that the course of justice in the Trial will be seriously

impeded or prejudiced. If so, it would not follow as a matter of course that an injunction should be granted. That would mean no more than that the jurisdiction of the court to grant an injunction had been established. I would then have to consider whether the remedy of an injunction was necessary and proportionate.

[The Judge then considered the background, including prior prejudicial coverage, following the failure of the jury to agree on one count and deliver verdicts on another. He noted that]

49. . . .The accused made applications that there should be no retrial, and for a stay, on the grounds that the jury had returned a verdict on the conspiracy to murder, and that a fair retrial would be impossible because of the adverse publicity. These submissions failed. . .

52. On 11 September every national newspaper reported that the seven accused were to face a retrial. Nevertheless, reporting continued. The Trial Judge said (at pp 17–20) that it was not possible to recite all the objectionable material that was published by the media, and he described it as 'an avalanche', including 'vast internet coverage which can be accessed with ease'. The essence of the vast majority was that all the accused were guilty of conspiracy to blow up aircraft. . .

[Tugenhadt then noted that despite this, the trial judge had concluded that a fair trial would be possible, with the passing of time, and fading of memories of the coverage. He then went on to find that, given the clear directions of the current trial judge, there was not a substantial risk that a juror would deliberately buy the book, read the pages in question and realise they applied to the current trial (paras 71–77). He then went on to consider the issue of impediment, rather than prejudice to the trial.]

78. Mr Whittam addressed me on what might happen if the Book were to be put back on sale. His submissions impliedly referred to matters of the kind set out in Archbold (2009 edition) para 4–419 (new information emerging after closure of the defence case).

79. First he submitted that it was inevitable that there would be an application to discharge the jury. The speeches for the defence will have finished, or nearly so, and it will be impossible for the accused to alter the way their defences are presented to take account of the Book (as might have been possible, perhaps, if the Book had been put on sale before, or at an earlier stage during, the Trial).

80. If the Trial Judge were not minded to discharge the jury, there would be applications that enquiries be made of the jurors to find out if any of them had read the Book. Any juror who had read it would be the subject of an application to discharge, with investigation whether he had contaminated other members of the jury. Fortunately, there are still all twelve jurors present, but losing any juror can put a trial at risk.

81. This is not a case in which the Trial Judge could be expected to exercise his power under the Juries Act 1974 s.13 to prohibit the jury from separating. The Trial has already been a very great interference in their private lives for many months. If they were not to be permitted to separate, then they would be expected to be in isolation for a period of up to eight weeks, of which two or three weeks would be before they retired to consider their verdicts.

82. The jury have been told to expect that the case should finish by the end of August. They are likely to require a substantial period in retirement. If there is a delay, then the Trial may continue into September. This court should have regard to the rights and interests of the jurors.

83. Ms Evans accepts that there may be some disruption to the Trial. But she submits that in such a long trial as this, where there have already been delays, I cannot be sure that there is a substantial risk that the Trial would be seriously impeded.

84. Having considered these submissions, I am sure that if the Book were put back on sale there would be a substantial risk that the course of justice would be seriously impeded. The impediments would include the applications to which Mr Whittam has referred. With so many accused, there is a substantial risk that these applications would take days. The jury would have to wait, when they had expected the summing up to start. The Trial Judge would be distracted from his summing up by having to deal with these applications. The extent to which these accused's submissions may be time consuming is clearly illustrated by the hearing that took place in December 2008. There is a substantial risk that much of that ground would be retraced, because the Book cannot be considered in isolation from other publications which the jury may be prompted to look at, if any of them reads the Book. After so long a trial, it is important that continuity be maintained. It would be difficult for the jury not start their deliberations, but by then they would not yet have the directions in the summing-up which were necessary for them to do so.

85. I am also sure that there is a substantial risk that Trial Judge would discharge the jury. He has a knowledge of the Trial which is of a different order to my knowledge. The fact that, on the limited material before me, I have reached the view I have reached as to the risk of prejudice, cannot require me to assume that there is no substantial risk of him taking a different view. I am sure that if he did not discharge the jury, then there is a substantial risk that that would found a ground of appeal. I am not sure that, if he did not discharge the jury, he would have to give an extreme direction. I expect that a form of words could be found. But it would not carry the same weight as the direction that he gave on 24 February (para 60 above). He would not be able to tell the jury that the information in the Book might not be accurately reported. Neither the defence, nor the prosecution, could be expected to submit that he should say that to the jury. This is not a case where a trial judge could be expected to exercise his powers under s. 13 of the Juries Act.

86. I have answered the questions in para 44 above as follows. I have answered Yes to question (i) in respect of both prejudice and impediment. In respect of questions (ii) and (iii) I have answered No on the subject of prejudice, but Yes on the subject of impediment. In short I am sure that the putting of the Book on sale again would create a substantial risk that the course of justice in the Trial will be seriously impeded, but I am not sure that that would create a substantial risk that it would be seriously prejudiced.

[The Justice then decided that s 5 of the Act did not apply (see below). He went on to consider whether an injunction should be granted]:

97. ...In *Ex p The Telegraph Group Ltd* [2001] 1 WLR 1983, 1991, para [22] the Court said that if the risk required by the Act was found to exist (the first question), two further questions arose. The second question was: would the order eliminate the risk? If not, obviously there could be no necessity to make the order, and that would be the end of the matter. Clearly that test is satisfied in the present case. The third question was:

> even if the judge is satisfied that an order would achieve the objective, he or she would still have to consider whether the risk could satisfactorily be overcome by some less restrictive means. If so it could not be said to be necessary. . .

99. Mr Sheldon submits that an injunction is necessary and proportionate, having regard to the unique circumstances of this case. . .In addition he stresses the short period, expected to be not more than about eight weeks, during which the injunction sought is to run. Further, he submits that the Publishers and the authors have already enjoyed the opportunity to express themselves in the form of the serialisation in the Times which did not

include the words complained of. And notwithstanding the difficulties encountered by the Publishers, the court may consider that the Book is of sufficient interest to the public for the Publishers to plan a fresh publication at a later date. These points are made by reference to s.12(4)(a)(i) HRA.

100. Detailed evidence has been given for the Publishers of the consequences of the grant of the injunction. . .If the injunction is not lifted immediately (and to some extent, even if it is) the damage to the marketing of the Book will be irreparable. . .It is difficult to persuade major retailers to provide space on their shelves. There is not empty space waiting for books. The vacant space left by books that are returned to a publisher are filled by something else. The retailers plan well in advance what books they will stock, and what they will not. The Publishers were fortunate to obtain for the Book initial subscription orders which were very strong indeed for a serious work of non-fiction. This was one of the biggest hardback non-fiction releases from the Publishers this year. The publicity campaign, which was crucial to stimulate sales during the week following serialisation and running up to the official publication day, 2 July 2009, had been carefully planned and very successfully orchestrated. . .The first week is the one in which publishers expect to make their maximum sales. If the injunction is upheld, the Publishers' evidence is that their entire publication of the Book might effectively be destroyed. They had expected a number of reprints. But experience has shown that booksellers are not interested in taking a book back once it has been returned, if much time goes by. This is partly because there is nervousness about any publication that has been returned as a result of legal action. In the present case the position has been made worse because reporting restrictions have prevented the Publishers from explaining why the injunction was granted. If the retailers are willing to take the Book back, new arrangements with them and new promotions would have to be made, at a cost. . . .

102. More important than any of this evidence, in my judgment, is the subject matter of the Book and the nature of the "expression" it represents. The courts have recognised different types of speech, some of which attract more protection than others. Political speech, or speech on public affairs is the category which attracts the most protection. The Book is in that category. I am satisfied that it would be in the public interest for the Book to be published. (s 12(4)(a)(ii) HRA).

103. Causing a publisher to recall a book (or any other publication) is always a major step to take. The costs will exceed by a very large measure the amount which the court might be expected to impose, following a committal for contempt, by way of fine in a case such as the present, assuming the facts were as I have set them out here. If the Book had been sold out and no application made to the court for an injunction, it is for consideration whether the Attorney-General would have thought it in the public interest in this case to apply to commit for contempt of court. That would have depended upon all the circumstances, which may have included what happened at the Trial. It is in any case not a matter for this court, so I shall assume that the Attorney-General would have applied to commit. If she had, and depending on the circumstances, it seems to me that the court might have taken a lenient view in this case. It is unlikely that the financial consequences would have been as great as the evidence shows the consequences of this injunction have been and, if it is continued, will be in the future.

104. I have considered what other measures might be to hand to address the risk which I have held to exist. A direction to the jury would not carry the weight that such directions usually carry, for reasons already discussed (para 85 above). The powers of the court under s 13 of the Juries Act have rarely been exercised in recent years. They should not be

overlooked, but nor should the difficulties in exercising those powers. There may be cases where that would be the proportionate response. If so, there would be difficulties, except in those rare cases where an injunction is sought from a High Court Judge during a trial, as happened in the *HTV Cymru* case. A circuit judge sitting in the Crown Court could not grant an injunction, and the judge of the High Court to whom the Attorney-General applied for an injunction cannot exercise the powers of the trial judge over the jury, nor require that any powers be exercised by him.

105. In my judgment the unique features of this case referred to at the start of this judgment put the case in a category of its own. It is important not to lose sight of what is at stake in the Trial. While I recall the finding that I have made as to the limited risk of prejudice that would be created in this case, what is at stake in the Trial makes it of the highest importance that the Trial be not seriously impeded.

106. The public interest in the Trial being fair could not be higher. If any of the accused is convicted on count 1, he will face the prospect of spending much if not all of the rest of his life in custody.

107. If any of the accused is innocent, and is nevertheless convicted, the scale of the injustice involved would be difficult to exaggerate. In addition, experience over the last 30 years shows that such injustice (on those occasions when it has occurred) has had a long lasting, and extremely adverse effect upon public confidence in the administration of justice. This is to the detriment of society as a whole.

108. On the other hand, if any of the accused did indeed take part in the conspiracy alleged in count 1, and if he is not convicted, or if his conviction has to be set aside on appeal and if he cannot be retried for a second time, the injustice and danger to the public is again difficult to exaggerate. In that event the lives of very many people may be put at risk.

109. In many cases less weight might be attached to the implications of any appeal and retrial that might follow if the jury were to be discharged, or any appeal against conviction succeeds. But in this case seven accused have been in custody for three years already, and there are three further accused (two in custody) whose trial is to follow the trial of these accused. If there is a retrial, they will have to wait for many more months before there is a verdict. Two juries have sat for many months in two separate trials. This places a very great strain on them and upon the administration of justice. There is not unlimited capacity in the criminal justice system. When one case is being tried, or retried, another case must be kept waiting. The cost to the public of each trial of the scale of the Trial runs into millions of pounds. The financial implications for the Publishers of a delay even as short as eight weeks are great. But they cannot be compared to the financial implications for the public at large of a delay to this trial, or an appeal. Even a trial of a single accused for a few days or weeks is expensive, but the administrative and financial implications of the trials of those accused of the airline plot is exceptional. The disparity of risk which exists between what the Publishers must suffer if this injunction is granted, and what the public must risk suffering if it is not, is beyond measurement, and is another unique feature of this case.

110. In my judgment, in the present case, for the reasons I have stated, it is necessary and proportionate that the injunction be granted.

Notes

1. The above case is of considerable interest, first because it illustrates a rare instance of a court granting an injunction to prevent interference with a trial, rather than punishing for contempt

91   See, e.g. G Zellick [1982] PL 343.

after the fact, second because it is based on impediment to the trial rather than a direct finding of a substantial risk of serious prejudice to it and third because it represents one of the few instances of a post-HRA case that deals comprehensively with the nature of the impediments created, in relation to the free speech considerations.

2. *Attorney-General v English*, above, is the leading case on s 5 and is generally considered to provide a good example of the kind of case for which s 5 was framed.[91] Lord Diplock's ruling was seen as giving a liberal interpretation to s 5. As he points out, a narrower interpretation of s 5 would have meant that all debate in the media on the topic of mercy killing would have been prevented for almost a year—the time during which the proceedings in Dr Arthur's case were active from charge to acquittal. (It may be noted that Dr Arthur was acquitted; therefore the article presumably did not influence the jurors against him. That fact, however, did not preclude a finding that there was a substantial risk of serious prejudice to his trial.) The proper interpretation of s 5 has also been considered in the following cases: *Attorney-General v Times Newspaper;*[92] *Attorney-General v Hislop;*[93] *Daily Express* case.[94] In *Attorney-General v TVS Television; Attorney-General v HW Southey and Sons,*[95] it was determined that a TVS programme concerned with the possibility that Rachmanism had arisen in the south of England but focused on landlords in Reading, which coincided with the charging of a Reading landlord with conspiring to defraud the DHSS, could not create a merely incidental risk. Lloyd L said that the judge should:

> look at the subject matter of the discussion and see how closely it relates to the particular legal proceedings. The more closely it relates the easier it will be for the Attorney-General to show that the risk of prejudice is not merely incidental to the discussion. The application of the test is largely a matter of first impression.

In the *Random House* case above, Tugendadt J found, at para 94 that:

> the impediment in the present case arises from the fact that the passages complained of [in the book] discuss the very acts which led to the Trial. On reflection, but not without hesitation, I am sure that these passages are not incidental to the discussion.

Intentionally prejudicing proceedings: common law contempt

Section 6(c) of the 1981 Act preserves liability for contempt at common law if intention to prejudice the administration of justice can be shown, although prosecutions under this form of contempt are very rare. 'Prejudice (to) the administration of justice' clearly includes prejudice to particular proceedings. Once the requirement of intent is satisfied it is easier to establish contempt at common law rather than under the Act, as it is only necessary to show at common law 'a real risk of prejudice', proceedings need only be 'imminent', not 'active', and there is no provision protecting free speech equivalent to that under s 5.

---

92   *The Times,* 12 February 1983.

93   [1991] 1 QB 514.

94   *The Times,* 19 December 1981.

95   *The Times,* 7 July 1989.

Liability can be established at common law in instances when it might also be established under the 1981 Act, as occurred in *Attorney-General v Hislop*,[96] but obviously common law liability is of most significance in instances in which the Act does not apply because proceedings are inactive. The *actus reus* of common law contempt will be satisfied by a publication which creates a real risk of prejudice to the administration of justice (*R v Thomson Newspapers*).[97] There may be a number of different methods of fulfilling this test, as *Hislop* demonstrated. From the Court of Appeal ruling in the *Spycatcher* case (below), it is clear that the *mens rea* for common law contempt is specific intent and therefore it cannot include recklessness. The test may be summed up as follows: did the defendant either wish to prejudice proceedings or foresee that such prejudice was a virtually inevitable consequence of publishing the material in question? This test is based on the meaning of intent arising from rulings on the *mens rea* for murder from *R v Hancock and Shankland*,[98] *R v Nedrick*[99] and *R v Woollin*.[100]

At common law the *sub judice* period began when proceedings could be said to be imminent (*R v Savundranayagan*).[101] However, it may not always be necessary to establish imminence. In *Attorney-General v Newsgroup Newspapers plc*,[102] it was held *obiter* that, where it is established that the defendant intended to prejudice proceedings, it is not necessary to show that proceedings are imminent. This was endorsed, *obiter*, in one of the rulings on imminence in *Attorney-General v Sport*.[103] However, that stance was not reaffirmed in *Punch*. Thus it appears that imminence should be established, although the issue still requires clarification.

The following cases illustrate an important variant of common law contempt in which one newspaper publishes material that another organ of the media has been barred by injunction from publishing.

Attorney-General v Times Newspapers and Another (Spycatcher case)
[1991] 2 WLR 994, 1000, 1003, 1004

As indicated above, in 1986 *The Guardian* and *The Observer* published reports which included some *Spycatcher* material and the Attorney-General obtained temporary *ex parte* injunctions preventing them from further disclosure of such material.[104] While the temporary injunctions were in force the *Independent* and two other papers published material covered by them. The question arose whether such actions could amount to common law contempt. In *Attorney-General v Newspaper Publishing plc, The Times*, 28 February 1990, the Court of Appeal found that the respondents' publications could amount to a contempt of court and remitted the case for trial. Just before that ruling the *Sunday Times* had published extracts from *Spycatcher*. The Attorney-General brought proceedings for contempt against the publishers and editors of the *Sunday Times*. At first instance it was found that the publishers and editors of the *Independent* and the *Sunday Times* had been guilty of contempt, and that finding was

---

96   [1991] 1 QB 514.

97   [1968] 1 All ER 268.

98   [1986] AC 455.

99   [1986] 1 WLR 1025.

100   [1999] AC 82. See further D Ormerod, *Smith & Hogan, Criminal Law*, 12th edn (2008), Part 1 Chapter 5.

101   [1968] 1 WLR 1761.

102   [1988] 2 All ER 906.

103   [1992] 1 All ER 503.

104   For discussion of this branch of the litigation, see pp 1026–1028, above.

confirmed by the Court of Appeal. Times Newspapers appealed to the House of Lords. The only matter still at issue was whether the appellants had committed the *actus reus* of common law contempt. The House of Lords found that it had.

Lord Brandon of Oakbrook: It is, in my opinion, of the utmost importance to formulate with precision the question which falls to be decided in this appeal. For the purpose of such formulation it is necessary to assume a situation in which one person, B, is a party to an action brought against him by another person, A, and the court grants A an injunction restraining B from doing certain acts. . . .The question for decision is whether, in the situation assumed, it is a contempt of court for C, with the intention of impeding or prejudicing the administration of justice by the court in the action between A and B, himself to do the acts which the injunction restrains B from committing. . . It remains to consider in what circumstances conduct by C, in knowingly doing acts which would, if done by B, be a breach of an injunction against him, is such as to impede or interfere with the administration of justice by the court in the action between A and B. I do not think that it would be wise, even if it were possible, to try to give an exhaustive answer to that question. A principal example, however, of circumstances which will have that effect is where the subject matter of the action is such that, if it is destroyed in whole or in part before the trial of the action, the purpose of the trial will be wholly or partly nullified.

The present case presents a similar situation. The claims of the Attorney General in the confidentiality actions were for permanent injunctions restraining the defendants from publishing what may conveniently be called *Spycatcher* material. The purpose of the Millett injunctions was to prevent the publication of any such material pending the trial of the confidentiality actions. The consequence of the publication of *Spycatcher* material by the publishers and editor of the Sunday Times before the trial of the confidentiality actions was to nullify, in part at least, the purpose of such trial, because it put into the public domain part of the material which it was claimed by the Attorney General in the confidentiality actions ought to remain confidential. It follows that the conduct of the publishers and editor of the Sunday Times constituted the *actus reus* of impeding or interfering with the administration of justice by the court in the confidentiality actions. *Mens rea* in respect of such conduct having been conceded by Mr Lester, both the necessary ingredients of contempt of court were present. . . In the result I would affirm the judgment of the Court of Appeal and dismiss the appeal. [The other four Law Lords concurred.]

Attorney-General v Punch Limited and Another (also referred to as A-G v Steen) [2003] 1 AC 1046 (extracts)

The editor of *Punch* magazine published an article by David Shayler, a former MI5 agent, containing confidential information on the operation of the security services. He had been subject to an interlocutory injunction restraining him until trial from disclosing information gained due to his employment with the security services, aside from information excepted by the Attorney General. The Attorney General argued that the editor of the magazine deliberately impeded or prejudiced the court's purpose in making the non disclosure order against Mr Shayler and was therefore in contempt of court.

Lord Nicholls of Birkenhead. . .
27 This appeal concerns a restraint on the freedom of expression. Freedom of expression includes, importantly, the right to impart information without interference by public authority, to use the language of article 10(1) of the European Convention for the Protection

of Human Rights. Restraints on the freedom of expression are acceptable only to the extent they are necessary and justified by compelling reasons. The need for the restraint must be convincingly established. Restraints on the freedom of the press call for particularly rigorous scrutiny.

28 This appeal also concerns protection of national security. National security is one of the reasons, set out in the familiar list in article 10(2) of the Convention, which may justify a restraint on freedom of expression. The interests of national security may furnish a compelling reason for preventing disclosure of information about the work of the Security Service.

29 But, let it also be said at once, the Security Service is not entitled to immunity from criticism. In principle the public has a right to know of incompetence in the Security Service as in any other government department. Here, as elsewhere where questions arise about the freedom of expression, the law has to strike a balance. On the one hand, there is the need to protect the nation's security. On the other hand, there is a need to ensure that the activities of the Security Service are not screened unnecessarily from the healthy light of publicity. In striking this balance the seriousness of the risk to national security and the foreseeable gravity of the consequences if disclosure occurs, and the seriousness of the alleged incompetence and errors sought to be disclosed, are among the matters to be taken into account.

30 The rule of law requires that the decision on where this balance lies in any case should be made by the court as an independent and impartial tribunal established by law. Clearly, if a decision on where the balance lies is to be effective, the court must be able to prevent the information being disclosed in the period which will necessarily elapse before the court is in a position to reach an informed decision after giving a fair hearing to both parties to the dispute. Once public disclosure occurs confidentiality is lost for ever. If disclosure were permitted to occur in advance of the trial serious and irreparable damage could be done to national security.

31 Thus, depending on all the circumstances of the case, a temporary injunction for a reasonable period pending the trial may be necessary for the protection of national security. Even a temporary restriction on the exercise of freedom of expression is not to be imposed lightly. News is a perishable commodity. Public and media interest in topical issues fades. But, when granted, such an injunction becomes an integral feature of the due administration of justice in the proceedings in which it was made.

32 Equally clearly, if a temporary injunction is to be effective the law must be able to prescribe appropriate penalties where a person deliberately sets the injunction at nought. Without sanctions an injunction would be a paper tiger. Sanctions are necessary to maintain the rule of law; in the language of the Convention, to maintain the authority of the judiciary. If the rule of law is to be meaningful, the decision of the court on how, and to what extent, the status quo should be maintained pending the trial must be respected. It must be respected by third parties as well as the parties to the proceedings. . . .

43 The reason why the court grants interim protection is to protect the plaintiff's asserted right. But the manner in which this protection is afforded depends upon the terms of the interlocutory injunction. The purpose the court seeks to achieve by granting the interlocutory injunction is that, pending a decision by the court on the claims in the proceedings, the restrained acts shall not be done. Third parties are in contempt of court if they wilfully interfere with the administration of justice by thwarting the achievement of this purpose in those proceedings. This is so, even if in the particular case, the injunction is drawn in seemingly over-wide terms.

44 The remedy of the third party whose conduct is affected by the order is to apply to the court for the order to be varied. Furthermore, there will be no contempt unless the act done has some significant and adverse effect on the administration of justice in the proceedings. This tempers the rigour of the principle.

45 Departure from this straightforward approach runs into serious practical difficulties. If, in this context, the purpose of the court in granting an interlocutory injunction means something other than the effect its terms show it was intended to have between the parties, how is a third party to know what it is? How is a third party to know what is the purpose, which he must respect, if it is something other than the purpose evident on the face of the order? Uncertainty is bound to follow, with consequential difficulties in proving that a third party knowingly impeded or prejudiced the purpose the court sought to achieve when granting the injunction. I see no justification or need to go down this route, which is not supported by authority. . .

47 On this basis I turn to consider the purpose of Hooper J's order. In my view, not only was the scope of the order clear, so also was its purpose; clear, indeed, beyond a peradventure. Self-evidently, the purpose of the judge in making the order was to preserve the confidentiality of the information *specified in the order* pending the trial so as to enable the court at trial to adjudicate effectively on the disputed issues of confidentiality arising in the action. This is apparent from merely reading the order. The Attorney General's claim for a permanent injunction might be defeated in advance of the trial if, before the trial, Mr Shayler was at liberty to put this information into the public domain. In other words, but to the same effect, the purpose of the court in making the order was to ensure that the court's decision on the claims in the proceedings should not be pre-empted by Mr Shayler disclosing any of the information specified in the order before the trial.

48 This being the purpose of the injunction, the *actus reus* of contempt lies in thwarting this purpose by destruction of the confidentiality of the material which it was the purpose of the injunction to preserve.

49 As already stated, Mr Steen accepts that the publication of the offending magazine article constituted the *actus reus* of contempt. He is right to do so. He did an act which Hooper J's order prohibited Mr Shayler from doing. Publication of the information by "Punch" was destructive in part of the purpose of Hooper J's order.

50 Although Mr Steen seems not to accept this, this is not a case where the conduct was inconsistent with the court's order in only a technical or trivial way. Disclosure of the three pieces of information mentioned above, not previously published, has had a significant and adverse effect on the trial of the action against Mr Shayler. Contrary to the court's object in granting the interlocutory injunction, the Attorney General's claim to keep these pieces of information confidential has now been thwarted in advance of the trial.

51 [On *mens rea*] Mr Steen's evidence was that he thought the purpose of the order was to prevent damage to national security, it was not his intention to damage national security in any way, and he did not consider he was doing so. . . . Accordingly, so the argument runs, the Attorney General did not establish that Mr Steen intended to thwart the court's purpose in making the interlocutory injunction.

52 I am not impressed by this argument. The facts speak for themselves. Mr Steen is an intelligent man and experienced journalist. He knew that the action against Mr Shayler raised confidentiality issues relating wholly or primarily to national security. He must, inevitably, have appreciated that by publishing the article he was doing precisely what the order was intended to prevent, namely, pre-empting the court's decision on these confidentiality issues. That is knowing interference with the administration of justice.

53 I do not see how on this issue, which is the relevant issue, the admitted or proved facts are susceptible of any other interpretation. The judge was entitled so to conclude, even though these conclusions were not put in so many words to Mr Steen in the course of his cross-examination. No credible alternative conclusion regarding Mr Steen's relevant beliefs or intentions has been advanced on his behalf. Mr Steen may have thought the order was intended to protect national security, and that publication would not damage national security. He may have had, as he says, no intention of damaging national security. Those beliefs and intentions are not inconsistent with an intention to take it upon himself to make a decision which, as he knew, the court had reserved to itself. I have to say, however, that even on the basis of his stated beliefs and intentions Mr Steen's conduct was surprisingly irresponsible. He frankly admitted, as is obvious, that he was not qualified to assess whether disclosure of any particular information would damage national security. Despite this he proceeded to publish information whose disclosure was, as he knew, asserted by the Attorney General to be damaging to national security.

Notes

1. The decision of the Court of Appeal in the *Punch* case sought to focus closely on the values and interests at stake and refused to allow an uncertain threat to the administration of justice to overcome freedom of expression. Although the ECHR was not relied on extensively, and there was virtually no recitation of the relevant jurisprudence, the Court showed itself determined to adopt a stance which relied on close examination of the necessity of the interference in question, eventually concluding that a pressing social need to allow such an interference with freedom of political expression was not present. The Court was not impressed by the claim that it was necessary to preserve this area of liability in order to prevent impediments to the administration of justice. Thus, the Court sought to identify another interest—in this instance national security—which could genuinely support the grave interference with freedom of expression represented by the *Spycatcher* doctrine, and found that the alleged harm was not serious enough to justify such a grave interference with media freedom. In some rare instances, it was noted, it might be possible to show that the journalist or other person in question, due to his or her background and/or specialist knowledge, did recognise that publication of the material in question would be likely to damage national security.

   This decision would have narrowed down and virtually destroyed the *Spycatcher* area of liability, since if the purpose of interim orders was accepted to be to prevent disclosure of any matter that arguably risked harming the national interest, then proof of *mens rea* for contempt would involve proving to the criminal standard that third parties, including editors and journalists, knew that materials published arguably risked harming that interest. That would probably have proved to be a difficult, if not impossible, task for the Crown in most instances. Editors would have been able to insist that they had no reason to believe that even arguable damage to national security might result from such publication. Since the *mens rea* required is specific intent, it would not be possible merely to show that a reasonable person in the defendant's position would have known that such a risk arose—a possible means of satisfying the test required under the Official Secrets Act 1989, s 5. Thus, the result would have been that the grant of such injunctions in most circumstances could not have lead to the imposition of criminal liability against third parties such as Mr Steen.

2. However, the House of Lords did not accept that the *mens rea* requirement demanded that the newspaper editor had deliberately subverted the underlying purpose of the injunction. The Lords reaffirmed that it required knowing interference with the administration of justice. This analysis proceeded on the basis that once a court had decided that material should be kept confidential before the trial of a permanent injunction and had imposed an interim injunction with that object

in mind, it would be likely that a court would view publication of a significant part of that material by another body as likely to have a significant and adverse effect on the administration of justice in that trial. In such circumstances the *mens rea* requirement would virtually always be satisfied since journalists would normally be aware that the material was covered by an injunction against another body or person. Thus, in both the *Spycatcher* and *Punch* cases establishing oblique intent was reasonably straightforward. In *Punch* it was found: 'The facts speak for themselves. Mr Steen . . . knew that the action against Mr Shayler raised confidentiality issues relating wholly or primarily to national security. He must, inevitably, have appreciated that by publishing the article he was doing precisely what the order was intended to prevent, namely, pre-empting the court's decision on these confidentiality issues. That is knowing interference with the administration of justice'.[105]

3. Lord Hope in *Punch* found that the requirements of proportionality were satisfied since the interim injunction allowed newspapers to apply to the Attorney-General to publish innocuous material. However, objection can be made to his findings on the basis that that this places—in effect—a power of censorship in the hands, not only of a member of the executive, but also in those of one party to the original and forthcoming actions, creating an appearance of bias. The Attorney-General is the very person (or office) whose rights are being upheld by the threat of the invocation of the contempt of court jurisdiction. To determine whether liability under that jurisdiction can be justified as an interference with freedom of expression, partly by reference to his powers to allow publication, does not appear to provide an adequate safeguard for the media. This was far from the hard look at the proportionality that one would expect of a court which took its duty under s 6(1) HRA seriously.

4. The requirements of both the *actus reus* and *mens rea*, as interpreted by the House of Lords in *Spycatcher* and *Punch*, did little to temper the rigour of this doctrine in terms of its impact on the media. In particular, the demands of proportionality do not appear to be satisfied when it is borne in mind that if the party to whom the interim injunction was originally addressed published material covered by it, it would only be subject to civil sanctions, whereas third parties such as *Punch* who published such material would be criminally liable. It is clearly anomalous that this should be the case. In the *Punch* case the Attorney-General had fair warning that *Punch* was likely to publish Shayler material and could have sought a separate injunction, backed up by civil sanctions, against it. (It is arguable that if a party violated an injunction as indicated, it could be punished under the law of criminal contempt in the sense that it had interfered with the administration of justice in the proceedings against itself, but since the civil sanction is available, this sanction is not used in such circumstances.)

5. The HRA appeared initially to have the potential to have a much greater effect on this form of common law contempt than on strict liability contempt. Development of a form of 'public interest defence' at common law appeared to be possible through the application of the Art 10(2) test under the HRA. The use of the common law doctrine can allow the provision under s 5 of the 1981 Act to be circumvented. Further, the imprecision of the common law as regards the *sub judice* period might have meant that the doctrine could not be viewed as being 'prescribed by law'. If the current test had been replaced by the 'active' test, this form of common law contempt might have become a dead letter. However, since the Lords in the *Punch* case reaffirmed the elements of common law contempt as determined in the *Spycatcher* case, without allowing Art 10, scheduled in the HRA, to have any significant impact on those elements, any radical change in the nature of common law contempt now seems unlikely.

6. The role of common law contempt in relation to causing prejudice to proceedings by influencing jurors may be becoming in any event a dead letter: there have been no post-HRA prosecutions in

---

105   *Ibid*, at paras 51 and 52 *per* Lord Nicholls.

that context. This is probably due to the difficulty of demonstrating that a risk of prejudice caused by influencing jurors could arise where the proceedings in question (the criminal trial) is so far in the future at the time of publication that the proceedings are inactive for the purpose of the 1981 Act. Thus prosecutions for common law contempt in those circumstances are not being brought. But after the *Punch* case, common law contempt retains an important role in relation to protecting information that the Government wishes to remain secret, since once an injunction against one media body has been obtained preventing the publication of confidential information, any media body that publishes the information covered by the injunction risks a prosecution for contempt. This position, it is argued, does not strike a satisfactory balance between protecting both freedom of expression and the administration of justice.

Orders restricting reporting of court proceedings

There are a large number of specific statutory restrictions on reporting of trials. Section 4(2) of the 1981 Act provides that during any legal proceeding held in public a judge may make an order post-poning reporting of the proceedings if such action 'appears necessary for avoiding a substantial risk of prejudice to the administration of justice in those proceedings', thus creating an exception to s 4(1).[106] This might typically involve the reporting of matters which the defence wished to argue should be ruled inadmissible. A right of appeal against such orders in relation to trials on indictment was created by s 159 of the Criminal Justice Act 1988 in order to take account of a challenge under Art 10 at Strasbourg.[107] The position of the media when a s 4(2) order is made in respect of reporting a summary trial is less clear. However, it was established in *R v Clerkenwell Metropolitan Stipendiary Magistrate ex parte The Telegraph and Others*[108] that in such circumstances the media have a right to be heard and must be allowed to put forward the case for discharging the order. Section 11 of the 1981 Act allows a court, which has power to do so, to make an order prohibiting publication of names or other matters if this appears necessary 'for the purpose for which it was so withheld'. Thus, s 11 does not itself confer such a power and therefore refers to other statutes[109] and to the imprecise common law powers. It allows a departure from the principles of free speech and of open justice since it allows a court to prohibit reporting of certain matters. However, as *Attorney-General v Leveller Magazine Ltd* made clear, the fundamental importance of open justice will be outweighed only if very clear detriment to the general public interest would be likely to flow from publication of the matters in question.[110] The following is the most recent decision in this area.

Attorney-General's Reference (No 3 of 1999), Re Also known as: BBC's Application to Set Aside or Vary a Reporting Restriction Order, Re [2009] 3 WLR 142 (extracts)

The BBC sought to set aside a restriction order in relation to the identity of a man acquitted of rape. The man was acquitted when DNA evidence was initially ruled inadmissible.

---

106   For comment on s 4 of the 1981 Act, see C Walker, I Cram and D Brogarth (1992) 55 MLR 647.

107   The journalist, Crook, attempted to challenge a s 11 anonymity order: *R v Central Criminal Court ex parte Crook, The Times*, 8 November 1984. When the challenge failed, Crook took the case to Strasbourg.

108   (1993) 2 All ER 183.

109   A number of statutory provisions impose restrictions such as allowing certain persons concerned in a case to remain anonymous. This is provided for in relation to complainants in rape cases under s 4 of the Sexual Offences (Amendment) Act 1976, as amended, and for children under s 39(1) of the Children and Young Persons Act 1933. For comment on s 11 of the 1981 Act, see Walker, Cram and Brogarth, n 106 above.

110   [1979] AC 440; [1979] 2 WLR 247. See also *R v Dover Justices ex parte Dover District Council and Wells* [1992] Crim LR 371.

Certain newspapers and magazines had revealed the man's identity. The BBC wanted to use the identity as part of a series on controversial acquittals but the order prevented disclosing the circumstances of the acquittal, and discussion of retrial, except anonymously.

Lord Hope of Craighead: [after deciding that the man's privacy rights under Art 8 were engaged, and therefore that the freedom of speech issue was to be decided under Art 8(2)]:
23 The tests that must be applied are well settled. They are whether publication of the material pursues a legitimate aim, and whether the benefits that will be achieved by its publication are proportionate to the harm that may be done by the interference with the right to privacy. Any restriction of the right of freedom of expression must be subjected to very close scrutiny. But so too must any restriction on the right to privacy. The protection of private life has to be balanced against the freedom of expression guaranteed by article 10: *Von Hannover v Germany* 40 EHRR 1, para 58. One must start from the position that neither article 8 nor article 10 has any pre-eminence over the other. The values that each right seeks to protect are equally important. The question is how far, as article 8(2) puts it, it is 'necessary' for the one to be qualified in order to protect the values that the other seeks to protect.
24 Further guidance as to the approach that is to be adopted was given in *Von Hannover v Germany*. The European court said, at para 60, that in the cases in which it has had to balance the protection of private life against freedom of expression it has always stressed the contribution that photographs or articles in the press make to a debate of general interest. It pointed out, at para 63, that a fundamental distinction had to be drawn between reporting facts which were capable of contributing to imparting information and ideas on matters of public interest and reporting details of the private life of an individual. It said, at para 76, that the decisive factor in balancing the protection of private life against freedom of expression should lie in the contribution that the published material makes to a debate of general interest. So the extent to which the programme that the BBC wish to make will satisfy that test must be examined with just as much care as the question whether the broadcast will engage D's right under article 8.
25 Lord Pannick suggested it would be open to the BBC to raise the issue of general interest without mentioning D's name or in any other way disclosing his identity. But I think that Mr Millar was right when he said that the BBC should not be required to restrict the scope of their programme in this way. The freedom of the press to exercise its own judgment in the presentation of journalistic material has been emphasised by the Strasbourg court. In *Jersild v Denmark* (1994) 19 EHRR 1, the court said, at para 31, that it was not for it, nor for the national courts for that matter, to substitute their own views for those of the press as to what technique of reporting should be adopted by journalists. It recalled that article 10 protects not only the substance of the ideas and the information expressed but also the form in which they are conveyed. In essence article 10 leaves it for journalists to decide what details it is necessary to reproduce to ensure credibility: see *Fressoz and Roire v France* (1999) 31 EHRR 28, para 54. So the BBC are entitled to say that the question whether D's identity needs to be disclosed to give weight to the message that the programme is intended to convey is for them to judge. As Lord Hoffmann said in *Campbell v MGN Ltd* [2004] 2 AC 457, para 59, judges are not newspaper editors. They are not broadcasting editors either. The issue as to where the balance is to be struck between the competing rights must be approached on this basis.
26 Will the revealing of D's identity in connection with the proposed programme pursue a legitimate aim? I would answer that question in the affirmative. In *Jersild v Denmark*, at para 31, it was recognised that there is a duty to impart information and ideas of public

interest which the public has a right to receive. The programme that the BBC wish to broadcast has been inspired by the removal of the double jeopardy rule. What this means in practice for our system of criminal justice is a matter of legitimate public interest. Among the issues which can be so described are the kinds of offences to which Part 10 of the 2003 Act applies, and the circumstances in which an application for a person who has been acquitted to be retried would be appropriate. These issues could, of course, be discussed in the abstract by reference to hypothetical facts and circumstances. But the arguments that the programme wishes to present will lose much of their force unless they can be directed to the facts and circumstances of actual cases. The point about D's name is that the producers of the programme believe that its disclosure will give added credibility to the account which they wish to present. This is a view which they are entitled to adopt and, given the content of the programme as a whole, it is an aim which can properly be regarded as legitimate.

27 There remains the question of proportionality. As against the public's right to receive information there is D's right to be protected against publication of details of his private life. But the weight that is to be given to his right has to be judged against the potential for harm if publication does take place. The fact that he was acquitted of the rape is already legitimately in the public domain. He cannot complain of a violation of his rights under article 8 if, as a result of the programme, an application is made for him to be put on trial again for that offence. This is because the statute provides for this, and because the interests of a democratic society in the prevention of crime and disorder lie in the bringing of those who have committed crimes before the courts so that, if convicted, they can be punished for them.

28 There is a risk, as Lord Pannick has pointed out, of D's being tried by the media. That, of course, is to be deprecated. If this happens it will add to the effects on his personality that will flow inevitably from the mention of his name in the broadcast. But I do not see this additional feature as a reason for holding that his article 8 right to the protection of his reputation outweighs the right of freedom of expression on a matter of legitimate public interest. It may increase the pressure on the authorities, which will be there anyway as a result of the broadcast, to take steps for him to be retried. If that happens, the system of justice will take its course. Procedures are available for protecting D's identity so that he can receive a fair trial: section 82 of the 2003 Act; see also *Montgomery v HM Advocate* [2003] 1 AC 641. The conclusion which I would draw is that the interference with D's article 8 right will be significant, but that it is proportionate when account is taken of the weight that must be given to the competing right to freedom of expression that the BBC wish to assert.

29 For these reasons I too agree that the order should now be discharged.

Notes

1. This decision confirms that free speech values, based on the open justice principle and couched in the Convention rights, post-HRA, will be difficult to overcome, based on countervailing arguments concerning the need to protect private life.[111] As this book went to press, one of the first decisions of the new Supreme Court (see Chapter 3, pp 153–156, for discussion of the new Court) was delivered, also overturning an anonymity order, this time granted to protect the identities of those subject to

---

111   See also *S Re (a child)* [2005] 1 AC 593. For discussion of that decision, of reporting restrictions intended to protect children, see H Fenwick and G Phillipson *Media Freedom under the HRA* (2006), Chapter 16.

freezing orders in respect of their assets under the Terrorism (United Nations Measures) Order 2006, Art 4: *Re Guardian News & Media Ltd* (also known as *HM Treasury v Youssef*) [2010] UKSC 1.

2. The interest in open justice is recognised under s 4(1) of the 1981 Act, which creates an exception to the strict liability rule, although under s 4(2) a judge may make an order postponing reporting of the proceedings in order to protect the administration of justice. The following rulings have suggested that s 4(2) should be used sparingly: *R v Horsham Magistrates ex parte Farquharson and Another*;[112] *R v Clerkenwell Metropolitan Stipendiary Magistrate ex parte the Telegraph and Others*;[113] *Re Central Independent Television plc and Others*.[114]

RESTRAINING FREEDOM OF EXPRESSION ON MORAL GROUNDS

Introduction

The Williams Committee,[115] convened in 1979 to report on obscenity (see *Pornography and Politics: The Williams Committee in Retrospect* (1983)), found that interference with the free flow of ideas and artistic endeavour was unacceptable since it amounted to ruling out in advance possible modes of human development, before it was known whether or not they would be desirable or necessary. Since they also reached the conclusion that 'no one has invented, or in our opinion could invent, an instrument that would suppress only [worthless pornography] and could not be turned against something. . .of [possibly] a more creative kind',[116] they concluded that the risk of suppressing worth-while creative art ruled out censorship of the written word. (They regarded standard photographic pornography as not expressing anything that could be regarded as an 'idea' and so as susceptible to regulation.) This liberal position is not reflected in UK law or in Art 10 of the ECHR, which allows restraint of freedom of speech on the ground of protection of morality. The development of UK law has been based on the suppression of speech to avoid the corruption of persons, particularly the more vulnerable.

R Dworkin, 'Is there a right to pornography?' (1981) *Oxford Journal of Legal Studies* 177

Pornography is often grotesquely offensive; it is insulting, not only to women but to men as well. But we cannot consider that a sufficient reason for banning it without destroying the principle that the speech we hate is as much entitled to protection as any other.

---

112 [1982] QB 762.

113 [1993] QB 462.

114 [1991] 1 All ER 347.

115 *Report of the Committee on Obscenity and Film Censorship* (Williams Committee), Cmnd 7772 (1979).

116 *Ibid*, para 5.24.

R Dworkin, Taking Rights Seriously (2005), p 257

Banning pornography abridges the freedom of authors, publishers and would-be readers. But if what they want to do is immoral, we are entitled to protect ourselves at that cost. Thus we are presented with a moral issue; does one have a moral right to publish or to read 'hard-core' pornography which can claim no value or virtue beyond its erotic effect? This moral issue should not be solved by fiat, nor by self-appointed ethical tutors, but by submission to the public. The public at present believes that hard-core pornography is immoral, that those who produce it are panderers, and that the protection of the community's sexual and related mores is sufficiently important to justify restricting their freedom.

Obscenity[117]

In the US, obscenity is defined, by *Miller v California* (1973) 413 US 15, 24 as:

> works which, taken as a whole, appeal to the prurient interest in sex, which portray sexual conduct in a patently offensive way, and which taken as a whole, do not have serious literary, artistic, political or scientific value.

This may be compared to the UK definition found in the following statute.

Obscene Publications Act 1959, as amended by the Obscene Publications Act 1964

1 Test of obscenity

(1)   For the purposes of this Act an article shall be deemed to be obscene if its effect or (where the article comprises two or more distinct items) the effect of any one of its items is, if taken as a whole, such as to tend to **deprave and corrupt** persons who are likely, having regard to all relevant circumstances, to read, see or hear the matter contained or embodied in it.

(2)   In this Act 'article' means any description of article containing or embodying matter to be read or looked at or both, any sound record, and any film or other record of a picture or pictures.

(3)   For the purposes of this Act a person publishes and article who—

(a)   distributes, circulates, sells, lets on hire, gives, or lends it, or who offers if for sale or for letting on hire; or

(b)   in the case of an article containing or embodying matter to be looked at or a record, shows, plays or projects it [or, where the matter is data stored electronically, transmits that data].

2 Prohibition of publication of obscene matter

(1)   Subject as hereinafter provided, any person who, whether for gain or not, publishes

---

117   See generally H Fenwick, *Civil Liberties and Human Rights,* 4th edn (2007), Chapter 6.3; see S Bailey, N Taylor, *Bailey, Harris and Jones: Civil Liberties Cases, Materials, and Commentary,* 6th edn (2009), Chapter 10; Robertson and Nichol, *Media Law* 5th edn (2007), Chapter 3.

an obscene article or who has an obscene article for publication for gain (whether gain to himself or gain to another) [commits an offence].

4 Defence of public good:

(1)   [Subject to subsection (1A) of this section] a person shall not be convicted of an offence against section two of this Act, and an order for forfeiture shall not be made under the foregoing section, if it is proved that publication of the article in question is justified as being for the public good on the ground that it is in the interests of science, literature, art or learning, or of other objects of general concern.

[(1A)   provides a like defence for films and soundtracks where it is proved that publication of the film or soundtrack is justified as being for the public good on the ground that it is in the interests of drama, opera, ballet or any other art, or of literature or learning.]

(2)   It is hereby declared that the opinion of experts as to the literary, artistic, scientific or other merits of an article may be admitted in any proceedings under this Act either to establish or negative the said ground.

Note
Leading cases on the interpretation of the Act follow.

R v Calder and Boyars [1969] 1 QB 151, 169

This description [in *Last Exit from Brooklyn* which had been prosecuted for obscenity] was compassionate and condemnatory. The only effect that it would produce in any but a mild lunatic fringe of readers would be horror, revulsion and pity; it was admittedly and intentionally disgusting, shocking and outrageous; it made the reader share in the horror it described and thereby so disgusted, shocked and outraged him that, being aware of the truth, he would do what he could to eradicate those evils and the conditions of modern society which so callously allowed them to exist. In short, according to the defence, instead of tending to encourage anyone to homosexuality, drug-taking or senseless brutal violence, it would have precisely the reverse effect.

. . . the proper direction on a defence under s 4 in a case such as the present is that the jury must consider on the one hand the number of readers they believe would tend to be depraved and corrupted by the book, the strength of the tendency to deprave and corrupt, and the nature of the depravity or corruption; on the other hand, they should assess the strength of the literary, sociological or ethical merit which they consider the book to possess. They should then weigh up all these factors and decide whether on balance the publication is proved to be justified as being for the public good.

R v Anderson [1972] 1 QB 304, 313, 314

At first instance it was found that a certain magazine, *Oz: 'School Kids' Issue,* was obscene.

Lord Widgery CJ: In the ordinary run of the mill cases. . .the issue 'obscene or no' must be tried by the jury without assistance of expert evidence on that issue, and we draw attention to the failure to observe that rule in this case in order that that failure may not occur again.

I turn now to criticisms which have been made. . .of the directions given by the judge in this case . . .It is said that in directing the jury as to the meaning of 'obscenity' under the Obscene Publications Act 1959, the judge did not make it clear that for the purpose of that Act 'obscene' means, and means only, a tendency to deprave or corrupt.

. . .we feel. . .that at least there is grave danger that the jury from that passage in the direction to them, took the view, or might have taken the view, that 'obscene' for all purposes including the purposes of the Obscene Publications Act 1959 included 'repulsive', 'filthy', 'loathsome' or 'lewd'.

The appeal was allowed, partly on this ground.

DPP v Whyte [1972] 3 All ER 12, 23

This decision concerned a book shop which sold pornographic material. The proprietors were prosecuted under s 1 of the 1959 Act. The defence argued that the customers in the shop could not be depraved and corrupted since they were regular readers of pornography; also it was argued that since they were mainly elderly men they were unlikely to engage in anti-social sexual conduct.

Lord Pearson: . . .in my opinion, the words 'deprave and corrupt' in the statutory definition, as in the judgment of Cockburn CJ in *Hicklin* [(1868) LR 3 QB 360], refer to the effect of pornographic articles on the mind, including the emotions, and it is not essential that any physical sexual activity (or any 'overt sexual activity', if that phrase has a different meaning) should result. According to the findings the articles did not leave the regular customers unmoved. On the contrary, they fascinated them and enabled them to engage in fantasies. Fantasies in this context must, I think, mean fantasies of normal or abnormal sexual activities. In the words of Cockburn CJ, the pornographic books in the respondents' shop suggested to the minds of the regular customers 'thoughts of a most impure and libidinous character. . . . Of course, bad conduct may follow from the corruption of the mind, but it is not part of the statutory definition of an obscene article that it must induce bad conduct.' (at p 864).

Lord Wilberforce: . . . the critical question to be asked is whether the effect of the articles is such to deprave and corrupt these likely readers. My Lords, I do not think that any extended discussion of the expression 'to deprave and corrupt' would be profitable, or is needed in the context of the present case (at p 861).

> . . . influence on the mind is not merely within the law, but is its primary target. (at p 863).
> . . . in every case, the magistrates, or the jury, are called upon to ascertain who are the likely readers and then to consider whether the article is likely to deprave and corrupt them (at p 860).

The majority in the House of Lords found that the respondents should have been convicted.

Knuller (Publishing, etc) Ltd v DPP [1972] 3 WLR 143

The House of Lords considered its earlier finding in *Shaw v DPP* [1962] AC 220,[118] that a common law offence known as conspiracy to corrupt public morals existed. Lord Reid said:

> I think that the meaning of the word 'corrupt' requires some clarification. One of my objections to the *Shaw* decision is that it leaves too much to the jury. I recognise

---

118   See also *R v Gibson* [1990] 2 QB 619.

that in the end it must be for the jury to say whether the matter published is likely to lead to corruption. . . . 'Corrupt' is a strong word and the jury ought to be reminded of that, as they were in the present case. I find nothing in the Act to indicate that Parliament thought or intended to lay down that indulgence in [homosexual acts between adult males in private] is not corrupting. I read the Act as saying that, even though it may be corrupting, if people choose to corrupt themselves in this way that is their affair and the law will not interfere. But no licence is given to others to encourage the practice. So if one accepts Shaw's case as rightly decided it must be left to each jury to decide in the circumstances of each case whether people were likely to be corrupted. In this case the jury were properly directed and it is impossible to say that they reached a wrong conclusion. It is not for us to say whether or not we agree with it.

The House of Lords upheld the conviction for conspiracy to corrupt public morals.

DPP v Jordan [1977] AC 699 (extracts)

. . . the structure of the section makes it clear that the other objects, or, which is the same argument, the nature of the general concern, fall within the same area, and cannot fall in the totally different area of effect on sexual behaviour and attitudes, which is covered in s 1. The judgment to be reached under s 4(1), and the evidence to be given under s 4(2), must be in order to show that publication should be permitted in spite of obscenity—not to negative obscenity. Section 4 has been diverted from its proper purpose, and indeed abused, when it has been used to enable evidence to be given that pornographic material may be for the public good as being therapeutic to some of the public' (*per* Lord Wilberforce).

R v Perrin [2002] EWCA Crim 747, CA (extracts)

This case concerned obscene material that was available as a free preview to a pay-per-view site. It was available to anyone able to access the internet.

Lord Justice Kennedy. . .
14. . . .The third ground of appeal is that the judge was wrong to reject the submission that the only relevant publication of the web page was to the officer who down-loaded it, and therefore it is wrong to test obscenity by reference to others who might have access to the preview page. Finally it is contended that. . .the judge was wrong not to say in clear terms that it was necessary for a significant proportion of those visiting the web page to be affected by it.
19. [Following *Barker*] the Court would still have to consider—

(1) whether any person or persons were likely to see the article, and if so –

(2) whether the effect of the article, taken as a whole, was such as to tend to deprave and corrupt the person or persons who were likely having regard to all relevant circumstances, to see the matter contained or embodied in it.

22. The publication relied on in this case is the making available of preview material to any viewer who may choose to access it (including of course vulnerable young people) and in such a situation the prosecution was entitled to invite the jury to look beyond PC Ysart and

to answer the two questions which we distilled from the decision in *Barker*. That was what was done in this case, and consequently in our judgment there is no substance in the third ground of appeal. Before parting with this ground of appeal we emphasise that section 1(1) of the 1959 Act only requires the jury to be satisfied that there is a likelihood of vulnerable persons seeing the material. The prosecution does not have to show that any such person actually saw it or would have seen it in the future.

30 [Re the 4th ground] . . .the submission that a clear reference to a tendency to corrupt more than a negligible number of viewers was a necessary part of a proper direction in the present case. We do not agree. . .. .

31 Nonetheless, despite the somewhat rambling nature of the judge's directions in response to the question posed by the jury, we consider that it was made clear that it was necessary for more than a negligible number of persons to be likely to see the material, and in our view that did not detract from the wording of the statute in any way disadvantageous to the appellant.

[His Lordship then considered and rejected an argument that the definition of obscenity was too vague for it to be 'prescribed by law' for the purposes of Art 10(2) and went on]:

49 No one has argued that the protection of minors and other vulnerable people is not an important issue to be addressed. On the other side of the balance sheet, apart from the general right to freedom of expression, there is no public interest to be served by permitting a business for profit to supply material which most people would regard as pornographic or obscene, using that word in its non-statutory sense. Yet, as Mr Patterson points out, the infringement of the appellant's freedom is limited, as can be seen by reference to the verdict of the jury on counts 2 and 3, and, although the protection to vulnerable people which is afforded by the 1959 Act may be limited, there is no reason why a responsible government should abandon that protection in favour of other limited remedies already available to parents and others as advocated by Mr Fulford.

Ground 1: Conclusion.

46. . . .Parliament was entitled to conclude that the prescription was necessary in a democratic society, and the publication shown by the evidence was sufficient to give jurisdiction to the court. We reject the suggestion that it is ever necessary for the Crown to show where the major steps in relation to publication were taken. . . . The appeal against conviction is therefore dismissed.

Handyside v United Kingdom (1976) 1 EHRR 737, 753–56

A book called *The Little Red Schoolbook,* which contained chapters on masturbation, sexual intercourse and abortion, was prosecuted under the 1959 Act on the basis that it appeared to encourage early sexual intercourse. The publisher applied for a ruling under Article 10 to the European Commission on Human Rights. The Commission referred the case to the Court.

Judgment

The Court points out that the machinery of protection established by the Convention is subsidiary to the national systems safeguarding human rights [*Belgian Linguistic case (No 2)* (1968) 1 EHRR 252, 296, para 10 in fine]. The Convention leaves to each contracting state, in the first place, the task of securing the rights and freedoms it enshrines. The institutions created by it make their own contribution to this task, but they become involved only through contentious proceedings and once all domestic remedies have been exhausted (Article 26).

These observations apply, notably, to Article 10(2). In particular, it is not possible to find in the domestic law of the various contracting states a uniform European conception of morals. The view taken by their respective laws of the requirements of morals varies from time to time and from place to place, especially in our era which is characterised by a rapid and far-reaching evolution of opinions on the subject. By reason of their direct and continuous contact with the vital forces of their countries, state authorities are in principle in a better position than the international judge to give an opinion on the exact content of these requirements as well as on the 'necessity' of a 'restriction' or 'penalty' intended to meet them. . . .it is for the national authorities to make the initial assessment of the reality of the pressing social need implied by the notion of 'necessity' in this context.

Consequently, Article 10(2) leaves to the contracting states a margin of appreciation. This margin is given both to the domestic legislator ('prescribed by law') and to the bodies, judicial amongst others, that are called upon to interpret and apply the laws in force [*Engel v The Netherlands* (1976) EHRR 684, para 100]. . . The Court's supervisory functions oblige it to pay the utmost attention to the principles characterising a 'democratic society'. Freedom of expression constitutes one of the essential foundations of such a society, one of the basic conditions for its progress and for the development of every man. Subject to Article 10(2), it is applicable not only to 'information' or 'ideas' that are favourably received or regarded as inoffensive or as a matter of indifference, but also to those that offend, shock or disturb the state or any sector of the population. Such are the demands of that pluralism, tolerance and broadmindedness without which there is no 'democratic society'. This means, amongst other things, that every 'formality', 'condition', 'restriction' or 'penalty' imposed in this sphere must be proportionate to the legitimate aim pursued.

From another standpoint, whoever exercises his freedom of expression undertakes 'duties and responsibilities' the scope of which depends on his situation and the technical means he uses. The Court cannot overlook such a person's 'duties' and 'responsibilities' when it enquires, as in this case; whether 'restrictions' or 'penalties' were conducive to the 'protection of morals' which made them 'necessary' in a 'democratic society'.

50 It follows from this that it is in no way the Court's task to take the place of the competent national courts but rather to review under Article 10 the decisions they delivered in the exercise of their power of appreciation.

52 The Court attaches particular importance to a factor to which the judgment of 29 October 1971 did not fail to draw attention, that is the intended readership of the Schoolbook. It was aimed above all at children and adolescents aged from 12 to 18. . . The applicant had made it clear that he planned a wide-spread circulation. . . the book included, above all in the section on sex and in the passage headed *'Be yourself'* in the chapter on pupils, sentences or paragraphs that young people at a critical stage of their development could have interpreted as an encouragement to indulge in precocious activities harmful for them or even to commit certain criminal offences. In these circumstances, despite the variety and the constant evolution in the UK of views on ethics and education, the competent English judges were entitled, in the exercise of their discretion, to think at the relevant time that the Schoolbook would have pernicious effects on the morals of many of the children and adolescents who would read it.

Paragraph 2 of Article 10 therefore applied; no breach of the Article was found.

Müller v Switzerland (1991) 13 EHRR 212, at [34]

Today, as at the time of the *Handyside* judgment . . . it is not possible to find in the legal and social orders of the Contracting States a uniform conception of morals. The view taken of the requirements of morals varies from time to time and from place to place, especially in our era, characterised by a far-reaching evolution of opinions on the subject. By reason of their direct and continuous contact with the vital forces of their countries, State authorities are in principle in a better position than the international judge to give an opinion on the exact content of these requirements as well as on the 'necessity' of a 'restriction' or 'penalty' intended to meet them.

Scherer v Switzerland (1993) A287 Com Rep

Where no adult is confronted unintentionally or against his will with filmed matter, there must be particularly compelling reasons to justify an interference.

Notes

1. The origins of the 'deprave and corrupt' test lie in the common law decision of *R v Hicklin*[119] where Lord Cockburn CJ stated that the test for obscene libel was a tendency 'to deprave and corrupt those whose minds are open to . . . immoral influences, and into whose hands a publication of this sort may fall.' The test can be applied to any material which might corrupt; it is clear from the ruling in *Calder, John (Publications) Ltd v Powell*[120] that it is not confined to descriptions or representations of sexual matters, and it could therefore be applied to a disturbing book on the drug-taking life of a junkie. This ruling was followed in *R v Skirving*,[121] which concerned a pamphlet on the means of taking cocaine in order to obtain maximum effect. In all instances the test for obscenity should not be applied to the type of behaviour advocated or described in the article in question but to the article itself. Thus, in *Skirving* the question to be asked was not whether taking cocaine would deprave and corrupt but whether the pamphlet itself would. To satisfy the test, the effect must be *more than* one of mere shock or revulsion—*Anderson*.[122] There must exist a possibility of *moral harm: Knuller v DPP*[123] points to the production of a 'real social evil.' In 1998 S. Edwards, 'On the contemporary application of the Obscene Publications Act 1959'[124] (quoting from a trial judge) found: '. . . "to deprave" means to make morally bad or morally worse; to pervert; to debase. "To corrupt" means to render morally unsound or rotten; to ruin a good quality; to defile . . . the test for obscenity depends on the article itself, and the purpose or intention of the distributor of the article are immaterial.'

2. The jury has to consider whether the article would be likely to deprave and corrupt a significant proportion of those likely to encounter it. It was determined in *R v Calder and Boyars Ltd*[125] that the jury must determine what is meant by a significant proportion, and this was approved in *DPP*

---

119   [1868] QB 360, at 371.

120   [1965] 1 QB 509.

121   [1985] QB 819.

122   [1972] 1 QB 304.

123   [1973] AC 435.

124   (1998) Crim LR 843, 849.

125   [1969] 1 QB 151.

v Whyte,[126] Lord Cross explaining that 'a significant proportion of a class means a part which is not numerically negligible but which may be much less than half'. This formulation was adopted in order to prevent sellers of pornographic material claiming that most of their customers would be unlikely to be corrupted by it.

3. The defence of public good, which arises under the 1959 Act, s 4, was intended to afford recognition to artistic merit and thus can be seen as a significant step in the direction of protecting freedom of speech. In *R v Penguin Books*,[127] it appeared that the jury found *Lady Chatterley's Lover* to be obscene but considered that the s 4 defence applied. In *Penguin Books* a two stage test was adopted: firstly, is the article obscene? Second, has the defendant established that it possesses sufficient merit—'in the interests of science, literature, art or learning, or of other objects of general concern'—to show that publication is for the public good? The defence will not be available if, as in *Knuller*, conspiracy to corrupt public morals is charged, thus circumventing the statutory protection for free speech.

4. Under s 3 of the Act, magazines and other material, such as videos, can be seized in forfeiture proceedings if they are obscene and have been kept for gain. No conviction is obtained; the material is merely destroyed and no other punishment is imposed, and therefore s 3 may operate at a low level of visibility. These proceedings may mean that the safeguards provided by the Act can be bypassed; in particular, consideration may not be given to the possible literary merits of such material because the public good defence need not be taken into account when the seizure warrant is issued. However, s 3 can be used only in respect of material which may be obscene rather than in relation to any form of pornography; it was held in *Darbo v DPP*[128] that a warrant issued under s 3 allowing officers to search for 'sexually explicit material' was bad on its face as such articles would fall within a much wider category of articles than those which could be called obscene.

5. At Strasbourg it is fair to say that artistic expression appears to have a lower place in the hierarchy of expression than political expression (see above, Chapter 7 p 329). Nevertheless, only one, aberrational, decision[129] defending restrictions on the freedom of expression of *adults* can be found, except in respect of 'hard core' pornography with no pretensions at all to artistic merit, or where a risk to children is also present, or in the context of offending religious sensibilities. In the *Handyside* case (extracted above), the European Court of Human Rights found that domestic law on obscenity was in harmony with Art 10 of the ECHR. In finding that para 2 applied, the judgment accepted that domestic legislators would be allowed a wide margin of appreciation in attempting to secure the freedoms guaranteed under the Convention in this area. This stance was again taken in *Müller v Switzerland* (also extracted above) in respect of a conviction arising from the exhibition of explicit paintings; the fact that the paintings had been exhibited in other parts of Switzerland and abroad did not mean that their suppression could not amount to a pressing social need. In contrast, in *Scherer v Switzerland*[130] it was found that the conviction of the proprietor of a sex shop for showing obscene and explicit videos had not breached Art 10 since access was restricted to adults and, further, no one was likely to confront them unwittingly.

6. Any prosecutions under the 1959 Act or forfeiture actions constitute interferences with freedom of expression under the HRA, although subject to justification. In relation to any particular decision,

---

126   [1973] AC 849.

127   [1961] Crim LR 176.

128   [1992] Crim LR 56.

129   Gibson v UK (known as *S. and G. v UK*) Appl No 17634/91. This was only an admissibility decision and can be seen as an aberration. See Fenwick (2007), p 1082, below, at pp 482–3; T Lewis [2002] 1 Ent. Law 50–71.

130   (1994) 18 EHRR 276. Note that the case was discontinued in the Court due to the death of the applicant.

the public authorities involved are bound by s 6 of the HRA to ensure that the tests under Art 10 are satisfied, while the provisions of the 1959 Act must be interpreted consistently with Art 10. Given the wide margin of appreciation afforded to the domestic authorities in the relevant decisions, little guidance as to the requirements of Art 10 in this context is available, especially where the material is directed at a willing adult audience. The domestic judiciary is therefore theoretically free to take a different stance. The decisions considered above at Strasbourg on the 1959 Act indicate that the statutory regime relating to publication of an obscene article under s 2 is broadly in harmony with Art 10 of the ECHR. Nevertheless, a specific decision might not meet the proportionality requirements, scrutinised more intensively than at Strasbourg.

7. The UK forfeiture regime has not been tested at Strasbourg. The HRA requirements may be especially pertinent in relation to forfeiture: the magistrates conducting the proceedings are, of course, bound by Art 10 and therefore would be expected to approach the task with greater rigour. In particular, it is arguably necessary to examine each item even where a large scale seizure has occurred, rather than considering a sample of items only.[131] But since, in practice, a vast amount of material is condemned as obscene in legal actions for forfeiture, the practical difficulties facing magistrates make it possible that the impact of the HRA is more theoretical than real.

8. There are, in practice, particular problems in applying the Obscene Publications Act to web-based material. For example, the definition of obscenity is a relative one, dependent on the susceptibilities of those who are likely to encounter the material.[132] Web-based erotic and pornographic material, including material from '18' or 'R18' rated films, is available on a range of websites to any user who possesses a computer of the correct specification, although a credit card would often have to be used to gain access to it. Children can therefore gain access to such material and images, and the question of the obscenity of the material might therefore have to be determined by reference to that likely audience, depending on the circumstances, including the nature of the website and the likelihood that children would be able to access it. It would be harder to establish the extent of the likelihood that children might access the information than it is to make the same calculation in relation to print material, although probably it would be as hard as it is in relation to videos. But videos are regulated by the BBFC and it is an offence in itself to publish an unclassified video, without reference to its obscenity or indecency. Further, the BBFC has already taken the decision to continue to censor video films beyond the demands of the criminal law, thereby obviating the possibility of a prosecution under the 1959 Act, a decision which is, in effect, a compromise between defending adult autonomy and risking the promulgation of pornography to children. Since the Internet is not subject to the policing of an equivalent regulator, this problem is more significant in that context.

9. Although the thrust of UK policy in relation to web-based pornography is against individual consumers under the OPA, where the manager of the ISP happens to be in this jurisdiction successful prosecution can occur. At least one successful prosecution has been brought against a web-page provider—*R v Perrin*[133] (extracted above). In that judgment, the Court of Appeal accepted that there was publication whenever anyone accessed the preview page. No evidence that children would be likely to access it or had accessed it was put forward, but the Court appeared to assume that this was a possibility and that therefore the obscenity of the material could be judged against that likely audience. The lack of interest in the evidence in relation to children could

---

131   It was found that such sampling was acceptable in *R v Snaresbrook Crown Court ex parte Commissioner of the Metropolis* (1984) 79 Cr App R 184.

132   See pp 1075–1076 above.

133   [2002] EWCA Crim 747, CA.

be viewed as creating an appearance of departure from the basic principle of relative obscenity. The Court also rejected the suggestion that a prosecution should only be brought against a publisher where the prosecutor could show that the major steps in relation to publication were taken within the jurisdiction of the court. The possibility that the main steps towards publication might have occurred in another jurisdiction with less restrictive laws (the US) was not accepted as relevant.

10. In general the gravest problem facing the UK authorities is the practical one of seeking to bring prosecutions against ISPs operating abroad. Clearly, jurisdictions differ greatly as to the speech that they criminalise. This potentially places both the national authorities and the Internet Service Providers in a difficult, almost impossible, position. If national laws *could* be enforced against ISPs regardless of jurisdiction, they would be forced to limit the provision of material on web-sites very severely since they would have to obey the most draconian and restrictive of the speech laws available.[134] As Barendt points out: 'Website operators and other senders may have no idea who picks up their messages and which jurisdiction they live in, so the law imposes a great burden of them if they can be prosecuted whenever, say, a sexually explicit communication is accessed by a child, or extremist speech is accessed by anyone living in a country with strict hate speech laws'.[135] The new offence of possession of extreme pornography introduced by The Criminal Justice and Immigration Act 2008, s 63, is aimed not at ISPs, but at the consumer in the UK of web-based pornography; it therefore addresses this issue to an extent. We do not consider it here for reasons of space and because the material it covers is already illegal to publish or distribute under the OPA. It therefore affects consumers of pornography, but not the media.[136]

FURTHER READING

SJ Bailey and N Taylor, *Bailey, Harris and Jones: Civil Liberties: Cases and Materials,* 6th edn (2009), Part Four

E Barendt, *Freedom of Speech* (2007)

R Clayton and H Tomlinson, *The Law of Human Rights* (2008), Chapter 15

D Feldman, *Civil Liberties and Human Rights,* 2nd edn (2002), Part IV

H Fenwick, *Civil Liberties and Human Rights,* 4th edn (2007), Part II

---

134 This was pointed out on behalf of the defence in *R v Perrin* [2002] EWCA Crim 747, CA, referring to 'the world wide accessibility of the internet' and the opinion of the United States Court of Appeal was relied on to the effect that (Third Circuit) in *ACLU v Reno (No 3)* [2000] 217 F 3d 162 at 168–69 any court or jury asked to consider whether there has been publication by a defendant of a web page which is obscene should be instructed to consider first where the major steps in relation to publication took place and only to convict if satisfied that those steps took place within the jurisdiction of the court. This argument was not accepted by the Court of Appeal.

135 See Barendt, *Freedom of Speech,* 2nd edn (2005), Chapter 13, p 452.

136 For details see C McGlynn and E Rackley, 'Striking a Balance: Arguments for the Criminal Regulation of Extreme Pornography' (2007) Crim LR 677–90 and 'Criminalising Extreme Pornography: A Lost Opportunity' (2009) Crim LR 245–60.

CHAPTER 19
FREEDOM OF ASSEMBLY, PUBLIC PROTEST AND PUBLIC ORDER

INTRODUCTION

Freedom of assembly, which is guaranteed under the Universal Declaration of Human Rights, Art 20 and in the European Convention on Human Rights (ECHR), Art 11, is a fundamental freedom which partly derives its legitimacy from its close association with freedom of expression. The exercise of freedom of assembly allows individuals to make their views known publicly and obtain public support. Free societies recognise the need to allow citizens to express views at variance with government views or 'mainstream' views, and to allow the public expression of such views. Allowing citizens to engage in public protest is seen as being one of the main distinctions between a totalitarian society and a democracy. Protest is valuable partly as demonstrating to the Government that it has strayed too far from the path of acceptability in policy making and partly in deterring it from doing so.

This chapter is concerned with the conflict between the legitimate interest of the state in maintaining order and the protection of freedom of protest and assembly. Therefore, it will focus on those legal provisions most applicable in the context of protests, demonstrations, marches or meetings. Many of these restraints are not aimed specifically at assemblies but generally at preserving public order or safety and keeping the peace. The legal regime aimed at preserving public order relies on the use of both prior and subsequent restraints. Prior restraint on protests and assemblies may mean that they cannot take place at all or can take place only under various limitations. Subsequent restraints, usually arrests and prosecutions for public order offences, may be used after the protest or assembly is in being. Although the availability of subsequent restraints may have a 'chilling' effect, they are used publicly and may receive publicity. If an assembly takes place and subsequently some of its members are prosecuted for public order offences, it will at least have achieved its end in gaining publicity, and may in fact have gained greater publicity due to the prosecutions. If the assembly never takes place, its object will probably be completely defeated.

An increasing mass of public order provisions

Prior and subsequent restraints arise from a large number of wide-ranging and sometimes archaic powers which spring partly from a mix of statutory provisions, partly from the common law and partly from the royal prerogative.[1] To an extent the number of restraints available is unsurprising because the range of state interests involved is wider than any other expressive activity would warrant: they include the possibilities of disorder, violence to citizens and damage to property. Clearly, the state has a duty to preserve order, protect citizens from the attentions of the mob and to maintain safety in public generally.[2]

Most of these restraints are not aimed specifically at assemblies and protesters, but generally at keeping the peace. Nevertheless, they severely affect the freedoms of protest and assembly. Therefore those seeking to exercise the freedoms of protest and assembly have historically been in a vulnerable position[3] and currently they are in an especially precarious legal position, since a web of overlapping and imprecise public order provisions now exists and is constantly increasing. The difficulty is

---

1   For discussion of the various offences, see *Smith and Hogan Criminal Law,* 12th edn (2008) (standard criminal law text), D Ormerod; D Feldman, *Civil Liberties and Human Rights,* 2nd edn (2002), Chapter 18; H Fenwick, *Civil Liberties and Human Rights,* 4th edn (2007), Chapter 9.

2   See the leading US case, *Hague v Committee for Industrial Organisation* 307 US 496 (1938).

3   See KD Ewing and CA Gearty, *The Struggle for Civil Liberties* (1999).

that, in furtherance of the interest in public order (which in itself protects freedom of assembly), the constitutional need to allow freedom of assembly in a democracy may be obscured. There has been a tendency in the UK over the last 30 years to react to particular forms of disorder and instances of public protest by introducing new provisions, even where existing ones might have proved adequate.

In the period leading up to the inception of the Public Order Act 1986 there were a series of disturbances beginning with the Brixton riots in 1981[4] and continuing with the disorder associated with the miners' strike in 1984–85, probably the most significant event in British public order history. The strike largely provided the justification for the introduction of the Public Order Act 1986, although it did not appear that further police powers to control disorder were needed. The police did not seem to have lacked powers to deal with the disturbances; on the contrary, a number of different common law and statutory powers were invoked, including powers to prevent a breach of the peace, s 3 of the Public Order Act 1936, offences of unlawful assembly, of obstruction of a constable and of watching and besetting under s 7 of the Conspiracy and Protection of Property Act 1875.[5] However, the Government took the view that the available powers were confused and fragmented and that there was scope for affording the police additional powers to prevent disorder before it occurred.[6] It therefore introduced a number of low level public order offences and created a cumbersome, unwieldy framework for the policing of processions and assemblies under the 1986 Act. The Act, as amended, remains the central public order statute.

Mass protest was not a hallmark of the 1990s, but the period did see an enormous growth in the use of direct action by a variety of groups, usually protesting about environmental and animal rights issues. These included hunt saboteurs, fishing saboteurs, motorway and bypass protesters, veal calf protesters. The protests at Newbury, Twyford Down and Oxleas Wood against bypasses[7] and at Brightlingsea and Shoreham Ferry Port against the export of veal calves were particularly notable. The rise in direct action suggested that the traditional aim of protest—to persuade—was being abandoned. The response of the Major Government was to introduce further repressive measures under the Criminal Justice and Public Order Act (CJPOA) 1994 aimed largely at direct action in order to suppress it.[8] The late 1980s and the early 1990s witnessed some similar protests, notably the anti-poll tax demonstrations, protests against The Satanic Verses and against the 1994 Act itself ('Kill the Bill' protests).

The coming into power of the Labour Government in 1997 did not herald any diminution of the direct action form of protest, on the Government's own analysis of its predicted prevalence.[9] The concerns of protesters against motorway or airport runway development, abuse of human rights and on environmental matters, including the introduction of genetically modified crops, continued to

---

4   See the inquiry by Lord Scarman, *The Brixton Disorders*, Cmnd 8427, 1981.

5   See S McCabe and P Wallington, *The Police, Public Order and Civil Liberties: Legacies of the Miners' Strike* (1988), esp. Appendix 1; P Wallington, 'Policing the Miners' Strike' (1985) 14 ILJ 145. During the miners' strike, over 10,000 offences were charged; see Wallington, *ibid*.

6   See: House of Commons, Fifth Report from the Home Affairs Committee, Session 1979–80, *The Law Relating to Public Order*, HC 756–1; Lord Scarman, *The Brixton Disorders*, Part VI, Cmnd 8427, 1981; Smith, ATH, 'Public Order Law 1974–1983: Developments and Proposals' [1984] Crim LR 643; White Paper, *Review of Public Order Law*, Cmnd 9510, 1985.

7   See B Bryant, *Twyford Down: Roads, Campaigning and Environmental Law*, 1996; 'Roads to Nowhere', Green Party Election Manifesto 1997, Transport section.

8   For the background to the 1994 Act, which received the royal assent on 3 November 1994, see the introduction in Wasik and Taylor's *Guide to the Act*, 1995, p 1. For discussion of the public order offences see ATH Smith (1995) Crim LR 19. See also D Mead (2009) n 64 below, Chapter 6.

9   *Legislation Against Terrorism: A Consultation Paper*, Cm 4178, 1998.

be expressed in this form.[10] Human rights groups, including Amnesty, attempted to protest against the abuse of human rights in China on the occasion of the visit of the Chinese President in October 1999,[11] but were met by heavy-handed policing. Diverse groups continued to view protest as a valuable means of drawing attention to viewpoints which tended to be excluded from what may be termed the mainstream communications market place, particularly the tabloid press.

In the first decade of the 21st century a rise in mass protest linked to the 'war on terror', religious extremism, and foreign policy was evident. Examples included the entry of Britain into the Iraq war, which sparked large-scale protests, demonstrations against capitalism and the impact of trading globalisation in London, marches protesting against the Danish cartoons of Muhammed in 2008 and the protests against Israel's action against Gaza in 2009. The availability of a range of other means of communication, particularly via the internet, did not appear to lead to the marginalisation of protest as a means of communicating and of participating in the democratic process. Indeed, the internet, far from providing an alternative means of communication, facilitates protest and publicises it.[12]

A blurring of the distinction between terrorist groups and direct action protest groups is a feature of post-2000 law and policy. Special terrorist offences and the special counter-terrorism stop and search, arrest and detention powers[13] may be used against protesters. The 9/11 attacks on the World Trade Centre in 2001, the entry of Britain into the Iraq war and the London bombings in 2005, also had an impact in leading to the introduction of a range of new offences aimed at stifling anti-war dissent, a number of which are relevant in this area. The Serious and Organised Crime Act 2005 ushered in severe restrictions on demonstrations in Parliament Square, which were clearly aimed mainly at anti-war demonstrators—and, contrary, to expectations, these were *not* repealed by the Constitutional Reform and Governance Act 2010 (below, p 1108). The Anti-Social Behaviour Act 2003 was employed to broaden a number of the already broad provisions in order to deploy them in a wider range of circumstances against protesters. The Act deleted reference to activity taking place in the 'open air' in s 68 of the Criminal Justice and Public Order Act 1994, a broad provision aimed originally at animal rights and environmental activists. It also reduced the number of persons who can constitute a 'public assembly' for the purpose of banning it or imposing conditions on it under the 1986 Act, from twenty to two. A number of the wide range of statutory provisions already in place, as well as the ancient common law doctrine of breach of the peace, were deployed against anti-war protesters. The broadening of the definition of 'public assembly' means that two people reading out names of those killed in the Iraq war are now subject to the 'assembly' provisions of the Public Order Act 1986. The Protection from Harassment Act 1997 was aimed at providing a remedy against stalkers, but has been used against protestors.[14] It emerged recently that the police had adopted a practice of taking photographs of

---

10   See the Newbury Bypass website: geocities.com/newburybypass/index.html; reports of protests at Newbury, *Daily Telegraph*, 11 January 1999 and 30 April 1999; the Greenpeace website: www.greenpeace.org.uk/.

11   The Home Office stated that it had not placed pressure on the Metropolitan Police to prevent demonstrators disrupting the visit of the Chinese President (national news reports 25 October 1999). A routine internal review was carried out which exonerated the police; report published on 17 March 2000. Eventually, in judicial review proceedings brought by lawyers for the Free Tibet campaign, the Metropolitan Police admitted that that the treatment of the demonstrators had been unlawful: news reports, 4 May 2000.

12   The Newbury Bypass website—www.geocities.com/newburybypass/index.html – for example, runs to 23 pages and has links to a mass of connected pages.

13   See Chapter 20. In particular, s 76 Counter Terrorism Act 2008 criminalises the taking of photos of police officers and could be used to harass journalists attending protests.

14   For a recent case, see *Novartis Pharmaceuticals UK Limited v Stop Huntingdon Animal Cruelty* [2009] EWHC 2716 (QB). For comment on the use of harassment powers generally against protestors, see J. Seymour, 'Who can be Harassed? Claims Against Animal Rights Protestors under Section 3 of the Protection from Harassment Act 1997' (2005) 64(1) CLJ 57–65.

'repeat' demonstrators, and storing them on a database, for the purposes of identifying 'trouble-makers'. This practice was very recently challenged by way of judicial review and found to be an unlawful interference with the privacy rights of the individuals concerned under Art 8 of the Convention.[15]

For the last 10 years the Human Rights Act has also been in force—an intriguing contradiction that forms one of the main themes of this chapter. But in exploring the tensions between statutory provisions curbing protest and rights under the European Convention on Human Rights, it must be remembered that the common law doctrine of breach of the peace overshadows all the statutory changes over the last ten years. Breathtakingly broad, bewilderingly imprecise in scope, it provides the police with such wide powers to use against protesters as to render the statutory frameworks almost redundant. As will be found below, the two key post-HRA House of Lords' decisions (*Laporte*[16] and *Austin*)[17] on the impact of the HRA in relation to police powers used against protesters, have both occurred in the breach of the peace context. The Liberal-Conservative government, which took office in 2010, has put forward the Freedom (Great Repeal) Bill to reverse Labour erosions of civil liberties: it may include protection for peaceful protest, but it needs to include consideration of common law powers, not just statutory ones.

The change in stance under the Human Rights Act—recognition of rights to freedom of assembly and protest in UK law

Prior to the inception of the Human Rights Act 1998 (HRA) there was some very limited recognition of a right to freedom of assembly in UK law. Under the Representation of the People Act 1983, local authorities are placed under a very limited positive obligation to allow election meetings to take place. The Education (No 2) Act 1986, s 43 provided protection for meetings in universities. Also a liberty to assemble appeared to exist. The Public Order Act 1986, ss 12 and 14 (see below) impliedly recognise the freedom to assemble so long as the statutory requirements are complied with. There are certain specific statutory prohibitions on meetings in certain places or at certain times, such as the Seditious Meetings Act 1817, s 3 which prohibits meetings of 50 or more in the vicinity of Westminster during a parliamentary session. Such restrictions impliedly supported the existence of a general negative freedom to meet or march which would exist if not specifically prohibited.[18]

However, when the Human Rights Act 1998 was introduced, it meant that for the first time in UK law, citizens were able to rely directly, in domestic courts, on an express recognition in domestic law of rights to protest and assemble within Arts 10 and 11 of the ECHR as afforded further effect in UK law under that Act. This constituted a potentially climactic break with the traditional UK constitutional position. That position was that citizens might do anything which the law did not forbid, whereas under the HRA they are able to exercise rights to protest and assembly, circumscribed, as Chapter 17 explains, only in a manner compatible with specified Convention exceptions or, exceptionally, by incompatible domestic legislation.[19]

---

15   See *Wood v Commissioner of Police of the Metropolis* [2009] EWCA Civ 414; [2010] EMLR 1, CA. For Article 8 ECHR, see chapter 7 at 317–328.

16   p 1125 below.

17   p 1128 below.

18   See DG Barnum (1977) PL 310 and (1981) 29 AJCL 59; LA Stein (1971) PL 115 for discussion of the constitutional status of public protest.

19   HRA 1998, s 3(2).

The focus of this chapter is on the mass of common law and statutory public order provisions, considered in the light of the rights to the freedoms of assembly and protest under Arts 10 and 11. It will evaluate the responses of the judiciary so far to the acceptance of the values underlying public expression under Arts 10 and 11 in UK public order law. It will be argued that the common law has failed to provide the recognition for the value of public protest as a form of political expression which is evident in respect of media expression. This is due, it will be contended, to the desire in the context of public protest to protect countervailing interests, particularly proprietorial rights, but the judiciary pre-HRA did not make this explicit: the express balancing act which may be carried out at Strasbourg between political expression and other societal interests tended to fail to occur in the judgments of domestic courts, often because the former value was merely afforded no recognition at all. The guarantees of freedom of expression and peaceful assembly under Arts 10 and 11 of the ECHR were hardly adverted to pre-HRA in the domestic courts in public protest cases, as certain of the decisions discussed below reveal. The close relationship between assembly and expression failed to receive recognition when low level public order offences, committed in the course of, or directly through, the exercise of political protest, were adjudicated upon.

In seeking to discover the limits of the legal acceptance of freedom of protest and assembly, and the value that the law places upon it, this chapter focuses on those provisions of the criminal and civil law most applicable in the context of demonstrations, marches, meetings, direct action. The central theme of this chapter will concern the impact that the ECHR under the HRA is having on the mass of restrictions on freedom of assembly. Lord Bingham tellingly described the impact that the HRA is having in this context in the House of Lords decision in *R (On the application of Laporte) (FC) v Chief Constable of Gloucestershire:*[20]

> The approach of the English common law to freedom of expression and assembly was hesitant and negative, permitting that which was not prohibited. Thus although Dicey in *An Introduction to the Study of the Law of the Constitution*[21] in Part II on the 'Rule of Law', included chapters VI and VII entitled 'The Right to Freedom of Discussion' and 'The Right of Public Meeting', he wrote of the first[22] that 'At no time has there in England been any proclamation of the right to liberty of thought or to freedom of speech' and of the second[23] that 'it can hardly be said that our constitution knows of such a thing as any specific right of public meeting'. Lord Hewart CJ reflected the then current orthodoxy when he observed in *Duncan v Jones*[24] that 'English law does not recognize any special right of public meeting for political or other purposes'. The Human Rights Act 1998, giving domestic effect to articles 10 and 11 of the European Convention, represented what Sedley LJ in *Redmond-Bate v Director of Public Prosecutions*,[25] aptly called a 'constitutional shift'.

---

20 [2006] UKHL 55, para 34. CA: *R (On the application of Laporte) v CC of Gloucester Constab* [2004] EWCA Civ 1639. See below for discussion, pp 1125–1128.

21 10th edn (1959).

22 At pp 239–240.

23 At p 271.

24 [1936] 1 KB 218, 222.

25 (1999) 163 JP 789, 795; for discussion of the decision see below at pp 1121–1125.

THE RIGHTS OF FREEDOM OF ASSEMBLY AND PROTEST PROTECTED UNDER THE HUMAN RIGHTS ACT 1998

Under s 6 of the HRA, those seeking to exercise rights of protest and assembly can rely on Arts 10 and 11 of the ECHR, and any other relevant right, in particular Art 5, against public authorities, usually the police. All the legislation already mentioned and discussed below must be interpreted compatibly with those rights, under s 3 of the HRA, taking the Strasbourg jurisprudence into account under s 2. So far s 3 has not played a significant part in decisions on legislation relating to the area of public protest; when one provision—s 11 Public Order Act 1986—was afforded a restrictive interpretation in 2008 in the House of Lords, s 3 was not relied on.[26] But in order to evaluate the impact of the Convention, it is necessary to consider the scope and content of the Arts 10 and 11 rights of protest and assembly. Article 5 is discussed in Chapter 7.[27]

Article 11 of the ECHR, received into UK law under the HRA, is specifically aimed at freedom of assembly. Forms of public protest as examples of both assembly and expression will fall within Art 10 also. Art 11 leaves a great deal of discretion to the judiciary. It is not a far-reaching provision since, as explained in Chapter 7, it protects only freedom of *peaceful* assembly and since, in common with Arts 8–10, it contains a long list of exceptions in para 2.[28] The key factor in determining whether a protest counts as a peaceful assembly appears to be whether it is disorderly in itself or whether any disorder or violence arises incidentally.[29] In applying Art 11, the UK judiciary is obliged, under s 2 HRA, to take the relevant Strasbourg jurisprudence into account. That jurisprudence is not, on the whole, of a radical nature, although the Court has found that the right to organise public meetings is 'fundamental'[30] and includes the right to organise marches, demonstrations and other forms of public protest. The cautious stance largely arises from the wide margin of appreciation that has been afforded to national authorities in determining what is needed to preserve public order at local level. It was a feature of the older Art 11 jurisprudence that applications did not reach the Court since the Commission tended to find them to be manifestly ill founded.[31]

Article 11 may impose limited positive duties on the state to ensure that an assembly or protest can occur even though it is likely to provoke others to violence; the responsibility for any harm caused appears to remain with the counter-demonstrators.[32] The acceptance of further positive duties, including a duty to require owners of private land to allow some peaceful assemblies on their property, has not been accepted under the Convention[33] despite the growth of quasi-public places such as large, enclosed shopping centres and the privatisation of previously public places. 'Direct action' used in a

---

26   See below pp 1094–1096.

27   See pp 304–310.

28   See Chapter 7, pp 315, 332.

29   *Christians against Racism and Fascism v UK* Application No 8440/78, (1980) 21 DR 138, 148.

30   *Rassemblement Jurassien Unite Jurassienne v Switzerland* Application No 819/78, (1979) 17 DR 93, 119. See for discussion D Mead, 'The Right to Peaceful Protest under the ECHR' (2007) EHRLR 345.

31   *Friedl v Austria* Application No 15225/89, (1992) unreported; *Christians Against Racism and Fascism v UK* Application No 8440/78, (1980) 21 DR 138.

32   *Plattform 'Ärtze für das Leben' v Austria*, Series A No 139; (1988) 13 EHRR 204.

33   See *Appleby v UK* (2003) 37 EHRR 783 for an unsuccessful application in relation to the owners of a private shopping mall.

symbolic sense has been found to fall within Art 11,[34] but currently the Court views such protest as falling most readily within Art 10. In *Steel and Others v UK* and *Hashman and Harrup v UK,* a violation of Art 10 was found in respect of public protest, and the Court therefore did not find it necessary to consider Art 11.

The Art 10 jurisprudence relating specifically to public protest is meagre, as this chapter will indicate. However, the extensive jurisprudence on expression generally, especially political expression, is clearly applicable to public protest.[35] The *content* of speech will rarely exclude it from Art 10 protection: thus, speech as part of a protest likely to cause such low level harm as alarm or distress may be protected, according to the *dicta* of the Court in *Müller v Switzerland*[36] to the effect that the protection of free speech extends equally to ideas which 'offend, shock or disturb'. The Court has repeatedly asserted that freedom of expression 'constitutes one of the essential foundations of a democratic society', that exceptions to it 'must be narrowly interpreted and the necessity for any restrictions-. . .convincingly established'.[37] As Chapter 18 indicates, it is a marked feature of the Strasbourg jurisprudence that political expression receives a high degree of protection. One of the leading works on the Convention concludes, 'It is clear that the Court ascribes a hierarchy of value' to different classes of speech, attaching 'the highest importance to the protection of political expression. . .widely understood'.[38]

Prima facie all forms of protest that can be viewed as the expression of an opinion fall within Art 10 according to the findings of the Court in *Steel and Others v UK.*[39] Thus, the direct action form of protest, such as symbolic or actual physical obstruction, does fall within the scope of Art 10,[40] a finding that was reiterated in *Hashman and Harrup v UK.*[41] In *Steel,* protesters who were physically impeding grouse shooters and road builders and had been arrested for breach of the peace, were found to be engaging in 'expression' within the meaning of Art 10. The findings in *Steel* suggest that while actual obstruction falls within Art 10, it may have a lower status than protest in the form of pure speech. In *Ziliberberg v Moldova*[42] the Court made the association between assembly and expression explicit: 'the right to freedom of assembly is a fundamental right in a democratic society and, like the right to freedom of expression, is one of the foundations of such a society.' This stance is appropriate given the deliberate adoption of the wider term 'expression' rather than 'speech' in Art 10; it also avoids the problems experienced in the US, in distinguishing between message-bearing conduct and conduct *simpliciter.*

Owing to the likelihood that, as indicated, most forms of protest will fall within Art 10 and probably

---

34 *G v Federal Republic of Germany* Application No 13079/87, (1989) 60 DR 256, 263.

35 *Steel and Others v UK* (1999) 28 EHRR 603.

36 (1991) 13 EHRR 212.

37 *The Observer and The Guardian v UK* Series A No 216; (1991) 14 EHRR 153, para 59.

38 Harris, O'Boyle and Warbrick, (1995), 'further reading' below, p 1138, at pp 397 and 414. The second rank is artistic speech, the third commercial speech, e.g. advertising. They acknowledge that these terms may be too narrow (at n 14 and associated text). In particular, the term 'artistic' is too restrictive since it does not cover all speech, including some forms of protest, which may be said to be supported by the free speech arguments. See also D Mead (2009), n 64 below, Chapter 2.

39 (1999) 28 EHRR 603.

40 See *Steel and Others v UK* (1999) 28 EHRR 603, para 92: 'It is true that the protests took the form of physically impeding the activities of which the applicants disapproved, but the Court considers nonetheless that they constituted expressions of opinion with the meaning of Article'.

41 *Hashman and Harrup v UK* (2000) 30 EHRR 241; (2000) BHRC 104 does not offer much guidance as to the scope of protection for direct action since, having found that a sanction applied to the applicants for blowing a horn with the intention of disrupting a hunt was a form or expression within Art 10, the Court went on to find that the interference was not 'prescribed by law': the domestic law—the *contra bonos mores* doctrine—was found to be insufficiently precise.

42 App No 61821/00, 4 May 2004, unreported, para 2.

also Art 11, the emphasis of Strasbourg findings is on the para 2 exceptions which include 'in the interests of national security. . .public safety . . . for the prevention of disorder or crime. . .for the protection of the. . .rights of others'.[43] In order to be justified, state interference with Art 10 and 11 guarantees must be prescribed by law, have a legitimate aim, be necessary in a democratic society and be applied in a non-discriminatory fashion (Art 14). In carrying out this assessment, the domestic courts are obliged to take the Strasbourg public protest jurisprudence into account, although they are not bound by it unless it is clear and constant.[44]

In freedom of expression cases, Strasbourg's main concern has been with the 'necessary in a democratic society' requirement; the notion of 'prescribed by law' has been focused upon to some extent but almost always with the result that it has been found to be satisfied. It was found in the context of protest not to be satisfied by the *contra bonos mores* (contrary to a good way of life) power arising under the Justices of the Peace Act 1361, due to its imprecision.[45] The legitimate aim' requirement will normally be readily satisfied; as Harris, O'Boyle and Warbrick point out, the grounds for interference are so wide that 'the State can usually make a plausible case that it did have a good reason for interfering with the right'.[46] The provision against non-discrimination arising under Art 14 is potentially very significant, especially in relation to minority public protests, but so far it has not been a significant issue in the relevant freedom of expression jurisprudence.

The Court tends to afford a wide margin of appreciation when reviewing the necessity of interferences with expression in the form of protest, viewing measures taken to prevent disorder or protect the rights of others as peculiarly within the purview of the domestic authorities, in contrast to its stance in respect of 'pure' speech. In finding that applications are manifestly ill founded, the Commission has been readily satisfied that decisions of the national authorities to adopt quite far-reaching measures, including complete bans, in order to prevent disorder are within their margin of appreciation.[47] The Court has also found 'the margin of appreciation extends in particular to the choice of the reasonable and appropriate mean to be used by the authority to ensure that lawful manifestations can take place peacefully'.[48] Thus, states are typically *not* required to demonstrate that lesser measures than those actually taken would have been inadequate to deal with the threats posed by demonstrations—disorder, interferences with the rights of others and so on.

However, in *Ezelin v France*[49] the Court took a 'hard look' at the issue of proportionality. The applicant, an advocate, took part in a demonstration against the judicial system generally and against particular judges, involving the daubing of slogans attacking the judiciary on court walls, and eventual violence. Ezelin did not himself take part in any illegal acts, but did not disassociate himself from the march, even when it became violent. He was disciplined by the Bar Association and eventually given a formal reprimand, which did not impair his ability to practice. No fine was imposed. The French Government's argument was that '[b]y not disavowing the unruly incidents that had occurred during the demonstration, the applicant had ipso facto approved them [and that] it was essential for judicial

---

43   See: *Plattform "Ärzte für das Leben" v Austria* (1988) 13 EHRR 204; *Djavit An v Turkey* (2003) Reports of Judgments and Decisions, 2003-III, p 233; *Christian Democratic People's Party v Moldova* (App No 28793/02, 14 May 2006, unreported); *Öllinger v Austria* (App No 76900/01, 29 June 2006, unreported).

44   See the discussion of the HRA 1998 in Chapter 17, s 2(1), p 972.

45   See *Hashman and Harrup v UK* (2000) 30 EHRR 241; (2000) 8 BHRC 104.

46   See n 38 above, ibid, p 290.

47   See *Christians against Racism and Fascism v UK* Application No 8440/78, (1980) 21 DR 138; and *Friedl v Austria* Application No 15225/89, (1992) unreported.

48   *Chorherr v Austria* Series A No 266-B; (1993) 17 EHRR 358, para 31.

49   (1991) 14 EHRR 362, para 53.

institutions to react to behaviour which, on the part of an 'officer of the court. . .seriously impaired the authority of the judiciary and respect for court decisions'.[50] The argument was rejected; Art 11 was found to have been violated. In an emphatic judgment, the Court found: '. . .the freedom to take part in a peaceful assembly—in this instance a demonstration that had not been prohibited—is of such importance that it cannot be restricted in any way, even for an advocate, so long as the person concerned does not himself commit any reprehensible act on such an occasion.'[51]

Somewhat similarly, in *Christian Democratic People's Party v Moldova*[52] the Court found that a peaceful meeting could not be the subject of a temporary ban on the ground that it was unauthorised. The Court considered the three grounds relied upon by the domestic authorities to justify the ban: that the CDDP had not obtained an authorisation for its gatherings in accordance with the Assemblies Law, that children were present at its gatherings and that some statements made at the gatherings amounted to calls to public violence and found that they were not relevant and sufficient reasons to justify imposing the ban on the CDPP's activities. The Court stressed that only very serious breaches, such as those which endanger political pluralism or fundamental democratic principles, could justify a ban on the activities of a political party. Since the CDPP's gatherings were entirely peaceful, there were no calls to violent overthrow of the Government or any other encroachment on the principles of pluralism and democracy, it could not reasonably be said that the measure applied to it was proportionate to the aim pursued and that it met a pressing social need.

The broad phrasing of Arts 10(2) and 11(2)[53] inevitably leaves a great deal of interpretative discretion to the UK judiciary in considering their application to existing law under the HRA. But certain conclusions can be drawn: the European Court of Human Rights will not tolerate the arrest and detention of purely peaceful protesters, even if the protest degenerates into violence, so long as the protesters in question have not themselves committed 'reprehensible acts'. The finding of the Court in *Steel v UK*, reiterated in *Hashman v UK*, that direct action protest such as physical obstruction does fall within the scope of Art 10,[54] is of great significance, as is the finding of the Commission that protesters engaged in a 'sit-in' blocking a road are covered by Art 11.[55] It appears to be the case that Strasbourg views such expression as having a lower status than 'purely' expressive and speech-based protest activities, but a distinction has not been drawn between actual and symbolic obstruction, although it may be inferred that actual obstruction might be viewed as reprehensible. Thus, apart from violent or threatening protest, most forms of protest and assembly are within the scope of both Arts 10 and 11, although ceremonious processions and assemblies will probably be considered only within Art 11,[56] while the recent tendency is to consider forms of direct action within Art 10. Thus, forms of protest, including those far removed from the classic peaceful assembly whose members hold up banners or hand out leaflets engage these Articles, but interference with direct action protest can be readily justified, even where it is primarily of a symbolic nature.

---

50   *Ezelin v France* (1991) 14 EHRR 362, para 49.

51   *Ibid*, para 53.

52   (App No 28793/02, 14 May 2006, unreported).

53   Arts 5 and 6 may also be relevant in some circumstances.

54   In *Steel and Others v UK* (1999) 28 EHRR 603, para 92: 'It is true that the protests took the form of physically impeding the activities of which the applicants disapproved, but the Court considers nonetheless that they constituted expressions of opinion within the meaning of Article 10.'

55   *G v FRG* Application No 13079/87, (1980) 21 DR 138.

56   See *Chorherr v Austria* (1993) 17 EHRR 358.

THE LEGAL CONTROL OF MEETINGS, MARCHES, DEMONSTRATIONS, PROTESTS—PRIOR RESTRAINTS IN DOMESTIC LAW

Controlling marches and assemblies

Public Order Act 1986, Part II, as amended

Processions and assemblies
Advance notice of public processions

11.–(1) Written notice shall be given in accordance with this section of any proposal to hold a public procession intended—

(a) to demonstrate support for or opposition to the views or actions of any person or body of persons,
(b) to publicise a cause or campaign, or
(c) to mark or commemorate an event,

unless it is not reasonably practicable to give any advance notice of the procession.

(2) Subsection (1) does not apply where the procession is one commonly or customarily held in the police area. . .

(3) The notice must specify the date when it is intended to hold the procession, the time when it is intended to start it, its proposed route, and the name and address of the person (or of one of the persons) proposing to organise it.

(4) Notice must be delivered to a police station—

(a) in the police area in which it is proposed the procession will start. . .

(5) If delivered not less than six clear days before the date when the procession is intended to be held, the notice may be delivered by post. . .

(6) If not delivered in accordance with subsection (5), the notice must be delivered by hand. . . .

(7) Where a public procession is held, each of the persons organising it is guilty of an offence if—

(a) the requirements of this section as to notice have not been satisfied, or
(b) the date when it is held, the time when it starts, or its route, differs from the date, time or route specified in the notice.

(8) It is a defence for the accused to prove that he did not know of, and neither suspected nor had reason to suspect, the failure to satisfy the requirements or (as the case may be) the difference of day, time or route.

(9) To the extent that an alleged offence turns on a difference of date, time or route, it is a defence for the accused to prove that the difference arose from circumstances

beyond his control or from something done with the agreement of a police officer or
by his direction.

Notes

1. The notice requirement under s 11 is likely to have some inhibiting effect on organisers of marches
   but, except in that sense, it cannot readily be characterised 'an interference' with freedom of
   expression or assembly under the HRA since it is not a request for *permission* to hold the march.
   However, as highlighted in the case of *Kay* in 2008, which is extracted below, there is one instance in
   which s 11 could, depending on its interpretation, in effect 'ban' marches which might not be
   viewed as spontaneous and cannot yet be said to be customarily held, but which have no predetermined route, since, for example, the route is to be determined by the organiser on the day
   itself. This is because s 11(3) provides that the proposed route must be notified to police and
   s 11(7) provides that deviation from the route notified is an offence, although a defence is provided. That point was discussed but not finally resolved in the *Kay* case. It is argued that it should
   be resolved in favour of taking the stance that marches with no predetermined route are outside the
   scope of s 11 since—as was discussed in *Kay*—s 13 provides a banning power for marches and
   it would appear to be contrary to Parliament's intention (as well as doubtfully compatible with
   Art 11 ECHR) to provide a further indirect banning power under s 11.

2. In *Austin and Saxby v Commissioner of Police of the Metropolis*[57] it was found at first instance
   that the organisers of a large Mayday protest in London in 2001 had complied with the notice
   requirement under s 11, but had stated that the march would start at 4.00 whereas in fact it
   began at 2.00. The police stated in court that this was a deliberate move designed to impede the
   policing operation. The march was ordered to cease and the protesters were trapped inside a
   police cordon in Oxford Square for seven hours. The assumption appeared to be—although this
   was not confirmed in the Court of Appeal decision—that the assembly was 'unlawful', partly
   because the notice requirement had not been fully complied with. However, the failure to comply
   with it could only give rise to liability on the part of the organisers, under s 11(7), not the
   participants. Also it is a notice requirement; it is not an application for *authorisation* of the march.
   Austin and Saxby indicates that s 11 can be of significance in terms of repressing protest. So
   s 11 probably does have a significant impact on organisers and on policing. *Austin and Saxby* is
   discussed fully below.[58]

3. Once notice is correctly given, the march can take place, although conditions may be imposed
   on it, the matter considered in the next section. As indicated above, prior restraints on marches,
   including complete bans, have been upheld at Strasbourg, although the margin of appreciation
   doctrine was influential.[59] Owing to its relatively minimal impact on marches, which means that
   the s 11 requirement is probably—depending on the circumstances of a particular case—proportionate to the aims pursued, the requirement, assuming that it exempts spontaneous marches,
   appears to be compatible with Arts 10 and 11. A march or procession intended to lend support to
   a cause or otherwise falls within s 11(1), but 'one commonly or customarily held in the police area
   (or areas)' is exempted from the notification requirement by s 11(2). The question of the meaning
   of s 11(2) and the general applicability of s 11 arose in the following significant case.

---

57 [2005] HRLR 20; 2005 WL 699571, QBD; (2005) 155 NLJ 515; [2005] EWHC 480; 23 March 2005, Queen's Bench Division of the High Court.

58 At p 1128–1135.

59 E.g. *Christians Against Racism and Fascism v UK* (1980) 21 DR 138.

Kay (FC) (Appellant) v Commissioner of Police of the Metropolis (Respondent)
House of Lords [2008] UKHL 69; on appeal from [2007] EWCA Civ 477 (extracts)

The case concerned a bike ride known as 'Critical Mass'; it takes place across the world and in various cities in the UK. The idea behind the ride appears to be to show support for cycling as an environmentally friendly way of travelling around cities and to campaign for better provision for cyclists. According to a Critical Mass website, some participants may intend to demonstrate opposition to car culture and to cause disruption. This case concerned the London ride which starts from the South Bank at about six o'clock in the evening on the last Friday of every month. The Metropolitan Police took the view that the ride had to comply with the notice requirement under s 11; if it did not a criminal offence would be committed. On behalf of the ride it was argued that s 11(2) applied but the Police Commissioner countered that argument by founding on the fact that, although all the rides began from the South Bank, they did not follow a fixed route but went to different places and down different streets from month to month. The Court of Appeal accepted that argument and found that therefore s 11(2) did not apply, meaning that the notice requirement had to be complied with. The case was appealed to the House of Lords.

LORD PHILLIPS OF WORTH MATRAVERS
Introduction
1. The facts of this case raise issues of public importance as to the ambit of section 11 of the Public Order Act 1986. . .
2. . . .'Critical Mass is not an organisation but the name given to a recurrent event. . . . It is in the nature of Critical Mass that there is no fixed, settled or predetermined route, end-time or destination; where Critical Mass goes, where and what time it ends, are all things which are chosen by the actions of the participants on the day.'
3. The spontaneity of the event and, in particular, of the route that it takes, is an important feature of Critical Mass. . . .

The narrow issue
12. Is Critical Mass a 'procession [which is] commonly or customarily held' in the Metropolitan Police Area? . . . The narrow issue is, in fact, an amalgam of two questions: (i) is the Critical Mass ride that takes place each month the same procession and (ii) is that procession 'commonly or customarily held' in the Metropolitan Police Area.
16. I am in no doubt that the Critical Mass cycle rides. . . have so many common features that any person would consider that each month the same procession takes place and, giving the English language its natural meaning, that it is a procession that is 'commonly or customarily held' in the Metropolitan Police Area.
21. Section 11 does not require notice to be given of every procession that is capable of creating a disturbance. The fact that, on their natural meaning, the words of section 11(2) are wide enough to exclude some processions in respect of which the police do not have all the information that they would wish is no reason to give those words an unnatural meaning. They should be given their natural meaning so as to apply to Critical Mass as a procession that is commonly or customarily held. For this reason I would allow this appeal.

The wider issues
23. What is the position where there are organisers who are proposing to hold, for the first time, a procession such as Critical Mass that has no predetermined route?

24. It was Mr Pannick's suggestion that the approach of your Lordships' House in *R (Quintavalle) v Secretary of State for Health* [2003] 2 AC 687 brings events such as Critical Mass within the ambit of section 11. I beg to differ.

25. There are a number of possible constructions of section 11 that do not involve outlawing a procession such as Critical Mass:

(i) The notification obligation does not apply to a procession that has no predetermined route.

(ii) There is no obligation to give notice of a procession that has no predetermined route because it is not reasonably practicable to comply with section 11(1).

(iii) The notification obligation is satisfied if a notice is given that states that the route will be chosen spontaneously.

It is not necessary to select between these, nor appropriate to do so without hearing argument on them. Any one would, however, be preferable to the construction urged by Mr Pannick.

26. If these observations are correct there is a more fundamental basis for allowing this appeal. I would, however, allow it simply on the narrow issue raised by the appellant.

The other Law Lords also agreed that the appeal should be allowed.

Note

The result of this decision is that s 11 *may* be found, if a suitable case arises, not to apply to marches or processions that have no predetermined route, even if they cannot be viewed as ones customarily held. If they *can* be viewed as 'customarily held' on the basis of a range of features that create similarity between the marches on different occasions so as to identify them as the same march, *despite the fact* that they follow different routes each time (or, possibly, show some other dissimilarity), then s 11(2) will apply to exempt them from the notice requirement. If the appeal in *Kay* had gone the other way the result would have meant that s 11 in effect banned such marches since in order to achieve the aim of the legislation—to allow the police to consider imposing conditions or take any other appropriate action—the notice would have to tell the police which route the procession would follow; that was one of the elements of the notice prescribed by s 11(3). Consistently with that intention, s 11(7)(b) provides that, if the procession takes a different route from the one specified in the notice, any organiser or organisers would be guilty of an offence. Thus it would have appeared that all marches without a predetermined route could no longer lawfully occur. The result is in accordance with Art 11 since leaders of marches that do not always follow a predetermined route may not incur liability due to the need to comply with s 11.

Public Order Act 1986

Imposing conditions on public processions

12.–(1) If the senior police officer, having regard to the time or place at which and the circumstances in which any public procession is being held or is intended to be held and to its route or proposed route, reasonably believes that—

(a) it may result in serious public disorder, serious damage to property or serious disruption to the life of the community, or

(b) the purpose of the persons organising it is the intimidation of others with a view to compelling them not to do an act they have a right to do, or to do an act they have a right not to do, he may give directions imposing on the persons organising or taking part in the procession such conditions as appear to him necessary to prevent such disorder, damage, disruption or intimidation, including conditions as to the route of the procession or prohibit it from entering any public place specified in the directions.

(2)   In subsection (1) 'the senior police officer' means—

(a)   in relation to a procession being held, or to a procession intended to be held in a case where persons are assembling with a view to taking part in it, the most senior in rank of the police officers present at the scene, and

(b)   in relation to a procession intended to be held in a case where paragraph (1) does not apply, the chief officer of police.

(4)   A person who organises a public procession and knowingly fails to comply with a condition imposed under this section is guilty of an offence, but it is a defence for him to prove that the failure arose from circumstances beyond his control.

(5)   A person who takes part in a public procession and knowingly fails to comply with a condition imposed under this section is guilty of an offence, but it is a defence for him to prove that the failure arose from circumstances beyond his control.

(6)   A person who incites another to commit an offence under subsection (5) is guilty of an offence.

(7)   A constable in uniform may arrest without warrant anyone he reasonably suspects is committing an offence under subsection (4), (5) or (6).

Prohibiting public processions
13.–(1) If at any time the chief officer of police reasonably believes that, because of particular circumstances existing in any district or part of a district, the powers under section 12 will not be sufficient to prevent the holding of public processions in that district or part from resulting in serious public disorder, he shall apply to the council of the district for an order prohibiting for such period not exceeding three months as may be specified in the application the holding of all public processions (or of any class of public procession so specified) in the district or part concerned.

. . .

(7)   A person who organises a public procession the holding of which he knows is prohibited by virtue of an order under this section is guilty of an offence.

(8)   A person who takes part in a public procession the holding of which he knows is prohibited by virtue of an order under this section is guilty of an offence.

(9)   A person who incites another to commit an offence under subsection (8) is guilty of an offence.

(10)   A constable in uniform may arrest without warrant anyone he reasonably suspects is committing an offence under subsection (7), (8) or (9).

Imposing conditions on public assemblies
[Section 14 essentially provides for the same power as s 12 in relation to public processions

but the conditions that can be imposed can only relate to place, duration, number of persons.]

Prohibiting trespassory assemblies[60]

14A.–(1) If at any time the chief officer of police reasonably believes that an assembly is intended to be held in any district at a place on land to which the public has no right of access or only a limited right of access and that the assembly—

(a)　is likely to be held without the permission of the occupier of the land or to conduct itself in such a way as to exceed the limits of any permission of his or the limits of the public's right of access, and

(b)　may result—

(i)　in serious disruption to the life of the community, or

(ii)　where the land, or a building or monument on it, is of historical, architectural, archaeological or scientific importance, in significant damage to the land, building or monument,

he may apply to the council of the district for an order prohibiting for a specified period the holding of all trespassory assemblies in the district or a part of it, as specified.

(5)　An order prohibiting the holding of trespassory assemblies operates to prohibit any assembly which—

(a)　is held on land to which the public has no right of access or only a limited right of access, and

(b)　takes place in the prohibited circumstances, that is to say, without the permission of the occupier of the land or so as to exceed the limits of any permission of his or the limits of the public's right of access.

(6)　No order under this section shall prohibit the holding of assemblies for a period exceeding 4 days or in an area exceeding an area represented by a circle with a radius of 5 miles from a specified centre.

(9)　In this section and ss 14B and 14C—

'assembly' means an assembly of 2 or more persons;
'land', means land in the open air;
'limited', in relation to a right of access by the public to land, means that their use of it is restricted to use for a particular purpose. . .

14B.–(1) A person who organises an assembly the holding of which he knows is prohibited by an order under section 14A is guilty of an offence.

(2)　A person who takes part in an assembly which he knows is prohibited by an order under section 14A is guilty of an offence.

(4)　A constable in uniform may arrest without a warrant anyone he reasonably suspects to be committing an offence under this section.

60　Inserted by the Criminal Justice and Public Order Act 1994, s 70.

Stopping persons from proceeding to trespassory assemblies

14C.–(1) If a constable in uniform reasonably believes that a person is on his way to an assembly within the area to which an order under section 14A applies which the constable reasonably believes is likely to be an assembly which is prohibited by that order, he may, subject to subsection (2) below —

    (a)   stop that person, and

    (b)   direct him not to proceed in the direction of the assembly.

  (2)   The power conferred by subsection (1) may only be exercised within the area to which the order applies.

  (3)   A person who fails to comply with a direction under subsection (1) which he knows has been given to him is guilty of an offence.

  (4)   A constable in uniform may arrest without a warrant anyone he reasonably suspects to be committing an offence under this section.

Notes

1. The phrase 'serious disruption to the life of the community', used in ss 12(1)(a), 14(1)(a) and now 14A(1)(b), is very broad and clearly offers police officers wide scope for interpretation. This 'trigger' has attracted particular criticism from commentators. It has been said that 'some inconvenience is the inevitable consequence of a successful protest. The Act. . .threatens to permit only those demonstrations that are so convenient that they become invisible'.[61] Bonner and Stone have warned of 'the dangers that lie in the vague line between serious disruption and a measure of inconvenience'.[62] That danger was realised, it is argued, in the post-HRA *Brehony case* discussed below. It has been noted that the term 'the community' used in ss 12, 14 and 14A is ambiguous. In the case of London, it is unclear whether the term could be applied to Oxford Street or inner London or the whole Metropolitan area.[63] The more narrowly the term is defined, the more readily a given march or assembly could be said to cause serious disruption.

2. Although the approach to public protest cases has changed under the HRA in that Arts 10 and 11 may be adverted to, the courts have as yet made little attempt to curb ss 12 and 14 as they impact upon protesters, although it should be noted that there has been very little litigation and it has often not reached the senior courts. In *R (Brehony) v Chief Constable of Greater Manchester*[64] a very light touch approach was taken to the demands of proportionality in the circumstances. A regular demonstration had occurred outside a Marks and Spencers, protesting about the firm's support for the Government of Israel; a counter-demonstration had also occurred, supporting the Government. The Chief Constable had issued a notice under s 14 requiring the demonstration to move to a different location due to the disruption it would be likely to cause to shoppers over the Xmas period when the number of shoppers was likely to treble in number. The demonstrators sought judicial review of this decision; the judge refused the application on the basis that, in Arts 10 and 11 terms, the restraint was proportionate to the aim, of maintaining public order, pursued. This decision confirms that 'serious disruption to the life of the community' can mean mere anticipated inconvenience to shoppers. The decision indicates that ss 12 and 14 provide the police with

---

61 Ewing and Gearty (1990) (see p 1139, below), p 121.

62 'The Public Order Act 1986: Steps in the Wrong Direction?' [1987] PL 202.

63 Ewing and Gearty, n 61 above.

64 [2005] EWHC 640. For discussion see D Mead (2009) p 1138, below, at pp 204–205.

extremely wide scope for interfering in demonstrations and marches, despite the inception of the HRA.

3. The conditions that can be imposed if one of the 'triggers' under s 12(1) or 14(1) is thought be present are limited in scope under s 14, but very wide in the case of marches under s 12. In *Director of Public Prosecutors v Jones*[65] (below) it was made clear that the possible conditions under s 12 cannot be imported into s 14. The use of such broad wording does not oust the jurisdiction of the courts to assess the legality of the decision made.[66] Thus, at least in theory, it is not the case that any decision which appears necessary to an officer will in fact be lawful. However, it must be noted that in dealing with police action to maintain public order, the courts have been very unwilling to find police decisions to have been unlawful.[67] Also, unless the conditions were imposed some time before the assembly, a challenge to them by way of judicial review would be pointless.

4. In *Austin and Saxby v Commissioner of Police of the Metropolis*[68] at first instance it was found that both ss 12 and 14 allow for the imposition of extremely broad and restrictive conditions. The case concerned a protest against globalisation in 2001, discussed in full below, which the police controlled by trapping all the protesters behind a police cordon in Oxford Square, London for seven hours. It was found that s 12 gives a power to bring a procession that is in progress to an end. The section refers to 'the circumstances in which any public procession is being held' and specifically states that directions may be 'as to the route of the procession or prohibiting it from entering any public place specified in the directions'. So, it was found, if a procession is intended to go to a certain destination, a direction prohibiting that falls within s 12(1). The judge did find in that instance that a condition imposed could not amount to a ban, but could be imposed—even if amounting to a ban on the continuance of the march—where the march had already taken place to an extent.

   It was found that if the conditions do no more than is necessary and proportionate in the circumstances of the case to achieve the statutory public order objectives, then bringing the procession to an end will not be unlawful. That point clearly raises the question of strict scrutiny of the police action in order to be certain that bringing the march to an end was proportionate, or whether a post facto justification is being put forward.[69] Section 12 also, it was found, includes a power to detain persons who are part of a protest if that is necessary in order to achieve the objectives of preventing disorder or disruption of the life of the community. This is discussed below under s 14; a fortiori it must be possible under s 12 if it was found to be possible under s 14 since a much broader range of conditions can be imposed under s 12 than under s 14. The Court of Appeal decision in *Austin* (extracts are set out from the House of Lords' decision below) did not overturn these findings since that was unnecessary to decide the case, although doubts were expressed about them.

5. It was further found in *Austin and Saxby* that a protest could have conditions applied to it, including far-reaching ones, even where the protest itself was not the source of the disruption. In other words, if counter-protesters were causing a disruption the police would be justified in imposing conditions on the original protest, not the counter-protest. This is technically correct; the wording of ss 12(1)(a) and 14(1)(a) does not refer to any need for the protest in question to be the *source* of the disruption, disorder etc. However, it is contrary to the principle enunciated in

---

65 [2002] EWHC Admin 110.

66 See, e.g. *Secretary of State for Education and Science v Tameside* [1977] AC 1014.

67 See *Kent v Metropolitan Police Commission, The Times*, 15 May 1981.

68 [2005] HRLR 20.

69 See the discussion of this case below in which it is suggested that since the police did not have s 12 in mind at the time of the march it is arguable that they were seeking to find justifications for their very controversial actions after the event.

Beatty v Gillbanks[70] to the effect that the responsibility for causing disruption should be placed on those who are disruptive, not on those who are peaceful but whose protest has provoked a disorderly counter-protest. That principle was also enunciated in *Redmond-Bate*[71] by Sedley LJ. It is also, it is argued, contrary to the pronouncements in *Ezelin*[72] on Art 11 of the Convention.

6. The conditions which may be imposed under s 14 are on their face much more limited in scope than those that can be imposed under s 12. In *DPP v Jones*[73] conditions as to the movement of the assembly had been imposed; and were found to be *ultra vires* on the basis that they could only have been imposed under s 12; they could not be imposed under s 14 since the demonstration in question was clearly a static assembly, not a march.

7. However, the first instance decision in *Austin and Saxby v Commissioner of Police of the Metropolis* gave an interpretation to the conditions that can be imposed under s 14 that gave them a much broader scope than their face value wording warrants. In *Austin* it was found that s 14 gives a power to detain people for a very substantial period of time, even when they have behaved peacefully. The judge noted that on its face, the section is aimed at limiting the numbers who may attend, or continue to attend, but that the purpose of the power is to prevent public disorder, damage, disruption and intimidation. He considered that if the only direction apt to achieve those ends in the particular circumstances is a controlled dispersal, which in turn involves a period of preliminary detention, then s 14 would allow for that condition also.

In coming to this conclusion he relied on *DPP v Meaden*.[74] In that instance, in finding that the search warrant in that case carried with it a power to detain the occupants of the premises, the judge found: 'The authority [to search premises and person], to be meaningful, had . . . to enable the search to be effective. It could not be effective . . . if the occupiers were permitted to move about freely within the premises while the search was going on'. Relying on this observation, the judge found that there may be a greater implied power to detain when the police act pursuant to ss 12 and 14 of the 1986 Act than there would be if they acted pursuant to their common law powers. The judge concluded that a direction under s 14 that some or all members of an assembly disperse, can include a direction that they disperse by a specified route, and that they stay in a specified place for as long as is necessary for the dispersal to be effected, consistently with the objective of preventing disorder, damage, disruption or intimidation, and of taking reasonable care for the safety of themselves and others.

This was, it is argued, a very doubtful extension of the law. Had Parliament wished to allow for the imposition of a broad range of conditions in s 14, as in s 12, the two sections could have been framed in the same terms. It was also found, somewhat less controversially, that a direction under s 14 may bring an existing assembly to an end. The judge said that this would be allowable since the section refers to 'the circumstances in which any public assembly is being held' and authorises a direction imposing the 'maximum duration'.

8. The Court of Appeal in *Austin* did not over-rule these findings on ss 12 and 14, but did express some doubts about them. The finding at first instance was doubtful since once a march becomes a static assembly it is subject to s 14 which does not on its face allow for detention of the assembly, and case law has established that the condition must be imposed under the right section.[75] But as

---

70   (1882) 15 Cox CC 138.

71   See p 1121 below.

72   See n 49 above.

73   [2002] EWHC 110.

74   [2003] EWHC 3005 (Admin); [2004] 1 WLR 945.

75   See *DPP v Jones* (2002), below p 1102.

discussed above, the judge found that s 14 could be interpreted to include a power to impose detention.[76]

Police v Lorna Reid [1987] Crim LR 702 (Commentary, Professor D Birch)

The defendant, with about 20 others, demonstrated outside South Africa House in Trafalgar Square on the occasion of a reception there. She shouted slogans through a megaphone and the others joined in, raising their arms towards the arriving guests as they did so. The slogans included 'Apartheid murderers, get out of Britain' and 'You are a dying breed'. One visitor turned to remonstrate with the demonstrators.

The chief inspector in charge decided that this was intimidatory and purported to impose a condition on the assembly, relying on s 14(1) of the Public Order Act 1986. He used a police megaphone to say, 'This is a police message. You are required to go to the mouth of Duncannon Street, north of the tree'. The defendant made a speech over her megaphone, saying that they would not move.

When the group reached the tree, the defendant refused to go further and her arresting officer said that she pushed against him saying 'I am going back to where I came from'. She was arrested and charged with knowingly failing to comply with a condition imposed on a public assembly, contrary to s 14(5) of the 1986 Act.

In cross-examination, the chief inspector said that he defined intimidation as 'putting people in fear or discomfort'.

Held, the question was whether these demonstrators acted with a view to compelling visitors not to go into South Africa House or merely with the intention of causing them discomfort so as to make them look again at what was going on in South Africa. The chief inspector had equated intimidation with discomfort. That was the wrong test. Causing someone to feel uncomfortable would not be intimidation. The officer needed to go further and reasonably believe that the organisers acted with a view to compelling. Since he had not said that he had done so in this case, there was no ground for imposing a condition on the assembly and the defendant had therefore not committed the offence.

Director of Public Prosecutors v Jones [2002] EWHC Admin 110, QBD (extracts)

. . .

The respondent was charged with an offence contrary to section 14(5) and (9) of the Public Order Act 1986, in that she. . .took part in a public assembly and knowingly failed to comply with a condition imposed by a senior police officer under section 14 of the Public Order Act 1986, that is she failed to remain in the designated demonstration area. The charge arose out of the respondent's alleged participation in a demonstration outside Huntingdon Life Services premises at Woolley, near Huntingdon. . . the Assistant Chief Constable issued a notice under section 14 of the Public Order Act 1986 imposing certain conditions upon the assembly to be held on 4th November 2000. The conditions prescribed and defined in writing (by reference to a map) the area within which the assembly could take place. The assembly was to be permitted to take place between seven in the morning and seven in the evening. The respondent was arrested . . .on 4th November 2000 outside the area in which the demonstration was permitted. When interviewed she admitted that she had been given a copy of the section 14 notice upon her arrival at the demonstration, and

76   See n 7, p 1101.

that she had been warned before her arrest that she was outside the area designated in the notice within which the assembly was permitted. She said at interview that she had no sense of direction and had got lost when trying to find her way back to the road . . .

10. It is three of the five conditions of the notice in this case which are said to be ultra vires the senior police officer's powers under section 14, and to render the notice unlawful in its entirety, as was found by the magistrates. . .it is contended by the respondent that the three conditions said to be ultra vires are permitted by section 12 of the 1986 Act but not section 14. . .

16. The contention for the respondent before the justices . . . states: 'It was contended by the Respondent that the document was unlawful in that it exceeded the powers of the Assistant Chief Constable under section 14 . . . The substance of the order went too far and invoked powers under section 12 of the Public Order Act 1986 namely, the route, rendering the order unlawful. The order whilst using conditions relevant to a notice under section 14 Public Order Act 1968 also used conditions relevant to a notice under section 12 of the Public Order Act 1968 thereby rendering the notice ultra vires.'. . .

20 . . .the question [for us] should be considered in two parts, namely are conditions [relating to the route] ultra vires of the Deputy Chief Constable's powers under section 14. . .? Secondly, if so, are they severable?

24. In my judgment, the magistrates were correct in concluding in this case that conditions [regarding the route], fell outside the Deputy Chief Constable's power under section 14. . .

32. . . . I conclude that the [*ultra vires*] conditions of the section 14 notice can be severed without invalidating the whole notice. . . . What remains on severance are the conditions dealing with the permitted area for assembly. This, in my judgment, is exactly what section 14 permits.

The appeal was allowed.

Director of Public Prosecutions v Jones and Another [1999] 2 AC 240, HL (extracts)

The defendants took part in a peaceful, non-obstructive assembly on a highway in respect of which there was in force an order under s 14A of the Public Order Act 1986 prohibiting the holding of trespassory assemblies. They were convicted before justices of taking part in a trespassory assembly knowing it to be prohibited, contrary to s 14B(2) of the 1986 Act, as inserted. The appeal came to the House of Lords.

Lord Irvine of Lairg LC: My Lords, this appeal raises an issue of fundamental constitutional importance: what are the limits of the public's rights of access to the public highway? Are these rights so restricted that they preclude in all circumstances any right of peaceful assembly on the public highway? On 1 June. . .Inspector Mackie counted 21 people on the roadside verge of the southern side of the A344, adjacent to the perimeter fence of the monument at Stonehenge. Some were bearing banners with the legends, 'Never Again' . . . 'Free Stonehenge'. He concluded that they constituted a 'trespassory assembly' and told them so. When asked to move off, many did, but some, including the defendants, Mr Lloyd and Dr Jones, were determined to remain and put their rights to the test. They were arrested for taking part in a 'trespassory assembly' and convicted . . . Their appeals to the Salisbury Crown Court, however, succeeded. The court held that neither of the defendants, nor any member of their group, was 'being destructive, violent, disorderly, threatening a breach of the peace or, on the evidence, doing anything other than reasonably using the highway'. . . An appeal by way of case stated to the Divisional Court [1998] QB 563 followed. It was assumed for the purposes of that appeal (per McCowan LJ, at p 568c) that (a) the grass verge constituted part of the public highway; and (b) the group was peaceful, did not create an obstruction and did not constitute or cause a public nuisance. The defendants had been charged with 'trespassory assembly'. . .

. . . The central issue in the case . . . turns on two interrelated questions: (i) what are the 'limits' of the public's right of access to the public highway at common law? and (ii) what is the 'particular purpose' for which the public has a right to use the public highway?

. . . in broad terms the basis of the Divisional Court's decision is the proposition that the public's right of access to the public highway is limited to the right to pass and repass, and to do anything incidental or ancillary to that right. Peaceful assembly is not incidental to the right to pass and repass. Thus peaceful assembly exceeds the limits of the public's right of access and so is conduct which fulfils the actus reus of the offence of 'trespassory assembly'.

The Divisional Court's decision is founded principally on three authorities. In *ex parte Lewis* (1888) 21 QBD 191 the Divisional Court held obiter that there was no public right to occupy Trafalgar Square for the purpose of holding public meetings. However, Wills J, giving the judgment of the court, had in mind, at p 197, an assembly 'to the detriment of others having equal rights. . .in its nature irreconcilable with the right of free passage. . .'. Such an assembly would probably also amount to a public nuisance, and, today, involve the commission of the offence of obstruction of the public highway contrary to section 137(1) of the Highways Act 1980. Such an assembly would probably also amount to unreasonable user of the highway. It by no means follows that this same reasoning should apply to a peaceful assembly which causes no obstruction nor any public nuisance.

Harrison v Duke of Rutland [1893] 1 QB 142. . .[established that using the highway], not for the purpose of using it in order to pass and repass, or for any reasonable or usual mode of using the highway as a highway, [is trespass]

. . .The question to which this appeal gives rise is whether the law today should recognise that the public highway is a public place, on which all manner of reasonable activities may go on. For the reasons I set out below in my judgment it should. Provided these activities are reasonable, do not involve the commission of a public or private nuisance, and do not amount to an obstruction of the highway unreasonably impeding the primary right of the general public to pass and repass, they should not constitute a trespass. Subject to these qualifications, therefore, there would be a public right of peaceful assembly on the public highway. . . Nor can I attribute any hard core of meaning to a test which would limit lawful use of the highway to what is incidental or ancillary to the right of passage. In truth very little activity could accurately be described as 'ancillary' to passing along the highway: perhaps stopping to tie one's shoe lace, consulting a street-map, or pausing to catch one's breath. But I do not think that such ordinary and usual activities as making a sketch, taking a photograph, handing out leaflets, collecting money for charity, singing carols, playing in a Salvation Army band, children playing a game on the pavement, having a picnic, or reading a book, would qualify. These examples illustrate that to limit lawful use of the highway to that which is literally 'incidental or ancillary' to the right of passage would be to place an unrealistic and unwarranted restriction on commonplace day-to-day activities. The law should not make unlawful what is commonplace and well accepted.

. . .If the right to use the highway extends to reasonable user not inconsistent with the public's right of passage, then the law does recognise (and has at least since Lord Esher MR's judgment in *Harrison v Duke of Rutland* [1893] 1 QB 142 recognised) that the right to use the highway, goes beyond the minimal right to pass and repass. That user may in fact extend, to a limited extent, to roaming about on the highway, or remaining on the highway. But that is not of the essence of the right.

I conclude therefore the law to be that the public highway is a public place which the public may enjoy for any reasonable purpose, provided the activity in question does not amount to a public or private nuisance and does not obstruct the highway by unreasonably impeding the primary right of the public to pass and repass: within these qualifications there is a public right of peaceful assembly on the highway. Since the law confers this public right, I deprecate any attempt artificially to restrict its scope. It must be for the magistrates in every case to decide whether the user of the highway under consideration is both reasonable in the sense defined and not inconsistent with the primary right of the public to pass and repass. In particular, there can be no principled basis for limiting the scope of the right by reference to the subjective intentions of the persons assembling.

. . .If, contrary to my judgment, the common law of trespass is not as clear as I have held it to be, then at least it is uncertain and developing, so that regard should be had to the Convention for the Protection of Human Rights and Fundamental Freedoms in resolving the uncertainty and in determining how it should develop. . .Article 11 confers a 'right to freedom of peaceful assembly' and then entitles the state to impose restrictions on that right. The effect of the Divisional Court's decision in this case would be that any peaceful assembly on the public highway, no matter how minor or harmless, would involve the commission of the tort of trespass.

Unless the common law recognises that assembly on the public highway may be lawful, the right contained in Article 11(1) of the Convention is denied. Of course the right may be subject to restrictions (for example, the requirements that user of the highway for purposes of assembly must be reasonable and non-obstructive, and must not contravene the criminal law of wilful obstruction of the highway). But in my judgment our law will not comply with the Convention unless its starting point is that assembly on the highway will not necessarily be unlawful. . . Thus, if necessary, I would invoke Article 11 to clarify or develop the common law in the terms which I have held it to be; but for the reasons I have given I do not find it necessary to do so. I would therefore allow the appeal.

Lord Slynn of Hadley: The question is what are the limits to the right (not, it should be noted, the practice) of the public to use or be on the highway. . . .

The right of assembly, of demonstration, is of great importance but in English law it is not an absolute right which requires all limitations on other rights to be set aside or ignored. These cases, in limiting or linking rights of user by the public of the highway to passage or repassage, in themselves exclude a right to stay on the highway other than for purposes connected with such passage. . .

The right is restricted to passage and reasonable incidental uses associated with passage. I am willing to assume that more people are now more conscious of the importance of assembly and demonstration than they were in previous centuries, but I do not see that this in itself is enough to justify changing the nature and scope of the public's right to use the highway. That it cannot in itself justify as of right assemblies or demonstrations on private land is obvious.

. . .the fact that an assembly is peaceful or unlikely to result in violence, or that it is not causing an obstruction at the particular time when the police intervene, [does not] in itself change what is otherwise a trespass into a legal right of access. . .Reference was also made to the European Convention for the Protection of Human Rights and Fundamental Freedoms. . .I am not satisfied that the existing law on highways is necessarily in conflict with article 11 of the Convention providing for a right of assembly, or of article 10 relating to freedom of expression. Both provide for exceptions to the rights created. . . . I am not satisfied that there was here such a violation either by the law relating to access to the highway as it stands, or in its application to the facts of this case, which should compel us to change the law as I believe it to be.

. . . .Put in the way in which the question is framed, ie whether such an assembly where there is no obstruction does exceed the public right of access to the highway so as to constitute a trespassory assembly contrary to section 14A of the Act of 1986, I would answer in the affirmative. I would accordingly dismiss the appeal.

In the event the Lords allowed the appeal by a majority of 3:2.

Notes

1. The above decision of the Lords is disappointing in that one would have expected a greater reliance on the Convention, given the imminent inception of the HRA. All the Lords in the majority delivered substantial and quite different speeches; therefore, it is a matter of some difficulty to identify the *ratio*, but the key finding in common was that since *the particular assembly in question* had been found by the tribunal of fact to be a reasonable user of the highway, it was therefore not trespassory and so not caught by the s 14A order. The conduct of the protesters, according to the majority, thus had the classic character of an English negative liberty: since it was not unlawful, it was permitted, and the police had 'no right' to remove the protesters. This was the basis of the judgment, not any finding that the protesters had a positive right to peaceful protest which the police were under a corresponding duty to respect.[77] The majority, therefore, apparently found a liberty to peaceful assembly on the highway. A liberty generally is precarious for two reasons: there is no duty upon the state (or anyone else) to respect it or facilitate its exercise, and the legislature (or the judiciary through the common law) may encroach upon it at any time. Not one of their Lordships was prepared to find that assemblies on the highway which were both peaceful and non-obstructive were invariably lawful.

2. The approach to public protest cases has changed, under the HRA in that Arts 10 and 11 should be adverted to, and the para 2 tests applied, but no radical change in approach to ss 12–14A has occurred due to the impact of the HRA. The findings of the House of Lords in *Jones* take a traditionally blinkered and deferential judicial approach to public protest; that stance is still influential, although the very recent decision in *Kay* (above) in the House of Lords suggests that a change of stance may be occurring. Challenges to ss 12–14A under the HRA present the judiciary with the chance of adopting a change of stance, since they are expected to construe existing law so that it complies with Arts 10 and 11 of the Convention, 'in so far as it is possible to do so' under s 3 of the HRA, and apply the law in any particular instance compatibly with those Articles under s 6 HRA. The courts' approach to this matter has undergone a change, at least in methodology, but the change does not, it is argued, reflect the values underpinning those articles fully. But *Laporte*, on common law powers (below), suggests that a change of stance, giving greater weight to the values underlying the ECHR, may also come about in this context.

3. Rather than focusing primarily upon the limitations upon otherwise lawful conduct that ss 11–14A create, the starting point ought to be the Convention rights in issue. Courts should find that a protest which is wholly peaceful falls within Art 11 and, following *Steel*, should also find Art 10 applicable. The first step is to determine whether *prima facie* interference with the right(s) has

---

77 Lord Hutton did appear to assert this ([1999] 2 WLR 625, 660), but his conclusion (at 666) upholds only the narrow and precarious liberty formulated by Lords Irvine and Clyde.

occurred, such as the imposition of conditions under s 12, and/or the arrests of the defendants and/or any convictions sustained.[78] Having made this determination, a court should then consider the exceptions within para 2 of those articles. It is bound under s 6 HRA to consider whether the interference was justified under the para 2 tests. Although it is also bound under s 3 HRA to find an interpretation of ss 12–14A which is compatible with the Convention, if at all possible, sections 11–14A appear to be compatible with the Convention on their face since they answer to the exceptions under Arts 10 and 11 to protect public order or the rights of others. So everything depends upon the proportionality of the interference in the particular instance, considered under s 6 HRA. The question of what is required in order to satisfy the demands of proportionality is open to interpretation, depending on the view of the Strasbourg jurisprudence adopted. It may be noted that although this is the approach one would *expect* the courts to follow under s 6 HRA in the post-HRA era, it was very clearly absent from the discussion in the 2002 case of *Jones,* above, on s 14 of the 1986 Act. In *Austin* the Court of Appeal implied that ss 12 and 14 were not as broad as the first instance judge had suggested, but evaded consideration of s 3 HRA in relation to them:

> 74. In these circumstances it is unnecessary to say much about the 1986 Act. . . . We only refer to the Act at all for two reasons. The first is that we are concerned that, if we do not, it may be thought that we would have reached the same conclusion as the judge and the second is to highlight the fact that, at any rate as it seems to us, the exceptional circumstances of this case suggest that sections 12 to 14 of the 1986 Act require further consideration and perhaps amendment for the future.

4. The power to prohibit public processions under s 13 is open to criticism in that once a banning order has been imposed it prevents all marches in the area it covered for its duration. Thus, a projected march likely to be of an entirely peaceful character would be caught by a ban aimed at a violent march. The Campaign for Nuclear Disarmament attempted unsuccessfully to challenge such a ban (under the predecessor of s 13—s 3 of the 1936 Act) after it had had to cancel a number of its marches: *Kent v Metropolitan Police Commissioner.*[79]

It might seem that the s 13 banning power would be in breach of Art 11 of the ECHR, in that the banning of a march expected to be peaceful would not appear to be justified under Art 11, para 2 in respect of the need to prevent disorder. However, in *Christians Against Racism and Fascism v UK,*[80] the applicants' argument that a ban imposed under s 3(3) of the Public Order Act 1936 infringed, *inter alia,* Art 11 was rejected by the Commission as manifestly ill founded, on the ground that the ban was justified under the exceptions to Art 11 contained in para 2, since there was a real danger of disorder which it was thought could not be 'prevented by other less stringent measures'. Thus, it may be irrelevant that a particular march affected by the ban was unlikely in itself to give rise to disorder. Nevertheless, the s 13 power may be open to amelioration under the HRA in order to achieve compatibility with Arts 10 and 11. A court confronted with the kind of situation that arose in *Christians Against Racism and Fascism* under the HRA could take a hard look at the question of proportionality. The court could take the view that the geographical or temporal scope of the ban had been greater than was needed to obviate the risk of serious disorder. Or it

---

78 Where an arrest and police detention took place but no charges were laid, or no conviction sustained, there would still be a *prima facie* violation of Arts 10 and 11, following *Steel and Others v UK* (1999) 28 EHRR 603: violations were found in relation to the third, fourth and fifth applicants who were arrested and detained but not tried (the prosecution adduced no evidence).

79 *The Times,* 15 May 1981.

80 (1984) 24 *Yearbook* 178.

could find that the ban need not have been imposed at all since the imposition of conditions under s 12 would have been sufficient.

5. In *Steel and Others v UK*,[81] the Court found that the interference with an entirely peaceful protest which had occurred was disproportionate to the aim of preventing disorder, and in *Ezelin v France*[82] the Court found that: 'the freedom to take part in a peaceful assembly. . .is of such importance that it cannot be restricted in any way. . .so long as the person concerned *does not himself* commit any reprehensible act on such an occasion.' On its face,[83] this finding would prohibit the application of criminal sanctions to peaceful protesters[84] as a result of the use of blanket bans, a possibility which, as noted above, is left open by *Jones*. It would also prohibit the imposition of conditions which can, depending on the circumstances, have an effect on an assembly almost as severe as that created by a ban. As indicated above, conditions can be imposed on peaceful assemblies where it is thought that a risk of disruption to the life of the community may arise. Following *Steel* and *Ezelin* it is open to the courts to impose a narrow interpretation on ss 12–14A, under s 3 of the HRA and to scrutinise the question of proportionality carefully in any particular instance under s 6 HRA.

6. The Serious and Organised Crime Act 2005, ss 132–38 provided controversial new powers which were introduced partly as a response to the presence near Parliament of a peace protester, Brian Haw, against the war in Iraq; he set up a peace protest site outside Parliament in 2001 which he maintained until it was largely dismantled under the new powers in 2005.[85] It appeared that the key provisions—the requirement to apply for permission to hold a demonstration from the Metropolitan Police Commissioner—was to be repealed by the Constitutional Reform and Governance Act 2010. Such provision was included in the Bill, but was removed from it during 'wash up'—the process of rushing Bills through Parliament to make them law before dissolution of Parliament in time for the May 2010 General Election.

THE LEGAL CONTROL OF MEETINGS, MARCHES, DEMONSTRATIONS, PROTESTS—SUBSEQUENT RESTRAINTS

Subsequent restraints arising from a variety of sources can be used as an alternative, or in addition, to the powers arising under the 1986 and 1994 Acts and, as will be seen, many of the powers overlap. It should be noted that the powers arising under ss 12 and 14 of the 1986 Act may be used during the assembly, not merely prior to it. The senior police officer present, who may of course be a constable, can impose the conditions mentioned if, after the assembly has begun, it is apparent that one of the 'triggers' is in being or is about to come into being.

---

81 (1999) 28 EHRR 603. The applicants had been holding a banner and giving out leaflets outside an arms exhibition.

82 (1991) 14 EHRR 362, para 53. See also *Cetinkaya v Turkey* (2006) App 75569/01.

83 The Crown might argue that it is inapplicable beyond its particular facts: it concerned professional disciplinary sanctions applied to a lawyer who took part in a march that became violent and disorderly, but who conducted himself peacefully.

84 It might be argued that a distinction should be drawn between protesters who take part in a peaceful demonstration which they know to be banned, arguably thereby committing a reprehensible act, and those who obey the ban by abandoning their proposed demonstrations, but bring proceedings to test its legality.

85 For discussion see I Loveland, 'Public Protest in Parliament Square' (2007) EHRLR 252. Also see *DPP v Haw* [2008] 1 WLR 379.

Violence, threats, abuse, insults

Public Order Act 1986

Fear or provocation of violence

4.–(1) A person is guilty of an offence if he—

(a)   uses towards another person threatening, abusive or insulting words or behaviour, or

(b)   distributes or displays to another person any writing, sign or other visible representation which is threatening, abusive or insulting,

with intent to cause that person to believe that immediate unlawful violence will be used against him or another by any person, or to provoke the immediate use of unlawful violence by that person or another, or whereby that person is likely to believe that such violence will be used, or it is likely that such violence will be provoked. . . .

(2)   An offence under this section may be committed in a public or a private place, except that no offence is committed where the words or behaviour are used, or the writing, sign or other visible representation is distributed or displayed, by a person inside a dwelling and the other person is also inside that or another dwelling.

(3)   A constable may arrest without warrant anyone he reasonably suspects is committing an offence under this section.

Intentional harassment, alarm or distress[86]

4A.–(1) A person is guilty of an offence if, with intent to cause a person harassment alarm or distress, he—

(a)   uses threatening, abusive or insulting words or behaviour, or disorderly behaviour, or

(b)   displays any writing, sign or other visible representation which is threatening, abusive or insulting, thereby causing that or another person harassment, alarm or distress. . . .

(2)   [as s 4(2) above]

(3)   It is a defence for the accused to prove—

(a)   that he was inside a dwelling and had no reason to believe that the words or behaviour used, or the writing, sign or other visible representation displayed, would be heard or seen by a person outside that or any other dwelling, or

(b)   that his conduct was reasonable.

(4)   A constable may arrest without warrant anyone he reasonably suspects is committing an offence under this section.

---

86   Inserted by the Criminal Justice and Public Order Act 1994, s 154.

Harassment, alarm or distress

5.–(1) A person is guilty of an offence if he—

[commits the same conduct as in s 4A above]

(2) [as s 4(3) above]

(3) [as s 4A(3) above]

(4) A constable may arrest a person without warrant if—

(a) he engages in offensive conduct which the constable warns him to stop, and
(b) he engages in further offensive conduct immediately or shortly after the warning.

(5) In subsection (4) 'offensive conduct' means conduct the constable reasonably suspects to constitute an offence under this section, and the conduct mentioned in paragraph (a) and the further conduct need not be of the same nature.

Mental element—miscellaneous

6.–(3) A person is guilty of an offence under section 4 only if he intends his words or behaviour, or the writing, sign or other visible representation to be threatening, abusive or insulting, or is aware that it may be threatening, abusive or insulting.

(4) A person is guilty of an offence under section 5 only if he intends his words or behaviour, or the writing, sign or other visible representation to be threatening, abusive or insulting, or is aware that it may be threatening, abusive or insulting or (as the case may be) he intends his behaviour to be or is aware that it may be disorderly.

Note

In these provisions the words/behaviour must be 'threatening, abusive or insulting'. The term 'insulting' was considered in *Brutus v Cozens* [1973] AC 854 in respect of disruption of a tennis match involving a South African player by an anti-apartheid demonstrator.

Brutus v Cozens **[1973] AC 854, 860–63**

Lord Reid: My Lords, the charge against the appellant is that on 28 June 1971, during the annual tournament at the All England Lawn Tennis Club, Wimbledon, he used insulting behaviour whereby a breach of the peace was likely to be occasioned, contrary to s 5 of the Public Order Act 1936, as amended.

While a match was in progress on No 2 Court he went on to the court, blew a whistle and threw leaflets around. On the whistle being blown nine or ten others invaded the court with banners and placards. I shall assume that they did this at the instigation of the appellant though that is not made very clear in the case stated by the magistrates. Then the appellant sat down and had to be forcibly removed by the police. The incident lasted for two or three minutes. This is said to have been insulting behaviour.

It appears that the object of this demonstration was to protest against the apartheid policy of the Government of South Africa. But it is not said that that Government was insulted. The insult is said to have been offered to or directed at the spectators. The spectators at No 2 Court were upset; they made loud shouts, gesticulated and shook their fists and, while the appellant was being removed, some showed hostility and attempted to strike him.

... the question of law in this case must be whether it was unreasonable to hold that the appellant's behaviour was not insulting. To that question there could in my view be only one answer—no. But as the divisional court [[1972] 1 WLR 484] have expressed their view as to the meaning of 'insulting' I must, I think, consider it. It was said, at p 487:

> It is, as I think, quite sufficient for the purpose of this case to say that behaviour which affronts other people, and evidences a disrespect or contempt for their rights, behaviour which reasonable persons would foresee is likely to cause resentment or protest such as was aroused in this case, and I rely particularly on the reaction of the crowd as set out in the case stated, is insulting for the purpose of this section.

I cannot agree with that. Parliament had to solve the difficult question of how far freedom of speech or behaviour must be limited in the general public interest. It would have been going much too far to prohibit all speech or conduct likely to occasion a breach of the peace because determined opponents may not shrink from organising or at least threatening a breach of the peace in order to silence a speaker whose views they detest. Therefore vigorous and it may be distasteful or unmannerly speech or behaviour is permitted so long as it does not go beyond any one of three limits. It must not be threatening. It must not be abusive. It must not be insulting. I see no reason why any of these should be construed as having a specially wide or a specially narrow meaning. They are all limits easily recognisable by the ordinary man. Free speech is not impaired by ruling them out. But before a man can be convicted it must be clearly shown that one or more of them has been disregarded.

The spectators may have been very angry and justly so. The appellant's conduct was deplorable.

Probably it ought to be punishable. But I cannot see how it insulted the spectators.

I would allow the appeal with costs.

Notes
1. The conviction of the defendant under the predecessor of s 4 of the 1986 Act was therefore overturned.
2. The test for 'insulting' appears to be whether an ordinary sensible person at whom the words in question are directed would find them insulting. The fact that the persons in question who hear the words are particularly likely to find them insulting may not preclude a finding that they are insulting, although whether or not the speaker knows that such persons will hear the words appears to be immaterial as far as this ingredient of ss 5, 4 and 4A is concerned (*Jordan v Burgoyne*).[87]
3. Section 5 is the lowest level public order offence contained in the 1986 Act and the most contentious, since it brings behaviour within the scope of the criminal law which was previously thought of as too trivial to justify the imposition of criminal liability.[88] In Northern Ireland, s 5 was used against a poster depicting youths stoning a British Saracen with a caption proclaiming 'Ireland: 20 years of resistance'.[89] In the so-called *Madame M* case, four students were prosecuted for putting up a satirical poster depicting Margaret Thatcher as a 'sadistic dominatrix';[90] the students were acquitted but it was disturbing that such a case was brought in a democracy.

---

87   [1963] 2 QB 744.

88   For background to s 5, see Law Commission Report No 123, *Offences Relating to Public Order* (1983); for comment see D Williams [1984] PL 12.

89   Reported in the *Independent*, 12 September 1988; mentioned in Ewing and Gearty (1990), p 1139, below, at p 123.

90   P Thornton, *Decade of Decline: Civil Liberties in the Thatcher Years* (1990), p 37.

4. In *DPP v Fidler and Moran*[91] the respondents were part of a group shouting at and talking to persons attending the clinic, displaying plastic models of human foetuses, photographs of dead foetuses and placards. On the basis of these findings, it was accepted on appeal that s 5 of the Public Order Act 1986 was satisfied since the expression could be viewed as insulting and likely to cause distress.

5. In *DPP v Orum*[92] the Divisional Court found that a police officer may be a person who is caused harassment, alarm or distress by the various kinds of words or conduct to which s 5(1) applies.

6. The criminalisation of speech which causes the low level of harm connoted by the terms 'alarm' or 'distress' does not comport with *dicta* of the European Court of Human Rights in *Müller v Switzerland*,[93] to the effect that the protection of free speech extends equally to ideas which 'offend, shock or disturb';[94] however, a conviction under s 5 would not be in breach of Art 10 so long as in the particular instance the tests under Art 10(2) were satisfied.

7. The number of prosecutions being brought under s 5 suggests that the police may not be showing restraint in using this area of the Act in relation to protest. The old s 5 offence under the 1936 Public Order Act, an offence with a higher harm threshold,[95] accounted for the majority of the 8,194 charges brought in connection with the miners' strike of 1984. In a survey of 470 1988 public order cases, conducted in two police force areas, it was found that 56% of the sample led to charges under s 5. Research has also shown that during the period 1986–88 the number of charges brought for public order offences doubled and this was thought to be due, not to increased unrest, but to the existence of new offences, particularly s 5 with its low level of harm.[96] Obviously most use of s 5 is in the context of public rowdiness and is not the concern of this chapter. But there clearly remains a tendency to use s 5 on occasion against protest, as certain post-HRA cases mentioned below indicate.

DPP v Clarke, Lewis, O'Connell and O'Keefe [1992] Crim LR 60 (extracts)

It was alleged against the respondents that they 'did display writing, a sign or visible representation which was threatening, abusive or insulting, within the hearing or sight of a person likely to be caused harassment, alarm or distress thereby contrary to ss 5(1)(b) and 6 of the Public Order Act 1986'.

The events which gave rise to these charges took place outside a licensed abortion clinic. On 16 December the respondents, who were opposed to the procuring of abortions, assembled on the pavement outside the clinic, each carrying a picture of an aborted foetus which they displayed to police officers who were on uniform patrol duty and, in one case, to passers-by. The respondents refused to comply with police requests not to display the pictures. The magistrates concluded that the pictures were abusive and insulting giving the words their ordinary everyday meaning, and that they were displayed in the sight of a person likely to be caused harassment alarm or distress, and did in fact cause alarm and

---

91   [1992] 1 WLR 91. For comment see JC Smith [1992] Crim LR 63.

92   [1988] 3 All ER 449.

93   (1991) 13 EHRR 212.

94   It should be noted that in *Brutus v Cozens* [1973] AC 854, Lord Reid said that s 5 of the previous 1936 Public Order Act was 'not designed to penalise the expressions of opinion that happen to be disagreeable, distasteful or even offensive, annoying or distressing'.

95   It was similar to the offence which replaced it, s 4 of the 1986 Act.

96   T Newburn *et al*, 'Policing the Streets' (1990) 29 HORB 10 and 'Increasing Public Order' (1991) 7 Policing 22; quoted in SH Bailey, DJ Harris and BL Jones, *Civil Liberties: Cases and Materials*, 4th edn (1995), pp 229–30.

distress to the police officer concerned. Applying an objective test to s 5(3)(c) they found that, in all the circumstances, the respondents' conduct was not reasonable; applying s 6 and using a subjective test they concluded that, on the balance of probabilities, none of the respondents intended the pictures to be threatening, abusive or insulting, nor was any of them aware that they might be. The respondents were therefore acquitted by the magistrates.

Held, dismissing the appeal;

(i) The two limbs of s 5(1) must be distinguished. First, the thing displayed must be threatening, abusive or insulting; secondly, the display must be within the sight of a person likely to be caused harassment, alarm or distress thereby. However, s 6(4) provided that a person was only guilty under s 5 if he intended the writing, sign or other visible representation to be threatening, abusive or insulting or was aware that it might be. It did not, therefore, avail the appellant to argue that the respondents must have intended the pictures to cause harassment, alarm or distress or been aware that they might do so; a picture might cause harassment, alarm or distress without being threatening, abusive or insulting and vice versa. The magistrates' conclusion that, although the pictures were abusive and insulting and the police officer found them so, the respondents lacked the necessary intention or awareness, was unassailable. The question whether the pictures were abusive or insulting was essentially one for the magistrates; *Brutus v Cozens* [1973] AC 854.

(ii) The magistrates were correct in applying an objective test to the defence of reasonable conduct in s 5(3)(c) of the Act.

(iii) The magistrates correctly imputed a subjective awareness to the words 'is aware that it may be threatening, abusive or insulting' in s 6(4) of the Act

R v Horseferry Road Magistrate ex parte Siadatan [1990] 3 WLR 1006 (extracts)

Watkins LJ: . . .Viking Penguin Books Ltd published a book entitled *The Satanic Verses*, the author of which is Mr Salman Rushdie. It is clear that many devout Muslims have found the book offensive. [The applicant's] solicitors. . .laid before the Horseferry Road Magistrates' Court an information in these terms:

> Penguin Books Limited on or before the 19th of June 1989 at 157 Kings Road, Chelsea SW3 and other places unknown distributed books entitled The Satanic Verses by Salman Rushdie containing abusive and insulting writing whereby it was likely that unlawful violence would be provoked contrary to s 4(1) of the Public Order Act, 1986.

. . . The issue is whether the words 'such violence', where they appear in that subsection, mean 'unlawful violence' or 'immediate unlawful violence'. . .

A consequence of construing the words 'such violence' in s 4(1) as meaning 'immediate unlawful violence' will be that leaders of an extremist movement who prepare pamphlets or banners to be distributed or carried in public places by adherents to that movement will not be committing any offence under s 4(1) albeit that they intend the words in the pamphlet or on the banners to be threatening, abusive and insulting, and it is likely that unlawful violence will be provoked by the words in the pamphlet or on the banners.

The context in which s 4(1) appears in the 1986 Act is the first matter which leads us to our conclusion. Section 4 appears in the first part of the Act together with the creation of new offences, namely riot by s 1, violent disorder by s 2, affray by s 3, harassment, alarm or distress by s 5. The provisions of those sections are such that the conduct of the defendants must produce, in an actual or notional person of reasonable firmness, fear in relation to ss 1, 2 and 3 which is contemporaneous with the unlawful violence being used by the defendants, or harassment, alarm or distress which is contemporaneous with the threatening, abusive or insulting conduct under s 5.

We consider it most unlikely that Parliament could have intended to include, among sections which undoubtedly deal with conduct having an immediate impact on bystanders, a section creating an offence for conduct which is likely to lead to violence at some unspecified time in the future.

A. . . very compelling reason for our conclusion on the correct construction of this subsection is that here we are construing a penal statute, of which there are, or may be, two possible readings. It is an elementary rule of statutory construction that, in a penal statute where there are two possible readings, the meaning which limits the scope of the offence thus created is that which the court should adopt.

For these reasons we hold that the magistrate was right to refuse to issue a summons. Finally, we consider it advisable to indicate our provisional view on the meaning of the word 'immediate'. It seems to us that the word 'immediate' does not mean 'instantaneous', that a relatively short time interval may elapse between the act which is threatening, abusive or insulting and the unlawful violence. 'Immediate' connotes proximity in time and proximity in causation, that it is likely that violence will result within a relatively short period of time and without any other intervening occurrence.

Application dismissed.

Percy v Director of Public Prosecutions (2002) 166 JP 93 (extracts)

The appellant was convicted of using threatening, abusive and insulting words or behaviour likely to cause harassment, alarm or distress contrary to s 5 of the Public Order Act 1986. The convictions arose from her behaviour at an American air base at RAF Feltwell. She had experience over many years of protesting against the use of weapons of mass destruction and against American military policy, including the Star Wars National Missile Defence System. She defaced the American flag by putting a stripe across the stars and by writing the words 'Stop Star Wars' across the stripes. She stepped in front of a vehicle and she placed the flag down in front of it and stood upon it. Those affected by her behaviour were mostly American service personnel or their families, five of whom gave evidence of their distress to varying degrees. They regarded her acts as a desecration of their national flag to which they attached considerable importance. The district judge found that the appellant's behaviour with the flag was insulting to American citizens at whom it was directed.

The appellant did, however, satisfy the court that her behaviour was motivated by strongly held beliefs that the 'Star Wars' project was misguided, posed a danger to international stability and was not in the best interests of the United Kingdom. She failed to persuade the court that her conduct on the balance of probabilities was reasonable. Having made his findings of fact. . .the District Judge then turned to the impact of Article 10 of the European Convention on Human Rights on section 5 of the Public Order Act. He highlighted. . .that under Article 10(2) the right is not unqualified. . . The court considered in this case the risk of disorder and criminal offences by others to be slight. His only concern, therefore, was as to the protection of the rights of others. He. . .went on to consider. 'The need to protect the rights of American service personnel and their families occupying the base to be free from gratuitously insulting behaviour. . .'

He concluded: The court finds the restrictions and penalties attached by section 5 to the defendant's article 10 right to freedom of expression to be necessary in a democratic society for the protection of the rights of others and proportionate to the need to protect such rights.' . . .

[The court found on appeal] Where the right to freedom of expression under Article 10 is engaged, as in my view is undoubtedly the case here, it is clear from the European authorities put before us that the justification for any interference with that right must be convincingly established. Article 10(1) protects in substance and in form a right to freedom of expression which others may find insulting. Restrictions under Article 10(2) must be narrowly construed. In this case, therefore, the court had to presume that the appellant's conduct in relation to the American flag was protected by Article 10 unless and until it was established that a restriction on her freedom of expression was strictly necessary.

There may well be a pressing social need to protect people from such behaviour. It is, therefore, in my view, a legitimate aim, provided of course that any restrictions on the rights of peaceful protesters are proportionate to the mischief at which they are aimed. . . A civilised society must strike an appropriate balance between the competing rights of those who may be insulted by a particular course of conduct and those who wish to register their protest on an important matter of public interest. The problem comes in striking that balance, giving due weight to the presumption in the accused's favour of the right to freedom of expression.

. . .The message [Ms Percy] wished to convey, namely 'Stop Star Wars' was a perfectly lawful, political message. It only became insulting because of the manner in which she chose to convey the message. That manner was only insulting because she chose to use a national flag of symbolic importance to some of her target audience. . .

The fact that the appellant could have demonstrated her message in a way which did not involve the use of a national flag of symbolic significance to her target audience was undoubtedly a factor to be taken into account when determining the overall reasonableness and proportionality of her behaviour and the state's response to it. But, in my view, it was only one factor.

Relevant factors in a case such as this, depending on the court's findings, might include the fact that the accused's behaviour went beyond legitimate protest; that the behaviour had not formed part of an open expression of opinion on a matter of public interest, but had become disproportionate and unreasonable; that an accused knew full well the likely effect of their conduct upon witnesses; that the accused deliberately chose to desecrate the national flag of those witnesses . . . that it amounted to a gratuitous and calculated insult, which a number people at whom it was directed found deeply distressing.

In my judgment, at the crucial stage of a balancing exercise under Article 10 the learned District Judge appears to have placed either sole or too much reliance on just the one factor, namely that the appellant's insulting behaviour could have been avoided. This seems to me to give insufficient weight to the presumption in the appellant's favour, to which I have already referred. On the face of it, this approach fails to address adequately the question of proportionality which should have been, and may well have been, uppermost in the District judge's mind. Merely stating that interference is proportionate is not sufficient. It is not clear to me from the District Judge's reasons, given in relation to his findings under Article 10, that he has in fact applied the appropriate test. Accordingly, in my view, it appears that the learned judge inadvertently, in the course of a very careful and thorough examination of the facts and the law, has fallen into error. I am driven to the conclusion, therefore, that this conviction is incompatible with the appellant's rights under the European Convention on Human Rights and I would answer the first question posed in the case stated [Was the appellant's conviction under s 5 of the Public Order Act 1986 compatible with Article 10 of the European Convention on Human Rights and Fundamental Freedoms?] 'No'.

I am satisfied that, in all the circumstances, the appropriate course, therefore, is simply to quash the convictions.

Notes

1. The post-HRA decision of *Hammond*[97] indicates that consideration of proportionality under Article 10 tends to be circumscribed under s 5. In *Hammond* the appellant took a placard with the words 'Stop Immorality' 'Stop Homosexuality' 'Stop Lesbianism' and 'Jesus is Lord' to the centre of Bournemouth and began preaching. This attracted a large group of people who were provoked by the preaching and who physically attacked the appellant. He was requested by two police officers to stop preaching. Upon refusing to comply with this request, the appellant was arrested and subsequently charged and convicted of a s 5 offence. It was found that the interference with the appellant's right to freedom of expression under s 5 was a proportionate response in view of the fact that the appellant's behaviour went beyond legitimate protest, was provoking violence and disorder and interfered with the rights of others. In those circumstances it was found that the appellant's conduct was not reasonable. The conclusion on appeal was that the lower court had embarked upon the necessary exercise and had reached a decision that was open for them to take, namely, that the defendant's conduct was not reasonable in the particular circumstances.[98] It was accepted that Art 10 considerations apply to the evaluation of a reasonableness defence.[99] Thus, although Art 10 was taken into account on appeal, it was again found that the conviction was proportionate to the harm sought to be averted.

2. Section 4A of the 1986 Act, as amended, provides an area of liability which to some extent overlaps with s 5. The *actus reus* under s 4A is the same as that under s 5, with the proviso that the harm in question must actually be caused. The *mens rea* differs somewhat from that under s 5 since the defendant must intend the person in question to suffer harassment, alarm or distress. Section 4A provides another possible level of liability with the result that using offensive words is now imprisonable, without any requirement (as under s 4) to show that violence was intended or likely to be caused. It may also therefore offend against the protection for freedom of speech under Art 10 of the ECHR, which clearly includes protection for forms of forceful or offensive speech; the test for proportionality under Art 10(2) would be less likely to be satisfied in any particular instance if imprisonment had been imposed in respect of speech covered by s 4A.

3. Section 4 of the Act overlaps with s 5 or s 4A in terms of the words or behaviour it covers (aside from disorderly behaviour which is not included in s 4), but it requires certain additional ingredients in terms of the intention of the defendant or in terms of the consequences which may flow from the words or behaviour used. Its applicability in almost all circumstances due to the

---

97   [2004] EWHC 69. For discussion, see D Mead (2009), n 64 above, at pp 226–227.

98   At [33].

99   At [22].

requirement of immediacy only in the public order context was established by *R v Horseferry Road Metropolitan Stipendiary Magistrate ex parte Siadatan*.[100] *Siadatan* is a highly significant decision since it means that ss 5, 4, 4A, in most circumstances that can be envisaged, are inapplicable to the media (using that term to include all media, including the internet).

4. Section 42 of the Criminal Justice and Police Act 2001 clearly draws on the ingredients of ss 5 and 4, although there are also significant differences. There are also similarities with the offences under s 14C of the 1986 Act and s 69 of the 1994 Act (see below). Section 42 allows a constable to give any direction to persons, including a direction to leave the scene where they are outside or in the vicinity of a dwelling, if the constable reasonably believes (a) that they are seeking to persuade a person living at the dwelling not to do something that he or she has a right to do or to do something she or he is not under any obligation to do, and (b) that the presence of the persons (normally protesters) is likely to cause harassment, alarm or distress to the person living at the residence. Disobedience to a direction is an arrestable offence. Section 42 is an offence with a minimal *actus reus,* as is apparent when it is compared with the requirements of s 5 of the 1986 Act or ss 69 and 68 of the 1994 Act. The requirement that the words or conduct should be abusive, etc, in s 5 is missing; the requirements of ss 69 or 68 that the persons in question should be trespassing and must do something intended to be obstructive or intimidatory or disruptive are also absent. But s 42 is similar to s 69 and a number of the other recent offences discussed in this chapter in that it conflates the exercise of police powers with the substantive offence. The key limiting requirement is that the persons must be outside or in the vicinity of a dwelling, although the term 'the vicinity' is open to quite a wide interpretation. The need for the introduction of this offence must be questioned, bearing in mind that s 5 or s 4A could be used against intimidation by protesters gathered outside the home of the person targeted.

5. The offences under ss 5, 4A and 4 of the 1986 Act can be charged as racially or religiously aggravated, as provided by ss 28 and 31 of the Crime and Disorder Act 1998 (as amended by s 39 of the Anti-terrorism, Crime and Security Act 2001), in which case they carry higher maximum penalties. According to ss 28(1)(b) and 31(1)(c) of the 1998 Act, an offence under the sections of the 1986 Act is 'racially or religiously aggravated' if it is 'motivated (wholly or partly) by hostility towards members of a racial or religious group based on their membership of that group'.

6. Consideration of the potential effects of the ECHR via the HRA on ss 5, 4A and 4 has already occurred, and may be contrasted with the limited impact the ECHR is having in practice, for reasons discussed by Geddis, below. Section 5 is the most problematic provision, as indicated. The similar offence under s 42 of the 2001 Act is also problematic in the sense that it hits directly at peaceful protest—protest that need not be abusive, etc, but is aimed only at persuading. The protesters need have no intention of causing harassment, alarm or distress so long as a constable reasonably believes that the target of the protest might experience those feelings. In catching peaceful protest, this offence comes directly into conflict with Arts 10 and 11, although incompatibility would not arise if the para 2 tests were satisfied in any particular instance. Section 41 can also be viewed as protecting Art 8 rights, but a court would be expected to consider the extent to which those rights could be said to be at stake and the proportionality of the police response, in using s 41 as opposed to a lesser measure. The use of ss 5, 4A and 4 in the context of public protest should be restrained in order to answer to the strict requirements of proportionality under Arts 10(2) and 11(2). *Percy v DPP,* above, illustrates an approach which appears to afford weight to Art

---

10(1) values in the context of protest and gives some weight to such requirements, taking account of 'the presumption in the accused's favour of the right to freedom of expression'. But it is notable that in reaching its conclusion, the court relied upon s 6 of the HRA rather than s 3. In suitable instances s 3 must be used instead; as pointed out in the decision of the House of Lords in *S (Children) and Re W (Care Orders)* [2002] 2 AC 291; [2002] UKHL 10 (see Chapter 17, p 963) its use is obligatory.

A Geddis, 'Free speech martyrs or unreasonable threats to social peace?— "Insulting" expression and section 5 of the Public Order Act 1986' [2004] *Public Law* 853

The courts—at the lower levels, anyway—still appear to be 'exhibit[ing] a preference for public peacefulness and the avoidance of incitement over freedom of expression' when considering whether the expression of some individual dissenter constitutes a breach of s 5 of the Act. Therefore, while the HRA now requires that the Art 10 process of balancing between competing values be carried out in relation to s 5, a thumb still seems to sit upon the side of finding reasons to restrict expression which is deemed to be both recklessly insulting and likely to cause mental upset in those observing it. . . . A first explanation for the courts' ongoing preparedness to convict individual dissenters under s 5 lies in the very structure of the offence, and the subsequent process of appealing any conviction. Section 5 requires that the trial court first determine whether some particular expressive conduct is intentionally or recklessly insulting, and likely to harass, annoy or distress anyone witnessing it. Only after a prima facie breach is established does the court turn to ask if the defendant's right to freedom of expression nevertheless should mean that the conduct at issue be considered 'reasonable' in nature. Thus, the trial court has to find reasons to allow the defendant to express herself in a deliberately or recklessly insulting fashion, rather than look for reasons why she should *not* be allowed to do so. This approach, of course, is the exact opposite to that required by Art 10 ECHR. Article 10 confers an individual right to express oneself, a right that exists until the state can demonstrate it is necessary to restrict the expression at issue in order to achieve some pressing social end. Inverting this approach under s 5—the court begins by considering how 'bad' the defendant's speech has been, before turning to consider if there are 'good' reasons to allow it—makes it much easier for the judges at trial to accept that a conviction under that provision forms a necessary limit on the defendant's freedom of expression as per Art 10(2).

Similarly, when the matter subsequently gets appealed, the Divisional Court is presented with a finding that the appellant has intentionally or recklessly acted in an insulting fashion likely to cause significant mental upset to those observing the conduct. Further, the trial court will have decided that the defendant's conduct cannot be considered reasonable, even taking into consideration his or her right to freedom of expression under Art 10(1). And because these determinations are considered factual in nature, the appeal court can only ask whether the lower tribunal has addressed all the proper matters when reaching them, and whether the particular findings are unreasonable in a *Wednesbury* sense. What is more, the issues that must be considered are judgment calls upon which a range of quite rationally defensible conclusions can be drawn by different, well-meaning observers. Therefore, it becomes very difficult to show that the trial court's determination that an individual defendant's insulting conduct was not reasonable as per s 5(3)(c) is itself 'unreasonable', always assuming that the trial court has appeared to follow the correct Art 10 methodology when approaching the question. The defendant's fate thus effectively becomes contingent on the ad hoc determination of the trial court whether the defendant's conduct would offend or insult, as opposed to just annoy or vex, those viewing it; and whether this would be likely to cause significant mental upset in such observers.

Such continuing deference to the magistrates' ruling at trial is inappropriate in a post-HRA era. Section 6 of that legislation instructs the courts *at each level* to act in a manner compatible with the rights in the Convention. Therefore, when considering the issues put to it by way of case stated, the Divisional Court is obliged to ensure that the answer given to each question does not breach the Convention rights of the accused (unless, of course, the plain wording of some legislative provision mandates otherwise). This obligation in turn requires that the Divisional Court ensure that the lower court has applied the *correct* interpretation (as per s 3 HRA) to the 'reasonable' defence in s 5(3)(c), not merely reached a *reasonable* decision on this matter. Simply put, following the coming into force of the HRA, the Divisional Court should now conduct its own analysis of the Convention-compatibility of convicting the accused for his or her insulting conduct; rather than, in effect, subcontracting this analysis to the trial court and intervening only where that body has failed to consider all the relevant issues, or has strayed so far as to have acted 'unreasonably'. Furthermore, subsequent levels of the appellate courts are obliged to formulate principles by which the 'reasonableness' of a dissenter's insulting conduct can be assessed, rather than just leaving this as a 'factual' matter to be determined on a case-by-case basis at trial.

However, while the very structuring of the tasks required of the court when considering whether s 5 has been breached weighs against the individual dissenter, the courts—at trial, and then when assessing this decision upon appeal—are still required to consider whether or not the defendant's Art 10(1) right to freedom of expression means that his or her insulting conduct nevertheless should be considered 'reasonable'. And as has been seen, the courts have (by and large) held that Art 10 does not have this consequence. The primary reason given is that the criminal penalty contained in s 5 constitutes a necessary—in terms of meeting a pressing social need in a proportionate fashion—limitation on the defendant's freedom of expression as per Art 10(2), because protecting an onlooker's right to be free from the mental upset occasioned by the defendant's recklessly insulting conduct outweighs the defendant's right to express herself in the fashion she would otherwise choose. Why this should be so is not really explained in the Divisional Courts' decisions; it is implied in the case outcomes rather than argued out in any meaningful fashion. Therefore, a degree of speculation as to what might lie behind the courts' reasoning process is required. In that light, I would suggest that the lower courts can be seen to be of much the same mind as Lord Hoffmann in *R. (On the application of ProLife Alliance) v BBC*. In this case, Lord Hoffmann accepted that Parliament was entitled to lay down limits – namely, a prohibition on broadcasting material 'which offends against good taste or decency or is likely . . . to be offensive to public feeling'—as to what will constitute generally acceptable forms of political discourse. . . ..the courts have undertaken a similar pragmatic balancing exercise with respect to the costs and benefits of 'insulting' expression when confronted with an individual dissenter charged under s 5 of the Act.

. . . the risk to settled social peace—whether inside the viewer's mind, or in the form of external unrest—resulting from the emotive nature of people's reactions to such insulting conduct outweighs the minimal contribution it makes to public dialogue about matters of communal interest. And in the absence of any real wider, practical social benefit resulting from the expression at issue, it is not 'reasonable' for the individual dissenter to exercise his or her autonomy by giving expression to his or her own personal beliefs in a fashion which recklessly or intentionally visits a significant mental hurt—in the form of 'harassment, alarm or distress'—to those fellow members of the community observing the conduct.

This approach can be designated as being 'pro-civility' in its aspirations. According to it, the state legitimately can require that anyone wishing to espouse or discuss matters of general public or political interest respect the sensibilities of others, and act in a fashion which preserves a measure of decorum in society as a whole. . . .

Whether this pro-civility approach is entirely satisfactory or desirable is, of course, another matter. It rests upon the claim that the mental upset suffered by observers of insulting expression about a matter of public importance ought to be considered a 'harm' which the state then has a legitimate interest in preventing. This assertion obviously is deeply contentious—Mill rejects it as follows: 'there is no parity between the feeling of a person for his own opinion and the feeling of another who is offended at his holding it . . .'.

Note

Controversy was aroused in September 2009 when the owners of a private guest house were prosecuted under s 5 after they had become embroiled in a row with two Muslim guests. The Christian owners were alleged to have said that Mohammed was a warlord, and the hijab a form of female bondage. They were acquitted on the facts by Liverpool magistrates.[101] The case indicates the enormous potential breadth of s 5.

Breach of the peace[102]

The common law power to prevent a breach of the peace[103] overlaps with a number of the powers arising under the 1986 Act and is more useful to the police than those powers as its definition is so broad and uncertain. This means that it can be used in such a way as to undermine attempts in statutory provisions to carve out more clearly defined areas of liability. Power to prevent a breach of the peace may be used to disperse or prevent a peaceful protest or meeting which may provoke others to violence or disorder. *Beatty v Gillbanks*[104] established the important principle that organisers of assemblies could not be held responsible for the actions of those opposed to them whose actions in expressing their opposition created a breach of the peace. However, in *Duncan v Jones*[105] it was found that speakers could be held responsible when persons in agreement with them might be induced to breach the peace. *Duncan* is indicative of the dismissive approach to public protest that was often taken pre-HRA.

---

101 *R v Vogelenzang* (2009) unreported. See 'Christian hoteliers charged with insulting Muslim guest', *Telegraph*, 19 September 2009.

102 For further explanation of what may amount to a breach of the peace see Chapter 20, p 1170. For comment on the doctrine generally, pre-HRA, see 'Breaching the Peace and Disturbing the Quiet' [1982] PL 212; DGT Williams, *Keeping the Peace: The Police and Public Order* (1967). For post-HRA discussion, see D Mead (2009), n 64 above, Chapter 7, at III.

103 It should be noted that breach of the peace, although arrestable, is not a criminal offence.

104 (1882) 9 QBD 308.

105 [1936] 1 KB 218.

Duncan v Jones [1936] 1 KB 218, 221–23[106]

Lord Hewart CJ: There have been moments during the argument in this case when it appeared to be suggested that the Court had to do with a grave case involving what is called the right of public meeting. I say 'called', because English law does not recognise any special right of public meeting for political or other purposes. The right of assembly, as Professor Dicey puts it [Dicey's *Law of the Constitution*, 8th edn, p 499], is nothing more than a view taken by the court of the individual liberty of the subject. If I thought that the present case raised a question which has been held in suspense by more than one writer on constitutional law—namely, whether an assembly can properly be held to be unlawful merely because the holding of it is expected to give rise to a breach of the peace on the part of persons opposed to those who are holding the meeting—I should wish to hear much more argument before I expressed an opinion. This case, however, does not even touch that important question.

The present case reminds one rather of the observations of Bramwell B in Prebble [1 F & F 325, 326], where, in holding that a constable, in clearing certain licensed premises of the persons thereon, was not acting in the execution of his duty, he said: 'It would have been otherwise had there been a nuisance or disturbance of the public peace, or any danger of a breach of the peace.' The case stated which we have before us indicates clearly a causal connection between the meeting of May 1933 and the disturbance which occurred after it—that the disturbance was not only post the meeting but was also prior to the meeting. In my view, the deputy-chairman was entitled to come to the conclusion to which he came on the facts which he found, and to hold that the conviction of the appellant for wilfully obstructing the respondent when in the execution of his duty was right. This appeal should, therefore, be dismissed.

Redmond-Bate v DPP (1999) 163 JP 789 (extracts)

The Human Rights Act 1998 was not in force at the time of this decision, although it was about to come into force and appeared to influence the findings. The appellant was one of three women Christian fundamentalists who had agreed with the police to preach from the steps of a cathedral. A crowd of more than one hundred gathered. Some members of that crowd were showing hostility. Fearing a breach of the peace, the police officer asked the women to stop preaching, and when they refused to do so, he arrested them all for wilfully obstructing him in the execution of his duty under s 89(2) of the Police Act 1996. The appellant was convicted and appealed. The issue which arose on appeal was whether it was reasonable for the police officer, in the light of what he perceived, to believe that the appellant was about to cause a breach of the peace.

Sedley LJ: Among the duties of a constable was the prevention of breaches of the peace. A member of the public who failed to comply with a reasonable request properly made to this end was guilty of obstructing the constable in the execution of his duty. The test of the reasonableness of a police officer's action was objective in the sense that it was for the court to decide not whether the view taken by the officer fell within the broad band of rational decisions, but whether, in the light of what the officer knew and perceived at the time, the court was satisfied that it was reasonable to fear an imminent breach of the peace. . . A judgment as to the imminence of a breach of the peace did not conclude the

---

police officer's task. The next critical question for the officer, and in turn for the court, was where the threat was coming from, because it was to there that the preventive action had to be directed; the common law should seek compatibility with the values of the European Convention on Human Rights in so far it did not already share them; . . . . regard had to be had also to the fact that free speech included not only the inoffensive, but the irritating, the contentious, the eccentric, the heretical, the unwelcome and the provocative provided it did not tend to provoke violence. Freedom only to speak inoffensively was not worth having. The world had seen too many examples of State control of unofficial ideas, a central purpose of the Convention had been to set close limits to any such assumed power; police officers in a situation like that in the present case had difficult on the spot judgments to make. As they were judgments which impinged directly on important civil liberties and human rights, the courts had in their turn to scrutinise them with care. There was, however, nothing particularly obscure in the law as it now stood and as the Human Rights Act would shortly reinforce it. The question for the police officer was whether there was a real threat of violence and if so, from whom it was coming. If there was no real threat, no question of breach of the peace arose. If the appellant and her companions were being so provocative that someone in the crowd, without behaving wholly unreasonably, might be moved to violence, he was entitled to ask them to stop and to arrest them if they would not. If the threat of disorder or violence was coming from passers-by who were taking the opportunity to react so as to cause trouble, then it was they and not the preachers who would be asked to desist and arrested if they would not; the court had to be alert to the fact that ours was a society of many faiths and none, and many opinions. If the public promotion of faith or opinion was conducted in such a way as to insult or provoke others in breach of statute or common law, then the fact that it was done in the name of religious manifestations or freedom of speech would not necessarily save it. It might forfeit the protection of Articles 9 and 10 by reason of the limitations permitted in both Articles, provided they were necessary and proportionate, in the interests of public order and the protection of the rights of others; the situation perceived and recounted by the police officer in the present case had not justified him in apprehending a breach of the peace, much less a breach of the peace for which the appellant would be responsible, accordingly he had not been acting in the execution of his duty when he required the women to stop preaching, and the appellant was therefore not guilty of obstructing him in the execution of his duty when she refused to comply . . . Free speech includes not only the inoffensive but the irritating, the contentious, the eccentric, the heretical, the unwelcome and the provocative provided it does not tend to provoke violence. Freedom to speak only inoffensively was not worth having.

The appeal was allowed.

Notes

1. The leading pre-HRA case on breach of the peace is *R v Howell*[107] in which it was determined that a breach of the peace will arise if an act is done or threatened to be done which either harms a person or, in his presence, his property, or is likely to cause such harm, or which puts a person in fear of such harm. Threatening words are not in themselves a breach of the peace but they may lead a police officer to apprehend a breach. In a later case, *R v Chief Constable for Devon and Cornwall ex parte CEGB*,[108] Lord Denning, dissenting, offered a rather different definition of the offence. His

---

107 [1981] 3 All ER 383.

108 [1982] QB 458.

view was that violence is unnecessary; he considered that 'if anyone unlawfully and physically obstructs a worker—by lying down or chaining himself to a rig or the like—he is guilty of a breach of the peace'.

2. *The issue of provoking a breach.* Despite Lord Hewart's comments, above, in *Duncan v Jones*, it is arguable that *Beatty v Gillbanks*[109] applies to instances in which a peaceful assembly triggers off a violent response, even where such a response was foreseen by members of the peaceful assembly. If the decision in *Beatty v Gillbanks* is interpreted in this way, the decision in *Duncan v Jones* is not in accord with it, in that the freedom of the speaker was infringed, not because of her conduct but because of police fears about the possible response of the audience. Similarly, in *Jordan v Burgoyne*[110] it was found that a public speaker could be guilty of breach of the peace if he spoke words which were likely to cause disorder amongst the particular audience present, even where the audience had come with the express intent of causing trouble. *Jordan*, however, is out of line with *Redmond-Bate*.

3. The decision in *Nicol v DPP*,[111] which concerned the behaviour of fishing protesters, has not brought much clarity into this area as regards provocation. The protesters' behaviour in blowing horns and in attempting to dissuade the anglers from fishing provoked the anglers so that they were on the verge of using force to remove the protesters. It was found that the protesters were guilty of conduct whereby a breach of the peace was likely to be caused since their conduct, although lawful, was unreasonable and was likely to provoke the anglers to violence. This finding places a curb on the use of breach of the peace in this context since it means that behaviour which has as its natural consequence the provoking of others to violence will not amount to a breach of the peace unless it is also unreasonable. However, the decision also affirms that this area of law is subject to a wide and uncertain test of reasonableness. The judiciary may be disinclined to find that the behaviour of groups such as hunt saboteurs or tree protesters, while lawful, is reasonable.

4. *Breach of the peace and the HRA.* The HRA has had some impact on the doctrine of breach of the peace as applied in this context due to the decision of the House of Lords in *Laporte*, below. The application of the doctrine to curb public protest may be compatible with the demands of Arts 10 and 11, but compatibility in any particular instance depends on whether the specific power used is 'prescribed by law', and on the proportionality of the interference. In *Steel and Others v UK*,[112] the European Court of Human Rights found that the breach of the peace doctrine provided sufficient guidance and was formulated with sufficient precision to satisfy the requirement of Art 5(1)(c) that arrest and detention should be in accordance with a procedure prescribed by law, and that the 'prescribed by law' requirement of Art 10 was also satisfied. In *McLeod v UK*,[113] the Court found that the breach of the peace doctrine was 'in accordance with the law' under Art 8. Thus, in respect of the key elements of 'prescribed by law'—legal basis, certainty and accessibility—the breach of the peace doctrine appears to meet Strasbourg standards (but see *Laporte*, below).

5. Reappraisal and reform of the doctrine of breach of the peace is perhaps most likely to occur by reference to the notion of what is 'necessary in a democratic society' within Arts 10 and 11, para 2, although no significant modification has yet occurred. This issue was extensively considered by the Court in *Steel*, but the findings were quite strongly influenced by the doctrine of the margin of

---

109   (1882) 15 Cox CC 138.

110   [1963] 2 QB 744. It should be noted that the case was concerned with breach of the peace under the Public Order Act 1936, s 5.

111   (1996) 1 *Journal of Civil Liberties* 75.

112   (1999) 28 EHRR 603.

113   (1998) 27 EHRR 493.

appreciation.[114] The first applicant had taken part in a protest against a grouse shoot and had stood in the way of participants to prevent them taking shots. Since this behaviour was likely to be provocative, the Court found that her arrest and detention, although constituting serious interferences with her freedom of expression, could be viewed as proportionate to the aim of preventing disorder and of maintaining the authority of the judiciary[115] and this could also be said of her subsequent detention in the police station for 44 hours,[116] bearing in mind the findings of the police or magistrates that disorder might have occurred. The Court made little attempt to evaluate the real risk of disorder, taking into account the margin of appreciation afforded to the domestic authorities in determining what is necessary to avoid disorder in the particular domestic situation (para 101).

The second applicant had taken part in a protest against the building of a motorway, placing herself in front of the earth-moving machinery in order to impede it. The Court found unanimously that her arrest also could be viewed as proportionate to the aim of preventing disorder, even though it accepted that the risk of immediate disorder was not so high as in the case of the first applicant (para 109). The Court accepted the finding of the magistrates' court that there had been such a risk. The third, fourth and fifth applicants were peacefully holding banners and handing out leaflets outside a fighter helicopter conference when they were arrested for breach of the peace. The Court found that there was no justification for their arrests at all since there was no suggestion of any threat of disorder (para 110). A violation of Art 10 was therefore found in respect of those applicants.

6. These findings suggest that interferences with protest as direct action may frequently fall within the national authorities' margin of appreciation. But, significantly, the findings also make it clear that such protest constitutes expressions of opinion and therefore falls within Arts 10 and 11. This was re-affirmed in *Hashman and Harrup v UK*.[117] Thus, the findings of the Court in *Steel* required a re-structuring of the domestic scrutiny of interference with such expression, which takes the primary right as the starting point. *Steel* clearly afforded the domestic judiciary a wide discretion in interpreting the requirements of the Convention in an analogous case. Following an activist approach, the domestic judiciary, faced with similar facts, but disapplying the margin of appreciation aspects of *Steel*, could find that the interference was unjustified since their review of the decisions of the police or of magistrates would be less restrained. Within this model, some interferences with freedom of expression would be allowed, where direct action was likely to provoke immediate disorder due to the degree of provocation offered, but the measures taken in response, such as the length of detention, would be much more strictly scrutinised for their proportionality with the aims pursued.

7. Until *Laporte* under the HRA it was not possible to discern a clear change in the approach taken to the use of the breach of the peace doctrine as a means of curbing public protest. *Austin and Saxby*, below, does not provide an example, it is argued, of a change of approach. Under an activist approach, greater protection could be afforded to peaceful protest, including insulting or offensive persuasion or symbolic direct action, following *Steel*, and this approach would also receive some endorsement from *Plattform 'Ärtze für das Leben' v Austria*[118] which adopted a version of the *Beatty v Gillbanks* approach.

---

114   This was acknowledged by the Court, *Steel and Others v UK* (1999) 28 EHRR 603, para 101.

115   *Ibid*, paras 104 and 107.

116   *Ibid*, para 105. The Commission acknowledged (para 156) 'some disquiet as to the proportionality of a detention of this length' which continued long after the grouse shoot was over.

117   (2000) 30 EHRR 241.

118   (1988) 13 EHRR 204.

8. *Article 10 and provoking a breach.* An activist approach to the decision in *Steel* was, in some respects, taken by Sedley LJ in *Redmond-Bate v DPP,* above, in the period before the HRA was fully in force. Applying *Steel,* the Divisional Court found that there were no sufficient grounds on which to determine that a breach of the peace was about to be caused or, moreover, on which to determine that the threat was coming from Ms Redmond-Bate, bearing in mind the tolerance one would expect to be extended to offensive speech. This decision simplified the tests from *Nicol* of determining which party was acting reasonably where one was provoked to violence, and as to which was exercising rights. The key question—*Redmond-Bate* found—was to determine where the threat was coming from in order to determine who was causing the breach.

R (on the application of Laporte) (FC) v Chief Constable of Gloucestershire [2006] UKHL 55[119] (extracts)

The claimant, a peace protester, wanted to protest against the policy and conduct of the United Kingdom and United States Governments in relation to the Iraq war, and wished to join a protest at RAF Fairford in order to do so. Laporte was in a coach with around 120 other would-be protesters travelling to the anti-war protest. The coach was stopped and searched by police near to the air-base they were bound for, and a few items found that could possibly have been used in a non-peaceful protest, such as masks. There was evidence that some protesters belonging to groups associated with violence were travelling with the other protesters.[120] The police decided that once the protesters had arrived at the air-base, a breach of the peace would then become 'imminent' and the protesters could then have been arrested. To avoid this, they decided to turn the coaches round and send them back to London, and as the protesters were not allowed to leave the coaches they were in effect detained on them for several additional hours on the way back.

The Chief Constable decided not to invoke the power and duty under section 13 of the Public Order Act 1986 to seek an order prohibiting all processions in the Fairford area for a period of time. He issued a direction under section 12 of the Act, prescribing (in accordance with the notification) the time, place of assembly and procession route.

A statutory stop and search authorisation under section 60 of the Criminal Justice and Public Order Act 1994 was issued.[121] It applied to an area around Fairford, and was extended on the following day. An authority under section 60AA of the 1994 Act, giving power to require the removal of disguises, was also issued.

The officer took the view that had the coaches been permitted to continue to RAF Fairford the protesters on the coaches would have been arrested upon arrival. . ., since a breach of the peace would then have been 'imminent'. The coaches were driven to the motorway, where police motorcycle outriders prevented them from stopping on the hard shoulder or turning off to motorway services, even to allow passengers to relieve themselves.

The claimant issued an application for judicial review, seeking to challenge the actions of the Chief Constable in (1) preventing her travelling to the demonstration in Fairford, and forcing her to leave the area, and (2) forcibly returning her to London, keeping her on the

---

119   CA: *R (On the application of Laporte) v CC of Gloucester Constab* [2004] EWCA Civ 1639.

120   Activists known as 'the Wombles'.

121   See Chapter 20, pp 1148–1149, 1157.

coach and preventing her from leaving it until she had reached London. At first instance her first complaint was rejected but her second was upheld.[122] In upholding the claimant's second claim, May LJ concluded that the claimant had been detained on the coach back to London and that such detention could not be held to be covered by article 5(1)(b) or 5(1)(c) of the Convention. The Court of Appeal (Lord Woolf CJ, Clarke and Rix LJJ) upheld the Divisional Court's decision, dismissing an appeal by the Chief Constable and a cross-appeal by the claimant.[123]

Lord Bingham:

[Relying on *Sunday Times v United Kingdom (No 2)*[124] and *Hashman and Harrup v United Kingdom,*[125] Lord Bingham found] any prior restraint on freedom of expression calls for the most careful scrutiny. . . . [He noted that the protection of the Articles may be denied] 'if the demonstration is unauthorised and unlawful (as in the case of *Ziliberberg*),[126] or if conduct is such as actually to disturb public order (as in *Chorherr v Austria*)'.[127] [He noted this finding in *Ziliberberg*]:

> an individual does not cease to enjoy the right to peaceful assembly as a result of sporadic violence or other punishable acts committed by others in the course of the demonstration, if the individual in question remains peaceful in his or her own intentions or behaviour.[128]

[The key argument on behalf of Laporte was that subject to Arts 10(2) and 11(2) of the European Convention, the claimant had a right to attend the lawful assembly at RAF Fairford in order to express her strong opposition to the war against Iraq. The conduct of the police, in stopping the coach on which the claimant was travelling at Lechdale, and not allowing it to continue its intended journey to Fairford, was an interference by a public authority (s 6 HRA) with the claimant's exercise of her rights under Arts 10 and 11. The burden of justifying an interference with the exercise of a Convention right such as those protected by Arts 10 and 11 was on the public authority which has interfered with such exercise, in this case the Chief Constable. It was argued that there is nothing in domestic authority to support the proposition that action short of arrest may be taken when a breach of the peace is not so imminent as would be necessary to justify an arrest. Here, the officer in charge did not think that a breach of the peace was so imminent as to justify an arrest. Counsel for the police relied on *Moss v McLachlan,*[129] in support of an argument that it is not necessary to show that the breach of the peace was so imminent as to justify an arrest. Lord Bingham found]:

---

122 The case came before the Queen's Bench Divisional Court (May LJ and Harrison J) [2004] EWHC 253 (Admin); [2004] 2 All ER 874.

123 [2004] EWCA Civ 1639; [2005] QB 678.

124 (1991) 14 EHRR 229, at para 51.

125 (1999) 30 EHRR 241, at para 32.

126 App No 61821/00, 4 May 2004, unreported.

127 (1993) 17 EHRR 358.

128 At para 2.

129 [1985] IRLR 76.

'Parliament conferred carefully defined powers and imposed carefully defined duties on chief officers of police and the senior police officer. Offences were created and defences provided. Parliament plainly appreciated the need for appropriate police powers to control disorderly demonstrations but was also sensitive to the democratic values inherent in recognition of a right to demonstrate. It would, I think, be surprising if, alongside these closely defined powers and duties, there existed a common law power and duty, exercisable and imposed not only by and on any constable but by and on every member of the public, bounded only by an uncertain and undefined condition of reasonableness.'[130] [He further found little support in the authorities for the proposition that action short of arrest may be taken to prevent a breach of the peace which is not sufficiently imminent to justify arrest. Since the police officer in charge did not consider that the claimant could properly be arrested when the coaches were stopped before reaching Fairford, it followed that action short of arrest could not be taken as an alternative. He also did not accept the finding of the Court of Appeal that the present case is 'very much on all fours with the decision in *Moss v McLachlan*'.[131] He found that *Moss* carried the notion of imminence to extreme limits, but that it was not unreasonable to view the apprehended breach as imminent. But he considered that the situation in *Moss* differed greatly from that in the instant case in which 120 passengers, by no means all of whom were or were thought to be Wombles members, had been prevented from proceeding to an assembly point which was some distance away from the scene of a lawful demonstration. So he concluded that the actions of the police in turning away the passengers on the coach and then detaining them on the coach were not prescribed by law.

Counsel for the claimant also contended that the police action at Lechlade failed the Convention test of proportionality because it was premature and indiscriminate. It was argued that the action was premature because there was no hint of disorder at Lechlade and no reason to apprehend an immediate outburst of disorder by the claimant and her fellow passengers when they left their coaches at the designated drop-off points in Fairford. Since the action was premature it was necessarily indiscriminate because the police could not at that stage identify those (if any) of the passengers who appeared to be about to commit a breach of the peace]. Lord Bingham found:

55. ... I cannot accept the Chief Constable's argument. It was entirely reasonable to suppose that some of those on board the coaches might wish to cause damage and injury to the base at RAF Fairford, and to enter the base with a view to causing further damage and injury. It was not reasonable to suppose that even these passengers simply wanted a violent confrontation with the police, which they could have had in the lay-by. Nor was it reasonable to anticipate an outburst of disorder on arrival of these passengers in the assembly area or during the procession to the base, during which time the police would be in close attendance and well able to identify and arrest those who showed a violent propensity or breached the conditions to which the assembly and procession were subject. It was wholly disproportionate to restrict her exercise of her rights under articles 10 and 11 because she was in the company of others some of whom might, at some time in the future, breach the peace.

56. I would accordingly allow the claimant's appeal, set aside the orders of the Court of Appeal and the Divisional Court dismissing the claimant's first complaint, and grant the

---

130   *Ibid* at para 46.

131   At para 45 of the judgment.

claimant a declaration that the Chief Constable's actions which are the subject of her first complaint were unlawful because they were not prescribed by law and were disproportionate.

Notes

1. *The extent of powers under the breach of the peace doctrine.* In *Laporte* the House of Lords accepted that there is nothing in domestic authority to support the proposition that action short of arrest may be taken when a breach of the peace is not so imminent as would be necessary to justify an arrest. Lord Bingham took this view partly on the basis that otherwise the common law doctrine would undermine the 1986 Act. In *Laporte*[132] the Divisional Court and the Court of Appeal both adopted the approach in *Moss*, which allowed for preventive action short of arrest in relation to apprehended breaches of the peace that were not imminent. The House of Lords has now rejected that possibility as representing an illegitimate broadening of the breach of the peace doctrine. In requiring a clear element of immediacy, this decision has created a strong inhibitory rule, not as to the powers that can be invoked under this doctrine, but as to the point at which it can be invoked.

2. The judgment of the House of Lords in *Laporte* took ss 2 and 6 HRA seriously. The Strasbourg jurisprudence was quite closely analysed and the facts in question were subjected to close scrutiny under the doctrine of proportionality. The very real possibility that the common law could undermine a carefully crafted statutory scheme was recognised and, at least to an extent, avoided. Interestingly, the actions of the police were found not only to be disproportionate to the aim pursued, they were also found not to be prescribed by law. The starting point was the significance of upholding rights to protest. *Laporte* has offered a check to further development of the doctrine of breach of the peace and has recognised the 'constitutional shift' that the HRA has brought about in this context. Had the judgment gone the other way, it would have left intact a position whereby the police had carte blanche to order peaceful protesters away from the scene of a protest, stop cars proceeding to it, and detain persons, without arresting them, whenever a few of the protesters appeared likely to cause disorder or were causing it. That would have continued to render much of the Public Order Act 1986, as amended, effectively redundant, since it would have continued to be unnecessary in most circumstances, to rely on ss 12 and 14. It would also have undermined the arrest power under s 24 PACE,[133] and the safeguards for arrest contained in PACE and in Code of Practice G, since in public order situations police could have continued to decide merely to use common law powers to detain short of arrest.

3. The impact of *Laporte* must not be over-stated. It curbed the use of common law powers *only* where a breach of the peace could not be said to be imminent. A range of interventions, including arrest or short of arrest, is still available to the police so long as it can be said that a breach of the peace is imminent. Thus the statutory scheme is still highly likely to be marginalised. If a large group of protesters appears to the police to contain some unruly or aggressive, or potentially aggressive, elements, the police appear, post-*Laporte*, to retain very broad powers to intervene.

Austin, Saxby v The Commissioner of Police of the Metropolis [2009] 2 WLR 372 (extracts)

The decision concerned a political demonstration against capitalism and globalization that was organised in the heart of the West End of London on May Day 2001. About

---

132 [2004] EWCA Civ 1639; [2005] QB 678.

133 See Chapter 20, pp 1170–1173.

3,000 people gathered in Oxford Circus and thousands more in the surrounding streets, apparently taking the police by surprise. Some groups in the demonstration were disorderly, and some were violent. Austin, however, participated peacefully in the demonstration and made political speeches using a megaphone.

In response to the disorder and potential public safety problems the police detained thousands of demonstrators for about seven hours in Oxford Circus by forming a cordon around them—the so-called 'kettling' tactic. The cordon was absolute, in that persons were completely trapped in the area for the whole seven hour period in cold and uncomfortable conditions and without recourse to any food or water or facilities such as toilets. The police tactics in 2001 were more interventionist than previously; they changed after very serious breakdowns in public order in London in relation to protests in 1999 and 2000. The police view was that this action was necessary in order to prevent a threatened imminent breach of the peace, and that they had planned a controlled release of the crowd, but that this was hindered by some outbreaks of disorder or violence, either from the trapped group or from persons outside the cordon. The claimant, Austin, asked to be released but was refused on the ground that some protesters were threatening a breach of the peace. She had not created a threat; nor had she provoked others, remaining peaceable throughout. The other claimant, Saxby, was a passer-by, caught up in the protest by accident when the police formed the cordon. (Saxby dropped out of the case before it reached the House of Lords.) The claimants brought a claim for damages, alleging false imprisonment and also deprivation of liberty, contrary to Article 5 of the European Convention, on behalf of some 150 others in what was effectively a test case.

In the House of Lords it was accepted on both sides that, if the appellant's (Austin's) detention was an unlawful deprivation of liberty contrary to Article 5(1) of the Convention, the finding that this was a lawful exercise of breach of the peace powers at common law could not stand—and the converse position also applied. But this stance meant that, apart from Article 5(1), the extensive use of those powers was not in issue. The whole argument centred on whether there was a deprivation of liberty at all in the trapping of the demonstrators in the cordon for seven hours, not on the extent of the powers or on the application of an exception to Article 5; the argument thus concentrated exclusively on the ambit of Article 5(1).

It was accepted by Lord Hope, giving the leading judgment with which all the other Law Lords agreed, that there was no direct guidance from the jurisprudence as to whether Article 5(1) is engaged at all in such circumstances. In a controversial finding, he considered that in making a determination as to the ambit of Article 5(1), the *purpose* of the interference with liberty could be viewed as relevant; if so, he found that it must be to enable a balance to be struck between what the restriction sought to achieve and the interests of the individual.[134]

Lord Hope: 26. The decision whether there was deprivation of liberty is, of course, highly sensitive to the facts of each case. Little value can be derived therefore from decisions on the application of article 5 that depend entirely on their own facts. But they are of value where they can be said to illustrate issues of principle. In the present context some assistance is to be derived from the cases as to the extent to which regard can be had to the aim or purpose of the measure in question when consideration is being given as to whether it is within the ambit of article 5(1) at all.

27. If purpose is relevant, it must be to enable a balance to be struck between what the restriction seeks to achieve and the interests of the individual. The proposition that there is a balance to be struck at the initial stage when the scope of the article is being considered was not mentioned in *Engel v The Netherlands (No 1)* (1976) 1 EHRR 647 or *Guzzardi v Italy* (1980) 3 EHRR 333. Nor can it be said to be based on anything that is to be found in the wording of the article. But I think that there are sufficient indications elsewhere in the court's case law that the question of balance is inherent in the concepts that are enshrined in the Convention and that they have a part to play when consideration is being given to the scope of the first rank of fundamental rights that protect the physical security of the individual.

28. In *X v Federal Republic of Germany* (1981) 24 DR 158, where the Commission had regard to the fact that the purpose for which the children were taken to the police head-quarters and kept there for about two hours was to question them, not to arrest or detain them. This led to the conclusion that the action in question did not constitute a deprivation of liberty in the sense of article 5(1).

29. In *Nielsen v Denmark* (1988) 11 EHRR 175 the applicant, who was a minor, com-plained about his committal to a child psychiatric ward of a state hospital at his mother's request. The question was whether this was a deprivation of his liberty in violation of article 5. The applicant said that it was, as the ward in which he was placed was a closed ward, he was unable to receive visitors except with the agreement of the staff, special permission was required for him to make telephone calls and for persons outside the hospital to get into contact with him and he was under almost constant surveillance: para 65. On those facts his situation was close to the paradigm case described in *Secretary of State for the Home Department v JJ and others* [2008] 1 AC 385, para 37, by Lord Hoffmann. But the court said in para 72 that it did not follow that the case fell within the ambit of article 5. The restrictions that were imposed on the applicant were not of a nature or degree similar to the cases of deprivation of liberty specified in article 5(1). He was not detained as a person of unsound mind so as to bring the case within paragraph (e). He was there at the request of his mother, as to whom there was no evidence of bad faith. The court summed the matter up in this way in para 72:

> Hospitalisation was decided upon by her in accordance with expert medical advice. It must be possible for a child like the applicant to be admitted to hospital at the request of the holder of parental rights, a case which is clearly not covered by paragraph (1) of article 5.

30. In *Soering v United Kingdom* (1989) 11 EHRR 439 one of the applicant's complaints was that the decision to extradite him to the United States of America, if implemented, would give rise to a breach of article 3 as, if he were to be sentenced to death, he would be exposed to inhuman and degrading treatment on death row. In para 89 the court stressed the need for a fair balance to be struck:

> . . .inherent in the whole of the Convention is a search for a fair balance between the demands of the general interest of the community and the requirements of the protection of the individual's fundamental rights. . . . it is increasingly in the interest of all nations that suspected offenders who flee abroad should be brought to justice.

. . .These considerations must also be included among the factors to be taken into account in the interpretation and application of the notions of inhuman and degrading treatment or punishment in extradition cases.

31. In *O'Halloran and Francis v United Kingdom* (2007) 46 EHRR 397 drivers whose vehicles had been caught on a speed camera complained under article 6(1) that they had been compelled to give incriminating information as to their identities in violation of their right to remain silent and the privilege against self-incrimination. They contended that this destroyed the very essence of the right to a fair trial.

In para 57, the court said [rejecting their argument] that those who choose to keep and drive motor cars can be taken to have accepted certain responsibilities as part of the regulatory framework relating to motor vehicles. In para 58 the court brought into account the limited nature of the inquiry which the police were authorised to undertake, that the relevant statute did not sanction prolonged questioning about facts giving rise to criminal offences and that, as Lord Bingham noted in *Brown v Stott* [2003] 1 AC 681, 705, the penalty for declining to answer was moderate and non-custodial.

33. In *Saadi v United Kingdom*, application no 13229/03, 29 January 2008, the Grand Chamber said that it is a fundamental principle that no detention that is arbitrary can be compatible with article 5(1) and that the notion of 'arbitrariness' extends beyond lack of conformity with national law. In para 74 it said that, to avoid being branded as arbitrary, such detention must be carried out in good faith and its length should not exceed that reasonably required for the purpose pursued. The ambit of article 5(1) was not the point at issue in that case. But it must follow from these observations that measures of crowd control which involve a restriction on liberty, if they are not to be held to be arbitrary, must be carried out in good faith and should not exceed the length that is reasonably required for the purpose for which the measure was undertaken.

34. I would hold therefore that there is room, even in the case of fundamental rights as to whose application no restriction or limitation is permitted by the Convention, for a pragmatic approach to be taken which takes full account of all the circumstances. No reference is made in article 5 to the interests of public safety or the protection of public order as one of the cases in which a person may be deprived of his liberty. The ambit that is given to article 5 as to measures of crowd control must, of course, take account of the rights of the individual as well as the interests of the community. So any steps that are taken must be resorted to in good faith and must be proportionate to the situation which has made the measures necessary. This is essential to preserve the fundamental principle that anything that is done which affects a person's right to liberty must not be arbitrary. If these requirements are met however it will be proper to conclude that measures of crowd control that are undertaken in the interests of the community will not infringe the article 5 rights of individual members of the crowd whose freedom of movement is restricted by them. . . .

Article 5(1)(b) and (c)

36. . . . But in my opinion it would be most unfortunate if the police were to have to rely on these sub-paragraphs, or either of them, when they were considering whether or not it was lawful for them to resort to measures of crowd control. It is obvious that neither of them were designed with that way of preserving public order in mind.

37. If measures of this kind are to avoid being prohibited by the Convention therefore it must be by recognising that they are not within the ambit of article 5(1) at all. In my opinion

measures of crowd control will fall outside the area of its application, so long as they are not arbitrary. This means that they must be resorted to in good faith, that they must be proportionate and that they are enforced for no longer than is reasonably necessary. . . .

Conclusion

38. This was not the kind of arbitrary deprivation of liberty that is proscribed by the Convention, so article 5(1) was not applicable in this case. I would respectfully endorse the further remarks of my noble and learned friend, Lord Walker of Gestingthorpe, with which I am in full agreement. I would dismiss the appeal.

Notes

1. *Use of police cordons against protesters.* Austin is a very significant and very worrying judgment for public protest. It means that the police can use the breach of the peace doctrine against protesters in order to: arrest them; detain them for several hours, without arresting them; or to stop an assembly or march or divert it, or to disperse most or all of it. The power to do all this arises if some members of the group have been involved in disorder in the past, or intelligence suggests that this is the case, and some members are disorderly, or are about to become disorderly.

2. *A mistaken view of Art 5 in Austin?* The key point, it is argued, at which the judgment in *Austin* fell into error was in finding that if protesters are in the company of other protesters who are disorderly or may become disorderly, even though they themselves have shown no propensity at all to disorder over a long period of time, they become liable to detention in a cordon—a detention which falls outside Art 5. ATH Smith takes the view, concurring with that of the Court of Appeal, that the police may impose directions on innocent persons in order to avert the possibility of a breach of the peace, such as creating a path through a group of by-standers to reach a scuffle.[135] But to impose a detention of seven hours on persons seeking to take part in a demonstration is it is argued qualitatively distinct from that example in terms of its impact on liberty and on assembly.

3. It is argued, contrary to the view of the Lords, that Art 5 *was* breached at some point during the seven hours of detention in relation to both Austin and Saxby. Strasbourg appears to take a less restrained view of the ambit of Art 5(1) than the Lords did, although its precise ambit remains somewhat elusive. A recent modern decision of the Court, *Storck v Germany*,[136] echoed the leading Court decisions, including *Guzzardi*,[137] in finding: 'the starting-point must be the specific situation of the individual concerned and account must be taken of a whole range of factors arising in a particular case, such as the type, duration, effects and manner of implementation of the measure in question'.[138] In support of this contention the Court relied on a range of cases in which various aspects of 'deprivation of liberty' were in doubt, including the question whether confinement in a large area could fall within the term 'deprivation'.[139] But none of the cases concerned the situation at issue in *Austin* where the detention imposed by the police was not in doubt, where the confinement was total and in a very small area, where the period of detention was not negligible and where the lack of consent of the applicant to the confinement was obvious.

---

135 See ATH Smith 'May Day, May Day: Policing Protest' [2008] 67(1) CLJ 10–12. Smith finds: '. . . The difficulty about any reliance upon the breach of the peace was that it was quite clear that the appellants ... had behaved lawfully throughout. That fact is not necessarily determinative. It is clearly the law that the police are entitled to take action against persons who are not themselves threatening a breach of the peace if such a course is necessary to prevent a breach either happening or about to do so'.

136 (2006) 43 EHRR 96 at [74].

137 (1980) 3 EHRR 333.

138 At [71].

139 See, *inter alia, Guzzardi v Italy,* judgment of 6 November 1980, Series A no 39, p 33, [92]; *Nielsen. Denmark,* judgment of 28 November 1988, Series A no 144, p 24, [67]; and *HM v Switzerland,* no 39187/98, [42], ECHR 2002-II.

4. It may be suggested that the Strasbourg and domestic case-law supports the following proposition—it is where an issue as to the fact of, the brevity of, or intensity of confinement, or as to the issue of best interests or consent arises, that a focus on all the surrounding circumstances has especial pertinence. Lord Hope considered that 'in the paradigm case of close confinement in a prison cell. . . there is no room for argument'.[140] But the case-law does not support the notion that in *all other* cases of severe restriction of movement, such as arrest or detention after arrest, the room for argument is equal to that in the borderline cases, such as *Guzzardi*; the restriction imposed on Austin consisted of total police detention for a substantial period and was therefore analogous to the near-paradigm cases, not the borderline ones. All of the incidents of paradigm cases of detention applied to Austin's situation, and in some respects amounted to greater violations of autonomy: the extreme crowding together of those in the cordon would not be duplicated in prison; since no provision for food or water was made by the police, she was forbidden any refreshment by her 'gaoler'; and a basic facility available in prison—access to a lavatory—was denied. *Conditions* of detention are not within the coverage of Art 5(1), but given that the right to liberty protects dignity and autonomy as underlying values, then it is argued that they were very much at stake in relation to the impact of the cordon. Clearly, the duration of the detention was shorter than that which Lord Hoffman may have envisaged, but Strasbourg has brought brief detentions of about one hour within Art 5(1).[141] It is contended that authority for using the purpose of an intervention to determine the ambit of Art 5 is lacking, and that the Lords' findings on 'deprivation of liberty' were incorrect.

5. *The impact of Austin on the breach of the peace doctrine.* Domestically, after *Austin* the purpose of a restriction on movement is now relevant to the ambit of Art 5. Apart from formal arrest, if the purpose is to answer to immediate safety concerns the restriction falls outside the ambit. But that means that the converse also applies: where the purpose of such a restriction is not or may not be connected to such concerns and the restriction involves police detention for a more than minimal period, the restriction *would* fall within Art 5. Thus, the use of 'kettling' for another purpose, such as indentifying peaceful protesters, *would* be within Art 5(1) and therefore would appear to create a violation of the right.

6. It was probably correct to decide, as Lord Hope did, that the exceptions under Art 5(1)(b)[142] and (c) would not apply in the circumstances, but that appeared to lead the Lords to assume that therefore Art 5(1) must be found not to apply, rather than leading to the finding that the actions that can be taken by police when they consider that a breach of the peace may be imminent can include creating brief restrictions on the movement of innocent protesters, but cannot include detaining for a very substantial length of time those who are not suspected of being about to breach the peace.

7. *Impact of Austin and Laporte.* As far as the extent of police powers under the breach of the peace doctrine are concerned, the outcome of the two decisions in *Laporte* and *Austin* is that the police cannot detain peaceful protesters on the basis of an apprehended breach of the peace that is not yet imminent, but they can detain them—or take other preventive action—on grounds of necessity, even for very substantial periods, when they are in the company of others who are causing or about to cause a breach of the peace. It also appears possible that preventive action, such as dispersing part of the demonstration or imposing an absolute cordon, can occur before any disorderliness has

---

140   At [18].

141   See *X and Y v Sweden* (1976) 7 DR 123.

142   Counsel for the police indicated that in the alternative it could be argued that the detention was justified to fulfil an obligation—the common law obligation to assist a constable in dealing with a breach of the peace. However, that would have been specific to the individuals concerned, making it difficult to argue that each and every one of them was subject to that obligation.

occurred, if intelligence suggests that along with peaceful protesters hard core activists are present who may at some point cause a breach. The police would have to claim that the breach was "imminent" (about to happen) in order to allow intervention and (probably) that that meant actual violence was about to occur. The lack of deference shown to police decisions in *Laporte* might have encouraged the police to be cautious in making that claim in this context had the contrary tendency not been evident in *Austin*. Lord Brown agreed with Lord Bingham in finding in *Laporte*: 'If indeed the police are to enjoy a power to prevent entirely innocent citizens from taking part in demonstrations already afoot, I have no doubt that it can only be a power conferred by primary legislation. It is certainly not to be found in the common law'.[143] Lords Mance, Rodger and Carswell, obiter, did not concur with this finding.[144] In so far as doubts arose as to the availability of powers under the breach of the peace doctrine to trap innocent protesters in a cordon for substantial periods if others are violent/disorderly, *Austin* has settled the matter.[145]

8. The judgment in *Austin* stressed the exceptional nature of the circumstances of the May Day protest, but obviously for the future left it up to the police to determine whether, in the circumstances, the basis for the use of the power is present or about to be present. The only safeguard for innocent protesters is that there must be a 'necessity' for its use based on the actual or imminent breach of the peace of others. This leaves an immense discretion to the police, accompanied by no checks under Art 5, to allow detention of peaceful protesters via absolute cordons where those they are in company with are or may be disorderly—and obviously the police may over-estimate the likelihood or extent of violence or disorder.[146] The reports of the police response to the G20 protests in London in April 2009 do not suggest that restraint is being used in relation to the imposition of cordons; it appears that they are becoming normal practice. For recent critical surveys of police practice in relation to public protest, see the Joint Committee on Human Rights, *Demonstrating respect for rights? A human rights approach to policing protest*, Seventh Report (2008–09) HL Paper 47-I; HC 320-I and a follow up report in July 2009: Twenty Second Report HL Paper 141; HC 522.

9. In *Laporte*, the House of Lords showed a hitherto rare insistence by a court upon compliance by police with real standards of 'prescribed by law', proportionality and necessity when disrupting peaceful protest; it can be viewed as an example of expansive judicial reasoning in relation to Strasbourg concepts used domestically. In aligning this common law power with Arts 10 and 11 in this fashion, the decision offered a much-needed check upon broad police discretion and expressly recognised the 'constitutional shift' that the HRA has brought about in this context. *Austin* in contrast shows a minimalist mode of reasoning,[147] in a decision which, it is contended, exemplifies all the worst strains of excessive judicial deference to the executive and includes a complete failure to apply any kind of meaningful proportionality test: the treatment of the human rights dimension

---

143   At [132].

144   At [83], [105] and [148].

145   See further H Fenwick, 'Marginalising Human Rights, Breach of the Peace, "Kettling", the HRA and Public Protest' [2009] PL 737; D Mead, 'Of Kettles, Cordons and Crowd Control—*Austin v Commissioner of Police for the Metropolis* and the Meaning of "Deprivation of Liberty"' (2009) EHRLR 376.

146   Evidence referred to in the 2009 JCHR Report noted disproportionate police responses to peaceful demonstrations and the use of armed units (para 54). A man, Ian Tomlinson, died during the 2009 G20 protest in London, allegedly due to an assault by riot police—see *The Observer* 5 April 2009, pp 1–2. From the available news reports, which relied on citizen journalism, it appeared that Tomlinson may have been assaulted because he accidentally approached a police cordon. Some news reports suggested that the police had infiltrated the G20 protesters and acted as agents provocateurs, creating disturbances and thereby justifying the use of harsh tactics. This matter formed the basis of some of the questions asked of the Chief Officer of the Metropolitan Police by the Home Affairs Select Committee—19 May 2009.

147   See for discussion of such reasoning in relation to Strasbourg concepts in this context, Fenwick and Phillipson, p 1139, below. See also Fenwick and Phillipsen (2001) n 154, below.

was one which sought its marginalisation. Although Lord Hope indicated that 'kettling' would only fall outside Art 5(1) where the demands of proportionality were satisfied, he failed to set out the *nature* of those demands in this context. *Laporte* had determined that such demands would not be satisfied where police intervention was premature or indiscriminate. In *Austin* the police action was not premature, but it was indiscriminate in that peaceful protesters and bystanders were trapped in the cordon. Thus, it is argued that the demands of proportionality as set out in *Laporte* were not satisfied in *Austin* and that therefore the use of kettling should have been found to fall within Art 5(1).

10. In controlling public protest it is argued that it would be preferable to rely on the scheme under POA 1986, ss 11–14A which is specifically aimed at marches and assemblies, rather than on common law powers or the non-dedicated statutory provisions. Currently, as Lord Bingham said in *Laporte*, the breach of the peace doctrine undermines the statutory scheme.

11. Reports of the April 2009 London G20 protests showed that police took photographs and demanded names and addresses of peaceful protesters being released; refusal meant re-trapping in the cordon.[148] Not only is the basis for demanding addresses etc unclear, but the practice of re-trapping in the cordon indicates that refusal to release peaceful protesters may not always be based on immediate public safety concerns. Since the judgment in *Austin* was based on the continued necessity to maintain the cordon for the seven-hour period, such re-trapping in a cordon would appear to bring it within the ambit of Art 5(1), even following the restrictive stance in *Austin,* since it could not be justified by an immediate need to preserve public safety.[149] Indeed, it follows from *Austin* that *any* use of 'kettling' for significant periods for a purpose falling outside the need to meet continuing, urgent safety concerns, would appear to fall within the ambit of Art 5(1) and would therefore be unlawful.

Criminal trespass

Criminal Justice and Public Order Act 1994

Offence of aggravated trespass

68.–(1) A person commits the offence of aggravated trespass if he trespasses on land in the open air and, in relation to any lawful activity which persons are engaging in or are about to engage in on that or adjoining land in the open air, does there anything which is intended by him to have the effect—

    (a)   of intimidating those persons or any of them so as to deter them or any of them from engaging in that activity,

    (b)   of obstructing that activity, or

    (c)   of disrupting that activity.

  (2)   Activity on any occasion on the part of a person or persons on land is 'lawful' for the purposes of this section if he or they may engage in the activity on the land on that occasion without committing an offence or trespassing on the land.

  (4)   A constable in uniform who reasonably suspects that a person is committing an offence under this section may arrest him without a warrant.

---

148   See further H Fenwick (2009) n 145 above. See also D Mead (2009) n 64 above, at pp 349–356.

149   Lord Neuberger made this explicit, at [63].

(5)   In this section 'land' does not include—

(a)   the highways and roads excluded from the application of section 61 by paragraph (b) of the definition of 'land' in subsection (9) of that section; or

(b)   a road within the meaning of the Roads (Northern Ireland) Order 1993.

Powers to remove persons committing or participating in aggravated trespass
69.—(1) If the senior police officer present at the scene reasonably believes—

(a)   that a person is committing, has committed or intends to commit the offence of aggravated trespass on land in the open air; or

(b)   that two or more persons are trespassing on land in the open air and are present there with the common purpose of intimidating persons so as to deter them from engaging in a lawful activity or of obstructing or disrupting a lawful activity,

he may direct that person or (as the case may be) those persons (or any of them) to leave the land.

(2)   A direction under subsection (1) above, if not communicated to the persons referred to in subsection (1) by the police officer giving the direction, may be communicated to them by any constable at the scene.

(3)   If a person knowing that a direction under subsection (1) above has been given which applies to him—

(a)   fails to leave the land as soon as practicable, or

(b)   having left again enters the land as a trespasser within the period of three months beginning with the day on which the direction was given, he commits an offence and is liable on summary conviction to imprisonment for a term not exceeding three months or a fine not exceeding level 4 on the standard scale, or both.

(4)   In proceedings for an offence under subsection (3) it is a defence for the accused to show—

(a)   that he was not trespassing on the land, or

(b)   that he had a reasonable excuse for failing to leave the land as soon as practicable or, as the case may be, for again entering the land as a trespasser.

(5)   A constable in uniform who reasonably suspects that a person is committing an offence under this section may arrest him without a warrant.

(6)   In this section 'lawful activity' and 'land' have the same meaning as in section 68.

Notes
1. The offence of aggravated trespass under s 68 was aimed at certain groups such as hunt saboteurs or motorway protesters, animal rights activists and the 'peace convoys' which gather for the summer solstice festival at Stonehenge. No defence is provided and it is not necessary to show

that the lawful activity was affected. This is a very broad power since a great many peaceful demonstrations are intended to have some impact of an obstructive nature on lawful activities (for example, export of veal calves or closure of schools or hospitals).

2. 'Land' is defined in s 61(9); it does not include metalled highway or buildings apart from certain agricultural buildings and scheduled monuments; common land and non-metalled roads are included. Thus, s 68 does not apply to demonstrations on a metalled highway or in most, but not all, buildings. It does apply to public paths, such as bridleways.

3. Where a person is in receipt of the direction under s 69, even though it was erroneously given (since in fact the person did not have the purpose of committing the s 68 offence), it would seem that he or she will still commit an offence if thereafter he or she re-enters the land in question during the specified time.

4. Section 68 has been used against hunt saboteurs and other protesters on a number of occasions and some of the decisions on the section have had the effect of widening the area of liability created still further. In *Winder v DPP*[150] the appellants had been running after the hunt. It was accepted that they did not intend to disrupt it by running but it was found that running after it was more than a preparatory act and that it was close enough to the contemplated action to incur liability. The willingness of the court to extend the boundaries of s 68 to catch such activities was all the more disturbing given that s 69 allows a direction to be given where it is suspected that the s 68 offence will be committed, a provision surely intended to cover precisely this set of circumstances.

5. Although s 68 may not lead to the criminalisation of persons who simply walk on to land as trespassers, s 69 has the potential to do so, depending on the interpretation given by the courts to the 'reasonable excuse' defence. *Capon v DPP*[151] made it clear that the offence under s 69 could be committed even though the offence under s 68 was not established. The defendants were videoing the digging out of a fox when they were threatened with arrest under s 68 by a police officer if they did not leave and were asked whether they were leaving the land. This exchange and question was found to be sufficient, in the circumstances, to constitute the direction necessary under s 69. Their intention in undertaking the videoing was not found to be to disrupt, intimidate or interfere with the activity in question. Despite the fact that the protesters had been peaceful and non-obstructive throughout, and it was very doubtful whether the officer had directed his mind towards all the elements of the offence, including the *mens rea*,[152] it was found that there was sufficient evidence. It was further found that there was no defence of 'reasonable excuse' in the circumstances,[153] even though the protesters were still in the process of trying to find out what offence they were being arrested for when they were, in fact, arrested, and genuinely believed that no direction under s 69(1) had been made against them.[154]

---

150   *The Times*, 14 August 1996.

151   *The Times*, 23 March 1998. Considered by D Mead, 'Will Peaceful Protesters be Foxed by the Divisional Court Decision in *Capon v DPP*?' [1998] Crim LR 870.

152   As Mead notes, *ibid*.

153   'The fact that the appellants were not. . .committing an offence under s 68 plainly. . .does not provide a reasonable excuse for not leaving the land. So to hold would emasculate the obvious intention of the section' (*per* Lord Bingham).

154   See further H Fenwick and G Phillipson, 'Direct Action, Convention Values and the Human Rights Act' (2001) 21(4) LS 535–68.

Questions

❶   In debate on the Criminal Justice and Public Order Bill in the House of Lords, it was said that these provisions 'act as an open invitation to the police to interfere in the legitimate activities of people'. Do you agree? Is this also true of the 1986 Act?

❷   The Criminal Justice and Public Order Act 1994 has undoubtedly increased the power of the authorities to prevent protest. Do you consider that eventually a declaration of incompatibility may have to be made between any of its public order provisions and Arts 10 or 11 of the ECHR, under s 4 of the HRA?

❸   'Taking the breach of the peace power and all the statutory provisions that can be used to repress protest, it may be argued that public protest may now take place only on the basis that it is so anodyne and emasculated that it can hardly be termed protest at all.' Is this a fair evaluation of the current scheme, or might it be argued that the restrictions placed on the use of some of the statutory provisions, such as the defence of reasonableness under s 5(3)(c) of the 1986 Act or under s 69(4)(b) of the 1994 Act, provide sufficient protection for peaceful protest, taking into account the need to interpret the defences compatibly with Arts 10 and 11 under s 3 of the HRA?

CONCLUSION

This chapter has looked at a vast range of over-lapping provisions curtailing protest. The Labour government that came into power in 1997 inherited a scheme of curbing protest that was both complex and repressive. The Labour governments of 1997–2010 proceeded to create greater repression of protest or to disregard over-expansive interpretations of their powers by police. Over-broad statutory provisions have been broadened still further by incremental extension. The breach of the peace doctrine has been used extensively by police against protesters over most of the HRA period with little attempt by the judiciary, except in *Laporte* and *Redmond-Bate*, to hold it in check, the low point being *Austin*. The finding in 2009 that three thousand mainly peaceful protesters could be trapped for seven hours in a London Square, and that an entirely peaceful protester had no redress for the detention, is one of the lowest points of the domestic public protest jurisprudence. But it is not enough to view the breach of the peace doctrine as far too broad and as needing a check. Many of the statutory provisions are also excessively broad and of uncertain, far-reaching scope, leaving too much to police interpretations of the discretion they offer for interference in protest. Far more recognition of the value of peaceful protest, and of expression and assembly generally, is still needed in this context. The judiciary are still too prone to accept police assessments of public order risks. The police continue to interpret their powers very widely, especially their powers of intervention in protests under the breach of the peace doctrine, and powers to exercise surveillance over peaceful protesters and journalists attending protests, which includes storing information gathered on databases.[155] The use (or misuse) of counter-terrorism powers against peaceful protesters post-2000[156] continues to raise serious concerns.

The Liberal-Conservative government that took power in May 2010 has plans for a Great Repeal (Freedom) Bill, announced in the 2010 Queen's Speech, intended to roll back Labour legislation

---

155   See p1086 above. See the case of *Wood v Commissioner of Police for the Metroplis* [2008] EWHC 1105 which concerned the taking of a photograph of a protester by police and its retention for purposes of data-sharing; it was successfully challenged under Article 8 ECHR, relying on the HRA. See further D Mead (2009) 'further reading' at pp 375–380. But surveillance, harassment, covert photography of protesters for purposes of data-sharing appears to be continuing (*The Guardian* 7 March 2009).

156   See Chap 20 pp 1153–1157. The criminalisation of photographing police officers under s76 Counter-terrorism Act 2008 is viewed by journalists as a means of harassing them when covering protests, as evidenced by the NUJ protest on this issue in February 2009.

invasive of civil liberties. It was expected in some quarters that it will include provision to give greater protection to peaceful protest[157] and to address the question of harassment and surveillance of peaceful protesters. Provision to restore the right of peaceful protest was included, but the detail has yet to emerge. The Human Rights Act may also continue to be relied upon to challenge police intervention in public protest, as in *Laporte,* and the recent, more activist jurisprudence at Strasbourg on protest may provide a stronger basis for doing so.[158]

FURTHER READING

For current discussion, see:

SH Bailey, DJ Harris and Bl Jones, *Civil Liberties: Cases and Materials,* 5th edn (2002), Chapter 3

D Feldman, *Civil Liberties and Human Rights in England and Wales* (2002), Chapter 17

H Fenwick, *Civil Liberties and Human Rights,* 4th edn (2007), Chapter 9

H Fenwick, *Civil Rights: New Labour, Freedom and the Human Rights Act* (2000), Chapter 4

R Clayton and H Tomlinson, *The Law of Human Rights,* 2nd edn (2006), Chapter 16

D Mead, *The New Law of Peaceful Protest—Rights and Regulation in the Human Rights Act Era* (2010)

D Harris, M O'Boyle and C Warbrick, *Law of the European Convention on Human Rights* (1995); 2nd edn (2009) D Harris, M O'Boyle, E Bates, C Buckley

N Whitty, T Murphy and S Livingstone, *Civil Liberties Law* (2001), Part V

H Fenwick, 'Marginalising Human Rights, Breach of the Peace, "Kettling", the HRA and Public Protest' [2009] PL 737

G Clayton, 'Reclaiming Public Ground: The Right to Peaceful Assembly' (2000) 63 MLR 252

H Fenwick, 'The Right to Protest, the Human Rights Act and the Margin of Appreciation' (1999) 62 MLR 491

I Loveland, 'Public Protest in Parliament Square' (2007) EHRLR 252

D Mead, 'Strasbourg Discovers the Right to Demonstrate' (2007) EHRLR 133

D Mead, 'The Right to Peaceful Protest under the ECHR' (2007) EHRLR 345

A Geddis, 'Free Speech Martyrs or Unreasonable Threats to Social Peace?—"Insulting" Expression and Section 5 of the Public Order Act 1986' [2004] PL 853

C Newman, 'Divisional Court: Public Order Act 1986, s. 4A: Proportionality and Freedom of Expression' (2006) 70 *Journal of Criminal Law* 191

For discussion and criticism of the Public Order Act 1986, see:

D Bonner and R Stone, 'The Public Order Act 1986: Steps in the Wrong Direction?' [1987] PL 202

C Gearty, 'Freedom of assembly and public order', in C McCrudden and G Chambers (eds), *Individual Rights and the Law in Britain* (1994) at 55

ATH Smith, 'The Public Order Act 1986 Part I' [1987] Crim LR 156

For discussion and criticism of the Criminal Justice and Public Order Act 1986, see:

MJ Allen and S Cooper, 'Howard's Way: A Farewell to Freedom?' (1995) 58(3) MLR 364

VT Bevan, 'Protest and Public Disorder' [1979] PL 163S

H Fenwick and G Phillipson, 'Public Protest, the Human Rights Act and Judicial Responses to Political Expression' [2000] PL 627–50

K Ewing and C Gearty, *Freedom under Thatcher* (1990), Chapter 4

K Ewing and C Gearty, *The Struggle for Civil Liberties* (1999)

---

157   See *The Guardian* 13 May 2010, p37.
158   See p 52 above. See further D Mead (2009) Chap 3, arguing that in the last 5 years a new activism in relation to protest has been evident in the Strasbourg jurisprudence.

CHAPTER 20
CRIME CONTROL AND COUNTER-TERRORISM: POLICE POWERS

INTRODUCTION[1]

The exercise of police powers, such as arrest and detention, represents an invasion of personal liberty which is tolerated in the interests of the prevention and detection of crime. However, in accepting the need to allow such invasion, the interest in personal liberty requires that it should be strictly regulated in accordance with due process values—in other words, procedures should be in place that ensure that suspects' rights are respected and that evidence obtained is reliable. Such due process requirements inevitably place curbs on police powers. Thus, the rights-based due process model seeks to recognise the 'primacy of the individual and the complementary concept of limitation of official power'.[2] It calls for the police to be subject to tightly defined and rigorous control and for clear, legally guaranteed safeguards for suspects, with clear remedies for abuse through the courts.[3] In contrast, the crime control model values an accurate and efficient fact-finding role over slow and less accurate judicial trials in order to repress crime. Current analysis of aspects of the criminal justice system continues to rely quite heavily on these two familiar models of crime control and due process.[4] But while a rhetorical commitment to due process is still evident,[5] there is a clear perception that the law does not fully reflect this model. As Sanders and Young put it: 'Police and Court officials need not abuse the law to subvert the principles of justice; they need only use it.'[6] This chapter sets out extracts from the very extensive rules that apparently regulate police conduct in investigating crime and terrorist activity. But, as will become apparent, there is a mismatch between appearance and reality.

In this chapter, the powers of the police under PACE, the Terrorism Act 2000, as amended, other statutory provisions, and the accompanying safeguards, are evaluated with a view to considering how far the suspects' rights granted by PACE and by other provisions have had an impact on police working practice and how far, if at all, changes have occurred or are occurring due to the impact of the Human Rights Act 1998 (HRA). This is followed by a consideration of the value of the means of redress available, as affected by the inception of the HRA, if the police fail to comply with the rules.

Police powers—developments

The rules governing the exercise of police powers are still largely contained in the scheme created under the Police and Criminal Evidence Act 1984 (PACE), which is made up of rules deriving from the Act itself, from the Codes of Practice made under it, and from the Notes for Guidance contained in the Codes. The exercise of police powers is also influenced by Home Office circulars.

---

1   Key texts referred to in this chapter: A Sanders and R Young, *Criminal Justice,* 3rd edn (2007); H Fenwick, *Civil Liberties and Human Rights,* 4th edn (2007), Chapters 11, 12, 13; SH Bailey and N Taylor, *Bailey, Harris and Jones: Civil Liberties: Cases and Materials,* 6th edn (2009), Chapter 4; M Zander, *The Police and Criminal Evidence Act 1984,* 4th edn (2008); H Fenwick and G Phillipson, *Media Freedom under the HRA* (2006).

2   H Packer, *The Limits of the Criminal Sanction* (1968). As Walker puts it: 'The primacy of individual autonomy and rights is central to the due process model', *Miscarriages of Justice* (1999), p 39.

3   See further Baldwin, 'Taking rules to excess: police powers and the Police and Criminal Evidence Bill 1984', in Brenton and Jones (eds), *The Year Book of Social Policy in Britain 1984–85* (1985), pp 9–29; P Jones, 'Police powers and political accountability: the Royal Commission on Criminal Procedure' P Hillyard, 'From Belfast to Britain: some critical comments on the Royal Commission on Criminal Procedure', both in *Politics and Power,* Vol 4 (1981); T Jefferson, 'Policing the miners: law, politics and accountability', in Brenton and Ungerson (eds), *The Year Book of Social Policy in Britain 1985–86* (1986), pp 265–86.

4   See Packer, *ibid* e.g. the two models are extensively relied on in C Walker and K Starmer (eds), *Miscarriages of Justice* (1999). For discussion and criticism of the two models see Sanders and Young, *Criminal Justice* (2007), Chapter 1, Part 5.

5   See, e.g. *Legislation Against Terrorism: A Consultation Paper,* Cm 4178, 1998, esp. para 8 of the Introduction.

6   Sanders and Young, n 1 above, fn 1, p 20 (2000) 2nd edn.

PACE was introduced in order to provide clear and broad police powers, but these were supposed to be balanced by greater safeguards for suspects. Such safeguards were in part adopted due to the need to ensure that miscarriages of justice, such as that which occurred in the *Confait* case,[7] in which two boys were wrongly convicted of murder, would not recur. The Royal Commission on Criminal Procedure,[8] whose report influenced PACE, was set up largely in response to the inadequacies of safeguards for suspects which were exposed in the *Confait* report.[9] The result was a scheme in which the broad discretionary powers granted were to be balanced by two central structuring constraints. First, there were general precedent conditions for the exercise of such powers, the most common and significant being the requirement of reasonable suspicion. Second, there was the provision of specific countervailing due process rights, in particular a general right of custodial access to legal advice, in most cases laid down in, or underpinned by, quasi- and non-legal rules—the Codes of Practice and Notes for Guidance made under PACE.[10] Redress for breaches of the due process safeguards was largely to be within the disciplinary rather than the judicial sphere: breach of the Codes constituted automatically a breach of the police disciplinary Code.[11]

Post-PACE, the discovery of a number of miscarriages of justice—the cases of the *Birmingham Six*,[12] the *Guildford Four*,[13] *Judith Ward*,[14] *Stefan Kiszko*,[15] the *Tottenham Three*,[16] the *Maguire Seven*[17]—raised due process concerns again. After the Birmingham Six were freed in 1992, another Royal Commission under Lord Runciman[18] was set up in order to consider further measures which could be introduced, but although there appeared to be a link between the announcement of the Royal Commission and the *Birmingham Six* case owing to proximity in time, the Commission interpreted its remit as not requiring an analysis of the miscarriage of justice in that case. The remit was to examine the efficacy of the criminal justice system in terms of securing the conviction of the guilty and the acquittal of the innocent.[19] Once again, a Royal Commission was seeking to reconcile potentially conflicting aims—concern to protect due process, but also to further crime control. After the Commission reported, the Major Government introduced legislation, most notably the Criminal Justice and Public Order Act 1994 (CJPOA), which increased police powers significantly while removing a number of safeguards for suspects. In particular, the 1994 Act curtailed the right of silence, although the Runciman Royal Commission had recommended that the right should be retained since its curtailment might lead to further miscarriages of justice. Thus, there were significant developments in police powers during the

---

7   See report of the inquiry by the Hon Sir Henry Fisher, HC 90 (1977–78).

8   Royal Commission on Criminal Procedure Report, Cmnd 8092 (1981) (RCCP Report).

9   HC 90 (1977–78).

10   PACE 1984, s 66, Codes of Practice.

11   *Ibid*, s 67(8). For the current position, see p 1236, n 325.

12   See *R v McIlkenny and Others* [1992] 2 All ER 417.

13   See *Report*, HC 449 (1993–94), Chapter 17.

14   *R v Ward* (1992) 96 Cr App R 1.

15   *R v Kiseka, The Times*, 18 February 1992.

16   *R v Silcott, The Times*, 9 December 1991.

17   See *R v Maguire* [1992] 2 All ER 433.

18   Runciman Report, Cm 2263 (1993).

19   Effectiveness in securing 'the conviction of those guilty of criminal offences and the acquittal of those who are innocent', *ibid*, Chapter 1, para 5.

Major years, and the balance PACE was supposed to strike between such powers and due process was, it will be argued, undermined.

Since the Labour Government took office in 1997, there have been, apart from the passing of the HRA, no indications of attempts to break with the criminal justice legislative policies of the Conservative Party. In particular, the Terrorism Act 2000 (TA), as amended in 2003, then by the Terrorism Act 2006 and the Counter-Terrorism Act 2008, has increased the period of time for which terrorism suspects can be detained, to 28 days. Amendations made to PACE by the Serious and Organised Crime Act 2005 have significantly extended the arrest power. Both before and after the general elections of 2001 and 2005, both major parties were seeking to outdo each other in encouraging and pandering to populist notions of crime control, although after the 2010 election the Liberal-Conservative government set out to roll-back some of the Labour criminal justice measures (the Great Repeal (Freedom) Bill). One especially evident tendency over the years 1997–2010 was the movement away from the need to show reasonable suspicion as a necessary condition for the exercise for police powers. Its abandonment in the introduction of recent stop, arrest and detention powers is indicative of a formal acceptance of a less fettered police discretion, as opposed to the discretion developed *de facto* in police practice. Section 44 TA and s 60 CJPOA exemplify this tendency.

PACE, the Terrorism Act 2000 and the Codes of Practice

At present, the rules governing the exercise of police powers in relation to non-terrorist suspects are largely contained in the scheme created under PACE, as amended, which is made up of rules deriving from the Act itself and from the Codes of Practice made under it. The Terrorism Act 2000, as amended, contains a number of police powers and safeguards relating to terrorism suspects. The difference in status between the statutory provisions and the provisions in the Codes and the significance of adopting this two-tiered approach is considered below. (It should be emphasised at this point that a number of further significant police powers are not contained in PACE, as will be indicated.) The PACE pre-trial scheme must be examined in conjunction with the scheme that was created under the Terrorism Act 2000, as amended, which creates at certain points greater police powers and a lesser level of protection for terrorist suspects.

The Codes of Practice were created with a view to providing the police with a complete guide to the procedures they should follow when exercising their powers, which would also be easier to change and develop than statutory provisions. The Codes have a quasi-legal status. Until 2006 there were six Codes of Practice: Code A, covering stop and search procedures, Code B, covering searching of premises, Code C, covering interviewing and conditions of detention, Code D, covering identification methods and Code E, covering tape recording. Code F covering visual recording of interviews was introduced in 2004, a new version coming into force in 2006. Thus, each covers a particular area of PACE, although not all areas were covered: arrest, for example, was, until 2006, governed only by statutory provisions.[20] The Codes have gone through a number of revisions post-PACE, becoming steadily longer and more cumbersome in the process (Code C, for example, now runs to over 80 pages). In 2006 new, revised versions of the existing Codes came into force and the Codes were also added to. A new Code G covering arrest was introduced, as was a special new Code—Code H. It was introduced to govern the rights of terrorist suspects in police questioning and detention, meaning that the provisions of Code C relating to such suspects were removed, reappearing in a revised form in Code H (although at various points Codes C and H are almost identical). Thus 2006 saw a very dramatic revision and extension

---

20   Report of the Inquiry by the Hon Sir Henry Fisher, HC 90 of 1977–78.

of the Codes. The Codes were revised again in 2008, but in terms of the aspects of police powers and duties that are the concern of this chapter, only minor changes were made.

If safeguards for suspects are taken seriously then why do they largely appear in the Codes rather than in PACE itself? It may be asked why all of the stop and search rules, for example, were not merely made part of the Act. The answer may partly lie in the need for some flexibility in making changes: the Codes are quicker and less cumbersome to amend than statutory provisions, so they can be adapted quite readily to changing needs in the stop and search sphere. However, it is also probable that the Government did not want to create rules which might give rise to liability on the part of the police if they were broken; rules which could operate at a lower level of visibility than statutory ones may have appeared more attractive. It has for some time been apparent that the police powers were contained in PACE, as amended, and other statutes, while suspects' rights were largely contained in the non-statutory Codes. That tendency has only become more marked in the post-PACE years. The proliferation of Code provisions, especially in 2006, has not been accompanied by any determination to deal with their very doubtful legal status.[21] At the same time certain safeguards of particular significance have always remained in the statute, in particular the provisions governing time limits on police detention. It is hard to escape the conclusion that the safeguards surrounding the questioning of suspects, contained mainly in Codes C and H, are viewed as of less significance.

Section 67(10) of PACE makes clear the intended distinction between Act and Codes in providing that no civil or criminal liability will arise from a breach of the Codes. But the question of civil liability in respect of a breach of PACE, as opposed to the Codes, is itself not without difficulty. Liability will arise where a police power is needed in order to render an act non-tortious that would otherwise be tortious. For example, an arrest would give rise to liability for false imprisonment if no power to arrest arose. Certain PACE rules have been treated by the courts as mandatory and therefore adherence to them is necessary in order to render the act in question lawful, as will be discussed below. So breach of *certain* PACE rules (not all) will give rise to civil liability because they operate in the context of existing areas of tortious liability, whereas breach of the Codes cannot give rise to liability, even within that context.

This distinction is of significance in relation to the stop and search, arrest and detention provisions of Parts I to IV of PACE,[22] in comparison with the Code provisions in those areas, in Codes A and G. However, this distinction does not seem to have any significance as far as the interviewing provisions of Part V PACE are concerned or their equivalents in the TA. The most important statutory safeguard for interviewing, the entitlement to legal advice, has not been affected by the availability of tortious remedies.[23] Thus statutory and Code provisions concerned with safeguards for suspects in police interviewing are in an *equally* weak position in the sense that a clear remedy is not available if they are breached. The context in which breaches of the interviewing provisions have been considered is that of exclusion of evidence.[24] In that context, the courts have not drawn a clear distinction between the

---

21   In *Delaney* (1989) 88 Cr App R 338; *The Times*, 20 August 1988, CA, the status of the Codes was considered. It was held that the mere fact that there had been a breach of the Codes of Practice did not of itself mean that evidence had to be rejected. Section 67(11) of the Act provides that '... if any provision of such Code appears to the court ... to be relevant to any question arising in the proceedings, it shall be taken into account in determining that question'.

22   In that respect, such claims are significant; eg in 1991, the Metropolitan Police faced an increase in claims of 40% over 1990. See HC Deb, Vol 193 Col 370w. For discussion of the use of tortious claims in this context, see below, pp 1230–1234.

23   The question whether an unlawful denial of access to legal advice amounts to a breach of statutory duty has been considered in an unreported case, 26 October 1985, QB (Rose J), which is cited by Clayton and Tomlinson in *Civil Actions Against the Police*, 1st edn (1992), p 359 (current edn 2005). It was held that the application would be refused even if jurisdiction to make the order sought existed as it would 'cause hindrance to police inquiries'.

24   Breach of a code provision is quite frequently taken into account in determining whether or not a confession should be excluded, usually under PACE, s 78. Breach of a code provision will not lead to automatic exclusion of an interview obtained thereby, but a substantial and significant breach may be the first step on the way to its exclusion (see *Walsh* [1989] Crim LR 822, CA, transcript from LEXIS).

provisions of the Act or of the Codes, except to require that breach of a Code provision should be of a substantial and significant nature[25] if exclusion of evidence is to be considered.

Role of the Human Rights Act

As indicated, under the Labour Governments from 1997–2010 there has been a very marked tendency to increase police powers. The Labour Government under Blair was also responsible for the introduction of the Human Rights Act 1998 (HRA). Thus, the UK has a benchmark—primarily Arts 5 and 6 of the European Convention on Human Rights (ECHR), scheduled in the HRA—by which to measure standards of procedural justice. The ECHR was intended to provide a series of minimum standards—a 'floor', not a 'ceiling' of rights—and the UK provides, mainly in PACE, the Terrorism Act 2000, as amended, and the PACE Codes of Practice, a number of rights for suspects that taken at face value appear to go beyond the basic standards set out in the Convention, taking the jurisprudence into account.

Nevertheless, given the current trend towards increasing police powers and away from protecting suspects' rights which this chapter will outline, the HRA could be perceived as providing a means of re-infusing due process into criminal procedure. It will be argued, however, that the impact of the HRA has been and is diluted and unpredictable in practice. It will be argued below at various points that this is partly due to the weakness of the Strasbourg jurisprudence in certain key areas, areas in which the common law has traditionally failed to protect due process; decisions under the HRA indicate that the inception of the HRA is having little impact in such areas. But the impact of the HRA has also been diluted, it will be argued, by the interpretations adopted by the police themselves, judges and by the police watchdog body, the Independent Police Complaints Commission (IPCC), of provisions governing police powers, of the Convention rights and of the duties placed upon the police and the IPCC by s 6 HRA.

Police culture

Judicial intervention and formal rules have always had an uncertain impact on the institutional culture of the criminal justice system, and it would probably be unduly optimistic to predict a clear change of stance under the HRA. As many scholars have argued, the impact of externally imposed rules on actual police practice is limited and uncertain.[26] In particular, researchers have highlighted the problems of rule-evasion—the avoidance of apparent safeguards through the use of informal practices[27]—and of deterrence.[28] There is general agreement that internal police governance and culture is highly

---

25 *Keenan* [1989] 3 All ER 598, CA.

26 See: the PSI Report's distinction between Presentational, Inhibitory and Working Rules; D Dixon, *Law and Policing: Legal Regulation and Police Practices* (1997).

27 See, e.g. A Goldsmith, 'Taking Police Culture Seriously: Police Discretion and the Limits of the Law' (1990) *Policing and Society* Vol 1, pp 91–114.

28 There is some evidence that use of exclusion of evidence where police have breached the rules in dealing with suspects may encourage police officers to observe suspects' rights. See Oldfield, 'The Exclusionary Rule and Deterrence: An Empirical Study of Chicago Narcotics Officers' (1987) 54 U Chicago L Rev 1016–69. In the context of PACE, this finding receives some support from research by Sanders, Bridges, Mulvaney and Crozier entitled 'Advice and assistance at police stations', November 1989; it was thought that unlawful denials of legal advice had been discouraged by the ruling in *R v Samuel* [1988] 2 All ER 135 (below, p 1215). The research found that in 1987, before the ruling, delay was authorised in around 50% of applicable cases; in 1990–91, in only one case out of 10,000. Such evidence cannot, however, be treated as conclusive of the issue; apart from other factors, police officers will be aware that the question of exclusion of evidence is unlikely to arise since the case is unlikely to come to a full trial; even if it does arise, a conviction may still be obtained. Any deterrent effect is therefore likely to be undermined.

significant in determining the extent to which suspects' rights are delivered, but it should also be emphasised that that culture is itself likely to be influenced by enhanced possibilities of external review of internal police decisions. There appears to be academic agreement that the relationship between external rules and police culture is a complex one and that rather than tending merely towards straightforward evasion of the legal rules, the institutional culture may encourage the development of strategies intended to adapt and accommodate the rules within the practices it has already fostered.[29] But it is also suggested that enhanced external review of such practices under the Human Rights Act (HRA) may be encouraging a shift from the working rules formulated by the police towards an infusion of the legal rules into their informal counterparts. As Dixon puts it: '[Rule] compliance has to be sought by skilfully blending negotiation and imposition.'[30]

STOP AND SEARCH POWERS

Current statutory stop and search powers are meant to maintain a balance between the interest of society as represented by the police in crime control and the interest of the citizen in personal liberty. The use of such powers may be a necessary part of effective policing and represents less of an infringement of liberty than an arrest, but on the other hand their exercise may create a sense of grievance and of violation of personal privacy. There was no general power at common law to detain without the subject's consent in the absence of specific statutory authority. Instead there was a miscellany of such powers, the majority of which were superseded under PACE.

The grant of further powers post-PACE has not been accompanied by a strengthening of the protection for the due process rights of suspects. One of the key structuring constraints, identified above as intended to protect due process under the Police and Criminal Evidence Act 1984, was the requirement of reasonable suspicion. This requirement has been eroded in the post-PACE developments; it has been dropped from the more recently introduced special powers, and under the Terrorism Act 2000 it continues to be unnecessary in respect of terrorist suspects.

The use of stop and search powers remains a contentious matter that continues to attract public attention, especially as it has frequently been suggested that they may be used in a racially or religiously discriminatory fashion. This issue was raised in relation to the *Stephen Lawrence* case in the MacPherson Report in 1999.[31] Their recorded use has more than trebled since PACE came into force in 1986[32] and, as indicated below, a large number of further powers have been introduced in the post-PACE period. The efficacy of such powers is debatable. Only around 10–14% of stops lead to an arrest and only around 3% to a charge.[33] There are, of course, other methods of measuring the crime control value of stop and search powers; in particular, they have some value in terms of information-gathering and, more controversially, as a means of asserting police authority on the streets.

---

29   See DJ Smith, 'Case Construction and the Goals of the Criminal Process' [1997] 37 Br Journal of Criminology 319; RV Ericson, *Making Crime: A Study of Detective Work* (1981).

30   In C Walker and K Starmer (eds), *Miscarriages of Justice* (1999), p 67.

31   Cm 4262–1 (1999).

32   Home Office Statistical Bulletin 21/93; Statistical Bulletin 27/97; see further Sanders and Young, *Criminal Justice* (2007), pp 98–101.

33   Home Office Statistical Bulletin 21/93.

Police and Criminal Evidence Act 1984 (as amended by the Criminal Justice Act 1988, s 140)

Part I—Powers to stop and search

Power of constable to stop and search persons, vehicles etc

1.–(1) A constable may exercise any power conferred in this section—

>   (a) in any place to which. . .the public or any section of the public has access. . .or
>   (b) in any other place to which people have ready access at the time when he proposes to exercise the power but which is not a dwelling.

(2) Subject to subsections (3) to (5) below, a constable—

>   (a) may search—
>
>   (i) any person or vehicle;
>   (ii) anything which is in or on a vehicle, for stolen or prohibited articles [or any article to which subsection 8A below applies] and
>
>   (b) may detain a person or vehicle for the purpose of such a search.

(3) This section does not give a constable power to search a person or vehicle or anything in or on a vehicle unless he has reasonable grounds for suspecting that he will find stolen or prohibited articles [or any article to which subsection 8A below applies]

. . .

(6) If in the course of such a search a constable discovers an article which he has reasonable grounds for suspecting to be a stolen or prohibited article, he may seize it.

(7) An article is prohibited for the purposes of this part of this Act if it is—

>   (a) an offensive weapon; or
>   (b) an article—
>
>   (i) made or adapted for use in the course of or in connection with an offence to which this sub-paragraph applies; or
>   (ii) intended by the person having it with him for such use by him or by some other person.

(8) The offences to which subsection (7)(b)(i) above applies are—

>   (a) burglary;
>   (b) theft;
>   (c) offences under section 12 of the Theft Act 1968 (taking motor vehicle or other conveyance without authority); and
>   (d) offences under section 15 of that Act (obtaining property by deception).

[(8A) This subsection applies to any article in relation to which a person has committed, or is committing, or is going to commit an offence under section 139 of the Criminal Justice Act 1988].

(9) In this part of this Act 'offensive weapon' means any article—

(a) made or adapted for use for causing injury to persons, or

(b) intended by the person having it with him for such use by him or by some other person;. . .

Provisions relating to search under s 1 and other powers

. . .

2.–(2) If a constable contemplates a search, other than a search of an unattended vehicle, in the exercise—

(a) of the power conferred by section 1 above; or

(b) of any other power. . .

(i) to search a person without first arresting him; or

(ii) to search a vehicle without making an arrest,

it shall be his duty, subject to subsection (4) below, to take reasonable steps before he commences the search to bring to the attention of the appropriate person—

(i) if the constable is not in uniform, documentary evidence that he is a constable; and

(ii) whether he is in uniform or not, the matters specified in subsection (3) below, and the constable shall not commence the search until he has performed that duty.

(3) The matters referred to in subsection (2)(ii) above are—

(a) the constable's name and the name of the police station to which he is attached;

(b) the object of the proposed search;

(c) the constable's grounds for proposing to make it; and

(d) the effect of section 3(7) or (8) below, as may be appropriate. . .

Duty to make records concerning searches

3.–(1) Where a constable has carried out a search. . . he shall make a record of it in writing unless it is not practicable to do so. . . .

(7) If a constable who conducted a search of a person made a record of it, the person who was searched shall be entitled to a copy of the record if he asks for one. . .

Criminal Justice and Public Order Act 1994, as amended

Powers to stop and search in anticipation of violence

60.–(1) Where a police officer of or above the rank of superintendent reasonably believes that—

(a)   incidents involving serious violence may take place in any locality in his area; and

(b)   it is expedient to do so to prevent their occurrence, he may give an authorisation that the powers to stop and search persons and vehicles conferred by this section shall be exercisable at any place within that locality for a period not exceeding 24 hours.

(2)   The power conferred by subsection (1) above may be exercised by a chief inspector or an inspector. . .

(3)   If it appears to the officer who gave the authorisation or to a superintendent that it is expedient to do so, having regard to offences which have, or are reasonably suspected to have, been committed in connection with any incident falling within the authorisation, he may direct that the authorisation shall continue in being for a further six hours.

(4)   This section confers on any constable in uniform power—

(a)   to stop any pedestrian and search him or anything carried by him for offensive weapons or dangerous instruments;

(b)   to stop any vehicle and search the vehicle, its driver and any passenger for offensive weapons or dangerous instruments.

(5)   A constable may, in the exercise of those powers, stop any person or vehicle and make any search he thinks fit whether or not he has any grounds for suspecting that the person or vehicle is carrying weapons or articles of that kind.

(6)   If in the course of a search under this section a constable discovers a dangerous instrument or an article which he has reasonable grounds for suspecting to be an offensive weapon, he may seize it. . .

(8)   A person who fails

[(a)   to stop or (as the case may be) to stop a vehicle; or

(b)   to remove any item worn by him][34] when required to do so by a constable in the exercise of his powers under this section shall be liable on summary conviction to imprisonment for a term not exceeding one month or to a fine not exceeding level 3 on the standard scale or both.

Terrorism Act 2000

44.–(1) An authorisation under this subsection authorises any constable in uniform to stop a vehicle in an area or at a place specified in the authorisation and to search—

(a)   the vehicle;

(b)   the driver of the vehicle;

(c)   a passenger in the vehicle;

(d)   anything in or on the vehicle or carried by the driver or a passenger.

---

34   As amended by the Crime and Disorder Act 1998, s 25(3).

(2)   An authorisation under this subsection authorises any constable in uniform to stop a pedestrian in an area or at a place specified in the authorisation and to search—

  (a)   the pedestrian;
  (b)   anything carried by him.

(3)   An authorisation under subsection (1) or (2) may be given only if the person giving it considers it expedient for the prevention of acts of terrorism. . .

Exercise of power

45.–(1) The power conferred by an authorisation under section 44(1) or (2)—

  (a)   may be exercised only for the purpose of searching for articles of a kind which could be used in connection with terrorism, and
  (b)   may be exercised whether or not the constable has grounds for suspecting the presence of articles of that kind.

(2)   A constable may seize and retain an article which he discovers in the course of a search by virtue of section 44(1) or (2) and which he reasonably suspects is intended to be used in connection with terrorism.

Duration of authorisation

46.–(1) An authorisation under section 44 has effect, subject to subsections (2) to (7), during the period—

  (a)   beginning at the time when the authorisation is given, and
  (b)   ending with a date or at a time specified in the authorisation.

(2)   The date or time specified under subsection (1)(b) must not occur after the end of the period of 28 days beginning with the day on which the authorisation is given.

(3)   The person who gives an authorisation shall inform the Secretary of State as soon as is reasonably practicable. . .

(6)   The Secretary of State may cancel an authorisation with effect from a specified time.

(7)   An authorisation may be renewed in writing by the person who gave it or by a person who could have given it; and subsections (1) to (6) shall apply as if a new authorisation were given on each occasion on which the authorisation is renewed.

Offences

47.–(1) A person commits an offence if he—

  (a)   fails to stop a vehicle when required to do so by a constable in the exercise of the power conferred by an authorisation under section 44(1);
  (b)   fails to stop when required to do so by a constable in the exercise of the power conferred by an authorisation under section 44(2);. . .

R (on the application of Gillan) v Commissioner of Police for the Metropolis
[2006] UKHL 12 (extracts)

House of Lords

The first appellant, Mr Gillan, came to London in September 2003 to protest peacefully against an arms fair being held at the ExCel Centre, Docklands, in east London. He was riding his bicycle near the Centre when he was stopped by two male police officers. They searched him and his rucksack and found nothing incriminating. They gave him a copy of the Stop/Search Form 5090 which recorded that he was stopped and searched under section 44 of the 2000 Act. The search was said to be for 'Articles concerned in terrorism'. The whole incident lasted about twenty minutes. The second appellant, Ms Quinton, was an accredited freelance journalist and went to the ExCel Centre in September 2003 to film the protests taking place against the arms fair. She was stopped by a female police officer near the Centre and asked to explain why she had appeared out of some bushes. Ms Quinton was wearing a photographer's jacket and carrying a small bag and a video camera. She explained she was a journalist and produced her press passes. The officer searched her, found nothing incriminating, and gave her a copy of Form 5090. Ms Quinton estimated that the search lasted for thirty minutes; the police five.

The appellants argued inter alia that the stops and searches had constituted a breach of Article 5, Sched 1 Human Rights Act; Article 5 provides: 1. Everyone has the right to liberty and security of the person. No one shall be deprived of his liberty save in the following cases and in accordance with a procedure prescribed by law: . . . (b) the lawful arrest or detention of a person for non-compliance with the lawful order of a court or in order to secure the fulfilment of any obligation prescribed by law . . . ". The other exceptions were deemed not relevant.

Lord Bingham, who gave the leading judgment, sought to determine firstly whether the stops and searches were 'a deprivation of liberty' in Art 5(1) terms. He found:

> the clearest exposition of principle by the Strasbourg court is to be found in *Guzzardi v Italy*,[35] an exposition repeatedly cited in later cases. In paragraphs 92–93 the Court observed: '92. The Court recalls that in proclaiming the 'right to liberty', paragraph 1 of Article 5 is contemplating the physical liberty of the person; its aim is to ensure that no one should be dispossessed of this liberty in an arbitrary fashion. As was pointed out by those appearing before the Court, the paragraph is not concerned with mere restrictions on liberty of movement; such restrictions are governed by Article 2 of Protocol No. 4 which has not been ratified by Italy. In order to determine whether someone has been 'deprived of his liberty' within the meaning of Article 5, the starting point must be his concrete situation and account must be taken of a whole range of criteria such as the type, duration, effects and manner of implementation of the measure in question . . . 93. The difference between deprivation of and restriction upon liberty is nonetheless merely one of degree or intensity, and not one of nature or substance.

[Lord Bingham found (in para 25) that there was no deprivation of liberty in Art 5(1) terms]:

---

35   (1980) 3 EHRR 333.

It is accordingly clear, as was held in *HL v United Kingdom*,[36] that in order to determine whether there has been a deprivation of liberty, the starting-point must be the concrete situation of the individual concerned and account must be taken of a whole range of factors arising in a particular case such as the type, duration, effects and manner of implementation of the measure in question. I would accept that when a person is stopped and searched under sections 44–45 the procedure has the features on which the appellants rely. On the other hand, the procedure will ordinarily be relatively brief. The person stopped will not be arrested, handcuffed, confined or removed to any different place. I do not think, in the absence of special circumstances, such a person should be regarded as being detained in the sense of confined or kept in custody, but more properly of being detained in the sense of kept from proceeding or kept waiting. There is no deprivation of liberty. That was regarded by the Court of Appeal as 'the better view' (para 46), and I agree.

[Article 8(1) was also viewed in a restrictive manner]: 'I am, however, doubtful whether an ordinary superficial search of the person can be said to show a lack of respect for private life. It is true that "private life" has been generously construed to embrace wide rights to personal autonomy. But it is clear Convention jurisprudence that intrusions must reach a certain level of seriousness to engage the operation of the Convention, which is, after all, concerned with human rights and fundamental freedoms, and I incline to the view that an ordinary superficial search of the person. . . can scarcely be said to reach that level'.[37]

[He did consider, conversely, the possibility that Art 8(1) might be engaged, but dealt with the issue of justification under Art 8(2) dismissively]:

'If, again, the lawfulness of the search is assumed at this stage, there can be little question that it is directed to objects recognised by article 8(2). The search must still be necessary in a democratic society, and so proportionate. But if the exercise of the power is duly authorised and confirmed, and if the power is exercised for the only purpose for which it may permissibly be exercised (ie. to search for articles of a kind which could be used in connection with terrorism: section 45(1)(a)), it would in my opinion be impossible to regard a proper exercise of the power, in accordance with Code A, as other than proportionate when seeking to counter the great danger of terrorism'.[38]

Notes

1. The concept of reasonable suspicion as the basis for the exercise of certain stop and search powers, including the PACE powers, is set out briefly in Code of Practice A on 'stop and search', para 2 (below). According to Code A there must normally be a concrete basis for this suspicion which relates to the particular person in question and could be evaluated by an objective observer. However, research in the area suggests that in practice there is a tendency to view reasonable suspicion as a flexible concept which may denote quite a low level of suspicion.[39]

   The case law is meagre, but suggests that an imprecise and inconsistent standard of 'reasonable

---

36   (2004) 40 EHRR 761, at para 89.

37   At [28].

38   At [29].

39   D Dixon (1989) 17 Int J Soc Law 185–206. See also D Mead (2009), n 42 below, at p 313 *et seq.*

suspicion' is maintained. In *Slade*,[40] the suspect was close to the house of a well known drug dealer; on noticing the officer, he put his hand in his pocket and smiled. This was found to give rise to reasonable suspicion. However, in *Black v DPP*,[41] the fact of visiting a well known drug dealer was found in itself to be insufficient as a basis for reasonable suspicion. In *Samuels v Commissioner of Police for the Metropolis*[42] S was ambling along, in a high crime area, with his hands in his pockets and did not tell the officer where he was going when asked. It was found that these facts could not give rise to reasonable suspicion. In *Francis*[43] the police purported to have reasonable suspicion to stop and search on the basis that the person in question was driving in an area known for drug use, with a passenger. The person had been stopped previously and her passenger at the time had been found to be in possession of drugs. Reasonable suspicion was not found to be established. This handful of cases clearly does very little to define the concept of reasonable suspicion, although it could be taken to indicate that extremely vague and broad bases for suspicion will not be sufficient.

2. Section 23 of the Misuse of Drugs Act 1971 provides a stop and search power which is frequently invoked. Under s 23, a constable may stop and search a person whom the constable has reasonable grounds to suspect is in possession of a controlled drug. Code A and ss 2 and 3 of PACE apply to this as they do to other statutory stop and search powers unless specific exceptions are made (see below).

3. A very broad power to stop vehicles arises under s 163 of the Road Traffic Act 1988 (RTA). Its ambit remains unclear. Section 163 provides a constable in uniform with power to stop vehicles, which may be unqualified as to purpose[44] and does not depend upon reasonable suspicion. Section 60 of the 1994 Act, as amended by s 8 of the Knives Act 1997 (extracted above), provides police officers with a further stop and search power which does not depend on showing reasonable suspicion of particular wrongdoing on the part of an individual. The powers under s 60 of the 1994 Act and ss 44–47 of the Terrorism Act 2000 (TA) arise in addition to the general PACE power to stop and search.

4. The Terrorism Act 2000 (TA), s 43 requires suspicion that a person is a terrorist (s 43) and the stop is to discover whether the person has in his/her possession anything which may constitute evidence that s/he is a terrorist. 'Being a terrorist' is not in itself an offence under the TA (unless the 'terrorist' group in question is also proscribed); therefore, this power is not dependent on suspicion of commission of an offence or of carrying prohibited articles.

5. Section 44 Terrorism Act 2000 (extracted above) provides a further stop and search power which is especially controversial since it is not based on reasonable suspicion once an authorisation has been given. Not only does the s 44 power arise independently of reasonable suspicion relating to objects suspected of being carried,[45] or of reasonable grounds to believe that acts of terrorism may occur in the area covered by the authorisation, but it is an offence in itself to refuse to comply with the search. (It is not an offence under PACE to refuse to comply with a s 1 search, or to obstruct it, although to do so would probably amount to the offence of obstructing a constable under s 89(2) of the Police Act 1996).[46] Authorisations apply to a specific area and are for a maximum of 28 days,

---

40   LEXIS CO/1678/96 (1996).

41   (1995) unreported, 11 May.

42   (1999) unreported, 3 March. See also news reports of the use of stop and search at the camp for climate action in 2008; in a judicial review challenge, the police admitted conducting illegal stops and searches: see *The Guardian* 12.1.10.

43   (1992) LEXIS CO/1434/91.

44   See HC Standing Committee E col 339 (13 December 1983).

45   Section 45(1)(b) provides that the powers 'may be exercised whether or not the constable has grounds for suspecting the presence of articles. . .' [connected with terrorism].

46   Reproducing the Police Act 1964, s 51(3).

but that period can be continually renewed. The authorisation has to stipulate both the area to which it applies and the period, not exceeding 28 days, for which it will remain in force. Under s 44(3) 'an authorisation under subsection (1) or (2) may be given only if the person giving it considers it expedient for the prevention of acts of terrorism'. The word 'expedient' is obviously significant—it is not necessary to demonstrate that terrorist acts are likely to occur or more likely to occur in the area covered by the authorisation than in other areas. Since the term 'expedient' is used, there is no requirement that the officer granting the authorisation should reasonably believe that it is *necessary* in order to prevent the commission of acts of terrorism. The term clearly connotes a less rigorous requirement.

If an authorisation is in force, an officer can stop any person or vehicle within the specified locality in order to look for articles which could be used for the commission of acts of terrorism. The area may be very large—it can include the whole of the police area in question, or part of it. The authorisation must be given by a senior police officer and confirmed by the Secretary of State within 48 hours of its being made, or it will cease to have effect. An authorisation confirmed by the Secretary of State can be renewed at the end of 28 days under s 46(7). Thus, theoretically, authorisations can be continually renewed, depending on the intervention of the Secretary of State. The tendency of this provision appears to be in effect to leave the authorisation power largely in police hands alone.

Section 44 remains a particularly controversial provision; it was used until 2009 to impose an authorisation to stop and search on the whole of London. During 2009 it was withdrawn to smaller selected areas in Central London—this appeared to be in the hope of avoiding an adverse ruling in the case of *Gillan v UK* (discussed below) which was about to be heard at Strasbourg. It has already been suggested that the reasonable suspicion requirement of a number of powers, including s 1 PACE, does not have a strong inhibitory effect. However, s 44 provides police officers with an even broader discretion, and clearly there is a danger that s 44 is being used in a racially or religiously discriminatory fashion. Sections 44–47 do not spell out what a police officer must have in mind before conducting a search; the power is therefore non-transparent and not based on objectively justifiable criteria.

6. There were also powers in s 16 and para 4(2) of Sched 5 to the PTA, which empowered the police and others to stop, question and search people about to enter or leave Great Britain or Northern Ireland, to determine whether they had been concerned in acts of terrorism. These powers were reproduced in Sched 7 to the TA and, again, they are not dependent on showing reasonable suspicion.

7. Since a number of these powers on their face allow for stop and search on subjective grounds, they may tend to be used disproportionately against the Muslim or black community. The same can also be said of the powers that demand reasonable suspicion since they appear in fact to be exercised on partially subjective grounds. Post-PACE research has consistently suggested that stop and search powers are used in a discriminatory fashion.[47] However, the amendments made to the Race Relations Act 1976 in 2000 by the Race Relations (Amendment) Act 2000 may be having some impact on police practice since discrimination on grounds of race in police operational decisions is now covered by the 1976 Act.

8. The Criminal Justice and Police Act 2001 (CJPA) introduced certain further seizure powers. The powers are significant since, *inter alia,* they allow the police officers to remove items from persons even where they are not certain that—apart from s 51—they have the power to do so. This power is

---

47 See Skogan, HO Research Study No 117, 1990, p 34; *Entry into the Criminal Justice System,* August 1998 and Statistics on Race and the Criminal Justice System, December 1998; MacPherson Report (1999), Cm 4262–1; Ministry of Justice *Statistics on Race and the Criminal Justice System 2006* (2007), Chapter 4.

'balanced' by the provisions of ss 52–61 which provide a number of safeguards. They are discussed below in relation to seizures from property since the same safeguards apply.

9. *Relevance and impact of the Human Rights Act.* Article 5 of the European Convention on Human Rights (ECHR), set out and discussed in Chapter 7,[48] provides a guarantee of 'liberty and security of person'. It appeared from the pre-2000 Strasbourg jurisprudence that the short period of detention represented by a stop and search might be sufficient to constitute a deprivation of liberty,[49] but it was found domestically in the House of Lords in *R (On the application of Gillan) v Commissioner of Police for the Metropolis*[50] that short detentions for stop and search purposes fall outside Art 5(1). The findings in *Gillan* left some leeway, but not very much, for finding that in different circumstances Art 5(1) could be engaged by a stop and search. Lord Bingham, having decided that the stop and search fell outside Art 5(1), went on to consider the question whether, had there been a deprivation of liberty, it would have been justified as within Art 5(1)(b). He found that the statutory regime and the authorisation itself were 'prescribed by law' and that 'the respondents bring themselves within the exception, for the public are in my opinion subject to a clear obligation not to obstruct a constable exercising a lawful power to stop and search for articles which could be used for terrorism and any detention is in order to secure effective fulfilment of that obligation'. Continual renewal of the authorisation was found acceptable under Art 5. Thus Art 5 was deemed inapplicable, but even if it had been found to be applicable, the stops and searches would have been justified. This judgment found not merely that the stops and searches were justified in Art 5 terms, it gave no encouragement to the raising of Art 5 arguments in relation to stop and search, in future. It is hard to see that Lord Bingham left the question of the engagement of Art 5(1) by stops and searches open since he found that there was no deprivation of liberty in unambiguous terms, but it could be suggested that since the case was considered and determined under Art 5(1)(b), that question could be re-raised in future.

Thus, a restrained view of the ambit of Art 5 was adopted which meant, it appeared, that s 44 stops and searches would be unlikely to fall within it. In contrast, when the *Gillan* case[51] reached Strasbourg, the European Court of Human Rights found: 'They were obliged to remain where they were and submit to the search and if they had refused they would have been liable to arrest, detention at a police station and criminal charges. This element of coercion is indicative of a deprivation of liberty within the meaning of Article 5(1).'[52] In the event, however, the Court did not finally have to determine that question in the light of its findings in relation to Art 8 of the Convention, discussed below. Strasbourg thus appeared to view the s 44 process as closer to the paradigm cases of deprivation of liberty—where the deprivation is total, as in arrest and detention—rather than the non-paradigm instances, of which *Guzzardi* is the leading example. The Court focused on the element of coercion which meant that the applicants had to remain on one spot, rather than on the range of criteria from *Guzzardi*. In *Gillan*, in considering the interference with the Art 8 guarantee, Lord Bingham also took a minimalist stance, marginalising Art 8. He appeared to be minded to carry out a minimalist audit of UK law against Convention law, finding that because the power was authorised and exercised for the right purpose, it was covered by Art 8(2); so there was no breach of the Convention.[53] Clearly, there was no real proportionality review.

---

48   At 304 *et seq.*

49   *X v Austria* (1979) 18 DR 154.

50   [2006] UKHL 12.

51   *Gillan and Quinton v UK* judgment of 12 Jan 2010, (Application No 4158/05).

52   The Court noted in support the example of *Foka v Turkey*, No 28940/09, §§ 74–79, 24 June 2008.

53   See further Fenwick and Phillipson (2006) n 1 above, Chapter 2, p 147.

10. The stance taken by Strasbourg in *Gillan and Quinton v UK*[54] as regards Art 8 could hardly present a stronger contrast to the stance of the House of Lords. Strasbourg found, not only that Art 8 had been breached but in so doing found—strikingly, not to say astonishingly—that ss 44–47 TA failed the 'prescribed by law' test. That was an unprecedented move in relation to a modern statute—the first time it had happened in the UK's history of engagement with the ECHR. The Court began by finding that Art 8(1) was engaged by the use of s 44: 'The individual can be stopped anywhere and at any time, without notice and without any choice as to whether or not to submit to a search.' That was found to constitute an interference with respect for private life under Art 8(1). The Court then turned to the question whether the interference was in accordance with the law and necessary in a democratic society under Art 8(2). Upholding the claimants' contention, the Strasbourg judges found that the powers vested in the police under ss 44–47 of the Act could not be regarded as 'in accordance with the law' because the power dispensed with the condition of reasonable suspicion: 'The powers of authorisation and confirmation as well as those of stop and search under sections 44 and 45 of the 2000 Act are neither sufficiently circumscribed nor subject to adequate legal safeguards against abuse,' the court ruled. The judges pointed, in particular, to the breadth of the discretion conferred on the individual police officer whose decision to stop somebody could be 'based exclusively on the 'hunch' or 'professional intuition' of the officer concerned'. The Court continued: 'There is a clear risk of arbitrariness in the grant of such a broad discretion to the police officer.'

   The UK Government is currently appealing the case to the Grand Chamber, but it is probable, especially as it was the easily satisfied 'in accordance with the law' test that was not met, that ultimately s 44 will have to be significantly modified to connect it much more closely with suspicion of terrorist activity. In *Gillan* Strasbourg showed a hitherto rare insistence upon compliance with real standards of 'prescribed by law'; it can be viewed as an example of expansive judicial reasoning in relation to ECHR principles. In demanding alignment of UK anti-terrorism stop and search powers with Art 8 standards, the decision offered a much-needed check upon the excessively broad police discretion provided by s 44. *Gillan* provides an important instance in which Strasbourg upheld higher human rights standards than the domestic judiciary, under the HRA, had done.

11. Under Art 5 a deprivation of liberty can occur only on a basis of law[55] and in certain specified circumstances, including, under Art 5(1)(b), the detention of a person in order to secure the fulfilment of any obligation prescribed by law and, under Art 5(1)(c), the lawful detention of a person effected for the purpose of bringing him before the competent legal authority on reasonable suspicion of having committed an offence. Both these provisions may cover temporary detention for the purposes of a search, but whether they would be required to do so would depend on whether if Art 5 was engaged at all. *Gillan v UK* (above) would suggest that stop and search probably engages Art 5.

12. Article 5(1)(b) has received a restrictive interpretation at Strasbourg. In *McVeigh, O'Neill and Evans v UK*[56] a requirement to submit to an examination on arrival in the UK was found not to violate Art 5(1)(b) since it was sufficiently specific and concrete, but it was emphasised that this was found on the basis that the obligation in question only arose in limited circumstances and had a limited purpose—to combat terrorism. In *Lawless*,[57] it was found that a specific and concrete obligation

---

54   For discussion, see D Mead, *The New Law of Peaceful Protest* (2009) at p 380.

55   See Art 5(1) p 304, above.

56   (1981) 5 EHRR 71.

57   (1961) 1 EHRR 15.

must be identified; once it has been, detention can in principle be used to secure its fulfilment. Following *Gillan*, it is clear that the term 'obligation' applies to the current statutory provisions. The requirements are to submit to a search, and, apart from the power under s 163 of the Road Traffic Act 1988, to remain under police detention for the period of time necessary to allow it to be carried out.[58] Under the interpretation in *Lawless,* following *Gillan,* the PACE, Misuse of Drugs Act, CJPOA and TA stop and search provisions appear on their face to fall within Art 5(1)(b). The CJPOA and s 44 TA powers are in very doubtful conformity with Art 5 and may not fall within Art 5(1)(b) due to the lack of specificity in the obligation imposed. S 60 CJPOA, after *Gillian*, may not be compatible with Art 8.

13. The PACE powers and the Misuse of Drugs Act power appear also to fall within Art 5(1)(c), which requires reasonable suspicion of the commission of an *offence*. This exception may not apply to the other powers, including s 43 of the TA, since no such suspicion is required. However, even if certain of the powers or their exercise in particular instances may not be covered by Art 5(1)(c), they would be likely, as discussed, to be covered by Art 5(1)(b).

14. The use of force in order to carry out a stop and search is permitted under s 117 of PACE, which provides: 'the officer may use reasonable force, if necessary, in the exercise of the [PACE] power.' The TA provides an equivalent provision in s 114(2). But, under Art 3, the use of force must be strictly in proportion to the conduct of the detainee.

Code of Practice A (revised 2008)

The Code applies to statutory powers to search a person or vehicle without first making an arrest.

1.5 An officer must not search a person, even with his or her consent, where no power to search is applicable. Even where a person is prepared to submit to a search voluntarily, the person must not be searched unless the necessary legal power exists, and the search must be in accordance with the relevant power and the provisions of this Code.

Searches requiring reasonable grounds for suspicion

2.2 Reasonable grounds for suspicion depend on the circumstances in each case. There must be an objective basis for that suspicion based on facts, information, and/or intelligence which are relevant to the likelihood of finding an article of a certain kind or, in the case of searches under section 43 of the Terrorism Act 2000, to the likelihood that the person is a terrorist. Reasonable suspicion can never be supported on the basis of personal factors. It must rely on intelligence or information about, or some specific behaviour by, the person concerned. For example, other than in a witness description of a suspect, a person's race, age, appearance, or the fact that the person is known to have a previous conviction, cannot be used alone or in combination with each other, or in combination with any other factor, as the reason for searching that person. Reasonable suspicion cannot be based on generalisations or stereotypical images of certain groups or categories of people as more likely to be involved in criminal activity. A person's religion cannot be considered as reasonable grounds for suspicion and should never be considered as a reason to stop or stop and search an individual.

2.3 Reasonable suspicion can sometimes exist without specific information or intelligence and on the basis of the behaviour of a person. . .

2.4 However, reasonable suspicion should normally be linked to accurate and current intelligence or information. . .

---

58   See *McVeigh, O'Neill and Evans v UK* (1981) 5 EHRR 71; the obligation imposed was a requirement to 'submit to examination'.

2.6 Where there is reliable information or intelligence that members of a particular group or gang habitually carry knives unlawfully or weapons or controlled drugs and wear a distinctive item of clothing or other means of identification to indicate their membership of the group or gang that distinctive item of clothing or other means of identification may provide reasonable grounds to stop and search a person.

Notes

1. All the stop and search powers mentioned that are not contained in PACE are still subject to the same procedural requirements under ss 2 and 3 of PACE (echoed in para 3.8 and para 4 of Code A) as those relating to the powers under s 1 of PACE. Information giving and record keeping is intended to ensure that officers do not overuse the stop and search powers, partly because it means that the citizen can make a complaint later, and partly because the police station will have a record of the number of stops being carried out.

2. The 2008 version of Code A (para 1.5) continues to forbid consensual searches: officers cannot ask members of the public to consent to a search where no power to search exists. Para 1.5 reflects the concern that voluntary contacts can have a sinister side: some people might 'consent' to a search in the sense of offering no resistance to it due to uncertainty as to the basis or extent of the police power in question.[59]

3. Failures to follow the procedural requirements under ss 2 and 3 of PACE may affect the legality of the search. There is no provision under the TA, PACE or Code A to the effect that if the procedural requirements are not complied with, the search will be unlawful, but if it is unlawful, tortious liability will be incurred since a search will normally amount to trespass to the person unless there is legal authority for it. A number of due process requirements are contained only in Code A[60] and therefore their breach cannot give rise to civil liability.[61] But breach of certain of the *statutory* procedural requirements will render searches unlawful, as will breach of the statutory powers. It has been held that a failure to make a written record of the search in breach of s 3 will not render it unlawful,[62] whereas a failure to give the grounds for it will do so, following *R v Fenelley*[63] and *Samuel v Commissioner of Police for the Metropolis*,[64] as will a failure to comply with the duties to provide identification under s 2(3), following *Osman v Director of Public Prosecutions*.[65]

4. The PACE and TA Codes are admissible in evidence.[66] It is possible for a defendant who claims that a search was conducted improperly or unlawfully to seek the limited form of redress represented by exclusion of evidence which has been obtained as a result of a breach of PACE or Code A. This possibility is discussed below (at pp 1228–1210). In practice this argument is unlikely to succeed.

---

59   See D Dixon, 'Consent and the Legal Regulation of Policing' (1990) Int J Soc Law 245–362.

60   Code A made under PACE 1984, s 66 and the TA Code made under the TA, ss 96 and 98 in respect of Northern Ireland and the Code introduced under Sched 14 in respect of the UK.

61   Under PACE 1984, s 67(10). The TA Codes will have the same status as the PACE Codes; under Sched 14, para 6(2) 'The failure by an officer to observe a provision of a code shall not of itself make him liable to criminal or civil proceedings', but under para 6(3) 'A code (a) shall be admissible in evidence in criminal and civil proceedings, and (b) shall be taken into account by a court or tribunal in any case in which it appears to the court or tribunal to be relevant'.

62   *Basher v DPP* (1993) unreported, 2 March.

63   [1989] Crim LR 142.

64   (1999) unreported, 3 March.

65   (1999) 163 JP 275; *The Times*, 29 September 1999.

66   PACE 1984, s 67(11); TA 2000, Sched 14, para 6(3).

Questions

❶   If, despite para 1.5 Code A, police officers stop and search a person on a consensual basis, without following the PACE procedure under ss 2 and 3, and find an article for which they would have been empowered to search under s 1 of PACE, what redress would the subject of the search have?

❷   Bearing *Gillan v UK* in mind, consider why the Code A safeguards for suspects were found unable to maintain, in practice, a balance between suspects' Art 8 rights and the increased police powers under s 44 TA? Would the same arguments apply to s 60 CJPOA?

POWERS OF ENTRY TO PREMISES, SEARCH AND SEIZURE[67]

In America, the Fourth Amendment to the Constitution guarantees freedom from unreasonable search and seizure, thus recognising the invasion of privacy which a search of premises represents. A search without a warrant will normally[68] be unreasonable; therefore an independent check is usually available on the search power. In contrast, the common law in Britain, despite some rulings asserting the importance of protecting the citizen from the invasion of private property,[69] allowed search and seizure on wide grounds, going beyond those authorised by statute.[70] Thus, the common law did not provide full protection for the citizen and PACE went some way towards remedying this by placing powers of entry and seizure on a clearer basis and ensuring that the person whose premises are searched understands the basis of the search and can complain as to its conduct if necessary.

Entry without warrant under the Police and Criminal Evidence Act 1984 (as amended)

Entry and search after arrest

18.–(1) Subject to the following provisions of this section, a constable may enter and search any premises occupied or controlled by a person who is under arrest for an indictable offence, if he has reasonable grounds for suspecting that there is on the premises evidence other than items subject to legal privilege, that relates—

(a)   to that offence; or

(b)   to some other indictable offence which is connected with or similar to that offence.

---

67   See generally RTH Stone, *Entry, Search and Seizure* (1989); SH Bailey, N Taylor, *Bailey, Harris and Jones: Civil Liberties: Cases and Materials,* 6th edn (2009), pp 172–96, R Clayton and H Tomlinson, *Civil Actions Against the Police,* 3rd edn (2005), Chapter 7.

68   *Coolidge v New Hampshire* 403 US 443 (1973); exception accepted where evidence might otherwise be destroyed.

69   See, e.g. rulings in *Entick v Carrington* (1765) 19 St Tr 1029; *Morris v Beardmore* [1981] AC 446.

70   The ruling in *Ghani v Jones* [1970] 1 QB 693 authorised seizure of a wide range of material once officers were lawfully on premises. The ruling in *Thomas v Sawkins* [1935] 2 KB 249 allowed a wide power to enter premises to prevent crime.

(2)   A constable may seize and retain anything for which he may search under sub-section (1) above. . . .

Search upon arrest

. . .

32.–(2) Subject to subsections (3) to (5) below, a constable shall also have power in any such case—

. . .

(b)   if the offence for which he was arrested is an indictable offence, to enter and search any premises in which he was when arrested or immediately before he was arrested for evidence relating to the offence . . . .

(6)   A constable may not search premises in the exercise of the power conferred by subsection (2)(b) above unless he has reasonable grounds for believing that there is evidence for which a search is permitted under that paragraph on the premises.

Note

If the requirements of the s18 power to enter and search without a warrant appear not to be satisfied, a search warrant would have to be obtained unless the provisions of s 32 applied.

Entry to premises under a search warrant or written authority under the Police and Criminal Evidence Act 1984

Police Powers

Part II—Powers of entry, search and seizure

8.–(1) If on an application made by a constable a justice of the peace is satisfied that there are reasonable grounds for believing—

(a)   that an indictable offence has been committed; and
(b)   that there is material on premises. . .which is likely to be of substantial value. . .to the investigation of the offence; and
(c)   that the material is likely to be relevant evidence; and
(d)   that it does not consist of or include items subject to legal privilege, excluded material or special procedure material; and
(e)   that any of the conditions specified in subsection (3) below applies, he may issue a warrant authorising a constable to enter and search the premises.

(2)   A constable may seize and retain anything for which a search has been authorised under subsection (1) above.

(3)   The conditions mentioned in subsection (1)(e) above are—

(a)   that it is not practicable to communicate with any person entitled to grant entry to the premises;
(b)   . . .it is not practicable to communicate with any person entitled to grant access to the evidence;
(c)   that entry to the premises will not be granted unless a warrant is produced;

(d)   that the purpose of a search may be frustrated or seriously prejudiced unless a constable arriving at the premises can secure immediate entry to them.

Search warrants—safeguards

15.(2)   Where a constable applies for any such warrant, it shall be his duty—

(a)   to state—

(i)   the ground on which he makes the application; and
(ii)   the enactment under which the warrant would be issued;

2A If the application relates to one or more sets of premises specified in the application, each set of premises which it is desired to enter and search; and

(c)   to identify, so far as is practicable, the articles or persons to be sought. . .

(5)   A warrant shall authorise an entry on one occasion only [unless it specifies that it authorises multiple entries. . . .]

Execution of warrants

16.–(5) . . .the constable—

(a)   shall identify himself to the occupier and, if not in uniform, shall produce to him documentary evidence that he is a constable;
(b)   shall produce the warrant to him; and
(c)   shall supply him with a copy of it. . . .

Terrorism Act 2000, as amended

Schedule 5—Terrorist Investigations: Information

Searches

1.–(1)   A constable may apply to a justice of the peace for the issue of a warrant under this paragraph for the purposes of a terrorist investigation.

(2)   A warrant under this paragraph shall authorise any constable—

(a)   to enter the premises specified in the warrant,
(b)   to search the premises and any person found there, and
(c)   to seize and retain any relevant material which is found on a search under paragraph (b).

(3)   For the purpose of sub-paragraph (2)(c) material is relevant if the constable has reasonable grounds for believing that—

(a)   it is likely to be of substantial value, whether by itself or together with other material, to a terrorist investigation, and
(b)   it must be seized in order to prevent it from being concealed, lost, damaged, altered or destroyed.

    (4)   A warrant under this paragraph shall not authorise—

        (a)   the seizure and retention of items subject to legal privilege. . .

    (5)   Subject to paragraph 2, a justice may grant an application under this paragraph if satisfied—

        (a)   that the warrant is sought for the purposes of a terrorist investigation,
        (b)   that there are reasonable grounds for believing that there is material on premises specified in the application which is likely to be of substantial value, whether by itself or together with other material, to a terrorist investigation and which does not consist of or include excepted material (within the meaning of paragraph 4 below), and

    . . .

    (5)   An authorisation under this paragraph shall not authorise—

        (a)   the seizure and retention of items subject to legal privilege. . .

    (7)   A person commits an offence if he wilfully obstructs a search under this paragraph.

Notes
1. The PACE search warrant provisions provide a scheme which is dependent on magistrates observing its requirements. Research suggests that in practice some magistrates make little or no attempt to ascertain whether the information a warrant contains may be relied upon, while magistrates who do take a rigorous approach to the procedure and refuse to grant warrants may not be approached again.[71]
2. Searching of premises other than under ss 17 and 18 PACE can also occur if a search warrant is issued under s 8 of PACE, as amended, by a magistrate, or if a warrant is applied for under other statutory powers, including post-PACE powers. Applications for all warrants by police officers, and the execution of the warrant must comply with the procedures set out in ss 15 and 16 of PACE. The application for the warrant must be supported, under s 15(3), by an 'Information' in writing. It must specify the enactment under which it is issued, the premises to be searched[72] and the articles or persons to be sought (s 15(6)). Section 8(1C), inserted by s 113(4) of the Serious and Organised Crime Act 2005 (SOCA), provides that multiple entry can be authorised. Section 15(5A), also introduced in 2005 by SOCA, provides that if the warrant authorises multiple entry it must specify whether the multiple entries are limited to a specified maximum or unlimited. Previously, the warrant authorised entry to premises on one occasion only. The 'all premises' warrant was introduced on the basis that the nature of crime and of technology have changed and 'moved on significantly since the introduction of PACE. Evidence and the proceeds of crime can be moved very quickly between locations to thwart investigations'.[73]
3. Section 16 governs the procedure to be followed in executing the warrant. The warrant must be produced to the occupier (although it seems that this need not be at the time of entry if

---

71   See D Dixon (1991) 141 NLJ 1586.

72   *Southwestern Magistrates' Court ex parte Cofie* [1997] 1 WLR 885.

73   The 2004 Consultation Paper *Modernising Police Powers to Meet Community Needs.*

impracticable in the circumstances)[74] under s 16(5)(b) and (c) and must identify the articles to be sought, although once the officer is on the premises, other articles may be seized under s 19 if they appear to relate to any other offence. The warrant does not necessarily allow for a general search of the premises[75] since the search can only be for the purpose for which the warrant was issued (s 16(8)). The extensiveness of the search depends upon that purpose.

Under s 16, the copy of the warrant issued to the subject of the search must identify the articles or persons sought and the offence suspected. The courts seem prepared to take a strict view of the importance of complying with this safeguard. In *Chief Constable of Lancashire ex parte Parker and McGrath*[76] police officers conducted a search of the applicant's premises in the execution of a search warrant issued under s 8 of PACE. However, after the warrant had been signed by the judge, the police detached part of it and reattached it to the other original documents. In purported compliance with s 16 of PACE, the police produced all these documents to the applicants. Thus, the police did not produce the whole of the original warrant and moreover, did not supply one of the documents constituting the warrant. The applicants applied for judicial review of both the issue and the execution of the warrants. It was determined that s 16(5)(b) of PACE had been breached in that the warrant produced to the applicants was not the original warrant as seen and approved by the judge and a declaration was granted to that effect. The police had admitted that there was a breach of the requirement under s 16(5)(c) that a copy of the warrant should be supplied to the occupier of the premises.

4. A warrant under s 8 will only be issued if there are reasonable grounds for believing that an indictable offence has been committed and where the material is likely to be of substantial value to the investigation of the offence and which will be admissible evidence at trial. A large number of other statutes also provide for the issuing of warrants to the police and to other public officials. Special provisions arise, *inter alia*, under s 27 of the Drug Trafficking Act 1994, s 2(4) of the Criminal Justice Act 1987 (in relation to serious fraud) and, as discussed below, in relation to the security and intelligence services under the Intelligence Services Act 1994. Section 8 covers 'all premises' searches and under certain circumstances, and as indicated, under changes introduced by s 113 Serious and Organised Crime Act 2005, multiple entries to the same premises are possible.

5. As revised, Code of Practice B made under PACE provides for an increase in the amount of information to be conveyed to owners of property to be searched by use of a standard form, the Notice of Powers and Rights. It covers certain information, including specification of the type of search in question, a summary of the powers of search and seizure arising under PACE and the rights of the subjects of searches. This notice must normally be given to the subject of the search before it begins, but under para 6 need not be if is reasonably believed that to do so would lead to frustration of the object of the search or danger to the police officers concerned, or to others.

Powers of seizure and retention under the Police and Criminal Evidence Act 1984

General power of seizure
19.–(2) The constable may seize anything which is on the premises if he has reasonable grounds for believing—

---

74   *Longman* [1988] 1 WLR 619, CA; for comment, see R Stevens, *Justice of the Peace* (1988), p 551.

75   See *Chief Constable of Warwick Constabulary ex parte Fitzpatrick* [1999] 1 WLR 564.

76   (1992) 142 NLJ 635.

(a)   that it has been obtained in consequence of the commission of an offence; and

(b)   that it is necessary to seize it in order to prevent it being concealed, lost, damaged, altered or destroyed.

(3)   The constable may seize anything which is on the premises if he has reasonable grounds for believing—

(a)   that it is evidence in relation to an offence which he is investigating or any other offence; and

(b)   that it is necessary to seize it in order to prevent the evidence being concealed, lost, altered or destroyed. . . .

Criminal Justice and Police Act 2001

Property seized by constables etc.

56.–(1) The retention of [seized property]—

. . .is authorised by this section if the property falls within subsection (2) or (3).

(2)   Property falls within this subsection to the extent that there are reasonable grounds for believing—

(a)   that it is property obtained in consequence of the commission of an offence; and

(b)   that it is necessary for it to be retained in order to prevent its being concealed, lost, damaged, altered or destroyed.

(3)   Property falls within this subsection to the extent that there are reasonable grounds for believing—

(a)   that it is evidence in relation to any offence; and

(b)   that it is necessary for it to be retained in order to prevent its being concealed, lost, altered or destroyed.

Notes

1.   Under s 22(1) of PACE, anything which has been so seized may be retained 'so long as is necessary in all the circumstances'. It was made clear in *R v Chief Constable of Lancashire ex p Parker and McGrath*[77] that the above provisions assume that the search itself is lawful; in other words, material seized during an unlawful search cannot be retained and if it is, an action for trespass to goods can arise.

2.   Under s 9 of PACE, excluded or special procedure material or material covered by legal privilege cannot be seized during a search not under warrant, and it is exempt from the s 8 search warrant procedure under s 8(1). However, the police may gain access to excluded or special procedure material (not legally privileged material) by making an application to a circuit judge in accordance with Sched 1 or, in the case of special procedure material only, to a magistrate for a search warrant. Access to excluded material may only be granted where it could have been obtained under the previous law relating to such material.

---

77   [1993] 2 WLR 428.

3. The ruling in *R v Guildhall Magistrates' Court ex parte Primlaks Holdings Co (Panama) Limited*[78] made it clear that a magistrate must satisfy him or herself that there were reasonable grounds for believing that the items covered by the warrant did not include material subject to the special protection. The magistrates had issued search warrants authorising the search of two solicitors' firms. Judicial review of the magistrates' decision to issue a warrant was successfully sought; it was found that the magistrate had merely accepted the police officer's view that s 8(1) was satisfied rather than independently considering the matter.

4. The strongest protection extends to items subject to legal privilege, since they cannot be searched for or seized by police officers and, therefore, the meaning of 'legal privilege' is crucial. Under s 10, it will cover communications between client and solicitor connected with giving advice or with legal proceedings. However, if items are held with the intention of furthering a criminal purpose they will not, under s 10(2), attract legal privilege. The House of Lords in *R v Central Criminal Court ex parte Francis and Francis*[79] found that material which figures in the criminal intentions of persons other than solicitor or client will not be privileged. A judge must give full consideration to the question whether particular documents have lost legal privilege.[80] This interpretation of s 10(2) was adopted on the basis that, otherwise, the efforts of the police in detecting crime might be hampered, but it may be argued that it gives insufficient weight to the need to protect the special relationship between solicitor and client and, as argued below, may be vulnerable to challenge under the HRA.

Impact of the Human Rights Act

In the following two cases, the European Court of Human Rights considered the compatibility of searches of property with the Convention rights.

Camenzind v Switzerland (1999) 28 EHRR 458 (extracts)

[As to the question whether there was an interference with the right to respect for the home under Art 8(1) in respect of the search. . .]
. . . the search of the room occupied by the applicant amounted to an interference, within the meaning of Article 8, with his right to respect for his home.

It accordingly has to be determined whether the interference was justified under paragraph 2 of Article 8, in other words whether it was 'in accordance with the law', pursued one or more of the legitimate aims set out in that paragraph and was 'necessary in a democratic society' to achieve the aim or aims in question.

Whether the interference was justified: 1 'In accordance with the law'. The Court reiterates that the expression 'in accordance with the law', within the meaning of Article 8(2) of the Convention, requires that the impugned measure should have some basis in domestic law and that the law in question should be accessible to the person concerned—who must moreover be able to foresee its consequences for him—and compatible with the rule of law. [FN35] In the instant case it notes, [the relevant offence under section 42 of the Federal Act of 1922]. . . The Court further notes. . .that the Act contains safeguards against

---

78   [1989] 2 WLR 841.

79   [1989] AC 346. For comment see Stevenson (1989) Law Soc Gazette, 1 February, p 26.

80   *R v Southampton Crown Court ex parte J and P* [1993] Crim LR 962.

arbitrary interference by the authorities with the right to respect for the home. . . the Court accepts that the measure complained of was 'in accordance with the law'.

2 Legitimate aim the search. . .pursued. . .the 'prevention of disorder or crime'.

3 'Necessary in a democratic society'. Under the Court's settled case law, the notion of 'necessity' implies that the interference corresponds to a pressing social need and, in particular, that it is proportionate to the legitimate aim pursued; in determining whether an interference is 'necessary in a democratic society', the Court will take into account that a margin of appreciation is left to the Contracting States.

If individuals are to be protected from arbitrary interference by the authorities with the rights guaranteed under Article 8, a legal framework and very strict limits on such powers are called for. Secondly, the Court must consider the particular circumstances of each case in order to determine whether, in the concrete case, the interference in question was proportionate to the aim pursued.

With regard to the safeguards provided by Swiss law, the Court notes that. . .a search may, subject to exceptions, only be effected under a written warrant. . . Searches can only be carried out in 'dwellings and other premises. . .if objects or valuables liable to seizure or evidence of the commission of an offence are to be found there' they cannot be conducted on Sundays, public holidays or at night 'except in important cases or where there is imminent danger'. At the beginning of a search the investigating official must produce evidence of identity and inform the occupier of the premises of the purpose of the search. . . In principle, there will also be a public officer present to ensure that '[the search] does not deviate from its purpose'. A record of the search is drawn up immediately. . . . Furthermore, searches for documents are subject to special restrictions. In addition, suspects are entitled, whatever the circumstances, to representation; anyone affected by an 'investigative measure' who has 'an interest worthy of protection in having the measure. . .quashed or varied' may complain to the Indictment Division of the Federal Court.

Having regard to the safeguards provided by Swiss legislation and especially to the limited scope of the search, the Court accepts that the interference with the applicant's right to respect for his home can be considered to have been proportionate to the aim pursued and thus 'necessary in a democratic society' within the meaning of Article 8. Consequently, there has not been a violation of that provision.

Özgür Gündem v Turkey (2001) 31 EHRR 49 (extracts)

This part of the ruling concerned the police operation at the Özgür Gündem (a newspaper) premises in Istanbul on 10 December 1993.

The Court finds that the operation, which resulted in newspaper production being disrupted for two days, constituted a serious interference with the applicants' freedom of expression. It accepts that the operation was conducted according to a procedure 'prescribed by law' for the purpose of preventing crime and disorder within the meaning of the second paragraph of Article 10. It does not, however, find that a measure of such dimension was proportionate to this aim. No justification has been provided for the seizure of the newspaper's archives, documentation and library. Nor has the Court received an explanation for the blanket apprehension of every person found on the newspaper's premises. . . .

As stated in the Commission's report, the necessity for any restriction in the exercise of freedom of expression must be convincingly established. The Court concludes that the search operation, as conducted by the authorities, has not been shown to be necessary, in a democratic society, for the implementation of any legitimate aim.

R (Rottman) v Commissioner of Police of the Metropolis
[2002] 2 WLR 1315 (extracts)

In 2000, a provisional warrant for the claimant's arrest was issued under s 8(1)(b) of the Extradition Act 1989. The claimant was arrested; thereafter the arresting officers entered and searched his house and removed items belonging to the claimant which they suspected might hold evidence of the alleged offences or proceeds of the offences, having acted in purported reliance on s 18 in Part II of PACE and in the belief that they had in any event power under the common law to search the premises of a suspect following his arrest on an extradition warrant. The claimant applied to the Divisional Court for an order directed to the Commissioner of Police of the Metropolis requiring the delivery up of all items seized and a declaration that the entry and search had been unlawful and in breach of the claimant's rights under Art 8 of the European Convention on Human Rights as scheduled to the Human Rights Act 1998. The Divisional Court held that the statutory powers of entry, search and seizure without a warrant in Part II of PACE did not extend to extradition cases, that any powers of search under the common law had been extinguished when the 1984 Act came into force and that accordingly the search and seizure had been unlawful and in violation of the claimant's rights under Art 8.

Lord Hutton: [having referred to and approved *Ghani v Jones* [1970] 1 QB 693]. . .if the police have power at common law to search the person of the individual whom they have arrested under a warrant issued pursuant to section 8(1)(b) PACE, it seems contrary to common sense to hold that they do not have power to seize material evidence present in the room where he is arrested and also to search other rooms in his house and seize material evidence found in them. Accordingly I would hold that the common law power of search and seizure after the execution of a warrant of arrest issued pursuant to section 8(1)(b) was not extinguished by PACE and that the police officers were entitled to exercise that power after the arrest of the respondent.

80 I am unable to accept the respondent's submission that the common law power of search and seizure after arrest constitutes a violation of his rights under article 8. The search and seizure was in accordance with the law which was clearly stated by Lloyd LJ in Osman [1990] 1 WLR 277. . . . The power has the legitimate aim in a democratic society of preventing crime, and is necessary in order to prevent the disappearance of material evidence after the arrest of a suspect. The power is proportionate to that aim because it is subject to the safeguards that it can only be exercised after a warrant of arrest has been issued by a magistrate or a justice of the peace in respect of an extradition crime and where the evidence placed before him would, in his opinion, justify the issue of a warrant for the arrest of a person accused of a similar domestic offence.

81 Accordingly I would answer the certified question 'Yes, a police officer who has arrested a person in or on his premises pursuant to a warrant of arrest issued under section 8 of the Extradition Act 1989 has power to search those premises for, and to seize, any goods or documents which he reasonably believes to be material evidence in relation to the extradition crime in respect of which the warrant was issued.' I would allow the appeal and would set aside the order of the Divisional Court.

The Lords agreed to allow the appeal, Lord Hope dissenting.

Notes

1. *Impact of the HRA.* As discussed in Chapter 7, Article 8(1) of the ECHR provides a right to respect for private and family life, the home and correspondence, subject to a number of exceptions enumerated in para 2.[81] As *Camenzind v Switzerland* (above) indicates, the European Court of Human Rights has found that entry, search and seizure can create interferences with all the Article 8 guarantees, apart from that of the right to respect for family life.[82] Search for and seizure of documents is covered by the term 'correspondence' and the documents do not have to be personal in nature.[83] Such interferences can be justified only if they are in accordance with the law (Art 8(2)). This requirement covers not only the existence of national law, but its quality.[84] The statutory and common law powers probably meet this requirement[85] and have the legitimate aim of preventing crime or protecting national security.

   Any interference with the Art 8(1) guarantees must also 'correspond to a pressing social need and, in particular, [must be] proportionate to the legitimate aim pursued'.[86] It was found in the context of intercept warrants in *Klass v FRG*[87] that judicial or administrative authority for warrants would provide a degree of independent oversight: sufficient safeguards against abuse were available. It could be argued that the arrangements whereby magistrates issue search warrants might fail to meet this requirement since, although in appearance an independent judicial check is available before the event, the 'check' may be almost a formality in reality.[88] As mentioned above, research suggests that in practice, some magistrates make little real attempt to ascertain whether the information a warrant contains should be relied upon.[89] Therefore, a breach of Art 8 might be established in respect of the practice of certain magistrates. It may be noted, however, that this argument failed in the Scottish case of *Birse v HM Advocate*.[90] *Gillan v UK* may signal the need, from 2010, onwards, to apply Art 8 with greater rigour.

2. A search of premises that is authorised but goes beyond the authorisation is likely to be viewed as disproportionate to the legitimate aim pursued. As indicated above, in *Camenzind v Switzerland*,[91] there were specific procedures in place and the search was of a limited scope: it was found, therefore, to be proportionate to the aim pursued.

3. Article 8 ECHR is able to influence this search and seizure scheme due to the use of arguments under s 7(1)(b) of the HRA, either raised in criminal proceedings, in civil actions against the police for trespass, trespass to goods or for conversion, or as freestanding actions under s 7(1)(a) of the

---

81 See Chapter 7, pp 314–328.

82 See also *Funke v France* (1993) 16 EHRR 297; *Mialhe v France* (1993) 16 EHRR 332.

83 See *Niemietz v Germany*, Series A No 251–B; (1992) 16 EHRR 97.

84 *Kopp v Switzerland* (1999) 27 EHRR 91, paras 70–71. See also *Gillan v UK*, p 1156, above.

85 In *McLeod v UK* (1998) 27 EHRR 493 powers to enter to prevent a breach of the peace were found to meet this requirement (paras 38–45).

86 *Olsson v Sweden*, Series A No 130; (1988) 11 EHRR 259, para 67.

87 (1978) 2 EHRR 214.

88 See R Clayton and H Tomlinson, *The Law of Human Rights*, 1st edn (2000), p 863.

89 See further *Bailey, Harris* and *Jones* (2009), n 1 above at pp 184–185.

90 (2000) unreported, 13 April.

91 (1997) 28 EHRR 458.

HRA. The PACE and CJPA schemes are subject to an Art 8-friendly interpretation, taking the Convention jurisprudence above into account, under s 3 of the HRA.

4. *R (Rottman) v Commissioner of Police of the Metropolis* confirms that broad common law powers can continue to supplement the statutory ones and that domestic judges consider such a position to be entirely compatible with Article 8.

POWERS OF ARREST AND DETENTION[92]

Introduction

Any arrest represents a serious curtailment of liberty; therefore, use of the arrest power requires careful regulation. An arrest is seen as *prima facie* illegal necessitating justification under a specific legal power. If an arrest is effected where no arrest power arises, a civil action for false imprisonment will lie. The powers are contained largely in PACE but common law powers remain, while some statutes create a specific power of arrest which may overlap with the PACE powers. All the powers must now be exercised within the constraints created by Art 5 ECHR given effect in domestic law under the HRA. As noted above in relation to stop and search, under Art 5 a deprivation of liberty can occur only on a basis of law[93] and in certain specified circumstances, including, under Art 5(1)(b), the detention of a person in order to secure the fulfilment of any obligation prescribed by law and, under Art 5(1)(c), the lawful detention of a person effected for the purpose of bringing him before 'the competent legal authority on reasonable suspicion of having committed an offence'.

The due process and crime control views of arrest and detention are diametrically opposed. Under the due process model, arrest should be based on strong suspicion that the individual has committed a specific offence, since arrest and subsequent detention represent a severe infringement of individual liberty. Under the crime control model, arrest and detention need not be sanctioned merely in relation to specific offences, but should be both an investigative tool and a means of asserting police authority over persons with a criminal record or of doubtful character, with a view to creating a general deterrent effect. Under this model, reasonable suspicion is viewed as a needless irrelevancy, an inhibitory rule standing in the way of an important police function.

PACE has not affected the power to arrest which arises at common law for breach of the peace.[94] Factors present in a situation in which breach of the peace occurs may also give rise to arrest powers under PACE, but may extend further than they do due to the wide definition of breach of the peace. The leading case on arrest under this doctrine is *R v Howell.*[95]

---

92   Relevant reading: the Home Office, *Modernising Police Powers to meet community needs—a consultation paper* (Aug 2004). For current comment on arrest powers under PACE and the Terrorism Act 2000, as amended, see A Ashworth, *The Criminal Process*, 3rd edn (2005); D Feldman, *Civil Liberties and Human Rights in England and Wales*, 2nd edn (2002), Chapters 5 and 9; A Sanders and R Young, *Criminal Justice*, 3rd edn (2007), Chapter 3; M Zander, *The Police and Criminal Evidence Act 1984* (2008); Clark, D Bevan and Lidstone's *The Investigation of Crime* (2004); K Starmer and A Hopkins, *Human Rights in the Investigation of Crime* (2007); M Ayres, L Murray and R Fiti (2003) *Arrests for Notifiable Offences*, Home Office Paper 17/03.

93   See Chapter 7, pp 305–306.

94   For commentary on breach of the peace generally see G Williams [1954] Crim LR 578. See Chapter 19, p 1120 *et seq* for further discussion of the powers under the doctrine of breach of the peace.

95   [1981] 3 All ER 383. For comment see G Williams (1982) 146 JPN 199–200, 217–19. See also the discussion of *Laporte* and *Austin* (2009) in Chapter 19, p 1125 *et seq.*

A range of powers of arrest

R v Howell [1981] 3 All ER 383 (extracts)

Watkins LJ: We hold that there is power of arrest for breach of the peace where:

(1) a breach of the peace is committed in the presence of the person making the arrest; or

(2) the arrestor reasonably believes that such a breach will be committed in the immediate future by the person arrested although he has not yet committed any breach; or

(3) where a breach has been committed and it is reasonably believed that a renewal of it is threatened.

The common law, we believe, whilst recognising that a wrongful arrest is a serious invasion of a person's liberty, provides the police with this power in the public interest. In those instances of the exercise of this power which depend on a belief that a breach of the peace is imminent it must, we think we should emphasise, be established that it is not only an honest, albeit mistaken, belief but a belief which is founded on reasonable grounds.

Power of arrest with warrant

Magistrates' Courts Act 1980, Part I

Issue of summons to accused or warrant for his arrest

1.–(1) Upon an information being laid before a justice of the peace for an area to which this section applies that any person has, or is suspected of having, committed an offence, the justice may. . . .

(a) issue a summons directed to that person requiring him to appear before a magistrates' court for the area to answer to the information, or

(b) issue a warrant to arrest that person and bring him before a magistrates' court for the area or such magistrates' court as is provided in subsection (5) below.

Powers of arrest without warrant

Police and Criminal Evidence Act 1984, as amended

Part III—Arrest

Arrest without warrant: constables

24.–(1) A constable may arrest without a warrant—

(a) anyone who is about to commit an offence;

(b) anyone who is in the act of committing an offence;

(c)   anyone whom he has reasonable grounds for suspecting to be about to commit an offence;

(d)   anyone whom he has reasonable grounds for suspecting to be committing an offence.

(2)   If a constable has reasonable grounds for suspecting that an offence has been committed he may arrest without warrant anyone whom he has reasonable grounds to suspect of being guilty of it.

(3)   If an offence has been committed a constable may arrest without warrant—

(a)   anyone who is guilty of the offence;

(b)   anyone whom he has reasonable grounds for suspecting to be guilty of it.

(4)   But the power of summary arrest conferred by sub-section (1), (2) or (3) is exercisable only if the constable has reasonable grounds for believing that for any of the reasons mentioned in sub-section (5) it is necessary to arrest the person in question.

(5)   The reasons are—

(a)   to enable the name of the person in question to be ascertained (in the case where the constable does not know and cannot readily ascertain the person's name or has reasonable grounds for doubting whether a name given by the person as his name is his real name);

(b)   correspondingly as regards the person's address;

(c)   to prevent the person in question—

(i)   causing physical harm to himself or any other person;

(ii)   suffering physical injury;

(iii)   causing loss of or damage to property;

(iv)   committing an offence against public decency. . . or

(v)   causing an unlawful obstruction of the highway;

(d)   to protect a child or other vulnerable person from the person. . .;

(e)   to allow the prompt and effective investigation of the offence or of the conduct of the person in question;

(f)   to prevent any prosecution of the offence from being hindered by the disappearance of the person in question.

Arrest under the Terrorism Act 2000

Terrorism Act 2000

Terrorist: interpretation

40.–(1) In this Part 'terrorist' means a person who—

(a)   has committed an offence under any of sections 11, 12, 15 to 18, 54 and 56 to 63, or

> (b)   is or has been concerned in the commission, preparation or instigation of acts
>   of terrorism.

Arrest without warrant

41.–(1) A constable may arrest without a warrant a person whom he reasonably suspects
to be a terrorist.

(2)   Where a person is arrested under this section the provisions of Schedule 8 (detention: treatment, review and extension) shall apply.

(3)   Subject to subsections (4) to (7), a person detained under this section shall (unless
detained under any other power) be released not later than the end of the period of
48 hours beginning—

> (a)   with the time of his arrest under this section, or
> (b)   if he was being detained under Schedule 7 when he was arrested under this
>   section, with the time when his examination under that Schedule began. . . .

Notes

1. For an arrest to be valid an arrest warrant must have been issued or there must be a power of arrest
without warrant. Section 110 of the Serious and Organised Crime Act 2005 introduced a new s 24
PACE, creating a single very broad arrest power, broader than that under the old s 25 power it
replaces. Under s 24 (above) a person can now be arrested by a constable on reasonable suspicion
of being in the act of committing (s 24(1)(d)), having committed (s 24(2)), or being about to
commit (s 24(1)(c)), an offence—any offence. Thus this power now allows an officer to arrest for
any offence so long as reasonable suspicion can be shown. A person can also be arrested by a
constable if in the act of committing (s 24(1)(b)), having committed, (s 24(3)(a)), or being about
to commit (s 24(1)(a)), an offence. In other words, the officer can arrest on a hunch so long as it
turns out to be justified. This possibility, which was also available prior to 2005, may tend to
undermine the reasonable suspicion requirement since police officers are aware that the likelihood
of being called to account for the false arrest is not high. Under the current s 24 the difference
between arrestable and non-arrestable offences has been abolished: *all* offences are arrestable so
long as certain other conditions are also satisfied.

2. In order to arrest under s 24, two steps must be taken: first, there must be reasonable suspicion
relating to the offence in question, unless s 24(1)(b), s 24(3)(a) or s 24(1)(a) applies (the 'hunch'
provisions). Second, there must be reasonable grounds for thinking that one of the arrest conditions is satisfied. The need for the officer to have reasonable suspicion relating to the offence in
question *and* as to the further requirement (previously—'general arrest conditions') was
emphasised on appeal in *Edwards v DPP*[96] in relation to the previous provisions, but the decision is
applicable to the new s 24. But, crucially, two new alternative arrest conditions have been added
under the new s 24. The police also have the further options of showing that the arrest is needed to
allow the prompt and effective investigation of the suspected offence in question, or to prevent
prosecution of the offence from being hindered by the suspect's disappearance (s 24(5)(e) and (f)).
These two current reasons were not available under s 25, and greatly broaden the ambit of this
current power.

It is highly probable that one of these reasons will be found to be satisfied in relation to most
arrests. Thus the police now have the broad power of arrest that would have been viewed as too
draconian had it been introduced in 1984. Some attempt at balancing this power with increased

---

safeguards for arrestees was made by the introduction of Code G, the arrest Code, in 2006. For example, s 1.3 Code G demands that the arrest must be proportionate to the objectives of the investigation. Section 1 also reminds police that arrest should not be resorted to readily; it should only be used if other means of achieving the objectives of the investigation are not feasible. However, breach of Code G does not give rise to civil liability, and it is probable that its safeguards are having little significant impact in practice on street policing.

3. There are a large number of statutory provisions allowing an arrest warrant to be issued, of which the most significant is that arising under s 1 of the Magistrates' Courts Act 1980. This provision limits the circumstances under which a warrant can be sought as an alternative to using the non-warrant arrest power under s 24 PACE.

4. A power of arrest in respect of the terrorist offences under the Terrorism Act 2000 (formerly contained in the Prevention of Terrorism (Temporary Provisions) Act 1989 (PTA)) arises under the TA itself or under s 24 of PACE. Section 41 TA read with s 40(1)(a) of the TA, covers arrest in respect of certain TA offences. If an arrest is effected under s 41 of the TA, as opposed to s 24 of PACE, this has an effect on the length of detention, as will be seen below.

5. Police discretion is particularly wide where no reasonable suspicion of any particular offence is necessary in order to arrest. Such a power is provided by s 41 of the TA read with s 40(1)(b). This power provides a completely separate power from the PACE power; it allows arrest without needing to show suspicion relating to a particular offence. This arrest is not for an offence but in practice for investigation, questioning and general intelligence gathering. Thus, this power represents a departure from the principle that liberty should be curtailed only on clear and specific grounds which connect the actions of the suspect with a specific offence under criminal law.[97]

6. *The Article 5(1)(c) exception.* In considering the exceptional circumstances in which liberty can be taken away, the requirements connoted by the general provision that they must have a basis in law under Art 5(1) are also implied into the 'prescribed by law' rubric of each sub-paragraph.[98] Article 5(1)(c) of the Convention sets out one of the circumstances in which an individual can be detained. It permits the lawful arrest or detention of a person effected for the purpose of bringing him before the competent legal authority on reasonable suspicion of having committed an offence, or where it is reasonably considered that an arrest is necessary to prevent the person in question from committing an offence or fleeing after having done so. In requiring arrest only for specific offences and not for general crime control purposes, Art 5(1)(c) adheres closely to the due process model of arrest indicated above. Section 24 of PACE and s 41 of the TA (in so far as it relates to certain specific terrorist offences under s 40(1)(a)) appear to comply with these provisions owing to their requirements of reasonable suspicion.

7. *'Reasonable suspicion'.* The requirements of the arrest power must be satisfied; usually this is the requirement of reasonable suspicion that the suspect is about to commit or has committed an offence. Section 24 of PACE and s 41 of the TA depend on the concept of reasonable suspicion; the idea behind the powers is that an arrest should take place at quite a late stage in the investigation. This limits the number of arrests and makes it less likely that a person will be wrongfully arrested. The term 'reasonable grounds' for suspicion indicates that a clear, objective basis for forming the view in question should exist. The objective nature of the suspicion required is echoed in various

---

97 For discussion of this arrest power under the PTA 1984, see C Walker (1984) 47 MLR 704–08; D Bonner, *Emergency Powers in Peace Time* (1985), pp 170–81.

98 *Winterwerp v Netherlands* (1980) Series A No 33; (1979) 2 EHRR 387, para 39.

decisions on the suspicion needed for an arrest.[99] In *Dallison v Caffrey*[100] Lord Diplock said the test was whether 'a reasonable man assumed to know the law and possessed of the information which in fact was possessed by the defendant would believe there were [reasonable grounds]'. Thus, it is not enough for a police officer to have a hunch that a person has committed or is about to commit an offence; there must be a concrete basis for this suspicion which relates to the particular person in question and could be evaluated by an objective observer.

8. The decisions on arrest endorse a fairly low level of suspicion; *Ward v Chief Constable of Somerset and Avon Constabulary*[101] suggested that a high level of suspicion was not required, and this might also be said of *Castorina v Chief Constable of Surrey*.[102] Detectives were investigating a burglary of a company's premises and on reasonable grounds came to the conclusion that it was an 'inside job'. The managing director told them that a certain employee had recently been dismissed and that the documents taken would be useful to someone with a grudge. However, she also said that she would not have expected the particular employee to commit a burglary. The detectives then arrested the employee, having found that she had no previous criminal record. She was detained for nearly four hours and then released without charge. She claimed damages for false imprisonment. The Court of Appeal found that the question was whether there was reasonable cause to suspect the plaintiff of burglary. Given that certain factors could be identified, including inside knowledge of the company's affairs and the motive of the plaintiff, the Court found that there was sufficient basis for the detectives to have reasonable grounds for suspicion.

9. *Castorina* may be compared with the findings of the Strasbourg Court in *Fox, Campbell and Hartley v UK*.[103] The applicants had been arrested in accordance with s 11 of the Northern Ireland (Emergency Provisions) Act 1978, which required only suspicion, not reasonable suspicion. The only evidence put forward by the Government for the presence of reasonable suspicion was that the applicants had convictions for terrorist offences and that when arrested, they were asked about particular terrorist acts. The Government said that further evidence could not be disclosed for fear of endangering life. The Court found that although allowance could be made for the difficulties of evidence-gathering in an emergency situation, reasonable suspicion which 'arises from facts or information which would satisfy an objective observer that the person concerned may have committed the offence'[104] had not been established. Moreover, 'the exigencies of dealing with terrorist crime cannot justify stretching the notion of reasonableness to the point where the essence of the safeguard secured by Art 5(1)(c) is impaired'.[105] The arrests in question could not, therefore, be justified. In *Murray v UK*,[106] this test was viewed as a lower standard for reasonable suspicion, applicable in terrorist cases, but it was again emphasised that an objective standard of reasonable suspicion was required,[107] although the information grounding the suspicion might

---

99   Eg, *Nakkuda Ali v Jayaratne* [1951] AC 66, 77; *Allen v Wright* (1835) 8 C & P 522.

100 [1965] 1 QB 348, 371.

101 *The Times*, 26 June 1986. *Cf Monaghan v Corbett* (1983) 147 JP 545, DC.

102 (1988) 138 NLJ 180.

103 A 182 (1990); 13 EHRR 157.

104 *Ibid*, para 32.

105 *Ibid*.

106 [1994] EHRR 193.

107 Para 50.

acceptably remain confidential in the exigencies of a situation such as that pertaining at the time of the arrest in question, in Northern Ireland.[108] It is debatable whether the UK courts are in general applying a test of reasonable suspicion under PACE or the TA which reaches the standards which the European Court had in mind, especially where terrorism is *not* in question. The departure which the HRA brings about is to encourage stricter judicial scrutiny of decisions to arrest.

10. The European Court of Human Rights in *O'Hara v UK*[109] commented on the nature of the reasonable suspicion required to satisfy Art 5(1)(c). The Court found that it requires the existence of some facts or information which would satisfy an objective observer that *the person concerned* may have committed the offence. However, the Court also accepted that the reasonable suspicion at the time of arrest need not be of the same level as that necessary to bring a charge.[110] As mentioned above, this statement accords with the test under Code A and with that under Code G. Unsurprisingly, it confirms the need for an objective test, but otherwise is generally likely to effect no radical change in the stance of the courts in relation to this concept.

But the later decision in *Cumming v Chief Constable of Northumbria Police*[111] appears to be out of line with that of the European Court. The five claimants worked for a local authority department concerned with monitoring recordings made by the town's closed circuit television cameras. They were arrested following the discovery of tampering with tapes showing the possible commission of an offence. They had no links with the suspected offender and were all of good character. Their claims for damages for wrongful arrest and false imprisonment were dismissed[112] and they appealed against this finding. The claimants submitted that mere opportunity could not found the requirements of reasonable suspicion under s 24(6) of the Police and Criminal Evidence Act 1984. However, it was found by the Court of Appeal that there was nothing in principle to prevent opportunity from amounting to reasonable grounds. It was also acceptable to arrest more than one person even if only one could have committed the offence (*Hussein v Chong Fook Kam*[113] was relied upon). In the instant case only a small number of people could be clearly identified as the ones with the opportunity of committing an offence. That could in principle, it was found, afford reasonable grounds for suspecting each of them in the absence of any information enabling further elimination. It was noted that in *Fox, Campbell and Hartley v United Kingdom*[114] the European Court had held that the protection of Art 5 of the Convention was met by the requirement that there be reasonable grounds for an arrest. Therefore, it was found, the Convention did not require the court to evaluate the exercise of police discretion in any different way from the exercise of any other executive discretion. Thus, the Court of Appeal found that where there were reasonable grounds to suspect that one out of a certain group of people had committed an offence, there could be said to be reasonable grounds for arresting all of them. This decision does not demand that the reasonable suspicion should relate to the specific person arrested, although the test laid down by the Strasbourg Court does make that demand.

---

108   Paras 58–59.

109   (2002) 34 EHRR 32.

110   *Ibid*, paras [34], [36].

111   [2003] EWCA Civ 1844.

112   By Judge Hewitt, sitting in Newcastle upon Tyne County Court on 27 January 2003.

113   [1970] AC 942.

114   (1990) 13 EHRR 157.

11. Research into the use of arrest suggests that, in practice, the concept of reasonable suspicion is interpreted very flexibly by the police, as it is in respect of stop and search powers. A wealth of academic research and analysis has established that the need for reasonable suspicion provides only uncertain protection against wrongful arrest. Somewhat doubtful grounds sometimes appear to be sufficient to provide reasonable grounds to justify deprivation of liberty. Further, only in exceptional instances will an officer's use of this power be found to have been wrongful; the courts are quite ready to find that these somewhat hazy tests have been satisfied.[115] As Sanders and Young observe, commenting on *Castorina*, 'The decision gives the police considerable freedom to follow crime control norms, in that it allows them to arrest on little hard evidence'.[116] Sanders and Young further speak of appearing 'suspicious' as being 'a key working rule' in arrests and stops, and observe that association with other criminals is also often the basis for arrest even where the police are 'entirely without reasonable suspicion', since the object is to obtain statements against associates.[117] The courts appear to be reluctant to interfere with the police interpretation and use of the arrest power. The post-PACE decisions discussed leave a great deal of leeway to officers to arrest where suspicion relating to the particular person is at a low level, but they want to further the investigation by gathering information.[118]

12. The reasonableness of the suspicion is to be judged by what the arresting officer had in mind at the time: *Redmond-Bate v DPP*.[119] In *O'Hara v Chief Constable of the RUC*,[120] a decision on s 12(1) of the PTA, the House of Lords found that a constable could form a suspicion based on what he had been informed of previously as part of a briefing by a superior officer, or otherwise. The question to be asked was whether a reasonable man would personally have formed the suspicion after receiving the relevant information. In *Raissi v Commissioner of Police of the Metropolis*[121] it was accepted that the arresting officer subjectively suspected the arrestee of being a terrorist, under s 41 TA 2000; the question was whether there were also objectively reasonable grounds for the suspicion. The arresting officer stated that senior officers probably had further information which they had not made known to him. It was found that the officer should have arrested on the basis of facts known to *him*, not on the basis of facts that superior officers may have been aware of. The facts known to the arresting officer did not provide reasonable grounds for suspicion.

13. *Purpose of arrest.* The *purpose* of the arrest should also be in compliance with Art 5(1)(c), even where reasonable suspicion is established, in that it should be effected in order to 'bring [the suspect] before the competent legal authority', although this does not mean that every arrest must lead to a charge.[122] It was found in *Chalkley and Jeffries*[123] that the existence of a collateral motive for an arrest would not necessarily render it unlawful. Under the HRA, a domestic court has to consider whether Art 5 is satisfied by an arrest with a 'mixed' purpose.

---

115   See C Ryan and K Williams, 'Police Discretion' [1986] PL 285, and D Brown, *PACE Ten Years On: A Review of the Research* (1997).

116   Sanders and Young, 2nd edn (2000), p 86 (current edition, 2007).

117   Sanders and Young, n 1 above, n 2 (2007), pp 143–48 esp at 144, based on research undertaken by Leng (Royal Commission on Criminal Justice Research Study No 10), 1993.

118   See *Ward v Chief Constable of Somerset and Avon Constabulary*, The Times, 26 June 1986; *Castorina v Chief Constable of Surrey* (1988) NLJ 180, transcript from LEXIS.

119   (1999) 163 JP 789; [1999] Crim LR 998 (see pp 1121–1122, above).

120   [1997] 2 WLR 1.

121   [2009] 2 WLR 1243.

122   *K-F v Germany* (1997) 26 EHRR 390.

123   [1998] 2 All ER 155.

14. *Reasonable suspicion unrelated to a specific offence.* The test under Art 5(1)(c) ECHR relies on reasonable suspicion regarding *an offence* and therefore calls into question s 41 of the TA, in so far as it relates to suspicion that a person is a terrorist in the sense of (under s 40(1)(b)) being concerned in the commission, preparation, or instigation of an act of terrorism. Section 41 therefore may allow for arrest in some circumstances without reasonable suspicion that a particular offence has been committed, depending on whether the relevant offences under the Terrorism Act 2006 would apply. The compatibility of s 41 and Art 5(1)(c) depends on the interpretation afforded to *Brogan and Others v UK*.[124] The Court applied two tests to the basis for the arrests in finding that the power of arrest was justified within Art 5(1)(c). First, the definition of acts of terrorism was 'well in keeping with the idea of an offence'.[125] Second, after arrest, the applicants were asked about specific offences. Thus, 'the Court decided the point on the basis that involvement in "acts of terrorism" indirectly meant the commission of specific criminal offences under Northern Irish law, which would appear to be the better approach on the facts'.[126] On either test, arrests under s 41 read with s 40(1)(b) might be in a more doubtful position given the breadth of the definition of terrorism under s 1 of the TA. The application of the second test would partly depend in practice on the particular instance which arose before a domestic court. If a person was arrested under s 41 as part of an investigation and was not asked about specific offences on arrest, the connection with the basis of the arrest, bearing in mind the width of the s 1 TA definition, might be viewed as too tenuous to be termed an arrest on reasonable suspicion of an offence.

15. *Volunteers.* There is nothing to prevent a police officer asking any person to come to the police station to answer questions, even where there is no legal power to do so. This creates something of a grey area as the citizen may not realise that he or she does not need to comply with the request.[127] The Government refused to include a provision in PACE requiring the police to inform citizens of the fact that they are not under arrest at the point when the request is made.

Procedural elements of arrest

Police and Criminal Evidence Act 1984

Information to be given on arrest
28.–(1) Subject to subsection (5) below, when a person is arrested otherwise than by being informed that he is under arrest, the arrest is not lawful unless the person arrested is informed that he is under arrest as soon as is practicable after his arrest. . . .

    (3)   Subject to subsection (5) below, no arrest is lawful unless the person arrested is informed of the ground for the arrest at the time of, or as soon as is practicable after, the arrest.

Notes
1. Article 5(2) ECHR, which provides that a person must be informed promptly of the reason for arrest, corresponds to s 28 of PACE. In *Fox, Campbell and Hartley v UK*,[128] the applicants, who were

---

124   (1989) 11 EHRR 117.

125   *Ibid*, para 51.

126   D Harris, K O'Boyle and C Warbrick, *Law of The European Convention on Human Rights*, 1st edn (1995), p 116.

127   See I McKenzie, R Morgan and R Reiner, 'Helping the Police with their Enquiries' [1990] Crim LR 22. 53

128   Series A No 182, (1990) 13 EHRR 157.

arrested on suspicion of terrorist offences, were not informed of the reason for the arrest at the time of it, but were told that they were being arrested under a particular statutory provision. Clearly, this could not convey the reason to them at that time. At a later point, during interrogation, they were asked about specific criminal offences. The European Court of Human Rights found that Art 5(2) was not satisfied at the time of the arrest, but that this breach was healed by the later indications made during interrogation of the offences for which they had been arrested. Under s 28 of PACE, the police also have a certain leeway as to informing the arrestee. A domestic court in the post-HRA era might be prepared to take a strict approach to the interpretation of s 28 in a non-terrorist case, under s 3 of the HRA, bearing Art 5(2) in mind.

2. For an arrest to be made validly, not only must the power of arrest exist, whatever its source, and its requirements be satisfied, but the procedural elements must be complied with. The fact that a power of arrest arises will not alone make the arrest lawful.

3. The procedural elements are of crucial importance due to the consequences which may flow from a lawful arrest which will not flow from an unlawful one.[129] Such consequences include the right of the officer to use force in making an arrest if necessary and the loss of liberty inherent in an arrest. If an arrest has not occurred, the citizen is free to go wherever he or she will and any attempt to prevent him or her doing so will be unlawful.[130] It is therefore important to convey the fact of the arrest to the arrestee and to mark the point at which the arrest comes into being and general liberty ceases.

4. Where the arrest is under s 24 of PACE, the offence the defendant is suspected of committing should be made known and so should the arrest condition which applies. The arrest cannot be said to be for breach of the condition. In *Ghafar v Chief Constable of West Midland Police*[131] (a case arising under the old s 25 PACE) the defendant was stopped for driving a car without wearing a seatbelt and failed to provide a name and address; he was arrested on that basis. It was found that both the relevant matters should have been communicated to him. Where there are grounds for the arrest, but the ulterior motive is to investigate the involvement of the suspect in a more serious offence, it is sufficient to inform the defendant of the apparent ground so long as it is a valid reason for the arrest: *R v Chalkley and Jeffries*.[132] But where it seems that the defendant is deliberately being misled into thinking he or she is in custody on a less serious charge (which may mean that he or she will not seek access to legal advice) the police should, having made the arrest, ensure, before questioning him or her about the more serious offence, that he or she is aware of the true nature of the investigation.[133] In general the private view of an officer as to the probability that a charge will result from an arrest is not relevant so long as he or she is acting in good faith.[134]

5. Conveying the reason for the arrest does not involve using a particular form of words,[135] but it appears that reasonable detail must be given so that the arrestee will be in a position to give a

---

129   The question as to the difference between a valid and invalid arrest has been much debated; see KW Lidstone [1978] Crim LR 332; D Clark and D Feldman [1979] Crim LR 702; M Zander (1977) 127 NLJ 352; JC Smith [1977] Crim LR 293.

130   *Rice v Connolly* [1966] 2 QB 414; *Kenlin v Gardner* [1967] 2 QB 510.

131   (2000) unreported, 21 May, CA.

132   [1998] QB 848, CA.

133   *R v Kirk* [1999] 4 All ER 698, CA.

134   *Martin v Metropolitan Police Commissioner* (2001) unreported, 18 June, CA.

135   The Court of Appeal confirmed this in *Brosch* [1988] Crim LR 743. In *Abassey and Others v Metropolitan Police Comr* [1990] 1 WLR 385, it was found that there was no need for precise or technical language in conveying the reason for the arrest; the question whether the reason had been given was a matter for the jury. See also *Nicholas v Parsonage* [1987] RTR 199.

convincing denial and therefore be more speedily released from detention.[136] Given the infringe-ment of liberty represented by an arrest and the need, therefore, to restore liberty as soon as possible, consistent with the needs of the investigation, it is unfortunate that s 28 did not make it clear that a reasonable degree of detail should be given. In *Mullady v DPP*,[137] where the arrest reasons were given as 'obstruction', it was held that where the reasons given to a suspect for his arrest are invalid or are the wrong reasons, then the arrest itself is unlawful. 'Obstruction' was not deemed sufficient since it is not an arrestable offence. It was found that where a police officer has given a reason for an arrest, another reason cannot be substituted, whether that involves the substitution of another offence or the inference that s 25(3)(a) of the 1984 Act was satisfied. This finding should also be applied to the conditions now applicable under s 24(5). The reason should be correct (*Wilson v Chief Constable of Lancashire Constab*).[138] In *Wilson* the arrestee was not given enough information to enable him to challenge the arrest, rendering the arrest unlawful.

6. The reason for the arrest need only be made known as soon as is 'practicable'. The meaning and implications of this provision in s 28 were considered in the following case.

DPP v Hawkins [1988] 3 All ER 673, 675, 676

A police officer took hold of the defendant to arrest him but did not give the reason. The youth struggled and was therefore later charged with assaulting an officer in the execution of his duty. The question which arose was whether the officer was in the execution of his duty as he had failed to give the reason for the arrest. If the arrest was thereby rendered invalid he could not be in the execution of his duty as it could not include effecting an unlawful arrest.

Simon Brown J: . . .is a police officer acting in the execution of his duty during the period of time between his arresting a person and it first thereafter becoming practicable for him to inform that person of the ground of arrest, given that, at this later time, he in fact gives the wrong ground or no ground at all? If so, then clearly an assault on him by the person arrested during that period of time would constitute a criminal offence. Otherwise not.

. . .by virtue of s 28(3) the arrest ultimately proved to be unlawful. But that is not to say that all the earlier steps taken during the course of events leading to that ultimate position must themselves be regarded as unlawful. Still less does it follow that conduct on the part of the police officer, which at the time was not only permitted but positively required of him in the execution of his duty, can become retrospectively invalidated by reference to some later failure (a failure which, I may add, could well have been that of some officer other than himself).

S28 says nothing in respect of the intermediate period during which it is not practicable to inform the person arrested of the ground for his arrest. . . .

Notes
1. The Court of Appeal found that the arrest became unlawful when the time came at which it was practicable to inform the defendant of the reason but he was not so informed. This occurred at the police station or perhaps in the police car, but did not occur earlier due to the defendant's

---

136 *Murphy v Oxford*, 15 February 1985, unreported, CA. This is out of line with the CA decision in *Abassey* [1990] 1 WLR 385, in which *Murphy* unfortunately was not considered.

137 [1997] COD 422; WL 1103678.

138 (2000) 23 November 2000, unreported.

behaviour. Thus, the officer in question *was* acting in the course of his duty during the period until informing of the reason for arrest became practicable, despite the fact that when so informing became practicable the officer failed to do so.

2. The police, therefore, have a certain leeway as to informing the arrestee; the lawfulness of the arrest will not be affected, and nor will other acts arising from it, until the time when it would be practicable to inform of the reason for it has come and gone. Following *Hawkins,* what can be said as to the status of the suspect *before* the time came and passed at which the requisite words should have been spoken? Was he or was he not under arrest at that time?

3. In *Murray v Ministry of Defence*[139] soldiers occupied a woman's house, thus clearly taking her into detention, but did not inform her of the fact of arrest for half an hour. The question arose whether she was falsely imprisoned during that half hour. The House of Lords found that delay in giving the requisite information was acceptable due to the alarm which the fact of arrest, if known, might have aroused in the particular circumstances—the unsettled situation in Northern Ireland. The European Court of Human Rights found (*Murray v United Kingdom*)[140] that no breach of Art 5(1) (which requires, *inter alia,* that deprivation of liberty can occur only if arising from a lawful arrest founded on reasonable suspicion) had occurred, even though the relevant legislation (s 14 of the Northern Ireland (Emergency Provisions) Act 1987) required only suspicion, not reasonable suspicion, since there was some evidence which would provide a basis for the suspicion in question.

No breach was found of Art 5(2), which provides that a person must be informed promptly of the reason for arrest. Mrs Murray was eventually informed during interrogation of the reason for the arrest, and it was found that allowing an interval of a few hours between arrest and informing of the reason for it could still be termed prompt. The violation of privacy fell within the exception under Art 8(2) in respect of the prevention of crime. No violation of the Convention was therefore found. It seems that, under UK law and under Art 5 of the Convention, an arrest which does not comply with all the procedural requirements can still be an arrest as far as all the consequences arising from it are concerned, for a period of time. It is therefore in a more precarious position than an arrest which from its inception complies with all the requirements, because it will cease to be an arrest at an uncertain point. It is clear that some departure has occurred from the principle that there should be a clear demarcation between the point at which the citizen is at liberty and the point at which his or her liberty is restrained. A domestic court in the post-HRA era may, however, be prepared to take a more activist approach to the application of Art 5(2), especially where a s 41 TA arrest, accompanied by delay in informing of the reason owing (apparently) to the terrorist context, occurred in circumstances which could not be compared in terms of volatility to the situation in Northern Ireland when *Murray* was decided.

Questions

❶   At what point after the police had detained him, if at all, could a suspect in the position of the suspect in *DPP v Hawkins* attempt lawfully to regain his liberty?

❷   Does the decision in *DPP v Hawkins* accept the existence of a concept of lawful detention as distinct from the concept of an arrest?

---

139   [1988] 2 All ER 521, HL. For comment see Williams (1991) 54 MLR 408.

140   (1994) 19 EHRR 193.

Use of force[141]

Criminal Law Act 1967

Use of force in making arrest, etc

3.–(1) A person may use such force as is reasonable in the circumstances in the prevention of crime, or in effecting or assisting in the lawful arrest of offenders or suspected offenders or of persons unlawfully at large.

Police and Criminal Evidence Act 1984

Power of constable to use reasonable force

117.   Where any provision of this Act—

(a)   confers a power on a constable, and does not provide that the power may only be exercised with the consent of some person, other than a police officer,

(b)   the officer may use reasonable force, if necessary, in the exercise of the power.

Notes

1. Force may include, as a last resort, the use of firearms; such use is governed by Home Office guidelines and the most recent version is the Association of Chief Officers of Police (ACPO), *Manual of Guidance on Police Use of Firearms* (2001).[142] It states that firearms should be used only where absolutely necessary, where conventional methods have been tried and have failed or would be likely to fail if tried, for example, if there is reason to suppose that a person to be apprehended is so dangerous that he or she could not be safely restrained otherwise.

2. Section 3 is in one sense wider than s 117, since it authorises the use of force by any person, although only in relation to making an arrest or preventing crime. The prevention of crime would include resistance to an unlawful arrest. Section 117 only applies to police officers and then only in relation to provisions under PACE which do not provide that the consent of someone other than a constable is required. Under the 1967 Act, the force can only be used if it is 'necessary' and the amount of force used must be 'reasonable'. 'Reasonable' is taken to mean 'reasonable in the circumstances'[143] and, therefore, allows extreme force if the suspect is also using, or appears to be about to use, extreme force.

DETENTION IN POLICE CUSTODY

The right to liberty provided under Art 5(1) ECHR is subject to certain exceptions which must have a basis in law. Not only must an exception apply, the requirements under Art 5(2), (3) and (4) must also be met. The current domestic arrest and detention scheme for non-terrorist suspects is, as one would expect, largely in harmony, formally speaking, with these provisions, and in some respects may afford a higher—or, at least, clearer—value to due process. But the use of Art 5 as an interpretative tool under

---

141   For comment see: [1982] Crim LR 475; *Report of Commissioner of Police of the Metropolis for 1983*, Cmnd 9268.

142   Available from www.acpo.police.uk.

143   See the ruling in *Farrell v Secretary of State for Defence* [1980] 1 All ER 166, HL.

s 3 HRA may have lead to a more rigorous judicial approach to the detention scheme. Breaches of Art 5 are most likely to be established in respect of the special counter-terrorist arrest and detention powers available under the Terrorism Act 2000, as amended in 2006 and 2008. At present detention in police custody for nearly a month is possible in relation to terrorism suspects.

Detention after arrest under the Police and Criminal Evidence Act 1984

Police and Criminal Evidence Act 1984, Part IV

Review of police detention[144]

40.–(1) Reviews of the detention of each person in police detention in connection with the investigation of an offence shall be carried out periodically in accordance with the following provisions of this section—

    (a)   in the case of a person who has been arrested and charged, by the custody officer; and

    (b)   in the case of a person who has been arrested but not charged, by an officer of at least the rank of inspector who has not been directly involved in the investigation. . .

  (3)   Subject to subsection (4) below—

    (a)   the first review shall be not later than six hours after the detention was first authorised;

    (b)   the second review shall be not later than nine hours after the first;

    (c)   subsequent reviews shall be at intervals of not more than nine hours.

  (12) Before determining whether to authorise a person's continued detention the review officer shall give—

    (a)   that person (unless he is asleep); or

    (b)   any solicitor representing him who is available at the time of the review, an opportunity to make representations to him about the detention.

Limits on period of detention without charge

41.–(1) Subject to the following provisions of this section and to sections 42 and 43 below, a person shall not be kept in police detention for more than 24 hours without being charged.

  (2)   The time from which the period of detention of a person is to be calculated (in this Act referred to as 'the relevant time')—

    (a)   in the case of a person to whom this section applies, shall be—

---

144   Section 40 applied with modifications by Police and Criminal Evidence Act 1984 (Application to Customs and Excise) Order 1985, SI 1985/1800, Arts 3–11, Scheds 1, 2.

(i)   the time at which that person arrives at the relevant police station, or

(ii) the time 24 hours after the time of that person's arrest, whichever is the earlier. . . .

Authorisation of continued detention

42.–(1) Where a police officer of the rank of superintendent or above who is responsible for the police station at which a person is detained has reasonable grounds for believing that—

(a)   the detention of that person without charge is necessary to secure or preserve evidence relating to an offence for which he is under arrest or to obtain such evidence by questioning him;

(b)   an offence for which he is under arrest is a serious arrestable offence; and

(c)   the investigation is being conducted diligently and expeditiously, he may authorise the keeping of that person in police detention for a period expiring at or before 36 hours after the relevant time.

Warrants of further detention

43.–(1) Where, on an application on oath made by a constable and supported by an information, a magistrates' court is satisfied that there are reasonable grounds for believing that the further detention of the person to whom the application relates is justified, it may issue a warrant of further detention authorising the keeping of that person in police detention.

(2) A court may not hear an application for a warrant of further detention unless the person to whom the application relates—

(a)   has been furnished with a copy of the information; and

(b)   has been brought before the court for the hearing.

(3) The person to whom the application relates shall be entitled to be legally represented at the hearing and, if he is not so represented, but wishes to be so represented—

(a)   the court shall adjourn the hearing to enable him to obtain representation; and

(b)   he may be kept in police detention during the adjournment.

(4) A person's further detention is only justified for the purposes of this section or section 44 below if—

(a)   his detention without charge is necessary to secure or preserve evidence relating to an offence for which he is under arrest or to obtain such evidence by questioning him;

(b)   an offence for which he is under arrest is a serious arrestable offence; and

(c)   the investigation is being conducted diligently and expeditiously.

Extension of warrants of further detention

44.–(1) On an application on oath made by a constable and supported by information, a magistrates' court may extend a warrant of further detention issued under section

43 above if it is satisfied that there are reasonable grounds for believing that the further detention of the person to whom the application relates is justified.

(2) Subject to subsection (3) below, the period for which a warrant of further detention may be extended shall be such period as the court thinks fit, having regard to the evidence before it.

(3) The period shall not—

(a) be longer than 36 hours; or
(b) end later then 96 hours after the relevant time.

(4) Where a warrant of further detention has been extended under subsection (1) above, or further extended under this subsection, for a period ending before 96 hours after the relevant time, on an application such as is mentioned in that sub-section, a magistrates' court may further extend the warrant if it is satisfied as there mentioned; and subsections (2) and (3) above apply to such further extensions as they apply to extensions under subsection (1) above. . . .

Notes

1. The detention scheme governed by Part IV of PACE put the power to hold for questioning on a clear basis and it was made clear under s 37(2) that the purpose of the detention is to obtain a confession.

2. Under s 41, the detention can be for up to 24 hours, but in the case of a person in police custody for an indictable offence (defined in s 116) it can extend to 96 hours. Part IV of PACE does not apply to detention under the Terrorism Act 2000 (below), as amended, or to detention by immigration officers.[145] Under s 42(1), a police officer of the rank of superintendent or above can sanction detention for up to 36 hours if the three conditions specified apply. After 36 hours, detention can no longer be authorised by the police alone. Under s 43(1), the application for authorisation must be supported by information and brought before a magistrates' court, which can authorise detention under s 44 for up to 96 hours if the conditions are met, as set out above in the extracts from PACE.

3. It may be noted that a person unlawfully detained can apply for a writ of habeas corpus in order to secure release from detention and this remedy is preserved in s 51(d). Its usefulness in practice is, however, very limited since the courts have developed a practice of adjourning applications for 24 hours in order to allow the police to present their case. Thus, detention can continue for that time allowing the police to carry out questioning or other procedures in the meantime.

4. The safeguards surrounding the powers to detain under ss 41–44 can be called into question. D Dixon in 'Safeguarding the Rights of Suspects in Police Custody'[146] suggests that the periodic review of detention and the right to make representations tend to be treated not as genuine investigations into the grounds for continuing the detention, but as formalities. Perhaps in recognition of the need for rigour in relation to reviews, a proposal made in 1999 by the Chief Constable of Kent Police that detention review should be by video link in the majority of cases was rejected in judicial review proceedings on the ground, discussed below, that it might undermine the protection for liberty they are intended to offer, taking Article 5 into account.[147] However, the

---

145 PACE 1984, s 51.

146 (1990) 1 *Policing and Society* 130–31.

147 *R v Chief Constable of Kent Constabulary ex parte Kent Police Federation Joint Branch Board and Another, The Times*, 1 December 1999.

Government then brought forward legislation—s 73 of the Criminal Justice and Police Act 2001 (CJPA)—to reverse the effect of this decision. Section 73 inserted current ss 40A and 45A into PACE to allow for the use of telephone and video links for reviews of detention. Clearly, these new provisions in relation to review of detention detracted from the face-to-face confrontation that was originally envisaged.

Detention under the Terrorism Act 2000, as amended by the Terrorism Act 2006 and the Counter-Terrorism Act 2008

41.–(2) Where a person is arrested under this section the provisions of Schedule 8 (detention: treatment, review and extension) shall apply.

(3) Subject to subsections (4) to (7), a person detained under this section shall (unless detained under any other power) be released not later than the end of the period of 48 hours beginning—

    (a) with the time of his arrest under this section, or

    (b) if he was being detained under Schedule 7 when he was arrested under this section, with the time when his examination under that Schedule began.

Schedule 8

Part II Review of Detention under Section 41

21.–(1) A person's detention shall be periodically reviewed by a review officer.

(2) The first review shall be carried out as soon as is reasonably practicable after the time of the person's arrest.

(3) Subsequent reviews shall, subject to paragraph 22, be carried out at intervals of not more than 12 hours.

(4) No review of a person's detention shall be carried out after a warrant extending his detention has been issued under Part III. . . .

Grounds for continued detention

23.–(1) A review officer may authorise a person's continued detention only if satisfied that it is necessary—

    (a) to obtain relevant evidence whether by questioning him or otherwise,

    (b) to preserve relevant evidence,. . .

    (ba) pending the result of an examination or analysis of any relevant evidence or of anything the examination or analysis of which is to be or is being carried out with a view to obtaining relevant evidence,

    (c) pending a decision whether to apply to the Secretary of State for a deportation notice to be served on the detained person,

    (d) pending the making of an application to the Secretary of State for a deportation notice to be served on the detained person,

    (e) pending consideration by the Secretary of State whether to serve a deportation notice on the detained person, or

(f)   pending a decision whether the detained person should be charged with an offence.

(3)   The review officer shall not authorise continued detention by virtue of sub-paragraph (1)(c) to (f) unless he is satisfied that the process pending the completion of which detention is necessary is being conducted diligently and expeditiously. . . .

Review officer
24.–(1) The review officer shall be an officer who has not been directly involved in the investigation in connection with which the person is detained.

(2)   In the case of a review carried out within the period of 24 hours beginning with the time of arrest, the review officer shall be an officer of at least the rank of inspector. . . .

Representations
26.–(1) Before determining whether to authorise a person's continued detention, a review officer shall give either of the following persons an opportunity to make representations about the detention—

(a)   the detained person, or
(b)   a solicitor representing him who is available at the time of the review. . . .

Extension of detention under section 41
29.–(2) A warrant of further detention—

(a)   shall authorise the further detention under section 41 of a specified person for a specified period, and
(b)   shall state the time at which it is issued.

(3)   [[Subject to sub-paragraph (3A) and paragraph 36], the] specified period in relation to a person shall [be] the period of seven days beginning—

(a)   with the time of his arrest under section 41, or
(b)   if he was being detained under Schedule 7 when he was arrested under section 41, with the time when his examination under that Schedule began.

(3A) A judicial authority may issue a warrant of further detention in relation to a person which specifies a shorter period as the period for which that person's further detention is authorised if—

(a)   the application for the warrant is an application for a warrant specifying a shorter period; or
(b)   the judicial authority is satisfied that there are circumstances that would make it inappropriate for the specified period to be as long as the period of seven days mentioned in sub-paragraph (3).

Time limit
30.–(1) An application for a warrant shall be made—

    (a)   during the period mentioned in section 41(3), or

    (b)   within six hours of the end of that period. . .

  (3)   For the purposes of this Schedule, an application for a warrant is made when written or oral notice of an intention to make the application is given to a judicial authority. . . .

Grounds for extension

32.–(1) A judicial authority may issue a warrant of further detention only if satisfied that—

    (a)   there are reasonable grounds for believing that the further detention of the person to whom the application relates is necessary [as mentioned in sub-paragraph (1A)], and

    (b)   the investigation in connection with which the person is detained is being conducted diligently and expeditiously.

  (1A) The further detention of a person is necessary as mentioned in this sub-paragraph if it is necessary—

    (a)   to obtain relevant evidence whether by questioning him or otherwise;

    (b)   to preserve relevant evidence; or

    (c)   pending the result of an examination or analysis of any relevant evidence or of anything the examination or analysis of which is to be or is being carried out with a view to obtaining relevant evidence.

  (2)   In [this paragraph] 'relevant evidence' means, in relation to the person to whom the application relates, evidence which—

    (a)   relates to his commission of an offence under any of the provisions mentioned in section 40(1)(a), or

    (b)   indicates that he is a person falling within section 40(1)(b).

Representation

33.–(1) The person to whom an application relates shall—

    (a)   be given an opportunity to make oral or written representations to the judicial authority about the application, and

    (b)   subject to sub-paragraph (3), be entitled to be legally represented at the hearing.

. . .

Extensions of warrants

36.–(1) . . . (d) in any part of the United Kingdom, a police officer of at least the rank of superintendent, may apply for the extension or further extension of the period specified in a warrant of further detention.

  (1A) The person to whom an application under sub-paragraph (1) may be made is—

    (a)   in the case of an application falling within sub-paragraph (1B), a judicial authority; and

    (b)   in any other case, a senior judge.

(1B) An application for the extension or further extension of a period falls within this sub-paragraph if—

    (a)   the grant of the application otherwise than in accordance with sub-paragraph (3AA)(b) would extend that period to a time that is no more than fourteen days after the relevant time; and

    (b)   no application has previously been made to a senior judge in respect of that period.

(2)   Where the period specified is extended, the warrant shall be endorsed with a note stating the new specified period.

(3)   Subject to sub-paragraph (3AA), the period by which the specified period is extended or further extended shall be the period which—

    (a)   begins with the time specified in sub-paragraph (3A); and

    (b)   ends with whichever is the earlier of—

        (i)   the end of the period of seven days beginning with that time; and

        (ii)   the end of the period of 28 days beginning with the relevant time.

Code of Practice H (The Terrorism Act 2000 is referred to in Code H as TACT)

Reviews and extensions of detention

14.2 For the purposes of reviewing a person's detention, no officer shall put specific questions to the detainee:

- regarding their involvement in any offence; or
- in respect of any comments they may make:

    – when given the opportunity to make representations; or
    – in response to a decision to keep them in detention or extend the maximum period of detention.

Such an exchange could constitute an interview as in *paragraph 11.1* and would be subject to the associated safeguards in *section 11* and in respect of a person who has been charged.

14.4 When an application for a warrant of further or extended detention is sought under Paragraph 29 or 36 of Schedule 8, the detained person and their representative must be informed of their rights in respect of the application. These include:

    (a)   the right to a written or oral notice of the warrant See *Note 14G*.

    (b)   the right to make oral or written representations to the judicial authority about the application.

    (c)   the right to be present and legally represented at the hearing of the application, unless specifically excluded by the judicial authority.

    (d)   their right to free legal advice (see section 6 of this Code).

Part 2 Post-charge questioning of terrorist suspects

22 Post-charge questioning: England and Wales

(1) The following provisions apply in England and Wales.

(2) A judge of the Crown Court may authorise the questioning of a person about an offence—

    (a) after the person has been charged with the offence or been officially informed that they may be prosecuted for it, or

    (b) after the person has been sent for trial for the offence, if the offence is a terrorism offence or it appears to the judge that the offence has a terrorist connection.

(4) The period during which questioning is authorised—

    (a) begins when questioning pursuant to the authorisation begins and runs continuously from that time (whether or not questioning continues), and

    (b) must not exceed 48 hours.

    This is without prejudice to any application for a further authorisation under this section.

Notes

1. The detention scheme adopted in respect of terrorist suspects allows for the suspect to be detained for much longer periods than for non-terrorist suspects, and for a lower level of due process safeguards to be applicable during detention.[148] The detention scheme for terrorist suspects has been through a number of revisions, as discussed below, which have been driven on the one hand by due process demands imposed in effect by the European Court of Human Rights and on the other by governmental crime control concerns; it is still under review. Essentially, the period of detention has become incrementally longer, but it is subject to judicial authorisation.

2. The current detention scheme for terrorist suspects is affected by certain previous decisions against the UK at Strasbourg. Article 5(3) ECHR confers a right to be brought promptly before the judicial authorities; in other words, not to be held for long periods without a hearing. It covers both arrest and detention. There will be some allowable delay in both situations; the question is therefore what is meant by 'promptly'. The UK had entered a derogation under Art 15 ECHR against the applicability of Art 5(3) to Northern Ireland, but withdrew that derogation in August 1984. Two months later, the *Brogan* case was filed. In *Brogan v UK*[149] the applicants complained *inter alia* of the length of time they were held in detention without coming before a judge, on the basis that it could not be termed prompt. The Court took into account the need for special measures to combat terrorism; such measures had to be balanced against the individual right to liberty. However, it found that detention for four days and six hours was too long on the ground that holding a person for longer than four days without judicial authorisation was a violation of the requirement that persons should be brought promptly before a judicial officer. The Court did not specify how long was acceptable; previously, the Commission had seen four days as the limit. The Government made no move to comply with this decision; instead, it entered a derogation under Art 15 to Art 5(3).

---

148   See below, pp 1218–1219 *et seq* for discussion of such safeguards.

149   (1989) 11 EHRR 117 (see Chapter 7, pp 336–340).

This derogation was challenged unsuccessfully in *Brannigan and McBride v UK*[150] as invalid. The European Court of Human Rights found that it was justified since the state of public emergency in Northern Ireland warranted exceptional measures. The Court found: 'a wide margin of appreciation [on the question] of the presence of an emergency . . . and on the nature and scope of derogations necessary to avert it [should be allowed].'[151] But is questionable whether the exigencies of the situation did require detention of six days without recourse to independent review. Possibly it was assumed on insufficient grounds that such review would prejudice the legitimate purpose of the investigation.

3. The *Brogan* decision clearly presented the Blair Government with a difficulty in formulating the Terrorism Act 2000. Although the HRA continued the derogation entered in *Brogan*, under s 14(1)(a) HRA, for a time, it was vulnerable to challenge at Strasbourg at some future point, in the light of the settlement in Northern Ireland. The Government put forward various justifications for producing new terrorist legislation in 2000, but it recognised that it might be in difficulties in arguing that a state of emergency sufficient to support the derogation could be said to exist post-2000.[152] Its solution, in the TA, was to make provision for judicial authorisation of detention, rather than to decrease the length of time during which terrorist suspects could be detained. In requiring judicial authorisation for detention for up to seven days under s 41 and Sched 7 of the TA, the Government sought to ensure that the detention provisions complied with Art 5(3) as interpreted in *Brogan* and *Brannigan*, meaning that it became possible to withdraw the derogation and, once this was accomplished, the HRA was accordingly amended; the derogation was no longer needed, and it was lifted on 19 March 2001.

4. *Detention of terrorist suspects with judicial authorisation—current scheme.* The maximum period of detention, applicable to a person arrested under s 41 of the TA, was seven days; it was extended to 14 days by amendment to s 41(7) and Sched 8 TA under the Criminal Justice Act 2003 and then, after the July 2005 bombings in London, it was extended again by further amendment under the Terrorism Act 2006, to 28 days. The Labour Government sought to extend the period of time to 90 days but was defeated in the House of Commons. The Government intended to seek to bring forward the 90-day period once again in the Counter-Terrorism Bill 2007. On 13 October 2008 this measure was dropped from the Bill by a vote in the House of Lords. However, a compromise was reached: the Counter-Terrorism Act 2008 Part 2 (below) allows for post-charge questioning, but the period of detention prior to charge was not extended beyond 28 days. Thus terrorism suspects can currently be held in detention for almost a month, in strong contrast to non-terrorist suspects, who can only be held for 96 hours, even for the most serious offences.

   The police can detain a person on their own authority for 48 hours under s 41(3); after 48 hours of detention judicial approval is needed. Paragraph 29, Sched 8 TA (above), provides that the detention must be under a warrant issued by a 'judicial authority'. The detainee or his solicitor has the right to make written or oral representations under para 33(1). Thus, authorisation may not be merely 'on the papers'. Such a possibility might not have satisfied the aim of achieving compliance with Art 5(3), despite the involvement of a judicial figure.

5. As part of the port and border controls regime, Sched 5 of the PTA provided a further power of detention in allowing a person to be detained for 12 hours before examination at ports of entry into Britain or Northern Ireland. The period could be extended to 24 hours if the person was suspected of involvement in the commission, preparation or instigation of acts of terrorism. These

---

150   Series A, 258-B (1993); (1993) 17 EHRR 594.

151   Para 207.

152   See *Legislation Against Terrorism* (1988) Cm 4178, para 8.2.

provisions are partially reproduced in Sched 7 to the TA; they are modified to take account of the abolition of the exclusion power.

6. *Duties imposed on public authorities under the HRA regarding arrest and detention of terrorist and non-terrorist suspects.* All the public authorities involved, including the police, are bound under s 6 of the HRA to abide by the Art 5 requirements. Article 5-based arguments under the HRA can be raised within the trial process, by means of a civil action or under the police complaints provisions. Judicial review, on Art 5 principles, of decisions within the police complaints process, or in respect of judicial authorisations within the PACE or TA schemes, or of police decisions relating to detentions, are also available under s 7(1) HRA.

The first and most essential requirement of Art 5 is that a person's detention is in accordance with a procedure prescribed by law. This means that the procedure should be in accordance with national law and with recognised Convention standards, including Convention principles and is not arbitrary.[153] Thus, where one of the Art 5(1) exceptions applies to a person's detention, this requirement will also have to be satisfied. The procedure covers the arrest provisions[154] and the procedure adopted by a court in authorisations of detention.[155] The requirement that the detention should be in accordance with the law was given a robust interpretation in one of the first domestic decisions in the pre-HRA period to place a heavy reliance on Art 5: *R v Chief Constable of Kent Constabulary ex parte Kent Police Federation Joint Branch Board and Another*[156] (note the discussion above). The court had to consider an application that the conduct of reviews of police detention under s 40(1)(b) of the 1984 Act should be, in the majority of cases, by video link. Lord Bingham concluded that Parliament had provided for a face-to-face confrontation between the review officer and the suspect and, if important rights enacted to protect the subject were to be modified, it was for Parliament after appropriate consultation so to rule and not for the courts. This decision indicated a determination to give real efficacy to Art 5. One question which may be raised eventually in the domestic courts under the HRA, or at Strasbourg, will be whether allowing a detention for 28 days, even with judicial authorisation, is in accordance with Art 5(3).

POLICE INTERVIEWING AND ACCESS TO LEGAL ADVICE[157]

The most crucial events during a person's contact with police will probably be the interviews, and therefore this section will concentrate on the various safeguards available for the suspect which are intended to ensure that interviews are fair and that admissions made can be relied upon, if necessary, in court. The safeguards for terrorist suspects are not as extensive as for non-terrorist suspects. In crime control and counter-terrorism terms, the police interview occupies a central position in the criminal justice system; it represents an effective use of resources, since if a confession becomes

---

153   *Winterwerp v Netherlands,* Series A No 33, (1979) 2 EHRR 387, para 39.

154   *Fox, Campbell and Hartley v UK,* Series A No 182, (1990) 13 EHRR 157.

155   *Weston v UK* (1981) 3 EHRR 402 (also known as *H v UK); Van der Leer v Netherlands,* Series A No 170–A, (1990) 12 EHRR 567.

156   *The Times,* 1 December 1999. See p 1184 above.

157   For further reading see: A Sanders and R Young, *Criminal Justice,* 3rd edn (2007); D Feldman, *Civil Liberties and Human Rights in England and Wales,* 2nd edn (2002), Chapters 5 and 9; D Clark, *Bevan and Lidstone's the Investigation of Crime* (2004); T Bucke and D Brown, *In Custody* (1997).

available, the criminal process is likely to be accelerated.[158] In particular, since *mens rea* is a requirement of most offences, admissions provide the most readily available means of establishing the state of mind of the suspect at the relevant time. The interview may also frequently play a part in general criminal intelligence gathering.[159] On their face, the crime control advantages of the interview are readily apparent, although, clearly, if an intimidating atmosphere and a lack of due process safeguards lead a suspect to make false admissions that cannot advance crime control ends.

From a due process perspective the police interview is largely unjustifiable, since its *raison d'être* is to secure admissions which probably would not otherwise be secured; it therefore undermines the privilege against self-incrimination. This due process norm traditionally underpinned criminal justice practice,[160] but it was gradually abandoned until it became accepted in the pre-PACE years that the purpose of the interview was to obtain admissions.[161] The precarious position of the interview from this perspective explains, it is suggested, why it seemed necessary, when PACE placed police interviews on a formal basis, to infuse due process elements into them. Such elements are intended to detract from any impression that the confession is involuntary. The police, however, remain the gatekeepers to these safeguards, a position that runs counter to their crime control role, and therefore they may not be observed or, more subtly, the weaknesses and loopholes in the interviewing scheme tend to be discovered and explored.

PACE strongly reflects this uneasy compromise between crime control and due process: the detainee can be detained for the purposes of obtaining a confession under s 37(2), but a number of safeguards were created which are influenced by due process concerns and are intended to lessen the coerciveness of the interview, and to ensure its integrity and reliability so that it can be used as evidence. The extensive and complex rules of Codes C and H which appear to surround police interviews with a range of safeguards, afford the interview an appearance of due process. A number of flaws, however, in due process terms, were built into the scheme when it was first introduced. Most significantly, there are no sanctions for breach of the interviewing rules, including those arising under PACE itself, apart from the possibility of disciplinary action.[162] There is uncertainty as to when an exchange with police becomes an interview so as to attract all the safeguards. There is scope for interviewing away from the police station, thereby evading the most significant safeguards, those of access to legal advice and tape recording. Virtually no guidance is given as to the acceptable limits of 'persuasive' interviewing, so long as it is not oppressive. This is particularly a matter of concern in respect of the questioning of terrorist suspects, especially bearing in mind the length of the detention to which they can be subjected—as indicated, up to 28 days at present.

This section does not concentrate only on interviews or exchanges *inside* the police station because contact between police and suspect may take place a long time before the police station is reached. This has been recognised in the provisions of Part V of PACE and Code of Practice C (the current version was revised in 2008) which govern treatment of suspects and interviewing, but have some application outside as well as inside the police station. Code of Practice H was introduced in 2006 to deal with the detention, treatment and questioning by police officers of persons under s 41, and Sched 8 to the Terrorism Act 2000, as amended.

---

158   See M McConville, RCCJ Research Study No 13, 1993; Baldwin (1993) 33 Br J Criminology 325.

159   Maguire and Morris, RCCJ Research Study No 5, 1992.

160   The 1912 Judges' Rules did not allow police interrogation, although the police could invite and receive voluntary statements.

161   *Holgate-Mohammed v Duke* [1984] 1 AC 437; [1984] 1 All ER 1054.

162   This possibility became even more remote when PACE, s 67(8), rendering breach of the Codes *automatically* a breach of the police Disciplinary Code, was repealed in 1994 by the Police and Magistrates' Courts Act 1994, s 37 and Sched 9.

As discussed below, the level of protection for due process applicable to terrorism suspects is lower at a number of points than for non-terrorist suspects. Code H, which governs their treatment in police questioning, does recognise to an extent that the lengthy detention periods to which terrorism suspects can be subject has particular implications in terms of its mental impact, but, although there are a number of provisions for obtaining medical aid in respect of such suspects, the problem of relying on admissions made after a lengthy period of detention are not, it is argued, afforded sufficient recognition.

Access to legal advice, discussed below, is generally viewed as the most important safeguard for the suspect.[163] The main safeguards available currently for interviews under the Codes of Practice include contemporaneous recording or tape recording,[164] the ability to read over, verify and sign the notes of the interview as a correct record, notification of legal advice, the right to have advice before and during questioning and, where appropriate, the presence of an adult. One of the most important issues in relation to these safeguards is the question *when* they come into play. There may be a number of stages in a particular investigation, beginning with first contact between police and suspect, and perhaps ending with the charge. Two factors can be identified which decide which safeguards should be in place at a particular time. First, it must be asked whether an exchange between police and suspect can be called 'an interview', and second whether it took place inside or outside the police station.

Interviews and exchanges with suspects

Code of Practice C (revised 2008)[165]

11. Interviews: general

(a) Action

11.1A An interview is the questioning of a person regarding their involvement or suspected involvement in a criminal offence or offences which, by virtue of paragraph 10.1 of Code C, must be carried out under caution. Whenever a person is interviewed they must be informed of the nature of the offence or further offence . . . .

11.1 Following a decision to arrest a suspect they must not be interviewed about the relevant offence except at a police station or other authorised place of detention unless the consequent delay would be likely—

   (a) to lead to

- interference with, or harm to, evidence connected with an offence;
- interference with, or physical harm to, other people; or
- serious loss of, or damage to, property.

11.2 Immediately prior to the commencement or re-commencement of any interview at a police station or other authorised place of detention, the interviewer should remind the suspect of their entitlement to free legal advice and that the interview can be delayed for legal advice to be obtained, unless one of the exceptions in *paragraph 6.6* applies. It is the interviewer's responsibility to make sure all reminders are recorded in the interview record.

---

163   See D Dixon in C Walker and K Starmer (eds), *Miscarriages of Justice* (1999), p 67.

164   Under Code E.

165   See for the 2006 revision The Police and Criminal Evidence Act 1984 (Code of Practice C and Code of Practice H) Order 2006, SI 2006/1938.

11.4 At the beginning of an interview the interviewer, after cautioning the suspect, see *section 10*, shall put to them any significant statement or silence which occurred in the presence and hearing of a police officer or other police staff before the start of the interview and which have not been put to the suspect in the course of a previous interview. See *Note 11A*. The interviewer shall ask the suspect whether they confirm or deny that earlier statement or silence and if they want to add anything.

11.4A A significant statement is one which appears capable of being used in evidence against the suspect, in particular a direct admission of guilt. A significant silence is a failure or refusal to answer a question or answer satisfactorily when under caution, which might, allowing for the restriction on drawing adverse inferences from silence, see *Annex C*, give rise to an inference under the Criminal Justice and Public Order Act 1994, Part III.

11.5 No interviewer may try to obtain answers or elicit a statement by the use of oppression. Except as in *paragraph 10.9*, no interviewer shall indicate, except to answer a direct question, what action will be taken by the police if the person being questioned answers questions, makes a statement or refuses to do either. If the person asks directly what action will be taken if they answer questions, make a statement or refuse to do either, the interviewer may inform them what action the police propose to take provided that action is itself proper and warranted.

11.6 The interview or further interview of a person about an offence with which that person has not been charged or for which they have not been informed they may be prosecuted, must cease when:

(a) interference with or harm to evidence connected with an offence or interference with or physical harm to other persons; or

(b) to lead to the alerting of other persons suspected of having committed an offence but not yet arrested for it; or

(c) to hinder the recovery of property obtained in consequence of the commission of an offence.

Interviewing in any of these circumstances should cease once the relevant risk has been averted or the necessary questions have been put in order to attempt to avert that risk.

11.7 (a) An accurate record must be made of each interview, whether or not the interview takes place at a police station. . . .

11.11 Unless it is impracticable, the person interviewed shall be given the opportunity to read the interview record and to sign it as correct or to indicate how they consider it.

11.13 A written record shall be made of any comments made by a suspect, including unsolicited comments, which are outside the context of an interview but which might be relevant to the offence. Any such record must be timed and signed by the maker. When practicable the suspect shall be given the opportunity to read that record and to sign it as correct or to indicate how they consider it inaccurate.

11.18 The following persons may not be interviewed unless an officer of superintendent rank or above considers delay will lead to the consequences in *paragraph 11.1(a)* to *(c)*, and is satisfied the interview would not significantly harm the person's physical or mental state (see Annex G):

(a) a juvenile or person who is mentally disordered or otherwise mentally vulnerable if at the time of the interview the appropriate adult is not present;

(b) anyone other than in (*a*) who at the time of the interview appears unable to:

- appreciate the significance of questions and their answers; or
- understand what is happening because of the effects of drink, drugs or any illness, ailment or condition.

(c) a person who has difficulty understanding English or has a hearing disability, if at the time of the interview an interpreter is not present.

Notes for Guidance
11C Although juveniles or people who are mentally disordered or otherwise mentally vulnerable are often capable of providing reliable evidence, they may, without knowing or wishing to do so, be particularly prone in certain circumstances to provide information that may be unreliable, misleading or self-incriminating. Special care should always be taken when questioning such a person. . . .

Code of Practice H (applies to terrorist suspects and repeats parts of Code C)

11 Interviews: general

(a) Action

11.1 An interview in this Code is the questioning of a person arrested on suspicion of being a terrorist which, under *paragraph 10.1*, must be carried out under caution.

11.2 Following a decision to arrest a suspect, they must not be interviewed about the relevant offence except at a place designated for detention under Schedule 8 paragraph 1 of the Terrorism Act 2000, unless the consequent delay would be likely to [have similar consequences to those set out in Code C] . . .

11.8 Interview records should be made in accordance with the Code of Practice issued under Schedule 8 Paragraph 3 to the Terrorism Act where the interview takes place at a designated place of detention.

Notes

1. *Notification of rights.* When the detainee arrives at the police station, he or she will be 'booked in'. The crucial nature of this stage in the proceedings is made clear below in relation to the discussion of the legal advice provisions. Under para 3 of Codes C and H, a person must be informed orally and by written notice of four rights on arrival at the police station after arrest: the right, arising under s 56 of PACE, to have someone informed of his or her detention;[166] the right to consult a solicitor and the fact that independent legal advice is available free of charge; the right to consult the other Codes of Practice, and the right to silence as embodied in the caution.

2. *'Interviews.'* The term 'interview' is currently defined in Code C para 11.1.A for non-terrorist suspects and under Code H para 11.1 for terrorist suspects. The term 'grounds to suspect' in para 10.1 (below) in both Codes, which is crucial in determining when an 'interview', as opposed to a general enquiry, has begun, is significant: there must be grounds for suspicion that an offence has been committed by the person in question, not a mere hunch or suspicion that somebody has committed the offence.[167]

---

166   Under Codes C and H para 5, if the person cannot be contacted, the person in charge of detention or of the investigation has discretion to allow further attempts until the information has been conveyed. Section 56 PACE is subject to exceptions, similar to those under s 58 in respect of access to legal advice.

167   *R v Shah* [1994] Crim LR 125; *R v James* (1996) unreported, 8 March; *R v Blackford* (2000) WL 362561.

3. Under s 30 PACE, as amended,[168] the suspect must be taken to the police station as soon as practicable after arrest. Under para 11.1 of Code C and para 11.2 Code H the suspect should be taken to the station (or a designated place of detention in the case of terrorist suspects) once the decision to arrest has been made, unless certain exceptions apply. Therefore Code C para 11.1 and Code H para 11.2 allow for some interviewing outside the police station due to this requirement, before it is necessary to proceed to the station, of a higher level of suspicion than that denoted by para 11.1A—since interviewing can continue until the decision to arrest is taken. The suspect interviewed outside the police station may be unaware of the right to legal advice[169] and it is also at present unlikely that the interview would be tape recorded; Code E does not envisage tape recording taking place anywhere but inside the police station.[170]

4. Once the suspect is inside the police station/designated place of detention under arrest or under caution,[171] any interview[172] should be tape recorded unless an exception under the tape recording code, Code E, applies. Interviews with certain groups of terrorist suspects need not be taped.

5. PACE does not attempt to regulate the conduct of the interview except in so far as such regulation can be implied from the provision of s 76 that confessions obtained by oppression or in circumstances likely to render them unreliable will be inadmissible (see also Code C, para 11.5, Code H para 11.6). It seems that use of a degree of intimidation, haranguing, and indirect threats is still quite common, especially in interviews with juveniles.[173]

Questions

❶ Does the definition of an interview in Codes C and H cover *all* exchanges between police and suspect when there are grounds to suspect him or her of an offence? Can an 'interview' be distinguished clearly from 'relevant' comments?

❷ Is the point at which the suspect must be taken to the police station/designated place of detention for further questioning clearly demarcated? Why is this a matter of significance?

The right to silence

The aspect of the ancient, common law 'right to silence' under discussion here denotes the right of suspects not to reply to some or all questions during a police interview in the knowledge that, if the case comes to trial, a jury or magistrate will not be allowed (formally speaking) to draw adverse

---

168 The Criminal Justice Act 2003 inserted s 30A into s 30 allowing an arrested person to be released on bail at any point before the police station is reached.

169 Notification of the right to legal advice is governed by Codes C and H, para 3.1 which is expressed to apply only within the police station.

170 Code E, para 3.1. Some police forces have experimented with hand-held tape recorders used outside the police station, but at present this is by no means common practice.

171 Under Code E, para 3.4, once a volunteer becomes a suspect (i.e. at the point when he should be cautioned) the rest of the interview should be tape recorded.

172 Under Code E, para 3.1(a), an interview with a person suspected of an offence triable only summarily need not be taped.

173 See R Evans, *The Conduct of Police Interviews with Juveniles*, Home Office Research Study No 8 (1993).

inferences from the silence. In other words, the right implies that jurors or magistrates are not, formally, invited to draw the inference that the refusal of the suspect to answer certain questions implies that he/she may be guilty of the offence in question, or at least that aspects of his or her 'story' may be fabricated.

As will be found below, the right has undergone very significant modification over the last 15 years. Basically, if the suspect in the police interview has had legal advice or the opportunity of access to it (and declined it), adverse inferences can be drawn if he/she remains silent. The suspect can still refuse to answer questions, but will be told that so doing is risky if the case comes to trial, since adverse inferences are likely to be drawn against him/her. If the suspect has been *denied* the opportunity of having advice, it is still possible to remain silent, knowing that no such risk will arise. The 'caution' given before police interviewing begins explains the right to remain silent to the suspect. The caution is contained in Codes C and H and, as will be explained below, two different cautions are now given, depending on whether adverse inferences could or could not be drawn later on.

There is general academic agreement that, as Sanders and Young have put it, 'it is over the right of silence that due process and crime control principles clash most fundamentally'.[174] The right to silence, in the sense of the immunity of an accused person from having adverse inferences drawn from failure to answer questions during police questioning, is central to the due process model. In contrast, adherence to crime control principles logically demands, not only that such inferences should be drawn, but that in some or all circumstances, refusal to answer police questions should be an offence in itself, on the ground that innocent persons would not thereby be disadvantaged and the burden on the prosecution would be eased. Within the due process camp, retention of the right to silence was advocated on the grounds of its value in protecting suspects, decreasing the risk of false admissions and also on the basis that it symbolises the presumption of innocence. In the crime control camp abolition was often advocated on the ground that only the guilty have something to hide; the innocent need fear nothing from speaking.[175]

The large body of writing on the right to silence generally came down on the side of its retention.[176] The 1993 Royal Commission on Criminal Justice favoured retention,[177] but considered that, once the prosecution case was fully disclosed, defendants should be required to offer an answer to the charges made against them at the risk of adverse comment at trial on any new defence they then disclosed. However, despite the proposals of the Royal Commission, the right to silence was curtailed under the Criminal Justice and Public Order Act 1994 (CJPOA) and this was reflected in the cautioning provisions introduced under the 1995 revision of Code C. The academic consensus is that the advantages of the curtailment in terms of crime control are doubtful, whereas the risk of miscarriages of justice has been increased.[178] The 1994 provisions were then modified under s 34(2A) CJPOA in 2003 (see below) in order to ensure that the scheme met Art 6 ECHR standards, by providing that inferences could *not* be drawn where the suspect had not had an opportunity to have legal advice before being interviewed and those modifications were carried through into the 2008 version of Code C and into Code H.

---

174   *Criminal Justice*, 3rd edn (2007), p 223.

175   See S Greer, 'The Right of Silence: A Review of the Current Debate' (1990) 53 MLR 709 .

176   See Philips Commission Report, Cmnd 8092 (1981); Report of the Home Office Working Group on the Right to Silence 1989 (in favour of modification of the right). For criticism of the report, see Zuckermann [1989] Crim LR 855. For review of the debate, see S Greer (1990) 53 MLR 709.

177   Cm 2263, Proposal 82.

178   See M Zander, *The Police and Criminal Evidence Act 1984* (1995), pp 303–23 (current edn 2008); H Fenwick [1995] Crim LR 132; M Jackson [1995] Crim LR 587; Pattenden [1995] Crim LR 602–11.

S Greer, 'The right to silence: a review of the current debate'
(1990) 53 *Modern Law Review* 709, 726–28

The following extract relates to the debate on the retention or abolition of the right to silence that preceded the inception of the curtailment of the right in the Criminal Justice and Public Order Act 1994; Greer examines the value of the right to silence.

Innocent suspects in England and Wales must currently balance two risks which police interviews pose for any subsequent trial: the risk that if they stay silent this may be taken as an indication of guilt even if no adverse comment is made about it in court, and the risk that if they talk they may inadvertently make a remark which is misinterpreted at the trial, thus damaging their defence. The abolition of the right to silence would tend to oblige them to take the latter option even if there were good reasons for staying silent. One of the key considerations in balancing these risks is that the suspect is likely to be at least partially ignorant of the police case against him and is thus open to manipulation. . . .This is not necessarily to imply bad faith on the part of the police, although the Guildford Four, Birmingham Six and West Midlands Serious Crime Squad scandals show that it can clearly no longer be ruled out. Police officers acting in good faith are likely to see themselves as being capable of skilfully manoeuvring a guilty offender into giving the game away. The problem is that police assumptions about the guilt or innocence of any given suspect can be fundamentally mistaken. Instead of winkling a crook out of his shell they may instead inadvertently trick an innocent suspect into compromising his position by making remarks which are open to misrepresentation at trial. It is now widely recognised that under pressure people are capable of confessing to offences which it would have been impossible for them to have committed.

The right to silence also provides an incentive for other evidence to be sought by the police and subsequently adduced at trial. Its removal might create a risk of a decline in policing standards. It also ensures that anything which the suspect does say will have added credibility because it was offered without fear of the consequences of staying silent.

Innocent reasons for silence

There are a number of legitimate reasons why an entirely innocent suspect may be well advised not to answer at least certain police questions. They may be in an emotional and highly suggestible state of mind. They may feel guilty when in fact they have not committed an offence. They may be ignorant of some vital fact which explains away otherwise suspicious circumstances. They may be confused and liable to make mistakes which could be interpreted as deliberate lies at the trial. . . . They may use loose expressions unaware of the possible adverse interpretations which could be placed upon them at trial. . .They may have already given an explanation in the police car on the way to the police station which was not believed and thus prove reluctant to repeat it in the formal interview. Their silence may be an attempt to protect others or a reluctance to admit to having done something discreditable but not illegal. Some suspects may not want to be tricked into giving information about others because this could result in being stigmatised as an informer with all the dangers which this label carries, particularly in Northern Ireland.

I Dennis, 'The evidence provisions' [1995] *Criminal Law Review* 4, 11–12, 15–16

Dennis considers the likely impact of the 1994 provisions curtailing the right to silence.

. . . the court or jury may draw such inferences as appear proper from the failure to mention facts relied on subsequently. However, the Act gives no further guidance on what inferences might be proper. . .The most obvious inference is that the previously undisclosed fact is untrue, a conclusion based on an argument that the accused did not mention the fact to the police because he knew that they would expose its falsity. Whether this inference can form part of a chain of reasoning leading to a conclusion that the accused is guilty rather depends on the issue in the case, the nature of the fact in question and the state of the other evidence. If the 'fact' is in the nature of a 'confession and avoidance' defence, whereby the accused admits the actus reus and mens rea of the offence but sets up some independent ground of justification or excuse such as self-defence, then the rejection of that defence is almost certain to lead to the conclusion that the accused has no defence at all and is guilty. On the other hand, if the issue is identity, and the other evidence against the accused is circumstantial, the rejection of one fact offered as an innocent explanation of one piece of circumstantial evidence may not necessarily yield a further inference of guilt. This suggests that it would be wrong for a court to conclude simply because an accused fails to mention a fact relied on subsequently that he is therefore guilty. Accordingly trial judges will have to direct juries carefully on the inferences which may fairly be drawn from such failures.

Criminal Justice and Public Order Act 1994, as amended in 2003

Effect of accused's failure to mention facts when questioned or charged.[179]

34.–(1) Where, in any proceedings against a person for an offence, evidence is given that the accused—

(a) at any time before he was charged with the offence, on being questioned under caution by a constable trying to discover whether or by whom the offence had been committed, failed to mention any fact relied on in his defence in those proceedings; or

(b) on being charged with the offence or officially informed that he might be prosecuted for it, failed to mention any such fact,

being a fact which in the circumstances existing at the time the accused could reasonably have been expected to mention when so questioned, charged or informed, as the case may be,

(c) the court, in determining whether there is a case to answer; and

(d) the court, in determining whether the accused is guilty of the offence charged,

may draw such inferences from the failure as appear proper.

(2A) Where the accused was at an authorised place of detention at the time of the failure, subsections (1) and (2) above do not apply if he had not been allowed an opportunity

---

179   In force, 1 February 1997.

to consult a solicitor prior to being questioned, charged or informed as mentioned in subsection (1) above.[180]

(3)   In section 36 (effect of accused's failure or refusal to account for objects, sub-stances or marks), after subsection (4) there shall be inserted—

> '(4A) Where the accused was at an authorised place of deten-tion at the time of the failure or refusal, subsections (1) and (2) above do not apply if he had not been allowed an opportunity to consult a solicitor prior to the request being made.'

(4)   In section 37 (effect of accused's failure or refusal to account for presence at a particular place), after subsection (3) there shall be inserted—

> '(3A) Where the accused was at an authorised place of detention at the time of the failure or refusal, subsections (1) and (2) do not apply if he had not been allowed an opportunity to consult a solici-tor prior to the request being made.'

. . .

36.–(1) Where—

(a)   a person is arrested by a constable and there is—

> (i)   on his person; or
> (ii)   in or on his clothing or footwear; or
> (iii) otherwise in his possession; or
> (iv) in any place in which he is at the time of his arrest,

any object, substance or mark, or there is any mark on any such object; and

(b)   that or another constable investigating the case reasonably believes that the presence of the object, substance or mark may be attributable to the partici-pation of the person arrested in the commission of an offence specified by the constable; and

(c)   the constable informs the person arrested that he so believes, and requests him to account for the presence of the object, substance or mark; and

(d)   the person fails or refuses to do so, then if, in any proceedings against the person for the offence so specified, evidence of those matters is given, subsection (2) below applies.

Effect of accused's failure or refusal to account for presence at a particular place
37.–(1) Where—

(a)   a person arrested by a constable was found by him at a place at or about the time the offence for which he was arrested is alleged to have been committed; and

---

180   Added by s 58 of the Youth Justice and Criminal Evidence Act 1999 in order to seek to ensure compliance with Art 6(1) of the ECHR. See below, pp 1201–1202, 1207.

(b) that or another constable investigating the offence reasonably believes that the presence of the person at that place and at that time may be attributable to his participation in the commission of the offence; and

(c) the constable informs the person that he so believes, and requests him to account for that presence; and

(d) the person fails or refuses to do so,

then if, in any proceedings against the person for the offence, evidence of those matters is given, subsection (2) below applies.

[Subsection (2) of ss 36 and 37 echoes s 34(2).]

Code of Practice C (Code H is in substantially the same terms)

10 Cautions

(a) When a caution must be given

10.1 A person whom there are grounds to suspect of an offence, see *Note 10A,* must be cautioned before any questions about an offence, or further questions if the answers provide the grounds for suspicion, are put to them if either the suspect's answers or silence, (i.e. failure or refusal to answer or answer satisfactorily) may be given in evidence to a court in a prosecution. A person need not be cautioned if questions are for other necessary purposes . . .

10.2 Whenever a person not under arrest is initially cautioned, or reminded they are under caution, that person must at the same time be told they are not under arrest and are free to leave if they want to . . .

10.4 As per *Code G, section 3,* a person who is arrested, or further arrested, must also be cautioned. . . .

(b) Terms of the cautions

10.5 The caution which must be given on:

(a) arrest;

(b) all other occasions before a person is charged or informed they may be prosecuted, should, unless the restriction on drawing adverse inferences from silence applies, see *Annex C,* be in the following terms:

'You do not have to say anything. But it may harm your defence if you do not mention when questioned something which you later rely on in Court. Anything you do say may be given in evidence.'

ANNEX C – RESTRICTION ON DRAWING ADVERSE INFERENCES FROM SILENCE AND TERMS OF THE CAUTION WHEN THE RESTRICTION APPLIES

(a) The restriction on drawing adverse inferences from silence

1. The Criminal Justice and Public Order Act 1994, sections 34, 36 and 37 as amended by the Youth Justice and Criminal Evidence Act 1999, section 58 describe the conditions under which adverse inferences may be drawn from a person's failure or refusal to say anything about their involvement in the offence when interviewed, after being charged or informed they may be prosecuted. These provisions are subject to an overriding restriction

on the ability of a court or jury to draw adverse inferences from a person's silence. This restriction applies:

(a)   to any detainee at a police station, see Note 10C who, before being interviewed, see *section 11* or being charged or informed they may be prosecuted, see section 16, has:

(i)   asked for legal advice, see *section 6, paragraph 6.1*;
(ii)   not been allowed an opportunity to consult a solicitor, including the duty solicitor, as in this Code; and
(iii) not changed their mind about wanting legal advice, see *section 6*, paragraph 6.6(d).

(b) Terms of the caution when the restriction applies
2. When a requirement to caution arises at a time when the restriction on drawing adverse inferences from silence applies, the caution shall be:

'You do not have to say anything, but anything you do say may be given in evidence.'

Notes for guidance
C1 The restriction on drawing inferences from silence does not apply to a person who has not been detained and who therefore cannot be prevented from seeking legal advice if they want to. . .

The following extracts from various cases give indications as to the response in the domestic courts and at Strasbourg to the curtailment of the right to silence.

R v Argent [1997] 2 Cr App R 27 (extracts)

Lord Bingham CJ: What then are the formal conditions to be met before the jury may draw such an inference?. . .the alleged failure must occur during questioning under caution by a constable. . .the constable's questioning must be directed to trying to discover whether or by whom the alleged offence had been committed. Here. . .[t]he Detective Constable was trying to discover who inflicted the fatal wound. . .the alleged failure by the defendant must be to mention any fact relied on in his defence in those proceedings. That raises two questions of fact: first, is there some fact which the defendant has relied on in his defence; and secondly, did the defendant fail to mention it to the constable when he was being questioned in accordance with the section? Being questions of fact these questions are for the jury as the tribunal of fact to resolve. Here it would seem fairly clear that there were matters which the appellant relied on in his defence which he had not mentioned. . . . The sixth condition is that the appellant failed to mention a fact which in the circumstances existing at the time the accused could reasonably have been expected to mention when so questioned. The time referred to is the time of questioning, and account must be taken of all the relevant circumstances existing at that time. The courts should not construe the expression 'in the circumstances' restrictively: matters such as time of day, the defendant's age, experience, mental capacity, state of health, sobriety, tiredness, knowledge, personality and legal advice are all part of the relevant circumstances. . .When reference is made to 'the accused' attention is directed not to some hypothetical, reasonable accused of ordinary phlegm and fortitude but to the actual accused with such qualities, apprehensions, knowledge and advice as he is shown to have had at the time. Like so many other questions in criminal trials this is a question to be resolved by the jury in the exercise of their collective common-sense, experience and understanding of human nature. Sometimes they may conclude that it was reasonable for the defendant to have held his peace for a host of reasons. . .

In other cases the jury may conclude. . .that he could reasonably have been expected to [answer].

Condron v UK (2001) 31 EHRR 1 (extracts)

Background

The decision in *Condron and Another*,[181] in relation to the treatment in court of legal advice to stay silent, was later found at Strasbourg (below) to have led to a breach of Article 6. The appellants were to be questioned by police at the police station on suspicion of being involved in the supply and possession of heroin. The police surgeon found that they were fit to be interviewed, but their solicitor considered that they were unfit, since they were suffering withdrawal symptoms, and so advised them not to answer any questions. They relied on that advice during the interview and remained silent. Argument that it would be improper to allow an inference to be drawn under s 34 because in making no comment they had only followed the bona fide advice of their solicitor was also rejected. The interviews were admitted and the prosecution then argued that they could reasonably have been expected to mention at interview the facts they now relied on in their defence; they were cross-examined on their failure to mention such facts. They gave the explanation that they had relied on the solicitor's advice. In summing up, the judge directed the jury that they must determine whether any adverse inferences should be drawn from the failure of the defendants to mention the facts in question during the police interview. The judge did not explain that the inferences could only be drawn if, despite the explanation, the jury concluded that the silence could only sensibly be attributed to the defendants having no satisfactory explanation to give. Thus, it is possible that the jury may have drawn adverse inferences despite accepting the defendants' explanations.

The appellants were convicted and argued on appeal that the jury should not have been directed that they could draw adverse inferences from the refusal to answer questions since they had followed the advice of their solicitor in so refusing. The Court of Appeal took into account an earlier case, *Cowan and Others*,[182] in finding that inferences can be drawn if the only sensible explanation of silence was that the suspect had no explanation, or none that would stand up to cross-examination. The judge's direction was criticised in that it did not make this clear. The court then considered the procedure to be followed in relation to s 34, where silence is on legal advice. The jury may draw an adverse inference from the failure unless the accused gives the reason for the advice being given. The reason for the advice is legally privileged, since it is part of a communication between solicitor and client, but once the client gives evidence of the nature of the advice, that will probably amount to a waiver of privilege so that the solicitor and/or client can then be asked about the reasons for the advice in court. The court found that if an accused gives as the reason for not answering questions in a police interview that he has been advised not to do so, this assertion without more will not amount to a sufficient reason for not mentioning relevant matters which may later be relied on in defence. The convictions

---

181   [1997] 1 Cr App R 185.

182   [1996] QB 373; [1995] 4 All ER 939.

were upheld on the basis of the overwhelming evidence of drug supply, despite the flaw in the summing up. The decision was then challenged at Strasbourg.

Judgment of the European Court of Human Rights:

'The Court observes that it must confine its attention to the facts of the case and consider whether the drawing of inferences against the applicants under section 34 of the Criminal Justice and Public Order Act 1994 ('the 1994 Act') rendered the applicants' trial unfair within the meaning of Article 6 of the Convention. . . .

56 The Court recalls that in its *John Murray* judgment it proceeded on the basis that the question whether the right to silence is an absolute right must be answered in the negative. It noted in that case that whether the drawing of adverse inferences from an accused's silence infringes Article 6 is a matter to be determined in the light of all the circumstances of the case having regard to the situations where inferences may be drawn, the weight attached to them by the national courts in their assessment of the evidence and the degree of compulsion inherent in the situation.

60. . . . For the Court, particular caution is required when a domestic court seeks to attach weight to the fact that a person who is arrested in connection with a criminal offence and who has not been given access to a lawyer does not provide detailed responses when confronted with questions the answers to which may be incriminating. At the same time, the very fact that an accused is advised by his lawyer to maintain his silence must also be given appropriate weight by the domestic court. There may be good reason why such advice may be given. The applicants in the instant case state that they held their silence on the strength of their solicitor's advice that they were unfit to answer questions. Their solicitor testified before the domestic court that his advice was motivated by his concern about their capacity to follow questions put to them during interview. . . .

61 . . . Admittedly the trial judge drew the jury's attention to this explanation. However he did so in terms which left the jury at liberty to draw an adverse inference notwithstanding that it may have been satisfied as to the plausibility of the explanation. It is to be observed that the Court of Appeal found the terms of the trial judge's direction deficient in this respect. In the Court's opinion, as a matter of fairness, the jury should have been directed that if it was satisfied that the applicants' silence at the police interview could not sensibly be attributed to their having no answer or none that would stand up to cross-examination it should not draw an adverse inference.

62 Unlike the Court of Appeal, the Court considers that a direction to that effect was more than merely 'desirable'. It notes that the responsibility for deciding whether or not to draw such an inference rested with the jury. As the applicants have pointed out, it is impossible to ascertain what weight, if any, was given to the applicants' silence. . . the Court considers that the trial judge's omission to restrict even further the jury's discretion must be seen as incompatible with the exercise by the applicants of their right to silence at the police station.

63 The Court does not agree with the Government's submission that the fairness of the applicants' trial was secured in view of the appeal proceedings . . . the Court of Appeal had no means of ascertaining whether or not the applicants' silence played a significant role in the jury's decision to convict.

R v Beckles [2005] 1 All ER 705 (extracts)

After seeing his solicitor, the defendant refused to answer any questions when interviewed. The judge did not direct the jury that they should not draw adverse inferences from the defendant's silence during the interview with the police if they considered that his silence was attributable to legal advice rather than to having no sensible answer to the questions. He was convicted and sentenced to a total of 15 years' imprisonment.

Court of Appeal:

46. In our judgment, in a case where a solicitor's advice is relied upon by the defendant, the ultimate question for the jury remains under section 34 whether the facts relied on at the trial were facts which the defendant could <u>reasonably</u> have been expected to mention at interview. If they were not, that is the end of the matter. If the jury consider that the defendant genuinely relied on the advice, that is not necessarily the end of the matter. It may still not have been reasonable for him to rely on the advice, or the advice may not have been the true explanation for his silence. In *Betts & Hall*, Lord Justice Kay was particularly concerned [at paragraph 54] with *'whether or not the advice was truly the reason for not mentioning the facts'*. In the same paragraph he also says *'A person, who is anxious not to answer questions because he has no or no adequate explanation to offer, gains no protection from his lawyer's advice because that advice is no more than a convenient way of disguising his true motivation for not mentioning facts'*. If, in the last situation, it is possible to say that the defendant genuinely acted upon the advice, the fact that he did so because it suited his purpose may mean he was not acting reasonably in not mentioning the facts. . .

47. Under the revised direction the jury will be asked to consider whether the defendant <u>genuinely and reasonably</u> relied on the legal advice to remain silent.

48. The summing up in the present case did not match up to these standards . . .

Notes

1. Curtailment of the right to silence had already been foreshadowed. It was abolished in Northern Ireland in 1988 and curtailed in Britain in cases involving serious fraud. *R v Saunders*[183] concerned the penalty for staying silent in serious fraud investigations. Inspectors of the Department of Trade and Industry interviewed Saunders, regarding allegations of fraud. They acted under s 437 of the Companies Act 1985 which provides for a sanction against the person being investigated if he refuses to answer questions. Thus, Saunders lost his privilege against self-incrimination, which he argued was unfair and amounted to an abuse of process. Saunders took his case to Strasbourg; a breach of Art 6 was found on the basis that he had in effect been compelled to speak.

2. *Saunders v UK*[184] establishes that the use of direct coercion to obtain statements from persons will clearly be incompatible with Art 6(1) if the statement is then used against him or her in criminal proceedings. It was found at Strasbourg that the applicant's right to freedom from self-incrimination had been infringed in that he had been forced to answer questions put to him by inspectors investigating a company take-over, or risk the imposition of a criminal sanction.

   Section 172 of the Road Traffic Act 1988 (RTA) makes it an offence for motorists not to tell police who was driving their vehicle at the time of an alleged offence. The coerced statement can then be used in evidence at trial for the RTA offence in question. The provision clearly contravenes the right against self-incrimination, as interpreted in *Saunders*, and this was found to be the case in

---

183 (1966) 1 Cr App R 464.

184 (1997) 23 EHRR 313, paras 69–75.

Scotland in *Stott v Brown*[185] during the period of time when the Convention was in force in Scotland, but not in England.[186] The defendant encountered the police officers after parking her car and was suspected of driving while intoxicated; she was asked under s 172 to reveal the name of the person driving the car at the relevant time. On pain of the penalty under s 172 she did so, revealing that she had been driving and was convicted of driving while intoxicated, after the coerced statement was admitted into evidence.

The Privy Council found (*Brown v Stott*)[187] that it was not necessary to declare that s 172 is incompatible with Art 6(1) or (2). They reached the decision that the two were compatible, despite the findings in *Saunders v UK*, on the basis that the requirements of Art 6 admit of implied restriction. The restriction, Lord Hope said, must have a legitimate aim in the public interest. It was found that this was the case, bearing in mind the need to promote road safety. If so, he went on to ask, 'is there a reasonable relationship of proportionality between the means employed and the aim sought to be realised'? He found that the answer to the question, in terms of limiting the right not to incriminate oneself under Art 6(1), was in the affirmative since the section demands a response to a single question, and does not allow prolonged questioning, as in *Saunders*. The decision in *Brown* rested on the finding that coercing a statement from the defendant was not a disproportionate response to the legitimate aim of seeking to address the problem of road safety.

3. The decision in *Murray (John) v UK*[188] may be contrasted with that in *Saunders* since it indicates that, depending on the circumstances of a case, Art 6 takes a very different stance towards imposing a formal penalty on silence and drawing adverse inferences from it. Murray was arrested. A detective superintendent, pursuant to the Northern Ireland (Emergency Provisions) Act 1987, decided to delay access to a solicitor for 48 hours. While being interviewed, Murray repeatedly stated that he had 'nothing to say'. After he had seen his solicitor, he stated that he had been advised not to answer the questions. The Criminal Evidence (Northern Ireland) Order 1988 enables a court in any criminal trial to exercise discretion to draw adverse inferences from an accused's failure to mention a fact during police questioning. Such inferences were drawn from Murray's silence in the police interviews once the prosecution had established a *prima facie* case against him, and he was convicted. The Strasbourg Court emphasised that its decision was confined to the particular facts of the case in finding that no breach of Art 6(1) or (2) had occurred where adverse inferences had been drawn. The Court placed emphasis on the fact that he had been able to remain silent; also, given the strength of the evidence against him, the matter of drawing inferences was one of common sense which could not be regarded as unfair.[189] But, crucially, the Court did find that Art 6(1) and (3)(c) had been breached by the denial of custodial access to a lawyer for 48 hours since it found that such access was essential where there was a likelihood that adverse inferences would be drawn from silence. The subsequent decisions in *Averill v UK* and *Brennan v UK*[190] confirmed the finding in *Murray*, although *Brennan* took a somewhat more restrictive view of the circumstances in which a breach of Art 6 would arise.

4. Section 34, Criminal Justice and Public Order Act 1994 (CJPOA), set out above, curtailed the right to silence for all suspects, though it did not impose a formal penalty for silence. The regime under

---

185   2000 SLT 379. See [2000] J Civ Lib 193.

186   The Convention rights were brought into force in Scotland under the Scotland Act 1998, s 57(2).

187   [2001] 2 WLR 817—see Chapter 17, pp 1000–1001.

188   (1996) 22 EHRR 29. For comment, see Munday [1996] Crim LR 370.

189   *Murray (John) v UK* (1996) 22 EHRR 29, para 54.

190   (2002) 34 EHRR 18.

the 1988 Order was, in essence, the same as that under s 34 of the CJPOA, which therefore became vulnerable to challenge at Strasbourg or under the HRA. *Murray* made it clear that drawing adverse inferences from silence *when the defendant had not had access to legal advice* prior to the failure to reply to questioning would breach Art 6. Thus *Murray* required a domestic answer, bearing in mind the curtailment of the right to silence that had already occurred under ss 34–37 CJPOA. The response to *Murray* was eventually provided by s 58 of the Youth Justice and Criminal Evidence Act 1999 (which came into force in 2003). Section 58 inserted s 34(2A) into the CJPOA to provide essentially that adverse inferences shall not be drawn from a suspect's silence under caution before or after charge at an authorised place of detention if he has not been allowed an *opportunity* to consult a solicitor before that point (emphasis added). Once the provisions of ss 34, 36 and 37 of the Criminal Justice and Public Order Act 1994 were made subject to an this overriding restriction, following from s 34(2A), that position was then reflected in Code C and Code H, Annex C.

5. The change to the caution originally introduced in 1995, which occurred to reflect s 34 of the CJPOA 1994,[191] means that the suspect is warned that refusing to answer questions may lead to the drawing of adverse inferences in court. That caution still applies in certain circumstances. It is used where an opportunity to have access to legal advice has been given, and as set out above is intended to warn the suspect that failing to mention a matter likely to be relied on later in defence may be harmful to that defence. In other words, the intention was and is to put pressure on the suspect to give explanations at this point. Drawing adverse inferences from silence in police interviewing does not necessarily breach Art 6(1) or (2), but the greater the reliance placed on such inferences at the trial, the greater the likelihood that a breach will occur. Under s 38(3) of the CJPOA, a conviction cannot be based 'solely' on silence. Art 6(1) and (2) might therefore be found to be breached in circumstances in which the other evidence against the defendant was less overwhelming than it was in *Murray*.

6. Codes C and H (above) reflect s 34(2A) in the sense that they provide in Annex C that a restriction on drawing adverse inferences applies when the suspect has not had an *opportunity* to have access to legal advice. The restriction is reflected in the use of the Annex C para 2 caution, encapsulating the traditional right to silence, which must be used where an opportunity to have legal advice has not been given. In other words, the original caution, reflecting the traditional right to silence was reintroduced where that opportunity was not in place. The detailed provisions setting out the caution and determining what amounts to an 'opportunity' are set out above. Section 34(2A) CJPOA may be likely to encourage the police to afford access to legal advice. This position accords with Art 6, following *Murray*.

7. The loopholes in the provision for restricting the circumstances in which adverse inferences can be drawn are canvassed below, in relation to rights of access to legal advice. Suffice it to say here that the suspect may well be cautioned that such inferences may be drawn in circumstances in which s/he has had no *true* opportunity to have access to legal advice. Thus, the restriction on drawing adverse inferences appears to adhere to the due process demands of Art 6 but, it is argued, falls short of them in practice.

8. *Adverse inference-drawing.* The case law on s 34 of the CJPOA establishes, following *R v Cowan*,[192] that the jury should only consider drawing inferences under s 34 if a *prima facie* case to answer has been made out by the prosecution. Inferences may only be drawn if a sound explanation for remaining silent is not proffered;[193] it cannot be inferred that the reason for silence was the need to

---

191   Now see Code C Paragraph 10.5; Code H para 10.4 (2008 revision).

192   [1996] 1 Cr App R 1.

193   This is implicit in *R v Cowan* [1996] 1 Cr App R 1; see also *R v Argent* [1997] Cr App R 27.

concoct a false explanation if the real and innocent reason for silence is put forward, so long as the reason is plausible. A number of circumstances can be taken into account. In *Argent*,[194] the Court of Appeal found that when considering whether, in the circumstances existing at the time, the defendant could reasonably have been expected to mention the fact he now relies on, the court should take into account matters such as the defendant's age, health, experience, mental capacity, sobriety, tiredness, personality and legal advice. It is a matter for the jury to resolve whether, bearing these matters in mind, the defendant could have been expected to mention the fact in question, although the judge may give them guidance. Any restrictive impact of these findings is doubtful; in *R v Friend*[195] adverse inferences were drawn under s 35 against a defendant aged 14, with a mental age of nine.

9. *The situation where the legal advisor advises silence.* The explanation often given for remaining silent is that the legal advisor advised silence, or at least a selective silence. This explanation has given rise to a problem that is still bedeviling the UK courts (as is apparent from the extracts above) and it is argued that they still have not dealt with it satisfactorily in Art 6 terms, despite more than one trip to Strasbourg, pre-HRA. From a crime control perspective the concern is that allowing this explanation would drive a coach and horses through the CJPOA provisions: legal advisors could merely advise silence in almost all circumstances and so doing would then normally preclude the drawing of adverse inferences.

10. From a due process perspective, accepting the drawing of adverse inferences when the solicitor has advised silence is equally problematic. The solicitor is there in the police station to represent the interests of his or her client; he or she may consider that the best recourse for the client is silence, if, for example, the client has been pressurised or intimidated, or is unable to cope with the questioning. So the solicitor, in seeking to further the best interests of the client, is clearly placed in a dilemma: if she advises silence this may turn out to be to the client's disadvantage. So the solicitor may be forced to advise a client to talk against her better judgement, for fear of the penalty attaching to silence later on. The domestic courts have tended to adopt the crime control stance in dealing with this issue.

11. In *Condron*[196] (above) the defendants acted on legal advice in refusing to answer questions. It was found on appeal that adverse inferences could nevertheless be drawn from their silence. It was found at Strasbourg (the decision is extracted above) that the applicants in *Condron v UK*[197] had failed to receive a fair trial under Article 6 on the basis that the appeal court should not have found that the conviction was safe, despite the erroneous direction of the judge to the jury. Since the Court could not know what part the drawing of adverse inferences played in the jury's decision, it should have allowed the appeal. That decision impliedly confirms that juries should be directed that they should not draw adverse inferences where they consider that there was a sound reason for advising silence *and* it was reasonable for the defendant to rely on the advice.

12. In *R v Beckles*[198] (extracted above) the applicant appealed on the ground that there had been a misdirection to the jury as to their right, under s 34 of the Criminal Justice and Public Order Act 1994, to draw adverse inferences from the defendant's silence during an interview with police. Lord Woolf found that in a case where a solicitor's advice was relied upon by the defendant in the police interview, the ultimate question for the jury, under s 34, remained whether the facts relied on at the

---

194   [1997] 2 Cr App R 27; *The Times*, 19 December 1996. See K Broome, 'An Inference of Guilt' (1997) 141 SJ 202.

195   [1997] 1 WLR 1433.

196   [1997] 1 Cr App R 185.

197   (2001) 31 EHRR 1; [2000] Crim LR 679.

198   [2004] EWCA 2766.

trial were facts which the defendant could reasonably have been expected to mention at interview. The trial judge had not directed the jury to consider the reasonableness or the genuineness of the defendant's reliance on his solicitor's advice as the reason why he did not answer questions in interview. It was found that that misdirection made the defendant's conviction unsafe. The appeal was allowed and a retrial was ordered. Thus Lord Woolf purported to take account of the Strasbourg decision in his findings. However, the emphasis on, in a sense, justifying the silence – even where it was genuinely in reliance on the legal advice—represents some departure from the ECHR decision. *Beckles* is indicative of a Court of Appeal tendency, after *Condron v UK*, to take an unsympathetic stance towards defendants who rely on legal advice in remaining silent.[199] Beckles took his case to Strasbourg.

13. The European Court of Human Rights confirmed its ruling in *Condron* in *Beckles v United Kingdom*.[200] The Court found that there had been a violation of Art 6(1) of the European Convention of Human Rights as to the trial judge's directions to the jury. The misdirection concerned the instruction to the jury as to their right, under s 34 of the 1994 Act, to draw adverse inferences from the defendant's silence during an interview with police. The Court had found that the jury should have been directed that if they considered that the defendant had genuinely remained silent on legal advice they should consider refusing to draw an adverse inference from his silence.

14. Since *Beckles v UK* the use of s 34 has remained a difficult and confusing area of law, and the problems are evident in the decision in *R v Bresa*.[201] In giving a direction to the jury on the effect of s 34 the judge failed to say that to draw adverse inferences the jury had to be *sure* that the defendant had remained silent, not because of the legal advice, but because he had no answer to give in the interview. The Court of Appeal found that the direction was flawed, the conviction therefore unsafe, and ordered a retrial. The Court said the judge should have given a direction in (broadly) the following terms: 'If you accept the evidence that he was so advised [to remain silent], this is obviously an important consideration; but it does not automatically prevent you from drawing any conclusion from his silence. . . a person given legal advice has the choice whether to accept or reject it. . . You have no explanation for the advice in this case. It is the defendant's right not to reveal the contents of any advice from his solicitor. . . The question for you is whether the defendant could reasonably have been expected to mention the facts on which he now relies and saying that he had legal advice without more cannot automatically make it reasonable. If, for example, you consider that he had or may have had an answer to give, i.e. that he was acting in self-defence, but genuinely and reasonably relied on the legal advice to remain silent, you should not draw any conclusion against him. But if, for example, you were sure that the defendant remained silent, not because of the legal advice, but because he had not acted in self-defence and that was a matter which he fabricated later, and merely latched on to the legal advice as a convenient shield behind which to hide, you would be entitled to draw a conclusion against him.'[202]

15. It is difficult to see how a jury could be *sure* that the defendant had genuinely and reasonably relied on the legal advice. The problem in essence is that if the solicitor and client do not breach the confidentiality of their consultations, they run the risk that the jury, without an explanation for the reasons behind the legal advice, will assume that the defence was fabricated later and that the advice is merely 'a convenient shield behind which to hide'.

---

199   See *R v Inman* [2002] EWCA 1950; *R v Chenia* [2003] 2 Cr App 6; *R v Hoare and Pierce* [2004] EWCA Crim 784; *R v Howell* [2003] Crim LR 405; *R v Turner* [2004] 1 All ER 1025.

200   (2002) 36 EHRR 162.

201   [2005] EWCA Crim 1414.

202   At [49].

Questions

❶   Are ss 34, 36 and 37 of the CJPOA confined to formal interviews within the police station? Why is this a matter of significance?

❷   Are there grounds for fearing that curtailment of the right to silence may lead to further miscarriages of justice?

❸   Is the current position in relation to the curtailment of the right to silence under ss 34, 36 and 37 of the CJPOA fully in harmony with Art 6 of the ECHR, as afforded further effect in domestic law under the HRA?

Access to legal advice

There is general agreement that the most significant protection for due process introduced for the first time by PACE[203] was that of the right of access to legal advice in the police station.[204] But this right is far from absolute. It is subject to a number of formal exceptions, which are broader in terrorist cases and it is dependent on a formal request to exercise it. It is also limited to interviewing in police stations and may be subverted informally in a variety of ways. Nevertheless, its impact in due process terms should not be under-estimated. It has been bolstered by the domestic response to the key decision at Strasbourg on the demands of Art 6, *Murray v UK*.[205] The legislative response to *Murray*, considered above, means that where suspects, including terrorist suspects, are in police detention and have been formally denied access to legal advice, adverse inferences cannot be drawn from silence.

Access to legal advice should have an impact in upholding due process which encompasses, but goes beyond, advising on making 'no comment' answers. How far it has such an impact in practice is debatable. The impact varies, depending on the contact with the suspect and the expertise of the advisor. The Sanders research in 1989 found that telephone advice alone had little impact on suspects: 50% of those who received telephone advice made admissions, as opposed to 59.6% of those who received no advice.[206] The research criticised the great variation in practice between advisors, and considered that too many duty solicitors gave telephone advice only, thereby depriving the client of most of the benefits of legal advice.[207] Subsequent research suggests that in 23% of cases when advice

---

203   The Criminal Law Act 1977, s 62 declared a narrow entitlement to have one reasonably named person informed of the arrest. It did not provide that the arrestee must be informed of this right, nor did it provide any sanction for non-compliance by a police officer. That statutory form of this right gave it no greater force than the non-statutory Judges' Rules (rules of practice for the guidance of the police: see *Practice Note* [1984] 1 All ER 237; 1 WLR 152). The Judges' Rules upheld the right of the suspect/arrestee in the police station to communicate with/consult a solicitor, but permitted the withholding of such access 'lest unreasonable delay or hindrance is caused to the process of investigation or the administration of justice'. Any officer, in relation to a person detained for any offence, could deny access to legal advice on these broad grounds; see *Lemsatef* [1977] 1 WLR 812; [1977] 2 All ER 835.

204   See, e.g. Sanders and Young, *Criminal Justice*, 3rd edn (2007), Chapter 4.5; D Dixon, *Miscarriages of Justice* (1999), p 67. The research studies mentioned in this chapter do not question the value of the legal right of access per se, although they do question its quality and the responses of the police.

205   (1996) 22 EHRR 29.

206   Sanders *et al*, *Advice and Assistance at Police Stations*, November 1989.

207   The Sanders research, *ibid*, found that only 50% of solicitors attended the police station: 25% gave advice over the telephone and 25% gave no advice. Even attendances at the police station were not always followed by attendance at the interview. A few solicitors merely put the police case to the suspect (p 150). It appeared that some advisors who did attend the interview disadvantaged the client by seeming to give their imprimatur to improper police behaviour.

is requested, telephone advice only continues to be given, and only around 12–14% of suspects in police interviews have an advisor present.[208]

Police and Criminal Evidence Act 1984

Access to legal advice

58.–(1) A person arrested and held in custody in a police station or other premises shall be entitled, if he so requests, to consult a solicitor privately at any time. . . .

(4) If a person makes such a request, he must be permitted to consult a solicitor as soon as is practicable except to the extent that delay is permitted by this section.

(5) In any case he must be permitted to consult a solicitor within 36 hours from the relevant time, as defined in section 41(2) above.

(6) Delay in compliance with a request is only permitted—

   (a) in the case of a person who is in police detention for a serious arrestable offence; and

   (b) if an officer of at least the rank of superintendent authorises it.

. . .

(8) Subject to sub-section (8A) below an officer may only authorise delay where he has reasonable grounds for believing that the exercise of the right conferred by subsection (1) above at the time when the person detained desires to exercise it—

   (a) will lead to interference with or harm to evidence connected with a serious arrestable offence or interference with or physical injury to other persons; or

   (b) will lead to the alerting of other persons suspected of having committed such an offence but not yet arrested for it; or

   (c) will hinder the recovery of any property obtained as a result of such an offence.

(8A) An officer may also authorise delay where the serious arrestable offence is a drug trafficking offence or an offence to which Part VI of the Criminal Justice Act 1988 applies and the officer has reasonable grounds for believing—

   (a) . . . that the recovery of the value of that person's proceeds of drug trafficking will be hindered by the exercise of the right conferred by subsection (1) above; and

   (b) . . . the recovery of the value of the property obtained by that person from or in connection with the offence or of the pecuniary advantage derived by him from or in connection with it will be hindered by the exercise of the right conferred by subsection (1) above.

(12) Nothing in this section applies to a person arrested or detained under the terrorism provisions.[209]

---

208   Brown, *PACE Ten Years On: A Review of the Research*, Home Office Research Study 155, 1997, at pp 94–95.

209   Substituted by the TA 2000, Sched 15, para 5(6).

Terrorism Act 2000

Schedule 8
Rights: England, Wales and Northern Ireland

7.–(1) Subject to paragraphs 8 and 9, a person detained under Schedule 7 or section 41 at a police station in England, Wales or Northern Ireland shall be entitled, if he so requests, to consult a solicitor as soon as is reasonably practicable, privately and at any time. . .

8.–(1) . . . an officer of at least the rank of superintendent may authorise a delay—

. . .

    (b)   in permitting a detained person to consult a solicitor under paragraph 7.

. . .

  (3) Subject to sub-paragraph (5), an officer may give an authorisation under sub-paragraph (1) only if he has reasonable grounds for believing—

    (a)   in the case of an authorisation under sub-paragraph (1)(a), that informing the named person of the detained person's detention will have any of the consequences specified in subparagraph (4), or

    (b)   in the case of an authorisation under sub-paragraph (1)(b), that the exercise of the right under paragraph 7 at the time when the detained person desires to exercise it will have any of the consequences specified in sub-paragraph (4).

  (4) Those consequences are—

    (a)   interference with or harm to evidence of a serious arrestable offence,

    (b)   interference with or physical injury to any person,

    (c)   the alerting of persons who are suspected of having committed a serious arrestable offence but who have not been arrested for it,

    (d)   the hindering of the recovery of property obtained as a result of a serious arrestable offence or in respect of which a forfeiture order could be made under section 23,

    (e)   interference with the gathering of information about the commission, preparation or instigation of acts of terrorism,

    (f)   the alerting of a person and thereby making it more difficult to prevent an act of terrorism, and

    (g)   the alerting of a person and thereby making it more difficult to secure a person's apprehension, prosecution or conviction in connection with the commission, preparation or instigation of an act of terrorism. . . .

Rights: Scotland

. . .

16.–(6) A person detained shall be entitled to consult a solicitor at any time, without delay.

(7) A police officer not below the rank of superintendent may authorise a delay in holding the consultation where, in his view, the delay is necessary on one of the grounds mentioned in paragraph 17(3). . .

17.–(3) The grounds mentioned in paragraph 16(4) and (7) and in sub-paragraph (1) are—

(a) that it is in the interests of the investigation or prevention of crime;

(b) that it is in the interests of the apprehension, prosecution or conviction of offenders;

(c) that it will further the recovery of property obtained as a result of the commission of an offence or in respect of which a forfeiture order could be made under section 23;

(d) that it will further the operation of Part VI of the Criminal Justice Act 1988, Part I of the Proceeds of Crime (Scotland) Act 1995 or the Proceeds of Crime (Northern Ireland) Order 1996 (confiscation of the proceeds of an offence).

Code of Practice C

6 Right to legal advice

(a) Action

6.1 Unless *Annex B* applies, all detainees must be informed that they may at any time consult and communicate privately with a solicitor, whether in person, in writing or by telephone, and that free independent legal advice is available. . . .

6.4 No police officer should, at any time, do or say anything with the intention of dissuading a detainee from obtaining legal advice.

6.5 The exercise of the right of access to legal advice may be delayed only as in *Annex B*.

6.5A In the case of a juvenile, an appropriate adult should consider whether legal advice from a solicitor is required.

6.6 A detainee who wants legal advice may not be interviewed or continue to be interviewed until they have received such advice unless:

(a) *Annex B* applies, when the restriction on drawing adverse inferences from silence in *Annex C* will apply because the detainee is not allowed an opportunity to consult a solicitor; or

(b) an officer of superintendent rank or above has reasonable grounds for believing that:

(i) the consequent delay might:

- lead to interference with, or harm to, evidence connected with an offence;
- lead to interference with, or physical harm to, other people;
- lead to serious loss of, or damage to, property;
- lead to alerting other people suspected of having committed an offence but not yet arrested for it;
- hinder the recovery of property obtained in consequence of the commission of an offence.

       (ii)   when a solicitor, including a duty solicitor, has been contacted and has agreed to attend, awaiting their arrival would cause unreasonable delay to the process of investigation.

Note: In these cases the restriction on drawing adverse inferences from silence in *Annex C* will apply because the detainee is not allowed an opportunity to consult a solicitor.

    (c) the solicitor the detainee has nominated or selected from a list:

       (i)   cannot be contacted;
       (ii)   has previously indicated they do not wish to be contacted; or
       (iii)   having been contacted, has declined to attend; and

the detainee has been advised of the Duty Solicitor Scheme but has declined to ask for the duty solicitor.

In these circumstances the interview may be started or continued without further delay provided an officer of inspector rank or above has agreed to the interview proceeding.

    Note: The restriction on drawing adverse inferences from silence in Annex C will not apply because the detainee is allowed an opportunity to consult the duty solicitor.

    (d) the detainee changes their mind, about wanting legal advice.

In these circumstances the interview may be started or continued without delay provided that:

       (i)   the detainee agrees to do so, in writing or on the interview record made in accordance with Code E or F; and
       (ii)   an officer of inspector rank or above has inquired about the detainee's reasons for their change of mind and gives authority for the interview to proceed.

In these circumstances the restriction on drawing adverse inferences from silence in *Annex C* will not apply because the detainee is allowed an opportunity to consult a solicitor if they wish.

Code of Practice H

6 Right to legal advice

(a) Action
6.1 Unless *Annex B* applies, all detainees must be informed that they may at any time consult and communicate privately with a solicitor, whether in person, in writing or by telephone, and that free independent legal advice is available from the duty solicitor.
    Where an appropriate adult is in attendance, they must also be informed of this right. . . .
6.4 The exercise of the right of access to legal advice may be delayed exceptionally only as in *Annex B*. . . .[6.4 goes on to repeat 6.5 Code C.]
6.5 An officer of the rank of Commander or Assistant Chief Constable may give a direction under TACT Schedule 8 paragraph 9 that a detainee may only consult a solicitor

within the sight and hearing of a qualified officer. Such a direction may only be given if the officer has reasonable grounds to believe that if it were not, it may result in one of the consequences set out in TACT Schedule 8 paragraphs 8(4) or 8(5)(c).

R v Samuel [1988] 2 WLR 920, 930, 931, 932, CA

The leading case determining the scope of the s 58 exceptions is *Samuel*. The appellant was arrested on suspicion of armed robbery and, after questioning at the police station, asked to see a solicitor. The request was refused, apparently on the grounds that other suspects might be warned[210] and that recovery of the outstanding stolen money might thereby be hindered;[211] the appellant subsequently confessed to the robbery and was later convicted. On appeal the defence argued that the refusal of access was not justifiable under s 58(8) and that therefore the confession obtained should not have been admitted into evidence as it had been obtained due to impropriety.

Hodgson J: . . .The right denied is a right 'to consult a solicitor privately'. The person denied that right is in police detention. In practice, the only way that the person can make any of [s 58(8)] (a) to (c) happen is by some communication from him to the solicitor. For (a) to (c) to be made to happen the solicitor must do something. If he does something knowing that it will result in anything in (a) to (c) happening he will, almost inevitably, commit a serious criminal offence. Therefore, inadvertent or unwitting conduct apart, the officer must believe that a solicitor will, if allowed to consult with a detained person, thereafter commit a criminal offence. Solicitors are officers of the court. We think that the number of times that a police officer could genuinely be in that state of belief will be rare. . . .

Mr Jones was unable to point to any inadvertent conduct by Mr Warner which could have led to any of the results in (a)–(c) save his transmission to someone of some sort of coded message. We do not know who made the decision at 4.45pm but we find it impossible to believe that whoever did had reasonable grounds for the belief required by s 58(8).

The more sinister side to the decision is, of course, this. The police had, over a period exceeding 24 hours, interviewed this young man four times without obtaining any confession from him in respect of the robbery. Time was running out for them. . . Thirty-six hours from the relevant time would expire in the early hours of the morning; then access to a solicitor would have to be permitted. On the following day the appellant would have to be taken before the magistrates' court (s 46). As he had already been interviewed four times and been in police custody for over 24 hours, the expectation would be that a solicitor might well consider that, at least for that evening, enough was enough and that he ought to advise his client not to answer further questions. There were, therefore, very few hours left for the police to interview the appellant without his having legal advice. And, as events showed, that was something the police very much wanted to do; this one knows because, within 37 minutes, he was in fact interviewed. . . The interview at 5.20pm was conducted by a detective inspector, the sergeant and detective being present, so that the appellant now faced a different questioner and a total of three police officers. At that interview he made the confession to the robbery. Regrettably we have come to the conclusion that whoever made the decision to refuse Mr Warner access at 4.45pm was very probably

---

210   See s 58(8)(b).

211   See s 58(8)(c).

motivated by a desire to have one last chance of interviewing the appellant in the absence of a solicitor.

. . .we find that the refusal of access to Mr Warner at 4.45pm was unjustified. That being so the interview, without a solicitor being present, should not have taken place: Code 6.3.

Notes

1. The consequence of the finding in *Samuel* that s 58 had been breached is considered below, p 1226.
2. *The right of access to legal advice.* This is really a bundle of rights. As the extracts above show, both PACE and the Terrorism Act 2000 entitle a suspect to consult an advisor privately,[212] although the TA provides in Sched 8, para 9 an exception to the privacy requirement. The statutory entitlement is therefore both to access to legal advice and to the preservation of the confidentiality of solicitor/client consultation. The access to legal advice is available under a publicly funded scheme;[213] under Codes C and H the suspect is entitled to be informed of this right;[214] given, if necessary, the name of the duty solicitor[215] and to be permitted to have the solicitor present during questioning.[216] The right to have a solicitor present in the interview, available only under Codes C and H, rather than PACE or the TA, is arguably the most significant right.[217]
3. The right of custodial access to legal advice is, as discussed above, also protected by Art 6 of the European Convention on Human Rights, under the HRA. Article 6(3)(c) provides that everyone charged with a criminal offence has the right to defend himself through legal assistance of his own choosing.[218] Access to legal advice in pre-trial questioning, as opposed to such access for the purposes of the trial, is not expressly provided for in Art 6 (see Chapter 7).[219] However, protection for such access has been implied into Art 6(1) and 6(3)(c). In *Murray (John) v UK*[220] the Court found that Art 6(1) and (3)(c) had been breached by the denial of custodial access to a lawyer for 48 hours, since such access was essential where there was a likelihood that adverse inferences would be drawn from silence. It found that Article 6 would normally require that the accused should be allowed to benefit from the assistance of a lawyer in the initial stages of police interrogation, although that right might be subject to restrictions for good cause. Where a violation of Art 6 is claimed in respect of a lack of access to legal advice in pre-trial questioning, a breach of both paras (1) and (3) will be in question. The judgment in *Imbrioscia v Switzerland*[221] suggests that if either the accused or his lawyer requests that the latter should be present in pre-trial questioning, this should be allowed if the answers to questions would be likely to prejudice the defence; it is now clear, as discussed below, that the ruling is applicable to police interviews.

---

212   PACE, s 58(1): 'A person in police detention shall be entitled, if he so requests, to consult a solicitor privately at any time.' For TA suspects, this right also arises under the TA, Sched 8, para 7.

213   See the Legal Aid Act 1988, Sched 6; the Access to Justice Act 1999. Everyone is entitled to free legal advice at the police station from a solicitor whose office is contracted with the Legal Services Commission, whatever their income and capital/savings. The Access to Justice Act provides for payment to franchised firms for most criminal legal aid work, on a fixed fee contract basis.

214   Codes C and H, para 3.1(ii).

215   Codes C and H, Note 6B.

216   Code C, para 6.8, Code H 6.9.

217   See further Saunders and Young (2007), n 1 above at pp 205–212.

218   See Chapter 7, p 310.

219   P 313.

220   (1996) 22 EHRR 29.

221   (1993) 17 EHRR 441; A 275 (1993).

4. *Access to legal advice where adverse inferences may be drawn from silence.* The Strasbourg Court went further than *Imbrioscia* in *Murray (John) v UK*,[222] which is also discussed above, in finding that Art 6(1) and (3)(c) had been breached by the denial of custodial access to a lawyer for 48 hours, since such access was essential where there was a likelihood that adverse inferences would be drawn from silence. It found that where such inferences could be drawn, Art 6 would normally require that the accused should be allowed to benefit from the assistance of a lawyer in the initial stages of a police interrogation, although that right might be subject to restrictions for good cause.

5. The findings in *Murray* were confirmed in *Averill v UK*.[223] The applicant was denied access to a solicitor during the first 24 hours of interrogation; he was then allowed to consult a solicitor, but the solicitor was not allowed to be present during subsequent interviews. Adverse inferences were drawn from his silence at trial under Art 3 of the Criminal Evidence (Northern Ireland) Order 1988. The Court found that no breach of Art 6(1) had occurred; he had been subject to 'indirect compulsion', due to the probability that adverse inferences would be drawn if he remained silent, but that in itself was not decisive.[224] The drawing of adverse inferences, it was found, did not render the trial unfair since the presence of incriminating fibres found on his clothing called for an explanation from him. Further, the drawing of adverse inferences was only one factor in the finding that the charges were proved. However, the Court did find a breach of Art 6(3)(c) read with Art 6(1) on the basis—which it noted in *Murray*—that, bearing in mind the scheme contained in the 1998 Order, it is of 'paramount importance for the rights of the defence that an accused has access to a lawyer at the initial stages of police interrogation'.[225] This was because, under the scheme, the accused is confronted with a dilemma from the outset. If he remains silent, adverse inferences may be drawn. If he breaks his silence, his defence may be prejudiced. In order to deal with this dilemma, the Court found, legal advice is needed at the initial stages of the interrogation.[226] Thus, a right of access to legal advice in custodial questioning may be implied into Art 6(3)(c) when read with Art 6(1) where the drawing of adverse inferences is a relevant issue.

    In *Brennan v UK*[227] the accused had been formally denied access to legal advice, but the denial of access was then lifted, although the accused did not in fact receive legal advice. At that point he made a confession. The European Court found that no adverse inferences had in fact been drawn from his silence at trial, and that he had made the confession at a time when the formal denial of access was no longer operative. Taking those factors into account, no breach of Art 6 was found. The limitations on access to legal advice and certain of the formal and informal loopholes in the access discussed below arguably may not fully accord with the requirements of Art 6(3)(c) in conjunction with Art 6(1) as interpreted in *Murray* and *Averill*.

6. *Access to legal advice: formal exceptions to the right, limitations and informal subversion of the right.* The rights of access to legal advice are limited in formal and informal terms. The formal PACE and TA exceptions are narrowly drawn and, following *R v Samuel* (above), have received a narrow interpretation. This cannot, however, be said of the formal Code C and H exceptions. Further, the factor which previously motivated the police to delay (or refuse) access to legal advice remains unchanged: the suspect still has the right to remain silent and the legal advisor may advise him or

---

222   (1996) 22 EHRR 29.

223   (2001) 31 EHRR 36; *The Times*, 20 June 2000. See also *Magee v UK* (2001) 31 EHRR 35; *The Times*, 20 June 2000.

224   Para 48.

225   Para 59.

226   Para 57.

227   (2002) 34 EHRR 18.

her to exercise it in the particular circumstances of the case, despite the risk that adverse inferences may be drawn later at court. Even if the solicitor does not advise silence, the police may think that they are more likely to obtain incriminating admissions from detainees in the absence of a solicitor and therefore at times may deny or delay access to one. Quite a large body of research suggests that the police prefer to interview suspects who have not had advice and without an advisor present.[228] Research confirms that the possibility of formally delaying access to legal advice is almost certainly not as significant as the more informal police influence on the notification and delivery of advice and on securing the presence of the advisor.[229]

7. *Delaying access to legal advice under s 58(8) PACE—non-terrorist suspects.* The most direct method of delaying legal advice involves invoking one of the s 58(8) PACE exceptions. The exceptions come into operation if the suspect is in police detention for an indictable offence. It used to be the case that the exceptions applied in respect of 'serious arrestable offences'. The concept of an arrestable offence under s 24 was abolished in 2005 when PACE was amended, so s 58(8) has now broadened to cover indictable offences.[230] Thus, the officer must believe on reasonable grounds that the exercise of the right at the time when the person in police detention desires to exercise it will lead to the solicitor acting as a channel of communication between the detainee and others—alerting them or hindering the recovery of stolen property or the products of drug trafficking, or the benefits of crime. These exceptions are repeated in Annex B of Code C, which also provides that if the exception is invoked the suspect must be allowed to choose another solicitor. The leading case determining the scope of the s 58 exceptions is *Samuel*[231] (extracted above). The court considered that only in the remote contingency that evidence could be produced as to the corruption or inexperience of a particular solicitor would a police officer be able to assert a reasonable belief that a solicitor would alert others. This interpretation of s 58(8) greatly narrowed its scope.

8. *Terrorism suspects—statutory exceptions.* Under the TA 2000, as amended, the access to legal advice can be delayed for up to 48 hours (see Sched 8, para 8(2)) on the grounds for delay mentioned above, with additional ones relating to terrorism. The right can be delayed if a superintendent reasonably believes that communication with an advisor will lead to interference with the gathering of information about the commission, preparation, or instigation of acts of terrorism or make it more difficult to prevent an act of terrorism or apprehend and prosecute the perpetrators of any such act. Delay can be for 48 hours, which is also the period of time for which the suspect can be detained on police authority alone, without recourse to judicial authorisation. The TA provisions largely continue the previous counter-terrorism regime and therefore do not address the concerns of those who view confessions obtained after 24 hours in detention as inherently fallible,[232] particularly where the detainee has also been held without access to legal advice and incommunicado. The wider possibilities of delaying access under the TA in relation to the terrorist, as opposed to the conventional suspect, are therefore open to question under Art 6, as discussed

---

228 The research undertaken by Sanders *et al, Advice and Assistance at Police Stations,* November 1989; Brown, *PACE Ten Years On: A Review of the Research,* Home Office Research Study 155, 1997, p 77.

229 The research undertaken by Sanders *et al, ibid,* put the figure at around 2%. In comparison, Brown, *ibid,* found that approximately 35% of suspects may have been influenced against advice by the police. The Government's *Consultation Paper on Terrorism* (1998) stated that it was not aware of any formal denial in terrorist cases over the last two years in Britain (para 8.31).

230 A serious arrestable offence was defined in s 116. The amendment was made to s 58(6) by the Serious and Organised Crime Act 2005, Sched 7(3), para 43(1)(b). The Criminal Justice Act 1988, s 99 extended the exceptions to drug trafficking offences.

231 [1988] QB 615; [1988] 2 All ER 135; [1988] 2 WLR 920, CA.

232 See, e.g. Walker, *Miscarriages of Justice* (1999), pp 39 and 18.

below. Code H reflects the TA exceptions in para 6.7(iii), and they are repeated in Annex B. If an exception is invoked the restriction on drawing adverse inferences applies under s 34(2)A CJPOA, and this is stated in Code H in para 6.7(b).

9. *Unavailability of nominated solicitor or delay.* Further powers to delay access and to interview the suspect without his having had legal advice arise under Codes C and H. Code C, para 6.6(b)(ii) provides that the interview can be started although the suspect has not received advice if 'a solicitor has agreed to attend, and awaiting his arrival would cause unreasonable delay to the process of the investigation'. This is repeated in Annex B. Code H contains the same exception in para 6.7. The restriction on drawing adverse inferences from silence applies. Sub-paragraph 6.6(c) Code C and 6.7(c) Code H provides two further exceptions: that the detainee can be interviewed without legal advice if the nominated solicitor is unavailable and, firstly notification of the duty solicitor scheme is given but the duty solicitor is unavailable, or second he or she is not required. In these instances the restriction on drawing adverse inferences from silence does *not* apply on the basis that the suspect has had an opportunity to have advice. The first exception does not, it is argued, accord with Art 6 as interpreted in *Murray* and *Averill* since where both the nominated and duty solicitor are unavailable, the suspect cannot be said to have had an opportunity to have legal advice.

10. *Consent to forgo advice.* The detainee who has decided to have advice can nevertheless change his or her mind; this is provided for by sub-para 6.6(d) of both Codes, if the consent is given in writing or on tape and an officer of the rank of inspector or above has inquired into the reason for the change of mind and gives authority for the interview to proceed. The ruling of the Court of Appeal in *Hughes*[233] suggested that if the police misled the suspect without bad faith, a resultant consent would be treated as genuine. The appellant, disappointed of obtaining advice from his own solicitor, inquired about the duty solicitor scheme but was informed, erroneously (but in good faith), that no solicitor was available. Under this misapprehension, he gave consent to be interviewed and the Court of Appeal took the view that his consent was not thereby vitiated. The restriction on drawing adverse inferences does not apply since the suspect has apparently consented to forego advice.

11. *Implied limitations and informal subversion of the rights.* Interviews outside the police station continue to be unaffected by rights of access to legal advice, in the sense that notification of the right under para 3.1 of Codes C and H is reserved for the police station, thus disadvantaging the inexperienced suspect who is not already aware of it at the point when admissions may be made.[234] The very significant reform of notification of legal advice on caution was omitted from all the Code C revisions, including the 2008 one, despite the fact of curtailment of the right to silence and of the findings discussed at Strasbourg to the effect that questioning accompanied by the risk of drawing adverse inferences from silence without access to legal advice breaches Art 6(1). The restriction on drawing adverse inferences from silence where no opportunity to have access to legal advice has been given (in Codes C and H, Annex C), goes only part of the way to meet those findings, it is argued, since the restriction only applies inside the police station. The lack of notification of legal advice outside the police station, combined with the leeway for interviewing before the police station is reached within Codes C and H, is probably one of the key flaws in the PACE scheme in due process terms.

---

233   [1988] Crim LR 519, CA, transcript from LEXIS.

234   Softley's research into the issue indicated that when suspects were informed of this right, requests for advice were three times as high as when they were not so informed (Softley, *Police Interrogations*, 1980).

REDRESS FOR POLICE IMPROPRIETY

Introduction

This chapter has been concerned so far with the question of the balance to be struck between the exercise of powers by the police in conducting an investigation on the one hand and safeguards for the suspect against abuse of power on the other. As we have seen, PACE, the TA and the Codes of Practice set out to maintain this balance by declaring certain standards for the conduct of criminal investigations. However, it may be that an investigation does not, at certain points, reach those standards. In such circumstances certain means of redress are available[235] and these are considered below.

Exclusion of evidence

Exclusion of evidence may occur if within the investigation that produced the evidence significant breaches of the relevant rules occur or in some other respect malpractice by the police has occurred. The key reason for excluding evidence in that circumstance is that it may be unreliable, but that is not the only reason. The rules on exclusion of evidence are complex, as the discussion below indicates. PACE provides four separate tests which can be applied to a confession to determine whether it is admissible in evidence. In theory, all four tests could be applied to a particular confession, although in practice it may not be necessary to consider all of them. They are the 'oppression' test (s 76(2)(a)), the 'reliability' test (s 76(2)(b)), and the 'fairness' test (s 78). PACE also preserves the residual common law discretion to exclude evidence, under s 82(3). The scheme in respect of non-confession evidence is less complex: only ss 78 and 82(3) can be applicable. In practice, s 78 is by far the most significant section to be considered in relation to the possibility of excluding evidence. In practice, confessions are rarely excluded under either head of s 76; this may be in part because the judges strongly wish to retain a discretion as to admissibility. Even where a confession is excluded, physical evidence found as a result of information given in it need not be, under s 76(4).[236] Therefore, it may be said that s 76 has had a limited impact in upholding due process. This stance has not changed under the HRA. Thus, s 78 has operated as a catch-all section, bringing within its boundaries many confessions which pass the tests contained in either head of s 76. Section 78, as will be seen below, is rarely employed to exclude non-confession evidence and again, that stance has hardly changed post-HRA, for reasons to be discussed below.

Police and Criminal Evidence Act 1984

Confessions

76.–(2) If, in any proceedings where the prosecution proposes to give in evidence a confession made by an accused person, it is represented to the court that the confession was or may have been obtained—

---

235   See generally D Birch, 'Confessions and Confusions under the 1984 Act' [1989] Crim LR 95; D Feldman [1990] Crim LR 452.

236   See further P Mirfield, *Silence, Confessions and Improperly Obtained Evidence* (1997); P Mirfield, 'Successive Confessions and the Poisonous Tree' [1996] Crim LR 554; Sharpe, *Judicial Discretion and Criminal Investigation* (1998).

   (a)   by oppression of the person who made it; or

   (b)   in consequence of anything said or done which was likely, in the circum-stances existing at the time, to render unreliable any confession which might be made by him in consequence thereof, the court shall not allow the confession to be given in evidence against him except in so far as the prosecution proves to the court beyond reasonable doubt that the confession (notwithstanding that it may be true) was not obtained as aforesaid.

. . .

(4)   The fact that a confession is wholly or partly excluded in pursuance of this section shall not affect the admissibility in evidence—

   (a)   of any facts discovered as a result of the confession;

. . . .

(8)   In this section 'oppression' includes torture, inhuman or degrading treatment, and the use or threat of violence (whether or not amounting to torture). . . .

Exclusion of unfair evidence
78.–(1) In any proceedings the court may refuse to allow evidence on which the prosecution proposes to rely to be given if it appears to the court that, having regard to all the circumstances, including the circumstances in which the evidence was obtained, the admission of the evidence would have such an adverse effect on the fairness of the proceedings that the court ought not to admit it.

(2)   Nothing in this section shall prejudice any rule of law requiring a court to exclude evidence.

R v Fulling [1987] 2 All ER 65, 67, 69, 70, CA[237]

Lord Lane CJ: 'Oppression' in s 76(2)(a) should be given its ordinary dictionary meaning. The Oxford English Dictionary as its third definition of the word runs as follows: 'Exercise of authority or power in a burdensome, harsh, or wrongful manner; unjust or cruel treatment of subjects, inferiors, etc; the imposition of unreasonable or unjust burdens.' One of the quotations given under that paragraph runs as follows: 'There is not a word in our language which expresses more detestable wickedness than oppression.'
We find it hard to envisage any circumstances in which such oppression would not entail some impropriety on the part of the interrogator. We do not think that the judge was wrong in using that test. What however is abundantly clear is that a confession may be invalidated under s76(2)(b) where there is no suspicion of impropriety.
   Appeal dismissed.

R v Keenan [1990] 2 QB 54 (extracts)

Hodgson J: . . .We think that in cases where there have been 'significant and substantial' breaches of the 'verballing' provisions of the code, the evidence so obtained will frequently be excluded. We do not think that any injustice will be caused by this. It is clear that not every breach or combination of breaches of the code will justify the exclusion of interview evidence under s 76 or s 78. They must be significant and substantial. If this were not the case, the courts would be undertaking a task which is no part of their duty; as Lord Lane CJ said in *Delaney* (at 341): 'It is no part of the duty of the court to rule a statement inadmissible simply in order to punish the police for failure to observe the codes of practice.'

R v Samuel [1988] 2 WLR 920, 933, 934

The Court of Appeal found that the appellant had been unlawfully denied access to a solicitor and that, if the right to such access is denied, this can lead to the exclusion of admissions obtained at unlawful interviews conducted after the denial by the exercise of the judge's power under s 78(1).

Hodgson J: [The solicitor in question] gave evidence. . .on this occasion, knowing that his client had already been interviewed on four occasions and at each had strenuously denied complicity in the robbery and had already been charged with two serious offences, he would probably, after consultation, have advised his client, for the time being at any rate, to refuse to answer further questioning.

In this case this appellant was denied improperly one of the most important and fundamental rights of a citizen. The trial judge fell into error in not so holding. If he had arrived at correct decisions on the two points argued before him he might well have concluded that the refusal of access and consequent unlawful interview compelled him to find that the admission of evidence as to the final interview would have 'such an adverse effect on the fairness of the proceedings' that he ought not to admit it. Such a decision would, of course, have very significantly weakened the prosecution case (the failure to charge earlier ineluctably shows this). In those circumstances this court feels that it has no alternative but to quash the appellant's conviction on count I in the indictment, the charge of robbery.

Attorney-General's Reference (No 3 of 1999) [2001] 2 AC 91, HL (extracts)

In this case the police had retained a DNA sample (arguably in breach of Art 8) in breach of s 64 of PACE; the question was whether such evidence should be admissible in the instant case—a very serious rape case. Lord Steyn in the House of Lords treated the possible breach of both Article 8 and PACE as *not* engaging Art 6(1); he looked only at the requirements of s 78 of PACE. The general conclusion was that regardless of the inception of the HRA, invocation of Article 6 did not aid the argument since the question of admissibility is a matter of national law

Lord Steyn: Article 6 provides, inter alia, that in the determination of any criminal charge against him everyone is entitled to a fair and public hearing within a reasonable time by an independent and impartial tribunal established by law. Under the general law the trial judge has adequate powers to ensure fairness: (1) he has jurisdiction to stay the proceedings as an abuse of the process and (2) he has a discretion to exclude evidence under section 78 if it would be unfair to admit the evidence 'having regard to all the circumstances, including the circumstances in which the evidence was obtained'. If trial is allowed to proceed, and the evidence is not excluded, the accused will have a full opportunity to contest the reliability and accuracy of the DNA evidence. In any event, the question of admissibility is a matter for regulation under national law. There is no principle of Convention law that unlawfully obtained evidence is not admissible: *Schenk v Switzerland* (1988) 13 EHRR 242, 265–266, para 46; *R v Khan (Sultan)* [1997] AC 558.

Notes

1. *Section 76(2)(a) of PACE: the 'oppression' test.* This test derives from the rule as it was at common law. Under it if it is put to the court that the confession was or may have been obtained by oppression of the person who made it, and the prosecution cannot prove beyond reasonable doubt that the police did not behave oppressively, the confession is inadmissible. The judge has no discretion in the matter. The wording derives from Art 3 of the Convention,[238] but it is not necessary for torture or inhuman or degrading treatment to be present, as discussed below. The idea behind the old common law rule, and now s 76(2)(a), is that threats of violence or other oppressive behaviour are so abhorrent that no further question as to the reliability of a confession obtained by such methods should be asked. But the principle of reliability underlies the rule, as does the principle of voluntariness.

2. In *R v Mushtaq* Lord Hutton said: 'It is clear that there are two principal reasons underlying the rule that a confession obtained by oppression should not be admitted in evidence. One reason, which has long been stated by the judges, is that where a confession is made as a result of oppression it may well be unreliable, because the confession may have been given, not with the intention of telling the truth, but from a desire to escape the oppression imposed on, or the harm threatened to, the suspect. A further reason, stated in more recent years, is that in a civilised society a person should not be compelled to incriminate himself, and a person in custody should not be subjected by the police to ill-treatment or improper pressure in order to extract a confession'.[239] He found that these principles were in harmony with those accepted under Art 6(1): 'These two reasons also underlie the decision of the European Court of Human Rights in *Saunders v The United Kingdom*.[240] This rule has the dual function of removing any incentive to the police to behave oppressively and of protecting the detainee from the consequences of oppressive behaviour if it has occurred.

3. *The meaning of oppression.* The only evidence given in the Act as to the meaning of oppression is the non-exhaustive definition contained in s 76(8): 'In this section "oppression" includes torture, inhuman or degrading treatment and the use or threat of violence (whether or not amounting to torture).' The word 'includes' ought to be given its literal meaning according to the Court of Appeal in *Fulling*.[241] Therefore, it appeared that the concept of oppression might be fairly wide: the question was whether it encompassed the old common law rulings on its width. In *Fulling*, the Court of Appeal held that PACE is a codifying Act and that, therefore, a court should examine the statutory language uninfluenced by pre-Act decisions. The court then proffered its own definition of oppression: '. . . the exercise of authority or power in a burdensome, harsh or wrongful manner; unjust or cruel treatment of subjects, inferiors, etc; the imposition of unreasonable or unjust burdens.' It thought that oppression would almost invariably entail impropriety on the part of the interrogator.

---

238   See Chapter 7, pp 301–302 for the wording of Art 3 and for Strasbourg case law on the meaning of the three terms used in it.

239   [2005] UKHL 25 at [7]. He relied on *Wong Kam-ming v The Queen* [1980] AC 247, 261 and *Lam Chi-ming v The Queen* [1991] 2 AC 212, 220 E–G.

240   [1996] 23 EHRR 313; [2005] UKHL 25 at [8]

241   [1987] QB 426; [1987] 2 All ER 65, CA.

4. The Court of Appeal in *Hughes*[242] held that a denial of legal advice, owing not to bad faith on the part of the police, but to a misunderstanding, could not amount to oppression. In *Alladice*[243] the Court of Appeal also took this view in suggesting, *obiter*, that an improper denial of legal advice, if accompanied by bad faith on the part of the police, would certainly amount to 'unfairness' under s 78 and probably also to oppression. In *Beales*,[244] rather heavy-handed questioning accompanied by misleading suggestions, although not on the face of it a very serious impropriety, was termed oppressive because it was obviously employed as a deliberate tactic. In *Paris*,[245] the case of the *Cardiff Three*, confessions made by one of the defendants after some 13 hours of highly pressured and hostile questioning were excluded on the ground of oppression. He was a man of limited intelligence, but the Court of Appeal thought that the questioning would have been oppressive even in relation to a suspect of normal intelligence.

5. The position may be summed up as follows. Oppression will arise if, firstly, improper behaviour of a certain level of seriousness has occurred. The behaviour in *Paris* was clearly oppressive; other improper behaviour might fall only just within the category of oppressive behaviour; second, the behaviour must be perpetrated deliberately. Improper treatment falling outside s 76(8) and of insufficient seriousness to be termed oppressive, or oppressive behaviour unaccompanied by bad faith could fall within s 76(2)(b) if the confession was likely to have been rendered unreliable thereby. The emphasis on bad faith or the lack of it at least gives an indication as to when improper behaviour on the part of the police will lead to automatic exclusion of the confession under s 76(2)(a) and when it will merely suggest the likelihood of unreliability under s 76(2)(b). But, since s 76(2)(a) only operates to exclude confessions obtained as a result of very serious impropriety on the part of the police, meaning that confessions are rarely excluded under the sub-section, its ability to protect due process is limited. However, its impact on due process should not be disregarded. It sets a basic standard for police behaviour, probably deterring police from forms of impropriety still relatively common in some jurisdictions.

6. *Burden of proof.* Under s 76(2)(a) once the defence has advanced a reasonable argument (*Liverpool Juvenile Court ex parte R*)[246] that the confession was obtained by oppression, it will not be admitted in evidence unless the prosecution can prove that it was not so obtained.

7. *Section 76(2)(b): the 'reliability' test.* The 'reliability' test of s 76(2)(b) is concerned with objective reliability: the judge must consider the situation at the time the confession was made and ask whether the confession would be *likely* to be unreliable, not whether it *is* unreliable. In *Wahab*[247] the defendant tried to negotiate the release of his family from arrest with the police by offering to confess. The police did not make the bargain but he confessed in any event and tried later to have the confession excluded under s 76(2)(b). This was refused partly on the ground that the confession was reliable, but also on the ground that the inducement to confess did not come from the police.

8. In most instances the 'something said or done' will consist of some impropriety on the part of the police. Having identified such a factor, a court will go on to consider whether any circumstances

---

242   [1988] Crim LR 519.

243   (1988) 87 Cr App R 380, CA.

244   [1991] Crim LR 118. See to the same effect *Heron* (1993) unreported; forceful questioning was accompanied by lies as to the identification evidence.

245   (1993) 97 Cr App R 99; [1994] Crim LR 361, CA.

246   [1987] All ER 688.

247   [2003] 1 Cr App R 15.

existed which rendered the impropriety particularly significant. The 'circumstances' could include the particularly vulnerable state of the detainee. In *Mathias*,[248] the defendant was particularly vulnerable because he had not been afforded legal advice although an offer of immunity from prosecution had been made to him. The Court of Appeal held that the offer had placed him in great difficulty and that this was a situation in which the police should have ensured that he had legal advice. From the judgment, it appears that if an inducement to confess is offered to the detainee, the police should ensure that he or she can discuss it with a solicitor, even if the police are entitled to deny access to legal advice, on the ground that the detainee falls within s 58(8) (see above). Thus in such instances s 76(2)(b) may be satisfied since the 'circumstances' will be the lack of legal advice and the 'something said or done', the inducement.

9. The vulnerability relied upon by the defence as a special circumstance may relate to a physical or mental state. In *Delaney*[249] the defendant was 17, had an IQ of 80 and, according to an educational psychologist, was subject to emotional arousal which would lead him to wish to bring a police interview to an end as quickly as possible. These were circumstances in which it was important to ensure that the interrogation was conducted with all propriety. In fact, the officers offered some inducement to the defendant to confess by playing down the gravity of the offence and by suggesting that if he confessed, he would get the psychiatric help he needed. They also failed to make an accurate, contemporaneous record of the interview in breach of Code C, para 11.3 (referring to version of Code C in force at the time). Failing to make the proper record was of indirect relevance to the question of reliability since it meant that the court could not assess the full extent of the suggestions held out to the defendant. Thus, in the circumstances existing at the time (the mental state of the defendant), the police impropriety did have the special significance necessary under s 76(2)(b). The decision in *Marshall*[250] was to similar effect, although it did not identify a specific breach of Code C: the defendant was on the borderline of sub-normality and therefore, after an interview accompanied by his solicitor, he should not have been re-interviewed unaccompanied about the same matters.

10. *Section 78: the 'fairness' test.*[251] Section 78 confers an exclusionary *discretion* on a judge and appears to have been conceived to cover the very narrow function of the old common law discretion[252] to exclude improperly obtained non-confession evidence. Section 78 provides a discretion to exclude evidence if admitting it would render the trial unfair. In adopting this formula, it was clear that the Government did not wish to import into this country a USA-type exclusionary rule. The Home Secretary informed the House of Commons[253] that the function of exclusion of evidence after police misconduct must not be disciplinary, but must be to safeguard the fairness of the trial. The idea behind this was that non-confession evidence obtained by improper means could still be admitted on the basis that police misconduct could be dealt with by internal disciplinary procedures.

---

248   *The Times*, 24 August 1989.

249   (1989) 8 Cr App R 338; *The Times*, 20 August 1988, CA.

250   *The Times*, 28 December 1992.

251   For discussion of the operation of s 78 see Allen [1990] CLJ 80; Gelowitz (1990) 106 LQR 327; May [1988] Crim LR 722; Stone (1995) 3 Web JCL 1; Sanders and Young, n 1 above, Chapter 11, Part 5; AL-T Choo and S Nash, 'What's the Matter with s 78?' [1999] Crim LR 929–40; M Hunter, 'Judicial Discretion: s 78 in Practice' (1994) Crim LR 558; D Ormerod and D Birch, 'The Evolution of the Discretionary Exclusion of Evidence' (2004) Crim LR 767.

252   See *Sang* [1980] AC 402; [1979] 2 All ER 1222, HL.

253   1983–84, HC Deb Col 1012, 29 October 1984.

11. *Section 78: excluding confessions.* Section 78 must be applied in accordance with the courts' duty under s 6 HRA to abide by Art 6 ECHR. Article 6(1) is silent as to the admissibility of improperly obtained evidence, including confessions. The Strasbourg Court has emphasised that the assessment of evidence is for the domestic courts[254] and that Art 6 does not require any particular rules of evidence. Thus, it has allowed the national authorities a wide margin of appreciation in this respect. But Article 6 standards in relation to legal advice and the right to silence (above) are a relevant factor under s 7.

12. In *Keenan*,[255] the Court of Appeal ruled under s 78 that once a breach of the PACE or Code rules can be identified, it will be asked whether it is substantial or significant. The Court found that a combination of breaches of the recording provisions satisfied this test. In contrast, a breach of para 10.2 requiring a police officer to inform a suspect that he is not under arrest, is free to go and may obtain legal advice, has been held to be insubstantial.[256] This view of para 10.2 also seems to have been implicit in the ruling of the Court of Appeal in *Joseph*,[257] although a breach of para 10.5 governing contemporaneous recording (now para 10.7), in contrast, was clearly found to be substantial and significant in order to merit exclusion of the confession. In *Walsh*,[258] the Court of Appeal held that what was significant and substantial would be determined by reference to the nature of the breach.

13. In *Samuel*,[259] extracted above, the Court of Appeal found that the confession should have been excluded under s 78 because it was causally linked to the police impropriety—a failure to allow the appellant access to legal advice. In order to establish this point, the solicitor in question gave evidence that had he been present, he would have advised his client to remain silent in the last interview, whereas in fact Samuel made damaging admissions in that interview which formed the basis of the case against him. It could not be said with certainty that he would have confessed in any event: he was not, it was determined, a sophisticated criminal who was capable of judging for himself when to speak and when to remain silent. Thus—although this was not made explicit—the Court of Appeal was in effect prepared to make the judgment that a trial would be rendered unfair if a court associated itself with a breach of the PACE interrogation procedure. The Court of Appeal in *Alladice*,[260] also faced with a breach of s 58, accepted that the key factor in exercising discretion under s 78 after a breach of the interviewing rules was the causal relationship between breach and confession (and, it appeared by implication, between breach and fairness at the trial). On the basis of this factor, it was determined that the confession had been rightly admitted despite the breach of s 58 because no causal relationship between the two could be established.[261]

14. Deciding that an impropriety is causally linked to the confession does not of itself explain why admission of the confession will render the trial unfair. In *Samuel*, for example, the Court of Appeal merely stated:

---

254 *Edwards v UK* A 247-B (1992).

255 [1989] 3 WLR 1193; [1989] All ER 598, CA.

256 *Rajakuruna* [1991] Crim LR 458.

257 [1993] Crim LR 206, CA.

258 [1989] Crim LR 822; (1989) 19 Cr App R 161.

259 [1988] QB 615; [1988] 2 All ER 315; [1988] 2 WLR 920, CA.

260 (1988) 87 Cr App R 380. The Court of Appeal appeared to have a similar test in mind in relation to a failure to caution in *Weerdesteyn* (1995) 1 Cr App R 405; [1995] Crim LR 239, CA.

261 See also *Dunford* (1990) 91 Cr App R 150; (1990) 140 NLJ 517, CA: the Court of Appeal determined that the criminally experienced appellant had made his own assessment of the situation in deciding to make certain admissions and legal advice would not have affected his decision; the failure to allow legal advice was not therefore causally linked to the confession.

'. . . the appellant was denied improperly one of the most important and fundamental rights of the citizen'.[262] Broadly, it could be argued that if the court refuses to
take the opportunity afforded by s 78 to put right what has occurred earlier in the
process, this will give an appearance of unfairness to the trial. Bearing in mind
the balance PACE is supposed to create between increased police powers and
safeguards for suspects, it can perhaps be argued that to accept evidence deriving
from an interview in which the police were able to use their powers to the full, but
the defendant was unable to take advantage of an important safeguard, would not
be perceived by most reasonable people as fair. The findings of the Privy Council in
Mohammed (Allie) v State[263] in respect of a denial of custodial access to legal advice
adopted this stance: 'The stamp of constitutionality on a citizen's rights is not
meaningless: it is clear testimony that added value is attached to the protection of
the right . . . Not every breach will result in a confession being excluded. But their
Lordships make clear that the fact that there has been a breach of a constitutional
right is a cogent factor militating in favour of the exclusion of the confession. In this
way the constitutional character of the infringed right is respected and accorded a
high value . . . '

This stance receives indirect support from Strasbourg.[264]

15. *Section 78: exclusion of non-confession evidence.*[265] The discussion has shown that the courts have
continued the common law tradition within the PACE scheme of excluding confessions tainted by
impropriety, but they have shown great reluctance to exclude other evidence which is equally
tainted. The general stance taken is that improperly obtained evidence is admissible in a criminal
trial subject to a discretion to exclude it. Except in one instance—that of identification evidence—
the discretion is viewed as very narrow, although where the impropriety consists of some forms of
trickery, it may be wider. This stance has not changed under the HRA. Pre-HRA the courts
demonstrated little inclination to take a different stance where the impropriety consisted of a
breach of a Convention right[266] and, following the Strasbourg jurisprudence, it is not necessary for
that approach to change under the HRA, as discussed below.

16. *Identification evidence* has been seen as particularly vulnerable and may therefore be treated in the
same way as a confession obtained in breach of PACE. If some doubt is raised as to the reliability of
the identification owing to delay,[267] or to a failure to hold an identification parade where one was
practicable,[268] the identification evidence is likely to be excluded. However, in the leading decision
on identification evidence, *Forbes*,[269] the House of Lords found that despite a breach of Code D,
para 2.3, there had been no need to exclude the evidence.

---

262   [1988] 2 WLR 920, p 934.

263   [1999] 2 WLR 552 (Trinidad and Tobago); judgment delivered by Lord Steyn on 8 December 1998.

264   See *Austria v Italy* 4 YB 112.

265   For discussion see Gelowitz (1990) 106 LQR 327; AL-T Choo and S Nash, 'What's the Matter with s 78?' [1999] Crim LR 929–40; Choo
        (1989) 9(3) LS 261; Allen [1990] CLJ 80; Choo (1993) Journal of Crim Law 195.

266   See the judgment of the House of Lords in *Khan* [1997] AC 558.

267   *Quinn* [1990] Crim LR 581, CA; *The Times*, 31 March 1990.

268   *Ladlow* [1989] Crim LR 219.

269   [2001] Crim LR 649.

17. *Other non-confession evidence.* According to *Thomas*[270] and *Quinn*,[271] physical evidence will be excluded only if obtained with deliberate illegality; the pre-PACE ruling of the House of Lords in *Fox*[272] would also lend support to this contention. In *Fox*, the police made a *bona fide* mistake as to their powers in effecting an unlawful arrest, and the House of Lords, in determining that the physical evidence obtained was admissible, considered that the unlawful arrest was merely part of the history of the case and not the concern of the court. This stance is in accord with that taken in *Sang*[273] and confirmed as correct in *Khan (Sultan)*.[274] It appears to be in accord with the general PACE scheme, since evidence obtained as a result of an inadmissible confession will be admissible under s 76(4).

18. The House of Lords decision in *Khan (Sultan)*[275] is the leading case on s 78 in relation to non-confession evidence. A bugging device had been secretly installed on the outside of a house which Khan was visiting. Khan was suspected of involvement in the importation of prohibited drugs and the tape recording obtained from the listening device clearly showed that he was so involved. The case against him rested wholly on the tape recording. The defence argued, first, that the recording was inadmissible as evidence because the police had no statutory authority to place listening devices on private property and that therefore, such placement was a trespass and, further, that admission of the recording would breach Art 8 of the European Convention on Human Rights, which protects the right to privacy. Second, it was argued that even if the recording was admissible, it should be excluded from evidence under s 78 because of the unfairness of admitting the evidence. It was accepted in the Court of Appeal that trespass to the building had occurred as well as some damage to it and that there had been an invasion of privacy. However, the Court of Appeal found,[276] supporting the trial judge, that these factors were of slight significance and therefore were readily outweighed by the facts that the police had largely complied with the Home Office guidelines and that the offences involved were serious. The House of Lords upheld the Court of Appeal. The Lords relied on the decision in *Sang*[277] to the effect that improperly obtained evidence other than 'involuntary' confessions is admissible in a criminal trial The House of Lords concluded that the circumstances in which the evidence was obtained, even if they involved a breach of Art 8, were not such as to require exclusion of the evidence.

19. In *Chalkley*,[278] the same stance was taken. The evidence consisted of incriminating statements made by the accused which were secretly recorded by the police. Despite the impropriety of the police actions, it was found that the evidence was rightly admitted. This stance did not change with the inception of the HRA. As *AG's Reference (No 3 of 1999)*,[279] (extracted above) found, evidence need not be excluded under s 78, despite a breach of PACE. It was not found that Art 6 affected the

---

270   [1990] Crim LR 269. See to the same effect *Wright* [1994] Crim LR 55.

271   [1990] Crim LR 581, CA.

272   [1986] AC 281; see to the same effect *DPP v Wilson* [1991] Crim LR 441. On similar facts, in *Matto v Wolverhampton Crown Court* [1987] RTR 337, physical evidence was excluded since the police had acted with *mala fides*.

273   [1980] AC 402; [1979] 2 All ER 1222, HL.

274   [1997] AC 558; [1996] 3 All ER 289.

275   [1996] 3 All ER 289; (1996) 146 NLJ 1024. For comment see Carter (1997) 113 LQR 468.

276   *Khan* [1996] 3 All ER 289; (1996) 146 NLJ 1024, HL; [1995] QB 27, CA.

277   [1980] AC 402; [1979] 2 All ER 1222.

278   [1998] 2 Cr App R 79.

279   [2001] 2 WLR 56.

position, since the Court has left the assessment of evidence to the national courts. This stance was affirmed in later decisions.[280] This position as regards unlawfully obtained non-confession is clearly based on crime control values.

20. *The position under Article 6 ECHR.* This current narrow interpretation of s 78 of PACE[281] means that improperly obtained non-confession evidence will rarely be excluded, whether or not the impropriety also amounted to a breach of a Convention right. In other words, the admission of evidence in such circumstances need not amount to a breach of Art 6. The findings in *AG's Reference (No 3 of 1999)*[282] suggest that at present, there is a tendency to reject the possibility of using exclusion of evidence to uphold fundamental rights. This seems to be the case even where such rights are recognised within a statutory scheme; and possibly also where the breach is of a Convention right. In *Schenk v Switzerland*[283] the Strasbourg Court found no breach of Art 6(1) when an illegally obtained incriminating tape recording was admitted in evidence, and made it clear that unlawfully obtained evidence is not necessarily inadmissible. The Court found: 'While Article 6 guarantees the right to a fair trial, it does not lay down any rules as to admissibility of evidence as such, which is therefore primarily a matter of regulation under national law'. The test is to ask whether the trial as a whole would be rendered unfair if the 'tainted' evidence was admitted.[284]

21. A Chamber of the Court continued to take this stance in its important decision on admission of non-confession evidence under Art 6 in *Khan v UK*,[285] despite finding a breach of Art 8. A fundamental breach of Art 8 (secret recording which was not in accordance with the law)[286] had occurred in obtaining the only evidence against the defendant, but, following *Schenk*,[287] no breach of Art 6 was found, owing to the admission of the evidence. The Court said that it was not its role to determine whether unlawfully obtained evidence should be admissible. The case of *Khan v UK*[288] therefore can be utilised by the courts to support their stance in relation to non-confession evidence, taking s 2 HRA into account.[289]

22. As indicated, under domestic practice, non-confession evidence gained through a very serious impropriety, including a breach of a Convention right, is admissible, as is, under s 76(4) of PACE, physical evidence uncovered through an inadmissible confession gained as a result of impropriety, not excluding Art 3 treatment. The discretion to exclude non-confession evidence is very narrow and the impact which s 78 has had in encouraging adherence to due process may be diminishing at the present time. As AL-T Choo observes: 'recent decisions of the Court of Appeal signal a movement away from focusing on the nature of the breach [of PACE or the Codes] and towards an

---

280   See *Button* [2005] Crim LR 571. See further D Ormerod 'Trial Remedies for Art 8 breaches?' [2003] Crim LR 61.

281   See *Chalkley* [1998] 2 All ER 155; *Khan* [1997] AC 558 and *Shannon* [2001] 1 WLR 51.

282   [2001] 2 WLR 56, p 64, *per* Lord Steyn, and p 65, *per* Lord Cook of Thorndon.

283   (1988) 13 EHRR 242.

284   A 140 (1988), para 46. This test was also used in *Khan v UK* (2000) 8 BHRC 310.

285   (2000) 8 BHRC 310; Commission decision: (1999) 27 EHRR CD 58. See also *Chalkley v UK* No 63831/00 (2002).

286   See Chapter 7, p 317.

287   (1988) 13 EHRR 242.

288   (2000) 8 BHRC 310.

289   See also *PG v UK* [2002] Crim LR 308.

approach which takes the nature of the evidence as its central consideration'.[290] In other words, the movement is away from due process values and towards acceptance of the crime control norm that the end—a conviction—justifies the means.

Questions

❶   The confession made in *Samuel* may have been truthful. Why was it excluded from evidence?

❷   What principles may underlie determinations as to the admissibility of physical evidence?

❸   Is it at all probable in future that the domestic courts could decide to rely on Art 6 under s 3 or s 6 of the HRA to exclude improperly obtained non-confession evidence? Would this be a desirable development?

Tort damages[291]

Introduction

Tort damages will be available as a result of some breaches of PACE, the TA and other relevant statutes if an officer acts in a manner that would be tortious if no power authorising the action is in place. For example, if a police officer arrests a citizen (potentially tortious) where no reasonable suspicion arises under s 24 PACE, an action for false imprisonment is available. Equally, such a remedy would be available if the Part IV provisions governing time limits on detention were breached[292] or if a detention review failed to occur for a period of time.[293] Trespass to land or to goods will occur if the statutory provisions providing powers to search premises or seize goods are not followed. If force is used in effecting a false arrest an action for assault is available. Malicious prosecution will be available where police have abused their powers in recommending prosecution to the Crown Prosecution Service. Also, one of the ancient 'malicious process torts' may be available where a malicious search or arrest has occurred, although in fact these actions are extremely rare and their continued existence is in doubt.[294] Such actions may not be brought because a claim of false imprisonment is preferred, but there is a distinction between malicious process torts and false imprisonment in that in the former case, but not the latter, all the proper procedural formalities will have been carried out. Actions for malicious prosecution are quite common, but the plaintiff carries quite a heavy burden in the need to prove that

---

290   AL-T Choo and S Nash, 'What's the Matter with s 78?' [1999] Crim LR 929–40.

291   See generally, R Clayton and H Tomlinson, *Civil Actions Against the Police*, 3rd edn (2005) 1st Supplement; Sanders and Young, n 1 above, at 12.3.

292   E.g. *Edwards v Chief Constable of Avon and Somerset* (1992) 9 March, unreported; the plaintiff was detained for 8 hours, 47 minutes following a lawful arrest. The detention was wrongful because it was 'unnecessary' compensation was awarded.

293   In *Roberts* [1999] 1 WLR 662 the review took place two hours after it should have done. The Court of Appeal found that Roberts had been falsely imprisoned during those two hours even though it was found that, had the review taken place, he would have remained in detention.

294   See R Clayton and H Tomlinson, *Civil Actions Against the Police*, 1st edn (1987), p 284. For discussion see Winfield, *History of Conspiracy and Abuse of Legal Process* (1921).

there was no reasonable or probable cause for the prosecution.[295] It may be that if the prosecution is brought on competent legal advice, this action will fail, but this is unclear.[296]

Almost the whole of the interviewing scheme, which is contained mainly in Codes C, E and H rather than in PACE or the TA, is unaffected by tortious remedies since section 67(10) of PACE provides that no civil or criminal liability arises from a breach of the Codes of Practice. This lack of a remedy also extends to some statutory provisions, in particular the most significant statutory interviewing provision, the entitlement to legal advice, arising under both PACE and the TA.[297] There is no tort of denial of access to legal advice; the only possible tortious action would be for breach of statutory duty. It might have been expected that an action for false imprisonment might lie where gross breaches of the questioning provisions had taken place, such as interviewing a person unlawfully held incommunicado. But this argument now seems to have been ruled out by the decision in *Weldon v Home Office*[298] in the context of lawful detention in a prison. It seems likely, therefore, that access to legal advice, like the rest of the safeguards for interviewing, will continue to be unaffected by the availability of the pre-HRA tortious remedies.

Where actions in tort *are* available against the police, they may be of particular value owing to the willingness of the courts to accept that exemplary or punitive damages may sometimes be appropriate. Such damages are awarded to punish the defendant and will be available only in two instances:[299] where there has been 'oppressive, arbitrary or unconstitutional behaviour by the servants of the government' or where the profit accruing to the defendant through his conduct may be greater than the compensation awarded to the plaintiff. Only the first of these two categories will be relevant in actions against the police, and in order that such damages should be available, the term 'servant of the government' has been broadly interpreted to include police officers.[300]

Examples of civil actions

Examples of the use of civil actions are given below (obviously the sums awarded must be considered in the light of inflation).

Ballard, Stewart-Park, Findlay v Metropolitan Police Commissioner (1983) 133 New Law Journal 1133; Legal Action, 10 January 1984

Westminster County Court, judge.
Facts: P1 and P2 had been hit over the head by police officers with truncheons in the course of a demonstration, P2 carried spread-eagled and dumped on ground from a height of four feet. P3 was lawfully arrested and was prodded in stomach, hit over eye with truncheon and, as a result suffered migrainous attacks.

---

295   See *Glinskie v McIver* [1962] AC 726.

296   *Abbott v Refuge Assurance Co Ltd* [1962] 1 QB 632.

297   See pp 1210–1216.

298   [1991] WLR 340, CA.

299   This limitation was imposed by the House of Lords in *Rookes v Barnard* [1964] AC 1129, p 1226. Note that the Law Commission, *Consultation Paper on Punitive Damages*, Consultation No 132, 1993, advocated, in its provisional conclusion, retention of such damages, but that they should be placed on a more principled basis. See also *Kuddus (AP) v Chief Constable of Leicestershire Constabulary* [2001] UKHL 29.

300   *Broome v Cassell and Co* [1972] AC 1027, at 1088.

Damages: P1—compensatory £400 including small sum for aggravated damages (1992 value: £660). P2—compensatory £600 including aggravated damages (1992 value: £990). P3—compensatory £3,000 including aggravated damages (1992 value: £4,950).

Lewis v Chief Constable of South Wales, 5 October 1989; unreported

Bridgend County Court, jury.
Facts: Ps' arrest unlawful as a result of their not being given reasons. The unlawfulness of these arrests was cured by subsequent giving of reasons, to P1 after 10 minutes and P2 after 23 minutes (Court of Appeal upheld judge's ruling on law [1991] 1 All ER 206).
Damages: £200 for each P (1992 value: £232).

Leigh-Williams v Chief Constable of Essex, The Guardian, 18 October 1990

High Court, Michael Davies J and a jury.
Facts: P, a former vicar, was unlawfully arrested and detained for 40 hours for breach of the peace. He had previously been lawfully arrested for assault on a 13-year old boy and was unlawfully arrested near the boy's home.
Damages: £4,000 (1992 value: £4,184).
(From R Clayton and H Tomlinson, *Civil Actions Against the Police*, 2nd edn (1992), pp 413, 420)

Jason Paul v Chief Constable of Humberside Police, unreported, 27 January 2006

A young black man, Mr Paul brought a claim for false imprisonment and malicious prosecution after he was arrested for murder and detained on 1st April 1998. The previous night he had tried to stop a fight between Mr Alder and another man. Mr Paul was arrested on suspicion of murder the next day when, after hearing that Mr Alder had died in police custody, he reported to police voluntarily, with his solicitor, as a potential witness. He was then charged with GBH with intent and denied bail on 2nd April 1998 in relation to the death of Mr Alder, another young black man. On 1st May 1998 magistrates granted him unconditional bail. On 30th June 1998 the CPS told Mr Paul the case against him was to be discontinued. Jason Paul claimed that Humberside police charged him to distract public attention away from their own behavior. The police, according to video footage, allowed Christopher Alder to die while lying on the floor in a police custody suite with his hands handcuffed behind his back.

The eight-strong jury ruled in favour of Mr Paul on a series of questions posed by the judge. They agreed unanimously that it was 'more likely than not that the police charged (Mr Paul) with causing GBH with intent to deflect potential criticism of the circumstances of Christopher Alder's death'. They also decided by a margin of seven to one that it was 'more likely than not that the instruction to arrest for murder was given to deflect potential criticism of the circumstances of Christopher Alder's death'.

Jason Paul was awarded £30,500 damages (and also costs) for false imprisonment and malicious prosecution.

Thompson v Commissioner of Police of the Metropolis [1998] QB 498 (extracts)

The plaintiff, having been lawfully arrested, was subsequently assaulted and manhandled by police officers and wrongly detained in a cell for about four hours. She claimed against the Commissioner damages for false imprisonment and malicious prosecution. She claimed both aggravated damages and exemplary damages. The only defendant was the Commissioner. No argument was presented to the court that exemplary damages should not be awarded in a vicarious liability case. So the court was entitled to proceed on the footing that exemplary damages as well as aggravated damages could be awarded.

Lord Woolf MR said, at p 512: The fact that the defendant is a chief officer of police also means that here exemplary damages should have a lesser role to play. Even if the use of civil proceedings to punish a defendant can in some circumstances be justified it is more difficult to justify the award where the defendant and the person responsible for meeting any award is not the wrongdoer, but his 'employer'. While it is possible that a chief constable could bear a responsibility for what has happened, due to his failure to exercise proper control, the instances when this is alleged to have occurred should not be frequent.

Notes

1. Civil actions against the police in the 1980s and early 1990s attracted high levels of damages. One of the highest awards was made in *White v Metropolitan Police Comr.*[301] Police officers unlawfully entered the home of a middle aged black couple at night and attacked the plaintiffs. The police then charged both plaintiffs with various offences in order to cover up their own conduct. The plaintiffs were awarded £20,000 exemplary damages each and, respectively, £6,500 and £4,500 aggravated damages. One of the highest awards was made in *Treadaway v Chief Constable of West Midlands:*[302] £50,000, which included £40,000 exemplary damages, was awarded in respect of a serious assault perpetrated in order to obtain a confession. In 1996, a number of very high awards were made against the Metropolitan Police. In *Goswell v Comr of Metropolitan Police*[303] the plaintiff was awarded £120,000 damages for assault, £12,000 for false imprisonment and £170,000 exemplary damages for arbitrary and oppressive behaviour. Mr Goswell, who is black, was waiting in his car when a police officer approached. Goswell complained about the lack of police activity over an arson attack on his home. He was handcuffed to and then struck by the officer; the blow left a permanent scar. Goswell was then arrested for assault and threatening behaviour. He was cleared of these charges and then brought the successful civil action. In *Hsu v Comr of Metropolitan Police,*[304] the plaintiff won £220,000 damages for assault and wrongful arrest at his home.

2. These high awards are no longer available. The question of the appropriate level of damages was addressed by the Court of Appeal in *Thompson v Comr of Police for the Metropolis.*[305] The court laid down guidelines for the award of damages which took as a starting point a basic award of £500 for the first hour of unlawful detention, with decreasing amounts for subsequent hours. It was

---

301   *The Times*, 24 April 1982.

302   *The Times*, 25 October 1994.

303   *The Guardian*, 27 April 1996.

304   [1997] 2 All ER 762.

305   *Ibid.*

found that aggravated damages could be awarded where there were special features of the case, such as oppressive or humiliating conduct at the time of arrest. Such damages would start at around £1,000 but would not normally be more than twice the level of the basic damages. Exemplary damages should only be awarded where aggravated and basic damages together would not appear to provide a sufficient punishment. Exemplary damages would be not less than £5,000, but the total figure awarded as exemplary damages would not be expected to amount to more than the basic damages multiplied by three. The overall award should not exceed £50,000. In accordance with these guidelines, the award made in *Hsu* was reduced to £50,000. Doubts were expressed in *Thompson* (above), and have been subsequently,[306] as to the award of exemplary damages where liability is vicarious since obviously the defendant did not bear direct responsibility for the oppressive behaviour.

3. In *Gerald v MPC*,[307] the Court of Appeal found that the guidelines in *Thompson* should not be applied in a rigid fashion. In *Rutherford v Chief Constable of Kent*,[308] an award of £50,000 was made where officers had falsified records and assaulted the claimant. Bailey and Taylor note that the police paid out over 44 million in compensation and damages in the period 2002–07.[309]

4. If a civil action against a police officer is successful, he or she will not be personally liable; s 48 of the Police Act 1964 provides that a chief constable will be vicariously liable in respect of torts committed by constables under his direction or control in the performance or purported performance of their functions.

5. Sections 6 and 8 of the HRA require the courts to offer a remedy where a public authority violates the Convention rights,[310] unless in so doing it is acting in accordance with incompatible legislation.[311] Articles 3, 5, 8 and 14 of the ECHR potentially cover certain pre-trial rights of suspects. Tortious liability arises and damages can be awarded under s 8 of the HRA if one or more of these Articles are found to have been breached in respect of police treatment of suspects. As indicated, some custodial treatment in breach of these Articles is already tortious under domestic law, and civil actions against the police have provided an increasingly significant means of creating some police accountability,[312] but this possibility is clearly of particular significance where domestic law currently fails to provide a tortious remedy in respect of the maltreatment of detainees. Some breaches of Article 8 provide an example.[313] However, if an existing tort action is available, as is usually the case, tort damages, as opposed to HRA damages, would normally be sought since the quantum of damages would be higher.[314]

---

306   See *Kuddus (AP) v Chief Constable of Leicestershire Constabulary* [2001] UKHL 29.

307   *The Times*, 26 June 1998.

308   Unreported, 15 May 2001.

309   SH Bailey, N Taylor, *Bailey, Harris and Jones: Civil Liberties: Cases and Materials*, 6th edn (2009), Chapter 4, p 101.

310   Sections 6(1), 7 and 8. For discussion, see Chapter 17, pp 976 *et seq*.

311   Section 6(2). Section 3 requires that the legislation should be rendered compatible with the Convention rights 'so far as it is possible to do so'.

312   See the Home Affairs Committee, First Report 1997–98, Police Disciplinary and Complaints Procedures, printed 16 December 1997, which noted (para 32) the 'striking rise in the cost of civil settlements for the Metropolitan Police, from £0.47m in 1991 to £2.69m in 1996. (This figure may decline owing to the decision in *Thompson* [1997] 2 All ER 762.) The Police Action Lawyers Group and the Commission for Racial Equality attributed the rise to disillusionment with the complaints process.

313   See the discussion in *Wainwright v HO* [2004] 2 AC 406.

314   See Chapter 17, pp 992–996.

Complaints against the Police and disciplinary action[315]

The current complaints and disciplinary scheme[316]
Background[317]

The police complaints and disciplinary system provides a potential method of ensuring that the police adhere to the safeguards created by PACE, as amended and the TA. PACE set up the Police Complaints Authority (PCA) as an independent body with an involvement in the complaints and disciplinary system, replacing the Police Complaints Board (PCB), which was set up under the Police Act 1976.[318] The idea was to afford an appearance of independence to the system. The scheme set up by PACE for dealing with complaints, contained in ss 83–106, was repealed and re-enacted in the Police Act 1996.[319] Under s 67(2) of the Police Act 1996, a complaint went in the first instance to the Chief Officer of Police of the force in question, who had to determine by reference to the section whether or not he was the appropriate person to deal with it and whether it, in fact, constituted a complaint about 'the conduct of an officer' and not about 'the direction or control' of a police force.[320] The decision as to the side of the dividing line on which a particular complaint fell was made by the police force complained about. Therefore, at the very outset, 'an issue of independence [arose]'.[321]

A complaint had to be referred to the PCA if it concerned serious misconduct.[322] Under s 75(3) of the 1996 Act, if the Chief Officer determined that the report on the complaints investigation indicated that a criminal offence might have been committed, he had to send a copy of it to the DPP. In addition, there was a discretionary power to refer complaints to the PCA. It did not carry out the investigation itself in such cases, but supervised it and received a report at the end of it under s 72. Thus, its role in relation to complaints was very limited. Independence was lacking in other respects: the remuneration system was under the control of the Home Secretary,[323] and under s 83 of the Police Act 1996, his guiding role was retained. Under s 69(5),[324] a member of the force which was the subject of the complaint could conduct the investigation.

---

315   See M Maguire, 'Complaints against the police: the British experience', in A Goldsmith (ed), *Complaints Against the Police: A Comparative Study* (1990); Greaves [1985] Crim LR; Khan (1984) 129 SJ 455; Williams [1985] Crim LR 115; L Lustgarten, *The Governance of Police* (1986), pp 139–40. The Runciman Commission considered that the existing arrangements probably do not command public confidence: Cm 2263, p 46; J Harrison, *Police Misconduct: Legal Remedies* (1987); Triennial Review of the PCA 1991–94, HC 396 (1994–95); Home Affairs Committee Fourth Report, HC 179 (1991–92); A Sanders and R Young, *Criminal Justice*, 3rd edn (2007), Chapter 12, Part 4; House of Commons Home Affairs Select Committee, Police Disciplinary and Complaints Procedure, First Report, HC 258–1 (1998).

316   See further R Stone, *Civil Liberties and Human Rights*, 6th edn (2006), Chapter 4.6.3; Complaints Against the Police: A Framework for a New System—available from the Home Office web-site: www.homeoffice.gov.uk.

317   See further: AJ Goldsmith, *Complaints Against the Police: The Trend to External Review* (1991); AJ Goldsmith, 'Necessary but not sufficient: The role of public complaints procedures in police accountability', in PC Stenning (ed), *Accountability for Criminal Justice* (1995), 110–34; T Prenzler and C Ronken, 'Models of police oversight: a critique', *policing and society* (2001) 11/3: 151–80.

318   The operation of the PCB did not create confidence in the complaints system: see Brown, *Police Complaints Procedure*, Home Office Research Study No 93, 1987.

319   Which came into force on 1 April 1999, replacing PACE 1984, Part IX.

320   PACE 1984, s 84(4) and (5). The requirement regarding 'the conduct of a police officer' then arose under s 65 of the 1996 Act.

321   Home Affairs Committee First Report (1997–98), para 47.

322   Police Act 1996, s 70, formerly PACE 1984, s 87(4).

323   See PCA Report 1998–99 Appendix C, para 5.

324   Which replaced PACE 1984, s 105(4).

Reform

The changes to the complaints procedure which occurred in the mid-1990s, partly in response to the Runciman Royal Commission Report, did not involve any radical reform. In particular, they did not include the introduction of a new, independent element into the process. The Police and Magistrates' Courts Act 1994, which was then consolidated in the Police Act 1996, made only limited changes to the functions and powers of the PCA. Under s 37(a) of the 1994 Act, a breach of the PACE Codes became no longer automatically a breach of the Police Discipline Code.[325] This change could be seen merely as legitimising police working practices, since it appeared that very few complaints in respect of breaches of the Codes were made; those that were rarely led to disciplinary proceedings. Unsurprisingly, this trend continued after the 1994 Act came into force.[326] Part IV of the Police Act 1996, which then created the scheme governing complaints and discipline, did not affect this position; it was merely a consolidating, not a reforming, measure.

The 1997 Report of the Select Committee on Home Affairs[327] made a number of recommendations, reflecting a number of the criticisms as to lack of independence and the then Home Secretary, Jack Straw, said that he had accepted the case for speedy reform. But the initial proposals for reform[328] mirrored the moderate changes proposed by the Conservative Government in 1993.[329] Racist language and behaviour is now a breach of the police code of conduct, but it is not yet possible to determine how far reaching such change might be. It might also lead to a breach of the Race Relations Act 1976, as amended. The Runciman Commission considered that the existing arrangements probably did not command public confidence.[330]

Prior to the introduction of the Police Reform Act 2002 a strong consensus had emerged that the independent element in the complaints and disciplinary process was too weak and was the key factor in the inefficacy of the system.[331] Maguire and Corbett commented in their 1991 review that an independent system might lead to an improvement in public confidence in the system, although they expressed doubts about its efficacy in other respects.[332] The MacPherson Report recommended that there should be an independent tribunal for serious complaints.[333] Morgan and Newburn found: 'The fact that most complaints . . . continue to be investigated exclusively by the police themselves is almost certainly an important factor in explaining why so few complaints are made compared with the proportion of members of the public who report having felt like making a complaint.'[334] The Police

---

325   Section 37(a) repealed PACE 1984, s 67(8).

326   E.g. the PCA Report for 1998–99 showed that there were 107 complaints relating to breach of Code A, governing stop and search in the period. One led to disciplinary charges (Table 5, p 13).

327   HC 258-I (1997–98).

328   HC 683 (1997–98).

329   The Government issued a consultation paper in April 1993 which included various proposals, including abolition of the criminal standard of proof in discipline cases and the double jeopardy rule, which meant that criminal proceedings against officers were not followed by disciplinary proceedings. See 143 NLJ 591; in its Triennial Review 1988–91, HC 352, 1991, the PCA also made this proposal. The Labour proposals also addressed the tendency of police officers who are facing disciplinary charges to take extended sick leave and/or early retirement, thereby evading the disciplinary process.

330   RCCJ Report, Cm 2263, p 46.

331   Sanders and Young, n 1 above, p 702; H Kennedy, in C Walker andK Starmer (eds), *Miscarriages of Justice: A Review of Justice in Error* (1999) at 374; SH Bailey, N Taylor, *Bailey, Harris and Jones: Civil Liberties: Cases and Materials,* 6th edn (2009), Chapter 3 at 108–9.

332   *A Study of the Police Complaints System,* 1991.

333   Cm 4262-I, 1999, Recommendation 58.

334   *The Future of Policing,* 1997, p 53; finding based on Skogan, *Contacts between Police and Public: Findings from the 1992 British Crime Survey,* HO Research Study No 134, 1994.

Action Lawyers Group stated: 'the fundamental problem . . . is the lack of independence in the system.'[335] The Home Office Consultation Paper 2000[336] accepted that the system had failed to win public confidence.

The Police Reform Act 2002

The result of the consultation was the Police Reform Act 2002 Part 2 and Sched 3, which came into force in April 2004 and made certain changes to the previous system, intended to increase public confidence in the police and in particular in the complaints system.[337] One of its aims was to make investigations more open, timely, proportionate and fair. It set up the Independent Police Complaints Commission (IPCC) in order to answer to the demand for an independent system. The cases extracted below provide an illustration of the current work of the IPCC and give indications as to the problems it still appears to face in maintaining the confidence of the public in itself and in the police.

The Police Reform Act 2002, as amended

Schedule 3

Investigations and subsequent proceedings

Power of the Commission to determine the form of an investigation

15 (1) This paragraph applies where—

   (a)   a complaint or recordable conduct matter is referred to the Commission; and
   (b)   the Commission determines that it is necessary for the complaint or matter to be investigated.

   (2)   It shall be the duty of the Commission to determine the form which the investigation should take.

   (3)   In making a determination under sub-paragraph (2) the Commission shall have regard to the following factors—

   (a)   the seriousness of the case; and
   (b)   the public interest.

   (4)   The only forms which the investigation may take in accordance with a determination made under this paragraph are—

   (a)   an investigation by the appropriate authority on its own behalf;
   (b)   an investigation by that authority under the supervision of the Commission;
   (c)   an investigation by that authority under the management of the Commission;
   (d)   an investigation by the Commission.

---

335   Home Affairs Committee Report, para 43.

336   London, Home Office, 2000.

337   For criticism of the new scheme see Sanders and Young, *Criminal Justice,* 3rd edn (2007), Chapter 12.4.

Investigations by the appropriate authority on its own behalf

16 (3) Subject to sub-paragraph (4), it shall be the duty of the appropriate authority to appoint—

(a) a person serving with the police (whether under the direction and control of the chief officer of police of the relevant force or of the chief officer of another force), or

(b) a member of the National Criminal Intelligence Service or the National Crime Squad,

to investigate the complaint or matter.

(4) The person appointed under this paragraph to investigate any complaint or matter—

(a) in the case of an investigation relating to any conduct of a chief officer, must not be a person under that chief officer's direction and control. . .

Investigations supervised by the Commission

17 (1) This paragraph applies where the Commission has determined that it should supervise the investigation by the appropriate authority of any complaint or recordable conduct matter.

(2) On being given notice of that determination, the appropriate authority shall, if it has not already done so, appoint—

(a) a person serving with the police (whether under the direction and control of the chief officer of police of the relevant force or of the chief officer of another force), or

(b) a member of the National Criminal Intelligence Service or the National Crime Squad,

to investigate the complaint or matter. . . .

(4) Where a person has already been appointed to investigate the complaint or matter, or is selected under this sub-paragraph for appointment, and the Commission is not satisfied with that person, the Commission may require the appropriate authority, as soon as reasonably practicable after being required to do so—

(a) to select another person falling within sub-paragraph (2)(a) or (b) to investigate the complaint or matter; and

(b) to notify the Commission of the person selected.

Investigations managed by the Commission

18 (1) This paragraph applies where the Commission has determined that it should manage the investigation by the appropriate authority of any complaint or recordable conduct matter.

(2) Sub-paragraphs (2) to (6) of paragraph 17 shall apply as they apply in the case of an investigation which the Commission has determined is one that it should supervise.

(3) The person appointed to investigate the complaint or matter shall, in relation to that investigation, be under the direction and control of the Commission.

Investigations by the Commission itself

19 (1) This paragraph applies where the Commission has determined that it should itself carry out the investigation of a complaint or recordable conduct matter.

(2) The Commission shall designate both—

(a) a member of the Commission's staff to take charge of the investigation on behalf of the Commission, and

(b) all such other members of the Commission's staff as are required by the Commission to assist him.

R (Dennis on the application of) v Independent Police Complaints Commission, Court of Appeal, Administrative Court, May 06, 2008, [2008] EWHC 1158 (Admin) (extracts)

In this instance a woman was mistakenly detained and searched by police.

4 Nicola Dennis [opened her door and] was faced with members of the Police Armed Response Unit. A gun was pointed at her and she was told to put her hands up and to move away from the house. She was made to lie on the floor; her hands were tied behind her back with plastic cuffs; all of this at gun point. She was aware that the safety catch was off. She was made to go to another area; people who had been apprehended were placed by her on the ground. She was terrified that she was going to be shot; she was crying and shaking. Her ordeal may have gone on for as long as 15 minutes before she was released.

9 Nicola Dennis made a complaint to the defendant alleging: an unauthorised entry into her premises; an unlawful arrest, if she was arrested; unauthorised use of force to detain her
. . .

10 The statutory framework for the investigation of complaints against the police is the Police Reform Act 2002 and Regulations and Guidance made pursuant to that Act. Schedule 3 deals with handling of complaints. The defendant decided in accordance with paragraph 15(4)(b) that the investigation of this complaint should be conducted by the police supervised by the defendant. . . .

15 The investigating officers concluded that the actions of PC Callan and the degree of force used were reasonable. . . .

17 Ms Dennis exercised her right to appeal these findings to the defendant [the IPCC]. Under paragraphs 25(2)(b) and (c) of Schedule 3 of the Police Reform Act 2002 she was entitled to appeal against the findings of the investigation . . .

18 . . . The conclusion of the review was that the appeal was partially successful. The caseworker did not find that any criminal allegations or misconduct allegations had been made out but concluded that some action was required, namely:

'Management words of advice to be given to PC Pilsbury in relation to the treatment of Ms Dennis, ie, cuffing Ms Dennis and placing her on the floor.'

21 Unhappily, the caseworker has been led into error because she has misunderstood important findings of fact made by the investigating officers. . . .

28 . . . observations by the caseworker clearly raise a question as to whether PC Pilsbury used only reasonable force.

30 . . . the caseworker has misunderstood the factual findings made by the investigating officers. The reason for the prolonged detention of Ms Dennis was for the purpose

of searching her, not so that PC Pilsbury could go off and do other things. These misunderstandings, in my view, go to the heart of the review.

32 I am satisfied that, taken as a whole, this appeal decision is fatally flawed and is irrational in that it is based upon a misunderstanding of the facts and lack of clarity in reasoning which renders the decision difficult to understand. It also includes criticisms of a police officer which are unjustified.

33 ... [the IPCC case-worker] has not considered an important area of the case as to whether it was reasonable for PC Callan to handcuff and then detain Ms Dennis in order to carry out a further search. This all formed part of the detention. Part of the complaint was that it was not lawful and that has been considered by the investigating officers.

34 Ms Dennis is entitled to have a proper review. It is important that the functions of the defendant are carried out properly to maintain public confidence in the system and the police force and to ensure that if there are lessons to be learned that that happens.

R (On the Application of Saunders) v Independent Police Complaints Commission; R (On the Application of Tucker) v Independent Police Complaints Commission, Administrative Court, 10 October 2008, [2008] EWHC 2372 (Admin)[338] (extracts)

Summary

In both claims for judicial review a young man was shot dead by police officers. In each of the cases the Independent Police Complaints Commission (IPCC) was pursuing an investigation into the circumstances of the shooting. In each case the victim's family believed that the investigation had not been properly conducted and brought claims for judicial review against the IPCC. The complaints concerned three main areas: first, it was accepted that in both cases no steps were taken either by the police or by the Commission's staff, to prevent the officers who were most centrally involved in the incidents from speaking to one another before they gave their first accounts of what had happened. It was also accepted that the officers did in fact collaborate; second, that the senior investigator did not seek to interview most of the principal officers, but relied entirely on their witness statements; and third, that the IPCC acted in breach of a statutory obligation under s 21 of the Police Reform Act 2002 to keep the claimant and her family properly informed about the progress of the investigation.

Underhill J:

38 In my view the judgment in Ramsahai v Netherlands (2008) 46 EHRR 43 demonstrates that in the case of a fatal shooting by police officers the state may be held to have violated art 2 if, in the course of the investigation required by the article, adequate steps were not taken to prevent the police officers directly concerned from conferring before producing their first accounts of the incident; and that that is so even if it cannot be shown that they in fact did confer. . . .

40 In my view the relevant statements of principle emerging from Ramsahai are that there must in every case of a killing by state agents be an effective investigation, and that in order to be effective such an investigation must be both independent and 'adequate'. . . .

---

52 [It was argued on behalf of the IPCC that] the Commission [did not have] an unqualified power to give general directions, binding on police officers, of the kind contended for [to forbid conferring]. Section 10 does not assist the claimants: it is no more than a standard-form powers—I found those submissions compelling. . . .

56 . . . the essential submission [on behalf of the IPCC] was that it was the Commission's genuine and reasonable view that directing the relevant chief officers to prohibit conferring (so far as possible), and in particular to countermand the ACPO guidance and prevent officers collaborating in producing their first accounts, would be more likely to prejudice than to assist an effective investigation.

. . .

62 the Commission's position is not one of passive acceptance of an unsatisfactory situation. On the contrary, it is actively pursuing the abolition of conferring/collaboration by agreement with ACPO. . . .

63 [It was argued for the claimants that it was for the judge, and not the Commission], to judge whether in the circumstances of these cases the failure to take steps to prohibit conferring or collaboration was incompatible with the obligation under art 2. I was referred to *Huang v Secretary of State for the Home Department* [2007] UKHL 11; [2007] 2 A.C. 167; [2007] H.R.L.R. 22, esp. per Lord Bingham at [13] (185). . . in making my decision I am entitled to give full weight to the Commission's own judgment. Adopting that approach, it is my conclusion that in not giving a direction of the kind contended for by the claimants the Commission was not acting incompatibly with their art 2 rights.

64 . . .The Commission's. . .job is to make reliable findings about what happened. If the officers give statements after conferring, that is not the best evidence; but that does not mean that it is bad evidence. . . and it is certainly preferable to having no evidence at all. . . .As already noted, officers who choose to remain silent will themselves be asserting a right under the Convention: this is not therefore a case of a public authority acquiescing for pragmatic reasons in another party's breach of duty.

. . .

72 . . .in my judgment it was not necessary for the purpose of an effective investigation that Mr Cummins [the IPCC investigator] should have interviewed D or the other officers present. . .

74 Section 21 of the 2002 Act (as amended by the 2005 Act) imposes duties on the Commission and others with regard to the supply to 'interested persons' (defined in subs (5)) of various specified kinds of information about investigations being carried out under Pt 2 of the Act.

. . .

80 I certainly do not accept that the Commission is under any obligation as such to disclose to interested persons the statements received from witnesses in the course of the investigation.

81 I see nothing in the phrase 'the progress of the investigation', or in the statutory context, to require it to be interpreted in the narrowly procedural manner submitted [on behalf of the IPCC]. . . . it is part of the policy of the Act that the Commission should be as open as is reasonably possible in the communication of information to interested persons.

. . .

Conclusion

84 The claim in *Tucker* is dismissed in its entirety. The claim in *Saunders* is dismissed save that the question whether there has been a breach by the Commission of its duty under s 21(6) of the 2002 Act is adjourned generally, with liberty to either party to apply for it to be restored.

Notes

1. Under Sched 3 Police Reform Act 2002, a complaint may be received in the first instance by the Chief Constable, the police authority, or the Independent Police Complaints Commission (IPCC). It must then be determined who is the 'appropriate authority' for the purposes of the investigation (Sched 3, para 1). This will normally be the Chief Constable of the force in question. The Chief Constable then appoints an officer to carry out a formal investigation, unless the complaint can be informally resolved. Therefore, it is still fair to say, despite the reforms, that an issue of independence arises at the beginning of the process.[339] Informal resolution can only occur if the complainant consents and the authority is satisfied that even if the complaint was proved no criminal or disciplinary proceedings would be appropriate (Sched 3, para 6). The provisions governing the IPCC's operation were significantly amended, with effect from 1 April 2006, by the provisions of Sched 12 to the Serious Organised Crime and Police Act 2005. Under the original provisions of the 2002 Act the Commission's role was limited to cases of complaints against the police or of 'conduct matters', but by amendments introduced by the 2005 Act its functions were extended to cover the investigation of 'death or serious injury matters'—see s 12(2A)–(2D).

2. A complaint must be referred to the IPCC if the alleged misconduct resulted in death or serious injury (Sched 3, para 6) or where the Secretary of State has provided by regulations that the investigation of the complaint must be supervised by the IPCC (intended to be in the case of more serious misconduct). In addition, there is a discretionary power to refer complaints to the PCA and it can require a complaint to be referred to it. Where a complaint is referred to it the IPCC decides on the procedure (Sched 3, para 15). It can carry out the investigation itself using its own staff where a complaint is referred to it. This is the key difference from the previous scheme. It can also supervise or manage the investigation by the appropriate authority and then receive a report at the end of it. The appropriate authority can also carry out the investigation on behalf of the IPCC. If it appears once an investigation has been completed that a criminal offence may have been committed, the case must be referred to the DPP.

3. The *procedure* at the hearing is now governed by the Police (Conduct) Regulations 2004 which repealed the regulations introduced in April 1999.[340] The 1999 regulations followed up the initial Labour proposals for reform,[341] including in particular abolition of the criminal standard of proof in disciplinary proceedings.[342] The 2004 Regulations do not create radical changes but do improve the position of the complainant to an extent. Under the procedure as governed by the 1999 Regs, the hearing was private, but the complainant could attend the proceedings, although not before his evidence was given.[343] Now he or she can attend for the full hearing but can be excluded on public interest grounds if there are sensitivities regarding the evidence.[344]

4. The key change under the reformed scheme is that the police are for the first time subject to external investigation. Nevertheless, it appears that in the majority of cases, due to lack of resources, the IPCC's role in relation to the investigation—as opposed to the supervision—of complaints remains limited. Many complaints will never be referred to the IPCC but will remain

---

339 Home Affairs Committee First Report (1997–98), para 47.

340 The Police (Conduct) Regulations 1999. The procedures operated alongside the 1995 ones until March 2000, when the transitional arrangements ended; all cases were then dealt with under the 1999 procedures. The 2004 Regulations are contained in SI No 845 and now govern the procedure.

341 HC 683 (1997–98).

342 *Ibid*, reg 27(3)(b) (previously 23(3)).

343 *Ibid*, reg 25(3).

344 A number of provisions, however, previously allowed for the exclusion of the complainant: under reg 25(5) the complainant could be removed if he interrupted. Now under reg 31 (previously reg 27) he can be excluded if matters arise which it would not be in the public interest to disclose to him.

in the hands of the police force in question. Thus, despite the involvement (albeit limited) of the Independent Police Complaints Commission, introduced by the Police Reform Act 2002, with a view to creating a stronger independent element in the system, the complaints procedure is still largely administered by the police themselves. Thus, now that the system contains this independent element, a number of problems remain even in relation to those exceptional cases in which independent investigation by civilian investigators occurs. Institutional factors, including obstruction of the system by the police and the possibility that civilian investigators will be affected by police culture, may continue to hamper the system; the success rate may remain low.[345] As Sanders and Young argue, the IPCC is in the same position as the PCA since in general it relies on reports of the facts of a case, compiled by police officers. The police concerned use various techniques to discredit a complaint, constructing the case in a manner that justifies no further action.[346]

5. Where officers are placed under investigation with a view to disciplinary charges, they may take early retirement or resign on medical grounds. After the MacPherson Report[347] into the *Stephen Lawrence* case, disciplinary charges were recommended against five officers involved. All, however, retired and therefore could not face charges. The Home Office has considered the possibility of disciplinary action up to five years after retirement.[348] In the wake of the MacPherson Report, and with the inception of the new complaints system, racist police behaviour may begin to lead more frequently to disciplinary charges,[349] as well as liability under the Race Relations Act 1976, as amended, although such a trend cannot yet be discerned.[350] There remains a disconnection between successful civil actions against the police and disciplinary action or prosecution.[351] For example, in the *Hsu* case,[352] it was found that Mr Hsu was assaulted, racially abused and falsely arrested. It was accepted that the police officers in question had lied on oath and fabricated notebook entries. Mr Hsu was awarded £200,000 damages (reduced on appeal to £35,000), but no officer was disciplined.[353]

6. Under the pre-2004 system, the overwhelming majority of complaints did not result in disciplinary proceedings: as many as 30% of complaints were dealt with by informal resolution,[354] and 50% of

---

345 See J Harrison and M Cuneen, *An Independent Police Complaints Commission* (2000); A Goldsmith and S Faran, 'Complaints against the police in Canada: a new approach' [1987] Crim LR 615.

346 See Sanders and Young, *Criminal Justice*, 3rd edn (2007) at 615.

347 Cm 4262-I, 1999.

348 MacPherson Report, Recommendations 55–57.

349 E.g. in February 2000 a police officer, PC Hutt, was disciplined and dismissed from the force for oppressive, racist behaviour (News report 22 February 2000).

350 The 1998–99 Annual Report of the PCA, Table 5: 2,415 complaints concerned assaults; 81 disciplinary charges were preferred. 203 complaints concerned racially discriminatory behaviour; three charges were preferred. There is quite a lot of evidence that stop and search is still carried out in a racially discriminatory fashion: see Sanders and Young, n 1 above (2007) at 2.3.

351 *The Butler Report*, 1998, criticised the CPS for its decision making in the *Treadaway* case; Derek Treadaway was awarded £50,000 in damages in respect of a serious assault by police officers while he was in custody: *R v DPP ex parte Treadaway, The Times*, 18 November 1997. The CPS decided not to prosecute the officers. Treadaway successfully sought judicial review of this decision and the case was remitted for reconsideration by the CPS.

352 *Thompson v Comr of Police for the Metropolis, Hsu v Comr of Police for the Metropolis* [1997] 2 All ER 762.

353 See further the Home Affairs Committee First Report (1998), Section B: 'The evidence from civil actions'. A further example, in which the disciplinary sanction was, in effect, rescinded, is provided by *Goswell v Comr of Metropolitan Police, The Guardian* Report, 27 April 1996. The officer who was found in that case to have perpetrated a serious assault, PC Trigg, was dismissed as a result of a complaint from Goswell. In the civil action Goswell had been awarded £120,000 for assault, £12,000 for false imprisonment and £170,000 for arbitrary and oppressive behaviour. Trigg appealed against his dismissal and was reinstated by the Home Secretary, Michael Howard. On the face of it, his reinstatement after it had been proved beyond reasonable doubt (in the disciplinary proceedings) that Trigg had perpetrated the assault in question appeared highly questionable.

354 PCA Triennial Review, HC 466 (1985–88), para 1.14, p 8.

complaints were withdrawn.[355] Clayton and Tomlinson noted that the 16,712 complaints dealt with in 1990 led to 305 criminal or disciplinary charges and advice or admonishment in 573 cases; thus, less than 2% of complaints led to any disciplinary action.[356] The Independent Police Complaints Commission published statistics for the number of complaints recorded by police in England and Wales, for the year ended 31 March 2005, after the IPCC had been responsible for public complaints and conduct issues since April 2004.[357] A total of 27,909 allegations were completed in 2004/05. These were dealt with as follows: 50% were dealt with by local resolution (13,936 compared with 8,914 informal resolutions in 2003/4); 20% were dealt with by formal investigation (5,585 compared with 7,761 in 2003/04); 17% by dispensation (4,737 compared with 5,863); 13% withdrawn (3,651 compared with 2,838). Of those allegations formally investigated, 745 (13%) were substantiated. In 2004/05 a total of 22,898 complaint cases were recorded, marking a 44% increase on the previous year. There was a great deal of variation across police forces, with some but not all experiencing very large increases in complaints.

7. In 2004/05 the IPCC received 768 valid appeals from complainants. Half (49%) were against the non-recording of a complaint, one-third (35%) about the outcome of a supervised or local investigation and 17% about the local resolution process. Nearly half (46%) of the appeals against non-recording were upheld, compared to one-fifth of those against the outcome of an investigation and 13% of those against the local resolution process. In 2004/05 misconduct sanctions were imposed on 1,204 police officers. For 80 of these officers the charges related to a public complaint. A total of 324 officers received sanctions resulting from a misconduct hearing. Of these, a total of 34 officers were dismissed and 57 officers were requested to resign. Since April 1 2004 the IPCC has used its powers to begin 87 independent and 322 managed investigations into the most serious complaints against the police. The IPCC considered that the increase in complaints was due to a number of factors. The Police Reform Act 2002 (PRA Act) widened the categories of complainant and those who could be subject to complaints. More significantly, in preparation for the PRA Act, police forces had made improvements in accessibility and recording procedures. Such improvements were likely to have resulted in more people being included in the complaints system who in the past would have had their complaint dealt with informally or, while aggrieved, would not have presented their complaint.

8. Once the 2002 Act had been in place for a year, in 2004/05, a total of 22,898 complaints were received; of the allegations formally investigated, 13% were substantiated. Appeals to the IPCC led to misconduct charges against 80 officers. Further charges related to misconduct not the subject of a public complaint. These figures demonstrate that a rise in the number of complaints has occurred and also in the number of substantiated complaints since the inception of the IPCC. But a 13% substantiation rate remains low; a large number are still withdrawn or informally resolved. The difference between the number of complaints and the number substantiated, and between those substantiated and those leading to disciplinary charges, remains dramatic. Under-resourcing of the IPCC may be one reason for lack of IPCC involvement in certain instances where arguably such involvement would be justified.

9. The IPCC is a public authority under s 6 HRA and is therefore bound to adhere to the ECHR. Its interpretation of its role may mean that it is not fully adhering to its duties under the Convention; this was a key issue in the *Saunders* and *Tucker* case, above. The case can be viewed as suggesting

---

355 See Triennial Review of the PCA 1991–94, HC 396, 1994–95; R Clayton and H Tomlinson, *Civil Actions Against the Police*, 2nd edn (1992), p 13.

356 Clayton and Tomlinson, *ibid*, p 13.

357 Police Complaints: Statistics for England and Wales 2004/05, Emily Gleeson and Tom Bucke, IPCC Research and Statistics Series: Paper 3, www.ipcc.gov.uk.

that the IPCC is taking an approach to its role as determined by the 2002 Act, as amended, which appears to be generous to the police but ungenerous to claimants. Its interpretation of its statutory duty put forward in that case as regards its ability to disallow conferring between officers and as to the provision of information to claimants appears to be a narrow one—'narrowly procedural'. In that case the judge found that the *Ramsahai* case on ECHR Art 2 cannot be viewed, as matter of domestic law, under s 6 HRA, as meaning that the IPCC is failing in its s 6 HRA duty where it does not disallow conferring between police officers involved in a fatal shooting. That point is debatable since it partly turns on whether conferring contaminates the evidence to the point that the investigation is unlikely to be effective. If so, and given that the IPCC, as the independent judge found, did have the power to disallow conferral, it is unclear that the IPCC were right to assume that forbidding conferral would have been more likely to hinder the investigation. The officers concerned had a Convention right to remain silent, but if they had had legal advice, then as far as the Convention, Art 6, is concerned, adverse inferences could be drawn from the silence without breaching their Art 6 rights.[358] The interpretation of Art 2 and of the HRA demands adopted by the judge in that case absolved the IPCC of breaching Art 2 in relation to its investigation of the fatal police shooting, but it is contended that, at the least, if the case reaches Strasbourg, the UK may have been found to breach Art 2.

10. The *Dennis* case (above) indicates that doubts are being raised as to the competence of the IPCC and its ability to maintain public confidence in the system, and the police force. In 2009 doubts were also raised over the independence shown by the IPCC in their initial response to the death of Ian Tomlinson, allegedly after an assault by a police officer, at the April G20 protests.[359] The widespread use of 'kettling' (a police strategy whereby thousands of protesters are trapped for hours in a police cordon, a tactic which the Metropolitan police have stood by for the last ten years as a means of controlling mass protest) and other aspects of the policing of the G20 protests was the subject of a large number of complaints to the IPCC. The IPCC reported that it had received more than 270 complaints over the G20 protests, of which about 52 appeared to be about police tactics.[360] The most serious, which the IPCC is currently investigating, concerns the death of bystander Ian Tomlinson who died after allegedly being assaulted by a police officer when he may inadvertently have approached a police cordon at the G20 protests.[361] The initial IPCC response was viewed in some media reports as one that too readily accepted the police version of events, which was that Tomlinson died of a heart attack and in which protesters impeded police efforts to aid him.[362] That version of events would have meant that no independent investigation was needed. One commentator argued that the case illustrates: 'The age-old dilemma—only police can investigate the police, but the police cannot investigate the police—is exacerbated by a tendency of the IPCC to allow the police to conduct investigations themselves, using their own resources. A

---

358   See above, p 1207.

359   See the IPCC evidence to the Home Affairs Select Committee which held an inquiry leading to a report on the policing of the G20 protests in April 2009, *Policing of the G20 Protests* 8th Report of Session 2008–09. See further H Fenwick, 'Marginalising Human Rights: Breach of the Peace, 'Kettling', the HRA and Public Protest' [2009] PL 737–65.

360   See A Hirsch, *The Guardian*, 14 April 2009.

361   The officer in question had reportedly concealed his identity but was subsequently suspended; he may also face manslaughter charges after a second post-mortem showed that Tomlinson died from internal bleeding. The Commission is also investigating further allegations of assault by police officers—one of a woman at a memorial protest for Tomlinson on April 2 (see the Independent Police Complaints Commission response, 7 May 2009 www.ipcc.gov.uk/jchr_submission_-_070509.pdf); the same officer is under investigation by the IPCC over a further assault during the protests, against a student whom he is alleged to have confronted in an alley off Bishopsgate, and thrown to the ground (see *The Guardian* 11 June 2009 'G20 police officer under investigation for alleged second assault').

362   See *The Guardian*, 18 April 2009.

"managed" investigation, where the police are supervised by a single member of the IPCC, is exactly that.'[363]

CONCLUSIONS

The previous 'balance' struck by PACE in 1984 and pre-PACE between state powers and individual rights—often pre-HRA—has, it is argued, been eroded over the last fifteen years. First, the rules themselves set out in this Chapter provide the police with a great deal of discretion due to the use of terminology such as 'reasonable suspicion' or due to the provision of powers, such as the stop and search power under s 44 of the Terrorism Act 2000, which are not dependent on the formation of such suspicion, and can in effect be exercised on a subjective basis—a hunch. Second, the redress if the rules are breached is either normally unavailable in practice (in relation to breaches of the Codes of Practice) or of doubtful efficacy (the impact of the IPCC and of redress via tort damages). The police are of course, as a public authority, bound by s 6 HRA to adhere to the ECHR; Articles 2, 3, 5, 6 and 8 are of especial pertinence. The Police and Criminal Evidence Act 1984, the Codes of Practice made under it, other statutory provisions should provide safeguards for suspects which go well beyond the minimum standards provided by the ECHR. However, it has been argued at certain points above that the ECHR standards could be utilised to improve such safeguards, but that in practice, in the ten years that the HRA has been in force, they have had little influence upon them. From both a crime control and a due process perspective this is an unfortunate situation since it means not only that police abuses of power may go unchecked, but also that public confidence in the police is undermined, resulting in a diminution in public co-operation with the police.

FURTHER READING

SH Bailey, N Taylor, *Bailey, Harris and Jones: Civil Liberties: Cases and Materials,* 6th edn (2009), Chapter 4
D Feldman, *Civil Liberties and Human Rights in England and Wales,* 2nd edn (2002), Chapters 6 and 10
H Fenwick, *Civil Liberties and Human Rights,* 4th edn (2007), Chapters 11, 12, 13
A Sanders and R Young, *Criminal Justice,* 3rd edn (2007)
M Zander, *The Police and Criminal Evidence Act 1984,* 4th edn (2008)

---

363 A Hirsh *ibid.* A change of culture at the IPCC may be becoming evident, however: their investigation of Commander Ali Dizaei appeared to be thorough and rigorous; it was apparently pivotal in securing a conviction against him in 2010. He was eventually convicted of misconduct in public office and perverting the course of justice (see the *Independent,* 8 February 2010).

Index

A

Abraham, Ann 886, 921; Ombudsman as part of UK constitution 891–3; PO accountability 921–2

Accountability; *see also* Individual Ministerial Responsibility; Executive 603–63; Parliamentary Ombudsmen 920–5; responsibility—distinction 628–32; to Parliament for using armed forces 565–71

Act of Settlement 174

Acts of Indemnity 174

Acts of State 588

Acts of Union 6, 235

Additional Member System 351

Advertising Standards Authority 739

Advocacy advertising 1036

Alternative Vote System 351, 354

Anti-poll tax protests 1085

Anti-Social Behaviour Act 2003 1086

Anti-Terrorism, Crime and Security Act 2001 308, 337–8

Armstrong Memorandum 618

Armstrong, Lord 642

Army Act 1955 327–8

Arrest and detention 1169–81; arrest conditions 1172; common law 1169; crime control model 1169; due process model 1169; exceptional circumstances 1173; false imprisonment 1180; information to be given 1177–80; procedural elements 1177–80; purpose of arrest 1176; range of powers of arrest 1170–81; reasonable grounds 1173–4, 1176; reasonable suspicion 1172, 1173–7; terrorism 1171–2, 1173, 1174–5, 1177; use of force 1181; validity 1172; volunteers 1177; with warrant 1170; without warrant 1170–1

Asylum and Immigration Act 2003 772–4

Audi alteram partem 799; *see also* Procedural Impropriety

Austin and Saxby case 1094, 1100–2, 1128–35

Australian Senate 78; lessons from overseas 457–8

Automatic disqualification rule 779–83

Axa General Insurance 250–4

B

Backbencher 363; *see also* House of Commons, Wright Committee

Reforms; ability to influence government policy 362; role enhancement 391

Bailiff 144

Basic Law (Germany) 9, 12

BBC 1032–3

Belmarsh case 1011, 1016

Bias, rules against 779–96; direct interest 779–83; impartiality of jurors' verdict 790–3; indirect interest 783–96; indirect interest, basic test 783–6; indirect interest, bias and informed observer 794–6; indirect interest, decisions taken by non-judicial bodies 793–6; indirect interest, institutional bias by overlap of roles 788–93; indirect interest, strong views expressed previously by a judge 787–8

Bill of Rights 86, 175, 186, 935, 944–8; arguments against 944–5; arguments for 945–6; civil liberties 935; coalition government, plans for 1015–16; comparisons with Germany and United States 949–50; Dworkin, R 944–5, 947–8; entrenched 935; Human Rights Act 1998 949–57, 959–61; Klug F, commentary 1012–15; methods of protection 947–8; Waldron, J 945–6, 947

Birmingham Six 1142

Blair, Tony 36–7, 367, 408, 605, 608; control/sidelining of cabinet 612–14; special advisers 617–18; war on Iraq 363–5, 569, 653–7, 661–2

Breach of confidence 1023–32; changes in doctrine 1025–32; changes in doctrine, *Spycatcher* litigation 1026–30; Human Rights Act 1998, and 1023–4; interim injunctions 1024–5

Breach of peace 1120–35

Brind case 939, 942, 943

British constitution *see* UK constitution

Brixton riots 1085

Brogan case 1189–90

Brown, Gordon 615

Bryce Commission 436

Butler Inquiry 614–16, 627, 661–2; national interest and politics of threat exaggeration 653–7

C

Cabinet 603–26; Blair, Tony 608, 612–14; changing role 608–10;

collective responsibility 73, 608, 621–6; committees 609, 611; consulting cabinet 612; core executive thesis 616; Crossman diaries 608; departmental evidence and response 408–10, 413–14; format of meetings 608, 609; government business and core executive 611–16; inner Cabinet 609; Ministerial Code 609–10; ministerial meetings 609; power 608–9; prerogative powers 551; Prime Ministerial patronage 610–11; secrecy of proceedings and papers 58–60; significance of bypassing 614; Thatcher, Margaret 609, 611–13

Calcutt report 887

Calman Commission 271–2

Campaign for Freedom of Information 699, 710

Canada 60–1

Canadian Senate 79; lessons from overseas 457, 458–9

Cane, Peter; public bodies 733–4

Cardiff Three 1224

Case of Proclamations 575

Central Executive; Cabinet 603–26; civil servants 603–26; Prime Minister 603–26; structures and accountability 603–63

Chilcott (Iraq) Inquiry 662

Children Act 1989 963

Civil liberties; Allan, TRS 937–8; Bill of Rights question 944–8; Dicey, AV 937, 938–9; influence of European Convention on Human Rights 941–4; judicial review 939–41; traditional definition 935–6; traditional protection 935–1017

Civil Procedure Rules; judicial review 734–5

Civil Servants 603–26; Constitutional Reform and Governance Act 2010 619–20; governance on statutory basis 619–20; individual ministerial responsibility 629–32; ministers and government agencies 617–20; misleading parliament 662–3; rules and principles 617–18; special advisers 617–18

Civil Service Code 617–18

CJPOA *see* Criminal Justice and Public Order Act

CLA *see* Commissioner for Local Administration

Clerk of the House of Commons 77–8